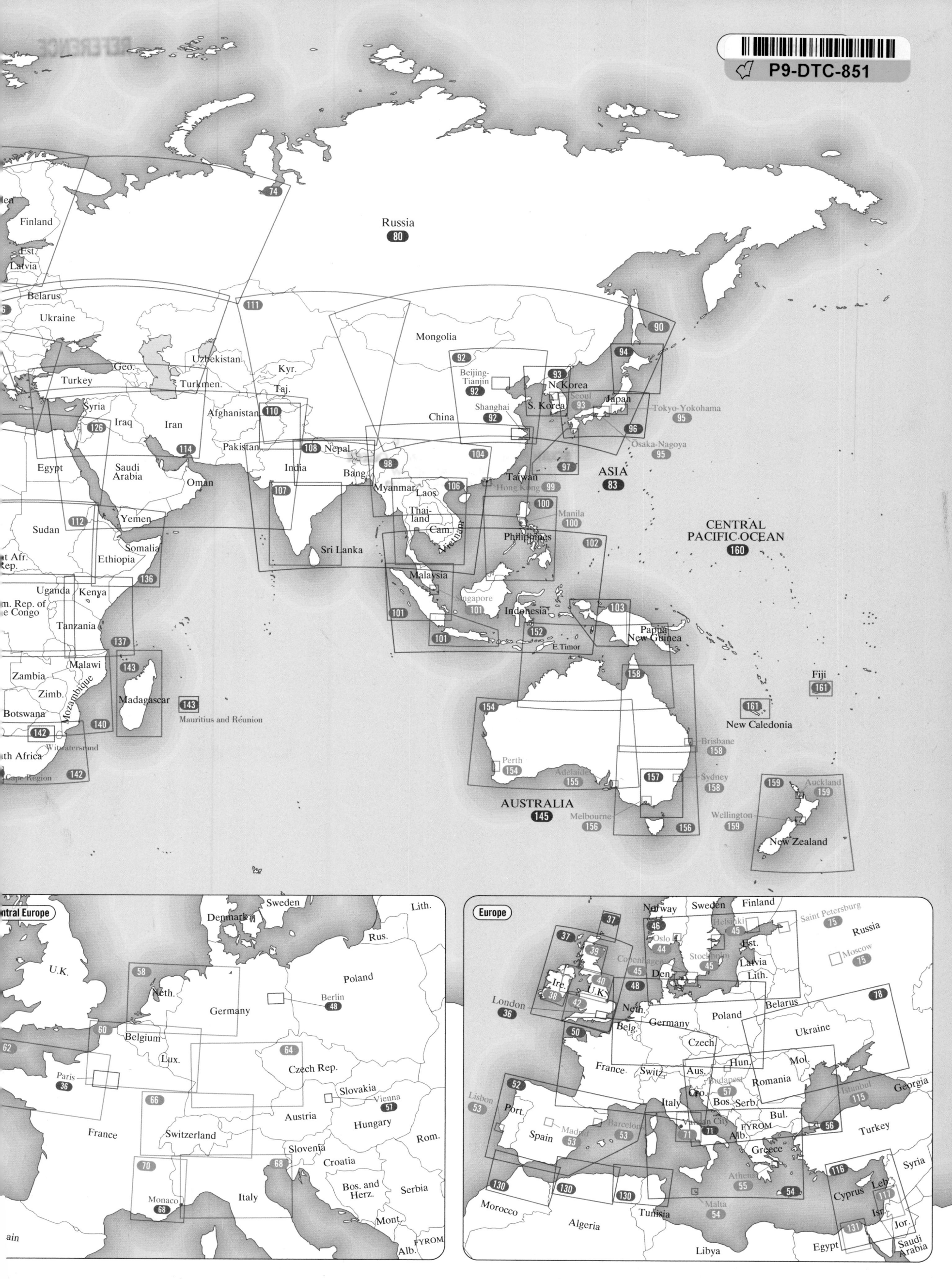

HAMMOND

— FIFTH EDITION —

WORLD ATLAS

"The first day or so we all pointed to our countries. The third or fourth day we were pointing to our continents. By the fifth day we were aware of only one Earth."

Discovery 5 Space Mission

15°

20°

HAMMOND
– FIFTH EDITION –
WORLD ATLAS

25°

30°

35°

40°

45°

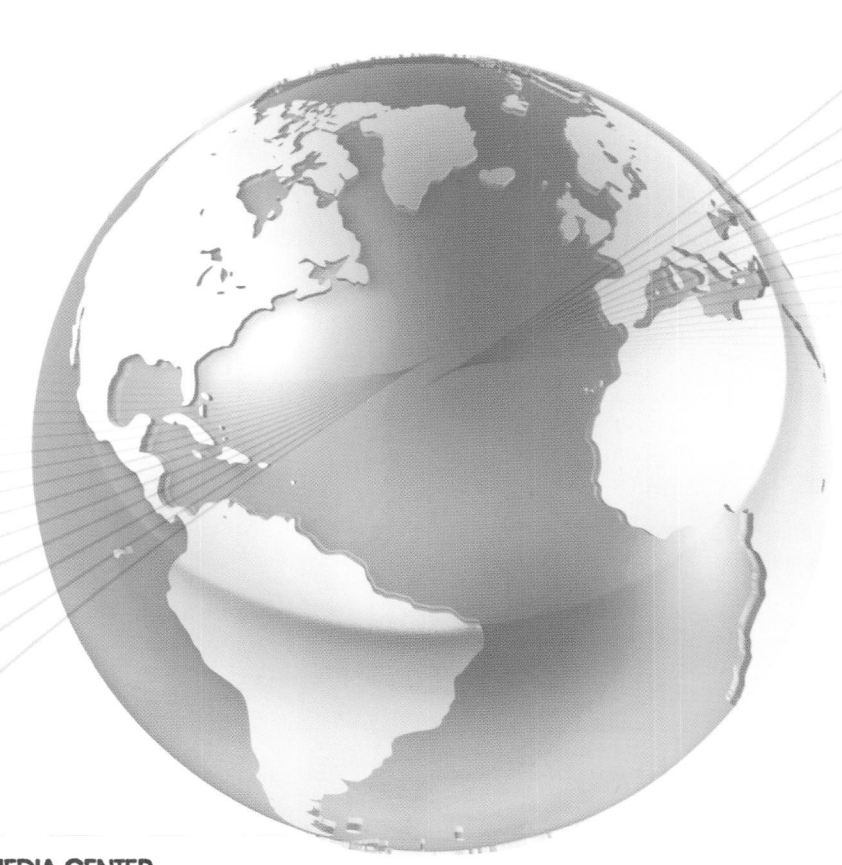

50°

55°

HAMMOND World Atlas Corporation

presenting the world

60°

Publisher **Hammond
World Atlas Corporation**

Chairman Andreas Langenscheidt
President Marc Jennings

VP Cartography Vera Lorenz

Director Cartography and Theophrastos E. Giouvanos
Database Resources

Cartography Walter H. Jones Jr.
Sharon Lightner
Harry E. Morin
James Padykula
Thomas R. Rubino
Thomas J. Scheffer

Layout and Composition John A. DiGiorgio
Maribel López Castillo

Cover Design Marian Purcell
Map Text Blocks Helmut Vieser;
Klartext Journalistenbüro, Stuttgart

Thematic Section
Conception and
Editorial Supervision Dr. Eva Maria Brugger
Writers Dr. Joachim Born,
Technische Universität Dresden
Dr. Eva Maria Brugger, Heidelberg
Prof. Dr. Eckart Ehlers, Universität Bonn
Dr. Horst Eichler, Universität Heidelberg
Dr. Gernot Gruber, Wiesbaden
Prof. Uwe Jäschke, Hochschule für Technik
und Wirtschaft Dresden
Wolfhard Keimer, Dossenheim
Prof. Dr. Wilhelm Lauer &
Daud Rafiqpoor, Universität Bonn
Prof. Dr. Franz-Dieter Miotke, Garbsen
Prof. Dr. Stefan Rahmsdorf, Institut für
Klimafolgenforschung Potsdam
Prof. Dr. Theo Sundermeier,
Universität Heidelberg
Layout and Composition Matthias Hugo;
Hugo Grafische Formgebung, Köln
Informational Graphics Matthias Hugo;
Hugo Grafische Formgebung, Köln
Joachim Knappe, Hamburg
Cartography Dipl.-Ing. (FH) Jörg Radtke
Dipl.-Ing. (FH) Manuela Lipp
Erika Korbien

Satellite Section
Conception and
Design Supervision Dipl.-Geogr. Ellen Astor
Consultation and
Photo Procurement Dr. Lothar Beckel; GEOSPACE, Salzburg
Layout and Composition Sigrid Hecker / doppelpack, Mannheim

Translation
German to English John S. Southard
Editorial Assistance Michael Venhoff
Ellen Astor
Technology Sigrid Hecker
Jörg Radtke

Author of Bibliographisches Institut & F. A.
Satellite Sections Brockhaus AG

Author of Bibliographisches Institut & F. A.
Thematic Sections Brockhaus AG
and Hammond World Atlas Corporation

Hammond World Atlas
Fifth Edition

Library of Congress
Cataloging-in-Publication Data

Hammond World Atlas Corporation.
Hammond world atlas. - 5th ed.
p. cm.
Relief shown by shading and gradient tints.
Includes statistic tables and index.
ISBN 9-780843-70967-7
1. Atlases.
I. Title: World Atlas
II. Title.
G1021. H2665   2000
912--dc21   2002068882

Introduction

Throughout the ages, humankind has been driven by a need to explore. From early on in our history, we recorded our explorations and marked our place in the world through the creation of maps. Although the art and science of cartography have evolved enormously, our sense of wonder at the world around us remains constant. Today, our need to know, and our demand for the latest information and sophisticated cartography, are satisfied with the help of computer technology that enables us to portray our planet with more accuracy, precision, and visual power than ever before.

The work you are holding in your hands is the definitive atlas for our rapidly changing world. It describes a world of breathtaking beauty and heart-breaking devastation. A world that exists as a benefit to mankind and endures in spite of us. A world of contrasts. A world of mysteries. As you leaf through the evocative maps and fascinating text in this Fifth Edition of the Hammond World Atlas you'll experience the excitement of exploration for yourself, of the world and of this book – the culmination of years of painstaking and dedicated labor.

At the heart of the atlas is the outstanding digital cartography that has become synonymous with the Hammond name. In the physical map section realistic computer simulated relief, enhanced with naturalistic coloration, gives a vivid, 3-dimensional impression of the forms and landscapes of the earth. Hypsometric tints for land elevations, and bathymetric tints to depict ocean depths, are used to dramatic effect in the world map section. The map image practically leaps off the page while the clear typography of the nomenclature makes places and other features easy to identify.

If the maps are the heart of the atlas, then the extensive collection of front matter and the 36 new pages of fascinating thematic text preceding the continent map sections are the soul. The maps will help you find your place in the world, while the text and images will draw you into the planet's mysteries, wonders, and ills. Filled with intellectually stimulating information and compelling photography and graphics, the thematic text will enhance your awareness of the interrelatedness of the earth and the living things that share its space.

The opulent satellite photography is nothing short of spectacular and further illustrates the concepts presented in the thematic text. Each of these photos, taken from the perspective of space, is accompanied by technical information and description that satisfies the intellectual curiosity of the reader. They offer a greater understanding of the technologies that allow us to explore the world in ways our ancestors never imagined.

You may have picked up this book for its utility – just to look up a place and continue on with your day. You may want to refer to the new 24-page section of world and country statistics for research, study, or business. If so, the clear organization and the comprehensive index will make it easy for you to quickly find what you need. Nevertheless, when the human need to explore stirs within you, we invite you to take the time to sit back and let the beauty of the atlas inspire you on a fascinating journey of the intellect and the imagination. We are confident you will find it a rewarding experience.

The Publisher

Table of Contents

Map Locator
Title
Attribution
Introduction
Contents
Map and Photo Credits

Thematic Section

Satellite Section

Map Section

Statistics and Index Section

Maps and Photo Credits

Maps in the Map Section: © Hammond World Atlas Corporation 2008, Springfield, New Jersey

Satellite Images: © GEOSPACE, Austria, 2000, Original Data: Eurimage – © GEOSPACE/World Sat International Corp. 2000 – © Deutsches Zentrum für Luft- und Raumfahrt, Oberpfaffenhofen

Theme Section and other pages in the atlas: action press, Hamburg – aisa, Archivo iconografico, Barcelona – Archiv für Kunst und Geschichte, Berlin – theartarchive, London – Art Publishers, Durban – Astrofoto Bildagentur, Sörth – Prof. Dr. J. Bähr, Altwittenbek – Prof. Dr. W. Barthlott, Bonn – J. Bautze, Berlin – BAVARIA Bildagentur, Gauting – Berliner Missionswerk – Hans Bertram Luftbildverlag, Munich – Bibliographisches Institut & F. A. Brockhaus, Mannheim – Bibliothèque Nationale de France, Paris – Bildarchiv Preußischer Kulturbesitz, Berlin – Bilderberg, Archiv der Fotografen, Hamburg – Prof. Dr. G. Bosinski, Neuwied – Prof. Dr. G. Bräuer, Hartenholm – British Library, London – Luftbildarchiv Albrecht Brugger im Hause Fotofachlabor Schnepf, Stuttgart – R. Brugger, Königswinter – Bundesanstalt für Geowissenschaften und Rohstoffe, Hanover – J.-L. Charmet, Paris – Prof. M. Deuchler, London – Deutscher Wetterdienst, Offenbach am Main – Deutsches Museum, Munich – Digimago, Eppelheim – dpa Bildarchiv, Frankfurt am Main und Stuttgart – Dr. H. Eichler, Heidelberg – Prof. Dr. Ch. Feest, Frankfurt am Main – Photo- und Presseagentur FOCUS, Hamburg – Photo- und Presseagentur Focus, Hamburg / B. Barbey / Magnum – Photo- und Presseagentur Focus, Hamburg / J. Blair – Photo- und Presseagentur Focus, Hamburg / B. Edmaier – M. Fries, Wiesbaden – Dr. K. Gallas, München – Studio X, Gamma, Limours – Dr. G. Gerster, Zumikon, Schweiz – Dr. S. von der Heide, Cologne – Prof. Dr. K. Heine, Regensburg – D. Heunemann, Starnberg – Prof. Dr. P. Höllermann, Bonn – IFA-Bilderteam, Taufkirchen – Prof. Dr. A. Jockenhövel, Münster – W. Keimer, Dossenheim – KNA Kath. Nachrichten Agentur, Frankfurt am Main – Dr. H.-J. Kress, Fulda – Helga Lade Fotoagentur, Frankfurt am Main – laenderpress, Mainz – J. Lauré, Woodfin Camp & Associates, New York – Löppert, Optik-Foto-Dia, Munich – Dr. L. Marfaing, Hamburg – Bildagentur Mauritius, Mittenwald – P. Meyer, Frankfurt. – MEV Verlag, Augsburg – Prof. Dr. F.-D. Miotke, Garbsen – W. Müller, Ettlingen – Museum für Völkerkunde, Vienna – NASA / Earth from Space Images, Washington D.C. – NASA /

JPL/RPIF/DLR – Neanderthal Museum, Mettmann – Prof. Dr. G. Niemz, Neu-Isenburg – Oberösterreichisches Landesmuseum, Linz – G. Dagli Orti, Paris – Österreichische Nationalbibliothek, Vienna – Physikalisch-Technische Bundesanstalt, Braunschweig und Berlin – Picture Press, Hamburg / Meyer-Andersen – J. Poupard – J. M. Prieto, Asunción – Dr. D. Rafiqpoor, Bonn – Prof. Dr. S. Rahmstorf, Potsdam – Agentur RAPHO, Paris – Rosgartenmuseum, Konstanz – Prof. Dr. H.-J. Sander, Bonn – K. Schlosser, Kiel – G. Schrüfer, Bayreuth – Forschungsinstitut und Natur-Museum Senckenberg, Frankfurt am Main – Silvestris Verlag, Bildarchiv, Kastl – Sipa Press, Paris – E. SLAWIK, Waldenburg – K. Stevens, USA – H. Stierlin, Genf – Dr. K.-H. Striedter, Frankfurt am Main – L. A. Thomas / Doug Peebles Photography, Hawaii – Tony Stone Bilderwelten, Munich – Uitgeverij Het Spectrum, Utrecht – Ullstein Bilderdienst, Berlin – Ulmer Museum, Ulm – Prof. Dr. W. H. Valentin, Berlin – Prof. Dr. M. Yaldiz, Berlin – ZEFA-Zentrale Farbbild Agentur, Düsseldorf – Carl Zeiss, Oberkochen

Locator maps based on MHM © 1993 Digital Wisdom, Inc.

Other graphic illustrations, maps, and drawings: Bibliographisches Institut & F. A. Brockhaus, Mannheim

The Galápagos Islands, *all Photos*
UNESCO Cultural Heritage - Asia,
The Great Wall of China
– Erika Gold

Australian Aborigines, *Dot Style Painting*
– John DiGiorgio

Thematic Section

The Universe - Our Place in Space

"The works of incredible grandeur are as glorious as on the First Day"

Lifting our gaze upward from the earth, we look into space, but we call what we see the sky. Hung there, so it seems, are all the lights that shine upon us — the warming sun during the day, the cool moon, and the twinkling stars at night.

Ages passed before we humans abandoned the concept of an existence beneath an all-encompassing protective sky and dared to venture, intellectually at first, then through experiment, and finally in concrete steps, into the vastness of space, into the world of worlds, into the universe.

A Grain of Sand in the Desert

How can we comprehend a phenomenon like the universe, something we cannot grasp because it is too large, too small, or too far away? Modern science relies on precise observation linked with proven principles to form explanatory hypotheses. If such hypotheses stand up to all theoretical and practical attempts to refute them, they are regarded as true, and we incorporate them into our fund of knowledge.

Applying this method, we have learned that our earth is like a grain of sand in the desert in comparison to the universe. We have also come to realize that earth is not the center of the universe – indeed, that the universe has no center at all. Does that mean that the earth could as easily be somewhere else? In another solar syste another star system, or another galaxy? Theoretica the answer is yes, but whether there would then be l on earth, or even human beings, is another questi altogether.

Ordinarily, being somewhere else means being in different place and a different environment. Mode cosmology tells us that place or position in the unive is generally inconsequential but that environment crucial. And the heavenly bodies nearest the earth sho that this must be true. Although very different from o another, the moon and our neighboring planets Ven and Mars have one thing in common which distinguish them from the earth: As far as we know, they are devo of life.

Galaxies – Structures of the Universe

Aside from the moon, our constant, though chang able companion, the most prominent features of t nighttime sky are stars and a nebulous, luminous ba known as the Milky Way. Despite all appearances, t band of light we perceive is a system of stars to whi the sun – one of millions upon millions of stars – al belongs, and with it the earth and we ourselves.

Horsehead Nebula

Named for its shape, a horsehead nebula is an extension of a huge, dark cloud of dust (seen in the upper left-hand portion of the picture) that has expanded in such a way that light from any star positioned behind it cannot penetrate it. The dark cloud covers a nebula that emits reddish light. The only stars visible in the vicinity of the dark cloud are those located in front of it. The reflective nebula of the dust cloud is visible on the left above the "horse's head," where a foreground star (which cannot be seen because it is swallowed up by the light coming from behind it) shines against the wall of dust from the front. The bright star that dominates the upper half of the picture is part of Orion's "belt."

Spherical Star Clusters

Spherical star clusters may contain as many as several million stars. They are among the very oldest objects in their respective galaxies and almost always appear – unlike open star clusters – outside the visible disks of the galaxy. This photo shows M 13, the most magnificent spherical star cluster in the northern sky.

The Hale-Bopp Comet

The Danish astronomer Tycho Brahe (1546–1601) discovered that comets are not objects within the earth's atmosphere but bodies moving through the solar system. Scientists now assume that they originate in the Kuiper Belt, a region beyond the dwarf planet Pluto, and from the Oort Cloud, which is much farther from the sun than Pluto. Orbiting comets do not begin to form tails until they approach the sun, as in the case of Hale-Bopp, shown here with a blue tail of ions and a reddish-white tail of dust. The Milky Way, with its characteristic dark clouds, extends across the photograph from the lower left to the upper right.

Spiral Galaxy

Our home galaxy, the Milky Way, would probably look much like this galaxy (NGC 2997) if observed along a line perpendicular to its central plane from a great distance. Easily recognizable in its spiral arms are the arrange- ment of open star clusters and t distribution of interstellar dust.

The Universe - Our Place in Space

...he idea that the earth and the sun are a part of the Milky Way seems somewhat more plausible if we consider that ...he band of the Milky Way encircles the earth complete-...y with roughly the same intensity of light at all points. ...et it would be wrong to conclude from this observa-...on that we are located at the center. The sun is actually ...ar from the middle and much nearer to the edge of the ...ystem. The insight that the earth is a part of the Milky ...Vay, the luminous band of stars we perceive, leads us to ... second, valid conclusion, however: that the stars are ...ery far apart, separated by distances much greater than ...aat between the earth and the sun. The star closest to ...s, Proxima Centauri, is seven thousand times farther ...om the sun than the dwarf planet Pluto, its most distant ...lanet, which is visible to us only through a telescope.

The universe comprises a multitude of star systems of ...ifferent types and sizes, generally referred to as galaxies. ...stronomers estimate that there are between several ...undred billion and several trillion of such galaxies. The ...piral galaxy closest to earth is 2.2 million light years ...way. Depending upon their type and size, galaxies may ...onsist of as few as a billion or as many as a trillion stars. ...Not all of these are single stars but may appear as double ...r multiple stellar systems and star clusters. We use the ...erm galaxy to distinguish our home star system from all ...thers.

The structural principle of larger objects composed of ...everal or many similar smaller objects can be applied ...vith respect to galaxies to derive the existence of both ...maller and larger objects.

Galaxies form galactic groups and galactic clusters ...vhich may contain as many as several thousand indi-...idual galaxies, and several dozen galactic clusters may ...orm a supercluster. Superclusters are immense cosmic ...tructures, some of which measure more than a million ...ght years across and are separated by equally large ...oids. A million light years is the distance light travels in ...ne million years (moving at a speed of about 300,000 ...ilometers per second). Our galaxy and the Androme-...a Galaxy are the largest members of a galactic cluster ...nown as the Local Group.

Some stars – including our sun – have their own solar ...lanet systems. Astronomers have determined that there ...re other planet systems in the Milky Way besides our ...olar system.

tars and Interstellar Matter

...alactic matter appears not only in highly condensed ...orm as stars but also as finely distributed particles in ...louds of dust and gas which are observed through ... telescope as luminous nebulas. There is a very close ...elationship between this kind of matter, which scien-...sts refer to as interstellar matter because it is distrib-...ted between stars, and the early and late phases – the ...irth and death – in the development of stars. Stars form ...n and from interstellar matter. The greater their initial ...ass, the shorter their lifespans and the more forceful ...nd violent their deaths, which often occur in explosions ...volving the release of huge quantities of gas and dust.

All of the stars we have observed and named as indi-...idual objects belong to the Milky Way system. To facili-...te their location in the sky, ancient observers of the ...eavens assigned the visible stars to certain prominent ...elestial constellations. Since 1933, astronomers have ...efined constellations as specific rectangular sectors on ...he celestial sphere, which is divided into eighty-eight ...uch areas.

We notice three things immediately when we gaze at ...he nighttime sky: that all stars twinkle, that some are ...righter than others, and that they appear in different ...olors ranging from bluish or whitish to reddish-yellow. ...he twinkling effect is not produced by the stars them-...elves but by turbulence in the earth's atmosphere, while ...erceived differences in brightness depend upon the

relative distance of stars from the earth and on such factors as a star's size and tempera-ture. The color of a star is also a function of its temperature and the direction in which it is moving – toward or away from the observer. Stars are catego-rized within light and spectral classes on the basis of these characteristics.

The fact that stars seem to hang motionless in the sky has to do with their great dis-tance from us. They actually move through space at tremendous speeds, and their positions in the heavens change accordingly over the course of millennia. The con-stellation we know as the Big Dipper looked much differ-ent 100,000 years ago than it does now, and its shape will have changed again in another 100,000 years. Many stars classified as "changeable" exhibit changes in brightness over periods of several days or less, some of them, the novas or supernovas, as a result of massive explosions.

During the greater part of their lives, stars emit energy generated by nuclear fusion in their interiors at tempera-tures of up to several million degrees Fahrenheit.

The Unity of Nature

We are moved emotionally by the beauty of the heavens. By observing and measuring celestial bodies, we gain insight into the nature of the universe. Through thou-sands of years of increasingly precise observation of plan-ets, stars, solar systems, and galaxies, we have learned that the laws of nature discovered on earth apply to the universe as well, and this principle has become very useful in the exploration of space. It was the basis for the heuristic hypothesis that the information we obtain about outer space can be explained with the aid of laws of nature discovered on earth – scientific explanation of the universe would be impossible otherwise. This is the theory of the unity of nature.

Particularly useful aids to our study of space are the laws of mechanics, the theory of gravitation, and the laws of nuclear physics, particularly as they apply to spectral

analysis. The currently accepted theory of gravitation is Einstein's General Theory of Relativity. The nature of atoms and their interaction both with one another and with electromagnetic radiation are described by various quantum theories, most notably the theory of quantum mechanics.

By applying the laws of mechanics and the theory of gravitation, we have succeeded in computing the move-ment of objects in the universe – both man-made and natural objects, from spacecraft to galaxies. The use of spectral analysis in combination with quantum theory has enabled us to explain cosmic structures, from elemen-tary particles to atoms and molecules, and to describe the structures of such bodies as stars, stellar systems, and superclusters. Our capacity to describe and explain cov-ers a broad spectrum of phenomena, beginning with the Big Bang, the earliest phase in the history of the universe, and extending practically to the origin of life on earth. We know that our solar system is five billion years old and that the Milky Way has existed for twelve billion years in a universe that is now fourteen billion years old. And we have learned that the universe and space itself have been expanding since the very first moment of their existence.

Northern Lights
Polar light, popularly known as the Northern or Southern Lights, is produced in the earth's atmosphere, most often near the polar circles. It is caused by electrically charged atomic particles entering the atmosphere from outer space. The photograph is a wide-angle exposure of a polar light display taken in Norway.

Gazing into the Universe
Breaking away from the medieval concept of the self-enclosed world, represented as an attempt to gaze beyond the sphere of the fixed stars by a late-nineteenth-century art-ist painting in the style of the period around 1520.

The Big Dipper
Constellations have been a source of fascination to mankind since time immemorial. It was their beauty that attracted Caroline Herschel to astro-nomy. Although stellar constellations appear fixed and unchangeable to us, they actually do change over long periods of time. The illustration shows how the Big Dipper probably looked 100,000 years ago, how we see it today, and how it can be expected to appear 100,000 years from now.

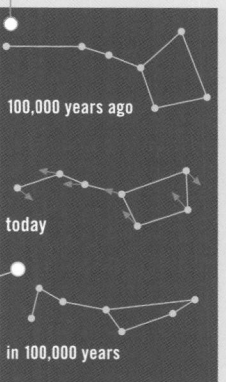

100,000 years ago

today

in 100,000 years

Caroline Herschel
"The object is a comet," she noted in her diary with respect to a new object she had discovered in the sky the night before. The astronomer Caroline Herschel (1750–1848) discovered several other comets during her lifetime. Her contribution helped shape the view of the world accepted by modern astronomers. She was awarded the Gold Medal of the London Astronomical Society in 1828.

The Solar System

Our Home Star and Its Orbiting Planets

The sun is just one star among billions in our galaxy, the Milky Way. The solar system comprises nine planets (and their moons): Mercury, Venus, Earth (one moon), Mars (2), Jupiter (16), Saturn (17), Uranus (15), Neptune (8), and the recently "demoted" Pluto (1) (see explanation on bottom of page 5), as well as numerous other smaller objects, such as comets, meteorites, and asteroids. Most asteroids are less than 100 km. in diameter, and nearly all of their paths pass between Mars and Jupiter. Unlike the stars, the planets, their moons, and the small celestial bodies emit no light and are visible to us only because they are illuminated by the sun.

Seen through a telescope, the planets appear as disks of various sizes. Images transmitted from spacecraft provide information about their surface features. The planets move along elliptical orbits on planes which deviate only slightly from that of the earth's orbit. Puzzled by apparent reversals of direction, ancient and medieval observers were unable to explain the motions of the planets as seen from the earth.

Key Data: The Sun	
Diameter:	1,392,000 km
Mass:	333,000 x earth mass
Mean density:	1.409 g/ccm
Distance from earth:	149.6 mill. km
Time of light travel sun–earth:	8 min 20 s

Key Data: The Moon	
Distance earth–moon:	384,403 km
Mass:	0.0123 x earth mass
Mean density:	3.341 g/ccm
Daytime temp.:	214°F
Nighttime temp.:	−240 °F

Planets	Mass (x earth mass)	Dens (g/cc
Mercury	0.055	5.43
Venus	0.815	5.24
Earth	1.000	5.52
Mars	0.107	3.93
Jupiter	318.0	1.33
Saturn	95.1	0.70
Uranus	14.4	1.3
Neptune	17.2	1.70
Pluto	0.002	1.7

Sizes and Distances

Because the inner, "earthlike" planets Mercury, Venus, Earth, and Mars are composed of metals and rock (rock planets), they are relatively dense. The outer, Jovian planets – Jupiter, Saturn, Uranus, Neptune – and the dwarf planet Pluto consist primarily of gases (including hydrogen, helium, and methane) and frozen water. The asteroid belt lies between the inner and outer planets. The distribution of light and heavy matter took place during the infancy of the solar system, as lighter materials condensed in the colder outer regions of the system. With the exception of Pluto, all of the other planets (known as giant planets) are considerably larger than the earth. The diameter of Jupiter is eleven times greater than that of the earth, that of Saturn almost ten times greater. The sun's diameter is ten times larger than Jupiter's. A comparison of the masses of the objects in the solar system reveals even more marked differences. Added together, the masses of all planets including Pluto amount to only 13% of the sun's mass, and Jupiter alone accounts for 70% of that total. Relative sizes and distances can be illustrated on the basis of the following example: The distance between the sun and Pluto is 5.9 billion kilometers. If the sun had a diameter of one meter, Pluto would measure two millimeters across, and the distance between the two would be four kilometers.

Born of a Cloud of Dust

Some five billion years ago, a cloud of interstellar dust began to condense, a reaction perhaps triggered by a nearby supernova. As gravitational forces increased, the core of the cloud grew increasingly dense, while the concentration of mass in the center accelerated the system's rotation. Gradually, a flat disk formed, from which the planets later emerged. Temperatures at the center of the disk approached eighteen million degrees F, generating nuclear fusion of the hydrogen atoms. The sun began to radiate. At its core, 655 million tons of hydrogen were converted into 650 million tons of helium every second, while five million tons of matter were transformed into energy. Five billion years from now, when its nuclear energy has been consumed, the sun will enter its final phase, at which point it will turn first into a red giant and later into a white dwarf.

The Earth's Reliable Heater

The sun produces temperatures of up to 27 million degrees F at its core. Pressure at that point is 200 billion times that recorded on the earth's surface. The visible surface of the sun is called the photosphere. It is about 400 km thick and has a mean temperature of 9,900 degrees F. Sunspots form where magnetic-field lines break through the surface. Granules (giant bubbles) measuring about 1,500 km in diameter form on the upper surface of the photosphere and bubble upward. Flames of gas (protuberances) shoot forth from the outer layer (the chromosphere), reaching heights up to tens of thousands of kilometers. The outer atmosphere of the sun (the corona) has a very low density and temperatures around 1.8 million degrees F. It extends beyond the photosphere to heights equivalent to several times the radius of the sun.

The Inner Planets

Mercury, the second-smallest planet after to Pluto, is closest to the sun. Humans could not possibly survive its surface temperatures of 780°F during the day and –325°F during the night. The atmosphere (helium, argon) above the moonlike, cratered landscape is extremely thin.

The surface of Venus is not visible from the earth. Thick clouds of carbon dioxide (96%), nitrogen (3%), and trace amounts of water vapor and other gases reflect 65% of the sun's rays, making Venus the third brightest object in the sky, after the sun and the moon. The greenhouse effect caused by its mantle of gases raises the surface temperatures of the planet's craters and lava fields (80%) to temperatures in the range of 850°F. There is no liquid water, and there are no rivers or oceans, only a few dunes.

The distance between the earth and the sun is favorable to life as we know it, and temperatures are neither too high nor too low.

People long assumed that there could be some form of life on Mars – intelligent or at least primitive life. The pattern of lines on the planet's surface thought to be a network of irrigation canals proved to be an optical illusion however, although valleys marked by meanders do suggest that rivers must have flowed through them at one time. The cold crater landscapes of the "Red Planet" (with lows at the winter polar caps reading -225°F) are marked by rocky deserts. The largest shield volcano on Mars is 700 km wide, 25 km high and presumably several hundred million years old.

The Smallest of the Group

Pluto, the planet in our solar system, was discovered in 1930. Its low surface temperature (−440 °F) cannot support a gaseous atmosphere, and existing gases were presumably frozen out long ago.

Middleweight 1

Little is known about Neptune's internal structure. Its density of 1.76 g/ccm suggests that it has a core of rock, probably surrounded by a mantle of frozen water, methane, ammonia, hydrogen and helium. Neptune's hydrogen atmosphere also contains helium and methane. Six of its eight moons were not discovered until 1989.

Predictable Relationships

The planets travel in elliptical orbits on planes which, unlike those of comet orbits, are "tilted" only slightly off the earth's orbital plane. The inner planets, Mercury, Venus, the earth, and Mars, are closest to the sun and receive more warming solar radiation than the distant outer planets, which accordingly much colder.

Middleweight 2

Seen through a telescope, Uranus appears as a blue-green disk without visible surface features. It was not until 1986 that Voyager 2 provided a more detailed picture, revealing cloud structures, the presence of a magnetic field, and ten previously undiscovered moons. The planet's greater density indicates a composition containing metals heavier than those on Saturn. Its atmosphere consists primarily of hydrogen and helium.

Our Moon

When Astronauts Armstrong and Aldrin took their first steps on the moon on July 21, 1969, they fulfilled an age-old human dream. Since then, plans have been in the making for a manned mission to Mars. Although that goal has yet to be achieved, a number of unmanned spacecraft have explored the depths of space as far away as Neptune.

The Blue Planet

The view from the porthole of a spacecraft shows how lost our planet is in space. Compared with the giant planets or the sun, it seems infinitely small. If mankind is to survive, we must manage our resources wisely. Viewed from outer space, our planet appears predominantly blue.

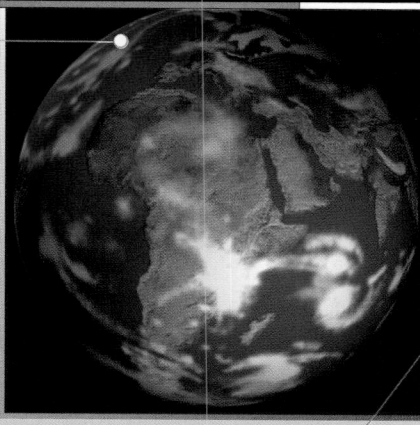

A Glaring Ball of Fire

Only when the sun is just above the horizon can we gaze at it without protecting our eyes. From this position, sunlight travels farther through the atmosphere, and the energy-laden blue rays are largely filtered out. Looking directly at the sun at midday without protection causes irreparable damage to the retina.

Giant Twins

The rings of Saturn and several of Jupiter's moons are clearly visible through even a small telescope. The giant planets Jupiter and Saturn are so large that the earth is dwarfed in comparison. Like other giant planets, Jupiter also has a system of rings, although it is not as prominent as that of Saturn. Both planets have many moons and are encircled by bands of clouds. Their atmospheres consist of hydrogen, helium and minute admixtures of methane and ammonia. Towards the interior, these gases pass through transitions from gaseous to liquid (on the planet's surface) to solid states (at their cores). The two giants have strong magnetic fields.

Io, the innermost planet of Jupiter, became famous through images sent back to earth by Voyager, which provided the first opportunity to observe extraterrestrial volcanic activity. Fountains of lava expelled at speeds of up to 1,000 m/s traveled as high as 300 m above the surrounding areas covered with multi-colored lava and frozen sulfur-dioxide.

It's not easy being Pluto

Originally considered an official planet, in August of 2006 the International Astronomical Union (IAU) downgraded Pluto to a dwarf planet.

According to new rules established by the IAU an offical planet must meet three criteria: 1) it must orbit the sun, 2) be large enough for gravity to have formed it into a sphere, and 3) it must have cleared other objects out of the way in its orbital neighborhood.

Since Pluto orbits among the many other icy objects of the Kuiper Belt – a distinct region beyond the orbit of Neptune – it does not meet the third criterion.

Mars

Venus

Mercury

Earth

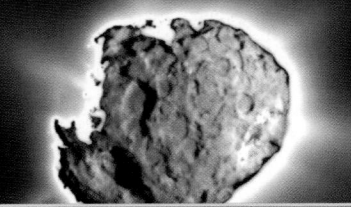

Comets & Asteroids

Space Dust, Science, and Superstition

Comets, and meteors – the streaks of light created by asteroids on a collision course with earth – have inspired awe and fear in cultures around the world since antiquity. To our ancestors, a blazing sword of fire tearing through the heavens was a message from angry, vengeful gods – a symbol of impending death and destruction. Babylonian mythology described fire, brimstone, and flood with the arrival of a comet. Roman prophecies told of a "great conflagration from the sky, falling to earth." Extensive Chinese comet atlases, dating back to at least 240 BC, chronicle the mysterious appearances and trajectories of hundreds of "long-tailed pheasant stars" and associate them with natural disasters. In 1456, Pope Calixtus III went so far as to excommunicate Halley's Comet as an instrument of the devil because it coincided with the Turkish invasion of the Balkans.

Eyes to the Skies

Although most comets are too small or too faint to be seen without the aid of a telescope, the characteristic cosmic glow of Halley's Comet or Comet Hyakutake is clearly visible to the naked eye. In 1997, the most active comet in more than 400 years, Hale-Bopp came to within 197 million kilometers of Earth and wowed scientists and casual observers alike with a spectacular display for some 500 days.

How do these interstellar objects light up the evening sky from hundreds of millions of kilometers away? Comets and asteroids are packed with rocks, ice, dust—and volumes of information about the beginnings of our solar system and the birth of our planet.

Anatomy of a Dirty Snowball

The core, or nucleus, of a comet is a solid ball of ice and gas interspersed with small amounts of dust. A black layer of dust and rock covers most of the ice, which is why comets are sometimes referred to as "dirty snowballs" or "icy mudballs." As the comet's orbit brings it closer to the sun, or inner solar system, ice on the surface of the nucleus is converted to gas and creates the coma – a dense cloud of water, carbon dioxide, and other gases present in the nucleus. The coma grows larger and fluoresces as the comet becomes hotter. The sun's radiation pushes dust particles away from the coma, creating the dust tail, while fast-moving electrically charged particles stream away from the coma to form the ion tail. The dust tail, which is the most visible part of a comet to the naked eye, can reach up to 10 million km; the ion tail can grow to over 100 million km.

Comets lose ice and dust during each journey around the sun and over time can become less active or dormant. If a comet burns off its entire core of ice, it may dissipate into clouds of dust or turn into an inactive rocky formation much like an asteroid.

Origins of Comets – The Oort Cloud and Kuiper Belt

Halley's Comet is not only the most famous "dirty snowball," it is also the first comet to be defined as periodic – it becomes visible to the naked eye once about every 76 years, as its orbit approaches the sun. In his book, A Synopsis of the Astronomy of Comets, Edmund Halley (1656–1742) asserted that the comets of 1531, 1607 and 1682 were in fact a single comet, and predicted that it would return in 1758. Halley was correct, and the comet was named in his honor.

Short-period comets, such as Halley's Comet, take than 200 years to orbit the sun and move along a p near the orbits of other planets. The gravitational of the outer planets can bump objects out of the Kui belt – a region beyond Neptune – toward the sun wh they become active comets. A dozen or so "new" con are discovered each year, most of which are short-pe comets that orbit the sun in periods ranging between and 200 years.

Comets that take more than 200 years to orbit the are known as long-period comets and are far less c mon than their short-period counterparts. Long-per comets are found in the Oort Cloud around the o edge of our solar system. Because the sun's phys and gravitational effects are extremely weak in the C Cloud – located 1,000 times farther away from the than Pluto – the billions of comets and other icy bo found there are easily nudged out of orbit by the for exerted by passing stars. Long-period comets bum out of their orbits in the Oort Cloud may be obser in the inner solar system on occasion, although they never be seen again – one trip around the sun can t as long as 30 million years.

Close Encounters with Asteroids and Meteorites

Sometimes called minor planets, asteroids are r nant rocks from the formation of the solar system 4.6 lion years ago. They are significantly smaller than con – the largest asteroid, Ceres, has a diameter of about 1 km. If the total mass of all asteroids was gathered i a single object, scientists estimate such an object wc be less than 1,500 km across (less than half the diame of our moon).

Asteroids orbit the sun in the Asteroid Belt or M Belt located between Mars and Jupiter. This area of solar system probably contains millions of astero

(Comet Neat)

Comet C/2001 Q4 (NEAT) was discovered on August 24, 2001, by the Near Earth Asteroid Tracking (NEAT) system operated by NASA's Jet Propulsion Laboratory, Pasadena, CA. In the image to the right, a brilliant cloud of dust and gas surround the tail of the comet as it passes through the inner solar system in 2004. The image was taken with the Mosaic I camera, which has a one-square degree field of view, or about five times the size of the Moon. Even with this large field of view, only the comet's coma and the inner portion of its tail are visible. This color image was assembled by combining images taken through blue, green and red filters.

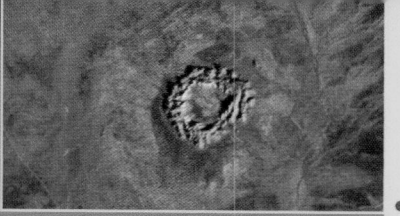

Comets & Asteroids

...ging in size from 1,000 km in diameter to bodies less ...n 1 km across. As asteroids orbit around the Sun, Jupi-...'s gravity and close encounters with Mars or nearby ...eroids can knock them out of the Main Belt toward ...e orbits of the planets. For example, some scientists ...ieve Mars' moons, Phobos and Deimos, may be cap-...ed asteroids. Near-Earth asteroids (NEAs) have orbits ...t bring them within 195 million km of the sun. It is ...ieved that most NEAs are fragments jarred from the ...in belt by a combination of asteroid collisions and the ...vitational influence of Jupiter. Some NEAs may be the ...clei of dead, short-period comets.

...Scientists classify asteroids according to how well ...y reflect or absorb light – bright objects reflect light; ...k objects absorb light. Using this system, asteroids are ...ted into 3 groups: C-type, S-type, M-type. Seventy-five ...cent of known asteroids are C-type (carbonaceous), ...ery dark rock with a composition similar to the sun. ...venteen percent are S-type (silicaceous), a relatively ...ght rock composed of metallic iron mixed with iron ...d magnesium silicates. The remaining asteroids are ...atively bright with a metallic iron composition and ...designated M-type (metallic).

...Much of our knowledge about asteroids comes from ...mining space debris that reaches the Earth. An aster-...or asteroid collision fragment with an orbit that will ...llide with the Earth's is called a meteoroid. The glow-...object that zips across the sky is a meteoroid. Often ...erred to as a falling star, "meteor" is the term for the ...eak of light that shoots through the sky. When the ...teoroid reaches the earth, it is called a "meteorite."

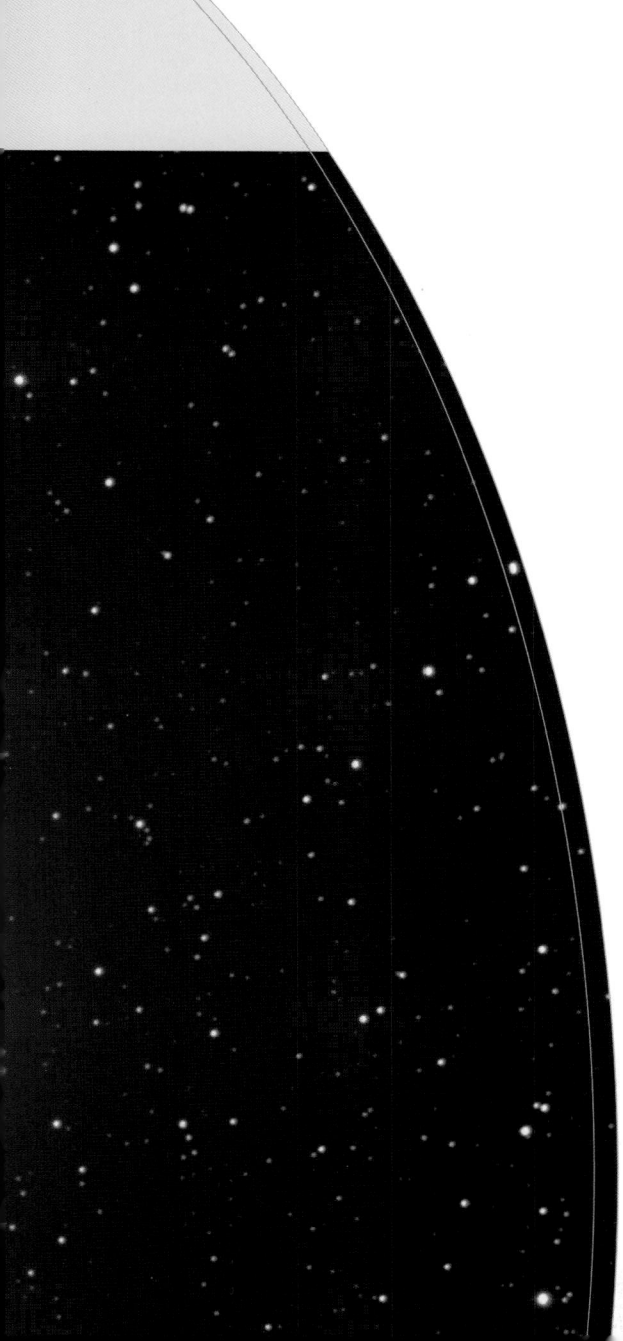

Comet Hale-Bopp is Discovered

On July 23, 1995, an unusually bright comet outside of Jupiter's orbit (7.15 AU!) was discovered independently by Alan Hale, New Mexico and Thomas Bopp, Arizona. The new comet, designated C/1995 O1, is the farthest ever discovered by amateurs and appeared 1000 times brighter than Comet Halley did at the same distance. Normally, comets are inert when they are beyond the orbit of Jupiter, so it has been speculated that Comet Hale-Bopp is either rather large, or experienced a bright outburst (or both). The comet is the brightest comet since Comet West in 1976. From Hubble Space Telescope images, the comet's diameter has been determined to be about 40 km.

Asteroid Ida

Ida is the second asteroid ever encountered by a spacecraft. It appears to be about 52 kilometers (32 miles) in length. Ida is an irregularly shaped asteroid placed by scientists in the S class (believed to be like stony or stony iron meteorites). It is a member of the Koronis family, presumed fragments left from the breakup of a precursor asteroid in a catastrophic collision.

Artist's Concept of Deep Impact

Comets are time capsules that hold clues about the formation and evolution of the solar system. They are composed of ice, gas and dust, primitive debris from the solar system's distant and coldest regions that formed 4.5 billion years ago. Deep Impact, a NASA Discovery Mission, is the first space mission to probe beneath the surface of a comet and reveal the secrets of its interior.

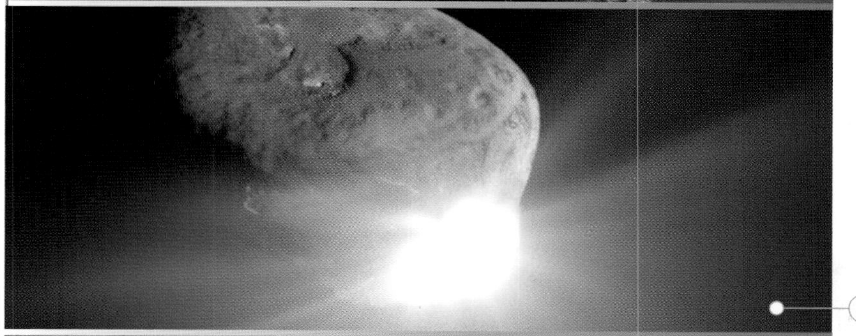

Deep Impact Mission Accomplished

On July 4, 2005, the Deep Impact spacecraft arrived at Comet Tempel 1 to impact it with a 370-kg (~820-lbs) mass, creating a crater estimated to be up to 800 feet in diameter. Deep Impact has yielded unexpected results about the structure and composition of comets. Mission scientists found the first definitive evidence of water ice on the surface of a comet. Analysis of the ejection plume indicated that comets contain a substantial amount of organic material and thus could have brought such material to Earth early in the planet's history.

Arizona's Impact Crater

The Meteor Crater in Arizona was the first crater to be identified as an impact crater. It is believed to have been formed 20,000 to 50,000 years ago when a small asteroid about 80 feet in diameter impacted the Earth. The crater is the best preserved crater on Earth and measures 1.2 km in diameter. For many years, scientists had doubted that there were any impact craters on Earth. The origin of this crater has been a source of controversy for many years. The discovery of fragments from the Canyon Diablo Meteorite helped prove that the feature is in fact an impact crater.

Planet Earth

... and it truly does move!

If we could look from a great distance at the supposedly firm and motionless ground on which we normally stand, we would see that it is anything but motionless. Our Earth is a dynamic celestial body which rotates on its own axis and revolves around the sun. The very point at which we stand moves along a complicated orbit through space.

Dancing on a Volcano

An entirely different kind of motion involving shifts in the positions of points on Earth relative to one another ordinarily takes place unnoticed and so slowly that extraordinarily precise instruments are required to prove that it occurs at all. Yet a time-lapse film in which 10 million years are compressed into a single second would provide striking evidence of how much the Earth's appearance has changed since prehistoric times and become the planet we know today. The key terms used to describe this process are "continental drift" and "plate tectonics." The only effects of these changes we perceive directly are the – often disastrous – earthquakes and seaquakes, frequently followed by massive tidal waves, that frequently accompany movements of the large plates in the uppermost layers of the Earth's crust.

Like our perceptions of the positions and movements of objects in the sky, much of what we experience on Earth – the alternation of day and night, the changing seasons – is caused by the motion of the Earth. The alternation of day and night would seem easy enough to explain: The Earth turns completely around its own axis every 24 hours, and thus every place on Earth experiences a sunrise and a sunset. But wait! There are regions on Earth in which the sun doesn't rise for months and doesn't set

again until more months have passed: the polar zones within the Arctic and Antarctic Circles. These periods of time are referred to as polar nights and polar days.

The cause of both – and for the changing seasons everywhere on Earth – is the fact that the Earth's rotational axis is inclined 23.5 degrees to the plane of the Earth's orbit around the sun. Because the angle of the Earth's axis does not change as it revolves around the sun – its northern extension always points towards the North Star – one hemisphere is always closer to the sun: the northern hemisphere during the northern summer and the southern hemisphere during the northern winter. Only at the spring and fall equinoxes, when days and nights are equally long, are the northern and southern hemispheres exposed to the same intensity of solar radiation.

Moon – Calendar – Clock

The Earth has a constant companion on its journey around the sun – the moon. The movements of the Earth and the moon are the basis for our reckoning of time, the rhythm of our clocks, and our calendar system. The corresponding units of time are days, months, and years – the interval between one arrival of the sun at its zenith and the next; the period between full moons, and the length of time it takes the Earth to complete a full revolution around the sun. Precise astronomical observations are required to measure the lengths of these periods. Ancient astronomers discovered that neither a revolution of the Earth around the sun nor of the moon around the Earth equated to a full number of revolutions of the Earth around its own axis. There are approximately 365 ¼ days in a year and about 29 ½ days in a (lunar) month. That is what makes designing a precise, reliable calendar such

a difficult matter. Sophisticated correction systems required to keep the calendar in step with the moveme of the celestial bodies. Depending upon the system in these systems involve the addition of additional day months to the calendar at regular intervals (in leap ye for example).

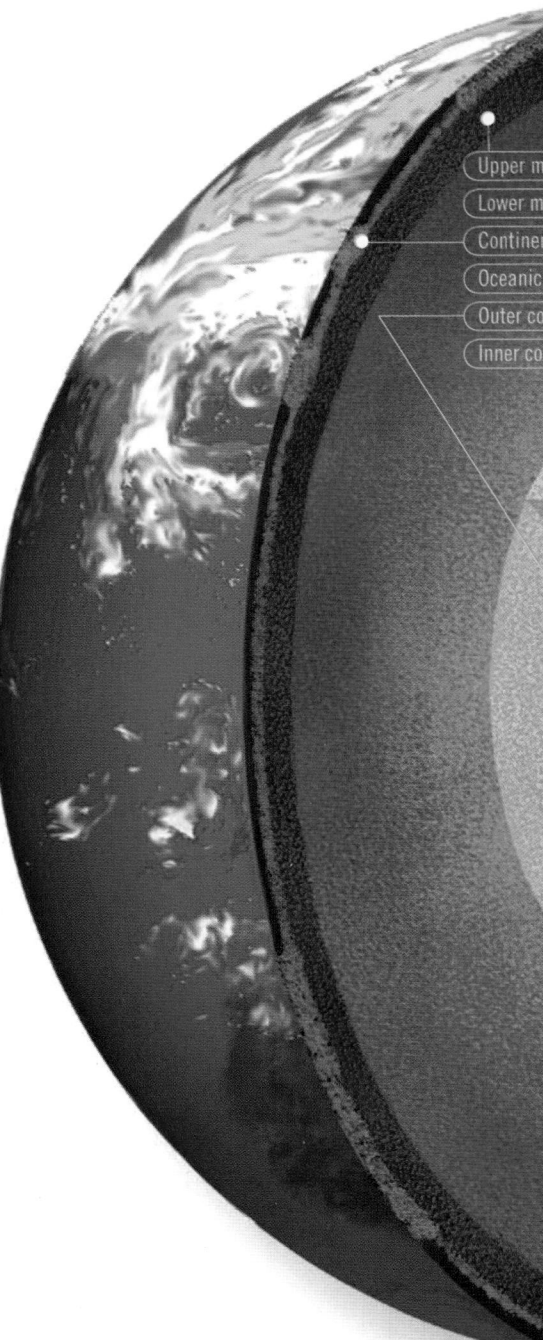

Upper ma
Lower ma
Continen
Oceanic
Outer cor
Inner cor

Light and Shadow

During a solar eclipse, the moon passes between the Earth and the sun, whereas a lunar eclipse occurs when the moon moves through the shadow cast by the Earth and thus grows dark. Depending upon their relative positions the sun and the moon may totally or only partially obscured. We can observe a total eclipse of the sun from a place at which the moon's umbra falls. During a total lunar eclipse, the moon is encompassed entirely within the Earth's umbra.

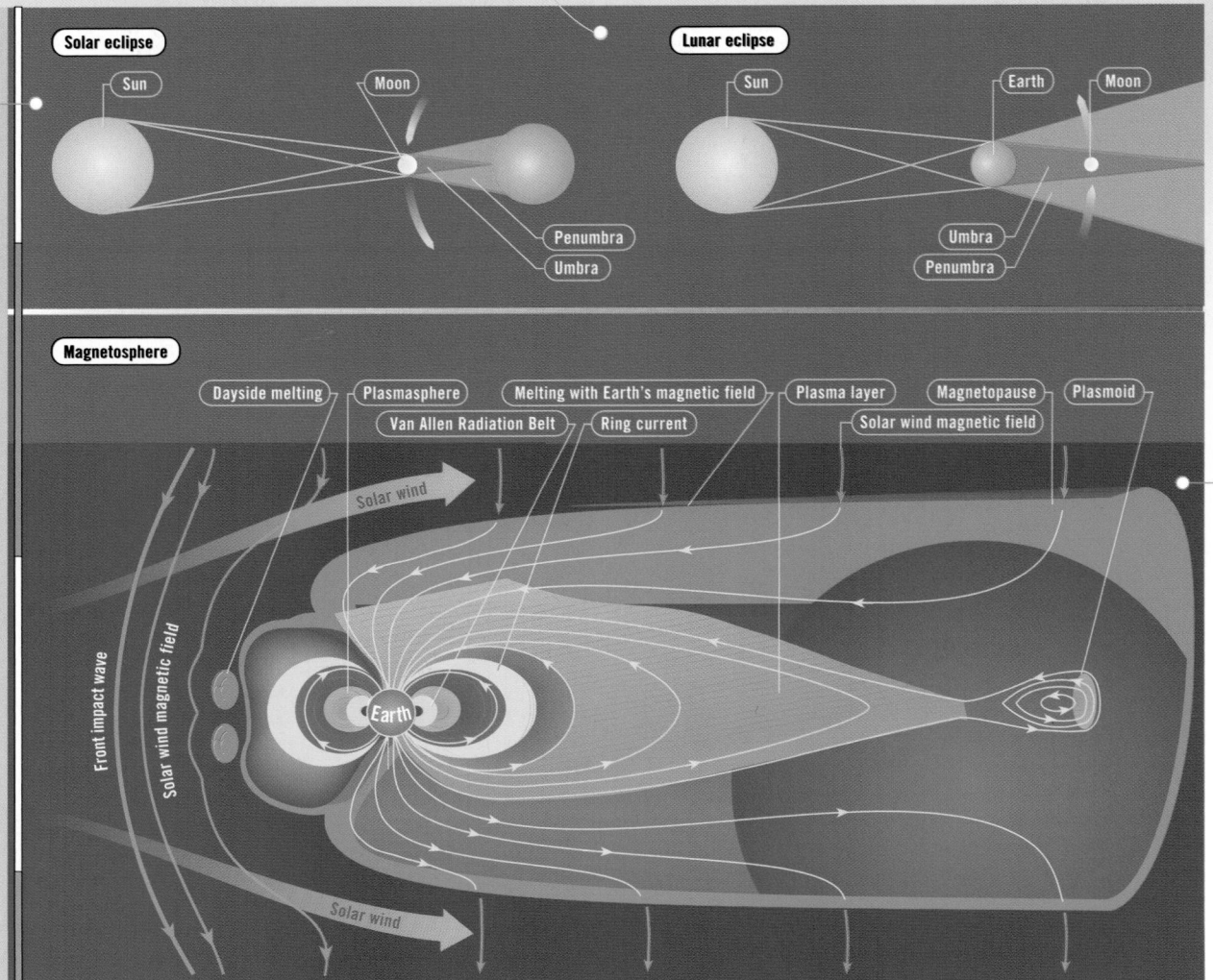

Solar eclipse

Sun | Moon

Penumbra
Umbra

Lunar eclipse

Sun | Earth | Moon

Umbra
Penumbra

Magnetosphere

Dayside melting | Plasmasphere | Melting with Earth's magnetic field | Plasma layer | Magnetopause | Plasmoid
Van Allen Radiation Belt | Ring current | Solar wind magnetic field

Solar wind

Front impact wave

Solar wind magnetic field

Earth

Solar wind

An Invisible Cloak

Generated within the Earth's core, the Earth magnetic field is shaped and limited by solar wind, a stream of electrically charged particles emitted by the sun. The space it encloses is known as the magnetosphere. On the side of the Earth facing the sun, the magnetosphere extends to a distance equivalent to between 10 and 20 Earth radii. On the opposite side of the Earth, it pulls a tail measuring some 1,000 Earth radii in length. In the Van Allen radiation belt, electrically charged particles captured from cosmic radiation by the magnetosphere move back and forth between the Earth's magnetic poles. The term "plasma" denotes a gas consisting of positively and negatively charged particles, whose charges offset one another. Plasmoids are lumps of plasma that are cut off and catapulted from tail of the magnetosphere.

ccasional corrections to clock time are required, usu-
ly in late June and/or late December, for a different
ason: the irregular rotation of the Earth. This irregu-
rity was not discovered until the 1930s, following the
vention of quarz clocks that were more exact than the
arth's own rotation. These smaller corrections involve
e addition of leap seconds.

The Earth Seen from Space

Although mankind has long
been aware that the Earth is an
object in space, like the sun and
the moon, people did not truly
appreciate that fact until the age
of space exploration began in the
early sixties. The image shows an
early docking maneuver during
the Gemini 8 mission in 1966.

**A Glowing Hot Core
inside a Cool Shell**

In terms of its static structure, the
Earth can be divided roughly into
a crust, a mantle, and a core. We
distinguish between the upper and
the lower mantle, while the core
consists of an outer and an inner
core. The crust and the mantle are
composed of rock, while the core
consists primarily of iron and nickel.
The outer core (iron and iron oxide)
is molten liquid. The inner core (iron
and nickel) is solid. The continental
crust is considerably thicker than
the oceanic crust.

The Seasons

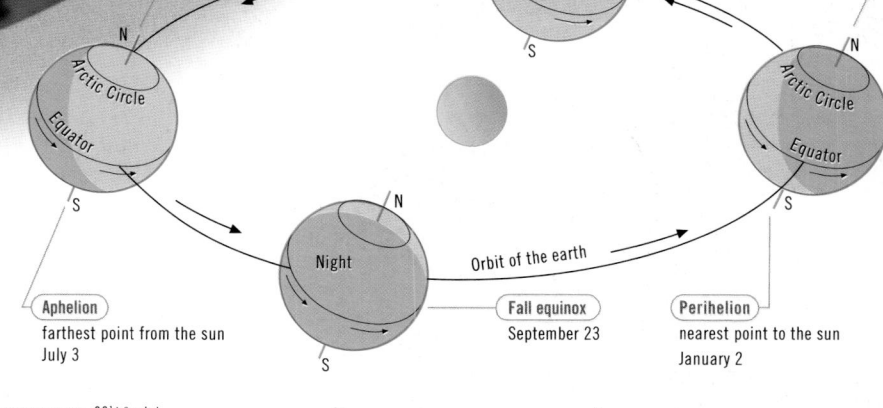

Summer solstice June 21	**Spring equinox** March 21 — Day — **Winter solstice** December 21
Arctic Circle / Equator / N / S	Night — Orbit of the earth
Aphelion farthest point from the sun July 3	**Fall equinox** September 23 — **Perihelion** nearest point to the sun January 2

e a Tilted Top

asonal temperature differences
e attributable to the fact that the
rth's rotational axis is not pre-
ely perpendicular to the plane
its orbit around the sun. As a
ult, the Earth tips its northern
ar region toward the sun during
e northern summer, while the
uthern polar region is inclined
ward the sun during the north-
n winter. In the first case, the
thern hemisphere is exposed
stronger solar radiation; in the
cond, it is the southern hemi-
here that is bathed in warmer
nlight. At the spring and autumn

equinoxes, when days and nights
are of equal length, the northern
and southern hemispheres are
exposed to the same amount of
solar radiation.

The larger figures representing the
Earth illustrate the distribution of
sunlight at the summer solstice
(around June 21st, on the left)
and at the winter solstice (around
December 21st, on the right).

The amount of warmth received by
the various regions of the globe,
and thus the temperature characteristics of the four seasons,
depend largely upon the angle at

which solar radiation reaches the
Earth, which is in turn a function
of the time of day, geographic latitude, and the time of year.

The elliptical shape of the Earth's
orbit also exerts a small influence
on temperatures. At the most
distant (aphelion) and the nearest
points (perihelion) to the sun, the
distance between the Earth and
the sun is 1.7 per cent greater or
smaller than its mean distance.
Thus at these points, solar radiation is also nearly 3.5 per cent
stronger or weaker, respectively.

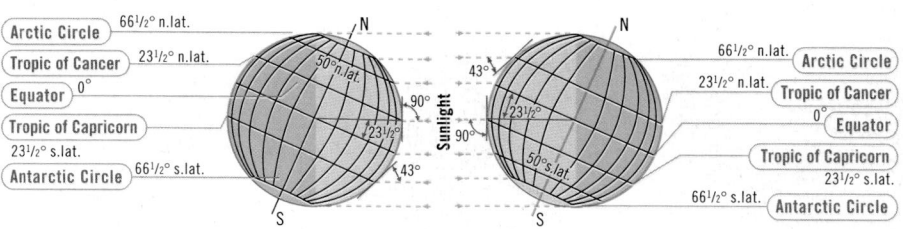

Arctic Circle	$66\frac{1}{2}°$ n.lat.			$66\frac{1}{2}°$ n.lat.	Arctic Circle
Tropic of Cancer	$23\frac{1}{2}°$ n.lat.			$23\frac{1}{2}°$ n.lat.	Tropic of Cancer
Equator	$0°$			$0°$	Equator
Tropic of Capricorn	$23\frac{1}{2}°$ s.lat.			$23\frac{1}{2}°$ s.lat.	Tropic of Capricorn
Antarctic Circle	$66\frac{1}{2}°$ s.lat.			$66\frac{1}{2}°$ s.lat.	Antarctic Circle

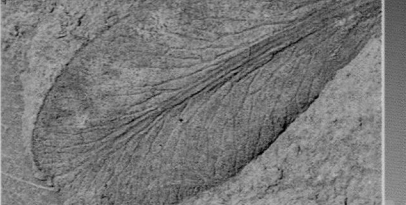

Drifting Lithospheric Plates

The Evolution of Continents and Oceans

Meteorologist Alfred Wegener first presented his hypothesis of continental drift at a geologists' conference in Frankfurt in 1912. He later published a detailed discussion of his theory of continental division and drift in his book Die Entstehung der Kontinente und Ozeane (The Origins of Continents and Oceans, 1915), showing evidence of astounding similarities between geological structures, rock, fossils, and fossilized climatic evidence on both sides of the Atlantic.

Seams in the Earth

Geologist Eduard Suess had previously postulated the existence of a huge Paleozoic continent (Gondwana). Based upon the same concept, Wegener now reconstructed a supercontinent called Pangaea, which originally encompassed all of the Earth's land masses and later broke apart. His bold ideas were almost unanimously rejected by geologists, and it was not until 50 years later that studies based on new research methods confirmed his work.

Plate Tectonics, the New View of the Earth

The lithosphere consists of about twelve large plates and a number of smaller ones, all of which drift over the upper crust of the Earth. In the course of geological history, they have collided, drifted past one another, separated, and broken up into new plate segments. Beneath the continents, they are between 80 and 120 km thick, but they are much thinner under the oceans (30–70 km). The largest plate (the Pacific Plate) measures 12,000 km in diameter. Given its expansive horizontal dimensions, the lithosphere is very thin. Plates move at speeds ranging

from one to 18 cm per year. Where their edges collide or overlap, the earth quakes, forming mountain ranges, faults, and volcanoes. Plates drifting apart create oceanic trenches, continental margins, and mid-oceanic ridges.

Beneath the lithosphere is the asthenosphere which in its upper region where it meets the lithosphere, is semi-plastic and near the melting point, and thus acts as a lubricant over which the plates can glide. The underlying crust is solid but not completely rigid. Slow movement is possible there under the influence of high temperatures and pressure.

Hot Currents Move Segments of the Earth's Crust

Convection currents in the mantle set the plates in motion. When one plate begins to drift, the others are moved as well. Some 500 million years ago, the continents were distributed widely over the surface of the Earth. But they later converged to form the supercontinent Pangaea. The remainder of the globe was covered by the superocean Panthalassa, which continued to expand into Pangaea north of the equator. The east-west arm of the sea (Tethys) eventually split the great land mass apart,

Remnants of Gondwana
Massive mainland deposits of sandstone dating primarily from the Carboniferous and the Permian periods are found on all of the continents of ancient Gondwana. In southern Africa, they are referred to as Karoo formations (photo: western rim of the Groot Karoo). They contain fossils from a variety of climates ranging from humid to arid, as the continents have drifted through many different climate zones.

forming Laurasia and Gondwana. These two continen[t] also broke apart as time passed. The present-day distr[i]bution of land and sea is only a momentary state. Ind[ia] has already joined Eurasia, and Africa is approaching [?] "Panta rhei" (everything is in flux), declared the Gree[k] philosopher Heraclitus with reference to this perpetu[al] process of growth, change, and decline.

Scientists began exploring the ocean floor with the a[id] of sonar in 1945. The mid-oceanic ridges were discove[r]ed, along with such phenomena as seafloor spreadi[ng] and subduction, the underthrusting of heavy ocean[ic] plates beneath lighter continental plates. More recentl[y] measurements of magnetic anomalies and radiometr[ic] rock dating techniques have shed new light on the pr[o]cesses involved in plate tectonics.

Disappearing Crust
When one oceanic plate slides beneath another in a process known as subduction, oceanic trenches and island chains are formed. Steeper subduction produces straighter trenches and island chains. Abrupt subduction triggers earthquakes at depths of up to 700 km. The underlying plate becomes soft and begins to melt. Cracks form in the overriding plate; parts break away and are thrust downward. The movement of the sinking plate may be blocked, forming bulges which in turn raise previously sunken volcanic islands to the surface again. Lighter

oceanic sediments are not carried deep into the Earth's crust. They accumulate along with rock from the volcanic chain in deep-sea trenches, some of which are more than 10,000 meters deep. Deformed, partially folded, and thrust above the ocean surface at certain points, this chaotic mass (mélange) builds an accretionary prism that can form a chain of islands off the main volcanic chain. Volcanoes are formed by rising granodoritic magma above the area where the sinking plate begins to melt. Interarc basins, in which spread zones sink or are forced apart, are created behind

the main chain. This opens channels through which lava flows to the surface.

Hot Spots and Wandering Volcanoes
In the lower crust, 2,900 m below the Earth's surface, matter along the boundary to the outer core is heated so intensely that basalt magma plumes are forced upward through the lower and upper crust. At the surface, shield volcanoes are formed above these hot spots (Hawaii is a good example). New volcanoes are created wherever oceanic crust drifts over the stationary hot spots. The extinct

volcanoes in a thus created island chain are eroded and gradually submerge. Hot spots are also found beneath continents.

Building New Crust
Hot streams of magma in the crust underneath mid-oceanic ridges thrust the relatively thin oceanic plate upward, breaking it apart. Basalt lava emerges beneath the sea and closes the fissures in the crust. On both sides of the fault line, the crust drifts in the direction of the subduction zone where it is melted deep inside the Earth. Since plates drift at different speeds, transform faults emerge

along the ridge. Larger volcanic islands (Iceland is an example) form at certain points. Mid-oceanic ridges can reach elevations of over 3,000 m. Oceanic crust in ocean basins is no more than 160 million years old. Only recently discovered, black smokers are hydrothermal vents – hot springs on the seafloor. They release water containing hydrogen sulphide at temperatures of over 630 °F, from which sulphide minerals precipitate in the cold water at the bottom of the ocean.

High Mountain Ranges at the Edges of Continental Plates
Deep-ocean trenches, accretiona[ry] ry prisms, and marginal trenches filled with sediment also form where oceanic plates subduct beneath continental plates. The continental crust is folded, broke[n] apart, and raised in some places[.] Intrusions of granite magma occ[ur] often forming magma chambers [?] from which magma is extruded and frequently rises to the surfac[e.] High mountain chains (orogenes) topped by shield volcanoes are created at these points. Plate se[g]ments drift apart in the spread

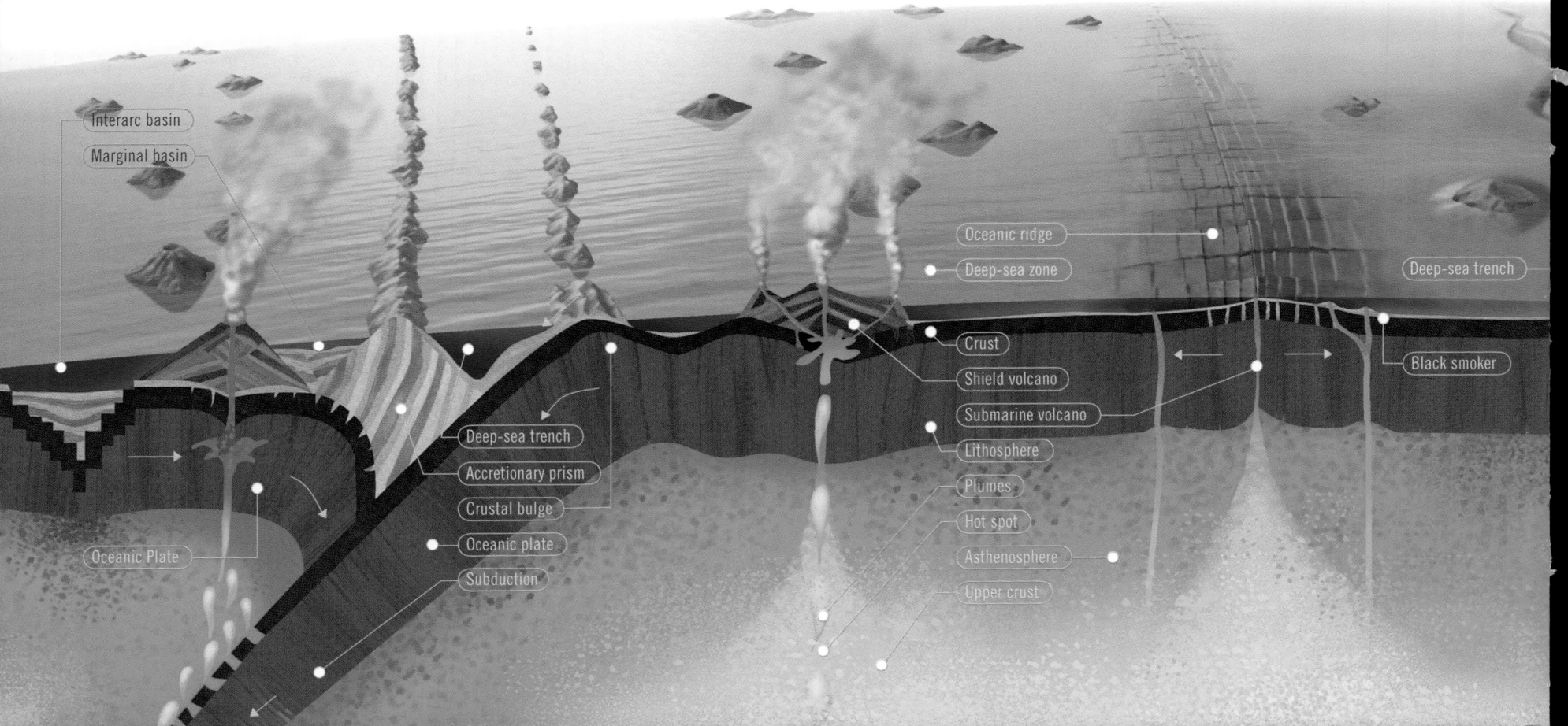

Interarc basin
Marginal basin
Oceanic ridge
Deep-sea zone
Deep-sea trench
Crust
Shield volcano
Submarine volcano
Lithosphere
Black smoker
Deep-sea trench
Accretionary prism
Plumes
Crustal bulge
Hot spot
Oceanic plate
Asthenosphere
Oceanic Plate
Subduction
Upper crust

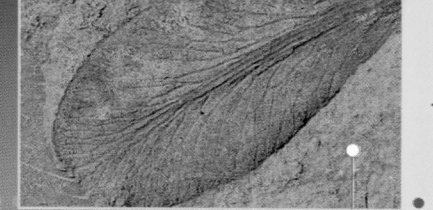

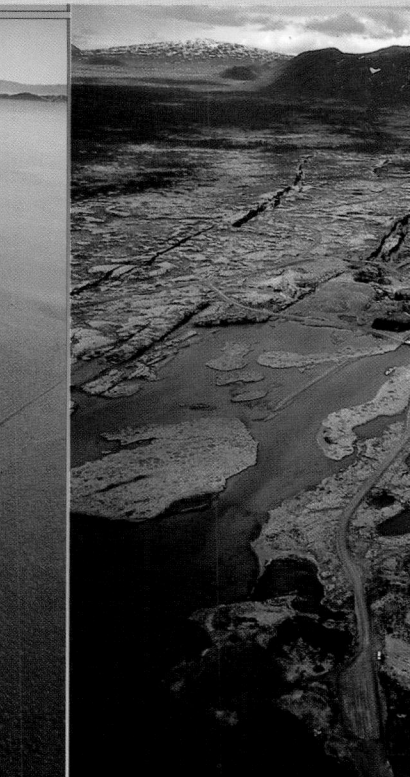

Prehistoric Evidence

A fossilized leaf of glossopteris, a tree-shaped fern that flourished in cool to temperate regions of Gondwana near the poles from the Carboniferous to the Jurassic. Its distribution is further evidence of the existence of the ancient continent as a contiguous land mass.

Plates Drifting Apart in Iceland

The Mid-Atlantic Ridge rises from the sea in Iceland. The North American Plate drifts toward the west, the Eurasian Plate toward the east. A young, still active volcanic zone runs through the middle of the island. The photo shows the Thingvellir Plain at the edge of the Almannagjá Gorge.

tes Drifting Past Each her in California

ng the San Andreas Fault California, the Pacific Plate ght-hand side of the illustra- n), which forms the edge the North American continent, ushed horizontally against North American Plate (on the c) towards the viewer – that to the northwest. Along the lt line, both plates are slightly vated and heavily scarred by sion.

es in the interior of the conti- t, producing rift valleys. Magma es at the rift lines, forming salt floors and volcanoes. These salt floors often reach massive d expansive proportions.

ung Oceans, Old Shields

eanic rifts eventually grow so le that new crust is formed by gma rising from below. This rks the birth of a new ocean. e rift often fills with fresh water g. the lakes of East Africa), ch is later mixed with inflow- seawater. The collision of two tinental plates may lead to

subduction when the rock is too light to penetrate into the heavier material of the upper crust. This causes overthrusting, which creates formations up to 80 km thick (as in the Himalayas). The continental plates have grown larger over the course of geological history. Only in the continental plates have crust segments (shields) several million years old survived as the only remaining evidence of the Earth's early history.

Continents in Motion

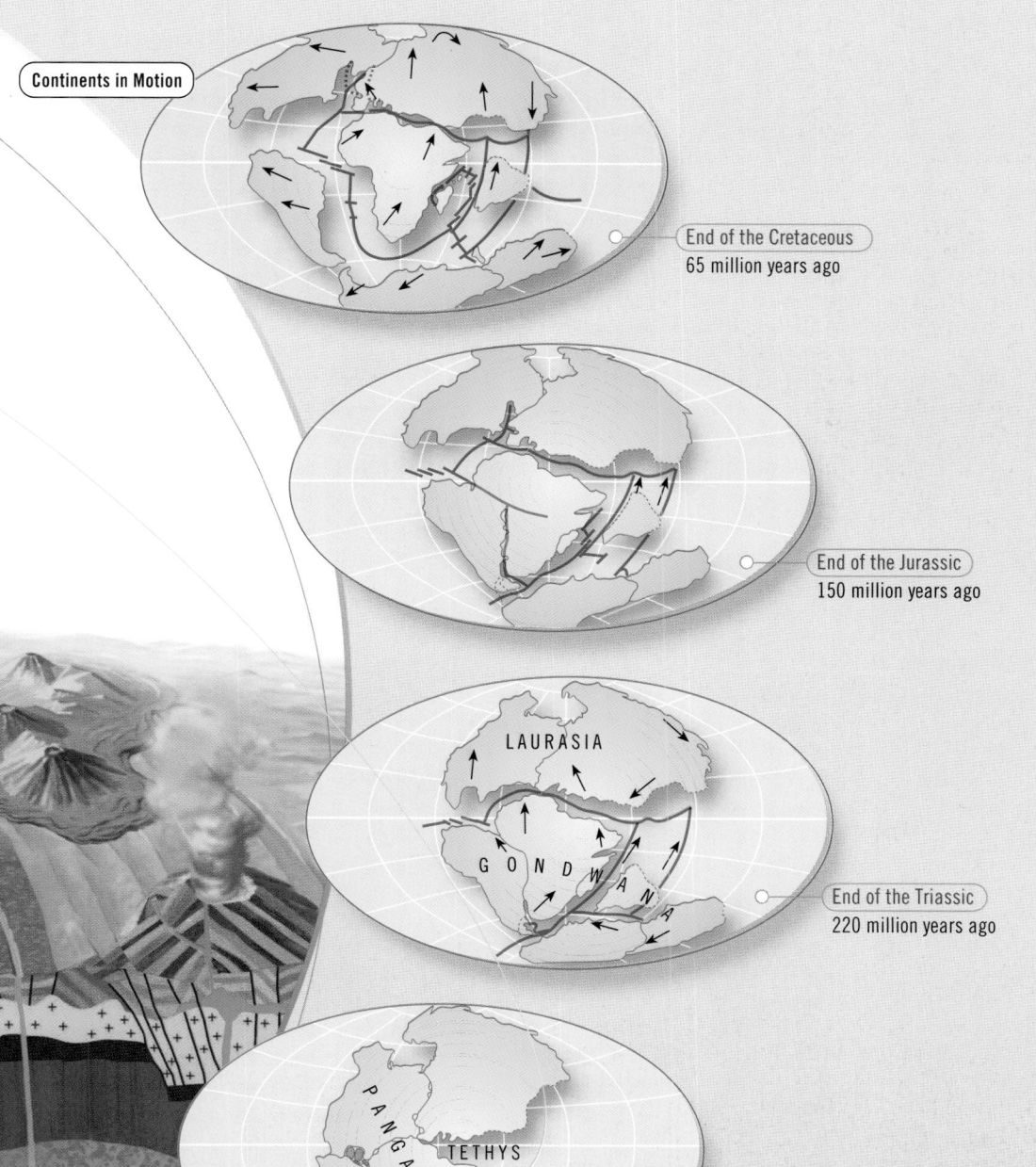

End of the Cretaceous
65 million years ago

End of the Jurassic
150 million years ago

LAURASIA

GONDWANA

End of the Triassic
220 million years ago

PANGAEA

TETHYS

End of the Paleozoic
250 million years ago

mountain ranges
Foothills
Coastal plain
Basalt floor
Stratovolcano
Granite
Fault tectonics
Magma chamber
Continental plate
Deep earthquake
Melt zone

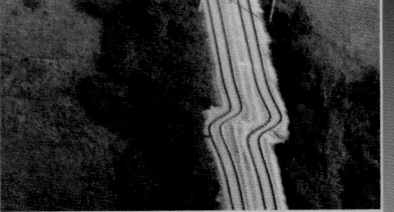

Earthquakes - Danger from the Depths

When the ground begins to shake beneath our feet

Well into the Middle Ages, earthquakes were regarded as the work of mythical, supernatural beings or signs of the wrath of God. The quake that destroyed Lisbon in cataclysmic waves of fire and flooding on November 1, 1775 caused many people to wonder about the validity of prevailing philosophical systems. Could anyone still look upon our world as the "best of all possible worlds," as a planet governed by reliable natural laws?

And why had Lisbon, of all places, a city of churches and monasteries devoted to piety, been singled out by God for such terrible punishment? That earthquake marked the beginning of the science of seismology. The Portuguese minister Pombal had reports compiled by observers all over the country. The British engineer John Michell computed the speed of the shock waves. Questions were raised about the origin and the causes of the quake.

The Restless Earth

Although we rarely notice it, the Earth's crust is constantly moving. The oceans and atmosphere are subject to patterns of natural motion, and so are the seemingly fixed landmasses of the continents, though their movements are so slow that we do not perceive them. Much more obvious – and dangerous – are the brief (lasting less than a minute), abrupt, and rapid shifts of larger segments of crust caused by tensions inside the Earth. The amplitude of these movements of ground may amount to as much as several decimeters. The energy released in the process spreads in the form of elastic waves through the Earth's interior: longitudinal and transverse waves. Longitudinal waves (also known as P or primary waves) move faster and arrive at a given distant point sooner than transverse waves (S or secondary waves). The slowest but most highly energized waves are surface waves (L and Rayleigh waves).

The source of an earthquake, known as the focus or hypocenter, may be near the surface or deep within the Earth's crust. Based upon its distance from the epicenter, the point of greatest surface movement, seismologists distinguish between shallow, intermediate, and deep-focus earthquakes. At depths below 720 km, rock is so soft and malleable that no abrupt shifts occur.

On average, 10,000 earthquakes classified as grade 4 or higher on the Richter Scale are recorded annually. Between 10 and 15 of these cause significant damage. In 1999, more than 22,000 people died as a result of earthquakes, while the average death toll for the preceding years is about 10,000. Some 15 percent of the Earth's land area is subject to severe earthquake activity. Another 40 percent is classified as virtually risk-free.

Measuring Earthquake Energy and Effects

Earthquakes are registered and recorded in seismograms using highly sensitive measuring instruments known as seismographs. The direction, distance, and energy of an earthquake can be derived from the data in the seismogram, i.e. the amplitude of the waves generated by an earthquake. Energy is expressed as magnitude, which is computed on the basis of ground amplitude, wave duration, and a calibration function. Earthquakes are classified on the Richter Scale of Earthquake Magnitude according to the maximum amplitude measured at a distance of 100 km from the epicenter. Magnitude values range from zero to between 7.7 and 8.6, but the scale has no upper limit.

California Awaits "The Big One"

The United States Geological Survey (USGS) estimates the probability of a major earthquake in northern California by the year 2020 at 70 per cent. USGS experts anticipate a seismic event comparable to the San Francisco earthquake of 1906, which measured 8.3 on the Richter Scale and laid much of the city to waste, causing numerous fires and killing some 2,000 people. The quake in Northridge near Los Angeles in 1994 took 60 human lives, and total damage was valued at $ 30–40 billion (a U.S. record). The American West Coast is one of the most severely endangered regions in the world. The Pacific Plate thrusts against the North American Plate along several fault lines, the best known of which is the San Andreas fault. These movements are not gradual and consistent but abrupt and violent, and they are responsible for a seemingly endless series of earthquakes. Some 7,800 earthquakes are registered in California each year, although most of them can only be detected by sensitive seismographic instruments.

Seismic Waves Explore the Earth's Interior

Physical bores are mere pinpricks in the Earth's crust (at about 13 km, the deepest bore ever made reached a depth equivalent to only about 0.2 per cent of the Earth's radius). We learn a great deal more about the structure of the Earth's interior from seismic waves that penetrate to the core and beyond. This method is the basis for the shell model of the Earth, with a crust (50–70 km thick beneath the continents, 5–10 km thick below the oceans), a mantle (2,900 km thick, divided in two by a transition zone), and a core (outer core to a depth of 5,200 km, inner core to a depth of 6,371 km). Correlations between wave speeds and experimental findings generate conclusions about the density, the temperature, and the chemical and mineral composition of the different zones.

Are Earthquakes Predictable?

People in ancient China observed unusual behavior in animals immediately preceding earthquake events, although they realized this only later. Today, even seismologists disagree about whether the location, time, and magnitude of an earthquake can be predicted. Researchers have been trying to identify reliable signs for decades. Using automatic recording devices, they systematically measure changes in specific characteristics – temperature, chemical composition, gas concentration (radon) and electrical groundwater resistance, groundwater levels and spring behavior, movements at fault lines, and deformations of the Earth's surface. All of these phenomena can – but do not necessarily – indicate impending earthquake activity.

Crisis Management – Emergency Disaster Aid

In industrialized countries threatened by earthquake such as Japan, the U. S. (especially California), and Ital plans have been made for responses to natural disaster Kindergarten and school children in Japan and Californ learn rules for behavior when danger threatens. Publ emergency disaster exercises are conducted on a broa basis in Japan. Plans are modified in response to experi ence gained in such emergencies. California has esta lished a network of decentralized emergency aid statio staffed and equipped to meet specific local needs. Th central Japanese authority failed to respond adequate during the Kobe earthquake.

Earthquake-Proof Construction – Only an Illusion?

The first building designed to resist earthquake sho was erected by American architect Frank Lloyd Wrig in Tokyo between 1916 and 1922. It survived the eart quake of 1923 virtually undamaged. In the years sinc architects have employed special methods of stable flexible construction at locations in Japan, Californ

Earthquake Epicenters and Plate Boundaries

120Y 150Y

Zones of Critical Seismic Activity

Ninety per cent of all earthquakes are caused by seismic activity (volcanism and collapsing hollow areas in the Earth account for the remainder). Thus the theory of plate tectonics has given rise to new insights into the causes and distribution of earthquakes. As this map of epicenters shows, seismic activity is most intense along plate margins. The Circum-Pacific Belt coincides primarily with subduction zones (these incline toward the continental interiors, which explains the locations of deep-focus earthquakes), while the Mediterranean-Transasian Belt is aligned with converging continental plates. Weaker earthquakes originate at the edges of plates moving away from another near mid-oceanic ridges.

Eurasian Plate

60Y

30Y

Seismic Waves

| Regional earthquake |
| 0 2 4 8 min |

| Nearby earthquake |
| 0 4 8 12 16 min |

| Nearby earthquake |
| 0 2 4 min |

| Local earthquake |
| 0 1 min |

S SS PP

Mantle

Shadow zone

Outer core

Inner core

Epi-center

Center of the Earth

Focal depth   Hypocenter

PMP
SSS
PPP
PKIKP

Longitudinal wave (P)
Transverse wave (P)

Spread of seismic waves
P(S) direct waves,
PP(SS) single reflection,
PPP(SSS) double reflection,
K part of wave passing through Earth's core,
KIK part of wave passing through the inner
Earth core
(Diagram is not to scale.)

Configuration of a vertical seismograph
Rotating drum
Pendulum weight

Where the Ball Rolls – the First Seismograph

The first device used to register earthquake activity was invented in China in the first century AD. The pot-bellied vessel is adorned with eight dragon figures, each facing a crouching toad positioned on the base below. When a tremor occurs, the pendulum inside begins to swing. The mouth of the dragon on the side opposite the direction of the shock wave opens and drops a ball into the mouth of the toad beneath it. This was believed to indicate the direction of the earthquake.

An Earthquake Exposes Weaknesses in Japanese Society

The quake that shook the Japa industrial and port city of Kobe in the early morning of January 17, 1995 lasted no more than few seconds. More than 20,00 buildings were heavily damage destroyed; 6,432 people were k and 350,000 lost their homes. The supports beneath 500 m o the Hanshin Highway collapse and the supposedly earthquake proof elevated road crashed to ground. The multi-story buildi nearby remained undamaged. The seemingly well-organized disaster aid and rescue system was largely ineffective.

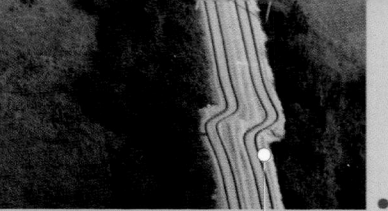

Earthquakes - Danger from the Depths

and other parts of the world. A number of countries have enacted corresponding building regulations in the past few years. Cellular construction techniques and "sandwich structures" comprised of steel and rubber plates built into the foundations of high-rise buildings absorb earthquake shocks. Steel structures are generally safer than stone or brick buildings. Wood-frame buildings may also offer satisfactory earthquake resistance if certain safety requirements are met. Schools, hospitals and other public buildings are subject to particularly stringent regulations. Recent experience has shown that many bridges, highway ramps, and similar structures need upgrading to meet safety requirements. Loose substrata, especially made-made fills or embankments, are very susceptible to earthquake damage. Much depends on the quality of construction – an issue of concern in developing countries. It is important to consider that the greatest damage incurred during major earthquakes (e.g. San Francisco, 1906 and Kobe, 1995) resulted from fire (broken gas lines). Although earthquakes cannot be prevented, precautionary measures reduce damage significantly.

A "Bend" in the Landscape
Only rarely are movements of the Earth's crust as obvious as in this photo: a bend of 3 to 5 meters in the railway line near Izmit, Turkey in August 1999.

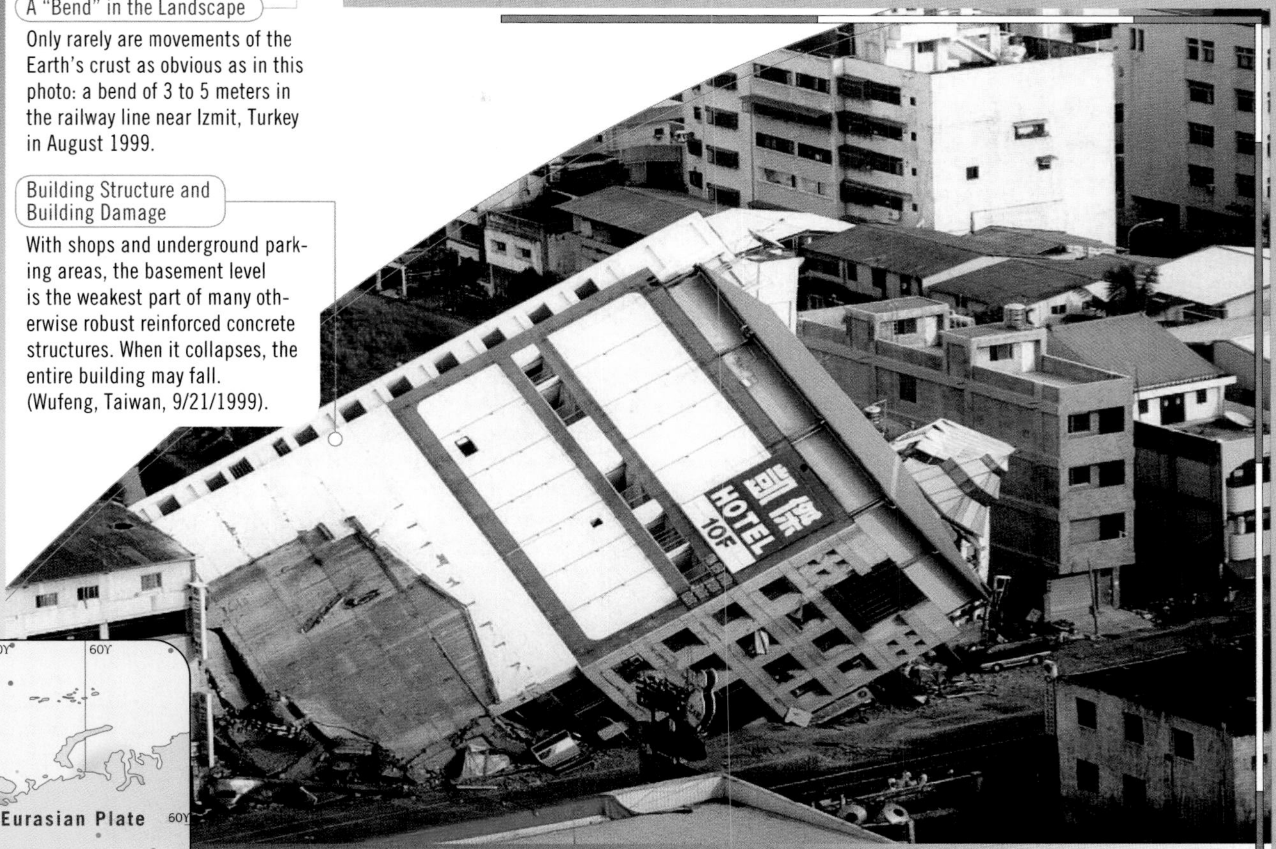

Building Structure and Building Damage
With shops and underground parking areas, the basement level is the weakest part of many otherwise robust reinforced concrete structures. When it collapses, the entire building may fall. (Wufeng, Taiwan, 9/21/1999).

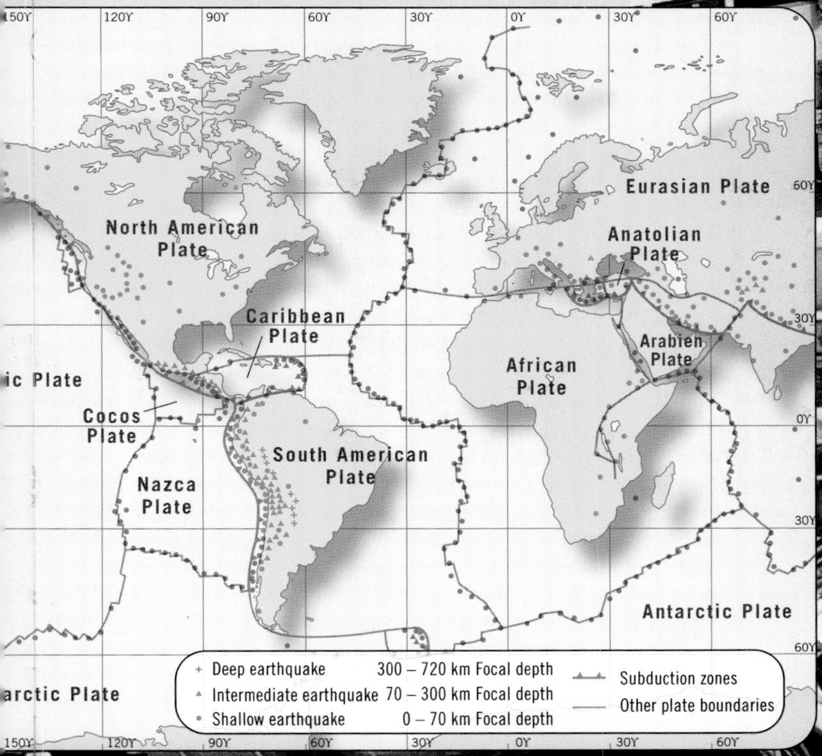

Map legend

+	Deep earthquake	300 – 720 km Focal depth
+	Intermediate earthquake	70 – 300 km Focal depth
•	Shallow earthquake	0 – 70 km Focal depth

Subduction zones
Other plate boundaries

Plate labels: Eurasian Plate, Anatolian Plate, North American Plate, Caribbean Plate, Arabien Plate, African Plate, Cocos Plate, South American Plate, Nazca Plate, Antarctic Plate

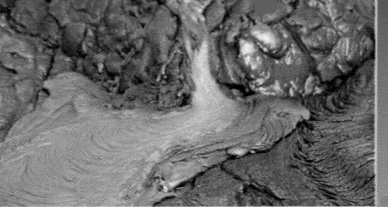
Fertile Soil – Ever-Present Danger

In the early morning hours of August 27, 1883, the small volcanic island of Krakatoa in the Sundra Strait was shaken by violent explosions which virtually blew the island paradise apart. The enormous bang was heard more than 5,000 km away, and atmospheric pressure rose by 1.45 millibars in Tokyo. Massive tremors that triggered tsunamis traveling at the speed of an airliner battered the coastlines of Java and Sumatra. Roughly 36,000 people lost their lives as a direct result of the eruptions. And this was by no means the worst volcanic disaster in history. Eruptions on the Indonesian island of Sumbawa in 1815 ejected more than 180 cubic km of lava and ash (compared to only 20 cubic km on Krakatoa). The volcano, the tidal waves, and the famine that followed were responsible for some 90,000 deaths. Dust in the atmosphere darkened the sky for weeks.

A Bubbling Inferno Beneath Us

The solid crust that floats on the hot molten rock of the upper mantle is actually very thin. Continental crust attains a maximum thickness of 70 km, while oceanic crust is ordinarily between 5 and 10 km thick. (Imagine

An Eruption in Hawaii

An eruption of Kilauea in Hawaii begins with a fountain of lava lasting several hours. Escaping gas catapults the red-hot molten mass hundreds of meters into the air.

"Rushing Stream"

This is the literal translation of the Islandic word for geyser (geysir). Rainwater seeping into the hot volcanic underground is heated and ejected – often at regular intervals – through fissures in the rock. (photo: geysers in the Rotorua region of New Zealand). The process is a part of the waning phase of volcanic activity.

Volcanic Breakthrough in a Glacier

In 1996, the volcano beneath the Vatnajökull Glacier in Iceland melted a hole in the ice cap, sending clouds of ash as high as 4,000 m into the air. The lava eruptions that followed were accompanied by severe earthquakes.

Aa and Pahoehoe Lava

A skin forms on the surface of the thin, red-hot pahoehoe lava as it flows. Once it has cooled and solidified, the lava may look much like lengths of intertwining twisted ropes or strings.

A Volcanic Blessing

Geothermal energy is a readily available alternative energy source in volcanically active regions like Italy, Iceland, and New Zealand.

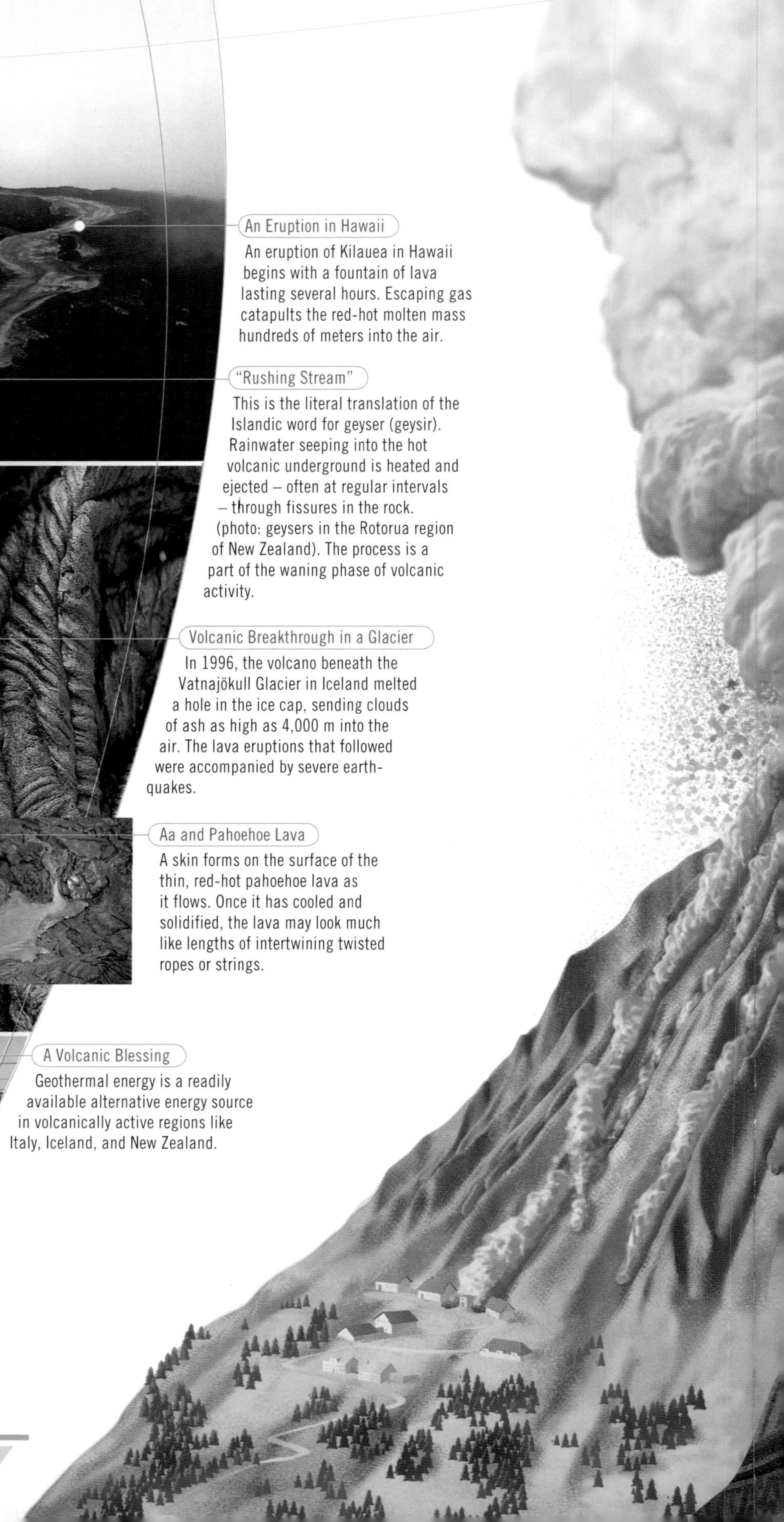

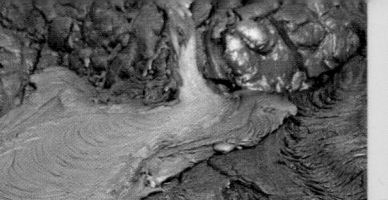
Volcanism - Unbridled Forces from the Earth's Interior

an orange measuring 12 cm in diameter with a peel only 0.3 mm thick!). And thus it is no wonder that the Earth's thin crust is extremely fragile. Molten rock accumulates in large magma chambers beneath the surface and rises where faults or openings develop. Magma that emerges at the surface is called lava.

Harmless and Dangerous Volcanoes

The flow characteristics of lava depend on its chemical composition and gas content. Thin, basaltic lava (50% SiO2) of the kind that erupts from Kilauea (Hawaii) is often ejected in towering fountains which then flow smoothly from the crater. Andesitic magma rich in silicic acid (60 % SiO2) is catapulted from volcanic Mount Saint Helens to heights of several kilometers. Gases escape easily from thin magma, whereas thick, highly gaseous magma builds up high pressures that are released suddenly and explosively near the surface, where outside pressure decreases rapidly. At these points, lava shoots from the volcano like champagne from a shaken bottle. Basaltic lava forms relatively flat (12 degrees) shield volcanoes like those in Hawaii, or basalt floors (Dekkan, India).

Acidic lava tends to erupt violently, although it may also flow quietly down volcanic slopes. Alternating deposits of lava and tuff form cone-shaped stratovolcanoes with slopes as steep as 30 degrees. The most famous volcano of this type is Fujiama in Japan. When underground pressure has no means of escape, domes of lava form, raising the overlying layers and the Earth's surface above. The destructive power of explosive eruptions makes living in these areas extremely dangerous. The worst outbreak of this kind occurred at the Montagne Pelée on the island of Martinique in 1902. Extremely hot air (1,440° F) loaded with ash enveloped the nearby city of Saint-Pierre in a red-hot cloud, killing 29,000 people. The only survivor was found at the island prison.

Volcanoes – Gigantic Dirt Canons

Volcanic eruptions also hurl huge blocks of rock (bombs) far into the surrounding countryside. Fine particles are shot up to 10 km into the atmosphere, where they may circulate around the Earth for years. Bombs, lapilli (fragments measuring from two to 64 mm), and fine ash fall to the ground, forming volcanic tuff. Fragments that have not cooled sufficiently fuse into clinkers. Rock baked from larger masses becomes volcanic breccia. Storms among the high clouds above the volcano bring heavy rains, often causing massive mudflows that obliterate everything in their paths to the valleys below.

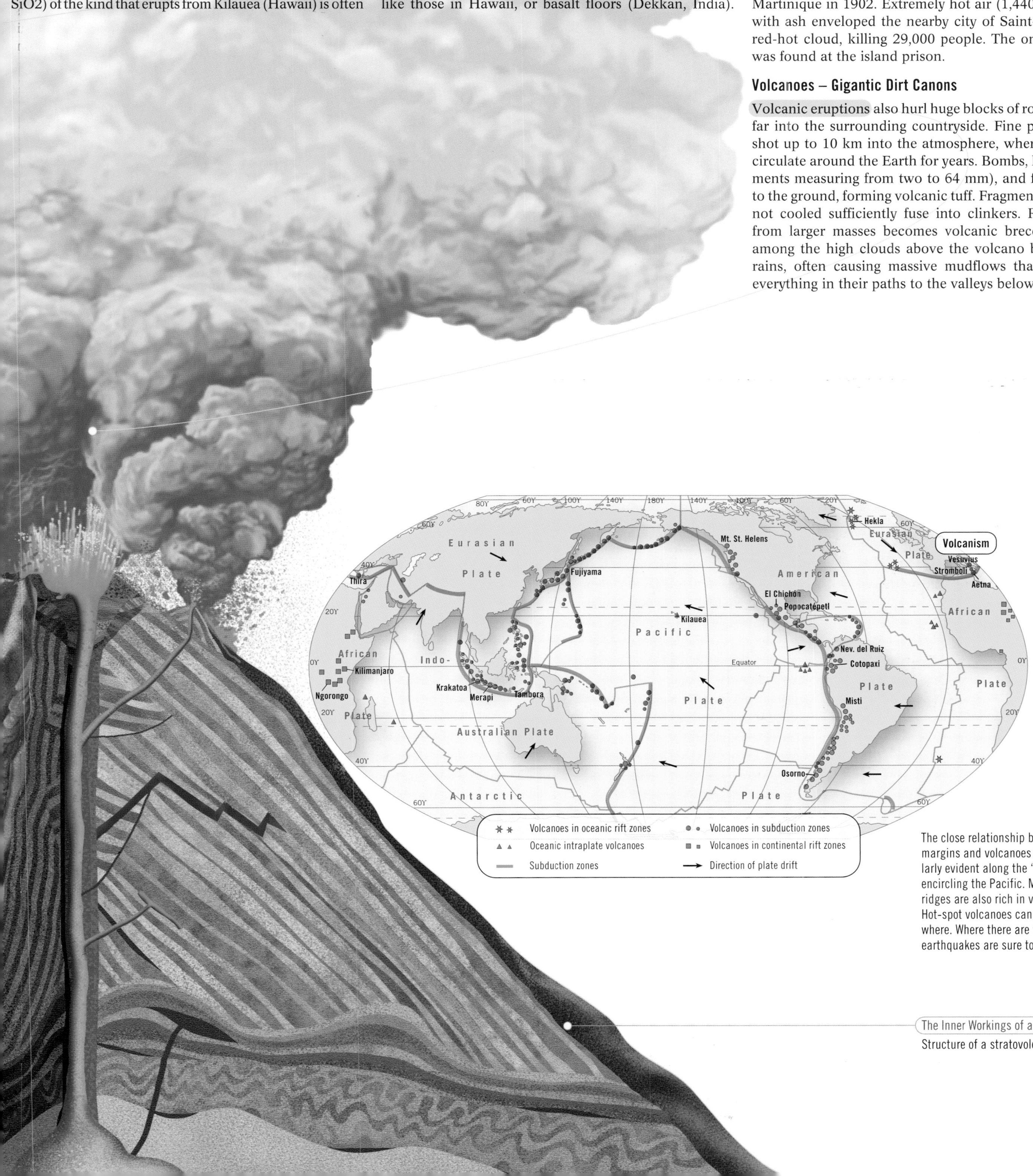

✱✱ Volcanoes in oceanic rift zones	•• Volcanoes in subduction zones
▲▲ Oceanic intraplate volcanoes	■■ Volcanoes in continental rift zones
— Subduction zones	→ Direction of plate drift

The close relationship between plate margins and volcanoes its particularly evident along the "Ring of Fire" encircling the Pacific. Mid-oceanic ridges are also rich in volcanoes. Hot-spot volcanoes can appear anywhere. Where there are volcanoes, earthquakes are sure to occur as well.

The Inner Workings of a Volcano:
Structure of a stratovolcano

Tsunamis

Seismic Shifts at Sea

Contrary to popular belief, a tsunami is not a "tidal wave," as its behavior has nothing to do with the movement of tides. And although the term comes from the Japanese word for "harbor wave," a tsunami should also not be confused with the kinds of wind-generated waves observed at the beach. So what exactly is a tsunami? Simply put, it is a series of enormous sea waves created when a large volume of water is displaced. Underwater disturbances such as earthquakes and accompanying landslides, violent volcanic eruptions, explosions, meteorite impacts, can all cause tsunamis.

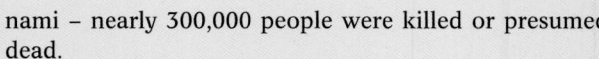

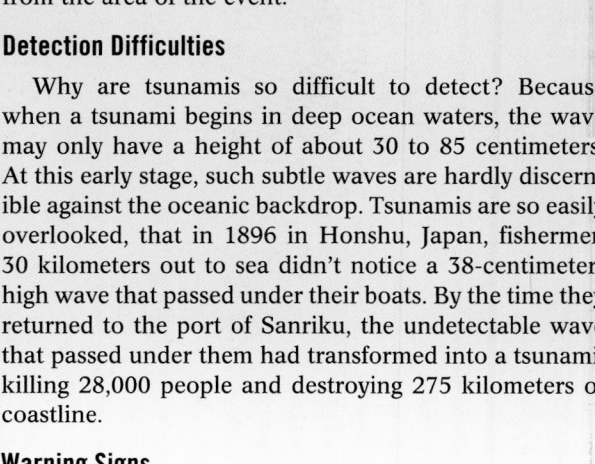

Shallow-Water Giants

To truly appreciate the awesome power of a tsunami, it helps to know a little bit about how more common types of waves behave. The wind-generated waves we see at the beach have a period – the amount of time that elapses between successive waves – that lasts between 5 and 20 seconds and a wavelength – the distance between two successive waves – of 100 to 200 meters. A tsunami's period can last for as little as 10 minutes, or as long as 2 hours and it can have a wavelength in excess of 500 km. It is because of these exceedingly long wavelengths that tsunamis behave as shallow-water waves and are able to travel great distances without losing much energy. For example, an unnoticed tsunami traveling across the ocean in water that is 6,100 meters deep will move at about 890 km/hr – the speed of a jet airplane! At this rate, the wave can move from one side of the Pacific Ocean to the other side in less than 24 hours.

Travel and Transformation

As a tsunami leaves the deeper water of the open sea and moves through shallow water near the coast, it undergoes a transformation. As the depth of the water decreases, the tsunami travels at reduced speeds and the height of the wave begins to increase. This means a tsunami that is imperceptible at sea can grow to a height of several meters as it nears the coast. The physical characteristics of the coastal region and topography of the ocean floor – the presence of reefs, bays, river deltas, undersea features and the slope of the beach – all affect the shape and size of the waves as they approach the shore.

Waves Crash the Coast

As a tsunami approaches shore, its speed gradually reduces as the water becomes shallow, and the wave grows in height. All waves lose energy as they break on the shore. And although the tsunami does lose some energy, it arrives at the coast with tremendous force and can devastate the land around the shore. It may appear as a rapidly rising or falling tide, a succession of breaking waves, or even a tidal bore – a large step-like wave or wall of water that has a steep breaking front. Onshore, tsunamis may reach heights between 10 and 30 meters. They are capable of flooding hundreds of meters inland and the fast-moving waters of breaking waves can destroy homes and other coastal structures, strip beaches of sand and unearth trees.

Origins Affect Outcomes

Tectonic earthquakes are the most common type of earthquake. When tectonic plates grind against each and other, stress builds up and is released through the Earth's surface as tremors or shakes—this causes the crust to break. A tsunami may occur when tectonic earthquakes in the ocean cause large areas of the sea floor to elevate or subside.

On December 6, 2004, the tsunami generated by the tectonic earthquake off the coast of northern Sumatra inundated coastal communities across South and Southeast Asia, including parts of Indonesia, Sri Lanka, India, and Thailand. This tsunami was recorded nearly worldwide and killed more people than any other tsunami in history. Over 1 million people were displaced by the combined effects of the earthquake and subsequent tsunami – nearly 300,000 people were killed or presumed dead.

In general, ocean-wide tsunamis caused by tectonic earthquakes are more destructive than tsunamis generated by non-seismic events. Landslides and cosmic-body impacts that disturb the water from above – by transferring momentum into the water with the falling debris – often dissipate quickly and rarely affect coastlines far from the area of the event.

Detection Difficulties

Why are tsunamis so difficult to detect? Because when a tsunami begins in deep ocean waters, the wave may only have a height of about 30 to 85 centimeters. At this early stage, such subtle waves are hardly discernible against the oceanic backdrop. Tsunamis are so easily overlooked, that in 1896 in Honshu, Japan, fishermen 30 kilometers out to sea didn't notice a 38-centimeter-high wave that passed under their boats. By the time they returned to the port of Sanriku, the undetectable wave that passed under them had transformed into a tsunami, killing 28,000 people and destroying 275 kilometers of coastline.

Warning Signs

Tsunami waves are difficult to detect out at sea, and warning signs are considered somewhat unreliable. Still, there are a couple worth mentioning.

- A tectonic earthquake that occurs in the ocean and that registers over 6.5 on the Richter scale may generate a tsunami.

- The first sign of an impending tsunami in coastal areas is often a sudden outrush of water, exposing the sea bed offshore and leaving boats and some marine life stranded. After a few minutes, a series of huge waves rush inland, the largest of which is usually between the third and the eighth to arrive.

Aceh, Sumatra Hit Hard

The Indonesian province of Aceh was hit hardest by the earthquake and tsunamis of December 26, 2004. Aceh is located on the northern tip of the island of Sumatra. On December 29, estimates of the death toll in Indonesia were over 80,000—more than half the total number of casualties. The town of Lhoknga, on the west coast of Sumatra near the capital of Aceh, Banda Aceh, was completely destroyed by the tsunami, except for the mosque (white circular feature) in the city's center. These high-resolution satellite images, acquired by Space Imaging's Ikonos satellite, show Lhoknga before (January 10, 2003) and after (December 29, 2004) the earthquake and tsunami. Almost all the trees, vegetation, and buildings in the area were washed away.

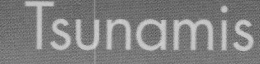

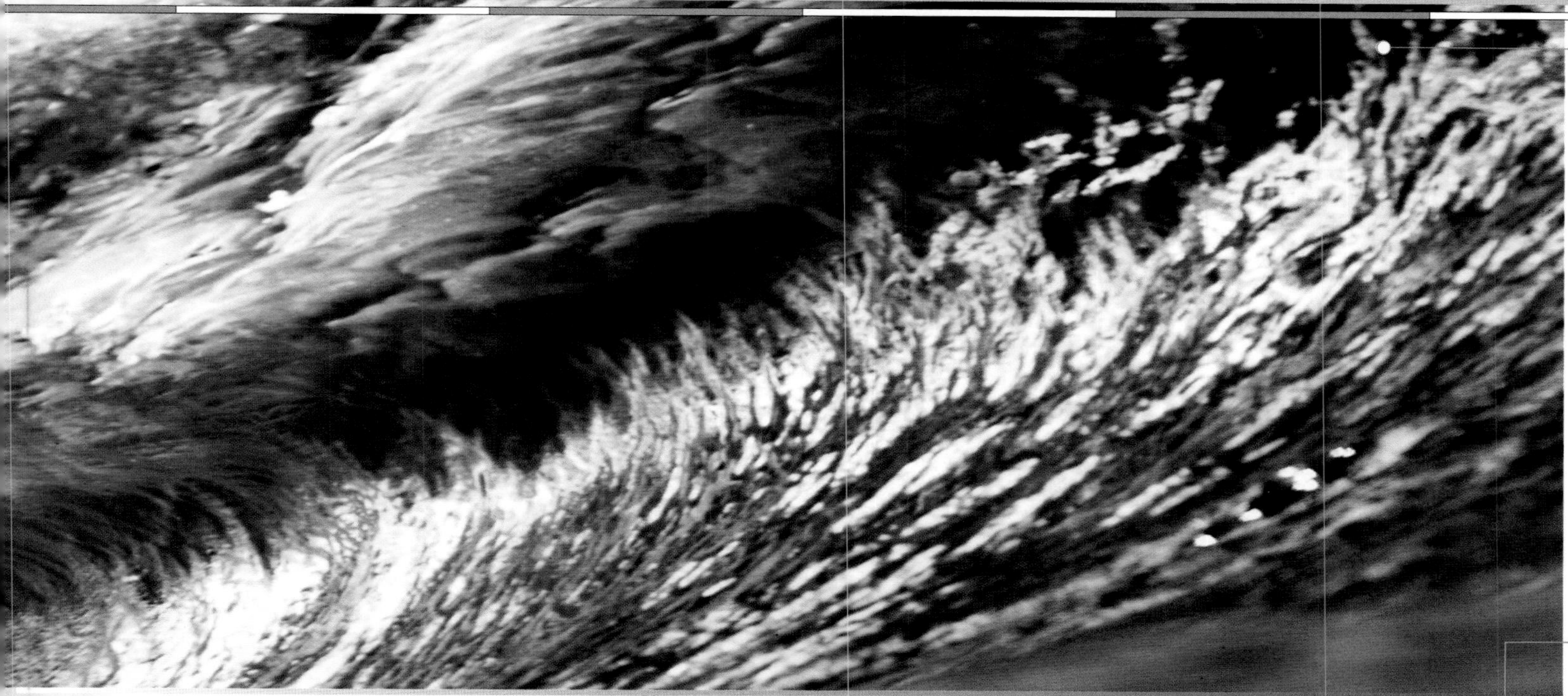

Wave of Destruction

A magnitude 9.4 Mw earthquake occurred off the west coast of Sumatra, Indonesia, on December 26, 2004. It was the fourth largest earthquake in the world since 1900 and the largest since the 1964 Prince William Sound, Alaska, earthquake. The earthquake generated a tsunami that caused more casualties than any other in recorded history. The tsunami was recorded nearly world-wide on tide gauges in the Indian, Pacific and Atlantic Oceans. In total, more than 283,1000 people were killed, and 14,1000 are still listed as missing. 1,126,900 were displaced by the earthquake and subsequent tsunami in 10 countries in South Asia and East Africa.

Aftermath

Community Groups Funded by USAID worked to help remove debris in Sri Lanka. In the aftermath, tsunamis leave behind a tangled mess of debris requiring a massive clean-up effort. In addition to the mess, the threat of diseases is a major concern.

Erosion in Sri Lanka

Natural sand dunes along Sri Lanka's coastal regions experienced extreme erosion as a result of the Indian Ocean tsunami. Sand dunes were washed away by the 5-to-10 meter waves, leaving deep craters once waters had receded.

Malé Battered by Tsunami

These onlookers see firsthand the awesome power of the tsunami that struck Malé in the Maldives on December 26, 2004.

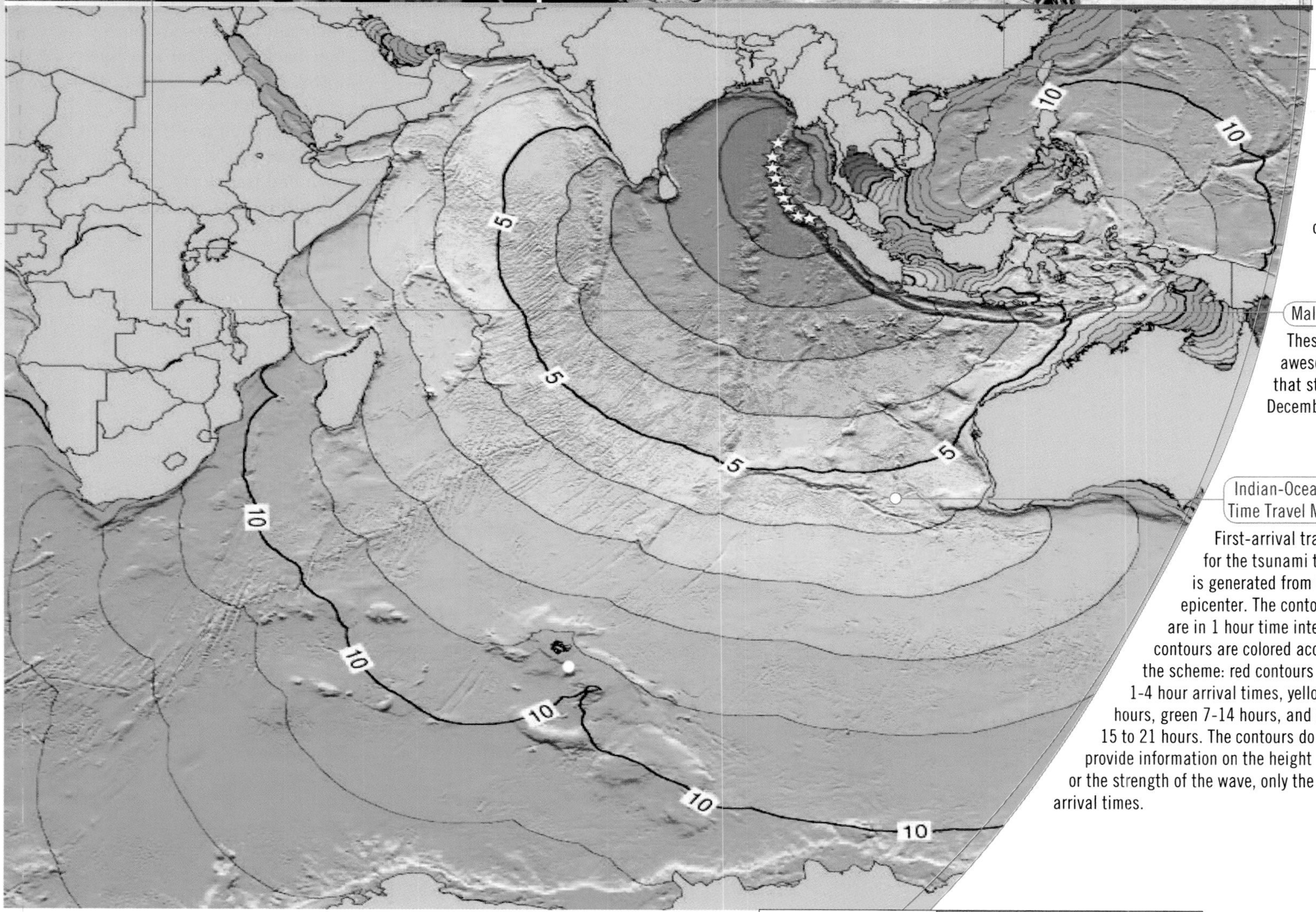

Indian-Ocean Tsunami Time Travel Map

First-arrival travel times on the grid for the tsunami time travel map is generated from the earthquake epicenter. The contours on the map are in 1 hour time intervals. The contours are colored according to the scheme: red contours are for 1-4 hour arrival times, yellow 5-6 hours, green 7-14 hours, and blue 15 to 21 hours. The contours do not provide information on the height or the strength of the wave, only the arrival times.

Water Molds the Landscape

Water's Journey from the Sea to the Mountains and Back

Life came to Earth with water, which entered the cloud of gas that surrounds our planet in the form of gas released from molten magma. The cooling process produced the first rains, and the seas began to form. In the protective watery environment and under the influence of rising oxygen concentrations, life burst forth explosively several hundred million years ago. We come from water, and we need water to live. The human body is 70 percent water. Although we can live for weeks without food, we would die within days without water. More than half of the human race suffers from a shortage of clean drinking water. Eighty percent of the diseases responsible for millions of deaths every year are carried by unclean water. Water is an essential, life-giving substance that is unequally distributed. Some people die of thirst, while others drown.

High into the Atmosphere and back to Earth. The Water Cycle

How does water find its way back to the sea? Raindrops falling to earth have several ways of returning to the bodies of water from which they came. They may evaporate, flow over the surface, or seep into the earth, emerging again later through springs. Water that remains on the surface reaches the sea in a matter of weeks. Yet water held captive in a freshwater lake can take years to return to the ocean. Water that falls as snow and turns to ice in cold regions of the Earth like the Antarctic, may not return to the sea for hundreds of thousands of years. Once there, it is ready to embark upon another long journey. Many water molecules take refuge at safe ocean depths, however, thus escaping the routine of constant travel.

The water cycle begins with the evaporation of liquid water, most of which takes place on the ocean surface. At a temperature of 77°F, this process consumes 583 calories per gram of water. Molecules of water vapor transport this kinetic energy over long distances. The water condenses again only after a journey of hours or even days through the air. At this point, raindrops are formed during the transition from the gaseous to the liquid state, and evaporation heat is released again. That is how warmth from the Caribbean, for example, travels via the Gulf Stream to Norway. When raindrops freeze (changing from liquid to solid), 79.4 calories are released per gram of water. Thus, as strange as it may seem, the freezing process generates heat. Molecules move more slowly in ice than in liquid water.

Water Shapes Mountains and Valleys by Day and by Night

With rare exceptions, water flows downhill toward the sea, quickly forming drainage lines on the surface. As the kinetic energy of water rushing downhill tears away material and carries it away, long cuts form in the earth – the valleys of streams and rivers. Naturally, elevated ridges are left standing between these valleys. The product is a relief of mountains and valleys. Depending upon elevation and slope, mountains of different heights are created and cut apart by water and/or ice (glaciers). The higher the mountain range, the steeper the forms carved by the water.

A Steady Drip Hollows the Stone

Water is the most important element in the weathering process that shapes rock – just as it is when automobiles succumb to rust (corrosion). Limestone is one of the most highly soluble types of rock, and large caves and other karsts are often found in limestone formations. Apart from its corrosive effect, moving water also works mechanically to hasten the process of rock destruction.

The effects of wind, water, and salt have combined to undercut a coastal rock formation on the island of Lanzarote.

Crashing waves strike steep coastal formations with incredible force (one cubic meter of water weighs roughly a ton), wielding sand and pebbles as abrasive weapons. Although these forces are weaker in rivers, a substantial amount of material is eroded and carried away from riverbeds and banks over the course of time. Deep, V-shaped valleys and gorges offer striking evidence of the destructive power of water. Bank and bed erosion caused by flowing water forms valleys in a multitude of different shapes.

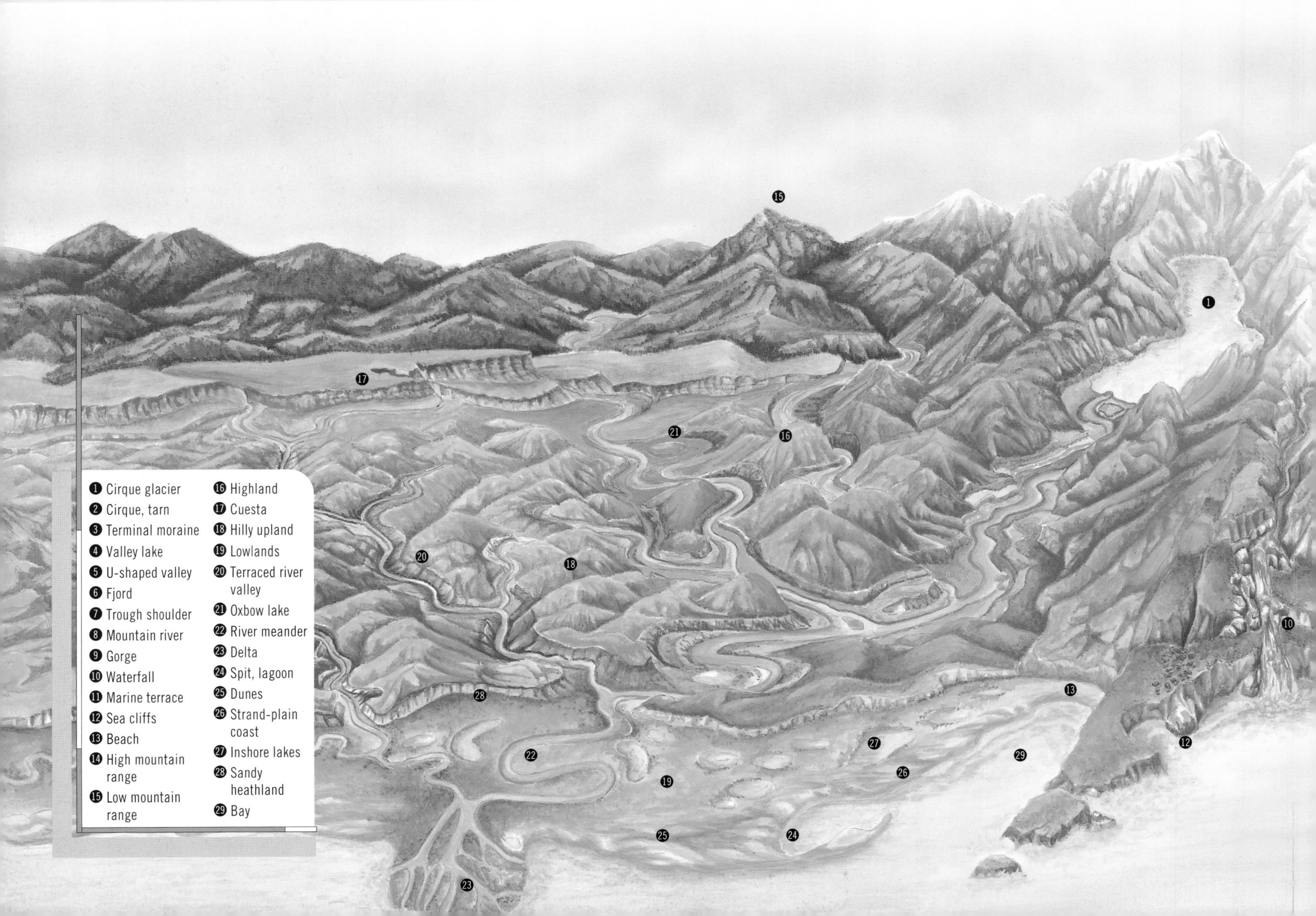

❶ Cirque glacier
❷ Cirque, tarn
❸ Terminal moraine
❹ Valley lake
❺ U-shaped valley
❻ Fjord
❼ Trough shoulder
❽ Mountain river
❾ Gorge
❿ Waterfall
⓫ Marine terrace
⓬ Sea cliffs
⓭ Beach
⓮ High mountain range
⓯ Low mountain range
⓰ Highland
⓱ Cuesta
⓲ Hilly upland
⓳ Lowlands
⓴ Terraced river valley
㉑ Oxbow lake
㉒ River meander
㉓ Delta
㉔ Spit, lagoon
㉕ Dunes
㉖ Strand-plain coast
㉗ Inshore lakes
㉘ Sandy heathland
㉙ Bay

Water Molds the Landscape

Glacial ice has even greater erosive power. The high pressure exerted by the ice causes severe erosion (detersion, exaration) even at low flow speeds. Blocks of stone the size of a house may be torn away and carried downward. This is how deep U-shaped valleys are formed. The eroded material is deposited in glacial moraines. Water and ice cover three-quarters of the Earth's surface. Although the total quantity of water on earth – some 1.4 billion square km – is almost impossible to imagine, this immense treasure is of little use to us, as 96.5 per cent of it is salty. Methods developed for desalinating seawater are too costly for most countries. And it is hardly practical to tow icebergs from the Antarctic to the arid regions of the world. We may expect future water shortages to reach life-threatening proportions in many places on Earth.

No Escape from Water

Although water is in short supply in many parts of the world, thousands die or lose their homes in water-related disasters every year. Floods, typhoons, and tsunamis ravage broad stretches of land. Melting snow and torrential rains cause rivers to swell and overflow their banks in low-lying areas. Dykes often do not hold or are simply not high enough.

When the ground freezes during the winter and is covered by a thick blanket of snow, it takes only a brief interlude of warm temperatures accompanied by heavy rainfall to melt the snow and cause severe flooding in the valleys. The frozen soil prevents water from seeping into the ground and accelerates the speed of surface runoff.

Spectacle of Nature
A thundering waterfall crashes over a steep drop in Iceland. The energy of flowing water, which mankind has not yet begun to exploit significantly, is a powerful force that here continues to erode the step in the terrain.

Planed and Leveled
The surf along the Basque coast near Saint-Jean-de-Luz has worn a flat abrasion plate in the terraced slopes of the Pyrenees.

Source of Life
Water is extremely scarce in deserts. Knowledge of the few, often hidden sources of water is crucial to survival in these extremely arid regions. Surface springs like this one in the Aïr Massif (Niger) are rare, and water must often be drawn from wells or water holes dug in the sands of dry riverbeds.

Unbridled Force
Water from melting snow and ice flows to the sea. In steep terrain, the milky glacial melt rushes unhindered to the valleys below. The fine sand dispersed in the water consists of rock material ground away under massive glacial pressure. In mountainous regions, the force of flowing water is strong enough to move even large blocks of stone.

Floods
When the snows melt in spring or rains are especially heavy in summer, flooding often occurs on the coastal plains and alpine piedmont regions of Europe.

In the Underworld
Underground erosion creates caves (photo: Wyandotte Cave, Indiana). Water acts as a solvent in limestone. This erosive action is enhanced by karst dissolution. In this process, carbon dioxide (CO_2) works as a catalyst in the conversion of calcium carbonate to highly soluble calcium hydrogen-carbonate, which is carried away in the karst water.

Natural Disasters - Human Catastrophes

Does Mankind Pose a Challenge to Nature?

The media provide news about a terrible natural disaster somewhere in the world virtually every day. Our television screens show us images of devastation and often of the dramatic events themselves as they unfold. Sober assessments of underlying causes are often overshadowed in the public mind by such sensational reports.

Yet there are several questions we cannot ignore: "To what extent are we humans at fault?" Is mankind inevitably doomed to destruction, or can we find a way to avert it?

A Devastating Christmas Present

On Christmas Day of 1974, Tropical Storm Tracy battered the city of Darwin in northern Australia. With average wind speeds of 140 kilometers per hour and gusts peaking at 260 kilometers per hour, the storm completely destroyed more than 5,000 of the 8,000 lightweight houses built on stilts. Forty-nine people died, and property damage amounted to 3 billion Australian dollars. Of Darwin's 45,000 inhabitants, 25,000 were evacuated by air, while 10,000 people fled the city by car toward the south. This was the greatest natural disaster in Australia's history.

Flight from the Inferno

In early April 1991, Pinatubo, a volcano on the Philippine island of Luzon, erupted again for the first time in human memory. In June, the mountain collapsed and lost 300 meters of elevation. Red-hot clouds spread like avalanches, covering distances of as much as 20 km. Ten cubic km of ash, gas, and other erupted matter were catapulted into the stratosphere to heights of up to 40 km. Torrential rains generated by a tropical storm turned the accumulated ash into massive streams of mud. More than 200,000 people fled the looming catastrophe; 400 lives were lost. The expulsion of ash and particles containing sulphuric acid caused average temperatures in the atmosphere near ground level to sink by as much as 0.9° F – worldwide.

Tornadoes – Dangerous Twisters

The narrow funnel of a tornado dips threateningly earthward. The air rising inside the funnel rotates at speeds that accelerate to a maximum of 200 kilometers per hour toward the inside. The suction force generated inside the funnel rips buildings apart and bursts lungs and blood vessels in human victims. Objects carried away become dangerous projectiles; dust and water are hurled high into the atmosphere. The path of the funnel, which moves at speeds between 50 and 60 kilometers per hour, is narrow and clearly delineated, and so is its wake of destruction – and destruction is almost always total. The extensive damage is attributable in part to the prevalence of lightweight, wood-frame buildings in the United States.

Disasters Mark the Course of the Earth's History

The history of the Earth teaches us that catastrophic events have always played a role in global and regional developments and have even impacted on the evolution of living organisms. Yet from our somewhat short-sighted present-day perspective, we tend to overlook the length of time involved in these processes. Experts continue to debate the question of whether the mass extinction of life forms some 65 million years ago was caused by a collision with an extraterrestrial body, a severe outbreak of volcanic activity, or other geological, perhaps tectonic events. Most agree, however, that the extinction of the dinosaurs (along with many other forms of animal life) paved the way for the development of mammals and thus ultimately for the origin of Homo sapiens. But when we speak of natural disasters, we are usually thinking of events that affect human beings directly.

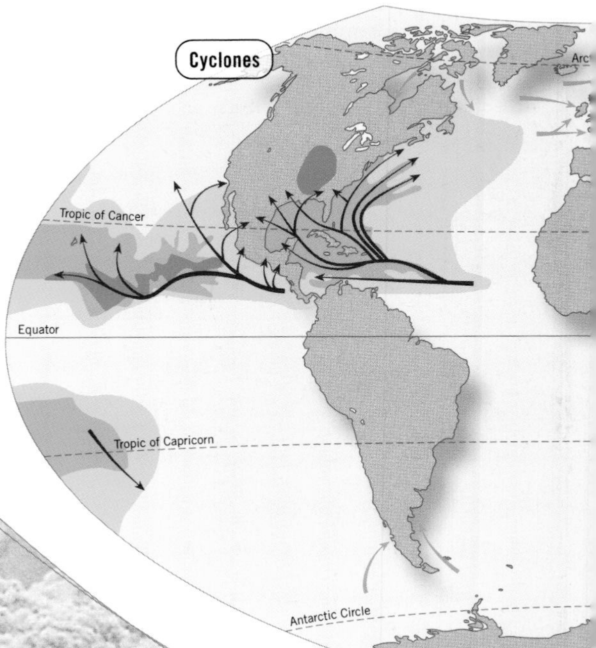

Natural Disasters - Human Catastrophes

The Earth's Vast Destructive Potential

The "restless Earth" poses many dangers. Earthquakes and volcanic eruptions are concentrated in certain regions. While it is impossible to prevent such events from occurring, precautions can be taken against their consequences. The number of severe earthquakes (measuring 7.0 or above on the Richter Scale) did not increase worldwide during the twentieth century. Yet the toll in human lives and property damage has risen steadily, due to increasing population and building density, to the spread of settlements into endangered areas people once avoided, to the increasing value of property and goods (concentrated primarily in metropolitan areas) that has accompanied the rise in living standards, and to the increased susceptibility of modern societies and technologies to damage. Explosive population growth is another significant factor. The Kobe earthquake (1995) clearly showed seismic activity affects not only devel-

oping countries but often industrialized nations as well. And much the same applies to volcanism. We find ourselves in the midst of a heated debate about the dangers posed by the Earth's atmosphere and waters. Is the number of incidents rising? Are they growing in severity? And what or who is to blame – nature or mankind? A closely related issue is the question of mankind's impact on climate. Hurricanes are not the only destructive climatic phenomenon. Extended periods of heavy rain or snow storms; hail, ice, droughts; heat waves and periods of extreme cold; forest, bush, and prairie fires caused by lightning; avalanches, fog and smog all leave destruction in their wake. Excessive precipitation causes floods, landslips, and mudslides.

Stormy Times

The most dangerous storms originate in the Tropics: hurricanes along the coasts of Central and North America, typhoons over the waters off East and Southeast Asia, and cyclones in the Bay of Bengal (Bangladesh). They often wander for days over the sea in a westerly direction, only to turn suddenly north or south just before landfall. Their low pressure areas measure between 300 and 1,000 km in diameter. The center (known as the eye) of such storms is virtually cloudless and calm. It is encircled by a spiral of clouds that rotates at speeds up to 400 kilometers per hour. Torrential rain falls from massive cloud formations towering to heights of more than 15,000 meters. Storms that reach land wreak tremendous destruction, to which tidal waves also contribute, but then quickly lose intensity and dissipate. Hurricane Andrew caused $30 billion in damage. Katrina, ultimately is expected to cost about $200 billion. In Bangladesh, more than 300,000 people lost their lives in flooding caused by cyclones in 1970. The energy bundled in such storms is equivalent to that of several atomic bombs.

The tornadoes that occur frequently in the Midwestern United States are born when warm, moist air from the Gulf of Mexico is overlayered by dry, cool air from the Rocky Mountains or the Arctic. The temperature differential (between 36° and 54°F) generates incredibly high wind speeds. An average of 750 tornadoes are registered in the U.S. every year. They have costs the lives of hundreds of people – despite the well-organized warning system.

Year in, Year out ...

Floods caused by high water on the Rhine (photo: Cologne) and its tributaries are practically a regular occurrence. Data gathered at water-level measuring stations enable authorities to issue advance warnings and initiate evacuation procedures. Dykes and ad hoc precautionary measures (such as mobile protective walls) can help prevent some but by no means all flood damage. Flooding in 1993 and 1995 caused total property damage estimated at five billion dollars.

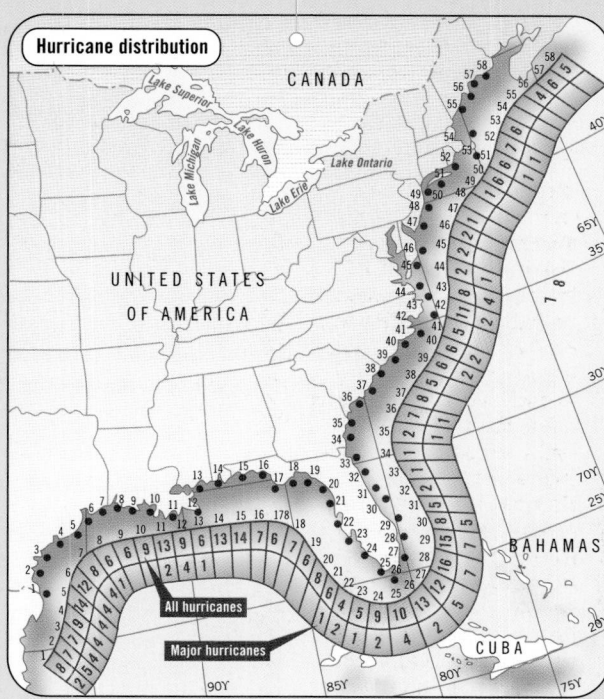

Hurricane distribution

Dangerous Tropical Storms

Tropical storms originate over waters with surface temperatures of at least 48°F in northern and southern latitudes between 5° and 30° during the late summer and early fall. A mass of moist, warm air with towering formations of cumulonimbus clouds gathers above the water. Condensation of the water vapor releases huge amounts of heat energy which accelerate the movement of rising air and the speed of the whirling mass of clouds. Tropical storms are generated by wavelike disruptions along the edge of the subtropical high-pressure belt or by the intrusion of low-pressure centers from the west-wind zone into the tropical circulation belt. Due to defrection caused by the Earth's rotation (Coriolis effect), storms spin clockwise in the southern hemisphere and counter-clockwise in the northern hemisphere. Cyclonic storms do not occur near the equator, as the Coriolis effect is too weak to accelerate the rotating masses of air.

When the Earth Slides Away

Saturation of debris or "soft," porous rock on mountain slopes or hillsides by heavy, sustained rainfall or melting snow can cause extensive landslips or mudslides. When these huge masses of mud and debris are carried into the valleys below, the descending wave cuts a broad path of destruction through the landscape. Mudslides of this kind occur often in the Apennines (photo taken near Sarno, east of Mt. Vesuvius), especially in areas where slopes have been stripped of vegetation through deforestation or overgrazing.

Tropical storms (cyclones)
- highly destructive
- severe to very severe
- weak to moderate
- Tornadoes

Major paths of movement
→ Tropical storms
→ Non-tropical storms

The Great Flood Yet to Come?

High water is ordinarily caused by unusually long periods of heavy precipitation or by rapid melting of winter snows. Repeated reports of catastrophic flooding evoke the impression that these disastrous events are becoming more frequent. Are they a by-product of global climatic changes that are reflected in increasingly heavy precipitation in Central Europe and the American Midwest? Catastrophic floods have occurred often in the past, as high-water marks show, but they had less far-reaching consequences, as agriculture and housing development were much less extensive than they are today. Various human interventions in the balance of nature have accelerated runoff activity and increased the danger of flooding. Prime examples are deforestation, ground-surface sealing (roads, housing developments, etc.), soil compaction (resulting from machine plowing and the conversion of meadowlands to fields), riverbed constriction with dams and dykes, river straightening, and the draining of wetlands (along the Mississippi, Missouri, and Red Rivers, for example), in combination with ground settlement and rising riverbed levels caused by accumulating silt deposits. Awakened from their lethargy by the increasing frequency and impact of floods, experts and regulatory authorities have instituted renaturation programs for river areas. Efforts to restore natural flood plains (retention areas) often encounter stiff opposition from local farmers, however.

Oceans and Marine Circulation Systems

The Global Climate Pump

Seen from space, the Earth is truly a blue planet, as more than two-thirds of its surface is covered by water. No other planet in our solar system has liquid water or the life it supports. The Earth's oceans are in constant motion, as water travels in powerful currents across them and circulate between the seafloor and the surface. Our seas are stirred by eddies and gyres and moved by winds and tidal forces. Visible waves on the surface are complemented by invisible ones in the ocean depths. The dynamics of the oceans have a significant impact on our planet's climate.

Driving Forces

Three different forces prevent the seas from ever coming to rest. The first is the gravitational pull of the Moon and (to a lesser extent) the Sun, which creates tidal action beneath which the Earth passes as it rotates. As a result, the seas shift in a twelve-hour (and in some places 24-hour) rhythm within their basins, rising and falling along their coasts (tidal action). Twice each month, the Moon, the Sun, and the Earth align with one another, causing particularly strong tidal action (spring and neap tides).

The second force that moves the seas is wind. It propels the major ocean surface currents, such as the Gulf and Brazil Currents in the Atlantic and the Kuroshio and Humboldt Currents in the Pacific. Highly characteristic, constant circulation patterns are sustained by prevailing winds – the trade winds in the subtropics and the West Wind Drift in the temperate zones – which are ultimately caused by the spheroid form and rotation of the Earth. Winds affect only the surface of the seas, and thus wind-driven circulation is restricted for the most part to the top 200 meters of water. However, the average depth of the world's oceans is about 4,000 meters, and their deepest

point (the Mariana Trench in the northwestern Pacific) is more than 11,000 meters below the surface.

The third driving force results from differences in sea-water density. Water density depends upon temperature and salt content (which ranges between 3.4% and 3.6% in most marine waters), and thus this motion is referred to as thermohaline circulation (from the Greek word háls, for salt). The densest, heaviest water tends to sink and is found most commonly in the European North Atlantic and near the Antarctic. The sinking masses of heavier water circulate around the Earth in the depths of the oceans, while warm surface water flows into the sinking regions. In this way, all of the water in all of the oceans on the globe circulates between the seafloor and the surface and is enriched with oxygen. On average, the journey of a single water molecule from the North Atlantic to the depths of the Pacific takes about a thousand years.

The rotation of the Earth (in the form of deflection caused by the Coriolis force) plays an important role in the dynamics of marine circulation systems, causing much stronger currents along the western rims of ocean basins.

The Effects of Climate

The uppermost two meters of the ocean can store as much heat as the entire atmosphere, since water has a very high heat-retention capacity. This storage capacity works like a buffer that partially evens out seasonal temperature fluctuations. The range of these fluctuations is therefore much narrower in coastal maritime climates than in continental inland areas. The average difference between summer and winter temperatures on the East Coast of the United States is about 60°F, but increases to 105°F in Edmonton, Canada. In addition, ocean currents transport stored solar heat over tremendous distances, normally from the tropics to the poles. In this way, they help to narrow temperature gaps caused by the unequal distribution of solar radiation on earth.

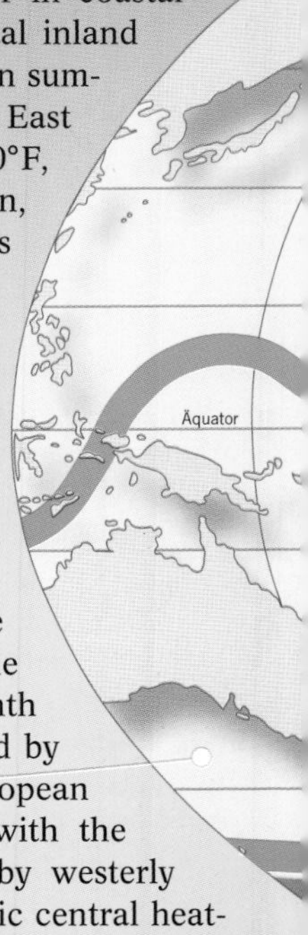

The Atlantic is unique in that heat is transported through its waters by thermohaline circulation from the southern hemisphere to regions off the coasts of Europe. There, this warmth ascends into the air, which is carried by prevailing westerly winds to the European mainland. Europeans are familiar with the mild winter temperatures brought by westerly winds from time to time. This Atlantic central heating system raises the average annual air temperature in northwestern Europe by more than 9° F (5° C) – an effect that was instrumental in the development of agriculture and the rise of northern European cultures.

El Niño, the Christ Child

The interaction of marine currents, waves, and trade winds in the Pacific tropics produces a natural climatic fluctuation known as El Niño – Southern Oscillation (ENSO). At intervals of between three and seven years, the trade winds dissipate, the cold, nutrient-rich Humboldt current slows, and unusually warm water accumulates off the Pacific coast of South America. The people of the region have named this phenomenon El Niño after the Christ Child, because the coastal waters ordinarily grow warmer around Christmas. El Niño generates waves beneath the surface of the ocean which travel across the entire Pacific along the Equator. They are reflected at its western edge and return to the east, where their arrival marks the beginning of the end of the warm phase. The reverse phase of this fluctuation – unusually cold temperatures in the eastern Pacific – is called La Niña. Occurrences of El-Niño cause massive fish death off the coasts of Peru and Ecuador and are responsible

The El Niño Phenomenon

A satellite image showing the unusual warming pattern. The white zone represents high-temperature associated with the highest surface elevation, ranging between 14 and 32 cm above the average level. The ocean surface in the purple zone is lower, and the red zones indicate unusually high heat retention.

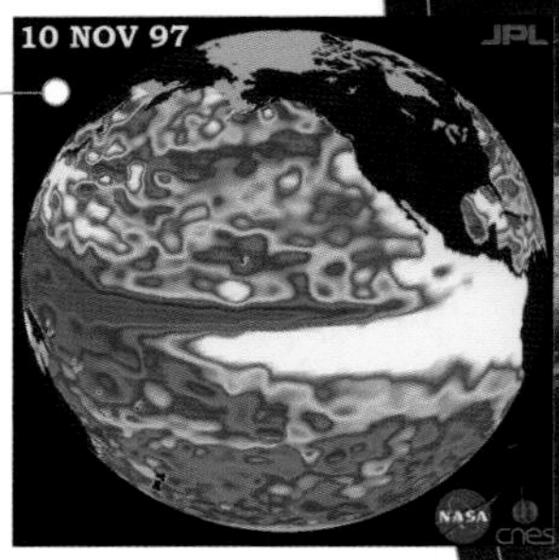

10 NOV 97

Research Vessel in Heavy Seas

Ships are still needed to survey marine currents, since satellite imagery captures only the ocean's surface. The photo shows the "Rapuhia," a vessel from New Zealand on a scientific expedition in the South Pacific. Unmanned probes that cross the oceans on programmed courses and transmit data to satellites are now being used more and more frequently.

Ocean Currents

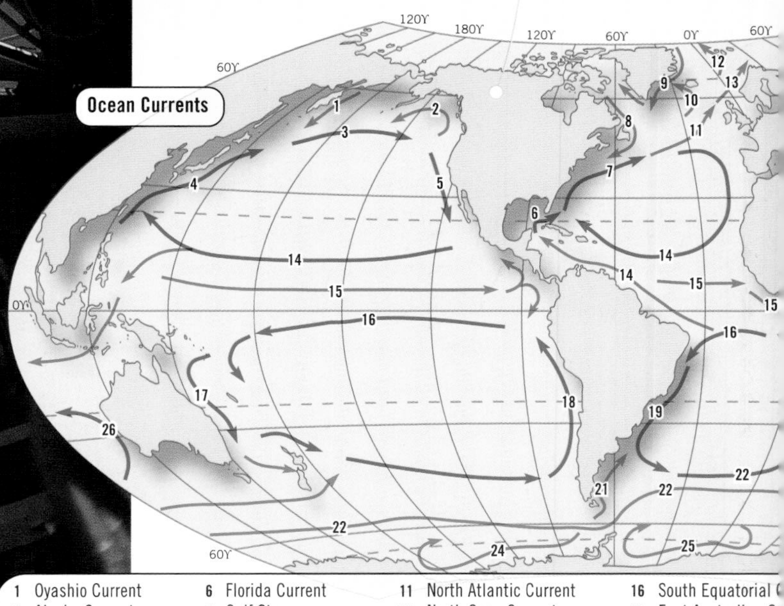

1 Oyashio Current	6 Florida Current	11 North Atlantic Current	16 South Equatorial C
2 Alaska Current	7 Gulf Stream	12 North Cape Current	17 East Australian Cu
3 North Pacific Current	8 Labrador Current	13 Norwegian Current	18 Humboldt Current
4 Kuroshio	9 East Greenland Current	14 North Equatorial Current	19 Brazil Current
5 California Current	10 Irminger Current	15 Equatorial countercurrents	20 Benguela Current

Oceans and Marine Circulation Systems

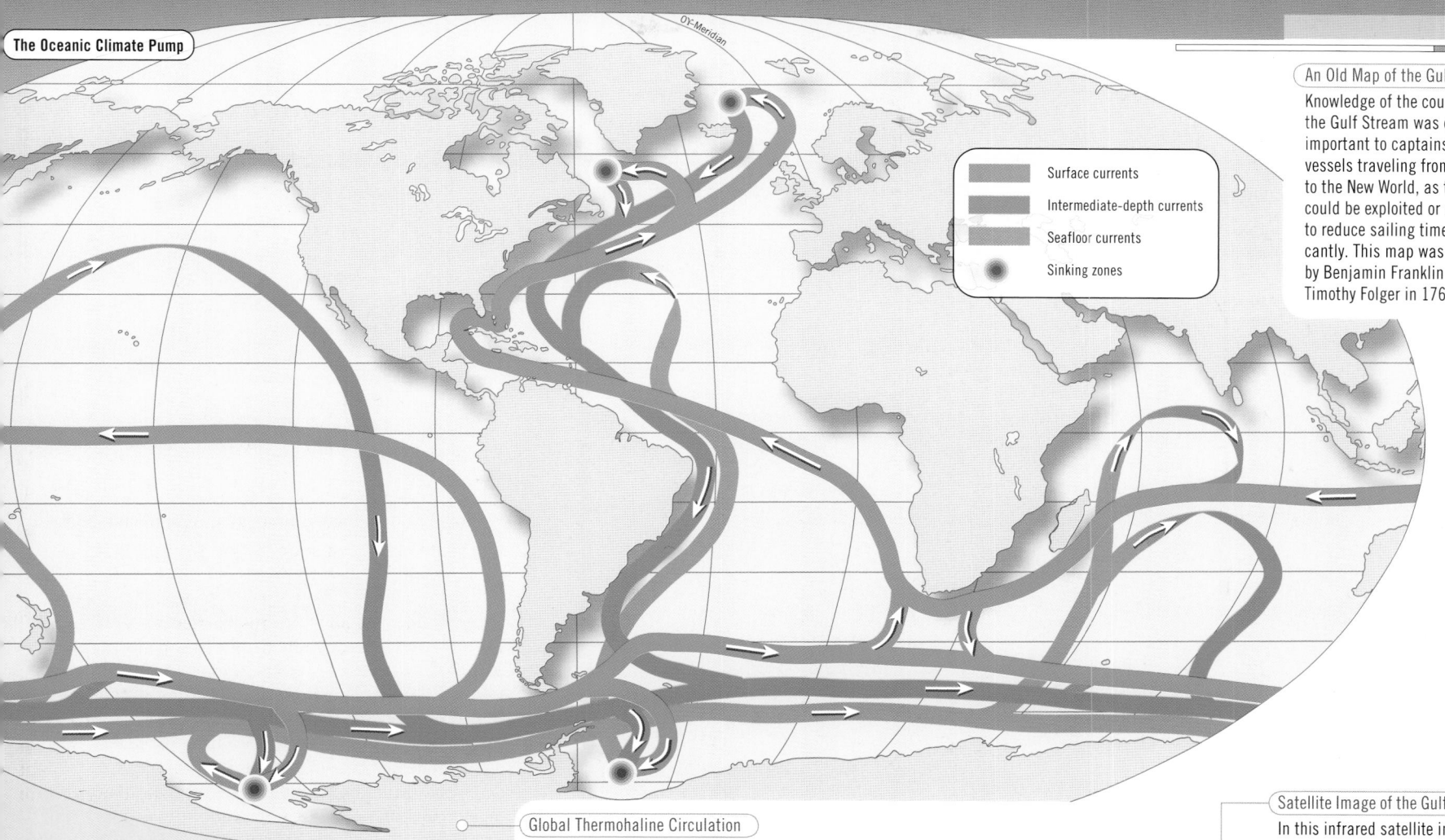

The Oceanic Climate Pump

Surface currents

Intermediate-depth currents

Seafloor currents

Sinking zones

Knowledge of the course of the Gulf Stream was extremely important to captains of ocean vessels traveling from Europe to the New World, as the current could be exploited or avoided to reduce sailing times significantly. This map was compiled by Benjamin Franklin and Timothy Folger in 1769.

for weather extremes all over the globe. Today, they can be predicted several months in advance on the basis of computer simulations. If farmers respond in time, crop failures can be avoided for the most part.

Currents of Life

Ocean currents circulate vast quantities of nutrients and trace substances and supply oxygen to the depths of the sea. Thus they are essential to marine life. Without currents, the oceans of the Earth would be nearly dead. The rich fishing grounds off the coast of Peru are fed by the Humboldt Current, and thermohaline circulation promotes especially vigorous algae growth in the North Atlantic. Currents also carry carbon dioxide into the depths of the sea, thus helping rid the atmosphere of man-made emissions that contribute to global warming.

Global Thermohaline Circulation

The pattern of thermohaline circulation driven by differences in water density spans the Earth like a gigantic conveyor belt. Thus warm water near the surface of the Atlantic flows northward from the southern tip of Africa through the Benguela Current, the Gulf Stream, and the North Atlantic Current into the sinking regions in the North Atlantic (these currents overlie wind-driven circulation patterns). From there, it flows as cold water at a depth of two to three kilometers back to the south. In the process, 1015 Watts of thermal energy are transported into the North Atlantic region – the equivalent of the output of 500,000 large power plants.

Satellite Image of the Gulf Stream

In this infrared satellite image, the Gulf Stream is clearly identifiable as a warm (black and red) band. It veers from the North American coast off Cape Hatteras and breaks apart, forming meanders and gyres. Its warm water flows with the North Atlantic Stream to regions off the coasts of northern Europe.

Surface Currents

Ocean currents which flow near the surface are largely wind-driven but may also be propelled by differences in seawater density. The prevailing trade and west winds are responsible for the largest subtropical gyre, along the western edge of which the strong boundary currents (including the Gulf Stream, the Kuroshio and the Brazil Current) flow toward the poles.

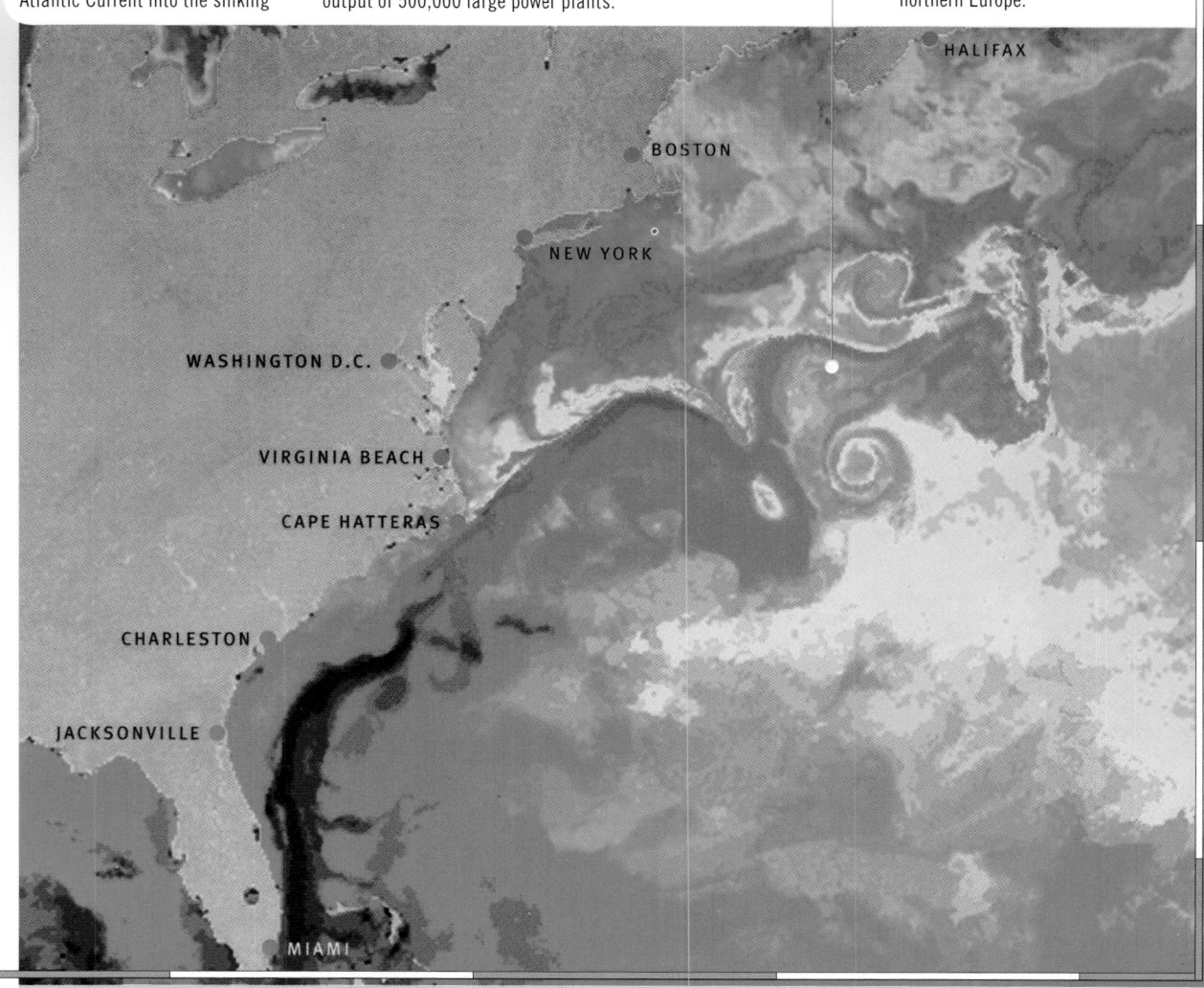

HALIFAX

BOSTON

NEW YORK

WASHINGTON D.C.

VIRGINIA BEACH

CAPE HATTERAS

CHARLESTON

JACKSONVILLE

MIAMI

60Y

4

30Y

14

15

0Y

16

26

30Y

22

60Y

lkland Current	25	Wedell Gyre
ntarctic Circum-	26	West Australien Current
lar Current	→	Major subtropical gyres
gulhas Current	→	Strong Currents
oss-Sea Gyre	*	Direction depends upon the season

The Earth's Ice - A Remnant of the Ice Age

Is Ice on Earth Melting or is a New Ice Age Coming?

Many people today are concerned that global warming will eventually melt all of the Earth's ice. Were this to happen, the sea level would rise as much as 70 meters. Coastal cities like New York, London, and Hamburg would be flooded completely. Many low-lying areas and countless islands would be submerged. On the other hand, the warming process could also produce heavier precipitation in the polar regions, adding to the existing Antarctic ice sheet. Yet the danger could come from another quarter. Oceanic warming could affect ocean currents. The Gulf Stream, our warm water heating system, could disperse, and the climate in the North Atlantic region would become much colder. Those who think in terms of geological time know that a new ice age will come sooner or later, as many warm periods lasted hardly longer than the Holocene, our own post-glacial era.

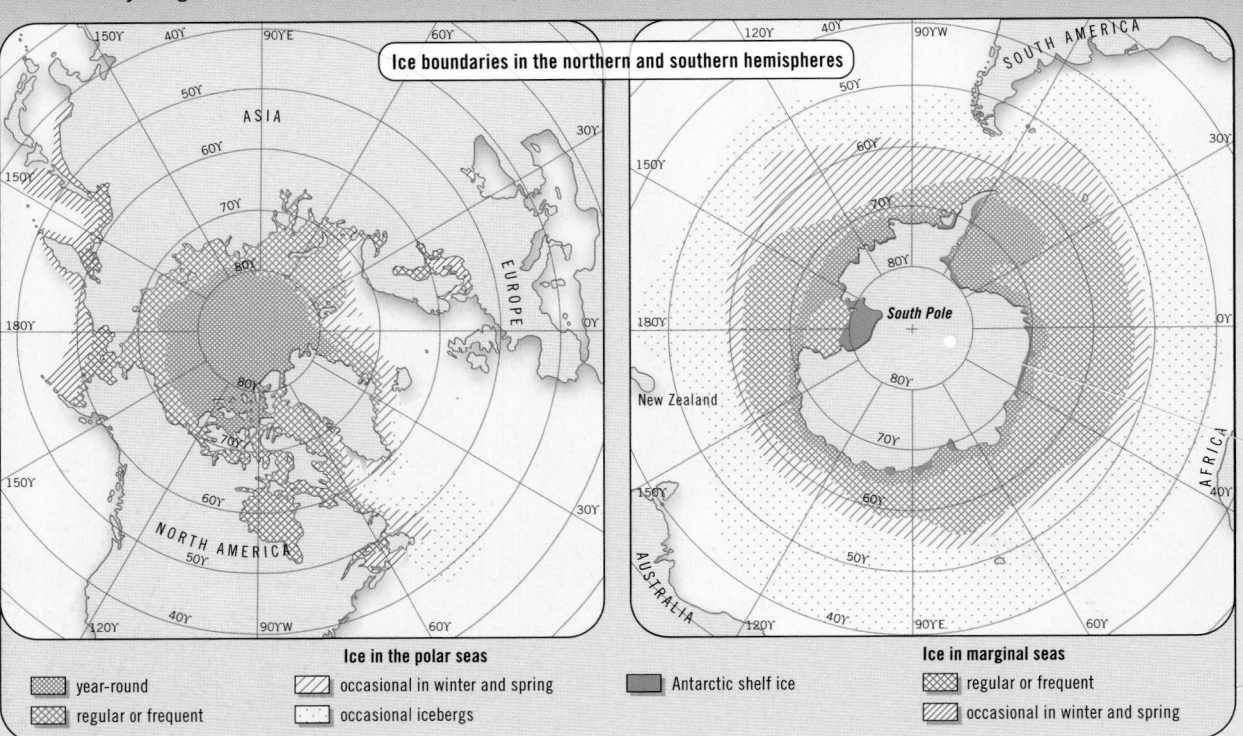

Ice boundaries in the northern and southern hemispheres

Ice in the polar seas
- year-round
- regular or frequent
- occasional in winter and spring
- occasional icebergs

Ice in marginal seas
- Antarctic shelf ice
- regular or frequent
- occasional in winter and spring

From Snow to Glacial Ice

Dry, fresh snow (density: 0.01–0.04 g/ccm) is 90 % air. Delicate ice crystals in snowflakes soon break down; the snow settles, melts to a certain degree, and freezes again (regelation). Developing grains of ice form firn snow (0.55 g/ccm), which contains 50 % air, and then firn ice (0.84 g/ccm), in which air bubbles account for only 30 % of total mass. The final phase is glacial ice (0.90 g/ccm), which is impermeable to air and water. Pure ice has a density of 0.917 g/ccm. In the Alps, ice grains measuring up to eight centimeters in diameter form after several years, while grains of ice at the South Pole can take 200 years to reach a diameter of one centimeter.

Ice Shapes the Topography

Although ice moves more slowly than flowing water, it exerts tremendous pressure on the underlying rock (100 to 5000 tons per square meter). Pressure and motion grind the rock away (detersion) and form roches moutonnées with flat ice-facing slopes and steeply inclined back sides. Rock fragments carried by the flow cut grooves in the smoothly ground rock, which later make it possible to trace the direction of glacial movement. V-shaped valleys carved by flowing water before the formation of ice are reshaped into U-shaped valleys. Rock debris broken away by the ice is transported to the edge of the ice flow, where it is melted out and deposited in terminal moraines. Unlike flowing water, ice is capable of moving huge boulders, which are left as erratics in the landscape after the ice recedes.

Flowing Glaciers

In contrast to rigid sea ice, glacial ice is granulated and becomes malleable and flowable under pressure. Regelation plays an important role in this process. The much colder ice in the Antarctic glides only as rigid block formations.

The Water Vapor – Ice – Water Cycle

Water evaporates from the warm oceans and rises with air currents into the high mountain regions. At these ice-cold elevations, it forms small ice crystals that fall to the ground as snow, even during the summer. This snow turns to ice, which then flows downward toward warmer areas, actually reaching the sea in some places. Icebergs are calved as inland ice slides into the sea. This cycle is driven by solar energy.

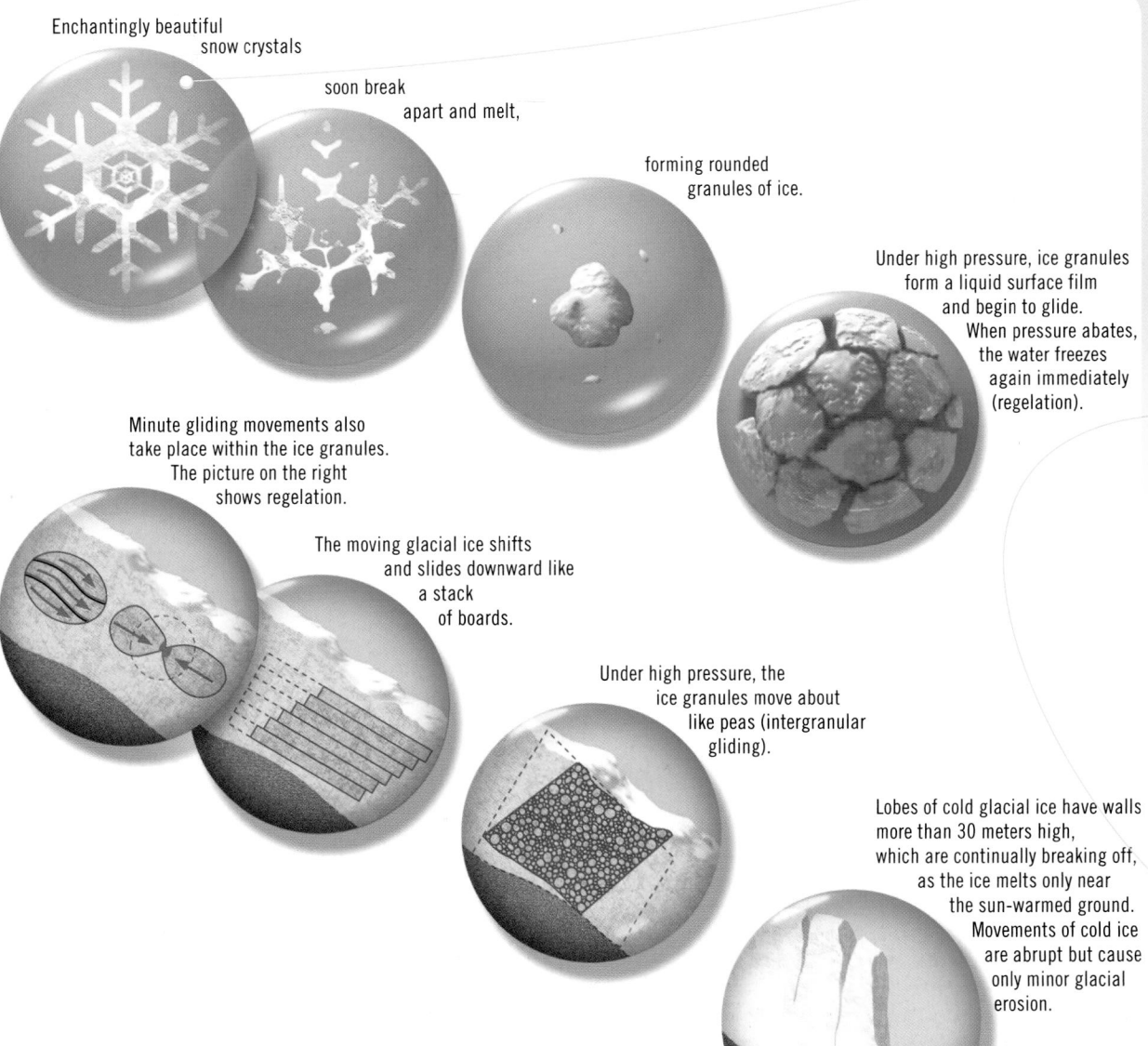

Enchantingly beautiful snow crystals

soon break apart and melt,

forming rounded granules of ice.

Under high pressure, ice granules form a liquid surface film and begin to glide. When pressure abates, the water freezes again immediately (regelation).

Minute gliding movements also take place within the ice granules. The picture on the right shows regelation.

The moving glacial ice shifts and slides downward like a stack of boards.

Under high pressure, the ice granules move about like peas (intergranular gliding).

Lobes of cold glacial ice have walls more than 30 meters high, which are continually breaking off, as the ice melts only near the sun-warmed ground. Movements of cold ice are abrupt but cause only minor glacial erosion.

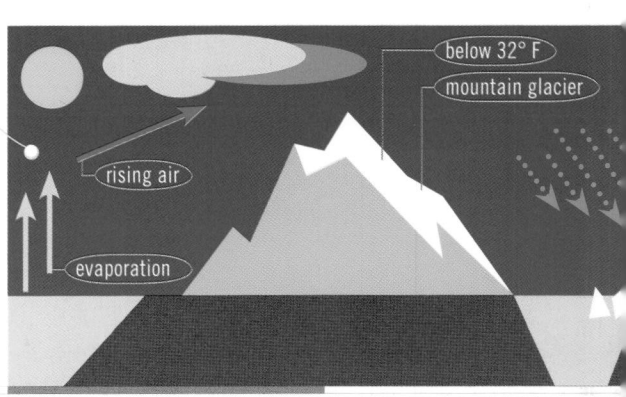

below 32° F
mountain glacier
rising air
evaporation

The Earth's Ice - A Remnant of the Ice Age

The Earth's Frozen Caps

The lower boundary of permanent ice in the mountains depends largely on the climate. The ice line lies at about 2,600 m on the northern face of the Alps, 4,800 m at the Equator, and over 6,000 m in dry subtropical regions, such as Tibet. Snow descends quickly to the valleys in avalanches from very steep terrain but forms glacial ice wherever it can accumulate.

The rocky summits of many of the world's highest mountains are hidden from view by ice caps. On steep slopes, the ice breaks apart, forming deep crevasses. Concealed by a covering of snow, these pose a particular danger to mountain climbers. Ice avalanches are common on extremely steep inclines.

There are hundreds of glaciers in north-western Canada and Alaska. The Malaspina Glacier in Alaska, the longest valley glacier in the world, is 115 km long. Glaciers are numerous in the Rocky Mountains of the United States and the Andes in South America.

When Islands Merge with the Mainland

Global sea levels fall as increasing amounts of water are captured in ice. During the last ice age, the sea level was 135 meters lower than it is today. Many areas now far below the ocean's surface were once dry land. A land bridge across the Bering Strait connected Asia with North America. England was not an island, and coral isles rose as small mountains from the sea. During warm periods, the ice melts and sea levels begin to rise again. The Antarctic ice sheet (12.6 million square km) has presumably existed for some 20 million years. Sea ice in the Arctic (2 million square km) is only three centimeters thick and tends to melt and regelate quickly. The massive Greenland ice sheet (1.7 million square km) is relatively stable.

When Water Freezes, Everything Changes

Liquid water assumes a solid state at temperatures below 32° F. Average temperatures remain below the freezing point the year round in the polar regions and in the high mountain areas above the snow line. The polar caps are exposed to insufficient warming solar radiation, and the thin air in the alpine regions grows increasingly colder at higher elevations. Temperatures fall by up to 1.8° F per 100 meters of elevation. At heights of 5,000 meters and above, mountain slopes are covered constantly with ice and snow, even in hot, tropical inland areas. In the coldest regions of the world, the ground is frozen permanently (permafrost), though not beneath the inland ice sheets.

Ice Sheets Cover Entire Continents

During glacial periods ice may bury entire mountain ranges and expand far into the surrounding landscape. In North America, the Laurentide Ice Sheet, which once covered Canada and northern parts of the United States, covered a total area of more than 13 million square km. Today, only two parts of the world remain covered by enormous inland ice sheets: Greenland and the Antarctic. Ice in the Antarctic is some 4,800 meters thick in some places. If the 30 million cubic km of ice in the Antarctic were distributed among five million people, each of them would receive a ton of ice every minute for ten years. The same quantity of ice would cover all the dry land on earth with a layer 180 meters thick.

Snow

Inland ice sheet

Montblanc

Sea Ice

Seawater freezes out fresh water, forming ice slush that later hardens into shelf ice. Wind and water currents break the solid ice masses into separate floes (pack ice). The ice insulates so effectively that pack ice reaches a thickness of no more than three meters even at the North Pole. Lateral ice compression forms pressure ridges as high as 20 meters.

Eternal Snow

The snow line becomes visible in the summer, when snow at lower mountain elevations melts completely. Above the snow line, precipitation falls almost exclusively in the form of snow, and more snow falls than melts in the course of the year. This surplus of snow turns to glacial ice. In the late fall, the snow line begins its gradual descent to lower elevations (temporary snow line).

Solid Ice

Column-shaped ice crystals give sheets of ice on fresh-water lakes considerable strength. These crystals grow downward from the surface. Rigid lake ice is inflexible and very strong. Depending upon its thickness, it can support skaters or even large cargo aircraft.

Ice in the Sky (Cirrus Clouds)

Fine ice crystals form from water vapor high in the atmosphere. Since cold air contains very little water, these clouds of ice crystals are very thin and thus transparent. Cirrus clouds often herald bad weather.

Ice-Cold Ground

Water contained in soil is completely frozen in permafrost regions. When the upper layer of ground thaws in the summer and liquid surface water seeps into fissures in the ground, it freezes immediately and seals the hollow spaces. (photo from an underground tunnel).

A Conveyor Belt of Ice

Rock debris that falls from mountain slopes or is stripped away by glacial ice (exaration, detraction) is carried over long distances before being melted out at the foot of the glacier and deposited in a terminal moraine.

Global Climate Zones

Stable or Constantly in Flux?

Today's climate patterns are certain to change. Just 5,000 years ago, average summer temperatures in North America were 36.5 degrees higher than today, and deciduous forests stood where conifers thrive today. The state of New Hampshire was covered by an ice sheet as recently as 18,000 years ago.

Core samples from the Greenland Ice Sheet show how abruptly climate can change. Scientists studying samples from a lake in southern Italy recently learned that local vegetation changed from dense forest to sparse steppe growth and back again within only 200 years about 75,000 years ago. The discovery came as a surprise to the many people who believed that the natural phenomenon of climate is constant over extended periods of time.

The Varying Intensity of Solar Heat

During the ice ages, plants, animals, and human beings were forced out of vast areas of the northern hemisphere. Life did not return to these regions until temperatures rose again and the ice gradually receded. We still do not know precisely what caused these drastic climatic changes, although experts agree that solar radiation is a crucial determinant of climate. Our planet is close enough to the sun to benefit from its warmth, yet far enough away that our atmosphere does not evaporate. The parallel rays of the sun strike the earth at a ninety-degree angle at the equator but reach the poles at a much flatter angle. Differences in pressure resulting from this unequal distribution of solar energy generate massive air currents. The influx of solar energy also differs from point to point depending upon the season and time of day, and this affects local weather as well. This results in part from the fact that the Earth's axis is not perpendicular to the plane of its orbit around the sun but is instead inclined at an angle of 23.5 degrees. The effects of this tilt are particularly noticeable in the polar regions (polar days and nights).

Global Respiration

Masses of air warmed in the tropics rise and drift into cooler northern or southern regions, while colder polar air flows toward the Equator. This general pattern of atmospheric circulation is a blessing that balances extremes in different climate zones. Yet a number of other factors also contribute to climate differences: elevation, topography, the distribution of land and seas, and cold or warm ocean currents. The macroclimates of specific climate zones can be broken down into mesoclimates (local weather patterns) and microclimates nearest the Earth's surface.

Weather activity takes place primarily in the troposphere, which lies beneath the stratosphere and extends to an altitude of about 13 km. The composition of our atmosphere is remarkably constant. Dry air is composed of nitrogen (78% by volume), oxygen (21%) and small amounts of argon (0.9%), carbon dioxide (0.03%), neon, helium, and other gases. It can also contain up to 4% water vapor. Terrestrial organisms have adapted to this mixture of gases. When oxygen concentration falls below 20% (at high altitudes or in poorly ventilated rooms, for example), we feel the unpleasant effects immediately.

Launch of a weather balloon equipped with a radio sensor that transmits readings from high altitudes. Special balloons rise to altitudes of 35 km. Satellites send back data and images from as high as 36,000 km above the earth.

Weather, Weather Patterns, and Climate

A look at the formations and movements of clouds in the sky tells us a great deal about local weather at any given moment. Average prevailing weather conditions at a specific location represent general weather patterns. Prevailing weather patterns that persist over long periods of time make up the climate of a particular region.

Adaptation – Creating Our Own Microclimates

Human beings depend on weather and climate more than any other living organisms. It is no coincidence that most ancient cultures had weather gods – Zeus in ancient Greece and Thor, the god of thunder in the Germanic world are just two examples. Yet unlike other living beings, humans possess the ability to protect themselves against extreme weather.

Humans have little difficulty coping with conditions in the warmer climate zones, as they adapt easily to high temperatures (due perhaps to their origin in the African savannahs). But to survive in the cold regions of the Earth, man had to gain command of fire, develop appropriate clothing, and learn to build tolerable microclimates – tents made of hides, igloos built with blocks of snow, wooden houses or urban housing developments.

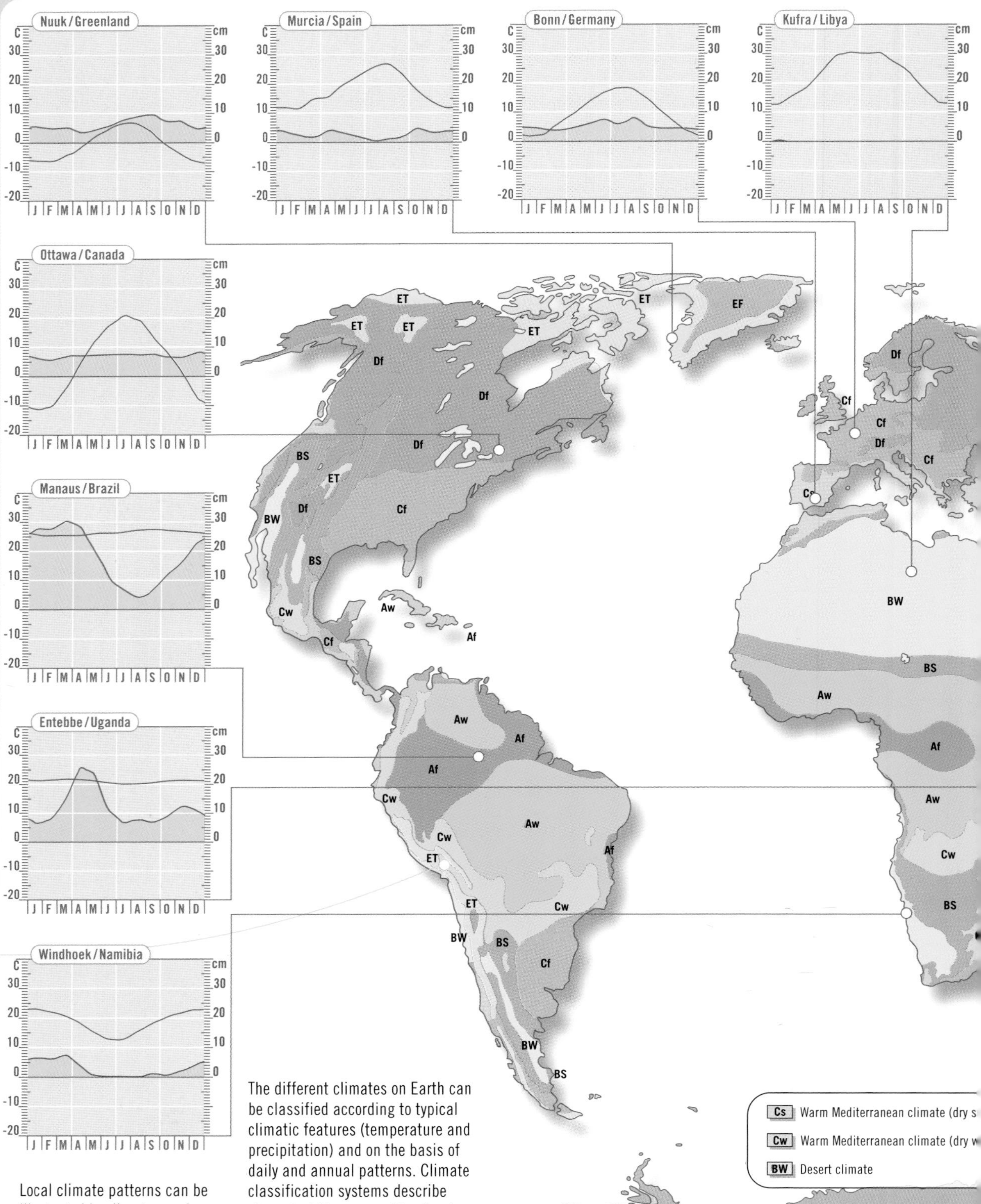

Local climate patterns can be illustrated in climate graphs. The graph for each station shows curves for average temperature (red) and precipitation (blue). A temperature curve that lies above the precipitation curve indicates arid conditions, while the reverse is an indicator of humidity.

The different climates on Earth can be classified according to typical climatic features (temperature and precipitation) and on the basis of daily and annual patterns. Climate classification systems describe characteristic geographic climate differences. The Köppen-Geiger Climate Chart is based primarily on the distribution of vegetation. Since climate conditions are among the most important factors affecting plant growth, vegetation is a good indicator of climate at a given location.

A simplified version of Köppen-Geiger's classification scheme distinguishes among tropical wet-dry and arid climates (A), desert and steppe climates (B), humid temperate climates (C), cold wet-dry continental climates (D) and tundra and snow-and-ice climates (E).

Cs	Warm Mediterranean climate (dry s...
Cw	Warm Mediterranean climate (dry w...
BW	Desert climate

Alpine Elevation Zones

Mountain climates grow increasingly inhospitable at higher altitudes. Temperatures fall, and the air becomes moister and stormier. Vegetation is also distributed in belts at different elevations depending upon local climate conditions. The upper vegetation boundary borders on a zone of debris, snow, and ice near the summit (photo taken near Haines, Alaska). The ground is covered by snow for longer periods at higher elevations, thus shortening vegetation periods during which photosynthesis is possible. This basic heat deficit is offset somewhat by solar radiation, which is filtered only slightly by the thin atmosphere (as mountain climbers learn when they experience their first severe case of ultra-violet sunburn). Not only are air and ground temperatures lower at high altitudes, atmospheric pressure falls as well, reducing the supply of life-giving oxygen, carbon dioxide and water vapor in the air. The unfavorable conditions in the high mountain regions restrict species diversity. Summer temperatures are a crucial factor. The tree line is highest where summer solar radiation is most intense. Although plants in polar and alpine regions have much in common, they also exhibit major differences, as these climates are subject to different annual climatic shifts to which living organisms must adjust accordingly.

Virtually Lifeless Regions of Snow and Ice

The polar regions are not only cold, they are among the most arid areas on Earth. The capacity of air to retain water vapor diminishes as it grows colder. Thus the high Antarctic Plateau is drier than the Sahara. Human beings living here consume an average of six liters of water per day (photo: Paradise Bay, Antarctica).

Tundra Climate in the Arctic North

With average annual temperatures of about 5° F, only the uppermost layer of permafrost thaws for a few months during the summer, allowing for a vegetation period of between 30 and 90 days. The photo shows a summer carpet of alpine Veronica on Ellesmere Island.

Hot, Arid Deserts with Little Vegetation

Most of the world's hot, arid zones (with less than 200 mm of precipitation per year) are found in the interiors of large continents (photo: Libyan Desert) or along the margins of cold ocean currents, where very little moisture is taken up by moving masses of air. Rainfall is also extremely sparse in trade wind belts with prevailing high pressure and on the leeward slopes of high mountain ranges.

Hot Days in the Tropics

Daily temperature fluctuations in the tropics are greater than seasonal ones. It is always hot in the lowlands. Temperatures fall only slightly during rainy periods, although humidity rises to extreme levels, creating a paradise for lush plants growth (photo: eucalyptus forest in NE Australia). Tropical wet zones merge along their boundaries with semi-arid savannahs, where wet and dry periods alternate.

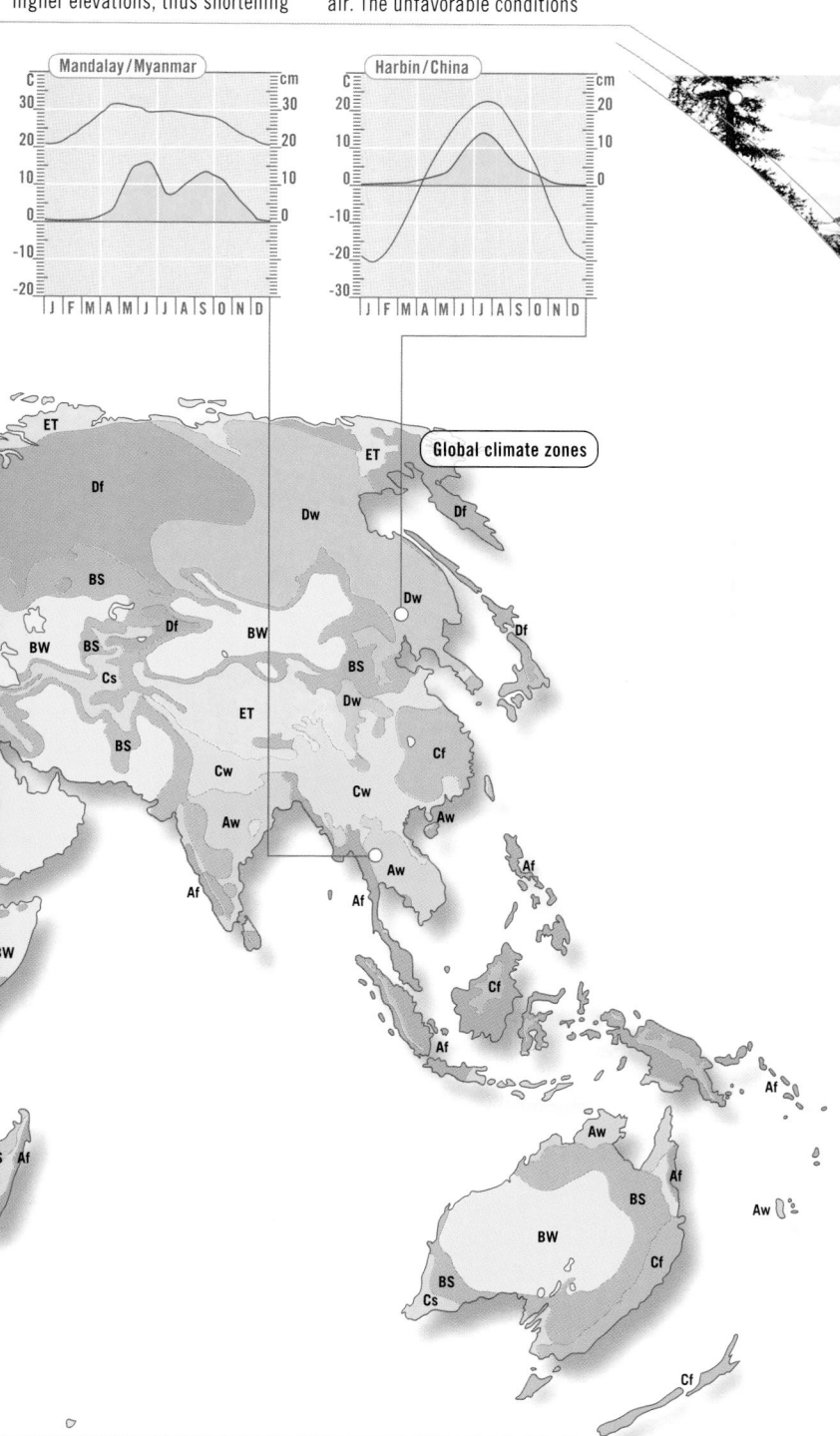

Global climate zones

	Mandalay/Myanmar		Harbin/China

BS	Steppe climate	Df	Cold continental climate (humid winters)	EF	Snow-and-ice climate
Aw	Savannah climate	Dw	Cold continental climate (dry winters)	ET	Tundra climate
Af	Wet equatorial climate	Cf	Humid temperate climate		

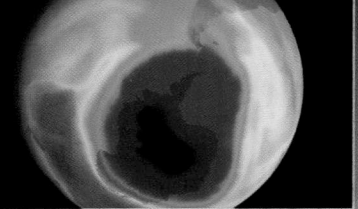

The Changing Global Climate

... and Mankind's Role in the Process

The history of the Earth's climate is one of changes, some gradual, others rapid and dramatic. Periods of relative stability and calm like the Holocene, which began some 10,000 years ago, are the exception rather than the rule. Yet it was precisely this climatic stability that allowed human civilization to develop. Today, the extent of human intervention in climatic processes is increasing. Are we merely a minor disruptive factor in the interplay of these powerful forces of nature, or does mankind pose a serious threat to the global climatic balance?

Variations in the Earth's Orbit

Some 20,000 years ago, at the peak of the last ice age, substantial portions of North America and northern Europe were covered by sheets of ice several thousand meters thick. This ice extended deep into the North American continent to the region now covered by the Great Lakes. The land south of the ice was arctic steppe, much like today's tundra regions. On the basis of bore samples taken from deposits thousands and even millions of years old, from layers of sediment on the ocean floor or from continental ice in Antarctica and Greenland, for example, it has been possible to reconstruct temperature patterns and many other characteristics of past climate. For at least two million years, the Earth's climate has been governed by relatively regular cycles. Ice ages lasting roughly 100,000 years have alternated with warm periods usually about 10,000 years long. These cycles are caused by subtle shifts in the Earth's orbit around the sun and in the inclination of the Earth's axis. These changes, known as Milankovitch variations, affect the seasonal and geographic distribution of solar radiation – although the total amount of radiation that reaches the Earth remains constant. It is not entirely clear why the Earth's climate reacts so dramatically to these changing radiation patterns. One crucial factor is apparently the intensity of summer sunlight over the continents of the northern hemisphere, for when the snows of the past winter do not melt completely, large sheets of ice begin to form. They reflect solar radiation and thus lead to further cooling. Our understanding of Milankovitch variations suggests that the Holocene is an unusually long warm phase, which would mean that a new ice age is not to be expected for several tens of thousands of years.

Abrupt Climatic Shifts

Scientists have learned only fairly recently that the last ice age was marked by a series of very abrupt and drastic changes in climate. In the course of these so-called Dansgaard-Oeschger Events (of which more than 20 are known to have occurred during the last ice age), average temperatures in the North Atlantic region rose rapidly – within only a few years – by between 11 and 14°F. These unusually warm periods lasted several hundreds or thousands of years. Their effects were felt around the globe – even in the Antarctic. Evidently, sudden shifts in the course of marine currents played a significant role in these sudden climatic changes.

Even the Holocene, the current, relatively stable warm period, has not been free of climatic changes. Some 5,500 years ago, the Sahara was transformed from a landscape of swamps, lakes and areas of vegetation inhabited by many large animals and human beings into the desert we know today. In all likelihood, this process was set in motion by a shift in the Earth's orbit which triggered a fatal chain of events: a gradual decrease in rainfall resulting in diminished plant growth which led in turn to further reduction in precipitation.

The Radiation Budget

The Earth's temperature is regulated by a simple radiation budget. On average, the energy received from the sun is equal to the energy radiated by the Earth into space. If too much energy is received, temperatures rise and the Earth radiates more heat until balance is

Frozen Lake, 1830

From the fifteenth to the eighteenth century, temperatures in Europe were 1.8 to 3.6°F cooler than today. This cool period is known as the "Little Ice Age." Lake Constance froze over completely about every 20 years during that period but only once during the twentieth century (1963). Inhabitants of the alpine regions often experienced failed harvests and famine during the "Little Ice Age." This View of Frozen Lake Constance was painted by the local artist Nicolaus Hug in 1830.

Aussicht auf dem Dam in Constanz nach dem überfrornen Bodensee im Jahre 1830.

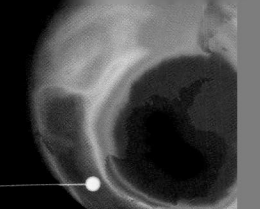

The Changing Global Climate

restored. If the Earth had no atmosphere, its average temperature would be somewhere near 0° F. The atmosphere inhibits thermal radiation from the Earth's surface, primarily due to the insulating effect of water vapor and carbon dioxide, the so-called greenhouse gases. Consequently, the Earth's surface warms until the radiation balance is restored at today's average temperature of about 59°F. It is this natural greenhouse effect that makes our planet inhabitable. Changes in the composition of the atmosphere or in the surface area of reflective ice and cloud masses can affect the radiation budget and thus raise or lower temperatures.

The Human Factor

Human impact on the global climate dates back to the Middle Ages, when people began clearing forests to make room for farmland, thereby increasing carbon dioxide levels in the atmosphere and creating lighter areas of surface that reflect more sunlight. But it was not until the Industrial Revolution in the first half of the nineteenth century that mankind developed the means to disrupt the delicate radiation balance significantly. The leading cause of these man-made changes is the use of fossil fuels – coal, petroleum, and natural gas. The fossil fuel we burn in a single year took roughly a million years to accumulate. The carbon contained in these materials oxidizes during

combustion and is released into the air as carbon dioxide (CO_2). About half of it remains in the atmosphere, while the remainder is absorbed by the oceans and the biosphere. Since the beginning of the Industrial Age, the carbon-dioxide concentration in the atmosphere has risen from 280 parts per million (ppm) to 360 ppm, and the greenhouse effect has grown stronger accordingly. Other gases released in the course of human activities intensify the greenhouse effect even further. Examples are methane and fluorocarbons, which are also responsible for the ozone hole.

Concentrations of greenhouse gases in the atmosphere have risen in recent years, raising average global temperatures by about 1.25° F – over both land and sea. Mountain glaciers are melting all over the world (total glacier volume in the Alps has already decreased by half). Artic Ice has become almost 40 per cent thinner over the past 30 years.

Using sophisticated pattern-recognition techniques, climatologists have attempted to determine the extent to which these trends are actually attributable to anthropogenic emissions and to identify other possible causes (such as fluctuations in the sun). Their findings indicate that, at the very least, the accelerated warming trend observed since 1970 is largely a man-made phenomenon.

Scientists warned as early as the late nineteenth century on the basis of simple computations that increasing concentrations of carbon dioxide in the atmosphere would lead to global warming. Today, the world's climate can be simulated with the aid of powerful computers, which make it possible both to reconstruct past climate patterns and to project scenarios for the future. If concentrations of greenhouse gases in the atmosphere continue to rise at the current pace, we can expect global temperatures to rise by between 2.7 and 9.9 degrees F over the next hundred years. Should this happen, the earth will be warmer than it has been at any time during the past 100,000 years. One consequence would be a rise in sea level of between 20 and 90 centimeters, which would persist for centuries even if the warming trend were halted. Warming would also lead to changes in precipitation patterns and thus possibly to drought and flooding, endangering many existing ecosystems in the process. Low-lying coastal regions would be threatened by flooding caused by storms, and several island nations in the Pacific would disappear beneath the sea.

In an effort to slow the process of global warming, most of the nations participating in the international conference in Kyōto, Japan in 1997 signed a Climate Treaty that obliges industrial nations to reduce emissions of greenhouse gases to five per cent below 1990 levels by the year 2012. The treaty is not yet in force, as only a few nations have ratified it, and it represents, at best, only a first small step toward effective climate protection.

The Radiation Budget and the Greenhouse Effect

Assuming a value of 100 % for the amount of solar radiation that actually effects the global radiation budget (342.5 Watts per square meter), only 45 % (on long-term, global average) actually reaches the Earth's surface. The remainder is absorbed or scattered. The total reflective capacity of the earth (including the atmosphere and clouds) is referred to as the Earth's albedo, and amounts to 30 % on a yearly average.
The effective heat radiated by the Earth's surface is 18 %. This equates to the difference between 114 % – the value which would be expected if the Earth had no atmosphere – and 96 % – for radiation reflected back by the atmosphere (the greenhouse effect). The difference between incoming solar radiation and outgoing terrestrial radiation (27 %) at the surface is offset by heat currents.

Threatening Hole

In 1985, British researchers discovered a hole in the ozone layer of the upper atmosphere – our shield against dangerous cosmic radiation. One of the causes identified was the release of industrially produced fluorocarbons, such as those used in spray cans, into the atmosphere. The Montreal Protocol of 1987 called for a global ban on these gases, to be achieved in a step-by-step process. They are hardly used at all today, and scientists now predict that the ozone hole will gradually close over the next several decades. It will probably take more than 100 years to restore the ozone layer completely, however.

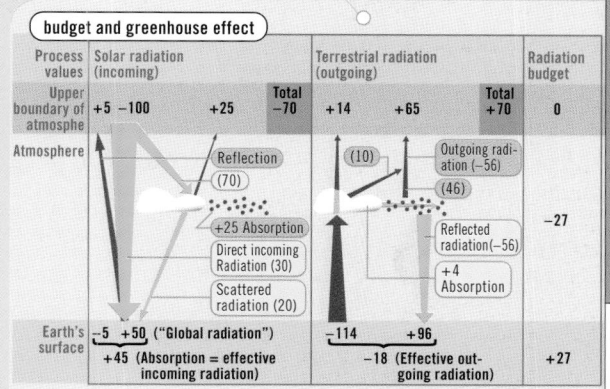

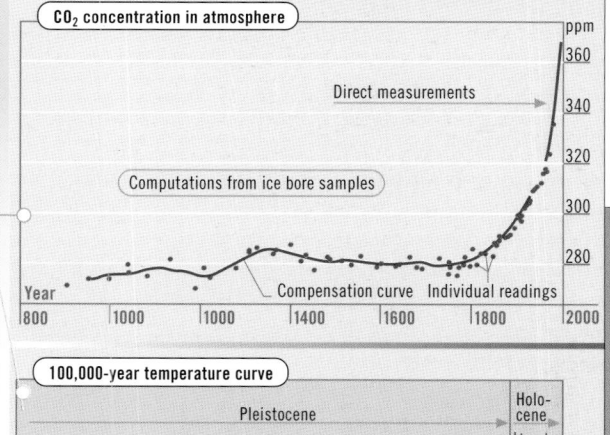

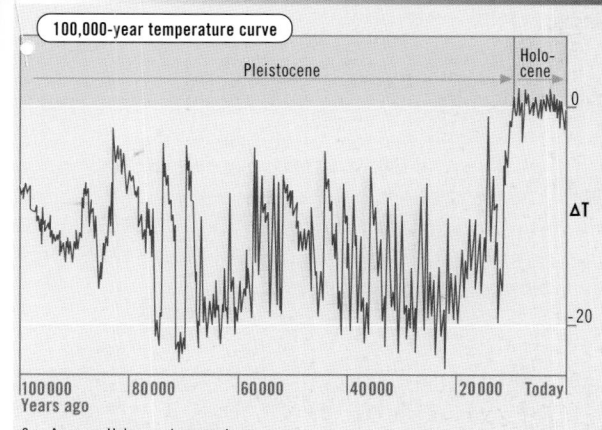

This climate curve from Greenland shows the consistently warm climate of the past 10,000 years, the Holocene period. During the preceding 100,000 ice-age years, the climate was not only much colder but also subject to sudden fluctuations.

Global warming trends, 1976 – 1999

Quelle: NCDC

in degrees Fahrenheit per century

14°F 17.6°F 21.2°F 24.8°F 28.4°F 32°F 35.6°F 39.2°F 42.8°F 46.4°F 50°F

Red dots on the map mark regions that have grown warmer. Blue dots show those that have cooled. Insufficient data is available for the remaining areas.

Saharan Rock Painting

Until about 6,000 years ago, the Sahara was much greener than it is today. A large number of rock drawings offer evidence of a much moister climate. The buffalo Homoioceras antiquus (Oued Djerat, Tassili n'Ajjer, Algeria) became extinct during the early Holocene.

Alarming Rise

Analyses of air bubbles in Antarctic ice and measurements taken at Mauna Loa (Hawaii) since 1957 tell us a great deal about carbon-dioxide concentration in the atmosphere: about 280 ppm during warm periods like the Holocene, 200 ppm during the ice ages, and more

THEMATIC SECTION

Global Warming and Climate Change

The Future of Our Planet

Evidence of global warming is everywhere. It is affecting physical and biological processes on every continent, and the far-reaching implications are alarming – rising sea levels, coastal flooding, more frequent heat waves, droughts and wildfires. In February 2007, the Intergovernmental Panel on Climate Change (IPCC) – an intergovernmental body of more than 1,200 authors and 2,500 scientific expert reviewers from more than 130 countries – reported that it is "very likely" that heat-trapping emissions from human activities have caused "most of the observed increase in globally averaged temperatures since the mid-20th century." By the end of the century, the IPCC projects temperature increases in the range of approximately 2°F to 11.5°F.

The Problem – In a Nutshell

Although "climate change" and "global warming" are often used interchangeably, according to the National Academy of Sciences, "the phrase 'climate change' is growing in preferred use to 'global warming' because it helps convey that there are [other] changes in addition to rising temperatures."

Global warming is the average increase in the temperature of the atmosphere near the Earth's surface and in the troposphere. It can occur as the result of natural factors or processes, such as the changes in the Earth's orbit around the sun or changes in ocean circulation. The natural warming of our planet's climate can also be affected by human activities that change the atmosphere's composition.

For over 200 years, the burning of fossil fuels, such as coal and oil, have caused the concentrations of "greenhouse" or heat-trapping gases to rise significantly in our atmosphere. These gasses prevent heat from escaping to space and ultimately contribute to human-influenced global warming and climate change.

Turning Up the Heat

Recent scientific data confirms that the earth's climate is not only changing, but that it's doing so quite quickly. Although temperatures do fluctuate naturally, global temperatures increased by about 1°F over the course of the last century, and will likely rise even more rapidly in coming decades. Since 1980, the earth has experienced 19 of its 20 hottest years on record, with 2005 and 1998 tied for the hottest and 2002 and 2003 coming in second and third.

Melting Glaciers and Floods

According to NASA scientists, the polar ice cap is now melting at the alarming rate of 9 percent per decade, and arctic ice thickness has decreased 40 percent since the 1960s. At this rate, all of the glaciers in Glacier National Park in Montana will be gone by 2070.

The current pace of sea-level rise is 3 times the historical rate and appears to be accelerating as a result of melting mountain glaciers and the Antarctic and Greenland ice caps. The consequences include loss of coastal wetlands and barrier islands, and a greater risk of flooding in coastal communities. Low-lying areas, such as the coastal region along the Gulf of Mexico are especially vulnerable. Flooding caused by sea-level rise will likely affect millions of additional people every year by the end of the century, with small islands and the crowded delta regions around large Asian rivers facing the highest risk.

Droughts

Hundreds of millions of people face water shortages that will worsen as temperatures rise. Most at risk are current drought-affected regions with heavily used water resources, and areas that get their water from glaciers. Scientists expect the land areas affected by drought to increase and water resources in such areas could decline as much as 30 percent by the year 2050. U.S. crops that are already near the upper end of their temperature tolerance range, or depend on heavily used water resources, could suffer with further warming.

Species at Risk

Many species and ecosystems may not be able to adapt as the effects of global warming and associated floods, droughts, wildfires, and insect infestations are compounded by stresses such as pollution and resource exploitation. As much as 30 percent of plant and animal species could face extinction if the global average temperature rises more than 3°F to 5°F relative to the 1980–1999 period.

The first comprehensive assessment of the extinction risk from global warming found that more than 1 million species could face extinction by 2050 if steps are not taken to address global warming pollution. A study published in the Nature journal found that at least 279 species of plants and animals are already responding to global warming. The geographic ranges of these species have shifted north and south toward the poles at an average rate of 6.4 kilometers per decade and their spring events occur earlier by an average of 2 days per decade.

Facing the Reality

Americans make up 4 percent of the world's population and produce 25 percent of the carbon dioxide pollution, burning fossil fuels such as coal–more than the emissions from China, India and Japan, combined. Coal-burning power plants are the largest U.S. source of carbon dioxide pollution, producing 2.5 billion tons every year. Automobiles, the second largest source, create nearly 1.5 billion tons of carbon dioxide annually. We have the technologies to build cars that run cleaner and burn less gas, modernize power plants to generate electricity from nonpolluting sources, and cut electricity use through energy efficiency. It's time to start putting these technologies to use – for the good of our planet.

What You Can Do

Visit the EPA's Climate Change Web site (http://www.epa.gov/climatechange) to learn about straightforward steps you can take to reduce your household's emission of greenhouse gasses. Taking a few minutes to replace the conventional bulbs in your house with ENERGY STAR bulbs, which use about 75 percent less energy, produce 75 percent less heat, and last up to 10 times longer. If every household in the U.S. took this simple initiative, 1 trillion pounds of greenhouse gas emissions would be prevented.

(Volcanic Aerosols)

Large-scale volcanic activity may last only a few days, but the massive outpouring of gases and ash can influence climate patterns for years. Sulfuric gases convert to sulfate aerosols, sub-micron droplets containing about 75 percent sulfuric acid. Following eruptions, these aerosol particles can linger as long as three to four years in the stratosphere. As a result, volcanic eruptions cause short-term climate changes and contribute to natural climate variability.

(Melting Ice-caps)

In March 2000, an iceberg the size of a small U.S. state cracked off the leading edge of Antarctica's Ross Ice Shelf. Originally the giant berg, named B-15, was about 300 kilometers long and 40 kilometers wide (186 miles long by 25 miles wide). The near-Connecticut-sized iceberg calved into many pieces over subsequent years; many of the "offspring" were themselves large enough to be named by the National Ice Center. On February 1, 2007, one of the original berg's descendants, B-15J, shed several smaller icebergs. This pair of images shows B-15J on January 29, 2007, and again on February 1. On February 1, three bergs have split off the southeastern quadrant of B-15J.

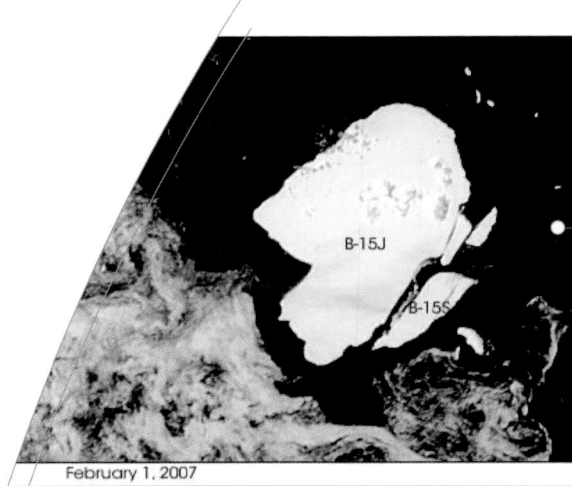

February 1, 2007

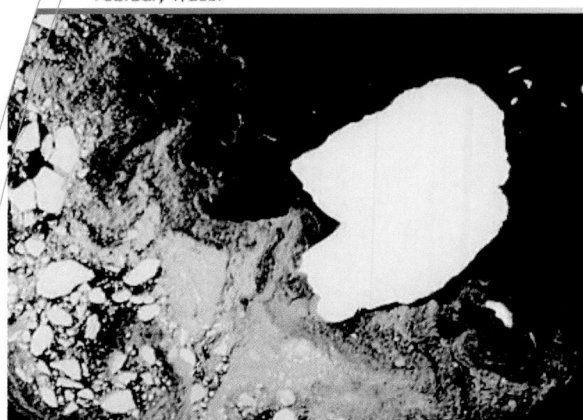

January 29, 2007

Global Warming and Climate Change

The ozone hole over the polar region of the Southern Hemisphere broke records for both area and depth in 2006. This image, made from data collected by the Ozone Monitoring Instrument on NASA's Aura satellite, shows the Antarctic ozone hole on September 24, 2006. The blues and purples that cover most of Antarctica illustrate where ozone levels were low, while greens, yellows, and red point to higher ozone levels.

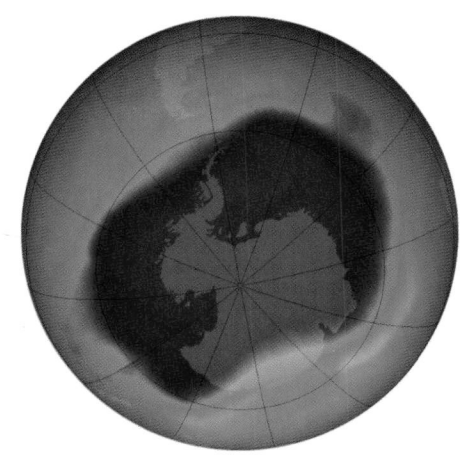

Total Ozone (Dobson Units)

| 110 | 220 | 330 | 440 | 550 |

The Sun's Heat

Many researchers believe the steady rise in sunspots and faculae since the late seventeenth century may be responsible for as much as half of the 0.6 degrees of global warming over the last 110 years. According to the 2001 report of the Intergovernmental Panel on Climate Change (IPCC), the imbalance between incoming solar radiation and outgoing thermal radiation will likely cause the Earth to heat up over the next century, possibly melting polar ice caps, causing sea levels to rise, creating violent global weather patterns.

Pollution from Power Plants

Fossil fuel-fired power plants, many of which were built before 1964, and long before pollution controls, are the largest source of air pollution in the U.S. By the year 2000, electric power plants produced 2.2 billion tons of carbon dioxide, 12 million tons of sulfur dioxide, and 7 million tons of nitrogen oxides. Of the 1,000 largest plants in the U.S., 77 percent are not subject to pollution controls under the Clean Air Act's New Source Review Requirements.

Green Power

During the process of photosynthesis plants convert sunlight, water from the soil, and carbon dioxide from the air into the energy they need to grow. In removing carbon dioxide from the atmosphere, plants contribute to the reduction of the greenhouse gases that are blamed for global warming.

Vegetation - The Earth's Botanical Cloak

Plant and Human Life – A Reassessment

According to the Book of Genesis, God created plants on the third day, calling upon the Earth to "bring forth grass, the herb yielding seed ... and the tree yielding fruit ... and God saw that it was good." (Genesis 1:11). Mankind arrived on the scene soon afterward. By current reckoning, human beings have since destroyed about 30 % of the original 62 million square kilometers of forest on Earth, transformed much of our planet's vast grasslands into arid wastelands (desertification) through overcultivation, and altered the character of natural vegetation in many regions of the world. We have intervened in natural patterns of growth and distribution, manipulated genetic makeup through breeding experiments, and replaced local flora with secondary growth over wide areas. Yet despite this massive human intervention in the plant kingdom, more than 99 % of the Earth's biomass – about 1.8 trillion tons of organic material (300 tons for every living human being) – is vegetable matter.

The Foundation of Human and Animal Life

In his famous "Canticle of the Sun," Saint Francis of Assisi spoke of "... Earth, our Mother, who feeds us in her sovereignty and produces various fruits and colored flowers and herbs." The words of Saint Francis reflect an uncomplicated view of nature and an implicit recognition of the close and vital cosmic relationship between all living organisms (the biosphere) and the Earth's inorganic crust (the lithosphere), a mystery that was not solved by modern biological science until many years later. Biologists, ecologists and biochemists agree that animal, and thus of course human life could not exist in its present form without the Earth's botanical cloak.

Plants as Chemical Factories and Nutrient Pumps

The leaves of plants contain chlorophyll (the pigment that makes them green), which they use to convert water taken up by their roots and carbon dioxide (CO_2) absorbed from the air into glucose (sugar) with the aid of light (solar energy) captured on their surfaces in a complicated process known as photosynthesis. Through their roots, which in some plants (wheat, for example) form networks of microscopically fine fibrous tendrils with combined lengths of up to several hundred kilometers, they absorb a wide variety of elements essential to all life on Earth from the soil. These they process along with the glucose into organic matter, referred to collectively as biomass (the dry weight of organic matter).

Through this process, a number of elements essential to many physiological processes, such as iron, phosphorus, calcium, magnesium, nitrogen, and sulfur, are incorporated into biomass and passed along through the food chain to herbivorous animal organisms and ultimately to carnivores (including humans as well, regardless of whether they actually eat meat or not, since the consumption of animal protein is virtually unavoidable for modern consumers).

In this way, the massive global nutrient pump of natural vegetation extracts more than two cubic kilometers per year – roughly six billion tons – of minerals and substances of all kinds from the Earth's crust and makes them available as sustenance to animals and human beings (approximately one ton for every living human being on Earth).

A root hair launches a biochemical attack on a calcite mineral: the first stage in the transition from mineral to chemical substance.

Soil-Building Vegetation

Vegetable biomass consumed by animal organisms is returned to the eternal mineral cycle as feces or in the bodies of dead organisms themselves. Unconsumed biomass is also remineralized when humus is formed through the decomposition of fallen leaves and dead plants. Mineral replacement resulting from biochemical and physical root activity, on the one hand, and the accumulation of biomass, on the other, are important soil-building processes which work within an ecological network in collaboration with such non-biological factors as the warmth and moisture of vegetation in a specific region.

Trees – Unsung "Environmental Helpers"

Trees are the largest forms of plant life. A deciduous tree between 15 and 20 meters high generates three million liters of oxygen annually (four times as much as a single human being needs in a year) through the process of photosynthesis. In one year, the same tree also filters as much as 7,000 kg of dust from the air with its foliage and extracts up to 7,000 liters of water from the soil through its root system, thus contributing significantly to the prevention of soil erosion – a problem that can assume catastrophic proportions in deforested areas. For every human being on Earth today, there are about 500 trees at work providing these important environmental services.

How Do the Little Flowers Grow, and How Do Plants Give Us Food?

The preceding description shows how very important the plant kingdom is. In light of the crucial role plants play in our lives, it is shocking to realize how little we know about them. Most people in the industrialized countries of the world can name at least 20 different makes of car but not nearly as many kinds of plants! Yet botanists have now identified more than 360,000 varieties, of which about 180,000 are blossoming plants.

It is not the species of so-called "higher plants" classified into families of trees, shrubs, flowers, and grasses that are so difficult to identify with certainty. The real difficulty and suspense begins with the attempt to establish clear scientific distinctions among the varieties of "lower plant organisms" or microflora: fungi, the various species of algae, lichens as symbiotic communities of fungi and algae, and even the types of bacteria that are classified as forms of plant life – the "little beasties" discovered and described by Antonie van Leewenhoek (1632–1723) with the aid of his home-made microscope.

Although between 10,000 and 50,000 edible varieties of plants are available for human consumption, only about 150 to 200 species (between 0.3 and 2 %) are actually used for nutritional purposes. Over 75 % of all energy consumed by human beings in the form of vegetable matter comes from only about ten crop plants (between 0.002 and 0.1 % of all edible species of plants).

The Earth's Coat of Brightly Colored Stripes

Plants have no means of locomotion, and thus the characteristics they exhibit as indicator plants at the present stage of evolutionary development are always evidence of their adaptation to prevailing conditions in their local environments (known as habitat conditions). These include such features as water-retention organs (in cactuses or agaves in arid regions), shallow, broad root systems (like those of the birch tree) in permafrost regions where soil thaws only for a few months during the summer, or a thick coat of hair as protection against evaporation in alpine regions (edelweiss is an example). Thus we understand why belts of vegetation corresponding generally to the Earth's climatic zones, communities of plants known by botanists as vegetation zones, cover the Earth like a brightly-colored striped coat. And the same explanation applies to the typical vegetation patterns in mountainous regions that reflect the increasing lack of heat at progressively higher elevations, a phenomenon described with specific reference to South America by Alexander von Humboldt as early as the late eighteenth century.

(2) Tundra Vegetation

With average annual temperatures normally below 5°F, permafrost soil thaws only briefly to a depth of a few centimeters in the summer. With a growth period of 30–90 days, this type of vegetation, which forms a continuous belt only in the northern hemisphere, is characterized by an extraordinary abundance of lichens (in the Arctic north) and treeless, summer-green, flower-covered meadows (in the subpolar south).

(11) Alpine Vegetation

The most impressive alpine vegetation is found in the Andes (see photographs). Here the hierarchy of vegetation levels, from the tropical rain forest to the Paramo to the high tropical grasslands (moist puna) and the frost-prone, high, cold puna at elevations of about 5,000 m, where grass is sparse but lichens are plentiful, reflect the effects of diminishing warmth at progressively higher elevations.

The upper layer of permafrost soil thaws in the early summer.

Tundra meadows blossom in mid-summer.

Soil erosion following deforestation in Peru

Vegetation - The Earth's Botanical Cloak

(5) Tropical deciduous forest

Despite annual precipitation often exceeding 1,000 mm, these forests of long-trunked trees that turn fully green only near their tops during the summer rainy season have a relatively short growth period, as water is scarce during the rest of the year (photo: Caprivi, Namibia). The monsoon forests of southern and Southeast Asia represent a special form of this class of vegetation.

Sparse cold puna with cushion grass and lichens

Moist puna of the Altiplano with grazing llamas

Transition from tropical mountain to mist forest

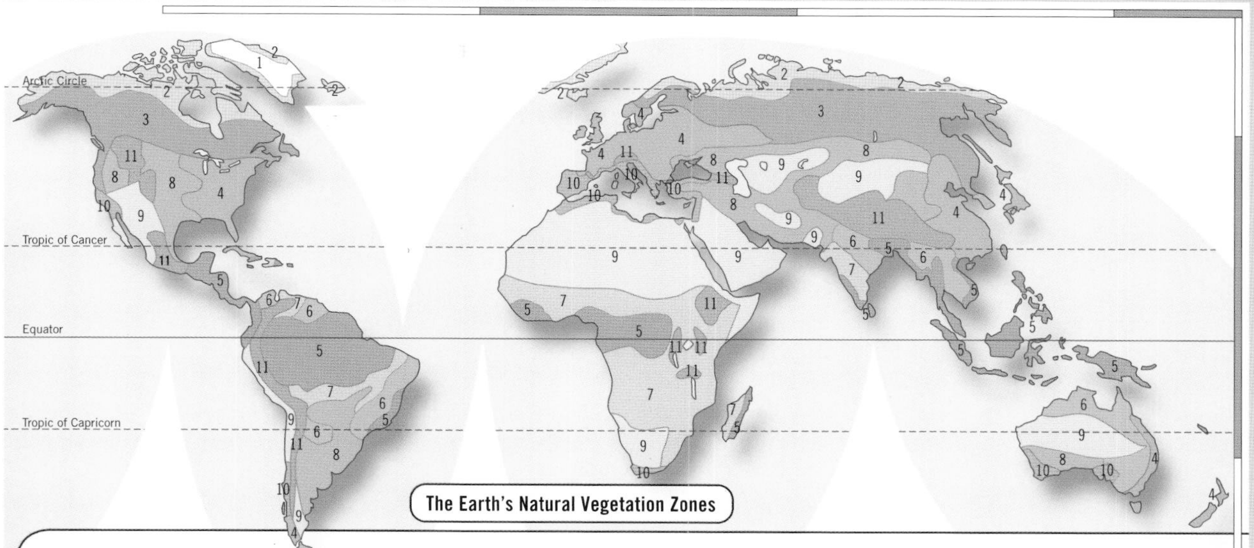

The Earth's Natural Vegetation Zones

1	Permanent ice cover	7	Tropical savanna and grassland
2	Polar barrens and Tundra	8	Subtropical grassland and steppe
3	Boreal forest, Taiga	9	Desert and semi-arid desert
4	Temperate forest and cultivated land	10	Mediterranean vegetation, sclerophyllous plants
5	Tropical rain forest	11	Alpine vegetation
6	Tropical deciduous forest		

(3) Taiga – the Northern Continental Vegetation Belt

Average annual temperatures in these regions covered by boreal evergreen and summer-green coniferous forests comprising only a few species, which span the globe only in the permafrost regions of the northern hemisphere, range near 32°F. Covering some 20 million square km (about 13 % of the Earth's dry land), they represent the world's largest forest formation.

(5) Tropical Rain Forest

In the tropics, where rain falls the year round and annual precipitation often exceeds 2,000 mm, temperatures determine the character of forests. Multi-tiered, evergreen equatorial rain forest – a habitat for a wide range of species – is predominant in low-lying areas with mean annual temperatures of 72–82°F. Mountain forests with fewer species are prevalent at elevations over 1,000 m and average temperatures of 57–72°F. Mist forests characterized by beard lichens, epiphytes, and tree ferns predominate only at elevations of over 2,000 m and at average temperatures of only 40–57°F. Together, these three forest types occupy a total area of about 12.5 million square km (approximately 8 % of the dry land on Earth). They are seriously endangered, particularly at lower elevations, by logging operations and large-scale deforestation. The most common natural form of vegetation along the tropical coasts are mangrove forests, although they have now been almost totally destroyed.

(7) Savannas – Maximum Landscape Diversity

Savannas are generally thought of as expansive tropical grasslands (like the Serengeti). Actually, they display a number of different faces. Although grass is the dominant ground cover in all savanna landscapes, the spectrum of plant formations encompasses dry, thorny shrub vegetation, flourishing bush growth, densely wooded areas, and even true forests (such as the gallery forests along riverbanks or the Mopane and Miombo woodlands of southern Africa). Common to all types of savannas are summer rainy seasons and the absence of a thermal winter.

(8) Steppes – Non-Tropical Grasslands Under the Plow

Where grasslands once stretched to the horizon in climates with dry summers and often extremely cold winters (on the North American prairies or the black-earth regions of southern Russia), human beings have replaced the natural vegetation of the dry, short-grass and moister, long-grass steppes with vast grain fields. In many places, such industrial-scale farming operations have contributed to soil deterioration by clearing the way for wind and water erosion.

(9) Desert Vegetation

Vegetation in deserts and semi-arid regions (where climates are only slightly more favorable), is ideally adapted to the extreme conditions of their environments (scarcity of water, heat, nocturnal or winter frost, sand storms, etc.). Higher forms of plant life have developed appropriate survival tools: water-retaining organs, leaf coverings that inhibit evaporation, suspension of metabolic activity during extremely dry periods ("latent life") or disproportionately large (relative to above-ground biomass) underground plant organs (primarily roots). Microflora – ordinarily overlooked by human beings – is represented in abundance on the surface in the form of algae, fungi, and blankets of lichens that can even be seen in satellite images.

(10) Mediterranean Vegetation

The original natural vegetation of the Mediterranean regions, which are classified as subtropical climate zones with wet winters, was evergreen sclerophyllous forest (holm oak forests in the actual Mediterranean region). Extreme overuse by humans has caused much of this original vegetation to be replaced by meager second-growth formations such as broad-leaved shrubs and small trees (matorral, chaparral or maquis) and even poorer scrubland vegetation (garrigue).

(4) Forests of the Temperate Zone

The summer-green deciduous and mixed forests that once prevailed throughout this climate zone, which with average annual temperatures of between 43 and 54°F and growth periods of 200 days or longer offers ideal conditions for agriculture, have fallen victim to large-scale deforestation and have been replaced in isolated areas by second-growth forests used primarily for wood production.

Biodiversity - Geodiversity - Ecodiversity

Species Diversity – the Earth's Living Treasure

Why is the survival of every species so important? What prompted the authors of the Old Testament to emphasize species diversity in the story of Noah, whom God commanded to bring "of every living thing of all flesh, two of every sort . . . into the ark . . . to keep them alive?" Biological diversity is an essential aspect of life on earth. Research on biological diversity will play an important role in the future of mankind as a basis for advances in the fields of nutrition, medical care, and even tourism.

The Number of Species – an Unsolved Puzzle

The study of biodiversity involves identification and analysis of the structural diversity of communities of living organisms. The process of identifying all species of plants and animals is far from complete. About 1.7 million species have been identified thus far, yet we can only speculate as to the actual number of species on earth, drawing conclusions based on analogy. Scientists assume the existence of some 20 million species. New ones are being discovered every day.

Geodiversity – A New Concept

The term "geodiversity" refers to the wide range of geographic factors and combinations of influences that have emerged in the course of the Earth's history. It is the product of interaction between the atmosphere, the lithosphere, the pedosphere (dry land) and the hydrosphere. It determines local conditions in the biosphere (flora and fauna) and the anthroposphere (human beings). Climate and its component elements (solar radiation, temperature, precipitation, humidity, evaporation, wind) are the most important determinants of species distribution in different regions of the world. Patterns of distribution are also shaped by topography, the configuration of land masses, their position with respect to the oceans of the world, and ocean surface temperatures. Developments in the Earth's history, including the evolution of living species, have contributed significantly to present patterns of species diversity.

One important factor is floral migration, a process that has taken place in the recent geological past (mostly during periods of transition between ice ages and warm periods) along mountain ranges aligned with meridians. Thus Antarctic floras have long since moved into the tropics along the Andes in South America. Non-tropical plant species have invaded the tropical regions along routes parallel to the mountain chains of Southeast Asia, enriching local flora significantly. Mountain ranges oriented along lines of latitude (the Alps, the Pyreneans, and the Himalayas) have blocked these migrations.

Diversity – a Regional View

The limited species diversity of subpolar tundra and boreal coniferous forest regions is attributable to unfavorable geographic conditions (freezing temperatures, long periods of snow cover, short annual growth periods). Diversity is similarly restricted in tropical and subtropical deserts, where high levels of solar radiation and a consistently negative radiation balance result in wide fluctuations in daily and seasonal temperatures and extreme aridity, creating a hostile living environment for flora and fauna, not to mention Homo sapiens. In the Sahara, mountain ranges (Hoggar, Tibesti, Aïr) rise up from surroundings virtually devoid of vegetation as climatically and geographically favorable zones for plant growth. Inland deserts (Atacama, Libyan Desert, Tanezrouft, Ténéré, Rub al-Chali), which receive only ephemeral precipitation at very irregular intervals, exhibit an absolute minimum of diversity. The same can be said of the subpolar regions around the Antarctic and Greenland ice sheets and the Tibetan Plateau, with its cold desert.

Generally speaking, species diversity increases from the poles to the Equator. Maximum diversity – more than 5,000 species per 10,000 square km – is found in the tropical rain and mountain forests of South America, Africa, Asia, and the Indo-Malaysian Archipelago, where tropical temperatures prevail year round and precipitation is heavy and non-seasonal. In tropical inland areas, a high degree of biodiversity is possible only in combination with maximum geodiversity. This applies in particular to tropical mountain regions where, within very small areas, topographic variations (elevation, exposure, slope steepness), mountain/valley winds, an enormous evaporation potential and high levels of latent evaporation heat, differing degrees of condensation and fog at mountain forest roofs (mist and cloud forests) favor plant diversity (Choco region in Costa Rica, eastern and western roofs of the Andes in Ecuador and

Unique Fynbos

The Cape Floral Kingdom of South Africa is home to one of the most diverse plant communities on Earth. Known as the fynbos vegetation belt, it has 8,600 plant species, 73% of which are found nowhere else on Earth. About the size of the Lüneburger Heide in Germany (photo above), it contains ten times as many plant species. Factors contributing this unusual degree of diversity include continual, relatively rapid climatic oscillations and the absence of major long-term climatic changes during the earlier geological epochs, both of which have exerted a favorable influence on evolutionary processes in this, the smallest phytogeographic kingdom on earth.

Interdependence of geodiversity, biodiversity, and ecodiversity

Ecodiversity

Geodiversity — Biodiversity

Interaction

Geodiversity and biodiversity are closely related and interdependent. Their interaction is responsible for ecodiversity.

Biodiversity - Geodiversity - Ecodiversity

Colombia, northeastern Brazil, eastern Himalayas / Yunnan, northern Borneo and New Guinea).

In Southeast Asia, plant diversity is supported by the monsoon-like character of the inner-tropical west wind circulation pattern, with maximum water-vapor accumulation over the warmest ocean basin of the Indo-Malaysian Archipelago. Similar conditions prevail off the western coast of Colombia and in the Gulf of Guinea.

Tropical trade wind currents blowing inland into the coastal mountain regions of the tropical-subtropical eastern continental margins (eastern Brazil, Middle America, northeastern Australia, Madagascar) also favor high levels of species diversity. In contrast, the divergent trade wind currents on the western sides of the continents tend to cause extreme aridity, although they also give impetus to the cold ocean currents. The result is a constant layer of fog over the cold ocean water, accompanied by local land/sea wind systems along the coasts. In the humid-air deserts ("fog oases"), this fog, combined with the cold ocean current, encourages the development of highly diverse flora, such as the Loma vegetation on the western coast of South America.

The subtropical regions with winter rainy seasons assume a unique status resulting from seasonal alternation of climatic factors (including most importantly rainfall) typical of tropical temperate zones. In the rainier mountainous countries, winter rains alternating with summer convection precipitation in combination with long thermal vegetation periods produce substantial phytodiversity, particularly at middle elevations, and create favorable living conditions for human beings (European Mediterranean region, Middle East, California, central Chile, the Cape Provinces of South Africa, and southwestern Australia).

Areas with high and low vascular-plant diversity are separated by transition zones. In the northern hemisphere, zones of diversity tend to run parallel to lines of latitude, much like the large landscape belts. In the southern hemisphere, they tend to align – depending upon the position and orientation of mountain ranges – concentrically in the direction of the major atmospheric currents and in response to lee/luff effects (Australia, southern Africa) or along north-south axes (South America).

Coral Reef Habitat

Coral reefs are home to an abundance of species. These often tiny organisms build huge reefs providing a wide range of different ecological niches.

A Diverse Cultivated Landscape

Natural vegetation has been almost totally destroyed in the European Mediterranean region. Yet this rich cultivated landscape, the cradle of advanced cultures since ancient times, exhibits a high degree of species diversity thanks to its favorable climatic and edaphic influences.

The World's Plant Reservoir

The tropics encompass regions of great species diversity. It is in the best interest of mankind to preserve them as reservoirs of new food and other crop plants.

Species-Poor Taiga

Despite their vast biomass potential, the boreal coniferous forests support only a meager selection of plant species. No more than five kinds of trees are found in the entire taiga. In the tropical rain forests, hundreds of species can be found in an area the size of that covered in the photo.

Cloud Forests

At the western roof of the Andes, trees at the cloud forest level (photo: Ecuador), are covered by an abundance of blossoming epiphytic plants.

Moist Coastal Forests

Kept moist by frequent coastal fog, the mountains along the coast of northern California are densely forested. The characteristic giant redwoods (Sequoia sempervirens) are joined here by other conifers (Douglas firs, etc.) and deciduous species.

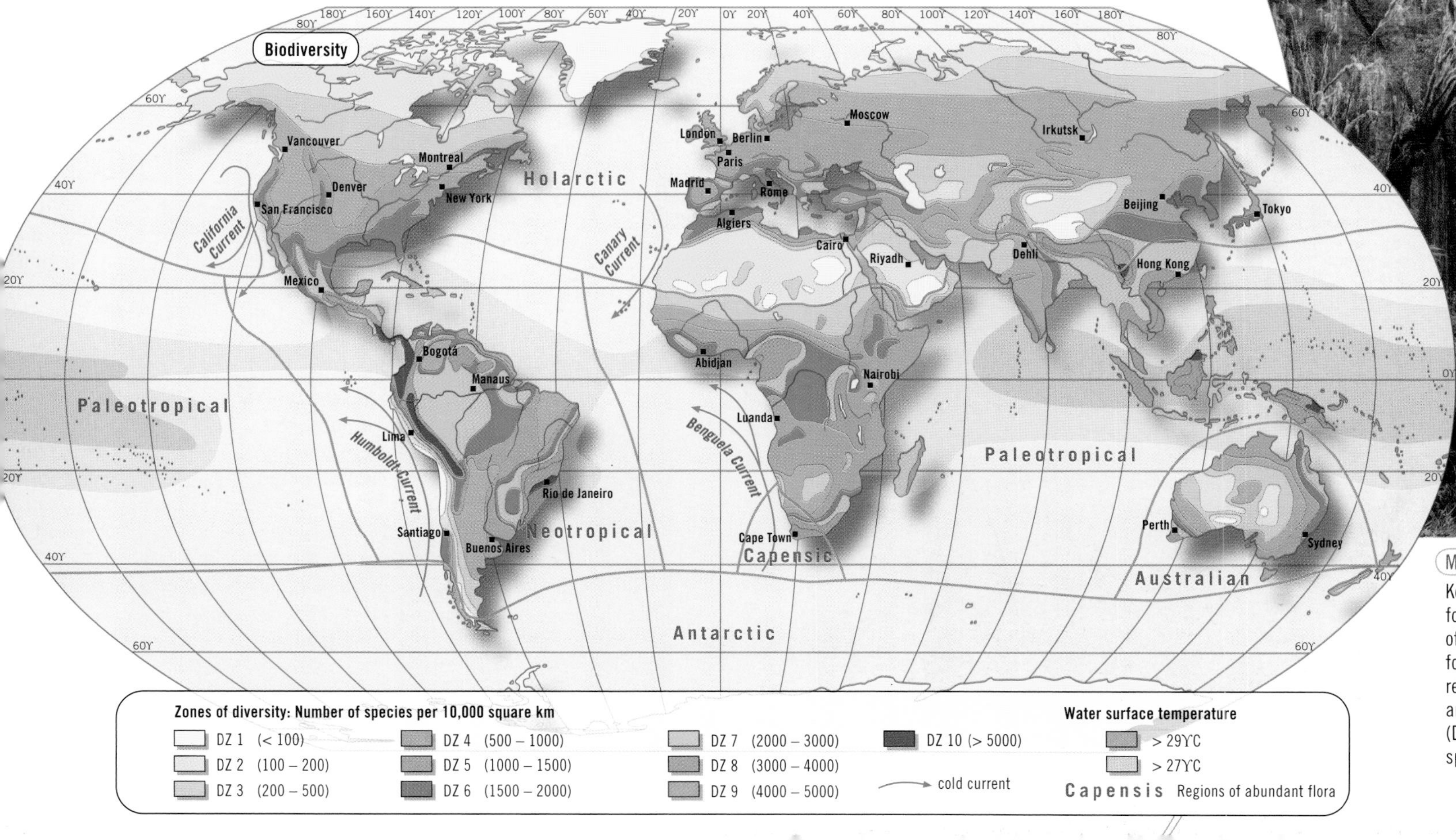

Biodiversity

Holarctic · Paleotropical · Neotropical · Capensic · Australian · Antarctic

California Current · Canary Current · Humboldt Current · Benguela Current

Zones of diversity: Number of species per 10,000 square km				Water surface temperature	
DZ 1 (< 100)	DZ 4 (500 – 1000)	DZ 7 (2000 – 3000)	DZ 10 (> 5000)	> 29°C	
DZ 2 (100 – 200)	DZ 5 (1000 – 1500)	DZ 8 (3000 – 4000)		> 27°C	
DZ 3 (200 – 500)	DZ 6 (1500 – 2000)	DZ 9 (4000 – 5000)	cold current	**Capensis** Regions of abundant flora	

Deserts and Desertification

Are We Turning the Earth into a Desert?

Public attention was first drawn to the endangered African Sahel region by the catastrophic drought and famine of 1968–1973. Steadily dwindling harvest yields and widespread livestock death cost the lives of 100,000–200,000 people. Nomads and farmers sought refuge in cities or less arid regions in the south, many of them never to return. Since then, the percentage of nomadic people among the total population of Mauritania has fallen from 70 % to 25 %. Other drought-endangered areas of the world have experienced similar fates. The UN has officially recognized the problem of "desertification," and programs have been devoted to solving it, most recently within the framework of the Agenda 21 resolution passed at the 1992 Earth Summit in Rio de Janeiro.

What is Desertification?

Desertification is a process involving natural and man-made influences by which land is transformed into desert. It affects all dry regions on Earth – not only existing deserts but especially steppes and dry savannas that could easily become or be turned into deserts. More than one-third of the dry land on our planet, and nearly a billion of its people, are threatened by desertification. The most severely endangered countries are among the poorest in the world. Between ten and fourteen million acres of farm and grazing land are lost to desertification every year.

A Constant Water Shortage

Regions with dry climates have fragile ecosystems and are thus naturally endangered. Precipitation is not only meager but seasonal as well. In tropical regions with both dry and rainy seasons, dry winters alternate with wet summers, and precipitation levels vary significantly. Dry or wet periods often last for several years. These factors influence the make-up of plant communities, determine plant survival strategies, and affect the production of vegetable biomass. Satellite images show that the southern boundary of the Sahara may drift northward or southward depending upon precipitation. Yet it is not true that the Sahara is steadily and progressively expanding. The climate in this region has not changed significantly since northern Africa began to turn arid over 4,000 years ago. The crucial factor is mankind's disruptive intervention in the delicate equilibrium of nature. Accordingly, desert-like conditions do not expand along broad fronts but tend instead to develop in spots.

Progressive Environmental Destruction

Failure to adapt land-use practices to natural circumstances in farming and grazing operations can have devastating consequences. Thus in the Sahel region, for example, the boundary of sustainable rain-fed farming (minimum precipitation of 500 mm per year in marginal tropical regions with summer rains and 300 mm in subtropical areas with winter wet seasons) was pushed into the desert during the extended humid period from 1950 to 1967 – up to 200 km in the Sahel region and 100 km in northwestern Africa. In the process, much natural vegetation, which, although sparse, was well adapted to changing moisture conditions, was thinned or eliminated entirely, causing extensive, irreparable damage. The grass cover was stripped away, and bushes and trees

were cut for firewood. The destruction of vegetation accelerates the rate of evaporation; soil grows drier and is subject to wind or water erosion. Where topsoil is completely stripped away, impermeable crusts of rock may be exposed, the soil water budget can be permanently affected, and the groundwater level may sink. Sand carried away by winds may accumulate in dunes. Sandstorms originating in the Sahel and the Sahara have been known to carry material as far away as the Caribbean and South America.

Intensive farming in the Sahel region went hand in hand with shorter fallow periods (fertilizers are ordinarily not used). Nomads who had used these fields as grazing areas were forced to move to inferior land, particularly since political boundaries have made wide-ranging migration more difficult or even impossible. Deep wells were drilled in many places to secure an adequate water supply for nomads and farmers – but this, too, produced negative effects. Herds grew larger, and the groundwater level sank even further.

Where precipitation is insufficient to support cultivation, farmers must irrigate, as they have done for thousands of years in the Valleys of the Nile, the Tigris and Euphrates, and the Indus, which are fed by heavy precipitation in the mountain along their upper reaches, and along the rivers that empty into the Aral Sea in the piedmont region of Central Asia or the Tarim Basin. Due to the high evaporation rate in dry regions, however, irrigation tends to cause excessive soil salinity, as examples from ancient history show. Damage of this kind has been much more severe in recent times, however (e.g. in Pakistan and the Al-Wadi al-Jadid in Egypt).

A Global Problem

Desertification is actually a by-product of the twentieth-century population explosion brought about in part by significant improvements in medical care. Farmers and nomads rank low in the political and economic ladders of developing countries. Since colonial times, governments have consistently encouraged or decreed market-oriented production (e.g. cotton, peanuts, meat) in order to increase tax and export revenues and ensure an adequate food supply for politically significant urban populations. Increasing economic globalization and requirements imposed by the World Bank and the International Monetary Fund have put rural populations under tremendous pressure to adapt. Worldwide, desertification is respon-

sible for production shortfalls valued at 40 billion dollars per year – more than the combined gross national products of all of the countries of the Sahel region, from Senegal to Somalia. Desertification not only jeopardizes the fulfillment of basic human needs – nutrition, health, and education – it also contributes to the spread of poverty, the dissolution of social bonds, political instability,

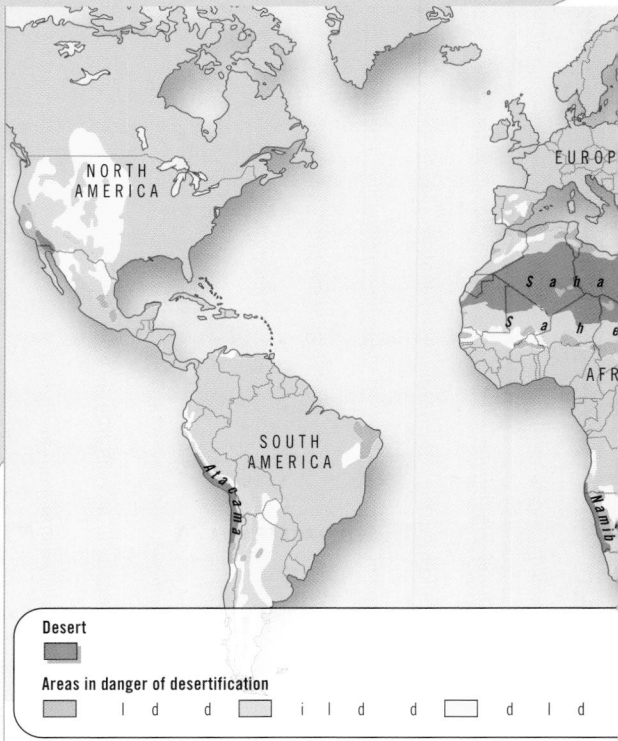

Desert

Areas in danger of desertification

First presented at the 1977 UN Conference in Nairobi, the World Desertification Map shows that areas immediately adjacent to existing deserts are often in less danger of desertification than somewhat moister region, where the burden of cultivation and population density is greater.

Fluctuations in annual precipitation levels recorded at various measuring stations in the western Sahel region between 1901 and 1990, entered as percentage deviations from the long-term average. Older records also document similar alternating periods of precipitation deficit (1820-40) and surplus (1870-95), as do variations in the shoreline of Lake Chad.

The Power of Water

Where the protective cover of vegetation in dry regions has been thinned or stripped away entirely through cultivation or grazing, brief but often very heavy rains wreak havoc on the exposed soil. Rapid runoff cuts grooves, troughs, and deep gorges in the ground, as can be seen in this photo taken in the Sierra Madre del Sur, Mexico. Badland formations of this kind are especially prevalent in areas with soft sediments.

Bread or Salt

Given sufficient water, the desert can be brought to bloom. But desert soil must be irrigated with great care, ensuring that it is well flushed in order to avoid salt accumulation. Numerous cases of excessive, irreversible soil salination have been recorded in Libya, for example, where extensive grain fields were laid out and irrigated (with long-armed rotary sprinklers) using water drawn from "fossil" reserves formed deep in the earth during wetter geological periods in the past.

Dying of Thirst

During extended periods of drought – this photo was taken in the degraded dry Kaokoveld savanna (Namibia) in the early 1980s – water becomes so scarce that many animals die of thirst.

Deserts and Desertification

and armed conflicts fueled by competition for dwindling resources. Soon, 100 million people will have joined the worldwide exodus from rural regions into the cities. The effects of this wave of migration will ultimately be felt in North America and Europe as well.

Desertification is not a new phenomenon. The ancient Romans destroyed their "granary" on the Tunisian steppe through overuse (Bedouin immigrants from Arabia reclaimed the land for grazing, and it eventually recovered, only to be converted to farmland again under French colonial rule, which hastened the process of degradation through desertification). Dust storms and soil

erosion on the U.S. Great Plains ("Dust Bowl") between 1930 and 1935 (affecting 650,000 farmers and 400,000 square km of land) offered striking proof that industrialized countries are not immune to desertification. But poor countries lack the resources to overcome these problems on their own. International aid is needed, especially in light of the fact that desertification poses not only social and economic dangers but environmental ones as well. If vegetation disappears from the dry regions, huge quantities of greenhouse gases (carbon dioxide, methane), now being absorbed by plants will be released into the atmosphere – 30 times the amount of CO_2 currently emitted every year.

Can Desertification Be Stopped?

Counteractive measures need time to take effect. Once an understanding of ecological relationships is achieved, the local population must be educated and encouraged to adapt farming and grazing practices to the environment. The use of alternative forms of energy can be helpful. Other effective measures include the planting of drought-resistant crop plants, the use of appropriate agricultural methods and technologies (e.g. dams to protect against erosion, terracing, the planting of trees), and accelerated development in the non-agrarian sector.

The Last Tree

In the absence of environmentally sounder energy alternatives (such as solar energy or biogas), the inhabitants of the Sahel zone, where wood is extremely scarce (photo: Tuareg tribespeople in Niger) must rely on firewood to prepare their daily meals. This results in the loss of as many as 200 savanna trees per family per year.

The Aral Sea Drama

The use of water from rivers feeding the Aral Sea for irrigation caused the sea to shrink from 68,000 to 17,000 square km. between 1960 and 2004. Salinity also rose to alarming levels (up to 30%), decimating the fish population. Many fishing boats were left high and dry. Salt and dust (75 million tons per year), along with accumulated toxic residues (pesticides, herbicides, fertilizers) are carried from the old seabed by winds and deposited on the surrounding fields (cotton, rice, etc.). These substances contaminate the groundwater and have led to a substantial rise in the incidence of disease, birth defects, and infant death.

Degradation

The grass cover in the savanna is often so heavily damaged by overuse that it cannot regenerate even during the rainy season and thus leaves the bare soil exposed (left: intact or only slightly damaged savanna; right: degraded savanna). Only trees with deep roots that reach the groundwater aquifer – Acacias, for the most part – can survive.

Driven by Hunger

After several years of drought, the ground in the Sahel region along the southern rim of the Sahara is severely desiccated and covered by a network of deep cracks. Desperately searching for nourishment, these women use long poles to loosen the hard clumps of soil in the hope of finding edible plants and roots beneath them.

Deserts and Desertification

ASIA
Tarim Basin Gobi
AUSTRALIA

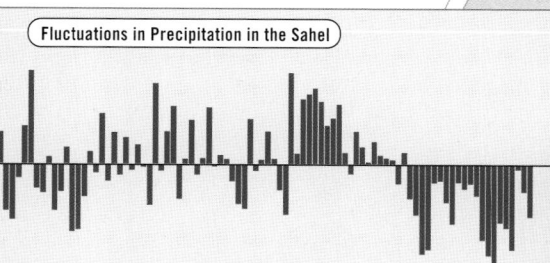

Fluctuations in Precipitation in the Sahel

%
+50

0

−50

|1900 |1910 |1920 |1930 |1940 |1950 |1960 |1970 |1980 |1990

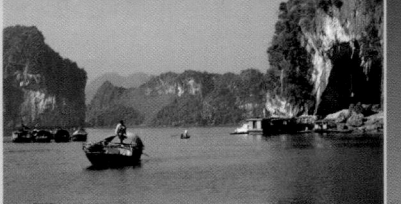

Protection of Natural Treasures through UNESCO

Will Our Natural Heritage Be Preserved for the Next Generation?

World Natural Heritage sites are chosen for their uniqueness and outstanding universal value. Thus the goal of the UNESCO World Heritage Convention is to identify the most outstanding examples of significant natural ecosystems and landscapes and the most important geological and paleontological sites from among the many applications received. Yet some countries fear that increasing publicity will increase the pressure of tourism on already fragile landscapes and have refrained from submitting applications.

The Threat Posed by Mankind

Environmental pollution, resource depletion, population pressure! Can we truly hope to pass the heritage entrusted to us on to succeeding generations? The Convention focuses particular attention on "endangered natural heritage sites," and thus the last remaining Australian rain forests have been saved from destruction. In other cases, however, such as that of the Srebarna Danube wetlands, rescue efforts almost came too late.

Does Conservation Make Sense in Our Time?

The static concept of conservation was long the dominant guiding principle in our thinking about protecting nature. We know today that all natural systems are highly dynamic. The Agenda 21 program passed at the UN Earth Summit Conference in Rio Janeiro strongly emphasized the concept of "sustainable use and development" as a guideline for thought and action.

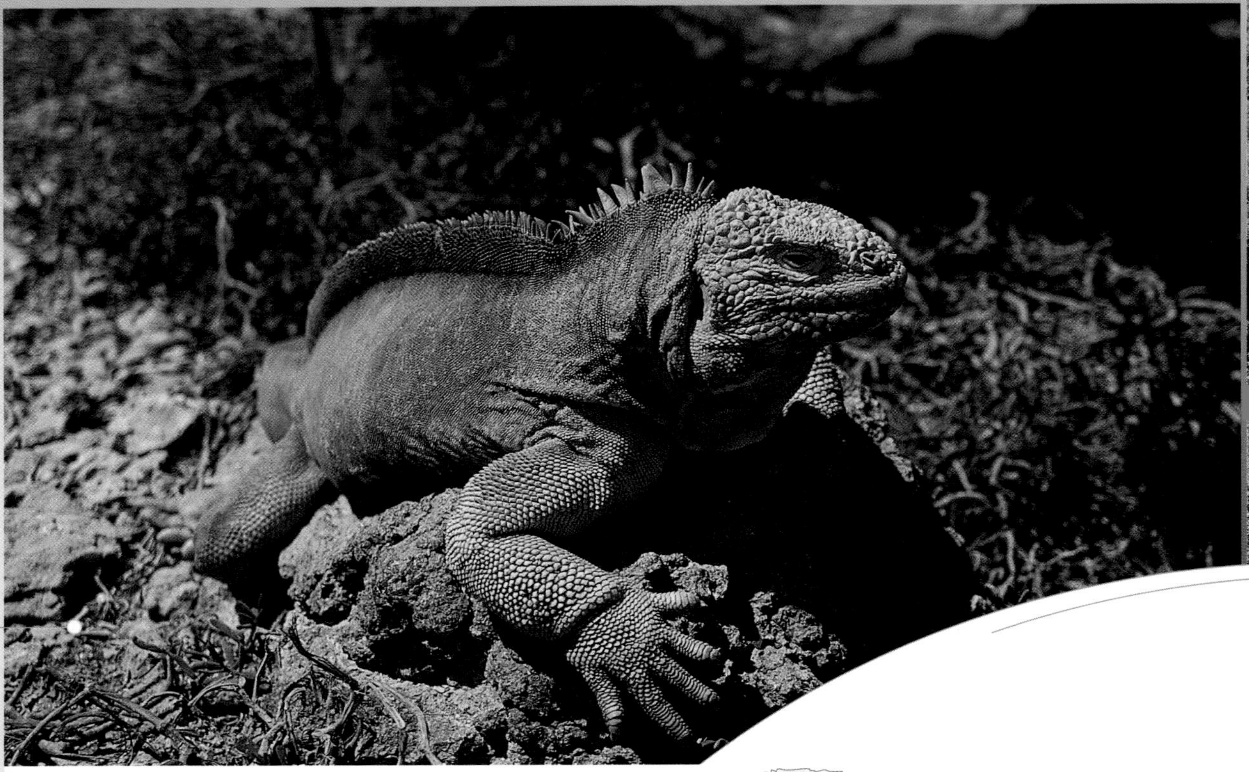

Home of Pele, Goddess of Fire

Kilauea is one of Hawaii's two active volcanoes (106). From deep in the Earth's upper mantle, the mountain brings liquid lava to the surface, where it emerges at a temperature of 2,160°F and spreads rapidly (at a speed of up to 40 km per hour) into the surrounding countryside.

Los Glaciares

The Moreno Glacier (30) flows eastward from the continental Patagonian ice sheet into Lago Argentino. The irregular advances of its broad tongue (more than two km wide) cause occasional flooding.

A Window on Evolution

The Galapagos Islands (25) were formed by a group of shield volcanoes whose peaks rise from the depth of the Pacific on both sides of the Equator. The land iguana belongs to the large group of endemic species.

Sinter Terraces

Yellowstone National Park (8) encompasses a caldera with a diameter of 79 km surrounded by high peaks in the Rocky Mountains. These sinter terraces were formed by hot springs, remnants of volcanic activity dating back 600,000 years.

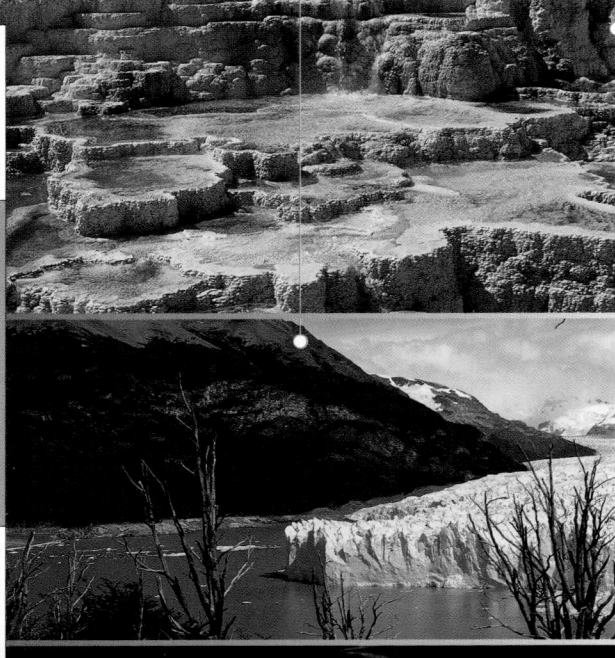

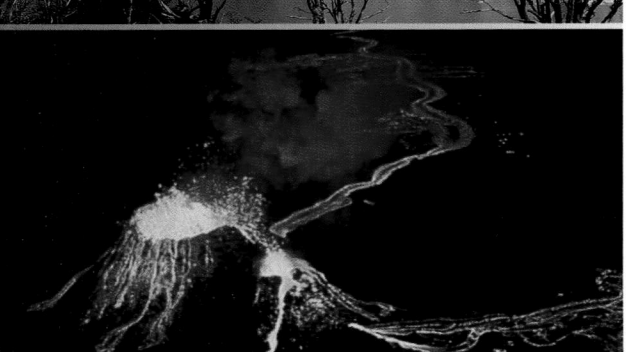

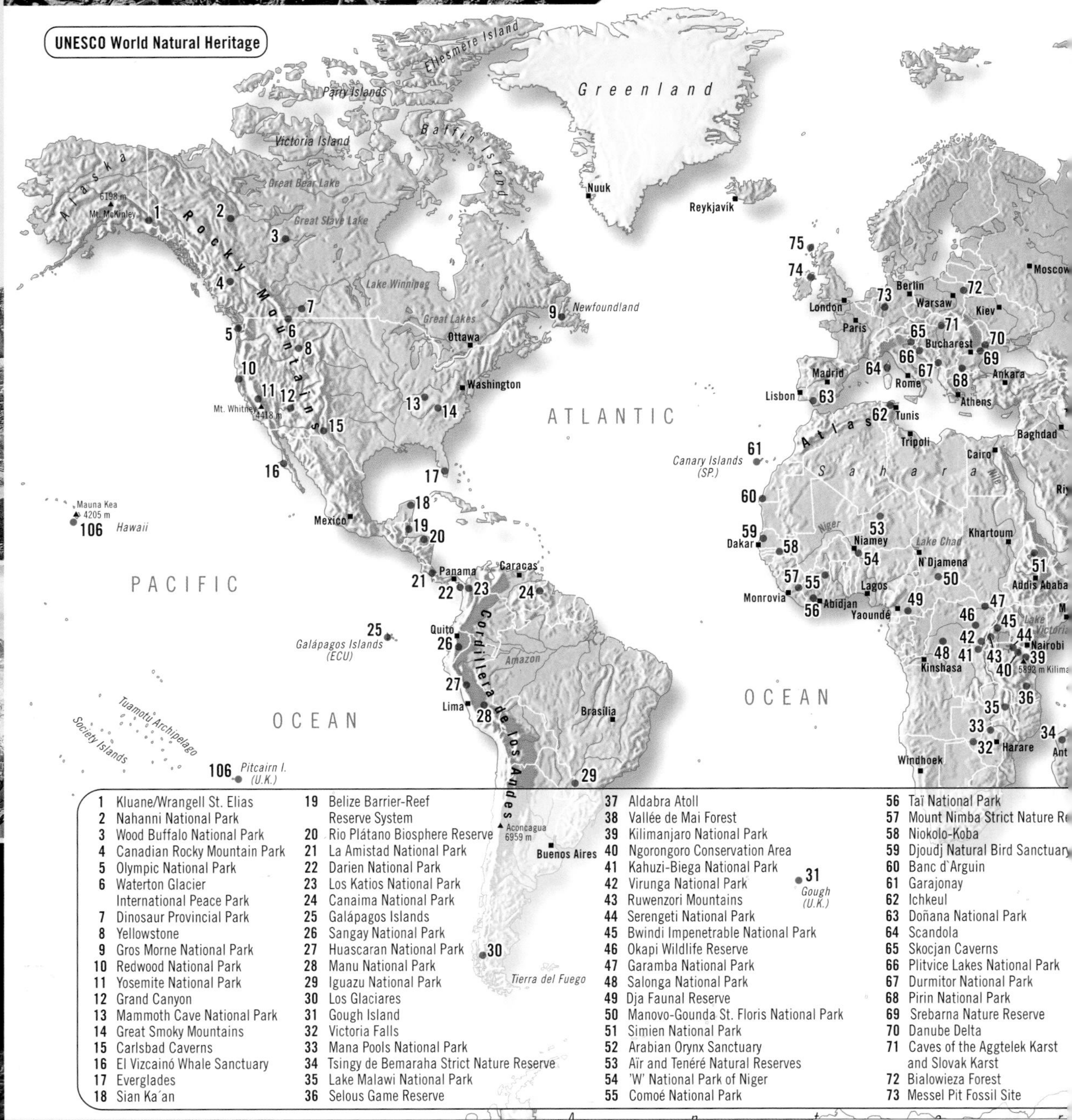
UNESCO World Natural Heritage
Greenland
Ellesmere Island
Parry Islands
Baffin Island
Victoria Island
Great Bear Lake
Great Slave Lake
Alaska
Rocky Mountains
Mt. McKinley
Lake Winnipeg
Great Lakes
Newfoundland
Nuuk
Reykjavik
Ottawa
Washington
Mt. Whitney
ATLANTIC
PACIFIC
OCEAN
Hawaii
Mauna Kea
Mexico
Panama
Caracas
Quito
Lima
Brasilia
Amazon
Cordillera de los Andes
Aconcagua
Buenos Aires
Tierra del Fuego
Galápagos Islands (ECU)
Tuamotu Archipelago
Society Islands
Pitcairn I. (U.K.)
Gough (U.K.)
Canary Islands (SP.)
London
Paris
Berlin
Warsaw
Kiev
Moscow
Madrid
Lisbon
Rome
Bucharest
Ankara
Athens
Tunis
Tripoli
Cairo
Baghdad
Sahara
Atlas
Niger
Dakar
Monrovia
Abidjan
Yaoundé
Lagos
Niamey
N'Djamena
Khartoum
Addis Ababa
Lake Chad
Nairobi
Kinshasa
Harare
Windhoek
1 Kluane/Wrangell St. Elias
2 Nahanni National Park
3 Wood Buffalo National Park
4 Canadian Rocky Mountain Park
5 Olympic National Park
6 Waterton Glacier International Peace Park
7 Dinosaur Provincial Park
8 Yellowstone
9 Gros Morne National Park
10 Redwood National Park
11 Yosemite National Park
12 Grand Canyon
13 Mammoth Cave National Park
14 Great Smoky Mountains
15 Carlsbad Caverns
16 El Vizcainó Whale Sanctuary
17 Everglades
18 Sian Ka'an
19 Belize Barrier-Reef Reserve System
20 Rio Plátano Biosphere Reserve
21 La Amistad National Park
22 Darien National Park
23 Los Katios National Park
24 Canaima National Park
25 Galápagos Islands
26 Sangay National Park
27 Huascaran National Park
28 Manu National Park
29 Iguazu National Park
30 Los Glaciares
31 Gough Island
32 Victoria Falls
33 Mana Pools National Park
34 Tsingy de Bemaraha Strict Nature Reserve
35 Lake Malawi National Park
36 Selous Game Reserve
37 Aldabra Atoll
38 Vallée de Mai Forest
39 Kilimanjaro National Park
40 Ngorongoro Conservation Area
41 Kahuzi-Biega National Park
42 Virunga National Park
43 Ruwenzori Mountains
44 Serengeti National Park
45 Bwindi Impenetrable National Park
46 Okapi Wildlife Reserve
47 Garamba National Park
48 Salonga National Park
49 Dja Faunal Reserve
50 Manovo-Gounda St. Floris National Park
51 Simien National Park
52 Arabian Oryx Sanctuary
53 Aïr and Ténéré Natural Reserves
54 'W' National Park of Niger
55 Comoé National Park
56 Taï National Park
57 Mount Nimba Strict Nature R
58 Niokolo-Koba
59 Djoudj Natural Bird Sanctuary
60 Banc d'Arguin
61 Garajonay
62 Ichkeul
63 Doñana National Park
64 Scandola
65 Skocjan Caverns
66 Plitvice Lakes National Park
67 Durmitor National Park
68 Pirin National Park
69 Srebarna Nature Reserve
70 Danube Delta
71 Caves of the Aggtelek Karst and Slovak Karst
72 Bialowieza Forest
73 Messel Pit Fossil Site

Protection of Natural Treasures through UNESCO

Sunken Karst Landscape

With its 1,600 islands and islets, Ha Long Bay (82) on the northern coast of Vietnam is one of the most beautiful examples of cone karst formations. It is the product of limestone dissolution – which began on the mainland – in a humid tropical climate. Over time, the coast has sunk, allowing the sea to inundate the karst landscape. Only the highest karst towers rise above sea level.

A Stairway of Lakes in Limestone Sinter

The Korana River built up massive bars of calcareous tufa in a deeply notched valley that cuts through the Croatian karst landscape, forming the Plitvice Lakes (66), a stairway of 16 small and larger lakes covering a distance of 7 km. Some of the many waterfalls that spill over the sinter barriers are nearly 80 m high.

Moso-oa-tunya, "Thundering Smoke"

Flowing slowly over a basalt plateau, the two-kilometer-wide Zambezi plunges 100 meters into a narrow gorge (only 40 m wide in some places) that cuts straight across its course. The broad water curtain of the Victoria Falls (32) is transformed into clouds of spray and fine mist that promote rich plant growth.

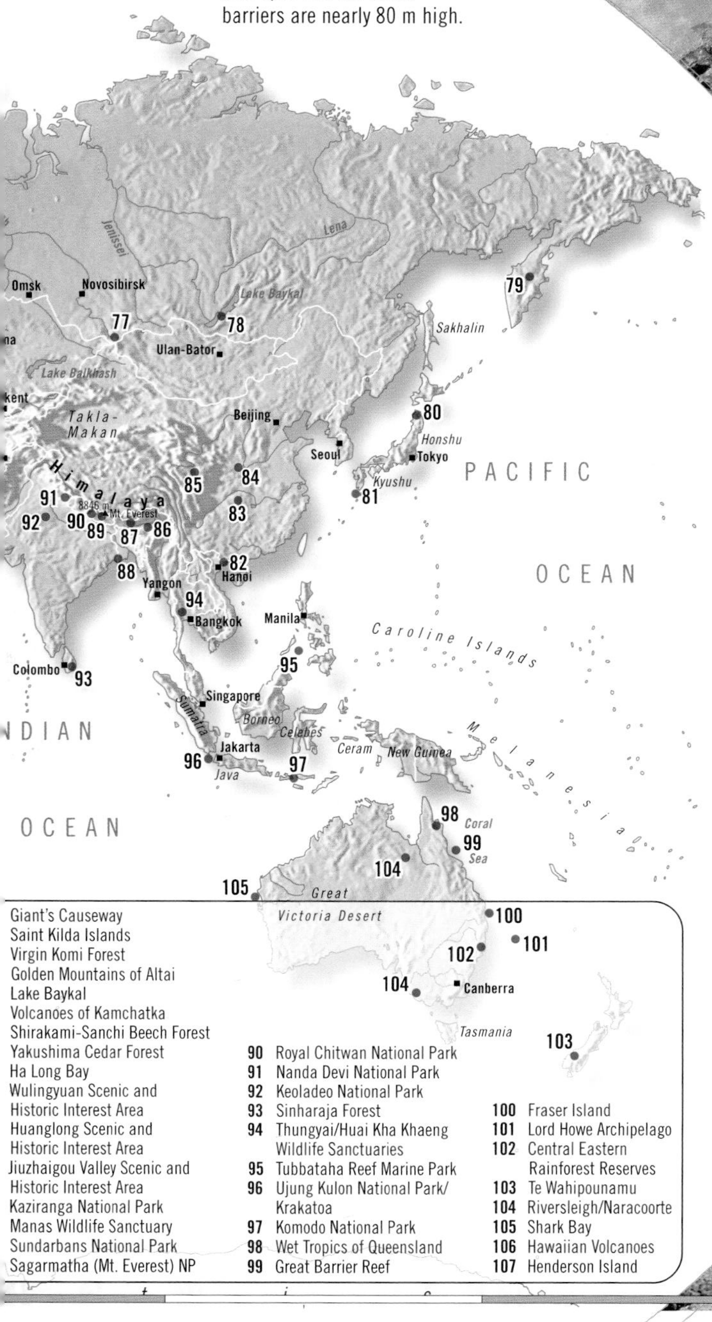

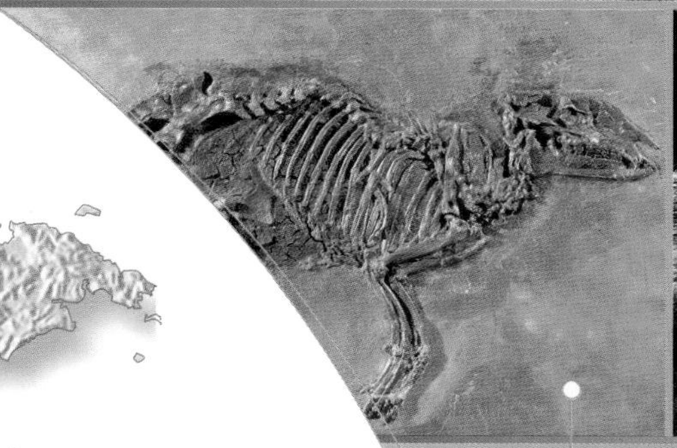

A Refuge for Rhinos

Chitwan National Park (90) in the wet lowlands of Nepal is a refuge (protected by the military) for 400 Indian Rhinos.

A Tiny Horse from a Warmer Era

Numerous fossils from the Eocene have been recovered from the oil shale layers of the Messel Pit (73) near Darmstadt, among them this well-preserved skeleton of the prehistoric horse Propalaeotherium parvulum. Fossil evidence of flora and fauna indicate a subtropical to tropical climate in the region some 40 to 50 million years ago.

Endangered Desert Landscape

The Aïr and Ténéré Natural Reserves (53) comprise two different natural landscapes. The sandstone base of the Aïr desert mountain range is riddled with plutonic ring intrusions (photo: Adrar Chiriet). To the east is the Ténéré, a desolate region through which the Tuareg have traditionally driven their camel caravans, bearing salt from Bilma and Fachi to distant markets.

Te Wahipounamu

The Te Wahipounamu Fiordland (103) on the western coast of New Zealand's South Island encompasses untouched stretches of coast, 28 mountains with peaks above 3,000 m, and glaciers that descend below the tree line.

Living Fossils

Cyanobacteria have been producing oxygen for at least 2.3 billion years. In Shark Bay (105), they are still forming bulbous, reef-like limestone deposits known as stromatolites today.

Early Human Development and Migration

Advancing to the Ends of the World

At least twice in the course of human history, our ancestors, hominids of the genus Homo, set out from Africa to conquer the world. Why did they abandon their familiar, warm, tropical homeland in the African savanna for an unknown and distant world full of surprises, challenges, and dangers – and new opportunities?
Were they forced to move – 1.8 million years ago – by population pressure, changes in climate, vegetation, or fauna, or was it curiosity and the urge to explore that drove them. Although the first sedentary communities did not appear until after the end of the last ice age 10,000 years ago, individuals are unlikely to have traveled far from their homes even long before then. Human migrations over long distances presumably took place over extended periods of time.

When Apes Came Down from the Trees – It all began with an upright posture

The earliest phase of human evolution and migration began during a period of environmental change along the East African Rift. About six million years ago, the rain forest began to give way to expanding tree savannas, forcing tree-dwelling primates to adopt an upright posture in order to facilitate travel over greater distances. Remains of Australopithecines, hominids which first appeared about four million years ago (example: Lucy), show jawbone modifications indicating adaptation to a diet no longer comprised of soft fruit and leaves of rain forest plants but primarily of harder seeds, roots, grass, and nuts found in the savannas. An upright posture enhanced mobility. Bones of Australopithecines about 3.5 million years old have been found from Ethiopia to South Africa and in

Chad. A period of global cooling about 2.5 million years ago caused increasing aridity accompanied by changes in flora and fauna, intensifying the selective influence of the environment. The first hominids of the genus Homo (Homo habilis, Homo rudolfensis) appeared at this point. They used simple stone tools (such as scrapers) to process the harder foodstuffs and butcher animals (slain game or carrion?). The use of tools made them less dependent on their environment.

The shift to a carnivorous diet evidently favored brain development. About two million years ago, hominids with larger, more robust skeletons began to appear in Africa. The brains of these hominids were larger, more humanoid in structure, and thus indicative of higher intelligence. Homo erectus (known as Homo ergaster in its earliest form) had arrived.

Quest for Fire – Early migration from Africa

Barely 100,000 years after the period marked by the oldest finds in Africa (at Lake Turkana, 1.9 million years BC), Homo erectus had already occupied new lands in western, eastern, and southeastern Asia, presumably favoring familiar, warm biotopes (savannas or steppes) at first. The oldest remains of non-African hominids were discovered in Java (Mojokerto), China (Longgupo), Georgia (Dmanisi, all circa 1.8 million BC), and Palestine (Ubaidiya, 1.4 million BC). More recent evidence has been found in India, Vietnam, and Japan. Artifacts 800,000 years old unearthed on Flores and Timor suggest the use of boats. The dating of tools found in Europe (Andalusia, 1.6–1.8 million BC) is disputed. Did these ancestors migrate across the Strait of Gibraltar?

Homo erectus later advanced across the high mountain ranges of Eurasia into much cooler and more humid climes. This required a command of fire (oldest evidence discovered in Africa dating to 1 – 1,5 million BC). Fire provided warmth and light, helped keep animal predators at bay, made cooking possible, and served a social function (campfires as central gathering places). Only a few of the bone and wooden implements used alongside stone tools have survived (among them wooden lances about 400,000 years old found in Schöningen in the German state of Lower Saxony).

The oldest reliable evidence of the presence of humans in Europe (at least one million years ago) consists only of isolated artifacts (found near Nice and in the Rhine Val-

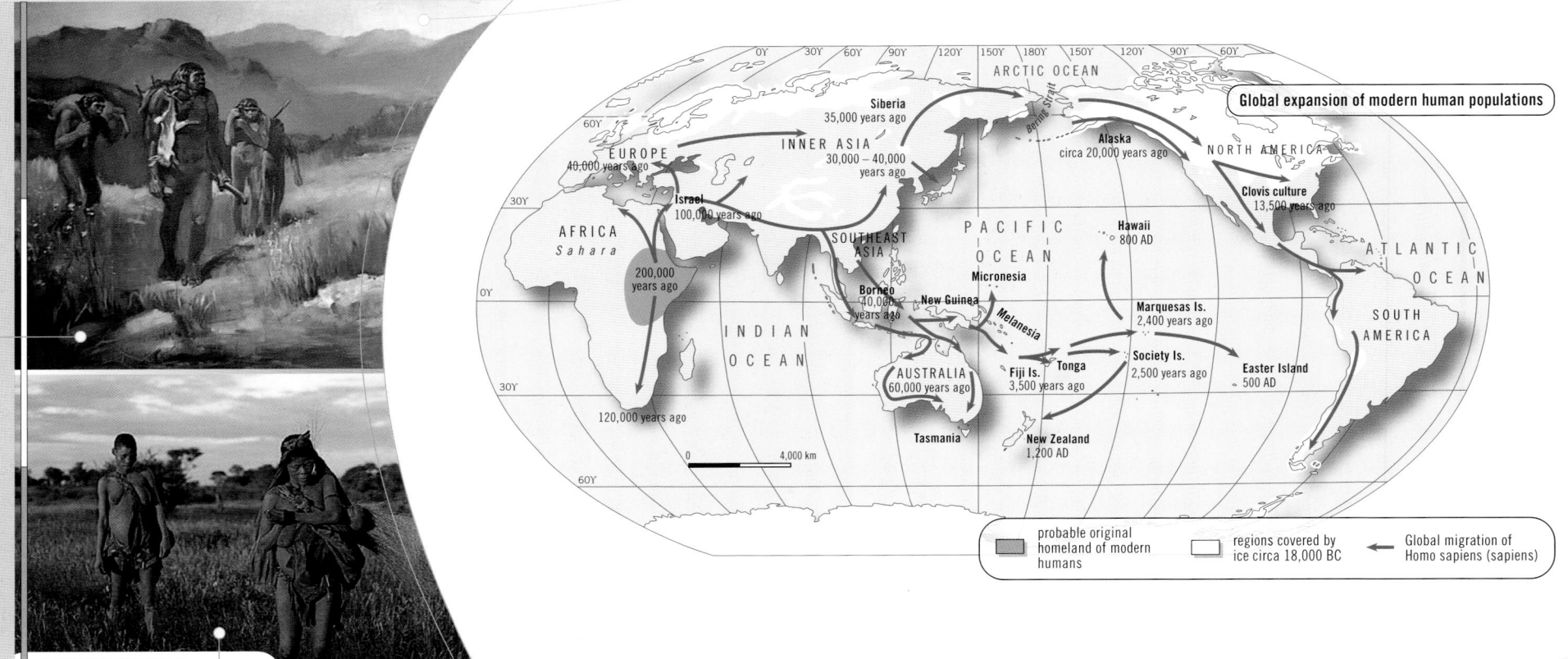

Global expansion of modern human populations

| probable original homeland of modern humans | regions covered by ice circa 18,000 BC | ← Global migration of Homo sapiens (sapiens) |

Stability and Change

Basic hunting and gathering economies have remained for the most part intact in a few small societies over a period of 1.5 million years, despite advances in weapon and tool technology, clothing, and housing. Men of the San culture (bushman) still bring their daily kill back to the community camp site just as Homo erectus (upper illustration) did ages ago. One can easily imagine early women gathering food plants with their babies strapped to their backs much like the San women (lower photo) of the Kalahari today.

The Unjustly Maligned Neanderthal

Once considered hardly more than a "wild animal," Neanderthal Man is now regarded as an intelligent human species that adapted successfully to an inhospitable ice-age climate – either as a direct ancestor of modern Homo sapiens in accordance with the multi-regional model (parallel, independent development of modern human beings in different regions) or as an evolutionary offshoot that culminated in a dead end.

ley). The oldest bones were found in Spain (Atepuerca, 780,000 BC). The finds uncovered in Mauer near Heidelberg (600,000 BC) and Bilzingsleben (400,000 BC) are much more recent. They have been classified along with other fossil remains as evidence of a species distinct from the humans of eastern Asia (true Homo erectus) known as Homo heidelbergensis. In general, European settlement patterns, especially in higher latitudes, reflect the influence of climatic changes associated with ice ages, which continually shifted the boundaries of inhabitable regions. It was never extremely cold south of the Alps, however. Changes in sea level impacted on settlement all over the world. During cold periods, continental shelf margins were dry and could be settled and traveled by human migrants.

Early Human Development and Migration

The Evolution of Homo Sapiens –
Are we all Africans by descent?

Archaic Homo sapiens emerged from Homo erectus or Homo heidelbergensis in all regions of the world. This phase of evolution probably began in Africa about 600,000 years ago and in Europe around 400,000 BC.

This early human form survived longest – until about 40,000 BC – in Southeast Asia. In Europe, primarily north of the Alps, a distinct form associated with the cold periods of the Pleistocene emerged from the late archaic Homo sapiens: the Neanderthal. The "classical" Neanderthal emerged from early Neanderthals after some 200,000 years, at the beginning of the last ice age, roughly 90,000 years ago. The sturdy, stocky build typical of the late Neanderthal presumably reflects adaptation to the cold climate of the period. Neanderthal populations appeared all over Europe, from the Iberian Peninsula to Central Asia (Uzbekistan) and did not die out until about 30,000 years ago. They advanced into western Asia about 80,000 BC. Long regarded as a direct ancestor of modern man, the Neanderthal is now seen as an evolutionary dead end, since fossil remains exhibiting the anatomical features of modern Homo sapiens (sapiens) found in Africa have been dated to about 200,000 BC, and it is only there that the evolutionary process can be traced in an unbroken line.

Out of Africa – Modern humans conquer the earth

As recently as 100,000 BC, modern man (as defined in anatomical terms) first appeared in western Asia, where he lived alongside Neanderthal groups for another 30,000 years. He was also a contemporary of the Neanderthal in Europe for 10,000 years, before emerging as the dominant species (Cro-Magnon People) 40,000 years ago. Isolated intermingling of the two types may have occurred.

Archaeological evidence of human settlements in Southeast Asia is dated to 40,000 BC, although humans must have arrived there much earlier, as they are known to have traveled by sea on boats or rafts to Australia more than 60,000 years ago.

Settlement in Oceania

After the settlement of New Guinea, the Bismarck Archipelago, and the Solomon Islands by forebears of the Papuans during the last ice age, Oceania – like the islands of Indonesia – witnessed an influx of Austronesian-speaking immigrants from Indochina, whose agrarian culture is identified by Lapita ceramics. The Austronesians who remained in Melanesia intermingled with the original dark-skinned population (Melanesians), and their language spread beyond the island of New Guinea. Other (light-skinned) Austronesians, who were experienced seafarers, soon moved with their food plants and domesticated animals to the islands of Polynesia. They continued to move eastward, reaching the Fiji Islands about 1,500 BC, Tonga in 1,400 BC, Samoa in 1,100 B.C, and the Society Islands in 500 BC, proceeding from there to Tahiti, Easter Island, Hawaii and New Zealand. Western Micronesia was probably settled by migrants from Indonesia or the Philippines as recently as 2,000 years ago, the remaining Micronesian islands from the south and east and the New Hebrides beginning about 1,300 BC (the Carolines were settled last, during the 3rd century AD).

The First Americans

The first humans to arrive on the American continent were anatomically modern. More than 20,000 years ago, people from hunting societies in northeastern Asia trekked over the land bridge across today's Bering Strait into the predominantly ice-free territory of Alaska.

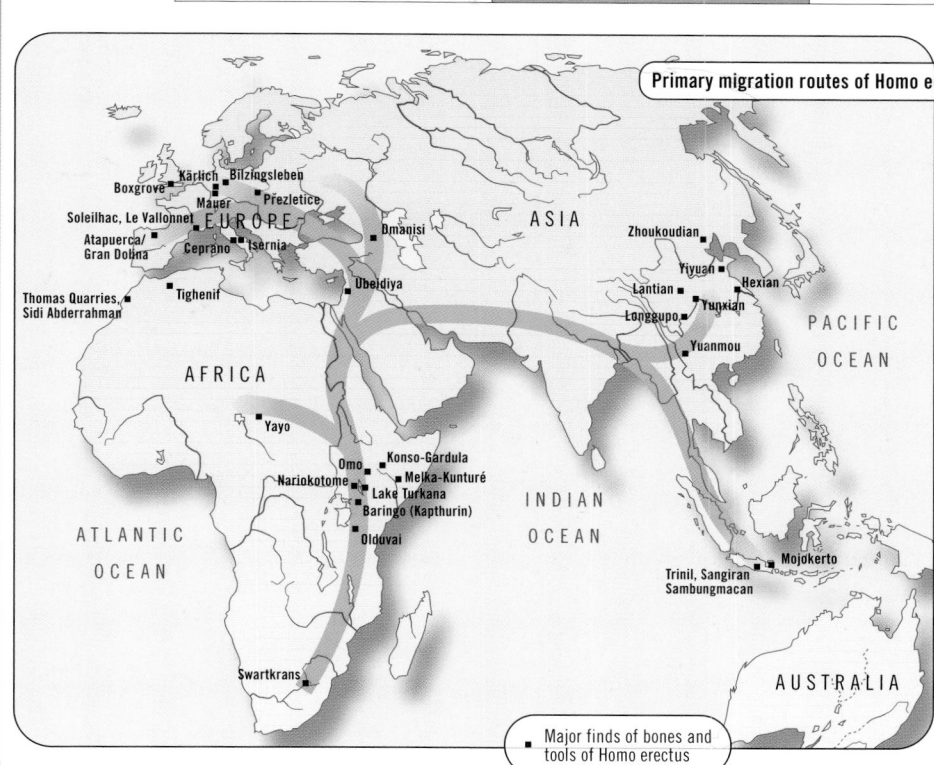

Primary migration routes of Homo erectus

Major finds of bones and tools of Homo erectus

Protection against Cold and Rain

Reconstruction of a house from the last phase of the Late Stone Age: walls and roof (wood) are covered with horse hides; inside, a mammoth thigh bone supports a roasting spit next to the fire place.

The "Lion King"

People living during the ice age more than 30,000 years ago regarded the lion not only as a dangerous enemy and a hunting rival but also as a symbol of strength and superiority. Does this ivory (female) human-lion figure discovered in Lonetal indicate belief in a magical unity of animal and human beings?

Adaptable hominid: Although the cranium of Australopithecus afarensis was no larger than that of contemporary chimpanzees, this hominid traveled on two legs through the savanna.

Following the movements of game animals (mammoth, bison, reindeer), they advanced into the continental interior along an ice-free corridor between the glacial ice of the Cordilleras and the Laurentide Ice Sheet. These Paleo-Indian peoples then spread rapidly over the American continents, advancing as far as Brazil, Patagonia and Chile. Since the Monte Verde archeological site (southern Chile) is about14,000 years old, migration into North America must have begun much earlier than the oldest finds uncovered in the region (artifacts of the Clovis Culture, named for its characteristic arrow and spear heads, from about 13,500 BC) would indicate. Was there a pre-Clovian culture whose people lived from plants and small animals and used different, more rudimentary implements? Evidence of human settlement in the Amazon Basin near the end of the last ice age points to the existence of such a culture. The significance of much older finds in South America (dating as far back as 40,000 BC) remains in dispute, however. Presumably, human populations initially spread along the coasts.

Three distinct waves of migration have been identified on the basis of linguistic and genetic evidence. The last wave brought the ancestors of the Eskimos (Inuit) to the northern regions of Canada and Greenland some 4,000 years ago. Well adapted to their arctic environment, they survived the "little ice age" that began in the 13th century BC and put an end to Viking settlements in Greenland.

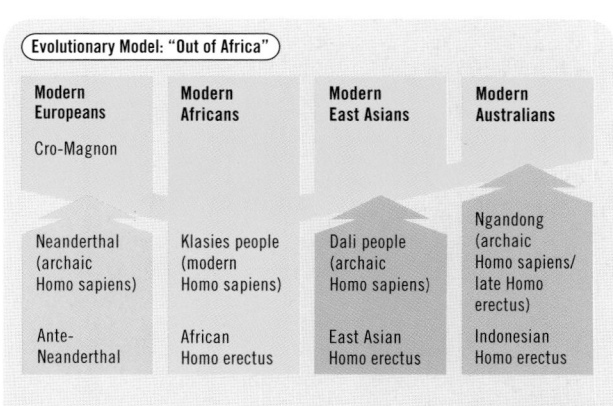

Evolutionary Model: "Out of Africa"

Modern Europeans	Modern Africans	Modern East Asians	Modern Australians
Cro-Magnon			
			Ngandong (archaic Homo sapiens/ late Homo erectus)
Neanderthal (archaic Homo sapiens)	Klasies people (modern Homo sapiens)	Dali people (archaic Homo sapiens)	
Ante-Neanderthal	African Homo erectus	East Asian Homo erectus	Indonesian Homo erectus

Exploration of the Earth's Surface

A Grand European Triumph?

The European seafarers of the 15th and 16th centuries were celebrated as great discoverers. And that they were, at least from the European perspective. Reports of their travels were circulated and analyzed by cartographers, and their knowledge was widely disseminated (with some valuable insights kept secret) thanks to the newly invented printing process. Yet other explorers had achieved great seafaring accomplishments long before. Perhaps the most ambitious adventure of all times was the settlement of Polynesia by Austronesians from Southeast Asia. The boldest of their advances took place in the 1st millennium BC and brought human settlements to Hawaii and Easter Island.

Ancient Discoveries

Egyptians are known to have voyaged to Punt (presumably Somalia) as early as 2,200 BC. Queen Hatshepsut sponsored a sea expedition to Punt in the 15th century BC. Phoenicians are believed to have circumnavigated the African continent under the flag of the Egyptian Pharaoh in the early 6th century BC. In the 5th century BC, Herodotus compiled a map of the known world on the basis of his own knowledge and accounts of voyages of exploration. The Greek seafarer Pytheas of Massalia (Marseilles) sailed the coasts of western and northern Europe in about 330 BC, and is thought to have reached Arctic drift ice.

The Arabs expanded the geographic knowledge amassed by the Greeks. In the Middle Ages, they had compiled the most detailed knowledge about Africa, western and southern Asia. The overland journeys of Ibn Battutah (14th century) took him to Timbuktu and China.

The Chinese first ventured to the shores of the Persian Gulf in the 5th century. Chinese naval exploration flourished in the 10th century and reached its zenith in the expeditions of Zheng He to East Africa in the 15th century. The European Age of Discovery began – after some forerunners like Marco Polo – with the great sea voyages of the 15th and 16th centuries. Under the leadership of Henry the Navigator, the Portuguese initially took the lead in ocean-going exploration, but were soon rivaled by the Spanish. Their goal was to eliminate Arab middlemen from the spice trade. Arab merchants had traveled as far as Southeast Asia, spreading the religion of Islam on their commercial crusades into these distant regions.

Who Discovered America?

Humans first set foot on the North American continent at least 20,000 years ago. Migrating over the land bridge between Alaska and northeastern Siberia across what is now the Bering Strait, they eventually settled the entire continent. The hunting societies on both sides of the Bering Strait remained in contact. The Vikings made a number of visits to the eastern coast of North America beginning in the 10th century AD, but their explorations had no lasting impact on early American or European societies. The arrival of Christopher Columbus had much more far-reaching consequences. The map of the known world grew larger. Europeans conquered the "New World." Native Americans were subjugated and their populations decimated in the centuries that followed.

"Show me Adam's will!"

This angry outburst by French King Francis I is indicative of the reactions of the English, Dutch, and Italians, who were compelled to look on passively while Spain and Portugal divided the world up between them, at first in the Treaty of Tordesillas in 1494 and later in the Treaty of Saragossa (1529). The nations of Europe did everything in their power to secure their share of the treasures of the "newly discovered" lands. The quest for northeast and northwest passages, short trade routes through Arctic waters to Asia, began under the English flag (Caboto) in the late 15th century.

"Replenish the earth, and subdue it!"

The "discovered" peoples might surely have posed the question of Adam's will with better reason. Why did the Europeans become the leading discoverers and conquerors? Why didn't the Aztecs or the Incas invade Spain? Why didn't the Chinese become a true sea power? A number of cultural, political, and technological factors combined to enable the Europeans to answer the biblical call to action. They were driven not only by hunger for power, gold, and riches, but also by missionary zeal and a curiosity about foreign lands that was alien to such cultures as the Chinese of the Middle Kingdom, for example.

By 1600, knowledge of geography had expanded immensely – as a by-product of exploration, so to speak. Scientific interest played an important role in the voyages of the last great seafaring explorer James Cook, and the continental explorations of Alexander von Humboldt, which also focused on vertical aspects of topography, were devoted exclusively to scientific inquiry.

The Wonders of the Distant Orient

Members of the Polo family traveled as merchants and trade representatives to China long before the age of European expansion. Printed in many European languages, Marco Polo's Il Milione, an account of his travels, was the most important source of information about Asia in the medieval world and is known to have influenced Columbus.

Objective Achieved

Only 28 years after the death of Henry the Navigator, Vasco da Gama discovered the sea route to India and weighed anchor off the Indian coast after a ten-month journey around Africa. He returned to Lisbon with a rich cargo of spices and jewels but with only a third of his original crew.

Prototype of an Explorer's Vessel

After the first voyages of discovery in small, agile caravels fitted with a triangular sail in the style of Arab dhows, explorers saw the need for larger ships capable of transporting troops, horses, cannons, and provisions. The new vessels were modeled after Nordic ships and powered by a square sail.

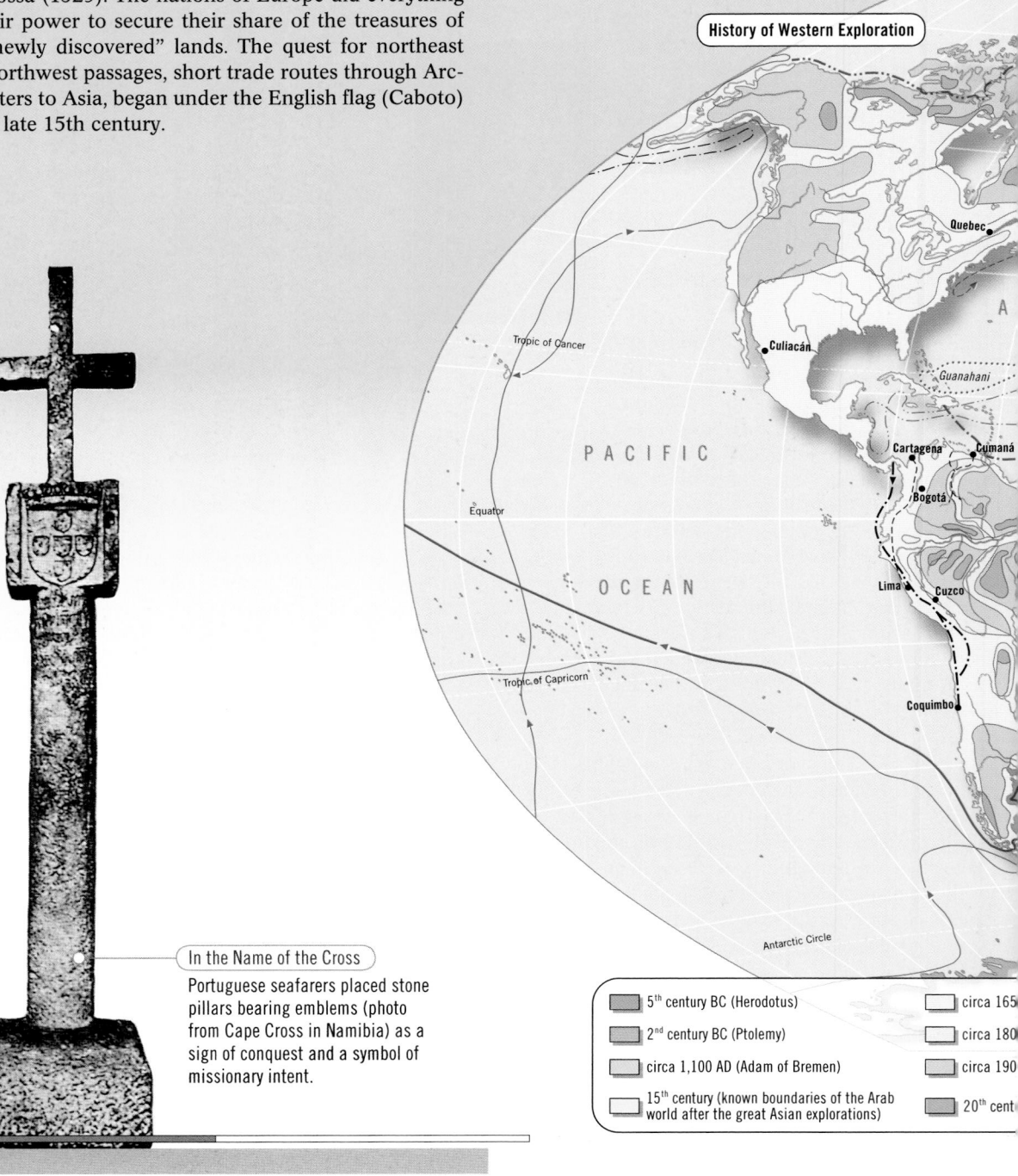

History of Western Exploration

In the Name of the Cross

Portuguese seafarers placed stone pillars bearing emblems (photo from Cape Cross in Namibia) as a sign of conquest and a symbol of missionary intent.

5th century BC (Herodotus)	circa 165
2nd century BC (Ptolemy)	circa 180
circa 1,100 AD (Adam of Bremen)	circa 190
15th century (known boundaries of the Arab world after the great Asian explorations)	20th cent

Exploration of the Earth's Surface

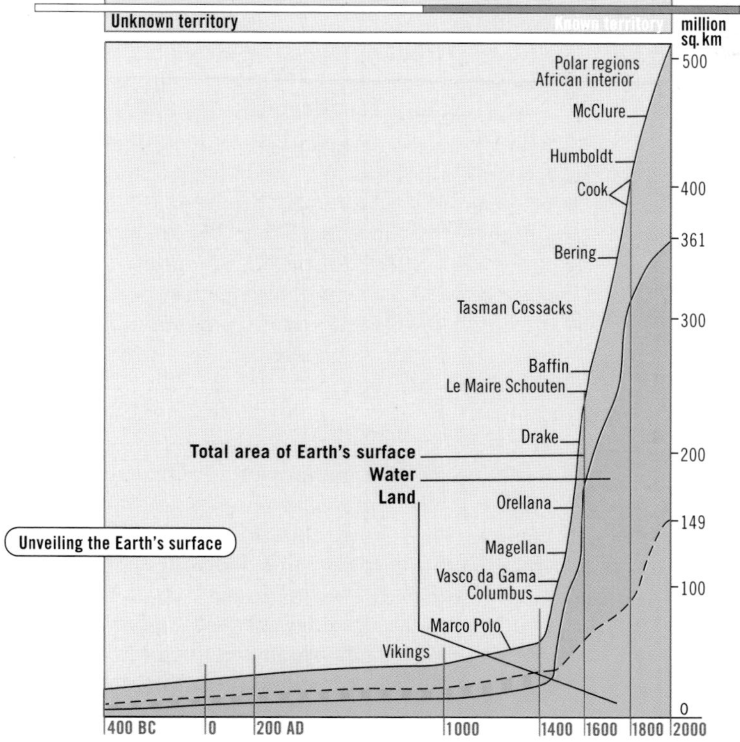

Unknown territory — **Known territory** — million sq. km

Polar regions	500
African interior	
McClure	
Humboldt	400
Cook	
Bering	361
Tasman Cossacks	300
Baffin	
Le Maire Schouten	
Drake	200
Total area of Earth's surface	
Water	
Land	149
Orellana	
Magellan	100
Vasco da Gama	
Columbus	
Marco Polo	
Vikings	0

Unveiling the Earth's surface

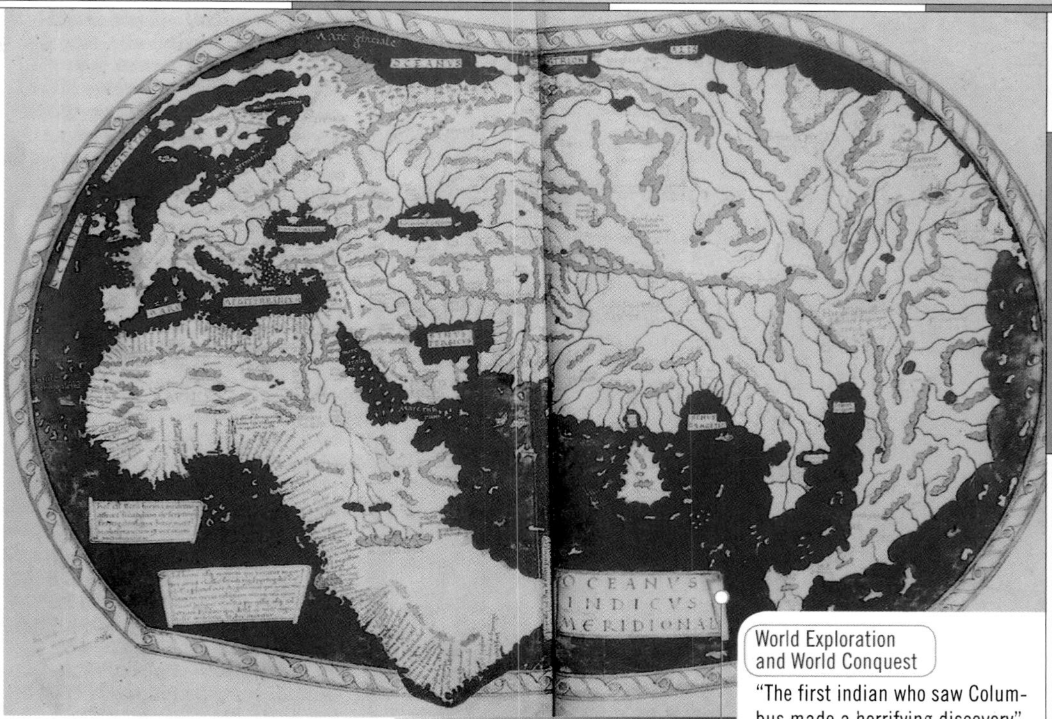

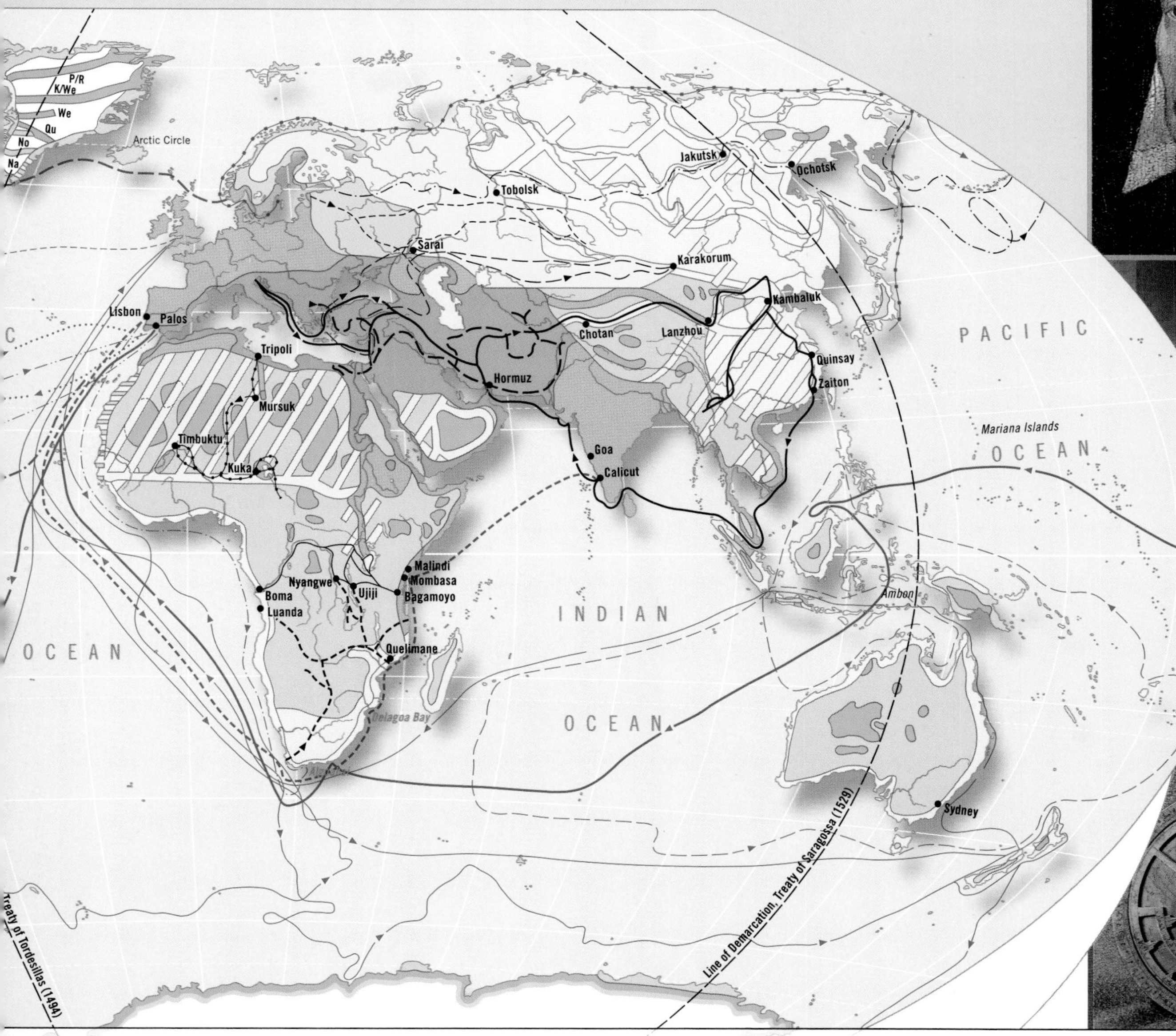

400 BC — 0 — 200 AD — 1000 — 1400 1600 1800 2000

World Exploration and World Conquest

"The first indian who saw Columbus made a horrifying discovery" (G. Lichtenberg). This statement offers a view of a milestone event in world history from the other side. The painting by Johann Theodor de Bry (1594) shows indians bringing gifts while Spanish soldiers erect a cross.

The World According to Ptolemy

This 15th-century map is based on the view of the world as envisioned by the Greek astronomer and geographer Ptolemy (2nd century AD), which was generally accepted until after the rounding of the African horn (1488) and the western voyage of Columbus (1492). Africa is linked to a continent in the south, Terra australis incognita, which almost completely encloses the Indian Ocean.

A Visionary Founds a Think Tank

Known by the misleading title of "Henry the Navigator," Portuguese Prince Dom Henrique established an interdisciplinary academy of navigation in Sagres, where available geographic knowledge was compiled — and kept strictly secret. Beginning in 1418, he promoted the exploration of unknown waters in hopes of discovering a sea route to India and its spices.

Planet of Seas

The myth of the vast southern continent of Terra australis incognita was finally put to rest by James Cook. Traveling more ocean routes than all of his predecessors together, Cook shed light on the configuration of the Earth's oceans.

An Arab Innovation

Portuguese seafarers owed much of their success to nautical instruments invented by Arabs. With the aid of the astrolabe, latitude and local time could be determined on the basis of celestial measurements.

Campaigns of Alexander the Great (334–324 BC)	Giovanni Caboto (1497–98)	James Cook (1768–79)	**Greenland expeditions:**
Norman Conquests (8th to 11th century AD)	Columbus, 3rd voyage (1498–1500)	Alexander v. Humboldt (1799–1804, 1829)	**No** Nordenskjöld (1883)
William of Rubrouck (1253–55)	Columbus, 4th voyage (1502–04)	Heinrich Barth (1850–55)	**Na** Nansen (1888)
Marco Polo (1271–95)	Magellan (1519–22)	Livingstone (1849–73)	**P/R** Peary (1892–95), Rasmussen (1912)
Bartolomeu Dias (1487)	Pizarro, Almagro (1531–37)	Stanley (1871–77, 1887–89)	**Qu** Quervain (1912)
Columbus, 1st voyage (1492–93)	Tasman (1642–44)	Nordenskjöld, Northeast Passage (1878–79)	**K/We** Koch-Wegener (1912–13)
Vasco da Gama (1497–98)	Bering (1728–43)	Amundsen, Northwest Passage (1903–06)	**We** Wegener (1930)

The Dynamic Global Population

Explosion versus Stagnation

The world's population is constantly growing. When Christ was born, some 300 million people lived on Earth. By the time Columbus discovered America, the number had risen to 500 million. In 1969, the first human to set foot on the moon looked back at a world with a population of 3.5 billion. The number has since grown to 6.6 billion and continues to rise at a rate of about 80 million every year.

Battling the "Black Death"

The flagellants sought to ward off the Plague, which was regarded as God's wrath judgment, through penance and self-mortification. The Plague epidemic that broke out in Genoa and Marseille in 1347 and eventually spread throughout Europe took the lives of more than 20 million people (one-third of the total population) from southern Italy to northern England and Scandinavia between 1348 and 1352.

A Demographic Time Bomb

Populations continue to grow at a virtually unbroken pace in many countries. Masses of humanity fill the streets of Bombay, India and many other major cities.

Phases of Growth

Population growth has proceeded slowly but steadily since the Neolithic revolution, when human communities first adopted a sedentary lifestyle some 12,000 years ago. Growth accelerated rapidly after the Industrial Revolution, which began in Europe around 1800. Industrialization led to significant improvements in living standards, nutrition, medical care, and disease prevention and thus unleashed a veritable population explosion. The Demographic Transition Model reflects the interdependence of birth and mortality rates as a crucial parameter of population growth. As a rule, the later a country enters the third phase, the more significant – although shorter – the period of explosive growth will be.

Global Developments

Comparisons in time and place support this statement. England, birthplace of the Industrial Revolution in the waning 18th century (Malthus published his pessimistic treatise on the Principle of Population in 1803), did not achieve balance between birth and death rates until nearly 200 years later, whereas it took Japan only 40 to 50 years to do so. Today, many countries in Asia and especially in Africa are in the midst of demographic transition. Apparently growing without end, their populations double about every 25 years (Great Britain every 423 years; Austria every 2,310 years; Japan every 318 years!). Yet demographers expect that global population growth will slow to a standstill in the mid-21st century at a level of between ten and twelve billion people.

Possible Growth Scenarios

To an increasing extent, global population is concentrated in the developing nations today. In 1950, only about two-thirds of the estimated 2.5 billion people on Earth were inhabitants of these countries. By the mid-21st century, this figure will have risen to 88% of a total world population of about ten billion. Rapid growth in these regions contrasts with stagnation or extremely slow growth in the industrialized countries. Both of these tendencies pose grave dangers to human societies.

Unbridled growth in Latin America, Asia, and especially Africa not only exacerbates the social and economic disparities between north and south, it also has a severe impact on the environment in the form of uncontrolled exploitation of available land, diminishing water

Planting, sedentary lifestyle

| 12000 | 9000 | 8000 | 7000 | 6000 |

The Dynamic Global Population

World population in 1999 – Growth and projection								
	Population in millions	Birth rate per thousand	Death rate per thousand	Natural growth per cent	Population doubling (in years at current growth rate)	Projected population in 2025 (millions)	Age distribution <15	>65
World	5 982	23	9	1.4	49	8 054	31	7
Africa	771	39	14	2.5	28	1 290	43	3
North America	303	14	8	0.6	119	374	21	13
Latin America	512	24	6	1.8	38	709	33	5
Australia – Oceania	30	18	7	1.1	64	41	26	10
Asia	3 637	23	8	1.5	46	4 923	32	6
Europe	728	10	11	−0.1	–	718	18	14
Examples of extremes:								
Dem. Rep. Congo	50.5	48	16	3.2	22	105.7	48	3
Austria	8.1	10	10	0.0	2 310	8.1	17	15
Germany	82.0	10	10	−0.1	–	79.9	16	16

reserves, deforestation, and desertification. The consequences include famine, waves of refugee migration, the expansion of slums in major urban centers, increasing poverty, and the spread of disease. The devastating effects of the AIDS epidemic on societies in Africa and other parts of the world speak much louder than words.

Yet stagnation and decline (populations in several industrialized nations such as Germany and Austria are currently shrinking) pose serious problems as well. As populations dwindle, they also tend to grow older, and both trends will have a lasting impact on many areas of life – the labor market and social security systems, education and housing, public health service, commerce and transportation, to name only a few.

Limits and Dangers: Quantitative and Qualitative Population Growth

Exploding populations in some places, stagnating or declining populations in others. This disparity in a world that is becoming more closely interconnected in time and space every day poses a significant problem in itself. The situation is made worse by severe inequalities in the distribution and use of limited natural resources. The question of the Earth's ability to accommodate its inhabitants can no longer be answered simply in terms of its potential to produce food but must also be examined in the light of environmental factors. It is not necessarily the sheer numbers of people that threaten the equilibrium of System Earth. More often than not, it is the rich (we ourselves!) who jeopardize the balance through our irresponsible and insatiable urge to consume in order to satisfy what we regard as essential needs!

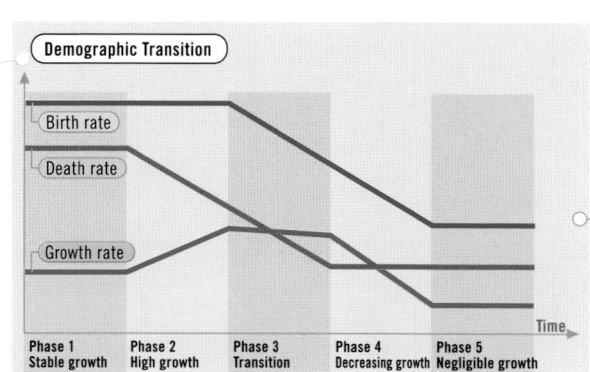

Demographic Transition

Birth rate
Death rate
Growth rate

Time

Phase 1 Stable growth | Phase 2 High growth | Phase 3 Transition | Phase 4 Decreasing growth | Phase 5 Negligible growth

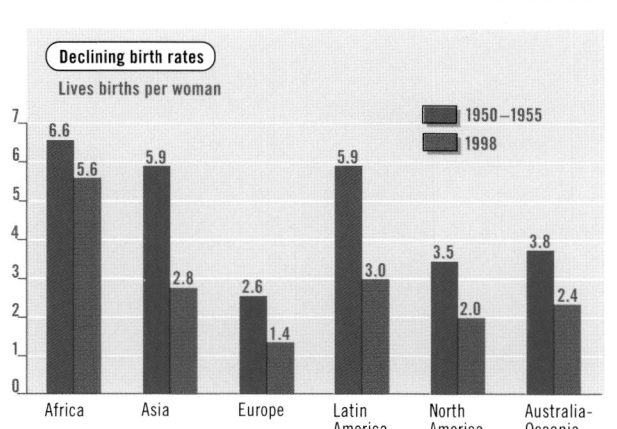

Declining birth rates

Lives births per woman

■ 1950–1955
■ 1998

Africa 6.6 / 5.6
Asia 5.9 / 2.8
Europe 2.6 / 1.4
Latin America 5.9 / 3.0
North America 3.5 / 2.0
Australia-Oceania 3.8 / 2.4

Future Fathers

With a growth rate of 2.3 % per annum (1990-98) South Africa is by no means the fastest-growing country on the African continent (that honor goes to Niger, with 3.9%). These school children in Johannesburg will probably be parents themselves in 15 years.

Unstoppable Growth?

The length of time it takes the global population to increase by one billion people has become increasingly shorter over the course of history. The one-billion mark was reached in 1804, and the total reached two million 123 years later. Successive billions were added at intervals of 33, 14, and 13 years, respectively. Only twelve years later – in October 1999 – world population reached six billion.

Changing Growth Rates

Demographic transition from an agrarian to an industrial society follows a predictable pattern. State 1 is characterized by high birth and death rates, with natural growth (the difference between the two) remaining relatively low. In State 2, death rates fall, birth rates remain stable, and the growth rate rises accordingly. In State 3, birth rates begin to fall as well. State 4 marks the transition from rapid to slow growth. In State 5, birth, death, and growth rates stabilize at a low level.

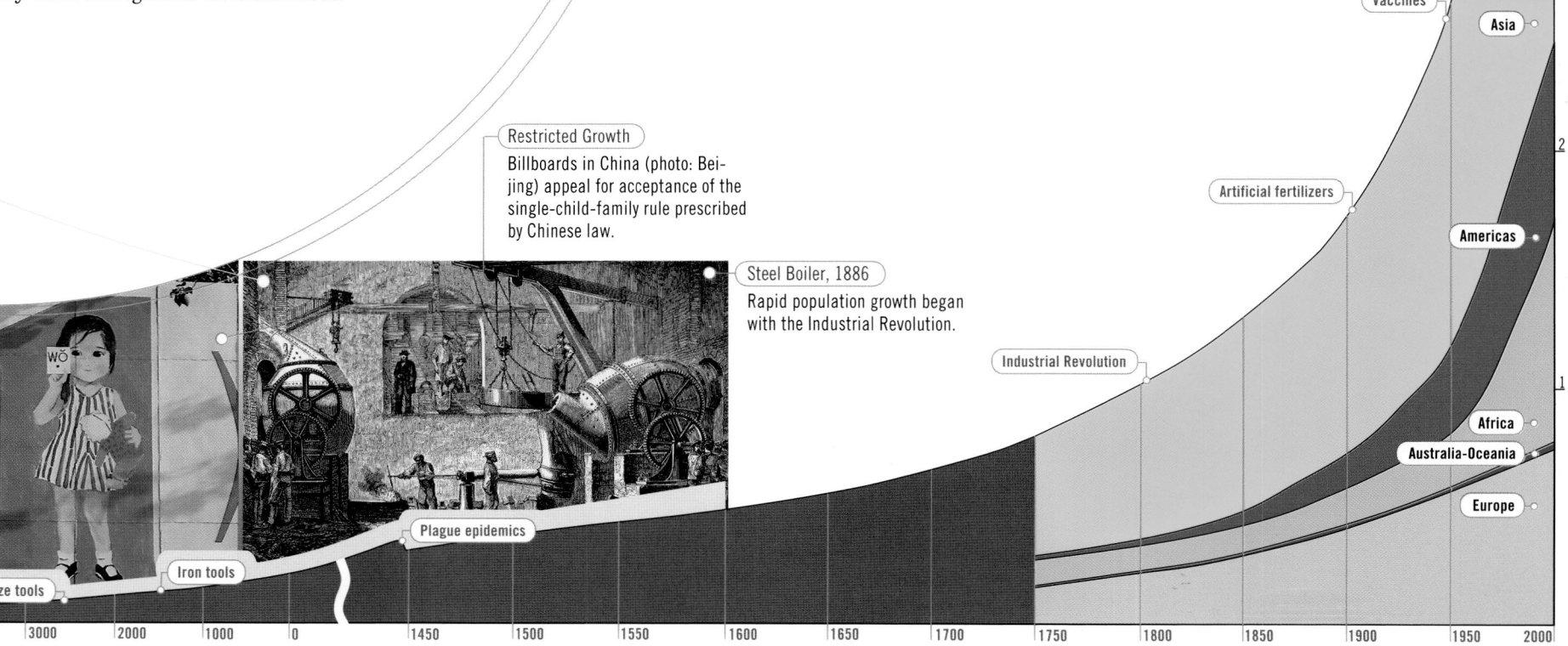

Restricted Growth

Billboards in China (photo: Beijing) appeal for acceptance of the single-child-family rule prescribed by Chinese law.

Steel Boiler, 1886

Rapid population growth began with the Industrial Revolution.

World population in billions

World population development

Vaccines
Artificial fertilizers
Industrial Revolution
Plague epidemics
Bronze tools
Iron tools

Asia
Americas
Africa
Australia-Oceania
Europe

6
5
4
3
2
1

3000 | 2000 | 1000 | 0 | 1450 | 1500 | 1550 | 1600 | 1650 | 1700 | 1750 | 1800 | 1850 | 1900 | 1950 | 2000

Human Migration

A Global View of Shifting Populations

The history of humanity is a history of migration – and has been since the first humans appeared on Earth. Immigrants and emigrants – invading hordes and war refugees – mass migrations: all of these terms describe aspects of a complex problem that is of crucial global importance today.

Causes of Popular Migration

In addition to the natural causes of many major population movements (floods, soil degradation, desertification, etc.), people have tended to migrate primarily for ideological and economic reasons. Aside from the many unfortunate cases of involuntary migration (banishment, deportation, flight from persecution, slavery, etc.), economic push-and-pull factors are among the most common causes of large-scale migration. Overpopulation, a shortage of work, and the corresponding economic and social misery that accompany these phenomena are and always have been important "push" factors contributing to regional migration and emigration. On the other hand, prosperity and an abundance of jobs in other countries attract workers and economic refugees, as "pull" factors, with the promise of better living conditions and opportunities for social advancement. A review of the economic and social history of the modern era clearly shows that political developments in many areas of the world have been shaped by major population movements – from the mass displacement of African slaves to the emigration of Europeans (primarily for economic or political reasons) to the New World, Australia, New Zealand, and South Africa. In the roughly one hundred years between 1830 to 1928, nearly six million Germans emigrated, about 90% of them to the U.S., the remainder to Canada, Brazil, Australia, Argentina, South Africa, and Asia.

Between Hostile Lines
In the fall of 1996, hundreds of thousands of Hutu refugees fled the war zone in eastern Zaire to return to their homelands in war-torn Rwanda.

Skills Wanted Abroad
Young emigrants from Germany in Brazil (1925): automotive knowledge and skills provide the basis for a new start.

Involuntary Exile
African captives were often chained together with their hands bound to a pole during their journey into slavery.

Boat People
Hundreds of thousands of Vietnamese fled their homeland, often in overloaded, unseaworthy boats, seeking refuge in non-communist countries in Southeast Asia even long after the Vietnam War. A favored destination was the former British Crown Colony of Hong Kong.

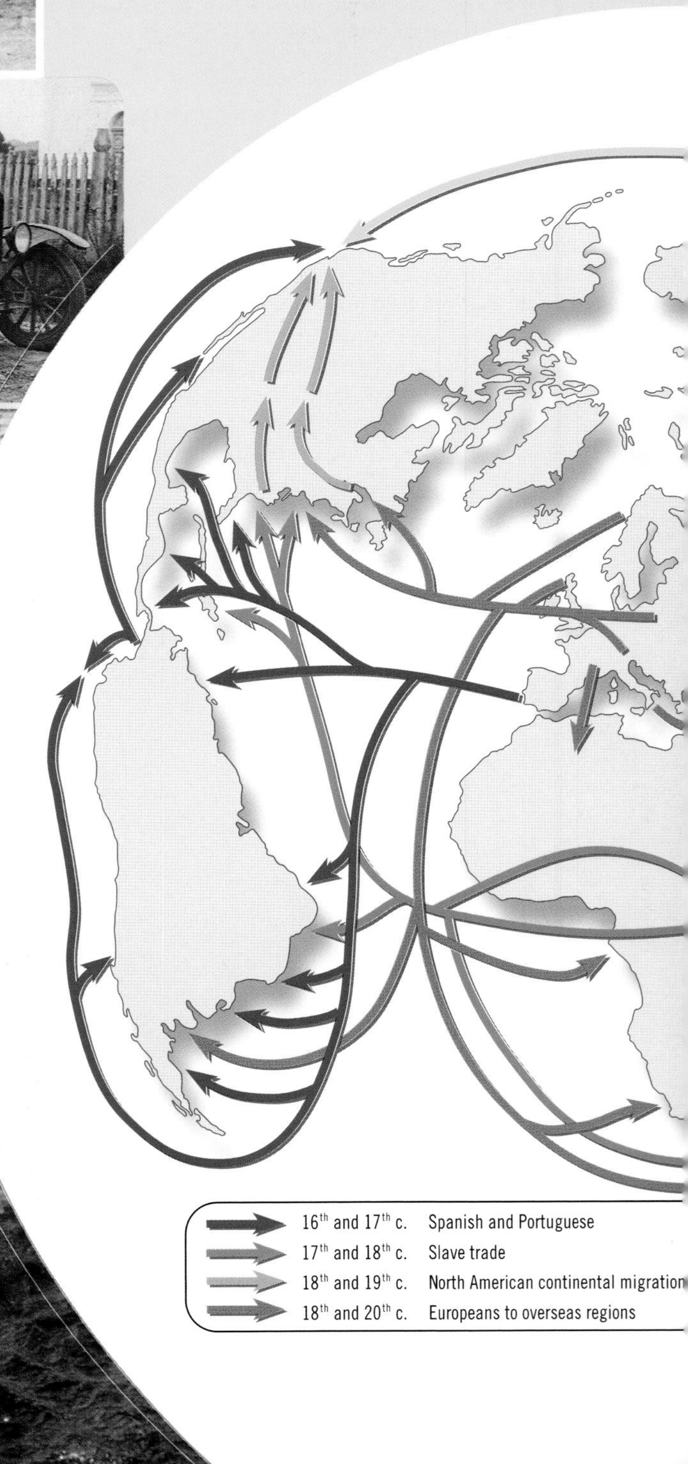

	16th and 17th c.	Spanish and Portuguese
	17th and 18th c.	Slave trade
	18th and 19th c.	North American continental migration
	18th and 20th c.	Europeans to overseas regions

Human Migration

Streams of Refugees

Probably the most frequent cause of often involuntary mass migrations is war. In addition to the two World Wars, a number of more recent local wars and hostilities have caused huge groups of refugees to leave their homelands in Africa (Congo, Rwanda, the Guineas), Afghanistan, and the Middle East (where unsolved political and military conflicts between Israelis and Palestinians and problems involving Kurdish populations have persisted for decades). Striking evidence that religious and ideological differences as well as ethnic hostilities can lead to major refugee migrations can be found in the Balkan states, Southeast Asia (Christian-Moslem antagonism), and the Indian sub-continent (conflicts between Moslems and Hindus).

Environmental refugees are people who have been compelled to move away from their familiar homelands due to degradation of their natural environments and the resulting deterioration or loss of traditional foundations of life. Water shortages and water pollution, soil erosion, deforestation, desertification, and changes affecting the diversity of animal and plant species are forcing increasing numbers of people, especially in the "Third World," to abandon their native lands.

Economic refugees are prompted to leave their native lands in search of better living conditions – primarily in western industrialized countries – by worsening social and, above all, economic imbalances of regional or global proportions. Noteworthy examples include the immigration of Mexicans into the U.S., the growing stream of eastern European migrants into central and western Europe, and the rising number of Africans and Asians smuggled illegally by organized gangs into the Member States of the European Union.

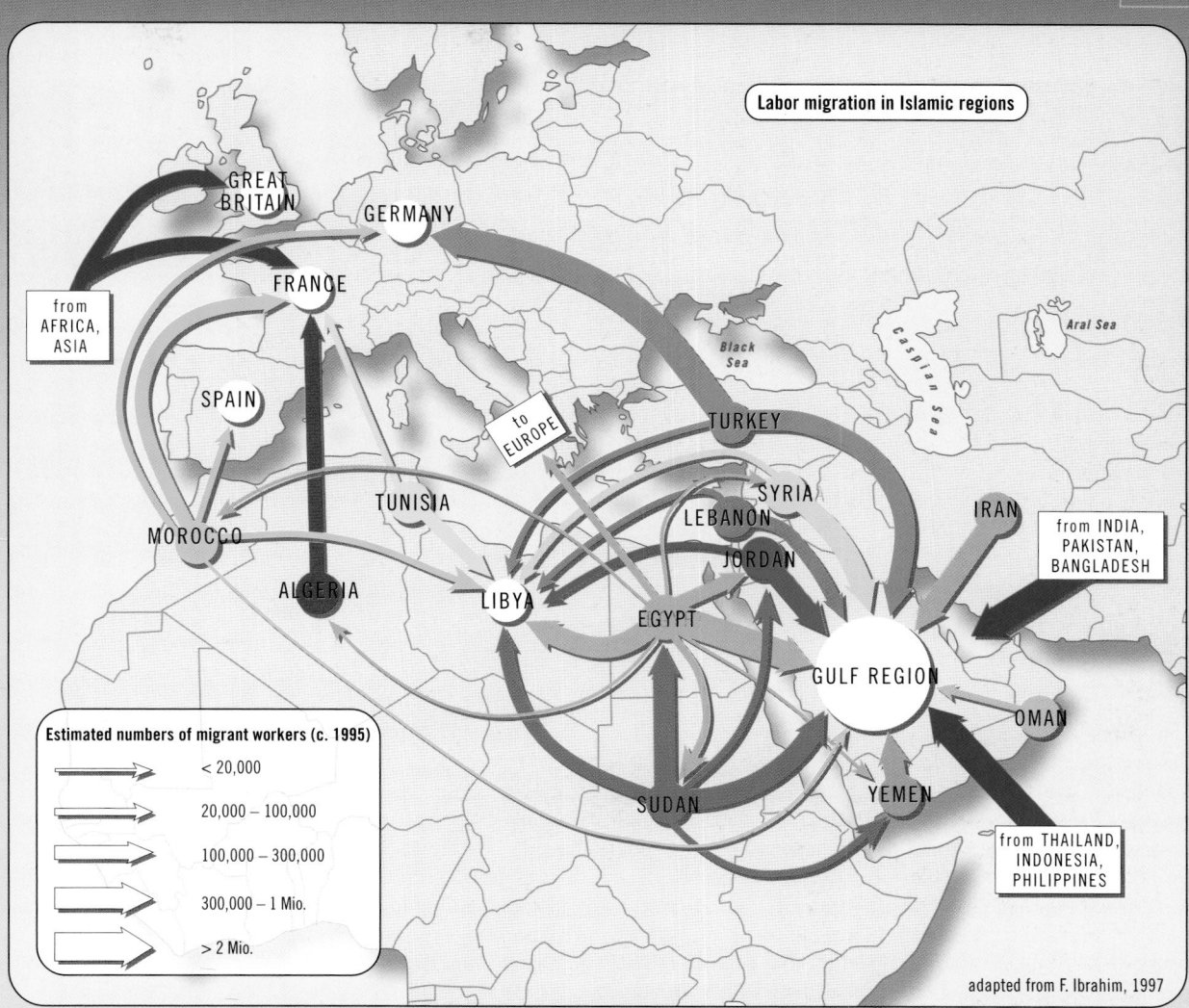

Labor migration in Islamic regions

Estimated numbers of migrant workers (c. 1995)

< 20,000
20,000 – 100,000
100,000 – 300,000
300,000 – 1 Mio.
> 2 Mio.

adapted from F. Ibrahim, 1997

Major migration streams of the past 500 years

19th c.	Indians
19th and 20th c.	Russians into Asia
19th and 20th c.	Chinese (and Japanese) to overseas regions

Effects of disasters on world population, 1969–1993				
Type of disaster	No. of persons affected	homeless	Death toll	No. of events
Drought and famine	57,906,000	23,000	74,000	438
Floods	47,850,000	3,178,000	12,000	1,366
Tropical storms	9,417,000	1,066,000	29,000	1,551
Earthquakes	1,765,000	224,000	22,000	640
Landslides	132,000	107,000	1,600	218
Volcanic eruptions	95,000	13,000	1,000	98
Technical accidents	53,000	8,400	600	310
Fire	33,000	88,000	3,300	583

On an Emigrant Ship

During the 19th century, thousands of Irish emigrants embarked on a quest for a better life in the New World, the majority of them fleeing during the Irish potato famine of 1845–50. This 1884 woodcut shows passengers on an emigrant ship being called to breakfast by a bell.

Labor Migration

Unlike the many and diverse groups of more or less involuntary migrants, migrants who leave their homelands in search of work ordinarily do so voluntarily on the basis of personal considerations. Two examples may serve to illustrate this phenomenon.

In North America, migrant workers are needed primarily as unskilled harvest laborers in the agricultural sector. Most of these people come from the south – from Mexico or the Caribbean. According to official estimates, there were approximately 8.5 million Mexicans living and working in the U.S. in 2001, about three million of them illegally. In most cases, these migrant workers have been smuggled into the country by organized gangs. Over the years, specific migration patterns have taken shape in the United States. A significant number of migrant laborers work as fruit pickers in Florida during the winter before moving north to the New England states to help harvest tomatoes, potatoes, and apples in the summer. A second stream of migrant workers moves from Texas into the Midwest or to the West Coast in search of jobs picking fruit, vegetables, sugar beets, or cotton. A third current flows northward along the West Coast from southern California to Washington, working during the fruit and vegetable harvests.

Migrant workers often contribute significantly to the maintenance of living standards and even to increasing prosperity, as the example of the small oil-producing countries along the Persian Gulf clearly shows. Not only do "guest laborers" account for up to 80% of their populations, social institutions and economic sectors – public services, schools, universities, hospitals, private households, national and municipal administrations, the construction business and to a certain extent even the oil industry itself – depend heavily upon foreign workers and could hardly function without them.

Prospects

Environmental catastrophes, rapid population growth, and economic stagnation in some regions; sluggish population growth accompanied by strong economic expansion in others; political disputes and regional conflicts, civil wars, and famines – all of these factors will continue to cause large-scale popular migrations and waves of refugees in the 21st century. In a global economy, hardly a single country will be spared the consequences of these developments.

Global Linguistic Diversity

One World – Thousands of Languages

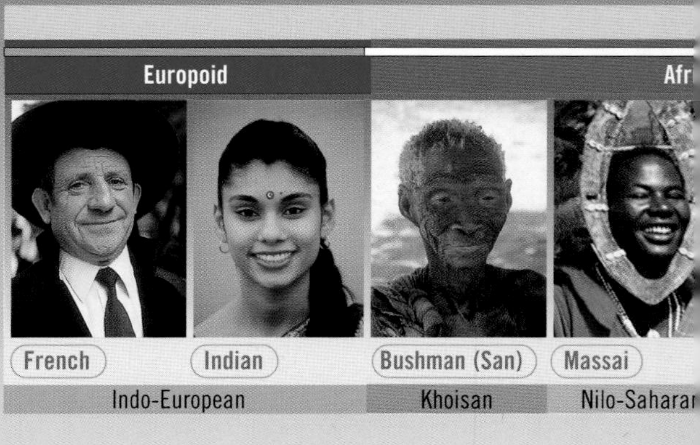

Depending upon the criteria applied in distinguishing them, between 2,500 and 6,500 languages are spoken on Earth. These widely diverging figures reflect both the difficulty involved in differentiating with certainty between a dialect and a language and our lack of knowledge about many languages spoken by very small groups in regions such as the Amazon Basin, New Guinea, and the African interior.

European languages account for only a small portion of the total. Somewhere between 70 and 165 different tongues are spoken on the continent. More languages (nearly 750!) are spoken in Papua New Guinea than in any other single country in the world. Only very few countries are completely unilingual (Iceland is one). Most countries are home to speakers of several or many different tongues and their variants. A number of languages die out every year, and discoveries of new languages are rare even today.

Europoid		Afr
French	Indian	Bushman (San)	Massai
Indo-European		Khoisan	Nilo-Saharan

Dead Languages – Living Legacies

Some languages die out with their last speakers, while others are preserved as funds of knowledge, taught in schools (classical Arabic), used only in religious contexts (Old Hebrew), or studied as fixed points of historical reference in linguistics (Sanskrit). Still others serve as a source of new scientific terminology (Greek, Latin) or retain their vitality as literary languages (classical Chinese).

English – A Dominant World Language

Languages are affected by globalization as well. English has become the dominant language worldwide, although it ranks far behind Chinese in terms of numbers of native speakers. In sports and culture, in the high-tech world of computers and telecommunication, in the realm of travel and leisure activities, in scientific discourse and business correspondence, English has attained a degree of appeal, prestige, and influence that is unrivalled by any other language at the global level. International organizations exert considerable influence on language policy in support of other tongues. At the UN, for example, Arabic, Chinese, French, Russian, and Spanish join English as official languages. The European Union has even awarded official status to the national languages of all its member states.

Ethnic Revival – Grass Roots Resistance

The emancipation movements of the sixties and seventies led to a reassessment of the importance of language within the context of ethnic revival. Emphasis suddenly shifted from "utility" and "suitability" in a global sense to concern for linguistic diversity. "Minority" languages and tongues spoken in now independent former colonies were recognized as worthy of equal status and treatment. Languages which for centuries had been preserved and passed from one generation to the next only in oral form were systematically analyzed and described, transposed into a standardized written form, and documented in learning and reference materials such as textbooks, teachers' guides, dictionaries, and grammars (examples include Faeroese, a Germanic island language, and Swahili, the lingua franca in Africa). Bilingual or trilingual traffic and street signs, multilingual billboards, and enhanced media presence now offer striking visible and audible evidence of the new status of many once-neglected languages.

Writing Systems – Keys to Language

Human beings have employed a wide range of different writing systems to present natural, spoken language in visual form for more than three millennia. People of the ancient Egyptian, Inuit, and Maya cultures developed various forms of hieroglyphics, the Sumerians created a cuneiform system, while people of other civilizations established systems comprised of signs for words or syllables. Most forms of writing employed today make use of letters or symbols representing specific sounds. The writing systems now used in Europe and North America derive from the Phoenician alphabet developed in the 10th century BC, which also provided the basis for both the Arabic and Hebrew writing systems. Linguists have identified four major groups of alphabets: Greek (Latin, Coptic, Cyrillic, Armenian, Georgian), Semitic (Arabic, Hebrew, Ethiopian), Indian (Devanagari, Bengali, Tibetan, Burman, Thai, Khmer), and East Asian (Chinese, Japanese, Korean).

Every human has a language, but not everyone has command of its written form. Illiteracy is actually quite widespread and is particularly prevalent in the Third World. In Haiti, for example, 55% of the population cannot read or write. Illiterates account for 40% of the population of the Central African Republic, and 62% of all Yemeneseare unable to read a newspaper or write even a short note. Even the rich industrialized countries of the world face the problem of illiteracy, with up to 5% of their inhabitants unable to read or express themselves in written form and thus virtually excluded from the mainstream of cultural and economic life.

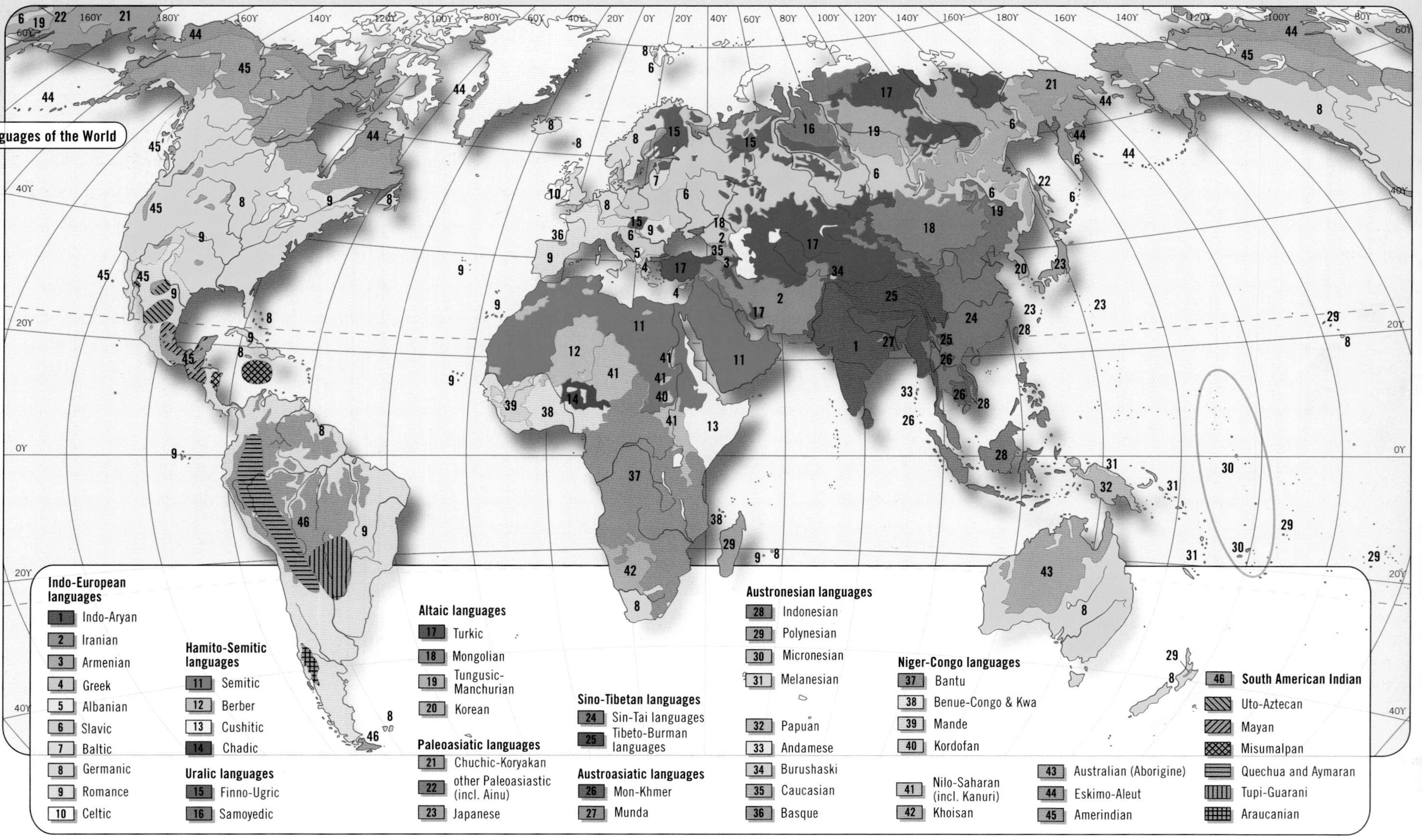

Languages of the World

Indo-European languages
- 1 Indo-Aryan
- 2 Iranian
- 3 Armenian
- 4 Greek
- 5 Albanian
- 6 Slavic
- 7 Baltic
- 8 Germanic
- 9 Romance
- 10 Celtic

Hamito-Semitic languages
- 11 Semitic
- 12 Berber
- 13 Cushitic
- 14 Chadic

Uralic languages
- 15 Finno-Ugric
- 16 Samoyedic

Altaic languages
- 17 Turkic
- 18 Mongolian
- 19 Tungusic-Manchurian
- 20 Korean

Paleoasiatic languages
- 21 Chuchic-Koryakan
- 22 other Paleoasiastic (incl. Ainu)
- 23 Japanese

Sino-Tibetan languages
- 24 Sin-Tai languages
- 25 Tibeto-Burman languages

Austroasiatic languages
- 26 Mon-Khmer
- 27 Munda

Austronesian languages
- 28 Indonesian
- 29 Polynesian
- 30 Micronesian
- 31 Melanesian
- 32 Papuan
- 33 Andamese
- 34 Burushaski
- 35 Caucasian
- 36 Basque

Niger-Congo languages
- 37 Bantu
- 38 Benue-Congo & Kwa
- 39 Mande
- 40 Kordofan
- 41 Nilo-Saharan (incl. Kanuri)
- 42 Khoisan

- 43 Australian (Aborigine)
- 44 Eskimo-Aleut
- 45 Amerindian
- 46 South American Indian
- Uto-Aztecan
- Mayan
- Misumalpan
- Quechua and Aymaran
- Tupi-Guarani
- Araucanian

East Asian			Arctic	Amerindian		Oceanian		Australian
Pygmy	Chinese	Tibetan	Inuit	Maya	Yanomami	Polynesian	Melanesian	Australian
Niger-Kordofan	Sino-Tibetan		Eskimo-Aleut	Amerindian		Austronesian		Australian

Linguistic Diversity – a Curse?

Did all humans originally speak a single language? The idea (no longer accepted) is expressed in the biblical story of the Tower of Babylon (painting by Pieter Bruegel the Elder, 1563), in which linguistic diversity is described as God's punishment for human pride and greed for power.

Linguistic Exchange – The Foreign Element

All languages have changed over the course of centuries. Apart from natural, organic evolution, languages are influenced significantly by contact among speakers of different linguistic communities – conquerors and conquered peoples, neighboring linguistic groups, etc. In this way, languages enrich one another with "foreign material" (adopted and adapted words and forms). These phenomena are referred to by historical linguistics as strata: Substrates are traces of the language of a conquered or exterminated people left behind in the language of the victors (e.g. remnants of Celtic in the Romance languages). Superstrata are elements introduced by a conquering group into the language of a subjugated people but which do not displace the original language (e.g. Franconian influences on French). Adstrata are linguistic influences which do not reflect hierarchical relationships (e.g. contacts between speakers of Germanic and Romance languages along linguistic boundaries).

The Birth of New Languages: Pidgin and Creole Forms

Pidgin and Creole languages are the products of a special form of linguistic interaction which takes place primarily when speakers of different native tongues communicate with each other. Such languages have developed through trading activity and in economies significantly influenced by slavery in the New World, Africa, Southeast Asia, and Oceania. Pidgin languages are characterized by markedly simplified structures that facilitate communication but are found in neither of the original native languages involved. Pidgin languages that become established and are passed on to succeeding generations are known as Creoles. Many Creole languages have been standardized and adopted as official national languages (in Haiti, Mauritius, and the Seychelles, for example) and thus contribute to local or national identity.

The Future of Languages

Though many have predicted the eventual demise of linguistic diversity, languages have proven astonishingly resilient. Even today, there are those who hope and believe that globalization will result in the establishment of English as the worldwide medium for communication. Yet efforts have also been undertaken to have the right to speak one's native language firmly anchored in international human rights conventions. Slowly but surely, people are beginning to realize that linguistic diversity has the capacity to enrich humanity and is not, as the Bible suggests, God's punishment for human pride, vanity, and greed. In the age of technology, languages that remain open to progress and capable of integrating it into their dynamic systems will survive and ensure the preservation of linguistic diversity in the 21st century.

A Monument to Language

A prime example of a literary language developed through deliberate effort is Afrikaans, which is spoken in South Africa. The unique monument to language erected in Paarl near Cape Town commemorates the linguistic movement founded by the Boers in 1875.

The Physiognomy of Diversity

Portraits of people from selected ethnic groups and their language families (lower print bar).

Geographic distribution of languages on Earth

- 32% Asia
- 3% Europe
- 15% America
- 19.5% Australia & Oceania
- 30.5% Africa

Most widely spoken languages by number of speakers
as native and second language

millions	
940	Chinese
475	English
395	Hindi
375	Spanish
300	Russian
215	Arabic
200	Bengali
185	Portuguese
155	Malayan-Indonesian
125	Japanese
122	French
118	German
100	Urdu

Overcoming Social Ostracism

Of the 880 million illiterates in the world, two thirds are women. 120 million children do not attend proper schools – due primarily to a lack of money. The photo shows a Massai "bush school" in East Africa.

Bilingual Street Sign

Increasing attention is now being given to linguistic minorities in many countries (photo: sign in French and Occitan in Agde). Distinctions are expressed in different print sizes.

Rue
Hôtel du cheval blanc
PORTA DE LA FONT

Religions of the World

One Divine Power? Many Concepts of Divinity

Religion is an expression of human responses to the experience of divinity in ritual and doctrine. It appears in different forms in different cultures and at different times, and though distinct from other manifestations of culture, it both reflects and shapes them at the same time. Religion is always community-oriented and always involves standards of ethics, although these may differ significantly from one set of beliefs and principles to another. Religion takes public form in rituals and pilgrimages, at specific places, and in the teachings of religious leaders. Religious faith informs and molds the lives of those who share it.

A Ubiquitous Phenomenon

All human societies since prehistoric times have embraced religious beliefs of some kind. We distinguish between two basic types of religion. The first is known as "primary religion." The origin and basis for all religions, it is still clearly evident today in "tribal religions" (frequently, though imprecisely and even inaccurately referred to as "natural" or "animistic" religions). These systems of belief have primarily local or regional relevance and generally govern communal life in small societies. They provide guidance and support at critical points in life – birth, puberty, marriage, death and mourning – through "rites of passage." Events marking seasonal transitions, such as planting and harvest or the winter and summer solstices, are also celebrated in rituals and serve as fixed points of reference for communal life, much like Christmas and Easter in western societies.

The second group, "secondary religions," comprises systems of belief and ritual which can be traced to the teachings or activities of founders, reformers, and charismatic leaders. They include the five major religions of the world: Judaism, Christianity, Islam, Buddhism, and Hinduism. They all pose the question of truth, which plays no role at all in primary religions, whose "natural" legitimacy is grounded in the specific societies that embrace them. Many secondary religions have sacred scriptures, which contain the basic tenets of ethics, faith, and behavior to which their adherents subscribe. Because they claim possession of universal truth, they tend to assume a missionary character, and their founders are the central focus of teaching and devotion. Buddhism, Christianity, and Islam are prime examples of this tendency. As they spread throughout the world, these secondary religions have had to come to grips with

Christian Africa

The majority of people in most of the countries of central and southern Africa are Christians. More than one-third of African Christians are members of the Catholic Church, which actively promotes the education and development of native clerics. The "Independent Churches" embody a form of Christianity that deliberately makes room for traditional aspects of African tribal cultures.

Religion by the Book

An Ethiopian monk demonstrates the art of manuscript illumination while writing a page of the Bible in Amharic, which becomes established as the liturgical language of the Ethiopian Church.

Sacred Waters

A bath in the sacred Ganges River is believed to purify the soul of a Hindu. The ghats (bathing steps) at the pilgrimage center in Varanasi provide easy access to the Ganges.

Traditional Healer

In many African religions, misfortune, disease, and death are attributed to evil spells cast by witches. Only the healer (photo: Susa Madela, Sorcerer of Lightning, 1902–1988) can provide protection.

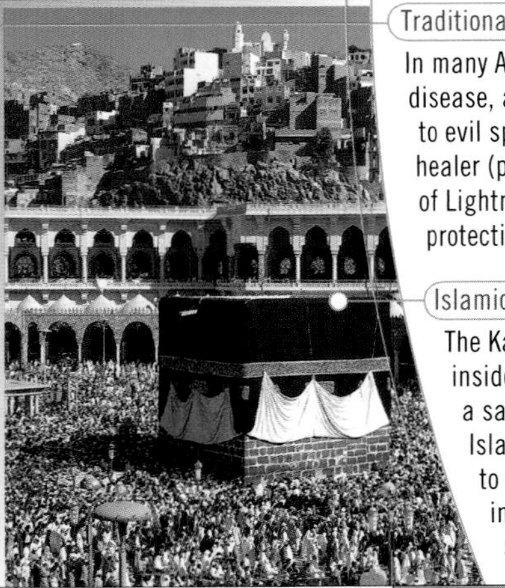

Islamic Pilgrimage

The Ka'bah, an empty, windowless building inside the Great Mosque in Mecca was a sacred shrine in the city even during pre-Islamic times. All Muslims are obliged to make at least one pilgrimage to Mecca in their lifetime. Pilgrims walk around the shrine seven times.

Religions of the World

Great Lakes

Salt Lake City

Tropic of Cancer

ATLANTIC

Guadalupe

PACIFIC

Equator

OCEAN

Tropic of Capricorn

Christianity		Islam
Protestantism	Judaism	Sunni
Roman Catholicism	Significant Jewish communities	Shi'a
Eastern Orthodox Churches		
Other Christian sects		Hinduis

primary religions. In the process, they have adopted and adapted existing sacred rituals, places and times, reinterpreting them and casting out whatever elements could not be reconciled with their teachings. Buddhism developed into Mahayana Buddhism in China, for example, in response to regional influences. Christianity split into an eastern (Orthodox) branch under the influence of the religions of Greece and Asia Minor and a western (Roman) form of Catholicism oriented toward the more dogmatic Roman religions. Islam adopted pre-Islamic and existing Judaic and Christian elements, as the life of Mohammed clearly shows.

When the great religions face a loss of vitality and begin to abandon their original doctrines under the influence of progressive enlightenment, modern patterns of thought, and the pressure of political systems, reformers appear, new sects are founded, and fundamentalist revival movements take shape, as we witness all over the world today. This tendency is reflected in new religious movements and sects in Japan (Tenrykyo and others), the United States (Mormons, Children of God, etc.), Latin America (Umbanda, voodoo cults), India (neo-Hinduism), and Africa (Kimbanguism, Aladura churches, etc.) as well as the emphatically pious New-Age religions.

Religion – a Source of Conflict?

All religions strive to control the lives of their members, and thus they play an important role in public life. Radical, often fundamentalist religious movements also seek to exert political influence, although they often expose themselves to manipulation by political forces as well. In view of the dangers all societies face in today's world, religions would do well to remember their humanitarian function and support the growth of a system of ethics that will enable human beings to live together in peace.

Religions of the World

Religions	Date of origin	Sacred scriptures	Number of adherents	% of world population
Christianity	30 AD	Bible	2 bn	33 % – increasing in the Third World
Islam	622 AD	Koran	1.3 bn	20 % – increasing
Hinduism and neo-Hinduism	c. 1,500 BC	Vedas, Upanishads	900 mil.	15 % – stagnant
Atheists and agnostics	–		900 mil.	15 % – decreasing
Buddhism	c. 530 BC	Tipitaka	360 mil.	6 % – stagnant
Chinese Religious Complex (ancestor and nature worship, Taoism, Confucianism*)	c. 1,500 BC	–	230 mil.	5 %
Tribal religions	prehistoric	Oral tradition	91 mil.	2 %
Yoruba religions: voodoo cults, Umbanda, etc.	?	–	30 mil.	< 1 %
New religious movements (Caodaism, Soka-Gakkai, Ananda Marge, etc.)	19th/20th c.	–	30 mil.	< 1 %
Sikhism	1500 AD	Adi Granth	18 mil.	< 1 %
Judaism	Babylonian exile (587– 538 BC)	Torah, Talmud	15 mil.	< 1 %
Shamanism	prehistoric	Oral tradition	12 mil.	< 1 %
Spiritism*	after 1800	–	10 mil.	< 1 %
Baha'i	1863 AD	The Most Holy Book	4 mil.	< 1 %
Shintō	6th c. AD	Kojiki, Nihongi, Fudoki	4 mil.	< 1 %
Jainism	6th/5th c.BC	Extensive canon in Prakrit literature	3 mil.	< 1 %
Parsiism	500 – 250 BC	Avesta	150,000	< 1 %

* not a religion in the strict sense

Jewish Marriage Rites

Bride and groom cover their heads with a tallit (prayer cloak) during the marriage ceremony.

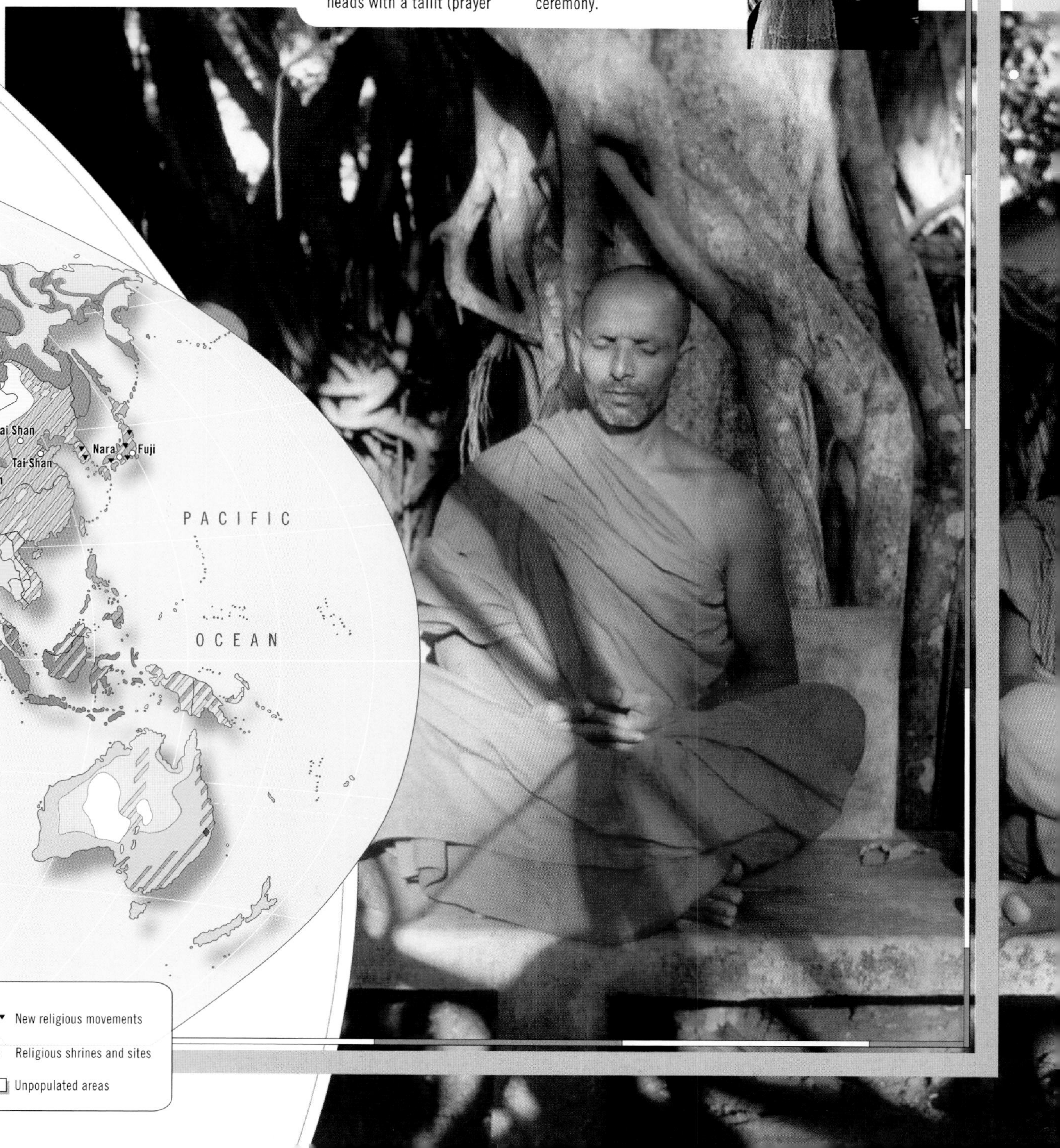

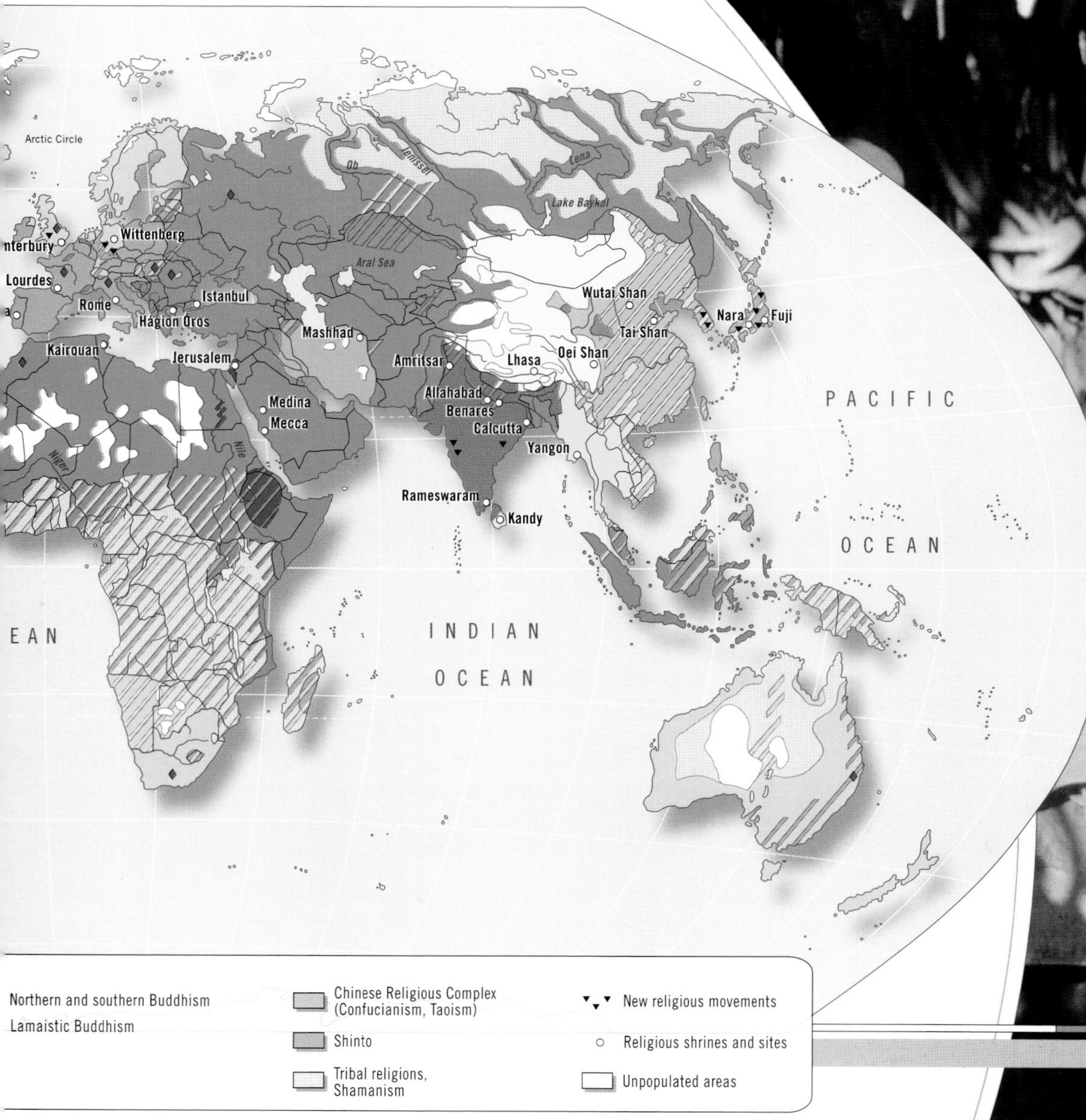

Northern and southern Buddhism
Lamaistic Buddhism

Chinese Religious Complex (Confucianism, Taoism)

Shinto

Tribal religions, Shamanism

New religious movements

Religious shrines and sites

Unpopulated areas

Arctic Circle

Ob

Lake Baikal

Aral Sea

nterbury
Wittenberg
Lourdes
Rome
Istanbul
Hagion Oros
Kairouan
Jerusalem
Mashhad
Medina
Mecca
Allahabad
Benares
Calcutta
Amritsar
Lhasa
Wutai Shan
Tai Shan
Nara
Fuji
Oei Shan
Yangon
Rameswaram
Kandy

PACIFIC OCEAN

INDIAN OCEAN

EAN

From Jericho to the Global City – The City as a Human Habitat?

Jericho and urban history are inseparably intertwined. Here, in the Jordan River Valley, the roots of urban culture can be traced back to the 7th millennium BC. But evidence of early city life can also be found beneath thousands of years of accumulated rubble in other parts of the world.

In the earliest phase in the history of cities, "city-dwellers" represented only a tiny segment of the world's population (estimated at roughly 80 million around the year 1000 BC). At the dawn of the third millennium AD, after nearly nine thousand years of urban history, the majority of the 6.6 billion people on earth live in urban settlements. The number of city residents is expected to rise by nearly 100% by the year 2030, increasing from 2.9 billion (48%) in the year 2000 to about five billion (about 60%) by 2030.

What is "urban" and what is "urbanity"?

Rome, the birthplace of Caesar and Cicero, has always been regarded in the western world as the prototype of the most advanced form of human communal life. During that period it was simply called "urbs" (the city) – and clearly understood as such throughout the ancient world. Rome was the capital of a world empire, a center of art and science, of architecture, of fashion and good taste – indeed of every aspect of life in all its diversity. Thus the adjective "urban" refers to the unique and specific characteristics of the city as human living space, features embodied in ancient Rome. The term "urbanity" encompasses the idea of city life as a whole. Writing in the 18th century, English author Samuel Johnson aptly described the essence of urbanity in his famous remark about the city of London: "When a man is tired of London, he is tired of life; for there is in London all that life can afford."

The Urbanization of the Earth

The invention of the steam engine (c. 1770) revolutionized the world and especially its cities. Coal began to replace water power as the most important source of energy. Nearly everywhere (but particularly in Europe), the Industrial Revolution inundated traditional urban structures with technical innovations as societies entered the Age of Industry. Massive industrial complexes spewing filth from smokestacks laid claim to both urban space and human labor. Impoverished through overpopulation, millions of people from rural areas streamed into the rapidly ballooning cities. Between 1851 and 1901, the population of London rose from 2.5 to six million, while those of Berlin and Leipzig grew by factors of four and eight, respectively, during the same period. Country people who found no room and no means of subsistence in the overcrowded cities of Europe sought refuge in the prospering urban centers of the New World (primarily in North America) in waves of migration beginning in the mid-19th century. Working class settlements and the misery endemic to them began to shape the physiogno-

my of entire metropolitan areas (Manchester, Liverpool, Chicago, New York, and the Ruhr region of Germany).

In the 20th century, coal largely gave way to oil – at least in the industrialized countries of the world. The gasoline-powered automobile gained popularity rapidly, and the resulting increase in mobility was accompanied by changes in attitudes about living conditions in the urban population. New suburban developments sprang up everywhere, spreading across administrative boundaries (urban sprawl) – either invading former rural areas (suburbanization) or mixing with neighboring urban districts (to form "conurbations").

Smog is an urban environmental problem. The quality of life in densely populated metropolitan regions is often severely impaired by air pollution caused by industrial emissions and automobile exhaust – as in São Paulo (a city with over five million passenger cars).

Unreliable Statistics – Confusing Terminology

According to statistics published by the UN, there are now about 320 "urban agglomerations" (each with more than one million inhabitants) in the world. Of these, only 20 are classified on the basis of census figures for the year 1995 as "megacities" (with over 10 million inhabitants). These include the metropolitan areas of Tokyo (26.8 million), São Paulo (16.4), New York (16.3), Mexico City (15.6), Bombay (15.1), Shanghai (15.1), Los Angeles (12.4), Beijing (12.3), Kolkata (Calcutta) (11.7) and Seoul (11.6). There is no agreement among urban experts as to the precise meaning of such once commonly used terms as "city" (minimum population of 100,000 for European cities), "metropolis" (a large city with a significant central function), or "megalopolis" (urban agglomeration). Yet one thing seems clear: Global urbanization is progressing at a rapid pace – much too fast for government administrations, statisticians and urban research to follow.

The Two Faces of Development

The pattern of global urbanization mirrors the global prosperity gap between industrialized and developing countries. Urban population in the industrialized nations as a group grew at a rate of only 0.6% per year between 1995 and 2000. The figure for all developing countries for the same period was 2.9%. Demographers estimate that the statistical increase in urban population by the year 2030 will be absorbed by the urban agglomerations of the developing countries alone. This trend will result in a dramatic deterioration of urban living conditions for the latecomers, as present developments already indicate. More than half of the urban population of the developing countries now lives below the poverty line in illegal slums and hut settlements – the "favelas," "shanty towns," "squatter settlements," "barriadas," and "Bidonvilles" that have encircled existing urban structures like a constricting noose in many parts of the world. Sociologists attribute this trend to push and pull factors. Push factors such as poverty, unemployment, infrastructure deficiencies, and the generally bleak prospects of rural life turn dazzling urban behemoths into enchanting magnets that generate hopes of social and economic betterment (the pull effect). Offering ostensibly sound reasons for abandoning rural homelands, these factors have led to a general exodus from the country into the cities in the developing nations.

The Global View

At present, the urban population is growing at a rate of 2.1 per year, much faster than the total world population (1.4%). Due to climatic conditions and factors affecting transportation, the region of heaviest urban agglomeration lies within a strip of territory between 80 and 120 km wide running parallel to the coasts in the temperate zones between about 20 and 60 degrees north latitude. In other words, total urbanization of the Earth's surface is highly unlikely.

Nor has the often-cited process of economic and (in the broadest sense) cultural "globalization" eradicated the integrity and unique character of the diverse types of urban communities in the different cultural regions of the world (many of which are firmly rooted in historical

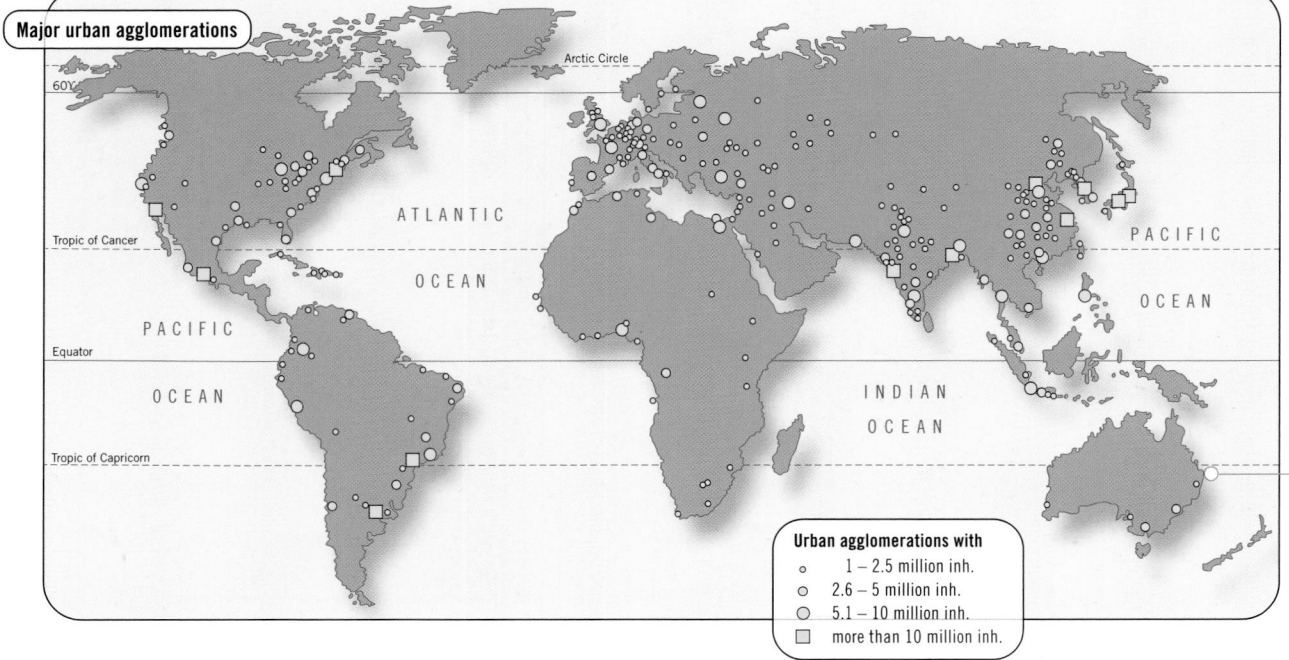

Major urban agglomerations

Arctic Circle
60°
ATLANTIC
OCEAN
Tropic of Cancer
PACIFIC
OCEAN
OCEAN
PACIFIC
OCEAN
Equator
OCEAN
INDIAN
OCEAN
Tropic of Capricorn

Urban agglomerations with
- ○ 1 – 2.5 million inh.
- ○ 2.6 – 5 million inh.
- ○ 5.1 – 10 million inh.
- □ more than 10 million inh.

The Dark Heart of the Continent

Satellite images of the Earth at night reveal points of light along continental coastlines – as shown in the map on the left – corresponding to major urban agglom-

erations. Approximately 50% of the earth's population is concentrated in regions less than 150 kilometers from the nearest coast.

Global Urbanization

Walls, a Standard Feature of Early Urban Settlements

City walls remain a typical feature of urban architecture even in our day. The photo shows the city wall in Nördlingen, Germany – built in the 14th century and still almost entirely intact today.

Traditional Cities Resist Globalization

Many cities and urban forms have retained their distinct physiognomy in spite of the current trend. One example of a type of Portuguese colonial city that has remained virtually unchanged since the 18th century is Ouro Preto in Brazil. Shibam, the "Desert Manhattan" located in the Wadi Hadhramaut (Yemen) exemplifies a form of high-rise, loam-construction typical of oriental cities, a tradition with roots in pre-Islamic times.

Life in the Vertical Dimension

The invention of reinforced concrete and the elevator, coupled with the high price of land, literally gave rise to upward growth in leaps and bounds in many cities in the early 20th century. Manhattan is a prime example. Skyscrapers, the modern temples of capitalism, now tower far above the church spires that once dominated the city profile.

Global City of the Fun Society

Cities serve their surrounding regions in many ways. Situated in the Nevada desert, Las Vegas – the wide world in a pocket-sized format – is perhaps the most bizarre manifestation of the "fun city" concept.

Ersatz Walls

The politically controversial Israeli settlement of Maale Adumim stands like a fortress in the desert of Judaea in the West Bank east of Jerusalem. The compact ring of buildings serves as a substitute for a protective city wall.

Misery on the Urban Fringe

Uncontrolled immigration creates more than a planning crisis for many cities. Visible here is the sea of tin-roofed huts in the squatter town of Windhoek (Namibia). Such settlements hinder controlled growth and cause severe environmental problems (photo: legalized, sanitized developments bordered on the right by a wild hut settlement).

The City as a Magnet

Everything life has to offer can be found in the big city – and affects the surrounding countryside like a population magnet with a pull so strong that it can hardly be controlled with administrative means. An impassable fence along the border is the only defense against the lure of Hong Kong's nocturnal aura.

tradition), despite the strong tendency toward uniformity in urban architecture. Only very few major metropolitan areas have achieved the status of "global cities," centers of international banking, global business management, international business and telecommunication, and world political power (those few include New York, London, Paris, Tokyo and the relative newcomers Río de Janeiro, Mexico City, Hong Kong, and Shanghai). These are the cities whose centers represent advanced forms of modern urban development almost everywhere in the world, although they often bear the indelible imprint of a randomly interchangeable physiognomy. Knowledgeable urban sociologists have identified in precisely these global control centers strong tendencies toward innerurban polarization and signs of social and ethnic segregation. In the "global cities," the dominant entrepreneurial culture shaped by a profit-oriented, transnational urban aristocracy stands in stark contrast to the masses of urban fringe groups that depend upon low-paid, labor intensive jobs – a contrast much like that of the glittering facades of dream metropolises and their slum districts, whose ceaseless growth has devoured some eight million acres of valuable farmland worldwide (enough to produce food for ten million people) between 1980 and 2000.

Water as a Resource & a Source of Problems & Conflicts

"Blue Gold" – Our Most Precious Resource

During the International Hydrological Decade (IHD, 1964-1974), a global effort to assess the world's water reserves was launched under the auspices of UNESCO. Based on the results, experts now agree: There is plenty of water in the world – yet not nearly enough to satisfy the needs of the entire human race in the 21st century. According to projections presented at the World Water Conference in The Hague in March 2000, some 3.3 billion people (37% of the world's population) will be directly confronted with a shortage of water by 2025 (the number has already reached two billion), because only about 0.29% of the total water supply on earth is available as fresh water suitable for human use (for drinking, hygiene, and the production of consumer goods), while the population continues to grow at a rapid pace. In the course of the 20th century, the human population grew from 1.6 billion to more than 6 billion people, who now share a maximum total of 4.2 million cubic kilometers of liquid fresh water – a supply that cannot be increased significantly. Thus every new addition to the world's population reduces the amount of water available to each person on earth.

How Much Water Does a Human Being Need?

Inhabitants of temperate climate zones – North Americans, for example – need between two and three liters of water per day to satisfy their basic physical and physiological needs. People who live in hot climes require six or more liters per day. For a worker in the oil fields of Saudi Arabia, a daily ration of twelve liters of liquids is just about sufficient. If he quenches his thirst with beer, the figure of twelve liters must be multiplied by 60 (bringing the total to 720 liters), since up to 60 liters of fresh water are required to produced a single liter of beer. A scholar who stills his thirst for knowledge with three books weighing one kilogram each and places them on his bookshelf must – like the beer-drinking oil field worker – accept responsibility for the consumption of at least 750 liters of water, as it takes roughly 250 liters to produce one kilogram of paper. In light of the worldwide water shortage, the fact that between 20,000 and 30,000 liters of water are required for the production of an average passenger car should give pause for thought, especially when one considers that there are currently 750 million cars on the world's roads and that a country like China (with one-fifth of the world's population) is

Water Shortage Caused by Population Density

There are more than 1,000 deep wells in Shanghai. Groundwater removal has caused the central districts of the city to sink by more than 13 cm annually in recent years.

Unequal Distribution

Global water resources are unfairly distributed. Only one-fourth of the world's population has access to a sufficient water supply.

World Water Resources

- water surplus
- sufficient supply
- increasing scarcity
- water shortage

CANADA · USA · MEXICO · ATLANTIC · BRAZIL · ARGENTINA · PACIFIC OCEAN · RUSSIA · KAZAKHSTAN · ALGERIA · LIBYA · SUDAN · CONGO · PR CHINA · INDIA · INDONESIA · INDIAN OCEAN · OCEAN · AUSTRALIA

Water from the Desert

Muammar Qaddafi's mammoth "Great-Man-Made-River" project has been under construction since 1984. More than 1,000 km of pipelines with a diameter of four meters convey fossil water from depths of 400 to 1,500 m in southeastern Libya to the coastal region.

Water as a Resource & a Source of Problems & Conflicts

motorizing in leaps and bounds. Even more alarming is the tremendous amount of fresh water needed to ensure an adequate supply of food for the growing global population. Depending upon climate conditions, the production of one kilogram of grain requires between 1,000 and 2,000 liters of fresh water (or 1,000 to 2,000 tons of water per ton of grain). Thus our daily bread or bowl of rice – like our daily minimum ration of fresh water – is a very important factor in the calculation of per capita consumption of water, although it is seldom given sufficient consideration. The published figures for "average daily water consumption per person per day" (128 liters in Germany and about twice that amount in the U.S.) reflect only measurable household consumption and thus give a false picture of actual water use, which – particularly when viewed from a global perspective – goes far beyond daily household needs.

Who Needs and Uses How Much Water?

According to the most recent precise calculation of the global demand for fresh water (in 1990), private households, which (combined with small businesses and public consumption) account for 7.6% of total consumption, are the smallest but most significant user group, followed in increasing size by industry (24.6%). At 67.8%, agriculture, in its role as the producer of food for the world, is far and away the largest consumer. In contrast to industry, which ordinarily uses water only briefly as utility or process water (which it usually returns to the water cycle as polluted waste water, however), agriculture consumes water in the production of biomass. Despite worldwide efforts to encourage economical use of water resources, the unbridled growth of the world's population is likely to make the water shortage the number-one global problem in the 21st century.

The Statistics of Scarcity

According to guidelines issued by the World Health Organization (WHO), a human being in the 21st century requires a minimum annual per capita ration of 1,000 cubic meters of fresh water (or 2,470 liters per day for food and energy production, industrial products, hygiene, education, traffic, and other purposes) to maintain a living standard appropriate in our time without endangerment to health (current per capita consumption is about 3,000 cubic meters per year in the U.S. and 1,500 cubic meters in other industrialized countries).

The water shortage is not necessarily restricted to specific climate zones. Much more important as a measure of scarcity is the quantity of renewable water resources (precipitation as well as inflowing river and groundwater) available in a given country relative to its population per year. Accordingly, countries with a fresh water supply of less than 1,000 cubic meters per person are classified as water emergency areas. Serious problems arise from water shortage where the natural supply of water falls below 1,700 – 2,000 cubic meters per person (the water stress level). Regions with renewable supplies of between 2,000 and 2,500 cubic meters and above per capita are regarded as non-critical. Africa has the largest number of water-poor countries, in which about 300 million people (one-third of the population) live under conditions of water emergency.

Reasons for Scarcity

Statistically speaking, the fresh water reserves on our "blue planet" are sufficient to serve the needs of humanity as a whole. Yet a number of factors contradict this naive statistical assessment. First of all, fresh water reserves are not equally distributed throughout the world. Nor does the presence of water in a given region necessarily mean that the other living conditions are favorable to human life. Secondly, fresh water that comes from the sky as precipitation rarely stays where it falls. The nature of water – its mobility – causes it to run off, evaporate, or seep to

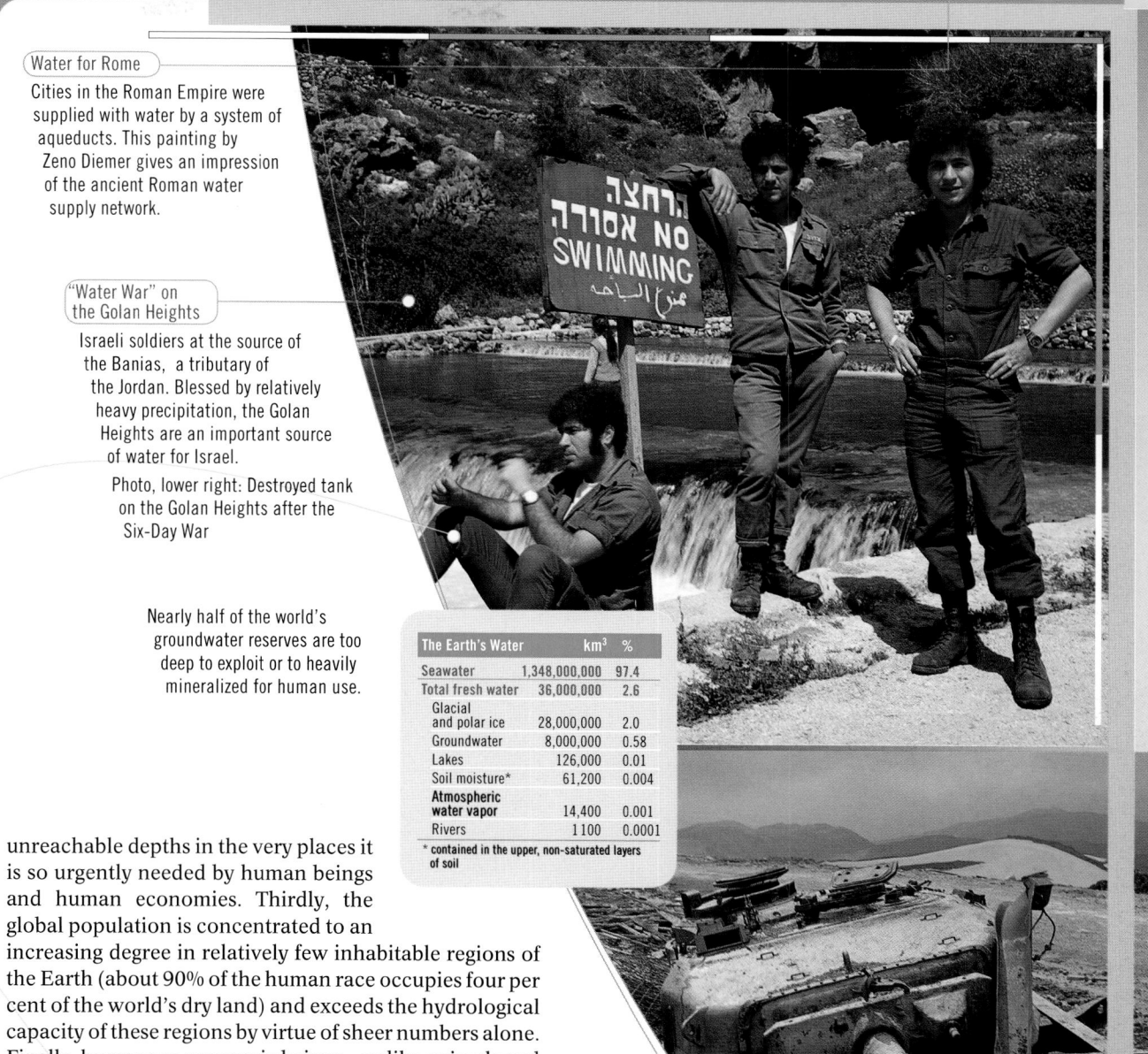

Water for Rome
Cities in the Roman Empire were supplied with water by a system of aqueducts. This painting by Zeno Diemer gives an impression of the ancient Roman water supply network.

"Water War" on the Golan Heights
Israeli soldiers at the source of the Banias, a tributary of the Jordan. Blessed by relatively heavy precipitation, the Golan Heights are an important source of water for Israel.
Photo, lower right: Destroyed tank on the Golan Heights after the Six-Day War

Nearly half of the world's groundwater reserves are too deep to exploit or to heavily mineralized for human use.

The Earth's Water	km³	%
Seawater	1,348,000,000	97.4
Total fresh water	36,000,000	2.6
Glacial and polar ice	28,000,000	2.0
Groundwater	8,000,000	0.58
Lakes	126,000	0.01
Soil moisture*	61,200	0.004
Atmospheric water vapor	14,400	0.001
Rivers	1 100	0.0001

* contained in the upper, non-saturated layers of soil

unreachable depths in the very places it is so urgently needed by human beings and human economies. Thirdly, the global population is concentrated to an increasing degree in relatively few inhabitable regions of the Earth (about 90% of the human race occupies four per cent of the world's dry land) and exceeds the hydrological capacity of these regions by virtue of sheer numbers alone. Finally, humans as economic beings – unlike animals and plants – tend to burden fresh water with many kinds of foreign substances (primarily chemicals) that make it unsuitable for reuse as drinking water and thus exacerbate the water shortage, particularly in densely populated urban agglomerations.

Relief Measures

Advanced cultures with large populations were forced to deal with the problem of water scarcity even in ancient times. Thus hydraulic engineering measures for the procurement and storage of scarce, life-giving water are among the oldest technical structures known to mankind. Remnants of irrigation systems from the 3rd millennium BC have been found in India, China, Yemen, and Egypt. As long ago as 1700 BC, the Babylonian King Hammurabi enacted important laws governing the use of the precious resource of water in the Code of Hammurabi.

Outstanding examples of early urban water supply systems involving technically sophisticated aqueducts are the ancient cities of Pergamum (western Anatolia) and Rome. In the 1st century AD, the Romans moved 600,000 cubic meters of water into their city daily, supplying every inhabitant with 600 liters per day. Modern water procurement systems make use of other means in addition to long-distance water conveyance via pipelines and canals (e.g. the California Aqueduct and the "Great-Man-Made-River" in Libya). Today, some 800,000 small and large dams all over the world prevent rapid water run-off, making more water available for drinking or use in farming or industrial operations than is contained in all of the rivers of the world.

Water Wars?

Experts anticipate population growth of between 30% and 70% in the water-poor regions of the world by the year 2025. It is highly likely that this will lead to increased competition for water, not only among cities and between agriculture and industry but between nations as well.

Forty per cent of the world's population live in regions fed by rivers that flow through more than two countries, and over 200 areas burdened by political conflict largely attributable to disputes over the use of water from such rivers clearly underscore the magnitude of the water shortage as a potential source of political conflict.

The most volatile regions of conflict over water with serious potential for armed hostilities are located along the Ganges (usage disputes between India and Bangladesh), the Tigris and Euphrates (Turkey, Syria, Iraq), the Jordan (Israel, Syria, the West Bank, Jordan), and the Nile (Egypt, Sudan, Ethiopia, Eritrea). "Real" water wars have occurred only rarely in history, but water scarcity has often been the spark that set off the powder keg of existing religious, ethnic, or territorial conflicts.

Fossil Fuels - Production and World Trade

Competition for the Earth's Energy Reserves

The recent rapid rise in prices for fuels and heating oil have reminded us how vulnerable our social and economic systems are and how dependent we are on the oil-producing countries. Our high-tech world consumes vast amounts of energy, and most industrialized countries do not have sufficient resources to cover their own needs. Cartels formed by the oil-producing countries ensure a certain degree of market stability, but they also underscore the dependence of importing countries on the suppliers of raw materials. Transnational and multinational firms operating in the raw materials markets have the power to circumvent cartel agreements more or less at will. Aside from the political and economic problems associated with fossil fuels, environmental issues are now becoming increasingly important.

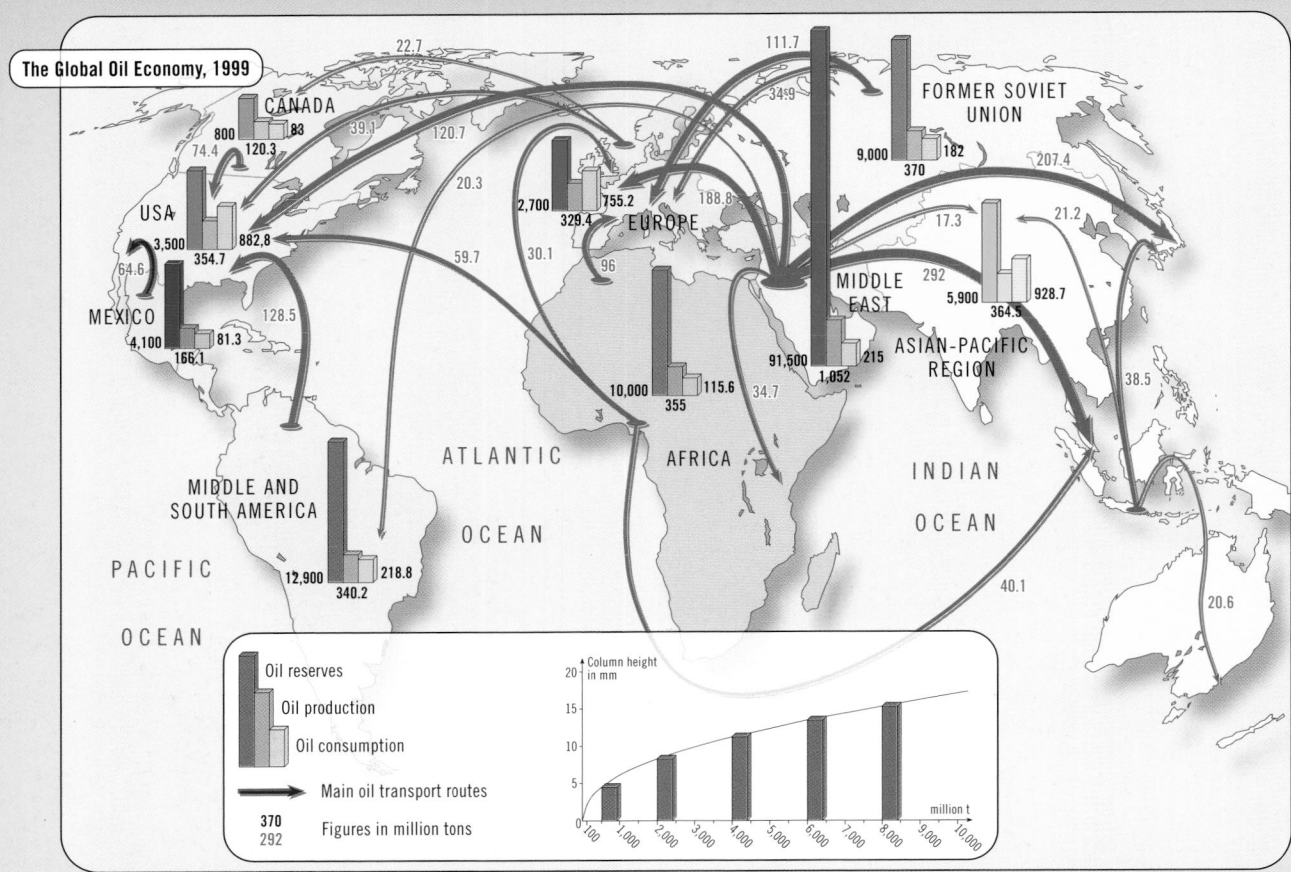

The Global Oil Economy, 1999

Oil reserves	
Oil production	
Oil consumption	
→ Main oil transport routes	
370 / 292 Figures in million tons	

The Growing Hunger for Energy

Hunting and gathering societies met all of their energy needs with wood, a renewable source of energy. This did not change significantly during the transition to farming and animal husbandry, although wood did become scarce in heavily deforested areas. It was not until humans began processing ores to make metal implements using wood or charcoal as fuels that dependence upon renewable energy sources began to pose serious problems. Forests, which had once seemed endless, were destroyed at a pace that far outstripped their capacity to recover. Water and wind mills facilitated the processing of agricultural products and were later employed by the textile industry. The advent of industrialization and mechanized vehicles (steam locomotives) brought the need for higher-energy fossil fuels (coal). In terms of energy output, one ton of coal equated to the annual yield of two acres of forest. Electrification intensified the demand for fossil fuels and also made energy easily transportable. But this applied only to "developed countries." Around 1900, wood, wind, water, and human and animal muscle power still covered two-thirds of the world's energy needs. Only a few decades ago, wood was the only available source of heating and cooking energy for one-third of the world's population. Today, energy consumption and management prognoses must take into account the anticipated rapid rise in energy demand in the Third World.

The Underground Forest

Bituminous coal was used occasionally in ancient civilizations and to an increasing extent during the Middle Ages. Large-scale exploitation, including underground mining, did not begin until the 19th century, when coal became an indispensable source of energy. Worldwide coal production rose rapidly from twelve million tons (1820) to 1.2 billion t (1910), when 85% of all coal produced in the world was mined in Germany, Great Britain, and the U.S.A. Although global production has stagnated in recent years (1998: 3.7 billion t) or grown only marginally, the focal points of mining activity shifted due to cost pressures. Difficult and thus expensive mining operations in the European Union (Great Britain, Germany, France) were cut back drastically in favor of cheaper coal from such countries as the U.S. The German bituminous coal-mining industry, for example, is highly subsidized, as coal costs more than $140 per ton there, while the price of imported coal is below $36. China, Australia, Colombia, South Africa, and other countries increased production, not only to cover domestic demand but for export as well. According to estimates, exploitable coal reserves amount to at least 550 billion tons of bituminous coal units, concentrated mostly in Russia, the U.S., China, Australia, and India. Due to its high water content and low energy output, brown coal is used primarily in the production of electricity and is not transported over long distances.

Petroleum, "Black Gold"

More than 140 years after the discovery of oil in Pennsylvania (1859), global economic and political developments are now more dependent than ever before on the availability of oil. This is primarily the consequence of motorization, and the rise in the use of motor vehicles to transport people and material, although petroleum is also used for heating, in power plants, and as an industrial raw material. After a modest beginning (1900: 20 million t), oil production increased dramatically following the Second World War (1950: 523 million; 1999: 4.1 billion t). Every day, nearly 10 million tons of oil are pumped from several thousand oil wells around the world. The amount of natural gas produced at the same time matches the energy value of six million tons of petroleum.

Devouring the Landscape

Brown coal deposits are usually not deep in the earth and are therefore mined almost exclusively in open pits. In the Rhenish brown-coal fields (photo), huge bucket-wheel excavators remove covering layers of sediment and mine the underlying coal. These machines can move more than 200,000 cubic meters of material a day.

Driving Force

The invention of the coal-burning steam engine launched the Industrial Revolution. The development of railroads (photo: steam locomotive built by George Stephenson, c. 1815) made it possible to transport coal, agricultural and industrial goods as well as people quickly, over long distances, and on a large scale. The loud, smoke-spewing engines gave rise to early complaints about environmental pollution.

Protection against Heat and Cold

The designers of the Alaska Pipeline (1,310 km long, 1974-77) had to find ways to protect the delicate permafrost ecosystem, in which soil thaws only near the surface in the summer and would shift if exposed to additional heat. The pipes were laid on supports above ground and equipped with automatic cooling units. But the oil entering the well-insulated pipeline at about 176° F must not cool excessively, as it would stop flowing. After four-and-a-half weeks, it arrives at the port of Valdez at about 86° F.

Fossil Fuels - Production and World Trade

From Crude Oil to the Consumer

Petroleum products such as heating oil, gasoline, diesel fuel, kerosene and bitumen are produced through distillation, refining, and cracking.

Man-Made Islands

Prospecting for oil and natural gas beneath ocean floors and exploiting discovered reserves requires the use of huge platforms, which are towed to the drilling site and anchored with massive steel or concrete constructions. They must be able to withstand heavy tides and severe storms – particularly in the North Sea. The oil or gas is brought to land via pipelines or by shuttle tankers.

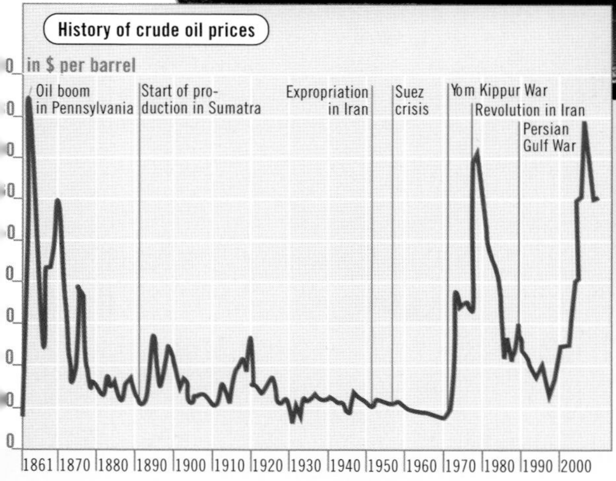

History of crude oil prices

in $ per barrel

Oil boom in Pennsylvania | Start of production in Sumatra | Expropriation in Iran | Suez crisis | Yom Kippur War | Revolution in Iran | Persian Gulf War

1861 1870 1880 1890 1900 1910 1920 1930 1940 1950 1960 1970 1980 1990 2000

The present tight oil supply situation and accompanying price explosion call to mind the oil crisis of 1973, when the oil price rose 600% as the result of deliberately induced shortages in the aftermath of the Arab-Israeli War. The consequence was a worldwide economic crisis. Years before, in 1960, seven oil-exporting countries formed OPEC (Organization of Petroleum Exporting Countries, which now has eleven members), in the hope of gaining a higher share of oil revenues and exerting greater political influence as a cartel.

The end of the Oil Age predicted by the Club of Rome in 1973 did not come to pass. The sudden rise in prices made it possible to tap petroleum reserves that had previously appeared too expensive to exploit. Thanks to new fields in the North Sea and Alaska, supply rose faster than demand. The power of OPEC waned temporarily.

Natural Gas, an Increasingly Popular Fuel

The demand for natural gas has risen steadily over the past 30 to 40 years. Easily transported via pipelines, it is used to heat buildings and generate electricity. Production is concentrated primarily in the CIS countries and the U.S. The United States, which also import natural gas from Canada and Mexico, consume more than one forth of total world production. The largest reserves are in Russia (36%), the other CIS countries, the Middle East, and Southeast Asia. More than 40% are held by the OPEC states. Germany imports nearly 80% of its natural gas (mainly from Russia, Norway, and the Netherlands).

Is an Energy Crisis Looming?

At present, 90% of the world's energy needs are covered by fossil fuels. Industrialized countries account for nearly 60% of total demand. Over the past 30 years, primary energy consumption has risen at a rate of 2% per year, although the collapse of the Eastern Bloc significantly reduced the pace of growth. Increasing motorization in the developing countries could raise the rate of increase to double that figure within the next 20 years.

Half of the energy consumed by the EU countries is imported (Germany: 60%). With only 4.5% of the world's population, the U.S. uses 25% of the annual production of primary energy. Europe (excluding the CIS countries) is not far behind at over 20%.

At present consumption levels, the known reserves of petroleum (approx. 150 billion t) would last for more than 40 years, natural gas reserves (at least 150 trillion cubic meters) for over 60 years. Moreover, new technologies favor more efficient exploitation of deposits and the discovery of new ones. This could result in a doubling of known reserves. And there are also a number of as yet untapped reserves of tar sand, oil shale, and heavy crude oil. These are expensive to exploit, however, and would raise the price of oil accordingly. Since two thirds of the easily exploitable reserves are located in the Persian Gulf region (chiefly in Saudi Arabia), the power of OPEC is a major factor in the global economy. The OPEC countries currently hold over 75% of known reserves and control 40% of global production. Yet the Middle East, like the oil-rich Caspian Sea region, is politically unstable, which means that disruptions of production are likely.

Protecting the Earth's Atmosphere

Two major themes have dominated discussion with regard to global energy management in recent years: the principle of sustainability and the threat – or reality – of global warming as a consequence of a man-made greenhouse effect. The joint resolution of nearly all industrialized countries (enacted 1992 without the U.S.) calling for reduction of the burning of oil, natural gas, and coal to the 1990 level by the year 2005 has born little fruit thus far. Resistance to nuclear energy (which accounts for 7.4% of primary energy worldwide) and the closing of nuclear power plants could actually result in higher CO_2 emissions due to the increased reliance of oil, gas, and coal. It is likely to take quite some time to achieve large-scale, effective use of renewable energy sources (currently 2.7% of primary energy, primarily from hydroelectric power) – photovoltaic solar cells, solar heating plants, fuel cells, wind and biomass power plants, geothermal energy, heat pumps, ocean energy (wave and tide energy, ocean warmth). It will also be necessary to seek new ways of conserving energy. Regardless of the actual size of current reserves of fossil fuels, they are ultimately limited.

Renewable Energy Sources and Technology

Photovoltaic solar cells. Passive solar heating. Windmill farms. Biopower plants. All of these technologies rely on renewable energy sources. And unlike facilities that burn fossil fuels such as coal and petroleum for power, these eco-friendly alternatives do not produce as many greenhouse gases and other pollutants. The reality of climate change and the risks associated with the use of fossil fuels and nuclear power are calling scientists, politicians, and environmental activists from around the world to take action. At present, only 7 percent of the total energy consumed in the United States comes from alternative sources. Fortunately, communities such as Somerset County, Pennsylvania – where wind farms generate clean electricity and provide economic growth for the region – are taking initiative and embracing ecologically friendly technologies. As more cities follow suit and go "green," energy systems using regenerative resources will become increasingly efficient and more affordable.

Solar Power

There are many technologies that have been designed to make use of the sun's energy cleanly and efficiently. Solar ovens can be used to heat food, air passing through a solar chimney can be heated or cooled, domestic solar thermal panels can be used to heat water and air in houses and buildings. Large-scale industrial factories, office buildings, and residential properties can all benefit from solar-powered energy systems. In the United States, solar water heating is used in 2.1 million buildings, while in Japan, the city of Tokyo alone has more than 1 million buildings using it.

Photovoltaic (PV), or solar cells, are made of materials that absorb the sun's light energy and use it to produce electricity. PV cells can be used to power calculators and watches or to recharge batteries. The next generation of power plants uses concentrating solar power systems (instead of fossil-fuel based facilities) to supply energy to generators that produce electricity.

Wind Power

The fastest growing of the renewable energy technologies, wind power is 100 percent renewable and produces no greenhouse gases during operation. In the United States, wind energy supplies less than one half of 1 percent of the country's electricity needs, whereas Denmark relies on wind for about 20 percent of its electrical energy.

Wind turbines with propeller-like blades can be used alone for water pumping or to provide electricity for a farm, ranch or domestic estate. Several electricity providers today use wind farms to supply power to their customers. Wind farms often include large numbers of turbines and can be connected to a power grid or combined with a solar cell system. They are most effective offshore and at high altitudes, where winds are stronger and more constant.

Water Power

There are many forms of water energy being explored. Hydroelectric energy usually refers to large-scale hydroelectric dams. Smaller-scale systems such as hydroelectric power installations are used in water-rich areas around the world as a Remote Area Power Supply (RAPS).

Biomass Energy

Burning plants and plant-derived materials produces biomass energy. Although wood is still the largest bio-

Soybeans

Biomass – food crops, grassy and woody plants, agriculture residues, and organic waste – can be used to make biofuels such as ethanol and biodiesel. In the United States, biodiesel is produced using oil from soybeans, canola, and other agricultural products.

Coconut Oil

During World War II, armies in the Philippines used coconut oil to run diesel engines. Since then, coconut oil has grown in popularity among Pacific Islanders as an inexpensive and eco-friendly substitute to diesel.

Solar Power Plant

Solar Two is a large scale thermal solar power plant in the Mojave Desert just east of Barstow, California. The plant has the capability of redirecting the equivalent of 600 suns and the ability to produce 10 megawatts. Solar Two uses molten salt, a combination of 60 percent sodium nitrate and 40 percent potassium nitrate, as an energy storage medium instead of water or oil. This helps in energy storage during brief interruptions in sunlight due to clouds.

The Future of Energy and the Environment

mass energy resource, food crops, grassy and woody plants, organic components of municipal and industrial wastes can also be tapped for energy. Even methane fumes from landfills can be used as a biomass energy source. Biopower plants burn biomass such as paper mill residue, lumber mill scrap, and municipal waste to produce steam. The steam then powers a turbine to turn a generator, converting energy into electricity.

Biofuels

Unlike other renewable energy sources, biomass can be converted directly into liquid biofuels, the two most common of which are biodiesel and ethanol. Biodiesel and ethanol are agriculturally produced and release energy when burned in internal combustion engines or boilers.

Biodiesel is made by combining alcohol (usually methanol) with vegetable oil, animal fat, or recycled cooking grease. A wide range of oils can be used to produce biodiesel, including soybean, coconut, and rapeseed oils, waste vegetable oil (WVO). Using biodiesel in modern diesel vehicles requires little or no modification to the engine and reduces emission of carbon monoxide and other hydrocarbons by 20 to 40 percent. Pure biodiesel is available at gas stations throughout Germany.

Corn, cornstalks, sugarbeets, sugar cane, and switchgrasses are grown to produce bioalcohols such as ethanol (also known as grain alcohol), a liquid biofuel that can be used in internal combustion engines and fuel cells. Ethanol is being phased into the current energy

infrastructure. At present E85, an alternative fuel composed of 85 percent ethanol and 15 percent gasoline, is available in many countries around the world. There are about 6 million E85 compatible vehicles in the United States and between 3 and 4 million in Brazil, where government-sponsored programs have encouraged its use.

Biogas

Fermenting organic mater such as manure, sewage, municipal solid waste, biodegradable waste and feedstock, under anaerobic conditions, produces biogas. This biofuel is comprised primarily of methane and carbon dioxide and can be used as vehicle fuel or for generating electricity. Existing gas networks can be used to distribute biogas over large distances and using minimal energy. Biogas can be burned directly for cooking, heating and lighting.

For more information about renewable energy technologies visit:
- The Renewable Energies Knowledge – Transfer Network
  (www.REnNow.Net)
- National Renewable Energy Laboratory
  (www.nrel.gov)
  U.S. Department of Energy Office of
  Energy Efficiency and Renewable Energy
  (www.eere.energy.gov)
- Department for Environment, Food and Rural Affairs
  (www. defra.gov.uk)

Solar panels and wind cowls at BedZED

The Beddington Zero Energy Development (BedZED) is the United Kingdom's largest carbon-neutral eco-village. Home to 100 individuals, all the houses, community centers, and workspaces in the development use energy derived from renewable sources – wind, sun, and water.

Wind Farms

Wind is the world's fastest growing energy resource. Wind farms, comprised of between 2 and 2,000 wind turbines, are increasingly common around the world. Regions such as Navarra, Spain, which derives up to 70 percent of its electricity from the wind and the sun, are capable of generating more electricity from renewable sources than European Union countries like France or Poland.

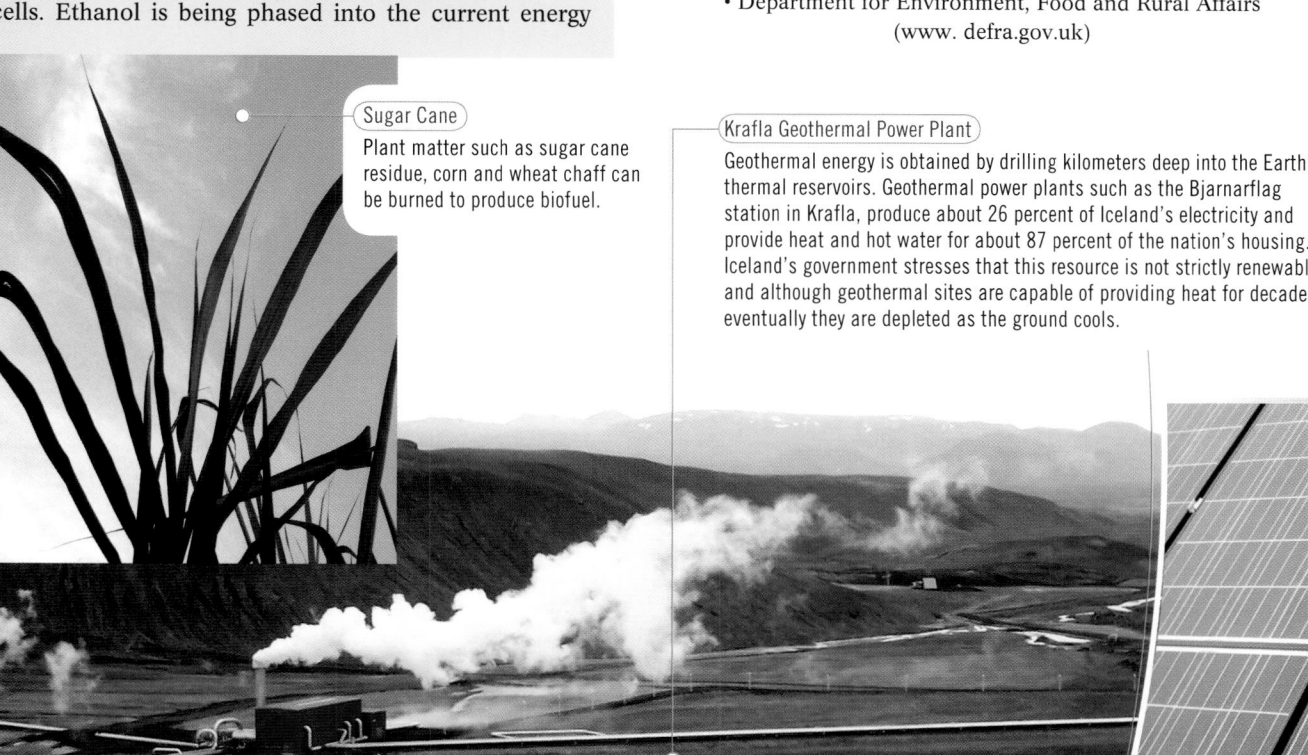

Sugar Cane

Plant matter such as sugar cane residue, corn and wheat chaff can be burned to produce biofuel.

Krafla Geothermal Power Plant

Geothermal energy is obtained by drilling kilometers deep into the Earth's thermal reservoirs. Geothermal power plants such as the Bjarnarflag station in Krafla, produce about 26 percent of Iceland's electricity and provide heat and hot water for about 87 percent of the nation's housing. Iceland's government stresses that this resource is not strictly renewable, and although geothermal sites are capable of providing heat for decades, eventually they are depleted as the ground cools.

Division of the Globe into Time Zones

The Stock Exchange is Always Open – Somewhere on Earth!

When we want to call someone in Europe, we need to consider the time difference in order to be sure that we don't wake up our party in the middle of the night. Business people and international airlines must be constantly alert to these time differences. Stock-market speculators are happy to know that trading is possible around the clock, as there is always a stock exchange open somewhere in the world, whether in Sydney, New York, or Frankfurt am Main.

Local Time vs. Zone Time

Long ago, local times were different virtually wherever one looked. After all, it is only natural for the noon bell to ring when the sun reaches its highest point in the sky. The time difference between two towns at the same latitude separated by only 50 km is three minutes. Before the railways were built, such discrepancies were of little significance, since travel was always slow at best. Nevertheless, local mean times were introduced toward the end of the 18th century and regarded as binding for a given center and its surrounding region – Geneva time in 1780, Berlin time in 1820, Paris time in 1826, Zurich time in 1832, Pulkow and Greenwich time in 1848, Warsaw and Bern time in 1853. North Americans, in particular, lent strong support to the plan to establish a global system for measuring time. In 1873, 71 different railroad times were still in effect here. That year, Sandford Fleming, Chief Engineer of the Canadian Pacific Railway, proposed setting up a system of 24 meridians spaced at intervals of 15 degrees – a time difference of one hour – and assigning a standard time to each. That would divide the world into 24 time zones. But where was one to start? Which meridian was to get the zero label?

Ignoring the different times in effect in the many different countries of the world, seafarers had generally agreed to go by Greenwich time. But there were also zero meridians in Ferro (now Hierro), in Venice, and in many other places as well. At the Washington conference of 1884, 27 countries agreed to establish the zero meridian at Greenwich and to divide the globe into two geographic hemispheres, the western and the eastern.

Time systems were also standardized in many other European countries in response to the increasing internationalization of travel and transport. In Germany, which was still comprised of many independent states, most of them small, the railroad system could function properly only if agreement was reached on a standard time system. This was achieved with the Reichsgesetz of 1893. France did not join the system until 1911.

Most time zones are 15 degrees wide and cover a section of the globe that lies 7.5 degrees to the east and west of one of the 24 meridians. The standard time is the same everywhere within a given time zone. In some regions, time zone boundaries do not run along lines of longitude but along national borders. This is meant to ensure that the same time applies at every location within a country. Yet , many countries are too large to be accommodated within a single time zone. The U.S. is divided into four time zones, for example.

People living in Los Angeles should call their relatives on the East Coast early in the evening in order to avoid waking them during the night. TV networks must determine the best times to broadcast programs in order to reach the largest possible number of viewers. Under certain circumstances, networks accept the need to broadcast certain programs ("breaking news") at unfavorable times. Countries spanning several time zones require a system that makes it clear which time is meant when times are announced. In the U.S. times are identified by the time zone names: Eastern, Central, Rocky Mountain, and Pacific.

Which Island Will Be the First?

As the new year 2000 approached, several island countries in the Pacific set their sights on being the first to ring in the year 2000. The Fiji Islands introduced daylight saving time, turning their clocks ahead in order to be the first to celebrate. Tonga shifted the International Date Line along the eastern edge of its territory, putting itself 13 hours ahead of Greenwich. But the island kingdom had no chance against Kiribati, with its extensive ocean territory measuring 3,870 km from west to east. The eastward protrusion of the Date Line runs along the eastern border of Kiribati. Caroline Island, the easternmost atoll, was given the name Millennium Island (14 hours ahead of Greenwich).

… and the living is easy

Daylight savings time, the practice of turning the clock ahead one hour during the summer months in the northern hemisphere, has existed in Great Britain and Ireland since 1916. In the U.S., it was reintroduced in 1967 after having been used during both World Wars as a means of conserving energy by taking advantage of daylight. The desired energy-saving effect was actually never achieved, but people enjoy having an extra hour of leisure time while the sun shines and see daylight saving time as an improvement in quality of life.

One Day Too Early

People first recognized the need for an international date line when the "Victoria," a ship from Magellan's fleet, returned to Spain after circumnavigating the globe on September 6, 1522. The entries in the ship's log were a day behind the correct date. The expedition had constantly "gained time" on its westward voyage, saving an entire day by the time it had completely circled the globe.

The First Pocket Watch

Peter Henlein is believed to have invented the spring-driven watch. Beginning in 1510, he produced a series of small, portable clocks shaped like a can – the first pocket watches.

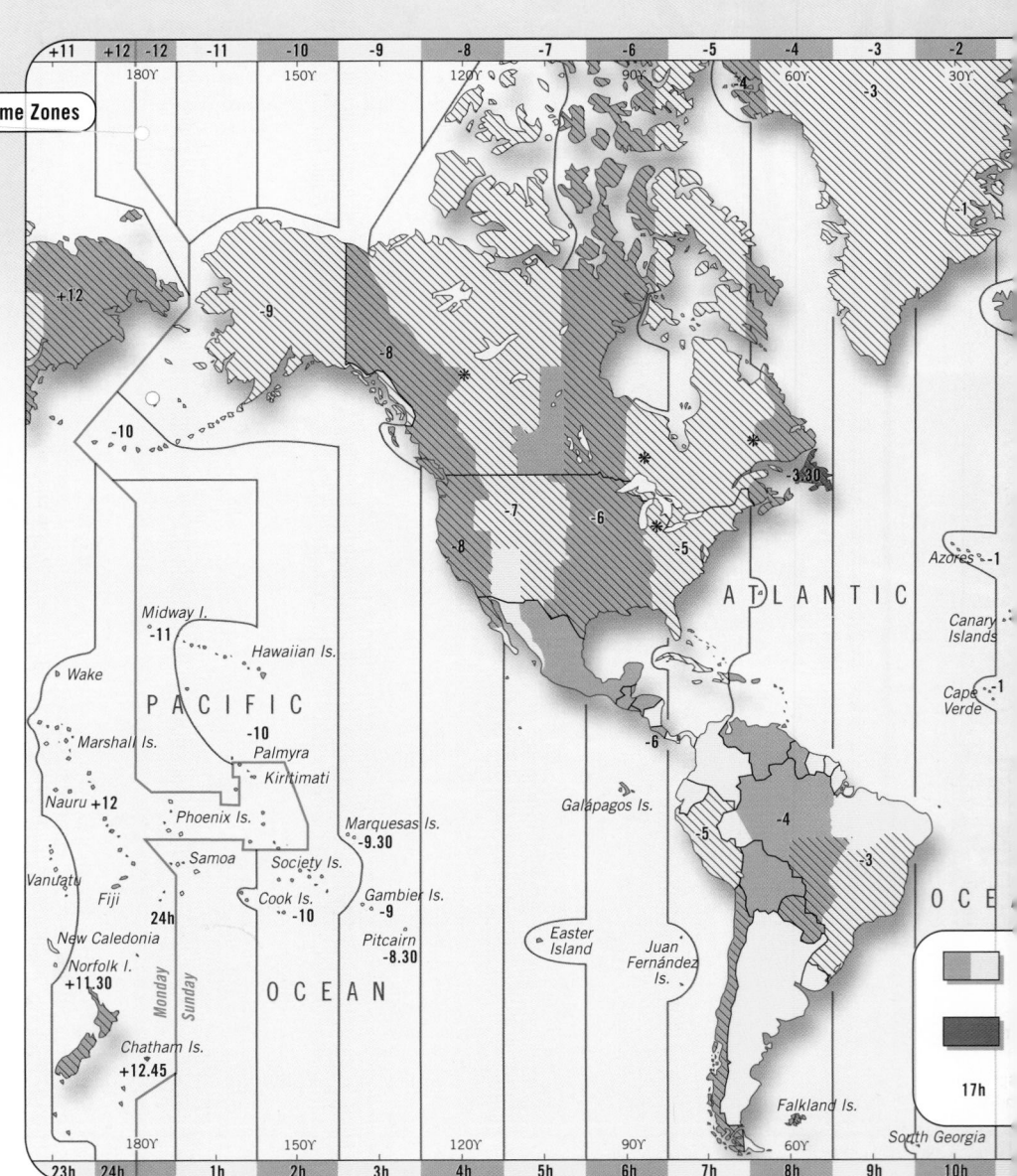

Time Zones

Division of the Globe into Time Zones

I and the Zero Meridian

The seam of our system of measuring time runs through the observatory in Greenwich (now Flamsteed House), which was established in 1675.

People who cross the International Date Line from east to west must move the calendar one day ahead. Those crossing in the reverse direction, from west to east, turn it back one day. A traveler who fails to heed this convention while circling the globe from west to east will find himself a day ahead of the local calendar upon arriving at his starting point. This happened to Phileas Fogg in Jules Verne's famous novel.

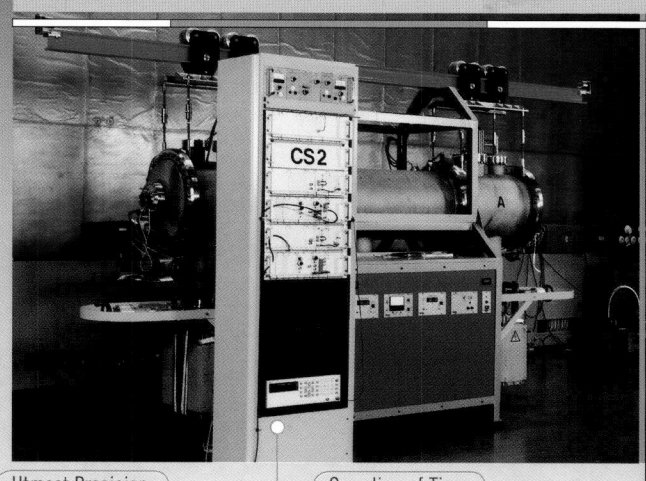

Utmost Precision

The CS 2 atomic clock at the Federal Office of Physics and Technology in Braunschweig, Germany is one of the most precise timepieces in the world. It is accurate to within a second even after two million years.

Guardian of Time

The ancient Egyptians amassed a wealth of astronomical knowledge. As early as 2750 BC, they had developed a lunar calendar and a solar calendar that divided the year into 365 days. The sciences and the calculation of time were the domain of the moon god Thot, who was often depicted as a human figure with the head of an ibis (c. 600 BC, Luxor).

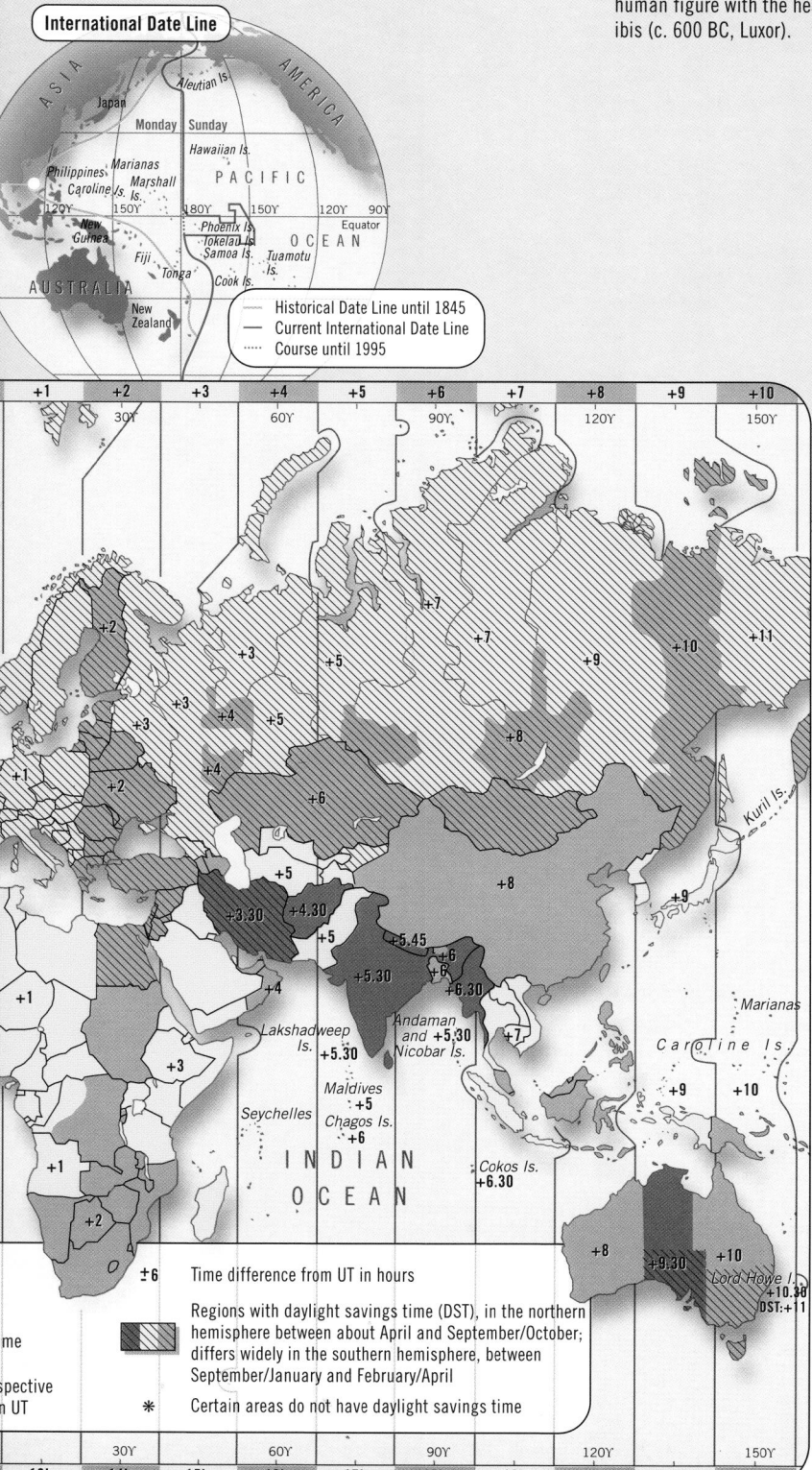

International Date Line

- — Historical Date Line until 1845
- — Current International Date Line
- ⋯ Course until 1995

±6   Time difference from UT in hours

Regions with daylight savings time (DST), in the northern hemisphere between about April and September/October; differs widely in the southern hemisphere, between September/January and February/April

✳   Certain areas do not have daylight savings time

An Ingenious Invention

Portable equatorial sundial made by Johann Georg Vogler (1750), with an adjustable hour ring. The clock is positioned facing north with the aid of a compass; the plane of the hour ring is aligned with a point on the curved latitude scale that conforms to the latitude of the measurement site. In this way, the shadow-casting rod of the sundial is positioned parallel to the Earth's axis, so that its tip points to the north celestial pole and the hour ring is parallel to the earth's equator.

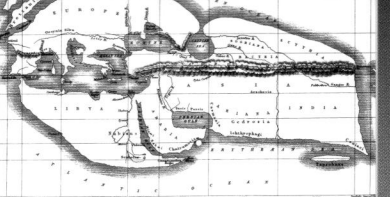
The Evolution of Cartography

Creating a Picture of the World

The first maps provided mankind with a means of creating a highly simplified, abstract image of the Earth. Long before aircraft were invented, the globe had already been depicted – from a bird's-eye view, so to speak – on a smaller, measurable scale in accordance with mathematical principles. Yet maps are never more than a reflection of social reality – of the knowledge, political visions, and religious beliefs of a given age. A map's claim to accuracy and reliability derives from the manner in which it was produced, from the degree of precision achieved by the engraver, lithographer, or draftsman, from the printer's command of his art, and from the ability of map-readers to recognize familiar aspects of their world.

Cartography

Since the mid-19th century, when the term "cartography" was first introduced, the art of map-making developed from a subdiscipline that served the needs of geodesy and geography into a science in its own right. By the early 20th century cartography had developed its own clearly defined concepts and methods.

Because of their military significance, the immense costs of making them, and the detailed nature of their contents, topographic maps remained a monopoly of the state in Europe until the latter half of the 19th century. Around the turn of the 18th to the 19th century, the nations of Europe began to establish statistical services and offices which published some of their data in topical maps intended for broad public use.

From the Disk to the Sphere

Even ancient cultures had maps of known territories showing possessions and boundaries. Excellent examples include the rock drawing of a Neolithic settlement in Çatal Hüyük dated about 6200 BC, the 3,500-year-old city map of Nippur in Babylon, and maps made by the ancient Greeks.

These early map-makers viewed the Earth as a flat disk, inhabited in the center and inaccessible at its outer edges. As knowledge increased, the disk expanded. New insights gained through the conquests of Alexander the Great and the observations of seafarers and scientists gave birth to the idea that the Earth is a sphere, for which Erastosthenes calculated a circumferences of 37,700 km (or 46,250 km, depending upon the conversion method applied) in c. 250 BC. He took his investigations a step further, projecting the three-dimensional segments of the sphere onto a flat surface and overlaying his map with a system of coordinates based on the length and width of the Mediterranean Sea.

Immortalized in a Choir Loft: A wood sculpture of Claudius Ptolemaeus (Ptolemy) in the choir loft of the cathedral in Ulm (Michael Erhart, c. 1470). The publication of his Geographia in Ulm in 1482 revived the ancient concept of the shape of the world.

In the 2nd century AD, the astronomer, astrologist, and cartographer Ptolemy of Alexandria developed the first north-oriented map projection with longitudinally true lines of latitude. Ptolemy's instructions for map-making were distributed in copies, commentaries, and translations to geographers and cartographers – and along with them his most glaring error: His globe had a circumference of only 29,000 km.

Mappae mundi – The Christian Image of the World

For the next several centuries, theology shaped mankind's view of the world and its representation on maps. Rome's influence waned, and the center of the new Christian world shifted to the east, to Jerusalem. Thus the maps of Christianity were oriented toward the east, and they depicted the earth once again as a flat disk. Like all works of art from this period, they proclaimed the greatness of God and the Church.

The emergence of Islam beginning in the 6th century AD posed a challenge to the dominant Christian view. Arab cartographers incorporated the ancient tradition of Ptolemy (the Earth as a sphere) into their scientific system and expanded their knowledge of the world through extensive travel and the use of astronomical instruments.

Unveiling the Earth

Maps used by seafarers and merchants were not documents of religious philosophy. Their maps were intended for practical use and were therefore as accurate as possible under the given circumstances. Portolan charts of the Mediterranean showed the coasts and major landmarks in detail, and, as studies have proven, contained only minor errors of distance.

However, maps of foreign countries and coastlines were usually kept locked away in the safes of rulers and merchants and were released for public use only after the existence of such regions had become widely known. Even Columbus lacked the most current maps on his journey of "discovery" to America. Although the Vikings had reached North America long before him, Columbus sailed westward into an "unknown" Atlantic (guided by Ptolemy's incorrect estimate of the earth's circumference) hoping to reach India. The newly discovered regions were presented on a world map made by Martin Waldseemüller as early as 1507.

Motivated by the prospect of finding new worlds beyond the horizon and by the lure of endless riches, the nations of Europe launched their campaign of worldwide exploration.

Surveying the Planet

The circumnavigation of the globe by Magellan's expedition had provided practical proof that the Earth is a sphere. Subsequent advances in science and the development of better instruments enabled cartographers to improve the accuracy and detail of their maps of the world over the course of the next several centuries. Unknown regions of the Earth were populated on maps with imaginary beings – an expression of horror vacui, the unwillingness of map-makers to reveal gaps in their knowledge to the general public. Later, they were simply entered as "white spots."

The era of cartographic precision based upon mathematical principles began in the latter half of the 18th century. In the nations of Europe, topographic surveys were carried out for military and administrative purposes, and the data obtained through these efforts serves even today as the basis for planning in modern countries.

Once it became possible to explore the Earth from space in the 20th century, the last remaining white spots disappeared from the maps of the world, and cartographers gained access to all the geographic data they could possibly need. Electronic data processing relieved map-makers of the arduous tasks of drawing and engraving maps, turning them into specialists in graphic communication.

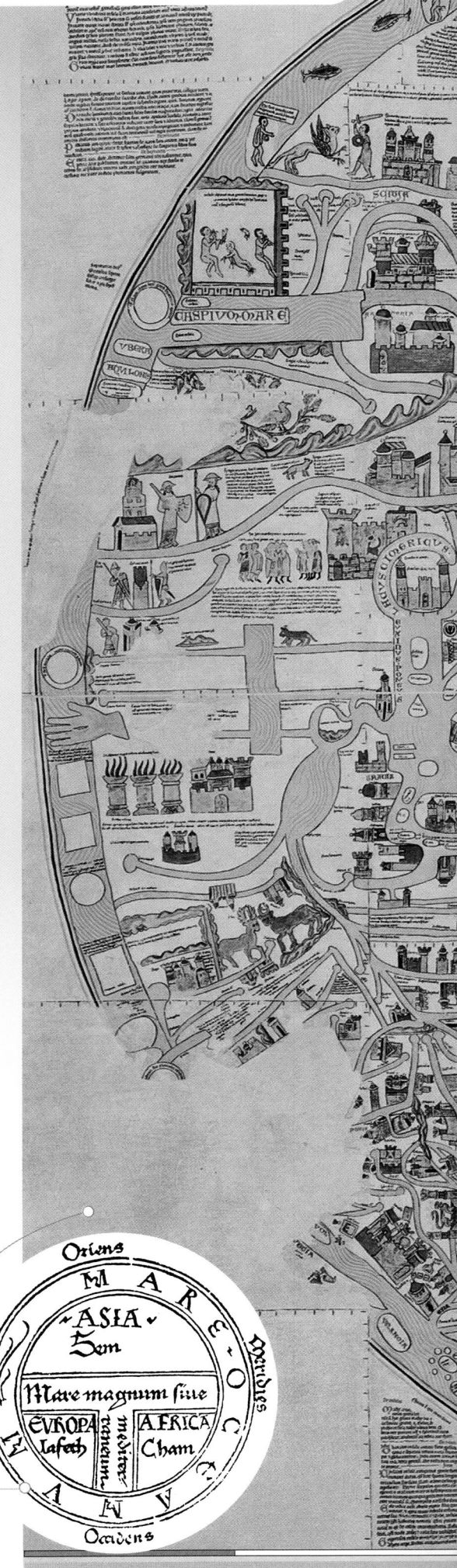

Image of the Medieval World

Produced between 1230 and 1240, the Ebstorf World Map is an example of medieval Christian cartography. Drawn in a TO configuration, it transposes the body of Christ onto the known world. Encircled by the O-shaped ocean, the Earth's landmasses are separated by the T (of the inland seas) – the symbol of Christ's death on the cross. The original map was destroyed by fire in a bombing raid on Hanover in 1943. A copy of the large map (358 x 356 cm) has survived in 30 parts.

The Schematic World

Schematic world map (TO map) by Isidor of Sevilla (1472), illustrating the Christian image of the world.

The Evolution of Cartography

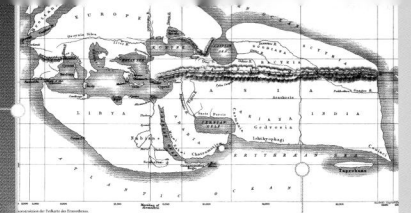

First Coordinate System

This reconstruction of a map by Eratosthenes (3rd c. BC) shows the known world in a coordinate system based upon the position of the Mediterranean Sea.

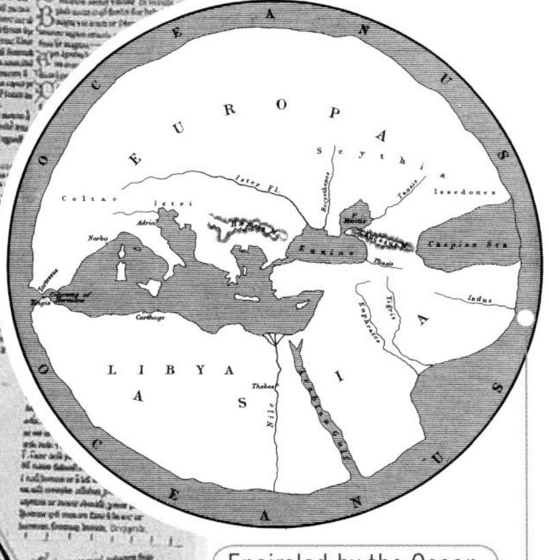

Encircled by the Ocean

Map by Hecataeus of Miletus (c.500 BC) reconstructed from texts, showing the Earth as a disk with the continents of Europe and Asia encircled by an ocean.

Roman Itinerary

The Tabula Peutingeriana illustrates the pragmatic approach of the Roman government. It depicts the network of roads as a schematic itinerary without scale, showing route markers, postal stations, and cities in signature form.

Birth of the Name "America"

Amerigo Vespucci and the regions of South America he discovered. Detail from a map by the Freiburg cartographer Martin Waldseemüller, on which the name "America" (in honor of Vespucci) appeared for the first time. The map was printed in Saint-Dié (Lorraine) in 1507.

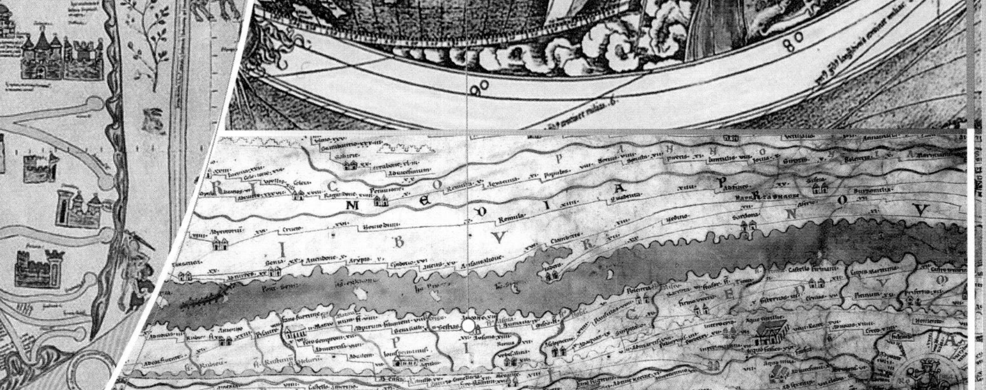

Tourism: Economics and the Environment

The Urge to Travel versus Environmental Awareness

Why do we travel, willingly accepting the costs and the risks it entails – disorientation and boredom, intestinal troubles and even malaria? Are we motivated to seek out new places less by curiosity than by the need to find ourselves? If so, the Greek philosopher Seneca reminds us that we cannot solve our problems by traveling to and fro, since "we always take ourselves along."

Aid or Exploitation

The tourist trade is the largest industry in the global economy in terms of both employees and investment volumes. The number of international tourists rose nearly 1000% between 1960 (69 million) and 2000 (670 million). If we add those who travel within their own countries, the total number of tourists increases to about 5.3 billion. The Germans take the lead in world travel, while the French tend to stay at home and plan accordingly. The 180-km-long Mediterranean coast of the Languedoc-Roussillon region has been under development on a grand scale since 1963.

Many developing countries see tourism as a panacea for their economic problems but are often disappointed, as only a small portion of profits from the tourist trade actually flows into local economies.

A New Form of Colonialism?
Rebellion in Host Countries

People long believed that travel promotes better understanding of foreign cultures and thus contributes to international peace. Yet it appears that it often has the opposite effect, as old prejudices are strengthened and new ones emerge through tourism. It has become increasingly clear since the 1970s that the influx of tourists can indeed cause grave social and environmental problems. Natural landscapes are damaged (by winter sports, for example), traditional cultural landscapes are permeated by functional architecture, long-standing customs give way to behavior patterns apparently imposed by foreign visitors. Lost local and regional cultural heritage cannot be replaced. The voices of those who are no longer willing to be marketed are growing stronger in many countries. Yet the potential positive effects of globalization through tourism should not be overlooked, as contact with tourists from abroad can provide encouragement for social and economic development.

The Hard Road to Soft Tourism

In some parts of the world, indigenous communities rely on cooperation with travel companies in the hope of generating income with innovative forms of environmental tourism without placing their own cultures and environments at risk. But to what extent is this kind of sustainable tourism really possible?

It would seem to call for a new breed of traveler. Tour organizers, airlines, and publishers of tourists' guides take an optimistic view. A number of them have joined forces in support of a code of ethics for travelers.

The Most on the Coast

Built in 1967–77 according to plans by French architect Jean Marie Balladour, La Grande-Motte, a vacation area on the coast of Languedoc near Montpellier, offers the "total beach experience."

Giddy Heights

Heliskiing in virtually unexplored terrain accessible only by helicopter. There are 43 officially recognized mountain landing sites for helicopters in Switzerland, 16 of them at elevations above 3,000 m.

Meeting of Two Worlds

Oblivious to tourist photographers, the Tuareg drive their salt caravans through the Ténéré Desert (Niger), traveling for months at a time to reach their markets in Nigeria.

Adventure tours in deserts, mountains, rainforests, in polar or other regions must be judged by the respect they show for local cultures and environments.

Satellite Section

Hurricane Floyd

From September 14 through 18, 1999, Hurricane Floyd swept the East Coast of the United States with heavy winds and rains, causing extensive flooding and storm damage. A state of emergency was decla-red in ten southeastern and mid-Atlantic states. This satellite image provides a vivid picture of the hurricane's vast breadth. Future hurricanes are identified while still in the embryonic phase with conventional satellite imaging techniques. Floyd was born in early September as "Tropical Low-Pressure System Number 8" near the Cape Verde Islands off the west coast of Africa.

Technical data relating to the satel-lite images presented in this section can be found in the small informa-tion insets provided with each image. The symbols in these insets have the follo-wing meanings:

Name of Satellite or Imaging Process		NOAA-AVHRR
Ground Resolution		1 000 m
Exposure Altitude		840 km
Date of Image		Sept. 15, 1999

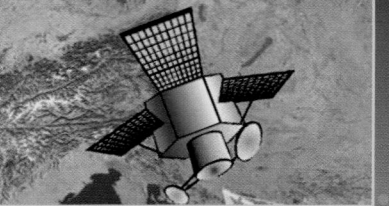

Remote Satellite Surveying

Graphic: Imaging Techniques

Most Earth survey satellites travel around the Earth at an altitude of between 600 and 900 km in an almost circular near-polar orbit. The time it takes to complete a single orbit ranges from 90 to 120 minutes. Depending upon the type of equipment used, satellite imaging systems scan the Earth's surface in strips varying in width from eleven to 2,000 km. Detail resolution ranges from one meter (high resolution, e.g. IKONOS) to one kilometer (medium resolution, e.g. NOAA-AVHRR weather satellites) per image pixel. The imaging sensors of some satellites can be rotated laterally or in a complete circle. This makes it possible to obtain multiple images of especially interesting regions or to produce stereoscopic images used to create digital terrain models. Image data are ordinarily transmitted by satellites to ground stations distributed around the world. Satellites also have the capacity to store image data from areas beyond the reception range of ground stations until they can be retrieved by the nearest ground receiving station.

How Do Earth Survey Satellites Work?

Panoramic View of Salzburg

New perspectives for regional imaging have emerged from the combination of satellite image data with digital terrain models (DTM), which are produced either from topographic maps or stereoscopic aerial or satellite photographs. They provide elevation data on every point on the Earth's surface. Such terrain models make it possible to derive through computation a wide range of panoramic views from vertical images. They serve as the basis for virtual flights through a landscape.

The picture below is a panorama developed in this way from Landsat TM and SPOT Pan data of the Salzburg lowlands, showing the Obertrum lakes in the foreground and the regional capital of Salzburg in the center. The summits of the Hagen Mountains rise along the horizon behind the high plateau of the Tennen Mountains. Visible in the background are the Central Alps and Austria's highest peak, the Grossglockner (3,798 m).

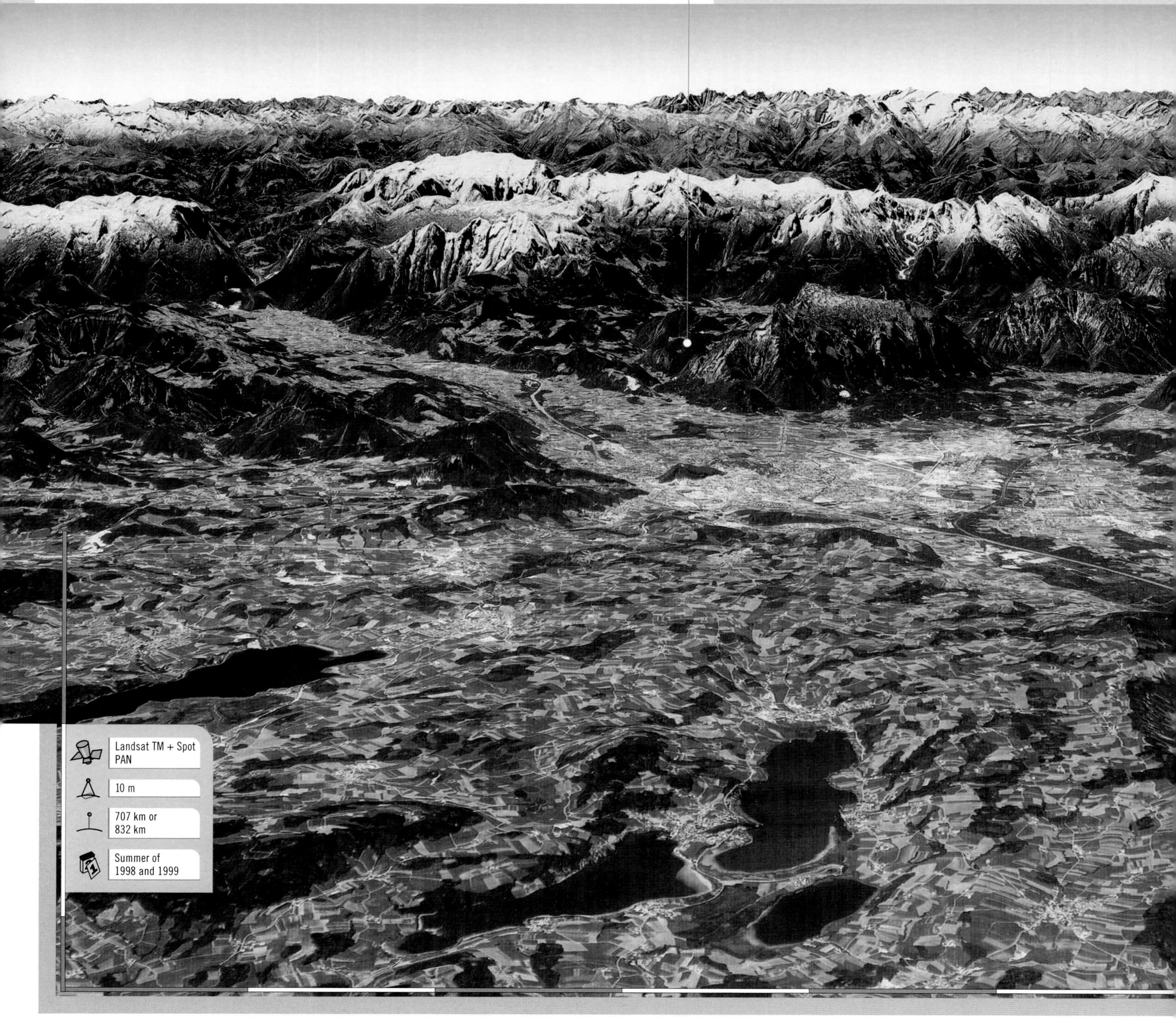

Landsat TM + Spot PAN	
10 m	
707 km or 832 km	
Summer of 1998 and 1999	

Austria

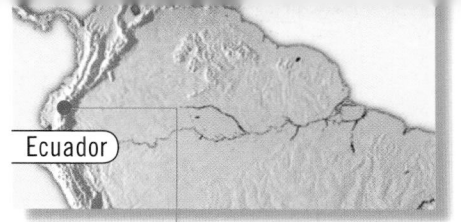

Ecuador

Digital Elevation Model of Cotopaxi

The Shuttle Radar Topography Mission (SRTM) achieved a new level of quality in the production of digital elevation models. In February 2000, the Space Shuttle Endeavor embarked on a mission devoted to setting up a system capable of producing a three-dimensional image of the Earth with the aid of multiple radar antennas attached to a 60-meter-long extendable mast. Using a radar interferometry technique, two radar images are taken from positions offset only slightly from one another. The differences between the two images are used to compute the elevation curves of the exposed terrain, which are then displayed on a map.

Our image shows Mount Cotopaxi in the Eastern Cordilleras of Ecuador, at 5,897 m the highest active volcano on Earth. The volcano has erupted 50 times since 1738, most recently in 1904 and 1928. The flow trenches of the cone-shaped volcano are clearly visible in the digital elevation model. As the snow line lies at an altitude of 4,000 m, the danger of mudslides in the flow trenches is great.

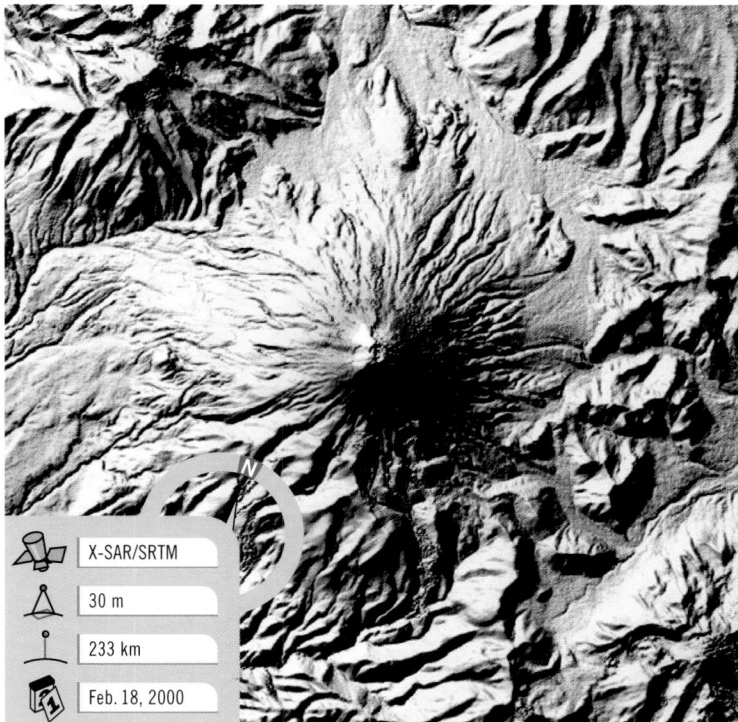

| X-SAR/SRTM |
| 30 m |
| 233 km |
| Feb. 18, 2000 |

Source: DLR

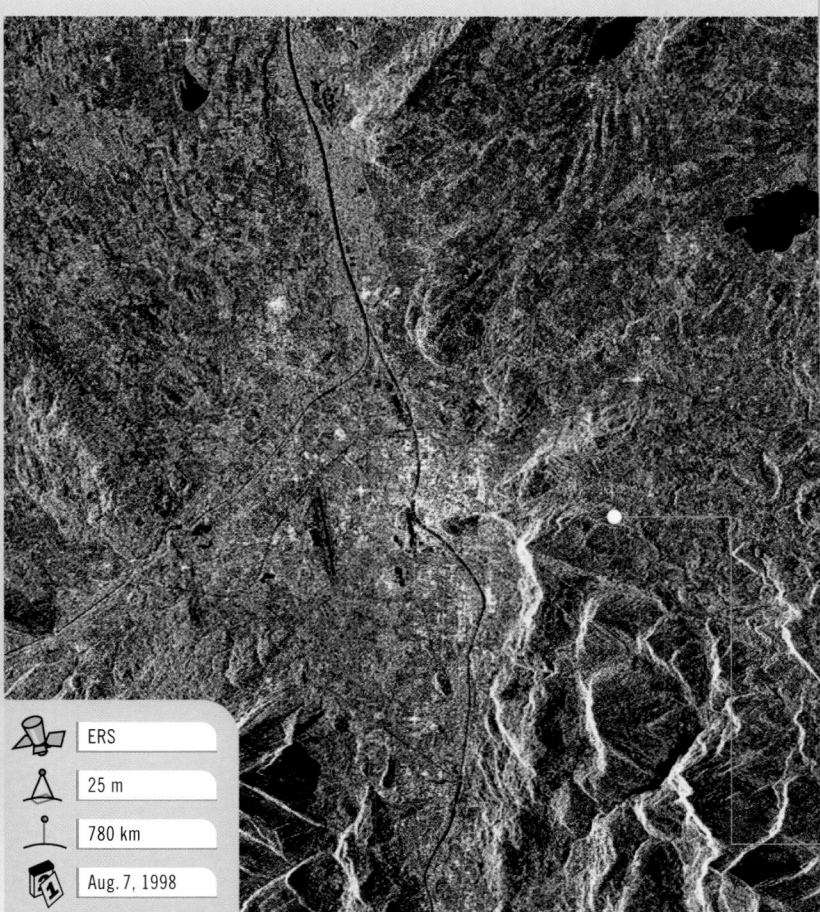

| ERS |
| 25 m |
| 780 km |
| Aug. 7, 1998 |

Radar Image of Salzburg

Radar image of the city of Salzburg showing parts of the Flachgau and the Tennengau. While "conventional" Earth survey satellites pick up solar radiation reflected by the Earth (passive sensing systems), many radar satellites have the capacity to emit electromagnetic impulses and measure their reflection (active sensor systems), from which "images" can be computed. The strongest reflection comes from topographic ridges. Radar images can also be obtained at night or through cloud cover.

Landsat Thematic Mapper Image of Salzburg

As an example of an image produced by optical sensors, this Landsat Thematic Mapper image of Salzburg presents a much more "realistic" picture of the Earth. Optical sensors ordinarily operate in the visible, proximate infrared range. Some sensor systems produce images in the middle or thermal infrared ranges, registering in the latter the thermal radiation from the Earth's surface. The reflected radiation picked up by sensors is broken down into multiple spectral ranges (4 in SPOT, 8 in LANDSAT 7), making it possible to produce images in natural colors or in infrared or false colors (which lend themselves better to scientific analysis) from the exposures by mixing the various wavelengths. The nature of ground cover can be interpreted with the support of computer-aided imaging processes, as every surface has distinctive reflective characteristics. This facilitates recognition of water surfaces, wooded areas (deciduous, mixed, and coniferous forest), residential developments, industrial areas, etc.

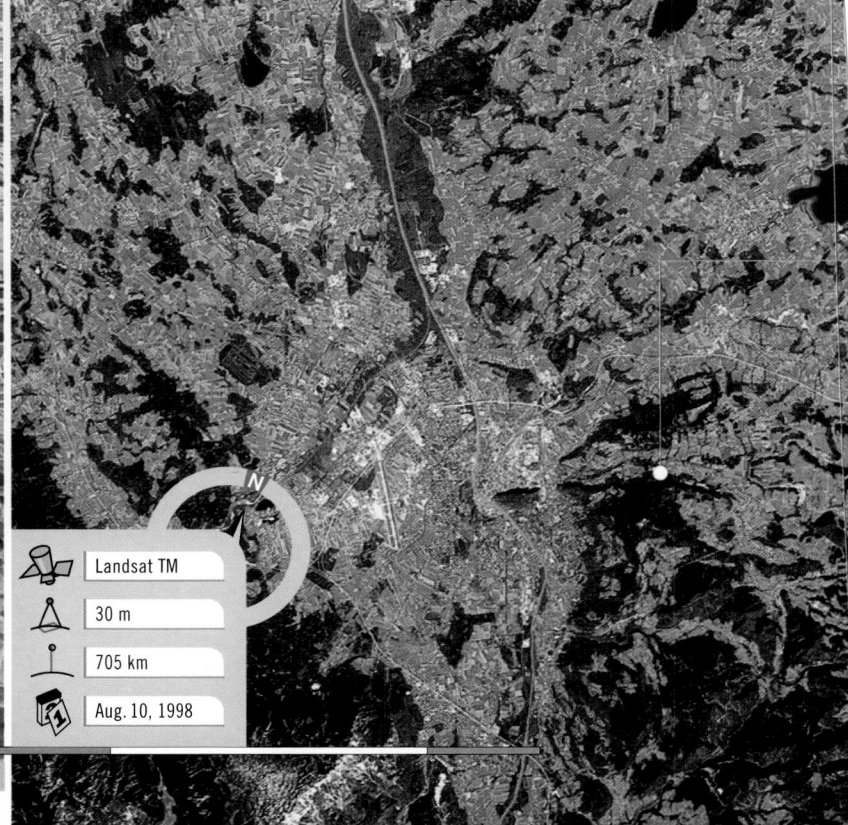

| Landsat TM |
| 30 m |
| 705 km |
| Aug. 10, 1998 |

Topographic Image

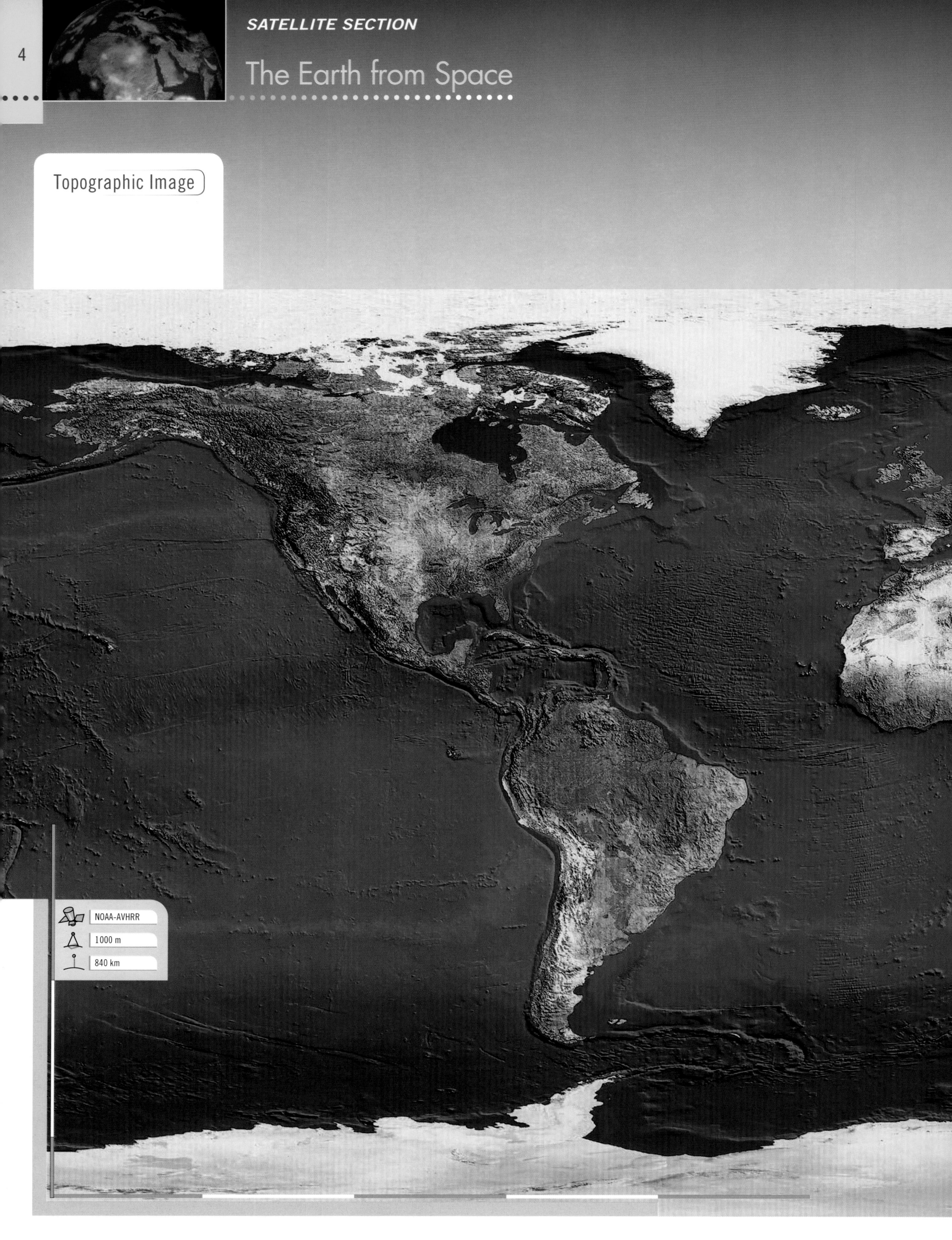

NOAA-AVHRR

1000 m

840 km

View of the Earth from Space

Several thousand images from the U.S. NOAA Satellite Series were required to compile this completely cloudless picture of the Earth.
In the projection selected for this satellite imagery map, the polar regions extend along the full length of the Equator. The continents are true to form to north and south latitudes of about 35 degrees, but distortion grows more extreme toward the poles.
This composite satellite image gives a good overview of major landscapes of the continents and their vegetation patterns. A particularly striking feature is the belt of deserts that encircles the globe.

(Copyright: GEOSPACE / World Sat International Corp. 2000)

Land and Seafloor Topography

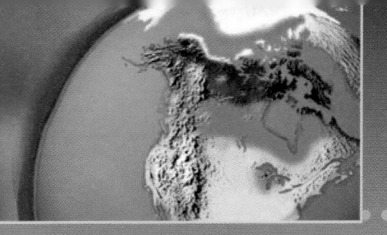

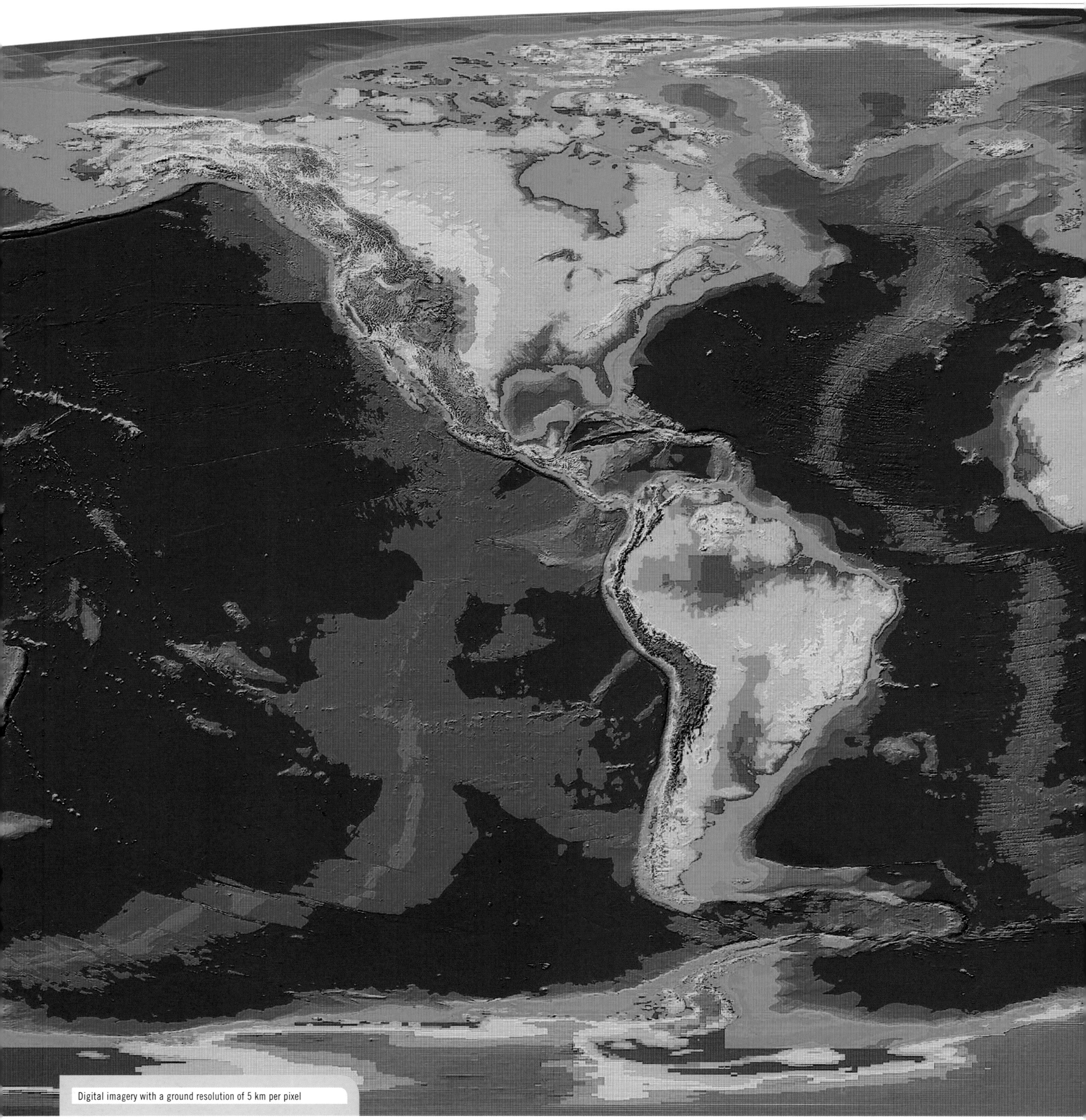

Digital imagery with a ground resolution of 5 km per pixel

The Earth's Surface

Shelf seas along the world's coastlines (light blue areas) trace the outlines of continental landmasses and highlight the topographic connections between offshore islands and their "parent" continents. The submerged oceanic ridges of the Atlantic and Indian Oceans stand out clearly as the longest continuous mountain ranges on Earth.

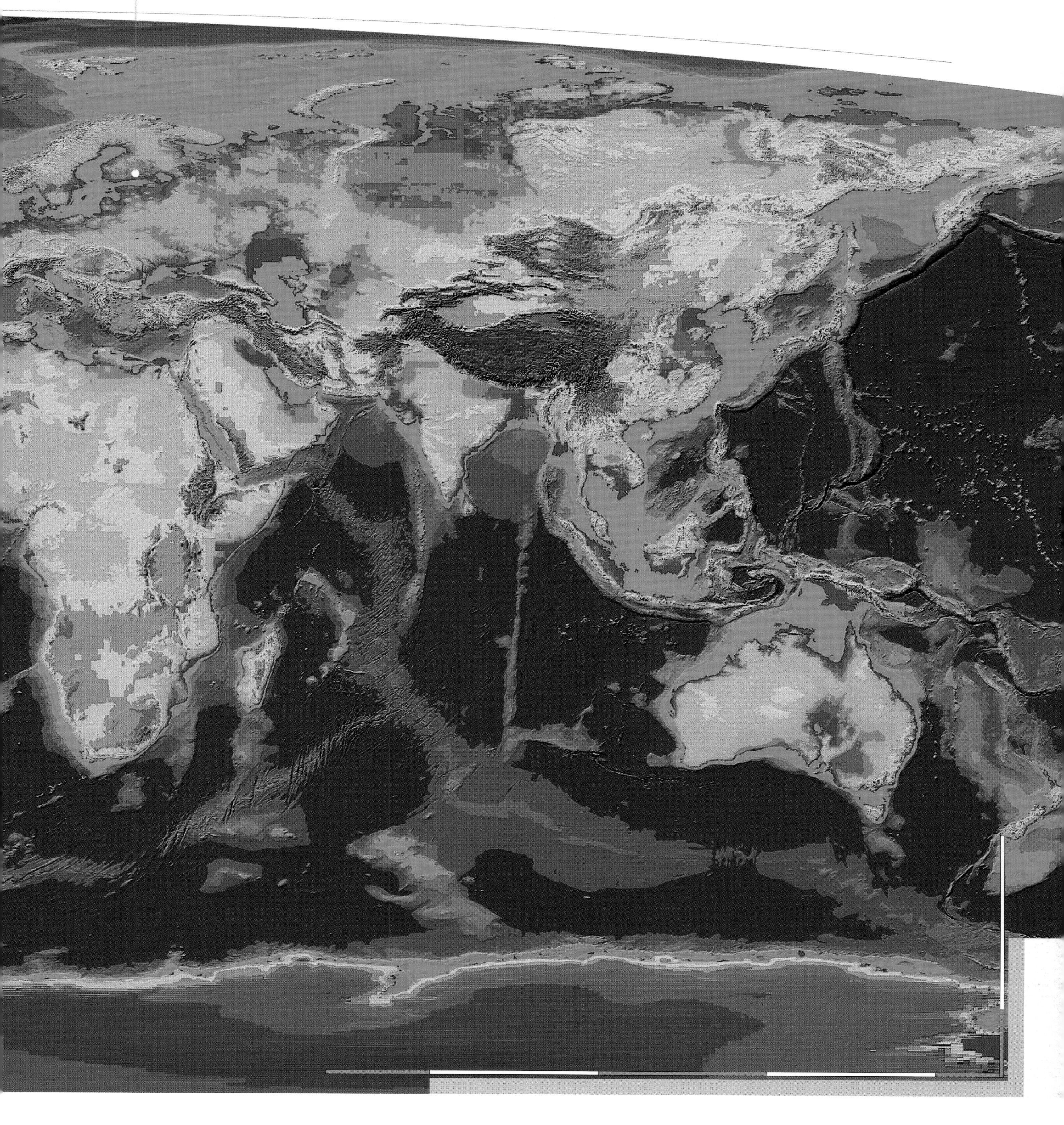

Volcanism

Living Links to the Earth's Core

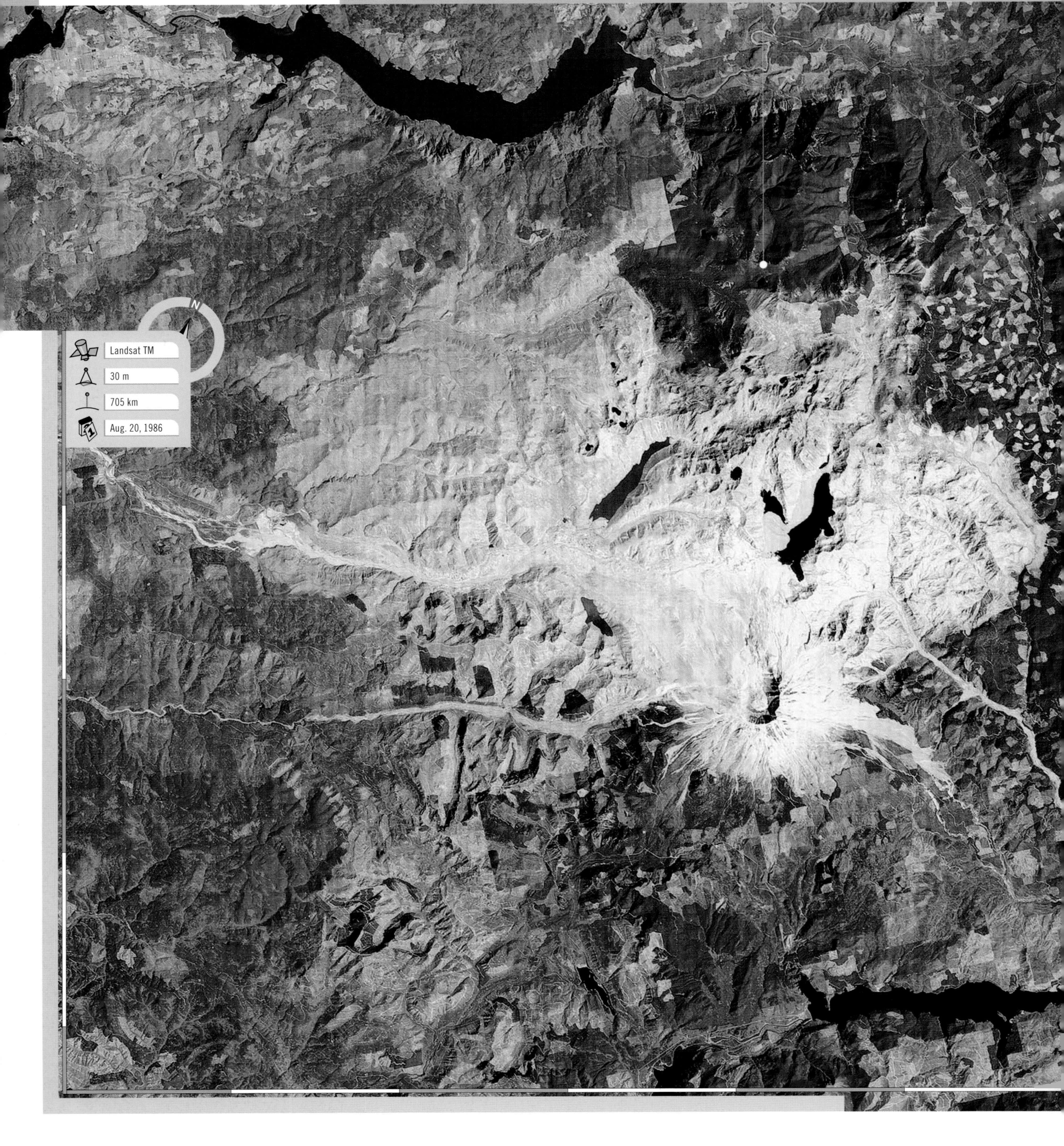

Landsat TM

30 m

705 km

Aug. 20, 1986

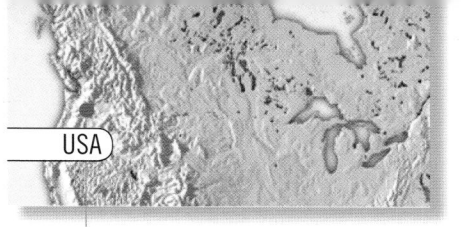
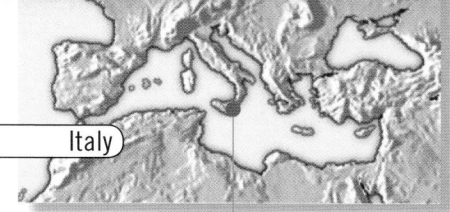

Mt. Saint Helens

One of the most spectacular natural events of the latter half of the 20th century was the eruption of Mount Saint Helens in the Cascade Range in the state of Washington. All of the active volcanoes of North America are located in this chain of mountains that extends from northern California to Canada. The region without vegetation in the center of the image is the area of volcanic devastation surrounding the collapsed oval crater (caldera) and Spirit Lake.

Originally 2,948 m high, the mountain known by the Indians as the "Guardian of Fire" lost about 400 m of elevation during the eruption on May 18, 1980. Avalanches of melted snow, mud, and rock debris rushed down two river valleys, sweeping away bridges and houses and cutting long swaths through the forests. A massive fountain of ash rose up to 23 km into the stratosphere from the mountain's fractured northern flank. The shockwave knocked down all trees within miles of the cone like matches. Sixty people died in the inferno.

Less violent eruptions occurred in 1984, 1986, 1989, and 1991.

Mount Aetna

Mount Aetna, the highest active volcano in Europe, towers above the eastern coast of Sicily between Catania and Taormina on the shores of the Ionian Sea.

The last major eruption of Mount Aetna (present elevation: 3,350 m) occurred in 2001 and threatened the village of Nicolosi. This thermal image shows the pattern of temperature distribution on the surface of the powerful volcano. Red indicates areas of high temperature; blue represents lower surface temperatures. Temperatures are markedly influenced by solar radiation (exposed versus shaded surfaces). Typical of Mount Aetna are its many parasite craters – the largest of which are clearly recognizable on the western and southeastern sides of the volcano. Also evident are the numerous fissures and steam springs through which magma gases are released.

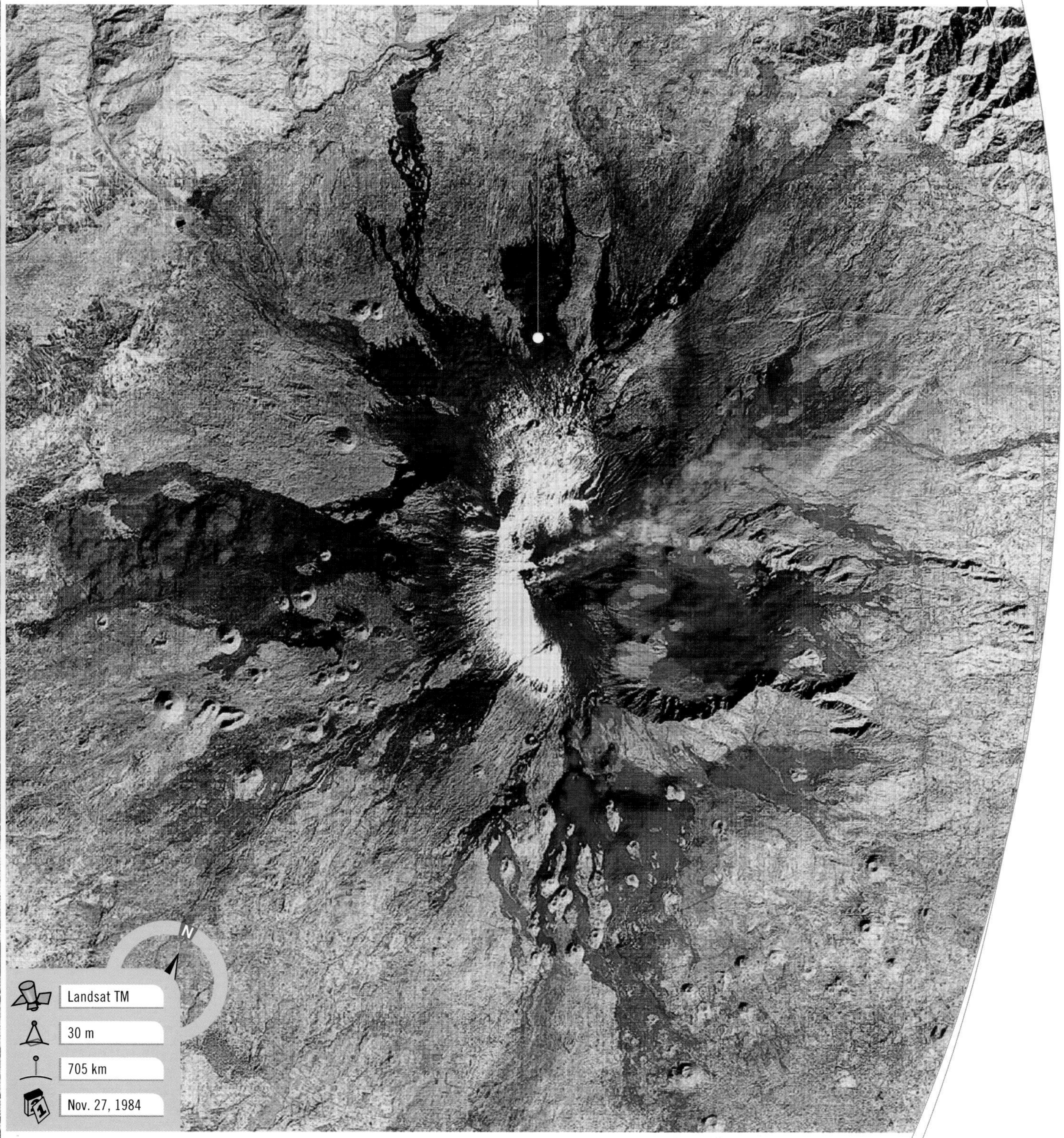

Landsat TM

30 m

705 km

Nov. 27, 1984

Threat from Outer Space

Clearwater Lake

This satellite image shows the two basins
of Clearwater Lake in the Canadian province
of Quebec. The lakebeds are the product of
an extremely rare event – the impact of "twin
meteorites" – that occurs only about once
every one million years, when two presumably
related meteorite fragments strike the earth
in succession. Complex craters formed by
impacts of large meteorites are characterized
by a central mountain formation.
The islands in the larger of the two lakes are
the visible remnants of such a central
mountain formation, left exposed after the
craters filled with water.
The impact that formed the lakes is presumed
to have occurred some 300 million years ago.

Landsat TM

30 m

705 km

Sept. 8, 1986

Canada

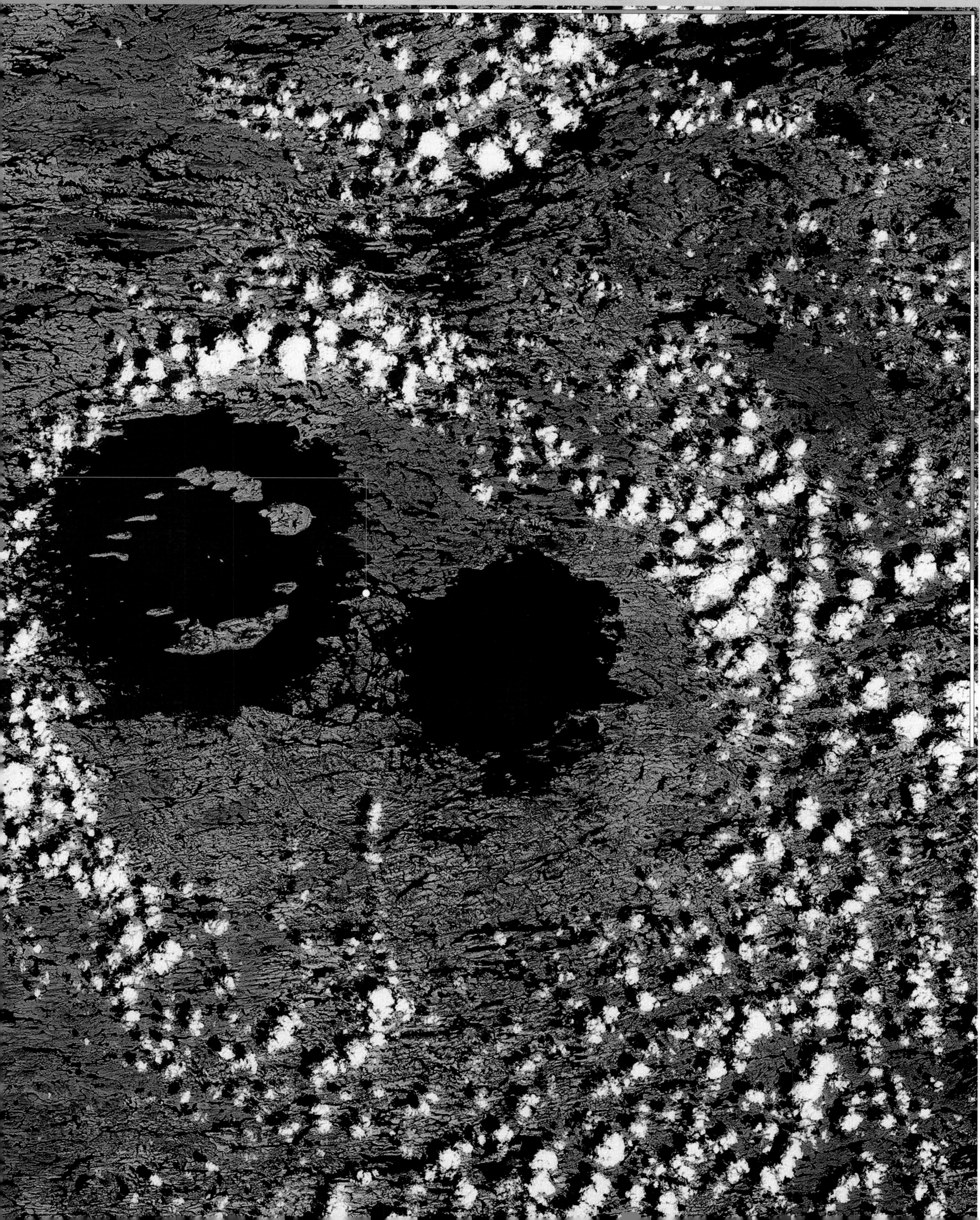

Storms and a Dangerous Christ Child

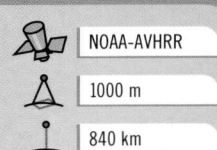

NOAA-AVHRR

1000 m

840 km

Temperature distribution
September 9, 1986

Temperature distribution
September 5, 1987

Temperature distribution
September 6, 1988

El Niño

The El Niño phenomenon appears in the Pacific around Christmas time at intervals of between four and 30 years. El Niño is Spanish for "the (Christ) Child."
It is the result of extreme pressure differences between the Australo-Asiatic low-pressure and the South Pacific high-pressure systems. These sefferences generate strong currents of warm water moving toward the west, which in turn produce cold reverse streams at lower depths along the path of the Humboldt current. When the pressure differential changes, the warmed water begins to flow eastward again, heating the air above it. This lieads to periods of heavy precipitation along the western coast of South America and corresponding droughts in large parts of Asia and Australia. One such El Niño year was registered in 1987. The phenomenon was particularly severe in 1997/98.
The thermal image of the Pacific shows masses of warm water (shades of yellow and red) approaching the South American coastline.

< 16.5 °C	21.0 – 21.5 °C	26.0 – 26.5 °C
16.5 – 17.0 °C	21.5 – 22.0 °C	26.5 – 27.0 °C
17.0 – 17.5 °C	22.0 – 22.5 °C	27.0 – 27.5 °C
17.5 – 18.0 °C	22.5 – 23.0 °C	27.5 – 28.0 °C
18.0 – 18.5 °C	23.0 – 23.5 °C	28.0 – 28.5 °C
18.5 – 19.0 °C	23.5 – 24.0 °C	28.5 – 29.0 °C
19.0 – 19.5 °C	24.0 – 24.5 °C	29.0 – 29.5 °C
19.5 – 20.0 °C	24.5 – 25.0 °C	29.5 – 30.0 °C
20.0 – 20.5 °C	25.0 – 26.5 °C	30.0 – 30.5 °C
20.5 – 21.0 °C	25.5 – 26.0 °C	> 30.5 °C

N

Landsat TM

30 m

705 km

Aug. 24, 1992

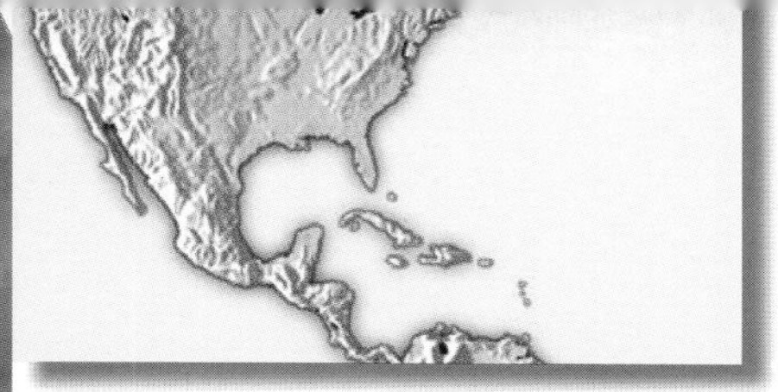

(Hurricane Andrew)

On August 24, 1992, Hurricane Andrew swept through the densely populated region of South Florida with peak wind speeds exceeding 270 km per hour, leaving a trail of devastation in its wake. Forty-seven people were killed, and some 350,000 lost their homes. The satellite image shows a vividly clear picture of the characteristic spiral cloud pattern and the virtually windless eye at the center of the hurricane. Hurricanes are born as low-pressure systems formed by storm cells. They become particularly dangerous when water temperatures reach 80° F or above. Moist, warm air rises, and water vapor condenses at high altitudes, releasing heat, which causes the air column to rise even higher. Air pressure immediately above the water's surface falls, and moist air flows at an accelerated pace into the storm system — a vicious circle that speeds the development of the hurricane.
Hurricanes generate wind speeds of up to 400 km per hour. Their paths are determined by prevailing global wind systems and major regional weather patterns.

Climate 〔 Changes in the Ozone Layer – The Ozone Hole 〕

The large quantities of chlorofluorocarbons (CFC), used in spray dispensers and as coolants in refrigerators for example) released into the atmosphere every year produce chemical changes in the stratosphere which destroy the protective shell of the ozone layer encircling the Earth. The ozone layer absorbs some of the harmful ultra violet B radiation emitted by the Sun and helps regulate the heat budget of the atmosphere. Ozone depletion is most severe above the southern hemisphere during the months of September and October. NASA and the Ozone Research Program of the European Union have been observing changes in the ozone layer for many years. Seasonal fluctuations are illustrated in the series of images below, which show that ozone concentrations can fall to half their normal levels in certain years.

Higher atmospheric temperatures above the Arctic (as compared to the south polar region) reduce the danger of ozone depletion, although the sequence of images shows an increase here as well. The ozone veil above the Arctic is not as thin as that in the Antarctic stratosphere. However, chemical analysis has shown that the composition of the atmosphere above the north polar regions has suffered nearly the same degree of disturbance as that above the Antarctic.

Many of the consequences of atmospheric ozone depletion for mankind are well known. The increased intensity of UV radiation causes a higher incidence of sunburn and skin cancer and a general impairment of the human immune system. High UV radiation levels also have a lasting impact on plant life.

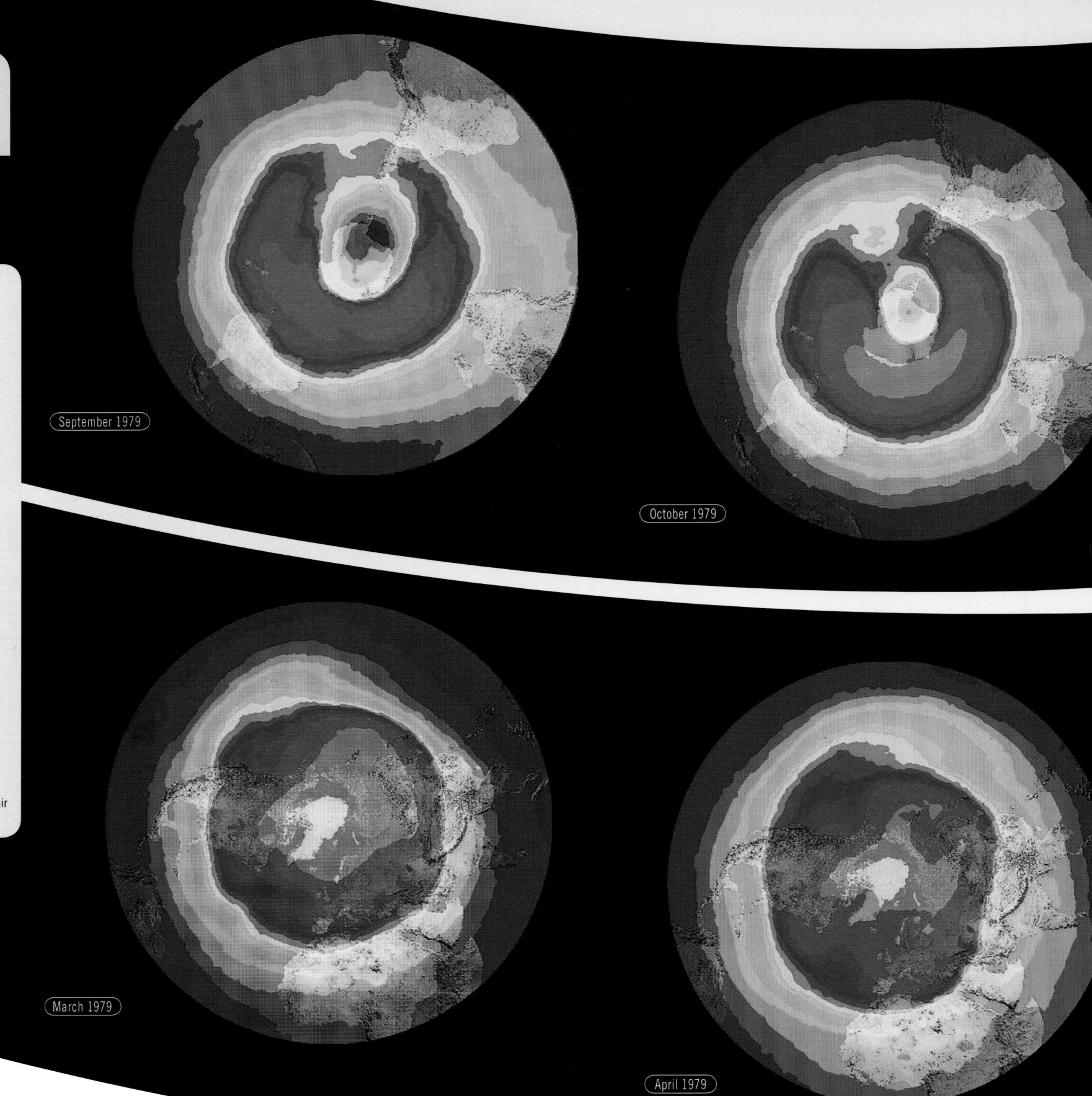

NOAA-AVHRR

1000 m

840 km

Ozone concentration in the atmosphere

	100 – 250
	250 – 260
	260 – 270
	270 – 280
	280 – 290
	290 – 300
	300 – 310
	310 – 320
	320 – 330
	330 – 340
	340 – 350
	350 – 360
	360 – 370
	370 – 380
	380 – 390
	390 – 400
	400 – 450
	450 – 500
	> 500

Ozone concentration per air column in Dobson Units

September 1979

October 1979

March 1979

April 1979

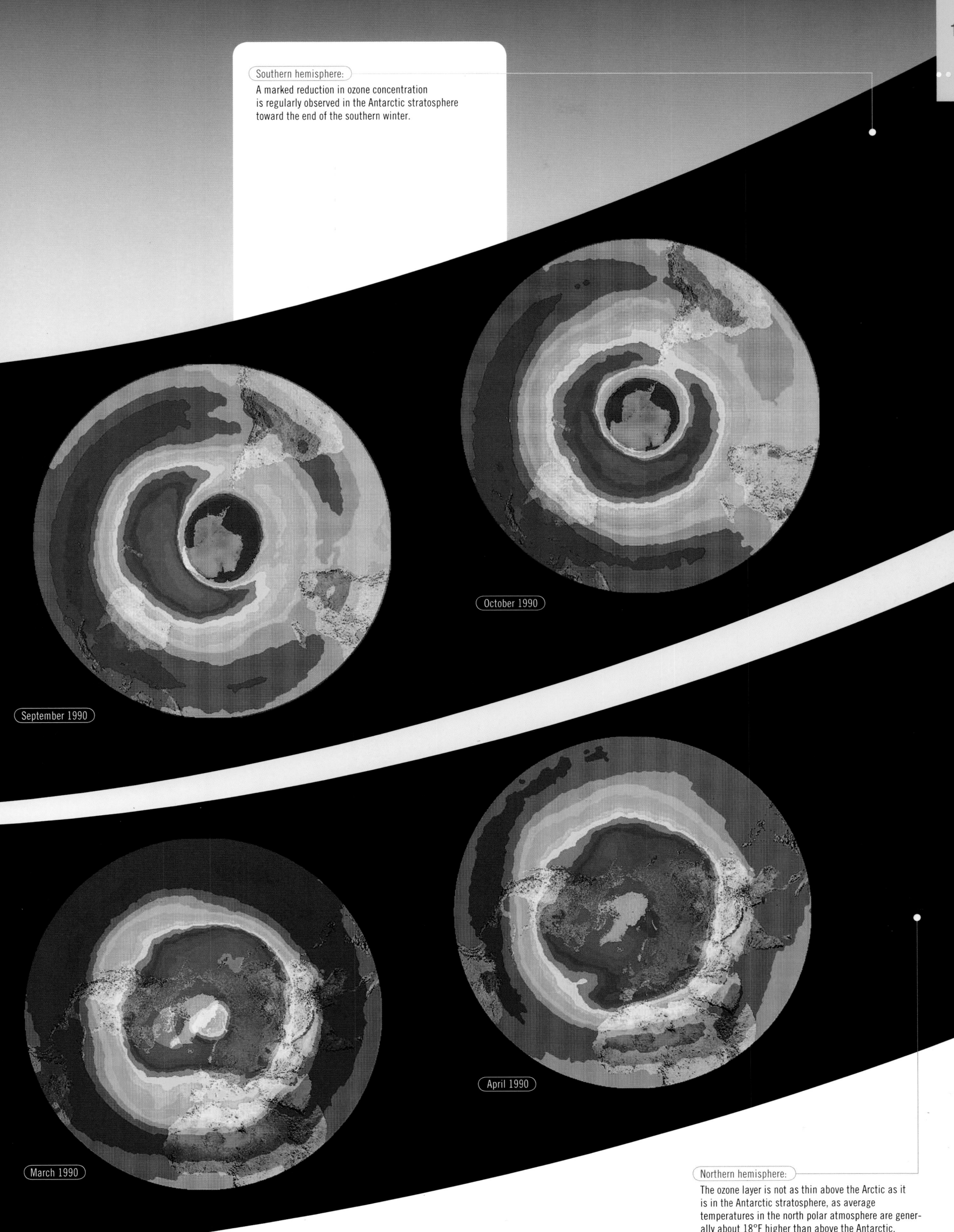

Southern hemisphere:

A marked reduction in ozone concentration is regularly observed in the Antarctic stratosphere toward the end of the southern winter.

September 1990

October 1990

March 1990

April 1990

Northern hemisphere:

The ozone layer is not as thin above the Arctic as it is in the Antarctic stratosphere, as average temperatures in the north polar atmosphere are generally about 18°F higher than above the Antarctic.

The Nile Near Cairo

The ancient Egyptian city of Cairo emerged where the Nile Valley expands to form the Nile Delta.

With an estimated population of ten million, Cairo is the largest city in Africa and the Arabian region. Surrounded by Egypt's most important agricultural landscape, the city has spread eastward into the desert at an increasingly rapid pace over the past several decades. The nine districts of the city are clearly delineated by their rectangular pattern of streets. The famous pyramids of Giza are located west of the Nile and connected to the ancient old city of Cairo by a broad band of residential settlements.

The contrast between the uninhabited desert and the Nile Valley could hardly be more dramatic. Measuring 6,671 km from source to mouth, the world's second longest river flows without tributaries in a flat-bottomed groove up to 20 km wide on the last 2,700 km of its course between the Arabian and Nubian deserts. Once it reaches the vast delta (24,000 sq. km), the river forks into two branches, the Rosetta and the Damietta, which empty into the Mediterranean Sea.

Both the Nile Valley and the Nile Delta are dotted with small settlements positioned at regular intervals between "central" towns. This Landsat image offers a striking picture of the city at the point where the fertile flood plain of the river begins to fan out into the delta.

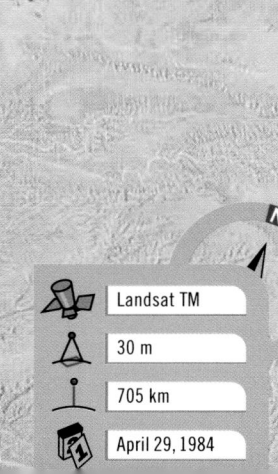

Landsat TM

30 m

705 km

April 29, 1984

Landsat ETM

15 m

705 km

Nov. 3, 1999

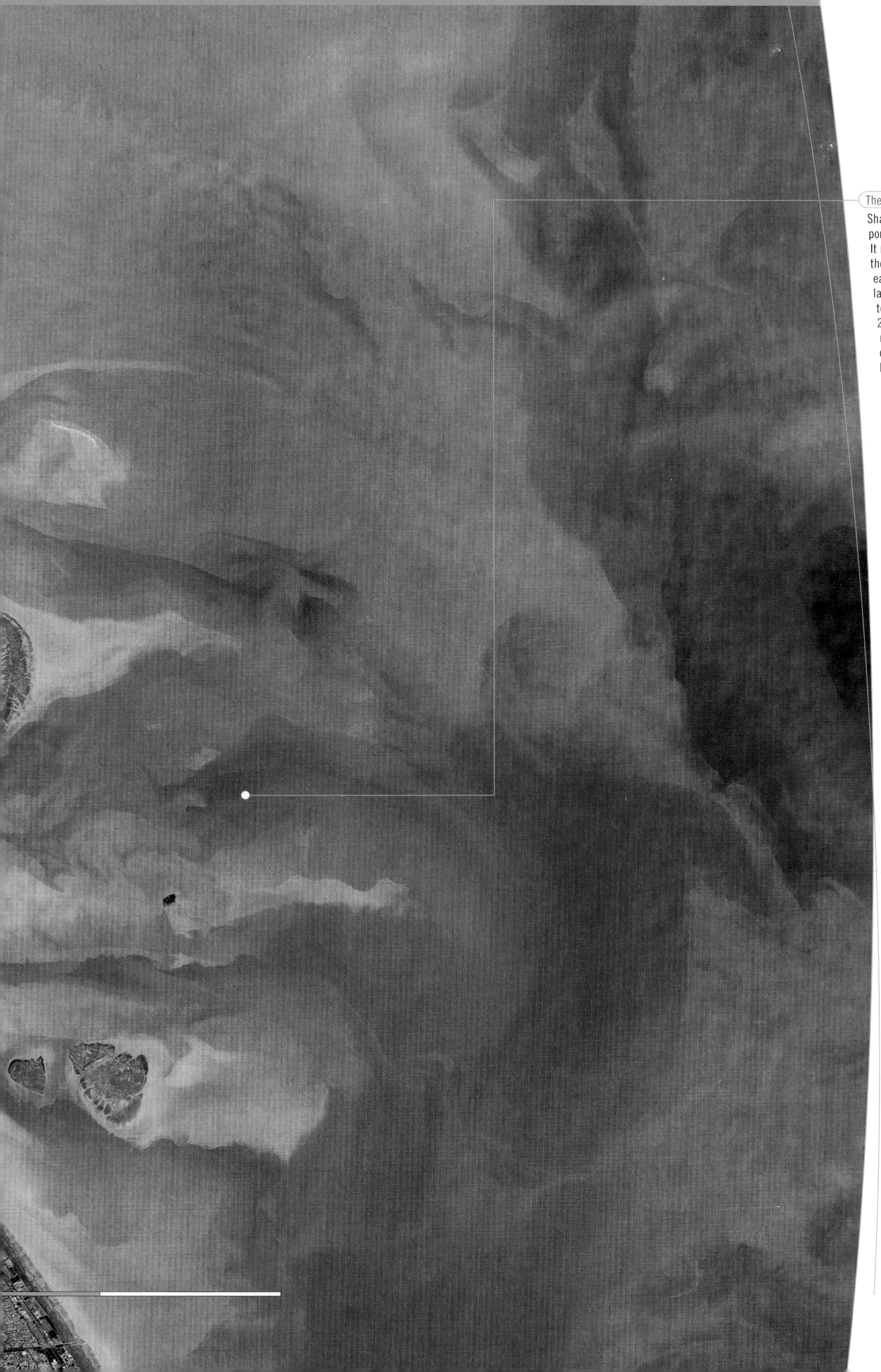

The Mouth of the Yangtze (Chang)

Shanghai is China's most important port and its largest metropolis. It radiates from the confluence of the Huang River and the Yangtze east of Tai Lake. At the turn of the last century, the city was home to some 12 million people, and nearly 20 million people live in greater metropolitan Shanghai. The opening of China to international trade has spurred rapid growth in the city in recent years, to which an expansive system of urban freeways and a number of new high-rise complexes bear witness. The amount of developed land nearly doubled between 1980 and 2000. In the process, the belt of vegetation that once encircled the city (visible in places as spots of light-green coloration in the satellite image) was obliterated. Development has been especially intensive in the Pudong district on the right bank the Huang, where large areas the old city were demolished and replaced by new business and industrial centers.

The Dead Sea

The surface of the Dead Sea, known as Yam
Ha-Melah (Salt Lake) in Hebrew,
lies an average of 396 m below the level
of the Mediterranean, making it the
lowest-lying inland sea in the world. It is 80
km long, 18 km wide, up to 794 m deep, and
covers an area of 940 sq. km. As recently as
the early 1970s, the Dead Sea still consisted
of two bodies of water connected by a narrow
channel at the tip of the Lisan Peninsula.
Increasing use of water from the sea for irrigation of fields along its tributaries, coupled
with industrial potassium-mining operations
in the southern basin, led to higher levels of
solid salt deposits and eventually divided the
sea into two separate bodies of water. The
sea is fed by numerous underground springs
which introduce valuable minerals
and trace elements, including calcium,
magnesium, silicic acid, potassium,
iron, bromides, and iodine. With a salinity
level of 25%, the Dead Sea is totally
devoid of plant and animal life. Due to the
warm climate, between two and 25 mm
of water surface evaporate every day, keep-
ing salt content high despite the influx of
fresh water. Potassium, bromides, and
magnesium salts are collected in the
evaporation basins. The industrial facilities are clearly identified by the walls of
the evaporation basins.
Located in the western part of the Jordan
Rift Valley are the Judaean Heights
(maximum elevation 1,014 m), a region
of intensive cultivation and irrigation
that slopes steeply toward the
Mediterranean. The capital of Israel,
Jerusalem, lies at the same latitude as
the northernmost shore of the Dead
Sea. The Tel Aviv-Yafo metropolitan
area is visible along the coast. The
Jordanian capital of Amman is
located northwest of the Dead Sea
along the edge of the steppe.

Landsat ETM

30 m

705 km

May 15, 1989

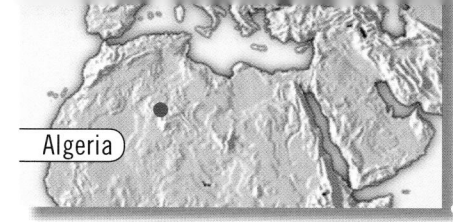

The Sahara near Amguid in Algeria

The Sahara presents a very different face in many places. Landscapes can be distinguished on the basis of differences in surface material — exposed rock, gravel, sand, or salt clay. A large portion of the image is occupied by the debris-covered surfaces of the Hamada de Tinrhert (light gray and reddish brown areas). This bolder-strewn desert is known as Serir in Algeria. The second type of desert in the Sahara is characterized by sand sheets and dunes. A prominent feature of the landscape in this satellite image is the tongue of sand in the upper portion of the picture, with its regular pattern of star-shaped figures. Salt clay plains (bluish-turquoise coloration) are found in the broad depressions where the wadis — dry valleys through which water flows only after heavy rains — grow wider. The dark brown areas are the northern fingers of the Tassili-n-Ajjer range, with peaks as high as 1,800 m.

Landsat ETM

30 m

705 km

Winter 1987

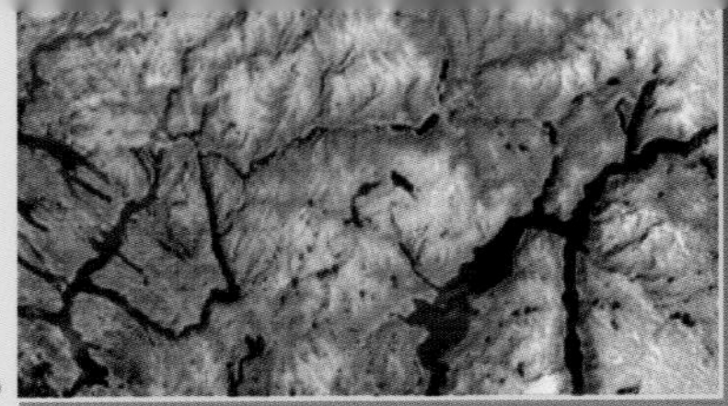

Coastal Formations (Fjords and Skerries)

Norway

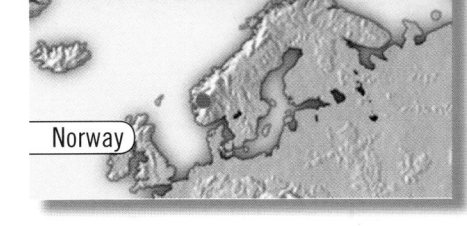

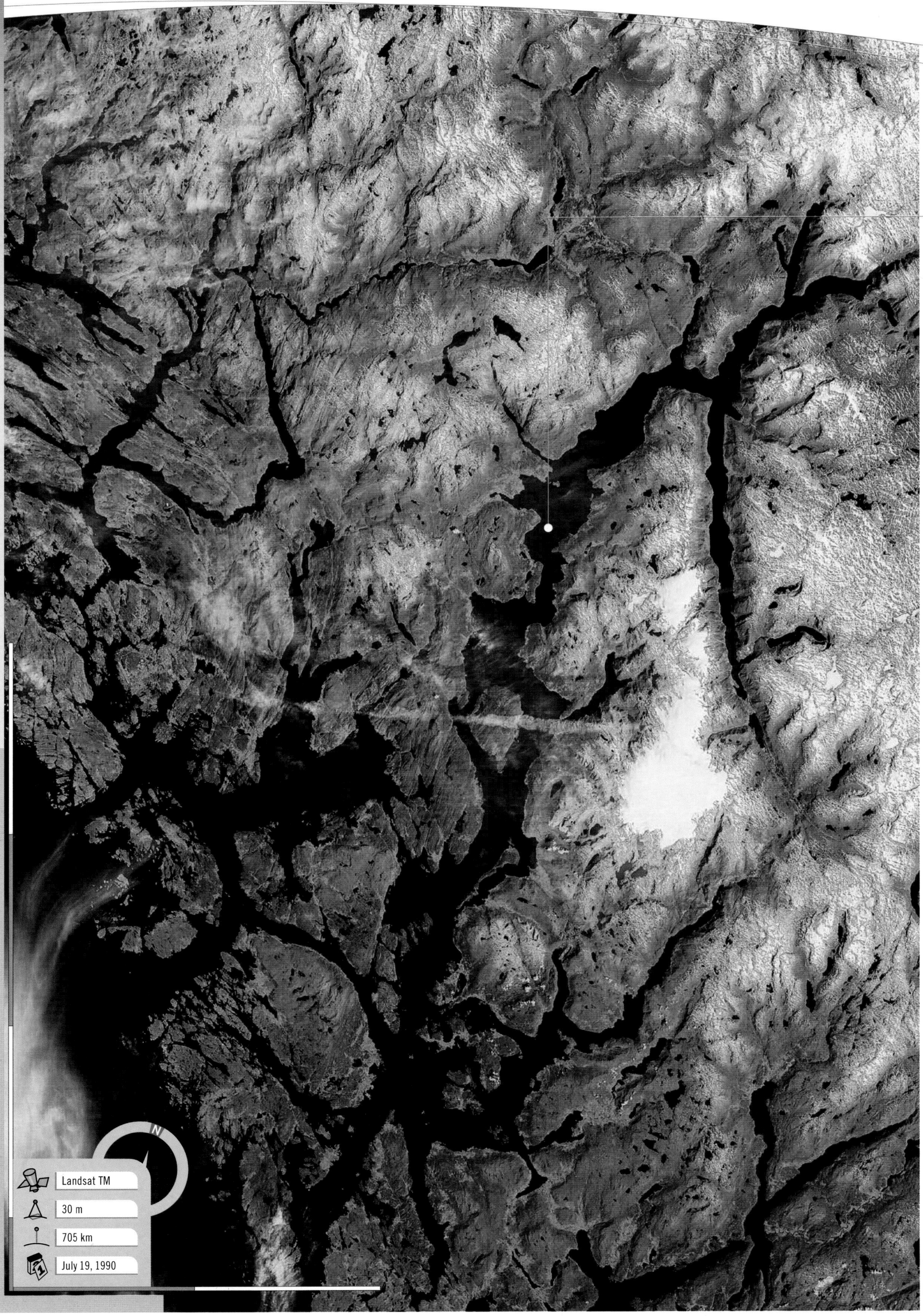
Hardangerfjorden
N
Landsat TM
30 m
705 km
July 19, 1990

Framed by the Hardangerfjorden and the eastern Numedal, the snow-covered Hardangervidda in southern Norway reaches elevations of between 1,200 and 1,400 m. Covering an area of 7,500 sq. km, it is 30 times the size of the Bavarian Forest in Germany. The intricate branching network of the Hardangerfjorden extends far into the hinterland of southwestern Norway. One of the best-known fjords in the world, the Hardangerfjorden was formed during the last ice age. Huge glaciers thrust far out into the sea, pushing large volumes of debris ahead of them. When the glaciers melted, they left behind a U-shaped valley with maximum depths of more than 1,000 m, which was flooded by the sea. The debris carried by the glaciers filled the entrance to the fjord, making it relatively shallow and restricting the exchange of seawater and fresh water entering the fjord from the interior. Favored by the mild climate, large plantations of apple and cherry orchards line the shores of the Hardangerfjorden.

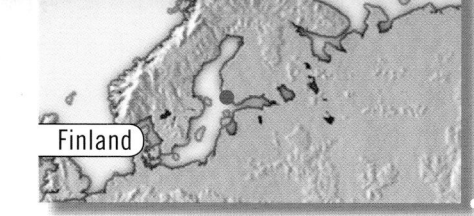
Skerry Landscape

The Åland Islands are located in the
Gulf of Bothnia between Turku
and Stockholm. The satellite image
highlights the typical features of
a skerry coast, a glacially formed
landscape of domed islets flooded by
the sea. Some of the numerous
small islands between the Åland
group and Turku are inhabited.
For generations, people have lived in
virtual isolation in the skerries.
There are very few roads, and water
routes are the most important
links to other islands and the
mainland. Fishing has been the
most important source of income for
centuries, although the skerry population also relies on farming, animal
husbandry, and forestry. Environmental tourism is one of the most
important sources of revenue
today.

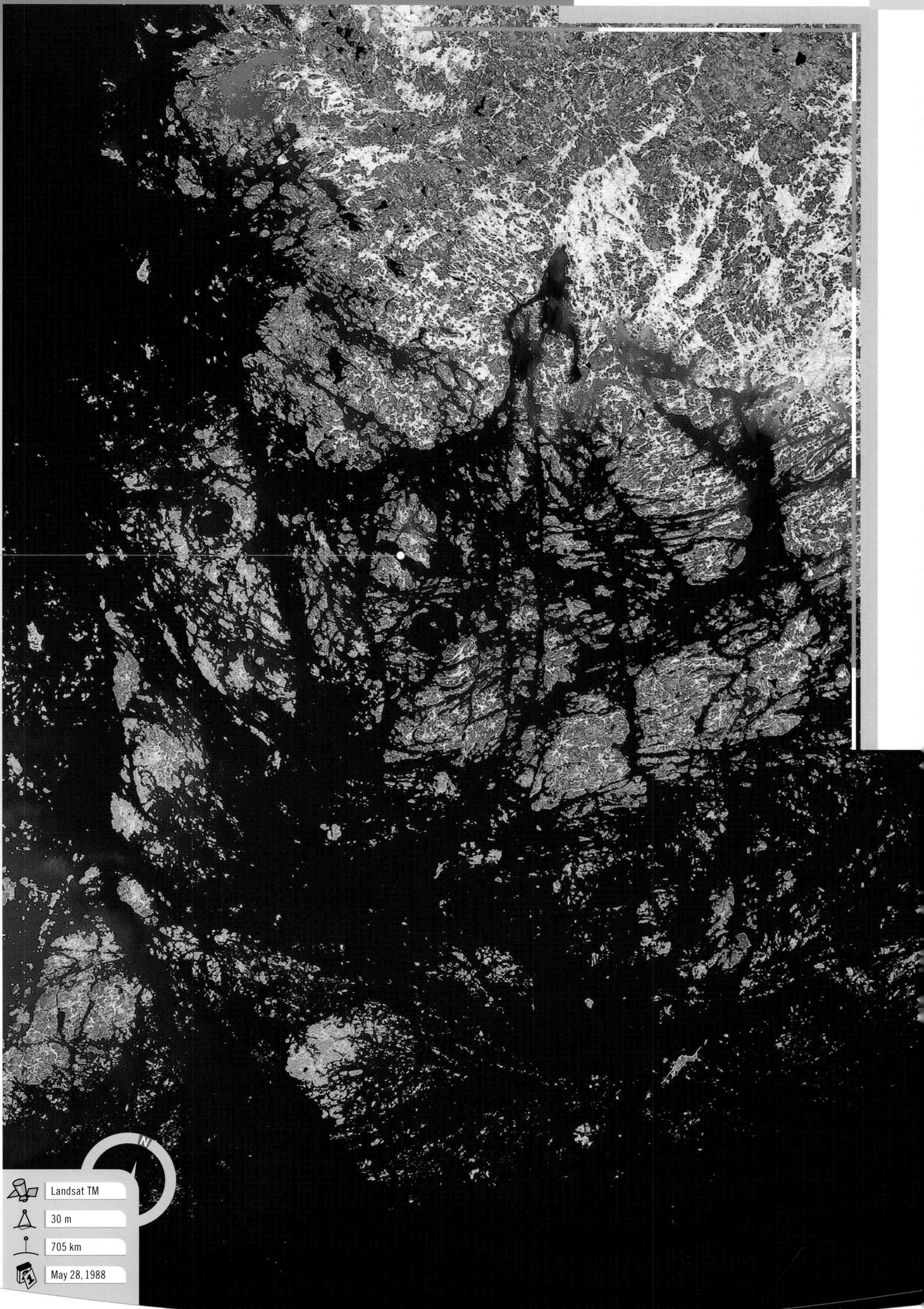

Landsat TM

30 m

705 km

May 28, 1988

Coastal Formations [The Largest Reef on Earth]

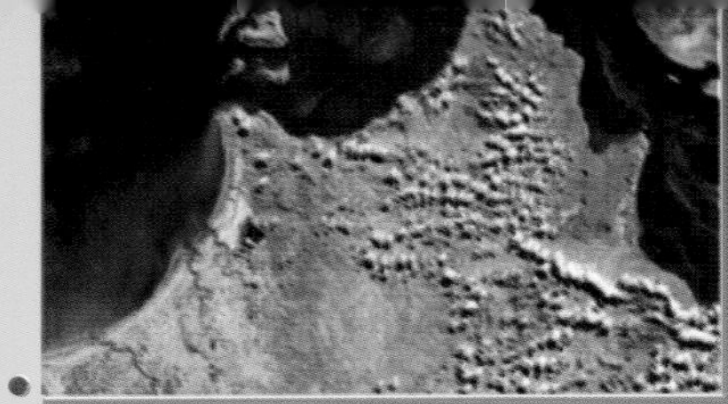

	Landsat TM
	30 m
	705 km
	July 13, 2000

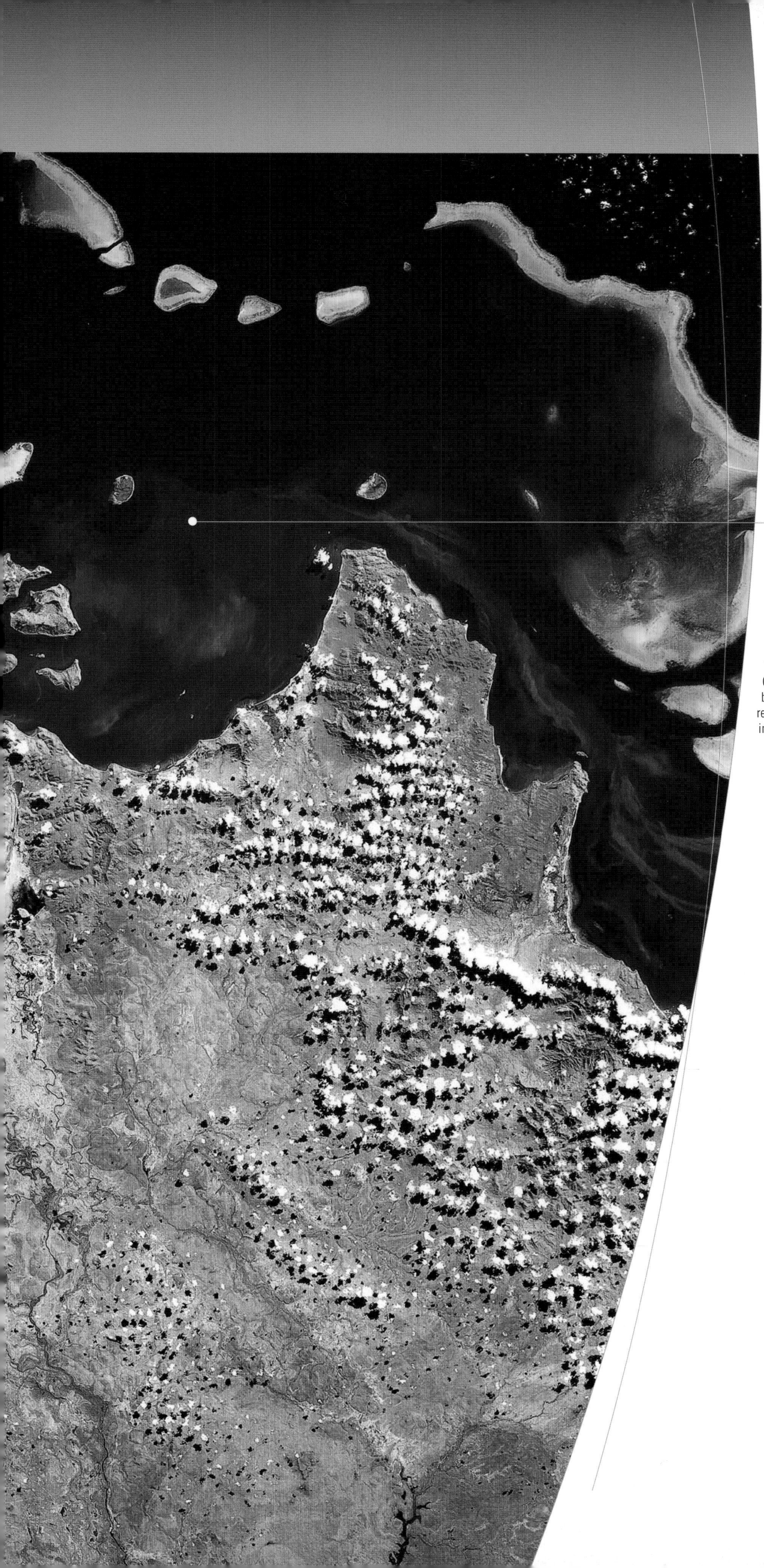

The Great Barrier Reef

The world's largest coral reef runs parallel to the coast of Australia off the shores of Queensland. This satellite image shows Princess Charlotte Bay on the southern coast of the Cape York Peninsula.

The chain of elongated, oval or circular coral reefs is discernable only from the air. Covered only by shallow waters, they appear as turquoise and light blue areas that stand out clearly against the deep blue of the open sea.

The view from the air tells us something else as well. The Great Barrier Reef is not a continuous, linear reef system but instead comprises a large number of individual reefs of different sizes distributed in a picturesque pattern in the lagoon.

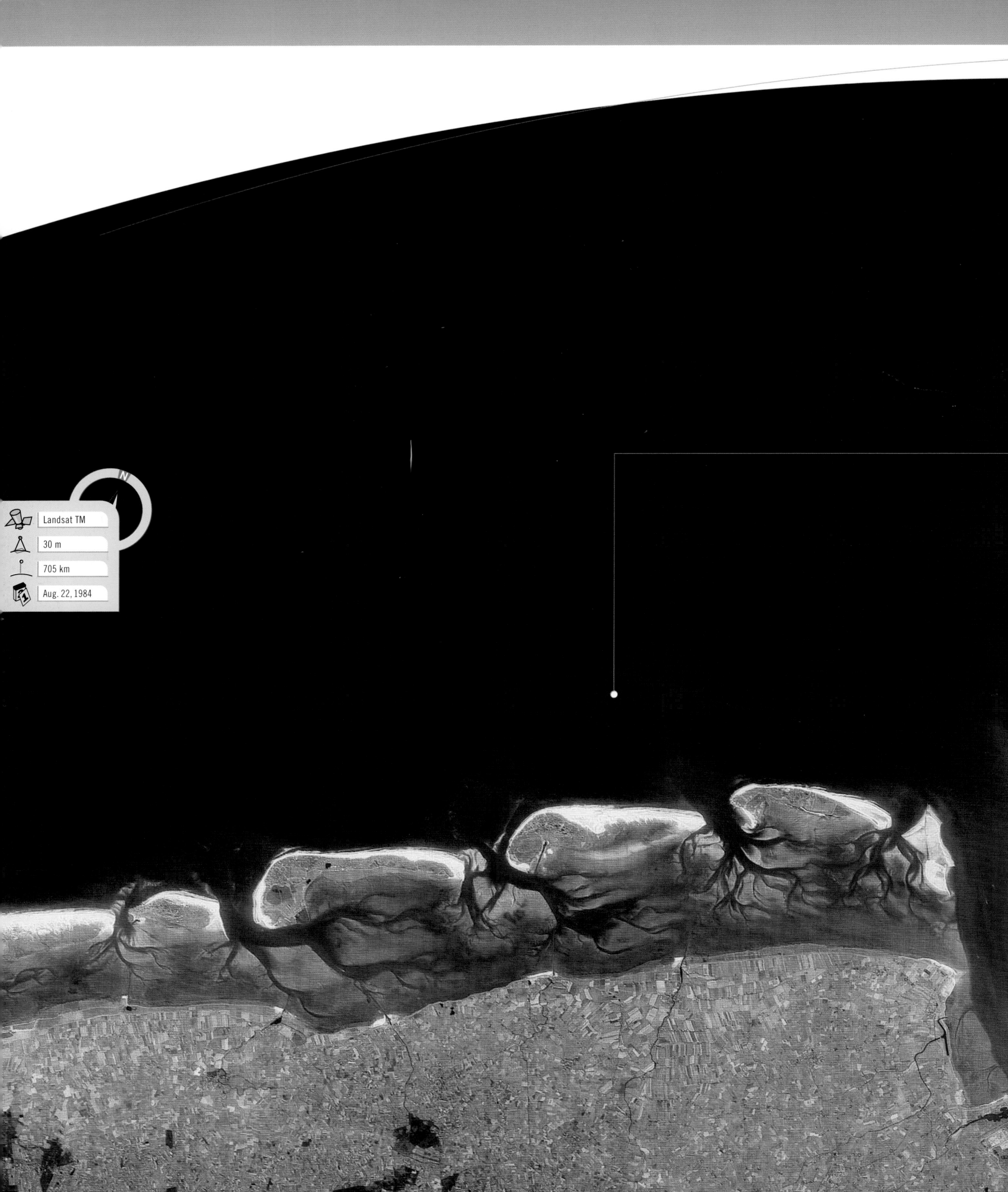

Landsat TM

30 m

705 km

Aug. 22, 1984

East Frisian Islands

The East Frisian Islands are massive dune islands built on foundations of sand. The different stages in their development are evident in this satellite image. Broad, light-colored beaches line the northern and eastern shores of the islands (rudimentary spits can be seen on the eastern side of the island of Juist). Behind them are rows of dunes — younger formations nearer the shore; older, more heavily vegetated ones farther inland. Situated inside the protective dune walls are marshlands used for grazing. Frequently flooded salt meadows lie between the beaches and the tidal flats.

The pattern of channels and flats exposed at low tide is clearly visible in this satellite image. Rising and falling by as much as 3 meters, the tides have cut gateways to depths of up to 20 meters between the islands. The tides are also responsible for the formation of arc and sickle ripples. A reddish tinge identifies the ecologically significant areas of salt meadow and tidal mud flats. The area known as "Niedersächsisches Wattenmeer" was declared a National Park in 1986 in order to preserve this sensitive biosphere.

Hamburg

The satellite image shows the Elbe River as a complex network of waterways that wind through the city of Hamburg. Clearly visible are the extensive, branching docklands of Hamburg Harbor, one of Europe's largest and commercially most significant seaports.

The harbor and its facilities account for about 10% of the total area of Hamburg. The characteristic finger-shaped configuration of the tidal harbor results from the dredging of artificial harbor basins to allow ships to dock directly in front of the city's warehouses. Germany's largest international harbor has always been a gateway for movement of goods to and from Europe. Once primarily a transfer point for bulk and piece goods, Hamburg Harbor has since developed into a major logistics center.

Landsat TM +
Spot PAN

30 m

705 km

May 15, 1988
May 2, 1986

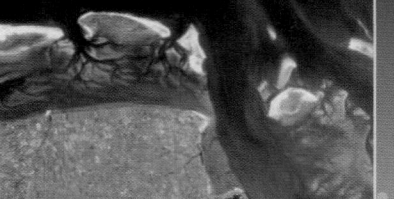

Continental Divides

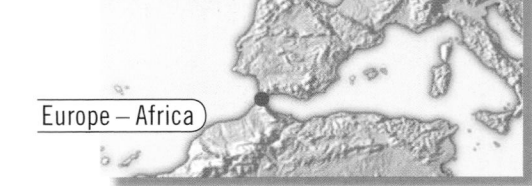

Europe – Africa

Natural Boundaries

Gibraltar

Roughly 60 km long, the Strait of Gibraltar narrows from west to east,
separating Spain and Morocco by only 15 km at its narrowest point.
Over the course of history, it has served as both a link between the continents
of Europe and Africa and a gateway between the New and Old Worlds.
Its strategic importance has made the Strait of Gibraltar a source of ceaseless political strife.

Landsat TM	
30 m	
705 km	
Aug. 10, 1998	

Bosporus

Measuring 31 km in length and between 660 and 3,000 m in width, the Bosporus, a narrow strait between Europe and Asia, connects the Black Sea with the Sea of Marmara. It is a flooded river valley that sank during the Würm (Wisconsin) glacial stage and eventually formed a strait linking the two seas.
The city of Istanbul sits astride the Bosporus. Like every metropolis, it is a mosaic of many different districts, each with its own distinctive character. The city center itself is divided into three parts, for which water is both a barrier and a connecting link: the Golden Horn, an arm of the sea that separates the old, formerly Greek-Byzantine Istanbul from the modern Beyoglu, and the Bosporus, which separates the European and Asian parts of the city. Although Turkey's capital was moved to Ankara in 1923, Istanbul remains the country's most important commercial and cultural center.
Suspension bridges built in 1973 and 1988 connect the European and Asian halves of the city.

N

Landsat ETM

15 m

705 km

Oct. 4, 1999

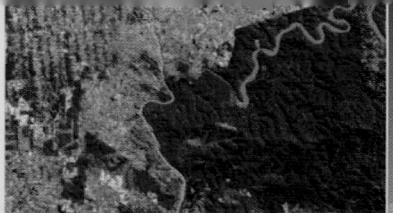

Carving New Settlements from the Rainforest

Rio Paraná

In 1975, Brazil and Paraguay began constructing the world's largest dam for the Itaipú hydroelectric power plant. Itaipú means "singing stone" in the Guaraní Indian language. Since 1982, the Rio Paraná has backed up over a length of 180 km, forming a huge lake that covers an area of 1,460 sq. km. before entering a long (60 km) canyon near the city of Foz do Iguaçu. Dam projects of this magnitude have a significant impact on the environment.

The power plant went into operation at full capacity in May 1991 and now provides much of the electricity consumed in Brazil. Paraguay, which covered half of the roughly 30-million-dollar construction bill, does not need that much electrical power. The country sells 98% of its energy share to its powerful neighbor. Experts fear that silt accumulation resulting from extensive deforestation operations along the upper eaches of the river will shorten the life of the power plant.

Clearly visible in the satellite image is the sharp boundary between heavily cultivated deforested areas and the remaining virgin rain forest, which is now protected as a national park.

Brazil · Paraguay

Landsat TM

30 m

705 km

June 25, 1987

Vegetation and Land Use Carving New Settlements from the Desert

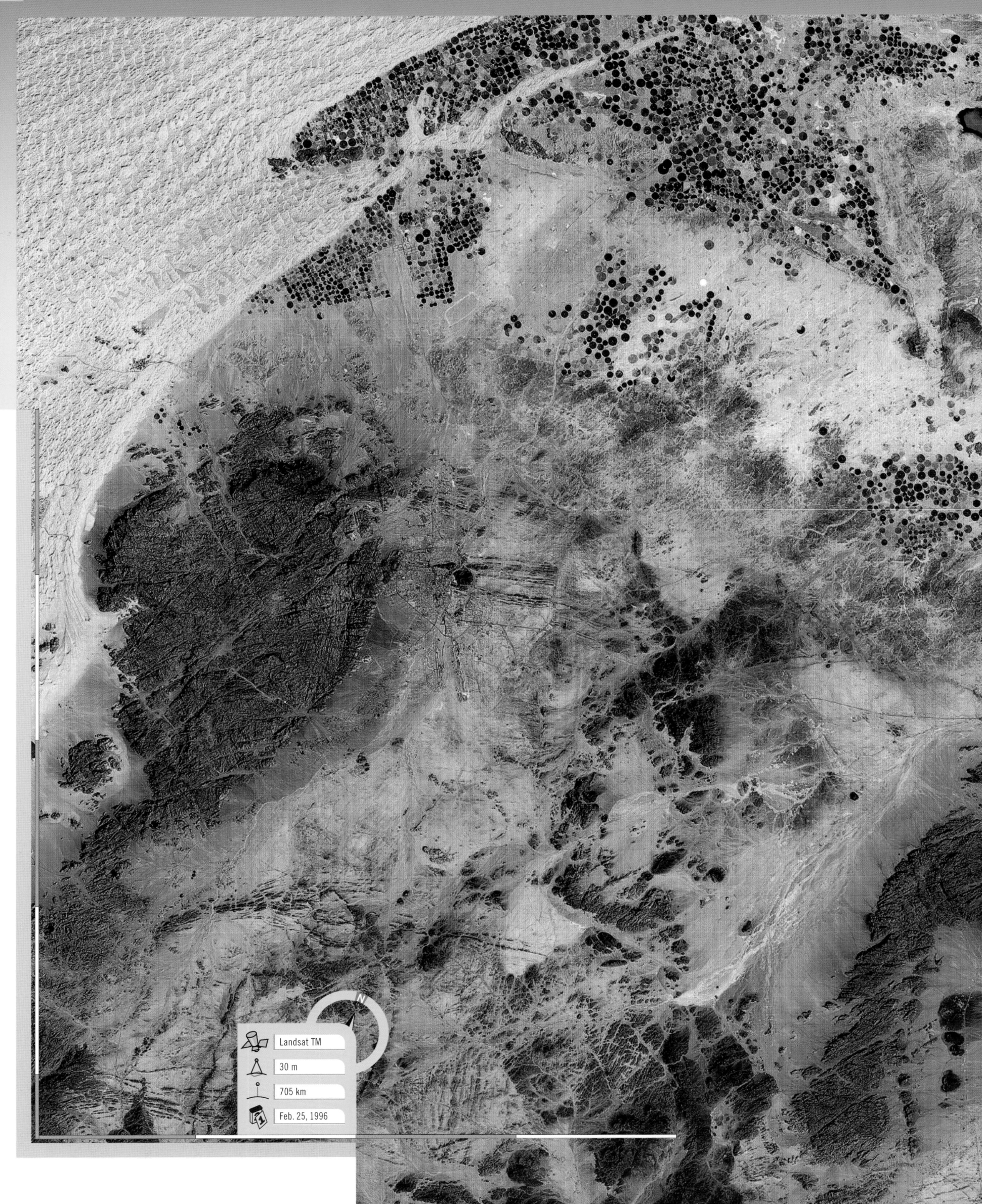

Landsat TM

30 m

705 km

Feb. 25, 1996

Saudi Arabia – Hā'il

Expansive plateaus irregularly interspersed with ranges of mountains and inselbergs characterize the topography of the Central Arabian Highlands. In the north, the crystalline highlands extend to the edge of the sand desert of An Nafūd. Circular patches are distributed like confetti over the yellow sand of the Wadi Ha'il – small areas of cultivation in the midst of the arid desert, irrigated with rotating sprinkler systems fed to a certain extent with fossil water. Conveyed by pumps and pipelines, the water is distributed for specified periods of time in fine veils of rain. This process enables farmers to fertilize their fields efficiently by adding plant nutrients to the water. Excessive irrigation creates swampy soil conditions, which make the fields difficult to tend. Evaporation rates are extremely high in the hot, arid regions of Saudi Arabia, and changing wind patterns can lead to unequal distribution of water vapor.

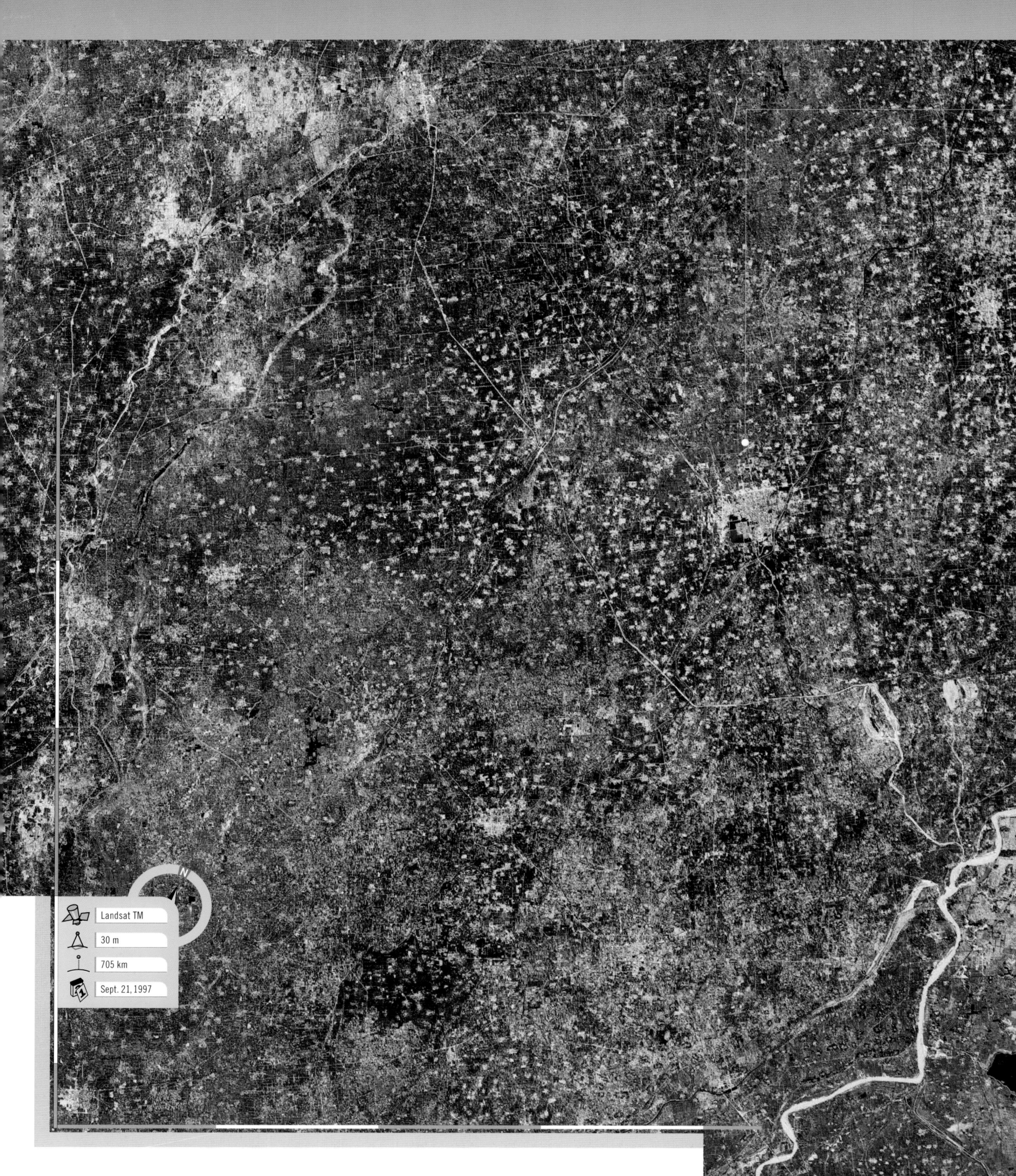

Landsat TM

30 m

705 km

Sept. 21, 1997

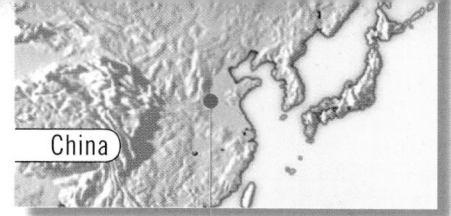

China | USA

Settlement Structure in Northern China

This satellite image shows a section of the low North China Plain, where elevations range between 5 m and 50 m above sea level. The plain was formed centuries ago by frequent flooding of the Huang River and the resulting accumulation of fertile loess deposits. Extensive river regulation measures have since greatly reduced the danger of flooding. The high fertility of the region is evident in the dense, regular pattern of small rural settlements and the intensive use of land for agriculture. The most important crops in this region of northern China are wheat, corn, soybeans, peanuts, and tobacco.

San Francisco

San Francisco is famous for its location on the northern tip of the peninsula at the entrance to San Francisco Bay. The city is bordered on the west by the Pacific Ocean, on the north by the Golden Gate Strait, on the east by San Francisco Bay, and on the south by the San Bruno Mountains. The Sacramento and San Joaquin valleys open to the Bay from the northeast. Covering an area of 120 sq. km, the city encompasses Angel, Treasure and Yerba Buena islands as well as the former island prison of Alcatraz. Central San Francisco is situated on a chain of hills with elevations of up to 285 m. Clearly visible in the image is the Golden Gate, the strait (8 km long and 3 km wide) that joins the Pacific and San Francisco Bay.

Landsat TM	
30 m	
705 km	
May 8, 1986	

Settlement Patterns

The Metropolis

Italy

Venice

Venice was built on more than 100 small islands in the Laguna Veneta north of the Po delta. The heart of the city is St. Mark's Square, situated at the southern end of the S-shaped Canal Grande. A four-kilometer-long road and railroad bridge connects Venice to the mainland.

Venetians have lived with the threat of floods and high water for centuries. Yet flooding has grown more frequent over the past fifty years, for many different reasons. The water level in the Adriatic Sea has risen by about eight centimeters during the last one hundred years, and the city itself has sunk farther into the lagoon over the past several decades as the result of groundwater depletion on the nearby mainland.

Ikonos	
1 m	
682 km	
Sept. 15, 2000	

Ikonos

1 m

682 km

Apr. 4, 1996

New York

From a colonial settlement to a modern megacity: Bordered by the Hudson, Harlem, and East rivers, the island of Manhattan is the heart of New York City.

With its many skyscrapers — concentrated heavily on the southern tip of the island and south of Central Park — Manhattan is the nation's commercial and financial hub and one of the most important cultural centers in the world. Defying the city's checkerboard street pattern, Broadway, New York's most famous thoroughfare, presents a changing face along its 20-km path from one end of the island to the other. The proportionately large "green island" of Central Park is clearly visible in the middle of Manhattan. A number of bridges connect the island with its neighboring boroughs.

Landsat TM +
Spot PAN

30 m

705 km

Aug. 14, 1993
July 7, 1993

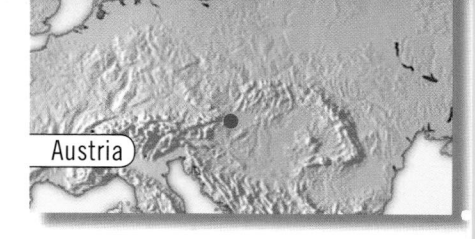

Austria

41

Vienna

Positioned favorably where the Alps descend to the Great
Hungarian Plain at a major crossroads of traditional
European trading routes from north to south, the Danube
metropolis developed from a village into a world city
within only few centuries.

The Danube, whose course has been artificially altered
twice during the past several centuries, forms the region's
natural axis. The former meanders of the Old Danube
in the northern part of the satellite image serve as important urban recreation areas today.

The New Danube, which runs parallel to the river, was
created in 1970 to prevent flooding. A by-product of this
water-regulation measure is the Danube Island, a
popular park and recreation area for the people of Vienna.

Neusiedler Lake

Despite its size – approximately 296 sq. km, including
120 sq. km of encircling reed growth, Neusiedler
Lake is neither fed nor drained by a river of significant
size. Its cloudy greenish-gray coloration is not
caused by pollution but is a sign of the presence of
billions of suspended particles that never sink
entirely to the bottom of the shallow, windswept lake.
The border between Austria and Hungary is vividly
documented in this satellite image. The landscape
in the Austrian state of Burgenland is covered by an
intricate quilt of small strip parcels indicating intensive cultivation. These stand in stark contrast to
the large block fields on the other side of the border
– remnants of the collective farms of a bygone era.

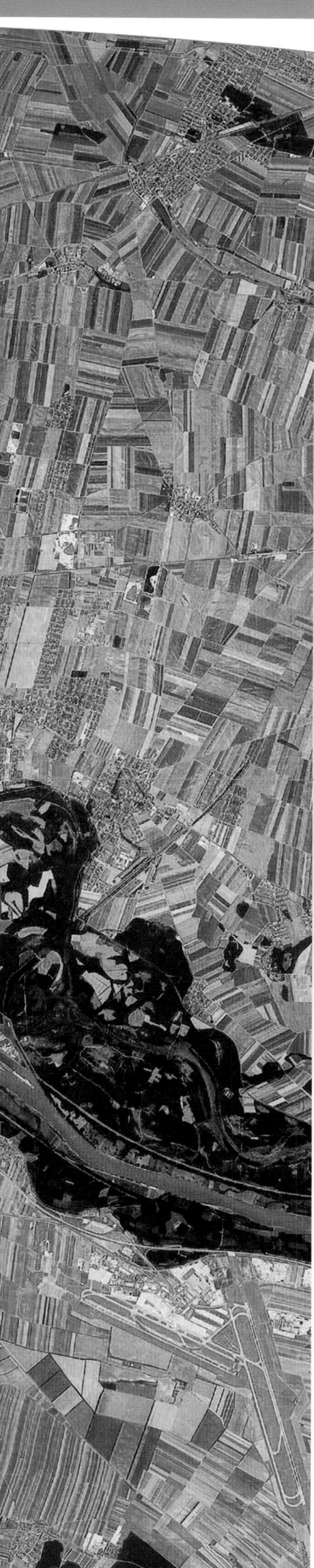

Landsat TM +
Spot PAN

30 m

705 km

Aug. 14, 1993
Aug. 10, 1992

Environmental Problems Natural Phenomena and Human Influences

Landsat TM

30 m

705 km

Sept. 9, 1989

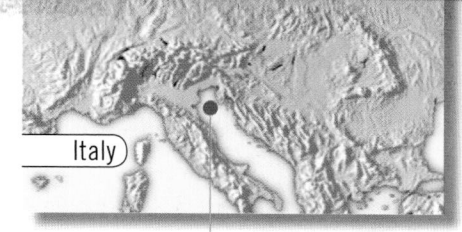
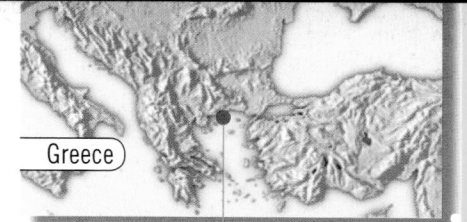
Carpet of Algae

The satellite image shows a stretch of the Italian Adriatic coastline between Chioggia in the north and Fano in the south. Particularly noticeable are the red streaks in the blue of the Adriatic Sea. Red hues indicate vegetation in the false-color image, and the streaks here represent accumulations of algae floating in the sea.

The formation of algae slime in the Mediterranean is a natural phenomenon that is intensified by long periods of good weather and placid seas. Now a common occurrence in many parts of the Mediterranean, the appearance of huge swarms of jellyfish is attributable to the influx of organic household, industrial, and agricultural waste water, which provides an abundance of nutrients for algae.

This satellite image offers impressive evidence of the expansion of the algae carpet. No other medium is capable of documenting such natural phenomena with this degree of clarity at a comparable cost.

Forest Fires on the Island of Thassos

With an area of 398 sq. km, Thassos is the second-largest island in the northern Aegean Sea and the northernmost Greek isle. The highest mountain on the rugged island is Ipsarion, which rises to an elevation of 1,203 m.

Vast areas of forest in Greece are regularly devastated by fires during the summer months. Such fires are primarily the result of dry periods that often last months at a time, although some are the work of arsonists. Disastrous forest fires on Thassos in 1985 and 1987 destroyed a large portion of the island's trees. Yet, despite the extensive damage caused by these fires, Thassos — once the most heavily forested island in Greece — has remained a green isle. The red areas visible in the southern part of the island show the regions destroyed by the fires of 1985.

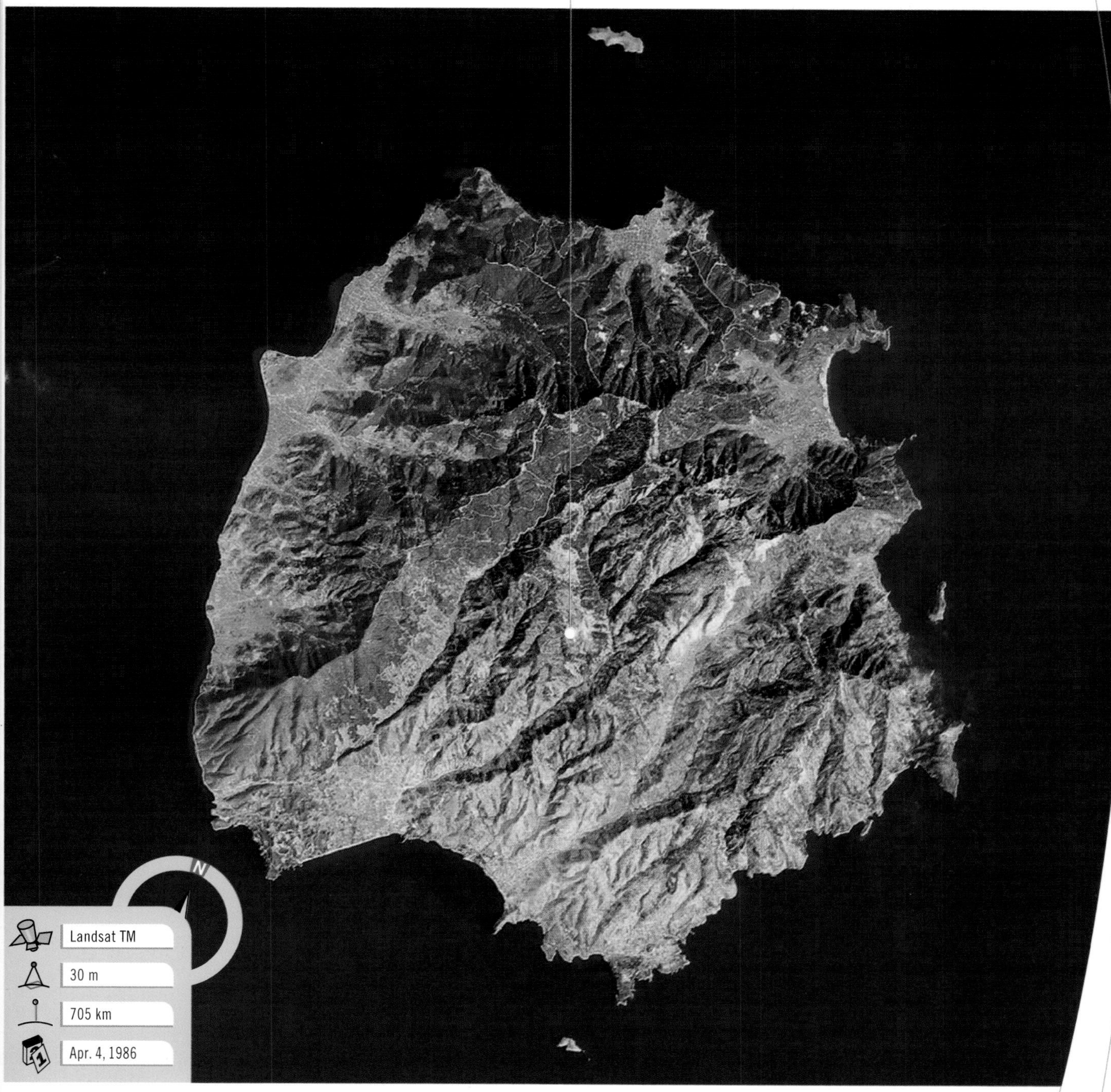

Landsat TM	
30 m	
705 km	
Apr. 4, 1986	

The Arctic

Landsat TM

30 m

705 km

Aug. 12, 1985

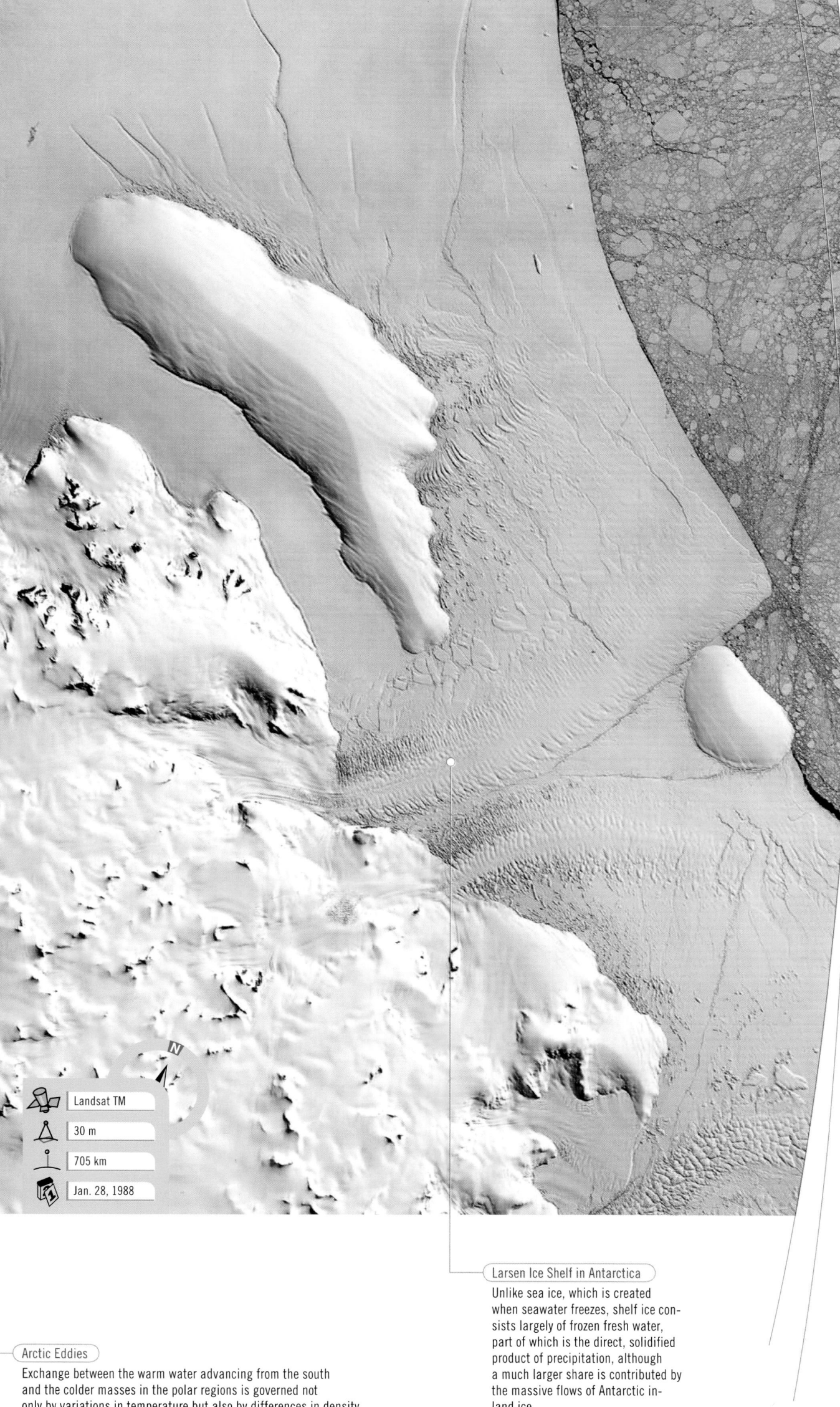

Landsat TM

30 m

705 km

Jan. 28, 1988

Larsen Ice Shelf in Antarctica

Unlike sea ice, which is created
when seawater freezes, shelf ice consists largely of frozen fresh water,
part of which is the direct, solidified
product of precipitation, although
a much larger share is contributed by
the massive flows of Antarctic inland ice.
Shelf ice reaches a thickness of up to
1,500 m at the line along which
it abuts with the Antarctic ice cap.

Arctic Eddies

Exchange between the warm water advancing from the south
and the colder masses in the polar regions is governed not
only by variations in temperature but also by differences in density
between masses of seawater with varying degrees of salinity.
The convergence of water masses with different properties – in
this case at the eastern coast of Greenland – triggers complex
interactions which in turn create marine gyres or so called eddies.

Landsat TM

30 m

705 km

Sept. 28, 1985

(The Aletsch Glacier)

The Aletsch Glacier stands out strikingly against the rugged terrain of the Bernese Alps in this satellite image. With a length of 24.1 km (measured in 1996) and a total area of nearly 87 sq. km (1975), it is both the longest and the most expansive glacier of the Alps. Known as the Great Aletsch, the main glacier flows generally southward from the junction of several other firn fields at Concordia Platz down to the Aletsch Forest.

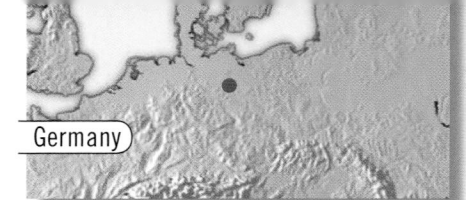
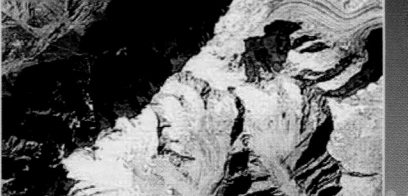

Mountains (Ancient Massifs)

(Harz)

The Harz Mountain region rises like an island above the North German Plain. A very old formation, it is also the highest central mountain range in Germany north of the Main River.

The numerous different types and formations of rock make this mountain landscape an ideal laboratory for students of geological history. Thus experts refer to the Harz as "Silverland," emphasizing its broad and fascinating geographic diversity. Although its ore deposits are now nearly depleted, the richly varied landscape, with its crystal clear mountain lakes and massifs, is an El Dorado for professional and amateur geologists alike.

Rugged, canyon-like valleys are interspersed among plateaus and heaths. Parts of the Upper Harz, including Mount Brocken, its highest peak (1,141 m), have been set aside as National Park areas.

	Landsat ETM
	30 m
	705 km
	Aug. 31, 1989

Map Section

Note: M=millions, K=thousands

Using the Map Section

The Contents and Functions of Geographic Maps

Offering a broad range of features and functions, this new Atlas of the World is not only an up-to-date reference work of superior quality but an ideal and thoroughly readable guide for virtual global exploration and armchair travel. The information provided below will help you to get the most enjoyment and benefit from its use.

Relief Maps

The relief maps of the continents – on pages 12–25 of the Map Section – provide a striking impression of the character of the entire Earth's surface, from the mountains of the continental mainlands to the depths of the ocean floor. Produced with the aid of state-of-the-art computer technology, these maps offer a vividly realistic picture of the diverse structures and forms of the global terrain.

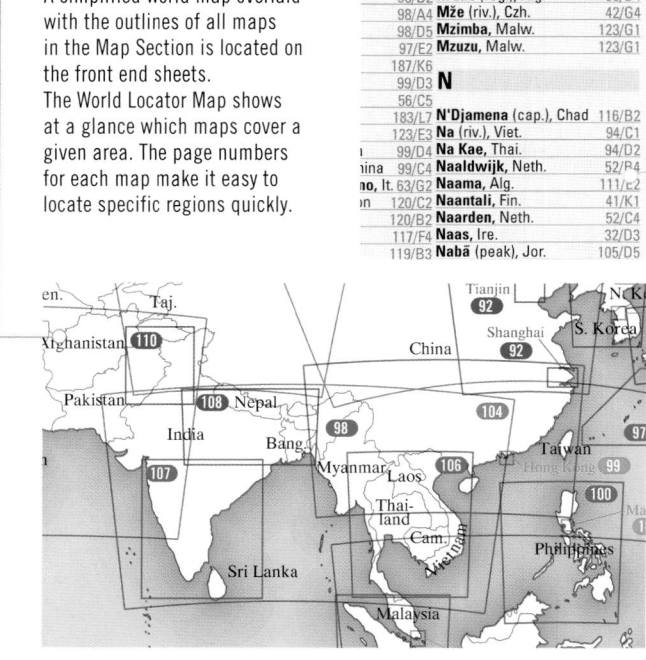

World Locator Map

A simplified world map overlaid with the outlines of all maps in the Map Section is located on the front end sheets.
The World Locator Map shows at a glance which maps cover a given area. The page numbers for each map make it easy to locate specific regions quickly.

Geographic Maps

The detailed maps of all regions of the Earth are arranged by continent. The chapters for each of the continents are introduced with a stunning satellite image and a political map. The continental maps show each country in a different color in order to facilitate recognition of political divisions.

A variety of different symbols, line patterns, surface colors, and textures highlight distinctive features such as mountains, national parks, urban areas, forests, and deserts. These maps also provide a wealth of information on roadways and canals, geographic features, and political divisions. All of the geographic maps and the complex information they contain are the product of modern computer-assisted map development and compilation techniques.

Map Frames

The map frames contain a number of graphic features that make the atlas much easier to use. The page numbers of each map are entered in the blue chapter markers at the right-hand edge of each map. An additional locator map in the upper corner shows the position of the individual map section within a larger geographic area. The blue arrows along the four edges of each map refer by page number to the adjacent map sections and thus make it easy to find neighboring areas quickly in the atlas. The letters and numerals in the red squares positioned along the frame are search coordinates used to locate places and objects listed in the map index. In addition, integrated legends and introductory texts provide basic information about the region covered by each map.

Map Scales

A map's scale describes the relationship of any length on the map to a corresponding length on the Earth's surface. A scale of 1:3,000,000 means that one cm on the map represents 3,000,000 cm (30 km) in nature. Thus a scale of 1:1,000,000 is larger than 1:3,000,000, just as 1/1 is larger than 1/3.
Most regions are shown at a scale of either 1:3,000,000 or 1:6,000,000. Areas of particular interest are shown at 1:1,000,000. Selected densely populated areas are covered by maps with a larger scale. Whole continents and large regions are shown at a smaller scale.

Boundary and Name Policies

The atlas shows the internationally recognized national boundaries. Boundary disputes, armistice lines, and de facto boundaries are indicated by special symbols where appropriate. Generally, the names of places and geographic objects appear in the language of the respective country. Accepted conventional names are used for certain major foreign places names. Name usage also tends to vary depending upon cultural factors, however, and is subject to change over time, not least of all for political reasons. In several cases where, for example, a new name has not gained universal acceptance or the use of a traditional name persists, a second name has been entered in parentheses. Thus the selection of names is not entirely systematic and reflects important aspects of common usage.

Index to the Map Section

The index facilitates the search for a specific place in the atlas. It contains an alphabetical list of more than 110,000 names of places and geographic objects entered in the maps. The page numbers and coordinates listed for each index entry show the location of the desired place or object in the map corresponding coordinate grid. A list of the abbreviations used in the index is found on the first index page.

Map Components

A brief text provides information about the geography, history, economy, or culture of the area shown on the map.

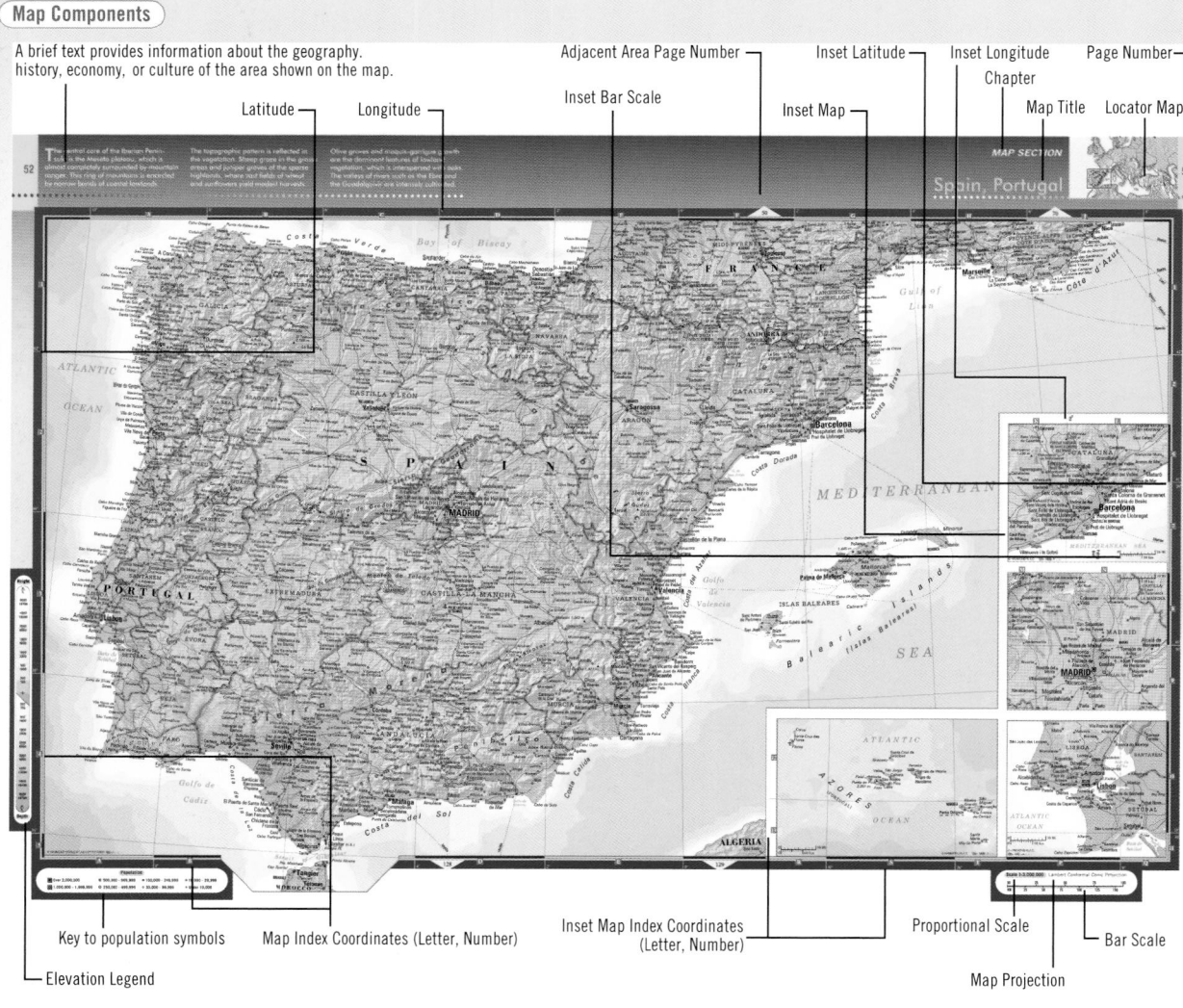

Adjacent Area Page Number — Inset Latitude — Inset Longitude — Page Number — Chapter — Map Title — Locator Map — Inset Bar Scale — Inset Map — Latitude — Longitude

Key to population symbols — Map Index Coordinates (Letter, Number) — Inset Map Index Coordinates (Letter, Number) — Proportional Scale — Bar Scale — Elevation Legend — Map Projection

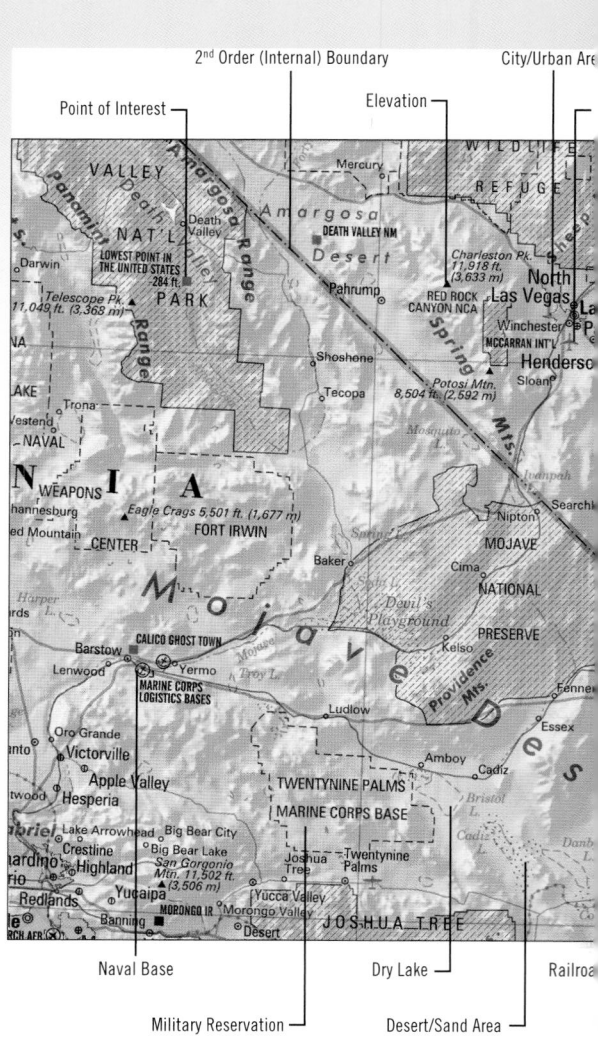

2nd Order (Internal) Boundary — City/Urban Area — Point of Interest — Elevation — Naval Base — Dry Lake — Railroad — Military Reservation — Desert/Sand Area

Map type faces

The use of different type faces helps the reader distinguish between types of map content.

Major Political Arenas
LUXEMBOURG

Internal Political Divisions
SAXONY-ANHALT

Historical Regions
Polabská Nížina

Cities and Towns
Norfolk Sumter Smyrna

Neighborhoods
BIGGIN HILL

Points of Interest
MISSION SAN BUENAVENTURA

Water Features
L. Elsinore

Capes, Points, Peaks, Passes
Cape Horn...Pt. La Jolla
Mt. Rainier

Islands, Peninsulas
Cape Breton I.

Mountain Ranges, Plateaus, Hills
Serra do Norte

Deserts, Plains, Valleys
San Fernando Valley

The spelling of geographic names conforms to the rules of the respective official language of each country. Where the official language is written in Latin characters, local spellings, including diacritical marks and modified letters, have been used. For countries with languages written in non-Latin characters, such as China, Russia or the Arabic-speaking countries, an international standard form is used, which may deviate in some cases from conventional American usage.

Symbols used on Maps of the World

First Order (National) Boundary
Demarcated Land Boundary
Demarcated Water Boundary
Disputed Boundary
Armistice Boundary
De Facto Boundary
Undefined

Second Order (Internal) Boundary
Land/Administrative District Boundary
Water Boundary

Third Order (Internal) Boundary
Land/Administrative District Boundary
Water Boundary

Cities and Towns
Stockholm First Order (National) Capital
Salt Lake City Second Order (Internal) Capital
Manchester Third Order (Internal) Capital
Towns
City District/Neighborhood
City and Urban Area Limits

Transportation
International Airport
Airport
Highways/Roads
Railroads
Ferries
Tunnels (Road, Railroad)

Drainage Features
Shoreline, River
Intermittend River
Canal
Lake, Reservoir
Intermittent Lake
Dry Lake
Salt Pan
Swamp/Marsh

Other Physical Features
▲ Elevation
⌒ Pass
● Falls
✳ Rapids
Desert/Sand Area
Lava Flow
Glacier/Ice Shelf

Cultural Features
Archeological Sites, Ruins
Dam
Park
Wildlife Area
Point of Interest
Well
Air Base
Naval Base
International Date Line

Ancient Walls
Native Reservation/Reserve
Military/Government Reservation
State Park/Recreation Area
National Park/Forest/Recreation/Wildlife Area

Elevation Legend
Height

| m./ft. |
| 6000 / 19700 |
| 4000 / 13000 |
| 2000 / 6500 |
| 1500 / 5000 |
| 1000 / 3300 |
| 500 / 1600 |
| 200 / 700 |
| 0 |
| 200 / 700 |
| 500 / 1600 |
| 1000 / 3300 |
| 2000 / 6500 |
| 3000 / 9800 |
| 4000 / 13000 |
| 5000 / 16400 |
| 6000 / 19700 |
| m./ft. |
Depth

The color tints in this bar represent both elevation of land areas and depth of the oceans. The changes between colors are labeled in meters and feet. Selective shading for the land areas highlights those regions with significant relief variations. The legend is entered next to each individual map.

Abbreviations used in the maps

Abor. Rsv.	Aboriginal Reserve	Fk.	Fork	NB	National Battlefield	PN	Park National
Admin.	Administration	For.	Forest	NBP	National Battlefield Park	Prom.	Promontory
AFB	Air Force Base	Ft.	Fort	NCA	National Conservation	Prsv.	Preserve
Amm. Dep.	Ammunition Depot	G.	Gulf		Area	Pt.	Point
Arch.	Archipelago	Govt.	Government	NHP	National Historical Park	R.	River
Aut.	Autonomous	Gd.	Grand	NHS	National Historic Site	Rec.	Recreation(al)
B.	Bay	Gt.	Great	NL	National Lakeshore	Ref.	Refuge
Bfld.	Battlefield	Har.	Harbor	NM	National Monument	Reg.	Region
Bk.	Brook	Hist.	Historic(al)	NMEM	National Memorial	Rep.	Republic
Br.	Branch	Hts.	Heights	NMILP	National Military Park	Res.	Reservoir, Reservation
C.	Cape	I., Is.	Island(s)	No.	Northern	Sa.	Sierra
Can.	Canal	Ind. Res.	Indian Reservation	NP	National Park	Sd.	Sound
Cap.	Capital	Int'l	International	NPP	National Park and	So.	Southern
C.G.	Coast Guard	IR	Indian Reservation		Preserve	SP	State Park
Chan.	Channel	Isth.	Isthmus	NPRSV	National Preserve	Spr., Sprgs.	Spring, Springs
Co.	County	Jct.	Junction	NRA	National Recreation Area	St.	State
Consv.	Conservation	L.	Lake	NRIV	National River	Sta.	Station
Cord.	Cordillera	Lag.	Lagoon	NRSV	National Reserve	Stm.	Stream
Cr.	Creek	Mem.	Memorial	NS	National Seashore	Str.	Strait
Ctr.	Center	Mil.	Military	NWR	National Wildlife Refuge	Terr.	Territory
Dep.	Depot	Mon.	Monument	Obl.	Oblast	Tun.	Tunnel
Depr.	Depression	Mt.	Mount	Occ.	Occupied	Twp.	Township
Des.	Desert	Mtn.	Mountain	Okr.	Okrug	UNDOF	United Nations
Dist.	District	Mts.	Mountains	Passg.	Passage		Disengagement Observer
DMZ	Demilitarized Zone	Nat.	Natural	Pen.	Peninsula		Force
Est.	Estuary	Nat'l	National	Pk.	Peak	Val.	Valley
Fed.	Federal	Nav.	Naval	Plat.	Plateau	Vill.	Village

Lake   National Park Area
Airport   Native Reservation   River
Native Reservation   Other Road
Canal   Intermittent River   Principal Highway

Quick Reference Guide

This concise alphabetical reference lists continents, countries, states, territories, possessions and other major geographical areas, including the size, population and capital or chief town of each. Blue page numbers and blue alpha-numeric reference keys (which refer to the grid squares of latitude and longitude on each map) are visible at a glance. The population figures are the latest and most reliable figures obtainable.

Place	Square Miles*	Square Kilometers*	Population	Capital or Chief Town	Page/Index
A					
Afghanistan	250,000	647,500	31,889,923	Kabul	113/H 2
Africa	11,701,147	30,306,000	935,813,000	....	157
Alabama, U.S.	52,237	135,293	4,447,100	Montgomery	173/J 5
Alaska, U.S.	615,230	1,593,444	626,932	Juneau	201
Albania	11,100	28,749	3,600,523	Tiranë	55/F 2
Alberta, Canada	255,285	661,185	3,290,350	Edmonton	170/E 3
Algeria	919,591	2,381,740	33,333,216	Algiers	129/F 3
American Samoa	77	199	57,663	Pago Pago	161/T10
Andorra	174	450	71,822	Andorra la Vella	53/F 1
Angola	481,351	1,246,700	12,263,596	Luanda	119/D 6
Anguilla, U.K.	35	91	13,677	The Valley	203/N 8
Antarctica	5,500,000	14,245,000	....		228
Antigua and Barbuda	170	440	69,481	St. John's	203/N 8
Argentina	1,068,296	2,766,890	40,301,927	Buenos Aires	209/C 6
Arizona, U.S.	114,006	295,276	5,130,632	Phoenix	179/F 3
Arkansas, U.S.	53,182	137,742	2,673,400	Little Rock	173/H 4
Armenia	11,506	29,800	2,971,650	Yerevan	77/H 5
Aruba, Netherlands	75	193	72,194	Oranjestad	216/D 1
Ascension Island, St. Helena	34	88	1,117	Georgetown	26/J 6
Asia	17,159,867	44,444,100	4,004,788,000	....	115
Australia	2,967,893	7,686,850	20,434,176	Canberra	145
Australian Capital Territory	938	2,430	280,132	Canberra	156/D 2
Austria	32,375	83,851	8,199,783	Vienna	51/L 3
Azerbaijan	33,436	86,600	8,120,247	Baku	77/H 4
Azores, Portugal	902	2,335	241,762	Ponta Delgada	53/R12
B					
Bahamas, The	5,382	13,939	305,655	Nassau	203/F 2
Bahrain	240	622	708,573	Manama	112/F 3
Balearic Islands, Spain	1,936	5,014	841,669	Palma	53/F 3
Bangladesh	55,598	144,000	150,448,339	Dhaka	109/G 4
Barbados	166	430	280,946	Bridgetown	203/P 8
Belarus	80,154	207,600	9,724,723	Minsk	29/G 3
Belgium	11,780	30,510	10,392,226	Brussels	48/C 3
Belize	8,865	22,960	294,385	Belmopan	206/D 2
Benin	43,483	112,620	8,078,314	Porto-Novo	133/F 4
Bermuda, U.K.	19	50	66,163	Hamilton	163/L 6
Bhutan	18,147	47,000	2,327,849	Thimphu	109/G 2
Bolivia	424,163	1,098,582	9,119,152	La Paz; Sucre	209/C 4
Bosnia & Herzegovina	19,781	51,233	4,552,198	Sarajevo	56/C 3
Botswana	231,803	600,370	1,639,131	Gaborone	119/E 7
Brazil	3,286,470	8,511,965	190,010,647	Brasília	209/D 3
British Columbia, Canada	365,946	947,800	4,113,487	Victoria	170/D 3
British Virgin Islands	59	153	23,098	Road Town	203/M7
Brunei	2,228	5,770	386,511	Bandar Seri Begawan	100/A 4
Bulgaria	42,823	110,912	7,322,858	Sofia	57/G 4
Burkina Faso	105,869	274,200	14,326,203	Ouagadougou	171/E 3
Burundi	10,745	27,830	8,390,505	Bujumbura	139/G 3
C					
California, U.S.	158,869	411,470	33,871,648	Sacramento	172/C 4
Cambodia	69,900	181,040	14,131,858	Phnom Penh	106/D 3
Cameroon	183,568	475,441	18,060,382	Yaoundé	119/D 4
Canada	3,851,787	9,976,139	33,390,141	Ottawa	170
Canary Islands, Spain	2,808	7,273	1,694,477	Las Palmas; Santa Cruz	128/A 3
Cape Verde	1,556	4,030	423,613	Praia	119/J 9
Cayman Islands, U.K.	100	259	46,600	George Town	207/F 2
Celebes, Indonesia	72,986	189,034	14,946,488	Ujung Pandang	103/E 4
Central African Republic	240,533	622,980	4,369,038	Bangui	134/C 4
Chad	495,752	1,283,998	10,238,807	N'Djamena	119/D 3
Channel Islands, U.K.	75	194	150,000	St. Helier; St. Peter Port	62/C 2
Chile	292,258	756,950	16,284,741	Santiago	209/B 6
China, People's Rep. of	3,705,386	9,596,960	1,321,851,888	Beijing	83/J 6
Christmas Island, Australia	52	135	1,520	The Settlement	27/Q 6
Cocos (Keeling) Islands, Australia	5.4	14	628	West Island	27/P 6
Colombia	439,733	1,138,910	44,227,550	Bogotá	216/C 4
Colorado, U.S.	104,100	269,618	4,301,261	Denver	172/E 4
Comoros	838	2,170	710,960	Moroni	143/G 5
Congo, Dem. Rep. of the	905,563	2,345,410	64,606,759	Kinshasa	119/E 5
Congo, Rep. of the	132,046	342,000	3,800,610	Brazzaville	138/C 3
Connecticut, U.S.	5,544	14,358	3,405,565	Hartford	191/K 4
Cook Islands, New Zealand	93	240	21,750	Avarua	161/J 6
Corsica, France	3,352	8,682	260,196	Ajaccio	54/A 1
Costa Rica	19,730	51,100	4,133,884	San José	207/F 4
Côte d'Ivoire	124,502	322,460	18,013,409	Yamoussoukro	132/D 5
Croatia	22,050	56,538	4,493,312	Zagreb	56/C 3
Cuba	42,803	110,860	11,416,987	Havana	207/F 1
Curaçao, Neth. Antilles	172	445	130,627	Willemstad	203/H 5
Cyprus	3,571	9,250	788,457	Nicosia	116/C 2
Czech Republic	30,387	78,703	10,228,744	Prague	49/H 4
D					
Delaware, U.S.	2,396	6,206	783,600	Dover	173/L 4
Denmark	16,629	43,069	5,468,120	Copenhagen	46/C 4
District of Columbia, U.S.	68	177	572,059	Washington	198/B 6
Djibouti	8,494	22,000	496,374	Djibouti	136/B 2
Dominica	290	751	68,925	Roseau	203/N 8
Dominican Republic	18,815	48,730	9,365,818	Santo Domingo	203/H 4
E					
East Timor	5,743	14,874	1,084,971	Dili	152/B 2
Eastern Cape, South Africa	65,858	170,616	6,436,763	Bisho	142/D 3
Ecuador	109,483	283,561	13,755,680	Quito	209/B 3
Egypt	386,659	1,001,447	80,264,543	Cairo	127/F 3
El Salvador	8,124	21,040	6,939,688	San Salvador	206/D 3
England, U.K.	50,356	130,423	49,138,831	London	37/K10
Equatorial Guinea	10,831	28,052	551,201	Malabo	138/B 2
Eritrea	46,842	121,320	4,906,585	Asmara	119/F 3
Estonia	17,413	45,100	1,315,912	Tallinn	47/L 2
Ethiopia	435,184	1,127,127	76,511,887	Addis Ababa	119/F 4
Europe	4,066,019	10,531,000	727,228,000	....	61

Place	Square Miles*	Square Kilometers*	Population	Capital or Chief Town	Page/Index
F					
Falkland Islands & Dependencies, U.K.	4,699	12,170	2,967	Stanley	227/M 8
Faroe Islands, Denmark	540	1,399	47,511	Tórshavn	29/D 2
Fiji	7,055	18,272	918,675	Suva	161/Y17
Finland	130,128	337,032	5,238,460	Helsinki	44/H 2
Florida, U.S.	59,928	155,214	15,982,378	Tallahassee	195/F 4
France	211,208	547,030	61,083,916	Paris	50/D 3
Free State, South Africa	49,963	129,437	2,706,775	Bloemfontein	142/D 3
French Guiana	35,135	91,000	203,321	Cayenne	218/C 2
French Polynesia	1,522	3,941	278,633	Papeete	161/W15
G					
Gabon	103,347	267,670	1,454,867	Libreville	138/B 3
Gambia, The	4,363	11,300	1,688,359	Banjul	132/B 3
Gauteng, South Africa	7,241	18,760	8,837,178	Johannesburg	142/Q12
Gaza Strip	139	360	1,482,405	Gaza	116/C 4
Georgia	26,911	69,700	4,646,003	T'bilisi	77/G 4
Georgia, U.S.	58,977	152,750	8,186,453	Atlanta	173/K 5
Germany	137,803	356,910	82,400,996	Berlin	48/E 3
Ghana	92,100	238,540	22,931,299	Accra	133/E 4
Gibraltar, U.K.	2.5	6.5	27,967	Gibraltar	52/C 4
Greece	50,942	131,940	10,706,290	Athens	55/G 3
Greenland, Denmark	840,000	2,175,600	56,344	Nuuk (Godthåb)	163/N 2
Grenada	131	340	89,971	St. George's	203/N 7
Guadeloupe & Dependencies, France	687	1,779	456,698	Basse-Terre	203/N 7
Guam, U.S.	209	541	173,456	Agaña	160/D 3
Guatemala	42,042	108,889	12,728,111	Guatemala	206/D 3
Guinea	94,927	245,860	9,947,814	Conakry	132/C 4
Guinea-Bissau	13,946	36,120	1,472,041	Bissau	132/B 3
Guyana	83,000	214,970	769,095	Georgetown	217/G 3
H					
Haiti	10,714	27,750	8,706,497	Port-au-Prince	207/H 2
Hawaii, U.S.	6,459	16,729	1,211,537	Honolulu	172/S10
Heard & McDonald Islands, Australia	159	412	....		228/E 7
Honduras	43,277	112,087	7,483,763	Tegucigalpa	206/E 3
Hong Kong, China	402	1,040	6,980,412	Victoria	99/G 4
Howland Island, U.S.	0.6	1.6	....		161/H 4
Hungary	35,919	93,030	9,956,108	Budapest	56/D 2
I					
Iceland	39,768	103,000	301,931	Reykjavík	44/N 7
Idaho, U.S.	83,574	216,456	1,293,953	Boise	172/C 3
Illinois, U.S.	57,918	150,007	12,419,293	Springfield	173/J 4
India	1,269,339	3,287,588	1,129,866,154	New Delhi	104/C 3
Indiana, U.S.	36,420	94,328	6,080,485	Indianapolis	173/J 4
Indonesia	741,096	1,919,440	245,452,739	Jakarta	103/E 4
Iowa, U.S.	56,275	145,752	2,926,324	Des Moines	185/G 2
Iran	636,293	1,648,000	65,397,521	Tehran	115/H 3
Iraq	168,753	437,072	27,499,638	Baghdad	114/E 3
Ireland	27,136	70,282	4,109,086	Dublin	37/G10
Isle of Man, U.K.	227	588	75,831	Douglas	40/C 3
Israel	8,019	20,770	6,426,679	Jerusalem	116/C 3
Italy	116,305	301,230	58,147,733	Rome	73/F 2
J					
Jamaica	4,243	10,990	2,780,132	Kingston	207/G 2
Jan Mayen, Norway	144	373	....		29/D 1
Japan	145,882	377,835	127,467,972	Tokyo	91/M 4
Java, Indonesia	48,842	126,500	121,352,608	Jakarta	101/E 4
Johnston Atoll, U.S.	1	2.8	....		161/J 3
Jordan	34,445	89,213	6,053,193	Amman	116/D 4
K					
Kansas, U.S.	82,282	213,110	2,688,418	Topeka	173/G 4
Kazakhstan	1,049,150	2,717,300	15,284,929	Aqmola	80/G 5
Kentucky, U.S.	40,411	104,665	4,041,769	Frankfort	192/E 2
Kenya	224,960	582,646	36,913,721	Nairobi	119/F 4
Kermadec Islands, New Zealand	13	33	....		160/G 8
Kiribati	277	717	107,817	Tarawa	160/H 5
Korea, North	46,540	120,539	23,301,725	P'yŏngyang	93/D 2
Korea, South	38,023	98,480	49,044,790	Seoul	93/D 4
Kuwait	6,880	17,820	2,505,559	Kuwait	115/F 4
KwaZulu Natal, South Africa	35,312	91,481	9,426,017	Pietermaritzburg	143/E 3
Kyrgyzstan	76,641	198,500	5,284,149	Bishkek	111/B 3
L					
Laos	91,428	236,800	6,521,998	Vientiane	106/C 2
Latvia	24,749	64,100	2,259,810	Riga	47/L 3
Lebanon	4,015	10,399	3,921,278	Beirut	116/D 3
Lesotho	11,718	30,350	2,012,649	Maseru	142/D 3
Liberia	43,000	111,370	3,193,942	Monrovia	132/C 5
Libya	679,358	1,759,537	6,036,914	Tripoli	126/C 2
Liechtenstein	62	160	34,247	Vaduz	67/F 3
Limpopo, South Africa	46,168	119,606	5,273,642	Pietersburg	141/F 4
Lithuania	25,174	65,200	3,575,439	Vilnius	47/K 4
Louisiana, U.S.	49,651	128,595	4,468,976	Baton Rouge	173/H 5
Luxembourg	999	2,587	480,222	Luxembourg	61/E 4
M					
Macau, China	6	16	456,989	Macau	99/G 4
Macedonia (F.Y.R.O.M.)	9,781	25,333	2,055,915	Skopje	55/G 2
Madagascar	226,657	587,041	19,448,815	Antananarivo	143/H 8
Madeira Islands, Portugal	307	794	245,012	Funchal	128/A 2
Maine, U.S.	33,741	87,388	1,274,923	Augusta	188/B 3
Malawi	45,745	118,480	13,603,181	Lilongwe	119/F 6
Malaya, Malaysia	50,806	131,588	18,523,632	Kuala Lumpur	101/C 1
Malaysia	127,316	329,750	24,821,286	Kuala Lumpur	102/C 2
Maldives	116	300	369,031	Male	83/F 9
Mali	478,764	1,240,000	11,626,219	Bamako	119/B 3
Malta	124	320	401,880	Valletta	54/L 7
Manitoba, Canada	250,946	649,951	1,148,401	Winnipeg	170/G 3
Marquesas Islands, French Polynesia	405	1,049	8,064	Atuona	161/M 5

*Includes land and water

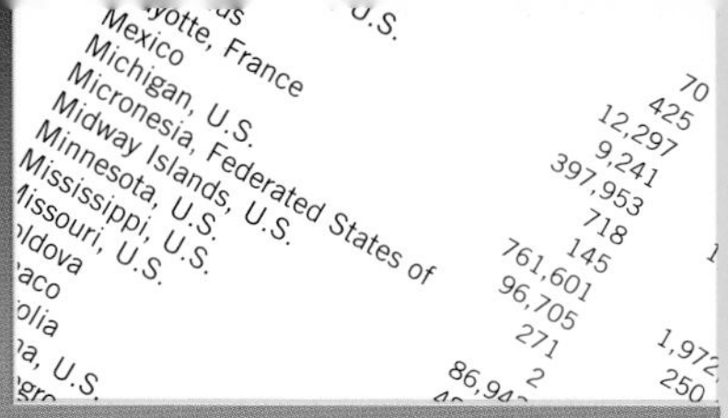

Place	Square Miles*	Square Kilometers*	Population	Capital or Chief Town	Page/ Index
Marshall Islands	70	181	61,782	Majuro	160/G 3
Martinique, France	425	1,100	439,202	Fort-de-France	203/N 8
Maryland, U.S.	12,297	31,849	5,296,486	Annapolis	173/L 4
Massachusetts, U.S.	9,241	23,934	6,349,097	Boston	173/M 3
Mauritania	397,953	1,030,700	3,270,065	Nouakchott	119/A 3
Mauritius	718	1,860	1,250,882	Port Louis	143/T15
Mayotte, France	145	375	208,807	Mamoutzou	143/H 6
Mexico	761,601	1,972,546	108,700,891	Mexico	163/G 7
Michigan, U.S.	96,705	250,465	9,938,444	Lansing	173/J 2
Micronesia, Federated States of	271	702	107,862	Palikir	160/D 4
Midway Islands, U.S.	2	5.2	40	....	160/H 2
Minnesota, U.S.	86,943	225,182	4,919,479	St. Paul	173/G 2
Mississippi, U.S.	48,286	125,060	2,844,658	Jackson	173/H 5
Missouri, U.S.	69,709	180,546	5,595,211	Jefferson City	143/H 4
Moldova	13,012	33,700	4,320,490	Chişinău	78/E 4
Monaco	0.7	1.9	32,671	....	68/J 8
Mongolia	606,163	1,569,962	2,874,127	Ulaanbaatar	90/D 2
Montana, U.S.	147,046	380,849	902,195	Helena	172/D 2
Montenegro	5,333	13,812	684,736	Podgorica	56/D 4
Montserrat, U.K.	39	100	9,538	Plymouth	203/N 7
Morocco	172,414	446,550	33,757,175	Rabat	128/D 2
Mozambique	309,494	801,590	20,905,585	Maputo	141/G 3
Mpumalanga, South Africa	31,581	81,816	3,122,990	Nelspruit	143/E 2
Myanmar (Burma)	261,969	678,500	47,373,958	Yangon; Nay Pyi Taw	105/G 2
N					
Namibia	318,694	825,418	2,055,080	Windhoek	119/D 7
Nauru	8	21	13,528	Yaren (district)	160/F 5
Nebraska, U.S.	77,358	200,358	1,711,263	Lincoln	184/D 3
Nepal	54,363	140,800	28,901,790	Kathmandu	108/D 1
Netherlands	14,413	37,330	16,570,613	The Hague; Amsterdam	58/B 5
Netherlands Antilles	371	960	223,472	Willemstad	216/D 1
Nevada, U.S.	110,567	286,367	1,998,257	Carson City	172/C 4
New Brunswick, Canada	28,355	73,440	729,997	Fredericton	188/D 2
New Caledonia & Dependencies, France	7,359	19,060	221,943	Nouméa	161/U11
Newfoundland & Labrador, Canada	156,649	405,721	505,469	St. John's	171/K 3
New Hampshire, U.S.	9,283	24,044	1,235,786	Concord	191/L 3
New Jersey, U.S.	8,215	21,277	8,414,350	Trenton	198/D 3
New Mexico, U.S.	121,598	314,939	1,819,046	Santa Fe	172/E 5
New South Wales, Australia	309,498	801,600	5,731,906	Sydney	156/C 1
New York, U.S.	53,989	139,833	18,976,457	Albany	191/J 3
New Zealand	103,736	268,676	4,115,771	Wellington	191
Nicaragua	49,998	129,494	5,675,356	Managua	207/E 3
Niger	489,189	1,267,000	12,894,865	Niamey	119/C 3
Nigeria	356,668	923,770	135,031,164	Abuja	119/C 4
Niue, New Zealand	100	259	2,166	Alofi	161/J 7
Norfolk Island, Australia	13.4	34.6	1,470	Kingston	160/F 7
North America	9,355,975	24,232,000	523,686,000	....	195
North Carolina, U.S.	52,672	136,421	8,049,313	Raleigh	193/G 3
North Dakota, U.S.	70,704	183,123	642,200	Bismarck	186/D 4
Northern Cape, South Africa	140,268	363,389	822,727	Kimberley	142/C 3
Northern Ireland, U.K.	5,459	14,138	1,685,267	Belfast	37/H 9
Northern Marianas, U.S.	184	477	84,546	Saipan	160/D 3
Northern Territory, Australia	519,784	1,346,241	175,876	Darwin	145/C 2
North Korea	46,540	120,539	23,301,725	P'yŏngyang	93/D 2
North-West, South Africa	45,347	117,450	3,669,349	Mmabatho	142/D 2
Northwest Territories, Canada	589,315	1,526,328	41,464	Yellowknife	170/E 2
Norway	125,181	324,220	4,627,926	Oslo	44/C 3
Nova Scotia, Canada	21,425	55,491	913,462	Halifax	188/E 3
Nunavut, Canada	733,590	1,900,000	29,474	Iqaluit	171/K 2
O					
Oceania	3,292,000	8,526,280	33,515,000	....	192
Ohio, U.S.	44,828	116,103	11,353,140	Columbus	173/K 3
Oklahoma, U.S.	69,903	181,048	3,450,654	Oklahoma City	183/E 3
Oman	82,031	212,460	3,204,897	Muscat	113/G 4
Ontario, Canada	412,580	1,068,582	12,160,282	Toronto	170/H 3
Oregon, U.S.	97,132	251,571	3,421,399	Salem	172/B 3
Orkney Islands, Scotland	376	974	19,210	Kirkwall	37/N13
P					
Pakistan	310,403	803,944	169,270,617	Islamabad	113/H 3
Palau	177	458	20,842	Koror	160/C 4
Panama	30,193	78,200	3,242,173	Panamá	207/F 4
Papua New Guinea	178,259	461,690	5,795,887	Port Moresby	160/D 5
Paraguay	157,047	406,752	6,667,147	Asunción	224/D 2
Pennsylvania, U.S.	46,058	119,291	12,281,054	Harrisburg	191/G 4
Peru	496,223	1,285,220	28,674,757	Lima	220/C 3
Philippines	115,830	300,000	91,077,287	Manila	132
Pitcairn Islands, U.K.	18	47	45	Adamstown	161/N 7
Poland	120,725	312,678	38,518,241	Warsaw	49/K 2
Portugal	35,552	92,080	10,642,836	Lisbon	52/A 3
Prince Edward Island, Canada	2,184	5,657	135,851	Charlottetown	188/F 2
Puerto Rico, U.S.	3,508	9,085	3,944,259	San Juan	203/M7
Q					
Qatar	4,247	11,000	907,229	Doha	112/F 3
Québec, Canada	594,857	1,540,680	7,546,131	Québec	171/J 3
Queensland, Australia	666,872	1,727,200	2,977,813	Brisbane	158/A 3
R					
Réunion, France	969	2,510	798,094	St-Denis	143/R15
Rhode Island, U.S.	1,231	3,189	1,048,319	Providence	191/L 4
Romania	91,699	237,500	22,276,056	Bucharest	57/F 3
Russia	6,592,735	17,075,200	141,377,752	Moscow	80/H 3
Rwanda	10,169	26,337	9,907,509	Kigali	139/G 3
S					
Sabah, Malaysia	28,460	73,711	2,603,485	Kota Kinabalu	103/E 2
Saint Helena & Dependencies, U.K.	158	410	7,543	Jamestown	26/J 6
Saint Kitts and Nevis	104	269	39,349	Basseterre	203/N 7
Saint Lucia	239	620	170,649	Castries	203/N 8
Saint Pierre & Miquelon, France	93.5	242	7,036	Saint-Pierre	189/J 2

Place	Square Miles*	Square Kilometers*	Population	Capital or Chief Town	Page/ Index
Saint Vincent & the Grenadines	131	340	118,149	Kingstown	203/N 8
Sakhalin, Russia	29,500	76,405	632,000	Yuzhno-Sakhalinsk	81/Q 4
Samoa	1,104	2,860	176,615	Apia	161/R 9
San Marino	23.4	60.6	29,615	San Marino	69/F 5
São Tomé and Príncipe	371	960	199,579	São Tomé	138/A 2
Sarawak, Malaysia	48,050	124,449	2,071,506	Kuching	102/D 3
Sardinia, Italy	9,301	24,090	1,631,880	Cagliari	54/A 2
Saskatchewan, Canada	251,865	652,330	968,157	Regina	170/F 3
Saudi Arabia	756,981	1,960,582	27,601,038	Riyadh	112/D 4
Scotland, U.K.	30,414	78,772	5,062,011	Edinburgh	37/J 8
Senegal	75,749	196,190	12,521,851	Dakar	132/B 3
Serbia	34,185	88,538	10,150,265	Belgrade	56/E 3
Seychelles	176	455	81,895	Victoria	27/M6
Shetland Islands, Scotland	552	1,430	21,940	Lerwick	37/N12
Sicily, Italy	9,926	25,708	4,968,991	Palermo	54/C 3
Sierra Leone	27,699	71,740	6,144,562	Freetown	132/B 4
Singapore	244	632.6	4,553,009	Singapore	101/H 6
Slovakia	18,859	48,845	5,447,502	Bratislava	49/K 4
Slovenia	7,836	20,296	2,009,245	Ljubljana	56/B 3
Society Islands, French Polynesia	677	1,753	117,703	Papeete	161/K 6
Solomon Islands	10,985	28,450	566,842	Honiara	160/E 6
Somalia	246,200	637,658	9,118,773	Mogadishu	119/G 4
South Africa	471,008	1,219,912	43,997,828	Cape Town; Pretoria	119/E 7
South America	6,879,916	17,819,000	380,017,000	....	209
South Australia, Australia	379,922	984,000	1,400,630	Adelaide	145/C 3
South Carolina, U.S.	31,189	80,779	4,012,012	Columbia	193/G 3
South Dakota, U.S.	77,121	199,744	754,844	Pierre	184/D 1
South Korea	38,023	98,480	49,044,790	Seoul	93/D 4
Spain	194,884	504,750	40,448,191	Madrid	52/C 2
Sri Lanka	25,332	65,610	20,926,315	Colombo	104/D 6
Sudan	967,494	2,505,809	42,292,929	Khartoum	119/E 3
Sumatra, Indonesia	182,811	473,481	43,259,707	Medan	101/D 3
Suriname	63,039	163,270	470,784	Paramaribo	218/B 1
Svalbard, Norway	23,957	62,049	2,701	Longyearbyen	80/C 2
Swaziland	6,703	17,360	1,133,066	Mbabane; Lobamba	143/E 2
Sweden	173,731	449,964	9,031,088	Stockholm	44/E 3
Switzerland	15,943	41,292	7,554,661	Bern	66/D 4
Syria	71,498	185,180	19,314,747	Damascus	114/D 3
T					
Tahiti, French Polynesia	402	1,041	150,707	Papeete	161/X15
Taiwan	13,892	35,980	23,174,294	T'aipei	99/J 3
Tajikistan	55,251	143,100	7,076,598	Dushanbe	80/H 6
Tanzania	364,699	945,090	38,139,640	Dar es Salaam; Dodoma	119/F 5
Tasmania, Australia	26,178	67,800	452,851	Hobart	156/C 4
Tennessee, U.S.	42,146	109,158	5,689,283	Nashville	192/D 3
Texas, U.S.	267,277	692,248	20,851,820	Austin	172/G 5
Thailand	198,455	513,998	65,068,149	Bangkok	106/C 3
Tibet, China	471,428	1,221,000	2,620,000	Lhasa	111/D 5
Togo	21,927	56,790	5,701,579	Lomé	133/F 4
Tokelau, New Zealand	3.9	10	1,392	....	161/H 5
Tonga	289	748	116,921	Nuku'alofa	161/H 7
Trinidad and Tobago	1,980	5,128	1,056,608	Port-of-Spain	203/N 9
Tristan da Cunha, St. Helena	38	98	284	Edinburgh	26/J 7
Tuamotu Archipelago, French Polynesia	266	690	15,370	Apataki	161/L 6
Tunisia	63,170	163,610	10,276,158	Tunis	129/H 2
Turkey	301,382	780,580	71,158,647	Ankara	114/C 2
Turkmenistan	188,455	488,100	5,136,262	Ashgabat	80/F 6
Turks and Caicos Islands, U.K.	166	430	21,746	Grand Turk	207/H 1
Tuvalu	10	26	11,992	Funafuti	160/G 5
U					
Uganda	91,135	236,040	30,262,610	Kampala	119/F 4
Ukraine	233,089	603,700	46,299,862	Kiev	78/F 4
United Arab Emirates	29,182	75,581	2,642,566	Abu Dhabi	112/F 4
United Kingdom	94,525	244,820	60,776,238	London	37
United States	3,618,765	9,372,610	301,139,947	Washington, D.C.	172
Uruguay	68,039	176,220	3,447,496	Montevideo	209/D 6
Utah, U.S.	84,904	219,902	2,233,169	Salt Lake City	172/D 4
Uzbekistan	172,741	447,400	27,780,059	Tashkent	80/G 5
V					
Vanuatu	5,699	14,760	211,971	Port-Vila	160/F 6
Vatican City	0.17	0.44	921	....	71/F 7
Venezuela	352,143	912,050	26,084,662	Caracas	217/E 3
Vermont, U.S.	9,614	24,900	608,827	Montpelier	191/K 3
Victoria, Australia	87,876	227,600	4,244,282	Melbourne	156/C 3
Vietnam	127,243	329,560	85,262,356	Hanoi	106/D 2
Virginia, U.S.	42,326	109,625	7,078,515	Richmond	193/H 2
Virgin Islands, British	59	153	23,552	Road Town	203/M7
Virgin Islands, U.S.	136	352	108,448	Charlotte Amalie	203/M7
W					
Wake Island, U.S.	2.5	6.5	200	....	160/F 3
Wales, U.K.	8,017	20,764	2,903,085	Cardiff	37/J10
Wallis and Futuna, France	106	275	16,309	Mata Utu	160/G 6
Washington, U.S.	70,637	182,949	5,894,121	Olympia	174/D 4
West Bank	2,263	5,860	2,535,927	....	117/C 4
Western Australia, Australia	975,096	2,525,500	1,587,050	Perth	145/B 3
Western Cape, South Africa	49,943	129,386	4,524,335	Cape Town	142/C 4
Western Sahara	102,703	266,000	382,617	....	128/B 4
West Virginia, U.S.	24,231	62,758	1,808,344	Charleston	173/K 4
Wisconsin, U.S.	65,499	169,643	5,363,675	Madison	173/H 3
World	(land) 57,505,734	148,940,000	6,605,047,000	....	58
Wyoming, U.S.	97,818	253,349	493,782	Cheyenne	172/E 3
Y					
Yemen	203,849	527,970	22,211,743	Sanaa	112/E 5
Yukon Territory, Canada	186,660	483,450	30,372	Whitehorse	170/C 2
Z					
Zambia	290,583	752,610	11,477,447	Lusaka	119/E 6
Zimbabwe	150,803	390,580	12,311,143	Harare	141/F 3

Sources: CIA Factbook; U.S. Bureau of the Census, International Data Base

Map Projections

A Difficult Problem Solved by Computers Today

A map projection is an image of the Earth or parts of the Earth on a flat plane. Every point on Earth can be identified with the aid of geographic coordinates, within a global coordinate grid, and this grid can be projected onto a flat surface. Today, computer cartography plays an important role in calculating the projection most appropriate for a particular purpose.

Basic Principles and Terms

The Earth rotates around its axis once a day. Its end points are the North and South poles; the line circling the Earth midway between the poles is the Equator. The arc from the Equator to each pole is divided into 90 degrees of latitude. The Equator itself represents 0° latitude and is divided into 360 degrees of longitude. Lines circling the globe from pole to pole which intersect with the Equator at 90-degree angles are called meridians, or great circles. The meridian passing through the Greenwich Observatory near London was chosen by international agreement as to prime meridian or 0° longitude in 1884. Meridians and lines of latitude (parallels) form the global coordinate grid, or graticule. The distance from the prime meridian to a given point to the west or east, expressed in degrees

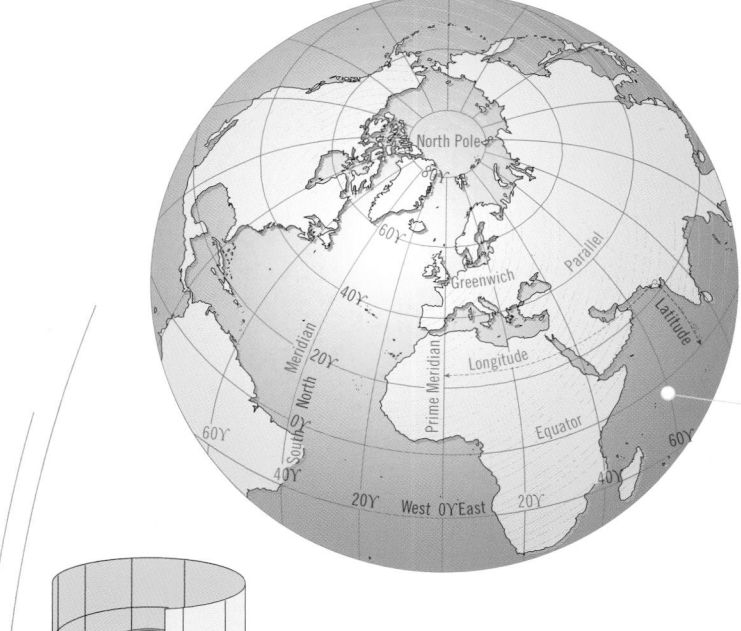

(coordinates) is its geographic longitude. Similarly, distances north or south of the Equator represent geographic latitude. Although all meridians are equal in length, parallels become shorter as they approach the poles. Thus, while the distance between two parallels (one degree of latitude) is approximately 112 km everywhere on Earth, the distance between two meridians (one degree of longitude) varies between 112 km at the Equator and zero at the poles where the meridians converge. Each degree of longitude and latitude is divided into 60 minutes. One minute of latitude equals one nautical mile (1.85 km).

Distortion

There is only one way to represent the sphere of the Earth with absolute precision: as a globe. All attempts to project our planet's curved surface onto a plane create distortion. Depending upon the map projection selected, distortions appear in shapes and area sizes, angles or distances between points on the Earth. Only parallels or meridians (or some other set of lines) can be represented in accurate proportion. All other lines must be either too long or too short. Accordingly, the scale on a flat map

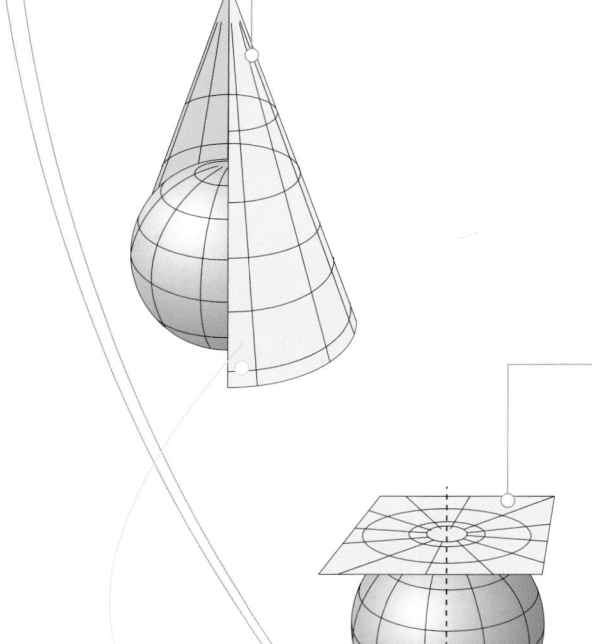

Cylindrical Projection

A cylinder of variable axis length is wrapped around the Earth. The cylinder can touch the Earth at the Equator, for example, or penetrate through the Earth, as is the case in the (conformal) Mercator projection.

Conic Projection

This projection is produced by capping the Earth with a cone. Axis length is variable. Normally, the cone axis is aligned with an Earth axis or with the Equator. In the conic projection shown here, the cone can be made tangent to any desired parallel. One popular version of the conic projection is the Lambert Conformal Conic, in which two parallels are represented in conforming lengths.

Azimuthal Projection

In azimuthal projections, the projection surface is a plane that touches the Earth at a single point. It is ordinarily used as a polar projection of the Earth – with a pole at the center of the projection. This type of projection can only show one hemisphere. Depending upon the distance from the projection axis to the Earth's axis, map projections are referred to as polar, equatorial or oblique-axis. A version frequently used for maps of continents is the Lambert Azimuthal Equal Area Projection, which shows areas with relatively little distortion of shapes.

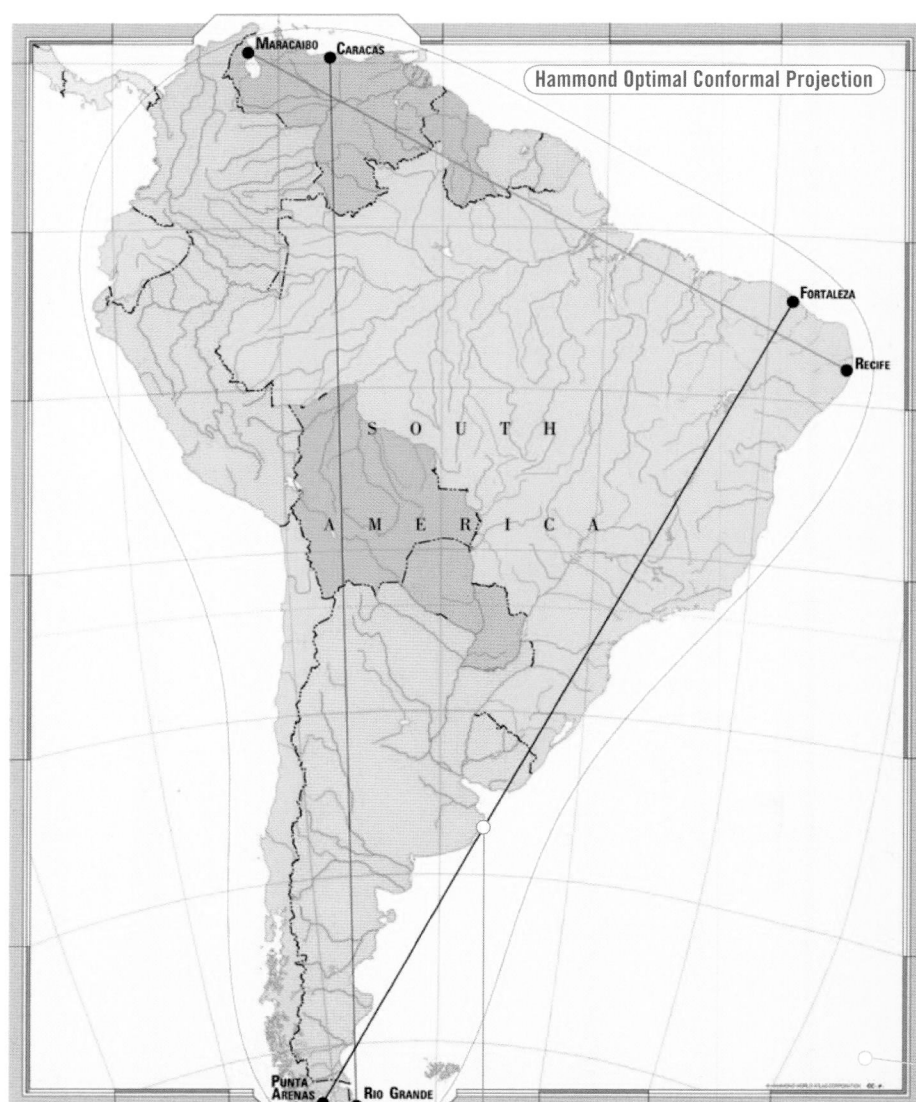

Hammond Optimal Conformal Projection

Cities	True Distance	Hammond Projection	Lambert Projection
Caracas – Rio Grande	7 149 km	7 126 km	6 944 km
Maracaibo – Recife	4 560 km	4 578 km	4 533 km
Fortaleza – Punta Arenas	6 246 km	6 266 km	6 163 km

Comparison of Accuracy

The use of the Lambert Azimuthal Equal Area Projection for maps of continents produces distortions ranging from 2.3% (Europe) to 15% (Asia). The Hammond Optimal Conformal reduces these distortions by half and improves the reliability of distance measurements based on these maps.

Map Projections

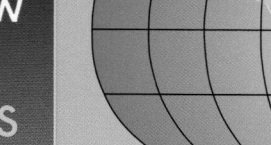

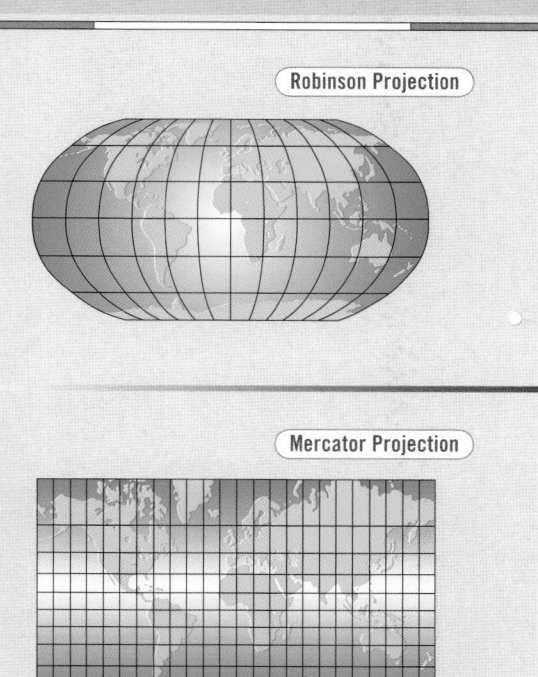

Robinson Projection

Mercator Projection

cannot be true everywhere. On world maps or very large areas, variations in scale may be extreme.

Projections: Selected Examples

The Mercator projection is a conformal, normal-axis cylindrical projection in which all meridians and parallels intersect at right angles. Because all compass directions appear as straight lines, the Mercator projection is still an important navigational tool. Moreover, every small region conforms to the shape on a globe – hence the name conformal. But because its meridians are evenly-spaced vertical lines that do not converge (unlike those on the globe), the horizontal parallels must be drawn farther apart as they approach the poles to maintain a correct relationship. Only the Equator is true to scale, and the size of areas in the higher latitudes is dramatically distorted.

The Robinson projection was used to create the two-page world map in the Map Section. It combines elements of both conformal and equal-area projections to show the whole earth with relatively true shapes and reasonably equal areas. This projection is a mediating pseudo-cylindrical representation.

The conic projection is used frequently for air navigation charts. It was used to create most of the national and regional maps in this atlas.

The Hammond Optimal Conformal projection presents an optimal view of an area by reducing shifts in scale over an entire region to the minimum degree possible. The concept underlying the Optimal Conformal projection is that, for any region on the globe, there is an ideal projection for which scale variations can be kept as small as possible. Consequently, unlike other projections, the Optimal Conformal does not use a standard formula to construct a map. Each map is a unique projection – the optimal projection for that specific area.

In practice, the cartographer first defines the map subject, then, working on a computer, draws a boundary around the region to be mapped. Next, a sophisticated software program evaluates the size and shape of the region to determine the most accurate way to project it. The result is a precise map with the minimum possible degree of distortion. All of the continent maps in this Atlas (with the exception of Antarctica) have been drawn using this projection.

Projections Compared

The following diagrams show the distortions produced by several commonly used projections. By using a simple face with familiar shapes (the Plan) as the starting point, it is easy to see the advantages and drawbacks of each. Areas or continents on a map change much like the shapes of the face in the diagram. The distortion appears not only in the features themselves, but also in the changing shapes, angles, and areas of the background grid, or graticule.

The Plan

The Plan shows the "continents" either as perfect circles or true straight lines on the Earth. They should appear that way on a "perfect" map.

Orthographic Projection (Parallel Projection)

This azimuthal view shows the "continents" on Earth as seen from space. The facial features occupy half of the Earth. Toward the edge, the eyes grow increasingly elliptical, the nose appears larger and less straight, and the mouth curves into a smile.

Mercator Projection

This cylindrical projection preserves angles exactly, but the mouth is now smiling broadly and shows extreme distortion at the map's outer edge. Typical of the rapid expansion of forms toward the outer edge is the extreme enlargement of Greenland on Mercator world maps.

Peters Projection

This equal-area cylindrical projection represents areas in their correct proportions, but it does not closely resemble the Plan. Angles, local shapes, and global relations are significantly distorted.

Gnomonic Projection

This strange-looking projection is neither conformal nor equal-area. It is a centrally positioned azimuthal projection, meaning that the center of projection lies in the center of the Earth. Although its outer regions are badly distorted, the straight mouth and precise triangle of the nose indicate a key advantage of this map: all great circles appear as straight lines. This enables the user to find the shortest path between any two points on the map simply by connecting them with a straight line.

Hammond Optimal Conformal Projection

As one can easily see, this projection minimizes inaccuracies between the angles and shapes of the Plan, yielding a near-perfect map of the given area, up to a complete hemisphere. Like all conformal maps, the Optimal projection preserves every angle exactly, but it is more successful than previous projections at spreading the inevitable curvature across the entire map. The sides of the triangle appear almost straight, although the sum of the angles is greater than 180°. Although the eyes are somewhat too large, this is the only map with eyes that appear concentric. Both mathematically and visually, it offers the best conformal map that can be made of the ideal Plan.

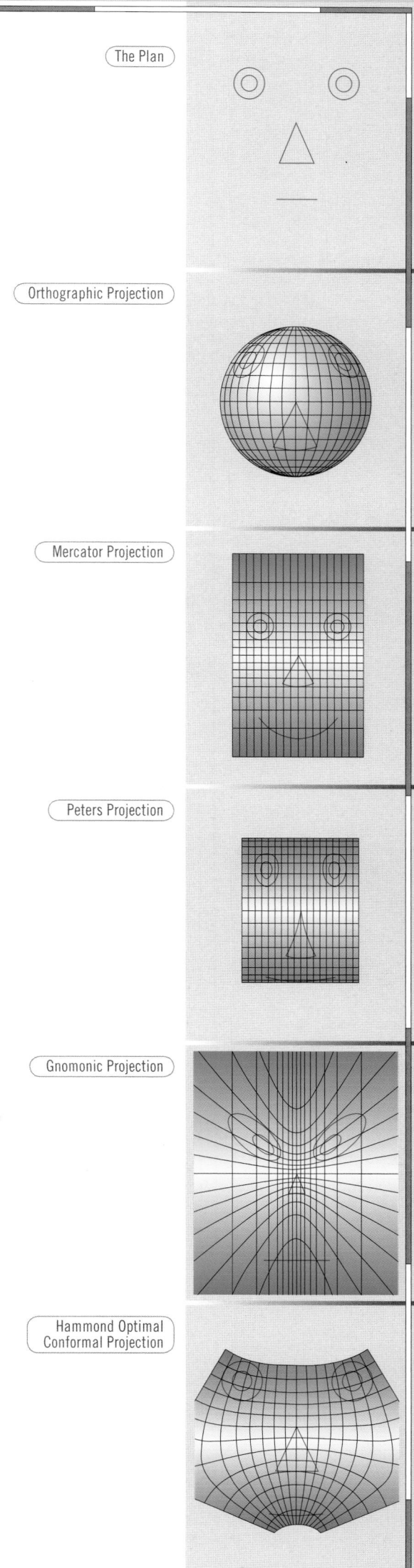

The Plan

Orthographic Projection

Mercator Projection

Peters Projection

Gnomonic Projection

Hammond Optimal Conformal Projection

"In every outthrust headland, in every curving beach, in every grain of sand there is a story of the earth."

Rachel Carson

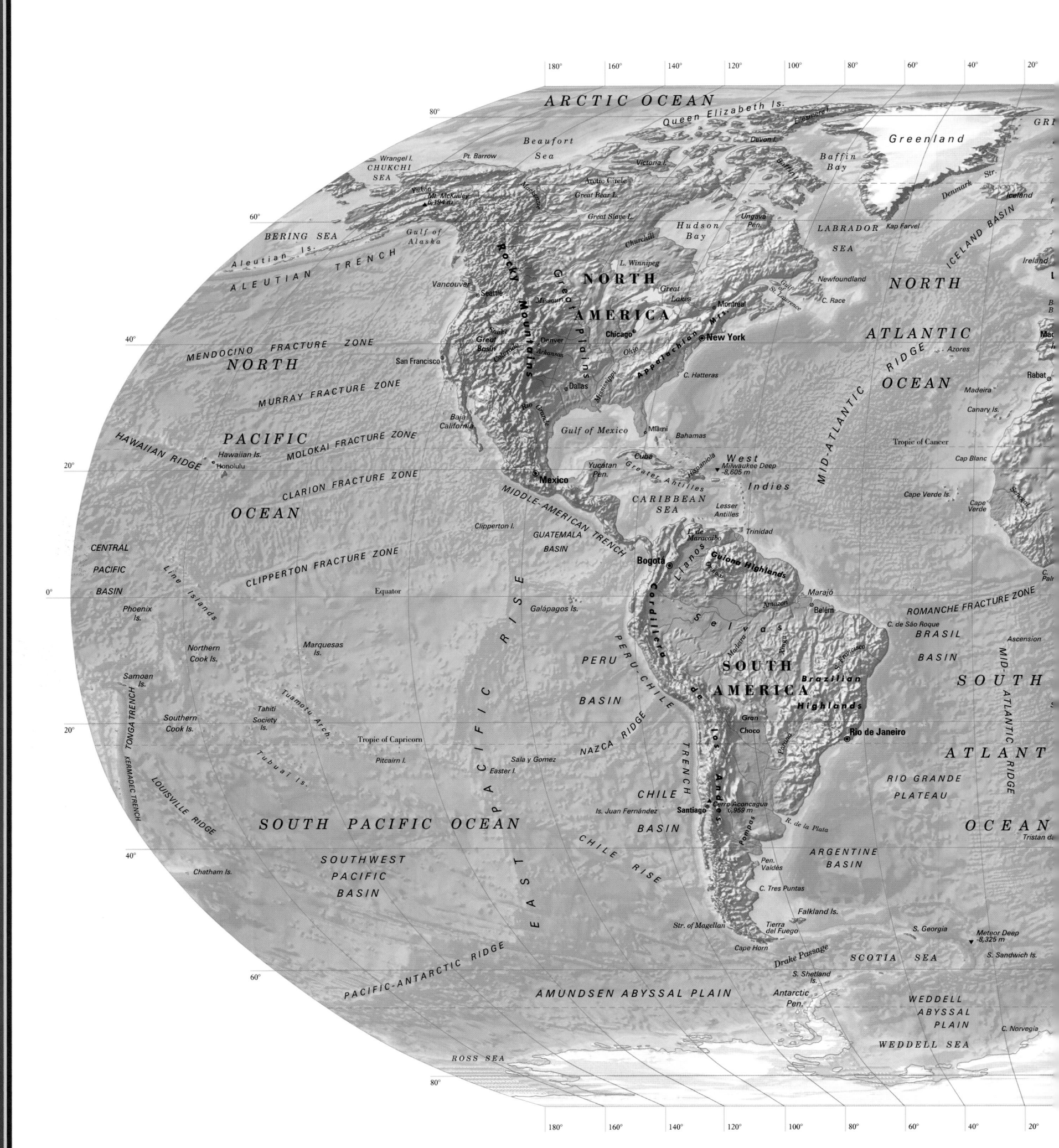

Height
m. ft.
6000 19700
4000 13000
2000 6500
1500 5000
1000 3300
500 1600
200 700
-0-
200 700
500 1600
1000 3300
2000 6500
3000 9800
4000 13000
5000 16400
6000 19700
m. ft.
Depth

ARCTIC OCEAN

Queen Elizabeth Is.
Ellesmere I.
Greenland
GR
Beaufort Sea
Baffin Bay
Devon I.
Wrangel I.
Pt. Barrow
Victoria I.
CHUKCHI SEA
Arctic Circle
Denmark
Str.
Iceland
Yukon
Mt. McKinley 6,194 m
Great Bear L.
Kap Farvel
ICELAND BASIN
BERING SEA
Great Slave L.
Hudson Bay
LABRADOR SEA
Ireland
Gulf of Alaska
Churchill
Ungava Pen.
Aleutian Is.
L. Winnipeg
Newfoundland
NORTH
Vancouver
NORTH AMERICA
Great Lakes
Montreal
G. St. Lawrence
C. Race
ATLANTIC
ALEUTIAN TRENCH
Seattle
Missouri
Chicago
MENDOCINO FRACTURE ZONE
Ohio
Azores
NORTH
Denver
Arkansas
Appalachian Mts.
C. Hatteras
OCEAN
San Francisco
New York
Ma
MURRAY FRACTURE ZONE
Great Basin
Colorado
Mississippi
Dallas
Rabat
PACIFIC
Rio Grande
Madeira
HAWAIIAN RIDGE
Hawaiian Is.
Baja California
Gulf of Mexico
Miami
Bahamas
Tropic of Cancer
Honolulu
MOLOKAI FRACTURE ZONE
Cuba
Cap Blanc
OCEAN
Mexico
Yucatan Pen.
Greater Antilles
Hispaniola
West
Milwaukee Deep -8,605 m
Cape Verde Is.
Cape Verde
CLARION FRACTURE ZONE
Indies
CENTRAL
CARIBBEAN SEA
Lesser Antilles
C. Pal
PACIFIC
Clipperton I.
GUATEMALA BASIN
Trinidad
BASIN
Phoenix Is.
L. de Maracaibo
Guiana Highlands
ROMANCHE FRACTURE ZONE
Equator
Galápagos Is.
Bogotá
Llanos
Orinoco
Marajó
Sch
CLIPPERTON FRACTURE ZONE
Line Islands
Cordillera
Belém
BRASIL
Ascension
Northern Cook Is.
Marquesas Is.
PERU
Selvas
Amazon
BASIN
Samoan Is.
BASIN
SOUTH
Brazilian
MID
PERU-CHILE
Madeira
AMERICA
Highlands
Tahiti
PACIFIC
Tropic of Capricorn
Society Is.
Gran Choco
ATLANTIC
TONGA TRENCH
Southern Cook Is.
Tubuai Is.
Pitcairn I.
NAZCA RIDGE
Rio de Janeiro
Sala y Gomez
SOUTH
RIDGE
Easter I.
Los Andes
S
KERMADEC TRENCH
CHILE
Paraguay
RIO GRANDE
ATLANT
TRENCH
Cerro Aconcagua 6,959 m
PLATEAU
LOUISVILLE RIDGE
Is. Juan Fernández
Santiago
R. de la Plata
BASIN
OCEAN
Pampas
SOUTH PACIFIC OCEAN
CHILE
ARGENTINE
Chatham Is.
SOUTHWEST
CHILE RISE
Pen. Valdés
BASIN
PACIFIC
Tristan da
BASIN
C. Tres Puntas
Str. of Magellan
Tierra del Fuego
Falkland Is.
S. Georgia
Meteor Deep -8,325 m
Cape Horn
Drake Passage
SCOTIA SEA
S. Sandwich Is.
PACIFIC-ANTARCTIC RIDGE
S. Shetland Is.
AMUNDSEN ABYSSAL PLAIN
Antarctic Pen.
WEDDELL ABYSSAL PLAIN
C. Norvegia
ROSS SEA
WEDDELL SEA

Population
⊕ Over 5,000,000
⊙ 500,000 - 1,999,999
⊙ 2,000,000 - 4,999,999
○ Under 500,000

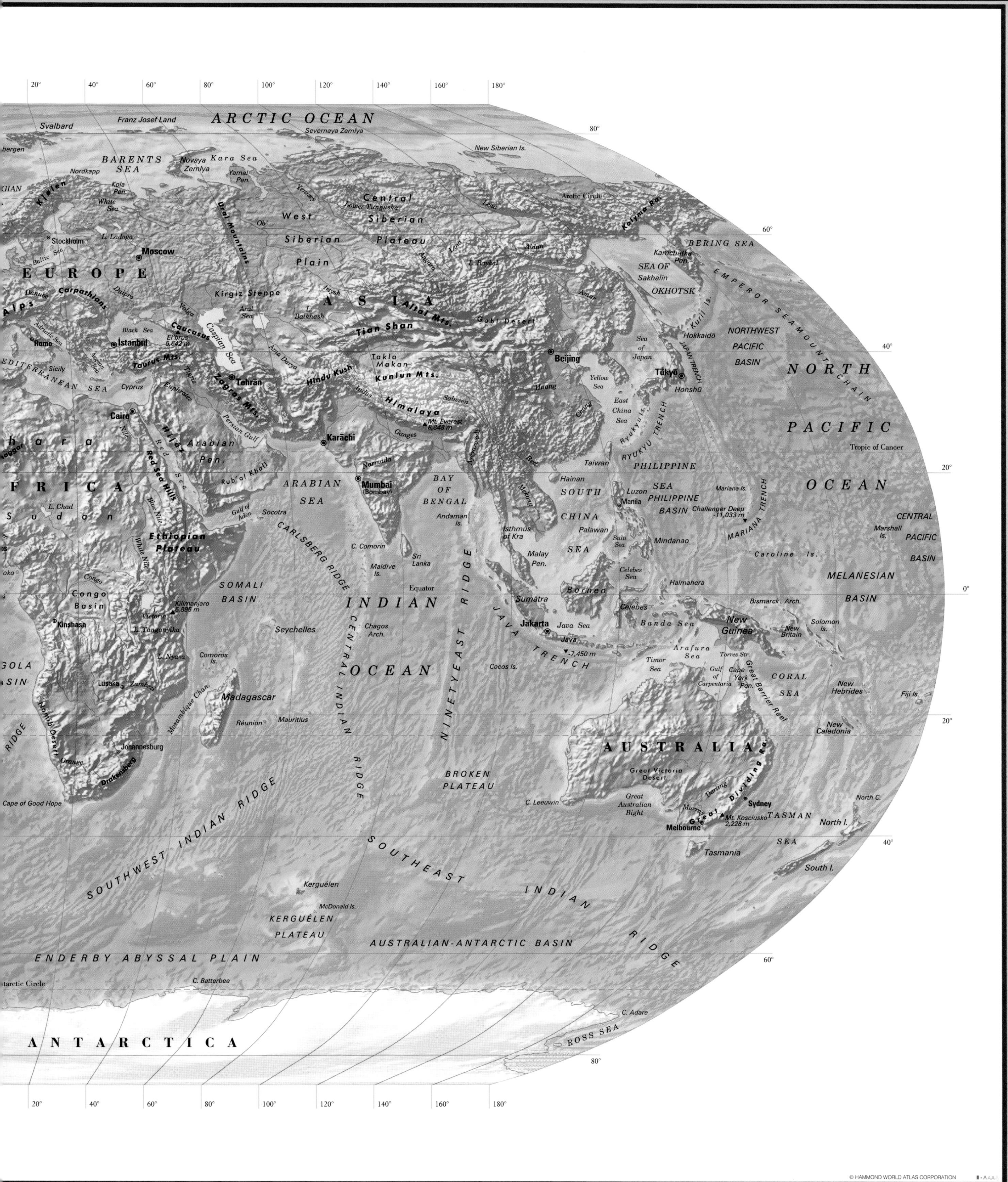

20° 40° 60° 80° 100° 120° 140° 160° 180°

Svalbard *Franz Josef Land* **ARCTIC OCEAN** *Severnaya Zemlya* *New Siberian Is.* 80°

bergen *Nordkapp* **BARENTS SEA** *Novaya Zemlya* *Kara Sea* *Yamal Pen.* *Arctic Circle* *Kolyma Ra.* 60°

GIAN *Kjølen* *Kola Pen.* *White Sea* *Ob'* *West Siberian Plain* *Yenisey* *Central Siberian Plateau* *Lower Tunguska* *Lena* **BERING SEA** *Kamchatka Pen.*

Stockholm *L. Ladoga* **Moscow** *Kirgiz Steppe* *Irtysh* **A S I A** *Angara* *L. Baikal* *Aldan* *Amur* **SEA OF OKHOTSK** *Sakhalin*

E U R O P E *Danube* **Carpathians** *Dnipro* *Volga* *Aral Sea* *L. Balkhash* **Altai Mts.** *Gobi Desert* *Hokkaidō* **NORTHWEST PACIFIC BASIN** **N O R T H** 40°

Alps *Black Sea* **Caucasus** *El'brus 5,642 m* *Caspian Sea* **Tian Shan** *Sea of Japan* *Kuril Is.* *JAPAN TRENCH*

Rome **İstanbul** **Taurus Mts.** *Amu Darya* **Beijing** *Honshū* **Tōkyō**

Sicily *Cyprus* **Zagros Mts.** **Tehrān** *Takla Makan* **Kunlun Mts.** *Huang* *Yellow Sea* **P A C I F I C**

MEDITERRANEAN SEA *Euphrates* **Hindu Kush** *Salween* **Himalaya** *East China Sea* *RYUKYU TRENCH* **O C E A N** 20°

Cairo *Nile* *Tigris* *Persian Gulf* *Indus* *Mt. Everest 8,848 m* **Karāchi** *Ganges* *Brahmaputra* *Taiwan* *Tropic of Cancer*

hara *agar* **Red Sea Hills** **Arabian Pen.** *Rub' al Khali* *Normada* **Mumbai (Bombay)** **BAY OF BENGAL** *Mekong* *Red* *Hainan* **SOUTH** *Luzon* **PHILIPPINE SEA** *Mariana Is.* **CENTRAL**

A F R I C A *Sudan* *Red Sea* *Gulf of Aden* *Socotra* **ARABIAN SEA** *Andaman Is.* **CHINA** *Manila* **PHILIPPINE BASIN** *Challenger Deep -11,033 m* **PACIFIC**

oko **Ethiopian Plateau** *C. Comorin* *Sri Lanka* *Isthmus of Kra* *Palawan* **SEA** *Mindanao* *MARIANA TRENCH* *Marshall Is.* **BASIN**

L. Chad *White Nile* *Blue Nile* **SOMALI BASIN** *Maldive Is.* *Malay Pen.* *Sulu Sea* *Caroline Is.* **MELANESIAN**

Congo **Congo Basin** *Kilimanjaro 5,895 m* *Equator* **INDIAN** **CARLSBERG RIDGE** *Chagos Arch.* *Sumatra* *Borneo* *Celebes Sea* *Halmahera* *Bismarck Arch.* **BASIN** 0°

Kinshasa *Victoria* *L. Tanganyika* *Seychelles* **OCEAN** *Java Sea* *Celebes* *Banda Sea* **New Guinea** *New Britain* *Solomon Is.*

GOLA *Lusaka* *Zamb.* *L. Nyasa* *Comoros Is.* **Jakarta** *Java ▼-7,450 m* *Arafura Sea* *Timor Sea* *Gulf of Carpentaria* **CORAL** *New Hebrides* *Fiji Is.*

SIN *Madagascar* *Mozambique Chan.* **CENTRAL INDIAN RIDGE** **JAVA TRENCH** *Cocos Is.* *Torres Str.* *Cape York Pen.* **SEA** 20°

RIDGE *Namib Desert* *Orange* **Johannesburg** *Réunion* *Mauritius* **NINETYEAST RIDGE** **BROKEN PLATEAU** **AUSTRALIA** **Great Dividing Ra.** *New Caledonia*

ASIN **Drakensberg** *Great Victoria Desert* *Darling* **Sydney** *North C.*

Cape of Good Hope *C. Leeuwin* *Great Australian Bight* *Murray* *Mt. Kosciusko 2,228 m* **TASMAN** *North I.*

SOUTHWEST INDIAN RIDGE **Melbourne** **SEA** 40°

SOUTHEAST *Tasmania* *South I.*

Kerguélen **INDIAN**

McDonald Is. **KERGUÉLEN PLATEAU** **AUSTRALIAN-ANTARCTIC BASIN** **RIDGE** 60°

ENDERBY ABYSSAL PLAIN

Antarctic Circle *C. Batterbee* *C. Adare*

A N T A R C T I C A **ROSS SEA** 80°

20° 40° 60° 80° 100° 120° 140° 160° 180°

Scale 1:70,000,000 Robinson Projection

MI	600	1200	1800	2400
KM	600 1200	2400	3000	3600

NORWEGIAN
BASIN

NORWEGIAN

VORING
PLATEAU

Vesterålen

Lofoten

Arctic Circle

Reykjavik

Iceland

Hekla

ICELAND BASIN

Faroe Is.

SEA

Trondheim

Glittertind
2,470 m

ROCKALL

PLATEAU

Rockall

HEBRIDIAN SHELF

Shetland Is.

Bergen

Lindesnes

Vesterås

Vänern

Stockholm

ATLANTIC

OCEAN

ROCKALL TROUGH

Hebrides

Orkney Is.

Moray Firth

Ben Nevis
1,343 m

Aberdeen

Glasgow

NORTH

SEA

Skagerrak

Göteborg

Vättern

Öland

PORCUPINE
BANK

Belfast

Ireland

I. of Man

Great

Jutland

Fyn

Copenhagen

Bornholm

Dublin

Irish
Sea

Pennine Chain

Liverpool

Britain

PORCUPINE ABYSSAL PLAIN

C. Clear

St. George's Chan.

Birmingham

Thames

London

Frisian Islands

Hamburg

Weser

Elbe

Berlin

CELTIC
SHELF

Land's End

English Channel

Channel
Is.

Amsterdam

The Hague

Brussels

Rhine

Cologne

Bonn

Leipzig

Oder

AREA OF OPTIMIZATION

Le Havre

Seine

Paris

BISCAY ABYSSAL
PLAIN

Nantes

Loire

Rhine

Stuttgart

Munich

Danube

Vienna

Bratislava

IBERIAN

ABYSSAL

PLAIN

Cabo Finisterre

Bay of
Biscay

Bordeaux

Garonne

Central

Lot

Massif

Lyon

Rhône

Mont Blanc
4,807 m

A L P S

Bern

Graz

Zagreb

Mino

Cordillera
Cantábrica

Bilbao

Pyrenees

Ebro

Marseille

G. of Lion

Ligurian

Sea

Turin

Milan

Venice

Po

Genoa

Dinaric

Madrid

Duero

Ródano

Saragossa

Corsica

Apennines

Adriatic

Lisbon

Tagus

Barcelona

Rome

Sierra Morena

Jucar

Valencia

Balearic Islands

Minorca

Sardinia

Tyrrhenian

Sea

Naples

Cádiz

Cerro de Mulhacén
3,478 m

Ibiza

Mallorca

ALGERIAN PLAIN

–3,630 m

Capo Teulada

Str. of Gibraltar

Málaga

Tangier

M E D I T E R R A

Palermo

Mt. Etna 3,323 m

Sicily

Algiers

Oran

Rabat

A F R I C A

Tunis

Pantelleria

Capo Passero

Malta

JAN MAYEN RIDGE

Rockall

Height

m.
ft.

6000
19700

4000
13000

2000
6500

1500
5000

1000
3300

500
1600

200
700

–0–

200
700

500
1600

1000
3300

2000
6500

3000
9800

4000
13000

5000
16400

6000
19700

m.
ft.

Depth

30°

50°

40°

30°

10°

The Mediterranean Sea is a remnant of the Thethys Sea that once separated Europe and Africa. The floor of the sea between the continents was squeezed and folded to form the high mountain ranges of the Mediterranean region. North of the Alps and the Black and Caspian Seas are the old, heavily eroded central mountain ranges and lowland plains of the European continent.

50°

60°

Murmansk

Hammerfest

Kola
Pen.

Arctic Circle

Torniojoki

Kemijoki

White Sea

Akhangel'sk

Northern Dvina

Tobol

Yekaterinburg

URAL
Mountains

Iijoki

Oulu

Onega

Kama

Perm'

Chelyabinsk

A
S
I
A

Lake
Onega

Rybinsk
Res.

Kama

Kazan'

Lake
Ladoga

Kuybyshev
Res.

Bothnia

St. Petersburg

Volga

Nizhniy
Novgorod

Samara

Gulf of Finland

Tallinn

Volga

50°

Hiiumaa

Lake
Peipus

L. Il'men

Oka

Volga

Saaremaa

Gulf of
Riga

Moscow

Central

Zhayyq (Ural)

A

Riga

Daugava

Russian

Emba

Vilnius

Minsk

Uplands

Volga
Uplands

Volga

Prikaspian Plai

CASPIAN SEA

European Plain

Bug

Pripyat'

Desna

Khoper

Don

Volgograd

Volga

Astrakhan'

Warsaw

Kharkiv

Kráków

L'viv

Kiev

Dnipro

Donets

Tsimlyansk
Res.

Don

Donets'k

Manych

Kuma

Vistula

San

Dniester

Pivdenniy Buh

Carpathian Mts.

Prut

Sea of
Azov

Kuban

Krasnodar

Caucasus

Baku

Great Alföld

Cluj-Napoca

Siret

Odesa

Crimean
Pen.

Tbilisi

Transylvanian
Alps

Olt

Bucharest

BLACK SEA

Aras

Belgrade

Danube

-2,211m

L. Urmia

Balkan Mts.

Sofia

Bosporus

Kizilirmak

L. Van

Skopje

Istanbul

Ankara

A   S   I   A

Tirane

Sea of
Marmara

Thessaloniki

L. Tuz

Pindus Mts.

Aegean

Évvoia

Lésvos

Izmir

Taurus Mts.

Tigris

Baghdad

Ionian

Sea

Athens

Cyclades

Euphrates

Islands

Peloponnesus

-5,150 m

Ákra Taínaron

Rhodes

Cyprus

Nicosia

© HAMMOND WORLD ATLAS CORPORATION

CC-A

Crete

Beirut

S   E   A

Damascus

40°

Asia

Although the Ural Mountains and the Caspian Sea form a boundary between Europe and Asia, geologists view both continents as part of the Eurasian Plate. The largest contiguous land mass on earth, this plate also comprises the Himalayas, the world's highest and most extensive mountain system. Deep ocean trenches sear the boundaries of the Pacific and Indo-Australian plates.

Scale 1:42,000,000   Lambert Azimuthal Equal-Area

Vast highland basins and deserts stand in marked contrast to the fertile plains of the region. Deserts, such as the Gobi, dominate the northwestern part of this region, while the waters and floodplains of great Huang Ho (Yellow) and the Yangtze (Chang) Rivers in the east provide the basis for the cultivation of food crops that feed millions of people.

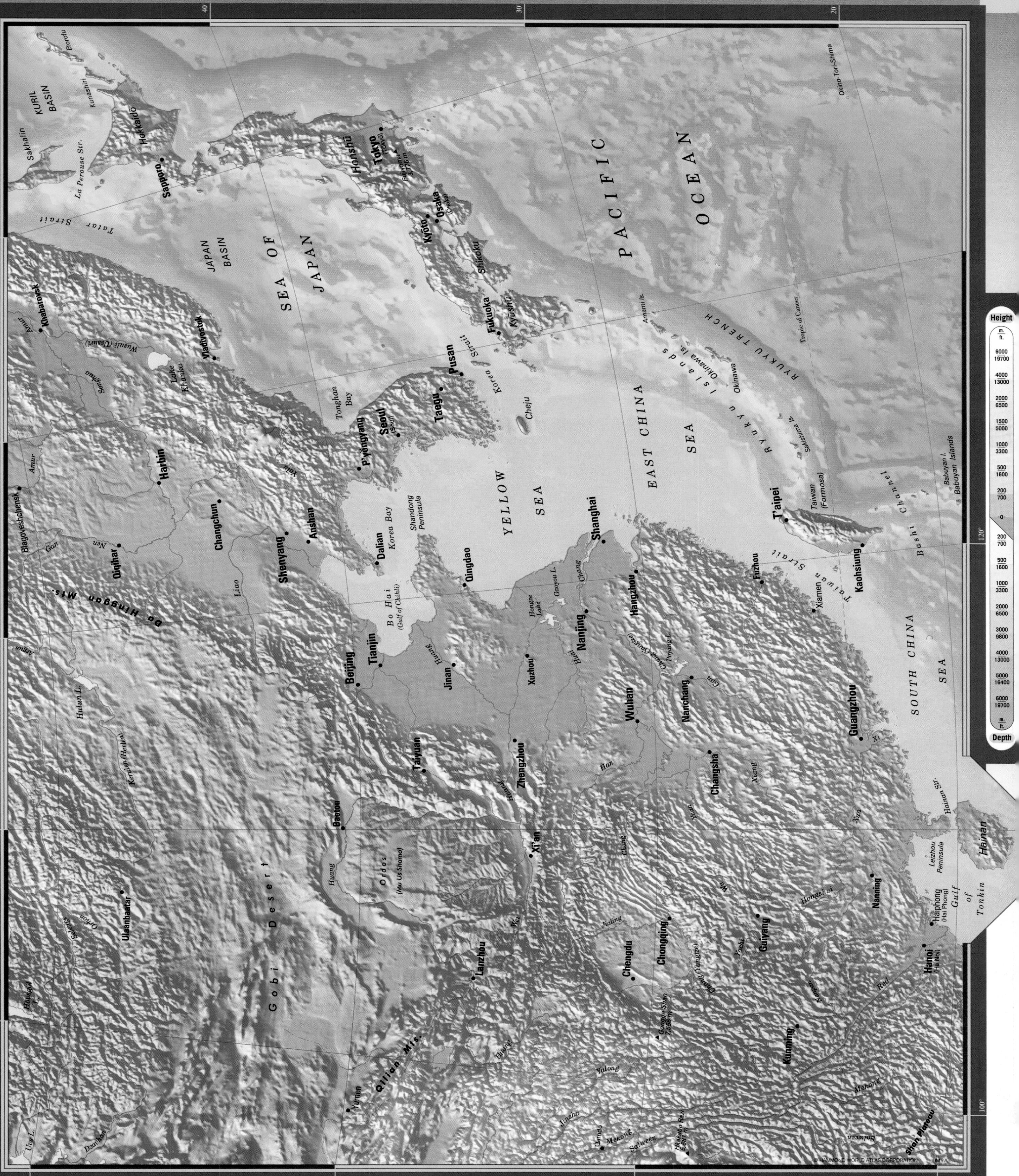

East Asia

KURIL BASIN

Sakhalin

Ecorofu

Kunashiri

Hokkaidō

Sapporo

La Perouse Str.

Tatar Strait

JAPAN BASIN

SEA OF JAPAN

Honshū

Tokyo

Yokohama

Fuji-san 3,776 m

Osaka

Kyoto

Shikoku

Okino-Tori-Shima

PACIFIC OCEAN

Khabarovsk

Amur

Wusuli (Ussuri)

Shangsui

Vladivostok

Lake Khanka

Tonghan Bay

Fukuoka

Kyūshū

Amami Is.

Korea Strait

Tropic of Cancer

RYUKYU TRENCH

Blagoveshchensk

Amur

Harbin

Nen

Gan

Pyongyang

Seoul

Taegu

Pusan

Cheju

Amami Is.

Okinawa

Sakishima Is.

Ryukyu Is.

Argun

Hulan L.

Qiqihar

Changchun

Anshan

Shenyang

Liao

Yalu

Dalian

Korea Bay

Shandong Peninsula

Qingdao

YELLOW SEA

EAST CHINA SEA

Taiwan (Formosa)

Taipei

Da Hinggan Mts.

Kerulen (Herlen)

Hulun L.

Beijing

Tianjin

Bo Hai (Gulf of Chihli)

Jinan

Huang

Shanghai

Hangzhou

Fuzhou

Xiamen

Kaohsiung

Bashi Channel

Babuyan Islands

Babuyan I.

Ulaanbaatar

Orhon

Selenga

Baotou

Ordos (Mu Us Shamo)

Taiyuan

Fen

Xuzhou

Zhengzhou

Huai

Nanjing

Hongze Lake

Gaoyou L.

Chang (Yangtze)

Wuhan

Han

Nanchang

Gan

Changsha

Xiang

Fuzhou

Taiwan Strait

SOUTH CHINA SEA

Gobi Desert

Huang

Wei

Xi'an

Jialing

Chengdu

Chongqing

Chang (Yangtze)

Guiyang

Wu

Yuan

Hongshui

Guilin

Nanning

You

Leizhou Peninsula

Hainan Str.

Hainan

Gulf of Tonkin

Qilian Shan

Yalong

Yangtze

Yalong

Hua Shan 5,881 m

Min

Xi

Hongshui

Red

Kunming

Haiphong (Hai Phong)

Hanoi (Ha Noi)

Dzuunbogd

Uigi L.

Hövsgöl Nuur

Qilian Mts.

Tumen

Mekong

Xinzhou

Salween

Hong (Red)

Shan Plateau

Yalong

Yangtze

RAYMOND WORLD ATLAS CORPORATION

Height	
m.	ft.
6000	19700
4000	13000
2000	6500
1500	5000
1000	3300
500	1600
200	700
0	0
200	700
500	1600
1000	3300
2000	6500
3000	9800
4000	13000
5000	16400
6000	19700
m.	ft.
Depth	

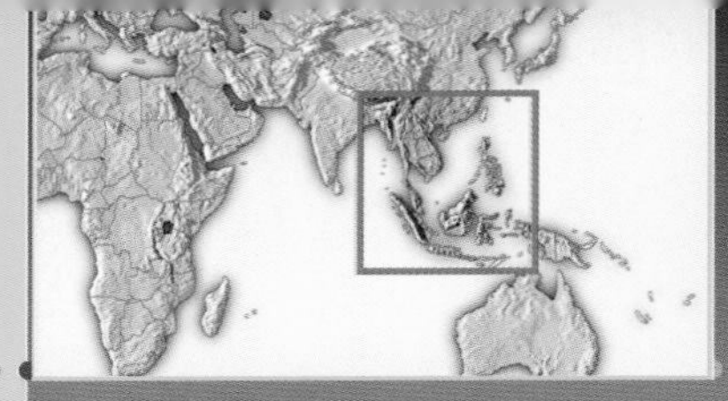

Several tectonic plates converge in Southeast Asia to form an extended arc of islands adjacent to deep ocean trenches. Many of the islands are characterized by extreme volcanic activity. Located on the continental shelf along the South China Sea is the vast delta (70,000 km2) of the Mekong, the "Mother of Waters," whose course from the Tibetan Plateau to the sea measures 4,500 km.

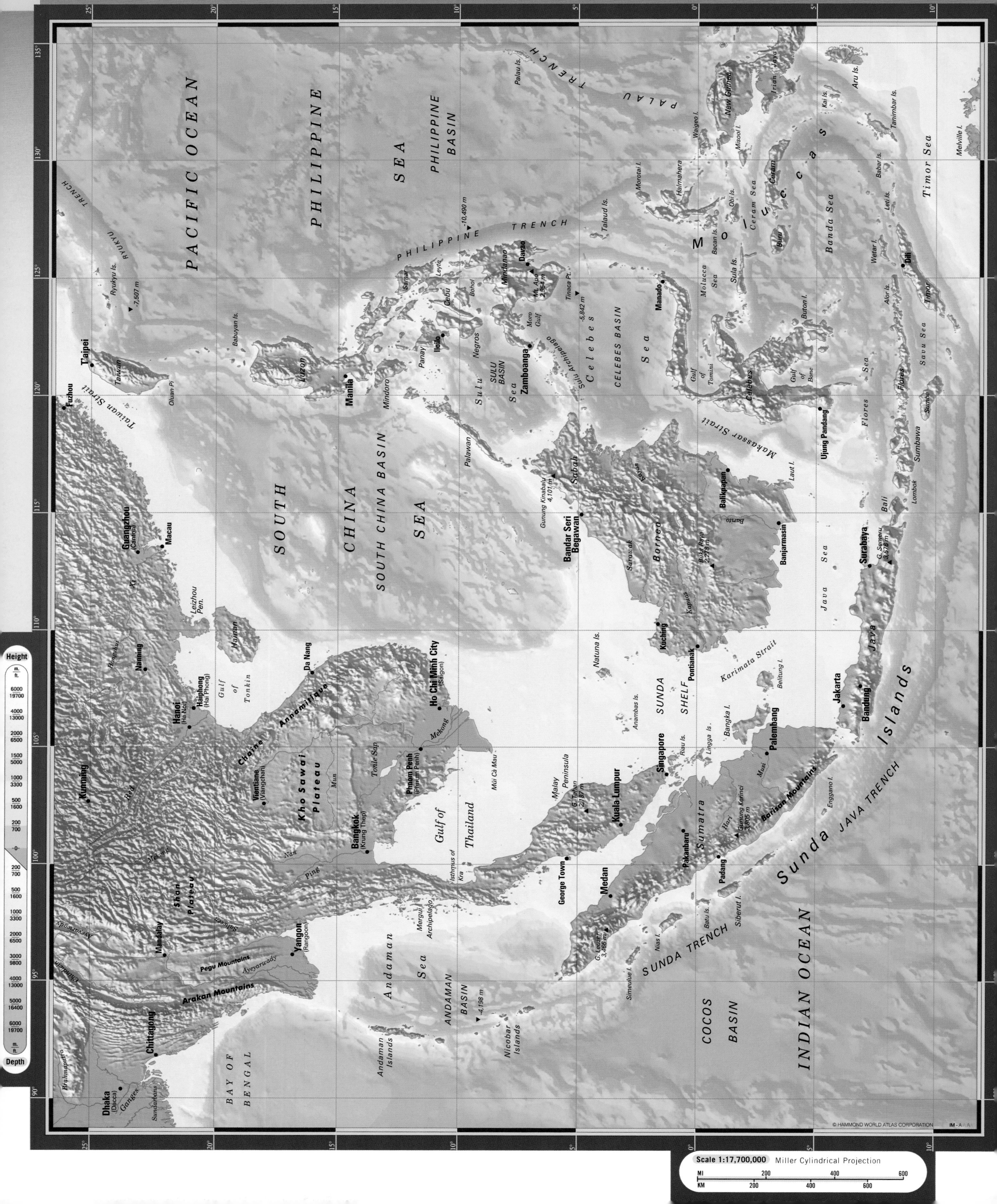

Height

m. / ft.
6000 / 19700
4000 / 13000
2000 / 6500
1500 / 5000
1000 / 3300
500 / 1600
200 / 700
-0-
200 / 700
500 / 1600
1000 / 3300
2000 / 6500
3000 / 9800
4000 / 13000
5000 / 16400
6000 / 19700
m. / ft.
Depth

PACIFIC OCEAN

RYUKYU TRENCH
-7,507 m

PHILIPPINE SEA

PHILIPPINE BASIN

PALAU TRENCH
Palau Is.

PHILIPPINE TRENCH
-10,490 m

Taipei
Fuzhou
Taiwan Strait
Oluan Pi
Babuyan Is.
Luzon
Samar
Leyte
Cebu
Bohol
Panay
Iloilo
Negros
Mindanao
Davao
Mt. Apo 2,954 m
Moro Gulf
Tinaca Pt.
-5,842 m
Sulu Archipelago
Manila
Mindoro
Palawan
Sulu Sea
SULU BASIN
Zamboanga
Manado

Taluad Is.
Morotai I.
Halmahera
Bacan Is.
Obi Is.
Sula Is.
CELEBES BASIN
Celebes Sea
Gulf of Tomini
Gulf of Bone
Celebes
Molucca Sea
M O L U C C A S
Ceram Sea
Ceram
Buru
Banda Sea
Obi Is.
Waigeo I.
Misool I.
New Guinea
Irian Jaya
Kai Is.
Aru Is.
Tanimbar Is.
Babar Is.
Leti Is.
Wetar I.
Alor Is.
Timor
Dili
Timor Sea
Melville I.

Ujung Pandang
Makassar Strait
Laut I.
Balikpapan
Banjarmasin
Barito
Bukit Raya 2,278 m
Borneo
Kapuas
Kayan
Sarawak
Gunung Kinabalu 4,101 m
Sabah
Bandar Seri Begawan

Flores Sea
Flores
Sumba
Savu Sea
Lombok
Sumbawa
Bali
Java Sea
Surabaya
G. Semeru 3,676 m
Java
Jakarta
Bandung
Sunda Islands
JAVA TRENCH

SOUTH CHINA SEA
SOUTH CHINA BASIN

Guangzhou (Canton)
Macau
Nanning
Fuzhou
Xi
Leizhou Pen.
Hainan
Gulf of Tonkin
Haiphong (Hai Phong)
Hanoi (Ha Noi)
Da Nang
Kunming
Annamite Range
Chaine Annamitique
Mekong
Ho Chi Minh City (Saigon)
Mui Ca Mau
Natuna Is.
Anambas Is.
SUNDA SHELF
Pontianak
Kuching
Karimata Strait
Belitung I.
Bangka I.
Riau Is.
Lingga Is.
Singapore
G. Tahan 2,187 m
Malay Peninsula
Kuala Lumpur
Palembang
Musi
Pekanbaru
Padang
Gunung Kerinci 3,805 m
Sumatra
Barisan Mountains
Enggano I.
Medan
George Town
G. Leuser 3,466 m
Batu Is.
Nias I.
Siberut I.
Simeulue I.
SUNDA TRENCH

Kho Sawai Plateau
Vientiane (Viangchan)
Phnom Penh (Phnum Penh)
Tonle Sap
Mun
Bangkok (Krung Thep)
Ping
Nan
Gulf of Thailand
Isthmus of Kra
Thailand
Mergui Archipelago

Andaman Sea
ANDAMAN BASIN
-4,198 m
Andaman Islands
Nicobar Islands

Shan Plateau
Mandalay
Salween
Ayeyarwady
Pegu Mountains
Yangon (Rangoon)
Arakan Mountains
Irrawaddy

BAY OF BENGAL
Dhaka (Dacca)
Ganges
Chittagong
Sundarbans
Brahmaputra

COCOS BASIN
INDIAN OCEAN

© HAMMOND WORLD ATLAS CORPORATION

Scale 1:17,700,000 Miller Cylindrical Projection

MI 200 400 600
KM 200 400 600

The collision of the Indian subcontinent with Eurasia about 50 million years ago gave birth to the Himalayas. Since that time, the Indian subcontinent has penetrated some 2,000 km into Eurasia, thrusting rock upward to form the world's loftiest mountain range, with peaks as high as 9,000 m. Today, such mighty rivers as the Ganges (2,700 km long) flow from sources in the Himalayas.

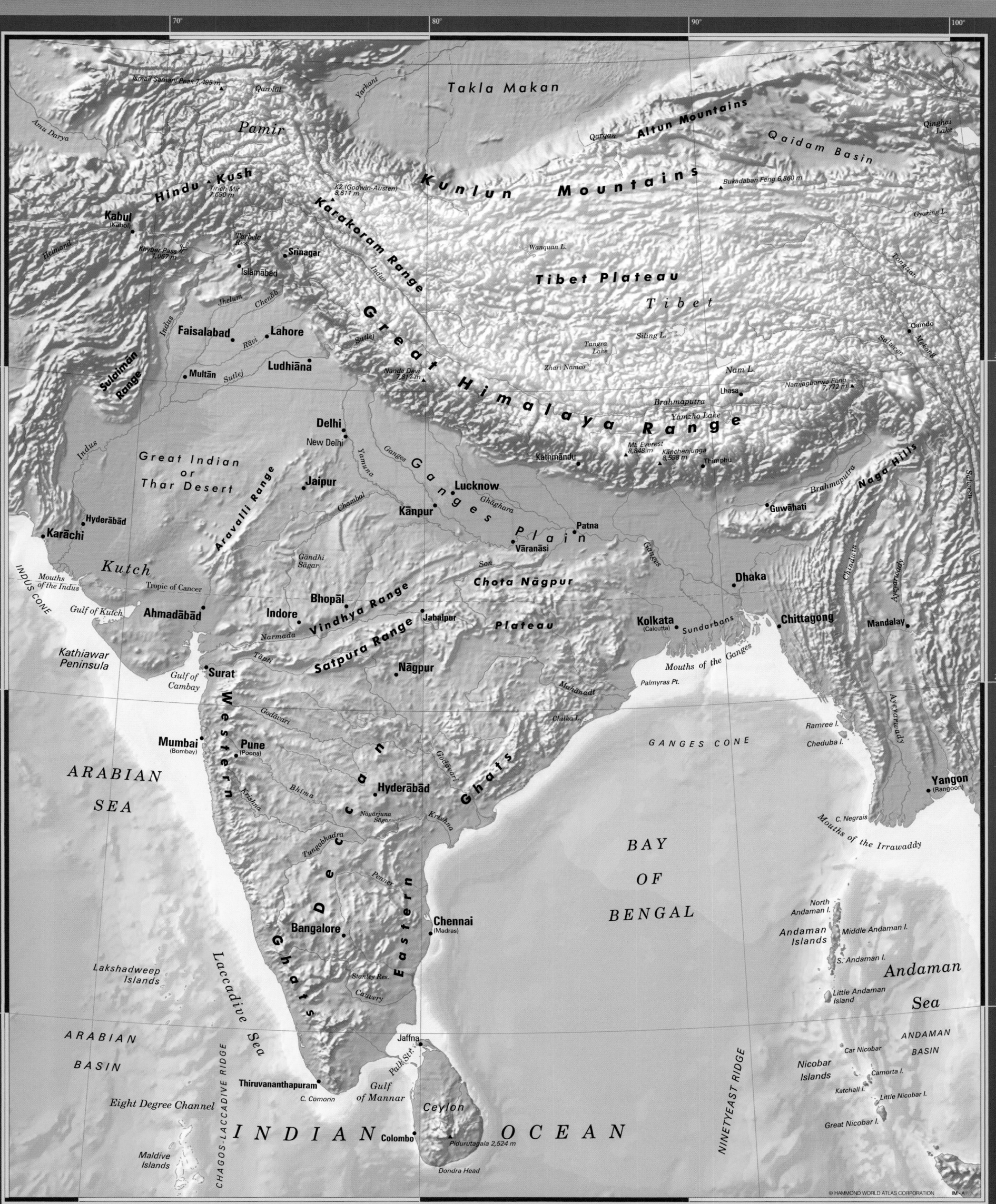

Height	
m.	ft.
6000	19700
4000	13000
2000	6500
1500	5000
1000	3300
500	1600
200	700
0	0
200	700
500	1600
1000	3300
2000	6500
3000	9800
4000	13000
5000	16400
6000	19700
m.	ft.
Depth	

© HAMMOND WORLD ATLAS CORPORATION

Scale 1:13,100,000 Lambert Conformal Conic Projection

MI		100	200	300	400
KM	100	200	300	400	600

Some 25 million years ago, the Red Sea opened, separating the Arabian Peninsula from Africa. At some time in the distant future, a new arm of the sea may extend from the southern Red Sea through the Afar Depression into continental Africa. Today, the oil fields along the Persian Gulf and around the Caspian seaport of Baku hold about two thirds of the world's known oil reserves.

Height	
m.	ft.
6000	19700
4000	13000
2000	6500
1500	5000
1000	3300
500	1600
200	700
-0-	
200	700
500	1600
1000	3300
2000	6500
3000	9800
4000	13000
5000	16400
6000	19700
m.	ft.
Depth	

© HAMMOND WORLD ATLAS CORPORATION

Scale 1:13,700,000 Lambert Conformal Conic Projection

MI 100 200 300 400

KM 100 200 300 400 500 600

Africa comprises some 30 million square kilometers – one-fifth of the world's total land area. Except for the young Atlas Mountains, the continent consists of an ancient shelf divided into basins by low rises. The African Sahara is the largest desert in the world. The East African Rift System, marked by the volcano Kilimanjaro (5,892 m) and other major peaks, runs north to south through the eastern half of the continent.

Scale 1:30,000,000   Hammond Optimal Conformal

MAP SECTION

Australia and Pacific Ocean

Situated on the Indo-Australian Plate, the continent of Australia lies on a largely stable foundation. The earth is considerably more active off the coasts of New Zealand and Japan and around the Aleutians. There, the subduction of oceanic crust is accompanied by lively volcanic activity caused primarily by the breakup of the East Pacific Rise extending from the Baja Peninsula in California to the Antarctic.

Scale 1:68,000,000 Miller Cylindrical Projection

| MI | 600 | 1200 | 1800 | 2400 |
| KM | 600 | 1200 | 1800 | 2400 | 3000 | 3600 |

© HAMMOND WORLD ATLAS CORPORATION

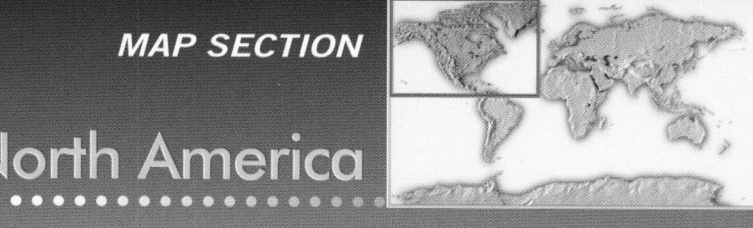

Two mountain ranges enclose the North American heartland: the old, heavily eroded Appalachian chain in the East and the Rocky Mountains of the Cordillera system in the West. The northernmost points of the continent are on Ellesmere Island and Greenland. Geographers place the southern continental boundary on the Isthmus of Tehuantepec in Mexico, although it is culturally a part of Central America.

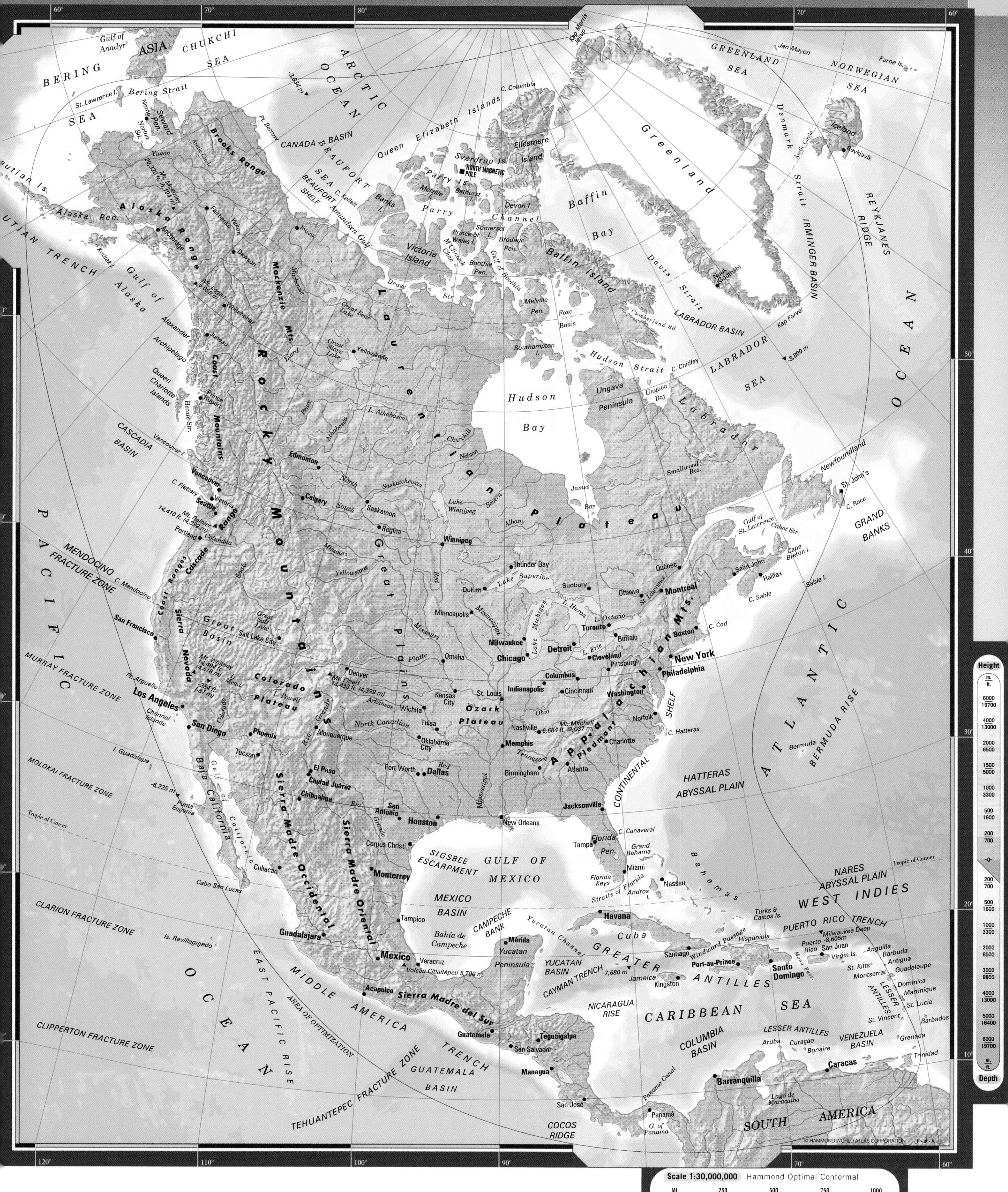

Height	
m.	ft.
6000	19700
4000	13000
2000	6500
1500	5000
1000	3300
500	1600
200	700
0	- 0 -
200	700
500	1600
1000	3300
2000	6500
3000	9800
4000	13000
5000	16400
6000	19700
m.	ft.
Depth	

Scale 1:30,000,000   Hammond Optimal Conformal

MI   0   250   500   750   1000
KM   0 250 500 750 1000 1250 1500

© HAMMOND WORLD ATLAS CORPORATION

Middle America

North and South America are connected only by a narrow land bridge. Actually, the two land masses are separated by the relatively small Caribbean Plate, whose western boundary is defined by the prominent East Middle America Trench, which reaches a depth of 6662 m off the coast of Chiapas in Mexico. There, the Cocos Plate is thrust under the Caribbean Plate, causing considerable earthquake and volcanic activity.

Scale 1:19,500,000   Lambert Conformal Conic Projection

© HAMMOND WORLD ATLAS CORPORATION

The Andes, extending 7200 km from north to south, are a product of the subduction of the Nazca Plate beneath the South American Plate. Some 130 million years ago, a 7000-km-wide strip of Pacific seafloor disappeared into the earth's crust. The rock melted, and the magma rising to the surface formed the Andes range, with snow-capped volcanoes rising to more than 6,000 meters above sea level.

CARIBBEAN SEA

Punta Gallinas

San José

Barranquilla

Maracaibo

L. de Maracaibo

Willemstad

Port-of-Spain

Caracas

Trinidad

G. of Paria

Panama Canal

Panamá

Pico Bolivar 5,007 m

Delta del Orinoco

Ciudad Guayana

DEMERARA ABYSSAL PLAIN

ATLANTIC

Gulf of Panama

Bucaramanga

Alto Ritacuba 5,493 m

Arauca

Orinoco

Georgetown

Paramaribo

MID-ATLANTIC RIDGE

PANAMA

Medellín

Nevado del Tolima 5,215 m

Meta

Salto del Angel

Mt. Roraima 2,772 m

Cayenne

PARA ABYSSAL PLAIN

OCEAN

Cabo Corrientes

Bogotá

Guaviare

Guiana Highlands

CEARA ABYSSAL PLAIN

Isla de Malpelo

Cali

Nevado del Huila 5,750 m

Salto Angostura

Yaupés

Orinoco

Rep. de Balbina

Ilha de Marajó

B. de Marajó

BASIN

Punta Galera

Pico de la Neblina 3,014 m

Branco

Pará

Belém

Equator

Quito

Salto Grande

Caquetá

Negro

Amazon

Equator

Chimborazo 6,267 m

Napo

Putumayo

Içá

Amazon

B. de São Marcos

São Luís

Guayaquil

Iquitos

Amazon

Manaus

Rep. de Tucuruí

Fortaleza

I. Fernando de Noronha

G. de Guayaquil

Marañón

Yavarí

Selvas

Madeira

Teresina

Punta Aguja

Pastaza

Ucayali

Juruá

Purus

Tapajós

Xingu

Natal

Cabo de São Roque

Trujillo

Huallaga

Nevado Huascarán 6,768 m

Madre de Diós

Rooseveld

Araguaia

Caatingas

Rep. de Sobradinho

Recife

PERU-CHILE TRENCH

La Montaña

Serra dos Parecis

Teles Pires

Tocantins

São Francisco

Maceió

PERU BASIN

Callao

Lima

Beni

Mamoré

Guaporé

Iténez

Juruena

Planalto do

Brazilian

Salvador

Cusco

Cordillera

Lake Titicaca

Nevado Ancohuma 6,550 m

Goiânia

Paraguaçu

NAZCA RIDGE

Apurímac

Arequipa

La Paz

Culuene

Mato Grosso

Brasília

Highlands

Jequitinhonha

PACIFIC

Altiplano

Arica

L. Poopó

Gran Chaco

Pilcomayo

Paranaíba

Campo Grande

Belo Horizonte

Pico da Bandeira 2,890 m

BRAZIL

OCEAN

-8,064 m

Antofagasta

Atacama Desert

Volcán Llullaillaco 6,723 m

Bermejo

Paraná

Grande

Tietê

São Paulo

Rio de Janeiro

Cabo de São Tomé

Santos

Cabo Frio

BASIN

Tropic of Capricorn

San Miguel de Tucumán

Cerro Ojos del Salado 6,880 m

Asunción

Represa de Itaipu

Cataratas del Iguazú

Iguaçu

Curitiba

Serra do Mar

Tropic of Capricorn

I. San Felix

I. San Ambrosio

Salado del Norte

Paraná

Uruguay

SANTOS PLATEAU

Is. Juan Fernández

Cordillera de los Andes

Cerro Aconcagua 6,959 m

L. Mar Chiquita

Santa Fe

Pôrto Alegre

RIO GRANDE

I. Alejandro Selkirk

I. Robinson Crusoe

Córdoba

Rosario

PLATEAU

CHALLENGER FRACTURE ZONE

Valparaíso

Mendoza

Pampas

Buenos Aires

La Plata

Montevideo

Río de la Plata

1500 5000

1000 3300

500 1600

200 700

Santiago

Salado

0

200 700

Concepción

Bahía Blanca

Colorado

Cabo San Antonio

Continental Shelf

ATLANTIC

500 1600

1000 3300

CHILE BASIN

Bahía Blanca

Negro

Limay

ARGENTINE

2000 6500

Puerto Montt

L. Nahuel Huapi

Golfo San Matías

Pen. Valdés

BASIN

3000 9800

CHILE RISE

Isla Chiloé

Chubut

OCEAN

4000 13000

G. Corcovado

Patagonia

Arch. de Los Chonos

Lago Buenos Aires

Golfo San Jorge

5000 16400

Pen. Taitao

Deseado

Cabo Tres Puntas

-6,098 m

6000 19700

Cabo Tres Montes

Chico

L. San Martín

Santa Cruz

Bahía Grande

FALKLAND ESCARPMENT

Isla Wellington

Arch. Reina Adelaida

West Falkland

Falkland Is.

East Falkland

Punta Arenas

Strait of Magellan

Tierra del Fuego

C. San Diego

© HAMMOND WORLD ATLAS CORPORATION

Cape Horn

Height

m. ft.

6000 19700

4000 13000

2000 6500

1500 5000

1000 3300

500 1600

200 700

0

200 700

500 1600

1000 3300

2000 6500

3000 9800

4000 13000

5000 16400

6000 19700

m. ft.

Depth

Scale 1:24,000,000   Lambert Azimuthal Equal-Area

MI   200   400   600   800

KM   200   400   600   800   1000 1200

According to an estimate published by the United Nations, roughly 8 billion people will be living on earth in the year 2025 – the majority of them in Asia and Africa. Their environment will have changed dramatically in the interim. The growing global population requires a constantly increasing supply of food, energy, and clean drinking water. Progressive land development threatens the survival of numerous animal and plant species. Even today, wars and migration can often be traced to deteriorating environmental conditions.

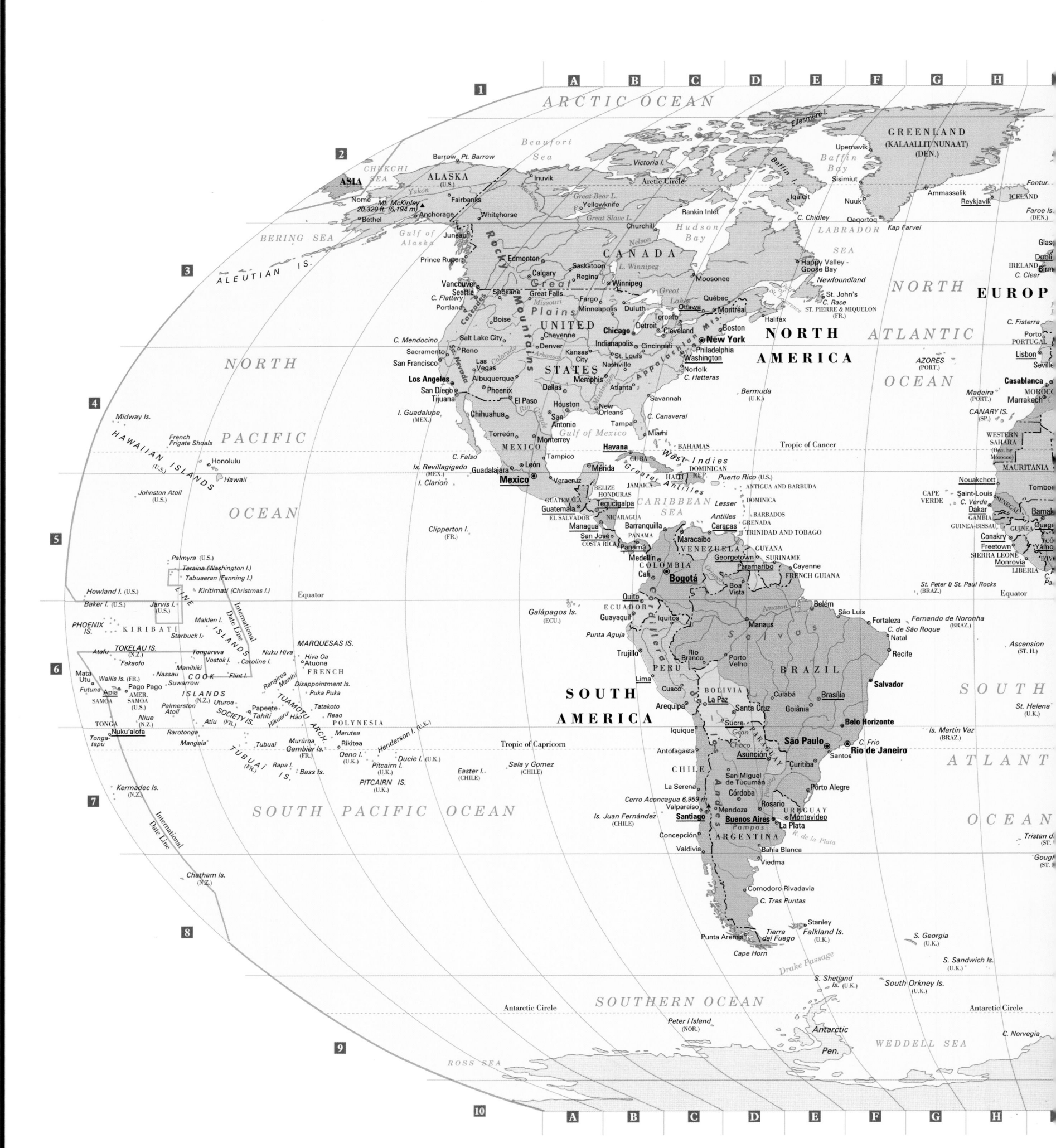

Population
- ⊛ Over 5,000,000
- ⊛ 2,000,000 - 4,999,999
- ⊙ 500,000 - 1,999,999
- ○ Under 500,000

L M N P Q R S T

ARCTIC OCEAN

FRANZ JOSEF LAND (RUS.)
Severnaya Zemlya
New Siberian Is.

BARENTS SEA
Novaya Zemlya
Kara Sea
Khatanga
Hammerfest
North Cape
Tromsø
Kirkenes
Murmansk
Nar'yan-Mar
Vorkuta
Noril'sk
Arctic Circle
Verkhoyansk
Anadyr'
Oulu
FINLAND
Archangel'sk
Salekhard
Yakutsk
Magadan
BERING SEA
Umeå
Tampere
Helsinki
St. Petersburg
Syktyvkar
Surgut
Tomsk
Siberia
Bodaybo
Okhotsk
Kamchatka
Petropavlovsk-Kamchatskiy
Mys Lopatka
Stockholm
Moscow
Nizhniy Novgorod
Perm'
Yekaterinburg
Nizhnevartovsk
Krasnoyarsk
Bratsk
Lensk
Komsomol'sk-na-Amure
SEA OF OKHOTSK
Göteborg
Berlin
Warsaw
Minsk
Yaroslavl'
Izhevsk
Nizhniy Tagil
Chelyabinsk
Novosibirsk
Novokuznetsk
Irkutsk
Chita
Ulan-Ude
Blagoveshchensk
Khabarovsk
Sakhalin
Int'l Date Line
Prague
RUSSIA
Kazan
Ufa
Magnitogorsk
Barnaul
L. Baykal
Vladivostok
Hokkaidō
Sapporo
KURIL IS.
Vienna
Budapest
UKRAINE
Kharkiv
Volgograd
Orenburg
Astana
KAZAKHSTAN
Ulaanbaatar
MONGOLIA
Choybalsan
Harbin
Jilin
Hakodate
Honshū
Sendai
Belgrade
Rostov
Astrakhan'
Qaraghandy
Almaty
Yining
Baotou
Changchun
Shenyang
Sea of Japan
Fukuoka
Tōkyō
Rome
Naples
İstanbul
Ankara
Baku
Bishkek
Ürümqi
Beijing
Tianjin
Dalian
P'yŏngyang
N. KOREA
Seoul
JAPAN
Kyōto
Yokohama
Athens
İzmir
Tbilisi
Tashkent
Takla Makan
Yumen
Yinchuan
Lanzhou
Taiyuan
S. KOREA
Pusan
Ōsaka
TURKEY
Adana
Tabriz
Mashhad
Dushanbe
Tibet
CHINA
Xi'an
Nanjing
Shanghai
EAST CHINA SEA
Kyūshū
İstanbul
Tehrān
Kabul
Islāmābād
Lhasa
Chengdu
Chongqing
Wuhan
Changsha
RYUKYU IS.
BONIN IS. (JAP.)
Iwo Jima
Baghdad
IRAN
Eşfahān
PAKISTAN
Lahore
Delhi
NEPAL
Mt. Everest 8,848 m
Kunming
Guiyang
Fuzhou
Guangzhou
Taipei
TAIWAN
Okinawa
VOLCANO IS. (JAP.)
Tropic of Cancer
Cairo
SAUDI ARABIA
Riyadh
Karāchi
Ahmadābād
New Delhi
BHUTAN
Dhaka
MYANMAR
Mandalay
Nanning
HONG KONG
Daito Is. (JAP.)
Minami-Tori-Shima (JAP.)
Mumbai
Pune
INDIA
Hyderābād
Kolkata
Hanoi
Hainan
C. Engaño
Okino-Tori-Shima (JAP.)
Farallon de Pajaros
Maug Is.
Wake I. (U.S.)
Mecca
Medina
ARABIAN SEA
Bangalore
BAY OF BENGAL
Yangon
THAILAND
VIETNAM
SOUTH CHINA SEA
Luzon
NORTHERN MARIANAS (U.S.)
Pagan
Alamagan
Anathan
Saipan
PHILIPPINE OCEAN
Khartoum
SUDAN
Asmara
ERITREA
Sanaa
YEMEN
Socotra (YEMEN)
Lakshadweep Is. (INDIA)
Coimbatore
Chennai
CAMBODIA
Bangkok
Phnom Penh
Ho Chi Minh City
Manila
PHILIPPINES
Samar
Hagåtña Guam (U.S.)
Yap Is.
Ulithi
Enewetak
Bikini
Rongelap
MARSHALL IS.
Maloelap
Addis Ababa
ETHIOPIA
Djibouti
Aden
Gulf of Aden
Gees Gwardafuy
C. Comorin
SRI LANKA
Colombo
Nicobar Is. (INDIA)
Andaman Is. (INDIA)
Mindanao
Ngulu
Babelthuap
Koror
PALAU
Sonsoral Is.
Namonuito
Hall Is.
Chuuk Is.
Lamotrek
Satawan
Senyavin
Kosrae
CAROLINE IS.
Butaritari
GILBERT IS.
Mogadishu
SOMALIA
MALDIVES
Male
Dondra Head
BRUNEI
Davao
Celebes Sea
Halmahera
Equator
FED. STATES OF MICRONESIA
Banaba
Tarawa
KIRIBATI
KENYA
Nairobi
Kampala
INDIAN OCEAN
BRITISH INDIAN OCEAN TERR.
Kuala Lumpur
MALAYSIA
SINGAPORE
Borneo
Celebes
Admiralty Is.
New Ireland
NAURU
Tabiteuea
Arorae
Kilimanjaro 5,895 m
Mombasa
Dar es Salaam
SEYCHELLES
Victoria
Mahé
Chagos Arch.
Diego Garcia
Medan
Sumatra
Palembang
Banjarmasin
Ujung Pandang
INDONESIA
Banda Sea
New Guinea
PAPUA NEW GUINEA
Jayapura
Bismarck Arch.
Bougainville
SOLOMON IS.
New Britain
Ontong Java
Nanumea
TUVALU
Funafuti
Lumumbashi
Kananga
Amirante Is.
Coetivy I.
Agalega Is. (MRTS.)
Java Sea
Jakarta
Bandung
Surabaya
Java
Bali
Sumba
EAST TIMOR
Arafura Sea
Port Moresby
Honiara
Guadalcanal
Sta. Isabel
Malaita
San Cristobal
Rennell I.
Sta. Cruz Is. (S.I.)
Espíritu Santo
Rotuma I. (FIJI)
Luanda
ANGOLA
COMOROS
Mayotte (FR.)
Aldabra Is. (SEY.)
Farquhar Group
Tanjon'i Bobaomby
Antsiranana
Christmas I. (AUSTL.)
Timor
Timor Sea
Darwin
Gulf of Carpentaria
Cape York Pen.
Cairns
CORAL SEA
VANUATU
Port-Vila
New Caledonia (FR.)
Nouméa
FIJI
Suva
Loyalty Is.
Benguela
Huambo
ZAMBIA
MALAWI
Lilongwe
MOZAMBIQUE
MADAGASCAR
Toamasina
Cocos Is. (AUSTL.)
Townsville
Rockhampton
Norfolk I. (AUSTL.)
C. Fria
NAMIBIA
ZIMBABWE
Harare
Antananarivo
Port Louis
MAURITIUS
Rodrigues (MRTS.)
Tropic of Capricorn
North West C.
Port Hedland
Great Sandy Desert
Brisbane
Lord Howe I. (AUSTL.)
Windhoek
BOTSWANA
Réunion (FR.)
Toliara
Tanjona Vohimena
AUSTRALIA
Alice Springs
Geraldton
Great Victoria Desert
Broken Hill
Newcastle
North C.
Kalahari
Gaborone
Pretoria
Maputo
SWAZILAND
LESOTHO
Johannesburg
Bloemfontein
Durban
SOUTH AFRICA
Amsterdam I. (FR.)
St. Paul I. (FR.)
Perth
Kalgoorlie
Whyalla
Great Australian Bight
Adelaide
Murray
Canberra
Sydney
TASMAN SEA
North I.
Auckland
Cape Town
Cape of Good Hope
C. Agulhas
Port Elizabeth
C. Leeuwin
Albany
Melbourne
Mt. Kosciusko 2,228 m
Wellington
NEW ZEALAND
Christchurch
South I.
Prince Edward Is. (S. AFR.)
Crozet Is. (FR.)
Kerguélen (FR.)
McDonald Is. (AUSTL.)
Macquarie I. (AUSTL.)
Auckland Is. (N.Z.)
Campbell I. (N.Z.)
Antipodes Is. (N.Z.)
Bounty Is. (N.Z.)
South East C.
Hobart
Tasmania
Dunedin
South C.

SOUTHERN OCEAN
C. Batterbee
Antarctic Circle
ANTARCTICA
C. Adare
ROSS SEA

NORTH PACIFIC OCEAN
PHILIPPINE SEA
RALIK CHAIN
Kwajalein
Majuro
Mili

1 2 3 4 5 6 7 8 9 10

© HAMMOND WORLD ATLAS CORPORATION

Scale 1:70,000,000 Robinson Projection

MI 600 1200 1800 2400

KM 600 1200 1800 2400 3000 3600

Europe

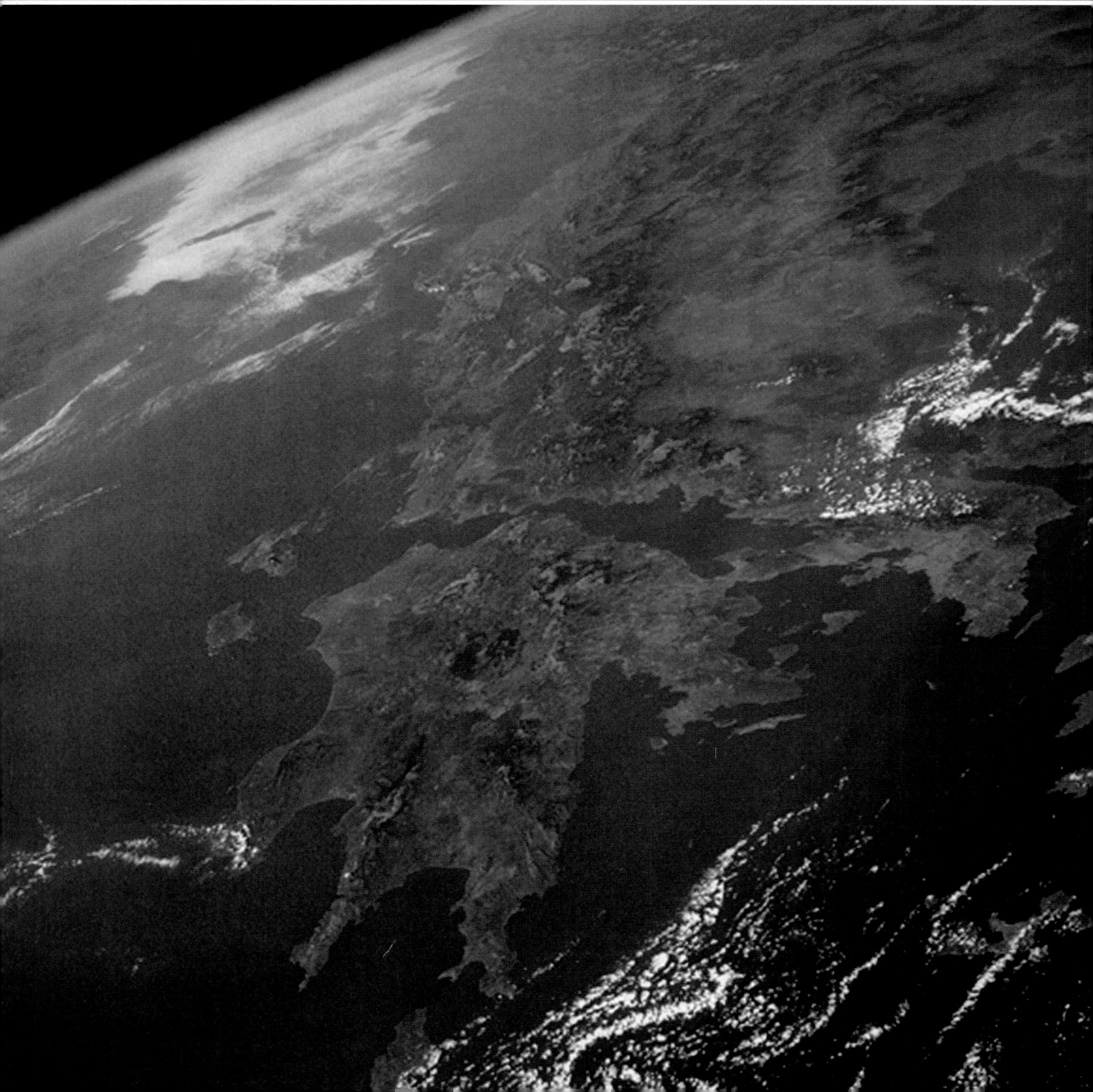

The four large peninsulas of Peloponnesus extend like fingers into the Mediterranean south of the Gulf of Corinth. The peninsula as a whole is bounded by the Ionian Sea to the west and the Mirtóön Sea to the east. The ancient Greeks regarded Cape Taínaron, located at the tip of the central peninsula, as the end of the world. The Peloponnesus, the Gulf of Corinth, and the Pindus Mountains to the north are excellent examples of the effects of the upward and downward thrust of segments of the earth's crust caused by the collision of the African and Eurasian Plates.

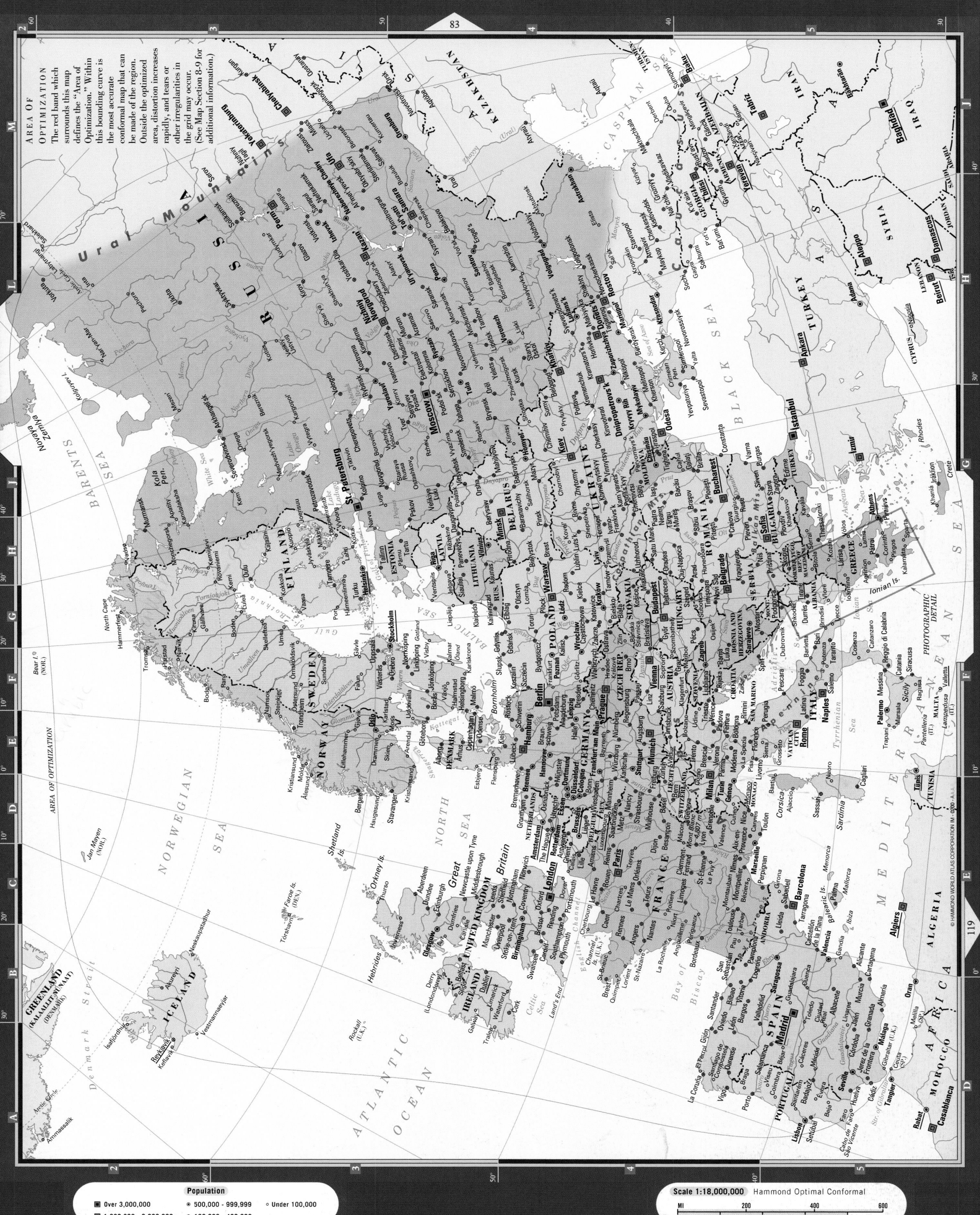

Population

■ Over 3,000,000 ● 500,000 - 999,999 ○ Under 100,000
■ 1,000,000 - 2,999,999 ⊙ 100,000 - 499,999

Scale 1:18,000,000 Hammond Optimal Conformal

MI   200   400   600

KM   200   400   600   800

UNESCO Protects World Cultural Heritage Sites

World Heritage Sites in EUROPE

Perspectives for the World Heritage Convention

Armed conflict ranks highest among the many dangers to which our cultural heritage is exposed. The impact of industrialization and urban development is also significant. Air pollution threatens building substance, tourism detracts from the authenticity of cultural sites, and the dynamics of technical and economic progress often impair the integrity of traditional cultural treasures.

Can Tourists Save the World Cultural Heritage?

Can the goal of protecting monuments of the World Cultural Heritage be achieved without neglecting the needs of people who live near them? It is not enough merely to list the necessary protective measures. It is equally important to consider marketing issues and to respond to the wishes and expectations of visitors. This applies in particular to the cultural landscape, the youngest category of the World Heritage List. The "sustainable cultural landscape" is classified as a region in which change must take place in order to ensure that its inhabitants can continue to live normal lives. But which elements of a cultural landscape can be changed without detracting from their outstanding character, and which must be preserved unaltered? The field of possibilities is broad.

Text continues on page 84 - UNESCO World Cultural Heritage Sites of Asia

Catharist Bastion

Fortified by two rings of walls, the medieval city of **Carcassonne (38)** crowns a hill above the Aude Valley. Situated along a route from the Atlantic to the Mediterranean, its position was of strategic importance during periods of Muslim and Frankish occupation. It was captured after a long siege during the Albigensian Wars in 1209.

Mysterious Religious Ritual

Rock drawing of a ship and two axe-wielding warriors from the Nordic Bronze Age in **Tanum (241)**, southern Sweden.

Early Christian Refuge

The rocky island of **Skellig Michael (86)** and ruins of the cloister of Saint Finan (9th c.). The structure is one of the earliest examples of Irish architecture.

Europe's First Mountain Railway

With many tunnels and viaducts, the **Semmering Railway (121)** crosses Semmering Pass (elevation: 985 m) between Lower Austria and the Steiermark. Built between 1848 and 1854, the line is a true adhesion railway with a maximum incline of 2.5%.

Bulgarian Renaissance Castle

The **Rila Monastery (181)** was a center of painting and literature in the 18th and 19th centuries and played an important role in the growth of a national identity. Thick, high external walls give the complex the look of a fortress.

Fortified Religious Architecture

The rich heritage of Transylvanian art is represented by a number of unique churches. These **fortified churches (195)** offered protection for the "Saxons" who settled in the border region. The choir tower was the defensive core of the complex.

"With Outspread Arms"

In just this way, according to Bernini's vision, the collonades surrounding St. Peter's Square in **Rome (146)** were to welcome visitors to the new Basilica of St. Peter (early 17th c.).

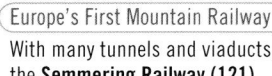

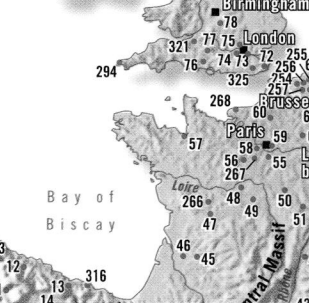

Moorish Art in Perfection

The architecture of the Alhambra of **Granada (27)** is less striking than its decorative embellishments. The intricate ornamentation of even a small niche bears witness to a tendency toward a dematerialization of objective representation.

Ancient Greek Religious Site

The Oracle of the Temple of Apollo at **Delphi (173)** was consulted by pilgrims about the prospects for success in business or political endeavors.

Northern Boundary of the Roman Empire

The borders of the empire were expanded and fortified to form a permanent defense line under Roman Emperor Hadrian. The photo shows part of **Hadrian's Wall (82)** in northern England.

Unique Silver Mines

The **Rammelsberg Mines (108)** in the Harz Mountains is the only mine complex in the world that boasts 1,000 years of continuous operation. They were closed in 1988. A shaft from the 12th century is well preserved.

UNESCO World Cultural Heritage Sites in Europe

1 City Center of Angra do Heroismo, Azores (not shown on map)
2 Cultural Landscape of Sintra
3 Hieronymite Monastery and Tower of Belem
4 Historic Center of Evora
5 Alcobaca Monastery
6 Batalha Monastery
7 Convent of Christ in Tomar
8 Rock-Art Sites in the Coa Valley
9 Historic Center of Porto
10 Historic Center of Santiago de Compostela
11 Las Medulas
12 Churches of the Kingdom of the Asturias
13 Altamira Cave
14 Cathedral of Burgos
15 San Millan Yuso and Suso Monasteries
16 Old Town of Salamanca
17 Old Town of Segovia
18 Old Town of Ávila
19 El Escorial
20 Historic Precinct of Alcalá de Henares
21 Historic City of Toledo
22 Monastery of Santa Maria de Guadalupe
23 Old Town of Cáceres
24 Roman Buildings in Mérida
25 Cathedral and Alcazar in Seville
26 Mosque of Córdoba
27 Granada
28 'La Lonja de la Seda' of Valencia
29 Ibiza
30 Rock Art of the Mediterranean Basin on the Iberian Peninsula
31 Historic Walled Town of Cuenca
32 Mudejar Architecture of Aragón
33 Poblet Monastery
34 Parque Guell and Case Mila, Barcelona
35 Palau de la Musica in Barcelona
36 Mont Perdu in the Pyrenees
37 Pilgrims' Route to Santiago de Compostela
38 Old City of Carcassonne
39 Le Canal du Midi
40 Pont du Gard (Roman Aqueduct)
41 Arles
42 Papal Palace of Avignon
43 Orange (Roman Theater, Triumphal Arch)
44 Historical Monuments of Lyon
45 Decorated Grottoes of the Vézère Valley
46 Saint-Émilion
47 Church of Saint-Savin-sur-Gartempe
48 Chambord Castle
49 Cathedral of Bourges
50 Abbey Church of Vézelay
51 Royal Saltworks of Arc-et-Senans
52 Cistercian Abbey of Fontenay
53 Sites in Nancy
54 Strasbourg, Grand Ile
55 Palace and Park of Fontainebleau
56 Chartres Cathedral
57 Mont Saint-Michel
58 Palace and Park of Versailles
59 Banks of the Seine, Paris
60 Cathedral of Amiens
61 Cathedral of Reims
62 Old City of Luxembourg
63 Medieval Belfries of Flanders, Wallonia
64 Four Lifts on the Canal de Centre
65 La Grande Place, Brussels
66 Flemish Beguinages
67 Mill Network of Kinderdijk-Elshout
68 Defense Line of Amsterdam
69 Beemster Polder
70 Shokland and Environs
71 Steam Pump Plant in Wouda
72 Canterbury Cathedral
73 Royal Greenwich Park
74 Westminster Abbey and Church of St. Margaret, London
75 Tower of London
76 Stonehenge and Avebury
77 Bath
78 Blenheim Palace
79 Monuments in Ironbridge Valley
80 Fortifications of Edward I in Wales
81 Fountains Abbey
82 Hadrian's Wall
83 Castle and Cathedral in Durham
84 Edinburgh
85 Orkney Islands
86 Skellig Michael
87 Bend of the Boyne
88 Jelling Mounds
89 Roskilde Cathedral
90 Hanseatic City of Lübeck
91 Cologne Cathedral
92 Roman Monuments, Cathedral in Trier
93 Castles in Brühl
94 Aachen Cathedral
95 Völklingen Ironworks
96 Speyer Cathedral
97 Abbey and Altenmünster of Lorsch
98 Maulbronn Monastery Complex
99 Pilgrimage Church of Wies
100 Residence in Würzburg
101 Old Town of Bamberg
102 Wartburg Castle
103 Classical Weimar
104 Luther Memorials in Eisleben, Wittenberg
105 Bauhaus Sites in Weimar and Dessau
106 Historic Sites in Quedlinburg
107 St. Mary's Cathedral, St. Michaels Church, Hildesheim
108 Mines of Rammelsberg and the Historic Town of Goslar
109 Palaces and Parks in Potsdam and Berlin
110 Museum Island, Berlin
111 Historic Center of Prague
112 Historic Center of Kutná Hora
113 Litomysl Castle
114 Gardens and Castle at Kroměříž
115 Lednice-Caltice Cultural Landscape
116 Pilgrimage Church at Zelen Hora in Zd'ár nad Sázavou
117 Historic Center of T?lc
118 Holasovice Historical Village Reservation
119 Historic Center of Krumau
120 Palace and Gardens of Schönbrunn
121 Semmering Railway
122 Old City of Graz
123 Salzkammergut Cultural Landscape
124 Historic Center, City of Salzburg
125 Convent of St. Gallen
126 Old City of Bern
127 Convent of St. John at Müstair
128 Rock Drawings in Valcamonica
129 Crespi d'Adda
130 Santa Maria delle Grazie in Milan
131 Residences of the Royal House of Savoy
132 Portovenere and Cinque Terre
133 Cathedral and Piazza Grande, Modena
134 Ferrara
135 Vicenza, Palladio and Villas on the Veneto
136 Botanical Gardens, Padua
137 Aquileia
138 Venice
139 Early Christian Monuments of Ravenna
140 Historic Center of Florence
141 Piazza del Duomo, Pisa
142 Historic Center of San Gimignano
143 Historic Center of Siena
144 Historic Center of Urbino
145 Historic Center of Pienza
146 Historic Center of Rome, Properties of the Holy See, and San Paolo Fuori le Mura
147 Villa Adriana
148 Su Nuraxi di Barumini
149 Royal Palace at Caserta
150 Historic Center of Naples
151 Costiera Amalfitana
152 Archeological Areas of Pompeii, Ercolano
153 Paestum and Certosa di Pavia
154 Castel del Monte
155 Trulli of Alberobello
156 I Sassi di Matera
157 Agrigento
158 Roman Villa of Casale
159 Megalithic Temples of Malta
160 City of Valletta
161 Hal Saflieni Hypogeum
162 Medieval City of Rhodes
163 Historical Sites, Island of Patmos
164 Island of Delos
165 Pythagoreion and Hereion of Samos
166 Monuments of Chios
167 Acropolis, Athens
168 Archeological Sites of Mycenae and Tiryns
169 Archeological Site of Epidaurus
170 Mystras
171 Temple of Apollo at Bassae
172 Archeological Site of Olympia
173 Archeological Site of Delphi
174 Meteora
175 Mount Athos
176 Monuments of Thessaloniki
177 Archeological Sites of Vergina
178 Butrint
179 City and Lake of Ohrid
180 Church of Boyana
181 Monastery of Rila
182 Thracian Tomb of Kazanlak
183 Rock-hewn Churches of Ivanovo
184 Ancient City of Nessebar
185 Madara Rider
186 Thracian Tomb of Sveshtari
187 Monastery of Studenica
188 Stari Ras and Sopocani Monastery
189 Historic Region of Kotor
190 Old City of Dubrovnik
191 Historic Complex of Split
192 Historic City of Trogir
193 Historic Center of Porec
194 Dacian Fortresses in Orastie Mountains
195 Fortified Churches in Transylvania
196 Horezu Monastery
197 Historic Center of Sighisoara
198 Churches of Moldavia
199 Wooden Churches of Maramures
200 Hortobágy National Park
201 Benedictine Monastery of Pannonhalma
202 Budapest
203 Holloko
204 Banska Stiavnica
205 Vlkolinec Reservation of Folk Architecture
206 Spissky Hrad and Environs
207 Historic Center of L'viv
208 Kiev
209 Old City of Zamosc
210 Wieliczka Salt Mine
211 Historic Center of Kraków
212 Kalwaria Zebrzydowska
213 Auschwitz Concentration Camp
214 Historic Center of Warsaw
215 Medieval Town of Torum
216 Malbork
217 Historic Center of Vilnius
218 Historic Center of Riga
219 Historic Center of Tallinn
220 Historic Center of St. Petersburg
221 Historic Monuments in Novgorod
222 Church of Anscension, Kolomenskoye
223 Kremlin and Red Square, Moscow
224 Monastery in Sergiev Possad
225 White Monuments of Vladimir and Suzdal
226 Kizhi Pogost in Lake Onega
227 Cultural and Historic Ensemble of the Solovetsky Islands
228 Verla Groundwood and Board Mill
229 Fortress of Suomenlinna
230 Old Rauma
231 Petäjävesi Old Church
232 Burial Site of Sammallahdenmäki
233 Laponian Area
234 Old City of Luleå
235 Engelsberg Ironworks
236 Skogskrykogården
237 Royal Domain of Drottningholm
238 Birka and Hovgården
239 Hanseatic Town of Visby
240 Naval Port of Karlskrona
241 Rock Carvings in Tanum
242 Bryggen, Old Hanseatic Quater of Bergen
243 Urnes Stave Church
244 Røros Mining Town
245 Rock Drawings of Alta
246 Museum-City of Gjirokastra
247 Madriu-Perafita-Claror Valley
248 Wachau Cultural Landscape
249 Fertö / Neusiedlersee Cultural Landscape
250 Historic Centre of Vienna
251 Mir Castle Complex
252 Complex of the Radziwill Family at Nesvizh
253 Struve Geodetic Arc (Belarus, Estonia, Finland, Latvia, Lithuania, Norway, Moldova, Russia, Sweden, Ukraine)
254 Historic Centre of Brugge
255 Major Town Houses of the Architect Victor Horta
256 Neolithic Flint Mines at Spiennes
257 Notre-Dame Cathedral in Tournai
258 Plantin-Moretus House-Workshops-Museum
259 Old Bridge Area of the Old City of Mostar
260 The Cathedral of St James in Šibenik
261 Holy Trinity Column in Olomouc
262 Tugendhat Villa in Brno
263 Jewish Quarter, St Procopius' Basilica in T?ebí?
264 Kronborg Castle
265 Vegaøyan - The Vega Archipelago
266 The Loire Valley
267 Provins, Town of Medieval Fairs
268 Le Havre, the City Rebuilt by Auguste Perret
269 Garden Kingdom of Dessau-Wörlitz
270 Monastic Island of Reichenau
271 Zollverein Coal Mine Industrial Complex in Essen
272 Historic Centres of Stralsund and Wismar
273 Upper Middle Rhine Valley
274 Dresden Elbe Valley
275 Muskauer Park / Park Muzakowski
276 Town Hall on the Marketplace of Bremen
277 Old Town of Regensburg with Stadtamhof
278 Early Christian Necropolis of Pécs (Sopianae)
279 Fertö / Neusiedlersee Cultural Landscape
280 Tokaj Wine Region Historic Cultural Landscape
281 Þingvellir National Park
282 Assisi, the Basilica of San Francesco
283 City of Verona
284 Villa d'Este, Tivoli
285 Late Baroque Towns of the Val di Noto
286 Sacri Monti of Piedmont and Lombardy
287 Etruscan Necropolises of Cerveteri and Tarquinia
288 Val d'Orcia
289 Syracuse and the Rocky Necropolis of Pantalica
290 Genoa: Le Strade Nuove and the Palazzi dei Rolli
291 Kernav? Archaeological Site
292 Rietveld Schröderhuis (Rietveld Schröder House)
293 Landscape of the Pico Island Vineyard Culture
294 Cornwall and West Devon Mining Landscape
295 Churches of Peace in Jawor and Swidnica
296 Wooden Churches of Southern Little Poland
297 Muskauer Park / Park Muzakowski
298 Centennial Hall in Wroclaw
299 Alto Douro Wine Region
300 Historic Centre of Guimarães
301 Curonian Spit
302 Ensemble of the Ferrapontov Monastery
303 Historic Complex of the Kazan Kremlin
304 Citadel, Ancient City and Buildings of Derbent
305 Ensemble of the Novodevichy Convent
306 Historical Centre of the City of Yaroslavl
307 Medieval Monuments in Kosovo
308 Bardejov Town Conservation Reserve
309 Archaeological Ensemble of Tárraco
310 Archaeological Site of Atapuerca
311 Catalan Romanesque Churches of the Vall de Boí
312 Palmeral of Elche
313 Roman Walls of Lugo
314 Aranjuez Cultural Landscape
315 Monumental Ensembles of Úbeda and Baeza
316 Vizcaya Bridge
317 Agricultural Landscape of Southern Öland
318 Mining of the Great Copper Mountain in Falun
319 Varberg Radio Station
320 Three Castles of the Market-Town of Bellinzone
321 Blaenavon Industrial Landscape
322 Derwent Valley Mills
323 New Lanark
324 Saltaire
325 Royal Botanic Gardens, Kew
326 Liverpool – Maritime Mercantile City

The European Union at a Glance

A Place in the Union

✧ The EU was set up in the aftermath of the Second World War to bring peace, stability and prosperity to Europe. Since its foundation more than 50 years ago, the EU has been a magnet, attracting a constant stream of new members, expanding from 15 to 27. Bulgaria and Romania are the latest countries to enter in 2007.

✧ Any European country may join, provided it has a stable democracy that guarantees the rule of the law, human rights and the protection of minorities. It must also have a functional market economy and a civil service capable of applying EU laws.

Symbols of the Union

✧ The countries that make up the EU remain independent sovereign nations, but they pool their sovereignty in order to gain strength and world influence.

✧ Entry negotiations began in 2005 with Turkey and Croatia. It can take up to 10 years or more before a country can enter the union, provided the application is ratified by the EU Parliament and by the national parliament of the cadidate country.

◉ **Flag:** The 12 stars in the a circle symbolize the ideals of perfection, completeness and unity

◉ **The European Anthem:** Melody from the Ninth Symphony by Beethoven (no words)

◉ **Europe Day:** May 9th

◉ **EU moto:** "United in diversity"

Fewer Frontiers

✧ The first right of a European citizen is the right to travel, work, live and retire in any EU country. These rights are gradually being extended to citizens from the 12 countries that have joined the EU since 2004.

✧ Citizens may travel across the EU without carrying a passport.

✧ Any person who is a national of an EU country may work in the health, education and other public services anywhere in the Union, except for public authorities (the police, armed forces, foreign affairs, etc.).

✧ You can shop in another country without paying any additional taxes.

✧ The single currency, the euro, allows shoppers to compare prices in the 13 countries that use it.

A _greener_ EU

✧ People in Europe are very environmentally conscious. The EU is trying to preserve the environment and promote sustainable development.

✧ The EU signed the Kyoto Protocol to reduce emissions of the "greenhouse gases" blamed for global warming and climate change.

✧ In 2005 the EU introduced an "emission trading scheme", which allows manufacturing companies to buy and sell a limited number of pollution permits.

Historic Dates

1951: The European Coal and Steel Community is established by the six founding members

1957: The Treaty of Rome establishes a common market

1973: The Community expands to nine member states and develops its common policies

1979: The first direct elections to the European Parliament

1981: The first Mediterranean expansion

1993: - Completion of the single market
- The Treaty of Maastricht establishes the European Union

1995: The EU expands to 15 members

2001: The Treaty of Nice sets policy for expanded European Union

2002: Euro notes and coins are introduced

2004: Ten more countries join the Union

2007: Two more countries join the Union

Euro Usage by Country

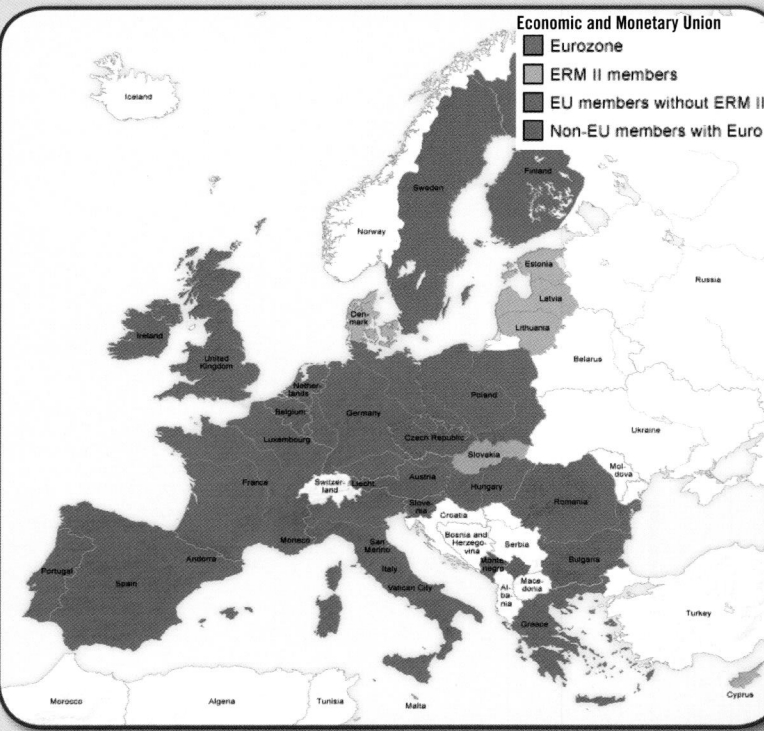

Economic and Monetary Union
- ◼ Eurozone
- ◼ ERM II members
- ◼ EU members without ERM II
- ◼ Non-EU members with Euro

✧ **EU countries using the euro:**
Austria, Belgium, Finland, France, Germany, Greece, Ireland, Italy, Luxembourg, the Netherlands, Portugal, Slovenia and Spain

✧ **EU countries not using the euro:**
Bulgaria, Cyprus, Czech Republic, Denmark, Estonia, Hungary, Latvia, Lithuania, Malta, Poland, Romania, Sweden and the United Kingdom

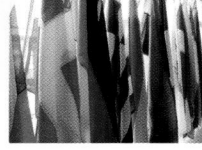

Member States of the EU
(year of entrance)

Austria (1995)
Belgium (1952)
Bulgaria (2007)
Cyprus (2004)
Czech Republic (2004)
Denmark (1973)
Estonia (2004)
Finland (1995)
France (1952)
Germany (1952)
Greece (1981)
Hungary (2004)
Ireland (1973)
Italy (1952)

Latvia (2004)
Lithuania (2004)
Luxembourg (1952)
Malta (2004)
Netherlands (1952)
Poland (2004)
Portugal (1986)
Romania (2007)
Slovakia (2004)
Slovenia (2004)
Spain (1986)
Sweden (1995)
United Kingdom (1973)

EU Member
Candidate Countries

© HAMMOND WAC

The European Union at a Glance

* The European Parliament (EP) is elected every 5 years by the citizens of the European Union.
* The main job of Parliament is to pass European laws.
* The present Parliament has 785 members from all 27 EU countries (only 736 members for the 2009-14 term).
* Members of the EU Parliament do not sit in national blocks, but in seven Europe-wide political groups.
* The EU Parliament has three centers of operation: Brussels (Belgium), Luxembourg and Strasbourg (France).
* It functions in all 23 official EU languages.

Parliament Members

Term Country	2009-14 ▼	04-09 ▼	Term Country	2009-14 ▼	04-09 ▼
Austria	17	18	Latvia	8	9
Belgium	22	24	Lithuania	12	13
Bulgaria	17	18	Luxembourg	6	6
Cyprus	6	6	Malta	5	5
Czech Rep.	22	24	Netherlands	25	27
Denmark	13	14	Poland	50	54
Estonia	6	6	Portugal	22	24
Finland	13	14	Romania	33	35
France	72	78	Slovakia	13	14
Germany	99	99	Slovenia	7	7
Greece	22	24	Spain	50	54
Hungary	22	24	Sweden	18	19
Ireland	12	13	U.K.	72	78
Italy	72	78	Total	736	785

EU Council

* The Council shares with Parliament the responsibility for passing laws and making policy decisions.
* It consists of ministers from the national governments of all the EU countries.
* Each country has a number of votes reflecting the size of their population, but weighted in favor of smaller ones.
* Decisions are taken by majority vote. Issues like taxation, asylum, immigration and security require unanimity.
* Presidents of member States meet up to four times a year as the EU Council. These "summits" set overall EU policy.

EU Commision

* The Commision represents and upholds the interest of all EU countries.
* It is independent of all national governments.
* It drafts proposals for new European laws, and manages policies and spending of EU funds.
* It consists of 27 members - one from each EU country. Most work in Brussels.
* Its President and members are appointed for 5 years. The term is the same period as for Parliament.

EURO BILLS

EURO COINS

EUROPEAN PARLIAMENT in STRASBOURG

INSIDE EU PARLIAMENT

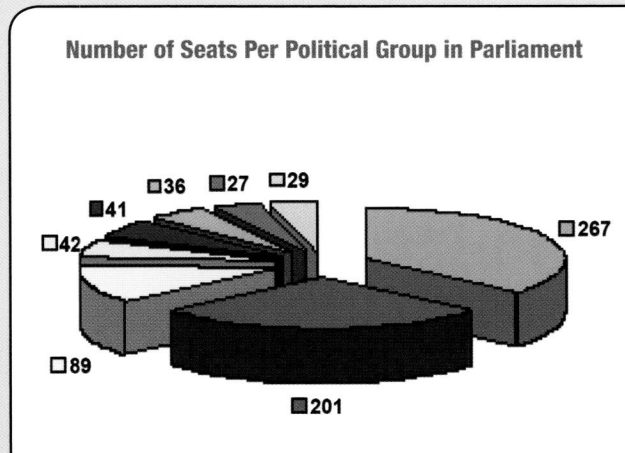

Number of Seats Per Political Group in Parliament

267, 201, 89, 42, 41, 36, 27, 29

Political Group	Abbreviation
European People's Party (Christian Democrats) and European Democrats	EPP-ED
Socialist Group	PES
Alliance of Liberals and Democrats for Europe	ALDE
Greens/European Free Alliance	Greens/EFA
European United Left - Nordic Green Left	GUE/NGL
Independence/Democracy	IND/DE
Union for Europe of the Nations	UEN
Non-attached	NI

Court of Justice

* Makes sure that EU law is interpreted and applied in the same way in all EU countries.
* It ensures that national courts do not give different rulings on the same issue.
* It makes sure that EU member states and institutions do what the law requires.
* It has one judge from each member country.
* The Court is based in Luxembourg.

Court of Auditors

* Checks that the EU's funds are spent legally, economically, and for their intended purposes.
* It has the right to audit any organization or company which handles EU funds.
* The Court is based in Luxembourg.

Committee of the Regions

* Is consulted on upcoming EU decisions.
* It has impact at the local and regional level in areas such as transportation.
* The Committee is based in Luxembourg.

Economic and Social Committee

* Has 344 members.
* It represents many interests, from employers to trade unionists, from consumers to ecologists.
* It gives its opinion on EU decisions about employment, social spending, vocational training, etc.

Central Bank

* Has responsibility for managing the euro.
* It sets interest rates.
* It ensures price stability so the EU economy is not damaged by inflation.
* It makes decisions independent of governments.
* The Central Bank is based in Frankfurt, Germany.

MAASTRICHT TREATY 1993

ECSC TREATY 1951

ROME TREATY 1957

EURO LAUNCH 2002

NICE TREATY 2001

Traveling Europe by Train

What to Expect

- Traveling by train can be an amazing exprience. It is convenient, reliable, and affordable. If you're planning a trip to Europe, try exploring the continent by train. If you are uncertain of how train travel works in Europe, we will show you how to get around. There is information about rail stations, what to do with your luggage, how to read timetables, get a ticket, get on the right train and find the right seat.

- It is a good idea to start your trip by flying into a European airport that offers direct links to major train stations (see list of **Airports with Train Stations**).

- Most train stations in Europe are unique, picturesque and have town personality - they are often tourist attractions themselves.

Services Found in Train Stations

- ▸ **Access to Metro/Subway Stations**
- ▸ **ATMs**
- ▸ **Bookstores (source of maps and city tour guides)**
- ▸ **Currency Exchange**
- ▸ **Gift Shops**
- ▸ **Information Desks (look for "i", universal symbol for "Information")**
- ▸ **Lockers**
- ▸ **Luggage Carts**
- ▸ **Postal Services**
- ▸ **Reservation Offices**
- ▸ **Restaurants**
- ▸ **Restrooms**
- ▸ **Taxi Stands**

Finding Your Train and Using Timetables

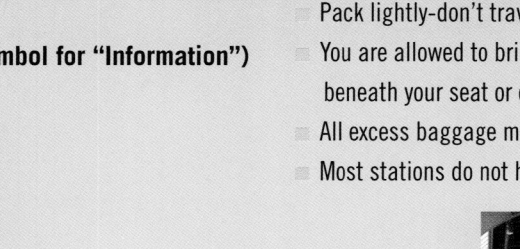

- Most timetables show departure, arrival and platform number.

- Usually, departure timetables are printed with yellow background while arrivals are printed in white.

- Major rail stations provide timetables on computerized boards.

- All trains are listed chronologically from 0 to 24 hours.

- Fast trains are shown in red rather than black type.

- Next to the time, the name and number of the important intermediate stops, as well as track and platform number from which the train departs and arrives can be found.

Luggage/Baggage

- Pack lightly–don't travel with more bags than you need.

- You are allowed to bring as many carry-on bags as can fit beneath your seat or on the baggage rack above you.

- All excess baggage must be checked.

- Most stations do not have porters.

Airports with Train Stations

Amsterdam Schiphol
Athens (Eleftherios Venizelos)
Barcelona Prat
Berlin Schönefeld
Birmingham
Brussels Nationaal
Copenhagen
Düsseldorf
Frankfurt am Main
Geneve Coitrin
London (Gatwick, Heathrow, Stansted)
Malaga
Manchester
München Franz Josef Strauss
Paris Charles de Gaulle
Rome Leonardo da Vinci
Stockholm
Stuttgart Echterdingen
Wien Schwechat
Zurich Kloten

Boarding the Right Car

- Each train car has an identification panel on its side to indicate:
  - ▸ **on top:** name of the city where it originated.
  - ▸ **on the bottom:** name of the final destination.
  - ▸ **in the middle:** names of the most important stops en route.
  - ▸ **beside the door:** a panel indicating the car number.

- It is very important to get on the right car.

- Some trains can split at certain junctions with each part heading in different directions.

- Passengers with reservations must match the number shown on the ticket with the correct car and seat number.

- If you are getting off a train at a small town or station not listed on the identification panel of the car, you need to find out from the conductor which car you should be on before or after boarding.

- Many train stations have diagrams that show the location of each car on the train. Use the diagrams to position yourself on the platform close to your car and seat.

- Each car is marked first-class or second-class with the number "1" or "2".

- Some trains may have a yellow stripe below the roof for first class and green for second-class.

RAIL SYSTEM IN EUROPE

EUROSTAR

Main stations for this highspeed trains: London (Waterloo Int'l), Ashford (Ashford Int'l, Kent), Calais (Calais-Frethun), Lille (Lille Europe), Brussels (Brussels-Midi/Zuid), Paris (Gare du Nord) - London to Paris takes 2 hours 35 minutes, London to Brussels 2 hours 15 minutes.

Rail Accommodations and Rail Passes

First-Class or Second-Class

- First-class is generally quieter, roomier, comfortable, efficient, safe and can even be an elegant experience.
- First-class tickets are only moderately more expensive than second-class tickets.
- There are fewer seats per car in first-class, and more space for luggage.
- Second-class may be more comfortable in some countries than in others.
- A meal might be included in the price of a first-class ticket on some Premier trains.
- The style of service on the train is as unique as the personality of each country.

On Day Trains

- **Coach car seating:** the car is open with a center aisle and seats on either side.
- First-class often has two seats on one side of the aisle and one on the other.
- Second-class has two seats on each side of the aisle.
- **Compartment seating:** The car is separated into enclosed cabins with a corridor along one side.
- First-class cabins can accommodate up to six passengers and second-class up to eight passengers.

On Night Trains

- **Sleepers:** The most comfortable way to travel by train at night.
- They contain berths, a private washstand, fresh linens and towels.
- First-class accommodates up to two people, and second-class up to four people.
- Couples, families and travelers of the same sex may share a sleeper.
- Sleeper charges are per person, and depend on the level of accommodations.

- **Couchettes:** These are simple overnight accommodations.
- They are open bunks in a compartment, each with a pillow and blanket.
- Offered in second-class, cabins accommodate up to six people with no distinction by sex.

MOST POPULAR PASSES

Eurail Global Pass	• Great flexibility for a wide range of travel. • Unlimited rail travel in 18 European countries [1]. • Travel for 10 days within a 3 month period. • Adult, Saver and Youth passes available.
Eurail Select Pass	• Great value in a three country pass. • Unlimited travel in your choice of 3, 4 or 5 countries [1]. • Travel for 5, 6, 8, 10 or 15 days within 2 months. • Adult, Saver and Youth passes available.
Eurail Regional Pass	• Best deal when traveling two or more countries. • Unlimited travel within one of the 20 available countries [2]. • Travel from 3 to 10 days within 2 months.
Eurail National Pass	• Unlimited travel within one single country [3]. • Travel for up to 15 days within a longer period of time.
Rail and Drive	• For the ultimate in adventure and flexibility. • Take the train for longer distances, then rent a car to explore locally. • See places you can't reach by train.
Point to Point Tickets	• Book a ticket for any of 3,500 cities in Europe, including high speed trains like Eurostar, Thalys or the TGVs.
Tour Britain and Europe	• BritRail, Eurail Global Pass, Eurail Select Pass

[1] [2] [3] *see below* Eurail Pass (country availability)

SPECIALTY TRAINS

High Speed Trains	• Up to 187.5 mph (300 kph) • Comfortable 1st and 2nd class • Widespread high speed network throughout Europe	
Scenic Trains	• Travel on Europe´s most picturesque routes • Breathtaking views • Some routes are even part of the UNESCO World Heritage List	
Hotel Trains	• More comfortable than regular night train • 1, 2 or more beds per compartment • Breakfast Included	

HIGH SPEED TRAINS

Alaris (Spain)
Altaria (Spain)
Artesia de jour (France, Italy)
AVE (Spain)
EC - Cisalpino (Switzerland, Italy)
Cisalpino (Germany, Switzerland, Italy)
Euromed (Spain)
Eurostar (Great Britain, France, Belgium)
Eurostar Italia (Italy)
ICE (Germany, Austria, Belgium, Netherlands, Switzerland)
TGV (France, Belgium, Switzerland)
Thalys (France, Belgium, Netherlands, Germany, Switzerland)
X2000 (Sweden)

SCENIC TRAINS

Arlbergline (Austria)
Bernina Express (Switzerland, Italy)
Centovalli Railway (Switzerland, Italy)
Flåm Railway (Norway)
Glacier-Express (Switzerland)
Golden Pass (Switzerland)
Rauma Line (Norway)
Wilhelm Tell Express (Switzerland)

HOTEL TRAINS

Allegro (Italy, Austria, Czech Republic)
Artesia de Nuit (France, Italy)
Berlin Night Express (Germany, Sweden)
CityNightLine (Germany, Austria, Switzerland)
Connex Norrlandståget (Sweden, Norway)
DB Nachtzug (Germany, Denmark)
Elipsos (Spain, France, Italy, Switzerland)
Hotel Train Lusitania (Spain, Portugal)
Riviera (France, Italy)

Dining & Bar Cars

- You can purchase food on almost every long-distance train at meal times.
- Trains with bar cars serve snacks and light meals in a social atmosphere.
- On Premier trains, first-class meals are served at the passenger's seat.
- On short trips, a food trolley passes through the aisles.

Reservations

- It is necessary to make a reservation in order to guarantee a seat.
- Sold on a first-come first-served basis, so reserve in advance (up to 60 days, 120 for Eurostar).
- Reservations required for Couchettes or sleepers on night trains.
- Required for all Premier trains, certain InterCity and EuroCity trains, and Swiss scenic trains.
- On most other trains, travelers can sit anywhere within the class designated on their pass/ticket.
- In Switzerland, reservations are available only on some specialty trains.
- Reserve locally in Bulgaria, Greece, Portugal or Romania (cannot be booked ahead from USA).
- In Eastern Europe reservations can be made only to and from major cities.
- Difficult to confirm in Spain and Italy in May and September, and for trains from Eastern to Western Europe.

Useful Hints

- Rail Passes do NOT include reservation costs, though you may upgrade for an additional fee.
- When using a CROSS BORDER train, be sure you have your identification papers ready.
- Check whether a VISA is required for any country that you are traveling through.

Purchasing Tickets

- Anyone is eligible to purchase a Eurail Pass or a Eurailticket, except residents from the countries of Europe, the Russian Federation, Turkey, Morocco, Algeria, or Tunisia.
- Check that your pass is valid for all countries you are traveling through.
- Contact the Eurail Aid offices for any problem with your pass; all capitals in member countries have one.
- Since Eurail passes are not intended for European residents, it is difficult to buy these passes in Europe, therefore, **buy your Eurail passes from an authorized agent or from www.eurail.com.**

EURAIL PASSES (country availability)

[1] Global and Select Passes *(countries or country combinations)*
- Austria (including Liechtenstein) - Belgium/Netherlands/Luxemburg - Bulgaria/Montenegro/Serbia - Croatia/Slovenia - Denmark - Finland - France (including Monaco) - Germany - Greece - Hungary - Italy - Norway - Portugal - Ireland - Romania - Spain - Sweden - Switzerland

[2] Regional Passes	
Austria-Czech Republic	France-Italy
Austria-Croatia-Slovenia	France-Spain
Austria-Germany	France-Switzerland
Austria-Hungary	Greece-Italy
Austria-Switzerland	Germany-Switzerland
Benelux-France	Germany-Poland
Benelux-Germany	Hungary-Croatia-Slovenia
Czech Republic-Germany	Hungary-Romania
Denmark-Germany	Italy-Spain
France-Germany	Portugal-Spain

[3] National Passes
Austria, Balkans, Britain, Croatia, Czech Republic, Eastern Europe, Finland, France, Germany, Greece, Hungary, Iberia, Ireland, Italy, Netherlands, Norway, Portugal, Romania, Scandinavia, Spain, Switzerland

...or some connections trains make use of ferry crossings (Puttgarden, Germany to Rodby Faerge, ...enmark and Villa S. Giouvanni, mainland Italy to Messina, Sicily).

MAP SECTION

London, Paris

Both of these major commercial centers are situated on the banks of major rivers: the Thames and the Seine. With more than seven million inhabitants, Greater London is one of the largest cities on earth.

Though Paris itself has a population of only 2.5 million, its greater metropolitan area is home to some ten million people. The Channel Tunnel has reduced travel time from Paris to London to only a few hours.

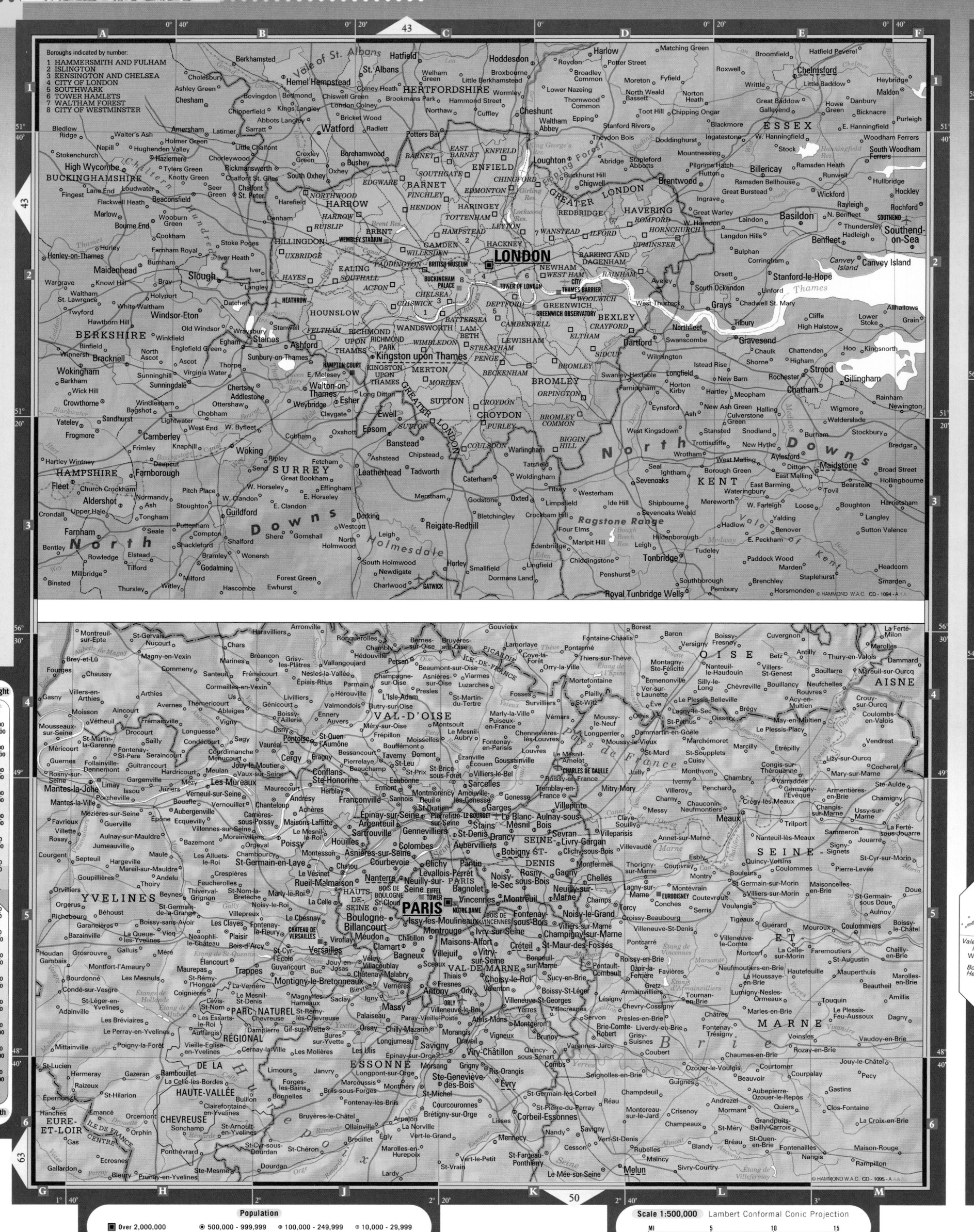

Population

■ Over 2,000,000	◉ 500,000 - 999,999	● 100,000 - 249,999	○ 10,000 - 29,999
▣ 1,000,000 - 1,999,999	◎ 250,000 - 499,999	◔ 30,000 - 99,999	○ Under 10,000

Scale 1:500,000   Lambert Conformal Conic Projection

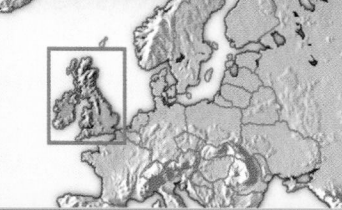
The British Isles are only 32 km from the European continent. Britain's isolated geographic position is due chiefly to its irregular coastline with its many very steep, towering cliffs, which offers only very few points of access for ships. The most important commercial centers of the United Kingdom and Ireland developed where fjords and estuaries extend far into the island interior.

Scale 1:3,000,000 Lambert Conformal Conic Projection

© HAMMOND WORLD ATLAS CORPORATION

MAP SECTION
Central and Southern Ireland

The "Emerald Isle" of Ireland derives its name from the lush, evergreen vegetation that flourishes in Ireland's oceanic climate. Low-pressure centers passing over the island from the Atlantic bring substantial precipitation, which falls more frequently in the west than in the east. Moreover, the influence of the Gulf Stream keeps temperatures relatively mild even during the winter months.

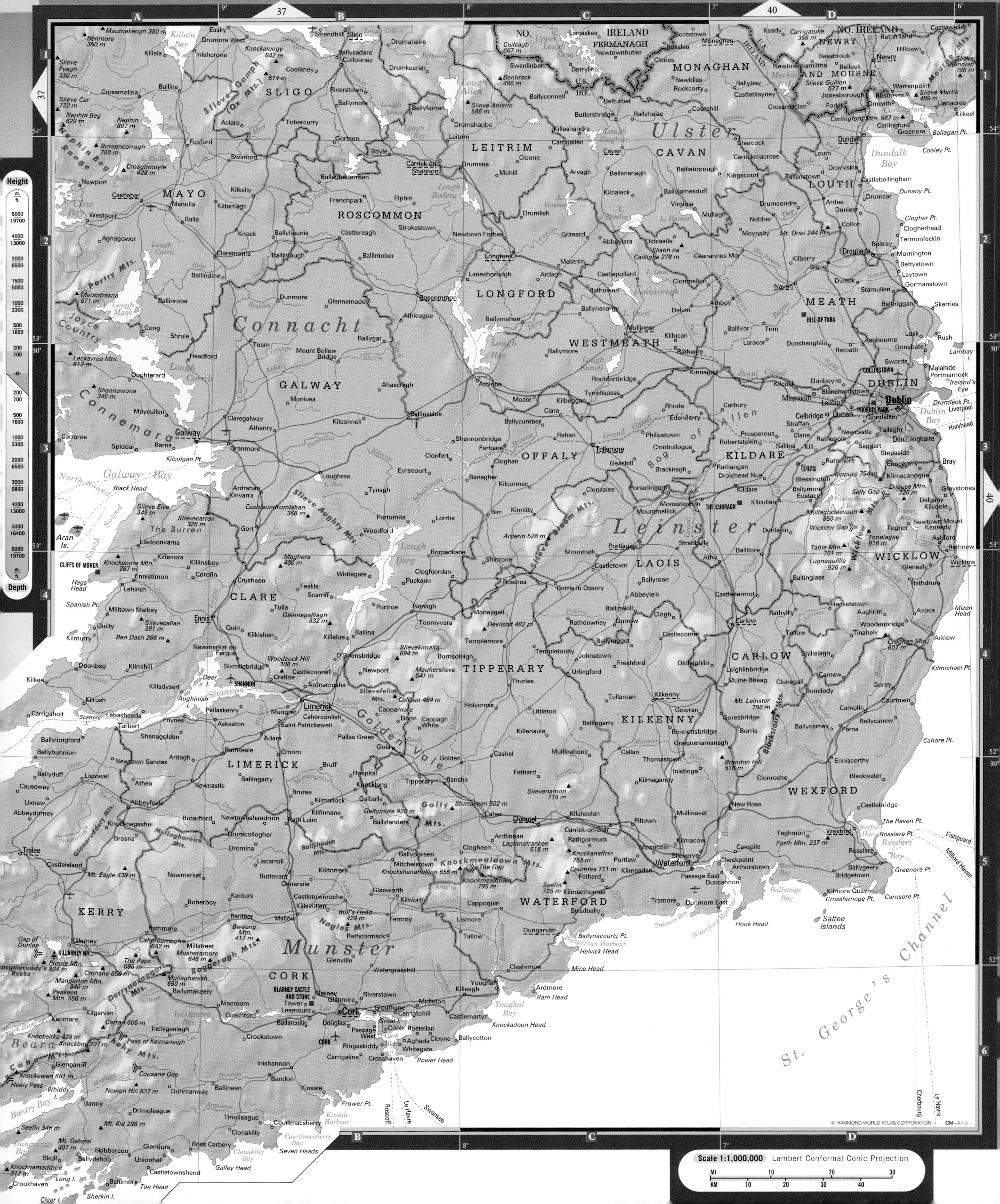

Height

m.	ft.
6000	19700
4000	13000
2000	6500
1500	5000
1000	3300
500	1600
200	700
~0	~0
200	700
500	1600
1000	3300
2000	6500
3000	9800
4000	13000
5000	16400
6000	19700

Depth

© Hammond World Atlas Corporation

CM-A-A-A

Scale 1:1,000,000   Lambert Conformal Conic Projection

MI 0 10 20 30

KM 10 20 30 40

Glen Mòr, the largest linear fault in northern Scotland, divides central Scotland into the Northern Highlands and the Grampian Mountains to the south. Ben Nevis (1,343 m) is the highest peak in the Grampian range. The sparsely forested highlands covered by broad moors and heaths provide ideal grazing areas for sheep. Farmland is found primarily in the lowlands and along the coast.

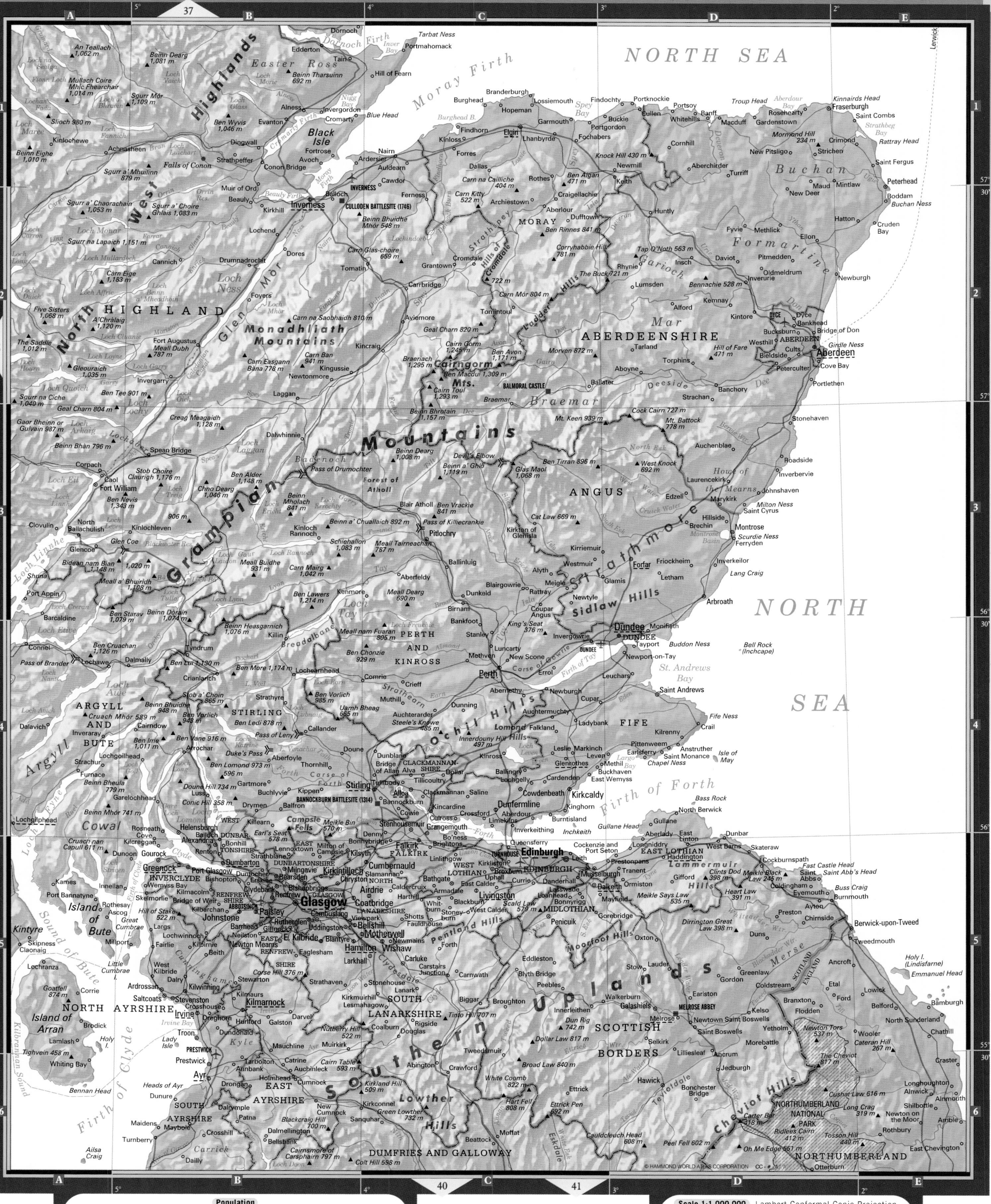

NORTH SEA

NORTH HIGHLAND

West Highlands

Easter Ross

Black Isle

Moray Firth

Inverness

Loch Ness

Glen Mòr

Monadhliath Mountains

MORAY

ABERDEENSHIRE

Aberdeen

Cairngorm Mts.

Braemar

Grampian Mountains

Forest of Atholl

Badenoch

Ben Nevis 1,343 m

Fort William

ANGUS

Strathmore

PERTH AND KINROSS

Dundee

NORTH SEA

Perth

St. Andrews Bay

FIFE

Firth of Forth

STIRLING

ARGYLL AND BUTE

Glasgow

Edinburgh

EAST LOTHIAN

WEST LOTHIAN

MIDLOTHIAN

Lammermuir Hills

NORTH AYRSHIRE

Island of Arran

SOUTH AYRSHIRE

EAST AYRSHIRE

SOUTH LANARKSHIRE

SCOTTISH BORDERS

Southern Uplands

Lowther Hills

Cheviot Hills

NORTHUMBERLAND NATIONAL PARK

DUMFRIES AND GALLOWAY

NORTHUMBERLAND

Firth of Clyde

© HAMMOND WORLD ATLAS CORPORATION

Population

■ Over 2,000,000	⊛ 500,000 - 999,999	◉ 100,000 - 249,999	⊙ 10,000 - 29,999
▣ 1,000,000 - 1,999,999	⊕ 250,000 - 499,999	⊖ 30,000 - 99,999	· Under 10,000

Scale 1:1,000,000 Lambert Conformal Conic Projection

MI 10 20 30
KM 10 20 30 40

Lake District National Park offers a striking display of the diversity of the landscape of the British Isles. The park contains not only England's largest lake, Lake Windermere, but also its highest peak, Seafell Pike (978 m). Sheep graze on the lush, green meadows of this area. Although the landscape seems almost alpine, many of the lakes here lie below sea level.

During the Ice Age, a land bridge connected Great Britain and Irland. When the waters rose again, the Irish Sea formed and separated the two large islands.

IRISH SEA

North Channel

Firth of Clyde

St. George's Channel

Cardigan Bay

SCOTLAND

NORTHERN IRELAND

IRELAND

Isle of Man (U.K.)

ISLE OF ANGLESEY

SNOWDONIA

WALES

Height

m. / ft.
6000 / 19700
4000 / 13000
2000 / 6500
1500 / 5000
1000 / 3300
500 / 1600
200 / 700
-0-
200 / 700
500 / 1600
1000 / 3300
2000 / 6500
3000 / 9800
4000 / 13000
5000 / 16400
6000 / 19700

Depth

Population

■ Over 2,000,000	⊛ 500,000 - 999,999
■ 1,000,000 - 1,999,999	⊛ 250,000 - 499,999
⊛ 100,000 - 249,999	⊚ 10,000 - 29,999
⊚ 30,000 - 99,999	○ Under 10,000

Scale 1:1,000,000 Lambert Conformal Conic Projection

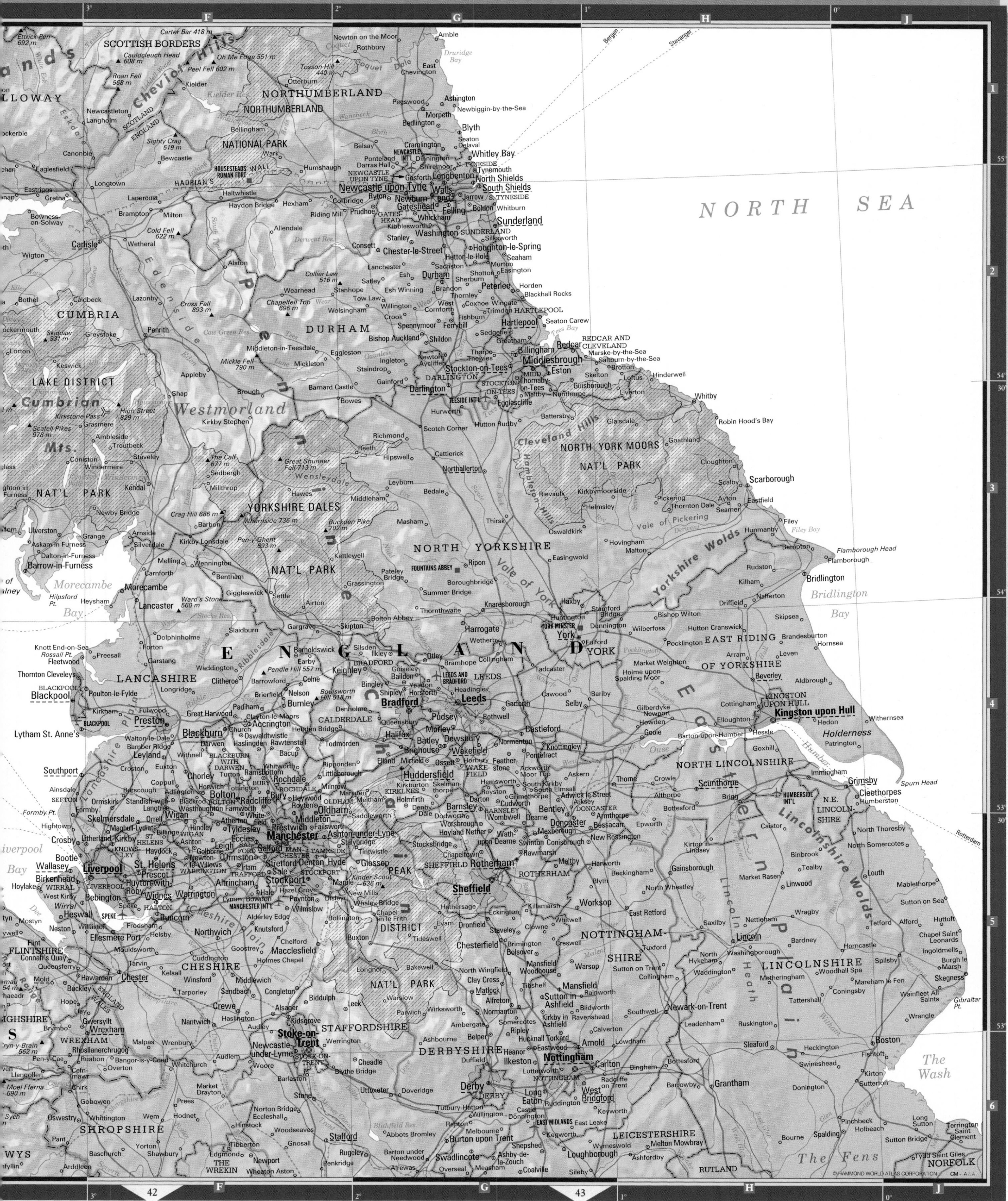

MI | 10 | 20 | 30
KM | 10 | 20 | 30 | 40

© Hammond World Atlas Corporation   CM - A.I.A.

Southern England and Wales

Southern Great Britain is traditionally divided into two regions characterized by yellow and green coloration. Yellow is the eastern region, where wheat is grown, and as in Spain, annual precipitation amounts

WALES

ENGLAND

GWYNEDD · POWYS · CEREDIGION · CARMARTHENSHIRE · PEMBROKESHIRE · SWANSEA · NEATH PORT TALBOT · BRIDGEND · VALE OF GLAMORGAN · RHONDDA CYNON TAFF · MERTHYR TYDFIL · CAERPHILLY · BLAENAU GWENT · TORFAEN · MONMOUTHSHIRE · NEWPORT · CARDIFF

SHROPSHIRE · WORCESTERSHIRE · HEREFORDSHIRE · GLOUCESTERSHIRE · SOUTH GLOUCESTERSHIRE · BATH AND N.E. SOMERSET · NORTH SOMERSET · SOMERSET · DEVON · DORSET · CORNWALL

SNOWDONIA NATIONAL PARK · PEMBROKESHIRE COAST NAT'L PARK · BRECON BEACONS NATIONAL PARK · EXMOOR NATIONAL PARK · DARTMOOR NATIONAL PARK

Cardigan Bay · Saint George's Channel · Bristol Channel · Celtic Sea · Barnstaple Bay (Bideford Bay) · Lyme Bay · Carmarthen Bay · Swansea Bay · Mount's Bay · Forest of Dean

Shrewsbury · Wolverhampton · Telford · Worcester · Hereford · Gloucester · Cheltenham · Bristol · Bath · Cardiff · Newport · Swansea · Port Talbot · Bridgend · Merthyr Tydfil · Pontypool · Cwmbran · Caerleon · Chepstow · Aberystwyth · Cardigan · Fishguard · Haverfordwest · Milford Haven · Pembroke · Tenby · Carmarthen · Llanelli · Neath · Taunton · Yeovil · Exeter · Plymouth · Truro · Penzance · Newquay · Bodmin · Barnstaple · Bideford · Okehampton · Dorchester · Weymouth · Bridport

Isle of Portland · Bill of Portland · The Lizard · Lizard Pt. · Land's End · Penwith · St. Peter Port · Roscoff · Rosslare · Cork

Population

■ Over 2,000,000	⊙ 500,000 - 999,999 · ● 100,000 - 249,999 · ◎ 10,000 - 29,999
▣ 1,000,000 - 1,999,999	◉ 250,000 - 499,999 · ◍ 30,000 - 99,999 · ○ Under 10,000

Height
m. / ft.
6000 / 19700
4000 / 13000
2000 / 6500
1500 / 5000
1000 / 3300
500 / 1600
200 / 700
0
Depth
200 / 700
500 / 1600
1000 / 3300
2000 / 6500
3000 / 9800
4000 / 13000
5000 / 16400
6000 / 19700
m. / ft.

...o no more than 500 mm in many places. ...Green is the western region, where ...louds moving in from the sea bring rain ...o the mountains. With elevations of over ...,000 m, the Welsh highlands extend as a broad peninsula far toward the west, forming a precipitation barrier that keeps the eastern lowlands dry. High humidity is the cause of frequent winter fog, which is thickened in places by air pollution.

Scale 1:1,000,000 Lambert Conformal Conic Projection

© HAMMOND WORLD ATLAS CORPORATION

Major labels: LEICESTERSHIRE, RUTLAND, LINCOLNSHIRE, NORFOLK, East Anglia, NORTHAMPTONSHIRE, CAMBRIDGESHIRE, SUFFOLK, WARWICKSHIRE, BEDFORDSHIRE, ENGLAND, HERTFORDSHIRE, ESSEX, BUCKINGHAMSHIRE, OXFORDSHIRE, GREATER LONDON, NORTH SEA, WEST BERKSHIRE, SURREY, KENT, HAMPSHIRE, WEST SUSSEX, EAST SUSSEX, The Weald, North Downs, South Downs, Strait of Dover, FRANCE, PAS-DE-CALAIS, PICARDIE, SOMME, ENGLISH CHANNEL, ISLE OF WIGHT, New Forest

Selected cities and towns: Leicester, Peterborough, Norwich, Great Yarmouth, Lowestoft, Cambridge, Bury Saint Edmunds, Ipswich, Northampton, Bedford, Milton Keynes, Luton, Oxford, London, Reading, Southampton, Portsmouth, Brighton and Hove, Dover, Folkestone, Canterbury, Margate, Ramsgate, Chelmsford, Colchester, Harwich, Basildon, Southend-on-Sea, Maidstone, Ashford, Guildford, Crawley, Winchester, Eastbourne, Hastings, Bournemouth, Swindon, Coventry, Birmingham, Solihull, Nuneaton, Rugby, Banbury, Boulogne-sur-Mer, Calais

Marked by fjords, deep valleys, and lakes, the landscape of northern Europe was clearly shaped during the Ice Age. Although glaciers have long since receded in this region, the picture in Iceland is very different. The Vatnajökull Ice Cap covers an area of some 8,410 square kilometers, and melt caused by subglacial eruptions poses a significant danger to coastal settlements.

Scale 1:6,000,000   Lambert Conformal Conic Projection

© HAMMOND WORLD ATLAS CORPORATION

Helsinki, Copenhagen and Stockholm are situated at strategically favorable points on the Baltic Sea coast. With its many bays and rocky islands as well as Finland's largest harbor, Helsinki commands the entrance to the Gulf of Finland, Copenhagen the Øresund. Stockholm, located where Lake Mälaren joins the Baltic Sea, is sometimes called the "Venice of the north" for its many waterways.

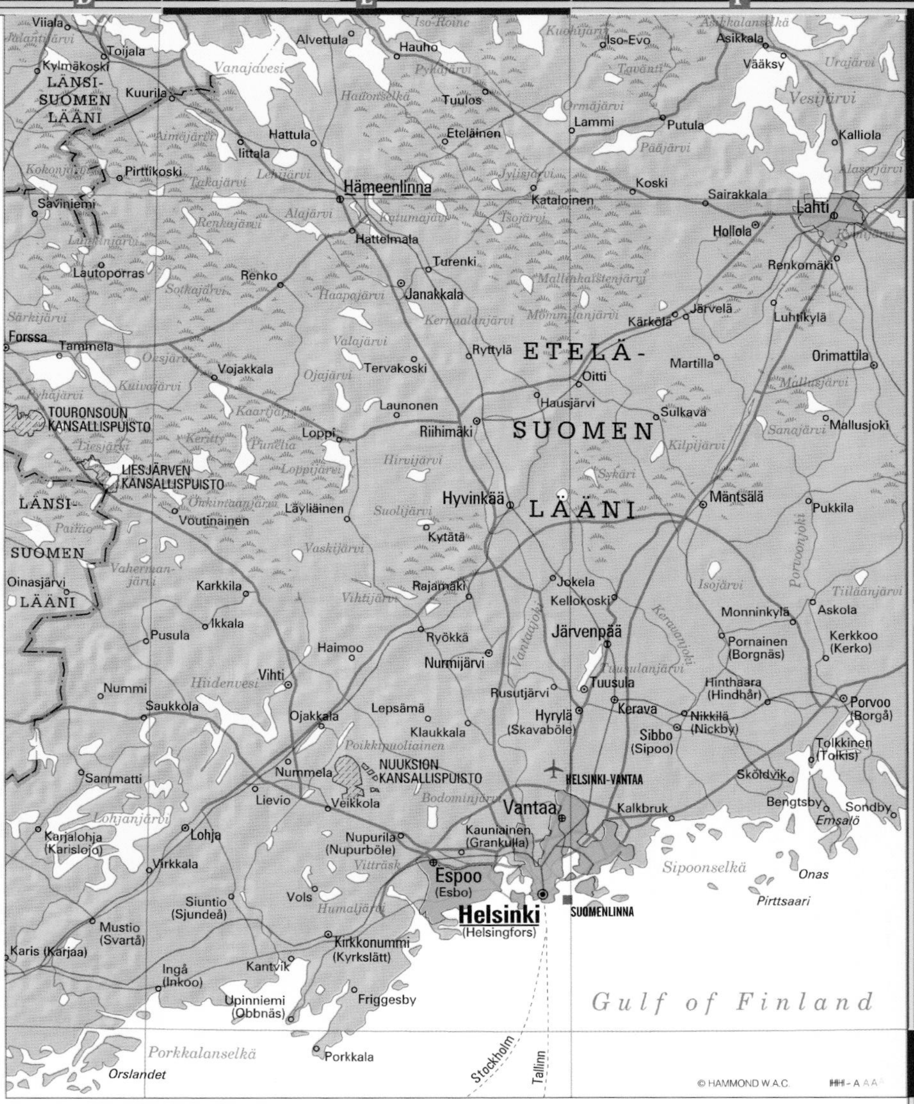

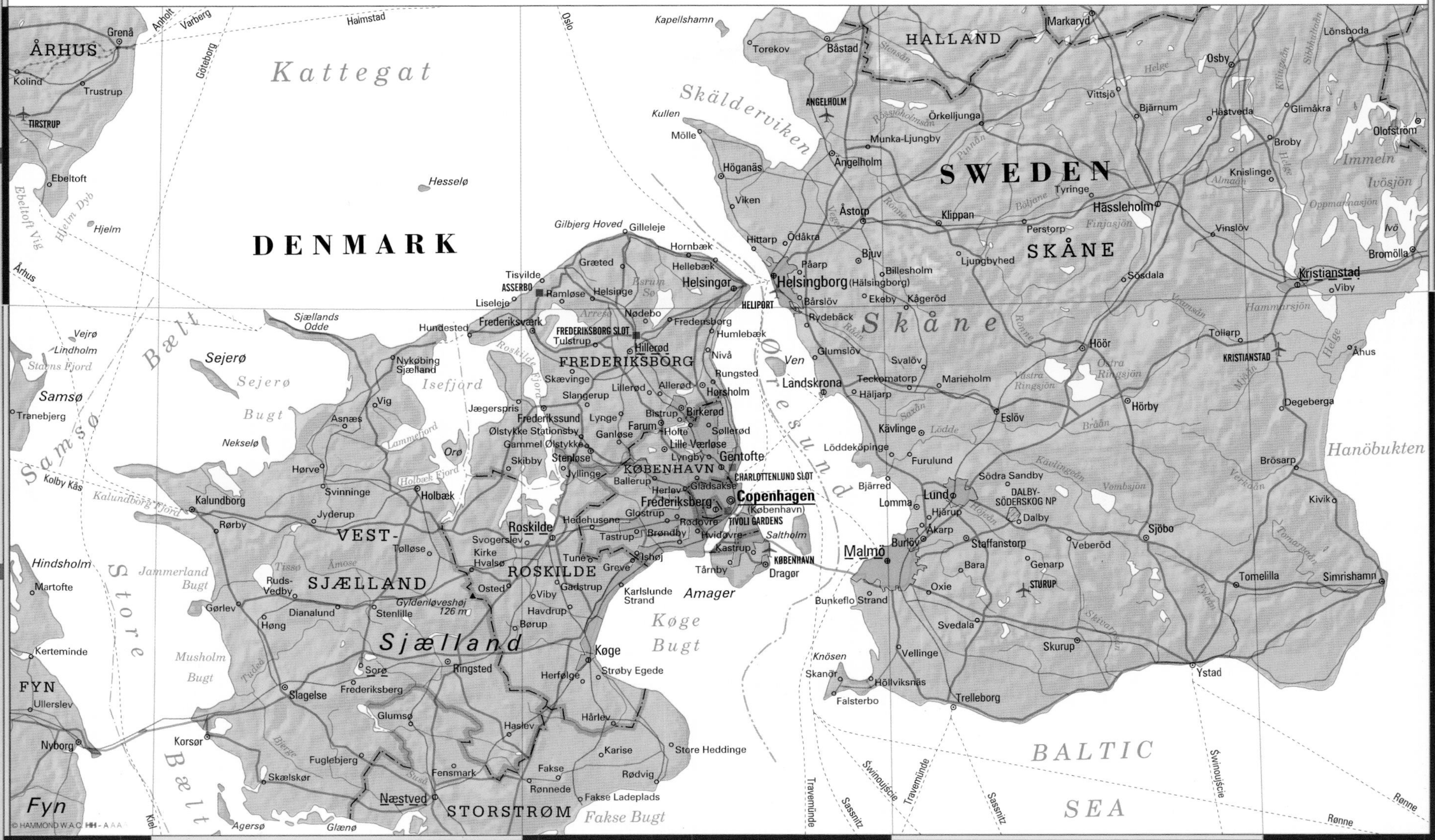

Population

- ■ Over 2,000,000
- ■ 1,000,000 - 1,999,999
- ● 500,000 - 999,999
- ● 250,000 - 499,999
- ◉ 100,000 - 249,999
- ○ 30,000 - 99,999
- ⊙ 10,000 - 29,999
- ∘ Under 10,000

Scale 1:1,000,000 Lambert Conformal Conic Projection

MI — 10 20 30
KM 10 20 30 40

Height
m. / ft.
6000 / 19700
4000 / 13000
1500 / 5000
1000 / 3300
500 / 1600
200 / 700
0 / —
200 / 700
1000 / 3300
2000 / 6500
3000 / 9800
4000 / 13000
5000 / 16400
6000 / 19700
m. / ft.
Depth

© HAMMOND W.A.C.   HH - A △ A

The Baltic Sea is connected to the North Sea by the Skagerrak and the Kattegat. Covering 390,000 square km (including the Kattegat), it has an average depth of 55 m, and measures 459 at its deepest point. Originally an inland lake, the Baltic is fed by the rivers of northern Europe and exchanges little water with the North Sea. Thus its salinity is low: 8 % at the surface. Tides play only a minor role in the region. At high tide, the water level rises no more than 40 cm in the Kattegat, between 20 and 30 cm in the Store Baelt, and only a few centimeters along the central coastlines.

Population

■ Over 2,000,000	● 500,000 - 999,999	◉ 100,000 - 249,999	○ 10,000 - 29,999
◻ 1,000,000 - 1,999,999	◉ 250,000 - 499,999	○ 30,000 - 99,999	○ Under 10,000

Gulf of Bothnia

FINLAND

LÄNSI SUOMEN LÄÄNI

ITÄ-SUOMEN LÄÄNI

ETELÄ-SUOMEN LÄÄNI

RESPUBLIKA KARELIYA

Lake Ladoga

LENINGRADSKAYA OBLAST'

St. Petersburg (Leningrad)

Helsinki (Helsingfors)

Åland
Ahvenanmaa

Gulf of Finland

Narva Bay

Tallinn

ESTONIA

Hiiumaa

Saaremaa

Gulf of Riga

Lake Peipus

Lake Pskov

Pskov

NOVGORODSKAYA OBLAST'

Novgorod

RUSSIA

PSKOVSKAYA OBLAST'

TVERSKAYA OBLAST'

BALTIC SEA

Riga LATVIA

Velikiye Luki

Vitsyebsk

LITHUANIA

Kaunas

Vilnius

VITSYEBSKAYA VOBLASTS'

BELARUS

RUSSIA

Kaliningrad

KALININGRADSKAYA OBLAST'

POLAND

WARMIŃSKO-MAZURSKIE

PODLASKIE

HRODZYENSKAYA VOBLASTS'

MINSKAYA VOBLASTS'

Minsk

MAHILYOWSKAYA VOBLASTS'

Mahilyow

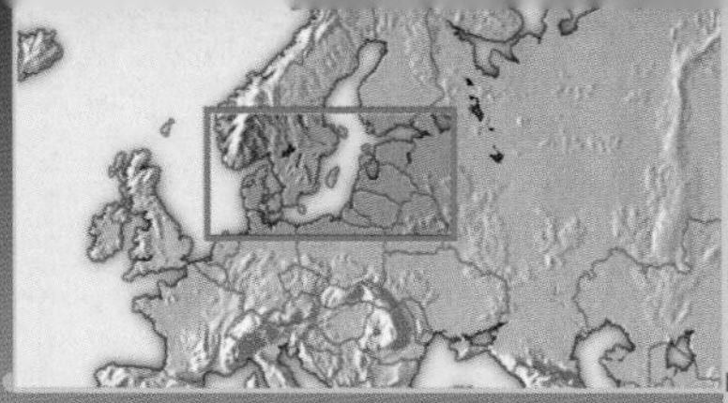

Scale 1:3,000,000   Lambert Conformal Conic Projection

Next to the Rhine, the Elbe (1,165 km) is the longest and busiest river in North Central Europe. Its drainage basin encompasses some 144,000 square km. The Elbe flows from its source at 1,500 m above sea level in the Riesengebirge Range in the Czech Republic to its mouth in the North Sea at Cuxhaven in Germany, where it reaches a width of 15 km. Hamburg marks the beginning of the long (100 km) Elbe estuary, in which tidal activity is significant as far upriver as Geesthacht. Although international treaties have brought some improvement in water quality, the Elbe is still one of the most heavily polluted rivers in Europe.

47

BALTIC SEA

RUSSIA
LITHUANIA
Kaunas
Vilnius

Kaliningrad
KALININGRADSKAYA OBLAST

BELARUS
Białystok
Brest

POLAND
Warsaw
Gdynia
Gdańsk
Szczecin
Poznań
Łódź
Wrocław
Lublin
Kraków
Katowice
Bydgoszcz

Dresden
Prague

CZECH REPUBLIC
Brno

SLOVAKIA
Košice

UKRAINE
L'viv

AUSTRIA
Vienna
Bratislava

HUNGARY
BUDAPEST

ROMANIA

Carpathian Mountains

Scale 1:3,000,000   Lambert Conformal Conic Projection

© HAMMOND WORLD ATLAS CORPORATION

About 1,200 km long and up to 250 km wide, the Alps are the largest mountain system in Europe. Their highest peak is Mont Blanc (4,807 m). The Alps occupy an area of 220,000 square km and form the watershed between the North Sea and the Mediterranean Sea along the north-south axis and between the Black Sea and the Mediterranean Sea to the east. Geologically speaking, the Alps are a young mountain system and continue to rise at a rate of several millimeters per year due to continental drift, growing higher as the African Plate presses against the European.

Height

m.	ft.
6000	19700
4000	13000
2000	6500
1500	5000
1000	3300
500	1600
200	700
0	0
200	700
500	1600
1000	3300
2000	6500
3000	9800
4000	13000
5000	16400
6000	19700

Depth

Population

- ■ Over 2,000,000
- ◉ 500,000 - 999,999
- ◉ 100,000 - 249,999
- ◎ 10,000 - 29,999
- ▣ 1,000,000 - 1,999,999
- ◉ 250,000 - 499,999
- ◎ 30,000 - 99,999
- ○ Under 10,000

The central core of the Iberian Peninsula is the Meseta plateau, which is almost completely surrounded by mountain ranges. This ring of mountains is encircled by narrow bands of coastal lowlands.

The topographic pattern is reflected in the vegetation. Sheep graze in the grassy areas and juniper groves of the sparse highlands, where vast fields of wheat and sunflowers yield modest harvests.

Olive groves and maquis-garrigue growth are the dominant features of lowland vegetation, which is interspersed with oaks. The valleys of rivers such as the Ebro and the Guadalquivir are intensely cultivated.

Height
m. / ft.
6000 / 19700
4000 / 13000
2000 / 6500
1500 / 5000
1000 / 3300
500 / 1600
200 / 700
0
200 / 700
500 / 1600
1000 / 3300
2000 / 6500
3000 / 9800
4000 / 13000
5000 / 16400
6000 / 19700

m. / ft. Depth

Population
- ■ Over 2,000,000
- ■ 1,000,000 - 1,999,999
- ● 500,000 - 999,999
- ● 250,000 - 499,999
- ● 100,000 - 249,999
- ● 30,000 - 99,999
- ○ 10,000 - 29,999
- ○ Under 10,000

© HAMMOND WORLD ATLAS CORPORATION CC·A

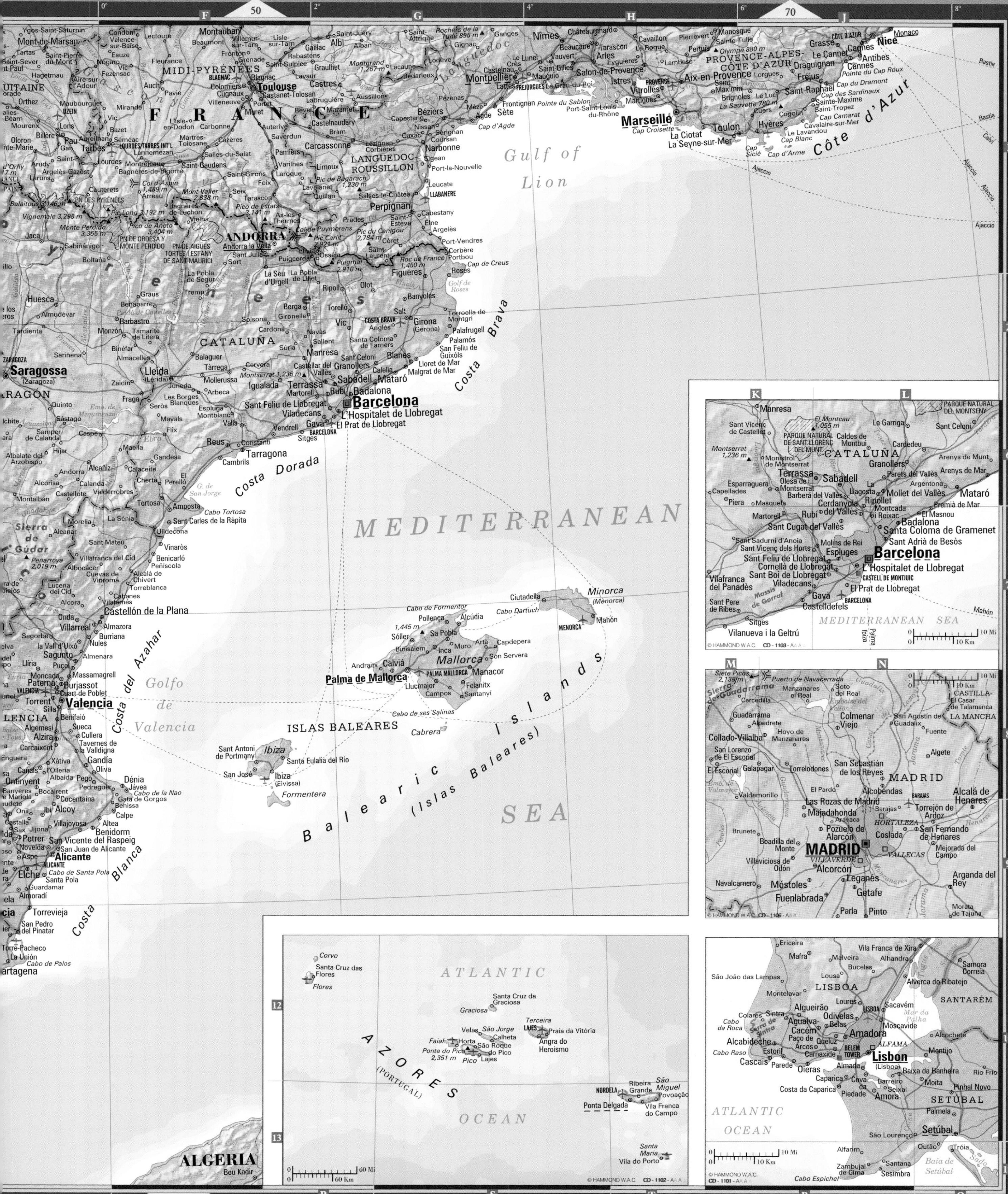

Scale 1:3,000,000   Lambert Conformal Conic Projection

© HAMMOND W.A.C.

The once remarkably fertile and heavily forested Mediterranean region suffers today from soil erosion and a severe shortage of water. Deforestation began with the ancient Greeks and Romans, who needed huge quantities of wood for heating and ship-building. Forest fires are still a regular summer occurrence today. The exposed soil is carried off by rain, thus depleting a valuable water storage medium. Rivers often run dry during the summer months, particularly in the south, where rain does not fall for as much as six months at a time.

ITALY

CORSE / Corsica (FRANCE)

SARDEGNA / Sardinia

TYRRHENIAN SEA

ADRIATIC

CROATIA

Rome

Naples (Napoli)

Bari

Sicily / SICILIA

Palermo

Messina

Catania

Siracusa

Reggio di Calabria

CALABRIA

BASILICATA

PUGLIA

CAMPANIA

MOLISE

ABRUZZO

MARCHE

UMBRIA

LAZIO

TOSCANA

Cagliari

Sassari

Isole Eolie (Lipari Islands)

MEDITERRANEAN

Strait of Sicily

Malta Channel

TUNISIA

Tunis

BIZERTE

ARIANA

SILIANA

ZAGHOUAN

KAIROUAN

MONASTIR

MAHDIA

SIDI BOU ZID

Gulf of Tunis

Golfe de Hammamet

MALTA

Gozo

Malta

Valletta

Population	
■ Over 2,000,000	⊕ 500,000 - 999,999 ● 100,000 - 249,999 ○ 10,000 - 29,999
◫ 1,000,000 - 1,999,999	⊙ 250,000 - 499,999 ◦ 30,000 - 99,999 ∘ Under 10,000

Height
m. / ft.
6000 / 19700
4000 / 13000
2000 / 6500
1500 / 5000
1000 / 3300
500 / 1600
200 / 700
0
200 / 700
500 / 1600
1000 / 3300
2000 / 6500
3000 / 9800
4000 / 13000
5000 / 16400
6000 / 19700
Depth

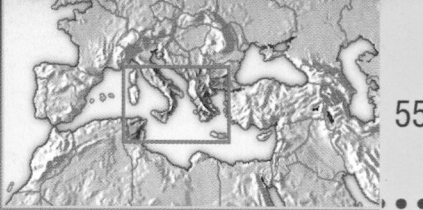

Scale 1:3,000,000 Lambert Conformal Conic Projection

© HAMMOND W.A.C.   C1 - 1108 - A A A

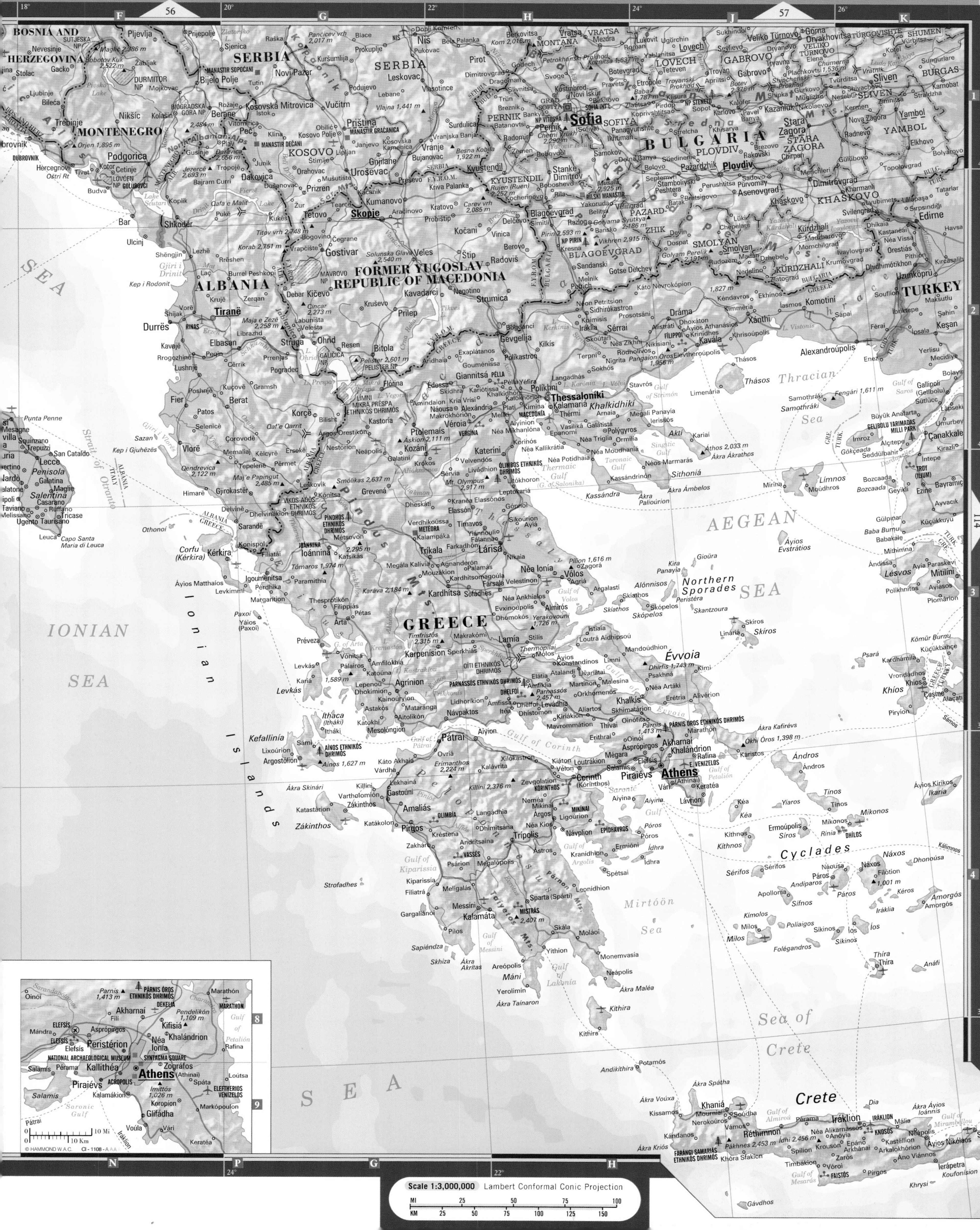

When the Alps and neighboring mountain ranges formed during the Tertiary some 65 million years ago, the folding process extended into the Mediterranean region, creating the Dinaric Alps on the western Balkan Peninsula. The ridges of these folds can be seen today along the Dalmatian coast, where they rise from the sea as elongated islands. The troughs of the folded range are covered by water.

The product of a similar upthrusting process, the Carpathians are cut by the Danube, which is 2,850 km long and second only to the Volga among the longest rivers of Europe.

Height
m.
ft.

6000
19700

4000
13000

2000
6500

1500
5000

1000
3300

500
1600

200
700

0

200
700

500
1600

1000
3300

2000
6500

3000
9800

4000
13000

5000
16400

6000
19700

m.
ft.

Depth

Population
- Over 2,000,000
- 1,000,000 – 1,999,999
- 500,000 – 999,999
- 250,000 – 499,999
- 100,000 – 249,999
- 30,000 – 99,999
- 10,000 – 29,999
- Under 10,000

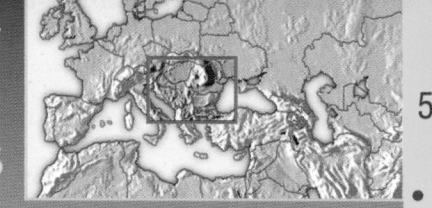

Scale 1:3,000,000 Lambert Conformal Conic Projection

In the 15th century, the Dutch began building a system of dykes to protect their land, much of which lies below sea level, from the sea. A massive seawall now separates the former North Sea bay of the Zuidersee from the North Sea, transforming it into a fresh-water lake – the IJsselmeer. Parts of the lake have been drained, creating new areas of dry land known as polders.

| A | 4° | B | 5° | C | 6° | D |

Juist
East

NORTH SEA

West Frisian Islands

Borkum
Borkum
Lütje
Oosterems
Juist
Rottumeroog
Rottumerplaat
Simonszand
Schiermonnikoog
Schiermonnikoog
Engelsmanplaat
Lauwers
Waddenzee
Ameland
Nes Buren
Hollum
Oosterend
Terschelling
West-Terschelling
Vliestroom
Wierum
Warffum
Uithuizen
Bierum
Delfzijl
Appin
Holwerd
Ferwerd
Oostmahorn
Anjum
Ulrum
Zoutkamp
Lauwersmeer

Oost-Vlieland
Vlieland
Waddenzee
Griend
Richel
Sint Jacobiparochie
Hallum
Menaldum
Stiens
Franeker
Leeuwarden
Dokkum
Damwoude
Kollum
Grijpsk
Winsum
Bedum
Ten Boer
GRONINGEN
Groningen
Hoogezand
Sappe
meer

Texel
De Cocksdorp
De Koog
Harlingen
Boxum
Makkum
Witmarsum
FRIESLAND
Grouw
Drachten
Marum
Leek
Eelde-Paterswolde
Zuidlaren
Veendam
DRENTHE

Noorderhaaks
Den Helder
Marsdiep Texelstroom
De Cocksdorp
LORENTZSLUIZEN
STEVINSLUIZEN
Gaast
Workum
Hindeloopen
IJlst
Sneek
Joure
Heerenveen
Oosterwolde
Appelscha
Assen
Rolde
Gieten

IJsselmeer

Breezand
Anna Paulowna
Hippolytushoef
Wieringerwerf
Den Oever
Staveren
Balk
Sloten
Lemmer
Wolvega
Diever
Beilen
Westerbork
Borger
Odoorn

Callantsoog
Schagen
Middenmeer
Winkel
Medemblik
Andijk
Enkhuizen
Rutten
Oldemarkt
Steenwijk
Ruinen
Hoogeveen

Bergen aan Zee
Bergen
Heerhugowaard
Langedijk
Opmeer
Hoogkarspel
Wognum
Bovenkarspel
Urk
Noordoostpolder
Nagele
Vollenhove
De Wijk
Zuidwolde
Coevorden

Egmond aan Zee
Alkmaar
Hoorn
Berkhout
Westerblokker
HOUTRIBDIJK
Emmeloord
Marknesse
Giethoorn
Blokzijl
Meppel
Staphorst

Heiloo
Castricum
NOORD-HOLLAND
Purmerend
Volendam
Edam
Monnickendam
Marken
Markerwaard
Lelystad
Swifterbant
Dronten
Oostelijk Flevoland
Kampen
IJsselmuiden
Nieuwleusen
Dedemsvaart
Hardenberg
Gramsbergen
Nieuw-Schoonebe

Heemskerk
Beverwijk
IJmuiden
Zaanstad
Zaandijk
Koog a. de Zaan
Wormer
Landsmeer
Broek in Waterland
FLEVOLAND
Almere
Zeewolde
Zuidelijk Flevoland
Zwolle
Dalfsen
Ommen
Hattem
Wijhe
Raalte
Hellendoorn
Wierden
Almelo

NATIONAAL PARK DE KENNEMERDUINEN
Bloemendaal
Haarlem
Amsterdam
Amstelveen
Diemen
Muiden
Naarden
Bussum
Huizen
Harderwijk
Nunspeet
Elburg
Oldebroek
Epe
Heerde
Nijverdal
Rijssen
Holten
Borne
Hengelo

Zandvoort
Hoofddorp
SCHIPHOL
Aalsmeer
Uithoorn
Weesp
's-Graveland
Laren
Eemnes
Spakenburg
Putten
Nijkerk
Apeldoorn
Twello
Deventer
Bathmen
Delden
Enschede

KEUKENHOF
Lisse
Sassenheim
Oegstgeest
Leiden
Leiderdorp
Bodegraven
Nieuwkoop
Ter Aar
Mijdrecht
Breukelen
Hilversum
Soest
Baarn
Amersfoort
Leusden-Zuid
Barneveld
Harskamp
Voorst
Otterlo
Eefde
Lochem
Haaksbergen

Noordwijkerhout
Noordwijk aan Zee
Noordwijk-Binnen
Katwijk aan Zee
Rijnsburg
Wassenaar
Voorschoten
Alphen aan den Rijn
UTRECHT
Maarssen
Maartensdijk
Bilthoven
De Bilt
Utrecht
Zeist
Driebergen
Doorn
Leersum
RIJKSMUSEUM KRÖLLER MÜLLER
NATIONAAL PARK VELUWEZOOM
Brummen
Zutphen
Vorden
Ruurlo
Eibergen
Neede
Borculo

The Hague ('s-Gravenhage)
Leidschendam
Voorburg
Rijswijk
Zoetermeer
Pijnacker
Berkel
Boskoop
Waddinxveen
Reeuwijk
Gouda
Woerden
Harmelen
Vleuten
Bunnik
Houten
Wijk bij Duurstede
Rhenen
Renkum
Oosterbeek
Westervoort
Duiven
Didam
Doesburg
Zelhem
Graafschap
Doetinchem
Lichtenvoorde
Winterswijk
Groenlo
Vreden

Scheveningen
Monster
Naaldwijk
Delft
Berkel
Moordrecht
Nieuwerkerk aan de IJssel
IJsselstein
Nieuwegein
Montfoort
Oudewater
Lopik
Schoonhoven
Culemborg
Buren
Tiel
Betuwe
Valburg
Elst
Bemmel
NETHERLANDS

Hoek van Holland
EUROPOORT
ZUID-HOLLAND
Maassluis
Vlaardingen
Schiedam
Rotterdam
Krimpen aan de IJssel
Capelle
Ridderkerk
Alblasserdam
Sliedrecht
Hardinxveld-Giessendam
Gorinchem
Brakel
Geldermalsen
Waardenburg
Druten
Beuningen
Wijchen
Nijmegen
Groesbeek
Kranenburg
Kleve
Bedburg-Hau
Rees
Isselburg
Bocholt
Borke

Harwich
Opstvoorne
Rozenburg
Brielle
Voorne
Spijkenisse
Portugaal
Barendrecht
Papendrecht
's Gravendeel
Dordrecht
Werkendam
Woudrichem
Kerkwijk
Zaltbommel
Vuren
Oss
Grave
Cuijk
Mook
Gennep
Goch
Uedem
Kalkar
Xanten
Schermbeck

Goeree
West-Nieuwland
Ouddorp
Oude-Tonge
Hoekse Waard
Zwijndrecht
Strijen
Numansdorp
Willemstad
Biesbosch
Aalburg
Heusden
Vlijmen
Drunen
Heesch
Schaijk
Oss
Uden
Sint Hubert
Boxmeer
Weeze
Uedem
Wesel
Hünxe
Dorsten

Sommelsdijk
Hellevoetsluis
Stellendam
Middelharnis
Dirksland
Overflakkee
Oltgensplaat
Dinteloord
Zevenbergen
Terheijden
Made
Raamsdonk
Waalwijk
Loon op Zand
Vught
Sint-Michielsgestel
Sint-Oedenrode
Veghel
Gemert
Boekel
Oploo
Overloon
Nieuw Bergen
Kevelaer
Alpen
Rheinberg

VOLKERAKDAM
BROUWERSDAM
Brouwershaven
Bruinisse
Zierikzee
GREVELINGENDAM
PHILIPSDAM
Sint Annaland
Nieuw-Vossemeer
Steenbergen
Oudenbosch
Prinsenbeek
Rijen
Dongen
Oisterwijk
Boxtel
Schijndel
NOORD-BRABANT
Helmond
Deurne
Venray
Arcen
Straelen
Kerken
Moers
Oberha

Schouwen
Haamstede
Renesse
OOSTERSCHELDEDAM
Oosterschelde
Colijnsplaat
Noord-Beveland
Kortgene
Tholen
Sint-Maartensdijk
Bergen op Zoom
Halsteren
Wouw
Roosendaal
Zundert
Etten-Leur
Breda
Ginneken
Gilze
Tilburg
Goirle
Hilvarenbeek
Eindhoven
EINDHOVEN
Nuenen
Geldrop
Someren
Weert
Nederweert
Helden
Venlo
Tegelen
Wachtendonk
LIMBURG
Kempen
Kamp-Lintfort
Bottrop
Ess

Domburg
Westkapelle
ZEELAND
Walcheren
Middelburg
Goes
Yerseke
Kruiningen
Krabbendijke
Bath
Woensdrecht
Ossendrecht
Putte
Essen
Kalmthout
Brecht
Rijsbergen
Baarle-Nassau
Baarle-Hertog
Poppel
Bladel
Eersel
Valkenswaard
Bergeyk
Waalre
Bree
Neerpelt
Budel
Weert
Horst
Sevenum
Maasbree
Blerick
Roermond
Swalmen
Beesel
Belfeld
Velden
Brüggen
Nettetal
Viersen
Willich
Meerbusch
Mettmann

Vlissingen
Borssele
Zuid-Beveland
Breskens
Cadzand-Bad
Oostburg
Sluis
Aardenburg
IJzendijke
Biervliet
Axel
Hoek
Terneuzen
Sas van Gent
Zelzate
Kloosterzande
Hulst
Kapellen
Ekeren
Stabroek
Zandvliet
Brasschaat
Schoten
Wuustwezel
Loenhout
Zoersel
Oud-Turnhout
Arendonk
Retie
Dessel
Mol
Lommel
Achel
Overpelt
Hamont
Weert
Nederweert
Heythuysen
Swalmen
Nieuwkrüchten
Krefeld
Neuss
Düsseldorf
Ratingen
Erkrath

Sheerness
Kingston Upon Hull

Ghent (Gent)
Lokeren
Sint-Niklaas
Beveren
Temse
Kruibeke
Hoboken
Burcht
Antwerp
Borgerhout
Mortsel
Lier
Nijlen
Herentals
Geel
Herenthout
Kasterlee
Tessenderlo
Leopoldsburg
Beringen
Kinrooi
Maaseik
Ophoven
Dilsen
Born
Sittard
Maasbracht
Tüddern
Heinsberg
Hückelhoven
Erkelenz
Jüchen
Grevenbroich
Rommerskirchen
Mönchengladbach
Wegberg
Schwalmtal
Waldfeucht
Wassenberg
Geilenkirchen

Aalter
Eeklo
Maldegem
Evergem
Wachtebeke
Zele
Dendermonde
Berlare
Wetteren
Aalst
Lebbeke
Buggenhout
Puurs
Bornem
Willebroek
Boom
Mechelen
Duffel
Heist-op-den-Berg
Aarschot
Diest
Tessenderlo
Ham
Lummen
Hasselt
Genk
As
Maasmechelen
Bilzen
Tongeren
Sittard
Geleen
LIMBURG

BELGIUM
OOST-VLAANDEREN
VLAAMS-BRABANT
ANTWERPEN

Deinze
Nazareth
Nevele
Zomergem
Lovendegem
Merelbeke
Melle
Wichelen
Zottegem
Herzele
Ninove
Opwijk
Londerzeel
Kapelle-op-den-Bos
Zemst
Kampenhout
Haacht
Tremelo
Begijnendijk
Tienen
Landen
Sint-Truiden
Borgloon
Gingelom
Waremme
Tongeren

Height
m. / ft.
6000 / 19700
4000 / 13000
2000 / 6500
1500 / 5000
1000 / 3300
500 / 1600
200 / 700
0
200 / 700
500 / 1600
1000 / 3300
2000 / 6500
3000 / 9800
4000 / 13000
5000 / 16400
6000 / 19700
m. / ft.
Depth

Population
■ Over 2,000,000
◉ 500,000 – 999,999
⊙ 100,000 – 249,999
○ 10,000 – 29,999
▪ 1,000,000 – 1,999,999
● 250,000 – 499,999
○ 30,000 – 99,999
∘ Under 10,000

Frisian Islands

NP SCHLESWIG-HOLSTEINISCHES WATTENMEER
Scharhörn
Neuwerk NP (HAMBURG)
NP HAMBURGISCHES WATTENMEER
Brunsbüttel

Helgoländer Bucht
Cuxhaven
NORDHOLZ
Elbe
Freiburg
Wilster
Krempe
Glückstadt
Barmstedt
Quickborn
Bargfeld-Stegen
Norderstedt
Bargteheide
Ahrensburg
Grosshansdorf
Trittau
Gudow
Zarrentin

Wangerooge
Wangerooge
Minsener Oog
Oldoog
Mellum
Schillighörn
NP NIEDERSÄCHSISCHES WATTENMEER

Langeoog
Spiekeroog
Baltrum
Langeoog
Norderney
Norderney

Jade
Weser
Jadebusen
BREMEN
BREMERHAVEN
BREMERHAVEN
Nordenham
Wilhelmshaven
Sande

Ostfriesland
Grosses Meer
Aurich
Westerholt
Wittmund
Jever
Schortens

HAMBURG
Hamburg
Wedel
Pinneberg
Schenefeld
Appen
Rellingen
SCHLESWIG-
HOLSTEIN
Reinbek
Börnsen
Geesthacht
MECKLENBURG-
VORPOMMERN

NIEDERSACHSEN

GERMANY

Lüneburger
Heide

Oldenburg
Delmenhorst
Hatten
Wardenburg
Wildeshausen

Osnabrück
Bielefeld
Gütersloh
Münster
Paderborn
Hamm
Dortmund
Bochum
Wuppertal

Hannover
Hannover
Garbsen
Langenhagen
Burgwedel

Braunschweig
Braunschweig
Wolfsburg
Wolfenbüttel
Salzgitter
Hildesheim

Göttingen
Kassel
HESSEN
THÜRINGEN

NORDRHEIN-
WESTFALEN

Münsterland

NATIONALPARK
HOCHHARZ
Brocken
1141 m
NATIONALPARK HARZ
Goslar
Wernigerode
SACHSEN-
ANHALT

NATIONALPARK HAINICH
Eisenach
Gotha

Scale 1:1,000,000   Lambert Conformal Conic Projection
MI   10   20   30
KM   10   20   30   40

© HAMMOND WORLD ATLAS CORPORATION

An extension of the Middle Rhine Highlands, the Ardennes form a high plateau that stretches across much of northeastern Central Europe. Its highest point (694 m) is in the Hautes Fagnes (Belgium). Exposed to the west, the heavily wooded, sparsely settled uplands dotted with numerous moors have a rugged climate. Average annual precipitation is 1,400 mm, and heavy snowfalls are common.

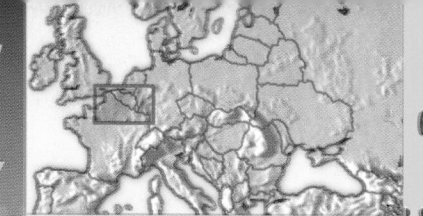

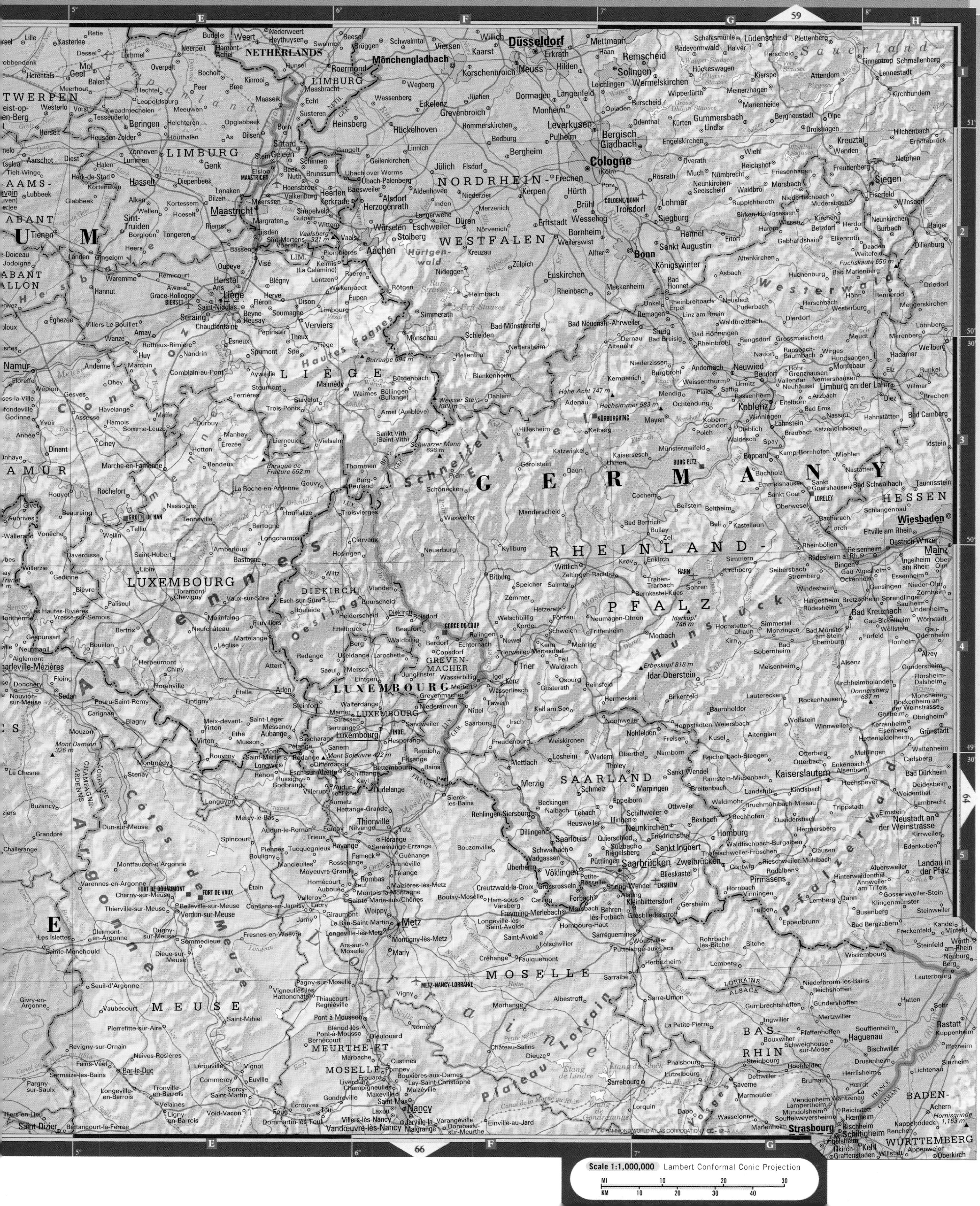
NETHERLANDS
BELGIUM
LUXEMBOURG
GERMANY
NORDRHEIN-WESTFALEN
RHEINLAND-PFALZ
SAARLAND
HESSEN
LORRAINE
ALSACE
MOSELLE
MEUSE
MEURTHE-ET-MOSELLE
BAS-RHIN
BADEN-WÜRTTEMBERG
LIMBURG
LIEGE
NAMUR
Ardennes
Eifel
Hunsrück
Westerwald
Sauerland
Pfälzerwald
Hautes Fagnes
Argonne
Plateau Lorrain
Düsseldorf
Mönchengladbach
Cologne
Bonn
Aachen
Koblenz
Trier
Saarbrücken
Kaiserslautern
Wiesbaden
Mainz
Liège
Maastricht
Metz
Nancy
Strasbourg
Luxembourg
Namur
Siegen
Scale 1:1,000,000
Lambert Conformal Conic Projection
MI 10 20 30
KM 10 20 30 40
©HAMMOND WORLD ATLAS CORPORATION

Tidal activity along the Channel coast of Normandy is unusually vigorous. In the Bay of Mont-Saint-Michel, the sea recedes several kilometers at low tide and rises roughly 15 m when the tide is in.

Normandy's gentle climate is favorable to agriculture, and vast fields of grain line the banks of the Seine and the Loire. The region is known for its orchards, which supply apples used in the production of cider and Calvados (apple brandy). Heaths, moors, and woodlands are prevalent in the highlands of Brittany, where the climate is much less agreeable.

Height

m.	ft.
6000	19700
4000	13000
2000	6500
1500	5000
1000	3300
500	1600
200	700
0	0
200	700
500	1600
1000	3300
2000	6500
3000	9800
4000	13000
5000	16400
6000	19700

m.
ft.
Depth

42

ENGLISH CHANNEL

Plymouth
Portsmouth
Weymouth
Southampton
Portsmouth

Alderney
Saint Anne
Cap de la Hague
Nez de Jobourg
Beaumont
Querqueville
Équeurdreville-Hainneville
Octeville
Cherbourg
Saint-Pierre-Église
Fermanville
Gatteville-le-Phare
Maupertus
Rev
Tourlaville
La Glacerie
Quettehou
Les Pieux
Valognes
Cotentin
Bricquebec
Montebo
Saint-Sauveur
UT

Guernsey
Vale
Saint Sampson's
Herm
Saint Peter Port
GUERNSEY
Torteval
Great Sark
Sark
Little Sark
Passage de la Déroute
Carteret
Barneville-Carteret
Picauvil
Portbail
La Haye-du-Puits
Saré
Car
MANCHE

CHANNEL ISLANDS
(U.K.)

Grosnez Pt.
Sorel Pt.
Saint John
Rozel
STATES
Saint Saviour
Saint Helier
FRANCE
U.K.
Lessay
Périers
St. Ouen's Bay
Corbière Pt.
Saint Aubin
Gorey
St. Ahlin's Bay
Saint-Sauveur-le
Gouville-sur-Mer
Coutances

Jersey

Pointe d'Agon

Les Minquiers
(U.K.)

Îles Chausey
(FR.)
Granville
Donville-les-Bains
Bréhal
Gavray
Pointe du Roc
Saint-Pair-sur-Mer
Thar
Jullouville
La Haye-Pe
Sartilly
Vill

Les Sept Îles
Pointe du Château
Îles d'Er
Île de Bréhat
Golfe de St-Malo
Cap Fréhel
Pointe du Grouin
Cancale
Baie du Mt-St-Michel
Avranch

Trégastel
Île Tomé
Pleubian
Pointe de l'Arcouest
Perros-Guirec
Penvénan
Plouézec
Trélévern
Ploubazlanec
Baie de St-Brieuc
Saint-Cast-le-Guildo
Saint-Coulomb
Saint-Malo

Île de Batz
Roscoff
Île Callot
Baie de Lannion
Lannion
Ploubezre
Tréguier
Plouha
Saint-Quay-Portrieux
Erquy
Saint-Lunaire
Dinard
Le Mont-Saint-Michel
Saint-Pol-de-Léon
Plougasnou
Locquirec
Servel
Étables-sur-Mer
Pléneuf-Val-André
Matignon
Saint-Briac-sur-Mer
Cherrueix
Dol
Pontorson

Kerlouan
Plouescat
Cléder
Lanmeur
Plestin-les-Grèves
Binic
Hénanbihen
Ploubalay
PLEURTUIT
Pleurtuit
Pleine-Fougères

Plouider
Plouvorn
Morlaix
Bégard
Pédernec
Pabu
Pordic
Lengueux
Plancoët
Créhen
Saint-Sauveur

Lesneven
Le Folgoët
Saint-Martin-des-Champs
Ploumilliau
Guingamp
Plérin
Pluduno
Corseul
Plancoët
Pleine-Fougères

St-Pabu
Lannilis
Plouzévédé
Plouigneau
Ploumagoar
Plouagat
Saint-Brieuc
Yffiniac
Quévert
Dinan
Lanvallay
Antrain

Plouguerneau
Landivisiau
Saint-Thégonnec
Plourin-les-Morlaix
Belle-Isle-en-Terre
Ploufragan
Trégueux
Plédran
Léhon
Combourg
Ploudaniel
Plabennec
La Roche-Maurice
Plougonven
Bourbriac
Le Faël
Plédran
Quessoy
Jugon
Plélan-le-Petit
Évran
Hédé
GUIPAVAS
Landerneau
Pleyber-Christ
Callac
CÔTES-D'ARMOR
Quintin
Plaintel
Plœuc-sur-Lié
Plestan
Moncontour
Broons
Plumaugat
Caulnes
Saint-Aubin

Gouesnou
Guilers
Huelgoat
Lanrivain
Monts de Bretagne
Tinténiac
Saint-Aubin

Brest
Guipavas
Signal de Toussaines 384 m
Montagne Saint-Michel 380 m
Saint-Nicolas
Uzel
Plouguenast-Langast
Médréac
Romillé
Melesse
Liffré

Loperhet
Daoulas
Hôpital-Camfrout
FINISTÈRE
Kergrist-Moëlou
Rostrenen
Gouarec
Mûr-de-Bretagne
Plémet
Montauban
Montfort-sur-Meu
Betton
Pacé
Cesson-Sévigné
ILLE-

Pointe de Saint-Mathieu
Le Relecq-Kerhuon
Plougastel
Carhaix-Plouguer
Plouguernével
Gourin
Saint-Méen-le-Grand
L'Hermitage
Acigné

Le Conquet
Plouzané
Camaret
Crozon
Lanvéoc
Pont-de-Buis-lès-Quimerch
Pleyben
Carhaix
Montagnes Noires
Canal de Nantes à Brest
Loudéac
Mordelles
Chantepie
Rennes
Noyal
Châteaub

Pointe de Penhir
Iroise
Telgruc-sur-Mer
Châteaulin
Châteauneuf-du-Faou
Plouray
Pontivy
Noyal-Pontivy
Plumieux
La Trinité-Porhoët
Mauron
Plélan-le-Grand
Saint-Jacques-de-la-Lande
Vern
Louvigné-de-
Châteaugiron
VILAIN

Cap de la Chèvre
Baie de Douarnenez
Briec
Gourin
Coray
Guémené-sur-Scorff
Le Faouët
Josselin
Bruz
Corps-Nuds
Guichen
Janzé

Pointe du Van
Douarnenez
Locronan
Ergué-Gabéric
Elliant
Scaër
Bubry
Guénin
Ploërmel
Guer
Guignen
Plechâtel
Retiers
La Gue

Pointe du Raz
Cléden-Cap-Sizun
Pont-Croix
Plogoff
Audierne
Quimper
PLUGUFFAN
Rosporden
Bannalec
Mellac
Plouay
Locminé
Lanouée
Maure-de-Bretagne
Piré
Martigné-Ferchaud

Plouhinec
Plozévet
Plogastel
Guilvinec
Rivière
Pouldreuzic
Plonéour-Lanvern
Combrit
Fouesnant
Bénodet
Concarneau
Riec-sur-Belon
Pont-Scorff
Intzinzac-Lochrist
Caudan
Languidic
Baud
MORBIHAN
La Gacilly
Malestroit
Pipriac
Messac
Bain-de-Bretagne
Rougé
Soudan

Baie d'Audierne
St-Guénolé
Penmarch
Pont-l'Abbé
Loctudy
Trégunc
Moëlan-sur-Mer
Quéven
Hennebont
Pluvigner
Elven
Rochefort-en-Terre
Peillac
Bains-sur-Oust
Grand-Fougeray
Sion-les-Mines
Chère
Châteaub

Pointe de Penmarc'h
Guidel
LANN-BIHOUÉ
Ploemeur
Larmor
Lorient
Lanester
Brech
Sainte-Anne-d'Auray
Saint-Avé
Sulniac
La Vraie-Croix
Allaire
Redon
Avessac
Saint-Vincent-de-
Guémené-Penfao
Derval

Îles de Glénan
Pointe du Talut
Port-Louis
Locoal-Mendon
Auray
Le Bono
Baden
Vannes
Questembert
Pénestin
BRETAGNE
PAYS DE LA LOIRE
Moisc
La-Riv

Île de Groix
Groix
Étel
LES ALIGNEMENTS DE CARNAC
Locmariaquer
Sarzeau
Golfe du Morbihan
La Roche-Bernard
Guenrouët
Plessé
Nozay
Grand Rés. de Vioreau
Abbaretz

Presqu'île de Quiberon
Saint-Pierre-Quiberon
Carnac
Muzillac
Saint-Gildas-des-Bois
Blain
Vay
Joué-sur-Erdre

Quiberon
Pointe du Grand Mont
Presqu'île de Rhuys
Herbignac
Pontchâteau
Campbon
Bouvron
Héric
Les Touches

Pointe du Conguel
Pointe des Poulains
Île de Houat
Sainte-Reine
La Chapelle-des-Marais
Sevenay
Nort
Carquefou

Passage de la Teignouse
Sauzon
Le Palais
Piriac-sur-Mer
Mesquer
La Turballe
Guérande
Saint-Joachim
Donges
La Chapelle
Le Loro
Orvault

BAY OF BISCAY
Belle-Île
Bangor
Pointe de Kerdonis
Passage des Sœurs
Île de Hoedic
Rade de Croisic
Le Croisic
Le Pouliguen
La Baule-Escoublac
Pornichet
Trignac
Saint-Malo-de-Guersac
Montoir
Saint-Nazaire
Paimbœuf
St-Étienne-de-Montluc
Sautron
Saint-Herblain
Rezé
Nantes
ATLANTIQUE
LOIRE-

Batz-sur-Mer
Saint-Michel-Chef-Chef
La Plaine-sur-Mer
Pointe du Croisic
Saint-Brevin-les-Pins
Saint-Père-en-Retz
Couëron
Le Pellerin
Saint-Jean
Sainte-Luce
Saint-Sébastien-sur-Loire
Chamopteceau

Population

- ■ Over 2,000,000
- ◉ 500,000 - 999,999
- ● 100,000 - 249,999
- ◎ 10,000 - 29,999
- ▣ 1,000,000 - 1,999,999
- ⊙ 250,000 - 499,999
- ○ 30,000 - 99,999
- ○ Under 10,000

SEINE-MARITIME

OISE

SOMME

Picardy

HAUTE-NORMANDIE

Pays de Caux

Baie de la Seine

Cap d'Antifer

Cap de la Hève

Le Havre

EURE

VAL-D'OISE

YVELINES

PARIS

ILE-DE-FRANCE

Normandy

CALVADOS

Collines de Normandie

BASSE-NORMANDIE

ORNE

ESSONNE

EURE-ET-LOIR

Maine

Collines du Maine

PAYS DE LA LOIRE

MAYENNE

SARTHE

LOIRET

CENTRE

Anjou

MAINE-ET-LOIRE

INDRE-ET-LOIRE

LOIR-ET-CHER

Orléanais

CHER

INDRE

OMAHA BEACH
GOLD BEACH
JUNO BEACH
SWORD BEACH

Dieppe

Fécam

Le Havre

Rouen

Caen

Bayeux

Saint-Lô

Lisieux

Évreux

Alençon

Le Mans

Laval

Angers

Tours

Chartres

Dreux

Orléans

Blois

Versailles

Beauvais

Saumur

La Flèche

Vierzon

© HAMMOND WORLD ATLAS CORPORATION

Scale 1:1,000,000 Lambert Conformal Conic Projection

MI   10   20   30
KM 10   20   40

At first glance, the three neighboring central ranges of the Franconian-Thuringian uplands appear quite similar. The Fichtelgebirge, the Thüringer Wald and the Frankenwald are all covered by dense mountain forests. Yet each has its own unique features: the granite massifs of the Fichtelgebirge, the deep valleys that cut through the higher elevations of the Thüringer Wald, and the high plateaus of the Frankenwald. The central uplands extend eastward through the Erzgebirge, whose old mixed forests, well adapted to the cold climate, were largely destroyed by intensive mining and gave way to less robust coniferous growth.

Population

- Over 2,000,000
- 1,000,000 – 1,999,999
- 500,000 – 999,999
- 250,000 – 499,999
- 100,000 – 249,999
- 30,000 – 99,999
- 10,000 – 29,999
- Under 10,000

Scale 1:1,000,000 Lambert Conformal Conic Projection

Switzerland is the most important source and reservoir of drinking water in Central Europe. It borders on the two largest Alpine lakes – Lake Constance and Lake Geneva – and pre-Alpine central

Switzerland is dotted with many smaller lakes. Major rivers such as the Rhine and the Rhône flow from sources in Switzerland. Glaciers also provide huge storehouses of water. Covering some 125 square km,

the Aletsch Glacier, which descends from the Jungfraujoch, is the largest in the Alps. Its tongue has receded more than 1,000 m since the early 20th century.

Central Alps Region

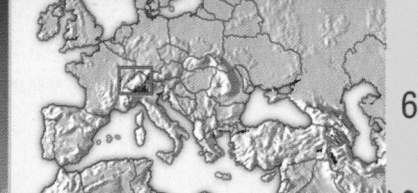

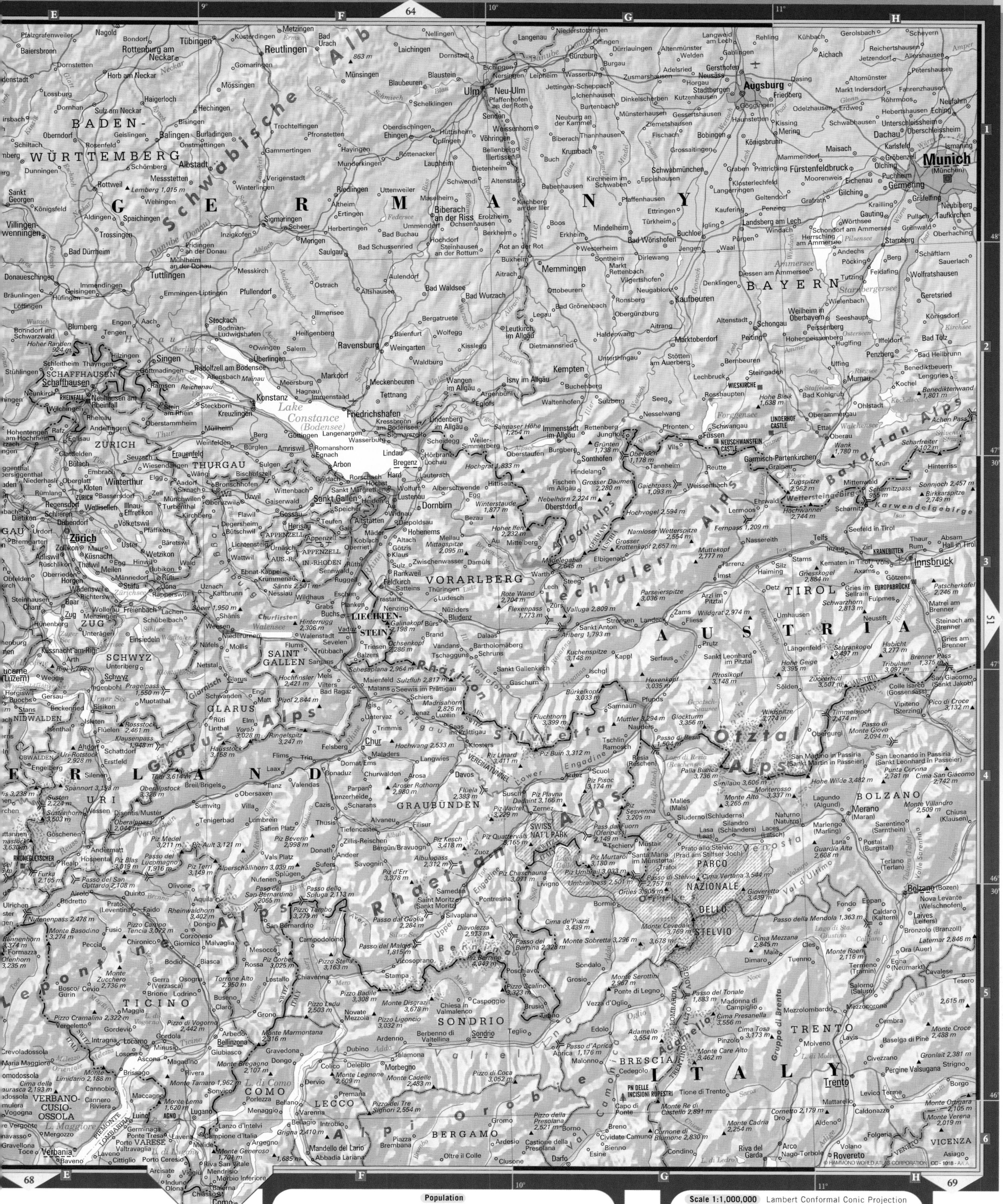

Population

■ Over 2,000,000	⊙ 500,000 - 999,999
▣ 1,000,000 - 1,999,999	◎ 250,000 - 499,999
⊕ 100,000 - 249,999	⊙ 10,000 - 29,999
⊙ 30,000 - 99,999	○ Under 10,000

Scale 1:1,000,000 Lambert Conformal Conic Projection

MI 0 10 20 30
KM 0 10 20 30 40

At the end of its course (652 km), the Po, the longest river on the Apennine Peninsula, empties into the Adriatic Sea south of Venice. Its drainage basin covers an area of about 75,000 square km.

Fast-flowing tributaries descending from the Alps and the Apennines deposit heavy loads of sediment in the Po delta, which extends some 80 m farther into the sea every year. Numerous dams along the

lower reaches of the river raise the riverbed above the level of the surrounding fertile plain. The Po often overflows its banks during periods of heavy rain in the spring and fall.

Height
m. / ft.
6000 / 19700
4000 / 13000
2000 / 6500
1500 / 5000
1000 / 3300
500 / 1600
200 / 700
0
200 / 700
500 / 1600
1000 / 3300
2000 / 6500
3000 / 9800
4000 / 13000
5000 / 16400
6000 / 19700
m. / ft.
Depth

Population

■ Over 2,000,000
□ 1,000,000 - 1,999,999
● 500,000 - 999,999
◉ 250,000 - 499,999
● 100,000 - 249,999
◎ 30,000 - 99,999
◉ 10,000 - 29,999
○ Under 10,000

SLOVENIA

CROATIA

Golfo di Venezia

Golfo di Trieste

ADRIATIC SEA

Mouths of the Po

Venice (Venezia)

UDINE
GORIZIA
TRIESTE
PORDENONE
TREVISO
BELLUNO
VICENZA
VERONA
PADOVA
VENEZIA
ROVIGO
FERRARA
BOLOGNA
RAVENNA
FORLÌ-CESENA
RIMINI
SAN MARINO
PESARO E URBINO
ANCONA
MACERATA
PERUGIA
AREZZO
SIENA
FIRENZE
PISTOIA
PRATO

Verona • Padova • Vicenza • Rovigo • Ferrara • Bologna • Modena • Ravenna • Florence (Firenze) • Rimini • Ancona • Pesaro • Fano • Senigallia

Appennino Tosco-Emiliano
Appennino Umbro-Marchigiano

Scale 1:1,000,000 Lambert Conformal Conic Projection

© HAMMOND WORLD ATLAS CORPORATION

The Alps dominated this region, with many peaks exceeding 3,000 meters in height. Provence, to the south, features rugged terrain, fragrant lavender fields, and a spectacular coastline. The famed French Riviera (Côte d'Azur), which stretches from St-Tropez through Cannes and Nice to the Italian border, boasts some of the most fashionable resorts in the world.

66

FRANCE

ITALY

AOSTA

TORINO

Turin

MONACO

RHÔNE
LOIRE
ARDÈCHE
ISÈRE
SAVOIE
DRÔME
VAUCLUSE
GARD
BOUCHES-DU-RHÔNE
VAR
HAUTES-ALPES
ALPES-DE-HAUTE-PROVENCE
ALPES-MARITIMES
CUNEO
CITTA DI TORINO

Lyon
Vienne
Grenoble
Valence
Montélimar
Gap
Avignon
Aix-en-Provence
Marseille
Nice
Cannes
Toulon

Provence

Côte d'Azur

Gulf of Lion

MEDITERRANEAN SEA

Mont Ventoux 1,909 m
Montagne de Lure
Montagne de Lubéron
Plateau de Valensole
Massif des Maures
Massif de l'Estérel

PARC NATIONAL DE LA VANOISE
PARC NATIONAL DES ÉCRINS
PARC NATIONAL DU MERCANTOUR
PARC NATIONAL DE PORT-CROS

CHÂTEAU D'IF
Iles d'Hyères
Iles de Lérins
Ile de Porquerolles
Ile du Levant

PARCO NAZIONALE DEL GRAN PARADISO

Mont Blanc

Height
m. / ft.
6000 / 19700
4000 / 13000
2000 / 6500
1500 / 5000
1000 / 3300
500 / 1600
200 / 700
0
200 / 700
500 / 1600
1000 / 3300
2000 / 6500
3000 / 9800
4000 / 13000
5000 / 16400
6000 / 19700
m. / ft.
Depth

Population
■ Over 2,000,000
● 500,000 - 999,999
◉ 100,000 - 249,999
◎ 10,000 - 29,999
□ 1,000,000 - 1,999,999
● 250,000 - 499,999
◉ 30,000 - 99,999
○ Under 10,000

Scale 1:1,000,000   Lambert Conformal Conic Projection
MI   10   20   30
KM   10   20   30   40

Central Italy

The Apennines, which cover an area roughly 1,500 km long and 150 km wide, have their own distinct climate. Average temperatures are lower while precipitation is heavier than elsewhere in the country.

In 1921, 292 square km in the southern reaches of this range of limestone formations were set aside as the Abruzzi National Park, which remains a refuge for bears, wolves, and golden eagles.

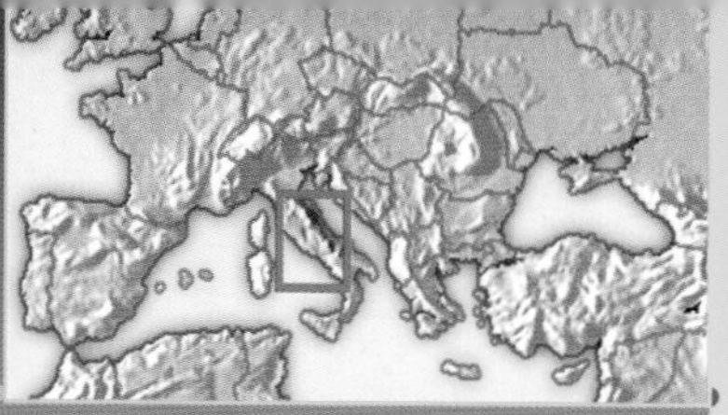

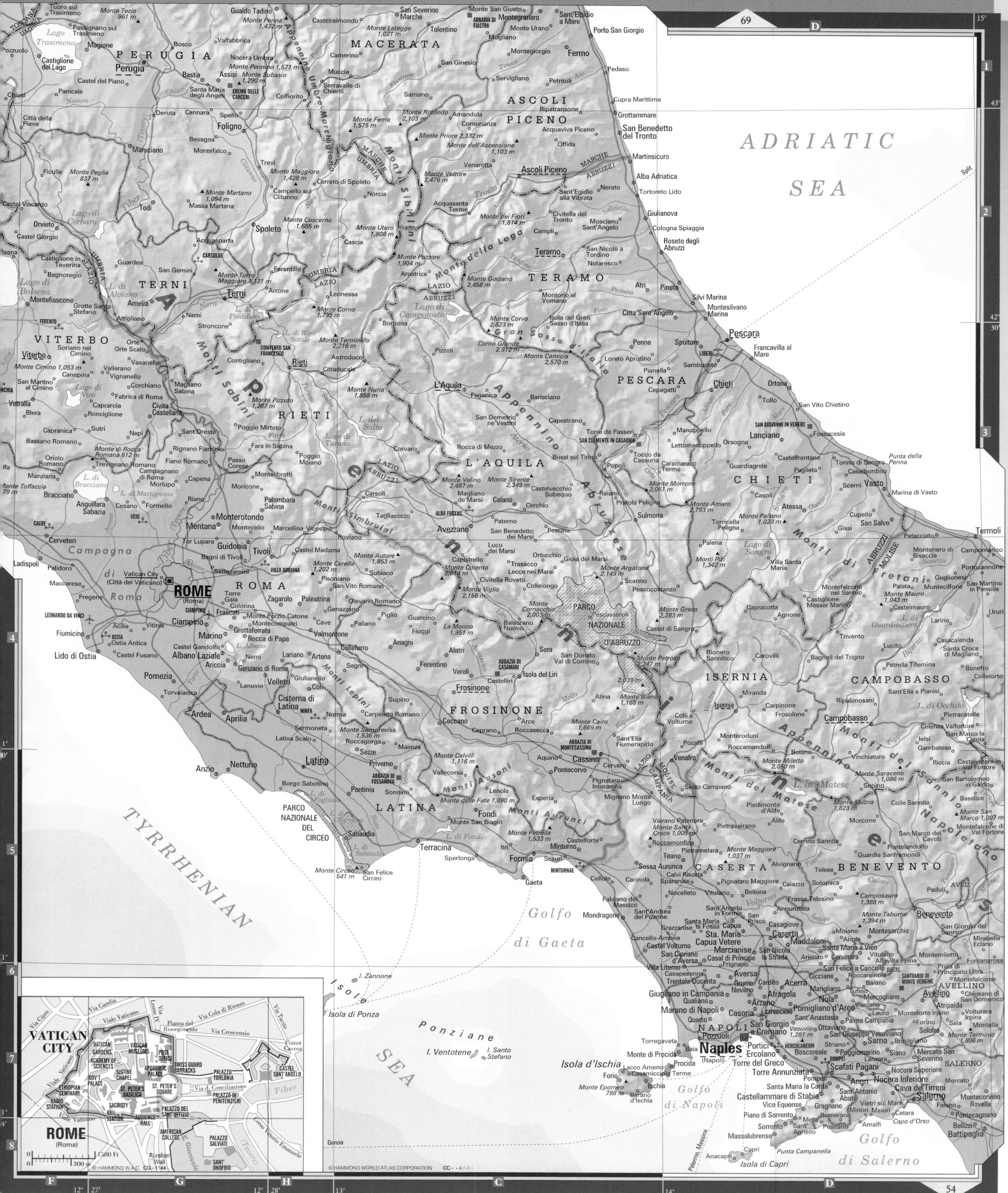

ADRIATIC SEA
TYRRHENIAN SEA
PERUGIA
MACERATA
ASCOLI PICENO
TERNI
TERAMO
VITERBO
RIETI
L'AQUILA
PESCARA
CHIETI
ROMA
ROME
FROSINONE
ISERNIA
CAMPOBASSO
LATINA
CASERTA
BENEVENTO
AVELLINO
NAPOLI
Naples
SALERNO
Golfo di Gaeta
Golfo di Napoli
Golfo di Salerno
Isole Ponziane
PARCO NAZIONALE D'ABRUZZO
PARCO NAZIONALE DEL CIRCEO
Appennino Abruzzese
Monti Sibillini
Gran Sasso d'Italia
Monti Sabini
Monti Simbruini
Monti Lepini
Monti Ausoni
Monti Aurunci
Monti del Matese
Monti del Sannio
Lago Trasimeno
Lago di Bolsena
Lago di Bracciano
VATICAN CITY
ROME (Roma)
© HAMMOND WORLD ATLAS CORPORATION

Population

- ■ Over 2,000,000
- ▣ 1,000,000 - 1,999,999
- ⊙ 500,000 - 999,999
- ⊙ 250,000 - 499,999
- ⊕ 100,000 - 249,999
- ⊙ 30,000 - 99,999
- ○ 10,000 - 29,999
- ○ Under 10,000

Scale 1:1,000,000 Lambert Conformal Conic Projection

MI 0 10 20 30
KM 0 10 20 30 40

The Mediterranean Sea is connected to the Atlantic by the Strait of Gibraltar. It covers a total surface area of 3.02 million square km and reaches a maximum depth of 5,121 m west of the Peloponnesus.

Due to more rapid evaporation, salinity in the Mediterranean (39.1 % in the east) is higher than in the Atlantic. Consequently, a strong surface current carries low-saline water into the Mediterranean from the Atlantic, while saltier water flows westward through the strait along the seafloor. The narrow passage between the two bodies of water also limits tidal activity in the Mediterranean.

Major features

Bay of Biscay

FRANCE

Ligurian Sea

Gulf of Lion

SPAIN

PORTUGAL

Corsica (FRANCE) — Mont Cinto 2,710 m

Sardinia (ITALY)

Balearic Islands — Mallorca (Majorca), Menorca (Minorca), Ibiza, I. de Formentera, I. de Cabrera

MEDITER R

MOROCCO

ALGERIA

TUNISIA

Atlas Mountains — Hauts Plateaux — Atlas Saharien

El Rif — Moyen Atlas — Al Maghrib

Grand Erg Oriental

Major cities

MADRID, Barcelona, Valencia, Seville, Málaga, Murcia, Zaragoza (Saragossa), Bilbao, Valladolid, Córdoba, Granada, Alicante, Cartagena, Lyon, Marseille, Toulouse, Bordeaux, Nantes, Montpellier, Nice, Turin (Torino), Milan (Milano), Genoa (Genova), Algiers (El Djezair), Oran, Constantine, Annaba, Tunis, Tangier, Fès, Meknès, Oujda, Zürich, Bern, Geneva

Legend

Height
m. / ft.
6000 / 19700
4000 / 13000
2000 / 6500
1500 / 5000
1000 / 3300
500 / 1600
200 / 700
0
200 / 700
500 / 1600
1000 / 3300
2000 / 6500
3000 / 9800
4000 / 13000
5000 / 16400
6000 / 19700
m. / ft.
Depth

Population

■ Over 2,000,000	◉ 500,000 - 999,999
■ 1,000,000 - 1,999,999	◉ 250,000 - 499,999
● 100,000 - 249,999	○ 30,000 - 99,999
● 10,000 - 29,999	○ Under 10,000

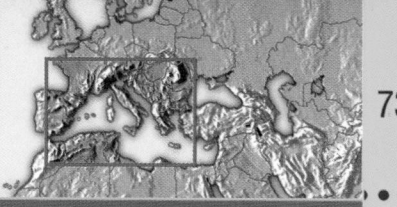

Seas and regions: BLACK SEA · ADRIATIC SEA · TYRRHENIAN SEA · IONIAN SEA · AEGEAN SEA · Sea of Marmara · Sea of Crete · Gulf of Sidra · Malta Channel · Strait of Sicily · Strait of Otranto

Countries: AUSTRIA · HUNGARY · SLOVENIA · CROATIA · BOSNIA AND HERZEGOVINA · SERBIA · MONTENEGRO · ROMANIA · BULGARIA · FORMER YUGOSLAV REP. OF MACEDONIA · ALBANIA · GREECE · TURKEY · ITALY · LIBYA · EGYPT · UKRAINE · MOLD. · MALTA (ITALY)

Capitals and cities: BUDAPEST · Cluj-Napoca · Timișoara · Brașov · Galați · Ljubljana · Zagreb · Belgrade · BUCHAREST · Ploiești · Craiova · Constanța · Sarajevo · Sofia · Varna · Plovdiv · Skopje · Tiranë · Durrës · Thessaloniki · İSTANBUL · Bursa · İZMIR · ROME · Naples · Bari · Taranto · Reggio di Calabria · Messina · Catania · Palermo · Siracusa · Venice (Venezia) · Ioánnina · Lárisa · Vólos · GREECE · Lamia · Athens · Piraiévs · Corinth · Pátra · Kalamáta · Tripolis · Sparta · Crete · Iráklion · KNOSSOS · Rhodes · Dodecanese · Cyclades · Náxos · Páros · Mílos · Tripoli (Ṭarābulus) · Benghāzi · MALTA · Valletta

Black Sea coast: Odesa · Dnistrovs'kyy · Kiliya · Delta of the Danube · Sfîntu Gheorghe · Navodari · Mangalia · Dobrich · Balchik

Physical features: Grossglockner 3,797 m · Mt. Olympus 2,917 m · Mt. Etna 3,323 m · Durmitor 2,522 m · Korab 2,751 m · Triglav 2,863 m · Botev 2,376 m · Idhi 2,456 m

Scale 1:6,000,000 Lambert Conformal Conic Projection

MI	50	100	150	200
KM	50 100	150	200 250	300

Receding ice left behind a landscape of lakes, morainic ridges, drumlins, and other glacial formations in northeastern Europe. The Finnish lake region alone comprises some 55,000 mostly shallow lakes. Northeastern Europe is known for its vast woodlands. With 68 per cent of its area covered by firs, pines, alders, and beeches, Finland is the most heavily forested country in Europe. The climate is continental for the most part, becoming subpolar in the north. Coastal waters begin to freeze over toward the end of the year. Tundra vegetation is predominant in the north.

Height

m.
ft.
6000
19700
4000
13000
2000
6500
1500
5000
1000
3300
500
1600
200
700
0
200
700
500
1600
1000
3300
2000
6500
3000
9800
4000
13000
5000
16400
6000
19700
m.
ft.
Depth

Population

■ Over 2,000,000   ● 500,000 - 999,999   ◉ 100,000 - 249,999   ○ 10,000 - 29,999
▣ 1,000,000 - 1,999,999   ● 250,000 - 499,999   ◉ 30,000 - 99,999   ○ Under 10,000

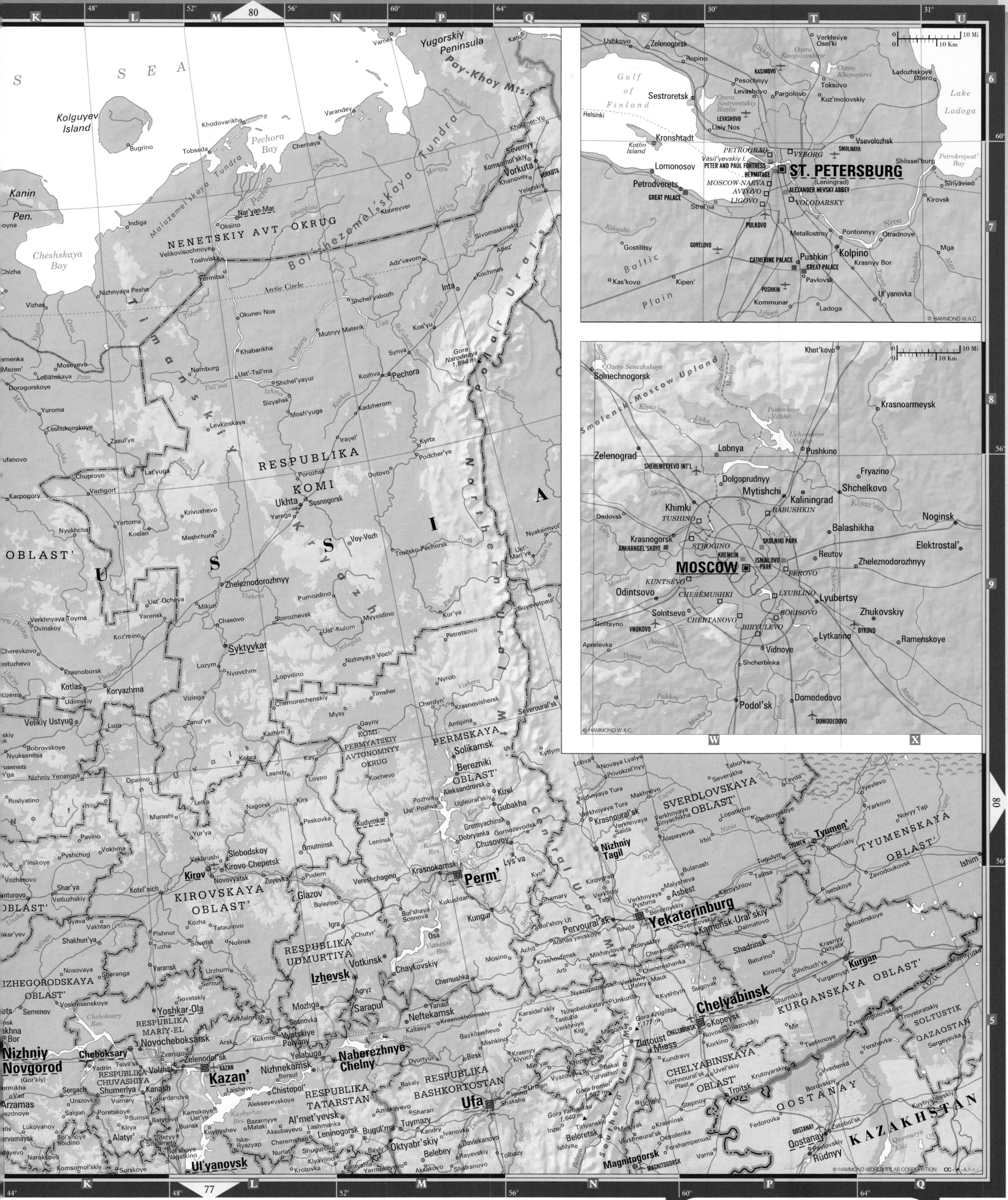

The Black Sea receives substantial flows of fresh water from such rivers as the Danube, the Don, and the Dnepr. Thus its salinity near the surface is only half that of the Atlantic. Salt-rich water also flows into the sea from the Mediterranean Sea along the floor of the Bosporus Strait. This stable layered configuration produces an oxygen shortage at the bottom of the Black Sea that is hostile to living organisms. By contrast, the Danube Delta teems with life. It is a paradise for birds – one of the last in Europe – and provides spawning grounds for over one hundred different species of fish.

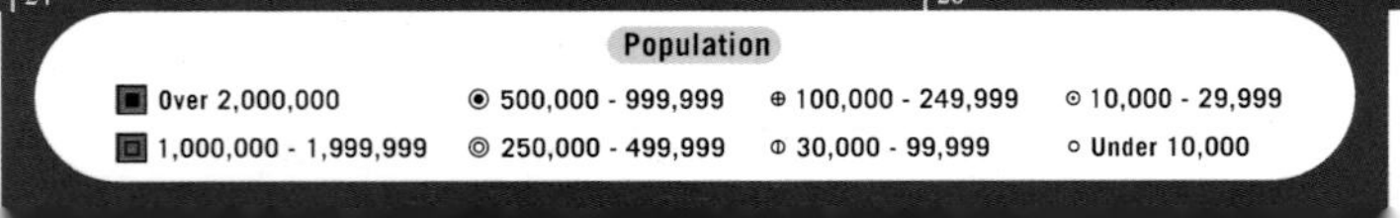

Height

m.	ft.
6000	19700
4000	13000
2000	6500
1500	5000
1000	3300
500	1600
200	700
0	
200	700
500	1600
1000	3300
2000	6500
3000	9800
4000	13000
5000	16400
6000	19700

Depth

Population

■ Over 2,000,000	● 500,000 – 999,999	● 100,000 – 249,999	○ 10,000 – 29,999
■ 1,000,000 – 1,999,999	● 250,000 – 499,999	○ 30,000 – 99,999	○ Under 10,000

RUSSIA

KAZAKHSTAN

UZBEKISTAN

TURKMENISTAN

GEORGIA

ARMENIA

AZERBAIJAN

IRAN

CASPIAN SEA

Aral Sea

Major cities and labels:

Ul'yanovsk, Dimitrovgrad, Tol'yatti, Samara, Novokuybyshevsk, Syzran', Penza, Saransk, Kuznetsk, Saratov, Engel's, Balashov, Volgograd, Volzhskiy, Volgodonsk, Astrakhan', Elista, Stavropol', Armavir, Cherkessk, Mineral'nyye Vody, Pyatigorsk, Kislovodsk, Nal'chik, Vladikavkaz, Groznyy, Makhachkala, Kaspiysk, Derbent, T'bilisi, Rust'avi, K'ut'aisi, Bat'umi, Zugdidi, Yerevan, Gyumri, Vanadzor, Sumqayit, Baku, Ganca, Mingacevir, Erzurum, Kars

Magnitogorsk, Sterlitamak, Salavat, Orenburg, Orsk, Novotroitsk, Aqtöbe, Oral, Atyraū, Aqtaū, Qostanay, Rūdnyy, Qostanay, Qyzylorda, Daşoguz

REPUBLIKA TATARSTAN, REPUBLIKA BASHKORTOSTAN, REPUBLIKA CHUVASHIYA, RESPUBLIKA MORDOVIYA, UL'YANOVSKAYA OBLAST', PENZENSKAYA OBLAST', SARATOVSKAYA OBLAST', SAMARSKAYA OBLAST', ORENBURGSKAYA OBLAST', VOLGOGRADSKAYA OBLAST', ASTRAKHANSKAYA OBLAST', RESPUBLIKA KALMYKIYA, STAVROPOL'SKIY KRAY, RESPUBLIKA KARACHAYEVO-CHERKESIYA, RESPUBLIKA KABARDINO-BALKARIYA, RESPUBLIKA SEVER. OSETIYA-ALANIYA, RESPUBLIKA INGUSHETIYA, RESPUBLIKA CHECHNYA, RESPUBLIKA DAGESTAN, CHELYABINSKAYA OBLAST'

BATYS QAZAQSTAN, ATYRAŪ, MANGGHYSTAŪ, AQTÖBE, QORAQALPOG'ISTON RESPUBLIKASI

Ustyurt Plateau, Mangghystaū Tübegi, Garabogazköl Aylagy, BALKAN, AHAL

CAUCASUS

Scale 1:6,000,000   Lambert Conformal Conic Projection

MI 50 100 150 200
KM 50 100 150 200 300

Northern Ukraine lies within a mixed-forest zone of oak, beech, and pine that gives way to a forest-steppe in the heartland, where the roots of trees reach groundwater at only a very few places.

The topography in the south is dominated by plains. The rich, black soil (chernozem) of the forest-steppes and plains yields bountiful harvests of wheat, barley, sugar beets, and sunflower seeds. Ukraine holds the world's largest reserves of anthracite coal in the Donets River Basin, as well as rich deposits of iron and manganese ore.

Height

m.	ft.
6000	19700
4000	13000
2000	6500
1500	5000
1000	3300
500	1600
200	700
- 0 -	
200	700
500	1600
1000	3300
2000	6500
3000	9800
4000	13000
5000	16400
6000	19700

m. ft.

Depth

Population

■ Over 2,000,000	⊛ 500,000 - 999,999
◉ 100,000 - 249,999	⊙ 10,000 - 29,999
▣ 1,000,000 - 1,999,999	⊚ 250,000 - 499,999
◦ 30,000 - 99,999	○ Under 10,000

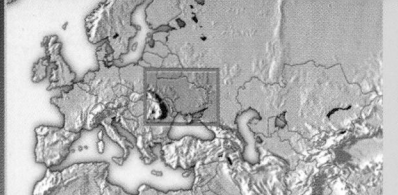

Scale 1:3,000,000   Lambert Conformal Conic Projection

MI 0 25 50 75 100
KM 0 25 50 75 100 125 150

Russia measures more than 4,000 km from north to south and stretches across 9,600 km of territory from west to east – spanning nearly half the globe in the northern latitudes. The Russian land-scape is dominated by vast plains west of the Yenisey River. The climate is predomi-nantly continental and cool. The coldest temperatures in the northern hemisphere have been recorded near the villages of Oimiakon and Verkojansk in eastern Siberia. Long winters with little snow keep the ground frozen for much of the year in about two-thirds of the country, while the climate along the Black Sea coast is subtropical.

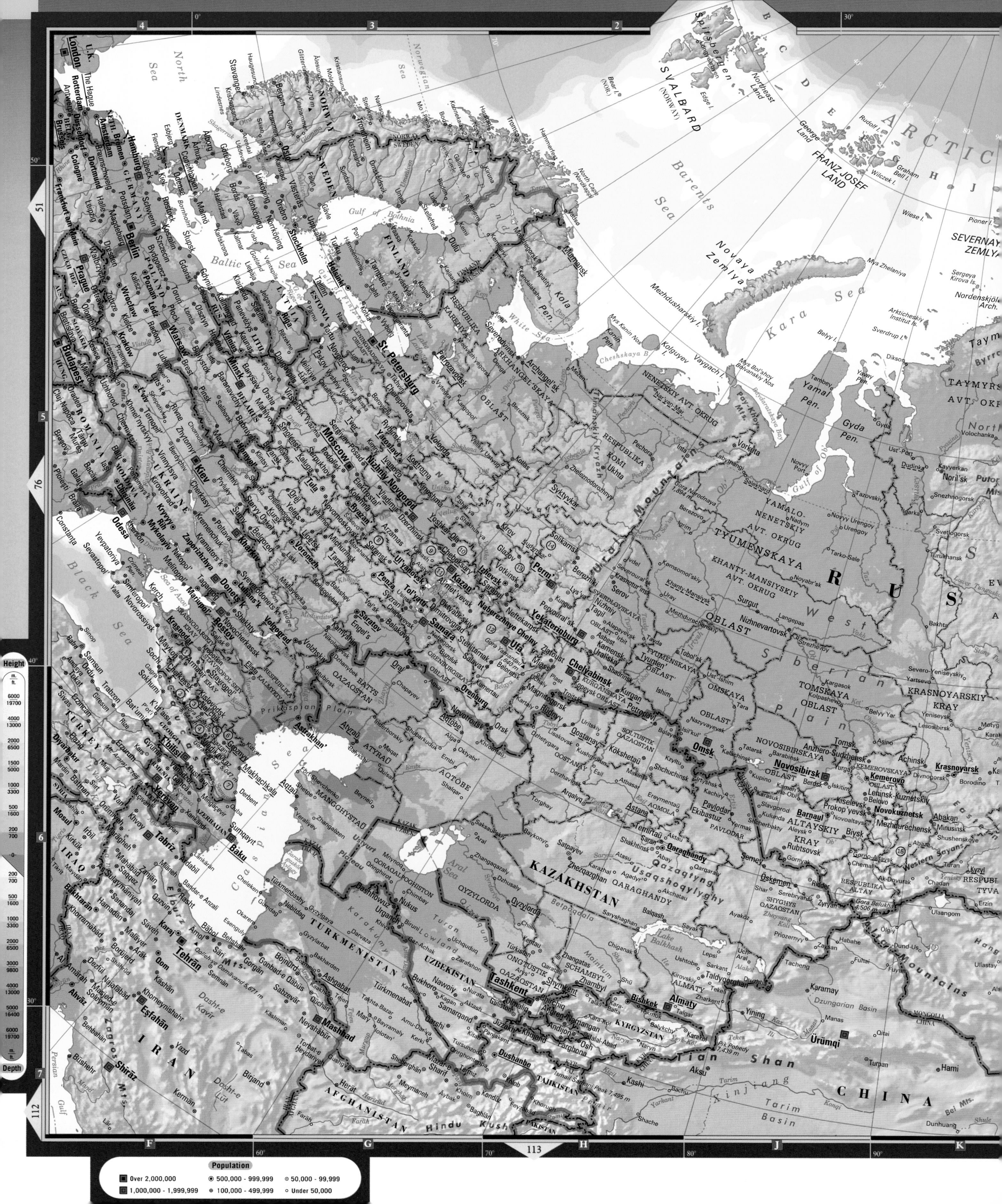

Height
m. / ft.
6000 / 19700
4000 / 13000
2000 / 6500
1500 / 5000
1000 / 3300
500 / 1600
200 / 700
0
200 / 700
500 / 1600
1000 / 3300
2000 / 6500
3000 / 9800
4000 / 13000
5000 / 16400
6000 / 19700
m. / ft.
Depth

Population
■ Over 2,000,000
◉ 500,000 - 999,999
● 50,000 - 99,999
■ 1,000,000 - 1,999,999
◉ 100,000 - 499,999
○ Under 50,000

[Physical map of Russia and surrounding regions, including Scandinavia, Eastern Europe, Central Asia, the Caucasus, Iran, Kazakhstan, and parts of China. Major features labeled include the Arctic Ocean, Barents Sea, Kara Sea, White Sea, Baltic Sea, Black Sea, Caspian Sea, Aral Sea, Ural Mountains, West Siberian Plain, Svalbard, Novaya Zemlya, Franz Josef Land, and cities such as Moscow, St. Petersburg, Kiev, Minsk, Novosibirsk, Omsk, Yekaterinburg, Chelyabinsk, Samara, Kazan, Perm, Ufa, Volgograd, Saratov, Rostov, Krasnoyarsk, Astana, Almaty, Tashkent, Baku, Tbilisi, Tehrān, Mashhad, and others.]

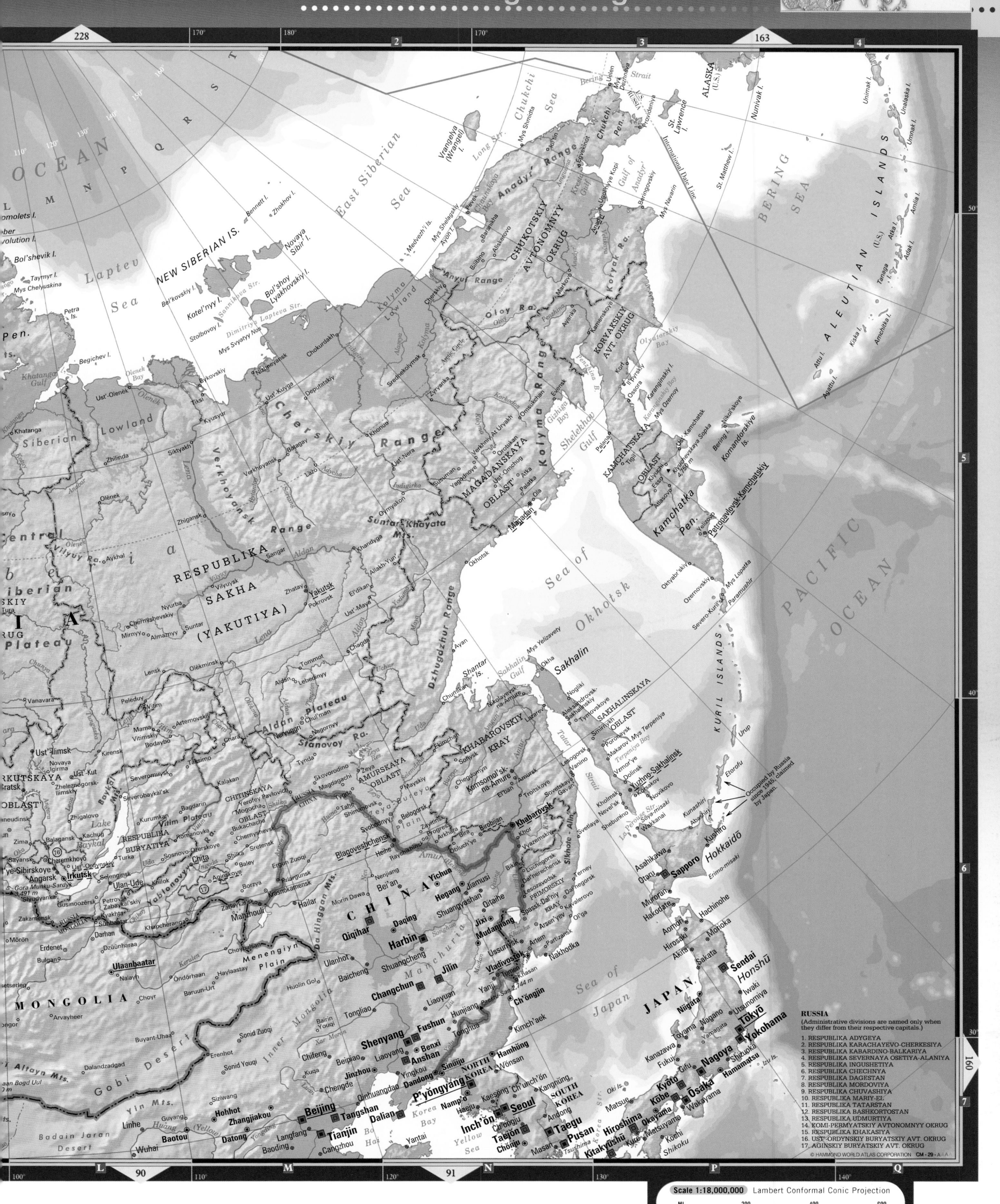

RUSSIA
(Administrative divisions are named only when
they differ from their respective capitals.)

1. RESPUBLIKA ADYGEYA
2. RESPUBLIKA KARACHAYEVO-CHERKESIYA
3. RESPUBLIKA KABARDINO-BALKARIYA
4. RESPUBLIKA SEVERNAYA OSETIYA-ALANIYA
5. RESPUBLIKA INGUSHETIYA
6. RESPUBLIKA CHECHNYA
7. RESPUBLIKA DAGESTAN
8. RESPUBLIKA MORDOVIYA
9. RESPUBLIKA CHUVASHIYA
10. RESPUBLIKA MARIY-EL
11. RESPUBLIKA TATARSTAN
12. RESPUBLIKA BASHKORTOSTAN
13. RESPUBLIKA UDMURTIYA
14. KOMI-PERMYATSKIY AVTONOMNYY OKRUG
15. RESPUBLIKA KHAKASIYA
16. UST'-ORDYNSKIY BURYATSKIY AVT. OKRUG
17. AGINSKIY BURYATSKIY AVT. OKRUG

© HAMMOND WORLD ATLAS CORPORATION   CM · 29 · A·A·A

Scale 1:18,000,000   Lambert Conformal Conic Projection

MI   200   400   600

KM   200   400   600   800

Asia

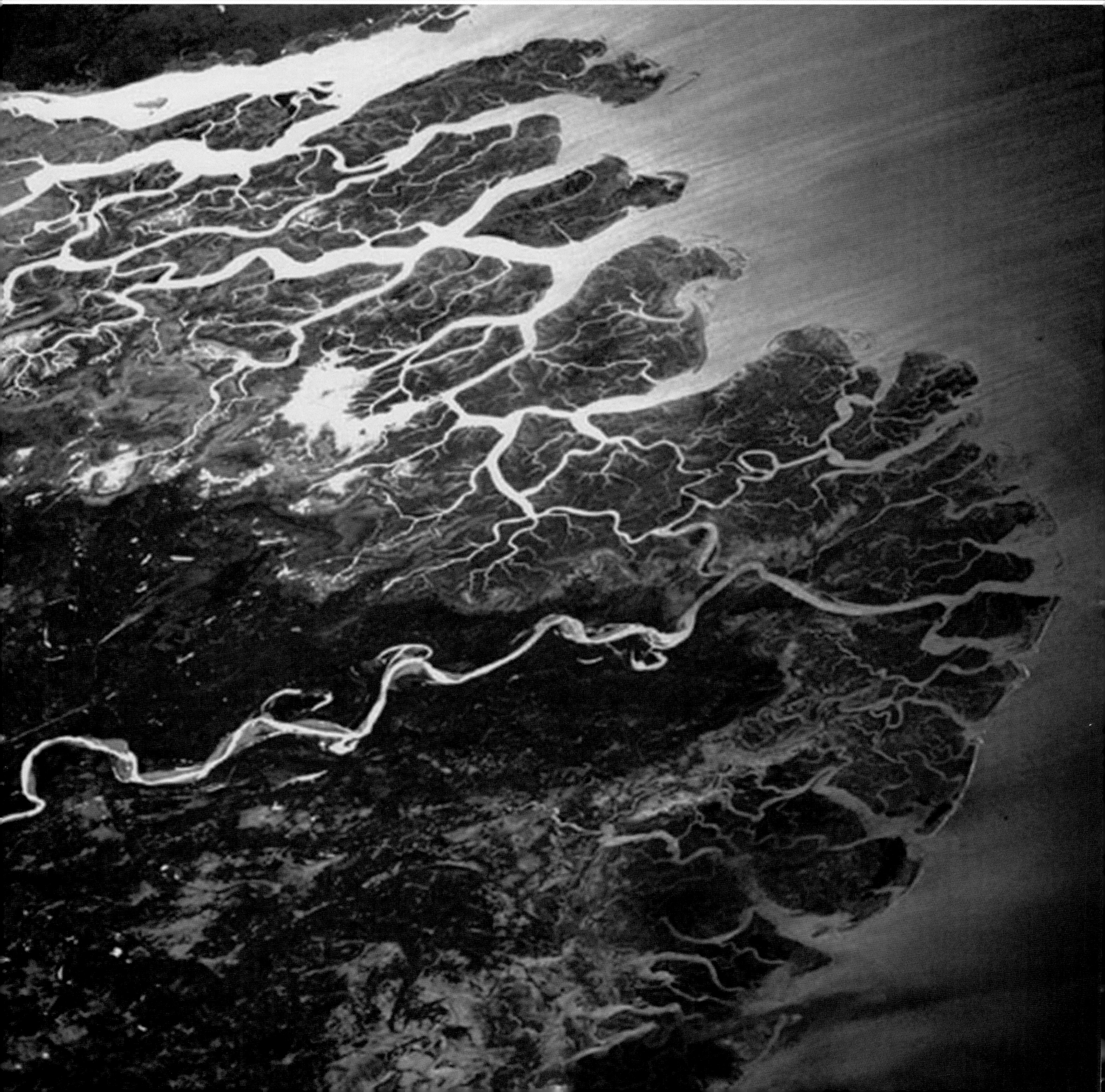

The Indus is the longest river in southwest Asia (3,200 km), and its delta covers an area of 7,800 square km. The river flows from its source at an elevation of 5,182 meters in the Trans-Himalayas

and is fed by snowmelt and glacial meltwater from the mountains of the Tibet Plateau. After leaving the Himalayas, it flows onto the Punjab Plain and through a vast alluvial lowland before emptying

into the Arabian Sea south of Hyderabad. Water levels on the Indus fluctuate with the rhythm of the monsoon rains. Dams and canals ensure a reliable supply of water to the world's largest irrigation zone.

83

AREA OF OPTIMIZATION

The red band which surrounds this map defines the "Area of Optimization." Within this bounding curve is the most accurate conformal map that can be made of the region. Outside the optimized area, distortion increases rapidly, and tears or other irregularities in the grid may occur. (See Map Section 8-9 for additional information.)

Population

■ Over 3,000,000	● 500,000 - 999,999	○ Under 100,000
■ 1,000,000 - 2,999,999	● 100,000 - 499,999	

Scale 1:42,000,000   Hammond Optimal Conformal

© HAMMOND WORLD ATLAS CORPORATION CM -1030- A.A

UNESCO Protects World Cultural Heritage Sites

World Heritage Sites in ASIA

Text continued from page 31 - UNESCO World Cultural Heritage Sites of Europe

To What Extent Is the World Cultural Heritage Endangered? The "Red List"

In addition to the World Heritage List, the World Heritage Committee maintains a list of endangered sites – properties in need of special attention and preservation efforts. The purpose of this list is to make both governments and the pubic aware of the natural and anthropogenic dangers to which World Heritage Sites are exposed.

The list of endangered properties currently contains 27 World Heritage Sites, among them the Natural and Cultural Region of Kotor (Yugoslavia), which was shaken by an earthquake in 1979, the Royal Palace of Abomey (Benin), which suffered serious hurricane damage in 1985, the sacred temples of Timbuktu (Mali), which are beset by the destructive forces of the desert, and the monuments of Hampi (India), which are threatened by road and bridge construction.

The World Heritage Committee collaborates with individual governments in preparing an action plan for endangered sites. It provides financial support and monitors the progress of work, which usually takes considerable time. Some countries seek the Committee's help for their problems, while others tend to resent such intervention. One of the few sites that has been restored and deleted from the list is Dubrovnik (Croatia).

Text continues on page 120 - UNESCO World Cultural Heritage Sites of Africa

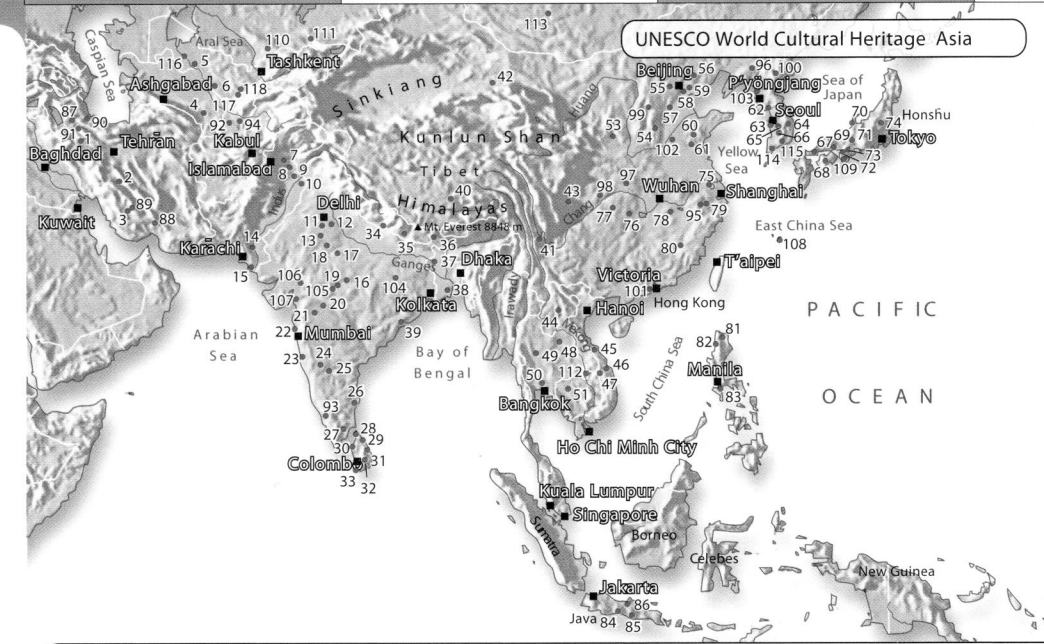

UNESCO World Cultural Heritage Asia

1 Tchogha Zanbil	33 Old Town of Galle	64 Sokkuram Grotto and Pulguksa Temple	93 Mountain Railways of India
2 Meidan Emam, Esfahan	34 Lumbini	65 Hwasong Fortress	94 Bamiyan Valle
3 Persepolis	35 Valley of Kathmandu	66 Chongmyo Shrine	95 Ancient Villages in Southern Anhui - Xidi and Hongcun
4 Ancient City of Merv	36 Darjeeling Himalayan Railway	67 Hiroshima Peace Memorial (Genbaku Dome)	96 Imperial Tombs, Ming and Qing Dynasties
5 Itchan Kala	37 Paharpur	68 Itsukushima Shrine	97 Longmen Grottoes
6 Historic Center of Bukhara	38 Historic Mosque City of Bagerhat	69 Himeji Castle	98 Mount Qingcheng and Dujiangyan Irrigation System
7 Ruins at Takht-i-Bahi	39 Sun Temple of Konarak	70 Shirakawa-Sanchi	99 Yungang Grottoes
8 Taxila	40 Potala Palace in Lhasa	71 Ancient Kyto	100 Capital Cities of Koguryo Kingdom
9 Rohtas Fort	41 Old Town of Lijiang	72 Buddhist Monuments in the Horyu-ji Area	101 Historic Centre of Macao
10 Fort in Lahore	42 Mogao Caves	73 Ancient Nara	102 Yin Xu
11 Qutb Minar in Delhi	43 Mt. Emei Scenic Area and Giant Buddha of Leshan	74 Shrines and Temples of Nikko	103 Complex of Koguryo Tombs
12 Humayun's Tomb Delhi	44 Luang Prabang	75 Classical Gardens of Suzhou	104 Mahabodhi Temple at Bodh Gaya
13 Fatehpur Sikri	45 Hue	76 Ancient Buildings in the Wudang Mountains	105 Rock Shelters of Bhimbetka
14 Archeological Ruins at Moenjodaro	46 Hoi An Ancient Town	77 Dazu Rock Carvings	106 Champaner-Pavagadh Archaeological Park
15 Historic Monuments of Thatta	47 My Son Sanctuary	78 Lushan National Park	107 Chhatrapati Shivaji Terminus
16 Agra, Red Fort	48 Ban Chiang	79 Mount Huangshan	108 Gusuku Sites of the Kingdom of Ryukyu
17 Agra, Taj Mahal	49 Sukhothai	80 Mount Wuyi	109 Sacred Sites in the Kii Mountain Range
18 Monuments at Khajuraho	50 Ayutthaya	81 Rice Terraces of the Ifugao	110 Mausoleum of Khoja Ahmed Yasawi
19 Buddhist Monuments at Sanchi	51 Angkor	82 Historic Town of Vigan	111 Petroglyphs of Tamgaly
20 Ajanta Caves	52 The Great Wall	83 Baroque Churches of the Philippines	112 Vat Phou
21 Ellora Caves	53 Mausoleum of the First Qing Emporer	84 Borobudur Temple Compounds	113 Orkhon Valley
22 Elephanta Caves	54 Ancient City of Ping Yao	85 Prambanan Temple Compounds	114 Gochang, Hwasun and
23 Churches and Convents of Goa	55 Imperial Palace in Beijing	86 Sangiran Early Man Site	115 Ganghwa Dolmen Sites
24 Monuments at Pattadakal	56 Chengde Mountain Resort	87 Takht-e Soleyman	116 Gyeongju Historic Areas Kunya-Urgench
25 Temple of Hampi	57 Peking Man Site at Zhoukoudian	88 Bam and its Cultural Landscape	117 Historic Centre of Shakhrisyabz
26 Monuments at Mahabalipuram	58 Summer Palace near Beijing	89 Pasargadae	118 Samarkand
27 Brihadisvara Temples Thanjavur	59 Temple of Heaven, Beijing	90 Soltaniyeh	
28 Sacred City of Anuradhapura	60 Mount Taishan	91 Bisotun	
29 Ancient City of Sigiriya	61 Temple of Confucious, Qufu	92 Minaret and Remains of Jam	
30 Golden Temple of Dambulla	62 Temple of Haeinsa		
31 Ancient City of Polonnaruwa	63 Palace Complex of Ch'angdokkung		
32 Sacred City of Kandy			

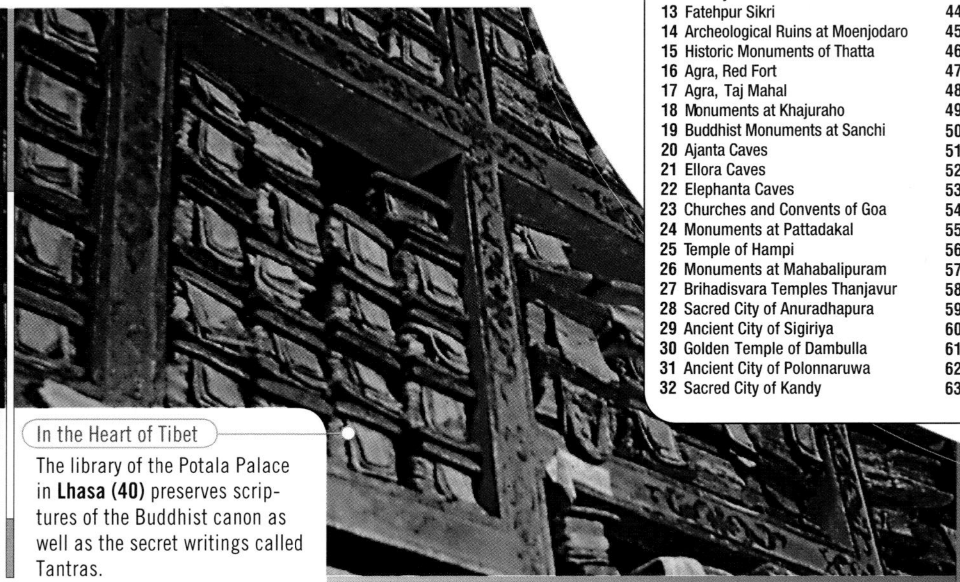

In the Heart of Tibet

The library of the Potala Palace in **Lhasa (40)** preserves scriptures of the Buddhist canon as well as the secret writings called Tantras.

Military Structure

In c. 220 B.C., under Qin Shi Huang, sections of earlier fortifications were joined to form a united defence system against invasions from the north. Construction continued up to the Ming dynasty (1368–1644), when the Great Wall of **China (52)** became the world's largest military structure.

Classical Mogul Architecture

The **Red Fort (16)** of Agra, India, comprises the Pearl Mosque (built between 1648 and 1654). The restrained decoration creates an impression of purity and clarity.

Ancient Stupa

The Dharmarajika stupa near Taxila, **Pakistan (8)**, originally a dome-shaped brick structure decorated with reliefs, dates to the 2nd century BC.

A Library of Wood

The repository of the Tripitaka Koreana (13th c.) at the temple of **Haeinsa (62)** near Taegu, South Korea provides natural air-conditioning for the more than 81,000 wooden printing blocks, testaments of extraordinary craftsmanship.

Camels for the King

The relief on the eastern stairs of the great reception hall in Persepolis, **Iran (3)**, shows Darius the Great receiving gifts.

The World's Largest Terrace System

The Rice Terraces of the Ifugao, **Philippines (81)**, are situated on steep mountain slopes in the northern part of the island of Luzon. Reaching heights of up to 15 meters, many of the heavy walls of stone, support terraces of only three meters wide.

Buddha Calls Upon the Earth Goddess

The sacred shrine of Wat Mahathat, containing sculptures from the 13th and 14th centuries, is located in the heart of the historic city of Sukhothai, **Thailand (49)**.

Ensemble of Bay, Island, and Shrine

The island of Miyajima in the Japanese inland sea is the site of a Shinto shrine built in the 6th and 7th centuries. Pilgrims arrived from the mainland (Hiroshima) at the foot of the **Itsukushima Shrine (68)** in boats. Only 160 meters from the shore, the entrance gate is submerged at high tide.

Towering Faces

The center of the Khmer Kingdom from the 9th to the 15th century, Angkor, **Cambodia (51)**, boasted not only an unparalleled urban architecture complemented by artificial lakes but a magnificent array of ornamentation on all exterior facades.

Measured Rhythm

The majestic roofs of the halls of the Imperial Palace in Beijing, **China (55)**, are aligned along the main axis of the palace.

The Indian Ocean Earthquake-Tsunami of 2004

Tsunami strikes Ao Nang, Thailand

History/Overview:

The 2004 Indian Ocean earthquake, known by the scientific community as the **Sumatra-Andaman earthquake**, was a great undersea event that occurred at 00:58:53 UTC (Coordinated Universal Time; 07:58:53 local time) December 26, 2004. It's epicenter was off the west coast of Sumatra, Indonesia.

The earthquake triggered a series of devastating tsunamis along the coasts of most land masses bordering the Indian Ocean, killing large numbers of people and inundating coastal communities across South and Southeast Asia, including parts of Indonesia, Sri Lanka, India and Thailand.

Estimates had put the death toll at over 275,000 with thousands of others missing. More recent totals by the United Nations indicate 229,866 people lost, including 186,983 dead and 42,883 missing.

One of the deadliest events in modern history, the disaster is known in Asia and the international media as the Asian Tsunami, and also the Boxing Day Tsunami in Australia, Canada, New Zealand, and United Kingdom.

The magnitude of the earthquake was originally recorded as 9.0 on the Richter scale, but has since been upgraded to between 9.1 and 9.3. It is the second largest earthquake ever recorded on a seismograph.

The earthquake was also reported to have had the longest duration of faulting ever observed, lasting between 500 and 600 seconds (8.3 to 10 minutes), and it was large enough to cause the entire planet to vibrate as much as half an inch, or over a centimeter.

The plight of the many affected people and countries prompted a widespread humanitarian response. In all, the worldwide community donated more than $7 billion in humanitarian aid.

The Earthquake:

The hypocenter of the main earthquake was at 3°19' N, 95°51'.24" E, approximately 160 km. (100 miles) west of Sumatra, at a depth of 30 km. (19 miles) below mean sea level.

The earthquake itself (apart from the tsunami) was felt as far away as Bangladesh, India, Malaysia, Myanmar, Thailand, Singapore and the Maldives.

Of all the seismic moment that has been released by earthquakes in the entire world in the 100 years from 1906 through 2005, roughly one-eighth was generated by this single event.

The earthquake covered a large geographic area. Nearly 1,600 km. (1,000 miles) of fault line slipped about 15 meters (50 feet) along the subduction zone where the India Plate slides under the Burma Plate.

Seismographic and acoustic data indicate that the first phase involved a rupture about 400 km. (250 miles) long and 100 km. (60 miles) wide, located 30 km. (19 miles) beneath the sea bed - the longest rupture ever known to have been caused by an earthquake.

The rupture proceeded at a speed of about 2.8 km./sec. (1.7 mi./sec.) or 10,000 kph (6,300 mph), beginning off the coast of Aceh and proceeding north-westerly over a period of about 100 seconds. A pause of about another 100 seconds took place before the rupture continued northwards towards the Andaman and Nicobar Islands. The northern rupture occurred more slowly than in the south, at about 2.1 km./sec. (1.3 mi./sec.) or 7,600 kph (4,700 mph), continuing north for another five minutes to a plate boundary where the fault changed from subduction to strike-slip (the two plates push past one another in opposite directions). This reduced the speed of the water displacement and so reduced the size of the tsunami that hit the northern part of the Indian Ocean.

The Tsunami:

The sudden vertical rise of the seabed by several meters during the earthquake displaced massive volumes of water, resulting in a tsunami that struck the coasts of the Indian Ocean.

The tsunami behaved very differently in deep water than in shallow water. In deep ocean water, tsunami waves form only a small hump, barely noticeable and harmless, which generally travels at a very high speed of 500 to 1,000 kph (310 to 620 mph); in shallow water, near coastlines, a tsunami slows down to only tens of kilometers an hour but also forms large destructive waves.

The force of the tsunami waves was equivalent to about five megatons of TNT. This is more than twice the total explosive energy used during all of World War II (including the two atomic bombs).

In many places the waves reached as far as 2 km. (1.24 miles) inland.

Because the nearly 1,600 km. (1,000 miles) of fault line affected by the earthquake was in a roughly north-south orientation, the greatest strength of the tsunami waves was in an east-west direction.

Bangladesh, which lies at the northern end of the Bay of Bengal, had very few casualties despite being a low-lying country relatively near the epicenter.

Coasts that have a landmass between them and the tsunami's location of origin are usually safe; however, tsunami waves can sometimes diffract around such land masses. Thus, the Indian state of Kerala was hit by the tsunami despite being on the western coast of India, and the western coast of Sri Lanka also suffered substantial impacts.

Distance alone is no guarantee of safety; Somalia was hit harder than Bangladesh despite being much farther away. Because of the distances involved, the tsunami took anywhere from fifteen minutes to seven hours (for Somalia) to reach the various coastlines. The northern regions of the Indonesian island of Sumatra were hit very quickly, while Sri Lanka and the east coast of India were hit roughly 90 minutes to two hours later. Thailand was struck about two hours later despite being closer to the epicenter, because the tsunami traveled more slowly in the shallow Andaman Sea off its western coast.

The tsunami was a succession of several waves, occurring in retreat and rise cycles with a period of over 30 minutes between each peak. The third wave was the most powerful and reached highest, occurring about an hour and a half after the first wave. Smaller tsunamis continued to occur for the rest of the day.

Without a Warning:

Despite a lag of up to several hours between the earthquake and the impact of the tsunami, nearly all of the victims were taken completely by surprise.

There were no tsunami warning systems in the Indian Ocean to detect tsunamis or to warn the general populace living around the ocean. Tsunami detection is difficult because while a tsunami is in deep water it has little height, and a network of sensors is needed to detect it.

Tsunamis are much more frequent in the Pacific Ocean because of earthquakes in the "Ring of Fire," and there an effective tsunami warning system has long been in place.

Unfortunately, although the extreme western edge of the Ring of Fire extends into the Indian Ocean (the point where this earthquake struck), no warning system existed in that area.

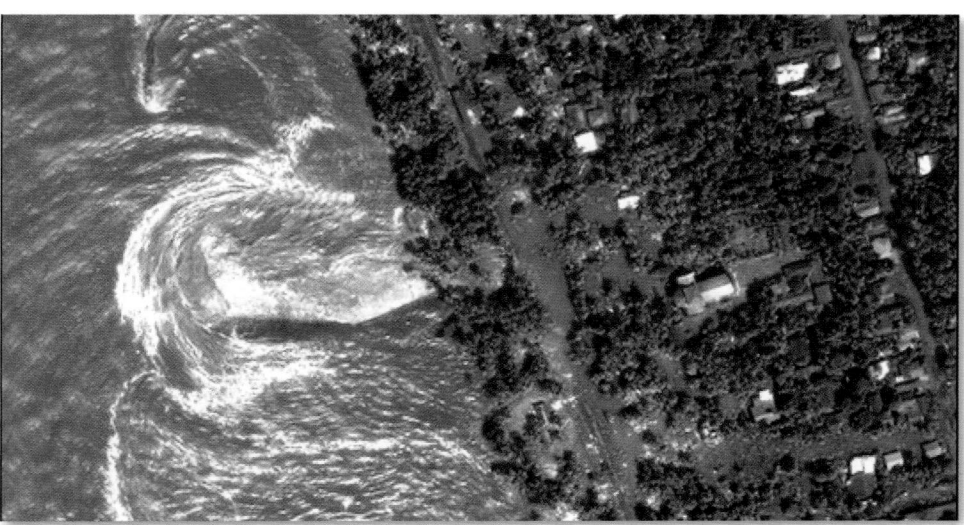

Sri Lanka before the tsunami (bottom) and the arrival of the tsunami waves (top)

Damage and Human Casualties:

Recent figures indicate that the actual casualties were 186,983 dead and 42,883 missing, for a total of 229,866, as more and more displaced survivors have been found and name duplications eliminated from the lists of victims.

Measured in lives lost, this is one of the ten worst earthquakes in recorded history, as well as the single worst tsunami in history.

As many as four times more women than men were killed in some regions because they were waiting on the beach for fishermen to return or looking after their children at home.

A village near the coast of Sumatra lies in ruin

In addition to the large number of local residents, up to 9,000 foreign tourists (mostly Europeans) enjoying the peak holiday travel season were among the dead or missing, especially people from the Nordic countries.

People gather under a helicopter to receive food and supplies

The European nation hardest hit may have been Sweden, whose death toll was 428 dead, with 116 missing.

States of emergency were declared in Sri Lanka, Indonesia and the Maldives. The United Nations estimated at the outset that the relief operation would be the costliest in human history.

UN Secretary-General Kofi Annan stated that reconstruction would probably take between five and ten years.

Human Caused Damage:

The human destruction of coral reefs played a significant role in the destruction caused by the tsunami. Many countries across Asia, including Indonesia, Sri Lanka and Bangladesh, have destroyed coral surrounding their beaches to make way for shrimp farms and other economic development.

On the Surin Island chain off Thailand's coast, many people were saved as the tsunami rushed against the coral reefs protecting the islands.

Loading plane with supplies to aid the tsunami survivors

Many reefs around the Indian Ocean have been exploded with dynamite because they are considered impediments to shipping, an important part of the South Asian economy.

The removal of coastal mangrove trees is also believed to have intensified the effect of the tsunami in some locations. These trees, which lined the coast but were removed to make way for coastal residences, might have blocked the force of the tsunami.

The removal of coastal sand dunes that were seen to be in the way of development were also a contributing factor.

Human Impact:

A great deal of humanitarian aid was needed because of widespread damage to the infrastructure, shortages of food and water and economic damage.

Epidemics were of special concern due to the high population density and tropical climate of the affected areas.

The main concern of humanitarian and government agencies was to provide sanitation facilities and fresh drinking water to contain the spread of diseases such as cholera, diphtheria, dysentery, typhoid and hepatitis A and B.

Economic Impact:

The impact on fishermen and their fishing communities, some of the poorest in the region, has been devastating, with high losses of income earners as well as boats and fishing gear.

Preliminary estimates indicate that two thirds of the fishing fleet and industrial infrastructure in coastal regions have been destroyed by the wave surges, which will have adverse

People take shelter in makeshift tents

economic effects both at local and national levels.

Both the earthquake and the tsunami may have affected shipping in the Malacca Straits by changing the depth of the seabed and by disturbing navigational buoys and old shipwrecks. Compiling new navigational charts may take months or years.

Humanitarian aid

Environmental Impact:

Beyond the heavy toll on human lives, the Indian Ocean earthquake has caused an enormous environmental impact that will affect the region for many years to come.

It has been reported that severe damage has been inflicted on ecosystems such as mangroves, coral reefs, forests, coastal wetlands, vegetation, sand dunes and rock formations, animal and plant biodiversity and groundwater.

The spread of solid and liquid waste and industrial chemicals, water pollution and the destruction of sewage collectors and treatment plants, threaten the environment even further in untold ways.

According to specialists, the worst damage is being caused by the poisoning of freshwater supplies and the soil by saltwater infiltration, and the deposit of a salt layer over arable land. More than a year after the tsunami struck, drinking water in Sri Lanka was still contaminated.

It has been reported that in the Maldives, 16 to 17 coral reef atolls that were overcome by sea waves are totally without fresh water and could be rendered uninhabitable for decades.

Uncountable wells that served communities were contaminated by sea, sand and earth; and aquifers were invaded through porous rock.

The Region Today:

The Deep-Ocean Assessment and Reporting of Tsunamis (DART) system has platforms that lie on the sea floor monitoring seismic activity and sending signals to buoys floating on the surface.

The buoys, provided by the United States, are able to detect sudden increases in pressure deep under the sea, and give coastal communities early warning of a tsunami.

The buoys then use satellite communication to pass on the gathered information to tsunami warning centers around the Indian Ocean.

In the event of an earthquake the system is designed to detect whether a tsunami will occur and pinpoint its height, location and when it will make landfall.

The first buoy has been placed between Thailand and Sri Lanka, two of the countries most seriously damaged by the worst tsunami in history.

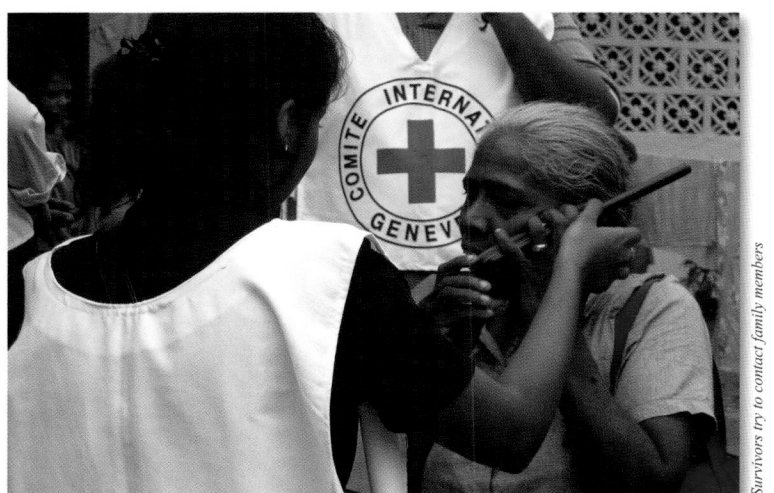

Survivors try to contact family members

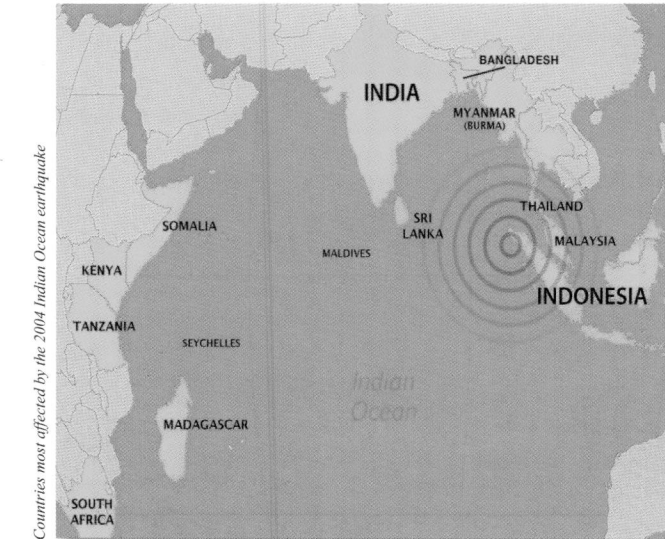

Countries most affected by the 2004 Indian Ocean earthquake

The Middle East Region

HISTORY/OVERVIEW: The Middle East is a political and cultural region traditionally referring to the lands between the Mediterranean Sea and the Persian Gulf, including the Arabian, Anatolian and Sinai peninsulas. The countries traditionally included are Bahrain, Cyprus, Egypt, Iran, Iraq, Israel, Jordan, Kuwait, Lebanon, Oman, Qatar, Saudi Arabia, Syria, Turkey and the United Arab Emirates (although sometimes the region is expanded to include North Africa in the west, and Afghanistan and Pakistan to the east). As a descriptive region, it does not have precise borders, and the lands included in the Middle East often depend on who is using the term.

For many Europeans, the term Near East originally referred to the Balkans and the Ottoman Empire, while the term Middle East referred to Persia, Afghanistan, Central Asia and the Caucasus, to distinguish that area from Far Eastern countries such as China, Japan, and Korea. During World War II the term Middle East came to be used as it is today. This change reflected new geopolitical realities, and a renewed sense of the Mediterranean Sea as a central feature of the region. In some ways the ambiguity of the term is an advantage, since it can be used in changing cultural and political circumstances. The term can point to a common history of shifting empires; from the Greco-Roman and Persian Empires to the vast Arab Caliphates and the long-lived Ottoman Empire. Other terms such as West Asia, Southwest Asia, Arab World and Greater Middle East are sometimes used to refer to the region.

In the west, "Middle Easterner" refers to someone who lives in this region. However, the region encompasses several cultural and ethnic groups including Iranians, Arabs, Greeks, Jews, Berbers, Assyrians, Kurds and Turks. Main language groups include Farsi, Arabic, Hebrew, Assyrian, Kurdish and Turkish.

Starting in the mid-20th century, the Middle East has been at the center of world affairs. Located at the crossroads of Asia, Africa and Europe, it possesses huge stocks of crude oil, which give it economic and strategic importance. It is also the birth-

Shrine of Imam Ali in Najaf, Iraq

place and spiritual center of Judaism, Christianity and Islam. These factors make the Middle East a place of great political and cultural sensitivity. Recent world events, and the threat of terrorist attacks, make understanding the history and culture of the Middle East vital to resolving present and future conflicts.

GEOGRAPHY: The Middle East has a variety of landscapes and climates. The region encompasses a land of extremes. The fertile river plains of the Nile, the Tigris and Euphrates, and the Indus were cradles of the earliest civilizations, providing agricultural sustenance for large numbers of people. But arable land is rare outside river valleys and narrow coastal plains. These lush areas are often surrounded by harsh, inhospitable areas such as the Sahara and the Arabian deserts which support little life. The heights of the Hindu Kush Mountains, separating the

Exploration work for oil and gas in the desert

Middle East from the rest of Asia, are among the highest in the world. The Dead Sea, located in a rift valley between Israel and Jordan, contains the lowest land on earth. Even though much of the Middle East is located in tropical latitudes, these extremes of elevation create a range of climates, from hot and dry desert heat to cool, snowy winters. Throughout the region, fresh water tends to be scarce. However, seas surround and bind the region together, and connect it with world trade.

Because of the difficulty of the rugged overland routes to the east, the Mediterranean Sea has served as the main highway for the Phoenician maritime colonies, as well as the imperial fleets of the Roman and Ottoman empires. The fertile North African coast provided food for several different cultures, as well as easy trade with Europe. In modern times, the opening of the Suez Canal in 1869 increased the importance of the Red Sea route to the Indian Ocean, and helped put the region back on the political map of Europe. However, outside of narrow coastal plains and fertile valleys, life in the Middle East is very different. The vast Sahara Desert in north central Africa, and the Arabian Desert which occupies most of the Arabian Peninsula, forced many people to adopt a nomadic or semi-nomadic lifestyle. For thousands of years, Bedouins herding camels, sheep and goats traveled from region to region, adapting to the intermittent and seasonal availability of water and pasture. After the 1950's, the discovery of huge amounts of oil throughout the

Weavers at Al-Janadriyah festival. Riyadh, Saudi Arabia

Middle East, and the shrinking of traditional grazing lands has shifted this pattern. Today most people live in densely populated cities. While the agricultural production of the Nile, Tigris and Euphrates valleys once supported vast ancient empires (and still is a major source of employment) the oil industry is the source of wealth and power in the Middle East today.

WATER RESOURCES: Several major aquifers provide water to large portions of the Middle East. In Saudi Arabia, two large

aquifers of Palaeozoic and Triassic origins are located beneath the Jabal Tuwayq mountains and areas west to the Red Sea. Cretaceous and Eocene-origin aquifers are located beneath large portions of central and eastern Saudi Arabia (including Wasia and Biyadh) which contain both fresh and saline water. The Nubian aquifer system underlies large areas of North Africa. Recharge for these deep rock aquifers is on the order of thousands of years; thus the aquifers are essentially non-renewable resources. Flood or furrow irrigation, as well as sprinkler methods, are extensively used for irrigation, covering millions of acres across the Middle East for agriculture.

LANGUAGES: Languages of the Middle East span many different families, including Indo-European, Afro-Asiatic and Altaic. Arabic in its numerous varieties, and Persian, are most widely spoken in the region, with Arabic being the major language in the Arab countries. Other languages spoken in the region include Armenian, Assyrian (a form of Aramaic), Azeri, Balochi or Baluchi, Berber languages, Circassian, Persian, Georgian, Hebrew in its numerous varieties, Kurdish, Luri, Turkish and other Turkic languages, Greek and Urdu. In Turkey, Kurdish, Dimli (or Zaza), Azeri, Kabardiaz, and Gagauz languages are spoken, in addition to the Turkish language.

English is also spoken, especially among the middle and upper

Oil Refinery in Saudi Arabia

class, in countries such as Egypt, Jordan, Israel and Kuwait. French is spoken in Israel, Lebanon, Syria and Egypt. Hindi and other Indian and South Asian languages are spoken in many Middle Eastern countries, such as the United Arab Emirates (UAE), Israel and Qatar, which have large numbers of South Asian immigrants.

ECONOMY: The Middle East has an oil-based economy with the largest proven oil reserves in the world; about 47% of the world's total. The region ranks as the largest producer as well as exporter of petroleum. It plays a leading role in world energy affairs, particularly in the Organization of Petroleum Exporting Countries (OPEC). Four countries, Saudi Arabia, UAE, Kuwait and Qatar account for about half of the total OPEC oil production. For the region, oil and gas exports represent three quarters of total export earnings. The oil and gas sector accounts for roughly two thirds of government revenues and more than 40% of GDP. The yearly average price for OPEC oil rose sharply, mainly attributed to strong demand for energy by the United States, China and other Asian countries. The region is continuing its economic reform program, and currently is focusing on attracting domestic and foreign private investment into oil and gas, power generation, telecommunications and real-estate sectors.

Petroleum and Natural Gas

CRUDE OIL AND NATURAL GAS RESERVES

OPEC Middle East Members	Members since	Crude Oil (billion barrels)		Natural Gas (trillion cubic feet barrels)	
		OGJ	WO	OGJ	WO
Iran	Sept. 1960	125.8	105.0	940.0	935.0
Iraq (Excluded from OPEC production quotas since 1998)	Sept. 1960	115.0	115.0	110.0	112.6
Kuwait	Sept. 1960	99.0	99.4	55.5	56.6
Qatar	Dec. 1961	15.2	27.4	910.0	913.4
Saudi Arabia	Sept. 1960	261.9	231.1	238.5	
United Arab Emirates	Nov. 1967	97.8	66.2	212.1	304.1

OGJ = Oil and Gas Journal, Dec. 2003   WO = World Oil, Sept.

Oil and Gas in the Persian Gulf:

The Persian Gulf and its coastal areas are the world's largest single source of crude oil, and related industries dominate the region.

Al-Safaniya, the world's largest offshore oil field, is located in the Persian gulf.

Large gas finds have also been made with Qatar and Iran sharing a giant field across the territorial median line (North Field in Qatar; South Pars Field in Iran).

Qatar has built up a substantial liquified natural gas (LNG) and petrochemical industry.

The oil-rich countries (excluding Iraq) that have a coastline on the Persian Gulf are referred to as the Persian Gulf States. Iraq's egress to the gulf is narrow and easily blockaded consisting of the marshy river delta of Arvandrud/Shatt al-Arab, which carries the waters of the Euphrates and the Tigris Rivers, where the left (East) bank is held by Iran.

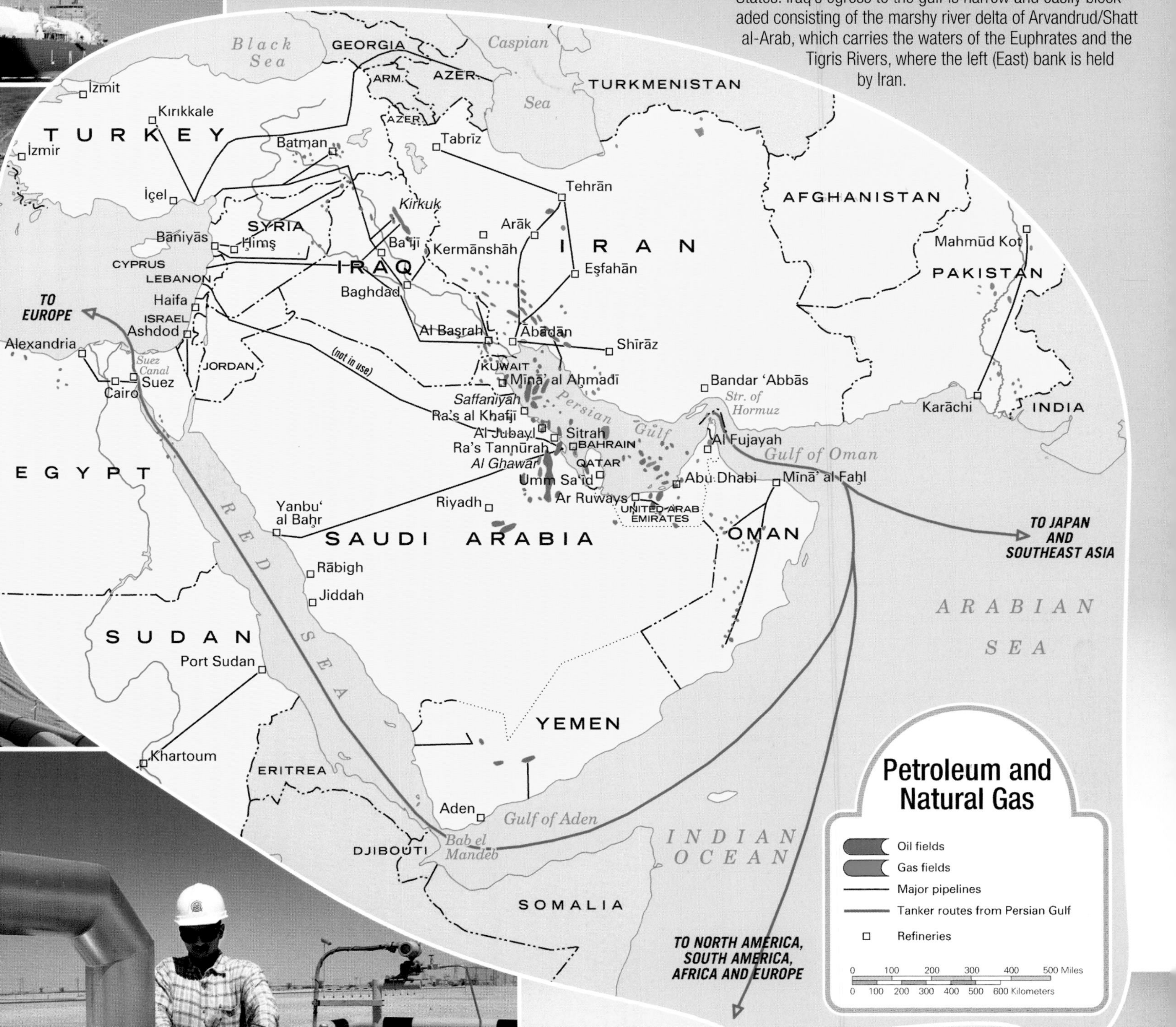

VLCC (very large crude carrier) oil tanker.

Liquid Natural Gas vessel.

Dukhan, Qatar oil gas field production process facilities.

A string of flowline sections traces the route that light crude oil will flow.

Production facilities in Central Saudi Arabia.

Oil spill containment floating buoy. (far right)

Petroleum and Natural Gas

- Oil fields
- Gas fields
- Major pipelines
- Tanker routes from Persian Gulf
- □ Refineries

0 100 200 300 400 500 Miles
0 100 200 300 400 500 600 Kilometers

TO EUROPE

TO JAPAN AND SOUTHEAST ASIA

TO NORTH AMERICA, SOUTH AMERICA, AFRICA AND EUROPE

Eastern Asia is the most populous region on Earth. Its most prominent topographic features are the high peaks of the Himalayas, the plains and deserts of the central highlands, and its broad, fertile loess plains. The climate is controlled by monsoon winds. In the winter, the East Asian monsoon carries dry, cold air – often accompanied by dust storms - from a cold high-pressure center in the Asian heartland to the Pacific. Temperatures in China drop to below freezing north of the Qinling Shan in the winter, while warm, moist air flows inland from the sea during the summer.

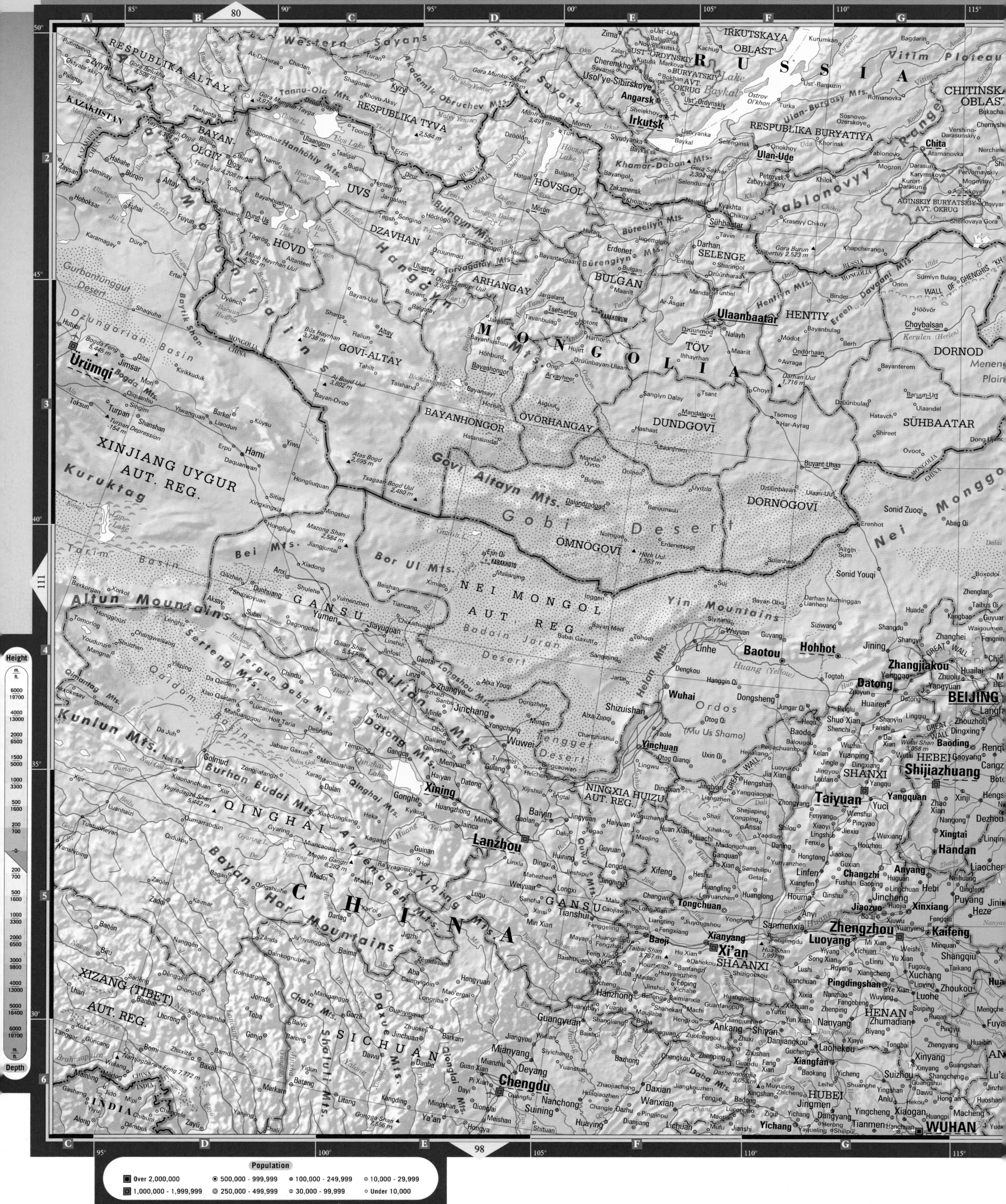

A B C D E F G
80
111
98
RUSSIA
MONGOLIA
CHINA
KAZAKHSTAN
INDIA
RESPUBLIKA ALTAY
RESPUBLIKA TYVA
RESPUBLIKA BURYATIYA
IRKUTSKAYA OBLAST'
CHITINSKAYA OBLAST'
UST'-ORDYNSKIY BURYATSKIY AVT. OKRUG
AGINSKIY BURYATSKIY AVT. OKRUG
BAYAN-ÖLGIY
UVS
HÖVSGÖL
DZAVHAN
HOVD
ARHANGAY
BULGAN
SELENGE
TÖV
HENTIY
DORNOD
GOVĬ-ALTAY
BAYANHONGOR
ÖVÖRHANGAY
DUNDGOVĬ
SÜHBAATAR
DORNOGOVĬ
ÖMNÖGOVĬ
XINJIANG UYGUR AUT. REG.
NEI MONGOL AUT. REG.
GANSU
QINGHAI
NINGXIA HUIZU AUT. REG.
SHANXI
HEBEI
SHAANXI
HENAN
HUBEI
SICHUAN
XIZANG (TIBET) AUT. REG.
Western Sayans
Eastern Sayans
Altay Mountains
Tannu-Ola Mts.
Akademik Obruchev Mts.
Hanhöhiy Mts.
Khamar-Daban Mts.
Ulan-Burgasy Mts.
Yablonovyy Range
Vitim Plateau
Bulnayn Mts.
Hangayn Mts.
Büteeliyn Mts.
Bürengiyn Mts.
Hentiyn Mts.
Govĭ Altayn Mts.
Gobi Desert
Dzungarian Basin
Gurbantünggüt Desert
Kuruktag
Tarim Basin
Bei Mts.
Bor Ul Mts.
Yin Mountains
Badain Jaran Desert
Tengger Desert
Helan Mts.
Ordos (Mu Us Shamo)
Altun Mountains
Serteng Mts.
Qaidam Basin
Tergun Daba Mts.
Qilian Mts.
Longshou Mts.
Datong Mts.
Qinghai Mts.
Kunlun Mts.
Burhan Budai Mts.
A'nyêmaqên Mts.
Bayan Har Mountains
Xiqing Mts.
Min Mts.
Chola Mts.
Daxue Mts.
Shaluli Mts.
Qionglai Mts.
Daba Mts.
Lake Baykal
Uvs Lake
Hövsgöl Lake
Qinghai Lake
Huang (Yellow)
GREAT WALL
WALL OF GHENGHIS KHAN
Irkutsk
Angarsk
Ulan-Ude
Chita
Ulaanbaatar
Ürümqi
Hami
Baotou
Hohhot
Zhangjiakou
Datong
BEIJING
Shijiazhuang
Taiyuan
Handan
Yinchuan
Lanzhou
Xining
Tongchuan
Baoji
Xianyang
Xi'an
Luoyang
Zhengzhou
Kaifeng
Pingdingshan
Xiangfan
Chengdu
WUHAN
Gora Belukha 4,506 m
Monh Sarĭdag 3,491 m
Gora Munku-Sasan 3,726 m
Otgon Tenger Uul 3,905 m
Turpan Depression -154 m
Bogda Feng 5,445 m
Qilian Shan 5,547 m
Mazong Shan 2,584 m
Amne Machin 6,282 m
Taibai Shan 3,767 m
Gongga Shan 7,556 m
Namjagbarwa Feng 7,772 m
50° 45° 40° 35° 30°
85° 90° 95° 100° 105° 110° 115°
Height
m. ft.
6000 19700
4000 13000
2000 6500
1500 5000
1000 3300
500 1600
200 700
-0-
200 700
500 1600
1000 3300
2000 6500
3000 9800
4000 13000
5000 16400
6000 19700
Depth
Population
Over 2,000,000
1,000,000 - 1,999,999
500,000 - 999,999
250,000 - 499,999
100,000 - 249,999
30,000 - 99,999
10,000 - 29,999
Under 10,000

Scale 1:9,000,000   Lambert Conformal Conic Projection

MI   100   200   300

KM   100   200   300   400

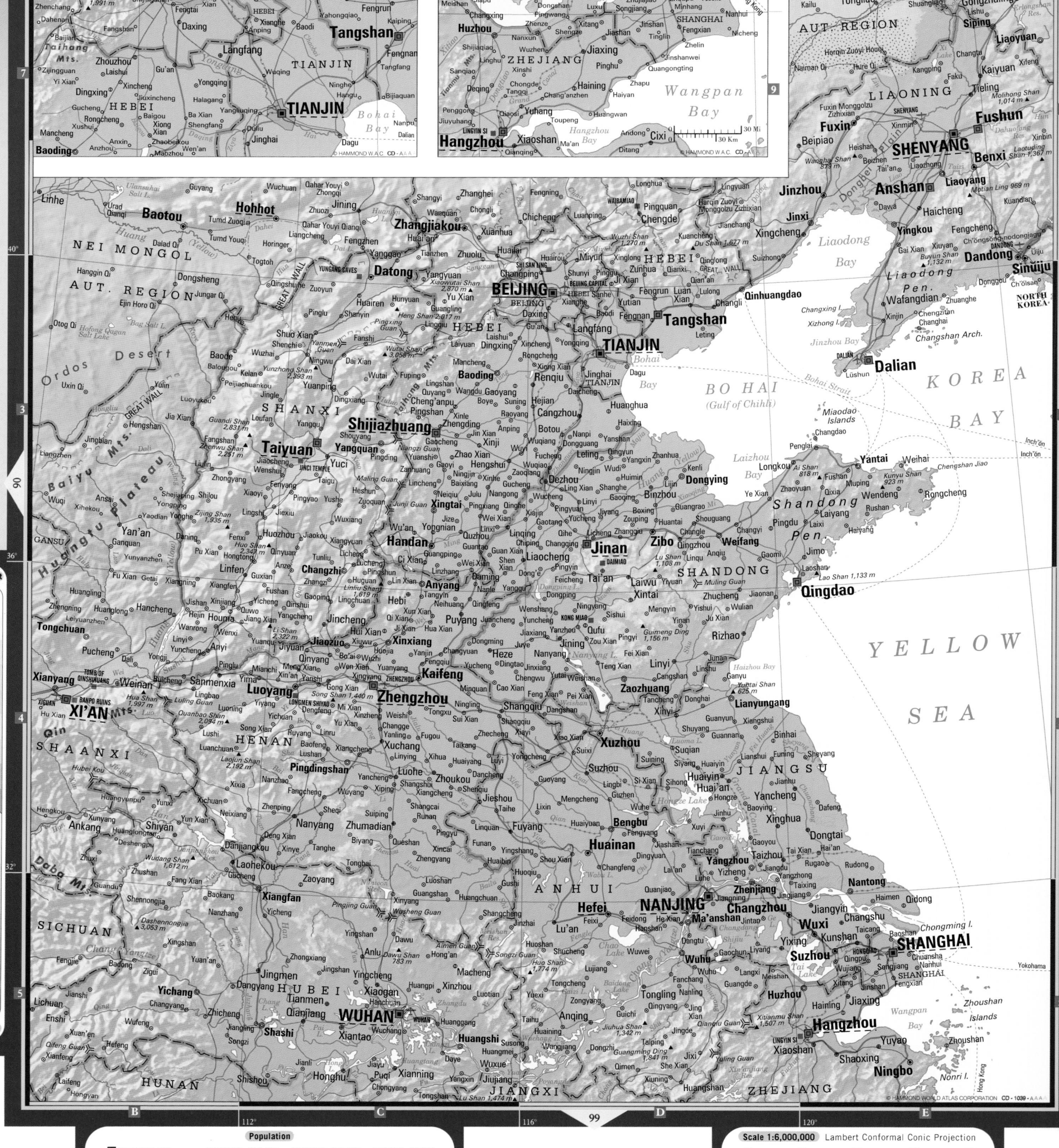

The alluvial plain created by the Huang (Yellow) River is the cradle of Chinese civilization. Now lined by levees along its lower reaches, the river lies up to 10 m above the surrounding land.

The Huang has often overflowed its banks, causing devastating floods, and even changed its course, emptying into the sea at different points north and south of the Shandong Peninsula.

Height
m. ft.
6000 19700
4000 13000
2000 6500
1500 5000
1000 3300
500 1600
200 700
0
200 700
500 1600
1000 3300
2000 6500
3000 9800
4000 13000
5000 16400
6000 19700
m. ft.
Depth

Population
■ Over 2,000,000
◉ 500,000 - 999,999
● 100,000 - 249,999
○ 10,000 - 29,999
□ 1,000,000 - 1,999,999
◎ 250,000 - 499,999
○ 30,000 - 99,999
○ Under 10,000

Scale 1:6,000,000   Lambert Conformal Conic Projection

MI   50   100   150   200
KM   50   100   150   200   250   300

The Korean peninsula is the home of a distinct culture that was influenced early on by China and bears the indelible imprint of Buddhism. Korea was annexed by Japan in 1910 and divided into a communist north and a pro-western south in 1948. In the years since the end of the Korean War (1950–1953), South Korea has become a major industrial power.

Population

- Over 2,000,000
- 1,000,000 – 1,999,999
- 500,000 – 999,999
- 250,000 – 499,999
- 100,000 – 249,999
- 30,000 – 99,999
- 10,000 – 29,999
- Under 10,000

Scale 1:3,000,000   Lambert Conformal Conic Projection

Northen Japan

Hokkaido, Japan's northernmost major island, is home to the Ainu, a people unrelated to the Japanese who also settled on Sakhalin and the Kuril Is-lands. Their origin is unknown. Long ago, the Ainu retreated to the fertile inland valleys to farm, hunt, and fish. Today, only 14,000 Ainu live on the island. Hokkaido hosted the Winter Olympics in 1972.

SEA OF OKHOTSK

SEA OF JAPAN

PACIFIC OCEAN

La Perouse Strait

RUSSIA
JAPAN

Kril'on Pen.
SAKHALINSKAYA OBLAST'
Aniva Bay
Tonino-Anivskiy Pen.
Mys Aniva

Mys Kril'on

Vulkan Chirip 1,589 m
Kuril'sk

Rebun-tō
Wakkanai
Sōya-misaki
Noshappu-misaki
Rebun
RISHIRI-REBUN-SAROBETSU NP
Rishiri-tō
Rishiri
Sarufutsu
L. Kutcharo
Hamatombetsu
Ōmu
Okoppe
Mombetsu

Etorofu

Gora Tyatya 1,819 m

Teshio
Esashi
Yakishiri-tō
Teuri-tō
Haboro
Tomamae
1,032 m
Nayoro
Shibetsu
Yūbetsu
Engaru
Kamikawa
Rubeshibe

Shiretoko-misaki
SHIRETOKO NP
Rausu

Kunashiri-tō
Yuzhno-Kuril'sk

Occupied by Russia since 1945; claimed by Japan

Enbetsu
Obira
Rumoi
Mashike

Hokkaidō

Fukagawa
Akabira
Shokanbetsu-dake 1,492 m
Takikawa
Ashibetsu
Sunagawa
Utashinai
Furano

Teshio-dake 1,558 m
Asahi-dake 2,290 m
Asahikawa
Ishikari Mts.
DAISETSUZAN NAT'L PARK

Tokoro
Abashiri
Shari
Bihoro
Kitami

Gora Golovnina 547 m
Golovnino

Habomai Islands
Shikotan-tō
Taraku-jima
Shpanberga Chan.
Shibotsu-jima
Suishō-tō
Yuri-tō

Kamui-misaki
Shakotan Pen.
Otaru
Yoichi
Ishikari
Ishikari Bay
Ebetsu
JŌZANKEI SPA
Sapporo
Tōbetsu
Mikasa
Iwamizawa
Kuriyama
Naganuma
Yubari
Shintoku
Shimukappu
Shimizu
Otofuke
HOKKAIDŌ
Me-akan-dake 1,503 m
AKAN NP
Ashoro
Teshikaga
Nakashibetsu
Shibecha

Konsen Plateau
Nemuro
Nemuro Pen.
Nosappu-misaki
Ochiishi-misaki
Akkeshi
Hamanaka
Kushiro
KUSHIRO-SHITSUGEN NP

Iwanai
Kutchan
Yōtei-san 1,893 m
SHIKOTSU-TOYA NP
Suttsu
Benkei-misaki
Kariba-yama 1,520 m
Motsuta-misaki
Setana
Oshamambe
Abuta
Date
Eniwa
Chitose
CHITOSE
Shiraoi
Noboribetsu
Tomakomai
Mukawa
Biratori
Hidaka
Hidaka Mts.
Horoshiri-dake 2,052 m

Horoshiri-dake
Urakawa
Samani
Erimo
Hiro'o
Urahoro
Obihiro
Ikeda
Shiranuka

Okushiri-tō
Okushiri
Kumaishi
Mori
Shikabe
Muroran
Yakumo
Uchiura Bay
Mombetsu
Shizunai
Taiki

Erimo-misaki

Esashi
Kaminoʻkuni
Kamiiso
Nanae
Minamikayabe
Esan-misaki

Oshima Peninsula
Dai-Segen-dake 1,072 m
Kikonai
Hakodate
Fukushima
Matsumae
Shirakami-misaki
Ōma-saki
Ōma
Ōhata
Mutsu
Shiriya-zaki

Tsugaru Strait
HOKKAIDŌ
TŌHOKU

Ō-shima

Tappi-zaki
Mimmaya
Kodomari
Tsugaru Pen.
Nakasato
Hiranai
Noheji
Rokkasho
Ogawara
Mutsu Bay

Shakotan
Shimokita Pen.

Goshogawara
Ajigasawa
Itayanagi
Kizukuri
Namioka
AOMORI
Misawa
Momoishi
Hachinohe

Iwaki-san 1,640 m
Hirosaki
Ōwani
Kuroishi
Hakkōda-san 1,585 m
TOWADA-HACHIMANTAI NP
Gonohe
Sannohe

Iwasaki
Henashi-zaki
Hachimori
Noshiro
Ōdate
Towada
Ichinohe
Kuji
Ninohe
Kuzumaki

Takanosu
Kazuno
Ani
Iwate
Tarō

Nyūdō-zaki
Oga Pen.
Oga
Gojōnome
TOWADA-HACHIMANTAI NP
Iwate-san 2,041 m
AKITA
Tazawako
Shizukuishi
Morioka
Hayachine-san 1,914 m
Miyako
Yamada

Akita
Kawabe
Kakunodate
Ōmagari
Yokote
Hanamaki
Kitakami
Tōno
Ōtsuchi
RIKUCHŪ-KAIGAN NP

Honjō
Kisakata
Yashima
Ōmagari
Yuzawa
Jūmonji
Esashi
Mizusawa
Kamaishi

Chōkai-san 2,237 m
Yuza
Sakata
Yuzawa
Kaneyama
Ōgachi
Ichinoseki
Rikuzentakata
Ōfunato

Amarume
Tsuruoka
Shinjō
Mogami
Kesen'numa
Gas-san 1,980 m
YAMAGATA
Obanazawa
Kurikoma-yama 1,628 m
Motoyoshi

Atsumi
Awa-shima
TŌHOKU CHŪBU BANDAI ASAHI NP
Higashine
Mutayama
Furukawa
Ogatsu
Tsukidate
Shizugawa

Murakami
Asahi-dake 1,870 m
Sagae
Tendō
Izumi
Yamoto
Onagawa
Ishinomaki

NIIGATA
Nakajō
Nagai
Kaminoyama
Zaō-san 1,841 m
Yamagata
Takajō
MIYAGI
Yamoto
Matsushima
Oshika Pen.

Sendai
SENDAI
Shiogama
Sendai Bay

© HAMMOND WORLD ATLAS CORPORATION   CC - 1036 - A.A

Population

◼ Over 2,000,000
◻ 1,000,000 - 1,999,999
● 500,000 - 999,999
● 250,000 - 499,999
● 100,000 - 249,999
● 30,000 - 99,999
◦ 10,000 - 29,999
◦ Under 10,000

Height

m. / ft.
6000 / 19700
4000 / 13000
2000 / 6500
1500 / 5000
1000 / 3300
500 / 1600
200 / 700
0
200 / 700
500 / 1600
1000 / 3300
2000 / 6500
3000 / 9800
4000 / 13000
5000 / 16400
6000 / 19700

Depth

Scale 1:3,000,000   Lambert Conformal Conic Projection

MI   25   50   75   100
KM   25   50   75   100   125   150

Tokyo is one of the most densely populated cities on Earth. This modern metropolis is also a major Japanese commercial center, and its industrial region spreads far beyond the city boundaries.

Osaka is the second-largest commercial and industrial center. The old capital, with its roughly 1,500 temples, is regarded as the heart of the Japanese culture.

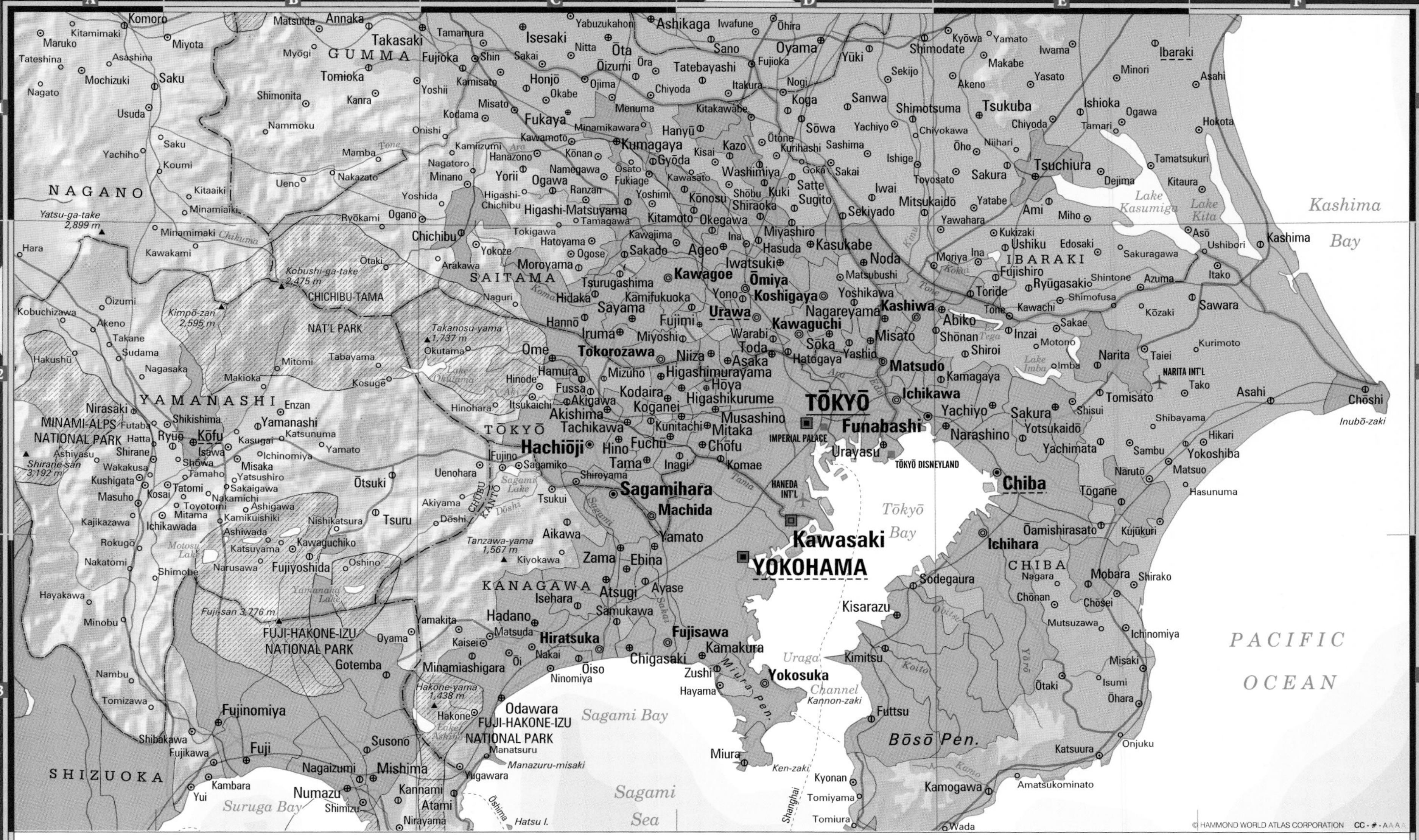

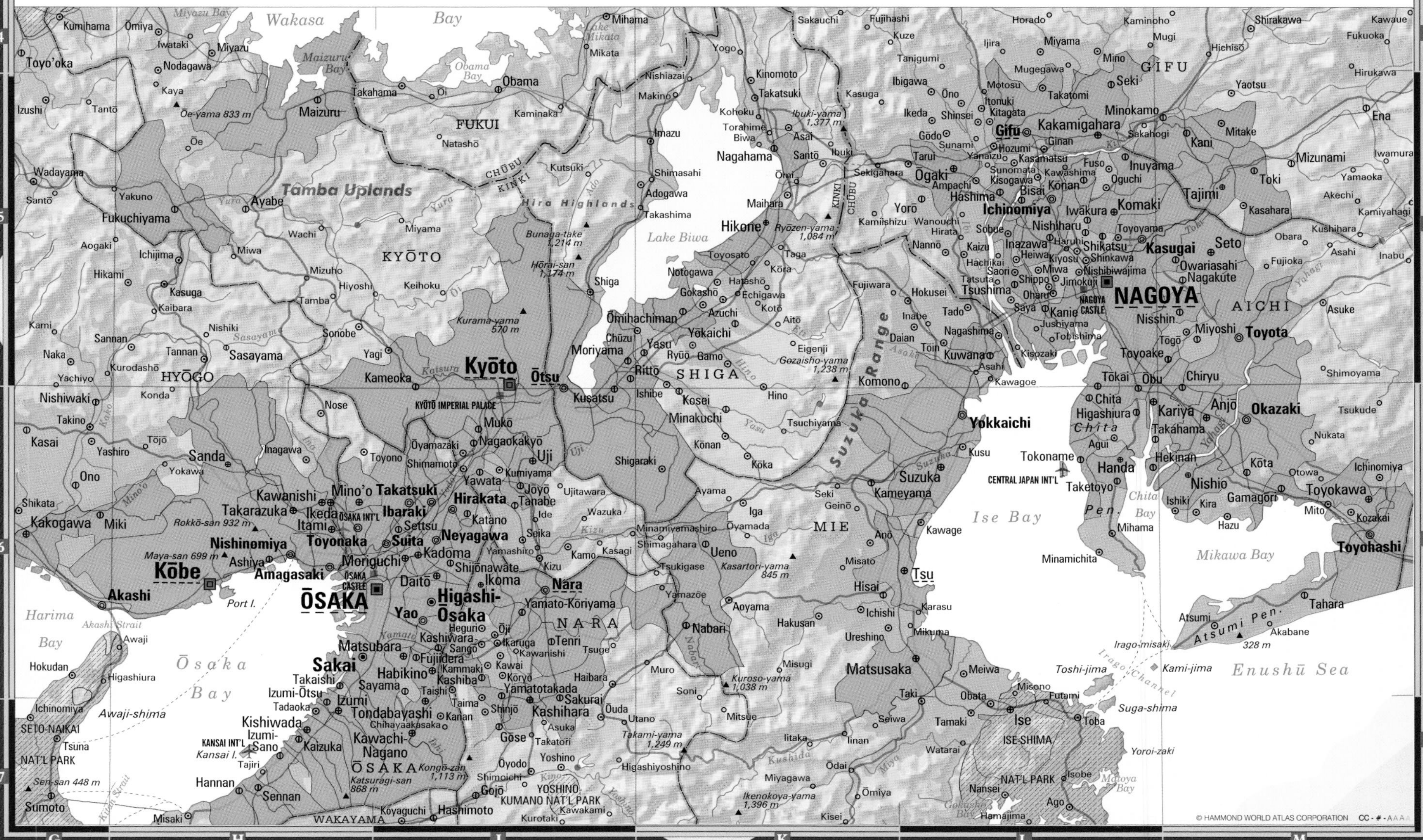

Population		
■ Over 2,000,000	● 500,000 - 999,999	● 100,000 - 249,999	● 10,000 - 29,999
■ 1,000,000 - 1,999,999	● 250,000 - 499,999	● 30,000 - 99,999	○ Under 10,000

Scale 1:1,000,000   Lambert Conformal Conic Projection

© HAMMOND WORLD ATLAS CORPORATION   CC - # - AAA

The heart of Japan's industrial might lies in four highly urbanized clusters, three of which are located on the southern coast of Honshu (Tokyo/Yokohama, Kōbe/Ōsaka, Nagoya), the fourth cluster is located in northern Kyushu. Despite its lack of iron ore, coal, and petroleum and its limited arable land, Japan has become a major economic power since the end of World War II.

Using imported raw materials, the highly skilled Japanese work force produces cars, electronics, optical equipment, and other quality products for the global market.

SEA OF JAPAN

SOUTH KOREA

KYŎNGSANG-BUKTO

TAEGU

KOREA

P'ohang

PUSAN

Western Channel

KOREA STRAIT

Eastern Channel

Tsushima

OKI ISLANDS

DAISEN-OKI NAT'L PARK

Matsue

SHIMANE

SAN'IN KAIGIN NATIONAL PARK

TOTTORI

Tottori

Fukui

FUKUI

KYŌTO

JAPAN

Kyōto

HYŌGO

KINKI

Himeji

Kōbe

ŌSAKA

OKAYAMA

CHŪGOKU MTS.

Kurashiki

Okayama

Akashi

HIROSHIMA

Fukuyama

Nara

WAKAYAMA

YAMAGUCHI

Hiroshima

PEACE MEMORIAL PARK

CHŪGOKU

Takamatsu

KAGAWA

TOKUSHIMA

Tokushima

Shimonoseki

Kitakyūshū

Fukuoka

SETO-NAIKAI NAT'L PARK

Matsuyama

EHIME

TOKUSHIMA

Sea of Suo

CHŪGOKU KYŪSHŪ NAT'L PARK

FUKUOKA

ŌITA

Ōita

SHIKOKU KYŪSHŪ

Kōchi

KŌCHI

Shikoku

SAGA

NAGASAKI

SAIKAI NAT'L PARK

GOTO ISLANDS

KUMAMOTO

ASO NAT'L PARK

Aso-san 1,592 m

Nagasaki

NAGASAKI PEACE PARK

Kumamoto

UNZEN-AMAKUSA NATIONAL PARK

Amakusa Sea

Kyūshū Highland

MIYAZAKI

Kirishima-yama 1,700 m

EAST CHINA SEA

KAGOSHIMA

Kagoshima

Miyazaki

Kyūshū

PACIFIC OCEAN

ŌSUMI ISLANDS

KIRISHIMA-YAKU NAT'L PARK

YAKU NAT'L PARK

Tanega-shima

Yaku-shima

Height
m.
ft.
6000 19700
4000 13000
2000 6500
1500 5000
1000 3300
500 1600
200 700
-0-
200 700
500 1600
1000 3300
2000 6500
3000 9800
4000 13000
5000 16400
6000 19700
m.
ft.
Depth

Continued on inset at right

Population
■ Over 2,000,000
◉ 500,000 - 999,999
◉ 100,000 - 249,999
◦ 10,000 - 29,999
□ 1,000,000 - 1,999,999
◉ 250,000 - 499,999
◉ 30,000 - 99,999
◦ Under 10,000

138°   F   140°   94   MIYAGI   142°   H   144°   J

38°

Sendai

E

Awa-shima

Hajiki-zaki

Higashine

Murakami   Sagae   Matsushima

YAMAGATA   Tendō   Shiogama

Asahi-dake   Zaō-san 1,841 m   Sendai

Aikawa   Ryōtsu   Nakajō   NP   Iwanuma   Bay

BANDAI-ASAHI   Nagai   Kaminoyama   Watari

Sado   **Niigata**   NIIGATA   Shibata   Takahata   Kakuda   SENDAI

Sawasaki-bana   Ogi   Niitsu   Gosen   **Fukushima**

Tsubame   Shirone   Yamato   Kitakata   Azuma-san 2,035 m   Nihonmatsu   Hobara   Haramachi

Toyama   Nagaoka   Sanjō   Mitsuke   Aizu-   BANDAI-ASAHI   Motomiya   Namie

Bay   Kashiwazaki   Ojiya   Tochio   **Kōriyama**

Itoigawa   Arai   Joetsu   Tōkamachi   Tajima   Nasu-dake 1,917 m   Shirakawa   Iwaki

Toyama   Myōkō-san 2,446 m   TŌHOKU   KANTŌ   Daigo

O C E A N

Honshū

Scale 1:3,000,000   Lambert Conformal Conic Projection

MI   25   50   75   100

KM   25   50   75   100   125   150

Southeastern China was once the most backward part of the country. Growth has accelerated in recent years, particularly in Guangzhou (Canton) – for many years the only city in China where foreign trade was possible – and Shenzhen, which benefits from its proximity to Hong Kong (a special administration of the People's Republic of China since 1997) and is now an autonomous economic district. Taiwan, the island refuge of the Nationalist Chinese government since 1949, has developed into a major industrial power.

Height

m.	ft.
6000	19700
4000	13000
2000	6500
1500	5000
1000	3300
500	1600
200	700
0	0
200	700
500	1600
1000	3300
2000	6500
3000	9800
4000	13000
5000	16400
6000	19700

Depth

Population
- ■ Over 2,000,000
- ■ 1,000,000 - 1,999,999
- ⬤ 500,000 - 999,999
- ⬤ 250,000 - 499,999
- ⊙ 100,000 - 249,999
- ⊙ 30,000 - 99,999
- ○ 10,000 - 29,999
- ○ Under 10,000

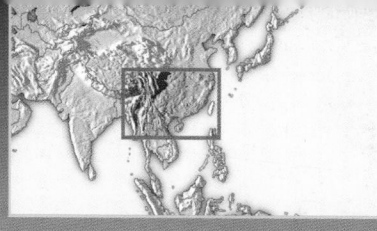

SHAANXI
HENAN
ANHUI
NANJING
JIANGSU
Hefei
Changzhou
Wuxi **Suzhou**
SHANGHAI
HUBEI
WUHAN
Hangzhou
Huangshi
ZHEJIANG
Ningbo
Yueyang
Changde
Nanchang
Jingdezhen
Changsha
Zhuzhou
Wenzhou
Xiangtan
HUNAN
Hengyang
JIANGXI
Fuzhou

EAST
CHINA
SEA

Guilin
Ganzhou
FUJIAN
T'AIPEI
Keelung
Hsinchu
Liuzhou
Shaoguan
Xiamen
TAIWAN
T'aichung
GUANGXI ZHUANGZU
Chaozhou
Shantou
Nanning AUTONOMOUS
GUANGDONG
Guangzhou (Canton)
Foshan **Dongguan**
T'ainan
Kaohsiung
REGION
Zhaoqing
Zhongshan
Shenzhen
Macau **Kowloon**
Victoria
Zhanjiang

SOUTH

Dongsha I.
(Pratas I.)
Pratas Reef
(CHINA)

CHINA SEA

Tropic of Cancer

Bashi Channel

Gulf of Tonkin

HAINAN
Haikou
Hainan
Dao

PHILIPPINES

Luzon

Hong Kong inset
GUANGDONG
Shenzhen
GUANGDONG
Sheung Shui
Fanling
Tin Shui Wai
Yuen Long
Tai Po
Tuen Mun
Tsuen Wan
Sha Tin
HONG KONG
New Kowloon
Kowloon
Victoria
Lantau Island
Lantau Peak
934 m
SOUTH
CHINA
SEA

Scale 1:6,000,000   Lambert Conformal Conic Projection

MI   50   100   150   200
KM   50   100   150   200   250   300

Philippines

Only ten percent of the 7,000 islands that comprise the Philippines are inhabited. The region was originally settled primarily by Malays. A Spanish dominion from 1565 until 1898, the islands be-came a bastion of Catholicism in Southeast Asia. The 48 years of U.S. rule that followed also left an indelible imprint on the island nation.

PHILIPPINE SEA

SOUTH CHINA SEA

CELEBES SEA

Sulu Sea

Luzon

Mindoro

Mindanao

Samar

Leyte

Negros

Panay

Cebu

Bohol

Palawan

Borneo

MALAYSIA

SARAWAK

BRUNEI

INDONESIA

PHILIPPINES

Sibuyan Sea

Visayan Sea

Mindanao Sea

Moro Gulf

Sulu Archipelago

Panay Gulf

Scarborough Shoal

Tubbataha Reefs

Babuyan Islands

Polillo Islands

Calamian Group

Cuyo Is.

Catanduanes I.

Quezon City
Manila
Pasig

Davao
Cebu
Bacolod
Iloilo
Zamboanga
Cagayan de Oro
General Santos
Baguio
Tuguegarao
Legaspi
Naga
Batangas
San Pablo
Lucena
Tarlac
Angeles
Cabanatuan
Dagupan
Laoag
Vigan
Tacloban
Ormoc
Dumaguete
Tagbilaran
Surigao
Butuan
Iligan
Pagadian
Cotabato
Puerto Princesa

Population

■ Over 2,000,000
■ 1,000,000 – 1,999,999
● 500,000 – 999,999
● 250,000 – 499,999
● 100,000 – 249,999
● 30,000 – 99,999
○ 10,000 – 29,999
○ Under 10,000

Scale 1:6,000,000   Lambert Conformal Conic Projection

Height
m. ft.
6000 19700
4000 13000
2000 6500
1500 5000
1000 3300
500 1600
200 700
0
Depth

© HAMMOND WORLD ATLAS CORPORATION

Malaya, Sumatra, Java

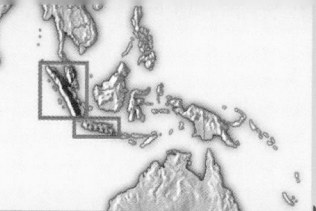

Malaysia and Indonesia are the easternmost outposts of Islam. Indonesia is now the most populous Islamic nation in the world. Only the island of Bali has a predominantly Hindu population. A major producer of wood, tin, and rubber positioned along important international shipping routes, Malaysia has developed one of the most productive economies in the region.

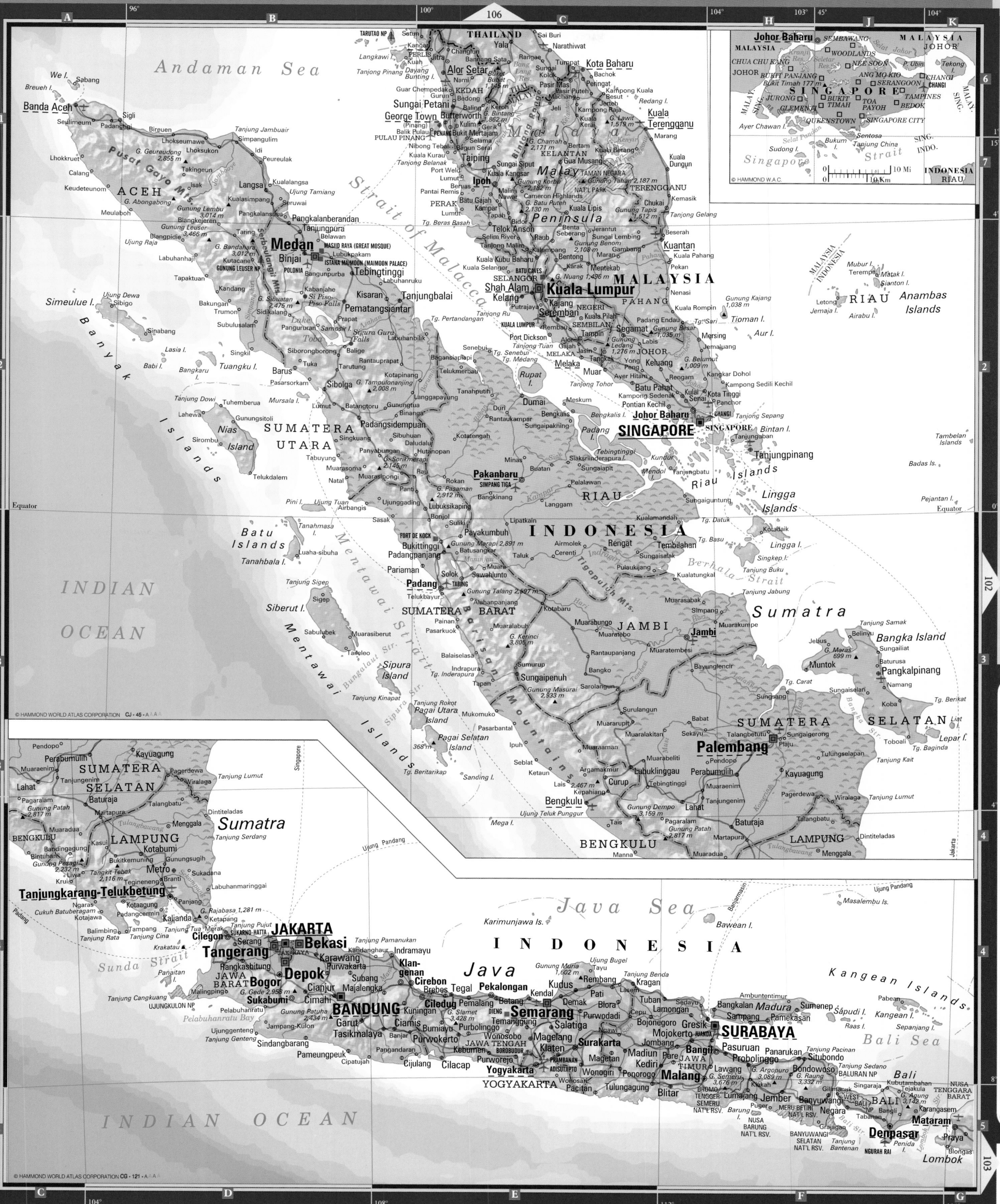

Population

- ■ Over 2,000,000
- ▣ 1,000,000 - 1,999,999
- ⦿ 500,000 - 999,999
- ◎ 250,000 - 499,999
- ⊕ 100,000 - 249,999
- ⊕ 30,000 - 99,999
- ⊙ 10,000 - 29,999
- ○ Under 10,000

Scale 1:6,000,000 Lambert Conformal Conic Projection

MI 0 50 100 150 200
KM 0 50 100 150 200 250 300

Indonesia covers most of the Malaysian archipelago. The Greater Sunda Islands of Sumatra and Java are characterized by "spines" of steep folded mountain ranges that tower above broad floodplains.

The hot, tropical climate, with annual rainfall of about 6,000 mm, supports flourishing rain-forest growth that once covered over 60 percent of the land surface. Today, the rain forest has given way to secondary forest, alang-alang grass, and ferns – the result of extensive logging and burning. The best known of the roughly 200 active volcanoes in the region is Krakatoa, which last erupted in 1883, causing thousands of deaths.

Height

m. / ft.
6000 / 19700
4000 / 13000
2000 / 6500
1500 / 5000
1000 / 3300
500 / 1600
200 / 700
0
200 / 700
500 / 1600
1000 / 3300
2000 / 6500
3000 / 9800
4000 / 13000
5000 / 16400
6000 / 19700

Depth

Population

- ◼ Over 2,000,000
- ◼ 1,000,000 - 1,999,999
- ◉ 500,000 - 999,999
- ◉ 250,000 - 499,999
- ○ 100,000 - 249,999
- ○ 30,000 - 99,999
- ○ 10,000 - 29,999
- ○ Under 10,000

Map of the Greater Sunda Islands region including Myanmar (Burma), Thailand, Cambodia, Vietnam, Malaysia, Singapore, Sumatra, Borneo, Java, and the Indian Ocean. Major cities labeled include Phnom Penh, Ho Chi Minh City, Kuala Lumpur, Singapore, Medan, Palembang, Jakarta, Bandung, Semarang, Surabaya, Bandar Seri Begawan, Pontianak, and Banjarmasin.

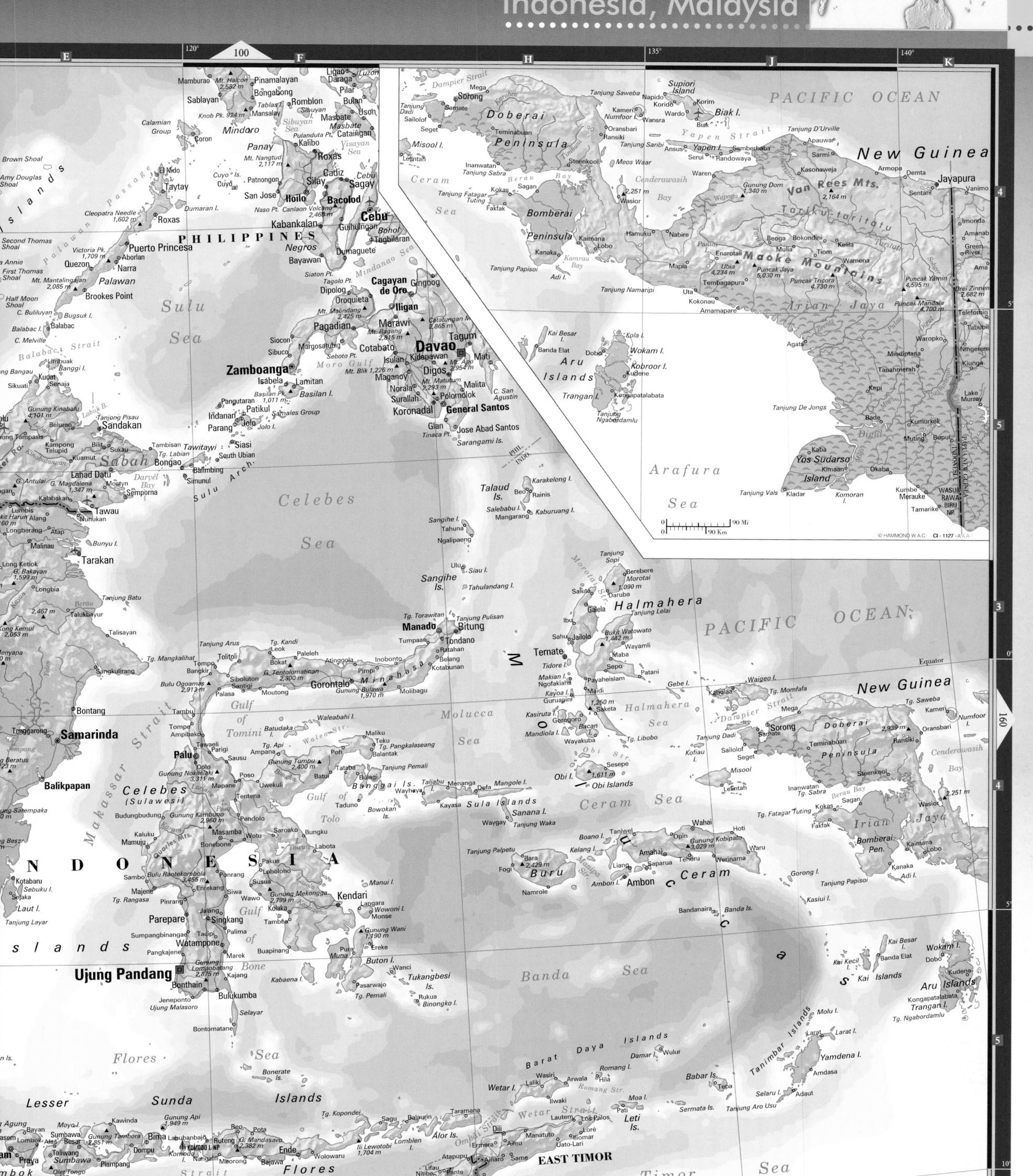

PACIFIC OCEAN

New Guinea

Doberai Peninsula

Van Rees Mts.

Jayapura

Maoke Mountains

Irian Jaya

Puncak Jaya 5,030 m

Puncak Mandala 4,700 m

Arafura Sea

Aru Islands

Yos Sudarso Island

PHILIPPINES

Mindoro

Panay

Roxas

Iloilo

Bacolod

Cebu

Negros

Bohol

Zamboanga

Davao

General Santos

Celebes Sea

Sulu Sea

Sabah

Tarakan

Sandakan

Tawau

Talaud Is.

Sangihe Is.

Halmahera

Ternate

Manado

Bitung

Gorontalo

M O L U C C A   S E A

Halmahera Sea

New Guinea

Doberai Peninsula

Sorong

Irian Jaya

Ceram Sea

Samarinda

Balikpapan

Palu

Celebes (Sulawesi)

Kendari

Buru

Ambon

Ceram

Banda Sea

Aru Islands

I N D O N E S I A

Ujung Pandang

Gulf of Bone

Flores Sea

Lesser   Sunda   Islands

Barat   Daya   Islands

Tanimbar Islands

Flores

Sumba

Sumbawa

Lombok

Timor

EAST TIMOR

Kupang

Timor Sea

© HAMMOND WORLD ATLAS CORPORATION   CD - 1047 - A A A

Scale 1:9,000,000   Lambert Conformal Conic Projection

MI   100   200   300

KM   100   200   300   400

The map shows the Asian monsoon region, through which expansive air currents move in an alternating, semi-annual rhythm. ("Monsoon" comes from the Arabic "mausim," or "season [suitable for sea voyages].") The southwest monsoon that comes from the sea brings life-giving rains to this densely populated region during the summer. A rainless monsoon season causes severe famine, while extreme monsoon precipitation often results in flood disasters. Roughly half of the world's population lives in monsoon regions. Most working people in this part of the world are employed in subsistence agriculture, primarily in rice cultivation.

Height

m. / ft.

6000 / 19700
4000 / 13000
2000 / 6500
1500 / 5000
1000 / 3300
500 / 1600
200 / 700
0
200 / 700
500 / 1600
1000 / 3300
2000 / 6500
3000 / 9800
4000 / 13000
5000 / 16400
6000 / 19700

m. / ft.

Depth

Population

- ■ Over 2,000,000
- ■ 1,000,000 – 1,999,999
- ● 500,000 – 999,999
- ● 250,000 – 499,999
- ● 100,000 – 249,999
- ● 30,000 – 99,999
- ○ 10,000 – 29,999
- ○ Under 10,000

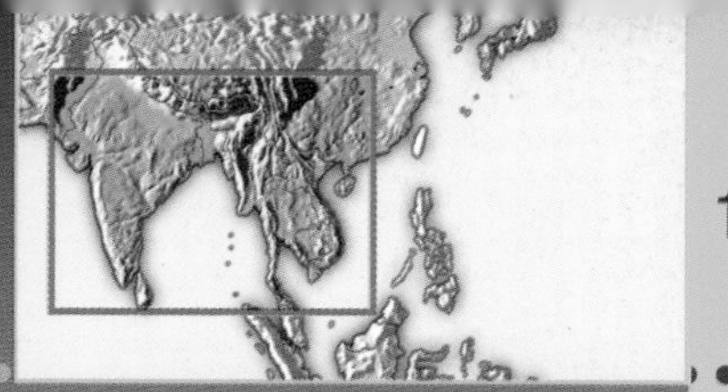

CHINA

MYANMAR
(BURMA)

LAOS

THAILAND

CAMBODIA

VIETNAM

MALAYSIA

CHITTAGONG

Mandalay

Kunming

Guiyang

Guangzhou

Changsha

Nanning

Liuzhou

Guilin

Hanoi
(Ha Noi)

Haiphong
(Hai Phong)

Haikou

YANGON
(Rangoon)

BANGKOK
(Krung Thep)

Vientiane
(Viangchan)

Nakhon Ratchasima

Phnom Penh
(Phnum Pénh)

HO CHI MINH CITY
(Saigon)

Da Nang

Kuala Terengganu

Kota Baharu

SICHUAN

YUNNAN

GUIZHOU

HUNAN

GUANGDONG

GUANGXI ZHUANGZU AUT. REG.

HAINAN

Hainan Dao

SOUTH
CHINA SEA

Gulf
of
Tonkin

Gulf
of
Thailand

Andaman
Sea

Strait of Malacca

Mouths
of the Ayeyarwady

Paracel Islands
(Sovereignty disputed)

INDOCHINA

Isthmus
of Kra

ANDAMAN AND NICOBAR
ISLANDS
(INDIA)

Port Blair

Phuket I.

© HAMMOND WORLD ATLAS CORPORATION

Scale 1:9,000,000   Lambert Conformal Conic Projection

| MI | 100 | 200 | 300 |
| KM | 100 | 200 | 300 | 400 |

The backbone of eastern India is formed by several mountain ranges to the southeast of the Himalayas which drain into the fertile plains of the Mekong, Salween, Irawadi, and Menam Chao Phraya rivers. The region has a monsoon climate, with rainfall decreasing toward the interior. The range of vegetation extends dense tropical rain forest to moist and arid savannahs farther inland.

Scale 1:6,000,000   Lambert Conformal Conic Projection

© HAMMOND WORLD ATLAS CORPORATION

Virtually no other country is as dependent upon monsoons as India. Monsoon rains are essential to the rice harvests that feed nearly a billion people. The southwest monsoon provides 90 percent of the region's precipitation (Cherrapunji holds the record, with 10,870 mm of rainfall per year). It also replenishes groundwater reserves that supply millions of people in India's metropolitan centers with drinking water.

Population		
■ Over 2,000,000	● 500,000 - 999,999	● 100,000 - 249,999	○ 10,000 - 29,999
■ 1,000,000 - 1,999,999	● 250,000 - 499,999	○ 30,000 - 99,999	○ Under 10,000

Scale 1:6,000,000 Lambert Conformal Conic Projection

Over 2,700 km long, the Ganges flows from headwaters 4,000 meters above sea level in the Himalayas. It joins the Brahmaputra in Bengal, forming a fertile delta comprising some 56,000 square km. Used intensively for irrigation, the river now carries much less water than in the past, especially during the dry months. The water shortage in the region is exacerbated by progressive deforestation in the Hima- layas, which has reduced the capacity to store monsoon rainwater. Water now runs off rapidly during the rainy season, causing frequent catastrophic flooding and taking thousands of lives.

Height	
m. ft.	
6000 19700	
4000 13000	
2000 6500	
1500 5000	
1000 3300	
500 1600	
200 700	
0	
200 700	
500 1600	
1000 3300	
2000 6500	
3000 9800	
4000 13000	
5000 16400	
6000 19700	
m. ft.	
Depth	

Population
- ■ Over 2,000,000
- ■ 1,000,000 - 1,999,999
- ◉ 500,000 - 999,999
- ◉ 250,000 - 499,999
- ◉ 100,000 - 249,999
- ○ 30,000 - 99,999
- ○ 10,000 - 29,999
- ○ Under 10,000

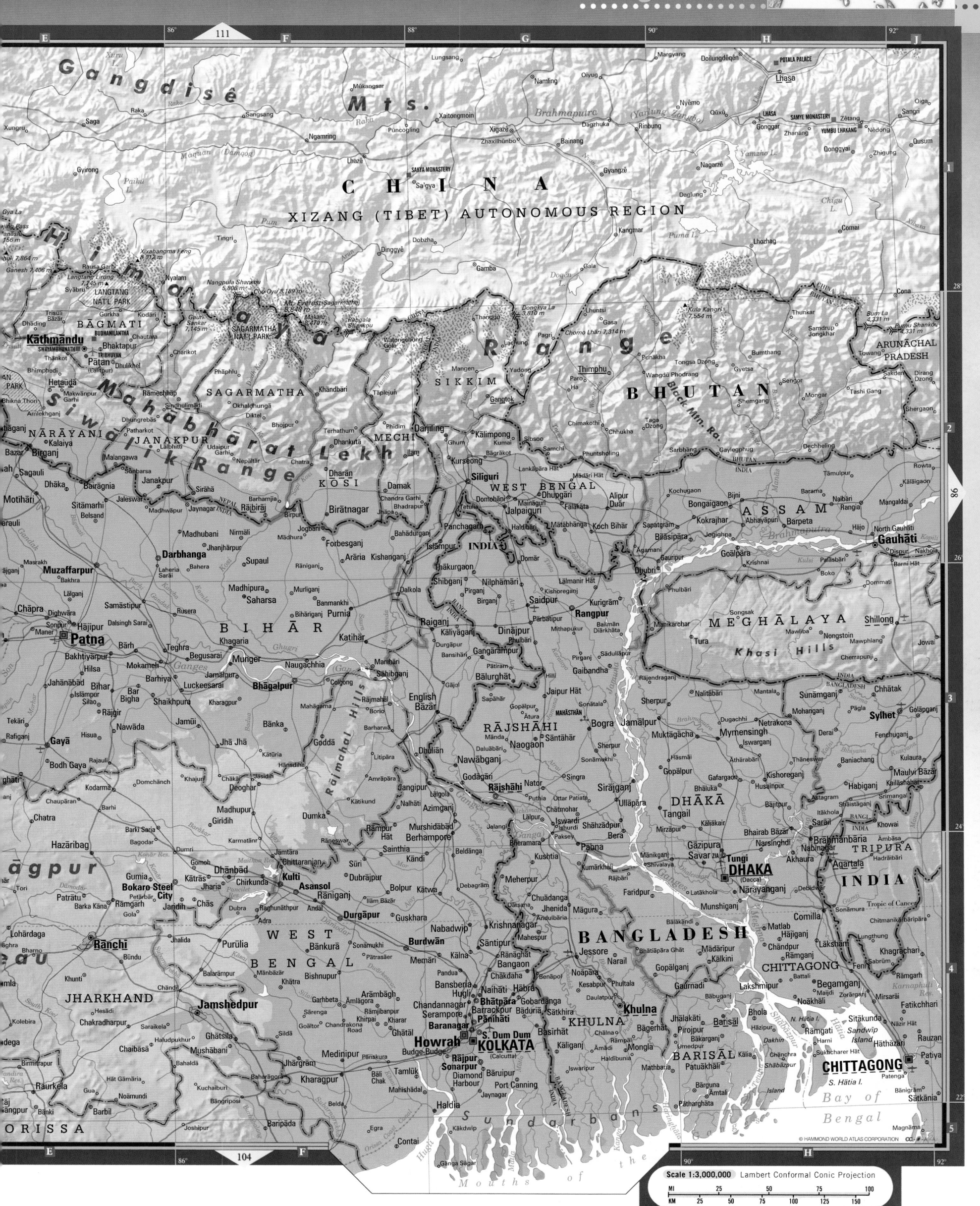

Scale 1:3,000,000   Lambert Conformal Conic Projection

MI   25   50   75   100
KM   25   50   75   100   125   150

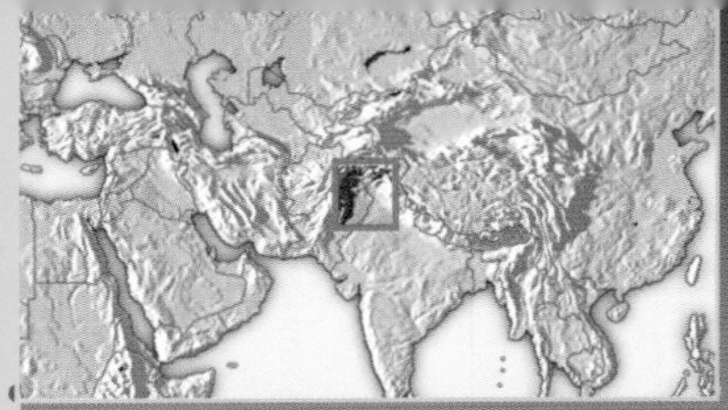

This plain, irrigated by a fan of eastern tributaries of the Indus, forms the granary of India and Pakistan. Over the course of thousands of years, a vast network of canals and dams has covered this plain. Thanks to this irrigation system, the Punjab is fertile agricultural land and the most productive wheat and cotton-growing region in western India. Most of the territory now belongs to Pakistan, which gained independence from India in 1947.

Height

m. / ft.
6000 / 19700
4000 / 13000
2000 / 6500
1500 / 5000
1000 / 3300
500 / 1600
200 / 700
0
200 / 700
500 / 1600
1000 / 3300
2000 / 6500
3000 / 9800
4000 / 13000
5000 / 16400
6000 / 19700

Depth

AFGHANISTAN
CHINA
NORTHERN AREAS*
NORTH-WEST FRONTIER
FEDERALLY ADMINISTERED TRIBAL AREAS
PAKISTAN
AZAD KASHMIR*
JAMMU AND KASHMIR
INDIA
HIMACHAL PRADESH
PUNJAB
HARYANA
UTTAR PRADESH
RAJASTHAN
Thal Desert
Punjab Plains
Thar Desert
Great Indian Desert

Peshāwar, Rāwalpindi, Islāmābād, Srinagar, Jammu, Siālkot, Gujrānwāla, Faisalābād, Lahore, Amritsar, Jalandhar, Ludhiana, Chandīgarh, Multān, Bahāwalpur, Patiāla, Delhi, New Delhi, Meerut, Faridabad

Mangla Dam, Tarbela Dam, Bhakra Dam, Beas Dam

Population

■ Over 2,000,000	◉ 500,000 - 999,999	◉ 100,000 - 249,999	◎ 10,000 - 29,999
▣ 1,000,000 - 1,999,999	● 250,000 - 499,999	◉ 30,000 - 99,999	○ Under 10,000

*AZAD KASHMIR AND THE NORTHERN AREAS ARE ADMINISTERED BY PAKISTAN BUT DO NOT HAVE PROVINCIAL STATUS.

Scale 1:3,000,000 Lambert Conformal Conic Projection

MI	25	50	75	100
KM	25 50	100	125	150

Central Asia

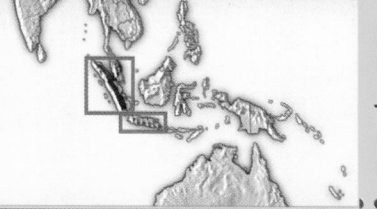

Known as the "Roof of the World," central Asia is dominated by the vast mountain systems of the Hindu Kush, the Pamir, the Tian Shan and the Himalayas, extending over 2,400 km from Pakistan to Bhutan. Here, the Indian plate thrusts beneath the Asian continent, pushing Tibet upward. The young mountain range is still rising at a rate of about one centimeter per year.

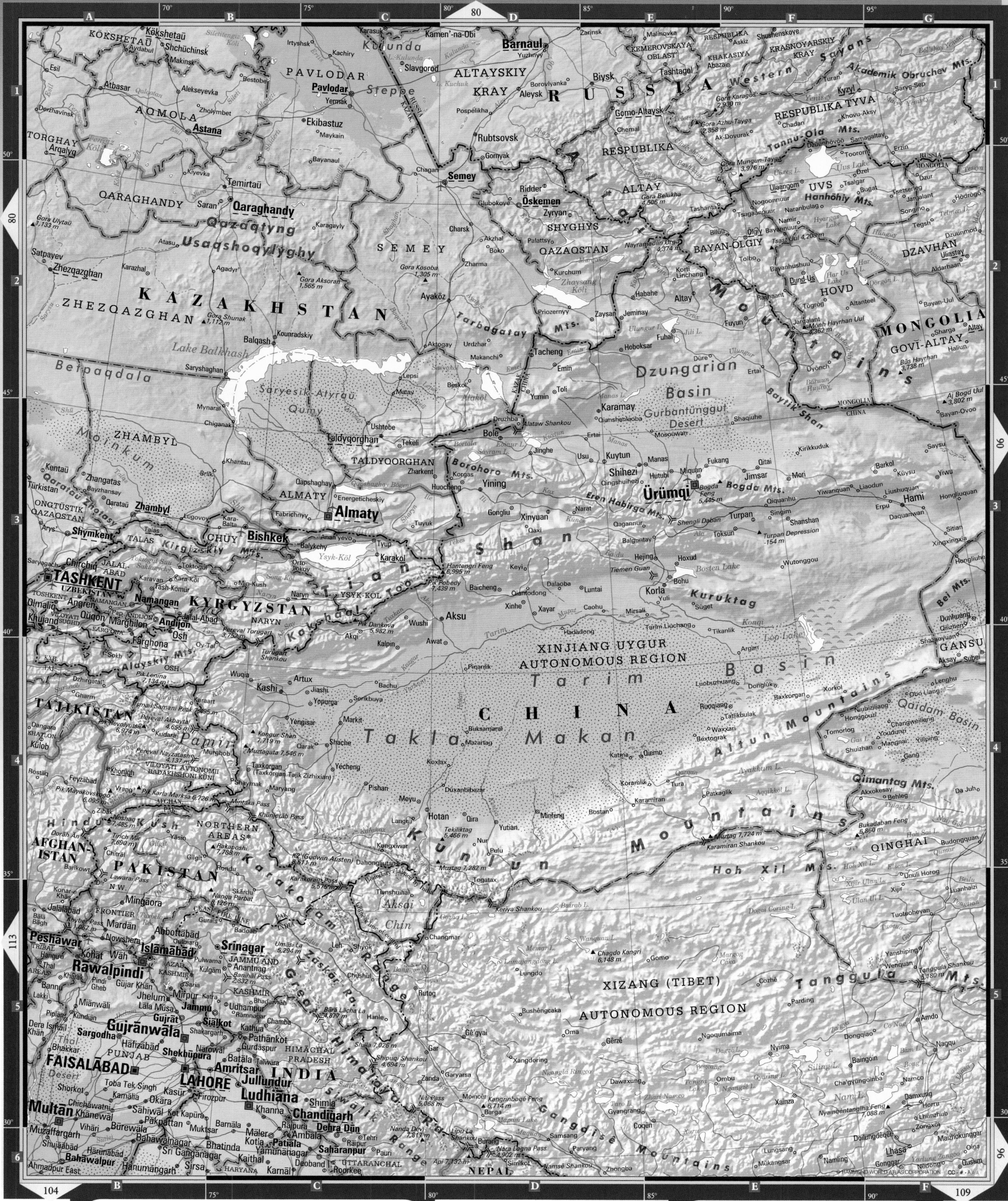

Population

■ Over 2,000,000	⊛ 500,000 - 999,999	⊕ 100,000 - 249,999	⊙ 10,000 - 29,999
▣ 1,000,000 - 1,999,999	◎ 250,000 - 499,999	⊙ 30,000 - 99,999	○ Under 10,000

*Azad Kashmir and the Northern Areas are administered by Pakistan but do not have provincial status.

Scale 1:9,000,000 Lambert Conformal Conic Projection

MI 0 100 200 300
KM 0 100 200 300 400

Height (m / ft.): 6000 19700; 4000 13000; 2000 6500; 1500 5000; 1000 3300; 500 1600; 200 700; 0; 200 700; 500 1600; 1000 3300; 2000 6500; 3000 9800; 4000 13000; 5000 16400; 6000 19700 — Depth

112

Saudi Arabia occupies most of the Arabian Peninsula. Arid plains and deserts, such as the Rub al Khali, cover ninety-nine percent of the country. Oases are found only at the foot of plateaus and near intermittently dry riverbeds known as wadis. The rift structure thrusts the southwestern edge of the peninsula abruptly upward from the Red Sea, forming an imposing escarpment from which it descends steeply toward the northeast. Water is extremely scarce. Sparse winter rains fall only in the north and in the Oman mountain region. The coastal areas, however, are very humid.

Both the Tigris and the Euphrates, the longest river in the Middle East (3,380 km), flow from sources in eastern Turkey and are of crucial geopolitical importance. Turkey uses the rivers for irrigation and hydroelectric power and can control the flow of water into neighboring countries with such large facilities as the Ataturk Dam. These two life-giving arteries of the Middle East converge to form the Shatt al Arab, which flows into the Persian Gulf. The world's largest oil reserves are located here in a total of 15 oil fields with known reserves of 1.5 billion tons each.

Height

ft.	m.
19700	6000
13000	4000
6500	2000
5000	1500
3300	1000
1600	500
700	200
0	0
200	700
500	1600
1000	3300
2000	6500
3000	9800
4000	13000
5000	16400
6000	19700

Depth

EGYPT
1. AL ISKANDARĪYAH
2. KAFR ASH SHAYKH
3. AL GHARBĪYAH
4. AL MINŪFĪYAH
5. AD DAQAHLĪYAH
6. DUMYĀŢ
7. BŪR SAĪD
8. ASH SHARQĪYAH
9. AL ISMĀ'ĪLĪYAH
10. AL QALYŪBĪYAH
11. AL QĀHIRAH
12. AL FAYYŪM
13. BANĪ SUWAYF

Population
- ■ Over 2,000,000
- ■ 1,000,000 - 1,999,999
- ◉ 500,000 - 999,999
- ◉ 250,000 - 499,999
- ◉ 100,000 - 249,999
- ◎ 30,000 - 99,999
- ◦ 10,000 - 29,999
- ○ Under 10,000

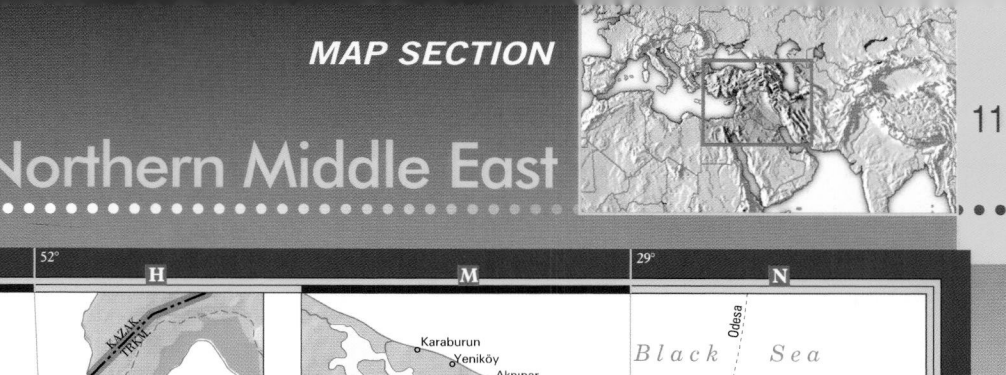

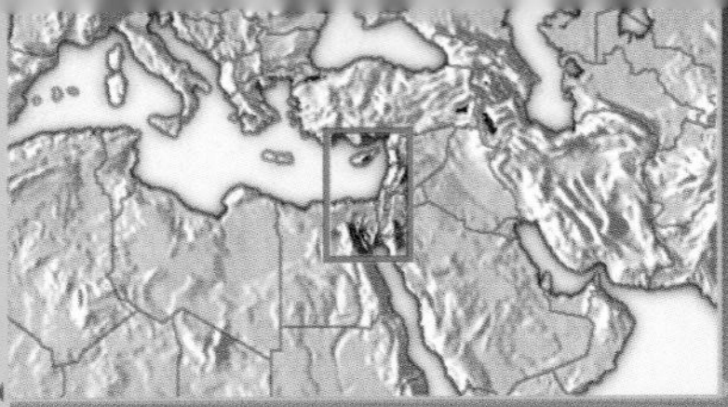

Eastern Mediterranean Region

The countries of the eastern Mediterranean region are faced with a constant shortage of water. Competition for water has always been a leading cause of conflicts in this part of the world. Citrus fruits are the most important products harvested in the narrow strips of heavily irrigated land along the coasts. Winter rains fall to the west of the uplands, while the higher, partially karst-ridden plateaus and mountain ridges offer only dry, sparse grazing.

114

Height

m.	ft.
6000	19700
4000	13000
2000	6500
1500	5000
1000	3300
500	1600
200	700
-0-	
200	700
500	1600
1000	3300
2000	6500
3000	9800
4000	16400
5000	
6000	19700

m. ft.

Depth

TURKEY

ANTALYA
Antalya
Gulf of Antalya
MUGLA
İÇEL
KONYA
KARAMAN
Adana
ADANA
Mersin
OSMANIYE
GAZIANTEP
HATAY
Antioch (Antakya)
HALAB
Aleppo (Halab)

CYPRUS
KYRENIA
NICOSIA
Nicosia
LIMASSOL
LARNACA
Famagusta
PAPHOS
Paphos
U.K. SOVEREIGN BASE AREA

MEDITERRANEAN SEA

SYRIA
Latakia (Al Lādhiqīyah)
AL LĀDHIQĪYAH
IDLIB
ḤAMĀH
Ḥamāh
ṬARṬŪS
Ṭarṭūs
ḤIMŞ
Ḥimş
Tripoli (Ṭarābulus)

LEBANON
Beirut (Bayrūt)
Sidon (Şaydā)
Tyre (Şūr)
AL JANUB
AL BIQĀ
DIMASHQ
Damascus (Dimashq)

ISRAEL
Haifa (Ḥefa)
HAIFA
CENTRAL
TEL AVIV
Tel Aviv-Yafo
Holon
Rishon LeZiyyon
Netanya
Hadera
Jerusalem (Yerushalayim)
Ashqelon
Ashdod
Beersheba (Be'er Sheva')
SOUTHERN
Negev
NORTHERN
Nazareth (Nazerat)
Tiberias
'Afula

WEST BANK
Nābulus
Jericho (Arīḥā)
Hebron (Al Khalīl)
Bethlehem (Bayt Laḥm)

GAZA STRIP
Gaza (Ghazzah)
Khān Yūnus
Rafah

JORDAN
Amman ('Ammān)
'AMMĀN
AL MAFRAQ
Az Zarqā'
AZ ZARQĀ'
Irbid
IRBID
DAR'Ā
Dar'a
AS SUWAYDĀ'
As Suwayda
AL KARAK
Al Karak
AṬ ṬAFĪLAH
MA'ĀN
Ma'an
Petra (Baṭrā')

AS SUWAYS
Suez (As Suways)
Gulf of Suez
SAUDI ARABIA
Al 'Aqabah

EGYPT
① AL GHARBĪYAH
② AL QALYŪBĪYAH
③ BŪR SA'ĪD
Nile Delta
ALEXANDRIA (Al Iskandarīyah)
Port Said (Būr Sa'īd)
Damietta (Dumyāṭ)
AL MANŞŪRAH
Al Maḩallah al Kubrā
Ṭanṭā
Az Zaqāzīq
Ismailia (Al Ismā'īlīyah)
AL JĪZAH
CAIRO (Al Qāhirah)
Shubrā al Khaymah
Al Fayyūm
SHAMAL SĪNĀ'
Sinai
JANŪB SĪNĀ'
Western Desert
MAṬRŪḤ
Gulf of Aqaba
ELAT

Population

■ Over 2,000,000	◉ 500,000 - 999,999	◎ 100,000 - 249,999	● 10,000 - 29,999
□ 1,000,000 - 1,999,999	◉ 250,000 - 499,999	◎ 30,000 - 99,999	○ Under 10,000

Scale 1:3,000,000 Lambert Conformal Conic Projection

MI 25 50 75 100
KM 25 50 75 100 125 150

© HAMMOND WORLD ATLAS CORPORATION

Two tectonic plates glide past each other in the Jordan River Valley. The eastern plate drifts northward along the western plate, creating a dislocation of about 105 km in the south. The fault line shifts west-ward in several places. There, the Earth's crust expands and sinks, a process that has given birth to the Lake of Genezareth and the Dead Sea, whose surface lies at 408 m below sea level – the lowest point on the surface of the Earth.

Scale 1:1,000,000   Lambert Conformal Conic Projection

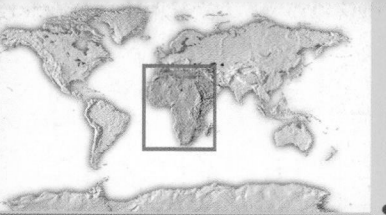

Taken from the southeast, this photograph shows the Nile Delta as a dark area in the foreground. It extends from Cairo at the apex of the delta to the Suez Canal (lower left), which connects the Mediterranean Sea and the Red Sea (upper middle). Desert-like areas are seen southwest of the delta and on the Sinai Peninsula. The Gulf of Aqaba protrudes like a spur from the Red Sea into the Arabian Peninsula. This depression extends into the Jordan River Valley and the Dead Sea toward the north and widens beneath the Red Sea in the south.

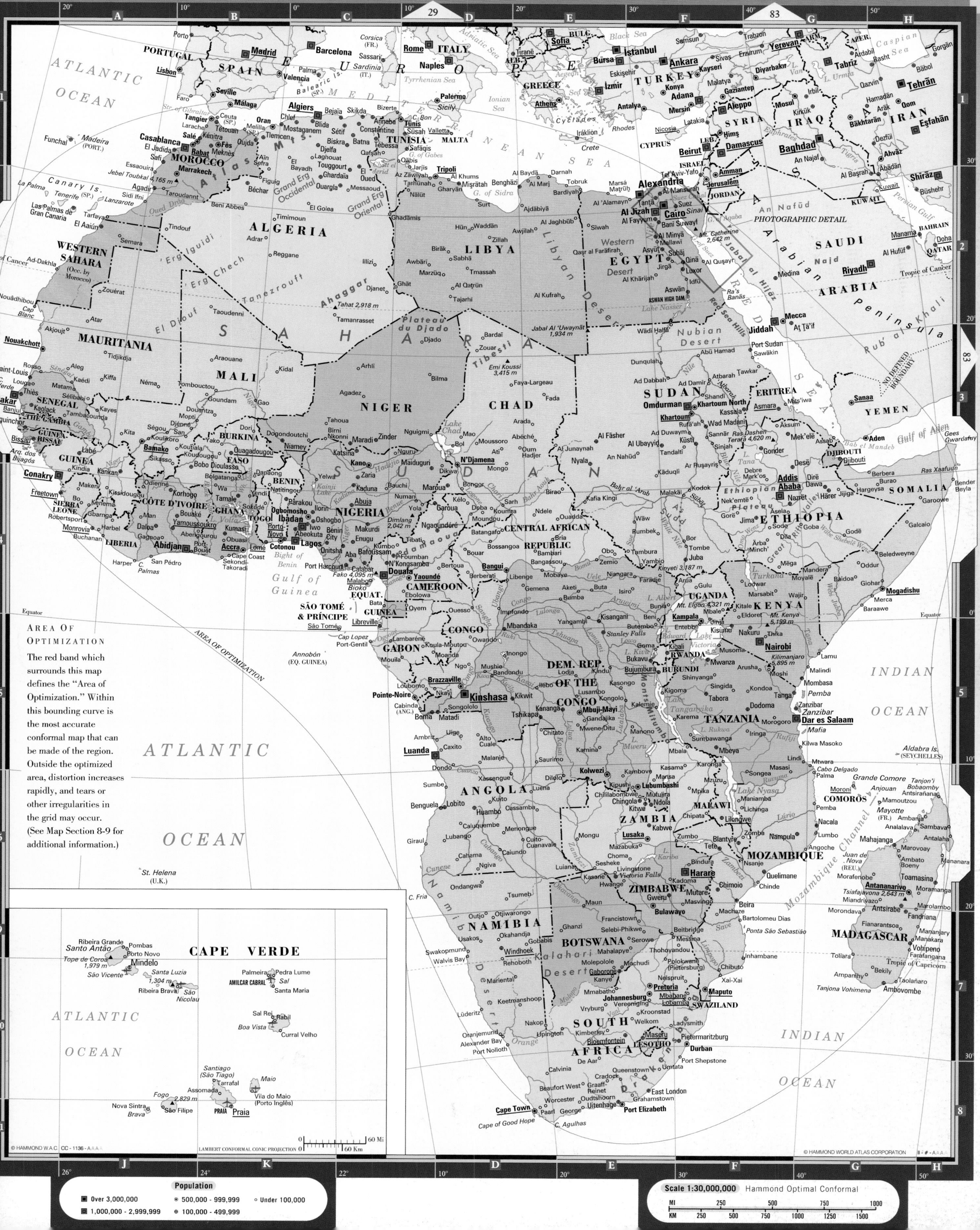

AREA OF OPTIMIZATION
The red band which surrounds this map defines the "Area of Optimization." Within this bounding curve is the most accurate conformal map that can be made of the region. Outside the optimized area, distortion increases rapidly, and tears or other irregularities in the grid may occur. (See Map Section 8-9 for additional information.)
AREA OF OPTIMIZATION
ATLANTIC OCEAN
INDIAN OCEAN
PHOTOGRAPHIC DETAIL
ALGERIA
LIBYA
EGYPT
SUDAN
CHAD
NIGER
MALI
MAURITANIA
NIGERIA
ETHIOPIA
SOMALIA
KENYA
TANZANIA
DEM. REP. OF THE CONGO
ANGOLA
ZAMBIA
NAMIBIA
BOTSWANA
ZIMBABWE
MOZAMBIQUE
MADAGASCAR
SOUTH AFRICA
SAUDI ARABIA
YEMEN
CAPE VERDE
© HAMMOND W.A.C. CC-1136-AAA
LAMBERT CONFORMAL CONIC PROJECTION
© HAMMOND WORLD ATLAS CORPORATION
Population
Over 3,000,000
1,000,000 - 2,999,999
500,000 - 999,999
100,000 - 499,999
Under 100,000
Scale 1:30,000,000 Hammond Optimal Conformal
MI 250 500 750 1000
KM 250 500 750 1000 1250 1500

World Heritage Sites in Africa and the Middle East

Text continued from page 84 - UNESCO World Cultural Heritage Sites of Asia

Criteria for Inclusion in the World Heritage List

A World Heritage Site must not only be authentic and intact, it must also be of outstanding universal value, as demonstrated by fulfillment of at least one of the following criteria:

• The site represents a unique artistic accomplishment, a masterpiece of human creative genius.

• The site has had a significant influence, over a span of time or within a cultural area of the world, on developments in architecture, monumental arts, town planning or landscape design.

• The site bears a unique or at least exceptional testimony to a cultural tradition or to a civilization which is living or which has disappeared.

Text continues on page 146 - UNESCO World Cultural Heritage Sites of Australia

• The site is an outstanding example of a type of building or architectural ensemble or landscape which illustrates a significant state in human history.

• The site is an outstanding example of a traditional human settlement or land use which is representative of a culture (or cultures), especially when it has become vulnerable under the impact of irreversible change.

• The site is directly or tangibly associated with events or living traditions, with ideas, or with beliefs, with artistic, or literary works of outstanding universal significance (this criterion should justify inclusion in the list only in exceptional circumstances and in conjunction with other criteria).

1 Sukur Cultural Landscape
2 Royal Palaces of Abomey
3 Asante Traditional Buildings
4 Colonial Coastal Forts
5 Old Towns of Djenné
6 Cliffs of Bandiagara
7 Timbuktu (Tombouctou)
8 Island of Gorée
9 Ouadane, Chinguetti, Tichitt and Oualata
10 San Cristóbal de La Laguna
11 Ksar of Ait-Ben-Haddou
12 Medina of Marrakesh
13 Medina of Fez
14 Historic City of Meknes
15 Archeological Site of Volubilis
16 Medina of Tétouan
17 Tipasa
18 Kasbah of Algiers
19 Djémila
20 Al Qala'a of Beni Hammand
21 Timgad
22 M'zab Valley
23 Dougga
24 Medina of Tunis
25 Archeological Site of Carthage
26 Medina of Kairouan
27 Punic Town of Kerkuane
28 Medina of Sousse
29 Amphitheater of El Jem
30 Archeological Site of Sabratha
31 Archeological Site of Leptis Magna
32 Old Town of Ghadames
33 Rock-Art Sites of Tassili n'Ajjer
34 Rock-Art Sites of Tadrart Acacus
35 Archeological Site of Cyrene
36 Abu Mena
37 Memphis and its Necropolis and Pyramids
38 Islamic Cairo
39 Ancient Thebes (Luxor)
40 Nubian Monuments from Abu Simbel to Philae
41 Paphos
42 Painted Churches in the Troodos Region
43 Neolithic Settlement of Choirokoitia
44 Xanthos-Letoon
45 Hierapolis-Pamukkale
46 Archeological Site Troy
47 Historic Areas of Istanbul
48 City of Safranbolu
49 Hattusha
50 Göreme National Park and the Rock Sites of Cappadocia
51 Great Mosque and Hospital of Divriği
52 Nemrut Dağ
53 Mountain Villages in Svaneti
54 Bagrati Cathedral and Gelati Monastery
55 Historic Churches of Mtskheta
56 Monasteries of Haghbat and Sanahin
57 Hatra
58 Ancient City of Aleppo
59 Site of Palmyra

60 Quadi Qadisha and the Forest of the Cedars of God
61 Byblos
62 Baalbek
63 Tyre
64 Anjar
65 Ancient City of Damascus
66 Ancient City of Bosra
67 Old City of Jerusalem and its Walls
68 Petra
69 Quseir Amra
70 Fort of Bahla
71 Archeological Sites of Bat, Al-Khutm and Al-Ayn
72 Old City of Sanaa
73 Medina of Zabid
74 Old Walled City of Shibam
75 Aksum
76 Fasil Ghebbi, Gondar Region
77 Rock-hewn Churches of Lalibela
78 Lower Awash Valley
79 Tiya
80 Lower Omo Valley
81 Ruins of Kilwa Kisiwani and Songo Mnara
82 Island of Mozambique
83 Khami Ruins
84 Great Zimbabwe
85 Fossil Hominid Sites of Sterkfontein, Swartkrans and Kromdraai
86 Robben Island
87 Harar Jugol, the Fortified Historic Town
88 James Island and Related Sites
89 Stone Circles of Senegambia
90 Lamu Old Town
91 Royal Hill of Ambohimanga
92 Chongoni Rock-Art Area
93 Tomb of Askia
94 Aapravasi Ghat
95 Osun-Osogbo Sacred Grove
96 Mapungubwe Cultural Landscape
97 Koutammakou, Land of the Batammarib
98 Tombs of Buganda Kings at Kasubi
99 Stone Town of Zanzibar
100 Kondoa Rock-Art Sites
101 Matobo Hills
102 uKhahlamba / Drakensberg Park
103 Qal'at al-Bahrain – Ancient Harbour and Capital of Dilmun
104 Saint Catherine Area
105 Ashur (Qal'at Sherqat)
106 Um er-Rasas (Kastrom Mefa'a)
107 Medina of Essaouira (formerly Mogador)
108 Portuguese City of Mazagan (El Jadida)
109 Land of Frankincense
110 Aflaj Irrigation Systems of Oman
111 Gebel Barkal and Sites of Napatan Region
112 Crac des Chevaliers and Qal'at Salah El-D
113 Tsodilo
114 Island of Saint Luis

Pearl of the Desert

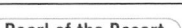

Protected by walls and towers, the city of **Ghadames (32)** is a masterpiece of Saharan architecture located along one of the trans-Sahara caravan routes. The three-story houses are connected by terraces — the women's realm.

Triumph of Will

From the 17th century until 1996, **Robben Island (86)**, located eight miles from Cape Town, was used as a whaling station, a camp for lepers and the mentally ill, a military base (World War II), and a penitentiary. Nelson Mandela was confined to the maximum security wing of the prison for 18 years and forced to work in the limestone quarry. The island is now an outdoor museum of human rights and one of the most popular tourist attractions on the Cape.

Treasures of Byzantine Art

Nowhere else are so many outstanding examples of Byzantine painting concentrated in a single region than in the **Troodos Mountains (42)** of Cyprus. The Archangel of Lagoudera (1192) is a particularly elegant work.

Puristic Islam

The Kutubiya Mosque (built between 1157 and 1197) is located in the pentagonal Medina of **Marrakesh (12)**. The early purism of the Almohad Dynasty is evident in the emphatic formal simplicity of the horseshoe arches in the prayer hall.

Dogon Religious Shrines

The **Cliffs of Bandiagara (6)** in Mali/Burkina Faso are home to the Dogons. Their rich cultural tradition is based upon a complex mythology of creation. Dogon shrines are built among the cliffs. The photo shows the house of the Hogon, the village religious leader.

NESCO World Cultural Heritage Sites in Africa and the Middle East

Desert Castle

The small castle of **Quseir Amra (69)** east of Amman, which dates from the Umayyad Dynasty (c. 715) features a splendidly furnished audience hall and luxurious baths.

Ancient Granite Seat of Kings

The largest stone architectural complex produced by black African cultures is **Great Zimbabwe (84)**, which means "houses of stone." Built of granite blocks fitted precisely without mortared joints, the massive ring of walls bears witness to the might of the Shona Kings of the 15th century. The solid, cone-shaped stone tower resembles the grain silos used by Shona farmers.

Loam Fortress

Built primarily of loam and straw, the fortress of **Bahla (70)** has towers as high as 50 m. Parts of the complex date back to pre-Islamic times. Bahla was the capital of the Sultanate of Oman at several different points in history.

City in Ruins with a Living Artistic Tradition

A dying city today, the former trading metropolis of **Oualata (9)** on the southern edge of the Sahara is still regarded as a center of Islamic scholarship. Some of the stone buildings covered with red loam are adorned with highly symbolic ornaments.

Late Stone Age Legacy

Some of the oldest rock paintings in the central Sahara are monumental works of static art. A prime example is the mysterious "Rain God Fresco" of Sefar in the **Tassili n'Ajjer (33)**.

Brilliant Architecture

The **Rock Churches of Lalibela (77)** were hewn from the exposed red tuff of the Ethiopian Plateau around 1200 AD. As imitations of existing architecture, they exhibit influences from the Byzantine and ancient Aksum civilizations.

Victorious Amazons

The kingdom of Dahomey rose to affluence and power (supported by a well-trained professional army) in the 17th century. The bas-relief on the walls of the **Royal Palaces of Abomey (2)** commemorates the Amazon Corps.

THE WONDER OF THE NILE: The confluence of two great rivers brought the desert sands to life - thus providing the backdrop to Egypt's rich history. Egypt only exists thanks to a bit of geographical serendipity. The line of least resistance for water escaping from two African lakes 1,600 km. (1,000 miles) apart, one of them actually straddling the equator, was not a quick dive into the Indian Ocean and Red Sea which lay close at hand. Instead, one went off as if looking to join the Congo River for its immense journey west to the Atlantic. The other went roughly south for hundreds of miles before that, too, proved to be a detour. Between them, the two rivers logged some 5,600 km. (3,500 miles) of idle wandering before combining their forces for a 3,200 km. (2,000 miles) mercy mission through what would otherwise have been one of the most barren places on earth.

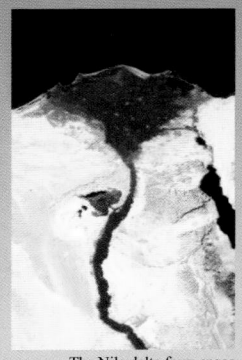

The Nile delta from space

Replenished by only one tributary, and hardly ever by rainfall, a lesser river than the unified streams of the White and Blue Niles would have petered out in the near insatiable sands of the desert long before it reached the Mediterranean. The Nile not only survived, but at the hottest and driest time of every year conjured up a tidal wave of flood water. The sheer volume of silt which the flood brought defied comprehension. In any one year it seemed sufficient to have stripped the lands from whence it came to skeletal bones, yet there was always more, year after year. Moreover, it was silt of great fertility, capable of turning a vast tract of desert into an agricultural paradise. In southern (Upper) Egypt, the miracle was confined to a narrow ribbon along the banks, but with only 160 km. (100 miles) to go, the river seemed of several minds about where to empty into the Mediterranean, and the result was what the Greeks recognized as the shape of their letter Delta, seven channels which merged during the floods into a coastal lake. Wherever the silt was deposited, all a farmer had to do was wait for the water to subside, scratch seeds into the ground, let his livestock trample them in, and sit back to watch them grow. The feeding of the people along the river more or less took care of itself.

TAMING THE NILE: Control of the annual flood has always been the key to the country's prosperity. Egyptian civilization relied on a paradox: at the hottest, driest time of the year, the Nile would break its banks with an ocean of water and rich silt. If the flood was too low, the amount of arable land could shrink disastrously; if too high, it washed away settlements that were supposedly on safe ground.

White waters in the Nile

Moreover, the secret of two or three consecutive crops was in having water on hand to refresh silt which would otherwise turn to stone in the searing heat. Thus control of the Nile was a challenge to Egyptian ingenuity.

EARLY ENGINEERING: This bold attempt is credited to Menes, the first king of a united Upper and Lower Egypt who, in about 3000 B.C., is said to have successfully diverted the river in order to build the new capital, Memphis, on reclaimed land.

The aquatic engineering feats of the pyramid builders were inspired by other considerations. Enormous granite blocks were floated down the river from Aswan on reed barges. The pyramids were generally built high above the flood plain so special canals were dug to reduce the distance over which the blocks had to be dragged on sledges. A curious lapse in the technical precocity that produced the pyramids was the failure to recognize the potential of the wheel, a concept already known to potters and shipwrights, for land transport.

FREE LABOR: Prisoners of war supplemented local labor, especially during the Middle Kingdom years (2040-1640 B.C.) at the tail end of the pyramid period. According to Herodotus, Sesostris III's prisoners were put to work on a network of canals that served to increase the amount of arable land. His impatience with the enemy in Nubia to the south was such that he cleared a passage for ships through the First Cataract, enabling him to mount successful punitive raids. King Amenemhet appreciated the extra crops that could be wrung out of the silt by efficient irrigation, so he initiated a bold program of canals and reservoirs. The 32 km. (20 miles) dam wall he built across the oasis lake in the al-Fayyum region was still functioning a millennium later, when Herodotus wrote: "The water in this lake does not spring from the soil. It is conveyed through a channel from the Nile, and for six months flows into the lake, and for six months out again into the Nile."

Herodotus was also impressed by a canal that joined the Nile and Red Sea. It was wide enough for triremes (warships) to pass abreast, and it reduced the fearsome overland journey to a comfortable four-day cruise. Some 120,000 laborers died working on the project, Herodotus noted, but it was only completed by Darius, the Persian conqueror, not long before Herodotus's visit.

ROMAN IMPROVEMENTS: The Romans, like the Persians and Greeks before them, improved the waterways of Egypt, and built a Red Sea canal that began near modern Cairo. At the time they considered but rejected the idea of a Suez canal because the Red Sea was thought to be 6 meters (30 feet) higher than the Mediterranean. The Arabs continued the good work: the Khalig canal dissected the capital they built at Cairo.

NAPOLEON'S COMPLAINT: The Mameluks the ruling cast neglected the waterways but Napoleon, who arrived in 1798, wanted to clear the canals and repair the hydraulic machine that lifted water into a tower to supply the citadel at Cairo. Napoleon planned a series of dams along the Nile but, like a proposed Suez canal, they did not materialize before his enforced departure.

VIRGIN SACRIFICES: The entrance to Cairo's canal was opposite the Nilometer on the island of Rawdah. Nilometers, maintained at key points along the river from pharaonic times measured the rise of the water, and in particular signaled the level (16 cubits) at which the farmers had to start paying tax on the land they worked. The annual cutting of the dam was observed with a tradition going back to pharaonic times: a young virgin was thrown into the river as a sacrifice. The victim was symbolized by a "Bride of the Nile" earth tower erected in front of the dam. The river rushed in to consummate the union, when washing away the tower the dam was breached.

By 1833 Muhammed Ali, the father of modern Egypt, had been persuaded by the Frenchman Mougel Bey to adopt a plan that would regulate the water level over the delta through a series of dams. The scheme faltered but was eventually revived during the British occupation and the dams were completed in 1891. The next major Nile project on the British agenda caused an outrage: a proposed dam at the First Cataract would drown the island of Philae. Though the island was only 450 meters (1,500 feet) long, it was the site of Egypt's finest Graeco-Roman works, notably the Temple of Isis. The height of the dam was adjusted to answer these objections and the old Aswan Dam was opened in 1902.

THE ASWAN DAM: The High Aswan Dam constructed in the 1960s created the world's largest artificial lake, the 6,000-sq.-km. (2,300 sq. mile) Lake Nasser, which stretches into Sudan. Its purpose was to protect Egypt from droughts or floods in Ethiopia and Sudan, as well as to provide water resources and cheap power needed by a rapidly growing population. The 280,000 hectares (700,000 acres) of land already cultivated could be harvested more than once a year, and more than 400,000 hectares (1 million acres) of desert land have been reclaimed for cultivation.

Lake Nasser wiped out Nubia; some 100,000 Nubians lost their land and most of their culture when they were resettled around Aswan and upriver. The dam traps the silt that formerly enriched the fields, so farmers now rely on chemical fertilizers, which enter the food chain and exhaust the soil. The perennial irrigation has caused soil salinity requiring extra drainage systems, which in turn provide breeding grounds for mosquitoes and bilharzia-carrying snails. This salinity of the soil, rising water tables and greater humidity also threaten the ancient monuments. The lack of silt deposits in the Delta area make the coastline more vulnerable to erosion.

UNESCO TO THE RESCUE: The decision in 1960 to build the High Dam at Aswan would have sandwiched Philae in destructive currents between the new dam and the older British dam downstream. A UNESCO rescue plan resulted in the nearby higher island of Agilqiyah being blasted into a semblance of Philae, after which the monuments of Philae were dismantled block by block and reassembled on their new home. For all the unfortunate side effects, a tamed Nile has removed the uncertainties which, at least 7,000 years ago, began with questions of the river's source and durability.

The Temple of Isis

Linked to control of the Suez Canal, the Aswan Dam was the apex of Nasser's dream for the future. It was an undertaking of pharaonic proportions: 30,000 Egyptians worked day and night for 11 years under Soviet supervision after the British and the United States governments withdrew their support in protest of Nasser's nationalist politics.

Power station of Aswan dam

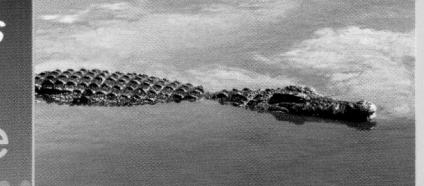

Nile Plant and Wildlife

The mild climate and rural expanse through which the river runs - unpolluted - offer a great habitat for wildlife. In pre-pharaonic times, most of Egypt was a savannah on which leopards, cheetahs and lions roamed freely. Herds of elephant, buffalo, onyx and gazelle fed on the wild grasses and drank from the river. In the Nile, crocodiles and hippopotamuses foraged from source to outlet. But with environmental changes and the growth of civilization, through which man began to dominate the Nile valley, local animals were pushed farther and farther south.

ANIMAL GODS: The ancient Egyptians had a strong connection to the natural world. Many of their gods were associated with animals: Sobek, god of al-Fayyum and Kom Ombo, was linked to the crocodile; Anubis, god of the dead, with the jackal; Thoth, god of wisdom, with the ibis. Hieroglyphic symbols included depictions of animals, birds, flowers and trees. Houses were decorated with paintings of flowers, and public buildings had pillars and colonnades in the form of papyrus and lotus.

By the time of the New Kingdom many of the Nile's indigenous species such as elephants, giraffes and monkeys, were disappearing from Egypt. The hippopotamus took longer to make its journey south. Hippos outlasted ancient Egypt and the Islamic medieval period, and were quite a novelty for European travelers of the Middle Ages. By the 20th century, of the great creatures, only crocodiles remained in Egyptian waters. The construction of the Aswan Dam in the 1960s pushed the crocodile into the Sudan, though a baby croc sometimes gets churned through the dam's sluice gates.

THE LONG MIGRATION: By contrast the country is still home to a tremendous variety of birds, whose numbers swell each winter as they are joined by

A bee-eater

additional species migrating to escape the winters of Europe and western Asia. The birds take to the air following a variety of migratory paths that take them over the Maghreb, Egypt, Saudi Arabia, Iraq, Iran and parts of Russia. Some birds travel nearly 2,000 km. (1,240 miles) before they reach their journey's end south of the Sahara, often exhausted and vulnerable to predators.

BIRDS OF PREY: Raptors (hawks, eagles and vultures) make their way south following land routes. These paths, sometimes known as flyways, begin in eastern Europe and Asia Minor. From the Sinai the migrating birds cut west over the Red Sea gulfs to the Egyptian coast, turn south and head to

Safaga. At Safaga they turn west again and soar over the Red Sea Mountains to Qena along the Nile. At Qena their journey continues south and, as they pass Luxor, Esna and Aswan, some birds settle, wintering on the Egyptian Nile. Two of the most exciting birds to be seen in the green areas along the Nile are the little green bee-eater and the hoopoe. Hoopoes have an orange and black feathery crown which opens like a fan when it is excited, and black and white striped wings.

Another garden resident is the Nile Valley sunbird. Once a year the male, resplendent in exotic iridescent purple-green plumages, yellow breast and long, slender tail feather, goes courting. Of African origin, this small bird is found in various habitats all along the Nile, from the lush Delta area to the desert. The sunbird is most frequently seen in flower gardens, particularly when hovering around trumpet-like flowers as it pierces the corolla and sips the nectar. In winter, the sunbird, along with other resident birds, shares the gardens with migrating wheatears, warblers and finches.

PURPLE PLUMAGE: Of the resident birds that enjoy the shores of the Nile, the most colorful and elusive is the purple gallinule, a stunning bird with blue, purple and green plumage and a red beak

Flamingos

and red legs. Both migrant and resident is the grey heron, a tall, elegant, shy bird that wades knee deep along the river's banks.

The water birds arrive in winter. Migrants include the white pelican, white stork, spoonbill, greater flamingo and numerous species of gull and duck. The sight of these birds flying over the Nile is a spectacular one: gulls follow boats, foraging for food, flocks of pelicans and storks fly high overhead, and the flamingo, graceful long neck outstretched and black striped wings flapping gracefully, flies at eye level past cruise boats.

Among the birds of prey that can be seen all year round are the kite, black-shouldered kite and kestrel. If you are in luck, you may see one of these birds hovering in the air as they hunt for field mice or insects.

ORNITHOLOGISTS' DELIGHT: Crocodile Island in Luxor is a good site for bird-watching, and a variety of birds can be seen in winter and summer alike. Aswan is a nature lover's paradise. Any

place along the river's edge is good for watching hundreds of birds; Salugah Island, now a protected natural area, is the best.

Lake Qarun in al-Fayyum is a spectacular natural

A heron about to take flight

habitat. The salt-water lake is situated in a pastoral environment with desert along its northern shore and farmland to the south. Protected by newly enforced laws, water birds winter in this area in the tens of thousands, with Senegal thick-knees flying in particularly graceful formations. At the shore of the lake smaller birds, from sandpipers to spotted shanks and pips, flutter. At night thousands of gulls roost in backwaters; during the day, accompanied by coots, grebes and an impressive variety of ducks, they dot the shores. In recent winters flamingos have returned to the western shores of Lake Qarun.

SHOOTING GAME: Given its abundance of wildlife, it's no surprise that the Nile Valley became a destination of game hunters. The white hunter, with his wide-brimmed hat, supplanted the intrepid explorer and his pith helmet in the first half of the 20th century, when the wholesale slaughter of some of Africa's finest animals began.

Unfortunately the Nile area still attracts hunters, despite the imposition of environmental restrictions. Gulf Arabs for instance train falcons to catch prey. In recent times, local environmental agencies have prevented European hunters from shooting birds on illegal hunts in Egypt.

FLOURISHING FLORA: Along the river, between acacia and tamarisk trees, are fields of sugar cane, banana groves and palm trees.

There is a variety of native acacia (mimosa) trees, all of which bloom with tiny yellow flowers. The

largest, the Nile acacia, rises high above the river. The delicate tamarisk with its blue-green feathery blooms, the thick-trunked mulberry with its light green leaves and edible fruit, the wind-breaking casuarina with its long pine needles, and the tall eucalyptus with its camphor-producing light green leaves also grace the shores of the Nile, as does

Papyrus still grows along the Nile

the sycamore, the ancient Egyptians' tree of love.

Cane fields exist all along the Nile. A government decree stipulates that all farmers must grow sugar cane. The date palm is the country's most important and prolific tree. There are a variety of date trees in Egypt (each of which bears a different kind of date) which are categorized as dry,

Harvesting the date palm

semi-dry, or soft. Brown and black dates are usually soft and sweet. At harvest time (September) the farmer climbs the palm tree and picks each date by hand.

Tomb paintings of a hunting scene

East Africa

An
Enchanted
World

- East Africa is one of the last refuges of wildlife forced from the rest of the continent by human incursions.

- There is a diversity and abundance of wildlife, from towering elephants to tiny spiders.

- There is a delicate balance between the East African people and wildlife, maintained by traditional values and ways of life.

- East Africa has every habitat imaginable, from savanna, woodland and rainforest to the highest mountain peaks via semi-arid zones to lakes, rivers and swamps.

- Thousands of African species face extinction, and human beings are the principal cause.

The list of endangered species is too long to enumerate, but even a cursory examination of some of the best-known examples illustrates both the extent of the problem and some measures that are being employed to stem the decline.

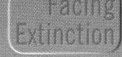
Rhino horns

A Vast and
Varied Land

Murchison Falls, Uganda

Kibo summit of Mt. Kilimanjaro

LIMITED JUNGLES: *Evergreen Forests* in East Africa are confined to belts around major mountains such as the Virunga volcanoes in Rwanda, the Ruwenzoris in Uganda, Mt. Kilimanjaro in Tanzania and Mt. Kenya in Kenya. *Ground Water Forests* occur where there is enough water seeping out of springs, such as at the base of the escarpment above Lake Manyara. *Riverine Forests* exist along major perennial water courses, along with remnant patches of low-lying *Coastal Forest*. Although tree species differ, the pattern is more or less the same: dense, layered canopies, trees up to 230 ft. high and relatively thin undergrowth.

THE SWEEPING PLAINS: Open grassland, such as the long grass plains of the Serengeti covered with red oat grass, is the backdrop. Add scattered shrubs, such as the patches of "toothbrush" bush in Queen Elizabeth National Park in Uganda, and one has bushed grassland. Replace the bushes with widely-spaced, flat-topped acacias and spiny desert dates, and the scene is wooded grassland.

THE SEASONS: The climate is a critical factor limiting the form and abundance of life in any ecosystem. In the Serengeti and Tanzania it rains in two peaks, April and November when powerful storms hurl down more rain than the soil can possibly absorb. In the long rains, usually April to May, there may be some constantly rainy days. But usually rainfall is discontinuous.

In regions where annual rainfall exceeds 47 inches - such as western Uganda and the Democratic Republic of the Congo - the seasons tend to merge, with no distinct rainy season, and forest vegetation tends to dominate. On the beaches of East Africa's coasts the sun is very intense.

Both plants and animals have to be adaptive, mobile or both. "Adaptive" implies the ability to breed quickly when there is sufficient moisture. "Mobile" means having the ability to move to places where the chance of reproduction and survival are better.

EAST AFRICA'S GEOLOGY: Much of East Africa looks unfinished: the gash of the Great Rift Valley which cuts through the country from the Red Sea to Zimbabwe has rugged step faults which drop 2,100 m. (6,900 ft.), from the Ngong Hills outside Nairobi, to the steaming soda of Lake Magadi at 610 m. (2,000 ft.). There are also active or recently extinct volcanoes: Virunga in Rwanda, Ol-Doinyo Lengai in Tanzania, Shetani and Teleki's in Kenya. Whole hill ranges are remnants of volcanic activities, such as the Ruwenzoris in Uganda and the Chyulu Hills in Kenya. Many of the soils in East Africa contain high amounts of volcanic ash - for example, the southern Serengeti from the Ngorongoro highlands, the Nairobi National Park and adjacent Athi-Kapiti plains from the Aberdares and Mt. Kenya, and others. Recent lava flows are common, and look like black treacle poured over the landscape. Older lava flows and granitic boulders are exposed as escarpments and are very picturesque. Much of the variety of plant and animal life is due to variation in elevation, from sea level to 6,000 m. (19,700 ft.).

PERIODIC DROUGHT: Failures of the annual rains happen at least once every 10 years, and some decades are drier than others. The effect is temporarily to change the relative numbers of species and the reproductive ability of those less tolerant to dry periods. When the rains return, the balance shifts back in favor of the perennials. The drought can have catastrophic effects on agriculture, drastically reducing cereal crop yields and decimating livestock. In the past, resulting widespread food shortages have triggered famine and massive international relief operations. Dry periods impact more on herbivores than carnivores since lions can live quite well off skinny wildebeest, but wildebeest cannot survive on dust. When the rains return and the vegetation is verdant, then herbivore populations, even elephants, are able to increase their numbers relatively quickly.

BUSH FIRES: African ecosystems are subjected to sporadic burning from natural causes such as lightning strikes. This is evidenced by the fact that many trees and shrubs are "fire-adapted," that is, they can not only withstand burning, but actually flourish or use the fire signal to produce flowers and seeds. Fire keeps many of the grasslands intact: if they were not burned periodically, they would start to develop towards bushland.

CONSERVATION CONSCIOUSNESS: Land management strategies must be practicable in the African setting, useful to African people, and linked to their society and economy. Wise conservation projects must involve local people, not just by informing them of critical issues, but by making them a direct part of the conservation process. At the simplest level this means getting some of the wildlife-generated revenue, such as game park fees, back to the landowners who bear the cost of having wildlife graze on their land.

The Mara river, Kenya

Great lake region

Forest in Marangu, Mt. Kilimanjaro

Garden of senecias

Moorelands

Tara river, Kenya - Nov. 27 2006

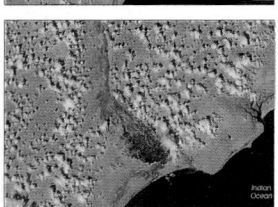
Tara river, Kenya (flooded) - Dec. 6 2006

Rhinos

While the white rhinoceros is under threat of extinction, its cousin, the black rhino, is also critically endangered, with fewer than 2,500 left in the wild. The largest population in East Africa (about 400) is in Kenya. The black rhino was hunted heavily for sport and for its horn. Today in many preserves, game scouts briefly capture rhinos and cut off their horns as a preventive measure.

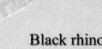
Black rhino

Highland Wolves and Painted Dogs

Extinction also threatens the Ethiopian wolf, a wild canid unjustifiably reviled by herdsmen for livestock predation; this shy predator feeds mainly on small rodents. The wolf also competes for food with domestic dogs and cross-breeds with them. Such hybridization could eventually wipe out the wolf as a true, distinct species; there may be as few as 400 pure Ethiopian wolves alive today.

Another endangered canid is the African wild dog, also known as the painted wolf. No more than 5,000 of these beautiful, piebald predators are left in all Africa. Although Kenya and Ethiopia have small populations, the only substantial wild dog population in East Africa is in southern Tanzania. Wild dogs are good hunters, but they suffer when they have to compete with larger, more aggressive predators such as lions. They are also less adept at dealing with traffic, and many wind up as road kill. However, the biggest threat facing them is disease from domestic animals. Aggressive measures are under way to protect wild dog populations, including captive breeding and reintroduction programs, road signs to warn motorists of their presence, and education campaigns to encourage greater tolerance by farmers.

Painted dog

Chimpanzees and Gorillas

Chimpanzees are highly valued for medical research, since they share most of our genome. Poachers usually obtain young animals for the medical trade by killing their mothers, a double tragedy. The destruction of their forest habitat by loggers and farmers has also contributed to the decline of chimps. There are fewer than 200,000 chimps living in the wild, many in some of Africa's poorest countries, where the temptation to poach wildlife is particularly acute.

Gorillas are also in serious trouble. While the two species of lowland gorilla number about 126,000, the mountain gorilla is on the brink of extinction; about 630 animals survive in the mountains at the borders of Rwanda, the Dem. Rep. of the Congo, and Uganda. Their forest habitat is threatened by agricultural demands. Also because of years of warfare in the region, rangers could not patrol the mountain gorilla sanctuaries, and poaching increased. However, the Rwandan and Ugandan governments, and communities living around protected areas in Virunga National Park, are committed to protecting the gorillas.

Gorilla

Cheetah

Serval cat

Wild cat

Zebra

Giraffe

Olive baboon

Chimpanzee

Spotted hyena

Hare

Golden jackal

Colubus monkey

Adult male lion

Ring-tailed lemur

Aard wolf

Warthog

Gazelle

African elephants

Hippopotamus

Wildebeest

Okapi

Leopard

The Tibesti range covers 100,000 square km of territory between northern Chad and the Libyan border. The range is a volcanic mountain system that rises steeply from the Sahara. This volcanic activity deep within the African continent is the result of a thermal anomaly in the earth's interior known as a hot spot. Hot springs and mud pools offer striking evidence of active geological activity in the region. Due to its height, the Tibesti range draws more rain than the surrounding areas and is known as the "emerald isle" of the Sahara.

73

MEDITERRANEAN

TUNISIA

KEBILI
EL OUED
MEDENINE
Ben Guerdane
Tataouine
Zeltun
Ra's Ajdir
Zuwārah
Al Jamil
Janzūr
SABRATHA
Sabrātah
Tripoli
(Ţarābulus)
TRIPOLI
Tajūra
Bin Ghashir
Ramādah
Ṣurmān
Zāwiyah
Al ʿAzīzīyah
Al Khums
LEPTIS MAGNA
Al Qaṣabāt
Zlīţan
Mişrātah
Adh Dhahibāt
Nālūt
Tījī
Kabaw
Jādū
Yafren
Gharyān
Tarhūnah
ALGERIA
OUARGLA
SIF FATIMA
TATAOUINE
Al Jmail
Bi'r al Ghanam
Jabal Nafūsah
981 m
Sabkhat Tāwurghā'
Tāwurghā'
Sabkhat al Hayshah
Mizdah
Bāni Walid

Al ʿInfāriḥ

Tripolitania
Ghadāmis
Sināwin
Bi'r Zeitūn
Diri
Qaryat Abū Qurayn
Zamzam
Bi'r umm al Ghirbāl
Bi'r as Sinīdah
Surt
As Sulţān
Gulf of Sidra
Al Qaryah al Gharbīyah
Al Qaryah ash Sharqīyah
Qaryat Abū Nujaym
Qaryat Abū Nujaym
An Nawfalīyah
Bin Jawwād
As Sidr
Marsa al Burayqah
Sirtica
Thamad Sidi Ṣāliḥ

Al Ḩamādah al Ḩamra
Bi'r al Ghnayyid
Hasy Berrez
Zarzaitine
In Amenas
Hassi el Mistane
Hasy in Aqulet
Hasy Timenocine
Zillah
LIBYA
Jabal Zaltan
Sabkhat al Milḥ
-42 m

671 m
Hūn
Sawknah
Waddān
840 m
Jabal as Sawdā'
Al Fuqahā'
Qarārat al Ḩayyirah
1,780 m
1,200 m

Al Harūj al Aswad

Zalţan

Şaḥrā Awbārī
Bi'r al Qaṭf
Adiri
Barqin
Birāk
Ashkidah
Rhat
Umm al ʿAbīd
Tamanhint
Samnū
Sabhā
Awbārī
Ghaddūwah
Fezzan
Ḩamādat Marzūq
Tasawāh
Marzūq
Trāghin
Majdūl
Umm al Arānib
Zawīlah
Tinassah
Wāw al Kabīr
740 m
Jabal Bin Ghunaymah

Şarir Kalanshiyū

Ghāt
1,428 m
Al Birkah
Tin Alkoum
Şaḥrā Marzūq
Bi'r al Masţūtah
Tajarhi
Bi'r Zāmūs

Sarir Kalanshiyū ar Ramli al Kabīr

Sarir Kalanshiyū

Tāzirbū
'Ayn Ath Tha'lab Oasis

Tadrart
Mesach Mellet

Şaḥrā' Rabyānah

TAMANGHASSET
In Ezzane
Erg d'Admer
AOUD
NIGER
Tropic of Cancer
Bi'r Musciuru
Sarir Tibasti

Kufrah
Al Jawf
Al Kufrah
At Tallāb Oasis

S A H

Plateau de Mangueni
Passé de Korizo
Aozou Strip
Asawanwah

Plateau du Djado
Madama
Tejerre
Plateau du Tchigai

Ténéré du Tafassasset
Djado
Chirfa
Fezzane
Bikkū Bittī
2,266 m
Aozou

Tibesti

AGADEZ
Séguédine
Wour
Bardai
Tiéboro
Aderké
Tarso Emissi
3,376 m
Ouri

Pic Toussidé
3,315 m
Yebbi-Bou
Aozi
Ma'tan as Sarra

Zouar
Tarso Tieroko
2,910 m

NIGER
Ténéré
Aney
Achegour
Dirkou
Séguédine
Tarso Ahon
3,325 m
Bini Erdi

Emi Koussi
3,415 m
Gouro

Bilma
Kanie
C H A D
Ounianga Kebir
Ounianga Sérir

Erg du Ténéré
Grand Erg de Bilma
Zoo Baba
Fachi
DIFFA
Tigui
Oyo-Yeska
Mataga
Borkou
Kaortchi
Erdi-Ma

ALGERIA
ILLIZI
Ténéré du Tafassasset

Al Jabal al Akhdar
CYRENE
APOLLONIA
Ra's al Hilāl
Al Ḩanīyah
PTOLEMAIS
Tūkrah
Al Bayḑā'
Shaḩḩāt
872 m
Darnah
Martūbah
Ra's at Tin
Al Marj
Abyār
Marāwah
At Tamimi
Al Qubbah
Khalīj al Bumbah
Taknis
Zāwiyat al Mukhaylī
Benghāzī
Madīnat al Abyār
BENINA
Ajdābiyā
Al Maqrūn
Sulūq
Qaminis
Qaryat az Zuwaytinah
Sabkhat ash Shuwayrib
Birak Mukhtara
Ayn Dahl
'Ayn al Ghazālah
Al 'Adam
Tobruk
QUSAYR AD DA
Tuḩruq
Al Jaght
Al Qatrūn
Al Ghrayfah
Al Harash
Bi'r al Harash
Bi'r al Ghanam

Cyrenaica

Libya

Ma'tan Bishrah

S A H A R A

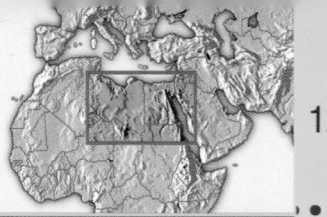

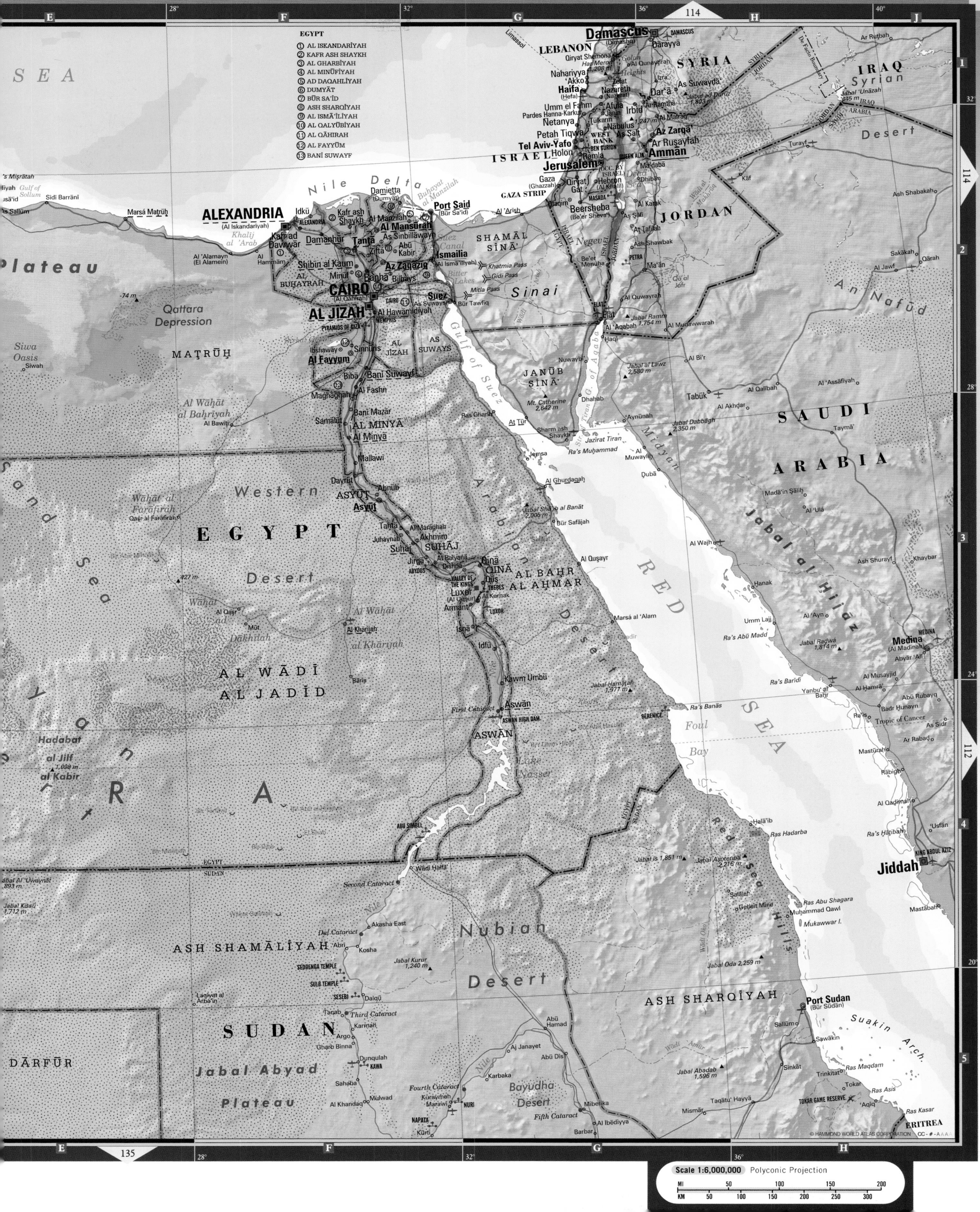

Scale 1:6,000,000 Polyconic Projection

The Sahara, the world's largest desert, covers some 9.1 million square km. It is 4,670 km long and 1,760 km wide. Evidence found in the Tassili-n-Ajjer mountains in Algeria shows that the region was once covered by lush green vegetation. Prehistoric drawings feature images of elephants, buffalo, hippos and crocodiles. The earliest of the more than 1,000 rock drawings are 8,000 years old. Fewer species are depicted as the drawings grow more recent. Thus the course of the Sahara's transformation into a desert can be traced from drawing to drawing. Temperatures of up to 136° F have been recorded in the region.

MOROCCO is divided into 7 non-administrative regions shown here. Scale does not permit showing the boundaries and names of Morocco's provinces and prefectures.

Population

■ Over 2,000,000	⊛ 500,000 - 999,999	⊙ 100,000 - 249,999	○ 10,000 - 29,999
▪ 1,000,000 - 1,999,999	⊜ 250,000 - 499,999	⊚ 30,000 - 99,999	○ Under 10,000

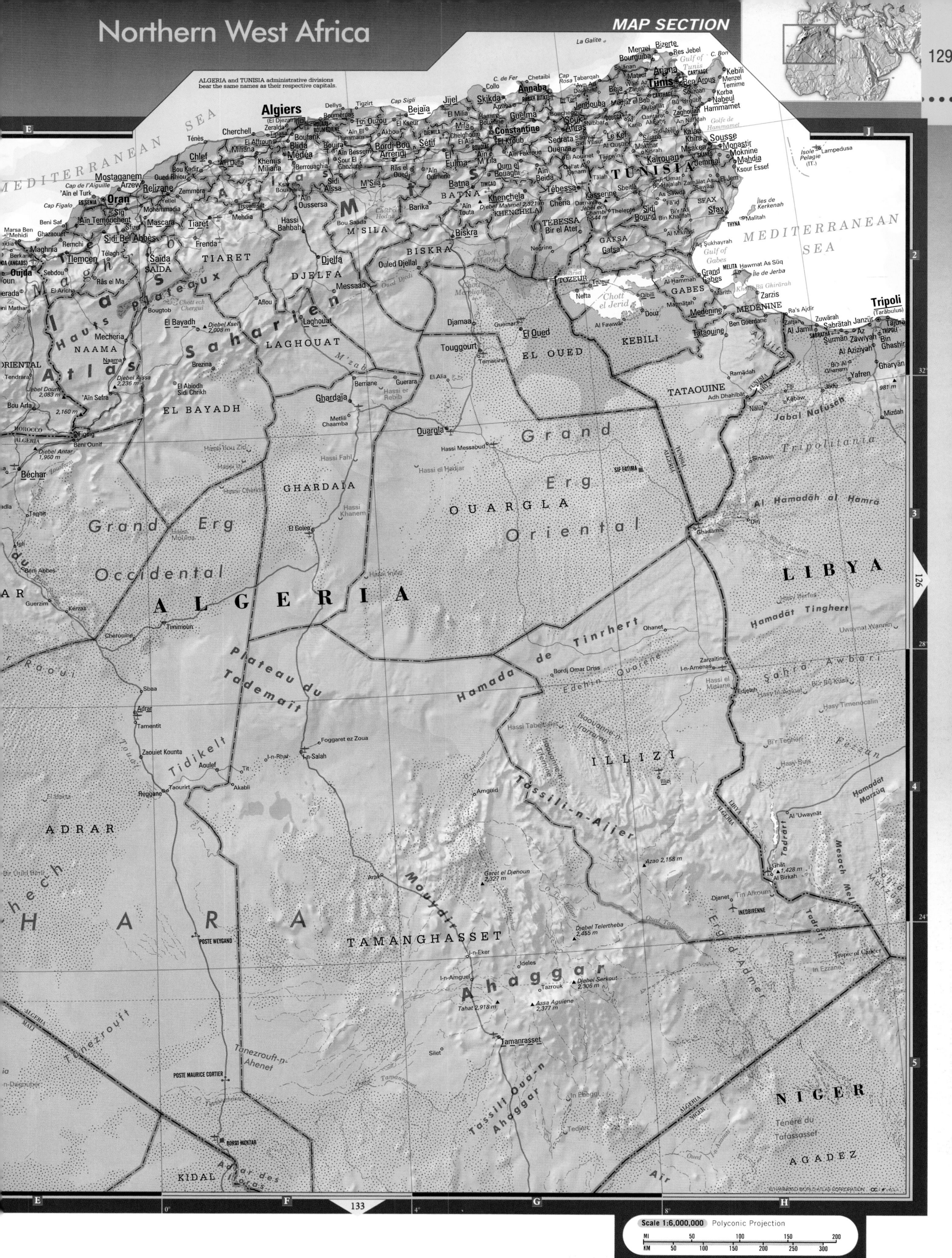

Scale 1:6,000,000 Polyconic Projection

MI   50   100   150   200
KM   50   100   150   200   250   300

MAP SECTION
Northern Morocco
Algeria, Tunisia

The Atlas Mountains of northern Africa are a protective wall that shields northern Morocco, Algeria, and Tunisia against encroachment by the desert to the south. Moist air from the sea brings welcome rains. Many of the ports along the coast lie in the lee of capes formed by steeply sloping mountain ridges that jut sharply into the sea.

Upper panel (Northern Morocco / Spain / western Algeria)

ATLANTIC OCEAN

MEDITERRANEAN SEA

SPAIN
- Barbate
- Cabo Trafalgar
- Los Barrios
- San Roque
- La Línea
- Gibraltar (U.K.)
- Europa Pt.
- Algeciras
- Tarifa
- NORTH FRONT

Alborán (SP.)

Málaga
Almería

- Pte. Malabata
- Cap Spartel
- Ceuta (SP.)
- Punta Almina
- Martil
- M'diq
- Tangier (Tanger)
- TANGIER (IBN BATOUTA)
- Tétouan
- TETOUAN
- Asilah
- Larache
- LIXUS
- LARACHE
- Ksar el Kebir
- Derdara
- Chefchaouene
- CHECHAOUENE
- Bab Taza
- Jebel Bouhalla 2,170 m
- Beni Ensar
- Penón de Vélez de la Gomera (SP.)
- Peñon de Al Hoceima (SP.)
- Al Hoceima (CHERIF AL IDRISSI)
- AL HOCEIMA
- Melilla (SP.)
- Islas Chafarinas (SP.)
- Cap des Trois Fourches
- Cap Noé
- Nador
- NADOR
- Beni Saf
- Cap Figalo
- Cap Falcon
- Oran
- ORAN
- ES SENIA INT'L
- Sig
- MASCARA
- Golfe d'Arzew
- Cap de l'Aiguille
- 'Aïn el Turk
- Arzew
- Cap Ferrat
- AÏN TEMOUCHENT
- 'Aïn Temouchent
- Sfizef
- Sidi Bel Abbès
- SIDI BEL ABBÈS
- Zelouane
- Beni Bouayach
- Zaïo
- Berkaoe
- Saïda
- Marsa Ben Mehidi
- Ahfir
- Maghnia
- Ghazaouet
- Remchi
- Tlemcen
- TLEMCEN
- Télagh
- SAÏDA
- Midar
- Targuist
- Ketama
- Taher Souk
- Aknoul
- Msoun
- OUJDA (ANGADS)
- Oujda
- OUJDA
- El Aioun
- Taourirt
- Jerada 1,726 m
- El Aricha
- Râs e! Ma
- Sebdou
- Barrage Mohammed V
- BARRAGE MOHAMMED V

MOROCCO
1. MOHAMMADIA-ZNATA
2. BEN MSIK-SIDI OTHMANE
3. CASABLANCA-ANFA
4. AÏN CHOK-HAY MOHAMMADIA

- Ouezzane
- KÉNITRA
- Sidi Kacem
- SIDI KACEM
- Mechra Bel Ksiri
- Morhrane
- Douar el Caïd el Gueddara
- Sidi Yahia el Gharb
- Mehdiya-Plage
- Kénitra
- KÉNITRA (RABAT SALE)
- Sidi Bou Knadel
- Salé
- Rabat
- RABAT (SALE)
- SALE
- Sidi Allal el Bahraoui
- SKHIRAT
- TEMARA
- Mohammedia
- Bouznika
- Ben Slimane
- BEN CENTRE
- CASABLANCA
- (Dar el Beida)
- Douar Toulal
- Meknès
- MEKNÈS
- FÈS (SAISS)
- Fès
- Sefrou
- El Menzel
- Bir Tamtam
- Taza
- TAZA
- Jebel Tazekka 1,980 m
- Jebel Bou Naceur 3,340 m
- BOULEMANE
- FIGUIG
- NAAMA
- Djebel-Amrag 1,225 m
- Mecheria
- El-Kasdir
- 'Aïn Beni Mathar
- Plateau du Rekkam
- Chott el Rharbi
- Atlas Mts.
- MOROCCO
- ALGERIA
- TAOUNATE
- VOLUBILIS
- BARRAGE IDRISS I
- El Hajeb
- Imouzzèr-Kandar
- Oulad-Rezzag
- Guercif
- Tissa
- Kana Ba Mohammed
- Taounate
- Jebel Boulhalla
- Sidi Lacem
- Dar Bel Hamri
- Tiflet
- Khémisset
- Aïn Taoujdat
- Moulay Idriss
- Moulay Yakoub

Middle panel (Algeria)

MEDITERRANEAN SEA

- Mostaganem
- MOSTAGANEM
- Cap Ferrat
- Cap de l'Aiguille
- Golfe d'Arzew
- Cap Falcon
- 'Aïn el Turk
- Arzew
- Oran
- ORAN
- ES SENIA INT'L
- Sig
- Cap Figalo
- Sebkha d'Oran
- Beni Saf
- AÏN TEMOUCHENT
- 'Aïn Temouchent
- Remchi
- Sidi Bel Abbès
- SIDI BEL ABBÈS
- Télagh
- Tlemcen
- TLEMCEN
- Sebdou
- Mohammadia
- Relizane
- RELIZANE
- Yellel
- Zemmora
- Oued Rhiou
- Oued Kadir
- CHLEF
- Chlef
- 'Aïn Defla
- AÏN DEFLA
- Khemis Miliana
- Miliana
- Ténès
- TIPAZA
- Hadjout
- Tipasa
- Boufarik
- BLIDA
- Blida
- El Affroun
- Médéa
- MÉDÉA
- Berrouaghia
- Cherchell
- Bou Ismaïl
- Zeralda
- 'Aïn Beniau
- Algiers (El Djezaïr)
- ALGER
- 'Aïn Taya
- Bordj el Kiffan
- Boumerdes
- BOUMERDES
- HOUARI BOUMEDIENE INT'L
- Khechna
- Bordj Ménaïel
- Dellys
- Tizirt
- Cap Corbelin
- Cap Sigli
- Cap Carbon
- Bejaïa
- BEJAIA
- 'Aïn El Hammam
- Tizi Ouzou
- TIZI OUZOU
- Akbou
- Bouira
- BOUIRA
- Sour El Ghozlane
- Ksar el Boukhari
- 'Aïn Bessem
- Larba
- Bougara
- BOURJ BOU ARRERIDJ
- Bordj Bou Arreridj
- Ras El Oued
- 'Aïn Oulmene
- Sidi Aïssa
- M'Sila
- M'SILA
- Barika
- Bou Saâda
- Zahrez Chergui
- Chott el Hodna
- SÉTIF
- Sétif
- DJEMILA
- Chelghoum
- El Eulma
- 'Aïn M'Lila
- OUM EL BOUAGHI
- Constantine
- MILA
- MOHAMED BOUDIAF INT'L
- CONST
- Mila
- Hamma-Bouziane
- Jijel
- JIJEL
- El Milia
- Collo
- SKIKDA
- 'Aïn Touta
- Batna
- BATNA
- TIMGAD
- Djebel Mahmel 2,321 m
- Biskra
- BISKRA
- Aurès
- TIARET
- Tiaret
- TISSEMSILT
- Tissemsilt
- Mehdia
- Frenda
- SAÏDA
- Saïda
- 'Aïn Oussersa
- Hassi Bahbah
- DJELFA
- Djelfa
- Aurès Mts
- Atlas Mts
- ALGERIA
- BEJAÏA
- BATNA
- JIJEL

Lower panel (Tunisia / eastern Algeria / Sicily / Malta)

MEDITERRANEAN SEA

- La Galite
- Cap Blanc
- Bizerte
- BIZERTE
- Ra's al Jabel
- Rafraf
- Lago di Bizerte
- Menzel Bourguiba
- Mateur
- Sajānan
- 'Ayn ad Darahim
- Tabarka
- Cap Serrat
- Cap Rosa
- Cap de Garde
- Cap Takouch
- Chetaïbi
- Cap de Fer
- Cap Bougar'oûn
- Collo
- El Milia
- Skikda
- SKIKDA
- Azzaba
- Jijel
- JIJEL
- Mila
- MILA
- Constantine
- CONSTANTINE
- MOHAMED BOUDIAF INT'L
- Chelghoum
- El Aid
- El Kroub
- Sedrata
- GUELMA
- Guelma
- Souk Ahras
- SOUK AHRAS
- Hamma-Bouziane
- 'Aïn M'Lila
- OUM EL BOUAGHI
- Oum El Boughi
- 'Aïn Beida
- 'Aïn Fakroun
- Batna
- BATNA
- TIMGAD
- Djebel Mahmel 2,321 m
- BISKRA
- Khenchela
- KHENCHELA
- Tébessa
- TÉBESSA
- Cheria
- Kasserine
- KASSERINE
- Sbeitla
- Jebel ech Chambi 1,544 m
- Thelepte
- Feriana
- Sidi Bou Zid
- SIDI BOU ZID
- Sidi 'Umar Bū Hajalah
- Zamālat As Sawāsī
- El Jem
- MAHDIA
- Mahdia
- Ksour Essef
- Moknine
- Jemmal
- Msaken
- SKANES INT'L
- MONASTIR
- Monastir
- Sousse
- SOUSSE
- Kalan Kbira
- Kairouan
- KAIROUAN
- Hammamet
- Hammamet
- Nabeul
- NABEUL
- Korba
- Beni Khiar
- Menzel Temime
- Kelibia
- Al Huwwāriyah
- Cap Bon
- Jazīrat Zembra
- Gulf of Tunis
- Golfe di Tunis
- La Marsa
- La Goulette
- CARTHAGE INT'L
- Carthage
- QARTAJANNAH
- Hammam Lif
- Soliman
- Menzel Bou Zelfa
- Grombalia
- Tunis
- TUNIS
- ARIANA
- Ariana
- Ettadhamen
- Douar Hicher
- Oued Ellil
- Mhamdia
- BEN AROUS
- Zaghouan
- ZAGHOUAN
- Uthīnah
- An Nafīdah
- Bū Fishah
- Enfidha
- Zaghouan
- SILIANA
- Siliana
- DOUGGA
- Gafour
- Nibbar
- El Fahs
- Bir Mcharga
- El Aroussa
- Medjez el Bab
- BEJA
- Béja
- Oued Zarga
- Testour
- Wadi Az Zarqā
- Al Fananah
- JENDOUBA
- Jendouba
- Ghardimaou
- Ghār Ad Dima
- Bou Salem
- Boucheghouf
- LE KEF
- Le Kef
- Ouenza
- 'Aïn Beida
- Tajūrīn
- Dahmani
- Kālat es Senam
- Al 'Aouinet
- Jerissa
- El Aouinet
- Al Quşūr
- Makthar
- Kisrāh
- Tālah
- Hāffir Al 'Uyūn
- Qartarat Qantarat
- Sidi Nāji
- Sbeitla
- ALGERIA
- TUNISIA
- Dorsal
- Mts de Tébessa
- Aurès Mts
- 'Aïn Fakroun
- Sidi Bou Zid

Sicily (IT.)
- Eraclea Minoa
- Agrigento
- Canicatti
- Favara
- Ravanusa
- Porto Empedocle
- Palma di Montechiaro
- Licata
- Gela
- Golfo di Gela
- Strait of Sicily
- Trapani
- Capigliano

- Pantelleria
- I. di Pantelleria (IT.)

MALTA
- Gozo
- Ras San Dimitri
- Rabat (Victoria)
- MALTA
- Linosa
- I. di Linosa (IT.)
- Isole di Pelagie (IT.)
- Lampedusa
- Isola di Lampedusa

ITALY / MALTA

ITALY / TUN.

Legend

Height
m. / ft.
6000 / 19700
4000 / 13000
2000 / 6500
1500 / 5000
1000 / 3300
500 / 1600
200 / 700
0
200 / 700
500 / 1600
1000 / 3300
2000 / 6500
3000 / 9800
4000 / 13000
5000 / 16400
6000 / 19700
m. / ft.

Depth

Population
- ■ Over 2,000,000
- ● 1,000,000 - 1,999,999
- ⊛ 500,000 - 999,999
- ⊛ 250,000 - 499,999
- ⊙ 100,000 - 249,999
- ○ 30,000 - 99,999
- ◦ 10,000 - 29,999
- · Under 10,000

Scale 1:3,000,000 Lambert Conformal Conic Projection

MI 25 50 75 100
KM 25 50 75 100 125 150

© HAMMOND W.A.C.

Measuring 6,671 km from source to mouth, the Nile is the longest river on Earth. Alternating periods of flooding and low water have shaped the lives of people in the region for millennia. A complex network of irrigation canals supplies the fertile Nile Delta with water. The Suez Canal in the northwest serves as a vital link between the Mediterranean and Red seas.

MAP SECTION
Nile River Delta

131

MEDITERRANEAN SEA

Al Burj
Baltim
Rosetta Mouth (Maṣabb Rashīd)
Damietta Mouth (Maṣabb Dumyāṭ)
Rās el-Barr
Buḥayrat al Burullus
'Izbat Jamāṣah al Gharbīyah
Kafr al Battīkh
Damietta (Dumyāṭ)
Izab al Başārītah
Port Said (Būr Sa'īd)
Būr Fu'ād

Rosetta Mouth (Maṣabb Rashīd)
Burj Mughayzil
Rosetta (Rashid)
Khalīj Abū Qīr
CANOPUS
Abū Qīr
Al Ma'mūrah
Idkū
Muṭūbis
Sīdī Sālim
Tidah
KAFR ASH SHAYKH
Al Ḥāmūl
Al Kafr ash Sharqī
DUMYĀṬ
Bilqās Qism Thānī
Fāriskūr
Kafr Sa'd
Mīt Abū Ghālib
Ra's Rahīminah
Buḥayrat al Manzilah

ALEXANDRIA
(Al Iskandarīyah)
ALEXANDRIA
Al Maks
Kafr Salīm
Kawm ash Shaykh Ishū
Buḥayrat Maryūṭ
Al Baslaqūn
Zāwiyat Sīdī Ghāzī
Balaqṭar

Kafr ad Dawwār
Birkat Ghiṭās
Abū Ḥummuṣ
Qāfilah
Ar Rahmānīyah
Shabās ash Shuhadā'
Shabās 'Umayr

Idfīnā
Barrīyat al Uṣayfir
Dayrūṭ
Fuwah
Al Mahmūdīyah
Disūq
Shabās al Milḥ
BUTO
Aryamūn
Sīdī Ghāzī
Al Kawm al Akhḍar

Port Said
BŪR SA'ĪD

Damanhūr
Al Kawm al Akhḍar
Nudaybah
Al Ghayatah
Abū al Maṭāmir
Hawsh 'Īsā
NAUCRATIS
Ṣā al Ḥajar (SAIS)
Ṣafṭ al Mulūk
Urein
Niklā al 'Inab
Basyūn
Damāt
Qutūr
Mahallat Minūf
Birmā
Al Mansūrah
Al Maḥallah al Kubrá
Samannūd
Ajā
AD DAQAHLĪYAH
TALL AR RUB' (MENDES)
TALL TIMAY (THMUIS)

AL BUḤAYRAH
Ad Dilinjāt
Iṭyāy al Bārūd
Shisht al An'ām
AL GHARBĪYAH
Abyār
Kafr az Zayyāt
Ad Daljamūn
Kawm Ḥamādah
Biban
Al Wafā'īyah
Qaṣr Baghdād
Kafr Rabī'
Bābil
Tanṭā
As Sanṭah
Mashalah
Zifta
Mīt Ghamr
Diyarb Najm
Ikwān
Hihyā
ASH SHARQĪYAH
Abū Kabīr
Fāqūs

AL ISKANDARĪYAH
Tala
Tūkh Dalakah
Al Batanūn
Birkat as Sab'
Muṣṭay
Farsīs
Ṣahrajat al Kubrá
Ibnaha
Az Zaqāzīq
Ismailia (Al Ismā'īlīyah)

Naṣr
Ash Shuhadā'
Ibnaha
Quwaysīnā
Shibīn al Kaum
BUBASTIS
Al 'Abbāsah ash Sharqīyah
Al Qurayn
Az Zankalūn
At Tall al Kabīr
PITHOM

AL MINŪFĪYAH
Terenūthis
Minūf
Istanhā
Miṣ ul Qamḥ
Nashwah
Kafr al 'A'id
AL ISMĀ'ĪLĪYAH
Abū Sulṭān

Sīrs al Layyānah
Zāwiyat Razīn
Madīnat as Sādāt
Shanshūr
Al Bājūr
Biltān
Marṣafā
Mashtūl as Sūq
Bilbays
Inshāṣ ar Raml
Az Zawāmil

Great Bitter Lake

Al Khaṭānbah
Ashmūn
Tamalay
Samadūn
Shanṭanūf
Talyā
Ṭūkh
Qāhā
Shibīn al Qanāṭir
Ma'mal
Zufaytat Mashtūl
'Abū Za'bal
Madīnat al 'Āshir min Ramadān
Fā'id
Fenārah

AL JĪZAH
Western Desert
Jabal Ḥadīd 185 m
Jabal Qanṭarah 198 m
Birqash
Burṭus
Al Manṣūrīyah
Awsīm
Berqash
AL QALYŪBĪYAH
Al Qanāṭir al Khayrīyah
Qalyūb
Al Khānkah
Ar Rubayqī
Jabal 'Uwaysīd
Jabal 'Uwaybid 510 m

Shubrā al Khaymah
HELIOPOLIS
CAIRO INT'L
Heliopolis (Miṣr al Jadīdah)
DĀR AL BAYḌĀ

Imbābah
CAIRO
(Al Qāhirah)

AL JĪZAH
PYRAMIDS OF JĪZAH
Abū an Numrūs
Turā
Al Ma'ādī
AL QĀHIRAH
Jabal Abū Shāmah 678 m

ABŪ ṢIR
Al Ḥawāmidīyah
MEMPHIS
Al Badrashayn
Al Ma'ṣarah
Hulwān

QAHSHŪR
Dahshūr
At Tabbīn
Al Minyā
Jabal Sadd an Na'ām 622 m
Arabian Desert
AS SUWAYS
Jabal Ruzzah 204 m
Qārat ar Raml 200 m
Jabal Abū Ghuṣūn

MAṬRŪḤ
Jabal Riṣṣū 217 m
Barnasht
Al 'Ayyāṭ
Al Ḥawṣ
AL JĪZAH
Naqb Ghul 861 m
Ayn Sukhnah

MADĪNET DIMAI (SOCNOPAIOS)
KWAM AWSHIM (KARANIS)
Al Lisht
Aṣ Ṣaff
As Su'ūdīyah
Al Widy
Kulet el-Qrein 897 m

Birkat Qārūn (-45 m)
EL-HAMMAM
Sanhūr
Az Zarbī
KWAM AL HAMĀM (PHILADELPHIA)
Ṭāmīyah
Ar Rawḍah
Maydūm
Al Qibābāt
Atfīḥ
Jabal al Jalālah al Baḥrīyah

Qaṣr Qārūn
DIONYSIAS
PHILOTERIS
KHARABAT HERIT (THEADELPHIA)
Ash Shawāshinah
Ibshawāy
Sinnūris
Maṭīr Ṭārīs
Saylah
Al Wāsiṭah
Al Burumbul
Wādī Rīshrāsh

Qārat Jahannam 224 m
AL FAYYŪM
CROCODILOPOLIS
An Nazlat
Al 'Ajamīyīn
Al Fayyum
Ḥawwārat al Maqṭa'
Al Maymūn
Ishmant
BANĪ SUWAYF
Gebel Ṭarbūl Abū Khashīrāt 310 m
Bi'r Burayd
El-Tarabīn 994 m

Al Minyā
Al Lāhūn
AL FAYYŪM
Qalamshāh
Dandīl
Būsh
AshShanāwīyah
Bani Suwayf
AL BAḤR AL AḤMAR
Al Gharaq as Sulṭānī
Tuṭūn
HERACLEOPOLIS MAGNA
TEBTUNIS
Ihnāsīyah al Madīnah
Tizmant ash Sharqīyah
Bayāḍ an Naṣārā

127

Height	
m. ft.	
6000	19700
4000	13000
2000	6500
1500	5000
1000	3300
500	1600
200	700
0	-
200	700
1000	3300
2000	6500
3000	9800
4000	13000
5000	16400
6000	19700
m. ft.	
Depth	

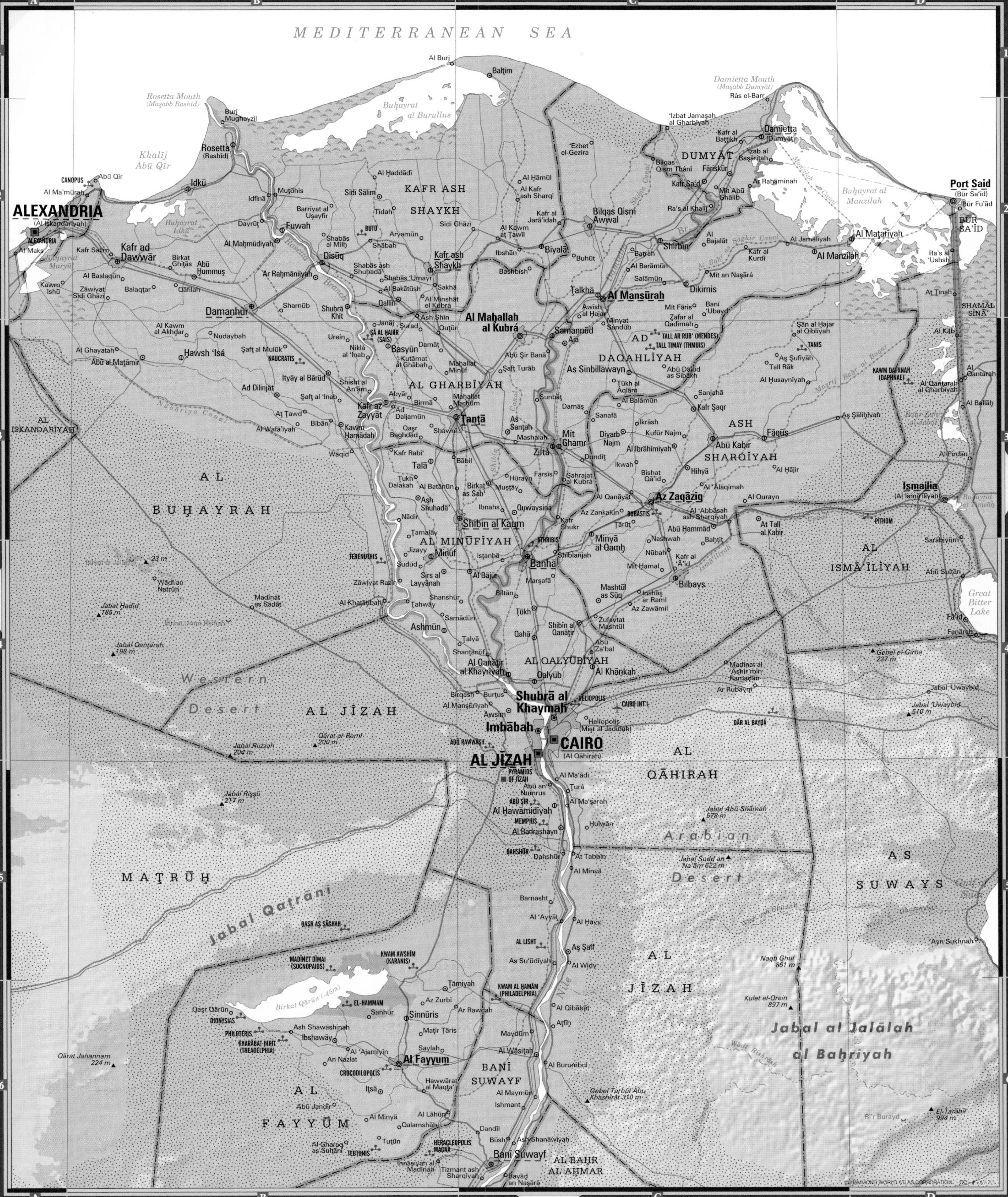

Population
- ■ Over 2,000,000
- ● 500,000 - 999,999
- ● 100,000 - 249,999
- ○ 10,000 - 29,999
- ■ 1,000,000 - 1,999,999
- ◉ 250,000 - 499,999
- ⊙ 30,000 - 99,999
- ○ Under 10,000

Scale 1:1,000,000 Lambert Conformal Conic Projection

MI 10 20 30
KM 10 20 30 40

The course of the Niger could hardly be more unusual. The river descends from the Loma Mountains on the border between Sierra Leone and Guinea, but rather than flowing directly to the Atlantic, it pursues a circuitous route through Mali, Niger, and Nigeria before finally emptying into the Gulf of Guinea. With a length of 4,184 km, it is the third-longest river in Africa. The Niger deposits massive quantities of sediment in its wide delta (20,000 square km), which lies above rich reserves of oil and natural gas. Nearly 90 percent Nigeria's income comes from petroleum exports.

Height

m. / ft.
6000 / 19700
4000 / 13000
2000 / 6500
1500 / 5000
1000 / 3300
500 / 1600
200 / 700
0

Depth

m. / ft.
200 / 700
500 / 1600
1000 / 3300
2000 / 6500
3000 / 9800
4000 / 13000
5000 / 16400
6000 / 19700

ATLANTIC OCEAN

Population

Symbol	Range	Symbol	Range
Over 2,000,000		500,000 - 999,999	
1,000,000 - 1,999,999		250,000 - 499,999	
100,000 - 249,999		10,000 - 29,999	
30,000 - 99,999		Under 10,000	

© HAMMOND WORLD ATLAS CORPORATION

Southern West Africa

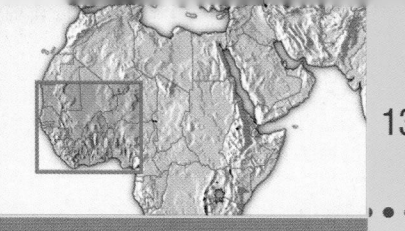

Like the bow of a ship, the Mandara Mountains of northern Cameroon extend into the arid plains of Nigeria and the swamplands of Chad. The wooded highland savannah is relatively fertile, as rainfall from May to November is sufficient to support agriculture. Some of this water flows into the riverless depression of the Chad Basin and Lake Chad, the large, shallow lake at its center. Lake Chad is one of the few fresh water reservoirs along the edge of the Sahel region, which encompasses substantial parts of Chad, Niger, and Sudan.

Height
m. / ft.
6000 / 19700
4000 / 13000
2000 / 6500
1500 / 5000
1000 / 3300
500 / 1600
200 / 700
0
200 / 700
500 / 1600
1000 / 3300
2000 / 6500
3000 / 9800
4000 / 13000
5000 / 16400
6000 / 19700
m. / ft.
Depth

Population
▪ Over 2,000,000
▫ 1,000,000 - 1,999,999
⊙ 500,000 - 999,999
⊙ 250,000 - 499,999
⊙ 100,000 - 249,999
⊙ 30,000 - 99,999
⊙ 10,000 - 29,999
∘ Under 10,000

North Central Africa

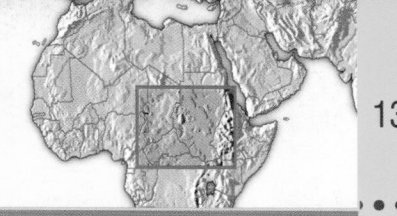

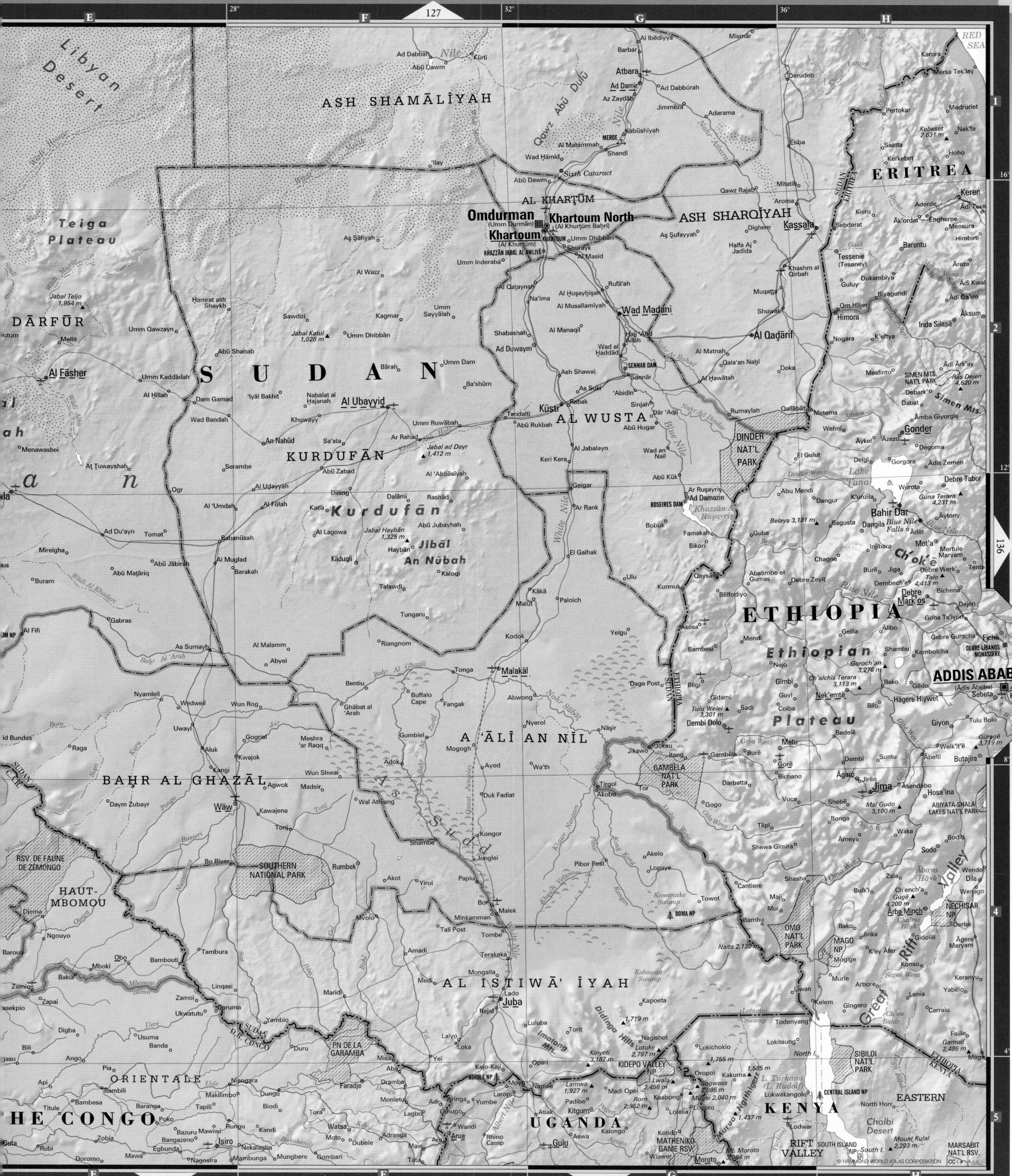

ERITREA

RED SEA

ASH SHAMĀLĪYAH

Libyan Desert

Teiga Plateau

DĀRFŪR

S U D A N

AL KHARṬŪM
Omdurman (Umm Durmān)
Khartoum North (Al Khurṭūm Baḥrī)
Khartoum (Al Khurṭūm)

ASH SHARQĪYAH

Kassala

Wad Madani

Al Qaḍārif

KURDUFĀN

Kurdufān

Al Ubayyid

Jibāl An Nūbah

AL WUSTA

DINDER NAT'L PARK

ETHIOPIA

Ethiopian Plateau

ADDIS ABABA (Ādīs Ābebā)

Lake Tana

Bahir Dar

Gonder

A 'ĀLĪ AN NĪL

Malakāl

BAHR AL GHAZĀL

Wāw

GAMBELA NAT'L PARK

Jima

AL ISTIWĀ' ĪYAH

Juba

SOUTHERN NATIONAL PARK

BOMA NP

OMO NAT'L PARK

MAGO NP

NECHISAR NP

HAUT-MBOMOU

RSV. DE FAUNE DE ZÉMONGO

PN DE LA GARAMBA

ORIENTALE

THE CONGO

UGANDA

Gulu

KENYA

EASTERN

Chalbi Desert

RIFT VALLEY

SIBILOI NAT'L PARK

Great Rift Valley

Scale 1:6,000,000   Polyconic Projection

MI   50   100   150   200
KM   50   100   150   200   250   300

© HAMMOND WORLD ATLAS CORPORATION

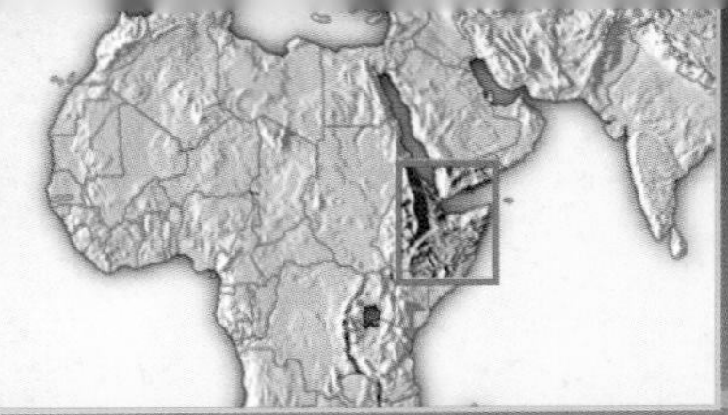

Ethiopia, Somalia

A hot spot beneath the Afar Depression in eastern Ethiopia gave birth to two young seas some 30 million years ago: the Gulf of Aden and the Red Sea. The volcanic islands in the Bab el Mandeb Strait bear witness to the geological forces that caused Africa and the Arabian Peninsula to drift apart. As they continue to diverge, the Red Sea is gradually becoming an ocean.

112

SAUDI ARABIA

RED SEA

YEMEN

Hadhramaut

ERITREA

Sanaa (San'a)

Aden ('Adan)

Gulf of Aden

DJIBOUTI

Djibouti

ADDIS ABABA (Adis Abeba)

ETHIOPIA

Ogadēn

SOMALIA

Hargeysa

Haud

Nugaaleed Valley

INDIAN OCEAN

NORTH EASTERN

EASTERN

KENYA

Mogadishu (Muqdisho)

© HAMMOND WORLD ATLAS CORPORATION

Height

m. / ft.
6000 / 19700
4000 / 13000
2000 / 6500
1500 / 5000
1000 / 3300
500 / 1600
200 / 700
0
200 / 700
500 / 1600
1000 / 3300
2000 / 6500
3000 / 9800
4000 / 13000
5000 / 16400
6000 / 19700
m. / ft.

Depth

Population
- Over 2,000,000
- 1,000,000 - 1,999,999
- 500,000 - 999,999
- 250,000 - 499,999
- 100,000 - 249,999
- 30,000 - 99,999
- 10,000 - 29,999
- Under 10,000

Scale 1:6,000,000   Polyconic Projection

MI   50   100   150   200
KM   50   100   150   200   250   300

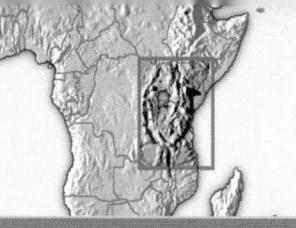

The East Africa Rift System runs from Ethiopia to Mozambique and splits into two branches at Lake Victoria. The many lakes in the region bear witness to plate rift that began some 40 million years ago and still in progress today. Its margin is lined by some of the highest mountains on the continent - most of them volcanoes like Kilimanjaro (5,895 m).

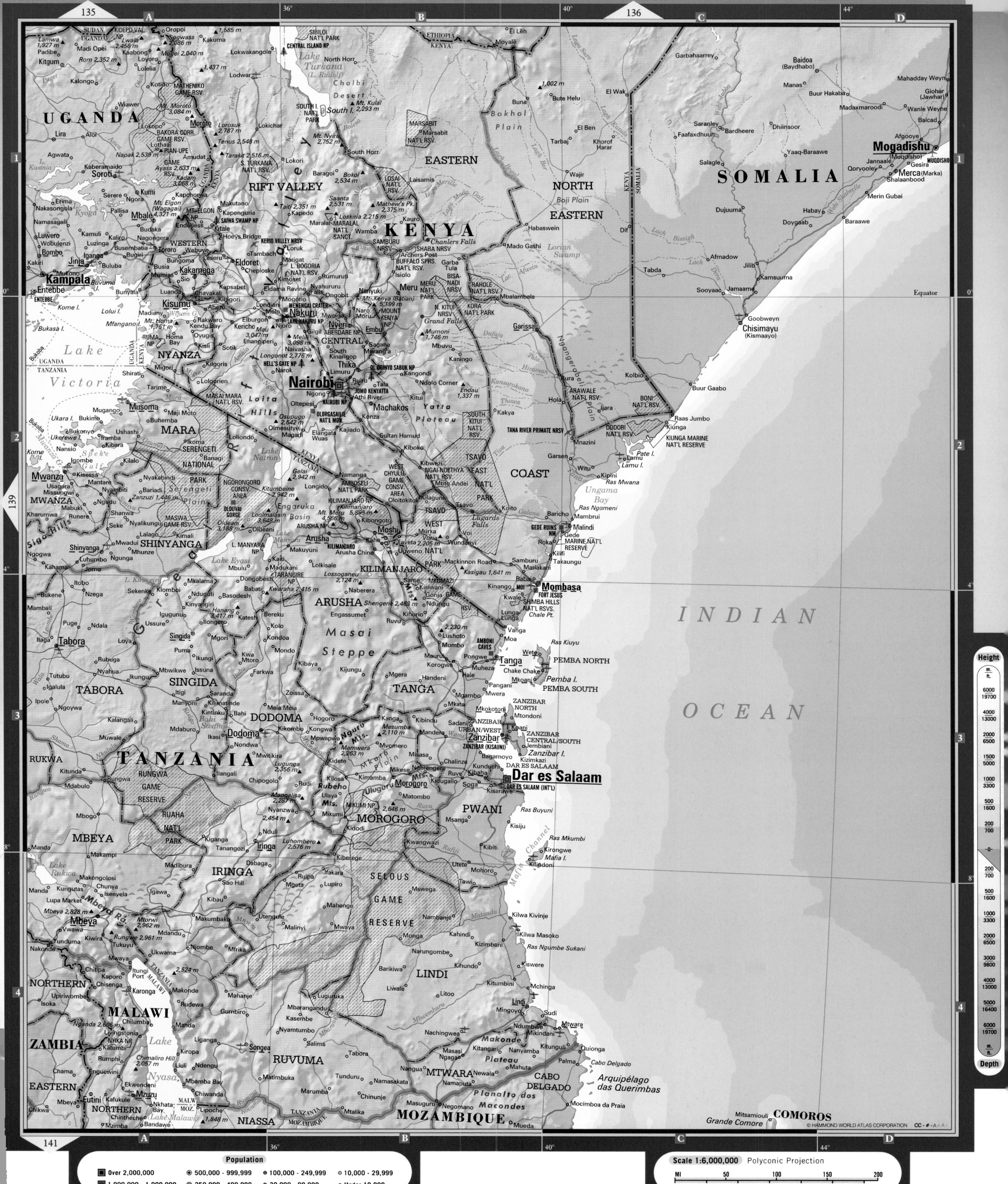

The Congo Basin encompasses the largest contiguous, evergreen rain forest in Africa. It lies between 300 and 450 meters above sea level and is encircled by high marginal ridges.

The Congo River cuts through this barrier in the west in a series of more than 30 waterfalls and rapids. This energy is harnessed by hydroelectric power plants. The Democratic Republic of The Congo (formerly Zaire) covers

NIGERIA

Niger Delta
Bight of Biafra
Gulf of Guinea

EQUATORIAL GUINEA

SÃO TOMÉ AND PRÍNCIPE

CAMEROON

CENTRAL AFRICAN REPUBLIC

Douala
Yaoundé

EQUATORIAL GUINEA
Bata

GABON

Libreville

Port-Gentil

CONGO

Brazzaville
KINSHASA

Pointe-Noire

CABINDA (ANGOLA)

Matadi
Boma

ZAIRE

BANDUNDU

ATLANTIC OCEAN

Luanda

ANGOLA

MALANJE

LUNDA NORT

BIÉ

Height
m. / ft.
6000 / 19700
4000 / 13000
2000 / 6500
1500 / 5000
1000 / 3300
500 / 1600
200 / 700
-0-
200 / 700
500 / 1600
1000 / 3300
2000 / 6500
3000 / 9800
4000 / 13000
5000 / 16400
6000 / 19700
m. / ft.
Depth

Population
■ Over 2,000,000
□ 1,000,000 - 1,999,999
● 500,000 - 999,999
◉ 250,000 - 499,999
● 100,000 - 249,999
○ 30,000 - 99,999
● 10,000 - 29,999
○ Under 10,000

2.3 million square km of territory and occupies most of the Congo Basin. An abundance of arable land and mineral resources make it potentially one of the richest countries of Africa. It is, however, one of the poorest.

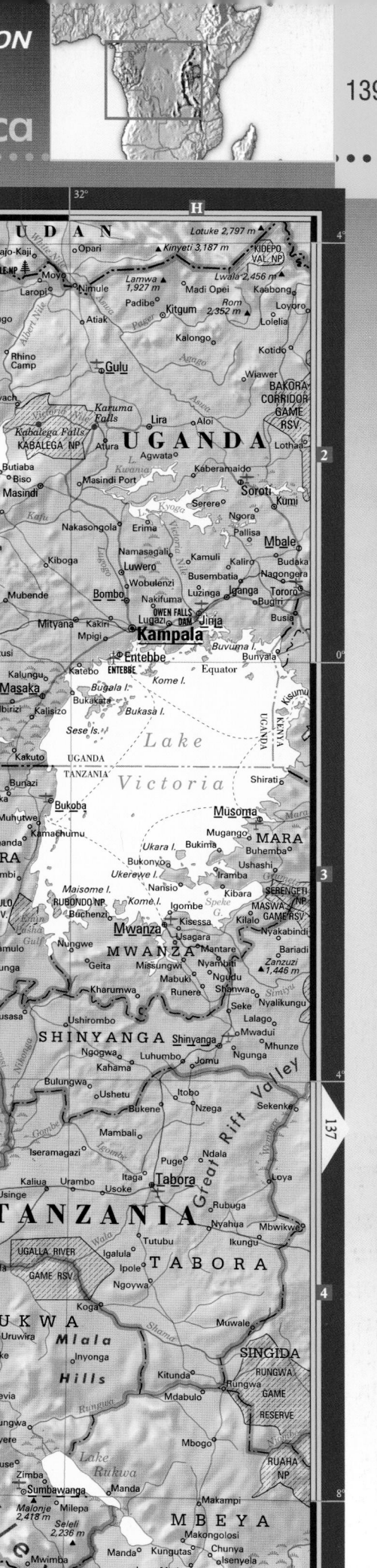

Scale 1:6,000,000   Polyconic Projection

One of the most arid regions of the world is the Namib, a desert that stretches for more than 2,000 km along the western coast of Africa from Angola to South Africa. Annual precipitation here rarely exceeds 50 mm. The desert owes its existence to the cold Benguela Current and cool prevailing winds that carry very little moisture. The Namib is a diverse desert landscape. A prominent topographic feature is the Namib-Naukluft Park south from Walvis Bay, which encompasses some 34,000 square km of sand dunes with an abundant array of forms. Some star dunes here rise to heights of 550 meters.

MAP SECTION

South Central Africa

141

139   139

137   137

143   143

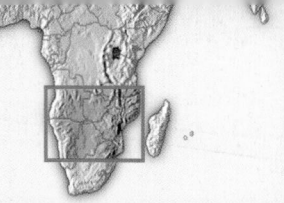

Scale 1:6,000,000 Polyconic Projection

© HAMMOND WORLD ATLAS CORPORATION

Extending from northern South Africa to the Cape Provinces, the Drakensberg mountains are among the most imposing and beautiful natural features of South Africa. Known as the Great Escarpment, the range comprises rock of different hardness that has been selectively eroded into impressive landscape formations. Billions of years old, the continental plate holds rich ore and diamond deposits that are intensively mined today. Madagascar – separated from the African continent – is the home of many plant and animal species that have developed in isolation and are found nowhere else in the world.

Height

m. ft.	
6000 19700	
4000 13000	
2000 6500	
1500 5000	
1000 3300	
200 700	
0	
200 700	
500 1600	
1000 3300	
2000 6500	
3000 9800	
4000 13000	
5000 16400	
6000 19700	
m. ft.	

Depth

Population

■ Over 2,000,000	◉ 500,000 - 999,999	◉ 100,000 - 249,999	○ 10,000 - 29,999
▣ 1,000,000 - 1,999,999	◉ 250,000 - 499,999	◉ 30,000 - 99,999	○ Under 10,000

© HAMMOND W.A.C. CD - 1141 - A A A

© HAMMOND W.A.C. CD - 1142 - A A A

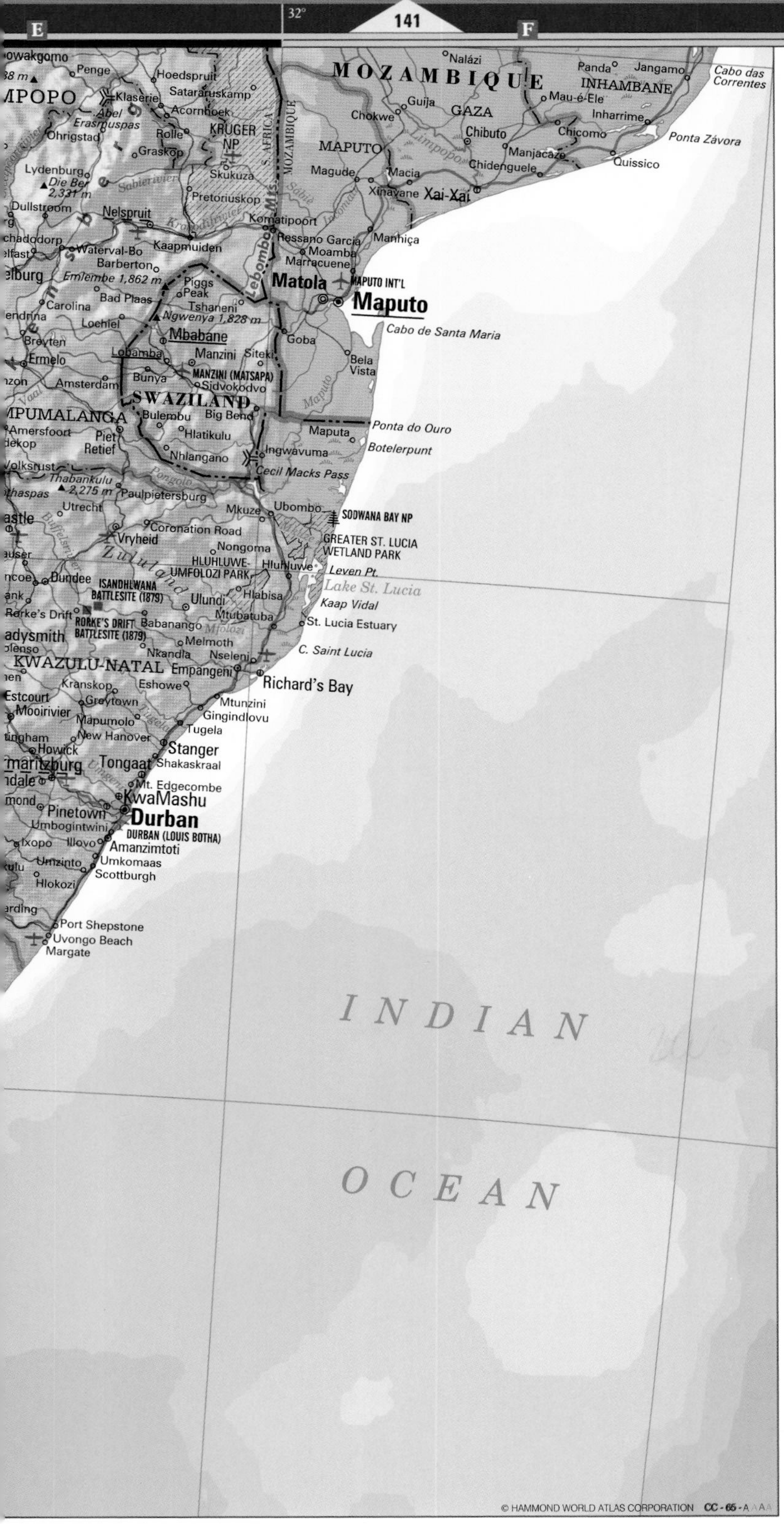

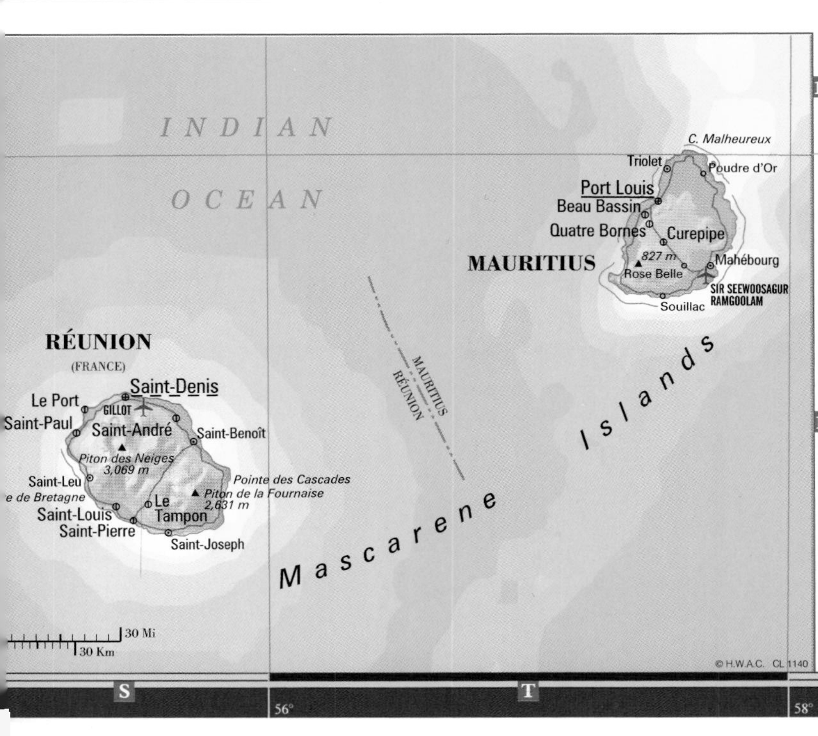

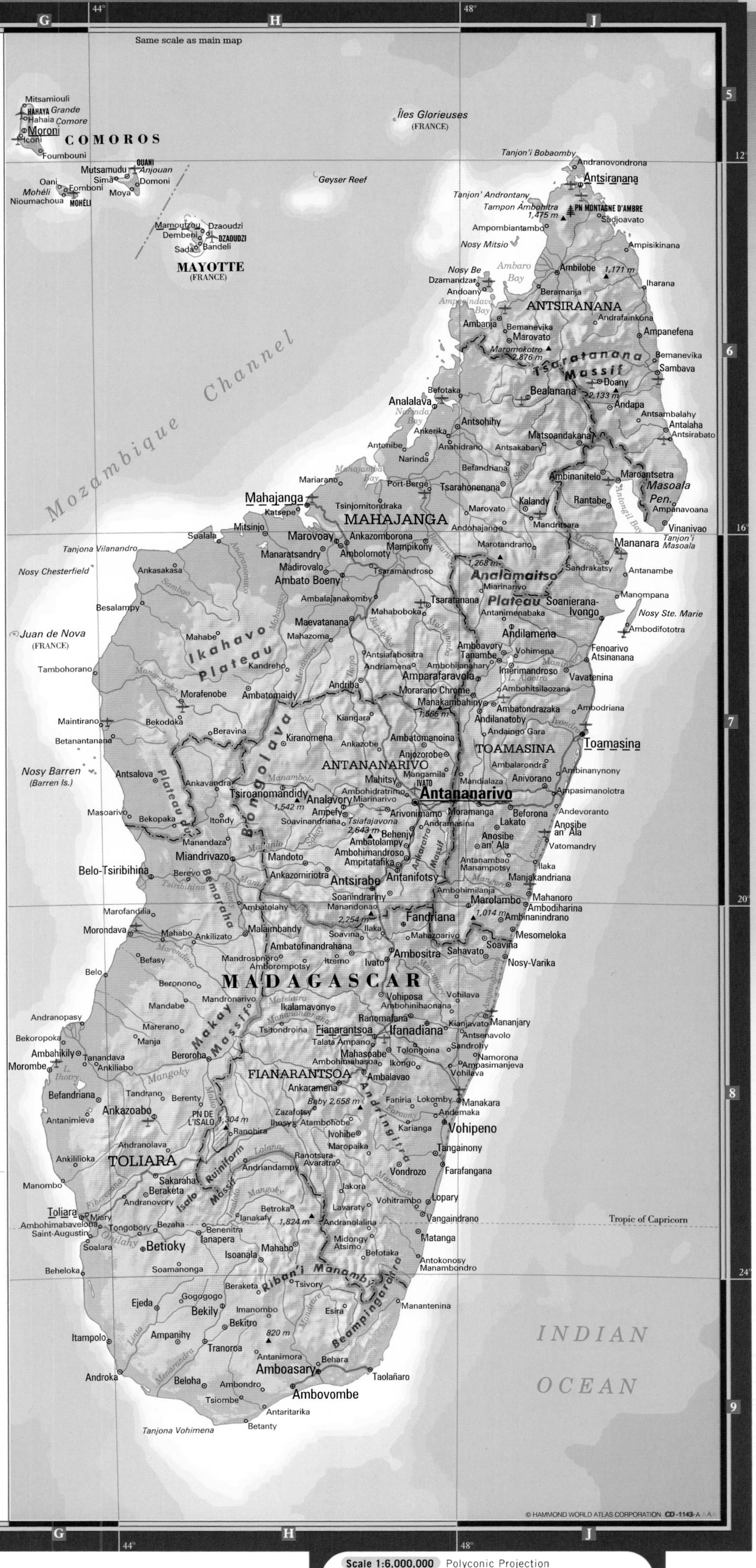

Same scale as main map

141

© HAMMOND WORLD ATLAS CORPORATION   CC-65

© HAMMOND WORLD ATLAS CORPORATION   CD-1143-A

H.W.A.C. CL 1140

Scale 1:6,000,000   Polyconic Projection

| MI | 50 | 100 | 150 | 200 |
| KM | 50 | 100 | 150 | 200 | 250 | 300 |

30 Mi
30 Km

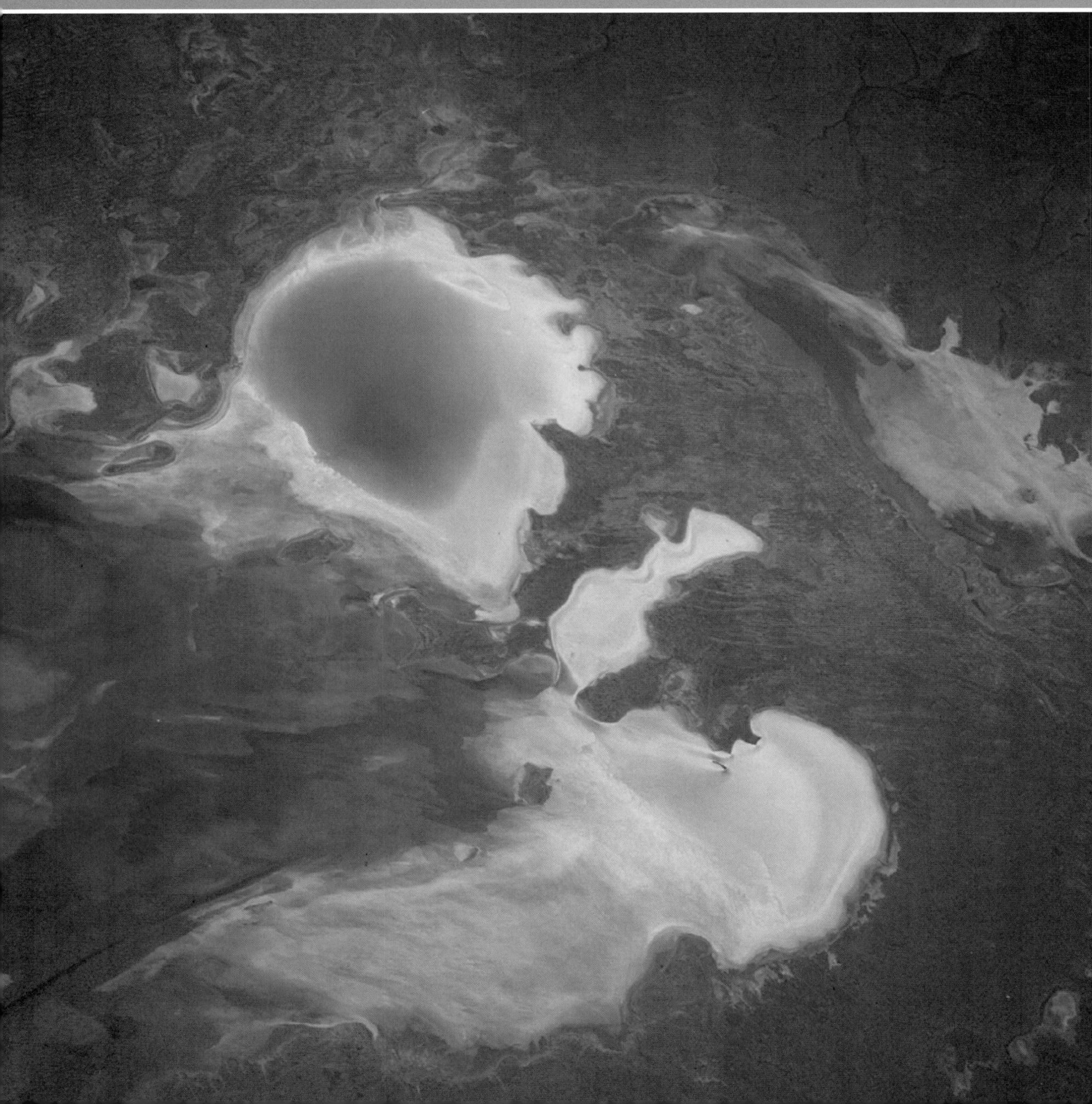

Lake Eyre, located at the edge of the Victoria Desert, is the largest lake basin on the continent (8,900 square km), although it fills with water only after heavy rains. For most of the year, the bed of this salt lake is dry. With depths of up to 16 m below sea level, it is the lowest point in Australia. The much larger northern basin shown on the left (the highly reflective areas) comprises two lakebeds. The western lobe is Belt Bay, and the eastern lobe is Madigan Bay. The coloration, especially of Madigan Bay, indicates that there was some water in this lobe at the time the image was taken.

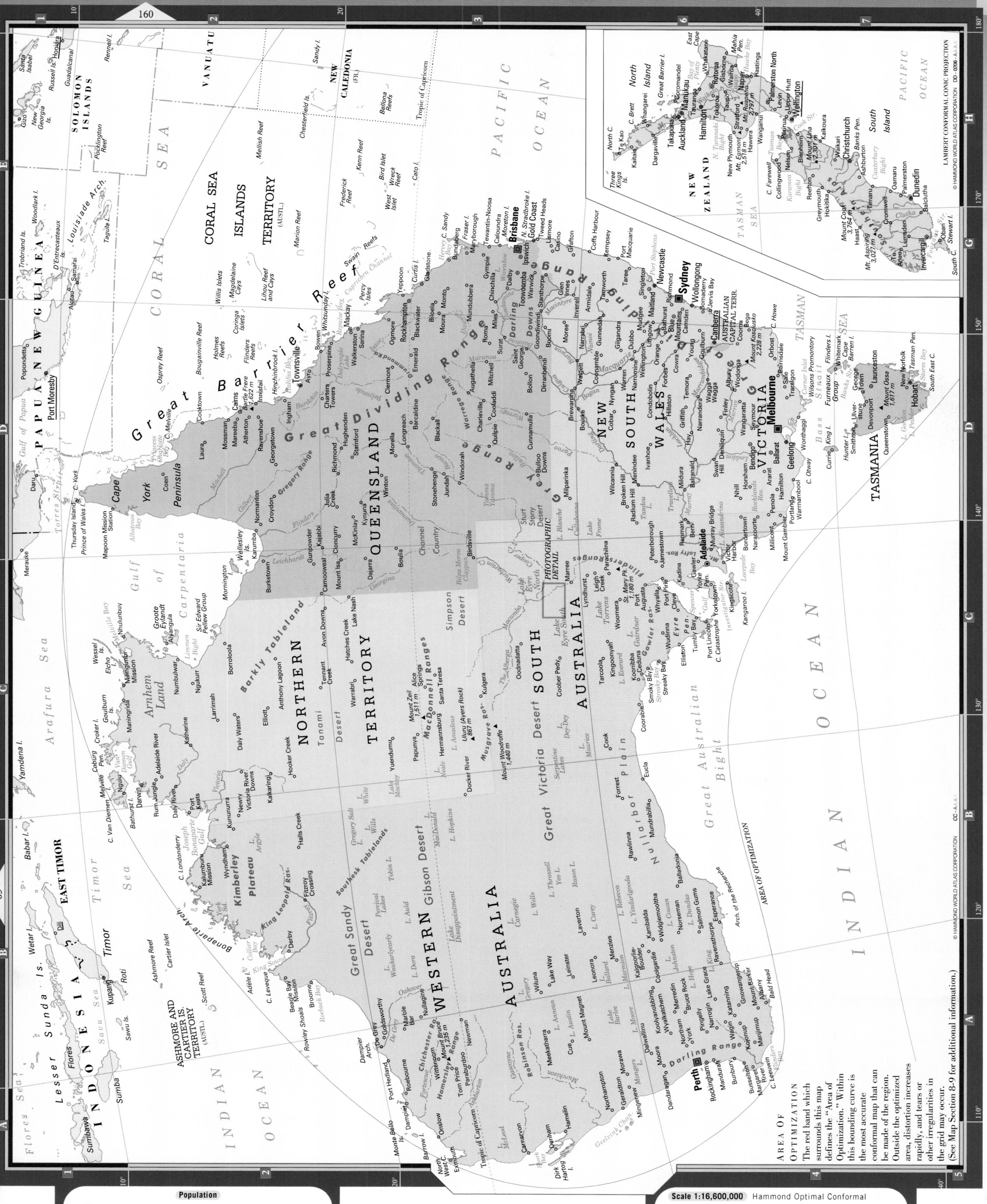

AREA OF OPTIMIZATION

The red band which surrounds this map defines the "Area of Optimization." Within this bounding curve is the most accurate conformal map that can be made of the region. Outside the optimized area, distortion increases rapidly, and tears or other irregularities in the grid may occur.

(See Map Section 8-9 for additional information.)

Population

- ■ Over 2,000,000
- ▢ 1,000,000 - 1,999,999
- ● 500,000 - 999,999
- ● 100,000 - 499,999
- ◦ 50,000 - 99,999
- ◦ Under 50,000

Scale 1:16,600,000 Hammond Optimal Conformal

MI 125 250 375 500
KM 125 250 500 625 750

LAMBERT CONFORMAL CONIC PROJECTION

© HAMMOND WORLD ATLAS CORPORATION

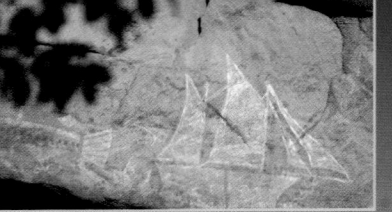

UNESCO Protects World Cultural Heritage Sites

World Heritage Sites in Australia and New Zealand

Text continued from page 120 - UNESCO World Cultural Heritage Sites of Africa

UNESCO's World Heritage mission is to:

- Encourage countries to sign the World Heritage Convention and to ensure the protection of their natural and cultural heritage;

- Encourage States Parties to the Convention to nominate sites within their national territory for inclusion on the World Heritage List;

- Encourage States Parties to establish management plans and set up reporting systems on the state of conservation of their World Heritage sites;

- Help States Parties safeguard World Heritage properties by providing technical assistance and professional training;

- Provide emergency assistance for World Heritage sites in immediate danger;

- Support States Parties' public awareness-building activities for World Heritage conservation;

- Encourage participation of the local population in the preservation of their cultural and natural heritage;

- Encourage international cooperation in the conservation of our world's cultural and natural heritage.

Text continues on page 164 - UNESCO World Cultural Heritage Sites of North America

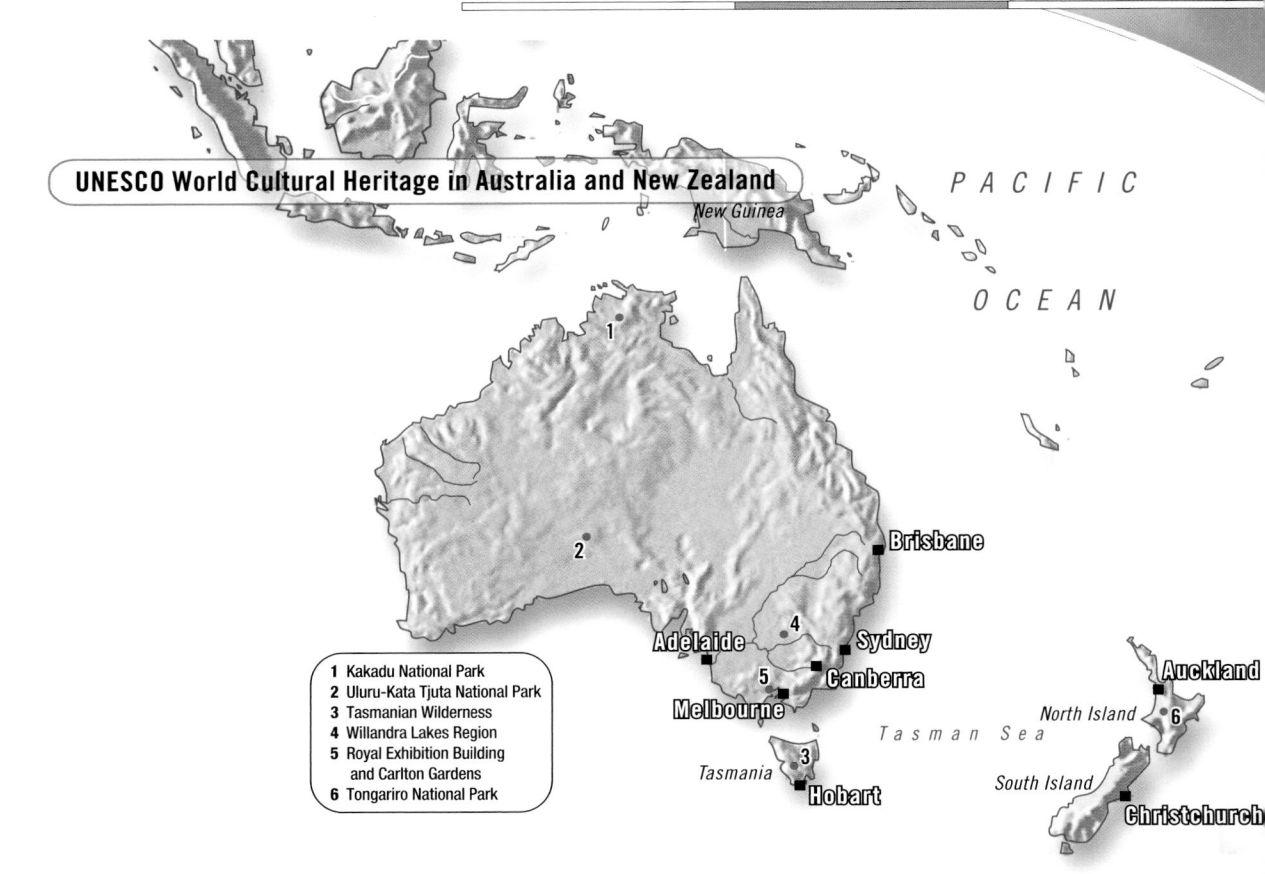

UNESCO World Cultural Heritage in Australia and New Zealand

1 Kakadu National Park
2 Uluru-Kata Tjuta National Park
3 Tasmanian Wilderness
4 Willandra Lakes Region
5 Royal Exhibition Building and Carlton Gardens
6 Tongariro National Park

Spiritual Region

The mountains at the heart of the Tongariro National Park, North Island, **New Zealand (6)**, have cultural and religious significance for the Maori people and symbolize the spiritual links between this community and its environment. The park has active and extinct volcanoes, a diverse range of ecosystems and some spectacular landscapes. It plays an important role in the mythical Aborigine "Time of Dreams."

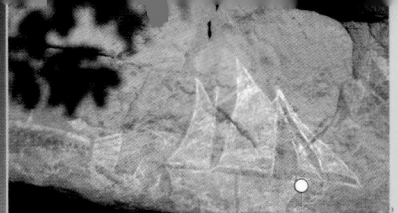

(Aboriginal Rock Art)

At Ubirr shelter in Kakadu NP, Northern Territory, **Australia (1)** , many of the paintings were made well before the last Ice Age, 8,000 years ago.

(Temperate Rainforest)

The **Tasmania Wilderness (3)** is one of the last expanses of temperate rainforest in the world. Remains found in limestone caves attest to the human occupation of the area for more than 20,000 years.

(Uluru – Kata Tjuta National Park)

The 36 rock domes comprised of Paleozoic conglomerate are known by the Aborigines as Kata Tjuta, Northern Territory, **Australia (2)**. Like Uluru (Ayers Rock), they play an important role in the mythical Aborigine "Time of Dreams."

(Fossils)

The fossil remains of a series of lakes and sand formations that date from the Pleistocene, can be found in Willandra Lakes Region, New South Wales, **Australia (4)**, together with archaeological evidence of human occupation dating from 45–60,000 years ago.

Visiting The Great Barrier Reef

Visiting the Reef

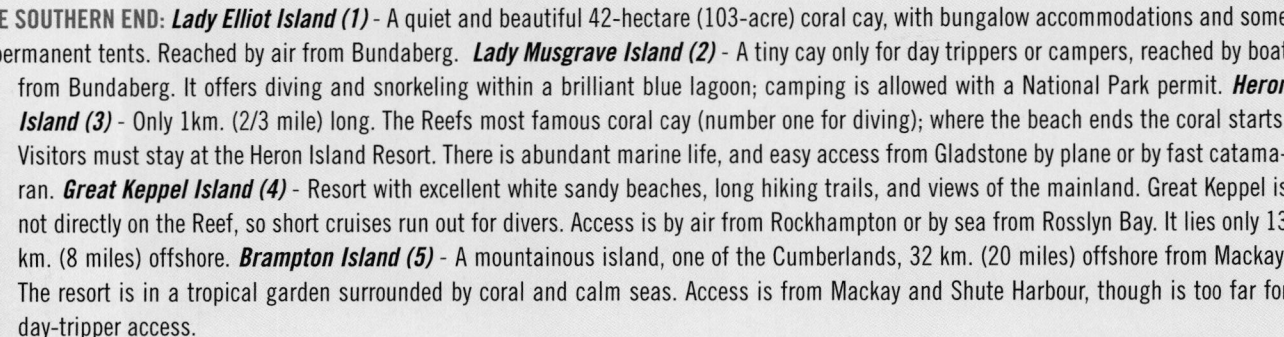

Regardless of your reason for visiting the Great Barrier Reef in Queensland, Australia's "Sunshine State," weather will play an important part in your enjoyment of its attractions. From late April through October it's at its best, the clear skies and moderate breezes offering perfect conditions for coral viewing, diving, swimming and fishing. In November the first signs of the approaching "Wet" appear: variable winds, increasing clouds and showers. By January it rains at least once nearly every day.

The easiest way to visit the Reef is not to stay on an offshore island but to take a day trip from Cairns or Port Douglas. Every morning dozens of fully equipped diveboats and catamarans head out from the two centers to various pre-selected sites. You can also take Reef trips from Cape Tribulation.

About an hour later, wherever you leave from, you'll be moored near the coral. Because the water is so shallow, snorkelling is good for seeing the marine life (in fact, many people prefer it to scuba diving).

Above the waves, the turquoise void might be broken only by a sand cay crowded with sea birds, but as soon as you poke your mask underwater, the world erupts. It's almost sensory overload: there are vast forests of staghorn coral, whose tips glow purple like electric Christmas-tree lights, brilliant blue clumps of mushroom coral, layers of pink plate coral and bulbous green brain coral.

Tropical fish with exotic names show off their fluorescent patterns: painted flutemouth, long-finned batfish, crimson squirrel fish, hump-headed Maori wrasse and cornflower sergeant-major.

Thrown into the mix are scarlet starfish and black sea cucumbers. You definitely don't pick up the sleek conus textile shells. They shoot darts into anything that touches them, each with enough venom to kill 300 people. There are 21 darts in each shell.

Almost all Reef trips follow a more or less similar format. There's a morning dive, followed by a buffet lunch then an afternoon dive. There should be a marine biologist on board, who will explain the Reef's ecology. Before you book, ask about the number of passengers the boat takes: they vary from several hundred on the famous Quicksilver fleet of catamarans to fewer than a dozen on smaller craft.

As a general rule, the farther out the boat heads, the more pristine the diving. But don't be conned by hype about the "Outer Reef" - as the edge of the continental shelf it may be the "real" Reef, but it looks the same as other parts. Even in the winter months, the water here is never cold, but it is worth paying to rent a wet suit anyway; most people find it hard not to snorkel for hours here.

Catamaran on the way to the reef

Major Islands

THE SOUTHERN END: *Lady Elliot Island (1)* - A quiet and beautiful 42-hectare (103-acre) coral cay, with bungalow accommodations and some permanent tents. Reached by air from Bundaberg. *Lady Musgrave Island (2)* - A tiny cay only for day trippers or campers, reached by boat from Bundaberg. It offers diving and snorkeling within a brilliant blue lagoon; camping is allowed with a National Park permit. *Heron Island (3)* - Only 1km. (2/3 mile) long. The Reefs most famous coral cay (number one for diving); where the beach ends the coral starts. Visitors must stay at the Heron Island Resort. There is abundant marine life, and easy access from Gladstone by plane or by fast catamaran. *Great Keppel Island (4)* - Resort with excellent white sandy beaches, long hiking trails, and views of the mainland. Great Keppel is not directly on the Reef, so short cruises run out for divers. Access is by air from Rockhampton or by sea from Rosslyn Bay. It lies only 13 km. (8 miles) offshore. *Brampton Island (5)* - A mountainous island, one of the Cumberlands, 32 km. (20 miles) offshore from Mackay. The resort is in a tropical garden surrounded by coral and calm seas. Access is from Mackay and Shute Harbour, though is too far for day-tripper access.

THE WHITSUNDAYS: *Lindeman Island (6)* - At the southern end of the archipelago is Lindeman's resort, Australia's first Club Med. Here the national park offers 20 km. (12 miles) of bushwalking trails through the national park. There are good views of other islands of the Whitsunday group. Access is from Mackay, Hamilton Island and Proserpine. *Long Island* - Has three very different resorts a short boat trip from Shute Harbour. Club Crocodile is a resort for all ages, and popular with the young. Peppers Palm Bay Resort is ideal for a back-to-nature holiday. It has lovely beaches, clear water and coral, and offers solitude. The self-catering Whitsunday Wilderness Lodge provides camping cabins. *Hamilton Island* -The group's largest resort, it has a floating marina, a jet airstrip with direct flights to major cities (and also the surrounding islands). With a pseudo-South Seas main street once described as "Daiquiri Disneyland", Hamilton Island is not the place for a quiet island sojourn. *Whitsunday Island* - The largest of the Whitsunday group, covering 109 sq. km. (42 sq. miles), with no resort, but the fabulous Whitehaven Beach. *South Molle Island* - Self-contained resort on a large, hilly island popular with families. Access from Shute Harbour or Hamilton Island. *Daydream Island* - A popular all-inclusive family resort with great beaches and a wide range of activities. Just 15 minutes by launch from Shute Harbour; access also from Hamilton Island. *Hook Island* - This is the second-largest island in the Whitsundays and provides camping and cabins. There is an excellent underwater observatory. *Hayman Island* - An exclusive five-star resort set in a coral-trimmed lagoon, close to the outer Reef. Fine beaches and fishing are complemented by the elegant resort facilities. Access from Hamilton Island, Proserpine, Shute Harbour and Townsville.

THE CENTER TO THE NORTH: *Magnetic Island (7)* - A large 5,000 hectare (12,400 acre) island and a national park, with a population of 2,300. It has a wide range of accommodations and facilities for day trippers. Plenty of walks in the rainforest, or hike up to 500 meters (1,640 foot) Mount Cook. There is also a koala and wildlife park at Horseshoe Bay. *Orpheus Island (8)* - In the Palm group northeast of Townsville and very close to the outer Reef. Wonderful sea shells can be found on the beaches. An exclusive resort hidden among the trees. Seaplane access from Townsville. *Hinchinbrook Island (9)* - A large and spectacular island, dominated by mountains dropping sheer to the waterline. Almost the whole island is devoted to national parkland, featuring rainforests, mangrove swamps and superb beaches. The small Hinchinbrook Island Wilderness Lodge is ideal for the bushwalker or naturalist. The 3 to 5 day Throsborne Trail trek is one of the best in the world. Access is from Cardwell. *Bedarra Island (10)* - A small fragment of the Family Islands, with an exclusive resort set in a rich rainforest. Lovely white beaches and tranquil coves; access is via Dunk Island. *Dunk Island (11)* - This was where the recluse E.J. Banfield lived for 26 years at the turn of the 20th century, writing his classic Confessions of a Beachcomber. A rich rainforested, national park with a large resort nestled in one corner and a campground along side; access is from Townsville, Cairns and Mission Beach. *Fitzroy Island (12)* - Totally surrounded by coral reef, it is a great place for diving and fishing. Access is from Cairns 6 km. (4 miles) offshore. *Green Island (13)* - A tiny coral cay just off Cairns with a good underwater observatory. Mostly for day trippers. *Lizard Island (14)* - The most northerly of the resorts and home, during the season, to the marlin boats. Lizard has access directly from the beach to the Reef and is the step-off point for the world-famous Cod Hole dive site. This small resort caters to wealthy sports fishermen and divers from all over the world.

Threats to a Fragile Ecosystem

There are a number of real threats to the Great Barrier Reef's fragile ecosystem. In the past 70 years, the Reef has suffered from increasing impacts from human activities. For example, anchoring sometimes causes significant damage to coral, and snorkellers or divers may brush against polyps killing or damaging them. The Reef is also under pressure from the effects of poor water quality, which is often caused by human land uses such as agriculture activities and coastal development.

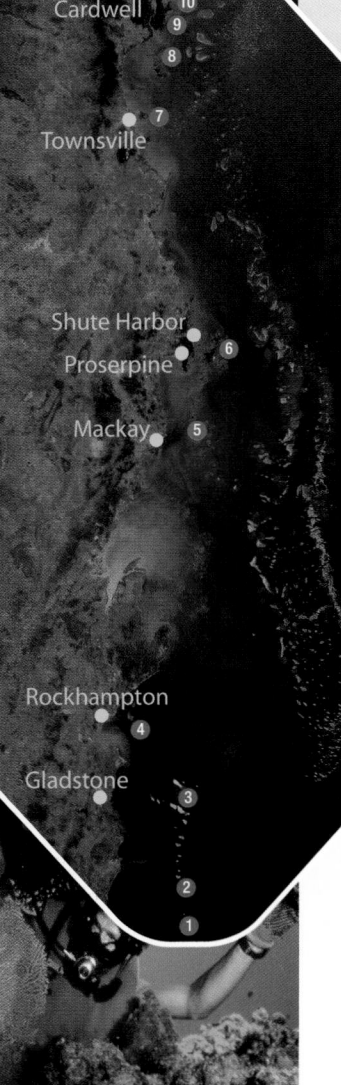

The World's Largest Living Thing

(A Natural Wonder)

(Complex and Diverse Ecosystem)

The Reef is not only Queensland's major tourist attraction, it is one of the natural wonders of the world. The largest coral reef on earth, it is also one of the most accessible.

The Reef consists of over 2,500 separate, interconnected reefs stretching over 2,300 km. (1,430 miles) from the northern tip of Australia's continental shelf to just north of Bundaberg in the south.

The Reef comprises layer upon layer of "stony coral" that use the sun's rays to produce food, and in turn energy, to form their calcium carbonate skeletons. It is these skeletons which over millions of years have formed coral reefs.

The Greater Barrier Reef Marine Park was established in the 1970's - the Park Authority manages the activities that may occur within it such as tourism, fishing and research.

The Reef was placed on the World Heritage List in 1981.

▲ BLOOMING FLOWER

Not all corals use the sun's rays to provide their food. Some, such as this Tubastrea, or sun coral, live in the shade in strong currents, and feed by filtering food from the water.

When the Reef was put forward for World Heritage listing, the nomination said: "Biologically, the Great Barrier Reef supports the most diverse ecosystem known to man. Its enormous diversity is thought to reflect the maturity of an ecosystem which has evolved over millions of years..."

At the heart of that ecosystem is the humble polyp, a tiny animal consisting of not much more than a mouth and surrounding tentacles to feed it, plus of course a limestone skeleton into which it withdraws during the day. It is the remains of these skeletons that form the basis of the reef. Individual polyps are linked by body tissue (to share the colony's food) but the main source of a photosynthetic coral's food is algae cells within its tissue called Zooxanthellae, which convert the sun's energy into nutrients for the coral. This massive accumulation of plant and animal life can truly be said to be the largest living thing in the world.

OTHER INHABITANTS: The Reef is home to a fantastic variety of marine life, including more than 1,000 species of fish, from the relatively plain to the ornately bizarre. They include sharks (such as the white-tipped reef shark, above), the huge but strictly vegetarian manta ray, and some of the largest black marlin in the world. There are thousands of different crustacea (crabs, lobsters and shrimp), starfish with feathery arms or brittle, spiny fingers, sea urchins and sea slugs, and a seemingly infinite variety of shellfish. Dugongs feed here, and it is a breeding area for the humpback whale and green and loggerhead turtles.

▲ A LURKING KILLER

For a moray eel, a coral cave is a convenient hiding place from which to ambush prey. The moray grows to 2 meters (6 ½ ft.) in length and is a ferocious predator, with sharp teeth and a savage bite.

▶ SEND IN THE CLOWNS

A family of pink clown fish live symbiotically with a sea anemone. The anemone is not a plant but an animal, closely related to coral, but consisting of one large polyp. Anemones feed on particles that drift by, helped in this case by the feeding activities of the clown fish.

▲ A KING-SIZE COD

The Cod Hole is a spot on the outer reef 40 minutes by boat from Lizard Island. It is noted for its concentration of very large fish, such as this giant potato cod, which probably weighs 60 kg. (130 lbs.).

▶ FAN WORSHIP

The sea fan belongs to a group known as Gorgonians (other members include sea whips and sea feathers). They all have a flexible spine of hornlike material, with the polyps living on the outside. The intricate colony that makes up a sea fan can grow up to 3 meters (10 ft.) in diameter.

▲ SUBMARINE STAGHORN

There are some 300 species of stony (hard) coral, of which Acropora or staghorn corals are the most common. They appear in many forms and colors, including the beautiful lilac version above.

▲ MARINE TURTLES

Six of the world's seven species of marine turtle live in the waters around Australia, and all occur within the Great Barrier Reef area. Some species such as the loggerhead and green turtle are seen frequently, while others such as the olive ridley and leatherback are known to occur in the Great Barrier Reef but are seldom seen.

◀ THE REEF'S GREATEST ENEMY?

For years, the most famous threat to the Reef was thought to be the crown-of-thorns starfish, an ugly creature that clamps on to coral and effectively spits its stomach out. Its digestive juices dissolve the polyps and leave great expanses of coral bleached and dead. The crown-of-thorns is poisonous to other fish and almost indestructible: it can regenerate to full size from a single leg and a small piece of intestine.

Altogether, it's an unpleasant creature but at least it was once relatively rare. With only a few around, it was easy to ignore its depredations on the Reef. But in the early 1960s the pattern changed. Instead of a few crown-of-thorns starfish, suddenly there were millions. Green Island was the first to see the plague, in 1962. From there it spread southward, reaching the reefs around Bowen by 1988. Surveys between 1985 and 1988 established that about 31 percent of the reefs examined had been affected. Even after millions of dollars worth of research, no one knows what caused the proliferation of the starfish. Furthermore, no economical way to get rid of the pest has presented itself.

Recently, however, marine biologists have decided to let the crown-of-thorns run its destructive course. The latest wisdom holds that it isn't a genuine threat at all but a natural, if poorly understood, part of the Reef's life cycle.

After more than 200 years of European settlement, Aboriginal Australians are the country's most disadvantaged group. Statistics show the sad results of the colonial experience: the average life expectancy for Aborigines is 15 years shorter than that of other Australians; they have three times the infant mortality rate and a far higher incidence of both communicable diseases, such as hepatitis B, and "lifestyle" diseases such as heart failure. They also have an unemployment rate six times the national average and half the average income. Most live in sub-standard housing or temporary shelters. Aborigines are also 16 times more likely to be imprisoned than other Australians. Aborigines today also have a keen

The traditional corroboree is still performed.

political consciousness, born of years of struggle to attain the basic rights and freedoms denied to them until the early 1970s.

THE COLONIAL CURSE: From 1788, the first British settlers to arrive on Australia's remote shores could not understand the Aborigines' nomadic lifestyle or the profound connection they had to their tribal lands. It seemed that the Aborigines came and went without reason across the sparse landscape. Terra Australis was conveniently declared a terra nullius - an uninhabited void that could be occupied without further thought.

As white settlers arrived by the boatload, Aboriginal communities were systematically pushed from their homes, leading to the disruption and destruction of their traditional culture and communal life.

The colonial governments had little interest in allowing the Aborigines to determine their own future. In the mid-19th century, bureaucrats and missionaries, well intentioned but believing in innate Aboriginal inferiority, sought to "protect" them from the expansion of what they saw as the superior Anglo-Saxon civilization. The most dramatic case was the removal of the Tasmanian Aborigines to Flinders Island in the Bass Strait in the 1830s. All over Australia, similar tragedies were acted out, as Aborigines were taken from their lands and grouped with other peoples with whom they shared neither language nor traditions.

A quasi-apartheid system was established in the Outback, with Aborigines segregated on reserves and given inferior legal status. When Australia became a federation in 1901, Aborigines were not allowed to vote: they were considered a "dying race" with no future.

Policies of assimilation were developed to integrate "half-caste" Aborigines into the lower strata of society, at the same time maintaining the strict segregation of "full-bloods" who, it was still felt, would disappear.

The Aborigines were not passive victims. Political activity began in order to obtain basic freedoms. Despite their enforced marginalization, many Aborigines had adapted to European society. As early as the 1860s, Aborigines had successfully engaged in farming enterprises. The development of the cattle industry in Outback Australia would not have been possible without Aborigine stockmen and boundary riders (paid, of course, considerably less than their white counterparts).

Aboriginal political awareness grew steadily from the 1930s, culminating in the Freedom Rides of the mid-1960s, when activists rode in buses through Outback Queensland and New South Wales bringing their message to the remotest communities. An "Aboriginal Embassy" was set up in front of Parliament House in Canberra; demonstrations resulted in violent clashes with police, pushing the Aboriginal plight on to the front pages and into white middle-class homes on television. Activists demanded that discriminatory legislation be repealed and that Aborigines be awarded basic freedoms enjoyed by other Australians.

TOWARDS SELF-DETERMINATION: This allowed Aborigines to make decisions affecting their own future, retain their cultural identity and values, and achieve greater economic and social equality.

The Department of Aboriginal Affairs was established in 1972, followed by the Aboriginal Development Commission (ADC) in 1980. The underlying concept was to develop programs that would bring increasing economic independence to Aboriginal people by fostering the development of business enterprises.

In 1988, while the rest of Australia celebrated 200 years of white settlement at the Bicenten-

nial, Aborigine activists took the opportunity to stage peaceful protest marches. In many ways, the events of 1988 pushed Aboriginal issues into the forefront of the national political agenda. More importantly, a wide range of organizations, from community-based medical and legal services to Land Councils (which govern the affairs of different regions), have been established; there are now over 1,200 Aboriginal community organizations.

LAND RIGHTS: For all Aboriginal groups, "land rights" have always been the top priority. The Northern Territory Land Rights Act, passed in 1975, allowed Aborigines to make claims to vast swaths of the Outback on the basis of traditional ownership. Royalties from mining operations were distributed to Aboriginal groups throughout the territory.

Land rights acts have been passed in various states, and in 1985 the federal government attempted to introduce national land rights legislation. Perhaps the most symbolic change occurred in 1992, when the High Court of Australia overturned the legal fiction of terra nullius that had been the basis of Australia's settlement. The judges agreed that "native title" had always existed for land that had been continuously occupied by Aborigines, and in 1993 the government set up a Native Title Tribunal to regulate claims.

As time went on, it appeared that the tribunal would achieve little in practice: since 19th-century missionaries had moved Aboriginal peoples around, often splitting up clans by force and lumping them together again in remote areas, few Aboriginal groups could prove continuous occupation of their lands. The lack of progress has been frustrating for many Aborigines, and the emotional land-rights debate remains one of the most contentious issues in Australia today.

DEALING WITH PROBLEMS: Inevitably, the growth of an "Aboriginal industry," comprising politicians, city-based do-gooders and opportunistic Aboriginal leaders, had been nurtured by the uneasy communal guilt that sprang from the endless reiteration of old injustices against Aborigines. These groups began competing with genuinely committed people and organizations for control of the rivers of cash flowing from government aid and mining rights, and some decisions were made that brought no long-term advantages to Aborigines at all.

ADC Chairman Charles Perkins once admitted in public: "We've funded over 150 projects, and they've all gone broke." The prominent and popular Aboriginal lawyer, Noel Pearson, said in 1999: "Welfare is a resource that is laced with poison, and the poison present is the money-for-nothing principle. Welfare is a parasitic exploiter." Pearson may have discovered a better foundation on which to build such businesses. Following the failures of earlier endeavors, and under more comprehensive guidance, a number of successful Aboriginal businesses have been established throughout Australia, from shopping centers and cattle stations to craft shops.

The Aboriginal and Torres Strait Islander Commission (ATSIC), which replaced the ADC, helped some communities buy their native lands (thus circumventing the land rights arguments), to build adequate housing and to take out home loans. Albert Namatjira, for example, was the first Aboriginal painter to interpret the rugged landscapes of central Australia in Western-style watercolors. While his work received international acclaim, Namatjira couldn't cope with the huge cultural differences between Aborigine and European societies. In the 1950s, official Australian citizenship and the accompanying right to drink alcohol were granted to him at a time when Aborigines were not normally afforded these privileges, and this man of dignity and great skill went from alcoholism to jail and premature death.

SUCCESS STORIES: Many Aborigines, have successfully entered Australian society on their own terms. Neville Bonner became a Senator of the Commonwealth Parliament, and pastor Sir Doug Nichols was appointed Governor of South Australia. Evonne Goolagong-Cawley became a Wimbledon tennis champion, and Oodgeroo Noonuccal (formerly Kath Walker), one of Australia's most prominent artists and authors. Writers such as Herb Wharton and Evelyn Crawford are immensely popular, as are sports stars, such as the "flying Ella brothers" in Rugby Union, and Olympic gold-medal winner, Cathy Freeman. In arts and entertainment, success stories include actors such as David Gulpilil; the television and film comedian and actor, Ernie Dingo; an Aboriginal and Islanders' Dance School; contemporary paint-

Olympic track star, Cathy Freeman

ers such as Trevor Nickolls and Danny Eastwood; the part-Aborigine photographer Tracey Moffatt, and the outstanding music group, Yothu Yindi, led by a former Australian of the Year, Mandawuy Yunupingu.

Where the Past Meets the Present

It's contemporary yet traditional. It's today but it's timeless. Attaching a label to modern Aboriginal art can be as difficult as establishing the meanings behind the symbols. But it does provide us with a unique cultural vision of Australia, as deep and enduring as any on earth. The international explosion in Australian Aboriginal art began in the early 1970s as a spark in Northern Territory, first among various groups in Arnhem Land and in the desert community of Papunya, west of Alice Springs. In Arnhem Land, missionaries encouraged tribal people to paint their designs, derived from traditional rock art and body decoration, on bark panels stripped from trees. Meanwhile, in central Australia, teacher Geoffrey Bardon introduced polymer paints to desert dwellers, producing an entirely new genre of art: the strongly symbolic dot style was born. Today the National Gallery in Canberra, the state galleries, and private galleries in all the major cities feature desert and Top End art.

THE EXPLOSION SPREADS: More recently, other northern Aboriginal communities have also earned distinguished reputations for their artisans: Tiwi Islanders for their carving and distinctive painting, Western Australia's Kimberley region, for the work by Rover Thomas and Paddy Carlton and Balgo Hills for the blazing acrylics from Eubana Nampitjin. Works by the late Emily Kngwarreye put the central Australian community of Utopia on the map. Her niece Kathleen Petyarre continues that tradition.

▲ TRIBAL INSPIRATION

Colorful murals decorate many public and private buildings. The work above was painted on an urban brick wall by Danny and Jamie Eastwood. Descendants of the Ngemba tribe of Western New South Wales, the artists' work reflect their ancestry – the Dreamtime stories passed on through generations – as well as nontraditional images.

▲ ABSTRACT EXPRESSIONS

Steeped in the tradition of her people and infused with spiritual meaning, the work of Emily Kngwarreye, a famous Aboriginal artist from Utopia in Central Australia, progressively developed from depicting traditional subjects to images of pure abstraction.

◄ FUNERAL POLES

Pukamani burial poles are still carved today as an enduring gesture of respect for the dead. The number of poles produced reflects the individual's standing in the community. A plethora of poles are erected at the funeral of an important elder.

▲ TRADITIONAL AND MODERN

Paintings in the dot style take their inspiration from the landscape, from traditional elements such as the snake, lizard, or tortoise, and often allude to ancient images found in Aboriginal rock art.

► A PICTURE BOOK OF HISTORY

Aboriginal rock art is recognized as the world's oldest and longest continuous living tradition. The ancient art is found all across Australia in the form of paintings or engravings on rock. Archaeologists continue to argue over their age, but some of the earliest paintings, in red ochre in northern sandstone shelters, could be 50,000 years old. In 1996 in the Kimberley region of Western Australia, an engraving site was dated at over 110,000 years old, sending archaeologists back to the drawing board and rewriting the history of modern human movement.

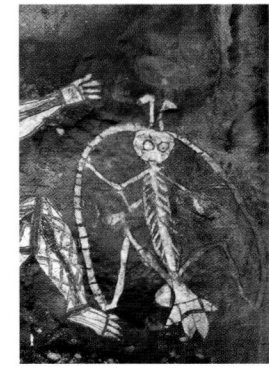

Arnhem Land and neighboring Kakadu National Park in the Northern Territory provide the finest Aboriginal rock art experiences. At Ubirr shelter in Kakadu, many of the paintings were made well before the last Ice Age, 8,000 years ago. A layer of animal depictions (some of species now extinct) lie beneath red dynamic figures racing across the shelter. Over them are splashed "X-ray" paintings of barramundi fish, their internal organs accurately detailed. Over them are sailing vessels, documenting the European arrivals in Australia. Each layer reads like a page in the history of the continent.

▲ Starry Night

An Aboriginal man and the ancient cave paintings of his ancestors at Cave Hill, Anangu Pitjantjara lands in North Western South Australia. The magnificent paintings illustrate the Seven Sisters creation story.

Papua New Guinea lies on the seam between the Indo-Australian and Pacific Plates. Consequently, it is a region of massive earthquakes, active volcanoes, and rugged mountain terrain that provides a unique natural refuge for plants and wildlife today. The tropical rain forest is home to rare birds of paradise and butterflies with wingspans of up to 25 cm. It is also the geographical boundary for many Australian species, including the duck-billed platypus of the order Monotremata. Most Papuans had no contact with modern civilization until 1933.

103

124°   128°   132°

A   **B**   **C**   **D**

Banda   Sea

I N D O N E S I A

SULAWESI   Buton
TENGGARA
1,570 m
Kabaena
Island
Kai Is.
Kai   Tual
Kecil I.   Banda Elat
Kai Besar I.   Dobo   Wokam I.
Tayandu   Kobroor I.
Is.   Aru
Islands
Kopapat
Jerdera
Trangan
I.   Nieuw
Krai

Flores   Tukangbesi   MALUKU
Sea   Is.

Daya   Islands
Barat   Nila I.
Molu I.
Damar I.   MALUKU
Wulur
Larat I.
Fordate I.
Tanjung Ngabordamlu
Enu I.

Kalaotoa I.

NUSA TENGGARA   Dai I.
TIMUR   Selu I.   Yamdena
Wetar   Babar   Isands   Sera I.   Island
Wasiri   Arwala   Wuliara I.   Watmuri
Lioppa   Laliki   Hila   Amdasa
Wetar I.   Tepa   Babar I.   Waslatan   Saumlaki
Ilwaki   Romang I.   Wetan I.   Masela I.   Adaut
Solor Is.   Kisar I.   Leti   Serwaru   Moa I.   Lakor I.   Sermata I.   Selaru I.
Alor   Is.   Taramana   Wonreli   Leti Is.   Pati I.   Sermata Is.
Sagu Ili Bolena   Baukau   Lautem   Tutuala   Tanjung Aro Usu
Solor I.   Ataúro I.   Manatuto   Mata Bia   Los Palos   MALUKU
Lamakera   Dili   Aileu   2,315 m   Loré   EAST TIMOR
Besar   Larantuka   Lamalera   Lomblen I.   Ermera   Lclubar   Uato-Lari   Timor
Keli   Tanjung   Tatá Mailau   Same   Vikeke   Arafura
Mutu   Margeta   Atapupu   Aúba   Sea
Maumere   EAST   2,980 m
TIMUR   Atambua
Ende   Lifau Wini   Mena   Suai   Ainaro   Timor
Ntibe   Pante Makasar
NUSA TENGGARA   Naikliu   Kefamenanu
TIMUR   Besikama
Gunung Mutis   Tilomar
2,427 m
Waingapu, Ujung Padang   Lelogama   Soe   Nikiniki
Barate   Camplong   Timor   Sea
Savu   Kolbano
Sea   Kupang   Kolbano
Semau I.   ELTARI   NUSA TENGGARA
TIMUR
Sawu   Tanjung Niuwudu
Is.   Seba   Eahun
Raijua   Sawu   Sawu I.
I.   Baa   Roti I.
Nembrala

INDONESIA
AUSTRALIA

Cape Van Diemen   Cape Croker
GURIG   Croker I.
NAT'L PARK   Cape Cockburn
Point Jahleel   Cobourg Pen   Mountnorris Bay
BATHURST   Milikapiti   N. Goulburn I.
Rocky Point   Melville I.   MURGENELLA   S. Goulburn I.
Bathurst I.   MELVILLE I.   C. Don   WILDLIFE   Braithwaithe Pt.
ABOR.   ABOR. LAND   Cape Keith   Endyalgout I.   SANCTUARY   Hawkesbury Pol
LAND   Nguiu   Cape Gambier   Oenpelli   Maningrida   Milingimbi
Cape Fourcroy   Cape   Field I.   Ramingini
Cape Hotham   Chambers
Van Diemen   Bay
Beagle Gulf   Gulf   Clarence Str.
Charles Point   DARWIN   Koolpinyah   ARNHEM LAND
Darwin   ABOR. LAND
Humpty Doo   KAKADU   Jabiru   Arnhem
Point Blaze   WAGAIT ABOR. LAND   Rum Jungle   Mt. Pa
N. Peron I.   Batchelor   NAT'L   Land
Anson Bay   Adelaide River   PARK
Cape Ford   Litchfield   Mainoru
Cape Scott   DALY RIVER   Pine Creek
WILD. SANCT.   Daly River   Douglas   KATHERINE
DALY   GORGE NP   BESWICK
RIVER   Katherine   Barnyili   ABOR. LAND
ABORIGINAL   Claravale   Beswick
LAND   Wingate Mts.   Urapunga
FORREST   Matarranka   ALAWA
RIVER   Roper Valley   NGANDI
ABOR. RSV.   Willeroo   ABOR. LAND
FORREST RIVER   Victoria   Moray   Larrimah
NAT'L PARK   Range   Birdum   NORTHERN
Forrest River   Coolibah   Nutwood Downs
Mission   Auvergne   Newry   Willeroo

INDIAN
OCEAN

Scott Reef

ASHMORE AND
CARTIER ISLANDS
TERRITORY
Ashmore Reef
Cartier Islet

Cape Londonderry
Napier   Cape Rulhieres
Broome   Cape Bougainville   Joseph   TERRITORY
Vansittart B.   CARSON   Bonaparte
KALUMBURU   RIVER.   Gulf   Cape Dombey
Cape Voltaire   ABOR. RSV.   ABOR.   Cape Hay   Rosewood   AMANBIDJI
Admiralty   KALUMBURU   RSV.   Buckle   Pearce Point   ABOR.
Gulf   Mission   Head   LAND
Bigge I.   ADMIRALTY   Lacross   Keying Inlet   Victoria River
Montague   GULF   Turtle Point   Downs
Cape Pond   ABOR. RSV.   Queens Chnl.   Top Springs
York Sd.   DRYSDALE   Wyndham   Ord   Killarney
Bonaparte   RIVER   Montejinni
Cape Brewster   ABOR. RSV.   Kununurra   O. T. Do
Arch.   FORREST   KEEP RIVER NP   Daly Waters
RIVER   Newry
Mavis   NAT'L PARK   DOON
Reef   Karunjie   DOON   Birrimbah   Daly Waters
Adèle I.   PRINCE   ABOR.
Camden Sd.   REGENT   Gibb River   LAND   NORTHERN
Hall Point   NATURE   Mt. Hann   Rosewood
Raft Point   Mt. Methuen   RSV.   779 m   Waterloo   TERRITORY
427 m   KUNMUNYA   BOW RIVER   Camfield
Collier B.   ABOR. RSV.   PANTIJAN   ABOR. LAND   Mistake Creek   Limbunya
ABOR.   VIOLET VALLEY   Turkey Creek   Wave Hill
Cape Leveque   LAND   ABOR. LAND   DAGURAGU
WOTJALUM   Karunjie   ABOR.   Kalkaringi
ABOR. LAND   Mt. Hart 661 m   Inverway   LAND   Top Springs
Kimberley   Ord River
PENDER BAY   Gogo   Mt. Napier
Pender Bay   ABOR. LAND   Plateau   Mt. Lush   Mt. Ord   487 m   HOOKER CR.   Montejinni
Emeriau Point   King   778 m   937 m   Tableland   ABOR.   ABOR. LAND
BEAGLE BAY   Sound   Nicholson   LAND   WARLMANPA
Cape Baskerville   ABOR.   Mt. Amhurst   Hooker Creek
Beagle Bay   RSV.   689 m   Halls Creek   Birrindudu
Mission   Derby   WINDJANA GORGE   Gordon Downs   Helen Springs
Mowanjum   NAT'L PARK   GEIKIE GORGE NP
COULOMB POINT   Mission   TUNNEL CREEK   Mt. Bertram   ABORIGINAL
NATURE RSV.   NAT'L PARK   382 m   CENTRAL DESERT
Cape Bossut   Yeeda   Ellendale   Christmas Creek   LAND   Banka Banka
Coulomb Point   Looma   Fitzroy Crossing   Tanami   Rockhampton
Cape Latouche Treville   NOONKANBAH   Gogo   LAND
FRAZIER   WOLFE CR. CRATER
DOWNS   Dampier Downs   NAT'L PARK   Eva Downs
False Cape Bossut   ABOR.   ABORIGINAL   LAND
Cape Bossut   LAND   Mt. Samuel
La Grange   435 m   Tennant Creek
Cape Jaubert   ABOR.   WESTERN   BILILUNA   Mt. Figg
Broome   LAND   ABOR. LAND   521 m
Gantheaume Point   AUSTRALIA   ABORIGINAL   Devenp
Roebuck Plains   GREGORY LAKE   LAND
Roebuck Bay   ABOR. LAND   TANAMI   MCLAREN CREEK
Eighty Mile Beach   Great Sandy Desert   Gregory Salt L.   DESERT   KAYTEJ   ABOR. LAND
Walal Downs   Southesk Tablelands   BALWINA ABORIGINAL RESERVE   Tee Brambles   ABORIGINAL   Warrabri
Anna Plains   NGARTI ABOR. LAND   436 m   LAND   Barrow Creek
De Grey   CENTRAL AUSTRALIA   WILDLIFE   Mt. Theo   Willowra   Mt. Strzelecki
ABOR. RSV.   SANCTUARY   584 m   Mt. Patricia   636 m
AUSTRALIA   LAKE MACKAY   578 m   WILLOWRA   ABOR. LAND
L. White   ABORIGINAL LAND   ABOR. LAND
L. Wills   Mt. Patricia

Flores   Sea

Timor

Timor
Sea

12°   8°   16°   20°

A   **B**   **C**   **D**
124°   128°   132°

Height

m.	ft.
6000	19700
4000	13000
2000	6500
1500	5000
1000	3300
500	1600
200	700
0	-
200	700
500	1600
1000	3300
2000	6500
3000	9800
4000	13000
5000	16400
6000	19700

Depth

Population

■ Over 2,000,000	◉ 500,000 - 999,999	● 100,000 - 249,999	○ 10,000 - 29,999
■ 1,000,000 - 1,999,999	◎ 250,000 - 499,999	○ 30,000 - 99,999	○ Under 10,000

Australia is covered by more desert for its size than any other inhabited continent. Known collectively as the "outback," these desert regions are located primarily in the west and the interior. Many of the rivers that flow sporadically into the central basin seldom reach their terminal lakes, which are dry salt flats for most of the year. The basin has enormous groundwater reserves left over from the ice age, however. These are tapped from artesian wells to water grazing lands for sheep. Cultivation is possible only in a few coastal areas concentrated primarily around Perth and Adelaide. The isolated monolith of Ayers Rock rises from the plain in the Northern Territory. It is sacred to the Aborigines, who call it Uluru.

Population

- ■ Over 2,000,000
- □ 1,000,000 - 1,999,999
- ◉ 500,000 - 999,999
- ◎ 250,000 - 499,999
- ● 100,000 - 249,999
- ⊚ 30,000 - 99,999
- ◍ 10,000 - 29,999
- ○ Under 10,000

Western and Central Australia

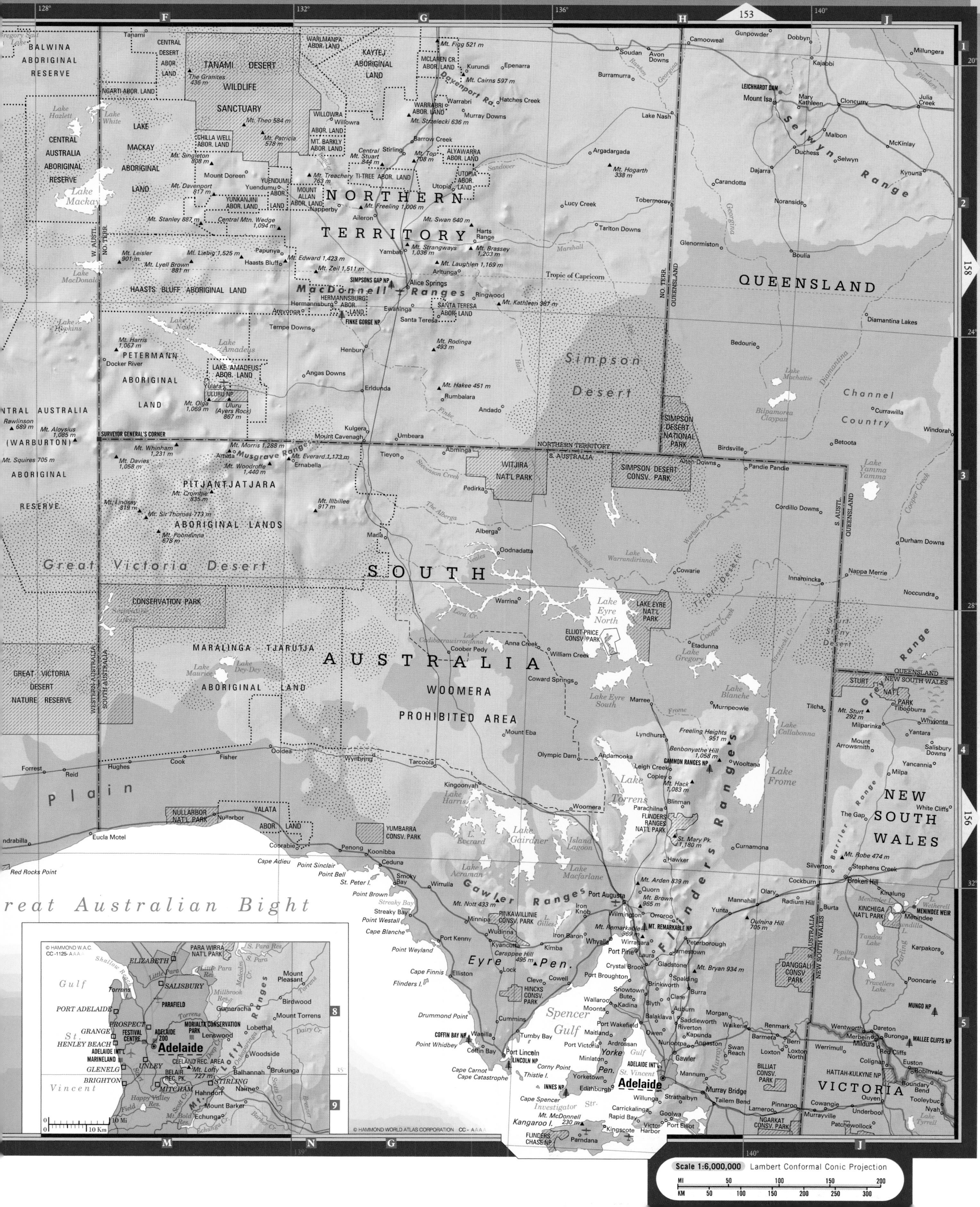
NORTHERN TERRITORY
QUEENSLAND
SOUTH AUSTRALIA
NEW SOUTH WALES
VICTORIA
Great Australian Bight
Great Victoria Desert
Simpson Desert
Channel Country
TANAMI DESERT WILDLIFE SANCTUARY
HAASTS BLUFF ABORIGINAL LAND
PETERMANN ABORIGINAL LAND
PITJANTJATJARA ABORIGINAL LANDS
MARALINGA TJARUTJA ABORIGINAL LAND
WOOMERA PROHIBITED AREA
GREAT VICTORIA DESERT NATURE RESERVE
CENTRAL AUSTRALIA ABORIGINAL RESERVE
MacDonnell Ranges
Musgrave Ranges
Flinders Ranges
Gawler Ranges
Selwyn Range
Barrier Range
Grey Range
Eyre Pen.
Yorke Pen.
Spencer Gulf
Gulf St. Vincent
Kangaroo I.
Lake Eyre North
Lake Eyre South
Lake Torrens
Lake Gairdner
Lake Frome
Lake Mackay
Lake Amadeus
Alice Springs
Tennant Creek
Mount Isa
Coober Pedy
Port Augusta
Port Pirie
Whyalla
Port Lincoln
Ceduna
Broken Hill
Mildura
Adelaide
Birdsville
Oodnadatta
Tropic of Capricorn
Scale 1:6,000,000 Lambert Conformal Conic Projection
© HAMMOND WORLD ATLAS CORPORATION

Tasmania lies within the cool-temperate West Wind Drift of the southern hemisphere. The resulting climate provides abundant precipitation and ideal conditions for fruit and berry cultivation. The northern area of southeastern Australia, where New South Wales merges with the monsoon region of Queensland, is much warmer. Areas of subtropical rain forests are also found along the northern coast.

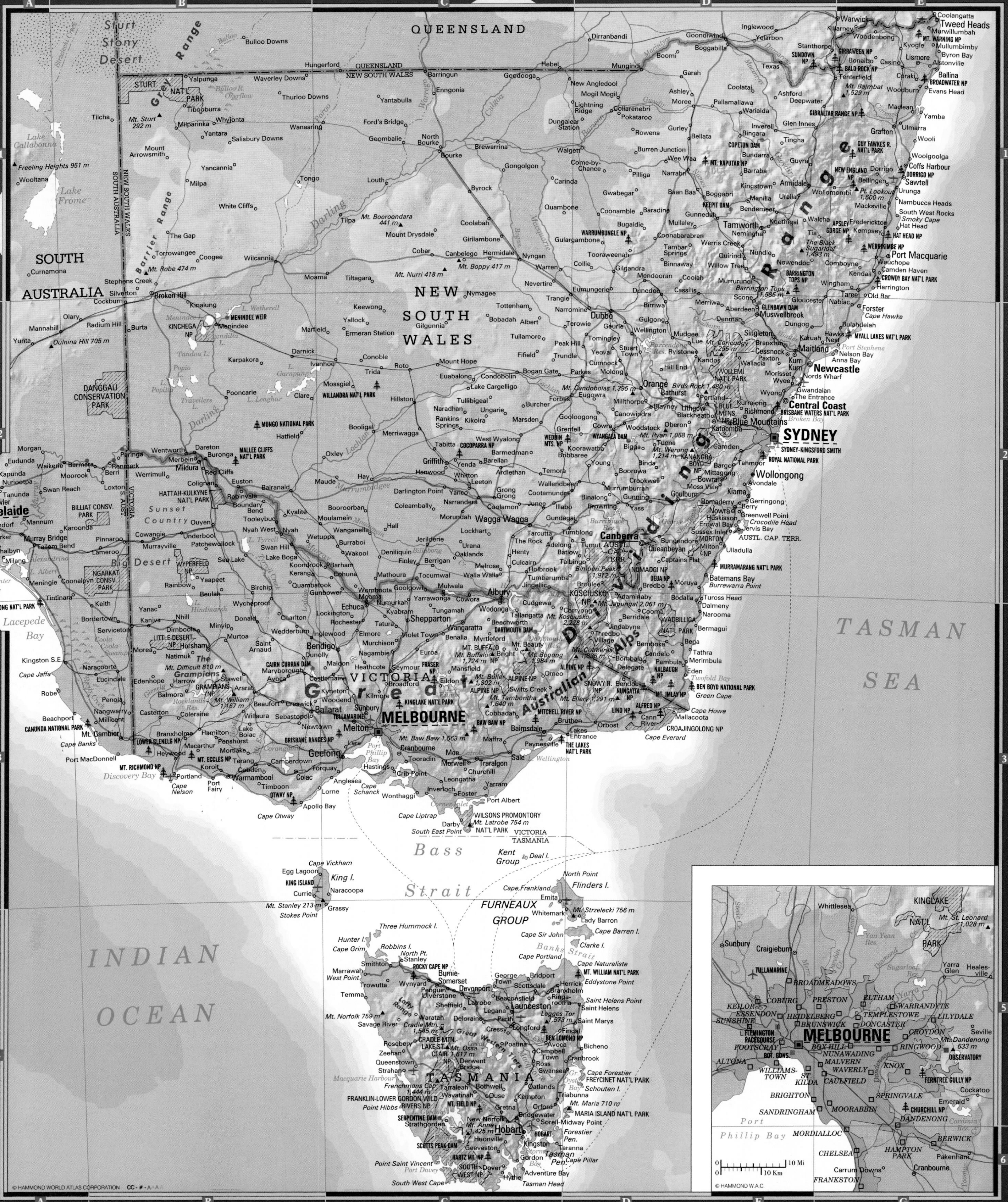

QUEENSLAND

NEW SOUTH WALES

SOUTH AUSTRALIA

VICTORIA

TASMANIA

SYDNEY
MELBOURNE
Adelaide
Canberra
Newcastle
Wollongong
Geelong
Hobart
Launceston

TASMAN SEA

INDIAN OCEAN

Bass Strait

Great Dividing Range

Australian Alps

Sturt Stony Desert

Barrier Range

Grey Range

FURNEAUX GROUP

KING ISLAND

Height

m.	ft.
6000	19700
4000	13000
2000	6500
1500	5000
1000	3300
200	700
0	0
200	700
500	1600
1000	3300
2000	6500
3000	9800
4000	13000
5000	16400
6000	19700

Depth

Population
- Over 2,000,000
- 1,000,000 – 1,999,999
- 500,000 – 999,999
- 250,000 – 499,999
- 100,000 – 249,999
- 30,000 – 99,999
- 10,000 – 29,999
- Under 10,000

Scale 1:6,000,000 Lambert Conformal Conic Projection

MI 50 100 150 200
KM 100 200 300

MELBOURNE (inset)

© HAMMOND WORLD ATLAS CORPORATION

Due to its relatively pleasant climate and reliable rainfall, the region between Sydney and Melbourne is home to most Australians. Lush forests of eucalyptus are found here, and the Blue Mountains west of Sydney are presumably named for the shimmering blue of indigenous eucalyptus trees. Mount Kosciusko, Australia's highest peak, rises to an elevation of 2,228 meters south of Canberra.

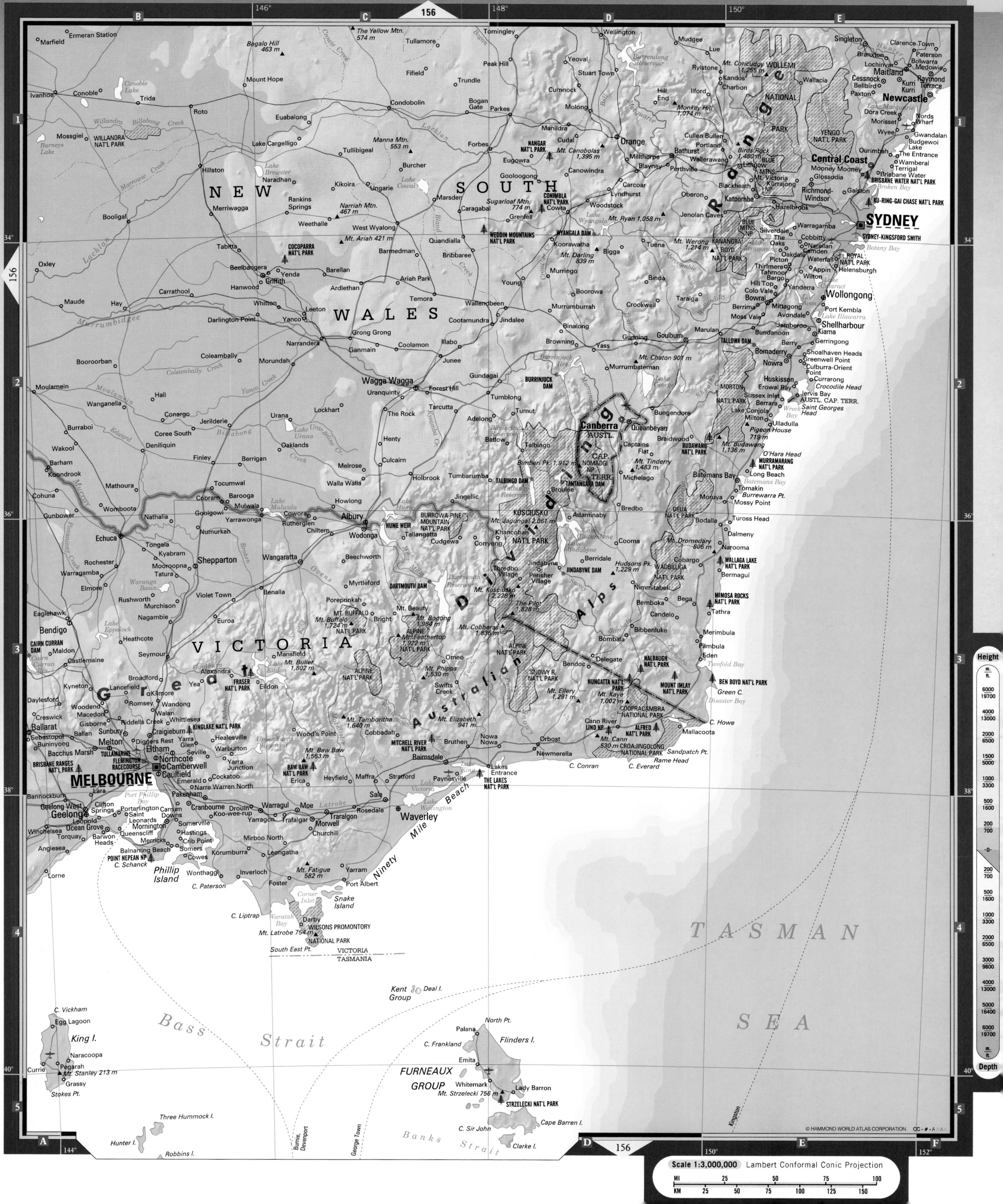

Scale 1:3,000,000   Lambert Conformal Conic Projection

© HAMMOND WORLD ATLAS CORPORATION

MAP SECTION
Northeastern Australia

The Great Barrier Reef is a complex of coral reefs, atolls, and shoals that runs along the northeastern coast of Australia for about 2,600 km. Its foundations lie on the shelf of the Coral Sea at depths of up to 180 m. Water levels and climatic conditions have a major impact on reef growth. A rapid rise in sea level endangers coral organisms, which cannot survive in depths below 55 m.

Cape York Peninsula

Gulf of Carpentaria

CORAL SEA

CORAL SEA ISLANDS TERRITORY

GREAT BARRIER REEF MARINE PARK

Osprey Reef
Bougainville Reef
Holmes Reef
Coringa Islets
Flinders Reefs
Abington Reef
Saumarez Reefs

QUEENSLAND

Great Dividing Range

Gregory Range

Selwyn Range

Beal Range

Grey Range

Warrego Range

Carnarvon Range

Chesterton Range

Great Barrier Reef

Swain Reefs

Tropic of Capricorn

Cairns
Townsville
Mackay
Rockhampton
Gladstone
Bundaberg
Hervey Bay
Maryborough
Brisbane
Gold Coast
Toowoomba

Fraser Island
Moreton I.
Curtis I.
Great Sandy Nat'l Park

NEW SOUTH WALES

Sturt Stony Desert

SOUTH AUSTRALIA

Brisbane inset
Moreton Island
Moreton Bay
Redcliffe
Brighton
Sandgate
Shorncliffe
Chermside
Mt. D'Aguilar 745 m
Mt. Glorious 635 m
Mt. Nebo 579 m
Brisbane Int'l
Newmarket
Indooroopilly
Wynnum
Morningside
Ipswich
Goodna
Logan
Peel Island
St. Helena I.
Coochiemudlo
Redland Bay
Russell

Sydney inset
Broken Bay
Palm Beach
Cowan
Ku-ring-gai Chase Nat'l Park
Hornsby
Mona Vale
Terrey Hills
Dee Why
Manly
SYDNEY
Parramatta
Penrith
Blacktown
Liverpool
Bankstown
Botany
Sydney-Kingsford Smith
Cronulla
Sutherland
Royal Nat'l Park
Tasman Sea

Height / Depth legend
Height	
m / ft	
6000 / 19700	
4000 / 13000	
2000 / 6500	
1500 / 5000	
500 / 1600	
200 / 700	
0	
Depth	

Population
■ Over 2,000,000	⊕ 500,000-999,999
■ 1,000,000-1,999,999	⊕ 250,000-499,999
⊕ 100,000-249,999	● 10,000-29,999
● 30,000-99,999	○ Under 10,000

Scale 1:6,000,000 Lambert Conformal Conic Projection

Active volcanoes, geysers, glaciers, fjords, sandy beaches, evergreen beach forests, ferns the size of trees, parrots – the list of New Zealand's natural beauties goes on and on.

The North Island lies along the Pacific "Ring of Fire" and is therefore subject to volcanic eruptions. The South Island, where glaciers descend far into forested areas, is much calmer.

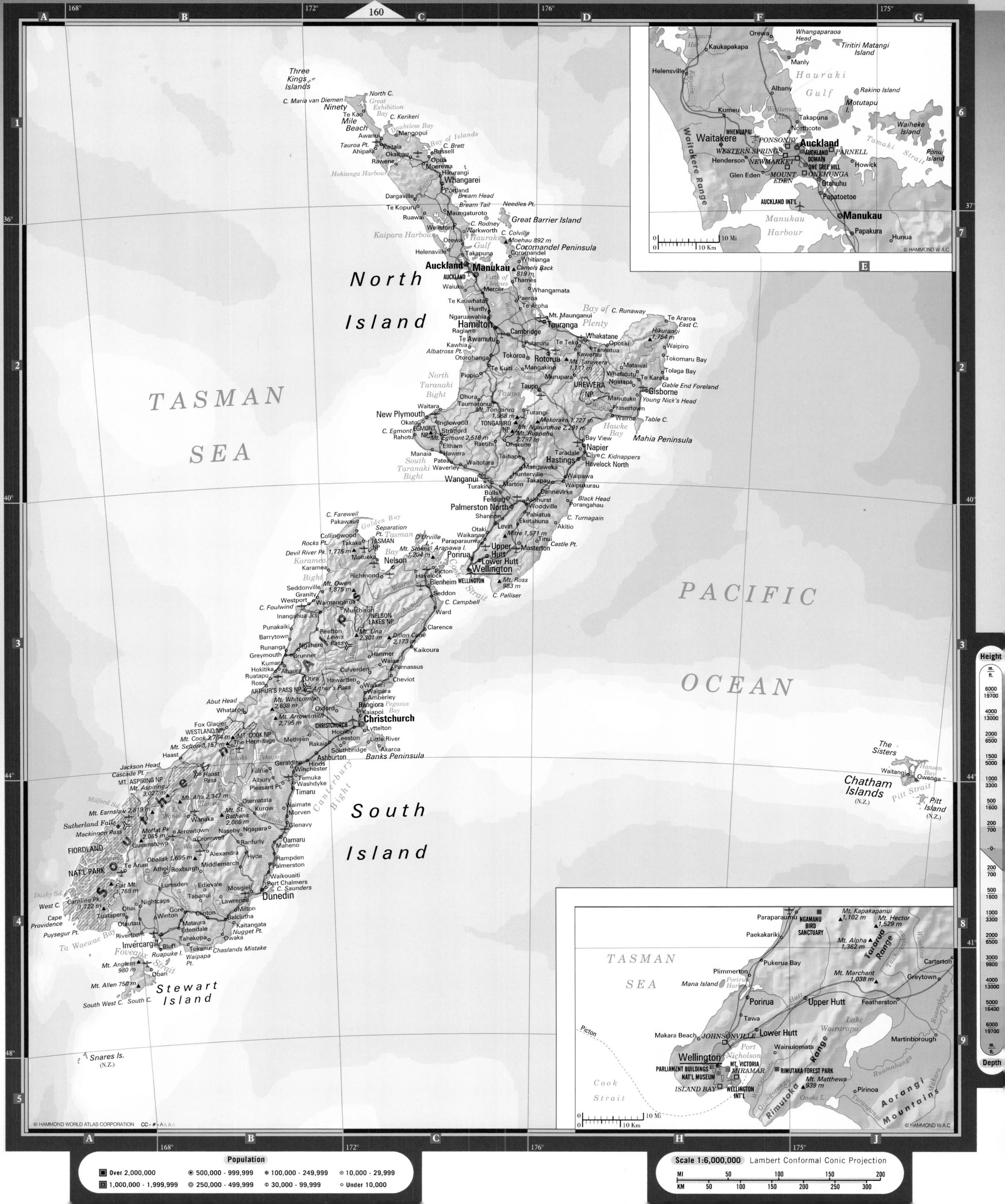

New Zealand

North Island

South Island

TASMAN SEA

PACIFIC OCEAN

Three Kings Islands

Ninety Mile Beach

Auckland
Manukau

Hamilton

Tauranga
Rotorua

Gisborne

New Plymouth

Napier
Hastings

Wanganui

Palmerston North

Upper Hutt
Lower Hutt
Wellington

Nelson
Blenheim

SOUTHERN ALPS

Greymouth

Christchurch

Fox Glacier
WESTLAND NP
Mt. Cook 3,764 m
MT. COOK NP

FIORDLAND
NAT'L PARK

Queenstown

Dunedin

Invercargill

Stewart Island

Chatham Islands (N.Z.)

The Sisters

Auckland inset
Auckland
Manukau
Waitakere

Hauraki Gulf

Manukau Harbour

Wellington inset
TASMAN SEA
Wellington
Porirua
Lower Hutt
Upper Hutt

Cook Strait

Scale 1:6,000,000 Lambert Conformal Conic Projection

Population
■ Over 2,000,000
□ 1,000,000 - 1,999,999
● 500,000 - 999,999
● 250,000 - 499,999
● 100,000 - 249,999
◉ 30,000 - 99,999
● 10,000 - 29,999
○ Under 10,000

Height
m. / ft.
6000 / 19700
4000 / 13000
2000 / 6500
1500 / 5000
1000 / 3300
500 / 1600
200 / 700
0
Depth

© HAMMOND WORLD ATLAS CORPORATION

The Pacific Ocean is the largest body of water on Earth. It covers about 166 million square km, while the world's total land area amounts to only 150 million square km. It is more than twice the size of the Atlantic and Indian oceans and holds roughly 46% of the Earth's water. The ocean is by no means as peaceful as its name suggests. Tropical storms known as typhoons generate waves up to 34 m high. Evidently, Ferdinand Magellan, who gave the ocean its name in 1520, enjoyed calm seas on his voyage across the Pacific.

CHINA

JAPAN

TAIWAN

PHILIPPINES

NORTHERN MARIANA ISLANDS (U.S.)

Guam (U.S.)

MARSHALL ISLANDS

PALAU

CAROLINE ISLANDS

FEDERATED STATES OF MICRONESIA

NAURU

GILBERT ISLANDS

TUVALU

MALAYSIA

INDONESIA

EAST TIMOR

PAPUA NEW GUINEA

BISMARCK ARCHIPELAGO

SOLOMON ISLANDS

VANUATU

NEW CALEDONIA (FR.)

NEW HEBRIDES

FIJI

WALLIS AND FUTUNA (FR.)

AUSTRALIA

CORAL SEA

TASMAN SEA

NEW ZEALAND

INDIAN OCEAN

NORTH PACIFIC

SOUTH PACIFIC

Micronesia

Melanesia

Polynesia

Height

m.	ft.
6000	19700
4000	13000
2000	6500
1500	5000
1000	3300
500	1600
200	700
-0-	
200	700
500	1600
1000	3300
2000	6500
3000	9800
4000	13000
5000	16400
6000	19700

Depth

Population
- Over 3,000,000
- 1,000,000 - 2,999,999
- 500,000 - 999,999
- 100,000 - 499,999
- Under 100,000

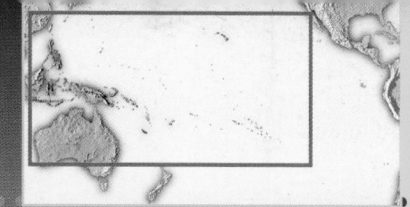
Scale 1:27,000,000 Lambert Azimuthal Equal-Area

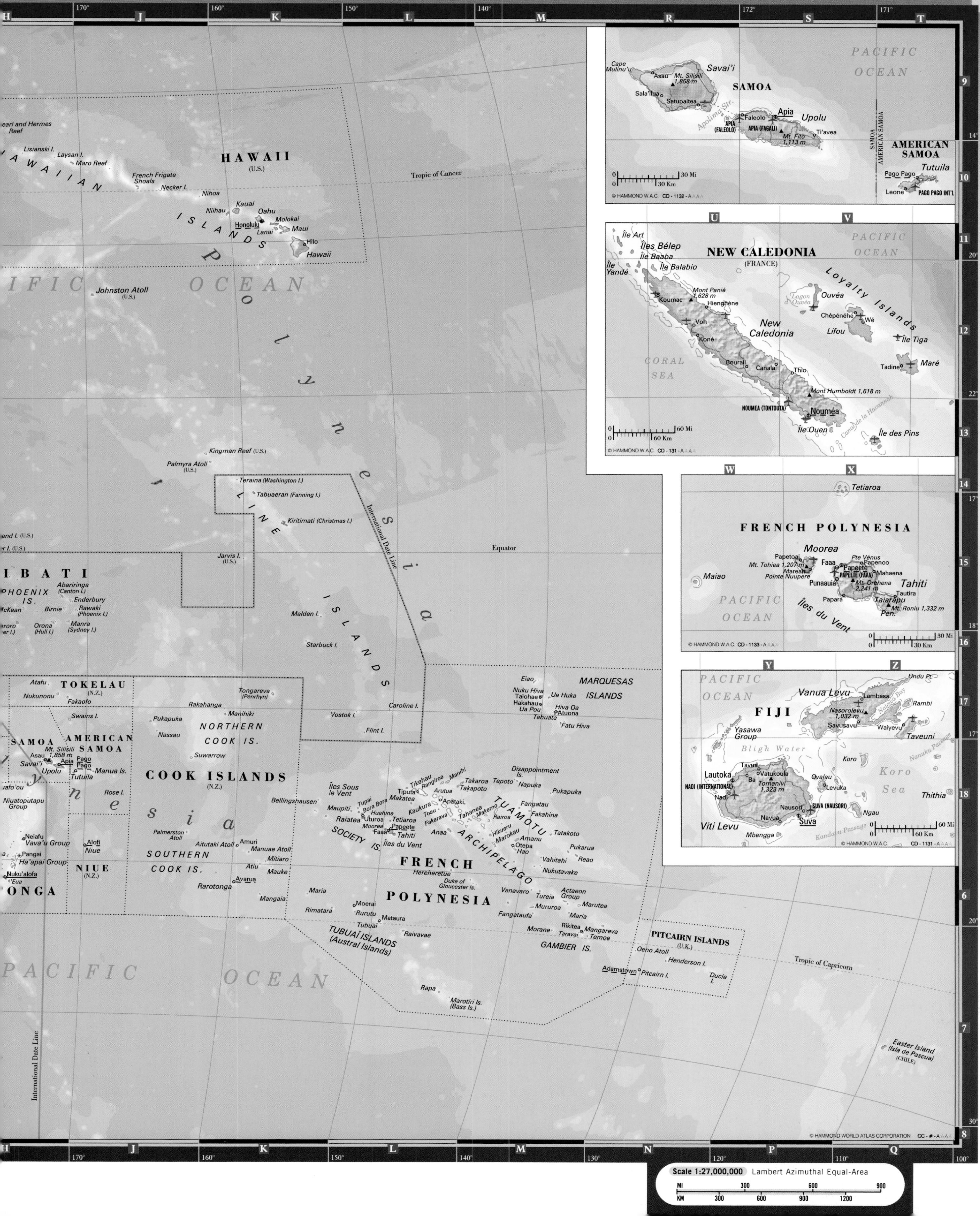

With a depth of 1.6 km, the Grand Canyon is one of the deepest river gorges in the world. This image taken toward the west shows the Colorado River, which has cut through rock billions of years old to form the canyon. The Grand Canyon is 260 km long and averages about 16 km in width at the top but narrows to as few as 15 m in places along the valley floor. The river flows over 150 rapids on its course through the canyon. The valley itself is only a few million years old. Visible in the image are the snow-covered Kaibab Plateau north of the canyon and the Coconino Plateau to the south.

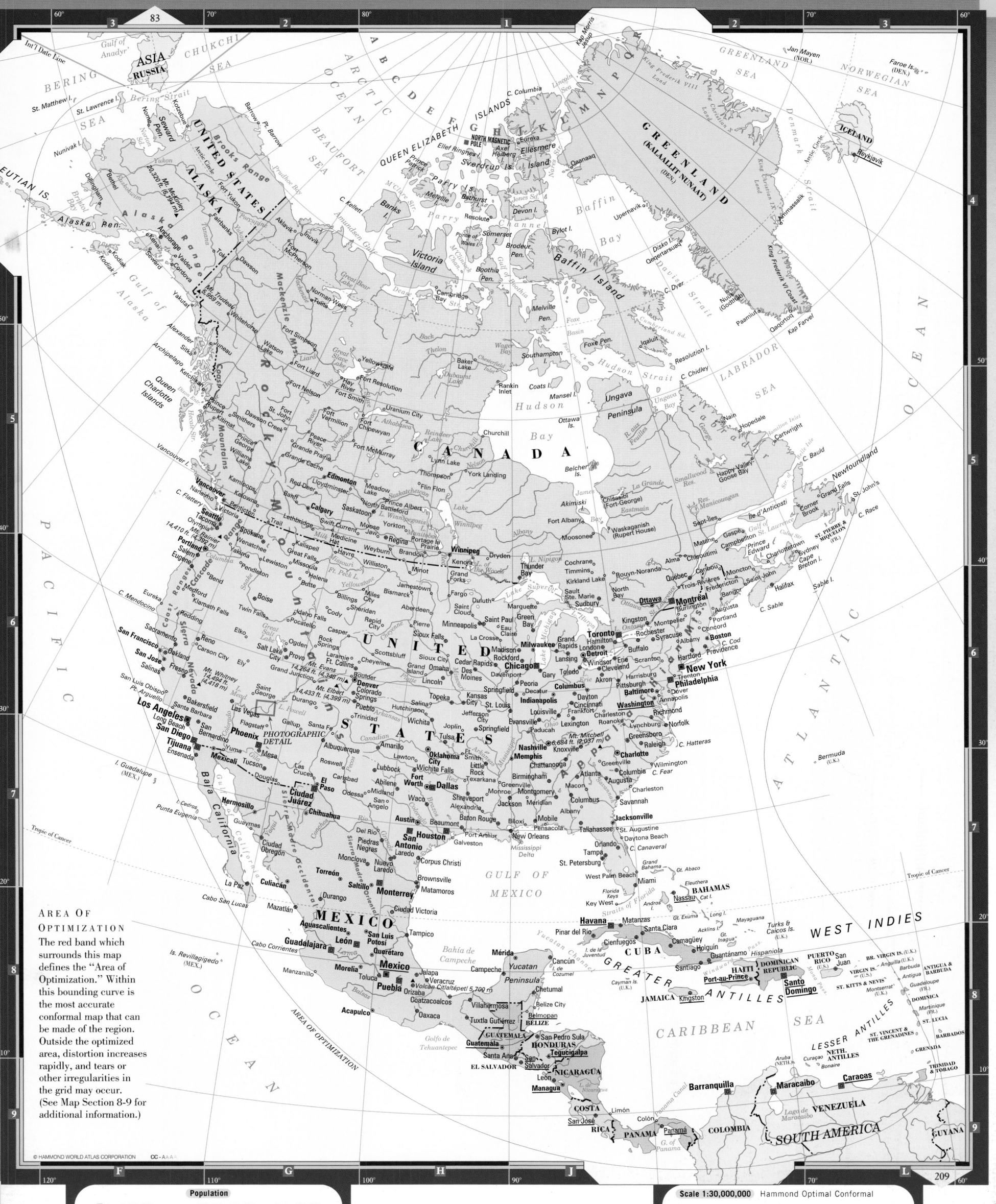

AREA OF OPTIMIZATION
The red band which surrounds this map defines the "Area of Optimization." Within this bounding curve is the most accurate conformal map that can be made of the region. Outside the optimized area, distortion increases rapidly, and tears or other irregularities in the grid may occur. (See Map Section 8-9 for additional information.)

© HAMMOND WORLD ATLAS CORPORATION

Population
■ Over 3,000,000
■ 1,000,000 - 2,999,999
● 500,000 - 999,999
● 100,000 - 499,999
○ Under 100,000

Scale 1:30,000,000   Hammond Optimal Conformal

MI   250   500   750   1000   1250   1500
KM   250   500   1000   1500

UNESCO Protects World Cultural Heritage Sites

World Heritage Sites in North America

Text continued from page 146 - UNESCO World Cultural Heritage Sites of Australia

The World Heritage Convention

The Convention on Preservation of the World Cultural and Natural Heritage was passed at the UNESCO General Assembly meeting of 1972. It has since been signed by 167 nations. Signatory countries accept the obligation to protect and preserve sites, recognized as part of the World Heritage, that lie within their borders.

The underlying principle is that sites of unique and universal value – be they architectural monuments, urban districts, or cultivated landscapes – should be recognized as the common heritage of all people on Earth and afforded international protection. The value of such objects may be aesthetic, historical, or scientific in nature.

Text continues on page 210 - UNESCO World Cultural Heritage Sites of South America

City of the Gods

Relief panels on the steps of the Quetzalcoatl Pyramid exhibit the heads of the Feathered Serpent and the god of rain or thunder. Temples erected on stepped pyramids in the ceremonial district of Teotihuacán, **Mexico (22)**, line both sides of the Avenue of the Dead for a distance of 2 km.

Impregnable Bastion

The fortress (16th c.) and Old Town of San Juan (38) in Puerto Rico were dominated by the massive Castillo de San Felipe del Morro. The photo shows the fortified tip of the peninsula.

Prehistoric Hunters

Prehistoric hunters in central North America killed game animals by driving them over high cliffs. (Photo: Head Smashed-in Bison Jump (2) in Alberta)

Historic City

A by-product of missionary work, Québec, **Canada (3)**, was founded by the French explorer Champlain in the early 17th century. The Upper Town and Lower Town with its ancient districts, forms an urban ensemble which is one of the best examples of a fortified colonial city in North America.

Model City

The colonial city of Santo Domingo, **Dominican Republic (37)**, founded in 1498, was laid out on a grid pattern that became the model for almost all town planners in the New World. Site of the first cathedral, hospital, customs house and university in the Americas.

Zoomorphic Altars

The Mayan city of Quiriguá, **Mexico (41)**, flourished between 500 and 800 AD. Hewn from sandstone blocks, the mythical animal figures with hieroglyphs were used as altars.

Havana, **Cuba (33)** was founded in 1519 by the Spanish. By the 17th century, it had become one of the Caribbean's main centers for ship-building.

Ancient Indian Housing Complex

Up to four stories high, the semicircular housing complex of Pueblo Bonito built by the Anasazi Indians in what is now Chaco Culture National Park, **USA (11)**, was occupied from 920 to 1120 AD. It comprised 800 living spaces and underground storage areas ("kivas"). Chaco Canyon was the hub of an extensive trading network and presumably a religious center in the 13th century.

UNESCO World Cultural Heritage in North America

1 Anthony Island	**19** Hospicio Cabanas, Guadalajara	**35** San Pedro de la Roca Fortress
2 Head Smashed-In Bison Jump	**20** Historic Center of Morelia	**36** Haiti National Historical Park
3 Historical Quebec	**21** Historic Center of Mexico City	**37** Colonial City of Santo Domingo
4 L'Anse aux Meadows	and Xochimilco	**38** Fortress and National Historic Site,
5 Old Town of Lunenburg	**22** Teotihuacán	San Juan
6 Statue of Liberty	**23** Xochicalco	**39** Brimstone Hill Fort
7 Independence Hall, Philadelphia	**24** Monasteries on the	**40** Tikal National Park
8 University of Virgunia Charlottesville	Slopes of Popocatépetl	**41** Quiriguá
9 Cahokia Mounds Historic Site	**25** Old Town of Puebla	**42** Copán
10 Mesa Verde National Park	**26** Oaxaca and Monte Albán	**43** Antigua, Guatemala
11 Chaco Culture National Historical Park	**27** Tlacotalpan	**44** Joya de Ceren
12 Pueblo de Taos	**28** Palenque	**45** Historic District of Panama
13 Paquime Archeological Zone	**29** Campeche	**46** Portobelo-San Lorenzo Fortifications
14 Rock Paintings, Sierra de San Francisco	**30** Uxmal	**47** Luis Barragán House and Studio
15 Historic Center of Zacatecas	**31** Chichén Itzá	**48** Agave Landscape and Ancient
16 Guanajuato	**32** Viñales Valley	Industrial Facilities of Tequila
17 El Taijin	**33** Old City of Havana	**49** Urban Historic Centre of Cienfuegos
18 Querétaro	**34** Trinidad	**50** First Coffee Plantations, South-East Cuba
		51 Ruins of León Viejo

Symbol of Liberty

Haiti Historic National Park (36) - The Palace of Sans Souci, the buildings at Ramiers and, in particular, the Citadel serve as universal symbols of liberty, being the first monuments to be constructed by black slaves who had gained their freedom.

Alaska

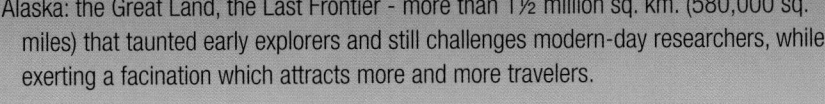

The Last Frontier

Alaska: the Great Land, the Last Frontier - more than 1½ million sq. km. (580,000 sq. miles) that taunted early explorers and still challenges modern-day researchers, while exerting a facination which attracts more and more travelers.

America's 49th state is broad, so unpeopled, and so roadless that small airplanes are more common here than taxi cabs in other states.

The population numbers just under 650,000, almost half of whom live in one city, Anchrorage. Nearly the entire state is raw, wondrous wilderness.

Alaska has lush, rain-drenched forests and fragile, windswept tundras. There are lofty mountains, still-active volcanoes, and spectacular glaciers, as well as three million lakes and endless swamps.

History Decisive Dates

Check used for the Alaska Purchase

THE EARLY ALASKANS: 30-10,000 B.C.- The migration of tribes from Asia occurs across a land bridge, which at the time linked Siberia and Alaska. The Aleuts settle in the Aleutian Islands. The name Alaska derived from their "Alaxsxag" meaning "the object toward which the action of the sea is directed."

THE RUSSIAN INVASION: 1741 - First Russian ships arrive; **1784** - Grigor Ivanovich Shelikof arrives on Kodiak Island. He enslaves the natives, then sets up the first permanent Russian settlements; **1790** - Alexander Baranof takes over the fur enterprise. He treats the natives more humanely, and moves the Russian colony to the site of the present city of Kodiak. The Tlingits raze to the ground the Russian town of Mikhailovsk. Later the Russians destroy the Tlingit village and establish New Achangel, capital of Russian America; **1799** - The Russian-American Company is formed. **1833** - The British Hudson's Bay Company establishes a fur-trading outpost in Alaska. **Mid-19th century** - Russian power diminishes. British and Americans undermine the fur monopoly and the Tlingits wage guerrilla war.

Totem pole

AMERICA TAKES OVER: 1867 - The U.S., at the instigation of Secretary of State William Seward, buys Alaska from the Russians for $7.2 million. **1870-80s** - Fish canneries are established around Nushagak Bay to exploit the huge runs of salmon. In the Aleutians, fur seals and otters are slaughtered ruthlessly. Whalers pursue their quarries to the high Arctic.

Trading post

THE GOLD RUSH: 1880 - Gold is discovered at Silver Bow Basin, and the town of Juneau is founded. **1896** - Gold is discovered in the Klondike River, a tributary of the Yukon. The White Pass and Chilkoot Trail to the gold fields are tackled by thousands, and Skagway becomes a thriving center. **1899** - Gold is discovered at Nome in the far northwest. **1902** - Felix Pedro strikes gold in the Tanana Hills. **1903** - The town of Fairbanks is founded. **Early 1900s** - Prospectors flock to Alaska from all over North America and Europe.

Gold panning

WORLD WAR II: The Alaska Highway (the Alcan) is constructed in under nine months as both a means of defense and an overland supply route to America's Russian allies. The Japanese land on the islands of Kiska and Attu. **1943** - After a two-week battle the Americans re-take Attu in May. In July the Americans bomb Kiska and the Japanese retreat.

Trans-Alaska pipeline

STATEHOOD AND OIL: 1957 - Oil is discovered at the Swanson River on the Kenai Peninsula. **1959** - Alaska becomes the 49th state in January. **1968** - Oil is discovered at Prudhoe Bay. **1971** - The Alaska Native Claims Settlements Act (ANCSA) gives natives title to 44 million acres of land, and $963 million, distributed among specially formed native corporations. **1971-77** - Construction of the Trans-Alaska pipeline to Valdez creates thousands of jobs, and the state economy booms. **1980** - President Jimmy Carter signs the Alaska National Interest Lands Conservation Act (ANILCA), which adds 106 million acres of conservation lands, in national parks, wildlife refuges, and forests. **1989** - The Exxon Valdez spills 11 million gallons of oil into Prince William Sound. Thousands of miles of coastline are affected, and thousands of birds and mammals are killed. **1990s** - The ecosystem of Prince William Sound largely recovers. Decline in oil production at Prudhoe Bay leads to lay-offs. Low-impact ecotourism flourishes. The logging and fishing industries are in steady decline. **Early 2000s** - Tourism continues to be one of the fastest-growing industries. State and federal governments officially recognize Alaska Native tribal governments. A fierce debate continues over the future of the Arctic National Wildlife Refuge's Coastal Plain. Developers want it to be opened to oil and gas exploration and development; environmentalists fight to have it preserved as wilderness, while Alaska's native people are split on the issue. There is talk of building a new pipeline to ship Alaska's rich reserves of natural gas to the Lower 48 states.

Cleaning oil spill

Tourist cruise

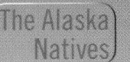
The Alaska Natives

Inuit woman

The Coastal Indians

These were probably in the first wave of immigrants to cross the land bridge from Siberia, although many initially settled in Canada. The Tlingits were the most numerous; they claimed most of the coastal Panhandle, leaving only a small southern portion to the less populous Haidas. In the late 1800s the Haidas were joined by the Tsimshians who emigrated from Canada to Annette Island. The Coastal Indians had great respect for the natural world. They believed that fish and animals gave themselves willingly to humans.

The Athabascans

The Athabascan Indians of Alaska's harsh interior were hunters and inland fishermen. Most lived in small nomadic bands along the region's rivers. They survived temperatures of -50F or less. Endurance and physical strength were prized; game was often run down on foot over difficult terrain. Athabascans hunted salmon, hares, birds, caribou, moose and bear with the help of snares, clubs and bows and arrows.

The Aleuts

This group settled the windswept islands of the Aleutian chain 10,000 years ago. They harvested the sea's bounty and contended with harsh weather, as well as earthquakes and volcanic eruptions. Aleut fishing technology included fish spears, weirs, nets, hooks and lines. Whales were killed with a poisoned stone-bladed lance. The job of women and children was to gather shellfish at low tide. Aleuts seldom journeyed far, but they made their ingenious skis from hairseal skins. Uphill the hair would dig into the snow. Downhill the hair would lay flat for speed.

The Alutiiqs

Close relatives of the Aleuts, Alutiiq people settled on the Alaska Peninsula, Kodiak Archipelago, and parts of the Kenai Peninsula and Prince William Sound. The Alutiiq were skilled maritime hunters and fishers. They paddled bidarkas while hunting sea lions, seals, sea otters and whales. The people collected all manner of items to make their clothes and build their homes and tools: animal skins, feathers, bones, sod, driftwood and grasses. Seal oil was used as fuel to light their lamps.

Alutiiq dancer

The Eyak

The tribe's oral history suggests that the Eyak people traveled south through Alaska's interior, then down the Copper River, to the Gulf of Alaska coast. A relatively small group, the Eyak were sometimes raided by other coastal tribes, particularly the Alutiiq. Over time much of the Eyak population and culture was assimilated by the Tlingit's larger and more dominant society. Today only a few hundred Eyak survive.

The Eskimos

Eskimos, the native group most familiar to non-Alaskans, were originally divided into two subgroups. The Inupiat Eskimos settled in Alaska's Arctic region, while the Yup'ik lived in the west. Life was a constant struggle against hunger and cold. Seasonal food was stored against future shortage and for long dark winters. Eskimo village sites were chosen for availability of food sources. Eskimos - known as the Nunamiut - lived on a diet of caribou, birds and small animals. They used boats called umiaks to hunt large sea animals. They also used smaller, one-man craft, called kayaks. Women were skilled in basketry and sewing. Their coats, called parkas, featured an attached hood and ruff. Eskimos are renowned for their fine ivory carving.

Alaskan Wildlife

Mountain goat

Caribou

Coyote

Lynx

Musk oxen

Red fox

Beaver

Ringed seal

Wolverine

Porcupine

Walrus

Black bear

River otter

Bold eagle

Spruce grouse

Artic fox

Snowtail rabbit

Willow ptarmigan

Oyster catcher

Salmon

Killer whales

Hurricane Katrina

History/Overview:

Hurricane Katrina was the deadliest since the 1928 Okeechobee hurricane and one of the costliest in the history of the United States. It was the third-strongest hurricane on record to make landfall in the United States, and the sixth-strongest Atlantic hurricane ever recorded.

On August 23, during the 2005 Atlantic hurricane season, Katrina formed over the Bahamas and crossed southern Florida as a moderate Category 1 hurricane, causing some deaths and flooding there. It then strengthened rapidly in the Gulf of Mexico and became one of the strongest hurricanes on record. The storm weakened before making its second and third landfall as a Category 3 storm on the morning of August 29. Due to its sheer size, Katrina devastated the Gulf Coast as far as 160 kilometers (100 miles) from the storm's center.

The most notable catastrophic effects were on the cities of Bay St. Louis, Waveland, Biloxi and Gulfport in Mississippi, as well as Mobile, Alabama, and Slidell, and New Orleans, Louisiana. Levees separating Lake Pontchartrain and several New Orleans canals were breached as Katrina passed slightly east of the city, subsequently flooding 80% of New Orleans and many areas of neighboring parishes for weeks.

At least 1,836 people lost their lives in Hurricane Katrina and in the subsequent floods.

Path of Hurricane Kat

Hurricane Katrina over the Gulf of Mexico

Formation:

Hurricane Katrina formed as Tropical Depression Twelve over the southeastern Bahamas on August 23, 2005. The system was upgraded to tropical storm status on the morning of August 24, and at this point the storm was given the name Katrina. The tropical storm continued to move towards Florida and became a hurricane only two hours before it made landfall between Hallandale Beach and Aventura on the morning of August 25. The storm weakened over land, but it regained hurricane status about one hour after entering the Gulf of Mexico.

The storm rapidly intensified after entering the Gulf, partly because of its movement over the warm waters of the Loop Current. On August 27, it reached Category 3 intensity on the Saffir-Simpson Hurricane Scale. An eye wall replacement cycle disrupted the intensification, but caused the storm to nearly double in size. Katrina again rapidly intensified, attaining Category 5 status on the morning of August 28, and reached its peak strength at 1:00 p.m. CDT that day, with maximum sustained winds of 280 kph (175 mph) and a minimum central pressure of 902 millibars.

Preparation:

By August 26, the possibility of an unprecedented cataclysm was already being considered. Many of the computer models had shifted the potential path of Katrina 150 miles westward from the Florida Panhandle, putting the city of New Orleans right in the center of their track probabilities. The chances of a direct hit were forecast at 17%, with strike probability rising to 29% by August 28. This scenario was considered a potential catastrophe because 80% of the city of New Orleans and the Metro area on the southern shore are below sea level along Lake Pontchartrain. Since the storm surge produced by the hurricane's right front quadrant (containing the strongest winds) was forecast to be 8.5 meters (28 feet), emergency management officials in New Orleans feared that the storm surge could go over the tops of levees protecting the city, causing major flooding.

At a news conference at 10:00 a.m. on August 28, shortly after Katrina was upgraded to a Category 5 storm, New Orleans mayor Ray Nagin ordered the first ever mandatory evacuation of the city, calling Katrina "a storm that most of us have long feared."

The city government also established several "refuges of last resort" for citizens who could not leave the city, including the massive Louisiana Superdome, which sheltered approximately 26,000 people and provided them with food and water for several days as the storm came ashore.

Retiring of Katrina:

Because of the large loss of life and property along the Gulf Coast, the name Katrina was officially retired on April 6, 2006 by the World Meteorological Organization at the request of the U.S. government. It was replaced by Katia on List III of the Atlantic hurricane naming lists, which will next be used in the 2011 Atlantic hurricane season.

Aftermath Tally:

As of May 19, 2006, the confirmed death toll of direct and indirect deaths stood at 1,836, mainly from Louisiana (1,577) and Mississippi (238). Many of the deaths are indirect, but it is almost impossible to determine the exact cause of some of the fatalities.

Federal disaster declarations covered 233,000 sq. km. (90,000 square miles) of the United States, an area almost as large as the United Kingdom.

The storm is estimated to have been responsible for $81.2 billion (2005 U.S. dollars) in damage, making it the costliest natural disaster in U.S. history.

The hurricane left an estimated three million people without electricity.

On September 3, 2005, Homeland Security Secretary Michael Chertoff described the aftermath of Hurricane Katrina as "probably the worst catastrophe, or set of catastrophes," in the country's history, referring to the hurricane itself plus the flooding of New Orleans.

Before Katrina hit (left) and after (right)

Hurricane Katrina Aftermath

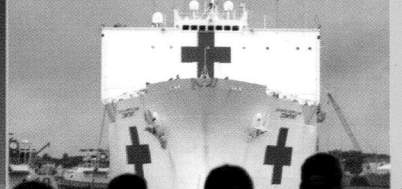

Economic Effects:

In 2006 the Bush Administration has sought more than $100 billion for repairs and reconstruction in the region. This does not take into account damage to the economy caused by potential interruption of the oil supply, destruction of the Gulf Coast's highway infrastructure, and the interrupted exports of commodities such as grain.

Katrina damaged or destroyed 30 oil platforms and caused the closure of nine refineries. The total lost oil production from the Gulf of Mexico in the six-month period following Katrina was approximately 24% of the annual production and the lost gas production for the same period was about 18%.

The forestry industry in Mississippi was also affected, as 1.3 million acres of forest lands were destroyed. The total loss to the forestry industry is estimated to be about $5 billion.

Population Effect:

Within six months less than half of the pre-storm population (about 200,000 people) were once again living in New Orleans.

In July, 2006, when new population estimates were calculated by the U.S. Census Bureau, the state of Louisiana showed a population decline of 219,563, or 4.87%.

Environmental Effects:

The storm surge caused substantial beach erosion, in some cases completely devastating coastal areas. On Dauphin Island, about 150 km. (90 miles) east of the point where the hurricane made landfall, the sands of the barrier island were transported across the island into the Mississippi Sound, pushing the island towards land.

The storm surge and waves from Katrina also obliterated the Chandeleur Islands, affecting many species of marine mammals.

Finally, as part of the cleanup effort, the flood waters that covered New Orleans were pumped into Lake Pontchartrain, a process that took 43 days to complete. These residual waters contained a mix of raw sewage, bacteria, heavy metals, pesticides, toxic chemicals and about 24.6 million liters (6.5 million U.S. gallons) of oil.

Controversy/Criticism of Response:

The criticisms of the government's response to Hurricane Katrina primarily consisted of condemnations of mismanagement and lack of leadership in the relief efforts in response to the storm and its aftermath.

The criticism focused on the delayed response to the flooding of New Orleans, and the subsequent state of chaos in the Crescent City.

The government was accused of making things worse, instead of making things better, by preventing help by others while delaying its own efforts.

In accordance with federal law, President George W. Bush directed the Secretary of the Department of Homeland Security, Michael Chertoff, to coordinate the Federal response. Chertoff designated Michael D. Brown, head of the Federal Emergency Management Agency (FEMA), as the principal official to lead the deployment and coordination of all federal response resources and forces in the Gulf Coast region.

Flooded streets

President Bush and Secretary Chertoff initially came under harsh criticism for what some perceived as a lack of planning and coordination. Eight days later, Brown was recalled to Washington and Coast Guard Vice Admiral Thad W. Allen replaced him as chief of hurricane relief operations.

Three days after the recall, Brown resigned as director of FEMA in spite of having received praise from President Bush.

Criticism from politicians, activists, pundits and journalists of all stripes was also directed at the local and state governments headed by Mayor Ray Nagin of New Orleans and Louisiana Governor Kathleen Blanco.

Nagin and Blanco were criticized for failing to implement New Orleans' evacuation plan and for ordering residents to a shelter of last resort without any provisions for food, water, security or sanitary conditions.

Perhaps the most important criticism of Nagin was that he delayed his emergency evacuation order until 19 hours before landfall, which led to the death of hundreds of people who by that time could not find any way out of the city.

New Orleans survivor search flyover

International Response:

Over seventy countries pledged monetary donations or other assistance.

Kuwait made the largest single pledge, $500 million; other large donations were made by Qatar ($100 million), South Korea ($30 million), India, China (both $5 million), Pakistan ($1.5 million), and Bangladesh ($1 million).

Cuba and Venezuela offered aid in the form of $1 million, 1,100 doctors, 26.4 metric tons of medicine, two mobile hospitals, 10 water purifying plants, 18 generators, 20 tons of bottled water, 50 tons of canned food and 66,000 barrels of heating oil. Their offers were refused by the U.S. government.

Countries including Canada, Mexico, Singapore and Germany sent supplies, relief personnel, troops, ships and water pumps to the aid.

Corporate Response:

Many corporations also contributed to relief efforts. By September 13, after only two weeks, it was reported that corporate donations had exceeded $400 million.

Red Cross emergency financial assistance was provided to 1.4 million families, which encompassed a total of 4 million people.

During and after the hurricanes Katrina, Wilma and Rita, the American Red Cross had opened 1,470 different shelters and registered 3.8 million overnight stays.

The Salvation Army donated more than $365 million to serve more than 1.7 million people.

Recovery: Mississippi

In partnership with the Mississippi Emergency Management Agency (MEMA), the U.S. Department of Homeland Security's Federal Emergency Management Agency (FEMA) obligated nearly $10 billion in disaster aid to Mississippi.

About $1.15 billion has been approved for public assistance (not including debris removal), and nearly a billion dollars have been disbursed for rebuilding projects including bridges, public buildings and utilities.

About $1.23 billion went to individuals and families.

More than $1.3 billion went to debris removal.

Recovery: Louisiana:

More than 600 vessels have been removed by the U.S. Coast Guard, under a FEMA-funded mission assignment. These wrecked vessels will no longer pose a health or safety threat from environmental pollution or impaired navigation.

There are more than 3,000 federal housing units occupied by hurricane evacuees in the State of Louisiana. Federal housing or housing vouchers from the Department of Housing and Urban Development, the U.S. Department of Agriculture and others were provided to displaced hurricane victims.

In addition to household debris removal from rights of way, the U.S. Army Corps of Engineers (USACE), along with private contractors working for some Louisiana Parishes, have removed more than 38 million cubic yards of debris.

More than two billion in federal dollars has already been allocated for Public Assistance (PA) projects, such as debris removal and emergency services in Louisiana parishes. FEMA has issued 1.5 million housing assistance checks, totaling more than $3.5 billion, to Louisiana victims in rental assistance and home repair grants.

FEMA Trailers

Canada's topography was shaped by glacial ice, and the country was completely covered by ice until only 18,000 years ago. As the ice receded, it left behind large basins that filled with melt water. Today,

Height

m.	ft.
6000	19700
4000	13000
2000	6500
1500	5000
1000	3300
500	1600
200	700
0	
200	700
500	1600
1000	3300
2000	6500
3000	9800
4000	13000
5000	16400
6000	19700

m. ft.

Depth

Population

■ Over 2,000,000	⊙ 500,000 - 999,999
▣ 1,000,000 - 1,999,999	⊙ 100,000 - 499,999
	⊙ 50,000 - 99,999
	○ Under 50,000

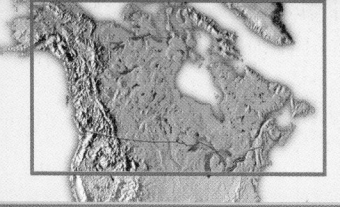

Canada has more than two million lakes. The country is larger than the United States but very thinly populated, as widespread settlement has been discouraged by the extremely short growing season north of the 55th parallel, the extremely poor, thin soils north of the St. Lawrence Valley, and low levels of precipitation in the northwestern coniferous forest and tundra region.

Scale 1:12,000,000   Lambert Conformal Conic Projection

© HAMMOND WORLD ATLAS CORPORATION

The Rocky Mountains, the Mississippi River system, which flows along a course of more than 6,400 km from the north to the Gulf of Mexico, and the Great Lakes along the border to Canada are the most striking major landscape features of the United States. The geologically young Rocky Mountains extend nearly 4,800 km from Alaska through Canada and into New Mexico. The five Great Lakes form the largest contiguous area of fresh water in the world, covering some 245,000 square km. Lake Ontario and Lake Erie are joined by the spectacular Niagara Falls.

Height

m.	ft.
6000	19700
4000	13000
2000	6500
1500	5000
1000	3300
500	1600
200	700
-0-	
200	700
500	1600
1000	3300
2000	6500
3000	9800
4000	13000
5000	16400
6000	19700

m. / ft.

Depth

Population

▣ Over 2,000,000	◉ 500,000 - 999,999	● 50,000 - 99,999
▫ 1,000,000 - 1,999,999	⊙ 100,000 - 499,999	○ Under 50,000

© HAMMOND W.A.C. CJ - 1158 - A A A

© HAMMOND W.A.C. CJ - 1157 - A A A

United States

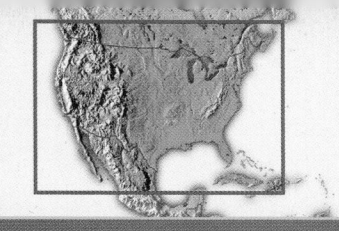

171

203

© HAMMOND WORLD ATLAS CORPORATION

Scale 1:12,000,000 Lambert Conformal Conic Projection

| MI | 100 | 200 | 300 | 400 |
| KM | 100 | 200 | 300 | 400 | 500 | 600 |

The glacier-covered Rocky Mountains, with peaks over 4,000 m high, and the volcanic Cascade Range are both products of a collision between the Pacific and North American plates. Over the course of the past several billion years, microplates have been pulverized, folded, thrust upward, or pressed deep into the earth along the line of convergence. Several thousand kilometers of the oceanic plate have disappeared beneath the North American continent. This rock melts and returns to the surface as lava through volcanoes like Mount Saint Helens and Mount Rainier.

Height	
m. / ft.	
6000 / 19700	
4000 / 13000	
2000 / 6500	
1500 / 5000	
1000 / 3300	
500 / 1600	
200 / 700	
-0-	
200 / 700	
500 / 1600	
1000 / 3300	
2000 / 6500	
3000 / 9800	
4000 / 13000	
5000 / 16400	
6000 / 19700	
m. / ft.	
Depth	

Population
- ■ Over 2,000,000
- ■ 1,000,000 - 1,999,999
- ● 500,000 - 999,999
- ● 250,000 - 499,999
- ◉ 100,000 - 249,999
- ◎ 30,000 - 99,999
- ○ 10,000 - 29,999
- ○ Under 10,000

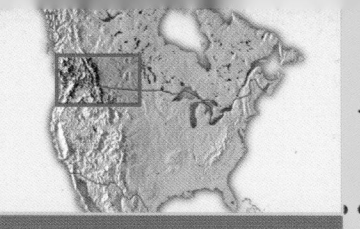

Southwestern Canada, Northwestern U.S.

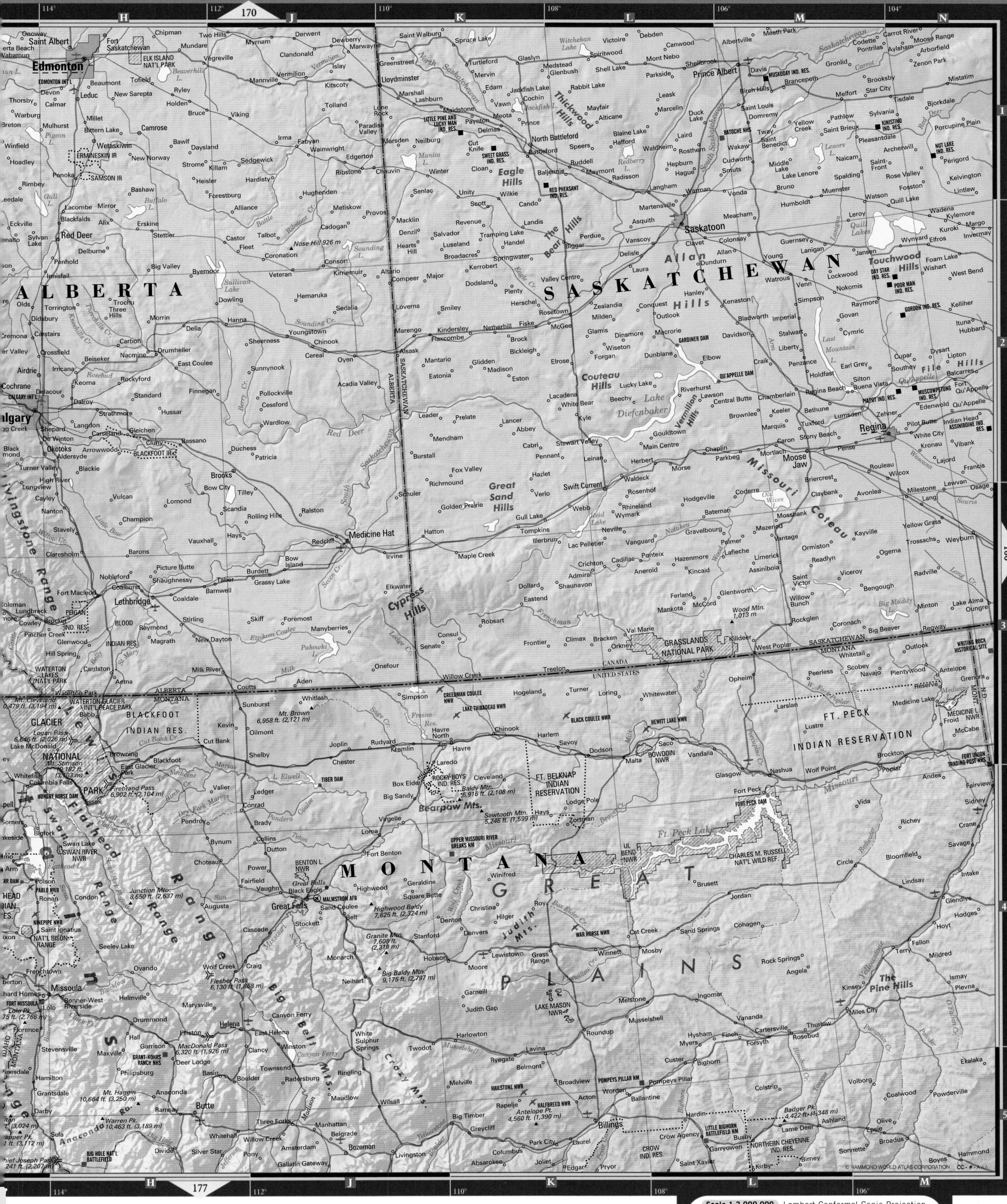

Scale 1:3,000,000 Lambert Conformal Conic Projection

Arid areas of North America like the Great Basin and the nearby salt lakes are most prevalent in the central western states, where high mountain chains hold back moisture-bearing winds. Thus annual precipitation west of the Sierra Nevada can be as high as 1,300 mm, while Reno on the rim of the Great Basin receives only about 150 mm of precipitation a year. The Great Salt Lake is a remnant of Lake Bonneville, an ice-age lake with depths of up to 330 m and a surface area of over 50,000 square km. Depending upon drainage, the Great Salt Lake covers some 5,000 square km with a mean depth of three meters.

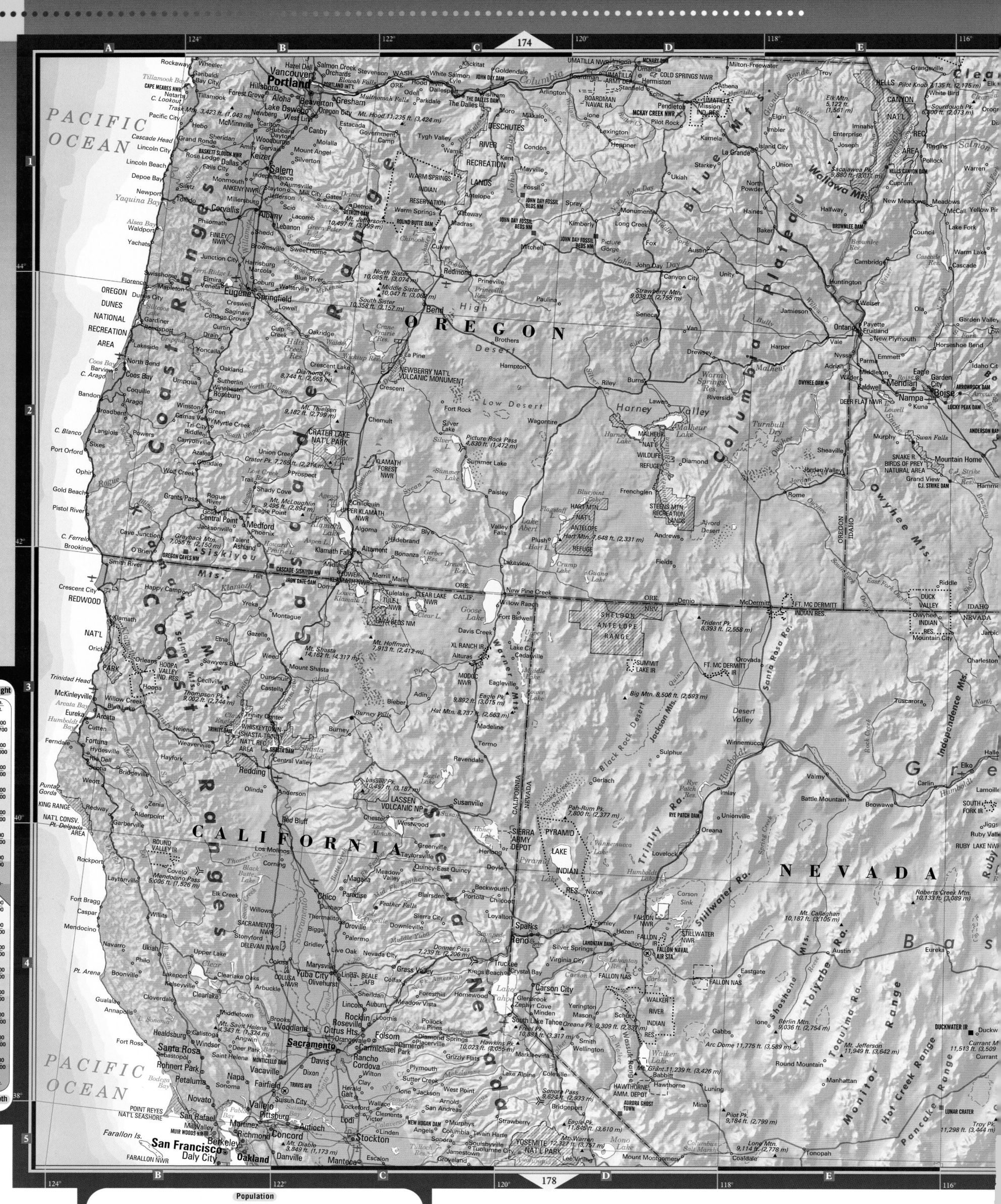

Height

m.	ft.
6000	19700
4000	13000
2000	6500
1500	5000
1000	3300
500	1600
200	700
-0-
200	700
500	1600
1000	3300
2000	6500
3000	9800
4000	13000
5000	16400
6000	19700

m.
ft.

Depth

Population

■ Over 2,000,000   ● 500,000 - 999,999   ⊚ 100,000 - 249,999   ○ 10,000 - 29,999
□ 1,000,000 - 1,999,999   ◉ 250,000 - 499,999   ⊙ 30,000 - 99,999   ∘ Under 10,000

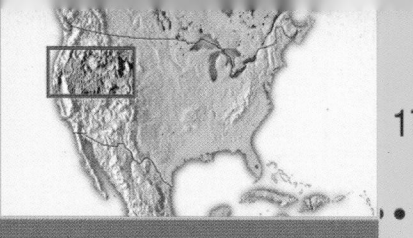

Central Pacific and Western U.S.

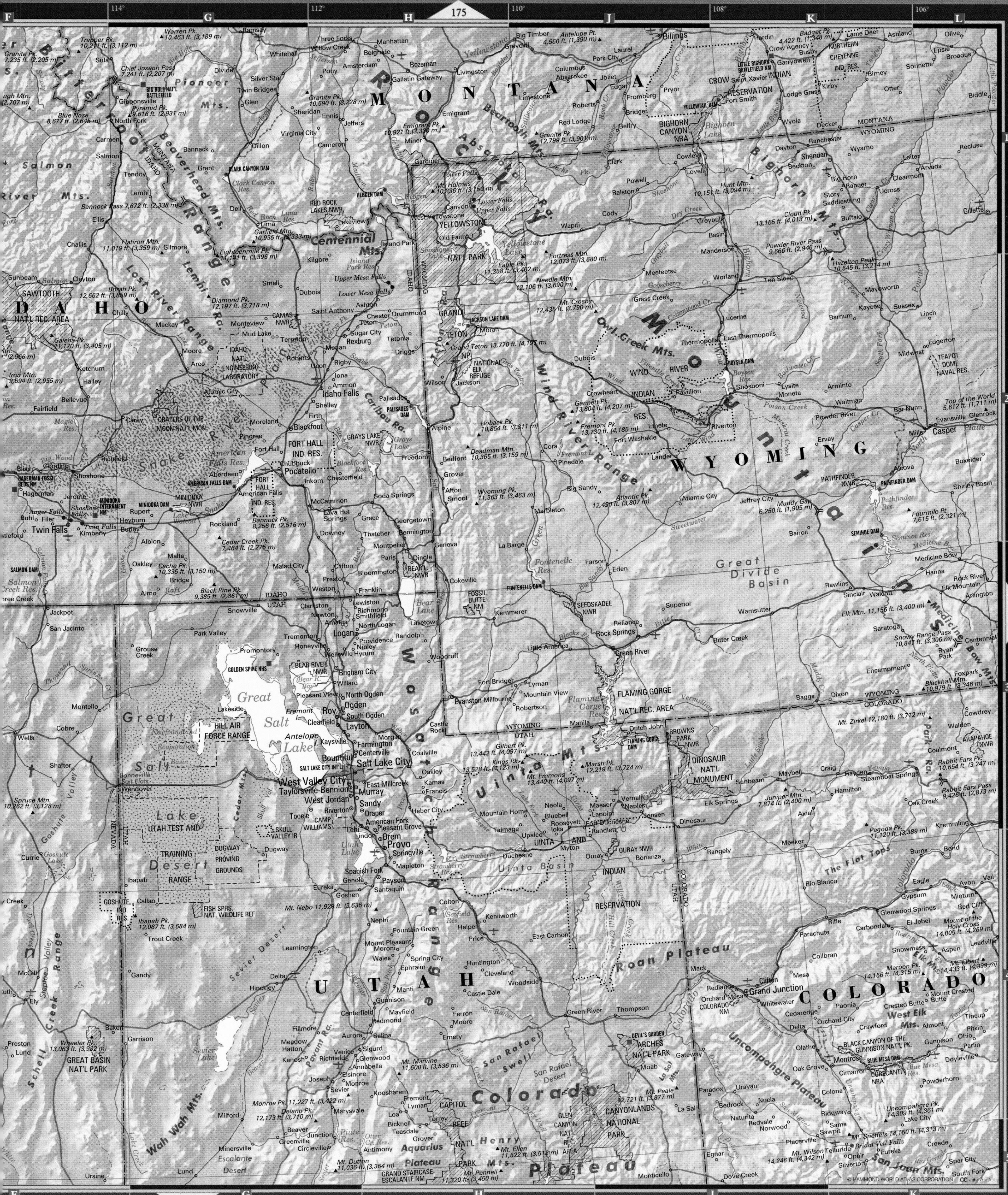

Scale 1:3,000,000   Lambert Conformal Conic Projection

MI   25   50   75   100
KM   25   50   75   100   125   150

© HAMMOND WORLD ATLAS CORPORATION

The world's most famous geologic fault runs straight through the state of California. The U.S. southwest is part of the Pacific Plate, which is drifting north-westward along the fault line at a rate of 5.6 cm per year. The San Andreas Fault is actually a bundle of parallel faults that extends north from the Gulf of Mexico to a point about 350 km north of San Francisco. The landscape bears the imprint of this plate movement: A number of valleys are sealed off; rain-water accumulates in the fracture zones and gives rise to characteristic bands of vegetation.

Southwestern United States

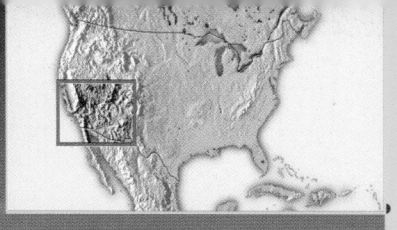

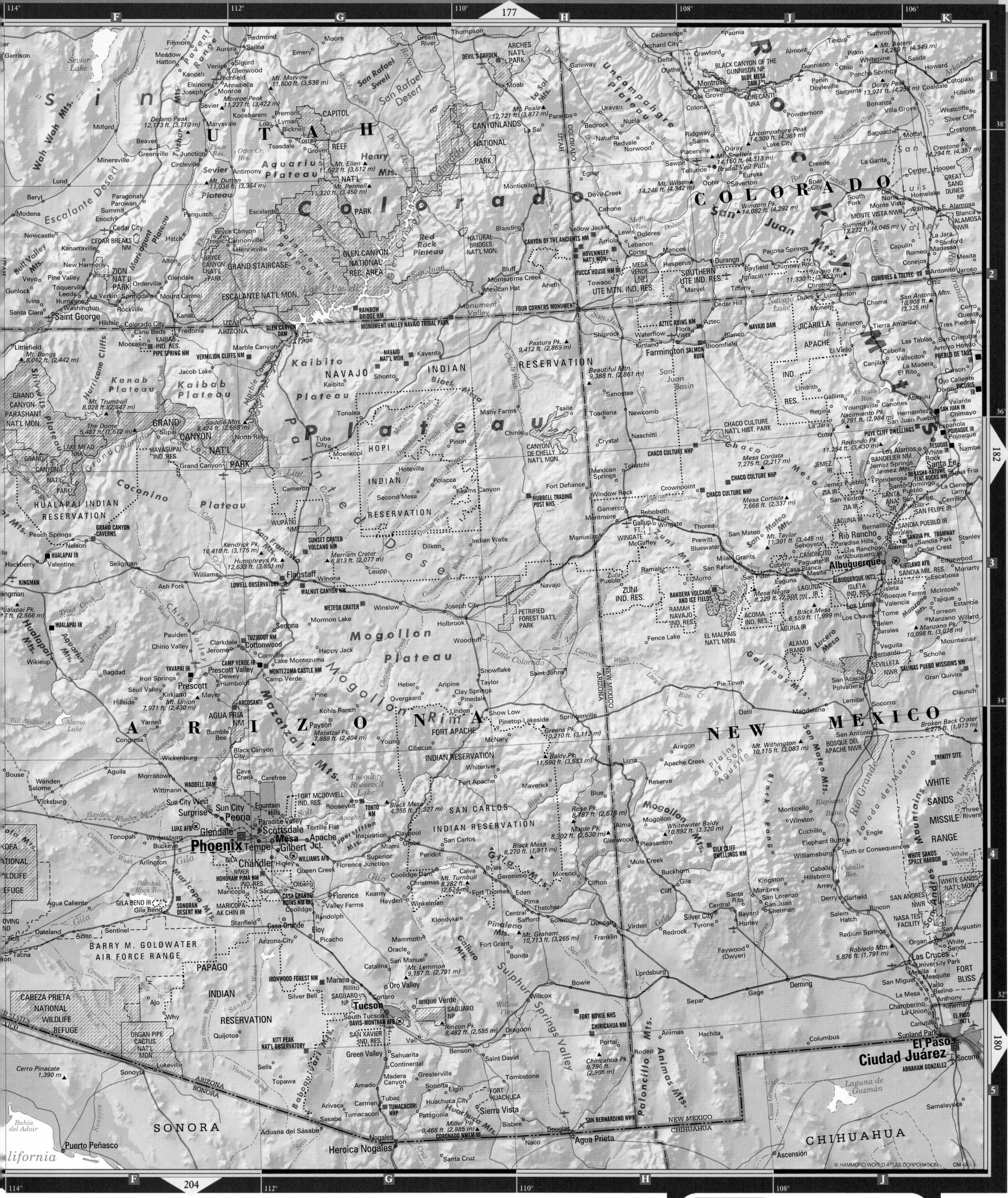

Scale 1:3,000,000 Lambert Conformal Conic Projection

MI 0 25 50 75 100

KM 0 25 50 75 100 125 150

The sensational discovery of the Spindletop Oil Field in 1901 made Texas the principal source of energy in the United States. The Mississippi, the Rio Grande, and other rivers that drain the continental interior have dumped vast quantities of sediment into a deep trough in the coastal plain and the Gulf of Mexico (with depths of up to 15 km). The rich deposits of oil and natural gas located there are the product of the intensive production of organic material and the sealing effect of the layers of sediment, which inhibited the natural process of decomposition.

Height

m.	ft.
6000	19700
4000	13000
2000	6500
1500	5000
1000	3300
500	1600
200	700
0	0
200	700
500	1600
1000	3300
2000	6500
3000	9800
4000	13000
5000	16400
6000	19700

m. / ft.

Depth

Population

- Over 2,000,000
- 1,000,000 - 1,999,999
- 500,000 - 999,999
- 250,000 - 499,999
- 100,000 - 249,999
- 30,000 - 99,999
- 10,000 - 29,999
- Under 10,000

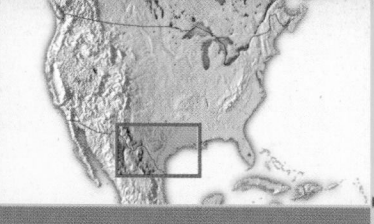

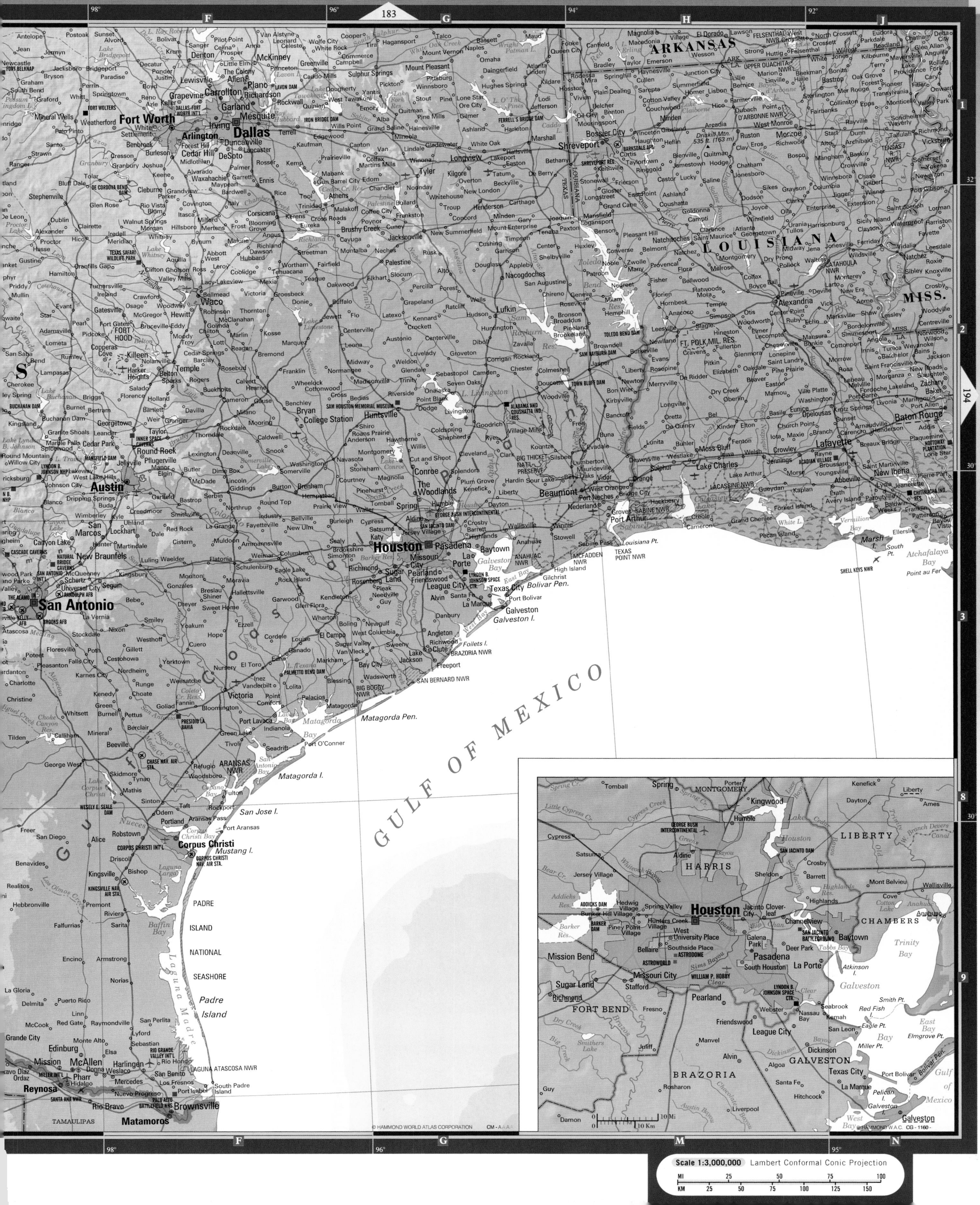

Scarcity of water is the dominant characteristic of the Great Plains. So much water has been drawn from the Ogallala aquifer beneath the plateaus of Texas and New Mexico during the past few centuries that it would take several thousand years to restore the ground-water to its original level. Geologists estimate that available reserves will be exhausted within a few years. Without this essential water supply, some five million acres of irrigated land — on which 12 percent of all the cotton, corn, wheat and millet produced in the U.S. are grown — would no longer be arable.

COLORADO

NEW MEXICO

KANSAS

OKLAHOMA

TEXAS

Great Plains

ROCKY MTS.

SANGRE DE CRISTO MTS.

SAN JUAN MTS.

Denver
Aurora
Lakewood
Westminster
Arvada
Colorado Springs
Pueblo
Albuquerque
Santa Fe
Los Alamos
Rio Rancho
Roswell
Clovis
Lubbock
Amarillo
Alamogordo
Las Cruces
El Paso
Midland
Abilene

WHITE SANDS MISSILE RANGE

FORT BLISS

CARLSBAD CAVERNS NP

GUADALUPE MTS. NP

Llano Estacado

The Caprock

Rolling Prairies

Rio Grande

Canadian

Height
m.
ft.
6000 19700
4000 13000
2000 6500
1500 5000
1000 3300
500 1600
200 700
0
200 700
500 1600
1000 3300
2000 6500
3000 9800
4000 13000
5000 16400
6000 19700
m.
ft.
Depth

Population
■ Over 2,000,000
▣ 1,000,000 - 1,999,999
◉ 500,000 - 999,999
◎ 250,000 - 499,999
● 100,000 - 249,999
◍ 30,000 - 99,999
• 10,000 - 29,999
○ Under 10,000

Scale 1:3,000,000 — Lambert Conformal Conic Projection

The Great Plains comprise one of the largest agricultural regions on Earth. Often plagued throughout their history by catastrophic droughts and erosion, the dry grasslands states of the "Dust Bowl" were hardest hit in 1935, the year in which 908 hours of dust storms – the infamous "Black Blizzards" - ravaged the region, carrying away much of the exposed topsoil and depositing it as far away as the Atlantic Ocean. Overcultivation and poor land management were to blame for this disaster, which took a heavy toll in soil and arable land.

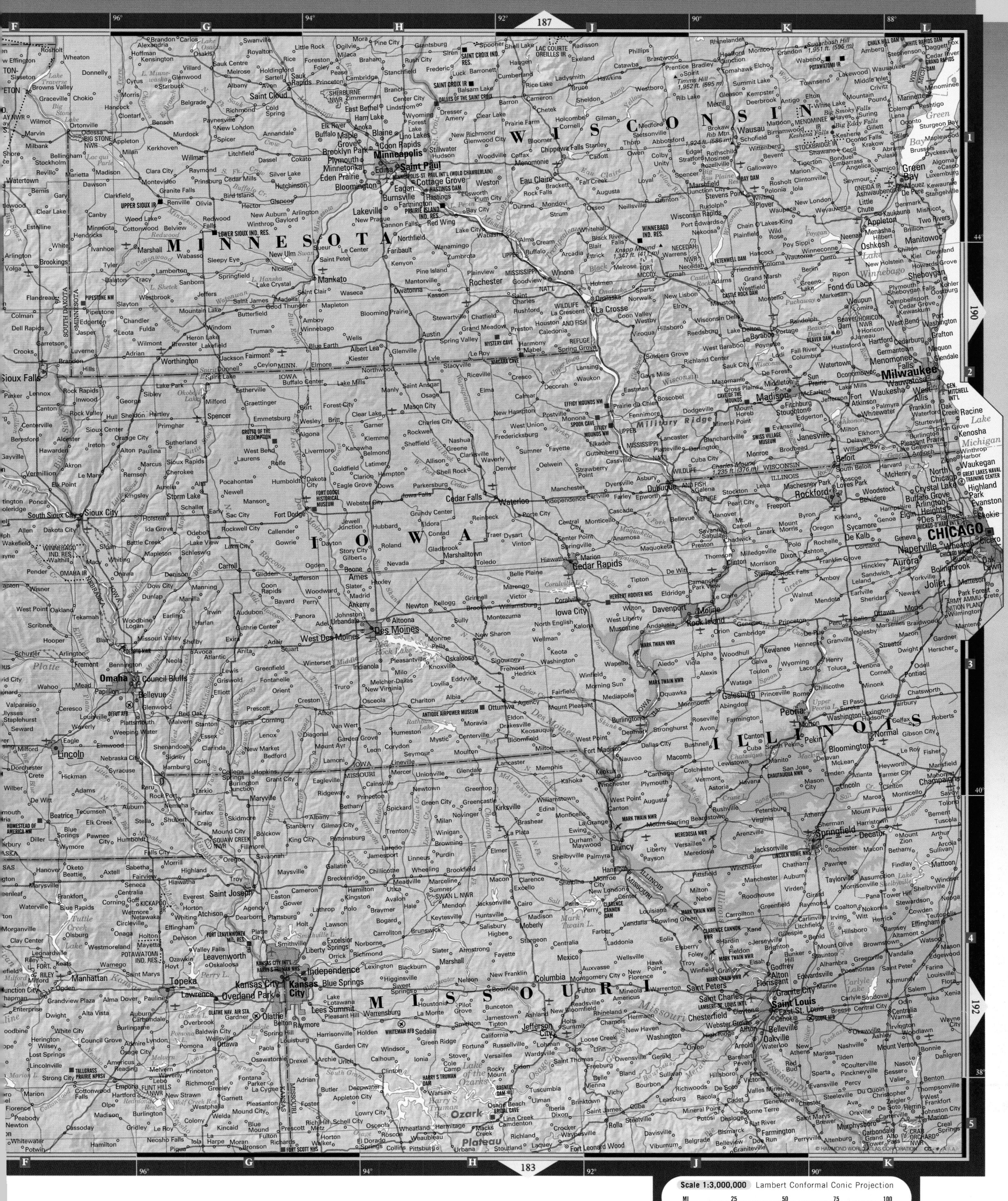

The drainage basins of the Hudson Bay, the Atlantic, and the Gulf of Mexico, to which the Mississippi flows, converge in Minnesota. The state's predominantly flat, rolling moraine topography and its continental climate are ideal for sheep and cattle grazing. The northern half of the state and much of the east are now densely forested again, the eastern region in particular having recovered from almost total deforestation in the early years of the 20th century. The fertile prairies of Manitoba and Saskatchewan to the north also offer prime land for wheat-farming and cattle-grazing.

Population

■ Over 2,000,000	● 500,000 - 999,999	◉ 100,000 - 249,999	○ 10,000 - 29,999
■ 1,000,000 - 1,999,999	● 250,000 - 499,999	○ 30,000 - 99,999	○ Under 10,000

Height

m.	ft.
6000	19700
4000	13000
2000	6500
1500	5000
1000	3300
500	1600
200	700
0	0
200	700
500	1600
1000	3300
2000	6500
3000	9800
4000	13000
5000	16400
6000	19700

Depth

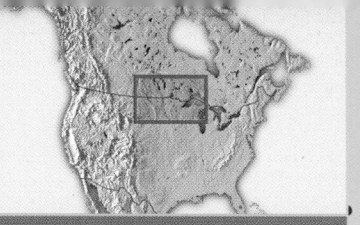

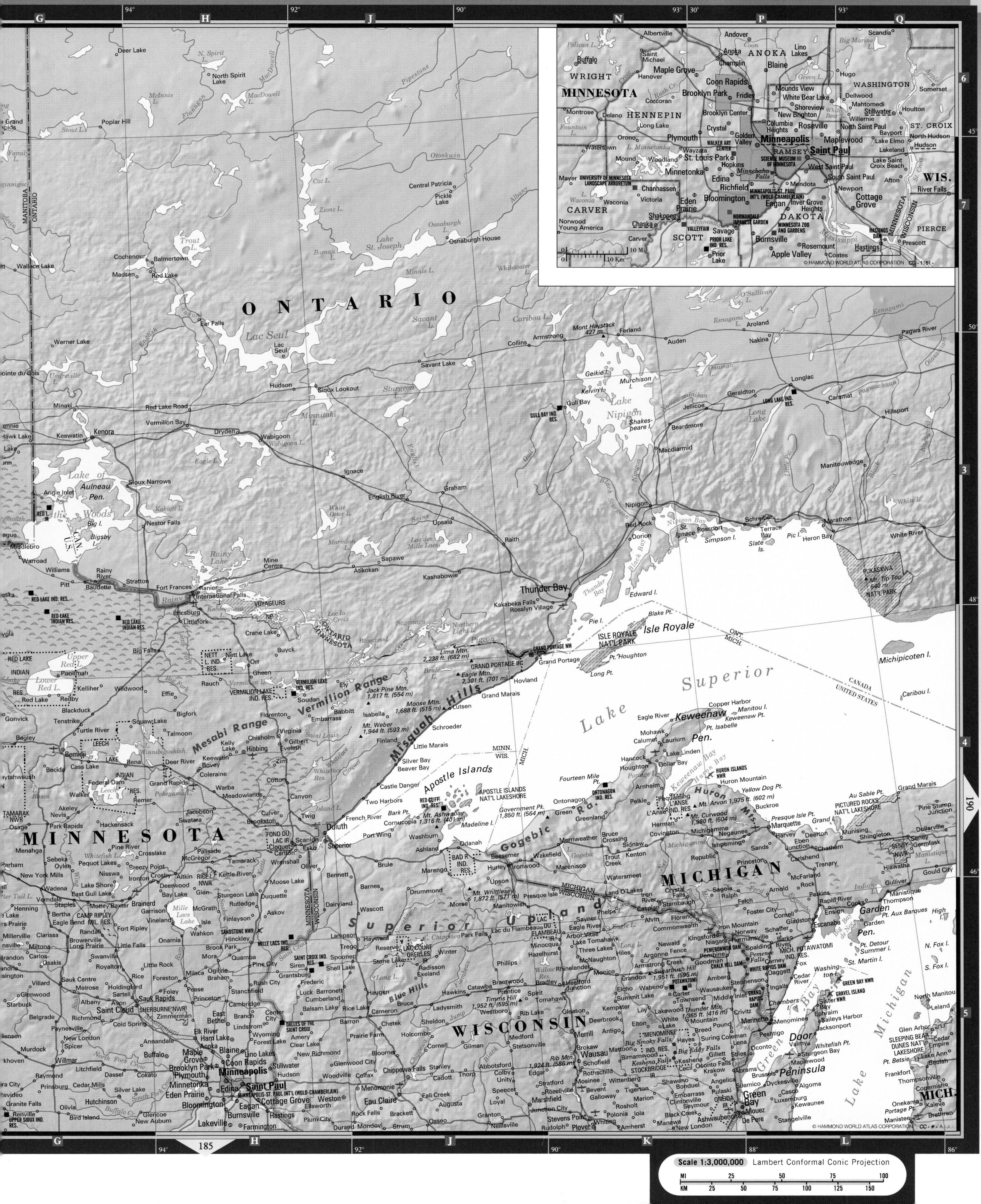

Scale 1:3,000,000   Lambert Conformal Conic Projection

© HAMMOND WORLD ATLAS CORPORATION

The low, undulating mountain chains of Newfoundland are part of the Appalachian system. Shaped by glacial action, the sparsely populated island highlands are covered by tundra and forest growth.

The waters around this island at the Gulf of St. Lawrence are rich in fish, as are those to further south of Nova Scotia. The strongest tides in the world have been measured at the funnel-shaped

mouth of the Bay of Fundy between Nova Scotia and Maine and New Brunswick to the east. The average difference between low and hide tides here is 14.5 m, with peaks of 16.3 m.

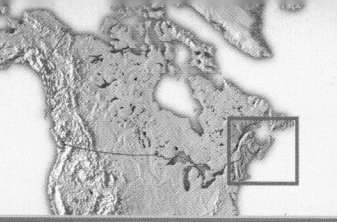

171

Gulf of St. Lawrence

Île d'Anticosti

NEWFOUNDLAND AND LABRADOR

Long Range Mts.

Annieopsquatch Mts.

Port au Port Peninsula

Bay of Islands

Middle Ridge

Bonavista Bay

Trinity Bay

Conception Bay

Avalon Peninsula

St. John's

Placentia Bay

Burin Peninsula

Hermitage Bay

Fortune Bay

ST. PIERRE AND MIQUELON (FRANCE)

Cabot Strait

Îles de la Madeleine (QUÉ.)

Cape Breton Highlands

Cape Breton I.

Sydney

SCOTIA

Sable I. (N.S.)

ATLANTIC OCEAN

Gulf of St. Lawrence

Montréal inset:

MIRABEL

LAVAL

VILLE DE MONTRÉAL

Montréal

MONTRÉAL-TRUDEAU

Longueuil

Toronto / Niagara inset:

ONTARIO

DUFFERIN

YORK

PEEL

WELLINGTON

HALTON

Brampton

Mississauga

TORONTO

SCARBOROUGH

NORTH YORK

ETOBICOKE

EAST YORK

PEARSON

Markham

Richmond Hill

Vaughan

Oshawa

Whitby

DURHAM

Hamilton

HAMILTON-WENTWORTH

BRANT

Brantford

Cambridge

Guelph

Oakville

Burlington

Lake Ontario

CANADA / UNITED STATES

NEW YORK / ONTARIO

Niagara Falls

Saint Catharines

NIAGARA

NEW YORK

ERIE

Buffalo

Cheektowaga

HALDIMAND-NORFOLK

Lake Erie

Scale 1:3,000,000   Lambert Conformal Conic Projection

MI 25 50 75 100

KM 25 50 75 100 125 150

© HAMMOND W.A.C. CG-2163

Thanks to a relatively mild climate and an abundance of natural resources, the Great Lakes region is one of the most heavily populated areas of North America. Ontario is situated on the Canadian Shield – a base of old ore-rich rock – and some of the world's largest deposits of nickel, copper, gold, silver, and platinum are located near Sudbury. The Appalachians farther south have large reserves of anthracite coal. Raw materials from these locations can be shipped easily through the Great Lakes or by river to the major industrial centers on the Atlantic Coast.

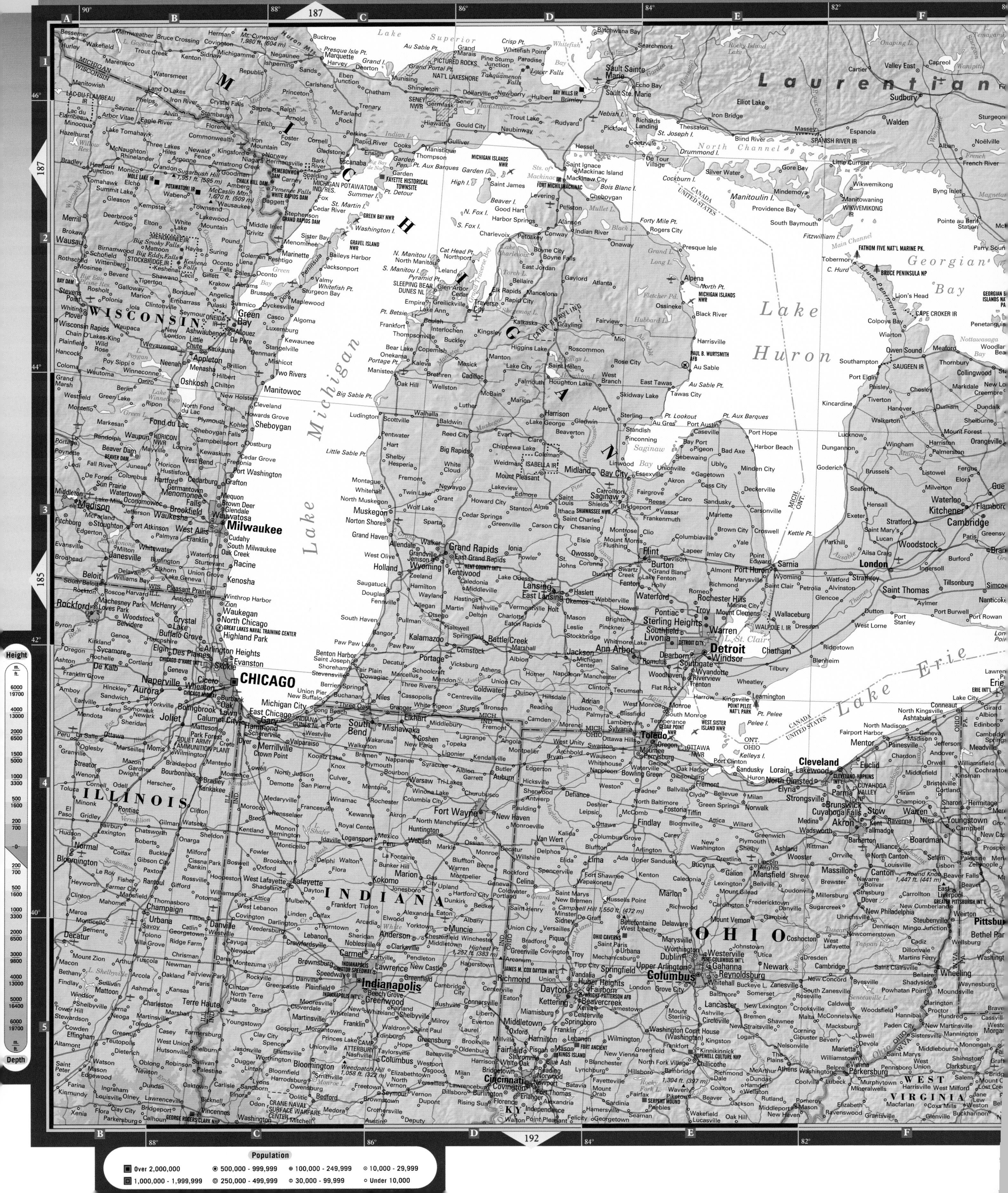

Population

■ Over 2,000,000
□ 1,000,000 - 1,999,999
● 500,000 - 999,999
◉ 250,000 - 499,999
● 100,000 - 249,999
◎ 30,000 - 99,999
◌ 10,000 - 29,999
○ Under 10,000

Height

m. / ft.
6000 / 19700
4000 / 13000
2000 / 6500
1500 / 5000
1000 / 3300
500 / 1600
200 / 700
0
200 / 700
500 / 1600
1000 / 3300
2000 / 6500
3000 / 9800
4000 / 13000
5000 / 16400
6000 / 19700
m. / ft.
Depth

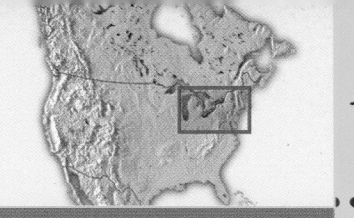

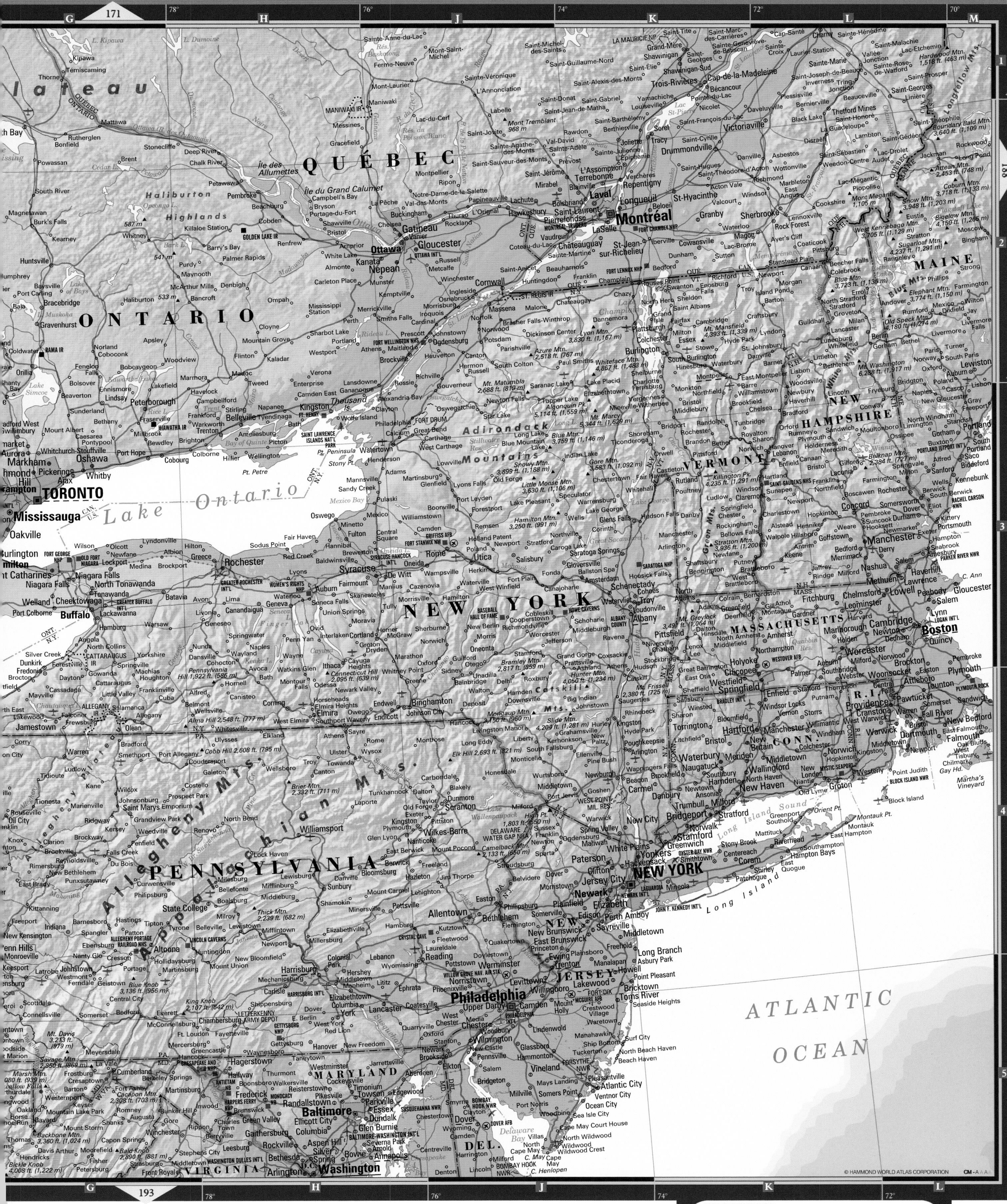

Scale 1:3,000,000   Lambert Conformal Conic Projection

© HAMMOND WORLD ATLAS CORPORATION

The mideastern region of the United States is dominated by the Appalachian Mountain system, a complex of low, rolling chains some 2,600 km long that separates the Atlantic coastal plain from the lowlands of the North American continent. They are broken by natural gaps in only a few places. Although the Appalachians bear a certain resemblance to the central mountain ranges of Europe, they are home to a much wider diversity of species – in part a consequence of the migration of animals toward the south along the northeast-southwest axis of the Appalachians during the last ice age.

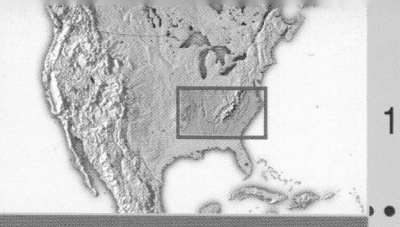

191

OHIO

WEST VIRGINIA

VIRGINIA

MARYLAND

DELAWARE

N.J.

Baltimore
Washington
Alexandria
Annapolis
Dover

Richmond
Lynchburg
Roanoke
Charlottesville
Newport News
Norfolk
Virginia Beach
Chesapeake
Portsmouth

NORTH CAROLINA

Charlotte
Raleigh
Durham
Greensboro
Winston-Salem
High Point
Chapel Hill
Fayetteville
Wilmington
Asheville
Gastonia

SOUTH CAROLINA

Columbia
Charleston
North Charleston
Mount Pleasant
Spartanburg
Greenville
Florence
Myrtle Beach
Hilton Head Island

Savannah

GEORGIA

Augusta

CAPE HATTERAS NAT'L SEASHORE
CAPE LOOKOUT NAT'L SEASHORE

Chesapeake Bay

ATLANTIC OCEAN

Atlanta (inset)

Atlanta
Marietta
Kennesaw
Roswell
Alpharetta
Sandy Springs
Dunwoody
Smyrna
Decatur
East Point
College Park
Douglasville

COBB
FULTON
GWINNETT
DEKALB
DOUGLAS
CLAYTON
HENRY
ROCKDALE
COWETA
FAYETTE
PAULDING

HARTSFIELD-JACKSON ATLANTA INT'L
SIX FLAGS OVER GEORGIA
KENNESAW MOUNTAIN NAT'L BATTLEFIELD PARK

© Hammond World Atlas Corporation

Scale 1:3,000,000   Lambert Conformal Conic Projection

MI 0 25 50 75 100
KM 0 25 50 75 100 125 150

195

The Mississippi is the mightiest river in North America and one of the longest in the world. Ordinarily, the river discharges more sediment into the Gulf of Mexico than waves, tides, and cur-rents can carry away. Yet the "bird's-foot delta" and its vast wetlands are actually shrinking. Dredging and dams are partly responsible for this, but so is the river it-self. The Mississippi has shifted its course back and forth several times during the last millennium and is now sending increasing amounts of sediment into an arm it abandoned some 3,800 years ago during the last ice age.

Height

m.
ft.
6000 19700
4000 13000
2000 6500
1500 5000
1000 3300
500   1600
200   700

200   700
500   1600
1000 3300
2000 6500
3000 9800
4000 13000
5000 16400
6000 19700
m.
ft.

Depth

Population

■ Over 2,000,000   ◉ 500,000 - 999,999   ⊙ 100,000 - 249,999   ● 10,000 - 29,999
▣ 1,000,000 - 1,999,999   ◎ 250,000 - 499,999   ⊚ 30,000 - 99,999   ○ Under 10,000

Northern Gulf Coast Region

Scale 1:3,000,000   Lambert Conformal Conic Projection

MI   25   50   75   100

KM   25   50   75   100   125   150

The sprawling metropolis of Los Angeles on California's West Coast extends over a distance of 184 km from Ventura to San Bernardino. The region is plagued by an increasingly severe shortage of water, since groundwater reserves are nearly exhausted. Even the many reservoirs in the area are barely able to meet the needs of local farmers and a rapidly growing population.

Population

- Over 2,000,000
- 1,000,000 - 1,999,999
- 500,000 - 999,999
- 250,000 - 499,999
- 100,000 - 249,999
- 30,000 - 99,999
- 10,000 - 29,999
- Under 10,000

Scale 1:1,000,000 Lambert Conformal Conic Projection

MI 10   20   30
KM 10   20   30   40

© HAMMOND WORLD ATLAS CORPORATION

Four different roads to the future: Seattle has grown steadily in recent years through a steady influx of people into the less densely populated northwest. New technologies have created new jobs here and in Silicon Valley, the region between San Francisco and San Jose. Detroit relies on the automobile industry, and Chicago is already one of the world's leading commercial centers.

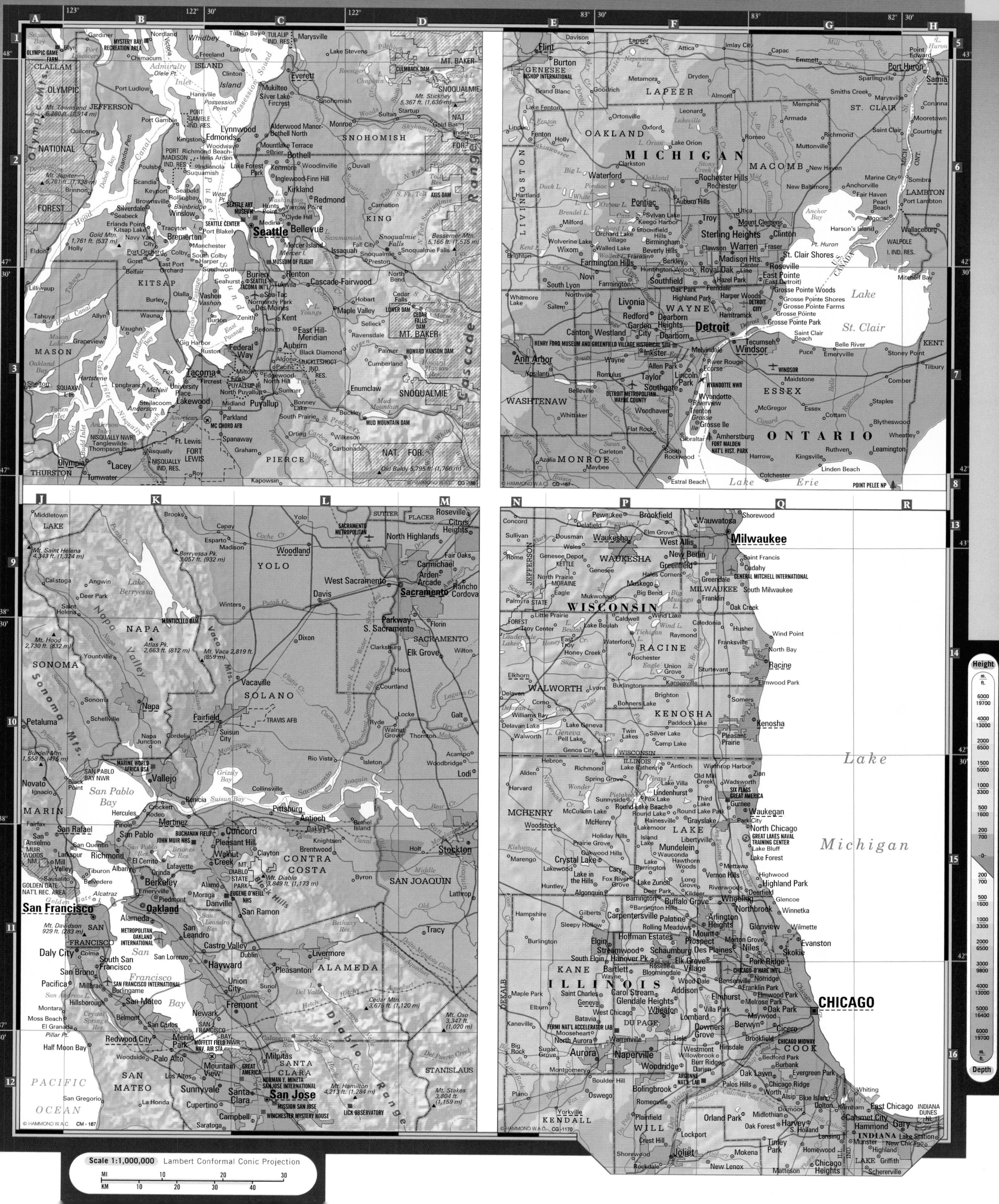

Scale 1:1,000,000   Lambert Conformal Conic Projection

Roughly 18,000 years ago, the sea level along the East Coast of the United States was about 100 meters lower than it is today. The old valleys along the coast were "drowned" when the waters rose again and flooded the coastal plain. These sunken valleys are still recognizable today as long, funnel-shaped bays on the northern and middle-Atlantic coasts. Raritan Bay at the mouth of the Hudson River and the Chesapeake and Delaware Bays are among the most prominent examples. They are actually estuaries with fluctuating salinity levels that provide a habitat for a unique range of fauna.

Population

| ■ Over 2,000,000 | ● 500,000 - 999,999 | ● 100,000 - 249,999 | ● 10,000 - 29,999 |
| ■ 1,000,000 - 1,999,999 | ● 250,000 - 499,999 | ● 30,000 - 99,999 | ○ Under 10,000 |

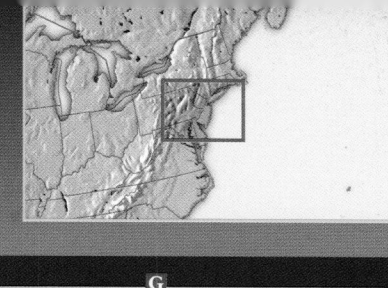

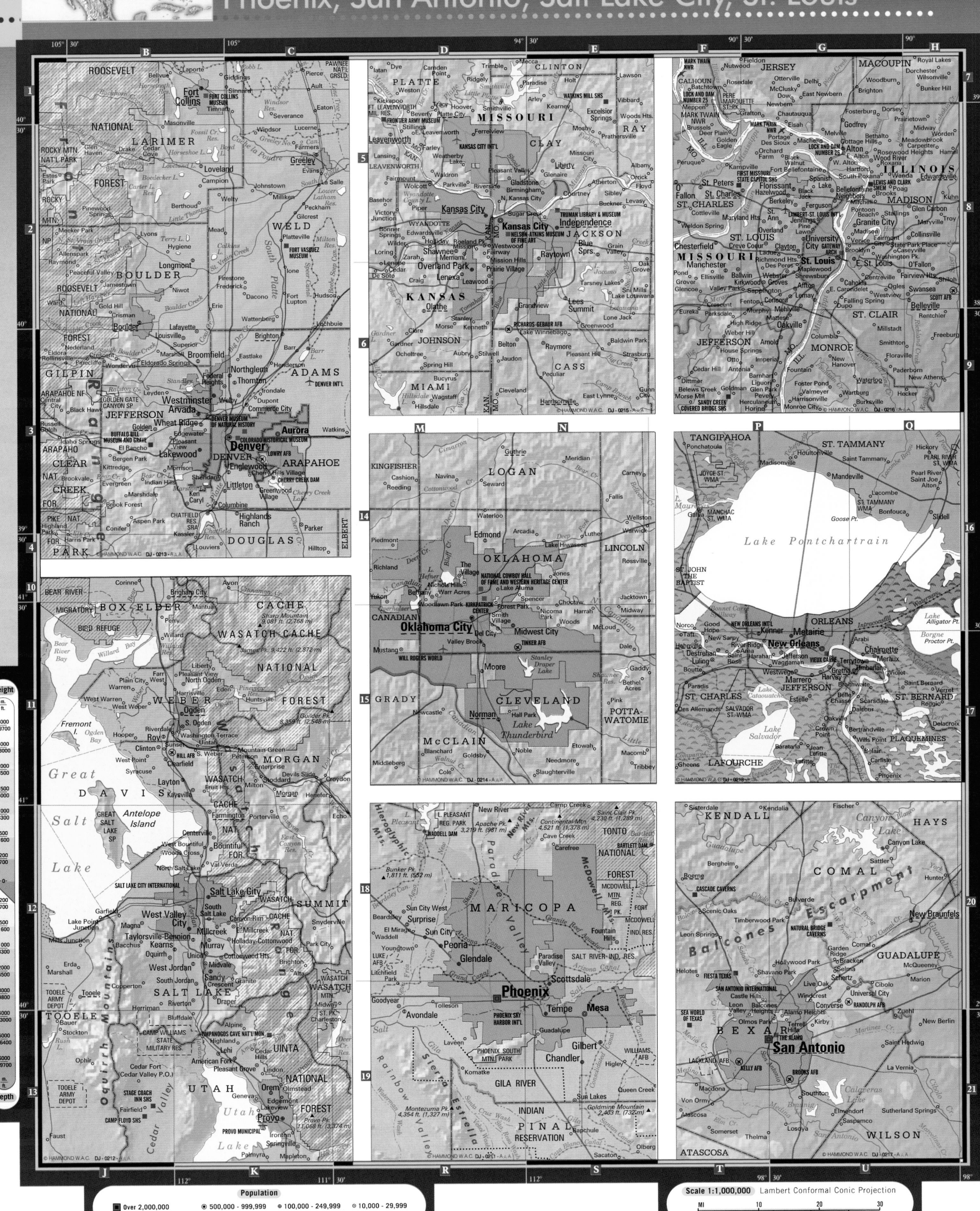

Alaska, the forty-ninth state of the U.S. In the south, the heavily glacialized Alaska Range extends along the Pacific coast, with its many fjords. Its highest peak is Mount McKinley, which at 6,198 meters is also the highest mountain in North America. The Brooks Range in the north extends eastward to the shores of the Beaufort Sea. The interior is dominated by the Yukon River system. The island chain of the Aleutians is the most geologically active area in the region. Here, the Pacific Plate submerges beneath the continental plate along the Aleutian Trench.

Population
■ Over 2,000,000   ◉ 500,000 - 999,999   ◎ 100,000 - 249,999   ⊙ 10,000 - 29,999
□ 1,000,000 - 1,999,999   ◉ 250,000 - 499,999   ◎ 30,000 - 99,999   ○ Under 10,000

Scale 1:9,000,000   Lambert Conformal Conic Projection

The isthmian tract between the United States and Colombia marks the transition from North America to South America. Geographically speaking, North America extends as far south as the Isthmus of Tehuantepec in Mexico. South America begins in the Rio Atrato Valley in Colombia. In the interest of simplicity and for statistical reasons, Mexico is treated as part of North America, all of Colombia

as part of South America. The countries in between and the islands of the Caribbean are referred to as Middle America.

ATLANTIC OCEAN

ATLANTIC OCEAN

CARIBBEAN SEA

DOMINICAN REPUBLIC

PUERTO RICO (U.S.)

Virgin Islands

Aguadilla · Isabela · Arecibo · **San Juan** · Carolina · Fajardo
Mayagüez · Utuado · Bayamón · Caguas · Yabucoa
Hormigueros · *I. Mona* · C. Rojo · Yauco · Ponce · Guayama
US I. de Vieques NAV. RES. (P.R.)

Tortola I. (U.K.) · Virgin Gorda · Anegada (U.K.)
Charlotte Amalie · St. Thomas (U.S.) · Road Town · St. John (U.S.)
Christiansted · *St. Croix* (U.S.)
Frederiksted · Anguilla (U.K.) · The Valley · Marigot · St-Martin (GUAD.)
Gustavia · St-Barthélemy · Barbuda
Sint Maarten (N.A.) · Codrington · **ANTIGUA AND BARBUDA**
Saba (N.A.) · Oranjestad · Basseterre · Saint John's · Falmouth
Sint Eustatius (N.A.) · St. Kitts · Nevis · Antigua
ST. KITTS AND NEVIS · BRIMSTONE HILL NP · Charlestown · Nevis Pk. 985 m · Boggy Pk. 402 m

Montserrat (U.K.) · Plymouth
Guadeloupe Passage · Grande-Terre
Port-Louis · **Guadeloupe** (FRANCE)
Basse-Terre · GUADELOUPE NP · Pointe-à-Pitre · Morne Constant
Soufrière 1,467 m · 205 m · Marie-Galante
Basse-Terre

Dominica Passage · Portsmouth · Marigot
DOMINICA · Morne Diablotin 1,447 m · Roseau

Martinique Passage
Mt. Pelée 1,397 m · Sainte-Marie
Saint-Pierre · **Martinique** (FRANCE)
FORT DESAIX · Fort-de-France

St. Lucia Channel
Castries · Gros Islet
Mt. Gimie 958 m · **ST. LUCIA** · Micoud
Vieux Fort

St. Vincent Passage
Soufrière 1,234 m · **BARBADOS**
Barrouallie · Georgetown · Mt. Hillaby 336 m · Bathsheba
St. Vincent · Kingstown · Bridgetown
ST. VINCENT AND THE GRENADINES · Bequia
Canouan
Carriacou
Sauteurs
Gouyave · Mt. St. Catherine 840 m
GRENADA · Saint George's

Leeward Islands
Lesser Antilles
Windward Islands

Tropic of Cancer

CUBA
Sagua la Grande · Caibarién · Arch. de Camagüey
Cabaiguán · Morón · Ciego de Ávila · Nuevitas · Puerto Maternillos
Sancti Spíritus · Carlos M. · Florida · Camagüey · Victoria de las Tunas
Santa Cruz del Sur · Contramaestre · Holguín · Mayarí
Bayamo · Palma · San Luis · Sagua de Tánamo · Cabo Maisí
Yara · Soriano · El Salvador · Guantánamo
Bartolomé Masó · Pico Turquino 4,131 m · **Santiago de Cuba** · GUANTANAMO BAY U.S. NAVAL BASE
Cabo Cruz

BAHAMAS
Grand Bahama · Freeport · Great Abaco
West Palm Beach · Bimini Is. · Berry Is.
Nassau · Eleuthera · Cat I.
New Providence I.
Andros I. · Great Bahama Bank · Exuma Sound
San Salvador (Watling I.)
Great Guana Cay · Rum Cay
Great Exuma · Long I. · Clarence Town
Acklins I. · Crooked I. · Northeast Pt.
Salina Pt. · Mayaguana
Caicos Is. · Little Inagua
Great Inagua · **Turks and Caicos Is.** (U.K.) · Grand Turk
Matthew Town · Southeast Pt. · Turks Is.

JAMAICA
Montego Bay · Ocho Rios · Saint Ann's Bay
Savanna-la-Mar · Spanish Town · Port Antonio
Mandeville · May Pen · Blue Mtn. Pk. 2,256 m · Portland Pt.
Kingston
Pedro Cays (JAM.)

HAITI
Port-de-Paix · Cap-Haïtien · Monte Cristi
St-Louis du Nord · Gonaïves · Santiago
Golfe de la Gonâve · Petite Rivière de l'Artibonite · Las Matas de Farfán · La Vega
Jérémie · Anse-d'Hainault · Anse-à-Galets · San Juan
Dame Marie · **Port-au-Prince** · Hinche
Pic de Macaya 2,300 m · Jacmel · Hato Mayor · Azua
Les Cayes · Chardonnières · Neiba · Barahona
Pointe à Gravois · Pedernales · Cabo Falso · Cabo Beata

DOMINICAN REPUBLIC
Mao · Cabo Frances Viejo
San Francisco · Cabo Samaná
Pico Duarte 3,175 m · El Seibo · Higüey
Hispaniola · San Pedro de Macorís
La Romana
SANTO DOMINGO

PUERTO RICO (U.S.)
San Juan · Bayamón · Carolina
Aguadilla · Utuado · Caguas
Mayagüez · Cabo Rojo · Ponce · Guayama · Christiansted

Virgin Is.
St. Thomas (U.S.) · St. John · Road Town · Tortola I. (U.K.) · Anegada (U.K.)
Charlotte Amalie · St. Croix (U.S.) · Saba (N.A.)
St. Maarten · Philipsburg · St-Martin (FR.) · Anguilla (U.K.) · The Valley
ANTIGUA AND BARBUDA · Codrington · Barbuda
ST. KITTS AND NEVIS · St. Kitts · Basseterre · Antigua · Saint John's
Charlestown
Montserrat (U.K.) · Plymouth
Basse-Terre · Grande-Terre
GUADELOUPE NP · **Guadeloupe** (FRANCE)
Soufrière 1,467 m · Pointe-à-Pitre
Basse-Terre · Marie-Galante
DOMINICA · Roseau · Marigot
Martinique Passage
Mont Pelée 1,397 m · Saint-Pierre · **Martinique** (FRANCE)
Fort-de-France
Castries · Gros Islet
ST. LUCIA · Micoud · Vieux Fort
Soufrière 1,234 m · Kingstown · Bridgetown · **BARBADOS**
ST. VINCENT AND THE GRENADINES
GRENADA · Carriacou · Saint George's · Mt. St. Catherine 840 m

CARIBBEAN SEA

Serranilla Bank (COL.)
Bajo Nuevo (COL.)
Serrana Bank (COL.)
Roncador Cay (COL.)

Lesser Antilles
Windward Is.

VENEZUELA
I. Blanquilla · Is. Los Testigos
La Asunción · NUEVA ESPARTA · Porlamar · PN PEN. DE PARIA · El Cerro del Aripo 940 m · Galera Pt. · Charlotteville
Cariaco · El Pilar · SUCRE · Irapa · Güiria · Chaguanas · Arima · Sangre Grande · Tobago · Roxborough · Scarborough
Casanay · Carúpano · **Port-of-Spain**
Gulf of Paria · San Fernando · Tabaquite · Río Claro
Caripito · Point Fortin · Siparia · Fullarton · *Trinidad* · **TRINIDAD AND TOBAGO**
Pedernales

© HAMMOND W.A.C. · CM-A-AAA

Aruba (NETH.) · Oranjestad
Punta Gallinas · Pen. de Paraguaná · Bonaire · NETH. ANTILLES · Curaçao · Willemstad · El Roque · I. La Orchila (VEN.)
Guajira Pen. · Cabo de la Vela · Carrizal · Cojoro · G. de Venezuela · Puerto Cardón · Santa Ana · Puerto Cumarebo · Islas Las Aves (VEN.) · Islas Los Roques (VEN.) · I. La Tortuga (VEN.) · I. de Margarita · La Asunción · Juangriego · Porlamar
Ríohacha · Punta Cardón · Coro · Jacura · Mirimire · Chichiriviche · Tucacas · Juangriego
Barranquilla · Malambo · Soledad · Ciénaga · PN SIERRA NEVADA DE SANTA MARTA · San Rafael · Seque · Cabure · Churuguara
Santa Marta · Pico Cristóbal Colón 5,775 m · San Francisco · **Maracaibo** · Coro · Siquisique
Cartagena · Turbaco · Pico Bolívar 5,007 m · Cabimas · Ciudad Ojeda · Mene Grande · Acarigua · San Carlos · San Juan de los Morros · **Caracas** · Petare · Los Teques · Barcelona · Puerto La Cruz · Maturín
COLOMBIA · Valledupar · Lago de Maracaibo · Trujillo · **Barquisimeto** · **Valencia** · **Maracay** · Turmero · Cumaná · Cariaco · San Antonio del Golfo · Pariaguán · Tucupita
Isthmus of Panama · **Panamá** · Colón · Tocumen · Cerro Chucantí 1,439 m

Scale 1:9,000,000 · Lambert Conformal Conic Projection

CARIBBEAN SEA

WEST INDIES

Lesser Antilles

Greater Antilles

Mexico has a unique blend of Native American and Spanish cultural heritages. Today, this Latin American culture is spreading north across the Rio Grande into the Anglo-American cultural region at an increasingly rapid pace. Bordered on the east and west by the parallel chains of the Sierra Madre Occidental and the Sierra Madre Oriental, Mexico's vast highlands are home to a large part of the Mexican population. The heavily urbanized area around Mexico City stretches from Guadalajara to Veracruz.

Map labels

United States: CALIF., ARIZONA, NEW MEXICO, San Diego, Tijuana, Chula Vista, El Cajon, El Centro, Mexicali, Calexico, Yuma, Tucson, El Paso, Ciudad Juárez, Las Cruces, Roswell, Carlsbad, CARLSBAD CAVERNS NP, ORGAN PIPE CACTUS NM, SAGUARO NP, CHIRICAHUA NM, BIG BEND NP, FORT DAVIS NHS, GUADALUPE MTS. NP, WHITE SANDS NM

Mexico states: BAJA CALIFORNIA, BAJA CALIFORNIA SUR, SONORA, CHIHUAHUA, COAHUILA DE ZARAGOZA, SINALOA, DURANGO, ZACATECAS, NAYARIT, JALISCO, AGUASCALIENTES

Cities and towns: Ensenada, Hermosillo, Chihuahua, Ciudad Delicias, Ciudad Camargo, Cd. Obregón, Navojoa, Los Mochis, Guasave, Guamúchil, Culiacán, Gómez Palacio, Torreón, Matamoros, Ciudad Lerdo, Durango, Mazatlán, La Paz, Ciudad Constitución, Ciudad Insurgentes, Loreto, Santa Rosalía, Mulegé, Guerrero Negro, San Ignacio, Cabo San Lucas, San José del Cabo, Todos Santos, Tepic, Zapopan, Guadalajara, Tlaquepaque, Puerto Vallarta, Colima, Manzanillo, Tecomán, Zacatecas, Jerez, Fresnillo, Sombrerete, Río Grande

Water features: PACIFIC OCEAN, Gulf of California, Bahía de Sebastián Vizcaíno, Bahía de La Paz, Bahía de Santa María, Tropic of Cancer

Islands: Islas Revillagigedo (MEXICO), I. Socorro, I. San Benedicto, I. Clarion, I. Roca Partida, Islas Tres Marías, I. María Madre, I. María Magdalena, I. María Cleofas, I. Cedros, I. Ángel de la Guarda, Isla Tiburón, I. San José, I. Cerralvo, I. Espíritu Santo, I. Santa Margarita, I. Santa Magdalena, I. Carmen

Mountains: Sierra Madre Occidental, Sierra de San Pedro Mártir, Sierra de la Giganta

Height / Depth scale
Height m. / ft.
6000 / 19700
4000 / 13000
2000 / 6500
1500 / 5000
1000 / 3300
500 / 1600
200 / 700
-0-
200 / 700
500 / 1600
1000 / 3300
2000 / 6500
3000 / 9800
4000 / 13000
5000 / 16400
6000 / 19700
Depth m. / ft.

Population
- ■ Over 2,000,000
- ▣ 1,000,000 - 1,999,999
- ⬤ 500,000 - 999,999
- ⬤ 250,000 - 499,999
- ⬤ 100,000 - 249,999
- ⬤ 30,000 - 99,999
- ○ 10,000 - 29,999
- ○ Under 10,000

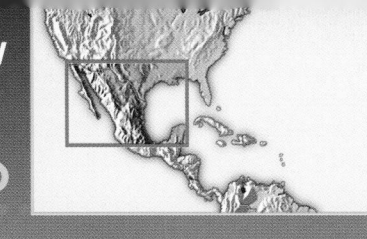

Northern and Central Mexico

183

TEXAS
North Central Plains
Edwards Plateau
Gulf Coastal Plain

HIDALGO
MÉXICO
Ecatepec
Naucalpan
MEXICO (Ciudad de México)
Tlalnepantla
Nezahualcóyotl
Toluca
DISTRITO FEDERAL
TLAXCALA
Cuernavaca
MORELOS
Puebla
PUEBLA
GUERRERO
Veracruz
VERACRUZ-LLAVE
Jalapa
OAXACA

Fort Worth · Arlington · Dallas
Austin
San Antonio
Corpus Christi
Padre Island
PADRE ISLAND NATIONAL SEASHORE

Nuevo Laredo · Laredo
NUEVO LEÓN
Monterrey
Guadalupe
San Nicolás de los Garza
Reynosa · Matamoros
Brownsville
Saltillo
Monclova

GULF

OF

MEXICO

Tropic of Cancer

TAMAULIPAS
Ciudad Victoria
Tampico · Ciudad Madero

SAN LUIS POTOSÍ
San Luis Potosí

GUANAJUATO
Querétaro
Celaya
Morelia
MEXICO
Toluca
Puebla
Cuernavaca

YUCATÁN
Mérida
Progreso
Cancún
Cozumel
Playa del Carmen
CHICHÉN ITZÁ

Campeche
CAMPECHE

QUINTANA ROO
Chetumal

Yucatan Peninsula

Bahía de Campeche

TABASCO
Villahermosa
Coatzacoalcos
Minatitlán

CHIAPAS

GUATEMALA
BELIZE
Belize City

Isthmus of Tehuantepec

Acapulco
GUERRERO
OAXACA

Scale 1:6,000,000 Lambert Conformal Conic Projection

© HAMMOND WORLD ATLAS CORPORATION

Costa Rica, the "Rich Coast," differs from its neighbors in many ways. Stable political relationships have enabled the country to preserve a large part of its tropical rain forest, which receives abundant precipitation from the northeast trade wind on the Caribbean side. Though much more dry in comparison, the Pacific coastal region is known around the world for its splendid orchids. The long (50 km) Valle Central in the interior highlands has a particularly mild climate and fertile volcanic soil. This is Costa Rica's traditional coffee-growing region.

Scale 1:6,000,000 Lambert Conformal Conic Projection

| MI | 50 | 100 | 150 | 200 |

| KM | 50 | 100 | 150 | 200 | 250 | 300 |

The highest mountain peak in the Americas, with an elevation of 6,959 meters, is glacier-covered Mount Aconcagua. This northeastward-looking image shows the north-south axis of the Andes along the border between Chile and Argentina. The narrow valley running east to west immediately south of Mount Aconcagua contains a section of the American Highway that connects Mendoza, Argentina, with Santiago, Chile. Although composed of volcanic material, Mount Aconcagua – unlike many of its neighbors in the Andes – is not a volcano itself.

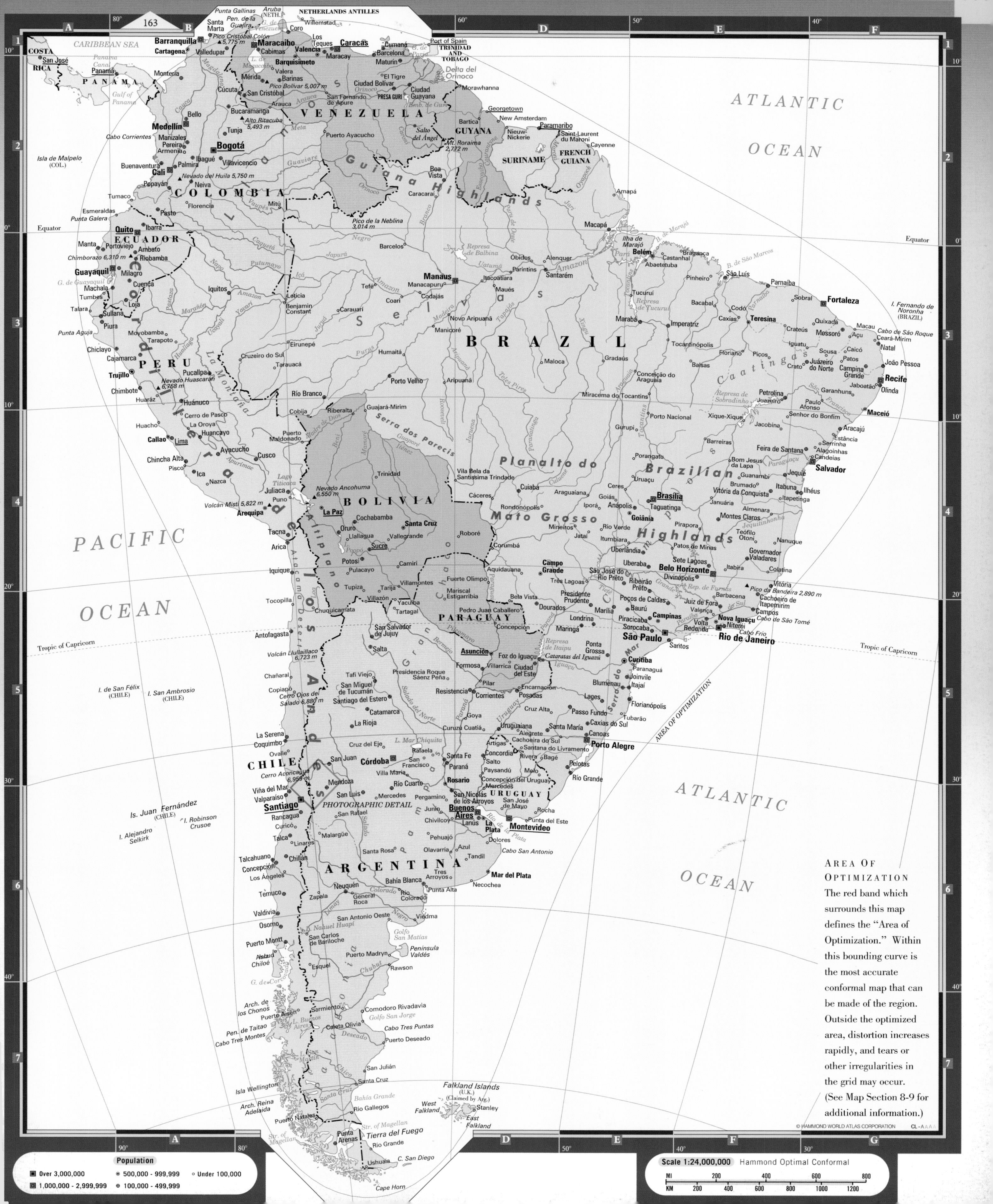

163

AREA OF OPTIMIZATION
The red band which surrounds this map defines the "Area of Optimization." Within this bounding curve is the most accurate conformal map that can be made of the region. Outside the optimized area, distortion increases rapidly, and tears or other irregularities in the grid may occur. (See Map Section 8-9 for additional information.)

Population
- ■ Over 3,000,000
- ● 500,000 - 999,999
- ○ Under 100,000
- ■ 1,000,000 - 2,999,999
- ◉ 100,000 - 499,999

Scale 1:24,000,000 Hammond Optimal Conformal

MI   200   400   600   800
KM 200 400 600 800 1000 1200

© HAMMOND WORLD ATLAS CORPORATION   CL - A A A

World Heritage Sites in South America

Text continued from page 164 - UNESCO World Cultural Heritage Sites of North America

World Heritage Committee

The World Heritage Committee is composed of delegates from 21 countries selected to represent all of the major cultural regions of the world. The committee convenes once each year to choose new sites for the World Heritage List from applications submitted by participating countries. The list currently contains 721 sites, of which 554 are identified as cultural legacies, 144 as natural heritage sites, and 23 as a combination of both. The Committee also makes decisions on the use of funds contributed by the signatory countries.

Differing Attitudes about the World Heritage List

As a matter of prestige, many countries are eager to have as many sites as possible entered in the list. Others regard recognition as more of a burden than an honor, as they fear a loss of control over their own national treasures.

City of the Gods

The Churches of Chiloé, **Chile (31)**, represent a unique example in Latin America of an outstanding form of ecclesiastical wooden architecture. Churches embody the intangible richness of the Chiloé Archipelago, and bear witness to a successful fusion of indigenous and European culture.

Stone Sentry

During the cultural bloom of San Agustín (6) (100–1000 AD), artists produced about 400 stone sculptures (mostly hybrid human-jaguar figures), each more than four meters tall. They stood at the entrances of burial chambers and temples.

Orthogonal Town Plan

Cuenca, **Ecuador (8)**, was founded in 1557 on the rigorous planning guidelines issued 30 years earlier by the Spanish King Charles V. Cuenca still observes the formal orthogonal town plan that it has respected for 400 years. (Photo: Cuenca Cathedral)

Unique Regional Baroque

A unique form of late baroque architecture emerged in the diamond and gold mining province of Minas Gerais, Brazil, in the 18th century. One of the most beautiful churches in the **Old City of Ouro Preto (24)** is São Francisco de Assis, designed by Aleijadinho and completed in 1794.

Like a Necklace

Diamantina, **Brazil (25)**, a colonial village set like a jewel in a necklace of inhospitable rocky mountains, recalls the exploits of diamond prospectors in the 18th century and testifies to the triumph of human cultural and artistic endeavour over the environment.

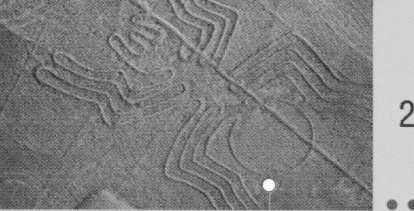

Art from the Air

On the coastal plain of Peru, the Nasca culture (200–600 AD) left behind **geoglyphs (15)** recognizable only from the air. This spider figure is 46 meters (151 ft.) long. The meaning and purpose of these ground figures remain an archeological puzzle.

Citadels or Palaces

The Chimu Kingdom, with **Chan Chan, Peru (10),** as its capital, reached its apogee in the 15th century, not long before falling to the Incas. The planning of this huge city, the largest in pre-Columbian America, reflects a strict political and social strategy, marked by the city's division into nine 'citadels' or 'palaces' forming autonomous units. (Photo: Fishnet ruins)

Amazing Urban Creation

Machu Picchu, Peru (13), stands 2,430 meters (7972 ft. above sea-level, in the middle of a tropical mountain forest, in an extraordinarily beautiful setting. It was probably the most amazing urban creation of the Inca Empire at its height; its giant walls, terraces and ramps seem as if they have been cut naturally in the continuous rock escarpments.

Stations of the Cross

The **Old City of Quito, Ecuador (7),** the oldest capital in South America (founded in 1534), has retained its colonial flavor. The stations of the cross at the monastery of La Merced are arranged on two stories and overlook a fountain.

Model States

A by-product of missionary work among the Guaranís, the **Jesuit Reductions (22)** were self-governing agricultural communities that survived for 160 years. (Photo: Church portal in Trinidad, Paraguay)

Sculptures

Rapa Nui (20), the indigenous name of Easter Island, bears witness to a unique cultural phenomenon. A society of Polynesian origin that settled there 300-400 A.D. and established a powerful, imaginative and original tradition of monumental sculpture and architecture, free from any external influence.

1 Colonial Cartagena
2 Willemstad
3 Coro
4 Santa Cruz de Mompox
5 Tierradentro National Archeological Park
6 San Agustín Archeological Park
7 Old City of Quito
8 Old City of Cuenca
9 Río Abiseo National Park
10 Chan Chan Archeological Zone
11 Chavín Archeological Site
12 Old City of Lima
13 Machu Picchu Historic Sanctuary
14 Cuzco
15 Lines and Geoglyphs of Nasca
16 Jesuit Missions of the Chiquitos
17 Samaipata Fortress
18 Historic City of Sucre
19 Potosí
20 Easter Island (NP Rapa Nui)
21 Colonia del Sacramento
22 Jesuit Mission of the Guaranís (Argentina, Brazil, Paraguay)
23 Sanctuary of Bom Jesus do Congonhas
24 Old City of Ouro Preto
25 Old City of Diamantina
26 Brasília
27 Old City of Salvador
28 Old City of Olinda
29 Serra da Capivara National Park
30 Old City of São Luís
31 Churches of Chiloé
32 Old City of Valparaíso
33 Humberstone and Santa Laura Saltpeter Works
34 Sewell Mining Town
35 Cueva de las Manos, Río Pinturas
36 Jesuit Block and Estancias of Córdoba
37 Quebrada de Humahuaca
38 Historic Centre of the Town of Goiás
39 Ciudad Universitaria de Caracas
40 Old City of Arequipa

UNESCO World Cultural Heritage in South America

The Amazon

Nature's Greatest Show

Elfin forest type

The forests and rivers of the Amazon are among the most fabulous sights in the world. The word "Amazon" stands for the world's mightiest rivers, as well as for the surrounding bio-geographic region, the tropical forests of the Amazon River system. These forests grow in the largest area on earth dominated by a moist tropical climate, and have evolved our planet's greatest diversity of plant and animal species. The Amazon is one of the earth's largest contiguous tracts of nature. Although more than 80 percent of these forests are still intact, at the current rate of deforestation they will no longer exist by the end of the century.

Geography

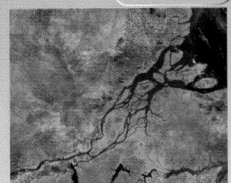

Amazon delta

The world's most diverse ecosystem is highly dependent on its geographical environment.

The vast lowland basin surrounding the Amazon River and its tributaries — Amazonia — covers 3.5 million sq. km. (1.4 million sq. miles).

Amazonia it is bordered by the Andes in the west, the Guayana shield in the north, the Brazilian shield in the south and the Atlantic Ocean in the east.

The area has a generally homogenous moist, warm climate, a prerequisite for the growth of tropical rainforests.

Climate and Diversity

A rainforest

This tropical climate changes at Amazonia's borders: to the west, to the cold mountain climate of the Andes, and to the north and south respectively, the dry climate of the llanos of Venezuela and the Cerrado, sertão and Chaco of Bolivia and Brazil.

Geological Influences

Orchid

One of the most important factors that influence the Amazon's flora and fauna was South America's long geographic isolation. For several tens of millions of years, throughout most of the tertiary era, South America existed as an island, without contact with other continents. Many families of animals and plants that became extinct elsewhere were preserved on this island continent. The temporary isolation is thought to have contributed to the immense biological richness of the Amazon basin, and areas of pronounced biodiversity are seen as remnants of previous moist refuges.

The Amazon Today

Waika man

The destruction of the Amazon's natural resources may leave the region not only devoid of its biodiversity but also of no sustainable economic use.

The mean annual deforestation rate from 2000 to 2005 (22,400 km² per year) was about 18% higher than in the previous five years (19,000 km² per year). At the current rate, in two decades the Amazon Rainforest will be reduced by 40%, and disappear by the end of the century.

The forces menacing the physical and cultural survival of the indigenous peoples of the region are the same as those threatening the destruction of the forest ecosystem and include above all, massive "development" schemes, large scale farming, and mining.

Over the past century, roughly one hundred vertebrate animal species have become extinct, and today even larger numbers are threatened.

Large sums of money change hands in the illegal trade of rare animal and plant species and, despite international legislation, the traffic continues.

Thanks to mounting pressure from governments and conservation groups many initiatives have been taken to encourage sustainable tourism.

Experts argue that the best hope for the conservation of the Amazonian forests maybe to put funding and control in the hands of indigenous peoples.

Angel Falls

The Amazon River

The Amazon River contributes almost one-fifth of the total annual amount of fresh water discharged into the oceans of the world.

It has a water flow five times that of the Congo, and 12 times that of the Mississippi.

The Amazon is the longest navigable natural waterway in the world.

You can travel 3,720 km. (2,310 miles) from the Atlantic to Iquitos, Peru.

The true source of the Amazon was discovered in 1953 to be a small stream, the Huarco, rising near the summit of Cerro Huagra in the Peruvian Andes.

The Huarco becomes the Río Toto, then the Río Santiago, then the Río Apurímac, followed by the Río Ene, then the Río Tambo, which flows into a main tributary of the Amazon, the Río Ucayali, still in Peru. The Amazon flows across Peru to Brazil, where it is known as the Rio Solimões, until it reaches the confluence with the large tributary, the Rio Negro near Manaus. The last 1,600 km. (1,000 miles) from Manaus to the mouth is the Rio Amazonas.

In the 990 km. (615 miles) from the source of the river to Atalaya, on the Río Tambo, it drops 4,450 meters (14,600 ft.) in altitude, but from Atalaya to the Atlantic, it drops only another 194 meters (636 ft.).

One of the most important features of the Amazon River system is the different types of water which occur within the basin. This can readily be seen near Manaus, where the Amazon and the Rio Negro flow together. The Amazon has a muddy brown color and is full of silt and alluvial matter. In local terminology, this is called a white water river. In contrast, the Rio Negro is the color of strong tea and has very little silt, and is an example of a black water river. Where these two large rivers converge at Manaus, the river water is clearly divided into two colors for 15-25 km. (9-15 miles) downstream until they eventually mix together.

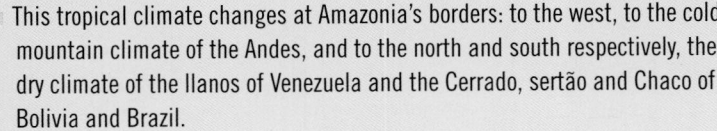

Deforestation patterns in Bolivia: Circle A - fish bone pattern; B satellite image from June 2006 and C - same area as B, satellite image from June 2002

June 2006

B

June 2002

C

A

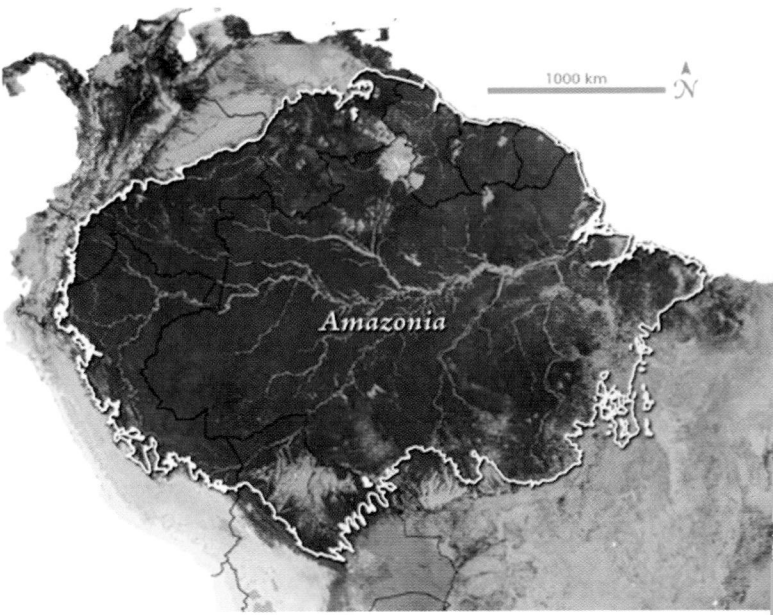

1000 km

Amazonia

Amazon Plant and Wildlife

Caiman

Capybara

Emperor tamarin

Jaquar

Sunbittern

Parrots

Silky anteater

Green iguana

Guarana

Emerald tree boa

Orchid

Victoria water lilies

Tree ferns

Wattled jacana

Big-eye frog

Macaws

Tree frog

Tarantula

Leaf fish

Red-bellied piranha

Red-breasted toucan

The Galápagos Islands

History: The first sighting by Europeans of the Galápagos Islands was in 1535, though it is possible that the ancient Mantans, Incas and even Polynesians visited the islands. The islands lie 600 miles (1,000 km.) off the Pacific coast of Ecuador. From their European discovery until their incorporation into Ecuador in 1832, the islands served as a refuge for European and American pirates, whalers and sealers, where they restocked supplies of firewood and water; and giant tortoises for meat, which could remain alive for a year in ships' holds.

Just as the islands were undergoing permanent settlement, the Beagle dropped anchor in **San Cristobal Bay (1)** and the 26-year-old naturalist Charles Darwin strode ashore. Previous scientific expeditions had been mounted, but with Darwin's visit, the enormous biological and geological significance of the Galápagos Islands was recognized. Although he stayed for only five weeks in 1835, Darwin made many of the observations upon which he based his theories of evolution and the mutability of species. He noticed 13 types of finch, each with a different beak designed to collect its particular food.

The islands' romantic appeal was tarnished over the next century, when a penal colony was established on the island of Floreana. Conditions were harsh. The original colonists, some 80 soldiers whose crimes of insurrection had been pardoned, fled the island, leaving the prisoners to their fate. As recently as 1944, a colony was established on Isabela to which increasingly hardened criminals were sent. It was dissolved following a riot and mass escape and, in 1959, the islands were declared a national park.

Galápagos Islands with a caldera

The Islands: There are 13 major islands, six small islands and 42 islets spread over an area of 80,000 sq. km. (30,000 sq. miles). The land consists of lava resting on a basalt base, volcanic refuse produced by successive underwater eruptions which continue today. The islands have never been connected with the mainland, but emerged from the water individually over a million years. The violence of the geological past is most evident on Isabela with its chain of five volcanoes as high as 1,700 meters (5,600 feet). One of them, the Sierra Negra, has the second largest crater in the world, measuring 10 km. (6 miles) in diameter.

Seeds were transported accidentally by birds and aboard ships. Today the six distinct vegetation zones of the islands, ranging from low level desert to the uppermost *pampa*, support almost 900 plant varieties, the most revered of which is the *Palo Santo* ("Holy Wood") found in abundance on *Isla Rábida (2)*.

On San Bartolomé, two horseshoe beaches are separated by a narrow strip of semi-tropical forest. From the island's summit, one of the best vantage points in the archipelago, the volcanic wasteland of Santiago stretches away to the west. Within this desert is a freshwater spring which quenched the thirst of many a pirate docked in **Buccaneer Cove**. Doubtless these early visitors watched the flamingos dance around the nearby lagoon, buried each other up to the neck in the coffee-colored sand of **Espumilla Beach** and, near **Puerto Egas (3)**, were confounded by the fur seals that swam through an underwater tunnel between the open sea and two small, clear pools.

Creatures of the Sea

Española (4), is the only place in the world in which the waved albatross breeds. In **Gardner Bay**, flapping manta rays share the spectacular waters with sea lions that can recognize the 290 individual varieties of fish in the water.

The Galápagos are home to the world's only marine iguanas, and the island of **Fernandina (5)** holds the largest colony. As inquisitive as the two related land species, they are much more dragon-like with their scaly skin (which turns from black to blue and red during mating season) and the row of spines along their back. Originally land dwellers, they

Sally Lightfoot Crab

can submerge for only a few minutes at a time, searching for algae; and upon re-surfacing, snort a salty spray into the air. Watching their antics beneath the smoldering **Volcán La Cumbre**, which erupted in September 1988, is a truly primal experience.

Directly opposite Fernandina is **Urbina Bay**, and one of the few coral reefs in the archipelago. Fish of every color steer clear of the Galápagos penguin, the world's northernmost species, whose clowning routines indicate its delight in the equatorial sun. The entrance to nearby **Elizabeth Bay** is protected by a cluster of islands which penguins share with nesting pelicans. En route to Floreana, schools of sperm and killer whales cruise the deep waters, and bottle-nosed dolphins surf the bow waves of boats. At **Devil's Crown (6)**, named after the jagged, truncated volcanic cone rising from the ocean, sea lions glide along strong currents.

The beach on **Point Cormorant**, Floreana's most beautiful location, is dotted with olivine crystals, while the adjacent lagoons teem with flamingos. Around the point is the **Bay of Sharks**; its ring of pristine white sand is popular with nesting tortoises. The name refers to the relatively harmless white-tipped shark, which is found mainly here and off San Bartolomé. It is, along with the enormous and equally docile whale shark, the only kind in these waters. On land, the unchallenged king of the islands is the giant tortoise, which can live for 200 years and weigh up to 270 kgs. (600 lbs.). On rocky, sparsely vegetated islands like Isabela and Española, its longer neck and legs and saddle-shaped carapace enable it to reach higher to obtain food. These features are absent from the more cumbersome species inhabiting fertile islands like Santa Cruz.

The **Charles Darwin Research Station** was established on Santa Cruz in 1959, on the centenary of the publication of The Origin of Species. One of its most important programs is the controlled hatching of tortoise eggs, a necessary step since the introduction by early settlers of feral dogs, cats, goats, pigs and rats. On Pinzón, not one young tortoise has been sighted for nearly 50 years. The feral species also destroy vegetation, but have participated in the evolutionary miracle of the islands in at least one respect: the goats on **Santa Fé (7)**, in the absence of freshwater, have developed a taste for sea water, and now live on it.

Scattered among the coves and hills are remnants of commercial ambition and military adventurism, which underline the inhospitable loneliness of these shores. In **Whale Bay (8)** on Santa Cruz, ceramic fragments conjure images of the famous buccaneer Henry Morgan with a blue-footed booby squawking on his shoulder. Pirates and whalers recorded their passage on the cliff faces of **Tagus Cove (9)** on Isabela: today the graffiti is read mainly by flightless cormorants. A more recent ruin is the incongruous skeleton of an abandoned salt mine dating from the 1960s which sits above Puerto Egas on Isla Santiago.

The Galápagos Islands are one of the few places in the world where animals still live undisturbed, and nowhere are the forces of evolution more clearly displayed.

A land iguana

A water iguana

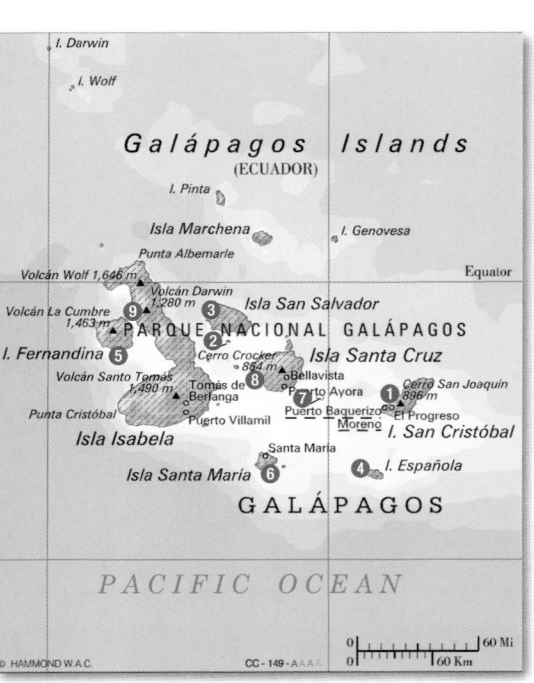

Birds of the Galápagos Islands

Evolution is Still Rich, Rare and Rewarding

Where else, but on these small islands off the coast of Ecuador, will birds come out to greet you? Life with no native predators has made the birds of the Galápagos fearless, which means that many of them are easy to spot. There are 58 resident species, of which 28 are endemic, as well as about 30 migratory birds. The seabirds are the most often seen: in the dry coastal areas one is likely to spot species of the booby family, the waved albatross (only found on the island of Española) and the world's only flightless seabirds, the Galápagos penguin and the flightless cormorant. Most migrants are visiting and birds are reproducing October to February. During that time a serious ornithologist might see 50 species in a week, and even a novice should be able to spot two dozen.

There are dangers in paradise, however: the introduction of domestic animals has been bad news. Some prey on the birds, others destroy or compete for their habitats. Farming on the inhabited islands also destroys habitats, and a natural phenomenon, the El Niño current, speads mosquito-carried disease and disrupts the food chain.

▲ FRIGATE BIRDS

The magnificent frigate bird (Fregata Magnificens) and its close relation, the great frigate bird, can be seen near the coasts of many islands. Both males and females have long forked tails and the male is remarkable for the red gular pouch which puffs in the mating season.

▶ BLUE-FOOTED BOOBY

The blue-footed booby (Sula Nebouxii Excisa) has a wonderful courtship ritual, in which the male ostentatiously displays his brightly colored feet in order to attract a mate. Two or three eggs are laid and both of the parents share the task of incubating them. Once they have become independent, the young birds leave the islands and do not return to breed until about three years later.

▶ GREATER FLAMINGO

The Greater Flamingos (Phoenicopterus ruber) (are large, pink, long necked birds that are instantly recognizable. They breed in small colonies year round but especially from January to May. They are mostly seen in salty lagoons in Floreana, Jervis and Santiago islands.

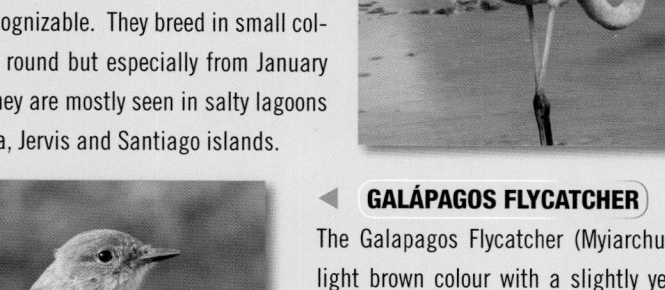

◀ GALÁPAGOS FLYCATCHER

The Galapagos Flycatcher (Myiarchus magnirostris) has a light brown colour with a slightly yellowish chest and, although common, is much harder to identify. They are aggressive, though not unfriendly, and have been known to recruit nest material of human hair from the head of tourists.

▶ SWALLOW-TAILED GULL

The Swallow-Tailed Gulls (Creagrus furcatus) are the only nocturnal gulls in the world. They have grey and white plumage with bright red feet and a crimson eye ring. They breed in a 9-10 month cycle and are found in large colonies on South Plaza, Tower, and Seymour islands.

▲ BROWN PELICAN

The brown pelican (Pelecanus Occidentalis Urinator) is a huge, cumbersome bird which can often be seen following fishing boats in search of food.

▲ GALÁPAGOS PENGUIN

The Galapagos penguin (Spheniscus mendiculus) is the most northerly penguin in the world, penguins otherwise being found in the colder regions of the southern hemisphere. Their existence on the equator at Galapagos is due to the cool Humboldt current which flows up the South American coast from the Antarctic to reach the Galapagos.

▶ THE SECRET OF DARWIN'S FINCHES

The finches of the Galápagos were vitally important in the development of Charles Darwin's ideas about evolution and the formation of species.

When he set off on his voyage around the world on HMS Beagle (1831-36), he believed, like most people of his time, in the fixity of species. But on the Galápagos he observed that 13 different species of the finch had evolved from a single ancestral group, and it was this (together with his observations of the islands' tortoises) which led to his contention that species could evolve over time, with those most suited to their natural environment surviving and passing on their characteristics to the next generation.

The main differences he noted between the finches was the size and shape of their beaks, leading him to conclude that the birds which survived were those whose beaks enabled them to eat the available food.

The 13 species of finch are divided into two groups: ground finches (pictured above is the large ground finch, Geospiza Magnirostris) and tree finches, of which the mangrove finch, found only in the swamps of Isabela Island, is the most rare.

▲ FLIGHTLESS CORMORANT

The flightless cormorant (Phalacrocorax harrisi) is the only grounded cormorant in the world. It makes up for the loss of its wings by being a terrific diver. The flightless cormorants are an endangered species and can only be found on the western islands of Isabela and Fernandina.

▲ GREAT BLUE HERON

The Great Blue Heron, (Ardea herodias) feeds in shallow water or at the water's edge during both the night and the day. It nests in trees or bushes that stand near a body of water.

The Orinoco is fed by the third-largest drainage basin in South America, a region that covers 70 percent of Venezuela and 25 percent of Colombia. Extreme topographic contrasts and a warm, humid climate make this one of the world's most diverse landscapes. Water flows from the heights of snow-covered Pico Bolivar (5,007 m) through tropical jungle, over virtually treeless plains known as Llanos, and on to the flood plain of the Orinoco. Here lie the oil reserves of Venezuela, which are among the largest in the world. Farther south, in the Guiana Highlands, water from plunges 979 meters from the top of a flat-topped plateau at Angel Falls, the highest waterfall in the world.

CARIBBEAN SEA

ATLANTIC OCEAN

GRENADA
Victoria
Saint George's
Point Salines
Mt. St. Catherine 840 m
Carriacou
Sauteurs

I. Blanquilla (VEN.)
Is. Los Testigos (VEN.)

Tobago 576 m
Charlotteville
Roxborough
Scarborough
CROWN POINT

NUEVA ESPARTA I. de Margarita
Juangriego La Asunción
PN LAGUNA DE LA RESTINGA Porlamar
GRAL. S. MARINO
PN CERRO EL COPEY
I. Cubagua Carúpano
I. de Coche

Las Aves (VEN.)
El Roque DEPENDENCIAS FEDERALES (VEN.)
Los Roques (VEN.)
I. La Tortuga C. Codera
I. La Orchila (VEN.)

Caracas
Petare
Los Teques MIRANDA
La Victoria Sabana de Uchire
Ocumare del Tuy
San José de los Morros
San Juan de los Morros
ARAGUA
de Cura

PN GUATOPO
Puerto La Cruz San Antonio del Golfo
Barcelona PN EL GUACHARO
Pozuelos GRAL.
Puerto Piritu J. A. ANZOÁTEGUI
Guanape San Antonio
ANZOÁTEGUI Caripito
Anaco Areo
Aragua de Barcelona Quiriquire
Onoto Punta de Mata

Cumaná SUCRE
Casanay El Pilar
Cariaco PN PENÍNSULA DE PARIA
Güiria
Yaguaraparo

TRINIDAD AND TOBAGO
Blanchisseuse
Toco Pta. Galera
Arima El Cerro del Aripo 940 m
Port-of-Spain Sangre Grande
Chaguanas PIARCO
Couva Tabaquite
San Fernando Rio Claro
Point Fortin Siparia
Fullarton Pta. Galeota

Gulf of Paria
Dragon's Mouth
Serpent's Mouth
Trinidad

Maturín MONAGAS
Aguasay
San Antonio de Tabasca
Temblador
Uracoa
Barrancas

Delta del Orinoco
La Horqueta
Tucupita
DELTA
Macareo Santo Niño
Piacoa
El Toro AMACURO
Los Costillos San José de Amacuro

VENEZUELA

Ciudad Guayana
Ciudad Bolívar
El Pao
Upata
El Palmar
Guasipati
Tumeremo
El Dorado
El Callao
Carabobo

PRESA GURI
Cerro Bolívar 802 m
Ciudad Piar
El Manteco
Embalse de Guri

BARIMA-WAINI
Mabaruma
Mount Everard
Baramanni
Charity
Baramita
POMEROON-SUPENAAM
Anna Regina
Queenstown
Suddie
Vreed-en-Hoop ESSEQUIBO IS.-W. DEMERARA
Paradise
Georgetown
TIMEHRI Mahaica
Mahaicony Village
Fort Wellington
DEMERARA-MAHAICA
MAHAICA-BERBICE
New Amsterdam
Rockstone Corriverton
Linden Nieuw-Nickerie

Guiana Highlands

BOLÍVAR
Salto Pará
Salto Hacha PARQUE
Salto del Angel (Angel Falls)
Auyán Tepui 2,950 m
Uruyén Cerro Venamo
NACIONAL 1,890 m
Uriman Rumán
Chimanta-Tepui 2,342 m
La Gran Sabana
CANAIMA
Santa Elena de Uairén
Icabaru

Cataratas de Kamaria
Bartica
Cataratas de Surwakwima
Kamarang CUYUNI-MAZARUNI
Aurora
Monte Roraima 2,772 m
Arabopó
Peraitepui
Monte Ayanganna 2,042 m
Kangaruma Ituni
Tumatumari
Kwakwani
Apoera
UPPER DEMERARA-BERBICE
E. BER.-COR.
Paradise
NICKERIE CORONIE
Totness
Calcutta Groningen
Lelydorp Paramaribo
Meerzorg
ZANDERIJ
PARA

PN JAUA SARISARINAMA
Santa María de Erebató
Guaina

PN DUIDA MARAHUACA
Cerro Marahuaca 2,579 m
Cerro Duida 2,400 m
La Esmeralda
Yerichaña
Uriranteriña
Guana

POTARO-SIPARUNI
PN KAIETEUR
Cataratas de Kaieteur
Kurupukari
Rera
Karasabai **GUYANA**
Kanuku Mts.
Wichabai
Kumaka
Lethem
Yupukarri
Annai
Isherton

SURINAME
PRESA AFOBAKA
Cataratas Tonckens
Hendrik Top 975 m
BROKO-PONDO
Juliana Top 1,230 m
Wilhelmina Gebergte
SIPALIWINI
Kayser Gebergte
Eilerts de Haan Gebergte
Oranje Gebergte
Tumuc-Humac Mts.
FRENCH GUIANA
Grand Santi-Papaïchton
St-Laurent-du-Maroni
Apatou
Majoli

AMAZONAS
PN YAPACANA
Buenos Aires
Pamoni
Tamatama
Capibara
Esperanza
San Carlos de Río Negro
Solano
Guayabal
Comunidad
Santa Isabel
El Carmen
Cucui
PARQUE NACIONAL SERRANÍA DE LA NEBLINA
Pico de la Neblina 3,014 m
PARQUE NACIONAL DO PICO DA NEBLINA

Serra Parima
Serra Pacaraima
Serra Grande
Serra Acaraí

UPPER TAKUTU-UPPER ESSEQUIBO
Amuku Mts.
Biloku
1,009 m
Kassikaityu
EAST BERBICE-CORENTYNE
Cataratas Frederik Willem IV
Cataratas Tiger
Maripasoula

RORAIMA
Boa Vista
Caracaraí
Serra Iricoumé

BRAZIL
PARÁ
Sauiá
AMAPÁ
Porto Poet

AMAZONAS
Barcelos
Represa de Balbina
Parintins
Oriximiná
Óbidos Monte Alegre
Alenquer
Nhamundá
Faro
Parque Nacional do Rio Jaú
Fonte Boa
Itapiranga
Urucará
Urucurituba
Silves
Itacoatiara
Manaus
Eduardo Gomes
Belterra
Santarém

Equator

Scale 1:6,000,000 Lambert Conformal Conic Projection
MI 50 100 150 200
KM 50 100 150 200 250 300

The Amazon Basin of northern Brazil comprises the world's largest rain forest, an area covering some 4.5 million square km. The Amazon, its more than 200 tributaries, and the vast rain forest are home to over one million different species of plants and animals. Millions of acres of this vital ecosystem are destroyed every year. Without its protective cover of foliage, the exposed, sensitive soil hardens into unfertile laterite and is subject to heavy erosion. The Amazon Basin region has an average relative humidity of 90 percent and receives up to 4,000 mm of precipitation per year.

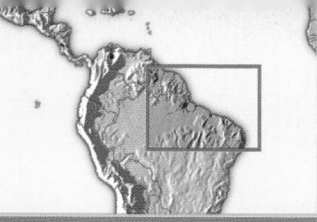

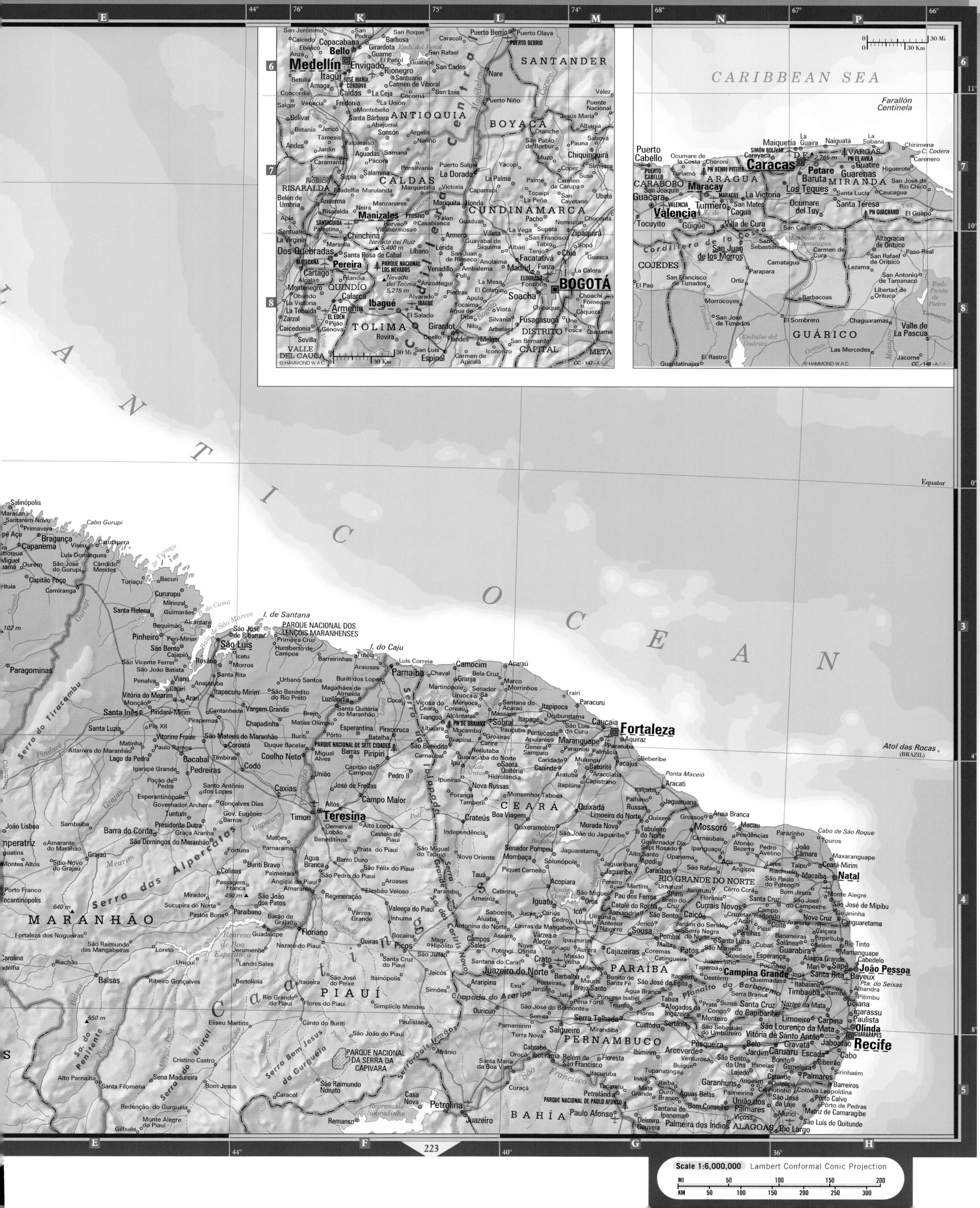
CARIBBEAN SEA
Caracas
Valencia
Maracay
Medellín
Manizales
Pereira
Ibagué
BOGOTÁ
ANTIOQUIA
BOYACÁ
CALDAS
CUNDINAMARCA
SANTANDER
TOLIMA
ARAGUA
CARABOBO
MIRANDA
GUÁRICO
COJEDES
ATLANTIC OCEAN
Equator
Fortaleza
Natal
João Pessoa
Recife
Olinda
Campina Grande
Teresina
São Luís
MARANHÃO
PIAUÍ
CEARÁ
RIO GRANDE DO NORTE
PARAÍBA
PERNAMBUCO
BAHÍA
ALAGOAS
Caatinga
Serra das Alpercatas
Chapada do Araripe
Atol das Rocas (BRAZIL)
PARQUE NACIONAL DOS LENÇÓIS MARANHENSES
PARQUE NACIONAL DA SERRA DA CAPIVARA
Scale 1:6,000,000 Lambert Conformal Conic Projection
© HAMMOND W.A.C.

223

A unique feature of the climate of the west coast of South America is the El Niño phenomenon, which occurs about every three to seven years. At these times, temperatures rise in the equatorial coastal waters, drastically reducing the amount of nutrient-rich cold water that ascends from the depths to the surface and thus decimating the fish population. The resulting unusually heavy rainfall in Peru and Ecuador has been known to cause severe landslides on the steep mountain slopes. The Andes reach their widest point in Bolivia, where the Cordillera Occidental and the Cordillera Oriental frame the expansive Bolivian highlands, the Altiplano, which grow progressively more arid south of Lake Titicaca and culminate in a high desert.

Height

m. ft.	
6000	19700
4000	13000
2000	6500
1500	5000
1000	3300
500	1600
200	700
0	
200	700
500	1600
1000	3300
2000	6500
3000	9800
4000	13000
5000	16400
6000	19700

Depth

Galápagos Islands
(ECUADOR)

I. Darwin
I. Wolf
I. Pinta
Isla Marchena
I. Genovesa
Punta Albemarle
Volcán Wolf 1,646 m.
Equator
Volcán Cumbre 1,463 m.
Volcán Darwin 1,280 m.
Isla San Salvador
PARQUE NACIONAL GALÁPAGOS
I. Fernandina
Cerro Crocker 864 m.
Isla Santa Cruz
Volcán Santo Tomás 1,490 m.
Bellavista
Cerro San Joaquin 896 m.
Tomás de Berlanga
Puerto Ayora
El Progreso
Punta Cristóbal
Puerto Villamil
Puerto Baquerizo Moreno
I. San Cristóbal
Isla Isabela
Santa María
I. Española
Isla Santa María
GALÁPAGOS

PACIFIC OCEAN

Population

◼ Over 2,000,000	⊛ 500,000 - 999,999	⦿ 100,000 - 249,999	⊙ 10,000 - 29,999
◻ 1,000,000 - 1,999,999	⊘ 250,000 - 499,999	⊙ 30,000 - 99,999	○ Under 10,000

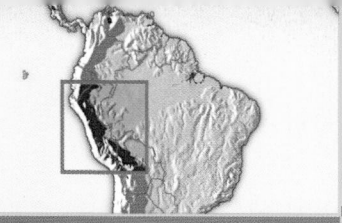

68°   64°   60°   56°

E   F   217   60°   G   56°   H

PARQUE NACIONAL
DO RIO JAÚ

Manaus
EDUARDO
GOMES
Manacapuru

Oriximiná   Óbidos   Alenquer
Faro   Santarém
Nhamundá   Belterra
Urucará   Parintins
Itapiranga   Urucurituba
Silves   Barreirinha
Itacoatiara   Nova Olinda
Autazes   do Norte   Juruti
Careiro   Maués   PARQUE
NACIONAL
Borba   DE AMAZÔNIA   Itaituba
(TAPAJÓS)

Tefé   Tefé
Codajás   Anori
Coari
L. de
Coari

A M A Z O N A S

Entre Rios

P A R Á

Carauari   Tapauá   Manicoré   Novo
Aripuaná   Jacareacanga

Canutama   Tapajós   RESERVA FLORESTAL
MUNDURUCÂNIA

B R A Z I L

Lábrea   Humaitá   Sumaúma

Bôca do Acre   Calama

Porto Velho   Santo Antônio   Alta Floresta

Rio Branco   Abunã   Ariquemes
Santos Mercado   Nuevo Mundo
Triunfo   Villa Bella   **R O N D Ô N I A**   Jaru
P A N D O   Guajará-Mirim   Ji-Paraná   Aripuanã   **RESERVA**
Guayaramerín   (Rondônia)   Presidente Médici   **FLORESTAL**
Riberalta   PARQUE   Cacoal   Espigão d'Oeste   **DO JURUENA**
RESERVA NACIONAL   NACIONAL   Pimenta Bueno
MANURIPI HEATH   DOS   Rolim de
AMAZÔNICA   PACAÁS   Moura
Sena   NOVOS   Sinop

Concepción   Alejandría
Tres Mapajos   Santa Rosa   Costa   Vilhena   **M A T O   G R O S S O**
San Lorenzo   Mayo Mayo   Marques
Fortaleza   El Perú   La Horquilla
Rosario   Versalles   Mateguá   Colorado do   Arenápolis   Diamantino
Remanso   Oeste   Nortelândia   Alto Paraguai
B E N I   Todos Santos   San Simón   Puerto Villazón   Tangará da Serra   Nobres
Cavinas   San Joaquín   Piso Firme   Bella Vista   Rosário
Llanos de Mojos   San Ramón   Puerto   Oeste   Nova Brasilândia
Magdalena   Saucedo   Puerto Alegre
Huacaraje   Porvenir   Acorizal
San Borja   Soberanía   Baurés   Huachi   Barra do Bugres
Chevejécure   San Miguel   La Esperanza   Vila Bela da   Várzea Grande
Santa Ana   El Carmen   San Ramón   Santíssima Trindade   Nossa Senhora
Trinidad   Puerto Leigue   La Esperanza   do Livramento   Chapada
San Javier   San Lorenzo   El Pensamiento   Monte   Puerto Frey   **Cuiabá**   dos Guimarães
B O L I V I A   Loreto   Perseverancia   Cristo   Pantes   Santo Antônio   Dom
Yaguarú   Urubichá   Puerto   e Lacerda   do Leverger   Aquino
PARQUE NACIONAL   Los Cusis   Arturo   Cáceres   Poxoréo
ISIBORO SÉCURE   Santa María   La Unión
Paz   San Pablo   Cuyuchi   Poconé   Barão   Rondonópolis
Ascención   San Diego   de Melgaço
Santa Rosa   **BRAZIL-**
COCHABAMBA   de la Roca   **BOLIVIA**
Yotaú   El Puente   San Javier   San Ignacio   Las   San Matías   **MATO GROSSO**
San Ignacio   Santa Ana   Petas   **DO SUL**
Cochabamba   **SANTA CRUZ**   San Rafael   Caucás   Itiquira

Scale 1:6,000,000   Lambert Conformal Conic Projection

MI   50   100   150   200
KM   50   100   150   200   250   300

Brazil is the fifth largest country on earth and covers nearly half of the South American continent. Its tropical-subtropical climate and extensive highlands provide ideal conditions for the cultivation of coffee.

The very old underlying rock is also rich in iron ore, gold, and diamonds. The most important energy source – water – is harnessed effectively in the Paraná River system (Itaipú hydroelectric plant). Substantial oil reserves have been

discovered off the coast near Rio de Janeiro. Eighty percent of the population lives in the cities, the largest of which are Sao Paulo and Rio de Janeiro.

Height

m.	ft.
6000	19700
4000	13000
2000	6500
1500	5000
1000	3300
500	1600
200	700
-0-	
200	700
500	1600
1000	3300
2000	6500
3000	9800
4000	13000
5000	16400
6000	19700

Depth

Population

■ Over 2,000,000	⊕ 500,000 - 999,999
■ 1,000,000 - 1,999,999	⊚ 250,000 - 499,999
● 100,000 - 249,999	⊙ 10,000 - 29,999
⊙ 30,000 - 99,999	○ Under 10,000

PARÁ
MARANHÃO
PIAUÍ
TOCANTINS
MATO GROSSO
Planalto do Mato Grosso
Serra do Cachimba
Serra Formosa
Serra do Roncador
GOIÁS
BRAZIL
Brasília
D.F.
PN DE BRASILIA
Goiânia
MINAS
BELO HORIZONTE
BOLIVIA
SANTA CRUZ
Pantanal
Parque Nacional Pantanal Matogrossense
Corumbá
Campo Grande
MATO GROSSO DO SUL
ALTO PARAGUAY
PRESIDENTE HAYES
CONCEPCIÓN
SAN PEDRO
PARAGUAY
Tropic of Capricorn
PARANÁ
Londrina
SÃO PAULO
Campinas
Guarulhos
Osasco
Santo André
São Bernardo do Campo
São Vicente
Santos
São José dos Campos
Jundiaí
Sorocaba
Ribeirão Prêto
São José do Rio Prêto
Uberlândia
Uberaba
Bauru
Marília
Presidente Prudente
Dourados
Cáceres
Cuiabá
Várzea Grande
Rondonópolis
Rio Verde
Araguaína
Gurupi
Porto Nacional
Palmas
Alta Floresta
Sinop

© HAMMOND WORLD ATLAS CORPORATION

219

E · 40° · F · 36° · G · 32° · H

ATLANTIC

OCEAN

PN DA SERRA DA CAPIVARA

PERNAMBUCO

Belém de São Francisco · Ibimirim · Planalto de Borborema · São Berito do Una · Ribeirão · Catende · Palmares

São Raimundo Nonato · Santa Maria da Boa Vista · Curaçá · Buíque · Lajedo · Garanhuns · Luminária · Sirinhaém

Jesus da Gurgueia · Casa Nova · PARQUE NACIONAL DE PAULO AFONSO · Mata Grande · Santana do Ipanema · São José da Laje · Colônia Leopoldina · Pôrto Calvo

Sa. Dois Irmãos · Petrolina · Paulo Afonso · Delmiro Gouveia · Palmeira dos Índios · Rio Largo · União dos Palmares

Pilão Arcado · Remanso · Juazeiro · 1,229 m · Olho d'Água das Flores · Arapiraca · ALAGOAS · **Maceió**

Represa de Sobradinho · Laje · Jeremoabo · Pão de Açúcar · São Miguel dos Campos · Marechal Deodoro

Barra · Xique-Xique · Central · Campo Formoso · Senhor do Bonfim · Euclides da Cunha · Pindobaçu · Uauá · Pôrto da Fôlha · Traipu · Penedo · Coruripe

Morpará · Ipupiara · Irecê · Jacobina · Queimadas · Tucano · Nossa Senhora da Glória · Propriá · Piaçabuçu

1,098 m · Morro do Chapéu · Piritiba · Ribeira do Pombal · Cícero Dantas · Simão Dias · SERGIPE · Itabaiana

AHÍA · Utinga · Conceição do Coité · Mairi · Riachão do Jacuípe · Serrinha · Tobias Barreto · Lagarto · Marium · Santo Amaro das Brotas

Ibotirama · Seabra · PN CHAPADA DIAMANTINA · Itaberaba · Santa Luz · Itabaianinha · São Cristóvão · **Aracajú**

BAHIA · Paratinga · Andaraí · Iaçu · Santo Amaro · Olindina · Rio Real · Estância

Bom Jesus da Lapa · Mucugê · Amargosa · Candeias · Camaçari · Acajutiba · Esplanada · Conde

Paramirim · Pico das Almas 1,850 m · Maracás · Santa Inês · Valença · Simões Filho · Alagoinhas · Entre Rios · Catu

1,129 m · Rio de Contas · Itiruçu · DOIS DE JULHO · **SALVADOR** · B. de Todos os Santos

Riacho de Santana · Livramento do Brumado · Jaguaquara · Ipiaú · Itubera · I. de Itaparica

Guanambi · Brumado · Poções · Jequié · Camamu · Ilha de Tinharé

Vitória da Conquista · Iguaí · Ibicaraí · Itabuna · Ubaitaba · Ponta do Mutá · Ilha de Boipeba

Espinosa · Condeúba · Belo Campo · Itambé · Itororó · Buerarema · Ilhéus · Itapitanga · Coaraci

Monte Azul · Mato Verde · São João do Paraíso · Itape · Una

Janaúba · Taiobeiras · Itapetinga · Canavieiras

Francisco Sá · Pedra Azul · Salto da Divisa · Belmonte

Capelinha · Joaíma · Guaratinga · Porto Seguro

Araçuaí · Almenara · Rubim · PN DE MONTE PASCOAL · Ponta Corumbaú

Turmalina · Águas Formosas · Pavão · Itamaraju

Pico de Itambé 2,033 m · Itambacuri · Medeiros Neto · Prado · Ponta da Baleia

Santa Maria do Suaçuí · Teófilo Otoni · Montanha · Alcobaça · Caravelas

Malacacheta · Pinheiros

Virgolândia · Frei Inocêncio

João Evangelista · Guanhães · Mantena · São Mateus

Governador Valadares · Inhapim · ESPÍRITO SANTO · São Gabriel da Palha

Ipatinga · Conselheiro Pena · Resplendor · Linhares

Timóteo · Coronel Fabriciano · Caratinga · Aimorés · Colatina

João Monlevade · Mutum · Baixo Guandu · Aracruz

Barão de Cocais · Raul Soares · Manhuaçu · Manhumirim · Santa Teresa · Pontal de Regência

Ouro Preto · Ponte Nova · Santa Bárbara · Serra

PARQUE NACIONAL DO CAPARAÓ · Pico da Bandeira 2,899 m · Vitória

Viçosa · Carangola · Guaçuí · Vila Velha · Argolas

Ervália · Alegre · Guarapari

Visconde do Rio Branco · Cachoeiro de Itapemirim · Anchieta

Ubá · Muriaé · Itapemirim

Cataguases · Miracema · Itaperuna

Santos Dumont · São Fidélis

Juiz de Fora · RIO DE JANEIRO · Conceição de Macabu · **Campos**

Matias Barbosa · Além Paraíba · Cabo de São Tomé

Paraíba do Sul · Cordeiro

Nova Friburgo · Macaé

Duque de Caxias · SANTOS DUMONT

Niterói · Cabo Frio

RIO DE JANEIRO · Tropic of Capricorn

E · 40° · F · 47° · J · K

(Inset – São Paulo / Rio de Janeiro region)

Arceburgo · Guaxupé · Muzambinho · Areado · Rep. de Furnas · Três Pontas · Itumirim · Represa de Camargos · Antônio Carlos · Guarani · Astolfo Dutra

Mococa · Cabo Verde · Alfenas · Divisa Nova · Varginha · Carmo da Cachoeira · Piedade do Rio Grande · Santos Dumont · São João Nepomuceno · Cataguases

São José do Rio Pardo · Caconde · Machado · Paraguaçu · Eloi Mendes · MAJOR BRIGADEIRO TROMPOWSKY · Madre de Deus de Minas · Andrelândia · Leopoldina

Casa Branca · Divinolândia · Botelhos · Campestre · Poço Fundo · Campanha · MINAS · GERAIS · Cambuquira · Conceição do Rio Verde · Cruzília · Lima Duarte · FRANCISCO DE ASSIS · **Juiz de Fora**

Poços de Caldas · Vargem Grande do Sul · Aguaí · da Prata · Caldas · São Gonçalo do Sapucaí · Lambari · Baependi · Aiuruoca · Bom Jardim de Minas · Matias Barbosa

São João da Boa Vista · POÇOS DE CALDAS · Andradas · Espírito Santo do Pinhal · Ouro Fino · Careaçu · Jesuânia · São Lourenço · Carmo

Conchal · Mogi-Guaçu · Itapira · Inconfidentes · Pouso Alegre · Santa Rita do Sapucaí · Cristina · Maria da Fé · Liberdade · Três Rios · Nova Friburgo

Mogi Mirim · Aguaí · de Lindóia · Borda da Mata · Conceição dos Ouros · Pedralva · Itamonte · Pico das Agulhas Negras 2,787 m · Valença · RIO DE JANEIRO

Artur Nogueira · Socorro · Bueno Brandão · Paraisópolis · Itajubá · Serra da Mantiqueira · Vassouras · Miguel Pereira · Teresópolis · Cachoeiras de Macacu

Cosmópolis · Amparo · Brazópolis · PN DE ITATIAIA · Resende · Barra do Piraí · Engenheiro Paulo de Frontin · Magé

Campinas · Jaguariúna · Paulínia · Pedreira · Cambuí · Piquete · Cruzeiro · Cachoeira Paulista · Volta Redonda · Rio Bonito

VIRACOPOS · Morungaba · Extrema · Camanducaia · Lorena · Bananal · **Nova Iguaçu** · Duque de Caxias

Valinhos · Bragança Paulista · Pindamonhangaba · Campos do Jordão · Piraí · São João de Meriti · São Gonçalo

Vinhedo · Itatiba · Louveira · Bom Jesus dos Perdões · Roseira · Guaratinguetá · Rio Claro · Nilópolis · **RIO DE JANEIRO** · Niterói · Maricá

Jundiaí · Atibaia · Nazaré Paulista · Aparecida · Piquerobi · PN SERRA DA BOCAINA · Angra dos Reis · PARQUE NACIONAL DA TIJUCA · CORCOVADO

Várzea Paulista · Campo Limpo Paulista · Igaratá · SÃO · PAULO · Cunha · Paraty · Ilha Marambaia

Francisco Morato · Mairiporã · Santa Isabel · São José dos Campos · B. da Ilha Grande · Ilha Grande

Franco da Rocha · Caieiras · Arujá · Jacareí · Ubatuba · Ponta de Juatinga · Tropic of Capricorn

Guarulhos · Itaquaquecetuba · Guararema · **ATLANTIC**

Carapicuíba · Mogi das Cruzes · Caraguatatuba · **OCEAN**

Osasco · **SÃO PAULO** · Biritiba-Mirim · Enseada de Caraguatatuba

Cotia · **Diadema** · **Santo André** · São Sebastião · Ilha dos Búzios

Ibiúna · **São Bernardo do Campo** · Cubatão · Ilha de São Sebastião

Juquitiba · **São Vicente** · **Santos** · I. de Santo Amaro

Praia Grande · Guarujá

Mongaguá · Ilha de Alcatrazes

Itanhaém

Peruíbe · Itariri

0 — 30 Mi · 0 — 30 Km

© HAMMOND WORLD ATLAS CORPORATION · CC-1150-A

E · 40° · F · 47° · J · K · 46° · L · 45° · M · N · 43° · P

Scale 1:6,000,000 Lambert Conformal Conic Projection

MI · 0 · 50 · 100 · 150 · 200
KM · 0 · 50 · 100 · 150 · 200 · 250 · 300

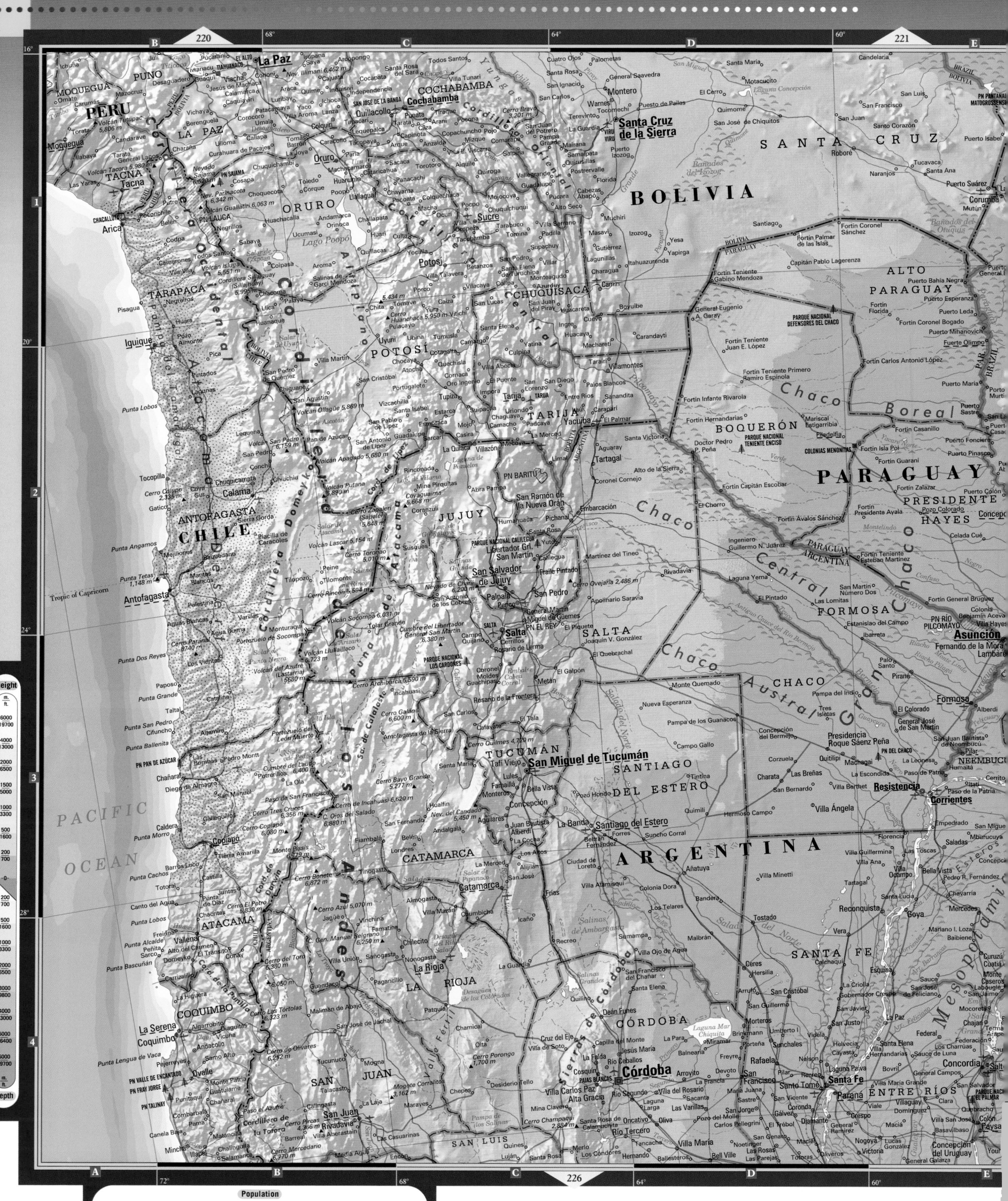

The Gran Chaco, South America's vast heartland, through which the many tributaries of the Paraguay and the Paraná flow, has a hot, subtropical climate with heavy precipitation in the east and much drier conditions in the west. The winds blowing inland from the Pacific travel over cold ocean currents and thus carry little moisture. The prevailing climate has produced coastal deserts in Chile and Peru, where average precipitation often falls below 4 mm. One such desert is the Atacama, an arid region rich in ore deposits where the mean annual temperature is a moderate 66° F.

Scale 1:6,000,000 Lambert Conformal Conic Projection

| MI | 50 | 100 | 150 | 200 |
| KM | 50 | 100 | 150 | 200 | 250 | 300 |

The expansive grasslands of Argentina, the Pampas, were probably covered with light forest growth before settlers began clearing the land for wheat farming and to provide grazing land for cattle. With good access to shipping routes, the area around the mouths of the Paraná and Uruguay rivers is one of South America's most important economic regions. Climatic conditions in the south are extreme, both in East Patagonia, with its salt swamps, and in Tierra del Fuego, where storms off Cape Horn have been the bane of seafarers for centuries.

Southern Chile and Argentina

Scale 1:6,000,000 Lambert Conformal Conic Projection

MAP SECTION
Arctic Regions, Antarctica

Polar climates fall within lines between the poles and the equator within which average temperatures during the warmest month do not exceed 40° F. Except for Greenland, the Arctic is a landless region of sea and ice. Antarctica is the coldest, driest continent on earth and also has the highest average elevation. A record low temperature of - 129.8° F was recorded at the Vostok Research Station, 3,500 m above sea level.

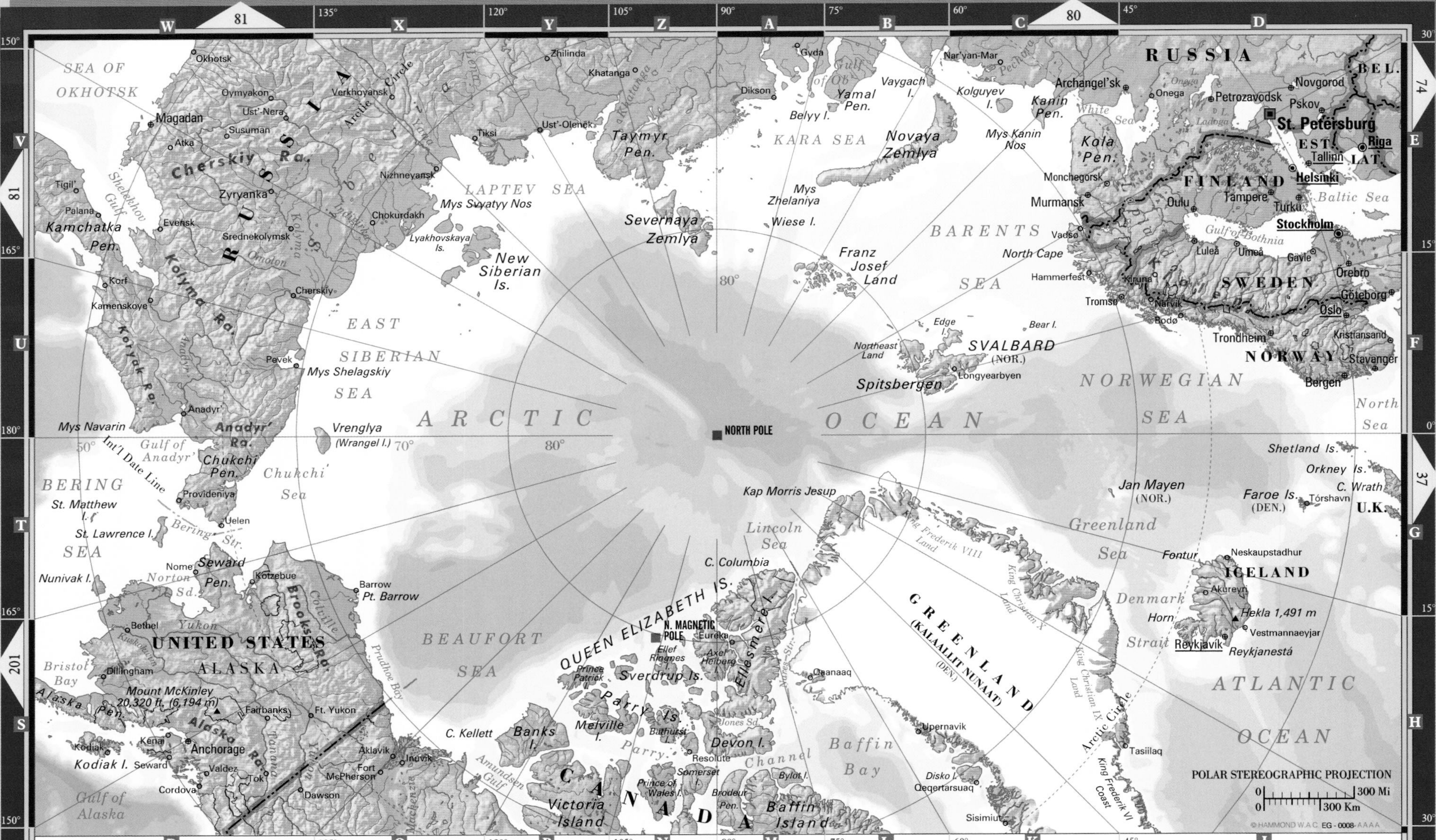

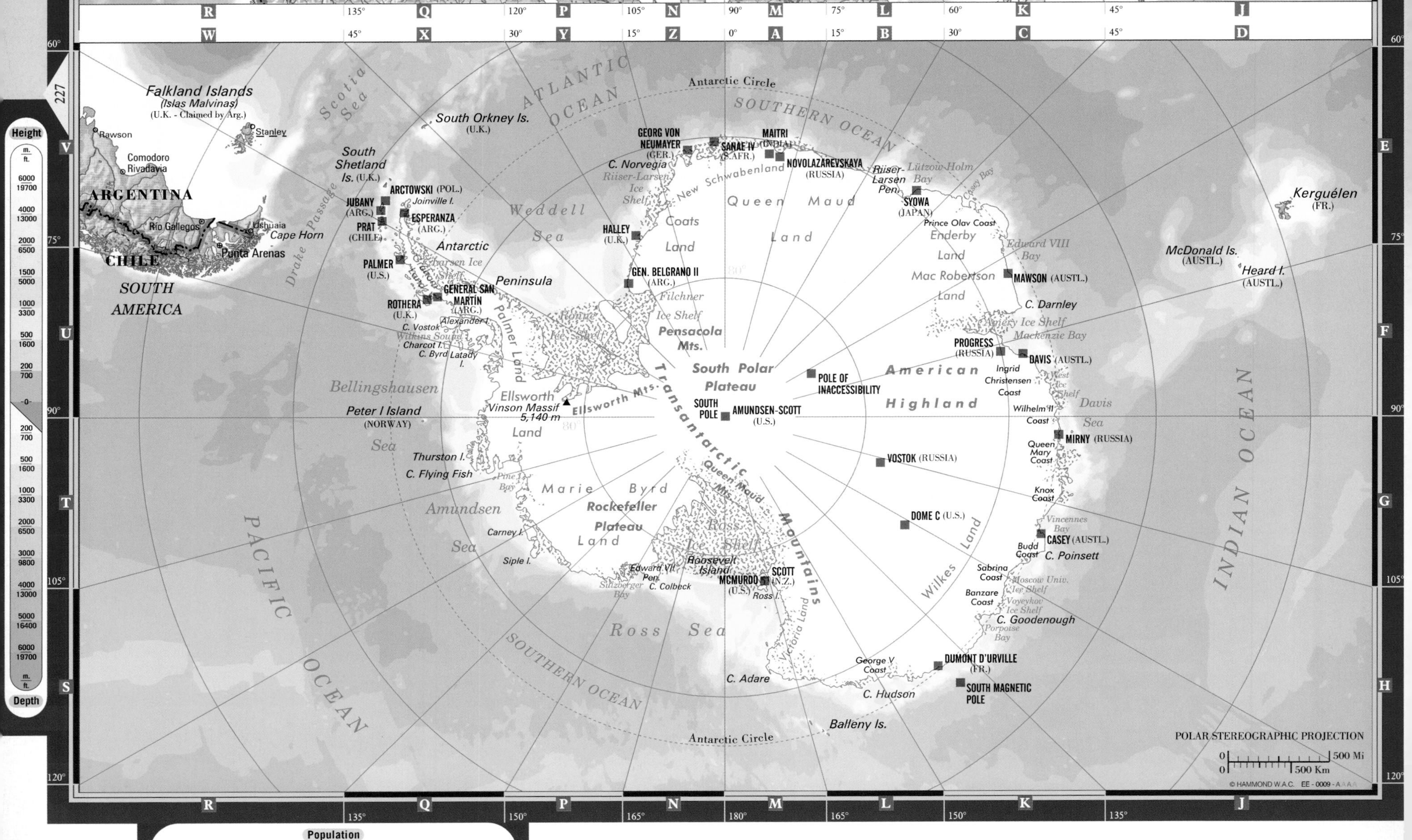

Height

m. / ft.	
6000 / 19700	
4000 / 13000	
2000 / 6500	
1500 / 5000	
1000 / 3300	
500 / 1600	
200 / 700	
0	
200 / 700	
500 / 1600	
1000 / 3300	
2000 / 6500	
3000 / 9800	
4000 / 13000	
5000 / 16400	
6000 / 19700	

Depth

POLAR STEREOGRAPHIC PROJECTION

0 — 300 Mi
0 — 300 Km

© HAMMOND W.A.C. EG - 0008- A-A-A

POLAR STEREOGRAPHIC PROJECTION

0 — 500 Mi
0 — 500 Km

© HAMMOND W.A.C. EE - 0009 - A-A-A

Population
- ■ Over 2,000,000
- ■ 1,000,000 - 1,999,999
- ● 500,000 - 999,999
- ● 100,000 - 499,999
- ○ 50,000 - 99,999
- ○ Under 50,000

Arctic Regions map labels

SEA OF OKHOTSK · Okhotsk · Oymyakon · Ust'-Nera · Susuman · Magadan · Atka · Verkhoyansk · Zhilinda · Khatanga · Gyda · Nar'yan-Mar · Pechora · **RUSSIA** · Novgorod · **BEL.** · Tigil · Palana · Zyryanka · Cherskiy Ra. · Nizhneyansk · Yamal Pen. · Kolguyev I. · Archangel'sk · Onega · Petrozavodsk · Pskov · Kamchatka Pen. · Korf · Chokurdakh · Taymyr Pen. · KARA SEA · Novaya Zemlya · Mys Kanin Nos · Kanin Pen. · Kola Pen. · Monchegorsk · **EST.** · Tallinn · **LAT.** · Riga · Kamenskoye · Anadyr' Ra. · Srednekolymsk · Lyakhovskaya Is. · Mys Svyatyy Nos · LAPTEV SEA · Severnaya Zemlya · Mys Zhelaniya · Wiese I. · Franz Josef Land · North Cape · Murmansk · Vadsö · **FINLAND** · Helsinki · Oulu · Tampere · Turku · Baltic Sea · Stockholm · Mys Navarin · Anadyr' · Chukchi Sea · New Siberian Is. · EAST SIBERIAN SEA · BARENTS SEA · Edge I. · Bear I. · SVALBARD (NOR.) · Hammerfest · Tromsö · Narvik · Bodö · **SWEDEN** · Luleå · Umeå · Gävle · Örebro · Int'l Date Line · Gulf of Anadyr · Providenlya · Uelen · ARCTIC · OCEAN · NORTH POLE · Northeast Land · Spitsbergen · Longyearbyen · NORWEGIAN SEA · Trondheim · **NORWAY** · Bergen · Oslo · Kristiansand · Stavanger · North Sea · BERING SEA · St. Matthew I. · St. Lawrence I. · Bering Strait · Seward Pen. · Nome · Kotzebue · Barrow · Pt. Barrow · Kap Morris Jesup · Shetland Is. · Orkney Is. · C. Wrath · **U.K.** · Jan Mayen (NOR.) · Faroe Is. (DEN.) · Törshavn · Nunivak I. · Norton Sd. · Bethel · Lincoln Sea · C. Columbia · Greenland Sea · Neskaupstadhur · Akureyri · **ICELAND** · Hekla 1,491 m · Reykjavik · Reykjanestá · Vestmannaeyjar · Bristol Bay · Dillingham · **UNITED STATES** · **ALASKA** · Brooks Ra. · Prudhoe Bay · N. MAGNETIC POLE · QUEEN ELIZABETH IS. · Ellef Ringnes I. · Prince Patrick I. · Eureka · Ellesmere I. · Sverdrup Is. · Axel Heiberg I. · Qaanaaq · **GREENLAND (KALAALLIT NUNAAT)** · Denmark Strait · Horn · Fontur · ATLANTIC OCEAN · Mount McKinley 20,320 ft. (6,194 m) · Fairbanks · Ft. Yukon · BEAUFORT SEA · C. Kellett · Banks I. · Melville I. · Bathurst I. · Devon I. · Oeanaaq · King Frederik VIII Land · Arctic Circle · Kodiak I. · Kenai · Seward · Valdez · Cordova · Anchorage · Tok · Dawson · McPherson · Aklavik · Inuvik · Resolute · Somerset I. · Baffin Bay · Upernavik · Disko I. · Qeqertarsuaq · King Christian IX Coast · Gulf of Alaska · Alaska Range · Yukon · Amundsen Gulf · Victoria Island · **CANADA** · Prince of Wales I. · Brodeur Pen. · Bylot I. · Baffin Island · Sisimiut · Tasiilaq · King Frederik VI Coast · Parry Is. · Parry Channel · Lancaster Sd. · Mackenzie

Antarctica map labels

Falkland Islands (Islas Malvinas) (U.K. - Claimed by Arg.) · Stanley · Rawson · Comodoro Rivadavia · **ARGENTINA** · Rio Gallegos · Ushuaia · Cape Horn · **CHILE** · Punta Arenas · **SOUTH AMERICA** · Scotia Sea · ATLANTIC OCEAN · South Orkney Is. (U.K.) · Antarctic Circle · SOUTHERN OCEAN · South Shetland Is. (U.K.) · ARCTOWSKI (POL.) · Joinville I. · JUBANY (ARG.) · ESPERANZA (ARG.) · PRAT (CHILE) · Weddell Sea · GEORG VON NEUMAYER (GER.) · SANAE IV (S.AFR.) · MAITRI (INDIA) · NOVOLAZAREVSKAYA (RUSSIA) · C. Norvegia · Riiser-Larsen Ice Shelf · Riiser-Larsen Pen. · Lützow-Holm Bay · New Schwabenland · SYOWA (JAPAN) · Prince Olav Coast · Enderby Land · Kerguélen (FR.) · PALMER (U.S.) · Larsen Ice Shelf · Antarctic Peninsula · Coats Land · Queen Maud Land · Edward VIII Bay · GENERAL SAN MARTIN (ARG.) · HALLEY (U.K.) · GEN. BELGRANO II (ARG.) · Filchner Ice Shelf · Mac Robertson Land · MAWSON (AUSTL.) · McDonald Is. (AUSTL.) · Heard I. (AUSTL.) · ROTHERA (U.K.) · C. Vostok · Alexander I. · Williams Sound · Charcot I. · C. Byrd Latady I. · Pensacola Mts. · C. Darnley · Amery Ice Shelf · Mackenzie Bay · PROGRESS (RUSSIA) · DAVIS (AUSTL.) · American Highland · Ingrid Christensen Coast · West Ice Shelf · Davis Sea · Bellingshausen Sea · Peter I Island (NORWAY) · Ellsworth Land · Vinson Massif 5,140 m · Ellsworth Mts. · SOUTH POLAR PLATEAU · POLE OF INACCESSIBILITY · Wilhelm II Coast · Thurston I. · C. Flying Fish · SOUTH POLE · AMUNDSEN-SCOTT (U.S.) · Transantarctic Mountains · MIRNY (RUSSIA) · Queen Mary Coast · Knox Coast · Amundsen Sea · Marie Byrd Land · Rockefeller Plateau · Pine Is. Bay · VOSTOK (RUSSIA) · Queen Maud Mts. · Carney I. · Siple I. · DOME C (U.S.) · Vincennes Bay · Budd Coast · CASEY (AUSTL.) · C. Poinsett · PACIFIC OCEAN · Ross Ice Shelf · Roosevelt Island · Edward VII Pen. · Sulzberger Bay · C. Colbeck · SCOTT (N.Z.) · McMURDO (U.S.) · Ross I. · Sabrina Coast · Moscow Univ. Ice Shelf · Banzare Coast · Voyeyko Ice Shelf · Porpoise Bay · C. Goodenough · INDIAN OCEAN · Ross Sea · Victoria Land · George V Coast · DUMONT D'URVILLE (FR.) · SOUTH MAGNETIC POLE · C. Adare · C. Hudson · Wilkes Land · Balleny Is. · Antarctic Circle

Statistics and Index Section

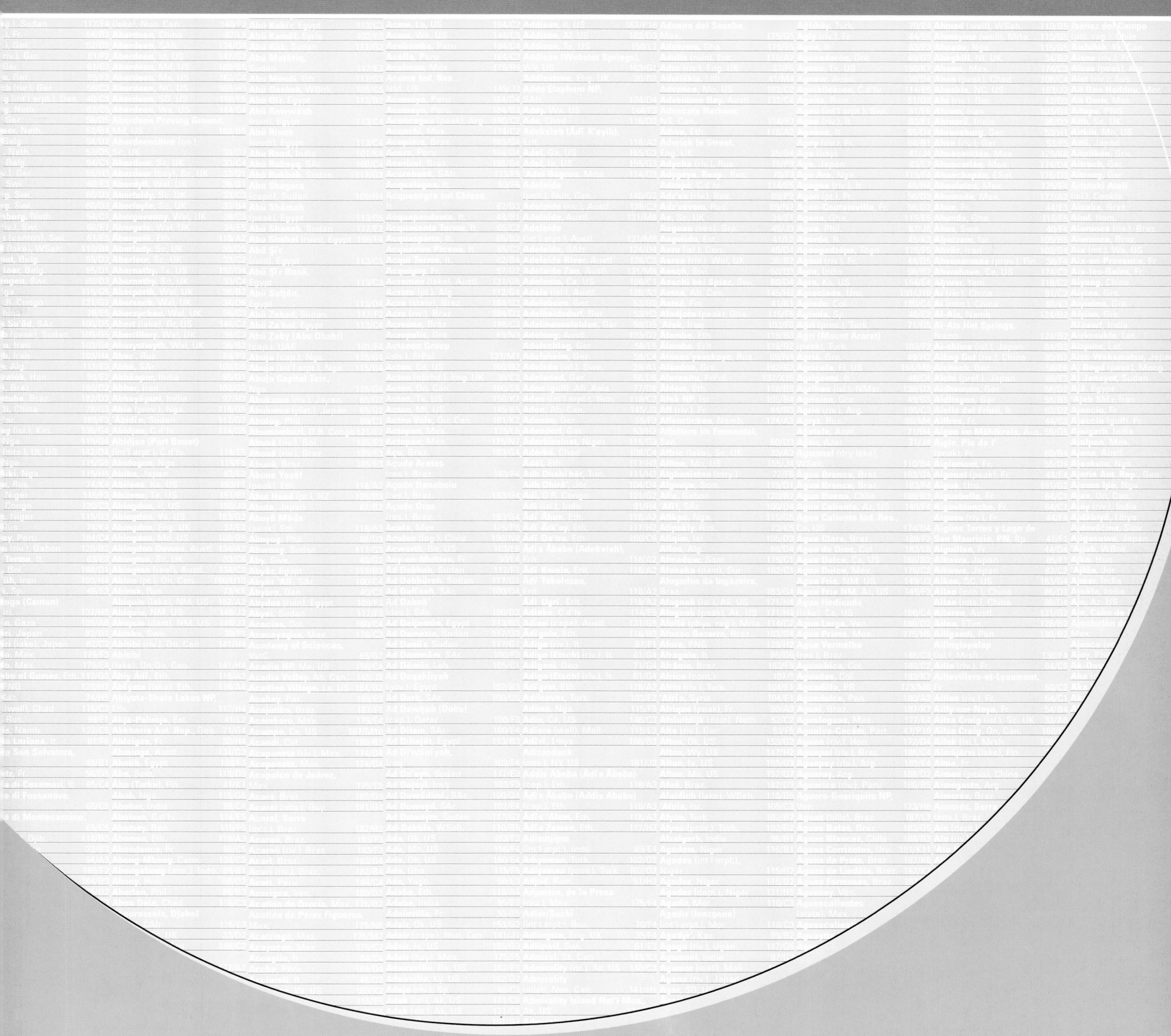

481,351	1,246,700	12,263,596
35	91	13,677
5,500,000	14,245,000	....
170	440	69,481
1,068,296	2,766,890	40,301,927
114,006	295,276	5,130,632
53,182	137,742	2,673,400
11,506	29,800	2,971,650
75	193	72,194
34	88	1,117
17,159,867	44,444,100	4,004,788,000

Population Rankings and Area, Top Languages

POPULATION AND LAND AREA OF THE WORLD, 1650–2008

Population Rank (2008)	Continent or Region	Population (estimated, in thousands)							Land Area		
		1650	1750	1850	1900	1950	2000	2008	(1,000 sq mi)	(1,000 sq km)	% of Earth Land Area
1.	Asia	335,000	476,000	754,000	932,000	1,411,000	3,689,169	4,004,788	12,000	31,000	29.5
2.	Africa	100,000	95,000	95,000	118,000	229,000	797,902	935,813	11,500	29,800	20.2
3.	Europe	100,000	140,000	265,000	400,000	392,000	730,029	727,228	8,800	22,800	7.0
4.	North America	5,000	5,000	39,000	106,000	221,000	485,347	523,686	8,300	21,400	16.2
5.	South America	8,000	7,000	20,000	38,000	111,000	348,337	380,017	6,800	17,500	11.9
6.	Australia, New Zealand, and the Pacific	2,000	2,000	2,000	6,000	12,000	30,745	33,515	3,200	8,400	5.8
7.	Antarctica	No indigenous inhabitants							5,400	14,000	9.4
	WORLD	550,000	725,000	1,175,000	1,600,000	2,556,000	6,081,528	6,605,047	57,506	148,940	100.0

Note: Areas are as defined by the U.S. Bureau of the Census and strictly apply only to 1950 and after; before then, areas may be defined differently. The Census Bureau area for Europe includes all of Russia (approximately 6,600,000 sq mi [17,100,000 sq km]); the area figure for Asia excludes Russia. Figures may not add to totals because of rounding.

LARGEST POPULATIONS

Rank	Country	Population	Persons per sq mi	Persons per sq km
1.	China[1]	1,321,851,888	367	142
2.	India	1,129,866,154	984	380
3.	United States	301,139,947	85	33
4.	Indonesia	245,452,739	348	134
5.	Brazil	190,010,647	58	22
6.	Pakistan	169,270,617	563	217
7.	Bangladesh	150,448,339	2,910	1,124
8.	Russia	141,377,752	22	8
9.	Nigeria	135,031,164	384	148
10.	Japan	127,467,972	881	340

[1]Excluding Hong Kong and Macau.

SMALLEST POPULATIONS

Rank	Country	Population	Persons per sq mi	Persons per sq km
1.	Vatican City	921	*	*
2.	Tuvalu	11,992	1,195	461
3.	Nauru	13,528	1,668	644
4.	Palau	20,842	118	45
5.	San Marino	29,615	1,253	484
6.	Monaco	32,671	43,394	16,754
7.	Liechtenstein	34,247	554	214
8.	Saint Kitts and Nevis	39,349	390	151
9.	Marshall Islands	61,782	883	341
10.	Dominica	68,925	237	91

*Area only 0.17 sq mi (0.44 sq km).

LARGEST LAND AREAS

Rank	Country	Land Area sq mi	Land Area (sq km)
1.	Russia	6,562,112	16,995,800
2.	China	3,600,946	9,326,410
3.	United States	3,537,437	9,161,923
4.	Canada	3,511,021	9,093,507
5.	Brazil	3,265,075	8,456,510
6.	Australia	2,941,298	7,617,930
7.	India	1,147,955	2,973,190
8.	Argentina	1,056,641	2,736,690
9.	Kazakhstan	1,030,815	2,669,800
10.	Algeria	919,595	2,381,740

SMALLEST LAND AREAS

Rank	Country	Land Area sq mi	Land Area (sq km)
1.	Vatican City	0.17	0.44
2.	Monaco	0.75	1.95
3.	Nauru	8	21
4.	Tuvalu	10	26
5.	San Marino	24	61
6.	Liechtenstein	62	160
7.	Marshall Islands	70	181
8.	Saint Kitts and Nevis	101	261
9.	Maldives	116	300
10.	Malta	122	316

TOP TEN LANGUAGES

Language	Major Countries Where Spoken	Native Speakers
Mandarin	China, Taiwan	874,000,000
Hindi	India	366,000,000
English	U.S., Canada, Britain	341,000,000
Spanish	Spain, Latin America	322,000,000
Arabic	Arabian Peninsula	207,000,000
Bengali	India, Bangladesh	207,000,000
Portuguese	Portugal, Brazil	176,000,000
Russian	Russia	167,000,000
Japanese	Japan	125,000,000
German	Germany, Austria	100,000,000

WORLD POPULATION THROUGH HISTORY

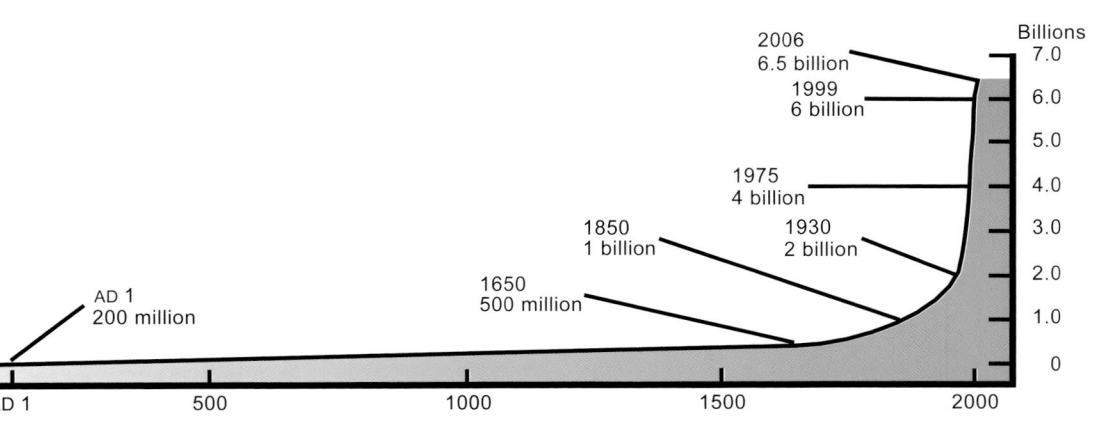

- AD 1 — 200 million
- 1650 — 500 million
- 1850 — 1 billion
- 1930 — 2 billion
- 1975 — 4 billion
- 1999 — 6 billion
- 2006 — 6.5 billion

35	91	13,677
5,500,000	14,245,000	....
170	440	69,481
1,068,296	2,766,890	40,301,927
114,006	295,276	5,130,632
53,182	137,742	2,673,400
11,506	29,800	2,971,650
75	193	72,194
34	88	1,117
17,159,867	44,444,100	4,004,788,000
2,967,893	7,686,850	20,434,176

231

Oceans, Ocean Depths, Islands and Lakes

AREAS AND AVERAGE DEPTHS OF OCEANS, SEAS, AND GULFS

Geographers and mapmakers recognize four major bodies of water: the Pacific, the Atlantic, the Indian, and the Arctic oceans. The Atlantic and Pacific oceans are considered divided at the equator into the North and South Atlantic and the North and South Pacific. The Arctic Ocean is the name for waters north of the continental landmasses in the region of the Arctic Circle.

	Area (sq mi)	Area (sq km)	Average Depth (ft)	Average Depth (m)
Pacific Ocean	64,186,300	166,241,800	12,925	3,940
Atlantic Ocean	33,420,000	86,557,400	11,730	3,575
Indian Ocean	28,350,500	73,427,500	12,598	3,840
Arctic Ocean	5,105,700	13,223,700	3,407	1,038
South China Sea	1,148,500	2,974,600	4,802	1,464
Caribbean Sea	971,400	2,515,900	8,448	2,575
Mediterranean Sea	969,100	2,510,000	4,926	1,501
Bering Sea	873,000	2,261,000	4,893	1,491
Gulf of Mexico	582,100	1,508,000	5,297	1,615
Sea of Okhotsk	537,500	1,392,000	3,192	973
Sea of Japan	391,100	1,013,000	5,468	1,667
Hudson Bay	281,900	730,100	305	93
East China Sea	256,600	664,600	620	189
Andaman Sea	218,100	564,900	3,667	1,118
Black Sea	196,100	507,900	3,906	1,191
Red Sea	174,900	453,000	1,764	538
North Sea	164,900	427,100	308	94
Baltic Sea	147,500	382,000	180	55
Yellow Sea	113,500	294,000	121	37
Persian Gulf	88,800	230,000	328	100
Gulf of California	59,100	153,000	2,375	724

PRINCIPAL OCEAN DEPTHS

Name of Area	Location (latitude)	Location (longitude)	Depth (m)	Depth (fathoms)	Depth (ft)
PACIFIC OCEAN					
Marianas Trench	11° 22′ N	142° 36′ E	10,924	5,973	35,840
Tonga Trench	23° 16′ S	174° 44′ W	10,800	5,906	35,433
Philippine Trench	10° 38′ N	126° 36′ E	10,057	5,499	32,995
Kermadec Trench	31° 53′ S	177° 21′ W	10,047	5,494	32,963
Bonin Trench	24° 30′ N	143° 24′ E	9,994	5,464	32,788
Kuril Trench	44° 15′ N	150° 34′ E	9,750	5,331	31,988
Izu Trench	31°05′ N	142°10′ E	9,695	5,301	31,808
New Britain Trench	06°19′ S	153°45′ E	8,940	4,888	29,331
Yap Trench	08°33′ N	138°02′ E	8,527	4,663	27,976
Japan Trench	36°08′ N	142°43′ E	8,412	4,600	27,599
Peru-Chile Trench	23°18′ S	71°14′ W	8,064	4,409	26,457
Palau Trench	07°52′ N	134°56′ E	8,054	4,404	26,424
Aleutian Trench	50°51′ N	177°11′ E	7,679	4,199	25,194
ATLANTIC OCEAN					
Puerto Rico Trench	19° 55′ N	65°27′ W	8,605	4,705	28,232
South Sandwich Trench	55°42′ S	25°56′ W	8,325	4,552	27,310
Romanche Gap	0°13′ S	18°26′ W	7,728	4,226	25,354

BIGGEST ISLANDS

Island	Area (sq mi)	Area (sq km)
Greenland (Denmark)	840,000	2,180,000
New Guinea (Indonesia, Papua New Guinea)	306,000	793,000
Borneo (Indonesia, Malaysia, Brunei)	280,100	725,500
Madagascar	226,658	587,040
Baffin (Canada)	195,928	507,450
Sumatra (Indonesia)	165,000	427,350
Honshu (Japan)	87,805	227,410
Great Britain (United Kingdom)	84,200	218,080
Victoria (Canada)	83,897	217,290
Ellesmere (Canada)	75,767	196,240
Celebes (Indonesia)	69,000	178,710
South (New Zealand)	58,384	151,210
Java (Indonesia)	48,900	126,650
North (New Zealand)	44,204	114,490
Cuba	42,804	110,860
Newfoundland (Canada)	42,031	108,860
Luzon (Philippines)	40,680	105,360

MAJOR NATURAL LAKES

Name	Continent	Area (sq mi)	Area (sq km)	Maximum Depth (ft)	Maximum Depth (m)
Caspian Sea[1]	Asia-Europe	143,244	371,000	3,363	1,025
Superior	North America	31,700	82,100	1,330	405
Victoria	Africa	26,828	69,484	270	82
Huron	North America	23,000	59,600	750	229
Michigan	North America	22,300	57,800	923	281
Aral Sea[1]	Asia	13,000[2]	33,700[2]	220	67
Tanganyika	Africa	12,700	32,900	4,823	1,470
Baykal	Asia	12,162	31,500	5,315	1,620
Great Bear	North America	12,096	31,330	1,463	446
Nyasa (Malawi)	Africa	11,150	28,880	2,280	695
Great Slave	North America	11,031	28,570	2,015	614
Erie	North America	9,910	25,670	210	64
Winnipeg	North America	9,417	24,390	60	18
Ontario	North America	7,340	19,010	802	244
Balkhash[1]	Asia	7,115	18,430	85	26
Ladoga	Europe	6,835	17,700	738	225

Note: A lake is generally defined as a body of water surrounded by land.

[1]Salt lake.

[2]Approximate figure, could be less. The diversion of feeder rivers since the 1960s has devastated the Aral—once the world's fourth-largest lake (26,000 sq mi [67,000 sq km]). By 2000, the Aral had effectively become three lakes, with the total area shown.

World Statistics

Rivers, Waterfalls, and Continental Altitudes

LONGEST RIVERS

River	Outflow	Length (mi)	Length (km)
Africa			
Congo	Atlantic Ocean	2,900	4,670
Niger	Gulf of Guinea	2,590	4,170
Nile	Mediterranean	4,160	6,690
Zambezi	Indian Ocean	1,700	2,740
Asia			
Amur	Tatar Strait	1,780	2,860
Brahmaputra	Bay of Bengal	1,800	2,900
Chang	East China Sea	3,964	6,380
Euphrates	Shatt al-Arab	1,700	2,740
Huang	Yellow Sea	3,395	5,460
Indus	Arabian Sea	1,800	2,900
Lena	Laptev Sea	2,734	4,400
Mekong	South China Sea	2,700	4,350
Ob	Gulf of Ob	2,268	3,650
Ob-Irtysh	Gulf of Ob	3,362	5,410
Yenisey	Kara Seav	2,543	4,090
Australia			
Murray-Darling	Indian Ocean	2,310	3,720
Europe			
Danube	Black Sea	1,776	2,860
Volga	Caspian Sea	2,290	3,690
North America			
Mississippi	Gulf of Mexico	2,340	3,770
Mississippi-Missouri-Red Rock	Gulf of Mexico	3,710	5,970
Missouri	Mississippi River	2,315	3,730
Missouri-Red Rock	Mississippi River	2,540	4,090
Rio Grande	Gulf of Mexico	1,900	3,060
Yukon	Bering Sea	1,979	3,180
South America			
Amazon	Atlantic Ocean	4,000	6,440
Japura	Amazon River	1,750	2,820
Madeira	Amazon River	2,013	3,240
Parana	Rio de la Plata	2,485	4,000
Purus	Amazon River	2,100	3,380
Sao Francisco	Atlantic Ocean	1,988	3,200

NOTABLE WATERFALLS

Name (Location)	Height (ft)	Height (m)
Africa		
Tugela# (South Africa)	2,014	614
Victoria, Zambezi River* (Zimbabwe-Zambia)	343	105
Australia, New Zealand		
Wallaman, Stony Creek# (Australia)	1,137	347
Wollomombi (Australia)	1,100	335
Sutherland, Arthur River# (New Zealand)	1,904	580
Europe		
Krimml# (Austria)	1,312	400
Gavarnie* (France)	1,385	422
Mardalsfossen (Northern) (Norway)	1,535	468
Mardalsfossen (Southern)# (Norway)	2,149	655
Skjeggedal, Nybuai River#** (Norway)	1,378	420
Trummelbach#(Switzerland)	1,312	400
North America		
Della# (Canada)	1,443	440
Niagara: Horseshoe (Canada)	173	53
Takakkaw, Daly Glacier# (Canada)	1,200	366
Niagara: American (U.S.)	182	55
Ribbon** (U.S.)	1,612	491
Silver Strand, Meadow Brook** (U.S.)	1,170	357
Yosemite#** (U.S.)	2,425	739
South America		
Iguazu (Argentina-Brazil)	230	70
Glass (Brazil)	1,325	404
Patos-Maribondo, Grande River (Brazil)	115	35
Paulo Afonso, Sao Francisco River (Brazil)	275	84
Urubupunga, Parana River (Brazil)	39	12
Great, Kamarang River (Guyana)	1,600	488
Kaieteur, Potaro River (Guyana)	741	226
Angel#* (Venezuela)	3,212	979
Cuquenan (Venezuela)	2,000	610

Note: If the river name is not shown, it is the same as that of the falls. "Height" is the total drop in one or more leaps. #Falls of more than one leap; *falls that diminish greatly seasonally; **falls that reduce to a trickle or are dry for part of each year.

The estimated mean annual flow, in cubic feet per second (cubic meters in parentheses), of major waterfalls is as follows: Niagara, 212,200 (6,000); Paulo Afonso, 100,000 (2,800); Urubupunga, 97,000 (2,700); Iguazu, 61,000 (1,700); Patos-Maribondo, 53,000 (1,500); Victoria, 35,400 (1,000); and Kaieteur, 23,400 (660).

HIGHEST CONTINENTAL ALTITUDES

Continent	Highest Point	Elevation (ft)	Elevation (m)
Asia	Mount Everest, Nepal-Tibet	29,035	8,850
South America	Mount Aconcagua, Argentina	22,834	6,960
North America	Mount McKinley, Alaska, U.S.	20,320	6,194
Africa	Kilimanjaro, Tanzania	19,340	5,895
Europe	Mount Elbrus, Russia	18,510	5,642
Antarctica	Vinson Massif	16,864	5,140
Australia	Mount Kosciusko, New South Wales	7,310	2,228

LOWEST CONTINENTAL ALTITUDES

Below Continent	Below Lowest Point	Feet Below Sea Level	Meters Below Sea Level
Asia	Dead Sea, Israel-Jordan	1,348	411
South America	Valdes Peninsula, Argentina	131	40
North America	Death Valley, California, U.S.	282	86
Africa	Lake Assal, Djibouti	512	156
Europe	Caspian Sea, Russia, Azerbaijan	92	28
Antarctica	Bentley Subglacial Trench	8,327[1]	2,538[1]
Australia	Lake Eyre, South Australia	52	16

[1]Estimated level of the continental floor. Lower points that have yet to be discovered may exist further beneath the ice.

Precipitation, Reservoirs, and Dams

HIGHEST AVERAGE ANNUAL PRECIPITATION

Continent or Region	Precipitation (in)	Precipitation (mm)	Place	Elevation (ft)	Elevation (m)	Years of Data
South America	523.6[1,2]	13,300[1,2]	Lloro, Colombia	520[3]	158[3]	29
Asia	467.4[1]	11,870[1]	Mawsynram, India	4,597	1,401	38
Oceania	460.0[1]	11,680[1]	Mt. Waialeale, Kauai, Hawaii	5,148	1,569	30
Africa	405.0	10,290	Debundscha, Cameroon	30	9	32
South America	354.0[2]	8,992[2]	Quibdo, Colombia	120	37	16
Australia	340.0	8,636	Bellenden Ker, Queensland	5,102	1,555	9
North America	256.0	6,502	Henderson Lake, British Columbia	12	4	14
Europe	183.0	4,648	Crkvica, Bosnia-Herzegovina	3,337	1,017	22

[1]The value given is continent's highest and possibly the world's depending on measurement practices, procedures, and period of record variations.

[2]The official greatest average annual precipitation for South America is 354 in (8,992 mm) at Quibdo, Colombia. The 523.6 in (13,300 mm) average at Lloro, Colombia (14 mi [23 km] SE and at a higher elevation than Quibdo) is an estimated amount.

[3]Approximate elevation.

LOWEST AVERAGE ANNUAL PRECIPITATION

Continent or Region	Precipitation (in)	Precipitation (mm)	Place	Elevation (ft)	Elevation (m)	Years of Data
South America	0.03	0.8	Arica, Chile	95	29	59
Africa	< 0.1	< 3	Wadi Halfa, Sudan	410	125	39
Antarctica	0.8[1]	20[1]	Amundsen-Scott South Pole Station	9,186	2,800	10
North America	1.2	30	Batagues, Mexico	16	5	14
Asia	1.8	46	Aden, Yemen	22	7	50
Australia	4.05	103	Mulka (Troudaninna), South Australia	160[2]	49[2]	42
Europe	6.4	163	Astrakhan, Russia	45	14	25
Oceania	8.93	227	Puako, Hawaii	5	2	13

[1]The value given is the average amount of solid snow accumulating in one year as indicated by snow markers. The liquid content of the snow is undetermined.

[2]Approximate elevation.

WORLD'S LARGEST RESERVOIRS

Rank	Name	Country	Capacity (1,000 acre-ft)	Capacity (1,000,000 cu m)
1.	Kariba	Zimbabwe/ Zambia	146,400	180,600
2.	Bratsk	Russia	137,000	169,000
3.	High Aswan	Egypt	131,300	162,000
4.	Akosombo	Ghana	119,950	147,960
5.	Daniel Johnson	Canada	115,000	141,851
6.	Xinfeng	China	112,660	138,960
7.	Guri	Venezuela	109,400	135,000
8.	W. A. C. Bennett	Canada	60,235	74,300
9.	Krasnoyarsk	Russia	59,425	73,300
10.	Zeya	Russia	55,450	68,400

WORLD'S HIGHEST DAMS

Rank	Name	Country	Height Above Lowest Formation (ft)	Height Above Lowest Formation (m)
1.	Nurek	Tajikistan	984	300
2.	Grand Dixence	Switzerland	935	285
3.	Inguri	Georgia	892	272
4.	Vajont	Italy	860	262
5.	Manuel M. Torres	Mexico	856	261
6.	Alvaro Obregon	Mexico	853	260
7.	Mauvoisin	Switzerland	820	250
8.	Mica	Canada	797	243
9.	Alberto Lleras C	Colombia	797	243
10.	Sayano-Shushensk	Russia	794	242

WORLD'S LARGEST-VOLUME EMBANKMENT DAMS

Rank	Name	Country	Volume (1,000 cu yd)	Volume (1,000 cu m)
1.	Tarbela	Pakistan	194,230	148,500
2.	Fort Peck	U.S.	125,630	96,050
3.	Tucurui	Brazil	111,400	85,200
4.	Ataturk	Turkey	111,200	85,000
5.	Yacireta	Argentina	105,900	81,000
6.	Rogun*	Tajikistan	98,750	75,500
7.	Oahe	U.S.	92,000	70,339
8.	Guri	Venezuela	91,560	70,000
9.	Parambikulam	India	90,460	69,165
10.	High Island West	China	87,600	67,000

*Under construction.

Temperatures, Highest Mountains and Deserts

AVERAGE GLOBAL TEMPERATURES, 1900–2000

Decade	Degrees Fahrenheit	Degrees Celsius
1900-09	56.52	13.62
1910-19	56.57	13.65
1920-29	56.74	13.74
1930-39	57.00	13.89
1940-49	57.13	13.96
1950-59	57.06	13.92
1960-69	57.05	13.92
1970-79	57.04	13.91
1980-89	57.36	14.09
1990-99	57.64	14.24
2000	57.60	14.22

HIGHEST MOUNTAINS

Peak	Place		(ft)	(m)	Height Rank Height
1.	Everest	Nepal-Tibet	29,035	8,850	
2.	K2 (Godwin Austen)	Kashmir	28,250	8,611	
3.	Kanchenjunga	India-Nepal	28,208	8,598	
4.	Lhotse I (Everest)	Nepal-Tibet	27,923	8,511	
5.	Makalu I	Nepal-Tibet	27,824	8,481	
6.	Lhotse II (Everest)	Nepal-Tibet	27,560	8,400	
7.	Dhaulagiri	Nepal	26,810	8,172	
8.	Manaslu I	Nepal	26,760	8,156	
9.	Cho Oyu	Nepal-Tibet	26,750	8,153	
10.	Nanga Parbat	Kashmir	26,660	8,126	

HIGHEST MEASURED TEMPERATURE

Continent or Region	Temperature (Fahrenheit)	Temperature (Celsius)	Place	Elevation (ft)	Elevation (m)	Date
Africa	136°	58°	El Azizia, Libya	367	112	Sept. 13, 1922
North America	134°	57°	Death Valley, California (Greenland Ranch)	−178	−54	July 10, 1913
Asia	129°	54°	Tirat Tsvi, Israel	−722	−220	June 21, 1942
Australia	128°	53°	Cloncurry, Queensland	622	190	Jan. 16, 1889
Europe	122°	50°	Seville, Spain	26	8	Aug. 4, 1881
South America	120°	49°	Rivadavia, Argentina	676	206	Dec. 11, 1905
Antarctica	59°	15°	Vanda Station, Scott Coast	49	15	Jan. 5, 1974

LOWEST MEASURED TEMPERATURE

Continent or Region	Temperature (Fahrenheit)	Temperature (Celsius)	Place	Elevation (ft)	Elevation (m)	Date
Antarctica	−129.0°	−89°	Vostok	11,220	3,420	July 21, 1983
Asia	−90.0°	−68°	Oimekon, Russia	2,625	800	Feb. 6, 1933
Asia	−90.0°	−68°	Verkhoyansk, Russia	350	107	Feb. 7, 1892
Greenland	−87.0°	−66°	Northice	7,687	2,343	Jan. 9, 1954
North America	−81.4°	−63°	Snag, Yukon, Canada	2,120	646	Feb. 3, 1947
Europe	−67.0°	−55°	Ust-Shchugor, Russia	279	85	Jan.*
South America	−27.0°	−33°	Sarmiento, Argentina	879	268	June 1, 1907
Africa	−11.0°	−24°	Ifrane, Morocco	5,364	1,635	Feb. 11, 1935
Australia	−9.4°	−23°	Charlotte Pass, New South Wales	5,758	1,755	June 29, 1994
Oceania	14.0°	−10°	Haleakala Summit, Maui, Hawaii	9,750	2,972	Jan. 2, 1961

* Exact day and year unknown.

NOTABLE DESERTS OF THE WORLD

Arabian (Eastern), 70,000 sq mi (181,000 sq km) in Egypt between the Nile River and Red Sea, extending southward into Sudan

Chihuahuan, 140,000 sq mi (363,000 sq km) in Texas, New Mexico, Arizona, and Mexico

Gibson, 120,000 sq mi (311,000 sq km) in the interior of Western Australia

Gobi, 500,000 sq mi (1,295,000 sq km) in Mongolia and China

Great Sandy, 150,000 sq mi (388,000 sq km) in Western Australia

Great Victoria, 150,000 sq mi (388,000 sq km) in South and Western Australia

Kalahari, 225,000 sq mi (583,000 sq km) in southern Africa

Kara Kum, 120,000 sq mi (311,000 sq km) in Turkmenistan

Kyzyl Kum, 100,000 sq mi (259,000 sq km) in Kazakhstan and Uzbekistan

Libyan, 450,000 sq mi (1,165,000 sq km) in the Sahara, extending from Libya through southwestern Egypt into Sudan

Nubian, 100,000 sq mi (259,000 sq km) in the Sahara in northeastern Sudan

Patagonia, 300,000 sq mi (777,000 sq km) in southern Argentina

Rub al-Khali (Empty Quarter), 250,000 sq mi (648,000 sq km) in the southern Arabian Peninsula

Sahara, 3,500,000 sq mi (9,065,000 sq km) in northern Africa, extending westward to the Atlantic; largest desert in the world

Sonoran, 70,000 sq mi (181,000 sq km) in southwestern Arizona and southeastern California extending into northwestern Mexico

Syrian, 100,000 sq mi (259,000 sq km) arid wasteland extending over much of northern Saudi Arabia, eastern Jordan, southern Syria, and western Iraq

Taklimakan, 140,000 sq mi (363,000 sq km) in Xinjiang Province, China

Thar (Great Indian), 100,000 sq mi (259,000 sq km) arid area extending 400 mi (640 km) along the India-Pakistan border

Energy and Environment

PRINCIPAL KNOWN CRUDE OIL AND NATURAL GAS RESERVES, JAN. 1, 2004

	Crude Oil (billion barrels)		Natural Gas (trillion cubic feet)			Crude Oil (billion barrels)		Natural Gas (trillion cubic feet)	
	OGJ	WO	OGJ	WO		OGJ	WO	OGJ	WO
NORTH AMERICA					Iraq	115.0	115.0	110.0	112.6
Canada	178.9	5.0	59.1	59.1	Kuwait	99.0	99.4	55.5	56.6
Mexico	15.7	14.6	15.0	20.7	Oman	5.5	5.7	29.3	31.0
United States	21.9	21.9	189.0	189.0	Qatar	15.2	27.4	910.0	913.4
SOUTH AMERICA					Saudi Arabia	261.9	261.8	231.1	238.5
Argentina	2.8	2.7	23.4	21.6	United Arab Emirates	97.8	66.2	212.1	204.1
Trinidad and Tobago	1.0	0.8	25.9	19.1	**AFRICA**				
Venezuela	77.8	52.5	148.0	149.2	Algeria	11.3	14.0	160.0	171.5
WESTERN EUROPE					Egypt	3.7	3.6	58.5	7.1
Netherlands	0.1	0.1	62.0	55.1	Libya	36.0	30.5	46.4	46.0
Norway	10.4	9.4	74.8	74.7	Nigeria	25.0	33.0	159.0	180.0
United Kingdom	4.7	4.3	22.2	21.8	**ASIA AND OCEANIA**				
EASTERN EUROPE AND FORMER USSR					Australia	3.5	4.0	90.0	142.9
Kazakhstan	9.0	NA	65.0	NA	China	18.3	15.5	53.3	47.9
Russia	60.0	65.4	1,680.0	2,340.5	India	5.4	4.0	30.1	14.6
Turkmenistan	0.5	NA	71.0	NA	Indonesia	4.7	5.5	90.3	67.7
Ukraine	0.4	NA	39.6	NA	Malaysia	3.0	3.1	75.0	57.6
Uzbekistan	0.6	NA	66.2	NA	Pakistan	0.3	0.3	26.8	28.2
MIDDLE EAST					**WORLD**				
Iran	125.8	105.0	940.0	935.0	TOTAL	1,265.0	1,050.7	6,078.6	6,508.8

OGJ = Oil and Gas Journal, Dec. 2003

WO = World Oil, Sept. 2004

NOTE: Data for Kuwait and Saudi Arabia include one-half of the reserves in the Neutral Zone between Kuwait and Saudi Arabia. All reserve figures except those for the former USSR and natural gas reserves in Canada are proved reserves recoverable with present technology and prices at the time of estimation. Former USSR and Canadian natural gas figures include proved and some probable reserves.

WORLD CARBON DIOXIDE EMISSIONS FROM THE USE OF FOSSIL FUELS, 2003

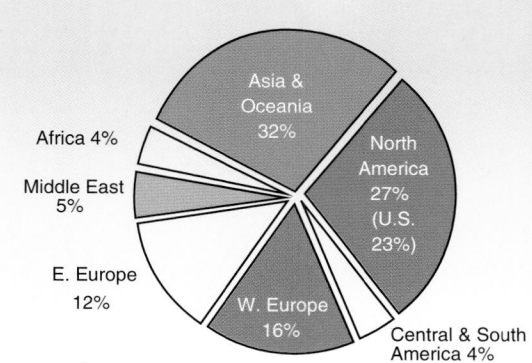

WORLD'S MAJOR PRODUCERS OF PRIMARY ENERGY, 2003
(quadrillion Btu)

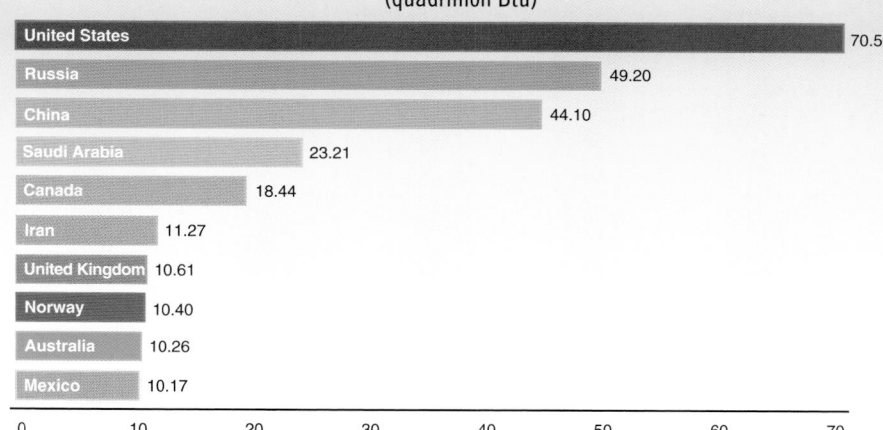

NATIONS MOST RELIANT ON NUCLEAR ENERGY, 2004
(nuclear energy generation as % of total electricity generated)

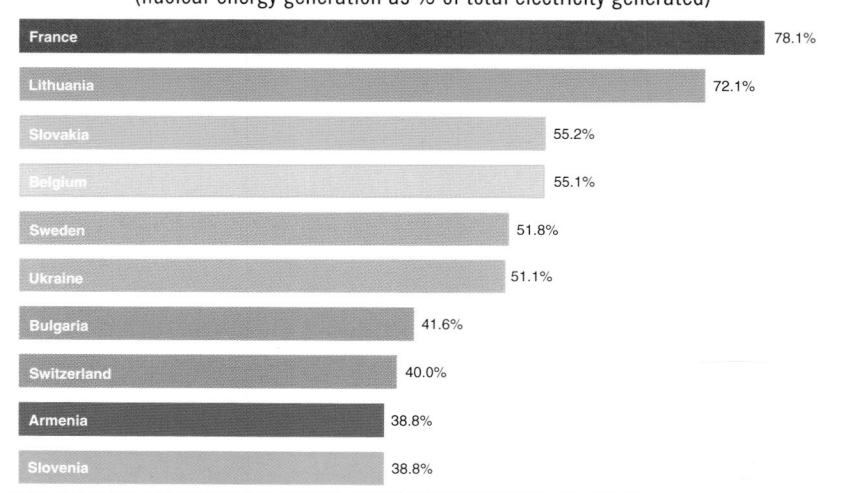

WORLD'S MAJOR CONSUMERS OF PRIMARY ENERGY, 2003
(quadrillion Btu)

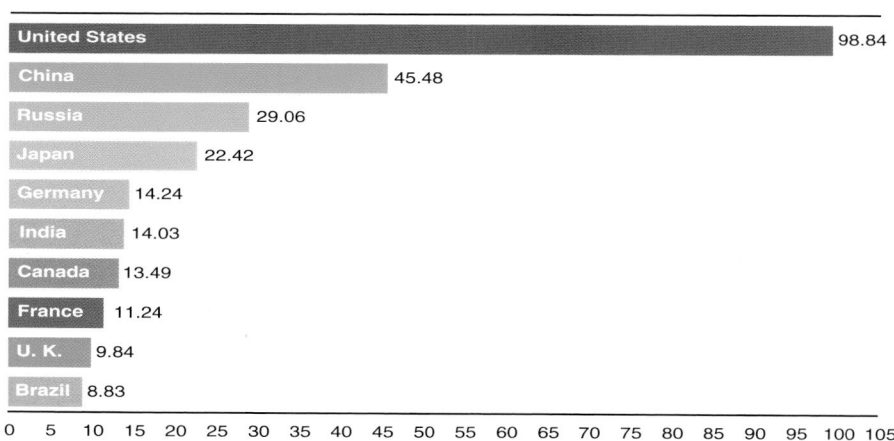

Countries of the World

AFGHANISTAN
Map page 113

Population: 31,889,923

Principal languages: Dari (Afghan Persian), Pashtu (both official); Turkic (including Uzbek, Turkmen), Balochi, Pashai, many others

Chief religions: Muslim (official; Sunni 85%, Shi'a 15%)

Area: 250,001 sq mi (647,500 sq km)

Capital: Kabul (pop., 2,956,000)

Independence date: August 19, 1919

Government type: transitional administration

Head of state and government: Pres. Hamid Karzai

Local divisions: 32 provinces

Monetary unit: afghani

GDP: $20 billion (2003 est.)

Per capita GDP: $700

Website: www.embassyofafghanistan.org

Did you know? Hamid Karzai won Afghanistan's first presidential election on October 9, 2004.

ALBANIA
Map page 55

Population: 3,600,523

Principal languages: Albanian (Tosk is the official dialect), Greek

Chief religions: Muslim 70%, Albanian Orthodox 20%, Roman Catholic 10%

Area: 11,100 sq mi (28,748 sq km)

Capital: Tiranë (pop., 367,000)

Independence date: November 28, 1912

Government type: republic

Head of state: Pres. Alfred Moisiu

Head of government: Prime Min. Sali Berisha

Local divisions: 36 districts, 1 municipality

Monetary unit: lek

GDP: $17.5 billion (2004 est.)

Per capita GDP: $4,900

Website: www.keshilliministrave.al/english

Did you know? Ancient people called the Illyrians lived in Albania around AD 1000.

ALGERIA
Map page 129

Population: 33,333,216

Principal languages: Arabic (official), French, Berber dialects

Chief religion: Sunni Muslim (official) 99%

Area: 919,595 sq mi (2,381,740 sq km)

Capital: Algiers (pop., 3,060,000)

Independence date: July 5, 1962

Government type: republic

Head of state: Pres. Abdelaziz Bouteflika

Head of government: Prime Min. Abdelaziz Belkhadem

Local divisions: 48 provinces

Monetary unit: dinar

GDP: $212.3 billion (2004 est.)

Per capita GDP: $6,600

Website: www.algeria-us.org

Did you know? Algeria was a colony of France from 1834 to 1963.

ANDORRA
Map page 53

Population: 71,822

Principal languages: Catalan (official), Castilian Spanish, French

Chief religion: mostly Roman Catholic

Area: 181 sq mi (468 sq km)

Capital: Andorra la Vella (pop., 21,000)

Independence date: 1278

Government type: parliamentary co-principality

Heads of state: president of France & bishop of Urgel (Spain), as co-princes

Head of government: Pres. Albert Pintat Santolària

Local divisions: 7 parishes

Monetary unit: euro

GDP: $1.9 billion (2003 est.)

Per capita GDP: $26,800

Website: www.andorra.ad/ang/home/index.htm

Did you know? The main sources of income for this tiny mountain nation are tourism and ski resorts.

ANGOLA
Map page 119

Population: 12,263,596

Principal languages: Portuguese (official), Bantu and other African languages

Chief religions: indigenous beliefs 47%, Roman Catholic 38%, Protestant 15%

Area: 481,353 sq mi (1,246,700 sq km)

Capital: Luanda (pop., 2,623,000)

Independence date: November 11, 1975

Government type: republic

Head of state: Pres. José Eduardo dos Santos

Head of government: Prime Min. Fernando da Piedade Dias dos Santos

Local divisions: 18 provinces

Monetary unit: new kwanza (AON)

GDP: $23.2 billion (2004 est.)

Per capita GDP: $2,100

Website: www.embangola-can.org

Did you know? Decades of civil war, now ended, left Angola with millions of land mines.

ANTIGUA AND BARBUDA
Map page 203

Population: 69,481

Principal languages: English (official), local dialects

Chief religions: predominantly Protestant, some Roman Catholic

Area: 171 sq mi (443 sq km)

Capital: Saint John's (pop., 28,000)

Independence date: November 1, 1981

Government type: constitutional monarchy with British-style parliament

Head of state: Queen Elizabeth II, represented by Gov.-Gen. James Carlisle

Head of government: Prime Min. Baldwin Spencer

Local divisions: 6 parishes, 2 dependencies

Monetary unit: East Caribbean dollar

GDP: $750 million (2002 est.)

Per capita GDP: $11,000

Website: www.antigua-barbuda.com

Did you know? Most of the people of these islands trace their roots to West Africa.

ARGENTINA
Map page 209

Population: 40,301,927

Principal languages: Spanish (official), English, Italian, German, French

Chief religion: Roman Catholic (official) 92%

Area: 1,068,302 sq mi (2,766,890 sq km)

Capital: Buenos Aires (pop., 13,047,000)

Independence date: July 9, 1816

Government type: republic

Head of state and government: Pres. Néstor Kirchner

Local divisions: 23 provinces, 1 federal district

Monetary unit: peso

GDP: $483.5 billion (2004 est.)

Per capita GDP: $12,400

Website: www.turismo.gov.ar/eng/menu.htm

Did you know? Argentina's central grasslands, "the Pampas," are one of the world's largest cattle-producing areas.

ARMENIA
Map page 77

Population: 2,971,650

Principal languages: Armenian (official), Russian

Chief religions: Armenian Apostolic 94%, other Christian 4%, Yezidi 2%

Area: 11,506 sq mi (29,800 sq km)

Capital: Yerevan (pop., 1,079,000)

Independence date: September 21, 1991

Government type: republic

Head of state: Pres. Robert Kocharian

Head of government: Prime Min. Andranik Markarian

Local divisions: 10 provinces, 1 city

Monetary unit: dram

GDP: $13.7 billion (2003 est.)

Per capita GDP: $4,600

Website: www.gov.am/enversion/index.html

Did you know? Dating to 783 BC, Yerevan is one of the oldest continuously occupied towns.

AUSTRALIA
Map page 145

Population: 20,434,176

Principal languages: English (official), aboriginal languages

Chief religions: Anglican 26%, Roman Catholic 26%, other Christian 24%

Area: 2,967,908 sq mi (7,686,850 sq km)

Capital: Canberra (pop., 373,000)

Independence date: January 1, 1901

Government type: democratic, federal state system

Head of state: Queen Elizabeth II, represented by Gov.-Gen. Michael Jeffery

Head of government: Prime Min. John Howard

Local divisions: 6 states, 2 territories

Monetary unit: Australian dollar

GDP: $611.7 billion (2004 est.)

Per capita GDP: $30,700

Website: www.australia.gov.au

Did you know? There are an estimated 50 million kangaroos in Australia.

AUSTRIA*
Map page 51

Population: 8,199,783

Principal languages: German (official), Serbo-Croatian, Slovenian

Chief religions: Roman Catholic 78%, Protestant 5%

Area: 32,382 sq mi (83,870 sq km)

Capital: Vienna (pop., 2,179,000)

Independence date: 1156

Government type: federal republic

Head of state: Pres. Heinz Fischer

Head of government: Chancellor Wolfgang Schüssel

Local divisions: 9 Bundesländer (federal states), each with a legislature

Monetary unit: euro

GDP: $255.9 billion (2004 est.)

Per capita GDP: $31,300

Website: www.austria.org

Did you know? Mozart, Strauss, Beethoven, Haydn, and Schubert all came to Vienna, still a center for classical music today.

AZERBAIJAN
Map page 77

Population: 8,120,247

Principal languages: Azeri (official), Russian, Armenian

Chief religions: Muslim 93%, Russian Orthodox 3%, Armenian Orthodox 2%

Area: 33,436 sq mi (86,600 sq km)

Capital: Baku (pop., 1,816,000)

Independence date: August 30, 1991

Government type: republic

Head of state: Pres. Ilham Aliyev

Head of government: Prime Min. Artur Rasizade

Local division: 59 rayons, 11 cities, 1 autonomous republic

Monetary unit: manat

GDP: $30.0 billion (2004 est.)

Per capita GDP: $3,800

Website: www.azembassy.us/

Did you know? Azerbaijan borders the Caspian Sea, the world's largest inland body of water.

THE BAHAMAS
Map page 203

Population: 305,655

Principal languages: English, Creole (among Haitian immigrants)

Chief religions: Baptist 32%, Anglican 20%, Roman Catholic 19%, other Christian 24%

Area: 5,382 sq mi (13,940 sq km)

Capital: Nassau (pop., 222,000)

Independence date: July 10, 1973

Government type: independent commonwealth

Head of state: Queen Elizabeth II, represented by Gov.-Gen. Arthur D. Hanna

Head of government: Prime Min. Perry Christie

Local divisions: 21 districts

*Member of the European Union

Monetary unit: Bahamas dollar

GDP: $5.3 billion (2004 est.)

Per capita GDP: $17,700

Website: www.bahamas.gov.bs

Did you know? Columbus first landed in the New World on San Salvador, an island in the Bahamas, in 1492.

BAHRAIN
Map page 112

Population: 708,573

Principal languages: Arabic (official), English, Farsi, Urdu

Chief religions: Muslim (official; Shi'a 70%, Sunni 30%)

Area: 257 sq mi (665 sq km)

Capital: Manama (pop., 139,000)

Independence date: August 15, 1971

Government type: constitutional monarchy

Head of state: King Hamad bin Isa al-Khalifa

Head of government: Prime Min. Khalifa bin Sulman al-Khalifa

Local divisions: 12 municipalities

Monetary unit: dinar

GDP: $13.0 billion (2004 est.)

Per capita GDP: $19,200

Website: www.bahrainembassy.org

Did you know? Only 1% of this island nation's land can be used for farming.

BANGLADESH
Map page 109

Population: 150,448,339

Principal languages: Bangla (official, also known as Bengali), English

Chief religions: Muslim (official) 83%, Hindu 16%

Area: 55,599 sq mi (144,000 sq km)

Capital: Dhaka (pop., 11,560,000)

Independence date: December 16, 1971

Government type: parliamentary democracy

Head of state: Pres. Iajuddin Ahmed

Head of government: Prime Min. Khaleda Zia

Local divisions: 6 divisions

Monetary unit: taka

GDP: $275.7 billion (2004 est.)

Per capita GDP: $2,000

Website: www.bangladesh.gov.bd

Did you know? A cyclone in Bangladesh in 1970 killed an estimated 300,000 people.

BARBADOS
Map page 203

Population: 280,946

Principal language: English

Chief religions: Protestant 67%, Roman Catholic 4%

Area: 166 sq mi (431 sq km)

Capital: Bridgetown (pop., 140,000)

Independence date: November 30, 1966

Government type: parliamentary democracy

Head of state: Queen Elizabeth II, represented by Gov.-Gen. Sir Clifford Husbands

Head of government: Prime Min. Owen Arthur

Local divisions: 11 parishes and Bridgetown

Monetary unit: Barbados dollar

GDP: $4.6 billion (2004 est.)

Per capita GDP: $16,400

Website: www.barbados.gov.bb

Did you know? Barbados is named for its bearded fig trees (from the Spanish barbados, meaning "bearded ones").

BELARUS
Map page 29

Population: 9,724,723

Principal languages: Belarusian, Russian

Chief religions: Eastern Orthodox 80%, other 20%

Area: 80,155 sq mi (207,600 sq km)

Capital: Minsk (pop., 1,705,000)

Independence date: August 25, 1991

Government type: republic

Head of state: Pres. Alexander Lukashenko

Head of government: Prime Min. Sergei Sidorsky

Local divisions: 6 oblasts and 1 municipality

Monetary unit: ruble

GDP: $70.5 billion (2004 est.)

Per capita GDP: $6,800

Website: www.belarusembassy.org

Did you know? Belarussian Bibles were some of the first books printed in Eastern Europe.

BELGIUM*
Map page 48

Population: 10,392,226

Principal languages: Dutch, French, German (all official); Flemish, Luxembourgish

Chief religions: Roman Catholic 75%; Protestant, other 25%

Area: 11,786 sq mi (30,528 sq km)

Capital: Brussels (pop., 998,000)

Independence date: October 4, 1830

Government type: parliamentary democracy under a constitutional monarch

Head of state: King Albert II

Head of government: Premier Guy Verhofstadt

Local divisions: 10 provinces and Brussels

Monetary unit: euro

GDP: $316.2 billion (2004 est.)

Per capita GDP: $30,600

Website: www.diplobel.us

Did you know? Belgium's second largest city, Antwerp, has been world-famous for diamond-cutting since the 16th century.

BELIZE
Map page 206

Population: 294,385

Principal languages: English (official), Spanish, Mayan, Garifuna (Carib), Creole

Chief religions: Roman Catholic 50%, Protestant 27%

Area: 8,867 sq mi (22,966 sq km)

Capital: Belmopan (pop., 9,000)

Independence date: September 21, 1981

Government type: parliamentary democracy

Head of state: Queen Elizabeth II, represented by Gov.-Gen. Sir Colville Young

Head of government: Prime Min. Said Musa

Local divisions: 6 districts

Monetary unit: Belize dollar

GDP: $1.8 billion (2004 est.)

Per capita GDP: $6,500

Website: www.embassyofbelize.org

Did you know? Belize is the only country in Central America without a Pacific coast.

BENIN
Map page 133

Population: 8,078,314

Principal languages: French (official), Fon, Yoruba, various tribal languages

Chief religions: indigenous beliefs 50%, Christian 30%, Muslim 20%

Area: 43,483 sq mi (112,620 sq km)

Capital: Porto-Novo (pop., 238,000)

Independence date: August 1, 1960

Government type: republic

Head of state and government: Pres. Boni Yayi

Local divisions: 6 departments

Monetary unit: CFA franc

GDP: $8.3 billion (2004 est.)

Per capita GDP: $1,200

Website: www.beninembassy.us/

Did you know? Sandbanks make access to the coast of Benin difficult.

BHUTAN
Map page 109

Population: 2,327,849

Principal languages: Dzongkha (official), Tibetan, Nepalese dialects

Chief religions: Lamaistic Buddhist (official) 75%, Hindu 25%

Area: 18,147 sq mi (47,000 sq km)

Capital: Thimphu (pop., 35,000)

Independence date: August 8, 1949

Government type: monarchy

Head of state and government: King Jigme Singye Wangchuk

Head of government: Prime Min. Lyonpo Sangay Ngedup

Local divisions: 18 districts

Monetary unit: ngultrum

GDP: $2.9 billion (2003 est.)

Per capita GDP: $1,400

Website: www.tourism.gov.bt

Did you know? The native name for Bhutan is Druk Yulm, which translates as "Kingdom of the Thunder Dragon."

BOLIVIA
Map page 209

Population: 9,119,152

Principal languages: Spanish, Quechua, Aymara (all official)

Chief religion: Roman Catholic (official) 95%

Area: 424,164 sq mi (1,098,580 sq km)

Capitals: La Paz (adminstrative) (pop., 1,477,000), Sucre (judicial) (pop., 212,000)

Independence date: August 6, 1825

Government type: republic

Head of state and government: Pres. Juan Evo Morales Aima

Local divisions: 9 departments

Monetary unit: boliviano

GDP: $22.3 billion (2004 est.)

Per capita GDP: $2,600

Website: www.embassyofbolivia.co.uk

Did you know? Bolivia and Paraguay are the only South American countries with no coastline.

BOSNIA AND HERZEGOVINA
Map page 56

Population: 4,552,198

Principal languages: Bosnian (official), Croatian, Serbian

Chief religions: Muslim 40%, Orthodox 31%, Roman Catholic 15%, Protestant 4%

Area: 19,741 sq mi (51,129 sq km)

Capital: Sarajevo (pop., 579,000)

Independence date: March 1, 1992

Government type: federal republic

Heads of state: collective presidency with rotating leadership

Head of government: Prime Min. Adnan Terzic

Local divisions: Muslim-Croat Federation, divided into 10 cantons; Republika Srpska

Monetary unit: converted marka (BAM)

GDP: $26.2 billion (2004 est.)

Per capita GDP: $6,500

Website: www.bhembassy.org

Did you know? Archduke Ferdinand's 1914 murder in Sarajevo triggered World War I.

BOTSWANA
Map page 119

Population: 1,639,131

Principal languages: English (official), Setswana

Chief religions: indigenous beliefs 85%, Christian 15%

Area: 231,804 sq mi (600,370 sq km)

Capital: Gaborone (pop., 199,000)

Independence date: September 30, 1966

Government type: parliamentary republic

Head of state and government: Pres. Festus Mogae

Local divisions: 10 districts, 4 town councils

Monetary unit: pula

GDP: $15.1 billion (2004 est.)

Per capita GDP: $9,200

Website: www.gov.bw

Did you know? The Kalahari Desert, a land of bush and grasslands, covers 84% of this country.

BRAZIL
Map page 209

Population: 190,010,647

Principal languages: Portuguese (official), Spanish, English, French

Chief religion: Roman Catholic (nominal) 80%

Area: 3,286,487 sq mi (8,511,965 sq km)

Capital: Brasília (pop., 3,099,000)

Independence date: September 7, 1822

Government type: federal republic

Head of state and government: Pres. Luis Inacio Lula da Silva

Local divisions: 26 states, 1 federal district (Brasília)

Monetary unit: real

GDP: $1,492 billion (2004 est.)

Per capita GDP: $8,100

Website: www.brasilemb.org

Did you know? Brazil, the world's 5th-largest country, produces about 40% of the world's coffee.

BRUNEI
Map page 100

Population: 386,511

Principal languages: Malay (official), English, Chinese

Chief religions: Muslim (official) 67%; Buddhist 13%; Christian 10%; indigenous beliefs, other 10%

Area: 2,228 sq mi (5,770 sq km)

Capital: Bandar Seri Begawan (pop., 61,000)

Independence date: January 1, 1984

Government type: independent sultanate

Head of state and government: Sultan Sir Muda Hassanal Bolkiah Mu'izzadin Waddaulah

Local divisions: 4 districts

Monetary unit: Brunei dollar (BND)

GDP: $6.8 billion (2003 est.)

Per capita GDP: $23,600

Website: www.gov.bn/index.htm

Did you know? This leading oil producer is in the Pacific, not in the Middle East.

BULGARIA
Map page 57

Population: 7,322,858

Principal languages: Bulgarian (official), Turkish

Chief religions: Bulgarian Orthodox 84%, Muslim 12%

Area: 42,823 sq mi (110,910 sq km)

Capital: Sofia (pop., 1,076,000)

Independence date: March 3, 1878

Government type: republic

Head of state: Pres. Georgi Parvanov

Head of government: Prime Min. Sergei Stanishev

Local divisions: 9 provinces

Monetary unit: lev

GDP: $61.6 billion (2004 est.)

Per capita GDP: $8,200

Website: www.government.bg/ fce/index. shtml?s=001&p=0023

Did you know? In 1989, more than 300,000 Turks fled Bulgaria to escape persecution.

BURKINA FASO
Map page 171

Population: 14,326,203

Principal languages: French (official), Sudanic languages

Chief religions: Muslim 50%, indigenous beliefs 40%, Christian (mainly Roman Catholic) 10%

Area: 105,869 sq mi (274,200 sq km)

Capital: Ouagadougou (pop., 821,000)

Independence date: August 5, 1960

Government type: republic

Head of state: Pres. Blaise Compaoré

Head of government: Prime Min. Paramanga Ernest Yonli

Local divisions: 45 provinces

Monetary unit: CFA franc

GDP: $15.7 billion (2004 est.)

Per capita GDP: $1,200

Website: www.burkinaembassy-usa.org

Did you know? As Upper Volta, this nation declared independence from France in 1960.

BURUNDI
Map page 139

Population: 8,390,505

Principal languages: Kirundi, French (both official); Swahili

Chief religions: Roman Catholic 62%, indigenous beliefs 23%, Muslim 10%, Protestant 5%

Area: 10,745 sq mi (27,830 sq km)

Capital: Bujumbura (pop., 378,000)

Independence date: July 1, 1962

Government type: in transition

Head of state and government: Pres. Pierre Nkurunziza

Local divisions: 15 provinces

Monetary unit: franc

GDP: $4.0 billion (2004 est.)

Per capita GDP: $600

Website: www.burundiembassy-usa.org

Did you know? Tutsi-Hutu ethnic violence killed 200,000 Burundians in the 1990s.

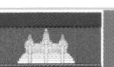

CAMBODIA
Map page 106

Population: 14,131,858

Principal languages: Khmer (official), French, English

Chief religion: Theravada Buddhist (official) 95%

Area: 69,900 sq mi (181,040 sq km)

Capital: Phnom Penh (pop., 1,157,000)

Independence date: November 9, 1953

Government type: constitutional monarchy

Head of state: King Norodom Sihamoni

Head of government: Prime Min. Hun Sen

Local divisions: 20 provinces and 3 municipalities

Monetary unit: riel

GDP: $27.0 billion (2004 est.)

Per capita GDP: $2,000

Website: www.cambodia.gov.kh

Did you know? Lake Tonle Sap expands from 1,200 to 3,000 sq. mi. in the wet season.

CAMEROON
Map page 119

Population: 18,060,382

Principal languages: English, French (both official); 24 African language groups

Chief religions: indigenous beliefs 40%, Christian 40%, Muslim 20%

Area: 183,568 sq mi (475,440 sq km)

Capital: Yaoundé (pop., 1,616,000)

Independence date: January 1, 1960

Government type: republic

Head of state: Pres. Paul Biya

Head of government: Prime Min. Ephraïm Inoni

Local divisions: 10 provinces

Monetary unit: CFA franc

GDP: $30.2 billion (2004 est.)

Per capita GDP: $1,900

Website: www.spm.gov.cm

Did you know? Cameroon was a German colony from the 1880s to 1919.

CANADA
Map page 170

Population: 33,390,141

Principal languages: English, French (both official)

Chief religions: Roman Catholic 46%, Protestant 36%, other 18%

Area: 3,855,101 sq mi (9,984,670 sq km)

Capital: Ottawa (pop., 1,093,000)

Independence date: July 1, 1867

Government type: confederation with parliamentary democracy

Head of state: Queen Elizabeth II, represented by Gov.-Gen. Michaëlle Jean

Head of government: Prime Min. Stephen Harper

Local divisions: 10 provinces, 3 territories

Monetary unit: Canadian dollar (CAD)

GDP: $1,023 billion (2004 est.)

Per capita GDP: $31,500

Website: www.canada.gc.ca/main_e.html

Did you know? In the War of 1812, U.S. forces tried unsuccessfully to invade Canada.

CAPE VERDE
Map page 119

Population: 423,613

Principal languages: Portuguese (official), Crioulo

Chief religions: Roman Catholic (infused with indigenous beliefs), Protestant (mostly Church of the Nazarene)

Area: 1,557 sq mi (4,033 sq km)

Capital: Praia (pop., 107,000)

Independence date: July 5, 1975

Government type: republic

Head of state: Pres. Pedro Pires

Head of government: Prime Min. José Maria Neves

Local divisions: 16 districts

Monetary unit: escudo

GDP: $600 million (2002 est.)

Per capita GDP: $1,400

Website: praia.usembassy.gov

Did you know? When the Portuguese arrived about 1460 these islands were uninhabited.

CENTRAL AFRICAN REPUBLIC
Map page 134

Population: 4,369,038

Principal languages: French (official), Sangho (national), tribal languages

Chief religions: indigenous beliefs 35%, Protestant 25%, Roman Catholic 25%, Muslim 15%

Area: 240,535 sq mi (622,984 sq km)

Capital: Bangui (pop., 689,000)

Independence date: August 13, 1960

Government type: in transition

Head of state: Pres. François Bozizé

Head of government: Prime Min. Élie Doté

Local divisions: 14 prefectures, 2 economic prefectures, 1 commune

Monetary unit: CFA franc

GDP: $4.2 billion (2004 est.)

Per capita GDP: $1,100

Website: state.gov/r/pa/ei/bgn/4007.htm

Did you know? Diamonds are the leading export of this developing nation.

CHAD
Map page 119

Population: 10,238,807

Principal languages: French, Arabic (both official); Sara; more than 120 different languages and dialects

Chief religions: Muslim 51%, Christian 35%, animist 7%, other 7%

Area: 495,755 sq mi (1,284,000 sq km)

Capital: N'Djamena (pop., 797,000)

Independence date: August 11, 1960

Government type: republic

Head of state: Pres. Idriss Déby

Head of government: Prime Min. Pascal Yoadimnadji

Local divisions: 14 prefectures

Monetary unit: CFA franc

GDP: $15.7 billion (2004 est.)

Per capita GDP: $1,600

Website: www.chadembassy.com

Did you know? Chad has cave paintings that are over 5,000 years old.

CHILE
Map page 209

Population: 16,284,741

Principal languages: Spanish (official), Araucanian

Chief religions: Roman Catholic 89%, Protestant 11%

Area: 292,260 sq mi (756,950 sq km)

Capital: Santiago (pop., 5,478,000)

Independence date: September 18, 1810

Government type: republic

Head of state and government: Pres. Verónica Michelle Bachelet Jeria

Local divisions: 13 regions

Monetary unit: peso

GDP: $169.1 billion (2004 est.)

Per capita GDP: $10,700

Website: www.chile-usa.org

Did you know? This "Shoestring Republic" is 2,650 mi. long but averages 110 mi. wide.

CHINA
Map page 83

(Statistical data for China do not include Hong Kong or Macau.)

Population: 1,321,851,888 (Hong Kong, 6,980,412; Macau, 456,989)

Principal languages: Mandarin (official), Yue (Cantonese), Wu (Shanghaiese), Minbei (Fuzhou), Minnan (Hokkien-Taiwanese), Xiang, Gan, Hakka, minority languages

Chief religions: officially atheist; Buddhism, Taoism; some Muslims, Christians

Area: 3,705,405 sq mi (9,596,960 sq km)

Capital: Beijing (pop., 10,848,000)

Independence date: 221 BC

Government type: Communist Party-led state

Head of state: Pres. Hu Jintao

Head of government: Premier Wen Jiabao

Local divisions: 22 provinces (not including Taiwan), 5 autonomous regions, and 4 municipalities, plus the special administrative regions of Hong Kong and Macau

Monetary unit: yuan (renminbi)

GDP: $7,262 billion (2004 est.)

Per capita GDP: $5,600

Website: www.china.org.cn

Did you know? The Great Wall of China once extended more than 1,500 miles.

COLOMBIA
Map page 216

Population: 44,227,550

Principal language: Spanish (official)

Chief religion: Roman Catholic 90%

Area: 439,735 sq mi (1,138,910 sq km)

Capital: Bogotá (pop., 7,290,000)

Independence date: July 20, 1810

Government type: republic

Head of state and government: Pres. Álvaro Uribe Vélez

Local divisions: 32 departments, capital district of Bogotá

Monetary unit: peso

GDP: $281.1 billion (2004 est.)

Per capita GDP: $6,600

Website: www.colombiaemb.org

Did you know? This is the only South American country with both Caribbean and Pacific coasts.

COMOROS
Map page 143

Population: 710,960

Principal languages: Arabic, French (both official); Shikomoro (a blend of Swahili and Arabic)

Chief religion: Muslim (official) 98%

Area: 838 sq mi (2,170 sq km)

Capital: Moroni (pop., 53,000)

Independence date: July 6, 1975

Government type: in transition

Head of state and government: Pres. Ahmed Abdallah Mohamed Sambi

Local divisions: 3 main islands with 4 municipalities

Monetary unit: franc

GDP: $441 million (2002 est.)

Per capita GDP: $700

Website: www.state.gov/r/pa/ei/bgn/5236.htm

Did you know? Comoros is made up of mountainous islands of volcanic origin.

CONGO, DEMOCRATIC REPUBLIC OF THE
Map page 119

Population: 64,606,759

Principal languages: French (official), Lingala, Kingwana (a Swahili dialect), Kikongo, Tshiluba

Chief religions: Roman Catholic 50%, Protestant 20%, Kimbanguist 10%, Muslim 10%

Area: 905,567 sq mi (2,345,410 sq km)

Capital: Kinshasa (pop., 5,277,000)

Independence date: June 30, 1960

Government type: republic with strong presidential authority (in transition)

Head of state and government: Pres. Joseph Kabila

Local divisions: 10 provinces, 1 city

Monetary unit: Congolese franc

GDP: $42.7 billion (2004 est.)

Per capita GDP: $700

Website: www.state.gov/r/pa/ei/bgn/2823.htm

Did you know? This country, the former Belgian Congo, lies east of the smaller Congo Republic.

CONGO, REPUBLIC OF
Map page 138

Population: 3,800,610

Principal languages: French (official), Lingala, Monokutuba, Kikongo, many local languages and dialects

Chief religions: Christian 50%, animist 48%, Muslim 2%

Area: 132,047 sq mi (342,000 sq km)

Capital: Brazzaville (pop., 1,080,000)

Independence date: August 15, 1960

Government type: republic

Head of state and government: Pres. Denis Sassou-Nguesso

Local divisions: 10 regions, 6 communes

Monetary unit: CFA franc

GDP: $2.3 billion (2004 est.)

Per capita GDP: $800

Website: state.gov/r/pa/ei/bgn/2825.htm

Did you know? Most people live in towns or cities. Rain forests remain mostly uninhabited.

COSTA RICA
Map page 207

Population: 4,133,884

Principal languages Spanish (official), English spoken around Puerto Limon

Chief religions: Roman Catholic (official) 76%, Protestant 14%

Area: 19,730 sq mi (51,100 sq km)

Capital: San José (pop., 1,085,000)

Independence date: September 15, 1821

Government type: republic

Head of state and government: Pres. Óscar Arias Sánchez

Local divisions: 7 provinces

Monetary unit: colon

GDP: $38.0 billion (2004 est.)

Per capita GDP: $9,600

Website: www.costarica-embassy.org

Did you know? More than 725 species of birds are native to Costa Rica.

CÔTE D'IVOIRE (IVORY COAST)
Map page 132

Population: 18,013,409

Principal languages: French (official), Dioula, many native dialects

Chief religions: Muslim 35-40%, Christian 20-30%, indigenous beliefs 25-40%

Area: 124,502 sq mi (322,460 sq km)

Official capital: Yamoussoukro (pop., 416,000); de facto capital, Abidjan (pop., 3,337,000)

Independence date: August 7, 1960

Government type: in transition

Head of state: Pres. Laurent Gbagbo

Head of government: Prime Min. Charles Konan Banny

Local divisions: 45 provinces

Monetary unit: CFA franc

GDP: $24.8 billion (2004 est.)

Per capita GDP: $1,500

Website: www.state.gov/r/pa/ei/bgn/2846.htm

Did you know? This nation is the world's leading producer of cocoa beans.

CROATIA
Map page 56

Population: 4,493,312

Principal languages Croatian (official), Serbian

Chief religions: Roman Catholic 88%, Orthodox 5%

Area: 21,831 sq mi (56,542 sq km)

Capital: Zagreb (pop., 688,000)

Independence date: June 25, 1991

Government type: parliamentary democracy

Head of state: Pres. Stipe Mesic

Head of government: Prime Min. Ivo Sanader

Local divisions: 21 counties

Monetary unit: kuna

GDP: $50.3 billion (2004 est.)

Per capita GDP: $11,200

Website: www.vlada.hr/default.asp?ru=2

Did you know? Croatia was part of Yugoslavia until its independence in 1991.

CUBA
Map page 207

Population: 11,416,987

Principal language: Spanish (official)

Chief religions: Roman Catholic, Santeria

Area: 42,803 sq mi (110,860 sq km)

Capital: Havana (pop., 2,189,000)

Independence date: May 20, 1902

Government type: Communist state

Head of state and government: Pres. Fidel Castro Ruz

Local divisions: 14 provinces, 1 special municipality

Monetary unit: peso

GDP: $33.9 billion (2004 est.)

Per capita GDP: $3,000

Website: www.cubagov.cu/ingles/

Did you know? Cuba was one of the islands Christopher Columbus visited in 1492.

CYPRUS*
Map page 116

Population: 788,457

Principal languages: Greek, Turkish (both official); English

Chief religions: Greek Orthodox 78%, Muslim 18%

Area: 3,571 sq mi (9,250 sq km)

Capital: Nicosia (pop., 205,000)

Independence date: August 16, 1960

Government type: republic

Head of state and government: Pres. Tassos Papadopoulos

Local divisions: 6 districts

Monetary unit: pound

GDP: Greek Cypriot area, $15.7 billion (2004 est.); Turkish Cypriot area, $4.5 billion (2004 est.)

Per capita GDP: Greek Cypriot area, $20,300; Turkish Cypriot area, $7,100

Website: www.cyprusembassy.net

Did you know? Center of a kingdom in the 7th century BC, Nicosia is one of the world's oldest cities.

CZECH REPUBLIC*
Map page 49

Population: 10,228,744

Principal languages: Czech (official), German, Polish, Romani

Chief religions: atheist 40%, Roman Catholic 39%, Protestant 5%, Orthodox 3%

Area: 30,450 sq mi (78,866 sq km)

Capital: Prague (pop., 1,170,000)

Independence date: January 1, 1993

Government type: republic

Head of state: Pres. Vaclav Klaus

Head of government: Prime Min. Jiri Paroubek

Local divisions: 13 regions, 1 capital city

Monetary unit: koruna

GDP: $172.2 billion (2004 est.)

Per capita GDP: $16,800

Website: www.czech.cz

Did you know? Prague is home to Europe's oldest synagogue (c. 1270).

DENMARK*
Map page 46

Population: 5,468,120

Principal languages: Danish (official), Faroese, Greenlandic (an Inuit dialect), German

Chief religions: Evangelical Lutheran (official) 95%, other Christian 3%, Muslim 2%

Area: 16,639 sq mi (43,094 sq km)

Capital: Copenhagen (pop., 1,066,000)

Independence date: 10th century

Government type: constitutional monarchy

Head of state: Queen Margrethe II

Head of government: Prime Min. Anders Fogh Rasmussen

Local divisions: 14 counties, 2 communes

Monetary unit: krone

GDP: $174.4 billion (2004 est.)

Per capita GDP: $32,200

Website: www.denmark.dk

Did you know? Denmark is on a peninsula but includes more than 400 islands.

DJIBOUTI
Map page 136

Population: 496,374

Principal languages: French, Arabic (both official); Afar, Somali

Chief religions: Muslim 94%, Christian 6%

Area: 8,880 sq mi (23,000 sq km)

Capital: Djibouti (pop., 502,000)

Independence date: June 27, 1977

Government type: republic

Head of state: Pres. Ismail Omar Guelleh

Head of government: Prime Min. Dileita Mohamed Dileita

Local divisions: 5 districts

Monetary unit: Djibouti franc (DJF)

GDP: $619 million (2003 est.)

Per capita GDP: $1,300

Website: www.state.gov/r/pa/ei/bgn/5482.htm

Did you know? French colonists started building Djibouti City, which is now the capital, in 1888.

DOMINICA
Map page 203

Population: 68,925

Principal languages: English (official), French patois

Chief religions: Roman Catholic 77%, Protestant 15%

Area: 291 sq mi (754 sq km)

Capital: Roseau (pop., 27,000)

Independence date: November 3, 1978

Government type: parliamentary democracy

Head of state: Pres. Nicholas Liverpool

Head of government: Prime Min. Roosevelt Skerrit

Local divisions: 10 parishes

Monetary unit: East Caribbean dollar

GDP: $384 million (2003 est.)

Per capita GDP: $5,500

Website: www.ndcdominica.dm/

Did you know? Banana plantations are vital to Dominica's economy.

DOMINICAN REPUBLIC
Map page 203

Population: 9,365,818

Principal language: Spanish (official)

Chief religion: Roman Catholic 95%

Area: 18,815 sq mi (48,780 sq km)

Capital: Santo Domingo (pop., 1,865,000)

Independence date: February 27, 1844

Government type: republic

Head of state and government: Pres. Leonel Fernández Reyna

Local divisions: 29 provinces and national district

Monetary unit: peso

GDP: $55.7 billion (2004 est.)

Per capita GDP: $6,300

Website: www.domrep.org/home.htm

Did you know? U.S. marines occupied this nation in 1916–24 and intervened in 1965.

EAST TIMOR
Map page 152

Population: 1,084,971

Principal languages: Tetum, Portuguese (both official); Indonesian, English, other native languages

Chief religions: Roman Catholic 90%, Muslim 4%, Protestant 3%

Area: 5,641 sq mi (14,609 sq km)

Capital: Dili (pop., 49,000)

Independence date: May 20, 2002

Government type: republic

Head of state: Pres. Jose Ramos-Horta

Head of government: Prime Min. Estanislau Aleixo da Silva (interim)

Local divisions: 13 administrative districts

Monetary unit: U.S. dollar and Indonesian rupiah

GDP: $370 million (2004 est.)

Per capita GDP: $400

Website: www.timor-leste.gov.tl

Did you know? During Indonesia's 25-year occupation of East Timor 25% of the population may have died.

ECUADOR
Map page 209

Population: 13,755,680

Principal languages: Spanish (official), Amerindian languages (especially Quechua)

Chief religion: Roman Catholic 95%

Area: 109,483 sq mi (283,560 sq km)

Capital: Quito (pop., 1,451,000)

Independence date: May 24, 1822

Government type: republic

Head of state and government: Pres. Rafael Correa

Local divisions: 21 provinces

Monetary unit: U.S. dollar

GDP: $49.5 billion (2004 est.)

Per capita GDP: $3,700

Website: www.ecuador.org/ecuador

Did you know? Quito is the oldest capital city in South America.

EGYPT
Map page 127

Population: 80,264,543

Principal languages: Arabic (official), English, French

Chief religions: Muslim (official; mostly Sunni) 94%, Coptic Christian and other 6%

Area: 386,662 sq mi (1,001,450 sq km)

Capital: Cairo (pop., 10,834,000)

Independence date: February 28, 1922

Government type: republic

Head of state: Pres. Hosni Mubarak

Head of government: Prime Min. Ahmed Nazif

Local divisions: 26 governorates

Monetary unit: pound

GDP: $316.3 billion (2003 est.)

Per capita GDP: $4,200

Website: www.egyptembassy.net

Did you know? About 20,000 ships go through Egypt's Suez Canal every year.

EL SALVADOR
Map page 206

Population: 6,939,688

Principal languages: Spanish (official), Nahua

Chief religions: Roman Catholic 83%, many Protestant groups

Area: 8,124 sq mi (21,040 sq km)

Capital: San Salvador (pop., 1,424,000)

Independence date: September 15, 1821

Government type: republic

Head of state and government: Pres. Antonio Elías Saca González

Local divisions: 14 departments

Monetary unit: colon

GDP: $32.4 billion (2004 est.)

Per capita GDP: $4,900

Website: www.elsalvador.org/home.nsf/home

Did you know? Casamiento, a mixture of rice and beans, is a common everyday food.

EQUATORIAL GUINEA
Map page 138

Population: 551,201

Principal languages: Spanish, French (both official); Fang, Bubi, pidgin English, Portuguese Creole, Ibo

Chief religions: nominally Christian and predominantly Roman Catholic, pagan practices

Area: 10,831 sq mi (28,051 sq km)

Capital: Malabo (pop., 95,000)

Independence date: October 12, 1968

Government type: republic

Head of state: Pres. Teodoro Obiang Nguema Mbasogo

Head of government: Prime Min. Miguel Abia Biteo Borico

Local divisions: 7 provinces

Monetary unit: CFA franc

GDP: $1.3 billion (2002 est.)

Per capita GDP: $2,700

Website: www.state.gov/r/pa/ei/bgn/7221.htm

Did you know? Equatorial Guinea won independence from Spain in 1968.

ERITREA
Map page 119

Population: 4,906,585

Principal languages: Arabic, Tigrinya (both official); Afar, Amharic, Tigre, Kunama, other Cushitic languages

Chief religions: Muslim, Coptic Christian, Roman Catholic, Protestant

Area: 46,842 sq mi (121,320 sq km)

Capital: Asmara (pop., 556,000)

Independence date: May 24, 1993

Government type: in transition

Head of state and government: Pres. Isaias Afwerki

Local divisions: 8 provinces

Monetary unit: nakfa

GDP: $4.2 billion (2004 est.)

Per capita GDP: $900

Website: www.state.gov/r/pa/ei/bgn/2854.htm

Did you know? Once a colony of Italy, Eritrea was occupied by Britain in World War II.

ESTONIA*
Map page 47

Population: 1,315,912

Principal languages: Estonian (official), Russian, Ukrainian, Finnish

Chief religions: Evangelical Lutheran, Russian Orthodox, Estonian Orthodox

Area: 17,462 sq mi (45,226 sq km)

Capital: Tallinn (pop., 391,000)

Independence date: August 20, 1991

Government type: republic

Head of state: Pres. Arnold Rüütel

Head of government: Prime Min. Andrus Ansip

Local divisions: 15 counties

Monetary unit: kroon

GDP: $19.2 billion (2004 est.)

Per capita GDP: $14,300

Website: www.riik.ee/en/valitsus/

Did you know? Estonia, along with Latvia and Lithuania, split from the Soviet Union in 1991.

ETHIOPIA
Map page 119

Population: 76,511,887

Principal languages: Amharic, Tigrinya, Oromigna, Guaragigna, Somali, Arabic, over 200 other languages

Chief religions: Muslim 45-50%, Ethiopian Orthodox 35-40%, animist 12%

Area: 435,186 sq mi (1,127,127 sq km)

Capital: Addis Ababa (pop., 2,723,000)

Independence date: more than 2,000 years ago (Aksum)

Government type: federal republic

Head of state: Pres. Girma Wolde Giorgis

Head of government: Prime Min. Meles Zenawi

Local divisions: 9 states, 2 chartered cities

Monetary unit: birr

GDP: $54.9 billion (2004 est.)

Per capita GDP: $800

Website: www.ethiopianembassy.org

Did you know? Ethiopian runners have won the Olympic marathon race 4 times.

FIJI
Map page 161

Population: 918,675

Principal languages: English (official), Fijian, Hindustani

Chief religions: Christian 52%, Hindu 38%, Muslim 8%

Area: 7,054 sq mi (18,270 sq km)

Capital: Suva (pop., 210,000)

Independence date: October 19, 1970

Government type: republic

Head of state: Pres. Ratu Josefa Iloilo

Head of government: Prime Min. Laisenia Qarase

Local divisions: 4 divisions comprising 14 provinces and 1 dependency

Monetary unit: Fiji dollar

GDP $5.2 billion (2004 est.)

Per capita GDP: $5,900

Website: www.fiji.gov.fj

Did you know? Wearing a hat is a sign of disrespect in Fijian culture.

FINLAND*
Map page 44

Population: 5,238,460

Principal languages: Finnish, Swedish (both official); Russian, Sami

Chief religion: Evangelical Lutheran 89%

Area: 130,128 sq mi (337,030 sq km)

Capital: Helsinki (pop., 1,075,000)

Independence date: December 6, 1917

Government type: republic

Head of state: Pres. Tarja Halonen

Head of government: Prime Min. Matti Vanhanen

Local divisions: 6 läänit (provinces)

Monetary unit: euro

GDP: $151.2 billion (2004 est.)

Per capita GDP: $29,000

Website: virtual.finland.fi

Did you know? Lapland in the North is home to the Saami (Lapps), a hunting, fishing, and reindeer-herding people.

FRANCE*
Map page 50

Population: 61,083,916

Principal languages: French (official), Italian, Breton, Alsatian (German), Corsican, Gascon, Portuguese, Provençal, Dutch, Flemish, Catalan, Basque, Romani

Chief religions: Roman Catholic 83-88%, Muslim 5-10%

Area: 211,209 sq mi (547,030 sq km)

Capital: Paris (pop., 9,794,000)

Independence date: 486

Government type: republic

Head of state: Pres. Nicholas Sarkozy

Head of government: Prime Min. François Fillon

Local divisions: 22 administrative regions containing 96 departments (overseas departments: French Guiana, Guadeloupe, Martinique, Réunion; overseas territorial collectivities: Mayotte, Saint Pierre and Miquelon)

Monetary unit: euro

GDP: $1,737 billion (2004 est.)

Per capita GDP: $28,700

Website: www.info-france-usa.org

Did you know? About one-fifth of the French people live in Paris or its suburbs.

GABON
Map page 138

Population: 1,454,867

Principal languages: French (official), Fang, Myene, Nzebi, Bapounou/Eschira, Bandjabi

Chief religion: Christian 55-75%

Area: 103,347 sq mi (267,667 sq km)

Capital: Libreville (pop., 611,000)

Independence date: August 17, 1960

Government type: republic

Head of state: Pres. Omar Bongo Ondimba

Head of government: Prime Min. Jean Eyeghe Ndong

Local divisions: 9 provinces

Monetary unit: CFA franc

GDP: $8.0 billion (2004 est.)

Per capita GDP: $5,900

Website: www.state.gov/r/pa/ei/bgn/2826.htm

Did you know? Libreville (French for "freetown") was founded in 1849 for freed slaves.

THE GAMBIA
Map page 132

Population: 1,688,359

Principal languages: English (official), Mandinka, Wolof, Fula, other native dialects

Chief religions: Muslim 90%, Christian 9%

Area: 4,363 sq mi (11,300 sq km)

Capital: Banjul (pop., 372,000)

Independence date: February 18, 1965

Government type: republic

Head of state and government: Pres. Yahya Jammeh

Local divisions: 5 divisions, 1 city

Monetary unit: dalasi

GDP: $2.8 billion (2004 est.)

Per capita GDP: $1,800

Website: www.visitthegambia.gm

Did you know? This narrow nation lies along both banks of the lower Gambia River.

GEORGIA
Map page 77

Population: 4,646,003

Principal languages: Georgian (official), Russian, Armenian, Azeri, Abkhaz (official in Abkhazia)

Chief religions: Georgian Orthodox 65%, Muslim 11%, Russian Orthodox 10%, Armenian Apostolic 8%

Area: 26,911 sq mi (69,700 sq km)

Capital: Tbilisi (pop., 1,064,000)

Independence date: April 9, 1991

Government type: republic

Head of state: Pres. Mikhail Saakashvili

Head of government: Prime Min. Zurab Noghaideli

Local divisions: 53 rayons, 9 cities, and 2 autonomous republics

Monetary unit: lari

GDP: $14.5 billion (2004 est.)

Per capita GDP: $3,100

Website: www.georgiaemb.org

Did you know? In 2004, the Georgian parliament adopted a new national flag.

GERMANY*
Map page 48

Population: 82,400,996

Principal languages: German (official), Turkish, Italian, Greek, English, Danish, Dutch, Slavic languages

Chief religions: Protestant 34%, Roman Catholic 34%, Muslim 4%

Area: 137,847 sq mi (357,021 sq km)

Capital: Berlin (pop., 3,327,000)

Independence date: January 18, 1871

Government type: federal republic

Head of state: Pres. Horst Köhler

Head of government: Chancellor Angela Merkel

Local divisions: 16 Länder (states)

Monetary unit: euro

GDP: $2,362 billion (2004 est.)

Per capita GDP: $28,700

Website: www.germany-info.org

Did you know? Aside from Russia, Germany is the most populous country in Europe.

GHANA
Map page 133

Population: 22,931,299

Principal languages: English (official); about 75 African languages, including Akan, Moshi-Dagomba, Ewe, and Ga

Chief religions: Christian 63%, indigenous beliefs 21%, Muslim 16%

Area: 92,456 sq mi (239,460 sq km)

Capital: Accra (pop., 1,847,000)

Independence date: March 6, 1957

Government type: republic

Head of state and government: Pres. John Agyekum Kufuor

Local divisions: 10 regions

Monetary unit: cedi

GDP: $48.3 billion (2004 est.)

Per capita GDP: $2,300

Website: www.ghana.gov.gh

Did you know? Led by Kwame Nkrumah, Ghana won independence from Great Britain in 1957.

 **GREECE***

Map page 55

Population: 10,706,290

Principal languages: Greek (official), English, French

Chief religions: Greek Orthodox (official) 98%, Muslim 1%

Area: 50,942 sq mi (131,940 sq km)

Capital: Athens (pop., 3,215,000)

Independence date: 1829

Government type: parliamentary republic

Head of state: Pres. Karolos Papoulias

Head of government: Prime Min. Costas Karamanlis

Local divisions: 13 regions comprising 51 prefectures

Monetary unit: euro

GDP: $226.4 billion (2004 est.)

Per capita GDP: $21,300

Website: www.greekembassy.org

Did you know? Ancient Greeks believed Mt. Olympus (9,570 ft. [2,917 m]), the highest point in Greece, was the home of the gods.

 **GRENADA**

Map page 203

Population: 89,971

Principal languages: English (official), French patois

Chief religions: Roman Catholic 53%, Anglican 14%, other Protestant 33%

Area: 133 sq mi (344 sq km)

Capital: Saint George's (pop., 33,000)

Independence date: February 7, 1974

Government type: parliamentary democracy

Head of state: Queen Elizabeth II, represented by Gov.-Gen. Daniel Williams

Head of government: Prime Min. Keith Mitchell

Local divisions: 6 parishes, 1 dependency

Monetary unit: East Caribbean dollar

GDP: $440 million (2002 est.)

Per capita GDP: $5,000

Website: www.grenadagrenadines.com

Did you know? Grenada is the world's second largest producer of nutmeg after Indonesia.

 GUATEMALA

Map page 206

Population: 12,728,111

Principal languages: Spanish (official); more than 20 Amerindian languages, including Quiche, Cakchiquel, Kekchi, Mam, Garifuna, and Xinca

Chief religions: mostly Roman Catholic; some Protestant, indigenous Mayan beliefs

Area: 42,043 sq mi (108,890 sq km)

Capital: Guatemala City (pop., 951,000)

Independence date: September 15, 1821

Government type: republic

Head of state and government: Pres. Oscar Berger Perdomo

Local divisions: 22 departments

Monetary unit: quetzal

GDP: $59.5 billion (2004 est.)

Per capita GDP: $4,200

Website: www.visitguatemala.com

Did you know? There are 23 Amerindian dialects spoken in Guatemala.

 **GUINEA**

Map page 132

Population: 9,947,814

Principal languages: French (official), many African languages

Chief religions: Muslim 85%, Christian 8%, indigenous beliefs 7%

Area: 94,926 sq mi (245,857 sq km)

Capital: Conakry (pop., 1,366,000)

Independence date: October 2, 1958

Government type: republic

Head of state: Pres. Gen. Lansana Conté

Head of government: Prime Min. Cellou Dalein Diallo

Local divisions: 4 administrative regions, 1 special zone

Monetary unit: franc

GDP: $19.5 billion (2004 est.)

Per capita GDP: $2,100

Website: www.state.gov/r/pa/ei/bgn/2824.htm

Did you know? Common animals in Guinea include parrots, snakes, and crocodiles.

 GUINEA-BISSAU

Map page 132

Population: 1,472,041

Principal languages: Portuguese (official), Crioulo, tribal languages

Chief religions: indigenous beliefs 50%, Muslim 45%, Christian 5%

Area: 13,946 sq mi (36,120 sq km)

Capital: Bissau (pop., 336,000)

Independence date: September 24, 1973

Government type: republic

Head of state: Pres. João Bernardo Vieira

Head of government: Prime Min. Aristides Gomes

Local divisions: 9 regions

Monetary unit: CFA franc

GDP: $1.0 billion (2004 est.)

Per capita GDP: $700

Website: state.gov/r/pa/ei/bgn/5454.htm

Did you know? At carnival time people wear masks of sharks, hippos, and bulls.

 **GUYANA**

Map page 217

Population: 769,095

Principal languages: English (official), Amerindian dialects, Creole, Hindi, Urdu

Chief religions: Christian 50%, Hindu 35%, Muslim 10%

Area: 83,000 sq mi (214,970 sq km)

Capital: Georgetown (pop., 231,000)

Independence date: May 26, 1966

Government type: republic

Head of state: Pres. Bharrat Jagdeo

Head of government: Prime Min. Samuel Hinds

Local divisions: 10 regions

Monetary unit: Guyana dollar

GDP: $2.9 billion (2004 est.)

Per capita GDP: $3,800

Website: www.guyana.org

Did you know? Dense forest makes up about 75% of this sparsely populated country.

 HAITI

Map page 207

Population: 8,706,497

Principal languages: French, Creole (both official)

Chief religions: Roman Catholic 80%, Protestant 16%; voodoo widely practiced

Area: 10,714 sq mi (27,750 sq km)

Capital: Port-au-Prince (pop., 1,961,000)

Independence date: January 1, 1804

Government type: in transition

Head of state: Pres. René Préval

Head of government: Prime Min. Jacques Édouard Alexis

Local divisions: 9 departments

Monetary unit: gourde

GDP: $12.1 billion (2004 est.)

Per capita GDP: $1,500

Website: www.haiti.org

Did you know? Haiti is the 2nd-oldest republic, after the United States, in the western hemisphere.

 **HONDURAS**

Map page 206

Population: 7,483,763

Principal languages: Spanish (official), Garífuna, Amerindian dialects

Chief religion: Roman Catholic 97%

Area: 43,278 sq mi (112,090 sq km)

Capital: Tegucigalpa (pop., 1,007,000)

Independence date: September 15, 1821

Government type: republic

Head of state: and government: Pres. José Manuel Zelaya Rosales

Local divisions: 18 departments

Monetary unit: lempira

GDP: $18.8 billion (2004 est.)

Per capita GDP: $2,800

Website: www.hondurasemb.org

Did you know? The marimba is Honduras's most popular musical instrument.

 **HUNGARY***

Map page 56

Population: 9,956,108

Principal languages: Hungarian (official), Romani, German, Slavic languages, Romanian

Chief religions: Roman Catholic 68%, Protestant 25%

Area: 35,919 sq mi (93,030 sq km)

Capital: Budapest (pop., 1,708,000)

Independence date: 1001

Government type: parliamentary democracy

Head of state: Pres. László Sólyom

Head of government: Prime Min. Ferenc Gyurcsány

Local divisions: 19 counties, 20 urban counties, 1 capital

Monetary unit: forint

GDP: $149.3 billion (2004 est.)

Per capita GDP: $14,900

Website: www.hungary.hu

Did you know? In 1872 the communities of Buda and Pest united as the city of Budapest.

 **ICELAND**

Map page 44

Population: 301,931

Principal language: Icelandic (official)

Chief religion: Evangelical Lutheran 93%

Area: 39,769 sq mi (103,000 sq km)

Capital: Reykjavík (pop., 184,000)

Independence date: June 17, 1944

Government type: constitutional republic

Head of state: Pres. Olafur Ragnar Grímsson

Head of government: Prime Min. Halldór Ásgrímsson

Local divisions: 23 counties, 14 independent towns

Monetary unit: krona

GDP: $9.4 billion (2004 est.)

Per capita GDP: $31,900

Website: www.iceland.is

Did you know? Underground (geothermal) energy heats 85% of Iceland's homes.

 **INDIA**

Map page 104

Population: 1,129,866,154

Principal languages: Hindi, English, Bengali, Telugu, Marathi, Tamil, Urdu, Gujarati, Malayalam, Kannada, Oriya, Punjabi, Assamese, Kashmiri, Sindhi, and Sanskrit (all official); Hindustani, a mix of Hindi and Urdu spoken in the north, is popular but not official

Chief religions: Hindu 82%, Muslim 12%, Christian 2%, Sikh 2%

Area: 1,269,345 sq mi (3,287,590 sq km)

Capital: New Delhi (pop. city proper, 300,000)

Independence date: August 15, 1947

Government type: federal republic

Head of state: Pres.
A. P. J. Abdul Kalam

Head of government: Prime Min. Manmohan Singh

Local divisions: 28 states, 6 union territories, 1 national capital territory

Monetary unit: rupee

GDP: $3,319 billion (2004 est.)

Per capita GDP: $3,100

Website: www.india.in

Did you know? India's population is larger than the next 5 biggest countries combined.

INDONESIA
Map page 103

Population: 245,452,739

Principal languages: Bahasa Indonesia (official, modified form of Malay), English, Dutch, Javanese, other dialects

Chief religions: Muslim 88%, Protestant 5%, Roman Catholic 3%, Hindu 2%, Buddhist 1%

Area: 741,100 sq mi (1,919,440 sq km)

Capital: Jakarta (pop., 12,296,000)

Independence date: August 17, 1945

Government type: republic

Head of state and government: Pres. Susilo Bambang Yudhoyono

Local divisions: 30 provinces, 2 special regions, 1 capital district

Monetary unit: rupiah

GDP: $827.4 billion (2004 est.)

Per capita GDP: $3,500

Website: www.embassyofindonesia.org

Did you know? Indonesia has 17,000 islands, but only 6,000 are inhabited.

IRAN
Map page 115

Population: 65,397,521

Principal languages: Farsi (Persian; official), Kurdish, Pashto, Luri, Balochi, Gilaki, Mazandarami, Turkic languages (including Azeri and Turkish), Arabic

Chief religions: Muslim (official; Shi'a 89%, Sunni 10%)

Area: 636,296 sq mi (1,648,000 sq km)

Capital: Tehran (pop., 7,190,000)

Independence date: April 1, 1979

Government type: Islamic republic

Religious head: Ayatollah Sayyed Ali Khamenei

Head of state and government: Pres. Mahmoud Ahmadinejad

Local divisions: 25 provinces

Monetary unit: rial

GDP: $516.7 billion (2004 est.)

Per capita GDP: $7,700

Website: www.salamiran.org

Did you know? Until the 1930s, Iran was known as Persia.

IRAQ
Map page 114

Population: 27,499,638

Principal languages: Arabic (official), Kurdish (official in Kurdish regions), Assyrian, Armenian

Chief religions: Muslim (official; Shi'a 60-65%, Sunni 32-37%)

Area: 168,754 sq mi (437,072 sq km)

Capital: Baghdad (pop., 5,620,000)

Independence date: October 3, 1932

Head of state: Pres. Jalal Talabani

Head of government: Prime Min. Nouri Kamel al-Maliki

Local divisions: 18 governorates (3 in Kurdish Autonomous Region)

Monetary unit: dinar

GDP: $54.4 billion (2004 est.)

Per capita GDP: $2,100

Website: baghdad.usembassy.gov

Did you know? Ancient Mesopotamia was located between the Tigris and Euphrates rivers in what is now Iraq.

IRELAND*
Map page 37

Population: 4,109,086

Principal languages: English, Irish Gaelic (both official); Irish Gaelic spoken by small number in western areas

Chief religions: Roman Catholic 92%, Anglican 3%

Area: 27,135 sq mi (70,280 sq km)

Capital: Dublin (pop., 1,015,000)

Independence date: December 6, 1921

Government type: parliamentary republic

Head of state: Pres. Mary McAleese

Head of government: Prime Min. Bertie Ahern

Local divisions: 26 counties

Monetary unit: euro

GDP: $126.4 billion (2004 est.)

Per capita GDP: $31,900

Website: www.irelandemb.org

Did you know? Ireland is known as the "Emerald Isle" for its brilliant green grass.

ISRAEL
Map page 116

Population: 6,426,679

Principal languages: Hebrew, Arabic (both official); English

Chief religions: Jewish 80%, Muslim (mostly Sunni) 15%, Christian 2%

Area: 8,019 sq mi (20,770 sq km)

Capital: Jerusalem (pop., 686,000)

Independence date: May 14, 1948

Government type: republic

Head of state: Pres. Moshe Katsav

Head of government: Prime Min. Ehud Olmert

Local divisions: 6 districts

Monetary unit: new shekel

GDP: $129.0 billion (2004 est.)

Per capita GDP: $20,800

Website: www.israelemb.org

Did you know? In 1979 Israel signed a peace treaty with Egypt, its first with an Arab nation.

ITALY*
Map page 73

Population: 58,147,733

Principal languages: Italian (official), German, French, Slovenian, Albanian

Chief religion: predominantly Roman Catholic

Area: 116,306 sq mi (301,230 sq km)

Capital: Rome (pop., 2,665,000)

Independence date: March 17, 1861

Government type: republic

Head of state: Pres. Giorgio Napolitano

Head of government: Prime Min. Romano Prodi

Local divisions: 20 regions divided into 94 provinces

Monetary unit: euro

GDP: $1,609 billion (2004 est.)

Per capita GDP: $27,700

Website: www.italiantourism.com

Did you know? The Renaissance, the 15th-16th-century revival of learning, began in Italy.

JAMAICA
Map page 207

Population: 2,780,132

Principal languages: English, patois English

Chief religions: Protestant 61%, Roman Catholic 4%, spiritual cults and other 35%

Area: 4,244 sq mi (10,991 sq km)

Capital: Kingston (pop., 575,000)

Independence date: August 6, 1962

Government type: parliamentary democracy

Head of state: Queen Elizabeth II, represented by Gov.-Gen. Kenneth Hall

Head of government: Prime Min. Portia Simpson Miller

Local divisions: 14 parishes

Monetary unit: Jamaican dollar

GDP: $11.1 billion (2004 est.)

Per capita GDP: $4,100

Website: www.visitjamaica.com

Did you know? Reggae, a mixture of native, rock, and soul music, is from Jamaica.

JAPAN
Map page 91

Population: 127,467,972

Principal languages: Japanese (official), Ainu, Korean

Chief religions: Shinto and Buddhist observed together by 84%

Area: 145,883 sq mi (377,835 sq km)

Capital: Tokyo (pop., 34,997,000)

Independence date: 660 BC

Government type: parliamentary democracy

Head of state: Emperor Akihito

Head of government: Prime Min. Junichiro Koizumi

Local divisions: 47 prefectures

Monetary unit: yen

GDP: $3,745 billion (2004 est.)

Per capita GDP: $29,400

Website: web-japan.org/factsheet/index.html

Did you know? No part of Japan is more than 100 miles from the sea.

JORDAN
Map page 116

Population: 6,053,193

Principal languages: Arabic (official), English

Chief religions: Muslim (official; mostly Sunni) 92%, Christian 6%

Area: 35,637 sq mi (92,300 sq km)

Capital: Amman (pop., 1,237,000)

Independence date: May 25, 1946

Government type: constitutional monarchy

Head of state: King Abdullah II

Head of government: Prime Min. Marouf al-Bakhit

Local divisions: 12 governorates

Monetary unit: dinar

GDP: $25.5 billion (2004 est.)

Per capita GDP: $4,500

Website: www.jordanembassyus.org

Did you know? The Dead Sea, on the Israel-Jordan border, is five to ten times saltier than ocean water.

KAZAKHSTAN
Map page 80

Population: 15,284,929

Principal languages: Kazakh, Russian (both official); Ukranian, German, Uzbek

Chief religions: Muslim 47%, Russian Orthodox 44%

Area: 1,049,155 sq mi (2,717,300 sq km)

Capital: Astana (pop., 332,000)

Independence date: December 16, 1991

Government type: republic

Head of state: Pres. Nursultan A. Nazarbayev

Head of government: Prime Min. Daniyal Akhmetov

Local divisions: 14 provinces, 3 cities

Monetary unit: tenge

GDP: $118.4 billion (2004 est.)

Per capita GDP: $7,800

Website: www.kazakhembus.com

Did you know? Kazakhstan is the world's ninth largest country in land area.

KENYA
Map page 119

Population: 36,913,721

Principal languages: English, Swahili (both official); numerous indigenous languages

Chief religions: Protestant 45%, Roman Catholic 33%, indigenous beliefs 10%, Muslim 10%

Area: 224,962 sq mi (582,650 sq km)

Capital: Nairobi (pop., 2,575,000)

Independence date: December 12, 1963

Government type: republic

Head of state and government: Pres. Mwai Kibaki

Local divisions: 7 provinces, 1 area (Nairobi)

Monetary unit: shilling

GDP: $34.7 billion (2004 est.)

Per capita GDP: $1,100

Website: www.kenyaembassy.com

Did you know? Kenya's diverse wildlife is protected in dozens of national parks.

KIRIBATI
Map page 160

Population: 107,817

Principal languages: English (official), I-Kiribati

Chief religions: Roman Catholic 52%, Protestant 40%

Area: 313 sq mi (811 sq km)

Capital: Tarawa (pop., 42,000)

Independence date: July 12, 1979

Government type: republic

Head of state and government: Pres. Anote Tong

Local divisions: 3 units, 6 districts

Monetary unit: Australian dollar

GDP: $79 million (2001 est.)

Per capita GDP: $800

Website: state.gov/r/pa/ei/bgn/1836.htm

Did you know? The island of Tarawa was the scene of fierce fighting in World War II.

KOREA, NORTH
Map page 93

Population: 23,301,725

Principal language: Korean (official)

Chief religions: activities almost nonexistent; traditionally Buddhist, Confucianist and Chondogyo

Area: 46,541 sq mi (120,540 sq km)

Capital: Pyongyang (pop., 3,228,000)

Independence date: September 9, 1948

Government type: Communist state

Leader: Kim Jong Il

Local divisions: 9 provinces, 4 special cities

Monetary unit: won

GDP: $40.0 billion (2004 est.)

Per capita GDP: $1,700

Website: www.korea-dpr.com/menu.htm

Did you know? Settled in 1122 BC, Pyongyang is the oldest city on the Korean Peninsula.

KOREA, SOUTH
Map page 93

Population: 49,044,790

Principal language: Korean (official)

Chief religions: Christian 49%, Buddhist 47%, Confucianist 3%

Area: 38,023 sq mi (98,480 sq km)

Capital: Seoul (pop., 9,714,000)

Independence date: August 15, 1948

Government type: republic

Head of state: Pres. Roh Moo-hyun

Head of government: Prime Min. Han Myung-sook

Local divisions: 9 provinces, 7 special cities

Monetary unit: won

GDP: $925.1 billion (2004 est.)

Per capita GDP: $19,200

Website: www.korea.net

Did you know? The Korean language is written in Han'gul, a language script created in the 1400s.

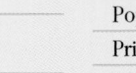
KUWAIT
Map page 115

Population: 2,505,559

Principal languages: Arabic (official), English

Chief religion: Muslim 85% (official; Sunni 70%, Shi'a 30%)

Area: 6,880 sq mi (17,820 sq km)

Capital: Kuwait City (pop., 1,222,000)

Independence date: June 19, 1961

Government type: constitutional monarchy

Head of state: Emir Sheikh Sabah al-Ahmed al-Jaber as-Sabah

Head of government: Prime Min. Sheikh Nasser al-Muhammad al-Ahmed al-Sabah

Local divisions: 5 governorates

Monetary unit: dinar

GDP: $48.0 billion (2004 est.)

Per capita GDP: $21,300

Website: www.kuwaitinfo.org.uk

Did you know? The Gulf War freed Kuwait from Iraqi forces who had invaded in 1990.

KYRGYZSTAN
Map page 111

Population: 5,284,149

Principal languages: Kyrgyz, Russian (both official); Uzbek

Chief religions: Muslim 75%, Russian Orthodox 20%

Area: 76,641 sq mi (198,500 sq km)

Capital: Bishkek (pop., 806,000)

Independence date: August 31, 1991

Government type: republic

Head of state: Pres. Kurmanbek Bakiyev

Head of government: Prime Min. Feliks Kulov

Local divisions: 6 oblasts, 1 city

Monetary unit: som

GDP: $8.5 billion (2004 est.)

Per capita GDP: $1,700

Website: www.cbtkyrgyzstan.kg/en/home_en

Did you know? This Central Asian country is almost entirely mountainous.

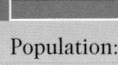
LAOS
Map page 106

Population: 6,521,998

Principal languages: Lao (official), French, English, and various ethnic languages

Chief religions: Buddhism 60%, animist and other 40%

Area: 91,429 sq mi (236,800 sq km)

Capital: Vientiane (pop., 716,000)

Independence date: July 19, 1949

Government type: Communist

Head of state: Pres. Khamtai Siphandon

Head of government: Prime Min. Boungnang Vorachith

Local divisions: 16 provinces, 1 municipality, 1 special zone

Monetary unit: kip

GDP: $11.3 billion (2004 est.)

Per capita GDP: $1,900

Website: www.laoembassy.com

Did you know? In the 1300s, Laos was named the Kingdom of the Million Elephants.

LATVIA*
Map page 47

Population: 2,259,810

Principal languages: Latvian (official), Russian, Belarusian, Ukrainian, Polish

Chief religions: Lutheran, Roman Catholic, Russian Orthodox

Area: 24,938 sq mi (64,589 sq km)

Capital: Riga (pop., 733,000)

Independence date: August 21, 1991

Government type: republic

Head of state: Pres. Vaira Vike-Freiberga

Head of government: Prime Min. Aigars Kalvitis

Local divisions: 26 counties, 7 municipalities

Monetary unit: lat

GDP: $26.5 billion (2004 est.)

Per capita GDP: $11,500

Website: www.latvia-usa.org

Did you know? For over 300 years, this area on the Baltic Sea was part of the domain of the Teutonic Knights.

LEBANON
Map page 116

Population: 3,921,278

Principal languages: Arabic (official), French, English, Armenian

Chief religions: Muslim 70%, Christian 30%

Area: 4,015 sq mi (10,400 sq km)

Capital: Beirut (pop., 1,792,000)

Independence date: November 22, 1943

Government type: republic

Head of state: Pres. Emile Lahoud

Head of government: Prime Min. Fouad Siniora

Local divisions: 5 governorates

Monetary unit: pound

GDP: $18.8 billion (2004 est.)

Per capita GDP: $5,000

Website: www.lebanonembassyus.org

Did you know? The Ottoman Turks ruled Lebanon for 400 years until World War I.

LESOTHO
Map page 142

Population: 2,012,649

Principal languages: Sesotho, English (both official); Zulu, Xhosa

Chief religions: Christian 80%, indigenous beliefs 20%

Area: 11,720 sq mi (30,355 sq km)

Capital: Maseru (pop., 170,000)

Independence date: October 4, 1966

Government type: modified constitutional monarchy

Head of state: King Letsie III

Head of government: Prime Min. Pakalitha Mosisili

Local divisions: 10 districts

Monetary unit: loti

GDP: $5.9 billion (2003 est.)

Per capita GDP: $3,200

Website: www.lesotho.gov.ls

Did you know? Diamonds are Lesotho's chief export.

LIBERIA
Map page 132

Population: 3,193,942

Principal languages: English (official), Mande, West Atlantic, and Kwa languages

Chief religions: indigenous beliefs 40%, Christian 40%, Muslim 20%

Area: 43,000 sq mi (111,370 sq km)

Capital: Monrovia (pop., 572,000)

Independence date: July 26, 1847

Government type: republic

Head of state and government: Pres. Ellen Johnson-Sirleaf

Local divisions: 13 counties

Monetary unit: Liberian dollar (LRD)

GDP: $2.9 billion (2004 est.)

Per capita GDP: $900

Website: state.gov/r/pa/ei/bgn/6618.htm

Did you know? Liberia is the oldest republic in Africa and one of the original member states of the UN.

LIBYA
Map page 126

Population: 6,036,914

Principal languages: Arabic (official), Italian, English

Chief religion: Muslim (official; mostly Sunni) 97%

Area: 679,362 sq mi (1,759,540 sq km)

Capital: Tripoli (pop., 2,006,000)

Independence date: December 24, 1951

*Member of the European Union

Government type: Islamic Arabic Socialist "Mass-State"

Head of state and government: Col. Muammar al-Qaddafi

Local divisions: 25 municipalities

Monetary unit: dinar

GDP: $37.5 billion (2004 est.)

Per capita GDP: $6,700

Website: state.gov/r/pa/ei/bgn/5425.htm

Did you know? Much of Libya lies within the great Sahara Desert.

LIECHTENSTEIN
Map page 67

Population: 34,247

Principal languages: German (official), Alemannic dialect

Chief religions: Roman Catholic 80%, Protestant 7%

Area: 62 sq mi (160 sq km)

Capital: Vaduz (pop., 5,000)

Independence date: January 23, 1719

Government type: hereditary constitutional monarchy

Head of state: Prince Hans-Adam II

Head of government: Otmar Hasler

Local divisions: 11 communes

Monetary unit: Swiss franc

GDP: $825 million (1999 est.)

Per capita GDP: $25,000

Website: www.liechtenstein.li/en

Did you know? The postal system in this tiny country is administered by Switzerland.

LITHUANIA*
Map page 47

Population: 3,575,439

Principal languages: Lithuanian (official), Belarusian, Russian, Polish

Chief religion: predominantly Roman Catholic

Area: 25,174 sq mi (65,200 sq km)

Capital: Vilnius (pop., 549,000)

Independence date: March 11, 1990

Government type: republic

Head of state: Pres. Valdas Adamkus

Head of government: Prime Min. Algirdas Brazauskas

Local divisions: 10 provinces

Monetary unit: litas

GDP: $45.2 billion (2004 est.)

Per capita GDP: $12,500

Website: www.president.lt/en

Did you know? Russians are Lithuania's largest ethnic minority.

LUXEMBOURG*
Map page 61

Population: 480,222

Principal languages: Luxembourgish (national), German, French (official)

Chief religion: majority is Roman Catholic; 1979

law forbids collection of such statistics

Area: 998 sq mi (2,586 sq km)

Capital: Luxembourg (pop., 77,000)

Independence date: 1839

Government type: constitutional monarchy

Head of state: Grand Duke Henri

Head of government: Prime Min. Jean-Claude Juncker

Local divisions: 3 districts

Monetary unit: euro

GDP: $27.3 billion (2004 est.)

Per capita GDP: $58,900

Website: www.luxembourg-usa.org

Did you know? Four Holy Roman emperors came from this tiny duchy.

MACEDONIA (F.Y.R.O.M.)
Map page 55

Population: 2,055,915

Principal languages: Macedonian (official), Albanian, Turkish, Romani, Serbo-Croatian

Chief religions: Macedonian Orthodox 67%, Muslim 30%

Area: 9,781 sq mi (25,333 sq km)

Capital: Skopje (pop., 447,000)

Independence date: September 17, 1991

Government type: republic

Head of state: Pres. Branko Crvenkovski

Head of government: Prime Min. Vlado Buckovski

Local divisions: 123 municipalities

Monetary unit: denar

GDP: $14.4 billion (2004 est.)

Per capita GDP: $7,100

Website: www.macedonianembassy.org.uk

Did you know? Alexander the Great conquered his vast empire after becoming King of Macedonia in 336 B.C.

MADAGASCAR
Map page 143

Population: 19,448,815

Principal languages: Malagasy, French (both official)

Chief religions: indigenous beliefs 52%, Christian 41%, Muslim 7%

Area: 226,657 sq mi (587,040 sq km)

Capital: Antananarivo (pop., 1,678,000)

Independence date: June 26, 1960

Government type: republic

Head of state: Pres. Marc Ravalomanana

Head of government: Prime Min. Jacques Sylla

Local divisions: 6 provinces

Monetary unit: ariary

GDP: $14.6 billion (2004 est.)

Per capita GDP: $800

Website: www.madagascar-embassy.ca

Did you know? The island is home to many unique wild animals, including the lemur and chameleon.

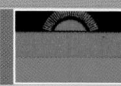

MALAWI
Map page 119

Population: 13,603,181

Principal languages: Chichewa, English (both official); several African languages

Chief religions: Protestant 55%, Roman Catholic 20%, Muslim 20%

Area: 45,745 sq mi (118,480 sq km)

Capital: Lilongwe (pop., 587,000)

Independence date: July 6, 1964

Government type: republic

Head of state and government: Pres. Bingu wa Mutharika

Local divisions: 3 regions, 26 districts

Monetary unit: kwacha

GDP: $7.4 billion (2003 est.)

Per capita GDP: $600

Website: www.malawi.gov.mw

Did you know? Malawi is one of Africa's most densely populated countries.

MALAYSIA
Map page 102

Population: 24,821,286

Principal languages: Malay (official), English, Chinese dialects, Tamil, Telugu, Malayalam, Panjabi, Thai; Iban and Kadazan in the east

Chief religions: Muslim (official) 60%, Buddhist 19%, Christian 9%, Hindu 6%, Confucianist/Taoist 3%

Area: 127,317 sq mi (329,750 sq km)

Capital: Kuala Lumpur (pop., 1,352,000)

Independence date: August 31, 1957

Government type: constitutional monarchy

Head of state: Paramount Ruler Syed Sirajuddin Syed Putra Jamalullail

Head of government: Prime Min. Datuk Seri Abdullah Ahmad Badawi

Local divisions: 13 states, 2 federal territories

Monetary unit: ringgit

GDP: $229.3 billion (2004 est.)

Per capita GDP: $9,700

Website: malaysia.embassyhomepage.com

Did you know? Malaysia's animal life includes elephants, tigers, and orangutans.

MALDIVES
Map page 83

Population: 369,031

Principal languages: Divehi (Sinhala dialect, Arabic script; official), English

Chief religion: Muslim (official; mostly Sunni)

Area: 116 sq mi (300 sq km)

Capital: Male (pop., 83,000)

Independence date: July 26, 1965

Government type: republic

Head of state and government: Pres. Maumoon Abdul Gayoom

Local divisions: 19 atolls and Male

Monetary unit: rufiyaa

GDP: $1.3 billion (2002 est.)

Per capita GDP: $3,900

Website: www.themaldives.com

Did you know? None of the Maldives' more than 1,000 islands is larger than 5 sq mi (13 sq km).

MALI
Map page 119

Population: 11,995,402

Principal languages: French (official), Bambara and other African languages

Chief religions: Muslim 90%, indigenous beliefs 9%

Area: 478,766 sq mi (1,240,000 sq km)

Capital: Bamako (pop., 1,264,000)

Independence date: September 22, 1960

Government type: republic

Head of state: Pres. Amadou Toumani Touré

Head of government: Prime Min. Ousmane Issoufi Maïga

Local divisions: 8 regions, 1 capital district

Monetary unit: CFA franc

GDP: $11.0 billion (2004 est.)

Per capita GDP: $900

Website: www.maliembassy.us

Did you know? Timbuktu was a great learning center in the 15th and 16th centuries.

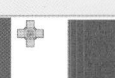

MALTA*
Map page 54

Population: 401,880

Principal languages: Maltese (a Semitic dialect), English (both official)

Chief religion: Roman Catholic (official) 91%

Area: 122 sq mi (316 sq km)

Capital: Valletta (pop., 83,000)

Independence date: September 21, 1964

Government type: parliamentary democracy

Head of state: Pres. Edward Fenech-Adami

Head of government: Prime Min. Lawrence Gonzi

Local divisions: 3 regions comprising 67 local councils

Monetary unit: Maltese lira

GDP: $7.2 billion (2004 est.)

Per capita GDP: $18,200

Website: www.gov.mt/index.asp?l=2

Did you know? Valletta is a 16th-century fortress-city that was built by the Knights of St. John.

MARSHALL ISLANDS
Map page 160

Population: 61,782

Principal languages: English, Marshallese (both official); Malay-Polynesian dialects, Japanese

Chief religion: mostly Protestant

Area: 70 sq mi (181 sq km)

Capital: Majuro (pop., 25,000)

Independence date: October 21, 1986

Government type: republic

Head of state and government: Pres. Kessai Note

Local divisions: 33 municipalities

Monetary unit: U.S. dollar

GDP: $115 million (2001 est.)

Per capita GDP: $1,600

Website: www.rmiembassyus.org

Did you know? Bikini Atoll, where the first hydrogen bomb was tested, is located here.

MAURITANIA
Map page 119

Population: 3,270,065

Principal languages: Hassaniya Arabic, Wolof (both official); Fulani, Pulaar, Soninke (all national); French

Chief religion: predominantly Muslim (official)

Area: 397,955 sq mi (1,030,700 sq km)

Capital: Nouakchott (pop., 600,000)

Independence date: November 28, 1960

Government type: Islamic republic

Head of state: Pres. Sidi Ould Cheikh Abdallahi

Head of government: Prime Min. Zeine Ould Zeidane

Local divisions: 12 regions, 1 capital district

Monetary unit: ouguiya

GDP: $5.5 billion (2004 est.)

Per capita GDP: $1,800

Website: www.mauritania-usa.org

Did you know? About forty percent of Mauritania's land area is covered by sand.

MAURITIUS
Map page 143

Population: 1,250,882

Principal languages: English (official), Creole, French, Hindi, Urdu, Hakka, Bhojpuri

Chief religions: Hindu 52%, Christian 28%, Muslim 17%

Area: 788 sq mi (2,040 sq km)

Capital: Port Louis (pop., 143,000)

Independence date: March 12, 1968

Government type: republic

Head of state: Pres. Anerood Jugnauth

Head of government: Prime Min. Navin Ramgoolam

Local divisions: 9 districts, 3 dependencies

Monetary unit: Mauritian rupee

GDP: $15.7 billion (2004 est.)

Per capita GDP: $12,800

Website: www.gov.mu

Did you know? The dodo became extinct here by 1681, 83 years after the Dutch arrived.

MEXICO
Map page 163

Population: 108,700,891

Principal languages: Spanish (official), Náhuatl, Maya, Zaptec, Otomi, Miztec, other indigenous

Chief religions: Roman Catholic 89%, Protestant 6%

Area: 761,606 sq mi (1,972,550 sq km)

Capital: Mexico (pop., 18,660,000)

Independence date: September 16, 1810

Government type: federal republic

Head of state and government: Pres. Felipe de Jesús Calderón Hinojosa

Local divisions: 31 states, 1 federal district

Monetary unit: new peso

GDP: $1,006 billion (2004 est.)

Per capita GDP: $9,600

Website: www.presidencia.gob.mx/en

Did you know? The Aztec capital of Tenochtitlán was destroyed by the Spanish in 1521.

MICRONESIA
Map page 160

Population: 107,862

Principal languages: English (official), Trukese, Pohnpeian, Yapese, Kosrean, Ulithian, Woleaian, Nukuoro, Kapingamarangi

Chief religions: Roman Catholic 50%, Protestant 47%

Area: 271 sq mi (702 sq km)

Capital: Palikir, on Pohnpei Island (pop., 7,000)

Independence date: November 3, 1986

Government type: republic

Head of state and government: Pres. Joseph J. Urusemal

Local divisions: 4 states

Monetary unit: U.S. dollar

GDP: $277 million (2004 est.)

Per capita GDP: $2,000

Website: www.fsmgov.org/info/index.html

Did you know? Micronesia is made up of more than 600 islands and islets.

MOLDOVA
Map page 78

Population: 4,320,490

Principal languages: Moldovan (official), Russian, Gagauz (a Turkish dialect)

Chief religion: Eastern Orthodox 99%

Area: 13,067 sq mi (33,843 sq km)

Capital: Chisinau (pop., 662,000)

Independence date: August 27, 1991

Government type: republic

Head of state: Pres. Vladimir Voronin

Head of government: Prime Min. Vasile Tarlev

Local divisions: 21 cities and towns, 48 urban settlements, more than 1,600 villages

Monetary unit: leu

GDP: $8.6 billion (2004 est.)

Per capita GDP: $2,600

Website: embassyrm.org/en/index.html

Did you know? Grapes are a major crop, and winemaking is a big industry.

MONACO
Map page 68

Population: 32,671

Principal languages: French (official), English, Italian, Monegasque

Chief religion: Roman Catholic (official) 90%

Area: 0.75 sq mi (1.95 sq km)

Capital: Monaco (pop., 32,000)

Independence date: 1419

Government type: constitutional monarchy

Head of state: Prince Rainier III

Head of government: Min. of State Patrick Leclercq

Local divisions: 4 quarters

Monetary unit: euro

GDP: $870 million (2000 est.)

Per capita GDP: $27,000

Website: www.monaco-consulate.com

Did you know? This rich but tiny country is the most densely populated in the world.

MONGOLIA
Map page 90

Population: 2,874,127

Principal languages: Khalkha Mongol, Turkic, Russian

Chief religion: Tibetan Buddhist Lamaism 96%

Area: 604,250 sq mi (1,565,000 sq km)

Capital: Ulaanbaatar (pop., 812,000)

Independence date: July 11, 1921

Government type: republic

Head of state: Pres. Nambaryn Enkhbayar

Head of government: Prime Min. Miyeegombo Enkhbold

Local divisions: 18 provinces, 3 municipalities

Monetary unit: tugrik

GDP: $5.3 billion (2004 est.)

Per capita GDP: $1,900

Website: www.mongolianembassy.us

Did you know? Rugged Mongolia is the world's most sparsely populated country.

MONTENEGRO
Map page 56

Population: 684,736

Principal language: Serbian of the Ijekavian dialect (official), Albanian

Chief religions: Orthodox 74%, Muslim 18%, Roman Catholic 2%

Area: 5,333 sq mi (13,812 sq km)

Capital: Podgorica (pop., 179,500)

Independence date: June 3, 2006

Government type: republic

Head of state: Pres. Filip Vujanovic

Head of government: Prime Min. Milo Dukanovic

Local divisions: 21 municipalities

Monetary unit: euro

GDP: $1.91 billion (2005 est.)

Per capita GDP: $3,100

Website: www.gom.cg.yu/eng

Did you know? Recently created Montenegro was once a part of Serbia.

MOROCCO
Map page 128

Population: 33,757,175

Principal languages: Arabic (official), Berber dialects, French, Spanish, English

Chief religion: Muslim (official) 99%

Area: 172,414 sq mi (446,550 sq km)

Capital: Rabat (pop., 1,759,000)

Independence date: March 2, 1956

Government type: constitutional monarchy

Head of state: King Mohammed VI

Head of government: Prime Min. Driss Jettou

Local divisions: 16 regions

Monetary unit: dirham

GDP: $134.6 billion (2004 est.)

Per capita GDP: $4,200

Website: www.mincom.gov.ma/english/e_page.html

Did you know? Morocco has the broadest plains and highest mountains in North Africa.

MOZAMBIQUE
Map page 143

Population: 20,905,585

Principal languages: Portuguese (official) and dialects, English

Chief religions: indigenous beliefs 50%, Christian 30%, Muslim 20%

Area: 309,496 sq mi (801,590 sq km)

Capital: Maputo (pop., 1,221,000)

Independence date: June 25, 1975

Government type: republic

Head of state: Pres. Armando Guebuza

Head of government: Prime Min. Pascoal Mocumbi

Local divisions: 10 provinces

Monetary unit: metical

GDP: $23.4 billion (2004 est.)

Per capita GDP: $1,200

Website: www.embamoc-usa.org

Did you know? Decades of civil war have left over a million land mines buried here.

MYANMAR (FORMERLY BURMA)
Map page 105

Population: 47,373,958

Principal languages: Burmese (official); many ethnic minority languages

Chief religions: Buddhist 89%, Christian 4%, Muslim 4%, animist 1%

Area: 261,970 sq mi (678,500 sq km)

Capitals: Yangon (Rangoon) (pop., 3,874,000), Nay Pyi Taw (administrative)

Independence date: January 4, 1948

Government type: military

Head of state : Gen. Than Shwe

Head of government: Lt. Gen. Soe Win

Local divisions: 7 states, 7 divisions

Monetary unit: kyat

GDP: $74.3 billion (2004 est.)

Per capita GDP: $1,700

Website: www.myanmar.com

Did you know? More than 100 native languages are spoken in Myanmar.

NAMIBIA
Map page 119

Population: 2,055,080

Principal languages: English (official), Afrikaans, German, Oshivambo, Herero, Nama

Chief religions: Lutheran 50%, other Christian 30%, indigenous beliefs 10-20%

Area: 318,696 sq mi (825,418 sq km)

Capital: Windhoek (pop., 237,000)

Independence date: March 21, 1990

Government type: republic

Head of state: Pres. Hifikepunye Pohamba

Head of government: Prime Min. Nahas Angula

Local divisions: 13 regions

Monetary unit: Namibia dollar (NAD)

GDP: $14.8 billion (2004 est.)

Per capita GDP: $7,300

Website: www.namibianembassyusa.org

Did you know? Windhoek is situated on a plateau more than a mile above sea level.

NAURU
Map page 160

Population: 13,528

Principal languages: Nauruan (official), English

Chief religions: Protestant 66%, Roman Catholic 33%

Area: 8 sq mi (21 sq km)

Capital: offices in Yaren District

Independence date: January 31, 1968

Government type: republic

Head of state and government: Pres. Ludwig Scotty

Local divisions: 14 districts

Monetary unit: Australian dollar

GDP: $60 million (2001 est.)

Per capita GDP: $5,000

Website: www.un.int/nauru

Did you know? Phosphates, from millions of years of bird droppings, are nearly used up.

NEPAL
Map page 108

Population: 28,901,790

Principal languages: Nepali (official); about 30 dialects and 12 other languages

Chief religions: Hindu (official) 86%, Buddhist 8%, Muslim 4%

Area: 54,363 sq mi (140,800 sq km)

Capital: Kathmandu (pop., 741,000)

Independence date: 1768

Government type: in transition

Head of state: King Gyanendra Bir Bikram Shah Dev

Head of government: Prime Min. Girija Prasad Koirala

Local divisions: 5 regions subdivided into 14 zones

Monetary unit: rupee

GDP: $39.5 billion (2004 est.)

Per capita GDP: $1,500

Website: www.nepalembassyusa.org

Did you know? Mt. Everest, the world's highest mountain, is partly in Nepal.

NETHERLANDS*
Map page 58

Population: 16,570,613

Principal languages: Dutch (official), Frisian, Flemish

Chief religions: Roman Catholic 31%, Protestant 21%, Muslim 4%

Area: 16,033 sq mi (41,526 sq km)

Capital: Amsterdam (pop., 1,145,000); seat of government, The Hague (pop., 741,000)

Independence date: 1579

Government type: parliamentary democracy under a constitutional monarch

Head of state: Queen Beatrix

Head of government: Prime Min. Jan Peter Balkenende

Local divisions: 12 provinces

Monetary unit: euro

GDP: $481.1 billion (2004 est.)

Per capita GDP: $29,500

Website: www.netherlands-embassy.org

Did you know? Much of the nation is below sea level, and is protected from flooding by dikes.

NEW ZEALAND
Map page 191

Population: 4,115,771

Principal languages: English, Maori (both official)

Chief religions: Protestant 52%, Roman Catholic 15%

Area: 103,738 sq mi (268,680 sq km)

Capital: Wellington (pop., 343,000)

Independence date: September 26, 1907

Government type: parliamentary democracy

Head of state: Queen Elizabeth II, represented by Gov.-Gen. Dame Anand Satyanand (pending)

Head of government: Prime Min. Helen Clark

Local divisions: 93 counties, 9 districts, 3 town districts

Monetary unit: New Zealand dollar

GDP: $92.5 billion (2004 est.)

Per capita GDP: $23,200

Website: www.govt.nz

Did you know? In 1893 New Zealand became the first country to grant women full voting rights.

NICARAGUA
Map page 207

Population: 5,675,356

Principal languages: Spanish (official), indigenous languages, English on Atlantic coast

Chief religion: Roman Catholic 85%

Area: 49,998 sq mi (129,494 sq km)

Capital: Managua (pop., 1,098,000)

Independence date: September 15, 1821

Government type: republic

Head of state and government: Pres. José Daniel Ortega Saavedra

Local divisions: 15 departments, 2 autonomous regions

Monetary unit: gold cordoba

GDP: $12.3 billion (2004 est.)

Per capita GDP: $2,300

Website: www.consuladodenicaragua.com

Did you know? The eastern shore is called Costa de Mosquitos (Mosquito Coast).

NIGER
Map page 119

Population: 12,894,865

Principal languages: French (official); Hausa, Djerma, Fulani (all national)

Chief religion: Muslim 80%

Area: 489,191 sq mi (1,267,000 sq km)

Capital: Niamey (pop., 890,000)

Independence date: August 3, 1960

Government type: republic

Head of state: Pres. Tandja Mamadou

Head of government: Prime Min. Hama Amadou

Local divisions: 7 departments, 1 capital district

Monetary unit: CFA franc

GDP: $9.7 billion (2003 est.)

Per capita GDP: $900

Website: www.nigerembassyusa.org

Did you know? Niger was part of noted ancient and medieval African empires.

NIGERIA
Map page 119

Population: 135,031,164

Principal languages: English (official), Hausa, Yoruba, Igbo (Ibo), Fulani

Chief religions: Muslim 50%, Christian 40%, indigenous beliefs 10%

Area: 356,669 sq mi (923,768 sq km)

Capital: Abuja (pop., 452,000)

Independence date: October 1, 1960

Government type: republic

Head of state and government: Pres. Umaru Musa Yar'Adua

Local divisions: 36 states, 1 capital territory

Monetary unit: naira

GDP: $125.7 billion (2004 est.)

Per capita GDP: $900

Website: www.nigeriaembassyusa.org

Did you know? Nigeria is the biggest oil-producing country in Africa.

NORWAY
Map page 44

Population: 4,627,926

Principal languages: Norwegian (official), Sami, Finnish

Chief religion: Evangelical Lutheran (official) 86%

Area: 125,182 sq mi (324,220 sq km)

Capital: Oslo (pop., 795,000)

Independence date: June 7, 1905

Government type: hereditary constitutional monarchy

Head of state: King Harald V

Head of government: Prime Min. Jens Stoltenberg

Local divisions: 19 provinces

Monetary unit: krone

GDP: $183.0 billion (2004 est.)

Per capita GDP: $40,000

Website: www.norway.org

Did you know? Norway has many steep-sided narrow inlets, called fjords, in its coastline.

OMAN
Map page 113

Population: 3,204,897

Principal languages: Arabic (official), English, Baluchi, Urdu, Indian dialects

Chief religion: Muslim 75% (official; mostly Ibadhi)

Area: 82,031 sq mi (212,460 sq km)

Capital: Muscat (pop., 638,000)

Independence date: 1650

Government type: absolute monarchy

Head of state and government: Sultan Qabus bin Said

Local divisions: 6 regions and 2 governorates

Monetary unit: rial Omani

GDP: $38.1 billion (2004 est.)

Per capita GDP: $13,100

Website: www.omanet.om/english/home.asp

Did you know? Oman has about 13 males for every 10 females.

PAKISTAN
Map page 113

Population: 169,270,617

Principal languages: English, Urdu (both official); Punjabi, Sindhi, Siraiki, Pashtu, Balochi, Hindko, Brahui, Burushaski

Chief religions: Muslim 97% (official; Sunni 77%, Shi'a 20%)

Area: 310,403 sq mi (803,940 sq km)

Capital: Islamabad (pop., 698,000)

Independence date: August 14, 1947

Government type: republic with strong military influence

Head of state: Pres. Pervez Musharraf

Head of government: Prime Min. Shaukat Aziz

Local divisions: 4 provinces and 1 capital territory, plus federally administered tribal areas

Monetary unit: rupee

GDP: $347.3 billion (2004 est.)

Per capita GDP: $2,200

Website: www.embassyofpakistan.org

Did you know? Pakistan is mostly Muslim; its neighbor India is mostly Hindu.

PALAU
Map page 160

Population: 20,842

Principal languages: English (official); Palauan, Sonsorolese, Tobi, Angaur, Japanese (all official in certain states)

Chief religions: Roman Catholic 49%, Modekngei 30%

Area: 177 sq mi (458 sq km)

Capital: Koror (pop., 14,000)

Independence date: October 1, 1994

Government type: republic

Head of state and government: Pres. Tommy Esang Remengesau, Jr.

Local divisions: 18 states

Monetary unit: U.S. dollar

GDP: $174 million (2001 est.)

Per capita GDP: $9,000

Website: www.visit-palau.com

Did you know? The islands of Palau are old coral reefs that have risen above the sea.

PANAMA
Map page 207

Population: 3,242,173

Principal languages: Spanish (official), English

Chief religions: Roman Catholic 85%, Protestant 15%

Area: 30,193 sq mi (78,200 sq km)

Capital: Panamá (pop., 930,000)

Independence date: November 3, 1903

Government type: republic

Head of state and government: Pres. Martín Torrijos Espino

Local divisions: 9 provinces, 3 territories

Monetary unit: balboa

GDP: $20.6 billion (2004 est.)

Per capita GDP: $6,900

Website: www.embassyofpanama.org

Did you know? Adventurer Richard Halliburton swam the Panama Canal in 1928, paying a toll of 36 cents.

PAPUA NEW GUINEA
Map page 160

Population: 5,795,887

Principal languages: English (official), pidgin English, Motu; 715 indigenous languages

Chief religions: indigenous beliefs 34%, Roman Catholic 22%, Protestant 44%

Area: 178,703 sq mi (462,840 sq km)

Capital: Port Moresby (pop., 275,000)

Independence date: September 16, 1975

Government type: parliamentary democracy

Head of state: Queen Elizabeth II, represented by Gov.-Gen. Sir Paulias Matane

Head of government: Prime Min. Sir Michael Somare

Local divisions: 20 provinces

Monetary unit: kina

GDP: $12.0 billion (2004 est.)

Per capita GDP: $2,200

Website: www.pngembassy.org

Did you know? Wild animals in Papua New Guinea include the tree kangaroo, wallaby, wild pig, and dingo.

PARAGUAY
Map page 224

Population: 6,667,147

Principal languages: Spanish, Guaraní (both official)

Chief religion: Roman Catholic 90%

Area: 157,047 sq mi (406,750 sq km)

Capital: Asunción (pop., 1,639,000)

Independence date: May 14, 1811

Government type: republic

Head of state and government: Pres. Nicanor Duarte Frutos

Local divisions: 18 departments and capital city

Monetary unit: guarani

GDP: $29.9 billion (2004 est.)

Per capita GDP: $4,800

Website: www.embaparusa.gov.py/index_english.html

Did you know? Itaipú dam, bordering Brazil, is the world's largest hydroelectric plant.

PERU
Map page 220

Population: 28,674,757

Principal languages: Spanish, Quechua (both official); Aymara

Chief religion: Roman Catholic (official) 90%

Area: 496,226 sq mi (1,285,220 sq km)

Capital: Lima (pop., 7,899,000)

Independence date: July 28, 1821

Government type: republic

Head of state: Pres. Alan García Pérez

Head of government: Prime Min. Jorge Alfonso Alejandro Del Castillo Gálvez

Local divisions: 12 regions containing 24 departments, and 1 constitutional province

Monetary unit: new sol

GDP: $155.3 billion (2004 est.)

Per capita GDP: $5,600

Website: www.peru.info/perueng.asp

Did you know? The Inca empire had its base in Peru's mountains.

PHILIPPINES
Map page 132

Population: 91,077,287

Principal languages: Filipino, English (both official); many dialects

Chief religions: Roman Catholic 83%, Protestant 9%, Muslim 5%

Area: 115,831 sq mi (300,000 sq km)

Capital: Manila (pop., 10,352,000)

Independence date: July 4, 1946

Government type: republic

Head of state and government: Pres. Gloria Macapagal Arroyo

Local divisions: 72 provinces, 61 chartered cities

Monetary unit: peso

GDP: $430.6 billion (2004 est.)

Per capita GDP: $5,000

Website: www.philippineembassy-usa.org

Did you know? Most Filipinos live on the 11 largest of the country's 7,100 islands.

POLAND*
Map page 49

Population: 38,518,241

Principal languages: Polish (official), Ukrainian, German

Chief religion: Roman Catholic 95%

Area: 120,728 sq mi (312,685 sq km)

Capital: Warsaw (pop., 2,200,000)

Independence date: November 11, 1918

Government type: republic

Head of state: Pres. Lech Kaczynski

Head of government: Prime Min. Kazimierz Marcinkiewicz

Local divisions: 16 provinces

Monetary unit: zloty

GDP: $463.0 billion (2004 est.)

Per capita GDP: $12,000

Website: www.poland.pl

Did you know? Germany invaded Poland on September 1, 1939, starting World War II.

PORTUGAL*
Map page 52

Population: 10,642,836

Principal language: Portuguese (official)

Chief religion: Roman Catholic 94%

Area: 35,672 sq mi (92,391 sq km)

Capital: Lisbon (pop., 1,962,000)

Independence date: 1143

Government type: republic

Head of state: Pres. Aníbal Cavaco Silva

Head of government: Prime Min. José Sócrates Carvalho Pinto de Sousa

Local divisions: 18 districts, 2 autonomous regions

Monetary unit: euro

GDP: $188.7 billion (2003 est.)

Per capita GDP: $17,900

Website: www.portugal.gov.pt/Portal/EN

Did you know? In 1497, Portuguese captain Vasco da Gama was the first to sail around the tip of Africa and into the Indian Ocean.

QATAR
Map page 112

Population: 907,229

Principal languages: Arabic (official), English

Chief religion: Muslim (official) 95%

Area: 4,416 sq mi (11,437 sq km)

Capital: Doha (pop., 286,000)

Independence date: September 3, 1971

Government type: traditional monarchy

Head of state: Emir Hamad bin Khalifa ath-Thani

Head of government: Prime Min. Abdullah bin Khalifa ath-Thani

Local divisions: 9 municipalities

Monetary unit: riyal

GDP: $19.5 billion (2004 est.)

Per capita GDP: $23,200

Website: www.qatarembassy.net

Did you know? Foreign workers outnumber the citizens of Qatar by more than three to one.

ROMANIA
Map page 57

Population: 22,276,056

Principal languages: Romanian (official), Hungarian, German, Romani

Chief religions: Romanian Orthodox 70%, Roman Catholic 6%, Protestant 6%

Area: 91,699 sq mi (237,500 sq km)

Capital: Bucharest (pop., 1,853,000)

Independence date: May 9, 1877

Government type: republic

Head of state: Pres. Traian Basescu

Head of government: Prime Min. Calin Constantin Anton Popescu-Tariceanu

Local divisions: 40 counties, 1 municipality

Monetary unit: lei

GDP: $171.5 billion (2004 est.)

Per capita GDP: $7,700

Website: www.roembus.org

Did you know? The real Dracula, Prince Vlad, lived in Romania in the 1400s.

RUSSIA
Map page 80

Population: 141,377,752

Principal languages: Russian (official), many others

Chief religions: Russian Orthodox, Muslim

Area: 6,592,769 sq mi (17,075,200 sq km)

Capital: Moscow (pop., 10,469,000)

Independence date: August 24, 1991

Government type: federal republic

Head of state: Pres. Vladimir Putin

Head of government: Prime Min. Mikhail Fradkov

Local divisions: 21 republics, 6 regions (kraya), 10 autonomous territories (okruga), 49 oblasts, 1 autonomous oblast, and 2 federal cities

Monetary unit: ruble

GDP: $1,408 billion (2004 est.)

Per capita GDP: $9,800

Website: www.russianembassy.org

Did you know? Record lows of –90° F have been recorded in Siberia.

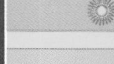

RWANDA
Map page 139

Population: 9,907,509

Principal languages: Kinyarwanda, French, English (all official); Swahili

Chief religions: Roman Catholic 57%, Protestant 26%, Adventist 11%, Muslim 5%

Area: 10,169 sq mi (26,338 sq km)

Capital: Kigali (pop., 656,000)

Independence date: July 1, 1962

Government type: republic

Head of state: Pres. Paul Kagame

Head of government: Prime Min. Bernard Makuza

Local divisions: 12 prefectures subdivided into 155 communes

Monetary unit: franc

GDP: $10.4 billion (2004 est.)

Per capita GDP: $1,300

Website: www.gov.rw

Did you know? The source of the Nile River has been located in Rwanda.

SAINT KITTS AND NEVIS
Map page 203

Population: 39,349

Principal language: English (official)

Chief religions: Anglican, other Protestant, Roman Catholic

Area: 101 sq mi (261 sq km)

Capital: Basseterre (pop., 13,000)

Independence date: September 19, 1983

Government type: constitutional monarchy

Head of state: Queen Elizabeth II, represented by Gov.-Gen. Sir Cuthbert M. Sebastian

Head of government: Prime Min. Denzil Llewellyn Douglas

Local divisions: 14 parishes

Monetary unit: East Caribbean dollar

GDP: $339 million (2002 est.)

Per capita GDP: $8,800

Website: www.stkitts-nevis.net

Did you know? St. Kitts was the first West Indies island settled by the British in 1623.

SAINT LUCIA
Map page 203

Population: 170,649

Principal languages: English (official), French patois

Chief religions: Roman Catholic 90%, Protestant 10%

Area: 238 sq mi (616 sq km)

Capital: Castries (pop., 14,000)

Independence date: February 22, 1979

Government type: parliamentary democracy

Head of state: Queen Elizabeth II, represented by

Gov.-Gen. Calliopa Pearlette Louisy

Head of government: Prime Min. Kenny Anthony

Local divisions: 11 quarters

Monetary unit: East Caribbean dollar

GDP: $866 million (2002 est.)

Per capita GDP: $5,400

Website: www.stlucia.gov.lc

Did you know? The island switched hands between the British and French 14 times.

SAINT VINCENT AND THE GRENADINES
Map page 203

Population: 118,149

Principal languages: English (official), French patois

Chief religions: Anglican 47%, Methodist 28%, Roman Catholic 13%

Area: 150 sq mi (389 sq km)

Capital: Kingstown (pop., 29,000)

Independence date: October 27, 1979

Government type: constitutional monarchy

Head of state: Queen Elizabeth II, represented by Gov.-Gen. Sir Frederick Nathaniel Ballantyne

Head of government: Prime Min. Ralph Gonsalves

Local divisions: 6 parishes

Monetary unit: East Caribbean dollar

GDP: $342 million (2002 est.)

Per capita GDP: $2,900

Website: www.svgtourism.com

Did you know? Black Caribs living here are descended from slaves and native Indians.

SAMOA (FORMERLY WESTERN SAMOA)
Map page 161

Population: 176,615

Principal languages: Samoan, English (both official)

Chief religion: Christian 99.7%

Area: 1,137 sq mi (2,944 sq km)

Capital: Apia (pop., 40,000)

Independence date: January 1, 1962

Government type: constitutional monarchy

Head of state: Malietoa Tanumafili II

Head of government: Prime Min. Tuilaepa Sailele Malielegaoi

Local divisions: 11 districts

Monetary unit: tala

GDP: $1.0 billion (2002 est.)

Per capita GDP: $5,600

Website: www.visitsamoa.ws/

Did you know? Most Samoans live in small seashore villages of 100–500 people.

SAN MARINO
Map page 69

Population: 29,615

Principal language: Italian (official)

Chief religion: predominantly Roman Catholic

Area: 24 sq mi (61 sq km)

Capital: San Marino (pop., 5,000)

Independence date: September 3, 301

Government type: republic

Heads of state and government: two co-regents appointed every 6 months

Local divisions: 9 castelli

Monetary unit: euro

GDP: $940 million (2001 est.)

Per capita GDP: $34,600

Website: www.visitsanmarino.com/defaulte.asp

Did you know? San Marino is the 5th-smallest country in the world and claims to be Europe's oldest country, founded in 301 A.D.

SÃO TOMÉ AND PRÍNCIPE
Map page 138

Population: 199,579

Principal languages: Portuguese (official), Creole, Fang

Chief religions: predominantly Roman Catholic

Area: 386 sq mi (1,001 sq km)

Capital: São Tomé (pop., 54,000)

Independence date: July 12, 1975

Government type: republic

Head of state: Pres. Fradique Melo de Menezes

Head of government: Prime Min. Tomé Vera Cruz

Local divisions: 2 provinces

Monetary unit: dobra

GDP: $214 million (2003 est.)

Per capita GDP: $1,200

Website: www.saotome.st

Did you know? Until 1975 Portugal ruled these islands for nearly 300 years.

SAUDI ARABIA
Map page 112

Population: 27,601,038

Principal language: Arabic (official)

Chief religion: Muslim (official)

Area: 756,985 sq mi (1,960,582 sq km)

Capital: Riyadh (pop., 5,126,000)

Independence date: September 23, 1932

Government type: constitutional monarchy with strong Islamic influence

Head of state and government: King Abdullah bin Abdul Aziz

Local divisions: 13 provinces

Monetary unit: riyal

GDP: $310.2 billion (2004 est.)

Per capita GDP: $12,000

Website: www.saudiembassy.net

Did you know? Mecca, the birthplace of Muhammad, is the holiest city of Islam.

SENEGAL
Map page 132

Population: 12,521,851

Principal languages: French (official), Wolof,

Pulaar, Jola, Mandinka

Chief religions: Muslim 94%, Christian 5%

Area: 75,749 sq mi (196,190 sq km)

Capital: Dakar (pop., 2,167,000)

Independence date: April 4, 1960

Government type: republic

Head of state: Pres. Abdoulaye Wade

Head of government: Prime Min. Macky Sall

Local divisions: 10 regions

Monetary unit: CFA franc

GDP: $18.4 billion (2004 est.)

Per capita GDP: $1,700

Website: www.senegalembassy.co.uk

Did you know? Senegal is among the world's largest producers of peanuts.

SERBIA
Map page 56

Population: 10,150,265

Principal languages: Serbian (official), Albanian

Chief religions: Orthodox 64%, Muslim 19%, Roman Catholic 4%

Area: 34,185 sq mi (88,538 sq km)

Capital: Belgrade (pop., 1,118,000)

Independence date: February 4, 2003

Government type: federal republic

Head of state and government: Pres. Svetozar Marović

Local divisions: 2 autonomous provinces

Monetary unit: new dinar

GDP: $26.3 billion (2004 est.)

Per capita GDP: $2,400

Website: www.srbija.sr.gov.yu/?change_lang=en

Did you know? Ruins of the Roman town of Singidunum can still be seen in Belgrade.

SEYCHELLES
Map page 27

Population: 81,895

Principal languages: English, French, Creole (all official)

Chief religions: Roman Catholic 87%, Anglican 7%

Area: 176 sq mi (455 sq km)

Capital: Victoria (pop., 25,000)

Independence date: June 29, 1976

Government type: republic

Head of state and government: Pres. James Michel

Local divisions: 23 districts

Monetary unit: rupee

GDP: $626 million (2002 est.)

Per capita GDP: $7,800

Website: www.seychelles.com

Did you know? This group of about 115 islands is the smallest country in Africa.

*Member of the European Union

SIERRA LEONE
Map page 132

Population: 6,144,562

Principal languages: English, Mende, Temne, Krio

Chief religions: Muslim 60%, indigenous beliefs 30%, Christian 10%

Area: 27,699 sq mi (71,740 sq km)

Capital: Freetown (pop., 921,000)

Independence date: April 27, 1961

Government type: republic

Head of state and government: Pres. Ahmad Tejan Kabbah

Local divisions: 3 provinces, 1 area

Monetary unit: leone

GDP: $3.1 billion (2003 est.)

Per capita GDP: $500

Website: www.embassyofsierraleone.org

Did you know? Portuguese explorer Pedro da Cintra named the area Serra Layoa, "Lion Mountains," in 1460.

SINGAPORE
Map page 101

Population: 4,553,009

Principal languages: Chinese, Malay, Tamil, English (all official)

Chief religions: Buddhist, Muslim, Christian, Taoist, Hindu

Area: 267 sq mi (693 sq km)

Capital: Singapore (pop., 4,253,000)

Independence date: August 9, 1965

Government type: republic

Head of state: Pres. S. R. Nathan

Head of government: Prime Min. Lee Hsien Loong

Monetary unit: Singapore dollar

GDP: $120.9 billion (2004 est.)

Per capita GDP: $27,800

Website: www.mfa.gov.sg/washington

Did you know? Singapore has one of the highest standards of living in Asia.

SLOVAKIA*
Map page 49

Population: 5,447,502

Principal languages: Slovak (official), Hungarian

Chief religions: Roman Catholic 60%, Protestant 8%, Orthodox 4%

Area: 18,859 sq mi (48,845 sq km)

Capital: Bratislava (pop., 425,000)

Independence date: January 1, 1993

Government type: republic

Head of state: Pres. Ivan Gašparovič

Head of government: Prime Min. Mikulás Dzurinda

Local divisions: 8 departments

Monetary unit: koruna

GDP: $78.9 billion (2004 est.)

Per capita GDP: $14,500

Website: www.slovakembassy-us.org

Did you know? Czechoslovakia split into Slovakia and the Czech Republic in 1993.

SLOVENIA*
Map page 56

Population: 2,009,245

Principal languages: Slovenian (official), Serbo-Croatian

Chief religion: Roman Catholic 71%

Area: 7,827 sq mi (20,273 sq km)

Capital: Ljubljana (pop., 256,000)

Independence date: June 25, 1991

Government type: republic

Head of state: Pres. Janez Drnovsek

Head of government: Prime Min. Janez Jansa

Local divisions: 136 municipalities, 11 urban municipalities

Monetary unit: tolar

GDP: $39.4 billion (2004 est.)

Per capita GDP: $19,600

Website: www.slovenia.info/intro/index.asp

Did you know? Slovenia is the most prosperous of the former Yugoslav republics.

SOLOMON ISLANDS
Map page 160

Population: 566,842

Principal languages: English (official), Melanesian pidgin, and 120 indigenous languages

Chief religions: Anglican 45%, Roman Catholic 18%, other Christian 35%

Area: 10,985 sq mi (28,450 sq km)

Capital: Honiara (pop., 56,000)

Independence date: July 7, 1978

Government type: in transition

Head of state: Queen Elizabeth II, represented by Gov.-Gen. Nathaniel Waena

Head of government: Prime Min. Manasseh Sogavare

Local divisions: 9 provinces and Honiara

Monetary unit: Solomon Islands dollar (SBD)

GDP: $800 million (2002 est.)

Per capita GDP: $1,700

Website: www.usvpp-solomonislands.org

Did you know? The island of Guadalcanal was the site of a key battle in World War II.

SOMALIA
Map page 119

Population: 9,118,773

Principal languages: Somali, Arabic (both official); Italian, English

Chief religion: Sunni Muslim (official)

Area: 246,201 sq mi (637,657 sq km)

Capital: Mogadishu (pop., 1,175,000)

Independence date: July 1, 1960

Government type: in transition

Head of state: Pres. Abdullahi Yusuf Ahmed

Head of government: Prime Min. Muhammad Abdi

Local divisions: 18 regions

Monetary unit: shilling

GDP: $4.6 billion (2004 est.)

Per capita GDP: $600

Website: state.gov/r/pa/ei/bgn/2863.htm

Did you know? Frankincense and myrrh are the major forestry products of Somalia.

SOUTH AFRICA
Map page 119

Population: 43,997,828

Principal languages: Afrikaans, English, Ndebele, Pedi, Sotho, Swazi, Tsonga, Tswana, Venda, Xhosa, Zulu (all official)

Chief religions: Christian 68%, indigenous beliefs and animist 29%

Area: 471,010 sq mi (1,219,912 sq km)

Capitals: Pretoria (administrative) (pop., 1,209,000), Cape Town (legislative) (pop., 2,967,000), Bloemfontein (judicial) (pop., 381,000)

Independence date: May 31, 1910

Government type: republic

Head of state and government: Pres. Thabo Mvuyelwa Mbeki

Local divisions: 9 provinces

Monetary unit: rand

GDP: $491.4 billion (2004 est.)

Per capita GDP: $11,100

Website: www.gov.za

Did you know? South Africa mines more gold than any other country in the world.

SPAIN*
Map page 52

Population: 40,448,191

Principal languages: Castilian Spanish, Catalan, Galician

Chief religion: Roman Catholic 94%

Area: 194,897 sq mi (504,782 sq km)

Capital: Madrid (pop., 5,103,000)

Independence date: 1492

Government type: constitutional monarchy

Head of state: King Juan Carlos I de Borbon y Borbon

Head of government: Prime Min. José Luis Rodríguez Zapatero

Local divisions: 17 autonomous communities

Monetary unit: euro

GDP: $937.6 billion (2004 est.)

Per capita GDP: $23,300

Website: www.spain.info/ TourSpain/ Informacion+practica

Did you know? Spanish rulers grew rich in the 1500s from New World gold and silver.

SRI LANKA
Map page 104

Population: 20,926,315

Principal languages: Sinhala, Tamil (both official); English

Chief religions: Buddhist 70%, Hindu 15%, Christian 8%, Muslim 7%

Area: 25,332 sq mi (65,610 sq km)

Capitals: Colombo (administrative) (pop., 648,000), Sri Jayawardenepura Kotte (legislative) (pop., 117,000)

Independence date: February 4, 1948

Government type: republic

Head of state: Pres. Mahinda Rajapaksa

Head of government: Prime Min. Ratnasiri Wickremanayake

Local divisions: 9 provinces

Monetary unit: rupee

GDP: $80.6 billion (2004 est.)

Per capita GDP: $4,000

Website: www.slembassyusa.org

Did you know? In 1960 Sri Lanka elected the world's first female prime minister.

SUDAN
Map page 119

Population: 42,292,929

Principal languages: Arabic (official), Nubian, Ta Bedawie; Nilotic, Sudanic dialects; English

Chief religions: Sunni Muslim 70%, indigenous beliefs 25%, Christian 5%

Area: 967,498 sq mi (2,505,810 sq km)

Capital: Khartoum (pop., 4,286,000)

Independence date: January 1, 1956

Government type: republic with strong military influence

Head of state and government: Pres. Gen. Omar Hassan Ahmad Al-Bashir

Local divisions: 26 states

Monetary unit: dinar (SDD)

GDP: $76.2 billion (2004 est.)

Per capita GDP: $1,900

Website: www.sudanembassy.org

Did you know? Sudan is the largest country in Africa in total area.

SURINAME
Map page 218

Population: 470,784

Principal languages: Dutch (official), English, Sranang Tongo (an English Creole), Hindustani, Javanese

Chief religions: Hindu 27%, Protestant 25%, Roman Catholic 23%, Muslim 20%

Area: 63,039 sq mi (163,270 sq km)

Capital: Paramaribo (pop., 253,000)

Independence date: November 25, 1975

Government type: republic

Head of state and government: Pres. Runaldo Ronald Venetiaan

Local divisions: 10 districts

Monetary unit: guilder

GDP: $1.9 billion (2004 est.)

Per capita GDP: $4,300

Website: www.surinameembassy.org

Did you know? In 1677, Britain "traded" Suriname to the Dutch for New York City.

*Member of the European Union

SWAZILAND
Map page 143

Population: 1,133,066

Principal languages: English, siSwati (both official)

Chief religions: Christian 60%, Muslim 10%, indigenous and other 30%

Area: 6,704 sq mi (17,363 sq km)

Capitals: Mbabane (administrative) (pop., 70,000), Lobamba (legislative) (pop., 5,000)

Independence date: September 6, 1968

Government type: constitutional monarchy

Head of state: King Mswati III

Head of government: Prime Min. Absalom Themba Dlamini

Local divisions: 4 districts

Monetary unit: lilangeni

GDP: $6.0 billion (2004 est.)

Per capita GDP: $5,100

Website: www.gov.sz

Did you know? Foreign people and companies own much of the country's land.

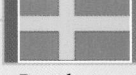

SWEDEN*
Map page 44

Population: 9,031,088

Principal languages: Swedish (official), Sami, Finnish

Chief religion: Lutheran 87%

Area: 173,732 sq mi (449,964 sq km)

Capital: Stockholm (pop., 1,697,000)

Independence date: June 6, 1523

Government type: constitutional monarchy

Head of state: King Carl XVI Gustaf

Head of government: Prime Min. Goran Persson

Local divisions: 21 counties

Monetary unit: krona

GDP: $255.4 billion (2004 est.)

Per capita GDP: $28,400

Website: www.sweden.se

Did you know? One of the world's oldest parliaments, the Riksdag dates back to 1435.

SWITZERLAND
Map page 66

Population: 7,554,661

Principal languages: German, French, Italian (all official); Romansch (semi-official)

Chief religions: Roman Catholic 46%, Protestant 40%

Area: 15,942 sq mi (41,290 sq km)

Capitals: Bern (pop., 320,000)

Independence date: August 1, 1291

Government type: federal republic

Head of state and government: The president is elected by the Federal Assembly to a nonrenewable 1-year term

Local divisions: 20 full and 6 half cantons

Monetary unit: franc

GDP: $251.9 billion (2003 est.)

Per capita GDP: $33,800

Website: www.swissemb.org

Did you know? Though home to the United Nations European headquarters, Switzerland did not join the UN until 2002.

SYRIA
Map page 114

Population: 19,314,747

Principal languages: Arabic (official), Kurdish, Armenian

Chief religions: Sunni Muslim 74%, other Muslims 16%, Christian 10%

Area: 71,498 sq mi (185,180 sq km)

Capital: Damascus (pop., 2,228,000)

Independence date: April 17, 1946

Government type: republic (under military regime)

Head of state: Pres. Bashar al-Assad

Head of government: Prime Min. Muhammad Naji al-Otari

Local divisions: 14 provinces

Monetary unit: pound

GDP: $60.4 billion (2004 est.)

Per capita GDP: $3,400

Website: www.syrianembassy.us

Did you know? Damascus may be the world's oldest continuously occupied city.

TAIWAN
Map page 99

Population: 23,174,294

Principal languages: Mandarin Chinese (official), Taiwanese (Min), Hakka dialects

Chief religions: Buddhist, Confucian, and Taoist 93%; Christian 5%

Area: 13,892 sq mi (35,980 sq km)

Capital: Taipei (pop., 2,624,000)

Independence date: 1949

Government type: democracy

Head of state: Pres. Chen Shui-bian

Head of government: Prime Min. Su Tseng-chang

Local divisions: 16 counties, 5 municipalities, 2 special municipalities (Taipei, Kaohsiung)

Monetary unit: Taiwan dollar (TWD)

GDP: $576.2 billion (2004 est.)

Per capita GDP: $25,300

Website: www.gio.gov.tw

Did you know? People fleeing Communist mainland China founded this "Republic of China" in 1949.

TAJIKISTAN
Map page 80

Population: 7,076,598

Principal languages: Tajik (official), Russian

Chief religion: Muslim (Sunni 85%, Shi'a 5%)

Area: 55,251 sq mi (143,100 sq km)

Capital: Dushanbe (pop., 554,000)

Independence date: September 9, 1991

Government type: republic

Head of state: Pres. Imomali Rakhmonov

Head of government: Prime Min. Akil Akilov

Local divisions: 2 viloyats, 1 autonomous viloyat

Monetary unit: somoni

GDP: $8.0 billion (2004 est.)

Per capita GDP: $1,100

Website: www.state.gov/r/pa/ei/bgn/5775.htm

Did you know? The Nurek Dam in Tajikistan is the highest in the world (984 ft [300 m]).

TANZANIA
Map page 119

Population: 38,139,640

Principal languages: Swahili, English (both official); Arabic, many local languages

Chief religions: Christian 30%, Muslim 35%, indigenous beliefs 35%; Zanzibar is 99% Muslim

Area: 364,900 sq mi (945,087 sq km)

Capital: Dodoma (pop., 155,000)

Independence date: April 26, 1964

Government type: republic

Head of state: Pres. Jakaya Mrisho Kikwete

Head of government: Prime Min. Edward Lowassa

Local divisions: 25 regions

Monetary unit: shilling

GDP: $23.7 billion (2004 est.)

Per capita GDP: $700

Website: www.tanzania.go.tz/index2E.html

Did you know? Kilimanjaro, the highest mountain in Africa (19,340 ft [5,895 m]), is in northeast Tanzania.

THAILAND
Map page 106

Population: 65,068,149

Principal languages: Thai, Chinese, Malay, Khmer

Chief religions: Buddhism (official) 95%, Muslim 4%

Area: 198,456 sq mi (514,000 sq km)

Capital: Bangkok (pop., 6,486,000)

Independence date: 1238

Government type: constitutional monarchy

Head of state: King Bhumibol Adulyadej

Head of government: Prime Min. Thaksin Shinawatra

Local divisions: 76 provinces

Monetary unit: baht

GDP: $524.8 billion (2004 est.)

Per capita GDP: $8,100

Website: www.thaiembdc.org

Did you know? Thailand is one of the world's largest tin producers, and a major source of rubies and sapphires.

TOGO
Map page 133

Population: 5,701,579

Principal languages: French (official), Ewe, Mina in the south; Kabye, Dagomba in the north

Chief religions: indigenous beliefs 51%, Christian 29%, Muslim 20%

Area: 21,925 sq mi (56,789 sq km)

Capital: Lomé (pop., 799,000)

Independence date: April 27, 1960

Government type: republic

Head of state: Pres. Faure Gnassingbé

Head of government: Prime Min. Edem Kodjo

Local divisions: 5 regions

Monetary unit: CFA franc

GDP: $8.7 billion (2004 est.)

Per capita GDP: $1,600

Website: www.state.gov/r/pa/ei/bgn/5430.htm

Did you know? About 70% of Togolese people practice traditional African religions.

TONGA
Map page 161

Population: 116,921

Principal languages: Tongan, English (both official)

Chief religions: Wesleyan 41%, Roman Catholic 16%, Mormon 14%

Area: 289 sq mi (748 sq km)

Capital: Nuku'alofa (pop., 35,000)

Independence date: June 4, 1970

Government type: constitutional monarchy

Head of state: King Taufa'ahau Tupou IV

Head of government: Prime Min. Feleti Sevele

Local divisions: 5 divisions, 23 districts

Monetary unit: pa'anga

GDP: $244 million (2002 est.)

Per capita GDP: $2,300

Website: www.tongaholiday.com

Did you know? Tonga is ruled by a King and a Prime Minister he appoints for life.

TRINIDAD AND TOBAGO
Map page 203

Population: 1,056,608

Principal languages: English (official), Hindi, French, Spanish, Chinese

Chief religions: Roman Catholic 29%, Hindu 24%, Protestant 14%, Muslim 6%

Area: 1,980 sq mi (5,128 sq km)

Capital: Port-of-Spain (pop., 55,000)

Independence date: August 31, 1962

Government type: parliamentary democracy

Head of state: Pres. George M. Richards

Head of government: Prime Min. Patrick Augustus Mervyn Manning

Local divisions: 8 counties, 3 municipalities, 1 ward

Monetary unit: Trinidad and Tobago dollar

GDP: $11.5 billion (2004 est.)

Per capita GDP: $10,500

Website: www.gov.tt

Did you know? East Indians, who came here in the 1800s, make up 40% of the population.

TUNISIA
Map page 129

Population: 10,276,158

Principal languages: Arabic (official), French prevalent

Chief religion: Muslim (official; mostly Sunni) 98%

Area: 63,170 sq mi (163,610 sq km)

Capital: Tunis (pop., 1,996,000)

Independence date: March 20, 1956

Government type: republic

Head of state: Pres. Gen. Zine al-Abidine Ben Ali

Head of government: Prime Min. Mohamed Ghannouchi

Local divisions: 23 governorates

Monetary unit: dinar

GDP: $70.9 billion (2004 est.)

Per capita GDP: $7,100

Website: www.tunisiaonline.com

Did you know? Tunisia's more than 800 miles of Mediterranean coastline is popular with European tourists.

TURKEY
Map page 114

Population: 71,158,647

Principal languages: Turkish (official), Kurdish, Arabic, Armenian, Greek

Chief religion: Muslim 99.8% (mostly Sunni)

Area: 301,383 sq mi (780,580 sq km)

Capital: Ankara (pop., 3,428,000)

Independence date: October 29, 1923

Government type: republic

Head of state: Pres. Ahmet Necdet Sezer

Head of government: Prime Min. Recep Tayyip Erdogan

Local divisions: 80 provinces

Monetary unit: new Turkish lira

GDP: $508.7 billion (2004 est.)

Per capita GDP: $7,400

Website: www.turkishembassy.org

Did you know? More than twenty of Turkey's mountains are over 10,000 ft. high.

TURKMENISTAN
Map page 80

Population: 5,136,262

Principal languages: Turkmen, Russian, Uzbek

Chief religions: Muslim 89%, Eastern Orthodox 9%

Area: 188,456 sq mi (488,100 sq km)

Capital: Ashgabat (pop., 574,000)

Independence date: October 27, 1991

Government type: republic with authoritarian rule

Head of state and government: Pres. Gurbankuly Berdymuhammedov

Local divisions: 5 regions

Monetary unit: manat

GDP: $27.6 billion (2004 est.)

Per capita GDP: $5,700

Website: www.turkmenistanembassy.org

Did you know? Turkmen are famed for the beautiful carpets they weave from sheep wool.

TUVALU
Map page 160

Population: 11,992

Principal languages: Tuvaluan, English, Samoan, Kiribati (on the island of Nui)

Chief religion: Church of Tuvalu (Congregationalist) 97%

Area: 10 sq mi (26 sq km)

Capital: Funafuti (pop., 6,000)

Independence date: October 1, 1978

Government type: parliamentary democracy

Head of state: Queen Elizabeth II, represented by Gov.-Gen. Filoimea Telito

Head of government: Prime Min. Maatia Toafa

Monetary unit: Australian dollar

GDP: $12.2 million (2000 est.)

Per capita GDP: $1,100

Website: www.timelesstuvalu.com

Did you know? These low-lying islands are threatened by rising sea levels.

UGANDA
Map page 119

Population: 30,262,610

Principal languages: English (official), Swahili, Ganda, many Bantu and Nilotic languages, Arabic

Chief religions: Protestant 33%, Roman Catholic 33%, indigenous beliefs 18%, Muslim 16%

Area: 91,136 sq mi (236,040 sq km)

Capital: Kampala (pop., 1,246,000)

Independence date: October 9, 1962

Government type: republic

Head of state: Pres. Yoweri Kaguta Museveni

Head of government: Prime Min. Apolo Nsibambi

Local divisions: 39 districts

Monetary unit: shilling

GDP: $39.4 billion (2004 est.)

Per capita GDP: $1,500

Website: www.ugandaembassy.com

Did you know? Bwindi Impenetrable National Park is home to endangered mountain gorillas.

UKRAINE
Map page 78

Population: 46,299,862

Principal languages: Ukrainian (official), Russian, Romanian, Polish, Hungarian

Chief religions: Ukrainian Orthodox (Kiev patriarchate and Russian patriarchate), Autocephalous Orthodox, Ukrainian Greek Catholic

Area: 233,090 sq mi (603,700 sq km)

Capital: Kiev (pop., 2,618,000)

Independence date: August 24, 1991

Government type: republic

Head of state: Pres. Viktor Yushchenko

Head of government: Prime Min. Yuriy Yekhanurov

Local divisions: 24 oblasts, 2 municipalities with oblast status, 1 autonomous republic

Monetary unit: hryvnia

GDP: $299.1 billion (2004 est.)

Per capita GDP: $6,300

Website: www.ukraineinfo.us

Did you know? In the 1840s, Russian rulers banned the Ukrainian language from schools.

UNITED ARAB EMIRATES
Map page 112

Population: 2,642,566

Principal languages: Arabic (official), Persian, English, Hindi, Urdu

Chief religion: Muslim 96% (official; Shi'a 16%)

Area: 32,000 sq mi (82,880 sq km)

Capital: Abu Dhabi (pop., 475,000)

Independence date: December 2, 1971

Government type: federation of emirates

Head of state: Pres. Sheik Khalifa ibn Zaid an-Nahayan

Head of government: Prime Min. Sheik Muhammad ibn Rashid al-Maktum

Local divisions: 7 autonomous emirates (Abu Dhabi, Ajman, Dubayy, Fujaira, Ras al-Khaimah, Sharjah, Umm al-Qaiwain)

Monetary unit: dirham

GDP: $63.7 billion (2004 est.)

Per capita GDP: $25,200

Website: www.uaeinteract.com

Did you know? A hereditary ruler, or emir, governs each of the 7 emirates of this country.

UNITED KINGDOM*
Map page 37

Population: 60,776,238

Principal languages: English (official), Welsh and Scottish Gaelic

Chief religions: Christian 72%, Muslim 3%, many others

Area: 94,525 sq mi (244,820 sq km)

Capital: London (pop., 7,619,000)

Independence date: 1801

Government type: constitutional monarchy

Head of state: Queen Elizabeth II

Head of government: Prime Min. Tony Blair

Local divisions: 467 local authorities, including England, 387; Wales, 22; Scotland, 32; Northern Ireland, 26

Monetary unit: pound

GDP: $1,782 billion (2004 est.)

Per capita GDP: $29,600

Website: www.britainusa.com

Did you know? The last successful invasion of England occurred in 1066.

UNITED STATES
Map page 172

Population: 301,139,947 (50 states and District of Columbia)

Principal languages: English, Spanish

Chief religions: Protestant 56%, Roman Catholic 28%, Jewish 2%

Area: 3,718,709 sq mi (9,631,418 sq km)

Capital: Washington, D.C. (pop., 4,098,000)

Independence date: July 4, 1776

Government type: federal republic

Head of state and government: Pres. George W. Bush

Local divisions: 50 states and District of Columbia

Monetary unit: U.S. dollar

GDP: $11,750 billion (2004 est.)

Per capita GDP: $40,100

Website: www.firstgov.gov

Did you know? Lake Michigan is the only one of the Great Lakes entirely within the United States.

URUGUAY
Map page 209

Population: 3,447,496

Principal languages: Spanish (official), Portunol/Brazilero (Portuguese-Spanish)

Chief religion: Roman Catholic 66%

Area: 68,039 sq mi (176,220 sq km)

Capital: Montevideo (pop., 1,341,000)

Independence date: August 25, 1825

Government type: republic

Head of state and government: Pres. Tabaré Ramón Vázquez Rosas

Local divisions: 19 departments

Monetary unit: peso

GDP: $49.3 billion (2004 est.)

Per capita GDP: $14,500

Website: www.uruwashi.org

Did you know? In 1930 Uruguay hosted and won soccer's first World Cup.

UZBEKISTAN
Map page 80

Population: 27,780,059

Principal languages: Uzbek (official), Russian, Tajik

Chief religions: Muslim 88% (mostly Sunni), Eastern Orthodox 9%

Area: 172,742 sq mi (447,400 sq km)

Capital: Tashkent (pop., 2,155,000)

Independence date: August 31, 1991

Government type: republic

Head of state: Pres. Islam A. Karimov

Head of government: Prime Min. Shavkat Mirziyaev

*Member of the European Union

Local divisions: 12 regions, 1 autonomous republic, 1 city

Monetary unit: som

GDP: $47.6 billion (2004 est.)

Per capita GDP: $1,800

Website: www.gov.uz

Did you know? Alexander the Great and Genghis Khan both conquered this region.

VANUATU
Map page 160

Population: 211,971

Principal languages: Bislama, English, French (all official); more than 100 local languages

Chief religions: Presbyterian 37%, Anglican 15%, Roman Catholic 15%, other Christian 10%, indigenous beliefs 8%

Area: 4,710 sq mi (12,200 sq km)

Capital: Port-Vila (pop., 34,000)

Independence date: July 30, 1980

Government type: republic

Head of state: Pres. Kalkot Mataskelekele

Head of government: Prime Min. Ham Lini

Local divisions: 6 provinces

Monetary unit: vatu (VUV)

GDP: $580 million (2003 est.)

Per capita GDP: $2,900

Website: www.vanuatutourism.com

Did you know? Before independence in 1980, Britain and France jointly ruled these islands.

VATICAN CITY (THE HOLY SEE)
Map page 71

Population: 921

Principal languages: Latin (official), Italian, French, Monastic Sign Language, various others

Chief religion: Roman Catholic

Area: 0.17 sq mi (0.44 sq km)

Independence date: February 11, 1929

Government type: ecclesiastical state

Sovereign: Pope Benedict XVI

Monetary unit: euro

Website: www.vatican.va/phome_en.htm

Did you know? The Vatican's Swiss Guards wear a style of uniform that dates from the 1500s.

VENEZUELA
Map page 217

Population: 26,084,662

Principal languages: Spanish (official), numerous indigenous dialects

Chief religion: Roman Catholic 96%

Area: 352,144 sq mi (912,050 sq km)

Capital: Caracas (pop., 3,226,000)

Independence date: July 5, 1811

Government type: federal republic

Head of state and government: Pres. Hugo Rafael Chávez Frías

Local divisions: 23 states, 1 federal district (Caracas), 1 federal dependency (72 islands)

Monetary unit: bolivar

GDP: $145.2 billion (2004 est.)

Per capita GDP: $5,800

Website: www.embavenez-us.org

Did you know? Angel Falls, the world's highest waterfall, drops 3,212 ft.

VIETNAM
Map page 106

Population: 85,262,356

Principal languages: Vietnamese (official), English, French, Chinese, Khmer

Chief religions: Buddhist, Roman Catholic

Area: 127,244 sq mi (329,560 sq km)

Capital: Hanoi (pop., 3,977,000)

Independence date: September 2, 1945

Government type: Communist

Head of state: Pres. Tran Duc Luong

Head of government: Prime Min. Phan Van Khai

Local divisions: 58 provinces, 3 cities, 1 capital region

Monetary unit: dong

GDP: $227.2 billion (2004 est.)

Per capita GDP: $2,700

Website: www.vietnamembassy-usa.org

Did you know? France took over Vietnam in 1854 and ruled there until 1954.

YEMEN
Map page 112

Population: 22,211,743

Principal language: Arabic (official)

Chief religions: Muslim (official; Sunni 60%, Shi'a 40%)

Area: 203,850 sq mi (527,970 sq km)

Capital: Sanaa (pop., 1,469,000)

Independence date: May 22, 1990

Government type: republic

Head of state: Pres. Ali Abdullah Saleh

Head of government: Prime Min. Abd-al-Qadir Bajamal

Local divisions: 17 governorates and capital region

Monetary unit: rial

GDP: $16.2 billion (2004 est.)

Per capita GDP: $800

Website: www.yemenembassy.org.uk

Did you know? "Mocha" coffee takes its name from a Yemeni seaport.

ZAMBIA
Map page 119

Population: 11,477,447

Principal languages: English (official), Bemba, Kaonda, Lozi, Lunda, Luvale, Nyanja, Tonga, 70 others

Chief religions: Christian 50-75%, Hindu and Muslim 24-49%

Area: 290,586 sq mi (752,614 sq km)

Capital: Lusaka (pop., 1,394,000)

Independence date: October 24, 1964

Government type: republic

Head of state and government: Pres. Levy Patrick Mwanawasa

Local divisions: 9 provinces

Monetary unit: kwacha

GDP: $9.4 billion (2004 est.)

Per capita GDP: $900

Website: www.zana.gov.zm

Did you know? Fossils show humans inhabited Zambia 100,000 years ago.

ZIMBABWE
Map page 141

Population: 12,311,143

Principal languages: English (official), Shona, Sindebele, numerous dialects

Chief religions: syncretic (Christian-indigenous mix) 50%, Christian 25%, indigenous beliefs 24%

Area: 150,804 sq mi (390,580 sq km)

Capital: Harare (pop., 1,469,000)

Independence date: April 18, 1980

Government type: republic

Local divisions: 8 provinces, 2 cities

Head of state and government: Pres. Robert Mugabe

Monetary unit: Zimbabwe dollar

GDP: $24.4 billion (2004 est.)

Per capita GDP: $1,900

Website: www.zimbabwe-embassy.us

Did you know? The beautiful Victoria Falls lie between Zimbabwe and Zambia.

ABOUT THIS SECTION

This section is based on data collected for The World Almanac® and The World Almanac for Kids® and represents the latest information available at the time of compilation.

Population figures for cities generally pertain to the entire metropolitan area.

GDP (gross domestic product) estimates are based on so-called purchasing power parity calculations, which make use of weighted prices in order to take into account differences in price levels between countries.

Please note that the addresses and content of websites are subject to change.

Principal Measurement Abbreviations

ft	foot, feet	mi	mile(s)
in	inch(es)	mm	millimeter(s)
km	kilometer(s)	sq	square
m	meter(s)		

*Member of the European Union

Population of Countries and Major Cities

The following pages include population figures for all countries, and cities with more than 100,000 inhabitants. All national capitals, regardless of size are also listed. Countries are listed alphabetically, and cities are grouped alphabetically within each country. Capitals are indicated with an asterisk (*). The population figures, given in thousands, represent the most current information available.

Country City	Population in thousands
A	
Afghanistan	**31,890**
Herāt	177
Kabul*	1,424
Mazār-e Sharīf	131
Qandahār	226
Albania	**3,601**
Tiranë*	244
Algeria	**33,333**
Algiers*	1,688
Annaba	228
Batna	185
Bechar	107
Bejaïa	118
Biskra	130
Blida	132
Chelif	130
Constantine	450
Mostaganem	115
Oran	599
Sétif	186
Sidi Bel-Abbes	155
Skikda	129
Tébessa	108
Tiaret	106
Tlemcen	108
Andorra	**72**
Andorra la Vella*	16
Angola	**12,264**
Luanda*	1,530
Antigua and Barbuda	**69**
Saint John's*	22
Argentina	**40,302**
Almirante Brown	514
Avellaneda	329
Bahía Blanca	275
Belén de Escobar	173
Berazateugi	287
Buenos Aires*	2,776
Catamaraca	141
Comodoro Rivadavia	136
Concordia	138
Córdoba	1,268
Corrientes	315
Florencio Varela	342
Formosa	198
General San Martín	403
General Sarmiento	253
Godoy Cruz	183
Lanús	453
La Plata	564
La Rioja	144
Las Heras	169
Lomas de Zamora	591
Mar del Plata	542
Mariano Moreno	379
Mendoza	111
Merlo	469
Morón	309
Neuquén	202
Paraná	236
Pilar	127
Posadas	253
Quilmes	519
Resistencia	274
Río Cuarto	144
Rosario	908
Salta	462
San Fernando	148
San Isidro	292
San Juan	113
San Luis	153
San Miguel de Tucumán	527
San Nicolás de los Arroyos	125
San Rafael	106
San Salvador de Jujuy	231
Santa Fé	369
Santiago del Estero	231
Tandil	101
Tigre	296
Vicente López	274
Villa Nueva	223
Armenia	**2,972**
Gyumri	159
Vanadzor	107
Yerevan*	1,104
Australia	**20,434**
Adelaide	957
Baulkham Hills	114
Brisbane	1146
Canberra*	276
Geelong	126
Gold Coast	226
Gosford	129
Hobart	127
Melbourne	2,762
Newcastle	262
Perth	1019
Salisbury	106
Stirling	173
Sydney	3,098
Townsville	101
Warringah	172
Waverley	118
Wollongong	211
Austria	**8,200**
Graz	226
Innsbruck	113
Linz	183
Salzburg	143
Vienna*	1,550
Azerbaijan	**8,120**
Baku*	1,874
Gäncä	306
Sumgayıt	267
B	
Bahamas, The	**306**
Nassau*	172
Bahrain	**709**
Manama*	140
Bangladesh	**150,448**
Barisāl	180
Chittagong	1,560
Comilla	184
Dhaka*	3,638
Dinājpur	137
Jamālpur	108
Jessore	176
Khulna	601
Mymensingh	189
Naogaon	105
Nārāyanganj	285
Nawābganj	130
Pābna	110
Rājshāhi	302
Rangpur	221
Saidpur	108
Sirājganj	100
Sylhet	110
Tangail	108
Barbados	**281**
Bridgetown*	7
Belarus	**9,725**
Babruysk	226
Baranavichy	170
Barysaw	152
Brest	287
Homyel'	503
Hrodna	295
Mahilyow	363
Mazyr	105
Minsk*	1,655
Orsha	125
Pinsk	128
Vitsyebsk	365
Belgium	**10,392**
Antwerp	468
Brugge	117
Brussels*	954
Charleroi	206
Ghent	230
Liège	195
Namur	103
Schaerbeek	103
Belize	**294**
Belmopan*	8
Benin	**8,078**
Cotonou	537
Djougou	134
Parakou	104
Porto-Novo*	179
Bhutan	**2,328**
Thimphu*	30
Bolivia	**9,119**
Cochabamba	404
El Alto	404
La Paz*	711
Oruro	183
Potosí	112
Santa Cruz de la Sierra	695
Sucre*	131
Bosnia & Herzegovina	**4,552**
Banja Luka	196
Doboj	103
Mostar	127
Prijedor	113
Sarajevo*	529
Tuzla	132
Zenica	146
Botswana	**1,639**
Gaborone*	175
Brazil	**190,011**
Alvorada	184
Americana	183
Anápolis	283
Aracaju	462
Araçatuba	169
Arapiraca	186
Araraquara	182
Barra Mansa	171
Baurú	316
Belém	1,281
Belo Horizonte	2,239
Betim	307
Blumenau	262
Boa Vista	201
Brasília*	2,051
Cachoeiro de Itapemirim	175
Campina Grande	335
Campinas	969
Campo Grande	664
Campos	407
Canoas	306
Carapicuíba	345
Cariacica	324
Caruaru	254
Cascavel	245
Caxias do Sul	360
Colombo	183
Contegem	538
Cuiabá	483
Curitiba	1,587
Diadema	357
Divinópolis	184
Dourados	165
Duque du Caxias	775
Embu	208
Feira de Santana	481
Florianópolis	342
Fortaleza	2,141
Foz do Iguaçu	259
Franca	288
Goiânia	1,093
Governador Valadares	247
Gravataí	233
Guarapuava	155
Guarujá	265
Guarulhos	1,073
Ilhéus	222
Imperatriz	231
Ipatinga	212
Itabuna	197
Itajaí	147
Itapevi	162
Itaquaquecetuba	273
Jaboatão dos Guarara	582
Jacareí	191
Jequié	147
João Pessoa	598
Joinvile	430
Juazeiro do Norte	212
Juiz de Fora	457
Jundiaí	323
Lages	158
Limeira	249
Londrina	447
Luziânia	141
Macapá	283
Maceió	798
Manaus	1,406
Marabá	168
Maracanau	180
Marília	197
Maringá	289
Mauá	363
Mogi das Cruzes	330
Montes Claros	307
Mossoró	214
Natal	712
Nilópolis	154
Niterói	459
Nova Friburgo	173
Nova Iguaçu	755
Novo Hamburgo	236
Olinda	368
Osasco	653
Passo Fundo	168
Parnaíba	132
Pelotas	321
Petrolina	219
Petrópolis	287
Piracicaba	329
Poços de Caldas	136
Ponta Grossa	274
Porto Alegre	1,361
Porto Velho	335
Presidente Prudente	189
Recife	1,423
Ribeirão Prêto	505
Rio Branco	253
Rio Claro	168
Rio de Janeiro	5,858
Rio Grande	187
Salvador	2,443
Santa Bárbara d'Oeste	170
Santa Maria	244
Santarém	263
Santo André	649
Santos	418
São Bernardo do Campo	703
São Caetano do Sul	140
São Carlos	193
São Gonçalo	891
São João de Meriti	449
São José do Rio Preto	359
São José dos Campos	539
São Leopoldo	210
São Luís	870
São Paulo	10,436
São Vicente	304
Sapucia do Sul	123
Sete Lagoas	185
Sorocaba	493
Suzano	229
Taboão da Serra	198
Taubaté	244
Teresina	715
Uberaba	252
Uberlândia	501
Uruguaiana	127
Várzea Grande	215
Viamão	227
Vila Velha Argolas	346
Vitória	292
Vitória da Conquista	262
Volta Redonda	242
Brunei	**387**
Bandar Seri Begawan*	46
Bulgaria	**7,323**
Burgas	196
Dobrich	104
Pleven	131
Plovdiv	341
Ruse	170
Sliven	106
Sofia*	1,114
Stara Zagora	150
Varna	309
Burkina Faso	**14,326**
Bobo Dioulasso	229
Ouagadougou*	442
Burundi	**8,391**
Bujumbura*	235
C	
Cambodia	**14,132**
Phnom Penh*	620
Cameroon	**18,060**
Bafoussam	140
Bamenda	130
Douala	1,030
Garoua	170
Maroua	150
Ngaoundéré	100
N'Kongsamba	110
Yaoundé*	654
Canada	**33,390**
Abbotsford	105
Barrie	128
Brampton	444
Burlington	164
Burnaby	203
Calgary	988
Cambridge	120
Coquitlam	102
Edmonton	730
Gatineau	239
Gloucester	104
Halifax	114
Hamilton	505
Kitchener	204
Laval	369
Lévis	130
London	352
Longueuil	229
Markham	262
Mississauga	669
Montréal	1,621
Oakville	166
Oshawa	142
Ottawa*	812
Québec	491
Regina	179
Richmond	174
Richmond Hill	163
Saguenay	144
Saint Catharines	132
Saint John's	102
Saskatoon	202
Sherbrooke	147
Surrey	395
Thunder Bay	109
Toronto	2,503
Vancouver	578
Vaughan	133
Windsor	216
Winnipeg	633
Cape Verde	**424**
Praia*	62
Central African Republic	**4,369**
Bangui*	597
Chad	**10,239**
Moundou	102
N'Djamena*	530
Sarh	113
Chile	**16,285**
Antofagasta	227
Arica	161
Barrancas	184
Calama	120
Chillán	146
Concepción	327
Coquimbo	115
Iquique	151
La Serena	109
Maipú	254
Osorno	114
Puente Alto	254
Puerto Montt	112
Punta Arenas	114
Quilpué	102
Rancagua	180
Renca	129
San Bernardo	191
Santiago*	4,298
Talca	161
Talcahuano	246
Temuco	211
Valdivia	114
Valparaíso	282
Viña del Mar	304
China	**1,321,852**
Acheng	193
Aksu	126
Anda	133
Ankang	129
Anqing	247
Anshan	1,215
Anshun	175
Anyang	395
Baicheng	214
Baiyin	199
Baoding	485
Baoji	325
Baotou	980
Bei'an	193
Beihai	116
Beijing*	5,715
Beipiao	190
Bengbu	441
Benxi	767
Binzhou	129
Cangzhou	222
Changchun	1,698
Changde	253
Changji	109
Changsha	1,077
Changshu	180
Changzhi	307
Changzhou	523
Chaoyang	218
Chaozhou	289
Chengde	243
Chengdu	1,719
Chenzhou	166
Chifeng	344
Chongqing	2,265
Chuzhou	120
Cixi	101
Da'an	124
Da Xian	185
Dali	134
Dalian	1,632
Dandong	525
Daqing	676
Datong	779
Deyang	171
Dezhou	183
Dongguan	271
Dongtai	131
Dongying	257
Dunhua	225
Duyun	130
Ezhou	137
Fengcheng	150
Foshan	291
Fuling	164
Fushun	1,210
Fuxin	623
Fuyang	161
Fuyu	174
Fuzhou	890
Ganzhou	219
Gejiu	212
Gongzhuling	218
Guangyuan	173
Guangzhou	2,892
Guigang	111
Guilin	371
Guiyang	1,009
Haicheng	196
Haikou	271
Hailar	176
Hailun	128
Hami	146
Handan	798
Hangzhou	1,119
Hanzhong	157
Harbin	2,468
Hebi	196
Hefei	733
Hegang	507
Hengyang	469
Heze	154
Hohhot	654
Honghu	130
Huadian	166
Huai'an	113
Huaibei	332
Huaihua	120
Huainan	674
Huaiyin	221
Huangshi	432
Huizhou	147
Hunjiang	475
Huzhou	398
Jiamusi	477
Ji'an	143
Jiangmen	219
Jiangyin	145
Jiaohe	172
Jiaozuo	386
Jiaxing	205
Jilin	1,038
Jinan	1,361
Jinchang	100
Jincheng	128
Jingdezhen	274
Jingmen	158
Jinhua	139
Jining (Nei Mong.)	248
Jining (Shandong)	190
Jinxi	349
Jinzhou	573
Jiujiang	284
Jiutai	173
Jixi	638
Kaifeng	503
Kaili	109
Kaiyuan	122
Karamay	194
Kashi	158
Korla	137
Kunming	1,108
Kunshan	100
Laiwu	186
Langfang	146
Lanzhou	1,205
Laohekou	108
Leiyang	129
Lengshuijiang	126
Leshan	333
Lianyuan	114
Lianyungang	352
Liaocheng	149
Liaoyang	485
Liaoyuan	341
Liling	107
Linchuan	161
Linfen	174
Linhe	131
Linyi	210
Liuzhou	602
Longyan	134
Loudi	121
Lu'an	137
Luohe	122
Luoyang	730
Lupanshui	342
Luzhou	262
Ma'anshan	297
Manzhouli	119
Maoming	162
Meihekou	205
Meizhou	120
Mianyang	250
Mudanjiang	562
Nanchang	1,026
Nanchong	179
Nanjing	2,114
Nanning	723
Nanping	188
Nantong	324
Nanyang	229
Neijiang	240
Ningbo	548
Panzhihua	407
Pingdingshan	442
Pingxiang	306
Puyang	120
Qingdao	1,317
Qingjiang	172
Qingyuan	134
Qinhuangdao	360
Qinzhou	105
Qiqihar	1,066
Qitaihe	218
Quanzhou	178
Qujing	163
Quzhou	105
Renqiu	128
Rizhao	109
Sanmenxia	114
Sanming	159
Shanghai	7,551
Shangqiu	159
Shangrao	127
Shangzhi	208
Shantou	558
Shaoguan	334
Shaoxing	180
Shaoyang	242
Shashi	277
Shenyang	3,588
Shenzhen	466
Sheung Shui-Fanling	201
Shihezi	160
Shijiazhuang	1,065
Shiyan	241
Shizuishan	245
Shuangyashan	392
Shuangcheng	131
Siping	310
Suihua	219
Suining	134
Suizhou	139
Suzhou (Anhui)	147
Suzhou (Jiangsu)	697
Tai'an	246
Taiyuan	1,514
Taizhou	151
Tangshan	1,042
Tianjin	4,521
Tianmen	138
Tianshui	238
Tieling	247
Tin Shui Wai	150
Tongchuan	259
Tonghua	321
Tongliao	247
Tongling	212
Tseung Kwan O	137
Ulanhot	152
Ürümqi	1071
Wafangdian	250
Wanxian	156
Weifang	359
Weinan	135
Wenzhou	204
Wuhai	261
Wuhan	3,177
Wuhu	419
Wuwei	125
Wuxi	806
Wuzhou	213
Xiamen	391
Xi'an	1,954
Xiangfan	390
Xiangtan	429
Xianning	110
Xiantao	124
Xianyang	328
Xiaogan	140
Xiaoshan	159
Xichang	133
Xingcheng	102
Xinghua	155
Xingtai	270
Xining	559
Xintai	209
Xinxiang	453
Xinyang	185
Xinyu	163
Xuchang	196
Xuzhou	795
Yan'an	106
Yancheng	239
Yangjiang	203
Yangquan	338
Yangzhou	306
Yanji	233

Country City	Population in thousands
Yantai	400
Yibin	241
Yichang	364
Yichun (Heilonjiang)	787
Yichun (Jiangxi)	134
Yinchuan	350
Yingkou	423
Yining	172
Yixing	186
Yiyang	180
Yong'an	109
Yuci	189
Yueyang	296
Yulin	130
Yumen	112
Yuyao	103
Zaozhuang	309
Zhangjiakou	525
Zhangzhou	178
Zhanjiang	384
Zhaodong	164
Zhaoqing	173
Zhengzhou	1,139
Zhenjiang	355
Zhongshan	256
Zhoukou	136
Zhuhai	162
Zhumadian	121
Zhuzhou	383
Zibo	864
Zigong	385
Zixing	107
Zunyi	269
Colombia	**44,257**
Armenia	211
Barrancabermeja	136
Barranquilla	1,109
Bello	260
Bogotá*	6,763
Bucaramanga	403
Buenaventura	187
Cali	2,040
Cartagena	576
Cúcuta	462
Dos Quebradas	115
Envigado	110
Floridablanca	177
Ibagué	336
Itagüí	168
Manizales	341
Medellín	2,187
Montería	182
Neiva	223
Palmira	189
Pasto	244
Pereira	329
Popayán	210
Santa Marta	211
Sincelejo	120
Soacha	181
Soledad	236
Tuluá	104
Tunjá	102
Valledupar	209
Villavicencio	190
Comoros	**711**
Moroni*	30
Congo, Dem. Rep. of the	**64,607**
Boma	264
Bukavu	210
Kananga	372
Kikwit	183
Kinshasa*	3,800
Kisangani	373
Kolwezi	545
Lubumbashi	739
Matadi	173
Mbandaka	166
Mbuji-Mayi	613
Panda-Likasi	146
Tshikapa	110
Congo, Rep. of the	**3,801**
Brazzaville*	938
Pointe-Noire	576
Costa Rica	**4,134**
San José*	279
Côte d'Ivoire	**18,013**
Abidjan	1,929
Bouaké	330
Daloa	122
Korhogo	109
Yamoussoukro*	107
Croatia	**4,493**
Rijeka	144
Split	175
Zagreb*	779
Cuba	**11,417**
Bayamo	138
Camagüey	249
Ciego de Ávila	101
Cienfuegos	130
Guantánamo	208
Havana*	2,176
Holguín	242
Las Tunas	127
Manzanillo	108
Marianao	128
Matanzas	123
Pinar del Río	129
Santa Clara	205
Santiago de Cuba	430
Victoria de las Tunas	115
Cyprus	**788**
Nicosia*	47
Czech Republic	**10,229**
Brno	379
Olomouc	103
Ostrava	319
Plzeň	166
Prague*	1,179
D	
Denmark	**5,468**
Ålborg	161
Århus	285
Copenhagen*	496
Odense	184
Djibouti	**496**
Djibouti*	200
Dominica	**69**
Roseau*	6
Dominican Republic	**9,366**
La Romana	140
San Francisco de Macorís	162
San Pedro de Macorís	125
Santiago de los Caballeros	365
Santo Domingo*	1,610
E	
East Timor	**1,085**
Dili*	13
Ecuador	**13,756**
Ambato	154
Cuenca	277
Eloy Alfaro	175
Guayaquil	1,985
Loja	119
Machala	205
Manta	183
Milagro	113
Portoviejo	172
Quito*	1,399
Riobamba	125
Santo Domingo de los Colorados	200
Egypt	**80,265**
Alexandria	3,380
Al Fayyum	250
Al Jīzah	2,144
Al Maḩallah al Kubrá	408
Al Manşūra	371
Al Minyā	208
Aswān	220
Asyūt	321
Az Zaqāzīq	287
Banhā	136
Banī Suwayf	179
Cairo*	6,663
Damanhūr	222
Ismailia	255
Kafr ad Dawwār	226
Luxor	146
Port Said	460
Qinā	141
Shibīn al Kaum	158
Shubrā al Khaymah	834
Suez	376
Suhāj	156
Tantā	380
El Salvador	**6,940**
Mejicanos	132
San Miguel	128
San Salvador*	415
Santa Ana	139
Soyapango	261
Equatorial Guinea	**551**
Malabo*	30
Eritrea	**4,907**
Asmara*	435
Estonia	**1,316**
Tallinn*	397
Tartu	114
Ethiopia	**76,512**
Ādīs Ābeba*	2,424
Bahir Dar	122
Debre Zeyit	106
Desē	124
Dirē Dawa	208
Gonder	142
Hārer	123
Jīma	114
Mek'elē	123
Nazrēt	164
F	
Fiji	**919**
Suva*	70
Finland	**5,238**
Esbo (Espoo)	191
Helsinki*	525
Oulu	109
Tampere	183
Turku	165
Vantaa	166
France	**61,084**
Aix-en-Provence	127
Amiens	136
Angers	146
Besançon	119
Bordeaux	213
Boulogne-Billancourt	102
Brest	153
Caen	116
Clermont-Ferrand	140
Dijon	152
Grenoble	154
Le Havre	197
Le Mans	148
Lille	178
Limoges	136
Lyon	422
Marseille	808
Metz	124
Montpellier	211
Mulhouse	110
Nancy	102
Nantes	252
Nice	346
Nîmes	134
Orléans	108
Paris*	2,175
Perpignan	108
Reims	185
Rennes	204
Rouen	105
Saint-Denis	122
Saint-Étienne	202
Strasbourg	256
Toulon	170
Toulouse	366
Tours	133
Villeurbanne	120
G	
Gabon	**1,455**
Libreville*	362
Gambia, The	**1,688**
Banjul*	42
Georgia	**4,646**
Bat'umi	136
K'ut'aisi	235
Rust'avi	159
Sokhumi	121
T'bilisi*	1,260
Germany	**82,401**
Aachen	242
Augsburg	257
Bergisch Gladbach	104
Berlin*	3,434
Bielefeld	319
Bochum	396
Bonn	292
Bottrop	119
Braunschweig	259
Bremen	551
Bremerhaven	130
Chemnitz	294
Cologne	954
Cottbus	126
Darmstadt	139
Dortmund	599
Dresden	491
Duisburg	535
Düsseldorf	576
Erfurt	209
Erlangen	102
Essen	627
Frankfurt am Main	645
Freiburg	191
Fürth	103
Gelsenkirchen	294
Gera	129
Göttingen	122
Hagen	214
Halle	310
Hamburg	1,652
Hamm	180
Hannover	513
Heidelberg	137
Heilbronn	116
Herne	178
Hildesheim	105
Ingolstadt	105
Jena	103
Karlsruhe	275
Kassel	194
Kiel	246
Koblenz	109
Köpenick	118
Krefeld	244
Leipzig	511
Leverkusen	161
Lübeck	215
Ludwigshafen	162
Magdeburg	279
Mainz	179
Mannheim	310
Moers	105
Mönchengladbach	259
Mülheim an der Ruhr	178
Munich	1,229
Münster	259
Neuss	147
Nürnberg	494
Oberhausen	224
Offenbach	115
Oldenburg	143
Osnabrück	163
Paderborn	121
Pforzheim	113
Potsdam	130
Recklinghausen	125
Regensburg	122
Remscheid	123
Reutlingen	104
Rostock	237
Saarbrücken	191
Salzgitter	118
Schwerin	122
Siegen	112
Solingen	166
Stuttgart	594
Ulm	115
Wiesbaden	271
Witten	106
Wolfsburg	128
Wuppertal	387
Würzburg	129
Zwickau	108
Ghana	**22,931**
Accra*	954
Kumasi	399
Tamale	136
Tema	100
Greece	**10,706**
Athens*	772
Iráklion	115
Kallithéa	114
Lárisa	113
Pátrai	153
Peristérion	137
Piraiévs	183
Thessaloníki	384
Grenada	**90**
Saint George's*	5
Guatemala	**12,728**
Guatemala*	823
Mixco	305
Quezaltenango	109
San Pedro Carchá	103
Villa Nueva	192
Guinea	**9,948**
Conakry*	1,093
Nzérékoré	107
Guinea-Bissau	**1,472**
Bissau*	109
Guyana	**769**
Georgetown*	72
Pickersgill	249
H	
Haiti	**8,706**
Port-au-Prince*	690
Honduras	**7,484**
San Pedro Sula	287
Tegucigalpa*	577
Hungary	**9,956**
Budapest*	2,017
Debrecen	212
Győr	129
Kecskemét	103
Miskolc	196
Nyíregyháza	114
Pécs	170
Szeged	175
Székesfehérvár	109
I	
Iceland	**302**
Reykjavík*	111
India	**1,129,866**
Abohar	124
Ādoni	156
Āgra	1,260
Agartala	189
Ahmadābād	3,515
Ahmadnagar	307
Aīzawl	230
Ajmer	485
Akola	400
Alīgarh	668
Allahābād	990
Alleppey	177
Alwar	260
Ambāla	139
Ambattūr	302
Amravati	549
Amritsar	976
Amroha	165
Anand	130
Anantapur	221
Arrah	203
Asansol	486
Aurangābād	873
Avadi	231
Bahraich	1168
Bally	262
Bālurghāt	136
Bangalore	4,292
Bānkurā	129
Baranagar	251
Bārāsat	232
Bareilly	700
Barrackpur	144
Basīrhāt	113
Beāwar	124
Belgaum	400
Bellary	317
Berhampur	280
Bhadrāvati	160
Bhāgalpur	340
Bharātpur	204
Bharuch	148
Bhatinda	217
Bhātpāra	442
Bhavnagar	511
Bhilai	554
Bhīlwāra	280
Bhimavaram	137
Bhind	154
Bhiwandi	599
Bhiwāni	169
Bhopāl	1,434
Bhubaneswar	647
Bhusawal	172
Bīdar	172
Bihar	232
Bījāpur	246
Bīkaner	529
Bilāspur	265
Bīr	138
Bokaro Steel City	394
Budaun	148
Bulandshahr	176
Burdwān	286
Burhānpur	194
Champdāni	103
Chandannagar	162
Chandīgarh	889
Chandrapur	298
Chāpra	179
Chennai (Madras)	4,216
Chittoor	153
Coimbatore	923
Cuddalore	159
Cuddapah	126
Cuttack	535
Darbhanga	267
Daryābād	270
Dasarahalli	264
Dāvangere	364
Dehra Dūn	448
Delhi	9,817
Dewās	231
Dhānbād	198
Dhūlia	341
Dibrugarh	123
Dindigul	197
Durg	231
Durgāpur	493
Elūrū	190
English Bāzār	161
Erode	151
Etāwah	211
Faizābād	145
Farīdābād	1,055
Farrukhābād	228
Fatehpur	152
Firozābād	279
Gadag-Betigeri	155
Gandhinagar	196
Gayā	283
Ghaziābād	969
Gondia	121
Gorakhpur	625
Gudivāda	112
Gulbarga	428
Guna	137
Guntakal	117
Guntūr	515
Gurgaon	174
Guwāhati	808
Gwalior	827
Hābra	128
Haldīa	171
Hālisahar	125
Hāpur	212
Hardwār	175
Hāthras	123
Hindupur	125
Hisār	257
Hoshiārpur	148
Howrah	1,009
Hubli-Dhārwār	768
Hugli	170
Hyderābād	3,450
Ichalkaranji	258
Imphāl	217
Indore	1,597
Jabalpur	951
Jaipur	2,324
Jalandhar	701
Jālgaon	369
Jālna	236
Jammu	378
Jāmnagar	478
Jamshedpur	570
Jaunpur	160
Jhānsi	383
Jodhpur	846
Junāgadh	169
Kākināda	290
Kalyān	1,193
Kāmārhāti	314
Kānchīpuram	153
Kanchrāpāra	126
Kānpur	2,532
Karīmnagar	204
Karnāl	210
Katihār	175
Khammam	158
Khandwa	172
Kharagpur	208
Kochi	596
Kolhāpur	485
Kolkata (Calcutta)	4,581
Korba	316
Kota	697
Kozhikode (Calicut)	437
Krishnanagar	139
Kulti	290
Kumbakonam	140
Kurnool	268
Kutakpalle	280
Lātūr	300
LB Nagar	262
Lucknow	2,207
Ludhiāna	1,395
Machilipatnam	183
Madurai	923
Mahbubnagar	131
Maheshtala	389
Mālegaon	409
Mandya	131
Mangalore	399
Mathurā	299
Maunath Bhanjan	210
Medinipur	153
Meerut	1,074
Mira-Bhayandar	520
Mirzāpur	205
Morādābād	641
Morena	151
Mumbai (Bombay)	11,914
Munger	187
Murwāra	187
Muzaffarnagar	316
Muzaffarpur	305
Mysore	742
Nabadwīp	115
Nadiād	193
Nāgercoil	208
Nāgpur	2,051
Naihāti	215
Nānded	431
Nandyāl	152
Nāsik	1,077
Navi Mumbai	704
Navsāri	134
Nellore	379
New Bombay	350
New Delhi*	295
Nizāmābād	287
Noida	284
North Barrackpur	124
Ongole	150
Ozhukarai	218
Pālghāt	131
Pāli	188
Pānīpat	262
Pānihāti	348
Parbhani	252
Pathānkot	160
Patiāla	303
Patna	1,377
Pīlībhīt	124
Pimpri-Chinchwad	1,006
Pondicherry	221
Porbandar	133
Proddatūr	165
Pune (Poona)	2,540
Purī	158
Purnia	171
Rāe Bareli	169
Raichūr	206
Raiganj	165
Raipur	605
Rājahmundry	313
Rājapālaiyam	122
Rajarhat Gopalpur	272
Rājkot	967
Rāj-Nāndagaon	144
Rāmagundam	236
Rāmpur	282
Rānchī	846
Ratlām	221
Raurkela	225
Rewa	183
Rishra	113
Rohtak	287
Sāgar	232
Sahāranpur	453
Salem	693
Sambalpur	154
Sambhal	183
Sāngli-Miraj	437
Sāntipur	138
Satna	225
Secunderābād	204
Serampore	198
Shāhjahānpur	298
Shillong	133
Shimoga	274
Shivpuri	147
Sholāpur	873
Sīkar	185
Silchar	142
Silīguri	470
Sirsa	160
Sītāpur	152
Sonīpat	216
South Dum Dum	394
Sri Gangānagar	211
Srīnagar	895
Surat	2,434
Surendranagar	156
Tenāli	150
Thāna	1,262
Thanjavur	216
Thiruvananthapuram	745
Tiruchchirāppalli	746
Tirunelveli	411
Tirupati	228
Tiruppūr	347
Tiruvannāmalai	130
Titāgarh	124
Tonk	136
Tumkūr	249
Tuticorin	216
Udaipur	389
Ujjain	430
Ulbāria	202
Ulhāsnagar	473
Unnāo	145
Uttarpara-Kotrung	150
Vadodara (Baroda)	1,306
Vārānasi	1,101
Vellore	177
Vijayawada	825
Visākhapatnam	970
Vizianagaram	174
Warangal	529
Wardha	111
Yamunānagar	190
Yavatmāl	123

Country City	Population in thousands
Indonesia	**245,453**
Ambon	205
Balikpapan	309
Banda Aceh	143
Bandung	2,026
Bangil	386
Banjarmasin	443
Bekasi	146
Bengkulu	170
Binjai	127
Blitar	113
Bogor	271
Ciamis	105
Cianjur	109
Cibinong	264
Cilacap	142
Ciedug	293
Cimahi	197
Ciparay	135
Cirebon	225
Denpasar	210
Depok	382
Garut	146
Gorontalo	133
Gresik	102
Jakarta*	8,228
Jambi	301
Jayapura	101
Jember	115
Karawang	143
Kediri	235
Klangenan	291
Klaten	120
Kudus	183
Kupang	111
Madiun	166
Magelang	123
Majalaya	177
Malang	650
Manado	321
Mataram	276
Medan	1,685
Padang	477
Pakanbaru	341
Palangkaraya	113
Palembang	1,084
Pangkalpinang	108
Parepare	109
Pasuran	134
Pekalongan	227
Pematangsiantar	203
Pontianak	397
Probolinggo	131
Purwokerto	158
Salatiga	103
Samarinda	335
Semarang	1,004
Sukabumi	120
Surabaya	2,410
Surakarta	504
Tanjungbalai	108
Tanjungkarang-Telukbetung	458
Tanjungpinang	106
Tasikmalaya	194
Tebingtinggi	117
Tegal	226
Ujung Pandang	913
Yogyakarta	412
Iran	**65,398**
Āmol	155
Ahvāz	828
Arāk	379
Ardabīl	330
Bābol	153
Bākhtarān	666
Bandar-e `Abbās	384
Bandar-e Mushehr	141
Bīrjand	115
Bojnūrd	126
Borūjerd	212
Būshehr	141
Dezfūl	202
Eşfahān	1,221
Eslāmshahr	240
Gorgān	178
Hamadān	406
Īlām	137
Karaj	588
Kāshān	166
Kermān	350
Khomeynīshahr	127
Khorramābād	277
Khvoy	153
Malāyer	150
Marāgheh	129
Mashhad	1,964
Masjed-e Soleymān	109
Najafābād	182
Neyshābūr	155
Orūmīyeh	396
Qā'emshahr	133
Qazvīn	299
Qom	780
Rasht	374
Sabzevār	161
Sanandaj	271
Sārī	186
Shīrāz	1,043
Sīrjān	120
Tabrīz	1,166
Tajrīsh	157
Tehrān*	6,750
Yazd	306
Zāhedān	420
Zanjān	281
Iraq	**27,500**
Ad Dīwānīyah	196
Al `Amārah	209
Al Başrah	406
Al Ḩillah	269
Al Karrādah	236
Al Kūt	183
An Najaf	309
An Nāşirīyah	266
Ar Ramādī	193
As Sulaymānīyah	364
Baghdad*	3,841
Ba`qūbah	115
Dīwānīyah	196
Irbīl	486
Karbalā'	297
Kirkūk	419
Mosul	664
Ireland	**4,109**
Cork	123
Dublin*	495
Israel	**6,427**
Ashdod	128
Bat Yam	142
Beersheba	153
Bene Beraq	129
Haifa	252
Holon	164
Jerusalem*	591
Netanya	148
Petah Tiqwa	153
Ramat Gan	122
Rishon LeZiyyon	165
Tel Aviv-Yafo	356
Italy	**58,148**
Ancona	103
Bari	341
Bergamo	116
Bologna	412
Bolzano	100
Brescia	197
Cagliari	212
Catania	330
Catanzaro	104
Cosenza	104
Ferrara	111
Florence	402
Foggia	155
Genoa	676
La Spezia	102
Lecce	102
Livorno	171
Messina	272
Mestre	182
Milan	1,371
Modena	176
Monza	121
Naples	1,025
Novara	103
Padova	215
Palermo	697
Parma	174
Perugia	110
Pescara	129
Piacenza	102
Prato	167
Reggio di Calabria	178
Reggio nell'Emilia	109
Rimini	115
Rome*	2,693
Salerno	153
Sassari	120
Siracusa	125
Taranto	232
Torre del Greco	101
Trieste	231
Turin	962
Verona	253
Vicenza	109
J	
Jamaica	**2,780**
Kingston*	104
Japan	**127,468**
Abiko	1288
Ageo	213
Aizu-Wakamatsu	118
Akashi	293
Akishima	107
Akita	318
Amagasaki	466
Anjō	159
Aomori	298
Asahikawa	360
Asaka	120
Ashikaga	163
Atsugi	218
Beppu	127
Chiba	887
Chigasaki	221
Chofū	205
Daitō	129
Ebetsu	124
Ebina	118
Fuchū	227
Fuji	234
Fujieda	128
Fujimi	103
Fujinomiya	120
Fujisawa	379
Fukaya	104
Fukui	252
Fukuoka	1,341
Fukushima	291
Fukuyama	379
Funabashi	550
Gifu	403
Habikino	119
Hachiōji	536
Hachinohe	242
Hadano	168
Hakodate	288
Hamamatsu	582
Handa	111
Higashi-Hiroshima	123
Higashikurume	113
Higashimurayama	142
Higashi-Ōsaka	515
Hikone	108
Himeji	478
Hino	168
Hirakata	403
Hiratsuka	255
Hirosaki	177
Hiroshima	1,126
Hitachi	193
Hitachineka	152
Hōfu	118
Hōya	103
Ibaraki	261
Ichihara	278
Ichikawa	449
Ichinomiya	274
Iida	107
Ikeda	102
Ikoma	113
Imabari	118
Iruma	148
Ise	100
Isesaki	126
Ishinomaki	120
Itami	192
Iwaki	360
Iwakuni	106
Iwatsuki	109
Izumi	173
Jōetsu	135
Kadoma	136
Kagoshima	552
Kakamigahara	132
Kakogawa	266
Kamagaya	103
Kamakura	168
Kanazawa	456
Kariya	132
Kashihara	125
Kashiwa	328
Kasuga	105
Kasugai	288
Kasukabe	203
Katsuta	110
Kawachi-Nagano	121
Kawagoe	331
Kawaguchi	460
Kawanishi	154
Kawasaki	1,250
Kiryū	115
Kisarazu	123
Kishiwada	200
Kitakyūshū	1,011
Kitami	112
Kōbe	1,493
Kōchi	331
Kōfu	196
Kōriyama	335
Kodaira	179
Koganei	112
Kokubunji	111
Komaki	143
Komatsu	109
Koshigaya	308
Kumagaya	156
Kumamoto	662
Kurashiki	430
Kure	203
Kurume	237
Kushiro	192
Kyōto	1,468
Machida	377
Maebashi	284
Matsubara	133
Matsudo	465
Matsue	153
Matsumoto	209
Matsusaka	124
Matsuyama	473
Mino'o	125
Misato	131
Mishima	111
Mitaka	172
Mito	247
Miyakonojō	132
Miyazaki	306
Moriguchi	152
Morioka	289
Muroran	103
Musashino	136
Nagano	360
Nagaoka	193
Nagareyama	151
Nagasaki	423
Nagoya	2,172
Naha	301
Nara	366
Narashino	154
Neyagawa	251
Niigata	501
Niihama	126
Niiza	150
Nishinomiya	438
Nishio	101
Nobeoka	125
Noda	120
Numazu	208
Obihiro	173
Odawara	200
Ōgaki	150
Ōita	436
Okayama	627
Okazaki	337
Okinawa	120
Ōme	141
Ōmiya	456
Ōmuta	139
Ōsaka	2,599
Ota	148
Ōta	140
Otaru	151
Ōtsu	288
Oyama	155
Saga	168
Sagamihara	606
Sakai	792
Sakata	101
Sakura	171
Sanda	112
Sapporo	1,822
Sasebo	241
Sayama	161
Sendai	1,008
Seto	132
Shimizu	237
Shimonoseki	252
Shizuoka	470
Sōka	225
Suita	348
Suzuka	186
Tachikawa	165
Takamatsu	333
Takaoka	172
Takarazuka	213
Takasaki	240
Takatsuki	357
Tama	146
Toda	108
Tokorozawa	330
Tokushima	268
Tokuyama	105
Tōkyō*	8,135
Tomakomai	172
Tondabayashi	127
Tottori	150
Toyama	326
Toyohashi	365
Toyokawa	117
Toyonaka	392
Toyota	351
Tsu	163
Tsuchiura	135
Tsukuba	166
Tsuruoka	101
Ube	174
Ueda	125
Uji	189
Urawa	485
Urasoe	103
Urayasu	133
Utsunomiya	444
Wakayama	387
Yachiyo	169
Yaizu	118
Yamagata	255
Yamaguchi	140
Yamato	213
Yao	275
Yatsushiro	106
Yokkaichi	291
Yokohama	3,427
Yokosuka	429
Yonago	139
Zama	126
Jordan	**6,053**
Amman*	970
Ar Ruşayfah	137
Az Zarqā'	351
Irbid	208
K	
Kazakhstan	**15,285**
Aqtöbe	264
Almaty	1,176
Atyraū	149
Aqmola*	287
Aqtaū	174
Atyraū	151
Ekibastuz	141
Kökshetaū	144
Oral	220
Öskemen	334
Pavlodar	349
Petropavl	248
Qaraghandy	596
Qostanay	234
Qyzylorda	164
Rudnyy	130
Semey	342
Shymkent	404
Taldyqorghan	125
Temirtaū	213
Zhambyl	317
Zhezqazghan	108
Kenya	**36,914**
Kisumu	185
Mombasa	465
Nairobi*	1,346
Nakuru	163
Kiribati	**108**
Tarawa*	2
Korea, North	**23,302**
Ch'ŏngjin	754
Haeju	131
Hamhŭng	775
Kaesŏng	346
Kimch'aek	281
Nampo	691
P'yŏngyang*	2,639
Sariwŏn	130
Sinŭiju	500
Wŏnsan	350
Korea, South	**49,045**
Andong	117
Ansan	252
Anyang	481
Ch'angwŏn	323
Ch'echŏn	102
Cheju	233
Chinhae	120
Chinju	256
Ch'ŏnan	211
Ch'ŏngju	478
Chŏnju	517
Ch'unch'ŏn	174
Ch'ungju	128
Inch'ŏn	2,203
Iri	203
Kangnŭng	153
Kimhae	106
Kohŭng	217
Kumi	206
Kunp'o	100
Kunsan	218
Kuri	109
Kwangju (Kwangju-Jikhalsi)	1,236
Kwangju (Kyŏnggi-Do)	906
Kwangmyŏng	329
Kyŏngju	142
Masan	494
Mokp'o	243
Nonsan	226
P'ohang	318
Puch'ŏn	668
Pusan	3,802
Seoul*	10,776
Sŏngnam	541
Sunch'ŏn	167
Suwŏn	665
Taegu	2,256
Taejŏn	1,183
Ŭijŏngbu	212
Ulsan	682
Wŏnju	173
Yŏsu	173
Kuwait	**2,506**
Al Jahrah	139
As Sālimīyah	116
Jalīb ash Shuyūkh	115
Kuwait*	31
Kyrgyzstan	**5,284**
Bishkek*	628
Osh	219
L	
Laos	**6,522**
Vientiane*	377
Latvia	**2,260**
Daugavpils	123
Liepāja	106
Riga*	865
Lebanon	**3,921**
Beirut*	1,000
Sidon	110
Tripoli	240
Lesotho	**2,013**
Maseru*	109
Liberia	**3,194**
Monrovia*	421
Libya	**6,037**
Benghāzī	446
Mişrātah	121
Tripoli*	590
Liechtenstein	**34**
Vaduz*	5
Lithuania	**3,475**
Kaunas	422
Klaipėda	204
Panevėžys	132
Šiauliai	148
Vilnius*	582
Luxembourg	**480**
Luxembourg*	75
M	
Macedonia, F.Y.R of	**2,056**
Gostivar	116
Skopje*	441
Madagascar	**19,449**
Amboasary	110
Ambovombe	144
Antananarivo*	676
Antsirabe	120
Betioky	140
Fandriana	135
Ifanadiana	102
Mahajanga	101
Toamasina	127
Vohipeno	106
Malawi	**13,603**
Blantyre	332
Lilongwe*	234
Malaysia	**24,821**
Alor Setar	125
George Town	219
Ipoh	383
Johor Baharu	329
Kelang	244
Kota Baharu	220
Kuala Lumpur*	1,145
Kuala Terengganu	229
Kuantan	198
Kuching	148
Petaling Jaya	255
Sandakan	126
Seremban	183
Shah Alam	102
Sibu	126
Sungai Petani	116
Taiping	183
Maldives	**369**
Male*	55
Mali	**11,995**
Bamako*	658
Malta	**402**
Valletta*	9
Marshall Islands	**62**
Majuro*	22
Mauritania	**3,270**
Nouakchott*	558
Mauritius	**1,251**
Port Louis*	144
Mexico	**108,701**
Acapulco de Juárez	621
Aguascalientes	594
Buenavista	194
Campeche	191
Cancún	397
Celaya	278
Chalco de Díaz Covarrubias	125
Chetumal	122
Chihuahua	658
Chilpancingo de los Bravos	143
Chimalhuacán	483
Ciudad Adolfo López Mateos	468
Ciudad Apodaca	270
Ciudad del Carmen	126
Ciudad General Escobedo	231
Ciudad Juárez	1,187
Ciudad Madero	182
Ciudad Obregón	251
Ciudad Valles	106
Ciudad Victoria	249
Coacalco de Berriozabal	252
Coatzacoalcos	226
Colima	120
Córdoba	134
Cuautitlán Izcalli	434
Cuautla Morelos	137
Cuernavaca	327
Culiacán Rosales	541
Durango de Victoria	427
Ecatepec de Morelos	1,622
Ensenada	223
Garza García	126
Gómez Palacio	210
Guadalajara	1,646
Guadalupe	670
Hermosillo	546
Heroica Matamoros	376
Heroica Nogales	157
Iguala de la Independencia	105
Irapuato	319
Ixtapaluca	236
Jalapa Enríquez	373
Jiutepec	142
La Paz	163
León	1,021
Los Mochis	201
Los Reyes Acaquilpan	211
Mazatlán	328
Mérida	663
Metepec	159
Mexicali	663
Mexico*	8,605
Minatitlán	109
Monclova	193
Monterrey	1,111
Morelia	550
Naucalpan de Juárez	835
Nezahualcóyotl	1,225
Nuevo Laredo	309
Oaxaca de Juárez	252
Orizaba	119
Pachuca de Soto	232
Piedras Negras	126
Poza Rica	151
Puebla de Zaragoza	1,272
Puerto Vallarta	151
Querétaro	536
Reynosa	404
Salamanca	137
Saltillo	563
San Cristóbal de las Casas	112
San Luis Potosí	629
San Luis Río Colorado	127
San Nicolás de los Garzas	497
San Pablo de las Salinas	147
Santa Catarina	226
Sánchez	170
Tampico	295
Tapachula	180
Tehuacán	205
Tepic	266
Texcoco de Mora	102
Tijuana	1,149
Tlalnepantla de Galeana	715
Tlaquepaque	459
Toluca de Lerdo	435

Country / City	Population in thousands
Tonalá	315
Torreón	503
Tuxtla Gutiérrez	425
Uruapan	226
Veracruz	412
Villahermosa	331
Villa Nicolás Romero	216
Zacatecas	114
Zamora de Hidalgo	123
Zapopan	911
Micronesia, Federated States of	**108**
Palikir*	6
Moldova	**4,320**
Bălţi	159
Chişinău*	665
Tighina (Bendery)	130
Tiraspol	182
Monaco	**33**
Monaco*	27
Mongolia	**2,874**
Ulaanbaatar*	575
Montenegro	**685**
Podgorica*	118
Morocco	**33,757**
Agadir	261
Beni Mallal	140
Casablanca	2,541
El Aaiún	137
El Jadida	119
Fès	508
Kénitra	293
Khouribga	152
Ksar el Kebir	107
Marrakech	521
Meknès	378
Mohammedia	169
Nador	208
Oujda	362
Rabat*	917
Safi	262
Salé	579
Témara	126
Tangier	519
Taza	121
Tétouan	278
Mozambique	**20,906**
Beira	397
Chimoio	171
Maputo*	967
Matola	425
Nacala	158
Nampula	303
Quelimane	150
Myanmar (Burma)	**47,374**
Akyab	108
Bago (Pegu)	151
Insein	144
Mandalay	533
Mawlamyine (Moulmein)	220
Monywa	107
Pathein (Bassein)	144
Sittwe (Akyab)	108
Taunggyi	108
Yangon* (Rangoon)	2,513
N	
Namibia	**2,055**
Windhoek*	147
Nauru	**14**
Yaren (district)	0.4
Nepal	**28,902**
Birātnagar	167
Kāthmāndu*	672
Pātan (Lalitpur)	163
Pokharā	156
Netherlands	**16,571**
Almere	150
Amersfoort	128
Amsterdam*	735
Apeldoorn	154
Arnhem	139
Breda	162
Dordrecht	120
Eindhoven	203
Enschede	147
Groningen	174
Haarlem	148
Leiden	117
Maastricht	122
Nijmegen	154
Rotterdam	595
The Hague*	442
Tilburg	161
Utrecht	256
Zaandam	130
Zaanstad	131
Zoetermeer	101
New Zealand	**4,115**
Auckland	404
Christchurch	348
Dunedin	119
Hamilton	129
Manukau	329
North Shore	206
Waitakere	156
Wellington*	179
Nicaragua	**5,675**
Chinandega	118
León	160
Managua*	883
Masaya	121
Niger	**12,895**
Maradi	109
Niamey*	392
Zinder	120
Nigeria	**135,031**
Aba	271
Abeokuta	387
Abuja*	306
Ado Ekiti	325
Akure	147
Awka	101
Benin City	207
Bida	114
Calabar	158
Deba Habe	125
Ede	278
Effon Alaiye	139
Enugu	286
Gusau	143
Ibadan	1,295
Ife	269
Ijebu Ode	142
Ikare	128
Ikerre	221
Ikire	112
Ikirun	164
Ikorodu	167
Ila Orangun	239
Ilawe - Ekiti	167
Ilesha	342
Ilobu	180
Ilorin	431
Inisa	108
Iseyin	197
Iwo	335
Jos	185
Kaduna	310
Kano	700
Katsina	187
Kuma	134
Lafia	111
Lagos	1,347
Maiduguri	289
Makurdi	111
Minna	126
Mushin	302
Offa	178
Ogbomosho	660
Oka	130
Ondo	154
Onitsha	337
Oshogbo	441
Owo	166
Oyo	237
Port Harcourt	371
Sapele	126
Shagamu	106
Shaki	161
Shomolu	136
Sokoto	186
Warri	114
Zaria	345
Norway	**4,628**
Bergen	203
Oslo*	508
Stavanger	108
Trondheim	143
O	
Oman	**3,204**
Muscat*	67
P	
Pakistan	**169,271**
Bahāwalpur	180
Chiniot	106
Dera Ghāzi Khān	102
Faisalābad	1,104
Gujrānwāla	659
Gujrāt	155
Hyderābād	752
Islāmābād*	204
Jhang Sadar	196
Jhelum	106
Karāchi	5,076
Kasūr	156
Lahore	2,953
Lārkāna	124
Mardān	148
Mirpur Khās	124
Multān	732
Nawābshāh	102
Okāra	127
Peshāwar	566
Quetta	286
Rahimyār Khān	119
Rāwalpindi	795
Sāhīwāl	151
Sargodha	291
Shekhūpura	141
Siālkot	302
Sukkur	191
Wāh	127
Palau	**21**
Koror*	9
Panama	**3,242**
Colón	174
Panamá*	680
San Miguelito	294
Papua New Guinea	**5,796**
Port Moresby*	193
Paraguay	**6,667**
Asunción*	547
Ciudad del Este	134
San Lorenzo	133
Peru	**28,675**
Arequipa	625
Ayacucho	106
Cajamarca	112
Callao	512
Chiclayo	412
Chimbote	269
Chincha Alta	110
Comas	287
Cusco	256
Huancayo	258
Huánuco	119
Ica	161
Iquitos	275
Juliaca	143
Lima*	376
Piura	278
Pucallpa	172
Santa	146
Sullana	147
Tacna	174
Trujillo	509
Philippines	**91,077**
Angeles	234
Antipolo	346
Bacolod	402
Bacoor	251
Bago	132
Baguio	227
Baliuag	103
Batangas	212
Biñan	160
Binangonan	141
Bislig	104
Butuan	247
Cabanatuan	201
Cadiz	126
Cagayan de Oro	428
Cainta	202
Calamba	219
Calbayog	129
Caloocan	1,023
Cebu	662
Concepcion	101
Cotabato	147
Dagupan	126
Dasmariñas	262
Davao	1,007
Digos	107
General Santos	327
Ilagan	107
Iligan	273
Iloilo	335
Imus	177
Kabankalan	139
Koranadal	118
Lapu-Lapu	174
Las Pinas	413
Legaspi	142
Lipa	178
Lubao	110
Lucena	178
Mabalacat	130
Makati	484
Malabon	347
Malasiqui	101
Malaybalay	112
Malolos	47
Mandaluyong	287
Mandaue	195
Manila*	1,655
Marawi	114
Marikina	357
Meycauayan	137
Muntinglupa	400
Naga	127
Navotas	229
Olongapo	180
Ormoc	144
Ozamiz	102
Pagadian	125
Panabo	131
Parañaque	391
Pasay	409
Pasig	471
Puerto Princesa	130
Quezon City	1,989
Roxas	119
Sagay	128
San Carlos (Negros Occ.)	101
San Carlos (Pangasinan)	134
San Fernando	193
San Jose	101
San Jose del Monte	201
San Juan del Monte	124
San Miguel	108
San Pablo	184
San Pedro	189
Santa Maria	161
Santa Rosa	138
Sariaya	101
Silang	124
Silay	123
Surigao	105
Tacloban	167
Taguig	381
Tagum	157
Talisay	120
Tanauan	104
Tarlac	230
Taytay	145
Toledo	121
Tuguegarai	107
Urdaneta	100
Valencia	129
Valenzuela	437
Zamboanga	511
Poland	**38,518**
Białystok	268
Bielsko-Biała	181
Bydgoszcz	380
Bytom	230
Chorzów	132
Częstochowa	257
Dąbrowa Górnicza	135
Elblag	126
Gdańsk	462
Gdynia	251
Gliwice	212
Gorzów Wielkopolski	123
Grudziądz	102
Jastrzębie Zdroj	102
Kalisz	106
Katowice	366
Kielce	213
Koszalin	108
Kraków	746
Legnica	104
Łódź	849
Lublin	349
Olsztyn	161
Opole	127
Płock	121
Poznań	587
Radom	226
Ruda Śląska	169
Rybnik	142
Rzeszów	151
Słupsk	100
Sosnowiec	259
Szczecin	411
Tarnów	121
Toruń	201
Tychy	190
Wałbrzych	142
Warsaw*	1,651
Włocławek	121
Wodzisław Śląski	111
Wrocław	641
Zabrze	203
Zielona Góra	113
Portugal	**10,643**
Lisbon*	818
Porto	330
Q	
Qatar	**907**
Doha*	217
R	
Romania	**22,276**
Arad	190
Bacău	205
Baia Mare	149
Botoşani	126
Brăila	234
Braşov	324
Bucharest*	2,068
Buzău	148
Cluj-Napoca	329
Constanţa	351
Craiova	304
Drobeta-Turnu Severin	115
Focşani	101
Galaţi	326
Iaşi	344
Oradea	223
Piatra Neamţ	123
Piteşti	179
Ploieşti	253
Reşiţa	106
Rîmnicu Vîlcea	114
Satu Mare	132
Sibiu	165
Suceava	114
Timisoara	334
Tîrgu Mures	164
Russia	**141,378**
Abakan	158
Achinsk	122
Al'met'yevsk	137
Angarsk	268
Anzhero-Sudzhensk	105
Arkhangel'sk	410
Armavir	161
Arzamas	111
Astrakhan'	508
Balakovo	207
Balashikha	136
Barnaul	595
Belgorod	314
Belovo	112
Berezniki	197
Biysk	233
Blagoveshchensk	212
Bratsk	260
Bryansk	456
Cheboksary	446
Chelyabinsk	1,130
Cherepovets	318
Cherkessk	118
Chita	365
Dimitrovgrad	131
Dzerzhinsk	286
Elektrostal'	152
Engel's	185
Glazov	107
Groznyy	354
Irkutsk	630
Ivanovo	474
Izhevsk	652
Kaliningrad (Kalin.)	413
Kaliningrad (Moscow)	136
Kaluga	344
Kamensk-Ural'skiy	206
Kamyshin	128
Kansk	111
Kazan'	1,086
Kemerovo	513
Khabarovsk	608
Khimki	136
Kineshma	103
Kirov	491
Kiselevsk	125
Kislovodsk	110
Kolomna	162
Kolpino	145
Komsomol'sk-na-Amure	314
Kostroma	281
Kovrov	162
Krasnodar	636
Krasnoyarsk	917
Kurgan	360
Kursk	434
Kuznetsk	102
Leninsk-Kuznetskiy	131
Lipetsk	466
Lyubertsy	164
Magadan	138
Magnitogorsk	439
Makhachkala	325
Maykop	162
Mezhdurechensk	108
Miass	170
Michurinsk	106
Moscow*	8,527
Murmansk	454
Murom	125
Mytishchi	153
Naberezhnye Chelny	527
Nakhodka	164
Nal'chik	236
Neftekamsk	117
Nevinnomyssk	127
Nizhnekamsk	206
Nizhnevartovsk	245
Nizhniy Novgorod	1,425
Nizhniy Tagil	431
Noginsk	121
Noril'sk	170
Novgorod	233
Novocheboksarsk	123
Novocherkassk	187
Novokuybyshevsk	113
Novokuznetsk	597
Novomoskovsk	144
Novorossiysk	193
Novoshakhtinsk	106
Novosibirsk	1,424
Novotroitsk	108
Obninsk	106
Odintsovo	131
Oktyabr'skiy	108
Omsk	1,164
Orekhovo-Zuyevo	135
Orël	343
Orenburg	554
Orsk	275
Penza	548
Perm'	1,091
Pervoural'sk	143
Petropavlovsk-Kamchatskiy	265
Petrozavodsk	279
Podol'sk	204
Prokop'yevsk	265
Pskov	207
Pyatigorsk	128
Rostov	1,013
Rubtsovsk	171
Ryazan'	524
Rybinsk	251
Saint Petersburg	4,329
Salavat	156
Samara	1,232
Saransk	321
Sarapul	110
Saratov	899
Sergiyev Posad	115
Serov	102
Serpukhov	140
Severodvinsk	249
Shakhty	227
Shchelkovo	108
Smolensk	349
Sochi	328
Solikamsk	109
Staryy Oskol'	190
Stavropol'	333
Sterlitamak	255
Surgut	261
Syktyvkar	226
Syzran'	175
Taganrog	290
Tambov	311
Tol'yatti	682
Tomsk	498
Tula	534
Tver'	449
Tyumen'	491
Ufa	1,092
Ukhta	112
Ulan-Ude	364
Ul'yanovsk	664
Usol'ye-Sibirskoye	107
Ussuriysk	161
Ust'-Ilimsk	113
Velikiye Luki	116
Vladikavkaz	308
Vladimir	335
Vladivostok	637
Volgodonsk	183
Volgograd	997
Vologda	290
Volzhskiy	282
Vorkuta	111
Voronezh	899
Votkinsk	105
Yakutsk	196
Yaroslavl'	628
Yekaterinburg	1,351
Yelets	118
Yoshkar-Ola	248
Yuzhno-Sakhalinsk	160
Zelenograd	179
Zhukovskiy	101
Zlatoust	207
Rwanda	**9,908**
Kigali*	233
S	
Saint Kitts and Nevis	**39**
Basseterre*	13
Saint Lucia	**171**
Castries*	13
Saint Vincent and the Grenadines	**118**
Kingstown*	15
Samoa	**177**
Apia*	39
San Marino	**30**
San Marino*	3
Sao Tome and Principe	**200**
São Tomé*	43
Saudi Arabia	**27,601**
Ad Dammām	350
Al Hufūf	101
Aṭ Ṭā'if	410
Jiddah	1,500
Mecca	630
Medina	400
Riyadh*	1,800
Senegal	**12,522**
Dakar*	1,641
Kaolack	193
Saint Louis	132
Thiès	216
Ziguinchor	162
Serbia	**10,150**
Belgrade*	1,555
Kragujevac	147
Niš	176
Novi Sad	179
Priština	125
Subotica	100
Uroševac	114
Seychelles	**82**
Victoria*	24
Sierra Leone	**6,145**
Freetown*	470
Singapore	**4,553**
Singapore*	3,462
Slovakia	**5,448**
Bratislava*	442
Košice	235
Slovenia	**2,009**
Ljubljana*	287
Maribor	105
Solomon Islands	**567**
Honiara*	30
Somalia	**9,119**
Mogadishu*	600
South Africa	**43,998**
Alexandra	125
Benoni	114
Bloemfontein	127
Boksburg	120
Botshabelo	178
Cape Town*	855
Carletonville	119
Daveyton	152
Diepmeadow	241
Durban	716
East London	102
Evaton	201
Germiston	134
Johannesburg	714
Katlehong	202
Kempton Park	107
Khayelitsa	190
KwaMashu	157
Lekoa	218
Mamelodi	155
Ntuzuma	102
Pietermaritzburg	156
Port Elizabeth	303
Pretoria*	526
Roodeport	163
Sandton	101
Soshanguve	146
Soweto	597
Tembisa	209
Umlazi	299
Virginia	118
Spain	**40,448**
Albacete	141
Alcalá de Henares	166
Alcorcón	142
Algeciras	104
Alicante	275
Almería	167
Badajoz	130
Badalona	219
Baracaldo	104
Barcelona	1,631
Bilbao	372
Burgos	166
Cádiz	155
Cartagena	180
Castellón de la Plana	139

Country / City	Population in thousands
Córdoba	316
Elche	191
Fuenlabrada	158
Getafe	144
Gijón	270
Granada	271
Huelva	145
Jaén	113
Jerez de la Frontera	190
La Coruña	255
La Laguna	125
Las Palmas de Gran Canaria	372
Leganés	178
León	147
L'Hospitalet de Llobregat	266
Lleida	114
Logroño	125
Madrid*	3,041
Málaga	531
Mataró	102
Móstoles	199
Murcia	342
Orense	109
Oviedo	202
Palma	322
Pamplona	182
Sabadell	189
Salamanca	167
San Sebastián	178
Santa Coloma de Gramenet	132
Santa Cruz de Tenerife	204
Santander	195
Saragossa	607
Seville	714
Tarragona	115
Terrassa	161
Valencia	764
Valladolid	337
Vigo	289
Vitoria	214
Sri Lanka	**20,927**
Colombo*	615
Dehiwala-Mount Lavinia	196
Galle	109
Jaffna	129
Kandy	104
Moratuwa	170
Sri Jayawardanapura (Kotte)	109
Sudan	**42,293**
Al Qaḍārif	189
Al Ubayyiḍ	228
Juba	115
Kassala	234
Khartoum*	925
Khartoum North	341
Nyala	112
Omdurman	229
Port Sudan	305
Wad Medanī	219
Suriname	**471**
Paramaribo*	180
Swaziland	**1,133**
Mbabane*	38
Sweden	**9,031**
Göteborg	478
Helsingborg	120
Jönköping	119
Linköping	136
Malmö	267
Norrköping	124
Örebro	126
Stockholm*	762
Umeå	108
Uppsala	181
Västerås	130
Switzerland	**7,555**
Basel	174
Bern*	127
Geneva	174
Lausanne	116
Zürich	344
Syria	**19,315**
Aleppo	1,542
Al Mamishlī	113
Ar Raqqah	138
Damascus*	1,549
Dar'ā	180
Dayr az Zawr	133
Dūmā	131
Ḥamāh	273
Ḥimṣ	558
Idlib	113
Jaramānah	138
Latakia	303
Ṭarṭūs	137
T	
Taiwan	**23,174**
Changhua	165
Chiai	266
Chungli	270
Chutung	105
Fengshan	291
Fengyüan	121
Hsinchu	396
Hsinchuang	299
Hsintien	226
Hualien	108
Kaohsiung	1,494
Keelung (Chilung)	388
P'ingchen	147
P'ingtung	172
Sanchung	376
Shulin	112
T'aichung	989
T'ainan	706
T'aipei*	2,624
T'aoyüan	241
Yungho	250
Tajikistan	**7,077**
Dushanbe*	602
Khujand	163
Tanzania	**38,140**
Dar es Salaam*	1,361
Dodoma*	204
Mbeya	194
Mwanza	223
Tabora	214
Tanga	188
Zanzibar	158
Thailand	**65,068**
Bangkok*	5,876
Chiang Mai	167
Chon Buri	187
Khon Kaen	206
Nakhon Ratchasima	278
Nakhon Sawan	152
Nakhon Si Thammarat	112
Nonthaburi	233
Sara Buri	107
Songkhla	243
Togo	**5,702**
Lomé*	450
Tonga	**117**
Nuku'alofa*	21
Trinidad and Tobago	**1,057**
Port-of-Spain*	51
Tunisia	**10,276**
Bizerte	114
Ettadhamen Douarhicher	118
Grand Gabes	116
Kairouan	118
Sfax	265
Sousse	173
Tūnis*	728
Turkey	**71,159**
Adana	1,113
Adapazarı	171
Adıyaman	179
Ankara*	3,203
Antakya (Antioch)	145
Antalya	606
Aydın	144
Balıkesir	215
Batman	248
Bursa	1,184
Çorum	161
Denizli	274
Diyarbakır	551
Edirne	119
Elazığ	270
Erzurum	267
Eskişehir	483
Gaziantep	862
Gebze	269
Iskenderun	164
Isparta	148
Istanbul	8,832
İzmir	2,250
İzmit	195
Kahramanmaraş	322
Karabük	101
Kayseri	525
Kırıkkale	205
Konya	761
Kütahya	168
Malatya	381
Manisa	214
Mersin	554
Ordu	113
Osmaniye	177
Sakarya	294
Samsun	363
Sivas	250
Tarsus	190
Trabzon	215
Urfa	384
Uşak	137
Van	284
Zonguldak	104
Turkmenistan	**5,136**
Ashgabat*	407
Chärjew	164
Dashhowuz	114
Tuvalu	**12**
Funafuti*	2
U	
Uganda	**30,263**
Kampala*	774
Ukraine	**46,300**
Alchevs'k	119
Bila Tserkva	200
Berdyans'k	122
Cherkasy	295
Chernihiv	305
Chernivtsi	241
Dniprodzerzhyns'k	256
Dnipropetrovs'k	1,065
Donets'k	1,016
Horlivka	292
Ivano-Frankivs'k	218
Kerch	157
Kharkiv	1,471
Kherson	328
Khmel'nytskyy	254
Kirovohrad	254
Kiev*	2,611
Kramators'k	181
Kremenchuk	234
Kryvyy Rih	669
Luhans'k	463
Luts'k	209
L'viv	733
Lysychans'k	115
Makiyivka	390
Mariupol'	492
Melitopol'	161
Mykolayiv	514
Nikopol'	136
Odesa	1,029
Pavlohrad	119
Poltava	318
Rivne	249
Sevastopol'	342
Simferopol'	344
Slov'yans'k	125
Sumy	293
Syeverodonets'k	120
Ternopil'	228
Uzhhorod	117
Vinnytsya	357
Yenakiyeve	104
Yevpatoriya	106
Zaporizhzhya	815
Zhytomyr	284
United Arab Emirates	**2,643**
Abu Dhabi*	243
Al 'Ayn	102
Ash Shāriqah	125
Dubayy	266
United Kingdom	**60,776**
Aberdeen	219
Basildon	101
Belfast	295
Birmingham	966
Blackburn	106
Blackpool	146
Bolton	139
Bournemouth	155
Bradford	289
Brighton	125
Bristol	408
Cardiff	272
Coventry	299
Derby	224
Dudley	192
Dundee	151
Edinburgh	448
Glasgow	618
Gloucester	114
Hillingdon	231
Huddersfield	144
Ipswich	130
Kingston upon Hull	311
Kingston upon Thames	132
Leeds	424
Leicester	319
Liverpool	482
London*	6,680
Luton	172
Manchester	403
Middlesbrough	147
Newcastle upon Tyne	189
Newport	116
Northampton	180
Norwich	171
Nottingham	270
Oldham	104
Oxford	119
Peterborough	135
Plymouth	245
Poole	138
Portsmouth	175
Preston	178
Reading	213
Rotherham	121
Saint Helens	106
Sheffield	432
Slough	111
Southampton	210
Southend-on-Sea	159
Stockport	133
Stoke-on-Trent	267
Sunderland	183
Sutton Coldfield	106
Swansea	171
Swindon	145
Thanet	117
Walsall	175
Watford	113
West Bromwich	146
Wolverhampton	258
York	125
United States	**301,140**
Abilene	116
Akron	217
Albuquerque	449
Alexandria	128
Allentown	107
Amarillo	174
Amherst	117
Anaheim	328
Anchorage	260
Ann Arbor	114
Arlington (Tex.)	333
Arlington (Va.)	189
Arvada	102
Athens	101
Atlanta	417
Augusta	200
Aurora (Colo.)	276
Aurora (Ill.)	143
Austin	657
Bakersfield	247
Baltimore	651
Baton Rouge	228
Beaumont	114
Bellevue	110
Berkeley	103
Birmingham	243
Boise	186
Boston	589
Bridgeport	140
Brownsville	140
Buffalo	293
Burbank	100
Cambridge	101
Cape Coral	102
Carrollton	110
Cedar Rapids	121
Chandler	177
Charlotte	541
Chattanooga	156
Chesapeake	199
Chicago	2,896
Chula Vista	174
Cincinnati	331
Citrus Heights	107
Clarksville	103
Clearwater	109
Cleveland	478
Colorado Springs	361
Columbia	116
Columbus (Ga.)	186
Columbus (Ohio)	711
Concord	122
Coral Springs	118
Corona	125
Corpus Christi	277
Costa Mesa	109
Dallas	1,189
Daly City	104
Dayton	166
Denver	555
Des Moines	199
Detroit	951
Downey	107
Durham	187
East Los Angeles	124
Elizabeth	121
El Monte	116
El Paso	564
Erie	104
Escondido	134
Eugene	138
Evansville	122
Fayetteville	121
Flint	125
Fontana	129
Fort Collins	119
Fort Lauderdale	152
Fort Wayne	206
Fort Worth	535
Fremont	203
Fresno	428
Fullerton	126
Garden Grove	165
Garland	216
Gary	103
Gilbert	110
Glendale (Ariz.)	219
Glendale (Calif.)	195
Grand Prairie	128
Grand Rapids	198
Green Bay	102
Greensboro	224
Hampton	146
Hartford	122
Hayward	140
Henderson	175
Hialeah	226
Hollywood	139
Honolulu	372
Houston	1,954
Huntington Beach	190
Huntsville	158
Independence	113
Indianapolis	792
Inglewood	113
Irvine	143
Irving	192
Jackson	184
Jacksonville	736
Jersey City	240
Joliet	106
Kansas City (Kans.)	147
Kansas City (Mo.)	442
Knoxville	174
Lafayette	110
Lakewood	144
Lancaster	119
Lansing	119
Laredo	177
Las Vegas	478
Lexington	261
Lincoln	226
Little Rock	183
Livonia	101
Long Beach	462
Los Angeles	3,695
Louisville	256
Lowell	105
Lubbock	200
Madison	208
Manchester	107
McAllen	106
Memphis	650
Mesa	396
Mesquite	125
Metairie	146
Miami	362
Milwaukee	597
Minneapolis	383
Mobile	199
Modesto	189
Montgomery	202
Moreno Valley	142
Naperville	128
Nashville	570
Newark	274
New Haven	124
New Orleans	485
Newport News	180
New York	8,008
Norfolk	234
North Las Vegas	115
Norwalk	103
Oakland	399
Oceanside	161
Oklahoma City	506
Omaha	390
Ontario	158
Orange	129
Orlando	186
Overland Park	149
Oxnard	170
Palmdale	117
Paradise	186
Pasadena (Calif.)	134
Pasadena (Tex.)	142
Paterson	149
Pembroke Pines	137
Peoria (Ariz.)	108
Peoria (Ill.)	113
Philadelphia	1,518
Phoenix	1,321
Pittsburgh	335
Plano	222
Pomona	149
Portland	529
Portsmouth	101
Providence	174
Provo	105
Pueblo	102
Raleigh	276
Rancho Cucamonga (Cucamonga)	128
Reno	180
Richmond	198
Riverside	255
Rochester	220
Rockford	150
Sacramento	407
Saint Louis	348
Saint Paul	287
Saint Petersburg	248
Salem	137
Salinas	151
Salt Lake City	182
San Antonio	1,145
San Bernardino	185
San Diego	1,223
San Francisco	777
San Jose	895
Santa Ana	338
Santa Clara	102
Santa Clarita	151
Santa Rosa	148
Savannah	132
Scottsdale	203
Seattle	563
Shreveport	200
Simi Valley	111
Sioux Falls	124
South Bend	108
Spokane	196
Springfield (Ill.)	111
Springfield (Mass.)	152
Springfield (Mo.)	152
Stamford	117
Sterling Heights	124
Stockton	244
Sunnyvale	132
Sunrise Manor	156
Syracuse	147
Tacoma	194
Tallahassee	151
Tampa	303
Tempe	159
Thousand Oaks	117
Toledo	314
Topeka	122
Torrance	138
Tucson	487
Tulsa	393
Vallejo	117
Vancouver	144
Ventura	101
Virginia Beach	425
Waco	114
Warren	138
Washington, D.C.*	572
Waterbury	107
West Covina	105
West Valley City	109
Westminster	101
Wichita	344
Wichita Falls	104
Winston-Salem	186
Worcester	173
Yonkers	196
Uruguay	**3,447**
Montevideo*	1,360
Uzbekistan	**27,780**
Andijon	297
Angren	133
Bukhoro	228
Chirchiq	159
Farghona	198
Jizzakh	108
Marghilon	125
Namangan	312
Nawoiy	110
Nukus	175
Olmaliq	116
Qarshi	163
Qŭqon	176
Samarqand	370
Tashkent*	2,094
Urganch	129
V	
Vanuatu	**212**
Port-Vila*	19
Vatican City	**1**
Vatican City*	1
Venezuela	**26,085**
Acarigua	117
Barcelona	222
Barinas	154
Barquisimeto	625
Baruta	183
Cabimas	166
Caracas*	2,080
Catia La Mar	100
Ciudad Bolívar	225
Ciudad Guayana	453
Coro	125
Cumaná	212
Guacara	101
Guarenas	134
Los Teques	141
Maracaibo	1,250
Maracay	354
Maturín	207
Mérida	171
Petare	338
Puerto Cabello	129
Puerto La Cruz	156
San Cristóbal	221
San Francisco	198
Turmero	174
Valencia	904
Vietnam	**85,262**
Bien Hoa	274
Cam Pha	105
Cam Ranh	118
Can Tho	208
Da Lat	103
Da Nang	370
Haiphong	450
Hanoi*	1,090
Ho Chi Minh City	2,900
Hong Gai	123
Hue	212
Long Xuyen	129
My Tho	105
Nam Dinh	166
Nha Trang	213
Phan Thiet	114
Qui Nhon	160
Rach Gia	138
Thai Nguyen	125
Vinh	111
Vung Tau	124
Y	
Yemen	**22,212**
Al Ḥudaydah	155
Al Mukallā	154
Aden	562
Sanaa*	972
Ta'izz	178
Z	
Zambia	**11,477**
Chingola	168
Kabwe	167
Kitwe	247
Lusaka*	982
Ndola	376
Zimbabwe	**12,311**
Bulawayo	622
Chitungwiza	275
Gweru	125
Harare*	1,189
Mutare	132
Uroševac	114
Areas of Special Sovereignty	
Hong Kong (China)	**6,980**
Kowloon	775
New Kowloon	1,527
Sha Tin	550
Tai Po	260
Tsuen Wan	700
Tuen Mun	432
Victoria*	1,251
Yuen Long	143
Macau (China)	**457**
Macau*	343
Puerto Rico (U.S.)	**3,944**
Bayamón	202
Carolina	162
Ponce	159
San Juan*	427

Foreign Term	Language	English Meaning
A		
Adrar	Berber	Mountains
Aiguille	French	Peak
Ákra	Greek	Cape
Altos	Spanish	Mountains
Älv, Älven	Swedish	River
Anse	French	Cove
Archipiélago	Spanish	Archipelago
Arcipelago	Italian	Archipelago
Arquipélago	Portuguese	Archipelago
Arrecife	Spanish	Reef
Arroyo	Spanish	Stream
'Ayn	Arabic	Spring
B		
Baai	Dutch	Bay
Bab	Arabic	Strait
Bach	German	Stream
Bælt	Danish	Strait
Bahia	Spanish	Bay
Baḥr	Arabic	River, Sea
Baia	Portuguese	Bay
Baie	French	Bay
Ballon	French	Dome
Bana	Japanese	Cape
Bañados	Spanish	Marsh
Bandar	Persian	Harbor
Barrage	French	Dam, Reservoir
Bassin	French	Basin
Bāçtlāq	Persian	Marsh
Be'er	Hebrew	Well
Belt	German	Strait
Ben, Beinn	Gaelic	Mountain
Berg	Afrikaans, German	Mountain
Bi'r	Arabic	Well
Birkat	Arabic	Lake
Boca	Spanish	River Mouth
Bogd	Mongolian	Range
Bolsón	Spanish	Depression
Botn	Norwegian	Bay
Brazo	Spanish	River Branch
Bucht	German	Bay
Bugt	Danish	Bay
Buhayrat	Arabic	Lake, Lagoon
Bukit	Malay	Mountain
Bukt, Bukten	Swedish	Bay
Bulu	Indonesian	Mountain
Burj	Arabic	Hill
Burnu, Burun	Turkish	Cape
Busen	German	Bay
C		
Cabo	Portuguese, Spanish	Cape
Cañada	Spanish	Stream
Canal	Portuguese, Spanish	Channel
Canale	Italian	Canal
Cap	French	Cape
Capo	Italian	Cape
Cataratas	Spanish	Waterfalls
Catena	Spanish	Range
Causse	French	Upland
Cayos	Spanish	Cays
Cerro(s)	Spanish	Hill(s)
Chaîne	French	Range
Chapada	Portuguese	Hills
Chott	Arabic	Intermittent Lakes, Marshes
Chroüy	Cambodian	Cape
Chute(s)	French	Waterfall(s)
Ciénaga	Spanish	Marsh
Cima	Italian, Spanish	Peak
Cime	French	Peak
Città	Italian	City
Ciudad	Spanish	City
Co	Tibetan	Lake
Col	French	Pass
Colina(s)	Spanish	Hill(s)
Colle	Italian	Pass
Colline	Italian	Hills
Collines	French	Hills
Cordillera	Spanish	Range
Corno	Italian	Peak
Costa	Portuguese, Spanish	Coast
Côte	French	Coast, Ridge
Coteau	French	Hills
Csatorna	Magyar	Canal
Cuchilla	Spanish	Hills
Cumbre	Spanish	Peak
D		
Dağ, Daği	Turkish	Mountain
Dake	Japanese	Mountain
Dal, Dalen	Swedish	Valley
Damágheh	Persian	Cape
Daryācheh	Persian	Lake
Dasht	Persian	Desert
Desierto	Spanish	Desert
Détroit	French	Strait
Dhar	Arabic	Escarpment
Diep	Dutch	Channel
Dijk	Dutch	Dike
Ding	Chinese	Hill
Djebel	Arabic	Mountain(s)
Doi	Thai	Mountain
Dyb	Danish	Strait
E		
Eiland	Dutch	Island
Elv	Norwegian	River
Embalse	Spanish	Reservoir
Emi	Berber	Mountain
Enseada	Portuguese	Cove
Ensenada	Spanish	Cove
Erg	Arabic	Desert
Estrecho	Spanish	Strait
Étang	French	Lagoon
F		
Falaise	French	Cliff
Feld	German	Plain
Feng	Chinese	Mountain
Firth	Gaelic	Estuary
Fjärden	Swedish	Bay, Sound
Fjord, Fjorden	Norwegian	Inlet
Fjördhur	Icelandic	Bay
Fljót	Icelandic	River
Flói	Icelandic	Bay
Foci	Italian	River Mouths
G		
Gat	Danish, Dutch	Marine Channel
Gebirge	German	Range
Geçidi	Turkish	Pass
Gobi	Mongolian	Desert
Göl	Turkish	Lake
Golfe	French	Gulf
Golfo	Italian, Spanish	Gulf
Gora	Russian	Mountain
Got	Korean	Cape
Graben	German	Ditch
Guan	Chinese	Pass
Guelb	Arabic	Mountain
Gunung	Indonesian	Mountain
H		
Hai	Chinese	Sea
Hamada	Arabic	Desert
Ḥammādat	Arabic	Plateau
Ḥāmūn	Persian	Intermittent Salt Lake
Har	Hebrew	Mountain
Havet	Norwegian	Bay
Ḥawḍ	Arabic	Oasis
Hāyk'	Amharic (Ethiopia)	Lake
Hegy	Magyar	Mountain
Heide	Arabic	Heath
Hoek	Dutch	Point
Höhe	German	Height
Holm	Danish, Swedish	Island
Horn	German	Point
Hornatina	Czech, Slovak	Plateau
Hory	Czech, Slovak	Range
Hügel	German	Hill
I		
Île(s)	French	Island(s)
Ilha(s)	Portuguese	Island(s)
Insel(n)	German	Island(s)
Irmak	Turkish	River
Isla(s)	Spanish	Island(s)
Isola, Isole	Italian	Island, Islands
J		
Jabal	Arabic	Mountains
Järvi	Finnish	Lake
Jazīrat, Jazā'ir	Arabic	Island, Islands
Jbel	Arabic	Mountain(s)
Jezero	Czech, Slovak	Lake
Jezioro	Polish	Lake
Jiao	Chinese	Cape
Jibāl	Arabic	Mountain(s)
Joki	Finnish	River
Jökull	Icelandic	Glacier
Jolgeh	Persian	Plain
K		
Kaap	Dutch	Cape
Kabīr	Persian	Mountains
Kanaal	Dutch	Canal
Kanal	German, Serbo-Croatian	Canal
Kangri	Tibetan	Peak
Kap	German	Cape
Kapp	Norwegian	Cape
Kavīr	Persian	Desert
Kawlat	Arabic	Mountain
Kawm	Arabic	Hill
Kep	Albanian	Cape
Khalīj	Arabic	Gulf
Khao	Thai	Mountain
Khatt	Arabic	Intermittent River
Khawr	Arabic	Intermittent River
Khazzān	Arabic	Dam
Khuan	Thai	Lake
Kloof	Dutch	Gap
Kogel	German	Mountain
Kop	Dutch	Peak
Kopf	German	Peak
Kreb	Arabic	Dune
Küh	Persian	Mountain
L		
La	Tibetan	Pass
Lac(s)	French	Lake(s)
Laem	Thai	Cape
Laga, Lagh	Swahili	Intermittent River
Lago(s)	Italian, Portuguese, Spanish	Lake(s)
Lagoa	Portuguese	Lake
Laguna	Spanish	Lagoon
Les	Czech	Mountains
Ling	Chinese	Mountain
Llano(s)	Spanish	Plain(s)
Loch, Lough	Gaelic	Inlet, Lake
M		
Mägi	Estonian	Mountain
Mare	Italian	Sea
Marsá	Arabic	Bay
Maṣabb	Arabic	River Mouth
Maṣrif	Arabic	Canal
Massif	French	Upland
Meer	Afrikaans, Dutch, German	Lake, Sea
Meseta	Spanish	Plateau
Mifraz	Hebrew	Bay
Misaki	Japanese	Cape
Mont(s)	French	Mountain(s)
Montagna	Italian	Mountain
Montagne(s)	French	Mountain(s)
Montaña(s)	Spanish	Mountain(s)
Monte	Italian, Portuguese, Spanish	Mountain
Montes	Portuguese, Spanish	Mountains
Monti	Italian	Mountains
Morne	French	Mountain
Morro	Portuguese, Spanish	Mountain
Mui	Vietnamese	Cape
Mys	Russian	Cape
N		
Nafūd	Arabic	Desert
Naḥal	Hebrew	River
Nahr	Arabic	River
Namakzār	Persian	Salt Flat
Neem	Estonian	Cape
Nek	Dutch	Pass
Nevado	Spanish	Snow-covered Peak
Nina	Estonian	Cape
Nos	Russian	Cape
Nosy	Malagasy	Island
O		
Ø, Øy	Norwegian	Island
Odde	Danish	Point
Óros	Greek	Mountain
Otok	Serbo-Croatian	Island
Ouadi, Oued	Arabic	Intermittent River
Ozero	Russian	Lake
P		
Pampa	Spanish	Plain
Pantanal	Portuguese, Spanish	Swamp
Pas	Dutch	Pass
Pas	French	Strait
Paso	Spanish	Pass
Passage	French	Marine Channel
Peña, Peñasco	Spanish	Peak
Pereval	Russian	Pass
Phnum	Cambodian	Mountain
Phou	Lao	Mountain
Pi	Chinese	Cape
Pic	French	Peak
Picacho	Spanish	Peak
Picco	Italian	Peak
Pico(s)	Portuguese, Spanish	Peak(s)
Pik	Russian	Peak
Pique	French	Peak
Piton	French	Mountain
Piz, Pizzo	Italian	Peak
Planalto	Portuguese	Plateau
Planina	Serbo-Croatian	Plain
Plato	Afrikaans	Plateau
Playa	Spanish	Beach
Plošina	Czech	Plateau
Pointe	French	Point
Ponta	Portuguese	Point
Presa	Spanish	Dam, Reservoir
Presqu'île	French	Peninsula
Prokhod	Bulgarian	Pass
Promontorio	Italian	Promontory
Puncak	Indonesian	Mountain
Punt	Dutch	Point
Punta	Italian, Spanish	Point
Q		
Qanāt	Arabic	Canal
Qiryat	Hebrew	City
Qolleh	Persian	Mountain
R		
Rada	Spanish	Anchorage
Rade	French	Anchorage
Rann	Hindi	Marsh
Rapides	French	Rapids
Ras, Ra's	Arabic	Cape
Recifes	Portuguese	Reefs
Represa	Portuguese	Dam, Reservoir
Retto	Japanese	Islands
Rio	Portuguese	River
Rio	Spanish	River
Rivier	Dutch	River
Rivière	French	River
Rosh	Hebrew	Cape
Rt	Serbo-Croatian	Cape
S		
Sabana	Spanish	Savanna
Sabkhat	Arabic	Lagoon, Salt Marsh
Sāgar	Hindi	Lake
Saguia	Arabic	Intermittent River
Ṣaḥrā'	Arabic	Desert
Saki	Japanese	Cape
Salar	Spanish	Salt Flat
Salina(s)	Spanish	Salt Flat(s)
Salto(s)	Portuguese, Spanish	Waterfall(s)
San	Japanese	Mountain
Sarīr	Arabic	Desert
Sebjet	Arabic	Dry Lake
Sebkha	Arabic	Salt Flat
See	German	Lake
Selkä	Finnish	Bay
Serra	Portuguese	Range
Serranía(s)	Spanish	Ridge(s)
Seto	Japanese	Strait
Sgurr	Gaelic	Mountain
Shan	Chinese	Mountain
Shankou	Chinese	Pass
Shaṭṭ	Arabic	Intermittent Lake
Shet'	Amharic (Ethiopia)	River
Shima	Japanese	Island
Shotō	Japanese	Islands
Sierra	Spanish	Range
Sistema	Spanish	Range
Sjö, Sjön	Swedish	Lake
Slieve	Gaelic	Mountain
Sø	Danish	Lake
Sommet	French	Peak
Sopka	Russian	Volcano
Spitze	German	Peak
Stausee	German	Reservoir
Stretto	Italian	Strait
Sund	Danish, Swedish	Sound
T		
Tal	German	Valley
Tall	Arabic	Mountain
Tanjona	Malagasy	Cape
Tanjong	Malay	Cape
Tanjung	Indonesian	Cape
Tassili	Berber	Plateau
Ténéré	Berber	Desert
Tepe	Turkish	Peak
Terara	Amharic (Ethiopia)	Mountain
Tō	Japanese	Island
Tó	Magyar	Lake
Tōge	Japanese	Pass
Tunturi	Finnish	Mountain
U		
Udde	Swedish	Point
Udolní	Czech	Reservoir
Uul	Mongolian	Mountain
Úval	Czech	Valley
V		
Val	French, Italian	Valley
Valle	Italian, Spanish	Valley
Vallée	French	Valley
Vallen	Dutch	Waterfall
Valli	Italian	Lagoon
Vatn	Norwegian	Lake
Veld	Dutch	Plain
Vig	Danish	Bay
Vik, Viken	Swedish	Bay
Vîrful	Romanian	Mountain
Vliet	Dutch	Channel
Vodoskhovyshche	Ukranian	Reservoir
Volcán	Spanish	Volcano
Vrch	Serbo-Croatian	Mountain
Vrchy	Czech, Slovak	Range
Vysočina	Czech, Slovak	Plateau
W		
Wabē	Amharic (Ethiopia)	River
Wādī	Arabic	Intermittent River
Wāḥāt	Arabic	Oasis
Wald	German	Forest, Mountains
Webi	Somali	River
Wenz	Amharic (Ethiopia)	River
Y		
Yam	Hebrew	Lake, Sea
Yama	Japanese	Mountain
Z		
Zaki	Japanese	Point
Zatoka	Ukranian	Gulf
Zee	Dutch	Lake, Sea
Zemlya	Russian	Land

Index of the World

This index is a comprehensive listing of the places and geographic features found in the atlas. Names are arranged in strict alphabetical order, without regard to hyphens or spaces. Every name is followed by the country or area to which it belongs. Except for cities, towns and cultural areas, all entries include a reference to feature type, such as province, river, island, peak, and so on. The page number and alpha-numeric code appear in blue to the right of each listing. The page number directs you to the largest scale map on which the name can be found. The code refers to the grid squares formed by the horizontal and vertical lines of latitude and longitude on each map. Following the letters from left to right and the numbers from top to bottom helps you to quickly locate the square containing the place or feature. Inset maps have their own alpha-numeric codes. Names on the map that are accompanied by a point symbol are indexed to the symbol's grid location. Other names are indexed in the grid in which the initial letter of the name falls. When a map name contains a subordinate or alternate name, both names are listed in the index. To conserve space and provide room for more entries, many abbreviations are used in this index. The primary abbreviations are listed below.

Index Abbreviations

A
Ab,Can — Alberta
Abor. — Aboriginal
Acad. — Academy
ACT — Australian Capital Territory
A.F.B. — Air Force Base
Afld. — Airfield
Afg. — Afghanistan
Afr. — Africa
Ak,US — Alaska
Al,US — Alabama
Alb. — Albania
Alg. — Algeria
Amm. Dep. — Ammunition Depot
And. — Andorra
Ang. — Angola
Angu. — Anguilla
Ant. — Antarctica
Anti. — Antigua and Barbuda
Ar,US — Arkansas
Arch. — Archipelago
Arg. — Argentina
Arm. — Armenia
Arpt. — Airport
Aru. — Aruba
ASam. — American Samoa
Ash. — Ashmore and Cartier Islands
Aus. — Austria
Austl. — Australia
Aut. — Autonomous
Az,US — Arizona
Azer. — Azerbaijan
Azor. — Azores

B
Bahm. — Bahamas, The
Bahr. — Bahrain
Bang. — Bangladesh
Bar. — Barbados
BC,Can — British Columbia
Bela. — Belarus
Belg. — Belgium
Belz. — Belize
Ben. — Benin
Berm. — Bermuda
Bfld. — Battlefield
Bhu. — Bhutan
Bol. — Bolivia
Bor. — Borough
Bosn. — Bosnia and Herzegovina
Bots. — Botswana
Braz. — Brazil
Brln. — British Indian Ocean Territory
Bru. — Brunei
Bul. — Bulgaria
Burk. — Burkina Faso
Buru. — Burundi
BVI — British Virgin Islands

C
Ca,US — California
CAfr. — Central African Republic
Camb. — Cambodia
Camr. — Cameroon
Can. — Canada
Can. — Canal
Canl. — Canary Islands
Cap. — Capital
Cap. Dist. — Capital District

Cap. Terr. — Capital Territory
Cay. — Cayman Islands
C.d'Iv. — Côte d'Ivoire
C.G. — Coast Guard
Chan. — Channel
Chl. — Channel Islands
Co. — County
Co,US — Colorado
Col. — Colombia
Com. — Comoros
Cont. — Continent
CpV. — Cape Verde Islands
CR — Costa Rica
Cr. — Creek
Cro. — Croatia
CSea. — Coral Sea Islands Territory
Ct,US — Connecticut
Ctr. — Center
Ctry. — Country
Cyp. — Cyprus
Czh. — Czech Republic

D
DC,US — District of Columbia
De,US — Delaware
Den. — Denmark
Depr. — Depression
Dept. — Department
Des. — Desert
DF — Distrito Federal
Dist. — District
Djib. — Djibouti
Dom. — Dominica
Dpcy. — Dependency
D.R.Congo — Democratic Republic of the Congo
DRep. — Dominican Republic

E
Ecu. — Ecuador
Emb. — Embankment
Eng. — Engineering
Eng,UK — England
EqG. — Equatorial Guinea
Erit.. — Eritrea
ESal. — El Salvador
Est. — Estonia
Eth. — Ethiopia
ETim. — East Timor
Eur. — Europe

F
Falk. — Falkland Islands
Far. — Faroe Islands
Fed. Dist. — Federal District
Fin. — Finland
Fl,US — Florida
For. — Forest
Fr. — France
FrAnt. — French Southern and Antarctic Lands
FrG. — French Guiana
FrPol. — French Polynesia
FYROM — Former Yugoslav Rep. of Macedonia

G
Ga,US — Georgia
Galp. — Galapagos Islands
Gam. — Gambia, The
Gaza — Gaza Strip
GBis. — Guinea-Bissau

Geo. — Georgia
Ger. — Germany
Gha. — Ghana
Gib. — Gibraltar
Glac. — Glacier
Gov. — Governorate
Govt. — Government
Gre. — Greece
Grld. — Greenland
Gren. — Grenada
Grsld. — Grassland
Guad. — Guadeloupe
Guat. — Guatemala
Gui. — Guinea
Guy. — Guyana

H
Har. — Harbor
Hi,US — Hawaii
Hist. — Historic(al)
Hon. — Honduras
Hts. — Heights
Hun. — Hungary

I
Ia,US — Iowa
Ice. — Iceland
Id,US — Idaho
Il,US — Illinois
IM — Isle of Man
In,US — Indiana
Ind. Res. — Indian Reservation
Indo. — Indonesia
Int'l — International
Ire. — Ireland
Isl., Isls. — Island, Islands
Isr. — Israel
Isth. — Isthmus
It. — Italy

J
Jam. — Jamaica
Jor. — Jordan

K
Kaz. — Kazakhstan
Kiri. — Kiribati
Ks,US — Kansas
Kuw. — Kuwait
Ky,US — Kentucky
Kyr. — Kyrgyzstan

L
La,US — Louisiana
Lab. — Laboratory
Lag. — Lagoon
Lakesh. — Lakeshore
Lat. — Latvia
Lcht. — Liechtenstein
Ldg. — Landing
Leb. — Lebanon
Les. — Lesotho
Libr. — Liberia
Lith. — Lithuania
Lux. — Luxembourg

M
Ma,US — Massachusetts
Madg. — Madagascar
Madr. — Madeira
Malay. — Malaysia
Mald. — Maldives
Malw. — Malawi
Mart. — Martinique

May. — Mayotte
Mb,Can — Manitoba
Md,US — Maryland
Me,US — Maine
Mem. — Memorial
Mex. — Mexico
Mi,US — Michigan
Micr. — Micronesia, Federated States of
Mil. — Military
Mn,US — Minnesota
Mo,US — Missouri
Mol. — Moldova
Mon. — Monument
Mona. — Monaco
Mong. — Mongolia
Mont. — Montenegro
Monts. — Montserrat
Mor. — Morocco
Moz. — Mozambique
Mrsh. — Marshall Islands
Mrta. — Mauritania
Mrts. — Mauritius
Ms,US — Mississippi
Mt. — Mount
Mt,US — Montana
Mtn., Mts. — Mountain, Mountains
Mun. Arpt. — Municipal Airport
Myan. — Myanmar

N
NAm. — North America
Namb. — Namibia
NAnt. — Netherlands Antilles
Nat'l — National
Nav. — Naval
NB,Can — New Brunswick
Nbrhd. — Neighborhood
NC,US — North Carolina
NCal. — New Caledonia
ND,US — North Dakota
Ne,US — Nebraska
Neth. — Netherlands
Nf,Can — Newfoundland and Labrador
Nga. — Nigeria
NH,US — New Hampshire
NI,UK — Northern Ireland
Nic. — Nicaragua
NJ,US — New Jersey
NKor. — North Korea
NM,US — New Mexico
NMar. — Northern Mariana Islands
Nor. — Norway
NS,Can — Nova Scotia
Nv,US — Nevada
Nun.,Can — Nunavut
NW,Can — Northwest Territories
NY,US — New York
NZ — New Zealand

O
Obl. — Oblast
Oh,US — Ohio
Ok,US — Oklahoma
On,Can — Ontario
Or,US — Oregon

P
Pa,US — Pennsylvania
PacUS — Pacific Islands, U.S.
Pak. — Pakistan

Pan. — Panama
Par. — Paraguay
Par. — Parish
PE,Can — Prince Edward Island
Pen. — Peninsula
Phil. — Philippines
Phys. Reg. — Physical Region
Pitc. — Pitcairn Islands
Plat. — Plateau
PNG — Papua New Guinea
Pol. — Poland
Port. — Portugal
Poss. — Possession
Pkwy. — Parkway
PR — Puerto Rico
Pref. — Prefecture
Prov. — Province
Prsv. — Preserve
Pt. — Point

Q
Qu,Can — Quebec

R
Rec. — Recreation(al)
Ref. — Refuge
Reg. — Region
Rep. — Republic
Res. — Reservoir, Reservation
Reun. — Réunion
RI,US — Rhode Island
Riv. — River
Rom. — Romania
Rsv. — Reserve
Rus. — Russia
Rvwy. — Riverway
Rwa. — Rwanda

S
SAfr. — South Africa
Sam. — Samoa
SAm. — South America
SaoT. — São Tomé and Príncipe
SAr. — Saudi Arabia
Sc,UK — Scotland
SC,US — South Carolina
SD,US — South Dakota
Seash. — Seashore
Sen. — Senegal
Serb. — Serbia
Sey. — Seychelles
SGeo. — South Georgia and Sandwich Islands
Sing. — Singapore
Sk,Can — Saskatchewan
SKor. — South Korea
SLeo. — Sierra Leone
Slov. — Slovenia
Slvk. — Slovakia
SMar. — San Marino
Sol. — Solomon Islands
Som. — Somalia
Sp. — Spain
Spr., Sprs. — Spring, Springs
SrL. — Sri Lanka
Sta. — Station
StH. — Saint Helena
Str. — Strait
StK. — Saint Kitts and Nevis
StL. — Saint Lucia

StP. — Saint Pierre and Miquelon
StV. — Saint Vincent and the Grenadines
Sur. — Suriname
Sval. — Svalbard
Swaz. — Swaziland
Swe. — Sweden
Swi. — Switzerland

T
Tah. — Tahiti
Tai. — Taiwan
Taj. — Tajikistan
Tanz. — Tanzania
Ter. — Terrace
Terr. — Territory
Thai. — Thailand
Tn,US — Tennessee
Tok. — Tokelau
Trg. — Training
Trin. — Trinidad and Tobago
Trkm. — Turkmenistan
Trks. — Turks and Caicos Islands
Tun. — Tunisia
Tun. — Tunnel
Turk. — Turkey
Tuv. — Tuvalu
Twp. — Township
Tx,US — Texas

U
UAE — United Arab Emirates
Ugan. — Uganda
UK — United Kingdom
Ukr. — Ukraine
Uru. — Uruguay
US — United States
USVI — U.S. Virgin Islands
Ut,US — Utah
Uzb. — Uzbekistan

V
Va,US — Virginia
Val. — Valley
Van. — Vanuatu
VatC. — Vatican City
Ven. — Venezuela
Viet. — Vietnam
Vill. — Village
Vol. — Volcano
Vt,US — Vermont

W
Wa,US — Washington
Wal,UK — Wales
Wall. — Wallis and Futuna
WBnk. — West Bank
Wi,US — Wisconsin
Wild. — Wildlife, Wilderness
WSah. — Western Sahara
WV,US — West Virginia
Wy,US — Wyoming

Y
Yem. — Yemen
Yk,Can — Yukon Territory

Z
Zam. — Zambia
Zim. — Zimbabwe

A'alī – Akok
261

A

A'alī an Nīl (pol. reg.), Sudan 135/F4
Aa (riv.), Fr. 60/B2
Aa (riv.), Ger. 58/D5
Aach (riv.), Ger. 67/F2
Aach, Ger. 67/E2
Aachen, Ger. 61/F2
Aalbach (riv.), Ger. 64/C3
Aalborg (int'l arpt.), Den. 46/C3
Aalburg, Neth. 58/C5
Aalen, Ger. 64/D5
Aalsmeer, Neth. 58/B4
Aalst, Belg. 60/D2
Aalten, Neth. 58/D5
Aalter, Belg. 60/C1
Aar (riv.), Ger. 61/H3
Aarau, Swi. 66/E3
Aarberg, Swi. 66/D3
Aarburg, Swi. 66/D3
Aardenburg, Neth. 60/C1
Aare (riv.), Swi. 72/E1
Aargau (canton), Swi. 67/E3
Aarred (lake), WSah. 128/B4
Aarschot, Belg. 61/D2
Aartselaar, Belg. 61/D1
Aarwangen, Swi. 66/D3
Aba, Nga. 133/G5
Aba, D.R. Congo 139/G2
Aba, China 90/E5
Abā as Su'ūd, SAr. 112/D5
Abadab (peak), Sudan 127/G5
Ābādān, Iran 115/G4
Ābādeh, Iran 115/H4
Abadla, Alg. 129/E3
Abádszalók, Hun. 56/E2
Abaeté, Braz. 222/D3
Abaetetuba, Braz. 218/D3
Abag Qi, China 90/G3
Abaí, Par. 225/F3
Abaiang (isl.), Kiri. 160/G4
Abaji, Nga. 133/G4
Abajo (mts.), Ut, US 172/D4
Abak, Nga. 133/G5
Abakaliki, Nga. 133/H5
Abakan, Rus. 80/K4
Abala, Congo 138/C3
Abala, Niger 133/F3
Abalak, Niger 133/G3
Aban, Rus. 80/K4
Abancay, Peru 220/C4
Abanga (riv.), Gabon 138/B2
Abano Terme, It. 69/E3
Abapó, Bol. 224/D1
Abar Kūh, Iran 115/H4
Abarán, Sp. 52/E3
Abariringa (Canton) (isl.), Kiri. 161/H5
'Abasān, Gaza 117/A6
Abashiri, Japan 94/D1
Abashiri (lake), Japan 94/C2
Abasolo, Mex. 205/F3
Abasolo, Mex. 205/E4
Abatimbo el Gumas, Eth. 135/G3
Abau, PNG 153/H2
Abay, Kaz. 80/H5
Abaya (well), Chad 134/C2
Abaza, Rus. 111/F1
Abbabis, Namb. 140/C5
Abbadia Lariana, It. 67/F6
Abbadia San Salvatore, It. 54/B1
Abbaretz, Fr. 62/D5
Abbazia di Casamari, It. 71/C4
Abbazia di Fossanova, It. 71/C5
Abbazia di Montecassino, It. 71/C5
Abbe (lake), Djib. 136/B3
Abbert (riv.), Ire. 38/B3
Abbeville, Fr. 60/A3
Abbeville, Al, US 195/F2
Abbeville, Ga, US 195/G2
Abbeville, La, US 194/B3
Abbeville, Ms, US 192/C3
Abbeville, SC, US 193/F3
Abbey (peak), Austl. 158/B1
Abbey, Sk, Can. 175/K2
Abbeydorney, Ire. 38/A5
Abbeyfeale, Ire. 38/A5
Abbeylara, Ire. 38/C2
Abbeyleix, Ire. 38/C4
Abbiategrasso, It. 68/B3
Abbot (mt.), Austl. 158/B3
Abbot (pt.), Austl. 153/H4
Abbots Bromley, Eng, UK 41/G6
Abbots Langley, Eng, UK 36/B1
Abbotsbury, Eng, UK 42/D5
Abbotsford, Wi, US 185/J1
Abbotsinch (int'l arpt.), Sc, UK 39/B5
Abbott, Tx, US 181/F2
Abbottābād, Pak. 110/B2
Abbottsburg, NC, US 193/H3
Abbottstown, Pa, US 198/B4
Abcoude, Neth. 58/B4
Ābdānān, Iran 112/E2
Abdul Hakīm, Pak. 110/B4
Abdulino, Rus. 77/K1
Abéché, Chad 134/D2
Abejorral, Col. 219/K7
Abel Erasmuspas (pass), SAfr. 141/F5
Ābeltī, Eth. 135/H3
Abemama (isl.), Kiri. 160/G4
Abenab, Namb. 140/C3
Abenberg, Ger. 64/D4
Abengourou, C.d'Iv. 132/E5
Åbenrå, Den. 46/C4
Abens (riv.), Ger. 48/F4
Abensberg, Ger. 65/E5
Abeokuta, Nga. 133/F5
Aber, Wal, UK 40/D5
Aber Wrac'h (riv.), Fr. 62/A3
Aberaeron, Wal, UK 42/B2
Aberangell, Wal, UK 42/C1
Aberarth, Wal, UK 42/B2
Abercarn, Wal, UK 42/C3
Aberchirder, Sc, UK 39/D1
Abercrombie, ND, US 186/F4
Abercrombie (riv.), Austl. 157/D2
Aberdare, Wal, UK 42/C3
Aberdare NP, Kenya 137/B2
Aberdaron, Wal, UK 40/D6
Aberdeen, Austl. 156/D2
Aberdeen (lake), Nun, Can. 170/F2
Aberdeen, China 99/L8
Aberdeen, Sc, UK 39/D2
Aberdeen (co.), Sc, UK 39/D2
Aberdeen, SAfr. 142/D4
Aberdeen, Id, US 177/G2
Aberdeen, Md, US 198/B5
Aberdeen, Ms, US 192/C4
Aberdeen, NC, US 193/H3
Aberdeen, SD, US 186/E5
Aberdeen, Wa, US 174/C4
Aberdeen Proving Ground, Md, US 198/B5
Aberdeenshire (co.), Sc, UK 39/D2
Aberdour, Sc, UK 39/C4
Aberdour (bay), Sc, UK 39/D1
Aberdyfi, Wal, UK 42/B1
Aberfeldy, Sc, UK 39/C3
Aberfoyle, Sc, UK 39/B4
Abergavenny, Wal, UK 42/C3
Abergele, Wal, UK 40/E5
Ābergelē, Eth. 136/A2
Aberlady, Sc, UK 39/D5
Aberlour, Sc, UK 39/C2
Abernathy, Tx, US 182/D4
Abernethy, Sc, UK 39/C4
Aberporth, Wal, UK 42/B2
Abersoch, Wal, UK 40/D6
Abersychan, Wal, UK 42/C3
Abert (lake), Or, US 176/C2
Abertillery, Wal, UK 42/C3
Aberystwyth, Wal, UK 42/B2
Abez', Rus. 75/P2
Abhá, SAr. 112/D5
Abhānpur, India 107/D1
Abhar, Iran 115/G2
Abhayāpuri, India 109/H2
Abia (prov.), Nga. 133/G5
'Ābidīn, Sudan 135/G2
Abidjan, C.d'Iv. 132/D5
Abidjan (Port Bouet) (int'l arpt.), C.d'Iv. 132/E5
Abidogun, Nga. 133/F5
Abiko, Japan 95/E2
Abilene, Ks, US 183/F1
Abilene, Tx, US 180/E1
Abingdon, Eng, UK 43/E3
Abingdon, Il, US 185/J3
Abingdon, Md, US 198/B5
Abingdon, Va, US 193/G2
Abingdon Downs, Austl. 158/A2
Abington, Sc, UK 39/C6
Abington (reef), Austl. 158/C2
Abino (pt.), On, Can. 190/U10
Abinsk, Rus. 79/K5
Abiquiu, NM, US 179/J2
Abiquiu (lake), NM, US 182/A2
Abiquiu (dam), NM, US 179/J2
Abisko, Swe. 44/F1
Abitibi (riv.), On, Can. 171/H4
Abitibi (lake), On,Qu, Can. 171/H4
Ābiy Ādī, Eth. 136/A2
Ābīyata (lake), Eth. 136/A4
Abiyata-Shala Lakes NP, Eth. 135/H4
Abja-Paluoja, Est. 47/L2
Abkhazia Aut. Rep., Geo. 77/G4
Ableiges, Fr. 36/H4
Abminga, Austl. 155/G3
Abnūb, Egypt 127/F3
Abo, Som. 136/D3
Åbo (Turku), Fin. 47/K1
Aboh, Nga. 133/G5
Abohar, India 110/C4
Aboisso, C.d'Iv. 132/E5
Abomey, Ben. 133/F5
Ābomsa, Eth. 136/A3
Abondance, Fr. 66/C5
Abong-Mbang, Camr. 138/C2
Abongabong (mtn.), Indo. 101/B1
Abony, Hun. 56/D2
Aborlan, Phil. 100/B3
Abou Deia, Chad 134/C3
Abourassein, Djebel (peak), CAfr. 134/E3
Aboyne, Sc, UK 39/D2
Abra Pampa, Arg. 224/C2
Abraham Lincoln Birthplace Nat'l Hist. Site, Ky, US 192/E2
Abraham's Bay, Bahm. 207/H1
Abraham Gonzalez (int'l arpt.), Mex. 204/D2
Abraka, Nga. 133/G5
Abrams, Wi, US 190/B2
Abrantes, Port. 52/A3
Abreojos (pt.), Mex. 204/B3
'Abrī, Sudan 127/F4
Abridge, Eng, UK 36/D2
Abrud, Rom. 57/F2
Abruzzi (pol. reg.), It. 71/C3
Abruzzi (prov.), It. 51/K5
Abruzzo, PN d', It. 54/C2
Absam, Aus. 67/H3
Absaroka (range), Mt,Wy, US 177/H1
Absarokee, Mt, US 177/J1
Absdorf, Aus. 57/N7
Absecon, NJ, US 198/D5
Abtsgmünd, Ger. 64/D5
Abū aḑ Ḑuhūr, Syria 116/E2
Abū al Maţāmīr, Egypt 131/B3
Abū 'Alī (isl.), SAr. 115/G5
Abū an Numrus, Egypt 131/C5
Abū 'Arīsh, SAr. 112/D5
Abū Dā'ūd as Sibākh, Egypt 131/C3
Abū Dawm, Sudan 135/F1
Abū Dawm, Sudan 135/G1
Abu Dhabi (int'l arpt.), UAE 113/F4
Abu Dhabi (Abū Ẓaby) (cap.), UAE 113/F4
Abū Dīs, Sudan 127/G5
Abū Ḩadrīyah, SAr. 115/G5
Abū Hamad, Sudan 127/G5
Abū Ḩammād, Egypt 131/C3
Abū Hugar, Sudan 135/G2
Abū Ḩummuş, Egypt 131/B2
Abū Jābirah, Sudan 135/E3
Abū Jandīr, Egypt 131/B6
Abū Jubayhah, Sudan 135/F3
Abū Kabīr, Egypt 131/C3
Abū Kamāl, Syria 114/E3
Abū Kūk, Sudan 135/G2
Abū Maţāriq, Sudan 135/E3
Abu Mendi, Eth. 135/G3
Abū Qashsh, WBnk. 117/C5
Abū Qīr, Egypt 131/B2
Abū Rawwāsh (ruin), Egypt 131/C4
Abū Rimth (wadi), Egypt 131/C4
Abu Road, India 113/K4
Abū Rubayq, SAr. 112/C4
Abū Rukbah, Sudan 135/G2
Abu Shagara (cape), Sudan 127/H4
Abū Shāmah (peak), Egypt 131/C5
Abū Shanab, Sudan 135/E2
Abu Simbel (ruin), Egypt 127/F4
Abū Şīr (ruin), Egypt 131/C5
Abū Şīr Banā, Egypt 131/C3
Abū Sulţān, Egypt 131/D4
Abū Zabad, Sudan 135/F2
Abū Za'bal, Egypt 131/C4
Abū Ẓaby (Abu Dhabi) (cap.), UAE 113/F4
Abuja (cap.), Nga. 133/G4
Abuja (int'l arpt.), Nga. 133/G4
Abuja Capital Terr., Nga. 133/G4
Abukuma (riv.), Japan 97/G2
Abukuma (plat.), Japan 97/G2
Abulog, Phil. 100/C1
Abumombazi, D.R. Congo 139/E2
Abuná (riv.), Bol. 221/E3
Abunã (riv.), Braz. 221/E3
Abunã, Braz. 221/E3
Ābune Yosēf (peak), Eth. 136/A2
Abut Head (pt.), NZ 159/B3
Abuta, Japan 94/B2
Ābuyē Mēda (peak), Eth. 136/A3
Abuyog, Phil. 100/D3
Abwong, Sudan 135/G3
Åby, Swe. 46/G2
Abyār, Egypt 131/B3
Abyār 'Alī, SAr. 112/C4
Åbybro, Den. 46/C3
Abydos (ruin), Egypt 127/F3
Abyei, Sudan 135/F3
Acacías, Col. 216/C4
Acacoyagua, Mex. 206/C3
Academy of Sciences, VatC. 71/G7
Acadia NP, Me, US 188/C4
Acadia Valley, Ab, Can. 175/J2
Acadian Village, La, US 194/B2
Acahay, Par. 225/E3
Acajutiba, Braz. 223/F1
Acámbaro, Mex. 205/E4
Acampo, Ca, US 197/M10
Acandí, Col. 216/B2
Acaponeta (riv.), Mex. 204/D4
Acaponeta, Mex. 204/D4
Acapulco de Juárez, Mex. 205/E5
Acará, Braz. 218/D3
Acarai (mts.), Guy. 217/G4
Acaraí, Serra (mts.), Braz. 218/B2
Acaraú, Braz. 219/F3
Acaraú (riv.), Braz. 219/F3
Acari, Braz. 219/G4
Acari (riv.), Braz. 218/B4
Acarí, Peru 220/C4
Acarigua, Ven. 216/D2
Acatlán de Osorio, Mex. 206/B2
Acatlán de Pérez Figueroa, Mex. 205/N8
Acatzingo, Mex. 205/M7
Acayucan, Mex. 206/C2
Acceglio, It. 70/C4
Accha, Peru 220/D4
Acciaroli, It. 54/D2
Accomac, Va, US 193/K2
Accra (cap.), Gha. 133/E5
Accrington, Eng, UK 41/F4
Aceguá, Uru. 225/F4
Aceh (prov.), Indo. 101/A1
Acerra, It. 71/D6
Aceuchal, Sp. 52/B3
Ach (riv.), Aus. 65/G6
Ach, Aus. 65/F6
Achaguas, Ven. 216/D3
Achalpur, India 107/C1
Achao, Chile 226/B4
Achar, Uru. 227/K10
Achegour (well), Niger 126/A5
Achen (pass), Ger. 67/H2
Acheng, China 91/K2
Achères, Fr. 36/J5
Acheron (riv.), Austl. 157/B3
Achhnera, India 108/A2
Achicourt, Fr. 60/B3
Achila, Bol. 220/D4
Achill (isl.), Ire. 36/N10
Achill Head (pt.), Ire. 36/N9
Achiltibuie, Sc, UK 37/R7
Achim, Ger. 59/G2
Achim, Ouadi (riv.), Chad 134/C1
Āchīn, Afg. 110/A2
Achinsk, Rus. 80/K4
Achit, Rus. 75/N4
Achmîm (well), Mrta. 132/D2
Achnasheen, Sc, UK 39/A1
Achoma, Peru 220/D4
A'chràlaig (peak), Sc, UK 39/A2
Achuapa, Nic. 206/E3
Achupallas, Ecu. 220/B1
Achuyevo, Rus. 79/J5
Achziv NP (ruin), Isr. 117/C2
Acigné, Fr. 62/D4
Acilia, It. 71/B4
Acireale, It. 54/D4
Ackerly, Tx, US 180/D1
Ackerman, Ms, US 192/C4
Acklins (isl.), Bahm. 203/G3
Ackworth Moor Top, Eng, UK 41/G4
Acland (mt.), Austl. 158/C4
Aclare, Ire. 38/B1
Acme, La, US 194/C2
Acme, Wa, US 174/C3
Acobamba, Peru 220/C4
Acolla, Peru 220/C3
Acolman, Mex. 205/R9
Acoma Ind. Res., NM, US 179/J3
Acomayo, Peru 220/D4
Acomayo, Peru 220/B3
Aconcagua (peak), Arg. 226/C2
Aconchi, Mex. 204/C2
Acopiara, Braz. 219/G4
Acora, Peru 220/D4
Acorizal, Braz. 221/G4
Acornhoek, SAfr. 141/F5
Acqualagna, It. 69/F6
Acquanegra sul Chiese, It. 68/D3
Acquapendente, It. 54/B1
Acquasanta Terme, It. 71/C2
Acquasparta, It. 71/B2
Acquaviva Piceno, It. 71/C2
Acqui Terme, It. 68/B4
Acquigny, Fr. 63/G2
Acraman (lake), Austl. 155/G5
Acrata (pt.), Alg. 130/G4
Acre (state), Braz. 220/D3
Acre (riv.), Braz. 220/D3
Acreúna, Braz. 222/C3
Acropolis, Gre. 55/N9
Actaeon Group (isls.), FrPol. 161/M7
Acton, Ca, US 196/B2
Acton (nbrhd.), Eng, UK 36/C2
Acton, On, Can. 190/S8
Acton, Tx, US 180/K7
Acton, Mt, US 175/K5
Acton Vale, Qu, Can. 191/K2
Actopan, Mex. 205/L6
Actopan, Mex. 205/N7
Açu, Braz. 219/G4
Açude Aratas (res.), Braz. 219/F4
Açude Banabuiu (res.), Braz. 219/G4
Açude Oros (res.), Braz. 219/G4
Acula, Mex. 205/P8
Aculeo (lag.), Chile 226/N8
Acworth, Ga, US 193/L6
Acy-en-Multien, Fr. 36/L4
Ad Dabbah, Sudan 135/F1
Ad Dabbūrah, Sudan 135/G1
Ad Dafīnah, SAr. 112/D4
Ad Dahnā' (des.), SAr. 112/D3
Ad Daljamūn, Egypt 131/B3
Ad Damazin, Sudan 135/G3
Ad Damīr, Sudan 135/G1
Ad Dammām, SAr. 112/F3
Ad Dāmūr, Leb. 117/C1
Ad Daqahliyah (gov.), Egypt 114/B3
Ad Darb, SAr. 112/D5
Ad Dawḩah (Doha) (cap.), Qatar 112/F3
Ad Dilam, SAr. 112/E4
Ad Dilinjāt, Egypt 131/B3
Ad Dīwānīyah, Iraq 115/F4
Ad Du'ayn, Sudan 135/E3
Ad Dujayl, Iraq 115/F3
Ad Duwādimī, SAr. 112/D4
Ad Duwayd, SAr. 114/E4
Ad Duwaym, Sudan 135/G2
Ad-Dakhla, WSah. 128/B5
Ada, Gha. 133/F5
Ada, Serb. 56/E3
Ada, Mn, US 186/F4
Ada, Oh, US 190/E4
Ada, Ok, US 183/F3
Ādaba, Eth. 136/A4
Adaba, India 107/E2
Adainville, Fr. 36/G5
Adair, Ok, US 183/G2
Adair (cape), Nun, Can. 171/J1
Adair, Ia, US 185/G3
Adair (bay), Mex. 205/F5
Adairsville, Ga, US 192/E3
Adairville, Ky, US 192/D2
Adaja (riv.), Sp. 52/C2
Adak (isl.), Ak, US 201/C6
Adak (str.), Ak, US 201/C6
Adam, Oman 113/G4
Adam (mt.), UK 227/E6
Adamantina, Braz. 225/G2
Adamaoua (prov.), Camr. 134/B4
Adamaoua (plat.), Camr., Nga. 119/D4
Adamawa (state), Nga. 134/B3
Adamello (peak), It. 67/G5
Adaminaby, Austl. 157/D3
Adamovka, Rus. 77/L2
Adams (lake), BC, Can. 174/E2
Adams (riv.), BC, Can. 174/E2
Adams, Ma, US 191/K3
Adams, Ne, US 185/F3
Adams, NY, US 191/H3
Adams (co.), Pa, US 198/A4
Adams, Tn, US 192/D2
Adams, Wi, US 185/K2
Adams (mt.), Wa, US 174/D4
Adams Run, SC, US 193/G4
Adamstown (cap.), Pitc. 161/M7
Adamstown, Pa, US 198/B3
Adamsville, Tn, US 192/C3
Adamsville, Tx, US 181/E2
Adamw (plat.), Nga. 133/H5
Aden ('Adan), Yem. 136/C2
'Adan (Aden), Yem. 136/C2
Adana, Turk. 114/C2
Adana (int'l arpt.), Turk. 114/C2
Adana (prov.), Turk. 114/C2
Adanhé, Gabon 138/B3
Adapazarı, Turk. 57/K5
Adarama, Sudan 135/G1
Adare, Ire. 38/B4
Adare (cape), Ant. 228/M
Adarza (peak), Fr. 52/E1
Adaut, Indo. 152/C2
Adavale, Austl. 158/B4
Add (riv.), Sc, UK 39/A4
Adda (riv.), Sudan 134/D3
Adda (riv.), It. 51/H4
Addicks (dam), Tx, US 181/M9
Addicks (res.), Tx, US 181/M9
Addis, La, US 194/C2
Addison, Il, US 197/P16
Addison, Al, US 192/D3
Addison, Tx, US 180/L7
Addison (Webster Springs), WV, US 193/G1
Addlestone, Eng, UK 36/B2
Addo Elephant NP, SAfr. 142/D4
Addy, Wa, US 174/F3
Adé, Chad 134/D2
Adekeieh (Ādī K'eyih), Erit. 136/A2
Adel, Ga, US 195/G2
Adel, Ia, US 185/G3
'Adel Bagrou, Mrta. 132/D3
Adelaide (pen.), Nun, Can. 170/G2
Adelaide (riv.), Austl. 152/C3
Adelaide, Austl. 155/M8
Adelaide (int'l arpt.), Austl. 155/M8
Adelaide, SAfr. 142/D4
Adelaide River, Austl. 152/C3
Adelaide Zoo, Austl. 155/M8
Adelanto, Ca, US 196/C1
Adèle (isl.), Austl. 152/A3
Adelebsen, Ger. 59/G5
Adelheidsdorf, Ger. 59/H3
Adelmannsfelden, Ger. 64/D5
Adelong, Austl. 157/D2
Adelschlag, Ger. 64/E5
Adelsheim, Ger. 64/C4
Adelsön (isl.), Swe. 45/A1
Adelsried, Ger. 64/D6
Aden (gulf), Afr.,Asia 83/D8
Aden, Ab, Can. 175/J3
Aden (int'l arpt.), Yem. 136/C2
Adenau, Ger. 61/F3
Adendorf, Ger. 59/H2
Aderbissinat, Niger 133/G3
Adèrké, Chad 126/C4
Ādēt, Eth. 135/H3
Adh Dhahībāt, Tun. 129/H2
Adh Dhirā', Jor. 116/D4
Adi, D.R. Congo 139/G2
Adi (isl.), Indo. 103/H4
Ādī Ābun, Eth. 136/A2
Ādī Ārk'ay, Eth. 135/H2
Ādī Da'iro, Eth. 112/C6
Ādīs Ābeba (Adekeieh), Erit. 136/A2
Ādī Kwala, Erit. 136/A2
Ādī Tekelezan, Erit. 136/A2
Ādī Ugrī, Erit. 136/A2
Adiaké, C.d'Iv. 132/E5
Adieu (cape), Austl. 155/G5
Ādīgala, Eth. 136/B3
Adige (riv.), It. 72/F1
Adige (Etsch) (riv.), It. 67/G4
Adigeni, Geo. 77/G4
Adigo (Etsch) (riv.), It. 67/G4
Ādīgrat, Eth. 136/A2
Adilcevaz, Turk. 115/E2
Adimo, Nga. 133/F5
Adin, Ca, US 176/C3
Adiora (well), Mali 133/E2
Adīrī, Libya 126/B3
Adirondack (mts.), NY, US 191/J2
Addis Ababa (Ādīs Ābeba) (cap.), Eth. 136/A3
Ādīs Ābeba (Addis Ababa) (cap.), Eth. 136/A3
Ādīs 'Alem, Eth. 136/A3
Ādīs Zemen, Eth. 135/H2
Adisutjipto (int'l arpt.), Indo. 101/E4
Adıyaman, Turk. 114/D2
Adiyaman (prov.), Turk. 114/D2
Adjud, Rom. 57/H2
Adjuntas, de la Presa (res.), Mex. 205/F4
Adler/Sochi (int'l arpt.), Rus. 76/F4
Adlington, Eng, UK 41/F4
Adliswil, Swi. 67/E3
Admiral, Sk, Can. 175/K3
Admirality (isl.), Ak, US 170/C3
Admirality (inlet), Nun, Can. 171/H1
Admirality Island Nat'l Mon., Ak, US 201/M4
Admiralty (inlet), Wa, US 197/B2
Admiralty (isls.), PNG 160/D5
Admiralty (gulf), Austl. 152/B3
Admiralty Gulf Abor. Rsv., Austl. 152/B3
Admire, Ks, US 183/F1
Adnan Menderes (int'l arpt.), Turk. 76/C5
Ado (riv.), Japan 95/J5
Ado Ekiti, Nga. 133/G5
Ado Odo, Nga. 133/F5
Adobe Creek (res.), Co, US 182/C1
Adogawa, Japan 95/K5
Adok, Sudan 135/F3
Adolfo López Mateos, Mex. 204/B3
Ādoni, India 107/C3
Adorf, Ger. 65/F2
Adoru, Nga. 133/G5
Adour (riv.), Fr. 72/D2
Adra, India 109/F4
Adra, Sp. 52/D4
Adranga, D.R. Congo 139/G2
Adrano, It. 54/D4
Adrar, Alg. 129/E4
Adrar (phys. reg.), Mrta. 132/B1
Adrar (pol. reg.), Mrta. 132/C1
Adrar (pol. reg.), Alg. 133/F1
Adrar (reg.), Mrta. 128/C5
Adrar (wilaya), Alg. 129/E4
Adrar bou Nasser (peak), Mor. 128/E2
Adrar Sotuf (mts.), WSah. 128/B5
Adré, Chad 134/D2
Adria, It. 69/F3
Adrian, Mo, US 183/G1
Adrian, Mi, US 190/D4
Adrian, Or, US 176/E2
Adrian, Mn, US 185/G2
Adrian, WV, US 193/G1
Adriatic (sea), Eur. 73/G2
Adro, It. 68/C2
Aduana del Sásabe, Mex. 205/G5
Adukrom, Gha. 133/E5
Adulis (ruin), Erit. 136/A2
Adur (riv.), Eng, UK 43/F5
Adutiškis, Lith. 47/M4
Advance, Mo, US 192/C2
Adventure Bay, Austl. 156/C4
Advocate Harbour, NS, Can. 188/E3
Ādwa, Eth. 136/A2
Adwick le Street, Eng, UK 41/G4
Adycha (riv.), Rus. 81/P3
Adygeya, Resp., Rus. 76/F3
Adzopé, C.d'Iv. 132/E5
Adz'va (riv.), Rus. 75/P2
Adz'vavom, Rus. 75/N2
Ae, Sc, UK 40/E1
Aegean (sea), Gre. 55/J3
Aegviidu, Est. 47/L2
Aerø (isl.), Den. 46/D4
Aeron (riv.), Wal, UK 42/B2
Aesch, Swi. 66/D3
Aeschi bei Spiez, Swi. 66/D4
Aetna, Ab, Can. 175/H3
Äetsä, Fin. 47/K1
Afadjoto (peak), Gha. 133/F5
'Afak, Iraq 115/F3
Āfambo, Eth. 136/B3
Āfambo, Erit. 136/B2
Afanas'yevskoye, Rus. 75/N4
Afándou, Gre. 114/B2
Afareaitu, FrPol. 161/X15
Āfdem, Eth. 136/B3
Afek NP, Isr. 117/B4
Aff (riv.), Fr. 50/B3
Affenrücken, Namb. 142/A3
Affoltern im Emmental, Swi. 66/D3
Affric (lake), Sc, UK 39/A2
Affton, Mo, US 185/J4
Afghanistan (ctry.) 113/H2
Afgooye, Som. 137/D1
Afia, Gabon 138/B2
'Afīf, SAr. 112/D4
Afikpo, Nga. 133/G5
Afipskiy, Rus. 79/K5
Afiqim, Isr. 117/D3
Aflou, Alg. 72/D4
Afmadow, Som. 137/C1
Afobaka (dam), Sur. 218/C1
Afogados da Ingàzeira, Braz. 219/G4
Afognak (isl.), Ak, US 201/H4
Afognak (peak), Ak, US 201/H4
Afollé (phys. reg.), Mrta. 132/C2
Afonso Bezerra, Braz. 219/G4
Afore, PNG 153/H2
Afragola, It. 71/D6
Afrânio, Braz. 219/F5
Africa (cont.) 119/*
Afrin (riv.), Turk. 116/E1
'Afrīn, Syria 116/E1
Afrique (peak), Fr. 66/A3
Afsluitdijk (dam), Neth. 58/C2
Afte (riv.), Ger. 59/F5
Afton, Ia, US 185/G3
Afton, Mn, US 187/Q7
Afton, Ok, US 183/G2
Afton, Wy, US 177/H2
Afuá, Braz. 218/D3
Afuidich (lake), WSah. 128/B5
'Afula, Isr. 117/C3
Afyon, Turk. 114/B2
Afyon (prov.), Turk. 114/B2
Afzalgarh, India 108/B1
Agadem, Niger 134/B1
Agades (int'l arpt.), Niger 133/G2
Agadez, Niger 133/G2
Agadez (dept.), Niger 129/H5
Agadir, Mor. 128/C3
Agadir (Inezgane) (int'l arpt.), Mor. 128/C3
Agadyr', Kaz. 111/B2
Agago (riv.), Ugan. 135/G5
Āgamani, India 109/G2
Agamor (well), Mali 133/F2
Agano (riv.), Japan 97/F2
Agar, SD, US 184/D1
Āgarfa, Eth. 136/A4
Āgaro, Eth. 135/H4
Agartala, India 109/H4
Agassiz Ice Cap (ice field), Nun, Can. 171/T6
Agassiz NWR, Mn, US 186/F3
Agate, Co, US 184/C4
Agate Fossil Beds Nat'l Mon., Ne, US 184/C2
Agats, Indo. 153/E1
Agattu (isl.), Ak, US 201/A5
Agattu (str.), Ak, US 201/A5
Agbabu, Nga. 133/G5
Agbor Bojiboji, Nga. 133/G5
Agboville, C.d'Iv. 132/D5
Ağcabädi, Azer. 115/F1
Ağdam, Azer. 115/F2
Ağdärä, Azer. 115/F1
Ağdaş, Azer. 77/H4
Agde, Fr. 50/E5
Agdz, Mor. 128/D3
Agen, Fr. 50/D4
Agency (lake), Or, US 176/B2
Agency, Mo, US 185/G4
Agency, Ia, US 185/H3
Ageo, Japan 95/D2
Ager (riv.), Aus. 65/G7
Ageræk, Den. 46/C4
Āgere Maryam, Eth. 136/A4
Agerisee (lake), Swi. 67/E3
Agersø (isl.), Den. 45/H7
Ageyevo, Rus. 76/F1
Agger (riv.), Ger. 61/G1
Aggteleki NP, Slvk. 56/E1
Āghā Jārī, Iran 115/G4
Aghada, Ire. 38/B6
Aghagallon, NI, UK 40/B3
Aghagower, Ire. 38/A2
Agiabampo, Mex. 204/C3
Ağın, Turk. 114/D2
Aginskiy Buryatskiy (aut. okrug), Rus. 90/G1
Aginskoye, Rus. 90/G1
Agivey, NI, UK 40/B1
Agjert, Mrta. 132/C2
Agliana, It. 69/D6
Ağlıköy, Turk. 76/E4
Agly (riv.), Fr. 50/E5
Agna, It. 69/E3
Agnanderón, Gre. 55/G3
Agnes, Tx, US 180/K7
Agnew, Austl. 154/D4
Agnibilékrou, C.d'Iv. 132/E5
Agnita, Rom. 57/G3
Agno (int'l arpt.), Swi. 67/E6
Agno (riv.), It. 69/E1
Agnone, It. 71/D4
Agny (riv.), Fr. 70/B1
Ago, Japan 95/L7
Ago Are, Nga. 133/F4
Agogna (riv.), It. 51/H4
Agon (pt.), Fr. 62/D3
Agon-Coutainville, Fr. 62/D2
Agona, Gha. 133/E5
Agoo, Phil. 99/J5
Agordo, It. 51/K3
Agougadzépe, Togo 133/F5
Agout (riv.), Fr. 50/D5
Āgra, India 108/B2
Agra, Ks, US 184/E4
Agraciada, Uru. 227/J10
Agrado, Col. 216/C4
Ágreda, Sp. 52/E2
Ağri (prov.), Turk. 77/G5
Ağrı (Mount Ararat) (peak), Turk. 115/F2
Agriá, Gre. 55/H3
Agricola, Fl, US 194/M8
Agrigento, It. 54/C4
Agrihan (isl.), NMar. 160/D3
Agrínion, Gre. 55/G3
Agrio (riv.), Arg. 226/C3
Agryz, Rus. 75/M4
Ağstafa, Azer. 77/H4
Ağsu, Azer. 77/J4
Agsumal (dry lake), WSah. 128/B4
Água Branca, Braz. 219/G4
Água Branca, Braz. 219/F4
Agua Buena, Chile 224/B3
Agua Caliente, Az, US 179/F4
Agua Caliente Ind. Res., Ca, US 178/D4
Água Clara, Braz. 225/F2
Agua de Dios, Col. 219/L8
Agua Dulce, Ca, US 196/B2
Agua Dulce, Mex. 206/C2
Agua Fria, NM, US 179/J3
Agua Fria NM, Az, US 179/F3
Agua Hedionda (lake), Ca, US 196/C4
Agua Larga, Ven. 216/D2
Agua Prieta, Mex. 205/H5
Agua Vermelha (res.), Braz. 222/C3
Aguachica, Col. 216/C2
Aguadas, Col. 219/K7
Aguadilla, PR 203/M8
Aguadulce, Pan. 216/A2
Aguaí, Braz. 223/K7
Agualeguas, Mex. 180/E7
Agualva-Cacém, Port. 53/P10
Aguan (riv.), Hon. 202/D4
Aguapeí (riv.), Braz. 222/C4
Aguapey (riv.), Arg. 225/E4
Aguaray, Arg. 224/D2
Aguarico (riv.), Peru 216/B5
Aguaro-Guariquito NP, Ven. 203/H6
Águas (hills), Braz. 223/L7
Águas Belas, Braz. 219/G5
Aguas Blancas, Chile 224/B3
Aguas Corrientes, Uru. 227/K11
Águas da Prata, Braz. 223/K6
Águas de Lindóia, Braz. 223/K7
Águas Formosas, Braz. 223/E3
Aguasay, Ven. 217/F2
Aguascalientes, Mex. 204/E4
Aguascalientes (state), Mex. 202/A3
Aguaytía (riv.), Peru 220/C3
Águeda, Port. 52/A2
Agueda (riv.), Sp. 52/B2
Aguelhok, Mali 133/F2
Agüenit, WSah. 128/B5
Aguêraktem (well), Mali 128/D5
Agugliano, It. 69/G6
Agui, Japan 95/L6
Aguié, Niger 133/G3
Aguijan (isl.), NMar. 160/D3
Aguila, Az, US 179/F4
Aguilâl Faï, Mrta. 132/B2
Aguilar, Co, US 182/B2
Aguilar, Sp. 52/C4
Aguilar de Campóo, Sp. 52/C1
Aguilares, Arg. 224/C3
Aguilas, Sp. 52/E4
Aguililla, Mex. 204/E5
Aguja (pt.), Peru 220/A2
Agulhas (cape), SAfr. 142/M11
Agulhas Negras, Pico das (peak), Braz. 223/M7
Agung (vol.), Indo. 101/F5
Agusan (riv.), Phil. 100/D3
Agustín Codazzi, Col. 216/C2
Agutaya, Phil. 100/C3
Agwata, Ugan. 137/A1
Agwok, Sudan 135/F4
Aha (hills), Bots. 140/D3
Ahaggar (mts.), Alg. 129/G5
Ahal (prov.), Trkm. 77/L5
Aham, Ger. 65/F5
Ahar, Iran 115/F2
Ahascragh, Ire. 38/B3
Ahau, Fiji 160/G6
Ahaura, NZ 159/B3
Ahaus, Ger. 58/E4
Aherlow (riv.), Ire. 38/B5
Ahero, Kenya 137/A2
Ahfir, Mor. 130/C2
Ahipara, NZ 159/C1
Ahırlı, Turk. 114/C2
Ahlat, Turk. 114/E2
Ahlen, Ger. 59/E5
Ahlerstedt, Ger. 59/G2
Ahmadābād, India 113/K4
Ahmadnagar, India 107/B2
Ahmadpur East, Pak. 110/A5
Ahmadpur Siāl, Pak. 110/A4
Ahmar (mts.), Eth. 136/B3
Ahmar, 'Erg el (des.), Mali 128/D4
Ahmed (well), WSah. 128/B5
Ahmeyine (well), Mrta. 128/B5
Ahoada, Nga. 133/G5
Ahoghill, NI, UK 40/B2
Ahome, Mex. 204/C3
Ahon (peak), Chad 126/C4
Ahoskie, NC, US 193/J2
Ahr (riv.), Ger. 48/D3
Ahram, Iran 115/G4
Ahraurā, India 108/D3
Ahrensburg, Ger. 59/H1
Ahse (riv.), Ger. 59/F5
Ahuacatitlán, Mex. 205/K8
Ahuacatlán, Mex. 204/D4
Ahuachapán, ESal. 206/D3
Ahualulco, Mex. 205/E4
Ahumada, Mex. 205/D2
Ahun, Fr. 50/E3
Ahunda, Gha. 133/F5
Åhus, Swe. 46/F4
Aḩuzzam, Isr. 117/B5
Ahvāz, Iran 115/G4
Ahvenanmaa (prov.), Fin. 44/F4
Ahwahnee, Ca, US 178/C2
Aḩwar, Yem. 136/C2
Ai (riv.), China 93/C2
Ai (mtn.), China 92/E3
Ai-Ais, Namb. 142/B2
Ai-Ais Hot Springs, Namb. 142/B2
Ai-shima (isl.), Japan 96/B3
Aichach, Ger. 64/E6
Aichi (pref.), Japan 97/E3
Aidhausen, Ger. 64/D2
Aidlingen, Ger. 64/B5
Aiello del Friuli, It. 69/G2
Aiffres, Fr. 50/C3
Aigen im Mühlkreis, Aus. 65/G5
Aigle, Pic de l' (peak), Fr. 66/B4
Aiglemont, Fr. 61/D4
Aigoual (peak), Fr. 50/E4
Aiguá, Uru. 227/G2
Aiguebelle, Fr. 70/C1
Aigueblanche, Fr. 70/C1
Aigues (riv.), Fr. 50/F4
Aigües Tortes y Lago de San Mauricio, PN, Sp. 53/F1
Aiguillon, Fr. 50/D4
Aikawa, Japan 97/F1
Aikawa, Japan 95/C2
Aiken, SC, US 193/G4
Ailao (mtn.), China 98/D3
Ailao (mts.), China 98/D4
Aileron, Austl. 155/G2
Aileu, ETim. 152/B2
Ailigandí, Pan. 216/B2
Ailinglapalap (isl.), Mrsh. 160/F4
Aille (riv.), Fr. 70/C6
Aillevillers-et-Lyaumont, Fr. 66/C2
Aillon (riv.), Fr. 70/C1
Ailly-sur-Noye, Fr. 60/B4
Ailsa Craig (isl.), Sc, UK 39/A6
Ailsa Craig, On, Can. 190/F3
Ailuk (isl.), Mrsh. 160/G3
Aimäjärvi (lake), Fin. 45/E3
Aime, Fr. 70/C1
Aimen (pass), China 92/C5
Aimogasta, Arg. 224/C4
Aimorés, Braz. 223/E3
Aimorés, Serra dos (mts.), Braz. 223/E3
Ain (dept.), Fr. 70/B1
Ain (riv.), Fr. 50/F4
'Aïn Beïda, Alg. 130/K7
Aïn Ben Tili, Mrta. 128/C4
'Aïn Beniau, Alg. 130/G4
'Aïn Bessem, Alg. 130/G4
Aïn Chok-Hay Mohammadia (prov.), Mor. 130/A2
'Aïn Defla, Alg. 130/F4
'Aïn Defla (wilaya), Alg. 130/F4
Aïn el Aouda, Mor. 130/A3
'Aïn El Bey (int'l arpt.), Alg. 130/K6
'Aïn El Hammam, Alg. 130/H4
'Aïn el Turk, Alg. 130/D2
'Aïn Fakroun, Alg. 130/K6
'Aïn M'lila, Alg. 130/K6
'Aïn Oulmene, Alg. 130/H5
'Aïn Oussersa, Alg. 130/G5
'Aïn Sefra, Alg. 129/E2
Aïn Taoujdat, Mor. 130/B3
'Aïn Taya, Alg. 130/G4
'Aïn Temouchent, Alg. 130/D2
'Aïn Touta, Alg. 130/H5
Ainaro, ETim. 152/B2
Ainaži, Lat. 47/L3
Aincourt, Fr. 36/H4
Aínos (peak), Gre. 55/G3
Aínos Ethnikós Dhrimós, (nat'l. park), Gre. 55/G3
Ainsdale, Eng, UK 41/E4
Ainslie (lake), NS, Can. 189/G2
Ainsworth, Ne, US 184/E2
Aiome, PNG 153/G1
Aipe, Col. 216/C4
Aiquile, Bol. 224/C1
Aïr (plat.), Niger 129/G5
Air Force (isl.), Nun, Can. 171/J2
Airabu (isl.), Indo. 101/D2
Airaines, Fr. 60/A4
Airasca, It. 70/D3
Airbangis, Indo. 101/B2
Airdrie, Sc, UK 39/C5
Airdrie, Ab, Can. 175/G2
Aire (riv.), Eng, UK 41/G3
Aire, Canal d' (canal), Fr. 60/B2
Aire-sur-la-Lys, Fr. 60/B2
Aire-sur-l'Adour, Fr. 50/C5
Airgin Sum, China 90/G3
Airmolek, Indo. 101/C3
Airola, It. 71/D5
Airolo, Swi. 67/E4
Airton, Eng, UK 41/F3
Airuno, It. 68/C2
Airvault, Fr. 50/C3
Aisch (riv.), Ger. 51/J2
Aiseau-Presles, Belg. 61/D3
Aisén del General Carlos Ibáñez del Campo (pol. reg.), Chile 226/B5
Aishihik, Yk, Can. 201/L3
Aisne (riv.), Fr. 48/B4
Aïssa (peak), Alg. 129/E2
Aist (riv.), Aus. 65/H6
Aït Ben Haddou, Mor. 128/D3
Aït Ourir, Mor. 128/D3
Aitape, PNG 160/D5
Aith, Sc, UK 37/W13
Aitkin, Mn, US 187/H4
Aitō, Japan 95/K5
Aitolikón, Gre. 55/G3
Aitrach, Ger. 67/G2
Aitrang, Ger. 67/G2
Aitutaki Atoll (isl.), Cookls. 161/J6
Aiuaba, Braz. 219/F4
Aiud, Rom. 57/F2
Aiuruoca (riv.), Braz. 223/M7
Aiuruoca, Braz. 223/M6
Aix (mt.), Wa, US 174/D4
Aix-en-Provence, Fr. 70/B5
Aix-les-Bains, Fr. 70/B1
Aiyang, China 93/C2
Aíyina, Gre. 55/H4
Aiyínion, Gre. 55/H2
Aíyion, Gre. 55/H3
Aīzawl, India 98/B4
Aizkraukle, Lat. 47/L3
Aizpute, Lat. 47/J3
Aizu-Wakamatsu, Japan 97/F2
Aj Bogd (peak), Mong. 90/D3
Aj Janayet, Sudan 127/G5
Ajā, Egypt 131/C3
'Ajab Shīr, Iran 115/F2
Ajaccio, Fr. 54/A2
Ajaccio (gulf), Fr. 72/E2
Ajaigarh, India 108/C3
Ajalpan, Mex. 205/M8
Ajana, Austl. 154/B3
Ajaokuta, Nga. 133/G5
Ajaria Aut. Rep., Geo. 77/G4
Ajasse Ipo, Nga. 133/G4
Ajax, On, Can. 190/U8
Ajay (riv.), India 109/F3
Ajdābiyā, Libya 126/D2
Ajdovščina, Slov. 51/K4
Ajigasawa, Japan 94/B3
'Ajjah, WBnk. 117/C4
Ajka, Hun. 56/C2
'Ajlūn, Jor. 117/D4
Ajmer, India 104/B2
Ajnāla, India 110/C4
Ajo, Az, US 179/F4
Ajo, Cabo de (cape), Sp. 50/B5
Ajuchitlán del Progreso, Mex. 202/A4
Ajusco (vol.), Mex. 205/Q10
Ajuy, Phil. 100/C3
Ak-Dovurak, Rus. 111/F1
Aka (riv.), Japan 97/F1
Aka Eze, Nga. 133/G5
Akabane, Japan 95/M6
Akabira, Japan 94/C2
Akabli, Alg. 129/F4
Akademik Obruchev (mts.), Rus. 90/C1
Akagera, PN de l', Rwa. 139/G3
Akaishi-dake (peak), Japan 97/F3
Āk'ak'ī Besek'a, Eth. 136/A3
Akālgarh, Pak. 110/B3
Akalkot, India 107/C2
Akaltara, India 108/D4
Akan (lake), Japan 94/D2
Akan NP, Japan 94/D2
Akana, Congo 138/C3
Akankpa, Nga. 133/H5
Akaroa, NZ 159/C3
Åkarp, Swe. 46/E4
Akarsu, Turk. 114/D2
Akasha East, Sudan 127/F4
Akashi, Japan 95/G6
Akashi (str.), Japan 95/G6
Akaska, SD, US 186/D5
Akbarpur, India 108/D2
Akbarpur, India 108/B2
Akbaytal (pass), Taj. 111/B4
Akbou, Alg. 130/H4
Akçaabat, Turk. 76/F4
Akçakale, Turk. 114/D2
Akçakoca, Turk. 57/K5
Akçaova, Turk. 57/J5
Akçapınar, Turk. 114/D2
Akçay, Turk. 116/A1
Akchâr (phys. reg.), Mrta. 128/B5
Akchatau, Kaz. 80/H5
Akdağmadeni, Turk. 76/E5
Akdar, Al Jabal al (mts.), Libya 126/D2
Akechi, Japan 95/M5
Akeley, Mn, US 187/G4
Akelo, Sudan 135/G4
Akeno, Japan 95/A2
Akeno, Japan 95/E1
Åkers styckebruk, Swe. 45/A1
Åkersberga, Swe. 46/H2
Akershus (co.), Nor. 44/D3
Akershus Castle, Nor. 44/S8
Aketi, D.R. Congo 139/E2
Akhalk'alak'i, Geo. 77/G4
Akhalts'ikhe, Geo. 77/G4
Akharnaí, Gre. 55/N8
Akhaura, Bang. 109/H4
Akhelóos (riv.), Gre. 55/G3
Akhiok, Ak, US 201/H4
Akhisar, Turk. 76/C5
Akhmeta, Geo. 77/H4
Akhmīm, Egypt 127/F3
Akhnūr, India 110/C3
Akhtopol, Bul. 57/H4
Akhtuba (riv.), Rus. 77/H3
Akhtubinsk, Rus. 77/H2
Akhtyrskiy, Rus. 79/K5
Aki, Japan 96/C4
Aki (riv.), Japan 95/C2
Akiachak, Ak, US 201/F3
Akiéni, Gabon 138/C3
Akigawa, Japan 95/C2
Akimiski (isl.), On, Can. 171/H3
Akıncı (pt.), Turk. 116/D1
Akıncılar, Turk. 114/D1
Akins, Ok, US 183/G3
Åkirkeby, Den. 46/F4
Akishima, Japan 95/C2
Akita, Japan 94/B4
Akita (pref.), Japan 94/B4
Akitio, NZ 159/D3
Akiyama, Japan 95/C2
Akjoujt, Mrta. 132/B2
Akka, Mor. 128/C3
Akkerhaugen, Nor. 46/C2
Akkeshi, Japan 94/D2
Acre ('Akko), Isr. 117/C3
'Akko (Acre), Isr. 117/C3
Akkrum, Neth. 58/C2
Akkystau, Kaz. 77/K2
Aklavik, NW, Can. 201/L2
'Aklé 'Aouâna (dune), Mrta. 132/D2
Aknīste, Lat. 47/L3
Aknoul, Mor. 130/C2
Akō, Japan 96/D3
Akoabas, Camr. 138/C2
Akobo, Sudan 135/G4
Ākobo Wenz (riv.), Eth. 135/G4
Akoga, Gabon 138/B2
Akok, Gabon 138/B2

Akom – Altai
262

Akom li, Camr. 138/B2
Akoma, PNG 153/G1
Akonolinga, Camr. 138/C2
Akora, Pak. 110/B2
Āk'ordat, Erit. 135/H2
Akören, Turk. 114/C2
Akosombo (dam), Gha. 133/F5
Akot, Sudan 135/F4
Akot, India 107/C1
Akoupé, C.d'Iv. 132/E5
Akpatok (isl.), Qu, Can. 171/K2
Akpınar, Turk. 115/M6
Akqi, China 111/C3
Akrab, Kaz. 77/K2
Akranes, Ice. 44/M7
Ákrathos (cape), Gre. 55/J2
Åkrehamn, Nor. 46/A2
Akrítas (cape), Gre. 55/G4
Akron, Al, US 192/D4
Akron, Co, US 184/C3
Akron, In, US 190/C4
Akron, Ia, US 185/F2
Akron, Mi, US 190/E3
Akron, NY, US 190/W9
Akron, Oh, US 190/F4
Akron, Pa, US 198/B3
Akrotiri, Cyp. 116/C2
Aksai Chin (reg.), India 111/C4
Aksakovo, Rus. 75/M5
Aksaray, Turk. 114/C2
Aksaray (prov.), Turk. 114/C2
Aksay, Rus. 79/K4
Aksay Kazakzu Zizhixian, China 90/C4
Akşehir, Turk. 114/B2
Akşehir (lake), Turk. 114/B2
Akseki, Turk. 114/B2
Aksoran (peak), Kaz. 111/C2
Aksu, Turk. 116/B1
Aksu (riv.), Turk. 116/B1
Aksu, China 111/D3
Aksu (riv.), Kaz. 111/C2
Aksubayevo, Rus. 75/L5
Āksum, Eth. 136/A2
Aktash, Uzb. 80/G6
Aktau, Kaz. 80/H4
Aktepe, Turk. 116/E1
Aktí (pen.), Gre. 76/C4
Aktogay, Kaz. 111/C2
Aktumsyk, Kaz. 77/L3
Aku, Nga. 133/G5
Akula, D.R. Congo 138/E2
Akune, Japan 96/B4
Akure, Nga. 133/G5
Akureyri, Ice. 44/N6
Akuse, Gha. 133/F5
Akutan (isl.), Ak, US 201/E5
Akutan, Ak, US 201/E5
Akutan Pass (str.), Ak, US 201/E5
Akwa Ibom (state), Nga. 133/G5
Akwanga, Nga. 133/H4
Akxokesay, China 90/C4
Akyab (Sittwe), Myan. 105/F3
Akyar, Rus. 77/L2
Akyazı, Turk. 57/K5
Akzhal, Kaz. 111/D2
Āl, Nor. 46/C1
Al 'Abbāsah ash Sharqīyah, Egypt 131/C3
Al 'Abbāsīyah, Sudan 135/F2
Āl 'Ābis, SAr. 112/D5
Al 'Adam, Libya 126/D2
Al Aḩmadī, Kuw. 115/G4
Al 'Ajamīyīn, Egypt 131/B6
Al Akhḑar, SAr. 127/H2
Al 'Āl, Jor. 117/D5
Al 'Alamayn (El Alamein), Egypt 127/F2
Al 'Alāqimah, Egypt 131/C3
Al 'Amārah, Iraq 115/F4
Al Anbār (gov.), Iraq 114/E3
Al 'Aqabah, Jor. 127/G2
Al 'Arīsh, Egypt 116/C4
Al Arţāwīyah, SAr. 112/E3
Al 'Assāfīyah, SAr. 127/H2
Al 'Awdah, SAr. 112/E3
Al 'Awsajīyah, SAr. 112/D3
Al 'Ayn, SAr. 127/H3
Al 'Ayn, UAE 113/G4
Al 'Ayyāţ, Egypt 131/C5
Al 'Azīzīyah, Iraq 115/F3
Al Azīzīyah, Libya 126/B1
Al Bāb, Syria 114/D2
Al Badrashayn, Egypt 131/C5
Al Baḩr Al Aḩmar (gov.), Egypt 127/G3
Al Bajalāt, Egypt 131/C2
Al Bājūr, Egypt 131/C4
Al Bakātūsh, Egypt 131/B2
Al Balāmūn, Egypt 131/C3
Al Ballāḩ, Egypt 131/D3
Al Balqā' (gov.), Jor. 116/D4
Al Balyanā, Egypt 127/G3
Al Bāqūrah, Jor. 117/D3
Al Barāmūn, Egypt 131/C2
Al Barrah, SAr. 112/E4
Al Baslaqūn, Egypt 131/B2
Al Başrah, Iraq 115/F4
Al Başrah (gov.), Iraq 115/F4
Al Batānūn, Egypt 131/C3
Al Batrūn, Leb. 116/D2
Al Bawīţī, Egypt 127/F2
Al Bayḑā, Libya 126/D1
Al Bayḑā, Yem. 136/C2
Al Biqā' (valley), Leb. 116/D3
Al Biqā (gov.), Leb. 117/D1
Al Bi'r, SAr. 127/H2
Al Bīrah, WBnk. 117/C5
Al Birk, SAr. 112/D5
Al Birkah, Libya 129/H4
Al Buḩayrah (gov.), Egypt 131/B3
Al Buraymī, Oman 113/G4
Al Burj, Egypt 131/B1
Al Burumbul, Egypt 131/C6
Al Buzūn, Yem. 136/D2
Al Fallūjah, Iraq 115/E3
Al Fanānahl, Tun. 130/L6
Al Farḑah, Yem. 136/D2
Al Fāsher, Sudan 135/E2
Al Fatḩah, Iraq 115/E3
Al Fāw, Iraq 115/G4
Al Fawwār, Tun. 129/H2
Al Fayyūm (gov.), Egypt 114/B3
Al Fayyum, Egypt 131/B6
Al Fāzah, Yem. 136/B2
Al Fifi, Sudan 135/E3
Al Firdān, Egypt 131/D3
Al Fuhūd, Iraq 115/F4
Al Fujayrah, UAE 113/G3
Al Fūlah, Sudan 135/F3
Al Fuqahā', Libya 126/C3
Al Gharaq as Sulţānī, Egypt 131/B6
Al Ghāriyah, Syria 117/F4
Al Ghāţ, SAr. 112/E3
Al Ghayatah, Egypt 131/B3
Al Ghayḑah, Yem. 112/F5
Al Ghayl, SAr. 112/E4
Al Ghurdaqah, Egypt 127/G3
Al Ḩaddādī, Egypt 131/B2
Al Ḩaddār, SAr. 112/E4
Al Ḩadīthah, SAr. 114/D4
Al Ḩadīthah, Iraq 114/E3
Al Ḩaḑr, Iraq 115/E3
Al Ḩaffah, Syria 116/E2
Al Ḩajar ash Sahrqī (mts.), Oman 113/G4
Al Hajarayn, Yem. 136/D2
Al Ḩājir, Egypt 131/C3
Al Ḩamādah al Ḩamrā (upland), Libya 126/A2
Al Ḩamar, SAr. 112/E4
Al Hamdab, Sudan 112/B5
Al Ḩammah, Tun. 129/H2
Al Hammām, Egypt 127/F2
Al Ḩamrā', SAr. 127/H4
Al Ḩāmūl, Egypt 131/C2
Al Hanākīyah, SAr. 112/D4
Al Ḩanīyah, Libya 126/D1
Al Hārithah, Iraq 115/F4
Al Ḩārrah, Syria 117/D2
Al Harūj al Aswad (hill), Libya 126/C3
Al Ḩasakah, Syria 114/E2
Al Ḩasakah (prov.), Syria 114/E2
Al Ḩawāmidīyah, Egypt 131/C5
Al Ḩawātah, Sudan 135/G2
Al Ḩawrah, Yem. 136/C2
Al Ḩawţah, SAr. 112/E3
Al Ḩawţah, Yem. 136/D2
Al Ḩayy, Iraq 115/F3
Al Ḩayy, Egypt 131/C5
Al Ḩayyānīyah, SAr. 114/E4
Al Ḩillah, Iraq 115/F3
Al Ḩillah, SAr. 112/E4
Al Ḩillah, Sudan 135/E2
Al Hindīyah, Iraq 115/F3
Al Hirmil, Leb. 116/E2
Al Ḩişn, Jor. 117/D4
Al Hoceima, Mor. 130/C2
Al Hoceima (prov.), Mor. 130/B2
Al Hoceima (Côte du Rif) (int'l arpt.), Mor. 130/C2
Al Ḩudaydah, Yem. 136/B2
Al Hufūf, SAr. 112/E3
Al Ḩulwah, SAr. 112/E4
Al Ḩumayshah, Yem. 136/C2
Al Ḩurayḑah, Yem. 136/D2
Al Ḩuşayḩişah, Sudan 135/G2
Al Ḩusaynīyah, Egypt 131/C3
Al Ḩuwaymī, Yem. 136/C2
Al Ḩuwayyiţ, SAr. 112/D3
Al Huwwārīyah, Tun. 130/M6
Al Ibēdiyya, Sudan 112/B5
Al Ibrāhīmīyah, Egypt 131/C3
Al 'Irqah, Yem. 136/C2
Al Iskandarīyah, Iraq 115/F3
Al Iskandarīyah (gov.), Egypt 114/B3
Al Iskandarīyah, Egypt 131/A2
Al Ismā'īlīyah (gov.), Egypt 116/C4
Al Ismā'īlīyah, Egypt 131/D3
Al Istiwā'īyah (pol. reg.), Sudan 135/F4
Al Jabal Akaur (mts.), Oman 113/G4
Al Jabal al Akhḑar (mts.), Libya 126/D2
Al Jabalayn, Sudan 135/G2
Al Jaghbūb, Libya 126/E2
Al Jamālīyah, Egypt 131/C2
Al Jamīl, Libya 126/B1
Al Janad (int'l arpt.), Yem. 136/C2
Al Janūb (gov.), Leb. 117/C2
Al Jawārah, Oman 113/G5
Al Jawf, SAr. 114/D4
Al Jawf, Libya 126/D3
Al Jibāb, Syria 117/E2
Al Jifārah (plain), Libya 129/H2
Al Jifārah, SAr. 112/E4
Al Jifārah (plain), Tun. 113/H2
Al Jīzah, Egypt 131/C4
Al Jīzah, Jor. 117/D5
Al Jubayl, SAr. 115/G5
Al Judaydah, Leb. 117/D1
Al Judayyidah, Jor. 117/D5
Al Junaynah, Sudan 134/D2
Al Junaynah, SAr. 112/D4
Al Kāb, Egypt 131/D3
Al Kafr ash Sharqī, Egypt 131/C2
Al Kahfah, SAr. 115/E5
Al Kāmil, Oman 113/G4
Al Karak (gov.), Jor. 116/D4
Al Karak, Jor. 127/G2
Al Karāmah, Jor. 117/D5
Al Karīb, Tun. 130/L6
Al Karnak, Egypt 127/G3
Al Kawd, Yem. 136/C2
Al Kawm al Akhḑar, Egypt 131/B3
Al Kawm aţ Ţawīl, Egypt 131/C2
Al Khabrā', SAr. 112/D3
Al Khābūrah, Oman 113/G4
Al Khalīl (Hebron), WBnk. 117/C5
Al Khāliş, Iraq 115/F3
Al Khandaq, Sudan 127/F5
Al Khānkah, Egypt 131/C4
Al Khārijah, Egypt 127/F3
Al Kharrārah, Qatar 112/F4
Al Kharţūm (pol. reg.), Sudan 135/G2
Al Kharţūm Baḩrī (Khartoum North), Sudan 135/G2
Al Khaţāţibah, Egypt 131/B4
Al Khiḑr, Iraq 115/F4
Al Khiyām, Leb. 117/D2
Al Khubar, SAr. 112/F3
Al Khums, Libya 126/B1
Al Khuraybah, Yem. 136/D2
Al Khurmah, SAr. 112/D4
Al Khurtum (Khartoum) (cap.), Sudan 135/G2
Al Kiswah, Syria 117/E2
Al Kittah, Jor. 117/D4
Al Kūfah, Iraq 115/F3
Al Kufrah, Libya 126/D3
Al Kūt, Iraq 115/F3
Al Lādhiqīyah (Latakia), Syria 116/D2
Al Lādhiqīyah (prov.), Syria 116/D2
Al Lagowa, Sudan 135/F3
Al Lāhūn, Egypt 131/B6
Al Lidām, SAr. 112/D4
Al Lisht (ruin), Egypt 131/C5
Al Līth, SAr. 112/D4
Al Luḩayyah, Yem. 136/B2
Al Ma'ādī, Egypt 131/C5
Al Madīnah, SAr. 112/C4
Al Madīyah (gov.)., Alg. 130/M7
Al Madwar, Jor. 117/D4
Al Mafraq, Jor. 117/E4
Al Maghārīm, Yem. 136/C2
Al Maghrib (reg.), Alg. 128/E2
Al Maghrib (reg.), Alg.,Mor. 72/C4
Al Maḩallah al Kubrá, Egypt 131/C3
Al Maḩmūdīyah, Iraq 115/F3
Al Maḩmūdīyah, Egypt 131/B2
Al Majdal, Jor. 117/D4
Al Majma'ah, SAr. 112/E3
Al Maks, Egypt 131/A2
Al Malamm, Sudan 135/F3
Al Mālikīyah, Syria 114/E2
Al Ma'mūrah, Egypt 131/B2
Al Manāmah (Manama) (cap.), Bahr. 112/F3
Al Manaqīl, Sudan 135/G2
Al Mansūrah, Egypt 131/C2
Al Manşūrīyah, Egypt 131/C4
Al Manzilah, Egypt 131/C2
Al Maqrūn, Libya 126/D2
Al Marāghah, Egypt 127/F3
Al Marj, Libya 126/D1
Al Ma'şarah, Egypt 131/C5
Al Masīd, Sudan 135/G2
Al Matammah, Sudan 135/G1
Al Maţarīyah, Egypt 131/D2
Al Matnah, Sudan 135/G2
Al Mawşil (Mosul), Iraq 115/E2
Al Mayādin, Syria 114/E3
Al Maymūn, Egypt 131/C6
Al Mazra'ah, Jor. 116/D4
Al Midhnab, SAr. 112/D3
Al Mīnā', Leb. 116/D2
Al Mindak, SAr. 112/D4
Al Minshāt el Kubrá, Egypt 131/B2
Al Minyā, Egypt 127/F2
Al Minyā, Egypt 131/C5
Al Minyā, Egypt 131/B6
Al Miqdādiyah, Iraq 115/F3
Al Mubarraz, SAr. 112/E4
Al Mudawwarah, Jor. 127/G2
Al Muglad, Sudan 135/E3
Al Mukallā, Yem. 136/D2
Al Munastīr (gov.), Alg. 130/M7
Al Musallamīyah, Sudan 135/G2
Al Musayjīd, SAr. 127/H3
Al Musayyib, Iraq 115/F3
Al Muthanná (gov.), Iraq 115/F4
Al Muwaqqar, Jor. 117/E5
Al Muwassam, SAr. 136/B1
Al Muwayh, SAr. 112/D4
Al Muwayliḩ, SAr. 127/G3
Al Qābil, Oman 113/G4
Al Qaḑārif, Sudan 135/G2
Al Qaḑīmah, SAr. 112/C4
Al Qādisīyah (gov.), Iraq 115/F4
Al Qāhirah (Cairo) (cap.), Egypt 131/C4
Al Qāhirah (gov.), Egypt 114/B3
Al Qaḩmah, SAr. 112/D5
Al Qā'im, Iraq 114/E3
Al Qāmishlī, Syria 114/E2
Al Qanāţir al Khayrīyah, Egypt 131/C4
Al Qanāyāt, Egypt 131/C3
Al Qantarah, Egypt 131/D3
Al Qanţarah al Gharbīyah, Egypt 131/D3
Al Qaryah al Sharqīyah, Libya 126/B2
Al Qaryāt, Libya 126/B2
Al Qaryatayn, Syria 116/E2
Al Qarẕabah, Libya 126/D1
Al Qaşabāt, Libya 126/B1
Al Qaşr, Egypt 127/F3
Al Qaşr, Jor. 117/D6
Al Qaţaynah, Sudan 135/G2
Al Qaţīf, SAr. 112/F3
Al Qaţrūn, Libya 126/B3
Al Qayşūmah, SAr. 115/F4
Al Qibābāt, Egypt 131/C6
Al Qubbah, Libya 126/D1
Al Qunayţirah (prov.), Syria 117/D2
Al Qunayţirah, Jor. 117/E5
Al Qunayţirah, Syria 117/D2
Al Qunfudhah, SAr. 112/D5
Al Qurayn, Egypt 131/C3
Al Qurnah, Iraq 115/F4
Al Quşayr, Syria 116/E2
Al Quşayr, Egypt 127/G3
Al Quşūr, Tun. 130/L7
Al Quţayfah, Syria 117/F1
Al Quway'id (well), Libya 126/D2
Al Quway'īyah, SAr. 112/E4
Al Quwayrah, Jor. 116/D5
Al 'Ubaylah, SAr. 112/F4
Al Ubayyiḑ, Sudan 135/F2
Al Uḑayyah, Sudan 135/F2
Al 'Ulá, SAr. 127/H3
Al 'Umdah, Sudan 135/F3
Al Uqaylah, Libya 126/C2
Al Uqşur, Egypt 127/G3
Al 'Uwaynāt (peak), Sudan 126/E4
Al 'Uwaynāt, Libya 129/H4
Al 'Uyūn, SAr. 112/D3
Al 'Uzayr, Iraq 115/F4
Al Wādī al Jadīd (wadi), Egypt 114/B5
Al Wafā'īyah, Egypt 131/B3
Al Wāḩāt al Baḩrtyah (reg.), Egypt 127/F2
Al Wāḩāt al Khārijah (reg.), Egypt 127/F3
Al Wajh, SAr. 127/H3
Al Wakrah, Qatar 112/F3
Al Wāsiţah, Egypt 131/C6
Al Wazz, Sudan 135/F2
Al Widy, Egypt 131/C5
Al Wusta (pol. reg.), Sudan 135/G2
Al Yādūdah, Jor. 117/D5
Al Yāmūn, WBnk. 117/C4
Ala (pt.), It. 54/B1
Ala, It. 69/E2
Ala (riv.), China 90/B3
Alabama (state), US 173/J5
Alabama (riv.), Al,Ga, US 173/J5
Alabama and Coushatta Ind. Res., Tx, US 181/G2
Alabaster, Al, US 192/D4
Alabat, Phil. 100/C2
Alaca, Turk. 114/C1
Alacalı, Turk. 57/J5
Alaçam, Turk. 76/E4
Alaçatı, Turk. 55/K3
Alachua, Fl, US 195/G3
Alacrán (reef), Mex. 206/D1
Alacranes (res.), Cuba 207/F1
Aladağ, Turk. 116/C1
Alaejos, Sp. 52/C2
Alafia (riv.), Fl, US 194/L8
Alagir, Rus. 77/H4
Alagna Valsesia, It. 68/A1
Alagnon (riv.), Fr. 50/E4
Alagoa Grande, Braz. 219/H4
Alagoas (state), Braz. 219/G5
Alagoinhas, Braz. 223/F2
Alagón, Sp. 53/E2
Alagón (riv.), Sp. 52/C2
Alah (riv.), Phil. 100/D4
Alahanpanjang, Indo. 101/C3
Alajärvi, Fin. 74/D3
Alajärvi (lake), Fin. 45/E4
Alajõe, Est. 47/M2
Alajuela, CR 207/E4
Alakanuk, Ak, US 201/F3
Alakol (lake), Kaz. 80/J5
Alakuko, Nga. 133/G5
Alalapadu, Sur. 218/B2
Alalaú (riv.), Braz. 217/F5
Alamaån (riv.), Swe. 45/K6
Alamagan (isl.), NMar. 160/D3
'Alāmarvdasht (riv.), Iran 115/H5
Ālamat'ā, Eth. 136/A2
Alameda, Sk, Can. 186/C3
Alameda (co.), Ca, US 197/L11
Alameda, Ca, US 197/K11
Alameda, NM, US 179/J3
Alameda (cr.), Ca, US 197/L11
Ālamgīr, Pak. 110/A4
Alamikamba, Nic. 207/E3
Alamito (cr.), Tx, US 180/B3
Alamo, Mex. 206/B1
Alamo (lake), Az, US 179/F3
Alamo, Ca, US 197/K11
Alamo, Ga, US 193/F4
Alamo (mtn.), NM, US 180/B1
Alamo, Nv, US 178/E2
Alamo, Tn, US 192/C3
Alamo Band Ind. Res., NM, US 179/J3
Alamo Village, Tx, US 180/D3
Alamor, Ecu. 220/A2
Álamos, Mex. 204/C3
Alamosa, Co, US 182/B2
Alamosa (cr.), NM, US 182/B3
Alamosa Nat'l Wild.Ref., Co, US 179/K2
Åland (isl.), Fin. 44/G3
Aland (riv.), Ger. 48/F2
Alang, Indo. 100/B4
Alanreed, Tx, US 182/D3
Alanson, Mi, US 190/D2
Alantika, Monts (mts.), Camr.,Nga. 134/B3
Alanya, Turk. 116/C1
Alaotra (lake), Madg. 143/J7
Alapaha, Ga, US 195/G2
Alapaha (riv.), Ga, US 195/G2
Alapayevsk, Rus. 75/P4
Alaplı, Turk. 57/K5
Alarcón (res.), Sp. 52/D3
Alarka, NC, US 193/F3
Alas, Indo. 103/E5
Alaşehir, Turk. 114/B2
Alaserjärvi (lake), Fin. 45/F3
Alashtar, Iran 115/G3
Alaska (gulf), Ak, US 201/J4
Alaska (pen.), Ak, US 201/F4
Alaska (range), Ak, US 201/H3
Alaska (state), US 201/*
Alassio, It. 68/B6
Ālāt, Azer. 115/G2
Alataw (pass), China 111/D2
Alatri, It. 71/C4
Alatyr', Rus. 75/K5
Alaverdi, Arm. 77/H4
Alavus, Fin. 74/D3
Alaw (riv.), Wal, UK 40/D5
Alawa Ngandi Abor. Land, Austl. 152/D3
'Ālayh, Leb. 117/D1
Alayor, Sp. 52/C3
Alayskiy (mts.), Kyr. 111/B4
Alazeya (riv.), Rus. 81/R3
Alb (riv.), Ger. 64/B5
Alba, Tx, US 183/G4
Alba (prov.), Rom. 57/F2
Alba Adriatica, It. 71/C2
Alba de Tormes, Sp. 52/C2
Alba Fucens (ruin), It. 71/C3
Alba Iulia, Rom. 57/F2
Albacete, Sp. 52/E3
Albaida, Sp. 53/E3
Albairate, It. 68/B3
Ålbæk, Den. 46/D3
Albalate del Arzobispo, Sp. 53/E2
Alban, On, Can. 190/F1
Alban, Fr. 50/E5
Albán, Col. 219/L8
Albania, Col. 219/M7
Albania (ctry.) 55/F2
Albanian Alps, North (mts.), Alb.,Mont. 56/D4
Albano (lake), It. 71/B4
Albano Laziale, It. 71/B4
Albany, Austl. 154/C5
Albany (riv.), On, Can. 171/H3
Albany, NZ 159/F6
Albany, Ca, US 197/K11
Albany, Ga, US 195/F2
Albany, In, US 190/D4
Albany, Ky, US 192/E2
Albany, Mn, US 187/G5
Albany, Mo, US 185/G3
Albany (cap.), NY, US 191/K3
Albany, Ok, US 183/F4
Albany, Or, US 176/B1
Albany, Tx, US 180/E1
Albaredo D'Adige, It. 69/E3
Albarine (riv.), Fr. 66/B5
Albarracín, Sp. 52/E2
Albatross (pt.), NZ 159/C2
Albatross (bay), Austl. 145/D2
Albatross Rock (pt.), Namb. 142/A2
Albbruck, Ger. 66/E2
Albemarle (pt.), Ecu. 220/J6
Albemarle, NC, US 193/G3
Albemarle (sound), NC, US 193/J3
Albenga, It. 68/B5
Alberche (riv.), Sp. 52/C2
Alberdi, Par. 224/E3
Alberga, Austl. 155/G3
Alberga (cr.), Austl. 145/C3
Alberhill, Ca, US 196/C3
Alberndorf in der Riedmark, Aus. 65/H6
Alberschwende, Aus. 67/F3
Albersdorf, Ger. 46/C4
Albersweiler, Ger. 64/B4
Albert, Austl. 156/C2
Albert (lake), Austl. 156/A2
Albert (lake), D.R.Congo, Ugan. 119/E4
Albert, Fr. 60/B3
Albert, Ks, US 182/E1
Albert Canyon, BC, Can. 174/F2
Albert Edward (mt.), PNG 153/G2
Albert Kanaal (riv.), Belg. 61/E2
Albert Lea, Mn, US 185/H2
Albert Nile (riv.), Ugan. 135/F5
Alberta (prov.), Can. 170/E3
Alberta, Al, US 192/D4
Alberta Beach, Ab, Can. 174/G1
Alberti, Arg. 226/E2
Albertinia, SAfr. 142/C4
Albertirsa, Hun. 56/D2
Alberto de Agostini, PN, Chile 227/B7
Alberton, PE, Can. 188/E2
Alberton, SAfr. 142/Q13
Alberton, Mt, US 174/G4
Albertshofen, Ger. 64/D3
Albertville, Sk, Can. 175/M1
Albertville, Fr. 70/C1
Albertville, Al, US 192/D3
Albertville, Mn, US 187/N6
Albestroff, Fr. 61/F6
Albeuve, Swi. 66/D4
Albi, Fr. 50/E5
Albia, Ia, US 185/H3
Albignasego, It. 69/E3
Albin, Wy, US 184/B3
Albina (pt.), Ang. 140/A2
Albina, Sur. 218/C1
Albinea, It. 68/D4
Albino, It. 68/C2
Albion, Id, US 177/G2
Albion, Il, US 192/C1
Albion, In, US 190/D4
Albion, Mi, US 190/D3
Albion, Ne, US 184/E3
Albion, NY, US 191/G3
Albion, Pa, US 190/F4
Albisola Marina, It. 68/B5
Albisola Superiore, It. 68/B5
Alblasserdam, Neth. 58/B5
Albocácer, Sp. 53/E2
Albon, Fr. 70/A2
Alborán (isl.), Mor. 128/E2
Alborán (isl.), Sp. 72/C4
Ålborg, Den. 46/C3
Ålborg (bay), Den. 46/D3
Albox, Sp. 52/D4
Albright Knox Art Gallery, NY, US 190/V10
Albrighton, Eng, UK 42/D1
Albristhorn (peak), Swi. 66/D5
Albufeira, Port. 52/A4
Albula (riv.), Swi. 51/H3
Albuñol, Sp. 52/D4
Albuquerque (int'l arpt.), NM, US 179/J3
Albuquerque, NM, US 179/J3
Alburquerque, Sp. 52/B3
Alburtis, Pa, US 198/C3
Albury, NZ 159/B4
Albury, Austl. 157/C3
Alby-sur-Chéran, Fr. 66/C6
Alca, Peru 220/C4
Alcabideche, Port. 53/P10
Alcácer do Sal, Port. 52/A3
Alcalá, Col. 219/K8
Alcalá de Chivert, Sp. 53/F2
Alcalá de Guadaira, Sp. 52/C4
Alcalá de Henares, Sp. 53/N9
Alcalá de los Gazules, Sp. 52/C4
Alcalá la Real, Sp. 52/D4
Alcalde (pt.), Chile 224/B4
Alcamo, It. 54/C4
Alcanadre (riv.), Sp. 53/E2
Alcanar, Sp. 53/E2
Alcañices, Sp. 52/B2
Alcañiz, Sp. 53/E2
Alcántara, Sp. 52/B3
Alcántara (res.), Sp. 52/B3
Alcântara, Braz. 219/E3
Alcântaras, Braz. 219/F3
Alcantarilla, Sp. 52/E4
Alcaraz, Sp. 52/D3
Alcaraz (range), Sp. 52/D3
Alcaraz, Sierra de (mts.), Sp. 72/C3
Alcatraz (isl.), Ca, US 197/K11
Alcatrazes (isl.), Braz. 223/L9
Alcaudete, Sp. 52/C4
Alcázar de San Juan, Sp. 52/D3
Alcester, SD, US 185/F2
Alcester, Eng, UK 43/E2
Alchevs'k, Ukr. 79/K3
Alcira, Sp. 53/E3
Alcira, Arg. 226/D2
Alçıtepe, Turk. 55/K2
Alco, Ar, US 183/H3
Alcoa, Tn, US 192/F3
Alcobaça, Braz. 223/F3
Alcobaça, Port. 52/A3
Alcobendas, Sp. 53/N8
Alcoche, Bol. 221/E4
Alcochete, Port. 53/Q10
Alcolu, SC, US 193/G4
Alcora, Sp. 53/E2
Alcorcón, Sp. 53/N9
Alcorisa, Sp. 53/E2
Alcoutim, Port. 52/B4
Alcova, Wy, US 177/K2
Alcoy, Sp. 53/E3
Alcúdia, Sp. 53/G3
Aldabra (isls.), Sey. 119/G5
Aldama, Mex. 204/D2
Aldama, Mex. 205/F4
Aldan (plat.), Rus. 81/N4
Aldan (riv.), Rus. 83/N3
Aldan, Rus. 81/N4
Aldar, Mong. 111/G2
Aldbourne, Eng, UK 43/E4
Aldbrough, Eng, UK 41/H4
Alde (riv.), Eng, UK 43/H2
Aldeburgh, Eng, UK 43/H2
Aldeia Formoza, Ang. 138/C5
Aldeia Nova de São Bento, Port. 52/B4
Aldeia Viçosa, Ang. 138/C5
Alden, Il, US 197/N15
Alden, NY, US 190/W10
Aldenhoven, Ger. 61/F2
Aldeno, It. 67/H6
Alder (lake), Wa, US 174/C4
Alder Flats, Ab, Can. 174/G1
Aldergrove, NI, UK 40/B2
Aldergrove (int'l arpt.), NI, UK 40/B2
Alderley Edge, Eng, UK 41/F5
Aldermaston, Eng, UK 43/E4
Alderney (isl.), Chl, UK 50/B2
Alderney (The Blaye) (arpt.), Chl, UK 62/C1
Alderpoint, Ca, US 176/B3
Aldershot, Eng, UK 43/F4
Aldershot, On, Can. 190/T9
Alderson, WV, US 193/G2
Aldersyde, Ab, Can. 175/H2
Alderwood Manor-Bothell North, Wa, US 197/C2
Aldine, Tx, US 181/M9
Aldingen, Ger. 67/E1
Aldred (lake), Pa, US 198/B4
Aldridge, Eng, UK 43/E1
Ale Water (riv.), Sc, UK 39/D6
Aledo, Il, US 185/J3
Aledo, Tx, US 180/K7
Aleg, Mrta. 132/B2
Alegre, Braz. 223/E4
Alegrete, Braz. 225/F4
Alejandría, Bol. 221/E4
Alejandro Gallinal, Uru. 227/G2
Alejandro Roca, Arg. 226/E2
Alejandro Selkirk (isl.), Chile 209/A6
Alejo Ledesma, Arg. 226/E2
Aleknagik, Ak, US 201/G4
Aleksandro-Nevskiy, Rus. 76/G1
Aleksandrov, Rus. 74/H4
Aleksandrov Gay, Rus. 77/J2
Aleksandrovac, Serb. 56/E4
Aleksandrovka, Rus. 79/K4
Aleksandrovsk, Rus. 75/N4
Aleksandrovsk-Sakhalinskiy, Rus. 91/N1
Aleksandrovskoye, Rus. 77/G3
Aleksandrów Kujawski, Pol. 49/K2
Aleksandrów Łódzki, Pol. 49/K3
Alekseyevka, Rus. 77/J1
Alekseyevka, Rus. 79/K2
Alekseyevka, Kaz. 111/B1
Alekseyevskoye, Rus. 75/L5
Aleksin, Rus. 74/H5
Aleksinac, Serb. 56/E4
Alem Maya, Eth. 136/B3
Além Paraíba, Braz. 223/P6
Alembé, Gabon 138/B3
Alemdar, Turk. 115/N6
Alençon, Fr. 63/F4
Alenquer, Braz. 218/C3
Alento (riv.), It. 71/D3
Alenuihaha (chan.), Hi, US 172/S9
Alépé, C.d'Iv. 132/E5
Aleppo (Ḩalab), Syria 116/E1
Alerce Andino, PN, Chile 226/B4
Aléria, Fr. 54/A1
Alert (pt.), Nun, Can. 171/S6
Alert, Nun, Can. 171/T6
Aleşd, Rom. 56/F2
Alessandria (prov.), It. 68/B3
Alessandria, It. 68/B4
Ålestrup, Den. 46/C3
Ålesund, Nor. 44/C3
Aletschhorn (peak), Swi. 66/D5
Aleutian (isls.), Ak, US 201/C5
Aleutian (range), Ak, US 201/G4
Alex, Ok, US 183/F3
Alexander (isl.), Ant. 228/V
Alexander (mt.), Austl. 154/B2
Alexander (pt.), Austl. 153/E3
Alexander, ND, US 186/C4
Alexander, Tx, US 181/E1
Alexander Archipelago (isls.), Ak, US 201/L4
Alexander Bay, SAfr. 142/B3
Alexander City, Al, US 192/E4
Alexander Graham Bell Nat'l Hist. Park, NS, Can. 189/G2
Alexander Nevsky Abbey, Rus. 75/T7
Alexandra, NZ 159/B4
Alexandra, Austl. 157/B3
Alexándria, Gre. 55/H2
Alexandria, Austl. 153/E4
Alexandria, Braz. 219/G4
Alexandria (int'l arpt.), Egypt 131/A2
Alexandria, Rom. 57/G4
Alexandria, SAfr. 142/D4
Alexandria, BC, Can. 174/C1
Alexandria, In, US 190/D4
Alexandria, Ky, US 192/E1
Alexandria, La, US 194/B2
Alexandria, Mn, US 187/G5
Alexandria, Ne, US 185/F3
Alexandria, Sc, UK 39/B5
Alexandria, SD, US 184/F2
Alexandria, Va, US 198/A6
Alexandria Bay, NY, US 191/J2
Alexandrina (lake), Austl. 145/C4
Alexandroúpolis, Gre. 55/J2
Alexeck (riv.), Namb. 140/C4
Alexis, Il, US 185/J3
Alexis Creek, BC, Can. 174/C1
Alexishafen, PNG 153/G1
Aley (riv.), Rus. 111/D1
Aleysk, Rus. 111/D1
Alfama (nbrhd.), Port. 53/P10
Alfarim, Port. 53/P11
Alfaro, Sp. 52/E1
Alfatar, Bul. 57/H4
Alfbach (riv.), Ger. 61/F3
Alfeld, Ger. 59/G5
Alfenas, Braz. 223/L6
Alfhausen, Ger. 59/E3
Alfiós (riv.), Gre. 55/G4
Alfonsine, It. 69/F4
Alfonso Bonilla Aragón (int'l arpt.), Col. 216/B4
Alford, Eng, UK 41/J5
Alford, Sc, UK 39/D2
Alford, Fl, US 195/F2
Alfred (mt.), BC, Can. 174/B2
Alfred, Me, US 191/L3
Alfred, NY, US 191/H3
Alfred NP, Austl. 157/D3
Alfreton, Eng, UK 41/G5
Alfriston, Eng, UK 43/G5
Alfter, Ger. 61/G2
Alga, Kaz. 77/L2
Algabas, Kaz. 77/K2
Ålgård, Nor. 46/A2
Algarrobito, Chile 224/B4
Algarrobo, Chile 226/N8
Algarve (reg.), Port. 52/A4
Algeciras, Col. 216/C4
Algeciras, Sp. 52/C4
Algemesí, Sp. 53/E3
Alger, Mi, US 190/D2
Alger (wilaya), Alg. 130/G4
Algeria (ctry.) 129/F3
Algermissen, Ger. 59/G4
Algete, Sp. 53/N8
Alghero, It. 54/A2
Algiers (El Djezair) (cap.), Alg. 130/G4
Algoa, Tx, US 181/M9
Algoa (bay), SAfr. 142/D4
Algodonales, Sp. 52/C4
Algoma, Ms, US 192/C3
Algoma, Or, US 176/C2
Algoma, Wi, US 190/C2
Algona, Ia, US 185/G2
Algona, Wa, US 197/C3
Algonac, Mi, US 197/G6
Algonquin (peak), NY, US 191/K2
Algonquin, Il, US 197/P14
Algood, Tn, US 192/E2
Algorta, Uru. 227/K10
Algueirão, Port. 53/P10
Algund (Lagundo), It. 67/H4
Alhama de Granada, Sp. 52/D4
Alhama de Murcia, Sp. 52/E4
Alhambra, Ca, US 196/F7
Alhambra, Il, US 185/K4
Alhandra, Port. 53/P10
Alhandra, Braz. 219/H4
Alhaurín el Grande, Sp. 52/C4
'Alī al Gharbī, Iraq 115/F3
'Alī ash Sharqī, Iraq 115/F3
Äli Bayramlı, Azer. 115/G2
'Ali Sabîeh, Djib. 136/B3
Alia, It. 54/C4
Alía, Sp. 52/C3
'Alīābād, Iran 115/H4
Aliade, Nga. 133/H5
Aliağa, Turk. 76/C5
Aliákmon (riv.), Gre. 55/G2
Aliákmonos (lake), Gre. 55/G2
Alíartos, Gre. 55/H3
Alibey (lake), Ukr. 78/F5
Alibey (riv.), Turk. 115/M6
Alibeyköy, Turk. 57/J5
Ālībo, Eth. 135/H3
Alicante (int'l arpt.), Sp. 53/E3
Alicante, Sp. 53/E3
Alice (riv.), Austl. 153/F3
Alice (pt.), It. 54/E3
Alice, SAfr. 142/D4
Alice, Tx, US 181/E4
Alice Springs, Austl. 155/G2
Aliceville, Al, US 192/C4
Aliceville (dam), Al, US 192/C4
Aliceville (lake), Al, US 192/C4
Alicia, Phil. 100/C4
Alicia, Ar, US 192/B3
Alicudi (isl.), It. 54/D3
Alicurá (res.), Arg. 226/C4
Alife, It. 71/D5
Alīganj, India 108/B2
Alīgarh, India 108/B2
Alijilán, Arg. 224/C4
Alijó, Port. 52/B2
Alīkadam, Bang. 105/F3
Alima (riv.), Congo 138/C3
Alindao, CAfr. 134/D4
Alingār (riv.), Afg. 110/A2
Alingsås, Swe. 46/E3
Alīpur, Pak. 110/A5
Alīpur Duār, India 109/G2
Alirājpur, India 113/K4
Aliskerovo, Rus. 81/S3
Alistráti, Gre. 55/H2
Alivérion, Gre. 55/J3
Aliwal North, SAfr. 142/D3
Alix, Ab, Can. 175/H1
Alixan, Fr. 70/B3
Aljezur, Port. 52/A4
Aljustrel, Port. 52/A4
Alkali Lake, BC, Can. 174/C2
Alken, Belg. 61/E2
Alkhan-Kala, Rus. 77/H4
Alkmaar, Neth. 58/B3
Alkoum (well), Alg. 129/H4
Alkoven, Aus. 65/H6
Alku (wadi), Sudan 135/E2
All American (canal), Ca, US 178/E4
Allada, Ben. 133/F5
Allagash (riv.), Me, US 188/C2
Allahābād, India 108/C3
Allaire, Fr. 62/C5
Allakaket, Ak, US 201/H2
Allakh-Yun', Rus. 81/P3
Allaman, Swi. 66/C5
Allan, Sk, Can. 175/L2
Allan (hills), Sk, Can. 175/L2
Alland, Aus. 57/N7
Allanmyo, Myan. 98/B5
Allanridge, SAfr. 142/D2
Allanson, Austl. 154/C5
'Allāq (well), Libya 126/A2
`Allāqt (wadi), Egypt 112/B4
Allariz, Sp. 52/B1
Allatoona (lake), Ga, US 192/E3
Allauch, Fr. 70/B6
Alldays, SAfr. 141/F4
Alle, Swi. 66/D3
Allegan, Mi, US 190/D3
Allegany, NY, US 191/G3
Allegheny (plat.), Pa, US 191/G4
Allegheny (riv.), Pa, US 191/G4
Allegheny (mts.), US 173/K4
Allegheny Portage Railroad Nat'l Hist. Site, Pa, US 191/G4
Allemands (lake), La, US 194/C3
Allen, Arg. 226/D3
Allen (mt.), NZ 159/A4
Allen (riv.), Eng, UK 42/B5
Allen, Ne, US 185/F2
Allen, Ok, US 183/F3
Allen, Tx, US 180/L6
Allen Park, Mi, US 197/F7
Allenby Bridge, Jor.,WBnk. 117/D5
Allendale, Eng, UK 41/F2
Allendale, Mi, US 190/D3
Allendale, NJ, US 199/J7
Allendale, SC, US 193/G4
Allende, Mex. 205/E2
Allende, Mex. 205/E3
Allendorf, Ger. 59/F6
Allensbach, Ger. 67/F2
Allentown, Pa, US 198/C2
Allentown-Bethlehem-Easton (arpt.), Pa, US 198/C2
Allentsteig, Aus. 49/H4
Allenwood, Pa, US 198/B1
Aller (riv.), Ger. 59/H3
Allerkanal (canal), Ger. 59/H4
Allerød, Den. 45/J7
Allersberg, Ger. 64/E4
Allershausen, Ger. 65/E6
Allevard, Fr. 70/C2
Allex, Fr. 70/A3
Allgäu Alps (range), Aus.,Ger. 48/F5
Allhallows, Eng, UK 36/F2
Alliance, Oh, US 190/F4
Alliance, Ne, US 184/C2
Alliance, Ab, Can. 175/J1
Allied War Cemetery, Myan. 106/B2
Allier (riv.), Fr. 72/D1
Allier, Montagne de l' (peak), Fr. 70/C4
Alligator (pt.), Austl. 153/F4
Alligator (lake), Fl, US 195/H3
Alligator (riv.), NC, US 193/J3
Allingåbro, Den. 46/D3
Allinge, Den. 46/F4
Allinges, Fr. 66/C5
Allingham, Austl. 153/E4
Allison, Ia, US 185/H2
Alliston, On, Can. 191/G2
Alloa, Sc, UK 39/C4
Allonnes, Fr. 63/F6
Allonnes, Fr. 63/F5
Allons, Tn, US 192/E2
Allora, Austl. 158/C5
Allos, Fr. 70/C4
Allouez, Wi, US 190/B2
Allow (riv.), Ire. 38/B5
Alloway, NJ, US 198/C4
Alloway (cr.), NJ, US 198/C4
Allschwil, Swi. 66/D2
Allumettes (isl.), Qu, Can. 191/H2
Alluvial City, La, US 194/D3
Allyn, Wa, US 174/C4
Alm (riv.), Aus. 65/G7
Alma, NS, Can. 188/E3
Alma, Qu, Can. 188/B1
Alma, Ar, US 183/G3
Alma, Ga, US 195/G2
Alma, Ks, US 183/F1
Alma, Mi, US 190/D3
Alma, Ne, US 184/E3
Alma, NM, US 179/H4
Alma (hill), NY, US 191/G3
Alma, Wi, US 185/J1
Almacelles, Sp. 53/F2
Almacén, Ven. 217/F2
Almada, Port. 53/P10
Almadén, Sp. 52/C3
Almafuerte, Arg. 226/D2
Almagro, Sp. 52/D3
Almanor (lake), Ca, US 176/C3
Almansa, Sp. 53/E3
Almanza, Sp. 52/C1
Almanzor, Pico de (peak), Sp. 52/C2
Almanzora (riv.), Sp. 52/D4
Almartha, Mo, US 183/H2
Almas, Braz. 222/D1
Almas, Pico das (peak), Braz. 223/E2
Almas, Rio das (riv.), Braz. 222/C2
Almaty Oblast, Kaz. 111/C3
Almaty (int'l arpt.), Kaz. 111/C3
Almazán, Sp. 52/D2
Almaznyy, Rus. 81/M3
Almazora, Sp. 53/E3
Almeida, Port. 52/B2
Almeirim, Port. 52/A3
Almeirim, Braz. 218/C3
Almelo, Neth. 58/D4
Almena, Ks, US 184/E4
Almenara (peak), Sp. 52/D3
Almenara, Sp. 53/E3
Almenara, Braz. 223/E3
Almendra (res.), Sp. 52/B2
Almendralejo, Sp. 52/B3
Almenno San Salvatore, It. 68/C2
Almere, Neth. 58/C4
Almería, Sp. 52/D4
Almería (gulf), Sp. 52/D4
Almese, It. 70/D2
Al'met'yevsk, Rus. 75/M5
Älmhult, Swe. 46/F3
Almina (pt.), Sp. 130/B2
Almirós, Gre. 55/H3
Almiroú (gulf), Gre. 55/J5
Almo, Id, US 177/G2
Almodôvar, Port. 52/A4
Almodóvar del Campo, Sp. 52/C3
Almodóvar del Río, Sp. 52/C4
Almoharín, Sp. 52/B3
Almond (riv.), Sc, UK 39/C4
Almont, ND, US 186/D4
Almont, Mi, US 190/E3
Almont (riv.), Fr. 36/L6
Almont, Co, US 179/J1
Almonte, On, Can. 191/H2
Almonte, Sp. 52/B4
Almora, India 108/B1
Almoradi, Sp. 53/E3
Almorox, Sp. 52/C2
Almte. Montt (gulf), Chile 227/B7
Almudévar, Sp. 53/E1
Almuñécar, Sp. 52/D4
Almunge, Swe. 45/B1
Almus, Turk. 114/D1
Alness, Sc, UK 39/B1
Alness (riv.), Sc, UK 39/B1
Alnmouth, Eng, UK 39/E6
Alnwick, Eng, UK 39/E6
Ålö (isl.), Swe. 45/B2
Alofi, NZ 161/J6
Alofi (isl.), Wall., Fr. 160/H6
Aloha, Or, US 176/B1
Aloi, Ugan. 137/A1
Aloja, Lat. 47/L3
Along, India 98/B2
Alongshan, China 91/J1
Alónnisos (isl.), Gre. 55/H3
Alonsa, Mb, Can. 186/E2
Alor (isl.), Indo. 152/B2
Alor (isls.), Indo. 152/B2
Alor Gajah, Malay. 101/C2
Alor Setar, Malay. 101/C1
Álora, Sp. 52/C4
Alotau, PNG 160/E6
Aloysius (mt.), Austl. 155/F3
Alpachiri, Arg. 226/E3
Alpaugh, Ca, US 178/C3
Alpe di Poti (peak), It. 69/E7
Alpe di Succiso (peak), It. 68/D5
Alpedrete, Sp. 53/M8
Alpen, Ger. 58/D5
Alpena, Mi, US 190/E2
Alpena, SD, US 184/E1
Alpercatas, Serra das (mts.), Braz. 219/E4
Alperschällihorn (peak), Swi. 67/F4
Alpes de Provence (range), Fr. 51/G5
Alpes-de-Haute-Provence (dept.), Fr. 70/C4
Alpes-Maritimes (dept.), Fr. 70/D5
Alpha, Austl. 158/B3
Alpha, Il, US 185/J3
Alpha (mt.), NZ 159/J8
Alpha, NJ, US 198/C2
Alpharetta, Ga, US 193/M6
Alphen aan de Rijn, Neth. 58/B4
Alpi Apuane (range), It. 51/J4
Alpi Dolomitiche (range), It. 51/J4
Alpi Orobie (range), It. 51/J3
Alpiarça, Port. 52/A3
Alpignano, It. 70/D2
Alpine, NJ, US 199/K8
Alpine, Tx, US 180/C2
Alpine, Wy, US 177/H2
Alpirsbach, Ger. 67/E1
Alpnach, Swi. 67/E4
Alps (mts.), Eur. 29/E4
Alqōsh, Iraq 115/E2
Alrewas, Eng, UK 43/E1
Alroy Downs, Austl. 153/E4
Als (isl.), Den. 48/F1
Alsace (dept.), Fr. 64/A5
Alsace (pol. reg.), Fr. 61/G6
Alsager, Eng, UK 41/F5
Alsask, Sk, Can. 175/K2
Alsasua, Sp. 50/B5
Alsdorf, Ger. 61/F2
Alsea (bay), Or, US 176/A1
Alsenz, Ger. 61/G4
Alsenz (riv.), Ger. 61/G4
Alsheim, Ger. 64/B3
Alsike, Swe. 45/A1
Alsip, Il, US 197/Q16
Alstahaug, Nor. 44/E2
Alstead, NH, US 191/K3
Alster (riv.), Ger. 59/H1
Alsting, Fr. 61/F5
Alston, Eng, UK 41/F2
Alstonville, Austl. 156/E1
Alsunga, Lat. 47/J3
Alt (riv.), Eng, UK 41/E4
Alta, Nor. 44/G1
Ålta, Swe. 45/B1
Alta (mt.), NZ 159/B4
Alta, Ia, US 185/G2
Alta Gracia, Arg. 224/C4
Alta Vista, Ks, US 183/F1
Altach, Aus. 67/F3
Altadena, Ca, US 196/F7
Altagracia, Nic. 206/E4
Altagracia de Orituco, Ven. 219/P8
Altai (mts.), Asia 83/H5

Altai (mts.), China 80/J5
Altamache (riv.), Ga, US 193/F5
Altamaha (riv.), Ga, US 195/H2
Altamira, Braz. 218/C3
Altamira, Chile 224/B3
Altamira, Mex. 206/B1
Altamira do Maranhão, Braz. 219/E4
Altamont, Il, US 192/C1
Altamont, Ks, US 183/G2
Altamont, Mb, Can. 186/E3
Altamont, Or, US 176/C2
Altamont, Tn, US 192/E3
Altamonte Springs, Fl, US 194/N6
Altamura, It. 54/E2
Altanteel, Mong. 90/C2
Altar (vol.), Ecu. 216/B5
Altar, Mex. 204/C2
Altar de los Sacrificios (ruin), Guat. 206/D2
Altar Wash (riv.), Az, US 179/G5
Altare, It. 68/B5
Altario, Ab, Can. 175/J2
Altavilla Irpina, It. 71/D6
Altavilla Vicentina, It. 69/E2
Altavista, Va, US 193/H2
Altay, China 111/E2
Altay, Mong. 90/D2
Altay, Mong. 90/B2
Altay Resp., Rus. 80/J4
Altayskiy Kray, Rus. 111/C1
Altdorf, Swi. 67/E4
Altdorf bei Nürnberg, Ger. 65/E4
Altea, Sp. 53/E3
Altedo, It. 69/E4
Altena, Ger. 59/E6
Altenahr, Ger. 61/G2
Altenau (riv.), Ger. 59/F5
Altenau, Ger. 59/H5
Altenbeken, Ger. 59/F5
Altenberg bei Linz, Aus. 65/H6
Altenburg, Ger. 48/G3
Altenburg, Mo, US 192/C2
Altenfelden, Aus. 65/G6
Altenglan, Ger. 61/G4
Altengottern, Ger. 59/H6
Altenkirchen, Ger. 61/G2
Altenmarkt an der Triesting, Aus. 57/N7
Altenmünster, Ger. 64/D6
Altenstadt, Ger. 67/G2
Altenstadt, Ger. 67/G1
Altenstadt, Ger. 64/B2
Altensteig, Ger. 64/B5
Altentreptow, Ger. 46/E5
Altepexi, Mex. 205/M8
Alter do Chão, Braz. 218/C3
Alter Rhein (riv.), Ger. 58/D5
Altes Land (phys. reg.), Ger. 59/G1
Altha, Fl, US 195/F2
Altheim, Aus. 65/G6
Altheim, Ger. 67/F1
Altheimer, Ar, US 183/J3
Althengstett, Ger. 64/B5
Althofen, Aus. 51/L3
Althorpe, Eng, UK 41/H4
Althütte, Ger. 64/C5
Alticane, Sk, Can. 175/L1
Altındere NP, Turk. 76/F4
Altınözü, Turk. 116/E1
Altıntaş, Turk. 114/B2
Altınyaka, Turk. 116/B1
Altınyayla, Turk. 114/B2
Altiplanicie del Payón (rocks), Arg. 226/C3
Altiplano (plat.), Bol.,Peru 209/C4
Altiplano (plat.), Peru 220/D4
Altkirch, Fr. 66/D2
Altlandsberg, Ger. 48/Q6
Altmark (phys. reg.), Ger. 48/F2
Altmühl (riv.), Ger. 51/J2
Altmünster, Aus. 65/G7
Altnaharra, Sc, UK 37/R7
Alto (peak), It. 67/G4
Alto, La, US 183/J4
Alto (peak), Braz. 222/D2
Alto, Tx, US 180/G2
Alto (mtn.), Tx, US 180/B2
Alto Araguaia, Braz. 222/B3
Alto Chicapa, Ang. 138/D5
Alto Cuale, Ang. 138/D4
Alto Cuilo, Ang. 138/D5
Alto de la Sierra, Arg. 224/D2
Alto de Tamar (peak), Col. 216/C3
Alto del Carmen, Chile 224/B4
Alto Garças, Braz. 222/B3
Alto Longá, Braz. 219/F4
Alto Lucero, Mex. 205/N7
Alto Molócuè, Moz. 141/H2
Alto Paraguai, Braz. 221/G4
Alto Paraguay (dept.), Par. 222/A4
Alto Paraná (dept.), Par. 225/F3
Alto Parnaíba, Braz. 219/E5
Alto Pass, Il, US 192/C2
Alto Pencoso, Arg. 226/D2
Alto Purús (riv.), Peru 220/D3
Alto Santo, Braz. 219/G4
Alto Seco, Bol. 224/C1
Alto Yuruá (riv.), Peru 220/C3
Altomünster, Ger. 64/E6
Alton, Eng, UK 43/F4
Alton, Il, US 185/J4
Alton, Ia, US 185/F2
Alton, Mo, US 183/J2
Alton, Ut, US 179/F2
Alton Downs, Austl. 155/H3
Altona, Mb, Can. 186/F3
Altona (nbrhd.), Austl. 156/F5
Altona, Ger. 59/G1
Altônia, Braz. 225/F2
Altoona, Ia, US 185/H3
Altoona, Pa, US 191/G4
Altopascio, It. 69/D6
Altos, Braz. 219/F4
Altos de Camapana NP, Pan. 216/B2
Altotonga, Mex. 205/M7
Altötting, Ger. 65/F6
Altrincham, Eng, UK 41/F5
Altrip, Ger. 64/B4
Altukhovo, Rus. 76/E1
Altun (mts.), China 83/H6
Altun Ha (ruin), Belz. 206/D2
Alturas, Ca, US 176/C3
Alturas, Fl, US 194/M8
Altus (A.F.B.), Ok, US 182/E3
Altus, Ok, US 182/E3
Altykarasu, Kaz. 77/K2
Altynivka, Ukr. 79/G2
Altynkul', Uzb. 77/L4
Altzayanca, Mex. 205/M7
Alucra, Turk. 114/D1
Aluk, Sudan 135/E3
Alūksne, Lat. 47/M3
Alum Fork (riv.), Ar, US 183/H3
Aluminé, Arg. 226/C3
Alunda, Swe. 46/H1
Alupka, Ukr. 76/E3
Ālūs, Iraq 114/E3
Alushta, Ukr. 79/H5
Aluta, D.R. Congo 139/F3
Alva, Fl, US 195/H4
Alva, Ok, US 183/E2
Alva, Sc, UK 39/C4
Alvalade, Port. 52/A4
Alvaneu-Bad, Swi. 67/F4
Älvängen, Swe. 46/E3
Alvarado, Col. 219/L8
Alvarado, Mex. 205/P8
Alvarado, Mn, US 186/F3
Alvarado, Tx, US 180/K7
Álvares Machado, Braz. 225/G2
Álvarez, Arg. 226/E2
Alvaro Obregón, Presa (dam), Mex. 204/C2
Alvdal, Nor. 44/D3
Älvdalen, Swe. 46/F1
Alvear, Arg. 225/E4
Alvechurch, Eng, UK 43/E2
Alverca, Port. 53/P10
Alveringem, Belg. 60/B1
Alvesta, Swe. 46/F3
Alviano (lake), It. 71/B2
Alvignano, It. 71/D5
Ålvik, Nor. 46/B1
Alvin, BC, Can. 174/C3
Alvin, Tx, US 181/M9
Alvin, Wi, US 187/K5
Alvinston, On, Can. 190/F3
Alvito, Port. 52/B3
Älvkarleby, Swe. 46/G1
Alvorada, Braz. 225/F4
Alvorada, Braz. 222/C2
Alvorada do Norte, Braz. 222/D2
Alvord, Tx, US 183/F4
Alvord (des.), Or, US 176/D2
Älvsborg (co.), Swe. 44/E4
Älvsbyn, Swe. 44/G2
Älvsjö, Swe. 45/B1
Alwen (riv.), Wal, UK 40/E5
Alxa Youqi, China 90/E4
Alxa Zuoqi, China 90/F4
Alyangula, Austl. 153/E3
Alyawarra Abor. Land, Austl. 155/G2
Alyth, Sc, UK 39/C3
Alytus, Lith. 47/L4
Alz (riv.), Aus. 56/A1
Alz (riv.), Ger. 48/G4
Alzada, Mt, US 184/B1
Alzano Lombardo, It. 68/C2
Alzenau in Unterfranken, Ger. 64/C2
Alzette (riv.), Lux. 61/F4
Alzey, Ger. 64/B3
Am Dam, Chad 134/D2
Am Djéména, Chad 134/C2
Am Timan, Chad 134/D3
Am Zoer, Chad 134/D2
Ama, PNG 103/K4
Amacayacú NP, Col. 220/D1
Amacuro (delta), Ven. 217/F2
Amacuro (riv.), Ven. 217/F2
Amacuzac (riv.), Mex. 205/K8
Amada Gaza, CAfr. 134/B4
Amadeus (lake), Austl. 145/C3
Āmādi, Bang. 109/G4
Amadi, Sudan 135/F4
Amadjuak (lake), Nun, Can. 171/J2
Amado, Az, US 179/G5
Amadora, Port. 53/P10
Amagá, Col. 219/K6
Amagansett, NY, US 199/F2
Amagansett Nat'l Wild. Ref., NY, US 199/F2
Amagasaki, Japan 95/H6
Amager (isl.), Den. 45/J7
Amagi, Japan 96/B4
Amagi-san (peak), Japan 97/F3
Amagon, Ar, US 183/J3
Amaguaña, Ecu. 216/B5
Amahai, Indo. 103/G4
Amajac (riv.), Mex. 205/N7
Amakusa (sea), Japan 91/K5
Åmål, Swe. 46/E2
Amala (riv.), Kenya 137/A2
Amalat (riv.), Rus. 90/G1
Amalfi, It. 71/D6
Amalfi, Col. 216/C3
Amalga, Ut, US 177/H3
Amalia, SAfr. 142/D2
Amaliás, Gre. 55/G4
Amalner, India 107/B1
Amaluza, Ecu. 220/B2
Amamapare, Indo. 103/J4
Amambaí, Braz. 225/F2
Amambaí (riv.), Braz. 222/B4
Amambay (dept.), Par. 222/A4
Amambay (dept.), Braz. 225/F2
Amambay, Serra (mts.), Braz.,Par. 225/F2
Amami (isls.), Japan 83/M7
Amami-O-Shima (isl.), Japan 97/K6
Amamula, D.R. Congo 139/F3
Amanã (lake), Braz. 217/E5
Amanab, PNG 103/K4
Amanbidji Abor. Land, Austl. 152/C4
Amance, Fr. 66/C2
Amanda Park, Wa, US 174/C4
Amandola, It. 71/C2
Amānganj, India 108/C3
Amāngarh, Pak. 110/A2
Amantea, It. 54/E3
Amanu (isl.), FrPol. 161/L6
Amanzimtoti, SAfr. 143/E3
Amapá, Braz. 218/D2
Amapá (state), Braz. 217/H4
Amarante, Braz. 219/F4
Amarante, Port. 52/A2
Amarante do Marahão, Braz. 219/E4
Amaranth, Mb, Can. 186/E2
Amarapura, Myan. 98/C4
Amareleja, Port. 52/B3
Amarete, Bol. 220/D4
Amargosa (range), Ca, US 178/D2
Amargosa (riv.), Ca,Nv, US 178/D2
Amargosa (des.), Nv, US 178/D2
Amargosa, Braz. 223/F2
Amarillo, Tx, US 182/D3
Amarkantak, India 108/C4
Amaro (peak), It. 71/D3
Amarpātan, India 108/C3
Amarume, Japan 94/A4
Amarwāra, India 108/B4
Amaseno (riv.), It. 71/C5
Amasra, Turk. 57/L5
Amasya, Turk. 76/E4
Amasya (prov.), Turk. 76/E4
Amata, Austl. 155/F3
Amatlán de Cañas, Mex. 204/D4
Amatrice, It. 71/C2
Amatsukominato, Japan 95/E3
Amawalk (res.), NY, US 199/E1
Amay, Belg. 61/E2
Amayuca, Mex. 205/L8
Amazar, Rus. 91/J1
Amazon (riv.), Braz. 209/C3
Amazon (Amazonas) (riv.), Braz. 209/C3
Amazonas, Cuba 207/G1
Amazonas (state), Braz. 216/C5
Amazonas (state), Ven. 217/E3
Amazonas (Amazon) (riv.), Braz. 209/C3
Amazônia (Tapajós), PN de, Braz. 221/G2
Amb, Pak. 110/B2
Āmba Gīyorgīs, Eth. 135/H2
Āmba Maryam, Eth. 136/A3
Ambāh, India 108/B2
Ambahikily, Madg. 143/G8
Ambajogai, India 107/C2
Ambāla, India 110/D4
Ambāla Sadar, India 110/D4
Ambalajanakomby, Madg. 143/H7
Ambalangoda, SrL. 107/D5
Ambalarondra, Madg. 143/J7
Ambalavao, Madg. 143/H8
Ambalema, Col. 219/L8
Ambam, Camr. 138/B2
Ambanja, Madg. 143/J6
Ambarnyy, Rus. 74/G2
Ambaro (bay), Madg. 143/J6
Āmbāsa, India 109/H4
Ambato, Ecu. 216/B5
Ambato Boeny, Madg. 143/H7
Ambatofinandrahana, Madg. 143/H8
Ambatolahy, Madg. 143/H8
Ambatolampy, Madg. 143/H7
Ambatomaidy, Madg. 143/H7
Ambatomanoina, Madg. 143/H7
Ambatondrazaka, Madg. 143/J7
Ambazac, Fr. 50/D4
Ámbelos (cape), Gre. 55/H3
Amber, Ok, US 183/F3
Amberg, Wi, US 187/L5
Amberg, Ger. 65/E4
Ambergate, Eng, UK 41/G5
Ambergris Cay (isl.), Belz. 206/E2
Ambérieu-en-Bugey, Fr. 66/B6
Amberley, NZ 159/C3
Amberloup, Belg. 61/E3
Ambidédi, Mali 132/C3
Ambikāpur, India 108/D4
Ambilobe, Madg. 143/J6
Ambinanindrano, Madg. 143/J8
Ambinanitelo, Madg. 143/J6
Ambinanynony, Madg. 143/J7
Ambla, Est. 47/L2
Amble, Eng, UK 39/E6
Ambler, Ak, US 201/G2
Ambler, Pa, US 198/C3
Ambleside, Eng, UK 41/F3
Amblève, Belg. 61/F3
Amblève (riv.), Belg. 48/C3
Ambo, Peru 220/B3
Amboasary, Madg. 143/H9
Amboavory, Madg. 143/J7
Ambodifototra, Madg. 143/J7
Ambodiharina, Madg. 143/J8
Ambodriana, Madg. 143/J7
Ambohidratrimo, Madg. 143/H7
Ambohijanahary, Madg. 143/J7
Ambohimahasoa, Madg. 143/H8
Ambohimahavelona, Madg. 143/G8
Ambohimandroso, Madg. 143/H7
Ambohimilanja, Madg. 143/H7
Ambohinihaonana, Madg. 143/H8
Ambohitsilaozana, Madg. 143/J7
Amboise, Fr. 63/F6
Ambolomoty, Madg. 143/H7
Ambon (isl.), Indo. 103/G4
Ambondro, Madg. 143/H9
Amboni Caves, Tanz. 137/B3
Amborompotsy, Madg. 143/H8
Amboseli NP, Kenya 137/B2
Ambositra, Madg. 143/H8
Ambouli (int'l arpt.), Djib. 136/B3
Ambovombe, Madg. 143/H9
Amboy, Ca, US 178/E3
Amboy, Il, US 185/K3
Amboy, Mn, US 185/G2
Amboy, Wa, US 174/C5
Ambrières-le-Grand, Fr. 63/E4
Ambriz, Ang. 138/C4
Ambrolauri, Geo. 77/G4
Ambrose, Ga, US 195/G2
Ambrym (isl.), Van. 160/F6
Ambuntentimur, Indo. 101/F4
Amchitka (isl.), Ak, US 81/T4
Amchitka Pass (str.), Ak, US 201/B6
'Amd, Yem. 136/C2
Amdasa, Indo. 152/C1
Amealco, Mex. 205/K6
Ameca, Mex. 204/D4
Amecameca de Juárez, Mex. 205/R10
Ameghino, Arg. 226/E2
Ameglia, It. 68/C5
Ameisberg (peak), Aus. 65/G5
Ameland (isl.), Neth. 58/C2
Amelia (isl.), Fl, US 195/H2
Amelia, It. 71/B2
Amelia City, Fl, US 195/H2
Amelia Court House, Va, US 193/J2
Ameliasburg, On, Can. 191/H2
Amelinghausen, Ger. 59/H2
Amenia, ND, US 186/F4
Amer (chan.), Neth. 58/B5
American (riv.), Ca, US 197/M9
American (lake), Wa, US 197/B3
American Bolder (peak), Wa, US 174/D3
American College, It. 71/G8
American Falls, Id, US 177/G2
American Falls (dam), Id, US 177/G2
American Falls (res.), Id, US 177/G2
American Fork, Ut, US 177/H3
American Highland (rocks), Ant. 228/F
American Samoa (terr.), US 161/T10
American, South Fork (riv.), Ca, US 176/C4
American, South Fork (riv.), Ca, US 179/J1
American, North Fork (riv.), Ca, US 176/C4
Americana, Braz. 225/H2
Americus, Ga, US 195/F1
Americus, Ks, US 183/F1
Americus, Mo, US 185/J4
Ameringkogel (peak), Aus. 51/L3
Amersfoort, Neth. 58/C4
Amersfoort, SAfr. 143/E2
Amersham, Eng, UK 43/F3
Amery, Wi, US 187/H5
Amery Ice Shelf, Ant. 228/E
Ames, Ks, US 184/F4
Ames, Ia, US 185/H2
Ames, Tx, US 181/N8
Amesbury, Eng, UK 43/E4
Amesbury, Ma, US 191/L3
Amet, India 104/B2
Amethi, India 108/C2
Āmeya, Eth. 135/H4
Amfíklia, Gre. 55/H3
Amfilokhía, Gre. 55/G3
Ámfissa, Gre. 55/H3
Amga (riv.), Rus. 81/N3
Amguema (riv.), Rus. 81/T3
Amguid, Alg. 129/G4
Amgun' (riv.), Rus. 81/P4
Amgun' (riv.), Rus. 91/M1
Amherst, NS, Can. 188/E3
Amherst (isl.), Qu, Can. 189/F2
Amherst, Ma, US 191/K3
Amherst, NY, US 190/V10
Amherst, Va, US 193/H2
Amherst, Wi, US 187/K5
Amherstburg, On, Can. 197/F7
Amherstdale-Robinette, WV, US 193/G2
Amhurst (mt.), Austl. 152/B4
Ami, Japan 95/E1
Amiata (peak), It. 54/B1
Amidon, ND, US 186/C4
Amiens, Fr. 60/B4
Amik (lake), Turk 116/E1
Amila (isl.), Ak, US 81/U4
Amilcar Cabral (int'l arpt.), CpV. 119/K10
Amillis, Fr. 36/M5
Amíndaion, Gre. 55/G2
Aminius, Namb. 140/C4
Aminu Kano (int'l arpt.), Nga. 133/H3
Amistad (dam), Tx, US 180/D3
Amistad (int'l. res), Mex.,US 180/D3
Amistad Nat'l Rec. Area, Tx, US 180/D3
Amite, La, US 194/C2
Amite (cr.), La, US 194/C2
Amity, Ar, US 183/H3
Amity (canal), Co, US 182/C1
Amity, Or, US 176/B1
Amityville, NY, US 199/M9
Amla, India 108/B5
Āmlāgora, India 109/F4
Amlash, Iran 115/G2
Amlekhganj, Nepal 109/E2
Åmli, Nor. 46/C2
Amlia (isl.), Ak, US 201/D6
Amlwch, Wal, UK 40/D5
'Ammān (gov.), Jor. 116/E4
Amman (riv.), Wal, UK 42/C3
'Ammān (Amman) (cap.), Jor. 112/C2
Amman ('Ammān) (cap.), Jor. 117/D5
Ammanford, Wal, UK 42/C3
Ammannsville, Tx, US 181/F3
Ammarfjället (peak), Swe. 44/E2
Ammassalik, Grld. 228/J
Ammer (riv.), Ger. 64/B5
Ammersee (lake), Ger. 51/J3
Ammon, Id, US 177/H2
Amnat Charoen, Thai. 106/D3
Amnéville, Fr. 61/F5
Amo (riv.), China 98/D4
Āmol, Iran 115/H2
Amora, Port. 53/P10
Amorbach, Ger. 64/C3
Amorgós, Gre. 55/J4
Amorgós (isl.), Gre. 73/K3
Amorinópolis, Braz. 222/C3
Amory, Ms, US 192/C4
Amos, Qu, Can. 171/J4
Åmose (riv.), Den. 45/H7
Åmot, Nor. 46/B2
Amotfors, Swe. 46/E2
Amourj, Mrta. 132/D2
Amozoc, Mex. 205/L7
Ampachi, Japan 95/L5
Ampana, Indo. 103/F4
Ampanavoana, Madg. 143/J6
Ampanefena, Madg. 143/J6
Ampangalana (canal), Madg. 143/J8
Ampanihy, Madg. 143/H9
Amparafaravola, Madg. 143/J7
Amparai, SrL. 107/D5
Amparo, Braz. 223/K7
Ampasimanjeva, Madg. 143/J8
Ampasimanolotra, Madg. 143/J7
Ampasindava (bay), Madg. 143/H6
Ampato (peak), Peru 220/D4
Ampefy, Madg. 143/H7
Amper (riv.), Ger. 65/E6
Amper, Nga. 133/H4
Ampfing, Ger. 65/F6
Ampflwang im Hausruckwald, Aus. 65/G6
Amphitrite Group (isls.), Asia 99/G5
Ampibako, Indo. 103/F4
Ampisikinana, Madg. 143/J6
Ampitatafika, Madg. 143/H7
Ampombiantambo, Madg. 143/J6
Amposta, Sp. 53/F2
Ampthill, Eng, UK 43/F2
Ampuis, Fr. 70/A2
Amqui, Qu, Can. 188/D1
'Amrān, Yem. 136/B2
Amrāpāra, India 109/F3
Amreli, India 113/K4
Amring, India 98/B3
'Amrīt (ruin), Syria 116/D2
Amritsar, India 110/C4
Amroha, India 108/B1
Amrūka, Pak. 110/B4
Amstel (riv.), Neth. 58/B4
Amstelveen, Neth. 58/B4
Amsterdam (isl.), Fr. 27/N7
Amsterdam (cap.), Neth. 58/B4
Amsterdam, SAfr. 143/E2
Amsterdam, Ga, US 195/F2
Amsterdam, NY, US 191/J3
Amsterdam (Schipol) (int'l arpt.), Neth. 58/B4
Amsterdam Rijnkan. (riv.), Neth. 58/C4
Amstetten, Aus. 51/L2
Āmtali, Bang. 109/H4
Amtkel, Geo. 77/G4
Amu Darya (riv.), Asia 83/F8
Amu Darya (riv.), Uzb. 77/L4
Amu Darya (riv.), Trkm. 80/G5
Amu-Dar'ya, Trkm. 80/G6
Amudālavalasa, India 107/D2
Amudar'ya (riv.), Trkm. 113/J1
Amudat, Ugan. 137/A1
Amukta Pass (str.), Ak, US 201/D5
Amuku (mts.), Guy. 217/G4
Amund Ringnes (isl.), Nun, Can. 171/S7
Amundsen (sea), Ant. 228/S
Amundsen (bay), Ant. 228/D
Amundsen (gulf), NW, Can. 170/D1
Amundsen-Scott, US, Ant. 228/A
Amunge (lake), Swe. 46/F1
Amur (riv.), Asia 83/M4
`Amūr (wadi), Sudan 127/G5
`Amur (wadi), Sudan 112/B5
Amur (Heilong) (riv.), China, Rus. 81/N4
Amur (Heilong) (riv.), China,Rus. 91/J1
Amuri, NZ 161/K6
Amurrio, Sp. 50/B5
Amursk, Rus. 91/M1
Amurskaya Oblast, Rus. 81/N4
Amvrosiyivka, Ukr. 79/K4
Amyūn, Leb. 116/D2
An Khe, Viet. 106/E3
An Nabaţīyah at Taḩtā, Leb. 117/C2
An Nabī Shīt, Leb. 117/E1
An Nafīḑah, Tun. 130/M6
An Nafūd (des.), SAr. 127/H2
An Nahūd, Sudan 135/F2
An Najaf, Iraq 115/F4
An Najaf (gov.), Iraq 115/E4
An Nāqūrah, Leb. 117/C2
An Nāşirīyah, Iraq 115/F4
An Nawfalīyah, Libya 126/C2
An Nazlat, Egypt 131/B6
An Nhon, Viet. 106/E3
An Nu'manīyah, Iraq 115/F3
An Phuoc, Viet. 106/E4
An Teallach (peak), Sc, UK 39/A1
An Uaimh, Ire. 38/D2
Ana María (gulf), Cuba 203/F3
Anaa (isl.), FrPol. 161/L6
Anabar (riv.), Rus. 81/L3
'Anabtā, WBnk. 117/C4
Anacapa (isl.), Ca, US 178/C4
Anacapri, It. 71/D6
Anachucuna (mtn.), Pan. 216/B2
Anaco, Ven. 217/E2
Anacoco, La, US 194/B2
Anaconda (range), Mt, US 175/H5
Anaconda-Deer Lodge County, Mt, US 175/H4
Anacortes, Wa, US 174/C3
Anadarko, Ok, US 183/E3
Anadia, Port. 52/A2
Anadyr', Rus. 81/T3
Anadyr' (riv.), Rus. 81/T3
Anadyr' (gulf), Rus. 81/U3
Anadyr' (range), Rus. 81/S3
Anáfi (isl.), Gre. 55/J4
Anafi (isl.), Gre. 73/K3
Anagni, It. 71/C4
'Ānah, Iraq 114/E3
Anaheim, Ca, US 196/G8
Anaheim Stadium, Ca, US 196/G8
Anahidrano, Madg. 143/H6
Anahim Lake, BC, Can. 174/B1
Anahim's Flat Ind. Res., BC, Can. 174/C1
Anáhuac, Mex. 180/D4
Anahuac, Mex. 204/D2
Anahuac, Tx, US 181/N9
Anahuac (lake), Tx, US 181/N9
Anahuac NWR, Tx, US 181/G3
Anai Mudi (peak), India 107/C4
Anajatuba, Braz. 219/E3
Anak, NKor. 93/C3
Anakāpalle, India 107/D2
Anaktuvuk Pass, Ak, US 201/H2
Analalava, Madg. 143/H6
Analamaitso (plat.), Madg. 143/J7
Analavory, Madg. 143/H7
Anambas (isls.), Indo. 102/C3
Anambra (state), Nga. 133/G5
Anamoose, ND, US 186/D4
Anamosa, Ia, US 185/J2
Anamur, Turk. 116/C1
Anamur (pt.), Turk. 116/C1
Anan, Japan 96/D4
Ananás, Braz. 218/D4
Anand, India 104/B3
Ananda Temple, Myan. 98/B4
Anandgarh, India 110/B5
Anandpur, India 110/D4
Anandpur, India 107/E1
Ananea, Bol. 220/D4
Ananea, Peru 220/D4
Anantapur, India 107/C3
Anantnag, India 110/C3
Anan'yevo, Kyr. 111/C3
Anan'yiv, Ukr. 78/E4
Anapa, Rus. 79/J5
Añapi (peak), Arg. 227/C6
Anápolis, Braz. 222/C3
Anapskaya, Rus. 79/J5
Anapu (riv.), Braz. 218/D3
Anār, Iran 115/H4
Anārak, Iran 115/H3
Anastasia (isl.), Fl, US 195/H3
Anastasiyevka, Rus. 79/K4
'Anātā, WBnk. 117/C5
Anathan (isl.), NMar. 160/D3
Anatolia (reg.), Turk. 76/D5
Añatuya, Arg. 224/D4
Anauá (riv.), Braz. 217/F4
Anbo, China 93/B3
Anbu, China 99/H4
Anbyŏn, NKor. 93/D3
Ancash (dept.), Peru 220/B3
Ancaster, On, Can. 190/T9
Ancenis, Fr. 63/D6
Anchangzhen, China 99/E2
Anchau, Nga. 133/H4
Anchieta, Braz. 223/E4
Anchor (bay), Mi, US 197/G6
Anchorage, Ak, US 201/J3
Anchorena, Arg. 226/D2
Anchor Point, Ak, US 201/H4
Anchorville, Mi, US 197/G6
Anchovy, Jam. 207/G2
Ancient Bristlecone Pine Forest, Ca, US 178/C2
Ancient City of Oc-Eo, Viet. 106/D4
Anclote (riv.), Fl, US 194/K7
Anclote, Fl, US 194/K7
Anclote Keys (isl.), Fl, US 194/K7
Ancoeur (riv.), Fr. 36/L6
Ancohuma (peak), Bol. 220/D4
Ancón, Peru 220/B3
Ancón de Sardinas (bay), Col. 216/B4
Ancona, It. 69/G6
Ancona (prov.), It. 69/G5
Ancoraimes, Bol. 220/D4
Ancre (riv.), Fr. 60/B3
Ancroft, Eng, UK 39/E5
Ancrum, Sc, UK 39/D5
Ancud, Chile 226/B4
Ancud (gulf), Chile 226/B4
Anda, China 91/K2
Andacollo, Arg. 226/C3
Andacollo, Chile 224/B4
Andado, Austl. 155/G3
Andagua, Peru 220/C4
Andahuaylas, Peru 220/C4
Andaingo Gara, Madg. 143/J7
Andāl, India 109/F4
Andalgalá, Arg. 224/C3
Åndalsnes, Nor. 44/C3
Andalusia (reg.), Sp. 72/B3
Andalusia, Al, US 195/E2
Andalusia, Il, US 185/J3
Andaman (sea), Asia 83/J8
Andaman (isls.), India 83/H8
Andaman and Nicobar (isls.), India 105/F5
Andaman, South (isl.), India 105/F5
Andamarca, Bol. 224/C1
Andamarca, Peru 220/C3
Andamooka, Austl. 155/H4
Andapa, Madg. 143/J6
Andara, Namb. 140/D3
Andaraí, Braz. 223/E2
Andau, Aus. 56/C2
Ande, China 106/D1
Andebu, Nor. 46/D2
Andechs, Ger. 67/H2
Andeer, Swi. 67/F4
Andelfingen, Swi. 67/E2
Andelle (riv.), Fr. 60/A5
Andelot-Blancheville, Fr. 66/B1
Andelsbach (riv.), Ger. 67/F2
Andelu, Fr. 36/H5
Andemaka, Madg. 143/H8
Andenne, Belg. 61/E3
Anderlues, Belg. 61/D3
Andermatt, Swi. 67/E4
Andernach, Ger. 61/G3
Anderson (riv.), NW, Can. 170/D2
Anderson, Ak, US 201/J3
Anderson, Ca, US 176/B3
Anderson, In, US 190/D4
Anderson, Mo, US 183/G2
Anderson, SC, US 193/F3
Anderson, Tx, US 181/G2
Anderson (isl.), Wa, US 197/B3
Anderson (inlet), Wa, US 197/B3
Anderson Ranch (res.), Id, US 177/F2
Anderson Ranch (dam), Id, US 176/F2
Andersonville, Ga, US 192/E4
Andersonville Nat'l Hist. Site, Ga, US 192/E4
Andes, Mt, US 186/B4
Andes (mts.), SAm. 209/C5
Andes, Col. 219/K7
Andevoranto, Madg. 143/J7
Andfjorden (chan.), Nor. 44/F1
Andhra Pradesh (state), India 104/C4
Andijk, Neth. 58/C3
Andijon, Uzb. 111/B3
Andikíthira (isl.), Gre. 73/J4
Andilamena, Madg. 143/J7
Andilanatoby, Madg. 143/J7
Andīmeshk, Iran 115/G3
Andíparos (isl.), Gre. 55/J4
Andira (riv.), Braz. 221/G1
Andira, Braz. 222/C4
Ándissa, Gre. 55/J3
Andoain, Sp. 50/B5
Andoany, Madg. 143/J6
Andoas, Peru 216/B5
Andohajango, Madg. 143/J6
Andong, China 92/L9
Andong, SKor. 96/A2
Andorf, Aus. 65/G6
Andorno Micca, It. 68/B2
Andorra, Sp. 53/E2
Andorra (ctry.) 53/F1
Andorra la Vella (cap.), And. 53/F1
Andover, Eng, UK 43/E4
Andover, Ks, US 183/F2
Andover, Me, US 191/L2
Andover, Mn, US 187/P6
Andover, NJ, US 198/D2
Andover, Oh, US 190/F4
Andøy, Nor. 44/F1
Andøya (isl.), Nor. 44/E1
Andradas, Braz. 223/K7
Andradina, Braz. 225/G2
Andrafainkona, Madg. 143/J6
Andraitx, Sp. 53/G3
Andramasina, Madg. 143/H7
Andranolalina, Madg. 143/H8
Andranolava, Madg. 143/H8
Andranomavo (riv.), Madg. 143/H7
Andranopasy, Madg. 143/G8
Andranovondrona, Madg. 143/J6
Andranovory, Madg. 143/H8
André Félix, PN, CAfr. 134/D3
Andreanof (isls.), Ak, US 201/C5
Andrelândia, Braz. 223/M6
Andrespol, Pol. 49/K3
Andrésy, Fr. 36/J5
Andrew Johnson Nat'l Hist. Site, Tn, US 193/F2
Andrews, NC, US 192/F3
Andrews, Or, US 176/D2
Andrews, Tx, US 180/C1
Andrews (A.F.B.), Md, US 198/B6
Andrews, SC, US 193/H4
Andreyevka, Rus. 77/K1
Andrezel, Fr. 36/L6
Andria, It. 54/E2
Andriamena, Madg. 143/H7
Andriandampy, Madg. 143/H8
Andriba, Madg. 143/H7
Andringitra (mts.), Madg. 143/H8
Andrítsaina, Gre. 55/G4
Andriyivka, Ukr. 79/J4
Androka, Madg. 143/H9
Androntany (cape), Madg. 143/J6
Andros (isl.), Bahm. 163/K7
Ándros, Gre. 55/J4
Ándros (isl.), Gre. 73/K3
Androscoggin (riv.), Me, US 188/B3
Androscoggin (riv.), NH, US 191/L2
Andrushivka, Ukr. 78/E2
Andújar, Sp. 52/C3
Āndulbāria, Bang. 109/G4
Andulo, Ang. 140/C1
Andytown, Fl, US 194/P10
Aneby, Swe. 46/F3
Anecón Grande (peak), Arg. 226/C4
Anefis I-n-Darane, Mali 133/F2
Anegada (isl.), UK 203/J4
Anegada (bay), Arg. 226/E4
Anegada Passage (chan), NAm. 203/J4
Aného, Togo 133/F5
Aneityum (isl.), Van. 160/F7
Añelo, Arg. 226/C3
Aneroid, Sk, Can. 175/L3
Anet, Fr. 63/G3
Aneta, ND, US 186/F4
Aneth, Ut, US 179/H2
Aneto, Pico de (peak), Sp. 53/F1
Aney, Niger 126/B5
Anfu, China 105/K2
Ang Mo Kio (nbrhd.), Sing. 101/J6
Ang Nam Ngum (lake), Laos 105/H4
Ang Thong, Thai. 106/C3
Angads (Oujda) (int'l arpt.), Mor. 130/D2
Angamma, Falaise d' (cliff), Chad 134/C1
Angamos (pt.), Chile 224/B2
Angara (riv.), Rus. 83/J4
Angarn, Swe. 45/B1
Angarsk, Rus. 90/E1
Angas Downs, Austl. 155/G3
Angaston, Austl. 155/H5
Angatuba, Braz. 225/G2
Angel (riv.), Ger. 59/E5
Ángel (falls), Ven. 217/F3
Ángel de la Guarda (isl.), Mex. 204/B2
Angela, Mt, US 175/L4
Angèle, Montagne d' (peak), Fr. 70/B4
Angeles, Phil. 100/C2
Angeles National Forest, Ca, US 196/B1
Angeles Nat'l Forest, Ca, US 196/F7
Ängelholm, Swe. 46/E3
Angelholm (int'l arpt.), Swe. 46/E3
Ängelholm, Den. 45/J6
Angelica, Wi, US 190/B2
Angelim, Braz. 219/G5
Angelina (riv.), Tx, US 181/G2
Angeln (reg.), Ger. 48/E1
Angelus (lake), Mi, US 197/F6
Angelus Oaks (Camp Angelus), Ca, US 196/D2
Angera, It. 68/B2
Ångermanalven (riv.), Swe. 44/E2
Angermünde, Ger. 49/H2
Angers, Fr. 63/E6
Angerville, Fr. 63/H4
Anghiari, It. 69/F6
Angical do Piauí, Braz. 219/F4
Angicos, Braz. 219/G4
Angie, La, US 194/D2
Angier, NC, US 193/H3
Angk Tasaom, Camb. 106/D4
Angkor (ruin), Camb. 106/C3
Anglais (bay), Qu, Can. 188/C1
Angle Inlet, Mn, US 187/G3
Angleine (riv.), Fr. 63/E4
Anglem (mt.), NZ 159/A4
Anglès, Sp. 53/G2
Anglesea, Austl. 157/B4
Anglesey (isl.), Wal, UK 40/D5
Anglet, Fr. 50/C5
Angleton, Tx, US 180/G3
Anglin (riv.), Fr. 50/D3
Ango, D.R. Congo 139/F1
Angoche, Moz. 141/H3
Angohrān, Iran 113/G3
Angol, Chile 226/B3
Angola (ctry.) 119/D6
Angola, In, US 190/D4
Angola, La, US 194/C2
Angola, NY, US 191/G3
Angoon, Ak, US 201/M4
Angostura (res.), Mex. 202/C4
Angostura (res.), SD, US 184/C2
Angostura (dam), SD, US 184/C2
Angostura, Mex. 204/C3
Angoulême, Fr. 50/D4
Angra do Heroísmo, Azor., Port. 53/S12
Angra dos Reis, Braz. 223/M7
Angren, Uzb. 111/B3
Angri, It. 71/D6
Ängsö NP, Swe. 45/B1
Ängsön (isl.), Swe. 45/B1
Angu, D.R. Congo 139/F2
Anguilla, Ms, US 192/B4
Anguilla (isl.), UK 203/N8
Anguillara Sabazia, It. 71/B3
Anguillara Veneta, It. 69/E3
Anguille (mts.), Nf, Can. 189/H2
Angul, India 107/E1
Angumu, D.R. Congo 139/F3
Angurugu, Austl. 153/E3
Angus (co.), Sc, UK 39/C3
Angus, Tx, US 181/F1
Angusville, Mb, Can. 186/D2
Angutikada Peak (mt.), Ak, US 201/G2
Angwa (riv.), Zim. 141/F3
Angwin, Ca, US 176/B4
Anhanduí (riv.), Braz. 222/B4
Anhée, Belg. 61/D3
Anholt (isl.), Den. 46/D3
Anhua, China 99/F2
Anhui (prov.), China 90/H5
Ani, Japan 94/B4
Aniak, Ak, US 201/G3
Aniakchak, Ak, US 201/G4
Aniakchak Nat'l Mon. and Preserve, Ak, US 201/G4
Anichab, Namb. 140/B4
Aniche, Fr. 60/C3
Anicuns, Braz. 222/C3
Aniene (riv.), It. 71/B4
Anikhovka, Rus. 77/M2
Anille (riv.), Fr. 63/F5
Animas, NM, US 179/H5
Animas (riv.), Co,NM, US 179/J2
Animas (mts.), NM, US 179/H5
Anin, Myan. 106/B3
Ānīn, WBnk. 117/C3
Anina, Rom. 56/E3
Anita, Ia, US 185/G3
Aniva (bay), Rus. 94/C1
Aniva (sea), Rus. 91/N2
Anivorano, Madg. 143/J7
Anizy-le-Château, Fr. 60/C4
Anjalankoski, Fin. 47/M1
Anjār, India 113/K4
'Anjar, Leb. 117/D1
'Anjarah, Jor. 117/D4
Anjō, Japan 95/M6
Anjou (reg.), Fr. 72/C1
Anjou, Qu, Can. 189/N6
Anjouan (isl.), Com. 143/H6
Anjozorobe, Madg. 143/H7
Anju, NKor. 93/C3
Anju, China 98/E2
Anjum, Neth. 58/D2
Ankang, China 90/F5
Ankara (prov.), Turk. 114/C1
Ankara (cap.), Turk. 114/C2
Ankaramena, Madg. 143/H8
Ankaratra (mass.), Madg. 143/H7
Ankarsrum, Swe. 46/G3
Ankasakasa, Madg. 143/H7
Ankavandra, Madg. 143/H7
Ankazoabo, Madg. 143/H8
Ankazobe, Madg. 143/H7
Ankazomborona, Madg. 143/H7
Ankazomiriotra, Madg. 143/H7
Ankeny, Ia, US 185/H3
Ankeny NWR, Or, US 176/B1
Ankerika, Madg. 143/H6
Ankiliabo, Madg. 143/G8
Ankililioka, Madg. 143/G8
Ankilizato, Madg. 143/H8
Anklam, Ger. 46/E5
Ānkober, Eh. 136/A3
Ankoro, D.R. Congo 139/F4
Ankpa, Nga. 133/G5
Ankum, Ger. 59/E3
Anliu, China 99/G4
Anloga, Gha. 133/F5
Anlong, China 105/J2
Anlong Bouyeizu Miaozu Zizhixian, China 98/E3
Anlong Veng, Camb. 106/D3
Anloo, Neth. 58/D2
Anlu, China 92/C5
Anma (isl.), SKor. 93/D5
Ann Arbor, Mi, US 190/E3
Anna, Rus. 79/L2
Anna, Il, US 192/C2
Anna, Tx, US 183/F4
Anna (lake), Va, US 193/J1
Anna Bay, Austl. 156/E2
Anna Creek, Austl. 155/H4
Anna Maria, Fl, US 195/G4
Anna Pavlowna, Neth. 58/B3
Anna Pink (bay), Chile 226/B5
Anna Plains, Austl. 152/A4
Anna Regina, Guy. 217/G3
Annaba, Alg. 130/K6
Annaba (wilaya), Alg. 130/K6
Annabella, Ut, US 179/F1
Annaberg-Buchholz, Ger. 65/G1
Annaclone, NI, UK 40/B3
Annai, Guy. 217/G4
Annaka, Japan 95/B1
Annalong, NI, UK 40/C3
Annan, Sc, UK 41/E2
Annan (riv.), Sc, UK 39/C6
Annandale, Mn, US 185/G1
Annandale, NJ, US 198/D2
Annandale, Va, US 198/A6
Annapolis (riv.), NS, Can. 188/E3
Annapolis, Ca, US 176/B4
Annapolis (cap.), Md, US 198/B6
Annapolis, Mo, US 183/J2
Annapolis Royal, NS, Can. 188/E3
Annapurna (peak), Nepal 108/D1
Annbank Station, Sc, UK 39/B6
Anne (mt.), Austl. 156/C4
Anne Arundel (co.), Md, US 198/B6
Annean (lake), Austl. 145/A3
Annecy (lake), Fr. 66/C6
Annecy, Fr. 66/C6
Annecy (Meythet) (arpt.), Fr. 66/C6
Annecy-le-Vieux, Fr. 66/C6
Annemasse, Fr. 66/C5
Anner (riv.), Ire. 38/C5
Annet-sur-Marne, Fr. 36/L5
Anneta, Tx, US 180/K7
Annette, Ak, US 201/M4
Anneyron, Fr. 70/A2
Annezin, Fr. 60/B2
Annieopsquatch (mts.), Nf, Can. 189/J1
Anning (riv.), China 98/D3
Anning, China 98/D3
Anniston, Al, US 192/E4
Anniston Army Depot, Al, US 192/D4
Annobón (isl.), EqG. 119/C5
Annonay, Fr. 70/A2
Annot, Fr. 70/C5
Annunziata, It. 71/D5
Annville, Pa, US 198/B3
Annweiler, Ger. 61/G5
Anō, Japan 95/K6
Año Nuevo (pt.), Ca, US 178/A2
Áno Viánnos, Gre. 55/J5
Anoia (riv.), Sp. 53/K7
Anoka, Mn, US 187/P6
Anoka (co.), Mn, US 187/P6
Anola, Mb, Can. 186/F3
Anolaima, Col. 219/L8
Anori, Braz. 221/F1
Anosibe An' Ala, Madg. 143/J7
Ânou-Zeggarene (riv.), Niger 133/G2
Anould, Fr. 66/C1
Anóyia, Gre. 55/J5
Anping, China 93/B2
Anping, China 92/C3
Anping, China 92/H7
Anpu, China 106/E1
Anqing, China 99/H2
Anqiu, China 92/D3
Anren, China 105/K2
Anrhomer (peak), Mor. 128/D3
Anröchte, Ger. 59/F5
Ans, Belg. 61/E2
Ansai, China 92/B3
Ansan, SKor. 93/F7
Anşār, Leb. 117/C2
Ansbach, Ger. 64/D4
Anse Rouge, Haiti 207/H2
Anse-à-Galets, Haiti 207/H2
Anse-d'Hainault, Haiti 207/H2
Anserma, Col. 219/K7
Ansfelden, Aus. 65/H6
Anshan, China 93/B2
Anshun, China 98/E3
Anshunchang, China 98/D2
Ansina, Uru. 225/F4
Ansley, Ne, US 184/E3
Anson (bay), Austl. 152/C3
Anson, Tx, US 180/E1
Ansŏng, SKor. 93/D4
Ansongo, Mali 133/F3
Ansonia, Ct, US 191/K4
Ansted, WV, US 193/G1
Anstruther, Sc, UK 39/D4
Ansus, Indo. 103/J4
Ant (isl.), Micr. 160/E4
Ant (riv.), Eng, UK 43/H1
Anta, Peru 220/C4
Antabamba, Peru 220/C4
Antakya, Turk. 116/E1
Antalaha, Madg. 143/J6
Antalya (gulf), Turk. 116/B1
Antalya (int'l arpt.), Turk. 116/B1
Antalya, Turk. 116/B1
Antalya (prov.), Turk. 114/B2
Antanambao Manampotsy, Madg. 143/J7
Antanambe, Madg. 143/J7
Antananarivo (cap.), Madg. 143/H7
Antananarivo (prov.), Madg. 143/H7
Antanifotsy, Madg. 143/H7
Antanimenabaka, Madg. 143/J7
Antanimieva, Madg. 143/G8
Antanimora, Madg. 143/H9
Antar (peak), Alg. 129/E3
Antarctic (pen.), Ant. 228/W
Antarctic Circle 228/Z
Antarctica (cont.) 228/*
Antaritarika, Madg. 143/H9
Antas, Rio das (riv.), Braz. 225/G4
Antella, It. 69/E6
Antelope, Mt, US 186/B3
Antelope (peak), Mt, US 175/K5
Antelope, Or, US 176/C1
Antelope, Tx, US 183/E4
Antelope (isl.), Ut, US 177/G3
Antelope Center, Ca, US 196/C1
Antelope Mine, Zim. 141/F4
Antenor Navarro, Braz. 219/G4

Asahi – Babat
265

Asahi, Japan 97/G3
Asahi, Japan 95/M5
Asahi, Japan 95/L5
Asahi, Japan 95/F1
Asahi-dake (peak), Japan 94/C2
Asahikawa, Japan 94/C2
Asai, Japan 95/K5
Asaka, Japan 95/D2
Asake (riv.), Japan 95/K5
'Asal (depr.), Djib. 136/B3
Āsalē, Eth. 136/B2
'Asalūyeh, Iran 115/H5
Asama-yama (peak), Japan 97/F2
Asamankese, Gha. 133/E5
Asan (bay), SKor. 93/D4
Asankrangwa, Gha. 133/E5
Asansol, India 109/F4
Asashi-dake (peak), Japan 97/F1
Asashina, Japan 95/A1
Asau, Sam. 161/R9
Asawanwah (well), Libya 126/C4
Āsayita, Eth. 136/B3
Asbach, Ger. 61/G2
Asbach-Bäumenheim, Ger. 64/D5
Āsbe Teferī, Eth. 136/B3
Asbest, Rus. 75/P4
Asbestos, Qu, Can. 191/L2
Asbestos. (mts.), SAfr. 142/C3
Asbury, Ia, US 185/J2
Asbury Park, NJ, US 199/D3
Ascención (bay), Mex. 202/D4
Ascensión, Arg. 226/E2
Ascención, Bol. 221/F4
Ascensión, Mex. 205/J5
Ascension, NAnt. 216/D1
Ascensione, Monte dell (peak), It. 71/C2
Aschach (riv.), Aus. 65/G6
Aschach an der Donau, Aus. 65/H6
Aschaffenburg, Ger. 64/C3
Aschau am Inn, Ger. 65/F6
Ascheberg, Ger. 59/E5
Aschendorf, Ger. 59/E2
Aschersleben, Ger. 48/F3
Ascog, Sc, UK 39/A5
Ascoli Piceno (prov.), It. 71/C1
Ascoli Piceno, It. 71/C2
Ascoli Satriano, It. 54/D2
Ascona, Swi. 67/E5
Ascope, Peru 220/B2
Ascot, Eng, UK 36/B2
Āsebot, Eth. 136/B3
Åseda, Swe. 46/F3
Aseki, PNG 153/G1
Āsela, Eth. 136/A4
Åsele, Swe. 44/F2
Āsendabo, Eth. 135/H4
Asendorf, Ger. 59/G2
Asendorf, Ger. 59/F3
Asenovgrad, Bul. 57/G4
Åseral, Nor. 46/B2
Aserei (peak), It. 68/C4
Asfeld, Fr. 61/D5
Ash, Eng, UK 36/A3
Ash, Eng, UK 36/D3
Ash Flat, Ar, US 183/J2
Ash Fork, Az, US 179/F3
Ash Shabakah, Iraq 114/E4
Ash Shāghūr, Jor. 117/D5
Ash Shamal (gov.), Leb. 116/E2
Ash Shamālīyah (pol. reg.), Sudan 127/E4
Ash Shāmīyah, Iraq 115/F4
Ash Shanāwīyah, Egypt 131/C6
Ash Shāriqah, UAE 113/G3
Ash Sharqāt, Iraq 115/E3
Ash Sharqīyah (prov.), Sudan 127/G5
Ash Shaṭrah, Iraq 115/F4
Ash Shawal, Sudan 135/G2
Ash Shawāshinah, Egypt 131/B6
Ash Shawbak, Jor. 116/D4
Ash Shaykh Sa'd, Syria 117/E3
Ash Shiḥr, Yem. 136/D2
Ash Shīn, Egypt 131/B2
Ash Shuhadā', Egypt 131/B3
Ash Shumlūl, SAr. 112/E3
Ash Shuqayq, SAr. 112/D5
Ash Shurayf, SAr. 112/C3
Asha, Nga. 133/F5
Ashampstead, Eng, UK 43/E4
Ashanti (pol. reg.), Gha. 133/E5
Ashanti (uplands), Gha. 132/E5
Asharoken, NY, US 199/M8
Ashbourne, Ire. 40/B4
Ashbourne, Eng, UK 41/G5
Ashburn, Ga, US 195/G2
Ashburton, NZ 159/B3
Ashburton, Eng, UK 42/C5
Ashburton (riv.), Austl. 145/A3
Ashburton Downs, Austl. 154/C2
Ashby, Mn, US 186/G4
Ashby (canal), Eng, UK 43/E1
Ashby-de-la-Zouch, Eng, UK 43/E1
Ashcroft, BC, Can. 174/D2
Ashdod, Isr. 117/B5
Ashdot Ya'aqov, Isr. 117/D3
Ashdown, Ar, US 183/G4
Asheboro, NC, US 193/H3
Asher, Ok, US 183/F3
Ashern, Mb, Can. 186/E2
Asherton, Tx, US 180/E3
Asheville, NC, US 193/F3
Ashfield, Austl. 157/E1
Ashford, Austl. 156/D1
Ashford, Eng, UK 36/B2
Ashford, Eng, UK 43/G4
Ashford, Ire. 40/B5
Ashford, Al, US 195/F2
Ashfordby, Eng, UK 43/F1
Ashgabat (cap.), Trkm. 113/G1
Ashgrove, On, Can. 190/T8
Ashhurst, NZ 159/C3
Ashibetsu, Japan 94/C2
Ashigawa, Japan 95/B2
Ashikaga, Japan 95/C1
Ashington, Eng, UK 41/G1
Ashino (lake), Japan 95/C3
Ashiwada, Japan 95/B3
Ashiya, Japan 95/H6
Ashiyasu, Japan 95/A2
Ashizuri-Misaki (cape), Japan 96/C4
Ashkelon NP, Isr. 117/B5
Ashkhabad (int'l arpt.), Trkm. 113/G1
Ashkīdah, Libya 126/B3
Ashland, Al, US 192/E4
Ashland, Ks, US 182/E2
Ashland, Ky, US 193/F1
Ashland, La, US 183/H4
Ashland, Mo, US 183/H1
Ashland, Ms, US 192/C3
Ashland, Mt, US 175/L5
Ashland, NY, US 191/J3
Ashland, Oh, US 190/E4
Ashland, Or, US 176/B2
Ashland, Pa, US 198/B2
Ashland, Tx, US 181/G1
Ashland, Wi, US 187/J4
Ashland City, Tn, US 192/D2
Ashley, ND, US 186/E4
Ashley, Austl. 156/D1
Ashley, Il, US 192/C1
Ashley, Pa, US 198/C1
Ashley Green, Eng, UK 36/B1
Ashmore, Il, US 190/B5
Ashmore and Cartier Islands (terr.), Austl. 145/B2
Ashmore (reef), Austl. 152/A3
Ashmūn, Egypt 131/B4
Ashnola Ind. Res., BC, Can. 174/D3
Ashoknagar, India 108/A3
Ashoro, Japan 94/C2
Ashqelon, Isr. 117/B5
Ashstead, Eng, UK 36/C3
Ashta, India 104/C3
Ashtabula, Oh, US 190/F4
Ashtarak, Arm. 77/H4
Ashti, India 107/C1
Āshtīān, Iran 115/G3
Ashton, SAfr. 142/M10
Ashton, Fl, US 194/N7
Ashton, Id, US 177/H1
Ashton, Il, US 185/K3
Ashton, SD, US 184/E1
Ashton-In-Makerfield, Eng, UK 41/F5
Ashton-under-Lyne, Eng, UK 41/F5
Ashuapmushuan (riv.), Qu, Can. 188/A1
Ashville, Oh, US 190/E5
Ashville, Al, US 192/D4
Ashwabay (mt.), Wi, US 187/J4
Ashwaubenon, Wi, US 190/B2
Ashwell, Eng, UK 43/F2
Asia (cont.) 83/*
Asia, Peru 220/B4
Asiago, It. 67/H6
Asidonhoppo, Sur. 218/C2
Asikkala, Fin. 47/L1
Asikkalanselkä (lake), Fin. 45/F3
Asilah, Mor. 130/A2
Asillo, Peru 220/D4
Asina, It. 71/C4
Asinara (gulf), It. 54/A2
Asinara (isl.), It. 54/A2
Asino, Rus. 80/J4
Asipovichy, Bela. 76/D1
`Asīr (mts.), SAr. 112/D5
Asis (cape), Sudan 127/H5
Aska, India 107/E2
Aşkale, Turk. 114/E2
Askam in Furness, Eng, UK 41/E3
Askaniya-Nova, Ukr. 79/G4
Askeaton, Ire. 38/B4
Asker, Nor. 46/D2
Askern, Eng, UK 41/G4
Askersund, Swe. 46/F2
Askew, Ms, US 192/B3
Askham, SAfr. 142/C2
Askim, Nor. 46/D2
Askim, Swe. 46/D3
Áskion (peak), Gre. 55/G2
Askiz, Rus. 111/F1
Askja (crater), Ice. 44/P6
Askö (isl.), Swe. 45/A2
Askola, Fin. 45/F4
Askot, India 108/C1
Askov, Den. 46/C4
Askov, Mn, US 187/H4
Askøy, Nor. 46/A1
Askvoll, Nor. 44/C3
Āsmār, Afg. 110/A2
Asmara (cap.), Erit. 136/A2
Asnæs, Den. 45/H7
Asnen (lake), Swe. 46/F3
Asnières-sur-Oise, Fr. 36/K4
Asnières-sur-Seine, Fr. 36/J5
Aso (riv.), It. 71/C1
Asō, Japan 95/E2
Aso NP, Japan 96/B4
Aso-san (peak), Japan 96/B4
Asola, It. 68/D3
Asolo, It. 69/E2
Āsosa, Eth. 135/G3
Asoteriba (peak), Sudan 127/H4
Asotin, Wa, US 174/F4
Aspach, Aus. 65/G6
Asparn, Aus. 57/N7
Aspatria, Eng, UK 41/E2
Aspe, Sp. 53/E3
Aspen (lake), Or, US 176/B2
Aspen Grove, BC, Can. 174/D3
Aspen Hill, Md, US 198/A5
Aspendos (ruin), Turk. 116/B1
Asperg, Ger. 64/C5
Aspermont, Tx, US 182/D4
Aspers, Pa, US 198/A4
Aspetuck (riv.), Ct, US 199/E1
Aspiring (mt.), NZ 159/B4
Aspres-sur-Buëch, Fr. 70/B3
Aspy (bay), NS, Can. 189/G2
Asquith, Sk, Can. 175/L1
Assa, Mor. 128/C3
Assa Aguiene (peak), Alg. 129/G5
Assab, Erit. 136/B2
Assam (state), India 105/F2
Assaouas, Niger 133/G2
Assaré, Braz. 219/G4
Assaria, Ks, US 183/F1
Assateague Island Nat'l Seashore, Md, US 193/K1
Asse, Belg. 61/D2
Assegairivier (riv.), SAfr. 141/F5
Assemini, It. 54/A3
Assen, Neth. 58/D3
Assenede, Belg. 60/C1
Assens, Den. 46/C4
Assens, Den. 46/D3
Assentoft, Den. 46/D3
Assesse, Belg. 61/E3
Assiniboia, Sk, Can. 175/M3
Assiniboine (riv.), Sk, Can. 186/D2
Assiniboine (riv.), Mb, Can. 170/F4
Assiniboine (mt.), Ab, Can. 174/G2
Assiniboine Ind. Res., Sk, Can. 186/C2
Assis, Braz. 225/G2
Assis Chateaubriand, Braz. 225/F3
Assisi, It. 71/B1
Assling, Ger. 65/F6
Asso, It. 68/C2
Assok-Ngoum, Gabon 138/B2
Assomada, CpV. 119/K10
Assou (riv.), Fr. 53/G1
Assumption, Il, US 185/K4
Astagram, Bang. 109/H3
Astakós, Gre. 55/G3
Astana (cap.), Kaz. 111/B1
Astara, Iran 115/G2
Astara, Azer. 77/J5
Astatula, Fl, US 194/M6
Asten, Aus. 65/H6
Asten, Neth. 58/C6
Asti (prov.), It. 68/B3
Astico (riv.), It. 69/E1
Astillero, Peru 220/D4
Astipálaia (isl.), Gre. 73/K3
Astipálaia, Gre. 73/K3
Astle, NB, Can. 188/D2
Aston, Eng, UK 43/E2
Aston on Clun, Eng, UK 42/D2
Astorga, Braz. 225/G2
Astoria (nbrhd.), NY, US 199/K8
Astoria, Il, US 185/J3
Astoria, Or, US 174/C4
Åstorp, Swe. 46/E3
Astra, Arg. 226/D5
Astrakhan', Rus. 77/J3
Astrakhanskaya Oblast, Rus. 77/H3
Astrodome, Tx, US 181/M9
Ástros, Gre. 55/H4
Astroworld, Tx, US 181/M9
Astudillo, Sp. 52/C1
Asturias (dist.), Sp. 52/B1
Astwood Bank, Eng, UK 43/E2
Asuka, Japan 95/J7
Asuke, Japan 95/M5
Asuncion (isl.), NMar. 160/D3
Asunción, Bol. 220/E3
Asunción (cap.), Par. 224/E3
Asunción (Silvio Pettirossi) (int'l arpt.), Par. 224/E3
Asunción Ixtaltepec, Mex. 202/B4
Asunden (lake), Swe. 46/F3
Asunta, Bol. 221/E5
Aswa (riv.), Ugan. 135/G5
Aswa, Ugan. 135/G5
Aswān (gov.), Egypt 127/G4
Aswān, Egypt 127/G3
Aswan High (dam), Egypt 127/G4
Asyūṭ (gov.), Egypt 127/F3
Asyūṭ, Egypt 127/F3
Asyūṭī (wadi), Egypt 127/F3
Aszód, Hun. 57/R9
At Ta'mīn (gov.), Iraq 115/E3
At Tabbīn, Egypt 131/C5
Aṭ Ṭafīlah (gov.), Jor. 116/D4
Aṭ Ṭafīlah, Jor. 116/D4
Aṭ Ṭā'if, SAr. 112/D4
At Tall, Syria 117/E1
At Tall al Kabīr, Egypt 131/C3
Aṭ Ṭallāb, Libya 126/D3
At Tamīmī, Libya 126/D1
Aṭ Ṭawd, Egypt 131/B3
Aṭ Ṭayyibah, Leb. 117/D2
Aṭ Ṭayyibah, Jor. 117/D3
Aṭ Ṭīnah, Egypt 131/D2
Aṭ Ṭunayb, Jor. 117/D5
Aṭ Ṭūr, Egypt 127/G2
Aṭ Ṭūr, WBnk. 117/C5
At Turbah, Yem. 136/C2
Aṭ Ṭuwayshah, Sudan 135/E2
Aṭ Ṭuwayyah, SAr. 114/E5
Atabapo (riv.), Ven. 217/E4
Atacama (des.), Chile 209/B4
Atacama (pol. reg.), Chile 224/B4
Atacames, Ecu. 216/B4
Atafu (isl.), Tok. 161/H5
Atakpamé, Togo 133/F5
Atalaia do Norte, Braz. 220/D2
Atalándi, Gre. 55/H3
Atalaya, Peru 220/C3
Atamanovka, Kaz. 90/G1
Atambohobe, Madg. 143/H8
Atambua, Indo. 152/B2
Atami, Japan 97/F3
Atap, Indo. 103/E3
Atapupu, Indo. 152/B2
'Atāq, Yem. 136/C2
Atarfe, Sp. 52/D4
Atarra, India 108/C3
Atas Bogd (peak), Mong. 90/D3
Atascadero, Ca, US 178/B3
Atascosa (riv.), Tx, US 181/E3
Atascosa, Tx, US 180/E3
Atasu, Kaz. 111/B2
Atatürk (dam), Turk. 114/D2
Ataturk (int'l arpt.), Turk. 115/M7
Atatürk (res.), Turk 114/D2
Atauro (isl.), ETim. 152/B2
Ātaya, Eth. 136/A3
Atbara (riv.), Eth. 135/H2
Atbara, Sudan 135/G1
Atbara (riv.), Sudan 119/F3
'Atbarah, Nahr (riv.), Sudan 112/B5
Atbasar, Kaz. 111/A1
Atchafalaya (riv.), La, US 181/J2
Atchafalaya (bay), La, US 181/J3
Atchison, Ks, US 185/G4
Atco, NJ, US 198/D4
Atebubu, Gha. 133/E5
Ateca, Sp. 52/E2
Ateelva (riv.), Nor. 44/G1
Atén, Bol. 220/D4
Atencingo, Mex. 205/L8
Atenco, Mex. 205/Q10
Atenco, Mex. 205/R9
Atengo (riv.), Mex. 204/D4
Aterno (riv.), It. 71/C3
Atessa, It. 71/D3
Aṭfīḥ, Egypt 131/C6
Atglen, Pa, US 198/C4
Ath, Belg. 60/C2
Athabasca (riv.), Ab, Can. 170/E3
Athabasca (lake), Ab,Sk, Can. 170/E3
Āthārabāri, Bang. 109/H3
Athboy, Ire. 38/D2
Athea, Ire. 38/A5
Athena, Or, US 174/E5
Athenry, Ire. 38/B3
Athens, On, Can. 191/J2
Athens (Athínai) (cap.), Gre. 55/N9
Athens, Al, US 192/D3
Athens, Ar, US 183/H3
Athens, Ga, US 193/F4
Athens, Il, US 185/K4
Athens, Mi, US 190/D3
Athens, NY, US 191/K3
Athens, Oh, US 190/E5
Athens, Pa, US 191/H4
Athens, Tn, US 192/E3
Athens, Tx, US 181/G1
Athens, WV, US 193/G2
Atherstone, Eng, UK 43/E1
Atherton, Eng, UK 41/F4
Atherton, Austl. 158/B2
Athgarh, India 107/E1
Athi (riv.), Kenya 137/B2
Athi River, Kenya 137/B2
Athienou, Cyp. 116/C2
Athínai (Athens) (cap.), Gre. 55/N9
Athis-Mons, Fr. 36/K5
Athleague, Ire. 38/B2
Athlone, Ire. 38/C3
Athok, Myan. 98/B5
Athol, Ma, US 191/K3
Athol, NZ 159/B4
Atholl (for.), Sc, UK 39/B3
Áthos (peak), Gre. 55/J2
Athribis (ruin), Egypt 131/C4
Athy, Ire. 38/D4
Ati, Chad 134/C2
Ati Ardébé, Chad 134/C2
Atiak, Ugan. 139/H2
Atibaia (riv.), Braz. 223/K7
Atibaia, Braz. 223/K8
Atico, Peru 220/C5
Atienza, Sp. 52/D2
Atikokan, On, Can. 187/J3
Atil, Mex. 204/C2
Atinggola, Indo. 103/F3
Atitlán (lake), Guat. 206/D3
Atiu (isl.), CookIs. 161/K7
Atizapan, Mex. 205/Q10
Atka, Rus. 81/R3
Atka (isl.), Ak, US 201/D5
Atka, Ak, US 201/D5
Atkarsk, Rus. 77/H2
Atkins, Ar, US 183/H3
Atkins, Va, US 193/G2
Atkinson (isl.), Tx, US 181/N9
Atlacomulco de Fabela, Mex. 205/K7
Atlanta, SAfr. 141/E5
Atlanta (cap.), Ga, US 193/M7
Atlanta, Il, US 185/K3
Atlanta, La, US 194/B2
Atlanta, Mi, US 190/D2
Atlanta, Tx, US 183/G4
Atlanta Botanical Garden, Ga, US 193/M7
Atlanta Nav. Air Sta., Ga, US 193/L7
Atlantic, NC, US 193/J3
Atlantic (ocean) 26/G3
Atlantic (peak), Wy, US 177/J2
Atlantic, Ia, US 185/G3
Atlantic (co.), NJ, US 198/D5
Atlantic Beach, Fl, US 195/H2
Atlantic Beach, NY, US 199/L9
Atlantic City, Wy, US 177/J2
Atlantic City, NJ, US 198/D5
Atlantic City International (arpt.), NJ, US 198/D5
Atlantic Highlands, NJ, US 199/J10
Atlantico (dept.), Col. 207/H4
Atlántida, Uru. 227/L11
Atlantique (prov.), Ben. 133/F5
Atlas (mts.), Afr. 72/C4
Atlas (peak), Ca, US 197/K10
Atlasovo, Rus. 81/R4
Atlatlahuaca, Mex. 205/Q10
Atlin, BC, Can. 201/M3
Atlin (lake), BC, Can. 201/M3
'Atlit, Isr. 117/B3
Atlixco, Mex. 205/L8
Atmore, Al, US 194/E2
Atnarko (riv.), BC, Can. 174/B1
Atocha, Bol. 224/C2
Atoka, Ok, US 183/F3
Atoka (res.), Ok, US 183/F3
Atoka, Tn, US 192/C3
Atome, Ang. 140/B1
Atomic City, Id, US 177/G2
Atondo, D.R. Congo 139/F3
Atotonilco, Mex. 205/L6
Atouila, 'Erg (des.), Mali 128/D5
Atoyac (riv.), Mex. 206/B2
Atoyac, Mex. 205/E5
Atqasuk, Ak, US 201/G1
Atrai (riv.), Bang. 109/G3
Atrak (riv.), Iran 80/F6
Ätran (riv.), Swe. 46/E3
Atrato (riv.), Col. 203/F6
Atrauli, India 108/B1
Atri, It. 71/C2
Atripalda, It. 71/D6
Atsugi, Japan 95/C3
Atsumi, Japan 95/M6
Atsumi (pen.), Japan 95/M6
Attalens, Swi. 66/C4
Attalla, Al, US 192/D3
Attapu, Laos 106/D3
Attapulgus, Ga, US 195/F2
Attawapiskat, On, Can. 171/H3
Attawapiskat (riv.), On, Can. 171/H3
Attean (mtn.), Me, US 191/L2
Attel (riv.), Ger. 65/F7
Attendorn, Ger. 59/E6
Atteridgeville, SAfr. 142/Q12
Attersee (lake), Aus. 51/K3
Attert, Belg. 61/E4
Attica, In, US 190/C4
Attica, Ks, US 183/E2
Attica, Mi, US 197/F5
Attica, Oh, US 190/E4
Attigliano, It. 71/B2
Attigny, Fr. 61/D5
'Attīl, WBnk. 117/C4
Attingal, India 107/C4
Attleboro, Ma, US 191/L4
Attleborough, Eng, UK 43/E1
Attnang-Puchheim, Aus. 65/G6
Attock, Pak. 110/B3
Attoyac (riv.), Tx, US 181/G2
Attu (isl.), Ak, US 201/A5
Āttūr, India 107/C4
Atuel (riv.), Arg. 226/D2
Atuntaqui, Ecu. 216/B4
Atuona, FrPol. 161/M5
Ātura, Bang. 109/G3
Atura, Ugan. 139/H2
Åtvidaberg, Swe. 46/G2
Atwater, Ca, US 178/B2
Atwood, Ok, US 183/F3
Atwood, Ks, US 184/D4
Atwood, Co, US 184/C3
Atyraū (int'l arpt.), Kaz. 77/J3
Atyraū, Kaz. 77/J3
Atyraū Oblast, Kaz. 77/J3
Atzcapotzalco (nbrhd.), Mex. 205/Q10
Au, Swi. 67/F3
Au, Aus. 67/F3
Au Gres, Mi, US 190/E2
Au in der Hallertau, Ger. 65/E5
Au Sable (riv.), Mi, US 190/E2
Au Sable (pt.), Mi, US 190/E2
Au Sable, Mi, US 190/E2
Auari (riv.), Braz. 217/E3
Auas, Hon. 207/E3
Auasbila, Hon. 207/E3
Aub, Namb. 140/C4
Aubá, ETim. 152/B2
Aubagne, Fr. 70/B6
Aubange, Belg. 61/E4
Aube, Fr. 63/F3
Aube (riv.), Fr. 48/C4
Aube (dept.), Fr. 61/D6
Aubepierre-Ozouer-le-Repos, Fr. 36/L6
Aubergenville, Fr. 36/H5
Auberry, Ca, US 178/C2
Aubert (peak), Swi. 66/C4
Aubervilliers, Fr. 36/K5
Aubetin (riv.), Fr. 60/C6
Aubette (riv.), Fr. 60/A5
Aubette de Magny (riv.), Fr. 36/H4
Aubevoye, Fr. 63/G2
Aubignon, Fr. 70/B4
Aubigny-en-Artois, Fr. 60/B3
Aubigny-sur-Nère, Fr. 50/E3
Aubin, Fr. 50/E4
Aubonne, Swi. 66/C5
Auboué, Fr. 61/E5
Aubrac (mts.), Fr. 50/E4
Aubrey, Ar, US 192/B3
Aubrives, Fr. 61/D3
Auburn, Austl. 155/H5
Auburn (nbrhd.), Austl. 158/H8
Auburn, Al, US 192/E4
Auburn, Ca, US 176/C4
Auburn, Ga, US 192/F3
Auburn, Il, US 185/K4
Auburn, In, US 190/D4
Auburn, Ks, US 183/G1
Auburn, Ky, US 192/D2
Auburn, Ma, US 191/L3
Auburn, Me, US 191/L2
Auburn, Ms, US 194/C2
Auburn, Ne, US 185/G3
Auburn, NY, US 191/H3
Auburn, Pa, US 198/B2
Auburn, Wa, US 174/C4
Auburn Hills, Mi, US 197/F6
Auburndale, Fl, US 194/M7
Aubusson, Fr. 50/E4
Aucá Mahuida (peak), Arg. 226/C3
Auce, Lat. 47/K3
Auch, Fr. 50/D5
Auchel, Fr. 60/B3
Auchenblae, Sc, UK 39/D3
Auchencairn, Sc, UK 40/E2
Auchi, Nga. 133/G5
Auchinleck, Sc, UK 39/B6
Auchterarder, Sc, UK 39/C4
Auchtermuchty, Sc, UK 39/C4
Auchy-lès-Hesdin, Fr. 60/B3
Aucilla (riv.), Fl, US 195/G2
Auckland (isls.), NZ 27/T8
Auckland (int'l arpt.), NZ 159/F6
Auckland, NZ 159/F6
Auckland Domain, NZ 159/F6
Aude (riv.), Fr. 72/D2
Auden, On, Can. 187/L2
Auderghem, Belg. 61/D2
Audet, Qu, Can. 188/B3
Audeux (riv.), Fr. 66/C3
Audience Hall, VatC. 71/G7
Audierne (bay), Fr. 50/A3
Audincourt, Fr. 66/C3
Audlem, Eng, UK 41/F6
Audley, Eng, UK 41/F5
Audo (range), Eth. 136/B4
Audruicq, Fr. 60/B2
Audubon, Ia, US 185/G3
Audubon NWR, ND, US 186/D4
Audun-le-Roman, Fr. 61/E5
Audun-le-Tiche, Fr. 61/E5
Aue (riv.), Ger. 59/E2
Aue, Ger. 65/F1
Auer (Ora), It. 67/H5
Auerbach, Ger. 65/F1
Auerbach in der Oberpfalz, Ger. 65/E3
Auersberg (peak), Ger. 65/F2
Aufess (riv.), Ger. 64/E3
Auffargis, Fr. 36/H5
Auffay, Fr. 63/G1
Augathella, Austl. 158/B4
Auger (falls), Id, US 177/F2
Augher, NI, UK 40/A3
Aughinish (isl.), Ire. 38/A4
Aughnacloy, NI, UK 40/B3
Aughrim, Ire. 40/B6
Auglaize (riv.), Oh, US 190/D4
Augrabies Falls NP, SAfr. 142/C3
Augrabiesvalle (falls), SAfr. 142/C3
Augsburg, Ger. 64/D6
Augsburg (Mühlhausen) (arpt.), Ger. 64/D6
Augub (peak), Namb. 142/A2
Augusta, Austl. 154/B5
Augusta, It. 54/D4
Augusta (gulf), It. 54/D4
Augusta, Ar, US 183/J3
Augusta, Ga, US 193/G4
Augusta, Il, US 185/J3
Augusta, Ks, US 183/F2
Augusta (cap.), Me, US 188/C3
Augusta, Mt, US 175/H4
Augusta, NJ, US 198/D1
Augusta, Wi, US 185/J1
Augusta, WV, US 191/G5
Augustdorf, Ger. 59/F5
Augustenborg, Den. 46/C4
Augustine Ind. Res., Ca, US 178/D4
Augusto César Sandino (int'l arpt.), Nic. 206/E3
Augustów, Pol. 47/K5
Augustus (mt.), Austl. 154/C3
Auk Bok (isl.), Myan. 106/B3
Aukam, Namb. 142/B2
Auki, Sol. 160/F5
Aukstatija NP, Lith. 47/M4
Aulander, NC, US 193/J2
Aulatsivik, North (isl.), Nf, Can. 171/K3
Aulatsivik, South (isl.), Nf, Can. 171/K3
Auld (lake), Austl. 145/B3
Auldearn, Sc, UK 39/C1
Aulencia (riv.), Sp. 53/M9
Aulendorf, Ger. 67/F2
Aulla, It. 68/C5
Aulnay-sous-Bois, Fr. 36/K5
Aulnay-sur-Mauldre, Fr. 36/H5
Aulne (riv.), Fr. 50/A2
Aulneau (pen.), On, Can. 187/G3
Aulnoy, Fr. 36/M5
Aulnoye-Aymeries, Fr. 60/C3
Aulnut (int'l arpt.), Fr. 50/E4
Ault, Fr. 60/A3
Ault (peak), Swi. 67/F4
Ault, Co, US 184/B3
Aumale, Fr. 60/A4
Aumetz, Fr. 61/E5
Aumsville, Or, US 176/B1
Aumühle, Ger. 59/H1
Auna, Nga. 133/G4
Aunay-sur-Odon, Fr. 63/E2
Aune (riv.), Fr. 63/F5
Auneau, Fr. 63/G4
Aunette (riv.), Fr. 60/B5
Auneuil, Fr. 60/B5
Auning, Den. 46/D3
Auob (riv.), Namb. 140/C5
Auobrivier (riv.), SAfr. 140/D5
Aups, Fr. 70/C5
Aur (isl.), Mrsh. 160/G4
Aur (isl.), Malay. 101/D2
Aura, NJ, US 198/C4
Aurach (riv.), Ger. 64/D3
Aurach, Ger. 64/D4
Auraiya, India 108/B2
Aurangābād, India 109/E3
Aurangābād, India 107/B2
Auray, Fr. 62/C5
Aureilhan, Fr. 50/D5
Aurelia, Ia, US 185/G2
Aurelian (wall), It. 71/G8
Aurès (mts.), Alg. 72/E4
Aurich, Ger. 59/E2
Auriflama, Braz. 225/G2
Aurillac, Fr. 50/E4
Auriol, Fr. 70/B6
Aurisina, It. 69/G2
Aurland, Nor. 46/B1
Aurolzmünster, Aus. 65/G6
Aurora, Braz. 219/G4
Aurora, On, Can. 191/G3
Aurora, Guy. 217/G3
Aurora, Phil. 100/C4
Aurora, Co, US 200/C3
Aurora, Il, US 190/B4
Aurora, Mo, US 183/H2
Aurora, NC, US 193/J3
Aurora, Ne, US 184/E3
Aurora, Ut, US 179/G1
Aurora Ghost Town, Nv, US 176/D4
Aurora Lodge, Ak, US 201/J3
Aurunci (mts.), It. 71/C5
Aus, Namb. 142/B2
Ausa (riv.), It. 69/G1
Ausable (riv.), On, Can. 190/F3
Auschwitz (Oświęcim), Pol. 49/K3
Ausert, WSah. 128/B5
Ausoni (mts.), It. 71/C5
Aussenkehr, Namb. 142/B3
Aussillon, Fr. 50/E5
Aust-Agder (co.), Nor. 44/C4
Austell, Ga, US 193/L7
Austin (lake), Austl. 145/A3
Austin, Mb, Can. 186/E3
Austin (isl.), Nun, Can. 170/G2
Austin, In, US 192/E1
Austin, Ky, US 192/D2
Austin, Mn, US 185/H2
Austin, Nv, US 176/E4
Austin, Or, US 176/D1
Austin (cap.), Tx, US 181/F2
Austin Bayou (riv.), Tx, US 181/M9
Austonio, Tx, US 181/G2
Austral (Tubuaï Islands) (isls.), FrPol. 161/K7
Australia (ctry.) 145/*
Australia (cont.) 145/*
Australian, BC, Can. 174/C1
Australian Capital Terr., Austl. 145/D4
Australind, Austl. 154/B5
Austria (ctry.) 51/L3
Austurhorn (pt.), Ice. 44/P7
Autaugaville, Al, US 192/D4
Autazes, Braz. 218/B3
Auterive, Fr. 50/D5
Authie (riv.), Fr. 48/B3
Authion (riv.), Fr. 63/E6
Authon-du-Perche, Fr. 63/F4
Autlán de Navarro, Mex. 204/D5
Automne (riv.), Fr. 60/B5
Autore (peak), It. 71/C4
Autreppe, Belg. 60/C3
Autun, Fr. 50/F3
Auvergne, Ar, US 183/J3
Auvergne (pol. reg.), Fr. 50/E4
Auvergne, Austl. 152/C3
Auvers-sur-Oise, Fr. 36/J4
Auvézère (riv.), Fr. 50/D4
Aux Barques (pt.), Mi, US 190/E2
Aux Barques (pt.), Mi, US 190/C2
Auxerre, Fr. 50/E3
Auxi-le-Château, Fr. 60/B3
Auxonne, Fr. 66/B3
Auxvasse, Mo, US 185/J4
Auyán-Tepuí (peak), Ven. 217/F3
Auyuittuq NP, Nun, Can. 171/K2
Auzangate (peak), Peru 220/D4
Ava, Il, US 192/C2
Ava, Mo, US 183/H2
Ava, Myan. 106/A1
Āvaj, Iran 115/G3
Avallon, Fr. 50/E3
Avaloirs (peak), Fr. 63/E4
Avalon, Ca, US 196/B4
Avalon (pen.), Nf, Can. 171/L4
Avalon, Mo, US 185/H4
Avalon, NJ, US 198/D5
Avanigadda, India 107/D2
Avanne-Aveney, Fr. 66/B3
Avaré, Braz. 225/G2
Avarua, NZ 161/K7
Avcilar, Turk. 115/M7
Avdiyivka, Ukr. 79/J3
Avebury, Eng, UK 43/E4
Avebury Stone Circle, Eng, UK 43/E4
Aveiro, Port. 52/A2
Aveiro (dist.), Port. 52/A2
Aveley, Eng, UK 36/D2
Avelgem, Belg. 60/C2
Avellaneda, Arg. 227/J11
Avellino, It. 71/D6
Avellino (prov.), It. 71/D6
Avelon (riv.), Fr. 60/A5
Aven (riv.), Fr. 62/B4
Avenal, Ca, US 178/B2
Avenches, Swi. 66/D4
Avenel, NJ, US 199/H9
Avernes, Fr. 36/H4
Aversa, It. 71/D6
Avery, Id, US 174/G4
Avery Island, La, US 194/C3
Aves (isl.), Ven. 203/J4
Avesnes-le-Comte, Fr. 60/B3
Avesnes-sur-Helpe, Fr. 60/C3
Avessac, Fr. 62/D5
Avesta, Swe. 46/G1
Aveyron (riv.), Fr. 50/D4
Avezzano, It. 71/C3
Avich (lake), Sc, UK 39/A4
Aviemore, Sc, UK 39/C2
Avigliana, It. 70/D2
Avignon, Fr. 70/A5
Aviẖayil, Isr. 117/B4
Ávila de los Caballeros, Sp. 52/C2
Avilés, Sp. 52/C1
Avio, It. 69/D2
Avion, Fr. 60/B3
Aviron (pt.), Nf, Can. 189/J2
Avis, Pa, US 198/A1
Avisio (riv.), It. 67/H5
Avize, Fr. 60/D6
Avlum, Den. 46/C3
Avoca (riv.), Ire. 40/B6
Avoca, Austl. 156/C4
Avoca, Austl. 156/B3
Avoca, Ia, US 185/G3
Avoca, NY, US 191/H3
Avoch, Sc, UK 39/B1
Avoine, Fr. 63/F6
Avola, It. 54/D4
Avola, BC, Can. 174/E2
Avon (lake), Austl. 157/E2
Avon (riv.), Fr. 36/L6
Avon (riv.), Eng, UK 42/C6
Avon (riv.), Sc, UK 39/C1
Avon, Al, US 195/F2
Avon, Il, US 185/J3
Avon, Mn, US 187/G5
Avon, Ms, US 192/B4
Avon, NC, US 193/K3
Avon, NY, US 191/H3
Avon Downs, Austl. 153/E5
Avon Park, Fl, US 194/M8
Avon Park Bombing Range, Fl, US 195/H4
Avon Valley NP, Austl. 154/C4
Avon Water (riv.), Sc, UK 39/B5
Avonbeg (riv.), Ire. 40/B6
Avondale, Co, US 182/B1
Avondale, Pa, US 198/C4
Avondale, Austl. 157/E2
Avonlea, Sk, Can. 186/B2
Avonmore (riv.), Ire. 40/B5
Avonmouth, Eng, UK 42/D3
Avraga, Mong. 90/F2
Avranches, Fr. 62/D3
Avre (riv.), Fr. 48/B4
Avrillé, Fr. 63/E5
Avrora, Azer. 115/G2
Avtovo (nbrhd.), Rus. 75/T7
Āvupalli, India 104/D4
Awa-shima (isl.), Japan 94/A4
Awaé, Camr. 138/B2
A'waj (riv.), Syria 116/E3
Awaji, Japan 95/H6
Awakaba, CAfr. 134/D3
Awans, Belg. 61/E2
Awantīpur, India 110/C3
Awanui, NZ 159/C1
Awara (plain), Kenya 136/B5
Āwarē, Eth. 136/C3
Āwasa, Eth. 136/A4
Āwash, Eth. 136/B3
Awash NP, Eth. 136/A3
Āwash Wenz (riv.), Eth. 135/H3
Awasibberge (peak), Namb. 140/B5
Awaso, Gha. 133/E5
Awat, China 111/D3
Awatere (riv.), NZ 159/C3
Awbārī (des.), Libya 129/H4
Awbārī, Libya 126/B3
Awbeg (riv.), Ire. 38/B5
Awdheegle, Som. 136/C5
Awe (lake), Sc, UK 39/A4
Awgu, Nga. 133/G5
Āwira Wenz (riv.), Eth. 136/A2
Awīsh al Ḩajar, Egypt 131/C2
Awjilah, Libya 126/D2
Awka, Nga. 133/G5
Awsīm, Egypt 131/C4
Ax-les-Thermes, Fr. 50/D5
Axamo (int'l arpt.), Swe. 46/F3
Axams, Aus. 67/H3
Axarfjördhur (inlet), Ice. 44/N6
Axbridge, Eng, UK 42/D4
Axel, Neth. 58/A6
Axel Heiberg (isl.), Nun, Can. 171/S7
Axial, Co, US 177/K3
Axim, Gha. 133/E5
Axios (riv.), Gre. 55/H2
Axis (dam), Wa, US 197/D2
Axixá do Tocantins, Braz. 218/E4
Axminster, Eng, UK 42/D5
Axochiapan, Mex. 205/L8
Axson, Ga, US 195/G2
Axtell, Ks, US 185/F4
Axtell, Ne, US 184/E3
Ay (riv.), Fr. 62/D2
Ay (riv.), Rus. 75/N5
Ay, Fr. 60/C5
Ayabaca, Peru 220/B2
Ayabe, Japan 95/H5
Ayacucho, Arg. 226/F3
Ayacucho, Peru 220/C4
Ayacucho (dept.), Peru 220/C4
Ayagöz, Kaz. 111/D2
Ayaguz (riv.), Kaz. 111/D2
Ayakkum (lake), China 111/E4
Ayama, Japan 95/K6
Ayamonte, Sp. 52/B4
Ayan, Rus. 81/P4
Ayancık, Turk. 76/E4
Ayanganna (mtn.), Guy. 217/G3
Ayangba, Nga. 133/G5
Ayanka, Rus. 81/S3
Ayapel, Col. 216/C2
Ayaş, Turk. 114/C1
Ayase, Japan 95/C3
Ayass (peak), Ugan. 137/A1
Ayaviri, Peru 220/D4
Āybak, Afg. 80/G6
Aybas, Kaz. 77/J3
Aybastı, Turk. 76/F4
Aydabul, Kaz. 111/A1
Ayden, NC, US 193/J3
Aydın, Turk. 114/A2
Aydin (prov.), Turk. 114/B2
Aydıncık, Turk. 114/C1
Aydıncık, Turk. 116/C1
Aydınkent, Turk. 116/B1
Aydinli, Turk. 115/N7
Āydora, Eth. 136/B3
Aydyrlinskiy, Rus. 77/L1
Āyelu (peak), Eth. 136/B3
Ayem, Gabon 138/B3
Ayer, Swi. 66/D5
Ayer Hitam, Malay. 101/C2
Ayer's Cliff, Qu, Can. 191/K2
Ayers Rock (Uluru) (peak), Austl. 155/F3
Ayeyarwady (div.), Myan. 105/F4
Ayiá, Gre. 55/H3
Ayía Paraskeví, Gre. 55/K3
Ayiásos, Gre. 55/K3
Ayina (riv.), Congo 138/C2
Áyios Athanásios, Gre. 55/J2
Áyios Evstrátios (isl.), Gre. 73/K3
Áyios Ioánnis (cape), Gre. 55/J5
Áyios Kírikos, Gre. 55/K4
Áyios Konstandínos, Gre. 55/H3
Áyios Matthaíos, Gre. 55/F3
Áyios Nikólaos, Gre. 55/J5
Āykel, Eth. 135/H2
Aykhal, Rus. 81/M3
Aylesbury, Eng, UK 43/F3
Aylesford, NS, Can. 188/E3
Aylesford, Eng, UK 43/G4
Aylesham, Eng, UK 43/H4
Ayllón, Sp. 52/D2
Aylmer, On, Can. 190/F3
Aylmer (lake), NW, Can. 170/F2
Aylsham, Eng, UK 43/H1
Aylsham, Sk, Can. 175/N1
'Ayn Ad Darāhim, Tun. 130/L6
'Ayn al 'Arab, Syria 114/D2
'Ayn al Ghazālah, Libya 126/D1
'Ayn Ath Tha'lab, Libya 126/D3
'Ayn Sukhnah, Egypt 131/D5
Ayna, Peru 220/C4
Aynor, SC, US 193/H4
'Aynūnah, SAr. 127/G2
Ayod, Sudan 135/F3
Ayolas, Par. 225/E3
Ayon (isl.), Rus. 81/S3
Ayora, Sp. 53/E3
Ayorou, Niger 133/F3
Ayos, Camr. 138/C2
Ayotzintepec, Mex. 206/B2
'Ayoûn 'Abd el Mâlek (well), Mrta. 128/D4
'Ayoûn el 'Atroûs, Mrta. 132/C2
Ayr (riv.), Sc, UK 39/B5
Ayr, Sc, UK 39/B6
Ayr, Austl. 158/B2
Āysha, Eth. 136/B3
Ayton, Sc, UK 39/D5
Ayton, Eng, UK 41/H3
Āytony, Eth. 135/H3
Aytos, Bul. 57/H4
Aytré, Fr. 50/C3
Ayubia NP, Pak. 110/B3
Ayutinskiy, Rus. 79/L4
Ayutla, Mex. 204/D4
Ayutla de los Libres, Mex. 202/B4
Ayutthaya (ruin), Thai. 106/C3
Ayvacık, Turk. 55/K3
Aywaille, Belg. 61/E3
Az Zabābidah, WBnk. 117/C4
Az Zabadānī, Syria 117/E1
Aẓ Ẓāhirīyah, WBnk. 117/B6
Az Zankalūn, Egypt 131/C3
Az Zaqāzīq, Egypt 131/C3
Az Zarqā' (gov.), Jor. 116/E3
Az Zarqā', Jor. 117/E4
Az Zawāmil, Egypt 131/C4
Az Zāwiyah, Libya 126/B1
Az Zaydāb, Sudan 135/G1
Az Zaydīyah, Yem. 136/B2
Az Zilfī, SAr. 112/D3
Az Zrārīyah, Leb. 117/C2
Az Zubayr, Iraq 115/F4
Az Zurbī, Egypt 131/B6
Azad Kashmir (terr.), Pak. 110/B3
Āzādshahr, Iran 115/G3
Azahar (coast), Sp. 53/F3
Azalea, Or, US 176/B2
Azalia, Mi, US 197/E7
Azamgarh, India 108/D2
Azángaro (riv.), Peru 220/D4
Azángaro, Peru 220/D4
Azao (peak), Alg. 129/H4
Azaouâd (phys. reg.), Mali 133/E2
Azapa, Chile 220/D5
Āzar Shahr, Iran 115/F2
Āzarān, Iran 115/F2
Āzarbāyjān-e Gharbī (gov.), Iran 115/F2
Āzarbāyjān-e Sharqī (gov.), Iran 115/F2
Azare, Nga. 133/H4
Azay-le-Rideau, Fr. 63/F6
A'zāz, Syria 116/E1
Azemmour, Mor. 128/C2
Azerbaijan (ctry.) 77/H4
Āzezo, Eth. 135/H2
Azhikal, India 107/B4
Azhu-Tayga (peak), Rus. 111/E1
Azilal, Mor. 128/D3
Azīmganj, India 109/G3
Azizbekov, Arm. 115/F2
Azle, Tx, US 180/K7
Aznā, Iran 115/G3
Aznakayevo, Rus. 75/M5
Azogues, Ecu. 216/B5
Azores (dpcy.), Port. 53/R12
Azourki (peak), Mor. 128/D3
Azov (sea), Rus.,Ukr. 80/D5
Azov, Rus. 79/K4
Azovs'ke, Ukr. 79/H5
Azoyú, Mex. 206/B2
Azpeitia, Sp. 50/B5
Azrou, Mor. 128/D2
Aztec, NM, US 179/J2
Aztec, Az, US 179/F4
Aztec Ruins Nat'l Mon., NM, US 179/H2
Azua de Compostela, DRep. 203/G4
Azuaga, Sp. 52/C3
Azuara, Sp. 53/E2
Azuay (dept.), Ecu. 216/B5
Azuchi, Japan 95/K5
Azuero (pen.), Pan. 203/E6
Azufre (vol.), Chile 224/B3
Azufre, Paso el (pass), Chile 224/B4
Azuga, Rom. 57/G3
Azul, Arg. 226/F3
Azul (peak), Arg. 224/B4
Azul (mtn.), CR 206/E4
Azul (riv.), Guat. 206/D2
Azul (riv.), Mex. 205/H5
Azul, Cordillera (mts.), Peru 220/B2
'Aẓūm (wadi), Sudan 134/D2
Azuma, Japan 95/E2
Azuma-san (peak), Japan 97/G2
Azumaya-san (peak), Japan 97/F2
Azurduy, Bol. 224/C1
Azure (mtn.), NY, US 191/J2
Azusa, Ca, US 196/C2
Azzaba, Alg. 130/K6
Azzano, It. 69/D3
Azzano Decimo, It. 69/F2
Azzano San Paolo, It. 68/C2
Azzate, It. 68/B2
'Azzūn, WBnk. 117/C4

B

Bà (riv.), Sc, UK 39/B3
Ba, Fiji 161/Y18
Bà (riv.), China 90/F5
Ba Illi, Chad 134/C3
Ba Lang An (cape), Viet. 106/E3
Ba Quan (cape), Viet. 106/D4
Ba Ra, Viet. 106/D4
Ba Xian, China 92/H7
Baa, Indo. 152/A2
Baan Baa, Austl. 156/D1
Baar, Swi. 67/E3
Baargaal, Som. 136/D3
Baarle-Hertog, Belg. 58/B6
Baarle-Nassau, Neth. 58/B6
Baarn, Neth. 58/C4
Bab Taza, Mor. 130/B2
Baba (mts.), Afg. 113/J2
Baba (peak), Bul. 57/F4
Baba (pt.), Turk. 57/K5
Baba Burnu (pt.), Turk. 55/K3
Bababé, Mrta. 132/B2
Babaçulândia, Braz. 218/E4
Babadag, Rom. 57/J3
Babadayhan, Trkm. 113/H1
Babaera, Ang. 140/B2
Babaeski, Turk. 57/H5
Babahoyo, Ecu. 216/B5
Babai Gaxun, China 90/E3
Babai Khola (riv.), Nepal 108/C1
Babakale, Turk. 55/K3
Babana, Nga. 133/F4
Babanango, SAfr. 143/E3
Babanūsah, Sudan 135/E3
Babar (isls.), Indo. 152/C1
Babar (isl.), Indo. 152/C1
Babat, Indo. 101/C3
Babati, Tanz. 137/A3

Babatorun, Turk. 116/E1
Babatpur (int'l arpt.), India 108/D2
Babayevo, Rus. 74/G4
Babb, Mt, US 175/H3
Babbacombe (bay), Eng, UK 42/C6
Babbitt, Mn, US 187/J4
Babbitt, Nv, US 176/D4
B'abdā, Leb. 117/D1
Babelthuap (isl.), Palau 160/C4
Babenhausen, Ger. 67/G4
Babenhausen, Ger. 64/B3
Baberu, India 108/C3
Babi (isl.), Indo. 101/B2
Babia (peak), Pol. 76/A2
Babian, China 105/H3
Bābil (gov.), Iraq 115/F3
Bābil, Egypt 131/B3
Bābil (Babylon) (ruin), Iraq 115/F3
Babīna, India 108/B3
Babinda, Austl. 158/B2
Babine (riv.), BC, Can. 170/D3
Bābol, Iran 115/H2
Bābol Sar, Iran 115/H2
Baboquivari (mts.), Az, US 179/G5
Baboua, CAfr. 134/B4
Babson Park, Fl, US 194/M8
Bābuganj, Bang. 109/H4
Babura, Nga. 133/H3
Babushkin (nbrhd.), Rus. 75/W9
Babuyan (isl.), Phil. 83/M8
Babuyan (chan.), Phil. 106/D1
Babylon, NY, US 199/E2
Babylon (Bābil) (ruin), Iraq 115/F3
Bac Can, Viet. 106/D1
Bac Giang, Viet. 106/D1
Bac Lieu, Viet. 106/D4
Bac Ninh, Viet. 98/E4
Bac Quang, Viet. 106/D1
Bacabal, Braz. 219/E4
Bacabal, Braz. 218/B4
Bacadéhuachi, Mex. 204/C2
Bacajá (riv.), Braz. 218/B4
Bacalar (lag.), Mex. 206/D2
Bacalar, Mex. 206/D2
Bacan (isl.), Indo. 103/G4
Bacarra, Phil. 106/D1
Bacău (prov.), Rom. 57/H2
Bacău, Rom. 78/D4
Baccarat, Fr. 66/C1
Bacchiglione (riv.), It. 69/E2
Bacchus Marsh, Austl. 157/B3
Bacerac, Mex. 204/C2
Bacharach, Ger. 61/G3
Bacheng, China 92/L6
Bachhraon, India 108/B1
Bachíniva, Mex. 204/D2
Bachok, Malay. 101/C1
Bachu, China 111/C4
Back (riv.), Nun, Can. 180/F2
Back, Md, US 196/B6
Back Bay, NB, Can. 188/D3
Back Bay Nat'l Wild. Ref., Va, US 193/K2
Bačka (reg.), Serb. 56/D3
Bačka Palanka, Serb. 56/D3
Bačka Topola, Serb. 56/D3
Backbone (mtn.), Md, US 191/G1
Bäckefors, Swe. 46/E2
Backnang, Ger. 64/C5
Backwell, Eng, UK 42/D4
Baco, Phil. 100/C3
Bacobampa, Mex. 204/C3
Bacolod, Phil. 100/C3
Bacoor, Phil. 100/E7
Bacqueville-en-Caux, Fr. 63/F1
Bácsalmás, Hun. 56/D2
Bács-Kiskun (prov.), Hun. 56/D2
Bacup, Eng, UK 41/F4
Bacuri, Braz. 219/E3
Bād, Iran 115/H3
Bad (riv.), SD, US 184/D1
Bad Abbach, Ger. 65/F5
Bad Axe, Mi, US 190/E3
Bad Bellingen, Ger. 64/B6
Bad Bergzabern, Ger. 64/A4
Bad Berneck, Ger. 65/E2
Bad Bocklet, Ger. 64/D2
Bad Brambach, Ger. 65/E2
Bad Breisig, Ger. 61/G3
Bad Brückenau, Ger. 64/D2
Bad Buchau, Ger. 67/F1
Bad Camberg, Ger. 64/D3
Bad Doberan, Ger. 46/D4
Bad Driburg, Ger. 59/G5
Bad Dürkheim, Ger. 64/B4
Bad Dürrheim, Ger. 67/E1
Bad Ems, Ger. 61/G3
Bad Endorf, Ger. 65/F7
Bad Essen, Ger. 59/F4
Bad Freienwalde, Ger. 49/H2
Bad Gandersheim, Ger. 59/H5
Bad Grund, Ger. 59/H5
Bad Hall, Aus. 65/H6
Bad Harzburg, Ger. 59/H5
Bad Heilbrunn, Ger. 67/H2
Bad Herrenalb, Ger. 64/C5
Bad Hofgastein, Aus. 51/K3
Bad Homburg vor der Höhe, Ger. 64/D3
Bad Honnef, Ger. 61/G3
Bad Hönningen, Ger. 61/G3
Bad Karlshafen, Ger. 59/G5
Bad Kissingen, Ger. 64/D2
Bad Kohlgrub, Ger. 67/H2
Bad Königshofen, Ger. 64/C3
Bad Kreuznach, Ger. 61/G4
Bad Krozingen, Ger. 64/B6
Bad Langensalza, Ger. 59/H6
Bad Lauterberg, Ger. 59/H5
Bad Leonfelden, Aus. 65/H4
Bad Liebenzell, Ger. 64/C5
Bad Lippspringe, Ger. 59/F5
Bad Marienberg, Ger. 61/G2
Bad Mergentheim, Ger. 64/D4
Bad Munder am Deister, Ger.
Bad Münster am Stein, Ger.
Bad Nauheim, Ger. 64/B2

Bad Nenndorf, Ger. 59/G4
Bad Neuenahr-Ahrweiler, Ger. 61/G2
Bad Neustadt an der Saale, Ger. 64/D2
Bad Oeynhausen, Ger. 59/F4
Bad Orb, Ger. 64/D2
Bad Peterstal-Griesbach, Ger. 64/C5
Bad Plaas, SAfr. 143/E2
Bad Pyrmont, Ger. 59/G5
Bad Ragaz, Swi. 63/E3
Bad Rappenau, Ger. 64/C4
Bad Reichenhall, Ger. 51/K3
Bägha Purāna, India
Bad Rothenfelde, Ger. 59/F4
Bad Sachsa, Ger. 59/H5
Bad Salzdetfurth, Ger. 59/G4
Bad Salzschlirf, Ger. 64/C1
Bad Salzuflen, Ger. 59/F4
Bad Salzungen, Ger. 64/D1
Bad Sankt-Leonhard im Lavanttal, Aus. 51/L3
Bad Sassendorf, Ger. 59/F5
Bad Schallerbach, Aus. 65/G6
Bad Schwalbach, Ger. 61/H3
Bad Schwartau, Ger. 46/D5
Bad Segeberg, Ger. 46/D5
Bad Soden-Salmünster, Ger. 64/C2
Bad Sooden-Allendorf, Ger. 59/G6
Bad Tölz, Ger. 67/H2
Bad Vilbel, Ger. 64/C3
Bad Waldsee, Ger. 67/F2
Bad Wildungen, Ger. 64/C4
Bad Wimpfen, Ger. 64/C4
Bad Wörishofen, Ger. 67/G1
Bad Wurzach, Ger. 67/F1
Bad Zell, Aus. 65/H6
Bad Zwischenahn, Ger. 59/F2
Badahe, China 105/H3
Badain Jaran (des.), China 81/L5
Badajós (lake), Braz. 221/F1
Badajoz, Sp. 52/B3
Badalona, Sp. 53/L7
Badalucco, It. 68/A5
Badanah, SAr. 112/D2
Badaojiang, China 71/B2
Badas (isls.), Indo. 101/D2
Baddeck, NS, Can. 189/G2
Baddeckenstedt, Ger. 59/H4
Baddomalhi, Pak. 110/C4
Badegg, Nga. 133/G4
Baden, Swi. 67/E3
Baden, Fr. 62/C5
Baden-Württemberg (state), Ger. 64/C5
Badenoch (reg.), Sc, UK 39/B3
Badenweiler, Ger. 64/B6
Bader (peak), Ger. 51/H2
Badgastein, Aus. 51/K3
Badger (cr.), Co, US 184/C4
Badger's Quay, Nf, Can. 189/L1
Badgingarra NP, Austl. 154/B4
Badhoevedorp, Neth. 58/B4
Badia Polesine, It. 69/E2
Badiar, PN de, Gui. 132/B3
Badile (peak), It. 67/F5
Badin, NC, US 193/G3
Badiraguato, Mex. 204/D3
Bado, Mo, US 183/H2
Badoğan, India 110/C2
Badonviller, Fr. 66/C1
Badou, Togo 133/F5
Badr Ḥunayn, SAr. 112/C4
Badrah, Iraq 115/F3
Bādshāhpur, India 108/D3
Badu, India 108/C5
Badu, China 99/H3
Badulla, SrL. 107/D5
Badw, China 98/E4
Bafang, Camr. 138/B1
Bafatá, GBis. 132/B3
Baffa, India 110/B2
Baffin (bay), Can. 163/K2
Baffin (isl.), Can. 163/K2
Bafilo, Togo 133/F4
Bāfq, Iran 115/H4
Bafra, Turk. 76/E4
Bafra, Turk. 76/E4
Bafra Bola (riv.), Chad 134/C3
Bāft, Iran 115/J4
Bafu, Libr. 132/C5
Bafwabalinga, D.R. Congo 139/E2
Bafwaboğo, D.R. Congo 139/E2
Bafwasende, D.R. Congo 139/E2
Baga, Nga. 134/B2
Baga Salt (lake), China 109/H2
Bagagnana, CR 207/E4
Bagamoyo, Tanz. 137/C2
Baganga, Phil. 100/D5
Bagansiapiapi, Indo. 101/B4
Bagarwa, Niger 133/G3
Baga, D.R. Congo 138/C3
Bai Thuong, Viet. 106/D2
Baia, It. 71/D6

Bagbag (cr.), Phil. 100/E6
Bagbiringula (pt.), Austl. 153/E3
Bagda (mts.), China 111/E3
Bagdad, Az, US 179/F3
Bagdadi, Geo. 77/G4
Bagé, Braz. 225/F4
Bagenkop, Den. 46/D4
Bägerhät, Bang. 109/G4
Baggs, Wy, US 177/K3
Bagheria, It. 71/D6
Bāghīn, Iran 115/H4
Baghlān (prov.), Afg. 113/J1
Bāghpat, India 108/B1
Baginda (cape), Indo. 101/D3
Baginton (arpt.), Eng, UK 43/E2
Bagirsdorf, Ger. 64/E3
Baifusi, China 99/F2
Baigorrita, Arg. 226/E2
Baigou (riv.), China 92/H7
Baigou, China 92/G7
Baihar, India 108/C4
Baihe (mtn.), China 92/G7
Baihe, China 99/F2
Baijian, China 92/G7
Baijiang, China 92/G7
Bā'ijī, Iraq 115/E3
Baikunthpur, India 108/D4
Bailadores, Ven. 216/D2
Bailén, Sp. 52/D3
Baile an Fheirtéaraigh, Ire.
Bailen, ...
Bāile Herculane, Rom. 56/F3
Bailhache (riv.), Qu, Can. 171/J1
Bailique, Ponta do (pt.), Braz. 218/B3
Bailleul, Fr. 60/B2
Bailey, Co, US 182/B1
Bailey, NC, US 193/H3
Baileys Harbor, Wi, US 190/C2
Bailiçtār, Iran
Bailicun, China 99/F3
Bailleau-le-Pin, Fr. 63/G4
Bailique, ...
Bailundo, Ang. 140/B2
Baima (riv.), D.R. Congo 135/F5
Baimangying, China 99/F3
Baimianxia, China 99/F2
Baimuru, PNG 153/G1
Bain-de-Bretagne, Fr. 62/C5
Bainang, China 109/G1
Bainbridge, Ga, US 195/F2
Bainbridge, NY, US 191/J3
Bainbridge, Oh, US 193/F3
Bainbridge, Pa, US 196/B3
Bainbridge Nav. Trg. Sta., Md, US 196/B6
Baines, West D.R. Congo
Baing, Indo. 101/F5
Baingoin, China 111/E5
Bains, La, US 194/C2
Bains-les-Bains, Fr. 66/C2
Bains-sur-Oust, Fr. 62/C5
Baiquan, China 91/K2
Bā'ir (wadi), Jor. 116/E4
Bairab (riv.), India 111/D4
Bairāgnia, India 109/E2
Baird, Fl, US 194/M8
Baird, Tx, US 180/E1
Bairi, Austl. 158/B2
Bairnsdale, Austl. 157/A3
Bais, Fr. 63/E4
Bais, Phil. 100/C3
Baisha, China 99/G4
Baisha, China 99/G4
Baishaguan, China 99/H3
Baishan, China 99/H3
Baishaling, China 99/H3
Baishe, China 99/H3
Baishi, China 99/H3
Baishui, China 99/H3
Baishui, China 90/G2
Baishui, China 99/G2
Baishuijiang, China 90/H3
Baisogala, Lith. 47/K4
Baisong (pass), China 99/H3
Baixa da Banheira, Port. 53/P10
Baixa Grande, Braz. 223/E2
Baixiang, China 99/G4
Baixo Guandu, Braz. 223/E3
Baiyang, China 92/H3
Baiyin River, PNG 153/G1
Baiyin (mts.), China 90/E4
Baiyu (mts.), China 98/C2
Baiyin (int'l arpt.), China 98/C2
Baiyun, China 99/H3
Baja, Hun. 56/D2
Baja California (pt.), Mex. 204/B2
Baja California (state), Mex.
Baja California Sur (state), Mex. 204/B2
Bajestān, Iran 115/H3
Bajil, Yem. 112/F3
Bajina Bašta, Serb. 56/D3
Bajitpur, Bang. 109/H3
Bajmat (mt.), Austl. 156/E1
Bajo Boquete, Pan. 207/F4
Bajo Kalāt, Iran 107/H3
Bajo de Gualicho (plain), Arg. 226/D4

Baia de Aramă, Rom. 57/F2
Baia dos Tigres, Ang. 140/A3
Baia Farta, Ang. 140/B2
Baia Mare, Rom. 57/F2
Baia Sprie, Rom. 57/F2
Baiano, It. 71/D6
Baibokoum, Chad 134/B4
Baicao (mts.), China 98/D3
Baicheng, China 111/D3
Baicheng, China 91/J2
Baidishi, China 99/F3
Baidoa (Baydhabo), Som. 136/B5
Baidong (riv.), China 92/D5
Baidu (riv.), China 99/H4
Baie Verte, Nf, Can. 171/L4
Baie-Saint-Paul, Qu., Can. 188/D1
Baie-Sainte-Anne, NB, Can. 188/E2
Baie-Trinité, Qu., Can. 189/D1
Baiersbronn, Ger. 64/B5
Baiersdorf, Ger. 64/E3
Baigou, China 99/F2
Bāile Govora, Rom. 57/G3
Bāile Olănești, Rom. 57/G3
Bāile Tuşnad, Rom. 57/G2
Bāileşti, Rom. 57/F3
Bailmān Diārkhāta, Bang. 109/G3
Bailundu, Ang. 140/B2
Baleine, Grand Rivière de la 171/J2
Baleine, Petite Rivière de la 171/J2
Baleine (riv.), Qu, Can. 171/J3
Balen, Belg. 61/E1
Baler, Phil. 100/C2
Balerna, Swi. 67/F6
Bālurghāt, Iran
Baleshwar (Balasore), India 109/H3
Baley, Rus. 90/H1
Baléyara, Niger 133/F3
Balezino, Rus. 75/M4
Balfour, BC, Can. 174/F3
Balfour, SAfr. 142/E2
Balfour, Sc, UK 39/W8
Balgatay, Mong. 90/D2
Balguntay, China 111/E3
Balhaf, Yem. 136/D2
Balhannah, Austl. 155/M8
Balholm, ...
Balıkesir (prov.), Turk. 76/C5
Balıkesir, Turk. 76/C5
Balikpapan, Indo. 103/J4
Balimbing, Indo. 101/C4
Balimbing, Phil. 101/E2
Balimo, PNG 153/F1
Baling, Malay. 101/C1
Baling, China 98/E1
Balingasag, Phil. 100/D3
Bālinge, Swe. 46/G2
Balingen, Ger. 67/E1
Balintang (chan.), Phil. 106/D1
Baliu, Indo. 101/C1
Baljennie, Sk, US 175/L1
Balk, Neth. 58/C3
Balkan (prov.), Trkm. 77/K3
Bālkāndi, Iran 115/H4
Balkassar, Pak. 110/C4
Balkhash (lake), Kaz. 75/J4
Balkhash, Kaz. 75/J4
Balkassa, Kaz. ...
Balla, Ire. 40/A4
Balladonia, Austl. 154/C4
Ballaghadereen, Ire. 40/A4
Ballan, Austl. 157/B3
Ballan-Miré, Fr. 63/F3
Ballangen, Nor. 44/F1
Ballantine, Mt, US 175/K5
Ballarat, Austl. 157/A3
Ballard (lake), Austl. 154/C3
Ballard, IM, UK 40/B3
Ballaugh, IM, UK 40/B3
Ballé, Mali 132/D2
Ballena, Ecu. 220/B1
Ballenita (pt.), Chile 224/B3
Ballens, Swi. 64/C4
Balleny (isls.), Ant. 228/L1
Ballesteros, Arg. 224/D5
Ballia, India 109/E3
Ballidu, Austl. 154/B4
Ballina, Ire. 40/A4
Ballinakill, Ire. 38/A6
Ballinalllard, NI, UK 37/Q9
Ballinasloe, Ire. 38/B2
Ballinderry, Ire. 38/A6
Ballinderry, NI, UK 38/B2
Ballindine, Ire. 40/A4
Ballina, Ire. 40/A4
Ballinger, Tx, US 180/E1
Ballingry, Sc, UK 39/C3
Ballinlough, Ire. 38/A2
Ballintober, Ire. 38/A2
Ballintoge, NZ 159/B4

Bajo Nuevo (bank), Col. 203/F4
Bajo Palena, Chile 226/B4
Bajone (pt.), Moz. 141/J2
Bajos Caracoles, Arg. 227/C5
Bajram Curri, Alb. 56/E4
Bajura, Nepal 108/C1
Baka, Slvk. 56/C2
Bakaba, Chad 134/C4
Bakal, Rus. 75/N4
Bakala, CAfr. 134/D4
Bakali (riv.), D.R. Congo 135/D3
Bakaly, Kaz. 75/N5
Bakanas (riv.), Kaz. 111/C2
Bakaoré, Chad 134/D2
Bakar, India 51/L4
Bakarganj, Bang. 109/H4
Bakayan (peak), Indo. 103/E3
Baker, Mi, US 190/D3
Baker, ND, US 186/D3
Baker, NY, US 199/L9
Baker City, Ks, US 183/G1
Baker Harbour, Baker (lake), Nun, Can. 170/G2
Baker (riv.), Chile 227/B5
Baker (isl.), Pac., US 161/H4
Baker, Ca, US 178/D3
Baker, Fl, US 194/E3
Baker, La, US 194/C2
Baker, Mt, US 186/B4
Baker, Nv, US 177/H4
Baker (peak), Ok, US 183/E3
Baker (mtn.), Mt, US 175/K3
Baker Hill, Al, US 195/F2
Baker Lake, Nun, Can. 170/F2
Bakere, D.R. Congo 139/E2
Bakers Mill, Fl, US 183/H7
Bakersfield, Mo, US 183/H2
Bakersfield, Ca, US 178/C3
Bakersville, NC, US 193/F2
Bakewell, Eng, UK 41/G5
Bakhchysaray, Ukr. 79/G2
Bakhma (riv.), India 109/E2
Bakhshāyesh, Iran 115/F2
Bakhtarān, Iran 115/F3
Bakhtegān, Iran 115/G4
Bakhtiārī, Iran
Bakia, CAfr. 135/C4
Bakkafloi (bay), Ice. 44/P6
Bako, Eth. 135/H4
Bako, Eth. 135/H4
Bako NP, Malay. 101/D2
Bakokandi, ...
Bakonyszombathely, Hun. 56/C2
Bakora Corridor Game Rsv., Ugan.
Bakori, Nga. 133/G4
Bakouma, CAfr. 134/D4
Bakovský Potok, Czh. 65/G2
Bala, Camr. 132/C4
Balabac (isl.), Phil. 101/E2
Balabac (str.), Malay./Phil. 101/E2
Balabanovo, Rus. 74/H5
Balad, Iraq 115/F3
Baladagh (mtn.), Iran 115/F3
Balagansk, Rus. 90/E1
Bālāghāt, India 108/D4
Balaguer, Sp. 53/F2
Balaiselasa, Indo. 101/B4
Balaitous (peak), Fr. 50/C5
Balak, Afg. 110/A2
Balakhna, Rus. 75/J4
Balaklava, Austl. 155/H5
Balaklava, Ukr. 79/J3
Balakliya, Ukr. 74/F2
Balakovo, Rus. 75/J1
Balambangan, Malay. 103/D4
Balamorghāb, Afg. 110/A2
Balan, Gui. 132/C4
Balan, Rom. 78/C4
Bālan, Rom. 78/C4
Balang, Phil. 100/C4
Balangala, D.R. Congo 134/D5
Balangero, It. 70/D2
Balāngīr, India 108/D4
Balantak, Indo. 103/G4
Balao, Ecu. 220/B1
Bālāqer, Egypt 129/B4
Balaram, India 109/F4
Balashikha, Rus. 75/W9
Balashov, Rus. 79/M2
Balasore (Baleshwar), India 109/H3
Balassagyarmat, Hun. 49/K4
Balatina, Mol. 78/D4
Balaton (lake), Hun. 73/H1
Balatonfenyves, Hun. 56/C2
Balatonfüred, Hun. 56/C2
Balatonlelle, Hun. 56/C2
Balatonszentgyörgy, Hun. 56/C2
Balbac, Phil. 100/C4
Balbieriškis, Lith. 47/K4
Balbina, Rus. ...
Balboa (nbrhd.), Ca, US 196/A2
Balbriggan, Ire. 40/B1
Balcarce, Arg. 224/D5
Balcarres, Sk, Can. 185/H3
Balch Springs, Tx, US 180/L7
Balchik, Bul. 57/J4
Balclutha, NZ 159/B4

Balcombe, Eng, UK 43/F4
Bald (hill), Il, US 192/C2
Bald (peak), Va, US 193/G2
Balfour, Iver, Ire. 38/D2
Bald (pt.), Austl. 154/C5
Bald (mtn.), Va, US 174/D4
Bald (peak), WV, US 193/H1
Bald Eagle (lake), Mn, US 187/M9
Bald Knob, Ar, US 183/J3
Bald Rock NP, Austl. 156/E1
Baldock, Eng, UK 43/F3
Baldone, Lat. 47/L3
Baldur, Mb, Can. 186/D3
Baldwin, Fl, US 195/H5
Baldwin, Ga, US 193/F3
Baldwin, La, US 194/C3
Baldwin, Mi, US 190/D3
Baldwin, ND, US 186/D4
Baldwin, NY, US 199/L9
Baldwin City, Ks, US 183/G1
Baldwin Park, Ca, US 178/D3
Baldwincumber, Ire. ...
Baldwinsville, NY, US 191/H3
Baldwyn, Ms, US 192/C3
Baldy (mtn.), Az, US 179/H4
Baldy (peak), Az, US 179/H4
Baldy (mtn.), Mt, US 175/K3
Baldy (mt.), Or, US 176/E1
Baldy Beacon, Belz. 206/D2
Bale (prov.), Eth. 136/D4
Bale Mountains NP, Eth. 136/C4
Bakere, D.R. Congo 139/E2
Baleares (Balearic) (isls.), Sp. 53/G3
Balearic (isls.), Sp. 72/D3
Baleares (Baleares) (isls.), Sp. 53/G3
Baleine, Grande Rivière de la 171/J2
Baleine, Petite Rivière de la 171/J2
Baleine (riv.), Qu, Can. 171/J3
Balen, Belg. 61/E1
Baler, Phil. 100/C2
Balerna, Swi. 67/F6
Baleshwar (Balasore), India 109/H3
Baley, Rus. 90/H1
Baléyara, Niger 133/F3
Balezino, Rus. 75/M4
Balfour, BC, Can. 174/F3
Balfour, SAfr. 142/E2
Balfour, Sc, UK 39/W8
Balgatay, Mong. 90/D2
Balguntay, China 111/E3
Balhaf, Yem. 136/D2
Balhannah, Austl. 155/M8
Balikesir (prov.), Turk. 76/C5
Balikesir, Turk. 76/C5
Balikpapan, Indo. 103/J4
Balimbing, Indo. 101/C4
Balimbing, Phil. 101/E2
Balimo, PNG 153/F1
Baling, Malay. 101/C1
Balingasag, Phil. 100/D3
Bālinge, Swe. 46/G2
Balingen, Ger. 67/E1
Balintang (chan.), Phil. 106/D1
Baljennie, Sk, Can. 175/L1
Balk, Neth. 58/C3
Balkan (prov.), Trkm. 77/K3
Balkassar, Pak. 110/C4
Balkhash (lake), Kaz. 75/J4
Balkhash, Kaz. 75/J4
Balla, La, US ...
Ball, Ire. 40/A4
Balla, Ire. 40/A4
Balladonia, Austl. 154/C4
Ballaghadereen, Ire. 40/A4
Ballan, Austl. 157/B3
Ballan, Ire. ...
Balş, Rom. 57/G3
Balsall Common, Eng, UK 43/E2
Balsam Lake, Wi, US 187/K5
Bálsamo, Braz. 216/A4
Balsas, Mex. 206/B2
Balsas, Braz. 219/E4
Balsas, Braz. 219/E4
Balsorano Nuovo, It. 71/C4
Balsta, Swe. 46/G2
Balsthal, Swi. 66/D3
Balta, ND, US 186/D3
Balta, Ukr. 78/E4
Bāltāl, India 110/C2
Baltanás, Sp. 52/C2
Baltasar Brum, Uru. 225/F2
Baltay, Rus. 77/J1
Balti, Mol. 78/C4
Baltic (plain), Eur. 47/L2
Baltic (sea), Eur. 44/F5
Baltic (bar), Pol./Rus. 47/L2
Baltimore, Md, US 196/B5
Baltimore (co.), Md, US 196/B5
Baltimore-Washington, Md, US 196/B5
Baltit, India 110/C2
Baltoji Voke, Lith. 47/L4
Baltra (isl.), SLeo. ...
Baltray, Ire. 40/B1
Baltrum (isl.), Ger. 59/E1

Ballintoy, NI, UK 40/B1
Ballivián, Bol. 220/D5
Ballivor, Ire. 38/B2
Balloch, Sc, UK 39/B5
Balls (mtn.), Va, US 193/H1
Balls Harbour, ...
Ballon d'Alsace, Fr. 67/F4
Ballon de Sevance, Fr. ...
Ballston Spa, NY, US 191/J1
Ballville, Oh, US 190/E4
Ballybay, Ire. 38/D1
Ballybunnion, Ire. 38/A4
Ballycanew, Ire. 38/D4
Ballycarney, Ire. 38/D4
Ballycarry, NI, UK 40/B1
Ballycastle, NI, UK 40/B1
Ballyclare, NI, UK 40/B2
Ballyconnell, Ire. 40/A2
Ballycotton, Ire. 38/B6
Ballycumber, Ire. 38/A6
Ballydehob, Ire. 38/A6
Ballyeaston, NI, UK 40/B2
Ballyfarnan, Ire. 38/B1
Ballygar, Ire. 38/A2
Ballygawley, NI, UK 40/A2
Ballygeary, Ire. ...
Ballyglass, NI, UK 38/B2
Ballyhaise, Ire. 40/A2
Ballyhalbert, NI, UK 40/C2
Ballyhaunis, Ire. 38/B2
Ballyheige, Ire. 36/P10
Ballyhoura (mts.), Ire. 38/B5
Ballyjamesduff, Ire. 40/A2
Ballykelly, NI, UK 40/A1
Ballylanders, Ire. 38/B5
Ballyliffin, Ire. 40/A1
Ballylongford, Ire. 38/A4
Ballymahon, Ire. 38/A2
Ballymakeery, Ire. 36/P10
Ballymena (dist.), NI, UK 40/B2
Ballymena, NI, UK 40/B2
Ballymoney, Ire. 38/C3
Ballymoney, NI, UK 40/A1
Ballymore Eustace, Ire. 38/D3
Ballymote, Ire. 38/A2
Ballynacargy, Ire. 38/C2
Ballynacourty (pt.), Ire. 38/C4
Ballynahinch, NI, UK 40/C2
Ballynure, NI, UK 40/B2
Ballyporeen, Ire. 38/B5
Ballyquintin (pt.), NI, UK 40/C2
Ballyragget, Ire. 38/C4
Ballyroan, Ire. 38/C4
Ballysadare, Ire. 38/B1
Ballyshannon, Ire. 40/A2
Ballyteige (bay), Ire. 38/D5
Ballywalter, NI, UK 40/C2
Balm, Fl, US 194/L8
Balma, Ca, US 196/A3
Balmaceda, Chile 227/B5
Balmaceda (peak), Chile 227/B6
Balmain, NSW, Aus. ...
Balmedie, Sc, UK 39/D2
Balmoral, NB, Can. 188/D2
Balmedianzi, China 93/C2
Balmoral, Mb, Can. 185/J3
Balmoral, Zam. 141/F2
Balmoral Castle, Sc, UK 39/C2
Balmorhea, Tx, US 180/B2
Balmorral Beach, ...
Balnarring Beach, Austl. ...
Balneária, Arg. 224/D4
Balneário Camboriú, Braz. 225/B3
Balneário Carrasco, ...
Balneario Claromecó, PN, Arg.
Balneario de los Novillos, PN, Mex.
Balneario Pico da Ibituruna, Braz.

Balwina Aboriginal Reserve, Austl. 152/B5
Balya, Turk. 76/C5
Balykchy, Kyr. 80/H5
Balykshi, Kaz. 77/J3
Balzar, Ecu. 216/B5
Balzers, Lcht. 67/F3
Bam (prov.), Burk. 132/E3
Bam (lake), China 111/F5
Bam, Iran 115/J4
Banc D'Arguin, Mrta. 91/J1
Banc D'Arguin, PN du, Mrta. 132/A2
Banchette, It. ...
Banchory, Sc, UK 39/D2
Banco Chinchorro (isls.), Mex. 202/D4
Bancroft, La, US 180/H2
Bancroft, On, Can. 191/H2
Bamba, Mali 133/E2
Bamba, D.R. Congo 135/E4
Bāndā, India 108/C3
Banda, India 108/B3
Banda (isls.), Indo. 83/M10
Banda Aceh, Indo. 101/A1
Banda Elat, Indo. 152/D2
Bandanaira (peak), Indo. 101/B2
Banda (sea), Indo. 83/M10
Bandama Blanc (riv.), C.d'Iv. 132/D4
Bandama Rouge (riv.), C.d'Iv. 132/D4
Bandar Abbas (int'l arpt.), Iran 115/J5
Bandar Seri Begawan (cap.), Bru. 100/A4
Bandar-e Anzalī, Iran 115/G2
Bandar-e Büshehr, Iran 115/G4
Bandar-e Chārak, Iran 115/H5
Bandar-e Deylam, Iran 115/G3
Bandar-e Gaz, Iran 115/H2
Bandar-e Kīāshahr, Iran 115/G2
Bandar-e Kong, Iran 115/H5
Bandar-e Lengeh, Iran 115/H5
Bandar-e Māhshahr, Iran 115/G3
Bandar-e Maqām, Iran 115/H5
Bandar-e Moghüyeh, Iran 115/H5
Bandar-e Rīg, Iran 115/G4
Bandar-e Torkeman, Iran 115/H2
Ban Chiang (ruin), Thai. 106/C2
Ban Dan Lan Hoi, Thai. 106/C2
Bāndarchua, India 108/D4
Bandawe, Malw. 141/G1
Bandeira do Sul, Braz. 223/K6
Bandeira, Pico da (peak), Braz. 223/E4
Bandeirantes, Braz. 225/F1
Bandeirantes, Braz. 225/G2
Bandelier Nat'l Mon., NM, US 179/J3
Banderilla, Mex. 205/N7
Bandhavgarh NP, India 108/C4
Bandholm, Den. 46/D2
Bandiagara, Mali 132/E3
Bandipur, Nepal 109/E2
Bandipur NP, India 107/C4
Bandirma (gulf), Turk. 57/H5
Bandirma, Turk. 57/H5
Bandol, Fr. 70/B6
Bandon, Or, US 176/A2
Bandon, Ire. 38/B6
Bandundu (pol. reg.), D.R. Congo 138/D2
Bandundu, D.R. Congo 138/D2
Bandung, Indo. 101/C4
Bandya, Austl. 154/D3
Banegas, Bol. 221/F5
Bañeres, Sp. 53/E3
Banfangzi, China 90/F5
Banff, Sc, UK 39/D1
Banff NP, Ab,BC, Can. 174/F2
Banfora, Burk. 132/D4
Banga, CAfr. 134/B4
Bangalow, Austl. 158/D2
Bangaon, India 109/G4
Bangau (cape), Malay. 100/B4
Bangazeno, China 139/F2
Banggai (isls.), Indo. 103/F4
Banggi (isl.), Malay. 103/D4
Bangka (isl.), Indo. 101/D4
Bangka (str.), Indo. 101/D4
Bangkalan, Indo. 102/D5
Bangkaru (isl.), Indo. 101/A3
Bangkinang, Indo. 101/B4
Bangko, Indo. 101/C4
Banat (reg.), Rom.,Serb. 56/E3
Banat (int'l arpt.), Thai. 106/C3
Bangkok (Krung Thep) (cap.), Thai. 106/C3

Banatsko Novo Selo, Serb. 56/E3
Banawe, Phil. 100/C1
Banaz, Turk. 114/B2
Banbar, China 98/B2
Banbishan, China 92/H6
Banbridge (dist.), NI, UK 40/B3
Banbridge, Eng, UK 43/E2
Banc D'Arguin, Mrta. 128/A5
Banc D'Arguin, PN du, Mrta. 132/A2
Banchette, It. 68/A2
Banchory, Sc, UK 39/D2
Banco Chinchorro (isls.), Mex. 202/D4
Bancroft, La, US 180/H2
Bancroft, On, Can. 191/H2
Band Mill, Ar, US 183/J2
Banda, D.R. Congo 135/E4
Bāndā, India 108/C3
Banda, India 108/B3
Banda (isls.), Indo. 83/M10
Banda Aceh, Indo. 101/A1
Banda Elat, Indo. 152/D2
Bandar Behestī, Iran 113/H3
Bandar Seri Begawan (cap.), Bru. 100/A4
Bandar-e Anzalī, Iran 115/G2
Bandar-e Büshehr, Iran 115/G4
Bandar-e Chārak, Iran 115/H5
Bandar-e Deylam, Iran 115/G3
Bandar-e Gaz, Iran 115/H2
Bandar-e Kīāshahr, Iran 115/G2
Bandar-e Kong, Iran 115/H5
Bandar-e Lengeh, Iran 115/H5
Bandar-e Māhshahr, Iran 115/G3
Bandar-e Maqām, Iran 115/H5
Bandar-e Moghüyeh, Iran 115/H5
Bandar-e Rīg, Iran 115/G4
Bandar-e Torkeman, Iran 115/H2
Bāndarchua, India 108/D4
Bandawe, Malw. 141/G1
Bandeira do Sul, Braz. 223/K6
Bandeira, Pico da (peak), Braz. 223/E4
Bandeirantes, Braz. 225/F1
Ban Houay Pamon, Laos 106/C2
Ban Houayxay, Laos 106/C2
Ban Kadian, Laos 106/D3
Ban Kantang, Thai. 107/H6
Ban Kapong, Thai. 106/C3
Ban Kariang, Thai. 106/B3
Ban Hong, Thai. 106/B2
Ban Kengkok, Laos 105/J4
Ban Kha, Laos 106/E3
Ban Khampho, Laos 106/D3
Ban Khlong Yai, Thai. 106/C4
Ban Khok Kloi, Thai. 107/G6
Ban Khon, Laos 106/D4
Ban Khuan Niang, Thai. 107/J6
Ban Kui Nua, Thai. 106/C3
Ban Laem, Thai. 106/C3
Ban Len, Laos 105/H4
Ban Loboy, Laos 106/D2
Ban Mdrack, Viet. 107/E3
Ban Mong, Viet. 106/D2
Ban Muangsen, Laos 106/D2
Ban Na Nang, Laos 106/D3
Ban Na Phao, Laos 106/D2
Ban Na San, Thai. 107/H6
Ban Nakala, Laos 106/D3
Ban Nambak, Laos 106/C1
Ban Pak Phanang, Thai. 106/D4
Ban Panghai, Thai. 106/D4
Ban Phai, Thai. 106/C2
Ban Phon, Laos 106/D3
Ban Rai, Thai. 106/C3
Ban Saka, Laos 106/C2
Ban Sieou, Laos 106/C1
Ban Ta Fa, Laos 106/C2
Ban Tak, Thai. 106/B2
Ban Thabok, Laos 106/D2
Ban Thieng, Laos 106/D3
Ban Tung, Laos 106/D2
Ban Woen, Laos 106/C1
Ban Xay, Laos 106/C1
Ban Xebang-Nouan, Laos 106/D3
Bang Lang NP, Thai. 106/D5
Bang Mun Nak, Thai. 106/C2
Bang Phli, Thai. 106/C3
Bang Saphan, Thai. 106/C3
Bang Yai, Thai. 106/C3
Bangalow, Austl. 158/D2
Bangaon, India 109/H4
Bangau (mt.), PNG 153/G1
Bangeta (mt.), PNG 153/G1
Banggai (isls.), Indo. 103/F4
Bangil, Indo. 101/H4
Bangka (isl.), Indo. 83/K10
Bangka (str.), Indo. 101/D4
Bangkalan, Indo. 102/D5
Bangkaru (isl.), Indo. 101/A3
Bangkinang, Indo. 101/B4
Bangko, Indo. 101/C4
Banat (reg.), Rom.,Serb. 56/E3
Banat (int'l arpt.), Thai. 106/C3
Bangkok (Krung Thep) (cap.), Thai. 106/C3

268
Beagle – Berni

Beagle Bay Abor. Rsv., Austl. 152/A4
Beagle Bay Mission, Austl. 152/A4
Beal (range), Austl. 158/A4
Béal Traversier, Pic du (peak), Fr. 70/C3
Bealanana, Madg. 143/J6
Beale AFB, Ca, US 176/C4
Beals (cr.), Tx, US 180/D1
Beaminster, Eng, UK 42/D5
Beampingaratra (ridge), Madg. 143/H9
Beamsville, On, Can. 190/U9
Bear (hills), Sk, Can. 175/K1
Bear (isl.), Nor. 80/B2
Bear (mt.), Ak, US 201/K3
Bear (mt.), Ak, US 201/K2
Bear (riv.), Ca, US 176/C4
Bear, De, US 198/C4
Bear (hill), Ne, US 184/D3
Bear (mtn.), SD, US 184/C2
Bear (lake), Ut, US 172/D3
Bear (cr.), Wy, US 184/B3
Bear Creek, Al, US 192/D3
Bear Lake, Mi, US 190/C2
Bear Lake NWR, Id, US 177/H2
Bear Lodge (mts.), Wy, US 184/B1
Bear River, NS, Can. 188/E3
Bear River (bay), Ut, US 177/G3
Bear River NWR, Ut, US 177/G3
Bear Town, Ms, US 194/C2
Beara (reg.), Ire. 38/A6
Bearden, Ar, US 183/H4
Bearden, Ok, US 183/F3
Beardmore, On, Can. 187/L3
Beardstown, Il, US 185/J3
Bearfort (mtn.), NJ, US 199/H7
Bearma (riv.), India 108/B4
Bearpaw (mts.), Mt, US 175/J3
Bearsden, Sc, UK 39/B5
Bearstead, Eng, UK 36/E3
Beartooth (mts.), Mt, US 177/H1
Beās (riv.), India 108/B3
Beas de Segura, Sp. 52/D3
Beasain, Sp. 50/B5
Beata (cape), DRep. 203/G4
Beata (pt.), DRep. 207/J2
Beata (isl.), Thai. 207/J2
Beatenberg, Swi. 66/D4
Beatrice, Zim. 141/F3
Beatrice, Ne, US 185/F3
Beatrice (cape), Austl. 153/E3
Beattie, Ks, US 185/F4
Beattock, Sc, UK 39/C6
Beatty, Nv, US 178/D2
Beattystown, NJ, US 198/D2
Beattyville, Ky, US 192/F2
Beau Bassin-Rose Hill, Mrts. 143/T15
Beaucaire, Fr. 70/A5
Beaucamps-le-Vieux, Fr. 60/A4
Beauceville, Qu, Can. 188/B2
Beauchamp, Fr. 36/J4
Beauchastel, Fr. 70/A3
Beaucourt, Fr. 66/C3
Beaudesert, Austl. 158/D4
Beaufort, Fr. 66/B4
Beaufort, Lux. 61/F4
Beaufort, Fr. 70/C1
Beaufort, Austl. 156/B3
Beaufort (sea), Can.,US 163/C2
Beaufort, Malay. 100/A4
Beaufort, SC, US 193/G4
Beaufort, NC, US 193/J3
Beaufort (inlet), NC, US 193/J3
Beaufort Castle (ruins), Leb. 117/D2
Beaufort Marine Corps Air Base, SC, US 193/G4
Beaufort West, SAfr. 142/C4
Beaufort-en-Vallée, Fr. 63/E6
Beaugency, Fr. 63/G5
Beauharnois, Qu, Can. 191/K2
Beauharnois (co.), Qu, Can. 189/M7
Beaujolais (mts.), Fr. 50/F4
Beaulieu, Eng, UK 43/E5
Beaulieu-sur-Mer, Fr. 70/D5
Beauly, Sc, UK 39/B2
Beauly (riv.), Sc, UK 39/B2
Beauly Firth (lake), Sc, UK 39/B2
Beaumaris, Wal, UK 40/D5
Beaumes-de-Venise, Fr. 70/B4
Beaumesnil, Fr. 63/F2
Beaumont, Fr. 62/D1
Beaumont, Belg. 61/D3
Beaumont, Ms, US 194/D2
Beaumont, Ca, US 196/D3
Beaumont, Fr. 50/E4
Beaumont, Ab, Can. 175/H1
Beaumont, Tx, US 181/G2
Beaumont-de-Lomagne, Fr. 50/D5
Beaumont-le-Roger, Fr. 63/F2
Beaumont-lès-Valence, Fr. 70/A3
Beaumont-sur-Oise, Fr. 36/J4
Beaumont-sur-Sarthe, Fr. 63/F4
Beaupréau, Fr. 63/E6
Beauquesne, Fr. 60/B3
Beauraing, Belg. 61/D3
Beaurainville, Fr. 60/A3
Beauregard, Ms, US 194/C2
Beaurepaire, Fr. 70/B2
Beaurevoir, Fr. 60/C4
Beausejour, Mb, Can. 186/F2
Beausoleil, Fr. 70/D5
Beautheil, Fr. 36/M5
Beautiful (mtn.), NM, US 179/H2
Beautor, Fr. 60/C4
Beauvais, Fr. 60/B5
Beauval, Fr. 60/B3
Beauvoir, Fr. 36/L6
Beaver (hills), Sk, Can. 186/C2
Beaver (riv.), Yk, Can. 170/D2
Beaver, Ak, US 201/J2
Beaver (lake), Ar, US 183/H2
Beaver (cr.), Co, US 184/C4
Beaver (cr.), Co,Ks, US 184/D4
Beaver, La, US 194/B2
Beaver (isl.), Mi, US 190/D2
Beaver (cr.), Ne, US 184/E3
Beaver, Oh, US 193/F1
Beaver, Ok, US 182/D2
Beaver, Pa, US 190/F4
Beaver, Ut, US 179/F1
Beaver (riv.), Ut, US 177/J4
Beaver, Wa, US 174/B3
Beaver (dam), Wi, US 185/K2
Beaver Bay, Mn, US 187/J4
Beaver City, Ne, US 184/E3
Beaver Creek, Yk, Can. 201/K3
Beaver Crossing, Ne, US 185/F3
Beaver Dam, Ky, US 192/D2
Beaver Dam, Wi, US 185/K2
Beaver Dam (lake), Wi, US 185/K2
Beaver Falls, Pa, US 190/F4
Beaver Meadows, Pa, US 198/C2
Beaver Springs, Pa, US 198/A2
Beaverbank, NS, Can. 188/F3
Beavercreek, Oh, US 190/D5
Beaverdam, Va, US 193/J2
Beaverdell, BC, Can. 174/E3
Beaverhead (mts.), Mt, US 177/G1
Beaverhead (riv.), Mt, US 177/G1
Beaverhill (lake), Ab, Can. 175/H1
Beaverton, On, Can. 191/G2
Beaverton, Mi, US 190/D3
Beaverton, Or, US 176/B1
Beavertown, Pa, US 198/A2
Beāwar, India 104/B2
Bebe, Tx, US 181/F3
Bébédjia, Chad 134/C3
Bebedouro, Braz. 225/G2
Beberibe, Braz. 219/G4
Bebington, Eng, UK 41/E5
Beboto, Chad 134/C3
Béboura Iii, CAfr. 134/C4
Bebra, Ger. 59/G7
Becal, Mex. 206/D1
Bécancour, Qu, Can. 191/K1
Beccles, Eng, UK 43/H2
Bečej, Serb. 56/E3
Becerreá, Sp. 52/B1
Bechar, Alg. 129/E3
Bechar (wilaya), Alg. 128/E3
Becharof (lake), Ak, US 201/G4
Bechhofen, Ger. 61/G5
Bechhofen, Ger. 64/D4
Bechtheim, Ger. 64/B3
Bechyně, Czh. 65/H4
Becida, Mn, US 187/G4
Beckdorf, Ger. 59/G2
Beckenham (nbrhd.), Eng, UK 36/D2
Beckenried, Swi. 67/E4
Becker, Ms, US 192/C4
Beckingen, Ger. 61/F5
Beckingham, Eng, UK 41/H5
Beckley, WV, US 193/G2
Beckton, Wy, US 177/K1
Beckum, Ger. 59/F5
Beckville, Tx, US 181/G1
Beckwourth, Ca, US 176/C4
Beclean, Rom. 57/G2
Bécon-les-Granits, Fr. 63/E5
Becs de Bosson (peak), Swi. 66/D5
Bedale, Eng, UK 41/G3
Bédaoyo, Chad 134/C4
Bédarieux, Fr. 50/E5
Bédarrides, Fr. 70/A4
Bedaya, Chad 134/C3
Bedburg, Ger. 61/F2
Bedburg-Hau, Ger. 58/D5
Beddau, Wal, UK 42/C3
Beddgelert, Wal, UK 40/D5
Bedelē, Eth. 135/H3
Beder, Den. 46/D3
Bederkesa, Ger. 59/G1
Bederkesa, Ger. 59/F1
Bedēsa, Eth. 136/B3
Bedford (cape), Austl. 158/B1
Bedford, Qu, Can. 191/K2
Bedford, SAfr. 142/D4
Bedford, Eng, UK 43/F2
Bedford, Ia, US 185/G3
Bedford, In, US 192/D1
Bedford, Ky, US 192/E1
Bedford, NH, US 191/L3
Bedford, Pa, US 191/G4
Bedford, Tx, US 180/K7
Bedford, Va, US 193/H2
Bedford, Wy, US 177/H2
Bedford Hills, NY, US 199/E1
Bedford Level (phys. reg.), Eng, UK 43/F2
Bedford Park, Il, US 197/Q16
Bedfordshire (co.), Eng, UK 43/F2
Bedias, Tx, US 181/G2
Bédiondo, Chad 134/C3
Bedlington, Eng, UK 41/G1
Bedmond, Eng, UK 36/B1
Bedok (nbrhd.), Sing. 101/J6
Bedong, Malay. 101/C1
Bedonia, It. 68/C4
Bédouaram, Niger 134/B2
Bedourie, Austl. 155/H3
Bedretto, Swi. 67/E5
Bedrock, Co, US 179/H1
Bedsted, Den. 46/C3
Bedum, Neth. 58/D2
Bedwas, Wal, UK 42/C3
Bedworth, Eng, UK 43/E2
Bee (cr.), Eng, UK 119/F6
Bee Branch, Ar, US 183/H3
Bee Spring, Ky, US 192/D2
Beebe, Ar, US 183/J3
Beech Grove, In, US 190/C5
Beecher Falls, Vt, US 191/L2
Beecher Island, Co, US 184/C4
Beechgrove, Tn, US 192/D3
Beechworth, Austl. 157/C3
Beechy, Sk, Can. 175/L2
Beek, Neth. 61/E2
Beek, Neth. 58/C5
Beekman, La, US 183/J4
Beelbangera, Austl. 157/C2
Beelen, Ger. 59/F5
Beeler, Ks, US 182/D1
Beelitz, Ger. 48/P7
Beenleigh, Austl. 158/D4
Beer, Eng, UK 42/C5
Beer (pt.), Eng, UK 42/C5
Be'er Menuẖa, Isr. 116/D4
Be'er Sheva' (Beersheba), Isr. 117/B6
Beerato, Som. 136/C3
Beerfelden, Ger. 64/B3
Be'eri, Isr. 117/A6
Beernem, Belg. 60/C1
Beersheba (Be'er Sheva'), Isr. 117/B6
Beerzel, Belg. 61/D1
Beesel, Neth. 58/D6
Beeville, Tx, US 180/F3
Befale, D.R. Congo 139/E2
Befandriana, Madg. 143/G8
Befandriana, Madg. 143/J6
Befasy, Madg. 143/H8
Befori, D.R. Congo 139/E2
Beforona, Madg. 143/J7
Befotaka, Madg. 143/H8
Befotaka, Madg. 143/J6
Beg (lake), NI, UK 40/B2
Bega, Austl. 157/D3
Bega (riv.), Ger. 59/F5
Bega Veche (riv.), Cro. 56/E3
Begamganj, India 108/B4
Begamganj, Bang. 109/H4
Bégard, Fr. 62/B3
Begarslan (peak), Trkm. 77/K4
Begejci, Serb. 56/E3
Beggs, Ok, US 183/F3
Bēgī, Eth. 135/G3
Begichev (isl.), Rus. 81/M2
Begna (riv.), Nor. 44/D3
Begoml', Bela. 47/N4
Begumpet (int'l arpt.), India 107/C2
Begunitsy, Rus. 47/N2
Begusarai, India 109/F3
Béhague (pt.), FrG. 218/D1
Behāla, India 104/E3
Behala (str.), Indo. 102/B4
Behamberg, Aus. 65/H6
Behara, Madg. 143/H9
Behat, India 110/D4
Behbahān, Iran 115/G4
Beheloka, Madg. 143/G8
Behenjy-Afovany, Madg. 143/H7
Behleg, China 90/C4
Béhoust, Fr. 36/H5
Behren-lès-Forbach, Fr. 61/F5
Behri (riv.), Nepal 108/C1
Behshahr, Iran 115/H2
Bei (mts.), China 80/K5
Bei'an, China 91/K2
Beiba, China 90/F5
Beibei, China 99/E2
Beida (riv.), China 90/D4
Beidianzi, China 93/A4
Beierfeld, Ger. 65/F1
Beigantang (isl.), Tai. 99/J3
Beigua (peak), It. 68/B5
Beiguo, China 92/L8
Beihai, China 99/F4
Beijing (prov.), China 90/H3
Beijing (cap.), China 92/H7
Beijing Capital (int'l arpt.), China 92/H6
Beilen, Neth. 58/D3
Beiling, China 99/G3
Beiliu, China 99/F4
Beilngries, Ger. 65/E4
Beilstein, Ger. 64/C4
Beilu (riv.), China 90/C5
Beilun (pass), China 99/E4
Bein Tharsuinn (peak), Sc, UK 39/B1
Beinamar, Chad 134/B3
Beinasco, It. 70/D2
Beindersheim, Ger. 64/B3
Beinn a' Chuallaich (peak), Sc, UK 39/B3
Beinn a' Ghlò (peak), Sc, UK 39/C3
Beinn a' Mheadhoin (lake), Sc, UK 39/B2
Beinn Bhàn (peak), Sc, UK 39/A3
Beinn Bheula (peak), Sc, UK 39/B4
Beinn Bhrotain (peak), Sc, UK 39/C2
Beinn Bhuidhe (peak), Sc, UK 39/B4
Beinn Bhuidhe Mhór (peak), Sc, UK 39/B2
Beinn Dearg (peak), Sc, UK 39/B1
Beinn Dearg (peak), Sc, UK 39/C3
Beinn Dòrain (peak), Sc, UK 39/B4
Beinn Eighe (peak), Sc, UK 39/A1
Beinn Heasgarnich (peak), Sc, UK 39/B3
Beinn Mholach (peak), Sc, UK 39/B3
Beinn Mhór (peak), Sc, UK 39/A4
Beinwil am See, Swi. 66/E3
Beipiao, China 92/E2
Beira (int'l arpt.), Moz. 141/G3
Beira, Moz. 141/G3
Beira Alta, Ang. 138/C5
Beirong, China 99/F2
Beiru (riv.), China 92/C4
Beirut (int'l arpt.), Leb. 117/C1
Beirut (Bayrūt) (cap.), Leb. 117/C1
Beiseker, Ab, Can. 175/H2
Beishan, China 90/D3
Beishan, China 99/F3
Beit Jann, Isr. 117/C3
Beitbridge, Zim. 141/F4
Beith, Sc, UK 39/B5
Beiuş, Rom. 56/F2
Beizhen, China 93/A2
Beja, Port. 52/B3
Beja (dist.), Port. 52/A4
Beja, Tun. 130/L6
Beja (gov.), Tun. 130/L6
Bejaïa, Alg. 130/H4
Bejaïa (wilaya), Alg. 130/H4
Béjar, Sp. 52/C2
Bejhi (riv.), Pak. 113/J3
Bekasi, Indo. 101/D4
Bekdash, Trkm. 77/K4
Békés (prov.), Hun. 56/E2
Békés, Hun. 56/E2
Békéscsaba, Hun. 56/E2
Bekilli, Turk. 114/B2
Bekily, Madg. 143/H9
Bekitro, Madg. 143/H9
Bekodoka, Madg. 143/H7
Bek'ojī, Eth. 136/A4
Bekopaka, Madg. 143/H7
Bekoropoka, Madg. 143/G8
Bekwai, Gha. 133/E5
Bel, La, US 194/B2
Bel Air, Md, US 198/B4
Bel Air South, Md, US 198/B5
Bel Aire, Ks, US 183/F2
Belá, Slvk. 49/K4
Bela, Pak. 113/J3
Bela, D.R. Congo 139/G2
Belā, India 104/D2
Bela Crkva, Serb. 56/E3
Bela Cruz, Braz. 219/F3
Bela Palanka, Serb. 56/F4
Bělá pod Bezdězem, Czh. 65/H1
Belā Pratāpgarh, India 108/C3
Bela Vista, Ang. 140/C2
Bela Vista, Braz. 225/E2
Bela Vista, Moz. 143/F2
Bela Vista de Goiás, Braz. 222/C3
Bela Vista do Paraíso, Braz. 225/G2
Belabérim (well), Niger 134/B2
Bélabo, Camr. 134/B4
Belair Rec. Pk., Austl. 155/M9
Belampalli, India 107/C2
Belan (riv.), India 108/D3
Belanak (cape), Malay. 101/C1
Belang, Indo. 103/F3
Belarus (ctry.) 29/G3
Belas, Port. 53/P10
Belawan, Indo. 101/B2
Belaya (riv.), Rus. 80/F4
Belaya (peak), Eth. 135/H3
Belaya Glina, Rus. 79/L4
Belaya Kalitva, Rus. 79/L3
Belbo (riv.), It. 68/B3
Bełchatów, Pol. 49/K3
Belchen (peak), Ger. 66/D2
Belcher, La, US 183/H4
Belcher (isls.), Can. 163/J4
Belcher (isls.), On, Can. 171/H3
Belcher (chan.), Nun, Can. 171/S7
Belchite, Sp. 53/E2
Belcourt, ND, US 186/E3
Belda, India 109/F4
Beldānga, India 109/G4
Belebey, Rus. 75/M5
Beled Weyne, Som. 136/C4
Belefuanai, Libr. 132/C5
Bélel, Camr. 134/B4
Belém, Braz. 219/H4
Belém, Braz. 218/D3
Belém de São Francisco, Braz. 219/G5
Belem Tower, Port. 53/P10
Belén, Arg. 224/C3
Belén, Bol. 221/E5
Belén, Chile 224/B1
Belén, Nic. 202/D5
Belen, Turk. 116/E1
Belen, Turk. 116/C1
Belén, Uru. 224/E4
Belen, NM, US 179/J3
Belén de Escobar, Arg. 227/J11
Belén de Umbría, Col. 219/K7
Belene, Bul. 57/G4
Bélep (isls.), NCal., Fr. 161/T11
Beles Wenz (riv.), Eth. 135/G3
Belesar (res.), Sp. 52/B1
Belev, Rus. 76/F1
Belfair, Wa, US 197/B3
Belfast (dist.), NI, UK 40/B2
Belfast (cap.), NI, UK 40/C2
Belfast, SAfr. 143/E2
Belfast Lough (bay), NI, UK 40/C2
Belfaux, Swi. 66/D4
Belfield, ND, US 186/C4
Bēlfodiyo, Eth. 135/G3
Belford, Eng, UK 39/E5
Belfort (dept.), Fr. 66/C2
Belfort, Fr. 66/C2
Belfountain, On, Can. 190/S8
Belfry, Mt, US 177/J1
Belgioioso, It. 68/C3
Belgium (ctry.) 48/C3
Belgorod, Rus. 79/J2
Belgorodskaya Oblast, Rus. 76/F2
Belgrade, Mn, US 187/G5
Belgrade, Mo, US 192/B2
Belgrade (Beograd) (cap.), Serb. 56/E3
Belgreen, Al, US 192/D3
Belhavel (lake), Ire. 38/B1
Belhaven, NC, US 193/J3
Beli Drim (riv.), Alb.,Serb. 56/E4
Beli Manastir, Cro. 56/D3
Beli Timok (riv.), Serb. 56/F4
Belidzhi, Rus. 77/J4
Bélinga, Gabon 138/C2
Belington, WV, US 193/H1
Belinskiy, Rus. 77/G1
Belinyu, Indo. 101/D3
Belitsa, Bul. 55/H2
Belitung (isl.), Indo. 102/C4
Belize, Ang. 138/C4
Belize (riv.), Belz. 206/D2
Belize (ctry.) 206/D2
Belize City, Belz. 206/D2
Bélizon, FrG. 218/C1
Beljanica (peak), Serb. 56/E3
Belk, Tx, US 183/G4
Belknap (mtn.), NH, US 191/L3
Bel'kovskiy (isl.), Rus. 81/N2
Bell, Ger. 61/G3
Bell (isl.), Nf, Can. 189/L2
Bell, Fl, US 195/G3
Bell, Ca, US 196/F8
Bell, Austl. 158/C4
Bell (pt.), Austl. 155/G5
Bell (riv.), Austl. 157/D1
Bell (riv.), Qu, Can. 171/J4
Bell (pen.), Nun, Can. 171/H2
Bell (pt.), PNG 153/F2
Bell Gardens, Ca, US 196/F8
Bell Rock (Inchcape) (isl.), Sc, UK 39/D4
Bell Ville, Arg. 224/D5
Bella Flor, Bol. 220/E3
Bella Vista, Arg. 224/E4
Bella Vista, Arg. 224/C3
Bella Vista, Bol. 221/F4
Bella Vista, Par. 225/E2
Bella Vista, Ar, US 183/G2
Bellac, Fr. 50/D3
Bellachat (peak), Fr. 70/C1
Bellaco, Uru. 227/K10
Bellaghy, NI, UK 40/B2
Bellagio, It. 67/F6
Bellaire, Mi, US 190/D2
Bellaire, Oh, US 190/F4
Bellaire, Tx, US 181/M9
Bellamy, Al, US 192/C4
Bellananagh, Ire. 38/C2
Bellano, It. 67/F5
Bellaria, It. 69/F5
Bellary, India 107/C3
Bellata, Austl. 156/D1
Bellavista (cape), It. 54/A3
Bellavista, Ecu. 220/J7
Bellavista, Peru 220/B2
Bellavista, Peru 220/B2
Bellbird, Austl. 157/E1
Belle, Mo, US 183/J1
Belle (riv.), On, Can. 197/G7
Belle, WV, US 193/G1
Belle Chasse, La, US 194/D3
Belle Fourche (res.), SD, US 186/C5
Belle Fourche, SD, US 184/C1
Belle Fourche (riv.), Wy,SD, US 184/"B2,
Belle Glade, Fl, US 195/H4
Belle Haven, Va, US 198/A6
Belle Isle, Fl, US 194/N7
Belle Isle (str.), NF, Can. 163/M4
Belle Plaine, Ks, US 183/F2
Belle Plaine, Ia, US 185/H3
Belle River, On, Can. 197/G7
Belle Terre, NY, US 199/E2
Belle Yella, Libr. 132/C5
Belle-Anse, Haiti 207/H2
Belle-Ile (isl.), Fr. 50/B3
Belle-Isle-en-Terre, Fr. 62/B3
Belleair, Fl, US 194/K8
Belleair Beach, Fl, US 194/K8
Belleair Bluffs, Fl, US 194/K8
Belleek, NI, UK 40/B3
Bellefontaine, Oh, US 190/E4
Bellefontaine, Ms, US 192/C4
Bellefonte, Ar, US 183/H2
Bellefonte, Pa, US 191/H4
Bellefonte, De, US 198/C4
Bellegarde-sur-Valserine, Fr. 66/B5
Bellême, Fr. 63/F4
Bellenberg, Ger. 67/G1
Bellencombre, Fr. 63/G1
Bellenden Ker NP, Austl. 158/B2
Belleoram, Nf, Can. 189/K2
Belleplain, NJ, US 198/D5
Bellerive-sur-Allier, Fr. 50/E3
Bellerose, NY, US 199/L9
Belleu, Fr. 60/C5
Belleview, Fl, US 195/G3
Belleview, Mo, US 192/B2
Belleville, On, Can. 191/H2
Belleville, Fr. 66/A5
Belleville, Ar, US 183/H3
Belleville, Il, US 192/C1
Belleville, Ks, US 184/F4
Belleville, Mi, US 197/E7
Belleville, NJ, US 199/J8
Belleville, Pa, US 191/H4
Belleville-sur-Meuse, Fr. 61/E5
Bellevue, Id, US 177/F2
Bellevue, Ia, US 185/J2
Bellevue, Md, US 198/B6
Bellevue, Ne, US 185/G3
Bellevue, Oh, US 190/E4
Bellevue, Wa, US 174/C4
Belley, Fr. 66/B6
Bellflower, Ca, US 196/F8
Bellheim, Ger. 64/B4
Bellignat, Fr. 66/B5
Bellinge, Den. 46/D4
Bellingen, Austl. 156/E1
Bellingham, Eng, UK 41/F1
Bellingham, Mn, US 185/F1
Bellingham, Wa, US 174/C3
Bellingrath Gardens and Home, Al, US 194/D2
Bellingshausen (sea), Ant. 228/U
Bellingshausen (isl.), FrPol. 161/K6
Bellingwolde, Neth. 59/E2
Bellinzago Novarese, It. 68/B2
Bellinzona, Swi. 67/F5
Belliveau Cove, NS, Can. 188/D3
Bellizzi, It. 71/D6
Bellmawr, NJ, US 198/C4
Bellmead, Tx, US 181/F2
Bellmore, NY, US 199/L9
Bello, Col. 219/K6
Bellona, It. 71/D5
Bellona Reefs (reef), NCal., Fr. 160/E7
Bellot (str.), Nun, Can. 170/G1
Bellows Falls, Vt, US 191/K3
Bellport, NY, US 199/F2
Bells, Tn, US 192/C3
Bells, Tx, US 183/F4
Bellsbank, Sc, UK 39/B6
Bellshill, Sc, UK 39/B5
Bellsite, Mb, Can. 186/D1
Belluno (prov.), It. 69/E1
Belluno, It. 51/K3
Bellville, SAfr. 142/L10
Bellville, Ga, US 193/G4
Bellville, Oh, US 190/E4
Bellville, Tx, US 180/F3
Bellwald, Swi. 66/E5
Bellwood, La, US 194/B2
Belly (riv.), Ab, Can. 175/H3
Belm, Ger. 59/F4
Belmar, NJ, US 199/D3
Bélmez, Sp. 52/C3
Belmond, Ia, US 185/H2
Belmont, Mb, Can. 186/E3
Belmont, NS, Can. 188/F3
Belmont, Ca, US 197/K11
Belmont, La, US 194/B2
Belmont, Ms, US 192/C3
Belmont, Mt, US 175/K4
Belmont, NC, US 193/G3
Belmont, Ne, US 184/C2
Belmont, NY, US 191/G3
Belmonte, Port. 52/B2
Belmonte, Sp. 52/D3
Belmonte, Braz. 223/F2
Belmopan (cap.), Belz. 206/D2
Belmullet, Ire. 37/P9
Belo, Madg. 143/G8
Belo Campo, Braz. 223/E2
Belo Horizonte, Braz. 222/E3
Belo Jardim, Braz. 219/G5
Belo-Tsiribihina, Madg. 143/H7
Beloeil, Belg. 60/C2
Beloeil, Qu, Can. 189/P6
Belogorsk, Rus. 91/K1
Beloha, Madg. 143/H9
Beloit, Ks, US 184/E4
Beloit, Wi, US 185/K2
Belokany, Azer. 77/H4
Béloko, CAfr. 134/B4
Belomorsk, Rus. 74/G2
Belondo-Kundu, D.R. Congo 138/D3
Beloomut, Rus. 74/H5
Beloozërsk, Bela. 76/C1
Belorado, Sp. 50/B5
Belorechensk, Rus. 79/K5
Belören, Turk. 114/C2
Beloretsk, Rus. 75/N5
Beloslav, Bul. 57/H4
Belovo, Bul. 55/J1
Belovo, Rus. 80/J4
Beloye (lake), Rus. 80/D3
Belozersk, Rus. 74/H3
Belozërskoye, Rus. 75/Q5
Belper, Eng, UK 41/G5
Belpre, Oh, US 190/F5
Belsand, India 109/E2
Belsay, Eng, UK 41/G1
Belt, Mt, US 175/J4
Belterra, Braz. 218/C3
Belterwijde (lake), Neth. 58/D3
Beltheim, Ger. 61/G3
Belton, Eng, UK 43/H1
Belton, Mo, US 183/G1
Belton, SC, US 193/F3
Belton, Tx, US 180/F2
Belton (lake), Tx, US 181/F2
Beltra (lake), Ire. 38/A2
Beltrán, Arg. 224/C3
Beltsville, Md, US 198/B5
Belturbet, Ire. 38/C1
Beltzville (lake), Pa, US 198/C2
Belukha (peak), Rus. 111/E2
Belumut (peak), Malay. 101/C2
Beluran, Malay. 100/B4
Belvedere, Ca, US 197/K11
Belvédère du Cirque, Fr. 70/D3
Belvedere Park, Ga, US 193/M7
Belvidere, SD, US 184/D2
Belvidere, Il, US 185/K2
Belvidere, NJ, US 198/C2
Belview, Mn, US 185/G1
Belvoir NP, Isr. 117/D3
Belwood, On, Can. 190/S8
Belyando (riv.), Austl. 145/D3
Belyayevka, Rus. 77/L2
Belynkovichi, Bela. 76/E1
Belyy (isl.), Rus. 80/G2
Belyy Yar, Rus. 80/J4
Belyye Berega, Rus. 76/E1
Belz, Ukr. 78/C2
Belzig, Ger. 48/G2
Belzoni, Ms, US 192/B4
Bełżyce, Pol. 49/M3
Bémal, CAfr. 134/C4
Bemanevika, Madg. 143/J6
Bemanevika, Madg. 143/J6
Bemaraha (plat.), Madg. 143/H7
Bemarivo (riv.), Madg. 143/H7
Bembe, Ang. 138/C4
Bembéréké, Ben. 133/F4
Bembezi (riv.), Zim. 141/F3
Bembibre, Sp. 52/B1
Bembo, Ang. 138/D5
Bemboka, Austl. 157/D3
Bembridge, Eng, UK 43/E5
Bemebesi, Zim. 141/F4
Bemetāra, India 107/D1
Bemidji, Mn, US 187/G4
Bemis, SD, US 185/F1
Bemmel, Neth. 58/C5
Bempton, Eng, UK 41/H3
Ben Aigan (hill), Sc, UK 39/C1
Ben Alder (peak), Sc, UK 39/B3
Ben Améra (well), Mrta. 128/B5
Ben Arous, Tun. 130/M6
Ben Arous (gov.), Tun. 130/M6
Ben Avon (peak), Sc, UK 39/C2
Ben Boyd NP, Austl. 157/E3
Ben Chonzie (peak), Sc, UK 39/C4
Ben Cleuch (peak), Sc, UK 39/C4
Ben Cruachan (peak), Sc, UK 39/A4
Ben Dash (peak), Ire. 38/A4
Ben Davis (pt.), NJ, US 198/C5
Ben Giang, Viet. 106/D3
Ben Guerdane, Tun. 129/H2
Ben Gurion (int'l arpt.), Isr. 117/B4
Ben Hope (peak), Sc, UK 37/R7
Ben Ime (peak), Sc, UK 39/B4
Ben Lawers (peak), Sc, UK 39/B3
Ben Ledi (peak), Sc, UK 39/B4
Ben Lomond (peak), Sc, UK 39/B4
Ben Lomond, Ca, US 178/A2
Ben Lomond NP, Austl. 156/C4
Ben Lui (peak), Sc, UK 39/B4
Ben Macdui (peak), Sc, UK 39/C2
Ben More (peak), Sc, UK 37/Q8
Ben More (peak), Sc, UK 39/B4
Ben More Assynt (peak), Sc, UK 37/R7
Ben Msik-Sidi Othmane (prov.), Mor. 130/A2
Ben Nevis (peak), Sc, UK 39/B3
Ben Quang, Viet. 106/D2
Ben Rinnes (peak), Sc, UK 39/C2
Ben Slimane, Mor. 128/D2
Ben Slimane (prov.), Mor. 130/A3
Ben Starav (peak), Sc, UK 39/A3
Ben Tee (peak), Sc, UK 39/B2
Ben Thuy, Viet. 98/E5
Ben Tirran (peak), Sc, UK 39/C3
Ben Tre, Viet. 106/D4
Ben Vane (peak), Sc, UK 39/B4
Ben Vorlich (peak), Sc, UK 39/B4
Ben Vrackie (peak), Sc, UK 39/C3
Ben Wyvis (peak), Sc, UK 39/B1
Ben Zohra (well), Alg. 128/E3
Bena, Mn, US 187/G4
Bena-Bendi, D.R. Congo 138/E4
Bena-Dibele, D.R. Congo 139/E4
Bena-Makima, D.R. Congo 139/E4
Benabarre, Sp. 53/F1
Benahmed, Mor. 128/D2
Benalla, Austl. 157/B3
Benalmádena, Sp. 52/C4
Benalto, Ab, Can. 174/G1
Benāpol, Bang. 109/G4
Benavente, Sp. 52/C1
Benavides, Bol. 221/E4
Benavides, Tx, US 181/E4
Benbane (pt.), NI, UK 40/B1
Benbecula (isl.), Sc, UK 37/Q8
Benbonyathe (peak), Austl. 155/H4
Benbrack (peak), Ire. 38/C1
Benbrook (lake), Tx, US 180/K7
Benbrook (dam), Tx, US 180/K7
Benbrook, Tx, US 180/K7
Benburb, NI, UK 40/B3
Benchley, Tx, US 181/F2
Bencubbin, Austl. 154/C4
Bend, Or, US 176/C1
Bend, Tx, US 181/E2
Benda (cape), Indo. 101/E4
Bende, Nga. 133/G5
Bendeleben (mt.), Ak, US 201/F2
Bendemeer, Austl. 156/D1
Bender Beyla, Som. 136/D3
Bender Cassim (Bosaaso), Som. 136/D3
Bendersville, Pa, US 198/A4
Bendery (Tighina), Mol. 78/E4
Bendigo, Austl. 157/B3
Bendoc, Austl. 157/D3
Bendorf, Ger. 46/C4
Bendugu, SLeo. 132/C4
Benduma, Libr. 132/C5
Bēne, Lat. 47/K3
Bene Beraq, Isr. 117/B4
Benedict (mt.), Nf, Can. 171/L3
Benediktbeuern, Ger. 67/H2
Benediktenwand (peak), Ger. 67/H2
Beneditinos, Braz. 219/F4
Benenitra, Madg. 143/H8
Benešov, Czh. 65/H3
Benevento (prov.), It. 71/D5
Benevento, It. 71/D5
Benfeld, Fr. 66/D1
Benga, Moz. 141/G3
Bengal (bay), Asia 83/H8
Bengal, Bay of (gulf), Asia 104/E4
Bengbis, Camr. 138/C2
Bengbu, China 92/D4
Benge, Wa, US 174/E4
Benghāzī, Libya 126/D1
Bengkalis, Indo. 101/C2
Bengkalis (isl.), Indo. 102/B3
Bengkayang, Indo. 102/C3
Bengkulu, Indo. 101/C3
Bengkulu (prov.), Indo. 101/C4
Bengo (riv.), Ang. 138/C5
Bengo (prov.), Ang. 138/C5
Bengo (bay), Ang. 138/C5
Bengough, Sk, Can. 186/B3
Bengtsby, Fin. 45/F4
Bengtsfors, Swe. 46/E2
Benguela, Ang. 140/B2
Benguela (prov.), Ang. 140/B2
Benguerir, Mor. 128/D2
Benguerua (isl.), Moz. 141/G4
Bengweulu (lake), Zam. 139/G5
Bengweulu (swamp), Zam. 139/G5
Beni (dept.), Bol. 221/E4
Beni (riv.), Bol. 209/C4
Beni, D.R. Congo 139/G2
Beni, Nepal 108/D1
Beni Abbes, Alg. 129/E3
Beni Bouayach, Mor. 130/C2
Beni Ensar, Mor. 130/B2
Beni Khiar, Tun. 130/M6
Beni Mellal, Mor. 128/D2
Beni Ounif, Alg. 129/E2
Beni Saf, Alg. 130/D2
Beni Tajit, Mor. 128/E2
Benicarló, Sp. 53/F2
Benicia, Ca, US 197/K10
Benidorm, Sp. 53/E3
Benifayó, Sp. 53/E3
Benin (ctry.) 133/F4
Benin City, Nga. 133/G5
Benina (int'l arpt.), Libya 126/D1
Benisa, Sp. 53/F3
Benisheikh, Nga. 134/B3
Benito, Mb, Can. 186/D2
Benito Juárez, Mex. 204/D2
Benjamin, Tx, US 182/E4
Benjamin Constant, Braz. 220/D2
Benjamín Hill, Mex. 204/C2
Benjamin, Isla (isl.), Chile 226/B5
Benkei-misaki (cape), Japan 94/B2
Benkelman, Ne, US 184/D3
Benld, Il, US 185/K4
Benllech, Wal, UK 40/D5
Benmore (peak), Ire. 38/A1
Bennachie (hill), Sc, UK 39/D2
Bennan (pt.), Sc, UK 39/A6
Benndale, Ms, US 194/D2
Benneckenstein, Ger. 59/H5
Bennett, BC, Can. 201/M3
Bennett (isl.), Rus. 81/Q2
Bennett, Co, US 184/B4
Bennett (peak), Co, US 182/A2
Bennett, Wi, US 187/J4
Bennettsbridge, Ire. 38/C4
Bennettsville, SC, US 193/H3
Bennichchab, Mrta. 132/B2
Bennington, Id, US 177/H2
Bennington, Ks, US 183/F1
Bennington, Ne, US 185/F3
Bennington, Ok, US 183/F3
Bennington, Vt, US 191/K3
Bénodet, Fr. 62/A5
Benoit, Ms, US 192/B4
Benom (peak), Malay. 101/C2
Bénoué (riv.), Camr. 134/B3
Bénoue, PN de la, Camr. 134/B3
Benover, Eng, UK 36/E3
Benoy, Chad 134/C3
Bensenville, Il, US 197/Q16
Bensheim, Ger. 64/B3
Benson, Sk, Can. 186/C3
Benson, Az, US 179/G5
Benson, La, US 180/H2
Benson, Mn, US 187/G5
Benson, NC, US 193/H3
Bensonhurst (nbrhd.), NY, US 199/K9
Benta (riv.), Hun. 57/Q10
Benta Seberang, Malay. 101/C1
Bentham, Eng, UK 41/F3
Bentheim, Ger. 59/E4
Benti, Gui. 132/B4
Bentiaba, Ang. 140/B2
Bentiaba (riv.), Ang. 140/B2
Bentinck (isl.), Austl. 153/E4
Bentiu, Sudan 135/F3
Bentley, Eng, UK 41/G4
Bentley, Eng, UK 36/A3
Bentley, ND, US 186/C4
Bentley, Ok, US 183/F3
Bento Gonçalves, Braz. 225/G4
Benton, Ar, US 183/H3
Benton, Il, US 192/C2
Benton, Ky, US 192/C2
Benton, La, US 183/H4
Benton, Ms, US 192/B4
Benton, Mo, US 192/C2
Benton, Pa, US 198/B1
Benton, Tn, US 192/E3
Benton Harbor, Mi, US 190/C3
Benton Lake NWR, Mt, US 175/J4
Bentong, Malay. 101/C2
Bentonia, Ms, US 192/B4
Bentonville, Ar, US 183/G2
Bentonville, Va, US 193/H1
Bent's Old Fort Nat'l Hist. Site, Co, US 182/C1
Benua Martinus, Indo. 102/D3
Benue (state), Nga. 133/H5
Benue (riv.), Nga. 119/C4
Benxi, China 93/B2
Benxi, China 93/C2
Beo, Indo. 103/G3
Beočin, Serb. 56/D3
Beoga, Indo. 103/J4
Beograd (int'l arpt.), Serb. 56/E3
Beograd (Belgrade) (cap.), Serb. 56/E3
Beohāri, India 108/C3
Béoumi, C.d'Iv. 132/D5
Béoux (riv.), Fr. 70/B3
Beowawe, Nv, US 176/E3
Beppu (bay), Japan 96/B4
Beppu, Japan 96/B4
Bequia (isl.), StV. 203/N9
Bequimão, Braz. 219/E3
Bera, Bang. 109/G3
Beragh, NI, UK 40/A2
Beraketa, Madg. 143/H8
Beraketa, Madg. 143/H9
Beramanja, Madg. 143/J6
Berane, Mont. 56/D4
Beras Basah (cape), Malay. 101/C2
Berasia, India 108/A4
Berat, Alb. 55/F2
Beratus (peak), Indo. 103/E4
Beratzhausen, Ger. 65/E4
Berau (bay), Indo. 103/H4
Berau (riv.), Indo. 103/E3
Beravina, Madg. 143/H7
Berbenno di Valtellina, It. 67/F5
Berbera, Som. 136/C3
Berbérati, CAfr. 134/B4
Berbice (riv.), Guy. 217/G3
Berceto, It. 68/C4
Berchem, Belg. 58/B6
Bercher, Swi. 66/C4
Berching, Ger. 65/E4
Berchogur, Kaz. 77/L2
Berchtesgaden, Ger. 51/K3
Berchtesgaden, NP Ger. 51/K3
Berck, Fr. 60/A3
Berclair, Tx, US 181/F3
Berdale, Som. 136/C4
Berdorf, Lux. 61/F4
Berdsk, Rus. 80/J4
Berdyans'k, Ukr. 79/J4
Berdyansk (bay), Ukr. 79/J4
Berdychiv, Ukr. 78/E3
Béré, Chad 134/C3
Bere Regis, Eng, UK 42/D5
Berea, Ky, US 192/E2
Berea, Les. 142/D3
Bereah, Fl, US 194/M8
Berebere, Indo. 103/G3
Bereguardo, It. 68/C3
Berehomet, Ukr. 78/C3
Berehove, Ukr. 49/M4
Bereina, PNG 153/G2
Bereku, Tanz. 137/A3
Berekum, Gha. 133/E5
Berenguela, Bol. 224/B1
Berenice (ruin), Egypt 127/G4
Berens (isl.), Mb, Can. 186/F1
Berens River, Mb, Can. 186/F1
Berenty, Madg. 143/H8
Beresford, NB, Can. 188/E2
Beresford, SD, US 185/F2
Bereşti, Rom. 57/H2
Berettyóújfalu, Hun. 56/E2
Berevo, Madg. 143/H7
Berezan', Ukr. 78/F2
Berezhany, Ukr. 78/C3
Berezhnoye, Rus. 74/H4
Berezino, Bela. 47/N5
Berezivka, Ukr. 78/F4
Bereznik, Rus. 74/J3
Berezniki, Rus. 75/N4
Berezovo, Rus. 80/G3
Berëzovskiy, Rus. 75/P4
Berezovyy, Rus. 91/L1
Berg, Ger. 64/B5
Berg, Ger. 67/H2
Berg, Lux. 61/F4
Berg (riv.), SAfr. 142/B4
Berg, Swi. 67/F2
Berg bei Rohrbach, Aus. 65/G5
Berg en Dal, Sur. 218/C1
Berga, Sp. 53/F1
Bergama, Turk. 76/C5
Bergamo, It. 68/C2
Bergamo (prov.), It. 67/F6
Bergara, Sp. 52/D1
Bergatruete, Ger. 67/F2
Bergedorf, Ger. 59/H2
Bergen, Ger. 46/E4
Bergen, Ger. 59/G3
Bergen, Neth. 58/B3
Bergen, Nor. 46/A1
Bergen (co.), NJ, US 199/D2
Bergen aan Zee, Neth. 58/B3
Bergen op Zoom, Neth. 58/B5
Bergenfield, NJ, US 199/K8
Berger, Nor. 44/S9
Bergerac, Fr. 50/D4
Bergeresse (riv.), Fr. 63/H5
Bergeyk, Neth. 58/C6
Bergheim, Aus. 65/G7
Bergheim, Ger. 61/F2
Bergheim, Tx, US 181/E3
Bergisch Gladbach, Ger. 61/G2
Bergkamen, Ger. 59/E5
Bergman, Ar, US 183/H2
Bergnäset, Swe. 74/D2
Bergneustadt, Ger. 61/G1
Bergrheinfeld, Ger. 48/F4
Bergsbrunna, Swe. 45/A1
Bergse Maas (riv.), Neth. 58/B5
Bergshamra, Swe. 46/H2
Bergsvatnet (lake), Nor. 44/R9
Bergsviken, Swe. 44/G2
Bergtheim, Ger. 64/D3
Berguent, Mor. 130/C2
Bergues, Fr. 60/B2
Bergum, Neth. 58/D2
Bergumermeer (lake), Neth. 58/D2
Bergün-Bravuogn, Swi. 67/F4
Bergviken (lake), Swe. 46/G1
Berh, Mong. 90/G2
Berhala (str.), Indo. 101/C3
Berhampore, India 109/G3
Berhampur, India 107/E2
Beri Khās, India 110/D5
Berikat (cape), Indo. 101/D3
Bering (sea), Asia,NAm. 201/D3
Bering (str.), Rus.,US 201/E3
Bering (isl.), Rus. 81/S4
Beringen, Belg. 61/E1
Beringovskiy, Rus. 81/T3
Beritarikap (cape), Indo. 101/C3
Berja, Sp. 52/D4
Berkane, Mor. 130/C2
Berkel (riv.), Ger. 48/D2
Berkel, Neth. 58/B5
Berkeley, Eng, UK 42/D3
Berkeley Heights, NJ, US 199/H9
Berkeley Lake, Ga, US 193/M7
Berkeley Springs (Bath), WV, US 191/G5
Berkhamsted, Eng, UK 36/B1
Berkheim, Ger. 67/G1
Berkhout, Neth. 58/B3
Berkley, Mi, US 197/F6
Berkovitsa, Bul. 57/F4
Berks (co.), Pa, US 198/C3
Berkshire (co.), Eng, UK 43/E3
Berkshire Downs (hills), Eng, UK 43/E3
Berlaimont, Fr. 60/C3
Berlanga de Duero, Sp. 52/D2
Berlare, Belg. 60/D1
Berleburg, Ger. 59/F6
Berlicum, Neth. 58/C5
Berlin (cap.), Ger. 48/Q6
Berlin (state), Ger. 48/Q6
Berlin, Ga, US 195/G2
Berlin, Md, US 193/K1
Berlin, NJ, US 198/D4
Berlin (mtn.), Nv, US 176/E4
Berlin, Wi, US 185/K2
Bermagui, Austl. 157/E3
Bermejillo, Mex. 204/E3
Bermejo (riv.), Arg. 209/D5
Bermejo, Arg. 226/D1
Bermeo, Sp. 50/B5
Bermillo de Sayago, Sp. 52/B2
Bermuda (isl.), UK 163/L6
Bermudian (cr.), Pa, US 198/A4
Bern (canton), Swi. 66/D4
Bern (cap.), Swi. 66/D4
Bern-Belp (int'l arpt.), Swi. 66/D4
Bernabé Rivera, Uru. 225/E4
Bernal, Peru 220/A2
Bernalda, It. 54/E2
Bernalillo, NM, US 179/J3
Bernard (riv.), NW, Can. 170/D1
Bernardo, NM, US 179/J3
Bernardo O'Higgins, PN, Chile 227/B6
Bernardston, Ma, US 191/K3
Bernardsville, NJ, US 198/D2
Bernau, Ger. 66/E2
Bernau, Ger. 48/Q6
Bernay, Fr. 63/F2
Bernbeuren, Ger. 67/G2
Bernburg, Ger. 48/F3
Berne, In, US 190/D4
Berne (riv.), Ger. 59/F2
Bernes-sur-Oise, Fr. 36/J4
Bernese Alps (mtn.), Swi. 51/G3
Bernhardswald, Ger. 65/F4
Bernice, La, US 183/H4
Bernie, Mo, US 192/C2
Bernier (isl.), Austl. 154/B3
Bernier (bay), Nun, Can. 170/G1
Bernières-sur-Mer, Fr. 63/E2
Bernierville, Qu, Can. 188/B2
Bernin, Fr. 70/B2
Bernina (mtn.), Swi. 67/F5
Bernina (peak), Swi. 67/F5
Bernina, Passo del (pass), Swi. 67/G5

Berni – Black
269

Bernissart, Belg. 60/C3
Bernkastel-Kues, Ger. 61/G4
Bernsbach, Ger. 65/F1
Bernville, Pa, US 198/B3
Beromünster, Swi. 66/E3
Béron (riv.), Fr. 63/E5
Beronono, Madg. 143/H8
Beroroha, Madg. 143/H8
Beroun, Czh. 65/H3
Berounka (riv.), Czh. 49/G4
Berovo, FYROM 55/H2
Berra, It. 69/E4
Berrara, Austl. 157/E2
Berre (lake), Fr. 50/F5
Berre-l'Étang, Fr. 70/B6
Berrechid, Mor. 128/D2
Berri, Austl. 155/J5
Berriane, Alg. 129/F2
Berridale, Austl. 157/D3
Berriedale, Sc, UK 37/S7
Berrien Springs, Mi, US 190/C4
Berriew, Wal, UK 42/C1
Berrigan, Austl. 157/B2
Berrima, Austl. 157/E2
Berriozábal, Mex. 206/C2
Berrondo, Uru. 227/K11
Berrotarán, Arg. 226/D2
Berrouaghia, Alg. 130/G4
Berry, Austl. 157/E2
Berry (isls.), Bahm. 203/F2
Berry (cr.), Ab, Can. 175/J2
Berry (pt.), NS, Can. 189/G3
Berry (canal), Fr. 63/G6
Berry (reg.), Fr. 72/D1
Berry (pt.), Eng, UK 42/C6
Berry, Ky, US 192/E1
Berry (mtn.), Pa, US 198/A2
Berryessa (peak), Ca, US 197/K9
Berryessa (lake), Ca, US 176/B4
Berryville, Ar, US 183/H2
Berryville, Va, US 193/J1
Berseba, Namb. 142/B2
Bersenbrück, Ger. 59/E3
Bershad', Ukr. 78/E3
Bersut, Rus. 75/L5
Bertam, Malay. 101/C1
Bertha, Mn, US 187/G4
Berthierville, Qu, Can. 191/K1
Berthold, ND, US 186/D3
Berthoud, Co, US 184/B3
Bertinoro, It. 69/F5
Bertiolo, It. 69/G2
Bertogne, Belg. 61/E3
Bertolínia, Braz. 219/F4
Bertoua, Camr. 134/B4
Bertram (mt.), Austl. 152/B4
Bertram, Tx, US 181/E2
Bertrand (peak), Arg. 227/B6
Bertrand, NB, Can. 188/E2
Bertrix, Belg. 61/E4
Bertry, Fr. 60/C3
Beru (isl.), Kiri. 160/G5
Beruas, Malay. 101/C1
Beruit (isl.), Malay. 102/D3
Beruwala, SrL. 107/C5
Bervie Water. (riv.), Sc, UK 39/D3
Berwa, India 104/B2
Berwick (nbrhd.), Austl. 156/G6
Berwick, NS, Can. 188/E3
Berwick, Me, US 191/L3
Berwick, Pa, US 198/B1
Berwick-Upon-Tweed, Eng, UK 39/D5
Berwyn (mts.), Wal, UK 40/E6
Berwyn, Il, US 197/Q16
Beryl, Ut, US 179/F2
Beryslav, Ukr. 79/G4
Berzence, Hun. 56/C2
Bès (riv.), Fr. 50/E2
Besalampy, Madg. 143/H7
Besançon, Fr. 66/C3
Bésao, Chad 134/B4
Besar (isl.), Indo. 152/A2
Besar (peak), Indo. 103/E4
Besar (peak), Malay. 101/C2
Besbre (riv.), Fr. 50/E3
Besedino, Rus. 79/J2
Beserah, Malay. 101/C2
Beshām Qala, Pak. 110/B2
Beshenkovichi, Bela. 47/N4
Beshlo Wenz (riv.), Eth. 136/A3
Beshneh, Iran 115/H4
Besikama, Indo. 152/B2
Beşiri, Turk. 114/E2
Beška, Serb. 56/E3
Beskids (mts.), Pol. 49/L4
Beskol', Kaz. 111/D2
Beşkonak, Turk. 116/B1
Beslan, Rus. 77/H4
Besna Kobila (peak), Serb. 56/F4
Besozzo, It. 68/B2
Bessacarr, Eng, UK 41/G5
Bessancourt, Fr. 36/J4
Bessarabia (reg.), Mol. 57/J2
Bessbrook, NI, UK 40/B3
Bessé-sur-Braye, Fr. 63/F5
Bessemer, Al, US 192/D4
Bessemer, Mi, US 187/J4
Bessemer (mtn.), Wa, US 197/D2
Bessines-sur-Gartempe, Fr. 50/D3
Best, Neth. 58/C5
Best, Tx, US 180/D2
Bestensee, Ger. 48/Q7
Bestobe, Kaz. 111/B1
Bestuzhevo, Rus. 75/K3
Bestwig, Ger. 59/F6
Beswick, Austl. 152/D3
Beswick Abor. Res., Austl. 152/D3
Bet Guvrin, Isr. 117/B5
Bet Qama, Isr. 117/B6
Bet She'an, Isr. 117/D3
Bet Shemesh, Isr. 117/B5
Betaghstown, Ire. 40/B4
Betanantanana, Madg. 143/H7
Betania, Col. 219/K7
Betanty, Madg. 143/H9
Betanzos, Sp. 52/A1
Betanzos, Bol. 224/C1
Bétaré-Oya, Camr. 134/B4
Bete Hor, Eth. 136/A3
Bétérou, Ben. 133/F4
Beth Alpha Synagogue (ruin), Isr. 117/C3
Beth She'an NP, Isr. 117/D3
Beth She'arim NP, Isr. 117/C3
Bethal, SAfr. 142/E2
Bethanie, SAfr. 141/E5
Bethanie, Namb. 142/B2
Bethany, On, Can. 191/G2
Bethany (res.), Ca, US 197/L11
Bethany, Mo, US 185/G3
Bethany, Il, US 185/K4
Bethany, La, US 180/G1
Bethel, Ak, US 201/F3
Bethel, Me, US 191/L2
Bethel, Ok, US 183/G3
Bethel, Pa, US 198/B3
Bethel, Vt, US 191/K3
Bethel Acres, Ok, US 183/F3
Bethel Island, Ca, US 197/L10
Bethel Park, Pa, US 190/F4
Bethelridge, Ky, US 192/E2
Bétheniville, Fr. 61/D5
Bétheny, Fr. 60/D5
Bethesda, Wal, UK 40/D5
Bethesda, Md, US 198/A6
Béthisy-Sainte-Pierre, Fr. 60/B5
Bethlehem, NH, US 191/L2
Bethlehem, SAfr. 142/E3
Bethlehem, Md, US 198/C6
Bethlehem, Pa, US 198/C2
Bethlehem (Bayt Laḩm), WBnk. 117/C5
Bethoncourt, Fr. 66/C2
Bethpage, NY, US 199/M9
Bethulie, SAfr. 142/D3
Béthune, Fr. 60/B2
Béthune (riv.), Fr. 50/D2
Bethune, Sk, Can. 175/M2
Betioky, Madg. 143/H8
Betoota, Austl. 158/A4
Betpaqdala (des.), Kaz. 80/G5
Betroka, Madg. 143/H8
Betschdorf, Fr. 64/A5
Betsiamites, Qu, Can. 188/C1
Betsiamites (riv.), Qu, Can. 188/C1
Betsiamites (riv.), Qu, Can. 171/J3
Betsiamites Ind. Res., Qu, Can. 188/C1
Betsiboka (riv.), Madg. 143/H7
Betsie (pt.), Mi, US 190/C2
Betsy Layne, Ky, US 193/F2
Bettancourt-la-Ferrée, Fr. 61/D6
Bette (peak), Libya 126/C4
Bettembourg, Lux. 61/F4
Betteravia, Ca, US 178/B3
Betterton, Md, US 198/B5
Bettiah, India 109/E2
Bettlach, Swi. 66/D3
Bettles, Ak, US 201/H2
Betton, Fr. 62/D4
Betūl, India 108/A5
Betulia, Col. 219/K6
Betuwe (phys. reg.), Neth. 58/C5
Betwa (riv.), India 108/B3
Betws-y-Coed, Wal, UK 40/E5
Betz, Fr. 36/L4
Betzdorf, Ger. 61/G2
Betzenstein, Ger. 65/E3
Béu, Ang. 138/C4
Beulah, Austl. 156/B2
Beulah, Mb, Can. 186/D2
Beulah, Co, US 182/B1
Beulah, Mi, US 190/C2
Beulah, Ms, US 192/B4
Beulah, ND, US 186/D4
Beulah (lake), Wi, US 197/P14
Beulah, Wy, US 184/B1
Beulakerwijde (lake), Neth. 58/C3
Beuningen, Neth. 58/C5
Beure, Fr. 66/C3
Beuvillers, Fr. 63/F2
Beuvray (peak), Fr. 50/F3
Beuvron (riv.), Fr. 50/D3
Beuvronne (riv.), Fr. 36/L5
Beuvry, Fr. 60/B2
Beuzeville, Fr. 63/F2
Bevagna, It. 71/B2
Bevensen, Ger. 59/H2
Bevent, Wi, US 185/K1
Bever (riv.), Ger. 59/E4
Bévera (riv.), Fr. 70/D5
Beveren, Belg. 58/B6
Beverin (peak), Swi. 67/F4
Beverley, Eng, UK 41/H4
Beverley, Austl. 154/C5
Beverly, Oh, US 190/F5
Beverly, WV, US 193/H1
Beverly Hills, Ca, US 196/F7
Beverly Hills, Mi, US 197/F6
Beverstedt, Ger. 59/F2
Beverungen, Ger. 59/G5
Beverwijk, Neth. 58/B4
Bevil Oaks, Tx, US 181/G2
Bewār, India 108/B3
Bewcastle, Eng, UK 41/F1
Bewdley, On, Can. 191/G2
Bewdley, Eng, UK 42/D2
Bewl Bridge (res.), Eng, UK 43/G4
Bex, Swi. 66/D5
Bexbach, Ger. 61/G5
Bexhill, Eng, UK 43/G5
Bexley (bor.), Eng, UK 36/D2
Bextograk, China 111/E4
Beyçayırı, Turk. 57/H5
Beycuma, Turk. 57/K5
Beykoz (nbrhd.), Turk. 115/N6
Beyla, Gui. 132/C4
Beylerbeyi Palace, Turk. 115/N6
Bēylul, Erit. 136/B2
Beyne-Heusay, Belg. 61/E2
Beynes, Fr. 36/H5
Beyneū, Kaz. 77/K3
Beyoglu (nbrhd.), Turk. 115/M6
Beyoneisu-Retsugan (isl.), Japan 97/F5
Beypazarı, Turk. 114/B1
Beypore, India 107/B4
Beyra, Som. 136/C4
Beyşehir, Turk. 116/E1
Beysug (bay), Rus. 79/K4
Bezaha, Madg. 143/H8
Bezau, Aus. 67/F3
Bezdan, Serb. 56/D3
Bezděz (peak), Czh. 65/H1
Bezdrev (lake), Czh. 65/H4
Bezhetsk, Rus. 74/H4
Bezhta, Rus. 77/H4
Béziers, Fr. 50/E5
Bhabua, India 108/D3
Bhadarwāh, India 110/C3
Bhadaur, India 110/C4
Bhadohī, India 108/D3
Bhādra, India 110/C5
Bhadrāchalam, India 107/D2
Bhadrak, India 104/E3
Bhadrapur, Nepal 109/G2
Bhadreswar, India 104/A3
Bhāgalpur, India 109/F3
Bhāi Pheru, Pak. 110/B4
Bhairab (riv.), Bang. 109/G4
Bhairab Bāzār, Bang. 109/H3
Bhairahawa, Nepal 108/D2
Bhairamgarh, India 107/D2
Bhakkar, Pak. 110/A4
Bhākra (dam), India 110/D4
Bhaktapur, Nepal 109/E2
Bhāluka, Bang. 109/H3
Bhalwāl, Pak. 110/B3
Bḩamdūn, Leb. 117/D1
Bhamo, Myan. 98/C3
Bhandāra, India 107/C1
Bhandāri, India 98/B3
Bhānder, India 108/B3
Bhānin, India 110/C5
Bhanjanagar, India 107/E2
Bhānrer (range), India 108/B4
Bhānwad, India 104/A3
Bharatpur, Nepal 109/E2
Bhārātpur, India 108/A2
Bhareli (riv.), India 98/B3
Bharno, India 109/E4
Bharthana, India 108/B2
Bhasāwar, India 108/A2
Bhātiāpāra Ghāt, Bang. 109/G4
Bhatinda, India 110/C4
Bhatkal, India 107/B3
Bhātpāra, India 109/G4
Bhaun, Pak. 110/B3
Bhavāni (riv.), India 107/C4
Bhavāni, India 107/C4
Bhavnagar, India 107/B1
Bhawāna, Pak. 110/B4
Bhawāni Mandi, India 104/C3
Bhawānīgarh, India 110/D4
Bhera, Pak. 110/B3
Bheramara, Bang. 109/G3
Bheri (zone), Nepal 108/C1
Bhīkhi, India 110/C4
Bhikkīwind Uttār, India 110/C4
Bhikna Thorī, Nepal 109/E2
Bhīlwāra, India 104/B2
Bhīma (riv.), India 113/L5
Bhima (riv.), India 104/C4
Bhīmavaram, India 107/D2
Bhīmmāl, India 113/K4
Bhīmphedi, Nepal 109/E2
Bhind, India 108/B2
Bhinga, India 108/C2
Bhiwandi, India 107/B2
Bhiwāni, India 110/D5
Bhojpur, Nepal 109/F2
Bhokardan, India 107/B1
Bhola, Bang. 109/H4
Bhongaon, India 108/B2
Bhopāl, India 104/C3
Bhopālpatnam, India 107/D2
Bhor, India 107/B2
Bhraoin (lake), Sc, UK 39/A1
Bhuban, India 107/E1
Bhūj, India 113/J4
Bhumibol (dam), Thai. 106/B2
Bhutan (ctry.) 109/G2
Bi (riv.), China 90/C5
Bi Doup (peak), Viet. 106/E3
Bia (riv.), C.d'Iv. 132/E5
Biá (riv.), Braz. 220/E2
Biaboye, D.R. Congo 139/G2
Biak (isl.), Indo. 103/J4
Biak (int'l arpt.), Indo. 103/J4
Biak, Indo. 103/J4
Biakowieski NP, Pol. 49/M2
Biała Podlaska, Pol. 49/M2
Białobrzegi, Pol. 49/L3
Białogard, Pol. 46/G4
Białowieski NP, Pol. 76/B1
Białowieski NP, Pol. 49/K4
Białystok, Pol. 49/M2
Bianca (peak), It. 67/G4
Biancavilla, It. 54/D4
Bianco, (peak), It. 71/C4
Biandrate, It. 68/B3
Biandronno, It. 68/B2
Bianga, CAfr. 134/D4
Biankouma, C.d'Iv. 132/D5
Bianya, China 98/E3
Bianyang, China 99/E3
Bianze, It. 68/B3
Biaro, D.R. Congo 139/F2
Biarritz, Fr. 50/C5
Biarvitz (Bayonne-Anglet) (arpt.), Fr. 50/C5
Biasca, Swi. 67/E5
Bibai, Japan 94/B2
Bibala, Ang. 140/B2
Bībān, Egypt 131/B3
Bibassé, Gabon 138/B2
Bibbenluke, Austl. 157/D3
Bibbiano, It. 68/D4
Bibbiena, It. 69/E6
Bibémi, Camr. 134/B3
Biberach, Ger. 66/E1
Biberach, Ger. 67/G1
Biberach an der Riss, Ger. 67/F1
Biberist, Swi. 66/D3
Bibione, It. 69/G2
Biblián, Ecu. 216/B5
Biblis, Ger. 64/B3
Bibrka, Ukr. 78/C3
Bicas, Braz. 223/N6
Bicas, Braz. 223/E3
Bicaz, Rom. 78/D4
Bicester, Eng, UK 43/E3
Bichano, Eth. 135/G4
Bicheno, Austl. 156/D4
Bichhia, India 108/C4
Bickerton (isl.), Austl. 153/E3
Bickle (peak), WV, US 193/H1
Bickleigh, Sk, Can. 175/K2
Bickleton, Wa, US 174/D5
Bicknacre, Eng, UK 36/E1
Bicknell, Ut, US 179/G1
Bicknell, In, US 192/D1
Bicske, Hun. 56/D2
Bīd Boland, Iran 115/G4
Bida, Nga. 133/G4
Bidadari (cape), Malay. 100/B4
Bidaga (rapids), C.d'Iv. 132/D5
Bīdar, India 107/C2
Biddeford, Me, US 191/L3
Biddinghuizen, Neth. 58/C4
Biddiyā, WBnk. 117/C4
Biddle, Mt, US 184/B1
Biddū, WBnk. 117/C5
Biddulph, Eng, UK 41/F5
Bidean nam Bian (peak), Sc, UK 39/A3
Bideford, Eng, UK 42/B4
Bideford (Barnstaple) (bay), Eng, UK 42/B4
Bidente (riv.), It. 69/F4
Bidford-on-Avon, Eng, UK 43/E2
Bidhūna, India 108/B2
Bīdokht, Iran 113/G2
Bidor, Malay. 101/C1
Bidouze (riv.), Fr. 53/E1
Bidrē, Eth. 136/A4
Bieber, Ca, US 176/C3
Biebesheim am Rhein, Ger. 64/B3
Biebzra (riv.), Pol. 49/M2
Biel, Swi. 66/D3
Bielawa, Pol. 49/J3
Bieldside, Sc, UK 39/D2
Bielefeld, Ger. 59/F4
Bieler (lake), Swi. 66/D3
Bieler (lake), Nun, Can. 171/J1
Biella, It. 68/B2
Bielsk Podlaski, Pol. 49/M2
Bielsko-Biała, Pol. 49/K4
Bien Hoa, Viet. 106/D4
Bien Son, Viet. 106/D1
Bienenbüttel, Ger. 59/H2
Bienfait, Sk, Can. 186/C3
Bienne (riv.), Fr. 66/B5
Bienno, It. 67/G6
Bientina, It. 68/D6
Bienvenue, FrG. 218/C2
Bienville, La, US 183/H4
Bienville (lake), Qu, Can. 171/J3
Bière, Swi. 66/C4
Bierset (int'l arpt.), Belg. 61/E2
Bierum, Neth. 58/D2
Bierutów, Pol. 49/J3
Biesbosch (reg.), Neth. 58/B5
Biesenthal, Ger. 48/Q6
Biesles, Fr. 66/B1
Biesme (riv.), Fr. 61/D5
Bieszczadzki NP, Pol. 76/B2
Bieszczadzkii NP, Pol. 49/M4
Bietigheim, Ger. 64/C5
Bietschhorn (peak), Swi. 66/D5
Bièvre, Belg. 61/E4
Bièvre (riv.), Fr. 36/J5
Bièvres, Fr. 36/J5
Biferno (riv.), It. 71/D4
Bifoun, Gabon 138/B3
Big (des.), Austl. 156/B2
Big (cr.), BC, Can. 174/C2
Big (riv.), NW, Can. 170/D1
Big (isl.), On, Can. 170/G4
Big (cr.), Ga, US 193/M6
Big (cr.), Ks, US 184/D4
Big (lake), Mi, US 197/E6
Big (riv.), Mo, US 184/J5
Big (mtn.), Nv, US 176/D3
Big (mtn.), WV, US 193/H1
Big Arm, Mt, US 174/G4
Big Bald (mtn.), NB, Can. 188/D2
Big Baldy (mtn.), Mt, US 175/J4
Big Bar Creek, BC, Can. 174/C2
Big Bear City, Ca, US 178/D3
Big Bear Lake, Ca, US 178/D3
Big Beaver, Sk, Can. 186/B3
Big Belt (mts.), Mt, US 175/J4
Big Bend, Swaz. 143/E2
Big Bend (dam), SD, US 184/E1
Big Bend, Wi, US 197/P14
Big Bend NP, Tx, US 180/C3
Big Black (riv.), Ms, US 192/B4
Big Blue (riv.), Ne, US 185/F3
Big Blue, West Fork (riv.), Ne, US 184/E3
Big Boggy NWR, Tx, US 181/G3
Big Cabin, Ok, US 183/G2
Big Canyon (riv.), Tx, US 180/C2
Big Creek, Ca, US 178/C2
Big Creek, Id, US 177/F1
Big Cypress (swamp), Fl, US 195/H4
Big Cypress National Preserve, Fl, US 195/H4
Big de Noc (bay), Mi, US 187/L5
Big Eau Plaine (res.), Wi, US 185/J1
Big Eddy (falls), Wi, US 185/K1
Big Falls, Mn, US 187/H3
Big Flat (brook), NJ, US 198/D1
Big Foot (pass), SD, US 184/C2
Big Fork (riv.), Mn, US 187/H4
Big Hole, SAfr. 142/D3
Big Hole (riv.), Mt, US 177/G1
Big Hole Nat'l Bfld., Mt, US 177/G1
Big Horn, Wy, US 177/K1
Big Indian, NY, US 191/J3
Big Lake, Tx, US 180/D2
Big Lake Nat'l Wild. Ref., Ar, US 192/B3
Big Lake Ranch, BC, Can. 174/D1
Big Lost (riv.), Id, US 177/G2
Big Marine (lake), Mn, US 187/Q6
Big Muddy (cr.), Mt, US 186/B3
Big Muddy (lake), Sk, Can. 175/M3
Big Muskego (lake), Wi, US 197/P14
Big Nemaha, North Fork (riv.), Ne, US 185/F3
Big Pine, Ca, US 178/C2
Big Pine (hill), Pa, US 198/C1
Big Pine Key, Fl, US 195/H5
Big Pines, Ca, US 196/C2
Big Piney, Mo, US 183/H2
Big Piney (riv.), Mo, US 192/B2
Big Pipe (cr.), Md, US 198/A4
Big Raccoon (riv.), In, US 190/C5
Big Rapids, Mi, US 190/D3
Big Rock (cr.), Il, US 197/N16
Big Rock, Il, US 197/N16
Big Rock, Va, US 193/F2
Big Sable (pt.), Mi, US 190/C2
Big Sandy (riv.), Wy, US 177/J3
Big Sandy (cr.), Co, US 184/C4
Big Sandy, Mt, US 175/J3
Big Sandy, Wy, US 177/J2
Big Satilla (cr.), Ga, US 195/G2
Big Sioux (riv.), Ia,SD, US 185/F2
Big Smoky (falls), Wi, US 187/K5
Big South Fork National River and Recreation Area, Tn, US 192/E2
Big Spring, Tx, US 180/D1
Big Stone (lake), Mn,SD, US 185/F1
Big Stone Gap, Va, US 193/F2
Big Stone NWR, Mn, US 185/F1
Big Sunflower (riv.), Ms, US 192/B4
Big Sur, Ca, US 178/B2
Big Thicket National Preserve, Tx, US 181/G2
Big Thompson (riv.), Co, US 184/B3
Big Timber, Mt, US 175/K5
Big Trout (lake), On, Can. 170/H3
Big Tujunga Canyon (canyon), Ca, US 196/B2
Big Valley, Ab, Can. 175/H1
Big Wells, Tx, US 180/E3
Big Wood (riv.), Id, US 177/F2
Biga, Turk. 57/H5
Bigadiç, Turk. 76/D5
Bigbury (bay), Eng, UK 42/C6
Bigelow (mtn.), Me, US 191/L2
Bigfoot, Tx, US 181/E3
Bigfork, Mn, US 187/H4
Bigfork, Mt, US 175/G3
Bigga, Austl. 157/D2
Biggar, Sk, Can. 175/L1
Biggar, Sc, UK 39/C5
Bigge (isl.), Austl. 152/B3
Bigge (riv.), Ger. 61/G1
Biggenden, Austl. 158/D4
Biggers, Ar, US 192/B2
Biggin Hill (nbrhd.), Eng, UK 36/D3
Biggleswade, Eng, UK 43/F2
Biggs, Ca, US 176/C4
Biggs Army Airfield, Tx, US 180/A2
Bighorn, Mt, US 175/L4
Bighorn (lake), Mt, US 177/J1
Bighorn (mts.), Wy, US 172/E3
Bighorn (riv.), Wy, US 172/E2
Bighorn (riv.), Wy, US 170/F4
Bighorn Canyon NRA, Mt, US 177/J1
Bight of Benin (bay), Afr. 119/C4
Bight of Biafra (bay), Afr. 138/A1
Bigi, D.R. Congo 139/E2
Biglerville, Pa, US 198/A4
Bignona, Sen. 132/A3
Bigosovo, Bela. 47/M4
Bigsby (isl.), On, Can. 187/G3
Biguaçu, Braz. 225/G3
Bihać, Bosn. 56/B3
Bīhar, India 109/E3
Bihār (state), India 104/D3
Biharamulo, Tanz. 139/G3
Biharamulo Game Rsv., Tanz. 139/G3
Bihārīganj, India 109/F3
Biharkeresztes, Hun. 56/E2
Bihor (co.), Rom. 49/M5
Bihorel, Fr. 63/G1
Bihoro, Japan 94/D2
Bijagós (arch.), GBis. 119/A3
Bijāpur, India 107/D2
Bījār, Iran 115/F3
Bijāwar, India 108/B3
Bijbiāra, India 110/C3
Bijeljina, Bosn. 56/D3
Bijelo Polje, Mont. 56/D4
Bijiang, China 98/C3
Bijiaquan, China 92/J7
Bijie, China 98/E3
Bijni, India 109/H2
Bijnor, India 108/B1
Bikar (isl.), Mrsh. 160/G3
Bikenibeu, Kiri. 160/G4
Bikfayyā, Leb. 117/D1
Bikin (riv.), Rus. 91/M2
Bikin, Rus. 91/L2
Bikini (isl.), Mrsh. 160/F3
Bikita, Zim. 141/F4
Bikori, Sudan 135/G3
Bikoro, D.R. Congo 138/D3
Bikramganj, India 109/E3
Bikuar, PN do, Ang. 140/B2
Bila Krynytsya, Ukr. 79/G4
Bila Tserkva, Ukr. 78/F3
Bilād Manaḩ, Oman 113/G4
Bilāra, India 104/B2
Bilāri, India 108/B1
Bilāsipāra, India 109/H2
Bilāspur, India 110/D4
Bilāspur, India 108/B1
Bilāspur, India 108/D4
Bilāsuvar, Azer. 115/G2
Bilauktaung (range), Myan.,Thai. 106/B3
Bilauri, Nepal 108/C1
Bilbao, Sp. 50/B5
Bilbays, Egypt 131/C4
Bileća, Bosn. 56/D4
Bilecik (prov.), Turk. 114/B1
Bīleh Savār, Iran 115/G2
Biłgoraj, Pol. 49/M3
Bilgrām, India 108/C2
Bilhaur, India 108/C2
Bilhorod-Dnistrovs'kyy, Ukr. 78/F4
Bili (riv.), D.R. Congo 134/D4
Bili, D.R. Congo 139/F1
Bilibino, Rus. 81/S3
Bilila, Malw. 141/G2
Bilin, Myan. 98/C5
Bilin (riv.), Myan. 106/B2
Bílina (riv.), Czh. 65/G2
Bílina, Czh. 65/G1
Biliran (isl.), Phil. 100/D3
Bilisht, Alb. 55/G2
Bilit, Malay. 100/B4
Biliu (riv.), China 93/B3
Bill, Wy, US 184/B2
Bill of Portland (pt.), Eng, UK 42/D5
Bill Williams (riv.), Az, US 179/F3
Billaouâr, Mrta. 132/C2
Bille (riv.), Ger. 59/H1
Billerbeck, Ger. 59/E5
Billère, Fr. 50/C5
Billericay, Eng, UK 36/E2
Billesholm, Swe. 45/K6
Billiat Consv. Park, Austl. 155/J5
Billiat Consv. Park, Austl. 156/B2
Billigheim, Ger. 64/C4
Billiluna Abor. Land, Austl. 152/B4
Billinge, Eng, UK 41/F4
Billingham, Eng, UK 41/G2
Billings, Mt, US 175/K5
Billings, Ok, US 183/F2
Billingsfors, Swe. 46/E2
Billingshurst, Eng, UK 43/F4
Billiton (isl.), Indo. 83/K10
Billund, Den. 46/C4
Billund (int'l arpt.), Den. 46/C4
Bilma, Niger 126/B5
Bīlo, Eth. 135/H3
Biloela, Austl. 158/C4
Bilohirs'k, Ukr. 79/H5
Biloku, Guy. 217/G4
Biloluts'k, Ukr. 79/K3
Bilopillya, Ukr. 79/H2
Bilovods'k, Ukr. 79/K3
Biloxi, Ms, US 194/D2
Bilpa Morea Claypan (lake), Austl. 155/H3
Bilqas Qism Awwal, Egypt 131/C2
Bilqas Qism Thânî, Egypt 131/C2
Bilsi, India 108/B1
Biltān, Egypt 131/C4
Bilthar, India 108/D2
Bilthoven, Neth. 58/C4
Biltine, Chad 134/D2
Biltine (pref.), Chad 134/D2
Biltmore, Tn, US 193/F2
Bilüü, Mong. 111/E2
Bilyayivka, Ukr. 78/F4
Bilyts'ke, Ukr. 79/J3
Bilzen, Belg. 61/E2
Bima, Indo. 103/E5
Bimberi (peak), Austl. 157/D2
Bimbo, CAfr. 134/C4
Bimini (isls.), Bahm. 203/F2
Bin Ghashīr, Libya 126/B1
Bin Jawwād, Libya 126/C2
Bin Yauri, Nga. 133/G4
Bina (riv.), Ger. 65/F6
Bina-Etāwa, India 108/B3
Binalong, Austl. 157/D2
Binanga, Indo. 101/B2
Binasco, It. 68/C3
Binatang, Malay. 102/D3
Binbrook, Eng, UK 41/H5
Binbrook, On, Can. 190/T9
Binche, Belg. 61/D3
Binchuan, China 98/D3
Binda, Austl. 157/D2
Binder Foulbé, Chad 134/B3
Bindki, India 108/C2
Bindoon, Austl. 154/C4
Bindoy, Phil. 100/C3
Bindu, D.R. Congo 138/D4
Bindungi, D.R. Congo 138/D4
Bindura, Zim. 141/F3
Binéfar, Sp. 53/F2
Binfield, Eng, UK 43/F4
Binford, ND, US 186/E4
Binga (mtn.), Moz. 141/G3
Binga, Zim. 141/E3
Bingara, Austl. 156/D1
Bingcaowan, China 90/E4
Bingen, Ger. 61/G4
Binger, Ok, US 183/E3
Bingerville, C.d'Iv. 132/E5
Bingham, Eng, UK 41/H6
Bingham, Me, US 191/M2
Binghamton, NY, US 191/J3
Bingley, Eng, UK 41/G4
Bingöl, Turk. 114/E2
Bingol (prov.), Turk. 114/E2
Binh Chanh, Viet. 106/D4
Binh Chau, Viet. 106/D4
Binh Son, Viet. 106/E3
Binhai, China 92/D4
Binhon (peak), Myan. 98/B5
Binic, Fr. 62/C3
Binisalem, Sp. 53/G3
Binjai, Indo. 101/B2
Binka, India 107/D1
Binkılıç, Turk. 57/J5
Binkolo, SLeo. 132/C4
Binnah (cape), Som. 136/D3
Binnaway, Austl. 156/D1
Binningen, Swi. 66/D2
Binongko (isl.), Indo. 103/F5
Binscarth, Mb, Can. 186/D2
Binsted, Eng, UK 36/A3
Bint Jubayl, Leb. 117/C2
Bintagoungou, Mali 132/E2
Bintan (isl.), Indo. 101/D2
Bintang (peak), Malay. 101/C1
Bintang (range), Malay. 101/C1
Bintimodouya, Gui. 132/B4
Bintuhan, Indo. 101/C3
Binyamina, Isr. 117/B3
Binyang, China 99/F4
Binza, D.R. Congo 138/C4
Binzhou, China 92/D3
Bío-Bío (riv.), Chile 226/B3
Bío-Bío (pol. reg.), Chile 226/B3
Biodi, D.R. Congo 139/G2
Biograd, Cro. 56/B4
Biogradska NP, Mont. 56/D4
Bioko (pol. reg.), EqG. 138/B2
Bioko (isl.), EqG. 119/C4
Bioko (Fernando Po) (isl.), EqG. 138/B2
Biola, Ca, US 178/B2
Biot, Fr. 70/D5
Biougra, Mor. 128/C3
Bipoint (Bissau) (int'l arpt.), GBis. 132/B4
Bippen, Ger. 59/E3
Bir (cape), Djib. 136/B3
Bīr, India 107/B2
Bîr Abu el-Husein (well), Egypt 127/F4
Bi'r Abu Hashim (well), Egypt 127/G4
Bîr Abu Minqâr (well), Egypt 127/E3
Bir Aïdiat (well), Mrta. 128/C4
Bi'r al Aḩmar (well), Libya 126/C2
Bi'r al 'Akkārīyah (well), Libya 126/C2
Bi'r Al Ghanam, Libya 126/B1
Bi'r al Ghuzayyil (well), Libya 126/A2
Bi'r al Ḩarash (well), Libya 126/D3
Bi'r Al Mashariqah, Tun. 130/L6
Bi'r al Mastūtah (well), Libya 126/B3
Bi'r al Mufaţţam (well), Libya 126/D2
Bi'r al Qāf (well), Libya 126/B2
Bi'r al Washkah (well), Libya 126/B2
Bi'r 'Alī, Yem. 136/D2
Bi'r as Sahl (well), Libya 126/B3
Bi'r as Sinidah (well), Libya 126/B2
Bi'r aţ Ţarfāwī (well), Libya 126/E2
Bir Bel Guerdâne (well), Mrta. 128/C4
Bi'r Burayd (well), Egypt 131/D6
Bîr Dibis (well), Egypt 127/F4
Bir el Ater, Alg. 113/H2
Bi'r Ghadir (well), Egypt 127/G3
Bîr Misâha (well), Egypt 127/E4
Bir Moghreïn, Mrta. 128/C4
Bîr Ounâne (well), Mali 128/E5
Bîr Safājah (well), Egypt 127/G3
Bir Tamtam, Mor. 130/B3
Bîr Tarfâwi (well), Egypt 127/F4
Bi'r Umm Hibal (well), Egypt 127/G4
Bi'r Zayt, WBnk. 117/C5
Bira, Rus. 91/L2
Birāk, Libya 126/B3
Birao, CAfr. 134/D3
Birātnagar, Nepal 109/F2
Biratori, Japan 94/C2
Birch (mts.), Ab, Can. 170/E3
Birch (cr.), Mt, US 175/H3
Birch Bay, Wa, US 174/C3
Birch Creek, Ak, US 201/J2
Birch Hills, Sk, Can. 175/M1
Birch River, Mb, Can. 186/D1
Birch Tree, Mo, US 183/J2
Birchenough Bridge, Zim. 141/G3
Birchip, Austl. 156/B2
Bircot, Eth. 136/B4
Bird (cr.), Ok, US 183/F2
Bird Island, Mn, US 185/G1
Bird Islet (isl.), Austl. 145/E3
Bird Point, Sk, Can. 186/C2
Birds Rock (peak), Austl. 157/E1
Birdsboro, Pa, US 198/C3
Birdsnest, Va, US 193/K2
Birdsville, Austl. 155/H3
Birdtail, Mb, Can. 186/D2
Birdum, Austl. 152/D3
Birdwood, Austl. 155/M8
Birecik, Turk. 114/D2
Bireuen, Indo. 101/B1
Bīrganj, Nepal 109/E2
Birganj, Bang. 109/G3
Birigui, Braz. 225/G2
Biritiba-Mirim, Braz. 223/K8
Bīrjand, Iran 113/G2
Birkat al Ja'ār (well), Egypt 131/B4
Birkat as Sab', Egypt 131/C3
Birkat Ghiţās, Egypt 131/B2
Birkat Umm Rīshah (well), Egypt 131/B4
Birkelane, Sen. 132/B3
Birken-Honigsessen, Ger. 61/G2
Birkenau, Ger. 64/B3
Birkenfeld, Ger. 61/G4
Birkenfeld, Ger. 64/B5
Birkenhead, Eng, UK 41/E5
Birkenhead, NZ 159/F6
Birkenheide, Ger. 64/B4
Birkenwerder, Ger. 48/Q6
Birkerød, Den. 45/J7
Birkirkara, Malta 54/L7
Birkkarspitze (peak), Aus. 67/H3
Birky, Ukr. 79/J3
Bîrlad (riv.), Rom. 76/C3
Bîrlad, Rom. 57/H2
Birmā, Egypt 131/B3
Birmāna, India 110/B5
Birmingham, Eng, UK 43/E2
Birmingham (co.), Eng, UK 43/E2
Birmingham (int'l arpt.), Eng, UK 43/E2
Birmingham, Al, US 192/D4
Birmingham, Mi, US 197/F6
Birmitrapur, India 109/E4
Birnam, Sc, UK 39/C3
Birnamwood, Wi, US 185/K1
Birney, Mt, US 177/K1
Birnhorn (peak), Aus. 51/K3
Birni Nkonni, Niger 133/G3
Birnie (isl.), Kiri. 161/H5
Birnin Gwari, Nga. 133/G4
Birnin Kebbi, Nga. 133/G3
Birnin Kudu, Nga. 133/H4
Birniwa, Nga. 133/H3
Birobjian, Rus. 91/L2
Bīrpur, India 109/F2
Birqash, Egypt 131/C4
Birr, Ire. 38/C3
Birreencorragh (peak), Ire. 38/A2
Birrimbah, Austl. 152/D4
Birrindudu, Austl. 152/C4
Birriwa, Austl. 156/D2
Birs (riv.), Swi. 51/G3
Birsk, Rus. 75/M5
Birstein, Ger. 64/C2
Birštonas, Lith. 47/L4
Birtle, Mb, Can. 186/D2
Biru, China 90/C5
Biruaca, Ven. 217/E3
Biruni, Uzb. 80/G5
Biryulevo (nbrhd.), Rus. 75/W9
Biržai, Lith. 47/L3
Birżebbuġa, Malta 54/M7
Bis (lake), Hun. 57/F4
Bisa-Nadi Nat'l Rsv., Kenya 137/B1
Bisagana, Nga. 134/B2
Bisai, Japan 95/L5
Bīsalpur, India 108/B1
Bisamberg, Aus. 57/N7
Bisauli, India 108/B1
Bisbee, ND, US 186/E3
Bisbee, Az, US 179/H5
Biscarrosse (lake), Fr. 50/C4
Biscarrosse, Fr. 50/C4
Biscay (bay), Fr.,Sp. 29/D4
Biscayne (bay), Fl, US 194/P11
Biscayne NP, Fl, US 203/E2
Bisceglie, It. 54/E2
Bischberg, Ger. 64/D3
Bischheim, Fr. 61/G6
Bischofsgrün, Ger. 65/E2
Bischofsheim, Ger. 64/B3
Bischofsheim an der Rhön, Ger. 64/D2
Bischofshofen, Aus. 51/K3
Bischofszell, Swi. 67/F3
Bischwiller, Fr. 66/D2
Biscoe, NC, US 193/H3
Biscoe (Fredonia), Ar, US 183/J3
Biscubio (riv.), It. 69/F5
Biscucuy, Ven. 216/D2
Bisenge, D.R. Congo 139/E2
Bīshah (riv.), SAr. 112/D4
Bīshat Qā'id, Egypt 131/C3
Bishkek (cap.), Kyr. 111/B3
Bishnupur, India 109/F4
Bisho, SAfr. 142/D4
Bishop, Ca, US 178/C2
Bishop, Tx, US 181/F4
Bishop Auckland, Eng, UK 41/G2
Bishop Ind. Res., Ca, US 178/C2
Bishop International (arpt.), Mi, US 197/E6
Bishop Wilton, Eng, UK 41/H4
Bishopbriggs, Sc, UK 39/B5
Bishops Castle, Eng, UK 42/D1
Bishops Cleeve, Eng, UK 42/D3
Bishop's Falls, Nf, Can. 189/K1
Bishop's Stortford, Eng, UK 43/G3
Bishops Waltham, Eng, UK 43/E5
Bishopton, Sc, UK 39/B5
Bishopville, SC, US 193/G3
Bishrah (well), Libya 126/D4
Bisingen, Ger. 64/B6
Biskra, Alg. 130/H5
Biskupiec, Pol. 47/J5
Bislig, Phil. 100/D3
Bismarck, On, Can. 190/U9
Bismarck (sea), PNG 160/D5
Bismarck (arch.), PNG 160/D5
Bismarck (range), PNG 153/G1
Bismarck, Ar, US 183/H3
Bismarck, Mo, US 192/B2
Bismarck (cap.), ND, US 186/D4
Bismil, Turk. 114/E2
Bismuna (lag.), Nic. 207/F3
Biso, Ugan. 139/G2
Bison, Ks, US 182/E1
Bison, SD, US 186/C5
Bispgarden, Swe. 44/F3
Bispingen, Ger. 59/G2
Bissau, India 110/C5
Bissau (cap.), GBis. 132/B4
Bissau (Bipoint) (int'l arpt.), GBis. 132/B4
Bissaula, Nga. 133/H5
Bissendorf, Ger. 59/F4
Bissett, Mb, Can. 187/G2
Bissingen, Ger. 64/D5
Bissingen an der Enz, Ger. 64/C5
Bissora, GBis. 132/B3
Bistagno, It. 68/B4
Bistriţa, Rom. 57/G2
Bistriţa (riv.), Rom. 57/G2
Bistriţa-Năsăud (prov.), Rom. 57/G2
Bistrup, Den. 45/J7
Biswān, India 108/C2
Bita (riv.), Col. 216/D3
Bitagron, Sur. 218/B1
Bitale, Tanz. 139/G4
Bitam, Gabon 138/B2
Bitburg, Ger. 61/F4
Bitche, Fr. 61/G5
Bitéa, Ouadi (riv.), Chad 134/D2
Bithnok, India 104/B2
Bitkin, Chad 134/C3
Bitlis, Turk. 114/E2
Bitlis (prov.), Turk. 114/E2
Bitola, FYROM 55/G2
Bitonto, It. 54/E2
Bitter (lake), Egypt 127/G2
Bitter (cr.), Wy, US 177/J3
Bitter Creek, Wy, US 177/J3
Bitter Lake Nat'l Wildlife Reserve, NM, US 182/B4
Bitterfontein, SAfr. 142/B3
Bittern Lake, Ab, Can. 175/H1
Bitterroot (range), Id, US 177/F1
Bitterroot (riv.), Mt, US 175/G4
Bitti, It. 54/A2
Bittou, Burk. 133/E4
Bitung, Indo. 103/G3
Bituruna, Braz. 225/G3
Biu, Nga. 134/B3
Biviers, Fr. 70/B2
Bivolari, Rom. 78/D4
Biwa, Japan 95/K5
Bixby, Ok, US 183/G3
Bixby, Mo, US 192/B2
Biyagundi, Erit. 135/H2
Biyalā, Egypt 131/C2
Biyang, China 92/C4
Biysk, Rus. 111/E1
Bizard (isl.), Qu, Can. 189/M7
Bizerte, Tun. 130/L6
Bizerte (lake), Tun. 130/L6
Bjärnum, Swe. 45/K6
Bjärred, Swe. 46/E4
Bjelovar, Cro. 56/C3
Bjerge (riv.), Den. 45/H7
Bjerkvik, Nor. 44/F1
Bjerringbro, Den. 46/C3
Bjorkdale, Sk, Can. 175/N1
Bjørkelangen, Nor. 46/D2
Björklinge, Swe. 46/G1
Björknäs, Swe. 45/B1
Björkö, Swe. 45/C1
Björkö (isl.), Swe. 45/C1
Björksund, Swe. 45/A2
Bjørnafjorden (estu.), Nor. 46/A1
Bjorne (pen.), Nun, Can. 171/S7
Björnlunda, Swe. 45/A1
Björnö, Swe. 45/B1
Bjugn, Nor. 44/D3
Bjuv, Swe. 46/E3
Blå Jungfrun NP, Swe. 46/G3
Blaby, Eng, UK 43/E1
Blace, Serb. 56/E4
Blachownia, Pol. 49/K3
Black (sea), Asia,Eur. 83/C5
Black (mts.), Bhu. 109/H2
Black (isl.), Mb, Can. 186/F2
Black (bay), On, Can. 187/K3
Black (riv.), On, Can. 187/M3
Black (mt.), Yk, Can. 201/M3
Black (riv.), China,Viet. 106/C1
Black (for.), Ger. 48/D5
Black (pt.), Namb. 140/B5
Black (pt.), NZ 159/D3
Black (pt.), Eng, UK 42/A6
Black (pt.), NI, UK 40/C2
Black (isl.), Sc, UK 39/B1
Black (mts.), Wal, UK 42/C3
Black (mtn.), Wal, UK 42/C3
Black (mts.), Az, US 178/E3
Black (pt.), Ct, US 199/F1
Black (mtn.), Id, US 174/G4
Black (mtn.), Ky, US 193/F2
Black (lake), Mi, US 190/D2
Black (cr.), Ms, US 194/D2
Black (mesa), NM, US 179/J3
Black (range), NM, US 179/J4
Black (mesa), Ok, US 182/C2
Black (cr.), Pa, US 198/B2
Black (hills), SD, US 172/F3
Black, Tx, US 182/C3
Black (mtn.), Tx, US 180/D3
Black (mtn.), Tx, US 180/C2
Black (riv.), Viet. 105/H3
Black (Da) (riv.), Viet. 98/E4
Black Bear (cr.), Ok, US 183/F2
Black Bourton, Eng, UK 43/E3
Black Butte (lake), Ca, US 176/B4
Black Canyon City, Az, US 179/F3
Black Canyon Of The Gunnison Nat'l Mon., Co, US 177/K4
Black Coulee Nat'l Wild. Ref., Mt, US 175/K3
Black Creek, Wi, US 187/K5
Black Diamond, Wa, US 197/C3
Black Diamond, Ab, Can. 175/G2
Black Eagle, Mt, US 175/J4
Black Forest, Co, US 182/B1
Black Forest (Schwarzwald) (for.), Ger. 64/B6
Black Fork (mtn.), Ok, US 183/G3
Black Hammer (hill), ND, US 186/E4
Black Head (pt.), Ire. 38/A3
Black Hills Caverns, SD, US 184/C1
Black Lake, Qu, Can. 188/B2
Black Lake Bayou (riv.), La, US 183/H4
Black Mesa (int), Az, US 179/G4
Black Mesa (int.), Az, US 179/H4
Black Mesa (mesa), Az, US 179/G2
Black Mountain, NC, US 193/F3
Black Mountain NP, Austl. 158/B1
Black Pine (peak), Id, US 177/G2
Black Point, Ca, US 197/K10
Black Reef (pt.), Namb. 140/B5
Black River, Mi, US 190/E2
Black River, Jam. 207/G2
Black River Falls, Wi, US 185/J1
Black Rock (des.), Nv, US 176/D3
Black Rock, Ar, US 192/B2
Black Rock (pt.), RI, US 199/G1
Black Sea Lowland (lowland), Ukr. 78/E4
Black Sea Lowlands (reg.), Ukr. 57/J3
Black Sturgeon (riv.), On, Can. 187/K3
Black Sugarloaf (peak), Austl. 156/D1
Black Volta (riv.), Burk. 119/B4
Black Warrior (riv.), Al, US 192/D4
Black Warrior, Locust Fk. (riv.), Al, US 192/D4
Blackadder Water. (riv.), Sc, UK 39/D5
Blackall, Austl. 158/B4
Blackbeard Island NWR, Ga, US 195/H2
Blackberry (cr.), Il, US 197/P16
Blackburn, Eng, UK 41/F4
Blackburn, Sc, UK 39/C5

Borme – Broko
271

Bormes-les-Mimosas, Fr. 70/C6
Bormida, It. 68/B5
Bormida (riv.), It. 51/H4
Bormida di Millesimo (riv.), It. 68/B4
Bormio, It. 67/G5
Born, Neth. 61/E1
Borna, Ger. 48/G3
Borndiep (chan.), Neth. 58/C2
Borne (riv.), Fr. 66/C6
Borne, Neth. 58/D4
Bornel, Fr. 60/B5
Bornem, Belg. 61/D1
Borneo (isl.), Indo.,Malay. 83/L9
Borneo (isl.), Indo. 103/E3
Bornheim, Ger. 61/G2
Bornholm (co.), Den. 46/F4
Bornholm (isl.), Den. 46/F4
Bornholmsgat (chan.), Den.,Swi. 49/H1
Borno, It. 67/G6
Borno (state), Nga. 134/B2
Bornos, Sp. 52/C4
Börnsen, Ger. 59/H2
Bornus (plain), Nga. 134/B2
Boro (riv.), Sudan 135/E3
Borobudur (ruin), Indo. 101/E4
Borodino, Rus. 80/K4
Borodino, Ukr. 57/J2
Borodyanka, Ukr. 78/E2
Borohoro (mts.), China 111/D3
Boromo, Burk. 132/E4
Boron, Ca, US 178/D3
Borongan, Phil. 100/D3
Borough Green, Eng, UK 36/D3
Boroughbridge, Eng, UK 41/G3
Borovany, Czh. 65/H5
Borovichi, Rus. 74/G4
Borovlyanka, Rus. 111/D1
Borovo, Cro. 56/D3
Borovo, Bul. 57/G4
Borovsk, Rus. 76/F1
Borovskiy, Rus. 75/Q4
Borovskoy, Kaz. 75/Q5
Borraan, Som. 136/D3
Borre, Nor. 46/D2
Borrego Springs, Ca, US 178/D4
Borris, Ire. 38/D4
Borris in Ossory, Ire. 38/C4
Borrisokane, Ire. 38/B4
Borrisoleigh, Ire. 38/C4
Bornida (riv.), It. 68/B3
Borroloola, Austl. 153/E4
Borroloola Abor. Land, Austl. 153/D4
Borşa, Rom. 57/F2
Borsec, Rom. 78/C4
Borshchiv, Ukr. 78/D3
Borshchovochnyy (mts.), Rus. 91/H1
Borso del Grappa, It. 69/E2
Borsod-Abaúj-Zemplén (co.), Hun. 49/L4
Borssele, Neth. 58/A6
Borstel, Ger. 59/F3
Bort-les-Orgues, Fr. 50/E4
Bortala (riv.), China 111/D3
Borth, Wal, UK 42/B2
Boruca, CR 207/F4
Borūjen, Iran 115/G4
Borūjerd, Iran 115/G3
Børup, Den. 45/H7
Boryslav, Ukr. 49/M4
Boryspil', Ukr. 78/F2
Borzna, Ukr. 78/G2
Borzonasca, It. 68/C5
Borzya, Rus. 90/H1
Bosa, It. 54/A2
Bosaaso (Bender Cassim), Som. 136/D3
Bosanska Dubica, Bosn. 56/C3
Bosanska Gradiška, Bosn. 56/C3
Bosanska Kostajnica, Bosn. 56/C3
Bosanska Krupa, Bosn. 56/C3
Bosanski Brod, Bosn. 56/D3
Bosanski Petrovac, Bosn. 56/C3
Bosanski Šamac, Bosn. 56/D3
Bošany, Slvk. 49/K4
Bosavi (mt.), PNG 153/F1
Bosc-le-Hard, Fr. 63/G1
Boscawen, NH, US 191/L3
Bosco, La, US 183/H4
Bosco, It. 71/B1
Bosco Mesola, It. 69/F4
Boscobel, Wi, US 185/J2
Bosconero, It. 68/A2
Boscoreale, It. 71/D6
Bose, China 99/E4
Bosham, Eng, UK 43/F5
Boshnyakovo, Rus. 91/N2
Boshof, SAfr. 142/D3
Boshrūyeh, Iran 115/J3
Boskoop, Neth. 58/B4
Boskovice, Czh. 49/J4
Bosler, Wy, US 184/B3
Bosna (riv.), Bosn. 56/D3
Bosnia and Herzegovina (ctry.) 56/C3
Bošnjaci, Cro. 56/D3
Bōsō (pen.), Japan 97/G3
Bosobolo, D.R. Congo 134/C4
Bososama, D.R. Congo 134/D4
Bosporus (str.), Turk. 76/D4
Bosporus (riv.), Turk. 115/N6
Bosque del Apache Nat'l Wild Ref., NM, US 179/J4
Bosque Farms, NM, US 179/J3
Bosques Petrificados, Mon. Natural, Arg. 227/C5
Boss, Mo, US 192/B2
Bossangoa, CAfr. 134/C4
Bossembele, CAfr. 134/C4
Bossentélé, CAfr. 134/C4
Bossier City, La, US 183/H4
Bosso, Niger 134/B2
Bossut (cape), Austl. 152/A4
Bostān, Iran 115/G4
Bostan, China 111/D4
Bostānābād-e Bālā, Iran 115/F2
Bosten (lake), China 111/E3
Boston (mts.), Ar, US 183/H3
Boston, Tx, US 183/G4
Boston, Eng, UK 41/H6
Boston, Ga, US 195/G2
Boston (cap.), Ma, US 188/B4
Bostwick, Fl, US 195/H3
Bosut (riv.), Cro. 56/D3
Boswell, In, US 190/C4
Boswil, Swi. 67/E3
Bot Makak, Camr. 138/B2
Botād, India 113/K4
Botany, Austl. 157/E1
Botelerpunt (pt.), SAfr. 143/F2
Botelhos, Braz. 223/K6
Botene, Laos 106/C1
Botev (peak), Bul. 57/G4
Botevgrad, Bul. 57/F4
Bothaspas (pass), SAfr. 143/E2
Bothaville, SAfr. 142/D2
Bothel, Eng, UK 41/E2
Bothel, Ger. 59/G2
Bothell, Wa, US 197/C2
Bothenhampton, Eng, UK 42/D5
Bothnia (gulf), Fin.,Swe. 44/G2
Bothwell, Austl. 156/C4
Botkyrka, Swe. 45/A1
Botletle (riv.), Bots. 140/D4
Botlikh, Rus. 77/H4
Botoşani, Rom. 78/D4
Botoşani (prov.), Rom. 57/H2
Botou, China 92/D3
Botrange (peak), Belg. 61/F3
Botrivier, SAfr. 142/L11
Botsford, Ct, US 199/E1
Botswana (ctry.) 119/E7
Bottanuco, It. 68/C2
Botte Donato (peak), It. 54/E3
Bottesford, Eng, UK 41/H6
Bottesford, Eng, UK 41/H4
Botticino, It. 68/D2
Bottineau, ND, US 186/D3
Bottineau Winter Park, ND, US 186/D3
Bottrighe, It. 69/F3
Bottrop, Ger. 58/D5
Botucatu, Braz. 225/G2
Botwood, Nf, Can. 189/K1
Bötzow, Ger. 48/Q6
Bou (riv.), C.d'Iv. 132/D4
Bou Arfa, Mor. 129/E2
Boû Djébéha (well), Mali 132/E2
Bou Hamdane, Oued (riv.), Alg. 130/K6
Bou Ismaïl, Alg. 130/G4
Bou Izakarn, Mor. 128/C3
Bou Kadir, Alg. 130/F4
Bou Laber (well), Alg. 128/D4
Boû Lanouâr, Mrta. 128/A5
Bou Naceur (peak), Mor. 130/C3
Bou Regreg (riv.), Mor. 130/A3
Bou Saâda, Alg. 130/H5
Bou Salem, Tun. 130/L6
Bou Sellam, Oued (riv.), Alg. 130/H4
Bouaflé, C.d'Iv. 132/D5
Bouafle, Fr. 36/H5
Bouaké, C.d'Iv. 132/D5
Bouali, CAfr. 134/C4
Bouanga, Congo 138/D3
Bouar, CAfr. 134/B4
Bouba Ndjida, PN de, Camr. 134/B3
Boubín (peak), Czh. 65/G5
Bouc-Bel-Air, Fr. 70/B6
Bouca, CAfr. 134/C4
Bouchain, Fr. 60/C3
Bouchegouf, Alg. 130/K6
Boucherville, Qu, Can. 189/P6
Bouches-du-Rhône (dept.), Fr. 70/A5
Bouchet (mtn.), Fr. 70/D3
Boucle Du Baoulé, PN de la, Mali 132/C3
Boudenib, Mor. 128/E3
Boudi, Eth. 136/B4
Boudreaux (lake), La, US 194/C3
Boudry, Swi. 66/C4
Bouenza (riv.), Congo 138/C3
Bouenza (pol. reg.), Congo 138/C3
Boufarik, Alg. 130/G4
Bouffémont, Fr. 36/J4
Bougainville (cape), Austl. 152/B3
Bougainville (reef), Austl. 145/D2
Bougainville (isl.), PNG 160/E5
Bougainville (reef), PNG 153/G3
Bougainville (cape), UK 227/F6
Bougara, Alg. 130/G4
Bougar'oûn (cape), Alg. 130/K6
Bough Beech (res.), Eng, UK 36/D3
Boughton, Eng, UK 36/E3
Bougouni, Mali 132/D4
Bougouriba (prov.), Burk. 132/E4
Bougtob, Alg. 72/D4
Bouguenais, Fr. 50/C3
Bouhachem (peak), Mor. 130/B2
Bouhalla (peak), Mor. 130/B2
Bouillancy, Fr. 36/L4
Bouillon, Belg. 61/E4
Bouira, Alg. 130/G4
Bouira (wilaya), Alg. 130/G4
Boujad, Mor. 128/D2
Boukhalf (Tangier) (int'l arpt.), Mor. 130/B2
Boukoko, CAfr. 138/D2
Boukoumbé, Ben. 133/F4
Boulaide, Lux. 61/E4
Boulaouane, Mor. 128/C2
Boulay-Moselle, Fr. 61/F5
Boulazac, Fr. 50/D4
Boulder (riv.), Mt, US 177/H1
Boulder, Co, US 200/B2
Boulder, Mt, US 175/H4
Boulder City, Nv, US 178/E3
Boulder Creek, Ca, US 178/A2
Boulder Hill, Il, US 197/P16
Boulemane, Mor. 128/D2
Boulemane (prov.), Mor. 130/C3
Bouleurs, Fr. 36/L5
Boulgo (prov.), Burk. 133/E4
Boulia, Austl. 155/H2
Boulieu-lès-Annonay, Fr. 70/A2
Bouligny, Fr. 61/E5
Boulkiemde (prov.), Burk. 133/E3
Boullarre, Fr. 36/M4
Boulogne (riv.), Fr. 50/C3
Boulogne-Billancourt, Fr. 36/J5
Boulogne-sur-Mer, Fr. 60/A2
Bouloire, Fr. 63/F5
Boulsa, Burk. 133/E3
Boulsworth (hill), Eng, UK 41/F4
Boumalne, Mor. 128/D3
Boumba (riv.), Camr. 138/C2
Boûmdeïd, Mrta. 132/C2
Boumerdas (wilaya), Alg. 130/G4
Boumerdas, Alg. 130/G4
Boun Nua, Laos 98/D4
Bouna, C.d'Iv. 132/E4
Bound Brook, NJ, US 198/D2
Boundary, Yk, Can. 201/K3
Boundary (peak), Nv, US 172/C4
Boundary Bald (mtn.), Me, US 191/L2
Boundary Bend, Austl. 156/B2
Boundiali, C.d'Iv. 132/D4
Boundji, Congo 138/C3
Bountiful, Ut, US 177/H3
Boupanda, Congo 138/C3
Bouquet (res.), Ca, US 196/B1
Bouquet (canyon), Ca, US 196/B2
Bourail, NCal., Fr. 161/U12
Bourbeuse (riv.), Mo, US 185/J4
Bourbon, In, US 190/C4
Bourbon, Mo, US 183/J1
Bourbon l'Archambault, Fr. 50/E3
Bourbonnais, Il, US 190/C4
Bourbonnais (reg.), Fr. 72/D1
Bourbonne-les-Bains, Fr. 66/B2
Bourbourg, Fr. 60/B2
Bourbre (riv.), Fr. 70/B1
Bourbriac, Fr. 62/B4
Bourdonné, Fr. 36/G5
Boureït, Mor. 130/B2
Bourem, Mali 133/E2
Bouressa (riv.), Mali 133/F2
Bourg, La, US 194/C3
Bourg-Achard, Fr. 63/F2
Bourg-de-Péage, Fr. 70/B2
Bourg-en-Bresse, Fr. 66/B5
Bourg-lès-Valence, Fr. 70/A3
Bourg-Saint-Andéol, Fr. 70/A4
Bourg-Saint-Maurice, Fr. 70/C1
Bourg-Saint-Pierre, Swi. 66/D6
Bourganeuf, Fr. 50/D4
Bourges, Fr. 50/E3
Bourget (lake), Fr. 66/B6
Bourgneuf (bay), Fr. 50/B3
Bourgogne (canal), Fr. 66/B3
Bourgogne (pol. reg.), Fr. 50/F3
Bourgoin-Jallieu, Fr. 70/B1
Bourgtheroulde-Infreville, Fr. 63/F2
Bourgueil, Fr. 63/F6
Bourke, Austl. 156/C1
Bourmont, Fr. 66/B1
Bourne (riv.), Fr. 70/B2
Bourne, Eng, UK 43/F1
Bourne (riv.), Eng, UK 43/E4
Bourne End, Eng, UK 43/F3
Bournemouth, Eng, UK 43/E5
Bournemouth (co.), Eng, UK 43/E5
Bournemouth (arpt.), Eng, UK 43/E5
Bournville, Eng, UK 43/E2
Bourquim (hill), Ne, US 184/D3
Bourscheid, Lux. 61/F4
Bourtanger Moor (reg.), Ger. 59/E3
Bourth, Fr. 63/F3
Bourton on the Water, Eng, UK 43/E3
Bousbecque, Fr. 60/C2
Bouse, Az, US 179/E4
Bousso, Chad 134/C3
Boussois, Fr. 60/D3
Boussouma, Burk. 133/E3
Boutilimit, Mrta. 132/B2
Bouvard (cape), Austl. 154/B5
Bouvet (isl.), Nor. 27/K8
Bouvron, Fr. 62/D6
Bouxières-aux-Dames, Fr. 61/F6
Bouxwiller, Fr. 61/G6
Bouza, Niger 133/G3
Bouzillé, Fr. 63/D6
Bouznika, Mor. 130/A3
Bouzonville, Fr. 61/F5
Bovalino, It. 54/E3
Bovegno, It. 68/D2
Boven Tapanahoni (riv.), Sur. 217/H4
Boven Tappanahoni (riv.), Sur. 218/C2
Boven-Hardinxveld, Neth. 58/B5
Bovenden, Ger. 59/G5
Bovenkarspel, Neth. 58/C3
Bovenwijde (lake), Neth. 58/D3
Boves, Fr. 60/B4
Boves, It. 70/D4
Bovey, Mn, US 187/H4
Bovey Tracey, Eng, UK 42/C5
Bovezzo, It. 68/D2
Bovina, Tx, US 182/C3
Bovingdon, Eng, UK 36/B1
Bovino, It. 56/B5
Bovolone, It. 69/E3
Bovril, Arg. 224/E4
Bow (riv.), Ab, Can. 170/E3
Bow (cr.), Ks, US 184/E4
Bow (riv.), Ab, Can. 175/H2
Bow City, Ab, Can. 175/H2
Bow Island, Ab, Can. 175/J3
Bow River Abor. Land, Austl. 152/B4
Bowbells, ND, US 186/C3
Bowdle, SD, US 186/E5
Bowdoin NWR, Mt, US 175/L3
Bowdon, ND, US 186/E4
Bowdon, Eng, UK 41/F5
Bowdon, Ga, US 192/E4
Bowen, Austl. 158/C3
Bowen, Arg. 226/D2
Bowen Island, BC, Can. 174/C3
Bowers Beach, De, US 198/C5
Bowes, Eng, UK 41/G3
Bowie, Tx, US 183/F4
Bowie, Az, US 179/H4
Bowie, Md, US 198/B6
Bowling Green, Oh, US 190/E4
Bowling Green, Fl, US 194/M8
Bowling Green (cape), Austl. 158/B2
Bowling Green, Ky, US 192/D2
Bowling Green, Mo, US 185/J4
Bowling Green, Va, US 193/J1
Bowling Green Bay NP, Austl. 158/B2
Bowman, ND, US 186/C4
Bowman (bay), Nun, Can. 171/J2
Bowman, Ga, US 193/F3
Bowman (mt.), BC, Can. 174/D2
Bowman-Haley (dam), ND, US 186/C5
Bowman-Haley (lake), ND, US 186/C4
Bowmansdale, Pa, US 198/B3
Bowmanstown, Pa, US 198/C2
Bowmansville, Pa, US 198/B3
Bowmanville, On, Can. 190/V8
Bowmore, Sc, UK 37/Q9
Bowness-on-Solway, Eng, UK 41/E2
Bowokan (isls.), Indo. 103/F4
Bowral, Austl. 157/E2
Bowring, Ok, US 183/F2
Bowron (riv.), BC, Can. 174/D1
Bowsman, Mb, Can. 186/D1
Bowutu (mts.), PNG 153/G1
Bowwood, Zam. 140/E3
Box Elder (riv.), Mt, US 186/B5
Box Elder (cr.), SD, US 184/C3
Box Elder (cr.), Co, US 184/B3
Box Elder, SD, US 184/C1
Box Elder, Mt, US 175/J3
Box Hill (nbrhd.), Austl. 156/G5
Box Springs, Ga, US 192/E4
Boxberg, Ger. 64/C4
Boxelder, Wy, US 184/B2
Boxholm, Swe. 46/F2
Boxing, China 92/D3
Boxley, Ar, US 183/H3
Boxmeer, Neth. 58/C5
Boxodoi, China 90/H3
Boxtel, Neth. 58/C5
Boxum, Neth. 58/C2
Boyabat, Turk. 76/E4
Boyabo, D.R. Congo 138/D2
Boyabo, D.R. Congo 134/C5
Boyaca (dept.), Col. 216/C3
Boyalık, Turk. 115/M6
Boyanup, Austl. 154/B5
Boyarka, Ukr. 78/F2
Boyce, La, US 194/B2
Boychinovtsi, Bul. 57/F4
Boyd, Tx, US 180/K6
Boydell, Ar, US 183/J4
Boyds, Wa, US 174/E3
Boydton, Va, US 193/H2
Boye, China 92/C3
Boyer (riv.), Ia, US 185/G2
Boyero, Co, US 184/C4
Boyertown, Pa, US 198/C3
Boyes, Mt, US 184/B1
Boyette, Fl, US 194/L8
Boykins, Va, US 193/J2
Boyle, Ire. 38/B2
Boyle, Ms, US 192/B4
Boyne (riv.), Ire. 40/B4
Boyne City, Mi, US 190/D2
Boyne Falls, Mi, US 190/D2
Boyne Island, Austl. 158/C3
Boynton, Ok, US 183/G3
Boynton Beach, Fl, US 194/P9
Boysen (res.), Wy, US 177/J2
Boysen (dam), Wy, US 177/J2
Boyuibe, Bol. 224/D2
Boyup Brook, Austl. 154/C5
Boz (pt.), Turk. 57/J5
Bozcaada, Turk. 55/K3
Bozcaada (isl.), Gre. 55/J3
Bozel, Fr. 70/C2
Bozeman, Mt, US 177/H1
Bozhai, China 99/F3
Bozkir, Turk. 114/C2
Bozkurt, Turk. 76/E4
Bozman, Md, US 198/B6
Bozoum, CAfr. 134/C4
Bozova, Turk. 114/D2
Bozüyük, Turk. 116/E1
Bozyazı, Turk. 116/C1
Bozzolo, It. 68/D3
Bra, It. 68/A3
Braan (riv.), Sc, UK 39/C3
Bråån (riv.), Swe. 45/K7
Brabourne Lees, Eng, UK 43/G4
Brač (isl.), Cro. 54/E1
Bracciano (lake), It. 54/B1
Bracciano, It. 71/B3
Bracebridge, On, Can. 191/G2
Bracieux, Fr. 63/G5
Bracigliano, It. 71/D6
Brackel, Ger. 59/H2
Bracken, Sk, Can. 175/K3
Brackenheim, Ger. 64/C4
Brackett, Wi, US 185/J1
Brackettville, Tx, US 180/D3
Brackley, Eng, UK 43/E2
Bracknagh, Ire. 38/C3
Bracknell, Eng, UK 43/F4
Bracknell Forest (co.), Eng, UK 43/F4
Brackwede, Ger. 59/F5
Braço do Norte, Braz. 225/G4
Braço Menor do Araguaia (riv.), Braz. 222/C2
Brad, Rom. 57/F2
Bradano (riv.), It. 56/B5
Bradda (pt.), IM, UK 40/D3
Braddock, ND, US 186/D4
Braden, Tn, US 192/C3
Bradenton, Fl, US 195/G4
Bradford, Eng, UK 41/G4
Bradford (co.), Eng, UK 41/G4
Bradford, Ar, US 183/J3
Bradford, Oh, US 190/D4
Bradford, Pa, US 191/G4
Bradford, Vt, US 191/K3
Bradford West Gwillimbury, On, Can. 191/G2
Bradford-on-Avon, Eng, UK 42/D4
Brading, Eng, UK 43/E5
Bradley, Wi, US 187/K5
Bradley, Ar, US 183/H4
Bradley (int'l arpt.), Ct, US 191/K4
Bradley, Il, US 190/C4
Bradley, Ca, US 178/B3
Bradley Beach, NJ, US 199/D3
Bradley Junction, Fl, US 194/M8
Bradner, Oh, US 190/E4
Brady, Mt, US 175/J3
Brady, Ne, US 184/D3
Brady, Tx, US 180/E2
Brady (cr.), Tx, US 180/E2
Braeburn, Yk, Can. 201/L3
Braemar (reg.), Sc, UK 39/C2
Braemar, Sc, UK 39/C2
Braeriach (peak), Sc, UK 39/C2
Braga, Port. 52/A2
Braga (dist.), Port. 52/A2
Bragado, Arg. 226/E2
Bragança, Port. 52/B2
Bragança (dist.), Port. 52/B2
Bragança, Braz. 219/E3
Bragança Paulista, Braz. 223/K7
Bragg Creek, Ab, Can. 174/G2
Braggs, Ok, US 183/G3
Bragin, Bela. 78/F2
Braham, Mn, US 187/H5
Brahmakund, India 98/C3
Brāhmanbāria, Bang. 109/H4
Brahmaputra (riv.), Asia 83/J7
Braich-y-Pwll (pt.), Wal, UK 40/D6
Braid (riv.), NI, UK 40/B2
Braidwood, Il, US 190/B4
Braidwood, Austl. 157/D2
Brăila, Rom. 57/H3
Brăila (prov.), Rom. 57/H3
Brainard, Ne, US 185/F3
Brainards, NJ, US 198/C2
Braine, Fr. 60/C5
Braine-l'Alleud, Belg. 61/D2
Braine-le-Comte, Belg. 61/D2
Brainerd, Mn, US 187/G4
Braintree, Eng, UK 43/G3
Braithwaithe (pt.), Austl. 152/D2
Brajarajnagar, India 107/D1
Brak (riv.), SAfr. 142/C3
Brak (riv.), SAfr. 142/D3
Brake, Ger. 59/F2
Brakel, Belg. 60/C2
Brakel, Ger. 59/G5
Brakel, Neth. 58/C5
Brakna (pol. reg.), Mrta. 132/B2
Brålanda, Swe. 46/E2
Bralorne, BC, Can. 174/C2
Bram, Fr. 50/E5
Bram (peak), It. 70/D4
Bramalea, On, Can. 190/T8
Braman, Ok, US 183/F2
Bramdrupdam, Den. 46/C4
Bramhope, Eng, UK 41/G4
Bramley, Eng, UK 36/B3
Bramley (mtn.), NY, US 191/J3
Brampton, Eng, UK 41/F2
Brampton, On, Can. 190/T8
Bramsche, Ger. 59/F4
Bramstedt, Ger. 59/F2
Bran (riv.), Sc, UK 39/A1
Branam, Gha. 133/E5
Brancaleone-Marina, It. 54/E4
Brancepeth, Sk, Can. 175/M1
Branch, Mn, US 187/H5
Branch, Nf, Can. 189/L2
Branch, La, US 194/B2
Branch Dale, Pa, US 198/B2
Branch, North (riv.), Md, US 198/B5
Branch, South (riv.), WV, US 193/H1
Branchville, NJ, US 198/D1
Branchville, Ct, US 199/E1
Branco (riv.), Braz. 209/C2
Brand, Aus. 67/F3
Brandberg (peak), Namb. 140/B4
Brandbu, Nor. 46/D1
Brande, Den. 46/C4
Brandenburg, Ger. 48/G2
Brandenburg (state), Ger. 48/P6
Brandenburg, Ky, US 192/D2
Brander, Pass of (pass), Sc, UK 39/A4
Branderburgh, Sc, UK 39/C1
Brandesburton, Eng, UK 41/H4
Brandfort, SAfr. 142/D3
Brandizzo, It. 68/A2
Brandon, Mb, Can. 186/E3
Brandon (peak), Ire. 38/D5
Brandon, Eng, UK 41/G2
Brandon, Eng, UK 43/G2
Brandon, Co, US 182/C1
Brandon, Fl, US 194/L8
Brandon, Mn, US 187/G5
Brandon, Ms, US 192/C4
Brandon, SD, US 185/F2
Brandon, Vt, US 191/K3
Brandsen, Arg. 227/J11
Brandsville, Mo, US 183/J2
Brandvlei, SAfr. 142/C3
Brandýs nad Labem, Czh. 65/H2
Brandywine, Md, US 198/B6
Brandywine (riv.), Pa, US 198/C4
Brandywine, WV, US 193/H1
Branford, Ct, US 199/F1
Branford, Fl, US 195/G3
Branges, Fr. 66/B4
Braniewo, Pol. 47/H4
Brannenburg, Ger. 51/K3
Bransgore, Eng, UK 43/E5
Branson, Mo, US 183/H2
Brant (co.), On, Can. 190/S9
Brant Beach, NJ, US 199/D4
Brantford, On, Can. 190/S9
Branti, Indo. 101/D4
Brantley, Al, US 195/E2
Brantwood, Wi, US 187/J5
Branxholm, Austl. 156/C4
Branxholme, Austl. 156/B3
Branxton, Austl. 157/E1
Branxton, Eng, UK 39/D5
Branzoll (Bronzolo), It. 67/H4
Brasfield, Ar, US 183/J3
Brashear, Mo, US 185/H3
Brasher Falls-Winthrop, NY, US 191/J2
Brasiléia, Braz. 220/D3
Brasília (cap.), Braz. 222/D2
Brasília de Minas, Braz. 222/D3
Brasilia, PN de, Braz. 222/C2
Braşov, Rom. 57/G3
Braşov (prov.), Rom. 57/G3
Brass, Nga. 133/G5
Brasschaat, Belg. 58/B6
Brassey (mt.), Austl. 155/G2
Brasstown Bald (peak), Ga, US 192/F3
Brastad, Swe. 46/D2
Braswell, Ga, US 192/E4
Brat (isl.), Cro. 73/H2
Bratislava (cap.), Slvk. 56/C1
Bratislava (Ivanka) (int'l arpt.), Slvk. 56/C1
Bratislavský (pol. reg.), Slvk. 49/J4
Bratsigovo, Bul. 55/J1
Bratsk, Rus. 81/L4
Brats'ke, Ukr. 78/F4
Bratslav, Ukr. 78/E3
Brattleboro, Vt, US 191/K3
Bratunac, Bosn. 56/D3
Braubach, Ger. 61/G3
Braulio Carrillo, PN, CR 202/E5
Braunau am Inn, Aus. 65/G6
Braunfels, Ger. 64/B1
Braunlage, Ger. 59/H5
Bräunlingen, Ger. 67/E2
Braunschweig, Ger. 59/H4
Braunschweig (arpt.), Ger. 59/H4
Braunton, Eng, UK 42/B4
Brava (coast), Sp. 53/G2
Brava (pt.), Chile 227/C7
Brava (isl.), CpV. 119/J11
Brava (pt.), Uru. 227/K11
Brave, Pa, US 190/F5
Bråviken (inlet), Swe. 46/G2
Bravo (peak), Bol. 224/C1
Bravo (peak), Peru 220/B2
Bravo del Norte (riv.), Mex. 202/A2
Brawley, Ca, US 178/E4
Bray (pt.), Ire. 40/B5
Bray, Ire. 40/B5
Bray, Eng, UK 36/A2
Bray (isl.), Nun, Can. 171/J2
Bray-Dunes, Fr. 60/B1
Braye (riv.), Fr. 50/D3
Braymer, Mo, US 185/H4
Brazeau (riv.), Ab, Can. 174/F1
Brazeau (mt.), Ab, Can. 174/F1
Brazey-en-Plaine, Fr. 66/B3
Brazil, In, US 190/C5
Brazil (ctry.) 209/D3
Brazil, Tn, US 192/C3
Brazilian Highlands (uplands), Braz. 209/E4
Brazo Casiquiare (riv.), Ven. 217/E4
Brazo Sur (riv.), Arg. 227/C6
Brazópolis, Braz. 223/L7
Brazoria (co.), Tx, US 181/M9
Brazoria NWR, Tx, US 181/G3
Brazos (riv.), Tx, US 181/G3
Brazos, Double Mountain Fork (riv.), Tx, US 182/D4
Brazos, Salt Fork (riv.), Tx, US 182/D4
Brazzaville (cap.), Congo 138/C4
Brčko, Bosn. 56/D3
Brda (riv.), Pol. 46/G5
Brdy (mts.), Czh. 49/G4
Brea, Ca, US 196/G8
Breadalbane (dist.), Sc, UK 39/B4
Breakenridge (mt.), BC, Can. 174/D3
Bream (pt.), NZ 159/C1
Bream, Eng, UK 42/D3
Bream Tail (pt.), NZ 159/C2
Breamish (riv.), Eng, UK 39/D6
Bréancon, Fr. 36/J4
Bréau, Fr. 36/L6
Breaux Bridge, La, US 194/C2
Breaza, Rom. 57/G3
Brebbia, It. 68/B2
Brebes, Indo. 101/E4
Brécey, Fr. 63/D3
Brech, Fr. 62/C5
Brêche (riv.), Fr. 60/B5
Brechen, Ger. 64/B2
Brechin, Sc, UK 39/D3
Brecht, Belg. 58/B6
Breckenridge, Mn, US 186/F4
Breckenridge, Mo, US 185/H4
Breckenridge, Tx, US 181/E1
Breckerfeld, Ger. 59/E6
Breckland (phys. reg.), Eng, UK 43/G2
Brecknock (pen.), Chile 227/C7
Brecon, Wal, UK 42/C3
Brecon Beacons (mts.), Wal, UK 42/C3
Bréda (riv.), Fr. 70/C2
Breda, Neth. 58/B5
Bredaryd, Swe. 46/E3
Bredasdorp, SAfr. 142/M11
Bredbo, Austl. 157/D2
Bredebro, Den. 46/C4
Bredene, Belg. 60/B1
Bredgar, Eng, UK 36/F3
Bredstedt, Ger. 46/C4
Bree, Belg. 61/E1
Breë (riv.), SAfr. 142/B4
Breeches (cr.), Pa, US 198/A3
Breed, Wi, US 187/K5
Breese, Il, US 192/C1
Breezand, Neth. 58/B3
Breezy Point, Mn, US 187/G4
Breg (riv.), Ger. 48/E5
Bregagno (peak), It. 67/F5
Bregalinca (riv.), FYROM 55/H2
Breganze, It. 69/E2
Bregenz, Aus. 67/F3
Bregenzer Ache (riv.), Aus. 67/F3
Bregovo, Bul. 56/F3
Brégy, Fr. 36/L4
Bréhal, Fr. 62/D3
Breidhafjördhur (bay), Ice. 44/M6
Breil-Brigels, Swi. 67/F4
Breil-sur-Roya, Fr. 70/D5
Breisach, Ger. 66/D1
Breitbrunn am Chiemsee, Ger. 65/F7
Breitenauriegel (peak), Ger. 65/G5
Breitenbach, Swi. 66/D3
Breitenbach, Ger. 61/G5
Breitenbrunn, Ger. 65/E4
Breitenbrunn, Ger. 65/F2
Breitenfurt bei Wien, Aus. 57/N7
Breitenworbis, Ger. 59/H6
Breithorn (peak), Swi. 66/D5
Breithorn (peak), Swi. 66/D6
Brejinho de Nazaré, Braz. 222/C1
Brejo, Braz. 219/F3
Brejo do Cruz, Braz. 219/G4
Brejo Santo, Braz. 219/G4
Brembate di Sopra, It. 68/C2
Brembilla, It. 68/C2
Brembio, It. 68/C3
Brembo (riv.), It. 67/F6
Bremen, Ger. 59/F2
Bremen (int'l arpt.), Ger. 59/F2
Bremen (state), Ger. 46/C5
Bremen, Ga, US 192/E4
Bremen, In, US 190/C4
Bremen, Oh, US 190/E5
Bremer (riv.), Austl. 158/E7
Bremerhaven, Ger. 59/F1
Bremerhaven (arpt.), Ger. 59/F1
Bremerton, Wa, US 174/C4
Bremervörde, Ger. 59/G2
Bremgarten, Swi. 67/E3
Bremgarten bei Bern, Swi. 66/D4
Bremnes, Nor. 46/A2
Bremond, Tx, US 181/F2
Bremsa (riv.), Nor. 44/R8
Brenchley, Eng, UK 36/E3
Brend (riv.), Ger. 64/D2
Brendel (lake), Mi, US 197/E7
Brendola, It. 69/E3
Brendon (hills), Eng, UK 42/C4
Brenham, Tx, US 181/F2
Brenne (riv.), Fr. 48/C5
Brenner (pass), Aus. 67/H4
Brenner (riv.), Austl. 155/N9
Brenno (riv.), Swi. 67/E5
Breno, It. 67/G6
Brent, On, Can. 191/G1
Brent (riv.), Eng, UK 36/B2
Brent (bor.), Eng, UK 36/C2
Brent (res.), Eng, UK 36/C2
Brent, Al, US 192/D4
Brenta (peak), It. 67/G5
Brenta (riv.), It. 51/J4
Brenton, WV, US 193/G2
Brentwood, Eng, UK 36/D2
Brentwood, Ca, US 197/L11
Brentwood, Tn, US 192/D2
Brentwood, NY, US 199/E2
Brenz (riv.), Ger. 64/D5
Brescello, It. 68/D4
Brescia (prov.), It. 67/G6
Brescia, It. 68/D2
Breskens, Neth. 60/C1
Breslau, Tx, US 181/F3
Bresle (riv.), Fr. 50/D1
Bresles, Fr. 60/B5
Bresque (riv.), Fr. 70/C5
Bressana, It. 68/C3
Bressanone, It. 51/J3
Bressay (isl.), Sc, UK 37/W13
Bressuire, Fr. 50/C3
Brest, Bela. 49/M2
Brest (int'l arpt.), Bela. 49/M2
Brest, Fr. 62/A4
Brestskaya Voblasts, Bela. 76/C1
Bretagne (pol. reg.), Fr. 50/B2
Bretagne (pt.), Reun., Fr. 143/S15
Bretagne, Monts de (mts.), Fr. 50/B2
Bretaña, Peru 220/C2
Breteuil, Fr. 63/F3
Breteuil, Fr. 60/B4
Brethren, Mi, US 190/C2
Brétigny-sur-Orge, Fr. 36/J6
Breton, Ab, Can. 174/G1
Breton (cape), NS, Can. 189/H3
Breton (isls.), La, US 194/D3
Breton (sound), La, US 194/D3
Breton Cove, NS, Can. 189/G2
Breton Nat'l Wild. Ref., La, US 194/D3
Brett (cape), NZ 159/C1
Brett (riv.), Eng, UK 43/G2
Brettach (riv.), Ger. 64/C4
Bretten, Ger. 64/B4
Bretteville-L'Orgueilleuse, Fr. 63/E2
Bretzenheim, Ger. 61/G4
Breuberg, Ger. 64/C3
Breueh (isl.), Indo. 101/A1
Breugel, Neth. 58/C5
Breuillet, Fr. 36/J6
Breukelen, Neth. 58/B4
Breuna, Ger. 59/G6
Breuvannes-en-Bassigny, Fr. 66/B1
Brevard, NC, US 193/F3
Breves, Braz. 218/D3
Brevig Mission, Ak, US 201/E2
Brevik, Nor. 46/C2
Brevik, Swe. 45/B1
Brevoort (isl.), Nun, Can. 171/K2
Brewarrina, Austl. 156/C1
Brewer, Mo, US 192/C2
Brewerton, NY, US 191/H3
Brewerville, Libr. 132/C5
Brewood, Eng, UK 42/D1
Brewster (cape), Austl. 152/B3
Brewster (lake), Austl. 157/C1
Brewster, Fl, US 194/M8
Brewster, Ks, US 184/D4
Brewster, Mn, US 185/G2
Brewster, Ne, US 184/E3
Brewster, Oh, US 190/F4
Brewster, Wa, US 174/E3
Brewton, Al, US 194/E2
Brey-et-Lû, Fr. 36/G4
Breyten, SAfr. 143/E2
Brežice, Slov. 56/B3
Brezina, Alg. 129/F2
Březnice, Czh. 65/G3
Breznik, Bul. 56/F4
Brezoi, Rom. 57/G3
Brézolles, Fr. 63/G3
Brezovo, Bul. 57/G4
Bria, CAfr. 134/D4
Briançon, Fr. 70/C3
Briar Creek, Pa, US 198/B1
Briare, Fr. 50/E3
Bribbaree, Austl. 157/C2
Bric de Rubren (peak), Fr. 70/C3
Bric Rosso (peak), It. 70/D3
Brice, Tx, US 182/D3
Briceni, Mol. 78/D3
Brick, NJ, US 199/D3
Brickerville, Pa, US 198/B3
Bricket Wood, Eng, UK 36/B1
Brickley (brook), Austl. 154/L7
Bricquebec, Fr. 62/D2
Bridal Cave, Mo, US 183/H1
Bridal Veil (falls), Co, US 179/J2
Bride, IM, UK 40/D3
Bride (riv.), Ire. 38/B5
Bridge, Id, US 177/G2
Bridge (riv.), BC, Can. 174/C2
Bridge City, Tx, US 181/H2
Bridge of Allan, Sc, UK 39/C4
Bridge of Don, Sc, UK 39/D2
Bridge of Weir, Sc, UK 39/B5
Bridgehampton, NY, US 199/F2
Bridgeman (mtn.), Ky, US 192/E2
Bridgend, Wal, UK 42/C3
Bridgend (co.), Wal, UK 42/C3
Bridgeport, Ca, US 176/D4
Bridgeport, Ct, US 199/E1
Bridgeport, Il, US 192/D1
Bridgeport, Mi, US 190/E3
Bridgeport, Ne, US 184/C3
Bridgeport, NJ, US 198/C4
Bridgeport, Tx, US 180/K6
Bridgeport (lake), Tx, US 181/F1
Bridgeport, Wa, US 174/E3
Bridgeport, WV, US 190/F5
Bridger, Mt, US 177/J1
Bridgeton, NJ, US 198/C5
Bridgetown, Ire. 38/D5
Bridgetown, NS, Can. 188/E3
Bridgetown, Oh, US 192/E1
Bridgetown, Austl. 154/C5
Bridgetown (cap.), Bar. 203/P9
Bridgeville, Qu, Can. 188/E1
Bridgeville, Ca, US 176/B3
Bridgeville, De, US 198/C6
Bridgewater, Austl. 156/C4
Bridgewater, NS, Can. 188/E3
Bridgewater, Va, US 193/H1
Bridgnorth, Eng, UK 42/D1
Bridgton, Me, US 191/L2
Bridgwater, Eng, UK 42/D4
Bridgwater (bay), Eng, UK 42/C4
Bridlington (bay), Eng, UK 41/H3
Bridlington, Eng, UK 41/H3
Bridport, Austl. 156/C4
Bridport, Eng, UK 42/D5
Bridport, Vt, US 191/K3
Brie (reg.), Fr. 48/B4
Brie-Comte-Robert, Fr. 36/K5
Briec, Fr. 62/A4
Brieg Brzeg, Pol. 49/J3
Brielle, Neth. 58/B5
Brielle, NJ, US 199/D3
Brienz, Swi. 66/E4
Brier (isl.), Ns., Can. 188/D3
Brier (cr.), Ga, US 193/G4
Brier (mtn.), Pa, US 191/H4
Brier, Wa, US 197/C2
Briercrest, Sk, Can. 175/M2
Brierfield, Eng, UK 41/F4
Brieselang, Ger. 48/Q6
Brig, Swi. 66/D5
Brigach (riv.), Ger. 64/B7
Brigantine, NJ, US 199/D5
Brigg, Eng, UK 41/H4
Briggs, Tx, US 180/F2
Briggs Corner, NB, Can. 188/E2
Brigham City, Ut, US 177/G3
Brighouse, Eng, UK 41/G4
Brighstone, Eng, UK 43/E5
Bright, Austl. 157/C3
Brightlingsea, Eng, UK 43/H3
Brighton (nbrhd.), Austl. 155/M9
Brighton (nbrhd.), Austl. 156/G5
Brighton (nbrhd.), Austl. 158/F6
Brighton, On, Can. 191/H2
Brighton, Eng, UK 43/F5
Brighton, Co, US 184/B4
Brighton, Il, US 185/J4
Brighton, Mi, US 190/E3
Brighton, Tn, US 192/C3
Brighton, Wi, US 197/P14
Brighton and Hove (co.), Eng, UK 43/F5
Brightons, Sc, UK 39/C5
Brignais, Fr. 70/A1
Brignoles, Fr. 70/C6
Brihante (riv.), Braz. 225/F2
Brihuega, Sp. 52/D2
Briis-sous-Forges, Fr. 36/J6
Brikama, Gam. 132/A3
Brilhante (riv.), Braz. 222/B4
Brill, Eng, UK 43/E3
Brillion, Wi, US 190/B2
Brilon, Ger. 59/F6
Brimington, Eng, UK 41/G5
Brimley, Mi, US 190/D1
Brimstone Hill NP, StK. 203/N8
Brindisi, It. 55/E2
Brinkley, Ar, US 183/J3
Brinkmann, Arg. 224/D4
Brinktown, Mo, US 183/H1
Brinkworth, Austl. 155/H5
Brinkworth, Eng, UK 42/E3
Brinnon, Wa, US 197/B2
Brinson, Ga, US 195/F2
Briny Breezes, Fl, US 194/P9
Brion (isl.), Qu, Can. 189/G2
Brión, Sp. 52/A1
Brione, Swi. 67/E5
Briones (res.), Ca, US 197/K11
Brionne, Fr. 63/F2
Briouze, Fr. 63/E3
Brisbane, Austl. 158/F6
Brisbane (int'l arpt.), Austl. 158/F6
Brisbane (riv.), Austl. 158/E7
Brisbane Forest Park, Austl. 158/E6
Brisbane Ranges NP, Austl. 157/B3
Brisbane Water, Austl. 157/E1
Brisbane Water NP, Austl. 157/E1
Brisco, BC, Can. 174/F2
Brisighella, It. 69/E5
Brissago, Swi. 67/E5
Bristol, NB, Can. 188/D2
Bristol, Qu, Can. 191/H2
Bristol, Eng, UK 42/D4
Bristol (co.), Eng, UK 42/D4
Bristol (chan.), Eng, Wal, UK 42/B4
Bristol (bay), Ak, US 201/F4
Bristol (lake), Ca, US 178/E3
Bristol, Co, US 182/C1
Bristol, Ct, US 191/K4
Bristol, Fl, US 195/F2
Bristol, Ga, US 195/G2
Bristol, NH, US 191/L3
Bristol, Pa, US 198/D3
Bristol, RI, US 191/L4
Bristol, SD, US 186/F5
Bristol, Tn, US 193/F2
Bristol, Tx, US 180/L7
Bristol, Vt, US 191/K2
Bristolville, Oh, US 190/F4
Bristow, Ok, US 183/F3
Britânia, Braz. 222/C2
British (mts.), Ak, US 201/K2
British Columbia (prov.), Can. 170/D3
British Empire (range), Nun, Can. 171/S6
British Indian Ocean Terr. (terr.), UK 83/G10
British Mountains (range), Can.,Ak, US 201/K2
British Museum, Eng, UK 36/C2
Brits, SAfr. 141/E5
Britstown, SAfr. 142/C3
Britt, Ia, US 185/H2
Brittany (reg.), Fr. 50/B3
Britton, SD, US 186/F5
Britton, Tx, US 180/K7
Brive-la-Gaillarde, Fr. 50/D4
Brives-Charensac, Fr. 50/E4
Briviesca, Sp. 50/B5
Brivio, It. 68/C2
Brixham, Eng, UK 42/C6
Brixworth, Eng, UK 43/F2
Brlik, Kaz. 111/B3
Brněnský (pol. reg.), Czh. 49/J4
Beneěov, Czh. 65/H3
Brnik (int'l arpt.), Slov. 51/L3
Brno, Czh. 49/J4
Broa (bay), Cuba 207/F1
Broad (riv.), Ga, US 193/F4
Broad Arrow, Austl. 154/D4
Broad Law (peak), Sc, UK 39/C6
Broad Sound (isls.), Austl. 158/C2
Broad Street, Eng, UK 36/E3
Broad Valley, Mb, Can. 186/F2
Broadacres, Sk, Can. 175/K1
Broadbent, Or, US 176/A2
Broaddus, Tx, US 181/G2
Broadford, Ire. 38/B5
Broadford, Austl. 157/B3
Broadkill (riv.), De, US 198/C6
Broadley Common, Eng, UK 36/D1
Broadmeadows (nbrhd.), Austl. 156/F5
Broadstairs, Eng, UK 43/H4
Broadstone, Eng, UK 42/E5
Broadus, Mt, US 184/B1
Broadview, Mt, US 175/K4
Broadwater, Ne, US 184/C3
Broadwater NP, Austl. 156/E1
Broadway (hill), Eng, UK 43/E3
Broadway, NJ, US 198/C2
Broadwindsor, Eng, UK 42/D5
Broby, Swe. 45/L6
Broc, Swi. 66/D4
Brocēni, Lat. 47/K3
Brochet, Mb, Can. 170/F3
Brock (isl.), NW, Can. 171/R7
Brock, Sk, Can. 175/K2
Brocken (peak), Ger. 59/H5
Brockenhurst, Eng, UK 43/E5
Brocket, ND, US 186/E3
Brocket, Ab, Can. 175/H3
Brockman (mt.), Austl. 154/C2
Brockport, NY, US 191/H3
Brockton, Mt, US 186/B3
Brockton, Ma, US 191/L3
Brockville, On, Can. 191/J2
Brockway, Pa, US 191/G4
Brocton, NY, US 191/G3
Brodeur (pen.), Nun, Can. 170/G1
Brodhead, Wi, US 185/K2
Brodhead (cr.), Pa, US 198/C1
Brodheadsville, Pa, US 198/C2
Brodick, Sc, UK 39/A5
Brodnica, Pol. 49/K2
Brody, Ukr. 78/C2
Broek in Waterland, Neth. 58/B4
Broek Op Langedijk, Neth. 58/B3
Brogden, NC, US 193/H3
Broglie, Fr. 63/F2
Bröhn (peak), Ger. 59/G4
Brokaw, Wi, US 185/K1
Broken (bay), Austl. 156/D2
Broken (riv.), Austl. 157/B3
Broken Arrow, Ok, US 183/G2
Broken Back (crater), NM, US 179/J4
Broken Bow (dam), Ok, US 183/G3
Broken Bow, Ok, US 183/G3
Broken Bow (lake), Ok, US 183/G3
Broken Bow, Ne, US 184/E3
Broken Hill, Austl. 156/B1
Brokenhead Ind. Res., Mb, Can. 186/F2
Brokeoff (mts.), NM, US 182/B4
Brokopondo, Sur. 218/C1
Brokopondo (dist.), Sur. 217/H3

Bylot – Caoqi
273

Bylot (isl.), Nun, Can. 171/J1
Byng, Ok, US 183/F3
Byng Inlet, On, Can. 190/F2
Bynum, Tx, US 181/F2
Bynum, Mt, US 175/H4
Bynum Run (riv.), Md, US 198/B4
Byram (lake), NY, US 199/L7
Byram (pt.), Ct, US 199/L8
Byram (riv.), Ct, US 199/E1
Byrd (cape), Ant. 228/U
Byrd, US, Ant. 228/S
Byrdstown, Tn, US 192/E2
Byremo, Nor. 46/B2
Byrock, Austl. 156/C1
Byromville, Ga, US 192/F4
Byron (isl.), Chile 227/B5
Byron, Ca, US 197/L11
Byron, Ga, US 192/F4
Byron, Il, US 185/K2
Byron Bay, Austl. 158/D5
Byrranga (mts.), Rus. 80/K2
Byrum, Den. 46/D3
Bystice (riv.), Czh. 65/F2
Bystrá (peak), Slvk. 49/K4
Bystřice, Czh. 65/H3
Bytantay (riv.), Rus. 81/N3
Bytom, Pol. 49/K3
Bytów, Pol. 46/G4
Byumba, Rwa. 139/G3

C

C (canal), Co, US 179/H1
C.F. Secada (int'l arpt.), Peru 220/C1
C.J. Strike (res.), Id, US 176/E2
C.J. Strike (dam), Id, US 176/E2
C.W. McConaughy (lake), Ne, US 184/C3
Ca (riv.), Viet. 105/J4
Ca Mau (cape), Viet. 106/D4
Ca Mau, Viet. 106/D4
Caacupé, Par. 225/E3
Caaguazú (dept.), Par. 225/E3
Caaguazú, Par. 225/E3
Caála, Ang. 140/B2
Caatingas (phys. reg.), Braz. 209/E3
Caazapá, Par. 225/E3
Caazapá (dept.), Par. 225/E3
Cabadbaran, Phil. 100/D3
Cabaiguán, Cuba 207/G1
Caballo, NM, US 179/J4
Caballo (res.), NM, US 179/J4
Caballococha, Peru 220/D1
Caban-Coch (res.), Wal, UK 42/C2
Cabana, Peru 220/B3
Cabanaconde, Peru 220/D4
Cabañaquinta, Sp. 52/C1
Cabanatuan, Phil. 100/C2
Cabanes, Sp. 53/F2
Cabannes, Fr. 70/A5
Cabano, Qu, Can. 188/C2
Cabarroguis, Phil. 100/C1
Cabatuan, Phil. 100/C3
Cabedelo, Braz. 219/H4
Cabella Ligure, It. 68/C4
Cabestany, Fr. 50/E5
Cabeza del Buey, Sp. 52/C3
Cabeza Lagarto (pt.), Peru 220/B3
Cabeza Prieta Nat'l. Wild. Ref., Az, US 179/F4
Cabezas, Bol. 224/D1
Cabezón de la Sal, Sp. 52/C1
Cabildo, Arg. 226/E3
Cabimas, Ven. 216/D2
Cabinda, Ang. 138/C4
Cabinda (prov.), Ang. 138/B4
Cabinet (mts.), Mt, US 174/G3
Cabiri, Ang. 138/C5
Cabo, Braz. 219/H5
Cabo Blanco, Arg. 227/D5
Cabo Blanco, Peru 220/A2
Cabo Bojador, WSah. 128/B4
Cabo Corrientes, Cabo (cape), Mex. 204/D4
Cabo de Hornos, PN, Chile 227/D7
Cabo Delgado (prov), Moz. 141/H2
Cabo do Norte (cape), Braz. 218/D2
Cabo Falso (bank), Hon. 207/F3
Cabo Frio, Braz. 223/E4
Cabo Gracias a Dios, Nic. 207/F3
Cabo Orange, PN do, Braz. 218/D2
Cabo San Lucas, Mex. 204/C4
Cabo Verde, Braz. 223/K6
Cabonga (res.), Qu, Can. 171/J4
Cabool, Mo, US 183/H2
Caboolture, Austl. 158/D4
Cabora Bassa (lake), Moz. 141/F2
Cabot, Ar, US 183/H3
Cabot (str.), NS,NF, Can. 171/K4
Cabourg, Fr. 63/E2
Cabra, Sp. 52/C4
Cabra Corral (res.), Arg. 224/C3
Cabra de Santo Cristo, Sp. 52/D4
Cabramatta (nbrhd.), Austl. 158/G8
Cabras, It. 54/A3
Cabrera, Isla de (isl.), Sp. 72/D3
Cabri, Sk, Can. 175/K2
Cabriel (riv.), Sp. 52/E3
Cabriès, Fr. 70/B6
Cabrillo Nat'l Mon., Ca, US 196/C5
Cabrobó, Braz. 219/G5
Cabruta, Ven. 217/E3
Cabudare, Ven. 216/D2
Cabugao, Phil. 100/C1
Cabure, Ven. 216/D2
Caçador, Braz. 225/G3
Čačak, Serb. 56/E4
Cacala, Ang. 140/B1
Cacalotán, Mex. 204/D4
Caçapava, Braz. 223/L8
Caçapava do Sul, Braz. 225/F4
Cacapon (mtn.), WV, US 191/G5
Cacapon (riv.), WV, US 193/H1
Caccia (cape), It. 54/A2
Cacequi, Braz. 225/F4
Cáceres, Col. 216/C3
Cáceres, Sp. 52/B3
Cáceres, Braz. 221/G5
Cachapoal (riv.), Chile 226/N9
Cacharí, Arg. 227/J12
Cache, Ok, US 183/E3
Cache (cr.), Ca, US 176/B4
Cache (peak), Id, US 177/G2
Cache Creek, BC, Can. 174/D2
Cache la Poudre (riv.), Co, US 184/B3
Cache Slough (riv.), Ca, US 197/L10
Cacheu, GBis. 132/A3
Cachicadán, Peru 220/B3
Cachimbo, Serra do (mts.), Braz. 218/B4
Cachingues, Ang. 140/C2
Cachipo, Ven. 217/E2
Cachoeira Alta, Braz. 225/G1
Cachoeira de Minas, Braz. 223/L7
Cachoeira do Arari, Braz. 218/D3
Cachoeira do Sul, Braz. 225/F4
Cachoeira Paulista, Braz. 223/L7
Cachoeiras de Macacu, Braz. 223/P7
Cachoeirinha, Braz. 225/G4
Cachoeiro de Itapemirim, Braz. 223/E4
Cachorras, Col. 216/C4
Cachos (pt.), Chile 224/B3
Cacoal, Braz. 221/F3
Cacolo, Ang. 138/D5
Caconda, Ang. 140/B2
Caconde, Braz. 223/K6
Cacongo, Ang. 138/C4
Caçu, Braz. 222/C3
Cacuaco, Ang. 138/C5
Cacula, Ang. 140/B2
Caculuvar (riv.), Ang. 140/B3
Cacuri, Ven. 217/E3
Cacuso, Ang. 138/C5
Cadaadle, Som. 136/C3
Čadca, Slvk. 49/K4
Caddo (mts.), Ar, US 183/H3
Caddo (riv.), Ar, US 183/H3
Caddo, Ok, US 183/F3
Caddo, Tx, US 181/E1
Caddo Mills, Tx, US 183/F4
Caddo Valley, Ar, US 183/H3
Cadelbosco di Sopra, It. 68/D4
Cadelle (peak), It. 67/F5
Cadenberge, Ger. 59/G1
Cadenet, Fr. 70/B5
Cader Idris (peak), Wal, UK 42/C1
Cadet, Mo, US 192/B2
Cadibarrawirracanna (lake), Austl. 155/G4
Cadillac, Mi, US 190/D2
Cadillac, Sk, Can. 175/L3
Cadiz, Oh, US 190/F4
Cádiz, Sp. 52/B4
Cádiz (gulf), Port.,Sp. 52/B4
Cadiz, Ca, US 178/E3
Cadiz, Ky, US 192/D2
Cadiz (lake), Ca, US 178/E3
Cadiz, Phil. 100/C3
Cadnam, Eng, UK 43/E5
Cadogan, Ab, Can. 175/J1
Cadolzburg, Ger. 64/D4
Cadomin, Ab, Can. 174/F1
Cadott, Wi, US 185/J1
Cadria (peak), It. 67/G6
Cadwell, Ga, US 193/F4
Cadzand-Bad, Neth. 60/C1
Caen, Fr. 63/E2
Caen (bay), Fr. 50/C2
Caerano di San Marco, It. 69/F2
Caerleon, Wal, UK 42/D3
Caernarfon, Wal, UK 40/D5
Caernarfon (bay), Wal, UK 40/D5
Caernarfon Castle, Wal, UK 40/D5
Caerphilly, Wal, UK 42/C3
Caerphilly (co.), Wal, UK 42/C3
Caersws, Wal, UK 42/C1
Caesarea, On, Can. 191/G2
Caesarea NP, Isr. 117/B3
Caeté, Braz. 223/E3
Cafarnaum, Braz. 223/E1
Cafasse, It. 70/D2
Cafayate, Arg. 224/C3
Cagayan (isls.), Phil. 100/C3
Cagayan de Oro, Phil. 100/D3
Cagayan Sulu (isl.), Phil. 100/B4
Cagayancillo, Phil. 100/C3
Cagli, It. 69/F6
Cagliari, It. 54/A3
Cagliari (gulf), It. 72/F3
Cagne (riv.), Fr. 70/D5
Cagnes-sur-Mer, Fr. 70/D5
Cagoyan (riv.), Phil. 100/C1
Cagua, Ven. 219/N7
Caguán (riv.), Col. 216/C4
Caguas, PR 203/M8
Caha (mts.), Ire. 38/A6
Cahaba, Al, US 192/D4
Cahaba (riv.), Al, US 192/D4
Cahama, Ang. 140/B3
Caher, Ire. 38/C5
Caherbarnagh (peak), Ire. 38/A5
Caherconlish, Ire. 38/B4
Cahirsiveen, Ire. 36/N11
Cahokia, Il, US 185/J4
Cahone, Co, US 179/H2
Cahore (pt.), Ire. 38/D4
Cahors, Fr. 50/D4
Cahuacan, Mex. 205/Q9
Cahuapanas, Peru 220/B2
Cahuilla Ind. Res., Ca, US 178/D4
Cahuinari (riv.), Col. 216/D5
Cahuita, PN, CR 207/F4
Cahul, Mol. 57/J3
Cai (riv.), Braz. 225/G4
Cai Nuoc, Viet. 106/D4
Caia, Moz. 141/G3
Caiabis, Serra dos (mts.), Braz. 221/G4
Caianda, Ang. 139/E5
Caiapó (riv.), Braz. 222/C3
Caiapó, Serra (mts.), Braz. 222/B3
Caiapônia, Braz. 222/C3
Caiazzo, It. 71/D5
Caibarién, Cuba 207/G1
Caiçara, Braz. 219/H4
Caicara, Ven. 217/F2
Caicara, Ven. 217/E3
Caicedo, Col. 219/K6
Caicedonia, Col. 219/K8
Caicó, Braz. 219/G4
Caicos (isls.), Uk 203/G3
Caicos Passage (chan.), Bahm. 207/H1
Caieiras, Braz. 223/K8
Caifuche, Ang. 140/D1
Cailloma, Peru 220/D4
Caillou (bay), La, US 194/C3
Caillou (lake), La, US 194/C3
Cailly (riv.), Fr. 60/A4
Caiman (pt.), Phil. 100/B2
Caimbambo, Ang. 140/B2
Cainde, Ang. 140/B2
Caine (riv.), Bol. 224/C1
Cainnyigoin, China 90/E5
Cainsville, Mo, US 185/H3
Cainta, Phil. 100/F6
Caio (peak), It. 68/D5
Caiongo, Ang. 138/C4
Cairate, It. 68/B2
Cairn (mt.), Ak, US 201/G3
Cairn Curran (res.), Austl. 157/A3
Cairn Curran (dam), Austl. 157/A3
Cairn Gorm (peak), Sc, UK 39/C2
Cairn Table (peak), Sc, UK 39/B6
Cairn Toul (peak), Sc, UK 39/C2
Cairndow, Sc, UK 39/B4
Cairngorm (mts.), Sc, UK 39/B2
Cairnryan, Sc, UK 40/C2
Cairns (int'l arpt.), Austl. 158/B2
Cairns, Austl. 158/B2
Cairns (mt.), Austl. 155/G2
Cairnsmore of Carsphairn (peak), Sc, UK 39/B6
Cairo (Al Qāhirah) (cap.), Egypt 131/C4
Cairo (int'l arpt.), Egypt 131/C4
Cairo, Ga, US 195/F2
Cairo (peak), It. 71/C4
Cairo, Il, US 192/C2
Cairo, Mo, US 185/H4
Cairo, Ne, US 184/E3
Cairo Montenotte, It. 68/B5
Caister-on-Sea, Eng, UK 43/H1
Caistor, Eng, UK 41/H5
Caistor Centre, On, Can. 190/T9
Caistorville, On, Can. 190/T9
Caitou, Ang. 140/B2
Caiuana (bay), Braz. 218/D3
Caiundo, Ang. 140/C2
Caixi, China 99/H3
Caiza, Bol. 224/C2
Caizi (lake), China 92/D5
Cajabamba, Ecu. 216/B5
Cajabamba, Peru 220/B2
Cajacay, Peru 220/B3
Cajamarca, Peru 220/B2
Cajamarca (dept.), Peru 220/B2
Cajamarca (ruin), Peru 220/B2
Cajapió, Braz. 219/E3
Cajari, Braz. 219/E3
Cajatambo, Peru 220/B3
Cajazeiras, Braz. 219/G4
Cajibío, Col. 216/B4
Cajidiocan, Phil. 100/C2
Cajon Junction, Ca, US 196/C2
Cajones (isl.), Nic. 207/F2
Caju (isl.), Braz. 219/F3
Cajuapara (riv.), Braz. 219/E4
Cajuata, Bol. 224/C1
Çal, Turk. 114/B2
Cala d'Oliva, It. 54/A2
Cala, Piombo, Punta di (pt.), It. 72/F3
Calabar (int'l arpt.), Nga. 133/H5
Calabar, Nga. 133/H5
Calabasas, Ca, US 196/B2
Calabash, NC, US 193/H4
Calabozo, Ven. 217/E2
Calabria (pol. reg.), It. 73/H3
Calabria, Parco Nazionale della, It. 54/D3
Calaburras (pt.), Sp. 52/C4
Calaceite, Sp. 53/F2
Calacoto, Bol. 220/D5
Calafat, Rom. 56/F4
Calagua (isls.), Phil. 100/C2
Calahorra, Sp. 52/E1
Calaí, Ang. 140/C3
Calais, Fr. 60/A2
Calais, Me, US 171/K4
Calais, Canal de (canal), Fr. 60/A2
Calama, Braz. 221/F3
Calama, Chile 224/B2
Calamar, Col. 216/C4
Calamar, Col. 216/C2
Calamarca, Bol. 224/B1
Calamba, Ang. 138/C5
Calambrone, It. 68/D6
Calamian Gr. (isls.), Phil. 103/E1
Calamian Group (isls.), Phil. 100/B2
Calamocha, Sp. 52/E2
Calamonte, Sp. 52/B3
Calamus (riv.), Ne, US 184/E2
Călan, Rom. 56/F3
Calañas, Sp. 52/B4
Calanda, Sp. 53/E2
Calang, Indo. 101/A1
Calangianus, It. 54/A2
Calapan, Phil. 100/C2
Calapooia (riv.), Or, US 176/B1
Călărași (prov.), Rom. 57/H3
Călărași, Rom. 57/H3
Călărași, Mol. 78/E4
Calarcá, Col. 219/K8
Calasparra, Sp. 52/E3
Calatayud, Sp. 52/E2
Calatorao, Sp. 52/E2
Calauag, Phil. 100/C2
Calaveras (res.), Ca, US 197/L12
Calaveras (riv.), Ca, US 176/C4
Calavite (cape), Phil. 100/C2
Calavon (riv.), Fr. 70/B5
Calayan (isl.), Phil. 100/C1
Calbayog, Phil. 100/D2
Calberlah, Ger. 59/H4
Calbiga, Phil. 100/D3
Calbuco, Chile 226/B4
Calca, Peru 220/D4
Calcasieu (lake), La, US 181/H3
Calcasieu (riv.), La, US 181/H2
Calceta, Ecu. 216/A5
Calchaquí, Arg. 224/D4
Calchaquí (riv.), Arg. 224/C3
Calci, It. 68/D6
Calcinate, It. 68/C2
Calcinato, It. 68/D3
Calcinelli, It. 69/F6
Calcio, It. 68/C3
Calcium, NY, US 191/J2
Calçoene, Braz. 218/D2
Calcutta, India 109/G4
Calcutta (int'l arpt.), India 109/G4
Calcutta, Sur. 217/H3
Caldaro (Kaltern), It. 51/J3
Caldas (dept.), Col. 216/C3
Caldas, Col. 219/K6
Caldas, Braz. 223/K6
Caldas da Rainha, Port. 52/A3
Caldas Novas, Braz. 222/C3
Caldbeck, Eng, UK 41/E2
Calden, Ger. 59/G6
Calder, Sk, Can. 186/D2
Calder (riv.), Eng, UK 41/F4
Calder (mt.), Ak, US 201/M4
Caldera, Chile 224/B3
Calderara di Reno, It. 69/E4
Calderas, Ven. 216/D2
Caldercruix, Sc, UK 39/C5
Calderdale (co.), Eng, UK 41/F4
Caldes de Montbui, Sp. 53/L6
Caldew (riv.), Eng, UK 41/F2
Caldicot, Wal, UK 42/D3
Caldiero, It. 69/E3
Çaldıran, Turk. 115/E2
Caldogno, It. 69/E2
Caldonazzo, It. 67/H6
Caldono, Col. 216/B4
Caldwell, Id, US 176/E2
Caldwell, NJ, US 199/H8
Caldwell, Oh, US 190/F5
Caldwell, Tx, US 180/F2
Caldwell, Wi, US 197/P14
Caldy (isl.), Eng, UK 42/B3
Caledon, NI, UK 40/B3
Caledon, SAfr. 142/L11
Caledon, On, Can. 190/T8
Caledon (riv.), SAfr. 142/D3
Caledon East, On, Can. 190/T8
Caledonia (hills), NB, Can. 188/E3
Caledonia, Mi, US 190/D3
Caledonia, Mn, US 185/J2
Caledonia, Ms, US 192/C4
Caledonia, NS, Can. 188/E3
Caledonia, Oh, US 190/E4
Caledonia, Wi, US 197/P14
Caledonian (canal), Sc, UK 39/B2
Calella, Sp. 53/G2
Calen, Austl. 158/C3
Calenzana, Fr. 54/A1
Calenzano, It. 69/E6
Calera, Ok, US 183/F4
Calera, Al, US 192/D4
Calera de Tango, Chile 226/N8
Calestano, It. 68/D4
Caleta Clarencia, Chile 227/C7
Caleta de Campos, Mex. 204/E5
Caleta Olivia, Arg. 226/D5
Caletones, Chile 226/N9
Calf of Man (isl.), IM, UK 40/C3
Calgary (int'l arpt.), Ab, Can. 175/G2
Calgary, Ab, Can. 175/G2
Calhan, Co, US 184/B4
Calheta, Port. 128/A2
Calheta, Azor., Port. 53/S12
Calhoun, Al, US 194/E1
Calhoun, Ga, US 192/E3
Calhoun, Il, US 192/C1
Calhoun, Ky, US 192/D2
Calhoun, Mo, US 183/H1
Calhoun City, Ms, US 192/C4
Calhoun Falls, SC, US 193/F3
Cali, Col. 216/B4
Calico Ghost Town, Ca, US 178/D3
Calico Rock, Ar, US 183/H2
Calicut (Kozhikode), India 107/B4
Calida (coast), Sp. 52/E4
Caliente, Nv, US 178/E2
Califon, NJ, US 198/D2
California (state), US 172/C4
California (gulf), Mex. 163/F6
California (aqueduct), Ca, US 178/B2
California, Md, US 193/J1
California, Mo, US 183/H1
California City, Ca, US 178/D3
Calilegua, Arg. 224/C2
Calilegua, PN, Arg. 224/C2
Călimănești, Rom. 57/G3
Calimaya, Mex. 205/Q10
Calimere (pt.), India 107/C4
Calimesa, Ca, US 196/C2
Calingasta, Arg. 224/B4
Calion, Ar, US 183/H4
Calipatria, Ca, US 178/E4
Calistoga, Ca, US 176/B4
Calitri, It. 54/D2
Calixa-Lavallée, Qu, Can. 189/P6
Calizzano, It. 68/B5
Calkiní, Mex. 206/D1
Çalköy, Turk. 114/B2
Callac, Fr. 62/B4
Callaghan (mt.), Nv, US 176/E4
Callaghan, Tx, US 180/E4
Callahan, Fl, US 195/H2
Callahonna (lake), Austl. 145/D3
Callalli, Peru 220/D4
Callan, Ire. 38/C4
Callander, Sc, UK 39/B4
Callantsoog, Neth. 58/B3
Callao, Peru 220/B4
Callao, Ut, US 177/G4
Callao, Va, US 193/J2
Callapa, Bol. 224/B1
Callaun (peak), Ire. 38/B4
Callaway, Mn, US 186/G4
Callaway, Fl, US 195/F2
Calle Larga, Chile 226/N8
Callender, Ia, US 185/G2
Callian, Fr. 70/C5
Calliham, Tx, US 181/E3
Callington, Eng, UK 42/B5
Calliope, Austl. 158/C4
Callosa de Segura, Sp. 53/E3
Calmar, Ia, US 185/J2
Calmar, Ab, Can. 175/H1
Calne, Eng, UK 42/E4
Calolziocorte, It. 68/C2
Calonga (riv.), Ang. 140/B2
Calonne (riv.), Fr. 63/F2
Calonne-Ricouart, Fr. 60/B3
Caloocan, Phil. 100/E6
Caloosahatchee (riv.), Fl, US 195/H4
Caloosahatchee Nat'l Wild. Ref., Fl, US 195/H4
Calore (riv.), It. 73/G2
Caloundra, Austl. 158/D4
Calpe, Sp. 53/F3
Calpulálpan, Mex. 205/L7
Calstock, Eng, UK 42/B6
Caltagirone, It. 54/D4
Caltanissetta, It. 54/D4
Caltavuturo, It. 54/C4
Caluango, Ang. 138/D5
Calucinga, Ang. 140/C1
Calueque (dam), Ang. 140/B3
Calulo, Ang. 138/C5
Calumbo, Ang. 138/C5
Calumet, Mi, US 187/K4
Calumet (riv.), Il, US 197/Q16
Calumet City, Il, US 190/C4
Calumet Sag (chan.), Il, US 197/Q16
Caluquembe, Ang. 140/B2
Caluso, It. 68/A2
Caluula (pt.), Som. 136/D3
Caluula, Som. 136/D3
Calva, Az, US 179/G4
Calvados (dept.), Fr. 63/E3
Calvary, Ga, US 195/F2
Calvello, It. 54/D2
Calvenzano, It. 68/C3
Calvert, Nf, Can. 189/L2
Calvert, Al, US 194/D2
Calvert, Tx, US 181/F2
Calvert City, Ky, US 192/C2
Calvert Hills, Austl. 153/E4
Calverton, Eng, UK 41/G5
Calverton, Md, US 198/B5
Calvi, Fr. 54/A1
Calvi (peak), It. 69/E5
Calvi Risorta, It. 71/D5
Calviá, Sp. 53/G3
Calvilli (peak), It. 71/C5
Calvillo, Mex. 204/E4
Calvin, Ok, US 183/F3
Calvinia, SAfr. 142/B3
Calvisano, It. 68/D3
Calvitero (peak), Sp. 52/C2
Calw, Ger. 64/B5
Calzada de Calatrava, Sp. 52/D3
Cam or Rhee (riv.), Eng, UK 43/F2
Cam Pha, Viet. 99/E4
Cam Ranh, Viet. 106/E4
Cam Thuy, Viet. 106/D1
Camabatela, Ang. 138/C5
Camaçari, Braz. 223/F2
Camacho, Bol. 224/C2
Camacho, Bol. 221/E3
Camacho, Mex. 204/E3
Camacupa, Ang. 140/C2
Camaguán, Ven. 217/E2
Camagüey (arch.), Cuba 203/F3
Camagüey, Cuba 207/G1
Camaiore, It. 68/D6
Camajuaní, Cuba 207/G1
Camalengue, Ang. 138/D5
Camalu, Mex. 204/A2
Camamu, Braz. 223/F2
Camaná, Peru 220/C5
Camanche (res.), Ca, US 176/C4
Camanche, Ia, US 185/J3
Camanducaia, Braz. 223/K7
Camanongue, Ang. 140/D1
Camapuã, Braz. 225/F1
Camaquã, Braz. 225/G4
Camaquã (riv.), Braz. 225/F4
Camarat (cape), Fr. 70/C6
Camaret-sur-Aigues, Fr. 70/A4
Camaret-sur-Mer, Fr. 62/A4
Camargo, Ok, US 182/E2
Camargo, Sp. 52/D1
Camargo, Bol. 224/C2
Camarillo, Ca, US 196/A2
Camariñas, Sp. 52/A1
Camarón (cape), Hon. 207/E3
Camarones (bay), Arg. 226/D5
Camarones, Arg. 226/D5
Camarones, Chile 224/B1
Camas, Sp. 52/B4
Camas NWR, Id, US 177/G2
Camas Prairie (grsld.), Id, US 174/F4
Camas Valley, Or, US 176/B2
Camatagua, Ven. 219/P8
Camaxilo, Ang. 138/D5
Cambados, Sp. 52/A1
Cambará, Braz. 225/G2
Cambay (gulf), India 104/B3
Cambé, Braz. 225/G2
Camberley, Eng, UK 36/A3
Camberwell (nbrhd.), Eng, UK 36/C2
Camberwell, Austl. 157/B3
Cambiano, It. 68/A3
Cambo (riv.), Ang. 138/D5
Cambo Camana, Ang. 138/D5
Cambodia (ctry.) 106/D3
Cambondo, Ang. 138/C5
Camborne, Eng, UK 42/A6
Cambrai, Fr. 60/C3
Cambria, Ca, US 178/B3
Cambrian (mts.), Wal, UK 40/E5
Cambridge (gulf), Austl. 152/C3
Cambridge, On, Can. 190/F3
Cambridge (int'l arpt.), Eng, UK 43/G2
Cambridge, Eng, UK 43/G2
Cambridge, NZ 159/C2
Cambridge, Id, US 176/E1
Cambridge, Il, US 185/J3
Cambridge, Ma, US 191/L3
Cambridge, Md, US 193/J1
Cambridge, Mn, US 187/H5
Cambridge, Ne, US 184/D3
Cambridge, Oh, US 190/F4
Cambridge, Vt, US 191/K2
Cambridge Bay, Nun, Can. 170/F2
Cambridge City, In, US 190/D5
Cambridge Springs, Pa, US 190/F4
Cambridge-Narrows, NB, Can. 188/E3
Cambridgeshire (co.), Eng, UK 43/F2
Cambrils, Sp. 53/F2
Cambuí, Braz. 223/K7
Cambulo, Ang. 139/E4
Cambuquira, Braz. 223/L6
Cambuslang, Sc, UK 39/B5
Cambutal (mtn.), Pan. 216/A3
Camden, Austl. 158/G9
Camden (sound), Austl. 152/A3
Camden (co.), Eng, UK 36/C2
Camden, Al, US 194/E2
Camden, Ar, US 183/H4
Camden, De, US 198/C5
Camden, Mi, US 190/D4
Camden, NC, US 193/J2
Camden, NJ, US 198/C4
Camden (co.), NJ, US 198/C4
Camden, NY, US 191/J3
Camden, SC, US 193/G3
Camden, Tn, US 192/C2
Camden, Tx, US 181/G2
Camden East, On, Can. 191/H2
Camden Haven, Austl. 156/E1
Camdenton, Mo, US 183/H1
Cameia, Ang. 140/D1
Cameia, PN da, Ang. 139/E5
Cameia, PN da, Ang. 140/D1
Camel (riv.), Eng, UK 42/B6
Camelback (mtn.), Pa, US 198/C1
Camelford, Eng, UK 42/B5
Camels Back (peak), NZ 159/C2
Camenca, Mol. 78/E3
Camerano, It. 69/G6
Cameri, It. 68/B3
Camerino, It. 71/C1
Camerón (riv.), Mex. 180/D4
Cameron (isl.), Nun, Can. 171/R7
Cameron, Az, US 179/G3
Cameron (peak), Co, US 184/B3
Cameron, La, US 194/B3
Cameron, Mo, US 185/G4
Cameron, Mt, US 177/H1
Cameron, Tx, US 181/F2
Cameron, Wi, US 187/J5
Cameron Highlands, Malay. 101/C1
Cameron Park, Ca, US 176/C4
Cameroon (ctry.) 119/D4
Cameroon Highlands (uplands), Nga. 134/A4
Cametá, Braz. 218/D3
Camey, Tx, US 180/L6
Camfield, Austl. 152/C4
Camicia (peak), It. 71/C3
Camiguin (isl.), Phil. 100/C1
Camiling, Phil. 100/C2
Camilla, Ga, US 195/F2
Camilo Aldao, Arg. 226/E2
Caminha, Port. 52/A2
Camiranga, Braz. 219/E3
Camiri, Bol. 224/D2
Camisano Vicentino, It. 69/E2
Camissombo, Ang. 139/E5
Çamlıdere, Turk. 76/E4
Çamlık NP, Turk. 114/C2
Camlin (riv.), Ire. 38/C2
Çamlıyayla, Turk. 116/D1
Camo-Camo, Moz. 141/G4
Camoapa, Nic. 207/E3
Camocim, Braz. 219/F3
Camogli, It. 68/C5
Camolin, Ire. 38/D4
Camon, Fr. 60/B4
Camooweal, Austl. 153/E4
Camopi, FrG. 218/C2
Camopi (riv.), FrG. 218/C2
Camorta (isl.), India 105/F6
Camoruco, Col. 216/D3
Camotes (sea), Phil. 100/D3
Camp Angelus (Angelus Oaks), Ca, US 196/D2
Camp Atterbury, In, US 192/D1
Camp Blanding Mil. Res., Fl, US 195/G3
Camp Grayling, Mi, US 190/D2
Camp Hill, Pa, US 198/B3
Camp J.T. Robinson, Ar, US 183/H3
Camp Lake, Wi, US 197/P14
Camp Lake Nat'l Wild. Ref., ND, US 186/D4
Camp Lejeune, NC, US 193/J3
Camp Lejeune Marine Base, NC, US 193/J3
Camp Pendleton, Ca, US 178/D4
Camp Ripley Mil. Res., Mn, US 187/G4
Camp Roberts, Ca, US 178/B3
Camp Shelby, Ms, US 194/D2
Camp Springs, Md, US 198/B6
Camp Verde, Az, US 179/G3
Camp Verde Ind. Res., Az, US 179/G3
Camp Williams, Ut, US 177/G3
Camp Wood, Tx, US 180/D3
Campagna di Roma (reg.), It. 71/B4
Campagna Lupia, It. 69/F3
Campagnano di Roma, It. 71/B3
Campagnola Emilia, It. 69/D4
Campamento, Uru. 225/E4
Campana, Arg. 227/J11
Campana (isl.), Chile 227/B6
Campanario, Sp. 52/C3
Campanario (peak), Arg. 226/C2
Campanella (cape), It. 71/D6
Campanha, Braz. 223/L6
Campania (prov.), It. 54/D2
Campbell (cape), NZ 159/C3
Campbell (isl.), NZ 27/T8
Campbell, Ca, US 197/L12
Campbell, Fl, US 194/N7
Campbell, Mn, US 186/F4
Campbell, Mo, US 192/B2
Campbell (hill), Oh, US 190/E4
Campbell, Oh, US 190/F4
Campbell, Ne, US 184/E3
Campbell, Tx, US 183/G4
Campbell Town, Austl. 156/C4
Campbellford, On, Can. 191/H2
Campbellpore, Pak. 110/B3
Campbell's Bay, Qu, Can. 191/H2
Campbellsport, Wi, US 190/B3
Campbellsville, Ky, US 192/E2
Campbellton, NB, Can. 188/D1
Campbellton, Fl, US 195/F2
Campbelltown (nbrhd.), Austl. 158/G9
Campbellville, On, Can. 190/T9
Campbeltown, Sc, UK 37/R9
Campbon, Fr. 62/D6
Campden, On, Can. 190/U9
Campeche (state), Mex. 202/C4
Campeche, Mex. 206/D2
Campeche (bay), Mex. 163/H7
Campello sul Clitunno, It. 71/B2
Camperdown, Austl. 156/B3
Camperville, Mb, Can. 186/D2
Campestre, Braz. 223/K6
Campi Bisenzio, It. 69/E6
Campidano (range), It. 54/A3
Campile, Ire. 38/D5
Campillo de Altobuey, Sp. 52/E3
Campillos, Sp. 52/C4
Campina da Lagoa, Braz. 225/F3
Campina Grande, Braz. 219/H4
Campina Verde, Braz. 222/C3
Campinas, Braz. 223/J7
Campione d'Italia, It. 67/E6
Campli, It. 71/C2
Camplong, Indo. 152/A2
Campo, Camr. 138/B2
Campo, Ca, US 178/D4
Campo (int'l arpt.), Braz. 220/C2
Campo Belo, Braz. 222/D4
Campo de Criptana, Sp. 52/D3
Campo de la Cruz, Col. 216/C2
Campo dei Fiori (peak), It. 68/B2
Campo Erê, Braz. 225/F3
Campo Florido, Braz. 225/G1
Campo Formoso, Braz. 223/E1
Campo Gallo, Arg. 224/D3
Campo Grande, Braz. 225/F2
Campo Ind. Res., Ca, US 178/D4
Campo Largo, Braz. 225/G3
Campo Ligure, It. 68/B4
Campo Limpo Paulista, Braz. 223/K8
Campo Maior, Port. 52/B3
Campo Maior, Braz. 219/F4
Campo Mourão, Braz. 225/F3
Campo Quijano, Arg. 224/C3
Campo Redondo, Braz. 219/G4
Campo Tencia (peak), Swi. 67/E5
Campo Tizzoro, It. 69/D5
Campoalegre, Col. 216/C4
Campobasso (prov.), It. 71/D4
Campobasso, It. 71/D4
Campobello (isl.), Ns., Can. 188/D3
Campodarsego, It. 69/E3
Campodolcino, It. 67/F5
Campogalliano, It. 69/D4
Campomorone, It. 68/B4
Camponogara, It. 69/F3
Camporosso, It. 68/A5
Camporredondo (res.), Sp. 52/C1
Camporredondo, Peru 220/B2
Campos (phys. reg.), Braz. 209/D5
Campos Belos, Braz. 222/D2
Campos de Hielo Norte (glacier), Chile 227/B5
Campos de Hielo Sur (glacier), Chile 227/B6
Campos del Puerto, Sp. 53/G3
Campos do Jordão, Braz. 223/L7
Campos dos Goytacazes, Braz. 223/E4
Campos Novos, Braz. 225/G3
Campos Sales, Braz. 219/F4
Camposampiero, It. 69/E2
Camposanto, It. 69/E4
Camposauro (peak), It. 71/D5
Campotosto (lake), It. 71/C3
Campsie Fells (hills), Sc, UK 39/B4
Campti, La, US 194/B2
Campton, Ky, US 193/F2
Camrose, Ab, Can. 175/H1
Çan, Turk. 76/C4
Can (riv.), Eng, UK 36/E1
Can Tho, Viet. 106/D4
Cana, Sk, Can. 186/C2
Canaan, Ar, US 183/H3
Canaan, Vt, US 191/L2
Canaan (riv.), NB, Can. 188/E2
Canaan, NH, US 191/K3
Canaan Game Ref., NB, Can. 188/E2
Canaçari (lake), Braz. 218/B3
Canada (ctry.) 170/*
Cañada de Gómez, Arg. 226/E2
Cañada Larga, Bol. 221/F5
Cañada Nieto, Uru. 227/J10
Cañada Rosquín, Arg. 226/E2
Canadensis, Pa, US 198/C1
Canadian, Tx, US 182/D3
Canadian (riv.), US 182/C3
Canadian, North (riv.), Ok, US 172/F4
Cañadón de las Vacas, Arg. 227/C6
Cañadon Grande (mts.), Arg. 226/C5
Cañadón Seco, Arg. 226/D5
Canaima, PN, Ven. 217/F3
Canajoharie, NY, US 191/J3
Çanakkale, Turk. 55/K2
Çanakkale (prov.), Turk. 76/C5
Canal Flats, BC, Can. 174/G2
Canal Point, Fl, US 195/H4
Canala, NCal., Fr. 161/U12
Canalbianco (riv.), It. 69/E2
Canale, It. 68/A3
Canale Cavour (canal), It. 68/B2
Canals, Sp. 53/E3
Canals, Arg. 226/E2
Canandaigua, NY, US 191/H3
Cananea, Mex. 204/C2
Canaos (riv.), Braz. 225/G3
Cañar (dept.), Ecu. 216/B5
Cañar, Ecu. 220/B1
Canard (riv.), On, Can. 197/G7
Canarsie (nbrhd.), NY, US 199/K9
Canary (isls.), Sp. 128/A3
Cañas, CR 207/E4
Cañasgordas, Col. 216/B3
Canatlán de las Manzanas, Mex. 204/D3
Canaveral (pen.), Fl, US 195/H3
Canaveral (cape), Fl, US 195/H3
Canaveral Nat'l Seashore, Fl., US 195/H3
Canavieiras, Braz. 223/F2
Canbelego, Austl. 156/C1
Canberra (cap.), Austl. 157/D2
Canby, Or, US 176/B1
Canby, Mn, US 185/F1
Cancale, Fr. 62/D3
Cance (riv.), Fr. 70/A2
Cancello-Arnone, It. 71/D5
Canchaque, Peru 220/B2
Canche (riv.), Fr. 50/E1
Cancun (int'l arpt.), Mex. 206/E1
Cancún, Mex. 206/E1
Candarave, Peru 224/B1
Çandarli (gulf), Gre. 114/A2
Candás, Sp. 52/C1
Candás, Sp. 52/B1
Candé, Fr. 63/D5
Candeias, Braz. 223/F2
Candela, Mex. 180/D4
Candelaria (riv.), Mex. 206/D2
Candelaria, Mex. 206/D2
Candelaria, Arg. 226/D2
Candelária, Braz. 225/F4
Candelaria, Bol. 224/E1
Candeleda, Sp. 52/C2
Candelo, It. 68/B2
Candelo, Austl. 157/D3
Candia Lomellina, It. 68/B3
Candiac, Qu, Can. 189/N7
Cândido Mendes, Braz. 219/E3
Cândido Mota, Braz. 225/G2
Canding (cape), Indo. 102/D5
Candiolo, It. 70/D3
Çandır, Turk. 114/C2
Candler-McAfee, Ga, US 193/M7
Candlewood, NJ, US 199/D3
Cando, ND, US 186/E3
Cando, Sk, Can. 175/K1
Candon, Phil. 100/C1
Cane (cr.), Ga, US 195/G2
Cane Beds, Az, US 179/F2
Canegrate, It. 68/B2
Canela, Braz. 225/G4
Canela Baja, Chile 224/B4
Canelli, It. 68/B4
Canelones (dept.), Uru. 227/F2
Canelones, Uru. 227/K11
Canepina, It. 71/B3
Cañete, Sp. 52/E2
Canete, Río de (riv.), Peru 220/B4
Caneva, It. 69/F2
Caney (cr.), Tx, US 181/G3
Caney, Ok, US 183/F3
Caney, Ks, US 183/G2
Caney (riv.), Ks,Ok, US 205/F2
Caneyville, Ky, US 192/D2
Canfield, Ar, US 183/H4
Canfield Lake Nat'l Wild. Ref., ND, US 186/D4
Cangallo, Peru 220/C4
Cangamba, Ang. 140/C2
Cangandala, Ang. 138/D5
Cangas, Sp. 52/A1
Cangas de Narcea, Sp. 52/B1
Cangas de Onís, Sp. 52/C1
Cangkuang (cape), Indo. 101/D4
Cango Caves, SAfr. 142/C4
Cangoa, Ang. 140/C2
Cangombe, Ang. 140/D2
Cangonga, Ang. 140/C2
Cangqian, China 99/H3
Cangrejo (peak), Arg. 227/B6
Cangshan, China 92/D4
Cangshan, China 91/J1
Canguaretama, Braz. 219/H4
Canguçu, Braz. 225/F4
Cangumbe, Ang. 140/C1
Cangwu, China 105/K3
Cangyuan (Cangyuan Vazu Zizhixian), China 98/C4
Cangzhou, China 92/D3
Canh Cuoc (isl.), Viet. 106/D1
Canhaua, Ang. 140/C3
Canhoca, Ang. 140/B2
Canhotinho, Braz. 219/G5
Cania Gorge NP, Austl. 158/C4
Caniapiscau (lake), Qu, Can. 171/K3
Caniapiskau (riv.), Qu, Can. 171/J3
Canicatti, It. 54/C4
Canigou, Pic du (peak), Fr. 50/E5
Canik (mts.), Turk. 114/C1
Caniles, Sp. 52/D4
Canim Lake, BC, Can. 174/D2
Canindé, Braz. 219/G4
Canindé (riv.), Braz. 219/F4
Canindeyú (dept.), Par. 222/B5
Canino, It. 54/B1
Canistear (res.), NJ, US 199/H7
Canisteo, NY, US 191/H3
Cañitas de Felipe Pescador, Mex. 204/E4
Canjáyar, Sp. 52/D4
Canje (riv.), Guy. 218/B1
Canjilon, NM, US 179/J2
Cankhor, Som. 136/C3
Çankırı, Turk. 76/E4
Çankırı (prov.), Turk. 76/E4
Canlaon (vol.), Phil. 100/C3
Canmore, Ab, Can. 174/G2
Cann (mtn.), Austl. 157/D3
Cann (riv.), Austl. 157/D3
Cann River, Austl. 157/D3
Canna (isl.), Sc, UK 37/Q8
Cannara, It. 71/B2
Canne (ruin), It. 54/E2
Cannel City, Ky, US 193/F2
Cannelton, In, US 192/D2
Canner (riv.), Fr. 61/F5
Cannero Riviera, It. 67/E5
Cannes, Fr. 70/D5
Canneto sull'Oglio, It. 68/D3
Cannich, Sc, UK 39/B2
Canning (peak), Austl. 154/C4
Canning (riv.), Austl. 154/K7
Canning (dam), Austl. 154/L7
Cannobio, It. 67/E5
Cannock, Eng, UK 42/D1
Cannon (A.F.B.), NM, US 182/C3
Cannon Ball, ND, US 186/D4
Cannon Beach, Or, US 174/C5
Cannon Falls, Mn, US 185/H1
Cannonball (riv.), ND, US 186/D4
Cannondale, Ct, US 199/E1
Cannonvale, Austl. 158/C3
Cannonville, Ut, US 179/F2
Caño Guaritico (riv.), Ven. 216/D3
Caño Negro Nat'l Wild. Ref., CR 207/E4
Canoas, Braz. 225/G4
Canobolas (mt.), Austl. 157/D1
Canoe, Al, US 194/E2
Canoe River, BC, Can. 174/E1
Canoga Park (nbrhd.), Ca, US 196/E7
Canoinhas, Braz. 225/G3
Canon City, Co, US 182/B1
Cañón de Río Blanco, PN, Mex. 205/M8
Cañón del Sumidero, PN, Mex. 206/C2
Cañon Largo (riv.), NM, US 179/J2
Canonbie, Sc, UK 41/F1
Cañoncito Ind. Res., NM, US 179/J3
Canones, NM, US 179/J2
Canoochee (riv.), Ga, US 195/G1
Canopus (ruin), Egypt 131/B2
Canora, Sk, Can. 186/C2
Canosa di Puglia, It. 54/E2
Canouan (isl.), StV. 203/N9
Canowindra, Austl. 157/D1
Cansado, Mrta. 128/A5
Canso, NS, Can. 189/G3
Canso (cape), NS, Can. 189/G3
Canta, Peru 220/B3
Cantabria (prov.), Sp. 50/B5
Cantabria (dist.), Sp. 52/C1
Cantal (mass.), Fr. 50/E4
Cantalejo, Sp. 52/D2
Cantanhede, Port. 52/A2
Cantanhede, Braz. 219/E3
Cantaura, Ven. 217/E2
Canteleu, Fr. 63/G2
Canterbury (nbrhd.), Austl. 158/H8
Canterbury, Eng, UK 43/H4
Canterbury Bight (bay), NZ 145/H7
Canterbury Cathedral, Eng, UK 43/H4
Cantiere, Eth. 135/G4
Cantil, Ca, US 178/D3
Cantilan, Phil. 100/D3
Cantillana, Sp. 52/C4
Canto del Agua, Chile 224/B4
Canto do Buriti, Braz. 219/F5
Canton, Ga, US 192/E3
Canton, Il, US 185/J3
Canton, Ks, US 183/F1
Canton, Mi, US 197/E7
Canton, Mo, US 185/J3
Canton, Ms, US 192/B4
Canton, NC, US 193/F3
Canton, NJ, US 198/C5
Canton, NY, US 191/J2
Canton, Oh, US 190/F4
Canton, Ok, US 183/E2
Canton (lake), Ok, US 183/E2
Canton, Pa, US 191/H4
Canton, SD, US 185/F2
Canton, Tx, US 181/G1
Canton (Abariringa) (isl.), Kiri. 161/H5
Cantoria, Sp. 52/D4
Cantù, It. 68/C2
Cantwell, Ak, US 201/J3
Cañuelas, Arg. 227/J11
Canumã (riv.), Braz. 218/B4
Canunda NP, Austl. 156/B3
Canutama, Braz. 221/E2
Canutillo, Tx, US 180/A2
Canvey (isl.), Eng, UK 36/E2
Canvey Island, Eng, UK 43/G3
Canwood, Sk, Can. 175/L1
Cany-Barville, Fr. 63/F1
Canyon, Mn, US 187/H4
Canyon (lake), Tx, US 181/E3
Canyon, Tx, US 182/D4
Canyon, Tx, US 182/D3
Canyon, Wy, US 177/H1
Canyon City, Or, US 176/D1
Canyon de Chelly Nat'l Mon., Az, US 179/H2
Canyon Ferry, Mt, US 175/J4
Canyon Lake, Tx, US 180/E3
Canyon of the Ancients Nat'l Mon., Co, US 179/H2
Canyonlands NP, Ut, US 177/J4
Canyonville, Or, US 176/B2
Canzo, It. 68/C2
Cao (riv.), China 93/C2
Cao Bang, Viet. 99/E4
Cao Lanh, Viet. 106/D4
Cao Xian, China 92/C4
Cao'e (riv.), China 99/J2
Caodu (riv.), China 99/E3
Caohecheng, China 93/C2
Caohekou, China 93/B2
Caohezhang, China 93/C2
Caohu, China 111/D3
Caojiawan, China 90/F5
Caol, Sc, UK 39/A3
Caoqiao, China 92/K8

Caorle, It. 69/F2
Caorso, It. 68/C3
Caoshi, China 93/C1
Cap (isl.), Phil. 100/C4
Cap Blanc (cape), Tun. 130/L6
Cap d'Agde (cape), Fr. 50/E5
Cap d'Antibes (cape), Fr. 70/D5
Cap d'Arguin (cape), Mrta. 128/A5
Cap d'Arme (cape), Fr. 70/C7
Cap de Fer (cape), Alg. 130/K6
Cap de Garde (cape), Alg. 130/K6
Cap de Gaspé (mtn.0, Qu, Can. 188/E1
Cap de l'Aigle (cape), Fr. 70/B6
Cap de l'Aiguille (cape), Alg. 130/E5
Cap de Saint-Tropez (cape), Fr. 70/C6
Cap des Mèdes (cape), Fr. 70/C6
Cap des Trois Fourches (cape), Mor. 130/C2
Cap du Dramont (cape), Fr. 70/C6
Cap Lopez (bay), Gabon 138/B3
Cap Lumière, NB, Can. 188/E2
Cap Rock Escarpment (cliff), Tx, US 182/D4
Cap-Chat, Qu, Can. 188/D1
Cap-D'Ail, Fr. 70/D5
Cap-de-la-Madeleine, Qu, Can. 191/K1
Cap-des-Rosiers, Qu, Can. 188/E1
Cap-Haïtien, Haiti 207/H2
Cap-Pelé, NB, Can. 188/E2
Cap-Rouge, Qu, Can. 188/B2
Cap-Saint-Ignace, Qu, Can. 188/B2
Cap-Santé, Qu, Can. 188/B2
Capa, SD, US 184/D1
Capac, Mi, US 197/G5
Capalonga, Phil. 100/C2
Capanaparo (riv.), Ven. 216/D3
Capanema, Braz. 219/E3
Capanne (peak), It. 54/B1
Capannoli, It. 69/D6
Capannori, It. 68/D6
Capão Bonito, Braz. 225/G3
Caparaó, PN do, Braz. 223/E4
Caparica, Port. 53/P10
Caparo (riv.), Ven. 216/D3
Caparrapí, Col. 219/L7
Capay, Ca, US 197/K9
Capbreton, Fr. 50/C5
Capdenac-Gare, Fr. 50/E4
Capdepera, Sp. 53/G3
Cape (riv.), Austl. 153/G5
Cape Alava (cape), Wa, US 174/B3
Cape Arid NP, Austl. 154/D5
Cape Barren (isl.), Austl. 145/D5
Cape Bougalinville Abor. Rsv., Austl. 152/B3
Cape Breton (isl.), NS, Can. 163/L5
Cape Breton Highlands (uplands), NS., Can. 189/G2
Cape Breton Highlands NP, Can. 189/G2
Cape Broyle, Nf, Can. 189/L2
Cape Canaveral (A.F.B.), Fl, US 195/H3
Cape Charles, Va, US 193/J2
Cape Cleveland NP, Austl. 158/B2
Cape Coast, Gha. 133/E5
Cape Cod (cape), Ma, US 188/B4
Cape Cod (bay), Ma, US 188/B5
Cape Cod Nat'l Seashore, Ma, US 188/C4
Cape Coral, Fl, US 195/H4
Cape Croker Ind. Res., On, Can. 190/F2
Cape Dorset, Nun, Can. 171/J2
Cape Fear (riv.), NC, US 193/H3
Cape Fear, Northeast (riv.), NC, US 193/J3
Cape Girardeau, Mo, US 192/C2
Cape Krusenstern Nat'l Mon., Ak, US 201/E2
Cape Le Grand NP, Austl. 154/D5
Cape May, NJ, US 198/D6
Cape May (co.), NJ, US 198/D5
Cape May County (arpt.), NJ, US 198/D6
Cape May Court House, NJ, US 198/D5
Cape May Lighthouse, NJ, US 198/D6
Cape Meares Nat'l Wild. Ref., Or, US 174/C5
Cape Melville NP, Austl. 158/B1
Cape Melville NP, PNG 153/G3
Cape Palmerston NP, Austl. 158/C3
Cape Range NP, Austl. 154/B2
Cape Romain NWR, SC, US 193/H4
Cape Sable (isl.), NS, Can. 188/E4
Cape Sable (cape), Fl, US 195/H5
Cape Saint Claire, Md, US 198/B5
Cape Smith, Nun, Can. 171/J2
Cape Town (cap.), SAfr. 142/L10
Cape Town (D.F. Malan) (int'l arpt.), SAfr. 142/L10
Cape Tribulation NP, Austl. 158/B2
Cape Upstart NP, Austl. 158/B2
Cape Verde (ctry.) 119/J9
Cape Yakataga, Ak, US 201/K3
Cape York, Austl. 153/F2
Cape York (pen.), Austl. 145/D2
Capel, Austl. 154/B5
Capel le Ferne, Eng, UK 43/H4
Capel Saint Mary, Eng, UK 43/H2
Capel-Curig, Wal, UK 40/E5
Capela, Braz. 223/F1
Capelinha, Braz. 223/E3
Capella, Austl. 158/C3
Capellades, Sp. 53/K6
Capena, It. 71/B3
Capenda-Camulemba, Ang. 138/D5
Capernaum (ruin), Isr. 117/D3
Capertree (riv.), Austl. 157/E1
Capestang, Fr. 50/E5
Capestrano, It. 71/C3
Capibara, Ven. 217/E4
Capicciola (pt.), Fr. 54/A2
Capilla del Monte, Arg. 224/C4
Capilla del Señor, Arg. 227/J11
Capim (riv.), Braz. 218/D3
Capinópolis, Braz. 222/C3
Capinota, Bol. 224/C1
Capinzal, Braz. 225/G3
Capioví, Arg. 225/F3
Capira, Ang. 140/B2
Capirara (res.), Braz. 225/G2
Capistrano, Braz. 219/G4
Capistrello, It. 71/C4
Capitan (mts.), NM, US 182/B4
Capitán Bado, Par. 225/F2
Capitán Curbelo (Punta del Este) (int'l arpt.), Uru. 227/G2
Capitán Pablo Lagerenza, Par. 224/D1
Capitão de Campos, Braz. 219/F4
Capitão Poço, Braz. 219/E3
Capitol, Mt, US 186/B5
Capitol Reef NP, Ut, US 177/H4
Capivara (res.), Braz. 222/C4
Capivari (riv.), Braz. 223/M6
Čapljina, Bosn. 56/C4
Caplone (peak), It. 68/D2
Capo di Ponte, It. 67/G5
Capo d'Orlando, It. 54/D3
Capoche (riv.), Moz. 141/G2
Capodichino (int'l arpt.), It. 71/D6
Capolo, Ang. 138/C5
Capolona, It. 69/E6
Capon Springs, WV, US 193/H1
Capote (peak), Tx, US 180/B2
Capoterra, It. 54/A3
Cappagh White, Ire. 38/B4
Cappamore, Ire. 38/B4
Cappella Maggiore, It. 69/F2
Cappoquin, Ire. 38/C5
Capracotta, It. 71/D4
Capraia (isl.), Fr. 54/A1
Capranica, It. 71/B3
Caprarola, It. 71/B3
Capreol, On, Can. 190/F1
Capri, It. 71/D6
Capri (isl.), It. 71/D6
Capricorn (cape), Austl. 158/C3
Capricorn (chan.), Austl. 158/C3
Caprino Veronese, It. 69/D2
Capriolo, It. 68/C2
Caprivi Strip (reg.), Namb. 140/D3
Caprock, NM, US 182/C4
Caprolace (lake), It. 71/B5
Caps, Tx, US 180/E1
Captain (har.), Ct, US 199/L7
Captainganj, India 108/D2
Captains Flat, Austl. 157/D2
Captiva, Fl, US 195/G4
Captiva (isl.), Fl, US 195/G4
Capua, It. 71/D5
Capulhuac, Mex. 205/Q10
Capulhuac, Mex. 205/Q10
Capulin, Co, US 179/J2
Capulin Volcano Nat'l Mon., NM, US 182/C2
Capulo, Ang. 138/C4
Capunda Cavilongo, Ang. 140/B2
Caputh, Ger. 48/Q7
Caquetá (dept.), Col. 216/C4
Caquetá (riv.), Col. 216/D5
Cáqueza, Col. 219/M8
Caquiaviri, Bol. 224/B1
Car Nicobar (isl.), India 105/F6
Carabobo (state), Ven. 216/D2
Carabobo, Ven. 217/F3
Caracal, Rom. 57/G3
Caracaraí, Braz. 217/F4
Caracas (cap.), Ven. 219/P7
Carache, Ven. 216/D2
Caracol, Braz. 219/F5
Caracolí, Col. 216/C3
Caracollo, Bol. 224/C1
Carácuaro de Morelos, Mex. 205/E5
Caradon (hill), Eng, UK 42/B5
Caraga, Phil. 100/D4
Caragabal, Austl. 157/C1
Caraglio, It. 70/D4
Caraguatatuba, Braz. 223/L8
Caraguatatuba (bay), Braz. 223/L8
Carahue, Chile 226/B3
Carajás, Braz. 218/D4
Carajás, Serra dos (mts.), Braz. 218/D4
Caramanico Terme, It. 71/D3
Caramanta, Col. 219/K7
Caramat, On, Can. 187/L3
Caramoan, Phil. 100/C2
Caramoran, Phil. 100/D2
Caranavi, Bol. 221/E4
Carandaí, Braz. 222/E4
Carandayti, Bol. 224/D2
Carandotta, Austl. 155/H2
Carangola, Braz. 223/E4
Caransebeş, Rom. 56/F3
Carantec, Fr. 62/B3
Carapari, Bol. 224/D2
Carapicuíba, Braz. 223/K8
Carapó, Braz. 225/F2
Carappee Hill (peak), Austl. 155/H5
Caraquet, NB, Can. 188/E2
Carare (riv.), Col. 219/L6
Caraş-Severin (prov.), Rom. 56/E3
Carasco, It. 68/C5
Carat (cape), Indo. 101/D3
Caratasca (lag.), Hon. 202/E4
Carate Brianza, It. 68/C2
Caratinga, Braz. 223/E3
Carauarí, Braz. 221/E2
Caraúbas, Braz. 219/G4
Caravaca de la Cruz, Sp. 52/E3
Caravaggio, It. 68/C3
Caravelas, Braz. 223/F3
Caravelí, Peru 220/C4
Caraway, Ar, US 192/B3
Carayaca, Ven. 219/N7
Caraz, Peru 220/B3
Carazinho, Braz. 225/F4
Carballino, Sp. 52/A1
Carballo, Sp. 52/A1
Carberry, Mb, Can. 186/E3
Carbo, Mex. 204/C2
Carbon (cape), Alg. 130/H4
Carbon, Ab, Can. 175/H2
Carbon (co.), Pa, US 198/C2
Carbon, Tx, US 181/E1
Carbon (riv.), Wa, US 197/C3
Carbon Hill, Al, US 192/D4
Carbonado, Wa, US 174/C4
Carbonara (peak), It. 54/D4
Carbonara (cape), It. 54/A3
Carbondale, Il, US 192/C2
Carbondale, Ks, US 183/G1
Carbondale, Pa, US 191/J4
Carbonear, Nf, Can. 189/L2
Carbonera, It. 69/F2
Carboneras, Mex. 205/F3
Carbonia, It. 54/A3
Carbonne, Fr. 50/D5
Carbost, Sc, UK 37/Q8
Carbury, Ire. 38/D3
Carcagente, Sp. 53/E3
Carcar, Phil. 100/C3
Carcarañá, Arg. 226/E2
Carcare, It. 68/B5
Carcassonne, Fr. 50/E5
Carcès, Fr. 70/C6
Carche (peak), Sp. 52/E3
Carchi (dept.), Ecu. 216/B4
Carcoar, Austl. 157/D1
Carcross, Yk, Can. 201/M3
Çardak, Turk. 57/H5
Cardal, Uru. 227/K11
Cardale, Mb, Can. 186/D2
Cardedeu, Sp. 53/L6
Cárdenas, Mex. 206/C2
Cárdenas, Cuba 207/F1
Cárdenas, Mex. 205/F4
Cardenden, Sc, UK 39/C4
Cardiel (lake), Arg. 227/C6
Cardiff (cap.), Wal, UK 42/C4
Cardiff (co.), Wal, UK 42/C4
Cardiff, Md, US 198/B4
Cardiff by the Sea, Ca, US 196/C4
Cardiff-Wales (arpt.), Wal, UK 42/C4
Cardigan, PE, Can. 189/F2
Cardigan (bay), PE, Can. 189/F2
Cardigan, Wal, UK 42/B2
Cardinal, On, Can. 191/J2
Cardington, Oh, US 190/E4
Cardito, It. 71/D6
Cardona, Sp. 53/F2
Cardona, Uru. 227/K10
Cardoso, Braz. 225/G2
Cardozo, Uru. 227/K10
Cardston, Ab, Can. 175/H3
Cardwell, Austl. 158/B2
Cardwell, Mo, US 192/B2
Care Alto (peak), It. 67/G5
Careaçu, Braz. 223/L7
Carefree, Az, US 179/G4
Carei, Rom. 49/M5
Careiro, Braz. 218/B3
Carelmapu, Chile 226/B4
Carencro, La, US 194/B2
Carenero, Ven. 219/P7
Carentan, Fr. 62/D2
Carev vrh (peak), FYROM 55/H1
Carey, Oh, US 190/E4
Carey, Id, US 177/G2
Carey (lake), Austl. 145/B3
Carhaix-Plouguer, Fr. 62/B4
Carhuamayo, Peru 220/B3
Carhuaz, Peru 220/B3
Carhué, Arg. 226/E3
Cariaco, Ven. 217/F2
Cariamanga, Ecu. 220/B2
Cariango, Ang. 138/C5
Cariati, It. 54/E3
Caribbean (sea), NAm,SAm. 203/G4
Cariboo (mts.), BC, Can. 174/D1
Cariboo (riv.), BC, Can. 174/D1
Caribou (mts.), Ab, Can. 170/E3
Caribou (lake), On, Can. 187/K2
Caribou (isl.), On, Can. 187/M4
Caribou, Yk, Can. 201/L3
Caribou (range), Id, US 177/H2
Caribou, Me, US 171/K4
Caridade, Braz. 219/G4
Carigara, Phil. 100/D3
Carignan, Fr. 61/E4
Carignan, Qu, Can. 189/P7
Carignano, It. 68/A3
Carinda, Austl. 156/C1
Cariñena, Sp. 52/E2
Carinhanha, Braz. 222/E2
Carinhanha (riv.), Braz. 222/D2
Carini, It. 54/C3
Carinola, It. 71/C5
Caripande, Ang. 140/D2
Caripito, Ven. 217/F2
Cariré, Braz. 219/F3
Caririaçu, Braz. 219/G4
Cariris Novos, Serra dos (mts.), Braz. 219/F4
Cariús, Braz. 219/G4
Carl Junction, Mo, US 183/G2
Carl Sandburg Home Nat'l Hist. Site, NC, US 193/F3
Carleton (mt.), NB, Can. 188/D2
Carleton, Qu, Can. 188/D1
Carleton (riv.), NS, Can. 188/E3
Carleton, Mi, US 197/F7
Carleton Place, On, Can. 191/H2
Carletonville, SAfr. 142/D2
Carlin, Nv, US 176/E3
Carlindie Abor. Land, Austl. 154/C2
Carling, Fr. 61/F5
Carlingford (lake), Ire. 40/B3
Carlingford (mtn.), Ire. 40/B3
Carlingford, Ire. 40/B3
Carlingford (nbrhd.), Austl. 158/H8
Carlinville, Il, US 185/K4
Carlisle, On, Can. 190/T9
Carlisle, Eng, UK 41/F2
Carlisle, Ar, US 183/J3
Carlisle, In, US 192/D1
Carlisle, Ky, US 192/E1
Carlisle, Ms, US 194/C1
Carlisle, Pa, US 191/H4
Carlisle, SC, US 193/G3
Carlisle Barracks Mil. Res., Pa, US 198/A3
Carlit (peak), Fr. 50/D5
Carlos, Mn, US 187/G5
Carlos Casares, Arg. 226/E2
Carlos Chagas, Braz. 223/E3
Carlos M. de Cespedes, Cuba 207/G1
Carlos Pellegrini, Arg. 224/D5
Carlow (co.), Ire. 40/B6
Carlow, Ire. 38/D4
Carloway, Sc, UK 37/Q7
Carlsbad, Ca, US 196/C4
Carlsbad, Tx, US 180/D2
Carlsbad, NM, US 180/B1
Carlsbad Caverns NP, NM, US 180/B1
Carlsberg, Ger. 64/B3
Carlsborg, Wa, US 174/C3
Carlsfeld, Ger. 65/F2
Carlshend, Mi, US 187/L4
Carluke, On, Can. 190/T9
Carlton, Eng, UK 41/G6
Carlton, Al, US 194/E2
Carlton, Ga, US 193/F3
Carlton, Mn, US 187/H4
Carlton, Or, US 176/B1
Carlton, Wa, US 174/D3
Carluke, Sc, UK 39/C5
Carlyle, Sk, Can. 186/C3
Carlyle, Mt, US 186/B4
Carlyle, Il, US 192/C1
Carlyle (lake), Il, US 185/K4
Carmacks, Yk, Can. 201/L3
Carmagnola, It. 68/A3
Carman, Mb, Can. 186/F3
Carmarthen (bay), Wal, UK 42/B3
Carmarthen, Wal, UK 42/B3
Carmarthenshire (co.), Wal, UK 42/B3
Carmaux, Fr. 50/E4
Carmel (pt.), Wal, UK 40/D5
Carmel, NY, US 191/K4
Carmel, In, US 190/C5
Carmel (Carmel-by-the-Sea), Ca, US 178/B2
Carmel Valley, Ca, US 178/B2
Carmelita, Guat. 206/D2
Carmelo, Uru. 227/J11
Carmen (isl.), Mex. 206/C2
Carmen, Az, US 179/G5
Carmen, Bol. 220/E3
Carmen, Id, US 177/G1
Carmen, Ok, US 183/E2
Carmen de Apicalá, Col. 219/L8
Carmen de Carupa, Col. 219/M7
Carmen de Cura, Ven. 219/P8
Carmen de Patagones, Arg. 226/E4
Carmen de Viboral, Col. 219/K6
Carmen, Río del (riv.), Mex. 180/A2
Carmensa, Arg. 226/D2
Carmi, Il, US 192/C1
Carmi, BC, Can. 174/E3
Carmichael, Ca, US 176/C4
Carmila, Austl. 158/C3
Carmo (peak), It. 68/B5
Carmo, Braz. 223/P6
Carmo da Cachoeira, Braz. 223/L6
Carmo da Mata, Braz. 222/D4
Carmo de Minas, Braz. 223/L7
Carmo do Cajuru, Braz. 225/H2
Carmo do Paranaíba, Braz. 222/D3
Carmo do Rio Claro, Braz. 222/D4
Carmona, Sp. 52/C4
Carn Ban (peak), Sc, UK 39/B2
Carn Easgann Bàna (peak), Sc, UK 39/B2
Càrn Eige (peak), Sc, UK 39/A2
Carn Glas-choire (peak), Sc, UK 39/C2
Carn Kitty (hill), Sc, UK 39/C2
Carn Mairg (peak), Sc, UK 39/B3
Carn Mór (peak), Sc, UK 39/C2
Carn na Cailliche (hill), Sc, UK 39/C1
Carn na Saobhaidhe (peak), Sc, UK 39/B2
Carnac, Fr. 62/B5
Carnago, It. 68/B2
Carnamah, Austl. 154/B4
Carnarvon, Austl. 145/A3
Carnarvon NP, Austl. 158/B4
Carnarvon, SAfr. 142/C3
Carnarvonleegte (riv.), SAfr. 142/C3
Carnation, Wa, US 197/D2
Carnaubais, Braz. 219/G4
Carnaubal, Braz. 219/F4
Carnaxide, Port. 53/P10
Carncastle, NI, UK 40/C2
Carndonagh, Ire. 40/A1
Carnduff, Sk, Can. 186/D3
Carnedd Llewelyn (peak), Wal, UK 40/E5
Carnegie, Ok, US 183/E3
Carnegie, Ga, US 195/F2
Carnegie (lake), Austl. 145/B3
Carnesville, Ga, US 193/F3
Carnew, Ire. 38/D4
Carney (isl.), Ant. 228/S
Carney, Mi, US 190/C2
Carney, Ok, US 183/F3
Carnforth, Eng, UK 41/F3
Carnlough, NI, UK 40/B2
Carnmore (Galway) (arpt.), Ire. 38/B3
Carnot, CAfr. 134/B4
Carnot (cape), Austl. 155/G5
Carnota, Sp. 52/A1
Carnoules, Fr. 70/C6
Carnoux-en-Provence, Fr. 70/B6
Carnsore (pt.), Ire. 38/D5
Carnwath, Sc, UK 39/C5
Carnwath (riv.), NW, Can. 170/D2
Caro, Mi, US 190/E3
Caroga Lake, NY, US 191/J3
Carol City, Fl, US 194/P11
Carol Stream, Il, US 197/P16
Carolina, Braz. 219/E4
Carolina, SAfr. 143/E2
Carolina, PR 203/M8
Carolina, Al, US 194/E2
Carolina Beach, NC, US 193/J3
Carolina Sandhills NWR, SC, US 193/G3
Caroline, Ab, Can. 174/G1
Caroline (isl.), Kiri. 161/K5
Caroline (isls), Micr. 160/D4
Caroline (peak), NZ 159/A4
Caroline (co.), Md, US 198/C6
Caromb, Fr. 70/B4
Caron, Sk, Can. 175/M2
Caroní (riv.), Ven. 209/C2
Carora, Ven. 216/D2
Carouge, Swi. 66/C5
Carovilli, It. 71/D4
Carp, Nv, US 178/E2
Carpaneto Piacentino, It. 68/C4
Carpathian (mts.), Eur. 29/G4
Carpegna, It. 69/F6
Carpegna (peak), It. 69/F6
Carpenedolo, It. 68/D3
Carpentaria (gulf), Austl. 145/C2
Carpenter, Wy, US 184/B3
Carpentersville, Il, US 197/P15
Carpentras, Fr. 70/B4
Carpi, It. 69/D4
Carpignano Sesia, It. 68/B2
Carpina, Braz. 219/H4
Carpineto Romano, It. 71/C4
Carpinone, It. 71/D4
Carpinteria, Ca, US 196/A2
Carpio, ND, US 186/D3
Carpiquet (int'l arpt.), Fr. 63/E2
Carquefou, Fr. 62/D6
Carqueiranne, Fr. 70/C6
Carr (inlet), Wa, US 197/B3
Carr Boyds (range), Austl. 152/C4
Carrabalci, Eth. 136/B3
Carrabelle, Fl, US 195/F3
Carraipía, Col. 216/C2
Carraiu, Eth. 135/H4
Carran (peak), Ire. 38/A6
Carrara, It. 68/D5
Carraroe, Ire. 38/A3
Carrasco (int'l arpt.), Uru. 227/K11
Carrasquero, Ven. 216/D2
Carrathool, Austl. 157/B2
Carrboro, NC, US 193/H3
Carrbridge, Sc, UK 39/C2
Carreg Ddu (pt.), Wal, UK 40/D6
Carriacou (isl.), Gren. 203/J5
Carrick, Mb, Can. 186/F3
Carrick (reg.), Sc, UK 39/B6
Carrick on Shannon, Ire. 38/B2
Carrick on Suir, Ire. 38/C5
Carrickalinga, Austl. 155/H5
Carrickfergus, NI, UK 40/C2
Carrickfergus (dist.), NI, UK 40/C2
Carrickmacross, Ire. 38/D2
Carrickmore, NI, UK 40/A2
Carriere, Ms, US 194/D2
Carrières-sous-Poissy, Fr. 36/J5
Carrigaholt, Ire. 38/A4
Carrigaline, Ire. 38/B6
Carrigallen, Ire. 38/C2
Carrigatuke (peak), NI, UK 38/D1
Carrigtwohill, Ire. 38/B6
Carrington, ND, US 186/E4
Carrión (riv.), Sp. 52/C1
Carrión de los Condes, Sp. 52/C1
Carrito, Bol. 221/E4
Carrizal, Col. 216/C1
Carrizalillo, Chile 224/B4
Carrizo (cr.), NM,Tx, US 182/C2
Carrizo (mts.), Az, US 172/D4
Carrizo Plain Nat'l Mon., Ca, US 178/C3
Carrizo Springs, Tx, US 180/E3
Carrizo Wash (riv.), Az, US 179/H3
Carrizozo, NM, US 182/B4
Carroll, Mb, Can. 186/D3
Carroll, Ia, US 185/G2
Carroll (co.), Md, US 198/A5
Carrollton, Al, US 192/C4
Carrollton, Ga, US 192/E4
Carrollton, Il, US 185/J4
Carrollton, Ky, US 192/E1
Carrollton, Mi, US 190/E3
Carrollton, Ms, US 192/C4
Carrollton, Mo, US 185/H4
Carrollton, Oh, US 190/F4
Carrollton, Tx, US 180/L7
Carrollwood Village, Fl, US 194/K7
Carron (lake), Sc, UK 39/A2
Carron (riv.), Sc, UK 39/A2
Carros, Fr. 70/D5
Carrot (riv.), Sk, Can. 175/M1
Carrot River, Sk, Can. 175/N1
Carrouges, Fr. 63/E3
Carrowdore, NI, UK 40/C2
Carrowkeel, Ire. 40/A1
Carrù, It. 68/A4
Carrum Downs, Austl. 156/G6
Carrumpa (cr.), NM,Ok, US 182/C2
Carry-le-Rouet, Fr. 70/B6
Carryduff, NI, UK 40/C2
Çarşamba, Turk. 76/F4
Carse of Forth (plain), Sc, UK 39/B4
Carse of Gowrie (plain), Sc, UK 39/C4
Carseland, Ab, Can. 175/H2
Carsoli, It. 71/C3
Carson, Ca, US 196/F8
Carson, Ms, US 194/D2
Carson, ND, US 186/D4
Carson, NM, US 182/B2
Carson (lake), Nv, US 176/D4
Carson (des.), Nv, US 176/D4
Carson (riv.), Nv, US 176/D4
Carson City, Mi, US 190/D3
Carson City (cap.), Nv, US 176/D4
Carson River Abor. Land, Austl. 152/B3
Carson Sink (sink), Nv, US 176/D4
Carsonville, Mi, US 190/E3
Carsphairn, Sc, UK 40/D1
Carstairs, Ab, Can. 175/G2
Carstairs Junction, Sc, UK 39/C5
Carsulae (ruin), It. 71/B2
Carswell (A.F.B.), Tx, US 183/F4
Carta Valley, Tx, US 180/D3
Cartagena, Col. 216/C2
Cartagena, Sp. 53/E4
Cartagena, Chile 226/N8
Cartago, Col. 219/K8
Cartago, CR 207/F4
Cartago, Ca, US 178/C2
Cártama, Sp. 52/C4
Cartaya, Sp. 52/B4
Cartecay, Ga, US 192/E3
Carter, Ok, US 182/E3
Carter, Wi, US 187/K5
Carter (mt.), Austl. 153/F3
Carter Bar (hill), Eng, UK 39/D6
Carteret (cape), Fr. 62/D2
Carteret, Fr. 62/D2
Carteret, NJ, US 199/J9
Cartersville, Ga, US 192/E3
Cartersville, Mt, US 175/L4
Carterton, NZ 159/J9
Carterton, Eng, UK 43/E3
Carterville, Il, US 192/C2
Carthage (int'l arpt.), Tun. 130/M6
Carthage, Ar, US 183/H3
Carthage, Il, US 185/J3
Carthage, Mo, US 183/G2
Carthage, Ms, US 192/C4
Carthage, NC, US 193/H3
Carthage, NY, US 191/J3
Carthage, Tn, US 192/E2
Carthage, Tx, US 181/G1
Carthage (Qarţājannah) (ruin), Tun. 130/M6
Cartí (mtn.), Pan. 216/B2
Cartier, On, Can. 190/F1
Cartier Islet (isl.), Austl. 145/B2
Cartwright, Mb, Can. 186/E3
Cartwright, Nf, Can. 171/L3
Caruaru, Braz. 219/H5
Carumás, Peru 220/D5
Carunjamba (riv.), Ang. 140/B2
Carúpano, Ven. 217/F2
Carutapera, Braz. 219/E3
Caruthers, Ca, US 178/C2
Caruthersville, Mo, US 192/C2
Carver (co.), Mn, US 187/N7
Carver, Mn, US 187/N7
Carvico, It. 68/C2
Carville, La, US 194/C2
Carvin, Fr. 60/B3
Carvoeiro (cape), Port. 52/A3
Cary, Il, US 197/P15
Cary, Ms, US 192/B4
Cary, NC, US 193/H3
Caryville, Fl, US 195/F2
Caryville, Tn, US 192/E2
Casa, Ar, US 183/H3
Casa Agapito, Col. 216/C4
Casa Blanca, NM, US 179/J3
Casa Branca, Braz. 223/J6
Casa de Piedra (res.), Arg. 226/D3
Casa Grande, Az, US 179/G4
Casa Grande Ruins Nat'l Mon., Az, US 179/G4
Casa Nova, Braz. 219/F5
Casabianca, Col. 219/K7
Casablanca, Chile 226/N8
Casablanca (Dar-El-Beida), Mor. 128/D2
Casablanca (Mohamed V) (int'l arpt.), Mor. 128/D2
Casablanca-Anfa (prov.), Mor. 130/A2
Casacalenda, It. 71/D4
Casagiove, It. 71/D5
Casal di Principe, It. 71/D5
Casalbordino, It. 71/D3
Casalbuttano, It. 68/C3
Casale di Scodosia, It. 69/E3
Casale Monferrato, It. 68/B3
Casale sul Sile, It. 69/F2
Casalecchio di Reno, It. 69/E5
Casaleone, It. 69/E3
Casalmaggiore, It. 68/D4
Casalpusterlengo, It. 68/C3
Casalserugo, It. 69/E3
Casamance (riv.), Sen. 132/A3
Casamicciola Terme, It. 71/C6
Casanare (dept.), Col. 216/D3
Casanare (riv.), Col. 216/D3
Casanay, Ven. 217/F2
Casapesenna, It. 71/D6
Casar de Cáceres, Sp. 52/B3
Casarano, It. 55/F2
Casarsa della Delizia, It. 69/F2
Casarza Ligure, It. 68/C5
Casas de Chacabuco, Chile 226/N8
Casas Grande (riv.), Mex. 179/J5
Casas Grandes (ruin), Mex. 204/C2
Casas Grandes, Mex. 204/D2
Casas-Ibáñez, Sp. 52/E3
Ca'Savio, It. 69/F3
Casazza, It. 68/C2
Cascada de Bassaseachic, PN, Mex. 204/C2
Cascade (pt.), NZ 159/B4
Cascade, Ia, US 185/J2
Cascade, Id, US 176/E1
Cascade (res.), Id, US 176/E1
Cascade, Mt, US 175/J4
Cascade (pt.), Or, US 176/A1
Cascade (range), Or,Wa, US 170/D4
Cascade, Va, US 193/H2
Cascade Caverns, Tx, US 181/E3
Cascade-Fairwood, Or, US 197/C3
Cascades (pt.), Reun., Fr. 143/S15
Cascade-Siskiyou Nat'l Mon., Or, US 176/B2
Cascais, Port. 53/P10
Cascapédia (riv.), Qu, Can. 188/D1
Cascas, Peru 220/B2
Cascavel, Braz. 225/F3
Cascia, It. 71/C2
Casciago, It. 68/B2
Casciana Terme, It. 68/D6
Cascina, It. 68/D6
Casco, Me, US 191/L2
Casco (bay), Me, US 188/B4
Casco, Wi, US 190/C2
Case (inlet), Wa, US 197/B3
Case Nuove, It. 69/E6
Casebier (hill), Wy, US 184/B2
Caselette, It. 70/D2
Casella, It. 68/B4
Caselle, It. 69/E3
Caselle Torinese, It. 70/D2
Caselton, Nv, US 178/E2
Casentino (valley), It. 69/E5
Caserta, It. 71/D5
Caserta (prov.), It. 71/D5
Caseville, Mi, US 190/E3
Casey, Austl., Ant. 228/H
Casey (bay), Ant. 228/D
Casey, Il, US 190/C5
Caseyr (cape), Som. 136/D3
Cash, Ar, US 183/J3
Cashel, Ire. 38/C4
Cashel, Zim. 141/G3
Cashion, Ok, US 183/F3
Cashlaundrumlahan (peak), Ire. 38/B3
Cashmere, Wa, US 174/D4
Cashtown, Pa, US 198/A4
Casigua, Ven. 216/C2
Casiguran, Phil. 100/C2
Casiguran, Phil. 100/C1
Casilda (pt.), Cuba 207/F1
Casilda, Arg. 226/E2
Casimiro Castillo, Mex. 204/D5
Casina, It. 68/D4
Casinalbo, It. 69/D4
Casino, Austl. 156/E1
Casino and Opera House, Mona. 68/J8
Casira, Bol. 224/C2
Casitas (lake), Ca, US 196/A2
Casitas Springs, Ca, US 196/A2
Casma, Peru 220/B3
Casmalia, Ca, US 178/B3
Casnigo, It. 68/C2
Casole d'Elsa, It. 69/E7
Casoli, It. 71/D3
Casorate Primo, It. 68/C3
Casorate Sempione, It. 68/B2
Casoria, It. 71/D6
Caspar, Ca, US 176/B4
Caspe, Sp. 53/E2
Casper (cr.), Wy, US 177/K2
Caspian (sea), Asia 83/E5
Caspian, Mi, US 187/K4
Caspoggio, It. 67/F5
Cass, Ar, US 183/H3
Cass (riv.), Mi, US 190/E3
Cass (lake), Mi, US 197/F6
Cass City, Mi, US 190/E3
Cass Lake, Mn, US 187/G4
Cassadaga, NY, US 191/G3
Cassai, Ang. 139/E5
Cassai (riv.), Ang. 139/E5
Cassamba, Ang. 140/D2
Cassanguidi, Ang. 139/E4
Cassano allo Ionio, It. 54/E3
Cassano d'Adda, It. 68/C2
Cassano Magnago, It. 68/B2
Cassano Spinola, It. 68/B4
Casscoe, Ar, US 183/J3
Cassel, Fr. 60/B2
Casselberry, Fl, US 194/N6
Casselton, ND, US 186/F4
Cássia, Braz. 225/H2
Cassiar, BC, Can. 201/N3
Cassiar (mts.), BC, Can. 170/C3
Cassilândia, Braz. 222/C3
Cassilis, Austl. 156/D1
Cassine, It. 68/B4
Cassinga, Ang. 140/C2
Cassino, It. 71/C5
Cassiporé (cape), Braz. 218/D2
Cassis, Fr. 70/B6
Cassoalala, Ang. 138/C5
Cassoday, Ks, US 183/F1
Cassolnovo, It. 68/B3
Cassongue, Ang. 140/B1
Cassopolis, Mi, US 190/C4
Cassville, Mo, US 183/H2
Cassville, WV, US 190/F5
Cassville, Wi, US 185/J2
Castagnaro, It. 69/E3
Castagneto Carducci, It. 51/J5
Castagnole delle Lanze, It. 68/B4
Castaic, Ca, US 196/B2
Castaic (lake), Ca, US 178/C3
Castalla, Sp. 53/E3
Castanet-Tolosan, Fr. 50/D5
Castanhal, Braz. 218/E3
Castaños, Mex. 180/D4
Casteau, Belg. 60/D2
Casteggio, It. 68/C3
Castegnato, It. 68/D2
Castel Bolognese, It. 69/E5
Castel d'Ario, It. 69/D3
Castel del Piano, It. 71/B1
Castel di Sangro, It. 71/D4
Castel Frentano, It. 71/D3
Castel Fusano, It. 71/B4
Castel Gandolfo, It. 71/B4
Castel Giorgio, It. 71/A2
Castel Goffredo, It. 68/D3
Castel Madama, It. 71/B4
Castel Mella, It. 68/D3
Castel NP, Isr. 117/C5
Castel San Giovanni, It. 68/C3
Castel San Lorenzo, It. 54/D2
Castel San Pietro Terme, It. 69/E5
Castel Viscardo, It. 71/B2
Castel Volturno, It. 71/C5
Castelbuono, It. 54/D4
Castelcovati, It. 68/C3
Castelfidardo, It. 69/G7
Castelfiorentino, It. 69/D6
Castelforte, It. 71/C5
Castelfranco di Sopra, It. 69/E6
Castelfranco Emilia, It. 69/E4
Castelfranco Veneto, It. 69/E2
Castelgomberto, It. 69/E2
Casteljaloux, Fr. 50/D4
Castell de Montjuic, Sp. 53/L7
Castella, Ca, US 176/B3
Castellammare (gulf), It. 54/C3
Castellammare di Stabia, It. 71/D6
Castellamonte, It. 68/A2
Castellane, Fr. 70/C5
Castellano (riv.), It. 71/C2
Castellanza, It. 68/B2
Castellar del Vallès, Sp. 53/G2
Castellarano, It. 69/D4
Castell'Arquato, It. 68/C4
Castellazzo Bormida, It. 68/B4
Castelldefels, Sp. 53/K7
Castelleone, It. 68/C3
Castelli, Arg. 227/K12
Castellina in Chianti, It. 69/E7
Castelliri, It. 71/C4
Castello di Godego, It. 69/E2
Castello di Miramare, It. 69/G2
Castello Eurialo (ruin), It. 54/D4
Castello, Monte il (peak), It. 69/E6
Castellón de la Plana, Sp. 53/E3
Castellote, Sp. 53/E2
Castellucchio, It. 68/D3
Castelmassa, It. 69/E3
Castelmauro, It. 71/D4
Castelnau-le-Lez, Fr. 50/E5
Castelnaudary, Fr. 50/D5
Castelnovo di Sotto, It. 68/D4
Castelnovo ne'Monti, It. 68/D5
Castelnuovo Berardenga, It. 69/E7
Castelnuovo di Garfagnana, It. 68/D5
Castelnuovo Don Bosco, It. 68/A2
Castelnuovo Scrivia, It. 68/B4
Castelo Branco (dist.), Port. 52/B2
Castelo Branco, Port. 52/B3
Castelo de Vide, Port. 52/B3
Castelo do Piauí, Braz. 219/F4
Castelraimondo, It. 71/C1
Castelsardo, It. 54/A2
Castelsarrasin, Fr. 50/D4
Castelvecchio Subequo, It. 71/C3
Castelverde, It. 68/C3
Castelvetere in Val Fortore, It. 71/D5
Castelvetrano, It. 54/C4
Castelvetro di Modena, It. 69/D4
Castelvetro Piacentino, It. 68/C3
Castenaso, It. 69/E4
Castenedolo, It. 68/D3
Casterton, Austl. 156/B3
Castiglioncello, It. 68/D7
Castiglione, It. 69/F5
Castiglione d'Adda, It. 68/C3
Castiglione dei Pepoli, It. 69/E5
Castiglione del Lago, It. 71/B1
Castiglione delle Stiviere, It. 68/D3
Castiglione in Teverina, It. 71/B2
Castiglione Messer Marino, It. 71/D4
Castiglione Torinese, It. 68/A2
Castilho, Braz. 225/G2
Castilla, Peru 220/A2
Castilla, Chile 224/B3
Castilla Y León (prov.), Sp. 50/B5
Castilla- La Mancha (pol. reg.), Sp. 53/N8
Castilla-La Mancha (dist.), Sp. 52/C3
Castilletes, Col. 216/D2
Castillo (peak), Arg. 226/C4
Castillo de San Marcos Nat'l Mon., Fl, US 195/H3
Castillon (lake), Fr. 70/C5
Castillos, Uru. 227/G2
Castione della Presolana, It. 67/G6
Castions, It. 69/F2
Castions di Strada, It. 69/G2
Castle (riv.), Ab, Can. 174/G3
Castle (pt.), NZ 159/D3
Castle Acre, Eng, UK 43/G1
Castle Cary, Eng, UK 42/D4
Castle Combe, Eng, UK 42/D4
Castle Dale, Ut, US 177/H4
Castle Danger, Mn, US 187/J4
Castle Donnington, Eng, UK 41/G6
Castle Douglas, Sc, UK 40/E2
Castle Hayne, NC, US 193/J3
Castle Hill (nbrhd.), Austl. 158/H8
Castle Hill Nat'l Hist. Park, Nf, Can. 189/K2
Castle Kennedy, Sc, UK 40/D2
Castle Rock, Ut, US 177/H3
Castle Rock (lake), Wi, US 185/J2
Castle Rock, Co, US 184/B4
Castle Rock, SD, US 184/C1
Castle Rock (dam), Wi, US 185/K2
Castle Rock, Wa, US 174/C4
Castle Tower NP, Austl. 158/C4
Castlebar, Ire. 38/A2
Castlebar (arpt.), Ire. 38/A2
Castlebay, Sc, UK 37/Q8
Castlebellingham, Ire. 40/B4
Castleberry, Al, US 194/E2
Castleblayney, Ire. 38/D1
Castlebridge, Ire. 38/D5
Castlecaufield, NI, UK 40/B3
Castlecomer, Ire. 38/C4
Castleconnell, Ire. 38/B4
Castledawson, NI, UK 40/B2
Castledermot, Ire. 38/D4
Castleford, Eng, UK 41/G4
Castleford, Id, US 177/F2
Castlegar, BC, Can. 174/F3
Castlegregory, Ire. 36/N10
Castleisland, Ire. 38/A5
Castlemaine, Austl. 157/B3
Castlemartyr, Ire. 38/B6
Castlepollard, Ire. 38/C2
Castlereagh, Ire. 38/B2
Castlereagh (nbrhd.), Austl. 158/G8
Castlerock, NI, UK 40/B1
Castleton, Vt, US 191/K3
Castletown, Ire. 38/C4
Castletown, IM, UK 40/D3
Castletownroche, Ire. 38/B5
Castletownsend, Ire. 38/A6
Castlewellan, NI, UK 40/C3
Castlewood, SD, US 185/F1
Castor (cr.), La, US 181/H1
Castor, La, US 183/H4
Castor, Ab, Can. 175/J1
Castor (riv.), Mo, US 192/B2
Castres, Fr. 50/E5
Castrezzato, It. 68/C2
Castricum, Neth. 58/B3
Castries (cap.), StL. 203/N9
Castro, Chile 226/B4
Castro, Braz. 225/G3
Castro Daire, Port. 52/B2
Castro de Rey, Sp. 52/B1
Castro del Río, Sp. 52/C4
Castro Verde, Port. 52/A4
Castro-Urdiales, Sp. 52/D1
Castrocaro Terme, It. 69/E5
Castrojeriz, Sp. 52/C1
Castrop-Rauxel, Ger. 59/E5
Castropol, Sp. 52/B1
Castrovillari, It. 54/E3
Castroville, Ca, US 178/B2
Castroville, Tx, US 181/E3
Castrovirreyna, Peru 220/C4
Castuera, Sp. 52/C3
Casupá, Uru. 227/G2
Çat, Turk. 114/E2
Cat (lake), On, Can. 187/J2
Cat (isl.), Bahm. 163/K7
Cat Ba (isl.), Viet. 99/E4
Cat Ba NP, Viet. 99/E4
Cat Creek, Mt, US 175/K4
Cat Head (pt.), Mi, US 190/D2
Cat Law (peak), Sc, UK 39/C3
Catabola, Ang. 140/C2
Catabola, Ang. 140/B2
Catacamas, Hon. 206/E3
Catacaos, Peru 220/A2
Catacocha, Ecu. 220/B2
Cataduanes (isl.), Phil. 100/D2
Cataguases, Braz. 223/P6
Catahoula (lake), La, US 194/B2
Catahoula NWR, La, US 181/H2
Cataiñgan, Phil. 103/F1
Çatak, Turk. 115/E2
Catala, Ang. 138/D5
Çatalağzı, Turk. 57/K5
Catalão, Braz. 222/D3
Çatalca, Turk. 115/M6
Çatalçam, Turk. 114/D2
Catalina, Nf, Can. 189/L1
Catalina, Chile 224/B3
Catalina, Az, US 179/G4
Catalone, NS, Can. 189/H3
Catalonia (reg.), Sp. 72/D2
Cataluña (prov.), Sp. 50/D5
Catamarca, Arg. 224/C4
Catamarca (prov.), Arg. 224/C3
Catamayo, Ecu. 220/B1
Catanauan, Phil. 100/C2
Catandica, Moz. 141/G3
Catanduanes (isl.), Phil. 100/D2
Catanduva, Braz. 225/G2
Catania, It. 54/D4
Catania (gulf), It. 54/D4
Catanzaro, It. 54/E3
Cataract (cr.), Az, US 179/F3
Cataract (lake), Austl. 157/E2
Cataratas (int'l arpt.), Braz. 225/F3
Cataratas del Iguazú (falls), Arg. 225/F3
Cataricahua, Bol. 224/C1
Catarina, Braz. 219/G4
Catarman, Phil. 100/D3
Catarman, Phil. 100/D2
Catarman (pt.), Phil. 100/D4
Catastrophe (cape), Austl. 155/G5
Catata Nova, Ang. 140/B2
Catatumbo (riv.), Col. 203/G6
Catatungan (mtn.), Phil. 100/D4
Catawba, Wi, US 187/J5
Catawba (dam), SC, US 193/G3
Catawba (riv.), NC, US 193/G3
Catawba, SC, US 193/G3
Catawba, South Fork (riv.), NC, US 193/G3
Catawissa, Pa, US 198/B2
Catbalogan, Phil. 100/D3
Cateco Cangola, Ang. 138/C5
Catedral (peak), Uru. 227/G2
Cateel, Phil. 100/D4
Catemaco (lake), Mex. 206/C2
Catemaco, Mex. 206/C2
Catende, Braz. 219/H5
Cateran (hill), Eng, UK 39/E5
Caterham, Eng, UK 36/C3
Caterham and Warlingham, Eng, UK 43/F4
Catete, Ang. 138/C5
Catfish (cr.), Fl, US 194/N8
Catharine, Ks, US 182/E1
Cathcart, SAfr. 142/D4
Cathedral (mtn.), Tx, US 180/C2
Cathedral City, Ca, US 178/D4
Cathédrale de Reims, Fr. 60/D5
Catherine (peak), Egypt 127/G2
Catherine, Al, US 192/D4
Catherine Palace, Rus. 75/T7
Cathlamet, Wa, US 174/C4
Ca'Tiepolo, It. 69/F4
Catierick, Eng, UK 41/G3
Catingueira, Braz. 219/G4
Catió, GBis. 132/B4
Cativá, Pan. 207/G4
Catlettsburg, Ky, US 193/F1
Catlin, Il, US 190/C4
Catmon, Phil. 100/D3
Cato (isl.), Aus. 145/E3

Chass – Chūha
276

Chassahowtzka Nat'l Wildlife Ref., Fl, US 195/G3
Chasse-sur-Rhône, Fr. 70/A1
Chassezac (riv.), Fr. 50/F4
Chastre-Villeroux-Blanmont, Belg. 61/D2
Chatanika, Ak, US 201/J2
Chatauqua (lake), Il, US 185/J3
Chatawa, Ms, US 194/C2
Château (pt.), Fr. 62/B3
Chateau de Mores Historical Site, ND, US 186/C4
Chateau de Versailles, Fr. 36/J5
Château d'If, Fr. 70/B6
Château-Arnoux, Fr. 70/C4
Château-d'Olonne, Fr. 50/C3
Château-du-Loir, Fr. 63/F5
Château-Gontier, Fr. 63/F5
Château-la-Vallière, Fr. 63/F5
Château-Porcien, Fr. 61/D4
Château-Renault, Fr. 63/F5
Château-Salins, Fr. 61/F6
Château-Thierry, Fr. 60/C5
Châteaubourg, Fr. 62/D4
Châteaubriant, Fr. 62/D5
Châteaudun, Fr. 63/G4
Chateaugay, NY, US 191/J2
Châteaugiron, Fr. 62/D4
Chateauguay (co.), Qu, Can. 189/N7
Châteauguay, Qu, Can. 189/N7
Châteaulin, Fr. 62/A4
Châteauneuf-de-Gadagne, Fr. 70/A5
Châteauneuf-de-Galaure, Fr. 70/A2
Châteauneuf-du-Faou, Fr. 62/B4
Châteauneuf-du-Pape, Fr. 70/A4
Châteauneuf-du-Rhône, Fr. 70/A4
Châteauneuf-en-Thymerais, Fr. 63/G3
Châteauneuf-les-Martigues, Fr. 70/B6
Châteauneuf-sur-Charente, Fr. 50/C4
Châteauneuf-sur-Isère, Fr. 70/A2
Châteauneuf-sur-Sarthe, Fr. 63/E5
Châteaurenard, Fr. 70/A5
Châteauroux, Fr. 50/D3
Châteauvillain, Fr. 66/A1
Châtel-Saint-Denis, Swi. 66/C4
Châtelaillon-Plage, Fr. 50/C3
Châtelet, Belg. 61/D3
Châtellerault, Fr. 50/D3
Châtenay-Malabry, Fr. 36/J5
Châtenois, Fr. 66/B1
Châtenois-les-Forges, Fr. 66/C2
Chatfield, Mn, US 185/H2
Chatham, NB, Can. 188/E2
Chatham, On, Can. 190/E3
Chatham (isls.), Chile 227/B6
Chatham (isls.), NZ 159/E4
Chatham, Eng, UK 43/G4
Chatham, Il, US 185/K4
Chatham, La, US 183/H4
Chatham, Mi, US 187/L4
Chatham, NJ, US 199/H9
Chatham, NY, US 191/K3
Chatham, Va, US 193/H2
Chathill, Eng, UK 39/E5
Châtillon, It. 70/D1
Châtillon, Fr. 36/J5
Châtillon-sur-Chalaronne, Fr. 66/A5
Châtillon-sur-Marne, Fr. 60/C5
Châtillon-sur-Seine, Fr. 50/F3
Chātmohar, Bang. 109/G3
Chatom, Al, US 194/D2
Chaton (mtn.), Austl. 157/D2
Chatou, Fr. 36/J5
Chatra, India 109/E3
Chatra, Nepal 109/F2
Châtres, Fr. 36/L5
Chatrūd, Iran 115/J4
Chatswood (nbrhd.), Austl. 158/H8
Chatsworth, Zim. 141/F3
Chatsworth (res.), Ca, US 196/B2
Chatsworth (nbrhd.), Ca, US 196/E7
Chatsworth, Ga, US 192/E3
Chatsworth, Il, US 190/B4
Chatsworth, NJ, US 198/D4
Chattahoochee, Fl, US 195/F2
Chattahoochee (riv.), Ga, US 192/E4
Chattahoochee (riv.), Ga, US 193/L7
Chattanooga, Ok, US 183/E3
Chattanooga, Tn, US 192/E3
Chattaroy, WV, US 193/F2
Chattaroy, Wa, US 174/F4
Chatte, Fr. 70/B2
Chattenden, Eng, UK 36/E2
Chatteris, Eng, UK 43/G2
Chattooga (riv.), Ga, US 193/F3
Chatuzange-le-Goubet, Fr. 70/B3
Chau Doc, Viet. 106/D4
Chaúa, Ang. 138/D5
Chaucey (isl.), Fr. 50/C2
Chauconin-Neufmontiers, Fr. 36/L5
Chaudfontaine, Belg. 61/E2
Chaudière (riv.), Qu, Can. 188/B2
Chauk, Myan. 98/B4
Chaukan (pass), India 98/C3
Chaulk, Eng, UK 36/E2
Chaumes-en-Brie, Fr. 36/L5
Chaumont, Fr. 66/B1
Chaumont-en-Vexin, Fr. 60/A5
Chaumont-sur-Lloire, Fr. 63/G6
Chaungwabyin, Myan. 106/B3
Chaungzon, Myan. 106/B2
Chaunskaya (bay), Rus. 81/T3
Chauny, Fr. 60/C4
Chaupāran, India 109/E3
Chaussin, Fr. 66/B4
Chaussy, Fr. 36/H4
Chausy, Bela. 76/D1
Chautara, Nepal 109/E2
Chautauqua (lake), NY, US 191/G3
Chautauqua Nat'l Wild. Ref., Il, US 185/J3
Chauvigny, Fr. 50/D3
Chauvin, Ab, Can. 175/J1
Chavakali, Kenya 137/A1
Chavakkad, India 107/C4
Chaval, Braz. 219/F3
Chavanay, Fr. 70/A2
Chavan'ga, Rus. 74/H2
Chavanoz, Fr. 66/B6
Chavarría, Arg. 224/E4
Chaves, Port. 52/B2
Chaves, Braz. 218/D3
Chavière, Montagne de la (peak), Fr. 70/B4
Chavies, Ky, US 193/F2
Chavín de Huantar (ruin), Peru 220/B3
Chaviña, Peru 220/C4
Chavinillo, Peru 220/B3
Chavornay, Swi. 66/C4
Chavuma (falls), Zam. 140/D2
Chawinda, Pak. 110/C3
Chay (riv.), Viet. 106/D1
Chayanta, Bol. 224/C1
Chayanta (riv.), Bol. 224/C1
Chaykovskiy, Rus. 75/M4
Chazuta, Peru 220/B2
Chazy, NY, US 191/K2
Chbar, Camb. 106/D3
Cheadle, Eng, UK 41/G6
Cheaha (mtn.), Al, US 192/E4
Cheam View, BC, Can. 174/D3
Cheat (riv.), WV, US 193/H1
Cheb, Czh. 65/F2
Cheben'ki, Rus. 77/K2
Cheboksary (res.), Rus. 75/K4
Cheboksary, Rus. 75/K4
Cheboygan, Mi, US 190/D2
Chechaouene (prov.), Mor. 130/B2
Chechaouene, Mor. 130/B2
Chechel'nyk, Ukr. 78/E3
Chechen' (isl.), Rus. 77/H3
Chechërsk, Bela. 76/D1
Chechevichi, Bela. 47/N5
Chechnya, Resp., Rus. 77/H4
Chech'ŏn, SKor. 93/E4
Checotah, Ok, US 183/G3
Chedabucto (bay), NS, Can. 189/G3
Cheddar, Eng, UK 42/D4
Cheduba (isl.), Myan. 105/F4
Cheduba (str.), Myan. 98/B5
Cheekpoint, Ire. 38/D5
Cheektowaga, NY, US 190/V10
Chefornak, Ak, US 201/F3
Chefumage (riv.), Ang. 140/D1
Chegdomyn, Rus. 91/L1
Chegutu, Zim. 141/F3
Chehalis (riv.), Wa, US 174/C4
Chehalis, Wa, US 174/C4
Chehalis Ind. Res., Wa, US 174/C4
Chehe, China 99/E3
Chehel Dokhtarān, Afg. 113/H1
Cheikh (well), Alg. 129/F3
Cheiron, Montagne du (mts.), Fr. 70/C5
Cheju (str.), SKor. 91/K5
Cheju, SKor. 91/K5
Cheju (int'l arpt.), SKor. 91/K5
Cheju, SKor. 91/K5
Chekhov, Rus. 76/F1
Chekhov, Rus. 91/N2
Chelan (lake), Wa, US 174/D3
Chelan, Wa, US 174/D4
Chelan NRA, Wa, US 174/D3
Cheleken, Trkm. 115/H2
Chelford, Eng, UK 41/F5
Chelghoum El Aïd, Alg. 130/J4
Chelles, Fr. 36/K5
Chełm, Pol. 49/M3
Chełmno, Pol. 49/K2
Chelmsford, Ma, US 191/L3
Chelmsford, Eng, UK 43/G3
Chelmuzhi, Rus. 74/G3
Chełmża, Pol. 49/K2
Chelsea (nbrhd.), Austl. 156/G6
Chelsea, Qu, Can. 191/J2
Chelsea (nbrhd.), Eng, UK 36/C2
Chelsea, Al, US 192/D4
Chelsea, Ok, US 183/G2
Chelsea, Vt, US 191/K3
Cheltenham, On, Can. 190/T8
Cheltenham, Eng, UK 42/D3
Chelva, Sp. 53/E3
Chelyabinsk, Rus. 75/P5
Chelyabinsk (int'l arpt.), Rus. 75/P5
Chelyabinskaya Oblast, Rus. 75/P5
Chelyuskina (cape), Rus. 81/L2
Chemaïa, Mor. 128/C2
Chemal, Rus. 111/E1
Chemax, Mex. 206/E1
Chemba, Moz. 141/G3
Chembe, Zam. 141/F1
Chemehuevi Ind. Res., Ca, US 178/E3
Chemillé, Fr. 63/E6
Chemnitz, Ger. 48/G3
Chemult, Or, US 176/C2
Chen (riv.), China 99/F3
Chen Baraq Qi, China 91/H2
Chenāb (riv.), Pak. 113/K2
Chenachane (well), Alg. 128/D4
Chena Hot Springs, Ak, US 201/J2
Chenango (riv.), NY, US 191/J3
Chenārān, Iran 113/G1
Ch'ench'a, Eth. 135/H4
Chencheng, China 99/H4
Cheney (res.), Ks, US 183/F2
Cheney, Wa, US 174/F4
Cheneyville, La, US 194/B2
Chenfang, China 99/H2
Cheng (lake), China 98/D3
Cheng'anpu, China 92/C3
Chengbu Miaozu Zizhixian, China 99/F3
Chengde, China 91/H3
Chengde, China 92/D2
Chengdu (int'l arpt.), China 98/D2
Chengdu, China 98/E2
Chengele, India 98/C2
Chengjiang, China 99/G3
Chengkou, China 99/H3
Chengkou, China 99/F2
Chengmai, China 99/F5
Chengshan Jiao (cape), China 93/B4
Chengwu, China 92/C4
Chengxiangzhen, China 99/H2
Chengzitan, China 93/B3
Chenîménil, Fr. 66/C1
Chenjiazhen, China 92/L8
Chennai (Madras), India 107/D3
Chennevières-lès-Louvres, Fr. 36/K4
Chenôve, Fr. 66/A3
Chenxi, China 99/F2
Chenxiangtun, China 93/B2
Chenzhou, China 99/G3
Chep Lak Kok (int'l arpt.), China 99/K7
Chepelare, Bul. 55/J2
Chepén, Peru 220/B2
Chépénéhé, NCal., Fr. 161/V12
Chepes, Arg. 224/C4
Chépica, Chile 226/C2
Chepigana, Pan. 216/B2
Cheploske, Kenya 137/A1
Chepo, Pan. 216/B2
Chepstow, Wal, UK 42/D3
Cheptsa (riv.), Rus. 75/M4
Cher (dept.), Fr. 63/H6
Cher (riv.), Fr. 72/D1
Chéran (riv.), Fr. 66/C6
Cherasco, It. 68/A3
Cherāt, Pak. 110/A3
Cheraw, Co, US 182/C1
Cheraw, Ms, US 194/D2
Cheraw, SC, US 193/H3
Cherbourg, Fr. 62/D1
Cherbourg, Austl. 158/C4
Cherchell, Alg. 130/G4
Cherdyn', Rus. 75/N3
Chère (riv.), Fr. 62/D5
Cheremisskoye, Rus. 75/P4
Cheremkhovo, Rus. 90/E1
Cheremshan, Rus. 75/L5
Cheremshanka, Rus. 75/P4
Cherëmushi (nbrhd.), Rus. 75/W9
Cherepovets, Rus. 74/H4
Cherevkovo, Rus. 75/K3
Cherf, Oued (riv.), Alg. 130/K6
Chergui (isl.), Tun. 73/F4
Cheria, Alg. 130/K7
Cherikov, Bela. 76/D1
Cherkas'ka Oblast, Ukr. 76/D2
Cherkasy, Ukr. 78/G3
Cherkessk, Rus. 79/M5
Chermignon, Swi. 66/D5
Chermside (nbrhd.), Austl. 158/F6
Chern', Rus. 76/F1
Chernaya, Rus. 75/M1
Chernaya (riv.), Rus. 75/N1
Cherni Lom (riv.), Bul. 57/H4
Cherni Vrŭkh (peak), Bul. 57/F4
Chernigovskaya, Rus. 79/K5
Chernihiv, Ukr. 78/F2
Chernihivs'ka Oblast, Ukr. 78/F2
Chernivets'ka Oblast, Ukr. 76/C2
Chernivtsi, Ukr. 78/C3
Chernomorskiy, Rus. 79/K5
Chernorechenskiy, Rus. 75/M3
Chernukha, Rus. 75/J5
Chernushka, Rus. 75/N4
Chernyakhiv, Ukr. 78/E2
Chernyakhovsk, Rus. 47/J4
Chernyanka, Rus. 79/J2
Chernyshevsk, Rus. 90/H1
Chernyshevskiy, Rus. 81/M3
Chernyy Otrog, Rus. 77/L2
Chernyy Yar, Rus. 77/H2
Cherokee, Al, US 192/D3
Cherokee, Ks, US 183/G2
Cherokee, Ia, US 185/G2
Cherokee, Ok, US 183/E2
Cherokee (lake), Tn, US 193/F2
Cherokee, Tx, US 181/E2
Cherrueix, Fr. 62/D3
Cherry (cr.), SD, US 184/D1
Cherry Creek, BC, Can. 174/D2
Cherry Creek, Nv, US 177/F4
Cherry Creek, SD, US 184/D1
Cherry Hill, Ar, US 183/H3
Cherry Hill, Md, US 198/C4
Cherry Hill, NJ, US 198/C4
Cherry Point MCAS, NC, US 193/J3
Cherry Valley, Ca, US 196/D3
Cherry Valley, Ar, US 192/B3
Cherryvale, Ks, US 183/G2
Cherryville, NC, US 193/G3
Cherski (range), Rus. 83/P3
Cherskiy, Rus. 81/R3
Chertanovo (nbrhd.), Rus. 75/W9
Chertkovo, Rus. 79/L3
Chertsey, Eng, UK 36/B2
Cherven', Bela. 47/N5
Cherven Bryag, Bul. 57/G4
Chervlënnaya, Rus. 77/H4
Chervone, Ukr. 79/H2
Chervonoarmiys'k, Ukr. 78/C2
Chervonohrad, Ukr. 78/C2
Chervonozavods'ke, Ukr. 79/G2
Cherwell (riv.), Eng, UK 43/E3
Chesaning, Mi, US 190/D3
Chesapeake (bay), US 173/L4
Chesapeake, WV, US 193/G1
Chesapeake, Va, US 193/J2
Chesapeake and Delaware (canal), De,Md, US 198/C4
Chesapeake and Ohio Nat'l Hist. Park, Md, US 191/H5
Chesapeake Bay Maritime Museum, Md, US 198/B6
Chesapeake City, Md, US 198/C4
Chesham, Eng, UK 43/F3
Cheshire (co.), Eng, UK 41/F5
Cheshire (plain), Eng, UK 41/F5
Cheshskaya (bay), Rus. 80/E3
Cheshunt, Eng, UK 36/C1
Chesilhurst, NJ, US 198/D4
Chesley, On, Can. 190/F2
Chester, Eng, UK 41/F5
Chester, Ar, US 183/G3
Chester, Ca, US 176/C3
Chester (riv.), De,Md, US 193/J1
Chester, Ga, US 193/F4
Chester, Id, US 177/H2
Chester, Il, US 192/C2
Chester (riv.), Md, US 198/B5
Chester, Mt, US 175/J3
Chester, Ne, US 184/F3
Chester, NJ, US 198/D2
Chester, Ok, US 182/E2
Chester, Pa, US 198/C4
Chester (cr.), Pa, US 198/C4
Chester (co.), Pa, US 198/C4
Chester, SC, US 193/G3
Chester, Tx, US 181/G2
Chester, Vt, US 191/K3
Chester Basin, NS, Can. 188/E3
Chester County G.O. Carlson (arpt.), Pa, US 198/C4
Chester Heights, Pa, US 198/C4
Chester Morse (lake), Wa, US 197/D3
Chester-le-Street, Eng, UK 41/G2
Chesterfield (inlet), Nun, Can. 163/H3
Chesterfield, Eng, UK 41/G5
Chesterfield (isls.), NCal., Fr. 160/E6
Chesterfield, Id, US 177/H2
Chesterfield, In, US 190/D4
Chesterfield, Mo, US 185/J4
Chesterfield, SC, US 193/G3
Chesterfield, Va, US 193/J2
Chesterfield Inlet, Nun, Can. 170/G2
Chesterton (range), Austl. 158/B4
Chestertown, NY, US 191/K3
Chestertown, Md, US 198/B5
Chesuncook (lake), Me, US 188/C2
Cheswold, De, US 198/C5
Chetaibi, Alg. 130/K6
Chetek, Wi, US 187/J5
Chéticamp, NS, Can. 189/G2
Chetopa, Ks, US 183/G2
Chetumal (bay), Mex. 202/D4
Chetumal, Mex. 206/D2
Chetwynd, BC, Can. 170/D3
Cheung Chau (isl.), China 99/J6
Chevak, Ak, US 201/E3
Cheval-Blanc, Fr. 70/B5
Chevejécure, Bol. 221/E4
Chevelon (cr.), Az, US 179/G3
Cheverny, Fr. 63/G5
Chevigny-Saint-Sauveur, Fr. 66/B3
Chevilly, Fr. 63/G4
Cheviot (hills), Sc, UK 39/D6
Cheviot, NZ 159/C3
Chèvre (cape), Fr. 62/A4
Chevreuse, Fr. 36/J5
Chèvreville, Fr. 36/L4
Chevry-Cossigny, Fr. 36/K5
Chew (riv.), Eng, UK 42/D4
Ch'ew Bahir (lake), Eth. 135/H4
Chew Valley (lake), Eng, UK 42/D4
Chewelah, Wa, US 174/F3
Chewore Game Rsv., Zim. 141/F2
Chexbres, Swi. 66/C5
Cheyenne, Ok, US 182/E3
Cheyenne (riv.), SD,Wy, US 184/D1
Cheyenne (cap.), Wy, US 184/B3
Cheyenne River Ind. Res., SD, US 184/E1
Cheyenne Wells, Co, US 182/C1
Cheyres, Swi. 66/C4
Chezacut, BC, Can. 174/B1
Chhabra, India 108/A3
Chhāīn, India 104/B2
Chhaprauli, India 110/D5
Chhāta, India 108/A2
Chhātak, Bang. 109/H3
Chhatarpur, India 108/B3
Chhatarpur, India 109/E3
Chhattisgarh (state), India 104/D3
Chhibrāmau, India 108/B2
Chhindwāra, India 108/B4
Chhukha, Bhu. 109/G2
Chi (riv.), Thai. 105/H4
Chi Ne, Viet. 98/E4
Chia, Col. 219/L8
Chiafua, Ang. 139/E5
Chiai, Tai. 99/J4
Ch'iak-san NP, SKor. 93/E4
Chiali, Tai. 99/J4
Chiampo, It. 69/E2
Chianciano Terme, It. 54/B1
Chiang Dao, Thai. 98/C5
Chiang Dao Caves, Thai. 98/C5
Chiang Kai Shek (int'l arpt.), Tai. 99/J3
Chiang Kham, Thai. 106/C2
Chiang Khan, Thai. 106/C2
Chiang Mai, Thai. 98/C5
Chiang Rai, Thai. 98/C5
Chiang Saen, Thai. 98/D4
Chiange, Ang. 140/B2
Chiani (riv.), It. 71/B2
Chianti (reg.), It. 69/E5
Chianti (mts.), It. 69/E5
Chiapa de Corzo, Mex. 206/C2
Chiapas (state), Mex. 202/C4
Chiappa (pt.), It. 68/C5
Chiaravalle, It. 69/G6
Chiari, It. 68/C2
Chiascio (riv.), It. 71/B1
Chiasso, Swi. 67/F6
Chiat'ura, Geo. 77/G4
Chiautempan, Mex. 205/L7
Chiautla, Mex. 205/R9
Chiautla de Tapia, Mex. 206/B2
Chiavari, It. 68/C5
Chiavenna, It. 67/F5
Chiawa, Zam. 141/F2
Chiba, Japan 97/G3
Chibabava, Moz. 141/G4
Chibakou, China 99/G2
Chibemba, Ang. 140/B2
Chibi, Zam. 141/F4
Chibia, Ang. 140/B2
Chibougamau, Qu, Can. 171/J4
Chibukak (pt.), Ak, US 201/D3
Chibuni, India 98/C2
Chibuto, Moz. 141/G5
Chibwe, Zam. 141/F2
Chic-Chocs (mts.), Qu, Can. 188/D1
Chicago, Il, US 190/C4
Chicago Heights, Il, US 197/Q16
Chicago Midway (int'l arpt.), Il, US 190/C4
Chicago Ridge, Il, US 197/Q16
Chicago Sanitary and Ship Canal, Il, US 197/P16
Chicago, North Branch (riv.), Il, US 197/Q15
Chicago-O'Hare (int'l arpt.), Il, US 190/C4
Chicala, Ang. 140/C1
Chicama, Peru 220/B2
Chicapa (riv.), Ang. 138/D5
Chichagof (isl.), Ak, US 170/C3
Chichaoua, Mor. 128/C3
Chīchāwatni, Pak. 110/B4
Chichén Itzá (ruin), Mex. 206/D1
Chicheng, China 90/H3
Chichester, Eng, UK 43/F5
Chichester (range), Austl. 145/A3
Chichibu, Japan 97/F3
Chichicastenango, Guat. 206/D3
Chichigalpa, Nic. 206/E3
Chichihualco, Mex. 205/F5
Chichiriviche, Ven. 216/D2
Chichishima (isls.), Japan 160/D2
Chichocane, Moz. 141/G4
Chichola, India 107/D1
Chickaloon, Ak, US 201/J3
Chickamauga, Ga, US 192/E3
Chickamauga (lake), Tn, US 192/E3
Chickamauga and Chattanooga Nat'l Mil. Park, Tn, US 192/E3
Chickasaw, Al, US 194/D2
Chickasaw Nat'l Rec. Area, Ok, US 183/F3
Chickasawhay (riv.), Ms, US 192/C5
Chickasha, Ok, US 183/F3
Chickerell, Eng, UK 42/D5
Chickies (cr.), Pa, US 198/B3
Chiclayo, Peru 220/B3
Chiclana de la Frontera, Sp. 52/B4
Chiclayo, Peru 220/B2
Chico (riv.), Arg. 209/B7
Chico, Ca, US 176/C4
Chico (riv.), Phil. 100/C1
Chicoloapan, Mex. 205/R10
Chicomo, Moz. 141/G5
Chicomostoc (ruin), Mex. 204/E4
Chicomuselo, Mex. 206/C3
Chiconcuac, Mex. 205/R9
Chicontepec de Tejeda, Mex. 206/B1
Chicopee, Ma, US 191/K3
Chicot (pt.), La, US 194/D3
Chicota, Tx, US 183/G4
Chicote, Ang. 140/D3
Chicoutimi, Qu, Can. 188/B1
Chicoutimi (riv.), Qu, Can. 188/B1
Chicualacuala, Moz. 141/F4
Chicului (riv.), Ang. 140/D2
Chicuma, Ang. 140/B2
Chidambaram, India 107/C4
Chiddingstone, Eng, UK 36/D3
Chidenguele, Moz. 141/G5
Chidester, Ar, US 183/H4
Chidley (cape), Nf, Can. 171/K2
Chido, SKor. 93/D5
Chiefland, Fl, US 195/G3
Chiem Hoa, Viet. 106/D1
Chiemsee (lake), Ger. 48/G5
Chieo Lan (res.), Thai. 105/G6
Chieri, It. 68/A2
Chierry, Fr. 60/C5
Chiers (riv.), Fr. 61/E5
Chiese (riv.), It. 51/J3
Chieti (prov.), It. 71/D3
Chieti, It. 71/D3
Chietla, Mex. 205/L8
Chieveley, Eng, UK 43/E4
Chièvres, Belg. 60/C2
Chifre, Serra do (mts.), Braz. 223/E3
Chiganak, Kaz. 111/B2
Chigasaki, Japan 97/F3
Chiginagak (mtn.), Ak, US 201/G4
Chignahuapan, Mex. 205/L7
Chignecto (bay), NB,NS, Can. 188/E3
Chignik, Ak, US 201/G4
Chignik Lake, Ak, US 201/G4
Chigorodó, Col. 216/B3
Chigu (lake), China 109/H1
Chiguana, Bol. 224/C2
Chigubo, Moz. 141/G4
Chigwell, Eng, UK 36/D2
Chihayaakasaka, Japan 95/J7
Chihli (Bo Hai) (gulf), China 81/M6
Chihuahua, Mex. 204/D2
Chihuahua (state), Mex. 204/D2
Chiili, Kaz. 80/G5
Chiipperfield, Eng, UK 36/B2
Chijiang, China 99/G3
Chikanda, Nga. 133/F4
Chikaskia (riv.), Ks,Ok, US 183/F2
Chikhachëvo, Rus. 47/N3
Chikhli, India 104/C3
Chikmagalūr, India 107/B3
Chikoy (riv.), Rus. 81/L5
Chikoy, Rus. 90/F1
Chikugo (riv.), Japan 96/B4
Chikuma (riv.), Japan 97/F2
Chikwa, Zam. 141/G1
Chikwawa, Malw. 141/G3
Chila, Ang. 140/B2
Chilac, Mex. 205/M8
Chilakalūrupet, India 107/D2
Chilanga, Zam. 141/F2
Chilanko Forks, BC, Can. 174/B1
Chilās, Pak. 110/C2
Chilbo-san (peak), NKor. 93/E2
Chilca, Peru 220/B4
Chilcoot, Ca, US 176/C4
Chilcotin (riv.), BC, Can. 170/D3
Chilcotin (riv.), BC, Can. 174/C2
Childers, Austl. 158/D4
Childersburg, Al, US 192/D4
Childress, Tx, US 182/D3
Chile (ctry.) 209/B6
Chile Chico, Chile 226/C5
Chile, Monte el (peak), Hon. 206/E3
Chilecito, Arg. 224/C4
Chilembwe, Zam. 141/F2
Chilete, Peru 220/B2
Ch'ilgap-san NP, SKor. 93/D4
Chililabombwe, Zam. 141/E2
Chilka (lake), India 104/E4
Chilko (lake), BC, Can. 170/D3
Chilko (riv.), BC, Can. 174/B2
Chilla Well Abor. Land, Austl. 155/F2
Chillagoe, Austl. 158/B2
Chillán, Chile 226/B3
Chillanes, Ecu. 220/B1
Chilleurs-aux-Bois, Fr. 63/H4
Chillicothe, Tx, US 182/E3
Chillicothe, Oh, US 190/E5
Chillicothe, Mo, US 185/H4
Chillicothe, Il, US 185/K3
Chillisquaque (cr.), Pa, US 198/B2
Chilliwack, BC, Can. 174/D3
Chillon, Swi. 66/C5
Chilly, Id, US 177/G1
Chilly-Mazarin, Fr. 36/J5
Chiloé (isl.), Chile 209/B7
Chiloé, PN, Chile 226/B4
Chilombo, Ang. 140/D2
Chiloquin, Or, US 176/C2
Chilpancingo de los Bravos, Mex. 205/F5
Chilpi, India 108/C4
Chiltern (hills), Eng, UK 43/E3
Chiltern, Austl. 157/C3
Chiltern Hundreds (reg.), Eng, UK 36/A2
Chilton, Wi, US 190/B2
Chilton, Tx, US 181/F2
Chiluage, Ang. 139/E5
Chilumba, Malw. 137/A4
Chilung (Keelung), Tai. 99/J3
Chilung La (pass), India 110/D3
Chilwa (lake), Malw. 141/G2
Chimacum, Wa, US 197/B1
Chimakothi, Bhu. 109/G2
Chimalhuacán, Mex. 205/R10
Chimaliro (hill), Malw. 137/A4
Chimaltenango, Guat. 206/D3
Chiman, India 110/C4
Chimán, Pan. 216/B2
Chimanimani, Zim. 141/G3
Chimanimani NP, Moz. 141/G3
Chimantá-Tepuí (peak), Ven. 217/F3
Chimay, Belg. 61/D3
Chimayo, NM, US 179/K2
Chimbay, Uzb. 80/F5
Chimboa, Ang. 140/B2
Chimborazo (dept.), Ecu. 216/B5
Chimborazo (vol.), Ecu. 216/B5
Chimbote, Peru 220/B3
Chimbu (prov.), PNG 153/G1
Chimichaqua, Col. 216/C2
Chimney (peak), NM, US 182/B4
Chimney Rock, Co, US 179/J2
Chimney Rock (peak), Ne, US 184/C3
Chimney Rock Nat'l Hist. Site, Ne, US 184/C3
Chimoio, Moz. 141/G3
Chin (hills), Myan. 98/B4
Chin (state), Myan. 105/F3
Chin (isl.), SKor. 91/K5
China (ctry.) 83/J6
China, Mex. 206/D2
China, Mex. 205/F3
China (cape), Sing. 101/J7
China Lake Nav. Weapons Ctr., Ca, US 178/D3
Chinácota, Col. 216/C3
Chinamba (hills), Bots. 140/E3
Chinan, SKor. 93/D5
Chinandega, Nic. 206/E3
Chinati (mts.), Tx, US 180/B3
Chinati (peak), Tx, US 180/B3
Chincha Alta, Peru 220/B4
Chinchaga (riv.), Ab,BC, Can. 170/E3
Chinchilla, Austl. 158/C4
Chinchilla, Sp. 52/E3
Chinchiná, Col. 219/K8
Chinch'ŏn, SKor. 93/D4
Chinchón, Sp. 52/D2
Chinchoua, Gabon 138/B2
Chincoteague, Va, US 193/K2
Chincoteague NWR, Md, US 193/K1
Chinde, Moz. 141/H3
Chindo, SKor. 93/D5
Chindrieux, Fr. 66/B6
Chindu, China 90/D4
Chindwin (riv.), Myan. 105/F3
Chinecto Game Sanctuary, NS, Can. 188/E3
Chineni, India 110/C3
Chingaza, PN, Col. 216/C3
Chingford (nbrhd.), Eng, UK 36/D2
Chingirlau, Kaz. 77/K2
Chingleput, India 107/C3
Chingola, Zam. 141/E2
Chinguar, Ang. 140/C2
Chinhae, SKor. 93/E5
Chinhoyi, Zim. 141/F3
Chinhoyi Caves, Zim. 141/F3
Chiniak (cape), Ak, US 201/H4
Chiñijo, Bol. 220/D4
Chiniot, Pak. 110/B4
Chinit (riv.), Camb. 106/D3
Chinju, SKor. 93/E5
Chinko (riv.), CAfr. 134/E4
Chinle, Az, US 179/H2
Chinle Wash (riv.), Az, US 179/H2
Chinnor, Eng, UK 43/F3
Chino, Ca, US 196/C2
Chino, Japan 97/F3
Chino (hills), Ca, US 196/G8
Chino (valley), Az, US 179/F3
Chino Valley, Az, US 179/F3
Chino Wash (riv.), Az, US 179/F3
Chinook (lake), Or, US 176/C1
Chinook, Wa, US 174/C4
Chinook, Mt, US 175/K3
Chinook, Ab, Can. 175/J2
Chinsali, Zam. 139/H5
Chintāmani, India 107/C3
Chintheche, Malw. 141/G1
Chinú, Col. 216/C2
Chinunje, Tanz. 141/H1
Chiny, Belg. 61/E4
Chinyama Litapi, Zam. 140/D2
Chinyingi, Zam. 140/D2
Chinyŏng, SKor. 93/E5
Chioggia, It. 69/F3
Chip (lake), Ab, Can. 174/G1
Chipaque, Col. 219/L8
Chipasanse, Zam. 139/G5
Chipata, Zam. 141/G2
Chipatá, Col. 216/C3
Chiperceni, Mol. 78/E4
Chiperone (peak), Moz. 141/G3
Chipeta, Ang. 140/C2
Chipindo, Ang. 140/B2
Chiping, China 92/D3
Chipinge, Zim. 141/G4
Chipiona, Sp. 52/B4
Chipley, Fl, US 195/F2
Chipman, NB, Can. 188/E2
Chipman, Ab, Can. 175/H1
Chipogolo, Tanz. 137/B3
Chipoka, Malw. 141/G2
Chipola (riv.), Fl, US 195/F2
Chiponde, Malw. 141/G2
Chippenham, Eng, UK 42/D4
Chippewa (riv.), Mn, US 185/G1
Chippewa (riv.), Wi, US 185/H1
Chippewa (lake), Wi, US 187/J5
Chippewa Falls, Wi, US 185/J1
Chippewa Lake, Mi, US 190/D3
Chippewa, East Branch (riv.), Mn, US 185/G1
Chipping Campden, Eng, UK 43/E2
Chipping Norton, Eng, UK 43/E3
Chipping Ongar, Eng, UK 36/D1
Chiprovtsi, Bul. 56/F4
Chipstead, Eng, UK 36/C3
Chīpurupalle, India 107/D2
Chiputneticook Lakes, NB, Can. 188/D3
Chiquián, Peru 220/B3
Chiquimula, Guat. 206/D3
Chiquimulilla, Guat. 206/D3
Chiquinquirá, Col. 219/M7
Chiquita (sea), Arg. 209/C6
Chira, Gha. 133/E5
Chiradzulu, Malw. 141/G2
Chirakkal, India 107/B4
Chiran (peak), Fr. 70/C5
Chīrāpātla, India 108/A4
Chirāwa, India 110/C5
Chirchiq, Uzb. 111/A3
Chire (riv.), Moz. 141/G3
Chiredzi, Zim. 141/F4
Chireno, Tx, US 181/G2
Chirfa, Niger 126/B4
Chīrgaon, India 108/B3
Chiri-san (peak), SKor. 93/D5
Chiri-san NP, SKor. 93/D5
Chiricahua (peak), Az, US 179/H5
Chiricahua Nat'l Mon., Az, US 204/C1
Chiriguaná, Col. 216/C2
Chirikof (isl.), Ak, US 201/G4
Chirimatá, Ven. 218/A1
Chirimena, Ven. 219/P7
Chirinos, Peru 220/B2
Chirip (peak), Rus. 94/E1
Chiripa (peak), Nic. 207/E4
Chiriquí (gulf), Pan. 202/E6
Chiriquí (lag.), Pan. 207/F4
Chiriquí Grande, Pan. 207/F4
Chirk, Eng, UK 41/E6
Chirkunda, India 109/F4
Chirnside, Sc, UK 39/D5
Chiromo, Malw. 141/G3
Chironico, Swi. 67/E5
Chirpan, Bul. 57/G4
Chirripó (mtn.), CR 207/F4
Chirripó, PN, CR 202/E6
Chirundu, Zim. 141/F3
Chiryu, Japan 95/M6
Chisamba, Zam. 141/F2
Chisana, Ak, US 201/K3
Chisasa, Zam. 140/E2
Chisasibi (Fort-George), Qu, Can. 171/J3
Chiseldon, Eng, UK 43/E3
Chisenga, Malw. 137/A4
Chishi, China 99/H2
Chisholm, Mn, US 187/H4
Chisholm, Tx, US 180/L7
Chishtiān Mandi, Pak. 110/B5
Chishui, China 98/E2
Chishui (riv.), China 98/E3
Chisimayu (Kismaayo), Som. 137/C2
Chisimba (falls), Zam. 139/G5
Chişinău (int'l arpt.), Mol. 78/E4
Chişinău (cap.), Mol. 78/E4
Chişineu Criş, Rom. 56/E2
Chisomo, Zam. 141/F2
Chisone (riv.), It. 70/D3
Chistochina, Ak, US 201/K3
Chistopol', Rus. 75/L5
Chiswell Green, Eng, UK 36/B1
Chiswick (nbrhd.), Eng, UK 36/C2
Chita, Bol. 224/C2
Chita, Col. 216/C3
Chita (pen.), Japan 95/L6
Chita (bay), Japan 95/L6
Chita, Japan 95/L6
Chita, Rus. 90/G1
Chita (int'l arpt.), Rus. 90/G1
Chitado, Ang. 140/B3
Chitato, Ang. 139/E4
Chitek (lake), Mb, Can. 186/E1
Chitembo, Ang. 140/C2
Chitimacha Ind. Res., La, US 194/C3
Chitina, Ak, US 201/K3
Chitinskaya Oblast, Rus. 90/G1
Chitipa, Malw. 137/A4
Chitmanikārbārīpāra, Bang. 109/J4
Chitobiço, Moz. 141/G4
Chitongo, Zam. 141/E3
Chitose, Japan 94/B2
Chitose (int'l arpt.), Japan 94/B2
Chitrakut, India 108/C3
Chitrāl, Pak. 110/A2
Chitral Gol NP, Pak. 110/A2
Chitré, Pan. 216/A3
Chittagong (pol. div.), Bang. 109/H4
Chittagong, Bang. 105/F3
Chittaranjan, India 109/F4
Chittaurgarh, India 104/B3
Chitungwiza, Zim. 141/F3
Chíuchíu, Chile 224/B2
Chiuduno, It. 68/C2
Chiueca, Ang. 140/C2
Chiumbe (riv.), Ang. 139/E5
Chiumbo, Ang. 140/C2
Chiume, Ang. 140/D2
Chiundaponde, Zam. 141/F2
Chiuppano, It. 69/E2
Chiusa (Klausen), It. 67/H4
Chiusa di Pesio, It. 68/A4
Chiusano di San Domenico, It. 71/D6
Chiusella (riv.), It. 68/A1
Chiusi, It. 71/A1
Chivacoa, Ven. 216/D2
Chivasso, It. 68/A2
Chivato (pt.), Mex. 204/C3
Chivay, Peru 220/D4
Chivé, Bol. 220/D4
Chivhu, Zim. 141/F3
Chivilcoy, Arg. 226/E2
Chivurúcua, Ang. 140/B2
Chiwanda, Tanz. 141/G1
Chixoy (riv.), Guat. 206/D3
Chiyoda, Japan 95/E1
Chiyoda, Japan 95/C1
Chiyokawa, Japan 95/D1
Chizarira (hills), Zim. 141/E3
Chizarira NP, Zim. 141/E3
Chizela, Zam. 140/E2
Chizha, Rus. 75/K2
Chkalovo, Ukr. 79/H4
Chkalovsk, Rus. 74/J4
Chlef (wilaya), Alg. 130/F4
Chlef (riv.), Alg. 130/F4
Chlef, Alg. 130/F4
Chloride, Az, US 179/E3
Chlum (peak), Czh. 65/H5
Chno Dearg (peak), Sc, UK 39/B3
Cho Moi, Viet. 106/D4
Cho Oyu (peak), Nepal 109/F1
Choachí, Col. 219/M8
Choam Khsant, Camb. 106/D3
Choapa (riv.), Chile 224/B4
Choate, Tx, US 181/F3
Chobe (riv.), Bots. 140/E3
Chobe (dist.), Bots. 140/E3
Chobe NP, Bots. 140/E3
Chobham, Eng, UK 36/B3
Chocaya, Bol. 224/C2
Choceň, Czh. 49/J4
Choch'iwŏn, SKor. 93/D4
Chocianów, Pol. 49/H3
Chocó (dept.), Col. 207/G5
Chocolate (mts.), Ca, US 178/E4
Chocolate Bayou (riv.), Tx, US 181/M9
Chocolate Mountains Aerial Gunnery Range, Ca, US 178/E4
Chocontá, Col. 216/C3
Chocope, Peru 220/B2
Choctaw Ind. Res., Ms, US 192/C4
Choctawhatchee (riv.), Fl, US 195/F2
Chodavaram, India 107/D2
Chodov, Czh. 65/F2
Chodzież, Pol. 49/J2
Choele Choel, Arg. 226/D3
Chōfu, Japan 97/F3
Ch'ŏgjin -si (prov.), NKor. 93/E2
Choiseul (isl.), Sol. 160/E5
Choisy-au-Bac, Fr. 60/B5
Choisy-le-Roi, Fr. 36/K5
Choix, Mex. 204/C3
Chojna, Pol. 49/H2
Chojnice, Pol. 46/G5
Chojnów, Pol. 49/H3
Chok Chai, Thai. 106/C3
Chokai-san (peak), Japan 94/B4
Ch'ok'ē (mts.), Eth. 135/H3
Choke Canyon (res.), Tx, US 181/E3
Chokio, Mn, US 186/F5
Chokoloskee, Fl, US 195/H5
Chokurdakh, Rus. 81/Q2
Chokwe, Moz. 141/G5
Chola (mts.), China 90/D5
Cholame, Ca, US 178/B3
Cholesbury, Eng, UK 36/B1
Cholila, Arg. 226/C4
Chŏlla-bukto (prov.), SKor. 93/D5
Ch'ŏlla-namdo (prov.), SKor. 93/D5
Ch'ŏlsan, NKor. 93/C3
Cholsey, Eng, UK 43/E3
Cholula de Rivadabia, Mex. 205/L7
Choluteca (riv.), Hon. 202/D5
Choluteca, Hon. 206/E3
Chom Bung, Thai. 106/B3
Chom Thong, Thai. 106/B2
Choma, Zam. 141/E3
Chŏmch'on, SKor. 93/E4
Chomérac, Fr. 70/A3
Chomo Lhāri (peak), Bhu. 109/G2
Chomutov, Czh. 65/G2
Chomutovka (riv.), Czh. 65/G2
Chon Buri, Thai. 106/C3
Chon Daen, Thai. 106/C2
Chon Thanh, Viet. 106/D4
Ch'ŏnan, SKor. 93/D4
Chōnan, Japan 95/E3
Chonchi, Chile 226/B4
Ch'ŏnch'ŏn, NKor. 93/D2
Chone, Ecu. 216/A5
Chong Kal, Camb. 106/C3
Ch'ŏng-yang, SKor. 93/D4
Ch'ŏngan, SKor. 93/D4
Ch'ŏngch'ŏn (riv.), NKor. 93/D2
Ch'ŏngdan, NKor. 93/C4
Chongde, China 92/L9
Ch'ŏngdo, SKor. 93/E5
Ch'ŏngjin, NKor. 93/E2
Chŏngju, SKor. 93/D5
Ch'ŏngju, SKor. 93/D4
Chŏngju, NKor. 93/C3
Chongkü, China 98/C2
Chongli, China 92/C2
Chongming (isl.), Asia 91/J5
Chongmyo Shrine, SKor. 93/G6
Chongo, Zam. 141/E3
Chongoroi, Ang. 140/B2
Chongoyape, Peru 220/B2
Chŏngp'yŏng, NKor. 93/D3
Chongqing, China 99/E2
Chongren, China 99/H3
Chŏngsŏn, SKor. 93/E4
Ch'ŏngsong, SKor. 96/A2
Ch'ŏngsŏng-Nodongjagu, NKor. 93/C2
Chongwe, Zam. 141/F2
Chongwu, China 99/H3
Chongyang, China 99/G2
Chongyi, China 105/K2
Chongzuo, China 99/E4
Chŏnju, SKor. 93/D5
Ch'ónma-san (peak), SKor. 93/G6
Ch'ŏnnae, NKor. 93/D3
Chonos, Archipiélago de los (arch.), Chile 226/B5
Chopan, India 108/D3
Choptank (riv.), Md, US 193/J1
Choquecamata, Bol. 221/E5
Choquecota, Bol. 224/C1
Chorcha (mtn.), Pan. 207/F4
Chorges, Fr. 70/C3
Chorhāt, India 108/C3
Chorley, Eng, UK 41/F4
Chorleywood, Eng, UK 36/B2
Chornobayivka, Ukr. 78/G4
Chornobyl', Ukr. 78/F2
Chornomors'ke, Ukr. 78/G5
Chornukhine, Ukr. 79/K3
Chornukhy, Ukr. 79/G2
Choroní, Ven. 219/N7
Choroszcz, Pol. 49/M2
Chortkiv, Ukr. 78/C3
Ch'ŏrwŏn, NKor. 93/D3
Ch'ŏrwŏn, SKor. 93/D3
Chorzele, Pol. 49/L2
Chorzów, Pol. 49/K3
Chos-Malal, Arg. 226/C3
Ch'osan, NKor. 93/C2
Chōsei, Japan 95/E3
Chōshi, Japan 97/G3
Choshui (riv.), Tai. 99/J4
Choszczno, Pol. 49/H2
Chota, Peru 220/B2
Chota Nagpur (plat.), India 104/D3
Choteau, Mt, US 175/H4
Chott el Rharbi (depr.), Alg. 130/D3
Chotýšanka (riv.), Czh. 65/H3
Choûm, Mrta. 128/B5
Choushuidun, China 90/D3
Chouteau, Ok, US 183/G2
Chouzé-sur-Loire, Fr. 63/F6
Chouzy-sur-Cisse, Fr. 63/G5
Chowagasberg (peak), Namb. 140/B5
Chowan (riv.), NC, US 193/J2
Chowchilla, Ca, US 178/B2
Chowchilla (riv.), Ca, US 178/B2
Choyang-nodongjagu, NKor. 93/D3
Choybalsan, Mong. 90/G2
Choyr, Mong. 90/F2
Chreïrik (well), Mrta. 128/B5
Chrisman, Il, US 190/C5
Christchurch (int'l arpt.), NZ 159/C3
Christchurch, Eng, UK 43/E5
Christchurch (bay), Eng, UK 43/E5
Christchurch, NZ 159/C3
Christian (sound), Ak, US 201/L4
Christiana, Jam. 207/G2
Christiana, SAfr. 142/D2
Christiana, De, US 198/C4
Christiana, Pa, US 198/C4
Christiansburg, Va, US 193/G2
Christiansfeld, Den. 46/C4
Christiansted, USVI 203/M8
Christina, Mt, US 175/K4
Christina (riv.), De, US 198/C5
Christine, ND, US 186/F4
Christine, Tx, US 180/E3
Christmas (isl.), Austl. 83/K11
Christmas (cr.), Austl. 152/B4
Christmas (isl.), Kiri. 161/K4
Christmas, Az, US 179/G4
Christopher, Il, US 192/C2
Christoval, Tx, US 180/D2
Chromo, Co, US 179/J2
Chrudim, Czh. 49/H4
Chrysler, Al, US 194/E2
Chryston, Sc, UK 39/B5
Chrzanów, Pol. 49/K3
Chu (riv.), Viet. 106/D2
Chu Yang Sin (peak), Viet. 106/E3
Chua Chu Kang (nbrhd.), Sing. 101/H6
Chuādanga, Bang. 109/G4
Chualar, Ca, US 178/B2
Chuanchang, China 99/H3
Chuansha, China 92/L8
Chuanshi, China 99/H3
Chuathbaluk, Ak, US 201/G3
Chuave, PNG 153/G1
Chubbuck, Id, US 177/G2
Chubut (riv.), Arg. 209/C7
Chubut (prov.), Arg. 226/C4
Chucanti (peak), Pan. 216/B2
Chuchkovo, Rus. 77/G1
Chudovo, Rus. 47/P2
Chūgoku (mts.), Japan 96/C3
Chūgoku (prov.), Japan 96/B4
Chugwater, Wy, US 184/B3
Chugwater (cr.), Wy, US 184/B3
Chūhar Kāna, Pak. 110/B4

Colne – Court
278

Colne (riv.), Eng, UK 43/G3
Colney Heath, Eng, UK 36/C1
Colo (riv.), Austl. 157/E1
Colo Vale, Austl. 157/E2
Cologna Spiaggia, It. 71/C2
Cologna Veneta, It. 69/E3
Cologne, It. 68/C2
Cologne, NJ, US 198/D5
Cologne (Kölm), Ger. 51/G1
Cologne/Bonn (int'l arpt.), Ger. 61/G2
Cologno Monzese, It. 68/C2
Coloma, Wi, US 185/K1
Colombelles, Fr. 63/E2
Colombes, Fr. 36/J5
Colombey-les-Belles, Fr. 66/B1
Colombia, Col. 216/C4
Colombia (ctry.) 216/C4
Colombia, Mex. 180/E4
Colombier, Swi. 66/C4
Colombine (peak), It. 68/D2
Colombis (peak), Fr. 70/C3
Colombo (peak), It. 70/D2
Colombo, Braz. 225/G3
Colombo (cap.), SrL. 107/C5
Colomiers, Fr. 50/D5
Colomoncagua, Hon. 206/D3
Colón, Arg. 226/E2
Colón, Arg. 224/E5
Colón, Cuba 207/F1
Colón (mts.), Hon. 207/E3
Colón, Pan. 207/G4
Colón, Uru. 227/G2
Colon Koret, D.R. Congo 139/E2
Colona, Co, US 179/J1
Colonche, Ecu. 220/A1
Colonelganj, India 108/C2
Colonia, Micr. 160/C4
Colonia, NJ, US 199/H9
Colonia (dept.), Uru. 226/F2
Colonia Barón, Arg. 226/E3
Colonia Benjamín Aceval, Par. 224/E3
Colonia del Sacramento, Uru. 227/K11
Colonia Dora, Arg. 224/D4
Colonia Gobernador Ayala, Arg. 226/C3
Colonia Josefa, Arg. 226/D3
Colonia Juárez, Mex. 204/C2
Colonia Las Heras, Arg. 226/C5
Colonia Lavalleja, Uru. 225/E4
Colônia Leopoldina, Braz. 219/H5
Colonia Presidente Stroessner, Par. 225/E2
Colonia Yby Yu, Par. 225/F2
Colonial Beach, Va, US 193/J1
Colonial Heights, Va, US 193/J2
Colonial NHP, Va, US 193/J2
Colonial Park, Pa, US 198/B3
Colonna, It. 71/B4
Colonsay (isl.), Sc, UK 37/Q8
Colonsay, Sk, Can. 175/M2
Colony, Ks, US 183/G1
Colony, Wy, US 184/B1
Colorado (peak), Arg. 227/C6
Colorado, Braz. 225/G2
Colorado, CR 207/F4
Colorado (riv.), Mex.,US 172/D5
Colorado (state), US 172/E4
Colorado (canal), Co, US 184/B4
Colorado (plat.), Ut, US 177/H4
Colorado City, Az, US 179/F2
Colorado City, Co, US 182/B2
Colorado City, Tx, US 180/D1
Colorado do Oeste, Braz. 221/F4
Colorado Nat'l Mon., Co, US 177/J4
Colorado River (aqueduct), Ca, US 178/E3
Colorado River Ind. Res., Az,Ca, US 178/E3
Colorado Springs, Co, US 182/B1
Colorno, It. 68/D4
Colostre (riv.), Fr. 70/B5
Colotlán, Mex. 204/E4
Colpoys Bay, On, Can. 190/F2
Colquechaca, Bol. 224/C1
Colquiri, Bol. 224/C1
Colquitt, Ga, US 195/F2
Colrain, Ma, US 191/K3
Colson (pt.), Belz. 206/D2
Colstrip, Mt, US 175/L5
Colt (hill), Sc, UK 39/B6
Coltauco, Chile 226/N9
Coltishall, Eng, UK 43/H1
Colton, Ca, US 196/C2
Colton, Ut, US 177/H4
Colton, Wa, US 174/F4
Colts Neck, NJ, US 199/D3
Coluene (riv.), Braz. 209/D4
Columbe, Ecu. 220/B1
Columbia (mt.), Ab, Can. 174/F1
Columbia (riv.), US 174/C5
Columbia, Al, US 195/F2
Columbia, Ky, US 192/E2
Columbia, La, US 183/H4
Columbia, Md, US 198/B5
Columbia, Mo, US 185/H4
Columbia, Ms, US 194/D2
Columbia, NC, US 193/J3
Columbia, NJ, US 198/C2
Columbia (co.), Pa, US 198/B1
Columbia, Pa, US 198/B3
Columbia (plat.), Or, US 170/E4
Columbia (plat.), Or, US 176/D2
Columbia (cap.), SC, US 193/G3
Columbia, Tn, US 192/D3
Columbia (riv.), Wa, US 172/B2
Columbia City, In, US 190/D4
Columbia City, Or, US 174/C5
Columbia Falls, Mt, US 175/G3
Columbia Heights, Mn, US 187/P6
Columbia NWR, Wa, US 174/E4
Columbia Reach (lake), BC, Can. 174/F2
Columbia Road (dam), SD, US 186/E5
Columbian White Tailed Deer Nat'l Wild. Ref., Or, US 174/C4
Columbiana, Al, US 192/D4
Columbiaville, Mi, US 190/E3
Columbine (cape), SAfr. 142/K10
Columbretes (isls.), Sp. 72/D3
Columbus, Ar, US 183/H4
Columbus, Ga, US 192/E4
Columbus, In, US 190/D5
Columbus, Ks, US 183/G2
Columbus, Ms, US 192/C4
Columbus (lake), Ms, US 192/C4
Columbus (A.F.B.), Ms, US 192/C4
Columbus, NC, US 193/F3
Columbus, Ne, US 185/F3
Columbus, NJ, US 198/D3
Columbus, NM, US 179/J5
Columbus (cap.), Oh, US 190/E5
Columbus, Wi, US 185/K2
Columbus, Tx, US 180/F3
Columbus Grove, Oh, US 190/D4
Columbus Salt Marsh (salt marsh), Nv, US 176/D4
Colunga, Sp. 52/C1
Colupo (peak), Chile 224/B2
Colusa, Ca, US 176/B4
Colusa NWR, Ca, US 176/B4
Colville (lake), NW, Can. 170/D2
Colville (cape), NZ 159/C2
Colville (riv.), Ak, US 201/H2
Colville, Wa, US 174/F3
Colville Ind. Res., Wa, US 174/E3
Colvos (passg.), Wa, US 197/B3
Colwall, Eng, UK 42/D2
Colwinston, Wal, UK 42/C4
Colwyn Bay, Wal, UK 40/E5
Comacchio, It. 69/F4
Comacchio (lag.), It. 51/K4
Comai, China 109/H1
Comala, Mex. 204/E5
Comalcalco, Mex. 206/C2
Comanche, Ok, US 183/F3
Comanche (cr.), Co, US 184/B4
Comanche (res.), Ca, US 178/B1
Comanche, Tx, US 180/E2
Comandante Luis Piedra Buena, Arg. 227/C6
Comandante Nicanor Otamendi, Arg. 226/F3
Comănești, Rom. 78/D4
Comar Gambon, Som. 136/C5
Comarapa, Bol. 224/C1
Comarnic, Rom. 57/G3
Comas, Peru 220/B3
Comas, Peru 220/C3
Comayagua, Hon. 206/E3
Comayagua (mts.), Hon. 206/D3
Combahee (riv.), SC, US 193/G4
Combapata, Peru 220/D4
Combarbalá, Chile 224/B4
Combe Martin, Eng, UK 42/B4
Combeaufontaine, Fr. 66/B2
Comber, On, Can. 197/G7
Comber, NI, UK 40/C2
Combermere (bay), Myan. 98/B5
Comblain-au-Pont, Belg. 61/E3
Combloux, Fr. 66/C6
Combourg, Fr. 62/D4
Comboyne, Austl. 156/E1
Combrée, Fr. 63/D5
Combrit, Fr. 62/A5
Combs (riv.), Fr. 62/C5
Combs, Ky, US 193/F2
Combs-la-Ville, Fr. 36/K6
Comé, Ben. 133/F5
Come-By-Chance, Austl. 156/D1
Comemoração (riv.), Braz. 221/F3
Comendador, DRep. 207/J2
Comer, Al, US 195/F1
Comfort, Tx, US 181/E3
Comilla, Bang. 109/H4
Comilla (pol. reg.), Bang. 109/H4
Comines, Fr. 60/C2
Comines, Belg. 60/B2
Comino (isl.), Malta 54/L6
Comitán de Domínguez, Mex. 206/C2
Commack, NY, US 199/E2
Commentry, Fr. 50/E3
Commeny, Fr. 36/H4
Commerce, Ca, US 196/F7
Commerce, Ga, US 193/F3
Commerce, Tx, US 183/G4
Commerce City, Co, US 184/B4
Commercy, Fr. 61/E6
Commewijne (dist.), Sur. 217/H3
Commissioner (isl.), Mb, Can. 186/F1
Committee (bay), Nun, Can. 171/H2
Commonwealth, Wi, US 187/K5
Como, It. 67/F6
Como (lake), It. 72/F1
Como (lake), Wi, US 197/P14
Como, Wi, US 197/P14
Como, Ms, US 192/C3
Comodoro Rivadavia, Arg. 226/D5
Comoé (prov.), Burk. 132/D4
Comoé, PN de la, C.d'Iv. 132/D4
Comorin (cape), India 107/C4
Comoros (ctry.) 143/G5
Comox, BC, Can. 174/B3
Company, Camr. 138/B1
Compeer, Ab, Can. 175/J2
Compiègne, Fr. 60/B5
Compomarino, It. 72/E4
Compostela, Mex. 204/D4
Comprida (isl.), Braz. 225/H3
Compton, Ca, US 196/F8
Compton, Eng, UK 36/B3
Comrat, Mol. 57/J2
Comrie, Sc, UK 39/C4
Comstock, Mi, US 190/D3
Comstock, Tx, US 180/D3
Comunanza, It. 71/C2
Comunidad, Ven. 217/E4
Con Cuong, Viet. 106/D2
Con Son (isl.), Viet. 105/J6
Cona, China 105/F2
Conaica, Peru 220/C4
Conakry (cap.), Gui. 132/B4
Conakry (pol. reg.), Gui. 132/B4
Conakry (int'l arpt.), Gui. 132/B4
Conambo (riv.), Ecu. 216/B5
Conargo, Austl. 157/B2
Conay, Chile 224/B4
Conboy NWR, Wa, US 174/D5
Conca (riv.), It. 69/F5
Concan, Tx, US 180/E3
Concarneau, Fr. 62/B5
Conceição das Alagoas, Braz. 225/G1
Conceição de Macabu, Braz. 223/E4
Conceição do Araguaia, Braz. 218/D5
Conceição do Coité, Braz. 223/F1
Conceição do Mato Dentro, Braz. 223/E3
Conceição do Rio Verde, Braz. 223/L6
Conceição dos Ouros, Braz. 223/L7
Concepción, Arg. 224/E4
Concepción, Arg. 224/C3
Concepción, Bol. 221/E3
Concepción, Bol. 221/F5
Concepción (lake), Bol. 221/F5
Concepción (lag.), Bol. 224/D1
Concepción, Chile 226/B3
Concepción (pt.), Mex. 204/C3
Concepción (bay), Mex. 204/B3
Concepción, Par. 224/E2
Concepción (dept.), Par. 222/A4
Concepción de La Vega, DRep. 203/G4
Concepción del Bermejo, Arg. 224/D3
Concepción del Oro, Mex. 205/E3
Concepción del Uruguay, Arg. 227/J10
Conception (bay), Nf, Can. 189/L2
Conception (pt.), Ca, US 178/B3
Conception (bay), Namb. 140/B4
Concesio, It. 68/D2
Concession, Zim. 141/F3
Conchal, Braz. 223/J7
Conchas (lake), NM, US 182/B3
Conches, Fr. 36/L5
Conches-en-Ouche, Fr. 63/F3
Conchi, Chile 224/B2
Conchillas, Uru. 227/J11
Concho (riv.), Tx, US 180/D2
Conchos (riv.), Mex. 163/G7
Concón, Chile 226/N8
Concord, Ar, US 183/J3
Concord, Fl, US 195/F2
Concord, NC, US 193/G3
Concord (cap.), NH, US 191/L3
Concord, Tx, US 180/G1
Concord, Va, US 193/H2
Concord, Wi, US 197/N13
Concordia, Arg. 224/E4
Concórdia, Braz. 225/F3
Concordia, Col. 219/K6
Concordia, Mex. 204/D4
Concordia, Peru 220/C2
Concordia, Ks, US 184/F4
Concordia Sagittaria, It. 69/F2
Concordia sulla Secchia, It. 69/D4
Concrete, Wa, US 174/D3
Condado, Cuba 207/G1
Condamine, Austl. 158/C3
Condamine (riv.), Austl. 145/E3
Condar, Col. 216/C5
Conde, SD, US 184/E1
Conde, Braz. 223/F1
Condé-sur-L'Escaut, Fr. 60/C3
Condé-sur-Noireau, Fr. 63/E3
Condé-sur-Sarthe, Fr. 63/F4
Condé-sur-Vesgre, Fr. 36/G5
Condé-sur-Vire, Fr. 63/D2
Condécourt, Fr. 36/H4
Condeúba, Braz. 223/E2
Condino, It. 67/G6
Condobolin, Austl. 157/C1
Condom, Fr. 50/D5
Condon, Or, US 176/C1
Condon, Mt, US 175/H4
Condor, Ab, Can. 174/G1
Condove, It. 70/D2
Condrieu, Fr. 70/A2
Condroz (plat.), Belg. 48/C3
Conecuh (riv.), Al, US 194/E2
Conegliano, It. 69/F2
Conehatta, Ms, US 192/C4
Conejos, Co, US 179/J2
Conejos (riv.), Co, US 179/J2
Conequh (riv.), Al, US 192/E5
Conesa, Arg. 226/E2
Conestoga (riv.), Pa, US 198/B3
Conewago (lake), Pa, US 198/A3
Conewago (cr.), Pa, US 198/B4
Coney Island (nbrhd.), NY, US 199/K9
Confins (int'l arpt.), Braz. 222/E3
Conflans-en-Jarnisy, Fr. 61/E5
Conflans-Sainte-Honorine, Fr. 36/J5
Confuso (riv.), Par. 224/E3
Cong, Ire. 38/A2
Congaree Swamp Nat'l Mon., SC, US 193/G4
Congers, NY, US 199/K7
Conghua, China 99/G4
Congis-sur-Thérouanne, Fr. 36/L4
Congjiang, China 99/F3
Congleton, Eng, UK 41/F5
Congo (riv.), Afr. 138/C4
Congo, Braz. 219/G4
Congo, Dem. Rep. (ctry.) 119/E5
Congo, Rep. (ctry.) 138/C3
Congonhal, Braz. 223/K7
Congonhas (int'l arpt.), Braz. 223/K8
Congonhas, Braz. 225/J2
Congress, Az, US 179/F3
Conguel (pt.), Fr. 62/B6
Conguillío, PN, Chile 226/C3
Conic (hill), Sc, UK 39/B4
Cónico (peak), Arg. 226/C4
Conie (riv.), Fr. 63/G4
Conil de la Frontera, Sp. 52/B4
Conimbla NP, Austl. 157/D1
Coningsby, Eng, UK 41/H5
Conisbrough, Eng, UK 41/G5
Coniston, Eng, UK 41/E3
Conley, Ga, US 193/M7
Conlie, Fr. 63/E4
Conlig, NI, UK 40/C2
Conn (lake), Nun, Can. 171/J1
Conn (lake), Ire. 38/A1
Connacht (reg.), Ire. 38/B2
Connah's Quay, Wal, UK 41/E5
Connantre, Fr. 60/C6
Conneaut, Oh, US 190/F4
Connecticut (riv.), US 188/A4
Connecticut (state), US 191/K4
Connecticut (hill), NY, US 191/H3
Connel, Sc, UK 39/A4
Connell, Wa, US 174/E4
Connellsville, Pa, US 191/G4
Connemara (dist.), Ire. 38/A3
Connemara NP, Ire. 37/P10
Conner, Phil. 100/C1
Connerré, Fr. 63/F4
Connersville, In, US 190/D5
Cono Grande (peak), Arg. 227/C6
Conoble, Austl. 157/B1
Conoble (lake), Austl. 157/B1
Conocoto, Ecu. 216/B5
Conodoguinet (cr.), Pa, US 198/A3
Conon, Falls of (falls), Sc, UK 39/B1
Cononbridge, Sc, UK 39/B1
Conondale NP, Austl. 158/D4
Čonoplja, Serb. 56/D3
Conover, NC, US 193/G3
Conquest, Sk, Can. 175/L2
Conrad, Ia, US 185/H2
Conrad, Mt, US 175/J3
Conran (cape), Austl. 157/D3
Conroe (lake), Tx, US 181/G2
Conroe, Tx, US 181/G2
Consandolo, It. 69/E4
Conscience Point Nat'l Wild. Ref., NY, US 199/F2
Consdorf, Lux. 61/F4
Conselheiro Lafaiete, Braz. 222/E4
Conselheiro Pena, Braz. 223/E3
Conselice, It. 69/E4
Conselve, It. 69/E3
Conservation Park, Austl. 155/F4
Consett, Eng, UK 41/G2
Conshohocken, Pa, US 198/C3
Consolación del Sur, Cuba 207/F1
Consort, Ab, Can. 175/J1
Constance (lake), Ger.,Swi. 67/F2
Constance (mt.), Wa, US 174/C4
Constance (Bodensee) (lake), Ger.,Swi. 67/F2
Constant (mtn.), Guad., Fr. 203/N9
Constanta (prov.), Rom. 57/H3
Constanța, Rom. 57/J3
Constantí, Sp. 53/F2
Constantina, Sp. 52/C4
Constantine, Alg. 130/K6
Constantine (cape), Ak, US 201/G4
Constitución (res.), Uru. 227/K10
Constitución, Chile 226/B2
Constitución de 1857, PN, Mex. 204/B2
Constitution, Ga, US 193/M7
Constitution de 1857, PN, Mex. 178/E5
Consuegra, Sp. 52/D3
Consul, Sk, Can. 175/K3
Contai, India 109/F5
Contamana, Peru 220/C2
Contarina, It. 69/F3
Contas, Rio de (riv.), Braz. 223/E2
Contegem, Braz. 222/D3
Contes, Fr. 70/D5
Conthey, Swi. 66/D5
Contigliano, It. 71/B3
Continental, Az, US 179/G5
Continentals (range), Ab, Can. 174/F1
Contoy (isl.), Mex. 206/E1
Contra Costa (canal), Ca, US 197/L10
Contra Costa (co.), Ca, US 197/L11
Contramaestre, Cuba 207/G1
Contratación, Col. 216/C3
Contrecoeur, Qu, Can. 189/P6
Contreras (res.), Sp. 52/E3
Contres, Fr. 63/G6
Contrexéville, Fr. 66/B1
Controller (bay), Ak, US 201/J3
Contulmo, Chile 226/B3
Contumazá, Peru 220/B2
Contwig, Ger. 61/G5
Contwoyko (lake), Nun, Can. 170/F2
Conty, Fr. 60/B4
Convención, Col. 216/C2
Convent, La, US 194/C2
Convento San Francesco, It. 71/B3
Conversano, It. 55/E2
Converse, La, US 180/H2
Conway (cape), Austl. 158/C3
Conwy, Wal, UK 40/E5
Conwy (co.), Wal, UK 40/E5
Conwy (riv.), Wal, UK 40/E5
Conwy (bay), Wal, UK 40/D5
Conway, Ar, US 183/H3
Conway, Fl, US 194/N6
Conway, Mi, US 190/D2
Conway, Mo, US 183/H2
Conway, NH, US 191/L3
Conway, SC, US 193/H4
Conway NP, Austl. 158/C3
Conyers, Ga, US 193/M7
Conyngham, Pa, US 198/B2
Coober Pedy, Austl. 155/G4
Cooch Behār, India 109/G2
Coochiemudlo (isl.), Austl. 158/F7
Coogee, Austl. 156/B1
Cook, Austl. 155/F4
Cook (bay), Chile 227/C7
Cook (str.), NZ 145/H7
Cook (mt.), NZ 159/B3
Cook (inlet), Ak, US 170/A3
Cook (co.), Il, US 197/Q16
Cook Is. (terr.), CookIs. 161/J6
Cooke (mt.), Austl. 154/C5
Cookeville, Tn, US 192/E2
Cookham, Eng, UK 36/A2
Cookhouse, SAfr. 142/D4
Cooks, Mi, US 190/C2
Cookshire, Qu, Can. 191/L2
Cookstown, NI, UK 40/B2
Cookstown (dist.), NI, UK 40/B2
Cooksville, Md, US 198/A5
Cooktown, Austl. 158/B1
Coola Coola (swamp), Austl. 156/B3
Coolabah, Austl. 156/C1
Cooladdi, Austl. 158/B4
Coolah, Austl. 156/D1
Coolamon, Austl. 157/C2
Coolaney, Ire. 38/B1
Coolangatta, Austl. 156/E1
Coolatai, Austl. 156/D1
Cooley (pt.), Ire. 40/B4
Coolgardie, Austl. 154/D4
Coolibah, Austl. 152/C3
Coolidge, Ga, US 195/G2
Coolidge (dam), Az, US 179/G4
Coolidge, Tx, US 181/F2
Coolidge Dam, Az, US 179/G4
Cooloola NP, Austl. 158/D4
Cooloongup (lake), Austl. 154/K7
Coolville, Oh, US 193/G1
Cooma, Austl. 157/D3
Coon (cr.), Il, US 197/N15
Coon (riv.), Mn, US 187/P6
Coon Rapids, Ia, US 185/G3
Coon Rapids, Mn, US 187/P6
Coon Valley, Wi, US 185/J2
Coon, East Branch (cr.), Mi, US 197/G6
Coonabarabran, Austl. 156/D1
Coonalpyn, Austl. 156/A2
Coonamble, Austl. 156/D1
Coonana Abor. Land, Austl. 154/D4
Coondapoor (Kundapura), India 113/K6
Coongan Abor. Land, Austl. 154/C2
Cooper, Tx, US 183/G4
Cooper (cr.), Austl. 155/J3
Cooper (mt.), BC, Can. 174/F2
Cooper City, Fl, US 194/P10
Cooper (brook), Austl. 145/C3
Coopersburg, Pa, US 198/C2
Cooperstown, ND, US 186/E4
Cooperstown, NY, US 191/J3
Coopracambra NP, Austl. 157/D3
Coorabie, Austl. 155/G4
Coordewandy (peak), Austl. 154/C3
Coorong NP, Austl. 156/A3
Coorow, Austl. 154/C4
Cooroy, Austl. 158/D4
Coos (bay), Or, US 176/A2
Coos Bay, Or, US 176/A2
Coosa, Ga, US 192/E3
Coosa (riv.), Al, US 192/D4
Coosawattee (riv.), Ga, US 192/E3
Coot (mtn.), Mo, US 183/J2
Cootamundra, Austl. 157/D2
Cootehill, Ire. 38/C1
Coot'tha (mt.), Austl. 158/E6
Copacabana, Col. 219/K6
Copacabana, Bol. 220/D5
Copachuncho, Bol. 224/C1
Copahué (vol.), Chile 226/C3
Copainalá, Mex. 206/C2
Copala, Mex. 202/B4
Copalis Beach, Wa, US 174/B4
Copan, Ok, US 183/G2
Copán (ruin), Hon. 206/D3
Copano (bay), Tx, US 181/F3
Cope (cape), Sp. 52/E4
Cope, Co, US 184/C4
Copeland (isl.), NI, UK 40/C2
Copemish, Mi, US 190/D2
Copenhagen (København) (cap.), Den. 45/J7
Coper, Col. 219/L7
Copertino, It. 55/F2
Copeton (dam), Austl. 156/D1
Copeville, Tx, US 180/L6
Copiague, NY, US 199/M9
Copiapó (peak), Chile 224/B3
Copiapó (riv.), Chile 224/B3
Copiapó, Chile 224/B3
Coplay, Pa, US 198/C2
Copley, Austl. 155/H4
Coporolo, Ang. 140/B2
Coporolo (riv.), Ang. 140/B2
Copparo, It. 69/E4
Coppell, Tx, US 180/K7
Coppename (riv.), Sur. 217/H3
Coppenbrügge, Ger. 59/G4
Copper (riv.), Ak, US 170/B2
Copper Center, Ak, US 201/J3
Copper Harbor, Mi, US 187/L4
Copperas Cove, Tx, US 180/F2
Copperbelt (prov.), Zam. 141/E2
Copperdahl (hill), ND, US 186/D3
Coppermine (riv.), NW,Nun, Can. 170/E2
Coppet, Swi. 66/C5
Coppolani, Mrta. 132/A2
Coppull, Eng, UK 41/F4
Copșa Mică, Rom. 57/G2
Coqên, China 111/E5
Coquet (riv.), Eng, UK 39/D6
Coquet Dale (valley), Eng, UK 41/G1
Coquille, Or, US 176/A2
Coquille (riv.), Or, US 176/A2
Coquimbo (pol. reg.), Chile 224/B4
Coquimbo, Chile 224/B4
Coquitlam, BC, Can. 174/C3
Cora, Wy, US 177/J2
Corabia, Rom. 57/G4
Coração de Jesus, Braz. 222/D3
Coracora, Peru 220/C4
Corail, Haiti 207/H2
Coraki, Austl. 156/E1
Coral (sea) 145/D2
Coral Gables, Fl, US 194/P11
Coral Harbour, Nun, Can. 171/H2
Coral Sea Islands Territory (terr.), Austl. 145/E2
Coral Springs, Fl, US 194/P10
Corales del Rosario, PN, Col. 216/C2
Coralville, Ia, US 185/J3
Coram, NY, US 199/E2
Corambá (riv.), Braz. 225/G1
Corani, Bol. 221/E5
Corantijne (riv.), Sur. 218/B1
Coranzulí, Arg. 224/C2
Corato, It. 54/E2
Coray, Fr. 62/B4
Corbara (lake), It. 71/B2
Corbeil-Essonnes, Fr. 36/K6
Corbélia, Braz. 225/F3
Corbelin (cape), Alg. 130/H4
Corbenay, Fr. 66/C2
Corbet (peak), Swi. 67/F5
Corbett NP, India 108/B1
Corbetta, It. 68/B3
Corbie, Fr. 60/B4
Corbière (pt.), Chl, UK 62/C2
Corbieres (mts.), Fr. 50/E5
Corbin, Ky, US 192/E2
Corbin City, NJ, US 198/D5
Corbridge, Eng, UK 41/F2
Corby, Eng, UK 43/F2
Corchiano, It. 71/B3
Corcoran, Ca, US 178/C2
Corcoran, Mn, US 187/N6
Corcovado, Braz. 223/N7
Corcovado, PN, CR 207/F4
Corcovado (gulf), Chile 209/B7
Corcovado (vol.), Chile 226/B4
Cord, Ar, US 183/J3
Cord. de la Punilla (mts.), Chile 224/B4
Cord. de Lipez (mts.), Bol. 224/C2
Cordata (mesa), NM, US 179/J3
Cordeiro, Braz. 223/E4
Cordele, Ga, US 195/G2
Cordele, Tx, US 181/F3
Cordelia, Ca, US 197/K10
Cordell (New Cordell), Ok, US 182/E3
Cordenons, It. 51/K4
Cordignano, It. 69/F2
Cordilheiras, Serra das (mts.), Braz. 218/D4
Cordillera (mts.), Sp. 72/B2
Cordillera (dept.), Par. 225/E3
Cordillera Central (mts.), Phil. 100/C1
Cordillera Darwin (mts.), Chile 224/B4
Cordillera de la Costa (mts.), Ven. 219/N8
Cordillera de los Andes (mts.), SAm. 224/B1
Cordillera de los Picachos, PN, Col. 216/C4
Cordillera Domeyko (mts.), Chile 224/B3
Cordillera Neo Volcanica (mts.), Mex. 205/Q10
Cordillera Occidental (mts.), Ecu. 216/B5
Cordillera Oriental (mts.), Col. 207/G7
Cordillera Oriental (mts.), SAm. 224/C1
Cordillera Real (mts.), Peru 220/C3
Cordillo Downs, Austl. 158/A4
Córdoba (dept.), Col. 207/H4
Córdoba, Sp. 52/C4
Córdoba (plain), SAm. 226/E2
Córdoba (prov.), Arg. 224/D4
Córdoba, Arg. 224/C4
Córdoba, Mex. 205/N8
Córdoba (Pajas Blancas) (int'l arpt.), Arg. 224/C4
Cordón. de la Totora (mts.), Arg. 224/B4
Córdova, Peru 220/C4
Cordova, Ak, US 201/J3
Cordova, Al, US 192/D4
Cordova, Md, US 198/C6
Cordova Peak (mt.), Ak, US 201/J3
Core Banks (isl.), NC, US 193/J3
Coreaú, Braz. 219/F3
Coree South, Austl. 157/B2
Corella, Sp. 52/E1
Coremas, Braz. 219/G4
Corentyne (riv.), Guy. 218/B2
Corfield, Austl. 158/A3
Corfu (Kérkira) (isl.), Gre. 73/H3
Corgémont, Swi. 66/D3
Corgo, Sp. 52/B1
Cori, It. 71/B4
Coria, Sp. 52/B3
Coria del Río, Sp. 52/B4
Coriano, It. 69/F6
Coribe, Braz. 222/D2
Coricudgy (mt.), Austl. 157/E1
Corigliano Calabro, It. 54/E3
Corinaldo, It. 69/G6
Corinda, Austl. 153/E4
Coringa Islets (isls.), Austl. 158/C2
Coringa Islets (isl.), Austl. 145/D2
Corinne, Ok, US 183/G3
Corinth (gulf), Gre. 73/J3
Corinth, Ms, US 192/C3
Corinth, NY, US 191/K3
Corinth, Tx, US 180/K6
Corinth (Kórinthos) (ruin), Gre. 55/H4
Corinto, Braz. 222/D3
Corinto, Nic. 206/E3
Corisco (bay), EqG. 138/B2
Corisco (isl.), EqG. 138/B2
Corixa Grande (riv.), Braz. 221/G5
Cork, Ire. 38/B6
Cork (har.), Ire. 38/B6
Cork (int'l arpt.), Ire. 38/B6
Corkscrew (swamp), Fl, US 195/H4
Corleone, It. 54/C4
Corleto Perticara, It. 54/E2
Çorlu, Turk. 57/H5
Cormeilles, Fr. 63/F2
Cormeilles-en-Vexin, Fr. 36/J4
Cormelles-le-Royal, Fr. 63/E2
Cormery, Fr. 63/F6
Cormons, It. 69/G2
Cormontreuil, Fr. 60/D5
Corn Palace, The, SD, US 184/E2
Cornaca, Bol. 224/C2
Cornacchia (peak), It. 71/C4
Cornaredo, It. 68/C3
Cornas, Fr. 70/A3
Cornberg, Ger. 59/G6
Corndon (peak), Wal, UK 42/C1
Cornedo Vicentino, It. 69/E2
Cornelia, Ga, US 193/F3
Cornélio Procópio, Braz. 225/G2
Cornelius Grinnel (bay), Nun, Can. 171/K2
Cornell, Ca, US 196/B2
Cornell, Mi, US 190/C2
Cornell, Wi, US 185/J1
Cornell, Il, US 185/K3
Cornella, Sp. 53/L7
Corner (inlet), Austl. 145/D4
Corner Brook, Nf, Can. 189/J1
Cornerstone, Ar, US 183/J3
Cornesti, Mol. 78/E4
Cornetto (peak), It. 67/H6
Cornfield (pt.), Ct, US 199/F1
Cornhill, Sc, UK 39/D1
Corniglio, It. 68/D5
Cornimont, Fr. 66/C2
Corning, Sk, Can. 186/C3
Corning, Ar, US 192/B2
Corning, Ca, US 176/B4
Corning, Ks, US 185/F4
Corning, Ia, US 185/G3
Corning, NY, US 191/H3
Corning, Oh, US 190/E5
Cornish (cr.), Austl. 158/B3
Corno (peak), It. 71/B2
Corno (riv.), It. 71/B2
Corno alle Scale (peak), It. 51/J4
Corno di Rosazzo, It. 69/G2
Cornone di Blumone (peak), It. 67/G6
Cornour (peak), It. 70/D3
Cornú (peak), Arg. 227/D7
Cornucopia, Wi, US 187/J4
Cornuda, It. 69/F2
Cornudas (mts.), NM, US 182/B4
Cornudas, Tx, US 180/B2
Cornville, Az, US 179/G3
Cornwall, On, Can. 191/J2
Cornwall (isl.), Nun, Can. 171/S7
Cornwall (co.), Eng, UK 42/A6
Cornwall (cape), Eng, UK 42/A6
Cornwall, Pa, US 198/B3
Cornwallis (isl.), Nun, Can. 171/S7
Cornwell, Fl, US 195/H4
Cornwerd, Neth. 58/C2
Corny (pt.), Austl. 155/H5
Coro, Ven. 216/D2
Coroatá, Braz. 219/E4
Corocoro, Bol. 224/B1
Corofin, Ire. 38/A4
Coroico, Bol. 220/E5
Coromandel, NZ 159/C2
Coromandel (pen.), NZ 159/C2
Coromandel (coast), India 104/D5
Coromandel, Braz. 222/D3
Coron (isl.), Phil. 100/C3
Coron, Phil. 100/C2
Corona, NM, US 182/B3
Corona, Ca, US 196/C3
Corona del Mar (nbrhd.), Ca, US 196/G8
Coronach, Sk, Can. 175/M3
Coronado, Ca, US 196/C5
Coronado (bay), CR 202/E6
Coronado Nat'l Mem., Az, US 179/G5
Coronation (gulf), Nun, Can. 170/E2
Coronation, Ab, Can. 175/J1
Coronation, SAfr. 143/E2
Coronda, Arg. 224/D4
Coronel, Chile 226/B3
Coronel Bogado, Par. 225/E3
Coronel Cornejo, Arg. 224/D2
Coronel Dorrego, Arg. 226/E3
Coronel Fabriciano, Braz. 223/E3
Coronel Moldes, Arg. 226/D2
Coronel Moldes, Arg. 224/C3
Coronel Oviedo, Par. 225/E3
Coronel Pringles, Arg. 226/E3
Coronel Suárez, Arg. 226/E3
Coronel Vidal, Arg. 226/F3
Coronel Vivida, Braz. 225/F3
Coronet, Fl, US 194/L8
Corongo, Peru 220/B3
Coronie (dist.), Sur. 217/G3
Coropuna (peak), Peru 220/C4
Çorovodë, Alb. 55/G2
Corozal, Belz. 206/D2
Corozal, Col. 216/C2
Corozo Pando, Ven. 217/E2
Corpach, Sc, UK 39/A3
Corps-Nuds, Fr. 62/D5
Corpus, Arg. 225/F3
Corpus Christi (lake), Tx, US 181/E3
Corpus Christi (bay), Tx, US 181/F4
Corpus Christi (int'l arpt.), Tx, US 205/F3
Corpus Christi, Tx, US 181/F4
Corpus Christi Nav. Air Sta., Tx, US 181/F4
Corque, Bol. 224/C1
Corral, Chile 226/B3
Corral de Almaguer, Sp. 52/D3
Corral de Bustos, Arg. 226/E2
Corrales, Col. 216/C3
Corrales, NM, US 179/J3
Corralillo, Cuba 207/F1
Corralitos (peak), Arg. 224/C4
Corre, Fr. 66/C2
Correa, Arg. 226/E2
Corredor, CR 207/F4
Correggio, It. 69/D4
Corrella (lake), Austl. 153/D4
Corrente (riv.), Braz. 222/C3
Corrente, Braz. 222/D1
Correntes (riv.), Braz. 221/H5
Correntes, Cabo das (cape), Moz. 141/G5
Corrib (lake), Ire. 38/A3
Corrie, Sc, UK 39/A5
Corrientes, Arg. 224/E3
Corrientes (prov.), Arg. 225/E4
Corrientes (pt.), Col. 216/B3
Corrientes (cape), Cuba 207/E1
Corrientes (riv.), Ecu. 216/B5
Corrientes (riv.), Peru 220/C1
Corrigan, Tx, US 181/G2
Corrigin, Austl. 154/C5
Corringham, Eng, UK 36/E2
Corris, Wal, UK 42/C1
Corriverton, Guy. 217/G3
Corry, Pa, US 191/G4
Corryhabbie (peak), Sc, UK 39/C2
Corryong, Austl. 157/C3
Corse (cape), Fr. 54/A1
Corse (hill), Sc, UK 39/B5
Corse (dept.), Fr. 51/H5
Corserine (peak), Sc, UK 40/D1
Corseul, Fr. 62/C4
Corsewall (pt.), NI, UK 40/C1
Corsham, Eng, UK 42/D4
Corsica, SD, US 184/E2
Corsica (isl.), Fr. 29/E4
Corsicana, Tx, US 181/F1
Corsico, It. 68/C3
Corsons (inlet), NJ, US 198/D5
Cortada (mesa), NM, US 179/J3
Cortaillod, Swi. 66/C4
Cortaro, Az, US 179/G4
Cortegana, Sp. 52/B4
Cortemaggiore, It. 68/C4
Cortemilia, It. 68/B4
Cortes, Phil. 100/D3
Cortez, Co, US 179/H2
Cortina d'Ampezzo, It. 51/K3
Cortines, Arg. 227/J11
Cortland, NY, US 191/H3
Cortland, Oh, US 190/F4
Cortland, Il, US 185/K3
Corubal (riv.), GBis. 132/B3
Coruche, Port. 52/A3
Çoruh (riv.), Turk. 77/G4
Çorum, Turk. 76/E4
Çorum (prov.), Turk. 76/E4
Corumbá, Braz. 224/E1
Corumbá (riv.), Braz. 222/C3
Corumbaú (pt.), Braz. 223/F3
Corumbiara (riv.), Braz. 221/F4
Corunna, Mi, US 190/D3
Corunna, On, Can. 197/H6
Coruripe, Braz. 223/F1
Corvallis, Or, US 176/B1
Corvaro, It. 71/C3
Corve (riv.), Eng, UK 42/D2
Corvo (peak), It. 71/C3
Corvo (isl.), Azor., Port. 53/R12
Corwen, Wal, UK 41/E6
Corydon, In, US 192/D1
Corydon, Ia, US 185/H3
Corzoneso, Swi. 67/E5
Corzuela, Arg. 224/D3
Cosalá, Mex. 204/D3
Cosamaloapan, Mex. 205/P8
Cosapa, Bol. 224/B1
Cosautlán, Mex. 205/N7
Coscapa, Bol. 220/D5
Coscerno (peak), It. 71/B2
Coscomatepec, Mex. 205/M7
Cosenza, It. 54/E3
Coshocton, Oh, US 190/F4
Cosigüina (pt.), Nic. 206/E3
Coslada, Sp. 53/N9
Cosmit Ind. Res., Ca, US 178/D4
Cosmo Newberry Aboriginal Rsv., Austl. 154/D3
Cosmópolis, Braz. 223/J7
Cosne d'Allier, Fr. 50/E3
Cosne-Cours-sur-Loire, Fr. 50/E3
Cosolapa, Mex. 205/N8
Cospeito, Sp. 52/B1
Cosquín, Arg. 224/C4
Cossa, Ang. 139/E4
Cossato, It. 68/B2
Cossé-le-Vivien, Fr. 63/E5
Cosson (riv.), Fr. 50/D3
Cossonay, Swi. 66/C4
Costa Azul, Uru. 227/G2
Costa Brava (int'l arpt.), Sp. 53/G2
Costa da Caparica, Port. 53/P10
Costa de Mosquitos (phys. reg.), Nic. 207/E4
Costa del Sol (coast), Sp. 72/B3
Costa di Rovigo, It. 69/E3
Costa Marques, Braz. 221/E4
Costa Masnaga, It. 68/C2
Costa Mesa, Ca, US 196/G8
Costa Rica (ctry.) 207/F4
Costa Rica, Bol. 220/D3
Costa Smeralda (int'l arpt.), It. 54/A2
Costa Volpino, It. 68/D2
Costabissara, It. 69/E2
Costello, Pa, US 191/G4
Costello (peak), SD, US 184/C1
Costessey, Eng, UK 43/H1
Costești, Rom. 57/G3
Costigliole d'Asti, It. 68/B4
Costiglione Saluzzo, It. 70/D3
Cosumnes (riv.), Ca, US 176/C4
Cotabambas, Peru 220/C4
Cotabato, Phil. 100/D4
Cotacachi (peak), Ecu. 216/B4
Cotacajes (riv.), Bol. 221/E5
Cotagaita, Bol. 224/C2
Cotahuasi, Peru 220/C4
Cotatumbo (riv.), Col. 207/H4
Cote Blanche (bay), La, US 194/C3
Côte d'Azur (coast), Fr. 53/J1
Côte d'Or (uplands), Fr. 50/F3
Côte d'Azur (int'l arpt.), Fr. 70/D5
Côte de Grace (coast), Fr. 63/F2
Côte de Hautmont (hill), Fr. 66/B1
Côte d'Ivoire (ctry.) 132/D5
Côte du Rif (Al Hoceima) (int'l arpt.), Mor. 130/C2
Côte-Saint-Luc, Qu, Can. 189/N7
Coteau des Prairies (plat.), SD, US 184/E1
Coteau du Missouri (plat.), SD, US 184/D1
Coteau-du-Lac, Qu, Can. 189/M7
Coteau-Landing, Qu, Can. 189/M7
Cotegipe, Braz. 222/D2
Cotentin (pen.), Fr. 50/C2
Cotento (peak), It. 71/C4
Côtes de Meuse (uplands), Fr. 48/C4
Côtes-D'Armor (dept.), Fr. 62/B4
Cothi (riv.), Wal, UK 42/B3
Cotia, Braz. 223/K8
Cotignac, Fr. 70/C5
Cotignola, It. 69/E5
Cotonou (int'l arpt.), Ben. 133/F5
Cotonou, Ben. 133/F5
Cotopaxi, Co, US 182/B1
Cotopaxi (vol.), Ecu. 216/B5
Cotopaxi (dept.), Ecu. 216/B5
Cotopaxi, PN, Ecu. 216/B5
Cotswolds (hills), Eng, UK 42/D3
Cottage Grove, Or, US 176/B2
Cottage Grove, Mn, US 187/Q7
Cottageville, SC, US 193/G4
Cottam, On, Can. 197/G7
Cottbus, Ger. 49/H3
Cottel (isl.), Nf, Can. 189/L1
Cottenham, Eng, UK 43/G2
Cotter, Ar, US 183/H2
Cottica, Sur. 218/C2
Cotton, Mn, US 187/H4
Cotton (lake), Tx, US 181/N9
Cotton Bowl (State Fair Park), Tx, US 180/L7
Cotton Plant, Ar, US 183/J3
Cotton Valley, La, US 183/H4
Cottondale, Fl, US 195/F2
Cottondale, Tx, US 180/K6
Cottonport, La, US 194/B2
Cottonton, Al, US 192/E4
Cottonwood, Al, US 195/F2
Cottonwood, Az, US 179/F3
Cottonwood, Id, US 174/F4
Cottonwood (riv.), Ks, US 185/F4
Cottonwood, Mn, US 185/G1
Cottonwood (riv.), Mn, US 185/G1
Cottonwood, Tx, US 181/F2
Cottonwood (cr.), Wy, US 177/J2
Cottonwood Falls, Ks, US 183/F1
Cottonwood Wash (riv.), Az, US 179/G3
Cottsloe (nbrhd.), Austl. 154/K6
Cotulla, Tx, US 180/E3
Couasnon (riv.), Fr. 63/E5
Coubert, Fr. 36/L6
Coublevie, Fr. 70/B2
Couch, Mo, US 183/J2
Couchey, Fr. 66/A3
Couchwood, La, US 183/H4
Coudekerque-Branche, Fr. 60/B1
Coudersport, Pa, US 191/G4
Coudoux, Fr. 70/B5
Couëron, Fr. 62/D6
Couesnon (riv.), Fr. 62/D4
Cougar, Wa, US 174/C4
Coulaines, Fr. 63/F4
Coulee City, Wa, US 174/E4
Coulee Dam, Wa, US 174/E4
Coulee Dam NRA, Wa, US 174/E3
Coulogne, Fr. 60/A2
Coulomb (pt.), Austl. 152/A4
Coulomb Pt. Nature Rsv., Austl. 152/A4
Coulombs-en-Valois, Fr. 36/M4
Coulommes, Fr. 36/L5
Coulommiers, Fr. 60/C6
Coulon (riv.), Fr. 70/B5
Coulonge (riv.), Qu, Can. 191/H1
Coulounieix-Chamiers, Fr. 50/D4
Coulsdon (nbrhd.), Eng, UK 36/C3
Coulterville, Ca, US 178/B2
Coulterville, Il, US 192/C1
Coumfea (peak), Ire. 38/C5
Counamama, FrG. 218/C1
Counce, Tn, US 192/C3
Council, Ak, US 201/F3
Council, Id, US 176/E1
Council Bluffs, Ia, US 185/G3
Council Grove, Ks, US 183/F1
Country Homes, Wa, US 174/F4
Coupar Angus, Sc, UK 39/C3
Coupeville, Wa, US 174/C3
Coupvray, Fr. 36/L5
Cour-Cheverny, Fr. 63/G5
Courantyne (riv.), Sur. 217/G3
Courantyne (riv.), Guy.,Sur. 209/D2
Courantyne (riv.), Guy. 218/B1
Courbevoie, Fr. 36/J5
Courcelles, Belg. 61/D3
Courcelles-sur-Seine, Fr. 63/G2
Courchevel (arpt.), Fr. 70/C2
Courcouronnes, Fr. 36/K6
Courdimanche, Fr. 36/H4
Courgenay, Swi. 66/D3
Courgent, Fr. 36/G5
Courmayeur, It. 66/C6
Cournon-d'Auvergne, Fr. 50/E4
Courpalay, Fr. 36/L6
Courrendlin, Swi. 66/D3
Courroux, Swi. 66/D3
Coursan, Fr. 50/E5
Courseulles-sur-Mer, Fr. 63/E2
Courtelary, Swi. 66/D3
Courtenay, ND, US 186/E4
Courtepin, Swi. 66/D4
Courthézon, Fr. 70/A4
Courtice, On, Can. 190/V8
Courtisols, Fr. 61/D6
Courtland, Ca, US 197/L10
Courtland, Ks, US 184/F4

Court – Dajar
279

Courtland, Va, US 193/J2
Courtmacsherry, Ire. 38/B6
Courtmacsherry (bay), Ire. 38/B6
Courtney, Tx, US 181/F2
Courtomer, Fr. 36/L6
Courtown, Ire. 38/D4
Courtright, On, Can. 197/H6
Courville-sur-Eure, Fr. 63/G4
Cousance, Fr. 66/B4
Cousane (pass), Ire. 38/A6
Coushatta, La, US 194/B1
Cousolre, Fr. 61/D3
Coutances, Fr. 62/D2
Couteau (hills), Sk, Can. 175/L2
Couterne, Fr. 63/E3
Coutevroult, Fr. 36/L5
Couto de Magalhães, Braz. 218/D5
Coutras, Fr. 50/C4
Coutts, Ab, Can. 175/J3
Couva, Trin. 217/F2
Couvet, Swi. 66/C4
Couvin, Belg. 61/D3
Couzeix, Fr. 50/D4
Covadonga, PN, Sp. 52/C1
Covasna (prov.), Rom. 57/G3
Covasna, Rom. 57/H3
Cove, Ar, US 183/G3
Cove, Sc, UK 39/B5
Cove, Tx, US 181/N9
Cove Bay, Sc, UK 39/D2
Cove Gap, WV, US 193/F1
Cove Neck, NY, US 199/L8
Covelo, Ca, US 176/B4
Covendo, Bol. 221/E4
Coventry, Eng, UK 43/E2
Coventry (co.), Eng, UK 43/E2
Coventry (canal), Eng, UK 43/E1
Covered, Turk. 115/M6
Covesville, Va, US 193/H2
Covilhã, Port. 52/B2
Covina, Ca, US 196/G7
Covington, Ga, US 192/F4
Covington, In, US 190/C4
Covington, Ky, US 192/E1
Covington, La, US 194/C2
Covington, Mi, US 187/K4
Covington, Ok, US 183/F2
Covington, Oh, US 190/D4
Covington, Tn, US 192/C3
Covington, Tx, US 181/F1
Covington, Va, US 193/H2
Covo, It. 68/C3
Cow (cr.), Or, US 176/B2
Cow Creek, Wy, US 184/B2
Cow Green (res.), Eng, UK 41/F2
Cowal (reg.), Sc, UK 39/A4
Cowal (lake), Austl. 157/C1
Cowal Creek Aboriginal Community, Austl. 153/F2
Cowan, Tn, US 192/D3
Cowan (nbrhd.), Austl. 158/H8
Cowan (lake), Austl. 145/B4
Cowangie, Austl. 156/B2
Cowansville, Qu, Can. 191/K2
Cowaramup, Austl. 154/B5
Coward Springs, Austl. 155/H4
Cowarie, Austl. 155/H3
Cowboy (hill), Ne, US 184/C3
Cowbridge, Wal, UK 42/C4
Cowden, Il, US 185/K4
Cowdenbeath, Sc, UK 39/C4
Cowee (mts.), NC, US 193/F3
Cowell, Austl. 155/H5
Cowes, Eng, UK 43/E5
Cowes, Austl. 157/B4
Cowessess Ind. Res., Sk, Can. 186/C2
Coweta (co.), Ga, US 193/L8
Cowhouse (cr.), Tx, US 181/E2
Cowichan (lake), BC, Can. 174/B3
Cowie, Sc, UK 39/C4
Cowlesville, NY, US 190/W10
Cowley, Ab, Can. 175/G3
Cowley, Wy, US 177/J1
Cowlitz (riv.), Wa, US 174/D4
Cowora, Austl. 157/C3
Cowpens Nat'l Bfld., SC, US 193/G3
Cowra, Austl. 157/D1
Cox City, Ok, US 183/F3
Coxhoe, Eng, UK 41/G2
Coxilha de Santana (hills), Braz. 225/F4
Coxim, Braz. 225/F1
Coxim (riv.), Braz. 222/B3
Cox's Bāzār, Bang. 105/F3
Cox's Cove, Nf, Can. 189/H1
Coxs Mills, WV, US 193/G1
Coxsackie, NY, US 191/K3
Coy, Al, US 194/E2
Coy Aike, Arg. 227/C6
Coya, Chile 226/N9
Coya Sur, Chile 224/B2
Coyah, Gui. 132/B4
Coyame, Mex. 180/B3
Coyanosa Draw (riv.), Tx, US 180/C2
Coye-la-Forêt, Fr. 36/K4
Coyoacán (nbrhd.), Mex. 205/R10
Coyote (cr.), Ca, US 197/L12
Coyotepec, Mex. 205/K7
Coyuca de Benítez, Mex. 205/E5
Coyutla, Mex. 205/M6
Cozad, Ne, US 184/E3
Cozhê, China 111/E5
Cozumel, Mex. 206/E1
Cozumel (int'l arpt.), Mex. 206/E1
Cozumel (isl.), Mex. 206/E1
Crab (cr.), Wa, US 174/E4
Crab Orchard Nat'l Wild. Ref., Il, US 185/K5
Crab Orchard NWR, Il, US 192/C2
Crabapple, Ga, US 193/M6
Cradle (mtn.), Austl. 156/C4
Cradock, SAfr. 142/D4
Craftsbury, Vt, US 191/K2
Crag (mt.), Yk, Can. 201/K3
Crag (peak), Eng, UK 41/F3
Craig, Ak, US 201/M4
Craig, Co, US 177/K3
Craig (mt.), Co, US 184/B3
Craig, Mo, US 185/G3
Craig, Mt, US 175/J4
Craig (cr.), Va, US 193/G2
Craigavad, NI, UK 40/C2
Craigavon (dist.), NI, UK 40/B3
Craigavon, NI, UK 40/B3
Craigellachie, Sc, UK 39/C2
Craigieburn, Austl. 156/F5
Craigsville, WV, US 193/G1
Craigsville, Va, US 193/H1
Craik, Sk, Can. 175/M2
Crail, Sc, UK 39/D4
Crailsheim, Ger. 64/D4
Craiova, Rom. 57/F3
Cramalina (peak), Swi. 67/E5
Cramlington, Eng, UK 41/G1
Cran-Gevrier, Fr. 66/C6
Crana (riv.), Ire. 40/A1
Cranborne Chase (for.), Eng, UK 42/D5
Cranbourne, Austl. 156/G6
Cranbrook, Austl. 156/D4
Cranbrook, Austl. 154/C5
Cranbrook, BC, Can. 174/G3
Cranbury, NJ, US 198/D3
Crandall, Mb, Can. 186/D2
Crandall, Tx, US 180/L7
Crandon, Wi, US 187/K5
Crane (lake), Il, US 185/J3
Crane, Mt, US 186/B4
Crane, Mo, US 183/H2
Crane, Tx, US 180/C2
Crane Hill, Al, US 192/D3
Crane Lake, Mn, US 187/H3
Crane Naval Weapons Support Center, In, US 190/C5
Crane Neck (pt.), NY, US 199/E2
Crane NWSC, In, US 192/D1
Crane Prairie (res.), Or, US 176/C2
Crane River, Mb, Can. 186/E2
Cranfills Gap, Tx, US 180/F2
Cranford, NJ, US 199/H9
Cranleigh, Eng, UK 43/F4
Cranston, RI, US 191/L4
Craon, Fr. 63/E5
Craponne (canal), Fr. 70/A5
Craponne, Fr. 70/A1
Crary, ND, US 186/E3
Crasna (riv.), Rom. 56/F2
Crasnoe, Mol. 78/E4
Craster, Eng, UK 39/E6
Crater (peak), Or, US 176/B2
Crater (lake), Or, US 176/B2
Crater Lake NP, Or, US 176/B2
Craters Of The Moon Nat'l Mon., Id, US 177/G2
Crateús, Braz. 219/F4
Crati (riv.), It. 54/E3
Cratloe, Ire. 38/B4
Crato, Port. 52/B3
Crato, Braz. 219/G4
Cravens, La, US 194/B2
Cravinhos, Braz. 225/H2
Crawford, Co, US 179/J1
Crawford, Ga, US 193/F4
Crawford, Ms, US 192/C4
Crawford, Ok, US 182/E3
Crawford, Sc, UK 39/C6
Crawford, Tx, US 181/F2
Crawford Bay, BC, Can. 174/F3
Crawfordsville, In, US 190/C4
Crawfordville, Fl, US 195/F2
Crawfordville, Ga, US 193/F4
Crawley, Eng, UK 43/F4
Cray (riv.), Eng, UK 36/D2
Crayford (nbrhd.), Eng, UK 36/D2
Crazy (mts.), Mt, US 175/J4
Crazy Horse Monument, SD, US 184/C2
Crazy Woman (cr.), Wy, US 177/K1
Creag Meagaidh (peak), Sc, UK 39/B3
Creagerstown, Md, US 198/A4
Creal Springs, Il, US 192/C2
Cream, Wi, US 185/J1
Creasy (Mifflinville), Pa, US 198/B1
Creazzo, It. 69/E3
Crêches-sur-Saône, Fr. 66/A5
Crécy-sur-Serre, Fr. 60/C4
Credit (riv.), On, Can. 190/T8
Crediton, Eng, UK 42/C5
Cree (riv.), Sc, UK 40/D2
Cree (lake), Sk, Can. 170/F3
Cree (riv.), Sk, Can. 170/F3
Creede, Co, US 179/J2
Creedman Coulee Nat'l Wild. Ref., Mt, US 175/K3
Creedmoor, Tx, US 181/F2
Creek (Pryor), Ok, US 183/G2
Creel, Mex. 204/D3
Creelman, Sk, Can. 186/C3
Creemore, On, Can. 190/F2
Creetown, Sc, UK 40/D2
Creglingen, Ger. 64/D4
Crégy-lès-Meaux, Fr. 36/L5
Créhange, Fr. 61/F5
Créhen, Fr. 62/C3
Creighton, Sk, Can. 170/F3
Creighton, Ne, US 184/F2
Creighton, SD, US 184/C1
Creignish, NS, Can. 189/G3
Creil, Fr. 60/B5
Crema, It. 68/C3
Crémieu, Fr. 66/B6
Cremlingen, Ger. 59/H4
Cremona, Ab, Can. 174/G2
Cremona, It. 68/D3
Cremona (prov.), It. 68/C2
Crenshaw, Ms, US 192/B3
Creola, Al, US 194/D2
Creole, La, US 194/B3
Crepaja, Serb. 56/E3
Crepori (riv.), Braz. 218/B4
Crépy, Fr. 60/C4
Creran (lake), Sc, UK 39/A3
Cres (isl.), Cro. 73/G1
Cres, Cro. 51/L4
Cresaptown, Md, US 191/G5
Cresbard, SD, US 184/E1
Crescent (lake), Fl, US 195/H3
Crescent, Ok, US 183/F3
Crescent, Or, US 176/C2
Crescent City, Ca, US 176/A3
Crescent City, Fl, US 195/H3
Crescent Group (isls.), Asia 99/F5
Crescent Lake, Or, US 176/C2
Crescent Lake Nat'l. Wild. Ref., Ne, US 184/C3
Crescentino, It. 68/B3
Cresco, Ia, US 185/H2
Cresco, Pa, US 198/C1
Crespano del Grappa, It. 69/E2
Crespellano, It. 69/E4
Crespières, Fr. 36/H5
Crespin, Fr. 60/C3
Crespo, Arg. 224/D5
Cresskill, NJ, US 199/K8
Cresson, Pa, US 191/G4
Cresson, Tx, US 180/K7
Cressona, Pa, US 198/B2
Cressy, Austl. 156/C4
Crest, Fr. 70/B3
Crest Hill, Il, US 197/P16
Crestline, Ca, US 196/C2
Crestline, Oh, US 190/E4
Creston, Nf, Can. 189/K2
Creston, Ca, US 178/B3
Creston, Ia, US 185/G3
Creston, BC, Can. 174/F3
Crestone, Co, US 182/B2
Crestone (peak), Co, US 182/B2
Crestview, Fl, US 194/E2
Crestwood Village, NJ, US 199/D4
Creswell, Eng, UK 41/G5
Creswell, Or, US 176/B2
Creswell Downs, Austl. 153/D4
Creswick, Austl. 157/A3
Crêt de la Neige (peak), Fr. 66/B5
Crêt du Nu (peak), Fr. 66/B5
Crêt du Rey (peak), Fr. 70/C1
Crete, Il, US 190/C4
Crete (sea), Gre. 73/K3
Crete, Ne, US 185/F3
Crete (isl.), Gre. 29/G5
Créteil, Fr. 36/K5
Cretin (cape), PNG 153/G1
Creuch (hill), Sc, UK 39/B5
Creus (cape), Sp. 53/G1
Creuse (riv.), Fr. 72/D1
Creussen (riv.), Ger. 65/E3
Creussen, Ger. 65/E3
Creutzwald-la-Croix, Fr. 61/F5
Creuzburg, Ger. 59/H6
Crevacuore, It. 68/B2
Crevalcore, It. 69/E4
Crèvecœur-le-Grand, Fr. 60/B4
Crevillente, Sp. 53/E3
Crevoladossola, It. 67/E5
Crewe, Eng, UK 41/F5
Crewe, Va, US 193/H2
Crewkerne, Eng, UK 42/D5
Crews (lake), Fl, US 194/K7
Crianlarich, Sc, UK 39/B4
Crib Point, Austl. 157/B4
Criccieth, Wal, UK 40/D6
Crichton, Sk, Can. 175/L3
Criciúma, Braz. 225/G4
Cricket, NC, US 193/G2
Crickhowell, Wal, UK 42/C3
Cricklade, Eng, UK 43/E3
Crieff, Sc, UK 39/C4
Criffell (hill), Sc, UK 40/E2
Crikvenica, Cro. 51/L4
Crillon (mt.), Ak, US 201/L4
Crimean (pen.), Rom. 57/L3
Crimean (mts.), Ukr. 79/H5
Crimond, Sc, UK 39/E1
Cripple Creek, Co, US 182/B1
Criquetot-L'Esneval, Fr. 63/F1
Crisenoy, Fr. 36/L6
Crisfield, Md, US 193/K2
Crisp (pt.), Mi, US 190/D1
Crisp, Tx, US 180/L7
Crissier, Swi. 66/C4
Crissiumal, Braz. 225/F3
Crissolo, It. 70/D3
Cristal, Monts de (mts.), Gabon 138/B2
Cristalândia, Braz. 222/C1
Cristalina, Braz. 222/D3
Cristalinho (riv.), Braz. 222/C2
Cristina, Braz. 223/L7
Cristino Castro, Braz. 219/E5
Cristóbal (pt.), Ecu. 220/J7
Cristóbal Colón (peak), Col. 216/C2
Cristoforo Colombo (int'l arpt.), It. 68/B5
Cristuru Secuiesc, Rom. 57/G2
Crişul Negru (riv.), Rom. 56/E2
Crişul Repede (riv.), Rom. 78/B4
Crivitz, Wi, US 190/B2
Crixás, Braz. 222/C2
Crixás-Açu (riv.), Braz. 222/C2
Crna Reka (riv.), FYROM 55/G2
Črnomelj, Slov. 56/B3
Croaghmoyle (peak), Ire. 38/A2
Croatia (ctry.) 56/C3
Croce (peak), It. 67/H5
Croce, Pico di (peak), It. 67/H4
Croche (peak), Fr. 66/C6
Croche (riv.), Qu, Can. 188/A1
Crocker, Mo, US 183/H2
Crocker (range), Malay. 103/E3
Crocker (peak), Ecu. 220/J7
Crocketford, Sc, UK 40/E1
Crockett, Ca, US 197/K10
Crockett, Tx, US 181/G2
Crockett Mills, Tn, US 192/C3
Crockham Hill, Eng, UK 36/D3
Crocodile (pt.), Austl. 157/E2
Crocodilopolis (ruin), Egypt 131/B6
Crodo, It. 67/E5
Crofton, Ky, US 192/D2
Crofton, Md, US 198/B6
Crofty, Wal, UK 42/B3
Croghan (mtn.), Ire. 40/B6
Crohane (peak), Ire. 38/A6
Croisette (cape), Fr. 70/B6
Croisic (bay), Fr. 62/C6
Croisic (pt.), Fr. 62/C6
Croisilles, Fr. 60/B3
Croissy-Beaubourg, Fr. 36/K5
Croix (lake), On, Can. 187/J3
Croix Rousse (peak), Fr. 70/D2
Croker (cape), Austl. 152/D2
Croker (isl.), Austl. 145/C2
Crolles, Fr. 70/B2
Cromarty, Sc, UK 39/B1
Cromarty Firth (bay), Sc, UK 39/B1
Crombie (mt.), Austl. 155/F3
Cromdale, Sc, UK 39/C2
Cromdale (hills), Sc, UK 39/C2
Cromer, Mb, Can. 186/D3
Cromer, Eng, UK 43/H1
Cromwell, NZ 159/B4
Cromwell, Al, US 192/C4
Cromwell, Ky, US 192/D2
Cromwell, Ok, US 183/F3
Crondall, Eng, UK 36/A3
Crong A Na (riv.), Viet. 106/D3
Cronulla (nbrhd.), Austl. 158/H9
Crook, Eng, UK 41/G2
Crooked (isl.), Bahm. 203/G3
Crooked (isl.), Fl, US 195/F3
Crooked (lake), Fl, US 195/H4
Crooked (cr.), Ks, US 182/D2
Crooked (riv.), Or, US 176/C1
Crooked Creek, Ak, US 201/G3
Crooked Island Passage (chan.), Bahm. 207/H1
Crookhaven, Ire. 38/A7
Crooks, SD, US 185/F2
Crooks Tower (peak), SD, US 184/C1
Crookston, Mn, US 186/F4
Crookstown, Ire. 38/B6
Crooksville, Oh, US 190/E5
Crookwell, Austl. 157/D2
Croom, Ire. 38/B4
Croom, Fl, US 194/L6
Crosby, Mn, US 187/H4
Crosby, ND, US 186/C3
Crosby, Eng, UK 41/E5
Crosby, Ms, US 194/C2
Crosby (mt.), Wy, US 177/J2
Crosby, Tx, US 181/M9
Crosbyton, Tx, US 182/D4
Cross (cape), Namb. 140/B4
Cross, Tx, US 181/F2
Cross Anchor, SC, US 193/G3
Cross City, Fl, US 195/G3
Cross Fell (peak), Eng, UK 41/F2
Cross Hill, SC, US 193/G3
Cross Plains, Tx, US 180/E1
Cross Plains, Wi, US 185/K2
Cross River (state), Nga. 133/H5
Cross River (res.), NY, US 199/E1
Cross Roads, Tx, US 181/G1
Cross Roads, Pa, US 198/B4
Crossett, Ar, US 183/J4
Crossfarnoge (pt.), Ire. 38/D5
Crossfield, Ab, Can. 175/G2
Crossford, Sc, UK 39/C4
Crossgar, NI, UK 40/C3
Crossgates, Wal, UK 42/C2
Crosshaven, Ire. 38/B6
Crosshill, Sc, UK 39/B6
Crosshouse, Sc, UK 39/B5
Crosskeys, Wal, UK 42/C3
Crosslake, Mn, US 187/G4
Crossmaglen, NI, UK 38/D1
Crossmichael, Sc, UK 40/E2
Crossmolina, Ire. 38/A1
Crossroads, Ire. 37/P9
Crossville, Il, US 192/C1
Crossville, Al, US 192/E3
Crossville, Tn, US 192/E3
Crosswicks (cr.), NJ, US 198/D3
Crostolo (riv.), It. 68/D3
Croston, Eng, UK 41/F4
Croswell, Mi, US 190/E3
Crothersville, In, US 192/E1
Croton-Harmon (Croton-On-Hudson), NY, US 199/E1
Croton-On-Hudson (Croton-Harmon), NY, US 199/E1
Crotone, It. 54/E3
Crottendorf, Ger. 65/F1
Croult (riv.), Fr. 36/K5
Crouy, Fr. 60/C5
Crouy-sur-Ourcq, Fr. 36/M4
Crow (cr.), Co, US 184/B3
Crow (riv.), Mn, US 187/N6
Crow (peak), SD, US 184/C1
Crow Creek Ind. Res., SD, US 184/E1
Crow Ind. Res., Mt, US 177/J1
Crow Ind. Res., Mt, US 175/K5
Crow Wing (riv.), Mn, US 187/G4
Crow, North Fork (riv.), Mn, US 187/G5
Crow, North Fork (riv.), Mn, US 185/G1
Crow, South Fork (riv.), Mn, US 187/G5
Crow, South Fork (riv.), Mn, US 185/G1
Crowborough, Eng, UK 43/G4
Crowder, Ok, US 183/G3
Crowdy Bay NP, Austl. 156/E1
Crowe (riv.), On, Can. 191/H2
Crowell, Tx, US 182/E4
Crowheart, Wy, US 177/J2
Crowie (cr.), Austl. 157/C1
Crowland, Eng, UK 43/F1
Crowle, Eng, UK 41/H4
Crowley (lake), Ca, US 178/C2
Crowley, La, US 194/B2
Crowley, Tx, US 180/K7
Crowley's (ridge), Ar, US 192/B3
Crown Point, In, US 190/C4
Crown Point (int'l arpt.), Trin. 217/F2
Crown Prince Frederik (isl.), Nun, Can. 171/H1
Crownpoint, NM, US 179/H3
Crows Nest (peak), SD, US 184/C1
Crows Nest Falls NP, Austl. 158/D4
Crowther (cr.), Austl. 157/D2
Crowthorne, Eng, UK 43/F4
Crowville, La, US 183/J4
Croxley Green, Eng, UK 36/B2
Croydon (bor.), Eng, UK 36/C2
Croydon (nbrhd.), Eng, UK 36/C2
Croydon, Austl. 158/A2
Croydon (nbrhd.), Austl. 156/G5
Croydon, Pa, US 198/D3
Crozet (isls.), Fr. 27/M8
Crozon, Fr. 62/A4
Cruach Mhór (peak), Sc, UK 39/A4
Cruach nan Capull (peak), Sc, UK 39/A5
Cruas, Fr. 70/A3
Crucero, Peru 220/D4
Cruden Bay, Sc, UK 39/E2
Cruger, Ms, US 192/B4
Cruick Water (riv.), Sc, UK 39/D3
Crum (mtn.), Ms, US 192/C3
Crumlin, NI, UK 40/B2
Crummock Water (lake), Eng, UK 41/E2
Crump (lake), Or, US 176/D2
Crump, Tn, US 192/C3
Crumpton, Md, US 198/C5
Cruseilles, Fr. 66/C5
Crusheen, Ire. 38/B4
Crusnes (riv.), Fr. 61/E5
Cruz (cape), Cuba 207/G2
Cruz Alta, Arg. 226/E2
Cruz Alta (peak), Port. 53/P10
Cruz Alta, Braz. 225/F4
Cruz del Eje, Arg. 224/C4
Cruz Grande, Mex. 206/B2
Cruzeiro, Braz. 223/M7
Cruzeiro do Oeste, Braz. 225/F2
Cruzeiro do Sul, Braz. 220/C2
Cruzeta, Braz. 219/G4
Cruzília, Braz. 223/M6
Crvenka, Serb. 56/D3
Cryn-y-Brain (peak), Wal, UK 41/E5
Crystal, Mn, US 187/P6
Crystal, NM, US 179/H2
Crystal (lake), Pa, US 198/C1
Crystal Bay, Nv, US 176/D4
Crystal Beach, Fl, US 194/K7
Crystal Brook, Austl. 155/H5
Crystal Cave, Pa, US 198/C2
Crystal City, Mb, Can. 186/E3
Crystal City, Tx, US 180/E3
Crystal Falls, Mi, US 187/K4
Crystal Hill, Va, US 193/H2
Crystal Lake, Fl, US 195/F2
Crystal Lake, Il, US 190/B3
Crystal River, Fl, US 195/G3
Crystal Springs, Ms, US 194/C2
Crystal Springs, Fl, US 194/L7
Crystal Springs (res.), Ca, US 197/K11
Csenger, Hun. 49/M5
Csepreg, Hun. 56/C2
Csongrád, Hun. 56/E2
Csorna, Hun. 56/C2
Csorvás, Hun. 56/E2
Csóványos (peak), Hun. 56/D2
Csurgó, Hun. 56/C2
Ctesiphon (ruin), Iraq 115/F3
Cu Lao (isl.), Viet. 106/E4
Cuajinicuilapa, Mex. 206/B2
Cualedro, Sp. 52/B2
Cuamba, Moz. 141/H2
Cuanavale (riv.), Ang. 140/C2
Cuando (riv.), Ang. 140/D3
Cuangar, Ang. 140/C3
Cuango, Ang. 138/D5
Cuango, Ang. 138/D4
Cuango (riv.), Ang. 138/D5
Cuanza (riv.), Ang. 119/D6
Cuanza Norte (prov.), Ang. 138/C5
Cuanza Sul (prov.), Ang. 138/C5
Cuareim (riv.), Braz. 225/E4
Cuaró, Uru. 225/F4
Cuart de Poblet, Sp. 53/E3
Cuarto (riv.), Arg. 226/D2
Cuatir (riv.), Ang. 140/C2
Cuatro Ojos, Bol. 224/D1
Cuauhtémoc, Mex. 204/E5
Cuauhtémoc, Mex. 204/D2
Cuautepec, Mex. 205/L6
Cuautitlán, Mex. 205/Q9
Cuautitlán Izcalli, Mex. 205/Q9
Cuautla, Mex. 205/L8
Cuba (ctry.) 207/F1
Cuba, Il, US 185/J3
Cuba, Ks, US 184/F4
Cuba, Mo, US 183/J1
Cuba, NM, US 179/J2
Cuba, NY, US 191/G3
Cuba, Port. 52/B3
Cuba City, Wi, US 185/J2
Cubagua (isl.), Ven. 217/E2
Cubal, Ang. 140/B2
Cubal (riv.), Ang. 140/B2
Cuballing, Austl. 154/C5
Cubango (riv.), Ang. 119/D6
Cubatão, Braz. 223/K8
Cubati, Braz. 219/G4
Cubero, NM, US 179/J3
Çubuk, Turk. 114/C1
Cuc Phuong NP, Viet. 98/E4
Cucamonga (Rancho Cucamonga), Ca, US 196/C2
Cuccurano, It. 69/F6
Cucharas (riv.), Co, US 182/B2
Cuchi, Ang. 140/C2
Cuchi (riv.), Ang. 140/C2
Cuchilla Caraguatá, Uru. 225/F5
Cuchillo, NM, US 179/J4
Cuchillo-Có, Arg. 226/D3
Cuchivero (riv.), Ven. 217/E3
Cuchumatanes (mts.), Guat. 206/D3
Cuckfield, Eng, UK 43/F4
Cuckmere (riv.), Eng, UK 43/G5
Cucuí, Braz. 217/E4
Cúcuta, Col. 216/C3
Cucuyagua, Hon. 206/D3
Cudahy, Wi, US 190/C3
Cudahy, Ca, US 196/F8
Cudal, Austl. 157/D1
Cuddalore, India 107/C4
Cuddington, Eng, UK 41/F5
Cudgewa, Austl. 157/C3
Cudillero, Sp. 52/B1
Cudrefin, Swi. 66/D4
Cudworth, Eng, UK 41/G4
Cudworth, Sk, Can. 175/M1
Cue, Austl. 154/C3
Cuebe (riv.), Ang. 140/C2
Cueio (riv.), Ang. 140/D2
Cueli (riv.), Ang. 140/C2
Cuéllar, Sp. 52/C2
Cuéllar-Baza, Sp. 52/D4
Cuenca, Ecu. 216/B5
Cuenca, Sp. 52/D2
Cuencamé de Ceniceros, Mex. 204/E3
Cuengo (riv.), Ang. 138/D5
Cuernavaca, Mex. 205/K8
Cuero, Tx, US 181/F3
Cuers, Fr. 70/C6
Cuesmes, Belg. 60/C3
Cueto, Cuba 207/H1
Cuetzalán, Mex. 205/M6
Cueva de la Quebrada del Toro, PN, Ven. 216/D2
Cuevas de Vinromá, Sp. 53/F2
Cuevas del Almanzora, Sp. 52/E4
Cuevo, Bol. 224/D2
Cuffley, Eng, UK 36/C1
Cufré, Uru. 227/K11
Cuges-les-Pins, Fr. 70/B6
Cugir, Rom. 57/F3
Cuglieri, It. 54/A2
Cugnaux, Fr. 50/D5
Cugo (riv.), Ang. 138/D4
Cuiabá, Braz. 222/A2
Cuiabá (riv.), Braz. 221/G5
Cuicas, Ven. 216/D2
Cuijk, Neth. 58/C5
Cuilapa, Guat. 206/D3
Cuilcagh (peak), NI, UK 38/C1
Cuilco (riv.), Guat. 206/C3
Cuillin (sound), Sc, UK 37/Q8
Cuilo, Ang. 138/D4
Cuilo (riv.), Ang. 138/C4
Cuilo Pombo, Ang. 138/C4
Cuima, Ang. 140/B2
Cuisance (riv.), Fr. 66/B4
Cuise-la-Motte, Fr. 60/C5
Cuiseaux, Fr. 66/B5
Cuisery, Fr. 66/A4
Cuisy, Fr. 36/L4
Cuité, Braz. 219/G4
Cuitláhuac, Mex. 205/N8
Cuito (riv.), Ang. 140/C2
Cuito-Cuanavale, Ang. 140/C2
Cuiuni (riv.), Braz. 217/E5
Cujmir, Rom. 56/F3
Cukuh Batuberagam (cape), Indo. 101/C4
Culasi, Phil. 100/C3
Culbertson (dam), Ne, US 184/D3
Culburra-Orient Point, Austl. 157/E2
Culcairn, Austl. 157/C2
Culdaff (riv.), Ire. 40/A1
Culdaff, Ire. 40/A1
Culebras, Peru 220/B3
Culemborg, Neth. 58/C5
Culfa, Azer. 115/F2
Culgoa (riv.), Austl. 145/D3
Culiacán Rosales, Mex. 204/D3
Culion (isl.), Phil. 100/B3
Culion Reservation, Phil. 100/C3
Culiseu (riv.), Braz. 222/B2
Cullen, Arg. 227/C7
Cullen, La, US 183/H4
Cullen, Sc, UK 39/D1
Cullen, Va, US 193/H2
Cullen Bullen, Austl. 157/E1
Cullenagh (riv.), Ire. 38/A4
Culleoka, Tx, US 180/L6
Cullera, Sp. 53/E3
Culleredo, Sp. 52/A1
Cullin (lake), Ire. 38/A2
Cullinan, SAfr. 141/F5
Cullman, Al, US 192/D3
Culloden Battlesite, Sc, UK 39/B2
Cullomburg, Al, US 194/D2
Cullompton, Eng, UK 42/C5
Cullowhee, NC, US 193/F3
Cully, Swi. 66/C5
Cullybackey, NI, UK 40/B2
Culmback (dam), Wa, US 197/D2
Culmore, NI, UK 40/A1
Culoz, Fr. 66/B6
Culp Creek, Or, US 176/B2
Culpeper, Va, US 193/J1
Culpina, Bol. 224/C2
Culross, Sc, UK 39/C4
Culta, Bol. 224/C1
Cultra (lake), Ire. 38/B3
Cults, Sc, UK 39/D2
Culuene (riv.), Braz. 221/H4
Culver (pt.), Austl. 154/E5
Culver, Ks, US 183/F1
Culver, In, US 190/C4
Culver, Mn, US 187/H4
Culver, Or, US 176/C1
Culver City, Ca, US 196/F7
Culverden, NZ 159/C3
Culvers (lake), NJ, US 198/D1
Culverstone Green, Eng, UK 36/E3
Cumã (bay), Braz. 219/E3
Cumaná, Ven. 217/E2
Cumane (riv.), Fr. 70/B2
Cumaría, Peru 220/C3
Cumba, Peru 220/B2
Cumbal, Col. 216/B4
Cumberland, BC, Can. 174/B3
Cumberland (pen.), Nun, Can. 171/K2
Cumberland (sound), Nun, Can. 171/K2
Cumberland (plat.), US 192/D3
Cumberland (isl.), Ga, US 195/H2
Cumberland, Ky, US 193/F2
Cumberland (falls), Ky, US 192/E2
Cumberland (lake), Ky, US 192/E2
Cumberland (riv.), Ky,Tn, US 173/J4
Cumberland, Md, US 191/G5
Cumberland (co.), NJ, US 198/A3
Cumberland, Va, US 193/H2
Cumberland, Wa, US 197/D3
Cumberland, Wi, US 187/H5
Cumberland Gap NHP, NC,Va, US 193/F2
Cumberland Island Nat'l Seashore, Ga, US 195/H2
Cumbernauld, Sc, UK 39/C5
Cumbi, Ang. 138/C4
Cumbre del Laudo (peak), Arg. 224/B3
Cumbre del Libertador General San Martín (peak), Arg. 224/C3
Cumbres and Toltec Railroad, Co, US 179/J2
Cumbres Bastonal, Cerro (peak), Mex. 206/C2
Cumbres de Majalca, PN, Mex. 204/D2
Cumbres de Monterrey, PN, Mex. 202/A2
Cumbres de Monterrey, PN, Mex. 204/E3
Cumbria (co.), Eng, UK 41/E2
Cumbrian (mts.), Eng, UK 41/E2
Cumbum, India 107/C3
Cumiana, It. 70/D3
Cumming, Ga, US 192/E3
Cummins, Austl. 155/G5
Cumnock, Sc, UK 39/B6
Cumnock, Austl. 157/D1
Cumpas, Mex. 204/C2
Çumra, Turk. 114/C2
Cuñapirú, Uru. 227/G1
Cuñaré, Col. 216/C4
Cunaviche, Ven. 217/E3
Cunco, Chile 226/B3
Cunde (riv.), Ang. 140/C2
Cundeelee Abor. Rsv., Austl. 154/D4
Cunderdin, Austl. 154/C4
Cundinamarca (dept.), Col. 216/C3
Cunduacán, Mex. 206/C2
Cunene (prov.), Ang. 140/B3
Cunene (riv.), Ang. 119/D6
Cuneo (prov.), It. 68/A3
Cuneo, It. 70/D4
Cuneo (prov.), Fr. 70/D3
Cuney, Tx, US 180/G1
Cung Son, Viet. 106/E3
Cunha, Braz. 223/M8
Cunhinga, Ang. 140/C2
Cunhinga (riv.), Ang. 140/C1
Cunjamba, Ang. 140/D2
Cunnamulla, Austl. 158/B5
Cunningham, Ks, US 183/E2
Cunningham, Ky, US 192/C2
Cunningham, Tx, US 183/G4
Cunninghame (reg.), Sc, UK 39/B5
Čuokkaraš'ša (peak), Nor. 44/H1
Cuorgnè, It. 70/D2
Cuozhen, China 99/H2
Cupar, Sk, Can. 186/B2
Cupar, Sc, UK 39/C4
Cupello, It. 71/D3
Cupertino, Ca, US 197/K12
Cupra Marittima, It. 71/C1
Cupramontana, It. 69/G7
Ćuprija, Serb. 56/E4
Cuprum, Id, US 176/E1
Cuquenán (riv.), Ven. 217/F3
Curaçá, Braz. 219/G5
Curaçao (isl.), Neth. 203/H5
Curacautín, Chile 226/C3
Curacaví, Chile 226/N8
Curahuara de Carangas, Bol. 220/D5
Curahuara de Pacajes, Bol. 224/B1
Curanilahue, Chile 226/B3
Curaray (riv.), Peru 216/C5
Curaray (riv.), Peru 216/B5
Curaray (riv.), Ecu.,Peru 220/C1
Curarén, Hon. 206/E3
Curaumilla (pt.), Chile 226/N8
Curcubăta (peak), Rom. 57/F2
Cure (riv.), Fr. 48/B5
Curecanti National Recreation Area, Co, US 177/K4
Curecanti Nat'l Rec. Area, Co, US 182/A1
Curepipe, Mrts. 143/T15
Curepto, Chile 226/B2
Curiche Grande (riv.), Bol. 221/G5
Curicó, Chile 226/C2
Curimatá, Braz. 222/D1
Curitiba, Braz. 225/G3
Curitibanos, Braz. 225/G3
Curnamona, Austl. 155/H4
Curno, It. 68/C2
Curoca (riv.), Ang. 140/B3
Curone (riv.), It. 68/C3
Currais Novos, Braz. 219/G4
Curral Velho, CpV. 119/K10
Curralinho, Braz. 218/D3
Currant (mtn.), Nv, US 176/F4
Currant, Nv, US 176/F4
Currarong, Austl. 157/E2
Currawilla, Austl. 158/A4
Current (riv.), Mo, US 192/B2
Currie, Austl. 157/A4
Currie, Sc, UK 39/C5
Currie, Nv, US 177/F3
Currituck, NC, US 193/J2
Currituck (sound), NC, US 193/K2
Curry, Ak, US 201/H3
Curtea de Argeş, Rom. 57/G3
Curtici, Rom. 56/E2
Curtin, Or, US 176/B2
Curtina, Uru. 225/E5
Curtis (riv.), Austl. 158/D4
Curtis (isl.), NZ 160/G8
Curtis, Sp. 52/A1
Curtis, Ar, US 183/H4
Curtis, La, US 183/H4
Curtis (pt.), Md, US 198/B6
Curú Nat'l Wild. Ref., CR 207/E4
Curuá (riv.), Braz. 218/C4
Curuá (isl.), Braz. 218/D2
Curuá (riv.), Braz. 217/H5
Curuá Una (riv.), Braz. 217/H5
Curuçá, Braz. 218/E3
Curuçú (riv.), Braz. 220/D2
Curup, Indo. 101/C3
Cururupu, Braz. 219/E3
Curuzú Cuatiá, Arg. 224/E4
Curvelo, Braz. 222/D3
Curwensville, Pa, US 191/G4
Curwood (mt.), Mi, US 187/K4
Cusco, Peru 220/D4
Cusco (dept.), Peru 220/C4
Cushendall, NI, UK 40/B1
Cusher (riv.), NI, UK 40/B3
Cushet Law (peak), Eng, UK 39/D6
Cushing, Ok, US 183/F3
Cushing, Tx, US 181/G2
Cushman, Ar, US 183/J3
Cusick, Wa, US 174/F3
Cusna (peak), It. 68/D5
Cussava (riv.), Ang. 140/B2
Cusse, Ang. 140/B2
Cusset, Fr. 50/E3
Cusseta, Ga, US 192/E4
Cusseta, Al, US 192/E4
Custer (peak), SD, US 184/C1
Custer, SD, US 184/C2
Custer, Mt, US 175/L4
Custer City, Ok, US 182/E3
Custines, Fr. 61/F6
Custódia, Braz. 219/G5
Cut (hill), Eng, UK 42/C5
Cut and Shoot, Tx, US 181/G2
Cut Bank, Mt, US 175/H3
Cut Bank (cr.), Mt, US 175/H3
Cut Knife, Sk, Can. 175/K1
Cut Off, La, US 194/C3
Cutato, Ang. 140/C2
Cutato, Ang. 140/C2
Cutato (riv.), Ang. 138/D5
Cutchogue, NY, US 199/F2
Cutenda, Ang. 140/B2
Cutervo, Peru 220/B2
Cuthbert, Ga, US 195/F2
Cutler Ridge, Fl, US 195/H5
Cutral-Có, Arg. 226/C3
Cutro, It. 54/E3
Cuttack, India 107/E1
Cutten, Ca, US 176/A3
Cuvelai, Ang. 140/B2
Cuvergnon, Fr. 36/L4
Cuvette (pol. reg.), Congo 138/C3
Cuvier (cape), Austl. 154/B3
Cuvo (riv.), Ang. 140/B1
Cuxac, Fr. 53/G1
Cuxhaven, Ger. 59/F1
Cuyabeno, Ecu. 216/C5
Cuyahoga (riv.), Oh, US 190/F4
Cuyahoga Falls, Oh, US 190/F4
Cuyahoga Valley Nat'l Park, Oh, US 190/F4
Cuyama (riv.), Ca, US 178/B3
Cuyapaipe Ind. Res., Ca, US 178/D4
Cuyo (isls.), Phil. 103/F1
Cuyo, Phil. 100/C3
Cuyo East Passage (chan.), Phil. 100/C3
Cuyo West Passage (chan.), Phil. 100/C3
Cuyocuyo, Peru 220/D4
Cuyuchi, Bol. 221/F4
Cuyuni (riv.), Guy. 217/G3
Cuyuni (riv.), Ven. 217/F3
Cuyuni-Mazaruni (pol. reg.), Guy. 217/F3
Cuzco (ruin), Peru 220/D4
Cwm, Wal, UK 42/C3
Cwmafan, Wal, UK 42/C3
Cwmbran, Wal, UK 42/C3
Cyangugu, Rwa. 139/G3
Cyclades (isls.), Gre. 73/K3
Cymric, Sk, Can. 186/B2
Cynthia, Ab, Can. 174/G1
Cynthiana, Ky, US 192/E1
Cynwyl Elfed, Wal, UK 42/B3
Cypress (hills), Ab, Can. 175/J3
Cypress, Al, US 192/D4
Cypress, Ca, US 196/F8
Cypress (lake), Fl, US 194/N7
Cypress, Tx, US 181/M9
Cypress (cr.), Tx, US 181/M8
Cypress Gardens, Fl, US 194/M8
Cyprus (ctry.) 116/C2
Cyrenaica (reg.), Libya 126/D2
Cyrene (ruin), Libya 126/D1
Cyril, Ok, US 183/E3
Cyrus, Mn, US 187/G5
Cysoing, Fr. 60/C2
Cywyn (riv.), Wal, UK 42/B3
Czaplinek, Pol. 49/J2
Czarna Białostocka, Pol. 49/M2
Czarnków, Pol. 49/J2
Czech Republic (ctry.) 49/H4
Częstochowa, Pol. 49/K3
Człuchów, Pol. 46/G5

D

D'Aguilar (range), Austl. 158/E6
D'Arcachon,Bassin di (lag.), Fr. 50/C4
D'Arcy, BC, Can. 174/C2
D' Ouvéa (lag.), NCal., Fr. 161/V12
D'Urville (isl.), NZ 159/C3
D. F. Malan (Cape Town) (int'l arpt.), SAfr. 142/L10
D.C. (fed. dist.), US 193/J1
Da (riv.), China 90/D5
Da (Black) (riv.), Viet. 98/E4
Da Hinggan (mts.), China 83/M5
Da Hoa, Viet. 106/D4
Da Juh, China 90/C4
Da Lat, Viet. 106/E4
Da Nang, Viet. 106/E2
Da Nang (cape), Viet. 106/E2
Da Qaidam, China 90/D4
Da Te, Myan. 106/B2
Da Xian, China 99/E2
Daaden, Ger. 61/G2
Da'an, China 91/J2
Daba (mts.), China 90/F5
Dabaga, Tanz. 137/A4
Dabai, Nga. 133/G4
Dabajuro, Ven. 216/D2
Dabakala, C.d'Iv. 132/D4
Dabas, Hun. 56/D2
Dabat, Eth. 135/H2
Dabeiba, Col. 216/B3
Dabeibu, China 99/H2
Dabein, Myan. 106/B2
Dabendorf, Ger. 48/Q7
Dabhoi, India 104/B3
Dabie (mts.), China 99/G2
Dabissé Kayati, Gui. 132/B4
Dabo, Fr. 61/G6
Dabob (bay), Wa, US 197/B2
Daboji, China 91/K3
Dabola, Gui. 132/C4
Daborow, Som. 136/D4
Dabou, C.d'Iv. 132/D5
Daboya, Gha. 133/E4
Dabra, India 108/B3
Dąbrowa Białostocka, Pol. 47/K5
Dąbrowa Górnicza, Pol. 49/K3
Dabu, China 99/G3
Dăbuleni, Rom. 57/G4
Dac Sut, Viet. 106/D3
Dac To, Viet. 106/D3
Dacca (Dhaka) (cap.), Bang. 109/H4
Dachang, China 92/L8
Dachang Huizu Zizhixian, China 92/H7
Dachau, Ger. 65/E6
Dacheng, China 99/G2
Dacono, Co, US 184/B3
Dadanawa, Guy. 218/B2
Dade (co.), Fl, US 194/P11
Dade City, Fl, US 194/L7
Dades, Oued (riv.), Mor. 128/D3
Dadeville, Al, US 192/E4
Dadi (cape), Indo. 103/H4
Ḑadnah, UAE 113/G3
Dadong, China 106/E1
Dādra and Nagar Haveli (state), India 104/B4
Dādri, India 110/D5
Dādu, Pak. 113/J3
Dadu (riv.), China 90/E5
Daduru (riv.), SrL. 104/C6
Daen Noi (peak), Thai. 106/B4
Dăeni, Rom. 57/J3
Daet, Phil. 100/C2
Dafang, China 98/E3
Dafanhe, China 93/B1
Dafeng, China 92/E4
Dafna, Isr. 117/D2
Dafu, China 98/D2
Dafu, China 99/H2
Dag, India 104/C3
Daga Medo, Eth. 136/B4
Daga Post, Sudan 135/G3
Dagaio, Eth. 136/B4
Dagana, Sen. 132/B2
Dağardı, Turk. 114/B2
Dağbaşı, Turk. 114/D2
Dagda, Lat. 47/M3
Dage, D.R. Congo 139/E2
Dagestan, Resp., Rus. 77/H4
Dagestanskiye Ogni, Rus. 77/J4
Daggaboersnek (pass), SAfr. 142/D4
Dagger (mtn.), Tx, US 180/C3
Daggett, Mi, US 190/C2
Daglung, China 109/H1
Dagmar Range NP, Austl. 158/B2
Dagneux, Fr. 66/B6
Dagny, Fr. 36/M5
Dagongcha, China 90/D4
Dagu, China 92/H7
Daguan, China 99/E3
Daguan, China 98/D3
D'Aguilar (mt.), Austl. 158/E6
Dagujia, China 93/C1
Daguokui (peak), China 91/K2
Dagupan, Phil. 100/C1
Daguragu Abor. Land, Austl. 152/C4
Dagxoi, China 105/G2
Dagzê (lake), China 111/E5
Dagzhuka, China 109/G1
Dahana (des.), SAr. 83/D7
Dāhānu, India 107/B2
Daharki, Pak. 104/A2
Dahei (riv.), China 92/B2
Daheiding (peak), China 91/K2
Dahekou, China 90/F5
Dahenan, China 92/G7
Dahlak (arch.), Erit. 136/B1
Dahlem, Ger. 61/F3
Dahlem, Ger. 48/Q7
Dahlenburg, Ger. 59/H2
Dahlgren, Il, US 192/C1
Dahlonega, Ga, US 192/F3
Dahmani, Tun. 130/L7
Dahme (riv.), Ger. 49/G3
Dahn, Ger. 61/G5
Dahongliutan, China 111/C4
Dahongqi, China 93/B2
Dahra, Sen. 132/B3
Dahshūr, Egypt 131/C5
Dahshūr (ruin), Egypt 131/C5
Dahūk, Iraq 115/E2
Dahūk (gov.), Iraq 115/E2
Dahuofang (res.), China 92/D2
Dahushan, China 93/B2
Dai (isl.), Indo. 152/C1
Dai (isl.), China 99/J2
Dai (lake), China 92/C2
Dai Loc, Viet. 106/E3
Dai Xian, China 92/C3
Dai-Segen-dake (peak), Japan 94/B3
Dai-sen (peak), Japan 96/C3
Daian, Japan 95/L5
Daicheng, China 92/D3
Daigo, Japan 97/G2
Daik-u, Myan. 106/B2
Dā'il, Syria 117/E3
Dailekh, Nepal 108/C1
Dailly, Sc, UK 39/B6
Daimiao, China 92/D3
Daimiel, Sp. 52/D3
Daingerfield, Tx, US 183/G4
Dainkognubma, China 90/D5
Daintree NP, Austl. 153/G4
Daiō-zaki (pt.), Japan 97/E3
Dāira Dīn Panāh, Pak. 110/A4
Daireaux, Arg. 226/E3
Dairy (cr.), Austl. 155/N8
Dairyland, Wi, US 187/H4
Daisen-Oki NP, Japan 96/C3
Daisetsuzan NP, Japan 94/C2
Daisy, Ok, US 183/G3
Daisy, Ar, US 183/H3
Daisy, Ky, US 193/F2
Daito (isl.), Japan 83/N7
Daitō, Japan 95/J6
Daiyun (peak), China 99/H3
Dajabón, DRep. 207/J2
Dajarra, Austl. 155/H2

280
Dajin – Derha

Dajing, China 105/K3
Dak Nhe, Viet. 106/D3
Dakar (cap.), Sen. 132/A3
Dakar (pol. reg.), Sen. 132/A3
Dakar (Yoff) (int'l arpt.), Sen. 132/A3
Dakeng, China 99/G3
Daketa Shet' (riv.), Eth. 136/B4
Dakhin Shābāzpur (isl.), Bang. 109/H4
Dakhlet Nouadhibou (pol. reg.), Mrta. 128/A5
Dakoro, Niger 133/G3
Dakota (co.), Mn, US 187/P7
Dakota City, Ia, US 185/G2
Dakota City, Ne, US 185/F2
Dakovica, Serb. 56/E4
Dakovo, Cro. 56/D3
Dal (riv.), Swe. 80/B3
Dal Cataract (falls), Sudan 127/F4
Dala, Ang. 138/E5
Dala-Järna, Swe. 46/F1
Dalaas, Aus. 67/F3
Dalaba, Gui. 132/B4
Dalad Qi, China 92/B2
Dalai (lake), China 90/H3
Dalaman, Turk. 114/B2
Dalaman (int'l arpt.), Turk. 114/B2
Dalāmī, Sudan 135/F3
Dalandzadgad, Mong. 90/E3
Dalangwan, China 99/G4
Dalaoba, China 111/D3
Dalarna (reg.), Swe. 44/E3
Dalarö, Swe. 45/B1
Dalatangi (pt.), Ice. 44/Q6
Dalavich, Sc, UK 39/A4
Dalbeattie, Sc, UK 40/E2
Dalby, Austl. 158/C4
Dalby, Swe. 46/E4
Dalby, Swe. 45/K7
Dalby-Söderskog NP, Swe. 45/K7
Dalcross (int'l arpt.), Sc, UK 39/B1
Dale, Nor. 46/A1
Dale, In, US 192/D1
Dale, Tx, US 180/F3
Dale, SC, US 193/G4
Dale City, Va, US 193/J1
Dale Hollow (lake), Tn, US 192/E2
Dalen, Nor. 46/C2
Dalen, Neth. 58/D3
Daleside, SAfr. 142/Q13
Daletme, Myan. 105/F3
Daleville, Al, US 195/F2
Dalfsen, Neth. 58/D3
Dalgan (riv.), Ire. 38/B2
Dalgaranger (mt.), Austl. 154/C3
Dalhart, Tx, US 182/C2
Dalhousie, NB, Can. 188/D1
Dalhousie, India 110/C3
Dalhousie (cape), NW, Can. 170/D1
Dali, China 92/B4
Dali (riv.), China 90/F4
Dali, China 98/D3
Dalian (bay), China 93/A3
Dalian, China 93/A3
Dalian (int'l arpt.), China 92/E3
Daliang, China 90/E4
Dalías, Sp. 52/D4
Daliburgh, Sc, UK 37/Q8
Dalidag (peak), Azer. 115/F2
Daling (riv.), China 91/H3
Dāliyat el Karmil, Isr. 117/C3
Dalizi, China 93/D2
Dalj, Cro. 56/D3
Dalkeith, Sc, UK 39/C5
Dalkola, India 109/F3
Dall (isl.), Ak, US 170/C3
Dall (lake), Ak, US 201/F3
Dallas, Sc, UK 39/C1
Dallas, Ga, US 192/E4
Dallas, Or, US 176/B1
Dallas (co.), Tx, US 180/L7
Dallas, Tx, US 180/L7
Dallas City, Il, US 185/J3
Dallas Love Field (arpt.), Tx, US 180/L7
Dallas-Fort Worth (int'l arpt.), Tx, US 180/K7
Dallastown, Pa, US 198/B4
Dalles of the Saint Croix, Mn, US 187/H5
Dallesport, Wa, US 176/C1
Dallgow, Ger. 48/Q6
Dallol Bosso (riv.), Mali,Niger 133/F3
Dalmally, Sc, UK 39/B4
Dalmatia (reg.), Cro. 73/G1
Dalmatia, Pa, US 198/B2
Dalmatovo, Rus. 75/P4
Dalmellington, Sc, UK 39/B6
Dalmeny, Austl. 157/E3
Dalmine, It. 68/C2
Dal'negorsk, Rus. 91/M3
Dal'nerechensk, Rus. 91/L2
Daloa, C.d'Iv. 132/D5
Dalol, Eth. 136/B2
Dalqū, Sudan 127/F4
Dalroy, Ab, Can. 175/H2
Dalry, Sc, UK 39/B5
Dalrymple, Sc, UK 39/B6
Dalrymple (lake), Austl. 145/D3
Dals Långed, Swe. 46/E2
Dalsingh Sarai, India 109/E3
Dalsjöfors, Swe. 46/E3
Dalton, Ar, US 192/B2
Dalton, Ga, US 192/E3
Dalton, Mn, US 186/G4
Dalton, Ma, US 191/K3
Dalton, Pa, US 191/J4
Dalton-in-Furness, Eng, UK 41/E3
Daltonganj, India 109/E3
Dalu, China 90/E4
Daluābāri, Bang. 109/G3
Daludalu, Indo. 101/C2
Daluo (peak), China 99/G4
Dalupiri (isl.), Phil. 100/C1
Dalvík, Ice. 44/N6
Dalwallinu, Austl. 154/C4
Dalwhinnie, Sc, UK 39/B3
Dalworthington Gardens, Tx, US 180/K7
Daly (bay), Nun, Can. 170/G2
Daly (riv.), Austl. 152/C3
Daly River Wild. Sanct., Austl. 152/C3
Daly River, Austl. 152/C3
Daly River Aboriginal Land, Austl. 152/C3
Daly Waters, Austl. 152/D4
Dalyup, Austl. 154/D5
Dam (riv.), China 111/F5
Dam Doi, Viet. 106/D4
Dam Gamad, Sudan 135/E2
Damagaram Takaya, Niger 133/H3
Damāgheh-ye Kūh (pt.), Iran 115/J5
Damak, Nepal 109/F2
Damān and Diu (state), India 104/B3
Damanhūr, Egypt 131/B2
Damara, CAfr. 134/C4
Damāş, Egypt 131/C3
Damasak, Nga. 134/B2
Damascus, Ar, US 183/H3
Damascus, Ga, US 195/F2
Damascus, Va, US 193/G2
Damascus (int'l arpt.), Syria 117/F2
Damascus, Md, US 198/A5
Damascus (Dimashq) (cap.), Syria 117/E1
Damāţ, Egypt 131/B3
Damaturu, Nga. 134/A3
Damavānd (mtn.), Iran 115/H3
Damāvand, Iran 115/H3
Damaying, China 99/G3
Damba, Ang. 138/C4
Dambach-la-Ville, Fr. 66/D1
Dambaslar, Turk. 57/H5
Dāmbuk, India 98/B2
Dame Marie (cape), Haiti 207/H2
Dame Marie, Haiti 207/H2
Damenglong, China 106/C1
Damerham, Eng, UK 43/E5
Dameron, Md, US 193/J1
Dāmghān, Iran 115/H2
Damietta (Dumyāţ) (mouth), Egypt 131/C1
Damietta Branch (riv.), Egypt 116/B4
Damigny, Fr. 63/F4
Daming (mtn.), China 99/F4
Daming, China 99/G3
Daming, China 92/C3
Damintun, China 93/B2
Damion (peak), Fr. 61/D4
Dāmiyā, Jor. 117/D4
Dammard, Fr. 36/M4
Dammartin-en-Goële, Fr. 36/L4
Dammastock (peak), Swi. 67/E4
Damme, Belg. 60/C1
Damme, Ger. 59/F3
Dāmodar (riv.), India 104/E3
Damoh, India 108/B4
Damon, Tx, US 181/M9
Damongo, Gha. 133/E4
Damparis, Fr. 66/B3
Dampier, Austl. 154/C2
Dampier (str.), Indo. 103/H4
Dampier (arch.), Austl. 145/A2
Dampier Downs, Austl. 152/A4
Dampierre, Fr. 66/B3
Dampierre, Fr. 36/H5
Dampierre-sur-Salon, Fr. 66/B2
Damprichard, Fr. 66/C3
Damqawt, Yem. 112/F5
Damqog (Maquan) (riv.), China 108/E1
Damrei (mts.), Camb. 106/C4
Damsterdiep (riv.), Neth. 58/D2
Damvant, Swi. 66/C3
Damville, Fr. 63/G3
Damwoude, Neth. 58/D2
Damxung, China 111/F5
Dan (riv.), China 90/G5
Dan, Isr. 117/D2
Dan (riv.), NC, US 192/H2
Dan Gulbi, Nga. 133/G4
Dan Sai, Thai. 106/C2
Dan Xian, China 99/F5
Ḑānā, Jor. 116/D4
Dana, In, US 190/C5
Dāna, Nepal 108/D1
Dana Point, Ca, US 196/C4
Danakil (reg.), Djib. 136/B3
Danané, C.d'Iv. 132/C5
Danao, Phil. 100/D3
Danba, China 98/D2
Danbury, Eng, UK 43/G3
Danbury, Ct, US 191/K4
Danbury, NC, US 193/G2
Danbury, Tx, US 180/G3
Danby, Vt, US 191/K3
Danby (lake), Ca, US 178/E3
Dancheng, China 92/C4
Dancing (pt.), Mb, Can. 186/E1
Dandaragan, Austl. 154/B4
Dande (riv.), Ang. 138/C5
Dandeldhurā, Nepal 108/C1
Dandenaong (cr.), Austl. 156/G5
Dandenong (nbrhd.), Austl. 156/G5
Dandenong (mt.), Austl. 156/G5
Danderhall, Sc, UK 39/C5
Dandīl, Egypt 131/C6
Dando, Ang. 140/C1
Dandong, China 93/C2
Dandridge, Tn, US 193/F2
Dane (riv.), Eng, UK 41/F5
Dang (riv.), China 90/D4
Dangal, Erit. 136/B2
Dangara, Taj. 111/A4
Dangayos (pt.), Phil. 99/J5
Dange, Nga. 133/G3
Dange, Ang. 138/C4
Dange-ia-Menha, Ang. 138/C5
Danger (pt.), SAfr. 142/L11
Danggali Conservation Park, Austl. 156/B2
Dangila, Eth. 135/H3
Dangkou, China 92/L8
Dangme (riv.), Bhu. 98/A3
Dangriga, Belz. 206/D2
Dangshan, China 92/D4
Dangtu, China 92/D5
Dangur, Eth. 135/H3
Dangyang, China 99/F2
Dania, Fl, US 194/P10
Danieb (riv.), Namb. 140/D4
Danielskuil, SAfr. 142/C3
Danielsville, Ga, US 193/F3
Danielsville, Pa, US 198/C2
Danilov, Rus. 74/J4
Daning, China 92/B3
Danjiangkou, China 92/B4
Danjiangkou (res.), China 90/G5
Danjoutin, Fr. 66/C2
Ḑank, Oman 113/G4
Dankaur, India 110/D5
Dankhar Gompa, India 113/L2
Dankov, Rus. 76/F1
Dankova (peak), Kyr. 111/C3
Danleng, China 98/D2
Danlí, Hon. 206/E3
Dannelly (res.), Al, US 192/D4
Dannemora, Swe. 46/G1
Dannemora, NY, US 191/K2
Dannenberg, Ger. 48/F2
Dannes, Fr. 60/A2
Dannevirke, NZ 159/D3
Dannhauser, SAfr. 143/E3
Dano, Burk. 132/E4
Dansville, NY, US 191/H3
Dantzler, Ms, US 194/D2
Danube (riv.), Eur. 29/G4
Danube (Donau) (riv.), Aus.,Ger. 67/E1
Danube, Delta of the (delta), Rom.,Ukr. 73/L1
Danube, Mouths of the (mouth), Rom.,Ukr. 76/D3
Danville, Qu, Can. 191/K2
Danville, Ar, US 183/H3
Danville, Il, US 190/C4
Danville, In, US 190/C5
Danville, Ky, US 192/E2
Danvers, Mt, US 175/K4
Danville, Oh, US 190/E4
Danville, Pa, US 198/B2
Danville, Va, US 193/H2
Danville, Vt, US 191/K2
Danville, Wa, US 174/E3
Dao, Phil. 100/C3
Dao Xian, China 99/F3
Daocheng, China 98/D2
Daodou'ao, China 99/J2
Daora, WSah. 128/B4
Daoshui, China 99/F4
D'Aosta (valley), It. 68/A1
Daotiandi, China 91/L2
Daoukro, C.d'Iv. 132/E5
Daoulas, Fr. 62/A4
Daoura, Oued ed (riv.), Alg. 128/D3
Daozhen, China 99/E2
Dapa, Phil. 100/D3
Dapaong, Togo 133/F4
Daphne, Al, US 194/E2
Dapingying, China 99/F2
Dapitan, Phil. 100/C3
Dapo, China 106/E2
Dapuzi, China 99/F3
Daqiao, China 98/D4
Daqiao, China 99/H3
Daqing, China 91/K2
Daqing (riv.), China 92/H7
Daqiu, China 99/H3
Daqu (isl.), China 99/J2
Daquanwan, China 90/C3
Dār al Bayḑā (ruin), Egypt 131/C4
Dār 'Aqīl, Sudan 135/G2
Dar Bel Hamri, Mor. 130/B2
Dar el Barka, Mrta. 132/B2
Dar es Salaam (prov.), Tanz. 137/B3
Dar es Salaam (int'l arpt.), Tanz. 137/B3
Dar es Salaam (cap.), Tanz. 137/B3
Dar Rounga (reg.), CAfr. 134/D3
Dar-e Rūd, Iran 115/J4
Dar-el-Beida (Casablanca), Mor. 128/D2
Dar'ā, Syria 117/E3
Dar'ā (prov.), Syria 117/E3
Dārāb, Iran 115/H4
Darāban, Pak. 110/A4
Darabani, Rom. 78/D3
Daraga, Phil. 100/C2
Daragodleh, Som. 136/C3
Darai (hills), PNG 153/F1
Daram, Phil. 100/D3
Dārān, Iran 115/G3
Darasun, Rus. 90/G1
Đaravica (peak), Serb. 56/E4
Dārayyā, Syria 117/E2
Darbatta, Eth. 135/G4
Darbėnai, Lith. 47/J3
Darbhanga, India 109/E2
Darby, Austl. 157/C4
Darby (cape), Ak, US 201/F3
Darby, Fl, US 194/L7
Darby, Mt, US 175/G4
Darby, Pa, US 198/C4
Darda, Cro. 56/D3
Dardanelle, Ar, US 183/H3
Dardanelle (dam), Ar, US 183/H3
Dardanelles (str.), Turk. 76/C4
Darebin (cr.), Austl. 156/G5
Darent (riv.), Eng, UK 36/D3
Dareton, Austl. 156/B2
Darfield, BC, Can. 174/D2
Darfo, It. 67/G6
Dārfūr (pol. reg.), Sudan 127/E5
Dargai, Pak. 110/A2
Dargaville, NZ 159/C1
Argentière, Aiguille d' (peak), Swi. 66/D6
Dargle (riv.), Ire. 40/B5
Dargo (riv.), Austl. 157/C3
D'Arguin (bay), Mrta. 132/A1
Darhan (peak), Mong. 90/F2
Darhan, Mong. 90/F2
Darhan Muminggan Lianheqi, China 90/G3
Darie (hills), Som. 136/C3
Darién (mts.), Pan. 207/G4
Darien, Ct, US 199/M7
Darien, Ga, US 195/H2
Darien, Il, US 197/P16
Darién, PN, Pan. 203/F6
Darjazīn, Iran 115/G3
Darjiling, India 109/G2
Darkan, Austl. 154/C5
Darlag, China 90/D5
Darling (lake), ND, US 186/D3
Darling, SAfr. 142/L10
Darling (mtn.), Austl. 157/D2
Darling (range), Austl. 145/A4
Darling (riv.), Austl. 145/D4
Darling Downs (range), Austl. 158/C3
Darling Downs (reg.), Austl. 145/D3
Darling Nat'l Wild. Ref., Fl, US 195/G4
Darlington, Eng, UK 41/G2
Darlington (co.), Eng, UK 41/G2
Darlington, In, US 190/C4
Darlington, Wi, US 185/J2
Darlington, SC, US 193/H3
Darlington, Md, US 198/B4
Darlington Point, Austl. 157/C2
D'Armainvilliers (pond), Fr. 36/L5
Darmstadt, Ger. 64/B3
Darmstadt, In, US 192/D1
Darnah, Libya 126/D1
Darnāyah, Tun. 130/L7
Darnétal, Fr. 63/G2
Darney, Fr. 66/C1
Darnick, Austl. 156/B2
Darnley (cape), Ant. 228/E
Darnley (bay), NW, Can. 170/D2
Daroca, Sp. 52/E2
Darongjiang, China 99/F3
Darongtang, China 99/F2
Darras Hall, Eng, UK 41/G1
Darregueira, Arg. 226/E3
Darreh Gaz, Iran 113/G1
Darreh-ye Shahr, Iran 115/F3
Darrington, Wa, US 174/D3
Dārsana, Bang. 109/G4
Darsser (cape), Ger. 46/E4
Dart (riv.), Eng, UK 42/C6
Dart, West (riv.), Eng, UK 42/C6
Dartford, Eng, UK 36/D2
Dartington, Eng, UK 42/C6
Dartmoor (upland), Eng, UK 42/B5
Dartmoor NP, Eng, UK 50/A1
Dartmouth (dam), Austl. 157/C3
Dartmouth, NS, Can. 188/F3
Dartmouth, Eng, UK 42/C6
Dartmouth, Ma, US 191/L4
Darton, Eng, UK 41/G4
Dartowo, Pol. 46/G4
Dartuch (cape), Sp. 53/G3
Daru, SLeo. 132/C5
Daru, PNG 153/F2
Daruba, Indo. 103/G3
Daruvar, Cro. 56/C3
Darvel, Sc, UK 39/B5
Darvel (bay), Malay. 103/E3
Darwen, Eng, UK 41/F4
Darwendale, Zim. 141/F3
Darwin, Austl. 152/C3
Darwin (int'l arpt.), Austl. 152/C3
Darwin, Ca, US 178/D2
Darwin (bay), Chile 226/B5
Darwin (isl.), Ecu. 220/J6
Darwin (vol.), Ecu. 220/J7
Darya Khan, Pak. 110/A4
Daryābād, India 108/C2
Dārzīn, Iran 113/G3
Dashahe, China 91/K3
Dashanzui, China 91/K3
Dashengtang (peak), China 91/H3
Dashennongjia (peak), China 92/B5
Dasher, Ga, US 195/G2
Dashhowuz, Trkm. 80/F5
Dashi, China 99/H2
Dashowuz (prov.), Trkm. 77/L4
Dasht Kaur (riv.), Pak. 113/H3
Dasht-e Kavīr (des.), Iran 80/F6
Dasht-e Lūt (des.), Iran 80/F6
Dasht-e Mārgow (des.), Afg. 113/H2
Dasima, Gha. 133/E4
Dasing, Ger. 64/E6
Daska, Pak. 110/C3
Daspalla, India 107/E1
Dassa-Zoumé, Ben. 133/F5
Dassel, Ger. 59/G5
Dassel, Mn, US 185/G1
Dassendorf, Ger. 59/H1
Dasseneiland (isl.), SAfr. 142/B4
Dasūya, India 110/C4
Dat Do, Viet. 106/D4
Datadian, Indo. 102/E3
Dātāganj, India 108/B1
Datchet, Eng, UK 36/B2
Date, Japan 94/B2
Dateland, Az, US 179/F4
Datia, India 108/B3
Datian (peak), China 99/F4
Datil, NM, US 179/J3
Datong, China 92/C2
Datong, China 90/E4
Datong, China 90/G3
Datong (mts.), China 90/D4
Datong (riv.), China 90/D4
Datteln, Ger. 59/E5
Dattohar, India 110/B5
Datu (cape), Indo.,Malay. 102/C3
Datuk (cape), Indo. 101/C2
Dāud Khel, Pak. 110/A3
Daugai, Lith. 47/L4
Daugava (riv.), Lat. 80/C4
Daugavpils, Lat. 47/M4
Daugherty Field (Long Beach) (arpt.), Ca, US 196/F8
Daulatpur, Bang. 109/G4
Daule (riv.), Ecu. 216/B5
Daule, Ecu. 216/B5
Daun, Ger. 61/F3
Daung (isl.), Myan. 106/B3
Dauphin, Mb, Can. 186/D2
Dauphin (riv.), Mb, Can. 186/E2
Dauphin (lake), Mb, Can. 186/E2
Dauphin (cape), NS, Can. 189/G2
Dauphin (co.), Pa, US 198/B3
Dauphin, Pa, US 198/B3
Dauphin Island, Al, US 194/D2
Dauphine (reg.), Fr. 72/E1
Dauphiné (range), Fr. 50/F4
Daura, Nga. 133/H3
Däväçi, Azer. 77/J4
Davao, Phil. 100/D4
Davao (gulf), Phil. 100/D4
Dāvarzan, Iran 115/J2
Davegoriale, Som. 136/C3
Davel, SAfr. 143/E2
Daveluyville, Qu, Can. 191/K1
Davenda, Rus. 91/H1
Davenport, ND, US 186/F4
Davenport, Ok, US 183/F3
Davenport, Fl, US 194/M7
Davenport, Ia, US 185/J3
Davenport, Ne, US 184/F3
Davenport (range), Austl. 152/D5
Davenport (mt.), Austl. 155/F2
Davenport, Wa, US 174/E4
Daventry, Eng, UK 43/E2
Daverdisse, Belg. 61/E3
Daveyton, SAfr. 142/E2
Davézieux, Fr. 70/A2
Davgaard-Jensen Land (phys. reg.), Grld. 171/T6
David, Pan. 207/F4
David City, Ne, US 185/F3
David-Gorodok, Bela. 78/D1
Davidson, Ar, US 183/G3
Davidson, Ok, US 182/E3
Davidson (mt.), Ca, US 197/J11
Davidson, Sk, Can. 175/M2
Davidson, NC, US 193/G3
Davie, Fl, US 194/P10
Davies (mt.), Austl. 155/F3
Davilla, Tx, US 181/F2
Daviot, Sc, UK 39/D2
Davis (sea), Ant. 228/F
Davis, Austl., Ant. 228/F
Davis (str.), Can.,Grld. 171/L2
Davis, Sk, Can. 175/M1
Davis (dam), Az, US 178/E3
Davis, Ca, US 176/C4
Davis (cr.), Mi, US 197/E7
Davis, Ok, US 183/F3
Davis (mt.), Pa, US 191/G5
Davis (mts.), Tx, US 172/F5
Davis, WV, US 193/H1
Davis Cove, Nf, Can. 189/K2
Davis Creek, Ca, US 176/C3
Davis Dam, Az, US 178/E3
Davis-Monthan (A.F.B.), Az, US 179/G4
Davisboro, Ga, US 193/F4
Davison, Mi, US 190/E3
Davisville, Mo, US 192/B2
Davlekanovo, Rus. 75/M5
Davo (riv.), C.d'Iv. 132/D5
Davos, Swi. 67/F4
Dawa, China 93/B2
Dawa Wenz (riv.), Eth. 136/B4
Dawan, China 99/F4
Dawangja (isl.), China 93/B3
Dawaxung, China 111/E5
Dawei (Tavoy), Myan. 106/B3
Dawen (riv.), China 90/H4
Dawlish, Eng, UK 42/C5
Dawqah, SAr. 112/D5
Dawson (riv.), Austl. 145/D3
Dawson (mt.), BC, Can. 174/F2
Dawson, Yk, Can. 201/L3
Dawson (isl.), Chile 227/C7
Dawson, Ga, US 195/F2
Dawson, Mo, US 183/H2
Dawson, Mn, US 185/F1
Dawson, Tx, US 181/F2
Dawson Creek, BC, Can. 170/D3
Dawson Springs, Ky, US 192/D2
Dawsonville, Ga, US 192/E3
Dawu, China 98/D2
Dawu, China 92/C5
Dawu (mtn.), China 92/C5
Dawujiang, China 99/E3
Dax, Fr. 50/C5
Daxin, China 106/D1
Daxing, China 99/F3
Daxing, China 92/H7
Daxue (mts.), China 90/E5
Day Star Ind. Res., Sk, Can. 186/B2
Dayang (riv.), China 93/B2
Dayang, China 99/F4
Dayang Bunting (isl.), Thai. 101/B1
Dayao, China 98/D3
Daye, China 99/G2
Dayi, China 98/D2
Daying, China 93/D1
Daying (riv.), China 105/G3
Daylesford, Austl. 157/B3
Daylight (pass), Ca, US 178/D2
Daym Zubayr, Sudan 135/E4
Daymán (riv.), Uru. 225/E4
Dayong, China 99/F3
Dayong, China 99/F2
Dayr Abū Sa'īd, Jor. 117/D3
Dayr al Balaḩ, Gaza 117/A6
Dayr al Ghuşūn, WBnk. 117/C4
Dayr al Qamar, Leb. 117/D1
Dayr 'Allā, Jor. 117/D4
Dayr az Zawr, Syria 114/E3
Dayr Az Zawr (prov.), Syria 114/D3
Dayr Ballūţ, WBnk. 117/C4
Dayr Dibwān, WBnk. 117/C5
Dayr Sharaf, WBnk. 117/C4
Dayrūt, Egypt 127/F3
Dayrūţ, Egypt 131/B2
Daysland, Ab, Can. 175/H1
Dayton, Ia, US 185/G2
Dayton, In, US 190/C4
Dayton, NJ, US 198/D3
Dayton, NY, US 191/G3
Dayton, Oh, US 190/D5
Dayton, Or, US 176/B1
Dayton, Tn, US 192/E3
Dayton, Tx, US 181/N8
Dayton, Va, US 193/H1
Dayton, Wa, US 174/F4
Dayton, Wy, US 177/K1
Daytona Beach, Fl, US 195/H3
Dayu (isl.), China 99/J3
Dayu, China 99/G3
Dayuan, China 99/J2
Dayushupu, China 93/A2
Dazey, ND, US 186/E4
Dazhengjiatun, China 93/B3
Dazhizhu Dau (isl.), China 99/K8
Dazhu, China 99/E2
De Aar, SAfr. 142/D3
De Bary, Fl, US 195/H3
De Berry, Tx, US 181/G1
De Bilt, Neth. 58/C4
De Cocksdorp, Neth. 58/B2
De Cordova Bend (dam), Tx, US 181/F1
De Doorns, SAfr. 142/L10
De Forest, Wi, US 185/K2
De Funiak Springs, Fl, US 195/E2
De Gaulle, CAfr. 134/B4
De Graff, Oh, US 190/E4
De Grey, Austl. 154/C2
De Grey (riv.), Austl. 152/A5
De Gray (lake), Ar, US 183/H3
De Haan, Belg. 60/C1
De Hart (res.), Pa, US 198/B3
De Hoge Veluwe, NP, Neth. 58/C4
De Jongs (cape), Indo. 153/E1
De Kalb (co.), Il, US 197/N16
De Kalb, Il, US 185/K3
De Kalb, Ms, US 192/C4
De Koog, Neth. 58/B2
De La Vassako-Bolo, Rsv. Nat. Int., CAfr. 134/C3
De Lacs (riv.), ND, US 186/D3
De Land, Fl, US 195/H3
De Las Ánimas (pt.), Mex. 204/B2
De Leijen (lake), Neth. 58/D2
De Leon (lake), Fr. 50/C4
De Leon, Tx, US 180/E1
De Lier, Neth. 58/B5
Délįne, NW, Can. 170/D2
De Luz, Ca, US 196/C4
De Meern, Neth. 58/C4
De Motte (Demotte), In, US 190/C4
De Panne, Belg. 60/B1
De Peel (phys. reg.), Neth. 58/C6
De Pere, Wi, US 190/B2
De Pinte, Belg. 60/C2
De Pue, Il, US 185/K3
De Queen, Ar, US 183/G3
De Quincy, La, US 194/B2
De Ridder, La, US 194/B2
De Smet, SD, US 184/F1
De Soto, Ga, US 195/F2
De Soto, Il, US 192/C2
De Soto, Mo, US 192/B1
De Soto, Ms, US 194/D2
De Tour Village, Mi, US 190/E2
De Valls Bluff, Ar, US 183/J3
De Wijk, Neth. 58/D3
De Winton, Ab, Can. 175/G2
De Witt, Ar, US 183/J3
De Witt, Ia, US 185/J3
De Witt, Ne, US 185/F3
De Witt, NY, US 191/H3
Dead (riv.), Ire. 38/B4
Dead (sea), Isr.,Jor. 117/C5
Dead (lake), Fl, US 195/F2
Deadhorse, Ak, US 201/J1
Deadman (peak), Austl. 154/C2
Deadman (mtn.), Wy, US 177/H2
Deadwood, SD, US 184/C1
Deal (isl.), Austl. 156/C3
Deal, NJ, US 199/D3
Deal Island, Md, US 193/K1
Deale, Md, US 198/B6
Dean (for.), Eng, UK 42/D3
Dean (riv.), BC, Can. 174/B1
Deán Funes, Arg. 224/C4
Deanmill, Austl. 154/C5
Deanville, Tx, US 180/F2
Dearborn, Mi, US 190/E3
Dearborn, Mo, US 185/G4
Dearborn Heights, Mi, US 197/F7
Dearing, Ga, US 193/F4
Dearne, Eng, UK 41/G4
Deary, Id, US 174/F4
Dease (riv.), BC, Can. 170/D3
Dease (str.), Nun, Can. 163/F3
Dease Lake, BC, Can. 201/M4
Death (valley), Ca, US 178/D2
Death Valley, Ca, US 178/D2
Death Valley NP, Ca,Nv, US 178/D2
Deauville, Fr. 63/F2
Deavgay (peak), Rus. 115/F1
Deba Habe, Nga. 134/A3
Debagrām, India 109/G4
Debar, FYROM 55/G2
Debark', Eth. 135/H2
Debauch (mt.), Ak, US 201/G3
Debaysīma, Erit. 136/B2
Debden, Sk, Can. 175/L1
Debelets, Bul. 57/G4
Deben (riv.), Eng, UK 43/H2
Debenham, Eng, UK 43/H2
Debert, NS, Can. 188/F3
Dębica, Pol. 49/L3
Debīdwār, Bang. 109/H4
Dęblin, Pol. 49/L3
Dębno, Pol. 49/H2
Deborah (mt.), Ak, US 201/J3
Debre Birhan, Eth. 136/A3
Debre Lībanos Monastery, Eth. 136/A3
Debre Mark'os, Eth. 135/H3
Debre Sīna, Eth. 136/A3
Debre Tabor, Eth. 135/H3
Debre Zebīt, Eth. 136/A3
Debre Zeyit, Eth. 136/A3
Debre Zeyit, Eth. 135/G3
Debrecen, Hun. 49/L5
Debub, Eth. 136/A2
Debundscha (pt.), Camr. 138/B1
DeBurgh (lake), Austl. 153/D4
Decatur, Al, US 192/D3
Decatur, Ga, US 193/M7
Decatur, Il, US 185/K4
Decatur, In, US 190/D4
Decatur, Mi, US 190/D3
Decatur, Ms, US 192/C4
Decatur, Tn, US 192/E3
Decatur, Tx, US 180/K6
Decaturville, Tn, US 192/C3
Decazeville, Fr. 50/E4
Deccan (plat.), India 104/C5
Dechang, China 98/D3
Dechheling, Bhu. 109/H2
Decima, It. 69/E4
Děčín, Czh. 49/H3
Décines-Charpieu, Fr. 66/A6
Decize, Fr. 50/E3
Decker, Mt, US 177/K1
Deckers, Co, US 182/B1
Deckerville, Mi, US 190/E3
Decorah, Ia, US 185/J2
Deddington, Eng, UK 43/E3
Dedemsvaart, Neth. 58/D3
Deder, Eth. 136/B3
Dedham, Ma, US 191/L3
Dedo (peak), Arg. 226/C5
Dédougou, Burk. 132/E3
Dedovichi, Rus. 47/N3
Dedovsk, Rus. 75/W9
Dedu, China 91/K2
Dedza, Malw. 141/G2
Dee (riv.), Sc, UK 39/C3
Dee Why (nbrhd.), Austl. 158/H8
Deel (riv.), Ire. 40/A4
Deep (cr.), Austl. 155/M8
Deep (cr.), De, US 198/C6
Deep (riv.), NC, US 193/H3
Deep Brook, NS, Can. 188/E3
Deep Creek Ind. Res., BC, Can. 174/C1
Deep Fork (riv.), Ok, US 183/F3
Deep Red (cr.), Ok, US 183/E3
Deep River, On, Can. 191/H1
Deep Springs, Ca, US 178/D2
Deepcut, Eng, UK 36/F3
Deeping Saint James, Eng, UK 43/F1
Deepwater, Mo, US 183/H1
Deepwater, Austl. 156/D1
Deepwater (pt.), De, US 198/C5
Deepwater, NJ, US 198/C4
Deer (isl.), Mb, Can. 186/F2
Deer (isl.), Ire. 38/A4
Deer (isl.), Ak, US 201/F5
Deer (cr.), Ms, US 183/J4
Deer Flat NWR, Id, US 176/E2
Deer Island, Or, US 174/C5
Deer Lake, On, Can. 187/G1
Deer Lake, Nf, Can. 189/J1
Deer Lake, Pa, US 198/B2
Deer Lodge, Mt, US 175/H4
Deer Park, Ca, US 176/B4
Deer Park, Il, US 197/P15
Deer Park, Md, US 198/B5
Deer Park, NY, US 199/E2
Deer Park, Tx, US 181/M9
Deer Park, Wa, US 174/F4
Deer River, Mn, US 187/H4
Deerbrook, Wi, US 187/K5
Deerfield, Ma, US 191/K3
Deerfield, Il, US 197/P15
Deerfield Beach, Fl, US 194/P10
Deering, Ak, US 201/F2
Deering, ND, US 186/D3
Deerlijk, Belg. 60/C2
Deerton, Mi, US 187/L4
Deerwood, Mn, US 187/H4
Deesa, India 113/K4
Deeside (valley), Sc, UK 39/D2
Deex Nugaaleed (riv.), Som. 136/C3
Defensores del Chaco, PN, Par. 224/D2
Defiance, Oh, US 190/D4
Deganwy, Wal, UK 40/E5
Dêgê, China 98/C2
Degeberga, Swe. 45/L7
Degeh Bur, Eth. 136/B3
Dégelis, Qu, Can. 188/C2
Degema, Nga. 133/G5
Degerfors, Swe. 46/F2
Degersheim, Swi. 67/F3
Deggendorf, Ger. 65/F5
Deggingen, Ger. 64/C5
Dego, It. 68/B5
Degoma, Eth. 135/H2
DeGrey (riv.), Austl. 154/C2
Dëgtevo, Rus. 79/L3
Deh Bīd, Iran 115/H4
Deh Dasht, Iran 115/G4
Deh-e Shīr, Iran 115/H4
Dehaj, Iran 115/H4
Dehalak (isl.), Erit. 136/A2
Dehalak Marine NP, Erit. 136/B2
Dehāqān, Iran 115/G4
Dehdez, Iran 115/G4
Deheq, Iran 115/G3
Dehlorān, Iran 115/F3
Dehri, India 109/E3
Dehua, China 99/H3
Dehui, China 91/K3
Deidesheim, Ger. 64/B4
Deil, Neth. 58/C5
Deinste, Ger. 59/G1
Deinze, Belg. 60/C2
Deister (mts.), Ger. 59/G4
Deiva Marina, It. 68/C5
Dej, Rom. 57/F2
Deje, Swe. 46/E2
Dejiang, China 99/F2
Dejima, Japan 95/E1
Dekalb (co.), Ga, US 193/M7
Dekelia (arpt.), Gre. 55/N8
Dekemhare (Dek'emhāre), Erit. 136/A2
Dek'emhāre (Dekemhare), Erit. 136/A2
Dekese, D.R. Congo 139/E3
Dekina, Nga. 133/G5
Dekle Beach, Fl, US 195/G3
Dékoa, CAfr. 134/C4
Del Campillo, Arg. 226/D2
Del Carril, Arg. 227/J11
Del Dios, Ca, US 196/C4
Del Gran Paradiso, It. 68/A2
Del Mar, Ca, US 196/C5
Del Norte, Co, US 179/J2
Del Puerte (cr.), Ca, US 197/M12
Del Rio, Tx, US 180/D3
Del Valle, Arg. 226/E2
Del Valle (lake), Ca, US 197/L11
Del Vallo Mazara (valley), It. 54/C4
Delacour, Ab, Can. 175/H2
Delacroix, La, US 194/D3
Delafield, Wi, US 197/P13
Delamar (lake), Nv, US 178/E2
Delano, Ca, US 178/C3
Delano, Mn, US 187/N6
Delano (peak), Ut, US 179/F1
Delareyville, SAfr. 142/D2
Delavan (lake), Wi, US 197/P14
Delavan, Il, US 185/K3
Delavan, Wi, US 185/K2
Delavan Lake, Wi, US 197/N14
Delaware (state), US 173/L4
Delaware (bay), US 193/K1
Delaware (riv.), US 191/J4
Delaware (riv.), Ks, US 185/G4
Delaware, NJ, US 198/C2
Delaware, Oh, US 190/E4
Delaware, Ok, US 183/G2
Delaware (co.), Pa, US 198/C4
Delaware (pass), Pa, US 198/C2
Delaware (mts.), Tx, US 180/B2
Delaware City, De, US 198/C4
Delaware Water Gap Nat'l Rec. Area, NJ,Pa, US 191/J4
Delbrück, Ger. 59/F5
Delburne, Ab, Can. 175/H1
Delčevo, FYROM 55/H2
Delcommune (lake), D.R. Congo 139/F5
Delden, Neth. 58/D4
Delebio, It. 67/F5
Delegate, Austl. 157/D3
Delémont, Swi. 66/D3
Delevan NWR, Ca, US 176/B4
Delft, Neth. 58/B4
Delfzijl, Neth. 58/D2
Delgada (pt.), Ca, US 176/A3
Delgada (pt.), Arg. 226/E4
Delgado (cape), Moz. 137/C4
Delgany, Ire. 40/B5
Delger (riv.), Mong. 90/D2
Delgī, Eth. 135/H2
Delhi, Ca, US 178/B2
Delhi, India 110/D5
Delhi, NY, US 191/J3
Delhi (state), India 104/C2
Déli, Chad 134/B3
Delia, Ab, Can. 175/H2
Delice, Turk. 114/C2
Delice (riv.), Turk. 76/E5
Délices, FrG. 218/C1
Delight, Ar, US 183/H3
Delījān, Iran 115/G3
Delingha, China 90/D4
Delisle, Qu, Can. 188/B1
Delisle, Sk, Can. 175/L2
Dell, Mt, US 177/G1
Dell City, Tx, US 180/B2
Dell Rapids, SD, US 185/F2
Delligsen, Ger. 59/G5
Dellwood, Mn, US 187/Q6
Dellys, Alg. 130/G4
Delmar, De, US 193/K1
Delmas, Sk, Can. 175/K1
Delmas, SAfr. 142/Q13
Delme (riv.), Ger. 59/F3
Delmenhorst, Ger. 59/F2
Delmiro Gouveia, Braz. 219/G5
Delmita, Tx, US 181/E4
Delmont, NJ, US 198/D5
Delnice, Cro. 51/L4
Deloraine, Mb, Can. 186/D3
Deloraine, Austl. 156/C4
Delphi, In, US 190/C4
Delphi (Dhelfoí) (ruin), Gre. 55/H3
Delphos, Oh, US 190/D4
Delphos, Ks, US 184/F4
Delportshoop, SAfr. 142/D3
Delran, NJ, US 198/D3
Delray Beach, Fl, US 194/P10
Delson, Qu, Can. 189/N7
Delta (state), Nga. 133/G5
Delta, Co, US 179/H1
Delta, Pa, US 198/B4
Delta, Ut, US 177/G4
Delta City, Ms, US 192/B4
Delta del Tigre, Uru. 227/K11
Delta du Saloum, PN du, Sen. 132/A3
Delta Junction, Ak, US 201/J3
Delta Nat'l Wild. Ref., La, US 194/D3
Delta-Mendota (canal), Ca, US 197/M11
Delton, Mi, US 190/D3
Deltona, Fl, US 195/H3
Delvin, Ire. 38/C2
Delvinë, Alb. 55/G3
Delyatyn, Ukr. 78/C3
Dëma (riv.), Rus. 75/M5
Demak, Indo. 101/E4
Demanda (range), Sp. 52/D1
Demarcation (pt.), Ak, US 201/K2
Demarest, NJ, US 199/K8
Demba, D.R. Congo 139/E4
Dembech'a, Eth. 135/H3
Dembeni, May., Fr. 143/H6
Dembī, Eth. 135/H3
Dembī Dolo, Eth. 135/G3
Dembia, CAfr. 134/E4
Demer (riv.), Belg. 48/C3
Demerara (riv.), Guy. 217/G3
Demerara-Mahaica (pol. reg.), Guy. 217/G3
Demerval Lobão, Braz. 219/F4
Deming, NM, US 179/J4
Demini (riv.), Braz. 217/F4
Demirci, Turk. 114/B2
Demirkent, Turk. 114/C2
Demirköy, Turk. 57/H5
Demirtaş, Turk. 57/J5
Demmin, Ger. 46/E5
Democratic Republic of the Congo (ctry.) 119/E5
Demone (valley), It. 54/D4
Demonte, It. 70/D4
Demopolis, Al, US 192/D4
Demotte (De Motte), In, US 190/C4
Dempo (peak), Indo. 101/C4
Dempster (pt.), Austl. 154/D5
Demta, Indo. 103/K4
Demuryne, Ukr. 79/J3
Den Burg, Neth. 58/B2
Den Chai, Thai. 106/C2
Den Ham, Neth. 58/D4
Den Helder, Neth. 58/B3
Den Oever, Neth. 58/C3
Denain, Fr. 60/C3
Denair, Ca, US 178/B2
Denakil (reg.), Eth. 112/D6
Denali National Park and Preserve, Ak, US 201/H3
Denan, Eth. 136/B4
Denbigh, On, Can. 191/H2
Denbigh, Wal, UK 41/E5
Denbighshire (co.), Wal, UK 41/E5
Denby Dale, Eng, UK 41/G4
Dendâra, Mrta. 132/D2
Dender (riv.), Belg. 48/B3
Denderleeuw, Belg. 61/D2
Dendermonde, Belg. 61/D1
Dendron, SAfr. 141/F4
Denekamp, Neth. 58/E4
Deng Xian, China 92/C4
Dengfeng, China 92/C4
Dengjiatang, China 99/G3
Dengkou, China 90/F3
Dêngqên, China 98/B2
Dengta, China 99/G3
Denguéno, CAfr. 134/C4
Denham, Eng, UK 36/B2
Denham (sound), Austl. 154/B3
Denham, Austl. 154/B3
Denholme, Eng, UK 41/G4
Denia, Sp. 53/F3
Deniliquin, Austl. 157/B2
Denio, Nv, US 176/D3
Denison (mt.), Ak, US 201/H4
Denison (dam), Ok, US 183/F4
Denison, Ks, US 185/G4
Denison, Ia, US 185/G2
Denison, Tx, US 183/F4
Denizli, Turk. 114/B2
Denizli (prov.), Turk. 114/B2
Denkendorf, Ger. 65/E5
Denklingen, Ger. 67/G2
Denman, Austl. 156/D2
Denmark (str.), Grld.,Ice. 163/R3
Denmark, Ia, US 185/J3
Denmark, Austl. 154/C5
Denmark (ctry.) 46/C4
Denmark, SC, US 193/G4
Denmark, Wi, US 190/C2
Dennard, Ar, US 183/H3
Dennilton, SAfr. 141/F5
Dennison, Oh, US 190/F4
Dennisville, NJ, US 198/D5
Denny, Sc, UK 39/C4
Denpasar, Indo. 101/F5
Dent de Cons (peak), Fr. 70/C1
Dent de Lys (peak), Swi. 66/C4
Dent d'Hérens (peak), It. 66/D6
Dentergem, Belg. 60/C2
Dentlein am Forst, Ger. 64/D4
Denton, Eng, UK 41/F5
Denton, Eng, UK 43/G5
Denton, Ga, US 195/G2
Denton, Md, US 198/C6
Denton, Mt, US 175/K4
Denton, Tx, US 180/K6
Denton (co.), Tx, US 180/K6
Denton (cr.), Tx, US 181/F1
D'Entrecasteaux (isls.), PNG 160/D5
D'Entrecasteaux (pt.), Austl. 154/B5
Dents du Midi (peak), Swi. 66/C5
Dentsville, SC, US 193/G3
Denver (cap.), Co, US 200/C3
Denver, Ia, US 185/H2
Denver, Pa, US 198/B3
Denver City, Tx, US 182/C4
Denver International (int'l arpt.), Co, US 200/C3
Denville, NJ, US 198/D2
Denzil, Sk, Can. 175/K1
Denzlingen, Ger. 66/D1
Deoband, India 110/D5
Deobhog, India 107/D2
Deoghar, India 109/F3
Deohā (riv.), India 108/B1
Deolāli, India 104/B4
Deoli, India 104/C2
Deoli, India 107/C1
Deolia, India 104/B2
Déols, Fr. 50/D3
Deora, Co, US 182/C2
Deorī, India 108/B4
Deoria, India 108/D2
Dependencias Federales (state), Ven. 217/E1
Depew, Ok, US 183/F3
Depew, NY, US 190/V10
Depoe Bay, Or, US 176/A1
Depok, Indo. 102/C5
Deport, Tx, US 183/G4
Deposit, NY, US 191/J3
Dépôt Lézard, FrG. 218/C1
Dépression de Mourdi (depr.), Chad 134/D1
Deptford (nbrhd.), Eng, UK 36/C2
Deputatskiy, Rus. 81/P3
Deputy, In, US 192/E1
Dêqên, China 98/C2
Deqing, China 92/L9
Dera, D.R. Congo 139/G2
Dera Ghāzi Khān, Pak. 110/A4
Dera Gopipur, India 110/D4
Dera Ismāīl Khān, Pak. 110/A4
Derā Nānak, India 110/C3
Dera Nawāb Sāhib, Pak. 110/A5
Derai, Bang. 109/H3
Deram Shet' (riv), Eth. 136/A3
Derazhnya, Ukr. 78/D3
Derbent, Rus. 77/J4
Derby, Austl. 152/A4
Derby, Eng, UK 41/G6
Derby (co.), Eng, UK 41/G6
Derby, Ct, US 199/E1
Derby, Ks, US 183/F2
Derbyshire (co.), Eng, UK 41/G6
Derdap NP, Serb. 56/F3
Derdara, Mor. 130/B2
Derdepoort, SAfr. 141/E5
Derecske, Hun. 56/E2
Dereköy, Turk. 57/H5
Dereköy (riv.), Turk. 115/M6
Derendingen, Swi. 66/D3
Deresgē, Eth. 136/A2
Dergachi, Rus. 77/J2
Derhachi, Ukr. 79/J2

Derik – Dorri
281

Derik, Turk. 114/E2
Derinkuyu, Turk. 114/C2
Derkul, Kaz. 77/J2
Derma, Ms, US 192/C4
Dermott, Ar, US 183/J4
Dernau, Ger. 61/G2
Déroute, Passage de la (Chan), Fr., UK 50/B2
Derravaragh (lake), Ire. 38/C2
Derreen (riv.), Ire. 38/D4
Derrevaragh (lake), Ire. 40/A4
Derry, NH, US 191/L3
Derry, NM, US 179/J4
Derryboy, NI, UK 40/C3
Derrylin, NI, UK 38/C1
Derrynasaggart (mts.), Ire. 38/A6
Dersingham, Eng, UK 43/G1
Derudeb, Sudan 135/H1
Deruta, It. 71/B2
Dervaig, Sc, UK 37/Q8
Derval, Fr. 62/D5
Derventa, Bosn. 56/C3
Dervio, It. 67/F5
Dervock, NI, UK 40/B1
Derwent (riv.), Austl. 156/C4
Derwent, Ab, Can. 175/J1
Derwent (res.), Eng, UK 41/F2
Derwent (riv.), Eng, UK 41/E2
Derwent Bridge, Austl. 156/C4
Derwent Water (lake), Eng, UK 41/E2
Derzhavīnsk, Kaz. 111/A1
Des Allemands, La, US 194/C3
Des Arc, Ar, US 183/J3
Des Arc, Mo, US 192/B2
Des Lacs NWR, ND, US 186/C3
Des Moines (riv.), Ia, Mn, US 173/H3
Des Moines (int'l arpt.), Ia, US 185/H3
Des Moines (cap.), Ia, US 185/H3
Des Moines, Wa, US 174/C4
Des Moines, East Fork (riv.), Ia, US 185/G2
Des Plaines, Il, US 190/C3
Desaguadero, Peru 224/B1
Desaguadero (riv.), Bol. 221/E9
Desagües de los Colorados, Arg. 224/C4
Desagües del Río Salvage, Arg. 224/C4
Desana, It. 68/B3
Desborough, Eng, UK 43/F2
Descabezado Grande (vol.), Chile 226/C2
Descalvado, Braz. 225/H2
Descartes, Fr. 50/D3
Deschutes (riv.), Or, US 176/C1
Deschutes River Recreation Lands, Or, US 176/C1
Desdunes, Haiti 207/H2
Dese (riv.), It. 69/F2
Desē, Eth. 136/A3
Deseado (riv.), Arg. 209/C7
Deseado (cape), Chile 227/B7
Desengaño (pt.), Arg. 227/D6
Desenzano del Garda, It. 68/D3
Deseret Depot, Ut, US 177/G3
Désert (riv.), Qu, Can. 191/H1
Desert (valley), Nv, US 176/D3
Desert (lake), Nv, US 178/E2
Desert Center, Ca, US 178/E4
Desert Hot Springs, Ca, US 178/D4
Désertines, Fr. 50/E3
Deshengpu, China 92/B4
Deshler, Oh, US 190/E4
Desiderio Tello, Arg. 224/C4
Desio, It. 68/C2
Desloge, Mo, US 192/B2
Desna (riv.), Rus. 75/W9
Desolación (isl.), Chile 227/B7
Desolation (pt.), Phil. 100/D3
Desoto, Tx, US 180/L7
Desoto Nat'l Wild.Ref., Ne, US 185/F3
Despatch, SAfr. 142/D4
Déssa, Niger 133/F3
Dessau, Ger. 48/G3
Dessel, Belg. 58/C6
Dessoubre (riv.), Fr. 66/C3
Destelbergen, Belg. 60/C1
Destêrro, Braz. 219/G4
Destin, Fl, US 194/E2
Destruction Bay, Can. 201/L3
Desulo, It. 54/A2
Desvres, Fr. 60/A2
Det Udom, Thai. 106/D3
Deta, Rom. 56/E3
Dete, Zim. 141/E3
Detern, Ger. 59/E2
Detmold, Ger. 59/F5
Detour (pt.), Mi, US 190/C2
Detrital Wash (riv.), Az, US 178/E3
Detroit (riv.), Can.,US 197/F7
Detroit, Mi, US 190/E3
Detroit, Or, US 176/B1
Detroit (dam), Or, US 176/B1
Detroit (lake), Or, US 176/B1
Detroit, Tx, US 183/G4
Detroit City (arpt.), Mi, US 197/G7
Detroit Lakes, Mn, US 186/G4
Detroit Metropolitan Wayne County (int'l arpt.), Mi, US 190/E3
Dettelbach, Ger. 64/D3
Dettifoss (falls), Ice. 44/P6
Dettwiller, Fr. 61/G6
Deua NP, Austl. 157/D2
Deuil-la-Barre, Fr. 36/J5
Deûle (riv.), Fr. 60/B2
Deurne, Belg. 58/B6
Deurne, Neth. 58/C6
Deurne (Antwerp) (int'l arpt.), Belg. 58/B6
Deustua, Peru 220/D4
Deutsch Evern, Ger. 59/H2
Deutsch Wagram, Aus. 57/P7
Deutschkreutz, Aus. 56/C2
Deutschlandsberg, Aus. 56/B2
Deux-Montagnes, Qu, Can. 189/N6
Deux-Montagnes (lake), Qu, Can. 189/M7
Deux-Montagnes (co.), Qu, Can. 189/M6
Deva, Rom. 56/F3
Dévaványa, Hun. 56/E2
Develi, Turk. 114/C2
Deventer, Neth. 58/D4
Deveron (riv.), Sc, UK 39/D2
Devil River (peak), NZ 159/C3
Devil's Playground (des.), Ca, US 178/E3
Deville, Fr. 61/D4
Deville, La, US 194/B2
Devil's (isl.), FrG. 218/C1
Devils (riv.), Mex. 205/E2
Devil's (pt.), SrL. 107/D4
Devils (lake), ND, US 186/E3
Devils (riv.), Tx, US 180/D3
Devil's Elbow (pass), Sc, UK 39/C3
Devil's Garden, Ut, US 179/H1
Devils Lake, ND, US 186/E3
Devils Paw (mt.), Ak, US 201/M4
Devils Postpile Nat'l Mon., Ca, US 178/C2
Devils Tower Nat'l Mon., Wy, US 184/B1
Devilsbit (peak), Ire. 38/C4
Devin, Bul. 55/J2
Devine, Tx, US 181/E3
Devizes, Eng, UK 42/E4
Devnya, Bul. 57/H4
Devola, Oh, US 190/F5
Devoll (riv.), Alb. 73/J2
Devoll (riv.), Alb.,Gre. 56/E5
Devon, Ab, Can. 175/H1
Devon (isl.), Nun, Can. 171/H1
Devon (riv.), Sc, UK 39/C4
Devon (co.), Eng, UK 42/C5
Devon-Berwyn, Pa, US 198/C3
Devonport, Austl. 156/C4
Devonport, NZ 159/F6
Devore, Ca, US 196/C2
Devoto, Arg. 224/D4
Devoys (peak), NM, US 182/C2
Devrek (riv.), Turk. 76/D4
Devrek, Turk. 76/D4
Devrez (riv.), Turk. 76/E4
Devure (riv.), Zim. 141/F3
Dewa (pt.), Indo. 101/A2
Dewa (mts.), Japan 94/B4
Dewar, Ok, US 183/G3
Dewās, India 104/C3
Dewberry, Ab, Can. 175/J1
Dewetsdorp, SAfr. 142/D3
Dewey, Ok, US 183/G2
Dewey, Az, US 179/F3
Deweyville, Tx, US 181/H2
Dewsbury, Eng, UK 41/G4
Dexter, Ga, US 193/F4
Dexter, Ks, US 183/F2
Dexter, Mo, US 192/C2
Dexter, NM, US 182/B4
Dey-Dey (lake), Austl. 145/C3
Deyang, China 98/E2
Deyhūk, Iran 115/J3
Deyyer, Iran 115/G5
Dez (riv.), Iran 80/E6
Dezfūl, Iran 115/G3
Dezhneva (cape), Rus. 172/W12
Dezhou, China 92/D3
Dhābān, India 110/C5
Dhabān Singh, Pak. 110/B4
Dhāding, Nepal 109/E2
Dhahab, Egypt 127/G2
Dhahabān, SAr. 112/C4
Dhahran (int'l arpt.), SAr. 112/F3
Dhahran, SAr. 112/D5
Dhākā (pol. div.), Bang. 109/G4
Dhāka, India 109/E2
Dhākā (pol. reg.), Bang. 109/H4
Dhākā (Dacca) (cap.), Bang. 109/H4
Dhaleswari (riv.), Bang. 109/H4
Dhali, Cyp. 116/C2
Dhamār, Yem. 136/C2
Dhāmpur, India 108/B1
Dhamtari, India 107/D1
Dhanaula, India 110/C4
Dhanaura, India 108/B1
Dhānbād, India 109/F4
Dhangadhī, Nepal 108/C1
Dhankutā, Nepal 109/F2
Dhār, India 104/C3
Dhar de Chinguetti (cliff), Mrta. 128/B5
Dhār Khurd, India 110/C3
Dhar Néma (cliff), Mrta. 132/D2
Dhar Oualâta (cliff), Mrta. 132/D2
Dhar Tîchît (cliff), Mrta. 132/C2
Dharampur, India 104/B3
Dharān, Nepal 109/F2
Dharchula, Nepal 108/C1
Dhāri, India 113/K4
Dhāriwāl, India 110/C4
Dharmapuri, India 107/C3
Dharmavaram, India 107/C3
Dharmjaygarh, India 108/D4
Dharmkot, India 110/C4
Dharmsāla, India 110/D3
Dhasan (riv.), India 108/B3
Dhaulāgiri (zone), Nepal 108/D1
Dhaulāgiri (peak), Nepal 108/D1
Dhaura, India 108/B3
Dhaurahra, India 108/C1
Dhekialjuli, India 98/B3
Dhelfoí, Gre. 55/H3
Dhelfoí (Delphi) (ruin), Gre. 55/H3
Dhelvinákion, Gre. 55/G3
Dheskáti, Gre. 55/G3
Dheune (riv.), Fr. 66/A4
Dhī Qār (gov.), Iraq 115/F4
Dhībān, Jor. 117/D5
Dhidhimótikhon, Gre. 57/H5
Dhiinsoor, Som. 137/C1
Dhíkaia, Gre. 57/H5
Dhílos (ruin), Gre. 55/J4
Dhimitsána, Gre. 55/H4
Dhírfis (peak), Gre. 55/H3
Dhístomon, Gre. 55/H3
Dhlo Dhlo (ruin), Zim. 141/F3
Dhofar (reg.), Oman 112/F5
Dhokímion, Gre. 55/G3
Dholipal, India 110/C5
Dholka, India 113/K4
Dholpur, India 108/A2
Dhomokós, Gre. 55/H3
Dhonoúsa (isl.), Gre. 55/J4
Dhorāji, India 113/K4
Dhorpātan, Nepal 108/D1
Dhoxáton, Gre. 55/J2
Dhronbach (riv.), Ger. 61/F4
Dhubāb, Yem. 136/B2
Dhubri, India 109/G2
Dhuizon, Fr. 63/G5
Dhūlia, India 107/B1
Dhuliān, Pak. 110/B3
Dhuliān, India 109/F3
Dhulikhel, Nepal 109/E2
Dhungrebās, Nepal 109/E2
Dhupgāri, India 109/G2
Dhūri, India 110/C4
Dhuudo, Som. 136/D3
Dhuudo (riv.), Som. 136/D3
Dhuusamarreeb (Dusa Marreb), Som. 136/C4
Di Linh, Viet. 106/E4
Dia (isl.), Gre. 55/J5
Diablo (mt.), Ak, US 201/H4
Diablo (range), Ca, US 178/B2
Diablo (mtn.), Tx, US 180/B2
Diablo (plat.), Tx, US 180/B2
Diablo, Punta del (pt.), Uru. 227/G2
Diablotin (peak), Dom. 203/N9
Diadema, Braz. 223/K8
Diadema Argentina, Arg. 226/D5
Diaganiao, Sen. 132/A3
Diagonal, Ia, US 185/G3
Diaguitas, Chile 224/B4
Dialakoto, Sen. 132/B3
Diamante (riv.), Arg. 226/D2
Diamante, Arg. 224/D5
Diamantina, Braz. 223/E3
Diamantina (riv.), Austl. 145/D3
Diamantina Lakes, Austl. 158/A3
Diamantina, Chapada (hills), Braz. 223/E1
Diamantino, Braz. 221/G4
Diamond (cr.), Austl. 156/G5
Diamond (peak), Id, US 177/G1
Diamond, Or, US 176/D2
Diamond (peak), Or, US 176/B2
Diamond Bar, Ca, US 196/G8
Diamond Harbour, India 109/G4
Diamond Springs, Ca, US 176/C4
Dian (lake), China 98/D3
Dianalund, Den. 46/D4
Dianbai, China 99/F4
Diancang (mtn.), China 98/D3
Dianjiang, China 99/E2
Diano Marina, It. 68/B6
Dianópolis, Braz. 222/D1
Dianshan (lake), China 92/L8
Diapaga, Burk. 133/F3
Diaroumé, Sen. 132/B3
Dias Creek, NJ, US 198/D5
Diavolezza (peak), Swi. 67/F5
Diaz, Ar, US 183/J3
Dibai, India 108/B1
Dibaya, D.R. Congo 139/E4
Dibaya-Lubwe, D.R. Congo 138/D4
Dibbin NP, Jor. 117/D4
Dibella (well), Niger 134/B1
Dibeng, SAfr. 142/C2
Dibiāpur, India 108/B2
Dībīlē, Eth. 136/B3
Diboll, Tx, US 180/G2
Dibrugarh, India 98/B3
Dibs, Iraq 115/F3
Dickens, Tx, US 182/D4
Dickens (pt.), RI, US 199/G1
Dickinson, ND, US 186/C4
Dickinson, Tx, US 181/M9
Dickinson Bayou (riv.), Tx, US 181/M9
Dickinson Center, NY, US 191/J2
Dickson, Ab, Can. 174/G1
Dickson, Ok, US 183/F3
Dickson, Tn, US 192/D2
Dicle (dam), Turk. 114/E2
Dicomano, It. 69/E6
Didam, Neth. 58/D5
Didcot, Eng, UK 43/E3
Didhav, Eth. 136/B2
Didiéni, Mali 132/C3
Didig Sala, Eth. 136/A2
Didinga (hills), Sudan 135/G4
Didsbury, Ab, Can. 175/G2
Dīdwāna, India 113/K3
Didyma (ruin), Turk. 114/A2
Die, Fr. 70/B3
Die Berg (peak), SAfr. 141/F5
Dieblich, Ger. 61/G3
Diébougou, Burk. 132/E4
Dieburg, Ger. 64/B3
Diedersdorf, Ger. 48/Q7
Diefenbaker (lake), Sk, Can. 170/F3
Diefenbaker (lake), Sk, Can. 175/L2
Diego de Almagro (isl.), Chile 227/B6
Diego de Almagro, Chile 224/B3
Diego Garcia (isl.), UK 83/G10
Diekirch, Lux. 61/F4
Diekirch (dist.), Lux. 61/E4
Diéma, Mali 132/C3
Diemen, Neth. 58/B4
Diemtigen, Swi. 66/D4
Dien Bien, Viet. 98/D4
Dien Chau, Viet. 106/D2
Dien Khanh, Viet. 106/E3
Dieng (ruin), Indo. 101/E4
Diepenbeek, Belg. 61/E2
Diepenveen, Neth. 58/D4
Diepholz, Ger. 59/F3
Diepoldsau, Swi. 67/F3
Dieppe, Fr. 63/G1
Dieppe, NB, Can. 188/E2
Dierdorf, Ger. 61/G2
Dieren, Neth. 58/D4
Dierks, Ar, US 183/G3
Diespeck, Ger. 64/D3
Diessen am Ammersee, Ger. 67/H2
Diest, Belg. 61/E2
Dietenheim, Ger. 67/G1
Dietenhofen, Ger. 64/D4
Dieterich, Il, US 192/C1
Dietersheim, Ger. 64/D3
Dietfurt an der Altmühl, Ger. 65/E4
Dietikon, Swi. 67/E3
Dietmannsried, Ger. 67/G2
Dietzenbach, Ger. 64/B2
Dieue-sur-Meuse, Fr. 61/E5
Dieulefit, Fr. 70/B3
Dieulouard, Fr. 61/F6
Dieuze, Fr. 61/F6
Dieveniškės, Lith. 47/L4
Diever, Neth. 58/D3
Diez, Ger. 64/B2
Dif, Kenya 137/C1
Diffa, Niger 134/B2
Diffa (dept.), Niger 134/B2
Differdange, Lux. 61/E4
Difficult (mt.), Austl. 156/B3
Dīg, India 108/A2
Digba, D.R. Congo 135/E4
Digboi, India 98/B3
Digby, NS, Can. 188/E3
Digby Neck (pen), Ns, Can. 188/D3
Diggers Rest, Austl. 157/B3
Dighem, Sudan 135/G2
Dighton, Ks, US 182/D1
Dighwāra, India 109/E3
Dīglūr, India 107/C2
Digne-les-Bains, Fr. 70/C4
Digoin, Fr. 50/E3
Digor, Turk. 115/E1
Digos, Phil. 100/D4
Digul (riv.), Indo. 103/K4
Digya NP, Gha. 133/E5
Dihang (riv.), India 98/B2
Dihun, Eth. 136/B4
Dijon, Fr. 66/A3
Dik, Chad 134/C3
Dikhil, Djib. 136/B3
Dikirnis, Egypt 131/C2
Diklosmta (peak), Geo. 77/H4
Diksmuide, Belg. 60/B1
Dikson, Rus. 80/J2
Diktel, Nepal 109/F2
Dikwa, Nga. 134/B2
Dīla, Eth. 136/A4
Dilbeek, Belg. 61/D2
Dilek Yarımadası NP, Turk. 114/A2
Dili (cap.), ETim. 152/B2
Dilijan, Arm. 77/H4
Dilkon, Az, US 179/G3
Dillenburg, Ger. 61/H2
Diller, Ne, US 185/F3
Dilley, Tx, US 180/E3
Dillia (riv.), Niger 134/A2
Dillikot, Nepal 108/C1
Dilling, Sudan 135/F2
Dillingen, Ger. 61/F5
Dillingen an der Donau, Ger. 64/D5
Dillingham, Ak, US 201/G4
Dillnås, Swe. 45/A1
Dillon, Mt, US 177/G1
Dillon, SC, US 193/H3
Dillon Cone (peak), NZ 159/C3
Dillonvale, Oh, US 190/F4
Dillsboro, In, US 192/E1
Dillsburg, Pa, US 198/A3
Dilolo, D.R. Congo 139/E5
Dilsen, Belg. 61/E1
Dimako, Camr. 134/B4
Dimāpur, India 98/B3
Dimaro, It. 67/G5
Dimas, Mex. 204/D4
Dimashq (prov.), Syria 117/E1
Dimashq (Damascus) (cap.), Syria 117/E1
Dimataling, Phil. 100/C4
Dimbaza, SAfr. 142/D4
Dimbelenge, D.R. Congo 139/E4
Dimbokro, C.d'Iv. 132/D5
Dimboola, Austl. 156/B3
Dîmbovița (prov.), Rom. 57/G3
Dîmbovița (riv.), Rom. 78/C5
Dimbulah, Austl. 158/B2
Dime Box, Tx, US 181/F2
Dimitriya Lapteva (str.), Rus. 81/P2
Dimitrovgrad, Bul. 57/G4
Dimitrovgrad, Rus. 77/J1
Dimitrovgrad, Serb. 57/F4
Dimlang (peak), Nga. 134/A3
Dimmitt, Tx, US 182/C3
Dimock, SD, US 184/F2
Dimovo, Bul. 57/F4
Dina, Pak. 110/B3
Dinach, Som. 136/D3
Dinagat, Phil. 100/D3
Dinagat (isl.), Phil. 103/G1
Dinājpur (pol. reg.), Bang. 109/G3
Dinājpur, Bang. 109/G3
Dinan, Fr. 62/C4
Dīnānagar, India 110/C3
Dinant, Belg. 61/D3
Dinar, Turk. 114/B2
Dinard, Fr. 62/C3
Dinaric Alps (mts.), Cro. 56/C3
Dinas (pt.), Wal, UK 42/B2
Dinas Powys, Wal, UK 42/C4
Dinder NP, Sudan 135/G2
Dinder Wenz (riv.), Eth. 135/G2
Dindima, Nga. 133/H4
Dindori, India 108/C4
Dinga, Pak. 110/B3
Ding'an, China 99/F5
Dingbian, China 90/F4
Dingelstädt, Ger. 59/H6
Dinggyê, China 109/F1
Dingjiang, China 99/G3
Dingjiasuo, China 91/J5
Dingle, Ire. 36/F10
Dingle (bay), Ire. 36/N10
Dingle, Id, US 177/H2
Dingmans Ferry, Pa, US 198/D1
Dingolfing, Ger. 65/F5
Dingras, Phil. 100/C1
Dingshuzhen, China 92/K8
Dingtao, China 92/C4
Dinguiraye, Gui. 132/C4
Dingwall, Sc, UK 39/B1
Dingwall, NS, Can. 189/G2
Dingxi, China 90/E4
Dingxiang, China 92/C3
Dingxing, China 92/G7
Dingyuan, China 92/D4
Dinh Lap, Viet. 106/D1
Dinkel (riv.), Ger. 59/E4
Dinkelsbühl, Ger. 64/D4
Dinkelscherben, Ger. 64/D6
Dinklage, Ger. 59/F3
Dinnebito Wash (riv.), Az, US 179/G2
Dinner (pt.), Fl, US 194/K7
Dinnington, Eng, UK 41/G1
Dinokana, SAfr. 140/E5
Dinosaur, Co, US 177/J3
Dinosaur Nat'l Monument, Co, US 177/J3
Dinslaken, Ger. 58/D5
Dinsmore, Sk, Can. 175/L2
Dintel Mark (riv.), Neth. 58/B5
Dintenloord, Neth. 58/B5
Dintiteladas, Indo. 101/D4
Dinuba, Ca, US 178/C2
Dinwiddie, Va, US 193/J2
Dinxperlo, Neth. 58/D5
Dioïla, Mali 132/D3
Diomandou, Gui. 132/C4
Dion (riv.), Gui. 132/C4
Dionysias (ruin), Egypt 131/B6
Diósd, Hun. 57/Q10
Diouloulou, Sen. 132/A3
Dioundiou, Niger 133/F3
Diourbel (pol. reg.), Sen. 132/A3
Diourbel, Sen. 132/A3
Dīpālpur, Pak. 110/B4
Diphu, India 98/B3
Diphu (pass), India 98/C2
Diplo, Pak. 113/J4
Dipni (dam), Turk. 114/E2
Dipolog, Phil. 100/C3
Dipperu NP, Austl. 158/C3
Dipperz, Ger. 64/C1
Dique (canal), Col. 207/H4
Dīr, Pak. 110/A2
Dira (well), Chad 134/B2
Dirang Dzong, India 109/J2
Diré, Mali 132/E2
Dirē Dawa, Eth. 136/B3
Direct, Tx, US 183/G4
Direction (cape), Austl. 153/F3
Diriamba, Nic. 206/E4
Dirico, Ang. 140/D3
Dirj, Libya 129/H3
Dirk Hartog (isl.), Austl. 145/A3
Dirkou, Niger 126/B5
Dirksland, Neth. 58/B5
Dirlewang, Ger. 67/G2
Dirranbandi, Austl. 158/C5
Dirrington Great Law (hill), Sc, UK 39/D5
Ḑirs, SAr. 112/D5
Dirty Devil (riv.), Ut, US 177/H4
Disappointment (lake), Austl. 145/B3
Disappointment (isls.), FrPol. 161/L6
Disappointment (cape), Wa, US 174/B4
Disaster (bay), Austl. 157/D3
Discovery (bay), Austl. 156/B3
Discovery Bay, Jam. 207/G2
Disentis-Mustér, Swi. 67/E4
Disgrazi (peak), It. 67/F5
Dishman, Wa, US 174/F4
Dishnā, Egypt 127/G3
Disko (isl.), Grld. 163/M3
Disko (Qeqertarsuaq) (isl.), Grld. 171/L2
Disley, Eng, UK 41/F5
Dismal (riv.), Ne, US 184/D3
Disna, Bela. 47/N4
Disney, Ok, US 183/G2
Disney Studios, Fl, US 194/M7
Disneyland, Ca, US 196/G8
Dison, Belg. 61/E2
Dispur, India 105/F2
Disraëli, Qu, Can. 188/B3
Diss, Eng, UK 43/H2
Dissen am Teutoburger Wald, Ger. 59/F4
Distington, Eng, UK 40/E2
Distrito Especial (cap. dist.), Col. 219/L8
Distrito Federal (fed. dist.), Braz. 222/D2
Distrito Federal (fed. dist.), Col. 216/C3
Distrito Federal (fed. dist.), Mex. 202/A5
Distrito Federal (fed. dist.), Ven. 217/E2
Disūq, Egypt 131/B2
Ditang, China 92/L9
Ditchling Beacon (hill), Eng, UK 43/F5
Dittaino (riv.), It. 54/D4
Dittelbrunn, Ger. 64/D2
Ditton, Eng, UK 36/E3
Ditzingen, Ger. 64/C5
Diu, India 104/B3
Diuata (mts.), Phil. 100/D3
Dīvān Darreh, Iran 115/F3
Divatte (riv.), Fr. 62/D6
Dive (riv.), Fr. 50/D3
Divénié, Congo 138/C3
Dives (riv.), Fr. 63/E2
Dives-sur-Mer, Fr. 63/E2
Divette (riv.), Fr. 62/D1
Divide, Co, US 182/B1
Divide, Mt, US 177/G1
Dividing Creek, NJ, US 198/C5
Divinolândia, Braz. 223/K6
Divinópolis, Braz. 222/D4
Divisa Nova, Braz. 223/K6
Divisões, Serra das (mts.), Braz. 222/C3
Divisor, Serra do (mts.), Braz.,Peru 220/C2
Divnogorsk, Rus. 80/K4
Divnoye, Rus. 77/G3
Divo, C.d'Iv. 132/D5
Divonne-les-Bains, Fr. 66/C5
Divriği, Turk. 114/D2
Divuma, D.R. Congo 139/E5
Dix (lake), Swi. 66/D5
Dixcove, Gha. 133/E5
Dixfield, Me, US 191/L2
Dixie, Al, US 194/E2
Dixie, Ga, US 195/G2
Dixie, Id, US 176/F1
Dixie, Wa, US 174/E4
Dixmoor, Il, US 197/Q16
Dixon, Ca, US 176/C4
Dixon, Il, US 185/K3
Dixon, Ky, US 192/D2
Dixon, Mt, US 174/G4
Dixon, NM, US 182/B2
Dixon, Mo, US 183/H2
Dixon, Wy, US 177/K3
Dixon Entrance (chan.), Can.,US 163/D4
Diyadin, Turk. 115/E2
Diyāla (gov.), Iraq 115/F3
Diyarb Najm, Egypt 131/C3
Diyarbakır, Turk. 114/E2
Diyarbakir (prov.), Turk. 114/E2
Dizangué, Camr. 138/B2
Dja (riv.), Camr. 134/B5
Djado, Niger 126/B4
Djado (plat.), Niger 119/D2
Djakotomé, Ben. 133/F5
Djamaa, Alg. 129/G2
Djamba, D.R. Congo 139/F2
Djambala, Congo 138/C3
Djamu, D.R. Congo 139/G2
Djanet, Alg. 129/H4
Djebel Tichka (peak), Mor. 128/C3
Djebel-Amrag (mtn.), Alg. 130/D3
Djébrène, Chad 134/C3
Djédaa, Chad 134/C2
Djedi, Oued (riv.), Alg. 129/G2
Djelfa, Alg. 72/D4
Djema, CAfr. 135/E4
Djemila (ruin), Alg. 130/H4
Djénné, Mali 132/D3
Djerem (riv.), Camr. 134/B4
Djermaya, Chad 134/B2
Djibo, Burk. 133/E3
Djibouti (cap.), Djib. 136/B3
Djibouti (ctry.) 136/B2
Djiguéni, Mrta. 132/C3
Djiouce (mtn.), Ire. 38/D3
Djiroutou, C.d'Iv. 132/D5
Djohong, Camr. 134/B4
Djouab (riv.), Congo 138/C2
Djoué (riv.), Congo 138/C3
Djougou, Ben. 133/F4
Djoum, Camr. 138/C2
Djugu, D.R. Congo 139/G2
Djúpivogur, Ice. 44/P7
Djurö, Swe. 45/B1
D'Lo, Ms, US 194/D2
Dmanisi, Geo. 77/H4
Dmitriyev-L'govskiy, Rus. 79/H1
Dmitriyevskiy, Kaz. 77/L2
Dmytrivka, Ukr. 79/G2
Dnepr (riv.), Rus. 80/D4
Dnestrovsc, Mol. 78/E4
Dnieper (lowland), Ukr. 78/F2
Dnieper (upland), Ukr. 78/E3
Dnipro (riv.), Ukr. 29/H3
Dniprodzerzhyns'ke Vodoskhovyshche (res.), Ukr. 79/H3
Dniprodzerzhyns'k, Ukr. 79/H3
Dnipropetrovs'k, Ukr. 79/H3
Dnipropetrovs'ka Oblast (Ukr. 76/E2
Dniprorudne, Ukr. 79/H4
Dniprovs'kyy Lyman (estu.), Ukr. 57/K2
Dnister (riv.), Eur. 80/C5
Dnister (riv.), Ukr. 48/M4
Dnistrovs'kyy Lyman (estu.), Ukr. 57/K2
Dno, Rus. 47/N3
Dnyapro (riv.), Bela. 47/P4
Do (lake), Mali 133/E3
Do (riv.), China 90/D5
Do Gonbadān, Iran 115/G4
Do Luong, Viet. 106/D2
Do Rāh (pass), Afg. 113/K1
Do Son, Viet. 106/D1
Doa, Moz. 141/G3
Doaktown, NB, Can. 188/D2
Doany, Madg. 143/J6
Doba, Chad 134/C3
Dobbins (A.F.B.), Ga, US 193/L7
Dobbs Ferry, NY, US 199/K7
Dobbyn, Austl. 153/F4
Dobele, Lat. 47/K3
Döbeln, Ger. 48/G3
Doberai (pen.), Indo. 103/H4
Dobiegniew, Pol. 49/H2
Dobo, Indo. 152/D1
Dobogo-kó (peak), Hun. 57/Q9
Doboj, Bosn. 56/D3
Dobřany, Czh. 65/G3
Dobre Miasto, Pol. 47/J5
Dobrich, Bul. 57/H4
Dobrinka, Rus. 77/G1
Dobrinka, Rus. 79/L1
Dobříš, Czh. 65/H3
Dobromyl', Ukr. 49/M4
Dobropillya, Ukr. 79/J3
Dobrovnik, Slov. 56/C2
Dobruja (reg.), Bul.,Rom. 73/K2
Dobrush, Bela. 76/D1
Dobryanka, Rus. 75/N4
Dobryanka, Ukr. 78/F1
Dobson, NC, US 193/G2
Dobzha, China 109/G1
Doce (riv.), Braz. 223/E3
Dochart (riv.), Sc, UK 39/B4
Dock Junction, Ga, US 195/H2
Docker River, Austl. 155/F3
Docking, Eng, UK 43/G1
Doctor Arroyo, Mex. 205/E4
Doctor Cecilio Báez, Par. 225/E3
Doctor Coss, Mex. 180/E5
Doctor González, Mex. 180/E5
Doctor Pedro P. Peña, Par. 224/D2
Doctor Petru Groza, Rom. 56/F2
Dod Ballāpur, India 107/C3
Doda (riv.), India 110/D3
Doda, India 110/C3
Doda Betta (peak), India 107/C4
Dodder (riv.), Ire. 40/B5
Doddinghurst, Eng, UK 36/D2
Dodge, Tx, US 181/G2
Dodge City, Ks, US 182/D2
Dodger Stadium, Ca, US 196/F7
Dodgeville, Wi, US 185/J2
Dodman (pt.), Eng, UK 42/B6
Dodola, Eth. 136/A4
Dodoma (prov.), Tanz. 137/A3
Dodoma, Tanz. 137/A3
Dodori Nat'l Rsv., Kenya 137/C2
Dodsland, Sk, Can. 175/K2
Dodson, La, US 194/B1
Dodson, Mt, US 175/K3
Dodwekon, Libr. 132/C5
Dodworth, Eng, UK 41/G4
Doe Run, Mo, US 192/B2
Doel, Belg. 58/B6
Doerun, Ga, US 195/G2
Doesburg, Neth. 58/D4
Doetinchem, Neth. 58/D5
Dofa, Indo. 103/G4
Dog (lake), Mb, Can. 186/E2
Dog (isl.), Fl, US 195/F3
Dog (riv.), BC, Can. 174/C2
Dogai Coring (lake), China 111/E5
Dogana, SMar. 69/F6
Doğanhisar, Turk. 114/B2
Doğankent (riv.), Turk. 76/F4
Doğanşar, Turk. 114/D1
Doğanşehir, Turk. 114/D2
Doğanyurt, Turk. 76/E4
Döğer, Turk. 114/B2
Dogliani, It. 68/A3
Dōgo (isl.), Japan 91/L4
Dogondoutchi, Niger 133/G3
Doğubayazıt, Turk. 115/F2
Doğukaradeniz (mts.), Turk. 114/D1
Doha (int'l arpt.), Qatar 112/F3
Doha (Ad Dawḩah) (cap.), Qatar 112/F3
Dohad, India 104/B3
Dohrīghāt, India 108/D2
Doi Inthanon NP, Thai. 98/C5
Doi Khun Tan NP, Thai. 106/B2
Doi Suthep-Pui NP, Thai. 98/C5
Doimara, India 98/B3
Doiras (res.), Sp. 52/B1
Dois Córregos, Braz. 225/G2
Dois de Julho (int'l arpt.), Braz. 223/F2
Dois Irmãos do Tocantins, Braz. 218/D5
Dois Irmãos, Serra (mts.), Braz. 219/F5
Dois Vizinhos, Braz. 225/F3
Doische, Belg. 61/D3
Doka, Sudan 135/G2
Dokka, Nor. 46/D1
Dokkum, Neth. 58/D2
Dokkumer Ee (riv.), Neth. 58/C2
Dokshitsy, Bela. 47/M4
Doksy, Czh. 65/H1
Dokuchayevs'k, Ukr. 79/J4
Dol-de-Bretagne, Fr. 62/D3
Dolan Springs, Az, US 178/E3
Dolbeau, Qu, Can. 188/A1
Dolcedorme (peak), It. 54/E3
Dole, Fr. 66/B3
Dolent (peak), Swi. 66/D6
Dolgellau, Wal, UK 42/C1
Dolgoprudnyy, Rus. 75/W9
Doli, India 104/B2
Dolianova, It. 54/A3
Dolinsk, Rus. 91/N2
Dolinskoye, Ukr. 78/E4
Dolj (prov.), Rom. 57/F3
Dollar, Sc, UK 39/C4
Dollar Bay, Mi, US 187/K4
Dollar Law (peak), Sc, UK 39/C5
Dollard, Sk, Can. 175/K3
Dollard (Dollart) (bay), Ger.,Neth. 59/E2
Dollard-des-Ormeaux, Qu, Can. 189/N7
Dollart (Dollard) (bay), Ger.,Neth. 59/E2
Dollarville, Mi, US 190/D1
Doller (riv.), Fr. 48/D5
Dollnstein, Ger. 64/E5
Dolmance Palace, Turk. 115/M6
Dolmar (peak), Ger. 64/D1
Dolmen (ruin), It. 54/E2
Dolna Banya, Bul. 57/F4
Dolni Dŭbnik, Bul. 57/G4
Dolní Kounice, Czh. 51/M2
Dolnośląskie (prov.), Pol. 49/J3
Dolo, Eth. 136/B4
Dolo, Indo. 103/E4
Dolo, It. 69/F3
Dolo (riv.), It. 68/D4
Dolo Odo, Eth. 136/B4
Dolobli, Libr. 132/C5
Dolomieu, Fr. 70/B1
Dolomite Alps (mts.), It. 73/F1
Dolon (riv.), Fr. 70/A2
Doloon, Mong. 90/F3
Dolores, Arg. 226/F3
Dolores, Bol. 220/D3
Dolores, Guat. 206/D2
Dolores, Phil. 100/D2
Dolores, Uru. 227/J10
Dolores, Co, US 179/H2
Dolores (riv.), Co, US 177/J4
Dolores, Ven. 216/D2
Dolphin (pt.), Namb. 140/B5
Dolphin (cape), UK 227/F6
Dolphin and Union (str.), Nun, Can. 170/E2
Dolphinholme, Eng, UK 41/F4
Dölsach, Aus. 51/K3
Dolton, Il, US 197/Q16
Dolyna, Ukr. 78/C3
Dolyns'ka, Ukr. 79/G3
Dolzhanskaya, Rus. 79/J4
Dom (peak), Indo. 103/J4
Dom (peak), Swi. 66/D5
Dom Aquino, Braz. 222/B2
Dom Carlos (pt.), Moz. 141/G4
Dom Noi (res.), Thai. 106/D3
Dom Pedrito, Braz. 225/F4
Doma, Zim. 141/F3
Domanivka, Ukr. 78/F4
Domār, Bang. 109/G2
Domariāganj, India 108/D2
Domasi, Malw. 141/G2
Domat-Ems, Swi. 67/F4
Domažlice, Czh. 65/F4
Dombarovskiy, Rus. 77/L2
Dombasle-sur-Meurthe, Fr. 61/F6
Dombay-Ul'gen (peak), Geo. 77/G4
Dombe Grande, Ang. 140/B2
Dombes (lake), Fr. 66/B5
Dombey (cape), Austl. 152/C3
Domboshawa, Zim. 141/F3
Dombóvár, Hun. 56/D2
Dombrád, Hun. 56/E1
Domburg, Sur. 218/C1
Domburg, Neth. 58/A5
Domchānch, India 109/E3
Dome, Az, US 178/E4
Dome (peak), Az, US 179/F2
Dome C, US, Ant. 228/J
Dôme de Barrot (peak), Fr. 70/C4
Dôme de l'Arpont (peak), Fr. 70/C2
Domène, Fr. 70/B2
Domérat, Fr. 50/E3
Domeyko, Chile 224/B4
Domfront, Fr. 63/E3
Domínguez, Arg. 224/E4
Dominica (ctry.) 203/N8
Dominica Passage (chan.), Dom.,Guad. 203/N9
Dominican Republic (ctry.) 203/H4
Dominion, NS, Can. 189/G2
Domiongo, D.R. Congo 139/E4
Dommartin-lès-Remiremont, Fr. 66/C2
Dommartin-lès-Toul, Fr. 61/E6
Dommati, India 109/H3
Dommel (riv.), Belg. 61/E1
Domo, Eth. 136/C4
Domodedovo, Rus. 75/W9
Domodedovo (int'l arpt.), Rus. 75/W9
Domodossola, It. 67/E5
Domohāni, India 109/G2
Domoni, Com. 143/H6
Domont, Fr. 36/J4
Dompu, Indo. 103/E5
Domremy, Sk, Can. 175/M1
Domrémy-la-Pucelle, Fr. 66/B1
Dömsöd, Hun. 56/D2
Domusnovas, It. 54/A3
Domuyo (vol.), Arg. 226/C3
Domvilk (mt.), Austl. 158/C5
Domžale, Slov. 51/L3
Don (cape), Austl. 152/C2
Don (riv.), Eng, UK 41/G5
Don (riv.), Sc, UK 39/D2
Don (ridge), Rus. 80/E5
Don (riv.), Rus. 29/J4
Don Benito, Sp. 52/C3
Don Pedro (res.), Ca, US 178/B2
Dona Ana, Moz. 141/G3
Donabate, Ire. 40/B5
Donada, It. 69/F3
Donaghadee, NI, UK 40/C2
Donaghmore, NI, UK 40/B2
Donald, Austl. 156/B3
Donald, BC, Can. 174/F2
Donaldson, Ar, US 183/H3
Donaldsonville, La, US 194/C2
Donalsonville, Ga, US 195/F2
Doñana, PN, Sp. 52/B4
Donath, Swi. 67/F4
Donau (Danube) (riv.), Aus.,Ger. 51/H2
Donaueschingen, Ger. 67/E2
Donauwörth, Ger. 64/D5
Doncaster (nbrhd.), Austl. 156/G5
Doncaster, Eng, UK 41/G4
Doncaster (co.), Eng, UK 41/G4
Donchery, Fr. 61/D4
Dondo, Ang. 138/C5
Dondo, D.R. Congo 134/D4
Dondo, Moz. 141/G3
Dondra Head (pt.), SrL. 107/D5
Donduseni, Mol. 78/D3
Donegal (bay), Ire. 37/P9
Donegal, Ire. 37/P9
Donegal (dist.), Ire. 40/A1
Doneraile, Ire. 38/B5
Donets (riv.), Rus. 77/G2
Donets' (riv.), Ukr. 79/J3
Donetsk (int'l arpt.), Ukr. 79/J3
Donets'ka Oblast, Ukr. 76/F3
Donetsk, Rus. 79/L3
Donets'k, Ukr. 79/J3
Dong (riv.), China 90/E3
Dong, India 105/G2
Dong (riv.), Viet. 105/J5
Dong Dang, Viet. 105/J3
Dong Ha, Viet. 106/D2
Dong Hoi, Viet. 106/D2
Dong Noi (riv.), Viet. 106/D4
Dong Tau, Viet. 106/D2
Dong Ujimqin Qi, China 90/H2
Donga, Nga. 133/H5
Donga (riv.), Nga. 133/H4
Dongai (riv.), Camr. 134/A4
Dongar Parāsia, India 108/B4
Dongara, Austl. 154/B4
Dongargarh, India 107/D1
Dongbei (plain), China 92/E2
Dongchuan, China 98/D3
Dong'e, China 92/D3
Dongen, Neth. 58/B5
Donges, Fr. 62/C6
Dongfang, China 106/E2
Dongfang, China 99/F5
Donggou, China 93/C3
Dongguan, China 99/G4
Dongguang, China 92/D3
Donghai, China 92/D4
Donghen, Laos 106/D2
Donghezhen, China 92/L8
Dongio, Swi. 67/E5
Dongjia, China 99/G2
Dongjing (riv.), China 99/G2
Dongjingling, China 93/B2
Dongkeng, China 99/H3
Dongkya (pass), China 109/G2
Dongli, China 105/K3
Dongliao (riv.), China 92/F2
Donglük, China 111/E4
Dongmen, China 106/D1
Dongming, China 92/C4
Dongnan (plat.), China 99/F4
Dongo, Ang. 140/B2
Dongo, D.R. Congo 138/D2
Dongo, D.R. Congo 139/E2
Dongo, It. 67/F5
Dongo-Kuma, D.R. Congo 138/E2
Dongobesh, Tanz. 137/A3
Dongola, Il, US 192/C2
Dongou, Congo 138/D2
Dongping, China 92/D4
Dongqiao, China 111/F5
Dongsha (isl.), China 99/H4
Dongsha (Pratas) (isl.), China 99/H4
Dongshajiao, China 99/J2
Dongshan (isl.), China 99/H4
Dongshan, China 92/L8
Dongshao, China 99/G3
Dongsheng, China 92/B3
Dongtai, China 92/E4
Dongtiao (riv.), China 92/L9
Dongting (lake), China 99/G2
Dongtingxi, China 99/F2
Dongue, Ang. 140/B2
Dongxing, China 106/D1
Dongxing, China 99/F3
Dongying, China 92/D3
Dongzhen, China 90/E4
Dongzhi, China 99/H2
Donie, Tx, US 181/F2
Donihue, Chile 226/N9
Donington, Eng, UK 41/H6
Doniphan, Mo, US 192/B2
Donjek (riv.), Yk, Can. 170/C2
Donji Komren, Serb. 56/E4
Donji Vakuf, Bosn. 56/C3
Donk, Neth. 58/C5
Donna, Tx, US 181/E4
Donnas, It. 68/A1
Donnelly, Mn, US 186/F5
Donner (pass), Ca, US 176/C4
Donner und Blitzen (riv.), Or, US 176/D2
Donnersberg (peak), Ger. 61/G4
Donnybrook, Austl. 158/D4
Donnybrook, Austl. 154/B5
Donnybrook, ND, US 186/D3
Donon (peak), Fr. 66/D1
Donora, Pa, US 191/G4
Donoratico, It. 51/J5
Donskoy, Rus. 79/L4
Donsol, Phil. 100/C2
Donville-les-Bains, Fr. 62/D3
Donyan (riv.), Myan. 98/B5
Donzdorf, Ger. 64/C5
Donzère, Fr. 70/A4
Donzy, Fr. 50/E3
Doole, Tx, US 180/E2
Dooleena (peak), Austl. 154/C2
Doomadgee Abor. Land, Austl. 153/E4
Doomadgee Aboriginal Community, Austl. 153/E4
Doon, Ire. 38/B4
Doon (lake), Sc, UK 39/B6
Doon (riv.), Sc, UK 39/B6
Doon Doon Abor. Land, Austl. 152/C4
Doonbeg (riv.), Ire. 38/A4
Doonbeg, Ire. 38/A4
Doonerak (mt.), Ak, US 201/H2
Door (pen.), Wi, US 187/L5
Door (pt.), La, US 194/D2
Doorn, Neth. 58/C4
Doorn (riv.), SAfr. 142/B3
Doppo (peak), It. 68/D2
Doqên (lake), China 109/G1
Dora (lake), Austl. 145/B3
Dora, Al, US 192/D4
Dora (lake), Fl, US 194/M6
Dora, Mo, US 183/H2
Dora Baltea (riv.), It. 70/D1
Dora Creek, Austl. 157/E1
Dora di Rhêmes (riv.), It. 70/D1
Dora Riparia (riv.), It. 51/G4
Dorada (coast), Sp. 53/F2
Dorāh Ān (pass), Pak. 111/B4
Doraville, Ga, US 193/M7
Dorchester, NB, Can. 188/E3
Dorchester (cape), Nun, Can. 171/J2
Dorchester, Eng, UK 42/D5
Dorchester, Ne, US 185/F3
Dorchester, NJ, US 198/D5
Dorchester, SC, US 193/G4
Dordabis, Namb. 140/C4
Dordogne (riv.), Fr. 72/D1
Dordrecht, Neth. 58/B5
Dordrecht, SAfr. 142/D3
Dore (mts.), Fr. 50/E4
Dore (riv.), Fr. 50/E4
Dores, Sc, UK 39/B2
Dores do Indaiá, Braz. 222/D3
Dorfen (riv.), Ger. 65/E6
Dorfen, Ger. 65/F6
Dorgali, It. 54/A2
Dörgön (lake), Mong. 90/C2
Dori, Burk. 133/E3
Doria, It. 68/B5
Dorion, On, Can. 187/K3
Dorion, Qu, Can. 189/M7
Dorking, Eng, UK 36/C3
Dorlisheim, Fr. 66/D1
Dormagen, Ger. 61/F1
Dormans, Fr. 60/C5
Dormans Land, Eng, UK 36/D3
Dornach, Swi. 66/D3
Dornakal, India 107/D2
Dornbirn, Aus. 67/F3
Dorney Park/ Wildwater Kingdom, Pa, US 198/C2
Dornhan, Ger. 67/E1
Dorno, It. 68/B3
Dornoch, Sc, UK 39/B1
Dornoch Firth (inlet), Sc, UK 39/B1
Dornod (prov.), Mong. 90/G2
Dornogovĭ (prov.), Mong. 90/F3
Dornstadt, Ger. 64/C6
Dornstetten, Ger. 64/B6
Doro, Mali 133/E2
Dorog, Hun. 57/Q9
Dorogobuzh, Rus. 74/G5
Dorogorskoye, Rus. 75/K2
Dorohoi, Rom. 78/D4
Doromo, D.R. Congo 139/F2
Doron de Chavière (riv.), Fr. 70/C2
Dorothy, NJ, US 198/D5
Dorowa Mining Lease, Zim. 141/F3
Dörpen, Ger. 59/E3
Dorra, Djib. 136/B2
Dorrance, Ks, US 183/E1
Dorre (isl.), Austl. 154/B3
Dorridge, Eng, UK 43/E2

Dorri – Eaton
282

Dorrigo, Austl. 156/E1
Dorrigo NP, Austl. 156/E1
Dorrington, Eng, UK 42/D1
Dorris, Ca, US 176/C3
Dorsale (mts.), Tun. 130/L7
Dorsbach (riv.), Ger. 64/B2
Dorset (co.), Eng, UK 42/D5
Dorsten, Ger. 58/D5
Dortan, Fr. 66/B5
Dortches, NC, US 193/J2
Dortmund, Ger. 59/E5
Dortmund (Wickede) (int'l arpt.), Ger. 59/E5
Dortmund-Ems (canal), Ger. 59/E4
Dörtyol, Turk. 116/E1
Dorum, Ger. 59/F1
Doruma, D.R. Congo 135/E4
Dorval, Qu, Can. 189/N7
Dörverden, Ger. 59/G3
Dos Bahias (cape), Arg. 226/D5
Dos de Mayo, Peru 220/C2
Dos Hermanas, Sp. 52/C4
Dos Palos, Ca, US 178/B2
Dos Pozos, Arg. 226/D4
Dos Puntas (cape), EqG. 138/B2
Dos Quebradas, Col. 219/K8
Dos Reyes (pt.), Chile 224/B3
Döşemealtı, Turk. 116/B1
Dosewallips (riv.), Wa, US 197/A2
Dōshi (riv.), Japan 95/C2
Dōshi, Japan 95/C2
Dosing, India 98/B3
Dospat, Bul. 55/J2
Dosse (riv.), Ger. 48/G2
Dosso (dept.), Niger 133/F3
Dosso, Niger 133/F3
Dosson, It. 69/F2
Dossor, Kaz. 77/K3
Dothan, Al, US 195/F2
Dot Lake, Ak, US 201/K3
Dötlingen, Ger. 59/F3
Dotnuva, Lith. 47/K4
Döttingen, Swi. 67/E2
Doty, Wa, US 174/C4
Douai, Fr. 60/C3
Douala, Camr. 138/B1
Douala (int'l arpt.), Camr. 138/B1
Douar el Câid el Gueddara, Mor. 130/A2
Douar Toulal, Mor. 130/B3
Douarnenez (bay), Fr. 50/A2
Douarnenez, Fr. 62/A4
Double Island (pt.), Austl. 158/D4
Double Mtn. Fork (riv.), Tx, US 205/E1
Double Springs, Al, US 192/D3
Doubs, Fr. 66/C4
Doubs (dept.), Fr. 66/C3
Doubs (riv.), Fr. 72/E1
Doubtful (bay), Austl. 152/B3
Doubtful Island (bay), Austl. 154/C5
Doubtless (bay), NZ 159/C1
Doucette, Tx, US 181/G2
Douchy-les-Mines, Fr. 60/C3
Doudeville, Fr. 63/F1
Doue, Fr. 36/M5
Doué-la-Fontaine, Fr. 63/E6
Douentza, Mali 132/E3
Dougga (ruin), Tun. 130/L6
Dougherty, Tx, US 183/G4
Douglas, Austl. 152/C3
Douglas (lake), BC, Can. 174/D2
Douglas, Ire. 38/B6
Douglas, SAfr. 142/C3
Douglas (cap.), IM, UK 40/D3
Douglas, Sc, UK 39/C5
Douglas (mt.), Ak, US 201/H4
Douglas, Az, US 179/H5
Douglas (co.), Ga, US 193/L7
Douglas, Ga, US 195/G2
Douglas, Mi, US 190/C3
Douglas, ND, US 186/D4
Douglas (lake), Tn, US 193/F3
Douglas, Wy, US 184/B2
Douglass, Ks, US 183/F2
Douglass, Tx, US 181/G2
Douglassville, Pa, US 198/C3
Douglastown, NB, Can. 188/E2
Douglasville, Ga, US 193/L7
Dougou, China 99/G1
Doujiang, China 99/F3
Doulaincourt-Saucourt, Fr. 66/B1
Doullens, Fr. 60/B3
Doumé, Camr. 134/B4
Doumé, Gabon 138/C3
Doumé (riv.), Camr. 134/B4
Dounby, Sc, UK 37/V14
Doune (peak), Sc, UK 39/B4
Doune, Sc, UK 39/B4
Doupovské Hory (mts.), Czh. 51/K1
Dour, Belg. 60/C3
Doura, Mali 132/D3
Dourada, Serra (mts.), Braz. 222/C2
Dourados, Braz. 225/F2
Dourados (riv.), Braz. 222/B4
Dourbali, Chad 134/B3
Dourdan, Fr. 36/J6
Dourdou (riv.), Fr. 50/E4
Dourdoura, Chad 134/D3
Dourh (peak), Mor. 129/E2
Douro (riv.), Port. 72/B2
Douron (riv.), Fr. 62/B3
Dousman, Wi, US 197/P13
Doussard, Fr. 66/C6
Douvaine, Fr. 66/C5
Douve (riv.), Fr. 62/D2
Douvrin, Fr. 60/B2
Doux (riv.), Fr. 50/F4
Douz, Tun. 129/H2
Douze (riv.), Fr. 50/C4
Dove Creek, Co, US 179/H2
Dover, Austl. 156/C4
Dover (pt.), Austl. 154/E5
Dover, Eng, UK 43/H4
Dover (str.), UK,Fr. 50/D1
Dover, Ar, US 183/H3
Dover (A.F.B.), De, US 198/C5
Dover (cap.), De, US 198/C5
Dover, Fl, US 194/L8
Dover, Ks, US 183/G1
Dover, NH, US 191/L3
Dover, NJ, US 198/D2
Dover, Oh, US 190/E1
Dover, Ok, US 183/F3
Dover, Pa, US 198/B4
Dover, Tn, US 192/D2
Dover Bluff, Ga, US 195/H2
Doveridge, Eng, UK 41/G6
Dovrefjell NP, Nor. 44/D3
Dovsk, Bela. 76/D1
Dow, Ok, US 183/G3
Dow City, Ia, US 185/G3
Dowagiac, Mi, US 190/C4
Dowerin, Austl. 154/C4
Dowghā'ī, Iran 113/G1
Dowi (cape), Indo. 101/B2
Dowlatābād, Iran 115/J4
Dowling, Ab, Can. 175/H2
Down (dist.), NI, UK 40/C3
Downers Grove, Il, US 197/P16
Downey, Ca, US 196/F8
Downey, Id, US 177/G2
Downham Market, Eng, UK 43/G1
Downieville, Ca, US 176/C4
Downingtown, Pa, US 198/C4
Downpatrick, NI, UK 40/C3
Downs, Ks, US 184/E4
Downsville, NY, US 191/J3
Downton, Eng, UK 43/E4
Dows, Ia, US 185/H2
Dowshī, Afg. 113/J1
Doygaab, Som. 137/C1
Doyle, Ca, US 176/C3
Doylestown, Pa, US 198/C3
Doyleville, Co, US 179/J1
Dōzen (isl.), Japan 96/C3
Dozier, Al, US 195/E2
Dozulé, Fr. 63/E2
Drâa (cape), Mor. 128/C3
Drâa, Oued (riv.), Mor. 119/B2
Drac (riv.), Fr. 50/F4
Dracena, Braz. 225/G2
Drachten, Neth. 58/D2
Drăgăneşti-Olt, Rom. 57/G3
Drăgăşani, Rom. 57/G3
Dragoman, Bul. 57/F4
Dragon's Mouth (str.), Trin.,Ven. 217/F2
Dragoon, Az, US 179/G4
Dragør, Den. 45/J7
Draguignan, Fr. 70/C5
Drain, Or, US 176/B2
Drake, ND, US 186/D4
Drake (passg.), SAm. 227/D8
Drakensberg (mts.), SAfr. 119/E8
Drakesville, Ia, US 185/H3
Dráma, Gre. 55/J2
Dramba, D.R. Congo 139/G2
Drammen, Nor. 46/D2
Drammensfjorden (fd.), Nor. 44/R8
Dramselva (riv.), Nor. 44/R8
Drance (riv.), Swi. 66/D5
Drancy, Fr. 36/K5
Drangedal, Nor. 46/C2
Dranse (riv.), Fr. 66/C5
Dransfeld, Ger. 59/G5
Drap, Fr. 70/D5
Draper, Ut, US 177/H3
Draperstown, NI, UK 40/B2
Drās, India 110/C2
Drau (riv.), Aus. 51/K3
Drava (riv.), Cro. 56/C2
Dráva (riv.), Hun. 56/C3
Drava (riv.), Slov. 51/L3
Draveil, Fr. 36/K5
Drawa (riv.), Pol. 49/H2
Drawienski NP, Pol. 49/H2
Drawsko Pomorskie, Pol. 49/H2
Drayton, ND, US 186/F3
Drayton Valley, Ab, Can. 174/G1
Dreghorn, Sc, UK 39/B5
Drei Zinnen (peak), PNG 103/K4
Dreiesselberg (peak), Ger. 65/G5
Dreisam (riv.), Ger. 66/D2
Drensteinfurt, Ger. 59/E5
Drenthe (prov.), Neth. 58/D3
Drentse Hoofdvaart (riv.), Neth. 58/D3
Drentwede, Ger. 59/F3
Dresano, It. 68/C3
Dresden, Ger. 80/B4
Dresden, Oh, US 190/E4
Dresden, On, Can. 190/E3
Dresden, Tn, US 192/C2
Dresser, Wi, US 185/H1
Dreux, Fr. 63/G3
Drew, Ms, US 192/B4
Drews (res.), Or, US 176/C2
Drewsey, Or, US 176/D2
Drexel, Mo, US 183/G1
Dreyer, Tx, US 181/F3
Drezdenko, Pol. 49/H2
Driebergen, Neth. 58/C4
Driedorf, Ger. 61/H2
Driffield, Eng, UK 41/H4
Drift Prairie (grsld.), ND, US 186/E4
Driggs, Id, US 177/H2
Drigh Road, Pak. 113/J4
Drimoleague, Ire. 38/A6
Drina (riv.), Bosn.,Serb. 56/D4
Drinit (gulf), Alb. 55/F2
Drinit (riv.), Alb. 55/F1
Dripping Springs, Tx, US 181/E2
Driscoll, ND, US 186/D4
Driscoll, Tx, US 181/F4
Driskill (mtn.), La, US 183/H4
Drniš, Cro. 56/C4
Dro, It. 67/G6
Drøbak, Nor. 46/D2
Drobeta-Turnu Severin, Rom. 56/F3
Drochia, Mol. 78/D3
Drochtersen, Ger. 59/G1
Drocourt, Fr. 36/H4
Drogheda, Ire. 40/B4
Drogichin, Bela. 78/C1
Drohobych, Ukr. 78/B3
Droichead Nuadh, Ire. 38/D3
Droitwich, Eng, UK 42/D2
Drolshagen, Ger. 61/G1
Dromahaire, Ire. 38/B1
Drôme (riv.), Fr. 63/E2
Drôme (dept.), Fr. 70/B3
Dromedary (mt.), Austl. 157/E3
Dromina, Ire. 38/B5
Dromiskin, Ire. 40/B4
Dromore (riv.), Ire. 40/A3
Dromore, NI, UK 40/B3
Dromore West, Ire. 38/B1
Dronero, It. 70/D4
Dronfield, Eng, UK 41/G5
Drongan, Sc, UK 39/B6
Dronne (riv.), Fr. 50/D4
Dronten, Neth. 58/C3
Drop, Tx, US 180/K6
Dropt (riv.), Fr. 50/D4
Drosh, Pak. 110/A2
Droskovo, Rus. 76/F1
Drottningholm Palace, Swe. 45/A1
Droué, Fr. 63/G4
Drouette (riv.), Fr. 60/A6
Drouin, Austl. 157/B4
Druento, It. 70/D2
Druid Hills, Ga, US 193/M7
Drum (inlet), NC, US 193/J3
Drumaness, NI, UK 40/C3
Drumbeg, NI, UK 40/C2
Drumcar, Ire. 40/B4
Drumcollogher, Ire. 38/B5
Drumcondra, Ire. 38/D2
Drumheller, Ab, Can. 175/H2
Drumkeeran, Ire. 38/B1
Drumleck (pt.), Ire. 40/B5
Drumlish, Ire. 38/C2
Drummond (mt.), Austl. 158/B4
Drummond (pt.), Austl. 155/G5
Drummond (range), Austl. 145/D3
Drummond, NB, Can. 188/D2
Drummond, Id, US 177/H2
Drummond (isl.), MI, US 190/E1
Drummond, Wi, US 187/J4
Drummonds, Tn, US 192/B3
Drummondville, Qu, Can. 191/K2
Drummore, Sc, UK 40/D2
Drumnadrochit, Sc, UK 39/B2
Drumnakilly, NI, UK 40/A2
Drumochter, Pass of (pass), Sc, UK 39/B3
Drumright, Ok, US 183/F3
Drumshanbo, Ire. 38/B1
Drumsna, Ire. 38/B2
Drunen, Neth. 58/C5
Drunken (pt.), Mb, Can. 186/F2
Druridge (bay), Eng, UK 41/G1
Drusenheim, Fr. 61/G6
Druskininkai, Lith. 47/K4
Druten, Neth. 58/C5
Druya, Bela. 47/M4
Druzhba, Kaz. 111/D2
Druzhba, Ukr. 79/G1
Druzhkivka, Ukr. 79/J3
Drvar, Bosn. 56/C3
Drwęca (riv.), Pol. 49/K2
Dry (lake), ND, US 186/E3
Dry (cr.), Ca, US 176/C4
Dry Cimarron (riv.), Ok, US 182/C2
Dry Creek, Yk, Can. 201/K3
Dry Creek, La, US 194/B2
Dry Fork (riv.), Wy, US 184/B1
Dry Fork Marias (riv.), Mt, US 175/H3
Dry Prong, La, US 194/B2
Dry Ridge, Ky, US 192/E1
Dry Run, Oh, US 193/F1
Dry Tortugas (isl.), Fl, US 195/G5
Dry Tortugas Nat'l Pk., Fl, US 195/G5
Dryanovo, Bul. 57/G4
Dryden, On, Can. 187/H3
Dryden, Mi, US 197/F6
Dryden, NY, US 191/H3
Dryden, Tx, US 180/C2
Dryden, Va, US 193/F2
Drygarn Fawr (peak), Wal, UK 42/C2
Drymen, Sc, UK 39/B4
Drysdale (riv.), Austl. 152/B3
Drysdale River NP, Austl. 152/B3
Du (riv.), China 90/G5
Du Bois, Pa, US 191/G4
Du Dja, Réserve, Camr. 134/B5
Du Long, Viet. 106/E4
Du Page (co.), Il, US 197/P16
Du Page (riv.), Il, US 197/P16
Du Page, East Branch (riv.), Il, US 197/P16
Du Quoin, Il, US 192/C1
Duaringa, Austl. 158/C3
Duarte (peak), DRep. 203/G4
Duarte, Ca, US 196/G7
Ḍubā, SAr. 127/G3
Dubach, La, US 183/H4
Dubai (int'l arpt.), UAE 113/G3
Dubăsari, Mol. 78/E4
Dubawnt (riv.), NW, Can. 170/F2
Dubawnt (lake), Nun, Can. 170/F2
Dubawnt (lake), Can. 163/G3
Dubayy, UAE 113/G3
Dubele, D.R. Congo 139/G2
Dübendorf, Swi. 67/E3
Dübener Heide (phys. reg.), Ger. 48/G3
Dubino, It. 67/F5
Dublin (cap.), Ire. 40/B5
Dublin (co.), Ire. 40/B5
Dublin, Ca, US 197/L11
Dublin, Ga, US 193/F4
Dublin, Md, US 198/B4
Dublin, Oh, US 190/E4
Dublin, Pa, US 198/C3
Dublin, Tx, US 181/E1
Dublin, Va, US 193/G2
Dubna, Rus. 76/F1
Dubna, Rus. 74/H4
Dubnica nad Váhom, Slvk. 49/K4
Dubno, Ukr. 78/C2
Dubois, Wy, US 177/J2
Dubois, Id, US 177/G1
Duboistown, Pa, US 198/A1
Dubossary (res.), Mol. 57/J2
Dubovskiy, Rus. 77/G2
Dubovskoye, Rus. 79/M4
Dubovyy Umët, Rus. 77/J1
Dubra, India 109/F4
Dubrājpur, India 109/F4
Dubréka, Gui. 132/B4
Dubrovka, Rus. 76/E1
Dubrovka, Rus. 47/P2
Dubrovnik, Cro. 56/D4
Dubrovnik (int'l arpt.), Cro. 56/D4
Dubrovno, Bela. 47/P4
Dubrovytsya, Ukr. 78/D2
Dubulu, D.R. Congo 134/D4
Dubuque, Ia, US 185/J2
Duc Lap, Viet. 106/D3
Duc Pho, Viet. 106/E3
Duc Phong, Viet. 106/D4
Duchcov, Czh. 65/G1
Duchesne, Ut, US 177/H3
Duchesne (riv.), Ut, US 177/H3
Duchess, Austl. 155/H2
Duchess, Ab, Can. 175/J2
Ducie (isl.), Pitc. 161/N7
Duck (lake), Mi, US 197/E7
Duck (cr.), Nv, US 177/F4
Duck (riv.), Tn, US 192/D3
Duck Bay, Mb, Can. 186/D1
Duck Hill, Ms, US 192/C4
Duck Lake, Sk, Can. 175/L1
Duck (mtn.), Mb, Can. 186/D2
Duck Valley Ind. Res., Id, US 176/E2
Duckabush (riv.), Wa, US 197/A2
Ducktown, Tn, US 192/E3
Duckwater, Nv, US 176/F4
Duckwater Ind. Res., Nv, US 178/E1
Duclair, Fr. 63/F2
Duda (riv.), Col. 216/C4
Duddon (riv.), Eng, UK 41/E3
Dudelange, Lux. 61/F5
Dudenhofen, Ger. 64/B4
Duderstadt, Ger. 59/H5
Dudh Kosi (riv.), Nepal 109/F2
Dūdhi, India 108/D3
Dudhwa NP, India 108/C1
Dudignac, Arg. 226/E2
Düdingen, Swi. 66/D4
Dudinka, Rus. 80/J3
Dudley, Eng, UK 42/D1
Dudley (co.), Eng, UK 42/D1
Dudub, Eth. 136/C4
Dudzele, Belg. 60/C1
Due, D.R. Congo 138/D4
Due West, SC, US 193/F3
Duékoué, C.d'Iv. 132/D5
Dueñas, Sp. 52/C2
Duenweg, Mo, US 183/G2
Dueré, Braz. 222/C1
Duette, Fl, US 194/L8
Dueville, It. 69/E2
Dufaja (riv.), Kenya 137/B2
Duff (isls.), Sol. 160/F5
Duffel, Belg. 61/D1
Dufferin (co.), On, Can. 190/S8
Duffield, Eng, UK 41/G6
Duff's Corners, On, Can. 190/S9
Dufftown, Sc, UK 39/C2
Dufour (Dufourspitze) (peak), Swi. 68/A1
Dufourspitze (Dufour) (peak), Swi. 68/A1
Dugachhi, Bang. 109/H3
Dugald, Mb, Can. 186/F3
Dugbia, D.R. Congo 139/F2
Dugdemona (riv.), La, US 181/H1
Dugger, In, US 192/D1
Dugi (isl.), Cro. 51/L4
Dugi Otok (isl.), Cro. 73/G2
Dugny-sur-Meuse, Fr. 61/E5
Dugo Selo, Cro. 56/C3
Dugu, Eth. 136/B3
Dugway, Ut, US 177/G3
Dugway Proving Grounds, Ut, US 177/G3
Duich (lake), Sc, UK 39/A2
Duida (peak), Ven. 217/E4
Duida Marahuaca, PN, Ven. 217/E4
Duifken (pt.), Austl. 153/F3
Duingen, Ger. 59/G4
Duino, It. 69/G2
Duisburg, Ger. 58/D6
Duitama, Col. 216/C3
Duiven, Neth. 58/D5
Duivendrecht, Neth. 58/B4
Dujuuma, Som. 137/C1
Duk Fadiat, Sudan 135/F4
Dukafulu, Eth. 136/A4
Dukambīya, Erit. 135/H2
Duke, Mo, US 183/H2
Duke of Gloucester (isls.), FrPol. 161/L7
Duke's (pass), Sc, UK 39/B4
Dukhān, Qatar 112/F3
Dukla Pass (Dukielska) (pass), Pol. 49/L4
Dūkštas, Lith. 47/M4
Dula, D.R. Congo 134/D4
Dulac, La, US 194/C3
Dulan, China 90/D4
Dulce (riv.), Arg. 224/D4
Dulce, NM, US 179/J2
Dulce (gulf), Pan. 207/F4
Dulce Nombre de Culmí, Hon. 207/E3
Dule, Erit. 136/A2
Duleek, Ire. 40/B4
Dŭlgopol, Bul. 57/H4
Duliu (riv.), China 105/J2
Duliu, China 92/H7
Dullewāla, Pak. 110/A4
Dullstroom, SAfr. 141/F5
Dülmen, Ger. 59/E5
Dulnain (riv.), Sc, UK 39/C2
Dulong (pass), China 98/B3
Dulovo, Bul. 57/H4
Dulunguin (pt.), Phil. 100/C4
Duluth, Mn, US 187/H4
Duluth, Ga, US 193/M6
Dulverton, Eng, UK 42/C4
Dūmā, Syria 117/E1
Dūmā, WBnk. 117/C4
Dumagasa (pt.), Phil. 100/C4
Dumaguete, Phil. 100/C3
Dumai, Indo. 101/C2
Dumalinao, Phil. 100/C4
Dumanjug, Phil. 100/C3
Dumaran, Phil. 100/B3
Dumaran (isl.), Phil. 103/E1
Dumas, Tx, US 182/D3
Dumas, Ar, US 183/J4
Ḍumayr, Syria 116/E3
Ḍumayr, Syria 117/F1
Dumbarton, Sc, UK 39/B5
Dumbi, D.R. Congo 138/D4
Dumbi, Ang. 140/B1
Ďumbier (peak), Slvk. 49/K4
Dumbleyung, Austl. 154/C5
Dumbrăveni, Rom. 57/G2
Dume (pt.), Ca, US 196/B2
Dumei, China 99/H3
Dumfries, Sc, UK 40/E1
Dumfries and Galloway (co.), Sc, UK 39/C6
Duminichi, Rus. 76/E1
Dumka, India 109/F3
Dumlu, Turk. 77/G4
Dummar, Syria 117/E1
Dümmer (lake), Ger. 59/F3
Dumoine (riv.), Qu, Can. 191/H1
Dumoine (lake), Qu, Can. 171/J4
Dumont, NJ, US 199/K8
Dumont d'Urville, Fr., Ant. 228/K5
Dumraon, India 109/E3
Dumri, India 109/F4
Dumyat (gov.), Egypt 114/B3
Dumyāţ (Damietta), Egypt 131/C2
Dumyāţ, Massabb (Damietta) (mouth), Egypt 131/C1
Dún Laoghaire, Ire. 40/B5
Dun Rig (peak), Sc, UK 39/C5
Dunaföldvár, Hun. 56/D2
Dunaharaszti, Hun. 57/R10
Dunajec (riv.), Pol. 49/L4
Dunakeszi, Hun. 57/R9
Dunany (pt.), Ire. 40/B4
Dunaszekcso, Hun. 56/D2
Dunaújváros, Hun. 56/D2
Dunavecse, Hun. 56/D2
Dunavtsi, Bul. 56/F4
Dunayivtsi, Ukr. 78/D3
Dunbar, Sc, UK 39/D5
Dunbar, Austl. 158/A2
Dunblane, Sk, Can. 175/L2
Dunblane, Sc, UK 39/C4
Dunboyne, Ire. 40/B5
Duncan, BC, Can. 174/C3
Duncan, Az, US 179/H4
Duncan, Ms, US 192/B3
Duncan, Ok, US 183/F3
Duncannon, Ire. 38/D5
Duncannon, Pa, US 198/A3
Duncansby Head (pt.), Sc, UK 37/V14
Duncanville, Tx, US 180/L7
Dund-Us, Mong. 90/C2
Dundaga, Lat. 47/K3
Dundalk, On, Can. 190/F2
Dundalk (bay), Ire. 40/B4
Dundalk, Ire. 40/B4
Dundalk, Md, US 198/B5
Dundas (lake), Austl. 154/D5
Dundas (str.), Austl. 152/C2
Dundas (pen.), NW, Can. 171/R7
Dundas, On, Can. 190/T9
Dundas, Oh, US 193/F1
Dundas, Il, US 192/C1
Dundee, SAfr. 143/E3
Dundee, Sc, UK 39/D4
Dundee (co.), Sc, UK 39/D4
Dundee (arpt.), Sc, UK 39/C4
Dundee, Fl, US 194/M7
Dundee, Ms, US 192/B3
Dundee, Tx, US 182/E4
Dundgovi (prov.), Mong. 90/F2
Dundīţ, Egypt 131/C3
Dundonald, Sc, UK 39/B5
Dundrum (bay), NI, UK 40/C3
Dundrum, NI, UK 40/C3
Dundurn, Sk, Can. 175/L2
Dundwa (range), Nepal 108/D2
Dundwārāganj, India 108/B2
Dunedin, NZ 159/B4
Dunedin, Fl, US 194/K7
Dunedoo, Austl. 156/D2
Dunellen, NJ, US 199/H9
Dunes City, Or, US 176/A2
Dunfanaghy, Ire. 37/Q9
Dunfermline, Sc, UK 39/C4
Dunga Bunga, Pak. 110/B5
Dungalear Station, Austl. 156/D1
Dungannon, NI, UK 40/B3
Dungannon (co.), NI, UK 40/B3
Dungannon, On, Can. 190/F3
Dungarpur, India 104/B3
Dungarvan, Ire. 38/C5
Dungarvan (har.), Ire. 38/C5
Dungau (reg.), Ger. 65/F5
Dungeness (pt.), Arg. 227/C7
Dungeness (pt.), Eng, UK 43/G5
Dungeness, Wa, US 174/C3
Dungiven, NI, UK 40/B2
Dunglow, Ire. 37/P9
Dungog, Austl. 156/D2
Dungu, D.R. Congo 139/G2
Dungu (riv.), D.R. Congo 135/F5
Dunham, Qu, Can. 191/K2
Dunhua, China 91/K3
Dunhuang, China 90/C3
Dunkeld, Sc, UK 39/C3
Dunkellin (riv.), Ire. 38/B3
Dunkerque (Dunkirk), Fr. 50/E1
Dunkery (hill), Eng, UK 42/C4
Dunkirk (Dunkerque), Fr. 50/E1
Dunkirk, In, US 190/D4
Dunkirk, NY, US 191/G3
Dunkley, BC, Can. 174/C1
Dunkwa, Gha. 133/E5
Dunlap, Tn, US 192/E3
Dunlap, Ia, US 185/G3
Dunlavin, Ire. 38/D3
Dunleath, Sk, Can. 186/C2
Dunleer, Ire. 40/B4
Dunloe, Gap of (pass), Ire. 38/A5
Dunloy, NI, UK 40/B2
Dunmanus (bay), Ire. 38/A6
Dunmanway, Ire. 38/A6
Dunmore, Ire. 38/B2
Dunmore, Pa, US 191/J4
Dunmore, WV, US 193/H1
Dunmore East, Ire. 38/C5
Dunmurry, NI, UK 40/B2
Dunn, La, US 183/J4
Dunn, NC, US 193/H3
Dunnamanagh, NI, UK 40/A2
Dunnamore, NI, UK 40/B2
Dunnell, Mn, US 185/G2
Dunnellon, Fl, US 195/G3
Dünnern (riv.), Swi. 66/D3
Dunnet Head (pt.), Sc, UK 37/V14
Dunning, Sc, UK 39/C4
Dunningen, Ger. 67/E1
Dunnington, Eng, UK 41/H4
Dunnsville, Va, US 193/J2
Dunnville, On, Can. 190/T10
Dunolly, Austl. 156/B3
Dunoon, Sc, UK 39/B5
Dunqulah, Sudan 127/F5
Dunqunāb, Sudan 112/C4
Dunragit, Sc, UK 40/D2
Duns, Sc, UK 39/D5
Dunsborough, Austl. 154/B5
Dunscore, Sc, UK 40/E1
Dunseith, ND, US 186/D3
Dunseverick, NI, UK 40/B1
Dunshaughlin, Ire. 40/B4
Dunsmuir, Ca, US 176/B3
Dunstable, Eng, UK 43/F3
Dunster, BC, Can. 174/E1
Duntocher, Sc, UK 39/B5
Dunure, Sc, UK 39/B6
Dunville, Nf, Can. 189/L2
Dunwoody, Ga, US 193/M7
Dunyāpur, Pak. 110/A5
Duobukur (riv.), China 91/J1
Duojing, China 99/E4
Duolun, China 90/H3
Dupont, In, US 192/E1
Dupont, Pa, US 198/C1
Dupree, SD, US 184/D1
Dupuy (cape), Austl. 154/B2
Duque Bacelar, Braz. 219/F4
Duque de Caxias, Braz. 223/N7
Duque de York (isl.), Chile 227/A6
Duquette, Mn, US 187/H4
Dūrā, WBnk. 117/C5
Durack (range), Austl. 152/B4
Durack (riv.), Austl. 152/B4
Durağan, Turk. 76/E4
Durak, Turk. 116/D1
Durand, Mi, US 190/E3
Durand, Wi, US 185/J1
Durango (state), Mex. 202/A3
Durango, Sp. 50/B5
Durango, Co, US 179/J2
Durango de Victoria, Mex. 204/D3
Duranillin, Austl. 154/C5
Durant, Ok, US 183/F4
Durant, Fl, US 194/L8
Durant, Ms, US 192/C4
Durazno (dept.), Uru. 227/F2
Durazno, Uru. 227/K10
Durban, SAfr. 143/E3
Durban (Louis Botha) (int'l arpt.), SAfr. 143/E3
Durbanville, SAfr. 142/L10
Durbe, Lat. 47/J3
Durbion (riv.), Fr. 66/C1
Durbuy, Belg. 61/E3
Dúrcal, Sp. 52/D4
Durdevac, Cro. 56/C2
Durdevo, Serb. 56/E3
Durdur (riv.), Som. 136/B3
Düre, China 111/E2
Dureji, Pak. 113/J3
Düren, Ger. 61/F2
Durg, India 107/D1
Durgāpur, India 109/G3
Durgāpur, India 109/F4
Durgerdam, Neth. 58/B4
Durham, On, Can. 190/F2
Durham (co.), On, Can. 190/V8
Durham (co.), Eng, UK 41/F2
Durham, Eng, UK 41/G2
Durham, Ca, US 176/C4
Durham, Ks, US 183/F1
Durham, Mo, US 185/J4
Durham, NC, US 193/H3
Durham, NH, US 191/L3
Durham Bridge, NB, Can. 188/D2
Durham Downs, Austl. 158/A4
Duri, Indo. 101/C2
Durlston (pt.), Eng, UK 42/E5
Ḍurmā, SAr. 112/E4
Durmitor NP, Mont. 56/D4
Durnford (pt.), WSah. 128/B5
Duror, Sc, UK 39/A5
Dürrenroth, Swi. 66/D3
Durrës, Alb. 55/F2
Durrington, Eng, UK 43/E4
Dürrlauingen, Ger. 64/D6
Durrow, Ire. 38/C4
Dürrwangen, Ger. 64/D4
Dursley, Eng, UK 42/D3
Dursunbey, Turk. 76/D5
Durtal, Fr. 63/E5
Duru, D.R. Congo 135/F4
Durugu, D.R. Congo 134/C4
Durukhsi, Eth. 136/C3
Durusu (lake), Turk. 115/M6
Durusu, Turk. 115/M6
Durūz (peak), Syria 127/H1
D'Urville (cape), Indo. 103/J4
Dusa Marreb (Dhuusamarreeb), Som. 136/C4
Dusanovac, Serb. 56/E4
Dusetos, Lith. 47/L4
Dushak, Trkm. 113/H1
Dushan, China 99/E3
Dushanbe (cap.), Taj. 80/G6
Dusheti, Geo. 77/H4
Dushui (riv.), China 99/E3
Dusky (sound), NZ 159/A4
Düsseldorf (int'l arpt.), Ger. 58/D6
Düsseldorf, Ger. 58/D6
Dusti, Taj. 113/J1
Dustin, Ok, US 183/F3
Duszniki-Zdrój, Pol. 49/J3
Dutch (riv.), Eng, UK 41/H4
Dutch (cr.), BC, Can. 174/F2
Dutch Harbor, Ak, US 201/E5
Dutch John, Ut, US 177/J3
Dutch Wonderland, Pa, US 198/B3
Dutlwe, Bots. 140/D4
Dutoitspiek (peak), SAfr. 142/L10
Dutovo, Rus. 75/N3
Dutse, Nga. 133/H4
Dutsen Wai, Nga. 133/H4
Dutsin-Ma, Nga. 133/G3
Dutton, On, Can. 190/F3
Dutton (mt.), Ut, US 179/F1
Dutton, Mt, US 175/J4
Dutukpene, Gha. 133/F4
Duvall, Wa, US 197/D2
Duvno, Bosn. 56/C4
Düxanbibazar, China 111/D4
Duxun, China 99/H4
Duyang, China 99/E3
Duyun, China 99/E3
Düzce, Turk. 57/K5
Düzici, Turk. 114/D2
Dve Mogili, Bul. 57/G4
Dvina (bay), Rus. 74/H2
Dvinskoy, Rus. 75/K3
Dvořiště (lake), Czh. 65/H4
Dvorníky, Slvk. 56/C1
Dwārka, India 113/J4
Dwārkeswar (riv.), India 109/F4
Dwight, Ks, US 183/F1
Dwight, Il, US 190/B4
Dworshak (res.), Id, US 174/F4
Dwyer (Faywood), NM, US 179/H4
Dwyfor (riv.), Wal, UK 40/D6
Dwyka (riv.), SAfr. 142/C4
Dyat'kovo, Rus. 76/E1
Dybvad, Den. 46/D3
Dyce, Sc, UK 39/D2
Dyce (int'l arpt.), Sc, UK 39/D2
Dyckesville, Wi, US 190/C2
Dyer (cape), Nun, Can. 171/K2
Dyer (cape), Chile 227/B6
Dyer, In, US 190/C4
Dyer, Nv, US 178/C2
Dyer, Tn, US 192/C2
Dyersburg, Tn, US 192/C2
Dyersville, Ia, US 185/J2
Dyess, Ar, US 192/B3
Dyess (A.F.B.), Tx, US 180/E1
Dyfed (co.), Wal, UK 42/B2
Dyffryn, Wal, UK 40/D6
Dyfi (riv.), Wal, UK 42/C1
Dyje (riv.), Czh. 49/J4
Dykan'ka, Ukr. 79/H3
Dyke Ackland (bay), PNG 153/H2
Dykh-tau (peak), Rus. 77/G4
Dyle (riv.), Belg. 48/C3
Dyleň (peak), Czh. 65/F3
Dylewska (peak), Pol. 49/K2
Dymchurch, Eng, UK 43/G4
Dymer, Ukr. 78/F2
Dymytrov, Ukr. 79/J3
Dysart, Sk, Can. 186/B2
Dysart, Austl. 158/C3
Dysart, Ia, US 185/H2
Dysseldorp, SAfr. 142/C4
Dyul'tydag (peak), Rus. 77/H4
Dyurtyuli, Rus. 75/M5
Dzalanyama (range), Moz. 141/G2
Dzamandzar, Madg. 143/J6
Dzaoudzi (cap.), May., Fr. 143/H6
Dzaoudzi (int'l arpt.), May., Fr. 143/H6
Dzavhan (riv.), Mong. 90/C2
Dzavhan (prov.), Mong. 90/D2
Dzel, Mong. 111/F2
Dzenzik (pt.), Ukr. 79/J4
Dzerzhinsk, Rus. 74/J4
Dzerzhinsk, Bela. 47/M5
Dzerzhyns'k, Ukr. 79/J3
Dzerzhyns'k, Ukr. 78/D2
Dzhalinda, Rus. 91/J1
Dzhambeyty, Kaz. 77/K2
Dzhanga, Trkm. 115/H1
Dzhankoy, Ukr. 79/H5
Dzhanybek, Kaz. 77/H2
Dzharylgach (gulf), Ukr. 57/L2
Dzhebel, Bul. 55/J2
Dzhebrail, Azer. 115/F2
Dzhirgatal', Taj. 111/B4
Dzhubga, Rus. 76/F3
Dzhugdzhur (range), Rus. 83/N4
Dzhusaly, Kaz. 80/G5
Działdowo, Pol. 49/L2
Dzibalchén, Mex. 206/D2
Dzibilchaltún (ruin), Mex. 206/D1
Dzidzantún, Mex. 206/D1
Dzierżoniów, Pol. 49/J3
Dzitbalché, Mex. 206/D1
Dziuché, Mex. 206/D2
Dzöölön, Mong. 90/D1
Dzukija NP, Lith. 47/L4
Dzungarian (basin), China 80/J5
Dzur, Mong. 90/D2
Dzüünbayan, Mong. 90/G3
Dzüünbulag, Mong. 90/G2
Dzüünharaa, Mong. 90/F2
Dzüünhövöö, Mong. 111/F1
Dzuunmod, Mong. 90/F2

E

E.D.F. (canal), Fr. 70/B5
Eads, Co, US 182/C1
Eagan, Mn, US 187/P7
Eagle (riv.), Nf, Can. 171/L3
Eagle (cr.), Sk, Can. 175/K2
Eagle (hills), Sk, Can. 175/K1
Eagle (mt.), Ire. 38/A5
Eagle, Ak, US 201/K3
Eagle (lake), Ca, US 176/C3
Eagle (mts.), Ca, US 178/E4
Eagle (peak), Ca, US 176/C3
Eagle (peak), Ca, US 176/D4
Eagle, Co, US 177/K4
Eagle (riv.), Co, US 177/K4
Eagle, Id, US 176/E2
Eagle (cr.), Ky, US 192/E1
Eagle (mtn.), Mn, US 187/J4
Eagle, Ne, US 185/F3
Eagle (peak), Tx, US 180/B2
Eagle (pt.), Tx, US 180/N9
Eagle, Wi, US 197/P14
Eagle (peak), Wy, US 177/H1
Eagle Bend, Mn, US 187/G4
Eagle Butte, SD, US 184/D1
Eagle Crags (peak), Ca, US 178/D3
Eagle Grove, Ia, US 185/H2
Eagle Lake, Fl, US 194/M8
Eagle Lake, Tx, US 180/F3
Eagle Mills, Ar, US 183/H4
Eagle Mountain (lake), Tx, US 183/F4
Eagle Pass, Tx, US 180/D3
Eagle Point, Or, US 176/B2
Eagle River, Mi, US 187/K4
Eagle River, Wi, US 187/K5
Eagle Rock, Va, US 193/H2
Eaglehawk, Austl. 157/B3
Eaglesfield, Sc, UK 41/E1
Eaglesham, Sc, UK 39/B5
Eagleton, Ar, US 183/G3
Eagletown, Ok, US 183/G3
Eagleville, Ca, US 176/C3
Eagleville, Mo, US 185/H3
Eahun, Indo. 152/A2
Eakly, Ok, US 183/E3
Ealing (bor.), Eng, UK 36/B2
Ear Falls, On, Can. 187/H2
Earby, Eng, UK 41/F4
Earith, Eng, UK 43/G2
Earl Grey, Sk, Can. 186/B2
Earl Stonham, Eng, UK 43/H2
Earle, Ar, US 192/B3
Earle Nav. Weapons Ctr., NJ, US 199/D3
Earlimart, Ca, US 178/C3
Earling, Ia, US 185/G3
Earlington, Ky, US 192/D2
Earls Barton, Eng, UK 43/F2
Earls Colne, Eng, UK 43/G3
Earl's Seat (peak), Sc, UK 39/B4
Earlsboro, Ok, US 183/F3
Earlsferry, Sc, UK 39/D4
Earlston, Sc, UK 39/D5
Earltown, NS, Can. 188/F3
Earlville, Ia, US 185/J2
Earlville, Il, US 185/K3
Early, Ia, US 185/G2
Early, Tx, US 180/E2
Earn (riv.), Sc, UK 39/C4
Earn (lake), Sc, UK 39/B4
Earnslaw (mt.), NZ 159/B4
Earp, Ca, US 178/E3
Easington, Eng, UK 41/G2
Easingwold, Eng, UK 41/G3
Easky, Ire. 38/B1
Easley, SC, US 193/F3
East (mt.), Austl. 154/D4
East (cape), NZ 159/D2
East (cape), Ak, US 201/B6
East (mesa), Ca, US 178/E4
East (cape), Fl, US 195/H5
East (pt.), NJ, US 198/C5
East (riv.), NY, US 199/K8
East (bay), Tx, US 181/G3
East (passg.), Wa, US 197/C3
East Alamosa, Co, US 182/B2
East Alligator (riv.), Austl. 152/D3
East Anglia (reg.), Eng, UK 43/H2
East Angus, Qu, Can. 191/L2
East Arrow Park, BC, Can. 174/F2
East Ayrshire (co.), Sc, UK 39/B6
East Baines (riv.), Austl. 152/C3
East Bangor, Pa, US 198/C2
East Barming, Eng, UK 36/E3
East Barnet (nbrhd.), Eng, UK 36/C2
East Berbice-Corentyne (pol. reg.), Guy. 217/G3
East Bergholt, Eng, UK 43/H3
East Berlin, Pa, US 198/B4
East Bernstadt, Ky, US 192/E2
East Berwick, Pa, US 198/B1
East Bethel, Mn, US 187/H5
East Bijou (cr.), Co, US 184/B4
East Brady, Pa, US 191/G4
East Brewton, Al, US 194/E2
East Brunswick, NJ, US 199/H10
East Cache (cr.), Ok, US 183/E3
East Caicos (isl.), UK 207/J1
East Calder, Sc, UK 39/C5
East Camden, Ar, US 183/H4
East Carbon, Ut, US 177/H4
East Chevington, Eng, UK 39/E6
East Chicago, In, US 190/C4
East China (sea), Asia 83/M6
East Clandon, Eng, UK 36/B3
East Coulee, Ab, Can. 175/H2
East Dart (riv.), Eng, UK 42/C5
East Dereham, Eng, UK 43/G1
East Detroit (East Pointe), Mi, US 197/G7
East Dismal (swamp), NC, US 193/J3
East Dublin, Ga, US 193/F4
East Dumbartonshire (co.), Sc, UK 39/B5
East Falkland (isl.), UK 209/D8
East Falmouth, Ma, US 191/L4
East Farmingdale, NY, US 199/M9
East Flat Rock, NC, US 193/F3
East Fork (riv.), Tx, US 183/F4
East Fork Chandalar (riv.), Ak, US 201/J2
East Fork Trinity (riv.), Tx, US 180/L6
East Frisian (isls.), Neth. 48/D2
East Frisian (isls.), Ger. 46/B5
East Ghor (canal), Jor. 117/D4
East Glacier Park, Mt, US 175/H3
East Glen (riv.), Eng, UK 41/H6
East Grand Rapids, Mi, US 190/D3
East Greenville, Pa, US 198/C3
East Griffin, Ga, US 192/E4
East Grinstead, Eng, UK 43/F4
East Gull Lake, Mn, US 187/G4
East Hampton, NY, US 199/F2
East Hampton (arpt.), NY, US 199/F2
East Hanningfield, Eng, UK 36/E2
East Haven, Ct, US 199/F1
East Helena, Mt, US 175/J4
East Hill-Meridian, Wa, US 197/C3
East Hills, NY, US 199/L8
East Hodge, La, US 194/B1
East Horseley, Eng, UK 36/B3
East Jordan, Mi, US 190/D2
East Kilbride, Sc, UK 39/B5
East Korea (bay), NKor. 91/K4
East Lamma (chan.), China 99/L8
East Lansing, Mi, US 190/D3
East Las Vegas, Nv, US 178/E2
East Leake, Eng, UK 41/G6
East Linton, Sc, UK 39/D5
East Liverpool, Oh, US 190/F4
East London, SAfr. 142/D4
East Los Angeles, Ca, US 196/F7
East Lothian (co.), Sc, UK 39/D5
East Malling, Eng, UK 36/E3
East Meadow, NY, US 199/L9
East Midlands (int'l arpt.), Eng, UK 41/G6
East Millcreek, Ut, US 177/H3
East Mojave Nat'l Scenic Area, Ca, US 178/E3
East Molesey, Eng, UK 36/B2
East Montpelier, Vt, US 191/K2
East Naples, Fl, US 195/H4
East Newark, NJ, US 199/J9
East Nishnabotna (riv.), Ia, US 185/G3
East Nodaway (riv.), Ia, US 185/G3
East Northport, NY, US 199/E2
East Olympia, Wa, US 174/C4
East Orange, NJ, US 199/J8
East Otis, Ma, US 191/K3
East Palatka, Fl, US 195/H3
East Palestine, Oh, US 190/F4
East Peckham, Eng, UK 36/E3
East Petersburg, Pa, US 198/B3
East Point, Ga, US 193/M7
East Point, La, US 180/H1
East Pointe (East Detroit), Mi, US 197/G7
East Port Orchard, Wa, US 197/B2
East Prairie, Mo, US 192/C2
East Prospect, Pa, US 198/B4
East Quogue, NY, US 199/F2
East Riding of Yorkshire (co.), Eng, UK 41/H4
East Renfrewshire (co.), Sc, UK 39/B5
East Retford, Eng, UK 41/H5
East Ridge, Tn, US 192/E3
East Rockaway, NY, US 199/L9
East Rockingham, NC, US 193/H3
East Rutherford, NJ, US 199/J8
East Saint Louis, Il, US 185/J4
East Siberian (sea), Rus. 81/S2
East Side, Pa, US 198/C1
East Stroudsburg, Pa, US 198/C2
East Sussex (co.), Eng, UK 43/G5
East Tampa, Fl, US 194/L8
East Tawas, Mi, US 190/E2
East Thermopolis, Wy, US 177/J2
East Timbalier Island Nat'l Wild. Ref., La, US 194/C3
East Timor (ctry.) 152/B2
East Troy, Wi, US 197/P14
East Walker (riv.), Ca, Nv, US 176/D4
East Wemyss, Sc, UK 39/C4
East Wenatchee, Wa, US 174/D4
East Windsor, NJ, US 198/D3
East Wittering, Eng, UK 43/F5
East York (city), On, Can. 190/U8
East-the-Water, Eng, UK 42/B4
Eastabuchie, Ms, US 194/D2
Eastbourne, Eng, UK 43/G5
Eastend, Sk, Can. 175/K3
Easter (pt.), Namb. 140/B5
Easter (Isla de Pascua) (isl.), Chile 161/Q7
Eastern (pt.), Nf, Can. 189/H2
Eastern (pol. reg.), Gha. 133/E5
Eastern (chan.), Japan 96/A4
Eastern (prov.), Kenya 137/B1
Eastern (prov.), SLeo. 132/C4
Eastern (prov.), SrL. 107/D5
Eastern (plain), Eng, UK 41/H4
Eastern (bay), Md, US 198/B6
Eastern Fields (reef), PNG 153/G2
Eastern Ghats (mts.), India 104/C5
Eastern Highlands (prov.), PNG 153/G1
Eastern Neck Island NWR, Md, US 198/B5
Eastern Sayans (mts.), Rus. 80/K4
Eastfield, Eng, UK 41/H3
Eastgate, Nv, US 176/E4
Eastland, Tx, US 181/E1
Eastleigh, Eng, UK 43/E5
Eastleigh (int'l arpt.), Eng, UK 43/E5
Eastmain (riv.), Can. 163/K4
Eastmain (riv.), Qu, Can. 171/J3
Eastman, Ga, US 193/F4
Eastman, Wi, US 185/J2
Easton, Eng, UK 42/D5
Easton, Ca, US 178/C2
Easton, Ct, US 199/E1
Easton (res.), Ct, US 199/E1
Easton, La, US 194/B2
Easton, Ma, US 191/L3
Easton, Md, US 193/J1
Easton, Mo, US 185/G4
Easton, Pa, US 198/C2
Easton, Tx, US 181/G1
Eastport, NY, US 199/F2
Eastriggs, Sc, UK 41/E2
Eastry, Eng, UK 43/H4
Eastsound, Wa, US 174/C3
Eastville, Va, US 193/K2
Eastwood, Eng, UK 41/G6
Eatington, Eng, UK 43/E2
Eaton, Co, US 184/B3
Eaton, In, US 190/D4
Eaton, Oh, US 190/D5
Eaton Park, Fl, US 194/M7

Eaton Rapids, Mi, US 190/D3
Eaton Socon, Eng, UK 43/F2
Eatonia, Sk, Can. 175/K2
Eatons Neck (pt.), NY, US 199/M8
Eatontown, NJ, US 199/D3
Eatonville, Fl, US 194/N6
Eatonville, Wa, US 184/B3
Eau Claire (lake), Qu, Can. 171/J3
Eau Claire (riv.), Wi, US 185/J1
Eau Claire, Wi, US 185/J1
Eau d'Heure (riv.), Belg. 61/D3
Eaubonne, Fr. 36/C5
Eaulne (riv.), Fr. 36/C4
Eauripik (isl.), Micr. 160/D4
Eauze, Fr. 54/C4
Ebalo (riv.), D.R. Congo 134/D5
Ebano, Mex. 206/B1
Ebble (riv.), Eng, UK 43/E4
Ebbw Vale, Wal, UK 42/C3
Ebebiyín, EqG. 138/B2
Ebeggi (well), Niger 129/G5
Ebéjico, Col. 219/K6
Ebeleben, Ger. 59/H6
Ebeltoft, Den. 46/D3
Ebeltoft Vig (bay), Swe. 45/G6
Eben Junction, Mi, US 187/L4
Ebensburg, Pa, US 191/G4
Ebensee, Aus. 56/A2
Eberbach, Ger. 64/B4
Ebergassing, Aus. 57/P7
Ebergötzen, Ger. 59/H5
Ebermannstadt, Ger. 64/E3
Ebern, Ger. 61/G4
Ebernburg, Ger. 61/G4
Ebersbach an der Fils, Ger. 64/C5
Ebersberg, Ger. 65/E6
Eberschwang, Aus. 65/G6
Ebersheim, Fr. 66/D1
Eberswalde-Finow, Ger. 64/G6
Ebetsu, Japan 94/B2
Ebian, China 105/H2
Ebina, Japan 94/B2
Ebingen, Ger. 67/F1
Ebinur (lake), China 111/D3
Ebnat-Kappel, Swi. 65/F6
Ebo (lake), Mali 132/E3
Ebola (riv.), D.R. Congo 134/D5
Ebolowa, Camr. 138/B2
Ebon (isl.), Mrsh. 160/F4
Ebony, Namb. 140/B4
Ebony, Va, US 193/J2
Eboro, Gabon 138/B2
Ebrach, Ger. 64/D3
Ebreichsdorf, Aus. 57/N8
Ebro, Mn, US 187/G4
Ebro, (riv.), Sp. 29/C4
Ebron (riv.), Fr. 70/B3
Ebstorf, Ger. 59/H2
Ecatepec, Mex. 205/Q9
Eccles, Eng, UK 41/E1
Eccles, WV, US 193/G2
Eccleshall, Eng, UK 42/D1
Echague, Phil. 100/C1
Echallens, Swi. 66/C4
Echarate, Peru 220/C4
Echaz (riv.), Ger. 64/C6
Éché Fadadinga (riv.), Niger 133/H3
Éché Téfidinga (riv.), Niger 134/D2
Echigawa, Japan 95/K5
Eching, Ger. 65/E6
Échirolles, Fr. 70/B2
Echo, La, US 194/B2
Echo (lake), NJ, US 198/D1
Echo Bay, On, US 187/L3
Echo Bay, NW, US 170/E2
Echols, Ky, US 192/D2
Echt, Neth. 61/E1
Echterdingen (int'l arpt.), Ger. 64/C5
Echternach, Lux. 61/F4
Echuca, Austl. 157/B3
Echunga (cr.), Austl. 155/M9
Echunga, Fr. 54/C4
Echzell, Ger. 64/D2
Écija, Sp. 52/C4
Ečka, Serb. 56/E3
Eckernförde, Ger. 46/C4
Eckerö, Fin. 47/H1
Eckerö (isl.), Fin. 47/H1
Eckington, Eng, UK 41/G5
Eckington, Eng, UK 43/E4
Eckville, Ab, Can. 174/E1
Eclectic, Al, US 192/D4
Eclipse Sound (bay), Nun, Can. 171/H2
Écommoy, Fr. 63/F5
Écorse, Mi, US 197/F5
Écorse (riv.), Mi, US 197/F5
Écos, Fr. 63/G2
Écouché, Fr. 63/F3
Écouen, Fr. 36/K4
Écquevilly, Fr. 36/H5
Écrins, PN, Fr. 51/G4
Écrosnes, Fr. 36/H6
Écrouves, Fr. 61/E6
Ecru, MS, US 192/C3
Ecuador (ctry.) 209/D3
Écublens, Swi. 66/C4
Ed, Erit. 136/B2
Ed, Neth. 58/C4
Edam, Neth. 58/C3
Edam, Sk, Can. 175/K1
Edapalli, India
Eday (isl.), Sc, UK 37/V14
Echera, Mor.
Edderton, Sc, UK 39/B1
Eddleston, Sc, UK 39/C5
Eddy (peak), Id, US 174/F3
Eddystone, Mb, Can.
Eddystone, Austl. 156/D4
Eddystone Rocks (isls.), Eng, UK 42/B6
Eddyville, Il, US 185/H3
Eddyville, Ky, US 185/H3
Ede, Nga. 133/G5
Ede, Neth. 58/C4
Edéa, Camr. 138/B2
Edéia, Braz. 225/D1

Edelény, Hun. 49/L4
Edemissen, Ger. 59/H4
Eden, Austl. 157/D3
Eden, Mb, Can. 186/E2
Eden (riv.), Sc, UK 39/H4
Edenbridge, Eng, UK
Edenbridge, Sk, Can.
Eden Prairie, Mn, US 187/P7
Edenton, NC, US 193/H2
Edenvale, SAfr. 142/D3
Edenville, SAfr.
Edenwold, Sk, Can. 186/B2
Eder (riv.), Ger.
Eder-Stausee
Edewecht, Ger. 59/F6
Effigy Mounds Nat'l Mon., (riv.), Ger. 58/D2
Edgar, Mt, US 177/J1
Edgar, Ne, US 184/F3
Edgar, Wi, US 185/K1
Edgar Springs, Mo, US 183/J2
Edgard, La, US 194/C2
Edgartown, Ma, US 188/B5
Edgcliff, Tx, US 180/K7
Edge (isl.), Sval. 80/C2
Edgefield, La, US 194/B1
Edgefield, SC, US 191/G3
Edgeley, ND, US 186/E4
Edgemere, Md, US 196/B5
Edgemont, Md, US
Edgemoor, De, US
Edgerton, Ab, Can. 175/J1
Edgerton, Mn, US 185/F2
Edgerton, Oh, US 190/D4
Edgerton, Wi, US 185/K2
Edgerton, Wy, US 184/A2
Edgewater, BC, Can. 174/F2
Egg Harbor City, NJ, US 196/D3
Edgewater, Fl, US 191/H5
Edgewater Park, NJ, US 198/D3
Edgewood, Fl, US 194/N6
Edgewood, Il, US 192/C1
Edgewood, Md, US 196/B5
Edgewood, NM, US 179/J3
Edgewood, Pa, US 191/G1
Edgewood, Tx, US 181/G1
Edgewood Arsenal, Md, US 196/B5
Eggnburg, Aus. 51/L2
Eggelsberg, Aus. 65/F6
Eggenfelden, Ger. 65/G6
Eggenstein-Leopoldshafen, Ger. 64/A4
Eggesin, Ger. 46/F5
Eggiwil, Swi. 66/D4
Egglescliffe, Eng, UK 41/G2
Eggleston, Eng, UK 41/G2
Egglhäm, Ger. 65/F7
Eggpenen, Aus. 65/F6
Eghezée, Belg. 61/D2
Egilsstadhir, Ice. 44/P6
Egiin, Ang. 140/B2
Egiyn (riv.), Mong. 90/E1
Egletons, Fr. 50/E4
Eglin, Ak, US 201/N4
Eglinton, NI, UK 40/A1
Eglinton (Londonderry) 40/A1
Eglisau, Swi. 67/E2
Egly, Fr. 36/J6
Egmond aan Zee, Neth. 58/B3
Egmont (bay), PE, Can. 188/E2
Egmont (mt.), NZ 159/G4
Egmont Key Nat'l Wild. Ref., Fl, US 194/N8
Egmont NP, NZ 159/C2
Egna (Neumarkt), It. 67/H5
Egnach, Swi. 67/F2
Egnar, Co, US 179/H3
Egoumbi, Gabon 138/B3
Egra, India 109/F5
Egremont, Eng, UK 40/E3
Égridir, Turk. 114/B2
Egridir (lake), Turk. 114/B2
Eguas, Rio das (riv.), Braz. 222/D3
Egvekinot, Rus. 81/U3
Egypt (ctry.) 127/F3
Egypt Lake, Fl, US 194/N8
Eha Amufu, Nga. 133/G5
Ehekirchen, Ger. 64/D3
Ehime (pref.), Japan 96/C4
Ehingen, Ger. 67/F1
Ehingen, Ger. 59/H6
Ehrenberg, Az, US 178/E4
Ehrenfriedersdorf, Ger. 64/B2
Ehrwald, Aus. 67/G3
Eiao (isl.), FrPol. 161/L5
Eibar, Sp. 50/B5
Eibelstadt, Ger. 64/C3
Eibenstock, Ger. 65/F1
Eibergen, Neth. 58/D4
Eich, Ger. 64/B3
Eichenau, Ger. 64/E6
Eichel (riv.), Fr.
Eichenbühl, Ger. 64/B3
Eichendorf, Ger. 65/F5
Eichenzell, Ger. 64/C2
Eichstätt, Ger. 64/E5
Eichwalde, Ger. 48/D7
Eicklingen, Ger. 59/H3
Eidelstedt, Ger. 59/G1
Eider (riv.), Ger. 46/E1
Eidfjord, Nor. 44/R9
Eidsfoss, Nor. 44/D4
Eidsvoll, Nor. 46/D1
Eifel (int'l arpt.), Ger. 48/D3
Eiffel Flats, Zim. 141/F3
Eiffel Tower, Fr.
Eiga (peak), Swi. 66/D4
Eigersund, Nor. 46/A2
Eigg (isl.), Sc, UK 37/Q8

Edwards, Ms, US 192/B4
Edwards (chan.), Ind.,Mald. 107/B5
Edwards (riv.), II, US 185/J3
Edwards (A.F.B.), Ca, US 178/C3
Edwardsville, Il, US 185/K4
Edwardsville, Pa, US 196/C1
Edwin, Al, US 193/K1
Edzná (ruin), Mex. 206/D2
Edzell, Sc, UK 39/D3
Eek, Ak, US 201/F3
Eekelo, Belg. 60/C1
Eel, South Fork (riv.), Ca, US 184/B3
Eelde-Paterswolde, Neth. 58/D2
Eemnes, Neth. 58/C4
Eems (Ems) (riv.), Ger., Neth. 58/D2
Eemshaven (har.), Neth. 58/D2
Eemskanaal (riv.), Neth. 58/D2
Eersel, Neth. 58/C6
Efate (isl.), Van. 160/F6
Eferding, Aus. 65/H6
Effingham, Eng, UK 36/B3
Effingham, Il, US 192/C1
Effingham, Ks, US 185/G4
Effingham, On, Can. 190/V9
Effingham Nat'l Hist. Site, On, US 187/L4
Effogi, PNG 153/G2
Eforie, Rom. 57/J3
Efringen-Kirchen, Ger. 66/D2
Egadi (isls.), It. 73/G3
Egan, Tx, US 180/K7
Egaña, Uru. 227/K10
Egbe, Nga. 133/G5
Egbunda, D.R. Congo 139/F2
Egeland, ND, US 186/E3
Egeln, Ger. 48/G3
Egeskov, Den. 46/D4
Egestorf, Ger. 59/H2
Egg, Swi. 67/E3
Egg Island (pt.), NJ, US 198/C5
Egg Lagoon, Austl. 157/A4
Egham, Eng, UK 36/B2
Eghezée, Belg.
Egilsstadhir, Ice. 44/P6
Egiin, Ang. 140/B2
Ein Mahil, Isr. 117/C3
Eina, Nor. 46/D1
Einbeck, Ger. 59/G5
Eindhoven (int'l arpt.), Neth. 58/C6
Eindhoven, Neth. 58/C6
Einsiedeln, Swi. 67/E3
Einville-au-Jard, Fr. 61/F6
Eirunepé, Braz. 220/D2
Eisack (Isarco) (riv.), It. 67/H4
Eisch (riv.), Lux. 61/E4
Eisenach, Ger. 59/H7
Eisenberg, Ger. 64/B3
Eisenerz, Aus. 51/L3
Eisenhower (mt.), Ab, Can. 174/G2
Eisenhower Nat'l Hist. Site, Pa, US 188/A4
Eisenhüttenstadt, Ger. 49/H2
Eisenstadt, Aus. 56/C2
Eisfeld, Ger. 64/D2
Eisingen, Ger. 64/C3
Eišiškės, Lith. 47/L4
Eislingen, Ger. 64/C5
Eitelborn, Ger. 61/G3
Eiter (riv.), Ger. 59/F3
Eitorf, Ger. 61/G2
Eitting, Ger. 65/E6
Ejea de los Caballeros, Sp. 53/E1
Ejeda, Madg. 143/H9
Ejido, Ven. 216/D2
Ejin Horo Qi, China 92/B3
Ejin Qi, China 90/E3
Ejule, Nga. 133/G5
Ejura, Gha. 133/E5
Ejutla de Crespo, Mex. 206/B2
Ekalaka, Mt, US 186/B5
Ekang, Nga. 133/H5
Ekata, Gabon 138/C2
Ekeby, Swe. 46/E3
Ekeny (riv.), Nor. 46/C4
Ekenäs (Tammisaari), Fin. 47/K2
Ekeren, Belg. 58/B6
Ekerö, Swe. 45/A1
Eketahuna, NZ 159/C3
Ekhinos, Gre. 55/J2
Ekibastuz, Kaz. 111/L1
Ekimchan, Rus. 91/L1
Ekma, India 109/E3
Ekoko, D.R. Congo 139/E2
Ekoli, D.R. Congo 139/F3
Ekoln (lake), Swe. 45/A1
Ekondo Titi, Camr. 138/B1
Ekpoma, Nga. 133/G5
Eksjö, Swe. 46/F3
Ekuk, Ak, US 201/G4
Ekukula, D.R. Congo 139/E3
Ekwan (riv.), On, Can. 171/H3
Ekwendeni, Malw. 141/G1
Ekwok, Ak, US 201/G4
El Aaiún, WSah. 128/B3
El Aaiún (Hassan) (int'l arpt.), WSah. 128/B3
El Aargub, WSah. 128/B5
El Aatf (reg.), WSah. 128/B5
El Abiodh Sidi Chrikh, Alg. 129/F2
El Ábrēd, Eth. 136/C3
El Affroun, Alg. 130/G4
El Aïoun, Mor. 130/D2
El Aïoun (pt.), Mor. 130/D3
El Alamein (Al 'Alamayan), Egypt 127/F2
El Alamo, Mex. 180/E4
El Alia, Alg. 129/G2
El Alto, Peru 220/A2
El Alto (int'l arpt.), Bol. 224/B1
El Amparo de Apure, Ven. 216/D3
El Anegado, Ecu. 216/A5
El Aouinet, Alg. 130/K7
El Arahal, Sp. 52/C4
El Arco, Mex. 180/C4
El Aricha, Alg. 130/D2
El Arrayán, Chile 226/N8
El Astillero, Sp. 50/D1
El Avila, PN, Ven. 219/F7
El Bagre, Col. 216/C2
El Banco, Col. 216/C2
El Barco, Col. 52/C2
El Barco de Ávila, Sp. 52/C2
El Baúl, Ven. 216/E2
El Bayadh (wilaya), Alg. 129/F2
El Bayadh, Alg. 129/F2
El Ben, Kenya 137/C1
El Bolsón, Arg. 226/C4
El Bonillo, Sp. 52/D3
El Boroug, Mor. 128/D2
El Burgo de Osma, Sp. 52/D2
El Cain, Arg. 226/C4
El Cajón (res.), Hon. 206/E3
El Calafate, Arg. 226/C6
El Callao, Ven. 217/F4
El Campo, Tx, US 181/F3
El Capitan (peak), Mt, US 177/F4
El Carmen, Bol. 221/F4
El Carmen, Chile 226/N8
El Carmen, Chile 226/N9
El Carmen, Peru 217/F4
El Carmen de Bolívar, Col. 216/B2
El Casabe, Ven. 217/F4
El Casar de Talamanca, Sp. 53/N8

Eight Degree (chan.), India,Mald. 107/B5
Eighteenmile (peak), Id, US 177/G1
Eighty Mile Beach (beach), Austl. 152/A4
Eijerlandse Gat (chan.), Neth. 58/B2
Eikelandsosen, Nor. 46/A1
Eil, Loch (inlet), Sc, UK 39/A3
Eilenburg, Ger. 48/D3
Eilerts de Haan (mts.), Sur. 217/G4
'Ein Mähil, Isr. 117/C3
Eina, Nor. 46/D1
Einbeck, Ger. 59/G5
Eindhoven (int'l arpt.), Neth. 58/C6
Eindhoven, Neth. 58/C6
El Cerrito, Col. 216/B4
El Cerro, Bol. 224/D3
El Cerro del Aripo (peak), Trin. 217/F2
El Cerrón (peak), Ven. 216/E2
El Chico, PN, Mex. 205/L6
El Chorro, Arg. 224/D2
El Cocuy, Col. 216/C3
El Cocuy (dept.), Col. 157/B3
El Colegio, Col. 219/L8
El Colorado, Arg. 224/E3
El Cóndor, Arg. 227/C7
El Cuy, Arg. 204/D4
El Der (riv.), Som. 136/B4
El Dere, Eth. 136/B4
El Descanso, Mex. 178/D4
El Difícil, Mex. 216/C2
El Djezaïr (Algiers) (cap.), Alg. 130/G4
El Djouf (des.), Alg. 128/D5
El Dorado, Ks, US 183/G3
El Dorado, Ok, US 183/F3
El Dorado (lake), Ks, US 183/F2
El Dorado (lake), Ks, US 204/D3
El Dorado Springs, Mo, US 183/G2
El Edén, Ecu. 216/B5
El Empedrado, Ven. 216/D2
El Escorial, Sp. 53/M8
El Espinar, Sp. 52/C2
El Eulma, Alg. 130/H4
El Fahs, Tun. 130/L6
El Ferrol, Sp. 52/A1
El Fuerte, Mex. 204/D3
El Fureidīs, Isr. 117/B3
El Galhak, Sudan 135/G3
El Galpón, Arg. 224/D2
El Gogorrón, PN, Mex. 202/A3
El Golea, Alg. 129/F2
El Golfete (lake), Guat. 206/D3
El Granada, Ca, US 197/K11
El Grullo, Mex. 204/D5
El Guachara, PN, Ven. 217/F2
El Guapo, Ven. 219/P7
El Gulut, Eth. 135/G2
El Had Harrara, Mor. 130/B3
El Hajeb, Mor. 130/D2
El Hank (cliff), Mali 128/D5
El Harino, Mex. 216/A2
El Harta (wilaya), Alg. 129/E4
El Higo, Mex. 206/B1
El Indio, Tx, US 180/D3
El Jadida, Mor. 128/C2
El Jem, Tun. 130/M7
El Kbab, Mor. 128/D2
El Kelaâ des Srarhna, Mor. 128/C2
El Kerê, Eth. 136/A1
El Khatt (depr.), Mrta. 132/C2
El Khnâchich (cliff), Mali 128/E5
El Kroub, Alg. 130/K6
El Kseur, Alg. 130/H4
El Limón, Mex. 216/D3
El Loco, Ven. 217/F4
El Lugar, Sp. 50/U8
El Mahia 46/F3
El Maitén, Arg. 226/C4
El Mallaile, Eth. 136/B4
El Malpais Nat'l Mon., NM, US 179/J4
El Manteco, Ven. 217/F3
El Manzano, Chile 226/N8
El Medera, Col. 216/B5
El Messir (well), Chad 134/C2
El Miamo, Ven. 217/F3
El Milia, Alg. 130/J4
El Mirage, Ca, US 196/C1
El Mirage, Az, US
El Mojar, Col. 221/F4
El Montcau (peak), Sp. 53/M6
El Morro (pt.), Chile 226/N9
El Morro, Mex. 179/J4
El Mrāyer (well), Mrta. 132/C2
El Mreyyé 128/D5
El Mzereb (well), Mali 128/E5
El Naranjo de Carlos Sarabia, Mex. 205/K4
El Nayar, Mex. 204/D4
El Nevado (peak), Arg. 216/C2
El Nido, Phil. 100/C3
El Nido, Phil. 216/A2
El Olivar Alto, Chile 226/N9
El Oro (dept.), Ecu. 220/A1
El Oso, Ven. 218/A1
El Oued (wilaya), Alg. 129/G2
El Oued, Alg. 129/G2
El Palmar, Mex. 204/D3
El Palmar, Ven. 217/F3
El Palmar, PN, Arg. 224/E4
El Pao, Ven. 217/F2
El Pao, Ven. 217/F3
El Paraíso, Col. 221/F4
El Paraíso, Hon. 206/E3
El Paraíso, Mex. 206/B2
El Pardo, Sp. 53/N8
El Paso, Il, US 185/J3
El Paso (peak), Ca, US 178/D3
El Paso International (int'l arpt.), Tx, US 180/C2
El Pensamiento, Bol. 221/F4
El Perú, Bol. 224/D3
El Pilar, Ven. 217/F2
El Pilar, Ven. 217/F2
El Pintado, Arg. 224/D3
El Piquete, Arg. 224/D2
El Plumerillo (Mendoza) (int'l arpt.), Arg. 226/C2
El Portal, Ca, US 186/C3
El Porvenir, Mex. 180/D3
El Porvenir, Pan. 216/B2

El Centro Nav. Air Facility, Ca, US 178/D4
El Cerrito, Ca, US 197/K11
El Cerrito, Col. 216/B4
El Prat de Llobregat, Sp. 53/L7
El Progreso, Ecu. 220/A1
El Progreso, Guat. 206/D3
El Progreso, Hon. 206/E3
El Progreso Industrial, Mex. 205/Q9
El Puente, Bol. 224/D2
El Puente, Bol. 224/D3
El Puerto de Santa María, Sp. 52/B4
El Quebrachal, Arg. 224/C3
El Quelite, Mex. 204/D4
El Quisco, Chile 226/N8
El Rama, Nic. 207/E3
El Rastro, Ven. 216/E2
El Remolino, Mex. 180/D3
El Reno, Ok, US 183/F3
El Rey, PN, Arg. 224/D2
El Rico (canal), Fl, US 194/P10
El Río, Ca, US 196/A2
El Rio (canal), Fl, US 192/D4
El Rito, NM, US 179/J2
El Roble, Pan. 216/A2
El Rosario de Arriba, Mex. 204/D3
El Sabinal, PN, Mex. 180/E4
El Sacromonte, PN, Mex. 205/L7
El Salado, Col. 219/K8
El Salado (pt.), Arg. 227/D6
El Salto, Mex. 204/D4
El Salvador, Cuba 211/H4
El Salvador (ctry.) 206/D3
El Samán de Apure, Ven. 216/E2
El Sauz, Mex. 180/A3
El Segundo, Ca, US 196/B3
El Socorro, Ven. 216/E2
El Sombrero, Arg. 226/C5
El Sombrero, Ven. 216/E2
El Sosneado, Arg. 226/N8
El Tabo, Chile 226/N8
El Tajín (ruin), Mex. 205/M6
El Tala, Arg. 224/C3
El Tama, PN, Ven. 216/C3
El Tarf (wilaya), Alg. 130/K6
El Tarf, Alg. 130/K6
El Teleno (peak), Sp. 52/B1
El Tepozteco, PN, Mex. 205/R10
El Tiemblo, Sp. 52/C2
El Tigre, Ven. 217/F2
El Tocuyo, Ven. 216/D2
El Toro, Ca, US 196/C4
El Toro, Tx, US 181/F3
El Toro, Chile 226/N8
El Tránsito, Chile 224/B3
El Trébol, Arg. 224/D4
El Triunfo, Mex. 204/D4
El Triunfo, Ecu. 220/A1
El Tucuche (peak), Trin. 217/F2
El Tuito, Mex. 204/D4
El Tuparro, PN, Col. 216/D3
El Turbio, Arg. 179/J2
El Valle, Ven. 216/E2
El Viejo (isl.), Nic. 207/F4
El Viejo (peak), Col. 216/C2
El Viejo, Nic. 216/D2
El Volcán, Chile 226/N8
El Wak, Kenya 137/C1
El Yunque (peak), PR 203/M8
El Zacatón, Mex. 204/C4
El Zurdo, Mex. 227/C6
Elaho (riv.), BC, Can. 174/C2
Elaine, Ar, US 185/H4
Elan (riv.), Wal, UK 42/C2
Élancourt, Fr. 36/H5
Elands (riv.), SAfr. 141/E5
Elandsrivier, SAfr.
Elángata Wuas, Kenya 137/D2
Elarmilon, Gabon 138/B2
Elassón, Gre. 55/H4
Elat (int'l arpt.), Isr. 116/D5
Elato (isl.), Micr. 160/D4
Élavagnon, Togo 133/F4
Elazığ, Turk. 114/D2
Elazıg (prov.), Turk. 114/D2
Elba, Al, US 195/E2
Elba (isl.), It. 54/E4
Elk (riv.), WV, US 193/G2
Elk City, Ks, US 183/G3
Elk City (dam), Ks, US 183/G2
Elbasan, Alb. 55/G2
Elbe (riv.), Ger. 29/D4
Elbe (Labe) (riv.), Czh.,Ger. 49/H2
Elbe-Seitenkanaal (canal), Ger. 59/H2

El Porvenir, Ven. 216/D3
El Potosí, Mex. 205/E3
El Potosí, PN, Mex. 197/K11
El Prat de Llobregat, Sp. 53/L7
El Progreso, Ecu. 220/A1
El Progreso, Guat. 206/D3
El Chorro, Arg. 224/D2
El Cocuy, Col. 216/C3
El Cocuy (dept.), Col. 157/B3
El Colegio, Col. 219/L8
El Colorado, Arg. 224/E3
El Cóndor, Arg. 227/C7
El Cuy, Arg. 204/D4
El Der (riv.), Som. 136/B4
Eindhoven, Neth. 58/C6
El Descanso, Mex. 178/D4
El Djezaïr (Algiers) (cap.), Alg. 130/G4
El Djouf (des.), Alg. 128/D5
El Rio, Ca, US 196/A2
El Rito, NM, US 179/J2
El Roble, Pan. 216/A2
El Rosario de Arriba, Mex. 204/D3
El Sabinal, PN, Mex. 180/E4
El Sacromonte, PN, Mex. 205/L7
El Salado, Col. 219/K8
El Salado (pt.), Arg. 227/D6
El Salto, Mex. 204/D4
Elela, Lat. 47/K3
Elek, Hun. 56/E2
Elektrénai, Lith. 47/L4
Elektrostal', Rus. 75/W9
Elele, Nga. 133/G5
Elena, Arg. 226/D2
Elena, Bul. 57/G4
Ellenwood, Ga, US 195/M7
Elephant (mtn.), Me, US 191/J2
Elephant Butte, NM, US 179/J4
Elephant Butte (res.), NM, US 179/J4
Elesbão Veloso, Braz. 219/F4
Eleşkirt, Turk. 115/E2
Eleuthera (isl.), Bahm. 163/K7
Eleven Point (riv.), Mo, US 183/J2
Elevtherón, Gre. 55/J2
Elevtheroúpolis, Gre. 55/J2
Elfers, Fl, US 194/K7
Elfershausen, Ger.
Elfin Cove, Ak, US 201/L4
Elfrida, On, Can.
Elgg, Swi. 67/E3
Elgin, Mb, Can. 186/D3
Elgin, Sc, UK 39/N5
Elgin, Az, US 179/G5
Elgin, Il, US 190/B3
Elgin, Mn, US 185/G2
Elgin, ND, US 186/D4
Elgin, Nv, US 178/E2
Elgin, Or, US 176/E1
Elgin, Austl. 152/A4
Elgin, SC, US 191/G3
Elgin, Tn, US 193/G1
Elgin, Tx, US 181/F3
Elgin Mills, On, Can. 190/U8
Elgóibar, Sp. 50/U8
Elgon (mt.), Uganda 137/D1
Eli (co.), Tx, US 180/C2
Elida, NM, US 182/C4
Elida, Oh, US 190/D3
Elie, Sc, UK 39/D4
Elila (riv.), D.R. Congo 139/E3
Elim, Sc, UK 39/D2
Elim, SAfr. 142/L11
Elimäki, Fin. 47/M1
Eliot, Me, US 191/J3
Elipa, D.R. Congo 139/E3
Elisenvaara, Rus. 47/N1
Eliseu Martins, Braz. 219/F5
Elista, Rus. 77/H3
Elizabeth (mtn.), Austl.
Elizabeth (bay), Namb. 140/B4
Elizabeth, Co, US 184/B4
Elizabeth, La, US 194/B2
Elizabeth, NJ, US 199/H9
Elizabeth, WV, US 193/G1
Elizabeth City, NC, US 193/J2
Elizabethan Village Hist. Site, (cr.), Tx, US 180/K6
Elizabethton, Tn, US 193/G1
Elizabethtown, Il, US 185/H4
Elizabethtown, Ky, US 190/C5
Elizabethtown, NC, US 193/H3
Elizabethtown, Pa, US 196/B3
Elizabethville, Pa, US 196/B2
Elizondo, Sp. 50/C5
Elk, Pol. 27/K2
Elk (riv.), BC, Can. 174/G2
Elk (riv.), Md, US 196/B5
Elbow (riv.), Ab, Can. 174/E2
Elbow, Sk, Can. 175/L2
Elbow Lake, Mn, US 186/E3
Elbow Lake, Mn, US 186/E3
Elburg, Neth. 58/C4
Elburn, Kenya 137/A2
Elburz (mts.), Iran 80/E7
Elche, Sp. 53/E3
Elche de la Sierra, Sp. 52/D3

Elchingen, Ger. 64/D6
Elkhart, Ks, US 182/D2
Elkhart, In, US 190/C3
Elkhart, Tx, US 181/G2
Elda (inlet), Wa, US 197/K5
Eldama Ravine, Kenya 137/A1
Elde (riv.), Ger. 48/G2
Eldersburg, Md, US 196/A5
Elderslie, La, US 194/C3
Elderslie, PE, Can. 188/F2
Eldikan, Rus. 81/P3
Eldon, NC, US 193/G2
Eldon, Ia, US 185/H3
Eldon, Mo, US 183/H1
Eldon, Wa, US 174/C2
Eldora, Ia, US 185/H2
Eldorado, NJ, US 198/D5
Eldorado, Va, US 193/H1
Eldorado, Arg. 224/E3
Eldorado, Braz. 225/D2
Eldorado, Il, US 185/J3
Eldorado, Ok, US 183/F3
Eldorado, Tx, US 180/D2
Eldoret, Kenya 137/A1
Eldridge, Al, US 192/D4
Eldridge, Ia, US 185/J3
Elef Ringnes (isl.),
Eleanor, WV, US 193/G2
Electra, Tx, US 183/F3
Elefsis, Gre. 55/N8
Elefsis (arpt.), Gre. 55/N8
Elefsís (ruin), Gre.
Elek, Hun. 56/E2
Elkhorn (isl.), Ne, US 173/G3
Elkhorn, Wi, US 185/K2
Elkhorn, Mb, Can. 186/D3
Elkhorn, Ne, US 185/G1
Elko (riv.), Chile 224/B4
Elko, Nv, US 178/E1
Eldon, Mo, US 183/H1
Elk River, Mn, US 185/H1
Elk Silver, NM, US 179/J4
Elk Slough (riv.), Ab, Can. 174/D2
Elk Valley, Tn, US 193/G1
Elkfield, BC, Can. 174/G2
Elkhart, Ks, US 182/D2
Elkhart, In, US 190/C3
Elkhart, Tx, US 181/G2
Elkhorn, Mb, Can. 186/D3
Elkhorn, Ne, US 185/G1
Elkhovo, Bul. 57/H4
Elklamar, Eth. 135/G2
Elkins, NC, US 193/H1
Elkins, WV, US 193/H1
Elkland, Pa, US 191/H4
Elko, Nv, US 178/E1
Elkó, Yk, US 201/L3
Elko New Market, Mn, US 185/H2
Elkton, Ky, US 192/C2
Elkton, Md, US 196/B5
Elkton, Mi, US 198/C4
Elkton, Or, US 184/C1
Elkton, SAfr. 142/L11
Elkton, Va, US 193/H1
Elkview, WV, US 193/G2
Elkwater, Ab, Can. 175/J3
Elland, Eng, UK 41/G4
Elle (riv.), Fr. 62/B5
Ellé (riv.), Fr.
Ellef Ringnes (isl.),
Ellefeld, Ger. 65/F2
Ellen (mt.), Ut, US 179/G1
Ellenabad, India 110/C5
Ellenberg, Ger. 64/D4
Ellendale, De, US 196/C5
Ellendale, ND, US 186/E4
Ellensburg, Wa, US 174/E4
Ellenton, Ga, US 195/G2
Ellenton, NY, US 191/J4
Ellenwood, Ga, US 195/M7
Ellerbe, NC, US 193/H3
Ellerslie, La, US 194/C3
Ellerslie, PE, Can. 188/F2
Ellery (mt.), Austl. 157/D3
Ellesmere Port, Eng, UK 41/F5
Ellesmere Port, Eng, UK 41/F5
Ellettsville, In, US 190/C5
Ellezelles, Belg. 60/C2
Elliant, Fr. 62/B4
Ellice (riv.), Nun, Can. 170/F2
Ellicott City, Md, US 196/B5
Ellijay, Ga, US 192/E3
Ellington, Mo, US 183/J2
Ellingon (int'l arpt.), Tx, US 181/G3
Ellinikón (int'l arpt.), Gre. 55/N9
Ellinwood, Ks, US 183/G2
Elliot (peak), Va, US 193/H1
Elliot Key (isl.), Fl, US 194/H5
Elliot Price Consv. Park, Austl. 155/H4
Elliott, Ia, US 185/G3
Elliott, SC, US 191/G3
Elliott, Austl. 152/L4
Elliott (peak), Va, US 193/H1
Ellis (co.), Tx, US 180/K8
Ellis Island, NJ,NY, US 199/J9
Ellisenvaara, Rus. 47/N1
Elliston, NM, US 182/C4
Elliston, Austl. 155/G5
Ellisville, Ms, US 194/D2
Elloree, SC, US 191/G3
Elloughton, Eng, UK 41/H4
Ellrich, Ger. 59/H5
Ellsworth (mts.), Ant. 234/G5
Ellsworth (A.F.B.), SD, US 184/C1
Ellsworth Land 234/C5
Ellwangen, Ger. 64/D5
Ellwood City, Pa, US 191/G4
Elm (lake), SD, US 185/K3
Elm (peak), Swaz. 143/E2
Elm, Nv, US 178/E2
Elm (lake), SD, US 185/K3
Elm City, NC, US 193/J3
Elm Creek, Mb, Can. 186/E3
Elm Fork (riv.), Ok, US 183/F3
Elm Fork (riv.), Tx, US 180/K5
Elm Grove, Wi, US 197/P13
Elm Grove, La, US 194/B1
Elma, NY, US 190/V10
Elma, Wa, US 184/C4
Elmali, Turk. 116/A1
Elma, NY, US
Elmer, La, US 194/B2
Elmer, Mo, US 185/H4
Elmer, NJ, US 196/C3
Elmhurst, Il, US 197/P16
Elmina, Gha. 133/E5
Elmira, NY, US 191/H3
Elmira Heights, NY, US 191/H3
Elmira, On, Can. 190/V9
Elmont, NY, US 199/L9
Elmora, (nbrhd.), NJ, US 199/G9
Elmsdale, PE, Can. 188/E2
Elmshorn, NY, US 191/H3
Elmsford, NY, US 199/J7
Elmswell, Eng, UK 43/G2
Elmvale, On, Can. 190/U9
Elmwood, Ok, US 183/F3
Elmwood Park, Il, US 197/Q16
Elmwood Park, Wi, US 197/Q14
Elmwood Park, NJ, US 199/H8
Elne, Fr.
Eloi Mendes, Braz. 194/M8
Elon College, NC, US 193/H1
Elora, Tn, US 192/E3
Elora, On, Can. 190/V9
Elordo (riv.), Ger. 50/A2
Elorn, Fr. 62/A2
Elortondo, Arg. 226/E2
Eloua Nat'l Rsv., Kenya 137/A2
Elowah (falls), Or, US 174/D5

Elkford, BC, Can. 174/G2
Elkhart, Ks, US 182/D2
Elkhart, In, US 190/C3
Elkhart, Tx, US 181/G2
Elkhorn, Mb, Can. 186/D3
Elkhorn (riv.), Ne, US 173/G3
Elkhorn, Wi, US 185/K2
Elkhovo, Bul. 57/H4
Elklamar, Eth. 135/G2
Elkins, NC, US 193/H1
Elkins, WV, US 193/H1
Elkland, Pa, US 191/H4
Elkó, Yk, US 201/L3
Elk New Market, Mn, US 185/H2
Elkton, Ky, US 192/C2
Elkton, Md, US 196/B5
Elkton, Mi, US 198/C4
Elkton, Or, US 184/C1
Elkton, SAfr. 142/L11
Elkton, Va, US 193/H1
Elkview, WV, US 193/G2
Elkwater, Ab, Can. 175/J3
Elland, Eng, UK 41/G4
Elle (riv.), Fr. 62/B5
Ellef Ringnes (isl.),
Ellefeld, Ger. 65/F2
Ellen (mt.), Ut, US 179/G1
Ellenabad, India 110/C5
Ellenberg, Ger. 64/D4
Ellendale, De, US 196/C5
Ellendale, ND, US 186/E4
Ellensburg, Wa, US 174/E4
Ellenton, Ga, US 195/G2
Ellenton, NY, US 191/J4
Ellenwood, Ga, US 195/M7
Ellerbe, NC, US 193/H3
Ellerslie, La, US 194/C3
Ellerslie, PE, Can. 188/F2
Ellery (mt.), Austl. 157/D3
Ellesmere Port, Eng, UK 41/F5
Ellettsville, In, US 190/C5
Ellezelles, Belg. 60/C2
Elliant, Fr. 62/B4
Ellice (riv.), Nun, Can. 170/F2
Ellicott City, Md, US 196/B5
Ellijay, Ga, US 192/E3
Ellington, Mo, US 183/J2
Ellington (int'l arpt.), Tx, US 181/G3
Ellinikón (int'l arpt.), Gre. 55/N9
Ellinwood, Ks, US 183/G2
Elliot (peak), Va, US 193/H1
Elliot Key (isl.), Fl, US 194/H5
Elliot Price Consv. Park, Austl. 155/H4
Elliott, Ia, US 185/G3
Elliott, SC, US 191/G3
Elliott, Austl. 152/L4
Ellis (co.), Tx, US 180/K8
Ellis Island, NJ,NY, US 199/J9
Elliston, NM, US 182/C4
Elliston, Austl. 155/G5
Ellisville, Ms, US 194/D2
Elloree, SC, US 191/G3
Elloughton, Eng, UK 41/H4
Ellrich, Ger. 59/H5
Ellsworth (mts.), Ant. 234/G5
Ellsworth (A.F.B.), SD, US 184/C1
Ellsworth Land 234/C5
Ellwangen, Ger. 64/D5
Ellwood City, Pa, US 191/G4
Elm (lake), SD, US 185/K3
Elm (peak), China 98/C3
Elm, Nv, US 178/E2
Elm City, NC, US 193/J3
Elm Creek, Mb, Can. 186/E3
Elm Fork (riv.), Ok, US 183/F3
Elm Fork (riv.), Tx, US 180/K5
Elm Grove, Wi, US 197/P13
Elm Grove, La, US 194/B1
Elma, NY, US 190/V10
Elma, Wa, US 184/C4
Elmali, Turk. 116/A1
Elmer, La, US 194/B2
Elmer, Mo, US 185/H4
Elmer, NJ, US 196/C3
Elmhurst, Il, US 197/P16
Elmina, Gha. 133/E5
Elmira, NY, US 191/H3
Elmira Heights, NY, US 191/H3
Elmira, On, Can. 190/V9
Elmont, NY, US 199/L9
Elmora, (nbrhd.), NJ, US 199/G9
Elmsdale, PE, Can. 188/E2
Elmshorn, Ger. 59/G1
Elmsford, NY, US 199/J7
Elmswell, Eng, UK 43/G2
Elmvale, On, Can. 190/U9
Elmwood, Ok, US 183/F3
Elmwood Park, Il, US 197/Q16
Elmwood Park, Wi, US 197/Q14
Elmwood Park, NJ, US 199/H8
Elne, Fr.
Eloi Mendes, Braz.
Elon College, NC, US 193/H1
Elora, Tn, US 192/E3
Elora, On, Can. 190/V9
Elorn, Fr. 62/A2
Elortondo, Arg. 226/E2
Eloua Nat'l Rsv., Kenya 137/A2
Elowah (falls), Or, US 174/D5

Eloy, Az, US 179/G4
Eloy Alfaro, Ecu. 216/B5
Éloyes, Fr. 66/C1
Elphin, Ire. 38/B2
Elphinstone, Mb, Can. 186/D2
Elqui (riv.), Chile 224/B4
Elrod, Al, US 192/D4
Elrose, Sk, Can. 175/K2
Elroy, Wi, US 185/J2
Elroy, NC, US 193/J3
Elsa, Yk, Can. 201/L3
Elsah, Il, US 185/K4
Elsberry, Mo, US 185/J3
Elsdorf, Ger. 61/F2
Elsdorf, Ger. 59/G2
Else (riv.), Ger. 59/F4
Elsenz, Ger. 64/B4
Elsfleth, Ger. 59/F2
Elsie, Mi, US 190/D3
Elsinore (lake), Ca, US 196/C3
Elsloo, Neth. 61/E2
Elspe, Eng, UK 43/E4
Elsnes-De, US 198/C4
Elst, Neth. 58/C5
Elstal, Ger. 48/Q6
Elstead, Eng, UK 43/F4
Elsterberg, Ger. 65/F2
Elstra, Ger. 64/D4
Eltari (int'l arpt.), Indo. 152/A2
Eltham (nbrhd.), Eng, UK 36/D2
Eltham, NZ 159/C2
Eltham, Austl. 157/B3
Elton, Wi, US 187/K5
Eltopia, Wa, US 174/E4
Eltville am Rhein, Ger. 64/B2
Elva, Est. 47/M2
Elvanlı, Turk. 116/C1
Elvas, Port. 52/B3
Elverum, Nor. 46/D1
Elvire (riv.), It. 68/B2
Elvo (riv.), It. 68/B2
Elwell (lake), Mt, US 175/J3
Elwood, In, US 190/D4
Elwood, Ne, US 184/E3
Elwood-Magnolia, NJ, US 196/D3
Elwy (riv.), Wal, UK 40/E5
Ely (riv.), Wal, UK 43/G2
Ely, Mn, US 187/J4
Ely, Nv, US 178/E2
Elyaqim, Isr. 117/C3
Elyashiv, Isr. 117/B4
Elyria, Oh, US 190/E4
Elysian Park, Ca, US 196/F7
Elz (riv.), Ger. 64/B6
Elz, Ger. 64/E1
Elze, Ger. 59/G4
Emām Taqī, Iran 113/G1
Emāmshahr, Iran 115/H2
Emán (riv.), Swe. 46/F3
Emas, PN das, Braz. 222/B3
Embarcación, Arg. 224/C2
Embarras (riv.), Il, US 185/J3
Embarrass, Mn, US 187/H4
Embarrass, Wi, US 185/K1
Embi, Kaz. 77/L2
Embi (riv.), Kaz. 80/F5
Embira (riv.), Braz. 220/D3
Embondo, D.R. Congo 138/D2
Embrach, Swi. 67/E2
Embrun, Fr. 70/D2
Embsen, Ger. 59/H2
Embu, Kenya 137/D2
Emden, Il, US 185/K3
Emden, Ger. 59/E2
Emei (peak), China 98/C3
Emeishan, China 98/C3
Emerald, Austl. 157/B3
Emerald, Austl. 158/C3
Emeriau (pt.), Austl. 152/A4
Emerson, Ar, US 183/H4
Emerson, NJ, US 199/J8
Emery (peak), NM, US 182/C2
Emery, SD, US 185/J2
Emery, Ut, US 179/G1
Emeryville, On, Can. 197/G7
Emet, Turk. 114/B2
Emida (peak), Mt, US 177/H1
Emida, Id, US 174/F4
Emigrant (peak), Mt, US 177/H1
Emigsville, Pa, US 196/B3
Emilia-Romagna (pol. reg.), It. 51/J4
Emiliano Zapata, Mex. 206/D2
Emin, China 111/D3
Emin (riv.), Kaz. 111/E2
Eminence, Mo, US 183/J2
Emināb, Pak. 110/C3
Emir Pasha (gulf), Tanz. 139/G3
Emirdağ, Turk. 114/B2
Emirgazi, Turk. 114/C2
Emissi, Tarso (peak), Chad 126/C4
Emlembe (peak), Swaz. 143/E2
Emlichheim, Ger. 58/D3
Emma (lake), SD, US 185/K3
Emma (peak), Id, US 174/E4
Emmaboda, Swe. 46/F3
Emmanuel Head (pt.), Eng, UK 39/E5
Emmaste, Est. 47/K2
Emmaus, Pa, US 196/C2
Emmaville, Austl. 157/D1
Emmeloord, Neth. 58/C3
Emmen, Neth. 58/D3
Emmendingen, Ger. 66/D1
Emmer (riv.), Ger. 59/F5
Emmer-Compascuum, Neth. 58/E3
Emmerbach (riv.), Ger. 59/F5

284
Emmer – Fairl

Emmerich, Ger. 58/D5
Emmet, Ar, US 183/H4
Emmet, Austl. 158/B4
Emmetsburg, Ia, US 185/G2
Emmett, Mi, US 197/G6
Emmett, Id, US 176/E2
Emmingen-Liptingen, Ger. 67/E2
Emmitsburg, Md, US 198/A4
Emmonak, Ak, US 201/F3
Emmons (mt.), Ut, US 177/H3
Emneth, Eng, UK 43/G1
Emód, Hun. 56/E2
Emory, Tx, US 183/G4
Emory (peak), Tx, US 180/C3
Emosson (lake), Swi. 66/C5
Empalme, Mex. 204/C3
Empangeni, SAfr. 143/E3
Empedrado, Chile 226/B2
Empedrado, Arg. 224/E3
Empire, Mi, US 190/C2
Empire, Ga, US 193/F4
Empoli, It. 69/D6
Emporia, Ks, US 183/F1
Emporia, Va, US 193/J2
Emporium, Pa, US 191/G4
'Emrānī, Iran 113/G2
Ems (riv.), Ger. 48/D2
Ems (Eems)
(riv.), Ger.,Neth. 58/D2
Ems-Jade (canal), Ger. 59/E2
Emsbüren, Ger. 59/E4
Emsdetten, Ger. 59/E4
Emskirchen, Ger. 64/D3
Emsland (reg.), Ger. 48/D2
Emstek, Ger. 59/F3
Emu, China 91/K3
Emu Park, Austl. 158/C3
Emumägi (hill), Est. 47/M2
Emur (riv.), China 91/J1
Emyvale, Ire. 40/B3
'En Gedi, Isr. 117/C6
'En Harod, Isr. 117/C3
Ena, Japan 97/E3
Enangiperi, Kenya 137/A2
Enarotali, Indo. 103/J4
Enbetsu, Japan 94/B1
Encampment, Wy, US 177/K3
Encantada, Cerro
(peak), Mex. 204/B3
Encantada, Cerro de la
(peak), Mex. 204/B2
Encarnación, Par. 225/F3
Encarnación de Díaz,
Mex. 204/E4
Enchi, Gha. 132/E5
Encinal, Tx, US 180/E3
Encinitas, Ca, US 196/C4
Encino (nbrhd.), Ca, US 196/E7
Encino, Tx, US 180/E4
Enciso, Col. 216/C3
Enciso, Col. 216/D4
Encón, Arg. 224/C5
Encontrados, Ven. 216/C2
Encounter (bay), Austl. 156/A2
Encruzilhada do Sul,
Braz. 225/F4
Encs, Hun. 49/L4
Endau (peak), Kenya 137/B2
Ende (isl.), Indo. 152/A2
Ende, Indo. 152/A2
Endeavour, Sk, Can. 186/C1
Endeavour (str.), Austl. 153/F2
Endeavour River NP,
Austl. 158/B1
Endebess, Kenya 137/A1
Enderbury (isl.), Kiri. 161/H5
Enderby, BC, Can. 174/E2
Enderby Land
(phys. reg.), Ant. 228/D
Enderlin, ND, US 186/F4
Endicott, NY, US 191/H3
Endicott, Wa, US 174/F4
Endingen, Ger. 66/D1
Endwell (Hooper),
NY, US 191/H3
Endyalgourt (isl.), Austl. 152/C2
Ene (riv.), Peru 220/C3
Eneabba, Austl. 154/B4
Enebakk, Nor. 46/D2
Enem, Rus. 79/K5
Energeticheskiy, Kaz. 111/C3
Energetik, Rus. 77/L2
Enewetak (isl.), Mrsh. 160/F3
Enez, Turk. 55/K2
Enfield, NS, Can. 188/F3
Enfield (nbrhd.), Eng, UK 36/C2
Enfield (bor.), Eng, UK 36/C2
Enfield, Ct, US 191/K4
Enfield, Il, US 192/C1
Enfield, NC, US 193/J2
Enfield, NH, US 191/K3
Enga (prov.), PNG 153/F1
Engaño (cape), Phil. 83/M8
Engaru, Japan 94/C1
Engaruka (basin), Tanz. 137/A2
Engassumet, Tanz. 137/B3
Engcobo, SAfr. 142/E3
Engelberg, Swi. 67/E4
Engelhartszell, Aus. 65/G5
Engel's, Rus. 77/H2
Engelskirchen, Ger. 61/G2
Engelsmanplaat
(isl.), Neth. 58/D2
Engen, Ger. 67/E2
Engenheiro Paulo de Frontin,
Braz. 223/N7
Enger, Ger. 59/F4
Engerwitzdorf, Aus. 65/H6
Enggano (isl.), Indo. 102/B5
Enghershatu
(peak), Erit. 112/C5
Enghien, Belg. 60/D2
Engi, Swi. 67/F4
England, Ar, US 183/J3
England, Eng, UK 41/F4
England, UK 42/D2
Engle, NM, US 179/J4
Englefield Green,
Eng, UK 36/B2
Englefontaine, Fr. 60/C3
Englevale, ND, US 186/F4
Englewood, Fl, US 195/G4
Englewood, NJ, US 199/K8
Englewood Cliffs,
NJ, US 199/K8
English (riv.), On, Can. 187/H2
English, In, US 192/D1
English (chan.), UK,Fr. 29/D4
English Bay, Ak, US 201/H4
English Bāzār, India 109/G3
English Creek, NJ, US 198/D5
English Harbour West,
Nf, Can. 189/K2
English River, On, Can. 187/J3
Englishtown, NJ, US 199/D3
Engong, Gabon 138/B2
Engucwini, Malw. 137/A4
Énguera, Sp. 53/E3
Engure, Lat. 47/K3
Enguri (riv.), Geo. 77/G4
Enhtal, Mong. 90/F2
Enid, Ok, US 183/F2
Enid (lake), Ms, US 192/C3
Enigma, Ga, US 195/G2
Eniwa, Japan 94/B2
Enka, NC, US 193/F3
Enkenbach-Alsenborn,
Ger. 61/G5
Enkhuizen, Neth. 58/C3
Enkirch, Ger. 61/G4
Enköping, Swe. 46/G2
Enna, It. 54/D4
Enné, Ouadi (riv.), Chad 134/C2
Ennedi (plat.), Chad 134/D1
Ennell, Lough (lake), Ire. 38/C3
Ennepe (riv.), Ger. 59/E6
Ennepetal, Ger. 59/E6
Enneri Bardagué
(riv.), Chad 126/C4
Enneri Blaka
(riv.), Niger 126/B4
Enneri Ké (riv.), Chad 126/C5
Enneri Maro
(riv.), Chad 126/C5
Enneri Yébiqué
(riv.), Chad 126/C4
Enneri Zergamouchi
(riv.), Niger 126/B4
Ennery, Fr. 36/J4
Enngonia, Austl. 156/C1
Enningerloh, Ger. 59/F5
Ennis, Ire. 38/B4
Ennis, Mt, US 177/H1
Ennis, Tx, US 181/F1
Enniscorthy, Ire. 38/D5
Enniskerry, Ire. 40/B5
Enniskillen, NI, UK 37/Q9
Ennismore, On, Can. 191/G2
Ennistimon, Ire. 38/A4
Enns (riv.), Aus. 49/H5
Enns, Aus. 65/H6
Ennuye (riv.), Fr. 70/B4
Enoch, Ut, US 179/F2
Enochs, Tx, US 182/C4
Enogger (res.), Austl. 158/E6
Enola, Ar, US 183/H3
Enola, Pa, US 198/B3
Enontekiö, Fin. 44/G1
Enoree, SC, US 193/G3
Enoree (riv.), SC, US 193/G3
Enosburg Falls, Vt, US 191/K2
Enping, China 99/G4
Enrekang, Indo. 103/E4
Enrick (riv.), Sc, UK 39/B2
Enrique Carbó, Arg. 227/J10
Enriquillo, DRep. 207/J2
Enschede, Neth. 58/D4
Ensdorf, Ger. 65/E4
Ense, Ger. 59/E5
Enseleni, SAfr. 143/F3
Ensenada, Arg. 227/K11
Ensenada, Mex. 204/A2
Ensheim (arpt.), Ger. 61/G5
Ensheim (Saarbrücken)
(arpt.), Ger. 61/G5
Enshi, China 99/F2
Ensign, Mi, US 190/C2
Ensisheim, Fr. 66/D2
Enskär (isl.), Swe. 45/A2
Ensley, Fl, US 194/E2
Ensuès-la-Redonne, Fr. 70/B6
Entebbe, Ugan. 139/H2
Entebbe
(int'l arpt.), Ugan. 139/H2
Entenbühl (peak), Ger. 65/F3
Enterprise, On, Can. 191/H2
Enterprise, Al, US 195/F2
Enterprise, Ks, US 183/F1
Enterprise, La, US 194/C2
Enterprise, Ms, US 192/C4
Enterprise, Ok, US 183/G3
Enterprise, Or, US 176/E1
Entiat, Wa, US 174/D4
Entlebuch, Swi. 66/E4
Entraigues-sur-Sorgue,
Fr. 70/A5
Entrance, Ab, Can. 174/F1
Entre Lagos, Chile 226/B4
Entre Ríos (prov.), Arg. 224/E4
Entre Ríos, Bol. 224/C2
Entre Rios, Braz. 218/C4
Entre Rios, Braz. 223/F1
Entre Ríos (mts.), Hon. 207/E3
Entre Rios de Minas,
Braz. 222/D4
Entre Vientos, Chile 227/C7
Entre-Deux-Guiers, Fr. 70/B2
Entre-Rios, Moz. 141/H2
Entrevaux, Fr. 70/C5
Entroncamento, Port. 52/A3
Entry (isl.), Qu, Can. 189/G2
Entwistle, Ab, Can. 174/G1
Entzheim, Fr. 66/D1
Entzheim (Strasbourg)
(int'l arpt.), Fr. 66/D1
Enu (isl.), Indo. 152/D1
Enugu, Nga. 133/G5
Enugu Ngwo, Nga. 133/G5
Enumclaw, Wa, US 197/D3
Enushū (sea), Japan 95/M6
Envermeu, Fr. 63/G1
Envigado, Col. 219/K6
Envira, Braz. 220/D2
Enyamba, D.R. Congo 139/F3
Enyang, China 99/E2
Enyellé, Congo 138/D2
Enz (riv.), Ger. 48/E4
Enza (riv.), It. 68/D4
Enzan, Japan 97/F3
Enzbach (riv.), Ger. 61/F4
Enzersdorf an der Fischa,
Aus. 57/P7
Enzklösterle, Ger. 64/B5
Eola, Tx, US 180/D2
Eolia, Mo, US 185/J4
Épaignes, Fr. 63/F2
Epalinges, Swi. 66/C4
Epáno Arkhánai, Gre. 55/J5
Epanomí, Gre. 55/H2
Epcot Center, Fl, US 194/M7
Epe, Nga. 133/F5
Epe, Neth. 58/C4
Épehy, Fr. 60/C3
Epéna, Congo 138/D2
Epenarra, Austl. 153/D5
Épernay, Fr. 60/C5
Épernon, Fr. 63/G3
Epfig, Fr. 66/D1
Ephesus (ruin), Turk. 73/K3
Ephraim, Wi, US 187/L5
Ephraim, Ut, US 177/H4
Ephrata, Pa, US 198/B3
Ephrata, Wa, US 174/E4
Epi (isl.), Van. 160/F6
Épiais-Rhus, Fr. 36/J4
Epídhavros (Epidaurus)
(ruin), Gre. 55/H4
Épinal, Fr. 66/C1
Épinal (Mirecourt)
(arpt.), Fr. 66/C1
Épinay-sur-Orge, Fr. 36/J6
Épinay-sur-Seine, Fr. 36/J5
Epira, Guy. 217/G3
Epirus (reg.), Gre. 73/J3
Epomeo (vol.), It. 71/C6
Épône, Fr. 60/A6
Eppalock (lake), Austl. 157/B3
Eppelborn, Ger. 61/F5
Eppelheim, Ger. 64/B4
Eppenbrunn, Ger. 61/G5
Eppeville, Fr. 60/C4
Epping, Eng, UK 36/D1
Epping (for.), Eng, UK 36/D2
Epping (nbrhd.), Austl. 158/H8
Epping Forest NP,
Austl. 158/B3
Eppingen, Ger. 64/B4
Eppishausen, Ger. 67/G1
Epps, La, US 183/J4
Epsie, Mt, US 175/M5
Epsom, Eng, UK 36/C3
Epsom and Ewell,
Eng, UK 43/F4
Epte (riv.), Fr. 60/A4
Epukiro, Namb. 140/C4
Epukiro (riv.), Namb. 140/D4
Epulu (riv.), D.R. Congo 139/G2
Epupa (falls), Ang. 140/B3
Epworth, Eng, UK 41/H4
Epworth, Ia, US 185/J2
Eqlīd, Iran 115/H4
Equateur
(pol. reg.), D.R. Congo 134/D5
Equator (fall), Ecu. 216/A4
Equatorial Guinea
(ctry.) 138/B2
Équeurdreville-Hainneville,
Fr. 62/D1
Équihen-Plage, Fr. 60/A2
Equimina, Ang. 140/B2
Er (lake), China 105/H2
Er (isl.), Fr. 62/B3
Er Rachidia, Mor. 128/D3
Er Reina, Isr. 117/C3
Er Rif (mts.), Mor. 72/B4
Era (riv.), It. 69/D5
Era (riv.), PNG 153/G1
Eraclea (ruin), It. 54/E2
Eraclea, It. 69/F2
Eraclea Minoa (ruin), It. 54/C4
Éragny, Fr. 36/J4
Eran, Phil. 100/B3
Erandique, Hon. 206/D3
Erath, La, US 194/B3
Erave (riv.), PNG 153/G1
Erave, PNG 153/F1
Erawan NP, Thai. 106/B3
Erba, It. 68/C2
Erbaa, Turk. 76/F4
Erbach, Ger. 64/B3
Erbendorf, Ger. 65/F3
Erbeskopf (peak), Ger. 61/G4
Ercan (int'l arpt.), Cyp. 116/C2
Ercé-en-Lamée, Fr. 62/D5
Erçek, Turk. 115/E2
Erçek (lake), Turk. 115/E2
Ercilla, Chile 226/B3
Erciş, Turk. 115/E2
Erciyes (peak), Turk. 114/C2
Erclin (riv.), Fr. 60/C3
Ercolano, It. 71/D6
Érd, Hun. 57/Q10
Erdao (riv.), China 91/K3
Erdek (gulf), Turk. 57/H5
Erdek, Turk. 57/H5
Erdemli, Turk. 116/D1
Erdenet, Mong. 90/E2
Erdenetsogt, Mong. 90/F3
Erdi (well), Chad 126/C4
Erdi-Ma (upland), Chad 126/D5
Erding, Ger. 65/E6
Erdre (riv.), Fr. 50/C3
Erdweg, Ger. 64/E6
Erechim, Braz. 225/F3
Ereen Davaanī
(mts.), Mong. 90/G2
Ereğli, Turk. 114/C2
Ereğli, Turk. 57/K5
Ereke, Indo. 103/F4
Eremo delle Carceri, It. 71/B1
Eremo di Camaldoli, It. 69/E6
Erenhaberga
(mts.), China 111/D3
Erenler, Turk. 57/K5
Erentepe, Turk. 114/E2
Erepecu (lake), Braz. 217/H5
Ērer Shet' (riv.), Eth. 136/B3
Eresma (riv.), Sp. 52/C2
Erétria, Gre. 55/H3
Erevan (int'l arpt.), Arm. 115/F1
Ereymentaū, Kaz. 80/H4
Érezée, Belg. 61/E3
Erfa (riv.), Ger. 64/C3
Erfoud, Mor. 128/D3
Erft (riv.), Ger. 48/D3
Erftstadt, Ger. 61/F2
Erfurt, Ger. 48/F3
'Erg Chech
(des.), Alg.,Mali 119/B2
Erg du Djourab
(des.), Chad 134/C2
'Erg Iguidi
(des.), Alg.,Mrta. 128/D4
Ergene Nehri (riv.), Turk. 57/H5
Ērgli, Lat. 47/L3
Ergué-Gabéric, Fr. 62/A4
Ergun (riv.), China,Rus. 91/J1
Ergun Youqi, China 91/J1
Ergun Zuoqi, China 91/J1
Erhard, Mn, US 186/F4
Erhlin, Tai. 99/J4
Erhulai, China 93/C2
Eriba, Sudan 135/H1
Erica, Neth. 58/D3
Erica, Austl. 157/C3
Ericeira, Port. 53/P10
Ericht (lake), Sc, UK 39/B3
Ericht (riv.), Sc, UK 39/B3
Erick, Ok, US 182/E3
Erickson, Mb, Can. 186/E2
Erickson, BC, Can. 174/F3
Ericsburg, Mn, US 187/H3
Erie, Ks, US 183/G2
Erie (int'l arpt.), Pa, US 190/F3
Erie, Pa, US 190/F3
Erie (lake), Can.,US 163/J5
Erie (canal), NY, US 190/V9
Erie (co.), NY, US 190/V10
Erie NWR, Pa, US 191/G4
Erigabo (Ceerigaabo),
Som. 136/C3
Eriksdale, Mb, Can. 186/E2
Eriksmalå, Swe. 46/F3
Erikub (isl.), Mrsh. 160/F4
Erima, Ugan. 139/H2
Erímanthos (peak), Gre. 55/G4
Erimo, Japan 94/C2
Erimo-misaki
(cape), Japan 94/C3
Erin, Tn, US 192/D2
Erin, On, Can. 190/S8
Erithraí, Gre. 55/H3
Eritrea (ctry.) 119/F3
Erkelenz, Ger. 61/F1
Erken (isl.), Swe. 47/H1
Erken (lake), Swe. 45/B1
Erkheim, Ger. 67/G1
Erkina (riv.), Ire. 38/C4
Erkner, Ger. 48/Q7
Erkrath, Ger. 58/D6
Erlach, Swi. 66/D3
Erlands Point-Kitsap Lake,
Wa, US 197/B2
Erlang (peak), China 98/D2
Erlangen, Ger. 64/E3
Erlanger, Ky, US 192/E1
Erlau (riv.), Ger. 65/G5
Erldunda, Austl. 155/G3
Erlenbach (riv.), Ger. 64/B4
Erlenbach am Main, Ger. 64/C3
Erlenbach bei
Marktheidenfeld, Ger. 64/C3
Erlenbach im Simmental,
Swi. 66/D4
Erlinsbach, Swi. 66/E3
Erlongshan, China 91/K2
Erlongshan (res.), China 92/F2
Erme (riv.), Eng, UK 42/C6
Ermelo, Neth. 58/C4
Ermelo, SAfr. 143/E2
Ermenek (riv.), Turk. 116/C1
Ermenek, Turk. 116/C1
Ermenonville, Fr. 36/L4
Ermera, ETim. 152/B2
Ermeran Station, Austl. 157/B1
Ermineskin Ind. Res.,
Ab, Can. 175/H1
Ermióni, Gre. 55/H4
Ermont, Fr. 36/J5
Ermoúpolis, Gre. 55/J4
Erms (riv.), Ger. 64/C6
Ernabella, Austl. 155/G3
Erndtebrück, Ger. 61/H2
Ernée, Fr. 63/E4
Ernée (riv.), Fr. 50/C2
Ernesto Cortissoz
(int'l arpt.), Col. 216/C2
Ernsthofen, Aus. 65/H6
Erode, India 107/C4
Erolzheim, Ger. 67/G1
Eromanga, Austl. 158/A4
Eros, La, US 183/H4
Erowal Bay, Austl. 157/E2
Erpe, Belg. 60/C2
Erpel, Ger. 61/G2
Erpengdianzi, China 93/C2
Erpu, China 90/C3
Erquelinnes, Belg. 61/D3
Erquy, Fr. 62/C3
Errego, Moz. 141/H3
Errigal (mtn.), Ire. 37/P9
Erris Head (pt.), Ire. 37/P9
Erro (riv.), It. 68/B4
Errochty (lake), Sc, UK 39/B3
Errol, Sc, UK 39/C4
Errol, NH, US 191/L2
Erromango (isl.), Van. 160/F6
Erse (riv.), Ger. 59/H4
Ersekë, Alb. 55/G2
Ershibadu, China 99/H2
Erskine, Mn, US 186/F4
Erskine, Ab, Can. 175/H1
Erstein, Fr. 66/D1
Erstfeld, Swi. 67/E4
Ertai, China 111/D3
Ertai, China 90/B2
Ertil', Rus. 79/L2
Ertingen, Ger. 67/F1
Ertis (riv.), Kaz. 80/H4
Ertix (riv.), China 90/B2
Ertvelde, Belg. 60/C1
Eruh, Turk. 114/E2
Erundu, Namb. 140/C4
Eruwa, Nga. 133/F5
Erval, Braz. 225/F5
Erval d'Oeste, Braz. 225/G3
Ervália, Braz. 223/E4
Ervay, Wy, US 177/K2
Erve (riv.), Fr. 63/E4
Ervia (riv.), It. 70/D5
Erwin, Tn, US 193/F2
Erwin, NC, US 193/H3
Erwitte, Ger. 59/F5
Eryuan, China 98/C3
Erzen (riv.), Alb. 55/F2
Erzgebirge (Krušné Hory)
(mts.), Czh.,Ger. 51/K1
Erzhausen, Ger. 64/B3
Erzin, Rus. 90/D1
Erzincan, Turk. 114/D2
Erzincan (prov.), Turk. 114/D2
Erzurum, Turk. 114/E2
Erzurum (prov.), Turk. 114/E1
Es Senia (int'l arpt.), Alg. 130/E5
Esa'ala, PNG 160/E5
Esambo, D.R. Congo 139/E3
Esan-misaki
(cape), Japan 94/B3
Esashi, Japan 94/B3
Esashi, Japan 94/C1
Esashi, Japan 94/B4
Esbiye, Turk. 76/F4
Esbjerg, Den. 46/C4
Esbjerg (int'l arpt.), Den. 46/C4
Esbly, Fr. 36/L5
Esbo (Espoo), Fin. 47/L1
Esbon, Ks, US 184/E4
Escabosa, NM, US 179/J3
Escada, Braz. 219/H5
Escalante, Ut, US 179/G2
Escalante (des.), Ut, US 177/G4
Escalante (riv.), Ut, US 179/G2
Escalón, Mex. 204/D3
Escalona, Sp. 52/C2
Escambia (riv.), Fl, US 194/E2
Escampobariou (pt.), Fr. 70/C6
Escanaba, Mi, US 190/C2
Escanaba (riv.), Mi, US 187/L4
Escarpada (pt.), Phil. 100/C1
Escatawpa
(riv.), Ms, US 194/D2
Escaudain, Fr. 60/C3
Escaut (riv.), Fr. 48/B3
Esch (riv.), Fr. 61/E6
Esch-sur-Alzette, Lux. 61/E4
Esch-sur-Sure, Lux. 61/E4
Eschach (riv.), Ger. 67/E1
Eschau, Fr. 66/D1
Eschborn, Ger. 64/B2
Eschede, Ger. 59/H3
Eschen, Lcht. 67/F3
Eschenbach, Ger. 64/C5
Eschenbach in der Oberpfalz,
Ger. 65/E3
Eschershausen, Ger. 59/G5
Esches (riv.), Fr. 60/B5
Escholzmatt, Swi. 66/D4
Eschwege, Ger. 59/H6
Eschweiler, Ger. 61/F2
Escobedo
(int'l arpt.), Mex. 180/D5
Escoma, Bol. 220/D4
Escondido, Ca, US 196/C4
Escondido (cr.), Ca, US 196/C4
Escoutay (riv.), Fr. 70/A3
Escudillas, Ven. 217/E3
Escuinapa de Hidalgo,
Mex. 204/D4
Escuintla, Guat. 206/D3
Esdraelon (plain), Isr. 117/C3
Eséka, Camr. 138/B2
Esenboga
(int'l arpt.), Turk. 114/C1
Esence (peak), Turk. 114/D2
Esenguly, Trkm. 115/H2
Esens, Ger. 59/E1
Esera (riv.), Sp. 53/F1
Eşfahān, Iran 115/G3
Eşfahān (gov.), Iran 115/H3
Esfandak, Iran 113/H3
Esfarāyen, Iran 115/J2
Esfarvarīn, Iran 115/G3
Esgair Ddu
(peak), Wal, UK 42/C1
Esh, Eng, UK 41/G2
Esh Winning, Eng, UK 41/G2
Esha Ness
(cape), Sc, UK 37/W13
Eshan Yizu Zizhixian,
China 98/D3
Esher, Eng, UK 36/B2
Eshimba, D.R. Congo 139/F4
Eshkol NP, Isr. 117/A6
Eshowe, SAfr. 143/E3
Eshtehārd, Iran 115/G3
Esil (riv.), Kaz. 83/F4
Esil, Kaz. 111/A1
Esine, It. 67/G6
Esino (riv.), It. 69/G6
Esira, Madg. 143/H9
Esk (riv.), Eng, UK 41/E2
Esk, North (riv.), Sc, UK 39/C5
Esk, South (riv.), Sc, UK 39/C5
Esk, South (riv.), Austl. 156/C4
Eskdale (valley), Sc, UK 39/C6
Eskifjördhur, Ice. 44/Q6
Eskil, Turk. 114/C2
Eskilstuna, Swe. 46/G2
Eskimalatya, Turk. 114/D2
Eskimo (lakes), NW,
Can. 170/C2
Eskipazar, Turk. 76/E4
Eskişehir, Turk. 114/B2
Eskişehir (prov.), Turk. 114/B2
Esko, Mn, US 187/H4
Esla (res.), Sp. 52/B2
Esla (riv.), Sp. 52/C1
Eslāmābād, Iran 115/F3
Eslāmābād, Iran 115/G2
Eslohe, Ger. 59/F6
Eslöv, Swe. 46/E4
Eslöv, Swe. 45/K7
Eşme, Turk. 114/B2
Esmeralda, Cuba 207/G1
Esmeraldas (dept.), Ecu. 216/B4
Esmeraldas, Ecu. 216/B4
Esmond, ND, US 186/E3
Esmont, Va, US 193/H2
Esmoraca, Bol. 224/C2
Esnagami (lake), On, US 187/L2
Esneux, Belg. 61/E2
Espada (pt.), Col. 216/D1
Espakeh, Iran 113/H3
Espalion, Fr. 50/E4
Espanola, On, Can. 190/F1
Española (isl.), Ecu. 220/K7
Española, NM, US 179/J3
Esparraguera, Sp. 53/K6
Esparta, Hon. 206/E3
Esparto, Ca, US 197/K9
Espejo, Sp. 52/C4
Espelkamp, Ger. 59/F4
Esperança, Braz. 219/H4
Esperance (bay), Austl. 154/D5
Esperance, Austl. 154/D5
Esperance (bay), Den. 46/E4
Esperancita, Bol. 221/F5
Esperantina, Braz. 219/F3
Esperantinópolis, Braz. 219/E4
Esperanza, Arg. 227/C6
Esperanza, Arg., Ant. 228/W
Esperanza (mts.), Hon. 206/E3
Esperanza, Mex. 205/M8
Esperanza, Mex. 204/C3
Esperanza, Peru 220/D3
Esperanza, Uru. 227/K10
Esperanza, Ven. 217/E4
Esperia, It. 71/C5
Espichel (cape), Port. 53/P11
Espigão d'Oeste, Braz. 221/F3
Espinal, Col. 216/C3
Espinal, Mex. 205/M6
Espinar, Peru 220/D4
Espinhaço, Serra do
(mts.), Braz. 223/E4
Espinho, Port. 52/A2
Espinillo (pt.), Uru. 227/F2
Espinosa, Braz. 223/E2
Espírito Santo
(state), Braz. 223/E3
Espíritu Santo
(bay), Mex. 206/E2
Espiritu Santo
(isl.), Mex. 204/C3
Espiritu Santo
(cape), Phil. 100/D2
Espiritu Santo
(isl.), Van. 160/F6
Espita, Mex. 206/D1
Esplanada, Braz. 223/F1
Espluga de Francolí, Sp. 53/E2
Espluges, Sp. 53/L7
Espoo (Esbo), Fin. 47/L1
Esposende, Port. 52/A2
Esprit-Saint, Qu, Can. 188/C1
Espungabera, Moz. 141/G4
Espy, Pa, US 198/B1
Esqueda, Mex. 204/C2
Esquel, Arg. 226/C4
Esquina, Arg. 224/E4
Esrum Sø (lake), Den. 45/J6
Essaouira, Mor. 128/C3
Esse (riv.), Ger. 59/G5
Essé, Camr. 138/B1
Essen, Belg. 58/B6
Essen, Ger. 59/E3
Essen, Ger. 58/E6
Essenbach, Ger. 65/F5
Essendon (mt.), Austl. 154/D3
Essendon
(nbrhd.), Austl. 156/F5
Essenheim, Ger. 61/H4
Essequibo (riv.), Guy. 209/D2
Essequibo Island-West
Demerara
(pol. reg.), Guy. 217/G3
Essex, On, Can. 197/G7
Essex (co.), On, Can. 197/G7
Essex (co.), Eng, UK 36/E1
Essex, Ca, US 178/E3
Essex, Ia, US 185/G3
Essex, Md, US 198/B5
Essex, Mt, US 175/H3
Essex (co.), NJ, US 199/D2
Essex, Vt, US 191/K2
Essex Fells, NJ, US 199/H8
Essexville, Mi, US 190/E3
Essie, Ky, US 193/F2
Esslingen, Ger. 64/C5
Esso, Rus. 81/R4
Essômes-sur-Marne, Fr. 60/C5
Essonne (riv.), Fr. 50/E2
Est (prov.), Camr. 134/B5
Est, Canal de l'
(canal), Fr. 61/E5
Estaca de Bares, Punta de la
(cape), Sp. 72/B2
Estacada, Or, US 176/B1
Estación Santa Engracia,
Mex. 205/F3
Eşţahbān, Iran 115/H4
Estaires, Fr. 60/B2
Estancia, NM, US 179/J3
Estância, Braz. 223/F1
Estancia Carmen, Arg. 227/D7
Estanislao del Campo,
Arg. 224/D3
Estarca, Bol. 224/C2
Estats, Pico de
(peak), Sp. 50/D5
Estavayer-le-Lac, Swi. 66/C4
Estcourt, SAfr. 143/E3
Este, It. 69/E3
Este, Punta del
(pt.), Cuba 202/E3
Esteio, Braz. 225/G4
Estelí, Nic. 206/E3
Estell Manor (Risley),
NJ, US 198/D5
Estella, Sp. 50/B5
Estelle (mtn.), Ca, US 196/C3
Estelline, Tx, US 182/D3
Estelline, SD, US 185/F1
Estepa, Sp. 52/C4
Estepona, Sp. 52/C4
Ester, Ak, US 201/J3
Esterel (upland), Fr. 70/C6
Esterhazy, Sk, Can. 186/C2
Esterias (cape), Gabon 138/B2
Esternay, Fr. 60/C6
Estero (pt.), Ca, US 178/B3
Estero de Agiabampo
(lag.), Mex. 204/C3
Estéron (riv.), Fr. 51/G5
Esteros de Iberá
(swamp), Arg. 224/E4
Esterwegen, Ger. 59/E3
Estes Park, Co, US 184/B3
Estevan, Sk, Can. 186/C3
Estherville, Ia, US 185/G2
Estill, SC, US 193/G4
Estill Springs, Tn, US 192/D3
Estinnes-au-Mont, Belg. 61/D3
Esto, Fl, US 195/F2
Eston, Sk, Can. 175/K2
Eston and South Bank,
Eng, UK 41/G2
Estonia (ctry.) 47/L2
Estoril, Port. 53/P10
Estrablin, Fr. 70/A1
Estral Beach, Mi, US 197/F8
Estrées-Saint-Denis, Fr. 60/B5
Estrêla, Braz. 225/G4
Estrella (pt.), Mex. 204/B2
Estremadura (reg.), Sp. 72/B3
Estremoz, Port. 52/B3
Estrondo, Serra do
(mts.), Braz. 218/D5
Estuna, Swe. 45/B1
Esturaire (prov.), Gabon 138/B3
Esvres, Fr. 63/F6
Esztergom, Hun. 56/D2
Eţ Ţaiyiba, Isr. 117/C4
Eţ Ţīra, Isr. 117/B4
Étables-sur-Mer, Fr. 62/C3
Etadunna, Austl. 155/H4
Etah, India 108/B2
Étain, Fr. 61/E5
Etaka (riv.), Namb. 140/B3
Etal, Eng, UK 39/D5
Etal (isl.), Micr. 160/E4
Étalle, Belg. 61/E4
Étampes, Fr. 63/H4
Étaples, Fr. 60/A2
Etāwah, India 108/B2
Etāwah Branch
(riv.), India 108/B2
Etchojoa, Mex. 204/C3
Etéké, Gabon 138/B3
Etel (riv.), Fr. 62/B5
Étel, Fr. 62/B5
Etelïnen, Fin. 45/E4
Etembue, EqG. 138/B2
Ethe, Belg. 61/E4
Ethel, Ar, US 192/B3
Ethel Creek, Austl. 154/D2
Ethelbert, Mb, Can. 186/D2
Ethete, Wy, US 177/J2
Ethiopia (ctry.) 119/F4
Ethiopian (plat.), Eth. 119/F4
Ethiopian Seminary,
VatC. 71/F7
Ethridge, Tn, US 192/D3
Eti (riv.), Japan 95/K5
Etili, Turk. 57/H6
Etinan, Nga. 138/A1
Etiro, Namb. 140/B4
Étival-Clairefontaine, Fr. 66/C1
Etive, Loch
(inlet), Sc, UK 39/A4
Etna (peak), It. 54/D4
Etna, Ca, US 176/B3
Etne, Nor. 46/A2
Etobicoke (co), On, Can. 190/T8
Étoile, D.R. Congo 141/E1
Étoile-sur-Rhône, Fr. 70/A3
Etolin (str.), Ak, US 201/E3
Eton, Eng, UK 36/B2
Eton, Ga, US 192/E3
Etorofu (isl.), Rus. 83/P5
Etosha NP, Namb. 140/B3
Etosha Pan
(salt pan), Namb. 140/C3
Etoumbi, Congo 138/C3
Etowah, Tn, US 192/E3
Etowah (riv.), Ga, US 192/E3
Étréchy, Fr. 63/H3
Etrek (riv.), Trkm. 115/H2
Étrelles, Fr. 63/D4
Étrépagny, Fr. 63/G2
Étrépilly, Fr. 36/L4
Étretat, Fr. 63/F1
Etropole, Bul. 57/G4
Etroubles, It. 66/D6
Etsch (Adigo) (riv.), It. 67/G4
Ettadhamen Douarhicher,
Tun. 130/M6
Ettelbruck, Lux. 61/F4
Etten-Leur, Neth. 58/B5
Ettenheim, Ger. 66/D1
Etterbeek, Belg. 61/D2
Etters (Goldsboro),
Pa, US 198/B3
Ettlingen, Ger. 64/B5
Ettrick, Sc, UK 39/C6
Ettrick, Wi, US 185/J1
Ettrick Pen
(peak), Sc, UK 39/C6
Ettrick Water
(riv.), Sc, UK 39/C5
Ettringen, Ger. 67/G1
Etzikom Coulee
(riv.), Ab, Can. 175/J3
Eu, Fr. 60/A3
'Eua (isl.), Tonga 161/H7
Euabalong, Austl. 157/C1
Eubenangee Swamp NP,
Austl. 158/B2
Euchiniko (riv.), BC, Can. 174/C1
Eucla, Austl. 155/F4
Euclid, Oh, US 190/F4
Euclides da Cuhna,
Braz. 223/F1
Eucumbene (lake),
Austl. 157/D3
Eudunda, Austl. 156/A2
Euerbach, Ger. 64/D2
Eufaula, Al, US 195/F2
Eufaula (dam), Ok, US 183/G3
Eufaula, Ok, US 183/G3
Eufaula (lake), Ok, US 173/G4
Eugendorf, Aus. 65/G7
Eugene, Or, US 176/B1
Eugene O'Neill NHS,
Ca, US 197/L11
Eugenia (pt.), Mex. 204/B3
Eugowra, Austl. 157/D1
Euharlee, Ga, US 192/E3
Euless, Tx, US 180/K7
Eulo, Austl. 158/B5
Eulonia, Ga, US 195/H2
Eume (res.), Sp. 52/B1
Eumungerie, Austl. 156/D1
Eungella NP, Austl. 158/C3
Eunice, La, US 194/B2
Eunice, NM, US 180/C1
Eupen, Belg. 61/F2
Euphrates
(riv.), Iraq,Syria 83/D6
Euphrates
(riv.), Syria,Iraq 112/C1
Eupora, Ms, US 192/C4
Eura, Fin. 47/K1
Eurajoki, Fin. 47/J1
Eure (dept.), Fr. 60/A5
Eure (riv.), Fr. 50/D2
Eure-et-Loir (dept.), Fr. 60/A6
Eureka
(sound), Nun, Can. 171/S7
Eureka, Co, US 179/J2
Eureka, Il, US 185/K3
Eureka, Ks, US 183/F2
Eureka, Mt, US 174/G3
Eureka, Nv, US 176/F4
Eureka, SD, US 186/E5
Eureka, Tx, US 181/F1
Eureka, Ut, US 177/G4
Eureka, Wa, US 174/E4
Eureka Springs, Ar, US 183/H2
Euroa, Austl. 157/B3
Eurodisney, Fr. 36/L5
Euron (riv.), Fr. 66/C1
Europa (pt.), EqG. 138/B2
Europa (isl.), Fr. 141/J4
Europa (pt.), Gib. 52/C4
Europabrücke, Aus. 67/H3
Europe (cont.) 29/*
Europoort, Neth. 58/B5
Euskirchen, Ger. 61/F2
Eussenheim, Ger. 64/C3
Eustis, Fl, US 195/H3
Eustis, Me, US 191/L2
Euston, Austl. 156/B2
Eutaw, Al, US 192/D4
Eutin, Ger. 46/D4
Eutini, Malw. 141/G1
Euville, Fr. 61/E6
Euxton, Eng, UK 41/F4
Eva, Fl, US 194/M7
Eva Downs, Austl. 152/D4
Evadale, Tx, US 181/G2
Evander, SAfr. 142/E2
Evans (mt.), Co, US 182/B1
Evans, La, US 194/B2
Evans (str.), Nun, Can. 171/H2
Evans, Co, US 184/B3
Evans, WV, US 193/G1
Evans, Ga, US 193/F4
Evans Head, Austl. 156/E1
Evansburg, Ab, Can. 174/G1
Evanston, Il, US 190/C3
Evanston, Wy, US 177/H3
Evansville, Ar, US 183/G3
Evansville, Il, US 192/C1
Evansville, In, US 192/D2
Evansville, Mn, US 187/G4
Evansville, Wi, US 185/K2
Evant, Tx, US 180/E2
Evanton, Sc, UK 39/B1
Evart, Mi, US 190/D3
Evaton, SAfr. 142/D2
Evaz, Iran 115/H5
Ève, Fr. 36/L4
Evel (riv.), Fr. 62/C5
Eveleth, Mn, US 187/H4
Even Yehuda, Isr. 117/B4
Evening Shade, Ar, US 183/J2
Evenlode (riv.), Eng, UK 43/E3
Evensk, Rus. 81/R3
Evenkiyskiy Aut. Okrug,
Rus. 81/R3
Evensville, Tn, US 192/E3
Everard (lake), Austl. 155/G4
Everard (mt.), Austl. 155/G3
Everard (cape), Austl. 157/D3
Evercreech, Eng, UK 42/D4
Everest, Ks, US 185/G4
Everest (Sagarmatha)
(mtn.), China,Nepal 109/F2
Everett, Ga, US 195/H2
Everett, Pa, US 191/G4
Everett, Wa, US 174/C4
Evergem, Belg. 60/C1
Everglades City, Fl, US 195/H5
Everglades NP, Fl, US 195/H5
Evergreen, Al, US 194/E2
Evergreen Park, Il, US 197/Q16
Everman, Tx, US 180/K7
Eversholt, Eng, UK 43/F3
Everson, Wa, US 174/C3
Everswinkel, Ger. 59/E5
Everton, Mo, US 183/H2
Everton, In, US 190/D5
Evesham, Eng, UK 43/E2
Évian-les-Bains, Fr. 66/C5
Evinayong, EqG. 138/B2
Évinos (riv.), Gre. 55/G3
Evje, Nor. 46/B2
Evolène, Swi. 66/D5
Évora (dist.), Port. 52/A3
Évora, Port. 52/B3
Évran, Fr. 62/D4
Evre (riv.), Fr. 63/D6
Évrecy, Fr. 63/E2
Évreux, Fr. 63/G2
Évron, Fr. 63/E4
Evrótas (riv.), Gre. 55/H4
Évry, Fr. 36/K6
Evvoia (gulf), Gre. 76/B5
Evvoia (isl.), Gre. 76/B5
Évvoia (gulf), Gre. 55/H3
Evxinoúpolis, Gre. 55/H3
Ewan, NJ, US 198/C4
Ewaninga, Austl. 155/G2
Ewarton, Jam. 207/G2
Ewaso Ng'iro
(riv.), Kenya 137/B1
Ewaso Ngiro
(riv.), Kenya 137/A2
Ewell, Eng, UK 36/C3
Ewell, Md, US 193/J2
Ewenkizu Zizhiqi, China 91/H2
Ewhurst, Eng, UK 36/B3
Ewing, Mo, US 185/J3
Ewing, Ky, US 192/F1
Ewing, Ne, US 184/E2
Ewing, NJ, US 198/D3
Ewo, Congo 138/C3
Exaltación, Bol. 221/E4
Exaplátanos, Gre. 55/H2
Excel, Al, US 194/E2
Excello, Mo, US 185/H4
Excelsior Springs,
Mo, US 185/G4
Excursion Inlet, Ak, US 201/L4
Exe (riv.), Eng, UK 42/C4
Exeland, Wi, US 187/J5
Exeter, On, Can. 190/F3
Exeter, Eng, UK 42/C5
Exeter (arpt.), Eng, UK 42/C5
Exeter, Ca, US 178/C2
Exeter, Mo, US 183/H2
Exeter, Ne, US 184/F3
Exeter, NH, US 191/L3
Exeter, Pa, US 191/J4
Exira, Ia, US 185/G3
Exminster, Eng, UK 42/C5
Exmoor
(upland), Eng, UK 42/C4
Exmoor NP, Eng, UK 42/C4
Exmore, Va, US 193/K2
Exmouth (gulf), Austl. 154/B2
Exmouth, Austl. 154/B2
Exmouth (pen.), Chile 227/B6
Exmouth, Eng, UK 42/C5
Experiment, Ga, US 192/E4
Exploits (riv.), Nf, Can. 189/J1
Extension, La, US 194/C2
Extension, BC, Can. 174/C3
Extrema, Braz. 223/K7
Extrême Nord
(prov.), Camr. 134/B3
Exu, Braz. 219/G4
Exuma (sound), Bahm. 203/F3
Eyach (riv.), Ger. 64/B6
Eyak, Ak, US 201/J3
Eyam, Eng, UK 41/G5
Eyangu, D.R. Congo 139/E3
Eyasi (lake), Tanz. 137/A2
Eyb (riv.), Ger. 64/C5
Eybens, Fr. 70/B2
Eydehamn, Nor. 46/C2
Eye, Eng, UK 43/H2
Eye (brook), Eng, UK 43/F1
Eyemouth, Sc, UK 39/D5
Eyguières, Fr. 70/B5
Eyl, Som. 136/D4
Eyn Hemed (ruin), Isr. 117/C5
Eyn Hemeo NP, Isr. 117/C5
Eynsford, Eng, UK 36/D2
Eyragues, Fr. 70/A5
Eyre, Austl. 154/E5
Eyre (pen.), Austl. 155/G5
Eyre, North (lake), Austl. 155/H4
Eyre, South (lake), Austl. 155/H4
Eyrecourt, Ire. 38/B3
Eyrieux (riv.), Fr. 70/A3
Eyüp (nbrhd.), Turk. 115/M6
Eyüp, Turk. 115/M6
Ézanville, Fr. 36/K4
Ezequiel Ramos Mexía
(res.), Arg. 226/C3
Ezhou, China 99/G2
Ezine, Turk. 55/K3
Ézy-sur-Eure, Fr. 63/G3
Ezzane (well), Alg. 126/A4
Ezzell, Tx, US 181/F3

F

F.E. Walter
(res.), Pa, US 198/C1
F.E. Warren
(A.F.B.), Wy, US 184/B3
Faaa, FrPol. 161/X15
Faaa (Papeete)
(int'l arpt.), FrPol. 161/X15
Faafaxdhuun, Som. 137/C1
Fabbrico, It. 69/D4
Fabens, Tx, US 180/A2
Fabero, Sp. 52/B1
Fåborg, Den. 46/D4
Fabrica di Roma, It. 71/B3
Fabrichnyy, Kaz. 111/C3
Fabyan, Ab, Can. 175/J1
Facatativá, Col. 219/L8
Faches-Thumesnil, Fr. 60/C2
Facundo, Arg. 226/C5
Fada (lake), Sc, UK 39/A1
Fada, Chad 134/D1
Fada-N'Gourma, Burk. 133/F3
Fadghamī, Syria 114/E3
Fadugu, SLeo. 132/C4
Faenza, It. 69/E5
Faetano, SMar. 69/F6
Fafa (riv.), CAfr. 134/C4
Fafe, Port. 52/A2
Fafen Shet' (riv.), Eth. 136/C4
Fagali (Apia)
(int'l arpt.), Sam. 161/S9
Făgăraş, Rom. 57/G3
Fagersta, Swe. 46/F2
Fagerstrand, Nor. 44/S8
Faggiola (peak), It. 69/E5
Faggo, Nga. 133/H4
Fagnano (lake), Arg. 227/D7
Fagnano Olona-Bergoro,
It. 68/B2
Fagnières, Fr. 61/D6
Faguibine (lake), Mali 132/D2
Fagundes, Braz. 218/C4
Fahl (well), Alg. 129/F3
Fahrenzhausen, Ger. 65/E6
Faial (isl.), Azor., Port. 53/S12
Faiano, It. 71/D6
Fā'id, Egypt 131/D4
Faido, Swi. 67/E5
Faille, Eth. 136/A4
Failsworth, Eng, UK 41/F4
Fains-Véel, Fr. 61/E6
Fair Bluff, NC, US 193/H3
Fair Grove, Mo, US 183/H2
Fair Haven, Mi, US 197/G6
Fair Haven, NY, US 191/H3
Fair Haven, Vt, US 191/K3
Fair Hill, Md, US 198/C4
Fair Isle (isl.), Sc, UK 37/W14
Fair Lawn, NJ, US 199/J8
Fair Oaks, Ca, US 197/M9
Fair Oaks, Ga, US 193/L7
Fair Plain, Mi, US 190/C3
Fair Play, Mo, US 183/H2
Fairbanks, Ak, US 201/J3
Fairbanks, La, US 183/H4
Fairborn, Oh, US 190/D5
Fairburn, Ga, US 193/L7
Fairburn, SD, US 184/C2
Fairbury, Il, US 185/K3
Fairbury, Ne, US 185/F3
Fairchild
(A.F.B.), Wa, US 174/F4
Fairdealing, Mo, US 192/B2
Fairfax, Ca, US 197/J11
Fairfax, Mb, Can. 186/D3
Fairfax, Mo, US 185/G3
Fairfax, Oh, US 192/F1
Fairfax, Ok, US 183/F2
Fairfax, SC, US 193/G4
Fairfax, SD, US 184/E2
Fairfax, Va, US 198/A6
Fairfax (co.), Va, US 198/A6
Fairfax, Vt, US 191/K2
Fairfield (nbrhd.), Austl. 158/G8
Fairfield, Ca, US 176/B4
Fairfield, Ct, US 199/E1
Fairfield (co.), Ct, US 199/L7
Fairfield, Ia, US 185/J3
Fairfield, Id, US 177/F2
Fairfield, Il, US 192/C1
Fairfield, Mt, US 175/J4
Fairfield, NC, US 193/J3
Fairfield, Ne, US 184/E3
Fairfield, NJ, US 199/H8
Fairfield, Oh, US 190/D5
Fairfield, Pa, US 198/A4
Fairfield, Tx, US 181/F2
Fairfield, Va, US 193/H2
Fairfield, Wa, US 174/F4
Fairfield Bay, Ar, US 183/H3
Fairford, Mb, Can. 186/E2
Fairford, Eng, UK 43/E3
Fairgrove, Mi, US 190/E3
Fairhope, Al, US 194/E2
Fairland, In, US 190/D5
Fairland, Md, US 198/B5
Fairland, Ok, US 183/G2
Fairlawn, Va, US 193/G2
Fairlee, Md, US 198/B5
Fairless Hills, Pa, US 198/D3

Fairl – Foley
285

Fairlie, Sc, UK 39/B5
Fairlie, NZ 159/B4
Fairlight, Sk, Can. 186/D3
Fairlight, Eng, UK 43/G5
Fairmead, Ca, US 178/B2
Fairmont, Mn, US 185/G2
Fairmont, NC, US 193/H3
Fairmont, WV, US 190/F5
Fairmont Hot Springs, BC, Can. 174/G2
Fairmount, ND, US 186/F4
Fairmount, NY, US 191/H3
Fairmount, Ga, US 192/E3
Fairplains, NC, US 193/G2
Fairplay, Ky, US 192/E2
Fairpoint, SD, US 184/C1
Fairport Harbor, Oh, US 190/F4
Fairton, NJ, US 198/C5
Fairvale, NB, Can. 188/E3
Fairview, Ab, Can. 170/E3
Fairview, Ga, US 192/E3
Fairview, Ks, US 185/G4
Fairview, Mt, US 186/B4
Fairview, Mo, US 183/G2
Fairview, Mi, US 190/D2
Fairview, NJ, US 199/K8
Fairview, Ok, US 183/E2
Fairview, Tn, US 192/D3
Fairview, Tx, US 180/L6
Fairview, Tx, US 180/D1
Fairview (peak), Zim. 141/G3
Fairview Park, In, US 190/C5
Fairweather (mt.), Can.,US 201/L4
Fairweather (cape), Ak, US 201/L4
Faisalābad, Pak. 110/B4
Faison, NC, US 193/H3
Faistós (ruin), Gre. 55/J5
Faizābād, India 108/D2
Fajardo, PR 203/M8
Fak Tha, Thai. 106/C2
Fakahina (isl.), FrPol. 161/M6
Fakaofo (isl.), Tok. 161/H5
Fakarava (isl.), FrPol. 161/L6
Fakfak, Indo. 103/H4
Fako (peak), Camr. 138/B1
Fakse, Den. 46/E4
Fakse Ladeplads, Den. 46/E4
Faku, China 92/E2
Fal (riv.), Eng, UK 42/B6
Falaba, SLeo. 132/C4
Falaise, Fr. 63/E3
Fālākāta, India 109/G2
Falam, Myan. 98/B4
Falāmah, WBnk. 117/C4
Falán, Col. 219/L7
Fálanna, Gre. 55/H3
Falciano del Massico, It. 71/C5
Fălciu, Rom. 57/J2
Falcon (cape), Alg. 130/D2
Falcon (res.), Mex., US 180/E4
Falcon (dam), Tx, US 180/E4
Falcón (state), Ven. 216/D2
Falcon Lake, Mb, Can. 187/G3
Falconara (arpt.), It. 69/G6
Falconara Marittima, It. 69/G6
Falconer, NY, US 191/G3
Falémé (riv.), Mali 132/C3
Faleolo, Sam. 161/S9
Faleolo (Apia) (int'l arpt.), Sam. 161/S9
Faleşti, Mol. 78/D4
Falfurrias, Tx, US 180/E4
Falissadé, Gui. 132/B4
Falkenberg, Swe. 46/E3
Falkensee, Ger. 48/Q6
Falkenstein, Ger. 65/F2
Falkenstein, Ger. 65/F4
Falkirk, Sc, UK 39/C5
Falkirk (co.), Sc, UK 39/C5
Falkland, Sc, UK 39/C4
Falkland (isls.), UK 209/C8
Falkland Sound (str.), UK 227/E7
Falköping, Swe. 46/E2
Falkville, Al, US 192/D3
Fall (riv.), Ks, US 183/F2
Fall City, Wa, US 197/D2
Fall Creek, Wi, US 185/J1
Fall River, Ks, US 183/F2
Fall River, Ma, US 191/L4
Fall River, Wi, US 185/K2
Fallbrook, Ca, US 196/C4
Fallere (peak), It. 66/D6
Fallingbostel, Ger. 59/G3
Fallon, Mt, US 186/B4
Fallon, Nv, US 176/D4
Fallon Ind. Res., Nv, US 176/D4
Fallon Naval Air Station, Nv, US 176/D4
Falls Church, Va, US 198/A6
Falls City, Ne, US 185/G3
Falls City, Or, US 176/B1
Falls City, Tx, US 181/E3
Falls Creek, Pa, US 191/G4
Falls Lake (res.), NC, US 193/H2
Falls of Rough, Ky, US 192/D2
Fallston, Md, US 198/B4
Falmey, Niger 133/F3
Falmouth, Anti. 203/N8
Falmouth, Eng, UK 42/A6
Falmouth (bay), Eng, UK 42/A6
Falmouth, Ky, US 192/E1
Falmouth, Ma, US 191/L4
Falmouth, Mi, US 190/D2
Falmouth, NS, Can. 188/E3
Falmouth, Va, US 193/J1
False Cape Bossut (cape), Austl. 152/A4
False Orford Ness (cape), Austl. 153/F2
False Pass, Ak, US 201/F5
Falshöft (pt.), Ger. 46/C4
Falso (cape), Hon. 207/F3
Falso Cabo de Hornos (cape), Chile 227/C7
Falso, Cabo (cape), Mex. 204/C4
Falster (isl.), Den. 44/E5
Falsterbo, Den. 45/J7
Falterona (peak), It. 69/E6
Fălticeni, Rom. 78/D4
Falun, Swe. 46/F1
Famagusta (dist.), Cyp. 116/C2
Famagusta, Cyp. 116/C2
Famagusta (bay), Cyp. 116/C2
Famaillá, Arg. 224/C3
Famakah, Sudan 135/G3
Fāmanīn, Iran 112/E1
Famatina, Arg. 224/C4
Fameck, Fr. 61/F5
Famenne (reg.), Belg. 61/E3
Family (lake), Mb, Can. 187/G2
Famoso, Ca, US 178/C3
Fan Si Pan (peak), Viet. 98/D4
Fana, Nor. 46/A1
Fana, Mali 132/D3
Fanārah, Egypt 131/D4
Fanchang, China 92/D5
Fancy Farm, Ky, US 192/C2
Fandriana, Madg. 143/H8
Fane (riv.), Ire. 38/D2
Fang, Thai. 106/B2
Fang Xian, China 92/B4
Fangak, Sudan 135/F3
Fangamandou, Gui. 132/C4
Fangatau (isl.), FrPol. 161/L6
Fangataufa (isl.), FrPol. 161/L7
Fangcheng, China 92/C4
Fangcheng Gezu Zizhixian, China 99/F4
Fangcun, China 99/H3
Fangdao, China 99/H3
Fangdou (mts.), China 99/E2
Fangjiatun, China 91/J3
Fangliao, Tai. 99/J4
Fangshan, China 92/B3
Fangshan, China 92/G7
Fangxi, China 99/G2
Faniria, Madg. 143/H8
Fanjing (peak), China 99/F3
Fannich (lake), Sc, UK 39/A1
Fannie (lake), Fl, US 194/M7
Fannin, Ms, US 192/C4
Fannin, Tx, US 181/F3
Fanning (Tabuaeran) (isl.), Kiri. 161/K4
Fanø (isl.), Den. 46/C4
Fano, It. 69/G6
Fanshan, China 99/J3
Fanshawe, Ok, US 183/G3
Fanshi, China 92/C3
Fanwood, NJ, US 199/H9
Faqīrwāli, Pak. 110/B5
Faqqū'ah, WBnk. 117/C3
Fāqūs, Egypt 131/C3
Far (mtn.), BC, Can. 174/B1
Far Rockaway (nbrhd.), NY, US 199/K9
Fara in Sabina, It. 71/B3
Fara Novarese, It. 68/B2
Faradje, D.R. Congo 139/G2
Farafangana, Madg. 143/H8
Farāh, Afg. 80/G6
Farāh (riv.), Afg. 80/G6
Fa'rah (wadi), WBnk. 117/C4
Farako, Mali 132/D3
Farallon (isls.), Ca, US 176/B5
Farallón Centinela (isl.), Ven. 219/P7
Farallon de Medinilla (isl.), NMar. 160/D3
Farallon de Pajaros (isl.), NMar. 160/D2
Farallon NWR, Ca, US 176/B5
Farallones de Cali, PN, Col. 216/B4
Faramana, Burk. 132/D3
Faranah, Gui. 132/C4
Faranah (pol. reg.), Gui. 132/C4
Farángi Samariás NP, Gre. 55/H5
Faraony (riv.), Madg. 143/H8
Farasan (isls.), Sudan 136/B1
Faraulep (isl.), Micr. 160/D4
Farber, Mo, US 185/J4
Farciennes, Belg. 61/D3
Fare (riv.), Fr. 63/F5
Fareham, Eng, UK 43/E5
Farellones, Chile 226/N8
Faremoutiers, Fr. 60/C6
Farentuna, Swe. 45/A1
Farewell (cape), NZ 159/C3
Farewell, Ak, US 201/H3
Farfa (riv.), It. 71/B3
Färgelanda, Swe. 46/D2
Farghona, Uzb. 111/B3
Fargo, Ga, US 195/G2
Fargo, ND, US 186/F4
Fargo, Ok, US 182/E2
Faribault, Mn, US 185/H1
Farīdābād, India 110/D5
Farīdkot, India 110/C4
Farīdpur, India 108/B1
Farīdpur (pol. reg.), Bang. 109/G4
Farīdpur, Bang. 109/G4
Farilhao (cape), Namb. 140/B4
Farim, GBis. 132/B3
Farina, Il, US 192/C1
Farindale, Ar, US 183/H3
Färingsö (isl.), Swe. 45/A1
Fāriskūr, Egypt 131/C2
Farit (peak), Eth. 136/A3
Färjestaden, Swe. 46/G3
Farkadhón, Gre. 55/H3
Farkasgyepú, Hun. 56/C2
Farkwa, Tanz. 137/A3
Farley, Ia, US 185/J2
Farlington, Ks, US 183/G2
Farmer City, Il, US 185/K3
Farmers Branch, Tx, US 180/L7
Farmersburg, In, US 190/C5
Farmersville, Tx, US 180/L6
Farmerville, La, US 183/H4
Farmingdale, NJ, US 199/D3
Farmingdale, NY, US 199/M9
Farmington, Ar, US 183/G2
Farmington, De, US 198/C6
Farmington, Il, US 185/J3
Farmington, Me, US 191/L2
Farmington, Mi, US 197/F7
Farmington, Mn, US 185/H1
Farmington, Mo, US 192/B2
Farmington, NH, US 191/L3
Farmington, NM, US 179/H2
Farmington, Ut, US 177/H3
Farmington, Wa, US 174/F4
Farmington Hills, Mi, US 197/E6
Farmoréya, Gui. 132/B4
Farmville, NC, US 193/J3
Farmville, Va, US 193/H2
Farnborough, Eng, UK 43/F4
Farnham (mt.), BC, Can. 174/F2
Farnham, Eng, UK 43/F4
Farnham (peak), Id, US 174/F3
Farnham Royal, Eng, UK 36/B2
Farningham, Eng, UK 36/D2
Farnworth, Eng, UK 41/F4
Faro, Braz. 218/B3
Faro (riv.), Camr. 134/B4
Faro, Yk, Can. 201/M3
Faro (int'l arpt.), Port. 52/B4
Faro, Port. 52/B4
Faro (dist.), Port. 52/A4
Faro, PN de, Camr. 134/B3
Faroe (isls.), Den. 29/D2
Fåron (isl.), Swe. 47/H3
Farösund, Swe. 47/H3
Farquhar (cape), Austl. 154/B2
Farragut, Tn, US 192/E3
Farranfore (arpt.), Ire. 38/A5
Farrāshband, Iran 115/H4
Farrokh Shahr, Iran 115/G3
Farroupilha, Braz. 225/G4
Farrukhābād, India 108/B2
Farrukhnagar, India 108/A1
Fārs (gov.), Iran 115/H4
Fársala, Gre. 55/H3
Fārsān, Iran 115/G3
Farsīs, Egypt 131/C3
Farsø, Den. 46/C3
Farson, Wy, US 177/J2
Farsund, Nor. 46/B2
Fartura, Braz. 225/G2
Farum, Swe. 45/J7
Farwell, Tx, US 182/C3
Fasā, Iran 115/H4
Fasano, It. 55/E2
Faşıkan (pass), Turk. 116/C1
Fassala-Néré, Mrta. 132/D3
Fassberg, Ger. 59/H3
Fast Castle (pt.), Sc, UK 39/D5
Fastiv, Ukr. 78/E2
Fatagar Tuting (cape), Indo. 103/H4
Fatahjang, Pak. 110/B3
Fate, Tx, US 180/L7
Fate, Monte delle (peak), It. 71/C5
Fatehābād, India 110/C5
Fatehgarh Chūriān, India 110/C4
Fatehpur, Pak. 110/A4
Fatehpur, India 108/C3
Fatehpur, India 108/C2
Fatëzh, Rus. 79/H1
Fathom Five NP, On, Can. 190/F2
Fatick (pol. reg.), Sen. 132/A3
Fatick, Sen. 132/A3
Fatigue (mt.), Austl. 157/C4
Fátima, Port. 52/A3
Fátima do Sul, Braz. 225/F2
Fātir (wadi), Leb. 117/D1
Fatoto, Gam. 132/B3
Fatsa, Turk. 76/F4
Fatu Hiva (isl.), FrPol. 161/M6
Fatunda, D.R. Congo 138/D4
Faucilles (mts.), Fr. 48/C4
Faughan (riv.), NI, UK 40/A2
Fauglia, It. 68/D6
Fauldhouse, Sc, UK 39/C5
Faulkton, SD, US 184/E1
Faulquemont, Fr. 61/F5
Faure (isl.), Austl. 154/B3
Făurei, Rom. 57/H3
Fauske, Nor. 44/E2
Fauville-en-Caux, Fr. 63/F1
Fauvillers, Belg. 61/E4
Favalto (peak), It. 69/F7
Favara, It. 54/C4
Fave (riv.), Fr. 66/C1
Faverges, Fr. 66/C6
Faverney, Fr. 66/C2
Faversham, Eng, UK 43/G4
Favières, Fr. 36/L5
Favignana, It. 54/C4
Favria, It. 68/A2
Favrieux, Fr. 36/G5
Fawley, Eng, UK 43/E5
Fawn (riv.), On, Can. 170/H3
Fawn Grove, Pa, US 198/B4
Fawumang, Gha. 133/E5
Faxaflói (bay), Ice. 44/M7
Faxinal, Braz. 225/G2
Faya-Largeau, Chad 134/C1
Fayd, SAr. 114/E5
Fayence, Fr. 70/C5
Fayette, Al, US 192/D4
Fayette (co.), Ga, US 193/M8
Fayette, Ia, US 185/J2
Fayette, Mo, US 185/H4
Fayette, Ms, US 194/C2
Fayette Historical Townsite, Mi, US 190/C2
Fayetteville, Ar, US 183/G2
Fayetteville, Ga, US 193/M8
Fayetteville, NC, US 193/H3
Fayetteville, Oh, US 192/F1
Fayetteville, Pa, US 191/H5
Fayetteville, Tn, US 192/D3
Fayetteville, Tx, US 181/F3
Fayetteville, WV, US 193/G1
Fayl-la-Forêt, Fr. 66/B2
Fayrā, Yem. 136/B2
Faywood (Dwyer), NM, US 179/H4
Fazao, Monts du (mts.), Togo 133/F4
Fazao, PN du, Togo 133/F4
Fazenda Nova, Braz. 222/C3
Fāzilka, India 110/C4
Fdérik, Mrta. 128/B5
Feakle, Ire. 38/B4
Feale (riv.), Ire. 38/A5
Fear (cape), NC, US 193/J4
Feasterville-Trevose, Pa, US 198/D3
Feather (riv.), Ca, US 176/C4
Feather (falls), Ca, US 176/C4
Feather, Mid. Fk. (riv.), Ca, US 176/C4
Featherston, NZ 159/J9
Featherstone, Eng, UK 41/G4
Featherstone, Zim. 141/F3
Feathertop (mt.), Austl. 157/C3
Fécamp, Fr. 63/F1
Fecht (riv.), Fr. 66/D1
Federación, Arg. 224/E4
Federal, Arg. 224/E4
Federal Dam, Mn, US 187/G4
Federal Hall Nat'l Mem., NY, US 199/K9
Federal Way, Wa, US 174/C4
Federally Admin. Tribal Areas, Pak. 110/A2
Federalsburg, Md, US 193/K1
Federsee (lake), Ger. 64/C6
Fedhaven, Fl, US 194/N8
Fedīs, Eth. 136/B3
Fedjaj (lake), Tun. 129/H2
Fedje, Nor. 46/A1
Fedorovka, Kaz. 75/P5
Fëdorovka, Kaz. 77/J2
Fedorovka, Rus. 77/J1
Fëdorovka, Rus. 79/K4
Fedscreek, Ky, US 193/F2
Feeny, NI, UK 40/A2
Feerfeer, Som. 136/C4
Fegersheim, Fr. 64/A6
Fégréac, Fr. 62/C5
Fehérgyarmat, Hun. 56/F2
Fehmarn (isl.), Den. 46/D4
Fehmarn Belt (str.), Den. 48/F1
Fei Huang (riv.), China 92/D4
Fei Xian, China 92/D4
Feia (lake), Braz. 223/E4
Feicheng, China 92/D3
Feidong, China 92/D5
Feignies, Fr. 60/C3
Feijó, Braz. 220/D3
Feilding, NZ 159/C3
Feillans, Fr. 66/A5
Feira, Port. 52/A2
Feira de Santana, Braz. 223/F2
Feistritz (riv.), Aus. 51/L3
Feixi, China 92/D5
Fejér (co.), Hun. 56/D2
Fejø (isl.), Ger. 46/D4
Feke, Turk. 114/C2
Feketić, Serb. 56/D3
Felanitx, Sp. 53/G3
Felch, Mi, US 187/L5
Feldafing, Ger. 67/H2
Feldaist (riv.), Aus. 65/H6
Feldberg (peak), Ger. 66/E2
Feldkirch, Aus. 67/F3
Feldkirchen an der Donau, Aus. 65/H6
Feldkirchen bei Graz, Aus. 56/B2
Feldkirchen in Kärnten, Aus. 51/L3
Feletto, It. 68/A2
Feletto Umberto, It. 69/G1
Feliciano, Arroyo (brook), Arg. 224/E4
Felicity, Oh, US 192/E1
Felino, It. 68/D4
Felipe Carrillo Puerto, Mex. 206/D2
Felix (riv.), NM, US 180/B1
Felixburg, Zim. 141/F3
Felixdorf, Aus. 56/C2
Felixlândia, Braz. 222/D3
Felixstowe, Eng, UK 43/H3
Felizzano, It. 68/B4
Fell, Ger. 61/F4
Fellbach, Ger. 64/C5
Felling, Eng, UK 41/G2
Fellows, Ca, US 178/C3
Fellsmere, Fl, US 195/H4
Felsberg, Ger. 59/G6
Felsberg, Swi. 67/F4
Felsenthal, Ar, US 183/H4
Felt, Ok, US 182/C2
Feltham (nbrhd.), Eng, UK 36/B2
Felton, Ca, US 178/A2
Felton, Ca, US 178/A2
Felton, De, US 198/C5
Felton, Mn, US 186/F4
Felton, Pa, US 198/B4
Feltwell, Eng, UK 43/G2
Fema (peak), It. 71/C2
Femø (isl.), Den. 46/D4
Femundsmarka NP, Nor. 44/D3
Fen (riv.), China 90/G5
Fénay, Fr. 66/B3
Fence, Wi, US 187/K5
Fence Lake, NM, US 179/H3
Fenchuganj, Bang. 109/H3
Fene, Sp. 52/A1
Fenelon Falls, On, Can. 191/G2
Fener (pt.), Turk. 116/D1
Feng Xian, China 92/D4
Feng Xian, China 90/F5
Fengári (peak), Gre. 55/J2
Fengcheng, China 93/C2
Fengchuihudie (peak), China 99/G3
Fenggeling, China 90/F5
Fenghuang, China 105/J2
Fenghuang, China 99/E3
Fengjie, China 99/F2
Fengkou, China 99/G2
Fengle (riv.), China 92/D5
Fengle, China 99/E2
Fengle, China 99/H3
Fenglin, Tai. 99/J4
Fenglingdu, China 90/G5
Fengnan, China 92/J7
Fengning, China 92/D2
Fengqing, China 98/C3
Fengqiu, China 92/C4
Fengrun, China 92/J7
Fengshan, China 105/J3
Fengshan, China 91/H3
Fengshan, China 99/F3
Fengshuba (res.), China 99/G3
Fengshui (peak), China 91/J1
Fengtai, China 92/H7
Fengtian, China 99/G3
Fengtian, China 99/G3
Fengxian, China 92/L9
Fengxiang, China 90/F5
Fengyang, China 92/D4
Fengyüan, Tai. 99/J3
Fengzhen, China 92/C2
Fengzhou, China 90/F5
Feni, Bang. 109/H4
Fenimore Pass (str.), Ak, US 201/C5
Fenner, Ca, US 178/E3
Fennimore, Wi, US 185/J2
Fennville, Mi, US 190/C3
Fenoarivo Atsinanana, Madg. 143/J7
Fenshui (pass), China 99/H3
Fenshui Guan (pass), China 99/H4
Fenshuizhen, China 99/F2
Fensmark, Den. 46/D4
Fensterbach (riv.), Ger. 65/F4
Fenton, La, US 194/B2
Fenton, Mi, US 190/E3
Fenton (lake), Mi, US 197/E7
Fenwick, WV, US 193/G1
Fenxi, China 92/B3
Fenyang, China 92/B3
Feodosiya, Ukr. 79/H5
Férai, Gre. 57/H5
Ferbane, Ire. 38/C3
Ferdinand, In, US 192/D1
Ferdinandshof, Ger. 49/G2
Ferdows, Iran 113/G2
Fère-Champenoise, Fr. 60/C6
Fère-en-Tardenois, Fr. 60/C5
Ferentillo, It. 71/B2
Ferentino, It. 71/C4
Ferento (ruin), It. 71/B3
Fereydūn Shahr, Iran 115/G3
Fergus (riv.), Ire. 38/B4
Fergus, On, Can. 190/F3
Fergus Falls, Mn, US 186/F4
Ferguson (lake), Nun, Can. 170/F2
Ferguson, Ky, US 192/E2
Ferihegy (int'l arpt.), Hun. 56/D2
Ferkéssédougou, C.d'Iv. 132/D4
Ferlach, Aus. 51/L3
Ferland, On, Can. 187/K2
Ferland, Sk, Can. 175/L3
Ferland-et-Boilleau, Qu, Can. 188/B1
Ferlo (valley), Sen. 132/B3
Fermanagh (dist.), NI, UK 40/A3
Fermanville, Fr. 62/D1
Ferme-Neuve, Qu, Can. 191/J1
Fermeuse, Nf, Can. 189/L2
Fermi Nat'l Accelerator Lab., Il, US 197/P16
Fermignano, It. 69/F6
Fermin (pt.), Ca, US 196/F8
Fermo, It. 71/C1
Fermoselle, Sp. 52/B2
Fermoy, Ire. 38/B5
Fern Park, Fl, US 194/N6
Fern Ridge (lake), Or, US 176/B1
Fernán-Núñez, Sp. 52/C4
Fernández, Arg. 224/D3
Fernandina (isl.), Ecu. 220/J7
Fernandina Beach, Fl, US 195/H2
Fernando de la Mora, Par. 224/E3
Fernando de Noronha (isl.), Braz. 209/F3
Fernando Po (Bioko) (isl.), EqG. 138/B2
Fernandópolis, Braz. 225/G2
Ferndale, Ca, US 176/A3
Ferndale, Fl, US 194/M6
Ferndale, Md, US 198/B5
Ferndale, Mi, US 197/F7
Ferndale, Pa, US 191/G4
Ferndale, Wa, US 174/C3
Ferndown, Eng, UK 43/E5
Ferness, Sc, UK 39/C2
Ferney-Voltaire, Fr. 66/C5
Fernie, BC, Can. 174/G3
Fernley, Nv, US 176/D4
Fernpass (pass), Aus. 67/G3
Ferns, Ire. 38/D4
Ferntree Gully NP, Austl. 156/G5
Fernwood, Id, US 174/F4
Ferrandina, It. 54/E2
Ferrara, It. 69/E4
Ferrara (prov.), It. 69/E3
Ferrat (cape), Fr. 70/D5
Ferrat (cape), Alg. 130/E5
Ferreira do Alentejo, Port. 52/A3
Ferreira Gomes, Braz. 218/D2
Ferrell's Bridge (dam), Tx, US 183/G4
Ferrelo (cape), Or, US 176/A2
Ferreñafe, Peru 220/B2
Ferret (cape), Fr. 50/C4
Ferrette, Fr. 66/D3
Ferriday, La, US 194/C2
Ferriere, It. 68/C4
Ferrière-la-Grande, Fr. 60/D3
Ferrières, Belg. 61/E3
Ferris, Tx, US 180/L7
Ferrisburg, Vt, US 191/K2
Ferron, Ut, US 177/H4
Ferrum, Va, US 193/G2
Ferry Pass, Fl, US 194/E2
Ferryden, Sc, UK 39/D3
Ferryfield (int'l arpt.), Eng, UK 43/G5
Ferryhill, Eng, UK 41/G2
Ferryland, Nf, Can. 189/L2
Ferryside, Wal, UK 42/B3
Fershampenuaz, Rus. 75/N5
Ferté-Bernard, Fr. 63/F4
Fertile, Mn, US 186/F4
Fertő (Neusiedler) (lake), Aus. 51/M3
Ferwerd, Neth. 58/C2
Fès (prov.), Mor. 130/B3
Fès, Mor. 130/B2
Fesches-le-Châtel, Fr. 66/C2
Feshi, D.R. Congo 138/D4
Feshie (riv.), Sc, UK 39/C2
Fessenden, ND, US 186/E4
Fessenheim, Fr. 66/D2
Festival Centre, Austl. 155/M8
Festus, Mo, US 192/B1
Fet, Nor. 44/T8
Fetcham, Eng, UK 36/B3
Feteşti, Rom. 57/H3
Fethaland (pt.), Sc, UK 37/W13
Fethard, Ire. 38/C5
Fethard, Ire. 38/C5
Fethiye, Turk. 114/B2
Fetsund, Nor. 44/T8
Feucherolles, Fr. 36/H5
Feucht, Ger. 64/E4
Feuchtwangen, Ger. 64/D4
Feuilles (lake), Qu, Can. 171/J3
Feuilles, Rivière aux (riv.), Qu., Can. 163/K4
Feuquières, Fr. 60/A4
Feuquières-en-Vimeu, Fr. 60/A3
Feurs, Fr. 50/F4
Fevzipaşa, Turk. 116/E1
Feyẕābād, Afg. 111/B4
Feyzin, Fr. 70/A1
Fez (Saiss) (int'l arpt.), Mor. 130/B3
Fezzane (well), Niger 126/B4
Ffestiniog, Wal, UK 40/E6
Fiambalá, Arg. 224/C3
Fianarantsoa, Madg. 143/H8
Fianarantsoa (prov.), Madg. 143/H8
Fianga, Chad 134/B3
Fiano Romano, It. 71/B3
Fiastrone (riv.), It. 71/C1
Ficarolo, It. 69/E4
Fichē, Eth. 136/A3
Fichtelberg (peak), Ger. 65/F2
Fichtelgebirge (mts.), Ger. 48/F3
Fichtelnaab (riv.), Ger. 65/E3
Ficksburg, SAfr. 142/D3
Ficulle, It. 71/B2
Fidenza, It. 68/D4
Fié (riv.), Gui. 132/C4
Field (isl.), Austl. 152/D3
Field (riv.), Austl. 155/M9
Field, Ab, Can. 174/F2
Field, On, Can. 190/F1
Fieldon, Il, US 185/J4
Fields, La, US 194/B2
Fields, Or, US 176/D2
Fieni, Rom. 57/G3
Fier, Alb. 55/F2
Fier (riv.), Fr. 66/B6
Fierzë (lake), Alb. 55/G1
Fiesch, Swi. 66/E5
Fiesole, It. 69/E6
Fiesso, It. 69/F3
Fiesso Umbertiano, It. 69/E4
Fife (co.), Sc, UK 39/D4
Fife, Wa, US 197/C3
Fife, Ga, US 193/L7
Fife Ness (pt.), Sc, UK 39/D4
Fifield, Austl. 157/C1
Fifth Cataract (falls), Sudan 127/G5
Fiftysix, Ar, US 183/H3
Figalo (cape), Alg. 130/D2
Figari, Fr. 54/A2
Figeac, Fr. 50/E4
Figg (mt.), Austl. 152/D5
Figline Valdarno, It. 69/E6
Figtree, Zim. 141/F4
Figueira da Foz, Port. 52/A2
Figueres, Sp. 53/G1
Figuig, Mor. 129/E2
Figuig (prov.), Mor. 130/C3
Figuil, Camr. 134/B3
Fiherenana (riv.), Madg. 143/G8
Fiji (ctry.) 161/Y17
Fik', Eth. 136/B3
Filabusi, Zim. 141/F4
Filadelfia, Col. 219/K7
Filadélfia, Braz. 219/E4
Filadelfia, Par. 224/D2
Filadelfia, Bol. 220/D3
Filandia, Col. 219/K8
Filattiera, It. 68/C5
Filchner Ice Shelf, Ant. 228/Y
File (hills), Sk, Can. 175/M2
Filer, Id, US 177/F2
Filey (bay), Eng, UK 41/H3
Filey, Eng, UK 41/H3
Filí, Gre. 55/N8
Filiaşi, Rom. 57/F3
Filiatái, Gre. 55/G3
Filiatrá, Gre. 55/G4
Filicudi (isl.), It. 54/D3
Filingué, Niger 133/F3
Filippiás, Gre. 55/G3
Fílippoi (ruin), Gre. 55/J2
Filipstad, Swe. 46/F2
Filisur, Swi. 67/F4
Fillière (riv.), Fr. 66/C6
Fillmore, Sk, Can. 186/C3
Fillmore, Ca, US 196/B2
Fillmore, Mo, US 185/G3
Fillmore, Ut, US 179/F1
Filo (mt.), Sam. 161/S9
Filomeno Mata, Mex. 205/M6
Filótion, Gre. 55/J4
Filottrano, It. 69/G7
Fils (riv.), Ger. 64/C5
Filsum, Ger. 59/E2
Filton, Eng, UK 42/D3
Fīltu, Eth. 136/B4
Fimi (riv.), D.R. Congo 138/D3
Fina, Rsv. de, Mali 132/C3
Finale Emilia, It. 69/E4
Finale Ligure, It. 68/B5
Fiñana, Sp. 52/D4
Fincastle, Va, US 193/H2
Finch, Mt, US 175/L4
Finch Hatton, Austl. 158/C3
Finchley (nbrhd.), Eng, UK 36/C2
Findel (int'l arpt.), Lux. 61/F4
Findhorn, Sc, UK 39/C1
Findhorn (riv.), Sc, UK 39/B2
Findlay, Oh, US 190/E4
Findlay, Il, US 185/K4
Findochty, Sc, UK 39/D1
Finesville, NJ, US 198/C2
Fingal, ND, US 186/F4
Fingal, Austl. 156/C4
Finger, Tn, US 192/C3
Finger Lakes, NY, US 191/H3
Fingest, Eng, UK 36/A2
Fíngoè, Moz. 141/F2
Finhaut, Swi. 66/C5
Finike, Turk. 116/B1
Finistère (dept.), Fr. 62/A4
Finisterre, Sp. 52/A1
Finisterre (cape), Sp. 52/A1
Finisterre (range), PNG 153/G1
Finjasjön (lake), Swe. 45/K6
Finke (riv.), Austl. 155/G3
Finke Gorge NP, Austl. 155/G3
Finkenwerder, Ger. 59/G1
Finksburg, Md, US 198/B5
Finland (ctry.) 44/H2
Finland (gulf), Eur. 80/C4
Finland, Mn, US 187/J4
Finlay (riv.), BC, Can. 170/D3
Finlay (mts.), Tx, US 180/B2
Finlayson, Mn, US 187/H4
Finley, Austl. 157/B2
Finley, ND, US 186/F4
Finley, Ok, US 183/G3
Finley, Tn, US 192/C2
Finley, Wa, US 174/E4
Finley NWR, Or, US 176/B1
Finn (riv.), Ire. 37/Q9
Finnegan, Ab, Can. 175/H2
Finnentrop, Ger. 59/E6
Finnigan (mt.), Austl. 158/B1
Finnis (cape), Austl. 155/G5
Finnmark (co.), Nor. 44/G1
Fino (riv.), It. 71/C2
Fino Mornasco, It. 68/C2
Fins, Oman 113/G4
Finschhafen, PNG 153/G1
Finsing, Ger. 65/E6
Finspång, Swe. 46/F2
Finsteraarhorn (peak), Swi. 66/E4
Finstown, Sc, UK 37/V14
Finström, Fin. 47/H1
Fintel, Ger. 59/G2
Fintona, NI, UK 40/A3
Fioio (riv.), It. 71/C4
Fionn Loch (lake), Sc, UK 39/A1
Fionnay, Swi. 66/D5
Fiora (riv.), It. 51/J5
Fiorano, It. 69/D4
Fiordland NP, NZ 159/A4
Fiorenzuola d'Arda, It. 68/C4
Fiori, Monte de (peak), It. 71/C2
Fīq, Syria 117/D3
Fircrest, Wa, US 197/C3
Fire Island Nat'l Seashore, NY, US 199/E2
Firebaugh, Ca, US 178/B2
Firebrand (pass), Mt, US 175/H3
Firenze (prov.), It. 69/E5
Firenze (Florence), It. 69/E6
Firenzuola, It. 69/E5
Firesteel (cr.), SD, US 184/E1
Firestone, Co, US 184/B3
Firmat, Arg. 226/E2
Firmi, Fr. 50/E4
Firminópolis, Braz. 222/C3
Firminy, Fr. 50/F4
Firozābād, India 108/B2
Firozpur, India 110/C4
First Cataract (falls), Egypt 127/G3
Firth, Id, US 177/G2
Firth of Forth (inlet), Sc, UK 39/C4
Firth of Lorn (inlet), Sc, UK 37/Q8
Firth of Tay (inlet), Sc, UK 39/C4
Firth of Thames (inlet), NZ 159/C2
Fīrūz Kūh, Iran 115/H3
Fīrūzābād, Iran 115/H4
Firyuza, Trkm. 113/G1
Fischa (riv.), Aus. 57/P7
Fischach, Ger. 67/G1
Fischamend Markt, Aus. 57/P7
Fischbacher Alpen (mts.), Aus. 51/L3
Fischbek, Ger. 59/G2
Fischen im Allgäu, Ger. 67/G3
Fisenge, Zam. 141/F2
Fish (riv.), Namb. 140/C5
Fish Camp, Ca, US 178/C2
Fishburn, Eng, UK 41/G2
Fisher, Austl. 155/F4
Fisher (bay), Mb, Austl. 186/F2
Fisher (mt.), BC, Can. 174/G3
Fisher (str.), Nun, Can. 171/H2
Fisher, Ar, US 192/B3
Fisher, Il, US 190/B4
Fisher, La, US 194/B2
Fisher, Mn, US 186/F4
Fisher, WV, US 193/H1
Fisher Bay, Mb, Can. 186/F2
Fisher Branch, Mb, Can. 186/F2
Fisherman (isl.), Austl. 158/F6
Fishermans Island Nat'l Wild. Ref., Va, US 193/K2
Fishers (isl.), NY, US 199/G1
Fishersville, Va, US 193/H1
Fishguard, Wal, UK 42/B3
Fishing (lake), Mb, Can. 187/G1
Fishing (cr.), NC, US 193/J2
Fisht (peak), Rus. 76/F4
Fishtoft, Eng, UK 41/J6
Fisk, Mo, US 192/B2
Fiske, Sk, Can. 175/K2
Fisksätra, Swe. 45/B1
Fismes, Fr. 60/C5
Fitchburg, Ma, US 191/L3
Fitchburg, Wi, US 185/K2
Fitful Head (pt.), Sc, UK 37/W14
Fitjar, Nor. 46/A2
Fittja, Swe. 45/A1
Fitton (mt.), Yk, Can. 201/L2
Fitz Roy, Arg. 226/D5
Fitzcarrald, Peru 220/D3
Fitzgerald, Ga, US 195/G2
Fitzgerald River NP, Austl. 154/C5
Fitzhugh, Ok, US 183/F3
Fitzroy (peak), Arg. 227/B6
Fitzroy, UK 227/F6
Fitzroy (riv.), Austl. 145/B2
Fitzroy Crossing, Austl. 152/B4
Fitzwilliam (isl.), On, Can. 190/E2
Fitzwilliam (str.), NW, Can. 171/R7
Fiuggi, It. 71/C4
Fiume Veneto, It. 69/F2
Fiumicino, It. 71/B4
Five Forks, Ga, US 193/M7
Five Islands, NS, Can. 188/E3
Five Sisters (peak), Sc, UK 39/A2
Fivemile (cr.), Wy, US 177/J2
Fivemiletown, NI, UK 40/A3
Fivizzano, It. 68/D5
Fizi, D.R. Congo 139/G4
Fizuli, Azer. 77/H5
Fjell, Nor. 46/A1
Fjellstrand, Nor. 44/S8
Fjerritslev, Den. 46/C3
Fjugesta, Swe. 46/F2
Flå, Nor. 46/C1
Flachslanden, Ger. 64/D4
Flackwell Heath, Eng, UK 36/A2
Fladungen, Ger. 64/D1
Flagler, Co, US 184/C4
Flagler Beach, Fl, US 195/H3
Flagler Museum, Fl, US 194/P9
Flagpole (peak), Tn, US 192/E2
Flagstaff, Az, US 179/G3
Flagstaff (lake), Or, US 176/D2
Flåm, Nor. 46/B1
Flambeau (riv.), Wi, US 187/J5
Flamborough Head (pt.), Eng, UK 41/H3
Flamborough, Eng, UK 41/H3
Flamborough, On, Can. 190/T9
Fläming (hills), Ger. 48/G2
Flaming Gorge (dam), Ut, US 177/J3
Flaming Gorge (res.), Ut.,Wy, US 177/J3
Flaming Gorge NRA, Wy, US 177/J3
Flamingo, Fl, US 195/H5
Flamingo Field (int'l arpt.), NAnt. 216/D1
Flanagan (riv.), On, Can. 187/H1
Flanders (reg.), Belg.,Fr. 60/B2
Flanders, NY, US 199/F2
Flandes, Col. 219/L8
Flandreau, SD, US 185/F1
Flärdlång (isl.), Swe. 45/B1
Flasher, ND, US 186/D4
Flat (mt.), NZ 159/A4
Flat Bay, Nf, Can. 189/H1
Flat Creek, Yk, Can. 201/L3
Flat Holm (isl.), Eng, UK 42/C4
Flat River, Mo, US 192/B2
Flat Rock, Mi, US 190/E3
Flat Rock, NC, US 193/G2
Flatbush (nbrhd.), NY, US 199/K9
Flateby, Nor. 44/T8
Flathead (lake), Mt, US 175/H4
Flathead (range), Mt, US 175/H3
Flathead (riv.), Mt, US 174/G4
Flathead Indian Res., Mt, US 174/G4
Flathead, South Fork (riv.), Mt, US 175/H4
Flatiron (mtn.), Id, US 177/G1
Flatonia, Tx, US 181/F3
Flattery (cape), Austl. 158/B1
Flattery (cape), Wa, US 172/A2
Flatwillow (cr.), Mt, US 175/K4
Flatwoods, La, US 194/B2
Flatwoods, Ky, US 193/F1
Flavio Alfaro, Ecu. 216/B5
Flawil, Swi. 67/F3
Flaxcombe, Sk, Can. 175/K2
Flaxlanden, Fr. 66/D2
Flayosc, Fr. 70/C5
Fleet, Eng, UK 43/F4
Fleet, Ab, Can. 175/J1
Fleetwood, Eng, UK 41/E4
Fleetwood, Pa, US 198/C3
Flekkefjord, Nor. 46/B2
Fleming, Sk, Can. 186/D2
Fleming, Co, US 184/C3
Fleming-Neon, Ky, US 193/F2
Flemingsberg, Swe. 45/A1
Flemingsburg, Ky, US 192/F1
Flemington, Mo, US 183/H2
Flemington, NJ, US 198/D2
Flemington Racecourse, Austl. 156/F5
Flemish Brabant (prov.), Belg. 61/D2
Flen, Swe. 46/G2
Flensburg, Ger. 46/C4
Flero, It. 68/D3
Fleron, Belg. 61/E2
Flers, Fr. 63/E3
Flesher (pass), Mt, US 175/H4
Flesk (riv.), Ire. 38/A5
Flesland (int'l arpt.), Nor. 46/A1
Fletcher, Ok, US 183/E3
Fletcher (pond), Mi, US 190/E2
Fletcher, NC, US 193/F3
Fletschhorn (peak), Swi. 66/D5
Fleurance, Fr. 50/D5
Fleurier, Swi. 66/C4
Fleurus, Belg. 61/D3
Fleury-les-Aubrais, Fr. 63/G5
Fleury-sur-Andelle, Fr. 63/G2
Fleury-sur-Orne, Fr. 63/E2
Flevoland (isl.), Neth. 48/C2
Flevoland (prov.), Neth. 58/C4
Flexenpass (pass), Aus. 67/G3
Flieden, Ger. 64/C2
Flieden (riv.), Ger. 64/C2
Fliess, Aus. 67/G3
Flimby, Eng, UK 40/E2
Flims, Swi. 67/F4
Flin Flon, Mb, Can. 170/F3
Flinders (range), Austl. 155/H5
Flinders (bay), Austl. 154/B5
Flinders (isl.), Austl. 145/D4
Flinders (riv.), Austl. 145/D2
Flinders Chase NP, Austl. 155/H5
Flinders Ranges (mts.), Austl. 145/C4
Flinders Ranges NP, Austl. 155/H4
Flinders Reefs (isls.), Austl. 158/C2
Flinders Reefs (reef), Austl. 153/H4
Flines-lez-Raches, Fr. 60/C3
Flint (lake), Nun, Can. 171/J2
Flint (isl.), Kiri. 161/K6
Flint, Wal, UK 41/E5
Flint (riv.), Ga, US 193/M8
Flint (hills), Ks, US 183/F2
Flint, Mi, US 190/E3
Flint City, Al, US 192/D3
Flint Hills Nat'l Wild. Ref., Ks, US 185/G4
Flint, South Branch (riv.), Mi, US 197/F5
Flintbek, Ger. 46/D4
Flinton, On, Can. 191/H2
Flintshire (co.), Wal, UK 41/E5
Flippen, Ga, US 193/M8
Flisa, Nor. 46/E1
Flitwick, Eng, UK 43/F2
Flix, Sp. 53/F2
Flixecourt, Fr. 60/B3
Flize, Fr. 61/D4
Flo, Tx, US 181/G2
Floby, Swe. 46/E2
Floda, Swe. 46/E3
Flodden, Eng, UK 39/D5
Flögelner See (riv.), Ger. 59/F1
Flöha (riv.), Ger. 49/G3
Floing, Fr. 61/D4
Flomaton, Al, US 194/E2
Flonheim, Ger. 64/B3
Flora (mt.), Austl. 154/C2
Flora, Nor. 44/C3
Flora, Il, US 192/C1
Flora, In, US 190/C4
Flora, La, US 194/B2
Flora, Ms, US 192/B4
Flora, Phil. 100/C1
Flora (mtn.), Wa, US 174/D3
Flora Vista, NM, US 179/H2
Floral, Ar, US 183/J3
Floral City, Fl, US 194/L6
Floral Park, NY, US 199/L9
Florala, Al, US 195/E2
Florange, Fr. 61/F5
Florânia, Braz. 219/G4
Floraville, Austl. 153/E4
Floreffe, Belg. 61/D3
Florence (Firenze), It. 69/E6
Florence, Al, US 192/D3
Florence, Ar, US 183/J4
Florence, Az, US 179/G4
Florence, Co, US 182/B1
Florence, Ks, US 183/F1
Florence, Ky, US 192/E1
Florence, Ms, US 192/B4
Florence, Mt, US 175/G4
Florence, Or, US 176/A2
Florence, SC, US 193/H3
Florence, SD, US 185/F1
Florence, Tx, US 181/F2
Florence, Wi, US 187/K5
Florence Junction, Az, US 179/G4
Florence Lake Nat'l Wild. Ref., ND, US 186/D4
Florence-Graham, Ca, US 196/F8
Florenceville, NB, Can. 188/D2
Florencia, Col. 216/C4
Florencia, Arg. 224/E4
Florennes, Belg. 61/D3
Florentino Ameghino, Arg. 226/D4
Florenton, Mn, US 187/H4
Florenville, Belg. 61/E4
Flores (isl.), Azor., Port. 53/R12
Flores, Braz. 219/G4
Flores, Guat. 206/D2
Flores (isl.), Indo. 83/M10
Flores (sea), Indo. 83/L10
Flores (dept.), Uru. 227/F2
Flores do Piauí, Braz. 219/F4
Flores, Arroyo de los (cr.), Arg. 226/E3
Floresta, Braz. 219/G5
Floreşti, Mol. 78/E4
Floresville, Tx, US 181/E3
Florham Park, NJ, US 199/H8
Floriano, Braz. 219/F4
Florianópolis, Braz. 225/G3
Florida, Bol. 220/D4
Florida, Bol. 224/D1
Florida, Col. 216/B4
Florida, Cuba 207/G1
Florida (str.), Cuba,US 173/K7
Florida, Hon. 206/D3
Florida, Peru 220/B2
Florida, Uru. 227/K11
Florida (dept.), Uru. 227/F2
Florida (state), US 195/F2
Florida (cape), Fl, US 194/P11
Florida, NY, US 199/D1
Florida City, Fl, US 195/H5
Florida Keys (isl.), Fl, US 195/H5
Florida Keys (isls.), Fl, US 163/J7
Florida Negra, Arg. 227/D6
Floridablanca, Col. 216/C3
Florida's Silver Springs, Fl, US 195/G3
Floridia, It. 54/D4
Florien, La, US 194/B2
Florin, Ca, US 197/M10
Flórina, Gre. 55/G2
Florissant, Mo, US 185/J4
Florissant Fossil Beds Nat'l Monument, Co, US 182/B1
Florissant Fossil Beds Nat'l Mon., Co, US 184/B4
Flörsbachtal, Ger. 64/C2
Flörsheim am Main, Ger. 64/B2
Flörsheim-Dalsheim, Ger. 64/B3
Florstadt, Ger. 64/B2
Flossenbürg, Ger. 65/F3
Flottsund, Swe. 45/A1
Flower Mound, Tx, US 180/K6
Floyd (riv.), Ia, US 185/F2
Floyd, Va, US 193/G2
Floyd, Ga, US 193/L7
Floydada, Tx, US 182/D4
Fluchthorn (peak), Aus. 67/G4
Flüelapass (pass), Swi. 67/F4
Flüelen, Swi. 67/E4
Fluessen (lake), Neth. 58/C3
Fluker, La, US 194/C2
Flume (riv.), Fr. 62/D4
Flums, Swi. 67/F3
Flushing, Mi, US 190/E3
Flushing (nbrhd.), NY, US 199/K8
Fluvanna, Tx, US 182/D4
Fly (riv.), PNG 153/F2
Fly River (delta), PNG 153/F2
Flying Fish (cape), Ant. 228/T
Fnjóská (riv.), Ice. 44/P6
Foam Lake, Sk, Can. 186/C2
Foard City, Tx, US 182/E4
Foča, Bosn. 56/D4
Fochabers, Sc, UK 39/C1
Fochville, SAfr. 142/P13
Fockbek, Ger. 46/C4
Focşani, Rom. 57/H3
Foëcy, Fr. 63/H6
Fog (bay), Austl. 152/C3
Fogang, China 105/K3
Foggaret ez Zoua, Alg. 129/F4
Foggia, It. 54/D2
Fogi, Indo. 103/G4
Foglia (riv.), It. 69/F5
Fogliano (lake), It. 71/B5
Foglizzo, It. 68/A2
Föglö (isl.), Fin. 47/J3
Fogo (isl.), CpV. 119/J10
Fohnsdorf, Aus. 51/L3
Föhren, Ger. 61/F4
Foix, Fr. 50/D5
Fokino, Rus. 76/E1
Folarskardnuten (peak), Nor. 46/B1
Folda (inlet), Nor. 44/E2
Földeák, Hun. 56/E2
Folégandros (isl.), Gre. 73/K3
Folembray, Fr. 60/C4
Foley, Mn, US 187/H5
Foley, Fl, US 195/G2

Foley – Fujie
286

Foley (isl.), Nun, Can. 171/J2
Foley, Mo, US 185/J4
Folgaria, It. 67/H6
Foligno, It. 71/B2
Foligno, It. 71/B2
Folkestone, Eng, UK 43/H4
Folkston, Ga, US 195/G2
Follainville-Dennemont, Fr. 36/H4
Follets (isl.), Tx, US 181/G3
Follonica (gulf), It. 51/J5
Folly Beach, SC, US 193/H4
Folschviller, Fr. 61/F5
Folsom (dam), Ca, US 178/B1
Folsom (lake), Ca, US 176/C4
Folsom, Ca, US 176/C4
Folsom, NJ, US 198/D4
Folteşti, Rom. 57/J3
Fomboni, Com. 143/G6
Fómeque, Col. 219/M8
Fomin, Rus. 77/G3
Fond de Peinin, Pic du (peak), Fr. 70/C3
Fond du Lac, Sk, Can. 170/F3
Fond du Lac (riv.), Sk, Can. 170/F3
Fond du Lac, Wi, US 185/K2
Fond du Lac Ind. Res., Mn, US 187/H4
Fonda, NY, US 191/J3
Fondettes, Fr. 63/F6
Fondi (lake), It. 71/C5
Fondi, It. 71/C5
Fondo, It. 67/H5
Fongen (peak), Nor. 44/D3
Fongolanbi, Sen. 132/B3
Fonni, It. 54/A2
Fonsagrada, Sp. 52/B1
Fonseca (gulf), Nic. 202/D5
Fonseca, Col. 216/C2
Font Sancte, Pic de la (peak), Fr. 70/C3
Fontaine, Fr. 70/B2
Fontaine-Châalis, Fr. 36/L4
Fontaine-lès-Dijon, Fr. 66/A3
Fontaine-lès-Luxeuil, Fr. 66/C2
Fontaine-l'Evêque, Belg. 61/D3
Fontana, Ca, US 196/C2
Fontana, Ks, US 183/G1
Fontana (lake), NC, US 192/F3
Fontanarossa, It. 71/E5
Fontanarossa (int'l arpt.), It. 54/D4
Fontanella, It. 68/C3
Fontanellato, It. 68/D4
Fontanelle, Ia, US 185/G3
Fontaniva, It. 69/E2
Fonte Boa, Braz. 217/E5
Fontenailles, Fr. 36/L6
Fontenais, Swi. 66/D3
Fontenay-en-Parisis, Fr. 36/K4
Fontenay-le-Comte, Fr. 50/C3
Fontenay-le-Fleury, Fr. 36/J5
Fontenay-le-Marmion, Fr. 63/E2
Fontenay-les-Briis, Fr. 36/J6
Fontenay-Saint-Père, Fr. 36/H4
Fontenay-sous-Bois, Fr. 36/K5
Fontenay-Trésigny, Fr. 36/L5
Fontenelle (res.), Wy, US 177/H2
Fontenelle (dam), Wy, US 177/H2
Fontibón, Col. 219/L8
Fontoy, Fr. 61/F5
Fontur (pt.), Ice. 44/P6
Fontvieille, Fr. 70/A5
Fontvieille, Mona. 68/J8
Footscray (nbrhd.), Austl. 156/F5
Foping, China 90/F5
Foraker (mt.), Ak, US 201/H3
Forbach, Fr. 61/F5
Forbach, Ger. 64/B5
Forbes, ND, US 186/E5
Forbes (mt.), BC, Can. 174/F2
Forbes, Austl. 157/D1
Forbesganj, India 109/F2
Forcados, Nga. 133/G5
Forcalquier, Fr. 70/B5
Forcarey, Sp. 52/A1
Forchheim, Ger. 64/E3
Ford (riv.), Mi, US 187/L4
Ford, Eng, UK 39/D5
Ford (cape), Austl. 152/C3
Ford City, Ca, US 178/C3
Fordate (isl.), Indo. 152/D1
Førde, Nor. 44/C3
Fordham (nbrhd.), NY, US 199/K8
Fordingbridge, Eng, UK 43/E5
Fordoche, La, US 194/C2
Fords, NJ, US 199/H9
Ford's Bridge, Austl. 156/C1
Fords Prairie, Wa, US 174/C4
Fordsville, Ky, US 192/D2
Fordville, ND, US 186/F3
Fordyce, Ar, US 183/H4
Forécariah, Gui. 132/B4
Foreland (pt.), Eng, UK 42/C4
Foreland, The (pt.), Eng, UK 43/E5
Foremost, Ab, Can. 175/J3
Foreness (pt.), Eng, UK 43/H4
Forest, La, US 183/J4
Forest (riv.), ND, US 186/F3
Forest, Ms, US 192/C4
Forest, Tx, US 181/G2
Forest City, Fl, US 194/N6
Forest City, Ia, US 185/H2
Forest City, NC, US 193/G3
Forest Green, Eng, UK 36/B3
Forest Grove, Me, US 176/B1
Forest Hill, Austl. 157/C2
Forest Hill, Md, US 198/B4
Forest Hill, Tx, US 180/K7
Forest Hill, WV, US 193/G2
Forest Hills (nbrhd.), NY, US 199/K9
Forest Hills, Tn, US 192/D2
Forest Lake, Mn, US 187/H5
Forest Park, Ga, US 193/M7
Forestbrook, SC, US 193/H4
Forestburg, Ab, Can. 175/H1
Foresthill, Ca, US 176/C4
Forestier (cape), Austl. 156/D4
Forestier (pen.), Austl. 156/D4
Foreston, Mn, US 187/H5
Forestport, NY, US 191/J3
Forestville, Qu, Can. 188/C1
Forestville, NY, US 191/G3
Forestville, Md, US 198/B6
Forét (bay), Fr. 62/B5
Forêt du Day NP, Djib. 136/B3
Forez (mts.), Fr. 50/E4
Forfar, Sc, UK 39/D3
Forgan, Ok, US 182/D2
Forgan, Sk, Can. 175/L2
Forges-les-Bains, Fr. 36/J6
Forges-les-Eaux, Fr. 63/G1
Forggensee (lake), Ger. 67/G2
Forillon NP, Qu, Can. 188/E1
Forino, It. 71/D6
Forio, It. 71/C6
Fork Res. (lake), Tx, US 181/G1
Fork River, Mb, Can. 186/D2
Forked Deer, South Fork (riv.), Tn, US 192/C3
Forked Island, La, US 194/B3
Forked River, NJ, US 199/D4
Forkill, NI, UK 40/B3
Forkland, Al, US 192/D4
Forks, Wa, US 174/B4
Forlì, It. 69/F5
Forlì (prov.), It. 69/F4
Forlimpopoli, It. 69/F5
Forman, ND, US 186/F4
Formartine (reg.), Sc, UK 39/D2
Formazza, It. 67/E5
Formby, Eng, UK 41/E4
Formby (pt.), Eng, UK 41/E4
Formello, It. 71/B3
Formentera, Isla de (isl.), Sp. 72/D3
Formentor (cape), Sp. 53/G3
Former Yugoslav Republic of Macedonia (Macedonia) (ctry.) 55/G2
Formerie, Fr. 60/A4
Formia, It. 71/C5
Formiga, Braz. 222/D4
Formigine, It. 69/D4
Formignana, It. 69/E4
Formosa (prov.), Arg. 224/D3
Formosa, Arg. 224/E3
Formosa, Braz. 222/D2
Formosa (isl.), GBis. 132/B4
Formosa (peak), SAfr. 142/C4
Formosa, Ar, US 183/H3
Formosa, Serra (mts.), Braz. 221/H4
Formoso (riv.), Braz. 222/C1
Formoso, Braz. 222/C2
Fornacelle, It. 69/E6
Fornaci di Barga, It. 68/D5
Fornæs (cape), Den. 46/D3
Fornebu (int'l arpt.), Nor. 46/D2
Forney, Tx, US 180/L7
Forno Canavese, It. 70/D2
Fornosovo, Rus. 47/P2
Fornovo di Taro, It. 68/D4
Foro (riv.), It. 71/D3
Foro Burunga, Sudan 134/D2
Foros, Ukr. 76/E3
Forres, Sc, UK 39/C1
Forres, Arg. 224/D3
Forrest, Austl. 155/F4
Forrest City, Ar, US 192/B3
Forrest River Abor. Rsv., Austl. 152/B3
Forrest River Mission, Austl. 152/B3
Forrest Station, Mb, Can. 186/E3
Forsan, Tx, US 180/D1
Forsand, Nor. 46/B2
Forsayth, Austl. 158/A2
Forshaga, Swe. 46/E2
Forssa, Fin. 47/K1
Forster, Austl. 156/E2
Forstern, Ger. 65/E6
Forstinning, Ger. 65/E6
Forsyth, Mo, US 183/H2
Forsyth (range), Austl. 158/A3
Forsyth, Ga, US 192/F4
Forsyth, Mt, US 175/L4
Forsythe NWR, NJ, US 199/D5
Fort Polk Mil. Res., La, US 181/H2
Fort A.P. Hill, Va, US 193/J1
Fort Abbās, Pak. 110/B5
Fort Albany, On, Can. 171/H3
Fort Ancient, Oh, US 190/D5
Fort Apache, Az, US 179/H4
Fort Apache Ind. Res., Az, US 179/G3
Fort Ashby, WV, US 191/G5
Fort Atkinson, Wi, US 185/K2
Fort Augustus, Sc, UK 39/B2
Fort Beaufort, SAfr. 142/D4
Fort Beauséjour Nat'l Hist. Park, NB, Can. 188/E3
Fort Belknap, Tx, US 183/E4
Fort Belknap Ind. Res., Mt, US 175/K3
Fort Belvoir, Va, US 198/A6
Fort Bend (co.), Tx, US 181/M9
Fort Benning, Ga, US 192/E4
Fort Benning Mil. Res., Ga, US 195/F1
Fort Benning South, Ga, US 192/E4
Fort Benton, Mt, US 175/J4
Fort Berthold Ind. Res., ND, US 186/C4
Fort Bidwell, Ca, US 176/C3
Fort Bliss (mil. res.), NM, US 179/J4
Fort Bowie Nat'l Hist. Site, Az, US 179/H4
Fort Bragg, Ca, US 176/B4
Fort Bragg, NC, US 193/H3
Fort Branch, In, US 192/D1
Fort Bridger, Wy, US 177/H3
Fort Buford Historical Site, ND, US 186/C4
Fort Campbell, Tn,Ky, US 192/D2
Fort Carson, Co, US 182/B1
Fort Carson, Co, US 184/B4
Fort Chambly Nat'l Hist. Park, Qu, Can. 189/P7
Fort Chipewyan, Ab, Can. 170/E3
Fort Clark Historical Site, ND, US 186/D4
Fort Collins, Co, US 200/B1
Fort Collins Museum, Co, US 200/B1
Fort Conde, Al, US 194/D2
Fort Davis, Al, US 192/E4
Fort Davis, Tx, US 180/C2
Fort Davis Nat'l Hist. Site, Tx, US 180/C2
Fort de Douaumont, Fr. 61/E5
Fort de Kock, Indo. 101/C3
Fort de Vaux, Fr. 61/E5
Fort Defiance, Az, US 179/H3
Fort Deposit, Al, US 194/E2
Fort Desaix Mil. Res., Fr. 203/N9
Fort Desoto Park, Fl, US 194/K8
Fort Dix, NJ, US 191/J4
Fort Dodge, Ia, US 185/G2
Fort Dodge Historical Museum, Ia, US 185/G2
Fort Donelson Nat'l Bfld., Tn, US 192/D2
Fort Drum, NY, US 191/J2
Fort Duchesne, Ut, US 177/J3
Fort Erie, On, Can. 190/V10
Fort Frances, On, Can. 187/H3
Fort Frederica Nat'l Mon., Ga, US 195/H2
Fort Gaines, Al, US 194/D2
Fort Gaines, Ga, US 195/F2
Fort Garland, Co, US 182/B2
Fort Gates, Tx, US 180/F2
Fort Gay, WV, US 193/F1
Fort George Nat'l Hist. Park, On, Can. 190/U9
Fort Gibson, Ok, US 183/G3
Fort Gibson (lake), Ok, US 183/G2
Fort Good Hope, NW, Can. 170/D2
Fort Gordon, Ga, US 193/F4
Fort Grant, Az, US 179/H4
Fort Green, Fl, US 194/M8
Fort Green Springs, Fl, US 194/M8
Fort Hall, Id, US 177/G2
Fort Hall Ind. Res., Id, US 177/G2
Fort Hancock, NJ, US 199/J10
Fort Hancock, Tx, US 180/B2
Fort Hood, Tx, US 181/F2
Fort Howard, Md, US 198/B5
Fort Huachuca, Az, US 179/G5
Fort Hunter Liggett, Ca, US 178/B3
Fort Independence Ind. Res., Ca, US 178/C2
Fort Irwin (mil. res.), Ca, US 178/D3
Fort Jackson, SC, US 193/G3
Fort Jesus, Kenya 137/B3
Fort Knox, Ky, US 192/E2
Fort Laramie (canal), Wy, US 184/B2
Fort Laramie Nat'l Hist.Site, Wy, US 184/B2
Fort Larned Nat'l Hist. Site, Ks, US 182/E1
Fort Lauderdale, Fl, US 194/P10
Fort Lauderdale-Hollywood (int'l arpt.), Fl, US 194/P10
Fort Lawn, SC, US 193/G3
Fort Leavenworth Mil. Res., Ks, US 183/G1
Fort Lee, NJ, US 199/K8
Fort Lennox Nat'l Hist. Park, Qu, Can. 191/K2
Fort Leonard Wood, Mo, US 183/H2
Fort Lewis, Wa, US 197/B3
Fort Liard, NW, Can. 170/D2
Fort Liberté, Haiti 207/J2
Fort Lonesome, Fl, US 194/L8
Fort Loudon, Pa, US 191/H5
Fort Lupton, Co, US 184/B3
Fort Lyon (canal), Co, US 184/C4
Fort Macleod, Ab, Can. 175/H3
Fort Madison, Ia, US 185/J3
Fort Malden Nat'l Hist. Park, On, Can. 197/F7
Fort Mandan Historical Site, ND, US 186/D4
Fort Matanzas Nat'l Mon., Fl, US 195/H3
Fort Mc Dermitt Ind. Res., Nv, US 176/D3
Fort McCoy, Fl, US 195/H3
Fort McCoy (fort), Wi, US 185/J1
Fort McDowell Ind. Res., Az, US 179/G4
Fort McHenry Nat'l Mon., Md, US 198/B5
Fort McMurray, Ab, Can. 170/E3
Fort McPherson, NW, Can. 201/M2
Fort Meade, Fl, US 194/M8
Fort Meade, Md, US 198/B5
Fort Michilimackinac, Mi, US 190/D2
Fort Mill, SC, US 193/G3
Fort Missoula, Mt, US 175/G4
Fort Monmouth, NJ, US 199/D3
Fort Mojave Ind. Res., Az,Ca, US 178/E3
Fort Morgan, Al, US 194/D2
Fort Morgan, Co, US 184/C3
Fort Morgan Museum, Co, US 184/C3
Fort Motte, SC, US 193/G4
Fort Moultrie, SC, US 193/H4
Fort Myers, Fl, US 195/H4
Fort Nelson, BC, Can. 170/D3
Fort Nelson (riv.), BC, Can. 170/D3
Fort Niobrara NWR, Ne, US 184/D2
Fort Nottingham, SAfr. 143/E3
Fort Payne, Al, US 192/E3
Fort Peck, Mt, US 175/L3
Fort Peck (dam), Mt, US 175/L4
Fort Peck (lake), Mt, US 163/G5
Fort Peck Ind. Res., Mt, US 175/L3
Fort Phantom Hill, Tx, US 180/E1
Fort Pierce, Fl, US 195/H4
Fort Pierre, SD, US 184/D1
Fort Plain, NY, US 191/J3
Fort Portal, Ugan. 139/G2
Fort Providence, NW, Can. 170/E2
Fort Pulaski Nat'l Mon., Ga, US 193/G4
Fort Qu'Appelle, Sk, Can. 186/C2
Fort Quitman Ruins, Tx, US 180/B2
Fort Raleigh Nat'l Hist. Site, NC, US 193/K3
Fort Randall (dam), SD, US 184/E2
Fort Ransom, ND, US 186/F4
Fort Ransom Historical Site, ND, US 186/F4
Fort Resolution, NW, Can. 170/E2
Fort Rice, ND, US 186/D4
Fort Rice Historical Site, ND, US 186/D4
Fort Riley (fort), Ks, US 185/F4
Fort Riley Mil. Res., Ks, US 183/F1
Fort Ripley, Mn, US 187/G4
Fort Rixon, Zim. 141/F4
Fort Rock, Or, US 176/C2
Fort Ross, Ca, US 176/B4
Fort Rucker Military Res., Al, US 195/f2
Fort Saint James, BC, Can. 170/D3
Fort Saint John, BC, Can. 170/D3
Fort Scott, Ks, US 183/G2
Fort Scott Nat'l Hist. Site, Ks, US 183/G2
Fort Seward Historical Site, ND, US 186/E4
Fort Seybert, WV, US 193/H1
Fort Shawnee, Oh, US 190/D4
Fort Sill Mil. Res., Ok, US 183/E3
Fort Simpson, NW, Can. 170/D2
Fort Smith, NW, Can. 170/E2
Fort Smith, Ar, US 183/G3
Fort Smith, Mt, US 177/K1
Fort Smith Nat'l Hist. Site, Ar, US 183/G3
Fort Stanwix Nat'l Mon., NY, US 191/J3
Fort Stewart, Ga, US 195/H2
Fort Stockton, Tx, US 180/C2
Fort Sumner, NM, US 182/B3
Fort Sumter Nat'l Mon., SC, US 193/H4
Fort Thomas, Az, US 179/H4
Fort Thomas, Ky, US 190/D5
Fort Tilden, NY, US 199/K9
Fort Totten, ND, US 186/E4
Fort Totten Indian Res., ND, US 186/E4
Fort Towson, Ok, US 183/G3
Fort Union Nat'l Mon., NM, US 182/B3
Fort Union Trading Post Nat'l Hist. Site, Mt, US 186/B3
Fort Valley, Ga, US 192/F4
Fort Vermilion, Ab, Can. 170/E3
Fort Wadsworth, NY, US 199/J9
Fort Walton Beach, Fl, US 194/E2
Fort Washakie, Wy, US 177/J2
Fort Washington (park), Md, US 198/A6
Fort Wayne, In, US 190/D4
Fort Wellington Nat'l Hist. Park, On, Can. 191/J2
Fort White, Fl, US 195/G3
Fort William, Sc, UK 39/A3
Fort Wingate, NM, US 179/H3
Fort Wingate (mil. res.), NM, US 179/H3
Fort Worth, Tx, US 180/K7
Fort Worth Museum of Science and History, Tx, US 180/K7
Fort Yates, ND, US 186/D4
Fort Yukon, Ak, US 201/J2
Fort Yuma Ind. Res., Ca, US 178/E4
Fort-de-France, Guad. 203/N9
Fort-Foureau, Camr. 134/B2
Fort-George (Chisasibi), Qu, Can. 171/J3
Fort-Mahon-Plage, Fr. 60/A3
Fort-Mardyck, Fr. 60/B1
Fort-Shevchenko, Kaz. 77/J3
Fortaleza, Bol. 221/E3
Fortaleza, Bol. 221/E4
Fortaleza, Braz. 219/G3
Fortaleza dos Nogueiras, Braz. 219/E4
Fortaleza Santa Teresa, Uru. 227/G2
Forte Cameia, Ang. 140/D1
Forte dei Marmi, It. 68/D6
Forte República, Ang. 138/D4
Fortescue (riv.), Austl. 154/C2
Fortescue, NJ, US 198/C5
Forth (mtn.), Ire. 38/D5
Forth (riv.), Sc, UK 39/B4
Forth, Sc, UK 39/C5
Fortín, Mex. 205/N8
Fortín Ávalos Sánchez, Par. 224/D2
Fortín Capitán Escobar, Par. 224/D2
Fortín Carlos Antonio López, Par. 224/E2
Fortín Casanillo, Par. 224/E2
Fortín Coronel Bogado, Par. 224/E2
Fortín Coronel Sánchez, Par. 224/E1
Fortín Florida, Par. 224/E2
Fortín General Bruguez, Par. 224/E3
Fortín Guaraní, Par. 224/E2
Fortín Hernandarias, Par. 224/D2
Fortín Infante Rivarola, Par. 224/D2
Fortín Isla Poi, Par. 224/E2
Fortín Palmar de las Islas, Par. 224/D1
Fortín Presidente Ayala, Par. 224/E2
Fortín Teniente Esteban Martínez, Par. 224/E3
Fortín Teniente Gabino Mendoza, Par. 224/D2
Fortín Teniente Juan E. López, Par. 224/D2
Fortín Teniente Primero Ramiro Espínola, Par. 224/D2
Fortín Uno, Arg. 226/D3
Fortín Zalazar, Par. 224/E2
Forton, Eng, UK 41/F4
Fortore (riv.), It. 54/D2
Fortress (mtn.), Wy, US 177/J1
Fortress of Louisbourg Nat'l Hist. Park, NS, Can. 189/G3
Fortrose, Sc, UK 39/B1
Fortuna, Arg. 226/D2
Fortuna, Braz. 219/E4
Fortuna, Ca, US 176/A3
Fortuna, Mo, US 183/H1
Fortuna, ND, US 186/C3
Fortuna Ledge, Ak, US 201/F3
Fortune (bay), Nf, Can. 189/K2
Fortune, Nf, Can. 189/K2
Fortuneswell, Eng, UK 42/D5
Fortville, In, US 190/D5
Forty Fort, Pa, US 198/C1
Forty Mile (pt.), Mi, US 190/E2
Forty Mile Scrub NP, Austl. 158/B2
Fortymile Wash (riv.), Nv, US 178/D2
Forūr (isl.), Iran 115/H5
Fos (gulf), Fr. 70/A6
Fos-sur-Mer, Fr. 70/A6
Fosca, Col. 219/M8
Foshan, China 99/G4
Fosheim (pen.), Nun, Can. 171/S7
Foso, Gha. 133/E5
Foss (riv.), Eng, UK 41/G3
Fossacesia, It. 71/D3
Fossalta di Piave, It. 69/F2
Fossalta di Portogruaro, It. 69/F2
Fossano, It. 68/A3
Fosses, Fr. 36/K4
Fosses-la-Ville, Belg. 61/D3
Fossil, Or, US 176/C1
Fossil Butte Nat'l Mon., Wy, US 177/H3
Fossò, It. 69/F3
Fossombrone, It. 69/F6
Fosston, Sk, Can. 186/C1
Fosston, Mn, US 186/G4
Foster, Austl. 157/C4
Foster, Mo, US 183/G1
Foster, Tx, US 182/C4
Foster City, Mi, US 187/L5
Fostoria, Oh, US 190/E4
Fót, Hun. 57/R9
Fotan, China 99/H3
Fotokol, Camr. 134/B2
Foucarmont, Fr. 60/A4
Foucherans, Fr. 66/B3
Fouesnant, Fr. 62/A5
Foug, Fr. 61/E6
Fougamou, Gabon 138/B3
Fougères, Fr. 62/D4
Fougerolles, Fr. 66/C2
Fouilloy, Fr. 60/B4
Fouke, Ar, US 183/H4
Foul (pt.), SrL. 107/D4
Foula (isl.), Sc, UK 37/V13
Foulness (riv.), Eng, UK 41/H4
Foulness (pt.), Eng, UK 43/G3
Foulness (isl.), Eng, UK 43/G3
Foulsham, Eng, UK 43/H1
Foulwind (cape), NZ 159/B3
Foum el Hassane, Mor. 128/C3
Foum Zguid, Mor. 128/D3
Foumbouni, Com. 143/G5
Foundiougne, Sen. 132/A3
Fountain, Co, US 182/B1
Fountain (cr.), Co, US 184/B4
Fountain, Fl, US 195/F2
Fountain (lake), Mn, US 187/N6
Fountain Green, Ut, US 177/H4
Fountain Hill, Pa, US 198/C2
Fountain Hills, Az, US 179/G4
Fountain Inn, SC, US 193/F3
Fountain Run, Ky, US 192/E2
Fountain Valley, Ca, US 196/G8
Fountains Abbey, Eng, UK 41/G3
Four Corners Monument, US 179/H2
Four Elms, Eng, UK 36/D3
Four Lakes, Wa, US 174/F4
Four Mountains (isls.), Ak, US 201/D5
Fourchambault, Fr. 50/E3
Fourche La Fave (riv.), Ar, US 183/H3
Fourcroy (cape), Austl. 152/C2
Fourges, Fr. 36/G4
Fourmies, Fr. 60/D4
Fourmile (peak), Wy, US 177/K2
Fourmile Draw (riv.), NM, US 180/B1
Fourneaux, Fr. 70/C2
Fourques, Fr. 70/A5
Fourteen Mile (pt.), Mi, US 187/K4
Fourth Cataract (falls), Sudan 127/G5
Fouta Djallon (phys. reg.), Gui. 132/B4
Foveaux (str.), NZ 145/G7
Fowey (riv.), Eng, UK 42/B6
Fowey, Eng, UK 42/B6
Fowler, Ca, US 178/C2
Fowler, Co, US 182/B1
Fowler, In, US 190/C4
Fowler, Mi, US 190/D3
Fowlkes, Tn, US 192/C3
Fowman, Iran 115/G2
Fownhope, Wal, UK 42/D2
Fox (mtn.), Yk., Can. 201/M3
Fox (isls.), Ak, US 201/E5
Fox, Ar, US 183/H3
Fox (lake), Il, US 185/K2
Fox, Mi, US 190/C2
Fox, Ok, US 183/F3
Fox, Or, US 176/D1
Fox (isl.), Wa, US 197/B3
Fox (riv.), Wi, US 187/K5
Fox (riv.), Wi,Il, US 185/"K2,
Fox Glacier, NZ 159/B3
Fox Harbour, Nf, Can. 189/L2
Fox Lake, Il, US 197/P15
Fox River Grove, Il, US 197/P15
Fox Valley, Sk, Can. 175/K2
Foxe (pen.), Nun., Can. 171/J2
Foxe (chan.), Nun., Can. 171/H2
Foxe Basin (bay), Nun., Can. 171/J2
Foxen (lake), Swe. 46/D2
Foxford, Ire. 38/A2
Foxton, Eng, UK 43/G2
Foyers, Sc, UK 39/B2
Foyle (riv.), Ire.,NI, UK 40/A2
Foynes, Ire. 38/A4
Foz, Sp. 52/B1
Foz do Breu, Braz. 220/C3
Foz do Cunene, Ang. 140/A3
Foz do Iguaçu, Braz. 225/F3
Frackville, Pa, US 198/B2
Fraga, Sp. 53/F2
Fraiburgo, Braz. 225/G3
Fraile Muerto, Uru. 225/F5
Fraile Pintado, Arg. 224/C2
Fraisans, Fr. 66/B3
Fraize, Fr. 66/D1
Frameries, Belg. 60/C3
Framlingham, Eng, UK 43/H2
Frammersbach, Ger. 64/C2
Franca, Braz. 225/H2
Francavilla al Mare, It. 71/D3
Francavilla Fontana, It. 55/E2
Francavilla in Sinni, It. 54/E2
France (ctry.) 50/D3
Frances (cape), Cuba 207/F1
Frances (lake), Yk, Can. 170/C2
Francés Viejo (cape), DRep. 203/H4
Francesville, In, US 190/C4
Franceville, Gabon 138/C3
Franche-Comté (pol. reg.), Fr. 66/B5
Francia, Uru. 227/K10
Francis, Sk, Can. 186/C2
Francis, Ok, US 183/F3
Francis, Ut, US 177/H3
Francis Case (lake), SD, US 184/E2
Francisco de Orellana, Peru 220/C1
Francisco Escárcega, Mex. 206/D2
Francisco I. Madero, Mex. 204/E3
Francisco Javier Mina, Mex. 204/C3
Francisco Portillo, Mex. 180/B3
Francisco Sá, Braz. 223/E3
Francisco Zarco, Mex. 204/A1
Francistown (int'l arpt.), Bots. 141/E4
Francistown, Bots. 141/E4
Franco da Rocha, Braz. 223/K8
Francolino, It. 69/E4
Franconville, Fr. 36/J5
Franeker, Neth. 58/C2
Frangy, Fr. 66/B5
Frank Hahn NP, Austl. 154/C5
Franken Wald (for.), Ger. 65/E2
Frankenau, Ger. 59/F6
Frankenberg-Eder, Ger. 59/F6
Frankenburg am Hausruck, Aus. 65/G6
Frankenhöhe (mts.), Ger. 48/F4
Frankenmarkt, Aus. 65/G7
Frankenmuth, Mi, US 190/E3
Frankenthal, Ger. 64/B3
Frankford, On, Can. 191/H2
Frankford, De, US 193/K1
Frankfort, SAfr. 142/E2
Frankfort, In, US 190/C4
Frankfort, Ks, US 185/F4
Frankfort (cap.), Ky, US 192/E1
Frankfort, Mi, US 190/C2
Frankfort, Oh, US 190/E5
Frankfurt (int'l arpt.), Ger. 64/B2
Frankfurt, Ger. 49/H2
Frankfurt am Main, Ger. 64/B2
Fränkische Alb (mts.), Ger. 48/F4
Fränkische Rezat (riv.), Ger. 64/D4
Fränkische Saale (riv.), Ger. 48/E3
Fränkische Schweiz (reg.), Ger. 48/F4
Fränkische Schweiz (reg.), Ger. 51/J2
Frankland (cape), Austl. 157/C4
Franklin (bay), NW, Can. 170/D2
Franklin (mts.), NW, Can. 170/D2
Franklin, Qu, Can. 191/K2
Franklin (cape), Ak, US 201/G1
Franklin, Az, US 179/H4
Franklin, Ga, US 192/E4
Franklin, Id, US 177/H2
Franklin, In, US 190/C5
Franklin, Ks, US 183/G2
Franklin, Ky, US 192/D2
Franklin, La, US 194/C3
Franklin, Mi, US 197/F6
Franklin, NC, US 193/F3
Franklin, Ne, US 184/E3
Franklin, NH, US 191/L3
Franklin, NJ, US 198/D1
Franklin, Oh, US 190/D5
Franklin, Pa, US 191/G4
Franklin, Tn, US 192/D3
Franklin, Tx, US 181/F2
Franklin, Va, US 193/J2
Franklin, Wi, US 190/B3
Franklin, WV, US 193/H1
Franklin D. Roosevelt (lake), Wa, US 174/E3
Franklin Grove, Il, US 185/K3
Franklin Lakes, NJ, US 199/J7
Franklin Mineral Museum, NJ, US 198/D1
Franklin Park, Il, US 197/Q16
Franklin Square, NY, US 199/L9
Franklin-Lower Gordon Wild Rivers NP, Austl. 156/C4
Franklinton, La, US 194/C2
Franklinton, NC, US 193/H2
Franklinville, NY, US 191/G3
Frankston (nbrhd.), Austl. 156/G6
Frankston, Tx, US 180/G1
Franksville, Wi, US 197/Q14
Frankville, Al, US 194/D2
Franois, Fr. 66/B3
Franquelin, Qu, Can. 188/D1
Franschhoek, SAfr. 142/L10
Fransfontein, Namb. 140/B4
Fransisco Beltrão, Braz. 225/F3
Fransisco Morato, Braz. 223/K8
Františkovy Lázně, Czh. 65/F2
Franz Josef Land (isls.), Rus. 80/F2
Franz Joseph Strauss (int'l arpt.), Ger. 65/E6
Franzburg, Ger. 46/E4
Frascati, It. 71/B4
Fraser (mt.), Austl. 154/C3
Fraser (isl.), Austl. 145/E3
Fraser (riv.), BC, Can. 174/D2
Fraser, Mi, US 197/G6
Fraser NP, Austl. 157/B3
Fraserburg, SAfr. 142/C3
Fraserburgh, Sc, UK 39/D1
Frasertown, NZ 159/D2
Fraserville, On, Can. 191/G2
Fraserwood, Mb, Can. 186/F2
Frasne, Fr. 66/C4
Frasnes-lez-Gosselies, Belg. 61/D2
Frassine (riv.), It. 69/E2
Frassino, It. 69/D3
Frasso Telesino, It. 71/D5
Frastanz, Aus. 67/F3
Frati, Monte dei (peak), It. 69/F6
Frauenfeld, Swi. 67/E2
Fraunberg, Ger. 65/F6
Fray Bentos, Uru. 227/J10
Fray Jorge, PN, Chile 224/B4
Fray Marcos, Uru. 227/L11
Frazier Downs Abor. Land, Austl. 152/A4
Frazier Park, Ca, US 178/C3
Frechen, Ger. 61/F2
Freckenfeld, Ger. 64/B4
Fred (mt.), Les. 142/E3
Fred, Tx, US 181/G2
Fredensborg, Den. 45/J7
Frederic, Wi, US 187/H5
Frederica, De, US 198/C6
Fredericia, Den. 46/C4
Frederick (reef), Austl. 145/E3
Frederick, Md, US 191/H5
Frederick (co.), Md, US 198/A5
Frederick, Ok, US 182/E3
Frederick, SD, US 184/E1
Fredericksburg, Ia, US 185/H2
Fredericksburg, Pa, US 198/B3
Fredericksburg, Tx, US 181/E2
Fredericksburg, Va, US 193/J1
Fredericksburg and Spotsylvania Nat'l Mil. Park, Va, US 193/J1
Frederickton, Austl. 156/E1
Fredericktown, Oh, US 190/E4
Fredericktown, Mo, US 192/B2
Frederico Westphalen, Braz. 225/F3
Fredericton (cap.), NB, Can. 188/D3
Fredericton Junction, NB, Can. 188/D3
Frederik Willem IV (falls), Sur. 217/G4
Frederiks, Den. 46/C3
Frederiksberg, Den. 45/H7
Frederiksberg, Den. 45/J7
Frederiksborg (co.), Den. 45/J7
Frederiksborg Slot (Frederiksborg Castle), Den. 46/E4
Frederikshavn, Den. 46/D3
Frederikssund, Den. 45/J7
Frederiksted, USVI 203/M8
Frederiksværk, Den. 45/J7
Fredersdorf bei Berlin, Ger. 48/Q7
Fredonia, ND, US 186/E4
Fredonia, Ks, US 183/G2
Fredonia, Wi, US 190/C3
Fredonia, NY, US 191/G3
Fredonia, Az, US 179/F2
Fredonia, Col. 219/K7
Fredonia (Biscoe), Ar, US 183/J3
Fredriksberg, Swe. 46/F1
Fredrikstad, Nor. 46/D2
Free State (prov.), SAfr. 142/P13
Freeburg, Mo, US 183/J1
Freeburg, Pa, US 198/B2
Freedom, Ok, US 182/E2
Freedom, Wy, US 177/H2
Freehold, NJ, US 199/D3
Freel (peak), Ca, US 176/D4
Freeland, Md, US 198/B4
Freeland, Pa, US 198/C1
Freeland, Wa, US 197/B1
Freeling (mt.), Austl. 155/G2
Freeling Heights (peak), Austl. 155/H4
Freelton, On, Can. 190/S9
Freeman, SD, US 184/F2
Freemansburg, Pa, US 198/C2
Freeport, Bahm. 203/F2
Freeport, Fl, US 195/E2
Freeport, Il, US 185/K2
Freeport, Me, US 191/L3
Freeport, NY, US 199/L9
Freeport, Pa, US 191/G4
Freeport, Tx, US 180/G3
Freer, Tx, US 181/E4
Freetown (cap.), SLeo. 132/B4
Freetown, In, US 192/D1
Freetown (Lungi) (int'l arpt.), SLeo. 132/B4
Fregenal de la Sierra, Sp. 52/B3
Fregene, It. 71/B4
Fréhel (cape), Fr. 62/C3
Frei Inocêncio, Braz. 223/E3
Freib Mulde (riv.), Ger. 48/G3
Freiberg, Ger. 49/G3
Freiburg, Ger. 66/D2
Freiburg, Ger. 59/G1
Freienbach, Swi. 67/E3
Freigné, Fr. 63/D5
Freihung, Ger. 65/E3
Freilassing, Ger. 65/F7
Freinsheim, Ger. 64/B3
Freire, Chile 226/B3
Freirina, Chile 224/B4
Freisen, Ger. 61/G4
Freising, Ger. 65/E6
Freistadt, Aus. 65/H5
Freital, Ger. 49/G3
Freixo de Espada à Cinta, Port. 52/B2
Frejorgues (int'l arpt.), Fr. 50/E5
Fréjus, Fr. 70/C6
Frekhaug, Nor. 46/A1
Frémainfille, Fr. 36/H4
Fremantle (nbrhd.), Austl. 154/K7
Fremdingen, Ger. 64/D5
Frémécourt, Fr. 36/J4
Fremington, Eng, UK 42/B4
Fremont, Ia, US 185/H3
Fremont, In, US 190/D4
Fremont, Mi, US 190/D3
Fremont, NC, US 193/J3
Fremont, Ne, US 185/F3
Fremont, Oh, US 190/E4
Fremont (riv.), Ut, US 177/H4
Fremont (isl.), Ut, US 177/G3
Fremont, Ut, US 179/G1
Fremont (lake), Wy, US 177/J2
Fremont (peak), Wy, US 177/J2
French (riv.), On, Can. 190/F1
French (cr.), Pa, US 198/C3
French Broad (riv.), Tn, US 193/F3
French Camp, Ms, US 192/C4
French Cr. SP, Pa, US 198/C3
French Frigate Shoals (bar), Hi, US 161/J2
French Guiana (dpcy.), FrG. 217/H3
French Lick, In, US 192/D1
French Polynesia (terr.), Fr. 161/L6
French River, On, Can. 190/F1
French River, Mn, US 187/J4
Frenchburg, Ky, US 192/F2
Frenchglen, Or, US 176/D2
Frenchman (riv.), Can.,US 170/F4
Frenchman (cr.), Co, US 184/C3
Frenchman (riv.), Sk, Can. 175/K3
Frenchman's (bay), On, Can. 190/U8
Frenchmans Cap (peak), Austl. 156/C4
Frenchpark, Ire. 38/B2
Frenchtown, Mt, US 174/G4
Frenchtown, NJ, US 198/C2
Frenda, Alg. 130/F5
Frêne, Pic du (peak), Fr. 70/C2
Frépillon, Fr. 36/J4
Freren, Ger. 59/E4
Fresco, C.d'Iv. 132/D5
Fresco (riv.), Braz. 218/D4
Freshford, Ire. 38/C4
Freshwater, Nf, Can. 189/L2
Freshwater, Eng, UK 43/E5
Fresia, Chile 226/B4
Fresnay-sur-Sarthe, Fr. 63/F4
Fresnes, Fr. 36/J5
Fresnes-en-Woëvre, Fr. 61/E5
Fresnillo, Mex. 204/E4
Fresno, Col. 219/K7
Fresno, Ca, US 178/C2
Fresno (riv.), Ca, US 178/B2
Fresno, Tx, US 181/M9
Fresno (res.), Mt, US 175/J3
Fresnoy-le-Grand, Fr. 60/C4
Fresse-sur-Moselle, Fr. 66/C2
Fressenneville, Fr. 60/A3
Fresta, Swe. 45/A1
Fretani (mts.), It. 71/D3
Fretin, Fr. 60/C2
Freuchie (lake), Sc, UK 39/C3
Freudenberg, Ger. 61/G2
Freudenberg, Ger. 65/E4
Freudenberg, Ger. 64/C3
Freudenburg, Ger. 61/F4
Freudenstadt, Ger. 67/E1
Frévent, Fr. 60/B3
Frewena, Austl. 153/D4
Frewsburg, NY, US 191/G3
Freycinet (har.), Austl. 154/B3
Freycinet NP, Austl. 156/D4
Freyming-Merlebach, Fr. 61/F5
Freyre, Arg. 224/D4
Freystadt, Ger. 65/E4
Freyung, Ger. 65/G5
Fria, Gui. 132/B4
Fria (cape), Namb. 140/B3
Friant, Ca, US 178/C2
Friant (dam), Ca, US 178/C2
Friant-Kern (canal), Ca, US 178/C3
Friars Point, Ms, US 192/B3
Frías, Peru 220/B2
Frías, Arg. 224/C4
Fribourg, Swi. 66/D4
Fribourg (canton), Swi. 66/D4
Frick, Swi. 66/E3
Frickenhausen am Main, Ger. 64/D3
Friday Harbor, Wa, US 174/C3
Fridingen an der Donau, Ger. 67/E1
Fridley, Mn, US 187/P6
Fridolfing, Ger. 65/F6
Friedberg, Ger. 64/B2
Friedberg, Ger. 64/D6
Friedeburg, Ger. 59/E2
Friedland, Ger. 59/G6
Friedrichsdorf, Ger. 64/B2
Friedrichshafen (arpt.), Ger. 67/F2
Friedrichshafen, Ger. 67/F2
Friedrichstadt, Ger. 46/C4
Friedrichsthal, Ger. 61/G5
Frielendorf, Ger. 59/G7
Friend, Ks, US 182/D1
Friend, Ne, US 185/F3
Friendship, Ar, US 183/H3
Friendship, Tn, US 192/C3
Friendship, Wi, US 185/K2
Friendswood, Tx, US 181/M9
Frierson, La, US 180/H1
Friesenhagen, Ger. 61/G2
Friesenheim, Ger. 66/D1
Friesland (prov.), Neth. 58/C2
Friesoythe, Ger. 59/E2
Friggesby, Fin. 45/E4
Frignano, It. 71/D6
Frignicourt, Fr. 61/D6
Friguiagbé, Gui. 132/B4
Frimley, Eng, UK 36/A3
Frinton, Eng, UK 43/H3
Frio (riv.), Tx, US 205/F2
Frio Draw (riv.), NM,Tx, US 182/C3
Friockheim, Sc, UK 39/D3
Friol, Sp. 52/B1
Friona, Tx, US 182/C3
Frisange, Lux. 61/F4
Frisco, Tx, US 180/L6
Frisco City, Al, US 194/E2
Frissell (mt.), Ct, US 191/K3
Fristad, Swe. 46/E3
Fritch, Tx, US 182/D3
Fritsla, Swe. 46/E3
Fritzlar, Ger. 59/G6
Friuli (reg.), It. 73/G1
Friuli-Venezia Giula (prov.), It. 51/K3
Friville-Escarbotin, Fr. 60/A3
Frizington, Eng, UK 40/E2
Frobisher (bay), Nun, Can. 171/K2
Frodsham, Eng, UK 41/F5
Frogmore, Eng, UK 36/A3
Frogue, Ky, US 192/E2
Frohavel (inlet), Nor. 44/D3
Frohnleiten, Aus. 51/L3
Froid, Mt, US 186/B3
Froid (mtn.), Fr. 70/C3
Froid-Chapelle, Belg. 61/D3
Froideconche, Fr. 66/C2
Froissy, Fr. 60/B4
Froland, Nor. 46/C2
Frolovo, Rus. 77/G2
Fromberg, Mt, US 177/J1
Frome (lake), Austl. 145/D4
Frome (riv.), Austl. 155/H4
Frome (riv.), Eng, UK 42/D2
Frome, Eng, UK 42/D4
Frome (riv.), Eng, UK 42/D5
Froncles, Fr. 66/B1
Front (range), Co, US 184/B3
Front Royal, Va, US 193/H1
Fronteira, Ang. 138/D4
Fronteira, Port. 52/B3
Frontenex, Fr. 70/C1
Frontenhausen, Ger. 65/F5
Frontera, Mex. 206/C2
Frontera Comalapa, Mex. 206/C3
Frontier, ND, US 186/F4
Frontier, Sk, Can. 175/K3
Frontignan, Fr. 50/E5
Fronton, Fr. 50/D5
Frosinone (prov.), It. 71/C4
Frosinone, It. 71/C4
Frösö, Swe. 44/E3
Frosolone, It. 71/D4
Frost, Tx, US 181/F1
Frostburg, Md, US 191/G5
Frostproof, Fl, US 194/M8
Frösunda, Swe. 45/B1
Frotey-lès-Vesoul, Fr. 66/C2
Frouard, Fr. 61/F6
Frövi, Swe. 46/F2
Frower (pt.), Ire. 38/B6
Frøya (isl.), Nor. 44/D3
Frozen (str.), Nun, Can. 171/H2
Fruges, Fr. 60/B2
Fruitdale, Al, US 194/D2
Fruitland, On, Can. 190/T9
Fruitland, Id, US 176/E1
Fruitland, Md, US 193/K1
Fruitvale, BC, Can. 174/F3
Fruitvale, Wa, US 174/D4
Frunze (int'l arpt.), Kyr. 111/B3
Frunzens'ke, Ukr. 79/H5
Frunzivka, Ukr. 78/E4
Fruška Gora (mts.), Cro.,Serb. 73/H1
Fruška Gora NP, Cro. 56/D3
Frutal, Braz. 225/G1
Frutigen, Swi. 66/D4
Frutillar, Chile 226/B4
Fruvik, Swe. 45/B1
Fryazino, Rus. 75/X9
Frýdek-Místek, Czh. 49/K4
Fryeburg, Me, US 191/L2
Fu Xian, China 92/B4
Fu'an, China 99/H3
Fubo, Ang. 138/C4
Fucecchio, It. 69/D6
Fuch, WSah. 128/B5
Fucheng, China 92/D3
Fuchū, Japan 96/C3
Fuchū, Japan 95/C2
Fuchun, China 99/H2
Fuchun (riv.), China 92/D5
Fude, China 99/H3
Fuding, China 99/J3
Fuengirola, Sp. 52/C4
Fuenlabrada, Sp. 53/N9
Fuensalida, Sp. 52/C2
Fuente, Sp. 53/N8
Fuente de Cantos, Sp. 52/B3
Fuente del Maestre, Sp. 52/B3
Fuente Obejuna, Sp. 52/C3
Fuentelapeña, Sp. 52/C2
Fuentes de Oñoro, Sp. 52/B2
Fuentesaúco, Sp. 52/C2
Fuerte (riv.), Mex. 204/C3
Fuerte Olimpo, Par. 224/E2
Fuerteventura (isl.), Canl., Sp. 128/B3
Fufang, China 99/H3
Fuga (isl.), Phil. 100/C1
Fuglebjerg, Den. 46/D4
Fugong, China 105/G2
Fugou, China 92/C4
Fuhai, China 111/E2
Fuhlsbüttel (Hamburg) (int'l arpt.), Ger. 59/G1
Fuhne (riv.), Ger. 48/F3
Fuhse (riv.), Ger. 59/H4
Fuji, Japan 97/F3
Fuji (riv.), Japan 97/F3
Fuji-Hakone-Izu NP, Japan 97/F3
Fuji-san (peak), Japan 97/F3
Fujian (prov.), China 99/H3
Fujieda, Japan 97/F3

Fujihashi, Japan 95/K4
Fujiidera, Japan 95/J6
Fujikawa, Japan 95/B3
Fujimi, Japan 95/D2
Fujino, Japan 95/C2
Fujinomiya, Japan 95/B3
Fujioka, Japan 97/F2
Fujioka, Japan 95/M5
Fujioka, Japan 95/D1
Fujisawa, Japan 97/F3
Fujishiro, Japan 95/E2
Fujiwara, Japan 95/K5
Fujiyoshida, Japan 97/F3
Fukagawa, Japan 94/C2
Fukang, China 111/E3
Fukaya, Japan 95/C1
Fukiage, Japan 95/C1
Fukuchiyama, Japan 95/H5
Fukue, Japan 96/A4
Fukue (isl.), Japan 91/K5
Fukui, Japan 96/E2
Fukui (pref.), Japan 96/E3
Fukuoka (pref.), Japan 96/B4
Fukuoka, Japan 96/B4
Fukuoka (int'l arpt.), Japan 96/B4
Fukuoka, Japan 95/M4
Fukuroi, Japan 97/E3
Fukushima, Japan 97/G2
Fukushima (pref.), Japan 97/F2
Fukushima, Japan 94/B3
Fukuyama, Japan 96/C3
Fulacunda, GBis. 132/B4
Fūlādī (mtn.), Afg. 113/J2
Fulbourn, Eng, UK 43/G2
Fulbright, Tx, US 183/G4
Fulda (riv.), Ger. 48/E3
Fulda, Ger. 64/C1
Fulda, Mn, US 185/G2
Fulford, Eng, UK 41/G4
Fuling, China 99/E2
Fullarton, Trin. 217/F2
Fullerton, La, US 194/B2
Fullerton, Ca, US 196/G8
Fullerton, Ne, US 184/F3
Fullerton (Whitehall), Pa, US 198/C2
Fully, Swi. 66/D5
Fulpmes, Aus. 67/H3
Fulton, Al, US 194/E2
Fulton, Ar, US 183/H4
Fulton (co.), Ga, US 193/M7
Fulton, Ky, US 192/C2
Fulton, Ks, US 183/G1
Fulton, Mo, US 183/J1
Fulton, Ms, US 192/C3
Fulton, NY, US 191/H3
Fulton, On, Can. 190/T9
Fulton, Tx, US 180/F3
Fultondale, Al, US 192/D3
Fulufjället (peak), Swe. 46/E1
Fuluo, China 99/F3
Fulwood, Eng, UK 41/F4
Fumaiolo (peak), It. 69/F6
Fumay, Fr. 61/D4
Fumel, Fr. 50/D4
Fumin, China 98/D3
Funabashi, Japan 95/D2
Funafuti (cap.), Tuv. 160/G5
Funafuti (isl.), Tuv. 160/G5
Funan, China 92/C4
Funchal (int'l arpt.), Port. 128/A2
Funchal, Port. 128/A2
Fundación, Col. 216/C2
Fundão, Port. 52/B2
Fundong, Camr. 133/H5
Fundy (bay), NB,NS, Can. 171/K4
Fundy NP, NB, Can. 188/E3
Funhalouro, Moz. 141/G4
Funing, China 92/D4
Funing, China 98/E4
Funshion (riv.), Ire. 38/B5
Funsi, Gha. 133/E4
Funston, Ga, US 195/G2
Funtua, Nga. 133/G4
Funza, Col. 219/L8
Fuorn, Pass dal (Ofenpass) (pass), Swi. 67/G4
Fuping, China 92/C3
Fuqiao, China 92/L8
Fuqū', Jor. 117/D6
Fuquan, China 105/J2
Fur (riv.), China 93/C2
Furan (riv.), Fr. 66/B6
Furancungo, Moz. 141/G2
Furano, Japan 94/C2
Fure (riv.), Fr. 70/B2
Fürfeld, Ger. 61/G4
Furmanov, Rus. 74/J4
Furmanovo, Kaz. 77/J2
Furnace, Sc, UK 39/A4
Furnas (res.), Braz. 209/E5
Furneaux Group (isls.), Austl. 145/D4
Fürstenau, Ger. 59/E3
Fürstenfeld, Aus. 56/C2
Fürstenfeldbruck, Ger. 64/E6
Fürstenwalde, Ger. 49/H2
Fürth, Ger. 64/B3
Furth, Ger. 65/F5
Fürth, Ger. 64/D4
Furth im Wald, Ger. 65/F4
Furtwangen im Schwarzwald, Ger. 66/E1
Furudal, Swe. 46/F1
Furukawa, Japan 94/B4
Furulund, Swe. 45/K7
Furusund, Swe. 45/B1
Fury and Hecla (str.), Nun, Can. 171/H2
Fusagasugá, Col. 219/L8
Fushan, China 92/B4
Fushan, China 92/E3
Fushi, China 99/H3
Fushi, China 99/F3
Fushu, China 99/H3
Fushun, China 93/B2
Fushun, China 98/E2
Fushuncheng, China 93/B2
Fusignano, It. 69/E5
Fusio, Swi. 67/E5
Fuso, Japan 95/L5
Fusong, China 91/K3
Fussa, Japan 95/C2
Füssen, Ger. 67/G2
Fusui, China 106/D1
Futaba, Japan 95/A2
Futaleufú, Chile 226/C4
Futami, Japan 95/L7
Futog, Serb. 56/D3
Futrono, Chile 226/B4
Futtsu, Japan 97/F3
Futuna (isl.), Wall., Fr. 160/H6
Fuveau, Fr. 70/B6
Fuwah, Egypt 131/B2
Fuxian (lake), China 105/H3
Fuxin, China 92/E2
Fuxin Monggolzu Zizhixian, China 92/E2
Fuxing, China 99/E2
Fuyang, China 92/C4
Fuyang, China 99/H4
Fuyi (riv.), China 99/F3
Fuyu, China 91/J2
Fuyu, China 91/J2
Fuyuan, China 98/E3
Fuyun, China 90/B2
Fuzhou, China 99/H3
Fuzhoucheng, China 93/A3
Fwamba, D.R. Congo 139/E4
Fyfield, Eng, UK 36/D1
Fyn (co.), Den. 46/D4
Fyn (isl.), Den. 46/D4
Fyne, Loch (inlet), Sc, UK 39/A5
Fyresdal, Nor. 46/C2
Fysingen (lake), Swe. 45/A1
Fyvie, Sc, UK 39/D2

G

Ga, Gha. 133/E4
Ga Vache (isl.), Haiti 207/H2
Gaalkacyo (Galcaio), Som. 136/C4
Gaast, Neth. 58/C2
Gabarus, NS, Can. 189/G3
Gabas (riv.), Fr. 50/C5
Gabbs, Nv, US 176/E4
Gabčíkovo, Slvk. 56/C2
Gabela, Ang. 138/C5
Gabes (gov.), Tun. 129/H2
Gabes (gulf), Tun. 129/H2
Gabia, D.R. Congo 138/D4
Gabicce Mare, It. 69/F6
Gable End (pt.), NZ 159/D2
Gablingen, Ger. 64/D6
Gablitz, Aus. 57/N7
Gabon (riv.), Gabon 138/B2
Gabon (ctry.) 138/B3
Gaborone (cap.), Bots. 140/E5
Gaborone (Sir Seretse Khama) (int'l arpt.), Bots. 140/E5
Gabras, Sudan 135/E3
Gabriel (mt.), Ire. 38/A6
Gabriel Leyva Solano, Mex. 204/C3
Gabrovo, Bul. 57/G4
Gaby, It. 68/A1
Gacé, Fr. 63/F3
Gachsārān, Iran 115/G4
Gackle, ND, US 186/E4
Gacko, Bosn. 56/D4
Gädäbäy, Azer. 115/F1
Gādarwāra, India 108/B4
Gadmen, Swi. 67/E4
Gadrut, Azer. 77/H5
Gadsden, Az, US 178/E4
Gadsden, Al, US 192/D3
Gadstrup, Den. 45/J7
Gadzema, Zim. 141/F3
Gadzi, CAfr. 134/C4
Găeşti, Rom. 57/G3
Gaeta, It. 71/C5
Gaeta (gulf), It. 54/C2
Gafargaon, Bang. 109/H3
Gaferut (isl.), Micr. 160/D4
Gaffney, SC, US 193/G3
Gafsa, Tun. 129/H2
Gafsa (gov.), Tun. 129/H2
Gagal, Chad 134/B3
Gagarawa, Nga. 133/H3
Gagarin, Rus. 74/G5
Gage, Ok, US 182/E2
Gage, NM, US 179/H4
Gagetown, NB, Can. 188/D3
Gagetown, Mi, US 190/E3
Gaggenau, Ger. 64/B5
Gaggio Montano, It. 69/D5
Gaglianico, It. 68/B2
Gagnoa, C.d'Iv. 132/D5
Gagny, Fr. 36/K5
Gagra, Geo. 76/G4
Gagret, India 110/D4
Gahanna, Oh, US 190/E4
Gahnpa, Libr. 132/C5
Gai Xian, China 93/B2
Gaibandha, Bang. 109/G3
Gaichtpass (pass), Aus. 67/G3
Gaidain'goinba, China 90/D4
Gail (riv.), Aus. 51/K3
Gail (riv.), It. 56/A2
Gail, Tx, US 180/D1
Gaildorf, Ger. 64/C5
Gaillac, Fr. 50/D5
Gaillefontaine, Fr. 63/G1
Gaillon, Fr. 63/G2
Gailtaler (mts.), Aus. 51/K3
Gaiman, Arg. 226/D4
Gaimersheim, Ger. 65/E5
Gainesboro, Tn, US 192/E2
Gainesville, Al, US 192/C4
Gainesville, Fl, US 195/G3
Gainesville, Ga, US 192/F3
Gainesville, Mo, US 183/H2
Gainesville, Tx, US 183/F4
Gainford, Eng, UK 41/G2
Gainsborough, Sk, Can. 186/D3
Gainsborough, Eng, UK 41/H5
Gairdner (lake), Austl. 145/C4
Gairezi (riv.), Zim. 141/G3
Gairn (riv.), Sc, UK 39/C2
Gais, Swi. 67/F3
Gaiserwald, Swi. 67/F3
Gaithersburg, Md, US 193/J1
Gaizina (peak), Lat. 47/L3
Gājol, India 109/G3
Gakarosa (peak), SAfr. 142/C2
Gakem, Nga. 133/H5
Gakona, Ak, US 201/J3
Gal Oya NP, SrL. 107/D5
Gala, China 109/G1
Galan (peak), Arg. 224/C3
Galana (riv.), Kenya 137/B2
Galand, Iran 115/H2
Galanga, Ang. 140/B2
Galangue, Ang. 140/C2
Galapagar, Sp. 53/M8
Galápagos (isls.), Ecu. 220/J6
Galápagos (dept.), Ecu. 220/J7
Galápagos, PN, Ecu. 220/J7
Galār, India 110/C3
Galashiels, Sc, UK 39/D5
Galaţi (prov.), Rom. 57/H3
Galaţi, Rom. 57/J3
Galatina, It. 55/F2
Galatiní, Gre. 55/G2
Galátista, Gre. 55/H2
Galatone, It. 55/F2
Galaure (riv.), Fr. 70/A2
Galax, Va, US 193/G2
Galb Azefal (hill), WSah. 128/B5
Galbally, Ire. 38/B5
Galbiate, It. 68/C2
Galcaio (Gaalkacyo), Som. 136/C4
Galdácano, Sp. 52/D1
Gáldar, Sp. 128/B3
Galeana, Mex. 205/E3
Galela, Indo. 103/G3
Galena, Ak, US 201/G3
Galena (peak), Id, US 177/F2
Galena, Il, US 185/J2
Galena, Ks, US 183/G2
Galena, Md, US 198/C5
Galena, Mo, US 183/H2
Galena Bay, BC, Can. 174/F2
Galena Park, Tx, US 181/M9
Galeota (pt.), Trin. 217/F2
Galera (pt.), Trin. 217/F2
Galera (pt.), Ecu. 216/A4
Galera (pt.), Chile 226/B3
Galesburg, Il, US 185/J3
Galeton, Pa, US 191/H4
Galey (riv.), Ire. 38/A5
Galga (riv.), Hun. 57/R9
Galgamácsa, Hun. 57/R9
Galgorm, NI, UK 40/B2
Gali, Geo. 77/G4
Gali Jāgīr, Pak. 110/B3
Galich, Rus. 74/J4
Galicia (reg.), Sp. 72/A2
Galičica NP, FYROM 55/G2
Galičica NP, Alb. 56/E5
Gālīkash, Iran 115/H2
Galilee (reg.), Isr. 117/C3
Galileo Galilei (int'l arpt.), It. 68/D6
Galim, Camr. 134/B4
Galinakopf (peak), Aus. 67/F3
Galinda, Ang. 138/C5
Galion, Oh, US 190/E4
Galiuro (mts.), Az, US 179/G4
Galiwinku, Austl. 153/D3
Gallan Head (pt.), Sc, UK 37/Q7
Gallarate, It. 68/B2
Gallardon, Fr. 63/G3
Gallatin (riv.), Mt, US 177/H1
Gallatin, Mo, US 185/H4
Gallatin, Tn, US 192/D2
Gallatin Gateway, Mt, US 177/H1
Gallegos (riv.), Arg. 227/C6
Galleguillos, Chile 224/B3
Galley Head (pt.), Ire. 38/B6
Galleyend, Eng, UK 36/E1
Galliano, La, US 194/C3
Galliate, It. 68/B3
Gallicano, It. 68/D5
Galliera Veneta, It. 69/E2
Gallina, NM, US 179/J2
Gallinas (pt.), Col. 216/D1
Gallinas (riv.), NM, US 182/B3
Gallinas (mts.), NM, US 179/J3
Gallion, Al, US 192/D4
Gallipoli, It. 55/E2
Gallipoli (pen.), Turk. 73/K2
Gallipolis, Oh, US 193/F1
Gällivare, Swe. 44/G2
Gallneukirchen, Aus. 65/H6
Gallo (lake), It. 67/G4
Gallo (cape), It. 54/C3
Galloway, Wi, US 185/K1
Gallspach, Aus. 65/G6
Galluis, Fr. 36/H5
Gallup, NM, US 179/H3
Gallur, Sp. 52/E2
Gally (riv.), Fr. 36/H5
Gålö (isl.), Swe. 45/B1
Gal'on, Isr. 117/B5
Galston, Sc, UK 39/B5
Galston (nbrhd.), Austl. 158/H8
Galston, Austl. 157/E1
Galt, Ca, US 176/C4
Galten, Den. 46/C3
Galty (mts.), Ire. 38/B5
Galtymore (peak), Ire. 38/B5
Galva, Ks, US 183/F1
Galva, Il, US 185/J3
Galvarino, Chile 226/B3
Galveston, Tx, US 181/N9
Galveston (bay), Tx, US 181/N9
Galveston (co.), Tx, US 181/M9
Galveston (isl.), Tx, US 181/G3
Gálvez, Sp. 52/C3
Gálvez, Arg. 224/D5
Galway, Ire. 38/A3
Galway (bay), Ire. 37/P10
Galway (co.), Ire. 38/B3
Galway (Carnmore) (arpt.), Ire. 38/B3
Galzignano, It. 69/E3
Gam (riv.), Viet. 105/J3
Gamaches, Fr. 60/A4
Gamagara (riv.), SAfr. 142/C2
Gamagōri, Japan 95/M6
Gamarra, Col. 216/C2
Gamay, Phil. 100/D2
Gamba, China 109/G1
Gamba, D.R. Congo 139/F4
Gamba, Gabon 138/B3
Gambaga, Gha. 133/E4
Gambaga Scarp (cliff), Gha. 133/E4
Gambais, Fr. 36/H5
Gambang, Malay. 101/C2
Gambara, It. 68/D3
Gambat, Pak. 104/A2
Gambatesa, It. 71/D5
Gambēla, Eth. 135/G3
Gambell, Ak, US 201/D3
Gambella NP, Eth. 135/G3
Gambellara, It. 69/E3
Gamber, Md, US 198/B5
Gambettola, It. 69/F5
Gambia (riv.), Afr. 132/A3
Gambia (ctry.) 132/B3
Gambier (cape), Austl. 152/C2
Gambier (isls.), FrPol. 161/M7
Gambier, Oh, US 190/E4
Gámbita, Col. 216/C3
Gambo, Nf, Can. 189/K1
Gambolò, It. 68/B3
Gamboma, Congo 138/C3
Gamboula, CAfr. 134/B4
Gambsheim, Fr. 64/A5
Gameleira, Braz. 219/H5
Gamerco, NM, US 179/H3
Gamewell, NC, US 193/G3
Gaming, Aus. 51/L3
Gamka (riv.), SAfr. 142/C4
Gamkab (riv.), Namb. 142/B3
Gamleby, Swe. 46/G3
Gamlingay, Eng, UK 43/F2
Gammel Ølstykke, Den. 45/J7
Gammelstad, Swe. 74/D2
Gammertingen, Ger. 67/F1
Gammon Ranges NP, Austl. 155/H4
Gamo, Japan 95/K5
Gamo Gofa (pol. reg.), Eth. 135/H4
Gampaha, SrL. 107/C5
Gampern, Aus. 65/G7
Gamtog, China 98/C2
Gamud (peak), Eth. 136/A4
Gan, Fr. 50/C5
Gan (riv.), China 91/J1
Gan Gan, Arg. 226/C4
Gan Hashlosha NP, Isr. 117/C4
Ganado, Tx, US 181/F3
Gananoque, On, Can. 191/H2
Ganāveh, Iran 115/G4
Ganbashao, China 99/E3
Gäncä, Azer. 77/H4
Gancheng, China 106/E2
Ganda, Ang. 140/B2
Gandajika, D.R. Congo 139/E4
Gandak (riv.), India 109/E2
Gandaki (zone), Nepal 108/D1
Gandara, Phil. 100/D2
Gāndarbal, India 110/C2
Gandarinha, Ang. 140/C1
Gandelin (riv.), Fr. 63/F5
Gander (lake), Nf, Can. 189/K1
Gander, Nf, Can. 189/K1
Ganderkesee, Ger. 59/F2
Gandesa, Sp. 53/F2
Gāndhi Sāgar (res.), India 104/B3
Gāndhīhām, India 113/K4
Gandhinagar, India 113/K4
Gandía, Sp. 53/E3
Gandino, It. 68/C2
Gandisê (mts.), China 109/E1
Gandjo, D.R. Congo 139/G3
Gandoca-Manzanillo Nat'l Wild. Ref., CR 207/F4
Gandy, Ut, US 177/G4
Ganeb (well), Mrta. 132/C2
Ganesh (mtn.), China 109/E1
Ganeshganj, India 104/C2
Gang, China 111/F4
Gang Ranch, BC, Can. 174/C2
Ganga (Ganges) (riv.), India 108/B1
Gānga Sāgar, India 109/G5
Gangala-Na-Bodio, D.R. Congo 134/D5
Gangāpur, India 104/C2
Gangara, Niger 133/H3
Gangārāmpur, India 109/G3
Gangaw, Myan. 98/B4
Gangca, China 90/E4
Gangdisê (mts.), China 111/D5
Gangelt, Ger. 61/F2
Ganges (riv.), Asia 83/A5
Ganges, BC, Can. 174/C3
Ganges, Fr. 50/E5
Ganges (Ganga) (riv.), India 108/B1
Ganges, Mouths of the (delta), India,Bang. 104/E3
Gangi, It. 54/D4
Gangkofen, Ger. 65/F6
Gango (riv.), Ang. 138/C5
Gangoh, India 110/D5
Gangtok, India 109/G2
Gangtou, China 99/H3
Ganjām, India 107/E2
Ganjingzi, China 93/A3
Ganløse, Den. 45/J7
Ganluo, China 105/H2
Ganmain, Austl. 157/C2
Gann Valley, SD, US 184/E1
Gannan, China 91/J2
Gannat, Fr. 50/E3
Gannett (peak), Wy, US 177/J2
Ganquan, China 92/B3
Gansbaai, SAfr. 142/L11
Gänserndorf, Aus. 57/P7
Gansu (prov.), China 90/D4
Gantheaume (pt.), Austl. 152/A4
Gantrisch (peak), Swi. 66/D4
Gantsevichi, Bela. 76/C1
Gantt, Al, US 195/E2
Gantt, SC, US 193/F3
Ganxitang, China 99/F3
Ganye, Nga. 134/A3
Ganyesa, SAfr. 142/D2
Ganyu, China 92/D4
Ganyushkino, Kaz. 77/J3
Ganzhou, China 99/G3
Ganzlin, Ger. 48/G2
Ganzourgou (prov.), Burk. 133/E3
Gao, Niger 133/G3
Gao, Mali 133/E2
Gao (pol. reg.), Mali 133/F2
Gao, D.R. Congo 139/G2
Gao Xian, China 98/E2
Gao'an, China 99/G2
Gaobei, China 99/G3
Gaocheng, China 92/C3
Gaochun, China 92/D5
Gaojian, China 99/J2
Gaolan (isl.), China 99/G4
Gaolan, China 90/E4
Gaoligong (mts.), Myan. 98/C3
Gaoling, China 93/A4
Gaomi, China 92/D3
Gaomutang, China 99/F3
Gaoping, China 92/C4
Gaoqiao, China 92/L8
Gaoqing, China 92/D3
Gaoqitou, China 99/F2
Gaor Bheinn (Gulvain) (peak), Sc, UK 39/A3
Gaotai, China 90/D4
Gaotang, China 92/D3
Gaotian, China 99/H3
Gaoua, Burk. 132/E4
Gaoual, Gui. 132/B4
Gaoxingxu, China 99/G3
Gaoyang, China 92/C3
Gaoyi, China 92/C3
Gaoyou (lake), China 91/H5
Gaoyou, China 92/D4
Gaozhou, China 99/F4
Gap, Fr. 70/C3
Gap, Pa, US 198/B4
Gap Mills, WV, US 193/G2
Gapeau (riv.), Fr. 70/B6
Gar, China 111/C5
Gar (riv.), China 90/C5
Gara (lake), Ire. 38/B2
Garabogazköl, Trkm. 77/K4
Garabogazköl (gulf), Trkm. 80/F5
Garacad, Som. 136/D4
Garachiné, Pan. 216/B2
Garachiné (pt.), Pan. 207/G4
Garah, Austl. 156/D1
Garai (riv.), Bang. 104/E3
Garaina, PNG 153/G1
Garajonay, PN de, Sp. 128/A3
Garalo, Mali 132/D4
Garamba, PN de la, D.R. Congo 135/F4
Garancières, Fr. 60/A6
Garango, Burk. 133/E4
Garanhuns, Braz. 219/G5
Garba, CAfr. 134/D3
Garba Tula, Kenya 137/B1
Garbahaarrey, Som. 136/B5
Garber, Ok, US 183/F2
Garberville, Ca, US 176/B3
Garbsen, Ger. 59/G4
Garça, Braz. 225/G2
Garças, Rio das (riv.), Braz. 222/B3
Garching an der Alz, Ger. 65/F6
Garcia, Co, US 182/B2
Garcia de Sota (res.), Sp. 52/C3
Gard (dept.), Fr. 70/A4
Gard (riv.), Fr. 72/E1
Garda, It. 69/D2
Garda (lake), It. 71/F1
Gardabani, Geo. 77/H4
Gardanne, Fr. 70/B6
Gardar, ND, US 186/F3
Gardelegen, Ger. 48/F2
Garden (isl.), Austl. 154/K7
Garden (pen.), Mi, US 187/L5
Garden (isl.), Mi, US 190/D2
Garden, Mi, US 190/C2
Garden (riv.), On, Can. 190/E1
Garden City, Ga, US 193/G4
Garden City, Id, US 176/E2
Garden City, Ks, US 182/D2
Garden City, Mi, US 197/F7
Garden City, Mo, US 183/G1
Garden City, NY, US 199/L9
Garden City, SD, US 184/F1
Garden City, Tx, US 180/D2
Garden City Beach, SC, US 193/H4
Garden City Park, NY, US 199/L9
Garden Grove, Ca, US 196/G8
Garden Grove, Fl, US 194/L7
Garden Grove, Ia, US 185/H3
Garden Valley, Id, US 176/F1
Garden View, Pa, US 198/A1
Gardena, Ca, US 196/F8
Gardendale, Al, US 192/D4
Gardenstown, Sc, UK 39/D1
Gardenton, Mb, Can. 186/F3
Gardēz, Afg. 113/J2
Gardhīwāla, India 110/C4
Gardi, Ga, US 195/H2
Gardiner (dam), Sk, Can. 175/L2
Gardiner, Mt, US 177/H1
Gardiner, Or, US 176/A2
Gardiner, Wa, US 197/B1
Gardiners (isl.), NY, US 199/F1
Gardiners (bay), NY, US 199/F1
Gardner, Fl, US 195/H4
Gardner, Ks, US 183/G1
Gardner, Il, US 190/B4
Gardner (lake), Me, US 188/D3
Gardner, Ma, US 191/L3
Gardner (mtn.), Wa, US 174/D3
Gardner (Nikumaroro) (isl.), Kiri. 161/H5
Gardone val Trompia, It. 68/D2
Gare Favre, Congo 138/C4
Gare Girard, Congo 138/C4
Gare Loch (inlet), Sc, UK 39/B4
Gareat el Tarf (salt pan), Alg. 130/K7
Garelochhead, Sc, UK 39/B4
Garéoult, Fr. 70/C6
Garessio, It. 68/B5
Garet el Djenoun (peak), Alg. 129/G4
Garfield (lake), Fl, US 194/M8
Garfield, Ga, US 193/F4
Garfield, Ks, US 182/E1
Garfield (mtn.), Mt, US 177/G1
Garfield, NJ, US 199/J8
Garfield, NM, US 179/J4
Garfield, Tx, US 181/F2
Garfield, Wa, US 174/F4
Gärflotta (isl.), Swe. 45/A2
Garforth, Eng, UK 41/G4
Gargaliánoi, Gre. 55/G4
Gargan (peak), Fr. 50/D4
Gargas, Fr. 70/B5
Gargenville, Fr. 60/A6
Garges-lès-Gonesse, Fr. 36/K5
Gargnano, It. 69/D2
Gargrave, Eng, UK 41/F4
Gargždai, Lith. 47/J4
Garh Mahārāja, Pak. 110/A4
Garhākotā, India 108/B4
Garhbeta, India 109/F4
Garhchiroli, India 107/C1
Garhi, India 108/C4
Garhmuktesar, India 108/B1
Garhshankar, India 110/D4
Garibaldi, Braz. 225/G4
Garibaldi, Or, US 174/C5
Garibaldi, BC, Can. 174/C3
Garies, SAfr. 142/B3
Garigliano (riv.), It. 71/C5
Garioch (reg.), Sc, UK 39/D2
Garissa, Kenya 137/B2
Garland, Mb, Can. 186/D2
Garland, Ks, US 183/G2
Garland, Tx, US 180/L7
Garland, NC, US 193/H3
Garlandville, Ms, US 192/C4
Garlasco, It. 68/B3
Garliava, Lith. 47/K4
Garlieston, Sc, UK 40/D2
Garmeh, Iran 115/J2
Garmisch-Partenkirchen, Ger. 67/H3
Garmouth, Sc, UK 39/C1
Garmsār, Iran 115/H3
Garmuda, Eth. 136/C4
Garneill, Mt, US 175/K4
Garner, Ia, US 185/H2
Garner, NC, US 193/H3
Garneton, Zam. 141/F2
Garnett, Ks, US 183/G1
Garnett, SC, US 193/G4
Garnish, Nf, Can. 189/K2
Garnpung (lake), Austl. 156/B2
Garonne (riv.), Fr. 72/D1
Garoowe, Som. 136/D3
Garopaba, Braz. 225/G4
Garou (lake), Mali 133/E2
Garoua, Camr. 134/B3
Garoua (int'l arpt.), Camr. 134/B3
Garoua Boulaï, Camr. 134/B4
Garphyttan, Swe. 46/F2
Garraf (mts.), Sp. 53/K7
Garreg, Wal, UK 40/D6
Garrel, Ger. 59/F3
Garretson, SD, US 185/F2
Garrett, In, US 190/D4
Garrett, Tx, US 181/F1
Garrett, Wy, US 184/B2
Garrison, Mo, US 183/H2
Garrison, Mn, US 187/H4
Garrison, ND, US 186/D4
Garrison (dam), ND, US 186/D4
Garrison, Ky, US 193/F1
Garrison, Mt, US 175/H4
Garrison, Tx, US 181/G2
Garrison, Ut, US 177/F4
Garron (pt.), NI, UK 40/C1
Garrovillas, Sp. 52/B3
Garry (lake), Sc, UK 39/B2
Garry (riv.), Sc, UK 39/A2
Garry (bay), Nun, Can. 171/H2
Garry (lake), Nun, Can. 170/F2
Gars am Inn, Ger. 65/F6
Gars am Kamp, Aus. 49/H4
Garsen, Kenya 137/C2
Garstang, Eng, UK 41/F4
Garsten, Aus. 65/H6
Garte (riv.), Ger. 59/H6
Gartempe (riv.), Fr. 50/D3
Garth, Wal, UK 42/C2
Gartmore, Sc, UK 39/B4
Gärtringen, Ger. 64/B5
Garut, Indo. 101/D4
Garvagh, NI, UK 40/B2
Garwa, India 108/D3
Garwolin, Pol. 49/L3
Garwood, NJ, US 199/H9
Garwood, Tx, US 180/F3
Gary, In, US 190/C4
Gary, SD, US 185/F1
Gary, Tx, US 181/G1
Gary, WV, US 193/G2
Garyarsa, China 111/D5
Garyi, China 98/C2
Garyville, La, US 194/C2
Garz, Ger. 46/E4
Garza García, Mex. 205/E3
Garzê, China 98/D2
Garzón, Col. 216/C4
Gas, Fr. 36/G6
Gas (lake), China 111/F4
Gas City, In, US 190/D4
Gas-san (peak), Japan 94/B4
Gasa, Bhu. 109/G2
Gæsafjöll (peak), Ice. 44/P6
Gasan, Phil. 100/C2
Gaschurn, Aus. 67/G4
Gasconade (riv.), Mo, US 185/J4
Gasconde (riv.), Mo, US 183/H2
Gascony (reg.), Fr. 72/D2
Gascoyne (mt.), Austl. 154/C3
Gascoyne (riv.), Austl. 145/A3
Gascoyne Junction, Austl. 154/B3
Gash (riv.), Erit. 135/H2
Gashaka, Nga. 134/A4
Gasheng, India 98/B2
Gasny, Fr. 63/G2
Gaspar (str.), Indo. 102/C4
Gaspard (riv.), BC, Can. 174/C2
Gasparilla (isl.), Fl, US 195/G4
Gaspé, Qu, Can. 188/E1
Gaspé (bay), Qu, Can. 188/E1
Gaspé (pen.), Qu, Can. 171/K4
Gaspoltshofen, Aus. 65/G6
Gasport, NY, US 190/V9
Gassin, Fr. 70/C6
Gassino Torinese, It. 68/A2
Gassville, Ar, US 183/H2
Gastins, Fr. 36/M6
Gaston, NC, US 193/J2
Gaston (lake), NC, US 193/H2
Gastonia, Tx, US 180/L7
Gastonia, NC, US 193/G3
Gastoúni, Gre. 55/G4
Gat, Isr. 117/B5
Gata (cape), Cyp. 116/C2
Gata (cape), Sp. 52/D4
Gata (mts.), Sp. 52/B2
Gata de Gorgos, Sp. 53/F3
Gatchina, Rus. 47/P2
Gate, Ok, US 182/D2
Gate City, Va, US 193/F2
Gatehouse-Of-Fleet, Sc, UK 40/D2
Gates, Or, US 176/B1
Gates of The Arctic NP and Prsv., Ak, US 201/G2
Gateshead (isl.), Nun, Can. 170/F1
Gateshead, Eng, UK 41/G2
Gateshead (co.), Eng, UK 41/G2
Gatesville, Tx, US 180/F2
Gatesville, NC, US 193/J2
Gateway, Co, US 179/H1
Gateway, Or, US 176/C1
Gateway NRA, NJ, US 199/K9
Gathright (dam), Va, US 193/H2
Gaths Mine, Zim. 141/F4
Gatico, Chile 224/B2
Gatineau, Qu, Can. 191/J2
Gatineau (riv.), Qu, Can. 191/J1
Gatlinburg, Tn, US 193/F3
Gatow, Ger. 48/Q7
Gattendorf, Aus. 51/M2
Gatteville-le-Phare, Fr. 62/D1
Gattianara, It. 68/B2
Gatton, Austl. 158/D4
Gatún (lake), Pan. 207/G4
Gatún (dam), Pan. 207/G4
Gatvand, Iran 115/G3
Gatwick (int'l arpt.), Eng, UK 36/C3
Gau Algesheim, Ger. 64/B3
Gau Bischofsheim, Ger. 64/B3
Gau Odernheim, Ger. 64/B3
Gaubickelheim, Ger. 61/H4
Gauchy, Fr. 60/C4
Gaucín, Sp. 52/C4
Gauja (riv.), Est.,Lat. 47/L3
Gauja NP, Lat. 47/L3
Gaujiena, Lat. 47/M3
Gaukönigshofen, Ger. 64/C3
Gauley (riv.), WV, US 193/G1
Gaunless (riv.), Eng, UK 41/G2
Gaupne, Nor. 44/C3
Gaur (riv.), Sc, UK 39/B3
Gauri Sankar (peak), Nepal 109/F2
Gauripur, India 109/G2
Gaurnadi, Bang. 109/H4
Gause, Tx, US 181/F2
Gausta (peak), Nor. 46/C2
Gauteng (prov.), SAfr. 141/F5
Gauting, Ger. 65/E6
Gavà, Sp. 53/L7
Gavardo, It. 68/D2
Gavāter, Iran 113/H3
Gāvbandī, Iran 115/H5
Gávdhos (isl.), Gre. 73/K4
Gave de Pau (riv.), Fr. 53/E1
Gavel-Långsjön (lake), Swe. 45/B1
Gavere, Belg. 60/C2
Gāvgān, Iran 115/F2
Gavi, It. 68/B4
Gavião, Port. 52/B3
Gavins Point (dam), SD, US 184/F2
Gaviota, Ca, US 178/B3
Gavirate, It. 68/B2
Gävle, Swe. 46/G1
Gävleborg (co.), Swe. 44/E3
Gavray, Fr. 62/D3
Gawai, Myan. 98/C3
Gawler, Austl. 155/H5
Gawler Ranges (mts.), Austl. 145/C4
Gawso, Gha. 133/E5
Gaxun (lake), China 90/D3
Gay, Rus. 77/L2
Gay (peak), WV, US 193/G1
Gaya, Niger 133/F4
Gayā, India 109/E3
Gaya (riv.), China 91/K3
Gayam, Chad 134/C3
Gayaza, Ugan. 139/G3
Gaylegphug, Bhu. 109/H2
Gaylord, Ks, US 184/E4
Gaylord, Mi, US 190/D2
Gaylord, Mn, US 185/G1
Gayndah, Austl. 158/C4
Gayny, Rus. 75/M3
Gays Mills, Wi, US 185/J2
Gayville, SD, US 185/F2
Gaz, Iran 115/G3
Gaz-Achak, Trkm. 80/G5
Gaza (prov.), Moz. 141/G4
Gaza (Ghazzah), Gaza 117/A5
Gaza Strip, Gaza 117/A6
Gazanjyk, Trkm. 77/K5
Gazanjyk, Trkm. 115/H2
Gazaoua, Niger 133/G3
Gazelle, Ca, US 176/B3
Gazeran, Fr. 36/H6
Gaziantep, Turk. 114/D2
Gaziantep (prov.), Turk. 114/D2
Gaziköy, Turk. 57/H5
Gazimur (riv.), Rus. 91/H1
Gazipaşa, Turk. 116/C1
Gazon de Faing (peak), Fr. 66/D1
Gazzaniga, It. 68/C2
Gbadolite, D.R. Congo 134/D4
Gbangbatok, SLeo. 132/B5
Gbarnga, Libr. 132/C5
Gboko, Nga. 133/H5
Gbongan, Nga. 133/G5
Gd Res de Vioreau (res.), Fr. 62/D5
Gdansk (gulf), Pol. 74/C5
Gdańsk, Pol. 46/H4
Gdov, Rus. 47/M2
Gdynia, Pol. 46/H4
Ge (lake), China 92/D5
Geal Charn (peak), Sc, UK 39/C2
Geal Charn (peak), Sc, UK 39/A3
Geary, NB, Can. 188/D3
Geary, Ok, US 183/E3
Geashill, Ire. 38/C3
Geba Wenz (riv.), Eth. 135/G3
Gebaberg (peak), Ger. 64/D1
Gebe (isl.), Indo. 103/G3
Gebeit Mine, Sudan 127/H4
Gebhardshain, Ger. 61/G2
Gebilu, Eth. 136/B3
Gebiz, Turk. 116/B1
Gebra-Hainleite, Ger. 59/H6
Gebre Guracha, Eth. 136/A3
Gedara (Umm Qays) (ruin), Jor. 117/D3
Gede (peak), Indo. 101/D4
Gede, Kenya 137/C2
Gedera, Isr. 117/B5
Gedern, Ger. 64/C2
Gedi (riv.), Turk. 73/K3
Gedi Ruins Nat'l Mon., Kenya 137/B2
Gedikbulak, Turk. 115/E2
Gedinne, Belg. 61/D4
Gediz, Turk. 114/B2
Gediz (riv.), Turk. 114/A2
Gedlegubē, Eth. 136/C4
Gēdo, Eth. 135/H3
Gedser, Den. 46/D4
Gedser (cape), Den. 46/D4
Gedsted, Den. 46/C3
Geel, Belg. 61/E1
Geelong, Austl. 157/B4
Geelong West, Austl. 157/B4
Geelvink (chan.), Austl. 145/A3
Geertruidenberg, Neth. 58/B5
Geeste (riv.), Ger. 59/F1
Geeste, Ger. 59/E3
Geestemünde, Ger. 59/F1
Geesthacht, Ger. 59/H2
Geeveston, Austl. 156/C4
Gefrees, Ger. 65/E2
Gegeya Shet' (riv.), Eth. 136/A2
Gê'gyai, China 111/D5
Gehrde, Ger. 59/F3
Gehrden, Ger. 59/G4
Geidam, Nga. 134/A2
Geifas (peak), Wal, UK 42/C2
Geigar, Sudan 135/G3
Geikie (isl.), On, Can. 187/K2
Geikie (riv.), Sk, Can. 170/F3
Geikie Gorge NP, Austl. 152/B4
Geilenkirchen, Ger. 61/F2
Geilo, Nor. 46/C1
Geinō, Japan 95/K6
Geiselhöring, Ger. 65/F5
Geiselwind, Ger. 64/D3
Geisenfeld, Ger. 65/E5
Geisenhausen, Ger. 65/F6
Geisenheim, Ger. 61/G4
Geislingen, Ger. 67/E1
Geislingen an der Steige, Ger. 64/C5
Geistown, Pa, US 191/G4
Geita, Tanz. 139/H3
Gejiu, China 98/D4
Gekeng, China 99/H3
Gel (riv.), Sudan 135/F4
Gela, It. 54/D4
Gela (gulf), It. 54/D4
Geladī, Eth. 136/C4
Gelai (peak), Tanz. 137/B2
Gelang (cape), Malay. 101/C1
Gelderland (prov.), Neth. 58/C4
Geldermalsen, Neth. 58/C5
Geldern, Ger. 58/D5
Geldersheim, Ger. 64/D2
Geldrop, Neth. 58/C6
Geleen, Neth. 61/E2
Gelemso, Eth. 136/B3
Gelendost, Turk. 114/B2
Gelendzhik, Rus. 79/K5
Gelibolu, Turk. 57/H5
Gelibolu Yarımadas NP, Turk. 55/K2
Gelīla, Eth. 135/H3
Gelincik (peak), Turk. 115/E2
Gelinggang, Indo. 102/D4
Gelligaer, Wal, UK 42/C3
Gelnhausen, Ger. 64/C2
Gelsenkirchen, Ger. 58/E5
Geltendorf, Ger. 67/H1
Gelterkinden, Swi. 66/D3
Gelting, Ger. 46/C4
Gemas, Malay. 102/B3
Gembloux, Belg. 61/D2
Gembogl, PNG 153/G1
Gemena, D.R. Congo 138/D2
Gémenos, Fr. 70/B6
Gemert, Neth. 58/C5
Gemlik (gulf), Turk. 57/J5
Gemlik, Turk. 57/J5
Gemona del Friuli, It. 51/K3
Gemsbok NP, Bots. 140/D5
Gemuk (mt.), Ak, US 201/G3
Gemünden am Main, Ger. 64/C2
Gen (riv.), China 90/J1
Genalē Wenz (riv.), Eth. 136/B4
Genappe, Belg. 61/D2
Genargentu (mts.), It. 54/A2
Genarp, Swe. 45/K7
Genay, Fr. 66/A6
Genazzano, It. 71/B4
Genç, Turk. 114/E2
Gendringen, Neth. 58/D5
Gendt, Neth. 58/C5
Genemuiden, Neth. 58/D3
General Acha, Arg. 226/D3
General Alfredo Vasquez Cobo (int'l arpt.), Col. 220/D2
General Alvear, Arg. 226/D2
General Alvear, Arg. 226/E3
General Arenales, Arg. 226/E2
General Artigas, Par 225/E3
General Belgrano, Arg. 226/F2
General Belgrano II, Arg., Ant. 228/X
General Bravo, Mex. 180/E5
General Cabrera, Arg. 226/E2
General Campos, Arg. 224/E4
General Carneiro, Braz. 222/B2
General Carrera (lake), Chile 226/B5
General Cepeda, Mex. 205/E3
General Conesa, Arg. 226/D4
General Deheza, Arg. 226/E2
General Edward Lawrence Logan (Logan Int'l) (int'l arpt.), Ma, US 191/L3
General Enrique Godoy, Arg. 226/D3
General Eugenio A. Garay, Par. 224/D2
General Francisco Villa, Mex. 205/F3
General Galarza, Arg. 227/J10
General Grant Grove, Ca, US 178/C2
General Grant Nat'l Mem., NY, US 199/K8
General José de San Martín, Arg. 224/E3
General Juan Álvarez, PN, Mex. 205/F5
General Juan José Rios, Mex. 204/C3
General Juan Madariaga, Arg. 227/F3
General La Madrid, Arg. 226/E3
General Lagos, Chile 224/B1
General Las Heras, Arg. 227/J11
General Lavalle, Arg. 227/K12
General Manuel Belgrano (peak), Arg. 224/C4
General Martín Miguel de Güemes, Arg. 224/C3
General Mitchell (int'l arpt.), Wi, US 190/C3
General Pico, Arg. 226/E2
General Pinto, Arg. 226/E2
General Ramírez, Arg. 224/D5
General Roca, Arg. 226/D3
General Saavedra, Bol. 224/D1
General Sampaio, Braz. 219/G4
General San Martín, Arg., Ant. 228/V
General San Martín, Arg. 226/E3
General San Martín, Arg. 227/J11
General Santiago Marino (int'l arpt.), Ven. 217/F2
General Santos, Phil. 100/D4
General Sherman Tree, Ca, US 178/C2
General Terán, Mex. 205/F3
General Treviño, Mex. 180/E4
General Trías, Mex. 180/A3
General Trias, Phil. 100/E7
General Viamonte, Arg. 226/E2
General Villalobas (int'l arpt.), Mex. 180/A3
General Villegas, Arg. 226/E2
General Zaragoza, Mex. 205/F4
General-Toshevo, Bul. 57/J4
Generoso (peak), Swi. 67/F6
Genesee, Id, US 174/F4
Genesee (co.), Mi, US 197/E6
Genesee (riv.), NY, US 191/G3
Genesee, Wi, US 197/P14
Genesee Depot, Wi, US 197/P14
Geneseo, Il, US 185/J3
Geneseo, Ks, US 183/E1
Geneseo, NY, US 191/H3
Genet, Eth. 136/A3
Geneva (Léman) (lake), Fr. 51/G3
Geneva (lake), Fr.,Swi. 72/E1
Geneva (Genève), Swi. 51/G3
Geneva (int'l arpt.), Swi. 66/C5
Geneva, Al, US 195/F2
Geneva, Id, US 177/H2
Geneva, Il, US 190/B4
Geneva, In, US 190/D4
Geneva, Ne, US 184/F3
Geneva, NY, US 191/H3
Geneva, Oh, US 190/F4
Geneva, Tx, US 181/H2
Genève, Swi. 66/C5
Genève (canton), Swi. 66/C5
Gengding (mtn.), China 99/E3
Gengenbach, Ger. 66/E1
Genglou, China 99/G4
Gengma Daizu Vazu Zizhixian, China 98/C4
Gengzhuang, China 93/B2
Génicourt, Fr. 36/J4
Genil (riv.), Sp. 72/B3
Genillé, Fr. 63/G6
Génissieux, Fr. 70/B2
Genk, Belg. 61/E2
Genlis, Fr. 66/B3
Gennach (riv.), Ger. 67/G2
Gennep, Neth. 58/C5
Gennevilliers, Fr. 36/J5
Genoa (riv.), Austl. 157/D3
Genoa (Genova), It. 68/B5
Genoa, Il, US 185/K2
Genoa, Ne, US 184/F3
Genoa, Oh, US 190/E4
Genoa City, Wi, US 197/P14
Genola, Ut, US 177/H4
Génova, Col. 219/K8
Genova (Genoa), It. 68/B5
Genova (prov.), It. 68/C4
Genova (gulf), It. 72/F1
Genovesa (isl.), Ecu. 220/K6
Gensingen, Ger. 61/G4
Gent (Ghent), Belg. 60/C1
Gent-Brugge Kanaal (canal), Belg. 60/C1
Genteng, Indo. 102/D5
Genteng (cape), Indo. 101/D4
Gentofte, Den. 45/J7
Gentry, Ar, US 183/G2
Genval, Belg. 61/D2
Genzano di Roma, It. 71/B4
Geographe (bay), Austl. 154/B5
Geographe (chan.), Austl. 154/B3
Geographical Center of North America, ND, US 186/D3
Geographical Center of the 48 Contiguous States, Ks, US 184/E4
Geographical Center of United States, SD, US 184/C1
Geok-Tepe, Trkm. 115/J2
Georg von Neumayer, Ger., Ant. 228/Z
George (pt.), Austl. 158/C3
George (lake), Austl. 154/D2
George (riv.), Can. 163/L4
George (riv.), Qu, Can. 171/K3
George, SAfr. 142/C4
George (lake), Ugan. 139/G3
George, Ia, US 185/F2
George, Wa, US 174/E4
George Land (isl.), Rus. 80/E2
George Rogers Clark Nat'l Hist. Park, In, US 192/D1
George Town, Austl. 156/C4
George Town (cap.), Cay. 207/F2
George Town, Malay. 101/C1
George V (coast), Ant. 228/L
George Washington Birthplace Nat'l Mon., Va, US 193/J1
George Washington Carver Nat'l Mon., Mo, US 183/G2
George West, Tx, US 181/E3
Georgensmünd, Ger. 64/E4
Georges (riv.), Austl. 158/G9
Georgetown, Austl. 158/A2
Georgetown, On, Can. 190/T8
Georgetown, PE, Can. 189/F2
Georgetown, Gam. 132/B3
Georgetown (cap.), Guy. 217/G3
Georgetown, StV. 203/N9
Georgetown, Co, US 184/B4
Georgetown, Ct, US 199/E1
Georgetown, De, US 193/K1
Georgetown, Fl, US 195/H3
Georgetown, Ga, US 195/F2
Georgetown, Ga, US 195/H2
Georgetown, Id, US 177/H2
Georgetown, Il, US 190/C5
Georgetown, Ky, US 192/E1
Georgetown, La, US 194/B2
Georgetown, Oh, US 192/F1

288
George – Gossen

Georgetown, SC, US 193/H4
Georgetown, Tx, US 181/F2
Georgi Traykov, Bul. 57/H4
Georgia (ctry.) 77/G4
Georgia (str.), BC, Can. 174/B3
Georgia (state), US 173/K5
Georgia Agrirama, Ga, US 195/G2
Georgian (bay), On, Can. 171/H4
Georgian Bay Islands NP, On, Can. 190/F2
Georgiana, Al, US 194/E2
Georgina (riv.), Austl. 145/C3
Georgsmarienhütte, Ger. 59/F4
Gepatsch (lake), Aus. 67/G4
Gera, Ger. 48/G3
Geraardsbergen, Belg. 60/C2
Geral de Goiás, Serra (mts.), Braz. 222/D1
Geral, Serra (mts.), Braz. 225/G3
Gerald, Sk, Can. 186/D2
Gerald, Mo, US 183/J1
Geraldine, NZ 159/B4
Geraldine, Mt, US 175/J4
Geraldton, Austl. 154/B4
Geraldton, On, Can. 187/L3
Gérardmer, Fr. 66/C1
Gerasdorf bei Wien, Aus. 57/N7
Gerāsh, Iran 115/H5
Gerber (res.), Or, US 176/C2
Gerbéviller, Fr. 66/C1
Gerbier de Jonc (peak), Fr. 50/F4
Gerbrunn, Ger. 64/C3
Gerdau (riv.), Ger. 59/H3
Gerdine (mt.), Ak, US 201/H3
Gère (riv.), Fr. 70/B2
Gerede, Turk. 76/E4
Geres, Iles D' (isls.), Fr. 72/E2
Geretsried, Ger. 67/H2
Gérgal, Sp. 52/D4
Gerger, Turk. 114/D2
Gerhards (cape), PNG 153/G1
Gerik, Malay. 101/C1
Gering, Ne, US 184/C3
Gerlach, Nv, US 176/D3
Gerlachovský Štít (peak), Slvk. 49/L4
Gerlafingen, Swi. 66/D3
Germantown, Md, US 198/A5
Germantown, Tn, US 192/C3
Germantown, Wi, US 190/B3
Germany (ctry.) 48/E3
Germering, Ger. 65/E6
Germersheim, Ger. 64/B4
Germfask, Mi, US 190/D1
Germigny-L'Evêque, Fr. 36/L5
Germinaga, It. 67/E6
Germiston, SAfr. 142/E2
Gernsbach, Ger. 64/B5
Geroldsgrün, Ger. 65/E2
Gerolsbach, Ger. 65/E5
Gerolstein, Ger. 61/F3
Gerolzhofen, Ger. 64/D3
Geronimo, Az, US 179/G4
Gerpinnes, Belg. 61/D3
Gerra (Verzasca), Swi. 67/E5
Gerrards Cross, Eng, UK 36/B2
Gerringong, Austl. 157/E2
Gers (riv.), Fr. 50/D5
Gersau, Swi. 67/E4
Gersfeld, Ger. 64/C2
Gersheim, Ger. 61/G5
Gerspenz (riv.), Ger. 64/B3
Gerstetten, Ger. 64/E5
Gerstheim, Fr. 66/D1
Gersthofen, Ger. 64/D6
Gerstungen, Ger. 59/H7
Gervais, Or, US 176/B1
Gervanne (riv.), Fr. 70/B3
Gervasio, Uru. 227/G2
Gerze, Turk. 76/E4
Gêrzê, China 111/D5
Gescher, Ger. 58/E5
Geseke, Ger. 59/F5
Gesher, Isr. 117/D3
Gesher Ha Ziw, Isr. 117/C2
Gesira, Som. 137/D1
Gespunsart, Fr. 61/D4
Gessertshausen, Ger. 64/D6
Gesso (riv.), It. 68/A4
Gesso (riv.), Fr. 70/D4
Gesves, Belg. 61/E3
Geta, Fin. 47/H1
Getafe, Sp. 53/N9
Getai, China 92/B4
Gete (riv.), Belg. 61/E2
Getinge, Swe. 46/E3
Gettorf, Ger. 46/C4
Gettysburg, Pa, US 191/H5
Gettysburg, SD, US 184/E1
Gettysburg Nat'l Mil. Park, Pa, US 198/A4
Getúlio Vargas, Braz. 225/F3
Geul (riv.), Neth. 61/E2
Geureudong (peak), Indo. 101/B1
Geurie, Austl. 156/D2
Gevar'am, Isr. 117/B5
Gevaş, Turk. 115/E2
Gevelsberg, Ger. 59/E6
Gevgelija, FYROM 55/H2
Gewanē, Eth. 136/B3
Gex, Fr. 66/C5
Geyer, Ger. 65/F1
Geyersberg (peak), Ger. 64/C3
Geyikli, Turk. 55/K3
Geysdorp, SAfr. 142/D2
Geyser (reef), Madg. 143/H6
Geyve, Turk. 57/K5
Gez (riv.), China 111/B4
Ghabāghib, Syria 117/E2
Ghābat al 'Arab, Sudan 135/F3
Ghadāmis, Libya 129/H3
Ghaddūwah, Libya 126/B3
Ghaggar (riv.), India 110/C5
Ghaghara (riv.), India 108/C2
Ghāghra, India 109/E4
Ghakhar, Pak. 110/C3
Ghana (ctry.) 133/E4
Ghantiāli, India 113/K3
Ghanzi, Bots. 140/D4
Ghanzi (dist.), Bots. 140/D4
Ghār Ad Dimā', Tun. 130/L6
Gharaunda, India 110/D5
Gharb Binna, Sudan 127/F5
Gharbah (wadi), Egypt 131/C5
Gharbi (isl.), Tun. 72/F4
Ghardaïa, Alg. 129/F2
Ghardaïa (wilaya), Alg. 129/F3
Ghardimaou, Tun. 130/L6
Gharghoda, India 108/D4
Gharībwāl, Pak. 110/B3
Gharm, Taj. 111/B4
Gharqābād, Iran 115/G3
Gharyān, Libya 126/B1
Ghāt, Libya 129/H4
Ghātāl, India 109/F4
Ghātampur, India 108/C2
Ghātsīla, India 109/F4
Ghayl Bā Wazīr, Yem. 136/D2
Ghazaouet, Alg. 130/D2
Ghaziābād, India 110/D5
Ghāzīpur, India 108/D3
Ghāzīpur, India 108/C3
Ghaznī, Afg. 113/J2
Ghazzah (Gaza), Gaza 117/A5
Ghedi, It. 68/D3
Gheen, Mn, US 187/H4
Ghemme, It. 68/B2
Ghent (Gent), Belg. 60/C1
Gheorghe Gheorghiu-Dej, Rom. 57/H2
Gheorgheni, Rom. 78/C4
Gherla, Rom. 57/F2
Gheura, India 113/K3
Ghilarza, It. 54/A2
Ghinda (Gīnda), Erit. 136/A2
Ghio (lake), Arg. 226/C5
Ghirārah (gulf), Tun. 129/H2
Ghisalba, It. 68/C2
Ghisonaccia, Fr. 54/A1
Gholson, Tx, US 181/F2
Ghora Bāri, Pak. 113/J4
Ghorāi, Nepal 108/D1
Ghost Town, Nv, US 178/D2
Ghotki, Pak. 104/A2
Ghugri (riv.), India 109/F3
Ghum, India 109/G2
Ghurayrah, SAr. 112/D5
Ghūriān, Afg. 113/H2
Ghuwaybah (wadi), Egypt 131/D5
Gia Lam (int'l arpt.), Viet. 98/E4
Gia Nghia, Viet. 106/D4
Gia Rai, Viet. 106/D4
Gia Vuc, Viet. 106/E3
Giaginskaya, Rus. 79/L5
Gianicolo (hill), It. 71/G8
Giannutri (isl.), It. 54/B1
Giant Sequoia Nat'l Mon., Ca, US 178/C2
Giant's Castle (peak), SAfr. 142/E3
Giant's Causeway, NI, UK 40/B1
Giarre, It. 54/D4
Giaveno, It. 70/D2
Giba`i Shet' (riv.), Eth. 136/A2
Gibb River, Austl. 152/B4
Gibbon, Ne, US 184/E3
Gibbonsville, Id, US 177/G1
Gibbstown, NJ, US 198/C4
Gībē Shet' (riv.), Eth. 135/H4
Gībē Wenz (riv.), Eth. 135/H3
Gibeon, Namb. 140/C5
Giberville, Fr. 63/E2
Gibloux (peak), Swi. 66/D4
Gibraleón, Sp. 52/B4
Gibraltar (cap.), Gib. 52/C4
Gibraltar (str.), Mor.,Sp. 29/D5
Gibraltar (pt.), Eng, UK 41/J5
Gibraltar (res.), Ca, US 196/A1
Gibraltar, Mi, US 197/F7
Gibraltar, Ven. 203/G6
Gibraltar Range NP, Austl. 156/E1
Gibsland, La, US 183/H4
Gibson, Austl. 154/D5
Gibson (des.), Austl. 145/B3
Gibson, Ga, US 193/F4
Gibson, NC, US 193/H3
Gibson City, Il, US 190/B4
Gibson Desert Nature Reserve, Austl. 154/E3
Gibsonburg, Oh, US 190/E4
Gibsonia, Fl, US 194/M7
Gibsons, BC, Can. 174/C3
Gibsonton, Fl, US 194/L8
Gīdamī, Eth. 135/G3
Giddarbāha, India 110/C4
Gidden (lake), Fl, US 194/L6
Giddings, Tx, US 181/F2
Gideon, Mo, US 192/C2
Gidollē, Eth. 135/H4
Giebelstadt, Ger. 64/C3
Gieboldehausen, Ger. 59/H5
Giedraičiai, Lith. 47/L4
Gien, Fr. 50/E3
Giengen an der Brenz, Ger. 64/D5
Gier (riv.), Fr. 50/F4
Giessbachfälle (falls), Swi. 66/E4
Giessen (riv.), Fr.,Ger. 66/D1
Giessen, Ger. 64/B1
Giessendam, Neth. 58/B5
Gieten, Neth. 58/D2
Giethoorn, Neth. 58/D3
Gif-sur-Yvette, Fr. 36/J5
Gīfān, Iran 115/J2
Gifford (riv.), Nun, Can. 171/H1
Gifford, Sc, UK 39/D5
Gifford, Fl, US 195/H4
Gifford, Il, US 190/B4
Gifford, SC, US 193/G4
Gifford (peak), Wa, US 174/D5
Giffre (riv.), Fr. 66/C5
Gifhorn, Ger. 59/H4
Gifu, Japan 95/L5
Gig Harbor, Wa, US 174/C4
Gigant, Rus. 79/L4
Gigante, Col. 216/C4
Giggleswick, Eng, UK 41/F3
Giglio (isl.), It. 72/F2
Gignac, Fr. 53/G1
Gignac-la-Nerthe, Fr. 70/B6
Gijón, Sp. 52/C1
Gikongoro, Rwa. 139/G3
Gil de Vilches, PN, Chile 226/C2
Gila (riv.), Az, NM, US 179/G4
Gila, NM, US 179/H4
Gila (mts.), Az, US 179/G4
Gila Bend, Az, US 179/F4
Gila Bend Ind. Res., Az, US 179/F4
Gila Cliff Dwellings Nat'l Mon., NM, US 179/H4
Gīlān (gov.), Iran 115/G2
Gīlān-e Gharb, Iran 115/F3
Gilat, Isr. 117/B6
Gilberdyke Newport, Eng, UK 41/H4
Gilbert (riv.), Austl. 145/D2
Gilbert (mt.), BC, Can. 174/B2
Gilbert (isls.), Kiri. 160/G5
Gilbert, Az, US 179/G4
Gilbert, Ia, US 185/H2
Gilbert, La, US 194/C1
Gilbert, Mn, US 187/H4
Gilbert (peak), Ut, US 177/H3
Gilbert Plains, Mb, Can. 186/D2
Gilbertown, Al, US 194/D2
Gilberts, Il, US 197/P15
Gilbjerg (pt.), Den. 45/J6
Gilbués, Braz. 219/E5
Gilby, ND, US 186/F3
Gilching, Ger. 64/E6
Gilchrist, Tx, US 181/G3
Gilé, Moz. 141/H3
Gilfach Gôch, Wal, UK 42/C3
Gilford, NI, UK 40/B3
Gilford, NH, US 191/L3
Gilford Park, NJ, US 199/D4
Gilgandra, Austl. 156/D1
Gilgil, Kenya 137/B2
Gilgit (riv.), Pak. 110/C1
Gilgit, Pak. 110/C2
Gilgit (riv.), India 111/B4
Gilgunnia, Austl. 156/C2
Gilimanuk, Indo. 101/F5
Gill, Ma, US 191/K3
Gill, Lough (lake), Ire. 38/B1
Gillam, Mb, Can. 170/G3
Gilleleje, Den. 45/J6
Gilles (lake), Austl. 155/H5
Gillespie, Il, US 185/K4
Gillett, Ar, US 183/J3
Gillett, Wi, US 190/B2
Gillett, Tx, US 181/F3
Gillette, Wy, US 184/B1
Gillies Bay, BC, Can. 174/B3
Gillingham, Eng, UK 43/G4
Gillot (int'l arpt.), Reun., Fr. 143/S15
Gilly, Swi. 66/C5
Gilly-sur-Isère, Fr. 70/C1
Gilman, Wi, US 187/J5
Gilman, Il, US 190/C4
Gilman City, Mo, US 185/H3
Gilman Hot Springs, Ca, US 196/D3
Gilmer, Tx, US 181/G1
Gilmore, Id, US 177/G1
Gīlo Wenz (riv.), Eth. 135/G4
Gilqit (riv.), Pak. 113/K1
Gilroy, Ca, US 178/B2
Giluwe (mt.), PNG 153/F1
Gilyuy (riv.), Rus. 91/K1
Gilze, Neth. 58/B5
Gīmbī, Eth. 135/G3
Gimbsheim, Ger. 64/B3
Gimel, Swi. 66/C4
Gimie (mt.), StL. 203/N9
Gimli, Mb, Can. 186/F2
Gimo, Swe. 46/H1
Gimone (riv.), Fr. 53/F1
Gin Gin, Austl. 158/C4
Ginan, Japan 95/L5
Gīnch'ī, Eth. 136/A3
Gīnda (Ghinda), Erit. 136/A2
Gingelom, Belg. 61/E2
Gingero, Eth. 135/H4
Gingin, Austl. 154/B4
Gingindlovu, SAfr. 143/E3
Gingoog, Phil. 100/D3
Gingst, Ger. 46/E4
Gīnīr, Eth. 136/B4
Ginneken, Neth. 58/B5
Ginnosar, Isr. 117/D3
Ginosa, It. 54/E2
Ginowan, Japan 97/J7
Gioia (gulf), It. 54/D3
Gioia dei Marsi, It. 71/C4
Gioia del Colle, It. 54/E2
Gioia Tauro, It. 54/D3
Giornico, Swi. 67/E5
Gioüra (isl.), Gre. 55/J3
Gioveretto (peak), It. 67/G5
Giovi (peak), It. 69/E6
Gipping (riv.), Eng, UK 43/G2
Gipsy, Mo, US 192/B2
Girard, Il, US 185/K4
Girard, Ks, US 183/G2
Girard, Pa, US 190/F3
Girardot, Col. 219/L8
Girardota, Col. 219/K6
Girardville, Qu, Can. 188/A1
Girardville, Pa, US 198/B2
Giraud (peak), Fr. 70/D4
Giraul, Ang. 140/B2
Giraul (riv.), Ang. 140/B2
Giraumont, Fr. 61/E5
Girawa, Eth. 136/B3
Girdle Ness (pt.), Sc, UK 39/D2
Giresun (prov.), Turk. 76/F4
Giresun, Turk. 76/F4
Girgnasco, It. 68/B2
Giri (riv.), D.R. Congo 138/D2
Gīrīdīh, India 109/F3
Girifalco, It. 54/E3
Girilambone, Austl. 156/C1
Girling (res.), Eng, UK 36/C2
Giromagny, Fr. 66/C2
Girón, Ecu. 216/B5
Girón, Col. 216/C3
Girona, Sp. 53/G2
Gironcourt-sur-Vraine, Fr. 66/B1
Gironde (riv.), Fr. 72/C1
Gironella, Sp. 53/F1
Girraween NP, Austl. 156/D1
Giru, Austl. 158/B2
Giruá, Braz. 225/F4
Girvan, Sc, UK 40/D1
Girvin, Tx, US 180/C2
Gisborne, NZ 159/D2
Gisborne, Austl. 157/B3
Gisenyi, Rwa. 139/G3
Gislaved, Swe. 46/E3
Gisors, Fr. 60/A5
Gissi, It. 71/D3
Gistel, Belg. 60/B1
Gistrup, Den. 46/D3
Gitarama, Rwa. 139/G3
Gitega, Buru. 139/G3
Gittsfjället (peak), Swe. 44/E2
Giubiasco, Swi. 67/F5
Giugliano in Campania, It. 71/D6
Giulianello, It. 71/B4
Giulianova, It. 71/C2
Giurgeni, Rom. 57/H3
Giurgiu, Rom. 57/G4
Giurgiu (prov.), Rom. 57/G3
Giussano, It. 68/C2
Giv'at Brenner, Isr. 117/B5
Giv'at Hayyim, Isr. 117/B4
Giv'atayim, Isr. 117/B4
Give, Den. 46/C4
Givet, Fr. 61/D3
Givors, Fr. 70/A1
Giwa, Nga. 133/G4
Giyani, SAfr. 141/F4
Gizhiga (bay), Rus. 81/R3
Gizo, Sol. 160/E5
Giżycko, Pol. 47/J4
Gjerdrum, Nor. 46/D1
Gjerlev, Den. 46/D3
Gjerstad, Nor. 46/C2
Gjirokastër, Alb. 55/G2
Gjoa Haven, Nun, Can. 170/G2
Gjøvik, Nor. 46/D1
Glabbeek, Belg. 61/E2
Glace Bay, NS, Can. 189/H2
Glacier, BC, Can. 174/F2
Glacier (peak), Wa, US 174/D3
Glacier Bay NP, Ak, US 201/L4
Glacier NP, BC, Can. 174/F2
Glacier NP, Mt, US 175/H3
Gladbeck, Ger. 58/D5
Gladbrook, Ia, US 185/H2
Glade Spring, Va, US 193/G2
Gladewater, Tx, US 181/G1
Gladsakse, Den. 45/J7
Gladsheim (peak), BC, Can. 174/F3
Gladstone, Austl. 158/C3
Gladstone, Austl. 155/H5
Gladstone, Mb, Can. 186/E2
Gladstone, Mi, US 190/C2
Gladstone, ND, US 186/C4
Gladwin, Mi, US 190/D3
Gladys, Va, US 193/H2
Glafsfjorden (lake), Swe. 46/D2
Glaisdale, Eng, UK 41/H3
Glamis, Sk, Can. 175/L2
Glamis, Sc, UK 39/D3
Glamis, Ca, US 178/E4
Glamsbjerg, Den. 46/D4
Glan (riv.), Ger. 48/D4
Glan, Phil. 100/D4
Glanamman, Wal, UK 42/C3
Glanaruddery (mts.), Ire. 38/A5
Glancy, Ms, US 194/C2
Gland, Swi. 66/C5
Gland (riv.), Fr. 61/D4
Glandon (riv.), Fr. 70/C2
Glandore, Ire. 38/A6
Glandorf, Ger. 59/F4
Glanmire, Ire. 38/B6
Glænø (isl.), Den. 45/H7
Glanworth, Ire. 38/B5
Glärnisch (range), Swi. 67/E3
Glarus, Swi. 67/F3
Glarus (canton), Swi. 67/E4
Glarus Alps (range), Swi. 51/H3
Glas Maol (peak), Sc, UK 39/C3
Glasbury, Wal, UK 42/C2
Glasco, Ks, US 184/F4
Glasgow, Sc, UK 39/B5
Glasgow (co.), Sc, UK 39/B5
Glasgow, De, US 198/C4
Glasgow, Ky, US 192/E2
Glasgow, Mt, US 175/L3
Glasgow, Va, US 193/H2
Glashütten, Ger. 64/B2
Glaslyn (riv.), Wal, UK 40/D6
Glaslyn, Sk, Can. 175/K1
Glass (lake), Sc, UK 39/B1
Glass (riv.), Sc, UK 39/B2
Glass (mts.), Tx, US 180/C2
Glassboro, NJ, US 198/C4
Glastonbury, Eng, UK 42/D4
Glatt (riv.), Swi. 67/E1
Glatt (riv.), Ger. 64/B6
Glattbach, Ger. 64/C3
Glattfelden, Swi. 67/E2
Glavinitsa, Bul. 57/H4
Glazoué, Ben. 133/F5
Glazov, Rus. 75/M4
Gleason, Wi, US 187/K5
Gleason, Tn, US 192/C2
Glebovka, Rus. 79/K4
Gleichen, Ab, Can. 175/H2
Gleisdorf, Aus. 56/B2
Glems (riv.), Ger. 64/C5
Glemsford, Eng, UK 43/G2
Glen, Mn, US 187/H4
Glen (riv.), Eng, UK 41/H6
Glen, Mt, US 177/G1
Glen (canyon), Ut, US 179/G2
Glen Allan, Ms, US 192/B4
Glen Allen, Va, US 193/J2
Glen Arbor, Mi, US 190/D2
Glen Burnie, Md, US 198/B5
Glen Canyon (dam), Az, US 179/G2
Glen Canyon Nat'l Rec. Area, Az,Ut, US 177/H4
Glen Coe (pass), Sc, UK 39/B3
Glen Cove, NY, US 199/L8
Glen Cove, Tx, US 180/E2
Glen Echo (park), Md, US 198/A6
Glen Eden, NZ 159/F6
Glen Elder, Ks, US 184/E4
Glen Flora, Tx, US 181/F3
Glen Gardner, NJ, US 198/D2
Glen Haven, Ga, US 193/M7
Glen Innes, Austl. 156/D1
Glen Lyon, Pa, US 198/B1
Glen Mòr (valley), Sc, UK 39/B2
Glen Ridge, NJ, US 199/J8
Glen Rock, NJ, US 199/J8
Glen Rock, Pa, US 198/B4
Glen Rose, Tx, US 181/F1
Glen Ullin, ND, US 186/D4
Glen Williams, On, Can. 190/T8
Glenan (isl.), Fr. 50/A3
Glenarm (riv.), NI, UK 40/C2
Glenarm, NI, UK 40/C2
Glenavon, Sk, Can. 186/C2
Glenavy, NI, UK 40/B2
Glenavy, NZ 159/B4
Glenbawn (dam), Austl. 156/D2
Glenboro, Mb, Can. 186/E3
Glenbrook, Nv, US 176/D4
Glenbrook (nbrhd.), Austl. 158/G8
Glenburn, ND, US 186/D3
Glenbush, Sk, Can. 175/L1
Glencaple, Sc, UK 40/E2
Glenclova, Zim. 141/F3
Glencoe, Ok, US 183/F2
Glencoe, Sc, UK 39/A3
Glencoe, On, Can. 190/F3
Glencoe, Il, US 197/Q15
Glencoe, Mn, US 185/G1
Glencoe, SAfr. 143/E3
Glencross, SD, US 186/D5
Glendale, Wi, US 190/C3
Glendale, Ca, US 196/F7
Glendale, Zim. 141/F3
Glendale, Az, US 179/F4
Glendale, Or, US 176/B2
Glendale, Ut, US 179/F2
Glendale, Ky, US 192/E2
Glendale, Mo, US 185/H3
Glendale, Tx, US 181/G2
Glendale Heights, Il, US 197/P16
Glenden, Austl. 158/C3
Glendive, Mt, US 186/B4
Glendo (dam), Wy, US 184/B2
Glendo (res.), Wy, US 184/B2
Glendo, Wy, US 184/B2
Glendon, NC, US 193/H3
Glendora, Ca, US 196/C2
Glendun (riv.), NI, UK 40/B1
Glenealy, Ire. 40/B6
Glenelg, Sc, UK 37/R8
Glenelg (riv.), Austl. 156/B3
Glenelg (nbrhd.), Austl. 155/M8
Glenelg, Md, US 198/B5
Glenella, Mb, Can. 186/E2
Glenelly (riv.), NI, UK 40/A2
Glenfield, NY, US 191/J3
Glengarriff, Ire. 38/A6
Glengarry (range), Austl. 154/C3
Glenluce, Sc, UK 40/D2
Glenmere (lake), NY, US 199/D1
Glenmora, La, US 194/B2
Glenmorgan, Austl. 158/C4
Glenn Heights, Tx, US 180/L7
Glennallen, Ak, US 201/J3
Glennamaddy, Ire. 38/B2
Glenns Ferry, Id, US 177/F2
Glennville, Ga, US 195/H2
Glennville, Ca, US 178/C3
Glenolden, Pa, US 198/C4
Glenoma, Wa, US 174/C4
Glenora, BC, Can. 201/M4
Glenorie, Austl. 158/H8
Glenormiston, Austl. 155/H2
Glenpool, Ok, US 183/F3
Glenrock, Wy, US 184/B2
Glenrothes, Sc, UK 39/C4
Glens Falls, NY, US 191/K3
Glenshane (pass), NI, UK 40/B2
Glenside, Pa, US 198/C3
Glenties, Ire. 37/P9
Glentrool, Sc, UK 40/D1
Glentworth, Sk, Can. 175/L3
Glenveagh NP, Ire. 37/Q9
Glenview, Il, US 197/Q15
Glenville, Ire. 38/B5
Glenville, Mn, US 185/H2
Glenville, WV, US 193/G1
Glenwood, Ab, Can. 175/H3
Glenwood, Al, US 195/E2
Glenwood, Ar, US 183/H3
Glenwood, Ga, US 193/F4
Glenwood, Ia, US 185/G3
Glenwood, Mn, US 187/G5
Glenwood, NM, US 179/H4
Glenwood, NJ, US 198/D1
Glenwood, Ut, US 179/G1
Glenwood City, Wi, US 185/H1
Gleouraich (peak), Sc, UK 39/A2
Glidden, Ia, US 185/G2
Glidden, Sk, Can. 175/K2
Glifádha, Gre. 55/N9
Glimåkra, Swe. 46/F3
Glina, Cro. 56/C3
Glinde, Ger. 59/H1
Glindow, Ger. 48/P7
Glitra (riv.), Nor. 44/R8
Glitrevatn (lake), Nor. 44/R8
Gliwice, Pol. 49/K3
Globe, Az, US 179/G4
Glockturm (peak), Aus. 67/G4
Glodeni, Mol. 78/D4
Gloggnitz, Aus. 49/H5
Głogów, Pol. 49/J3
Głogówek, Pol. 49/J3
Glomma (riv.), Nor. 44/D3
Glonn (riv.), Ger. 64/E6
Gloria (bay), Cuba 207/G1
Glorious (mt.), Austl. 158/E6
Glory of Russia (cape), Ak, US 201/D3
Glossodia, Austl. 157/E1
Glossop, Eng, UK 41/G5
Gloster, La, US 180/H1
Gloster, Ms, US 194/C2
Gloster, Ga, US 193/M7
Glostrup, Den. 45/J7
Glotovka, Rus. 77/H1
Gloucester, Ma, US 191/L3
Gloucester, On, Can. 191/J2
Gloucester, Austl. 156/D1
Gloucester, PNG 153/H1
Gloucester, Eng, UK 42/D3
Gloucester (co.), NJ, US 198/C4
Gloucester (Gloucester Court House), Va, US 193/J2
Gloucester City, NJ, US 198/C4
Gloucester Court House (Gloucester), Va, US 193/J2
Gloucester Point, Va, US 193/J2
Gloucestershire (co.), Eng, UK 42/D3
Glouster, Oh, US 190/E5
Glouthane, Ire. 38/B6
Glover, Ok, US 183/G3
Glover (isl.), Nf, Can. 189/J1
Glovers Reef (reef), Belz. 206/E2
Gloversville, NY, US 191/J3
Glovertown, Nf, Can. 189/K1
Głowno, Pol. 49/K3
Głubczyce, Pol. 49/J3
Glubokiy, Rus. 79/L3
Glubokoye, Kaz. 111/D1
Głuchołazy, Pol. 49/J3
Glücksburg, Ger. 46/C4
Glückstadt, Ger. 59/G1
Glumslöv, Swe. 45/J7
Glumsø, Den. 45/H7
Glyde (riv.), Ire. 38/D2
Glyn Heath, Wal, UK 42/C3
Glyncorrwg, Wal, UK 42/C3
Glyndon, Mn, US 186/F4
Glyndon, Md, US 198/B5
Glyngøre, Den. 46/C3
Glynn, NI, UK 40/C2
Gmünd, Aus. 49/H4
Gmunden, Aus. 65/G7
Gnagna (prov.), Burk. 133/E3
Gnarrenburg, Ger. 59/G2
Gnesta, Swe. 45/A1
Gnezdovo, Rus. 76/D1
Gniew, Pol. 47/H5
Gniezno, Pol. 49/J2
Gnjilane, Serb. 56/E4
Gnosall, Eng, UK 42/D1
Gnowangerup, Austl. 154/C5
Gō (riv.), Japan 96/C3
Go Cong, Viet. 106/D4
Go Dau Ha, Viet. 106/D4
Go Quao, Viet. 106/D4
Goa (state), India 104/B4
Goageb, Namb. 142/B2
Goālpāra, India 109/H2
Goāltor, India 109/F4
Goat Fell (peak), Sc, UK 39/A5
Goat River, BC, Can. 174/D1
Goathland, Eng, UK 41/H3
Goba, Eth. 136/A4
Goba, Moz. 143/F2
Gobabeb, Namb. 140/B4
Gobabis, Namb. 140/C4
Gobardānga, India 109/G4
Gobernador Castro, Arg. 226/F2
Gobernador Costa, Arg. 226/C5
Gobernador Crespo, Arg. 224/D4
Gobernador Duval, Arg. 226/D3
Gobernador Gregores, Arg. 227/C6
Gobernador Ingeniero Valetín Virasoro, Arg. 225/E4
Gobernador Mansilla, Arg. 227/J10
Gobi (des.), China,Mong. 83/K5
Gobindpur, India 109/E5
Göblberg (peak), Aus. 65/G6
Gobō, Japan 96/D4
Gobowen, Eng, UK 41/E6
Goch, Ger. 58/D5
Gochas, Namb. 142/B2
Gochsheim, Ger. 64/D2
Goda, Eth. 136/B4
Godāgāri, Bang. 109/G3
Godalming, Eng, UK 43/F4
Godāvari (riv.), India 83/G8
Godbout, Qu, Can. 188/D1
Goddā, India 109/F3
Godē, Eth. 136/B4
Godeanu (peak), Rom. 56/F3
Godech, Bul. 56/F4
Goderich, On, Can. 190/F3
Godfrey, Il, US 185/J4
Godhra, India 104/B3
Godinlabe, Som. 136/C4
Godinne, Belg. 61/D3
Godley, Tx, US 180/K7
Godmanchester, Eng, UK 43/F2
Gōdo, Japan 95/L5
Gödöllő, Hun. 49/K5
Godolphin Cross, Eng, UK 42/A6
Godoy Cruz, Arg. 226/C2
Gods (lake), Mb, Can. 170/G3
Gods (riv.), Mb, Can. 170/G3
Gods Mercy (bay), Nun, Can. 171/H2
Godstone, Eng, UK 36/C3
Godthåb (Nuuk), Grld. 163/M3
Godwin Austen (K2) (peak), Pak. 110/D2
Goeree (isl.), Neth. 58/A5
Goes, Neth. 58/A5
Goessel, Ks, US 183/F1
Goetzville, Mi, US 190/D1
Goff, Ks, US 185/G4
Goffstown, NH, US 191/L3
Gofitskoye, Rus. 77/G3
Gogebic (range), Mi, US 187/J4
Gogebic (lake), Mi, US 187/K4
Göggingen, Ger. 64/D6
Gogland (isl.), Rus. 47/M1
Gogo, Eth. 135/G4
Gogo, Austl. 152/B4
Gogogogo, Madg. 143/H9
Gogōme, Japan 94/B4
Gogounou, Ben. 133/F4
Gogra (riv.), India 104/D2
Gogrial, Sudan 135/F3
Goha Ts'iyon, Eth. 136/A3
Gohad, India 108/B2
Gohāna, India 110/D5
Goharganj, India 108/A4
Gohbach (riv.), Ger. 59/G3
Goiana, Braz. 219/H4
Goiandira, Braz. 222/C3
Goianésia, Braz. 222/C2
Goiânia, Braz. 222/C3
Goianinha, Braz. 219/H4
Goianira, Braz. 222/C3
Goiás, Braz. 222/C2
Goiás (state), Braz. 222/C2
Goiatuba, Braz. 222/C3
Goil (lake), Sc, UK 39/B4
Goinsargoin, China 98/C2
Goio-Erê, Braz. 225/F3
Goirle, Neth. 58/C5
Góis, Port. 52/A2
Goito, It. 69/D3
Gojam (prov.), Eth. 135/H3
Gojeb Wenz (riv.), Eth. 135/H4
Gojō, Japan 96/D3
Gojra, Pak. 110/B4
Gok (riv.), Turk. 76/E4
Goka, Japan 95/D1
Gokāk, India 107/B2
Gokase (riv.), Japan 96/B4
Gokashō, Japan 95/K5
Gokasho (bay), Japan 95/L7
Gökçeada (isl.), Turk. 114/A1
Gökçebey, Turk. 57/L5
Gökçekaya (dam), Turk. 114/B1
Göksu (riv.), Turk 114/D2
Göksun, Turk. 114/D2
Gokteik, Myan. 106/B1
Göktepe, Turk. 116/C1
Gokwe, Zim. 141/F3
Gol, Nor. 46/C1
Gola, India 109/E4
Gola Gokarannāth, India 108/C1
Golan Hts. (reg.), Syria 116/D3
Golasecca, It. 68/B2
Gölbaşı, Turk. 114/D2
Gölbaşı, Turk. 114/C2
Golbey, Fr. 66/C1
Golborne, Eng, UK 41/F5
Golconda, Il, US 192/C2
Gölcük, Turk. 57/J5
Gold (coast), Gha. 133/E5
Gold (mtn.), Wa, US 197/B2
Gold (cr.), BC, Can. 174/G3
Gold Bar, Wa, US 197/D2
Gold Beach, Fr. 63/E2
Gold Beach, Or, US 176/A2
Gold Bridge, BC, Can. 174/C2
Gold Coast, Austl. 158/D5
Gold Hill, Or, US 176/B2
Gold Point, Nv, US 178/D2
Goldach, Swi. 67/F3
Gołdap, Pol. 47/K4
Goldbach, Ger. 64/C3
Goldberg, Ger. 46/E5
Golden, NM, US 182/A3
Golden, Ire. 38/B4
Golden (bay), NZ 159/C3
Golden, Co, US 184/B4
Golden, BC, Can. 174/F2
Golden Beach, Fl, US 194/P11
Golden City, Mo, US 183/G2
Golden Gate, Fl, US 195/H4
Golden Gate (chan.), Ca, US 197/J11
Golden Gate Highlands NP, SAfr. 142/D3
Golden Gate Nat'l Recreation Area, Ca., US 178/A2
Golden Lake Ind. Res., On, Can. 191/H2
Golden Prairie, Sk, Can. 175/K2
Golden Spike Nat'l Hist. Site, Ut, US 177/G3
Golden Temple, India 110/C4
Golden Vale (plain), Ire. 38/B4
Golden Valley, Zim. 141/F3
Golden Valley, Mn, US 187/P6
Goldendale, Wa, US 174/D5
Goldene Aue (reg.), Ger. 48/F3
Goldenrod, Fl, US 194/N6
Goldenstedt, Ger. 59/F3
Goldfield, Nv, US 178/D2
Goldfield, Ia, US 185/H2
Goldkronach, Ger. 65/E2
Goldlauter, Ger. 64/D1
Goldonna, La, US 194/B1
Goldsboro, Md, US 198/C5
Goldsboro, NC, US 193/J3
Goldsboro, Tx, US 180/E1
Goldsboro (Etters), Pa, US 198/B3
Goldsworthy, Austl. 154/C2
Goldthwaite, Tx, US 181/E2
Göle, Turk. 77/G4
Goleniów, Pol. 46/F5
Golfito Nat'l Wild. Ref., CR 207/F4
Golfo Aranci, It. 54/A2
Golfo de Santa Clara, Mex. 204/B2
Gölhısar, Turk. 114/B2
Goliad, Tx, US 181/F3
Golinda, Tx, US 181/F2
Golitsyno, Rus. 75/W9
Gölköy, Turk. 76/F4
Gollach (riv.), Ger. 64/D3
Göllheim, Ger. 64/B3
Gölmarmara, Turk. 114/A2
Golmud, China 90/C4
Gololcha, Eth. 136/B3
Golomoti Station, Malw. 141/G2
Golovanovo, Rus. 74/J5
Golovin, Ak, US 201/F3
Golovino, Rus. 74/J5
Golovnina (peak), Rus. 94/D2
Golovnino, Rus. 94/D2
Golpāyegān, Iran 115/G3
Gölpazarı, Turk. 57/K5
Gols, Aus. 51/M3
Gol'shany, Bela. 47/M4
Goltry, Ok, US 183/E2
Golts, Md, US 198/C5
Golub-Dobrzyń, Pol. 49/K2
Golubovci (int'l arpt.), Mont. 56/D4
Golungo Alto, Ang. 138/C5
Golva, ND, US 186/C4
Golyam Perelik (peak), Bul. 55/J2
Golyama Kamchiya (riv.), Bul. 57/H4
Golyama Syutkya (peak), Bul. 55/J2
Goma (int'l arpt.), D.R. Congo 139/G3
Goma, D.R. Congo 139/G3
Gomantong Caves, Malay. 100/B4
Gomaringen, Ger. 64/C6
Gomati (riv.), India 108/C2
Gombari, D.R. Congo 139/G2
Gombe (riv.), Tanz. 139/G4
Gombe, Ang. 138/C4
Gombe NP, Tanz. 139/G4
Gombe-Matadi, D.R. Congo 138/C4
Gomera (isl.), Sp. 128/A4
Gomez (peak), Tx, US 180/B2
Gómez Farías, Mex. 204/D2
Gómez Palacio, Mex. 204/E3
Gomīshān, Iran 112/F1
Gommern, Ger. 48/F2
Gomo, China 111/E5
Gomoh, India 109/F4
Goms (valley), Swi. 66/E5
Gomshall, Eng, UK 36/B3
Gomshall, Eng, UK 43/F4
Gona, PNG 153/H2
Gonābād, Iran 113/G2
Gonaïves, Haiti 207/H2
Gonarezhou NP, Zim. 141/F4
Gonâve (gulf), Haiti 203/G4
Gonâve (isl.), Haiti 207/H2
Gonbad-e Qābūs, Iran 115/H2
Gönc, Hun. 49/L4
Gonçalves Dias, Braz. 219/E4
Gondā, India 108/C2
Gondal, India 113/K4
Gondelsheim, Ger. 64/B4
Gonder, Eth. 135/H2
Gonder (pol. reg.), Eth. 135/H2
Gondola Point, NB, Can. 188/E3
Gondomar, Port. 52/A2
Gondomar, Sp. 52/A1
Gondrecourt-le-Château, Fr. 66/B1
Gondreville, Fr. 61/E6
Gondrexange (lake), Fr. 61/F6
Gönen, Turk. 76/C4
Gonesse, Fr. 36/K5
Gonfaron, Fr. 70/C6
Gonfreville-L'Orcher, Fr. 63/F1
Gong Xian, China 105/H2
Gong Xian, China 92/C4
Gong'an, China 99/F3
Gongbo'gyamda, China 105/F2
Gongchangling, China 93/B2
Gongche, China 99/F4
Gongga (peak), China 98/D2
Gonggar, China 109/H1
Gongguan, China 99/F4
Gonghe, China 90/E4
Gongliu, China 111/D3
Gongo, D.R. Congo 138/D4
Gongola (riv.), Nga. 133/H4
Gongolgon, Austl. 156/C1
Gongping, China 99/G4
Gongshan Drungzu Nuzu Zizhixian, China 105/G2
Gongtian, China 99/G2
Gongwan (mts.), China 98/D3
Gongxi, China 99/G3
Gongzhuling, China 92/F2
Goñi, Uru. 227/K10
Gonja, Tanz. 137/B3
Gonjo, China 98/C2
Gónnoi, Gre. 55/H3
Gonohe, Japan 94/B3
Gonubie, SAfr. 142/D4
Gonvick, Mn, US 187/G4
Gonyú, Hun. 56/C2
Gonzaga, It. 69/D4
Gonzaga, Phil. 100/C1
Gonzales, Ca, US 178/B2
Gonzales, La, US 194/C2
Gonzales, Tx, US 181/F3
González, Mex. 205/F4
Gonzalez, Fl, US 194/E2
Goobweyn, Som. 137/C2
Goochland, Va, US 193/J2
Good Hart, Mi, US 190/D2
Good Hope, Cape of (cape), SAfr. 142/L11
Good Spirit (lake), Sk, Can. 186/C2
Goodenough (cape), Ant. 228/J
Goodes, Ga, US 193/L7
Goodfellow (A.F.B.), Tx, US 180/D2
Goodhope, Bots. 140/E5
Gooding, Id, US 177/F2
Goodland, Fl, US 195/H5
Goodland, Ks, US 184/D4
Goodman, Mo, US 183/G2
Goodman, Wi, US 187/K5
Goodna (nbrhd.), Austl. 158/E7
Goodnews Bay, Ak, US 201/F4
Goodooga, Austl. 156/C1
Goodrich, Mi, US 197/F6
Goodrich, ND, US 186/D4
Goodrich, Tx, US 181/G2
Goodridge, Mn, US 186/G3
Goodview, Mn, US 185/J1
Goodwater, Al, US 192/D4
Goodwell, Ok, US 182/D2
Goodwick, Wal, UK 42/B2
Goodwin, Ar, US 192/B3
Goodwood, SAfr. 142/L10
Gooimeer (lake), Neth. 58/C4
Goole, Eng, UK 41/H4
Goolgowi, Austl. 157/B2
Gooloogong, Austl. 157/D1
Goolwa, Austl. 155/H5
Goomalling, Austl. 154/C4
Goombalie, Austl. 156/C1
Goombungee, Austl. 158/C4
Goondiwindi, Austl. 158/C5
Goongarrie NP, Austl. 154/D4
Goor, Neth. 58/D4
Goose (riv.), ND, US 186/F4
Goose (lake), Ca, US 172/B3
Goose (cr.), Id, US 177/G2
Goose (pt.), De, US 198/C5
Goose Creek, SC, US 193/G4
Goose Green, UK 227/F6
Gooseberry (cr.), Wy, US 177/J1
Goostrey, Eng, UK 41/F5
Gopālganj, India 109/E2
Gopālganj, Bang. 109/G4
Gopālpur, Bang. 109/G3
Gopat (riv.), India 108/D3
Göppingen, Ger. 64/C5
Góra, Pol. 49/J3
Góra Kalwaria, Pol. 49/L3
Gorakhpur, India 108/D2
Gorakhpur, India 108/C4
Goras, India 108/A3
Goražde, Bosn. 56/D4
Gorchs, Arg. 227/J11
Gorczański NP, Pol. 49/L4
Gorda (pt.), Cuba 207/F1
Gorda (pt.), Nic. 207/F3
Gorda (pt.), Nic. 207/F4
Gorda (pt.), Ca, US 176/A3
Gordes, Fr. 70/B5
Gordevio, Swi. 67/E5
Gordeyevka, Rus. 76/D1
Gordil, CAfr. 134/D3
Gørding, Den. 46/C4
Gordo, Al, US 192/D4
Gordola, Swi. 67/E5
Gordon, Austl. 156/C4
Gordon (lake), Austl. 145/D5
Gordon, Sc, UK 39/D5
Gordon, Al, US 195/F2
Gordon, Ga, US 193/F4
Gordon (cr.), Ne, US 184/D2
Gordon Downs, Austl. 152/C4
Gordon Ind. Res., Sk, Can. 186/B2
Gordonsbaai, SAfr. 142/L11
Gordonsville, Va, US 193/H1
Gordonvale, Austl. 158/B2
Gore, Va, US 191/G5
Gore (mtn.), NY, US 191/J3
Goré, Chad 134/C4
Gorē, Eth. 135/G3
Gore, NZ 159/B4
Gore Bay, On, Can. 190/E2
Gore Point (cape), Ak, US 201/H4
Gorebridge, Sc, UK 39/C5
Goree, Tx, US 182/E4
Görele, Turk. 76/F4
Gorelovo (arpt.), Rus. 75/T7
Goresbridge, Ire. 38/D4
Goreville, Il, US 192/C2
Gorey, Ire. 38/D4
Gorey, Chl, UK 62/C2
Gorgān, Iran 115/H2
Gorgān (riv.), Iran 115/H2
Gorge du Loup, Lux. 61/F4
Gorges du Verdon, Fr. 70/C5
Gorges du Ziz, Mor. 128/D2
Gorgol (riv.), Mrta. 132/B2
Gorgol (pol. reg.), Mrta. 132/B3
Gorgona, Isola di (isl.), It. 68/C6
Gorgonzola, It. 68/C2
Gorgora, Eth. 135/H2
Gorham, Me, US 191/L3
Gorham, NH, US 191/L2
Gori, Geo. 77/H4
Gorinchem, Neth. 58/B5
Goring, Eng, UK 43/E3
Goring-by-Sea, Eng, UK 43/F5
Goris, Arm. 115/F2
Gorizia, It. 69/G2
Gorizia (prov.), It. 69/G1
Gorj (prov.), Rom. 57/F3
Gor'kiy (res.), Rus. 74/J4
Gørlev, Den. 45/H7
Gorlice, Pol. 49/L4
Görlitz, Ger. 49/H3
Gorllwyn (peak), Wal, UK 42/C2
Gorman, Ca, US 178/C3
Gorman, Tx, US 181/E1
Gormanstown, Ire. 40/B4
Gormī, India 108/B2
Gormley, On, Can. 190/U8
Gorna Oryakhovitsa, Bul. 57/G4
Gorner (glacier), Swi. 66/D6
Gornji Milanovac, Serb. 56/E3
Gornji Vakuf, Bosn. 56/C4
Gorno-Altaysk, Rus. 111/E1
Gornozavodsk, Rus. 75/N4
Gornyak, Rus. 76/F1
Gornyak, Rus. 111/D1
Gornyatskiy, Rus. 79/L3
Gornyy, Rus. 91/L3
Gornyy Balykley, Rus. 77/H2
Gornyy Zerentuy, Rus. 91/H1
Goro, It. 69/F4
Goro, Eth. 136/B4
Goroch'an (peak), Eth. 135/H3
Gorodets, Rus. 75/J4
Gorodok, Bela. 47/N4
Gorodovikovsk, Rus. 79/L4
Gorogoro, Indo. 103/G4
Goroka, PNG 153/G1
Gorom Gorom, Burk. 133/E3
Goromonzi, Zim. 141/F3
Gorong (isl.), Indo. 103/H4
Gorongoza, Moz. 141/G3
Gorongoza, PN da, Moz. 141/G3
Gorontalo, Indo. 103/F3
Goronyo, Nga. 133/G3
Gorredijk, Neth. 58/D3
Gorreh, Iran 115/G4
Gorron, Fr. 63/E4
Gorseinon, Wal, UK 42/B3
Gorshechnoye, Rus. 79/K2
Gorskoye, Ukr. 79/K3
Gorssel, Neth. 58/D4
Gorst, Wa, US 197/B2
Gort, Ire. 38/B3
Gorteen, Ire. 38/B2
Gortin, NI, UK 40/A2
Görwihl, Ger. 66/E2
Goryachiy Klyuch, Rus. 79/K5
Goryn' (riv.), Ukr. 76/C2
Gorzano (peak), It. 71/C2
Gorzów Wielkopolski, Pol. 49/H2
Gos, Eth. 136/C3
Gosainganj, India 108/D2
Göschenen, Swi. 67/E4
Gōse, Japan 95/J7
Gosen, Japan 97/F2
Gosford, Austl. 157/E1
Gosforth, Eng, UK 41/G2
Goshen, NS, Can. 189/G3
Goshen, In, US 190/D4
Goshen, NJ, US 198/D5
Goshen, NY, US 191/J4
Goshen, Ut, US 177/H4
Goshen Hole (lowland), Ne, Wy, US 184/B4
Goshogawara, Japan 94/B3
Goshute (lake), Nv, US 177/F3
Goshute (valley), Nv, US 177/F3
Goshute Ind. Res., Nv,Ut, US 177/F4
Goslar, Ger. 59/H5
Gosnell, Ar, US 192/C3
Gospić, Cro. 56/B3
Gosport, Eng, UK 43/E5
Gosport, Al, US 194/E2
Gosport, In, US 190/C5
Gossas, Sen. 132/A3
Gossau, Swi. 67/F3
Gossensass (Colle Isarco), It. 67/H4

Gosse – Gross
289

Gossersweiler-Stein, Ger. 61/G5
Gostepriimnyy, Rus. 77/M2
Gostilitsy, Rus. 75/S7
Gostishchevo, Rus. 79/J2
Gostivar, FYROM 55/G2
Gostyń, Pol. 49/J3
Gostynin, Pol. 49/K2
Göta (riv.), Swe. 46/G2
Gota, Eth. 136/B3
Götaland (reg.), Swe. 46/E3
Gotebo, Ok, US 182/E3
Göteborg, Swe. 46/D3
Göteborg Och Bohus (co.), Swe. 44/D4
Gotel (mts.), Cam.,Nga. 134/A4
Gotemba, Japan 97/F3
Götene, Swe. 46/E2
Gotha, Ger. 59/H7
Gothenburg, Ne, US 184/D3
Gothèye, Niger 133/F3
Gotland (isl.), Swe. 80/B4
Gotland (co.), Swe. 44/F4
Gotō (isls.), Japan 91/K5
Gotse Delchev, Bul. 55/H2
Gotska Sandön (isl.), Swe. 47/H2
Gotska Sandön NP, Swe. 47/H2
Gōtsu, Japan 96/C3
Gottenheim, Ger. 66/D1
Göttingen, Ger. 59/G5
Gottmadingen, Ger. 67/E2
Gottolengo, It. 68/D3
Gottröta, Swe. 45/B1
Götzis, Aus. 67/F3
Gouarec, Fr. 62/B4
Goubangzi, China 93/A2
Gouda, SAfr. 142/L10
Gouda, Neth. 58/B4
Goudiry, Sen. 132/B3
Gouesnou, Fr. 62/A4
Gouessant (riv.), Fr. 62/C4
Gouet (riv.), Fr. 62/C4
Gough (isl.), StH 26/J7
Gough, Ga, US 193/F4
Gouin (res.), Qu, Can. 171/J4
Goulais (riv.), On, Can. 190/D1
Goulburn, Austl. 157/D2
Goulburn (isls.), Austl. 145/C2
Goulburn, North (isl.), Austl. 152/D2
Goulburn, South (isl.), Austl. 152/D2
Gould (mt.), Austl. 154/C3
Gould, Ar, US 183/J4
Gould, Ok, US 182/E3
Gould City, Mi, US 190/D1
Gouldbusk, Tx, US 180/E2
Goulds, Nf, Can. 189/L2
Gouldsboro, Pa, US 198/C1
Gouldtown, Sk, Can. 175/L2
Goulfey, Camr. 134/B2
Goulimine, Mor. 128/C3
Goulmima, Mor. 128/D3
Goulou (peak), China 99/E3
Goulou (mts.), China 99/F4
Goumbou, Mali 132/D3
Gouménissa, Gre. 55/H2
Goundam, Mali 132/E2
Goundi, Chad 134/C3
Gounou Gaya, Chad 134/B3
Goupillières, Fr. 36/H5
Gouraye, Mrta. 132/B3
Gourcy, Burk. 133/E3
Gourdon, Fr. 50/D4
Gouré, Niger 133/H3
Gourin, Fr. 62/B4
Gourits (riv.), SAfr. 142/C4
Gourma (prov.), Burk. 133/F3
Gourma (phys. reg.), Burk. 133/F3
Gourma Rharous, Mali 133/E2
Gournay-en-Bray, Fr. 60/A5
Gouro, Chad 126/C5
Gourock, Sc, UK 39/B5
Goussainville, Fr. 36/K4
Gouvêa, Braz. 223/E3
Gouveia, Port. 52/B2
Gouverneur, NY, US 191/J2
Gouvieux, Fr. 36/K4
Gouville-sur-Mer, Fr. 62/D2
Gouvy, Belg. 61/E3
Gouyave, Gren. 203/N9
Govan, Sk, Can. 186/B2
Govardhan, India 108/A2
Gove (Gove City), Ks, US 182/D1
Goverla (peak), Ukr. 78/C3
Governador Archer, Braz. 219/E4
Governador Celso Ramos, Braz. 225/G3
Governador Dix-Sept Rosado, Braz. 219/G4
Governador Eugênio Barros, Braz. 219/E4
Governador Valadares, Braz. 223/E3
Government (hill), SD, US 186/C5
Government (peak), Mi, US 187/K4
Government (peak), Wy, US 184/B3
Government Camp, Or, US 176/C1
Government Palace, VatC. 71/G7
Governor Generoso, Phil. 100/D4
Governors (isl.), NY, US 199/J9
Govĭ Altayn (mts.), Mong. 81/K5
Govi-Altay (prov.), Mong. 90/D2
Govind Sāgar (res.), India 110/D4
Govindapalle, India 107/D2
Govindgarh, India 108/C3
Govindpur, India 107/E1
Gowanda, NY, US 191/G3
Gower (pen.), Wal, UK 42/B3
Gower, Mo, US 185/G4
Gower's Corner, Fl, US 194/L7
Gowk, Iran 113/G3
Gowna (lake), Ire. 38/C2
Gowran, Ire. 38/C4
Gowrie, Ia, US 185/G2
Goxhill, Eng, UK 41/H4
Goya, Arg. 224/E4
Göyçay, Azer. 77/H4
Goyen (riv.), Fr. 62/A4
Goyllarisquizga, Peru 220/B3
Göynük, Turk. 57/K5
Goyt (riv.), Eng, UK 41/F5
Göytäpä, Azer. 115/G2
Goz Beïda, Chad 134/D2
Goz Sassulko (dune), CAfr. 134/D3
Gozaisho-yama (peak), Japan 95/K5
Gözeli, Turk. 114/D2
Gozha (lake), China 111/D5
Gozo (isl.), Malta 73/G3
Gozzano, It. 68/B2
Graaff-Reinet, SAfr. 142/D4
Graafschap (phys. reg.), Neth. 58/D4
Græsted, Den. 45/J6
Graauw, Neth. 58/B6
Graben, Ger. 67/G1
Graberberg (peak), Namb. 142/B2
Grabouw, SAfr. 142/L11
Grabow, Ger. 48/F2
Graça Aranha, Braz. 219/E4
Gračac, Cro. 56/B3
Gračanica, Bosn. 56/D3
Grace, Id, US 177/H2
Grace City, ND, US 186/E4
Gracefield, Qu, Can. 191/H1
Gracemere, Austl. 158/C3
Gracemont, Ok, US 183/E3
Graceville, Fl, US 195/F2
Graceville, Mn, US 186/F5
Grächen, Swi. 66/D5
Grachev Kust, Rus. 77/J2
Grachëvka, Rus. 79/M5
Gracias, Hon. 206/D3
Gracias a Dios (cape), Hon. 207/F3
Graciosa (isl.), Azor., Port. 53/S12
Gradačac, Bosn. 56/D3
Gradaús, Braz. 218/D4
Gradaús, Serra dos (mts.), Braz. 218/D5
Gradisca d'Isonzo, It. 69/G2
Grado, It. 69/G2
Grädö, Swe. 45/C1
Grado, Sp. 52/B1
Grady, Al, US 195/E2
Grady, Ar, US 183/J3
Grady, Ok, US 183/F3
Graettinger, Ia, US 185/G2
Gräfelfing, Ger. 65/E6
Grafenau, Ger. 65/G5
Gräfenberg, Ger. 64/E3
Grafenrheinfeld, Ger. 64/D3
Gräfentonna, Ger. 59/H6
Grafenwöhr, Ger. 65/E3
Graffignana, It. 68/C3
Grafing bei München, Ger. 65/E6
Gråfjell (peak), Nor. 46/C1
Graford, Tx, US 183/E4
Grafrath, Ger. 67/H1
Grafton, Austl. 156/E1
Grafton, NB, Can. 188/D2
Grafton, Il, US 185/J4
Grafton, ND, US 186/F3
Grafton, Wi, US 190/C3
Grafton, WV, US 190/F5
Grafton Passage, Austl. 158/B2
Gragnano, It. 71/D6
Graham (isl.), BC, Can. 170/C3
Graham (isl.), Nun, Can. 171/S7
Graham, On, Can. 187/J3
Graham (mt.), Az, US 179/H4
Graham, Fl, US 195/G3
Graham (lake), Me, US 188/C3
Graham, NC, US 193/H2
Graham, Ok, US 183/F3
Graham, Tx, US 183/E4
Graham Bell (isl.), Rus. 80/G1
Graham Land (phys. reg.), Ant. 228/V
Grahamdale, Mb, Can. 186/E2
Grahamstown, SAfr. 142/D4
Grahamsville, NY, US 191/J4
Graian Alps (range), Fr. 72/E1
Graiguenamanagh, Ire. 38/D4
Grain (coast), Libr. 132/C5
Grain, Eng, UK 43/G4
Grainau, Ger. 67/H3
Grainfield, Ks, US 184/D4
Grajagan, Indo. 101/F5
Grajaú, Braz. 219/E4
Grajaú (riv.), Braz. 219/E4
Grajewo, Pol. 47/K5
Gram, Den. 46/C4
Gramada, Bul. 56/F4
Gramastetten, Aus. 65/H6
Gramat (plat.), Fr. 50/D4
Gramat, Fr. 50/D4
Gramatneusiedl, Aus. 57/N7
Grammont (peak), Fr. 70/D5
Grampian (mts.), Sc, UK 39/B3
Grampians NP, Austl. 156/B3
Gramsbergen, Neth. 58/D3
Gramsh, Alb. 55/G2
Gran, Nor. 46/D1
Gran (des.), Mex. 178/E4
Gran Altiplanicie Central (plat.), Arg. 227/C6
Gran Bajo de San Julián (plain), Arg. 227/C6
Gran Bajo Oriental (plain), Arg. 226/C5
Gran Canaria (int'l arpt.), Sp. 128/B4
Gran Canaria (isl.), Sp. 128/B4
Gran Chaco (plain), SAm. 209/C5
Gran Isla del Maíz (isl.), Nic. 207/F3
Gran Laguna Salada (lag.), Arg. 226/D5
Gran Paradiso (peak), It. 70/D1
Gran Paradiso, PN (Nat'l Parc), It. 51/G4
Gran Piedra (hill), Cuba 207/H2
Gran Pilastro (peak), It. 51/J3
Gran Quivira, NM, US 179/J3
Gran Sasso d'Italia (mts.), It. 71/C3
Gran Vilaya (ruin), Peru 220/B2
Grana (riv.), It. 70/D4
Granada, Co, US 182/C1
Granada, Col. 216/C4
Granada, Nic. 206/E4
Granada, Sp. 52/D4
Granadilla de Abona, Sp. 128/A3
Granados, Mex. 204/C2
Granard, Ire. 38/C2
Granarolo dell'Emilia, It. 69/E4
Granbury (lake), Tx, US 181/F1
Granbury, Tx, US 181/F1
Granby (riv.), BC, Can. 174/E3
Granby, Qu, Can. 191/K2
Granby, Co, US 184/B3
Granby, Mo, US 183/G2
Grand (lake), Nb, Can. 188/E2
Grand (canal), China 92/D4
Grand (lake), Nf, Can. 171/L4
Grand (falls), Kenya 137/B2
Grand (riv.), Ia,Mo, US 185/G3
Grand (isl.), Mi, US 187/L4
Grand Aféri, C.d'Iv. 132/E5
Grand Arc (peak), Fr. 70/C1
Grand Bahama (isl.), Bahm. 163/K7
Grand Bank, Nf, Can. 189/K2
Grand Bassa (co.), Libr. 132/C5
Grand-Bassam, C.d'Iv. 132/E5
Grand Bay, NB, Can. 188/D3
Grand Bay, Al, US 194/D2
Grand Bérard (peak), Fr. 70/C4
Grand Blanc, Mi, US 190/E3
Grand Brière (swamp), Fr. 62/C6
Grand Calumet (isl.), Qu, Can. 191/H2
Grand Canal d'Alsace (canal), Fr. 66/D2
Grand Cane, La, US 180/H1
Grand Canyon, Az, US 179/F2
Grand Canyon (canyon), Az, US 179/F2
Grand Canyon Caverns, Az, US 179/F3
Grand Canyon Nat'l Park, Az, US 179/F2
Grand Canyon-Parashant Nat'l Mon., Ut, US 179/F2
Grand Cape Mount (co.), Libr. 132/C5
Grand Cayman (isl.), Cay. 202/E4
Grand Centre, Ab, Can. 170/E3
Grand Cess, Libr. 132/C5
Grand-Charmont, Fr. 66/C2
Grand Chenier, La, US 194/B3
Grand Colombier (peak), Fr. 66/B6
Grand Combine (peak), Swi. 66/D6
Grand Coulee (dam), Wa, US 174/E4
Grand Coulee, Wa, US 174/E4
Grand-Couronne, Fr. 63/G2
Grand Drumont (peak), Fr. 66/C2
Grand Erg de Bilma (des.), Niger 126/B5
Grand Erg Occidental (des.), Alg. 119/C1
Grand Erg Oriental (des.), Alg. 119/C1
Grand Eyvia (riv.), It. 70/D1
Grand Falls, NB, Can. 188/D2
Grand Falls, Nf, Can. 189/K1
Grand Forks, BC, Can. 174/E3
Grand Forks (A.F.B.), ND, US 186/F4
Grand Forks, ND, US 186/F4
Grand-Fort-Philippe, Fr. 60/B2
Grand-Fougeray, Fr. 62/D5
Grand Gabes, Tun. 129/H2
Grand Galibier (peak), Fr. 70/C2
Grand Goâve, Haiti 207/H2
Grand Gorge, NY, US 191/J3
Grand Harbour, NB, Can. 188/D3
Grand Haven, Mi, US 190/C3
Grand Island, Ne, US 184/E3
Grand Isle, La, US 194/D3
Grand Isle, Vt, US 191/K2
Grand Jide (co.), Libr. 132/D5
Grand Junction, Co, US 177/J4
Grand Junction, Tn, US 192/C3
Grand-Lahou, C.d'Iv. 132/D5
Grand Manan (isl.), NB, Can. 188/D3
Grand Marais, Mn, US 187/J4
Grand Marais, Mb, Can. 186/F2
Grand Marsh, Wi, US 185/K2
Grand Meadow, Mn, US 185/H2
Grand Mont (pt.), Fr. 62/C5
Grand Mont Ruan (peak), Fr. 66/C5
Grand Mound, Wa, US 174/C4
Grand Muveran (peak), Swi. 66/D5
Grand North Fork (riv.), SD, US 186/C5
Grand Parpaillon (peak), Fr. 70/C4
Grand Pic de Belledonne (peak), Fr. 70/B2
Grand Pinier (peak), Fr. 70/C3
Grand-Popo, Ben. 133/F5
Grand Portage, Mn, US 187/K4
Grand Portage Ind. Res., Mn, US 187/J4
Grand Portage Nat'l Mon., Mn, US 187/K4
Grand Portal (pt.), Mi, US 190/C1
Grand Prairie, Tx, US 180/L7
Grand Prairie (plain), Ar, US 192/B3
Grand Pré Nat'l Hist. Park, NS, Can. 188/E3
Grand Queyron (peak), Fr. 70/D3
Grand Rapids, Mn, US 187/H4
Grand Rapids, ND, US 186/E4
Grand Rapids (dam), Mi, US 190/C2
Grand Rapids, Mi, US 190/D3
Grand Rhône (riv.), Fr. 50/F5
Grand Ronde, Or, US 176/B1
Grand Ronde (riv.), Wa, US 174/F4
Grand Russel (chan.), UK 62/C2
Grand Saline, Tx, US 181/G1
Grand Santi, FrG. 218/C1
Grand South Fork (riv.), SD, US 186/C5
Grand Staircase-Escalante Nat'l Mon., Ut, US 179/F2
Grand Taureau (peak), Fr. 66/C4
Grand Teton (peak), Wy, US 177/H2
Grand Teton NP, Wy, US 177/H2
Grand Tower, Il, US 192/C2
Grand Traverse (bay), Mi, US 190/D2
Grand Valley, On, Can. 190/S8
Grand Veymont (peak), Fr. 70/B3
Grand View, Id, US 176/E2
Grand, East Fork (riv.), Ia, Mo, US 185/G3
Grand, South Fork (riv.), SD, US 184/C1
Grandcamp-Maisy, Fr. 63/D2
Grandcour, Swi. 66/C4
Grande (bay), Arg. 209/C8
Grande (isl.), Braz. 222/B4
Grande (lake), Braz. 217/H5
Grande (pt.), Chile 224/B3
Grande (peak), It. 54/C4
Grande (peak), It. 71/C3
Grande (pt.), Pan. 207/G4
Grande (riv.), Uru. 227/K10
Grande (peak), NM, US 182/C2
Grande Autane (peak), Fr. 70/C3
Grande Cache, Ab, Can. 170/E3
Grande Comore (isl.), Com. 143/G5
Grande de Curuaí (lake), Braz. 218/C3
Grande de Gurupá (isl.), Braz. 218/D3
Grande de Manacapuru (lake), Braz. 218/A3
Grande de Tierra del Fuego (isl.), Chile,Arg. 227/D7
Grande do Curuaí (lake), Braz. 217/H5
Grande Miquelon (isl.), StP., Fr. 189/J2
Grande Pointe, Mb, Can. 186/F3
Grande Prairie, Ab, Can. 170/E3
Grande Ronde (riv.), Or, US 176/E1
Grande Saline, Haiti 207/H2
Grande Sassière (peak), Fr. 70/D1
Grande Séolane (peak), Fr. 70/C4
Grande, Serra (mts.), Braz. 217/F4
Grande-Anse, Qu, Can. 188/A2
Grande-Cascapédia, Qu, Can. 188/E1
Grande-Entrée, Qu, Can. 189/G2
Grande-Rivière, Qu, Can. 188/E1
Grande-Synthe, Fr. 60/B1
Grande-Terre (isl.), Guad. 203/J4
Grande-Vallée, Qu, Can. 188/E1
Grandes Jorasses (peak), It. 66/D6
Grandes Rousses (range), Fr. 70/C2
Grandfalls, Tx, US 180/C2
Grandfield, Ok, US 183/E3
Grandfresnoy, Fr. 60/B5
Grandin, Mo, US 192/B2
Grândola, Port. 52/A3
Grandpuits-Bailly-Carrois, Fr. 36/L6
Grandson, Swi. 66/C4
Grandview, Mb, Can. 186/D2
Grandview, Tx, US 181/F1
Grandview, Wa, US 174/E4
Grandview Park, Pa, US 191/G4
Grandview Plaza, Ks, US 183/F1
Grandvillars, Fr. 66/C2
Grandville, Mi, US 190/D3
Grandvilliers, Fr. 60/A4
Grâne, Fr. 70/A3
Graneros, Chile 226/N9
Graney (riv.), Ire. 38/B4
Granfjället (peak), Swe. 46/E1
Grange (nbrhd.), Austl. 155/M8
Grange (riv.), Ire. 38/B3
Grange, Eng, UK 41/F3
Grange, Mont de (peak), Fr. 66/C5
Grangemouth, Sc, UK 39/C4
Granger (mt.), Yk, Can. 201/L3
Granger, In, US 190/C4
Granger, Tx, US 181/F2
Granger, Wa, US 174/D4
Granges-sur-Vologne, Fr. 66/C1
Grängesberg, Swe. 46/F1
Grangeville, Id, US 174/F5
Granier (peak), Fr. 70/B2
Granite, Ok, US 182/E3
Granite (peak), Mt, US 177/J1
Granite (peak), Mt, US 177/G1
Granite (mtn.), Mt, US 175/J4
Granite Bay, BC, Can. 174/B2
Granite Canon, Wy, US 184/B3
Granite City, Il, US 185/J4
Granite Falls, Mn, US 185/G1
Granite Shoals, Tx, US 181/E2
Graniteville, Mo, US 192/B2
Granity, NZ 159/B3
Granja, Braz. 219/F3
Grankulla (Kauniainen), Fin. 45/E4
Grannis, Ar, US 183/G3
Granollers, Sp. 53/L6
Grans, Fr. 70/B5
Grant, Al, US 192/D3
Grant, Co, US 182/B1
Grant, Mi, US 190/D3
Grant, Mt, US 177/G1
Grant, Ne, US 184/D3
Grant (range), Nv, US 176/F4
Grant (mt.), Nv, US 176/D4
Grant City, Mo, US 185/G3
Grant-Kohrs Ranch Nat'l Hist. Site, Mt, US 175/H4
Grantham, Eng, UK 41/H6
Granton, Wi, US 185/J1
Grantown-on-Spey, Sc, UK 39/C2
Grants, NM, US 179/J3
Grants Pass, Or, US 176/B2
Grantsboro, NC, US 193/J3
Grantsburg, Wi, US 187/H5
Grantsdale, Mt, US 175/G4
Grantsville, WV, US 193/G1
Grantville, Ga, US 192/E4
Granville, Fr. 62/D3
Granville (lake), Mb, Can. 170/F3
Granville, Il, US 185/K3
Granville Ferry, NS, Can. 188/E3
Grapeland, Tx, US 181/G2
Grapeview, Wa, US 197/B3
Grapeview, Wa, US 174/C4
Grapevine, Ar, US 183/H3
Grapevine (lake), Tx, US 180/K6
Grapevine, Tx, US 180/K7
Gras-Ellenbach, Ger. 64/B3
Grasberg, Ger. 59/F2
Grasbrunn, Ger. 65/E6
Graskö (isl.), Swe. 45/C1
Graskop, SAfr. 141/F5
Grasmere, BC, Can. 174/G3
Grasmere, Eng, UK 41/E3
Grasmere, SAfr. 142/P13
Grasø (isl.), Swe. 46/H1
Grasonville, Md, US 198/B6
Grass (lake), Il, US 197/P15
Grass Creek, Wy, US 177/J2
Grass Range, Mt, US 175/K4
Grass Valley, Ca, US 176/C4
Grasse, Fr. 70/C5
Grassie, On, Can. 190/T9
Grassina, It. 69/E6
Grassington, Eng, UK 41/G3
Grasslands NP, Sk, Can. 175/L3
Grassy (peak), WV, US 193/G1
Grassy, Austl. 157/B5
Grassy Butte, ND, US 186/C4
Grassy Key (isl.), Fl, US 195/H5
Grassy Lake, Ab, Can. 175/J3
Grassy Park, SAfr. 142/L11
Grästorp, Swe. 46/E2
Grates Cove, Nf, Can. 189/L1
Gratkorn, Aus. 56/B2
Gratz, Pa, US 198/B2
Graubünden (canton), Swi. 67/F4
Graulhet, Fr. 50/E5
Graus, Sp. 53/F1
Gravatá, Braz. 219/H5
Grave, Neth. 58/C5
Grave of Sitting Bull, SD, US 186/D5
Gravedona, It. 67/F5
Gravel Island Nat'l Wild. Ref., Wi, US 190/C2
Gravelbourg, Sk, Can. 175/L3
Gravelines, Fr. 60/B2
Gravellona Toce, It. 67/E6
Gravelly, Ar, US 183/H3
Gravelotte, SAfr. 141/F4
Gravenhurst, On, Can. 191/G2
Grävenwiesbach, Ger. 64/B2
Gravesend, Eng, UK 36/E2
Graveson, Fr. 70/A5
Gravigny, Fr. 63/G2
Gravina di Puglia, It. 54/E2
Gray, Fr. 66/B3
Gray, Me, US 191/L3
Gray, Ga, US 193/F4
Grayback (mtn.), Or, US 176/B2
Grayland, Wa, US 174/B4
Grayling, Ak, US 201/F3
Grayling, Mi, US 190/D2
Grays, Eng, UK 36/E2
Grays (lake), Id, US 177/H2
Grays (har.), Wa, US 174/B4
Grays Lake NWR, Id, US 177/H2
Grayslake, Il, US 197/P15
Grayson, Sk, Can. 186/C2
Grayson, La, US 194/B1
Grayson, Ky, US 193/F1
Graysville, Al, US 192/D4
Grayville, Il, US 192/D1
Graz, Aus. 56/B2
Grazalema, Sp. 52/C4
Grazzanise, It. 71/D5
Greåker, Nor. 46/D2
Gréasque, Fr. 70/B6
Great (lake), Austl. 156/C4
Great (plain), US 182/D1
Great (isl.), Ire. 38/B6
Great (falls), Mt, US 175/J4
Great (bay), NH, US 188/B4
Great (falls), NJ, US 199/J8
Great (basin), Nv, US 172/C4
Great Abaco (isl.), Bahm. 163/K7
Great Alföld (plain), Hun., Serb. 56/D2
Great America, Ca, US 197/L12
Great Australian Bight (bay), Austl. 145/B4
Great Baddow, Eng, UK 36/E1
Great Bahama (bank), Bahm. 203/F2
Great Barford, Eng, UK 43/F2
Great Barrier (isl.), NZ 145/H6
Great Barrier (reef), Austl. 145/D2
Great Barrier Reef Marine Park, Austl. 153/G3
Great Barrington, Ma, US 191/K3
Great Barton, Eng, UK 43/G2
Great Basin NP, Nv, US 177/F4
Great Bear (lake), NW, Can. 170/D2
Great Bend, Ks, US 183/E1
Great Bend, NY, US 191/J2
Great Bitter (lake), Egypt 116/C4
Great Bookham, Eng, UK 36/B3
Great Brak (riv.), SAfr. 142/C3
Great Britain (isl.), UK 29/D3
Great Burstead, Eng, UK 36/E2
Great Cedar (swamp), NJ, US 198/D5
Great Coco (isl.), Myan. 105/F5
Great Cornard, Eng, UK 43/G2
Great Cumbrae (isl.), Sc, UK 39/B5
Great Dismal Swamp NWR, Va, US 193/J2
Great Divide (basin), Wy, US 177/J2
Great Dividing (range), Austl. 145/D2
Great Dunmow, Eng, UK 43/G3
Great Egg (har.), NJ, US 198/D5
Great Egg Harbor (riv.), NJ, US 198/D4
Great Exhibition (bay), NZ 159/C1
Great Exuma (isl.), Bahm. 163/K7
Great Falls, Mb, Can. 186/F2
Great Falls, Mt, US 175/J4
Great Falls, SC, US 193/G3
Great Fish (riv.), SAfr. 142/D4
Great Fish (pt.), SAfr. 142/D4
Great Gransden, Eng, UK 43/F2
Great Guana Cay (isl.), Bahm. 203/F3
Great Harwood, Eng, UK 41/F4
Great Himalaya (range), Asia 104/D2
Great Inagua (isl.), Bahm. 163/K7
Great Indian (des.), India,Pak. 104/B2
Great Karoo (plat.), SAfr. 142/C4
Great Kei (riv.), SAfr. 142/D4
Great Lakes Nav. Trg. Sta., Il, US 190/C3
Great Miami (riv.), Oh, US 190/D4
Great Milton, Eng, UK 43/E3
Great Mis Tor (hill), Eng, UK 42/B5
Great Missenden, Eng, UK 43/F3
Great Moose (lake), Me, US 188/C3
Great Mosque (Masjid Raya), Indo. 101/B2
Great Neck, NY, US 199/L8
Great Nicobar (isl.), India 105/F6
Great Ouse (riv.), Eng, UK 43/E2
Great Palace, Rus. 75/S7
Great Palace, Rus. 75/T7
Great Peconic (bay), NY, US 199/F2
Great Pee Dee (riv.), SC, US 193/H3
Great Piece Meadows (swamp), NJ, US 199/H8
Great Rift (valley), Afr. 139/G4
Great Ruaha (riv.), Tanz. 137/A3
Great Sacandara (lake), NY, US 191/J3
Great Salt (lake), Ut, US 163/F5
Great Salt Lake (des.), Ut, US 172/D3
Great Salt Plains (lake), Ok, US 183/E2
Great Sand (hills), Sk, Can. 175/K2
Great Sand Dunes Nat'l Park, Co, US 179/K2
Great Sand Sea (des.), Egypt,Libya 126/D2
Great Sandy (des.), Austl. 145/B2
Great Scarcies (riv.), SLeo. 132/B4
Great Shelford, Eng, UK 43/G2
Great Shunner Fell (peak), Eng, UK 41/F3
Great Slave (lake), NW, Can. 163/F3
Great Smoky Mountains NP, Tn, US 192/F3
Great South (bay), NY, US 199/E2
Great Stour (riv.), Eng, UK 43/G4
Great Torrington, Eng, UK 42/B5
Great Victoria (des.), Austl. 145/B3
Great Victoria Desert Nature Reserve, Austl. 155/E4
Great Village, NS, Can. 188/F3
Great Wall (wall), China 90/F4
Great Warley, Eng, UK 36/D2
Great Wass (isl.), Me, US 188/D3
Great Western Tiers (mts.), Austl. 156/C4
Great White Heron Nat'l Wildlife Refuge, Fl, US 195/H5
Great Winterhoek (peak), SAfr. 142/L10
Great Witley, Eng, UK 42/D2
Great Yarmouth, Eng, UK 43/H1
Great Zab (riv.), Iraq 115/E2
Great Zimbabwe (ruin), Zim. 141/F4
Greater Accra (pol. reg.), Gha. 133/F5
Greater Antilles (isls.), NAm. 163/J7
Greater Barsuki (des.), Kaz. 77/L3
Greater Buffalo (int'l arpt.), NY, US 190/V10
Greater Cincinnati (int'l arpt.), Oh, US 192/E1
Greater London (co.), Eng, UK 36/D2
Greater Manchester (co.), Eng, UK 41/F4
Greater Pittsburgh (int'l arpt.), Pa, US 190/F4
Greater Rochester (int'l arpt.), NY, US 191/H3
Greater Sunda (isls.), Indo. 102/C4
Greaterville, Az, US 179/G5
Greatham, Eng, UK 41/G2
Grebenhain, Ger. 64/C2
Grebenstein, Ger. 59/G6
Grébon (peak), Niger 133/H2
Grecco, Uru. 227/K10
Greco (cape), Cyp. 116/D2
Greco (peak), It. 71/C4
Greding, Ger. 65/E4
Gredos (mts.), Sp. 52/C2
Grée (riv.), Fr. 63/D6
Greece (ctry.) 55/G3
Greece, NY, US 191/H3
Greeley, Co, US 200/C2
Greeley, Ks, US 183/G1
Greeley (Greeley Center), Ne, US 184/E3
Greeleyville, SC, US 193/H4
Greely Ford (ford), Nun, Can. 171/S6
Green, Mi, US 187/K4
Green (lake), Wi, US 190/B3
Green (mts.), Vt, US 191/K3
Green (pond), NJ, US 199/H7
Green (riv.), Ut,Wy, US 172/E4
Green, Or, US 176/B2
Green (bay), Wi, US 185/L1
Green, Tx, US 181/F3
Green (swamp), NC, US 193/H3
Green (cape), Austl. 157/E3
Green Bay, Wi, US 190/B2
Green Bay Nat'l Wild. Ref., Wi, US 190/C2
Green City, Mo, US 185/H3
Green Cove Springs, Fl, US 195/H3
Green Creek, NJ, US 198/D5
Green Forest, Ar, US 183/H2
Green Haven, Md, US 198/B5
Green Hill, Tn, US 192/D2
Green Lake, Tx, US 180/F3
Green Lake, Wi, US 185/K2
Green Lane (res.), Pa, US 198/C3
Green Lowther (peak), Sc, UK 39/C6
Green Peter (lake), Or, US 176/B1
Green Pond, Al, US 192/D4
Green Pond, NJ, US 198/D1
Green Ridge, Mo, US 183/H1
Green River, On, Can. 190/U8
Green River, PNG 103/K4
Green River (hill), Ky, US 192/E2
Green River (lake), Ky, US 192/E2
Green River, Ut, US 179/G1
Green River, Wy, US 177/J3
Green Springs, Oh, US 190/E4
Green Valley, Az, US 179/G5
Green Valley, Ca, US 196/B1
Green Valley, Md, US 191/H5
Green Valley Lake, Ca, US 196/C2
Green Village, NJ, US 199/H9
Greenacres, Ca, US 178/C3
Greenacres City, Fl, US 194/P9
Greenbelt (park), Md, US 198/B6
Greenbelt, Md, US 198/B6
Greenbrier, Ar, US 183/H3
Greenbrier (riv.), WV, US 193/G2
Greenbush, Mn, US 186/F3
Greenbushes, Austl. 154/C5
Greencastle, Ire. 40/B1
Greencastle, In, US 190/C5
Greencastle, Pa, US 191/H5
Greencastle, Mo, US 185/H3
Greendale, Wi, US 197/Q14
Greene, NY, US 191/J3
Greene, Ia, US 185/H2
Greeneville, Tn, US 193/F2
Greenfield, Ca, US 178/B2
Greenfield, Ia, US 185/G3
Greenfield, Il, US 185/J4
Greenfield, In, US 190/D5
Greenfield, Mo, US 183/H2
Greenfield, Ma, US 191/K3
Greenfield, Nf, Can. 188/E3
Greenfield, Oh, US 190/E5
Greenfield, Tn, US 192/C2
Greenfield, Wi, US 197/P14
Greenfield Park, Qu, Can. 189/P7
Greenisland, NI, UK 40/C2
Greenland, Mi, US 187/K4
Greenland (sea) 163/R2
Greenland (Kalaallit Nunaat) (dpcy.), Den. 163/N2
Greenlaw, Sc, UK 39/D5
Greenleaf, Ks, US 185/F4
Greenmount, Md, US 198/B4
Greenock, Sc, UK 39/B5
Greenore (pt.), Ire. 38/D5
Greenore, Ire. 40/B3
Greenough (riv.), Austl. 154/B4
Greenough (mt.), Ak, US 201/K2
Greenport, NY, US 199/F1
Greens (peak), Az, US 179/H3
Greens Bayou (riv.), Tx, US 181/M9
Greensboro, Al, US 192/D4
Greensboro, Fl, US 195/F2
Greensboro, Ga, US 193/F4
Greensboro, Md, US 198/C6
Greensboro, NC, US 193/H2
Greensburg, In, US 190/D5
Greensburg, Ks, US 182/E2
Greensburg, Ky, US 192/E2
Greensburg, La, US 194/C2
Greensburg, Pa, US 191/G4
Greenspond, Nf, Can. 189/L1
Greenstreet, Sk, Can. 175/K1
Greensville, On, Can. 190/T9
Greentop, Mo, US 185/H3
Greenup, Ky, US 193/F1
Greenup, Il, US 192/C1
Greenvale, Austl. 158/B2
Greenville, Libr. 132/C5
Greenville, Al, US 194/E2
Greenville, Ca, US 176/C3
Greenville, Fl, US 195/G2
Greenville, Ga, US 192/E4
Greenville, Ky, US 192/D2
Greenville, Il, US 185/K4
Greenville, Mi, US 190/D3
Greenville, Mo, US 192/B2
Greenville, Ms, US 192/B4
Greenville, NC, US 193/J3
Greenville, Oh, US 190/D4
Greenville, SC, US 193/F3
Greenville, Tx, US 183/F4
Greenville, Ut, US 179/F1
Greenwater (riv.), Wa, US 197/D3
Greenwell Point, Austl. 157/E2
Greenwich, Oh, US 190/E4
Greenwich (pt.), Ct, US 199/L8
Greenwich (bor.), Eng, UK 36/D2
Greenwich, Ct, US 199/L7
Greenwich Observatory, Eng, UK 36/D2
Greenwich Village (nbrhd.), NY, US 199/K9
Greenwood, On, Can. 190/U8
Greenwood, Ar, US 183/G3
Greenwood, De, US 198/C6
Greenwood, Fl, US 195/F2
Greenwood, In, US 190/C5
Greenwood, Ms, US 192/B4
Greenwood, SC, US 193/F3
Greenwood (lake), SC, US 193/F3
Greenwood Lake, NY, US 199/D1
Greenwood Village, Co, US 182/B1
Greer, SC, US 193/F3
Greers Ferry (dam), Ar, US 183/J3
Greers Ferry, Ar, US 183/H3
Greers Ferry (lake), Ar, US 192/A3
Greeson (lake), Ar, US 183/H3
Grefrath, Ger. 58/D6
Gregoire Kayibanda (Kigali) (int'l arpt.), Rwa. 139/G3
Gregório (riv.), Braz. 220/D2
Gregory (peak), NC, US 192/F3
Gregory, SD, US 184/E2
Gregory (riv.), Austl. 153/E4
Gregory (range), Austl. 145/D2
Gregory (lake), Austl. 145/B3
Gregory Lake Abor. Land, Austl. 152/B5
Greifswald, Ger. 46/E4
Greifwalder Bodden (bay), Ger. 49/G1
Greilickville, Mi, US 190/D2
Greimberg (peak), Aus. 51/L3
Gremikha, Rus. 74/H1
Gremyachinsk, Rus. 75/N4
Grenå, Den. 46/D3
Grenada (ctry.) 203/N9
Grenada, Ms, US 192/C4
Grenada (lake), Ms, US 192/C4
Grenade, Fr. 50/D5
Grenay, Fr. 60/B3
Grenchen, Swi. 66/D3
Grenfell, Sk, Can. 186/C2
Grenfell, Austl. 157/D1
Grennach (riv.), Ger. 64/D6
Grenoble, Fr. 70/B2
Grenola, Ks, US 183/F2
Grenora, ND, US 186/C3
Grenville (cape), Austl. 153/F2
Grenzach-Wyhlen, Ger. 66/D2
Gréoux-les-Bains, Fr. 70/B5
Gresham, Or, US 176/B1
Gresham Park, Ga, US 193/M7
Gresik, Indo. 101/F4
Gressåmoen NP (nat'l park), Nor. 74/B2
Gressåmoen NP, Nor. 44/E2
Gressan, It. 70/D1
Gresse (riv.), Fr. 70/B3
Gresston, Ga, US 195/G1
Grésy-sur-Aix, Fr. 70/B1
Greta (riv.), Eng, UK 41/E2
Gretna, Austl. 156/C4
Gretna, Mb, Can. 186/F3
Gretna, Sc, UK 41/E2
Gretna, Fl, US 195/F2
Gretna, La, US 194/C3
Gretna, Va, US 193/H2
Gretton, Eng, UK 43/F1
Grettstadt, Ger. 64/D3
Gretz-Armainvilliers, Fr. 36/L5
Greve (riv.), It. 69/E5
Greve, Den. 45/J7
Greve in Chianti, It. 69/E6
Grevelingendam (dam), Neth. 58/B5
Greven, Ger. 59/E4
Grevená, Gre. 55/G2
Grevenbroich, Ger. 61/F1
Grevenmacher (dist.), Lux. 61/F4
Grevenmacher, Lux. 61/F4
Grevesmühlen, Ger. 48/F2
Grevlingen (chan.), Neth. 58/A5
Grey (cape), Austl. 153/E3
Grey (range), Austl. 145/D3
Grey (riv.), Nf, Can. 189/J2
Grey (pt.), NI, UK 40/C2
Grey Abbey, NI, UK 40/C2
Grey Peaks NP, Austl. 158/B2
Grey River, Nf, Can. 189/J2
Greybull (riv.), Wy, US 177/J1
Greybull, Wy, US 177/J1
Greycliff, Mt, US 175/K5
Greylingstad, SAfr. 142/E2
Greylock (mt.), Ma, US 191/K3
Greymouth, NZ 159/B3
Greystoke, Eng, UK 41/F2
Greystones, Ire. 40/B5
Greytown, NZ 159/J9
Greytown, SAfr. 143/E3
Grez-Doiceau, Belg. 61/D2
Grezzana, It. 69/E2
Gribanovskiy, Rus. 79/L2
Gribbin (pt.), Eng, UK 42/B6
Gribingui (riv.), CAfr. 134/C4
Gribingui (pref.), CAfr. 134/C4
Gribingui-Bamingui, Rsv. de Faune du, CAfr. 134/C4
Gridley, Ca, US 176/C4
Gridley, Il, US 185/K3
Gridley, Ks, US 183/G1
Griefensee (lake), Swi. 67/E3
Griekwastad, SAfr. 142/C3
Griend (isl.), Neth. 58/C2
Gries am Brenner, Aus. 67/H3
Griesheim, Ger. 64/B3
Grieskirchen, Aus. 65/G6
Griesskogel (peak), Aus. 67/H3
Griesstätt, Ger. 65/F7
Griffin, Sk, Can. 186/C3
Griffin (lake), Fl, US 194/M6
Griffin, Ga, US 192/E4
Griffiss (A.F.B.), NY, US 191/J3
Griffith, Austl. 157/C2
Griffith, In, US 197/R16
Griffith Park, Ca, US 196/F7
Griffithville, Ar, US 183/J3
Grifton, NC, US 193/J3
Griggs, Ok, US 182/C2
Grigna (peak), It. 67/F6
Grignan, Fr. 70/A4
Grignano Polesine, It. 69/E3
Grignon, Fr. 70/C1
Grigny, Fr. 70/A1
Grigny, Fr. 36/K6
Grigoriopol, Mol. 78/E4
Grigor'yevskoye, Rus. 74/H5
Grijalva (riv.), Mex. 206/C2
Grijpskerk, Neth. 58/D2
Grillby, Swe. 45/A1
Grillon, Fr. 70/A4
Grim (cape), Austl. 156/C4
Grimari, CAfr. 134/D4
Grimaud (riv.), Fr. 70/C6
Grimaud, Fr. 70/C6
Grimbergen, Belg. 61/D2
Grimesland, NC, US 193/J3
Grimethorpe, Eng, UK 41/G4
Grimisuat, Swi. 66/D5
Grimmen, Ger. 46/E4
Grimsby, Eng, UK 41/H4
Grimsby, On, Can. 190/T9
Grimselpass (pass), Swi. 67/E4
Grimsey (isl.), Ice. 44/N6
Grimsley, Tn, US 192/E2
Grimstad, Nor. 46/C2
Grindavík, Ice. 44/M7
Grindelwald, Swi. 66/E4
Grindsted, Den. 46/C4
Grinnel (pen.), Nun, Can. 171/S7
Grinnell, Ia, US 185/H3
Grintavec (peak), Slov. 51/L3
Griqualand East (reg.), SAfr. 142/E3
Griqualand West (reg.), SAfr. 142/C2
Gris-Nez (cape), Fr. 60/A2
Grise Fiord, Nun, Can. 171/S7
Grisslehamn, Swe. 47/H1
Griswold, Ia, US 185/G3
Grisy-les-Plâtres, Fr. 36/J4
Grisy-Suisnes, Fr. 36/L5
Grivaï Pamia, CAfr. 134/C4
Grivette (riv.), Fr. 36/L4
Grizzly (bay), Ca, US 197/K10
Grizzly (mtn.), Id, US 174/F4
Grizzly Flats, Ca, US 176/C4
Grmeč (mts.), Bosn. 56/C3
Groaíras, Braz. 219/F3
Grobbendonk, Belg. 58/B6
Gröben, Ger. 48/Q7
Gröbenzell, Ger. 65/E6
Grobiņa, Lat. 47/J3
Groblersdal, SAfr. 141/F5
Groblershoop, SAfr. 142/C3
Grödby, Swe. 45/A1
Grodków, Pol. 49/J3
Grodzisk Wielkopolski, Pol. 49/J2
Grodzyanka, Bela. 47/N5
Groenlo, Neth. 58/D4
Groesbeck, Tx, US 181/F2
Groesbeek, Neth. 58/C5
Groix, Fr. 62/B5
Groix (isl.), Fr. 50/B3
Grójec, Pol. 49/L3
Grömitz, Ger. 46/D4
Grombalia, Tun. 130/M6
Gromo, It. 67/F6
Gronau, Ger. 59/G4
Gronau, Ger. 58/E4
Grong Grong, Austl. 157/C2
Groningen (prov.), Neth. 58/D2
Groningen, Sur. 218/C1
Groningen, Neth. 58/D2
Gronlait (peak), It. 67/H5
Gronlid, Sk, Can. 175/M1
Grono, Swi. 67/F5
Groom, Tx, US 182/D3
Groot Kleeberg (mts.), Namb. 140/C4
Groot Marico (riv.), SAfr. 141/E5
Groot Waterberg (mts.), Namb. 140/C4
Groot-Letabarivier (riv.), SAfr. 141/F4
Groot-Marico, SAfr. 140/E5
Groot-Marico (riv.), SAfr. 142/D2
Grootberg (peak), Namb. 140/B4
Grootdraaidam (res.), SAfr. 142/Q13
Groote Eylandt (isl.), Austl. 145/C2
Grootegast, Neth. 58/D2
Grootfontein, Namb. 140/C3
Grootgeluk, SAfr. 141/E4
Grootvloer (salt pan), SAfr. 142/C3
Gropello Cairoli, It. 68/B3
Gros Islet, StL. 203/N9
Gros Morne (peak), Nf, Can. 171/L4
Gros Morne NP, Nf, Can. 189/J1
Gros Ventre (riv.), Wy, US 177/H2
Gros-Morne, Qu, Can. 188/E1
Grosbliederstroff, Fr. 61/G5
Grosio, It. 67/G5
Grosne (riv.), Fr. 50/F3
Grosnez (pt.), Chl, UK 62/C2
Grosrouvre, Fr. 36/H5
Gross Barmen, Namb. 140/C4
Gross Bieberau, Ger. 64/B3
Gross Oesingen, Ger. 59/H3
Gross Spitzkoppe (peak), Namb. 140/B4
Gross Unstadt, Ger. 64/B3
Gross-Enzersdorf, Aus. 57/P7
Gross-Gerungs, Aus. 49/H4
Gross-Zimmern, Ger. 64/B3
Grossa (pt.), Braz. 218/D2
Grossaitingen, Ger. 67/G1
Grossalmerode, Ger. 59/G6
Grossbeeren, Ger. 48/Q7
Grossbottwar, Ger. 64/C5

Halim – Heesl
291

Halim Perdana Kusuma (int'l arpt.), Indo. 101/D4
Haliun, Mong. 90/D2
Haljala, Est. 47/M2
Häljarp, Swe. 45/J7
Halkett (cape), Ak, US 201/H1
Hall, Austl. 157/B2
Hall (pt.), Austl. 152/B3
Hall (isls.), Micr. 160/E4
Hall (pen.), Nun, Can. 171/K2
Hall (isl.), Ak, US 201/D3
Hall, Mt, US 175/H4
Hall Beach, Nun, Can. 171/H2
Hall Park, Ok, US 183/F3
Halla-san (peak), SKor. 91/K5
Halladale (riv.), Sc, UK 37/S7
Hallam (peak), BC, Can. 174/E1
Hallam (Hellam), Pa, US 198/B4
Halland (co.), Swe. 44/E4
Hallandale, Fl, US 194/P11
Hällbybrunn, Swe. 46/G2
Halle, Ger. 80/B4
Halle, Belg. 61/D2
Halle, Ger. 59/F4
Halle-Neustadt, Ger. 48/F3
Halleck, Nv, US 176/F3
Hällefors, Swe. 46/F2
Hälleforsnäs, Swe. 46/G2
Hallein, Aus. 51/K3
Hallenberg, Ger. 59/F6
Hallertau (reg.), Ger. 65/E5
Hallettsville, Tx, US 181/F3
Halley, UK, Ant. 228/Y
Halliday, ND, US 186/C4
Halling, Eng, UK 36/E3
Hallingdalselvi (riv.), Nor. 46/C1
Hallock, Mn, US 186/F3
Halls, Tn, US 192/C3
Halls Creek, Austl. 152/B4
Hallsberg, Swe. 46/F2
Hallstahammar, Swe. 46/G2
Hallstavik, Swe. 46/H1
Hallsville, Tx, US 181/G1
Hallu (riv.), Fr. 48/B4
Halluin, Fr. 60/C2
Hallum, Neth. 58/C2
Hallwang, Aus. 65/G7
Hallwilersee (lake), Swi. 66/E3
Hallyŏ Haesang NP, SKor. 96/A3
Halmahera (isl.), Indo. 83/M9
Halmahera (sea), Indo. 103/G4
Halmstad, Swe. 46/E3
Hals, Den. 46/D3
Hälsingborg (Helsingborg), Swe. 46/E3
Halstead, Ks, US 183/F1
Halstead, Eng, UK 43/G3
Halsteren, Neth. 58/B5
Haltang (riv.), China 90/C4
Haltemprice, Eng, UK 41/H4
Haltern, Ger. 59/E5
Haltom City, Tx, US 180/K7
Halton (co.), On, Can. 190/T8
Halton (co.), Eng, UK 41/F5
Halton Hills, On, Can. 190/T8
Haltwhistle, Eng, UK 41/F2
Haludpukhur, India 109/F4
Halver, Ger. 59/E6
Halverder Aa (riv.), Ger. 59/E4
Ham, Fr. 60/C4
Ham, Chad 134/B3
Ham Lake, Mn, US 187/H5
Ham River, Namb. 142/B3
Ham, Oued El (riv.), Alg. 130/G5
Ham-sous-Varsberg, Fr. 61/F5
Hamada, Japan 96/C3
Hamada de Tinrhert (plat.), Alg. 129/G4
Hamada du Drâa (plat.), Alg. 128/D3
Hamada Safia (plat.), Mali 128/D5
Hamadān, Iran 115/G3
Hamadān (gov.), Iran 115/G3
Hamādat Marzūq (plat.), Libya 129/H4
Ḩamādat Tinghert (uplands), Libya 129/H3
Ḩamāh, Syria 116/E2
Ḩamāh (prov.), Syria 116/E2
Hamajima, Japan 95/L7
Hamakita, Japan 97/E3
Hamam, Turk. 116/E1
Hamamatsu, Japan 97/E3
Hamami (reg.), Mrta. 128/C5
Hamanaka, Japan 94/D2
Hamar, Nor. 46/D1
Ḩamāţah (peak), Egypt 127/G3
Hamath Tiberias NP, Isr. 117/D3
Hamatombetsu, Japan 94/C1
Hambergen, Ger. 59/F2
Hamble, Eng, UK 43/E5
Hambleton (hills), Eng, UK 41/G3
Hambühren, Ger. 59/G3
Hamburg, Ar, US 183/J4
Hamburg, Ger. 59/G1
Hamburg (state), Ger. 46/D5
Hamburg, Ia, US 185/G3
Hamburg, NJ, US 198/D1
Hamburg, NY, US 191/G3
Hamburg, Pa, US 198/C2
Hamburg (Fuhlsbüttel) (int'l arpt.), Ger. 59/G1
Ḩamḑ (wadi), SAr. 112/C3
Ḩamḑah, SAr. 112/D5
Ḩamdānah, SAr. 112/D5
Hamden, Ct, US 191/K4
Hamden, NY, US 191/J3
Hamden, Oh, US 193/F1
Häme (prov.), Fin. 44/G3
Hämeenkyrö, Fin. 47/K1
Hämeenlinna, Fin. 47/L1
Hamelin, Austl. 154/B3
Hamelin Pool (bay), Austl. 154/B3
Hameln, Ger. 59/G4
Hamero Hadad, Eth. 136/B4
Hamersley (range), Austl. 145/A3
Hamersley Range NP, Austl. 154/C2
Hamersville, Oh, US 192/F1
Hamford Water (inlet), Eng, UK 43/H3
Hamgyŏng (mts.), NKor. 91/K3
Hamgyŏng-bukto (prov.), NKor. 93/E2
Hamgyŏng-namdo (prov.), NKor. 93/D2
Hamhŭ-si (prov.), NKor. 93/D3
Hamhŭng, NKor. 93/D3
Hami, China 90/C3
Ḩamīdīyeh, Iran 115/G4
Hamill, SD, US 184/E2
Hamilton, Austl. 156/B3
Hamilton, On, Can. 190/T9
Hamilton (har.), On, Can. 190/T9
Hamilton (inlet), Nf, Can. 163/M4
Hamilton, NZ 159/C2
Hamilton, Sc, UK 39/B5
Hamilton, Al, US 192/D3
Hamilton (mt.), Ca, US 197/L12
Hamilton, Co, US 177/K3
Hamilton (lake), Fl, US 194/M7
Hamilton, Ga, US 192/E4
Hamilton, Ks, US 183/F2
Hamilton, Mi, US 190/C3
Hamilton, Mo, US 185/H4
Hamilton, Mt, US 175/G4
Hamilton, NY, US 191/J3
Hamilton (mtn.), NY, US 191/J3
Hamilton, Oh, US 190/D5
Hamilton, Tx, US 181/E2
Hamilton Mil. Res., NY, US 199/J9
Hamilton-Wentworth (co.), On, Can. 190/S9
Ḩamīm (wadi), Libya 126/D2
Hamina, Fin. 47/M1
Hamiota, Mb, Can. 186/D2
Hamīrpur, India 110/D4
Hamīrpur, India 108/C3
Hamju, NKor. 93/D3
Hamlet, NC, US 193/H3
Hamlin, Tx, US 182/D4
Hamlin, WV, US 193/F1
Hamm, Ger. 61/G2
Hamm, Ger. 64/B3
Hamm, Ger. 59/E5
Hamma-Bouziane, Alg. 130/K6
Hammam Lif, Tun. 130/M6
Hammamet, Tun. 130/M6
Hammamet (gulf), Tun. 130/M6
Hammanskraal, SAfr. 141/F5
Hammarland, Fin. 47/H1
Hammarön (isl.), Swe. 46/E2
Hammarsjön (lake), Swe. 45/L7
Hammarstrand, Swe. 44/F3
Hamme, Belg. 61/D1
Hamme (riv.), Ger. 59/F2
Hammel, Den. 46/C3
Hammelburg, Ger. 64/C2
Hammer (cr.), Pa, US 198/B3
Hammerfest, Nor. 44/G1
Hammershus, Den. 46/F4
Hammersmith and Fulham (bor.), Eng, UK 36/A1
Hammett, Id, US 176/F2
Hamminkeln, Ger. 58/D5
Hammon, Ok, US 182/E3
Hammonasset (pt.), Ct, US 199/F1
Hammond, In, US 190/C4
Hammond, La, US 194/C2
Hammond, Mt, US 184/B1
Hammond Street, Eng, UK 36/C1
Hammonton, NJ, US 198/D4
Hamnvik, Nor. 44/F1
Hamois, Belg. 61/E3
Hamon, Congo 138/C4
Hamont-Achel, Belg. 58/C6
Hamoud, Mrta. 132/C3
Hampden, ND, US 186/E3
Hampden, NZ 159/B4
Hampden Sydney, Va, US 193/H2
Hampshire, Il, US 185/K2
Hampshire Downs (hills), Eng, UK 43/E4
Hampstead (nbrhd.), Eng, UK 36/C2
Hampstead, Md, US 198/B4
Hampton, Ar, US 183/H4
Hampton, Fl, US 195/G3
Hampton, Ia, US 185/H2
Hampton, NB, Can. 188/E3
Hampton, NH, US 191/L3
Hampton, Or, US 176/C2
Hampton, Pa, US 198/A4
Hampton, SC, US 193/G4
Hampton, Tn, US 193/F2
Hampton, Va, US 193/J2
Hampton Bays, NY, US 199/F2
Hampton Court, Eng, UK 36/C2
Hampton Nat'l Hist. Site, Md, US 198/B5
Hampton Park (nbrhd.), Austl. 156/G6
Hampton Roads (est.), Va, US 193/J2
Hamp'yŏng, SKor. 93/D5
Ḩamrat ash Shaykh, Sudan 135/E2
Hamtramck, Mi, US 197/F7
Hamuku, Indo. 103/J4
Hamura, Japan 95/C2
Hamyang, SKor. 93/D5
Hamyŏl, SKor. 93/D4
Han (riv.), China 83/M6
Hana (riv.), India 108/C5
Hanahan, SC, US 193/G4
Hanainef, Erit. 136/B2
Hanak, Turk. 77/G4
Ḩanak, SAr. 127/H3
Hanamaki, Japan 94/B4
Hanan, Eth. 136/C4
Hanang (peak), Tanz. 137/A3
Hanau, Ger. 64/B2
Hanazono, Japan 95/C1
Hanceville, Al, US 192/D3
Hancheng, China 92/B4
Hanches, Fr. 63/G3
Hancock (lake), Fl, US 194/M8
Hancock, Md, US 191/G5
Hancock, Mi, US 187/K4
Hancock, Mn, US 186/G5
Hancock, NY, US 191/J4
Hancock, Wi, US 185/K1
Hancocks Bridge, NJ, US 198/C5
Handa, Japan 95/L6
Handae-ri, NKor. 93/D2
Handan, China 92/C3
Handawor, India 110/C2
Handel, Sk, Can. 175/K1
Handeloh, Ger. 59/G2
Handen, Swe. 45/B1
Handeni, Tanz. 137/B3
Handiā, India 108/D3
Handsworth, Sk, Can. 186/C3
Handsworth, Eng, UK 43/E1
Hanford, Ca, US 178/C2
Hanford Reach Nat'l Mon., Wa, US 174/E4
Hanford Site, Wa, US 174/E4
Hangayn (mts.), Mong. 80/K5
Hanggin Qi, China 92/B3
Hanging Rock (mtn.), NC, US 193/G2
Hangingstone (hill), Eng, UK 42/C5
Hangklip (cape), SAfr. 142/L11
Hangman (cr.), Wa, US 174/F4
Hangö (Hanko), Fin. 47/K2
Hangu, Pak. 110/A3
Hangu, China 92/H7
Hangzhou, China 92/L9
Hangzhou (bay), China 92/L9
Hanhofen, Ger. 64/B4
Hanhöhiy (mts.), Mong. 90/C2
Hani, Turk. 114/E2
Haninge, Swe. 46/H2
Hanja (riv.), Ang. 140/B2
Hanjalipan, Indo. 102/D4
Hanjiang, China 99/H3
Hankensbüttel, Ger. 59/H3
Hankey, SAfr. 142/D4
Hankinson, ND, US 186/F4
Hanko (Hangö), Fin. 47/K2
Hanle, India 111/C5
Hanley, Sk, Can. 175/L2
Hanmer, NZ 159/C3
Hann (mt.), Austl. 152/B3
Hanna, La, US 194/B2
Hanna, Ab, Can. 175/J2
Hannaford, ND, US 186/E4
Hannah, ND, US 186/E3
Hannahs Mill, Ga, US 192/E4
Hannan, Japan 95/H7
Hannibal, Mo, US 185/J4
Hannibal, NY, US 191/H3
Hannibal, Oh, US 190/F5
Hanningfield (res.), Eng, UK 36/E2
Hannō, Japan 95/C2
Hannover, Ger. 59/G4
Hannover (int'l arpt.), Ger. 59/G4
Hannut, Belg. 61/E2
Hanöbukten (bay), Swe. 44/E5
Hanoi (Ha Noi) (cap.), Viet. 98/E4
Hanover, On, Can. 190/F2
Hanover (isl.), Chile 227/B6
Hanover, SAfr. 142/D3
Hanover, Il, US 185/J2
Hanover, In, US 192/E1
Hanover, Ks, US 185/F4
Hanover, Mn, US 187/N6
Hanover, NH, US 191/K3
Hanover, Pa, US 198/B4
Hanover, Va, US 193/J2
Hanover Park, Il, US 197/P16
Hānsdiha, India 109/F3
Hansen (dam), Ca, US 196/F7
Hanshan, China 92/D5
Hānsi, India 110/C5
Hanska (lake), Mn, US 185/G1
Hanson (bay), NZ 159/E3
Hanstedt, Ger. 59/H2
Hanstholm, Den. 46/C3
Hanston, Ks, US 182/E1
Hansville, Wa, US 197/B2
Hantengri Feng (peak), China 111/D3
Hantsport, NS, Can. 188/E3
Hantzsch (riv.), Nun, Can. 171/J2
Hanumāngarh, India 110/C5
Hanuy (riv.), Mong. 90/E2
Hanwood, Austl. 157/C2
Hanyū, Japan 95/D1
Hanyuan, China 98/D2
Hanza, Ang. 138/C5
Hanzhong, China 90/F5
Hao (isl.), FrPol. 161/L6
Haoshan, China 99/G3
Haouach, Ouadi (riv.), Chad 134/D1
Håøya (isl.), Nor. 44/S8
Haparanda, Swe. 74/E2
Hapch'ŏn, SKor. 93/E5
Hapeville, Ga, US 193/M7
Happy Camp, Ca, US 176/B3
Happy Jack, Az, US 179/G3
Happy Jack, La, US 194/D3
Happy Valley (res.), Austl. 155/M9
Happy Valley-Goose Bay, Nf, Can. 171/K3
Haptŏk, SKor. 93/D4
Hāpur, India 108/A1
Ḩaql, SAr. 127/G2
Haquira, Peru 220/C4
Har (lake), Mong. 90/C2
Har Karmel (peak), Isr. 117/C3
Har Meron (peak), Isr. 117/C3
Har Nur, China 91/J2
Har Ramon (peak), Isr. 116/D4
Har Tavor (peak), Isr. 117/C3
Har Us (lake), Mong. 90/C2
Har-Ayrag, Mong. 90/F2
Har-Us (riv.), Mong. 90/D2
Hara, Japan 95/A2
Haraa (riv.), Mong. 90/F2
Ḩaraḑ, SAr. 112/E4
Ḩaraḑ, Yem. 136/B1
Ḩarajah, SAr. 112/D5
Haramachi, Japan 97/G2
Harappa (ruin), Pak. 110/B4
Harare (cap.), Zim. 141/F3
Harare (int'l arpt.), Zim. 141/F3
Haravilliers, Fr. 36/J4
Haraz, Chad 134/C2
Haraze-Mangueigne, Chad 134/D3
Harbel, Libr. 132/C5
Harbeson, De, US 198/C6
Harbin, China 91/K2
Harbiye, Turk. 116/E1
Harbonnières, Fr. 60/B4
Harboøre, Den. 46/C3
Harbor Beach, Mi, US 190/E3
Harbor City (nbrhd.), Ca, US 196/F8
Harbor Springs, Mi, US 190/D2
Harbour Breton, Nf, Can. 189/K2
Harbour Grace, Nf, Can. 189/L2
Harbour Main, Nf, Can. 189/L2
Harburg, Ger. 59/G2
Harburg, Ger. 64/D5
Harbury, Eng, UK 43/E2
Hårby, Den. 46/D4
Hard, Aus. 67/F3
Hardā, India 104/C3
Hardangervidda NP, Nor. 46/B1
Hardap (dam), Namb. 140/C5
Hardau (riv.), Ger. 59/H3
Hardaway, Al, US 192/E4
Hardee (co.), Fl, US 194/M8
Hardeeville, SC, US 193/G4
Hardegsen, Ger. 59/G5
Hardelot-Plage, Fr. 60/A2
Harden City, Ok, US 183/F3
Hardenberg, Neth. 58/D3
Harderwijk, Neth. 58/C4
Hardesar, India 110/C5
Hardheim, Ger. 64/C3
Hardin, Ky, US 192/C2
Hardin, Il, US 185/J4
Hardin, Mt, US 175/L5
Hardin, Tx, US 181/G2
Harding, SAfr. 143/E3
Harding (res.), Ga, US 192/E4
Hardinsburg, Ky, US 192/D2
Hardisty, Ab, Can. 175/J1
Hardoi, India 108/C2
Hardoi Branch (riv.), India 108/C2
Hardricourt, Fr. 36/H4
Hardscrabble Wash (riv.), Az, US 179/H3
Hardtner, Ks, US 183/E2
Hardwār, India 113/L3
Hardwick, Ga, US 193/F4
Hardwood (mtn.), Me, US 191/L1
Hardy, Ar, US 183/J2
Hardy, Ne, US 184/F3
Hardy (pen.), Chile 227/C7
Hare Bay, Nf, Can. 189/K1
Hare Dimona (peak), Isr. 116/D4
Harefield, Eng, UK 36/B2
Harelbeke, Belg. 60/C2
Haren, Ger. 59/E3
Haren, Neth. 58/D2
Hārer, Eth. 136/B3
Harerge (prov.), Eth. 136/B3
Harewa, Eth. 136/B3
Harfleur, Fr. 63/F1
Harford (co.), Md, US 198/B4
Hargele, Eth. 136/B4
Hargesheim, Ger. 61/G4
Hargeville, Fr. 36/H5
Hargeysa, Som. 136/C3
Hargeysa (int'l arpt.), Som. 136/C3
Harghita (prov.), Rom. 57/G2
Harghita (peak), Rom. 57/G2
Hargīgo, Erit. 136/A2
Harhorin, Mong. 90/E2
Hari (str.), Est. 47/K2
Hari (river), Indo. 101/C3
Hari (riv.), Indo. 102/B4
Ḩarīb, Yem. 136/C2
Haribes, Namb. 140/C5
Harihar, India 107/B3
Hariharganj, India 109/E3
Harīke, India 110/C4
Ḩārim, Syria 116/E1
Harima (sea), Japan 96/D3
Harima (bay), Japan 95/G6
Harima, Japan 95/G6
Ḩarīmā, Jor. 117/D3
Haringey (bor.), Eng, UK 36/C2
Haringhāta (riv.), Bang. 109/G4
Haringvliet (chan.), Neth. 58/B5
Haringvlietdam (dam), Neth. 58/B5
Harīpur, Pak. 110/B3
Harīrūd (riv.), Afg. 83/F6
Ḩāris, WBnk. 117/C4
Harisal, India 104/C3
Harjavalta, Fin. 47/K1
Harker Heights, Tx, US 181/F2
Harlan, Ky, US 193/F2
Harlan, Ia, US 185/G3
Harlan Co. (lake), Ne, US 184/E3
Harlan County (dam), Ne, US 184/E3
Harlech, Wal, UK 40/D6
Harlem, Ga, US 193/F4
Harlem, Mt, US 175/K3
Harlem (nbrhd.), NY, US 199/K8
Harleston, Eng, UK 43/H2
Harleton, Tx, US 181/G1
Hårlev, Den. 45/J7
Harleyville, SC, US 193/G4
Harlingen, Neth. 58/C2
Harlingen, Tx, US 180/F4
Harlington, Eng, UK 43/F3
Harlow, ND, US 186/E3
Harlow, Eng, UK 36/D1
Harlowton, Mt, US 175/K4
Harmannsdorf, Aus. 57/N7
Harmelen, Neth. 58/B4
Harmony, Mn, US 185/H2
Harnātānr, India 109/E2
Harnes, Fr. 60/B3
Harney, Md, US 198/A4
Harney (valley), Or, US 176/D2
Harney (lake), Or, US 176/D2
Harney (peak), SD, US 184/C2
Harni, Bang. 109/H4
Harnoli, Pak. 110/A3
Harö (isl.), Swe. 45/B1
Haro, Sp. 50/B5
Haro (cape), Mex. 204/C3
Harold, Ca, US 196/B1
Harpenden, Eng, UK 43/F3
Harper (mt.), Yk, Can. 201/L3
Harper, Libr. 132/D5
Harper (mt.), Ak, US 201/K3
Harper (lake), Ca, US 178/D3
Harper, Ks, US 183/E2
Harper, Or, US 176/E2
Harper, Tx, US 180/E2
Harper, Wa, US 197/B2
Harper Woods, Mi, US 197/F7
Harpers Ferry Nat'l Hist. Park, WV, US 191/H5
Harpersville, Al, US 192/D4
Harperville, Ms, US 192/C4
Harpeth (riv.), Tn, US 192/D2
Harpstedt, Ger. 59/F3
Harqin Qi, China 91/H3
Harqin Zuoyi Monggolzu Zizhixian, China 92/D2
Ḩarrah, Yem. 136/D2
Harrai, India 108/B4
Harran, Turk. 114/D2
Ḩarrān al 'Awāmīd, Syria 117/F2
Harrell, Ar, US 183/H4
Harricana (riv.), Qu, Can. 171/J4
Harrietsham, Eng, UK 36/F3
Harrietts Bluff, Ga, US 195/H2
Harriman, NY, US 199/D1
Harriman, Tn, US 192/E3
Harrington, Austl. 156/E1
Harrington, De, US 198/C6
Harrington Park, NJ, US 199/K8
Harris (isl.), Sc, UK 37/Q8
Harris (lake), Austl. 155/G4
Harris (mtn.), Tn, US 192/E2
Harris (mt.), Austl. 155/F3
Harris (co.), Tx, US 181/M9
Harrisburg, Ar, US 192/B3
Harrisburg, Il, US 192/C2
Harrisburg, Ne, US 184/C3
Harrisburg, Or, US 176/B1
Harrisburg (cap.), Pa, US 198/B3
Harrisburg (arpt.), Pa, US 198/B3
Harrislee, Ger. 46/C4
Harrismith, SAfr. 142/E3
Harrison (cape), Nf, Can. 171/L3
Harrison (lake), BC, Can. 174/C3
Harrison (bay), Ak, US 201/H1
Harrison, Ar, US 183/H2
Harrison, Ga, US 193/F4
Harrison, Id, US 174/F4
Harrison, Mi, US 190/D2
Harrison, Ne, US 184/C2
Harrison, NJ, US 199/J9
Harrison, NY, US 199/L8
Harrison, Oh, US 190/D5
Harrison, Tn, US 192/E3
Harrisonburg, La, US 194/C2
Harrisonburg, Va, US 193/H1
Harrisonville, Mo, US 183/G1
Harriston, On, Can. 190/F3
Harriston, Ms, US 194/C2
Harristown, Il, US 185/K4
Harrisville, Ms, US 194/C2
Harrisville, Mi, US 190/E2
Harrisville, WV, US 193/G1
Harrodsburg, In, US 192/D1
Harrodsburg, Ky, US 192/E2
Harrogate, Eng, UK 41/G4
Harrogate-Shawnee, Tn, US 192/F2
Harrold, Tx, US 182/E3
Harrow, On, Can. 190/E3
Harrow (bor.), Eng, UK 36/B2
Harrow (nbrhd.), Eng, UK 36/C2
Harrow, Austl. 156/B3
Harry S Truman (dam), Mo, US 183/H1
Harry S Truman (res.), Mo, US 185/H4
Harry S Truman Nat'l Hist. Site, Mo, US 185/G4
Harsefeld, Ger. 59/G2
Harsewinkel, Ger. 59/F5
Harskamp, Neth. 58/C4
Harson's Island, Mi, US 197/G6
Hart, Tx, US 182/C3
Hart, Mi, US 190/C3
Hart (riv.), Eng, UK 36/A3
Hart (isl.), NY, US 199/K8
Hart (lake), Or, US 176/C2
Hart (riv.), Yk, Can. 170/C2
Hart (mtn.), Or, US 176/D2
Hart (mt.), Austl. 152/B4
Hart Fell (peak), Sc, UK 39/C6
Hart Mtn. Nat'l Antelope Refuge, Or, US 176/D2
Ḩartā, Jor. 117/D3
Hartbeesrivier (riv.), SAfr. 142/C3
Harte (mtn.), Can. 186/D1
Hårteigen (peak), Nor. 46/B1
Hartelkanaal (riv.), Neth. 58/B5
Hartford, Libr. 132/C5
Hartford, Al, US 195/F2
Hartford (cap.), Ct, US 191/K4
Hartford, Ks, US 183/G1
Hartford, Ky, US 192/D2
Hartford, NJ, US 198/D4
Hartford, Wi, US 190/B3
Hartford City, In, US 190/D4
Hartheim, Ger. 66/D2
Harthill, Sc, UK 39/C5
Hartington, Ne, US 185/F2
Hartkirchen, Aus. 65/H6
Hartland, NB, Can. 188/D2
Hartland, Eng, UK 42/B4
Hartland (pt.), Eng, UK 42/B4
Hartland, Mi, US 197/E6
Hartland, Vt, US 191/K3
Hartlebury, Eng, UK 42/D2
Hartlepool, Eng, UK 41/G2
Hartlepool (co.), Eng, UK 41/G2
Hartleton, Pa, US 198/A2
Hartley, Eng, UK 36/D2
Hartley, Ia, US 185/G2
Hartley Bay, BC, Can. 201/N5
Hartley Wintney, Eng, UK 36/A3
Hartly, De, US 198/C5
Hartmannberge (mts.), Namb. 140/B3
Hartney, Mb, Can. 186/D3
Harts, WV, US 193/F1
Harts (riv.), SAfr. 140/E5
Harts Range, Austl. 155/G2
Hartsdale, NY, US 199/K7
Hartselle, Al, US 192/D3
Hartsfield Atlanta Int'l (int'l arpt.), Ga, US 193/M7
Hartshill, Eng, UK 43/E1
Hartshorn, Mo, US 183/J2
Hartshorne, Ok, US 183/G3
Hartsön (isl.), Swe. 45/A2
Hartstene (isl.), Wa, US 197/B3
Hartsville, SC, US 193/G3
Hartsville, Tn, US 192/D2
Hartville, Mo, US 183/H2
Hartwell (dam), Ga, US 193/F3
Hartwell, Ga, US 193/F3
Hartwell (res.), SC, US 193/F3
Hartz Mountain NP, Austl. 156/C4
Haruhi, Japan 95/L5
Harun (peak), Indo. 100/A4
Hārūnābād, Pak. 110/B5
Hārūt (riv.), Afg. 113/H2
Harvard, Ma, US 191/L3
Harvard, Il, US 185/K2
Harvard, Ne, US 184/E3
Harvest, Al, US 192/D3
Harvey, Austl. 154/B5
Harvey, NB, Can. 188/E3
Harvey, Il, US 197/Q16
Harvey, Mi, US 187/L4
Harvey, ND, US 186/E4
Harveys (lake), Pa, US 198/B1
Harwich, Eng, UK 43/H3
Harwood, ND, US 186/F4
Harworth, Eng, UK 41/G5
Haryana (state), India 111/C6
Harz (mts.), Ger. 48/F3
Hasan (peak), Turk. 114/C2
Hasan Abdāl, Pak. 110/B3
Hasanpur, India 108/B1
Ḩāşbayyā, Leb. 117/D2
Hasbrouck Heights, NJ, US 199/J8
Hascombe, Eng, UK 36/B3
Hasdo (riv.), India 108/D4
Hase (riv.), Ger. 48/D2
Hasel (riv.), Ger. 64/D1
Haselünne, Ger. 59/E3
Hasenmatt (peak), Swi. 66/D3
Hashaat, Mong. 90/E2
Hashima, Japan 95/L5
Hashimoto, Japan 96/D3
Hashtgerd, Iran 115/G3
Hasi el Farsía (well), WSah. 128/C4
Hāsilpur, Pak. 110/B5
Haskell, Ok, US 183/G3
Haskell, Tx, US 182/E4
Haskell, Ar, US 183/H3
Haslach an der Mühl, Aus. 65/H5
Haslach im Kinzigtal, Ger. 66/E1
Hasle bei Burgdorf, Swi. 66/D3
Haslemere, Eng, UK 43/F4
Hasler (cr.), Mi, US 197/F6
Haslet, Tx, US 180/K7
Haslett, Mi, US 190/D3
Haslev, Den. 45/H7
Haslingden, Eng, UK 41/F4
Haslington, Eng, UK 41/F5
Hasloh, Ger. 59/G1
Hāsmāi, Bang. 109/G3
Haspra, Ukr. 79/H5
Haspres, Fr. 60/C3
Hassa, Turk. 116/E1
Hassan (El Aaiún) (int'l arpt.), WSah. 128/B4
Hassayampa (riv.), Az, US 179/F3
Hassberge (hills), Ger. 64/D2
Hasse, Tx, US 180/E2
Hassel, Ger. 59/G3
Hassel Sound (str.), Nun, Can. 171/S7
Hasselt, Belg. 61/E2
Hasselt, Neth. 58/D3
Hassfurt, Ger. 64/D2
Hassi Bahbah, Alg. 130/G5
Hassi bou Zid (well), Alg. 129/F3
Hassi el Hadjar (well), Alg. 129/G3
Hassi el Mislane (well), Alg. 129/H4
Hassi er Rebib (well), Alg. 129/G2
Hassi Messaoud, Alg. 129/G3
Hässleholm, Swe. 46/E3
Hasslo (int'l arpt.), Swe. 46/G2
Hassloch, Ger. 64/B4
Haste, Ger. 59/G4
Hastings, Fl, US 195/H3
Hastings, Mi, US 190/D3
Hastings, Pa, US 191/G4
Hastings, SLeo. 132/B4
Hastings, NZ 159/D2
Hastings, Ne, US 184/E3
Hastings, Mn, US 187/Q7
Hastings (dam), Mn, US 187/Q7
Hastings, Eng, UK 43/G5
Hastings, Austl. 157/B4
Hastings Battlesite, Eng, UK 43/G5
Hastings-On-Hudson, NY, US 199/K7
Hästveda, Swe. 45/K6
Hasuda, Japan 95/D2
Hasunuma, Japan 95/E2
Hasvik, Nor. 44/G1
Haswell, Co, US 182/C1
Hat (mtn.), Ca, US 176/C3
Hat Chao Mai NP, Thai. 106/B5
Hāt Gāmāria, India 109/E4
Hat Head, Austl. 156/E1
Hat Head NP, Austl. 156/E1
Hat Nai Yang NP, Thai. 106/B5
Hat Yai, Thai. 106/C5
Hat Yai (int'l arpt.), Thai. 106/C5
Hatansuudal, Mong. 90/E3
Hatashō, Japan 95/K5
Hatavch, Mong. 90/G2
Hatay (prov.), Turk. 116/D1
Hatboro, Pa, US 198/C3
Hatch, Ut, US 179/F2
Hatch, NM, US 179/J4
Hatchechubbee, Al, US 192/E4
Hatcher (peak), Arg. 227/B6
Hatches Creek, Austl. 155/G2
Hatchie (riv.), Tn, US 192/C3
Hatchie NWR, Tn, US 192/C3
Hatchineha (lake), Fl, US 195/H3
Haţeg, Rom. 56/F3
Hatfield, Austl. 156/B2
Hatfield, Eng, UK 36/C1
Hatfield, Ar, US 183/G3
Hatfield, Pa, US 198/C3
Hatfield Peverel, Eng, UK 36/E1
Hatgal, Mong. 90/E1
Hāthāzāri, Bang. 109/H4
Hathersage, Eng, UK 41/G5
Hāthras, India 108/B2
Hātia (riv.), Bang. 109/H4
Hātia, North (isl.), Bang. 109/H4
Hātia, South (isl.), Bang. 109/H4
Hato (int'l arpt.), NAnt. 216/D1
Hato Corozal, Col. 216/D3
Hato Mayor, DRep. 203/H4
Hatogaya, Japan 95/D2
Hatoyama, Japan 95/C2
Hatsu (isl.), Japan 95/C3
Hatta, India 108/B3
Hatta, Japan 95/A2
Hattah-Kulkyne NP, Austl. 155/J5
Hattelmala, Fin. 45/E4
Hattem, Neth. 58/D4
Hatten, Fr. 61/G6
Hatten, Ger. 59/F2
Hatteras, NC, US 193/K3
Hatteras (isl.), NC, US 193/K3
Hattersheim am Mein, Ger. 64/B2
Hattiesburg, Ms, US 194/D2
Hattieville, Belz. 206/D2
Hattingen, Ger. 59/E6
Hatton, ND, US 186/F4
Hatton, Sc, UK 39/E2
Hatton, Eng, UK 41/G6
Hatton, Ut, US 179/F1
Hatton, Al, US 192/D3
Hatton, Sk, Can. 175/K2
Hattula, Fin. 47/L1
Håtuna, Swe. 45/A1
Hatvan, Hun. 56/D2
Hatzenbühl, Ger. 64/B4
Hatzfeld, Ger. 59/F6
Hau Bon, Viet. 106/E3
Hau Giang (riv.), Viet. 106/D4
Haubourdin, Fr. 60/B2
Haubstadt, In, US 192/D1
Haud (reg.), Eth. 136/C4
Hauge, Nor. 46/B2
Haugen, Wi, US 187/J5
Haugesund, Nor. 46/A2
Haughton, La, US 183/H4
Hauho, Fin. 45/E3
Haukeligrend, Nor. 46/B2
Haukipudas, Fin. 74/E2
Haune (riv.), Ger. 48/E3
Haunsberg (peak), Aus. 65/F7
Haunstetten, Ger. 64/D6
Hauonselkä (lake), Fin. 45/E3
Hauppauge, NY, US 199/E2
Hauraki (gulf), NZ 159/C2
Haus, Nor. 46/A1
Hausach, Ger. 66/E1
Hausjärvi, Fin. 47/L1
Hausleiten, Aus. 57/N7
Hausstock (peak), Swi. 67/F4
Haut Atlas (mts.), Mor. 128/D3
Haut-Ogooue (prov.), Gabon 138/C3
Haut-Rhin (dept.), Fr. 66/D2
Haut-Zaïre, D.R. Congo 139/F2
Haute-Kotto (pref.), CAfr. 134/D4
Haute-Normandie (pol. reg.), Fr. 50/D2
Haute-Sangha (pref.), CAfr. 134/B4
Haute-Saône (dept.), Fr. 66/B2
Haute-Savoie (dept.), Fr. 66/C5
Hautefeuille, Fr. 36/L5
Hautes Fagnes (uplands), Belg. 61/E3
Hautes-Alpes (dept.), Fr. 70/C3
Hauteurs de Gâtine (uplands), Fr. 50/C3
Hauteville-Lompnes, Fr. 66/B6
Hautmont, Fr. 60/C3
Hautsx (plat.), Alg. 129/E2
Hautsx (plat.), Alg.,Mor. 72/C4
Havana, ND, US 186/F5
Havana, Fl, US 195/F2
Havana, Il, US 185/J3
Havannah, Canal de la (chan.), NCal., Fr. 161/V13
Havant, Eng, UK 43/F5
Havasu (lake), Az, Ca, US 178/E3
Havasu Nat'l Wild Ref., Az, US 178/E3
Havasupai Ind. Res., Az, US 179/F2
Havdhem, Swe. 46/H3
Havdrup, Den. 46/E4
Havel (riv.), Ger. 49/G2
Havel (canal), Ger. 48/P6
Havelange, Belg. 61/E3
Haveli, Pak. 110/B4
Haveliān, Pak. 110/B2
Havelländischer Grosser Hauptkanal (canal), Ger. 48/P6
Havelock, NB, Can. 188/E2
Havelock, On, Can. 191/H2
Havelock, NZ 159/C3
Havelock, NC, US 193/J3
Havelock North, NZ 159/D2
Havelte, Neth. 58/D3
Haven, Ks, US 183/F2
Havencore (isl.), Eng, UK 43/G3
Haverfordwest, Wal, UK 42/B3
Haverhill, Eng, UK 43/G2
Haverhill, Fl, US 194/P9
Haverhill, Ma, US 191/L3
Haverhill, NH, US 191/K2
Havering (bor.), Eng, UK 36/D2
Haviland, Ks, US 182/E2
Ḩavīq, Iran 115/G2
Havířov, Czh. 49/K4
Havixbeck, Ger. 59/E5
Havlíčkuv Brod, Czh. 49/H4
Havneby, Den. 46/C4
Havnehage (isl.), Den. 45/G7
Hâvre (riv.), Fr. 62/D6
Havre, Mt, US 175/K3
Havre de Grace, Md, US 198/B4
Havre North, Mt, US 175/K3
Havre-Aubert, Qu, Can. 189/G2
Havre-Saint-Pierre, Qu, Can. 171/K3
Havsa, Turk. 57/H5
Havza, Turk. 76/E4
Haw (peak), NC, US 192/E3
Haw (riv.), NC, US 193/H2
Hawaii (state), US 172/S10
Hawaii (isl.), Hi, US 172/U11
Hawaii Volcanoes Nat'l Pk., Hi, US 172/U11
Hawaiian (isls.), Hi, US 161/H2
Hawaiian Gardens, Ca, US 196/F8
Ḩawallī, Kuw. 115/G4
Hawarden, Wal, UK 41/E5
Hawarden, NZ 159/C3
Hawarden, Ia, US 185/F2
Hawea (lake), NZ 159/B4
Hawera, NZ 159/C2
Hawes, Eng, UK 41/F3
Hawesville, Ky, US 192/D2
Haweswater (res.), Eng, UK 41/F2
Hawick, Sc, UK 39/D6
Hawk Point, Mo, US 185/J4
Hawke (bay), NZ 145/H6
Hawke (cape), Austl. 156/E2
Hawker, Austl. 155/H4
Hawkesbury, On, Can. 191/J2
Hawkesbury (pt.), Austl. 152/D2
Hawkesbury (riv.), Austl. 158/G8
Hawkins, Wi, US 187/J5
Hawkins (peak), Ca, US 176/D4
Hawkinsville, Ga, US 193/F4
Hawks Nest (peak), ND, US 186/E4
Hawks Nest, Austl. 156/E2
Hawksbill (mtn.), Va, US 193/H1
Hawley, Mn, US 186/F4
Hawley, Co, US 182/C2
Hawley, Tx, US 180/E1
Haworth, Ok, US 183/G4
Haworth, NJ, US 199/K8
Hawr al Ḩammār (lake), Iraq 115/F4
Ḩawsh 'Isá, Egypt 131/B3
Hawston, SAfr. 142/L11
Hawthorn Hill, Eng, UK 36/A2
Hawthorn Woods, Il, US 197/P15
Hawthorne, Ca, US 196/F8
Hawthorne, Fl, US 195/G3
Hawthorne, NJ, US 199/J8
Hawthorne, NY, US 199/K8
Hawthorne, Nv, US 176/D4
Hawthorne, Tx, US 181/G2
Hawthorne Ammunition Depot, Nv, US 176/D4
Ḩawwārah, Jor. 117/D3
Hawwārat al Maqţa', Egypt 131/B6
Hawzēn, Eth. 136/A2
Haxby, Eng, UK 41/G3
Haxtun, Co, US 184/C3
Hay, Austl. 157/B2
Hay (cape), Austl. 152/C3
Hay (pt.), Austl. 158/C3
Hay (riv.), Austl. 155/H3
Hay (riv.), Can. 163/F4
Hay (riv.), Ab, BC, Can. 170/E3
Hay, Wal, UK 42/C2
Hay, Wa, US 174/F4
Hay River, NW, Can. 170/E2
Hay Springs, Ne, US 184/C2
Hayachine-san (peak), Japan 94/B4
Hayakawa, Japan 95/A3
Hayama, Japan 95/D3
Hayange, Fr. 61/F5
Haybān (peak), Sudan 135/F3
Haybān, Sudan 135/F3
Haybes, Fr. 61/D4
Haycock, Ak, US 201/F2
Haydān (wadi), Jor. 117/D5
Hayden, Az, US 179/G4
Hayden, Co, US 177/K3
Hayden, Id, US 174/F4
Hayden-Rhodes (aqueduct), Az, US 179/F4
Haydock, Eng, UK 41/F5
Haydon Bridge, Eng, UK 41/F2
Hayes (riv.), Mb, Can. 170/G3
Hayes (nbrhd.), Eng, UK 36/B2
Hayes (pen.), Grld. 171/T7
Hayes (mt.), Ak, US 201/J3
Hayes, SD, US 184/D1
Hayes, Wi, US 190/B2
Hayes Center, Ne, US 184/D3
Hayesville, NC, US 192/F3
Hayfork, Ca, US 176/B3
Hayingen, Ger. 67/F1
Hāyk' (lake), Eth. 135/H4
Haylaastay, Mong. 81/M5
Hayle (riv.), Eng, UK 42/A6
Hayle, Eng, UK 42/A6
Hayling (isl.), Eng, UK 43/F5
Haylow, Ga, US 195/G2
Haymana, Turk. 114/C2
Haynes, ND, US 186/C5
Haynes, Ar, US 192/B3
Haynesville, La, US 183/H4
Hayneville, Al, US 192/D4
Haynin, Yem. 136/D2
Hayrabolu, Turk. 57/H5
Hays, Ks, US 182/E1
Hays, Ab, Can. 175/J2
Hays, Mt, US 175/K4
Haystack (peak), On, Can. 187/K2
Haysville, Ks, US 183/F2
Haysville, In, US 192/D1
Haysyn, Ukr. 78/E3
Hayti, Mo, US 192/C2
Hayti, SD, US 185/F1
Hayvoron, Ukr. 78/E3
Hayward, Wi, US 187/J4
Haywards Heath, Eng, UK 43/F5
Haywood, Ok, US 183/G3
Hazār (mtn.), Iran 115/J4
Hazard, Ky, US 193/F2
Hazāribag, India 109/E4
Hazebrouck, Fr. 60/B2
Hazel, SD, US 184/F1
Hazel, Ky, US 192/C2
Hazel Dell, Wa, US 174/C5
Hazel Green, Al, US 192/D3
Hazel Grove, Eng, UK 41/F5
Hazel Hill, NS, Can. 189/G3
Hazel Park, Mi, US 197/F7
Hazelbrook, Austl. 157/E1
Hazeldean, NB, Can. 188/D2
Hazelhurst, Wi, US 187/K5
Hazelton, ND, US 186/D4
Hazelton, Ks, US 183/E2
Hazelton (peak), Wy, US 177/K1
Hazen (str.), NW,Nun, Can. 171/R7
Hazen (bay), Ak, US 201/E3
Hazen, Ar, US 183/J3
Hazen, ND, US 186/D4
Hazen, Nv, US 176/D4
Hazenmore, Sk, Can. 175/L3
Hāzipur, Bang. 109/H4
Hazlehurst, Ga, US 195/G2
Hazlehurst, Ms, US 194/C2
Hazlemere, Eng, UK 36/A2
Hazlet, NJ, US 199/J10
Hazlet, Sk, Can. 175/K2
Hazleton, Pa, US 198/C2
Hazlett (lake), Austl. 155/F2
Ḩazor, Isr. 117/D3
Hazratbal Mosque, India 110/C2
Hazro, Pak. 110/B3
Hazu, Japan 95/M6
He (riv.), China 105/K2
He Xian, China 99/F3
He Xian, China 92/D5
Heacham, Eng, UK 43/G1
Head of Bay d'Espoir, Nf, Can. 189/K2
Head of Saint Margarets Bay, NS, Can. 188/F3
Headcorn, Eng, UK 43/G4
Headford, Ire. 38/A3
Headingley, Eng, UK 41/G4
Headland, Al, US 195/F2
Headlands, Zim. 141/G3
Headquarters, Id, US 174/G4
Heads of Ayr (pt.), Sc, UK 39/B6
Heafford Junction, Wi, US 187/K5
Healdsburg, Ca, US 176/B4
Healdton, Ok, US 183/F3
Healesville, Austl. 156/G5
Healy (pass), Ire. 38/A6
Healy, Ak, US 201/J3
Healy, Ks, US 182/D1
Heanor, Eng, UK 41/G6
Heany Junction, Zim. 141/F4
Heard (isl.), Austl. 228/E
Hearne, Tx, US 181/F2
Hearst, On, Can. 171/H4
Heart (riv.), ND, US 186/C4
Heart Butte (dam), ND, US 186/D4
Heart Law (hill), Sc, UK 39/D5
Hearts Hill, Sk, Can. 175/K1
Heath (pt.), QU, Can. 189/G1
Heath, Tx, US 180/L7
Heathcote, Austl. 157/B3
Heathcote NP, Austl. 158/G9
Heatherton, Nf, Can. 189/H1
Heathfield, Eng, UK 43/G5
Heathrow, Fl, US 194/N6
Heathrow (int'l arpt.), Eng, UK 36/B2
Heathsville, Va, US 193/J2
Hebbronville, Tx, US 181/E4
Hebbs Cross, NS, Can. 188/E3
Hebden Bridge, Eng, UK 41/F4
Hebei (prov.), China 90/G4
Hebel, Austl. 156/C1
Heber, Az, US 179/G3
Heber, Ca, US 178/E4
Heber City, Ut, US 177/H3
Heber Springs, Ar, US 183/H3
Hebert, La, US 194/C1
Hebertshausen, Ger. 65/E6
Hebgen (lake), Mt, US 177/H1
Hebgen (dam), Mt, US 177/H1
Hebi, China 92/C4
Hebo, Or, US 176/B1
Hebrides (sea), Sc, UK 37/Q8
Hebrides (isls.), UK 29/D3
Hebron, NS, Can. 188/D4
Hebron, Il, US 197/P15
Hebron, ND, US 186/C4
Hebron, Ne, US 184/F3
Hebron, Tx, US 180/L6
Hebron (Al Khalīl), WBnk. 117/C5
Heby, Swe. 46/G2
Hecate (str.), BC, Can. 163/D4
Hecelchakán, Mex. 206/D1
Hechi, China 99/F3
Hechingen, Ger. 64/B6
Hechtel, Belg. 61/E1
Hechthausen, Ger. 59/G1
Hechuan, China 99/E2
Heckington, Eng, UK 41/H6
Hecla, SD, US 186/E5
Hecla (isl.), Mb, Can. 186/F2
Hecla and Griper (bay), NW, Can. 171/R7
Hector (mt.), Ab, Can. 174/F2
Hector (mt.), NZ 159/J8
Hector, Ar, US 183/H3
Hector, Mn, US 185/G1
Hecun, China 99/H2
Heddal, Nor. 46/C2
Hédé, Fr. 62/D4
Hedehusene, Den. 45/J7
Hedel, Neth. 58/C5
Hedemora, Swe. 46/F1
Hedensted, Den. 46/C4
Hedi (res.), China 99/F4
Hedley, Tx, US 182/D3
Hedmark (co.), Nor. 44/D3
Hedo-misaki (cape), Japan 97/K7
Hedon, Eng, UK 41/H4
Hédouville, Fr. 36/J4
Hedrick, Ia, US 185/H3
Hedwig Village, Tx, US 181/M9
Heede, Ger. 59/E3
Heek, Ger. 59/E4
Heemskerk, Neth. 58/B3
Heemstede, Neth. 58/B4
Heerde, Neth. 58/D4
Heerenveen, Neth. 58/C3
Heerhugowaard, Neth. 58/B3
Heerlen, Neth. 61/E2
Heers, Belg. 61/E2
Heesch, Neth. 58/C5
Heeslingen, Ger. 59/G2

Holly – Hutub
293

Hollywood, Ar, US 183/H3
Hollywood (nbrhd.), Ca, US 196/F7
Hollywood, Fl, US 194/P10
Hollywood, SC, US 193/G4
Hollywood Bowl, Ca, US 196/F7
Hollywood Park, Tx, US 180/E3
Holm, Ger. 59/G1
Holman, NM, US 182/B2
Holman, NW, Can. 170/E1
Hólmavík, Ice. 44/N6
Holmdel, NJ, US 199/D3
Holme upon Spalding Moor, Eng, UK 41/H4
Holmen, Wi, US 185/J2
Holmenkollen, Nor. 44/S8
Holmer Green, Eng, UK 36/A2
Holmes (riv.), BC, Can. 174/E1
Holmes (mt.), Wy, US 177/H1
Holmes Chapel, Eng, UK 41/F5
Holmes Reef (reef), Austl. 153/H4
Holmes Reefs (isl.), Austl. 145/D2
Holmesdale (valley), Eng, UK 36/C3
Holmestrand, Nor. 46/D2
Holmfirth, Eng, UK 41/G4
Holmhead, Sc, UK 39/B6
Holmsbu, Nor. 44/S9
Holmsjön (lake), Swe. 44/F3
Holmsund, Swe. 44/G3
Holmsvatnet (lake), Nor. 44/R9
Hölö, Swe. 45/A1
Holoby, Ukr. 78/C2
Holon, Isr. 117/B4
Holoog, Namb. 142/B2
Holroyd, Austl. 157/E1
Holsfjorden (lake), Nor. 44/R8
Holstebro, Den. 46/C3
Holstein, Ia, US 185/G2
Holston (riv.), Tn, US 192/F3
Holston Ordnance Works Fed. Govt. Res., Tn, US 193/F2
Holston, North Fork (riv.), Va, US 193/F2
Holsworthy, Eng, UK 42/B5
Holt, Eng, UK 43/H1
Holt, Al, US 192/D4
Holt, Ca, US 197/M11
Holt, Fl, US 194/E2
Holt, Mi, US 190/D3
Holt, Mo, US 185/G4
Holtålen, Nor. 44/D3
Holte, Den. 45/J7
Holten, Neth. 58/D4
Holtland, Ger. 59/E2
Holton, Ks, US 185/G4
Holts Summit, Mo, US 183/H1
Holtsville, NY, US 199/E2
Holtville, NB, Can. 188/D2
Holtville, Ca, US 178/E4
Holwerd, Neth. 58/C2
Holy (isl.), Sc, UK 39/A5
Holy Cross, Ak, US 201/G3
Holy Trinity, Al, US 192/E4
Holycross, Ire. 38/C4
Holyhead, Wal, UK 40/D5
Holyoke, Ma, US 191/K3
Holyoke, Co, US 184/C3
Holyport, Eng, UK 36/A2
Holyrood, Ks, US 183/E1
Holyrood, Nf, Can. 189/L2
Holywell, Wal, UK 41/E5
Holywood, NI, UK 40/C2
Holzminden, Ger. 59/G5
Holzwickede, Ger. 59/E5
Hom (riv.), Namb. 142/B3
Homa (mt.), Kenya 137/A2
Homa Bay, Kenya 137/A2
Homathko (riv.), BC, Can. 174/B2
Homberg, Ger. 59/G6
Homberg, Ger. 58/D6
Hombori, Mali 133/E3
Hombori Tondo (peak), Mali 133/E3
Hombourg-Haut, Fr. 61/F5
Homburg, Ger. 61/G5
Home (bay), Nun, Can. 171/K2
Home Hill, Austl. 158/B2
Homécourt, Fr. 61/E5
Homelake, Co, US 179/J2
Homeland, Ca, US 196/C3
Homeland, Fl, US 194/M8
Homeland, Ga, US 195/G2
Homer, Ak, US 201/H4
Homer, Ga, US 193/F3
Homer, La, US 183/H4
Homer, Mi, US 190/D3
Homer, NY, US 191/H3
Homerville, Ga, US 195/G2
Homestead, Fl, US 195/H5
Homestead, Austl. 158/B3
Homestead of America Nat'l Mon., Ne, US 185/F3
Homewood, Il, US 197/Q16
Homewood, Ca, US 176/C4
Homewood, Al, US 192/D4
Homib (riv.), Erit. 112/C5
Hommersåk, Nor. 46/A2
Homochitto (riv.), Ms, US 192/B5
Homoíne, Moz. 141/G4
Homonhon (isl.), Phil. 100/D3
Homosassa (bay), Fl, US 194/K6
Homosassa, Fl, US 194/K6
Homosassa Springs, Fl, US 194/K6
Homosassa Springs Nature World, Fl, US 194/K6
Homyel', Bela. 76/D1
Homyel'skaya Voblasts, Bela. 76/D1
Hon, Ar, US 183/G3
Hon Chong, Viet. 106/D4
Hon Quan, Viet. 106/D4
Honbetsu, Japan 94/C2
Honda, Col. 219/L7
Honddu (riv.), Wal, UK 42/C2
Hondeklipbaai, SAfr. 142/B3
Hondo, Japan 96/B4
Hondo (riv.), Belz. 206/D2
Hondo, Tx, US 180/E3
Hondo (cr.), Tx, US 180/E3
Hondschoote, Fr. 60/B2
Hondsrug (hills), Neth. 48/D2
Hondsrug (reg.), Neth. 58/D3
Honduras (gulf), NAm. 202/D4
Honduras (ctry.) 206/E3
Honea Path, SC, US 193/F3
Hønefoss, Nor. 46/D1
Honesdale, Pa, US 191/J4
Honey (cr.), Wi, US 197/N14
Honey (lake), Ca, US 176/C3
Honey Brook, Pa, US 198/C3
Honey Creek, Wi, US 197/P14
Honey Grove, Tx, US 183/G4
Honeybourne, Eng, UK 43/E2
Honeyville, Ut, US 177/G3
Honfleur, Fr. 63/F2
Hong (isl.), SKor. 93/C5
Høng, Den. 45/H7
Hong (lake), China 92/C5
Hong (riv.), China 92/C4
Hong (Red) (riv.), Viet. 98/E4
Hong Gai, Viet. 99/E4
Hong Kong (dpcy.), China 99/K7
Hong Kong (see Chep Lak Kok) (int'l. arpt.), China */*
Hong Kong (isl.), China 99/L7
Hongam-nodongjagu, NKor. 93/E1
Hong'an, China 92/C5
Hongchang, China 93/B2
Hongch'ŏn, SKor. 93/D4
Hongdu (riv.), China 105/J2
Hongdu, China 99/F4
Honggouzi, China 90/C4
Hongguo, China 98/E3
Honghu, China 99/G2
Hongjiang, China 99/F3
Honglai, China 99/H3
Hongliu (riv.), China 90/F4
Hongliuhe, China 90/C3
Hongliuquan, China 90/D3
Honglu, China 99/H3
Hongqi, China 93/B2
Hongqiao, China 99/J2
Hongqiao (int'l arpt.), China 92/L8
Hongqizhen, China 106/E2
Hongshui (riv.), China 105/J3
Hongsŏng, SKor. 93/D4
Hongtian, China 99/H3
Hongtong, China 92/B3
Honguedo Passage, (chan.), Qu, Can. 171/K4
Honguedo Passage, Qu, Can. 188/E1
Hongwŏn, NKor. 93/D2
Hongya, China 98/D2
Hongyan, China 99/F2
Hongyang, China 99/H4
Hongyuan, China 90/E5
Hongze (lake), China 91/H5
Hongze, China 92/D4
Hœnheim, Fr. 61/G6
Honiara (cap.), Sol. 160/E5
Honiton, Eng, UK 42/C5
Honjō, Japan 94/B4
Honjō, Japan 95/C1
Honobia, Ok, US 183/G3
Honolulu (cap.), Hi, US 172/W13
Honoraville, Al, US 195/E2
Hönow, Ger. 48/Q6
Honshu (isl.), Japan 81/Q6
Honshū (isl.), Japan 83/P6
Hontianske Nemce, Slvk. 56/D1
Hoo, Eng, UK 36/E2
Hood, Ca, US 197/L10
Hood (pt.), Austl. 154/C5
Hood (pt.), PNG 153/G2
Hood (mt.), Ca, US 197/J10
Hood (mt.), Or, US 176/C1
Hood (co.), Tx, US 180/K7
Hood (canal), Wa, US 197/B2
Hood River, Or, US 174/D5
Hoofddorp, Neth. 58/B4
Hoogeloon, Neth. 58/C6
Hoogeveen, Neth. 58/D3
Hoogeveense Vaart (canal), Neth. 58/D3
Hoogezand, Neth. 58/D2
Hooghly (riv.), India 109/F5
Hooghly-Chinsura, India 109/G4
Hoogkarspel, Neth. 58/C3
Hooglede, Belg. 60/C2
Hoogstraten, Belg. 58/B6
Hook (sound), Austl. 158/C3
Hook, Eng, UK 43/F4
Hook Head (pt.), Ire. 38/D5
Hooker, Ok, US 182/D2
Hooker Creek, Austl. 152/C4
Hooker Creek Abor. Land, Austl. 152/C4
Hooksett, NH, US 191/L3
Hoonah, Ak, US 201/L4
Hoopa, Ca, US 176/B3
Hoopa Valley Ind. Res., Ca, US 176/B3
Hooper, Co, US 182/B2
Hooper, Ne, US 185/F3
Hooper (Endwell), NY, US 191/H3
Hooper Bay, Ak, US 201/E3
Hoopeston, Il, US 190/C4
Hoople, ND, US 186/F3
Hoopstad, SAfr. 142/D2
Höör, Swe. 46/E4
Hoorn, Neth. 58/C3
Hoornse Hop (bay), Neth. 58/C3
Hoosick Falls, NY, US 191/K3
Hoover (dam), Az, US 172/D4
Hoover (peak), WV, US 193/F2
Hoover, SD, US 184/C1
Höövör, Mong. 90/G2
Hopa, Turk. 77/G4
Hopatcong, NJ, US 198/D2
Hopatcong (lake), NJ, US 198/D2
Hope (lake), Austl. 145/A4
Hope, BC, Can. 174/D3
Hope, Wal, UK 41/E5
Hope, Ak, US 201/J3
Hope, Ar, US 183/H4
Hope, In, US 190/D5
Hope, Ks, US 183/F1
Hope, ND, US 186/F4
Hope, NJ, US 198/D2
Hope, Tx, US 181/F3
Hope Mills, NC, US 193/H3
Hope Vale Abor. Land, Austl. 153/G3
Hope Vale Aboriginal Community, Austl. 158/B1
Hope-under-Dinmore, Eng, UK 42/D2
Hopedale, Nf, Can. 171/K3
Hopelchén, Mex. 206/D2
Hopeman, Sc, UK 39/C1
Hopes Advance (cape), Qu, Can. 171/K2
Hope's Nose (pt.), Eng, UK 42/C6
Hopetoun, Austl. 154/D5
Hopetown, SAfr. 142/D3
Hopewell, NS, Can. 189/F3
Hopewell, NJ, US 198/D3
Hopewell, Va, US 193/J2
Hopewell Cape, NB, Can. 188/E3
Hopewell Culture Nat'l Mon., Oh, US 190/E5
Hopewell Furnace NHS, Pa, US 198/C3
Hopi Ind. Res., Az, US 179/G2
Hopin, Myan. 98/C3
Hôpital-Camfrout, Fr. 62/A4
Hopkins (lake), Austl. 155/F3
Hopkins (riv.), Austl. 156/B3
Hopkins, Mo, US 185/G3
Hopkins, Mn, US 187/P7
Hopkinsville, Ky, US 192/D2
Hopkinton, RI, US 191/L4
Hopkinton, NH, US 191/L3
Hoppecke (riv.), Ger. 59/F6
Hoppegarten, Ger. 48/Q6
Hopper Mtn. NWR, Ca, US 196/B2
Hoppstädten-Weiersbach, Ger. 61/G4
Hopsten, Ger. 59/E4
Hoquiam, Wa, US 174/C4
Hor, China 90/E4
Horace (mt.), Ak, US 201/J2
Horace, ND, US 186/F4
Horadiz, Azer. 115/F2
Horado, Japan 95/L4
Hōrai-san (peak), Japan 95/J5
Horasan, Turk. 114/E1
Horatio, Ar, US 183/G4
Horažďovice, Czh. 65/G4
Horb am Neckar, Ger. 64/B6
Horbat Qesari (ruin), Isr. 116/D3
Horbourg-Wihr, Fr. 66/D1
Hörbranz, Aus. 67/F2
Horbury, Eng, UK 41/G4
Hörby, Swe. 45/K7
Horche, Sp. 52/D2
Horconcitos, Pan. 207/F4
Horcones (riv.), Arg. 224/C3
Hordaland (co.), Nor. 44/C3
Horden, Eng, UK 41/G2
Hœrdt, Fr. 61/G6
Hördt, Ger. 64/B4
Horezu, Rom. 57/G3
Horgau, Ger. 64/D6
Horgen, Swi. 67/E3
Hörh (peak), Mong. 90/F3
Horicon, Wi, US 185/K2
Horicon NWR, Wi, US 185/K2
Horinger, China 92/B2
Horiult, Mong. 90/E2
Horizontina, Braz. 225/F3
Horley, Eng, UK 36/C3
Horlivka, Ukr. 79/K3
Hormigüeros, PR 203/M8
Hormozgān (gov.), Iran 115/J5
Hormūd-e Mīr Khūnd, Iran 115/H5
Hormuz (str.), Oman 113/G3
Horn (cape), Arg. 227/D8
Horn (pt.), Ice. 44/M6
Horn (isl.), Ms, US 194/D2
Horn Lake, Ms, US 192/B3
Horn-Bad Meinberg, Ger. 59/F5
Hornachuelos, Sp. 52/C4
Hornád (riv.), Slvk. 49/L4
Hornavan (lake), Swe. 44/F2
Hornbach, Ger. 61/G5
Hornbæk, Den. 45/J6
Hornbeck, Ab, Can. 174/F1
Hornbeck, La, US 194/B2
Hornberg, Ger. 67/E1
Hornburg, Ger. 59/H4
Hornby, NZ 159/C3
Hornby, On, Can. 190/T8
Hornby Island, BC, Can. 174/B3
Horncastle, Eng, UK 41/H5
Hornchurch (nbrhd.), Eng, UK 36/D2
Horndal, Swe. 46/G1
Horné Saliby, Slvk. 56/C1
Horneburg, Ger. 59/G1
Hornell, NY, US 191/H3
Hornersville, Mo, US 192/B2
Horní Bříza, Czh. 65/G3
Horní Slavkov, Czh. 65/F2
Hornisgrinde (peak), Ger. 64/B5
Hornitos, Ca, US 178/B2
Hornos, (cape), Chile 227/D7
Hornoy-le-Bourg, Fr. 60/A4
Hornsby (nbrhd.), Austl. 158/H8
Hornsea, Eng, UK 41/H4
Hornslet, Den. 46/D3
Hörnum (cape), Ger. 46/C4
Horodenka, Ukr. 78/C3
Horodnya, Ukr. 78/F2
Horodok, Ukr. 78/D3
Horodok, Ukr. 78/B3
Horodyshche, Ukr. 78/F3
Horokhiv, Ukr. 78/C2
Horoshiri-dake (peak), Japan 94/C2
Hořovice, Czh. 65/G3
Horqin Youyi Zhongqi, China 91/J2
Horqin Zuoyi Houqi, China 92/E2
Horqin Zuoyi Zhongqi, China 92/E1
Horqueta, Par. 225/E2
Horrabridge, Eng, UK 42/B5
Hörsching, Aus. 65/H6
Horse (cr.), Co, US 184/B4
Horse (mtn.), Tx, US 180/C2
Horse Cave, Ky, US 192/E2
Horse Creek, Wy, US 184/B3
Horse Shoe Run, WV, US 191/G5
Horsefly, BC, Can. 174/D1
Horsefly (riv.), BC, Can. 174/D1
Horsefly (lake), BC, Can. 174/D1
Horseheads, NY, US 191/H3
Horsens, Den. 46/C4
Horseshoe Beach, Fl, US 195/G3
Horseshoe Bend, Ar, US 183/J2
Horseshoe Bend, Id, US 176/E2
Horseshoe Bend Nat'l Mil. Park, Al, US 192/E4
Horsethief (cr.), BC, Can. 174/F2
Horsey (isl.), Eng, UK 43/H3
Horsforth, Eng, UK 41/G4
Horsham, Austl. 156/B3
Horsham, Eng, UK 43/F4
Horsham, Pa, US 198/C3
Hørsholm, Den. 45/J7
Horsmonden, Eng, UK 36/E3
Horšovský Týn, Czh. 65/F3
Horst, Ger. 59/H2
Horst, Neth. 58/D6
Hörstel, Ger. 59/E4
Horstmar, Ger. 59/E4
Horta, Azor., Port. 53/S12
Hortaleza (nbrhd.), Sp. 53/N9
Horten, Nor. 46/D2
Hortense, Ga, US 195/H2
Hortes, Fr. 66/B2
Hortobágyi NP, Hun. 76/B3
Horton, Mo, US 183/G2
Horton (riv.), NW, Can. 170/D2
Horton, Ks, US 185/G4
Horton (pt.), NY, US 199/F1
Horton Kirby, Eng, UK 36/D2
Høruphav, Den. 46/C4
Horusický Rybník (lake), Czh. 65/H4
Hørve, Den. 46/D4
Hørve, Den. 45/H7
Horvot 'Avedat (ruin), Isr. 116/D4
Horvot Dor, Isr. 117/B3
Horw, Swi. 67/E3
Horwich, Eng, UK 41/F4
Hosa'ina, Eth. 135/H4
Hösbach, Ger. 64/C2
Hosdrug, India 107/B3
Hosenfeld, Ger. 64/C1
Hosenofu (well), Libya 126/D4
Hoséré Vokré (peak), Camr. 134/B3
Hosford, Fl, US 195/F2
Hoshāb, Pak. 113/H3
Hoshangābād, India 108/A4
Hoshcha, Ukr. 78/D2
Hoshiārpur, India 110/C4
Hosingen, Lux. 61/F3
Hosmer, SD, US 186/E5
Hosmer, BC, Can. 174/G3
Hospental, Swi. 67/E4
Hospital, Ire. 38/B5
Hospital, Chile 226/N8
Hosston, La, US 183/H4
Hosszúpereszteg, Hun. 56/C2
Hoste (isl.), Chile 227/C7
Hostomel', Ukr. 78/F2
Hoswick, Sc, UK 37/W13
Hot, Thai. 106/B2
Hot Creek (range), Nv, US 176/E4
Hot Springs, SD, US 184/C2
Hot Springs NP, Ar, US 183/H3
Hot Springs Village, Ar, US 183/H3
Hot Sulphur Springs, Co, US 184/A3
Hotaka, Japan 97/E2
Hotaka-dake (peak), Japan 97/E2
Hotan (riv.), China 111/D4
Hotan, China 111/C4
Hotazel, SAfr. 142/C2
Hotevilla, Az, US 179/G3
Hotham (cape), Austl. 152/C3
Hoti, Indo. 103/H4
Hot'kovo, Rus. 75/W8
Hotont, Mong. 90/E2
Hottah (lake), NW, Can. 170/E2
Hottentot (bay), Namb. 142/A2
Hottentots (pt.), Namb. 140/B5
Hotton, Belg. 61/E3
Hou (riv.), China 90/F5
Houamuang, Laos 98/D4
Houari Boumedienne (int'l arpt.), Alg. 130/G4
Houat (isl.), Fr. 62/C6
Houchang, China 99/E3
Houdain, Fr. 60/B3
Houdan, Fr. 63/G3
Houdan, Fr. 36/G5
Houet (prov.), Burk. 132/D4
Houffalize, Belg. 61/E3
Houghton (pt.), Mi, US 187/K4
Houghton, SD, US 186/E5
Houghton (dam), SD, US 186/E5
Houghton, Mi, US 187/K4
Houghton (lake), Mi, US 190/D2
Houghton, NY, US 191/G3
Houghton Lake, Mi, US 190/D2
Houghton-le-Spring, Eng, UK 41/G2
Houilles, Fr. 36/J5
Houlgate, Fr. 63/E2
Houlton, Me, US 171/K4
Houlton, Wi, US 187/Q6
Houma, La, US 194/C3
Houma, China 92/B4
Houndé, Burk. 132/E4
Houplines, Fr. 60/B2
Hourn, Loch (inlet), Sc, UK 39/A2
Hourtin, Fr. 50/C4
Housatonic (riv.), Ct, US 199/E1
House (range), Ut, US 172/D4
Housesteads Roman Fort, Eng, UK 41/F1
Houssen, Fr. 66/D1
Houston, De, US 198/C6
Houston, Fl, US 195/G2
Houston, Mn, US 185/J2
Houston, Mo, US 183/J2
Houston, Ms, US 192/C4
Houston, Tx, US 181/M9
Houston (lake), Tx, US 181/G2
Houston Intercontinental (int'l arpt.), Tx, US 181/M9
Houston Ship (chan.), Tx, US 181/M9
Houstonia, Mo, US 183/H1
Houtbaai, SAfr. 142/L11
Houten, Neth. 58/C4
Houthalen, Belg. 61/E1
Houthulst, Belg. 60/B2
Houtman Abrolhos (isl.), Austl. 154/B4
Houtribdijk (dam), Neth. 58/C3
Houtskär (isl.), Fin. 47/J1
Houyet, Belg. 61/E3
Houyingzi, China 93/B2
Houzhenzi, China 90/F5
Hov, Nor. 46/D1
Hova, Swe. 46/F2
Hovd (prov.), Mong. 90/C2
Hove, Eng, UK 43/F5
Hövelhof, Ger. 59/F5
Hoven, SD, US 184/E1
Hovenweep Nat'l Mon., Co, US 179/H2
Hoveton, Eng, UK 43/H1
Hovfjället (peak), Swe. 46/E1
Hovingham, Eng, UK 41/H3
Hovland, Mn, US 187/K4
Hovmantorp, Swe. 46/F3
Hövsgöl (prov.), Mong. 111/G2
Hövsgöl (lake), Mong. 90/E1
Hovsta, Swe. 46/F2
Howa, Oued (riv.), Chad 134/D2
Howar (wadi), Sudan 135/E1
Howard, Austl. 158/D4
Howard (isl.), Austl. 153/D2
Howard, NB, Can. 188/E2
Howard, Co, US 182/B1
Howard, Fl, US 194/P11
Howard, Ks, US 183/F2
Howard (co.), Md, US 198/B5
Howard, SD, US 184/F1
Howard Beach (nbrhd.), NY, US 199/K9
Howard City, Mi, US 190/D3
Howard Draw (riv.), Tx, US 180/D2
Howard Hanson (res.), Wa, US 197/D3
Howard Hanson (dam), Wa, US 197/D3
Howard Prairie (lake), Or, US 176/B2
Howards Grove, Wi, US 190/C3
Howden, Eng, UK 41/H4
Howe, Ok, US 183/G3
Howe, Tx, US 183/F4
Howe (sound), BC, Can. 174/C3
Howe (cape), Austl. 157/D3
Howe Caverns, NY, US 191/J3
Howe Green, Eng, UK 36/E1
Howe of the Mearns (reg.), Sc, UK 39/D3
Howell, Mi, US 190/E3
Howell, NJ, US 199/D3
Howey-in-the-Hills, Fl, US 194/M6
Howick, NZ 159/F6
Howick, SAfr. 143/E3
Howison, Ms, US 194/D2
Howland (isl.), Pac., US 161/H4
Howley, Nf, Can. 189/J1
Howlong, Austl. 157/C2
Howrah, India 109/G4
Howser, BC, Can. 174/F2
Hoxie, Ks, US 184/D4
Hoxie, Ar, US 192/B2
Höxter, Ger. 59/G5
Hoxud, China 111/E3
Hoy (isl.), Sc, UK 37/V14
Hoya, Ger. 59/G3
Hōya, Japan 95/D2
Høyanger, Nor. 46/B1
Hoyerswerda, Ger. 49/H3
Hoylake, Eng, UK 41/E5
Hoyland Nether, Eng, UK 41/G4
Hoyo de Manzanares, Sp. 53/N8
Hoyos, Sp. 52/B2
Hoyoux (riv.), Belg. 61/E3
Hoyt, NB, Can. 188/D3
Hoyt, Ks, US 185/G4
Hoyt, Mt, US 186/B4
Hoyt, Ok, US 183/G3
Hoyt Tamir (riv.), Mong. 90/E2
Hozumi, Japan 95/L5
Hracholusky (res.), Czh. 65/F3
Hradec Králové, Czh. 49/H3
Hradište (peak), Czh. 65/G2
Hradyz'k, Ukr. 79/G3
Hranice, Czh. 65/F2
Hrasnica, Bosn. 56/D4
Hrastnik, Slov. 56/B2
Hrazdan, Arm. 115/F1
Hrebinka, Ukr. 79/G1
Hrebinky, Ukr. 78/F3
Hřivice, Czh. 65/G2
Hrodna, Bela. 47/K5
Hrodzyenskaya Voblasts, Bela. 74/E5
Hrolleifsborg (peak), Ice. 44/M6
Hron (riv.), Slvk. 76/A2
Hronov, Czh. 49/J3
Hrubieszów, Pol. 78/B2
Hrubý Jeseník (mts.), Czh.,Pol. 49/J3
Hrútafjöll (peak), Ice. 44/P6
Hrymayliv, Ukr. 78/D3
Hsenwi, Myan. 105/G3
Hsi-hseng, Myan. 98/C4
Hsinchu, Tai. 99/J3
Hsipaw, Myan. 106/B1
Hsüeh (peak), Tai. 99/J3
Htawgaw, Myan. 105/G2
Hts-de-Seine (dept.), Fr. 63/H3
Hu Xian, China 90/F5
Hua (peak), China 92/B4
Hua Hin, Thai. 106/B3
Hua Sai, Thai. 106/C4
Hua Xian, China 92/C4
Huab (riv.), Namb. 140/B3
Huacaraje, Bol. 221/F4
Huacareta, Bol. 224/D2
Huacaya, Bol. 224/D2
Huacaybamba, Peru 220/B3
Huachacalla, Bol. 224/B1
Huacheng, China 99/G3
Huachi, China 90/F4
Huachi, Bol. 221/F4
Huacho, Peru 220/B3
Huachón, Peru 220/C3
Huachuan, China 91/L2
Huachuca (mts.), Az, US 179/G5
Huachuca City, Az, US 179/G5
Huacrachuco, Peru 220/B3
Huade, China 90/G3
Huadian, China 91/K3
Huadianzi, China 93/C2
Huahine (isl.), FrPol. 161/K6
Huai (riv.), China 92/C4
Huai Yot, Thai. 106/B5
Huai'an, China 92/C2
Huai'an, China 92/D4
Huaibei, China 90/H5
Huaibin, China 92/C4
Huaihua, China 99/F3
Huaiji, China 99/G4
Huailai, China 92/G6
Huainan, China 92/D4
Huaining, China 99/H2
Huairen, China 92/C3
Huairou, China 92/H6
Huaiyang, China 92/C4
Huaiyin, China 92/D4
Huaiyin, China 92/D4
Huaiyuan, China 92/D4
Huajicori, Mex. 204/D4
Huajuapan de León, Mex. 206/B2
Hualahuises, Mex. 205/F3
Hualañé, Chile 226/C2
Hualapai (peak), Az, US 179/F3
Hualapai (mts.), Az, US 179/F3
Hualapai Ind. Res., Az, US 179/F3
Hualfín, Arg. 224/C3
Hualgayoc, Peru 220/B2
Hualien, Tai. 99/J4
Hualla, Peru 220/C4
Huallaga (riv.), Peru 209/B3
Huallanca, Peru 220/B3
Huamachuco, Peru 220/B2
Huamantanga, Peru 220/B3
Huamantla, Mex. 205/M7
Huambo, Ang. 140/B2
Huambo (dist.), Ang. 140/B2
Huambos, Peru 220/B2
Huan (riv.), China 92/C5
Huan Xian, China 90/F4
Huanan, China 91/L2
Huanaque, Bol. 224/B2
Huancané, Peru 220/D4
Huancapi, Peru 220/C4
Huancaspata, Peru 220/B3
Huancavelica, Peru 220/C4
Huancavelica (dept.), Peru 220/C4
Huancayo, Peru 220/C4
Huanchaca (peak), Bol. 224/C2
Huang (riv.), China 83/L6
Huang (Yellow) (riv.), China 90/G4
Huangbayi, China 90/F5
Huangbei, China 99/H3
Huangchuan, China 92/C4
Huangcun, China 99/F3
Huanggang (peak), China 99/H3
Huanggang, China 99/G2
Huanghua, China 92/D3
Huangjinbu, China 99/H2
Huangjinggou, China 98/E2
Huangli, China 92/K8
Huangling, China 92/B4
Huangliu, China 99/F5
Huanglong, China 92/B4
Huanglong, China 99/G3
Huanglongtan, China 92/B4
Huangmao (peak), China 99/H3
Huangmei, China 99/G2
Huangniupu, China 90/F5
Huangpi, China 99/G2
Huangping, China 105/J2
Huangqi (lake), China 92/C2
Huangshan, China 99/H2
Huangshi, China 99/G2
Huangshidu, China 99/H3
Huangtang (lake), China 92/C5
Huangtianpu, China 99/F3
Huangtu (plat.), China 92/B4
Huangtudian, China 99/F2
Huanguelén, Arg. 226/E3
Huangwan, China 92/L9
Huangyunpu, China 92/B4
Huangzhai, China 99/H2
Huangzhan, China 99/G2
Huangzhong, China 90/E4
Huaning, China 98/D3
Huanjiang, China 105/J3
Huanren, China 93/C2
Huanta, Peru 220/C4
Huantai, China 92/D3
Huántar, Peru 220/B3
Huantunas (lake), Bol. 221/E4
Huánuco, Peru 220/B3
Huánuco (dept.), Peru 220/C3
Huanuni, Bol. 224/C1
Huanxi, China 99/G3
Huapi (mts.), Nic. 207/E3
Huaping, China 98/D3
Huaqiaozhen, China 90/F5
Huaquechula, Mex. 205/L8
Huaquillas, Ecu. 220/A1
Huara, Chile 224/B1
Huaral, Peru 220/B3
Huaraz, Peru 220/B3
Huari, Bol. 224/C1
Huari, Peru 220/B3
Huaricolca, Peru 220/C3
Huarina, Bol. 220/D5
Huarmey, Peru 220/B3
Huarochirí, Peru 220/B4
Huarocondo, Peru 220/C4
Huásabas, Mex. 204/C2
Huasahuasi, Peru 220/C3
Huascarán (peak), Peru 220/B3
Huascaran, PN, Peru 220/B3
Huasco (riv.), Chile 224/B4
Huashi (mts.), China 99/G3
Huashi, China 99/G3
Huatabampo, Mex. 204/C3
Huatong, China 93/A2
Huatuxco, Mex. 205/N7
Huauchinango, Mex. 205/L6
Huaura, Peru 220/B3
Huautla de Jiménez, Mex. 206/B2
Huayacocotla, Mex. 205/L6
Huayang, China 99/J2
Huayangzhen, China 90/F5
Huaying, China 99/E2
Huaylas, Peru 220/B3
Huayllay, Peru 220/B3
Huayopata, Peru 220/C4
Huayuan, China 93/D1
Huayuan, China 105/J2
Huayuan, China 99/G2
Huazhaizi, China 90/E4
Huazhou, China 105/K3
Huazi, China 93/B2
Hub, Ms, US 194/D2
Hubbard, Sk, Can. 186/C2
Hubbard (mt.), Ak, US 201/L3
Hubbard, Ia, US 185/H2
Hubbard (lake), Mi, US 190/E2
Hubbard, Or, US 176/B1
Hubbard, Tx, US 181/F2
Hubbard Creek (res.), Tx, US 180/E1
Hubbards, NS, Can. 188/E3
Hubbell Trading Post Nat'l Hist. Site, Az, US 179/H3
Hubei (pass), China 92/B4
Huber Heights, Oh, US 190/D5
Hubli-Dhārwār, India 107/B3
Huch'ang, NKor. 93/D2
Hückelhoven, Ger. 61/F1
Hückeswagen, Ger. 61/G1
Hucknall, Eng, UK 41/G5
Hudai, China 92/L8
Huddersfield, Eng, UK 41/G4
Huddinge, Swe. 46/G2
Hude, Ger. 59/F2
Hudiksvall, Swe. 46/G1
Hudson (cape), Ant. 228/L
Hudson (bay), Can. 163/J3
Hudson, On, Can. 187/H2
Hudson, Qu, Can. 189/M7
Hudson (str.), Nun,Qu, Can. 171/J2
Hudson, Fl, US 194/K7
Hudson, Il, US 185/K3
Hudson, Mi, US 190/D4
Hudson, NC, US 193/G3
Hudson (co.), NJ, US 199/J9
Hudson, NY, US 191/K3
Hudson (riv.), NJ, NY, US 191/K3
Hudson (lake), Ok, US 183/G2
Hudson, Tx, US 181/G2
Hudson, Wi, US 187/Q7
Hudson Bay, Sk, Can. 170/F3
Hudson Falls, NY, US 191/K3
Hudson Oaks, Tx, US 180/K7
Hudsons (peak), Austl. 157/D3
Hudson's Hope, BC, Can. 170/D3
Hue, Viet. 106/D2
Hueco (mts.), Tx, US 180/B2
Huedin, Rom. 57/F2
Huehuetenango, Guat. 206/D3
Huehuetla, Mex. 205/L6
Huehuetlán, Mex. 205/L8
Huejotzingo, Mex. 205/L7
Huejuquilla el Alto, Mex. 204/E4
Huejutla de Reyes, Mex. 206/B1
Huelgoat, Fr. 62/B4
Huelma, Sp. 52/D4
Huelva, Sp. 52/B4
Huelva (riv.), Sp. 52/B4
Huequi (vol.), Chile 226/B4
Huercal-Overa, Sp. 52/E4
Huerfano (riv.), Co, US 184/B5
Huesca, Sp. 53/E1
Huéscar, Sp. 52/D4
Huesos (stream), Arg. 226/F3
Huetamo de Nuñez, Mex. 205/E5
Huete, Sp. 52/D2
Huexoculco, Mex. 205/R10
Hüfingen, Ger. 67/E2
Huger, SC, US 193/H4
Hugh Town, Eng, UK 37/Q12
Hughenden, Austl. 158/B3
Hughenden, Ab, Can. 175/J1
Hughenden Valley, Eng, UK 36/A2
Hughes, Arg. 226/E2
Hughes, Austl. 155/F4
Hughes, Ak, US 201/H2
Hughes, Ar, US 192/B3
Hughes Springs, Tx, US 183/G4
Hughesville, Pa, US 198/B1
Hughson, Ca, US 178/B2
Huglfing, Ger. 67/H2
Hugli (riv.), India 104/E3
Hugo, Co, US 184/C4
Hugo, Mn, US 187/Q6
Hugo, Ok, US 183/G3
Hugo (lake), Ok, US 183/G3
Hugo (dam), Ok, US 183/G3
Hugoton, Ks, US 182/D2
Huguan, China 92/C3
Hui (riv.), China 91/H2
Hui Xian, China 92/C4
Huib-Hock (plat.), Namb. 142/B2
Huichapan, Mex. 205/K6
Hŭich'ŏn, NKor. 93/D2
Huila (dept.), Col. 216/C4
Huila (dept.), Ang. 140/B2
Huilango, Mex. 205/Q9
Huili, China 105/H2
Huimanguillo, Mex. 206/C2
Huimin, China 92/D3
Huinan, China 91/K3
Huinca Renancó, Arg. 226/D2
Huining, China 90/F4
Hŭisaek-pong (peak), NKor. 93/D2
Huishui, China 105/J2
Huisne (riv.), Fr. 50/D2
Huisseau-sur-Cosson, Fr. 63/G5
Huissen, Neth. 58/C5
Huitong, China 105/J2
Huittinen, Fin. 47/K1
Huitzilan, Mex. 205/M7
Huitzuco, Mex. 205/K8
Huixcolotla, Mex. 205/M8
Huixquilucan, Mex. 205/Q10
Huixtla, Mex. 206/C3
Huize, China 98/D3
Huizen, Neth. 58/C4
Huizhou, China 99/G4
Hujirt, Mong. 90/E2
Hujra, Pak. 110/B4
Hŭksan (arch.), SKor. 91/J5
Hukuntsi, Bots. 140/D4
Hulah (dam), Ok, US 183/F2
Hulah (lake), Ok, US 183/F2
Hulan, China 91/K2
Hulan (riv.), China 91/K2
Hulbert, Ok, US 183/G3
Hulbert, Mi, US 190/D1
Hulett, Wy, US 184/B1
Hull (riv.), Eng, UK 41/H4
Hull, Ia, US 185/F2
Hull (Orona) (isl.), Kiri. 161/H5
Hullbridge, Eng, UK 36/E2
Hüllhorst, Ger. 59/F4
Hullo, Est. 47/K2
Hulst, Neth. 58/B6
Hultsfred, Swe. 46/F3
Hulu (riv.), China 90/F4
Hulun (lake), China 90/H2
Ḩulwān, Egypt 131/C5
Hulyaypole, Ukr. 79/J4
Huma (riv.), China 81/N4
Huma, China 91/K1
Humahuaca, Arg. 224/C2
Humaitá, Par. 224/E3
Humaitá, Braz. 221/F2
Humaitá, Bol. 221/E3
Humaljärvi (lake), Fin. 45/E4
Humansdorp, SAfr. 142/D4
Humansville, Mo, US 183/H2
Humay, Peru 220/C4
Humbe, Ang. 140/B3
Humber (riv.), Eng, UK 41/H4
Humber (riv.), Nf, Can. 188/J1
Humber (bay), On, Can. 190/U8
Humber, West (riv.), On, Can. 190/T8
Humberside (arpt.), Eng, UK 41/H4
Humberston, Eng, UK 41/H4
Humberto de Campos, Braz. 219/F3
Humble, Tx, US 181/M9
Humboldt, Sk, Can. 175/M1
Humboldt (bay), Col. 207/G5
Humboldt (peak), NCal., Fr. 161/V12
Humboldt, Az, US 179/F3
Humboldt (bay), Ca, US 176/A3
Humboldt, Ks, US 183/G2
Humboldt, Ia, US 185/G2
Humboldt, Mn, US 186/F3
Humboldt, Ne, US 185/G3
Humboldt (lake), Nv, US 176/D3
Humboldt (riv.), Nv, US 172/C3
Humboldt, Tn, US 192/C3
Humboldt, North Fork (riv.), Nv, US 176/F3
Hume (dam), Austl. 157/C3
Hūmedān, Iran 113/G3
Humenné, Slvk. 49/L4
Humeston, Ia, US 185/H3
Humlebæk, Den. 45/J7
Humlum, Den. 46/C3
Hummels Wharf, Pa, US 198/B2
Hummelstown, Pa, US 198/B3
Humnoke, Ar, US 183/J3
Humphrey, Ar, US 183/J3
Humphrey, Ne, US 184/F3
Humphrey, On, Can. 191/G2
Humphrey Point (cape), Ak, US 201/K2
Humphreys (peak), Az, US 179/G3
Humphreys (mt.), Ca, US 178/C2
Humpty Doo, Austl. 152/C3
Humshaugh, Eng, UK 41/F1
Hūn, Libya 126/B2
Hun (riv.), China 91/J3
Húnaflói (bay), Ice. 44/N6
Hunan (prov.), China 105/K2
Hunchun, China 91/L3
Hundested, Den. 45/H7
Hundewāli, Pak. 110/B4
Hundred, WV, US 190/F5
Hundred Fifty Mile House, BC, Can. 174/D1
Hundred Mile House, BC, Can. 174/D2
Hundsangen, Ger. 61/G3
Hunedoara (prov.), Rom. 56/F3
Hunedoara, Rom. 56/F3
Hünenberg, Swi. 67/E3
Hung Yen, Viet. 106/D1
Hungaroring, Hun. 57/R9
Hungary (ctry.) 56/D2
Hungen, Ger. 64/B2
Hungerford, Austl. 156/C1
Hungerford, Eng, UK 43/E4
Hŭnghae, SKor. 93/E4
Hŭngnam, NKor. 93/D3
Hŭngnyŏng-nodongjagu, NKor. 93/D3
Hungry (peak), Id, US 174/G4
Hungry Horse (dam), Mt, US 175/G3
Hungulo, Ang. 140/C2
Hüngüy (riv.), Mong. 90/C2
Hunjiang, China 93/D2
Hunkui, Nga. 133/G4
Hunmanby, Eng, UK 41/H3
Hunnebostrand, Swe. 46/D2
Hunsel, Neth. 58/C6
Hunsrück (mts.), Ger. 48/D4
Hunstanton, Eng, UK 43/G1
Hunt (mtn.), Wy, US 177/K1
Hunte (riv.), Ger. 48/E2
Hunter (mt.), Ak, US 201/H3
Hunter, ND, US 186/F4
Hunter (mtn.), NY, US 191/J3
Hunter (riv.), Austl. 156/D2
Hunter, Tx, US 180/E3
Hunter (isl.), Austl. 145/D5
Hunter Army Afld., Ga, US 195/H1
Hunterdon (co.), NJ, US 198/C2
Hunters, Wa, US 174/E3
Hunters Creek Village, Tx, US 181/M9
Huntersville, NC, US 193/G3
Hunterville, NZ 159/C2
Huntingburg, In, US 192/D1
Huntingdon, Qu, Can. 191/J2
Huntingdon, Eng, UK 43/F2
Huntingdon, Pa, US 191/G4
Huntingdon, Tn, US 192/C2
Huntington, Eng, UK 41/G4
Huntington, In, US 190/D4
Huntington, NY, US 199/M8
Huntington (bay), NY, US 199/M8
Huntington, Or, US 176/E1
Huntington (cr.), Pa, US 198/B1
Huntington, Tx, US 180/G2
Huntington, Ut, US 177/H4
Huntington, WV, US 193/F1
Huntington Bay, NY, US 199/M8
Huntington Beach, Ca, US 196/G8
Huntington Park, Ca, US 196/F8
Huntington Station, NY, US 199/M8
Huntington Woods, Mi, US 197/F7
Huntland, Tn, US 192/D3
Huntley, Il, US 197/P15
Huntly, Sc, UK 39/D2
Huntly, NZ 159/C2
Hunts Inlet, BC, Can. 201/M4
Hunts Point, Wa, US 197/C2
Huntsville, On, Can. 191/G2
Huntsville, Al, US 192/D3
Huntsville, Ar, US 183/H2
Huntsville, Mo, US 185/H4
Huntsville (res.), Pa, US 198/B1
Huntsville, Tn, US 192/E2
Huntsville, Tx, US 181/G2
Huntsville, Wa, US 174/E4
Hunua, NZ 159/G7
Hunucmá, Mex. 206/D1
Hünxe, Ger. 58/D5
Hunyuan, China 92/C3
Huo (mtn.), China 92/B3
Huo (mtn.), China 92/D5
Huocheng, China 111/D3
Huojia, China 92/C4
Huolin Gol, China 91/H2
Huolongmen, China 91/K2
Huolupu, China 99/E2
Huon (gulf), PNG 153/G1
Huon (pen.), PNG 153/G1
Huong Hoa, Viet. 106/D2
Huong Khe, Viet. 106/D2
Huong Son, Viet. 106/D2
Huong Thuy, Viet. 105/J4
Huonville, Austl. 156/C4
Huoqiu, China 92/D4
Huoshan, China 92/D5
Huotong, China 99/H3
Huozhou, China 92/B3
Ḩuraymilā, SAr. 112/E3
Hūrayn, Egypt 131/B3
Hurd (cape), On, Can. 190/F2
Hurdal, Nor. 46/D1
Hurdiyo, Som. 136/D3
Hurdle Mills, NC, US 193/H2
Hure Qi, China 92/E2
Hurepoix (reg.), Fr. 36/H6
Hurley, Eng, UK 36/A2
Hurley (riv.), Ire. 40/B4
Hurley, Ms, US 194/D2
Hurley, NY, US 191/J4
Hurley, NM, US 179/H4
Hurley, Wi, US 187/J4
Hurlford, Sc, UK 39/B5
Hurlock, Md, US 193/K1
Huron (lake), Can.,US 163/J5
Huron, Ca, US 178/B2
Huron (bay), Mi, US 187/K4
Huron (mts.), Mi, US 187/K4
Huron, Oh, US 190/E4
Huron (pt.), Mi, US 197/G6
Huron (riv.), Mi, US 197/E7
Huron, SD, US 184/E1
Huron Islands Nat'l Wild. Ref., Mi, US 187/K4
Huron Mountain, Mi, US 187/L4
Hurricane (lake), ND, US 186/E3
Hurricane, Al, US 194/E2
Hurricane (cliffs), Az, US 179/F2
Hurricane, Ut, US 179/F2
Hurricane, WV, US 193/F1
Hurshat Tal NP, Isr. 117/D2
Hurst, Tx, US 180/K7
Hurstville, Austl. 157/E1
Hurtaut (riv.), Fr. 60/D4
Hürtgenwald (reg.), Ger. 61/F2
Hürth, Ger. 61/F2
Hurtsboro, Al, US 192/E4
Hurum, Nor. 44/S9
Hurup, Den. 46/C3
Huruta, Eth. 136/A3
Hurworth, Eng, UK 41/G3
Hurzuf, Ukr. 76/E3
Husainābād, India 109/E3
Husainpur, Bang. 109/H3
Huslia, Ak, US 201/G2
Húsavík, Ice. 44/P6
Ḩusayyāt al Fawākhir (well), Libya 126/D2
Husbands Bosworth, Eng, UK 43/E2
Husby-Långhundra, Swe. 45/B1
Hushan, China 99/H2
Husher, Wi, US 197/Q14
Hushi, China 99/H3
Huşi, Rom. 78/E4
Huskisson, Austl. 157/E2
Husnes, Nor. 46/A2
Hussar, Ab, Can. 175/H2
Hussigny-Godbrange, Fr. 61/E5
Hustisford, Wi, US 185/K2
Husum, Ger. 46/C4
Husum, Swe. 44/F3
Husyatyn, Ukr. 78/D3
Hutag, Mong. 90/E2
Hutanopan, Indo. 101/C2
Hutchins, Tx, US 180/L7
Hutchinson, Ks, US 183/F1
Hutchinson (isl.), Fl, US 195/H4
Hutchinson, Mn, US 185/G1
Ḩūth, Yem. 136/B1
Hutiaoxia, China 98/D3
Hutsonville, Il, US 190/C5
Hutt (riv.), NZ 159/J9
Huttig, Ar, US 183/H4
Hüttisheim, Ger. 67/F1
Hüttlingen, Ger. 64/D5
Huttoft, Eng, UK 41/J5
Hutton, Eng, UK 36/E2
Hutton (mt.), Austl. 158/C4
Hutton Cranswick, Eng, UK 41/H4
Hutton Lake Nat'l Wild. Ref., Wy, US 184/B3
Hutton Rudby, Eng, UK 41/G3
Huttonville, On, Can. 190/T8
Huttwil, Swi. 66/D3
Hutubi, China 111/E3

294
Hutuo – Irico

Hutuo (riv.), China 92/C3
Huveane (riv.), Fr. 53/H1
Huveaune (riv.), Fr. 70/B6
Huwan, China 99/G2
Ḩuwwārah, WBnk. 117/C4
Huxi, China 99/G3
Huxley, Tx, US 181/H2
Huxley, Ia, US 185/H3
Huy, Belg. 61/E2
Huyton-with-Roby, Eng, UK 41/F5
Hūzgān, Iran 115/G4
Huzhou, China 92/L9
Hvammstangi, Ice. 44/N6
Hvannadalshnúkur (peak), Ice. 44/P7
Hvar, Cro. 56/C4
Hvar (isl.), Cro. 73/H2
Hvardiys'ke, Ukr. 79/H5
Hvide Sande, Den. 46/C4
Hvidovre, Den. 45/J7
Hvítá (riv.), Ice. 44/N7
Hvitsten, Nor. 44/S9
Hvittingfoss, Nor. 44/R9
Hvolsvöllur, Ice. 44/N7
Hwach'ŏn, SKor. 93/D3
Hwadae, NKor. 93/E2
Hwange, Zim. 141/E3
Hwange (Wankie) NP, Zim. 141/E3
Hwanghae-bukto (prov.), NKor. 93/D3
Hwanghae-namdo (prov.), NKor. 93/C3
Hwangju (riv.), NKor. 93/C3
Hwangju, NKor. 93/C3
Hwap'yŏng, NKor. 93/D2
Hwasun, SKor. 93/D5
Hyades (peak), Chile 226/B5
Hyak, Wa, US 174/D4
Hyangsan, NKor. 93/D2
Hyannis, Ne, US 184/D2
Hyargas (lake), Mong. 90/C2
Hyattstown, Md, US 198/A5
Hyattsville, Md, US 198/B6
Hyco (res.), NC, US 193/H2
Hydaburg, Ak, US 201/M4
Hyde, Eng, UK 41/F5
Hyde, NZ 159/B4
Hyde Park, Vt, US 191/K2
Hyde Park, NY, US 191/K4
Hyden, Ky, US 193/F2
Hyden, Austl. 154/C5
Hyder, Ak, US 201/M4
Hyderābād, India 107/C2
Hyderābād, Pak. 113/J3
Hydesville, Ca, US 176/A3
Hyères (riv.), Fr. 62/B4
Hyères (bay), Fr. 70/C6
Hyères, Fr. 70/C6
Hyères, Iles d' (isls.), Fr. 72/E2
Hyesan, NKor. 93/E2
Hyland (riv.), Yk, Can. 170/D2
Hyllestad, Nor. 46/A1
Hyltebruk, Swe. 46/E3
Hylton (hill), Ky, US 193/F2
Hyō-no-sen (peak), Japan 96/D3
Hyōgo (pref.), Japan 96/D3
Hyŏndŭng-san (peak), SKor. 93/G6
Hypoluxo, Fl, US 194/P9
Hyrra Banda, CAfr. 134/D4
Hyrum, Ut, US 177/H3
Hyrylä (Skavaböle), Fin. 45/F4
Hysham, Mt, US 175/L4
Hythe, Austl. 156/C4
Hythe, Eng, UK 43/E5
Hythe, Eng, UK 43/H4
Hytop, Al, US 192/D3
Hyūga, Japan 96/B4
Hyvinkää, Fin. 47/L1

I

I-n-Amenas, Alg. 129/H3
I-n-Amguel, Alg. 129/G5
I-n-Azaoua, Oued (riv.), Niger 129/H5
I-n-Chaouâg (wadi), Mali 133/F2
I-n-Dagouber (well), Mali 129/E5
I-n-Échaï (well), Mali 133/E1
I-n-Eker, Alg. 129/G4
I-n-Farba, Mrta. 132/C3
I-n-Gall, Niger 133/G2
I-n-Guezzâm, Alg. 133/G2
I-n-Milach (well), Mali 133/E2
I-n-Rhar, Alg. 129/F4
I-n-Sâkâne, 'Erg (des.), Mali 133/E1
I-n-Salah, Alg. 129/F4
I-n-Tassik (well), Mali 133/F2
I-n-Tebezas, Mali 133/F2
I-n-Tilelt, Mali 133/E3
Iabalo, Eth. 136/B4
Iacanga, Braz. 225/G2
Iaco (riv.), Braz. 220/D3
Iaçu, Braz. 223/E2
Iâf di Montasio (peak), It. 51/K3
Iakora, Madg. 143/H8
Ialibu, PNG 153/F1
Ialomiţa (riv.), Rom. 76/C3
Ialomita (prov.), Rom. 57/H3
Ianakafy, Madg. 143/H8
Ianapera, Madg. 143/H8
Iargara, Mol. 78/E4
Iaşi (prov.), Rom. 57/H2
Iaşi, Rom. 78/D4
Íasmos, Gre. 55/J2
Iatt (lake), La, US 194/B2
Iba, Phil. 100/B2
Ibadan, Nga. 133/F5
Ibagué, Col. 219/K8
Ibaiti, Braz. 225/G2
Ibajay, Phil. 100/C3
Ibanda, Ugan. 139/G3
Ibans (lake), Hon. 207/E3
Ibapah (peak), Ut, US 177/G4
Ibapah, Ut, US 177/G3
Ibar (riv.), Serb. 56/E4
Ibara, Japan 96/C3
Ibaraki (pref.), Japan 97/F2
Ibaraki, Japan 95/E1
Ibaraki, Japan 95/J6
Ibarra, Ecu. 216/B4
Ibarreta, Arg. 224/E3
Ibb, Yem. 136/C2
Ibba (riv.), Sudan 135/F4
Ibbenbüren, Ger. 59/E4
'Ibbīn, Jor. 117/D4
Ibdekkene (riv.), Mali 133/F2
Ibenga (riv.), Congo 138/D2
Iberia, Mo, US 183/H1
Iberia, Peru 220/D3
Iberia, Peru 220/C2
Ibérico, Sistema (mts.), Sp. 72/C2
Iberville, Qu, Can. 189/P7
Ibeto, Nga. 133/G4
Ibi, Nga. 133/H4
Ibi, Sp. 53/E3
Ibi (riv.), Japan 91/M4
Ibiapada, Serra da (mts.), Braz. 219/F3
Ibiapina, Braz. 219/F3
Ibicaraí, Braz. 223/F2
Ibicuí (riv.), Braz. 225/E4
Ibicuy, Arg. 227/J10
Ibigawa, Japan 95/L5
I'billīn, Isr. 117/C3
Ibimirim, Braz. 219/G5
Ibirapuitã (riv.), Braz. 225/F4
Ibirubá, Braz. 225/F4
Ibitinga, Braz. 225/G2
Ibiúna, Braz. 223/J8
Ibiza (isl.), Sp. 53/F3
Ibiza, Sp. 53/F3
Ibiza (isl.), Sp. 29/E5
Ibnahs, Egypt 131/C3
Ibo (riv.), Japan 96/D3
Ibo, Moz. 141/J2
Ibondo, D.R. Congo 139/G3
Iboro, Nga. 133/F5
Ibotirama, Braz. 223/E2
Iboundji (peak), Gabon 138/B3
Ibrā', Oman 113/G4
Ibrah (wadi), Sudan 135/E3
Ibrány, Hun. 49/L4
'Ibrī, Oman 113/G4
İbriktepe, Turk. 57/H5
Ibshān, Egypt 131/C2
Ibshawāy, Egypt 131/B6
Ibstock, Eng, UK 43/E1
Ibu, Indo. 103/G3
Ibuki, Japan 95/K5
Ibuki-yama (peak), Japan 95/K5
Iça (riv.), SAm. 209/D3
Ica, Peru 220/C4
Ica (dept.), Peru 220/C4
Icabarú, Ven. 217/F3
Içana (riv.), Braz. 216/E4
Icaño, Arg. 224/C4
Icaraíma, Braz. 225/F2
Icatu, Braz. 219/E3
Icel (prov.), Turk. 116/C1
Iceland (ctry.) 44/N7
Ichalkaranji, India 107/B2
Ichāmati (riv.), Bang. 109/G3
Ichenhausen, Ger. 64/D6
Icheu, Nga. 133/G5
Ichhāwar, India 108/A4
Ichihara, Japan 95/E3
Ichijima, Japan 95/H5
Ichikawa, Japan 95/D2
Ichikawada, Japan 95/B2
Ichilo (riv.), Bol. 221/E5
Ichinohe, Japan 94/B3
Ichinomiya, Japan 95/G7
Ichinomiya, Japan 95/L5
Ichinomiya, Japan 95/E3
Ichinomiya, Japan 95/B2
Ichinomiya, Japan 95/M6
Ichinoseki, Japan 94/B4
Ichishi, Japan 95/K6
Ichkeul (lake), Tun. 130/L6
Ichnya, Ukr. 79/G1
Ichoca, Bol. 224/C1
Ich'ŏn, SKor. 93/D4
Ich'ŏn, NKor. 93/D3
Ichtegem, Belg. 60/C1
Ichuña, Peru 224/B1
Ickesburg, Pa, US 198/A3
Icó, Braz. 219/G4
Icod de los Vinos, Sp. 128/A3
Iconi, Com. 143/G5
Icononzo, Col. 219/L8
Icy (bay), Ak, US 170/B3
Icy (cape), Ak, US 201/F1
Icy (pt.), Ak, US 201/L4
Icy (str.), Ak, US 201/L4
Ida Grove, Ia, US 185/G2
Idabel, Ok, US 183/G4
Idabo, Eth. 136/B4
Idah, Nga. 133/G5
Idaho (state), US 172/C3
Idaho City, Id, US 176/F2
Idaho Falls, Id, US 177/G2
Idaho Nat'l Engineering Laboratory, Id, US 177/G2
Idalia, Co, US 184/C4
Idalou, Tx, US 182/D4
Idanha-a-Nova, Port. 52/B3
Idāppādi, India 107/C4
Idar, India 104/B3
Idar-Oberstein, Ger. 61/G4
Idarkopf (peak), Ger. 61/G4
Idaville, In, US 190/C4
Idaville, Pa, US 198/A3
Ide, Japan 95/J6
Ide Hill, Eng, UK 36/D3
Ideal, Ga, US 192/E4
Idel', Rus. 74/G2
Ideles, Alg. 129/G5
Ider, Al, US 192/E3
Ider, Mong. 90/D2
Ider (riv.), Mong. 90/D2
Idfīnā, Egypt 131/B2
Idfū, Egypt 127/G3
Ídhi (peak), Gre. 55/J5
Ídhra, Gre. 55/H4
Idi, Indo. 101/B1
Idice (riv.), It. 69/E4
Idiofa, D.R. Congo 138/D4
Idiroko, Nga. 133/F5
Idkū (lake), Egypt 131/B2
Idkū, Egypt 131/B2
Idle (riv.), Eng, UK 41/H5
Idlib, Syria 116/E2
Idlib (prov.), Syria 116/E2
Idnah, WBnk. 117/B5
Idrija, Slov. 51/L4
Idriss I (dam), Mor. 130/B2
Idritsa, Rus. 47/N3
Idro (lake), It. 68/D1
Idstein, Ger. 64/B2
Idyllwild-Pine Cove, Ca, US 178/D4
Ie (isl.), Japan 97/J7
Iecava, Lat. 47/L3
Iema, Ang. 138/C4
Ieper, Belg. 60/B2
Ierápetra, Gre. 55/J5
Ierissós, Gre. 55/H2
Ierna, Slvk. 78/B3
Iesolo, It. 69/F2
Ifakara, Tanz. 137/B4
Ifaki, Nga. 133/G5
Ifalik (isl.), Micr. 160/D4
Ifanadiana, Madg. 143/H8
Ife, Nga. 133/G5
Iferfes (well), Libya 129/H3
Iferouâne, Niger 133/H2
Iffeldorf, Ger. 67/H2
Iffezheim, Ger. 64/B5
Ifon, Nga. 133/G5
Iforas, Adrar des (mts.), Alg.,Mali 129/F5
Ifrane, Mor. 128/D2
Ifs, Fr. 63/E2
Iga, Japan 95/K6
Iga (riv.), Japan 95/K6
Igal, Hun. 56/C2
Igalula, Tanz. 139/H4
Iganga, Ugan. 137/A1
Igara Paraná (riv.), Col. 216/C5
Igarapava, Braz. 225/H2
Igarapé Açu, Braz. 219/E3
Igarapé Água Preta (riv.), Braz. 221/E1
Igarapé Grande, Braz. 219/E4
Igarapé-Miri, Braz. 218/D3
Igarassu, Braz. 219/H4
Igaratá, Braz. 223/K8
Igarka, Rus. 80/J3
Igarra, Nga. 133/G5
Igawa, Tanz. 137/A4
Igbetti, Nga. 133/G4
Igboho, Nga. 133/F4
Igdet (peak), Mor. 128/C3
Iğdır, Turk. 115/F2
Igel, Ger. 61/F4
Iggesund, Swe. 46/G1
Ightham, Eng, UK 36/D3
Igikpak (mt.), Ak, US 201/H2
Igis, Swi. 67/F4
Igiugig, Ak, US 201/G4
Iglesias, It. 54/A3
Igli, Alg. 129/E3
Igling, Ger. 67/G1
Iglino, Rus. 75/N5
Igloolik, Nun, Can. 171/H2
Ignace, On, Can. 187/J3
Ignacio, Ca, US 197/J10
Ignacio, Co, US 179/J2
Ignacio de la Llave, Mex. 205/P8
Ignacio Zaragoza, Mex. 204/D2
Ignalina, Lith. 47/M4
İğneada, Turk. 57/H5
İğneada Burnu (cape), Turk. 57/J5
Igney, Fr. 66/C1
Ignon (riv.), Fr. 66/A2
Igny, Fr. 36/J5
Igombe (riv.), Tanz. 137/A3
Igombe, Tanz. 139/H3
Igor I. Sikorsky Memorial (arpt.), Ct, US 199/E1
Igora Paraná (riv.), Col. 220/C1
Igoumenítsa, Gre. 55/G3
Igra, Rus. 75/M4
Igreja Nova, Braz. 223/F1
Igrim, Rus. 80/G3
Iguaçu (riv.), Braz. 209/D5
Iguaçu, PN do, Braz. 225/F3
Iguaí, Braz. 223/E2
Iguala, Mex. 205/K8
Igualada, Sp. 53/F2
Iguape, Braz. 225/H3
Iguape, Ribeira do (riv.), Braz. 222/C5
Iguatemi (riv.), Braz. 222/B4
Iguatu, Braz. 219/G4
Iguazú (int'l arpt.), Arg. 225/F3
Iguéla, Gabon 138/B3
Iguetti (lake), Mrta. 128/C4
Igugunu, Tanz. 137/A3
Iharana, Madg. 143/J6
Iheya (isl.), Japan 97/J7
Ihhayrhan, Mong. 90/F2
Ihiala, Nga. 133/G5
Ihnāsiyah al Madīnah, Egypt 131/B6
Ihosy, Madg. 143/H8
Ihotry (lake), Madg. 143/G8
Ihu, PNG 153/G1
Ihuari, Peru 220/B3
Ihuo, Nga. 133/G5
Ii, Fin. 74/E2
Ii (riv.), Fin. 80/C3
Iida, Japan 97/E3
Iidaan, Som. 136/D4
Iide-san (peak), Japan 97/F2
Iijoki (riv.), Fin. 74/F2
Iinan, Japan 95/K7
Iisaku, Est. 47/M2
Iisalmi, Fin. 74/E3
Iitaka, Japan 95/K7
Iittala, Fin. 45/E3
Iitti, Fin. 47/M1
Iiyama, Japan 97/F2
Iizuka, Japan 96/B4
Ijara, Kenya 137/C2
Ijebu Ode, Nga. 133/F5
Ijill (lake), Mrta. 128/B5
Ijill (peak), Mrta. 128/B5
Ijira, Japan 95/L4
IJlst, Neth. 58/C2
IJmeer (bay), Neth. 58/C4
IJmuiden, Neth. 58/B4
Ijnaoun (well), Mrta. 132/B2
Ijoki (riv.), Fin. 44/H2
Ijoubbane, 'Erg (des.), Mali 128/D5
IJssel (riv.), Neth. 58/C3
Ijsselmeer (lake), Neth. 48/C2
Ijsselmuiden, Neth. 58/C3
Ijsselstein, Neth. 58/C4
Ijuí (riv.), Braz. 225/F4
Ijuí, Braz. 225/F4
Ijūin, Japan 96/B5
Ijzendijke, Neth. 60/C1
Ijzer (riv.), Belg. 48/B3
Ik (riv.), Rus. 75/M5
Ikahavo (plat.), Madg. 143/H7
Ikalamavony, Madg. 143/H8
Ikali, D.R. Congo 139/E3
Ikamba, Tanz. 139/G4
Ikanda Nord, D.R. Congo 139/E3
Ikang, Nga. 138/B1
Ikare, Nga. 133/G5
Ikaría (isl.), Gre. 73/K3
Ikaría (isl), Gre. 114/A2
Ikaruga, Japan 95/J6
Ikasi, Tanz. 137/A3
Ikeda, Japan 96/C3
Ikeda, Japan 94/C2
Ikeda, Japan 95/H6
Ikeda, Japan 95/L5
Ikeja, Nga. 133/F5
Ikela, D.R. Congo 139/E3
Ikelemba (riv.), D.R. Congo 138/D2
Ikelemba, Congo 138/D2
Ikem, Nga. 133/G5
Ikenokoya-yama (peak), Japan 95/K7
Ikerre, Nga. 133/G5
Ikhtiman, Bul. 57/F4
Iki (isl.), Japan 96/A4
Iki (chan.), Japan 96/A4
Iki-Burul, Rus. 77/H3
Ikire, Nga. 133/G5
Ikirun, Nga. 133/G5
İkizce, Turk. 114/C2
İkizdere, Turk. 77/G4
Ikkala, Fin. 45/E4
Ikole, Nga. 133/G5
Ikom, Nga. 133/H5
Ikoma, Tanz. 137/A2
Ikoma, Japan 95/J6
Ikongo, Madg. 143/H8
Ikopa (riv.), Madg. 143/H7
Ikorodu, Nga. 133/F5
Ikot Ekpene, Nga. 133/G5
Ikot Okpora, Nga. 133/H5
Ikozi, D.R. Congo 139/F3
Ikrāsh, Egypt 131/C3
Iksāl, Isr. 117/C3
Ikungi, Tanz. 137/A3
Ikungu, Tanz. 137/A3
Ikuno, Japan 96/D3
Ikwah, Egypt 131/C3
Ila Orangun, Nga. 133/G4
Ilabaya, Peru 224/B1
Ilagala, Tanz. 139/G4
Ilagan, Phil. 100/C1
Ilaka, Madg. 143/H8
Ilaka, Madg. 143/J7
Īlām, Iran 115/F3
Ilam, Nepal 109/F2
Īlām (gov.), Iran 115/F3
Ilām Bāzār, India 109/F4
Ilan, Tai. 99/J3
Ilangali, Tanz. 137/A3
Ilanz, Swi. 67/F4
Ilaro, Nga. 133/F5
Ilave, Peru 220/D5
Iława, Pol. 49/K2
Ilawe-Ekiti, Nga. 133/G5
'Ilay, Sudan 135/F1
Ilchester, Eng, UK 42/D4
Ile (riv.), Kaz. 83/G5
Ile Art (isl.), NCal., Fr. 161/T11
Ile aux Coudres (isl.), Qu, Can. 188/B2
Ile aux Grues (isl.), Qu, Can. 188/B2
Ile aux Lièvres (isl.), QU, Can. 188/C2
Ile Baaba (isl.), NCal., Fr. 161/T11
Ile Balabio (isl.), NCal., Fr. 161/U12
Ile Callot (isl.), Fr. 62/B3
Ile d' Orléans (isl.), Qu, Can. 188/B2
Ile d'Anticosti (isl.), Can. 163/L5
Ile de Bagaud (isl.), Fr. 70/C7
Ile de Batz (isl.), Fr. 62/A3
Ile de Bréhat (isl.), Fr. 62/C3
Ile de Levant (isl.), Fr. 70/C6
Ile de Porquerolles (isl.), Fr. 70/C7
Ile de Riou (isl.), Sp. 70/B6
Ile des Pins (isl.), NCal., Fr. 160/F7
Ile Esumba (isl.), D.R. Congo 139/E2
Ile Idjwe (isl.), D.R. Congo 139/G3
Ile Tidra (isl.), Mrta. 132/A2
Ile Tiga (isl.), NCal., Fr. 161/V12
Ile Yandé (isl.), NCal., Fr. 161/T12
Île-à-la-Crosse, Sk, Can. 170/F3
Île-de-France (pol. reg.), Fr. 60/A6
Ile-de-Montréal (co.), Qu, Can. 189/N6
Ile-Jésus (co.), Qu, Can. 189/N6
Île-Perrot (isl.), Qu, Can. 189/N7
Ilebo, D.R. Congo 139/E4
Ilek, Rus. 77/K2
Ilek (riv.), Rus. 77/K2
Ilen (riv.), Ire. 38/A6
Iles Chausey (isl.), Fr. 62/D3
Iles de la Madeleine (isl.), Qu, Can. 189/F2
Iles de Lérins (isls.), Fr. 70/D5
Iles du Vent (isls.), FrPol. 161/L6
Îles Ehotilés, PN des, C.d'Iv. 132/E5
Iles Glorieuses (isls.), Reun., Fr. 143/H5
Iles sous le Vent (isls.), FrPol. 161/K6
Iles Tristao (isls.), Gui. 132/B4
Ilesha, Nga. 133/G5
Ilfacombe, Austl. 158/B3
Ilfis (riv.), Swi. 66/D4
Ilford (nbrhd.), Eng, UK 36/D2
Ilford, Austl. 157/D1
Ilfracombe, Eng, UK 42/B4
Ilgaz, Turk. 76/E4
Ilgın, Turk. 114/B2
Ilha Caravela (isl.), GBis. 132/A4
Ilha de Jeta (isl.), GBis. 132/A4
Ilha de Marajó (isl.), Braz. 209/D3
Ilha do Bazaruto (isl.), Moz. 141/G4
Ilha Grande (bay), Braz. 222/D4
Ilha Solteira (res.), Braz. 222/C3
Ilhabela, Braz. 223/L8
Ilhas Desertas (isl.), Port. 128/A2
Ilhas Selvagens (isl.), Sp. 128/A3
Ílhavo, Port. 52/A2
Ilhea (pt.), Namb. 140/B4
Ilhéus, Braz. 223/F2
Iliamna, Ak, US 201/H4
Iliamna (lake), Ak, US 201/G4
Iliamna (mt.), Ak, US 201/H3
İliç, Turk. 114/D2
Ilıca, Turk. 77/G5
Ilicínea, Braz. 222/D4
Iliff, Co, US 184/C3
Iligan, Phil. 100/D3
Iligan (bay), Phil. 100/C3
Ilijaš, Bosn. 56/D4
Iliniza (peak), Ecu. 216/B5
Il'inskiy, Rus. 91/N2
Il'inskoye, Rus. 75/K4
Iliomar, ETim. 152/B2
Ilirska Bistrica, Slov. 51/L4
Ilısu (dam), Turk. 114/E2
Ilisu (res.), Turk. 114/E2
Ilium (Troy) (ruin), Turk. 55/K3
Ilkeston, Eng, UK 41/G6
Īlkhchī, Iran 115/F2
Ilkley, Eng, UK 41/G4
Ill (riv.), Fr. 51/G3
Ill (riv.), Aus. 51/H3
Illabo, Austl. 157/C2
Illana, Sp. 52/D2
Illapel, Chile 224/B4
Illasi (riv.), It. 69/E1
Illawarra (lake), Austl. 157/E2
Illbillee (mt.), Austl. 155/G3
Ille (riv.), Fr. 62/D4
Ille-et-Vilaine (dept.), Fr. 62/D4
Illéla, Niger 133/G3
Illela, Nga. 133/G3
Iller (riv.), Ger. 51/J2
Illerbrun, Sk, Can. 175/K3
Illertissen, Ger. 67/G1
Illescas, Sp. 52/D2
Illet (riv.), Fr. 62/D4
Illichivs'k, Ukr. 78/F4
Illiers-Combray, Fr. 63/G4
Illigh (pt.), Som. 136/D4
Illimani (peak), Bol. 224/C1
Illingen, Ger. 61/G5
Illinois (riv.), Il, US 173/J3
Illinois (state), US 173/J4
Illinois (riv.), Il, US 185/K3
Illizi, Alg. 129/H4
Illizi (wilaya), Alg. 129/G4
Illkirch-Graffenstaden, Fr. 66/D1
Illmensee, Ger. 67/F2
Illnau, Swi. 67/E3
Illogan, Eng, UK 42/A6
Illora, Sp. 52/D4
Illovo, SAfr. 143/E3
Illushi, Nga. 133/G5
Illyungmadja (pt.), Austl. 153/E3
Illzach, Fr. 66/D2
Ilm (riv.), Ger. 48/F4
Ilmajoki, Fin. 44/G3
Ilme (riv.), Ger. 59/G5
Il'men (lake), Rus. 80/D4
Ilmenau (riv.), Ger. 59/H2
Ilminster, Eng, UK 42/D5
Ilo, Peru 220/D5
Ilobu, Nga. 133/G5
Iloca, Chile 226/B2
Iloilo, Phil. 100/C3
Ilongero, Tanz. 137/A3
Ilorin, Nga. 133/G4
Ilovays'k, Ukr. 79/K4
Ilovlya, Rus. 77/G2
Ilovlya (riv.), Rus. 77/H2
Ilpendam, Neth. 58/B4
Il'pyrskiy, Rus. 81/S4
Ilsan, SKor. 93/F6
Ilse (riv.), Ger. 59/H5
Ilsede, Ger. 59/H4
Ilsenburg, Ger. 59/H5
Ilsfeld, Ger. 64/C4
Ilshofen, Ger. 64/C4
Il'skiy, Rus. 79/K5
Īlubabor (pol. reg.), Eth. 135/G4
Ilūkste, Lat. 47/M4
Ilwaco, Wa, US 174/B4
Ilwaki, Indo. 152/B1
Ilyas Burnu (pt.), Turk. 57/H5
Ilych (riv.), Rus. 75/N3
Ilz (riv.), Ger. 49/G4
Imabari, Japan 96/C3
Imaichi, Japan 97/F2
Imaloto (riv.), Madg. 143/H8
İmamoğlu, Turk. 114/C2
Imandra (lake), Rus. 44/J2
Imanombo, Madg. 143/H9
Imari, Japan 96/A4
Imatong (mts.), Sudan 135/G4
Imatra, Fin. 47/N1
Imazu, Japan 95/K5
Imba (lake), Japan 95/E2
Imba, Japan 95/E2
Imbābah, Egypt 131/C4
Imbabura (prov.), Ecu. 216/B4
Imbaimadai, Guy. 218/A1
Imbituba, Braz. 225/G4
Imbler, Or, US 176/E1
Imeni 26 Bakinskikh Komissarov, Trkm. 77/K5
Imeni Chapayeva, Trkm. 113/H1
Imeni Karla Libknekhta, Rus. 79/H2
Imeni Moskvy (canal), Rus. 75/W8
Imerimandroso, Madg. 143/J7
Imese, D.R. Congo 138/D2
Īmī, Eth. 136/B4
Imi n'tanout, Mor. 128/C3
İmişli, Azer. 115/G2
Imittós (peak), Gre. 55/N9
Imja (isl.), SKor. 93/C5
Imjin (riv.), NKor. 91/K4
Imlay, Nv, US 176/D3
Imlay City, Mi, US 190/E3
Immeln (lake), Swe. 45/L6
Immendingen, Ger. 67/E2
Immenhausen, Ger. 59/G6
Immenstaad am Bodensee, Ger. 67/F2
Immenstadt im Allgäu, Ger. 67/G2
Immingham, Eng, UK 41/H4
Immokalee, Fl, US 195/H4
Imnaha (riv.), Or, US 176/E1
Imnaha, Or, US 176/E1
Imnavait (mt.), Ak, US 201/J2
Imo (state), Nga. 133/G5
Imola, It. 69/E5
Imonda, PNG 103/K4
Imouzzer des Marmoucha, Mor. 128/D2
Imouzzèr-Kandar, Mor. 130/B3
Imperatriz, Braz. 219/E4
Imperia, It. 68/B6
Imperia (prov.), It. 70/D5
Imperial, Sk, Can. 175/M2
Imperial, Peru 220/B4
Imperial (dam), Az, US 178/E4
Imperial (res.), Az,Ca, US 178/E4
Imperial (valley), Ca, US 178/E4
Imperial, Ne, US 184/D3
Imperial, Tx, US 180/C2
Imperial Beach, Ca, US 196/C5
Imperial Nat'l Wild Ref., Az,Ca, US 178/E4
Imperial Palace, Japan 95/D2
Impero (riv.), It. 68/B5
Impfondo, Congo 138/D2
Imphāl, India 98/B3
Imphy, Fr. 50/E3
Impora, Bol. 224/C2
Impruneta, It. 69/E6
Impulo, Ang. 140/B2
İmrali (isl.), Turk. 57/J5
İmranlı, Turk. 114/D2
İmroz, Gre. 55/J2
Imshil, SKor. 93/D5
Imst, Aus. 67/G3
Imuris, Mex. 204/C2
Imus, Phil. 100/E7
Imus (riv.), Phil. 100/E7
Imusho, Zam. 140/D3
In Agiuel (well), Libya 126/A3
Ina, Japan 97/E3
Ina, Japan 95/E2
Ina, Japan 95/D2
Ina (riv.), Japan 95/H6
Ina (riv.), Pol. 46/F5
Inabanga, Phil. 100/D3
Inabe, Japan 95/L5
Inabu, Japan 95/M5
Inagawa, Japan 95/H6
Inagi, Japan 95/D2
Inaha, Ga, US 195/G2
Inajá, Braz. 219/G5
Inaja Ind. Res., Ca, US 178/D4
Inambari (riv.), Peru 220/D4
Inambari, Peru 220/D4
Inami, Japan 95/G6
Inangahua Junction, NZ 159/B3
Inanwatan, Indo. 103/H4
Inaouene (riv.), Mor. 130/B2
Iñapari, Peru 220/D3
Inarjärvi (lake), Fin. 44/H1
Inău (peak), Rom. 57/G2
Inawashīro (lake), Japan 97/F2
Inazawa, Japan 95/L5
Inca, Sp. 53/G3
Incahuasi, Arg. 224/C3
Incahuasi, Cerro de (peak), Chile 224/B3
Incekum (pt.), Turk. 116/C1
Inch'on-jikhalsi (prov.), SKor. 93/D4
Inchcape (Bell Rock) (isl.), Sc, UK 39/D4
Inchelium, Wa, US 174/E3
Incheville, Fr. 60/A3
Inchigeelagh, Ire. 38/A6
Inchinnan, Sc, UK 39/B5
Inchkeith (isl.), Sc, UK 39/C4
Inchnadamph, Sc, UK 37/R7
Inch'ŏn, SKor. 93/F7
Inchope, Moz. 141/G3
İncirliova, Turk. 114/A2
Incisa in Val d'Arno, It. 69/E6
Incomati (riv.), Moz. 141/G5
Inconfidentes, Braz. 223/K7
Incudine, Mont l' (peak), Fr. 54/A2
Ind. Dunes NL, In, US 190/C4
Inda Silasē, Eth. 112/C6
Indaiatuba, Braz. 225/H2
Indalsälven (riv.), Swe. 44/E3
Indanan, Phil. 100/C4
Indaw, Myan. 98/C4
Indawgyi (lake), Myan. 98/C3
Inde (riv.), Ger. 61/F2
Inden, Ger. 61/F2
Independence, Belz. 206/D2
Independence, Ca, US 178/C2
Independence, Ia, US 185/J2
Independence, Ks, US 183/G2
Independence, Ky, US 192/E1
Independence, La, US 194/C2
Independence, Mo, US 185/G4
Independence (mts.), Nv, US 176/E3
Independence, Or, US 176/B1
Independence (cr.), Tx, US 180/C2
Independence, Va, US 193/G2
Independence Nat'l Hist. Park, Pa, US 198/C4
Independencia, Peru 220/B4
Independencia, Bol. 224/C1
Independência, Braz. 219/F4
Inder (lake), Kaz. 77/K2
Inderapura (cape), Indo. 101/C3
Inderborskiy, Kaz. 77/J2
Index, Wa, US 197/D2
India (ctry.) 104/C3
Indian (lake), Mi, US 187/L4
Indian (ocean) 27/N6
Indian (hill), Ne, US 184/D2
Indian (cr.), Ga, US 193/M7
Indian Brook, NS, Can. 189/G2
Indian Church, Belz. 206/D2
Indian Echo Caverns, Pa, US 198/B3
Indian Harbour Beach, Fl, US 195/H3
Indian Head, Sk, Can. 186/C2
Indian Lake, NY, US 191/J3
Indian Lake Estates, Fl, US 194/N8
Indian Pictographs, Tx, US 180/E2
Indian River, Mi, US 190/D2
Indian Rocks Beach, Fl, US 194/K8
Indian Springs, Ga, US 192/F4
Indian Valley, Va, US 193/G2
Indian Wells, Az, US 179/G3
Indiana, Pa, US 191/G4
Indiana (state), US 173/J4
Indianapolis (cap.), In, US 190/C5
Indianapolis (int'l arpt.), In, US 190/C5
Indianapolis Motor Speedway, In, US 190/C5
Indianola, Ga, US 195/G2
Indianola, Ia, US 185/H3
Indianola, Ms, US 192/B4
Indianola, Tx, US 180/F3
Indianola, Wa, US 197/B2
Indiantown, Fl, US 195/H4
Indiaporã, Braz. 225/G1
Indicatore, It. 69/E7
Indiga, Rus. 75/L2
Indigirka (riv.), Rus. 83/P3
Inđija, Serb. 56/E3
Indio, Ca, US 178/D4
Indira Gandhi (int'l arpt.), India 110/D5
Indochina (reg.), Asia 106/C1
Indonesia (ctry.) 103/E4
Indooroopilly (nbrhd.), Austl. 158/E7
Indore, India 104/C3
Indragiri (riv.), Indo. 102/B4
Indragiri (river), Indo. 101/C3
Indramayu, Indo. 101/E4
Indramayu (cape), Indo. 102/C5
Indrapura, Indo. 101/C3
Indrāvati (riv.), India 104/D4
Indre (dept.), Fr. 63/G6
Indre (riv.), Fr. 50/D3
Indre Arna, Nor. 46/A1
Indre-et-Loire (dept.), Fr. 63/F5
Indrois (riv.), Fr. 50/D3
Indungo, Ang. 140/C2
Induno Olona, It. 67/E6
Indus (riv.), Asia 83/G6
Industry, Ca, US 196/G7
Industry, Tx, US 180/F3
İnebolu, Turk. 76/E4
İnece, Turk. 57/H5
İnecik, Turk. 57/H5
Inedbirenne (int'l arpt.), Alg. 129/H4
Iner (riv.), Ger. 64/C3
Ineu, Rom. 56/E2
Inez, Ky, US 193/F2
Inez, Tx, US 181/F3
Inezgane, Mor. 128/C3
Inezgane (Agadir) (int'l arpt.), Mor. 128/C3
Infanta (cape), SAfr. 142/C4
Infante dom Henrique, SaoT. 138/A2
Infiernillo (res.), Mex. 202/A4
Infiernillo, Presa del (dam), Mex. 204/E5
Infiesto, Sp. 52/C1
Ingá, Braz. 219/H4
Ingå (Inkoo), Fin. 45/E4
Ingalls, Mi, US 187/L5
Ingalls, Ar, US 183/H4
Inganda, D.R. Congo 139/E3
Ingapirca (ruin), Ecu. 216/B5
Ingarö (isl.), Swe. 45/B1
Ingarö, Swe. 45/B1
Ingasu, D.R. Congo 139/F2
Ingatestone, Eng, UK 36/E2
Ingelmunster, Belg. 60/C2
Ingende, D.R. Congo 138/D3
Ingeniero Guillermo N. Juárez, Arg. 224/D2
Ingeniero Jacobacci, Arg. 226/C4
Ingeniero Luiggi, Arg. 226/D2
Ingenio, Sp. 128/B4
Ingersheim, Fr. 66/D1
Ingersoll, On, Can. 190/F3
Ingettolgoy, Mong. 90/E2
Inggen, China 90/E3
Ingham, Austl. 158/B2
Ingleburn (nbrhd.), Austl. 158/G9
Ingleside, On, Can. 191/J2
Ingleside, Md, US 198/C5
Ingleton, Eng, UK 41/G2
Inglewood, Austl. 156/B3
Inglewood, Austl. 158/C5
Inglewood, On, Can. 190/T8
Inglewood, NZ 159/C2
Inglewood, Ca, US 196/F8
Inglewood-Finn Hill, Wa, US 197/C2
Inglis, Fl, US 195/G3
Ingmarsö (isl.), Swe. 45/B1
Ingoda (riv.), Rus. 81/M4
Ingoldmells, Eng, UK 41/J5
Ingolstadt, Ger. 65/E5
Ingomar, Mt, US 175/L4
Ingonish, NS, Can. 189/G2
Ingonish Beach, NS, Can. 189/G2
Ingraham, Il, US 192/C1
Ingram, Tx, US 180/E2
Ingrave, Eng, UK 36/E2
Ingré, Fr. 63/G5
Ingre, Bol. 224/D2
Ingrid Christianson (coast), Ant. 228/F
Ingulets (riv.), Ukr. 79/G3
Ingushetia, Resp., Rus. 81/Q6
Ingwavuma, SAfr. 143/E2
Ingwiller, Fr. 61/G6
Inhacalunga, Ang. 139/E5
Inhambane, Moz. 141/G4
Inhambane (prov.), Moz. 141/G4
Inhaminga, Moz. 141/G3
Inhapim, Braz. 223/E3
Inharrime, Moz. 141/G5
Inhassoro, Moz. 141/G4
Inhuca, Ang. 138/C4
Inhulets', Ukr. 79/G4
Inhuma, Braz. 219/F4
Inhumas, Braz. 222/C3
Iniesta, Sp. 52/E3
Inifel (well), Alg. 129/F3
Inini (riv.), FrG. 217/H4
Inini, FrG. 218/C2
Inírida (riv.), Col. 216/D4
Inishannon, Ire. 38/B6
Inishbofin (isl.), Ire. 36/N10
Inishcarra (res.), Ire. 38/A6
Inishcrone, Ire. 38/A1
Inishmaan (arpt.), Ire. 38/A3
Inishmeer (arpt.), Ire. 38/A3
Inishowen (pt.), Ire. 40/B1
Inishowen (pen.), Ire. 40/A1
Inistioge, Ire. 38/C5
Inje, SKor. 93/E3
Injibara, Eth. 135/H3
Injune, Austl. 158/C4
Inkerman, NB, Can. 188/E2
Inkhil, Syria 117/E2
Inkisi (riv.), D.R. Congo 138/C4
Inkom, Id, US 177/G2
Inkoo (Ingå), Fin. 45/E4
Inkster, Mi, US 197/F7
Inland (sea), Japan 96/C4
Inle (lake), Myan. 105/G3
Inman, Ks, US 183/F1
Inman, SC, US 193/F3
Inn (riv.), Aus. 51/J3
Inn (riv.), Aus.,Ger. 48/G5
Inn (riv.), Eur. 50/J3
Inn (riv.), Ger. 51/K2
Inn (riv.), Swi. 51/J3
Innamincka, Austl. 158/A4
Innbach (riv.), Aus. 65/H6
Innellan, Sc, UK 39/B5
Inner (sound), Sc, UK 37/R8
Inner (chan.), Belz. 206/D2
Inner Hebrides (isls.), Sc, UK 37/Q8
Inner Mongolia (reg.), China 83/L5
Inner Space Caverns, Tx, US 181/F2
Innerdouny (hill), Sc, UK 39/C4
Innerleithen, Sc, UK 39/C5
Innerste (riv.), Ger. 59/G4
Innertkirchen, Swi. 67/E4
Innes NP, Austl. 155/H5
Innichen (San Candito), It. 51/K3
Innis, La, US 194/C2
Innisfail, Austl. 158/B2
Innisfail, Ab, Can. 175/H1
Innoko (riv.), Ak, US 201/G3
Innsbruck, Aus. 67/H3
Innviertel (reg.), Aus. 65/G6
Inny (riv.), Ire. 38/C2
Inny (riv.), Eng, UK 42/B5
Ino, Japan 96/C4
Inobonto, Indo. 103/F3
Inocência, Braz. 225/G1
Inola, Ok, US 183/G2
Inongo, D.R. Congo 138/D3
İnönü, Turk. 114/B2
Inowrocław, Pol. 49/K2
Inquisivi, Bol. 224/C1
Insch, Sc, UK 39/D2
Inscription (cape), Austl. 154/B3
Insein, Myan. 98/C5
Inshāş ar Raml, Egypt 131/C4
Insinger, Sk, Can. 186/C2
Insiza, Zim. 141/F3
Insjön, Swe. 46/F1
Inspiration, Az, US 179/G4
Insu, Gha. 133/E5
International Amistad (res.), Mex.,US 180/D3
Inta, Rus. 75/N2
Intagaw, Myan. 106/B2
Intaing, Myan. 106/B2
Intake, Mt, US 186/B4
Intelewa, Sur. 218/C2
Intendente Alvear, Arg. 226/E2
İntepe, Turk. 55/K2
Intercession City, Fl, US 194/M7
Intercourse, Pa, US 198/B3
Interior, SD, US 184/D2
Interior (plat.), BC, Can. 174/B1
Interlaken, Swi. 66/D4
Interlaken, NY, US 191/H3
Interlochen, Mi, US 190/D2
Internacional (int'l arpt.), Braz. 220/D2
Internacional (int'l arpt.), Mex. 205/E5
International Falls, Mn, US 187/H3
International Peace Garden, ND, US 186/D3
Inthanon (peak), Thai. 98/C5
Intich'o, Eth. 136/A2
Întorsura Buzăului, Rom. 57/H3
Intragna, Swi. 67/E5
Introbio, It. 67/F6
Intuto, Peru 220/C1
Inubō-zaki (pt.), Japan 97/G3
Inukjuak, Qu, Can. 171/J3
Inutil (bay), Chile 227/C7
Inuvik, Yk, Can. 201/M2
Inuyama, Japan 95/L5
Inver (bay), Sc, UK 39/C1
Inver Grove Heights, Mn, US 187/P7
Inveraray, Sc, UK 39/A4
Inverbervie, Sc, UK 39/D3
Invercargill, NZ 159/B4
Inverclyde (co.), Sc, UK 39/B5
Inverell, Austl. 156/D1
Invergarry, Sc, UK 39/B2
Invergordon, Sc, UK 39/B1
Invergowrie, Sc, UK 39/C4
Inverie, Sc, UK 37/R8
Inverigo, It. 68/C2
Inverkeilor, Sc, UK 39/D3
Inverkeithing, Sc, UK 39/C4
Inverloch, Austl. 157/B4
Invermay, Sk, Can. 186/C2
Invermere, BC, Can. 174/F2
Invermoriston, IM, UK 40/D3
Inverness, NS, Can. 189/G2
Inverness, Qu, Can. 188/B2
Inverness, Sc, UK 39/B2
Inverness, Al, US 195/F1
Inverness, Fl, US 195/G3
Inveruno, It. 68/B2
Inverurie, Sc, UK 39/D2
Inverway, Austl. 152/C4
Investigator (str.), Austl. 145/C4
Invorio, It. 68/B2
Inwood, Ia, US 185/F2
Inwood, NY, US 199/L9
Inwood, WV, US 191/G5
Inyan Kara (mtn.), Wy, US 184/B1
Inyanga, Zim. 141/G3
Inyangani (peak), Zim. 141/G3
Inyati, Zim. 141/F3
Inyo (mts.), Ca, US 178/D2
Inyokern, Ca, US 178/D3
Inyonga, Tanz. 139/H4
Inza, Rus. 77/H1
Inzai, Japan 95/E2
Inzer, Rus. 75/N5
Inzhavino, Rus. 77/G1
Inzia (riv.), D.R. Congo 138/D4
Inzigkofen, Ger. 67/F1
Inzing, Aus. 67/H3
Inzinzac-Lochrist, Fr. 62/B5
Iō-shima (isl.), Japan 96/B5
Ioánnina, Gre. 55/G3
Ioánnina (int'l arpt.), Gre. 55/G3
Ioka, Ut, US 177/H3
Iola, Ks, US 183/G2
Iola, Wi, US 185/K1
Iolotan', Trkm. 113/H1
Ioma, PNG 153/G2
Iona (isl.), Sc, UK 37/Q8
Iona, Ang. 140/B3
Iona, Id, US 177/H2
Iona, PN da, Ang. 140/A3
Ione, Nv, US 176/E4
Ione, Or, US 176/D1
Ione, Ca, US 176/C4
Ione, Wa, US 174/F3
Ione Wash (riv.), Nv, US 178/D1
Iongo, Ang. 138/D5
Ionia, Mo, US 183/H1
Ionia, Mi, US 190/D3
Ionian (sea), Gre. 73/H3
Ionian (isls.), Gre. 29/F5
Íos (isl.), Gre. 73/K3
Iota, La, US 194/B2
Iouîk, Mrta. 132/A2
Iouîk (cape), Mrta. 132/A2
Iowa (state), US 185/G2
Iowa (riv.), Ia, US 185/H2
Iowa, La, US 194/B2
Iowa City, Ia, US 185/J3
Iowa Falls, Ia, US 185/H2
Iowa Park, Tx, US 183/E4
Ipameri, Braz. 222/C3
Ipanema, Braz. 223/E3
Ipanguaçu, Braz. 219/G4
Iparia, Peru 220/C3
Ipatinga, Braz. 223/E3
Ipatovo, Rus. 77/G3
Ipaumirim, Braz. 219/G4
Ipel' (riv.), Slvk. 49/K4
Ipel' (riv.), Hun. 56/D1
Iphofen, Ger. 64/D3
Ipiales, Col. 216/B4
Ipiaú, Braz. 223/F2
Ipirá, Braz. 223/F2
Ipixuna (riv.), Braz. 221/G2
Ipoh, Malay. 101/C1
Ipole, Tanz. 139/H4
Ipoly (riv.), Hun. 49/K4
Ipolyszög, Hun. 56/D1
Iporá, Braz. 222/C3
Iporã, Braz. 225/F2
Ippy, CAfr. 134/D4
İpsala, Turk. 57/H5
Ipsheim, Ger. 64/D3
Ipswich, SD, US 186/E5
Ipswich (nbrhd.), Austl. 158/E7
Ipswich, Eng, UK 43/H2
Ipu, Braz. 219/F4
Ipueiras, Braz. 219/F4
Ipuh, Indo. 101/C3
Ipuiúna, Braz. 223/K7
Ipumba (hill), Tanz. 139/G4
Ipun, Isla (isl.), Chile 226/B5
Ipupiara, Braz. 223/E1
Iqaluit, (cap.), Nun, Can. 171/K2
Iquique, Chile 224/B2
Iquitos, Peru 220/C1
Ira, Tx, US 180/D1
Iraan, Tx, US 180/D2
Iracoubo, FrG. 218/C1
Irago (chan.), Japan 95/L6
Irago-misaki (cape), Japan 95/M6
Iraí, Braz. 225/F3
Iráklia, Gre. 55/H2
Iráklia (isl.), Gre. 55/J4
Iráklion (int'l arpt.), Gre. 55/J5
Iráklion, Gre. 55/J5
Iramba, Tanz. 137/A2
Iran (ctry.) 115/H3
Iran (mts.), Indo.,Malay. 102/D3
Īrān Shāh, Iran 115/F2
Irapa, Ven. 217/F2
Irapuato, Mex. 205/E4
Iraq (ctry.) 114/E3
Irati, Braz. 225/G3
Irauçuba, Braz. 219/G3
Irayel', Rus. 75/M2
Irbid, Jor. 117/D3
Irbid (gov.), Jor. 116/D3
Irbīl, Iraq 115/F2
Irbit, Rus. 75/P4
Irdyn', Ukr. 78/F3
Irecê, Braz. 223/E1
Iredell, Tx, US 180/F2
Ireland (ctry.) 37/G10
Ireland, Tx, US 180/F2
Ireland's Eye (isl.), Ire. 40/B5
Iremel' (peak), Rus. 75/N5
Irene, SAfr. 141/F5
Ireton, Ia, US 185/F2
Irfon (riv.), Wal, UK 42/C2
Irgiz, Kaz. 77/M2
Irharhar, Oued (riv.), Alg. 129/G4
Irhazer Oua-n-Agadez (riv.), Niger 133/G2
Irherm, Mor. 128/C3
Irherm n'Ougdal, Mor. 128/D3
Iri, SKor. 93/D5
Irian Jaya (reg.), Indo. 103/H4
Irian Jaya (prov.), Indo. 153/E1
Iriba, Chad 134/D2
Iricoume (mts.), Braz. 217/G4

Kaise – Kawam
297

Kaiserslautern, Ger. 61/G5
Kaisheim, Ger. 64/D5
Kaišiadorys, Lith. 47/L4
Kait (cape), Indo. 101/D3
Kaitaia, NZ 159/C1
Kaitangata, NZ 159/B4
Kaithal, India 110/D5
Kaiti, Tanz. 137/A2
Kaiwi (chan.), Hi, US 172/T10
Kaiyang, China 105/J2
Kaiyuan, China 92/F2
Kaiyuan, China 98/D4
Kaizu, Japan 95/L5
Kaizuka, Japan 95/H7
Kajaani, Fin. 80/C3
Kajabbi, Austl. 153/F5
Kajang (peak), Malay. 101/D2
Kajang, Malay. 101/C2
Kajang, Indo. 103/F5
Kaji-san (peak), SKor. 96/A3
Kajiado, Kenya 137/B2
Kajikazawa, Japan 95/A2
Kajo-Kaji, Sudan 139/G2
Kajuru, Nga. 133/G4
Kākā, Sudan 135/G3
Kakabeka Falls, On, Can. 187/K3
Kakada (well), Chad 134/B1
Kakadu NP, Austl. 152/D3
Kakagi (lake), On, Can. 187/H3
Kakamas, SAfr. 142/C3
Kakamega, Kenya 137/A1
Kakamigahara, Japan 95/L5
Kakanj, Bosn. 56/D3
Kakata, Libr. 132/C5
Kākdwīp, India 109/G5
Kake, Ak, US 201/M4
Kaketsa (mt.), BC, Can. 201/M4
Kākhk, Iran 113/G2
Kakhovka, Ukr. 78/G4
Kakhovs'ke Vodoskhovyshche (res.), Ukr. 76/E3
Kakielo, D.R. Congo 141/F2
Kākināda, India 107/D2
Kakiri, Ugan. 139/H2
Kakkirigumma, India 107/D2
Kako (riv.), Japan 95/G6
Kakogawa, Japan 95/G6
Kakonga, Zam. 140/D2
Kakonko, Tanz. 139/G3
Kākori, India 108/C2
Kakrāla, India 108/B2
Kakrima (riv.), Gui. 132/B4
Kaktovik, Ak, US 201/K1
Kaku, India 104/B2
Kakuda, Japan 97/G2
Kakuma, Kenya 135/G5
Kakumbi, Zam. 141/F2
Kakuna, D.R. Congo 139/E4
Kakunodate, Japan 94/B4
Kakuri, Nga. 133/G4
Kakuto, Ugan. 139/G3
Kakya, Kenya 137/B2
Kāl-e Shūr (riv.), Iran 115/J2
Kalā Chāy, Iran 115/G2
Kala-i-Mor, Trkm. 113/H1
Kalaa Kbira, Tun. 130/M7
Kalaallit Nunaat (Greenland) (dpcy.), Den. 163/N2
Kalaat el Andalous, Tun. 130/M6
Kālābāgh, Pak. 110/A3
Kalabahi, Indo. 152/B2
Kalabakan, Malay. 100/B4
Kalabo, Zam. 140/D2
Kalabyin, Myan. 98/B5
Kalach, Rus. 79/L2
Kalach-na-Donu, Rus. 77/G2
Kalachinsk, Rus. 80/H4
Kaladan (riv.), Myan. 105/F3
Kaladar, On, Can. 191/H2
Kālāgarh, India 108/B1
Kalahari (des.), Namb. 119/D7
Kalahari-Gemsbok NP, SAfr. 142/C2
Kalaiya, Nepal 109/E2
Kalakan, Rus. 81/M4
Kalalé, Ben. 133/F4
Kalāleh, Iran 115/H2
Kalaloch, Wa, US 174/B4
Kalām, Pak. 110/B2
Kalama, Wa, US 174/C4
Kalamákion, Gre. 55/N8
Kalamaloué, PN de, Camr. 134/B2
Kalamare, Bots. 141/E4
Kalamariá, Gre. 55/H2
Kalamáta, Gre. 55/H4
Kalamazoo, Mi, US 190/D3
Kalamazoo (riv.), Mi, US 190/D3
Kalamitsk (bay), Ukr. 79/G5
Kalampáka, Gre. 55/G3
Kalanchak, Ukr. 79/G4
Kalandy, Madg. 143/J6
Kalangali, Tanz. 137/A3
Kalanguy, Rus. 90/H1
Kālānwāli, India 110/C5
Kalaotoa (isl.), Indo. 152/A1
Kalasin, Thai. 106/C2
Kalāswāla, Pak. 110/C3
Kalāt, Pak. 113/J3
Kalaupapa, Hi, US 172/T10
Kalávrita, Gre. 55/H3
Kalaw, Myan. 98/C4
Kalbā, UAE 113/G3
Kälbäcär, Azer. 115/F1
Kalbach, Ger. 64/B2
Kalbar, Austl. 158/D4
Kalbarri, Austl. 154/B3
Kalbarri NP, Austl. 154/B3
Kaldakvísl (riv.), Ice. 44/N7
Kale, Turk. 116/A1
Kale, Turk. 114/D1
Kalecik, Turk. 114/C1
Kaleden, BC, Can. 174/E3
Kaledupa (isl.), Indo. 152/A1
Kalefeld, Ger. 59/H5
Kalehe, D.R. Congo 139/G3
Kalema, D.R. Congo 139/F4
Kalemie (int'l arpt.), D.R. Congo 139/G4
Kalemie, D.R. Congo 139/G4
Kalemyo, Myan. 98/B4
Kalenda, D.R. Congo 139/E5
Kalety, Pol. 49/K3
Kaleva, Mi, US 190/C2
Kalevala, Rus. 74/F2
Kalewa, Myan. 98/B4
Kaleya, Zam. 141/E2
Kalgoorlie-Boulder, Austl. 154/D4
Kāli (riv.), India 108/B1
Kali (riv.), India 108/B2
Kāli (riv.), Nepal 108/D2
Kālia, Bang. 109/H4
Kāliākair, Bang. 109/H3
Kalianda, Indo. 101/D4
Kalibo, Phil. 100/C3
Kalida, Oh, US 190/D4
Kālīganj, Bang. 109/G4
Kālikot, Nepal 108/C1
Kalima, D.R. Congo 139/F3
Kalimala, India 107/D2
Kalimantan (reg.), Indo. 102/D4
Kálimnos, Gre. 73/K3
Kālimpong, India 109/G2
Kaliningrad, Rus. 75/W9
Kaliningrad, Rus. 47/J4
Kaliningradskaya Oblast, Rus. 74/D5
Kalinino, Rus. 79/K5
Kalininsk, Rus. 77/H2
Kalinkavichy, Bela. 78/E1
Kalinko, Gui. 132/C4
Kalinovka, Rus. 79/H2
Kaliro, Ugan. 137/A1
Kalis, Som. 136/D3
Kalisizo, Ugan. 139/G3
Kalispel Ind. Res., Wa, US 174/F3
Kalispell, Mt, US 174/G3
Kalisz, Pol. 49/K3
Kaliua, Tanz. 139/G4
Kalix, Swe. 74/D2
Kalixälven (riv.), Swe. 44/G2
Kāliyāganj, India 109/G3
Kālka, India 110/D4
Kalkaringi, Austl. 152/C4
Kalkaska, Mi, US 190/D2
Kalkbruk, Fin. 45/F4
Kalkfeld, Namb. 140/C4
Kalkfontein, Bots. 140/D4
Kalkhügel, Namb. 140/C5
Kālkini, Bang. 109/H4
Kalkrand, Namb. 140/C5
Kallar Kahār, Pak. 110/B3
Kallaste, Est. 47/M2
Kallham, Aus. 65/G6
Kallinge, Swe. 46/F3
Kallinge (int'l arpt.), Swe. 46/F3
Kalliola, Fin. 45/F4
Kallithéa, Gre. 55/N9
Kallsjön (lake), Swe. 44/E3
Kalmalo, Nga. 133/G3
Kalmar (co.), Swe. 44/F4
Kalmar (int'l arpt.), Swe. 46/G3
Kalmar, Swe. 46/G3
Kalmar, Swe. 45/A1
Kalmarsund (sound), Swe. 46/G3
Kalmthout, Belg. 58/B6
Kalmykia, Resp., Rus. 80/E5
Kalmykovo, Kaz. 77/J2
Kālna, India 109/G4
Kalnai, India 108/D4
Kalnciems, Lat. 47/K3
Kalni (riv.), Bang. 109/H3
Kalnibolotskaya, Rus. 79/L4
Kalocsa, Hun. 56/D2
Kalofer, Bul. 55/J1
Kalokhórion, Gre. 55/H2
Kaloko, D.R. Congo 139/F4
Kālol, India 113/K4
Kalole, D.R. Congo 139/F3
Kalombo, Zam. 140/D2
Kalomo, Zam. 141/E3
Kalona, Ia, US 185/J3
Kalongan, Indo. 100/D4
Kalongo, Ugan. 137/A1
Kaloqi, Sudan 135/F3
Kālpi, India 108/B2
Kalpin, China 111/C3
Kalpitiya, SrL. 107/C4
Kalsdorf bei Graz, Aus. 56/B2
Kaltag, Ak, US 201/G3
Kaltasy, Rus. 75/M5
Kaltbrunn, Swi. 67/F3
Kaltenleutgeben, Aus. 57/N7
Kaltennordheim, Ger. 64/D1
Kaltern (Caldaro), It. 51/J3
Kalu (riv.), SrL. 104/D6
Kaluga, Rus. 74/H5
Kaluku, Indo. 103/E4
Kalulushi, Zam. 141/F2
Kalumburu Abor. Rsv., Austl. 152/B3
Kalumburu Mission, Austl. 152/B3
Kalumpang, Malay. 101/C2
Kalundborg, Den. 46/D4
Kalundborg (inlet), Den. 45/G7
Kalungu, Ugan. 139/G3
Kalungwishi (riv.), Zam. 139/G5
Kalūr Kot, Pak. 110/A3
Kalush, Ukr. 78/C3
Kaluzhkaya Oblast, Rus. 74/G5
Kalvarija, Lith. 47/K4
Kalwelwe, Zam. 141/F2
Kalyān, India 104/B4
Kalyazin, Rus. 74/H4
Kalynivka, Ukr. 78/E3
Kama (res.), Rus. 75/M4
Kama, D.R. Congo 139/F3
Kama, Myan. 98/B5
Kama (riv.), Rus. 29/K3
Kamachumu, Tanz. 139/G3
Kamagaya, Japan 95/E2
Kamaishi, Japan 94/B4
Kamajai, Lith. 47/L4
Kamakura, Japan 95/D3
Kamakusa, Guy. 218/A1
Kamakwie, SLeo. 132/B4
Kamalampaka, Tanz. 139/G4
Kamālia, Pak. 110/B4
Kaman, Turk. 114/C2
Kāman, India 108/A2
Kamande, D.R. Congo 139/G3
Kamango (lake), Mali 132/E2
Kamango, D.R. Congo 139/G2
Kamanjab, Namb. 140/B3
Kamanyola, D.R. Congo 139/G3
Kamaran (isl.), Yem. 136/B2
Kamarang, Guy. 217/F3
Kāmāreddi, India 107/C2
Kāmārhāti, India 104/E3
Kamaria (falls), Guy. 217/G3
Kamas, Ut, US 177/H3
Kamāsin, India 108/C3
Kamativi, Zim. 141/E3
Kamba, Nga. 133/G3
Kamba-Poko, D.R. Congo 138/D4
Kambalda, Austl. 154/D4
Kambam, India 107/C4
Kambar, Pak. 104/A2
Kambara, Japan 95/B3
Kambaswana, D.R. Congo 139/E4
Kambia, SLeo. 132/B4
Kambja, Est. 47/M2
Kambove, D.R. Congo 139/F5
Kambuno (peak), Indo. 103/F4
Kamchatka (pen.), Rus. 83/Q4
Kamchatskaya Oblast, Rus. 81/R4
Kamchiya (riv.), Bul. 76/C4
Kamela, Or, US 176/D1
Kamen, Ger. 59/E5
Kamen'-na-Obi, Rus. 111/D1
Kamena, D.R. Congo 139/F4
Kamende, D.R. Congo 139/F4
Kamenets, Bela. 49/M2
Kameničná, Slvk. 56/D2
Kamenjak, Rt (cape), Cro. 51/K4
Kamenka, Kaz. 77/J2
Kamenka, Rus. 77/H1
Kamenka, Rus. 75/K2
Kamenka, Rus. 79/K2
Kamenka, Rus. 91/M3
Kamennogorsk, Rus. 47/N1
Kamennomostskaya, Rus. 79/L5
Kameno, Bul. 57/H4
Kamenolomni, Rus. 79/L4
Kamensk-Shakhtinskiy, Rus. 79/L3
Kamensk-Ural'skiy, Rus. 75/P4
Kamenskoye, Rus. 81/S3
Kameoka, Japan 95/J5
Kameri, Indo. 103/H4
Kames, Sc, UK 39/A5
Kameyama, Japan 95/K6
Kami, Japan 95/G5
Kami (isl.), Japan 95/M6
Kami-koshiki (isl.), Japan 96/A5
Kamiah, Id, US 174/F4
Kamień Pomorski, Pol. 46/F5
Kamieskroon, SAfr. 142/B3
Kamifukuoka, Japan 95/D2
Kamiisco, Japan 94/B3
Kamiishizu, Japan 95/K5
Kamiizumi, Japan 95/C1
Kamiji, D.R. Congo 139/E4
Kamikawa, Japan 94/C2
Kamikuishiki, Japan 95/B2
Kamin'-Kashyrs'kyy, Ukr. 78/C2
Kamina, D.R. Congo 139/F5
Kaminaka, Japan 95/J5
Kaminoho, Japan 95/M4
Kaminoyama, Japan 97/G1
Kamisato, Japan 95/C1
Kamishak (bay), Ak, US 201/H4
Kamiyahagi, Japan 95/M5
Kamiyaku, Japan 97/L5
Kamla (riv.), India 109/F3
Kamloops, BC, Can. 174/D2
Kamlot, Camb. 106/C4
Kammaki, Japan 95/J6
Kamnik, Slov. 51/L3
Kamo, Arm. 115/F1
Kamo, Japan 97/F2
Kamo, Japan 95/J6
Kamo (riv.), Japan 95/E3
Kamogawa, Japan 97/G3
Kamojima, Japan 96/D3
Kāmoke, Pak. 110/C4
Kamonia, D.R. Congo 139/E4
Kamp (riv.), Aus. 49/H4
Kamp-Bornhofen, Ger. 61/G3
Kamp-Lintfort, Ger. 58/D5
Kampala (cap.), Ugan. 139/H2
Kampalili (mt.), Phil. 100/D4
Kampar, Malay. 101/C1
Kampar (riv.), Indo. 102/B3
Kampar (river), Indo. 101/C2
Kampen, Ger. 46/C4
Kampen, Neth. 58/C3
Kampene, D.R. Congo 139/F3
Kamphaeng Phet, Thai. 106/C5
Kamphaeng Phet (ruin), Thai. 106/B2
Kamp'o, SKor. 93/E5
Kampong Cham, Camb. 106/D4
Kampong Chhnang, Camb. 106/D3
Kampong Kadok, Malay. 106/C5
Kampong Khleang, Camb. 106/D3
Kampong Kuala Besut, Malay. 101/C1
Kampong Raja, Malay. 101/C1
Kampong Saom (bay), Camb. 102/B1
Kampóng Saom, Camb. 106/C4
Kampong Sedenak, Malay. 101/C2
Kampong Sedili Kechil, Malay. 101/D2
Kampong Spoe, Camb. 106/D4
Kampong Tampasis, Malay. 103/E2
Kampong Telupid, Malay. 100/B4
Kampong Thum, Camb. 106/D3
Kampong Trabek, Camb. 106/D4
Kampot, Camb. 106/D4
Kampti, Burk. 132/E4
Kamrau (bay), Indo. 103/H4
Kamsack, Sk, Can. 186/D2
Kamsar, Gui. 132/B4
Kamsdorf, Ger. 65/E1
Kamskoye Ust'ye, Rus. 75/L5
Kamsuuma, Som. 137/C1
Kamtsha (riv.), D.R. Congo 138/D4
Kamui-misaki (cape), Japan 94/B2
Kámuk (mtn.), CR 207/F4
Kamuli, Ugan. 137/A1
Kamuzu (Lilongwe) (int'l arpt.), Malw. 141/G2
Kamwandu, D.R. Congo 139/E4
Kam'yanets'-Podil's'kyy, Ukr. 78/D3
Kam'yanka, Ukr. 79/G3
Kam'yanka-Buz'ka, Ukr. 78/C2
Kam'yanka-Dniprovs'ka, Ukr. 79/H4
Kāmyārān, Iran 115/F3
Kamyshevatskaya, Rus. 79/J4
Kamyshin, Rus. 77/H2
Kamyshla, Rus. 75/M5
Kamyshlov, Rus. 75/P4
Kamyzyak, Rus. 77/J3
Kanaaupscow (riv.), Qu, Can. 171/J3
Kanab, Ut, US 179/F2
Kanab (plat.), Az, US 179/F2
Kanab (cr.), Az, US 179/F2
Kanaga (mt.), Ak, US 201/C6
Kanairiktok (riv.), Nf, Can. 171/K3
Kanākir, Syria 117/E2
Kanan, Japan 95/J7
Kananga, D.R. Congo 139/E4
Kanaoudi, India 108/C4
Kanarraville, Ut, US 179/F2
Kanash, Rus. 75/K5
Kanasin, Mex. 206/D1
Kanata, On, Can. 191/J2
Kanawake Ind. Res., Qu, Can. 189/N7
Kanawha, Ia, US 185/H2
Kanawha (riv.), WV, US 193/F1
Kanazawa, Japan 97/E2
Kanazi, Tanz. 139/G3
Kanchanaburi, Thai. 106/B3
Kanchanadit, Thai. 106/B4
Kānchenjunga (peak), Nepal 104/E2
Kānchīpuram, India 107/C3
Kandahār, Afg. 113/J2
Kanda-Kanda, D.R. Congo 139/E4
Kandalaksha, Rus. 74/G2
Kandalaksha (gulf), Rus. 44/K2
Kandale, D.R. Congo 138/D4
Kandang, Indo. 101/B2
Kandanghaur, Indo. 101/D4
Kándanos, Gre. 55/H5
Kandava, Lat. 47/K3
Kandavu Passage, Fiji 161/Y18
Kandé, Togo 133/F4
Kandel, Ger. 64/B4
Kandel (peak), Ger. 66/E1
Kandep, PNG 153/F1
Kander (riv.), Swi. 66/D4
Kandern, Ger. 66/D2
Kandersteg, Swi. 66/D5
Kandhkot, Pak. 113/J3
Kāndhla, India 110/D5
Kandi, Ben. 133/F4
Kāndi, India 109/G4
Kandi, D.R. Congo 139/G2
Kandi (cape), Indo. 103/F3
Kandıra, Turk. 57/K5
Kandos, Austl. 157/D1
Kandrāch, Pak. 113/J3
Kandreho, Madg. 143/H7
Kandry, Rus. 75/M5
Kandukūr, India 107/C3
Kandy, SrL. 107/D5
Kane, Pa, US 191/G4
Kane (co.), Il, US 197/P16
Kane, Il, US 185/J4
Kane (basin), Grld. 171/T7
Kanem (reg.), Chad 134/B2
Kanem (pref.), Chad 134/B2
Kaneohe, Hi, US 172/W13
Kaneville, Il, US 197/N16
Kanëvka, Rus. 74/H2
Kanevskaya, Rus. 79/K4
Kaneyama, Japan 94/B4
Kang, Bots. 140/D4
Kanga (riv.), Bang. 109/G5
Kanga, D.R. Congo 139/G2
Kanga, Tanz. 137/B3
Kangaba, Mali 132/C4
Kangal, Turk. 114/D2
Kangān, Iran 115/H5
Kangān, Iran 113/G3
Kangan Abor. Land, Austl. 154/C2
Kanganpur, Pak. 110/C4
Kangar, Malay. 106/C5
Kangaré, Mali 132/C4
Kangaroo (isl.), Austl. 145/C4
Kangaruma, Guy. 217/G3
Kangasala, Fin. 47/L1
Kangāvar, Iran 115/F3
Kangbao, China 90/G3
Kangding, China 98/D2
Kangdong (nbrhd.), SKor. 93/G6
Kangean (isl.), Indo. 101/F4
Kangean (isls.), Indo. 101/F4
Kangen (riv.), Sudan 135/G4
Kangendala, PN da, Ang. 138/D5
Kanggye, NKor. 93/D2
Kanggyŏng, SKor. 93/D4
Kanghwa, SKor. 93/F6
Kangi, Sudan 135/E3
Kangiqcliniq (Rankin Inlet), Nun, Can. 170/G2
Kangiqsualujjuaq, Qu, Can. 171/K3
Kangiqsujuaq, Qu, Can. 171/J2
Kangirsuk, Qu, Can. 171/J2
Kangjin, SKor. 93/D5
Kangkar Dohol, Malay. 101/C2
Kangmar, China 109/G1
Kangnam (mts.), NKor. 93/C2
Kangnam, NKor. 93/C3
Kangnam (nbrhd.), SKor. 93/G6
Kangnŭng, SKor. 96/A2
Kangnyŏng, NKor. 93/C4
Kango, Gabon 138/B2
Kangondi, Kenya 137/B2
Kangping, China 92/E2
Kāngra, India 110/D3
Kangrinboqê (peak), China 111/D5
Kangsŏ, NKor. 93/C3
Kangsŏ (nbrhd.), SKor. 93/F6
Kangto (peak), China 98/B3
Kangu, D.R. Congo 138/C4
Kangwŏn-do (prov.), NKor. 93/D3
Kangwŏn-do (prov.), SKor. 96/A2
Kangxiwar, China 111/C4
Kanha NP, India 108/C4
Kanhān (riv.), India 104/C3
Kanholmsfjärden (sound), Swe. 45/B1
Kani, C.d'Iv. 132/D4
Kani, Japan 95/M5
Kani, Myan. 98/B4
Kaniama, D.R. Congo 139/F4
Kanie, Japan 95/L5
Kanin (pen.), Rus. 75/K1
Kanin Nos, Rus. 74/J1
Kanin Nos (pt.), Rus. 80/E3
Kaningo, Kenya 137/B2
Kaniv, Ukr. 78/F3
Kaniva, Austl. 156/B3
Kanivs'ke Vodoskhovyshche (res.), Ukr. 78/F2
Kanjiža, Serb. 56/E2
Kankakee, Il, US 190/C4
Kankakee (riv.), Il, US 190/C4
Kankan (pol. reg.), Gui. 132/C4
Kankan, Gui. 132/C4
Kānker, India 107/D1
Kankesanturai, SrL. 107/D4
Kankossa, Mrta. 132/C3
Kanmen, China 99/J2
Kanmuri-yama (peak), Japan 96/C3
Kannami, Japan 95/B3
Kannapolis, NC, US 193/G3
Kannauj, India 108/B2
Kannon-zaki (pt.), Japan 95/D3
Kannus, Fin. 74/D3
Kano (state), Nga. 133/H4
Kano, Nga. 133/H4
Kano Vlei, Namb. 140/C3
Kanona, Zam. 141/F2
Kanoneiland, SAfr. 142/C3
Kan'onji, Japan 96/C3
Kanopolis, Ks, US 183/E1
Kanopolis (lake), Ks, US 184/E4
Kanosh, Ut, US 179/F1
Kanouse (mtn.), NJ, US 199/H7
Kanowit, Malay. 102/D3
Kanoya, Japan 96/B5
Kānpur, India 108/C2
Kanra, Japan 95/B1
Kansai (int'l arpt.), Japan 95/H7
Kansai (isl.), Japan 95/H7
Kansarokana (riv.), Kenya 137/B2
Kansas (state), US 173/G4
Kansas (riv.), US 173/G4
Kansas, Al, US 192/D4
Kansas, Il, US 190/C5
Kansas City, Ks, US 200/D5
Kansas City (int'l arpt.), Mo, US 200/D5
Kansas City, Mo, US 200/D5
Kansas Cosmosphere and Space Center, Ks, US 183/F1
Kansasville, Wi, US 197/P14
Kansenia, D.R. Congo 139/F5
Kansk, Rus. 80/K4
Kansŏng, SKor. 93/E3
Kantābānji, India 107/D1
Kantchari, Burk. 133/F3
Kantemirovka, Rus. 79/K3
Kānth, India 108/B1
Kantharalak, Thai. 106/D3
Kantō (prov.), Japan 97/F2
Kantunilkin, Mex. 206/E1
Kanturk, Ire. 38/B5
Kantvik, Fin. 45/E4
Kanuku (mts.), Guy. 217/G4
Kanuma, Japan 97/F2
Kanyanga, Gha. 133/E4
Kanye, Bots. 140/E5
Kanyilombi, Zam. 140/E2
Kanyutkwin, Myan. 106/B2
Kanzenze, D.R. Congo 139/F5
Kanzi, China 93/B3
Kaoh Nhek, Camb. 106/D3
Kaohsiung (int'l arpt.), Tai. 99/J4
Kaohsiung, Tai. 99/J4
Kaolack (pol. reg.), Sen. 132/B3
Kaolack, Sen. 132/A3
Kaolinovo, Bul. 57/H4
Kaoma, Zam. 140/E2
Kaongweshi (riv.), D.R. Congo 139/E5
Kaortchi (well), Chad 126/C5
Kaouadja, CAfr. 134/D4
Kaouar (reg.), Niger 126/B5
Kapa, Myan. 106/B3
Kapakapanui (mt.), NZ 159/J8
Kapalala, Zam. 141/F2
Kapalong, Phil. 100/D4
Kapambwe, D.R. Congo 139/E4
Kapan, Arm. 115/F2
Kapanga, D.R. Congo 139/E5
Kapaonik (mts.), Serb. 56/E4
Kapchorwa, Ugan. 137/A1
Kapedo, Kenya 137/B1
Kapellen, Belg. 58/B6
Kapellshamn (isl.), Swe. 45/J6
Kapellskär, Swe. 45/C1
Kapenguria, Kenya 137/A1
Kapengwe, Zam. 141/F2
Kapfenberg, Aus. 51/L3
Kapidaği (pen.), Turk. 57/H5
Kapingamarangi (isl.), Micr. 160/E4
Kapiri Mposhi, Zam. 141/F2
Kapiskau (riv.), On, Can. 171/H3
Kaplan, La, US 194/B3
Kaplice, Czh. 65/H5
Kapoe, Thai. 106/B4
Kapoeta, Sudan 135/G4
Kapona, D.R. Congo 139/G4
Kaporo, Malw. 137/A4
Kapos (riv.), Hun. 56/C2
Kaposvár, Hun. 56/C2
Kapowsin, Wa, US 174/C4
Kapp, Nor. 46/D1
Kappeln, Ger. 46/C4
Kappl, Aus. 67/G3
Kapsabet, Kenya 137/A1
Kapsan, NKor. 93/E2
Kapuas (riv.), Indo. 102/C4
Kapuas Hulu (mts.), Indo.,Malay. 102/D3
Kapunda, Austl. 155/H5
Kapūrthala, India 110/C4
Kapuskasing, On, Can. 171/H4
Kaputa, Zam. 139/G5
Kapuvár, Hun. 56/C2
Kapydzhik (peak), Azer. 115/F2
Kap'yŏng, SKor. 93/D4
Kara (riv.), Rus. 75/Q1
Kara, Rus. 75/Q1
Kara (sea), Rus. 80/G2
Kara, Togo 133/F4
Kara K'orē, Eth. 136/A3
Kara-Balta, Kyr. 111/B3
Kara-Kala, Trkm. 115/J2
Kara-Köl, Kyr. 111/B3
Kara-Saki (pt.), Japan 96/A3
Karaali, Turk. 114/C2
Karaart, Taj. 111/B4
Karabau, Kaz. 77/K2
Karabiğa, Turk. 57/H5
Karabra (riv.), Indo. 103/H4
Karabudakhkent, Rus. 77/H4
Karabük, Turk. 76/E4
Karabula, Rus. 80/K4
Karabulak, Rus. 77/H4
Karaburun, Turk. 57/J5
Karaca (peak), Turk. 114/D2
Karacadağ, Turk. 57/H5
Karacaköy, Turk. 57/J5
Karaçal (peak), Turk. 116/C1
Karacaoğlan, Turk. 57/H5
Karachala, Azer. 77/J5
Karachayevo-Cherkesiya, Resp., Rus. 81/Q6
Karachev, Rus. 76/E1
Karachi (int'l arpt.), Pak. 113/J4
Karāchi, Pak. 113/J4
Karād, India 107/B2
Karadere, Turk. 57/K5
Karagayly, Kaz. 111/C2
Karaginskiy (isl.), Rus. 83/R4
Karagoš (peak), Rus. 111/E1
Karaidel'skiy, Rus. 75/N5
Kāraikkudi, India 107/C4
Karaj, Iran 115/G3
Karak, Malay. 101/C2
Karakax (riv.), China 111/C4
Karakelong (isl.), Indo. 103/G3
Karakhoto (ruin), China 90/E3
Karakol, Kyr. 111/C3
Karakoram (pass), India 110/D2
Karakoram (range), India 111/C4
Karakoro (riv.), Mali 132/C3
Karakorum (pass), China 113/L1
Karakorum (ruin), Mong. 90/E2
Karaköse, Turk. 115/E2
Karaköy, Turk. 114/E2
Karakul', Uzb. 80/G6
Karakul' (lake), Taj. 111/B4
Karakumy (des.), Trkm. 80/F5
Karakuwisa, Namb. 140/C3
Karakyon (peak), Trkm. 115/H1
Karakyr (peak), Trkm. 113/H1
Karam (riv.), Indo. 103/E4
Karamagay, China 90/B2
Karaman, Turk. 114/C2
Karaman (prov.), Turk. 114/C2
Karamay, China 111/D2
Karambi, Tanz. 139/G3
Karamea, NZ 159/C3
Karamea Bight (bay), NZ 145/H7
Karamet-Niyaz, Trkm. 113/H1
Karamiran, China 111/E4
Karamiran (pass), China 111/E4
Karamiran (riv.), China 111/D4
Karamürsel, Turk. 57/J5
Karamyshevo, Rus. 47/N3
Karangasem, Indo. 101/F5
Karanginskiy (isl.), Rus. 81/S4
Karanginskiy (bay), Rus. 81/S4
Karanjia, India 107/E1
Karanpur, India 110/B5
Karapelit, Bul. 57/H4
Karapınar, Turk. 114/C2
Karasabai, Guy. 217/G3
Karaşar, Turk. 76/E4
Karasburg, Namb. 142/B3
Karasjohka-Karasjok, Nor. 44/H1
Karasu, Turk. 57/K5
Karasu, Japan 95/L6
Karasuk, Rus. 111/C1
Karatá (lag.), Nic. 207/F3
Karatal (riv.), Kaz. 111/C2
Karataş, Turk. 116/D1
Karatau (mts.), Kaz. 111/A3
Karathuri, Myan. 106/B4
Karatobe, Kaz. 77/K2
Karaton, Kaz. 77/K3
Karatoya (riv.), Bang. 109/G3
Karatsu, Japan 96/A4
Karauli, India 108/A2
Karaurgan, Turk. 114/E1
Karáva (peak), Gre. 55/G3
Karavan, Kyr. 111/B3
Karawang, Indo. 101/D4
Karayaka, Turk. 76/F4
Karayazı, Turk. 114/E2
Karazhal, Kaz. 111/B2
Karbaka, Sudan 127/G5
Karbalā', Iraq 115/F3
Karbalā (gov.), Iraq 115/E3
Karben, Ger. 64/B2
Karcag, Hun. 56/E2
Kardhámila, Gre. 55/K3
Kardhítsa, Gre. 55/G3
Kardhitsomagoúla, Gre. 55/G3
Kärdla, Est. 47/K2
Kareha (riv.), India 109/E3
Karelī, India 108/B4
Karelia (reg.), Rus. 44/J2
Kareliya, Resp., Rus. 80/D3
Karema, Tanz. 139/G4
Karenga (riv.), Rus. 90/H1
Karera, India 108/B3
Karesuando, Swe. 44/G1
Karêt (reg.), Mrta. 128/D4
Kärevere, Est. 47/M2
Kargala, Rus. 77/K2
Kargasok, Rus. 80/J4
Kargı, Turk. 76/E4
Kargil, India 110/D2
Kargopol', Rus. 74/H3
Karhal, India 108/B2
Karhijärvi (lake), Fin. 47/K1
Karhula, Fin. 47/M1
Kariá, Gre. 55/G3
Karia Ba Mohammed, Mor. 130/B2
Kariaí, Gre. 55/J2
Karianga, Madg. 143/H8
Kariba, Zam.,Zim. 141/F3
Kariba (dam), Zim. 141/F3
Kariba (lake), Zim. 119/E6
Kariba-yama (peak), Japan 94/A2
Karibib, Namb. 140/B4
Karibumba, D.R. Congo 139/G2
Karikal, India 107/C4
Karimama, Ben. 133/F3
Karimata (str.), Indo. 102/C4
Karimata (isl.), Indo. 102/D4
Karīmnagar, India 107/C2
Karimui, PNG 153/G1
Karimunjawa (isls.), Indo. 101/E4
Karin, Som. 136/C3
Karin, Som. 136/D3
Kariótissa, Gre. 55/H2
Karis (Karjaa), Fin. 45/D4
Karise, Den. 46/E4
Karisimbi (vol.), D.R. Congo 139/G3
Karislojo (Karjalohja), Fin. 45/D4
Káristos, Gre. 55/J3
Kariya, Japan 95/L6
Karjaa (Karis), Fin. 45/D4
Karjalohja (Karislojo), Fin. 45/D4
Karkaar (mts.), Som. 136/D3
Karkar (isl.), PNG 160/D5
Karkinits'ka Zatoka (gulf), Ukr. 76/D3
Karkkila, Fin. 47/L1
Kärkölä, Fin. 45/F4
Karkonski NP, Pol. 49/H3
Karkur, Isr. 117/B4
Karl E. Mundt NWR, SD, US 184/E2
Karla Marksa (peak), Taj. 111/B4
Karleby (Kokkola), Fin. 74/D3
Karlholmsbruk, Swe. 46/G1
Karlino, Pol. 46/F4
Karlivka, Ukr. 79/H3
Karlo-Libknekhtovsk, Ukr. 79/K3
Karlovac, Cro. 56/B3
Karlovo, Bul. 57/G4
Karlovy Vary, Czh. 65/F2
Karlovy Vary (arpt.), Czh. 65/F2
Karlovarský (pol. reg.), Czh. 48/G3
Karlsdorf-Neuthard, Ger. 64/B4
Karlsfeld, Ger. 65/E6
Karlshamn, Swe. 46/F3
Karlshuld, Ger. 64/E5
Karlskoga, Swe. 46/F2
Karlskron, Ger. 65/E5
Karlskrona, Swe. 46/F3
Karlslunde Strand, Den. 45/J7
Karlsruhe, ND, US 186/D3
Karlsruhe, Ger. 64/B4
Karlstad, Swe. 46/E2
Karlstad, Mn, US 186/F3
Karlstadt, Ger. 64/C3
Karlstein am Main, Ger. 64/C2
Karluk, Ak, US 201/H4
Karmah, Sudan 127/F5
Karmāla, India 107/B2
Karmatānr, India 109/F3
Karmi'el, Isr. 117/C3
Karnāl, India 110/D5
Karnali (zone), Nepal 108/C1
Karnali (riv.), Nepal 108/C1
Karnaphuli (res.), Bang. 109/H4
Karnataka (state), India 104/C4
Karnes City, Tx, US 181/F3
Karnobat, Bul. 57/H4
Kärnten (prov.), Aus. 51/K3
Karo, Chad 134/C3
Karoi, Zim. 141/F3
Karomatan, Phil. 100/C4
Karonga, Malw. 137/A4
Karoo NP, SAfr. 142/D4
Karoo NP, SAfr. 142/C4
Karoonda, Austl. 156/A2
Karor, Pak. 110/A4
Karora, Sudan 112/C5
Karoso (cape), Indo. 103/E5
Karpakora, Austl. 156/B2
Kárpathos, Gre. 73/K4
Kárpathos (isl.), Gre. 114/A3
Karpatskiy NP, Ukr. 78/C3
Karpenísion, Gre. 55/G3
Karpogory, Rus. 75/K3
Karratha, Austl. 154/C2
Kars (prov.), Geo. 115/E1
Kars (riv.), SAfr. 142/M11
Kars, Turk. 115/E1
Kars (riv.), Turk. 77/G4
Kars (prov.), Turk. 77/G4
Kärsämäki, Fin. 74/E3
Karsantı, Turk. 114/C2
Kārsava, Lat. 47/M3
Kårsta, Swe. 45/B1
Kartaly, Rus. 77/M1
Kartārpur, India 110/C4
Kartushi, D.R. Congo 139/F4
Kartuzy, Pol. 46/H4
Karuah, Austl. 156/D2
Karuma (falls), Ugan. 139/H2
Karumba, Austl. 158/A2
Karūn (riv.), Iran 80/E6
Karunjie, Austl. 152/B4
Karup, Den. 46/C3
Karūr, India 107/C4
Karushe, D.R. Congo 139/F3
Karval, Co, US 182/C1
Karviná, Czh. 49/K4
Karwar, India 107/B3
Karymskoye, Rus. 90/G1
Kaş, Turk. 116/A1
Kås, Den. 46/C3
Kas, Sudan 134/E2
Kasaan, Ak, US 201/M4
Kasagi, Japan 95/J6
Kasahara, Japan 95/M5
Kāsai (riv.), India 109/F4
Kasai, Japan 96/D3
Kasai (riv.), D.R. Congo 119/D5
Kasai Occidental (pol. reg.), D.R. Congo 139/E4
Kasai Oriental (pol. reg.), D.R. Congo 139/E3
Kasaji, D.R. Congo 139/E5
Kasakalawe, Zam. 139/G5
Kasalu, Zam. 141/E2
Kasama, Japan 97/G2
Kasama, Zam. 139/G5
Kasamatsu, Japan 95/L5
Kasane, Bots. 140/E3
Kasanga (falls), Zam. 140/E3
Kasanga, Tanz. 139/G5
Kasangulu, D.R. Congo 138/C4
Kasanka NP, Zam. 141/F2
Kasaoka, Japan 96/C3
Kasar (cape), Sudan 127/H5
Kasartori-yama (peak), Japan 95/K6
Kasba (lake), NW,Nun, Can. 170/F2
Kasba Tadla, Mor. 128/D2
Kaseda, Japan 96/B5
Kaseke, D.R. Congo 141/E1
Kasembe, Tanz. 137/B4
Kasempa, Zam. 140/E2
Kasenga, D.R. Congo 139/G5
Kasenyi, D.R. Congo 139/G2
Kasese, Ugan. 139/G2
Kasese, D.R. Congo 139/F3
Kaset Wisai, Thai. 106/C3
Kāsganj, India 108/B2
Kashabowie, On, Can. 187/J3
Kashaf (riv.), Iran 113/H1
Kasha-Katuwe Tent Rocks Nat'l Mon., NM, US 179/J3
Kāshān, Iran 115/G3
Kashary, Rus. 79/L3
Kashi, China 111/C4
Kashiba, Zam. 139/G5
Kashiba, Japan 95/J6
Kashihara, Japan 95/J6
Kashima, Japan 97/G3
Kashima, Japan 96/B4
Kashima (bay), Japan 95/F1
Kashin, Rus. 74/H4
Kāshīpur, India 108/B1
Kashiwa, Japan 95/D2
Kashiwara, Japan 95/J6
Kashiwazaki, Japan 97/F2
Kāshmar, Iran 113/G1
Kashmūnd Ghar (range), Afg. 110/A2
Kashof (riv.), Iran 115/J2
Kashofu, D.R. Congo 139/G3
Kasia, India 108/D2
Kasidiji (riv.), D.R. Congo 139/E5
Kasigau (peak), Kenya 137/B2
Kasigluk, Ak, US 201/F3
Kasilof, Ak, US 201/H3
Kasimov, Rus. 74/J5
Kasimovo (arpt.), Rus. 75/T6
Kasindi, D.R. Congo 139/G2
Kasinge, D.R. Congo 139/F4
Kasiruta (isl.), Indo. 103/G4
Kasiui (isl.), Indo. 103/H4
Kasiya, Malw. 141/G2
Kaskaskia (riv.), Il, US 185/K4
Kas'kovo, Rus. 47/N2
Kaslo, BC, Can. 174/F3
Kasonaweja, Indo. 103/J4
Kasongan, Indo. 102/D4
Kasongo, D.R. Congo 139/F4
Kasongo-Lunda, D.R. Congo 138/D4
Kasonguele, D.R. Congo 139/F4
Kásos (isl.), Gre. 114/A3
Kaspi, Geo. 77/H4
Kaspichan, Bul. 57/H4
Kaspiysk, Rus. 77/H4
Kaspiyskiy, Rus. 77/H3
Kassala, Sudan 135/H2
Kassándra (pen.), Gre. 76/B5
Kassándria, Gre. 55/H2
Kassel, Ger. 59/G6
Kasserine, Tun. 130/L7
Kasserine (gov.), Tun. 130/L7
Kassikaityu (riv.), Guy. 217/G4
Kasson, Mn, US 185/H1
Kastamonu (prov.), Turk. 76/E4
Kastamonu, Turk. 76/E4
Kastanéai, Gre. 57/H5
Kaštel Stari, Cro. 56/C4
Kaštel Sućurac, Cro. 56/C4
Kastellaun, Ger. 61/G3
Kastéllion, Gre. 55/J5
Kasterlee, Belg. 58/B6
Kastl, Ger. 65/E4
Kastön (isl.), Swe. 45/B1
Kastoría, Gre. 55/G2
Kastornoye, Rus. 79/K2
Kastrakíou (lake), Gre. 55/G3
Kastrup, Den. 45/J7
Kasuga, Japan 95/K5
Kasuga, Japan 95/H5
Kasugai, Japan 95/B2
Kasugai, Japan 95/L5
Kasui, Indo. 101/D4
Kasukabe, Japan 97/F3
Kasuku (riv.), D.R. Congo 139/F3
Kasulu, Tanz. 139/G4
Kasumiga (lake), Japan 97/G2
Kasungu, Malw. 141/G2
Kasungu NP, Malw. 141/G2
Kasupe, Malw. 141/G2
Kasūr, Pak. 110/C4
Kat O Chau (isl.), China 99/M6
Kataba, Zam. 140/E3
Katagum (riv.), Nga. 134/A2
Katako-Kombe, D.R. Congo 139/F3
Katákolon, Gre. 55/G4
Katale, D.R. Congo 139/G3
Kataloinen, Fin. 45/E4
Katana, D.R. Congo 139/G3
Katanda, D.R. Congo 139/E4
Katanda, D.R. Congo 139/G3
Katanga, (pol. reg.), D.R. Congo 139/F5
Katangi, India 108/B4
Katanning, Austl. 154/C5
Katano, Japan 95/J6
Katanti, D.R. Congo 139/F3
Katarniān Ghāt, India 108/C1
Katastárion, Gre. 55/G4
Katavi NP, Tanz. 139/G4
Katchall (isl.), India 105/F6
Katea, D.R. Congo 139/F4
Katea, D.R. Congo 139/E4
Katebo, Ugan. 139/H3
Katemcy, Tx, US 180/E2
Katenga, D.R. Congo 139/G4
Kateríni, Gre. 55/H2
Kates Needle (mt.), Ak, US 201/M4
Katesh, Tanz. 137/A3
Katete, Malw. 141/G2
Katete, Zam. 141/G2
Katghora, India 108/D4
Katha, Myan. 98/C3
Katherine, Az, US 178/E3
Katherine, Austl. 152/D3
Katherine (riv.), Austl. 152/D3
Katherine Gorge NP, Austl. 152/D3
Kāthgodām, India 108/B1
Kathiawar (pen.), India 113/K4
Kathleen, Ga, US 195/G1
Kathleen, Fl, US 194/L7
Kathleen (mt.), Austl. 155/G2
Kāthmāndu (cap.), Nepal 109/E2
Kathryn, ND, US 186/F4
Kathua, India 110/C3
Kati, Mali 132/C3
Katiéna, Mali 132/D3
Katihār, India 109/F3
Kātikund, India 109/F3
Katiola, C.d'Iv. 132/D4
Katla, Sudan 135/F3
Katlehong, SAfr. 142/E2
Katlenburg-Lindau, Ger. 59/H5
Katma, China 111/E4
Katmai (mt.), Ak, US 201/H4
Katmai NP, Ak, US 201/G4
Káto Akhaía, Gre. 55/G3
Káto Nevrokópion, Gre. 55/H2
Katoba, Tanz. 139/G4
Katokhí, Gre. 55/G3
Katombe, D.R. Congo 139/E4
Katonah, NY, US 199/E1
Katonga (riv.), Ugan. 139/G2
Katoomba, Austl. 157/E1
Katoúna, Gre. 55/G3
Katowice, Pol. 49/K3
Katra, India 110/C3
Katra, India 108/C3
Kātrās, India 109/F4
Katrichev, Rus. 77/H2
Katrine (lake), Sc, UK 39/B4
Katrineholm, Swe. 46/G2
Katsepe, Madg. 143/H6
Katshi, D.R. Congo 139/F4
Katsikás, Gre. 55/G3
Katsina (state), Nga. 133/G3
Katsina, Nga. 133/G3
Katsina Ala (riv.), Nga. 133/H5
Katsina Ala, Nga. 133/H5
Katsunuma, Japan 95/B2
Katsura (riv.), Japan 95/J5
Katsuragi, Japan 96/D3
Katsuragi-san (peak), Japan 95/H7
Katsuta, Japan 97/G2
Katsuura, Japan 97/G3
Katsuyama, Japan 96/E2
Katsuyama, Japan 95/B3
Kattegat (str.), Den. 46/D3
Katua, Gha. 133/E4
Katul (mtn.), Sudan 135/F2
Katumajävi (lake), Fin. 45/E4
Katumbi, Malw. 137/A4
Katun' (riv.), Rus. 90/B1
Katunayake (int'l arpt.), SrL. 107/C5
Katun'chuya (riv.), Rus. 111/E1
Katundu, Zam. 140/E3
Kātūria, India 109/F3
Katuta Kampemba, Zam. 139/G5
Kātwa, India 109/G4
Katwa, D.R. Congo 139/G2
Katwe-Kabatooro, Ugan. 139/G3
Katwijk aan Zee, Neth. 58/B4
Katy, Tx, US 181/G3
Katzenbach (riv.), Ger. 64/B4
Katzenbuckel (peak), Ger. 64/C4
Katzenelnbogen, Ger. 61/G3
Katzhütte, Ger. 64/D1
Katzwinkel, Ger. 61/F3
Kau-ye (isl.), Myan. 106/B4
Kauai (isl.), Hi, US 172/S9
Kauai (chan.), Hi, US 172/S10
Kaudum (riv.), Namb. 140/D3
Kaudum Game Park, Namb. 140/D3
Kaufbeuren, Ger. 67/G2
Kaufering, Ger. 67/G1
Kaufman, Tx, US 181/F1
Kaufman (co.), Tx, US 180/L7
Kaufungen, Ger. 59/G6
Kauhava, Fin. 74/D3
Kauiki (pt.), Hi, US 172/U10
Kaukapakapa, NZ 159/F6
Kaukauna, Wi, US 190/B2
Kaukaveld (uplands), Namb. 140/B3
Kaukura (isl.), FrPol. 161/L6
Kaulashishi (hill), Zam. 141/F2
Kaulsdorf, Ger. 65/E1
Kaumba, D.R. Congo 139/F5
Kaunas (res.), Lith. 47/L4
Kaunas, Lith. 47/K4
Kaunas (int'l arpt.), Lith. 47/K4
Kauniainen (Grankulla), Fin. 45/E4
Kaupanger, Nor. 46/B1
Kaura Namoda, Nga. 133/G3
Kauro, Kenya 137/B1
Kauttua, Fin. 47/K1
Kavadarci, FYROM 55/H2
Kavajë, Alb. 55/F2
Kavála, Gre. 55/J2
Kavalerovo, Rus. 91/M3
Kāvali, India 107/C3
Kavango (riv.), Namb. 140/C3
Kavār, Iran 115/H4
Kavarna, Bul. 57/J4
Kavarskas, Lith. 47/L4
Kavgolovskoye (lake), Rus. 75/T6
Kavieng, PNG 160/E5
Kavimba, Bots. 140/E3
Kavīr-e Bāfq (Salt pan), Iran 115/H4
Kavīr-e Namak (Salt pan), Iran 115/J3
Kävlinge, Swe. 46/E4
Kävlingeån (riv.), Swe. 45/K7
Kaw, FrG. 218/C1
Kaw (lake), Ok, US 183/F2
Kaw (dam), Ok, US 183/F2
Kaw City, Ok, US 183/F2
Kawa (ruin), Sudan 127/F5
Kawa, Myan. 98/C5
Kawabe, Japan 94/B4
Kawachi, Japan 95/E2
Kawachi-Nagano, Japan 95/J7
Kawage, Japan 95/L6
Kawagoe, Japan 97/F3
Kawagoe, Japan 95/L5
Kawaguchi, Japan 97/F3
Kawaguchiko, Japan 95/B3
Kawai, Japan 95/J6
Kawajena, Sudan 135/F4
Kawajima, Japan 95/C2
Kawakami, Japan 95/B2
Kawakami, Japan 95/J7
Kawamata, Japan 97/G2

Kimry – Koran
299

Kimry, Rus. 74/H4
Kinabalu (peak), Malay. 100/B4
Kinabalu NP, Malay. 100/B4
Kinabatangan (riv.), Malay. 103/E2
Kinaliada (isl.), Turk. 115/M7
Kinalung, Austl. 156/B2
Kinango, Kenya 137/B3
Kinapat (cape), Indo. 101/B3
Kinard, Fl, US 195/F2
Kinards, SC, US 193/G3
Kinarut, Malay. 100/B4
Kinbasket (lake), BC, Can. 174/E1
Kinbrace, Sc, UK 37/S7
Kincaid, Sk, Can. 175/L3
Kincaid, Ks, US 183/G1
Kincardine, Sc, UK 39/C4
Kincardine, On, Can. 190/F2
Kinchafoonee (cr.), Ga, US 195/F1
Kincolith, BC, Can. 201/N4
Kincraig, Sc, UK 39/C2
Kinda, D.R. Congo 139/F5
Kindambi, D.R. Congo 138/E4
Kindberg, Aus. 51/L3
Kindembe, D.R. Congo 138/D4
Kinder, La, US 194/B2
Kinder Scout (peak), Eng, UK 41/G5
Kindersley, Sk, Can. 175/K2
Kindia (pol. reg.), Gui. 132/B4
Kindia, Gui. 132/B4
Kinding, Ger. 65/E5
Kindred, ND, US 186/F4
Kindsbach, Ger. 61/G5
Kindu, D.R. Congo 139/F3
Kinel', Rus. 77/J1
Kineshma, Rus. 74/J4
Kineton, Eng, UK 43/E2
King (isl.), Austl. 145/D4
King (lake), Austl. 154/C5
King (mt.), Austl. 158/B4
King (riv.), Austl. 157/C3
King (sound), Austl. 145/B2
King (mt.), BC, Can. 201/N4
King (isl.), NZ 145/H6
King, NC, US 193/G2
King (hill), Pa, US 191/G4
King (mtn.), Tx, US 180/C2
King (co.), Wa, US 197/D2
King Abdul Aziz (int'l arpt.), SAr. 127/H4
King And Queen Court House, Va, US 193/J2
King Christian (isl.), Nun, Can. 171/R7
King Christian IX Land (reg.), Grld. 163/P3
King Christian X Land (reg.), Grld. 163/Q2
King City, Ca, US 178/B2
King City, Mo, US 185/G3
King City, On, Can. 190/T8
King Cove, Ak, US 201/F4
King Frederik VI Coast (reg.), Grld. 163/N3
King Frederik VIII Land (reg.), Grld. 163/Q2
King George (isls.), FrPol. 161/L6
King George (mt.), BC, Can. 174/G2
King George, Va, US 193/J1
King George Is. (isls.), Qu, Can. 171/J3
King George's (res.), Eng, UK 36/C2
King Hussein (arpt.), Jor. 117/E4
King Khaled (int'l arpt.), SAr. 112/E4
King Leopold (range), Austl. 152/B4
King of Prussia, Pa, US 198/C3
King Peak (mt.), Yk, Can. 201/K3
King Salmon, Ak, US 201/G4
King William (isl.), Nun, Can. 170/G2
King William, Va, US 193/J2
King William's Town, SAfr. 142/D4
Kinganga, D.R. Congo 138/C4
Kingaroy, Austl. 158/C4
Kingfisher, Ok, US 183/F3
Kinghorn, Sc, UK 39/C4
Kingisepp, Rus. 47/N2
Kinglake NP, Austl. 156/G5
Kingman, Ks, US 183/E2
Kingman, Az, US 179/E3
Kingman (reef), Pac., US 161/J4
Kingombe, D.R. Congo 139/F3
Kingoonyah, Austl. 155/G4
Kings (peak), Ut, US 177/H3
Kings, Ms, US 192/B4
Kings (riv.), Ca, US 178/C2
Kings (cr.), Tx, US 180/L7
Kings Beach, Ca, US 176/C4
Kings Canyon NP, Ca, US 178/C2
Kings Island, Oh, US 190/D5
Kings Langley, Eng, UK 36/B1
King's Lynn, Eng, UK 43/G1
Kings Mountain, NC, US 193/G3
Kings Mountain Nat'l Mil. Park, SC, US 193/G3
Kings Park, Austl. 154/K6
Kings Point, NY, US 199/L8
King's Seat (hill), Sc, UK 39/C4
Kings Sutton, Eng, UK 43/E2
Kingsbridge, Eng, UK 42/C6
Kingsburg, Ca, US 178/C2
Kingsbury, Tx, US 181/F3
Kingsclere, Eng, UK 43/E4
Kingscote, Austl. 155/H5
Kingscourt, Ire. 38/D2
Kingsdown, Ks, US 182/E2
Kingsford, Mi, US 187/K5
Kingsland, Eng, UK 42/D2
Kingsland, Ar, US 183/H4
Kingsland, Ga, US 195/H2
Kingsland, Tx, US 181/E2
Kingsley, Ia, US 185/G2
Kingsley, Mi, US 190/D2
Kingsley (dam), Ne, US 184/D3
Kingsnorth, Eng, UK 36/E2
Kingsport, Tn, US 193/F2
Kingston, Austl. 156/C4
Kingston, Austl. 160/F7
Kingston, On, Can. 191/H2
Kingston (cap.), Jam. 207/G2
Kingston, La, US 194/B1
Kingston, Mo, US 185/G4
Kingston, NM, US 179/J4
Kingston, NY, US 191/K4
Kingston, Oh, US 190/E5
Kingston, Ok, US 183/F4
Kingston, Pa, US 198/C1
Kingston, RI, US 191/L4
Kingston, Tn, US 192/E3
Kingston, Wa, US 197/B2
Kingston S.E., Austl. 156/A3
Kingston Springs, Tn, US 192/D2
Kingston upon Hull, Eng, UK 41/H4
Kingston upon Hull (co.), Eng, UK 41/H4
Kingston upon Thames, Eng, UK 36/C2
Kingston Upon Thames (bor.), Eng, UK 36/C2
Kingstown, Austl. 156/D1
Kingstown (cap.), StV. 203/N9
Kingstree, SC, US 193/H4
Kingsville, Md, US 198/B5
Kingsville, On, Can. 190/E3
Kingsville, Tx, US 181/F4
Kingsville Nav. Air Sta., Tx, US 181/F4
Kingswear, Eng, UK 42/C6
Kingswood, Ky, US 192/D2
Kingswood, Eng, UK 42/D4
Kington, Eng, UK 42/D2
Kingushi, D.R. Congo 138/D4
Kingussie, Sc, UK 39/B2
Kingwood, Tx, US 181/M8
Kingwood, WV, US 191/G5
Kiniama, D.R. Congo 141/F1
Kiniati, D.R. Congo 138/D4
Kınık, Turk. 76/C5
Kinistino Ind. Res., Sk, Can. 175/M1
Kinkaid (mt.), Ak, US 201/L4
Kinkaid (lake), Il, US 192/C2
Kinkala, Congo 138/C4
Kinki (prov.), Japan 96/D3
Kinkosi, D.R. Congo 138/C4
Kinloch Rannoch, Sc, UK 39/B3
Kinlochewe, Sc, UK 39/A1
Kinlochleven, Sc, UK 39/B3
Kinloss, Sc, UK 39/C1
Kinmel, Wal, UK 40/E5
Kinmundy, Il, US 192/C1
Kinna, Swe. 46/E3
Kinnairds (pt.), Sc, UK 39/D1
Kinnegad, Ire. 38/C3
Kinnelon, NJ, US 199/H8
Kinnelon (lake), NJ, US 199/H8
Kinneret, Isr. 117/D3
Kinnikinnick, Oh, US 190/E5
Kinnitty, Ire. 38/C3
Kino (riv.), Japan 96/D3
Kinomoto, Japan 95/K5
Kinrooi, Belg. 61/E1
Kinross, Sc, UK 39/C4
Kinsach (riv.), Ger. 65/F4
Kinsale (har.), Ire. 38/B6
Kinsale, Ire. 38/B6
Kinsale, On, Can. 190/U8
Kinsarvik, Nor. 46/B1
Kinsey, Mt, US 175/M4
Kinshasa (pol. reg), D.R. Congo 138/C4
Kinshasa (cap.), D.R. Congo 138/C4
Kinsley, Ks, US 182/E2
Kinsman, Oh, US 190/F4
Kinston, Al, US 195/E2
Kinston, NC, US 193/J3
Kinta, Ok, US 183/G3
Kintampo, Gha. 133/E4
Kintinku, Tanz. 137/A3
Kintnersville, Pa, US 198/C2
Kintore, Sc, UK 39/D2
Kintyre, ND, US 186/E4
Kintyre (isl.), Sc, UK 37/R8
Kintzheim, Fr. 66/D1
Kinu (riv.), Japan 97/F2
Kinvarra, Ire. 38/B3
Kinwow (bay), Mb, Can. 186/F2
Kinyangiri, Tanz. 137/A3
Kinyeti (peak), Sudan 135/G5
Kinzig (riv.), Ger. 48/E4
Kiomboi, Tanz. 137/A3
Kiowa, Ok, US 183/G3
Kiowa, Ks, US 183/E2
Kiowa (cr.), Co, US 184/B4
Kiowa, Co, US 184/B4
Kipange, D.R. Congo 139/F4
Kiparissía, Gre. 55/G4
Kiparissía (gulf), Gre. 73/J3
Kipawa (lake), Qu, Can. 191/G1
Kipawa, Qu, Can. 191/G1
Kipen', Rus. 75/S7
Kipili, Tanz. 139/G4
Kipilingu, D.R. Congo 141/F2
Kipini, Kenya 137/C2
Kipkarren (riv.), Kenya 137/A1
Kipling, Sk, Can. 186/C2
Kipnuk, Ak, US 201/F4
Kippel, Swi. 66/D5
Kippen, Sc, UK 39/B4
Kippens, Nf, Can. 189/H1
Kippure (peak), Ire. 40/B5
Kipti, Ukr. 78/F2
Kipushi, D.R. Congo 141/E1
Kira, Japan 95/M6
Kira Panayía (isl.), Gre. 55/H3
Kirakira, Sol. 160/F6
Kirandul, India 107/D2
Kiranomena, Madg. 143/H7
Kīratpur, India 108/B1
Kirawa, Nga. 134/B3
Kirazlı, Turk. 55/K2
Kirbla, Est. 47/K2
Kirby, Ar, US 183/H3
Kirby, Mt, US 177/K1
Kirbyville, Tx, US 181/H2
Kırcasalih, Turk. 57/H5
Kirchberg, Ger. 61/G4
Kirchberg, Ger. 65/F1
Kirchberg, Swi. 66/D3
Kirchberg, Swi. 67/F3
Kirchberg an der Iller, Ger. 67/G1
Kirchberg an der Jagst, Ger. 64/C4
Kirchdorf, Ger. 59/F3
Kirchdorf an der Krems, Aus. 65/H7
Kirchen, Ger. 61/G2
Kirchenlamitz, Ger. 65/E2
Kirchenthumbach, Ger. 65/E3
Kirchheim, Ger. 67/G1
Kirchheim bei München, Ger. 65/E6
Kirchheim unter Teck, Ger. 64/C5
Kirchheimbolanden, Ger. 64/B3
Kirchhundem, Ger. 59/F6
Kirchlengern, Ger. 59/F4
Kirchlinteln, Ger. 59/G3
Kirchsee (lake), Ger. 67/H2
Kirchseeon, Ger. 65/E6
Kirchweidach, Ger. 65/F6
Kirchzarten, Ger. 66/D2
Kirchzell, Ger. 64/C3
Kircubbin, NI, UK 40/C3
Kircudbright (bay), Sc, UK 40/D2
Kirensk, Rus. 81/L4
Kirgiz Steppe (upland), Kaz. 80/F5
Kirgizskiy (mts.), Kyr. 111/B3
Kiri, D.R. Congo 138/D3
Kiriákion, Gre. 55/H3
Kiribati (ctry.) 160/H5
Kırık, Turk. 114/E1
Kırıkhan, Turk. 116/E1
Kırıkkale, Turk. 114/C2
Kırıkkale (prov.), Turk. 114/C2
Kirikkuduk, China 90/C3
Kirillov, Rus. 74/H4
Kirishi, Rus. 47/Q2
Kirishima-Yaku NP, Japan 96/B5
Kirishima-yama (peak), Japan 96/B5
Kiritimati (Christmas) (isl.), Kiri. 161/K4
Kırkağaç, Turk. 76/C5
Kirkburton, Eng, UK 41/G4
Kirkby, Eng, UK 41/F5
Kirkby in Ashfield, Eng, UK 41/G5
Kirkby Lonsdale, Eng, UK 41/F3
Kirkby Stephen, Eng, UK 41/F3
Kirkbymoorside, Eng, UK 41/H3
Kirkcaldy, Sc, UK 39/C4
Kirkcolm, Sc, UK 40/C2
Kirkconnel, Sc, UK 39/C6
Kirkcowan, Sc, UK 40/D2
Kirkcudbright, Sc, UK 40/D2
Kirke Hvalsø, Den. 45/H7
Kirkee, India 104/B4
Kirkenær, Nor. 46/E1
Kirkham, Eng, UK 41/F4
Kirkhill, Sc, UK 39/B2
Kirkinner, Sc, UK 40/D2
Kirkintilloch, Sc, UK 39/B5
Kirkkonummi (Kyrkslätt), Fin. 47/L1
Kirkland, Qu, Can. 189/N7
Kirkland (hill), Sc, UK 39/C6
Kirkland, Az, US 179/F3
Kirkland, Il, US 185/K2
Kirkland, Wa, US 174/C4
Kirkland Lake, On, Can. 171/H4
Kırklar (peak), Turk. 76/C5
Kırklareli, Turk. 57/H5
Kırklareli (prov.), Turk. 57/H5
Kirklees (co.), Eng, UK 41/G4
Kirkliston, Sc, UK 39/C5
Kirkmichael, IM, UK 40/D3
Kirkmuirhill, Sc, UK 39/C5
Kirkstone (pass), Eng, UK 41/F3
Kirksville, Mo, US 185/H3
Kirkton of Glenisla, Sc, UK 39/C3
Kirkūk, Iraq 115/F3
Kirkwall, Sc, UK 37/V14
Kirkwood, SAfr. 142/D4
Kirkwood, De, US 198/C4
Kirn, Ger. 61/G4
Kirongwe, Tanz. 137/B3
Kiropa, Tanz. 137/A4
Kirov, Rus. 75/L4
Kirov, Rus. 76/E1
Kirovo-Chepetsk, Rus. 75/L4
Kirovohrad, Ukr. 79/G3
Kirovohrads'ka Oblast, Ukr. 76/D2
Kirovsk, Bela. 76/D1
Kirovsk, Rus. 74/G2
Kirovsk, Rus. 75/U7
Kirovs'k, Ukr. 79/K3
Kirovskaya Oblast, Rus. 75/P5
Kirovs'ke, Ukr. 79/H5
Kirovs'ke, Ukr. 79/K3
Kirovskiy, Kaz. 80/H5
Kirovskiy, Rus. 77/J3
Kirovskiy, Rus. 91/L2
Kirriemuir, Ab, Can. 175/J2
Kirriemuir, Sc, UK 39/D3
Kirrweiler, Ger. 64/B4
Kirs, Rus. 75/M4
Kirsanov, Rus. 77/G1
Kırşehir, Turk. 114/C2
Kırşehir (prov.), Turk. 114/C2
Kirtland, NM, US 179/H2
Kirtland (A.F.B.), NM, US 179/J3
Kirtley, Wy, US 184/B2
Kirton, Eng, UK 41/H6
Kirton in Lindsey, Eng, UK 41/H5
Kiruna, Swe. 44/G2
Kirundu, D.R. Congo 139/F3
Kirwin (res.), Ks, US 184/E4
Kirwin, Ks, US 184/E4
Kirwin Nat'l Wildlife Res., Ks, US 182/E1
Kirya, Rus. 75/K5
Kiryū, Japan 97/F2
Kisa, Swe. 46/F3
Kisai, Japan 95/D1
Kisakata, Japan 94/A4
Kisangani, D.R. Congo 139/F2
Kisangani (int'l arpt.), D.R. Congo 139/F2
Kisantu, D.R. Congo 138/C4
Kisar (isl.), Indo. 152/B1
Kisaran, Indo. 101/B2
Kisarawe, Tanz. 137/B3
Kisarazu, Japan 97/F3
Kisauni (Zanzibar) (int'l arpt.), Tanz. 137/B3
Kisber, Hun. 49/K5
Kisbey, Sk, Can. 186/C3
Kisei, Japan 95/K7
Kiselevsk, Rus. 80/J4
Kisenda, D.R. Congo 138/D4
Kisenge, D.R. Congo 139/E5
Kisessa, Tanz. 137/A2
Kīsh, Iran 115/H5
Kīsh (isl.), Iran 115/H5
Kishanda, Tanz. 139/G3
Kishanganj, India 109/F2
Kishangarh, India 108/A2
Kishangarh, India 104/B2
Kishi, Nga. 133/F4
Kishiwada, Japan 95/H7
Kishoreganj, Bang. 109/G3
Kishorganj, Bang. 109/H3
Kishtwar, India 110/C3
Kishwaukee (riv.), Il, US 197/N15
Kisi, D.R. Congo 139/G3
Kisigo (riv.), Tanz. 137/A3
Kisii, Kenya 137/A2
Kisiju, Tanz. 137/B3
Kisiwani, Tanz. 137/B3
Kiska (isl.), Ak, US 81/T4
Kiska (mt.), Ak, US 201/B5
Kiskissink, Qu, Can. 188/A2
Kiskőrös, Hun. 56/D2
Kiskunfélegyháza, Hun. 56/D2
Kiskunhalas, Hun. 56/D2
Kiskunmajsa, Hun. 56/D2
Kiskunsági Nemzeti NP, Hun. 56/D2
Kislovodsk, Rus. 77/G4
Kismaayo, Som. 137/C2
Kismaayo (Chisimayu), Som. 137/C2
Kiso (riv.), Japan 97/E3
Kisogawa, Japan 95/L5
Kisoro, Ugan. 139/G3
Kisozaki, Japan 95/L5
Kisrah, Tun. 130/L7
Kíssamos, Gre. 55/H5
Kissee Mills, Mo, US 183/H2
Kissidougou, Gui. 132/C4
Kissimmee, Fl, US 194/N7
Kissimmee (lake), Fl, US 195/H4
Kissimmee (riv.), Fl, US 195/H4
Kissing, Ger. 64/D6
Kisslegg, Ger. 67/F2
Kissū (peak), Sudan 126/E4
Kissy, SLeo. 132/B4
Kist, Ger. 64/C3
Kisújszállás, Hun. 56/E2
Kisumu, Kenya 137/A2
Kisvárda, Hun. 49/M4
Kiswere, Tanz. 137/B4
Kit Carson, Co, US 182/C1
Kita, Mali 132/C3
Kita (lake), Japan 97/G2
Kita-Ibaraki, Japan 97/G2
Kitaaiki, Japan 95/B1
Kitab, Uzb. 80/G6
Kitadaitō (isl.), Japan 97/L8
Kitagata, Japan 95/L5
Kitakami, Japan 94/B4
Kitakami (mts.), Japan 94/B4
Kitakami (riv.), Japan 94/B4
Kitakata, Japan 97/F2
Kitakawabe, Japan 95/D1
Kitakyūshū, Japan 96/B4
Kitale, Kenya 137/A1
Kitami, Japan 94/C2
Kitami (mts.), Japan 91/N2
Kitamimaki, Japan 95/A1
Kitamoto, Japan 95/D1
Kitan (str.), Japan 95/G7
Kitangari, Tanz. 137/B4
Kitangiri (lake), Tanz. 137/A3
Kitaura, Japan 95/F1
Kitchener, On, Can. 190/F3
Kite, Ga, US 193/F4
Kitendwe, D.R. Congo 139/G4
Kitengo, D.R. Congo 139/F4
Kitgum, Ugan. 139/H2
Kíthira, Gre. 55/H4
Kíthira (isl.), Gre. 73/J3
Kíthnos, Gre. 55/J4
Kíthnos (isl.), Gre. 73/K3
Kithor, India 108/A1
Kitim, Jor. 117/D4
Kitimat, BC, Can. 170/D3
Kitkatla, BC, Can. 201/M5
Kitomesa, D.R. Congo 138/C4
Kitsap (co.), Wa, US 197/B3
Kitscoty, Ab, Can. 175/J1
Kitsman', Ukr. 78/C3
Kitt Peak National Observatory, Az, US 179/G5
Kittanning, Pa, US 191/G4
Kittatinny (mts.), NJ, US 198/C1
Kittery, Me, US 191/L3
Kitty Hawk, NC, US 193/K2
Kitu, D.R. Congo 139/F4
Kitui, Kenya 137/B2
Kitui Nat'l Rsv., Kenya 137/B2
Kitumala (pt.), PNG 153/G1
Kitumbeine (peak), Tanz. 137/B2
Kitumbini, Tanz. 137/B4
Kitunda, Tanz. 137/A3
Kitunguli, Tanz. 137/C4
Kitwe, Zam. 141/F2
Kitzbühel, Aus. 51/K3
Kitzingen, Ger. 64/D3
Kiunga, Kenya 137/C2
Kiunga, PNG 153/F1
Kiunga Marine Nat'l Res., Kenya 137/C2
Kiuruvesi, Fin. 74/E3
Kiuyu (pt.), Tanz. 137/B3
Kivalina, Ak, US 201/F2
Kivalo (mts.), Fin. 44/H2
Kivertsi, Ukr. 78/C2
Kivi-Vigala, Est. 47/L2
Kivijärvi (lake), Fin. 47/M1
Kivik, Swe. 45/L7
Kiviõli, Est. 47/M2
Kivu (lake), D.R. Congo 119/E5
Kiwai (isl.), PNG 153/F2
Kiwela, D.R. Congo 139/F4
Kiwira, Tanz. 137/A4
Kiyevka, Rus. 77/G3
Kiyevka, Kaz. 111/B1
Kıyıköy, Turk. 57/J5
Kiyokawa, Japan 95/C3
Kiyosu, Japan 95/L5
Kizamba, D.R. Congo 138/D5
Kizel, Rus. 75/N4
Kizëma, Rus. 75/K3
Kizhaba, Azer. 115/G2
Kizil (riv.), China 80/H6
Kızılcadağ, Turk. 116/A1
Kızılcahamam, Turk. 76/E4
Kızıldag NP, Turk. 114/B2
Kızılhisar, Turk. 114/B2
Kızılırmak (riv.), Turk. 76/E4
Kizil'skoye, Rus. 77/L1
Kızıltepe, Turk. 114/E2
Kızılyaka, Turk. 114/C2
Kizimbani, Tanz. 137/B4
Kizimkazi, Tanz. 137/B3
Kizlyar, Rus. 77/H4
Kizu (riv.), Japan 96/E3
Kizu, Japan 95/J6
Kizukuri, Japan 94/B3
Kizyl-Aatrek, Trkm. 115/H2
Kizyl-Su, Trkm. 115/H2
Kjeller, Nor. 44/T8
Kjerkestinden (peak), Nor. 44/F1
Kjevik (int'l arpt.), Nor. 46/C2
Kjølen (mts.), Nor. 44/E2
Klabava (riv.), Czh. 65/G3
Kladanj, Bosn. 56/D3
Kladar, Indo. 153/E2
Kladno, Czh. 65/H2
Kladovo, Serb. 56/F3
Klaeng, Thai. 106/C3
Klagenfurt, Aus. 51/L3
Klaipėda, Lith. 47/J4
Klakah, Indo. 101/F5
Klamath (riv.), Ca, US 172/B3
Klamath, Ca, US 176/A3
Klamath (mts.), Ca,Or, US 176/B2
Klamath Falls, Or, US 176/C2
Klamath Forest NWR, Or, US 176/C2
Klåmmingen (lake), Swe. 45/A1
Klangenan, Indo. 101/E4
Klapmuts, SAfr. 142/L10
Klar (riv.), Swe. 80/B4
Klarälven (riv.), Swe. 44/E3
Klarup, Den. 46/D3
Klaserie, SAfr. 141/F5
Klášterec nad Ohří, Czh. 65/G2
Klaten, Indo. 101/E4
Klatovy, Czh. 65/G4
Klaukkala, Fin. 45/E4
Klaus, Aus. 67/F3
Klausen (Chiusa), It. 67/H4
Klausenpass (pass), Swi. 67/E4
Klawock, Ak, US 201/M4
Klaza (mt.), Yk, Can. 201/L3
Klazienaveen, Neth. 58/E3
Kleena Kleene, BC, Can. 174/B2
Klein Karas, Namb. 142/B2
Klein Spitzkoppe (peak), Namb. 140/B4
Klein Vaaldoorn, Namb. 142/B3
Klein-Letabarivier (riv.), SAfr. 141/F4
Kleinblittersdorf, Ger. 61/G5
Kleinburg, On, Can. 190/T8
Kleine Elster (riv.), Ger. 49/G3
Kleine Emme (riv.), Swi. 66/E4
Kleine Gete (riv.), Belg. 61/D2
Kleine Laber (riv.), Ger. 65/F5
Kleine Nete (riv.), Belg. 61/D1
Kleinheubach, Ger. 64/C3
Kleinlützel, Swi. 66/D3
Kleinmachnow, Ger. 48/Q7
Kleinmond, SAfr. 142/L11
Kleinolifants (riv.), SAfr. 142/Q12
Kleinrinderfeld, Ger. 64/C3
Kleinsee, SAfr. 142/B3
Kleinwallstadt, Ger. 64/C3
Kleinwinternheim, Ger. 64/B3
Klemme, Ia, US 185/H2
Kleppe, Nor. 46/A2
Kleppestø, Nor. 46/A1
Klerksdorp, SAfr. 142/D2
Klesiv, Ukr. 78/D2
Klet' (peak), Czh. 65/H5
Kletnya, Rus. 76/E1
Kletskiy, Rus. 79/M3
Kleve, Ger. 58/D5
Klichev, Bela. 47/N5
Klichka, Rus. 91/H1
Klickitat, Wa, US 174/D5
Klickitat (riv.), Wa, US 174/D4
Klimovichi, Bela. 76/D1
Klimovo, Rus. 76/E1
Klina, Serb. 56/E4
Klinaklini (riv.), BC, Can. 174/B2
Kling, Phil. 100/D4
Klingenberg am Main, Ger. 64/C3
Klingenmünster, Ger. 64/B4
Klingenthal, Ger. 65/F2
Klínovec (peak), Czh. 65/F2
Klintehamn, Swe. 46/H3
Klintsy, Rus. 76/E1
Klip (riv.), SAfr. 142/E2
Klippan, Swe. 46/E3
Klipplaat, SAfr. 142/D4
Klisura, Bul. 57/G4
Klitmøller, Den. 46/C3
Kljajićevo, Serb. 56/D3
Ključ, Bosn. 56/C3
Kłodawa, Pol. 49/K2
Kłodzko, Pol. 49/J3
Klondike, Ga, US 193/M7
Klondyke, Az, US 179/G4
Klöntaler-See (lake), Swi. 67/E3
Kloosterzande, Neth. 58/B6
Kloster, Ger. 46/E4
Klosterbach (riv.), Ger. 59/F3
Klosterlechfeld, Ger. 67/G1
Klosterneuburg, Aus. 57/N7
Klosters, Swi. 67/F4
Klosterwappen (peak), Aus. 49/H5
Kloten, Swi. 67/E3
Klothuhta Zayat, Myan. 98/C5
Klötze, Ger. 48/F2
Kluane, Yk, Can. 201/L3
Kluane NP, Yk, Can. 201/K3
Kluczbork, Pol. 49/K3
Klundert, Neth. 58/B5
Klukshu, Yk, Can. 201/L3
Klukwan, Ak, US 201/L3
Klyavlino, Rus. 75/M5
Klyaz'ma (riv.), Rus. 74/J4
Klyuchevskaya (peak), Rus. 81/S4
Klyuchi, Rus. 81/R4
Knaphill, Eng, UK 36/B3
Knapp (hill), Wi, US 185/J1
Knappa, Or, US 174/C4
Knapstad, Nor. 44/T9
Knäred, Swe. 46/E3
Knaresborough, Eng, UK 41/G3
Knebworth, Eng, UK 43/F3
Kneehills (cr.), Ab, Can. 175/H2
Knetzgau, Ger. 64/D3
Knezha, Bul. 57/G4
Knife (riv.), ND, US 186/C4
Knife River Indian Villages Nat'l Hist. Site, ND, US 186/D4
Knight (inlet), BC, Can. 174/B2
Knighton, Wal, UK 42/C2
Knights, Fl, US 194/L7
Knightsen, Ca, US 197/L11
Knin, Cro. 56/C3
Knippa, Tx, US 180/E3
Knislinge, Swe. 45/L6
Knittelfeld, Aus. 51/L3
Knittlingen, Ger. 64/B4
Knivsta, Swe. 46/G2
Knížecí Stolec (peak), Czh. 65/H5
Knížecí Strom (peak), Czh. 65/F3
Knjaževac, Serb. 56/F4
Knob (cape), Austl. 154/C5
Knob (peak), Phil. 103/F1
Knobby (pt.), Austl. 154/B4
Knobel, Ar, US 192/B2
Knoch (hill), Sc, UK 39/D1
Knock, Ire. 38/B2
Knockadoon Head (pt.), Ire. 38/C6
Knockalongy (peak), Ire. 38/B1
Knockanaffrin (peak), Ire. 38/C5
Knockanore (mtn.), Ire. 38/A4
Knockboy (peak), Ire. 38/A6
Knockcloghrim, NI, UK 40/B2
Knockeirke (peak), Ire. 38/A6
Knocklong, Ire. 38/B5
Knockmealdown (peak), Ire. 38/C5
Knockmealdown (mts.), Ire. 38/B5
Knocknagashel, Ire. 38/A5
Knocknamaddree (peak), Ire. 38/A7
Knockowen (peak), Ire. 38/A6
Knockshanahullion (peak), Ire. 38/B5
Knoll (pt.), Namb. 140/B5
Knøsen (peak), Den. 46/D3
Knösen (pt.), Swe. 46/E4
Knosós (Knossos) (ruin), Gre. 55/J5
Knossos (Knosós) (ruin), Gre. 55/J5
Knott, Tx, US 180/D1
Knott End, Eng, UK 41/F4
Knottingley, Eng, UK 41/G4
Knott's Berry Farm, Ca, US 196/G8
Knotts Island, NC, US 193/K2
Knotty Green, Eng, UK 36/B2
Knowl Hill, Eng, UK 36/A2
Knowsley (co.), Eng, UK 41/F5
Knox (coast), Ant. 228/G
Knox (nbrhd.), Austl. 156/G5
Knox (cape), BC, Can. 170/C3
Knox, In, US 190/C4
Knox, ND, US 186/E3
Knox, Pa, US 191/G4
Knox City, Tx, US 182/E4
Knoxville, Ga, US 192/F4
Knoxville, Ia, US 185/H3
Knoxville, Ms, US 194/C2
Knoxville, Tn, US 192/F3
Knutby, Swe. 45/B1
Knutsford, Eng, UK 41/F5
Knysna, SAfr. 142/C4
Ko (riv.), Sen. 132/B3
Ko (peak), Rus. 91/M2
Ko Samut NP, Thai. 106/C3
Ko-saki (pt.), Japan 96/A3
Koanaka (hills), Bots. 140/D4
Koani, Tanz. 137/B3
Koāth, India 109/E3
Koba, Indo. 101/D3
Kobar Sink (depr.), Eth. 136/B2
Kobayashi, Japan 96/B5
Kōbe, Japan 95/H6
Kobelyaky, Ukr. 79/H3
København (int'l arpt.), Den. 46/E4
København (co.), Den. 45/J7
København (Copenhagen) (cap.), Den. 45/J7
Kobenni, Mrta. 132/C3
Kobern-Gondorf, Ger. 61/G3
Kobipato (peak), Indo. 103/G4
Koblach, Aus. 67/F3
Koblenz, Swi. 67/E2
Koblenz, Ger. 61/G3
K'obo, Eth. 136/A2
Kobowan (swamp), Sudan 135/G4
Kobozha, Rus. 74/G4
Kobra, Rus. 75/L3
Kobroor (isl.), Indo. 103/H5
Kobryn, Bela. 76/C1
Kobu, SKor. 93/D5
Kobuchizawa, Japan 95/A2
Kobuk, Ak, US 201/G2
Kobuk (riv.), Ak, US 201/G2
Kobuk Valley NP, Ak, US 201/G2
K'obulet'i, Geo. 77/G4
Kobushi-ga-take (peak), Japan 97/F3
Kocába (riv.), Czh. 65/H3
Kocaeli (prov.), Turk. 76/D4
Koçalı, Turk. 114/D2
Kočani, FYROM 55/H2
Kocapınar, Turk. 115/E2
Kočevje, Slov. 51/L4
Koch (isl.), Nun, Can. 171/J2
Koch'ang, SKor. 93/D5
Koch'ang, SKor. 93/D5
Kochel am See, Ger. 67/H2
Kochelsee (lake), Ger. 67/H2
Kochen'ga, Rus. 75/J3
Kocher (riv.), Ger. 51/H2
Kocherinovo, Bul. 55/H1
Kochetovka, Rus. 77/G1
Kochevo, Rus. 75/M4
Kōchi (pref.), Japan 96/C4
Kōchi, Japan 96/C4
Kochmes, Rus. 75/P2
Kochubey, Rus. 77/H3
Kochubeyevskoye, Rus. 79/L5
Kochugaon, India 109/H2
Kodaira, Japan 95/C2
Kodala, India 107/E2
Kodama, Japan 95/C1
Kodāri, Nepal 109/E2
Kodarmā, India 109/E3
Kodiak, Ak, US 201/H4
Kodiak (isl.), Ak, US 201/H4
Kodinār, India 113/K4
Kodomari, Japan 94/B3
Kodry (hills), Mol. 57/H2
Kodyma, Ukr. 78/E3
Koekelare, Belg. 60/B1
Koel (riv.), India 104/D3
Koes, Namb. 142/B2
Koesan, SKor. 93/D4
Koetari (riv.), Sur. 217/G4
Kofa (mts.), Az, US 179/E4
Kofa NWR, Az, US 179/E4
Kofçaz, Turk. 57/H5
Kofelē, Eth. 136/A4
Koffiefontein, SAfr. 142/D3
Kofiau (isl.), Indo. 103/G4
Koforidua, Gha. 133/E5
Kōfu, Japan 97/F3
Koga, Japan 97/F2
Koga, Tanz. 139/H4
Koganei, Japan 95/D2
Kogarah, Austl. 157/E1
Køge (bay), Den. 46/E4
Kogi, Nga. 133/G4
Kogon (riv.), Gui. 132/B4
Kŏgum (isl.), SKor. 93/D5
Kohāt, Pak. 110/A3
Kohila, Est. 47/L2
Kohīma, India 98/B3
Kohkīlūyeh and Bovīr Aḩmadi (gov.), Iran 115/G4
Kohler, Wi, US 190/C3
Kohls Ranch, Az, US 179/G3
Kohoku, Japan 95/K5
Kohout (peak), Czh. 65/H5
Kohtla-Järve, Est. 47/M2
Kohŭng, SKor. 93/D5
Kohunlich (ruin), Mex. 206/D2
Koichab (riv.), Namb. 140/B5
Koidern, Yk, Can. 201/K3
Koidu, SLeo. 132/C4
Koigi, Est. 47/L2
Koihoa, India 105/F6
Koilābās, Nepal 108/D2
Koímisis, Gre. 55/H2
Koindu, SLeo. 132/C4
Koito, Kenya 137/B2
Koito (riv.), Japan 95/D3
Koiva (riv.), Lat. 47/M3
Kŏje (isl.), SKor. 96/A3
Kojonup, Austl. 154/C5
Kojšovská (peak), Slvk. 49/L4
Kok (riv.), Myan. 106/B1
Kōka, Japan 95/K6
K'ok'a Gidib (dam), Eth. 136/A3
Kokai (riv.), Japan 95/E2
Kökar (isl.), Fin. 47/J3
Kokas, Indo. 103/H4
Kokemäenjoki (riv.), Fin. 47/J1
Kokhonak, Ak, US 201/H4
Kokhanovo, Bela. 47/N4
Kokkola (Karleby), Fin. 74/D3
Koknese, Lat. 47/L3
Koko, Nga. 133/G5
Koko, Nga. 133/G4
Kokoda, PNG 153/G2
Kokofata, Mali 132/C3
Kokola, D.R. Congo 139/G2
Kokomo, In, US 190/C4
Kokonau, Indo. 103/J4
Kokong, Bots. 140/D5
Kokonjärvi (lake), Fin. 45/D3
Kokrajhar, India 109/H2
Koksan, NKor. 93/D3
Kokshaal-Tau (mts.), Kyr. 111/C3
Kökshetaū, Kaz. 111/A1
Koksijde, Belg. 60/B1
Koksoak (riv.), Qu, Can. 171/K3
Koksovyy, Rus. 79/L3
Kokstad, SAfr. 142/E3
Kokubu, Japan 96/B5
Kokuy, Rus. 91/H1
Kol, PNG 153/G1
Kola (isl.), Indo. 103/H5
Kola (riv.), Rus. 74/G1
Kola (pen.), Rus. 74/H1
Kolachel, India 107/C4
Kolahun, Libr. 132/C4
Kolaka, Indo. 103/F4
Kolāras, India 108/A3
Kolašin, Mont. 56/D4
Kolbäck, Swe. 46/G2
Kolbano, Indo. 152/B2
Kolbio, Kenya 137/C2
Kolbotn, Nor. 44/S8
Kolbus, Sudan 134/D2
Kolbuszowa, Pol. 49/L3
Kolda, Sen. 132/B3
Kolda (pol. reg.), Sen. 132/B3
Kolding, Den. 46/C4
Kole, D.R. Congo 139/F2
Kolebira, India 109/E4
Kölen (mts.), Swe. 44/E2
Kolenté, Gui. 132/B4
Kolepom (Yos Sudarso) (isl.), Indo. 160/C5
Kolezhma, Rus. 74/G2
Kolgaküla, Est. 47/L2
Kolgompya (cape), Rus. 47/N2
Kolguyev (isl.), Rus. 75/K1
Koliba (riv.), Gui. 132/B3
Koliganek, Ak, US 201/G4
Kolín, Czh. 49/H3
Kolind, Den. 45/G6
Koliya, Gui. 132/B4
Kolka, Lat. 47/K3
Kolkasrags (pt.), Lat. 47/K3
Kolkhozabad, Taj. 113/J1
Kollbach (riv.), Ger. 65/F5
Kollnburg, Ger. 65/F4
Kollum, Neth. 58/D2
Kolmanskop, Namb. 142/A2
Köln (Cologne), Ger. 61/F2
Kolno, Pol. 49/L2
Koło, Pol. 76/A1
Kolo, Tanz. 137/A3
Kołobrzeg, Pol. 46/F4
Kolofata, Camr. 134/B3
Kologriv, Rus. 75/K4
Kolokani, Mali 132/C3
Kololo, Eth. 136/B4
Kolomna, Rus. 74/H5
Kolomyya, Ukr. 78/C3
Kolondiéba, Mali 132/D4
Kolongotomo, Mali 132/D3
Kolonnawa, SrL. 107/C5
Kolosib, India 98/B3
Kolossa (riv.), Mali 132/D3
Kolpashevo, Rus. 80/J4
Kolpino, Rus. 75/T7
Kolpny, Rus. 76/F1
Kolpyta, Ukr. 78/F2
Kolsva, Swe. 46/F2
Kolubara (riv.), Serb. 56/D3
Koluszki, Pol. 49/K3
Koluton (riv.), Kaz. 111/A1
Kolva (riv.), Rus. 75/N2
Kolwezi, D.R. Congo 139/F5
Kolyma (riv.), Rus. 83/Q3
Kolyma (range), Rus. 83/Q3
Kolyma Lowland (plain), Rus. 81/R2
Kolyshley, Rus. 77/H1
Kom (peak), Bul. 57/F4
Kom (riv.), Gabon 138/C2
Koma, Myan. 106/B3
Koma (riv.), Japan 95/C2
Komádi, Hun. 56/E2
Komadugu Gana (riv.), Nga. 133/H4
Komadugu Yobe (riv.), Nga. 133/H3
Komae, Japan 95/D2
Komagane, Japan 97/E3
Komaki, Japan 95/L5
Komaki (arpt.), Japan 95/L5
Komanda, D.R. Congo 139/G2
Komandorskiye (isls.), Rus. 83/R4
Komarichi, Rus. 79/H1
Komarin, Bela. 78/F2
Komárno, Slvk. 56/D2
Komárom, Hun. 56/D2
Komárom-Esztergom (prov.), Hun. 56/D2
Komatipoort, SAfr. 141/F5
Komatirivier (riv.), SAfr. 142/Q13
Komatlapeta, India 107/D2
Komatsu, Japan 96/E2
Komatsu (int'l arpt.), Japan 96/E2
Komatsushima, Japan 96/D3
Komba, D.R. Congo 139/E2
Kombat, Namb. 140/C3
Kombe, D.R. Congo 139/F4
Kombissiri, Burk. 133/E3
Kome (isl.), Ugan. 137/A2
Komering (riv.), Indo. 101/D4
Komi-Permyatskiy Aut. Okrug, Rus. 75/M2
Komjatice, Slvk. 49/K4
Komló, Hun. 56/D2
Kommetjie, SAfr. 142/L11
Kommunar, Rus. 47/P2
Komo, PNG 153/F1
Komodo (isl.), Indo. 103/E5
Komodo Island NP, Indo. 103/E5
Komodougou, Gui. 132/C4
Komoé (riv.), C.d'Iv. 132/E5
Komono, Congo 138/C3
Komono, Japan 95/L5
Komoran (isl.), Indo. 103/J5
Komoro, Japan 95/A1
Komotiní, Gre. 55/J2
Kompasberg (peak), SAfr. 142/D3
Kompiam, PNG 153/F1
Komsomolets (isl.), Rus. 83/J1
Komsomol's'k, Ukr. 79/G3
Komsomol'sk-na-Amure, Rus. 91/M1
Komsomol's'ke, Ukr. 79/J3
Komsomol's'ke, Ukr. 79/K4
Komsomol'skiy, Rus. 75/P2
Komsomol'skiy, Rus. 75/K5
Komsomol'skiy, Kaz. 77/K3
Komsomol'skiy, Rus. 80/G3
Komsomol'skiy, Rus. 77/H3
Komsomol'skoye, Rus. 77/H2
Komukanti, Namb. 140/C3
Kömür (pt.), Turk. 55/K3
Komysh-Zorya, Ukr. 79/J4
Komyshnya, Ukr. 79/G2
Kon (riv.), Kaz. 111/A2
Kon Plong, Viet. 106/E3
Kon Tum, Viet. 106/D3
Konabonou, C.d'Iv. 132/D5
Konakovo, Rus. 74/H4
Kōnan, Japan 95/K6
Kōnan, Japan 95/L5
Kōnan, Japan 95/C1
Konar (riv.), Afg. 110/A2
Konār (riv.), India 109/E4
Konār (res.), India 109/E4
Konar-e Khāş, Afg. 110/A2
Konārak, Iran 113/H3
Konārak, India 107/E2
Konawa, Ok, US 183/F3
Konaweha (riv.), Indo. 103/F4
Konda (riv.), Rus. 90/G1
Konda, Japan 95/H6
Kondagaon, India 107/D2
Kondé Sounga, Congo 138/B4
Kondinin, Austl. 154/C5
Kondoa, Tanz. 137/A3
Kondopoga, Rus. 74/G3
Kondūz, Afg. 80/G6
Koné, NCal., Fr. 161/U12
Konetsgor'ye, Rus. 74/J3
Kong (isl.), Camb. 106/C4
Kong, C.d'Iv. 132/D4
Kong (riv.), Laos 106/D3
Kong Kong (riv.), Sudan 135/G4
Kong Krailat, Thai. 106/B2
Kong Miao, China 92/D4
Kongapatalabata, Indo. 152/D1
Kongbo, CAfr. 134/D4
Kongiganak, Ak, US 201/F4
Kongju, SKor. 93/D4
Kongnŭg (riv.), SKor. 93/F6
Kongō-zan (peak), Japan 95/J7
Kongola, Namb. 140/D3
Kongolo, D.R. Congo 139/F4
Kongor, Sudan 135/F4
Kongoussi, Burk. 133/E3
Kongsberg, Nor. 46/C2
Kongsvinger, Nor. 46/E1
Kongtan, China 98/E2
Kongué, Chutes de (falls), Gabon 138/C2
Kongur (peak), China 111/C4
Kongwa, Tanz. 137/B3
Koniecpol, Pol. 49/K3
Königs Wusterhausen, Ger. 48/Q7
Königsberg in Bayern, Ger. 64/D2
Königsberg-Stein, Ger. 64/B5
Königsbronn, Ger. 64/D5
Königsbrunn, Ger. 67/G1
Königsdorf, Ger. 67/H2
Königsfeld im Schwarzwald, Ger. 67/E1
Königslutter am Elm, Ger. 59/H4
Königstein im Taunus, Ger. 64/B2
Königswinter, Ger. 61/G2
Konin, Pol. 49/K2
Konindou, Gui. 132/C4
Konispol, Alb. 55/G3
Kónitsa, Gre. 55/G2
Köniz, Swi. 66/D4
Konjic, Bosn. 56/C4
Könkämäeno (riv.), Fin. 74/D1
Konkiep (riv.), Namb. 140/C5
Konkiep, Namb. 142/B2
Konkola, Zam. 141/E2
Konkori, Gha. 133/E4
Konkouré (riv.), Gui. 132/B4
Konkourou-Bamingui, Rsv. de Faune du, CAfr. 134/D4
Konnevesi, Fin. 74/E3
Konobougou, Mali 132/D3
Konolfingen, Swi. 66/D4
Konosha, Rus. 74/J3
Kōnosu, Japan 95/D1
Konotop, Ukr. 79/G2
Konqi (riv.), China 80/J5
Konsen (plat.), Japan 94/D2
Końskie, Pol. 49/L3
Konso, Eth. 135/H4
Konstancin-Jeziorna, Pol. 49/L2
Konstantinovka, Ukr. 79/H3
Konstantinovsk, Rus. 79/L4
Konstantynówłódzki, Pol. 49/K3
Konstanz, Ger. 67/F2
Kontagora, Nga. 133/G4
Kontcha, Camr. 134/B4
Konteyevo, Rus. 74/J4
Kontich, Belg. 61/D1
Kontiolahti, Fin. 74/F3
Konuralp, Turk. 57/K5
Kóny, Hun. 56/C2
Konya, Turk. 114/C2
Konya (prov.), Turk. 114/C2
Konz, Ger. 61/F4
Konza, Kenya 137/B2
Koo-wee-rup, Austl. 157/B4
Koocenusa (lake), Mt, US 174/G3
Koog aan de Zaan, Neth. 58/B4
Koolpinyah, Austl. 152/C3
Koolyanobbing, Austl. 154/C4
Koondrook, Austl. 157/B2
Koonga, Est. 47/L2
Koonibba, Austl. 155/G4
Koontz Lake, In, US 190/C4
Kooparmora, Swe. 45/B1
Koorawatha, Austl. 157/D2
Koorda, Austl. 154/C4
Koosa, Est. 47/M2
Koosharem, Ut, US 179/G1
Kooskia, Id, US 174/G4
Kootenai Nat'l Wild. Ref., Id, US 174/F3
Kootenay (lake), BC, Can. 170/E3
Kootenay (riv.), BC, Can. 174/G2
Kootenay NP, BC, Can. 174/F2
Kootingal, Austl. 156/D1
Kop (pass), Turk. 114/E1
Kopāganj, India 108/D2
Kopaigo, PNG 153/F1
Kopargaon, India 107/B2
Kopargo, Ben. 133/F4
Kópavogur, Ice. 44/N7
Kope (peak), C.d'Iv. 132/D5
Köpenick, Ger. 48/Q7
Koper, Slov. 51/K4
Kopervik, Nor. 46/A2
Kopeysk, Rus. 75/P5
Kopfing im Innkreis, Aus. 65/G6
Kopia, D.R. Congo 139/E2
Kopili (riv.), India 98/B3
Köping, Swe. 46/G2
Koplik, Alb. 55/F1
Kopondei (cape), Indo. 152/A2
Koporskiy (bay), Rus. 47/N2
Koppang, Nor. 46/D1
Kopparberg (co.), Swe. 44/E3
Kopparberg, Swe. 46/F2
Koppi (riv.), Rus. 91/M2
Koppies, SAfr. 142/D2
Koprivnica, Cro. 56/C2
Koprivshtitsa, Bul. 57/G4
Kopru (riv.), Turk. 116/B1
Köprülü, Turk. 116/C1
Köprülü Kanyon NP, Turk. 114/B2
Kop'ung, NKor. 93/C2
Kopyl', Bela. 76/C1
Kopys', Bela. 47/P4
Kor (riv.), Iran 112/F2
Kora, India 108/C2
Kōra, Japan 95/K5
Kora NP, Kenya 137/B2
Korab (peak), Alb. 55/G2
Koráb (peak), Czh. 65/G4
Korablino, Rus. 76/G1
K'orahē, Eth. 136/C4
Korakuen Garden, Japan 96/C3
Koraluk (riv.), Nf, Can. 171/K3
Koramlik, China 111/E4
Korana (riv.), Cro. 51/L4

Kyritz, Ger. 48/G2
Kyrkslätt (Kirkkonummi), Fin. 47/L1
Kyrösjärvi (lake), Fin. 47/L1
Kyrta, Rus. 75/N2
Kyrykuduk, Kaz. 77/J2
Kyrylivka, Ukr. 79/H4
Kyshtym, Rus. 75/P5
Kythrea, Cyp. 116/G2
Kytlym, Rus. 75/N4
Kytäta, Fin. 45/E4
Kyūshū (isl.), Japan 83/M6
Kyūshū Highlands (uplands), Japan 96/B4
Kyusyur, Rus. 81/N2
Kywebwe, Myan. 98/B5
Kyyiv (Kiev) (cap.), Ukr. 78/F2
Kyyivs'ka Oblast, Ukr. 76/D2
Kyyivs'ke Vodoskhovyshche (res.), Ukr. 76/D2
Kyzyl, Rus. 90/C1
Kyzltu, Kaz. 80/H4

L

L'Achigan (riv.), Qu. Can. 189/N6
L'Anguille (riv.), Ar, US
L'Anse, Mi, US 187/K4
L'Aquila (prov.), It. 71/C3
L'Aquila, It. 71/C3
L' Ariana (lake), Fl, US 194/M7
L'Artois, Collines de (hills), Fr. 48/A3
L'Assomption (riv.), Qu. Can. 189/P6
L'Assomption (co.), Qu. Can. 189/N6
L'Hongrin (lake), Swi. 66/D5
L'Oriental (pol. reg.), Mor. 129/E2
La Algaba, Sp. 52/B4
La Almunia de Doña Godina, Sp.
La Amistad Int'l Park, CR 202/E6
La Araucanía (pol. reg.), Chile 226/B3
La Ascensión, Mex. 205/F3
La Asturiana, Col. 217/F2
La Asunción, Ven. 217/F2
La Aurora (int'l arpt.), Guat. 206/D3
La Baie, Qu. Can. 188/B1
La Banda, Arg. 224/C3
La Bañeza, Sp. 52/C1
La Barge, Wy, US 177/H2
La Barra, Nic. 207/F3
La Barra, Uru. 191/G2
La Barre-en-Ouche, Fr. 63/F3
La Bassée, Fr. 70/C1
La Bâthie, Fr. 70/C1
La Bâtie-Neuve, Fr. 70/C3
La Baule-Escoublac, Fr. 62/C6
La Belle, Fl, US 195/H4
La Birse (riv.), Swi.
La Blanquilla (isl.), Ven. 217/E2
La Bocana, Mex. 204/B3
La Bonneville-sur-Iton, Fr. 63/G3
La Bouilladisse, Fr. 70/B6
La Bresse, Fr. 66/C2
La Broque, Fr. 66/D1
La Broquerie, Mb, Can. 186/F2
La Cadière-d'Azur, Fr. 70/B6
La Caldera de Taburiente, PN, Sp.
La Calera, Col. 219/M8
La Calera, Chile
La Campana, Sp. 52/C4
La Campana, PN, Chile 226/N8
La Cañada (peak), Cuba 207/H4
La Canada-Flintridge, Ca, US 196/F7
La Canoa, Ven. 217/F2
La Capelle, Fr. 60/C4
La Carlota, Arg.
La Carlota, Arg. 226/E2
La Carolina, Sp. 52/D3
La Catedral (peak), Mex. 205/O9
La Ceiba, Hon. 206/E3
La Ceiba (int'l arpt.), Hon. 206/E3
La Ceja, Col. 219/K6
La Celle-les-Bordes, Fr. 36/H6
La Celle-Saint-Cloud, Fr. 36/C5
La Celle-sur-Morin, Fr. 36/L2
La Center, Ky, US 192/C2
La Chapelle-de-Guinchay, Fr. 66/A5
La Chapelle-des-Marais, Fr.
La Chapelle-Saint-Luc, Fr. 62/C6
La Chapelle-sur-Erdre, Fr. 62/D6
La Chartre-sur-le-Loir, Fr. 63/F5
La Chaussée-Saint-Victor, Fr.
La Chaux-de-Bonds, Swi. 66/C3
La Chinita (int'l arpt.), Ven. 216/D2
La Chorrera, Col.
La Cienega, NM, US 179/J3
La Ciotat, Fr. 70/B6
La Ciudad, PN, Mex. 204/D4
La Clusaz, Fr.
La Cocha, Arg. 224/D4
La Colle-sur-Loup, Fr.
La Concepción, Pan. 207/F4
La Concepción, Nic. 206/E4
La Concepcion, Ven. 216/D2
La Condamine (nbrhd.), Mona. 68/J8
La Coronilla, Uru. 191/G4
La Coruña, Sp. 52/A1
La Côte-Saint-André, Fr.
La Couronne, Fr.
La Couture-Boussey, Fr. 63/G3
La Crau, Fr. 70/C6
La Crèche, Fr.
La Crescent, Mn, US 185/J2
La Crescenta-Montrose, Ca, US
La Criolla, Arg. 224/D4
La Croche, Qu. Can.
La Croix-en-Brie, Fr. 36/M6
La Croix-Valmer, Fr.
La Crosse, Va, US 193/H4
La Crosse, Wi, US 185/J2

La Cruz, Chile 226/N8
La Cruz, Col. 216/B4
La Cruz, CR 206/E4
La Cruz, Mex. 204/D4
La Cruz, Uru. 191/K10
La Cuchilla, Uru.
La Cumbre (vol.), Ecu. 220/J7
La Dôle (peak), Swi. 66/C5
La Dorada, Col. 219/L7
La Doré, Qu. Can. 188/A1
La Dormida, Arg. 226/D2
La Durande (peak), Fr. 72/D1
La Embocada, Bol. 221/E4
La Escondida, Arg. 224/C3
La Escondida, Arg. 226/C3
La Esmeralda, Ven. 217/E4
La Esperanza, Bol. 221/F4
La Esperanza, Bol. 221/F5
La Esperanza, Bol. 221/F5
La Esperanza, Hon. 206/D3
La Esperanza, Hon. 206/D3
La Estanzuela, Arg. 191/K11
La Estrada, Sp.
La Estrella, Chile 226/N9
La Falda, Arg. 224/C4
La Fare-les-Oliviers, Fr. 70/B5
La Farlède, Fr. 70/C6
La Fayette, Ga, US 187/K4
La Fayette, Fr.
La Fère, Fr. 60/C4
La Ferrière-aux-Étangs, Fr. 63/E3
La Ferté-Gaucher, Fr. 60/C6
La Ferté-Imbault, Fr. 63/G6
La Ferté-Macé, Fr. 63/E3
La Ferté-Milon, Fr. 36/M7
La Ferté-Sous-Jouarre, Fr. 60/C6
La Ferté-St-Aubin, Fr.
La Ferté-Vidame, Fr. 63/F3
La Flèche, Fr. 63/E5
La Follette, Tn, US 192/E2
La Fontaine, In, US 190/D4
La Francia, Arg. 224/D4
La Fría, Ven. 216/C2
La Gacilly, Fr. 62/C5
La Galite (isl.), Tun. 130/L6
La Garde, Fr. 70/C6
La Garde-Adhémar, Fr. 70/A4
La Garde-Freinet, Fr.
La Garita (mts.), Co, US 182/A2
La Garita, Col. 179/J2
La Garriga, Sp. 53/L6
La Gineta, Sp. 52/E3
La Glacerie, Fr. 62/D1
La Gloria, Col. 216/C2
La Gran Sabana (plain), Ven. 217/F3
La Grande (riv.), Qu. Can. 171/J3
La Grande Rochette, Fr.
La Grande Ruine, Fr.
La Grange, Austl. 152/A4
La Grange, Ca, US 196/C3
La Grange, Ky, US 192/E1
La Grange, Mo, US 185/J3
La Grange, NC, US 193/J3
La Grange, Tx, US 181/F3
La Grange, Wy, US 184/B3
La Grave, Fr. 70/C2
La Grivola (peak), It. 70/D1
La Grue Bayou,
La Guadeloupe (lake), Swi. 66/D4
La Guaira, Ven. 217/E1
La Guajira (pen.), Col. 207/H4
La Guajira (dept.), Col. 207/H4
La Guardia, Arg. 224/C3
La Guardia, Bol. 224/D1
La Guardia, Sp. 52/A2
La Guardia, Sp. 52/D2
La Guardia, Bol.
La Guerche-de-Bretagne, Fr. 62/D5
La Habana (Havana) (cap.), Cuba
La Habra, Ca, US 196/G8
La Harpe, Ks, US 183/G2
La Have, Fr.
La Have (riv.), NS, Can. 188/E3
La Haye-du-Puits, Fr. 62/D2
La Haye-Pesnel, Fr. 62/D3
La Higuera, Chile
La Honda, Ca, US 197/K12
La Horqueta, Arg. 217/F2
La Horqueta, Ven. 217/F2
La Horquilla, Bol. 224/C1
La Houssaye-en-Brie, Fr. 36/L5
La Huaca, Peru 220/A2
La Huerta, Mex. 205/F5
La Huacana, Mex. 205/E5
La Isla, Mex. 205/Q10
La Jalca, Peru 220/B2
La Jara, NM, US 179/K2
La Jara, Sp.
La Javie, Fr. 70/C4
La Jolla Ind. Res.,
La Joya, Bol. 224/C1
La Joya, Arg. 226/D5
La Joya de los Sachas, Ecu. 220/B1
La Junta, Co, US 182/C2
La Junta, Mex. 204/D2
La Juventud (isl.), Cuba 163/J7
La Laguna, Sp. 128/A3
La Laja, Arg.
La Léchère, Fr. 70/C1
La Libertad, Ecu. 216/A5
La Libertad, Guat. 206/D2
La Libertad, Hon. 206/E3
La Libertad (dept.), Peru 50/A4
La Ligua, Chile 63/G3
La Linea de la Concepción, Sp.
La Llagosta, Sp. 53/L6
La Lobería, Arg.
La Loche, Sk, Can. 170/F3
La Loggia, It. 68/A3
La Londe-les-Maures, Fr. 70/C6
La Loupe, Fr. 63/F3
La Louvière, Belg. 61/D3
La Luisiana, Sp.
La Machine, Fr. 50/E3

La Maddalena, It. 54/A2
La Madeleine, Fr. 60/C2
La Madera, NM, US 179/J2
La Magdalena, Col. 219/L6
La Malbaie, Qu. Can. 188/B2
La Mancha (reg.), Sp. 72/C3
La Margarita, Ven. 217/F2
La Marque, Tx, US 181/N9
La Marsa, Tun. 130/M6
La Martre, Fr.
La Masica, Hon. 206/E3
La Media Luna, Bol. 221/D4
La Meije (peak), Fr. 70/C2
La Mensura (peak), Col. 217/E4
La Merca, Sp. 52/B1
La Merced, Arg. 224/C4
La Merced, Bol. 221/F5
La Merced, Hon. 206/D3
La Mesa (int'l arpt.), Hon. 206/E3
La Mesa, Ven. 217/E2
La Mesa, Ca, US 196/C5
La Mesa, NM, US 180/A1
La Mira, Mex. 204/E5
La Montaña (phys. reg.), Peru
La Monte, Mo, US 183/H1
La Motte (mtn.), Tx, US 180/C3
La Motte, Fr. 62/C4
La Motte-d'Aveillans, Fr. 70/B3
La Motte-du-Caire, Fr. 70/B1
La Motte-Servolex, Fr. 70/B1
La Moure, ND, US 184/G2
La Mula, Mex. 180/D3
La Mure, Fr. 63/E5
La Negra, Arg. 226/C3
La Neuveville, Swi. 66/D3
La Trinité-des-Monts,
La Ola, Chile 226/C2
La Orchila (isl.), Ven. 203/H5
La Oroya, Peru 220/C3
La Palma, Fr. 207/G4
La Palma (isl.), Sp. 119/A2
La Paloma, Uru. 191/G2
La Para, Arg. 224/E4
La Paragua, Ven. 217/F3
La Paz, Arg. 226/D2
La Paz, Col. 224/E4
La Paz, Peru 220/B2
La Paz (cap.), Bol. 224/E4
La Paz (dept.), Bol. 220/D4
La Paz, Col. 216/C3
La Paz, Hon. 206/E3
La Paz, Mex. 204/C3
La Paz (bay), Mex. 204/C3
La Paz, Phil. 100/D3
La Paz, Uru. 191/K11
La Pêche, Qu. Can. 191/H2
La Pedrera, Col. 216/D5
La Peña, Pan. 202/G6
La Peña, Col. 219/L7
La Penne-sur-Huveaune, Fr.
La Perla, Mex. 180/B3
La Perouse, Austl. 207/J4
La Petite-Raon, Fr.
La Piedad Cavadas, Mex. 204/E4
La Pine, Or, US 176/C2
La Place, La, US 194/C2
La Plant, SD, US 184/F3
La Plata, Arg. 219/P7
La Plata, Col. 216/C4
La Plata (riv.), Co, US 179/H2
La Plata, Mo, US 185/H3
La Pobla de Lillet, Sp. 53/F1
La Pocatière, Qu. Can. 188/B2
La Pola de Gordón, Sp. 52/C1
La Porte, In, US 190/C4
La Porte, Tx, US 181/M9
La Porte City, Ia, US 185/H2
La Posta Ind. Res.,
La Prairie (co.), Qu. Can. 189/N7
La Prairie, Qu. Can. 189/P7
La Pryor, Tx, US 180/D3
La Puebla de Almoradiel, Sp.
La Puebla de Cazalla, Sp.
La Puebla de Montalbán, Sp. 52/C2
La Puente, Ca, US 196/G7
La Puntilla (pt.), Ecu. 220/A2
La Quebrada, Ven. 216/D2
La Quiaca, Arg. 224/C2
La Rambla, Sp. 52/C4
La Ravoire, Fr. 70/B1
La Reforma, Mex. 204/D3
La Reforma, Sp.
La Rinconada, Sp. 52/C4
La Rioja, Arg. 224/C3
La Rioja (prov.), Arg. 224/C3
La Robla, Sp. 52/C1
La Roche, Swi. 66/D4
La Roche-Bernard, Fr. 62/C5
La Roche-de-Glun, Fr. 70/A3
La Roche-en-Ardenne, Fr.
La Roche-Maurice, Fr. 62/A3
La Roche-sur-Foron, Fr. 70/C3
La Roche-sur-Yon, Fr. 62/C6
La Rochelle, Fr. 62/C6
La Rochette, Fr. 70/C2
La Roda, Sp. 53/L6
La Romana, DRep. 203/H4
La Ronge, Sk, Can. 170/F3
La Rotta, It. 68/D6
La Rúa, Sp. 52/B1
La Rumorosa, Mex. 178/D4
La Sabana, Ven. 217/F3
La Sal, Ut, US 179/H1

La Sal (mts.), Ut, US 177/J4
La Salle, Mb, Can. 186/F3
La Salle, Co, US 179/J2
La Salle, Il, US 185/L5
La Salle les Alpes, Fr. 70/C3
La Salute di Livenza, It. 69/F2
La Sarraz, Swi. 66/C4
La Saussaye, Fr.
La Sauvette (peak), Fr. 63/F2
La Serena, Chile 224/B4
La Serville (peak), Fr.
La Sierpe, Cuba 207/G6
La Silueta (peak), Chile 191/B7
La Solana, Sp. 52/D3
La Souterraine, Fr. 50/D3
La Spezia (prov.), It. 68/C5
La Spezia, It. 69/D2
La Sûre (peak), Fr. 70/B2
La Suze-sur-Sarthe, Fr. 63/E5
La Tabatière, Qu. Can. 171/L3
La Tebaida, Col. 219/K8
La Teste, Fr. 50/C4
La Tête à l'Âne (peak), Fr. 66/C6
La Thuile, It. 70/C1
La Tigra, PN, Hon. 206/E3
La Toma, Arg. 226/D2
La Tortue (isl.), Haiti 217/E2
La Tortuga (isl.), Ven. 217/E2
La Tour-de-Peilz, Swi. 66/C5
La Tour-du-Trême, Swi. 66/D4
La Tour-du-Pin, Fr. 70/B1
La Tranca, Arg. 226/D2
La Tremblade, Fr. 50/C4
La Trinidad, Phil. 100/C1
La Trinitaria, Mex. 206/C2
La Trinité, Fr. 70/D5
La Trinité-Porhoët, Fr.
La Troncal, Ecu. 216/B5
La Troya (riv.), Arg. 224/B4
La Turballe, Fr. 62/C6
La Unión, ESal. 206/E3
La Unión, Col. 216/B3
La Unión, Chile 189/N7
La Unión, Qu. Can. 220/B2
La Unión, Peru 221/F4
La Unión, Bol. 216/E2
La Unión, Ven. 180/A2
La Union, NM, US 205/E5
La Union, Mex. 217/E2
La Urbana, Ven. 191/G5
La Vale, Md, US 70/B6
La Valette-du-Var, Fr. 52/C1
La Vecilla, Sp. 219/L8
La Vega, Col. 192/D2
La Vergne, Tn, US 179/F2
La Verkin, Ut, US 69/E6
La Verne, It.
La Verne, Ca, US 196/C2
La Verrière, Fr. 36/H5
La Victoria, Col. 216/B4
La Victoria, Ven. 217/E1
La Victoria, Ven. 216/D3
La Vieille-Lyre, Fr. 63/F3
La Vieja (riv.), Col. 219/K8
La Virginia, Col. 219/K8
La Voulte-sur-Rhône, Fr. 70/A3
La Vraie-Croix, Fr. 62/C5
La Wantzenau, Fr. 66/D1
Laa an der Thaya, Aus. 51/M2
Laaber, Ger. 65/E4
Laage, Ger. 48/G5
Laakirchen, Aus. 51/K3
Laarne, Belg. 60/C1
Laas (Lasa), It. 53/F1
Laas Caanood, Som. 136/D5
Laas Dhaareed, Som. 136/H2
Laas Qoray, Som. 136/H3
Lado, Sudan 135/H3
Ladoga, Rus. 75/T7
Ladoga, In, US 181/W1
Ladoix-Serrigny, Fr. 66/A3
Ladon (riv.), Gre. 55/G3
Ladozhskoye Ozero, Rus. 75/U6
Ladrillero (mtn.), Chile 189/P7
Ladson, SC, US 193/G4
Ladva-Vetka, Rus. 74/G3
Lādwa, India 110/D3
Lady Barron, Austl. 156/D3
Lady Isle (isl.), Sc, UK 39/C5
Lady Lake, Fl, US 195/H3
Ladybrand, SAfr. 141/E3
Ladybower (res.), Eng, UK 40/E3
Labian (cape), Malay. 100/D4
Labin, Cro. 51/L4
Labinsk, Rus. 79/G5
Labis, Malay. 106/B3
Labná (ruin), Mex. 206/D1
Laborde, Phil. 100/C4
Laborec (riv.), Slvk. 71/L2
Labota, Indo. 103/F4
Labouheyre, Fr. 62/C4
Laboulaye, Arg. 226/D2
Labrador (riv.), Nf, Can. 171/K11
Labrador (sea), Can. 163/M4
Labrador City, Nf, Can. 171/K3
Labré, Braz.
Labruguière, Fr. 50/E5
Labry, Fr. 61/F5
Labuan (terr.), Bru. 100/A4
Labuan, Phil. 100/C4
Labuanbajo, Indo. 103/F5
Labuhan, Indo. 106/C5
Labuhanbilik, Indo. 106/A3
Labuhanhaji, Indo. 101/B2
Labuhanruku, Indo. 101/B2
Labuk (bay), Malay. 103/F3
Labuništa, FYROM 55/G2
Labutta, Myan. 98/B5
Labytnangi, Rus. 80/G2
Laç, Alb. 55/F2
Laç (pref.), Chad 134/C2
Lac Afwein (riv.), Kenya 137/D1

Lac Court Oreilles Ind. Res., 177/J4
Lac du Bonnet, Mb, Can. 186/F3
Lac du Flambeau, 187/K5
Lac du Flambeau Ind. Res., 187/K5
Lac Vaart (canal), Neth. 58/C4
Lac La Biche, Ab, Can. 170/E3
Lac La Hache, BC, Can. 171/J4
Lac La Martre, NW, Can. 170/E2
Lac Pelletier, Sk, Can. 170/C6
Lac Seul, On, Can. 187/H2
Lac Son, Viet. 106/D1
Lac-Alouette, Qu. Can. 189/N6
Lac Kutulo (riv.), Kenya 137/C1
Lac-au-Saumon, 188/D1
Lac-aux-Sables, 188/A2
Lac-Beauport, Qu. Can. 188/A1
Lac-Bouchette, Qu. Can. 188/A1
Lac-des-Aigles, Qu. Can. 188/C2
Lac-du-Cerf, Qu. Can. 188/B3
Lac-Édouard, Qu. Can. 191/J1
Lac-Etchemin, Qu. Can. 188/B2
Lac-Mégantic, Qu. Can. 66/C6
Lacadena, Sk, Can. 175/K2
Lacantún (riv.), Mex. 206/D2
Lacassine Nat'l Wild. Ref., 181/H2
Lacaune, Fr. 50/E5
Laccadive (sea), Asia 104/B5
Lacchiarella, It. 68/C5
Lacco Ameno, It. 71/C6
Laceby, Eng, UK 41/C6
Lacepede (bay), Austl. 145/C4
Lacerdónia, Moz. 141/G3
Laces (Latsch), It. 67/G4
Lacey, Wa, US 174/C4
Lach Bissagh (riv.), Som. 137/C1
Lach Dera (riv.), Som. 137/C1
Lacha (lake), Rus. 74/H3
Lachay (pt.), Peru 224/B4
Lachen, Swi. 67/E3
Lachendorf, Ger. 59/H3
Lachhmangarh, India 108/A2
Lachi, Pak. 110/A3
Lachlan (riv.), Austl. 145/C4
Lachute, Qu. Can. 191/J2
Lachung, India 109/G2
Lackawanna, NY, US 190/V10
Lackawanna, 205/E5
Lackland (A.F.B.), Tx, US 181/E3
Läckö, Swe. 46/F3
Laclubar, ETim. 152/B2
Lacoi ti-Duyong 219/L8
Lacombe, La, US 194/D2
Lacombe, Ab, Can. 175/H1
Laconia, NH, US 191/K3
Laconia (gulf), Gre. 55/H4
Lacroix-Saint-Ouen, Fr. 60/D5
Lacrosse (isl.), Austl. 152/A3
Lacy-Lakeview, Tx, US 181/E2
Ladakh (mtn.), India 113/C2
Ladário, Braz. 224/E1
Ladbergen, Ger. 59/E4
Ladderhills, Pol. 49/J3
Ladenburg, Ger. 64/B4
Ladera Heights, Ca, US 196/F8
Ladismith, SAfr. 142/C4
Ladispoli, It. 71/B4
Ladoga, Sudan 135/H3
Ladha, Rus.

Lagan (riv.), NI, UK 40/B3
Lagan (riv.), Swe. 46/E3
Lagarto, Braz. 223/F1
Lagawe, Phil. 100/C1
Lagdo, D.R. Congo 139/G2
Lagdo (lake), Camr. 134/B3
Lajas, Peru 220/B2
Lajas, Azor., Port. 53/S12
Lajatico, It. 69/D7
Laje, Braz. 223/F1
Laje, Braz. 225/G4
Lajeado, Braz. 225/G4
Lajedo, Braz. 223/G5
Lajes, Azor., Port. 53/S12
Lajes, Braz. 225/G3
Lajes 53/S12
Lajes (int'l arpt.), Azor., Port.
Lajes (pass), Nepal 109/E2
Lajord (pass), Nepal 186/B2
Lajosmizse, Hun. 56/D2
Lāju, India 97/E5

Laixi, China 92/E3
Laiyang, China 92/E3
Laizhou (bay), China 92/D3
Laja (int'l arpt.), Chile 226/C3
Lagos, D.R. Congo
Lajamane, Mali 132/C3
Lagnò (isl.), Swe. 45/J3
Lagny-le-Sec, Fr. 36/L4
Lagny-sur-Marne, Fr. 36/L5
Lago da Pedra, Braz. 219/E4
Lago de Atitlán, PN, 206/D3
Lago Minchumina, 201/H3
Lago Posadas, Arg. 191/C5
Lago Puelo, PN, Arg. 226/C4
Lago Verde, Chile 226/C5
Lago Viedma, Arg. 191/B6
Lagoa da Prata, Braz. 225/H2
Lagoa Formosa, Braz. 222/D3
Lagoa Vermelha, Braz. 225/G3
Lagoda (lake), Rus. 44/J3
Lagona Larga, Arg. 224/D4
Lagos, Nga. 133/F5
Lagos (state), Nga. 133/F5
Lagos, Port. 52/A4
Lagos de Moreno, Mex. 204/E4
Lagosanto, It. 69/F4
Laguardia, Sp. 52/D1
Laguiole, Fr. 50/E4
Laguna, Braz. 225/G4
Laguna (bay), Phil. 100/F7
Laguna, Az, US 178/D4
Laguna (mts.), Ca, US 178/D4
Laguna (cr.), Ca, US 197/M10
Laguna (riv.), Austl. 145/D4
Laguna Atascosa NWR, 181/F4
Laguna Beach, Ca, US 196/C3
Laguna Blanca, PN, Arg. 226/C3
Laguna de Duero, Sp. 52/C2
Laguna de la Restinga, PN, 198/C1
Laguna del Laja, PN, 217/E2
Laguna del Rey, Mex. 204/D3
Laguna Grande, Arg. 191/C6
Laguna Hills, Ca, US 196/C3
Lagunas, Peru 220/B2
Lagunas, Chile 224/B2
Lagunas de Chacahua, PN, 206/C2
Lagunas de Montebello, PN, 206/D2
Lagunas de Zempoala, PN, 205/Q10
Lagundo (Algund), It. 67/H3
Lagunillas, Ven. 216/D2
Lagunillas, Chile 226/N8
Lagunillas, Bol. 224/D1
Lahad Datu, Malay. 100/B4
Lahaina, Hi, US 180/T12
Lahang, Thai. 79/K5

Laju 187/J5
Lake Placid, Fl, US 195/H4
Lake Placid, NY, US 191/K2
Lake Pleasant, NY, US 191/J3
Lake Preston, SD, US 185/F1
Lake Ronkonkoma, 226/C3
Lake, NY, US 199/E2
Lake Saint Croix Beach, 187/Q7
Lake Shore, Mn, US 187/G4
Lake Shore, Md, US 198/M5
Lake Station, In, US 197/R16
Lake Stevens, Wa, US 174/C3
Lake Success, ND, US 199/L8
Lake Tanglewood, 109/J7
Lake Thibadeau Nat'l Wild.
Lake Tomahawk, Wi, US 187/K5
Lake Toxaway, NC, US 193/F3
Lake View, Ia, US 185/G2
Lake Villa, Il, US 197/P15
Lake Waccamaw, NC, US 193/H3
Lake Wales, Fl, US 194/M8
Lake Worth, Fl, US 195/H5
Lake Zahl Nat'l Wild. Ref.,
Lake Woodruff Nat'l Wild. Ref.,
Lake Alice NWR, 185/G2
Lake Alma, Sk, Can. 86/B3
Lake Alpine, Ca, US 176/C4
Lake Amadeus Abor. Land, 155/F3
Lake Andes, SD, US 184/F2
Lake Andes Nat'l Wild. Ref.,
Lake Ann, Mi, US 190/D2
Lake Arrowhead, Ca, US 196/C2
Lake Arthur, NM, US 182/B4
Lake Arthur, La, US 194/B2
Lake Barrington, Il, US 197/P15
Lake Beulah, Wi, US 197/O15
Lake Bluff, Il, US 197/Q15
Lake Bolac, Austl. 156/B2
Lake Bolac, Austl. 156/B3
Lake Buena Vista, 225/G4
Lake Butler, Fl, US 195/G4
Lake Cargelligo, Austl. 157/C1
Lake Catherine, Il, US 197/P15
Lake Charles, La, US 194/B2
Lake City, Ar, US 192/B3
Lake City, Co, US 179/J1
Lake City, Fl, US 195/G2
Lake City, Ia, US 185/G2
Lake City, Mi, US 190/D2
Lake City, Mn, US 185/H1
Lake City, SD, US 184/F1
Lake Clark NP, Ak, US 201/H3
Lake Clarke Shores, Fl, US
Lake Conjola, Austl. 157/C2
Lake Cowichan, BC, Can. 174/B3
Lake Crystal, Mn, US 185/G1
Lake Dallas, Tx, US 180/K6
Lake Delton, Wi, US 185/K2
Lake District NP, 40/B3
Lake Elmo, Mn, US 187/Q7
Lake Elsinore, Ca, US 196/C3
Lake Fenton, Mi, US 190/D3
Lake Fern, Fl, US 194/K7
Lake Forest, Il, US 197/Q15
Lake Forest Park, 205/Q10
Lake Fork (riv.), Ut, US 177/H3
Lake Fork, Id, US 176/E1
Lake Garfield, Fl, US 194/M8
Lake Geneva, Wi, US 190/B3
Lake George, NY, US 191/K3
Lake George NWR, 195/H2
Lake Grace, Austl. 154/C5
Lake Hamilton, Ar, US 192/E3
Lake Hamilton, Fl, US 194/M7
Lake Havasu City, Az, US
Lake Helen, Fl, US 195/H3
Lake Hughes, Ca, US 196/C2
Lake Ilo NWR, ND, US 184/E4
Lake in the Hills, Il, US 197/P15
Lake Isom Nat'l Wild. Ref.,
Lake Jackson, Tx, US 180/K7
Lake Jem, Fl, US 194/M7
Lake King, Austl. 154/C5
Lake Lenore, Sk, Can. 175/K2
Lake Linden, Mi, US 187/K4
Lake Louise, Ab, Can. 174/F2
Lake Lucerne, Fl, US 194/P11
Lake Macleod, Austl. 152/A3
Lake Malawi NP, Malw. 141/G2
Lake Mary, Fl, US 194/N6
Lake McDonald, Mt, US 175/H3
Lake Mead Nat'l Rec. Area,
Lake Meredith Nat'l
Rec. Area, Tx, US 179/F2
Lake Mills, Ia, US 185/H2
Lake Mills, Wi, US 185/H2
Lake Mohawk, NJ, US 199/D1
Lake Montezuma, Az, US 179/G3
Lake Murray, PNG 147/F1
Lake Nakuru NP, Kenya 137/D2
Lake Nettie Nat'l Wild. Ref.,
Lake Odessa, Mi, US 190/D3
Lake Orion, Mi, US 190/D3
Lake Oswego, Or, US 176/C3
Lake Panasoffkee, Fl, US 194/L6
Lake Park, Fl, US 195/H5
Lake Park, Mn, US 186/F4

Lamas, Peru 220/B2
Lamastre, Fr. 70/A3
Lamāyūrū, India 110/D2
Lambach, Aus. 65/G6
Lamballe, Fr. 62/C4
Lambaré, Par. 224/E3
Lambaréné, Gabon 138/B3
Lambari, Braz. 223/L6
Lambasa, Fiji 161/Z17
Lambay (isl.), Ire. 40/B5
Lambayeque, Peru 220/A2
Lambayeque (dept.), Peru 220/A2
Lambayeque, Peru 220/B2
Lambè Coda (riv.), Mali 132/C3
Lambeg, NI, UK 40/B3
Lambert, Ms, US 192/B3
Lambert-St. Louis (int'l arpt.), Mo, US 200/G8
Lambert's Bay, SAfr. 142/B4
Lambertville, Mi, US 190/E4
Lambertville, NJ, US 198/D3
Lambesc, Fr. 70/B5
Lambeth (bor.), Eng, UK 36/C2
Lambhumn, Eng, UK 43/E3
Lambrama, Peru 220/C4
Lambrecht, Ger. 64/B4
Lambrecht, Ger. 68/D2
Lambourn (riv.), It. 59/E4
Lambsborg, Austl. 64/B3
Lambsheim, Ger. 64/B3
Lambton, Qu. Can. 188/B1
Lambton (co.), On, Can. 197/H6
Lame Deer, Mt, US 175/L5
Lameque, NB, Can. 188/E2
Lamego, Port. 52/B2
Lamero, Austl. 155/J5
Lamesa, Tx, US 180/D1
Lamia, Gre. 55/H3
Lamine (riv.), Mo, US 183/H1
Lamington NP, Austl. 158/D2
Lamington, NJ, US 198/C2
Lamitan, Phil. 100/C4
Lamlash, Sc, UK 39/A5
Lamma (isl.), China 92/K8
Lammefjord (inlet), Den. 45/H7
Lammermuir, 39/D5
Lammi, Fin. 47/L1
Lamming Mills, 174/G3
Lamoille, Nv, US 176/F3
Lamoille (riv.), Vt, US 191/J2
Lamon, Sol. Is. 161/Z17
Lamon (bay), Phil. 100/C2
Lamone (riv.), It. 69/E5
Lamoni, Ia, US 185/H3
Lamont, Ca, US 196/C3
Lamont, Ok, US 183/F2
Lamont, Fl, US 195/G2
Lamont, Ab, Can. 175/H2
Lamont, Ia, US 178/C3
Lamont, Wa, US 174/E4
Lamongan, Indo. 101/F4
Lamont (riv.), It. 51/J4
Lamorlaye, Fr. 36/K4
Lamotrek (isl.), Micr. 160/D4
Lamotte-Beuvron, Fr. 63/H5
Lampa, Chile 226/N8
Lampa, Peru 220/C4
Lampang, Thai. 106/B2
Lampasas, Tx, US 181/E2
Lampaul-Plouarzel, Fr. 62/A4
Lampazos de Naranjo, Mex. 180/D4
Lampedusa, It. 54/C5
Lampedusa (isl.), It. 54/C5
Lampeter, Wal, UK 42/B2
Lampeter, Wal, UK 43/D4
Lampertheim, Ger. 64/B3
Lamphun, Thai. 106/B2
Lampman, Sk, Can. 175/K3
Lamporecchio, It. 69/D6
Lampung (prov.), Indo. 101/D4
Lamstedt, Ger. 59/F1
Lamu (isl.), Kenya 137/C2
Lamu, Kenya 137/C2
Lamud (riv.), Peru 220/B2
Lamwa (peak), Ugan. 135/G5
Lamy, NM, US 182/B3
Lan (isl.), Tai. 99/J4
Lan Sang NP, Thai. 106/B2
Lana, Rio de la
Lāna‘i (isl.), Hi, US 180/T12
Lanaken, Belg. 61/E2
Lanark, Il, US 185/K2
Lanark, Sc, UK 39/C5
Lanark (co.), Eng, UK 41/E4
Lanark, Fl, US 195/F2
Lanberis, Wal, UK 40/B5
Lanbi (isl.), Myan. 105/G5
Lancang (riv.), China 98/C2
Lancang (Mekong),
Lancashire, 40/D3
Lancashire (co.), Eng, UK 41/F4
Lancaster, 198/B4
Lancaster (int'l arpt.), Ca, US
Lancaster, Ca, US 196/C2
Lancaster, Ky, US 192/E2
Lancaster, Mo, US 185/H3
Lancaster, NY, US 190/V10
Lancaster, Oh, US 190/E4
Lancaster (co.), Pa, US 198/B3
Lancaster, Pa, US 198/B3
Lancaster, Tx, US 180/L7
Lancaster, Wi, US 185/J2
Lance Creek, Wy, US 184/B2
Lancebranlette (peak), Fr. 70/C1
Lancefield, Austl. 157/B3
Lancelin, Austl. 154/B4
Lancenigo, It. 69/F2
Lanchester, Eng, UK 41/G2
Lanchkhut'i, Geo. 77/G4
Lanciano, It. 71/D3
L'Ancienne-Lorette,
Lanco, Chile 226/B3

Lanço – Lente
302

Lançon-Provence, Fr. 70/B5
Łańcut, Pol. 49/M3
Lancy, Swi. 66/C5
Land Between The Lakes Recreation Area, Ky, US 192/C2
Land Kehdingen (reg.), Ger. 59/G1
Land O'Lakes, Fl, US 194/L7
Land O'Lakes, Wi, US 187/K4
Landau an der Isar, Ger. 65/F5
Landau in der Pfalz, Ger. 64/B4
Landeck, Aus. 67/G3
Landen, Belg. 61/E2
Lander, Wy, US 177/J2
Landerneau, Fr. 62/A4
Landes (reg.), Fr. 50/C4
Landes de Lanvaux (mts.), Fr. 50/B3
Landesbergen, Ger. 59/G3
Landi Kotal, Pak. 110/A2
Landis, Sk, Can. 175/K1
Landis Valley Museum, Pa, US 198/B3
Landisburg, Pa, US 198/A3
Landivisiau, Fr. 62/A3
Landivy, Fr. 63/D4
Landrecies, Fr. 60/C3
Landri Sales, Braz. 219/F4
Landriano, It. 68/C3
Landrum, SC, US 193/F3
Land's End (pt.), Eng, UK 42/A6
Landsberg, Ger. 67/G1
Landsborough (cr.), Austl. 158/B3
Landser, Fr. 66/D2
Landshut, Ger. 65/F5
Landskrona, Swe. 46/E4
Landsmeer, Neth. 58/B4
Landstuhl, Ger. 61/G5
Landvetter (int'l arpt.), Swe. 46/E3
Landza, Congo 138/D2
Lane (riv.), Fr. 63/F6
Lane End, Eng, UK 36/A2
Lanercost, Eng, UK 41/F2
Lanesborough, Ire. 38/C2
Lanester, Fr. 62/B5
Lanett, Al, US 192/E4
Lang, Sk, Can. 186/B3
Lang Craig (pt.), Sc, UK 39/D3
Lang Kha Tuk (peak), Thai. 106/B4
Lang Son, Viet. 99/E4
Lang Suan, Thai. 106/B4
Langadhás, Gre. 55/H2
Langádhia, Gre. 55/H4
Langano (lake), Eth. 136/A4
Langara, Indo. 103/F4
Langdon, ND, US 186/E3
Langdon, Ab, Can. 175/H2
Langdon Hills, Eng, UK 36/E2
Langeac, Fr. 50/E4
Langeais, Fr. 63/F6
Langebaanweg, SAfr. 142/L10
Langeberg (mts.), SAfr. 142/L10
Langeland (isl.), Ger. 46/D4
Langelsheim, Ger. 59/H5
Langen (lake), Nor. 44/S8
Langen, Ger. 64/B3
Langen, Ger. 59/F1
Langenaltheim, Ger. 64/D5
Langenargen, Ger. 67/F2
Langenau, Ger. 64/D5
Langenbach, Ger. 65/E6
Langenberg, Ger. 59/E6
Langenburg, Sk, Can. 186/D2
Längenfeld, Aus. 67/G3
Langenfeld, Ger. 61/F1
Langenhagen, Ger. 59/G4
Langenhorn, Ger. 46/C4
Langenlois, Aus. 49/H4
Langenpreising, Ger. 65/E6
Langenselbold, Ger. 64/C2
Langenstein, Aus. 65/H6
Langenthal, Swi. 66/D3
Langenwang, Aus. 51/L3
Langenzenn, Ger. 64/D3
Langenzersdorf, Aus. 57/N7
Langeoog (isl.), Ger. 59/E1
Langeoog, Ger. 59/E1
Langepas, Rus. 80/H3
Langerringen, Ger. 67/G1
Langeskov, Den. 46/D4
Langesund, Nor. 46/C2
Langeten (riv.), Swi. 66/D3
Langfang, China 92/H7
Langford, SD, US 186/F5
Langfurth, Ger. 64/D4
Langgam, Indo. 101/C2
Langgapayung, Indo. 101/B2
Langgar, China 90/C6
Langham, Eng, UK 43/F1
Langham, Sk, Can. 175/L1
Langhirano, It. 68/D4
Langholm, Sc, UK 41/F1
Langhorne, Pa, US 198/D3
Langjökull (glacier), Ice. 44/N7
Langkawi (isl.), Thai. 105/G6
Langkon, Malay. 100/B4
Langley, Eng, UK 36/E3
Langley, Eng, UK 36/B2
Langley, Wa, US 197/C1
Langley (A.F.B.), Va, US 193/J2
Langlois, Or, US 176/A2
Langnau im Emmental, Swi. 66/D4
Langney (pt.), Eng, UK 43/G5
Langogne, Fr. 50/E4
Langon, Fr. 62/D5
Långön (isl.), Swe. 45/A2
Langon, Fr. 50/C4
Langøya (isl.), Nor. 44/E1
Langqên (riv.), China 111/C5
Langquaid, Ger. 65/F5
Langres, Fr. 66/B2
Langres, de (plat.), Fr. 72/E1
Langru, China 111/C4
Langrune-sur-Mer, Fr. 63/E2
Langsa, Indo. 101/B1
Langshyttan, Swe. 46/G1
Langstaff, On, Can. 190/U8
Langston, Ok, US 183/F3
Langtang, Nga. 133/H4
Langtang, China 99/F2
Langtang Lirung (peak), Nepal 109/E1
Langtang NP, Nepal 109/E1
Langtou, China 93/C2
Langtry, Tx, US 180/D3
Languedoc (reg.), Fr. 72/D2
Languedoc-Roussillon (pol. reg.), Fr. 50/E5
Langueux, Fr. 62/C3
Languidic, Fr. 62/B5
Langwedel, Ger. 59/G3
Langweid an Lech, Ger. 64/E6
Langwies, Swi. 67/F4
Langxi, China 92/D5
Lanham-Seabrook, Md, US 198/B6
Lanigan (riv.), Sk, Can. 175/M2
Lanigan, Sk, Can. 175/M2
Lanin (vol.), Arg. 226/C3
Lanin, PN, Arg. 226/C3
Lankāpāra Hāt, India 109/G2
Länkärän, Azer. 115/G2
Lankin, ND, US 186/F3
Lankou, China 99/G4
Lanlacuni Bajo, Peru 220/D4
Lanmeur, Fr. 62/B3
Länna, Swe. 45/A1
Lannemezan (plat.), Fr. 50/D5
Lannemezan, Fr. 53/F1
Lanner, Eng, UK 42/A6
Lannilis, Fr. 62/A3
Lannion, Fr. 62/B3
Lannion (bay), Fr. 50/B2
Lannion (Servel) (arpt.), Fr. 62/B3
L'Annonciation, Qu, Can. 191/J1
Lanouée, Fr. 62/C4
Lans, Montagne de (mts.), Fr. 70/B3
Lansdale, Pa, US 198/C3
Lansdowne, On, Can. 191/H2
Lansdowne, India 108/B1
Lansdowne, Pa, US 198/C4
Lansdowne-Baltimore Highlands, Md, US 198/B5
L'Anse Ind. Res., Mi, US 187/K4
Lansford, ND, US 186/D3
Lansford, Pa, US 198/C2
Lanshan, China 99/G3
Lansing, Yk, Can. 201/M3
Lansing, Il, US 197/Q16
Lansing, Ia, US 185/J2
Lansing (cap.), Mi, US 190/D3
Lanslebourg-Mont-Cenis, Fr. 70/C2
Lanta (isl.), Thai. 105/G6
Lantana, Fl, US 194/P9
Lantang, China 99/G4
Lantau (isl.), China 99/K7
Lantau (peak), China 99/K8
Lantau (chan.), China 99/K8
Lanterne (riv.), Fr. 66/C2
Lantosque, Fr. 70/D5
Lantouy, Laos 98/D4
Lantry, SD, US 184/D1
Lantz, NS, Can. 188/F3
Lantzville, BC, Can. 174/B3
Lanús, Arg. 191/J11
Lanusei, It. 54/A3
Lanuvio, It. 71/B4
Lanuza, Phil. 100/D3
Lanvallay, Fr. 62/C4
Lanvéoc, Fr. 62/A4
Lanxi, China 91/K2
Lanxi, China 99/H2
Lanza, Bol. 224/C1
Lanzara, It. 71/D6
Lanzarote (int'l arpt.), Sp. 128/B3
Lanzarote (isl.), Canl., Sp. 119/A2
Lanžhot, Czh. 49/J4
Lanzhou, China 90/E4
Lanzo d'Intelvi, It. 67/F6
Lanzo Torinese, It. 70/D2
Lao (mts.), China 93/D2
Lao (riv.), China 99/G2
Lao (peak), China 92/E3
Lao Cai, Viet. 98/D4
Lao Fu Chai, Laos 106/C1
Laoag, Phil. 100/C1
Laobian, China 93/B2
Laocheng, China 90/F5
Laodao (riv.), China 99/G2
Laodaodian, China 91/K1
Laoguanzui, China 99/G2
Laoha (riv.), China 91/H3
Laohekou, China 92/B4
Laohutun, China 93/A3
Laojun (mtn.), China 92/B4
Laoling, China 93/D2
Laon, Fr. 60/C4
Laos (ctry.) 106/C2
Laoshan, China 92/E3
Laotuding (peak), China 93/C2
Laou (riv.), Mor. 130/B2
Lapa, Braz. 225/G3
Lapalud, Fr. 70/A4
Lapataia, Arg. 191/C7
Lapeer, Mi, US 190/E3
Lapeer (co.), Mi, US 197/F6
Lapia, Nga. 133/G4
Lapine, Al, US 195/E2
Lapinlahti, Fin. 74/E3
Lapithos, Cyp. 116/C2
Lapland (reg.), Eur. 44/F1
Lapoint, Ut, US 177/J3
Laporte, Pa, US 191/H4
Laporte, Co, US 184/B3
Lapotina (mtn.), Rus. 91/N1
Lappeenranta, Fin. 47/N1
Lappersdorf, Ger. 65/F4
Lappi (prov.), Fin. 44/H2
Lâpseki, Turk. 55/K2
Laptev (sea), Rus. 83/M2
Lapua, Fin. 74/D3
Lapundra, India 113/K3
Lăpuşna, Mol. 78/E4
Łapy, Pol. 49/M2
Laqīyat al Arbaʻīn, Sudan 159/F4
Laquey, Mo, US 183/H2
Lār, Iran 115/H5
Lara (state), Ven. 216/D2
Lara, Austl. 157/B4
Laracha, Sp. 52/A1
Larache (prov.), Mor. 130/B2
Larache, Mor. 130/A2
Laracor, Ire. 38/D2
Laragne-Montéglin, Fr. 70/B4
Lārak (isl.), Iran 115/J5
Laramie (mts.), Wy, US 184/B2
Laramie, Wy, US 184/B3
Laramie (riv.), Wy, US 184/B3
Laramie (peak), Wy, US 184/B2
Laranjeiras do Sul, Braz. 225/F3
Larantuka, Indo. 152/A2
Larat (isl.), Indo. 103/H5
Larat, Indo. 152/C1
Larba, Alg. 130/G4
Larchmont, NY, US 199/K8
L'Arcouest (pt.), Fr. 62/B3
Lærdalsøyri, Nor. 46/B1
Lardier (cape), Fr. 70/C6
Laredo, Sp. 50/B5
Laredo, Mo, US 185/H3
Laredo, Peru 220/B3
Laredo, Mt, US 175/K3
Laredo, Tx, US 180/E4
Laredo (int'l arpt.), Tx, US 180/E4
Laren, Neth. 58/C4
Lares, Peru 220/C4
Larga (lag.), Tx, US 181/F4
L'Argentière-la-Bessée, Fr. 70/C3
Largo (bay), Sc, UK 39/D4
Largo, Fl, US 194/K8
Largo (cr.), NM, US 179/H3
Largo, Md, US 198/B6
Largs, Sc, UK 39/B5
Largue (riv.), Fr. 66/D2
Lariang (riv.), Indo. 103/E4
Lariano, It. 71/B4
Larino, It. 71/D4
Lárisa, Gre. 55/H3
Lark (riv.), Eng, UK 43/G2
Lark Harbour, Nf, Can. 189/H1
Lārkāna, Pak. 113/J3
Larkhall, Sc, UK 39/C5
Larkspur, Ca, US 197/J11
Larkspur, Co, US 184/B4
L'Arly, PN de, Burk. 133/F4
Larmor-Plage, Fr. 62/B5
Larnaca, Cyp. 116/C2
Larnaca (int'l arpt.), Cyp. 116/C2
Larnaca (dist.), Cyp. 116/C2
Larne, NI, UK 40/C2
Larne (dist.), NI, UK 40/C2
Larne Lough (inlet), NI, UK 40/C2
Larned, Ks, US 182/E1
Larochette, Lux. 61/F4
Laropi, Ugan. 139/G2
Laroque-d'Olmes, Fr. 50/D5
Larose, La, US 194/C3
Larreynaga, Nic. 206/E3
Larrimah, Austl. 152/D3
Larroque, Arg. 191/J10
Larrys (cr.), Pa, US 198/A1
Larry's River, NS, Can. 189/G3
Larsen Bay, Ak, US 201/H4
Larsen Ice Shelf, Ant. 228/V
Larsen Sound (bay), Nun, Can. 170/G1
Larslan, Mt, US 175/L3
Larto, La, US 194/C2
Laruns, Fr. 50/C5
Larvik, Nor. 46/D2
Las Animas, Co, US 182/C1
Las Aves (isls.), Ven. 203/H5
Las Bayas, Arg. 226/C4
Las Bombas, Chile 224/B3
Las Breñas, Arg. 224/D3
Las Cabezas de San Juan, Sp. 52/C4
Las Cabras, Chile 226/N9
Las Casuarinas, Arg. 224/B4
Las Cruces, NM, US 179/J4
Las Delicias, Ven. 216/C3
Las Esperanzas, Mex. 180/D4
Las Flores, Arg. 226/F3
Las Guacamayas, Mex. 204/E5
Las Hermosas, PN, Col. 216/C4
Las Higueras, Arg. 226/D2
Las Juntas, Col. 216/C4
Las Lajas (peak), Arg. 226/C3
Las Lajas, Arg. 226/C3
Las Lajitas, Ven. 217/E3
Las Lomas, Peru 220/A2
Las Lomitas, Arg. 224/D3
Las Margaritas, Mex. 206/D2
Las Martinas, Cuba 207/E1
Las Mercedes, Ven. 217/E2
Las Minas (peak), Hon. 206/D3
Las Montañitas, Ven. 216/D3
Las Navas, Phil. 100/D2
Las Nieves, Mex. 204/D3
Las Orquídeas, PN, Col. 216/B3
Las Palmas, Pan. 207/F4
Las Palmas (riv.), Mex. 178/D4
Las Palmas de Cocalán, PN, Chile 226/N9
Las Palmas de Gran Canaria, Sp. 128/B3
Las Pampitas, Bol. 221/E4
Las Parejas, Arg. 224/D5
Las Pedroñeras, Sp. 52/D3
Las Perdices, Arg. 226/E2
Las Perlas (arch.), Pan. 207/G4
Las Petas, Bol. 221/E4
Las Petas, Bol. 221/G5
Las Piedras, Bol. 221/E3
Las Piedras, Peru 220/D4
Las Piedras, Uru. 191/K11
Las Piedras, Ven. 216/C2
Las Piedras, Ven. 217/F2
Las Pinas, Phil. 100/E7
Las Pipinas, Arg. 191/F2
Las Plumas, Arg. 226/D4
Las Rosas, Mex. 206/C2
Las Rosas, Arg. 224/D5
Las Rozas de Madrid, Sp. 53/N9
Las Tablas, Pan. 216/A3
Las Tablas, NM, US 179/J2
Las Tórtolas (peak), Chile 224/B4
Las Toscas, Uru. 225/F5
Las Toscas, Arg. 224/E4
Las Trincheras, Ven. 217/E3
Las Varas, Mex. 204/D4
Las Varillas, Arg. 224/D4
Las Vegas, NM, US 182/B3
Las Vegas, Nv, US 178/E2
Las Vegas Nat'l Wildlife Reserve, NM, US 182/B3
Las Yaras, Peru 224/B1
Lasa (Laas), It. 67/G4
Lasahau, Indo. 152/A1
Lasalle, Qu, Can. 189/N7
Lasan, Indo. 102/E3
Lasanbāri, India 98/B3
Lasberg, Aus. 65/H6
Lascano, Uru. 191/G2
Lascar (vol.), Chile 224/C2
Lascar, Co, US 182/B2
Lasem, Indo. 101/E4
Lashburn, Sk, Can. 175/K1
Lashio, Myan. 98/C4
Lashkar Gāh, Afg. 113/H2
Lashmanka, Rus. 75/L5
Lasia (isl.), Indo. 101/B2
Lasne-Chapelle-Saint-Lambert, Belg. 61/D2
Læsø (isl.), Den. 46/D3
Lasolo (riv.), Indo. 103/F4
Lassay-les-Châteaux, Fr. 63/E4
Lassen (peak), Ca, US 176/C3
Lassen Volcanic NP, Ca, US 176/C3
L'Assomption, Qu, Can. 189/P6
Lasswade, Sc, UK 39/C5
Last Mtn. (lake), Sk, Can. 175/M2
Lastoursville, Gabon 138/C3
Lastovo (isl.), Cro. 54/E1
Lastovo, Cro. 56/C4
Lastovski Kanal (canal), Cro. 54/E1
Lastra a Signa, It. 69/E6
Lästringe, Swe. 45/A2
Lastrup, Ger. 59/E3
Lat Yao, Thai. 106/B3
Lata, Sol. 160/F6
Latacunga, Ecu. 216/B5
Latady (isl.), Ant. 228/U
Latākhola, Bang. 109/H4
Latakia (Al Lādhiqīyah), Syria 116/D2
L'Atakora (prov.), Ben. 133/F4
Lātehār, India 109/E4
Latemar (peak), It. 67/H5
Laterrière, Qu, Can. 188/B1
Laterza, It. 54/E2
Latexo, Tx, US 181/G2
Latham, Ks, US 183/F2
Lathan (riv.), Fr. 50/C3
Lathrop, Ca, US 197/M11
Lathrop, Mo, US 185/G4
Latimer, Eng, UK 36/B2
Latimer, Ia, US 185/H2
Latina, It. 71/B5
Latina (prov.), It. 71/C5
Latina Scalo, It. 71/B4
Latisana, It. 69/G2
Latium (reg.), It. 73/G2
Laton, Ca, US 178/C2
Latorica (riv.), Slvk.,Ukr. 49/M4
Latouche Treville (cape), Austl. 152/A4
Latrobe, Pa, US 191/G4
Latrobe, Austl. 156/C4
Latrobe (mt.), Austl. 157/C4
Latsch (Laces), It. 67/G4
Lattes, Fr. 50/E5
Lattingtown, NY, US 199/L8
Lātūr, India 107/C2
Latvia (ctry.) 47/L3
Lat'yuga, Rus. 75/L2
Lau Group (isl.), Fiji 160/H6
Laubach, Ger. 64/B1
Lauca, PN, Chile 220/D5
Lauca, PN, Chile 224/B1
Lauch (riv.), Fr. 51/G3
Lauchert (riv.), Ger. 64/C6
Lauchheim, Ger. 64/D5
Lauda-Königshofen, Ger. 64/C3
Lauder, Mb, Can. 186/D3
Lauder, Sc, UK 39/D5
Lauderdale (lakes), Wi, US 197/N14
Lauderdale, Ms, US 192/C4
Lauderdale Lakes, Fl, US 194/P10
Lauderdale-by-the-Sea, Fl, US 194/P10
Lauderhill, Fl, US 194/P10
Laudun, Fr. 70/A4
Lauenbrück, Ger. 59/G2
Lauenburg, Ger. 59/H2
Lauenen, Swi. 66/D5
Lauenförde, Ger. 59/H5
Lauer (riv.), Ger. 64/D2
Lauf, Ger. 64/E3
Laufach, Ger. 64/C2
Laufen, Swi. 66/D3
Laufen, Ger. 65/F7
Laufenburg, Swi. 66/E2
Lauffen am Neckar, Ger. 64/C4
Laugharne, Wal, UK 42/B3
Laughlen (mt.), Austl. 155/G2
Laughlin (A.F.B.), Tx, US 180/D3
Lauhanvuoren NP, Fin. 74/D3
Lauhkaung, Myan. 98/C3
Lauingen, Ger. 64/D5
Laukuva, Lith. 47/K4
Launceston, Austl. 156/C4
Launceston, Eng, UK 42/B5
Laune (riv.), Ire. 38/A5
Launette (riv.), Fr. 36/L4
Launglon, Myan. 106/B3
Launonen, Fin. 45/E4
Laupen, Swi. 66/D4
Lauperswil, Swi. 66/D4
Laupheim, Ger. 67/F1
L'Aupillon (peak), Fr. 70/C4
Laura, Austl. 158/B1
Laura, Austl. 155/H5
Laura, Sk, Can. 175/L2
Laureana di Borrello, It. 54/E3
Laurel, De, US 193/K1
Laurel, Fl, US 195/G4
Laurel, In, US 190/D5
Laurel, Md, US 198/B5
Laurel, Ms, US 194/D2
Laurel, Ne, US 185/F2
Laurel, Va, US 193/J2
Laurel Bay, SC, US 193/G4
Laurel Hill, Fl, US 195/E2
Laurel Springs, NJ, US 198/C4
Laureldale, Pa, US 198/C3
Laurelton, Pa, US 198/A2
Laurelvale, NI, UK 40/B3
Laurence Harbor, NJ, US 199/J10
Laurencekirk, Sc, UK 39/D3
Laurens, Ia, US 185/G2
Laurens, SC, US 193/F3
Laurentian (plat.), On, Can. 170/G3
Laurentides, Qu, Can. 189/N6
Laurier, Mb, Can. 186/E2
Laurier-Station, Qu, Can. 188/B2
Laurieston, Sc, UK 40/D2
Laurinburg, NC, US 193/H3
Lauris, Fr. 70/B5
Laurium, Mi, US 187/K4
Lauriya Nandangarh, India 109/E2
Lauro, It. 71/D6
Lausanne, Swi. 66/C4
Lauscha, Ger. 64/E2
Laut (isl.), Indo. 103/E4
Lautaro, Chile 226/B3
Lautem, ETim. 152/B2
Lauter (riv.), Ger. 48/E3
Lauter (riv.), Fr.,Ger. 64/B4
Lauter, Ger. 65/F1
Lauterach (riv.), Ger. 65/E4
Lauterbach (riv.), Ger. 64/E2
Lauterbach, Ger. 64/C1
Lauterbourg, Fr. 64/B5
Lauterbrunnen, Swi. 66/D4
Lauterecken, Ger. 61/G4
L'Authion (peak), Fr. 70/D4
Lautoka, Fiji 161/Y18
Lautoporras, Fin. 45/E4
Lauve, Nor. 46/D2
Lauwers (chan.), Neth. 58/D1
Lauwersmeer (lake), Neth. 58/D2
Lava Beds Nat'l Mon., Ca, US 176/C3
Lava Hot Springs, Id, US 177/G2
Lavaca (riv.), Tx, US 181/F3
Lavaca (bay), Tx, US 181/F3
Lavaca, Al, US 192/C4
Lavagna, It. 68/C5
Lavagna (riv.), It. 68/C4
Laval, Fr. 63/E4
Laval, Qu, Can. 189/N6
Lavalleja (dept.), Uru. 191/G2
Lavallette, NJ, US 199/D4
Lāvān (isl.), Iran 115/H5
Lavans-lès-Saint-Claude, Fr. 66/B5
Lavant (riv.), Aus. 51/L3
Lavapié (pt.), Chile 226/B3
Lavaraty, Madg. 143/H8
Lavassaare, Est. 47/L2
Lavaur, Fr. 50/D5
Lavelanet, Fr. 50/D5
Lavello, It. 54/D2
Lavena, It. 67/E6
Laveno, It. 67/E6
Laverne, Ok, US 182/E2
Laverton, Austl. 154/D4
Lavey, Swi. 66/D5
Lavezzola, It. 69/E4
Lavik, Nor. 46/A1
Lavillette, NB, Can. 188/E2
Lavina, Mt, US 175/K4
Lavino (riv.), It. 69/E4
Lavis, It. 67/H5
Lavon (dam), Tx, US 180/L6
Lavon, Tx, US 180/L6
Lavonia, Ga, US 193/F3
Lavos, Port. 52/A2
Lavras, Braz. 222/D4
Lavras da Mangabeira, Braz. 219/G4
Lávrion, Gre. 55/J4
Lavushi Manda NP, Zam. 141/F2
Lawa (riv.), FrG.,Sur. 218/C2
Lawa (riv.), FrG. 217/H4
Lawabauk, Myan. 98/C5
Lawang, Indo. 101/F4
Lāwar Khās, India 108/A1
Lawarai (pass), Pak. 110/A2
Lawas, Malay. 100/A4
Lawdar, Yem. 136/C2
Lawen, Or, US 176/D2
Lawit (peak), Malay. 101/C1
Lawit (mtn.), Indo. 102/D3
Lawksawk, Myan. 106/B1
Lawn, Nf, Can. 189/K2
Lawn, Tx, US 180/E1
Lawn Hill, Austl. 153/E4
Lawn Hill NP, Austl. 153/E4
Lawndale, Ca, US 196/F8
Lawnhill, BC, Can. 201/M5
Lawqah, SAr. 115/E4
Lawra, Gha. 132/E4
Lawrence, NZ 159/B4
Lawrence, In, US 190/C5
Lawrence, Ks, US 183/G1
Lawrence, Ma, US 191/L3
Lawrence, NY, US 199/L9
Lawrence, Ne, US 184/E3
Lawrence, Tx, US 180/L7
Lawrence Park, Pa, US 190/F3
Lawrence Station, NB, Can. 188/D3
Lawrenceburg, In, US 192/E1
Lawrenceburg, Ky, US 192/E1
Lawrenceburg, Tn, US 192/D3
Lawrencetown, NI, UK 40/B3
Lawrenceville, Ga, US 193/N7
Lawrenceville, Il, US 192/D1
Lawrenceville, NJ, US 198/D3
Lawrenceville, Va, US 193/J2
Lawson, Sk, Can. 175/L2
Lawson, Ar, US 183/H4
Lawson, Mo, US 185/G4
Lawtey, Fl, US 195/G2
Lawton, Ok, US 183/E3
Lawu (peak), Indo. 102/D5
Lax, Ga, US 195/G2
Laxå, Swe. 46/F2
Laxey, IM, UK 40/D3
Laxou, Fr. 61/F6
Lay (riv.), Fr. 50/C3
Lay-Saint-Christophe, Fr. 61/F6
Laya (riv.), Rus. 75/N2
Layar (cape), Indo. 103/E4
Laye (riv.), Fr. 70/B4
Layjūn, Yem. 136/D2
Laylān, Iraq 115/F3
Läyliäinen, Fin. 45/E4
Layon (riv.), Fr. 50/C3
Laysan (isl.), Hi, US 161/H2
Layton, Fl, US 195/H5
Layton, Ut, US 177/H3
Layton, NJ, US 198/D1
Laytonville, Ca, US 176/B4
Laytown, Ire. 40/B4
Lazarev, Rus. 81/Q4
Lazarevac, Serb. 56/E3
Lázaro Cárdenas, Mex. 178/E5
Lázaro Cárdenas, Mex. 204/B2
Lázaro Cárdenas, Mex. 204/E5
Lazdijai, Lith. 47/K4
Lazi, Phil. 100/C3
Lazio (prov.), It. 51/J5
Lazise, It. 69/D3
Lazo, Rus. 81/P3
Lazonby, Eng, UK 41/F2
Le Ban-Saint-Martin, Fr. 61/F5
Le Beausset, Fr. 70/B6
Le Bic, Qu, Can. 188/C1
Le Blanc, Fr. 50/D3
Le Blanc-Mesnil, Fr. 36/K5
Le Bono, Fr. 62/C5
Le Bourg-d'Oisans, Fr. 70/C2
Le Bourget (Paris) (Arpt.), Fr. 36/K5
Le Bourget-du-Lac, Fr. 70/B1
Le Breuil, Fr. 50/F3
Le Cannet, Fr. 70/D5
Le Cannet-des-Maures, Fr. 70/C6
Le Castellet, Fr. 70/B6
Le Cateau-Cambrésis, Fr. 60/C3
Le Center, Mn, US 185/H1
Le Chasseral (peak), Swi. 66/D3
Le Chasseron (peak), Swi. 66/C4
Le Chesnay, Fr. 36/J5
Le Chesne, Fr. 61/D4
Le Cheval Blanc (peak), Fr. 66/C5
Le Cheval Noir (peak), Fr. 70/C2
Le Cheylard, Fr. 50/F4
Le Claire, Ia, US 185/J3
Le Conquet, Fr. 62/A4
Le Cornate (peak), It. 51/J5
Le Coudray, Fr. 63/G4
Le Crès, Fr. 53/G1
Le Creusot, Fr. 50/F3
Le Croisic, Fr. 62/C6
Le Crotoy, Fr. 60/A3
Le Duffre (peak), Fr. 70/B4
Le Faouët, Fr. 62/B4
Le Fœil, Fr. 62/C4
Le Folgoët, Fr. 62/A3
Le Gore, Md, US 198/A4
Le Goulet, NB, Can. 188/E2
Le Grammont (peak), Swi. 66/C5
Le Grand (peak), Fr. 70/C1
Le Grand, Ca, US 178/B2
Le Grand (cape), Austl. 154/D5
Le Grand Ballon (peak), Fr. 66/D2
Le Grand Charnier (peak), Fr. 70/C2
Le Grand Coyer (peak), Fr. 70/C4
Le Grand-Lemps, Fr. 70/B2
Le Grand-Lucé, Fr. 63/F5
Le Grand-Quevilly, Fr. 63/G2
Le Grau-du-Roi, Fr. 50/F5
Le Grazie, It. 68/C5
Le Harve-Octeville (arpt.), Fr. 63/F1
Le Havre, Fr. 63/F1
Le Kef, Tun. 130/L6
Le Kef (gov.), Tun. 130/L6
Le Landeron, Swi. 66/D3
Le Lauzet-Ubaye, Fr. 70/C4
Le Lavandou, Fr. 70/C6
Le Lion-D'Angers, Fr. 63/E5
Le Locle, Swi. 66/C3
Le Loroux-Bottereau, Fr. 62/D6
Le Luc, Fr. 70/C6
Le Lude, Fr. 63/F5
Le Mans, Fr. 63/F4
Le Mars, Ia, US 185/F2
Le Mée-sur-Seine, Fr. 36/K6
Le Mêle-sur-Sarthe, Fr. 63/F3
Le Mesnil-Amelot, Fr. 36/K4
Le Mesnil-Aubry, Fr. 36/K4
Le Mesnil-Esnard, Fr. 60/A5
Le Mesnil-le-Roi, Fr. 36/J5
Le Mesnil-Saint-Denis, Fr. 36/H5
Le Mesnil-sur-Oger, Fr. 60/D6
Le Molay-Littry, Fr. 63/E2
Le Môle (peak), Fr. 66/C5
Le Monêtier-les-Bains, Fr. 70/C3
Le Mont-Saint-Michel, Fr. 62/D3
Le Morond (peak), Fr. 66/C4
Le Moure de la Gardille (peak), Fr. 50/E4
Le Mourre Froid (peak), Fr. 70/C3
Le Murge (mts.), It. 54/E2
Le Muy, Fr. 70/C6
Le Noirmont (peak), Fr. 66/C4
Le Noirmont, Swi. 66/C3
Le Noirmont (peak), Swi. 66/C5
Le Nouvion-en-Thiérache, Fr. 60/C3
Le Palais, Fr. 62/B6
Le Palais-sur-Vienne, Fr. 50/D4
Le Palyvestre (arpt.), Fr. 70/C6
Le Passage, Fr. 50/D4
Le Pellerin, Fr. 62/D6
Le Perray-en-Yvelines, Fr. 36/H5
Le Petit Ballon (peak), Fr. 66/D2
Le Petit Ferrand (peak), Fr. 70/C4
Le Plessis-Belleville, Fr. 36/L4
Le Plessis-Feu-Aussoux, Fr. 36/M5
Le Plessis-Placy, Fr. 36/L4
Le Pont-de-Beauvoisin, Fr. 70/B1
Le Pont-de-Claix, Fr. 70/B2
Le Pontet, Fr. 70/A5
Le Port, Reun., Fr. 143/S15
Le Portel, Fr. 60/A2
Le Pouliguen, Fr. 62/C6
Le Pouzin, Fr. 70/A3
Le Pradet, Fr. 70/C6
Le Puy-en-Velay, Fr. 50/E4
Le Puy-Sainte-Réparade, Fr. 70/B5
Le Quesnoy, Fr. 60/C3
Le Rateau (peak), Fr. 70/C2
Le Relecq-Kerhuon, Fr. 62/A4
Le Rocher Blanc (peak), Fr. 70/C2
Le Rouret, Fr. 70/D5
Le Rove, Fr. 70/B6
Le Roy, Ks, US 183/G1
Le Roy, Mn, US 185/H2
Le Roy, Il, US 185/K3
Le Russey, Fr. 66/C3
Le Sap, Fr. 63/F3
Le Suchet (peak), Swi. 66/C4
Le Sueur, Mn, US 185/H1
Le Tampon, Reun., Fr. 143/S15
Le Teil, Fr. 70/A3
Le Teilleul, Fr. 63/E3
Le Theil, Fr. 63/F4
Le Tholonet, Fr. 70/B5
Le Tholy, Fr. 66/C1
Le Thor, Fr. 70/A5
Le Thuit-Signol, Fr. 63/F2
Le Touquet-Paris-Plage, Fr. 60/A2
Le Touvet, Fr. 70/B2
Le Tréboux (peak), Fr. 70/B4
Le Trélod (peak), Fr. 70/C1
Le Tréport, Fr. 60/A3
Le Val, Fr. 70/C6
Le Val-d'Ajol, Fr. 66/C2
Le Vésinet, Fr. 36/J5
Le Vigan, Fr. 50/E5
Le'an (riv.), China 99/H2
Lea (riv.), Eng, UK 43/F3
Lea (Lee) (riv.), Eng, UK 36/C1
Leach, Camb. 106/C3
Leach (riv.), Eng, UK 43/E3
Leacock-Leola-Bareville, Pa, US 198/B3
Lead, SD, US 170/F4
Lead Hill, Ar, US 183/H2
Leaday, Tx, US 180/E2
Leadbetter (pt.), Wa, US 174/B4
Leadenham, Eng, UK 41/H5
Leader, Sk, Can. 175/K2
Leader Water (riv.), Sc, UK 39/D5
Leadon (riv.), Eng, UK 42/D3
Leaf, Ms, US 194/D2
Leaf (riv.), Ms, US 192/C5
Leaghur (lake), Austl. 156/B2
League City, Tx, US 181/M9
Leah, Ga, US 193/F4
Leakesville, Ms, US 194/D2
Leakey, Tx, US 180/E3
Lealui, Zam. 140/D2
Leam (riv.), Eng, UK 43/E2
Leamington, On, Can. 190/E3
Leamington, Ut, US 177/G4
Leander (pt.), Austl. 154/B4
Leander, Tx, US 181/F2
Leandro N. Alem, Arg. 225/F3
Leane (lake), Ire. 38/A5
Leaota (peak), Rom. 57/G3
Learmonth, Austl. 154/B2
Leary, Ga, US 195/F2
Leasburg, Mo, US 183/J1
Leask, Sk, Can. 175/L1
Leatherhead, Eng, UK 36/C3
Leavenworth, Ks, US 185/G4
Leavenworth, Wa, US 174/D4
Łeba, Pol. 46/G4
Lebach, Ger. 61/F5
Lebak, Phil. 100/D4
Lebam, Wa, US 174/C4
Lébamba, Gabon 138/B3
Lebane, Serb. 56/E4
Lébango, Congo 138/C2
Lebanon (ctry.) 116/D3
Lebanon (mts.), Leb. 116/D3
Lebanon (co.), Pa, US 198/B3
Lebanon, Co, US 179/H2
Lebanon, In, US 190/C4
Lebanon, Ks, US 184/E4
Lebanon, Ky, US 192/E2
Lebanon, Mo, US 183/H2
Lebanon, NH, US 191/K3
Lebanon, NJ, US 198/D2
Lebanon, Oh, US 190/D5
Lebanon, Or, US 176/B1
Lebanon, Pa, US 198/B3
Lebanon, Tn, US 192/D2
Lebanon, Va, US 193/F2
Lebanon Junction, Ky, US 192/E2
Lebbeke, Belg. 61/D2
Lebeau, La, US 194/C2
Lebec, Ca, US 178/C3
Lebedinyy, Rus. 81/N4
Lebedyan', Rus. 76/F1
Lebedyn, Ukr. 79/H2
Lebene (riv.), Mor. 130/B2
Lébény, Hun. 56/C2
Lébiga, Congo 138/C3
Lebo, Ks, US 183/G1
Lebombo (mts.), SAfr. 141/F5
Lębork, Pol. 46/G4
Lebowakgomo, SAfr. 141/F5
Lebrija, Sp. 52/B4
Lebu, Chile 226/B3
Leça da Palmeira, Port. 52/A2
Lecce, It. 55/F2
Lecce nei Marsi, It. 71/C4
Lecco (lake), It. 68/C1
Lech, Aus. 67/G3
Lech (riv.), Ger. 73/F1
Lechang, China 105/K2
Lechbruck, Ger. 67/G2
Leche (lake), Cuba 207/G1
Lechlade, Eng, UK 43/E3
Lechtaler Alps (mts.), Aus. 67/G3
Leck, Ger. 46/C4
Leckavrea (mtn.), Ire. 38/A3
Lecompte, La, US 194/B2
Léconi, Gabon 138/C3
Lectoure, Fr. 50/D5
Łęczna, Pol. 49/M3
Leda (riv.), Ger. 59/E2
Ledang (peak), Malay. 101/C2
Ledbury, Eng, UK 42/D2
Lede, Belg. 60/C2
Ledegem, Belg. 60/C2
Ledesma, Sp. 52/B2
Ledge Point, Austl. 154/B4
Ledger, Mt, US 175/J3
Lediba, D.R. Congo 138/D3
Lêdo (cape), Ang. 138/C5
Ledong, China 99/F5
Ledro (lake), It. 67/G6
Ledu (peak), It. 67/F5
Leduc, Ab, Can. 175/H1
Lee (riv.), Ire. 38/A6
Lee (Lea) (riv.), Eng, UK 36/C1
Lee, Fl, US 195/G2
Lee, Ma, US 191/K3
Lee (mtn.), Pa, US 198/B1
Lee Creek, Ar, US 183/G3
Leech (lake), Mn, US 173/H2
Leedale, Ab, Can. 174/G1
Leedey, Ok, US 182/E3
Leeds, Eng, UK 41/G4
Leeds (co.), Eng, UK 41/G4
Leeds, Al, US 192/D4
Leeds, ND, US 186/E3
Leeds, Ut, US 179/F2
Leeds and Bradford (int'l arpt.), Eng, UK 41/G4
Leeds and Liverpool (canal), Eng, UK 41/G4
Leeds Point, NJ, US 198/D5
Leegebruch, Ger. 48/Q6
Leek, Eng, UK 41/F5
Leek, Neth. 58/D2
Leeman, Austl. 154/B4
Leemount, Ire. 38/B6
Leer, Ger. 59/E2
Leerdam, Neth. 58/C5
Leersum, Neth. 58/C4
Lees Crossing, Ga, US 192/E4
Lees Summit, Mo, US 183/G1
Leesburg, Fl, US 194/M6
Leesburg, Ga, US 195/F2
Leesburg, NJ, US 198/D5
Leesburg, Va, US 193/J1
Leesdale, Ms, US 194/C2
Leese, Ger. 59/G3
Leesport, Pa, US 198/C3
Leeston, NZ 159/C3
Leesville, La, US 194/B2
Leesville (lake), Va, US 193/H2
Leesville (dam), Va, US 193/H2
Leeton, Austl. 157/C2
Leeu (riv.), SAfr. 142/L10
Leeudoringstad, SAfr. 142/D2
Leeuwarden, Neth. 58/C2
Leeuwin (cape), Austl. 154/B5
Leeuwin-Naturaliste NP, Austl. 154/B5
Leeville, La, US 194/C3
Leeward (isls.), NAm. 203/J4
Leff (riv.), Fr. 50/B2
Leffe, It. 68/C2
Léfini (riv.), Congo 138/C3
Lefka, Cyp. 116/C2
Lefo (peak), Camr. 133/H5
Lefor, ND, US 186/C4
Lefroy (lake), Austl. 154/D4
Left Hand, WV, US 193/G1
Legana, Austl. 156/C4
Leganés, Sp. 53/N9
Legaspi, Phil. 100/C2
Legau, Ger. 67/G2
Legazpia, Sp. 50/B5
Legges Tor (peak), Austl. 156/C4
Legionowo, Pol. 49/L2
Léglise, Belg. 61/E4
Legnago, It. 69/E3
Legnaro, It. 69/E3
Legnica, Pol. 49/J3
Legnone (peak), It. 67/F5
Léguer (riv.), Fr. 62/B3
Leh, India 110/D2
Leh Palace, India 110/D2
Lehi, Ut, US 177/H3
Lehigh, Ok, US 183/F3
Lehigh (riv.), Pa, US 191/J4
Lehigh (co.), Pa, US 198/C2
Lehigh Acres, Fl, US 195/H4
Lehighton, Pa, US 198/C2
Lehijärvi (lake), Fin. 45/E3
Lehinch, Ire. 38/A4
Léhon, Fr. 62/C4
Lehr, ND, US 186/E4
Lehrberg, Ger. 64/D4
Lehrte, Ger. 59/G4
Lehututu, Bots. 140/D4
Lei (riv.), China 105/K2
Leia (riv.), It. 71/A3
Leiah, Pak. 110/A4
Leiblfing, Ger. 65/F5
Leibnitz, Aus. 56/B2
Leibo, China 105/H2
Leicester, Eng, UK 43/E1
Leicester (co.), Eng, UK 43/E1
Leicestershire (co.), Eng, UK 41/H6
Leichhardt (dam), Austl. 155/H2
Leichhardt (falls), Austl. 153/E4
Leichhardt (riv.), Austl. 153/F4
Leichlingen, Ger. 61/G1
Leiden, Neth. 58/B4
Leiderdorp, Neth. 58/B4
Leidschendam, Neth. 58/B4
Leigh, Eng, UK 41/F5
Leigh, Eng, UK 36/D3
Leigh, Eng, UK 36/C3
Leigh Creek, Austl. 155/H4
Leighlinbridge, Ire. 38/D4
Leighton Buzzard, Eng, UK 43/F3
Leigong (mtn.), China 99/F3
Leimebamba, Peru 220/B2
Leimen, Ger. 64/B4
Leimersheim, Ger. 64/B4
Leinan, Sk, Can. 175/L2
Leine (riv.), Ger. 48/D3
Leinefelde, Ger. 59/H6
Leinfelden-Echterdingen, Ger. 64/C5
Leinster (reg.), Ire. 40/A5
Leinster (mt.), Ire. 38/D4
Leinster, Austl. 154/D3
Leintwardine, Eng, UK 42/D2
Leipheim, Ger. 64/D6
Leipsic, Oh, US 190/E4
Leipsic (riv.), De, US 198/C5
Leipsic, De, US 198/C5
Leipzig, Ger. 80/B4
Leira, Nor. 46/C1
Leiranger, Nor. 44/E2
Leiria, Port. 52/A3
Leiria (dist.), Port. 52/A3
Leirsund, Nor. 44/T8
Leirvik, Nor. 46/A2
Leisi, Est. 47/K2
Leisler (mt.), Austl. 155/F2
Leiston-cum-Sizewell, Eng, UK 43/H2
Leisure City, Fl, US 195/H5
Leitchfield, Ky, US 192/D2
Leiter, Wy, US 184/A1
Leith, Sc, UK 39/C5
Leith (hill), Eng, UK 36/B3
Leitha (riv.), Aus. 49/J5
Leitrim (co.), Ire. 38/C2
Leitrim, Ire. 38/B2
Leixlip, Ire. 40/B5
Leiyang, China 99/G3
Leiyuanzhen, China 92/B4
Leizhou (pen.), China 105/J3
Lejasciems, Lat. 47/M3
Lejpalingis, Lith. 47/K4
Lek (riv.), Neth. 48/C3
Lékana, Congo 138/C3
Lekhainá, Gre. 55/G4
Lekhcheb, Mrta. 132/C2
Lekkerkerk, Neth. 58/B5
Lekki (lag.), Nga. 133/G5
Lékoli-Pandaka, Rsv. de Faune de la, Congo 138/C2
Lekoni, Gabon 138/C3
Lekóti (riv.), Congo 138/C3
Lekoumou (pol. reg.), Congo 138/C3
Leksands-Noret, Swe. 46/F1
Leksozero (lake), Rus. 44/J3
Leku, Eth. 136/A4
Lelai (cape), Indo. 103/G3
Leland, Il, US 185/K3
Leland, Mi, US 190/D2
Leland, Ms, US 192/B4
Leland, NC, US 193/H3
Lelång (lake), Swe. 46/E2
Lel'chitsy, Bela. 78/E2
Leleque, Arg. 226/C4
Lelia Lake, Tx, US 182/D3
Leling, China 92/D3
Lelintah, Indo. 103/H4
Lelogama, Indo. 152/A2
Lelu, Micr. 160/F4
Lelydorp, Sur. 218/C1
Lelystad, Neth. 58/C3
Lem, Den. 46/C3
Lema (peak), It. 67/E5
Lema Shilindi, Eth. 136/B4
Léman (Geneva) (lake), Fr. 66/C5
Lemberg (peak), Ger. 67/E1
Lemberg, Sk, Can. 186/C2
Lemberg, Ger. 61/G5
Lembu (peak), Indo. 101/B1
Leme, Braz. 225/H2
Lemenjoen NP, Fin. 44/H1
Lemeshkino, Rus. 77/H2
Lemgo, Ger. 59/F4
Lemhi, Id, US 177/G1
Lemhi (range), Id, US 177/G1
Lemitar, NM, US 179/J3
Lemland (isl.), Fin. 47/H2
Lemland, Fin. 47/J1
Lemmer, Neth. 58/C3
Lemmon, SD, US 186/C5
Lemmon (mt.), Az, US 179/G4
Lemon Grove, Ca, US 196/C5
Lemon Springs, NC, US 193/H3
Lemoore, Ca, US 178/C2
Lemoore Nav. Air Sta., Ca, US 178/B2
Lemoyne, Ne, US 184/D3
Lempa (riv.), ESal. 206/D3
Lempäälä, Fin. 47/K1
Lempdes, Fr. 50/E4
Lemro (riv.), Myan. 98/B4
Lemsid, WSah. 128/B4
Lemva (riv.), Rus. 75/P2
Lemvig, Den. 46/C3
Lemwerder, Ger. 59/F2
Lemyethna, Myan. 98/B5
Lena, Mb, Can. 186/E3
Lena, Nor. 46/D1
Lena (riv.), Rus. 83/M3
Lena, Il, US 185/K2
Lena, Ne, US 184/D3
Lena, SC, US 193/G4
Lena, Wi, US 190/B2
Lenape (lake), NJ, US 198/D5
Lençóis Maranhenses, PN dos, Braz. 219/F3
Lençóis Paulista, Braz. 225/G2
Lendery, Rus. 74/F3
Lendinara, It. 69/E3
Lene (lake), Ire. 38/C2
Lengau, Aus. 65/G6
Lengdorf, Ger. 65/F6
Lenge, D.R. Congo 139/F4
Lengede, Ger. 59/H4
Lengenfeld, Ger. 65/F1
Lengerich, Ger. 59/E4
Lenggries, Ger. 67/H2
Lenghu, China 90/C4
Lengnau, Swi. 66/D3
Lengshuijiang, China 99/F3
Lengshuitan, China 99/F3
Lengua de Vaca (pt.), Chile 224/B4
Lengué Namobessie (riv.), Camr. 138/C2
Lengwe NP, Malw. 141/G3
Lengzipu, China 93/B2
Lenhartsville, Pa, US 198/C2
Lenia, Eth. 135/H4
Lenina (lake), Ukr. 79/H3
Lenina (peak), Taj. 111/B4
Leninabad (int'l arpt.), Taj. 111/A3
Lenine, Ukr. 79/H5
Leningradskaya, Rus. 79/K4
Leningradskaya Oblast, Rus. 74/G3
Leningradskiy, Rus. 172/U12
Leninogor, Kaz. 111/D1
Leninogorsk, Rus. 75/M5
Leninsk, Rus. 75/M4
Leninsk-Kuznetskiy, Rus. 80/J4
Leninskiy, Rus. 76/F1
Leninskoye, Kaz. 77/L2
Leninskoye, Rus. 91/L2
Leninváros, Hun. 49/L5
Lenk, Swi. 66/D5
Lenne (riv.), Ger. 61/G1
Lennestadt, Ger. 59/F6
Lenningen, Ger. 64/C5
Lennox (isl.), Chile 191/D7
Lennox (hills), Sc, UK 39/B5
Lennox, Ca, US 196/F8
Lennox, SD, US 185/F2
Lennoxtown, Sc, UK 39/B5
Lennoxville, Qu, Can. 191/L2
Leno, It. 68/D3
Lenoir, NC, US 193/G3
Lenoir City, Tn, US 192/E3
Lenola, It. 71/C5
Lenora, Ks, US 184/D4
Lenore, Mb, Can. 186/D3
Lenore (lake), Sk, Can. 175/M1
Lenox, Ga, US 195/G2
Lenox, Ia, US 185/G3
Lenox, Ma, US 191/K3
Lens, Swi. 66/D5
Lens, Fr. 60/B3
Lens, Belg. 60/C2
Lensahn, Ger. 46/D4
Lensk, Rus. 81/M3
Lenswood, Mb, Can. 186/D1
Lenswood, Austl. 155/M8
Lent, Neth. 58/C5
Lentekhi, Geo. 77/G4

Name	Ref.	Name	Ref.	Name	Ref.	Name	Ref.	Name	Ref.	Name	Ref.	Name	Ref.	Name	Ref.
Lenting, Ger.	65/E5	Les Gets, Fr.	66/C5	Leven (pt.), SAfr.	143/F2	Liangting, China	90/F5	Liebenau, Aus.	65/H5	Limavady, NI, UK	40/B1	Linden, NJ, US	199/J9	Lion (gulf), Fr.,Sp.	72/E2
Lentini, It.	54/D4	Les Haudères, Swi.	66/D6	Levens, Fr.	70/D5	Liangwan (mts.), China	98/D3	Liebenbergsvlei		Limay, Fr.	63/G3	Linden, Tn, US	192/D3	Lion Country Safari,	
Lentvaris, Lith.	47/L4	Les Hautes-Rivières, Fr.	61/D4	Leventina (Prato), Swi.	67/E5	Liangzhen, China	90/F4	(riv.), SAfr.	142/E2	Limay (riv.), Arg.	209/C7	Linden, Tx, US	183/G4	FI, US	194/P9
Lenvik, Nor.	44/F1	Les Herbiers, Fr.	50/C3	Leveque (cape), Austl.	152/A4	Liangzi (lake), China	92/C5	Liebenthal, Ks, US	182/E1	Limay Mahuida, Arg.	226/D3	Linden Beach, On, Can.	197/G7	Lion-sur-Mer, Fr.	63/E2
Lenwood, Ca, US	178/D3	Les Islettes, Fr.	61/E5	Lever (riv.), Braz.	222/C1	Lianhua (mts.), China	99/G4	Liebig (mt.), Austl.	155/F2	Limbach, Ger.	65/F1	Lindenberg im Allgäu,		Lions Den, Zim.	141/F3
Leny, Pass of		Les Mées, Fr.	70/B4	Leverburgh, Sc, UK	37/Q8	Lianhua, China	105/K2	Liechtenstein (ctry.)	67/F3	Limbang (riv.), Malay.	100/A4	Ger.	71/F2	Lion's Head, On, Can.	190/F2
(pass), Sc, UK	53/J4	Les Mesnuls, Fr.	39/B4	Levering, Mi, US	190/D2	Lianjiang, China	99/H3	Liedekerke, Belg.	60/C2	Limbani, Peru	220/D4	Lindenfels, Ger.	64/B3	Lioppa, Indo.	152/B1
Lenya, Myan.	106/B4	Les Minquier (isl.), UK	62/C2	Leverkusen, Ger.	61/F1	Lianjiang, China	99/G4	Liège, Belg.	61/E2	Limbara (peak), It.	54/A2	Lindenhurst, Il, US	197/P15	Lioto, CAfr.	134/D4
Lenzburg, Swi.	66/E3	Les Molières, Fr.	36/J6	Lèves, Fr.	63/G4	Lianjiangkou, China	99/G3	Liège (prov.), Belg.	61/E2	Limbaži, Lat.	47/L3	Lindenhurst, NY, US	199/E2	Liozno, Bela.	47/P4
Lenzing, Aus.	65/G2	Les Monges (peak), Fr.	70/C4	Levice, Slvk.	56/I1	Liannan Yaozu Zizhixian,		Lieksa, Fin.	74/F3	Limbdi, India	107/K3	Lindenwold, NJ, US	198/D4	Lipari, It.	54/D3
Lenzkirch, Ger.	70/B4	Les Mureaux, Fr.	60/A6	Levico Terme, It.	67/H5	China	99/G3	Lielvarde, Lat.	47/L3	Limbe, Camr.	138/B1	Lindern, Ger.	59/E3	Lipari (isl.), It.	73/G3
Léo, Burk.	133/E4	Les Orres, Fr.	70/C4	Levier, Fr.	66/C4	Lianping, China	99/H3	Lienden, Neth.	58/C5	Limbe, Malw.	141/G2	Lindesberg, Swe.	46/F2	Lipari (isls.), It.	73/G3
Leoben, Aus.	51/L3	Les Pennes-Mirabeau, Fr.	70/B6	Levin, NZ	159/C3	Lianpu, China	99/H3	Lienen, Ger.	59/E4	Limbé, Haiti	207/H2	Lindesnes (cape), Nor.	46/B3	Lipcani, Mol.	101/C3
Leográ (riv.), It.	69/E1	Les Pieux, Fr.	62/D2	Lévis-Saint-Nom, Fr.	36/H5	Lianshui, China	99/D3	Lienz, Aus.	51/K3	Limbiate, It.	68/B2	Lindesnes (cape), Nor.	46/B2	Lipetsk (int'l arpt.), Rus.	194/P11
Leok, Indo.	103/F3	Les Ponts-de-Cé, Fr.	63/E6	Levittown, Pa, US	199/U3	Liantang, China	106/C4	Liepa, Lat.	47/M3	Limbourg, Belg.	61/E2	Lindgren Acres, FI, US	100/B4	Lipetsk, Rus.	76/F1
Leola, SD, US	186/E5	Les Ponts-de-Martel, Swi.	66/C4	Levittown, Pa, US	198/D3	Liantang, China	99/F3	Liepāja, Lat.	47/J4	Limbuak, Malay.	100/B4	Lindholm (isl.), Den.	152/C4	Lipetskaya Oblast, Rus.	76/F1
Leola, Ar, US	183/H3	Les Rosiers, Fr.	63/E6	Levkás, Gre.	55/G3	Liantang, China	92/L8	Lierbyen, Nor.	46/D1	Limbunya, Austl.	152/C4	Lindi (riv.), D.R. Congo	139/F2	Lipez (riv.), Bol.	224/C2
Leominster, Ma, US	191/L3	Les Rousses, Fr.	66/D5	Levkás (isl.), Gre.	73/J3	Lianyun, China	99/D3	Lierneux, Belg.	61/E3	Limburg (prov.), Belg.	61/E2	Lindi (prov.), Tanz.	137/B4	Lipin Bor, Rus.	74/H3
Leominster, Eng, UK	42/D2	Les Sables-d'Olonne, Fr.	50/C4	Levkimmi, Gre.	55/F3	Lianyungang, China	99/D3	Lierre (riv.), China	92/D4	Limburg an der Lahn,		Lindian, China	91/J2	Lipljan, Serb.	56/E4
León, Mex.	205/E4	Les Salines,		Levkinskaya, Rus.	75/J2	Liao (riv.), China	83/M5	Lieser (riv.), Ger.	61/F3	Ger.	64/B2	Lindlar, Ger.	61/G1	Lipno, Pol.	49/K2
Leon (int'l arpt.), Mex.	204/C3	Les Sept Iles (isl.), Fr.	62/B3	Levоča, Slvk.	49/L4	Liaodong (pen.), China	93/A3	Liesjärven NP, Fin.	47/K1	Limedsforsen, Swe.	46/E1	Lindley, SAfr.	142/D2	Lipno (res.), Czh.	65/H5
León, Nic.	206/E3	Les Touches, Fr.	62/D6	Levrier (bay), Mrta.	128/A5	Liaodong (isls.), China	93/A3	Liesse-Notre-Dame, Fr.	60/D4	Limehouse, On, Can.	190/T8	Lindlar, Ger.	61/G1	Lipova, UN (lake), Austl.	190/B2
Leon, Sp.	52/C1	Les Ulis, Fr.	36/J5	Levuka, Fiji	161/Y18	Liaodong (gulf), China	91/J3	Liestal, Swi.	66/D3	Limeira, Braz.	222/F2	Lindome, Swe.	46/E3	Lipova, UN (lake), Austl.	51/L2
Leon, Ia, US	185/H3	Les Verrières, Swi.	66/C4	Levy (lake), FI, US	195/G3	Liaodun, China	90/C3	Lieto, Fin.	47/K1	Limekilns, Sc, UK	39/C4	Lindome, Swe.	46/E3	Lipova, Rom.	56/E2
Leon, Ok, US	183/F4	Lesa, It.	68/B2	Lewellen, Ne, US	184/C3	Liaoning (prov.), China	91/J3	Liéury, Fr.	63/F2	Limena, It.	69/E3	Lindon, Ut, US	177/H3	Lipovka (riv.), Az, US	179/H3
Leon (riv.), Tx, US	181/E2	L'Escarène, Fr.	70/D5	Lewes, Eng, UK	43/G5	Liaoping, China	92/L8	Liévin, Fr.	60/B3	Limentra, It.	55/L2	Lindsborg, Ks, US	184/C4	Lipovka, Moz.	141/G2
León Muerto		Leselidze, Geo.	76/G4	Lewin Brzeski, Pol.	49/J3	Liaoyang, China	91/K3	Lievio, Fin.	45/E4	Limerick, Sk, US	175/L3	Lindsay (lake), Ab, Can.	61/F6	Lippe (riv.), Ger.	68/C2
(pass), Chile	224/B3	Leseru, Kenya	137/A1	Lewis (hill), Nf, Can.	189/H1	Liaozhong, China	93/B2	Lièvre (riv.), Qu, Can.	189/N1	Limerick (co.), Ire.	38/B4	Lindrith, NM, US	179/J2	Lipova, Rom.	179/J2
Leon Valley, Tx, US	181/E3	Leshan, China	98/D2	Lewis (hills), Nf, Can.	189/H1	Liaquatpur, Pak.	110/A5	Liez (lake), Fr.	66/B2	Limerick (co.), Ire.	38/B5	Lindsay, Austl.	154/C5	Lippe (riv.), Ger.	48/B3
Leon-Guanajuato		Leshukonskoye, Rus.	75/K2	Lewis (isl.), Sc, UK	37/Q7	Liard (riv.), Can.	163/E3	Liezen, Aus.	51/L3	Limerick, Ire.	38/B4	Lindsay, On, Can.	190/F3	Lipscomb, Tx, US	182/D2
(int'l arpt.), Mex.	205/E4	Lésigny, Fr.	36/K5	Lewis (pass), NZ	159/C3	Liard (isl.), Indo.	101/D3	Lifake, D.R. Congo	139/E2	Limestone (lake), Tx, US	181/F2	Lindsay, Ca, US	178/C3	Lipsko, Pol.	78/A2
Leona, Tx, US	181/G2	Lesima (peak), It.	68/C4	Lewis, Co, US	179/H2	Libaçao, Phil.	100/C3	Lifau, ETim.	152/B2	Limestone, Mt, US	177/J1	Lindsay, Mt, US	186/B4	Lisala, D.R. Congo	139/E2
Leonardokovskoye, Rus.	75/K2	Lesja, Nor.	44/D3	Lewis, Ia, US	185/G3	Libano, Col.	216/C3	Liffey (riv.), Ire.	40/B5	Lindroth, NM, US	134/B4	Lindsay, Ok, US	183/F3	Liptovská Lúžna, Slvk.	49/K4
Leona (riv.), Tx, US	196/B1	Lesjöfors, Swe.	46/F2	Lewis, Ks, US	182/E2	Libau, Mb, Can.	186/F2	Liffol-le-Grand, Fr.	66/B1	Limidario (peak), It.	67/E5	Lindsborg, Ks, US	183/F3	Liptovský Svätý Mikuláš,	
Leona Valley, Ca, US	196/C2	Lesko, Pol.	49/M4	Lewis (riv.), Wa, US	174/D4	Libby, Mt, US	174/G3	Lifford, Ire.	37/Q9	Limite, It.	69/D6	Lindsdal, Swe.	46/G3	Slvk.	201/E2
Leonard, Mi, US	197/F6	Leskovac, Serb.	56/E4	Lewis and Clark		Libby (lake), Austl.	154/C3	Liffré, Fr.	62/D4	Limite, It.	66/B3	Line (isls.), Kiri.	161/J4	Little Andaman	
Leonard, ND, US	186/F4	Leskovik, Alb.	55/G2	(lake), SD,Ne, US	55/G2	Libenge, D.R. Congo	138/D2	Lifou (riv.), Swi.	161/V12	Limmат (riv.), Swi.	66/E3	Line Mountain		Little Andaman	
Leonardo da Vinci		Leslie, Ar, US	183/H3	Lewis and Clark NWR,		Liberal, Mo, US	183/G2	Lifton, Eng, UK	42/B5	Limmen Bight	153/D3	Lipu La (pass), India	111/D5	(isl.), India	105/F6
(int'l arpt.), It.	71/B4	Leslie, Ga, US	195/F2	On, US	77/C4	Liberal, Ks, US	182/D2	Liganga, Tanz.	137/A4	Limmen Bight	153/D3	Lira, Ugan.	139/H2	Little Arkansas	105/F1
Leonardtown, Md, US	193/J1	Leslie, Sc, UK	39/C4	Lewis Smith		Libercourt, Fr.	60/C2	Liganga, Tanz.	137/A4	Limneos de Nazca, Peru	145/C2	Liranga, Congo	138/D3	Little Arkansas	
Leonardville, Namb.	140/C4	Leslie, Wa, US	39/C4	(lake), Al, US	192/D3	Liberdade, Braz.	223/M7	Lгtane, Lat.	55/H3	Limni, Gre.	55/H3	Lirangwe, Malw.	141/G2	(riv.), Ks, US	183/F1
Leonardville, Ks, US	187/J3	Lewis Smith		Lewisberg, Ky, US	192/D3	Liberdade (riv.), Braz.	194/B2	Lighthouse, China	195/F3	Limoeiro, Braz.	219/H4	Lircay, Peru	220/C4	Little Ferry, NJ, US	199/J8
Leonberg, Ger.	64/C5	Lesmahagow, Sc, UK	39/C5	Lewisburg, Pa, US	198/B2	Libercý, Czh.	49/H3	Lighthouse Point,		Limoeiro do Norte,		Liré, Fr.	63/D6	Little Fishing (cr.),	
Leonding, Aus.	65/H6	Lesneven, Fr.	62/A3	Lewisburg, Tn, US	192/D3	Liberecký (pol. reg.), Czh.	49/H3	FI, US	194/P10	Braz.	219/H4	Linfen, China	92/B3	Pa, US	198/B1
Leone (peak), It.	66/D5	Leśnica, Serb.	56/D3	Lewisburg, WV, US	192/L3	Liberі (arpt.), It.	71/D3	Lightning Ridge, Austl.	156/C1	Braz.	219/H4	Lindford, Eng, UK	92/B3	Little Fork (riv.), Mn, US	187/L1
Leone, ASam.	161/T10	Lesnoy, Rus.	75/M4	Lewisham (bor.), Eng, UK	36/C2	Liberia (ctry.)	71/D3	Lightwater, Eng, UK	36/B3	Limoges, Fr.	50/D4	Liria, Sp.	53/E3	Little Fort, BC, Can.	174/D2
Leones, Arg.	226/E2	Lesogorsk, Rus.	91/N2	Lewisport, Nf, Can.	189/K1	Liberia, CR	207/E4	Lignan Sabbiadoro, It.	69/G2	Limogne (plat.), Fr.	50/D4	Lira (riv.), It.	67/F5	Little Gombi, Nga.	134/B3
Leonessa, It.	71/B2	Lesopil'noye, Rus.	91/L2	Lewiston, Nf, Can.	189/K1	Libertad, Belz.	206/D2	Lignite, MO, China	186/C3	Limón, CR	207/F4	Ling Xian, China	92/D3	Little Grand Rapids,	
Leongatha, Austl.	157/B4	Lesosibirsk, Rus.	80/K4	Lewiston, Me, US	188/B3	Libertad, Uru.	191/K11	Ligny-en-Barrois, Fr.	61/E6	Limon, Co, US	184/C3	Ling Xian, China	105/K2	Mb, Can.	187/G1
Leonia, NJ, US	199/K8	Lesozavodsk, Rus.	91/L2	Lewiston, NY, US	190/U9	Libertad, Ven.	216/C2	Ligonсio (peak), It.	67/F5	Limon, Co, US	184/C3	Lingao, China	105/J2	Little Heart's Ease,	
Leonidhion, Gre.	55/H4	Lesparre-Médoc, Fr.	50/C4	Lewiston, Ut, US	177/H3	Libertad de Orituco, Ven.	219/P8	Ligonha (riv.), Moz.	141/H2	Limone Piemonte, It.	70/D4	Lingayen (gulf), Phil.	100/B1	Nf, Can.	189/L1
Leonora, Austl.	55/H4	Lessay, Fr.	62/D2	Lewiston Woodville,		Libertador General		Ligionier, In, US	190/D4	Limone sul Garda, It.	69/D2	Lingayen (gulf), Phil.	53/P10	Lisboa (dist.), Port.	52/A3	Little Inagua (isl.),	
Leopold, Austl.	157/B4	Lessebo, Swe.	46/F3	NC, US	193/J2	San Martin, Arg.	224/C2	Ligoúrion, Gre.	55/H4	Limoquije, Bol.	221/E4	Lisboa (int'l arpt.), Port.	53/P10	Bahm.	203/G3
Leopoldina, Braz.	223/P6	Lesser Antilles		Lewistown, Il, US	185/J3	Liberty, Il, US	185/J4	Ligovo (nbrhd.), Rus.	75/T7	Limours, Fr.	36/J6	Lisboa, La, US	183/H4	Little Kanawha	
Leopoldkanaal (riv.),		(isls.), NAm.	203/H5	Lewistown, Mt, US	175/K4	Liberty, In, US	190/D5	Liguria (pol. reg.), It.	68/C5	Limousin (mts.), Fr.	50/D4	Lisbon, Md, US	198/A5	(riv.), WV, US	193/G2
Belg.	60/C1	Lesser Caucasus		Lewistown, Pa, US	191/H4	Liberty, Ky, US	192/E2	Ligurian (sea), Eur.	72/E2	Limousin (pol. reg.), Fr.	50/D4	Lisbon, ND, US	186/F4	Little Karoo (valley),	
Leopoldsburg, Belg.	61/E1	(mts.), Asia	77/G4	Lewisville (lake), Tx, US	181/F1	Liberty, Mo, US	185/G4	Lihou Reef and Kays		Limoux, Fr.	50/E5	Lisbon, Oh, US	190/F4	SAfr.	142/C4
Leopoldsdorf, Aus.	57/N7	Lesser Slave		Lewisville, Tx, US	183/F4	Liberty, Ms, US	194/C2	(isl.), Austl.	145/G2	Limpopo (prov.), SAfr.	141/F4	Lisbon, NH, US	58/C5	Little Lake, Ca, US	178/D3
Leopoldsdorf im Marchfelde,		(lake), Ab, Can.	170/E3	Lewotobi (peak), Indo.	152/A2	Liberty, NC, US	193/H3	Lihue, Hi, US	172/S10	Limpopo (riv.), Afr.	141/G5	Lisbon, Oh, US	59/E3	Little Lehigh (riv.),	
Aus.	57/P7	Lesser Sunda (isls.),		Lexa, Ar, US	192/B2	Liberty, NY, US	191/J1	Lijiang Naxizu Zizhixian,		Limu (mtn.), China	99/F5	Lisboa (Lisbon)		Pa, US	198/D2
Leopoldshöhe, Ger.	64/D2	Indo.	152/A4	Lexham, Belg.	60/C2	Liberty, Ok, US	183/F4	China	98/D3	Lin (mtn.), China	99/F5	(cap.), Port.	53/P10	Little Manatee	
Leota, Mn, US	185/F2	Lessines, Belg.	60/C2	Lexington, Il, US	185/K3	Liberty, Sc, Can.	175/M2	Lijin, China	92/D3	Limu, China	99/F5	Lisburn, NI, UK	40/B2	(riv.), FI, US	194/L8
Leoti, Ks, US	182/D1	Lessley, Ms, US	194/C2	Lexington, Ky, US	192/E1	Liberty, Tx, US	181/G2	Likasi, D.R. Congo	139/F5	Limulunga, Zam.	140/D2	Lisburne (cape),		Little Manatee, South Fork	
Leova, Mol.	78/E4	Lesterville, Mo, US	192/B2	Lexington, Mo, US	185/H3	Liberty Grove, Md, US	198/B4	Likati, D.R. Congo	139/E2	Limuru, Kenya	137/B2	Ak, US	162/E2	(riv.), FI, US	194/L8
Lepaera, Hon.	206/D3	Lesung (peak), Indo.	102/D3	Lexington, Ne, US	184/D3	Likely, BC, Can.	174/D1	Lin'an, China	99/H2	Lingel, Wy, US	184/B2	Liscarroll, Ire.	38/B5	Little Marais, Mn, US	187/J4
Lépanges-sur-Vologne,		Lesungbatu, Indo.	102/D3	Lexington, NC, US	193/H3	Likati, D.R. Congo	139/E2	Linakamari, Rus.	74/F1	Lingelstown, Pa, US	198/B3	Liscomb Game Sanctuary,		Little Minch (str.), Sc, UK	37/Q8
Fr.	62/B5	Les, China	192/E1	Lexington, Oh, US	190/E4	Likhoslavl', Rus.	74/G4	Linakhamari, Rus.	74/F1	Lingelsheim, Fr.	66/D1	NS, Can.	189/F1	Little Missouri	
Lepanto, It.	192/B3	Leswalt, Sc, UK	40/C2	Lexington, SC, US	193/H3	Likhovskoy, Rus.	79/H3	Linao, Arg.	45/B1	Lingmap, D.R. Congo	139/E2	Liseleje, Den.	46/D3	Little Missouri	
Lepar (isl.), Indo.	101/D3	Leszno, Pol.	49/J3	Lexington Park, Md, US	193/J1	Likimi, D.R. Congo	139/E2	Linao (pt.), Phil.	100/C4	Lingqiu, China	92/C3	Lisha (riv.), China	105/H2	(riv.), Ar, US	183/H3
Lepe, Indo.	52/B4	Letaba, SAfr.	141/F4	Leyburn, Eng, UK	41/G3	Libin, Belg.	61/E4	Likoma (isl.), Malw.	141/G2	Lingshan, China	105/H2	Lishan, China	92/D3	Little Moose	
Lepenoú, Gre.	55/G3	L'Étang-du-Nord,		Leye, China	99/E3	Libmanan, Phil.	100/C3	Likoto, D.R. Congo	139/E3	Lingshan, China	99/F4	Lisha (riv.), WV, US	98/D3	(mtn.), NY, US	191/J3
Lephepe, Bots.	140/E4	Qu, Can.	189/G2	Leydsdorp, SAfr.	141/F4	Libobo (cape), Indo.	103/G4	Likoualа (pol. reg.), Congo	138/D2	Lingshi, China	99/H2	Lishui, China	99/H2	Little Muddy	
Lepi, Braz.	140/B2	Lete, It.		Leysdown, Eng, UK	43/G4	Libochovice, Czh.	65/H2	Likouala aux Herbes		Linares, Sp.	52/D3	Lishui, China	99/H2	(riv.), ND, US	186/C3
L'Epine (pond), Fr.	36/K4	Letegge (peak), It.	71/C1	Leysin, Swi.	66/D5	Libon, Phil.	100/C3	(riv.), Congo	139/E2	Linares, Chile	226/C2	Lisieux, Fr.	63/F2	Little Muncy (cr.),	
Leping, China	99/H2	Letetkhi, SD, US	184/E2	Leyton (nbrhd.), Eng, UK	36/C2	Liboko, D.R. Congo	139/E2	Likouala Mossaka		Linares, Mex.	205/F3	Lisiar, Fr.	161/H2	Pa, US	198/B2
L'Épiphanie, Qu, Can.	189/P6	Letchworth, Eng, UK	43/F3	Lezama, Ven.	192/C3	Liboko, D.R. Congo	139/E2	(riv.), Congo	138/D2	Linaría, Gre.	55/J3	Linguère, Sen.	132/B3	Lisiy Nos, Rus.	75/T6	Little Neck (bay), NY, US	199/K8
Lepontine Alps		Lete,		Lezhë, Alb.	55/F2	Libon, Phil.	100/C3	Likova, Rus.	75/W9	Lincheng, China	92/C3	Lingwu, China	90/F4	Lisa, Rus.	99/J3	Little Nemaha	
(mts.), Swi.	72/F1	Letham, Sc, UK	39/D3	Lezhi, Moz.	141/G2	Libramont (riv.), Rus.	75/W9	Lincheng, China	99/H3	Lingyun, China	99/H3	Lisle, Il, US	197/P16	(riv.), Ne, US	199/K8
Lepreau Game Ref.,		Lethbridge, Ab, Can.	175/H3	Lexington Blue Grass		Libres, Mex.	205/M7	Likstammen (lake), Swe.	45/A2	Lichuan, China	99/H3	Lingyun Si, China	92/L9	L'Isle-Adam, Fr.	36/J4	Little Nicobar (isl.), India	105/F6
NB, Can.	188/D3	Lethe (riv.), Ger.	59/F2	Army Depot, Ky, US	192/E1	Libreville (cap.), Gabon	138/B2	Liku, Indo.	102/C3	Linchuan, China	99/H3	Linguyan, China	99/H3	L'Isle-d'Abeau, Fr.	70/B2	Little Ocmulgee	
Lepsämä, Fin.	42/H4	Lethem, Guy.	217/G2	Leyburn, Eng, UK	41/G3	Libya (int'l arpt.), Gabon	138/B2	Liku, Indo.	102/C3	Lincoln (sea), Can.	163/L1	Lingyuan, China	105/J3	L'Isle-en-Dodon, Fr.	50/D5	Little Para (res.), Austl.	155/M8
Lepsi, Kaz.	111/C2	Leti (isl.), Indo.	152/B2	Li, China	99/G3	Libya, China	99/H4	Libourn, Mo, US	192/C2	Lincoh, On, Can.	190/T10	Linhai, China	99/J2	L'Isle-sur-la-Sorgue, Fr.	70/B5	Little Patuxent	
Lepsy (riv.), Kaz.	111/C2	Leticia, Col.	220/D2	Leyland, Eng, UK	41/F4	Libya (ctry.)	127/C2	Lincoln, Eng, UK	193/M7	Linhares, Braz.	223/E3	L'Isle-sur-le-Doubs, Fr.	66/C3	(riv.), Md, US	
Leptis Magna (Labdah)		Leting, China	92/D3	Leysdown, Eng, UK	41/F4	Libyan (des.),		L'île-Perrot, Qu, Can.	189/N7	Lincoln, De, US	198/C5	Linière, Qu, Can.	188/B2	L'Islet, Qu, Can.	188/B2	Little Payne (cr.), FI, US	194/M8
(ruin), Libya	126/B1	Letlhakane, Bots.	140/E4	Leyte (isl.), Phil.	83/M8	Libyan (plat.), Egypt,Libya	126/D3	L'île-Rousse, Fr.	54/A1	Lincoln, Il, US	185/K3	Linköping, Swe.	46/F2	L'Isle-Verte, Qu, Can.	188/C1	Little Peconic	
Leptokariá, Gre.	55/H2	Letlhakeng, Bots.	140/E5	Leyte (gulf), Phil.	100/D4	Egypt,Libya		Lilianí, Gre.	110/B3	Lincoln, Ks, US	183/K1	Linkuva, Lith.	47/K3	Lismore, Austl.	156/E1	Little Pee Dee	
Leque, Bol.	221/E5	Letong, Indo.	101/D2	Leyton (nbrhd.), Eng, UK	36/C2	Licata, It.	54/C4	Lincoln, La, US	185/K3	Lincoln, Mo, US	183/J1	Linlithgow, Sc, UK	39/C5	Lismore, Sc, UK	38/D5	(riv.), SC, US	193/H3
Lequena, Chile	224/C1	Letnitsa, Bul.	132/A6	L'Étoile, Fr.	60/B3	Licciana Nardi, It.	68/D5	Lincoln, NM, US	179/K2	Linmo, US	183/J1	Linliu (mtn.), China	99/H3	Lisnaskea, NI, UK	38/B2	Little Pend Orielle NWR,	
Lequire, Ok, US	183/G4	Letong, Indo.	101/D2	Leytron, Swi.	66/D5	Lice, Turk.	114/E2	Lincoln, NH, US	191/L2	Linmo, US	183/J1	Liniu, Mo, US	183/J1	Lismore, SAfr.	155/F2	Wa, US	174/G3
Lera (peak), It.	70/D2	Letsin, Bul.	49/H2	Lez (riv.), Fr.	50/F4	Lille, Fr.	60/C2	Lincoln, Tx, US	181/F3	Linney (lake), Wal, UK	42/A3	Little Pic (riv.), On, US	187/N3
Léraba (riv.), Burk.	132/D4	Letschin, Ger.	49/H2	Lezama, Ven.	219/P8	Lille Bælt (chan.), Ger.	46/C4	Lincoln (Lincoln Center),		Linn Creek, Mo, US	183/J1	Lispeszentadorján, Hun.	56/C2	Little Pine and Lucky Man	
Lercara Friddi, It.	54/C4	Letsok-Aw (isl.), Myan.	102/A1	Lèze (riv.), Fr.	70/E5	Lille Værløse, Den.	46/C4	US	37/K4 S5	Linn, Pineus, Wa, US	185/M4	Liss, Neth.	58/B4	Little Pisgah	
Lerdo de Tejada, Mex.	206/C2	Letong, Indo.	101/D2	Lezhë, Alb.	55/F2	Lichfield, Eng, UK	43/E1	Lincoln Beach, Or, US	176/A1	Linney (lake), Wal, UK	43/A3	Liss, Neth.	58/B4	(mtn.), NC, US	193/G3
Léré, Chad	134/B3	Letterkenny, Ire.	37/Q9	Lezhi, Moz.	141/G2	Lichinga, Moz.	141/G2	Lincoln Boyhood Nat'l Mem.,		Linney (lake), Wal, UK	43/A3	List, Ger.	59/E1	Little Powder	
Lere, Nga.	133/H4	Letterkenny Army Depot,		Lézignan-Corbières, Fr.	50/E5	Lichtenau, Ger.	59/F5	In, US	190/C5	Linnich, Ger.	61/F2	Lista, Ger.	59/E1	(riv.), Wy, US	
Léré, Mali	132/D3	Pa, US	191/H4	Lézignan-Corbières, Fr.	50/E5	Lichtenau, Ger.	65/F4	Lincoln Caverns, Pa, US	191/H4	Lino Lakes, Mn, US	187/P6	Listowel, Ire.	38/A5	Little Prairie, Wi, US	197/N14
Leribe, Les.	142/E3	Lettonmanoppello, It.	71/D3	Lézignan-Corbières, Fr.	50/E5	Lichtenburg, SAfr.	142/D2	Lincoln Center (Lincoln),		Linnich, Ger.	59/E3	Listowel, On, Can.	190/F3	Little Red (riv.), Ar, US	183/J3
Lerici, It.	68/C5	Leu, China	191/H4	Lézignan-Corbières, Fr.	50/E5	Lichtenfels, Ger.	64/D2	US	183/E1	Linosa, It.	54/C5	Listowel, On, Can.	190/F3	Little River, NZ	159/C3
Lérida, Col.	216/C4	Leu Botanical Gardens,		Lhari, China	98/B2	Lichtensteig, Swi.	67/F3	Lincoln City, Or, US	176/A1	Linosa (isl.), It.	130/N7	Lit. Scarcies (riv.), SLeo.	132/B4	Little River, Ks, US	183/E1
Lérida, Col.	219/L8	FI, US	194/N6	Lhasa, China	109/H1	Lichtenstein, Swi.	67/F3	Lincoln Heath		Linqasi, Sudan	135/G4	Litang (riv.), China	105/H2	Little River, SC, US	193/H3
Lerik, Azer.	115/G2	Leuca, It.	55/F3	Lhasa (int'l arpt.), China	109/H1	Lillington, NC, US	193/H3	Lincoln Heights, Oh, US	190/C5	Linqing, China	92/C3	Litang, China	105/H2	Little Rock (cap.), Ar, US	183/H3
Lerín, Sp.	52/E1	Leuchars, Sc, UK	39/D4	Lhatog, China	98/C2	Lilliwaup, Wa, US	197/A3	Lincoln Home Nat'l		Linqu, China	92/D3	Litāni (riv.), FrG.,Sur.	218/D2	Little Rock, SC, US	193/H3
Lerma (riv.), Mex.	163/G7	Leukerbad, Swi.	66/D5	Lhazê, China	109/F1	Lillkyrka, Swe.	45/A1	Hist. Site, Il, US	185/K4	Linquan, China	92/C4	Litchfield, Austl.	152/C3	Little Rock (cap.), It, US	197/N16
Lerma, Mex.	205/Q10	Leun, Ger.	64/B2	L'Hermitage, Fr.	62/D4	Lillo, Sp.	52/D3	Lincoln Park, Co, US	179/K2	Linru, Braz.	92/C4	Litchfield, Il, US	185/K4	Little Rock, Mn, US	187/K3
Lermoos, Aus.	71/G1	Leupp, Az, US	179/G3	Lhokkruet, Indo.	101/A1	Lilooet, BC, Can.	174/C2	Lincoln Park, Mi, US	197/F7	Linru, Braz.	225/G4	Litchfield, Mn, US	185/K4	Little Sable (pt.), Mi, US	190/C3
Lérouville, Fr.	61/E6	Leusbost, Sc, UK	37/Q7	Lhokseumawe, Indo.	101/A1	Lilooet, BC, Can.	174/C2	Lincoln Park, NJ, US	199/H8	Linshu, China	92/D3	Litchfield, Ne, US	184/D3	Little Salmon, Yk, Can.	162/L3
Leroux Wash (riv.),		Leusden-Zuid, Neth.	58/C4	Lhoksukon, Indo.	101/B1	Lilongwe (cap.), Malw.	141/G2	Lincolnshire		Linthnu, China	92/C3	Litchfield, Ne, US	184/D3	Little Sark (isl.), Fr.	62/C2
Az, US	179/G3	Leuterhausen, Ger.	64/D3	L'Hospitalet de Llobregat,		Lilongwe (Kamuzu)		(co.), Eng, UK	41/H5	Linthou, China	92/C3	Litherland, Eng, UK	41/F5	Little Schuylkill	
Leroy, ND, US	186/F4	Leutkirch im Allgäu, Ger.	67/G2	Sp.	53/L7	Lincoln Park, NJ, US	199/U3	Lincolnshire Wolds		Linthou, China	90/F4	Litava (riv.), Czh.	66/B6	(riv.), Pa, US	198/D2
Leroy, Al, US	194/E2	Leuven (Louvain), Belg.	60/C2	Lhozhag, China	109/H2	Licking, Mo, US	192/C1	Lincolnshire Wolds		Linyi, China	92/D3	Liteta, Zam.	141/F2	Little Sioux	
Leroy, Sk, Can.	175/M1	Léry, Qu, Can.	189/K6	Lhuntsi, Bhu.	109/H2	Licking (riv.), Ky, US	192/E1	Lily, Ky, US	192/E2	Linyi, China	92/D3	Lith, Ger.	199/K8	Litomyšl, Czh.	49/J3	(riv.), Ia, US	185/F2
Leroy, Ks, US	181/F2	Léry, Qu, Can.	189/K6	Lhünzê, China	109/H2	Licquеs, Fr.	60/A2	Lily, Ky, US	192/E2	Linz, Ger.	64/F3	Lith, Ger.	59/E2	Little Sioux, West Fork	
Lerum, Swe.	46/E3	Les Alignements de Carnac,		Li (riv.), China	105/G2	Licungo (riv.), Moz.	141/H2	Lilydale (nbrhd.), Austl.	156/L6	Linz, Aus.	65/H6	Lithgow, Austl.	157/E1	(riv.), Ia, US	185/F2
Lerwick, Sc, UK	37/W13	Fr.	62/B5	Li (mtn.), China	98/C4	Lida, Bela.	47/L5	Lim (riv.), Mont.,Serb.	56/D4	Lincolnton, NC, US	193/G3	Lithgow, Austl.	157/E1	Little Sitkin (isl.), Ak, US	201/G5
Léry, Qu, Can.	189/K6	Les Alluets-le-Roi, Fr.	36/H5	Li Xian, China	99/F2	Lidao, China	105/K2	Lima, Peru	220/C4	Lincolnville, Ks, US	193/G3	Lithia Springs, Ga, US	193/L7	Little Snake (riv.), Co, US	177/J3
Les Alignements de Carnac,		Les Angles, Fr.	70/A5	Liddel Water (riv.),		Lima, Az, US	69/D6	Lima, Az, US	179/K1	Lind, Ger.	153/M3	Lithuania (ctry.)	41/H5	Little St. George	
Fr.	62/B5	Les Arcs, Fr.	70/C6	Li Xian, China	99/F2	Liddes, Swi.	66/D6	Lima (cap.), Peru	220/C4	Lind NP, Austl.	157/D3	Linwood, Ga, US	193/L7	Lithuania (ctry.)	195/F2
Les Avenières, Fr.	70/B1	Liddon (gulf), NW, Can.	71/T	Lidgerwood, ND, US	186/F4	Lima (riv.), Port.	52/A2	Linda, Ca, US	178/B2	Lindale, Ga, US	193/L7	Linwood, Mi, US	190/D3	Lituya (riv.), India	51/L3	Little Stour, Eng, UK	43/H4
Les Bauges (upland), Fr.	70/C1	Lavanto, It.	68/C5	Lidhoríkion, Gre.	55/G3	Lidgewood, ND, US	186/F4	Lidice, Czh.	65/H2	Lindau, Mn, US	187/P6	Linwu, China	99/G4	Litítpara, India	105/H2	Little Stukeley, Eng, UK	43/F2
Les Bois, Swi.	66/D3	Levashovo (arpt.), Rus.	75/T6	Lidice, Czh.	65/H2	Lidkoping, Swe.	46/E2	Lindau, Swi.	67/E3	Linxi, China	92/C4	Lítókhoron, Gre.	55/H2	Little Swatara	
Les Breuleux, Swi.	66/D3	Level, China	99/B2	Liancourt Rocks		Lidköping, Swe.	46/E2	Lindau, Ger.	71/E2	Linxia, China	90/E4	Litochoro, Gre.	55/H2	(cr.), Pa, US	198/B3
Les Bréviaires, Fr.	36/H5	Levee No. 33		(isls.), Asia	194/P10	Lidzbark, Pol.	49/K2	Linden (riv.), Neth.	58/D3	Linyanti (swamp), Bots.	140/D3	Litoo, Tanz.	141/G2	Little Tallapoosa	
Les Cayes, Haiti	207/H2	(canal), Il, US	197/P15	Liang, China	105/H2	Lidzbark Warmiński, Pol.	47/J4	Lindeman (chan.), Austl.	153/H5	Linyi, China	92/D3	Litovko, Rus.	91/M2	(riv.), Ga, US	192/E4
Les Cèdres, Qu, Can.	189/M7	Levan, Asia	194/P10	Liangcheng, China	103/G4	Lié (riv.), Fr.	62/C4	Lindenberg (peak), It.	226/C2	Linying, China	92/C4	Little Valley, NY, US	191/G3
Les Clayes-sous-Bois,		Levanger, Nor.	44/D3	Liangcun, China	99/F4	Liebenau, Aus.	65/H2	Lima Duarte, Braz.	223/N6	Linz am Rhein, Ger.	61/G2	Little Wabash (riv.),	
Fr.	36/H5	Levanna Centrale		Liangdang, China	99/F1	Liman, Rus.	77/H2	Limadkan, Ut, US	153/H5	Littabella NP, Austl.	158/D4	Il, US	192/C1
Les Contamines-Montjoie,		(mtn.), It.	70/D2	Liddell Water (riv.),		Liman, Rus.	77/H2	Limanowa, Pol.	49/L4	Linz, Aus.	65/H6	Littau, Swi.	67/E3	Little White (riv.),	
Fr.	66/C6	Levante, Riviera di		(riv.), Sc, UK	41/F2	Lima, Mt, US	177/G1	Linz (int'l arpt.), Aus.	65/H6	Littau, Swi.	67/E3	SD, US	184/D2
Les Diablerets		(coast), It.	68/C5	Lian Xian, China	99/G3	Limache, Bol.	224/C1	Linz am Rhein, Ger.	61/G2	Little Wichita (riv.),	
(range), Fr.	66/D5	Levanto, It.	68/C5	Liancourt, Fr.	60/B5	Limache, Chile	226/B2	Lizard (pt.), Eng, UK	42/A6	Little Wichita (riv.),		Tx,Ok, US	183/F4
Les Échelles, Fr.	70/B1	Levashovo (arpt.), Rus.	75/T6	Liancourt Rocks		Lido di Iesolo, It.	69/G2	Limal, Bol.	224/C2	Lizard (pt.), Eng, UK	42/A6	Little Wind (riv.), Wy, US	177/J3,J2
Les Escoumins, Qu, Can.	188/C1	Leven (lake), Sc, UK	39/C4	Liangjiadian, China	93/A3	Lido di Ostia, It.	71/B4	Liman, Rus.	77/H2	Limassol (dist.), Cyp.	116/C2	Little Wood (riv.), Id, US	177/F2
Les Essarts-le-Roi, Fr.	36/H5	Leven (lake), Sc, UK	39/C4	Liangshui, China	93/C2	Lizbark, Rus.	49/L2	Limassol, Cyp.	116/C2	Limavady (dist.), NI, UK	40/A2	Lioma, Moz.	141/H2		

Little Zab (riv.), Iraq	115/E3	Ljusterö, Swe.	45/B1
Littleborough, Eng. UK	41/F4	Lkst (peak), Mor.	128/C3
Littlefield, Tx, US	182/C4	Llabanere (int'l arpt.), Fr.	50/E5
Littlefield, Az, US	179/F2	Liaillay, Ch.	226/C3
Littlefork, Mn, US	187/H3	Llaima (vol.), Chile	226/C3
Littlehampton, Eng. UK	43/F5	Llallagua, Bol.	224/C1
Littleport, Eng. UK	43/G2	Llalli, Peru	220/C4
Littlerock, Ca, US	196/C1	Llanberis, Wal. UK	40/D4
Littlerock, Pa, US	198/A4	Llanberis, Pass of	
Littleton, Ire.	38/C4	Llandeilo, Wal. UK	40/C5
Littleton, NH, US	191/L2	Llandenny, Wal. UK	42/D3
Littleton, Co, US	184/B4	Llandovery, Wal. UK	40/C5
Littoral (prov.), Camr.	134/A4	Llandrillo, Wal. UK	40/E6
Litvinov, Czh.	65/G1	Llandrindod Wells,	
Lityn, Ukr.	78/E3	Wal. UK	42/C1
Liu (riv.), China	81/N6	Llandudno, Wal. UK	40/E5
Liuba, China	90/F5	Llandyssul, Wal. UK	40/E5
Liuche, China	99/G3	Llanelltyd, Wal. UK	40/D5
Liuchen, China	99/G3	Llanenddwyn, Wal. UK	40/D6
Liucheng, China	105/J3	Llanerchymedd, Wal. UK	40/C4
Liudongqiao, China	99/H2	Llanes, Sp.	52/C1
Liuduo, China	91/J5	Llanfair-Pwllgwyngyll,	
Liuhe, China	91/K3	Austl.	158/A1
Liuheng (isl.), China	99/M2	Lockhart River Aboriginal	
Liujing, China	106/E1	Community, Austl.	140/C1
Liukou, China	99/H2	Lockney, Tx, US	182/D3
Liukuei, Tai.	99/J4	Locknitz (riv.), Ger.	48/F2
Liuli, Tanz.	137/A4	Lockport, Mb, Can.	186/F2
Liulin, China	92/B3	Lockport, La, US	194/C3
Liushi, China	99/M2	Lockport, Il, US	197/P16
Liushuquan, China	111/F3	Lockwood (res.),	181/E2
Liuxi (riv.), China	99/G4	Lockwood, Eng. UK	
Liuyang, China	105/K2	Llano (riv.), Tx, US	180/E2
Liuyang (riv.), China	99/G2	Llano Estacado	
Liuzhou, China	99/F3	Locmariaquer, Fr.	62/C5
Liuzigang, China	99/G2	Llanos (plain), Col.,Ven.	209/B2
Livádhion, Gre.	55/H3	Llanquihue (lake), Chile	226/B4
Livanátai, Gre.	55/H3	Llanreaadr, Wal. UK	42/A3
Līvāni, Lat.	47/M3	Llanrian, Wal. UK	42/A3
Live Oak, Fl, US	195/G2	Llanrwst, Wal. UK	40/E5
Live Oak, Ca, US	176/C4	Llanthony, Wal. UK	40/E5
Livengood, Ak, US	201/J3	Llanuwchllyn, Wal. UK	40/D5
Livenza (riv.), It.	69/F2	Liata, Peru	220/B3
Liverdun, Fr.	61/F6	Llay, Wal. UK	41/F5
Liverdy-en-Brie, Fr.	36/L5	Locust Grove, Ok, US	193/H3
Livermore, Ca, US	184/B3	Lleida, Sp.	53/F2
Livermore, Me, US	191/L2	Llera de Canales, Mex.	205/F4
Livermore, Ky, US	192/D2	Llerena, Sp.	52/C3
Livermore, Ia, US	185/J6	Lleyn (pen.), Wal. UK	40/D6
Livermore (mt.), Tx, US	180/B2	Llica, Bol.	224/F1
Livermore Falls, Me, US	191/L2	Llico, Chile	226/B3
Liverpool (nbrhd.), Austl.	158/G8	Llivia, Sp.	50/D5
Liverpool, NS, Can.	188/E3	Llobregat (riv.), Sp.	53/F1
Liverpool (bay),		Llodio, Sp.	50/B5
NW, UK	170/C1	Llorente, Phil.	100/D3
Liverpool		Llosa, Gui.	
(cape), Nun, Can.	171/J1	Lodge Grass, Mt, US	177/K1
Liverpool, Eng. UK	41/F5	Lloyd (pt.), NY, US	199/M8
Liverpool (co.), Eng. UK	41/F5	Lloyd Harbor, NY, US	199/M8
Liverpool (bay), Wal. UK	41/E5	Lloydminster, Sk., US	175/K1
Liverpool, Pa, US	198/B2	Lloyds (riv.), Nf, Can.	189/J1
Liverpool, Tx, US	181/M9	Lluchmayor, Sp.	53/G3
Liverton, Eng. UK	41/H2	Llullaillaco	
Livet-et-Gavet, Fr.	70/B2	(vol.), Arg.,Chile	224/B3
Livilliers, Fr.	36/J4	Llwchwr (riv.), Wal. UK	42/B3
Livingston, Guat.	206/D3	Wal. UK	
Livingston, Sc, UK	39/C5	Llyn Brenig	
Livingston, Al, US	192/C4	(lake), Wal. UK	40/E5
Livingston, Tn, US	192/E1	Llyn Brianne	
Livingston (lake), Fl, US	194/M8	(res.), Wal. UK	42/C2
Livingston, Ky, US	192/E2	Llyn Efyrnwy	
Livingston, La, US	194/C2	(lake), Wal. UK	40/E6
Livingston (co.), Mi, US	190/F4	Llyn Tegid (lake), Wal. UK	40/E6
Livingston, Mt, US	177/H1	Llyn Trawsfynydd	
Livingston, NJ, US	199/H8	(lake), Wal. UK	40/D6
Livingston, Tn, US	192/E2	Llynfni (riv.), Wal. UK	42/C2
Livingston, Tx, US	181/G2	Lo Wu, China	99/G1
Livingston (lake), Tx, US	181/G2	Loa (riv.), Chile	209/C5
Livingston Manor,		Loanen, Neth.	
NY, US	191/J4	Loanda, Gabon	138/B3
Livingstone, Zam.	140/E3	Loano, Braz.	225/B2
Livingstone		Loange (riv.), D.R. Congo	138/D4
(range), Ab, Can.	174/G2	Loango Buele,	
Livingstone Memorial,		D.R. Congo	138/C4
Zam.	141/F2	Loanhead, Sc, UK	39/C5
Livingstone, Chutes de		Loano, It.	68/B5
(falls), Congo	138/C4	Loaoya (canal), Sp.	53/F2
Livingstonia, Malw.	137/A4	Loashi, D.R. Congo	139/G3
Livno, Bosn.	56/C4	Lobanskaya, Rus.	75/K2
Livny, Rus.	76/F1	Lobatse, Bots.	140/E5
Livojoki (riv.), Fin.	44/H2	Lobbes, Belg.	61/D3
Livonia, Mi, US	190/E3	Lobelville, Tn, US	192/D3
Livonia, La, US	194/C2	Lobenstein, Ger.	65/E2
Livonia, NY, US	191/H3	Loberia, Arg.	226/F3
Livorno, It.	68/D6	Lobethal, Austl.	155/M8
Livorno (prov.), It.	68/D6	Lobez, Pol.	49/H2
Livorno Ferraris, It.	68/B3	L'Obiou (peak), Fr.	70/B3
Livramento do Brumado,		Logan, Ut, US	177/H3
Braz.	223/E2	Lobitos, Peru	220/A2
Livron-sur-Drôme, Fr.	70/A2	Lobnya, Rus.	75/W8
Livry-Gargan, Fr.	36/K5	Lobo, Pic., C.d'Iv.	132/D5
L'ivs'ke (riv.), Ukr.	49/M4	Lobo, Tx, US	180/B2
Liwa, Chad	134/B2	Lobos, Arg.	191/J11
Liwa, Indo.	101/D4	Lobos (pt.), Chile	224/B2
Liwale, Tanz.	137/B4	Lobos Lake, BC, Can.	224/B4
Liwan, Sudan	135/G4	Lobos, Punta de	
Liwonde, Malw.	141/G2	(pt.), Chile	226/M9
Liwonde NP, Malw.	141/G2	Lobva, Rus.	75/P4
Lixin, China	99/H3	Loc (riv.), Fr.	
Lixin, China	92/C4	Loc Ninh, Viet.	106/D4
Lixnaw, Ire.	38/A5	Locana, It.	70/D2
Lixoúrion, Gre.	55/G3	Locarno, Swi.	67/E5
Lixus (ruin), Mor.	130/D2	Loch Haven Center,	
Liyang, China	92/D5	Fl, US	194/N6
Liyong, China	99/F3	Loch na Sealga	
Lizard, Eng. UK	42/A7	(inlet), Sc, UK	39/A1
Lizard (pt.), Eng. UK	42/A7	Loch Raven	
Lizard Point Ind. Res.,		(res.), Md, US	198/B5
Sk, Can.	186/D2	Lochaber (reg.), Sc, UK	39/A3
Lizella, It.	55/H3	Lochans, Sc, UK	40/E1
Lizifang, China	93/B3	Locharbriggs, Sc, UK	40/E1
Liziping, China	91/D6	Lochau, Aus.	67/F2
Lizy-sur-Ourcq, Fr.	60/C5	Lochawe, Sc, UK	39/A4
Ljubic, Serb.	56/C3	Lochboisdale, Sc, UK	37/Q8
Ljubija, Bosn.	56/C3	Lochearnhead, Sc, UK	39/B4
Ljubinje, Bosn.	56/D4	Lochem, Neth.	58/D4
Ljubljana (cap.), Slov.	51/L3	Loches, Fr.	50/D3
Ljubuški, Bosn.	56/C4	Lochgelly, Sc, UK	39/C4
Ljungan (riv.), Swe.	44/F3	Lochgilphead, Sc, UK	39/A4
Ljungby, Swe.	46/E3	Lochgoilhead, Sc, UK	39/A4
Ljungbyhed, Swe.	45/K6	Lochindorb, Sc, UK	39/C2
Ljungskile, Swe.	46/C2	Lochiel, SAfr.	143/E2
Ljusnan (riv.), Swe.	44/F3	Lochinvar, Austl.	157/K3
Ljusne, Swe.	46/G1	Lochinvar NP, Zam.	141/F2
Ljusterö (isl.), Swe.	47/H2	Lochmaben, Sc, UK	40/E1

Lochmaddy, Sc, UK	37/Q8	Lohman, Mo, US	183/H1
Lochów, Pol.	49/L2	Lohmar, Ger.	61/G2
Lochranza, Sc, UK	39/A5	Lohn, Tx, US	180/E2
Lochristi, Belg.	60/C1	Löhnberg, Ger.	64/B1
Lochwinnoch, Sc, UK	39/B5	Löhne, Ger.	59/F4
Lochy (lake), Sc, UK	39/B3	Lohne, Ger.	59/F3
Lochy (riv.), Sc, UK	39/B3	Loholoho, Indo.	103/F4
Lock, Austl.	155/G4	Loi-kaw, Myan.	98/C5
Lock Haven, Pa, US	191/H4	Loiano, It.	69/E5
Locke, Austl.	197/L10	Loica, Chile	226/N9
Locke (is.), Tx, US	195/G4	Loile (riv.), D.R. Congo	139/E3
Lockeford, Ca, US	176/C4	Loing (riv.), Fr.	60/B6
Lockeport, NS, Can.	188/E4	Loir (riv.), Fr.	50/D3
Lockerbie, Sc, UK	41/E1	Loir-et-Cher (dept.), Fr.	63/G5
Lockesburg, Ar, US	183/G4	Loire (dept.), Fr.	70/A2
Lockettville, Tx, US	182/C4	Loire (riv.), Fr.	29/E4
Lockhart, Fl, US	194/N6	Loire-Atlantique	
Lockhart, Tx, US	181/N7	(dept.), Fr.	62/D6
Lockhart Abor. Land,		Loiret (dept.), Fr.	60/B6
Austl.	139/H3	Loiron, Fr.	63/E4
Lockhart Abor. Rsv.,		Loita (hills), Kenya	137/A2
Austl.	158/A1	Loja, Ecu.	220/B2
Lockhart River Aboriginal		Loja (prov.), Ecu.	220/B2
Community, Austl.	140/C1	Løjt Kirkeby, Den.	46/C4
Lockney, Tx, US	182/D3	Loka, Sudan	135/F4
Locknitz (riv.), Ger.	48/F2	Lokandu, D.R. Congo	139/F3
Lockport, Mb, Can.	186/F2	Lökaö (isl.), Swe.	45/B1
Lockport, La, US	194/C3	Lökbatan, Azer.	115/G1
Lockport, Il, US	197/P16	Lökeren, Belg.	60/D1
Lockwood (res.),	181/E2	Lokhvytsya, Ukr.	79/G2
Lockwood, Eng. UK		Lokichar, Kenya	137/A1
Llano (riv.), Tx, US	180/E2	Lokichokio, Kenya	135/G4
Llano Estacado		Lokitaung, Kenya	135/G4
Locmariaquer, Fr.	62/C5	Lokka, Fin.	74/E2
Llanos (plain), Col.,Ven.	209/B2	Løkken, Den.	46/C3
Llanquihue (lake), Chile	226/B4	Lokoja, Rus.	47/P3
Llanreaadr, Wal. UK	42/A3	Loko, Nga.	133/G5
Llanrian, Wal. UK	42/A3	Lokofe, D.R. Congo	139/E3
Llanrwst, Wal. UK	40/E5	Lokoja, Nga.	133/G5
Llanthony, Wal. UK	40/E5	Lokoja (riv.), Ire.	38/A7
Llanuwchllyn, Wal. UK	40/D5	Lokolama, D.R. Congo	138/D3
Liata, Peru	220/B3	Lokolo, D.R. Congo	139/E3
Llay, Wal. UK	41/F5	Lokolo (str.), D.R. Congo	139/E3
Locust Grove, Ok, US	193/H3	Lokoti, Thai.	106/B2
Lleida, Sp.	53/F2	Lokomby, Madg.	143/H8
Llera de Canales, Mex.	205/F4	Lokomo, Camr.	138/C2
Llerena, Sp.	52/C3	Lokopo, Ugan.	137/A1
Lleyn (pen.), Wal. UK	40/D6	Lokori, Kenya	137/B1
Llica, Bol.	224/F1	Lökösháza, Hun.	56/E2
Llico, Chile	226/B3	Lokossa, Ben.	133/F5
Llivia, Sp.	50/D5	Lokot', Rus.	76/E1
Llobregat (riv.), Sp.	53/F1	Loks (isl.), Nun, Can.	171/K2
Llodio, Sp.	50/B5	Loksa, Est.	47/L2
Llorente, Phil.	100/D3	Lokwakangole, Kenya	135/G4
Lodge Grass, Mt, US	177/K1	Lola, Gui.	132/C5
Lloyd (pt.), NY, US	199/M8	Lolelia, Ugan.	137/A1
Lloyd Harbor, NY, US	199/M8	Lolgorien, Kenya	137/A2
Lloydminster, Sk., US	175/K1	Lolimo, D.R. Congo	139/E2
Lluchmayor, Sp.	53/G3	Loliondo, Tanz.	137/A2
Llullaillaco		Lolita, Tx, US	181/F3
(vol.), Arg.,Chile	224/B3	Lolkisale, Tanz.	137/B2
Llwchwr (riv.), Wal. UK	42/B3	Lollar, Ger.	64/B3
Wal. UK		Lolo (riv.), Gabon	138/C3
Llyn Brenig		Lolo, Mo, US	192/B2
(lake), Wal. UK	40/E5	Lolo, Mt, US	175/G4
Llyn Brianne		Lolo (peak), Mt, US	174/G4
(res.), Wal. UK	42/C2	Lolodorf, Camr.	138/B2
Llyn Efyrnwy		Lolui (isl.), Ugan.	137/A2
(lake), Wal. UK	40/E6	Lom, Bul.	57/F4
Llyn Tegid (lake), Wal. UK	40/E6	Lom (riv.), Camr.	134/B4
Llyn Trawsfynydd		Lomami, Kenya	137/A1
(lake), Wal. UK	40/D6	Lom Sak, Thai.	106/C2
Llynfni (riv.), Wal. UK	42/C2	Loma, Mt, US	177/J4
Lo Wu, China	99/G1	Loma, Co, US	180/F3
Loa (riv.), Chile	209/C5	Loenen, Neth.	
Loanen, Neth.		Loma, D.R. Congo	139/F4
Loanda, Gabon	138/B3	Loma Alta, Tx, US	180/D3
Loano, Braz.	225/B2	Loma Bonita, Mex.	206/C2
Loange (riv.), D.R. Congo	138/D4	Loma Linda, Ca, US	196/C2
Loango Buele,		Loma Mansa	
D.R. Congo	138/C4	(peak), SLeo.	132/C5
Loanhead, Sc, UK	39/C5	Löffingen, Ger.	67/E2
Loano, It.	68/B5	Loma Negra, Arg.	226/E3
Loaoya (canal), Sp.	53/F2	Lofoten (isle.), Nor.	44/D2
Loashi, D.R. Congo	139/G3	Loftus, Eng. UK	41/H2
Lobanskaya, Rus.	75/K2	Lofty (range), Austl.	154/C3
Lobatse, Bots.	140/E5	Loga, Niger	
Lobbes, Belg.	61/D3	Logan (Trudeau) (mt.)	
Lobelville, Tn, US	192/D3	Lombard, Il, US	197/P16
Lobenstein, Ger.	65/E2	Lombarda, Serra	
Loberia, Arg.	226/F3	Logan, Ks, US	184/E4
Lobethal, Austl.	155/M8	Lombardia (pol.reg.), It.	175/C3
Lobez, Pol.	49/H2	Logan, NM, US	180/C3
L'Obiou (peak), Fr.	70/B3	Lombardia, Mex.	204/E5
Logan, Ut, US	177/H3	Lombez, Fr.	52/C1
Lobitos, Peru	220/A2	Logan, Oh, US	197/H3
Lobnya, Rus.	75/W8	Logan, WV, US	193/G2
Lobo, Pic., C.d'Iv.	132/D5	Logan Int'l (General Edward	
Lobo, Tx, US	180/B2	Lawrence Logan)	
Lobos, Arg.	191/J11	(int'l arpt.), Ma, US	199/L3
Lobos (pt.), Chile	224/B2	Logan Lake, BC, Can.	191/L3
Lobos Lake, BC, Can.	224/B4	Logan Martin	
Lobos, Punta de		(lake), Al, US	192/D4
(pt.), Chile	226/M9	Logansport, La, US	180/F4
Lobva, Rus.	75/P4	Loganton, Pa, US	198/A1
Loc (riv.), Fr.		Logar (riv.), Afg.	147/J4
Loc Ninh, Viet.	106/D4	Loge (riv.), Ang.	138/C5
Locana, It.	70/D2	Logo, Ang.	138/C5
Locarno, Swi.	67/E5	Logone (riv.), Chad	134/B4
Loch Haven Center,		Logone Birni (pref.), Camr.	134/B3
Fl, US	194/N6	Logone Occ. (riv.), Chad	134/B3
Loch na Sealga		Logone-Occidental	
(inlet), Sc, UK	39/A1	(pref.), Chad	134/C3
Loch Raven		Logone-Oriental	
(res.), Md, US	198/B5	(pref.), Chad	134/C4
Lochaber (reg.), Sc, UK	39/A3	Lograto, It.	68/D3
Lochans, Sc, UK	40/E1	Logroño, Sp.	53/E1
Locharbriggs, Sc, UK	40/E1	Logrosán, Sp.	52/C3
Lochau, Aus.	67/F2	Lögstør, Den.	46/C3
Lochawe, Sc, UK	39/A4	Lögstrup, Den.	46/C3
Lochboisdale, Sc, UK	37/Q8	Løgstør, Den.	46/C3
Lochearnhead, Sc, UK	39/B4	Lohals, Den.	46/D4
Lochem, Neth.	58/D4	Lohärdaga, India	109/E4
Loches, Fr.	50/D3	Lohāru, India	107/B2
Lochgelly, Sc, UK	39/C4	Lohatlha, SAfr.	142/C3
Lochgilphead, Sc, UK	39/A4	Lohberg, Ger.	42/C3
Lochgoilhead, Sc, UK	39/A4	Londerzeel, Belg.	61/D2
Lochindorb, Sc, UK	39/C2	Lohfelden, Ger.	59/G6
Lochiel, SAfr.	143/E2	Lohiani, Kenya	137/A2
Lochinvar, Austl.	157/K3	Lohja, Fin.	47/L1
Lochinvar NP, Zam.	141/F2	Lohjanjärvi (lake), Fin.	47/K1
Lochmaben, Sc, UK	40/E1	London, On, Can.	190/F3

London (cap.), UK	36/C2	Longhua (pass), China	99/F3
London, Ky, US	192/E2	Longhua, China	92/D2
London, Oh, US	190/E5	Longhui, China	99/F3
London, Tanz.	137/B2	Longido, Tanz.	137/B2
London Bridge, Az, US	174/D4	Longjiang, China	91/J2
London Colney, Eng. UK	36/C1	Longjie, Phil.	100/D3
London (reef), Nic.	207/F3	Longjumeau, Fr.	36/J5
London, City of		Longkou, China	92/F3
		Longlac, On, Can.	187/L3
Londonderry (dist.),		Longli, China	105/J2
NI, UK	40/A2	Longmen, China	106/E1
Londonderry, NI, UK	40/A2	Longmen Shiyao, China	99/D3
Londonderry		Longmont, Co, US	184/B3
Longmen Shiyao, China		Longnan, China	99/G3
Londonderry (isl.), Chile	191/C7	Longnan, Eng. UK	99/G3
Londonderry (Eglinton)		Longnor, Eng. UK	41/F5
Londres, Arg.	224/C3	Longny-au-Perche, Fr.	63/F2
Londrina, Braz.	225/G2	Longo, Congo	138/D2
Londuimbali, Ang.	140/B2	Longojo, Ang.	140/B2
Lone, Ger.		Longonot (peak), Kenya	137/B2
Lone Butte, BC, Can.	174/D2	Lorian (swamp), Kenya	137/B1
Lone Grove, Ok, US	183/F3	Loriano, Col.	
Lone Pine, Ca, US	178/C2	Lorient, Fr.	62/B5
Lone Pine Ind. Res.,		Lorient (Lann-Bihoué)	
Fr.	60/A3	(arpt.), Fr.	62/B5
Lone Pine Sanct., Austl.	158/B3	L'Oriental	
Lone Rock, Sk, US	175/K1	(pol. reg.), Mor.	130/C3
Lone Star, Tx, US	183/G4	L'Orignal, On, Can.	191/J2
Lone Wolf, Ok, US	182/E4	Lorillard, Nun, Can.	170/G2
Longan, China	99/F2	Longriba, China	90/E5
Long (lake), Sc, UK	39/A2	Loriol-sur-Drôme, Fr.	70/A3
Long (mtn.), Wal. UK	42/C1	Loris, SC, US	193/H3
Long (pt.), Mi, US	181/G1	Lorman, Ms, US	194/C2
Long, Ak, US	201/G3	Lorne, Austl.	157/J3
Long (lake), Mi, US	186/D4	Lorne Park, On, Can.	190/T8
Longview, La, US	194/C2	Loro Ciuffenna, It.	69/E6
Longugué-Jumelles, Fr.	63/E6	Lorosquel (peak), Kenya	137/A2
Longué, Rus.	175/M3	Lorquin, Fr.	61/G6
Longueil-Annel, Fr.	60/B5	Lörrach, Ger.	66/C2
Longuenesse, Fr.	53/F1	Lorraine (plat.), Fr.	48/D4
Longuesse, Fr.	36/H4	Lorraine (pol. reg.), Fr.	36/D4
Longuyon, Fr.	61/E5	Lorraine (reg.), Fr.	61/E5
Longview, Ms, US	39/A2	Lorraine (pol.reg.), Fr.	61/E5
Longview, Tx, US	181/G1	Lorrha, Ire.	38/B3
Longview, Ab, Can.	174/G2	Lorsch, Ger.	64/B3
Lorton, Eng. UK	41/E2	Loro, D.R. Congo	139/E3
Longwa, China	99/G3	Lorton, Va, US	193/J1
Longwood, Fl, US	194/N6	Lorup, Ger.	59/E3
Longwood, NC, US	193/H3	Los Alamitos, Ca, US	196/C3
Longwood Gardens,		Los Álamos, Mex.	180/D3
Pa, US	198/C3	Los Álamos, NM, US	180/B3
Longworth, Tx, US	180/D1	Los Aldamas, Mex.	182/A2
Longxi, China	90/E4	Los Alerces, PN, Arg.	226/C4
Longxingkshi, China	99/G3	Los Altos, Arg.	224/C3
Longyan, China	99/H3	Los Altos, Ca, US	196/K12
Longyearbyen, Nor.	80/D3	Loubomo, Congo	138/C4
Longyou, China	99/H2	Los Amates, Guat.	206/D3
Longzhou, China	103/H3	Los Andes, Col.	216/B4
Loni, India	110/D5	Los Andes, Chile	226/N8
Lonigo, It.	69/E3	Los Angeles	
Löningen, Ger.	59/F4	Los Angeles (co.), Ca, US	
Lonkin, Myan.	98/C3	Los Angeles, Ca, US	196/B2
Lonneker, Neth.	58/D4	Los Angeles (riv.), Ca, US	196/B2
Lonoke, Ar, US	183/J3	Los Angeles, Chile	226/B3
Lonquimay, Arg.	226/B3	Los Angeles (int'l arpt.), Ca, US	196/F8
Lons-le-Saunier, Fr.	66/B4	Los Angeles, Chile	226/B3
Lonsee, Ger.	46/F3	Louessé (riv.), Congo	
Lonton, Myan.	98/C3	Los Angeles (aqueduct), Ca, US	178/C3
Long Eaton, Eng. UK	41/G6	Los Angeles Outer	
Long Grove, Il, US	197/P15	(har.), Ca, US	196/F9
Long Hill, Ct, US	199/E1	Looc, Phil.	100/C2
Long Island, Ks, US	184/E4	Los Aquijes, Peru	220/C4
Long Island MacArthur		Los Aztecas, Mex.	205/F4
(arpt.), NY, US	199/M8	Los Barrios, Sp.	52/C4
Long Ketiok, Indo.	103/E3	Los Canarreos	
Long Key (isl.), Fl, US	195/H5	(arch.), Cuba	207/F1
Long Lake, SD, US	186/D5	Los Cardales, Arg.	191/J11
Long Lake Ind. Res.,		Los Castillos, PN, Arg.	224/C2
Lookout (cape), NC, US	193/J3	Los Cerrillos, Uru.	191/K1
Long Lake NWR, ND, US	186/D4	Los Charrúas, Arg.	224/E4
Long Lane, Mo, US	183/H2	Los Chaves, NM, US	179/J3
Long Lelang, Malay.	100/A5	Los Chonos (arch.),	
Long Mynd, The		Chile	209/B7
(hill), Eng. UK	42/D1	Los Cóndores, Arg.	224/C4
Long op Zand, Neth.	58/C5	Los Corrales de Buelna,	
Long Phu, Viet.	106/D4	Louisa, Chile	193/F1
Long Plain Ind. Res.,		Louisa, Va, US	193/H1
Long Pond, Me, US	191/L2	Los Coyotes Ind. Res.,	
Loos, Fr.	60/C2	Ca, US	196/D3
Long Prairie, Mn, US	187/G5	Loose Creek, Mo, US	183/J1
Loose, BC, Can.	174/D1	Los Cusis, Bol.	221/E4
Long Range		Los Fresnos, Tx, US	182/A4
(mts.), Nf, Can.	189/H2	Los Glaciares, PN, Arg.	171/B6
Lop (lake), China	90/C3	Los Herreras, Mex.	180/E5
Lop Buri, Thai.	106/C3	Louisiade (arch.), PNG	160/E2
Long Semado, Malay.	100/H2	Los Katios, PN, Col.	216/B3
Long Sutton, Eng. UK	41/J6	Los Lagos, Chile	226/B3
Long Valley, NJ, US	199/D2	Los Lagos	
Lomblen (isl.), Indo.	103/F5	(pol. reg.), Chile	226/B4
Long Xian, China	90/F5	Louisiana, La, US	191/H3
Long Xuyen, Viet.	106/D4	Louisiana (state), US	188/E4
Long, Loch (inlet), Sc, UK	39/A4	Louisiana, Mo, US	185/J4
Longa, Ang.	140/C2	Los Llanos de Aridane,	
Lomé (cap.), Togo	133/F5	Sp.	128/A3
Longá (riv.), Braz.	219/F3	Louisville, Co, US	184/B4
Lomé (int'l arpt.), Togo	133/F5	Los Lunas, NM, US	179/J3
Long'an, China	105/J3	Louisville, Ga, US	191/G1
Lopez, Phil.	100/C2	Louisville, Il, US	192/C1
Long Beach (Daugherty Field)		Lopez (cape), Gabon	138/C4
(arpt.), Ca, US	196/B2	Los Mármoles, PN,	
Long Branch, NJ, US	199/E3	Mex.	206/B3
Long Buckby, Eng. UK	43/E2	Los Menucos, Arg.	205/F4
Long Cay (isl.), Bahm.	207/F2	Los Mochis, Mex.	204/C3
Long Chau, Viet.	98/C3	Lopik, Neth.	58/C5
Long Crag (hill), Eng. UK	39/E6	Los Molinos, Ca, US	176/B3
Long Creek, Or, US	176/D1	Los Monos, Arg.	226/C5
Long Crendon, Eng. UK	43/F3	Lopori (riv.), D.R. Congo	139/E2
Long Ditton, Eng. UK	36/C2	Los Mosquitos,	
Long Eaton, Eng. UK	41/G6	Loppa, Nor.	44/G1
Long Grove, Il, US	197/P15	Los Muermos, Chile	226/B4
Long Hill, Ct, US	199/E1	Loppi, Fin.	47/L1
Long Island, Ks, US	184/E4	Lopurankovka, Rus.	77/H4
Los Navalmorales, Sp.	52/C3	Loum, Camr.	138/B1
Los Navaluciilos, Sp.	52/C3	Loup (riv.), Fr.	70/C5
Longchamps, Belg.	61/E3	Los Nevados, PN, Col.	219/K8
Longchuan, China	105/G3	Lora del Rio, Sp.	52/C4
Lomme, Fr.	60/C2	Los Olmos, Tx, US	184/E3
Longchuan (riv.), China	58/C6	Loraine, Oh, US	180/D1
Lomnice, Czh.	49/J3	Los Órganos, Peru	220/A2
Lomnice nad Lužnicí,		Loup City, Ne, US	184/E3
Czh.	65/H4	Los Padres National Forest,	
Longdale, Oh, US	183/E2	Ca, US	196/B1
Longde, China	90/F4	Loralai, Pak.	113/J2
Lomond (lake), Sc, UK	39/C4	Loral, Ca, US	196/K12
Lomond (hills), Sc, UK	39/C4	Los Palacios y Villafranca,	
Lomond, Ab, Can.	175/H2	Sp.	52/C4
Lomonosov, Rus.	75/S7	Lorch, Ger.	64/C5
Lomonosovka, Rus.	75/R9	Lord Howe (isl.), Austl.	151/J7
Lomontai, It.	68/D3	Lorch, Ger.	67/F1
Longeville-en-Barrois, Fr.	61/E6	Longovicz, Pol.	
Longeville-lès-Metz, Fr.	61/F5	Lordsburg, NM, US	179/H4
Longeville-lès-Saint-Avold,		Los Pingüinos, PN, Chile	191/C7
Fr.	61/F5	Los Pinos (riv.), Co, US	180/B3
Longfellow, It.	68/B3	Lords Lake Nat'l Wild. Ref.,	
Lomomoc, Cu.	49/L2	ND, US	186/D3
Longfield, Eng. UK	36/D2	Los Ranchos de Albuquerque,	
Lomża, Pol.	49/M2	NM, US	179/J3
Longfield (co.), Eng. UK	43/F3	Los Reyes, Mex.	205/R10
Longford, Austl.	156/D4	Los Reyes de Salgado,	
Lönaväle, India	107/B2	Mex.	204/E5
Longford, Ire.	38/C2	Lorengau, PNG	160/D5
Longford (co.), Ire.	38/C2	Lorenz (riv.), Indo.	103/J5
Lomcopué, Arg.	226/C3	Los Ríos (prov.), Ecu.	220/B1
Loncoche, Chile	226/B3	Lorentz (riv.), Indo.	103/J5
Londiani, Kenya	137/A2	Los Roques (isls.), Ven.	216/D5
Londiani, Kenya	137/A2	Longguang, China	99/F3
Londinières, Fr.	63/G3	Lorenzo, SC, US	182/D4
London, On, Can.	190/F3	Longhoughton, Eng. UK	39/E6
Longguan, China	99/F5	Lorenzo Geyres, Uru.	226/F2

Loreo, It.	69/F3	Los Sauces, Chile	226/B3
Lorestān (gov.), Iran	115/G3	Louts (riv.), Fr.	53/E1
Los Tamariscos, Arg.	226/C5	Loútsa, Gre.	55/P9
Loreto, Ecu.	216/D2	Louvain (Leuven), Belg.	61/D2
Loreto (state), Peru	69/G7	Los Teques, Ven.	
Loreto, Phil.	100/D3	Los Telares, Arg.	192/E4
Loreto, Braz.	219/E4	Louveira, Braz.	223/K8
Loreto, Col.	220/D1	Los Vientos, Chile	
Loreto, Bol.	221/E4	Los Vilos, Chile	184/B4
Loreto, Par.	225/E2	Louviers, Co, US	63/G2
Loreto Nat'l Rsv., Kenya	204/C3	Lousheim, Ger.	61/F4
Loreto, Mex.	204/C3	Loskharévka, Ukr.	79/H4
Loreto (int'l arpt.), Mex.	204/C3	Louvroil, Fr.	60/C3
Loreto Aprutino, It.	184/B3	Lovaart (riv.), Belg.	60/B1
Lorette, Mb, Can.	186/F3	Lovat' (riv.), Bela.,Rus.	47/P3
Loretteville, Qu, US	188/A1	Lovčenac, Serb.	56/D3
Loretto, Tn, US	192/D3	Love, Fr.	66/B3
Loretto, Ky, US	192/E2	Lovech (prov.), Bul.	55/J1
Lorgues, Fr.	67/E1	Lovech, Bul.	55/J1
Lorian (swamp), Kenya	137/B1	Losser, Neth.	58/E4
Lorica, Col.	36/K4	Lossie (riv.), Sc, UK	39/C1
Lorient, Fr.	62/B5	Lossiemouth, Sc, UK	184/B3
Lorient (Lann-Bihoue)		Lössnitz, Ger.	65/F1
(arpt.), Fr.	62/B5	Lost (lake), Ca, US	177/J1
L'Oriental		Lossoganeu (hill), Tanz.	137/B3
(pol. reg.), Mor.	130/C3	Lost (riv.), Or, US	176/C2
L'Orignal, On, Can.	191/J2	Lost Creek (res.), Or, US	176/C2
Lorillard, Nun, Can.	170/G2	Lost Creek, WV, US	193/G1
Longriba, China	90/E5	Loverna, Sk, Can.	175/K2
Loriol-sur-Drôme, Fr.	70/A3	Loves Park, Il, US	185/K2
Loris, SC, US	193/H3	Lovilia, Ia, US	185/H3
Lorman, Ms, US	194/C2	Loving, NM, US	180/B1
Lorne, Austl.	157/J3	Lovington, Va, US	193/H2
Lorne Park, On, Can.	190/T8	Lovington, NM, US	182/C4
Loro Ciuffenna, It.	69/E6	Lovios, Sp.	52/A2
Lorosquel (peak), Kenya	137/A2	Lost River (range),	
Lorquin, Fr.	61/G6	Id, US	177/G1
Lörrach, Ger.	66/C2	Lost River Caverns,	
Lorraine (plat.), Fr.	48/D4	Lóvua, Ang.	138/E4
Lorraine (pol. reg.), Fr.	36/D4	Lost Springs, Ks, US	183/F1
Lorraine (reg.), Fr.	61/E5	Lost (des.), Or, US	176/C2
Lorraine (pol.reg.), Fr.	61/E5	Low (cape), Nun, Can.	171/H2
Lorrha, Ire.	38/B3	Lostallo, Swi.	
Lorsch, Ger.	64/B3	Lostwithiel, Eng. UK	42/B6
Loro, D.R. Congo	139/E3	Lowa (riv.), D.R. Congo	119/E5
Lorton, Va, US	193/J1	Lostwood NWR, ND, US	186/C3
Lorup, Ger.	59/E3	Lowdham, Eng. UK	41/H6
Los Alamitos, Ca, US	196/C3	Lowe Farm, Mb, Can.	186/F3
Los Álamos, Mex.	180/D3	Löwe (riv.), Ger.	
Los Álamos, NM, US	180/B3	Lowell, In, US	190/C4
Los Aldamas, Mex.	182/A2	Lowell, Oh, US	190/F5
Los Alerces, PN, Arg.	226/C4	Lowell (lake), Id, US	176/E2
Los Altos, Arg.	224/C3	Lowell, Or, US	176/C2
Los Altos, Ca, US	196/K12	Lowell, Id, US	176/F4
Loubomo, Congo	138/C4	Lowell Observatory,	
Los Amates, Guat.	206/D3	Az, US	179/G3
Los Andes, Col.	216/B4	Löwenstein, Ger.	64/C4
Los Andes, Chile	226/N8	Lower (lake), Nf, Namb.	142/B2
Los Angeles		Lowestoft, Eng. UK	43/J2
Los Angeles (co.), Ca, US	196/B2	Lowick, Eng. UK	39/E5
Los Angeles, Ca, US	196/B2	Lower Ganges	
Los Angeles (riv.), Ca, US	196/B2	(canal), India	108/B2
Los Angeles, Chile	226/B3	Lower Granite	
Los Angeles (int'l arpt.), Ca, US	196/F8	(gorge), Az, US	50/F3
Los Angeles, Chile	226/B3	Lower Heyford, Eng. UK	43/E3
Louessé (riv.), Congo		Lower Hutt, NZ	159/H9
Los Angeles (aqueduct), Ca, US	178/C3	Lower Kalskag, Ak, US	201/F3
Los Angeles Outer		Lower Klamath	
(har.), Ca, US	196/F9	NWR, Ca, US	176/C2
Looc, Phil.	100/C2	Lower Klamath	
Los Aquijes, Peru	220/C4	NWR, Ca, US	176/C2
Los Aztecas, Mex.	205/F4	Lower Mesa	
Los Barrios, Sp.	52/C4	(falls), Id, US	177/H1
Los Canarreos		Lower Monumental	
(arch.), Cuba	207/F1	(dam), Wa, US	174/E4
Los Cardales, Arg.	191/J11	Lower Nazeing, Eng. UK	36/D1
Los Castillos, PN, Arg.	224/C2	Lower Otay	
Los Cerrillos, Uru.	191/K1	(lake), Ca, US	196/D5
Los Charrúas, Arg.	224/E4	Lower Peach Tree,	
Los Chaves, NM, US	179/J3	Al, US	194/E2
Los Chonos (arch.),		Lower Red	
Chile	209/B7	(lake), Mn, US	187/G4
Los Cóndores, Arg.	224/C4	Lower Rhine, Neth.	58/C5
Los Corrales de Buelna,		Lower Rouge	
Chile	193/F1	(riv.), Mi, US	197/E7
Louisa, Va, US	193/H1	Lower Sioux Ind. Res.,	
Los Coyotes Ind. Res.,		Mn, US	185/G1
Ca, US	196/D3	Lower Stoke, Eng. UK	36/E2
Loose Creek, Mo, US	183/J1	Lower Suwannee Nat'l	
Los Cusis, Bol.	221/E4	Wild. Ref., Fl, US	195/G3
Los Fresnos, Tx, US	182/A4	Lower Trajan's Wall	
Los Glaciares, PN, Arg.	171/B6	(wall), Mol.,Ukr.	57/J3
Los Herreras, Mex.	180/E5	Lower Tunguska	
Louisiade (arch.), PNG	160/E2	(riv.), Rus.	83/J3
Los Katios, PN, Col.	216/B3	Lower Wedgeport,	
Los Lagos, Chile	226/B3	NS, Can.	188/E4
Los Lagos		Lower West Pubnico,	
(pol. reg.), Chile	226/B4	NS, Can.	188/E4
Louisiana, La, US	191/H3	Lower Zambezi NP, Zam.	141/F2
Louisiana (state), US	188/E4	Loxa (riv.), Wa, US	194/M7
Louisiana, Mo, US	185/J4	Lowick, Eng. UK	39/E5
Los Llanos de Aridane,		Lowicz, Pol.	49/K2
Sp.	128/A3	Lowman, Id, US	176/F1
Louisville, Co, US	184/B4	Lowell, In, US	
Los Lunas, NM, US	179/J3	Lower City, Mo, US	183/G1
Louisville, Ga, US	191/G1	Lowther (hills), Sc, UK	39/C6
Louisville, Il, US	192/C1	Loxton, SAfr.	142/C3
Los Mármoles, PN,		Lourches, Fr.	
Mex.	206/B3	Lourdes, Nf, Can.	189/H1
Los Menucos, Arg.	205/F4	Loxton, SAfr.	142/C3
Los Mochis, Mex.	204/C3	Loxton North, Austl.	
Lopik, Neth.	58/C5	Lourdes, Fr.	50/C5
Los Molinos, Ca, US	176/B3	Lourdes/Tarbes	
Los Monos, Arg.	226/C5	(int'l arpt.), Fr.	
Lopori (riv.), D.R. Congo	139/E2	Loya, Tanz.	137/A3
Los Mosquitos,		Loyal, Wi, US	185/J1
Loppa, Nor.	44/G1	Loyal, Ky, US	193/F2
Los Muermos, Chile	226/B4	Loyalton, Ca, US	176/C3
Loppi, Fin.	47/L1	Loyalton, Pa, US	198/B2
Lopurankovka, Rus.	77/H4	Loyalty (isls.), NCal., Fr.	160/F7
Los Navalmorales, Sp.	52/C3	Loyalty (isls.), NCal., Fr.	160/F7
Los Navaluciilos, Sp.	52/C3	Loyes, Bela.	78/F2
Longchamps, Belg.	61/E3	Loyne (lake), Qu, US	75/M4
Los Nevados, PN, Col.	219/K8	Loysburg, Pa, US	198/A3
Lora del Rio, Sp.	52/C4	Loysville, Pa, US	198/A3
Los Olmos, Tx, US	184/E3	Loxstedt, Ger.	59/F2
Loup City, Ne, US	184/E3	Lozanne, Fr.	
Los Padres National Forest,		Lourdes, Fr.	
Ca, US	196/B1	Loxton, SAfr.	142/C3
Loralai, Pak.	113/J2	Loyno (lake), Rus.	54/D2
Loral, Ca, US	196/K12	Loznica, Bul.	57/H4
Los Palacios y Villafranca,		Loznitsa, Bul.	57/H4
Sp.	52/C4	Lozova, Ukr.	79/J3
Lorch, Ger.	64/C5	Lozovik, Serb.	56/D3
Lord Howe (isl.), Austl.	151/J7		

Column 1

Lozym, Rus. 75/L3
Lü (isl.), Tai. 99/J4
Lu (mtn.), China 92/C5
Lu (peak), China 99/G2
Lu Xian, China 105/J2
Lua (riv.), D.R. Congo 138/D2
Lua Dekere (riv.), D.R. Congo 140/D1
Luabo, Moz. 141/H3
Luacano, Ang. 140/D1
Luachimo, Ang. 139/E4
Luachimo (riv.), Ang. 139/E5
Luaco, Ang. 139/E4
Luaha-Sibuha, Indo. 101/B3
Luala (riv.), D.R. Congo 119/E5
Lualaba (riv.), D.R. Congo 139/E2
Luali, D.R. Congo 138/C4
Luambe NP, Zam. 141/G2
Luampa, Zam. 140/E2
Luampa (riv.), Zam. 140/E2
Luan (riv.), China 81/M5
Lu'an, China 92/D5
Luan Xian, China 92/D3
Luancheng, China 99/F4
Luanchuan, China 92/B4
Luanco, Sp. 52/C1
Luanda (prov.), Ang. 138/C5
Luanda, Kenya 137/A1
Luanda (cap.), Ang. 138/C5
Luando (riv.), Ang. 138/D5
Luando, Rsv. Nat. do, Ang. 140/C1
Luang (peak), Thai. 106/B4
Luang (lag.), Malay. 105/H6
Luangue (riv.), Ang. 138/D5
Luangue, Ang. 138/D5
Luanginga (riv.), Ang. 140/D2
Luangwa (riv.), Zam. 139/G5
Luanhaizi, China 90/C5
Luano (int'l arpt.), D.R. Congo 141/E2
Luanping, China 92/D2
Lüderitz, Namb. 142/A2
Luanshya, Zam. 141/F2
Luao (riv.), D.R. Congo 139/E5
Luao, Ang. 139/E5
Luapula (riv.), Zam. 139/G5
Luapula (prov.), Zam. 139/G5
Luarca, Sp. 52/B1
Luashi, D.R. Congo 139/F3
Luatize (riv.), Moz. 141/F2
Luau (riv.), Ang. 139/E5
Luba, EqG. 138/B2
Lubaantun (ruin), Belz. 206/D2
Lubaczów, Pol. 49/M3
Lubalo, Ang. 138/D5
Lubań, Pol. 49/H3
Lubāna, Lat. 47/M3
Lubang (isl.), Phil. 100/B2
Lubang, Phil. 100/C2
Lubango, D.R. Congo 139/F3
Lubango, Ang. 140/B2
Lubansenshi (riv.), Zam. 139/G5
Lubao, D.R. Congo 139/F4
Lubartów, Pol. 49/K2
Lubawa, Pol. 49/K2
Lübbecke, Ger. 61/D2
Lubbock, Tx, US 187/H4
Lubefu, D.R. Congo 139/E4
Lubefu (riv.), D.R. Congo 139/F4
Lubelska (uplands), Pol. 49/M3
Lubelskie (prov.), Pol. 49/M3
Lubenka, Kaz. 77/K2
Lubero, D.R. Congo 139/G3
Lubero (riv.), D.R. Congo 139/G3
Lubéron, Montagne de (mts.), Fr. 70/B5
Lubi (riv.), D.R. Congo 139/F4
Lubień Kujawski, Pol. 49/K2
Lubika, D.R. Congo 139/G4
Lubilash (riv.), D.R. Congo 139/E4
Lubue (riv.), D.R. Congo 138/D4
Lubukianggau, Indo. 101/C3
Lubukpakam, Indo. 101/C2
Lubuksikaping, Indo. 101/C2
Lubumbashi, D.R. Congo 141/E1
Lubunda, D.R. Congo 139/F4
Lubunza, D.R. Congo 139/F3
Lubuskie (prov.), Pol. 49/H2
Lubutu, D.R. Congo 139/F3
Lubwe, Zam. 139/F3
Luc An Chau, Viet. 106/D1
Luc-en-Diois, Fr. 70/B3
Luc-sur-Mer, Fr. 63/E2
Lucala, Ang. 138/C5
Lucala (riv.), Ang. 138/C5
Lucan, Ire. 40/B5
Lucan, On, Can. 193/N7
Lucania (mt.), Yk, Can. 201/K3
Lücaoshan, China 90/D4
Lucapa, Ang. 139/E4
Lucas, Ks, US 187/H2
Lucas, Tx, US 180/L6
Lucas González, Arg. 191/J10
Lucasville, Oh, US 193/H2
Lucca, It. 68/D6
Lucciana, Fr. 54/A1
Lucé, Fr. 59/H2
Luce (bay), Sc, UK 40/D2
Luce Bayou (riv.), Tx, US 181/M8
Lucedale, Ms, US 203/G3
Lucélia, Braz. 225/G2
Lucena, Phil. 100/C2
Lucena del Cid, Sp. 53/E2
Lucena, Sp. 52/C4
Lučenec, Slvk. 49/K4
Lucens, Swi. 66/C4

Column 2

Lucerna, Peru 220/D4
Lucerne (lake), Ca, US 196/C1
Lucerne, Wv, US 177/J2
Lucerne, Wa, US 174/D3
Lucerne (Luzern), Swi. 51/H3
Lucerne (Vierwaldstättersee) (lake), Swi. 67/E3
Lucero (lake), NM, US 182/A4
Lucero (mesa), NM, US 179/K4
Luché-Pringé, Fr. 63/F3
Luchegorsk, Rus. 91/L2
Lucheng, China 92/C3
Lucheng, China 99/F3
Lucheringo (riv.), Moz. 141/G2
Lüchow, Ger. 48/F2
Luchuan, China 105/K3
Lucia, It. 68/D4
Lucia, Ca, US 178/B4
Lucija (bay), Ang. 140/B2
Lucindale, Austl. 156/B3
Lucira, Ang. 140/B2
Lucisant, Fr. 63/G4
Luíza, D.R. Congo 139/E4
Luján, Arg. 191/J11
Luján, Arg. 224/C5
Lujiang, China 92/D5
Lukavac, Bosn. 56/D3
Luke (A.F.B.), Az, US 179/F4
Lukeni (mt.), Austl. 154/C3
Lukeville, Az, US 179/F5
Lukhovitsy, Rus. 74/H5
Lukhovo (riv.), D.R. Congo 139/E5
Lukolela, D.R. Congo 138/D3
Lukolela, D.R. Congo 139/F4
Lukovit, Bul. 57/G4
Luków, Pol. 49/M3
Lukoyanov, Rus. 75/K5
Lukuga, D.R. Congo 139/G4
Lukula, D.R. Congo 138/C4
Lukula, D.R. Congo 138/C4
Lukulu, Zam. 140/D2
Lükün, D.R. Congo 139/E4
Lukunor (isl.), Micr. 160/F4
Lukusashi (riv.), Zam. 141/F2
Lukusuzi NP, Zam. 141/G2
Lukwesa, India 108/A3
Lukwesa, D.R. Congo 139/G5
Luleå, Swe. 74/D2
Luleälven (riv.), Swe. 44/G2
Lüleburgaz, Turk. 57/H5
Lules, Arg. 224/C3
Luling, China 105/H2
Lüliáni, Pak. 110/C4
Luliang, China 105/H2
Ludell, Ks, US 184/D4
Lüdenscheid, Ger. 59/E6
Lüderitz, Namb. 142/A2
Ludesar, India 110/C5
Ludershall, Eng, UK 43/E4
Ludhiāna, India 110/C4
Ludian, China 105/H2
Luding, China 98/D2
Luding, China 105/H2
Ludingen, China 59/E5
Ludington, Mi, US 190/C3
Ludlow, Ca, US 186/E4
Ludlow, Pa, US 191/G4
Ludlow, Vt, US 191/K3
Ludlow, Eng, UK 43/E4
Ludowici, Ga, US 195/H3
Ludvika, Swe. 46/E1
Ludwigshausen, Ger. 59/E5
Ludwigs (canal), Ger. 65/E4
Ludwigsburg, Ger. 64/C5
Ludwigsfelde, Ger. 48/G2
Ludwigshafen, Ger. 67/F2
Ludwigslust, Ger. 48/F2
Ludwigsstadt, Ger. 65/E2
Ludza, Lat. 47/M3
Lüdza, D.R. Congo 139/F4
Luebo, D.R. Congo 139/E4
Lueders, Tx, US 187/H5
Lueki, D.R. Congo 139/F4
Luena (riv.), Zam. 139/G5
Luena (flats), Zam. 140/D2
Luena, D.R. Congo 139/F4
Luengue (riv.), Ang. 140/D3
Luengue (riv.), Moz. 141/G3
Lueta (riv.), D.R. Congo 139/E4
Lüeyang, China 90/F5
Lufeng, China 99/G4
Lufico, D.R. Congo 138/C4
Lumigny-Nesles-Ormeaux, Fr. 36/C5
Lufira, D.R. Congo 139/F5
Lufkin, Tx, US 180/G2
Lufu, D.R. Congo 138/C4
Lufupa (riv.), Zam. 139/G4
Lufupa (riv.), Zam. 139/G2
Luga, Rus. 47/N2
Luga (riv.), Rus. 47/N2
Lugano, Swi. 69/D2
Lugagnano Val d'Arda, It. 67/E6
Lugano (lake), It. 67/E6
Lugu, Swi. 67/E6
Lumut, Malay. 101/C1
Lugards (falls), Kenya 137/B2
Lugavčina, Serb. 56/E3
Lugazi, Ugan. 139/H2
Lügde, Ger. 59/H5
Lügenda (riv.), Moz. 141/H2
Luganache, Ang. 140/D2
Lunahuaná, Peru 220/B4
Lunar Crater, Nv, US 186/E3
Lunay, Fr. 63/F5
Luncarty, Sc, UK 39/C4
Lund, Swe. 46/E4
Lund, Nv, US 177/F4
Lund, Ut, US 180/D1
Lundazi, Zam. 141/G2

Column 3

Lui (riv.), Zam. 140/D2
Luia, Ang. 139/E5
Luia (riv.), Moz. 141/G2
Luia (riv.), Moz. 140/D1
Luiana, Ang. 140/D3
Luichart (lake), Sc, UK 39/B1
Luidaogou, China 105/K3
Luigi Ridolfi (arpt.), It. 69/F5
Luilaka (riv.), D.R. Congo 139/E3
Luilu (riv.), D.R. Congo 139/E4
Luino, It. 69/F6
Luis B. Sánchez, Mex. 204/D1
Luis Correia, Braz. 219/F3
Luís Domingues, Braz. 219/F3
Luisant, Fr. 63/G4
Luíza, D.R. Congo 139/E4
Luján, Arg. 191/J11
Luján, Arg. 224/C5
Lujiang, China 92/D5
Lúkácsháza, Hun. 56/C2
Lukala, D.R. Congo 138/C4
Lukanga (swamp), Zam. 140/E2
Luke (A.F.B.), Az, US 179/F4
Luke (mt.), Austl. 154/C3
Lukenie (riv.), D.R. Congo 139/E3
Lukinjärvi (lake), Fin. 45/L4
Lünne, Ger. 59/E4
Luntai, China 111/D2
Lunz, Nv, US 176/D4
Lunzu, China 141/G2
Luo (riv.), China 92/B4
Luobei, China 91/L2
Luobuzhuang, China 111/E4
Luocheng, China 99/F3
Luodian, China 105/H3
Luoding, China 99/F4
Luofu (peak), China 99/F4
Luohe, China 92/C4
Luojing, China 105/K3
Luoma (lake), China 92/D4
Luonan, China 92/B4
Luong (riv.), Zam. 139/G5
Luoning, China 92/B4
Luoping, China 98/E3
Luoqiao (riv.), China 99/H3
Luoqing (riv.), China 99/F4
Luoshan, China 92/C4
Luoshuikan, China 105/H3
Luotian, China 99/G2
Luoxu, China 99/H1
Luoyang, China 99/F3
Luoyang, China 99/F3
Luoyukou, China 92/B3
Luozi, D.R. Congo 138/C4
Lupa Market, Tanz. 137/A4
Lupane, Zim. 140/D2
Lupanshui, China 98/E3
Lupeni, Rom. 57/F3
Lupire, Ang. 140/C2
Lupiro, Tanz. 141/G4
Lupon, Phil. 100/D4
Luputa, D.R. Congo 139/F4
Luqa (int'l arpt.), Malta 53/S16
Luqu, China 90/E5
Luquan, China 98/D3
Luquembo, Ang. 138/D5
Luremo (falls), Ang. 139/G5
Luráville, Fl, US 195/G2
Luray, Ks, US 184/E4
Luray, Va, US 193/G1
Lure, Fr. 66/C2
Lure, Montagne de (mts.), Fr. 70/B4
Lureco (riv.), Moz. 141/H2
Lurgan, NI, UK 40/B3
Luri, Fr. 54/A1
Luribay, Bol. 224/C1
Lurín, Peru 220/B4
Lúrio, Moz. 141/J2
Lúrio (riv.), Moz. 141/H2
Lurnfeld, Aus. 51/K3
Lurøy, Nor. 44/E2
Lurton, Ar, US 183/H3
Lusahunga, Tanz. 139/H3
Lusaka (cap.), Zam. 141/F2
Lusaka (int'l arpt.), Zam. 141/F2
Lusaka (prov.), Zam. 141/F2
Lusambo, D.R. Congo 139/E4
Lusange, Ang. 139/H4
Lusanga, D.R. Congo 138/D4
Lusenga NP, Zam. 139/G5
Lusengo, D.R. Congo 138/D2
Lush (mt.), Austl. 152/B4
Lushan, China 92/B4
Lushi, China 92/B4
Lushnjë, Alb. 55/F5
Lushoto, Tanz. 137/B3
Lushui, China 98/C3
Lüshun, China 98/D3
Lusignan, Fr. 50/D3
Lusk, Ire. 40/B5
Lusk, Wy, US 184/B2
Luso, Ang. 140/C1
Luss, Sc, UK 39/B4
Lustenau, Aus. 51/H3
Lustre, Mt, US 175/M3
Lutembo (riv.), Ang. 140/D2
Luther (pass), Ca, US 178/B1
Luther, Mt, US 190/D2
Luther, Tx, US 180/C4
Lutherans, Swi. 66/D3
Lutherville, Md, US 196/B5
Lützjenburg, Ger. 48/F1
Lütjenburg (isl.), Ger. 48/F1
Luton (co.), Eng, UK 43/F3
Luton, Eng, UK 43/F3
Lutong, Malay. 102/D3
Lutry, Swi. 66/C4
Lutselk'e, NW, Can. 170/G2
Lutsen, Mn, US 187/J4
Lutshima, D.R. Congo 138/D4
Lutshima (riv.), D.R. Congo 138/D4
Luts'k, Ukr. 44/F2
Lutterbach, Fr. 63/F5
Lutsetter, Ger. 59/H2
Lutterworth, Eng, UK 41/G1
Lutuhyne, Ukr. 44/F2
Lutz, Fr. 67/K3

Column 4

Lunenburg, NS, Can. 188/E3
Lunenburg, Vt, US 191/L2
Lunenburg, Va, US 193/H2
Lunestedt, Ger. 59/F2
Lunéville, Fr. 51/G2
Lung (riv.), Ire. 38/B7
Lung Kwu Chau (isl.), China 99/V7
Lunga (riv.), Zam. 141/F2
Lunga, West (riv.), Zam. 141/E2
Lunga-Lunga, Kenya 137/B3
Lungdo, China 111/D5
Lungi (Freetown) (int'l arpt.), SLeo. 132/B4
Lunglei, India 105/F4
Lungsang, China 111/E6
Lungtian, India 98/B4
Luni (riv.), India 104/B3
Luninets, Bela. 76/C1
Lunino, Rus. 77/H1
Luninyets, Bela. 76/C1
Lunita, La, US 193/M7
Lunkinjärvi (lake), Fin. 45/L4
Lüntai, China 111/D2
Lunzu, Malw. 141/G2
Luo (riv.), China 92/A2
Luobei, China 91/L2
Luobuzhuang, China 111/E4
Luoye, China 99/G2
Luyi, China 92/C4
Lysyye Gory, Rus. 77/H2
Luynes, Fr. 63/F5
Luz (coast), Port.,Sp. 52/B4
Luz, Braz. 222/D3
Luza, Braz. 75/L3
Luza, Braz. 75/K3
Luzarches, Fr. 36/K4
Luzein, Swi. 67/E3
Luzern (canton), Swi. 66/E3
Luzern (co.), Pa, US 198/B1
Luzhai, China 105/J3
Luzhou, China 92/C4
Lüzhi (riv.), China 98/E3
Luzhou, China 98/E2
Luziânia, Braz. 219/D3
Luzilândia, Braz. 219/F3
Lužnice (riv.), Czh. 49/H4
Luzon (isl.), Phil. 100/C1
Luzon (str.), Phil. 160/A3
Lužnice (riv.), Czh. 51/L2
Luzzara, It. 69/D4
Luzzi, It. 54/E3
L'viv, Ukr. 78/C3
L'vivs'ka Oblast, Ukr. 78/B2
Lwala (peak), Ugan. 139/G5
Lwena Mission, Zam. 139/G5
Lwi (riv.), Myan. 106/C2
Lwela (riv.), Zam. 139/G5
Lyady, Rus. 47/N2
Lyakhovichi, Bela. 76/C1
Lyantonde, Ugan. 139/G3
Lyapin (riv.), Rus. 75/P2
Lychett Matravers, Eng, UK 42/D5
Lycksele, Swe. 44/F2
Lycoming (co.), Pa, US 198/A1
Lydd, Eng, UK 43/G5
Lydia, La, US 194/C3
Lydney, Eng, UK 41/E3
Lyell (mt.), BC, Can. 174/F2
Lyell Brown (mt.), Austl. 155/F2
Lyepel', Bela. 47/N4
Lyford, Tx, US 181/F4
Lykens, Pa, US 185/B2
Lyle, Mn, US 185/H2
Lyle, Wa, US 174/D5
Lyles, Tn, US 192/D3
Lyleton, Mb, Can. 186/D3
Lyman, Ms, US 177/H3
Lyman, Ut, US 179/G1
Lyman, Wy, US 184/B1
Lyman, SC, US 192/C3
Lyme (bay), Eng, UK 50/B1
Lyme Regis, Eng, UK 41/E5
Lymington, Eng, UK 43/E5
Lynbrook, NY, US 199/L9
Lynch, Ky, US 188/D3
Lynch, Md, US 198/B5
Lynch Station, Va, US 193/H2
Lynchburg, Ms, US 192/B3
Lynchburg, Oh, US 193/G1
Lynchburg, Tn, US 192/F1
Lynches (riv.), SC, US 193/H3
Lynd, Austl. 154/B2
Lynden, Wa, US 174/C3
Lyndhurst, NJ, US 197/J8
Lyndhurst, Austl. 155/H4
Lyndhurst, Austl. 157/D1
Lyndon, Ks, US 185/F2
Lyndon, Vt, US 191/K2
Lyndon B. Johnson (lake), Tx, US 181/E4
Lyndon B. Johnson Nat'l Hist. Park, Tx, US 181/E4
Lyndon B. Johnson Space Center, Tx, US 181/M9
Lyndonville, Vt, US 191/K2
Lyne, Eng, UK 41/F1
Lyness, Sc, UK 37/G2
Lyngby, Den. 45/J7
Lyngdal, Nor. 45/J7
Lynge, Den. 45/J7
Lyngen (inlet), Nor. 44/G1
Lynher (riv.), Eng, UK 42/B6
Lynn, Ma, US 191/G3
Lynn, In, US 193/G3
Lynn Haven, Fl, US 195/C4
Lynnwood, Wa, US 174/C4
Lynton, Eng, UK 42/C4
Lyntupy, Bela. 47/M4
Lynx (lake), NW, Can. 170/G2
Lynx, Fr. 70/A1

Column 5

Lutz, Fl, US 194/L7
Lützow-Holm (bay), Ant. 227/C
Luuk, Phil. 100/C5
Luumäki, Fin. 47/M1
Luoyang, Wu, US 191/L2
Luvern, Al, US 195/G4
Luverne, Mn, US 185/G2
Luvo, Ang. 138/C4
Luvozero, Rus. 42/H3
Luvuei, D.R. Congo 140/D2
Luvua (riv.), D.R. Congo 139/F5
Luwego (riv.), Tanz. 141/G3
Luwembe, Zam. 141/F2
Luwero, Ugan. 139/H2
Luwingu, Zam. 139/G5
Lux, Fr. 66/A2
Luxapallila (cr.), Al, US 192/C4
Luxembourg (ctry.) 61/E4
Luxembourg (cap.), Lux. 61/F4
Luxembourg (prov.), Belg. 61/E4
Luxembourg, Wi, US 190/C2
Luxeuil-les-Bains, Fr. 66/C2
Luxi, China 99/F2
Luxi, China 98/C3
Luxico (riv.), Ang. 138/D5
Luxikou, China 99/G2
Luxor (int'l arpt.), Egypt 124/B2
Luxora, Ar, US 192/C3
Luxu, China 99/J2
Luy (riv.), Fr. 53/E1
Lüyang, China 93/A2
Luye, Fr. 70/C3
Luyi, China 92/C4
Lysyye Gory, Rus. 77/H2
Lytham Saint Anne's, Eng, UK 41/E4
Lytkarino, Rus. 75/W9
Lytle (cr.), Ca, US 183/H4
Lytle Creek, Ca, US 196/C2
Lyttelton, NZ 159/C3
Lytton (canton), Swi. 66/E3
Lytton, BC, Can. 174/D2
Lytton, Ia, US 187/H1
Lyuban', Bela. 76/D1
Lyubar, Ukr. 78/F2
Lyubech, Ukr. 78/F2
Lyubertsy, Rus. 75/W9
Lyubeshiv, Ukr. 78/C2
Lyubimets, Bul. 57/H5
Lyubinovo, Rus. 76/E1
Lyubotyn, Ukr. 79/H3
Lyudinovo, Rus. 76/E1
Lyud (riv.), Wal, UK 42/C3

Column 6

Lyon (Satolas) (int'l arpt.), Fr. 66/B6
Lyon, Peru 220/D4
Lyon (lake), Sc, UK 39/B3
Lyon (canal), Co, US 182/C1
Lyon (mtn.), NY, US 191/K2
Lyon (cap.), Fr. 68/F6
Lyon (cr.), Mi, US 197/F6
Lyonne (riv.), Fr. 70/B2
Lyons (riv.), Austl. 154/C3
Lyons, Ga, US 193/F4
Lyons, In, US 192/F1
Lyons, Ks, US 185/E3
Lyons, NY, US 191/H3
Lyons, Wi, US 197/P14
Lyons Falls, NY, US 188/E3
Lys (reef), PNG 160/E5
Lyra (reef), PNG 41/F5
Lys-lez-Lannoy, Fr. 60/C2
Lysá (peak), Czh. 49/K4
Lysá nad Labem, Czh. 65/H2
Lysaker, Nor. 46/D2
Lysaya (hill), Bela. 47/M4
Lysekil, Swe. 46/C2
Lyseren (lake), Nor. 44/B8
Lysica (peak), Pol. 49/L3
Lysina (peak), Czh. 65/F2
Lys'va, Rus. 75/N4
Lytham Saint Anne's, Eng, UK 41/E4

Column 7 (Macareo / M)

Macareo Santo Niño, Ven. 217/F2
Macari, Peru 220/D4
Macarthur, Austl. 156/B3
Macau, Braz. 219/G4
Macau (dpcy.), China 83/L7
Macau (cap.), Macau 99/G4
Macau (mesa), Mi, US 197/G6
Macau, North Branch (cr.), Mi, US 197/E7
Macauley (isl.), NZ 160/G7
Macaya (riv.), Col. 216/C4
Macaya, Pic de (peak), Haiti 207/H2
Macaya (riv.), Col. 216/C4
Macclenny, Fl, US 195/G2
Macclesfield (canal), Eng, UK 41/F5
Macclesfield, Eng, UK 41/F5
Maccomb (co.), Mi, US 197/G6
Macomb, Il, US 185/J3
Macomer, It. 54/A2
Mâcon, Fr. 68/F6
Macon, Ga, US 195/F3
Macon, Il, US 185/K4
Macon (cr.), Mi, US 197/E7
Macon, Mo, US 185/H4
Macon, Ms, US 192/C4
Macon, North Branch (cr.), Mi, US 197/E7
Maconcourt, Fr. 66/B1
Macondo, Ang. 140/D2
Macondo (riv.), Ang. 140/D2
Macosquin, Sp. 40/B1
Macotera, Sp. 52/C2
Macoun, Sk, Can. 186/G3
Macoupin (cr.), Il, US 185/K4
Macouria, Fr.Gu. 217/J2
Macovane (pt.), Moz. 141/G4
Macquarie (isl.), Port. 128/A2
Macquarie (lake), Austl. 157/E1
Macquarie (riv.), Austl. 155/F2
Macroom, Ire. 38/B6
Macrorie (mt.), Sk, Can. 175/L2
MacTier, On, Can. 191/G2
Macuelizo, Hon. 206/D3
Macuira, PN, Col. 216/D1
Macuma (riv.), Ecu. 222/C4
Macumba (riv.), Austl. 145/C3
Macusani, Peru 220/D4
Macuspana, Mex. 206/C2
Macuzari, Presa (res.), Mex. 204/C3
Macy, Ne, US 185/F2
Madaba, Jor. 117/D3
Mādabā, Jor. 117/C3
Madagali, Nga. 134/B3
Madagascar (ctry.) 143/H8
Madā'in Ṣāliḥ, SAr. 125/M7
Madā'in Ṣāliḥ, SAr. 125/M7
Madama, Niger 126/B4
Madan, Bul. 55/J2
Madanapalle, India 107/C3
Madang (int'l arpt.), PNG 153/G4
Madang (prov.), PNG 153/G4
Madaoua, Niger 133/G3
Madaripur, Bang. 109/G4
Madaroúnfa, Niger 133/G3
Madawaska, Me, US 189/G1
Madawaska (riv.), On, Can. 191/H2
Madaya, Myan. 106/B1
Madayeno (riv.), Rus. 91/K1
Maddaket, Ma, US 188/D5
Madden (dam), Pan. 216/B2
Maddock, ND, US 186/E4
Made, Neth. 58/B5
Madeir, Sudan 135/E4
Madeira (isl.), Port. 128/A2
Madeira (riv.), Bol. 225/E2
Madeira, Iles de la (isl.), Qu, Can. 171/K4
Madeira Beach, Fl, US 194/K8
Madeira Park, BC, Can. 174/B3
Madelegabel (peak), Ger. 67/G3
Madeleine, Magd. 143/H7
Madeleine, Iles de la (isl.), Qu, Can. 171/K4
Madelia, Mn, US 185/G1
Madeline, Fl, US 195/E1
Madeline (isl.), Wi, US 187/J4
Maden, Turk. 114/D2
Madera, Mex. 204/C3
Madera, Ca, US 186/B3
Madera Canyon, Az, US 179/G5
Maderas (vol.), Nic. 207/E4
Madgaon (Margao), India 107/C3
Madhipura, India 109/F3
Madhira, India 107/D2
Madhubani, India 109/F3
Madhupur, India 109/F3
Madhvapur, India 108/A3
Madhwāpur, India 108/A3
Madhya Pradesh (state), India 104/C3
Madi Opei, Ugan. 139/G3
Madibogo, SAfr. 142/J7
Madibira, Tanz. 137/A4
Madidi (riv.), Bol. 224/C1
Madikwe, SAfr. 141/G5
Madill, Ok, US 183/H5
Madimba, D.R. Congo 138/C4
Madín al Abyār (ruin), Libya 126/D2
Madīnat al 'Āshir min Ramaḍān (cap.), Egypt 131/N4
Madīnat as Sādāt, Egypt 131/N4
Madīnat ash Sha'b, Yem. 136/C2
Madīnat ash Thawrah, Syria 114/D3
Madīnat Dīmai (ruin), Egypt 131/B5
Madingo-Kayes, Congo 138/C2
Madingou, Congo 138/C2
Madiravalo, Madg. 143/H7
Madison, Sk, Can. 175/K2
Madison, Al, US 192/D3
Madison, Ar, US 192/B3
Madison, Ct, US 197/E2
Madison, Fl, US 195/G2
Madison, In, US 188/C3
Madison, Mn, US 185/F1
Madison, Mo, US 185/K4
Madison, Mt, US 172/D2

Column 8 (Macomb / Madison)

Macomb (co.), Mi, US 197/G6
Macomb, Il, US 185/J3
Macomer, It. 54/A2
Mâcon, Fr. 68/F6
Macon, Ga, US 195/F3
Macon, Il, US 185/K4
Macon (cr.), Mi, US 197/E7
Macon, Mo, US 185/H4
Macon, Ms, US 192/C4
Maconcourt, Fr. 66/B1
Macondo, Ang. 140/D2
Macondo (riv.), Ang. 140/D2
Macosquin, Sp. 40/B1
Macotera, Sp. 52/C2
Macoun, Sk, Can. 186/G3
Macoupin (cr.), Il, US 185/K4
Macouria, Fr.Gu. 217/J2
Macovane (pt.), Moz. 141/G4
Macquarie (isl.), Port. 128/A2
Macquarie (lake), Austl. 157/E1
Macquarie (riv.), Austl. 155/F2
Macroom, Ire. 38/B6
Macrorie (mt.), Sk, Can. 175/L2
MacTier, On, Can. 191/G2
Macuelizo, Hon. 206/D3
Macuira, PN, Col. 216/D1
Macuma (riv.), Ecu. 222/C4
Macumba (riv.), Austl. 145/C3
Macusani, Peru 220/D4
Macuspana, Mex. 206/C2
Macuzari, Presa (res.), Mex. 204/C3
Macy, Ne, US 185/F2
Madaba, Jor. 117/D3
Mādabā, Jor. 117/C3
Madagali, Nga. 134/B3
Madagascar (ctry.) 143/H8
Madā'in Ṣāliḥ, SAr. 125/M7
Madama, Niger 126/B4
Madan, Bul. 55/J2
Madanapalle, India 107/C3
Madang (int'l arpt.), PNG 153/G4
Madang (prov.), PNG 153/G4
Madaoua, Niger 133/G3
Madaripur, Bang. 109/G4
Madaroúnfa, Niger 133/G3
Madawaska, Me, US 189/G1
Madawaska (riv.), On, Can. 191/H2
Madaya, Myan. 106/B1
Madden (dam), Pan. 216/B2
Maddock, ND, US 186/E4
Made, Neth. 58/B5
Madeir, Sudan 135/E4
Madeira (isl.), Port. 128/A2
Madeira (riv.), Bol. 225/E2

Column 9 (far right — Madison / Madre)

Madison, Ne, US 184/F2
Madison, NJ, US 199/H9
Madison, Oh, US 190/E4
Madison, SD, US 185/F1
Madison, Va, US 193/H1
Madison, Wi, US 198/K3
Madison, WV, US 193/G1
Madison Heights, Mi, US 197/F6
Madison Heights, Va, US 193/H2
Madisonville, Ky, US 192/D2
Madisonville, Tn, US 194/C2
Madisonville, Tn, US 192/E3
Madisonville, Tx, US 181/G1
Madiun, Indo. 101/E4
Madjingo, Gabon 138/C2
Mado Gashi, Kenya 137/B1
Madoc, On, Can. 191/H2
Madoi, China 90/D5
Madona, Lat. 47/M3
Madone d'Utelle (peak), Fr. 70/D5
Madong, China 105/K3
Madongchuan, China 90/F4
Madras, Or, US 176/C1
Madras (Chennai), India 107/D3
Madre (lag.), Mex. 205/F3
Madre de Deus de Minas, Braz. 223/M6
Madre de Dios (riv.), Bol.,Peru 209/C4
Madre de Dios (isl.), Chile 191/A6
Madre de Dios (dept.), Peru 220/D3
Madredeiras, Bol. 221/F5
Madrid, Col. 219/L8
Madrid (dist.), Sp. 52/C2
Madrid, Sp. 52/C2
Madridejos, Sp. 52/D3
Madrigal, Peru 220/D4
Madrigal de las Altas Torres, Sp. 52/C2
Madrigalejo, Sp. 52/C3
Madrisahorn (peak), Swi. 67/F4
Madroñera, Sp. 52/C3
Madsen, On, Can. 187/H2
Maduda, D.R. Congo 138/C4
Madugula, India 107/D2
Madura (isl.), Indo. 83/L10
Madura, Austl. 154/E4
Madurai, India 107/C4
Madzharovo, Bul. 57/J5
Mae Chan, Thai. 106/B1
Mae Charim, Thai. 106/C2
Mae Hong Son, Thai. 106/B1
Mae Ping NP, Thai. 106/B2
Mae Ramat, Thai. 106/B2
Mae Sai, Thai. 106/B1
Mae Sariang, Thai. 106/B2
Mae Sot, Thai. 106/B2
Mae Taeng, Thai. 106/B2
Mae Tho (peak), Thai. 106/B2
Mae Ya (mtn.), Thai. 106/B2
Maebashi, Japan 97/F2
Maella, Sp. 53/F2
Maengsan, NKor. 93/D3
Maenza, It. 71/C4
Maep'o, SKor. 93/E4
Maerne, It. 69/F2
Maeser, Ut, US 177/J3
Maevatanana-Ambanivohitra, Madg. 143/H7
Maewo (isl.), Van. 160/F6
Mafeking, Mb, Can. 186/D1
Mafeteng, Les. 142/G3
Maffe, Belg. 61/E3
Maffra, Austl. 157/C3
Mafia (chan.), Tanz. 137/B4
Mafia (isl.), Tanz. 137/B4
Mafikeng, SAfr. 142/P12
Máfil, Chile 226/B3
Mafou (riv.), Gui. 132/C4
Mafra, Port. 53/P10
Mafra, Braz. 225/F1
Mafungabusi (plat.), Zim. 141/F3
Magadanskaya Oblast, Rus. 81/R4
Magadi, Kenya 137/B2
Magadino, Swi. 67/G5
Magalhães de Almeida, Braz. 219/F3
Magalia, Ca, US 176/C4
Magalies Berg (mts.), SAfr. 142/P12
Magaliesburg, SAfr. 142/P12
Magallanes, Phil. 100/C2
Magallanes y Antártica Chilena (prov.), Chile 191/C7
Magamba, CAfr. 134/C4
Magangué, Col. 216/C2
Magaria, Niger 133/H3
Magat (riv.), Phil. 100/C1
Magazine, Ar, US 183/H3
Magazine (mtn.), Ar, US 183/H3
Magdagachi, Rus. 91/K1
Magdalena, Arg. 191/K11
Magdalena, Bol. 221/E4
Magdalena (dept.), Col. 216/C2
Magdalena, Bol. 221/F4
Magdalena (peak), Malay. 100/B4
Magdalena, Mex. 204/C2
Magdalena de Kino, Mex. 204/C2
Magdeburger Börde (ledge), Ger. 48/F3
Magdalena Cays (isl.), Austl. 145/C2
Magdalene Cays (isl.), Austl. 145/C2
Magé, Braz. 223/N7
Mage-shima (isl.), Japan 96/B5
Magee, Ms, US 194/D2
Magee (isl.), NI, UK 40/C2
Magee, Ms, US 194/D2
Magellan (str.), Arg.,Chile 209/B8
Magenta, It. 68/B3
Magenta (lake), Austl. 154/C5

Mager – Manza
306

Magerøya (isl.), Nor. 44/H1
Magetan, Indo. 101/E4
Maggia (riv.), Swi. 67/E5
Maggia, Swi. 67/E5
Maggio (peak), It. 69/E7
Maggiorasca (peak), It. 68/C4
Maggiore (peak), It. 71/D5
Maggiore (peak), It. 71/B2
Maggiore (peak), It. 69/E6
Maggiore (lake), It. 72/F1
Maghāghah, Egypt 159/F2
Maghama, Mrta. 132/B3
Maghar, India 108/D2
Maghār, Isr. 117/C3
Maghdūshah, Leb. 117/C1
Maghera (peak), Ire. 38/B4
Maghera, NI, UK 40/B2
Magherafelt, NI, UK 40/B2
Magherafelt (co.), NI, UK 40/B2
Maghila (peak), Tun. 130/L7
Maghnia, Alg. 130/D2
Magic (res.), Id, US 177/F2
Magic Kingdom, Fl, US 194/M7
Magilligan, NI, UK 40/B1
Magilligan (pt.), NI, UK 40/B1
Magione, It. 71/B1
Maglaj, Bosn. 56/D3
Magliano de'Marsi, It. 71/C3
Magliano Sabina, It. 71/B3
Maglić (peak), Mont. 56/D4
Maglie, It. 55/F2
Maglod, Hun. 57/R10
Magnac-Laval, Fr. 50/D3
Magnet, Ga, US 193/M7
Magnetawan, On, Can. 191/G2
Magnetawan (riv.), On, Can. 190/F2
Magnetic Passage, Austl. 158/B2
Magnitka, Rus. 75/N5
Magnitogorsk, Rus. 75/N5
Magnitogorsk (int'l arpt.), Rus. 75/N5
Magnolia, Ar, US 183/H4
Magnolia, Ms, US 194/C2
Magnolia, Tx, US 181/G2
Magnolia, De, US 198/C5
Magny-en-Vexin, Fr. 60/A5
Magny-les-Hameaux, Fr. 36/J5
Mago NP, Eth. 135/H4
Mágoè, Moz. 141/F2
Magog, Qu, Can. 191/K2
Magor, Wal, UK 42/D3
Magoye, Zam. 141/E3
Magra (riv.), It. 68/C4
Magrath, Ab, Can. 175/H3
Magreta, It. 69/D4
Magsaysay, Phil. 100/D3
Maguan, China 106/D1
Maguarinho (cape), Braz. 218/D3
Magude, Moz. 141/G5
Magugnano, It. 69/D2
Māgura, Bang. 109/G4
Magway (Magwe), Myan. 98/B4
Magway (div.), Myan. 105/F4
Magyichaung, Myan. 105/F3
Maha Sarakham, Thai. 106/C2
Mahābād, Iran 115/F2
Mahabe, Madg. 143/H7
Mahabe, Madg. 143/H8
Mahābhārat (range), Nepal 108/C1
Mahabo, Madg. 143/H8
Mahaboboka, Madg. 143/H7
Mahād, India 107/B2
Mahadday Weyn, Som. 136/C5
Mahadeo (range), India 108/A4
Mahaena, FrPol. 161/X15
Mahāgama, India 109/F3
Mahagi, D.R. Congo 139/G2
Mahagi-Port, D.R. Congo 139/G2
Mahaica, Guy. 217/G3
Mahaica-Berbice (pol. reg.), Guy. 217/G3
Mahaicony Village, Guy. 217/G3
Mahajamba (bay), Madg. 143/H6
Mahajamba (riv.), Madg. 143/H7
Mahajanga, Madg. 143/H6
Mahajanga (prov.), Madg. 143/H6
Mahajilo (riv.), Madg. 143/H7
Mahakali (zone), Nepal 108/C1
Mahakam (riv.), Indo. 103/E3
Mahalapye, Bots. 141/E4
Mahale Mts. NP, Tanz. 139/G4
Maḩallāt, Iran 115/G3
Maḩallat Marḩūm, Egypt 131/B3
Maḩallat Minūf, Egypt 131/B3
Mahalpur, India 110/D4
Maham, India 110/D5
Māhān, Iran 115/J4
Māhān (riv.), India 108/D4
Mahānadī (riv.), India 104/D3
Mahananda (riv.), India 109/F3
Mahandiabani (riv.), C.d'Iv. 132/D4
Mahanje, Tanz. 137/A4
Mahanoro, Madg. 143/J7
Mahanoy (cr.), Pa, US 198/B2
Mahanoy City, Pa, US 198/B2
Mahantago (cr.), Pa, US 198/B2
Mahantango (mtn.), Pa, US 198/B2
Mahao, China 91/K3
Mahārājganj, India 109/E2
Mahārājganj, India 108/D2
Mahārajpur, India 104/C2
Mahārāshtra (state), India 104/B4
Mahāsamund, India 107/D1
Mahāshān (ruin), Bang. 109/G3
Mahasoabe, Madg. 143/H8
Maḩaţţat Ḑab'ah, Jor. 117/E5
Mahavavy (riv.), Madg. 143/H7
Mahawa (riv.), India 108/B1
Mahaxai, Laos 98/E5
Mahazoarivo, Madg. 143/H8
Mahazoma, Madg. 143/H7
Mahbūbābād, India 107/D2
Mahd adh Dhahab, SAr. 112/D4
Mahdia, Guy. 217/G3
Mahdia, Tun. 130/M7
Mahdia (gov.), Tun. 130/M7
Mahe, India 113/L2
Mahébourg, Mrts. 143/T15
Mahendragiri (peak), India 107/E2
Mahendranagar, Nepal 108/C1
Mahenge, Tanz. 137/B4
Maheno, NZ 159/B4
Mahesāna, India 113/K4
Mahespur, Bang. 109/G4
Mahezhen, China 90/E4
Mahgawān, India 108/B2
Mahia (pen.), NZ 145/H6
Mahilyow, Bela. 47/P5
Mahilyow (int'l arpt.), Bela. 47/P5
Mahilyowskaya Voblasts, Bela. 47/P5
Mahīshādal, India 109/F4
Mahitsy, Madg. 143/H7
Mahlaing, Myan. 98/B4
Mahlberg, Ger. 66/D1
Mahlow, Ger. 48/Q7
Mahmel (peak), Alg. 72/E4
Maḩmūd-e 'Erāqī, Afg. 113/J1
Mahmūdābād, India 108/C2
Mahmudiye, Turk. 114/B2
Mahnomen, Mn, US 186/G4
Mahoba, India 108/B3
Mahon (riv.), Ire. 38/C5
Mahón, Sp. 53/H3
Mahone Bay, NS, Can. 188/E3
Mahoning (riv.), Oh, US 190/F4
Mahroni, India 108/B3
Mahtomedi, Mn, US 187/Q6
Mahuanggou, China 90/D4
Mahur, India 98/B3
Mahusekwa, Zim. 141/F3
Mahuta, Tanz. 137/B4
Mahuva, India 107/A1
Mahwah, India 108/A2
Mahwah, NJ, US 199/J7
Mai-Ndombe (lake), D.R. Congo 138/D3
Maia, Port. 52/A2
Maiala Nat'l Pk., Austl. 158/E6
Maials, Sp. 53/F2
Maiana (isl.), Kiri. 160/G4
Maiao (isl.), FrPol. 161/W15
Maicao, Col. 216/C2
Maîche, Fr. 66/C3
Maicuru (riv.), Braz. 217/H5
Maiden (cr.), Pa, US 198/C2
Maiden Newton, Eng, UK 42/D5
Maidenhead, Eng, UK 43/F3
Maidens, Sc, UK 39/B6
Maidi, Indo. 103/G3
Maidstone, On, Can. 197/G7
Maidstone, Eng, UK 43/G4
Maidstone, Sk, Can. 175/K1
Maiduguri, Nga. 134/B3
Maie, D.R. Congo 139/G2
Maienfeld, Swi. 67/F4
Maigatari, Nga. 133/H3
Maigue (riv.), Ire. 38/B4
Maihar, India 108/C3
Maihara, Japan 95/K5
Maijdi, Bang. 109/H4
Maikala (range), India 108/C4
Maiko (riv.), D.R. Congo 139/F3
Maiko, PN de la, D.R. Congo 139/F3
Maikoor (riv.), Indo. 152/D1
Maikoro, Chad 134/C3
Mailāni, India 108/C1
Mailly-le-Camp, Fr. 61/D6
Mailsi, Pak. 110/B5
Maimoon Palace (Istana Maimoon), Indo. 101/B2
Main (riv.), NI, UK 40/B2
Main (riv.), Ger. 48/E4
Main (chan.), On, Can. 190/F2
Mā'īn, Jor. 117/D5
Main Centre, Sk, Can. 175/L2
Main Range NP, Austl. 158/C5
Main-à-Dieu, NS, Can. 189/H2
Main-Donau (canal), Ger. 64/D3
Maināguri, India 109/G2
Mainbernheim, Ger. 64/D3
Maincy, Fr. 36/L6
Maine (riv.), Ire. 38/A5
Maine (reg.), Fr. 50/C2
Maine (gulf), US 188/C4
Maine (state), US 188/B3
Maine, Collines du (hill), Fr. 50/C2
Maine-et-Loire (dept.), Fr. 63/E6
Maïné-Soroa, Niger 134/B2
Maingkwan, Myan. 105/G2
Maingnyaung, Myan. 98/B4
Mainhardt, Ger. 64/C4
Mainhausen, Ger. 64/B2
Maini, Pak. 110/B2
Mainit, Phil. 100/D3
Mainkung, China 98/C2
Mainland (isl.), Sc, UK 37/V14
Mainling, China 98/B2
Mainoru, Austl. 152/D3
Mainpurī, India 108/B2
Mainstockheim, Ger. 64/D3
Maintenon, Fr. 63/G3
Maintirano, Madg. 143/H7
Mainvilliers, Fr. 63/G4
Mainz, Ger. 64/B3
Maio (isl.), CpV. 119/K10
Maiori, It. 71/D6
Maipo (riv.), Chile 226/N8
Maipo (vol.), Chile 226/P9
Maipú, Arg. 226/F3
Maipú, Chile 226/N8
Maiquetía, Ven. 219/P7
Maira (riv.), It. 51/G4
Mairana, Bol. 224/D1
Maire (str.), Arg. 191/D7
Mairi, Braz. 223/E1
Mairiporã, Braz. 223/K8
Mairwa, India 109/E2
Mais Gate (int'l arpt.), Haiti 207/H2
Maisach, Ger. 64/E6
Maisí (cape), Cuba 203/G3
Maišiagala, Lith. 47/L4
Maiskhāl, Bang. 98/A4
Maisome (isl.), Tanz. 139/G3
Maison-Rouge, Fr. 36/M6
Maisoncelles-en-Brie, Fr. 36/M5
Maisons-Alfort, Fr. 36/K5
Maisons-Laffitte, Fr. 36/J5
Maitengwe, Bots. 141/E4
Maithon (res.), India 109/F4
Maitland, On, Can. 191/J2
Maitland (riv.), On, Can. 190/F3
Maitland, NS, Can. 188/F3
Maitland, Fl, US 194/N6
Maitland, Austl. 155/H5
Maitland, Austl. 157/E1
Maitri, India, Ant. 228/A
Maitum, Phil. 100/D4
Maizières-lès-Metz, Fr. 61/F5
Maizuru (bay), Japan 95/H4
Maizuru, Japan 95/H5
Maja e Zezë (peak), Alb. 55/G2
Majadahonda, Sp. 53/N9
Majagual, Col. 216/C2
Majalengka, Indo. 101/E4
Majardah (mts.), Alg. 130/K6
Majarr (wadi), Syria 117/E1
Majd el Kurūm, Isr. 117/C3
Majdal 'Anjar, Leb. 117/D1
Majdanpek, Serb. 56/E3
Majdūl, Libya 126/B3
Majene, Indo. 103/E4
Majhgawān, India 108/C3
Majī, Eth. 135/G4
Maji Moto, Tanz. 137/A2
Majia (riv.), China 92/D3
Majiang, China 105/K3
Majītha, India 110/C4
Majoli, Sur. 218/C2
Major, Sk, Can. 175/K2
Majorca (isl.), Alg. 53/G3
Majorca (isl.), Sp. 29/E5
Majorca (Mallorca) (isl.), Sp. 72/D3
Majrūr (wadi), Sudan 135/E2
Mājuli, India 98/B3
Majur, Serb. 56/D3
Majuro (cap.), Mrsh. 160/G4
Makabana, Congo 138/C3
Makabe, Japan 95/E1
Makak, Camr. 138/B2
Makalamabedi, Bots. 140/D4
Makālu (peak), China 109/F2
Makālu (peak), Nepal 104/E2
Makampi, Tanz. 137/A4
Makanchi, Kaz. 111/D2
Makapaanstad, SAfr. 141/F5
Makara (riv.), NZ 159/J9
Makara Beach, NZ 159/H9
Makari, Camr. 134/B2
Makaroff, Mb, Can. 186/D2
Makarov, Rus. 91/N2
Makarska, Cro. 56/C4
Makar'yev, Rus. 75/J4
Makasa, Zam. 139/G5
Makassar (str.), Indo. 83/L10
Makatea (isl.), FrPol. 161/L6
Makati, Phil. 100/F6
Makaw, Myan. 98/C3
Makay (mass.), Madg. 143/H8
Makaya, D.R. Congo 138/D3
Makemo (isl.), FrPol. 161/L6
Makeni, SLeo. 132/B4
Makgadikgadi Pans (salt pans), Bots. 140/E4
Makgadikgadi Pans Game Reserve, Bots. 140/E4
Makhachkala, Rus. 77/H4
Makhambet, Kaz. 77/J3
Makhdūmpur, Pak. 110/B4
Makhfar al Busayyah, Iraq 115/F4
Makhmūr, Iraq 115/E3
Makhnëvo, Rus. 75/P4
Makhrūq (wadi), Jor. 114/D4
Makian (isl.), Indo. 103/G3
Makilimbo, D.R. Congo 139/G2
Makin (isl.), Kiri. 160/G4
Makinak, Mb, Can. 186/E2
Makino, Japan 95/K5
Makinsk, Kaz. 111/B1
Makioka, Japan 95/B2
Makiyivka, Ukr. 79/J3
Makkah (Mecca), SAr. 112/C4
Makkovik, Nf, Can. 171/L3
Makkum, Neth. 58/C2
Makó, Hun. 56/E2
Makofi, D.R. Congo 139/G2
Makokou, Gabon 138/C2
Makonde, Tanz. 137/A4
Makonde (plat.), Tanz. 137/B4
Makongolosi, Tanz. 137/A4
Makorako (peak), NZ 159/D2
Makota, Ugan. 139/G3
Makoua, Congo 138/C2
Maków Mazowiecki, Pol. 49/L2
Makrakómi, Gre. 55/H3
Makran (coast), Iran 113/G3
Makran (reg.), Iran 113/H3
Makrokhórion, Gre. 55/H2
Maksudangarh, India 108/A3
Maksutlu, Turk. 57/H5
Makteir (reg.), Mrta. 128/C5
Makthar, Tun. 130/L7
Mākū, Iran 115/F2
Makumbako, Tanz. 137/A4
Makumbi, D.R. Congo 139/E4
Makung, Tai. 99/H4
Makunka, Zam. 140/E3
Makurazaki, Japan 96/B5
Makurdi, Nga. 133/H5
Makushin (mt.), Ak, US 201/E5
Makutano, Kenya 137/A1
Makuyuni, Tanz. 137/B2
Makwānpur Garhi, Nepal 109/E2
Makwiro, Zim. 141/F3
Mæl, Nor. 46/C2
Mal, Mrta. 132/B2
Mal Abrigo, Uru. 191/K11
Mala, CAfr. 134/C4
Mala (pt.), CR 206/E4
Mala (pt.), Pan. 216/B3
Mala, Peru 220/B4
Mala Vyska, Ukr. 78/F3
Malabang, Phil. 100/D4
Malabar, Fl, US 195/H3
Malabar (coast), India 104/B5
Malabata (pt.), Mor. 130/B2
Malabo (cap.), EqG. 138/B2
Malabon, Phil. 100/E6
Malabuñgan, Phil. 100/B3
Malacacheta, Braz. 223/E3
Malacanang Pal., Phil. 100/F6
Malacca (str.), Asia 83/J9
Malacky, Slvk. 49/J4
Malad (riv.), Id, US 177/G2
Malad City, Id, US 177/G2
Maladers, Swi. 67/F4
Maladi-Mukedi, D.R. Congo 138/D4
Maladzyechna, Bela. 47/M4
Málaga, Sp. 52/C4
Málaga (int'l arpt.), Sp. 52/C4
Malaga, NM, US 180/B1
Malaga, NJ, US 198/C4
Malaga Cove (bay), Ca, US 196/F8
Malagarasi (riv.), Tanz. 139/G4
Malagarasi, Tanz. 139/G4
Malagón, Sp. 52/D3
Malagueta (bay), Cuba 207/G1
Malahide, Ire. 40/B5
Malaimbandy, Madg. 143/H8
Malaita (isl.), Sol. 160/F5
Malakāl, Sudan 135/F3
Malakand, Pak. 110/A2
Mālākhera, India 108/A2
Malakoff, Tx, US 181/F1
Malakwāl, Pak. 110/B3
Malalaua, PNG 153/G2
Malalhue, Chile 226/B3
Malambo, Col. 216/C2
Malang, Indo. 101/F4
Malangawa, Nepal 109/E2
Malanje, Ang. 138/D5
Malanje (prov.), Ang. 138/D5
Malans, Swi. 67/F4
Malanville, Ben. 133/F4
Malapatan, Phil. 100/D4
Malār, Pak. 113/H3
Mälaren (lake), Swe. 45/A1
Malargüe, Arg. 226/C2
Malasoro (pt.), Indo. 103/E5
Malaspina, Arg. 226/D5
Malatya, Turk. 114/D2
Malatya (prov.), Turk. 114/D2
Malaucène, Fr. 70/B4
Malaut, India 110/C4
Malawali (isl.), Malay. 100/B4
Malawi (ctry.) 119/F6
Malay (pen.), Asia 102/B2
Malaya (reg.), Malay. 83/K9
Malaya Belozërka, Ukr. 79/H4
Malaya Vishera, Rus. 47/Q2
Malaybalay, Phil. 100/D3
Malāyer, Iran 115/G3
Malaysia (ctry.) 102/C2
Malazemel'skaya (tundra), Rus. 75/L2
Malazgirt, Turk. 114/E2
Malbaie (riv.), Qu, Can. 188/B2
Malbaza, Niger 133/G3
Malbon, Austl. 155/J2
Malbork, Pol. 47/H4
Malbrán, Arg. 224/D4
Malcaras, Pic de (peak), Fr. 53/F1
Malcesine, It. 69/D2
Malchin, Ger. 46/E5
Malcolm, Al, US 194/D2
Malcolm (cr.), Austl. 155/M8
Malcontenta, It. 69/F3
Maldegem, Belg. 60/C1
Malden (isl.), Kiri. 161/K5
Malden, Mo, US 192/C2
Malden, Wa, US 174/F4
Maldives (ctry.) 83/F9
Maldive (isls.), Mald. 104/B6
Maldon, Eng, UK 43/G3
Maldon, Austl. 157/B3
Maldonado, Uru. 191/G2
Maldonado (dept.), Uru. 191/G2
Male (cap.), Mald. 83/G9
Maléa (cape), Gre. 55/H4
Malebo (pool), D.R. Congo 138/C4
Malegaon, India 107/C1
Malek, Sudan 135/F4
Malek Kandī, Iran 115/F2
Malekula (isl.), Van. 160/F6
Malemba-Nkulu, D.R. Congo 139/F5
Malemort-sur-Corrèze, Fr. 50/D4
Malente, Ger. 46/D4
Maleny, Austl. 158/D4
Maleo, It. 68/C3
Māler Kotla, India 110/C4
Malesína, Gre. 55/H3
Malestroit, Fr. 62/C5
Malesus, Tn, US 192/C3
Malfa, It. 54/D3
Malgis (riv.), Kenya 137/B1
Malgobek, Rus. 77/H4
Malgrat de Mar, Sp. 53/G2
Malgrate, It. 68/C2
Malheur (riv.), Or, Id, US 176/E2
Malheur (lake), Or, US 176/D2
Malheur Nat'l Wildlife Refuge, Or, US 176/D2
Malheureux (cape), Mrts. 143/T14
Mali (ctry.) 119/B3
Mali, D.R. Congo 139/F3
Mali, Gui. 132/B3
Mali (isl.), Myan. 106/B3
Mali (riv.), Myan. 105/G2
Mali Lošinj, Cro. 51/L4
Mália, Gre. 55/J5
Malian (riv.), China 90/F4
Malianjing, China 90/E3
Malibu, Ca, US 196/B2
Malicorne-sur-Sarthe, Fr. 63/E5
Malīhābād, India 108/C2
Malijai, Fr. 70/C4
Malik (wadi), Sudan 135/F1
Maliku, Indo. 103/F4
Maliku, Indo. 102/D4
Målilla, Swe. 46/F3
Malim Nawar, Malay. 101/C1
Malimán de Abajo, Arg. 224/B4
Malin, China 99/F3
Malin, Ire. 40/A1
Malin, Or, US 176/C2
Malin Head (pt.), Ire. 37/Q9
Malinau, Indo. 103/E3
Malindang (mt.), Phil. 100/C3
Malindi, Kenya 137/C2
Maling (pass), China 92/C3
Malinga, Gabon 138/C3
Malingping, Indo. 101/D4
Malinovka, Rus. 79/M2
Malinovka, Rus. 111/E1
Malinvern (peak), Fr. 70/D4
Malinyi, Tanz. 137/B4
Malio (riv.), Madg. 143/H8
Malipo, China 106/D1
Malīr Cantonment, Pak. 113/J4
Malissard, Fr. 70/A3
Malita, Phil. 100/D4
Maliwun, Myan. 106/B4
Malka Mari NP, Kenya 136/B4
Malkāpur, India 107/C1
Malkara, Turk. 57/H5
Malkiyya, Isr. 117/D2
Malko Tŭrnovo, Bul. 57/H5
Mallacoota, Austl. 157/D3
Mallaig, Sc, UK 37/R8
Mallānwān, India 108/C2
Mallasvesi (lake), Fin. 47/K1
Mallawī, Egypt 159/F3
Mallee Cliffs NP, Austl. 156/B2
Mallemort, Fr. 70/B5
Mallén, Sp. 52/E2
Malleray, Swi. 66/D3
Mallero (riv.), It. 67/F5
Mallersdorf-Pfaffenberg, Ger. 65/F5
Malles (Mals), It. 67/G4
Mallín Grande, Chile 226/B5
Mallinkaistenjärvi (lake), Fin. 45/E4
Malloa, Chile 226/N9
Mallorca (Majorca) (isl.), Sp. 72/D3
Mallory (swamp), Fl, US 195/G3
Mallow, Ire. 38/B5
Mallusjärvi (lake), Fin. 45/F4
Mallusjoki, Fin. 45/F4
Mallusk, NI, UK 40/B2
Malmanoury, FrG. 218/C1
Malmberget, Swe. 44/G2
Malmédy, Belg. 61/F3
Malmesbury, SAfr. 142/L10
Malmesbury, Eng, UK 42/D3
Malmköping, Swe. 46/G2
Malmö, Swe. 46/E4
Malmöhus (co.), Swe. 44/E5
Malmöhus (co.), Den. 46/E4
Malmslätt, Swe. 46/F2
Malmstrom (A.F.B.), Mt, US 175/J4
Malmyzh, Rus. 75/L4
Malnate, It. 68/B2
Malo, It. 69/E2
Malo, Wa, US 174/E3
Maloarkhangel'sk, Rus. 76/F1
Maloca, Braz. 218/C4
Maloelap (isl.), Mrsh. 160/G4
Malolos, Phil. 100/E6
Malombe (lake), Malw. 141/G2
Malone, NY, US 191/J2
Malone, Fl, US 195/F2
Malone (riv.), It. 70/D2
Malone, Tx, US 181/F2
Malong, China 98/D3
Malonga, D.R. Congo 138/E4
Malonga, D.R. Congo 139/E5
Malonje (peak), Tanz. 139/G5
Malonno, It. 67/G5
Małopolska (uplands), Pol. 49/K3
Małopolskie (prov.), Pol. 49/K4
Malorita, Bela. 49/N3
Maloyaroslavets, Rus. 74/H5
Malpais (lava flow), NM, US 182/A4
Malpartida de Cáceres, Sp. 52/B3
Malpartida de Plasencia, Sp. 52/B3
Malpas, Eng, UK 41/F5
Malpelo (isl.), Col. 209/A2
Malpensa (int'l arpt.), It. 68/B2
Malpeque (bay), PE, Can. 188/F2
Malpica, Sp. 52/A1
Mals (Malles), It. 67/G4
Malsch, Ger. 64/B5
Malsch (riv.), Aus. 65/H5
Malše (riv.), Czh. 49/H4
Mälstek (peak), Czh. 65/G4
Malta (ctry.) 54/L7
Malta, Braz. 219/G4
Malta, Lat. 47/M3
Malta (chan.), Malta 54/C4
Malta (isl.), Malta 54/L7
Malta, Id, US 177/G2
Malta, Mt, US 175/L3
Malta, Oh, US 190/F5
Maltahöhe, Namb. 140/C5
Maltam, Camr. 134/B2
Maltby, Eng, UK 41/G5
Maltby, Eng, UK 41/G3
Maltepe (nbrhd.), Turk. 115/N7
Malters, Swi. 66/E3
Malton, Eng, UK 41/H3
Malton, On, Can. 190/T8
Maltorne (riv.), Fr. 36/G6
Malu, China 90/F5
Maluku, D.R. Congo 138/C4
Maluku (prov.), Indo. 152/B1
Ma'lūlā, Syria 117/F1
Malumba, D.R. Congo 139/F3
Malummaduri, Nga. 133/H3
Malung, Swe. 46/E1
Maluso, Phil. 100/C4
Malūt, Sudan 135/G3
Malvaglia, Swi. 67/E5
Malveira, Port. 53/P10
Malvern (nbrhd.), Austl. 156/G5
Malvern, Al, US 195/F2
Malvern, Ar, US 183/H3
Malvern, Ia, US 185/G3
Malvern, Pa, US 198/C3
Malverne, NY, US 199/L9
Malvinas (Falkland) (isls.), UK 191/E7
Malvy Uzen' (riv.), Rus. 77/H2
Malyn, Ukr. 78/E2
Malysheva, Rus. 75/P4
Malyy Yenisey (riv.), Rus. 90/D1
Malzéville, Fr. 61/F6
Mama, Rus. 81/M4
Mamanguape, Braz. 219/H4
Mamaroneck, NY, US 199/L8
Mamarr al Jadī (pass), Egypt 116/C4
Mamarr Mitlā (pass), Egypt 116/C4
Mamba, Zam. 141/E3
Mamba, Japan 95/B1
Mambajao, Phil. 100/D3
Mambali, Tanz. 139/H4
Mambare (riv.), PNG 153/G2
Mambasa, D.R. Congo 139/G2
Mamberamo (riv.), Indo. 103/J4
Mambéré (riv.), CAfr. 134/B4
Mambij, Syria 114/D2
Mambiya, Gui. 132/B4
Mamborê, Braz. 225/F3
Mambova, Zam. 140/E3
Mambrui, Kenya 137/C2
Mambunga, D.R. Congo 139/F2
Mamburao, Phil. 100/C2
Mamedkala, Rus. 77/J4
Mamelodi, SAfr. 141/F5
Mamer, Lux. 61/F4
Mamers, Fr. 63/F4
Mamfé, Camr. 133/H5
Mamlyutka, Kaz. 80/G4
Mammendorf, Ger. 67/H1
Mamming, Ger. 65/F5
Mammoth, Az, US 179/G4
Mammoth Cave NP, Ky, US 192/D2
Mammoth Lakes, Ca, US 178/C2
Mammoth Site, SD, US 184/C2
Mammoth Spring, Ar, US 183/J2
Mamonovo, Rus. 47/H4
Mamoré (riv.), Bol.,Braz. 209/C4
Mamoré (riv.), Braz. 221/E3
Mamou, La, US 194/B2
Mamou, Gui. 132/B4
Mamoutzou, May., Fr. 143/H6
Mampikony, Madg. 143/H7
Mampoko, D.R. Congo 138/D2
Mampong, Gha. 133/E5
Mamry (lake), Pol. 47/J4
Mamuju, Indo. 103/E4
Ma'mūnīyeh, Iran 115/G3
Mamuno, Bots. 140/D4
Mamuru (riv.), Braz. 221/G1
Mamwera (peak), Tanz. 137/B3
Man, C.d'Iv. 132/D5
Man Hpang, Myan. 106/B1
Man Mia (peak), Thai. 106/B4
Mān Ming, Myan. 98/C3
Mān Si, Myan. 105/G3
Mān Tha, Myan. 98/C3
Mān Wein, Myan. 98/C3
Man, Isle of (isl.), IM, UK 40/D3
Mana (isl.), NZ 159/H9
Mana, FrG. 218/C1
Mana (riv.), FrG. 217/H3
Mana Pools NP, Zim. 141/F2
Manabl (prov.), Ecu. 216/A5
Manacapurú (lake), Braz. 217/F5
Manacle (pt.), Eng, UK 42/A6
Manacor, Sp. 53/G3
Manado, Indo. 103/F3
Manage, Belg. 61/D3
Managua (cap.), Nic. 206/E3
Managua (lake), Nic. 206/E3
Manahawkin, NJ, US 199/D4
Manaia, NZ 159/C2
Manakambahiny, Madg. 143/J7
Manakara, Madg. 143/J8
Manākhah, Yem. 136/B2
Manalapan, Fl, US 194/P9
Manalapan, NJ, US 198/D3
Manāli, India 110/D3
Manama (Al Manāmah) (cap.), Bahr. 112/F3
Manambaho (riv.), Madg. 143/H7
Manambolo (riv.), Madg. 143/H7
Mananantanana (riv.), Madg. 143/H8
Mananara, Madg. 143/J7
Mananara (riv.), Madg. 143/H8
Manandaza, Madg. 143/H7
Manandona, Madg. 143/H8
Manangbhot, Nepal 109/E1
Mananjary, Madg. 143/J8
Mananjary (riv.), Madg. 143/H8
Manankoro, Mali 132/D4
Manantenina, Madg. 143/H9
Manantiales, Chile 191/C7
Mānānwāla, Pak. 110/B4
Manapire (riv.), Ven. 219/P8
Manappārai, India 107/C4
Manara (pt.), It. 68/C5
Manaratsandry, Madg. 143/H7
Manas (riv.), China 80/J5
Manās (riv.), India 109/H2
Manas, Som. 136/B5
Manas (lake), China 111/E2
Manas, China 111/E3
Manāslu (peak), Nepal 109/E1
Manasquan, NJ, US 199/D3
Manasquan (riv.), NJ, US 199/D3
Manassa, Co, US 179/K2
Manassas, Va, US 193/J1
Manassas Nat'l Bfld. Park, Va, US 193/J1
Manastir Dečani, Serb. 55/G1
Manastir Gračanica, Serb. 56/E4
Manastir Sopoćani, Serb. 56/E4
Manatang, Indo. 152/B2
Manatee (lake), Fl, US 195/G4
Manatee (co.), Fl, US 194/L8
Manatsuru, Japan 95/C3
Manatuto, ETim. 152/B2
Manau, PNG 153/G2
Manaung, Myan. 106/B3
Manaus, Braz. 218/B3
Manavgat, Turk. 116/B1
Manawa, Wi, US 187/K5
Manay, Phil. 100/D4
Mañazo, Peru 220/D4
Manazuru-misaki (cape), Japan 95/C3
Mānbāzār, India 109/F4
Mance (riv.), Fr. 66/B2
Mancelona, Mi, US 190/D2
Mancha Real, Sp. 52/D4
Manchang, China 99/E3
Manche (dept.), Fr. 62/D2
Mancheng, China 92/G7
Mancherāl, India 107/C2
Manchester (lake), Austl. 158/E7
Manchester, Eng, UK 41/F5
Manchester (co.), Eng, UK 41/F5
Manchester, Al, US 192/D4
Manchester, Ct, US 191/K4
Manchester, Ga, US 192/E4
Manchester, Ia, US 185/J2
Manchester, Il, US 185/J4
Manchester, Ky, US 192/F2
Manchester, Md, US 198/B4
Manchester, Mi, US 190/D3
Manchester, NH, US 191/L3
Manchester, Oh, US 192/F1
Manchester, Ok, US 183/E2
Manchester, Pa, US 198/B3
Manchester, Tn, US 192/D3
Manchester, Wa, US 197/B2
Manchester, Vt, US 191/K3
Manchester (Ringway) (int'l arpt.), Eng, UK 41/F5
Manchuria (reg.), China 81/N5
Mancieulles, Fr. 61/E5
Máncora, Peru 220/A2
Mancos, Co, US 179/H2
Mancos (riv.), Co, US 179/H2
Mand, Pak. 113/H3
Mand (riv.), Iran 113/F3
Manda, Chad 134/C3
Mānda, Bang. 109/G3
Manda, Tanz. 137/A4
Manda (peak), Sudan 134/E3
Manda, Tanz. 139/H5
Manda, Tanz. 139/H4
Manda, PN de, Chad 134/C3
Mandabe, Madg. 143/H8
Mandaguari, Braz. 225/G2
Mandal, Nor. 46/B2
Mandal, India 104/B3
Mandal, Mong. 90/F2
Mandal-Ovoo, Mong. 90/E3
Mandala (peak), Indo. 103/K4
Mandalay, Myan. 98/C4
Mandalay (div.), Myan. 105/G3
Mandalay Palace, Myan. 98/C4
Mandalgovĭ, Mong. 90/F2
Mandalī, Iraq 115/F3
Mandaluyong, Phil. 100/F6
Mandan, ND, US 186/D4
Mandara (mts.), Afr. 134/B3
Mandasavu (peak), Indo. 103/F5
Mandaue, Phil. 100/C3
Mandeb (str.), Afr.,Asia 119/G3
Mandela, India 110/C5
Mandelieu-la-Napoule, Fr. 70/C5
Mandello del Lario, It. 67/F6
Mandera, Tanz. 137/B3
Mandera, Kenya 136/B5
Manderson, Wy, US 177/K1
Mandeure, Fr. 66/C3
Mandeville, La, US 194/C2
Mandeville, Jam. 207/G2
Māndi, India 110/D4
Mandi Bahāuddīn, Pak. 110/B3
Mandi Būrewāla, Pak. 110/B4
Mandi Dabwāli, India 110/C5
Mandi Sādiqganj, Pak. 110/B4
Mandialaza, Madg. 143/J7
Mandiana, Gui. 132/C4
Mandié, Moz. 141/G3
Mandimba, Moz. 141/G2
Mandiola (isl.), Indo. 103/G4
Mandira (res.), India 109/E4
Mandje, D.R. Congo 139/G4
Mandji, Gabon 138/B3
Mandla, India 108/C4
Mandø (isl.), Den. 46/C4
Mando, Nga. 133/G4
Mandoc (falls), EqG. 138/B2
Mándok, Hun. 49/M4
Mandoto, Madg. 143/H7
Mandoúdhion, Gre. 55/H3
Mandouri, Togo 133/F4
Mándra, Gre. 55/N8
Mandrare (riv.), Madg. 143/H9
Mandritsara, Madg. 143/J6
Mandronarivo, Madg. 143/H8
Mandrosonoro, Madg. 143/H8
Mandsaur, India 104/C3
Mandumai, Indo. 102/D4
Mandurah, Austl. 154/B5
Manduria, It. 55/E2
Māndvi, India 113/J4
Mandya, India 107/C3
Mane (pass), Nepal 108/D1
Mane, Fr. 70/B5
Manea, Eng, UK 43/G2
Manendragarh, India 108/D4
Maner, India 109/E3
Manerbio, It. 68/D3
Manevychi, Ukr. 78/C2
Manfred, ND, US 186/E4
Manfredonia, It. 54/D2
Manfredonia (gulf), It. 73/H1
Mang (riv.), China 92/B4
Manga, Braz. 222/E2
Manga, Burk. 133/E4
Manga (reg.), Chad,Nga. 134/B2
Manga Grande, Ang. 138/C4
Mangabeiras, Chapada das (hills), Braz. 222/D1
Mangai, D.R. Congo 138/D4
Mangaia (isl.), CookIs. 161/K7
Mangakino, NZ 159/C2
Mangalagiri, India 107/D2
Mangaldai, India 105/F2
Mangaldan, Phil. 100/C1
Mangalia, Rom. 57/J4
Mangalisa (peak), Tanz. 137/B3
Mangalmé, Chad 134/C2
Mangamila, Madg. 143/H7
Mangania, D.R. Congo 139/E2
Mangarang, Indo. 103/G3
Mangaratiba, Braz. 223/M7
Mangareva (isl.), FrPol. 161/M7
Mangaweka, NZ 159/C2
Mange, SLeo. 132/B4
Mangeigne, Chad 134/D3
Mangembo, D.R. Congo 138/C4
Mangen, India 109/G2
Manger, Nor. 46/A1
Mangerton (mtn.), Ire. 38/A6
Mangghystau, Kaz. 80/F5
Mangghystaū Oblast, Kaz. 80/F5
Mangham, La, US 183/J4
Mangin (range), Myan. 98/B4
Mangkalihat (cape), Indo. 103/E3
Mangla (dam), Pak. 110/B3
Mangla, Pak. 110/B3
Mangla (res.), Pak. 110/B3
Manglaralto, Ecu. 220/A1
Manglares (pt.), Col. 216/B4
Manglaur, India 108/A1
Mangles (bay), Austl. 154/K7
Mangnai, China 90/C4
Mango, Togo 133/F4
Mango, Fl, US 194/L8
Mangoche, Malw. 141/G2
Mangoky (riv.), Madg. 143/H8
Mangole (isl.), Indo. 103/G4
Mangombe, D.R. Congo 139/F3
Mangonui, NZ 159/C1
Mangoro (riv.), Madg. 143/J7
Mangotsfield, Eng, UK 42/D4
Māngrol, India 113/K4
Mangualde, Port. 52/B2
Mangueira (lake), Braz. 191/G2
Manguéné, Gabon 138/B3
Mangui, China 91/J1
Mangum, Ok, US 182/E3
Manguredjipa, D.R. Congo 139/G2
Mangwe, Zim. 141/F4
Man'gyŏngdae, NKor. 93/C3
Mangyshlak, Kaz. 77/J4
Mangyshlak (pen.), Kaz. 77/J3
Mangyshlak (plat.), Kaz. 77/K4
Mānhairu, India 110/D5
Manhasset (bay), NY, US 199/L8
Manhasset, NY, US 199/L8
Manhattan (isl.), NY, US 199/K9
Manhattan, Nv, US 176/E4
Manhattan, Ks, US 185/F4
Manhattan, Mt, US 175/J5
Manhattan Beach, Ca, US 196/F8
Manhay, Belg. 61/E3
Manheim, Pa, US 198/B3
Manhiça, Moz. 141/G5
Manhuaçu, Braz. 223/E4
Manhumirim, Braz. 223/E4
Mania (riv.), Madg. 143/H7
Maniamba, Moz. 141/G2
Manianga, D.R. Congo 138/C4
Maniāri (riv.), India 108/C4
Manica, Moz. 141/G3
Manica (prov.), Moz. 141/G3
Manicaland (prov.), Zim. 141/F3
Manicoré, Braz. 221/F2
Manicoré (riv.), Braz. 218/A4
Manicouagan (riv.), Qu, Can. 171/K3
Manicouagan (res.), Can. 163/L4
Manicouagan (res.), Qu, Can. 171/K3
Manifold (cape), Austl. 158/C3
Maniganggo, China 98/C2
Manigotagan, Mb, Can. 186/F2
Manihāri, India 109/F3
Manihi (isl.), FrPol. 161/L6
Manihiki (isl.), CookIs. 161/J6
Manikarchar, India 109/G3
Mānikganj, Bang. 109/G4
Manila, Ut, US 177/J3
Manila, Ar, US 192/B3
Manila, Phil. 100/C2
Manila (cap.), Phil. 100/E6
Manila (bay), Phil. 100/E6
Manildra, Austl. 157/D1
Manilla, Austl. 156/D1
Manilla, Ia, US 185/G3
Manimpé, Mali 132/D3
Maniña, Ven. 217/E3
Maningory (riv.), Madg. 143/J7
Maningrida, Austl. 152/D3
Maninjau (lake), Indo. 101/C3
Manipa (str.), Indo. 103/G4
Manipat (hills), India 108/D4
Manipur (state), India 105/F3
Manisa (prov.), Turk. 76/D5
Manises, Sp. 72/C3
Manistee (riv.), Mi, US 190/D2
Manistee, Mi, US 190/C2
Manistique (lake), Mi, US 187/M4
Manistique, Mi, US 190/C2
Manito, Il, US 185/K3
Manito (lake), Sk, Can. 175/K1
Manitoba (lake), Can. 163/G4
Manitoba (prov.), Can. 170/G3
Manitou (isl.), Mi, US 187/L4
Manitou Springs, Co, US 182/B1
Manitoulin (isl.), On, Can. 190/E2
Manitouwadge, On, Can. 187/M3
Manitowaning, On, Can. 190/F2
Manitowish, Wi, US 187/J4
Manitowoc, Wi, US 190/C2
Manitsauá-Missu (riv.), Braz. 221/H3
Maniwaki, Qu, Can. 191/J1
Maniwaki Ind. Res., Qu, Can. 191/H1
Manizales, Col. 219/K7
Manjā, Jor. 117/D5
Manja, Madg. 143/H8
Manjacaze, Moz. 141/G5
Manjakandriana, Madg. 143/J7
Manjeri, India 107/C4
Manjiang, China 93/D2
Manjīl, Iran 115/G2
Manjimup, Austl. 154/C5
Mānjra (riv.), India 104/C4
Mankato, Ks, US 184/E4
Mankato, Mn, US 185/H1
Mankayane, Swaz. 141/F5
Mankera, Pak. 110/A4
Manki Ii, Camr. 134/A4
Mankim, Camr. 134/B4
Mankono, C.d'Iv. 132/D4
Mankota, Sk, Can. 175/L3
Manley Hot Springs, Ak, US 201/H2
Manlius, NY, US 191/J3
Manlleu, Sp. 52/D1
Manly, Ia, US 185/H2
Manly, NZ 159/F6
Manly (nbrhd.), Austl. 158/H8
Manlyutka, Rus. 75/R4
Manna, Indo. 102/B4
Manna (mtn.), Austl. 157/C1
Mannahill, Austl. 155/H5
Mannar (gulf), India,SrL. 83/G9
Mannar, SrL. 107/C4
Mannārgudi, India 107/C4
Männedorf, Swi. 67/E3
Mannetjiesberg (peak), SAfr. 142/C4
Mannford, Ok, US 183/F2
Mannheim, Ger. 64/B4
Mannheim (Neu-Ostheim) (arpt.), Ger. 64/B4
Manning, Ab, Can. 170/E3
Manning (cape), NW, Can. 171/Q7
Manning, Ar, US 183/H3
Manning, Ks, US 182/D1
Manning, Ia, US 185/G3
Manning, ND, US 186/C4
Manning, SC, US 193/G4
Manning Park, BC, Can. 174/D3
Mannington, WV, US 190/F5
Mannington Meadow (lake), NJ, US 198/C4
Manningtree, Eng, UK 43/H3
Männlifluh (peak), Swi. 66/D4
Mannsville, NY, US 191/H3
Mannum, Austl. 155/H5
Mannville, Ab, Can. 175/J1
Mano (riv.), Libr. 132/C5
Manoa, Bol. 221/E3
Manokotak, Ak, US 201/G4
Manokwari, Indo. 103/K5
Manombo, Madg. 143/G8
Manompana, Madg. 143/J7
Manono, D.R. Congo 139/F4
Manonwa, D.R. Congo 139/F4
Manoppello, It. 71/D3
Manor, Ga, US 195/G2
Manor, Tx, US 181/F2
Manorville, NY, US 199/F2
Manosque, Fr. 70/B5
Manp'o, NKor. 93/D2
Manp'o, NKor. 93/D2
Manra (Sydney) (isl.), Kiri. 161/H5
Manresa, Sp. 53/K6
Mānsa, India 110/C5
Mansa Konko, Gam. 132/B3
Mansalay, Phil. 100/C2
Mānsehra, Pak. 110/B2
Mansel (isl.), Can. 163/J3
Mansel (isl.), Nun, Can. 171/H2
Mansfield, Austl. 157/C3
Mansfield, Eng, UK 41/G5
Mansfield, Ar, US 183/G3
Mansfield, La, US 180/H1
Mansfield, Oh, US 190/E4
Mansfield, SD, US 184/E1
Mansfield, Tx, US 180/K7
Mansfield (dam), Tx, US 181/F2
Mansfield (mt.), Vt, US 191/K2
Mansfield, Wa, US 174/E4
Mansfield Woodhouse, Eng, UK 41/G5
Mansilla de las Mulas, Sp. 52/C1
Mansôa, GBis. 132/B3
Manson, Ia, US 185/G2
Mansouria, Mor. 130/A3
Mansura, La, US 194/B2
Manta, It. 70/D3
Manta, Ecu. 216/A5
Mantachie, Ms, US 192/C3
Mantala, Bang. 109/H3
Mantalingajan (mt.), Phil. 100/B3
Mantantale, D.R. Congo 138/E3
Mantare, Tanz. 137/A2
Mantario, Sk, Can. 175/K2
Mantaro (riv.), Peru 220/C3
Mantecal, Ven. 217/E3
Mantecal, Ven. 216/D3
Mantee, Ms, US 192/C4
Manteigas, Port. 52/B2
Mantena, Braz. 223/E3
Manteno, Il, US 190/C4
Manteo, NC, US 193/K3
Mantes-la-Jolie, Fr. 63/G3
Mantes-la-Ville, Fr. 63/G3
Manthani, India 107/C2
Manti, Ut, US 177/H4
Mantiqueira, Serra do (mts.), Braz. 222/D4
Manton, Mi, US 190/D2
Mantorp, Swe. 46/F2
Mantorville, Mn, US 185/H1
Mantos Blancos, Chile 224/B2
Mantova (prov.), It. 68/D2
Mantova, It. 69/D3
Mäntsälä, Fin. 47/L1
Mantua, Cuba 207/E1
Mantua, NJ, US 198/C4
Manturovo, Rus. 75/K4
Mäntyharju, Fin. 47/M1
Mäntyluoto, Fin. 47/J1
Manu (riv.), India 109/H3
Manu (riv.), Peru 220/D3
Manú, Peru 220/D4
Manú, PN, Peru 220/D3
Manua (isls.), ASam. 161/J6
Manuae Atoll (atoll), CookIs. 161/K6
Manuel Alves da Natividade (riv.), Braz. 222/C1
Manuel Benavides, Mex. 180/C3
Manuel J. Cobo, Arg. 191/K11
Manuelito, NM, US 179/H3
Manui (isl.), Indo. 103/F4
Manūjān, Iran 113/G3
Manuk (riv.), Indo. 102/C5
Manukan, Phil. 100/C3
Manukau, NZ 159/F7
Manulla, Ire. 38/A2
Manumbai (riv.), Indo. 152/D1
Manumuskin (riv.), NJ, US 198/D5
Manuripe (riv.), Bol. 220/D3
Manuripe Heath Amazonica, Res. Nacional, Bol. 220/E3
Manus (isl.), PNG 160/D5
Manutuke, NZ 159/D2
Manvel, ND, US 186/F3
Manvel, Tx, US 181/M9
Manville, Wy, US 184/B2
Manville, NJ, US 198/D2
Many, La, US 194/B2
Many Farms, Az, US 179/H2
Manyame (riv.), Zim. 141/F3
Manyanga, Congo 138/C4
Manyara (lake), Tanz. 137/A2
Manyara NP, Tanz. 137/A2
Manyberries, Ab, Can. 175/J3
Manych (riv.), Rus. 80/E5
Manych-Gudilo (lake), Rus. 77/G3
Manyoni, Tanz. 137/A3
Manzai, Pak. 110/A3
Manzanar, Chile 226/C3
Manzanares, Sp. 52/D3
Manzanares, Col. 219/K7
Manzanares (riv.), Sp. 53/N8
Manzanares el Real, Sp. 53/N8
Manzanillo, Cuba 207/G1
Manzanillo, Mex. 204/D5
Manzanillo (int'l arpt.), Mex. 204/D5
Manzanita, Or, US 174/C5
Manzanita Ind. Res., Ca, US 178/D4
Manzano, It. 69/G2
Manzano (peak), NM, US 179/J3
Manzano, NM, US 179/J3

Manzano (mts.), NM, US 179/J3
Manzanola, Co, US 182/C1
Manzanza, D.R. Congo 139/G4
Manzhouli, China 91/H2
Manziana, It. 71/B3
Manzilah (lake), Egypt 116/B4
Manzilah (canal), Egypt 131/C2
Manzini, Swaz. 143/E2
Manzini (Matsapa) (int'l arpt.), Swaz. 143/E2
Mao, Chad 134/B2
Mao Songsang, India 98/B3
Maoba, China 105/J2
Maobaguan, China 90/F5
Maodianzi, China 93/C2
Mao'ergai, China 90/E5
Maojing, China 90/F4
Maoke (mts.), Indo. 103/J4
Maoming, China 99/F4
Maoniushan, China 90/D4
Maoshan, China 92/H6
Maotian, China 90/F5
Maotou (peak), China 98/D3
Maowen Qiangzu Zizhixian, China 98/D2
Maoyang, China 99/H3
Maozhou, China 92/H7
Mapai, Moz. 141/F4
Mapam (lake), China 111/D5
Mapane, Indo. 103/F4
Mapastepec, Mex. 206/C3
Mapi (riv.), Indo. 103/J5
Mapia, Indo. 103/J4
Mapimí, Bolsón de (depr.), Mex. 204/D3
Mapire, Ven. 217/E3
Mapiri, Bol. 221/E3
Mapiri, Bol. 220/D4
Maple (peak), Az, US 179/H4
Maple (riv.), Ia, US 185/G2
Maple, On, Can. 190/T8
Maple Creek, Sk, Can. 175/K3
Maple Grove, Qu, Can. 189/N7
Maple Grove, Mn, US 187/P6
Maple Park, Il, US 197/N16
Maple Ridge, BC, Can. 174/C3
Maple River Nat'l Wild. Ref., ND, US 186/E4
Maple Shade, NJ, US 198/D4
Maple Valley, Wa, US 197/C3
Maples, Mo, US 183/J2
Maplesville, Al, US 192/D4
Mapleton, Ut, US 177/H3
Mapleton, Or, US 176/B1
Mapleton, Ia, US 185/G2
Mapleton, Mn, US 185/H2
Maplewood, Wi, US 190/C2
Maplewood, NJ, US 199/H9
Maplewood, Mn, US 187/P6
Map'o (nbrhd.), SKor. 93/F6
Mapoon Aboriginal Reserve, Austl. 153/F2
Mapoon Mission Station, Austl. 153/F2
Maporal, Ven. 216/D3
Mappsville, Va, US 193/K2
Mapuera (riv.), Braz. 217/G5
Mapumolo, SAfr. 143/E3
Maputa, SAfr. 143/F2
Maputo (int'l arpt.), Moz. 143/F2
Maputo (riv.), Moz. 141/G5
Maputo (prov.), Moz. 141/G5
Maputo (cap.), Moz. 143/F2
Maqat, Kaz. 77/K3
Maqdam (cape), Sudan 159/H5
Maqên, China 90/D5
Maquan (riv.), China 111/D6
Maquan (Damqog) (riv.), China 108/E1
Maquela do Zombo, Ang. 138/C4
Maquinchao, Arg. 226/C4
Maquoketa, Ia, US 185/J2
Maquoketa (riv.), Ia, US 185/J2
Maquoketa, North Fork (riv.), Ia, US 185/J2
Mar (reg.), Sc, UK 39/D2
Mar (mts.), Braz. 209/E5
Mar Chiquita (lag.), Arg. 224/D4
Mar de Ajó, Arg. 191/F3
Mar del Plata, Arg. 226/F3
Mar del Tuyú, Arg. 191/F3
Mar-Mac, NC, US 193/H3
Mara (riv.), Tanz. 137/A2
Mara (prov.), Tanz. 137/A2
Mara, Guy. 218/B1
Mara Creek, BC, Can. 174/E2
Maraã, Braz. 221/E1
Marabá, Braz. 218/D4
Maracá (isl.), Braz. 218/D2
Maracaibo (lake), Ven. 209/B2
Maracaibo, Ven. 216/D2
Maracaju, Braz. 225/F2
Maracaju, Serra de (mts.), Braz. 222/B4
Maracanã, Braz. 219/E3
Maracanaquará (plat.), Braz. 218/C3
Maracás, Braz. 223/E2
Maracay, Ven. 219/N7
Maracena, Sp. 52/D4
Marādah, Libya 126/C2
Maradi (dept.), Afr. 133/G2
Maradi, Niger 133/G3
Marāgheh, Iran 115/F2
Mārahra, India 108/B2
Marahuaca (peak), Ven. 217/E4
Maraira (pt.), Phil. 100/C1
Marais de St-Gond (swamp), Fr. 60/C6
Marais des Cygnes (riv.), Ks, Mo, US 183/G1
Marajó (bay), Braz. 209/E3
Maralal, Kenya 137/B1
Maralal Nat'l Sanct., Kenya 137/B1
Marali, CAfr. 134/C4
Maralik, Arm. 115/E1
Maralinga-Tjarutja Aboriginal Land, Austl. 155/F4
Maramag, Phil. 100/D4
Marambaia (isl.), Braz. 223/N8
Marampa, SLeo. 132/B4
Maramureş (co.), Rom. 49/M5
Maran, Malay. 101/C2
Marana (lag.), Cro. 69/G1
Marana, Az, US 179/G4
Marand, Iran 115/F2
Marandet, Niger 133/G2
Marang, Malay. 101/C1
Marangani, Peru 220/D4
Maranguape, Braz. 219/G3
Maranhão (riv.), Braz. 222/C2
Maranhão (state), Braz. 219/E5
Marano di Napoli, It. 71/D6
Marano Lagunare, It. 69/G2
Marano sul Panaro, It. 69/D5
Marano Vicentino, It. 69/E2
Maranoa (riv.), Austl. 145/D3
Marañón (riv.), Peru 209/B3
Marans, Fr. 50/C3
Maraoue, PN de la, C.d'Iv. 132/D5
Marapanim, Braz. 218/E3
Marapi (peak), Indo. 101/C3
Maras (peak), Indo. 101/D3
Mărăşeşti, Rom. 57/H3
Marathón, Gre. 55/N8
Marathón (arpt.), Gre. 55/N8
Marathon, Fl, US 195/H5
Marathon, On, Can. 187/L3
Marathon, NY, US 191/H3
Marathon, Tx, US 180/C2
Marau, Braz. 225/F4
Marauliānwāla, Pak. 110/B3
Maravatío de Ocampo, Mex. 205/E5
Maravilha, Braz. 225/F3
Maravillas, Bol. 221/E3
Maravillas (cr.), Tx, US 180/C3
Marāwah, Libya 126/D1
Marawaka, PNG 153/G1
Marawī, Sudan 159/F5
Marawi, Phil. 100/D3
Marayes, Arg. 224/C4
Marazion, Eng, UK 42/A6
Marbach, Swi. 66/D4
Marbach am Neckar, Ger. 64/C5
Marbache, Fr. 61/F6
Marbella, Sp. 52/C4
Marble (canyon), Az, US 179/G2
Marble, NC, US 192/F3
Marble Bar, Austl. 154/C2
Marble Canyon, Az, US 179/G2
Marble Falls, Tx, US 180/E2
Marble Hall, SAfr. 141/F5
Marble Hill, Mo, US 192/C2
Marblemount, Wa, US 174/D3
Marbleton, Qu, Can. 191/L2
Marbleton, Wy, US 177/H2
Marburg (lake), Pa, US 198/B4
Marbury, Al, US 192/D4
Marcali, Hun. 56/C2
Marcallo, It. 68/B3
Marcapata, Peru 220/D4
Marcelin, Sk, Can. 175/L1
Marceline, Mo, US 185/H4
Marcelino Ramos, Braz. 225/G3
Marcella, Ar, US 183/J3
Marcellina, It. 71/B3
Marcellus, Mi, US 190/D3
March (A.F.B.), Ca, US 196/C3
March, Eng, UK 43/G1
Marchant (mt.), NZ 159/J9
Marche (pol. reg.), It. 71/C2
Marche, Congo 138/C4
Marche (mts.), Fr. 50/d3
Marche-en-Famenne, Belg. 61/E3
Marchémoret, Fr. 36/L4
Marchena, Sp. 52/C4
Marchena (isl.), Ecu. 220/J6
Marcheno, It. 68/D2
Marches (reg.), It. 73/G2
Marchiennes, Fr. 60/C3
Marchin, Belg. 61/E3
Marchinbar (isl.), Austl. 153/E2
Marchtrenk, Aus. 65/H6
Marchwell, Sk, Can. 186/D2
Marciana Marina, It. 54/B1
Marcianise, It. 71/D5
Marcilly, Fr. 36/L4
Marcilly-sur-Tille, Fr. 66/B2
Marck, Fr. 60/A2
Marckolsheim, Fr. 66/D1
Marco, Fl, US 195/H5
Marco (isl.), Fl, US 195/H5
Marco, Braz. 219/F3
Marco Polo (int'l arpt.), It. 69/F3
Marcoing, Fr. 60/C3
Marcola, Or, US 176/B1
Marcon, It. 69/F2
Marcona, Peru 220/C4
Marconi (mt.), BC, Can. 174/G2
Marcos Juárez, Arg. 226/E2
Marcosli (riv.), BC, Can. 174/C1
Marcoussis, Fr. 36/J6
Marcovia, Hon. 206/E3
Marcq-en-Barœul, Fr. 60/C2
Marcus, Ia, US 185/G2
Marcus Baker (mt.), Ak, US 201/J3
Marcy (mt.), NY, US 191/K2
Mardān, Pak. 110/B2
Marden, Eng, UK 36/E3
Mardeuil, Fr. 60/C5
Mardin, Turk. 114/E2
Mardin (prov.), Turk. 114/E2
Maré (isl.), NCal., Fr. 161/W12
Marecchia (riv.), It. 69/F5
Marechal Cândido Rondon, Braz. 225/F3
Marechal Deodoro, Braz. 223/G1
Maree (lake), Sc, UK 37/R8
Mareeba, Austl. 158/B2
Mareham le Fen, Eng, UK 41/H5
Mareil-sur-Mauldre, Fr. 36/H5
Marek, Indo. 103/F4
Maréna, Mali 132/C3
Marengo, Wi, US 187/J4
Marengo, Il, US 197/N15
Marengo, Ia, US 185/H3
Marengo, Sk, Can. 175/K2
Marengo, In, US 192/D1
Marenisco, Mi, US 187/K4
Marennes, Fr. 50/C4
Mareolaboom, Namb. 140/C3
Marerano, Madg. 143/H8
Maresfield, Eng, UK 43/G5
Mareuil-sur-Ourcq, Fr. 36/M4
Marfa, Tx, US 180/B2
Marfield, Austl. 157/B1
Marfino, Rus. 77/J3
Margalla Hills NP, Pak. 110/B3
Margam, Wal, UK 42/C3
Marganets', Ukr. 79/H4
Margao (Madgaon), India 107/B3
Margaree, NS, Can. 189/G2
Margaree Valley, NS, Can. 189/G2
Margaret, Tx, US 182/E3
Margaret (riv.), Austl. 152/B4
Margaret (mt.), Austl. 154/C2
Margaret River, Austl. 154/B5
Margarita (peak), Ca, US 196/C4
Margarita (isl.), Ven. 217/F2
Margarita, Isla de (isl.), Trin. 203/J5
Margarítion, Gre. 55/G3
Margate, Eng, UK 43/H4
Margate, Fl, US 194/P10
Margate, SAfr. 143/E3
Margate City, NJ, US 198/D5
Margeride (mts.), Fr. 50/E4
Margeta (cape), Indo. 152/B2
Margherita (peak), Ugan. 139/G2
Marghilon, Uzb. 111/B3
Marghita, Rom. 56/F2
Margny-lès-Compiègne, Fr. 60/B5
Margo, Sk, Can. 186/C2
Margog Caka (lake), China 111/E5
Margos, Peru 220/B3
Margosatubig, Phil. 100/C4
Margraten, Neth. 61/E2
Marguareis (peak), It. 70/D4
Marguerite, BC, Can. 174/C1
Margyang, China 109/H1
Mari, PNG 153/F2
Mari, Braz. 219/H4
Maria, Qu, Can. 188/E1
Maria (mt.), Austl. 156/D4
Maria (isl.), Austl. 153/D3
Maria Aurora, Phil. 100/C2
María Cleófas (isl.), Mex. 204/D4
Maria da Fé, Braz. 223/L7
Maria Island NP, Austl. 156/D4
Maria Juana, Arg. 224/D4
María Madre (isl.), Mex. 204/D4
María Magdalena (isl.), Mex. 204/D4
Maria van Diemen (cape), NZ 159/C1
Mariāhū, India 108/D3
Mariakani, Kenya 137/B2
Mariakerke, Belg. 60/B1
Marialva, Braz. 222/C4
Marian, Austl. 158/C3
Marianao, Cuba 207/F1
Marianna, Fl, US 195/F2
Marianna, Ar, US 192/B3
Mariano Comense, It. 68/C2
Mariano I. Loza, Arg. 224/E4
Mariánské Lázně, Czh. 65/F3
Mariarano, Madg. 143/H6
Marias (riv.), Mt, US 175/H3
Mariato (pt.), Pan. 216/A3
Ma'rib, Yem. 136/C2
Maribo, Den. 46/D4
Maribor, Slov. 56/B2
Maricá, Braz. 223/P7
Maricopa, Ca, US 178/C3
Maricopa, Az, US 179/F4
Maricopa (mts.), Az, US 179/F4
Maricopa Ak Chin Ind. Res., Az, US 179/F4
Maridalsvatn (lake), Nor. 44/S8
Marīdī, Sudan 135/F4
Marié (riv.), Braz. 217/E5
Marie Byrd Land (phys. reg.), Ant. 228/S
Marie-Galante (isl.), Dom. 203/J4
Mariefred, Swe. 45/A1
Mariehamn (int'l arpt.), Fin. 47/H1
Mariehamn (Maarianhamina), Fin. 47/H1
Marieholm, Swe. 45/K7
Mariel, Cuba 207/F1
Marienbourg, Belg. 61/D3
Mariënburg, Sur. 218/C1
Mariendorf, Ger. 48/Q7
Marienfelde, Ger. 48/Q7
Marienhafe, Ger. 59/E1
Marienheide, Ger. 61/G1
Mariental, Namb. 140/C5
Marienville, Pa, US 191/G4
Mariestad, Swe. 46/E2
Marietta, Ga, US 193/L7
Marietta, Mn, US 185/F1
Marietta, Ms, US 192/C3
Marietta, Oh, US 190/F5
Marietta, Ok, US 183/F4
Marietta, Pa, US 198/B3
Marieval, Sk, Can. 186/C2
Marigat, Kenya 137/A1
Marigliano, It. 71/D6
Marignane, Fr. 70/B6
Marigot, Guad., Fr. 203/N8
Marigot, Dom. 203/N9
Marihatag, Phil. 100/D3
Marijampolė, Lith. 47/K4
Marikina, Phil. 100/F6
Marikina (riv.), Phil. 100/F6
Marilao, Phil. 100/E6
Marília, Braz. 225/G2
Mariluz, Braz. 225/F3
Marín, Mex. 180/D5
Marín, Sp. 52/A1
Marin (co.), Ca, US 197/J10
Marin-Epagnier, Swi. 66/D3
Marina, It. 54/D3
Marina, Ca, US 178/B2
Marina del Rey (harbor), Ca, US 196/F8
Marina del Rey, Ca, US 196/F8
Marina di Andora, It. 68/B6
Marina di Carrara, It. 68/D5
Marina di Massa, It. 68/D5
Marina di Montemarciano, It. 69/G6
Marina di Pisa, It. 68/D6
Marina di Ravenna, It. 69/F5
Marina di Vasto, It. 71/D3
Mar'ina Gorka, Bela. 47/N5
Marinduque (isl.), Phil. 100/C2
Marine, Il, US 185/K4
Marine City, Mi, US 190/E3
Marine Nat'l Res., Kenya 137/C2
Marine World Africa USA, Ca, US 197/K10
Marineland, Austl. 155/M8
Marineland of Florida, Fl, US 195/H3
Marines, Fr. 36/H4
Marinette, Wi, US 190/C2
Maringa (riv.), D.R. Congo 139/E2
Maringá, Braz. 225/G2
Maringouin, La, US 194/C2
Marínguè, Moz. 141/G3
Marinha Grande, Port. 52/A3
Marinhas, Port. 52/A2
Marino, It. 71/B4
Marion (reef), Austl. 145/E2
Marion, Al, US 192/D4
Marion, Ar, US 192/B3
Marion (cr.), Fl, US 194/M7
Marion (lake), Fl, US 194/M7
Marion, Ia, US 185/J2
Marion, Il, US 192/C2
Marion, In, US 190/D4
Marion, Ks, US 183/F1
Marion, Ky, US 192/C2
Marion, La, US 183/H4
Marion, Mi, US 190/D2
Marion, Ms, US 192/C4
Marion, NC, US 193/F3
Marion, ND, US 186/E4
Marion, Oh, US 190/E4
Marion, SC, US 193/H3
Marion (lake), SC, US 173/K5
Marion, SD, US 185/F2
Marion, Va, US 193/G2
Marion, Wi, US 185/K1
Marion Bridge, NS, Can. 189/G3
Marion Junction, Al, US 192/D4
Marionville, Mo, US 183/H2
Maripa, Ven. 217/E3
Maripa, FrG. 218/D2
Maripasoula, FrG. 218/C2
Mariposa, Ca, US 178/C2
Mariposa Grove, Ca, US 178/C2
Mariquita, Col. 219/L7
Mariscal Estigarribia, Par. 224/D2
Mariscal Sucre (int'l arpt.), Ecu. 216/B5
Marissa, Il, US 192/C1
Mārith, Tun. 129/H2
Maritime Alps (mts.), Fr. 72/E1
Maritsa (riv.), Bul. 76/C4
Maritsa (riv.), Turk. 57/H5
Mariupol', Ukr. 79/J4
Mariupol (int'l arpt.), Ukr. 79/J4
Mariy-El, Resp., Rus. 80/E4
Marj 'Uyūn, Leb. 117/D2
Märjamaa, Est. 47/L2
Mark (riv.), Belg. 58/B6
Mark Twain (lake), Mo, US 185/H4
Mark Twain Nat'l Wild. Ref., Il, Ia, US 185/J3
Mark Twain Nat'l Wild. Ref., Il, Mo, US 185/J4
Marka (riv.), Ger. 59/E3
Marka, Som. 137/D1
Mārkā, Jor. 117/D5
Markagunt (plat.), Ut, US 179/F2
Markākasa, India 107/D1
Markakol (lake), Kaz. 90/D4
Markam, China 98/C2
Mārkāpur, India 107/C3
Markaryd, Swe. 46/E3
Markazī (gov.), Iran 115/G3
Markdale, On, Can. 190/F2
Markdorf, Ger. 67/F2
Marked Tree, Ar, US 192/B3
Markelsdorfer (pt.), Ger. 46/D4
Marken (isl.), Neth. 58/C4
Markerwaard (polder), Neth. 58/C3
Markesan, Wi, US 185/K2
Market Bosworth, Eng, UK 43/E1
Market Deeping, Eng, UK 43/F1
Market Drayton, Eng, UK 41/F6
Market Harborough, Eng, UK 43/F2
Market Rasen, Eng, UK 41/H5
Market Weighton, Eng, UK 41/H4
Markethill, NI, UK 40/B3
Markgroningen, Ger. 64/C5
Markha, India 110/D3
Markham, On, Can. 189/S8
Markham (bay), Nun, Can. 171/J2
Markham (riv.), PNG 153/G1
Markham, Tx, US 181/F3
Marki, Pol. 49/L2
Markinch, Sc, UK 39/C4
Markit, China 111/C4
Markivka, Ukr. 79/K3
Markle, In, US 190/D4
Markleeville, Ca, US 176/D4
Marknesse, Neth. 58/C3
Markneukirchen, Ger. 65/F2
Markópoulon, Gre. 55/N9
Markounda, CAfr. 134/C4
Markova, Rus. 90/E1
Markovac, Serb. 56/E3
Markovo, Rus. 81/S3
Markoye, Burk. 133/F3
Marks, Rus. 77/H2
Marks, Ms, US 192/B3
Marksville, La, US 194/B2
Markt Bibart, Ger. 64/D3
Markt Erlbach, Ger. 64/D4
Markt Indersdorf, Ger. 65/E6
Markt Rettenbach, Ger. 67/G2
Markt Sankt Florian, Aus. 65/H6
Markt Schwaben, Ger. 65/E6
Marktbreit, Ger. 64/D3
Marktheidenfeld, Ger. 64/C3
Marktl, Ger. 65/F6
Marktoberdorf, Ger. 67/G2
Marktredwitz, Ger. 65/F3
Marl, Ger. 59/E5
Marla, Austl. 155/G3
Marlboro, Ab, Can. 174/F1
Marlboro, NJ, US 199/D3
Marlboro (Upper Marlboro), Md, US 198/B6
Marlborough, Ma, US 191/L3
Marlborough, Austl. 158/C3
Marlborough, Eng, UK 43/E4
Marle, Fr. 60/C4
Marlengo (Marling), It. 67/H4
Marlenheim, Fr. 61/G6
Marles-en-Brie, Fr. 36/L5
Marles-les-Mines, Fr. 60/B3
Marlette, Mi, US 190/E3
Marlin, Tx, US 181/F2
Marling (Marlengo), It. 67/H4
Marlinton, WV, US 193/G1
Marlow, Ok, US 183/F3
Marlow, Ger. 46/E4
Marlow, Eng, UK 43/F3
Marlow, Ga, US 193/G4
Marlpit Hill, Eng, UK 36/D3
Marlton, NJ, US 198/D4
Marly, Fr. 60/C3
Marly, Fr. 61/F5
Marly-la-Ville, Fr. 36/K4
Marly-le-Roi, Fr. 36/J5
Marmaduke, Ar, US 192/B2
Marmagão, India 107/B3
Marmande, Fr. 50/D4
Marmara (sea), Turk. 76/D4
Marmara (isl.), Turk. 73/K2
Marmara, Turk. 57/H5
Marmaraereğlisi, Turk. 57/H5
Marmaris, Turk. 114/B2
Marmarth, ND, US 186/C4
Marmelos, Rio dos (riv.), Braz. 218/A4
Marmet, WV, US 193/G1
Marmion (lake), On, Can. 187/J3
Marmion (lake), Austl. 154/D4
Marmirolo, It. 69/D3
Marmolada (peak), It. 51/J3
Marmolejo, Sp. 52/C3
Marmontana (peak), It. 67/F5
Marmora, On, Can. 191/H2
Marmora, NJ, US 198/D5
Marmot (peak), Mt, US 174/G4
Marmoutier, Fr. 61/G6
Marnay, Fr. 66/B3
Marnaz, Fr. 66/C5
Marne, Ger. 46/C5
Marne (dept.), Fr. 60/C6
Marne (riv.), Fr. 48/C4
Marne au Rhin, Canal de la (canal), Fr. 61/D6
Marneuli, Geo. 77/H4
Marnhull, Eng, UK 42/D5
Maro, Chad 134/C3
Maro (reef), Hi, US 161/H2
Maroa, Ven. 217/E4
Maroa, Il, US 185/K3
Maroantsetra, Madg. 143/J6
Marofandilia, Madg. 143/H8
Marokau (isl.), FrPol. 161/L6
Marolambo, Madg. 143/J8
Maroldsweisach, Ger. 64/D2
Marolles, Fr. 36/M4
Marolles-en-Brie, Fr. 36/M5
Marolles-en-Hurepoix, Fr. 36/J6
Maromme, Fr. 63/G2
Maromokotro (peak), Madg. 143/J6
Marondera, Zim. 141/F3
Marone, It. 68/D2
Maroni (riv.), FrG.,Sur. 209/D2
Maroni (riv.), FrG.,Sur. 218/C1
Maroni (riv.), Sur. 217/H3
Maroochydore-Mooloolaba, Austl. 158/D4
Maroon Town, Jam. 207/G2
Maropaika, Madg. 143/H8
Marostica, It. 69/E2
Marotandrano, Madg. 143/J7
Marotiri (Bass Is.) (isl.), FrPol. 161/L7
Marotta, It. 69/G6
Maroua, Camr. 134/B3
Marouini (riv.), FrG. 217/H4
Marovato, Madg. 143/J6
Marovato, Madg. 143/J6
Marovoay, Madg. 143/H7
Marowijne (dist.), Sur. 217/H3
Marpingen, Ger. 61/G5
Marple, Eng, UK 41/F5
Marqên Gangri (peak), China 90/D5
Marquan (riv.), China 104/E2
Marquand, Mo, US 192/B2
Marquard, SAfr. 142/D3
Marquarie (riv.), Austl. 156/C1
Marquesas (isls.), FrPol. 161/M5
Marquesas Keys (isls.), Fl, US 195/G5
Marquetalia, Col. 219/K7
Marquette, Ks, US 183/F1
Marquette, Mb, Can. 186/F2
Marquette, Mi, US 187/L4
Marquez, Tx, US 181/F2
Marquis, Sk, Can. 175/M2
Marquise, Fr. 60/A2
Marracuene, Moz. 143/F2
Marradi, It. 69/E5
Marrah (peak), Sudan 134/E2
Marrakech, Mor. 128/D3
Marrakech (Menara) (int'l arpt.), Mor. 128/C3
Marrawah, Austl. 156/C4
Marree, Austl. 155/H4
Marromeu, Moz. 141/G3
Marrowbone, Ky, US 192/E2
Marrowie (cr.), Austl. 157/B1
Marrupa, Moz. 141/H2
Mars, Pa, US 190/F4
Mars (peak), It. 68/A1
Mars Hill, NC, US 193/F3
Marsá al 'Alam, Egypt 159/G3
Marsá al Burayqah, Libya 126/C2
Marsa Ben Mehidi, Alg. 130/C2
Marsá Matrūh, Egypt 159/E2
Marsabit, Kenya 137/B1
Marsabit Nat'l Rsv., Kenya 135/H5
Marsabit National Reserve, Kenya 136/A5
Marşafā, Egypt 131/C4
Marsala, It. 54/C4
Marsange (riv.), Fr. 36/L5
Marsannay, Fr. 66/A3
Marsberg, Ger. 59/F6
Marsciano, It. 71/B2
Marsden, Eng, UK 41/G4
Marsden, Sk, Can. 175/K1
Marsden, Austl. 157/C1
Marsdiep Texelstroom (chan.), Neth. 58/B3
Marseille, Fr. 70/B6
Marseille au Rhône (canal), Fr. 70/A5
Marseille-en-Beauvaisis, Fr. 60/A4
Marseilles, Il, US 185/K3
Marsella, Col. 219/K8
Marsh (mtn.), Md, US 191/G5
Marsh (isl.), La, US 181/J3
Marsh (cr.), Pa, US 198/A4
Marsh (peak), Ut, US 177/J3
Marsh Gibbon, Eng, UK 43/E3
Marshall (riv.), Austl. 155/H2
Marshall, Sk, Can. 175/K1
Marshall, Libr. 132/C5
Marshall, Ar, US 183/H3
Marshall, Il, US 190/C5
Marshall, Mi, US 190/D3
Marshall, Mn, US 185/G1
Marshall, Mo, US 185/H4
Marshall, NC, US 193/F3
Marshall, Ok, US 183/F2
Marshall, Tx, US 181/G1
Marshall Islands (ctry.) 160/G3
Marshallton, De, US 198/C4
Marshalltown, Ia, US 185/H2
Marshallville, Ga, US 192/F4
Marshfield, Mo, US 183/H2
Marshfield, Wi, US 185/J1
Marshyhope (cr.), Md, US 198/C6
Marske-by-the-Sea, Eng, UK 41/G2
Marsland, Ne, US 184/C2
Märsta, Swe. 46/G2
Marston, Mo, US 192/C2
Marsyandi (riv.), Nepal 109/E1
Marta, It. 54/B1
Marta (mts.), Col. 207/H4
Martaban, Myan. 106/B2
Martaban (gulf), Myan. 106/B2
Martano (peak), It. 71/B2
Martap, Camr. 134/B4
Martapura, Indo. 101/D4
Martapura, Indo. 102/D4
Marte R. Gomez, Mex. 204/C3
Martelange, Belg. 61/E4
Martellago, It. 69/F2
Martensville, Sk, Can. 175/L1
Martfeld, Ger. 59/G3
Martha, Ok, US 182/E3
Martha, Ky, US 193/F1
Martha's Vineyard (isl.), Ma, US 188/B5
Martignacco, It. 69/G1
Martigné-Ferchaud, Fr. 62/D5
Martigné-sur-Mayenne, Fr. 63/E4
Martigny, Swi. 66/D5
Martigny-les-Bains, Fr. 66/B1
Martigues, Fr. 70/B6
Martil, Mor. 130/B2
Martilla, Fin. 45/F4
Martin, ND, US 186/D4
Martin, La, US 194/B1
Martin, Mi, US 190/D3
Martin, SD, US 184/D2
Martin (dam), Al, US 192/E4
Martin, Tn, US 192/C2
Martin (lake), Al, US 192/E4
Martín Chico, Uru. 191/J11
Martin Luther King, Jr. Nat'l Hist. Site, Ga, US 193/M7
Martina Franca, It. 55/E2
Martinborough, NZ 159/J9
Martindale, Tx, US 180/F3
Martinengo, It. 68/C2
Martinez, Ca, US 176/B4
Martinez, Ga, US 193/F4
Martínez de la Torre, Mex. 205/M6
Martínez del Tineo, Arg. 224/C2
Martinique (isl.), Fr. 203/N9
Martinique Passage (chan.), Dom.,Mart. 203/N9
Martínon, Gre. 55/H3
Martinópole, Braz. 219/F3
Martins, Braz. 219/G4
Martins Creek, Pa, US 198/C2
Martins Ferry, Oh, US 190/F4
Martins Mills, Tx, US 181/G1
Martinsburg, WV, US 191/H5
Martinsburg, Pa, US 191/G4
Martinsburg, NY, US 191/J3
Martinsicuro, It. 71/C2
Martinsville, Il, US 190/C5
Martinsville, In, US 190/C5
Martinsville, Ms, US 194/C2
Martinsville, Va, US 193/H2
Martock, Eng, UK 42/D5
Martofte, Den. 46/D4
Marton, NZ 159/C3
Martorell, Sp. 53/K7
Martos, Sp. 52/D4
Martovce, Slvk. 56/D2
Martres-Tolosane, Fr. 50/D5
Martūba, Libya 126/D1
Martuk, Kaz. 77/L2
Martuni, Arm. 77/H4
Marty, SD, US 184/E2
Martynovo, Kaz. 77/J2
Maru, Nga. 133/G3
Marudi, Malay. 100/A4
Marugame, Japan 96/C3
Maruim, Braz. 223/F1
Maruko, Japan 97/F2
Marulan, Austl. 157/E2
Marulanda, Col. 219/K7
Marum, Neth. 58/D2
Marumba, Tanz. 141/H1
Marungu (mts.), D.R. Congo 139/G5
Maruoka, Japan 96/E2
Marutea (isl.), FrPol. 161/M7
Marv Dasht, Iran 115/H4
Marvel, Co, US 179/H2
Marvell, Ar, US 192/B3
Marvin, SD, US 185/F1
Marvine (mt.), Ut, US 179/G1
Marwayne, Ab, Can. 175/J1
Marxheim, Ger. 64/D5
Mary (lake), Ms, US 194/C2
Mary, Trkm. 113/H1
Mary Anne Passage, Austl. 154/B2
Mary Esther, Fl, US 194/E2
Mary Kathleen, Austl. 155/H2
Mary-sur-Marne, Fr. 36/M4
Maryānaj, Iran 115/G3
Maryang, China 111/C4
Maryborough, Austl. 158/D4
Maryborough, Austl. 156/B3
Marydale, SAfr. 142/C3
Marydel, Md, US 198/C5
Maryfield, Sk, Can. 186/D3
Mar'yinka, Ukr. 79/J4
Marykirk, Sc, UK 39/D3
Maryland (co.), Libr. 132/C5
Maryland (state), US 173/L4
Maryland City, Md, US 198/B5
Maryland Junction, Zim. 141/F3
Maryland Line, Md, US 198/B4
Maryneal, Tx, US 180/D1
Maryport, Eng, UK 40/E2
Marystown, Nf, Can. 189/K2
Marysvale, Ut, US 179/F1
Marysville, Ca, US 176/C4
Marysville, Ks, US 185/F4
Marysville, Mi, US 190/E3
Marysville, Mt, US 175/H4
Marysville, Oh, US 190/E4
Marysville, Pa, US 198/B3
Marysville, Wa, US 174/C3
Maryūt (lake), Egypt 131/A2
Maryvale, Austl. 158/D5
Maryville, Mo, US 185/G3
Maryville, Tn, US 192/F3
Marzabotto, It. 69/E5
Marzano (peak), It. 54/D2
Marzo (pt.), Col. 216/B3
Marzūq, Libya 126/B3
Marzūq (des.), Libya 126/B3
Masabit Nat'l Rsv., Kenya 137/B1
Masada (ruin), Isr. 159/G2
Masada NP, Isr. 117/C6
Masagan (riv.), Som. 136/C3
Masai Mara Nat'l Rsv., Kenya 137/A2
Masai Steppe (grsld.), Tanz. 137/B3
Masaka, Ugan. 139/G3
Masalembu Besar (isl.), Indo. 101/F4
Masallı, Azer. 115/G2
Masamagrell, Sp. 53/E3
Masamba, Indo. 103/F4
Masan, SKor. 93/E5
Masan-ni, SKor. 93/F7
Masanga, D.R. Congo 139/E3
Masangwe (hill), Tanz. 139/G4
Masaryktown, Fl, US 194/L7
Masasi, Tanz. 137/B4
Masavi, Bol. 224/D1
Masaya, Nic. 206/E4
Masbate, Phil. 100/C2
Masbate (isl.), Phil. 100/C2
Mascara, Alg. 130/F5
Mascarene (isls.), Mrts. 143/T15
Mascot, Tn, US 192/F2
Mascota, Mex. 204/D4
Mascotte, Fl, US 194/M6
Mascouche, Qu, Can. 189/N6
Mase, D.R. Congo 139/F4
Masela (isl.), Indo. 152/C2
Maselheim, Ger. 67/F1
Maserà di Padova, It. 69/E3
Masereka, D.R. Congo 139/G3
Maseru (cap.), Les. 142/D3
Maseru (Moshoeshoe) (int'l arpt.), Les. 142/D3
Masevaux, Fr. 66/D2
Masfjorden, Nor. 46/A1
Masha, China 99/H3
Mashaba, Zim. 141/F4
Mashad (int'l arpt.), Iran 113/G1
Mashala, D.R. Congo 139/E4
Mashalah, Egypt 131/C3
Masham, Eng, UK 41/G3
Mashhad, Iran 113/G1
Mashike, Japan 94/B2
Mashivka, Ukr. 79/H3
Mashīz, Iran 115/J4
Māshkīd (riv.), Iran 113/H3
Mashonaland Central (prov.), Zim. 141/F3
Mashonaland East (prov.), Zim. 141/F3
Mashonaland West (prov.), Zim. 141/F3
Mashqharah, Leb. 117/D1
Mashtūl as Sūq, Egypt 131/C4
Mashū (lake), Japan 94/D2
Masiaca, Mex. 204/C3
Maside, Sp. 52/A1
Masīlah (wadi), Yem. 136/D2
Masim (peak), Rus. 77/L1
Masindi, Ugan. 139/G2
Masindi Port, Ugan. 139/H2
Masinloc, Phil. 100/B2
Masis, Arm. 115/F1
Masisea, Peru 220/C3
Masisi, D.R. Congo 139/G3
Masjed-e Soleymān, Iran 115/G4
Masjid Raya (Great Mosque), Indo. 101/B2
Mask (lake), Ire. 38/A2
Maskall, Belz. 206/D2
Maskan (cape), Som. 136/B3
Masker (peak), Mor. 128/D2
Maskin, Oman 113/G4
Maskūtān, Iran 113/G3
Masnou, Sp. 53/L7
Masoala (pen.), Madg. 143/J6
Masoala (cape), Madg. 143/J6
Masoarivo, Madg. 143/H7
Mason, Il, US 192/C1
Mason, Mi, US 190/D3
Mason, Nv, US 176/D4
Mason, Oh, US 190/D5
Mason, Ok, US 183/F3
Mason, Tx, US 180/E2
Mason (co.), Wa, US 197/A3
Mason (lake), Wa, US 197/B3
Mason, WV, US 193/F1
Mason and Dixon Line, Pa, US 198/B4
Mason City, Il, US 185/K3
Mason City, Ia, US 185/H2
Masonboro, NC, US 193/J3
Masone, It. 68/B5
Masontown, Pa, US 191/G5
Masonville, Ky, US 192/D2
Masquefa, Sp. 53/K6
Masrakh, India 109/E2
Maşrif Baḩr al Baqar (canal), Egypt 131/C3
Massa, It. 68/D5
Massa Finalese, It. 69/E4
Massa Fiscaglia, It. 69/F4
Massa Lombarda, It. 69/E5
Massa Lubrense, It. 71/D6
Massa Marittima, It. 54/B1
Massa Martana, It. 71/B2
Massa-Carrara (prov.), It. 68/C4
Massachusetts (bay), Ma, US 188/B4
Massachusetts (state), US 173/M3
Massaciuccoli (lake), It. 68/D5
Massafra, It. 55/E2
Massaguet, Chad 134/B2
Massakory, Chad 134/B2
Massandra, Ukr. 79/H5
Massangena, Moz. 141/G4
Massapê, Braz. 219/F3
Massapequa, NY, US 199/M9
Massapequa Park, NY, US 199/M9
Massarosa, It. 68/D6
Massbach, Ger. 64/D2
Massena, NY, US 191/J2
Massenya, Chad 134/C3
Masset, BC, Can. 201/M4
Massey, On, Can. 190/E1
Massey (sound), Nun, Can. 171/S7
Massey, Md, US 198/C5
Massibi, Ang. 139/E5
Massif Central (upland), Fr. 72/D1
Massif de Beaufort (mass.), Fr. 70/C1
Massif de Champsaur (mass.), Fr. 70/C3
Massif de Guéra (peak), Chad 134/C3
Massif de la Chartreuse (mass.), Fr. 70/B2
Massif de la Vanoise (mass.), Fr. 70/C2
Massif de l''Assâba (mass.), Mrta. 132/C2
Massif de Pelvoux (mass.), Fr. 70/C3
Massif de Termit (mass.), Niger 134/A1
Massif des Bongos (uplands), CAfr. 134/D3
Massif des Maures (mass.), Fr. 70/C6
Massif du Manéngouba (peak), Camr. 133/H5
Massif du Tamgue (mass.), Gui. 132/B3
Massigui, Mali 132/D4
Massillon, Oh, US 190/F4
Massinga, Moz. 141/G4
Massingir, Moz. 141/G4
Massy, Fr. 36/J5
Mastābah, SAr. 112/C4
Mastadon (mtn.), Id, US 174/G4
Maştağa, Azer. 77/J4
Masterton, NZ 159/C3
Mastgat (chan.), Neth. 58/B5
Mastic, NY, US 199/F2
Mastic Beach, NY, US 199/F2
Mastník (riv.), Czh. 65/H3
Mastūj (riv.), Pak. 110/A2
Mastung, Pak. 113/J3
Mastūrah, SAr. 112/C4
Masuda, Japan 96/B3
Masuguru, Tanz. 141/H1
Masuho, Japan 95/A2
Masurai (peak), Indo. 101/C3
Masvingo, Zim. 141/F4
Masvingo (prov.), Zim. 141/F4
Maswa Game Rsv., Tanz. 137/A2
Maşyāf, Syria 116/E2
Mat (riv.), Alb. 55/F2
Mata, D.R. Congo 139/E4
Mata Bia (peak), ETim. 152/B2
Mata de Guanábano, Ven. 216/D3
Mata Grande, Braz. 219/G5
Mata Mata, SAfr. 142/C2
Mata Utu, Wall., Fr. 161/H6
Matabeleland North (prov.), Zim. 141/E3
Matabeleland South (prov.), Zim. 141/F4
Mātābhānga, India 109/G2
Matadi, D.R. Congo 138/C4
Matador, Tx, US 182/D3
Matagalpa, Nic. 206/E3
Matagorda, Tx, US 181/G3
Matagorda (pen.), Tx, US 181/G3
Matagorda (bay), Tx, US 181/F3
Matagorda (isl.), Tx, US 181/F3
Matak (isl.), Indo. 101/D2
Matala, Ang. 140/B2
Matam, Sen. 132/B3
Matamba, D.R. Congo 139/E4
Mataméye, Niger 133/H3
Matamoras, Pa, US 198/D1
Matamoros, Mex. 204/E3
Ma'ţan as Sarra (well), Libya 126/D4
Matancilla, Chile 224/B4
Matanda, Zam. 141/F1
Matandu (riv.), Tanz. 137/B4
Matane, Qu, Can. 188/D1
Matane (riv.), Qu, Can. 188/D1
Matanga, Madg. 143/H8
Matanzas, Cuba 202/E3
Matão, Braz. 225/G2
Matape (riv.), Mex. 204/C2
Matapédia, Qu, Can. 188/D2
Mataquito (riv.), Chile 226/C2
Matara (ruin), Erit. 112/C6
Matara, Erit. 136/A2
Mataram, Indo. 103/E5
Mataránga, Gre. 55/G3
Matarani, Peru 220/C5
Mataranka, Austl. 152/D3
Mataró, Sp. 53/L6
Matatiele, SAfr. 142/E3
Mataura, FrPol. 161/L7
Mataura, NZ 159/B4
Mataura (riv.), NZ 159/B4
Matawai, NZ 159/D2
Matawan, NJ, US 199/J10
Matawin (riv.), Qu, Can. 188/A2
Matay, Kaz. 77/L3
Matay, Kaz. 111/C2
Matching Green, Eng, UK 36/D1
Matecaña (int'l arpt.), Col. 219/K8
Mateguá, Bol. 221/F4
Matehuala, Mex. 205/E4
Mateke (hills), Zim. 141/F4
Matera, It. 54/E2
Matéri, Ben. 133/F4
Maternillos (pt.), Cuba 203/F3
Matese (lake), It. 71/D5
Matese (mts.), It. 71/D5
Mátészalka, Hun. 49/M5
Matetsi, Zim. 140/E3
Mateur, Tun. 130/L6
Mathay, Fr. 66/C3
Mathbaria, Bang. 109/G4
Matheniko Game Rsv., Ugan. 135/G5
Matheson Island, Mb, Can. 186/F2
Mathews, La, US 194/C3
Mathews (lake), Ca, US 196/C3
Mathew's (peak), Kenya 137/B1
Mathews, Va, US 193/J2
Mathi, It. 70/D2
Mathis, Tx, US 181/F3
Mathiston, Ms, US 192/C4
Mathoura, Austl. 157/B2
Mathurā, India 108/A2
Mati, Phil. 100/D4
Matias Barbosa, Braz. 223/N6
Matias Olímpio, Braz. 219/F3
Matías Romero, Mex. 206/C2
Matignon, Fr. 62/C3
Matíguas, Nic. 207/E3
Matilija (dam), Ca, US 196/A2
Matimbuka, Tanz. 137/A4
Matinha, Braz. 219/E4
Matinicock (pt.), NY, US 199/L8
Maţir Ţāris, Egypt 131/B6
Matiyuri (riv.), Ven. 216/D3
Matkuli, India 108/B4
Mātla (riv.), India 109/G5
Matlock, Eng, UK 41/G5
Maţmāţah, Tun. 129/H2
Matn (riv.), Leb. 117/D1
Mato Grosso (plat.), Braz. 209/D4
Mato Grosso (state), Braz. 218/A5
Mato Grosso do Sul (state), Braz. 221/G5
Mato Grosso, Meseta do (plat.), Braz. 221/G4
Mato Verde, Braz. 223/E2
Matobo (Matopos) NP, Zim. 141/F4
Matões, Braz. 219/F4
Matolo-Rio, Moz. 143/F2
Matomb, Camr. 138/B2
Matombo, Tanz. 137/B3
Matopos, Zim. 141/F4
Matopos (Matobo) NP, Zim. 141/F4
Matosinhos, Port. 52/A2
Matoury, FrG. 218/C1
Matouti (pt.), Gabon 138/B3
Matoya (bay), Japan 95/L7
Maţraḩ, Oman 113/G4
Matrei am Brenner, Aus. 67/H3
Matrei in Osttirol, Aus. 51/K3
Matriz de Camaragibe, Braz. 219/H5
Matroosberg (peak), SAfr. 142/L10
Matsalu (gulf), Est. 47/K2
Matsapa (Manzini) (int'l arpt.), Swaz. 143/E2
Matsiatra (riv.), Madg. 143/H8
Matsoandakana, Madg. 143/J6
Matsubara, Japan 95/J6
Matsubushi, Japan 95/D2
Matsuda, Japan 95/C3
Matsudo, Japan 95/D2
Matsue, Japan 96/C3
Matsuida, Japan 95/B1
Matsumae, Japan 94/B3
Matsumoto, Japan 97/E2
Matsuo, Japan 95/E2
Matsusaka, Japan 95/L6
Matsushima, Japan 94/B4
Matsutō, Japan 96/E2
Matsuyama, Japan 96/C4
Matt, Swi. 67/F4
Mattamuskeet (lake), NC, US 193/J3
Mattamuskeet Nat'l Wild. Ref., NC, US 193/J3
Mattaponi (riv.), Va, US 193/J2
Mattarello, It. 67/H6
Mattawa, On, Can. 191/G1
Mattawa, Wa, US 174/E4
Matterhorn (peak), It.,Swi. 66/D6
Mattertal (valley), Swi. 66/D5
Matteson, Il, US 190/C4
Matthew Town, Bahm. 207/H1
Matthews, Mo, US 192/C2
Matthews (mt.), NZ 159/J9
Matthews, NC, US 193/G3
Matthews Dome (mt.), Ak, US 201/H2
Mattie (lake), Fl, US 194/M7
Mattig (riv.), Aus. 65/G6
Mattighofen, Aus. 65/G6
Mattituck, NY, US 199/F2
Mattmarksee (lake), Swi. 66/D5
Mattō, Japan 96/E2
Mattock (riv.), Ire. 40/B4
Mattoon, Wi, US 185/K1
Mattsee, Aus. 65/G7
Matucana, Peru 220/B3
Matumbla (mt.), NY, US 191/J2
Matundwe (range), Malw.,Moz. 141/G3
Maturín, Ven. 217/F2
Matusadona NP, Zim. 141/F3
Matutum (mt.), Phil. 103/G2
Matveyev Kurgan, Rus. 79/K4
Matzen, Aus. 57/P7
Mau, India 108/C3
Mau, India 108/C4
Mau (peak), Kenya 137/A2
Maú (riv.), Guy. 217/G3
Maú (riv.), Guy.,Ven. 218/B1
Mau Aimma, India 108/C3
Mau Rānīpur, India 108/B3
Mau-é-Ele, Moz. 141/G5
Maúa, Moz. 141/H2
Maubert-Fontaine, Fr. 61/D4
Maubeuge, Fr. 60/C3
Maubourguet, Fr. 50/D5
Mauchline, Sc, UK 39/B5
Maud, Ok, US 183/F3
Maud, Tx, US 183/G4
Maud, Sc, UK 39/D1

Maud (pt.), Austl. 154/B2
Maudaha, India 108/C3
Maude, Austl. 157/B2
Maudlow, Mt, US 175/J4
Mauerbach, Aus. 57/N7
Mauerkirchen, Aus. 65/G6
Maués, Braz. 218/B3
Maués Açu (riv.), Braz. 218/B4
Maug (isls.), NMar. 160/D2
Mauganj, India 108/C3
Maughold, IM, UK 40/D3
Maughold (pt.), IM, UK 40/D3
Mauguio, Fr. 50/F5
Mauherslieve (peak), Ire. 38/B4
Maui (isl.), Hi, US 172/T10
Mauk, Rus. 75/P5
Mauke (isl.), CookIs. 161/K7
Maukkadaw, Myan. 98/B4
Maulbronn, Ger. 64/B5
Mauldre (riv.), Fr. 60/A6
Maule, Fr. 36/H5
Maule (riv.), Chile 226/C2
Maule (pol. reg.), Chile 226/B2
Mauléon, Fr. 50/C3
Maullín, Chile 226/B4
Maulvi Bāzār, Bang. 109/H3
Maumakeogh (peak), Ire. 38/A1
Maumee, Oh, US 190/E4
Maumere, Indo. 152/A2
Maumtrasna (peak), Ire. 38/A2
Maun, Bots. 140/D3
Maun (int'l arpt.), Bots. 140/D3
Mauna Kea (peak), Hi, US 172/U11
Mauna Loa (peak), Hi, US 172/U11
Maunath Bhanjan, India 108/D3
Maunatlala, Bots. 141/E4
Maungaturoto, NZ 159/C2
Maungdaw, Myan. 105/F3
Mauperthuis, Fr. 36/M5
Maupertus (int'l arpt.), Fr. 62/D1
Maupiti (isl.), FrPol. 161/K6
Maur, Swi. 67/E3
Maur, India 110/C4
Maurāwān, India 108/C2
Maurecourt, Fr. 36/J5
Maurepas, Fr. 60/A6
Maurepas (lake), La, US 194/C2
Mauriac, Fr. 50/E4
Maurice (riv.), NJ, US 198/C5
Maurice (lake), Austl. 145/C3
Mauricetown, NJ, US 198/D5
Mauriceville, Tx, US 181/H2
Mauricie, PN de la, Qu, Can. 191/K1
Maurienne (valley), Fr. 51/G4
Maurilândia, Braz. 222/C3
Maurine, SD, US 184/C1
Mauritania (ctry.) 119/A3
Mauriti, Braz. 219/G4
Mauritius (ctry.) 143/T15
Mauro (peak), It. 71/D4
Mauron, Fr. 62/C4
Maurui, Tanz. 137/B3
Maury City, Tn, US 192/C3
Mauston, Wi, US 185/J2
Mauthausen, Aus. 65/H6
Maverick, Az, US 179/H4
Mavila, Peru 220/D3
Mavinga, Ang. 140/D2
Mavis (reef), Austl. 152/A3
Mavqi'im, Isr. 117/B5
Mavrommátion, Gre. 55/H3
Mavrovo NP, FYROM 55/G2
Mavuradonha (mts.), Zim. 141/F3
Maw (pt.), NC, US 193/J3
Maw Daung (pass), Thai. 106/B4
Mawa, D.R. Congo 139/F2
Mawāna, India 108/A1
Mawanga, D.R. Congo 138/D4
Mawasangka, Indo. 152/A1
Mawei, China 99/E3
Mawhun, Myan. 98/C3
Mawiwi, D.R. Congo 139/F2
Māwiyah, Yem. 136/C2
Mawjib (wadi), Jor. 117/D6
Mawkmai, Myan. 98/C4
Mawlaik, Myan. 98/B4
Mawlamyine (Moulmein), Myan. 106/B2
Mawliba, India 109/H3
Mawshij, Yem. 136/B2
Mawson, Austl., Ant. 228/E
Max, ND, US 186/D4
Max Meadows, Va, US 193/G2
Maxah Ind. Res., Wa, US 174/B3
Maxaranguape, Braz. 219/H4
Maxcanú, Mex. 206/D1
Maxdorf, Ger. 64/B4
Maxéville, Fr. 61/F6
Maxhütte-Haidhof, Ger. 65/F4
Maxie, Ms, US 194/D2
Maxie, La, US 194/B2
Maxixe, Moz. 141/G4
Maxton, NC, US 193/H3
Maxville, Mt, US 175/H4
Maxwell (A.F.B.), Al, US 192/D4
Maxwell Nat'l Wildlife Reserve, NM, US 182/B2
Maxwelton, Austl. 158/A3
May, Tx, US 180/E2
May (cape), NJ, US 198/D5
May Pen, Jam. 207/G2
May, Isle of (isl.), Sc, UK 39/D4
May-en-Multien, Fr. 36/M4
Maya (riv.), Rus. 83/N4
Maya (mts.), Guat. 206/D2
Maya (isl.), Indo. 102/C4
Maya Beach, Belz. 206/D2
Maya Maya (int'l arpt.), Congo 138/C4
Maya-san (peak), Japan 95/H6
Mayaguana (isl.), Bahm. 163/K7
Mayaguana Passage (chan.), Bahm. 207/H1
Mayagüez, PR 203/M8
Mayahi, Niger 133/G3
Mayakovskogo (peak), Taj. 111/B4
Mayala, D.R. Congo 138/D4
Mayama, Congo 138/C3
Mayamba, D.R. Congo 138/D4
Mayāmey, Iran 115/H2
Mayan, China 90/F5
Mayang, China 105/J2
Mayāng Imphāl, India 98/B3
Mayaoyao, Phil. 100/C1
Mayarí, Cuba 207/H1
Maybee, Mi, US 197/E8
Maybell, Co, US 177/J3
Maybole, Sc, UK 39/B6
Maych'ew, Eth. 136/A2
Maydān, Iraq 115/F3
Maydh, Som. 136/C3
Maydī, Yem. 136/B1
Maydolong, Phil. 100/D3
Maydūm, Egypt 131/C6
Mayébout, Gabon 138/C2
Mayen, Ger. 61/G3
Mayenne (dept.), Fr. 63/E4
Mayenne, Fr. 63/E4
Mayenne (riv.), Fr. 50/C3
Mayer, Az, US 179/F3
Mayer, Mn, US 187/N7
Mayesville, SC, US 193/G4
Mayet, Fr. 63/F5
Mayetta, Ks, US 185/G4
Mayfa'ah, Yem. 136/C2
Mayfair, Sk, Can. 175/L1
Mayfield, Sc, UK 39/C5
Mayfield, Ut, US 177/H4
Mayfield, Ky, US 192/C2
Mayhill, NM, US 182/B4
Maykain, Kaz. 111/C1
Maykop, Rus. 79/L5
Mayland, Eng, UK 43/G3
Maymont, Sk, Can. 175/L1
Maymyo, Myan. 98/C4
Mayna, Rus. 77/H1
Maynard, Ar, US 192/B2
Maynardville, Tn, US 192/F2
Maynooth, Ire. 38/D3
Maynooth, On, Can. 191/H2
Mayo (riv.), Arg. 226/C5
Mayo (co.), Ire. 38/A2
Mayo, Yk, Can. 201/L3
Mayo (riv.), Mex. 204/C3
Mayo, Fl, US 195/G2
Mayo, Md, US 198/B6
Mayo (res.), NC, US 193/H2
Mayo Belwa, Nga. 134/B3
Mayo Kébi (riv.), Chad 134/B3
Mayo Mayo, Bol. 221/E4
Mayo Oulo, Camr. 134/B3
Mayo-Kébbi (pref.), Chad 134/B3
Mayoko, Congo 138/C3
Mayon (vol.), Phil. 100/C2
Mayotte (dpcy.), Fr. 143/H6
Mayoworth, Wy, US 177/K2
Maypearl, Tx, US 181/F1
Mayport Nav. Air Sta., Fl, US 195/H2
Mays Landing, NJ, US 198/D5
Mays Lick, Ky, US 192/F1
Maysān (gov.), Iraq 115/F4
Mayskiy, Rus. 77/H4
Mayskiy, Rus. 79/L4
Mayskiy, Rus. 91/K1
Maysville, Ky, US 192/F1
Maysville, Mo, US 185/G4
Maysville, Ok, US 183/F3
Maythalūn, WBnk. 117/C4
Mayuka, Zam. 141/F1
Mayumba, Gabon 138/B3
Mayuram, India 107/C4
Mayville, ND, US 186/F4
Mayville, NY, US 191/G3
Mayville, Wi, US 190/B3
Mayville, Or, US 176/C1
Maywood, Ca, US 196/F8
Maywood, Il, US 197/Q16
Maywood, Mo, US 185/J4
Maywood, Ne, US 184/D3
Maywood, NJ, US 199/J8
Mazabuka, Zam. 141/E2
Mazagão, Braz. 218/D3
Mazama, Wa, US 174/D3
Mazamet, Fr. 50/E5
Mazan, Fr. 70/B4
Mazán, Peru 220/C1
Mazandaran (gov.), Iran 115/H2
Mazār-e Sharīf, Afg. 113/J1
Mazara del Vallo, It. 54/C4
Mazarrón, Sp. 52/E4
Mazartag, China 111/D4
Mazaruni (riv.), Guy. 217/G3
Mazatán, Mex. 204/C2
Mazatenango, Guat. 206/D3
Mazatlán, Mex. 204/D4
Mazatzal (peak), Az, US 179/G3
Mazatzal (mts.), Az, US 179/G3
Mazé, Fr. 63/E6
Mažeikiai, Lith. 47/K3
Mazenod, Sk, Can. 175/L3
Mazeppa NP, Austl. 158/B3
Mazetown, NI, UK 40/B3
Mazgirt, Turk. 114/D2
Mazie, Ok, US 183/G2
Mazıkıran (pass), Turk. 114/D2
Mazinda, D.R. Congo 138/D4
Mazingarbe, Fr. 60/B3
Mazingu, D.R. Congo 138/D4
Mazirbe, Lat. 47/K3
Mazocruz, Peru 224/B1
Mazoe, Zim. 141/F3
Mazoe (riv.), Moz. 141/G3
Mazomanie, Wi, US 185/K2
Mazomeno, D.R. Congo 139/F4
Mazon, Il, US 190/B4
Mazong (peak), China 90/D3
Mazowe (riv.), Zim. 141/F3
Mazowieckie (prov.), Pol. 49/L2
Mazsalaca, Lat. 47/L3
Mazunga, Zim. 141/F4
Mazury (reg.), Pol. 49/L2
Māzūz (well), Libya 126/D2
Mazyr, Bela. 78/E1
Mbabala (isl.), Zam. 139/G5
Mbabala, Zam. 141/E3
Mbabane (cap.), Swaz. 143/E2
Mbabo (peak), Camr. 134/B4
Mbacké, Sen. 132/B3
Mbagne, Mrta. 132/B2
Mbahiakro, C.d'Iv. 132/D5
Mbaïki, CAfr. 138/D2
Mbakaou, Camr. 134/B4
Mbakaou (lake), Camr. 134/B4
Mbala, Zam. 139/G5
Mbalabala, Zim. 141/F4
Mbalam, Camr. 138/C2
Mbalambala, Kenya 137/B2
Mbale, Ugan. 137/A1
Mbali, D.R. Congo 138/D3
Mbali-Iboma, D.R. Congo 138/D3
Mbalmayo, Camr. 138/B2
Mbam (riv.), Camr. 134/A4
Mbam Minkoum (peak), Camr. 138/B2
Mbamba Bay, Tanz. 141/G1
Mban (riv.), Camr. 138/B1
Mbandaka, D.R. Congo 138/D2
Mbandjok, Camr. 134/A4
Mbang, Camr. 138/C2
Mbanga, Camr. 138/B1
Mbanio (lag.), Gabon 138/B3
Mbanza Congo, Ang. 138/C4
Mbanza-Ngungu, D.R. Congo 138/D2
Mbaranganda (riv.), Tanz. 137/B4
Mbarangandu, Tanz. 137/B4
Mbarara, Ugan. 139/G3
Mbari (riv.), CAfr. 134/D4
Mbata, CAfr. 138/D2
Mbé, Camr. 134/B4
Mbengga (isl.), Fiji 161/Y18
Mberengwa, Zim. 141/F4
Mbereshi Mission, Zam. 139/G5
Mbeya, Tanz. 137/A4
Mbeya, Zam. 141/G1
Mbeya (prov.), Tanz. 137/A3
Mbeya (range), Tanz. 137/A4
Mbeya (peak), Tanz. 137/A4
M'Bigou, Gabon 138/B3
Mbii, CAfr. 134/D4
Mbinda, Congo 138/C3
Mbingué, C.d'Iv. 132/D4
Mbini (riv.), EqG. 138/B2
Mbini, EqG. 138/B2
Mbirira, Tanz. 139/G4
Mbirizi, Ugan. 139/G3
Mbizi, Zim. 141/F4
Mbogo, Tanz. 137/A3
Mboki, CAfr. 135/E4
Mboko, D.R. Congo 139/G3
Mboloma, Zam. 141/F2
Mbomo, Congo 138/C3
Mbomou (pref.), CAfr. 134/D4
Mbomou (riv.), CAfr. 135/E4
Mbonda (pt.), EqG. 138/B2
Mboro, Sen. 132/A3
Mborong, Indo. 103/F5
Mbouda, Camr. 138/B1
Mboula, CAfr. 134/C4
Mbouomo, Congo 138/C3
M'Bour, Sen. 132/A3
M'Bout, Mrta. 132/B2
Mbres, CAfr. 134/C4
Mbuji-Mayi, D.R. Congo 139/E4
Mbulu, Tanz. 137/A2
Mburucuya, Arg. 224/E4
Mbuvu, Kenya 137/B2
Mbuzi, Zam. 141/G2
Mbwemburu (riv.), Tanz. 137/B4
Mbwikwe, Tanz. 137/A3
McAdam, NB, Can. 188/D3
McAdoo, Pa, US 198/C2
McAdoo, Tx, US 182/D4
McAfee, NJ, US 198/D1
McAlester, Ok, US 183/G3
McAlisterville, Pa, US 198/A2
McAllen, Tx, US 181/E4
McAndrews, Ky, US 193/F2
McArthur, Oh, US 193/F1
McArthur Mills, On, Can. 191/H2
McBain, Mi, US 190/D2
McBean, Ga, US 193/G4
McBee, SC, US 193/G3
McBride, BC, Can. 174/D1
McBride, Ok, US 183/F4
McCabe, Mt, US 186/B3
McCall, Id, US 176/E1
McCall Creek, Ms, US 194/C2
McCamey, Tx, US 180/C2
McCammon, Id, US 177/G2
McCarran (int'l arpt.), Nv, US 178/E2
McCarthy, Ak, US 201/K3
McCarthy's Rust, Bots. 142/C2
McCaslin (mtn.), Wi, US 190/B2
McCaulley, Tx, US 180/D1
McCaysville, Ga, US 192/E3
McChord (A.F.B.), Wa, US 174/C4
McClanahan, Tx, US 181/F2
McClave, Co, US 182/C1
McClellan (cr.), Tx, US 182/D3
McClellanville, SC, US 193/H4
McCloud (riv.), Ca, US 176/B3
McClure, Il, US 192/C2
McClure, Pa, US 198/A2
McClusky, ND, US 186/D4
McColl, SC, US 193/H3
McComb, Ms, US 194/C2
McComb, Oh, US 190/E4
McConnell (A.F.B.), Ks, US 183/F2
McConnell, Tn, US 192/C2
McConnellsburg, Pa, US 191/H5
McConnelsville, Oh, US 190/F5
McCook, Ne, US 184/D3
McCook, Tx, US 181/E4
McCord, Sk, Can. 175/L3
McCormick, SC, US 193/F4
McCracken, Ks, US 182/E1
McCreary, Mb, Can. 186/E2
McCrory, Ar, US 183/J3
McCullom Lake, Il, US 197/P15
McCullough, Al, US 194/E2
McCune, Ks, US 183/G2
McCurtain, Ok, US 183/G3
McDade, Tx, US 180/F2
McDaniel, Md, US 198/B6
McDavid, Fl, US 194/E2
McDermitt, Nv, US 176/E3
McDonald (isls.), Austl. 228/E
McDonald (mt.), Ak, US 201/F3
McDonald Observatory, Tx, US 180/B2
McDonnell (mt.), Austl. 155/H5
McDonough, Ga, US 193/M8
McDougall (pass), NW, Yk., Can. 201/L2
McElhattan, Pa, US 198/A1
McEwen, Tn, US 192/D2
McFadden NWR, Tx, US 181/G3
McFarland, Ca, US 178/C3
McFarland, Mi, US 187/L4
McFarland, Wi, US 185/K2
McGaffey, NM, US 179/H3
McGee, Sk, Can. 175/K2
McGee Creek (lake), Ok, US 183/G3
McGehee, Ar, US 183/J4
McGhee Tyson (int'l arpt.), Tn, US 192/F3
McGill, Nv, US 177/F4
McGrath, Ak, US 201/G3
McGrath, Mn, US 187/H4
McGraw, NY, US 191/H3
McGraw Brook, NB, Can. 188/D2
McGregor, On, Can. 197/G7
McGregor, Mn, US 187/H4
McGregor, ND, US 186/C3
McGregor, Tx, US 181/F2
McGuire (A.F.B.), NJ, US 198/D3
McHenry, Il, US 190/B3
McHenry (co.), Il, US 197/N15
McHenry, Ky, US 192/D2
McHenry, Ms, US 194/D2
McHinga, Tanz. 137/B4
McHinji, Malw. 141/G2
McInnis (lake), On, Can. 187/H1
McIntosh, Mn, US 186/G4
McIntosh, SD, US 186/D5
McIntosh, Al, US 194/D2
McIntosh, NM, US 179/J3
McKay Creek Nat'l Wild. Ref., Or, US 176/D1
McKay Creek NWR, Or, US 174/E5
McKean (isl.), Kiri. 161/H5
McKeand (riv.), Nun, Can. 171/K2
McKee, Ky, US 192/F2
McKee City, NJ, US 198/D5
McKeesport, Pa, US 191/G4
McKellar, On, Can. 190/G2
McKenzie, Al, US 194/E2
McKenzie (riv.), Or, US 176/B1
McKenzie, Tn, US 192/C2
McKinlay, Austl. 158/A3
McKinley (mt.), Ak, US 201/H3
McKinley Park (Denali National Park), Ak, US 201/J3
McKinleyville, Ca, US 176/A3
McKinney, Tx, US 180/L6
McKinney Bayou (riv.), Tx,Ar, US 183/G4
McKittrick, Ca, US 178/C3
McLain, Ms, US 194/D2
McLaren Creek Abor. Land, Austl. 152/D5
McLaughlin, SD, US 186/D5
McLaurin, Ms, US 194/D2
McLean, Tx, US 182/D3
McLean, Il, US 185/K3
McLean, Va, US 198/A6
McLeansboro, Il, US 192/C1
McLeod (bay), NW, Can. 170/E2
McLeod (riv.), Ab, Can. 174/F1
McLeod (lake), Austl. 154/B3
McLoughlin (mt.), Or, US 176/B2
M'Clure (str.), NW, Can. 170/E2
McLure, BC, Can. 174/D2
McMillan, Ok, US 183/F3
McMinnville, Or, US 176/B1
McMinnville, Tn, US 192/E3
McMunn, Mb, Can. 187/G3
McMurdo, US, Ant. 228/M
McNab, Ar, US 183/H4
McNamee, NB, Can. 188/D2
McNary, Az, US 179/H3
McNary (dam), Or, US 174/E5
McNary NWR, Wa, US 174/E4
McNaughton, Wi, US 187/K5
McNeil, Ar, US 183/H4
McNeil (isl.), Wa, US 197/B3
McNeill, Ms, US 194/D2
McOcha, Malw. 141/G2
McPhee (res.), Co, US 179/H2
McPherson, Ks, US 183/F1
McQueeney, Tx, US 181/E3
McRae, Ar, US 183/J3
McRae, Ga, US 195/G1
McVille, ND, US 186/E4
McWilliams, Al, US 194/E2
Mdabulo, Tanz. 137/A3
Mdaburo, Tanz. 137/A3
Mdandu, Tanz. 137/A4
Mdantsane, SAfr. 142/D4
M'diq, Mor. 130/B2
Mê (riv.), China 90/E5
Me-akan-dake (peak), Japan 94/C2
Meacham, Sk, Can. 175/M1
Mead (lake), Az,Nv, US 163/F6
Mead, Ne, US 185/F3
Meade (riv.), Ak, US 201/G2
Meade, Ks, US 182/D2
Meadow, Tx, US 182/C4
Meadow, SD, US 186/C5
Meadow, Ut, US 179/F1
Meadow Lake, Sk, Can. 170/F3
Meadow Valley, Ca, US 176/C4
Meadow Valley Wash (riv.), Nv, US 178/E2
Meadow Vista, Ca, US 176/C4
Meadowlands, Mn, US 187/H4
Meadowlands Sports Complex, NJ, US 199/J8
Meadows, Id, US 176/E1
Meadows, Md, US 198/B6
Meadowvale, On, Can. 190/T8
Meadville, Ms, US 194/C2
Meadville, Pa, US 190/F4
Meadville, Mo, US 185/H4
Meaford, On, Can. 190/F2
Mealhada, Port. 52/A2
Meall a' Bhuiridh (peak), Sc, UK 39/B3
Meall Buidhe (peak), Sc, UK 39/B3
Meall Dearg (peak), Sc, UK 39/C3
Meall Dubh (peak), Sc, UK 39/B2
Meall nam Fuaran (peak), Sc, UK 39/C4
Meall Tairneachan (peak), Sc, UK 39/C3
Mearim (riv.), Braz. 219/E4
Measham, Eng, UK 43/E1
Meat (mt.), Ak, US 201/F2
Meath (co.), Ire. 40/B4
Meath Park, Sk, Can. 175/M1
Méaulte, Fr. 60/B4
Meaux, Fr. 36/L5
Mebenda (peak), Gabon 138/B3
Mebridege (riv.), Ang. 138/C4
Mecapalapa, Mex. 205/M6
Mècatina, Rivière du Petit (riv.), Nf,Qu, Can. 171/K3
Mecca (Makkah), SAr. 112/C4
Mecca, Ca, US 178/D4
Mechanicsburg, Oh, US 190/E4
Mechanicsburg, Pa, US 198/A3
Mechanicsburg Nav. Res., Pa, US 198/B3
Mechanicsville, Va, US 193/J2
Mechant (lake), La, US 194/C3
Mechara, Eth. 136/B3
Mechelen, Belg. 61/D1
Mecheria, Alg. 129/E2
Mechi (zone), Nepal 109/F2
Méchiméré, Chad 134/B2
Mechra-Bel-Ksiri, Mor. 130/B2
Mechrâ-Saf-Saf, Mor. 130/C2
Mecidiye, Turk. 57/H5
Mecitözü, Turk. 114/C1
Meckenbeuren, Ger. 67/F2
Meckenheim, Ger. 61/G2
Mecklenburg-Vorpommern (state), Ger. 46/E5
Mecklenburger (bay), Ger. 48/F1
Meconta, Moz. 141/H2
Mecoya, Bol. 224/C2
Mecsek (mts.), Hun. 73/H1
Mecuburi (riv.), Moz. 141/H2
Mecúfi, Moz. 141/J2
Mecuia (peak), Moz. 141/G2
Mecula, Moz. 141/H2
Meda, It. 68/C2
Medak, India 107/C2
Medan, Indo. 101/B2
Medang (cape), Indo. 101/C2
Médanos, Arg. 226/E3
Medanos de Coro, PN, Ven. 216/D2
Medanosa (pt.), Arg. 191/D6
Medaryville, In, US 190/C4
Medbourne, Eng, UK 43/F1
Mede Lomellina, It. 68/B3
Médéa (wilaya), Alg. 130/G4
Médéa, Alg. 130/G4
Medebach, Ger. 59/F6
Medeiros Neto, Braz. 223/E3
Medel (peak), Swi. 67/E4
Medellín, Col. 219/K6
Medemblik, Neth. 58/C3
Meden (riv.), Eng, UK 41/G5
Medenine, Tun. 129/H2
Medenine (gov.), Tun. 129/H2
Mederdra, Mrta. 132/B2
Medesano, It. 68/D4
Medetsiz (peak), Turk. 114/C2
Medford, NY, US 199/E2
Medford, Ok, US 183/F2
Medford, Or, US 176/B2
Medford, Wi, US 187/J5
Medford Lakes, NJ, US 198/D4
Medgidia, Rom. 57/J3
Medi, Sudan 135/F4
Media, Pa, US 198/C4
Media Agua, Arg. 224/B4
Medianeira, Braz. 225/F3
Mediapolis, Ia, US 185/J3
Mediaş, Rom. 57/G2
Medical Lake, Wa, US 174/F4
Medicina, It. 69/E5
Medicine (cr.), Mo, US 185/H3
Medicine (cr.), Ne, US 184/D3
Medicine (lake), Mt, US 175/M3
Medicine (riv.), Ab, Can. 174/G1
Medicine Bow (mts.), Wy, US 172/E3
Medicine Bow (riv.), Wy, US 177/K2
Medicine Bow (peak), Wy, US 184/A3
Medicine Hat, Ab, Can. 175/J2
Medicine Knoll (cr.), SD, US 186/E5
Medicine Lake, Mt, US 186/B3
Medicine Lake NWR, Mt, US 186/B3
Medicine Lodge, Ks, US 183/E2
Medicine Lodge (riv.), Ks,Ok, US 182/E2
Medika, Mb, Can. 186/G3
Medina, Col. 216/C3
Medina (int'l arpt.), SAr. 159/H3
Medina (riv.), Eng, UK 43/E5
Medina, ND, US 186/E4
Medina, NY, US 191/G3
Medina, Oh, US 190/F4
Medina, Tn, US 192/C3
Medina, Tx, US 180/E3
Medina (riv.), Tx, US 181/E3
Medina, Wa, US 197/C2
Medina de Pomar, Sp. 50/B5
Medina de Rioseco, Sp. 52/C2
Medina del Campo, Sp. 52/C2
Médina Gonassé, Sen. 132/B3
Medina-Sidonia, Sp. 52/C4
Medinaceli, Sp. 52/D2
Medininkai, Lith. 47/L4
Medinipur, India 109/F4
Medio (cr.), Tx, US 181/F3
Mediodía, Col. 216/C5
Mediouna, Mor. 128/D2
Mediterranean (sea) 29/E5
Medjaz el Bab, Tun. 130/L6
Medje, D.R. Congo 139/F2
Mednogorsk, Rus. 77/L2
Mêdog, China 98/B2
Medole, It. 68/D3
Medolla, It. 69/E4
Medora, In, US 192/D1
Medora, ND, US 186/C4
Médouneu, Gabon 138/B2
Medowie, Austl. 157/E1
Medstead, Sk, Can. 175/K1
Medulla, Fl, US 194/M8
Medveditsa (riv.), Rus. 80/E5
Medvedovskaya, Rus. 79/K5
Medvënka, Rus. 79/J2
Medvezh'i (isls.), Rus. 81/S2
Medvezh'yegorsk, Rus. 74/G3
Medvode, Slov. 51/L3
Medway (co.), Eng, UK 43/G4
Medyn', Rus. 74/G5
Medzilaborce, Slvk. 78/A3
Meekatharra, Austl. 154/C3
Meeker, Co, US 177/K3
Meelpaeg (lake), Nf, Can. 189/J1
Meenambarkkam (int'l arpt.), India 107/D3
Meer, Belg. 58/B6
Meerbusch, Ger. 58/D6
Meerhout, Belg. 61/E1
Meersburg, Ger. 67/F2
Meerssen, Neth. 61/E2
Meerut, India 108/A1
Meeteetse, Wy, US 177/J1
Meeuwen, Belg. 61/E1
Mēga, Eth. 136/A4
Mega (isl.), Indo. 101/C4
Mega, Indo. 103/H4
Megála Kalívia, Gre. 55/G3
Megáli Panayía, Gre. 55/H2
Megalo, Eth. 136/B4
Megálon Khoríon, Gre. 114/A2
Megalópolis, Gre. 55/H4
Meganom (cape), Ukr. 79/H5
Megantic (peak), Qu, Can. 188/B3
Mégara, Gre. 55/H3
Megargel, Tx, US 182/E4
Megargel, Al, US 194/E2
Megève, Fr. 66/C6
Megezez (peak), Eth. 136/A3
Meghalaya (state), India 105/F2
Meghna (riv.), Bang. 109/H4
Megiddo, Isr. 117/C3
Megista (isl.), Gre. 116/A1
Megrega, Rus. 47/Q1
Megri, Arm. 115/F2
Meguzalala, Moz. 141/F4
Mehaigne (riv.), Belg. 61/E2
Mehal Mēda, Eth. 136/A3
Mehamn, Nor. 44/H1
Meharry (mt.), Austl. 154/C2
Mehdia, Alg. 130/F5
Mehdīshahr, Iran 115/H3
Mehdiya-Plage, Mor. 130/A2
Mehe (riv.), Ger. 59/G1
Mehedinti (co.), Rom. 78/B5
Meherpur, Bang. 109/G4
Meherrin (riv.), Va, US 193/H2
Mehikoorma, Est. 47/M2
Mehlingen, Ger. 61/G4
Mehndāwal, India 108/D2
Mehrabad (int'l arpt.), Iran 115/G3
Mehrabān, Iran 115/F2
Mehrān (riv.), Iran 113/F3
Mehring, Ger. 61/F4
Mehrīz, Iran 115/H4
Mehrnbach, Aus. 65/G6
Mehtar Lām, Afg. 110/A2
Mei (riv.), China 99/G3
Meia Meia, Tanz. 137/A3
Meia Ponte (riv.), Braz. 222/C3
Meidougou, Camr. 134/B4
Meiganga, Camr. 134/B4
Meighen (isl.), Nun, Can. 171/R7
Meigle, Sc, UK 39/C3
Meigs, Ga, US 195/F2
Meigu, China 105/H2
Meihekou, China 91/K3
Meikle Bin (peak), Sc, UK 39/B4
Meikle Black Law (hill), Sc, UK 39/D5
Meikle Says Law (peak), Sc, UK 39/D5
Meikou, China 99/H3
Meiktila, Myan. 98/B4
Meilen, Swi. 67/E3
Meine, Ger. 59/H4
Meiners Oaks, Ca, US 196/A2
Meinersen, Ger. 59/H4
Meinerzhagen, Ger. 61/G1
Meiningen, Ger. 64/D1
Meiringen, Swi. 66/E4
Meisenheim, Ger. 61/G4
Meishan, China 98/D2
Meishan, China 99/H3
Meishan (res.), China 92/C5
Meishan, China 99/H3
Meishan, China 92/K8
Meishuikeng, China 99/H3
Meissen, Ger. 49/G3
Meissner (peak), Ger. 59/G6
Meitian, China 99/G3
Meitingen, Ger. 64/D5
Meiwa, Japan 95/L6
Meix-Devant-Virton, Belg. 61/E4
Meizhou, China 99/H3
Mejaniga, It. 69/E3
Mejaouda (well), Mrta. 128/D5
Mejillones, Chile 224/B2
Mejorada del Campo, Sp. 53/N9
Mekambo, Gabon 138/C2
Mekane Selam, Eth. 136/A3
Mek'elē, Eth. 136/A2
Mékhé, Sen. 132/A3
Mek'ī, Eth. 136/A3
Mekinock, ND, US 186/F3
Meknès, Mor. 130/B3
Meknès (prov.), Mor. 130/B3
Meko, Nga. 133/F5
Mekong (riv.), Asia 106/C1
Mekongga (peak), Indo. 103/F4
Mekoryuk, Ak, US 201/E3
Melaka, Malay. 101/C2
Melaka (state), Malay. 101/C2
Melanesia (reg.) 160/E5
Melappālaiyam, India 107/C4
Melawi (riv.), Indo. 102/D4
Melbeck, Ger. 59/H2
Melbourn, Eng, UK 43/G2
Melbourne, Austl. 156/G5
Melbourne (isl.), Nun, Can. 170/F2
Melbourne, Eng, UK 41/G6
Melbourne, Ar, US 183/J2
Melbourne, Fl, US 195/H3
Melbu, Nor. 44/E1
Melcher-Dallas, Ia, US 185/H3
Melchor (isl.), Chile 226/B5
Melchor Múzquiz, Mex. 180/D4
Melchor Ocampo, Mex. 180/E4
Melchor Ocampo, Mex. 205/Q9
Melcombe Regis, Eng, UK 42/D5
Meldola, It. 69/F5
Meldorf, Ger. 46/C4
Mele (cape), It. 68/B6
Meleb, Mb, Can. 186/F2
Melegnano, It. 68/C3
Melenci, Serb. 56/E3
Melenki, Rus. 74/J5
Melesse, Fr. 62/D4
Meleuz, Rus. 77/K1
Mélèzes (riv.), Qu, Can. 171/J3
Melezza (riv.), It. 67/E5
Melfa (riv.), It. 71/C4
Melfi, Chad 134/C3
Melfi, It. 54/D2
Melfort, Sk, Can. 175/M1
Melgaço, Port. 52/A1
Melgar, Col. 219/L8
Melgar de Fernamental, Sp. 52/C1
Melhus, Nor. 44/D3
Melibocus (peak), Ger. 64/B3
Melide, Swi. 67/E6
Meligalás, Gre. 55/G4
Melíki, Gre. 55/H2
Melili (peak), Kenya 137/B2
Melilla, Sp. 130/C2
Melimoyu (peak), Chile 226/B5
Melinca, Chile 226/B4
Melipilla, Chile 226/N8
Mélisey, Fr. 66/C2
Melissano, It. 55/F3
Melita, Mb, Can. 186/D3
Melita (int'l arpt.), Tun. 73/F4
Melito di Porto Salvo, It. 54/D4
Melitopol', Ukr. 79/H4
Melitota, Md, US 198/B5
Melka Guba, Eth. 136/A4
Melka Meri, Eth. 136/B4
Melkasa, Eth. 136/A3
Melkbosstrand, SAfr. 142/L10
Melksham, Eng, UK 42/D4
Mella (riv.), It. 68/D2
Mellac, Fr. 62/B5
Mellan Fryken (lake), Swe. 46/E2
Melle, Belg. 60/C2
Melle, Ger. 59/F4
Mellea (riv.), It. 68/A3
Mellègue (wadi), Tun. 130/L6
Mellègue, Oued (riv.), Alg. 130/K7
Mellerud, Swe. 46/E2
Mellette, SD, US 184/E1
Mellid, Sp. 52/A1
Mellieħa, Malta 54/L7
Melling, Eng, UK 41/F3
Mellingen, Swi. 67/E3
Mellit, Sudan 135/E2
Mellizo Sur (peak), Chile 191/B6
Mellrichstadt, Ger. 64/D2
Mellum (isl.), Ger. 59/F1
Melmoth, SAfr. 143/E3
Melnik, Bul. 55/H2
Mělník, Czh. 65/H2
Mel'nytsya-Podil's'ka, Ukr. 78/D3
Melo, Uru. 225/F5
Melocheville, Qu, Can. 189/N7
Melolo, Indo. 103/F5
Mélong, Camr. 138/B1
Melrose, Austl. 157/C2
Melrose, Sc, UK 39/D5
Melrose, La, US 194/B2
Melrose, Mn, US 187/G5
Melrose, Md, US 198/B4
Melrose, Wi, US 185/J1
Melrose Abbey, Sc, UK 39/D5
Melrose Bombing Range, NM, US 182/C3
Melrose Park, Il, US 197/Q16
Mels, Swi. 67/F3
Melstone, Mt, US 175/L4
Melsungen, Ger. 59/G6
Meltham, Eng, UK 41/G4
Melton, Austl. 157/B3
Melton Mowbray, Eng, UK 43/F1
Melúli (riv.), Moz. 141/H2
Melun, Fr. 36/K6
Melunga, Ang. 140/C3
Melvern, Ks, US 183/G1
Melvern (lake), Ks, US 185/G4
Melville (bay), Austl. 145/C2
Melville (cape), Austl. 158/B1
Melville (nbrhd.), Austl. 154/K7
Melville (lake), Nf, Can. 171/L3
Melville (pen.), Can. 163/J3
Melville (isl.), Can. 145/C2
Melville (cape), Phil. 100/B4
Melville, Sk, Can. 186/C2
Melville, La, US 194/C2
Melville, NY, US 199/M8
Melville, Mt, US 175/K4
Melville Abor. Land, Austl. 152/C2
Melvin, Al, US 194/D2
Melvin, Tx, US 180/E2
Melvindale, Mi, US 197/F7
Mélykút, Hun. 56/D2
Melzo, It. 68/C3
Memaliaj, Alb. 55/F2
Memar (lake), China 111/D5
Memāri, India 109/G4
Memba, Moz. 141/J2
Membalong, Indo. 102/C4
Même (riv.), Fr. 63/F4
Memmert (isl.), Ger. 58/D1
Memmingen, Ger. 67/G2
Memot, Camb. 106/D4
Memphis, Tx, US 182/D3
Memphis, Mi, US 197/G6
Memphis, Mo, US 185/H3
Memphis, Tn, US 192/B3
Memphis (int'l arpt.), Tn, US 192/C3
Memphis (ruin), Egypt 131/C5
Memphis Nav. Air Sta., Tn, US 192/C3
Memphrémagog (lake), Qu, Can. 188/A3
Mena, Ar, US 183/G3
Mèna, Mali 132/D3
Mena, Ukr. 78/G2
Mena, Eth. 136/A4
Mena, Indo. 152/B2
Menafra, Uru. 191/K10
Menaggio, It. 67/F5
Menahga, Mn, US 187/G4
Menai (str.), Wal, UK 40/D5
Menai Bridge, Wal, UK 40/D5
Ménaka, Mali 133/F3
Menaldum, Neth. 58/C2
Menan, Id, US 177/H2
Menanga, Indo. 103/F4
Menara (Marrakech) (int'l arpt.), Mor. 128/C3
Menarandra (riv.), Madg. 143/H9
Menard, Tx, US 180/E2
Menasalbas, Sp. 52/C3
Menasha, Wi, US 185/K1
Menavava (riv.), Madg. 143/H7
Menawashei, Sudan 135/E2
Mencué, Arg. 226/C4
Mendawai (riv.), Indo. 102/D4
Mende, Fr. 50/E4
Mendebo (mts.), Eth. 136/A4
Menden, Ger. 59/E6
Mendenhall (cape), Ak, US 201/E4
Mendenhall, Ms, US 194/D2
Mendes, Braz. 223/N7
Méndez, Mex. 205/F3
Mendham, Sk, Can. 175/K2
Mendham, NJ, US 198/D2
Mendī, Eth. 135/G3
Mendi, PNG 153/F1
Mendig, Ger. 61/G3
Mendip (hills), Eng, UK 42/D4
Mendocino, Ca, US 176/B4
Mendocino (pass), Ca, US 176/B4
Mendocino (cape), Ca, US 172/A3
Mendol (isl.), Indo. 101/C2
Mendon, Mi, US 190/D3
Mendon, Mo, US 185/H4
Mendooran, Austl. 156/D1
Mendota, Ca, US 178/B2
Mendota, Il, US 185/K3
Mendota, Mn, US 187/P7
Mendoza (prov.), Arg. 226/C2
Mendoza, Arg. 226/C2
Mendoza, Cuba 207/E1
Mendoza, Uru. 191/K11
Mendoza, Peru 220/B2
Mendoza (El Plumerillo) (int'l arpt.), Arg. 226/C2
Mendrisio, Swi. 67/E6
Mene Grande, Ven. 216/D2
Menegosa (peak), It. 68/C4
Menemen, Turk. 76/C5
Menen, Belg. 60/C2
Menengai Crater, Kenya 137/B2
Menengiyn (plain), Mong. 81/M5
Menfi, It. 54/C4
Meng Xian, China 92/C4
Mengcheng, China 92/D4
Mengen, Ger. 67/F1
Mengen, Turk. 76/E4
Mengersgereuth-Hämmern, Ger. 64/D2
Mengerskirchen, Ger. 64/B1
Mengeš, Slov. 51/L3
Menggala, Indo. 101/D4
Menggatal, Malay. 100/B4
Menghai, China 106/C1
Mengibar, Sp. 52/D4
Mengjian, China 99/F4
Mengkofen, Ger. 65/F5
Mengla, China 106/C1
Menglian Daizu Lahuzu Vazu Zizhixian, China 98/C4
Mengman, China 106/C1
Mengshan, China 99/F3
Mengxing, China 106/C1
Mengyin, China 92/D4
Mengzi, China 98/D4
Ménilles, Fr. 63/G2
Menindee (dam), Austl. 156/B2
Menindee, Austl. 156/B2
Menindee (lake), Austl. 155/J5
Meningie, Austl. 156/A2
Menlo, Ga, US 192/E3
Menlo Park, Ca, US 197/K12
Menlo Park, NJ, US 199/H9
Menlolat (peak), Chile 226/B5
Mennecy, Fr. 36/K6
Mennetou-sur-Cher, Fr. 63/G6
Menoken Indian Village Historical Site, ND, US 186/D4
Menominee (riv.), Mi, Wi, US 187/L5
Menominee, Mi, US 190/C2
Menominee Ind. Res., Wi, US 185/K1
Menomonee Falls, Wi, US 190/B3
Menomonie, Wi, US 185/J1
Menongue, Ang. 140/C2
Menonitas Colonias, Par. 224/E2
Menorca (int'l arpt.), Sp. 53/H3
Menorca (Minorca) (isl.), Sp. 53/H2
Mentana, It. 71/B3
Mentasta Lake, Ak, US 201/K3
Mentawai (isls.), Indo. 83/J10
Mentawai (str.), Indo. 102/A4
Mentekab, Malay. 101/C2
Menteroda, Ger. 59/H6
Menthon-Saint-Bernard, Fr. 66/C6
Mentmore, NM, US 179/H3
Menton, Fr. 70/D5
Mentone, Ca, US 196/C2
Mentone, In, US 190/C4
Mentone, Tx, US 180/C2
Mentor, Mn, US 186/F4
Mentor, Oh, US 190/F4
Mentougou, China 92/H7
Mentue (riv.), Swi. 66/C4
Menucourt, Fr. 36/H4
Menuma, Japan 95/C1
Menyamya, PNG 153/G1
Menyapa (peak), Indo. 103/E3
Menyuan Huizu Zizhixian, China 90/E4
Menzel Bou Zelfa, Tun. 130/M6
Menzel Bourguiba, Tun. 130/L6
Menzel Temime, Tun. 130/M6
Menzie (mt.), Yk, Can. 201/M3
Menzies, Austl. 154/D4
Menziken, Swi. 66/E3
Menzingen, Swi. 67/E3
Menznau, Swi. 66/E3
Meolo, It. 69/F2
Meon (riv.), Eng, UK 43/E5
Meopham, Eng, UK 36/E2
Meoquí, Mex. 180/B3
Meos Waar (isl.), Indo. 103/H4
Meota, Sk, Can. 175/K1
Méouge (riv.), Fr. 70/B4
Mepala, Ang. 138/C4
Mepistskaro (peak), Geo. 77/G4
Meppel, Neth. 58/D3
Meppen, Ger. 59/E3
Mequinenzo (res.), Sp. 53/E2
Mequon, Wi, US 190/C3
Mer, Fr. 63/G5
Mer Rouge, La, US 183/J4
Mera (riv.), It. 67/F5
Merak, Indo. 101/D4
Meramec (riv.), Mo, US 185/J5
Merano, It. 67/H4
Merasheen (isl.), Nf, Can. 189/K2
Merate, It. 68/C2
Meratus (mts.), Indo. 102/D4
Merauke, Indo. 153/F2
Merauke (riv.), Indo. 153/F2
Merbein, Austl. 156/B2
Mercaderes, Col. 216/B4
Mercantour, PN, Fr. 51/G4
Mercatello sul Metauro, It. 69/F6
Mercato, It. 71/D6
Mercato San Severino, It. 71/D6
Mercato Saraceno, It. 69/F6
Merced, Ca, US 178/B2
Merced (peak), Ca, US 178/C2
Merced (riv.), Ca, US 178/B2
Merced Grove, Ca, US 178/C2
Mercedario (peak), Arg. 224/B4
Mercedes, Arg. 226/D2
Mercedes, Arg. 191/J11
Mercedes, Arg. 224/E4
Mercedes, Uru. 191/J10
Mercedes, Tx, US 181/F4
Mercer, NZ 159/C2
Mercer, Mo, US 185/H3
Mercer (co.), NJ, US 198/D3
Mercer, Pa, US 190/F4
Mercer (isl.), Wa, US 197/C2
Mercer County (arpt.), NJ, US 198/D3
Mercer Island, Wa, US 197/C2
Mercersburg, Pa, US 191/H5
Mercerville-Hamilton Square, NJ, US 198/D3
Merchtem, Belg. 61/D2
Mercier, Qu, Can. 189/N7
Mercoal, Ab, Can. 174/F1
Mercogliano, It. 71/D6
Mercury, Nv, US 178/E2
Mercury, Tx, US 180/E2
Mercy (cape), Nun, Can. 171/K2
Mercy-le-Bas, Fr. 61/E5
Merdereau (riv.), Fr. 63/E4
Merderet (riv.), Fr. 62/D2
Merdrignac, Fr. 62/C4
Mere, Belg. 60/C2
Méré, Fr. 36/H5
Mere, Eng, UK 42/D4
Méreau, Fr. 63/H6
Mereb Wenz (riv.), Erit. 135/H2
Meredith (lake), Co, US 182/C1
Meredith, NH, US 191/L3
Meredith (cape), UK 191/E7
Meredosia, Il, US 185/J4
Meredosia Nat'l Wild. Ref., Il, US 185/J4
Mereeg, Som. 136/C5
Merefa, Ukr. 79/J3
Merelbeke, Belg. 60/C2
Merenberg, Ger. 64/B1
Mereuch, Camb. 106/D3
Méréville, Fr. 63/H4
Mereworth, Eng, UK 36/E3
Mergel (riv.), China 91/J2
Mergozzo, It. 67/E6
Mergui (arch.), Myan. 105/G5
Mergui (Myeik), Myan. 106/B3
Meriç, Turk. 57/H5
Meriç (riv.), Turk. 73/K2
Merichleri, Bul. 57/G4
Méricourt, Fr. 60/B3
Méricourt, Fr. 36/G4
Mérida, Mex. 206/D1
Mérida, Ven. 216/D2
Mérida (state), Ven. 216/D2
Mérida, Sp. 52/B3
Mérida, Cordillera de (mts.), Ven. 216/D3
Meriden, Ct, US 191/K4
Meriden, Wy, US 184/B3
Meridian, Ok, US 183/F3
Meridian, Pa, US 190/G4
Meridian, Ga, US 195/H2
Meridian, Id, US 176/E2
Meridian, Ms, US 192/C4
Meridian, Tx, US 180/F2
Meridian Nav. Air Sta., Ms, US 192/C4
Meridian Station, Ms, US 192/C4
Meridianville, Al, US 192/D3
Mérignac, Fr. 50/C4
Merignac (int'l arpt.), Fr. 50/C4
Merimbula, Austl. 157/D3
Merin Gubai, Som. 137/D1
Merinda, Austl. 158/C3
Mering, Ger. 64/D6
Meringa, Nga. 134/B3
Merino, Co, US 184/C3
Merinos, Uru. 191/K10
Merja Zerga (lake), Mor. 130/A2
Mérk, Hun. 56/F2
Merkel, Tx, US 180/D1
Merkendorf, Ger. 64/D4
Merkinė, Lith. 47/L4
Merksem, Belg. 58/B6
Merksplas, Belg. 58/B6
Merkus (cape), PNG 153/H1
Merlimont, Fr. 60/A3
Merlo, Arg. 191/J11
Merlo, Arg. 224/C5
Meroe (ruin), Sudan 135/G1
Merone, It. 68/C2
Merouane, Chott (lake), Alg. 72/E4
Merredin, Austl. 154/C4
Merri (cr.), Austl. 156/F5
Merriam (crater), Az, US 179/G3
Merrick (peak), Sc, UK 40/D1
Merrick, NY, US 199/L9
Merricks, Austl. 157/B4
Merrickville, On, Can. 191/J2
Merricourt, ND, US 186/E4
Merrill, Or, US 176/C2
Merrill, Wi, US 187/K5
Merrill Creek (res.), NJ, US 198/C2
Merrillville, In, US 190/C4

Merri – Mistr
309

Merrimack, NH, US 191/L3
Merrimack (riv.), NH, US 188/B4
Merriman, Ne, US 184/D2
Merriott, Eng, UK 42/D5
Merritt, BC, Can. 174/D2
Merritt (isl.), Fl, US 195/H3
Merritt (dam), Ne, US 184/D2
Merritt (res.), Ne, US 184/D2
Merritt Island, Fl, US 195/H3
Merritt Island Nat'l Wild. Ref., Fl, US 195/H3
Merriwa, Austl. 156/D2
Merriwagga, Austl. 157/B1
Merriweather, Mi, US 187/K4
Merryville, La, US 194/B2
Mers-les-Bains, Fr. 60/A3
Mersa Fatma, Erit. 136/B2
Mersa Gulbub, Erit. 136/A1
Mersa Tek'lay, Erit. 112/C5
Mersch, Lux. 61/F4
Merse (reg.), Sc, UK 39/D5
Mersey (riv.), Eng, UK 41/F5
Merseyside (co.), Eng, UK 41/F5
Mershon, Ga, US 195/G2
Mersin, Turk. 116/D1
Mersin Galgalo, Eth. 136/C4
Mersing, Malay. 101/C2
Mērsrags, Lat. 47/K3
Merstham, Eng, UK 36/C3
Mertens, Tx, US 181/F1
Mertert, Lux. 61/F4
Mertesdorf, Ger. 61/F4
Merthyr Tydfil, Wal, UK 42/C3
Merthyr Tydfil (co.), Wal, UK 42/C3
Mértola, Port. 52/B4
Merton (bor.), Eng, UK 36/C2
Mertzon, Tx, US 180/D2
Mertzwiller, Fr. 61/G6
Méru, Fr. 60/B5
Meru, Kenya 137/B1
Meru (mt.), Tanz. 137/B2
Meru NP, Kenya 137/B1
Meruoca, Braz. 219/F3
Merville, Fr. 60/B2
Mervin, Sk, Can. 175/K1
Merwedekanaal (riv.), Neth. 58/C5
Méry-sur-Oise, Fr. 36/J4
Merzen, Ger. 59/E4
Merzenich, Ger. 61/F2
Merzifon, Turk. 76/E4
Merzig, Ger. 61/F5
Mesa (peak), Arg. 191/C6
Mesa (mt.), Ak, US 201/G3
Mesa, Az, US 200/S19
Mesa, Co, US 177/J4
Mesa Prieta (mesa), NM, US 182/A3
Mesa Verde NP, Co, US 179/H2
Mesabi (range), Mn, US 187/H4
Mesach Mellet (hills), Libya 129/H4
Mesagne, It. 55/E2
Mesaména, Camr. 138/C2
Mesarás (gulf), Gre. 55/J5
Mescalero (ridge), NM, US 182/C4
Mescalero Sands (des.), NM, US 182/B4
Meschede, Ger. 59/F6
Mesco, Punta di (pt.), It. 68/C5
Mescolino (peak), It. 69/F6
Meseta de Montemayor (plat.), Arg. 226/D5
Mesfinto, Eth. 135/H2
Meshchura, Rus. 75/L3
Meshgīn Shahr, Iran 115/F2
Meshra'ar Raqq, Sudan 135/F3
Mesick, Mi, US 190/D2
Mesilla, NM, US 179/J4
Mesita, Co, US 182/B2
Mesita, NM, US 179/J3
Meskum, Indo. 101/C2
Meslay-du-Maine, Fr. 63/E5
Mesola, It. 69/F4
Mesolóngion, Gre. 55/G3
Mesomeloka, Madg. 143/J8
Mesopotamia (reg.), Iraq 112/D2
Mesopotamia (reg.), Arg 224/E4
Mesoraca, It. 54/E3
Mespelbrunn, Ger. 64/C3
Mesquer, Fr. 62/C6
Mesquite, NM, US 179/J4
Mesquite, Tx, US 180/L7
Mesrouh (peak), Mor. 128/E2
Messaad, Alg. 72/D4
Messac, Fr. 62/D5
Messalo (riv.), Moz. 141/H2
Messancy, Belg. 61/E4
Messei, Fr. 63/E3
Messel, Ger. 64/B3
Messina, It. 54/D3
Messina (str.), It. 73/G3
Messina, SAfr. 141/F4
Messines, Qu, Can. 191/H1
Messinge (riv.), Moz. 141/G2
Messíni, Gre. 55/H4
Messini (gulf), Gre. 73/J3
Messkirch, Ger. 67/F2
Messstetten, Ger. 67/E1
Messum Crater (peak), Namb. 140/B4
Messy, Fr. 36/L5
Mesta (riv.), Bul. 57/F5
Mestia, Geo. 77/G4
Město, Czh. 65/F3
Mestre, It. 69/F3
Mestrino, It. 69/E3
Mesudiye, Turk. 76/F4
Mesumba (peak), Tanz. 137/B3
Mesurado (cape), Libr. 132/C5
Meta (dept.), Col. 216/C4
Meta (riv.), Col.,Ven. 209/C2
Meta, It. 71/D6
Meta Incognita (pen.), Nun, Can. 171/K2
Metabetchouan, Qu, Can. 188/B1
Métabetchouane (riv.), Qu, Can. 188/B2
Metacáua (pt.), Moz. 141/J2
Metahāra, Eth. 136/A3
Metairie, La, US 194/C3
Metaline Falls, Wa, US 174/F3
Metallifere, Colline (mts.), It. 69/D6
Metallostroy, Rus. 75/T7
Metamora, Mi, US 197/F6
Metán, Arg. 224/C3
Metangula, Moz. 141/G2
Metapontum (ruin), It. 54/E2
Metauro (riv.), It. 51/K5
Metcalfe, On, Can. 191/J2
Metcalfe, Ms, US 192/B4
Meteghan, NS, Can. 188/D3
Meteghan River, NS, Can. 188/D3
Metelen, Ger. 59/E4
Metema, Eth. 135/H2
Meteor Crater, Az, US 179/G3
Metéora, Gre. 55/G3
Metepec, Mex. 205/Q10
Metheringham, Eng, UK 41/H5
Methil, Sc, UK 39/C4
Methlick, Sc, UK 39/D2
Methow (riv.), Wa, US 174/D3
Methuen, Ma, US 191/L3
Methuen (mt.), Austl. 152/B3
Methven, Sc, UK 39/C4
Methven, NZ 159/B3
Metica (riv.), Col. 216/C4
Metiskow, Ab, Can. 175/J1
Metković, Cro. 56/C4
Metlakatla, BC, Can. 201/M4
Metlakatla, Ak, US 201/M4
Metlatonoc, Mex. 206/B2
Metlili Chaamba, Alg. 129/F2
Metoro, Moz. 141/H2
Metro, Indo. 101/D4
Metro Toronto Zoo, On, Can. 190/U8
Metro-Dade Cultural Center, Fl, US 194/P11
Metropolis, Il, US 192/C2
Metropolitana de Santiago (pol. reg.), Chile 226/N8
Metrozoo, Fl, US 194/P11
Métsovon, Gre. 55/G3
Mettawa, Il, US 197/Q15
Mettenheim, Ger. 65/F6
Metter, Ga, US 193/F4
Mettet, Belg. 61/D3
Mettingen, Ger. 59/E4
Mettlach, Ger. 61/F4
Mettler, Ca, US 178/C3
Mettmach, Aus. 65/G6
Mettmann, Ger. 58/D6
Mettūr, India 107/C4
Metu, Eth. 135/G3
Metuchen, NJ, US 199/H9
Metulla, Isr. 117/D2
Metz, Mo, US 183/G2
Metz, Fr. 61/F5
Metz-Nancy-Lorraine (int'l arpt.), Fr. 61/F6
Metzingen, Ger. 64/C5
Metztitlán, Mex. 205/L6
Meu (riv.), Fr. 62/C4
Meudon, Fr. 36/J5
Meudt, Ger. 61/G3
Meulaboh, Indo. 101/B1
Meulan, Fr. 36/H4
Meulebeke, Belg. 60/C2
Meung-sur-Loire, Fr. 63/G5
Meurthe (riv.), Fr. 66/C1
Meurthe-et-Moselle (dept.), Fr. 61/E6
Meuse (riv.), Fr. 48/C4
Meuse (dept.), Fr. 61/E6
Meuvette (riv.), Fr. 63/F3
Meuzin (riv.), Fr. 66/A3
Mevasseret Ẕiyyon, Isr. 117/C5
Mexborough, Eng, UK 41/G5
Mexia, Tx, US 181/F2
Mexiana (isl.), Braz. 218/D2
Mexicalcingo, Mex. 205/Q10
Mexican Hat, Ut, US 179/H2
Mexican Springs, NM, US 179/H3
Mexico (ctry.) 163/G7
México (state), Mex. 202/A5
Mexico (Ciudad de México) (cap.), Mex. 205/Q10
Mexico (gulf), NAm. 163/H7
Mexico, In, US 190/C4
Mexico, Me, US 191/L2
Mexico, Mo, US 185/J4
Mexico, NY, US 191/H3
Mexico (bay), NY, US 191/H3
Mexico Beach, Fl, US 195/F3
Meximieux, Fr. 66/B6
Meybod, Iran 115/H3
Meycauayan, Phil. 100/E6
Meydān-e Gel (lake), Iran 115/H4
Meyers Chuck, Ak, US 201/M4
Meyersdale, Pa, US 191/G5
Meyerton, SAfr. 142/Q13
Meylan, Fr. 70/B2
Meymaneh, Afg. 113/H1
Méyo Kyé, Gabon 138/B2
Meyrargues, Fr. 70/B5
Meyrin, Swi. 66/C5
Meythet, Fr. 66/C6
Meythet (Annecy) (arpt.), Fr. 66/C6
Meyzieu, Fr. 66/A6
Mezaligon, Myan. 98/B5
Mezdra, Bul. 57/F4
Mèze, Fr. 50/E5
Mézel, Fr. 70/C5
Mezen', Rus. 75/K2
Mezen' (bay), Rus. 75/J2
Mezen' (riv.), Rus. 80/E3
Mezha (riv.), Bela. 47/P4
Mezhdurechensk, Rus. 80/J4
Mezhdurechenskiy, Rus. 80/G4
Mezhdusharskiy (isl.), Rus. 80/E2
Mezhova, Ukr. 79/J3
Mézidon-Canon, Fr. 63/E2
Mézières-sur-Seine, Fr. 36/H5
Mezoberény, Hun. 56/E2
Mezokovácsháza, Hun. 56/E2
Mezókövesd, Hun. 49/L5
Mezótúr, Hun. 56/E2
Mezquital (riv.), Mex. 204/D4
Mézy, Fr. 36/H5
Mezzana (peak), It. 67/G5
Mezzocorona, It. 67/H5
Mezzogoro, It. 69/F4
Mezzolombardo, It. 67/H5
Mfangano (isl.), Kenya 137/A2
Mfou, Camr. 138/B2
Mfrika, Tanz. 137/A4
Mga, Rus. 75/U7
Mga (riv.), Rus. 75/U7
Mgachi, Rus. 91/N1
Mgambo, Tanz. 137/B3
Mgera, Tanz. 137/B3
Mgeta, Tanz. 137/B4
Mglin, Rus. 76/E1
Mgori, Tanz. 137/A3
M'goun (peak), Mor. 128/D3
Mhamdia Fouchana, Tun. 130/M6
Mhòr (lake), Sc, UK 39/B2
Mhow, India 104/C3
Mhunze, Tanz. 137/A2
Mi (riv.), China 92/D3
Mi Xian, China 92/C4
Mi-shima (isl.), Japan 96/B3
Miahuatlán de Porfirio Díaz, Mex. 206/B2
Miajadas, Sp. 52/C3
Miaméré, CAfr. 134/C3
Miami, Tx, US 182/D3
Miami, Mb, Can. 186/E3
Miami, Ok, US 183/G2
Miami (canal), Fl, US 195/H4
Miami, Az, US 179/G4
Miami, Fl, US 194/P11
Miami (int'l arpt.), Fl, US 194/P11
Miami (riv.), Oh, US 192/E1
Miami Beach, Fl, US 194/P11
Miami Shores, Fl, US 194/P11
Miami Springs, Fl, US 194/P11
Miamisburg, Oh, US 190/D5
Miān Channūn, Pak. 110/B4
Miāna, India 108/A3
Miancaowan, China 90/D4
Mianchi, China 92/B4
Mīāndasht, Iran 115/J2
Mīāndoāb, Iran 115/F2
Miandrivazo, Madg. 143/H7
Mīāneh, Iran 115/F2
Mianhu, China 99/H4
Miāni, Pak. 110/B3
Mianmian (mts.), China 98/D2
Mianning, China 98/D2
Mianus (riv.), Ct, US 199/E1
Miānwāli, India 110/B5
Miānwāli, Pak. 110/A3
Mianyang, China 98/E2
Mianzhu, China 98/E2
Miāo, India 98/C3
Miao'er (peak), China 99/F3
Miaoshi, China 99/F2
Miarinarivo, Madg. 143/H7
Miarinarivo, Madg. 143/J7
Miary, Madg. 143/G8
Miass, Rus. 75/P5
Miass (riv.), Rus. 75/P5
Miastko, Pol. 46/G4
Miazal, Ecu. 220/B1
Mibenge, D.R. Congo 138/D3
Miberika, Sudan 159/G5
Mica Creek, BC, Can. 174/E1
Micanopy, Fl, US 195/G3
Micay, Col. 216/B4
Micco, Fl, US 195/H4
Miccosukee, Fl, US 195/F2
Miccosukee Ind. Res., Fl, US 195/H4
Michalovce, Slvk. 49/L4
Michaud (pt.), NS, Can. 189/G3
Michel (bay), Fr. 50/C2
Michelago, Austl. 157/D2
Michelfeld, Ger. 65/E3
Michelson (mt.), Ak, US 201/K2
Michelstadt, Ger. 64/C3
Michendorf, Ger. 48/Q7
Michie, Tn, US 192/C3
Michigamme (lake), Mi, US 187/K4
Michigamme, Mi, US 187/K4
Michigan, ND, US 186/E3
Michigan (lake), US 163/J5
Michigan (state), US 173/J2
Michigan Center, Mi, US 190/D3
Michigan City, In, US 190/C4
Michigan City, Ms, US 192/C3
Michigan Islands Nat'l Wild. Ref., Mi, US 190/D2
Michipicoten (isl.), On, Can. 187/M4
Michoacán de Ocampo (state), Mex. 202/A4
Michurin, Bul. 57/H4
Michurinsk, Rus. 77/G1
Mickle Fell (peak), Eng, UK 41/F2
Mickleton, Eng, UK 41/F2
Mico (riv.), Nic. 202/E5
Miconje, Ang. 138/C4
Micoud, StL. 203/N9
Micronesia (ctry.) 160/D4
Micronesia (reg.) 160/E3
Mid Yell, Sc, UK 37/W13
Midal (well), Niger 133/G2
Midale, Sk, Can. 186/C3
Midar, Mor. 130/C2
Middelburg, Neth. 58/A5
Middelburg, SAfr. 142/D3
Middelburg, SAfr. 143/E2
Middelharnis, Neth. 58/B5
Middelkerke, Belg. 60/B1
Middenmeer, Neth. 58/B3
Middle (ridge), Nf, Can. 189/K1
Middle (lake), Ca, US 176/C3
Middle (bay), NY, US 199/L9
Middle (mtn.), WV, US 193/G1
Middle Andaman (isl.), India 105/F5
Middle Caicos (isl.), UK 207/J1
Middle Concho (riv.), Tx, US 180/D2
Middle Fabius (riv.), Mo, US 185/H3
Middle Inlet, Wi, US 190/C2
Middle Lake, Sk, Can. 175/M1
Middle Loup (riv.), Ne, US 184/D3
Middle Pease (riv.), Tx, US 182/D3
Middle Raccoon (riv.), Ia, US 185/G3
Middle River, Mn, US 186/F3
Middle River, Md, US 198/B5
Middle Sister (peak), Or, US 176/C1
Middle Stewiacke, NS, Can. 188/F3
Middle Yuba (riv.), Ca, US 176/C4
Middlebourne, WV, US 190/F5
Middlebro, Mb, Can. 187/G3
Middleburg, Fl, US 195/H2
Middleburg, Pa, US 198/A2
Middleburg, Md, US 198/A4
Middleburgh, NY, US 191/J3
Middlebury, Vt, US 191/K2
Middlebury, In, US 190/D4
Middlefield, Oh, US 190/F4
Middlefield, Ma, US 191/K3
Middleham, Eng, UK 41/G3
Middlemarch, NZ 159/B4
Middlemount, Austl. 158/C3
Middleport, Oh, US 193/F1
Middleport, NY, US 190/W9
Middleport, Pa, US 198/B2
Middlesboro, Ky, US 192/F2
Middlesbrough, Eng, UK 41/G2
Middlesex (reg.), Eng, UK 43/F4
Middlesex, NJ, US 198/D2
Middlesex (co.), NJ, US 198/D3
Middlesex, NC, US 193/H3
Middleton, Eng, UK 41/F4
Middleton, NS, Can. 188/E3
Middleton, Id, US 176/E2
Middleton, Wi, US 185/K2
Middleton, Tn, US 192/C3
Middleton Cheney, Eng, UK 43/E2
Middleton-in-Teesdale, Eng, UK 41/F2
Middletown, NI, UK 40/B3
Middletown, NY, US 191/J4
Middletown, In, US 190/D4
Middletown, Ct, US 191/K4
Middletown, Oh, US 190/D5
Middletown, RI, US 191/L4
Middletown, NJ, US 199/J10
Middletown, Ca, US 176/B4
Middletown, Pa, US 198/B3
Middletown, Va, US 193/H1
Middletown, De, US 198/C5
Middleville, Mi, US 190/D3
Middlewich, Eng, UK 41/F5
Middlewood, NS, Can. 188/E3
Midelt, Mor. 128/D2
Midhurst, Eng, UK 43/F5
Midi (canal), Fr. 50/D5
Midi-Pyrénées (pol.reg.), Fr. 50/D4
Midkiff, WV, US 193/F1
Midland (nbrhd.), Austl. 154/L6
Midland, Mi, US 190/D3
Midland, On, Can. 191/G2
Midland, Or, US 176/C2
Midland, SD, US 184/D1
Midland, Tx, US 180/C2
Midland, Wa, US 197/C3
Midland City, Al, US 195/F2
Midland Park, NJ, US 199/J8
Midlands (prov.), Zim. 141/F3
Midleton, Ire. 38/B6
Midlothian (co.), Sc, UK 39/C5
Midlothian, Il, US 197/Q16
Midlothian, Tx, US 180/L7
Midlum, Ger. 59/F1
Midnight, Ms, US 192/B4
Midongy Atsimo, Madg. 143/H8
Midou (riv.), Fr. 50/C5
Midsayap, Phil. 100/D4
Midsomer Norton, Eng, UK 42/D4
Midu, China 105/H2
Midville, Ga, US 193/F4
Midway (isls.), Pac., US 160/H2
Midway, BC, Can. 174/E3
Midway, Al, US 195/F1
Midway, De, US 198/C6
Midway, Fl, US 195/F2
Midway, Ga, US 195/H2
Midway, Ky, US 192/E1
Midway, La, US 194/B2
Midway, Ne, US 184/E2
Midway, NM, US 182/B4
Midway, Tx, US 181/G2
Midwest, Wy, US 184/A2
Midwest City, Ok, US 183/F3
Midyan (reg.), SAr. 112/C3
Midyat, Turk. 114/E2
Midžor (peak), Serb. 57/F4
Mie (pref.), Japan 96/E3
Mie, Japan 96/B4
Miechów, Pol. 76/B2
Międzychód, Pol. 49/H2
Międzylesie, Pol. 49/J3
Międzyrzec Podlaski, Pol. 49/M3
Międzyrzecz, Pol. 49/H2
Międzyzdroje, Pol. 46/F5
Miehlen, Ger. 61/G3
Miéle I, Congo 138/C2
Mielec, Pol. 49/L3
Mier, Mex. 180/E4
Miercurea Ciuc, Rom. 57/G2
Mieres, Sp. 52/C1
Miesbach, Ger. 51/J3
Mī'ēso, Eth. 136/B3
Mifflin, Pa, US 198/A2
Mifflinburg, Pa, US 198/A2
Mifflintown, Pa, US 191/H4
Mifflinville (Creasy), Pa, US 198/B1
Mifraẕ Ḥefa (bay), Isr. 117/B3
Migdal, Isr. 117/D3
Migdal Ha'emeq, Isr. 117/C3
Migdol, SAfr. 142/D2
Migennes, Fr. 50/E3
Migliarino, It. 68/D6
Mignanego, It. 68/B4
Mignano Monte Lungo, It. 71/C5
Mignovillard, Fr. 66/C4
Migori (riv.), Kenya 137/A2
Migori, Kenya 137/A2
Miguel Alemán, Mex. 204/C2
Miguel Aleman, Presa (dam), Mex. 205/M8
Miguel Alves, Braz. 219/F4
Miguel Auza, Mex. 204/E3
Miguel Calmon, Braz. 223/E1
Miguel Hidalgo (int'l arpt.), Mex. 204/E4
Miguel Hidalgo (res.), Mex. 204/C3
Miguel Pereira, Braz. 223/N7
Miguel Riglos, Arg. 226/E3
Miguelete, Uru. 191/K11
Miguelópolis, Braz. 225/G2
Miguelturra, Sp. 52/D3
Migŭm, SKor. 93/G6
Mihama, Japan 96/D3
Mihama, Japan 95/L6
Mihara, Japan 96/C3
Mihara, Japan 95/J6
Miharu, Japan 97/G2
Mihintale (ruin), SrL. 107/D4
Mihla, Ger. 59/H6
Miho, Japan 95/E2
Mihrābpur, Pak. 113/J3
Mijares (riv.), Sp. 53/E2
Mijas, Sp. 52/C4
Mijdāḥah, Yem. 136/D2
Mijdrecht, Neth. 58/B4
Mikasa, Japan 94/B2
Mikashevichi, Bela. 76/C1
Mikata, Japan 95/J4
Mikata (lake), Japan 95/J4
Mikawa (bay), Japan 95/M6
Mikengere, D.R. Congo 139/F5
Mikese, Tanz. 137/B3
Mikhaylov, Rus. 76/F1
Mikhaylovka, Rus. 79/M2
Mikhaylovsk, Rus. 75/N4
Mikhmoret, Isr. 117/B4
Miki, Japan 95/G6
Mikínai, Gre. 55/H4
Mikínai (Mycenae) (ruin), Gre. 55/H4
Mikindani, Tanz. 137/C4
Mikkalo, Or, US 176/C1
Mikkeli (prov.), Fin. 44/H3
Mikomeseng, EqG. 138/B2
Míkonos, Gre. 55/J4
Míkonos (isl.), Gre. 55/J4
Mikope, D.R. Congo 139/E4
Mikri Prespa NP, Gre. 55/G2
Mikuma, Japan 95/L6
Mikumi, Tanz. 137/B3
Mikumi NP, Tanz. 137/B3
Mikun', Rus. 75/L3
Mikuni, Japan 96/E2
Mikuni-tōge (pass), Japan 97/F2
Mikura (isl.), Japan 97/F4
Mila, Alg. 72/E3
Mila (wilaya), Alg. 130/H4
Milaca, Mn, US 187/H5
Milagres, Braz. 219/G4
Milagro, Ecu. 216/B5
Milak, India 108/B1
Milakpur, India 108/A2
Milam, Tx, US 181/H2
Milan (Milano), It. 51/H4
Milan, Ga, US 195/G1
Milan, In, US 192/E1
Milan, Mn, US 185/G1
Milan, Mo, US 185/H3
Milan, NH, US 191/L2
Milan, NM, US 179/J3
Milan, Oh, US 190/E4
Milan, Tn, US 192/C3
Milando, Ang. 138/D5
Milang, Austl. 156/A2
Milange, Moz. 141/G3
Milano (Milan), It. 51/H4
Milano (prov.), It. 68/C2
Milano, Tx, US 181/F2
Milas, Turk. 114/A2
Milazzo, It. 54/D3
Milbank, SD, US 185/F1
Milborne Port, Eng, UK 42/D5
Milburn, Ne, US 184/E3
Milburn, Ok, US 183/F3
Milden, Sk, Can. 175/L2
Mildenhall, Eng, UK 43/G2
Mildred, Mt, US 186/B4
Mildura, Austl. 156/B2
Mīlē, Eth. 136/B3
Mile, China 98/D3
Mīlē Wenz (riv.), Eth. 136/B3
Milepa, Tanz. 139/G5
Miles, Austl. 158/C4
Miles, Tx, US 180/D2
Miles City, Mt, US 175/M4
Milesburg, Pa, US 191/H4
Milešovka (peak), Czh. 65/G1
Milestone, Sk, Can. 186/B3
Miletto (peak), It. 71/D5
Milevsko, Czh. 65/H4
Milford, Ire. 38/B4
Milford (sound), NZ 159/A4
Milford, NI, UK 40/B3
Milford, Ct, US 199/E1
Milford, De, US 198/C6
Milford, Ga, US 195/F2
Milford, Ia, US 185/G2
Milford, Il, US 190/C4
Milford, Ks, US 185/F4
Milford (lake), Ks, US 185/F4
Milford, Ma, US 191/L3
Milford, Mi, US 197/E6
Milford, Ne, US 185/F3
Milford, NH, US 191/L3
Milford, NJ, US 198/C2
Milford, Pa, US 191/J4
Milford, Tx, US 181/F1
Milford, Ut, US 179/F1
Milford Haven (inlet), Wal., UK 42/A3
Milford Haven, Wal, UK 42/A3
Milford Station, NS, Can. 188/F3
Milford-on-Sea, Eng, UK 43/E5
Mili (isl.), Mrsh. 160/G4
Miliana, Alg. 130/G4
Milicz, Pol. 49/J3
Milikapiti, Austl. 152/C2
Milingimbi Mission, Austl. 152/D3
Military (ridge), Wi, US 185/J2
Milk (riv.), Mt, Can., US 170/F4
Milk (hill), Eng, UK 43/E4
Milk River, Ab, Can. 175/H3
Mill (isl.), Nun, Can. 171/J2
Mill, Neth. 58/C5
Mill (riv.), Ct, US 199/E1
Mill Bay, BC, Can. 174/C3
Mill City, Or, US 176/B1
Mill Creek, Ok, US 183/F3
Mill Creek, WV, US 193/H1
Mill Neck, NY, US 199/L8
Mill Shoals, Il, US 192/C1
Mill Spring, Mo, US 192/B2
Mill Village, NS, Can. 188/E3
Millaa Millaa, Austl. 158/B2
Millau, Fr. 50/E4
Millboro, SD, US 184/E2
Millboro, Va, US 193/H2
Millbrae, Ca, US 197/K11
Millbridge, Eng, UK 36/A3
Millbrook, On, Can. 191/G2
Millbrook, Al, US 192/D4
Millbrook (res.), Austl. 155/M8
Millbrook, Eng, UK 42/B6
Millburn, NJ, US 199/H9
Millburne, Wy, US 177/H3
Mille Îles (riv.), Qu, Can. 189/N6
Mille Lacs (lake), Mn, US 173/H2
Mille Lacs Ind. Res., Mn, US 187/H4
Milledgeville, Ga, US 193/F4
Milledgeville, Il, US 185/K3
Milledgeville, Tn, US 192/C3
Millen, Ga, US 193/G4
Miller (peak), Az, US 179/G5
Miller, SD, US 184/E1
Miller (pt.), Tx, US 181/N9
Miller (int'l arpt.), Tx, US 205/F3
Millerovo, Rus. 79/L3
Millers Creek (res.), Tx, US 180/E1
Millers Ferry, Al, US 194/E1
Millers Ferry (dam), Al, US 194/E1
Millersburg, Oh, US 190/F4
Millersburg, Or, US 176/B1
Millersburg, Pa, US 198/B2
Millerstown, Pa, US 198/A2
Millersview, Tx, US 180/E2
Millersville, Pa, US 198/B4
Millerton (lake), Ca, US 178/C2
Millertown, Nf, Can. 189/J1
Millerville, Mn, US 187/G4
Millesimo, It. 68/B5
Millet, Ab, Can. 175/H1
Millett, Tx, US 180/E3
Milleur (pt.), Sc, UK 40/C1
Millevaches (plat.), Fr. 50/D4
Millgrove, On, Can. 190/T9
Millicent, Austl. 156/B3
Milligan, Fl, US 194/E2
Milliken, Co, US 184/B3
Millingen aan de Rijn, Neth. 58/D5
Millington, Md, US 198/C5
Millington, Tn, US 192/C3
Millinocket, Me, US 171/K4
Millisle, NI, UK 40/C2
Millmerran, Austl. 158/C4
Millmont, Pa, US 198/A2
Millom, Eng, UK 41/E3
Millport, Sc, UK 39/B5
Millport, Al, US 192/C4
Millry, Al, US 194/D2
Mills, NM, US 182/B2
Millsboro, De, US 193/K1
Millstone, WV, US 193/G1
Millstone (riv.), NJ, US 198/D3
Millstream-Chichester NP, Austl. 154/C2
Millstreet, Ire. 38/A5
Millthorpe, Austl. 157/D1
Millthrop, Eng, UK 41/F3
Milltown, In, US 192/D1
Milltown, NJ, US 199/H10
Milltown Malbay, Ire. 38/A4
Milltown-Head of Bay d'Espoir, Nf, Can. 189/K2
Millungera, Austl. 158/A2
Millville, Oh, US 190/D5
Millville, NJ, US 198/C5
Millville, Pa, US 198/B1
Millwood (dam), Ar, US 183/H4
Millwood (lake), Ar, US 183/G4
Millwood, Ga, US 195/G2
Millwood, WV, US 193/G1
Milmay, NJ, US 198/D5
Milnathort, Wal, UK 41/E5
Milne (bay), PNG 160/E5
Milngavie, Sc, UK 39/B5
Milnor, ND, US 186/F4
Milnrow, Eng, UK 41/F4
Milo (riv.), Gui. 132/C4
Milo, Ia, US 185/H3
Mílos, Gre. 55/J4
Mílos (isl.), Gre. 73/K3
Milpa, Austl. 156/B1
Milpa Alta (nbrhd.), Mex. 205/Q10
Milparinka, Austl. 155/J4
Milroy, In, US 190/D5
Milroy, Pa, US 191/H4
Milseburg (peak), Ger. 64/C1
Milstead, Ga, US 193/N7
Miltenberg, Ger. 64/C3
Milton, Austl. 157/E2
Milton, On, Can. 190/T8
Milton, Eng, UK 41/F2
Milton, Eng, UK 43/G4
Milton, NZ 159/B4
Milton, Fl, US 194/E2
Milton, Ia, US 185/H3
Milton, Il, US 185/J4
Milton, ND, US 186/E3
Milton, NH, US 191/L3
Milton, Pa, US 198/B1
Milton, Vt, US 191/K2
Milton, Wa, US 197/C3
Milton, Wi, US 185/K2
Milton Heights, On, Can. 190/T8
Milton Keynes, Eng, UK 43/F2
Milton Keynes (co.), Eng, UK 43/F2
Milton Ness (pt.), Sc, UK 39/D3
Milton of Campsie, Sc, UK 39/B5
Milton-Freewater, Or, US 174/E5
Miltona, Mn, US 187/G4
Miltonvale, Ks, US 184/F4
Miluo (riv.), China 99/G2
Milverton, On, Can. 190/F3
Milverton, Eng, UK 42/C4
Milwaukee, Wi, US 190/C3
Milwaukee (co.), Wi, US 197/P14
Milz (riv.), Ger. 64/D2
Mimbres, NM, US 179/J4
Mimbres (riv.), NM, US 179/J4
Mimet, Fr. 70/B6
Mimi (riv.), Japan 96/B4
Mimizan, Fr. 50/C4
Mimmaya, Japan 94/B3
Mimongo, Gabon 138/B3
Mimongo, Gabon 138/B3
Mimosa Rocks NP, Austl. 157/D3
Min (riv.), China 90/E5
Min Xian, China 90/E5
Min-Kush, Kyr. 111/B3
Mîna (riv.), Alg. 130/F5
Mina, Mex. 180/D4
Mina, Nv, US 176/D4
Mina Clavero, Arg. 224/C4
Mina Pirquitas, Arg. 224/C2
Mīnā' Su'ūd, Kuw. 115/G4
Mīnāb, Iran 115/J5
Minaçu, Braz. 222/C2
Minahasa (isl.), Indo. 103/F3
Minaki, On, Can. 187/G3
Minakuchi, Japan 95/K6
Minamata, Japan 96/B4
Minami Alps NP, Japan 97/F3
Minami-tori-shima (isl.), Japan 160/E2
Minamiaiki, Japan 95/B1
Minamiashigara, Japan 95/C3
Minamichita, Japan 95/L6
Minamidaitō (isl.), Japan 97/L8
Minamiiō (isl.), Japan 160/D2
Minamikawara, Japan 95/C1
Minamimaki, Japan 95/A2
Minamiyamashiro, Japan 95/J6
Minano, Japan 95/C1
Minas, Cuba 207/G1
Minas (peak), Ecu. 216/B5
Minas, Uru. 191/G2
Minas, Indo. 101/C2
Minas de Barroterán, Mex. 180/D4
Minas de Corrales, Uru. 225/F4
Minas de Matahambre, Cuba 207/F1
Minas de Ríotinto, Sp. 52/B4
Minas Gerais (state), Braz. 222/D3
Minatitlán, Mex. 206/C2
Minbu, Myan. 98/B4
Minbya, Myan. 98/B4
Minch, The (North Minch) (str.), Sc, UK 37/Q8
Mincha, Chile 224/B4
Minchinābād, Pak. 110/B4
Minchinhampton, Eng, UK 42/D3
Minchinmávida (vol.), Chile 226/B4
Mincio (riv.), It. 69/D2
Minco, Ok, US 183/F3
Mindanao (isl.), Phil. 83/M9
Mindanao (sea), Phil. 103/F2
Mindel (riv.), Ger. 48/F4
Mindelheim, Ger. 67/G1
Mindelo, CpV. 119/J10
Mindemoya, On, Can. 190/E2
Minden, Ger. 59/F4
Minden, La, US 183/H4
Minden, Ne, US 184/E3
Minden, Nv, US 176/D4
Minden, Tx, US 181/G1
Minden City, Mi, US 190/E3
Mindif, Camr. 134/B3
Mindiptana, Indo. 153/F1
Mindoro (isl.), Phil. 83/L8
Mindoro (str.), Phil. 100/C2
Mindouli, Congo 138/C4
Mindyak, Rus. 75/N5
Mine Centre, On, Can. 187/H3
Mine Head (pt.), Ire. 38/C6
Minehead, Eng, UK 42/C4
Mineiros, Braz. 222/B3
Mineola, NY, US 199/L8
Mineola, Mo, US 185/J4
Mineola, Tx, US 181/G1
Miner, Mt, US 177/H1
Miner, Mo, US 192/C2
Mineral, Tx, US 180/F3
Mineral, Wa, US 174/C4
Mineral del Monte, Mex. 205/L6
Mineral Point, Mo, US 192/B2
Mineral Point, Wi, US 185/J2
Mineral Springs, Ar, US 183/H4
Mineral Wells, Tx, US 181/E1
Mineral'nye Vody, Rus. 77/G3
Mineralnyye Vody (int'l arpt.), Rus. 77/G3
Mineralwells, WV, US 193/G1
Minerbe, It. 69/E3
Minerbio, It. 69/E4
Minerbio (pt.), Fr. 51/H5
Minersville, Ut, US 179/F1
Minersville, Pa, US 198/B2
Minetto, NY, US 191/H3
Mineville-Witherbee, NY, US 191/K2
Minfeld, Ger. 64/B4
Minfeng, China 111/D4
Ming (riv.), China 105/J3
Mingäçevir, Azer. 77/H4
Mingäçevir Su Anbari (res.), Azer. 77/H4
Mingala, CAfr. 134/D4
Mingāora, Pak. 110/B2
Mingenew, Austl. 154/B4
Mingin, Myan. 98/B4
Minglanilla, Sp. 52/E3
Mingo, Congo 138/C3
Mingo, Ks, US 184/D4
Mingo Junction, Oh, US 190/F4
Mingo NWR, Mo, US 192/B2
Mingouli, Chutes de (falls), Gabon 138/C2
Mingoyo, Tanz. 137/B4
Mingshan, China 98/D2
Mingshui, China 90/D3
Mingshui, China 91/K2
Mingun, Ancient City of, Myan. 98/B4
Minhang, China 92/L8
Minhe, China 90/E4
Minhla, Myan. 98/B5
Minhla, Myan. 98/B5
Minho (riv.), Port. 52/A1
Miniāri, India 104/B2
Minidoka (dam), Id, US 177/G2
Minidoka Internment Nat'l Mon., Id, US 177/F2
Minigwal (lake), Austl. 154/D4
Minilya, Austl. 154/B2
Minīn, Syria 117/E1
Miniota, Mb, Can. 186/D2
Ministro Pistarini (Buenos Aires) (int'l arpt.), Arg. 191/J11
Minitonas, Mb, Can. 186/D1
Minj, PNG 153/G1
Minkamman, Sudan 135/F4
Minkébé, Montagne de (peak), Gabon 138/C2
Minlaton, Austl. 155/H5
Minle, China 90/E4
Minna, Nga. 133/G4
Minneapolis, Ks, US 184/F4
Minneapolis, Mn, US 187/P7
Minneapolis-St.Paul (Wold-Chamberlain) (int'l arpt.), Mn, US 187/P7
Minnedosa, Mb, Can. 186/E2
Minnehaha (lake), Fl, US 194/M6
Minnehaha (falls), Mn, US 187/P7
Minneola, Ks, US 182/D2
Minneola, Fl, US 194/M6
Minneola (lake), Fl, US 194/M6
Minneota, Mn, US 185/G1
Minnequa (canal), Co, US 184/B4
Minnesota (state), US 173/G2
Minnesota (riv.), Mn, US 185/G1
Minnesota Zoo and Gardens, Mn, US 187/P7
Minnetonka, Mn, US 187/P7
Minnetonka (lake), Mn, US 187/N7
Minnewaska (lake), Mn, US 185/G1
Minnewaukan, ND, US 186/E3
Minnigaff, Sc, UK 40/D2
Minnipa, Austl. 155/G5
Minnis (lake), On, Can. 187/J2
Minnitaki (lake), On, Can. 187/H3
Miño (riv.), Sp. 52/A1
Mino, Japan 95/L4
Mino'o (riv.), Japan 95/H6
Minobu, Japan 97/F3
Minocqua, Wi, US 187/K5
Minokamo, Japan 95/M5
Minonk, Il, US 185/K3
Mino'o, Japan 95/H6
Minorca (Menorca) (isl.), Sp. 53/H2
Minori, It. 71/D6
Minori, Japan 95/E1
Minot, ND, US 186/D3
Minot (A.F.B.), ND, US 186/D3
Minqin, China 90/E4
Minqing, China 99/H3
Minquan, China 92/C4
Minsener Oog (isl.), Ger. 59/F1
Minsk (cap.), Bela. 47/M5
Minsk (int'l arpt.), Bela. 47/M5
Minskaya Voblasts, Bela. 47/M5
Mińsk Mazowiecki, Pol. 49/L2
Minster, Eng, UK 43/H4
Minster, Oh, US 190/D4
Mint Hill, NC, US 193/G3
Minta, Camr. 134/B4
Minter, Al, US 194/E1
Mintlaw, Sc, UK 39/E1
Minto, Mb, Can. 186/D3
Minto, NB, Can. 188/D2
Minto (inlet), NW, Can. 170/E1
Minto, Yk, Can. 201/L3
Minto, Ak, US 201/J2
Minto, ND, US 186/F3
Mintom Li, Camr. 138/C2
Minton, Sk, Can. 186/B3
Minturnae (ruin), It. 71/C5
Minturno, It. 71/C5
Mīnūdasht, Iran 115/H2
Minūf, Egypt 131/B4
Minusinsk, Rus. 80/K4
Minusio, Swi. 67/E5
Minutang, India 98/C2
Minvoul, Gabon 138/C2
Minwakh, Yem. 112/E5
Minxiao, China 99/F3
Minyā al Qamḩ, Egypt 131/C3
Min'yar, Rus. 75/N5
Minyat Sandūb, Egypt 131/C3
Minyip, Austl. 156/B3
Mio, Mi, US 190/D2
Mions, Fr. 70/A1
Miory, Bela. 47/M4
Mipi, India 98/B2
Miquan, China 111/E3
Miquelon, StP., Fr. 189/J2
Mir, Rus. 75/P5
Mira, La, US 183/H4
Mira (riv.), NS, Can. 188/G3
Mira (riv.), Col. 216/B4
Mira (riv.), Port. 52/A4
Mira, Port. 52/A2
Mira Loma, Ca, US 196/C2
Mira Monte, Ca, US 196/A2
Mira Taglio, It. 69/F3
Mirabel (int'l arpt.), Can. 189/M6
Mirabel, Qu, Can. 189/M6
Mirabella Eclano, It. 71/D5
Mirabello, It. 69/E4
Miracema, Braz. 223/E4
Miradolo Terme, It. 68/C3
Mirador (pass), Chile 226/C4
Mirador, Braz. 219/E4
Miraflores, Col. 216/C4
Miraflores, Col. 216/C3
Miraflores, Peru 220/B3
Miraflores, Mex. 204/C4
Miragoâne, Haiti 207/H2
Miraj, India 107/B2
Miramar, Ca, US 196/C5
Miramar, Arg. 226/F3
Miramar (nbrhd.), NZ 159/H9
Miramar, Arg. 224/D4
Miramar, Fl, US 194/P11
Miramar Naval Air Station, Ca, US 196/C5
Miramare (arpt.), It. 69/F5
Miramas, Fr. 70/A5
Mirambéllou (gulf), Gre. 55/J5
Miramichi (bay), NB, Can. 188/E2
Miramichi, South West (riv.), NB, Can. 188/D2
Miramont-de-Guyenne, Fr. 50/D4
Mīrān, Pak. 110/A4
Miranda, It. 71/D4
Miranda, SD, US 184/E1
Miranda, Braz. 225/E2
Miranda (riv.), Braz. 222/A3
Miranda de Ebro, Sp. 50/B5
Miranda do Corvo, Port. 52/A2
Miranda do Douro, Port. 52/B2
Mirande, Fr. 50/D5
Mirandela, Port. 52/B2
Mirandiba, Braz. 219/G5
Mirando City, Tx, US 180/E4
Mirandópolis, Braz. 225/G2
Mirano, It. 69/F3
Miranorte, Braz. 218/D5
Mīrānpur, India 108/A1
Mirassol, Braz. 225/G2
Miravalles (vol.), CR 207/E4
Miravalles (peak), Sp. 52/B1
Mirbāṭ, Oman 113/F5
Mirboo North, Austl. 157/C4
Mirebalais, Haiti 207/H2
Mirebeau, Fr. 66/B3
Mirecourt, Fr. 66/C1
Mirecourt (Épinal) (arpt.), Fr. 66/C1
Mireigha, Sudan 135/E3
Mirendi, Gabon 138/B3
Mirfield, Eng, UK 41/G4
Miri, Malay. 102/D3
Miriam Vale, Austl. 158/C4
Mirim (lake), Braz. 225/F5
Mirimire, Ven. 216/D2
Mírina, Gre. 55/J3
Miriñay (riv.), Arg. 224/E4
Mirinzal, Braz. 219/E3
Miritiparaná (riv.), Col. 216/D5
Mirna (riv.), Cro. 69/G5
Mirnyy, Rus. 81/M3
Mirnyy, Rus., Ant. 228/G
Mirow, Ger. 48/G2
Mīrpur, Pak. 110/B3
Mirria, Niger 133/H3
Mirror, Ab, Can. 175/H1
Mirror (lake), NJ, US 198/D4
Mirsali, China 111/E3
Mirthal, India 110/C3
Mirtóön (sea), Gre. 55/H4
Miryang, SKor. 96/A3
Mirzaani, Geo. 77/H4
Mirzāpur, Bang. 109/H3
Mirzāpur, India 108/D3
Misa (riv.), It. 69/G5
Misa, D.R. Congo 139/G1
Misaka, Japan 95/B2
Misaki, Japan 96/D3
Misaki, Japan 95/E3
Misano Adriatico, It. 69/F6
Misantla, Mex. 205/N7
Misasa, Tanz. 137/B3
Misato, Japan 95/D2
Misato, Japan 95/C1
Misato, Japan 95/K6
Misawa, Japan 94/B3
Miscano (riv.), It. 71/D5
Miscou (pt.), Qu, Can. 188/E1
Miscou (isl.), NB, Can. 188/E2
Miscou Centre, NB, Can. 188/E2
Misere (lake), La, US 194/B3
Misgār, Pak. 113/K1
Mishagua, Peru 220/C3
Mishan, China 91/L2
Mishawaka, In, US 190/C4
Misheguk (mt.), Ak, US 201/F2
Mishicot, Wi, US 190/C2
Mishima, Japan 97/F3
Mishkino, Rus. 75/M5
Mishmar Hanegev, Isr. 117/B6
Mishmar Hayarden, Isr. 117/D3
Misilmeri, It. 54/C3
Misiones (dept.), Arg. 225/E3
Miskolc, Hun. 49/L4
Mismār, Sudan 112/C5
Misono, Japan 95/L6
Misool (isl.), Indo. 103/H4
Misquah (hills), Mn, US 187/J4
Mişr al Jadīdah, Egypt 131/C4
Mişrātah, Libya 126/B1
Mişrātah (pt.), Libya 127/E1
Missão Velha, Braz. 219/G4
Missillac, Fr. 62/C6
Missinaibi (riv.), On, Can. 171/H3
Mission, BC, Can. 174/C3
Mission (bay), Ca, US 196/C5
Mission (mtn.), Ok, US 183/G2
Mission, Or, US 176/D1
Mission, Tx, US 181/E4
Mission Beach, Austl. 158/B2
Mission Bend, Tx, US 181/M9
Mission Ind. Res., Ca, US 196/C4
Mission Ridge, SD, US 184/D1
Mission San Buenaventura, Ca, US 196/A2
Mission San Jose, Ca, US 197/L12
Mission San Juan Capistrano, Ca, US 196/C3
Mission San Luis Obispo de Tolosa, Ca, US 178/B3
Mission San Miguel Arcangel, Ca, US 178/B3
Mission Viejo, Ca, US 196/C3
Mississagi (riv.), On, Can. 190/E1
Mississauga, On, Can. 190/T8
Mississippi (pt.), Austl. 154/D5
Mississippi (delta), La, US 194/D3
Mississippi (riv.), US 163/H6
Mississippi (state), US 173/H5
Mississippi (sound), Al,Ms, US 194/D2
Mississippi Sandhill Crane NWR, Ms, US 194/D2
Mississippi Station, On, Can. 191/H2
Missoula, Mt, US 175/H4
Missouri (riv.), US 173/G3
Missouri (state), US 173/H4
Missouri City, Tx, US 181/M9
Missouri Valley, Ia, US 185/G3
Missungwi, Tanz. 137/A2
Mist, Or, US 174/C5
Mistake (cr.), Austl. 158/B3
Mistake Creek, Austl. 152/C4
Mistaken (pt.), Nf, Can. 189/L2
Mistassini, Qu, Can. 188/A1
Mistassini (lake), Qu, Can. 171/J3
Mistatim, Sk, Can. 175/N1
Misti (vol.), Peru 220/D5
Mistissini, Qu, Can. 171/J3
Mistley, Eng, UK 43/H3
Mistrás (ruin), Gre. 55/H4
Mistretta, It. 54/D4

Misty – Morav
310

Misty Fjords Nat'l Mon., Ak, US 201/M4
Misugi, Japan 95/K6
Miswa, Zam. 141/F2
Mīt Abū Ghālib, Egypt 131/C2
Mīt an Naşārā, Egypt 131/C2
Mīt Fāris, Egypt 131/C2
Mīt Ghamr, Egypt 131/C3
Mīt Ḩamal, Egypt 131/C4
Mita, Punta de (pt.), Mex. 204/D4
Mitaka, Japan 95/D2
Mitake, Japan 95/M5
Mitama, Japan 95/B2
Mitare, Ven. 216/D2
Mitatib, Sudan 135/H1
Mitcham (nbrhd.), Austl. 155/M9
Mitcheldean, Eng, UK 42/D3
Mitchell, Ar, US 183/H2
Mitchell, Austl. 158/B4
Mitchell, Or, US 176/C1
Mitchell, Ne, US 184/C3
Mitchell (dam), Al, US 192/D4
Mitchell, SD, US 184/E2
Mitchell (mt.), NC, US 193/F3
Mitchell, In, US 192/D1
Mitchell (range), Austl. 153/D3
Mitchell (riv.), Austl. 145/D2
Mitchell (lake), Al, US 192/D4
Mitchell and Alice Rivers NP, Austl. 153/F3
Mitchell Bay, On, Can. 197/H7
Mitchell River NP, Austl. 157/C3
Mitchellville, Ar, US 183/J4
Mitchelstown, Ire. 38/B5
Mitha Tiwāna, Pak. 110/B3
Mithankot, Pak. 110/A5
Mithapukur, Bang. 109/G3
Mithi, Pak. 113/J4
Míthimna, Gre. 55/K3
Mitiaro (isl.), Cookls. 161/K6
Mitilíni, Gre. 55/K3
Mitla (ruin), Mex. 206/B2
Mito, Japan 97/G2
Mito, Japan 95/M6
Mitomi, Japan 95/B2
Mitre (pen.), Arg. 191/D7
Mitra (peak), EqG. 138/B2
Mitre (peak), NZ 159/C3
Mitre (peak), Tx, US 180/C2
Mitrofanovka, Rus. 79/K3
Mitry-Mory, Fr. 36/K5
Mitsamiouli, Com. 143/G5
Mitshibu, D.R. Congo 139/E4
Mitsinjo, Madg. 143/H7
Mits'iwa, Erit. 136/A2
Mitsue, Japan 95/K7
Mitsukaidō, Japan 97/F2
Mitsuke, Japan 97/F2
Mitta Mitta (riv.), Austl. 157/C3
Mittagong, Austl. 157/E2
Mittagspitze (peak), Aus. 67/F3
Mittainville, Fr. 36/G5
Mittelberg, Aus. 67/G3
Mittelland (canal), Ger. 59/F4
Mittelradde (riv.), Ger. 59/E3
Mittenwald, Ger. 67/H3
Mittersill, Aus. 51/K3
Mitterteich, Ger. 65/F3
Mitti, Gui. 132/B4
Mittlere-Isar (canal), Ger. 65/E6
Mittweida, Ger. 48/G3
Mitú, Col. 216/D4
Mituas, Col. 216/D4
Mitumba, Monts (mtns.), D.R. Congo 139/G3
Mituosi, China 99/G2
Mitwaba, D.R. Congo 139/F5
Mitwitz, Ger. 64/E2
Mityana, Ugan. 139/H2
Mitzic, Gabon 138/B2
Miura, Japan 95/D3
Miura (pen.), Japan 95/D3
Mivtaḩim, Isr. 117/A6
Miwa, Japan 95/L5
Miwa, Japan 95/H5
Mixco Viejo (ruin), Guat. 206/D3
Mixquiahuala, Mex. 205/K6
Mixteco (riv.), Mex. 206/B2
Miya (riv.), Japan 95/K7
Miyagawa, Japan 95/K7
Miyagi (pref.), Japan 94/B4
Miyake (isl.), Japan 97/F3
Miyako, Japan 94/B4
Miyako (isls.), Japan 97/H8
Miyako (isl.), Japan 97/H8
Miyakonojō, Japan 96/B5
Miyaly, Kaz. 77/K2
Miyama, Japan 95/L4
Miyama, Japan 95/J5
Miyanojō, Japan 96/B5
Miyashiro, Japan 95/D2
Miyazaki, Japan 96/B5
Miyazaki (pref.), Japan 96/B4
Miyazu (bay), Japan 95/H4
Miyazu, Japan 95/H4
Miyi, China 105/H2
Miyoshi, Japan 96/C3
Miyoshi, Japan 95/D3
Miyoshi, Japan 95/D2
Miyoshi, Japan 95/M5
Miyota, Japan 95/B1
Miyun (res.), China 92/H6
Miyun, China 92/H6
Mizdah, Libya 126/B2
Mizen (pt.), Ire. 40/B6
Mizhhir'ya, Ukr. 78/B3
Mizil, Rom. 57/H3
Miziya, Bul. 57/F4
Mizoch, Ukr. 78/D2
Mizoram (state), India 105/F3
Mizpah (cr.), Mt, US 186/B5
Mizpah, NJ, US 198/D5
Mizpe Ramon, Isr. 116/D4
Mizque, Bol. 224/C1
Mizuho, Japan 95/C2
Mizuho, Japan 95/H5
Mizunami, Japan 95/M5
Mizusawa, Japan 94/B4
Mjöån (riv.), Swe. 45/K7
Mjölby, Swe. 46/F2
Mjøndalen, Nor. 46/D2
Mjörn (lake), Swe. 46/E3
Mjøsa (lake), Nor. 44/D3
Mkalama, Tanz. 137/A3
Mkata, Tanz. 137/B3
Mkata (plain), Tanz. 137/B3
Mkoani, Tanz. 137/B3
Mkokotoni, Tanz. 137/B3
Mkomazi Game Rsv., Tanz. 137/B3
Mkombo (riv.), Tanz. 139/G4
Mkondoa (riv.), Tanz. 137/B3
Mkorn (peak), Mor. 128/D3
Mkumbi (pt.), Tanz. 137/B3
Mkushi, Zam. 141/F2
Mkushi (riv.), Zam. 141/F2
Mkuze (riv.), SAfr. 143/F2
Mkuze, SAfr. 143/F2
Mladá Boleslav, Czh. 65/H2
Mladá Vožice, Czh. 65/H3
Mladenovac, Serb. 56/E3
Mlala (hills), Tanz. 139/G4
Mława, Pol. 49/L2
Mljet (isl.), Cro. 73/H2
Mljet NP, Cro. 56/C4
Mlolo, Zam. 141/G2
Mmabatho, SAfr. 142/D2
Mmadinare, Bots. 141/E4
Mmamabula, Bots. 141/E4
Mmathethe, Bots. 140/E5
Mnazini, Kenya 137/C2
Mnyera (riv.), Tanz. 137/A4
Mo Duc, Viet. 106/E3
Moa (riv.), SLeo. 132/C5
Moa, Tanz. 137/B3
Moa, Cuba 207/H1
Moa (isl.), Indo. 152/B2
Moab, Ut, US 179/H1
Moabi, Gabon 138/B3
Moala Group (isl.), Fiji 160/G6
Moama, Austl. 156/C1
Moamba, Moz. 143/F2
Moaña, Sp. 52/A1
Moanda, Gabon 138/C3
Moanda, D.R. Congo 138/B4
Moapa River Ind. Res., Nv, US 178/E2
Moate, Ire. 38/C3
Mobara, Japan 95/E3
Mobārakeh, Iran 115/G3
Mobaye, CAfr. 134/D4
Mobeetie, Tx, US 182/D3
Moberly, Mo, US 185/H4
Mobile, Al, US 194/D2
Mobile (bay), Al, US 194/D2
Mobile (pt.), Al, US 194/D2
Mobridge, SD, US 186/D5
Moc Chau, Viet. 98/E4
Moc Hoa, Viet. 106/D4
Moca (pass), Turk. 116/C1
Mocache, Ecu. 216/B5
Mocajuba, Braz. 218/D3
Moçambique, Moz. 141/J2
Mocanaqua, Pa, US 198/B1
Mocassin, Az, US 179/F2
Mocha (riv.), Rus. 75/W9
Mocha, Yem. 136/B2
Moche (ruin), Peru 220/B3
Mochima, PN, Ven. 217/E2
Mochizuki, Japan 95/A1
Mochudi, Bots. 140/E5
Mochumí, Peru 220/B2
Mociu, Rom. 57/G2
Möckeln (lake), Swe. 46/E3
Mockfjärd, Swe. 46/F1
Möckmühl, Ger. 64/C4
Mocksville, NC, US 193/G3
Moclín, Sp. 52/D4
Moclips, Wa, US 174/B4
Mocoa, Col. 216/B4
Mococa, Braz. 223/J6
Mocoretá, Arg. 224/E4
Mocorito, Mex. 204/D3
Moctezuma, Mex. 205/E4
Moctezuma, Mex. 204/C2
Mocuba, Moz. 141/H3
Modane, Fr. 70/C2
Modāsa, India 104/B3
Modbury, Eng, UK 42/C6
Modderrivier (riv.), SAfr. 142/D3
Model Village, Ire. 38/B6
Modena, It. 69/D4
Modena (prov.), It. 69/D4
Modena, Ut, US 179/F2
Moder (riv.), Fr. 51/G2
Modesto, Ca, US 178/B2
Modica, It. 54/D4
Modigliana, It. 69/E5
Modjamboli, D.R. Congo 139/E2
Modjeska, Ca, US 196/C3
Modjigo (reg.), Niger 134/B1
Mödling, Aus. 57/N7
Modoc, SC, US 193/F4
Modoc NWR, Ca, US 176/C3
Modot, Mong. 90/F2
Modriča, Bosn. 56/D3
Modugno, It. 54/E2
Moe, Austl. 157/C4
Moeb (bay), Namb. 142/A2
Moehau (hill), NZ 159/C2
Moel Fammau (peak), Wal, UK 41/E5
Moel Fferna (peak), Wal, UK 41/E6
Moel Hywel (peak), Wal, UK 42/C2
Moel Sych (peak), Wal, UK 41/E6
Moel-y-Llyn (peak), Wal, UK 42/C2
Moëlan-sur-Mer, Fr. 62/B5
Moelfre (peak), Wal, UK 42/C1
Moelv, Nor. 46/D1
Moen, Nor. 44/F1
Moen, Micr. 160/E4
Moengo, Sur. 218/C1
Moenkopi, Az, US 179/G2
Moenkopi Wash (riv.), Az, US 179/G2
Moerai (isl.), FrPol. 161/K7
Moerbeke, Belg. 60/C1
Moerdijk, Neth. 58/B5
Moerewa, NZ 159/C1
Moers, Ger. 58/D6
Moervaart (riv.), Belg. 60/C1
Moesa (riv.), Swi. 67/F5
Moffat, Sc, UK 39/C6
Moffat (peak), NZ 159/B4
Moffat, Co, US 179/K2
Moffett Field Nav. Air Sta., Ca, US 197/K12
Moffit, ND, US 186/D4
Moga, India 110/C4
Mogadishu (cap.), Som. 136/C5
Mogadouro, Port. 52/B2
Mogalo, D.R. Congo 138/D2
Mogami, Japan 94/B4
Mogami (riv.), Japan 94/B4
Mogapinyana, Bots. 141/E4
Mogaung, Myan. 98/C3
Mogent (riv.), Sp. 53/L6
Mögglingen, Ger. 64/C5
Moghul Gardens, India 110/C3
Mogi das Cruzes, Braz. 223/K8
Mogi-Guaçu (riv.), Braz. 223/K7
Mogi-Guaçu, Braz. 223/K7
Mogi-Mirim, Braz. 223/K7
Mogige, Eth. 135/H4
Mogil Mogil, Austl. 156/D1
Mogilno, Pol. 49/J2
Mogincual, Moz. 141/J2
Moglia, It. 69/D4
Mogliano, It. 71/C1
Mogliano Veneto, It. 69/F2
Möglingen, Ger. 64/C5
Mogna, Arg. 224/B4
Mogocha, Rus. 91/H1
Mogogh, Sudan 135/F3
Mogok, Myan. 98/C4
Mogollon, NM, US 179/H4
Mogollon (rim), Az, US 179/G3
Mogollon (plat.), Az, US 179/G3
Mogollon (mts.), NM, US 179/H4
Mogolrivier (riv.), SAfr. 141/E4
Mogoro, It. 54/A3
Mogotes (pt.), Arg. 226/F3
Mogotio, Kenya 137/A2
Mogotón (peak), Nic. 206/E3
Mogoytuy, Rus. 90/G1
Moguer, Sp. 52/B4
Mogzon, Rus. 90/G1
Mohács, Hun. 56/D3
Mohaeli (isl.), Com. 143/G6
Mohales Hoek, Les. 142/D3
Mohall, ND, US 186/D3
Mohamed V (dam), Mor. 130/C2
Mohamed V (Casablanca) (int'l arpt.), Mor. 128/D2
Moḩammadābād, Iran 115/J3
Mohammadia, Alg. 130/F5
Mohammadia-Znata (prov.), Mor. 130/A2
Mohammedia, Mor. 130/A3
Mohanganj, Bang. 109/H3
Mohaniā, India 108/D3
Mohave (lake), Nv, US 178/E3
Mohawk, Mi, US 187/K4
Mohawk (riv.), NY, US 191/J3
Mohawk (lake), NJ, US 198/D1
Moheda, Swe. 46/F3
Mohembo, Bots. 140/D3
Mohican (cape), Ak, US 201/E3
Mohill, Ire. 38/C2
Mohindargarh, India 110/D5
Möhlin, Swi. 66/D2
Möhne (riv.), Ger. 59/F6
Möhnestausee (lake), Ger. 59/F5
Mohnton, Pa, US 198/C3
Mohnyin, Myan. 105/G3
Moho, Peru 220/D4
Mohoro, Tanz. 137/B4
Mohrsville, Pa, US 198/C3
Mohyliv-Podil's'kyy, Ukr. 78/D3
Moi, Nor. 46/B2
Moi (int'l arpt.), Kenya 137/B3
Moiano, It. 71/D5
Moie, It. 69/G6
Moincêr, China 111/D5
Moineşti, Rom. 78/D4
Moinkum (des.), Kaz. 80/H5
Moinsi (hills), Gha. 133/E5
Moira (riv.), On, Can. 191/H2
Moirans, Fr. 70/B2
Moirans-en-Montagne, Fr. 66/B5
Mõisaküla, Est. 47/L2
Moisant Field (New Orleans) (int'l arpt.), La, US 194/C3
Moisdon-la-Rivière, Fr. 62/D5
Moisie (riv.), Qu, Can. 171/K3
Moislains, Fr. 60/B4
Moissac, Fr. 50/D4
Moïssala, Chad 134/C3
Moisselles, Fr. 36/K4
Moisson, Fr. 36/G4
Moita, Port. 53/Q10
Moitaco, Ven. 217/E3
Möja (isl.), Swe. 45/B1
Möja, Swe. 45/B1
Mojácar, Sp. 52/E4
Mojave (des.), Ca, US 172/C5
Mojave, Ca, US 178/C3
Mojave (riv.), Ca, US 178/D3
Mojiang Hanizu Zizhixian, China 98/D4
Mojkovac, Mont. 56/D4
Mojo, Bol. 224/C2
Mojo, Eth. 136/A3
Mojocoya, Bol. 224/C1
Mojokerto, Indo. 101/F4
Mojos, Bol. 220/D4
Mojos, Llanos de (plain), Bol. 221/E4
Moju (riv.), Braz. 218/D3
Moju, Braz. 218/D3
Mōka, Japan 97/F2
Mokameh, India 109/E3
Mōkampur, India 110/B5
Mokelumne (aqueduct), Ca, US 197/M11
Mokelumne (riv.), Ca, US 176/C4
Mokena, Il, US 197/Q16
Mokhotlong, Les. 142/E3
Mokhovoye, Rus. 76/F1
Mokil (isl.), Micr. 160/E4
Mokine, Tun. 130/M7
Mokochu (peak), Thai. 106/B3
Mokokchūng, India 98/B3
Mokolo, Camr. 134/B3
Mokolo, D.R. Congo 138/D2
Mokp'o, SKor. 93/D5
Mokrin, Serb. 56/E3
Moksha (riv.), Rus. 77/G1
Mokumbusu, D.R. Congo 139/E2
Mokwa, Nga. 133/G4
Mol, Belg. 58/C6
Mol, Serb. 56/E3
Mola di Bari, It. 55/E2
Molalla, Or, US 176/B1
Moláoi, Gre. 55/H4
Molard Noir (peak), Fr. 70/B1
Molare, It. 68/B4
Molas, Punta (pt.), Mex. 206/E1
Molat (isl.), Cro. 56/B3
Molatón (peak), Sp. 52/E3
Molbergen, Ger. 59/E3
Mold, Wal, UK 41/E5
Moldavia (reg.), Rom. 57/H2
Moldavian Carpathian (range), Rom. 57/G2
Molde, Nor. 44/C3
Moldova (ctry.) 78/E4
Moldova (riv.), Rom. 57/G2
Moldova Nouă, Rom. 56/E3
Moldoveanu (peak), Rom. 57/G3
Mole, D.R. Congo 139/G3
Môle (riv.), Fr. 70/C6
Mole (riv.), Eng, UK 42/C5
Mole (riv.), Eng, UK 36/B3
Mole Lake Ind. Res., Wi, US 190/B2
Mole NP, Gha. 133/E4
Môle Saint-Nicolas, Haiti 207/H2
Molegbe, D.R. Congo 134/D4
Molena, Ga, US 192/E4
Molepolole, Bots. 140/E5
Molėtai, Lith. 47/L4
Molfetta, It. 54/E2
Molibagu, Indo. 103/F3
Molina, Sp. 52/E2
Molina, Chile 226/C2
Molina de Segura, Sp. 52/E3
Moline, Ks, US 183/F2
Moline, Il, US 185/J3
Molinella, It. 69/E4
Molines-en-Queyras, Fr. 70/C3
Molinfaing, Belg. 61/E4
Molinicos, Sp. 52/D3
Molino, Fl, US 194/E2
Molino de Flores, PN, Mex. 205/R9
Molins de Rei, Sp. 53/L7
Moliro, D.R. Congo 139/G5
Molise (reg.), It. 73/G2
Molkom, Swe. 46/E2
Möll (riv.), Aus. 51/K3
Mollakänd, Azer. 115/G1
Mölle, Swe. 45/J6
Møllebjerg (peak), Den. 44/D5
Mollendo, Peru 220/C5
Mollerussa, Sp. 53/F2
Molles (pt.), Chile 226/C2
Molles, Uru. 191/K10
Mollet del Vallès, Sp. 53/L6
Mollis, Swi. 67/F3
Mölnbo, Swe. 45/A1
Mölndal, Swe. 46/E3
Mölnlycke, Swe. 46/E3
Molo, Kenya 137/A2
Molo, Myan. 98/C4
Molochans'k, Ukr. 79/H4
Molochnoye (lake), Ukr. 79/H4
Molócue (riv.), Moz. 141/H3
Molodezhnaya, Rus., Ant. 228/D
Molodohvardiys'k, Ukr. 79/K3
Mologa (riv.), Rus. 74/G4
Molokai (isl.), Hi, US 172/T10
Molokovo, Rus. 74/H4
Moloma (riv.), Rus. 75/L4
Molong, Austl. 157/D1
Molopo (riv.), Bots. 119/E7
Moloporivier (riv.), SAfr. 140/D5
Mólos, Gre. 55/H3
Moloundou, Camr. 138/C2
Molsheim, Fr. 66/D1
Molteno, SAfr. 142/D3
Molu (isl.), Indo. 103/H5
Molucca (sea), Asia 83/M10
Molucca (isls.), Indo. 83/M10
Moluccas (arch.), Indo. 103/G3
Molveno, It. 67/G5
Molveno (lake), It. 67/G5
Moma, D.R. Congo 139/E3
Moma, Moz. 141/H3
Mombaça, Braz. 219/G4
Mombango Li, D.R. Congo 139/F2
Mombasa, Kenya 137/B3
Mombetsu, Japan 94/C1
Mombetsu, Japan 94/C2
Mombo, Tanz. 137/B3
Momboyo (riv.), D.R. Congo 138/D3
Mömbris, Ger. 64/C2
Momchilgrad, Bul. 57/G5
Momence, Il, US 190/C4
Momfafa (cape), Indo. 103/H4
Momignies, Belg. 61/D3
Mömlingen, Ger. 64/C3
Mommilanjärvi (lake), Fin. 45/E4
Momo, It. 68/B2
Momoishi, Japan 94/B3
Mompós, Col. 216/C2
Mompoto, D.R. Congo 138/D3
Møn (isl.), Den. 46/E4
Mon, Myan. 106/B2
Mon (state), Myan. 105/G4
Mon (riv.), Myan. 105/F3
Mon (state), Viet. 98/C5
Mona (passg.), NAm. 203/H4
Mona (isl.), PR 203/M8
Mona Quimbundo, Ang. 138/D5
Mona Vale (nbrhd.), Austl. 158/H8
Monaco (ctry.) 68/J8
Monaco (cap.), Mona. 68/J8
Monaco, Port of (har.), Mona. 68/J8
Monadhliath (mts.), Sc, UK 39/B2
Monaepa (pt.), Moz. 141/H3
Monagas (state), Ven. 217/F2
Monaghan (co.), Ire. 40/A3
Monaghan, Ire. 38/D1
Monagrillo, Pan. 216/A3
Monagrillo (ruin), Pan. 216/A2
Monahans, Tx, US 180/C2
Monango, ND, US 186/E4
Monapo, Moz. 141/J2
Monar (lake), Sc, UK 39/A2
Monaragala, SrL. 107/D5
Monarch, Mt, US 175/J4
Monashee (mts.), BC, Can. 174/E2
Monasterevin, Ire. 38/C3
Monastir, Tun. 130/M7
Monatélé, Camr. 138/B1
Moncada, Sp. 53/E3
Moncalvo, It. 68/B3
Monção, Braz. 219/E3
Moncayo (range), Sp. 52/E2
Mönch (peak), Swi. 66/D4
Monchegorsk, Rus. 74/G2
Mönchengladbach, Ger. 58/D6
Monchique (mts.), Port. 52/A4
Monchique, Port. 52/A4
Moncks Corner, SC, US 193/G4
Monclova, Mex. 180/D4
Moncontour, Fr. 62/C4
Moncton, NB, Can. 188/E2
Mondego (riv.), Port. 52/A2
Mondego (cape), Port. 52/A2
Mondéjar, Sp. 52/D2
Mondeville, Fr. 63/E2
Mondimbi, D.R. Congo 139/E2
Mondo, Chad 134/B2
Mondo, Tanz. 137/A3
Mondolfo, It. 69/G6
Mondoñedo, Sp. 52/B1
Mondorf-les-Bains, Lux. 61/F4
Mondovi, It. 68/A4
Mondovi, Wi, US 185/J1
Mondragon, Fr. 70/A4
Mondragón, Sp. 50/B5
Mondragone, It. 71/C5
Mondsee (lake), Aus. 65/G7
Mondsee, Aus. 65/G7
Mondy, Rus. 90/E1
Moneglia, It. 68/C5
Monemvasía, Gre. 55/H4
Monero, NM, US 179/J2
Mones Cazón, Arg. 226/E3
Monesterio, Sp. 52/B3
Moneta, Wy, US 177/K2
Monett, Mo, US 183/H2
Monette, Ar, US 192/B3
Money (pt.), Sc, UK 40/C2
Moneygall, Ire. 38/C4
Moneymore, NI, UK 40/B2
Moneyreagh, NI, UK 40/C2
Monferrato (reg.), It. 51/H4
Monforte, Port. 52/B3
Monforte, Sp. 52/B1
Mong Cai, Viet. 99/E4
Möng Hang, Myan. 106/B1
Möng Hpāyak, Myan. 106/B1
Möng Hsat, Myan. 106/B1
Möng Hsu, Myan. 98/C4
Möng Küng, Myan. 98/C4
Möng Long, Myan. 106/B1
Möng Maü, Myan. 106/B2
Möng Nai, Myan. 98/C4
Möng Pan, Myan. 106/B1
Möng Pawn, Myan. 98/C4
Möng Ping, Myan. 106/B1
Möng Tön, Myan. 106/B1
Möng Tūm, Myan. 106/B1
Möng Yai, Myan. 98/C4
Möng Yang, Myan. 98/C4
Möng Yawng, Myan. 98/D4
Möng Yu, Myan. 98/C4
Monga, Tanz. 137/B4
Monga, D.R. Congo 134/D4
Mongaguá, Braz. 223/K9
Mongala (riv.), D.R. Congo 139/E2
Mongalla, Sudan 135/F4
Mongandjo, D.R. Congo 139/F2
Mongar, Bhu. 109/H2
Mongaup (mtn.), NY, US 191/J3
Mongers (lake), Austl. 154/C4
Monggŭmp'o, NKor. 93/C3
Monghidoro, It. 69/E5
Mongioia (peak), It. 70/C3
Mongo, Chad 134/C2
Mongo (riv.), Gui. 132/C4
Mongolia (ctry.) 90/D2
Mongomo, EqG. 138/B2
Mongororo, Chad 134/D2
Mongoumba, CAfr. 138/D2
Mongoungou, Gabon 138/B3
Mongu, Zam. 140/D2
Mônguel, Mrta. 132/B2
Mönh Hayrhan (peak), Mong. 90/C2
Mönh Sarĭdag (peak), Mong. 90/E1
Monhegan (isl.), Me, US 188/C4
Monheim, Ger. 61/F1
Monheim, Ger. 64/D5
Moni, Cyp. 116/C2
Moni, China 98/E3
Moniaive, Sc, UK 40/E1
Monico, Wi, US 187/K5
Monietu, D.R. Congo 139/G2
Monifieth, Sc, UK 39/D4
Moniquirá, Col. 216/C3
Monistrol de Montserrat, Sp. 53/K6
Monistrol-sur-Loire, Fr. 50/F4
Monitor (range), Nv, US 176/E4
Monitor, Wa, US 174/D4
Monivea, Ire. 38/B3
Monkayo, Phil. 100/D4
Monkey (pt.), Nic. 207/F4
Monkey (mtn.), Austl. 157/D1
Monkey Bay, Malw. 141/G2
Monkey Jungle, Fl, US 194/P11
Monkey Mia, Austl. 154/B3
Monkey River Town, Belz. 206/D2
Mońki, Pol. 49/M2
Monkoto, D.R. Congo 139/E3
Monks (isl.), Md, US 198/B5
Monkton, Vt, US 191/K2
Monmouth, Il, US 185/J3
Monmouth, Or, US 176/B1
Monmouth Beach, NJ, US 199/E3
Monmouth Junction, NJ, US 198/D3
Monmouthshire (co.), Wal, UK 42/D3
Monmow (riv.), Eng, UK 42/C2
Monnaie, Fr. 63/F5
Monnickendam, Neth. 58/C4
Monninkylä, Fin. 45/F4
Mono (prov.), Ben. 133/F5
Mono (riv.), Togo 133/F5
Mono (cr.), Ca, US 196/A1
Mono (lake), Ca, US 176/D4
Mono Road, On, Can. 190/T8
Monocacy (riv.), Md, US 198/A4
Monocacy Nat'l Bfld., Md, US 191/H5
Monon, In, US 190/C4
Monona, Ia, US 185/J2
Monongah, WV, US 190/F5
Monongahela (riv.), WV, US 190/G5
Monopoli, It. 55/E2
Monor, Hun. 56/D2
Monóvar, Sp. 53/E3
Monreal del Campo, Sp. 52/E2
Monreale, It. 54/C3
Monroe, La, US 183/H4
Monroe, In, US 190/D4
Monroe, Mi, US 190/E4
Monroe, Wa, US 197/C2
Monroe (peak), Ut, US 179/F1
Monroe, Ut, US 179/F1
Monroe, Ia, US 185/H3
Monroe, Ga, US 192/F4
Monroe, Wi, US 185/K2
Monroe, Ct, US 199/E1
Monroe, NY, US 199/D1
Monroe, NC, US 193/G3
Monroe (lake), In, US 192/D1
Monroe City, Mo, US 185/J4
Monroe City, In, US 192/D1
Monroe Mil. Res., Va, US 193/J2
Monroeville, In, US 190/D4
Monroeville, Al, US 194/E2
Monroeville, Pa, US 191/G4
Monroeville, NJ, US 198/C4
Monrovia (cap.), Libr. 132/C5
Monrovia, Ca, US 196/G7
Monrovia (Roberts) (int'l arpt.), Libr. 132/C5
Mons, Belg. 60/C3
Monsanto, Port. 52/B2
Monschau, Ger. 61/F2
Monse, Indo. 103/F4
Monsefú, Peru 220/B2
Monsenhor Hipólito, Braz. 219/F4
Monsenhor Tabosa, Braz. 219/F4
Monsey, NY, US 199/J7
Monsheim, Ger. 64/B3
Monster, Neth. 58/B4
Mönsterås, Swe. 46/G3
Monsummano Terme, It. 69/D6
Mont Belvieu, Tx, US 181/N9
Mont Fouri, Rsv. Du, Congo,Gabon 138/B3
Mont Nebo, Sk, Can. 175/L1
Mont Peko, PN du, C.d'Iv. 132/D5
Mont Sangbé, PN du, C.d'Iv. 132/D4
Mont Ventoux (range), Fr. 70/B4
Mont-Carmel, Qu, Can. 188/C2
Mont-de-Marsan, Fr. 50/C5
Mont-Joli, Qu, Can. 188/C1
Mont-Laurier, Qu, Can. 191/J1
Mont-Près-Chambord, Fr. 63/G5
Mont-Royal, Qu, Can. 189/N6
Mont-Saint-Aignan, Fr. 63/G2
Mont-Saint-Martin, Fr. 61/E4
Mont-Saint-Michel, Qu, Can. 191/J1
Mont-Sous-Vaudrey, Fr. 66/B4
Montà, It. 68/A3
Monta Fon (mts.), Aus. 67/F3
Montabaur, Ger. 61/G3
Montagnana, It. 69/E3
Montagne d'Ambre NP, Madg. 143/J6
Montagny-Sainte-Félicité, Fr. 36/L4
Montague (sound), Austl. 152/B3
Montague, PE, Can. 189/F2
Montague (isl.), Mex. 178/E5
Montagu, SAfr. 142/M10
Montague, Yk,Can. 201/L3
Montague (isl.), Ak, US 201/J4
Montague (str.), Ak, US 201/J4
Montague, Ca, US 176/B3
Montague, Ma, US 191/K3
Montague, Mi, US 190/C3
Montague, NJ, US 198/D1
Montague, Tx, US 183/F4
Montaigu, Fr. 50/C3
Montaione, It. 69/D6
Montalba, Tx, US 180/G2
Montalbán, Sp. 53/E2
Montalbano Jonico, It. 54/E2
Montale, It. 69/E6
Montale, It. 69/D4
Montalieu-Vercieu, Fr. 66/B6
Montalvão, Port. 52/B3
Montalvo, Ca, US 196/A2
Montana, Swi. 66/D5
Montana (prov.), Bul. 55/H1
Montana (prov.), Slov. 57/F4
Montana, Bul. 57/F4
Montana (state), US 172/D2
Montanaro, It. 68/A2
Montanha, Braz. 223/E3
Montara, Ca, US 197/J11
Montargis, Fr. 50/E2
Montataire, Fr. 60/B5
Montauban, Fr. 62/C4
Montauban, Fr. 50/D4
Montauk, NY, US 199/G1
Montauk (pt.), NY, US 199/G1
Montauroux, Fr. 70/C5
Montbard, Fr. 50/F3
Montbazon, Fr. 63/F6
Montbéliard, Fr. 66/C2
Montblanc, Sp. 53/F2
Montcada i Reixac, Sp. 53/L7
Montcalm, WV, US 193/G2
Montceau-les-Mines, Fr. 50/F3
Montclair, Ca, US 196/C2
Montclair, NJ, US 199/J8
Montcornet, Fr. 60/D4
Montdidier, Fr. 60/B4
Monte Albán (ruin), Mex. 206/B2
Monte Alegre, Braz. 219/H4
Monte Alegre, Braz. 218/C3
Monte Alegre de Goiás, Braz. 222/D2
Monte Alegre de Minas, Braz. 222/C3
Monte Alegre do Piauí, Braz. 219/E5
Monte Alto, Braz. 225/G2
Monte Alto, Tx, US 181/F4
Monte Azul, Braz. 223/E2
Monte Belo, Ang. 140/B2
Monte Carmelo, Ven. 216/D2
Monte Carmelo, Braz. 222/D3
Monte Caseros, Arg. 224/E4
Monte Comán, Arg. 226/D2
Monte Cristo, Bol. 221/F4
Monte di Procida, It. 71/D6
Monte Dourado, Braz. 218/C3
Monte Escobedo, Mex. 204/E4
Monte Etna (Mount Etna) (vol.), It. 54/D4
Monte León, Arg. 191/C6
Monte Maíz, Arg. 226/E2
Monte Pascoal, PN de, Braz. 223/F3
Monte Patria, Chile 224/B4
Monte Porzio Catone, It. 71/B4
Monte Quemado, Arg. 224/D3
Monte Rosa (mts.), It. 66/D6
Monte San Biagio, It. 71/C5
Monte San Giusto, It. 71/C1
Monte San Savino, It. 69/E7
Monte Sant'Angelo, It. 54/D2
Monte Urano, It. 71/C1
Monte Verde, Bol. 220/D3
Monte Vista, Co, US 179/J2
Monte Vista Nat'l Wild. Ref., Co, US 179/J2
Monte-Carlo, Mona. 68/J8
Monteagudo, Bol. 224/D1
Montealegre, Sp. 52/E3
Montebello, Ca, US 196/F7
Montebello, Col. 219/K7
Montebello (isls.), Austl. 145/A3
Montebello Vincentino, It. 69/E3
Montebelluna, It. 69/F2
Montebourg, Fr. 62/D2
Montebruno, It. 68/C4
Montecarlo, Arg. 225/F3
Montecassiano, It. 69/G7
Montecatini Terme, It. 69/D6
Montecavolo, It. 68/D4
Montecchio, It. 69/F6
Montecchio Magiore, It. 69/E2
Montecelio, It. 71/B3
Montechiaro d'Asti, It. 68/B3
Montecilfone, It. 71/D4
Montecito, Ca, US 196/A2
Montecompatri, It. 71/B4
Montecorvino Rovella, It. 71/D6
Montecristo (isl.), It. 54/B1
Montecristo, PN, ESal. 206/D3
Montefalco, It. 71/B2
Montefalcone, It. 71/D6
Montefalcone di Val Fortore, It. 71/E5
Montefalcone nel Sannio, It. 71/D4
Montefeltro (reg.), It. 69/F5
Monteforte D'Alpone, It. 69/E3
Monteforte Irpino, It. 71/D6
Montefrío, Sp. 52/C4
Montegiorgio, It. 71/C1
Montego Bay, Jam. 207/G2
Montegranaro, It. 71/C1
Montegrotto Terme, It. 69/E3
Montehermoso, Sp. 52/B2
Monteiro, Braz. 219/G4
Montejinni, Austl. 152/C4
Montelavar, Port. 53/P10
Montelibretti, It. 71/B3
Montélimar, Fr. 70/A3
Montelindo (riv.), Par. 222/A4
Montell, Tx, US 180/D3
Montellano, Sp. 52/C4
Montello, Nv, US 177/F3
Montello, Wi, US 185/K2
Montelupo Fiorentino, It. 69/E6
Montemagno, It. 68/B4
Montemarciano, It. 69/G6
Montemiletto, It. 71/D5
Montemor-o-Novo, Port. 52/A3
Montemor-o-Velho, Port. 52/A2
Montemorelos, Mex. 205/F3
Montemuro (peak), Port. 52/A2
Montenay, Fr. 63/E4
Montendre, Fr. 50/C4
Montenegro, Braz. 225/G4
Montenegro, Chile 226/N8
Montenegro, Col. 219/K8
Montenegro (ctry.) 56/D4
Montenero di Bisaccia, It. 71/D4
Montepuez (riv.), Moz. 141/H2
Montepuez, Moz. 141/H2
Montepulciano, It. 54/B1
Montereau-sur-le-Jard, Fr. 36/L6
Monterey (bay), Ca, US 172/B4
Monterey, La, US 194/C2
Monterey, Tn, US 192/E2
Monterey, Va, US 193/H1
Monterey Park, Ca, US 196/F7
Montería, Col. 216/C2
Montero, Bol. 224/D1
Monteroduni, It. 71/D4
Monteros, Arg. 224/C3
Monterosso (peak), It. 67/G4
Monterosso al Mare, It. 68/C5
Monterotondo, It. 71/B3
Monterrey, Sp. 52/B2
Monterrey, Mex. 205/E3
Montes (pt.), Arg. 191/C6
Montes Altos, Braz. 219/E4
Montes Claros, Braz. 222/E3
Montesano, Wa, US 174/C4
Montesarchio, It. 71/D5
Montescaglioso, It. 54/E2
Montesilvano Marina, It. 71/D2
Montespertoli, It. 69/E6
Montesson, Fr. 36/J5
Monteux, Fr. 70/A4
Montevallo, Al, US 192/D4
Montevarchi, It. 69/E6
Montevideo, Mn, US 185/G1
Montevideo (dept.), Uru. 191/K11
Montevideo (cap.), Uru. 191/K11
Monteview, Id, US 177/G2
Montévrain, Fr. 36/L5
Montezuma, Ks, US 182/D2
Montezuma, In, US 190/C5
Montezuma (slough), Ca, US 197/K10
Montezuma, Ia, US 185/H3
Montezuma (cr.), Ut, US 179/H2
Montezuma, Ga, US 192/E4
Montezuma Castle Nat'l Mon., Az, US 179/G3
Montezuma Creek, Ut, US 179/H2
Montfermeil, Fr. 36/K5
Montferrand-le-Château, Fr. 66/B3
Montferrat, Fr. 70/C5
Montfoort, Neth. 58/B4
Montfort, Fr. 62/D4
Montfort (ruin), Isr. 117/C2
Montfort-L'Amaury, Fr. 60/A6
Montfort-sur-Risle, Fr. 63/F2
Montfrin, Fr. 70/A5
Montgenèvre, Fr. 70/C3
Montgeron, Fr. 36/K5
Montgomery, Ga, US 195/H2
Montgomery, La, US 194/B2
Montgomery, Il, US 197/P16
Montgomery, WV, US 193/G1
Montgomery (cap.), Al, US 192/D4
Montgomery, Wal, UK 42/C1
Montgomery, Tx, US 181/G2
Montgomery, Pa, US 198/B1
Montgomery (co.), Md, US 198/A5
Montgomery City, Mo, US 185/J4
Montgomery Village, Md, US 198/A5
Montgomeryville, Pa, US 198/C3
Montgrand (peak), Fr. 50/E5
Monthermé, Fr. 61/D4
Monthey, Swi. 66/C5
Monthureux-sur-Saône, Fr. 66/B1
Monthyon, Fr. 36/L4
Monticelli d'Ongina, It. 68/C3
Monticelli Terme, It. 68/D4
Monticello, Ar, US 183/J4
Monticello, La, US 183/J4
Monticello, In, US 190/C4
Monticello, Ms, US 194/C2
Monticello, Fl, US 195/G2
Monticello, NY, US 191/J4
Monticello (dam), Ca, US 176/B4
Monticello, Ut, US 179/H2
Monticello, Ia, US 185/J2
Monticello, Ky, US 192/E2
Monticello, Ga, US 192/F4
Monticello, Mo, US 185/J3
Monticello, NM, US 179/J4
Monticello, Va, US 193/H2
Monticello Conte Otto, It. 69/E2
Montichiari, It. 68/D3
Montier-en-Der, Fr. 66/A1
Montignies-le-Tilleul, Belg. 61/D3
Montigny-en-Gohelle, Fr. 60/B3
Montigny-le-Bretonneux, Fr. 36/J5
Montigny-le-Roi, Fr. 66/B2
Montigny-les-Metz, Fr. 61/F5
Montijo, Sp. 52/B3
Montijo, Port. 53/Q10
Montilla, Sp. 52/C4
Montivilliers, Fr. 63/F1
Montlebon, Fr. 66/C3
Montlhéry, Fr. 36/J6
Montluçon, Fr. 50/E3
Montluel, Fr. 66/B6
Montmagny, Qu, Can. 188/B2
Montmartre, Sk, Can. 186/C2
Montmédy, Fr. 61/E4
Montmélian, Fr. 70/C1
Montmerle-sur-Saône, Fr. 66/A5
Montmeyran, Fr. 70/A3
Montmirail, Fr. 60/C6
Montmorency, Fr. 36/J5
Montmorillon, Fr. 50/D3
Montmorot, Fr. 66/B4
Monto, Austl. 158/C4
Montodine, It. 68/C3
Montoir-de-Bretagne, Fr. 62/C6
Montoire-sur-le-Loir, Fr. 63/F5
Montois-la-Montagne, Fr. 61/F5
Montone (riv.), It. 69/E4
Montopoli, It. 69/D6
Montorio al Vomano, It. 71/C2
Montorio Veronese, It. 69/E3
Montoro, Sp. 52/C3
Montour (ridge), Pa, US 198/B2
Montour, Pa, US 198/B1
Montour Falls, NY, US 191/H3
Montoursville, Pa, US 198/B1
Montpelier, Id, US 177/H2
Montpelier, In, US 190/D4
Montpelier, Ms, US 192/C4
Montpelier, ND, US 186/E4
Montpelier, Oh, US 190/D4
Montpelier (cap.), Vt, US 191/K2
Montpellier, Qu, Can. 191/J2
Montpellier, Fr. 50/E5
Montréal, Qu, Can. 189/N6
Montréal-Est, Qu, Can. 189/N6
Montréal-la-Cluse, Fr. 66/B5
Montréal-Nord, Qu, Can. 189/N6
Montréjeau, Fr. 50/D5
Montreuil, Fr. 60/A3
Montreuil, Fr. 36/K5
Montreuil-Bellay, Fr. 50/C3
Montreuil-sur-Epte, Fr. 36/G4
Montreux, Swi. 66/C5
Montreux-Château, Fr. 66/C2
Montrevault, Fr. 63/D6
Montrevel-en-Bresse, Fr. 66/B5
Montrichard, Fr. 63/G6
Montricher, Swi. 66/C4
Montrose (lake), Mo, US 183/G1
Montrose, Ar, US 183/J4
Montrose (basin), Sc, UK 39/D3
Montrose, Sc, UK 39/D3
Montrose, Mi, US 190/E3
Montrose, Pa, US 191/J4
Montrose, Co, US 179/J1
Montrose, Mn, US 187/N6
Montross, Va, US 193/J1
Montrouge, Fr. 36/J5
Montry, Fr. 36/L5
Monts, Fr. 63/F6
Montseny, PN, Sp. 53/L6
Montserrado (co.), Libr. 132/C5
Montserrat (peak), Sp. 72/D2
Montserrat (dpcy.), UK 203/N8
Montserrat (isl.), Monts., UK 203/N8
Montsinéry, FrG. 218/C1
Montsoult, Fr. 36/J4
Montsûrs, Fr. 63/E4
Monturaqui, Chile 224/B3
Montvale, NJ, US 199/J7
Montverde, Fl, US 194/M6
Montville, NJ, US 199/H8
Monument, Co, US 182/B1
Monument, Or, US 176/D1
Monument (valley), Ut, US 179/G2
Monument Draw (riv.), Tx, US 180/C1
Monument Rocks, Ks, US 182/D1
Monument Valley Navajo Tribal Park, Ut, US 179/G2
Monveda, D.R. Congo 139/E2
Monywa, Myan. 98/B4
Monza, It. 68/C2
Monze, Zam. 141/E3
Monzingen, Ger. 61/G4
Monzón, Sp. 53/F2
Monzón, Peru 220/B3
Moody, Mo, US 183/J2
Moody, Tx, US 181/F2
Moodys, Ok, US 183/G2
Mooirivier, SAfr. 143/E3
Mook, Neth. 58/C5
Mookane, Bots. 141/E4
Mool (riv.), SAfr. 142/P13
Mooloo Downs, Austl. 154/C3
Moomaw (lake), WV, US 193/G2
Mooncoin, Ire. 38/C5
Mooney Mooney, Austl. 157/E1
Moonie, Austl. 158/C4
Moonta, Austl. 155/H5
Moora, Austl. 154/C4
Moorabbin (nbrhd.), Austl. 156/G5
Moorcroft, Wy, US 184/B1
Moordrecht, Neth. 58/B5
Moore, Ok, US 183/F3
Moore, Id, US 177/G2
Moore, Ut, US 179/G1
Moore, Mt, US 175/K4
Moore (lake), Austl. 145/A3
Moore Haven, Fl, US 195/H4
Moore River NP, Austl. 154/B4
Moorea (isl.), FrPol. 161/K6
Moorefield, WV, US 193/H1
Mooreland, Ok, US 182/E2
Moorenweis, Ger. 67/H1
Moores Creek Nat'l Bfld., NC, US 193/H3
Moorestown, NJ, US 198/D4
Mooresville, In, US 190/C5
Mooresville, NC, US 193/G3
Mooreton, ND, US 186/F4
Mooretown, On, Can. 197/H6
Moorfoot (hills), Sc, UK 39/C5
Moorhead, Mn, US 186/F4
Mooring, Tx, US 180/F2
Mooringsport, La, US 180/H1
Moorook, Austl. 156/B2
Mooroopna, Austl. 157/B3
Moorpark, Ca, US 196/B2
Moorreesburg, SAfr. 142/L10
Moorslede, Belg. 60/C2
Moosburg, Ger. 65/E6
Moose (mtn.), Mn, US 187/J4
Moose (isl.), Mb, Can. 186/F2
Moose (riv.), Me, US 188/B3
Moose Creek, Ak, US 201/J3
Moose Heights, BC, Can. 174/C1
Moose Jaw, Sk, Can. 175/M2
Moose (mtn.), Sk, Can. 186/C3
Moose Pass, Ak, US 201/J3
Moose Range, Sk, Can. 175/N1
Moosehead (lake), Me, US 173/N2
Mooseheart (mt.), Ak, US 201/H3
Mooseheart, Il, US 197/P16
Moosehorn, Mb, Can. 186/E2
Moosehorn NWR, Me, US 188/D3
Moosinning, Ger. 65/E6
Moosomin, Sk, Can. 186/D2
Moosonee, On, Can. 171/H3
Moosseedorf, Swi. 66/D3
Moosthenning, Ger. 65/F5
Mopeia, Moz. 141/G3
Mopipi, Bots. 140/E4
Mopti, Mali 132/D3
Mopti (pol. reg.), Mali 132/E3
Moqor, Afg. 113/J2
Moquegua, Peru 220/D5
Moquegua (dept.), Peru 220/D5
Moquehuà, Arg. 191/J11
Mor (riv.), India 109/F4
Mór, Hun. 56/D2
Mora, NM, US 182/B3
Mora, Mn, US 187/H5
Mora (riv.), NM, US 182/B3
Mora, Swe. 46/F1
Mora, La, US 194/B2
Mora, Camr. 134/B3
Mora, Sp. 52/D3
Mora, Port. 52/A3
Mora de Rubielos, Sp. 53/E2
Morača (riv.), Mont. 56/D4
Morada Nova, Braz. 219/G4
Morādābād, India 108/B1
Morado, PN, Chile 226/P8
Morafenobe, Madg. 143/H7
Morąg, Pol. 47/H5
Moraga, Ca, US 197/K11
Mórahalom, Hun. 56/D2
Morainvilliers, Fr. 36/H5
Moral de Calatrava, Sp. 52/D3
Moraleda, Canal de (chan.), Chile 226/B5
Moraleja, Sp. 52/B2
Morales, Guat. 206/D3
Moramanga, Madg. 143/J7
Moran, Ks, US 183/G2
Moran, Tx, US 180/E1
Moran, Wy, US 177/H2
Moranbah, Austl. 158/C3
Morane (isl.), FrPol. 161/M7
Morangis, Fr. 36/K5
Morannes, Fr. 63/E5
Morano Calabro, It. 54/E3
Morant Bay, Jam. 207/G2
Morar (lake), Sc, UK 37/R8
Morarano Chrome, Madg. 143/J7
Morat (lake), Swi. 66/D4
Morata de Tajuña, Sp. 53/N9
Moratalla, Sp. 52/E3
Moratuwa, SrL. 107/C5
Morava (riv.), Czh. 49/J4
Morava (riv.), Serb. 56/E4
Morāveh Tappeh, Iran 115/H2
Moravia (reg.), Czh. 49/J4

Morav – Mundu
311

Moravia, Ia, US 185/H3
Moravia, NY, US 191/H3
Moravia, Tx, US 181/F3
Moravian Falls, NC, US 193/G2
Moravská Třebová, Czh. 49/J4
Moravské Budějovice, Czh. 49/H4
Morawa, Austl. 154/C4
Moray (range), Austl. 152/C3
Moray (co.), Sc, UK 39/C2
Moray Firth (inlet), Sc, UK 39/B1
Morbach, Ger. 61/G4
Morbegno, It. 67/F5
Morbier, Fr. 66/C4
Morbihan (gulf), Fr. 62/C5
Morbihan (dept.), Fr. 62/B5
Morbio Inferiore, Swi. 67/F6
Morbras (riv.), Fr. 36/K5
Mörbylanga, Swe. 46/G3
Morcenx, Fr. 50/C4
Morciano di Romagna, It. 69/F6
Morclan, Pic de (peak), Fr. 66/C5
Morcone, It. 71/D5
Mordelles, Fr. 62/D4
Morden, Mb, Can. 186/E3
Morden (nbrhd.), Eng, UK 36/C2
Mordialloc (nbrhd.), Austl. 156/G6
Mordoviya Resp., Rus. 80/E4
Mordovo, Rus. 77/G1
Mordves, Rus. 74/H5
Møre Og Romsdal (co.), Nor. 44/C3
Morea, Austl. 156/B3
Moreau (riv.), SD, US 184/C1
Moreau, North Fork (riv.), SD, US 184/C1
Moreau, South Fork (riv.), SD, US 184/C1
Morebattle, Sc, UK 39/D5
Morecambe (bay), Eng, UK 41/E3
Morée, Fr. 63/G5
Moree, Austl. 156/D1
Morehead, Ky, US 193/F1
Morehead, PNG 153/F2
Morehead City, NC, US 193/J3
Morehouse, Mo, US 192/C2
Mörel, Swi. 66/E5
Moreland, Id, US 177/G2
Morelia, Mex. 205/E5
Morell, PE, Can. 189/F2
Morella, Austl. 158/A3
Morella, Sp. 53/E2
Morelos, Mex. 180/D3
Morelos (state), Mex. 202/A5
Moremi Wildlife Reserve, Bots. 140/D3
Morena, India 108/B2
Morena (range), Sp. 52/C4
Morenci, Mi, US 190/D4
Morenci, Az, US 179/H4
Moreni, Rom. 57/G3
Moreno Valley, Ca, US 196/C3
Moreno, Sierra (mts.), Sp. 72/B3
Moresby (isl.), BC, Can. 170/C3
Morestel, Fr. 70/B1
Moreton, Eng, UK 36/D1
Moreton (cape), Austl. 158/D4
Moreton (bay), Austl. 158/F6
Moreton (isl.), Austl. 145/E3
Moreton Island NP, Austl. 158/D4
Moreton-in-Marsh, Eng, UK 43/E3
Moretonhampstead, Eng, UK 42/C5
Moretta, It. 70/D3
Moreuil, Fr. 60/B4
Moreyu (riv.), Rus. 75/P2
Morez, Fr. 66/C4
Morgan, Ga, US 195/F2
Morgan, Vt, US 191/K2
Morgan, Ut, US 177/H3
Morgan, Austl. 155/H5
Morgan, Tx, US 180/F1
Morgan (pt.), Ct, US 199/F1
Morgan Brake NWR, Ms, US 192/B4
Morgan City, La, US 194/C3
Morgan Hill (town), Ca., US 3/B2
Morganfield, Ky, US 192/D2
Morganito, Ven. 216/E3
Morgantina (ruin), It. 54/D4
Morganton, Ga, US 192/E3
Morganton, NC, US 193/G3
Morgantown, WV, US 190/G5
Morgantown, In, US 190/C5
Morgantown, Ky, US 192/D2
Morgantown, Pa, US 198/C3
Morganville, Ks, US 185/F4
Morganza, La, US 194/C2
Morge (riv.), Fr. 50/E3
Morgenzon, SAfr. 143/E2
Morges, Swi. 66/C4
Morgex, It. 66/D6
Morghāb (riv.), Afg. 113/H1
Morgon, Pic de (peak), Fr. 70/C3
Morgongåva, Swe. 46/G2
Morguilla (pt.), Chile 226/B3
Morhange, Fr. 61/F6
Morhar (riv.), India 109/E3
Morhrane, Mor. 130/A2
Mori, Japan 94/B2
Mori Kazak Zizhixian, China 90/C3
Morialta Conservation Park Consv. Area, Austl. 155/M8
Moriarty, NM, US 179/J3
Moribaya, Gui. 132/C4
Morichal, Col. 216/D3
Morichal, Col. 216/D4
Moricone, It. 71/B3
Morie (lake), Sc, UK 39/B1
Morigny-Champigny, Fr. 63/H4
Moriguchi, Japan 95/J6
Morija, Les. 142/D3
Morin Dawa Daurzu Zizhiqi, China 91/J2
Moringen, Ger. 59/G5
Moringside (nbrhd.), Austl. 158/F6
Morioka, Japan 94/B4
Morisset, Austl. 157/E1
Moriston (riv.), Sc, UK 39/B2
Moriya, Japan 95/D2
Moriyama, Japan 95/J5
Mörkö (isl.), Swe. 45/A2
Mörkö, Swe. 45/A1
Morlaix (bay), Fr. 62/B3
Morlaix, Fr. 62/B3
Morland, Ks, US 184/D4
Morlanwelz, Belg. 61/D3
Mörlenbach, Ger. 64/B3
Morley, Eng, UK 41/G4
Morley, Tn, US 192/E2
Morlupo, It. 71/B3
Mormant, Fr. 36/L6
Mormon (peak), Nv, US 178/E2
Mormon (mts.), Nv, US 178/E2
Mormon Lake, Az, US 179/G3
Mormond (hill), Sc, UK 39/D1
Mornaguia, Tun. 54/B4
Mornant, Fr. 70/A1
Mornas, Fr. 70/A4
Morning Sun, Ia, US 185/J3
Morningstar (riv.), Ire. 38/B5
Mornington, Ire. 40/B4
Mornington (isl.), Chile 191/A6
Mornington, Austl. 157/B4
Mornington (isl.), Austl. 145/C2
Mornington Abor. Land, Austl. 153/E4
Mörnsheim, Ger. 64/D5
Moro (riv.), It. 71/D3
Moro, Pak. 113/J3
Moro (gulf), Phil. 100/C4
Moro, Ar, US 192/B3
Moro (cr.), Ar, US 183/H4
Moro, Or, US 176/C1
Morobe (prov.), PNG 153/G1
Morobe, PNG 153/G1
Morocco (ctry.) 128/D2
Morocco, In, US 190/C4
Morocelí, Hon. 206/E3
Morochata, Bol. 221/E5
Morococha, Peru 220/B3
Morogoro (prov.), Tanz. 137/B3
Morogoro, Tanz. 137/B3
Morokweng, SAfr. 142/C2
Morombe, Madg. 143/G8
Morón, Cuba 207/G1
Morón, Ven. 216/D2
Mörön, Mong. 90/E2
Morón, Arg. 191/J11
Morón de la Frontera, Sp. 52/C4
Morona, Ecu. 220/B1
Morona (riv.), Peru 220/B1
Morona-Santiago (dept.), Ecu. 216/B5
Morondara (riv.), Madg. 143/H8
Morondava, Madg. 143/H8
Morondo, C.d'Iv. 132/D4
Morongo Ind. Res., Ca, US 178/D4
Morongo Valley, Ca, US 178/D3
Moroni (cap.), Com. 143/G5
Moroni, Ut, US 177/H4
Morotai (isl.), Indo. 83/M9
Morotai (str.), Indo. 103/G3
Moroto, Ugan. 137/A1
Moroto (mt.), Ugan. 137/A1
Moroyama, Japan 95/C2
Morozovsk, Rus. 79/L3
Morpará, Braz. 223/E1
Morpeth, Eng, UK 41/G1
Morphou (bay), Cyp. 116/C2
Morphou, Cyp. 116/C2
Morra (lake), Neth. 58/C3
Morrill, Ne, US 184/C3
Morrill, Ks, US 185/G4
Morrilton, Ar, US 183/H3
Morrin, Ab, Can. 175/H2
Morrinhos, Braz. 222/C3
Morrinhos, Braz. 219/F3
Morris (riv.), Mb, Can. 186/F3
Morris, Mn, US 186/G5
Morris, Mb, Can. 186/F3
Morris, Ok, US 183/G3
Morris, NY, US 191/J3
Morris, Il, US 190/B4
Morris (res.), Ca, US 196/C2
Morris (mt.), Austl. 155/F3
Morris (co.), NJ, US 198/D2
Morris Jesup (cape), Grld. 228/J
Morris Plains, NJ, US 199/H8
Morrisburg, On, Can. 191/J2
Morrison, Ok, US 183/F2
Morrison, Il, US 185/K3
Morrison, Tn, US 192/E3
Morrisonville, Il, US 185/K4
Morriston, On, Can. 190/S9
Morriston, Wal, UK 42/C3
Morristown, SD, US 186/D5
Morristown, Az, US 179/F4
Morristown, Tn, US 193/F2
Morristown, NJ, US 198/D2
Morristown NHP, NJ, US 198/D2
Morrisville, NY, US 191/J3
Morrisville, Pa, US 198/D3
Morro (pt.), Chile 224/B3
Morro Agudo, Braz. 225/G2
Morro Bay, Ca, US 178/B3
Morro da Igreja (peak), Braz. 225/G4
Morro de Môco (peak), Ang. 140/B2
Morro de Puercos (pt.), Pan. 207/F5
Morro do Capão Doce (hill), Braz. 225/G3
Morro do Chapéu, Braz. 223/E1
Morro, Punta del (pt.), Mex. 205/N7
Morrocoy, PN, Ven. 216/D2
Morrocoyes, Ven. 219/N8
Morrone (peak), It. 71/C3
Mórrope, Peru 220/A2
Morropón, Peru 220/B2
Morros, Braz. 219/E3
Morrosquillo (gulf), Col. 207/G4
Morrow, La, US 194/B2
Morrow, Ga, US 193/M7
Morrow Point (dam), Co, US 179/J1
Mörrum, Swe. 46/F3
Morrumbala, Moz. 141/G3
Morrumbene, Moz. 141/G4
Mørs (isl.), Den. 46/C3
Morsang-sur-Orge, Fr. 36/K6
Morsbach, Fr. 61/F5
Morsbach, Ger. 61/G2
Morschwiller-le-Bas, Fr. 66/D2
Morse, Wi, US 187/J4
Morse, La, US 194/B2
Morse, Sk, Can. 175/L2
Morshansk, Rus. 77/G1
Morskoy (isl.), Kaz. 77/J3
Morsum, Ger. 59/G3
Mortagne (riv.), Fr. 66/C1
Mortagne-au-Perche, Fr. 63/F3
Mortagne-sur-Sèvre, Fr. 50/C3
Mortain, Fr. 63/E3
Mortara, It. 68/B3
Mortcerf, Fr. 36/L5
Morte (riv.), Fr. 66/B3
Morte (pt.), Eng, UK 42/B4
Morteau, Fr. 66/C3
Mortefontaine, Fr. 36/K4
Mortegliano, It. 69/G2
Morteros, Arg. 224/D4
Mortes, Rio das (riv.), Braz. 221/H4
Mortimer, Eng, UK 43/E4
Mortlach, Sk, Can. 175/L2
Mortlake, Austl. 156/B3
Morton, Tx, US 182/C4
Morton, Ms, US 192/C4
Morton, Il, US 185/K3
Morton, Wa, US 174/C4
Morton Grove, Il, US 197/Q15
Morton Nat'l Wild. Ref., NY, US 199/F2
Morton NP, Austl. 156/D2
Mortrée, Fr. 63/F3
Mortsel, Belg. 58/B6
Morundah, Austl. 157/C2
Morungaba, Braz. 223/K7
Moruya, Austl. 157/E2
Moruya (riv.), Austl. 157/D2
Morvan (plat.), Fr. 50/E3
Morven (peak), Sc, UK 39/C2
Morven, Ga, US 195/G2
Morven, Austl. 158/B4
Morven, NZ 159/B4
Morvi, India 113/K4
Morvillars, Fr. 66/C2
Morvin, Al, US 194/E2
Morwell, Austl. 157/C4
Morzine, Fr. 66/C5
Mos, Sp. 52/A1
Mosbach, Ger. 64/C4
Mosby, Mt, US 175/L4
Moscavide, Port. 53/P10
Mosciano Sant'Angelo, It. 71/C2
Moscovskaya Oblast, Rus. 74/H5
Moscow, Ar, US 183/J3
Moscow, Me, US 191/M2
Moscow, Tn, US 192/C3
Moscow, Id, US 174/F4
Moscow (Moskva) (cap.), Rus. 74/H5
Moscow U. Ice Shelf, Ant. 228/J
Moscow Upland (upland), Rus. 74/F5
Moscow-Narva (nbrhd.), Rus. 75/T7
Mosel (riv.), Ger. 48/D3
Moselebe (riv.), Bots. 140/E5
Moselle (dept.), Fr. 61/F5
Moselotte (riv.), Fr. 66/C2
Moser River, NS, Can. 189/F3
Moses (lake), Wa, US 174/E4
Moses Lake, Wa, US 174/E4
Mosetse, Bots. 141/E4
Moseyevo, Rus. 75/K2
Mosfellsbær, Ice. 44/N7
Mosgiel, NZ 159/B4
Moshaweng (riv.), SAfr. 142/C2
Moshchnyy (isl.), Rus. 47/M2
Moshi, Tanz. 137/B2
Moshi, China 99/F2
Moshoeshoe (Maseru) (int'l arpt.), Les. 142/D3
Moshupa, Bots. 140/E5
Mosh'yuga, Rus. 75/M2
Mosi-oa-Tunya NP, Zam. 140/E3
Mosina, Pol. 49/J2
Mosinee, Wi, US 185/K1
Mosino, Rus. 75/N4
Mosite, D.R. Congo 139/E2
Moskalëvka, Kaz. 77/M1
Moskva (riv.), Rus. 74/G5
Moskva (Moscow) (cap.), Rus. 74/H5
Mosley (riv.), BC, Can. 174/B2
Mosolovo, Rus. 77/G1
Mosomane, Bots. 140/E5
Mosonmagyaróvár, Hun. 56/C2
Mosouwan, China 111/E3
Mospyne, Ukr. 79/K4
Mosquera, Col. 216/B4
Mosquero, NM, US 182/C3
Mosquitia (phys. reg.), Hon. 207/E3
Mosquito (pt.), Pan. 207/G4
Mosquito (cr.), Ia, US 185/G3
Mosquito (lake), Ca, US 178/E3
Mosquitos (gulf), Pan. 202/E6
Moss, Nor. 46/D2
Moss Beach, Ca, US 197/J11
Moss Bluff, La, US 194/B2
Moss Point, Ms, US 194/D2
Moss Vale, Austl. 157/E2
Moss-Side, NI, UK 40/B1
Mossaka, Congo 138/D3
Mossbank, Sk, Can. 175/M3
Mosselbaai, SAfr. 142/C4
Mossendjo, Congo 138/C3
Mossgiel, Austl. 157/B1
Mossi Highlands (uplands), Burk. 132/E4
Mössingen, Ger. 64/C6
Mossley, NI, UK 40/C2
Mossman, Austl. 158/B2
Mossoró, Braz. 219/G4
Mossuril, Moz. 141/J2
Mossy Head, Fl, US 195/E2
Mossy Point, Austl. 157/E2
Mossyrock, Wa, US 174/C4
Most, Czh. 65/G1
Mostaganem, Alg. 130/F5
Mostaganem (wilaya), Alg. 130/F4
Mostar, Bosn. 56/C4
Mostardas, Braz. 225/G4
Mostki, Ukr. 79/K3
Móstoles, Sp. 53/N9
Mostovskoy, Rus. 79/L5
Mostrim, Ire. 38/C2
Mostyn, Wal, UK 41/E5
Mostyn, Malay. 100/B4
Mostys'ka, Ukr. 49/M4
Mosu, Bots. 140/E4
Mosul (Al Mawşil), Iraq 115/E2
Mot'a, Eth. 135/H3
Mota del Cuervo, Sp. 52/D3
Motacucito, Bol. 224/D1
Motagua (riv.), Guat. 202/D4
Motala, Swe. 46/F2
Moter, India 104/D4
Motherwell, Sc, UK 39/C5
Motian (mtn.), China 92/E2
Motīhāri, India 109/E2
Motilla del Palancar, Sp. 52/E3
Motley, Mn, US 187/G4
Motloutse, Bots. 141/E4
Motloutse (riv.), Bots. 141/E4
Moto, D.R. Congo 139/G2
Motobu, Japan 97/J7
Motokhovo, Rus. 47/Q2
Motokwe, Bots. 140/D5
Motol', Bela. 76/C1
Motomiya, Japan 97/G2
Motono, Japan 95/E2
Motosu (lake), Japan 95/B3
Motosu, Japan 95/L5
Motovskiy (gulf), Rus. 44/K1
Motoyoshi, Japan 94/B4
Motozintla de Mendoza, Mex. 206/C3
Motril, Sp. 52/D4
Motsuta-misaki (cape), Japan 94/A2
Mott, ND, US 186/C4
Motta di Livenza, It. 69/F2
Motta Visconti, It. 68/B3
Mottarone (peak), It. 68/B2
Motueka, NZ 159/C3
Motul de Carrillo Puerto, Mex. 206/D1
Motupe, Peru 220/B2
Motutapu (isl.), NZ 159/F6
Motygino, Rus. 80/K4
Mouangko, Camr. 138/B2
Mouans-Sartoux, Fr. 70/C5
Mouchard, Fr. 66/B4
Mouchoir Passage (chan.), UK 207/J1
Moúdhros, Gre. 55/J3
Moudjéria, Mrta. 132/B2
Moudon, Swi. 66/C4
Mougins, Fr. 70/D5
Mougris (well), Mrta. 132/B2
Mouhoun (prov.), Burk. 132/E3
Mouila, Gabon 138/B3
Mouïna (well), Alg. 129/F3
Moujiaba, China 90/F5
Mouka, CAfr. 134/D4
Moukoumbi, Gabon 138/C3
Moulamein, Austl. 157/B2
Moulay Idriss, Mor. 130/B2
Moulay Yakoub, Mor. 130/B2
Mould Bay, NW, Can. 171/R7
Mouldsworth, Eng, UK 41/F5
Moulins, Fr. 50/E3
Moulmein (Mawlamyine), Myan. 106/B2
Moulouya (riv.), Mor. 130/C2
Moulouya, Oued (riv.), Mor. 72/C4
Moulton, Ia, US 185/H3
Moulton, Al, US 192/D3
Moulton, Eng, UK 43/G2
Moulton, Tx, US 181/F3
Moultonboro, NH, US 191/L3
Moultrie, Ga, US 195/G2
Moultrie (lake), SC, US 193/G4
Mound, Mn, US 187/N7
Mound Bayou, Ms, US 192/B4
Mound City, SD, US 186/D5
Mound City, Ks, US 183/G1
Mound City, Il, US 192/C2
Mound City, Mo, US 185/G3
Moundou, Chad 134/C3
Moundridge, Ks, US 183/F1
Mounds, Ok, US 183/F3
Mounds, Il, US 192/C2
Mounds View, Mn, US 187/P6
Moundsville, WV, US 190/F5
Moundville, Mo, US 183/G2
Moundville, Al, US 192/D4
Moung Roessei, Camb. 106/C3
Mounlapamok, Laos 106/D3
Mount Aberdeen NP, Austl. 158/B3
Mount Abu, India 113/K4
Mount Airy, NC, US 193/G2
Mount Airy, Md, US 198/A5
Mount Albert, On, Can. 191/G2
Mount Allan Abor. Land, Austl. 155/G2
Mount Angel, Or, US 176/B1
Mount Arayat NP, Phil. 100/C2
Mount Arrowsmith, Austl. 156/B1
Mount Ayliff, SAfr. 142/E3
Mount Ayr, Ia, US 185/G3
Mount Baker-Snoqualmie Nat'l. For., Wa, US 197/D3
Mount Baldy, Ca, US 196/C2
Mount Barclay, Libr. 132/C5
Mount Barker, Austl. 154/C5
Mount Barker, Austl. 155/M9
Mount Barkly Abor. Land, Austl. 155/G2
Mount Beauty, Austl. 157/C3
Mount Bellew Bridge, Ire. 38/B3
Mount Bold (res.), Austl. 155/M9
Mount Carmel, Ut, US 179/F2
Mount Carmel, Il, US 192/D1
Mount Carmel, Pa, US 198/B2
Mount Carroll, Il, US 185/K2
Mount Cavenagh, Austl. 155/G3
Mount Clare, WV, US 193/G1
Mount Clemens, Mi, US 190/E3
Mount Currie, BC, Can. 174/C2
Mount Dora, Fl, US 194/M6
Mount Doreen, Austl. 155/F2
Mount Douglas, Austl. 158/B3
Mount Drysdale, Austl. 156/C1
Mount Eba, Austl. 155/G4
Mount Eccles NP, Austl. 156/B3
Mount Eden (nbrhd.), NZ 159/F6
Mount Edgecombe, SAfr. 143/E3
Mount Elliot NP, Austl. 158/B2
Mount Emu (cr.), Austl. 156/B3
Mount Enterprise, Tx, US 181/G2
Mount Etna (Monte Etna) (vol.), It. 54/D4
Mount Everard, Guy. 217/G3
Mount Field NP, Austl. 156/C4
Mount Fletcher, SAfr. 142/E3
Mount Forest, On, Can. 190/F3
Mount Gambier, Austl. 156/B3
Mount Garnet, Austl. 158/B2
Mount Gay-Shamrock, WV, US 193/F2
Mount Gilead, Oh, US 190/E4
Mount Hagen, PNG 153/G1
Mount Hermon, La, US 194/C2
Mount Holly, NC, US 193/G3
Mount Holly, NJ, US 198/D4
Mount Holly Springs, Pa, US 198/A3
Mount Hope, Ks, US 183/F2
Mount Hope, WV, US 193/G2
Mount Hope, On, Can. 190/T9
Mount Hope, Austl. 157/B1
Mount Horeb, Wi, US 185/K2
Mount Ida, Ar, US 183/H3
Mount Imlay NP, Austl. 157/D3
Mount Isa, Austl. 155/H2
Mount Jackson, Va, US 193/H1
Mount Joy, Pa, US 198/B3
Mount Judea, Ar, US 183/H3
Mount Kaputar NP, Austl. 156/D1
Mount Kenya NP, Kenya 137/B2
Mount Kisco, NY, US 199/E1
Mount Larcom, Austl. 158/C3
Mount Laurel, NJ, US 198/D4
Mount Magnet, Austl. 154/C4
Mount Maunganui, NZ 159/D2
Mount Mistake NP, Austl. 158/D4
Mount Molloy, Austl. 158/B2
Mount Morgan, Austl. 158/C3
Mount Morris, Mi, US 190/E3
Mount Morris, Il, US 185/K2
Mount Nebo, WV, US 193/G1
Mount Nebo, Austl. 158/E6
Mount Olive, Ms, US 194/D2
Mount Olive, Il, US 185/K4
Mount Olive, NC, US 193/H3
Mount Olivet, Ky, US 192/E1
Mount Orab, Oh, US 192/F1
Mount Pearl, Nf, Can. 189/L2
Mount Penn, Pa, US 198/C3
Mount Pleasant, Ar, US 183/J3
Mount Pleasant, Tx, US 183/G4
Mount Pleasant, Mi, US 190/D3
Mount Pleasant, Ut, US 177/H4
Mount Pleasant, Ia, US 185/J3
Mount Pleasant, Austl. 155/N8
Mount Pleasant (int'l arpt.), UK 191/F6
Mount Pleasant, SC, US 183/H4
Mount Pleasant, De, US 198/C4
Mount Plymouth, Fl, US 194/M6
Mount Pocono, Pa, US 198/C1
Mount Prospect, Il, US 197/P15
Mount Pulaski, Il, US 185/K3
Mount Rainier, Md, US 198/B6
Mount Remarkable NP, Austl. 155/H5
Mount Richmond NP, Austl. 156/B3
Mount Rushmore Nat'l Mem., SD, US 184/C2
Mount Selinda, Zim. 141/G4
Mount Shasta, Ca, US 176/B3
Mount Spec NP, Austl. 158/B2
Mount Sterling, Oh, US 190/E5
Mount Sterling, Il, US 185/J4
Mount Sterling, Ky, US 192/F1
Mount Stewart, PE, Can. 189/F2
Mount Storm, WV, US 191/G5
Mount Surprise, Austl. 158/B2
Mount Torrens, Austl. 155/M8
Mount Uniacke, NS, Can. 188/F3
Mount Union, Pa, US 191/H4
Mount Vernon, Ar, US 183/H3
Mount Vernon, Mo, US 183/H2
Mount Vernon, Tx, US 183/G4
Mount Vernon, Oh, US 190/E4
Mount Vernon, Al, US 194/D2
Mount Vernon, NY, US 199/K8
Mount Vernon, Il, US 192/C1
Mount Vernon, Ga, US 193/F4
Mount Vernon, SD, US 184/E2
Mount Vernon, In, US 192/D2
Mount Vernon, Ky, US 192/E2
Mount Vernon, Austl. 154/C3
Mount Vernon, Wa, US 174/C3
Mount Vernon, Va, US 198/A6
Mount Vernon, Md, US 193/K1
Mount Victoria, Austl. 157/E1
Mount Walsh NP, Austl. 158/C4
Mount Warning NP, Austl. 158/D5
Mount William NP, Austl. 156/D4
Mount Wolf, Pa, US 198/B3
Mount Zion, Il, US 185/K4
Mount's (bay), Eng, UK 42/A6
Mountain, Wi, US 187/K5
Mountain, ND, US 186/F3
Mountain (riv.), NW, Can. 170/D2
Mountain (cr.), Tx, US 180/K7
Mountain (cr.), Pa, US 198/A3
Mountain Ash, Wal, UK 42/C3
Mountain Brook, Al, US 192/D4
Mountain City, Nv, US 176/F3
Mountain City, Tn, US 193/G2
Mountain Creek (lake), Tx, US 180/L7
Mountain Grove, Mo, US 183/H2
Mountain Grove, On, Can. 191/H2
Mountain Home, Ar, US 183/H2
Mountain Home, Ut, US 177/H3
Mountain Home, Id, US 176/F2
Mountain Lake, Mn, US 185/G2
Mountain Lake Park, Md, US 191/G5
Mountain Lakes, NJ, US 199/H8
Mountain Park, Ga, US 193/M7
Mountain Park, Ab, Can. 174/F1
Mountain Pine, Ar, US 183/H3
Mountain Point, Ak, US 201/M4
Mountain Rest, SC, US 193/F3
Mountain Top, Pa, US 198/C1
Mountain View, Ar, US 183/H3
Mountain View, Ok, US 183/E3
Mountain View, Mo, US 183/J2
Mountain View, Ca, US 197/K12
Mountain View, Wy, US 177/H3
Mountain Village, Ak, US 201/F3
Mountain Zebra NP, SAfr. 142/D4
Mountainair, NM, US 179/J3
Mountainburg, Ar, US 183/G3
Mountainhome, Pa, US 198/C1
Mountainside, NJ, US 199/H9
Mountlake Terrace, Wa, US 197/C2
Mountmellick, Ire. 38/C3
Mountnessing, Eng, UK 36/E2
Mountnorris (bay), Austl. 152/D2
Mountrath, Ire. 38/C4
Mountville, Pa, US 198/B3
Moura, Chad 134/D2
Moura, Austl. 158/C4
Moura, Port. 52/B3
Mourão, Port. 52/B3
Mourdiah, Mali 132/D3
Mourenx, Fr. 50/C5
Mouriès, Fr. 70/A5
Mourindi, Gabon 138/B3
Mourmelon-le-Grand, Fr. 61/D5
Mourmelon-le-Petit, Fr. 61/D5
Mourne (mts.), NI, UK 40/B3
Mourniaí, Gre. 55/J5
Mouroux, Fr. 36/M5
Mourre Nègre (peak), Fr. 70/B5
Mours-Saint-Eusèbe, Fr. 70/B2
Mousâ'alli (peak), Djib. 136/B2
Mouscron, Belg. 60/C2
Moussayah, Gui. 132/B4
Mousseaux-sur-Seine, Fr. 36/G4
Mousso (well), Chad 134/C1
Moussoro, Chad 134/C2
Moussy-le-Neuf, Fr. 36/K4
Moussy-le-Vieux, Fr. 36/K4
Moustiers-Sainte-Marie, Fr. 70/C5
Mouth of the Severn (mouth), Wal, UK 42/C4
Mouthcard, Ky, US 193/F2
Mouths of the Irrawaddy (delta), Myan. 105/F4
Mouths of the Mekong (delta), Viet. 105/J6
Moutier, Swi. 66/D3
Moûtiers, Fr. 70/C2
Moutong, Indo. 103/F3
Mouvaux, Fr. 60/C2
Mouy, Fr. 60/B5
Mouydir (plat.), Alg. 129/G4
Mouyondzi, Congo 138/C3
Mouzákion, Gre. 55/G3
Mouzarak, Chad 134/B2
Mouzon (riv.), Fr. 66/B1
Mouzon, Fr. 61/E4
Moville, Ire. 40/A1
Mowanjum Mission, Austl. 152/A4
Möwe (bay), Namb. 140/B3
Moxico (prov.), Ang. 139/E5
Moy, NI, UK 40/B3
Moy (riv.), Ire. 38/B1
Moya, Com. 143/H6
Moyale, Kenya 136/A5
Moyalē, Eth. 136/A5
Moyamba, SLeo. 132/B4
Moycullen, Ire. 38/A3
Moye (isl.), China 93/B4
Moyen Atlas (mts.), Mor. 72/B4
Moyen-Chari (pref.), Chad 134/C3
Moyen-Ogooué (prov.), Gabon 138/B3
Moyenmoutier, Fr. 66/C1
Moyenne-Sido, CAfr. 134/C3
Moyers, Ok, US 183/G3
Moyeuvre-Grande, Fr. 61/F5
Moygashel, NI, UK 40/B3
Moyie (riv.), Id, US 174/F3
Moyie, BC, Can. 174/G3
Moyie Springs, Id, US 174/F3
Moyle (dist.), NI, UK 40/B1
Moynalty, Ire. 38/D2
Moyo, Ugan. 139/G2
Moyo (isl.), Indo. 103/E5
Moyobamba, Peru 220/B2
Moyowosi (riv.), Tanz. 139/G3
Moyto, Chad 134/C2
Moyu, China 111/C4
Moyuta, Guat. 206/D3
Mozambique (pt.), La, US 194/D3
Mozambique (chan.), Afr. 119/F7
Mozambique (ctry.) 141/G3
Mozarlândia, Braz. 222/C2
Mozdok, Rus. 77/H4
Mozhaysk, Rus. 74/H5
Mozhga, Rus. 75/M4
Mozogo-Gokoro, PN de, Camr. 134/B3
Mozzanica, It. 68/C3
Mozzecane, It. 69/D3
Mpal, Sen. 132/A3
Mpalapata, Zam. 139/G5
Mpama (riv.), Congo 138/C3
Mpanda, Tanz. 139/G4
Mpangu, Namb. 140/C3
Mpese, D.R. Congo 138/C4
Mpessoba, Mali 132/D3
Mphoengs, Zim. 141/E4
Mpigi, Ugan. 139/H2
Mpika, Zam. 141/F1
Mpo, Congo 138/C3
Mpoko, D.R. Congo 138/D3
Mpoko (riv.), CAfr. 134/C4
Mporaloko, Gabon 138/B3
Mporokoso, Zam. 139/G5
Mpoumé (falls), Camr. 138/B2
M'pouya, Congo 138/D3
Mpraeso, Gha. 133/E5
Mpulungu, Zam. 139/G5
Mpumalanga (prov.), SAfr. 143/E2
Mpwapwa, Tanz. 137/B3
Mrągowo, Pol. 47/J5
Mrkonjić Grad, Bosn. 56/C3
Msaken, Tun. 130/M7
Msanga, Tanz. 137/B3
M'sila (riv.), Alg. 130/H5
M'sila, Alg. 130/H5
Msoro, Zam. 141/F2
Msoun, Mor. 130/C2
Msoun (riv.), Mor. 130/C2
Msta (riv.), Rus. 74/G4
Mstislavl', Bela. 74/F5
Mswega, Tanz. 137/B4
Mszana Dolna, Pol. 49/L4
Mt-St-Michel (bay), Fr. 62/D3
Mt. Apo NP, Phil. 100/D4
Mt. Aspiring NP, NZ 159/A4
Mt. Baker-Snoqualmie, Wa, US 197/D1
Mt. Buffalo NP, Austl. 156/C3
Mt. Cook NP, NZ 159/B3
Mt. Diablo St. Park, Ca, US 197/L11
Mt. Elgon NP, Ugan. 137/A1
Mt. Lofty (range), Austl. 155/M9
Mt. Rainier NP, Wa, US 174/D4
Mt. Revelstoke NP, BC, Can. 174/E2
Mt. Rogers, Va, US 193/G2
Mt. St. Helens, Wa, US 174/C4
Mt. Victoria, NZ 159/H9
Mt. Welcome Abor. Land, Austl. 154/C2
Mtakuja, Tanz. 139/G4
Mtalika, Tanz. 141/H1
Mtarazi (falls), Zim. 141/G3
Mtarazi Falls NP, Zim. 141/G3
Mtito Andei, Kenya 137/B2
Mtondoni, Tanz. 137/B3
Mtorwi (peak), Tanz. 137/A4
Mtsensk, Rus. 76/F1
Mtubatuba, SAfr. 143/F3
Mtunzini, SAfr. 143/E3
Mtwara (prov.), Tanz. 137/B4
Mtwara, Tanz. 137/C4
Mu Ko Similan NP, Thai. 106/B4
Mu Ko Surin NP, Thai. 106/B4
Mu Us Shamo (Ordos) (des.), China 90/F4
Mu-kawa (riv.), Japan 94/C2
Muadiala, D.R. Congo 139/E4
Mualama, Moz. 141/H3
Muan, SKor. 93/D5
Muaná, Braz. 218/D3
Muang Dakchung, Laos 106/D3
Muang Gnommarat, Laos 106/D2
Muang Hay, Laos 98/D4
Muang Hinboun, Laos 106/D2
Muang Hounxianghoung, Laos 106/C1
Muang Kenthao, Laos 106/C2
Muang Khammouan, Laos 106/D2
Muang Khong, Laos 106/D3
Muang Khongxedon, Laos 106/D3
Muang Khoua, Laos 106/C1
Muang Lakhonpheng, Laos 106/D3
Muang May, Laos 106/D3
Muang Mok, Laos 106/D2
Muang Ou Tai, Laos 98/D4
Muang Pak-lay, Laos 106/C2
Muang Paktha, Laos 106/C1
Muang Pakxan, Laos 106/C2
Muang Pakxong, Laos 106/D3
Muang Phin, Laos 106/D2
Muang Sam Sip, Thai. 106/D3
Muang Sing, Laos 98/D4
Muang Soukhouma, Laos 106/D3
Muang Soy, Laos 106/D1
Muang Tahoi, Laos 106/D2
Muang Thadua, Laos 106/C2
Muang Thathom, Laos 106/C2
Muang Vangviang, Laos 106/C2
Muang Vapi, Laos 106/D3
Muang Xaignabouri, Laos 106/C2
Muang Xamteu, Laos 106/D2
Muang Xay, Laos 98/D4
Muang Xepon, Laos 106/D2
Muang Xon, Laos 106/C1
Muar (river), Malay. 101/C2
Muar, Malay. 101/C2
Muara, Indo. 101/C3
Muaraaman, Indo. 101/C3
Muarabeliti, Indo. 101/C3
Muarabenangin, Indo. 102/E4
Muarabungo, Indo. 101/C3
Muaradua, Indo. 101/D4
Muaraenim, Indo. 101/C3
Muarakumpe, Indo. 101/D3
Muaralabuh, Indo. 101/C3
Muaralakitan, Indo. 101/C3
Muararupit, Indo. 101/C3
Muarasabak, Indo. 101/C3
Muarasiberut, Indo. 101/B3
Muarasipongi, Indo. 101/B2
Muarasoma, Indo. 101/B2
Muaratebo, Indo. 101/C3
Muaratembesi, Indo. 101/C3
Muāri (pt.), Pak. 113/J4
Muatechissengue, Ang. 139/E5
Mubale, Ang. 138/D5
Mubārakpur, India 108/D2
Mubayira, Zim. 141/F3
Mubende, Ugan. 139/G2
Mubi, Nga. 134/B3
Mubur (isl.), Indo. 101/D2
Mucajaí (riv.), Braz. 217/F4
Mucambo, Braz. 219/F3
Muccia, It. 71/C1
Much, Ger. 61/G2
Much Wenlock, Eng, UK 42/D1
Muchanes, Bol. 221/E4
Muchinga (mts.), Zam. 139/G5
Muchinga Escarpment (cliff), Zam. 141/F2
Muchiri, Bol. 224/D1
Muchkapskiy, Rus. 77/G2
Muck (isl.), Sc, UK 37/Q8
Muckamore Abbey, NI, UK 40/B2
Muckleshoot Ind. Res., Wa, US 197/C3
Muckleshoot Ind. Res., Wa, US 174/C4
Muckno (lake), Ire. 38/D1
Mucojo, Moz. 141/J2
Mucope, Ang. 140/B3
Mucugê, Braz. 223/E2
Mucula, Ang. 138/C4
Mucupina (mtn.), Hon. 206/E3
Mucur, Turk. 114/C2
Mucuri (riv.), Braz. 223/E3
Mucusso, Ang. 140/D3
Mucussueje, Ang. 139/E5
Mud (lake), Mn, US 186/F3
Mud (cr.), Ne, US 184/E3
Mud Bay, BC, Can. 174/B3
Mud Lake, Id, US 177/G2
Mud Lake (res.), SD, US 184/E1
Mud Mountain (dam), Wa, US 197/D3
Mud Mountain (lake), Wa, US 197/D3
Mudanjiang, China 91/K3
Mudanya, Turk. 57/J5
Mudau, Ger. 64/C3
Mudaysīsāt (wadi), Jor. 117/E5
Mudbach (riv.), Ger. 64/C3
Muddan (riv.), China 81/N5
Muddas NP, Swe. 44/G2
Muddy (cr.), Ut, US 177/H4
Muddy Gap (pass), Wy, US 177/K2
Muddy (riv.), Nv, US 178/E2
Muddy Boggy (cr.), Ok, US 183/F3
Muddy Run (res.), Pa, US 198/B4
Müden, Ger. 59/H3
Mudersbach, Ger. 61/G2
Mudgee, Austl. 157/D1
Mudjatik (riv.), Sk, Can. 170/F3
Mudon, Myan. 106/B2
Mudu, China 92/L8
Mudurnu, Turk. 57/K5
Muecate, Moz. 141/H2
Mueda, Moz. 141/H1
Muela (peak), Chile 191/B7
Mueller (range), Austl. 152/B4
Muenster, Tx, US 183/F4
Muenster, Sk, Can. 175/M1
Muerte, Cerro de la (peak), CR 207/F4
Muff, Ire. 40/A1
Mufjir (wadi), Isr. 117/C4
Mufu (peak), China 99/G2
Mufu, China 99/F2
Mufulira, Zam. 141/F2
Mufulwe (hills), Zam. 141/F2
Mugango, Tanz. 137/A2
Mugardos, Sp. 52/A1
Mugegawa, Japan 95/L4
Mugei (peak), Ugan. 135/G5
Muggelheim, Ger. 48/Q7
Muggia, It. 51/K4
Mughal Sarai, India 108/D3
Mugi, Japan 95/L4
Mugia, Sp. 52/A1
Muğla, Turk. 114/B2
Muğla (prov.), Turk. 114/B2
Müglizh, Bul. 57/G4
Mugodzharskoye (mts.), Kaz. 77/L2
Mugombazi, Tanz. 139/G4
Mūḩ (lake), Syria 114/D3
Muhala, D.R. Congo 139/G4
Muhamdi, India 108/C2
Muḩammad Qawl, Sudan 159/H4
Muhammadābad, India 108/D3
Muhavura (vol.), Rwa. 139/G3
Muheza, Tanz. 137/B3
Muhila, Monts (mts.), D.R. Congo 139/F5
Mühlacker, Ger. 64/B5
Mühlbach (riv.), Ger. 64/A2
Mühldorf, Ger. 65/F6
Mühleberg, Swi. 66/D4
Mühlenbeck, Ger. 48/Q6
Mühlhausen, Ger. 65/E4
Mühlhausen (Augsburg) (arpt.), Ger. 64/D6
Mühlheim am Main, Ger. 64/B2
Mühlheim an der Donau, Ger. 67/E1
Mühltroff, Ger. 65/E1
Mühlviertel (reg.), Aus. 49/G4
Muhos, Fin. 74/E2
Muhu (isl.), Est. 74/D4
Muhulu, D.R. Congo 139/F3
Muhutwe, Tanz. 139/G3
Mui, Eth. 135/G4
Muiden, Neth. 58/C4
Muine Bheag, Ire. 38/D4
Muir of Ord, Sc, UK 39/B1
Muir Woods Nat'l Mon., Ca, US 197/J11
Muirkirk, Sc, UK 39/B5
Muizenberg, SAfr. 142/L11
Muizon, Fr. 60/C5
Muju, SKor. 93/D4
Mukacheve, Ukr. 49/M4
Mükangsar, China 109/F1
Mukawa, Japan 94/B2
Mukāwir, Jor. 117/D5
Mukāwir (Machaerus) (ruin), Jor. 117/D5
Mukawwar (isl.), Sudan 159/H4
Mukdahan, Thai. 106/D2
Mukden, Bol. 220/D3
Muke T'urī, Eth. 136/A3
Mukeriān, India 110/C4
Mukhayyam al Yarmūk, Syria 117/E2
Mukhmās, WBnk. 117/C5
Mukilteo, Wa, US 174/C4
Mukinbudin, Austl. 154/C4
Mukishi, D.R. Congo 139/E4
Muko, Ugan. 139/G3
Mukō, Japan 95/J6
Mukomuko, Indo. 101/C3
Mukono, Ugan. 137/A1
Mukope (riv.), Ang. 140/B2
Mukoshima (isls.), Japan 160/D2
Muktāgācha, Bang. 109/H3
Muktsar, India 110/C4
Mukuku, Zam. 141/F2
Mukunsa, Zam. 139/G5
Mukwakwa, Zam. 139/G5
Mukwe, Namb. 140/D3
Mukwikile, Zam. 141/F1
Mukwonago, Wi, US 197/P14
Mula, Sp. 52/E3
Mulan, China 91/K2
Mulanje, Malw. 141/G3
Mulbekh, India 110/D2
Mulberry (cr.), Tx, US 182/D3
Mulberry, Ar, US 183/G3
Mulberry, Ks, US 183/G2
Mulberry, In, US 190/C4
Mulberry, Fl, US 194/M8
Mulberry, NC, US 193/G2
Mulberry Fk. (riv.), Al, US 192/D4
Mulchatna (riv.), Ak, US 201/G4
Mulchén, Chile 226/B3
Mulde (riv.), Ger. 48/G3
Muldoon, Tx, US 181/F3
Mule Creek, NM, US 179/H4
Mulegé, Mex. 204/C3
Muleshoe, Tx, US 182/C3
Muleshoe Nat'l Wildlife Res., Tx, US 182/C3
Muleta (peak), Eth. 136/B3
Mulgŏn, SKor. 93/E5
Mulgrave, NS, Can. 189/G3
Mulgrave (isl.), Austl. 153/F2
Mulhacén, Cerro de (peak), Sp. 52/D4
Mülhausen, Ger. 59/H6
Mülheim an der Ruhr, Ger. 58/D6
Mulhouse, Fr. 66/D2
Mulhurst, Ab, Can. 175/H1
Muli (riv.), Indo. 103/J5
Muli Zangzu Zizhixian, China 98/D3
Mulia, Indo. 103/J4
Mulilansolo Mission, Zam. 139/H5
Mulima, D.R. Congo 139/G4
Muling (riv.), China 91/L2
Muling (pass), China 92/D3
Mulinu'u (cape), Sam. 161/R9
Mulkear (riv.), Ire. 38/B4
Mull (isl.), Sc, UK 37/R8
Mull of Galloway (pt.), Sc, UK 40/D2
Mull of Kintyre (pt.), Sc, UK 40/C1
Mull of Logan (pt.), Sc, UK 40/D2
Mullach Coire Mhic Fhearchair (peak), Sc, UK 39/A1
Mullagh, Ire. 38/D2
Mullaghanish (peak), Ire. 38/A6
Mullaghareirk (mts.), Ire. 38/A5
Mullaghcleevaun (peak), Ire. 40/B5
Mullaghmore (peak), NI, UK 40/B2
Mullaley, Austl. 156/D1
Mullan, Id, US 174/G4
Mullardoch (lake), Sc, UK 39/A2
Mullen, Ne, US 184/D2
Mullens, WV, US 193/G2
Muller (mts.), Indo. 102/D4
Muller (range), PNG 153/F1
Mullet (lake), Mi, US 190/D2
Mullet Key (isl.), Fl, US 194/K8
Mullewa, Austl. 154/B4
Müllheim, Ger. 66/D2
Müllheim, Swi. 67/F2
Mullica (riv.), NJ, US 198/D4
Mullica Hill, NJ, US 198/C4
Mullin, Tx, US 181/E2
Mullinahone, Ire. 38/C4
Mullinavat, Ire. 38/C5
Mullingar, Ire. 38/C2
Mullins, SC, US 193/H3
Mullinville, Ks, US 182/E2
Mullion, Eng, UK 42/A6
Mullumbimby, Austl. 156/E1
Mulobezi, Zam. 140/E3
Mulondo, Ang. 140/B2
Mulongo, D.R. Congo 139/F4
Multai, India 108/B5
Multān, Pak. 110/A4
Multeen (riv.), Ire. 38/B4
Mulu (peak), Malay. 100/A4
Mulumba, D.R. Congo 139/E4
Mulungu, Braz. 219/G4
Mulungushi, Zam. 141/F2
Mulungwishi, D.R. Congo 139/F5
Mulwad, Sudan 159/F5
Mulwala, Austl. 157/C2
Mulwala (lake), Austl. 157/C2
Mum Nauk (pt.), Thai. 106/B5
Mumbai (Bombay), India 113/K5
Mumbondo, Ang. 138/C5
Mumbotuta (falls), Zam. 141/F2
Mumbué, Ang. 140/C2
Mumbwa, Zam. 141/E2
Mumena, D.R. Congo 141/E1
Mumeng, PNG 153/G1
Mumias, Kenya 137/A1
Mümling (riv.), Ger. 64/B3
Mumoni (peak), Kenya 137/B2
Mumra, Rus. 77/H3
Mun (riv.), Thai. 105/H4
Muna (isl.), Indo. 103/F4
Muna, Mex. 206/D1
Munamägi (hill), Est. 47/M3
Muñani, Peru 220/D4
Munayly, Kaz. 77/K3
Munbura, Austl. 158/C3
Muncar, Indo. 102/D5
Münchberg, Ger. 65/E2
München (Munich), Ger. 65/E6
Münchenstein, Swi. 66/D2
Munchique (peak), Col. 216/B4
Munchique, PN, Col. 216/B4
Münchmünster, Ger. 65/E5
Munch'ŏn, NKor. 93/D3
Muncie, In, US 190/D4
Muncy (cr.), Pa, US 198/B1
Muncy, Pa, US 198/B1
Mundabullangana, Austl. 154/C2
Mundare, Ab, Can. 175/H1
Mundaring, Austl. 154/L6
Munday, Tx, US 182/E4
Mundelein, Il, US 197/Q15
Mundemba, Camr. 133/H5
Münden, Ger. 59/G6
Munderfing, Aus. 65/G6
Munderkingen, Ger. 67/F1
Mundesley, Eng, UK 43/H1
Mundford, Eng, UK 43/G1
Mundiwindi, Austl. 154/D2
Mundo Novo, Braz. 225/F2
Mundŏk, NKor. 93/C3
Mundrabilla, Austl. 155/E4
Mundubbera, Austl. 158/C4
Mundurucânia, Res. Florestal, Braz. 221/G2

312
Munen – Nassa

Munenga, Ang. 138/C5
Munera, Sp. 52/D3
Munford, Tn, US 192/C3
Munfordville, Ky, US 192/E2
Mungaba, Braz. 218/C3
Mungaolī, India 108/B3
Mungbere, D.R. Congo 139/G2
Mungeli, India 108/C4
Munger, India 109/F3
Mungindi, Austl. 156/D1
Mungo, Ang. 140/C1
Mungo NP, Austl. 156/B2
Mungret, Ire. 38/B4
Mungun-Tayga (peak), Rus. 111/F1
Mun'gyŏng, SKor. 93/E4
Munhango, Ang. 140/C2
Munhino, Ang. 140/B2
Munich, ND, US 186/E3
Munich (München), Ger. 65/E6
Munising, Mi, US 187/L4
Muniungu, D.R. Congo 138/D4
Munjor, Ks, US 182/E1
Munka-Ljungby, Swe. 45/J6
Munkebo, Den. 46/D4
Munkedal, Swe. 46/D2
Munkfors, Swe. 46/E2
Munku-Sardyk (peak), Rus. 81/L4
Munku-Sasan (peak), Rus. 90/D1
Münnerstadt, Ger. 64/D2
Muñoz Gamero (pen.), Chile 191/B7
Munsan, SKor. 93/F6
Münsingen, Swi. 66/D4
Münsingen, Ger. 64/C6
Munsön (isl.), Swe. 45/A1
Munster, Fr. 66/D1
Münster, Swi. 67/E5
Munster (riv.), Ire. 38/C4
Munster (reg.), Ire. 38/B5
Münster, Ger. 64/B3
Munster, On, Can. 191/J2
Munster, Ger. 59/H3
Munster, In, US 197/R16
Münster, Ger. 59/E5
Münster/Osnabrück (int'l arpt.), Ger. 59/E4
Münstereifel, Ger. 61/F2
Münsterhausen, Ger. 64/D6
Münsterland (reg.), Ger. 48/D2
Münstermaifeld, Ger. 61/G3
Muntele Mare (peak), Rom. 57/F2
Muntendam, Neth. 58/D2
Muntinglupa, Phil. 100/F7
Muntok, Indo. 101/D3
Müntschemier, Swi. 66/D4
Muntu, D.R. Congo 138/D3
Münzenberg, Ger. 64/B2
Münzkirchen, Aus. 65/G6
Munzur Vadisi NP, Turk. 114/D2
Muong Het, Laos 106/D1
Muong Hin, Viet. 98/E5
Muong Khuong, Viet. 106/D1
Muong Lat, Viet. 98/E4
Muonio, Fin. 44/G2
Muonioälven (riv.), Swe. 44/G1
Muotathal, Swi. 67/E4
Mupa, Ang. 140/B3
Mupa, PN da, Ang. 140/B2
Muping, China 92/E3
Muqaddan (wadi), Sudan 135/F1
Muqaţţa', Sudan 135/G2
Muqeibila, Isr. 117/C3
Müqtädir, Azer. 77/J4
Mur (riv.), Aus. 73/G1
Mûr-de-Bretagne, Fr. 62/C4
Mur-de-Sologne, Fr. 63/G6
Mura (riv.), Hun.,Slov. 56/C2
Muradiye, Turk. 115/E2
Murādnagar, India 110/D5
Murakami, Japan 97/F1
Murallón (peak), Chile 191/B6
Muramgaon, India 107/D1
Muramvya, Buru. 139/G3
Murang'a, Kenya 137/B2
Murano, It. 69/F3
Murashi, Rus. 75/L4
Murat (peak), Turk. 114/B2
Muratlı, Turk. 114/E2
Muratlı, Turk. 57/H5
Murayama, Japan 94/B4
Mūrcheh Khvort, Iran 115/G3
Murchison (isl.), On, Can. 187/K3
Murchison, NZ 159/C3
Murchison, Austl. 157/B3
Murchison (mt.), Austl. 154/C3
Murchison (riv.), Austl. 145/A3
Murchison Downs, Austl. 154/C3
Murcia (pol. reg.), Sp. 52/E4
Murcia, Sp. 53/E4
Murderkill (riv.), De, US 198/C6
Murdo, SD, US 184/D2
Murdochville, Qu, Can. 188/E1
Murdock (pt.), Austl. 158/B1
Murdock, Mn, US 185/G1
Mürefte, Turk. 57/H5
Mureş (riv.), Rom. 76/B3
Mureş (prov.), Rom. 57/G2
Muret, Fr. 50/D5
Murewa, Zim. 141/F3
Murfreesboro, Ar, US 183/H3
Murfreesboro, Tn, US 192/D3
Murfreesboro, NC, US 193/J2
Murg (riv.), Ger. 61/H6
Murgap (riv.), Trkm. 80/G6
Murgenella Wildlife Sanctuary, Austl. 152/D2
Murghob, Taj. 111/B4
Murgon, Austl. 158/C4
Murgoo, Austl. 154/C3
Muri, Swi. 67/E3
Muri, China 90/D4
Muri bei Bern, Swi. 66/D4
Muria (peak), Indo. 101/E4
Muriaé, Braz. 223/E4
Murias de Paredes, Sp. 52/B1
Murici, Braz. 219/H5
Murīdke, Pak. 110/C4
Muriege, Ang. 139/E5
Müritz (lake), Ger. 48/G2
Murka, Kenya 137/B2
Murle, Eth. 135/H4
Murlīganj, India 109/F3
Murmansk (int'l arpt.), Rus. 74/G1
Murmansk, Rus. 74/G1
Murmanskaya Oblast Rus. 44/J1
Murmashi, Rus. 74/G1
Murnau, Ger. 67/H2
Murnpeowie, Austl. 155/H4
Muro, Sp. 53/G3
Muro, Japan 95/K6
Muro Lucano, It. 54/D2
Murom, Rus. 74/J5
Murongo, Tanz. 139/G3
Muroran, Japan 94/B2
Muros, Sp. 52/A1
Muroto, Japan 96/D4
Muroto-zaki (pt.), Japan 96/D4
Murowana Goślina, Pol. 49/J2
Murphy, Id, US 176/E2
Murphy, NC, US 192/E3
Murphy, Tx, US 180/L6
Murphys, Ca, US 176/C4
Murphysboro, Il, US 192/C2
Murphytown, WV, US 193/G1
Murr (riv.), Ger. 64/C5
Murra, Nic. 206/E3
Murramarang NP, Austl. 157/E2
Murray, Ut, US 177/H3
Murray, Ky, US 192/C2
Murray (lake), PNG 153/F1
Murray (range), PNG 153/F1
Murray, Id, US 174/G4
Murray (riv.), Austl. 145/D4
Murray Bridge, Austl. 155/H5
Murray Downs, Austl. 155/G2
Murray River, PE, Can. 189/F2
Murraysburg, SAfr. 142/C3
Murrayville, Austl. 156/B2
Murrayville, Ga, US 192/F3
Murree, Pak. 110/B3
Mürren, Swi. 66/D4
Murrhardt, Ger. 64/C5
Murrieta, Ca, US 196/C3
Murrieta Hot Springs, Ca, US 196/C3
Murringo, Austl. 157/D2
Murrumbateman, Austl. 157/D2
Murrumbidgee (riv.), Austl. 145/D4
Murrumburrah, Austl. 157/D2
Murrupula, Moz. 141/H2
Murrurundi, Austl. 156/D1
Mursala (isl.), Indo. 101/B2
Murshidābād, India 109/G3
Murska Sobota, Slov. 56/C2
Murtala Muhammed (int'l arpt.), Nga. 133/F5
Murtaröl (peak), Swi. 67/G4
Murten, Swi. 66/D4
Murtle (riv.), BC, Can. 174/D1
Murtoa, Austl. 156/B3
Murton, Eng, UK 41/G2
Murua, PNG 153/G1
Murua Ngithigerr (mts.), Kenya 135/G5
Murud (peak), Malay. 100/A5
Murud, India 107/C2
Murupara, NZ 159/D2
Mururoa (isl.), FrPol. 161/M7
Murwāra, India 108/C4
Murwillumbah, Austl. 158/D5
Mürz (riv.), Aus. 49/H5
Mürzzuschlag, Aus. 49/H5
Muş, Turk. 114/E2
Muş (prov.), Turk. 114/E2
Musa, D.R. Congo 138/D2
Musa Khel, Pak. 110/A3
Musabeyli, Turk. 116/E1
Musāfirkhāna, India 108/C2
Musā'id, Libya 126/E2
Musala (peak), Bul. 55/H1
Musan, NKor. 93/E1
Musanda, D.R. Congo 138/C4
Musandam (pen.), Oman 115/H5
Musasa, Tanz. 139/G3
Musashino, Japan 95/D2
Musay'īd, Qatar 112/F4
Musaymir, Yem. 136/C2
Muscat (cap.), Oman 113/G4
Muscatatuck NWR, In, US 192/E1
Muscatine, Ia, US 185/J3
Musciuru (well), Libya 126/B4
Musconetcong (riv.), NJ, US 198/C2
Muscoot (res.), NY, US 199/E1
Muscowpetung Ind. Res., Sk, Can. 186/B2
Muscoy, Ca, US 196/C2
Muse, Ok, US 183/G3
Muse, Tanz. 139/G4
Museum of Flight, Wa, US 197/C2
Musgrave (range), Austl. 145/C3
Musgrave, Austl. 158/A1
Musgravetown, Nf, Can. 189/L1
Mushābani, India 109/F4
Mushāsh (wadi), Isr. 117/C5
Mushaway (peak), Tx, US 180/D1
Musheramore (peak), Ire. 38/B5
Mushie, D.R. Congo 138/D3
Mushin, Nga. 133/F5
Musholm (bay), Den. 45/H7
Musi (riv.), Indo. 101/C3
Musile di Piave, It. 69/F2
Musinga (peak), Col. 216/B3
Muskego, Wi, US 197/P14
Muskegon, Mi, US 190/C3
Muskegon (riv.), Mi, US 190/D3
Muskingum (riv.), Oh, US 190/E4
Muskirā, India 108/B3
Muskö (isl.), Swe. 45/B1
Muskoday Ind. Res., Sk, Can. 175/M1
Muskogee, Ok, US 183/G3
Muskrat (cr.), Wy, US 177/K2
Muslimīyah, Syria 116/E1
Musofu, Zam. 141/F2
Musoka (lake), On, Can. 191/G2
Musoma, Tanz. 137/A2
Musone (riv.), It. 69/G6
Musquodoboit Harbour, NS, Can. 188/F3
Mussau (isl.), PNG 160/D5
Mussel Fk. (riv.), Mo, US 185/H3
Musselburgh, Sc, UK 39/C5
Musselshell (riv.), Mt, US 172/E2
Musselshell, Mt, US 175/K4
Mussende, Ang. 138/D5
Musserra, Ang. 138/C4
Mussomeli, It. 54/C4
Musson, Belg. 61/E4
Mussuco, Ang. 138/D5
Mussuma (riv.), Ang. 140/D2
Mustafābād, Pak. 110/B4
Mustafābād, India 108/C3
Mustafakemalpaşa, Turk. 76/D4
Mustahīl, Eth. 136/C4
Müstair, Swi. 67/G4
Mustāng, Nepal 108/D1
Mustang, Ok, US 183/F3
Mustang (isl.), Tx, US 181/F4
Muşţāy, Egypt 131/C3
Mustayevo, Rus. 77/K2
Musters (lake), Arg. 226/C5
Mustio (Svartå), Fin. 45/D4
Mustvee, Est. 47/M2
Musu-dan (pt.), NKor. 93/E2
Musún (mtn.), Nic. 207/E3
Müsüslü, Azer. 115/F1
Mušutište, Serb. 56/E4
Muswellbrook, Austl. 156/D2
Mūt, Egypt 159/F3
Mut, Turk. 116/C1
Mutá, Ponta do (pt.), Braz. 223/F2
Mutambara, Zim. 141/G3
Mutango, Ang. 140/D3
Mutare, Zim. 141/G3
Mutenge, Zam. 141/F2
Mutepatepa, Zim. 141/F3
Muthill, Sc, UK 39/C4
Muting, Indo. 153/F1
Mutis (peak), Indo. 152/B2
Mutkyi, Myan. 106/B2
Mutnyy Materik, Rus. 75/M2
Mutoko, Zim. 141/G3
Mutombo, D.R. Congo 139/E4
Mutombo-Dibwe, D.R. Congo 139/E4
Mutombo-Mukulu, D.R. Congo 139/F4
Mutria (peak), It. 71/D5
Mutsamudu, Com. 143/H6
Mutshatsha, D.R. Congo 139/F5
Mutsu, Japan 94/B3
Mutsu (bay), Japan 94/B3
Mutsuzawa, Japan 95/E3
Muttaburra, Austl. 158/B3
Muttekopf (peak), Aus. 67/G3
Muttenz, Swi. 66/D2
Mutters, Aus. 67/H3
Mutterstadt, Ger. 64/B4
Muttler (peak), Swi. 67/G4
Muttonville, Mi, US 197/G6
Mutu (mtn.), Indo. 152/A2
Muţūhis, Egypt 131/B2
Mutum, Braz. 223/E3
Mutumbo, Ang. 140/C2
Mutumieque, Ang. 140/B3
Mutún, Bol. 224/E1
Mutur, SrL. 107/D4
Mutwanga, D.R. Congo 139/G2
Mutzig, Fr. 66/D1
Muwale, Tanz. 137/A3
Muyezerskiy, Rus. 74/F3
Muyinga, Buru. 139/G3
Müynoq, Uzb. 80/F5
Muyuka, Camr. 138/B1
Muyumba, D.R. Congo 139/F4
Muyuya, D.R. Congo 139/F5
Muzaffarābād, Pak. 110/B2
Muzaffargarh, Pak. 110/A4
Muzaffarnagar, India 110/D5
Muzaffarpur, India 109/E2
Muzambinho, Braz. 223/K6
Muzat (riv.), China 111/D3
Muzillac, Fr. 62/C5
Muzo, Col. 219/L7
Muzoka, Zam. 141/E3
Muzon (cape), Ak, US 201/M4
Muztag (peak), China 111/D4
Muztagata (peak), China 111/C4
Muzzana del Turgnano, It. 69/G2
Mvadhi-Ousyé, Gabon 138/C2
Mvangane, Camr. 138/B2
Mvolo, Sudan 135/F4
Mvomero, Tanz. 137/B3
Mvoung (riv.), Gabon 138/C2
M'vouti, Congo 138/C4
Mvuma, Zim. 141/F3
Mwadi-Kalumbu, D.R. Congo 138/D4
Mwadingusha, D.R. Congo 139/F5
Mwadui, Tanz. 137/A2
Mwami, Zim. 141/F3
Mwana (cape), Kenya 137/C2
Mwana-Ndeke, D.R. Congo 139/F4
Mwanza (gulf), Tanz. 137/A2
Mwanza, Malw. 141/G2
Mwanza (prov.), Tanz. 139/H3
Mwanza, Tanz. 139/H3
Mwanza, D.R. Congo 139/F4
Mwase Lundaz, Zam. 141/G2
Mwaya, Tanz. 137/B4
Mwaya, Tanz. 137/A4
Mweelrea (peak), Ire. 37/P10
Mweiga, Kenya 137/B2
Mweka, D.R. Congo 139/E4
Mwenda, Zam. 139/G5
Mwene-Ditu, D.R. Congo 139/E4
Mwenezi, Zim. 141/F4
Mwenezi (riv.), Zim. 141/F4
Mwenga, D.R. Congo 139/G3
Mwense, Zam. 139/G5
Mwenzo Mission, Zam. 139/H5
Mwera, Tanz. 137/B3
Mweru (lake), D.R. Congo 119/E5
Mweru-Wantipa (lake), D.R. Congo 139/G5
Mweru-Wantipa NP, Zam. 139/G5
Mwesi (mtn.), Tanz. 139/G4
Mwesi, Tanz. 139/G4
Mwimba, Tanz. 139/G5
Mwimba, D.R. Congo 139/E5
Mwinilunga, Zam. 140/E1
Mwitikira, Tanz. 137/A3
Mwombezhi (riv.), Zam. 140/E2
My Son Temples (ruin), Viet. 106/E3
My Tho, Viet. 106/D4
Myaksa, Rus. 74/H4
Myall Lakes NP, Austl. 156/E2
Myanaung, Myan. 98/B5
Myanmar (Burma) (ctry.) 105/G2
Myatlevo, Rus. 74/G5
Myaungmya, Myan. 98/B5
Myawadi, Myan. 106/B2
Mycenae (Mikínai) (ruin), Gre. 55/H4
Myebon, Myan. 105/F3
Myeik (Mergui), Myan. 106/B3
Myers, Mt, US 175/L4
Myerstown, Pa, US 198/B3
Myggenäs, Swe. 46/D2
Myingyan, Myan. 98/B4
Myintha, Myan. 98/B3
Myitinge (riv.), Myan. 98/C4
Myitkyinā, Myan. 98/C3
Myitta, Myan. 106/B3
Myittha, Myan. 106/B1
Myittha (riv.), Myan. 98/B4
Myjava, Slvk. 49/J4
Mykhaylivka, Ukr. 79/H4
Mykolayiv, Ukr. 78/B3
Mykolayiv, Ukr. 79/G4
Mykolayiv (int'l arpt.), Ukr. 78/G4
Mykolayivka, Ukr. 79/G5
Mykolayivs'ka Oblast, Ukr. 76/D3
Mykulyntsi, Ukr. 78/C3
Mylau, Ger. 65/F1
Mymensingh, Bang. 109/H3
Mymensingh (pol. reg.), Bang. 109/H3
Mynämäki, Fin. 47/J1
Mynaral, Kaz. 111/B2
Mynydd Eppynt (mts.), Wal, UK 42/C2
Mynydd Pencarreg (peak), Wal, UK 42/B2
Mynydd Preseli (mtn.), Wal, UK 42/B3
Myōgi, Japan 95/B1
Myohaung, Myan. 98/B4
Myohla, Myan. 98/C4
Myōkō-san (peak), Japan 97/F2
Myŏngch'ŏn, NKor. 93/E2
Myŏnggan, NKor. 93/E2
Myrhorod, Ukr. 79/G3
Myrnam, Ab, Can. 175/J1
Myronivka, Ukr. 78/F3
Myrtle, Ms, US 192/C3
Myrtle (isl.), Md, US 193/K2
Myrtle Beach, SC, US 193/H4
Myrtle Creek, Or, US 176/B2
Myrtleford, Austl. 157/C3
Mysen, Nor. 46/D2
Mysingen (bay), Swe. 45/B2
Myślenice, Pol. 49/K4
Myślibórz, Pol. 49/H2
Myslivna (peak), Czh. 65/H5
Mysore, India 107/C3
Mystery Bay Rec. Area, Wa, US 197/B1
Mystery Cave, Mn, US 185/H2
Mystic, Ga, US 195/G2
Mystic, Ia, US 185/H3
Mystic Island, NJ, US 198/D4
Mystic Seaport, Ct, US 191/L4
Mysy, Rus. 75/M3
Myszków, Pol. 49/K3
Mytishchi, Rus. 75/W9
Mýto, Czh. 65/G3
Myton, Ut, US 177/H3
Myyeldino, Rus. 75/M3
M'zab (reg.), Alg. 72/D4
Mže (riv.), Czh. 48/G4
Mzimba, Malw. 141/G1
Mzuzu, Malw. 141/G1

N

N'Djamena (cap.), Chad 134/B2
Na (riv.), Viet. 106/C1
Na Kae, Thai. 106/D2
Naaldwijk, Neth. 58/B4
Naama, Alg. 129/E2
Naantali, Fin. 47/K1
Naarden, Neth. 58/C4
Naarn im Machlande, Aus. 65/H6
Naas, Ire. 38/D3
Nabā (peak), Jor. 117/D5
Nababeep, SAfr. 142/B3
Nabadwīp, India 109/G4
Nabalat al Ḩajanah, Sudan 135/F2
Nabari, Japan 95/K6
Nabari (riv.), Japan 95/K6
Nabberu (lake), Austl. 154/D3
Nabburg, Ger. 65/F4
Naberera, Tanz. 137/B3
Naberezhnye Chelny, Rus. 75/M5
Nabeul, Tun. 130/M6
Nabeul (gov.), Tun. 130/M6
Nābha, India 110/D4
Nabiac, Austl. 156/E2
Nabīnagar, Bang. 109/H4
Nabire, Indo. 103/J4
Nabón, Ecu. 220/B1
Naboomspruit, SAfr. 141/F5
Nabua, Phil. 100/C2
Nābulus, WBnk. 117/C4
Nabunturan, Phil. 100/D4
Nacala, Moz. 141/J2
Nacaome, Hon. 206/E3
Nacebe, Bol. 221/E3
Nachi-Katsuura, Japan 96/D4
Nachingwea, Tanz. 137/B4
Náchod, Czh. 49/J3
Nachrodt-Wiblingwerde, Ger. 59/E6
Nachtigal, Chutes de (falls), Camr. 138/B1
Nachuge, India 105/F5
Nacimiento, Chile 226/B3
Nacimiento (peak), NM, US 179/J2
Nacimiento (res.), Ca, US 178/B3
Nacka, Swe. 45/B1
Nackawic, NB, Can. 188/D2
Nacmine, Ab, Can. 175/H2
Naco, Mex. 179/H5
Nacogdoches, Tx, US 181/G2
Nácori Chico, Mex. 204/C2
Nacozari de García, Mex. 204/C2
Nadadores, Mex. 180/D4
Nādbai, India 108/A2
Nadder (riv.), Eng, UK 42/D4
Nadi, Fiji 161/Y18
Nadi (int'l arpt.), Fiji 161/Y18
Nadiād, India 104/B3
Nādir, Egypt 131/B3
Nădlac, Rom. 56/E2
Nador, Mor. 130/C2
Nador (prov.), Mor. 130/C2
Nadur, Malta 54/L6
Nadvirna, Ukr. 78/C3
Nadvoitsy, Rus. 74/G3
Nadym, Rus. 80/H3
Naejang-san NP, SKor. 93/D5
Näfels, Swi. 67/F3
Nafferton, Eng, UK 41/H4
Nafī, SAr. 112/D3
Naftalan, Azer. 115/F1
Naga, Phil. 100/C2
Naga (hills), India 98/B3
Nagagami (riv.), On, Can. 187/M3
Nagahama, Japan 96/C4
Nagahama, Japan 95/K5
Nagai, Japan 97/G1
Nagaizumi, Japan 95/B3
Nagakute, Japan 95/M5
Nāgāland (state), India 105/F2
Nagambie, Austl. 157/B3
Nagano, Japan 97/F2
Nagano (pref.), Japan 97/E3
Naganuma, Japan 94/B2
Nagaoka, Japan 97/F2
Nagaokakyō, Japan 95/J6
Nagaon (Nowgong), India 98/B3
Nagappattinam, India 107/C4
Nagar, India 108/A2
Nagar Pārkar, Pak. 113/K4
Nagar Untāri, India 108/D3
Nagara (riv.), Japan 97/E3
Nagara, Japan 95/E3
Nagareyama, Japan 95/D2
Nāgārjuna Sāgar (res.), India 104/C4
Nagarote, Nic. 202/D5
Nagarzê, China 109/H1
Nagasaka, Japan 95/A2
Nagasaki, Japan 96/A4
Nagasaki (int'l arpt.), Japan 96/A4
Nagasaki (pref.), Japan 96/A4
Nagasaki Peace, Japan 96/A4
Nagashima, Japan 95/L5
Nagato, Japan 96/B3
Nagato, Japan 95/A1
Nagatoro, Japan 95/C1
Nāgaur, India 104/B2
Nāgda, India 104/C3
Nagele, Neth. 58/C3
Nāgercoil, India 107/C4
Nagīna, India 108/B1
Nagir, Pak. 113/K1
Nagishot, Sudan 135/G4
Nagles (mts.), Ire. 38/B5
Nago, Japan 97/J7
Nago-Torbole, It. 67/G6
Nāgod, India 108/C3
Nagold, Ger. 64/B5
Nagold (riv.), Ger. 64/B5
Nagongera, Ugan. 137/A1
Nagorno-Karabakh (prov.), Arm. 77/H5
Nagornyy, Rus. 81/N4
Nagorsk, Rus. 75/L4
Nagosira, D.R. Congo 139/F2
Nagoya, Japan 95/L5
Nagoya Castle, Japan 95/L5
Nagpula (pass), China 109/F1
Nāgpur, India 110/C5
Nāgpur, India 107/C1
Nagqu (riv.), China 90/C5
Nagqu, China 98/B2
Nags Head, NC, US 193/K3
Nagu (Nauvo), Fin. 47/J1
Naguri, Japan 95/C2
Nagy-Milic (peak), Hun. 49/L4
Nagyatád, Hun. 56/C2
Nagybatony, Hun. 56/D2
Nagyecsed, Hun. 49/M5
Nagyhalász, Hun. 56/E1
Nagykanizsa, Hun. 56/C2
Nagykáta, Hun. 56/D2
Nagykőrös, Hun. 56/D2
Naha, Japan 97/J7
Nahabuan, Indo. 102/D3
Naḩal Shillo (wadi), Isr. 117/C4
Nāhan, India 110/D4
Nahanni NP, NW, Can. 170/D2
Nāhar, India 110/D5
Nahariyya, Isr. 117/C3
Nahatlatch (riv.), BC, Can. 174/C3
Nahāvand, Iran 115/G3
Naḩel Soreq (riv.), Isr. 117/B5
Naḩḩālīn, WBnk. 117/C5
Nahol'no-Tarasivka, Ukr. 79/K3
Nahouri (prov.), Burk. 133/E4
Nahr Ad Dindar (riv.), Sudan 135/G2
Nahr Ar Rahad (riv.), Sudan 135/G2
Nahr aş Şafā (riv.), Leb. 117/C1
Nahr Ouassel (riv.), Alg. 130/F5
Nahuel Huapi (lake), Arg. 209/B7
Nahuel Huapí, PN, Arg. 226/C4
Nahuelbuta, PN, Chile 226/B3
Nahuentúe, Chile 226/B3
Nahunta, Ga, US 195/H2
Naica, Mex. 204/D3
Naicam, Sk, Can. 175/M1
Naiguatá, Ven. 219/P7
Naihāti, India 109/G4
Naij Gol (riv.), China 90/C4
Naij Tal, China 90/C4
Naikliu, Indo. 152/A2
Naila, Ger. 65/E2
Nailsea, Eng, UK 42/D4
Nailsworth, Eng, UK 42/D3
Nā'im (well), Libya 126/C2
Na'īma, Sudan 135/G2
Naiman Qi, China 92/E2
Nā'īn, Iran 115/H3
Nain, Nf, Can. 171/K3
Nainital, India 108/B1
Nainpur, India 108/C4
Naintré, Fr. 50/D3
Nairn (riv.), Sc, UK 39/B2
Nairn, Sc, UK 39/C1
Nairne, Austl. 155/M9
Nairobi (cap.), Kenya 137/B2
Nairobi NP, Kenya 137/B2
Naita (peak), Eth. 135/G4
Naivasha, Kenya 137/B2
Naives-Rosières, Fr. 61/E6
Najafābād, Iran 115/G3
Najd (des.), SAr. 114/E5
Nájera, Sp. 52/D1
Naju, SKor. 93/D5
Naka (riv.), Japan 96/D4
Naka, Japan 95/G5
Nakadōri (isl.), Japan 96/A4
Nakai, Japan 95/C3
Nakajō, Japan 97/F1
Nakamichi, Japan 95/B2
Nakaminato, Japan 97/G2
Nakamura, Japan 96/C4
Nakano, Japan 97/F2
Nakano (lag.), Japan 96/C3
Nakasato, Japan 94/B3
Nakashibetsu, Japan 94/D2
Nakasongola, Ugan. 139/H2
Nakatane, Japan 97/L5
Nakatomi, Japan 95/A3
Nakatsu, Japan 96/B4
Nakatsugawa, Japan 97/E3
Nakazato, Japan 95/B1
Nak'fa, Erit. 112/C5
Nakhodka, Rus. 91/L3
Nakhola, India 109/J2
Nakhon Nayok, Thai. 106/C3
Nakhon Pathom, Thai. 106/C3
Nakhon Phanom, Thai. 106/D2
Nakhon Ratchasima, Thai. 106/C3
Nakhon Sawan, Thai. 106/C3
Nakhon Si Thammarat, Thai. 106/B4
Nakhon Thai, Thai. 106/C2
Nakhtarāna, India 113/J4
Nakifuma, Ugan. 139/H2
Nakina, On, Can. 187/L2
Nakkila, Fin. 47/J1
Nakło nad Notecią, Pol. 49/J2
Naknek, Ak, US 201/G4
Nakodar, India 110/C4
Nakonde, Zam. 139/H5
Nakong, Gha. 133/E4
Nakop, Namb. 142/B3
Naksan-sa, SKor. 93/E3
Nakskov, Den. 46/D4
Naktong, SKor. 93/E4
Naktong (riv.), SKor. 96/A3
Nakūr, India 110/D5
Nakuru, Kenya 137/B2
Nakusp, BC, Can. 174/F2
Nāl (riv.), Pak. 113/J3
Nalao, China 98/E3
Nalayh, Mong. 90/F2
Nalázi, Moz. 141/G5
Nalbach, Ger. 61/F5
Nalbāri, India 109/H2
Nalbaugh NP, Austl. 157/D3
Nal'chik, Rus. 77/G4
Nalchik (int'l arpt.), Rus. 77/G4
Nale, Laos 106/C2
Nalgonda, India 107/C2
Nalhāti, India 109/F3
Nalitābāri, Bang. 109/H3
Naliya, India 113/J4
Nallıhan, Turk. 57/K5
Nalón (riv.), Sp. 52/B1
Nalong, Myan. 98/C3
Nālūt, Libya 129/H3
Nam (riv.), SKor. 93/D5
Nam (riv.), NKor. 93/D3
Nam (lake), China 111/E5
Nam Can, Viet. 106/D4
Nam Cum, Viet. 98/D4
Nam Dinh, Viet. 99/E4
Nam Nao NP, Thai. 106/C2
Nam Pat, Thai. 106/C2
Nam Phong, Thai. 106/C2
Nam Un (res.), Thai. 106/C2
Namacunde, Ang. 140/B3
Namacurra, Moz. 141/H3
Namadzi, Malw. 141/G2
Namāi, Nepal 108/D2
Namak (lake), Iran 115/G3
Namakzār-e Shahdād (salt pan), Iran 115/J4
Namang, Indo. 101/D3
Namanga, Kenya 137/B2
Namangan, Uzb. 111/B3
Namansansong Provicial Park, SKor. 93/G7
Namanyere, Tanz. 139/G4
Namapa, Moz. 141/H2
Namaputa, Tanz. 137/B4
Namaqualand (reg.), SAfr. 142/B3
Namari, Sen. 132/B3
Namaripi (cape), Indo. 103/J4
Namarrói, Moz. 141/H2
Namasagali, Ugan. 137/A1
Namasakata, Tanz. 141/H1
Namatanai, PNG 160/E5
Nambanje, Tanz. 137/B4
Nambe, NM, US 179/K3
Namborn, Ger. 61/G4
Nambour, Austl. 158/D4
Nambu, Japan 95/A3
Nambuangongo, Ang. 138/C5
Nambucca Heads, Austl. 156/E1
Nambung NP, Austl. 154/B4
Namco, China 111/F5
Namdae (riv.), NKor. 93/E2
Namdalseid, Nor. 44/D2
Nämdö (isl.), Swe. 45/B1
Nämdöfjärden (sound), Swe. 45/B1
Namegawa, Japan 95/C1
Namekagon (riv.), Wi, US 187/J4
Namentenga (prov.), Burk. 133/E3
Namerikawa, Japan 97/E2
Nametil, Moz. 141/H2
Namewaminikan (riv.), On, Can. 187/L3
Namhae (isl.), SKor. 93/D5
Namhae, SKor. 93/D5
Nami, Malay. 101/C1
Namib (des.), Namb. 119/D6
Namib-Naukluft Park, Namb. 140/B4
Namibe (int'l arpt.), Ang. 140/B2
Namibe, Ang. 140/B2
Namibe (dist.), Ang. 140/B2
Namibia (ctry.) 119/D7
Namie, Japan 97/G2
Namioka, Japan 94/B3
Namir, Mong. 90/C2
Namitete, Malw. 141/G2
Namja (pass), Nepal 111/D6
Namjagbarwa (peak), China 98/B2
Namlan, Myan. 106/B1
Namling, China 111/E6
Namloser Wetterspitze (peak), Aus. 67/G3
Nammoku, Japan 95/B1
Namnoi (peak), Myan. 106/B4
Namoi (riv.), Austl. 145/D4
Namonuito (isl.), Micr. 160/D4
Namorik (isl.), Mrsh. 160/F4
Namorona, Madg. 143/J8
Nampa, Id, US 176/E2
Nampala, Mali 132/D3
Namp'o, NKor. 93/C3
Nampula, Moz. 141/H2
Nampula (prov.), Moz. 141/H2
Namp'yŏng, SKor. 93/D5
Namrole, Indo. 103/G4
Nāmrup, India 98/B3
Namsa-ri, NKor. 93/D2
Namsang, Myan. 106/B1
Namsê (pass), China 111/D6
Namsos, Nor. 44/D2
Namtok Mae Surin NP, Thai. 98/C5
Namu (isl.), Mrsh. 160/F4
Namúli (mts.), Moz. 141/H2
Namuno, Moz. 141/H2
Namur (prov.), Belg. 61/D3
Namur, Belg. 61/D3
Namutoni, Namb. 140/C3
Namwala, Zam. 141/E2
Namwŏn, SKor. 93/D5
Namysłów, Pol. 49/J3
Nan, Thai. 106/C2
Nan (mts.), China 99/G3
Nan (riv.), China 90/F5
Nan (riv.), Thai. 99/F4
Nan'ao (isl.), China 99/H4
Nana Barya (riv.), Chad 134/C4
Nana Barya, Rsv. de Faune, CAfr. 134/C4
Nana Candundo, Ang. 140/D1
Nana-Mambéré (pref.), CAfr. 134/B4
Nanae, Japan 94/B3
Nanafalia, Al, US 192/D4
Nanaimo, BC, Can. 174/C3
Nanam, NKor. 93/E2
Nanango, Austl. 158/D4
Nanao, Japan 97/E2
Nanauta, India 110/D5
Nanay (riv.), Peru 220/C1
Nanbaozhen, China 92/L8
Nancagua, Chile 226/C2
Nancha, China 91/K2
Nanchang, China 99/G2
Nancheng, China 99/H3
Nanchong, China 98/E2
Nanchong, China 99/E2
Nanchuan, China 99/E2
Nancy, Fr. 61/F6
Nanda Devi (peak), India 111/C5
Nandan, China 105/J3
Nandashan, China 99/G2
Nānded, India 107/C2
Nandi Mill, Zim. 141/F4
Nandigāma, India 107/D2
Nanding (riv.), China 105/G3
Nandonge, Ang. 138/D5
Nandrin, Belg. 61/E3
Nandu, China 99/F4
Nandu (riv.), China 99/F5
Nandy, Fr. 36/K6
Nandyāl, India 107/C3
Nanfen, China 93/B2
Nanfeng, China 99/H3
Nang (isl.), Phil. 99/J4
Nang Rong, Thai. 106/C3
Nang Xian, China 98/B2
Nanga Parbat (peak), Pak. 110/C2
Nanga-Eboko, Camr. 134/B4
Nangalili, Indo. 103/F5
Nangamahap, Indo. 102/D4
Nangamentebah, Indo. 102/D3
Nangapinoh, Indo. 102/D4
Nangar NP, Austl. 157/D1
Nangata (pt.), Moz. 141/J2
Nangin, Myan. 106/B4
Nangis, Fr. 36/M6
Nangnim (mts.), NKor. 93/D2
Nangnim, NKor. 93/D2
Nangong, China 92/C3
Nangqên, China 90/D5
Nangtud (mt.), Phil. 100/C3
Nangua, Tanz. 137/B4
Nanguanling, China 93/A3
Nangwarry, Austl. 156/B3
Nanhsi, Tai. 99/J4
Nanhuang, China 93/A4
Nanhui, China 92/L8
Nanikelako, Zam. 140/D2
Nanjian Yizu Zizhixian, China 98/D3
Nanjiangkou, China 99/F4
Nanjing, China 92/D4
Nanka (riv.), Myan. 98/C4
Nankāna Sāhib, Pak. 110/B4
Nankoku, Japan 96/C4
Nankou, China 99/H3
Nankova, Ang. 140/C3
Nanlan (riv.), China 98/D4
Nanle, China 92/C3
Nanling, China 99/H2
Nanlinqiao, China 99/G2
Nanliu (riv.), China 105/J3
Nanlou (peak), China 91/K3
Nannestad, Nor. 46/D1
Nannine, Austl. 154/C3
Nanning, China 99/F4
Nannō, Japan 95/L5
Nannup, Austl. 154/B5
Nanny (riv.), Ire. 40/B4
Nanpan (riv.), China 98/E3
Nānpāra, India 108/C2
Nanpi, China 92/D3
Nanping, China 99/H3
Nanpu, China 92/J7
Nans-les-Pins, Fr. 70/B6
Nansei, Japan 95/L7
Nansemond Nat'l Wild. Ref., Va, US 193/J2
Nansen (sound), Nun, Can. 171/S6
Nansheng, China 99/H3
Nansio, Tanz. 137/A2
Nant (riv.), Fr. 63/G5
Nant (lake), Sc, UK 39/A4
Nantai, China 93/B2
Nantai-san (peak), Japan 97/F2
Nanterre, Fr. 36/J5
Nantes, Fr. 62/D6
Nantes à Brest (canal), Fr. 62/B4
Nanteuil-le-Haudouin, Fr. 36/L4
Nanteuil-lès-Meaux, Fr. 60/B6
Nantian, China 99/H3
Nantian, China 99/J2
Nanticoke, On, Can. 190/F3
Nanticoke, Pa, US 198/B1
Nanton, Ab, Can. 175/H2
Nantong, China 92/E4
Nantong, China 99/J1
Nantou, China 99/K6
Nantua, Fr. 66/B5
Nantucket, Ma, US 188/B5
Nantucket (isl.), Ma, US 188/C5
Nantucket (sound), Ma, US 188/B5
Nantucket Nat'l Wild. Ref., Ma, US 188/B5
Nantúpi, Moz. 141/H2
Nantwich, Eng, UK 41/F5
Nanty-Glo, Pa, US 191/G4
Nanuet, NY, US 199/J7
Nanuku Passage (chan.), Fiji 161/Y18
Nanumanga (isl.), Tuv. 160/G5
Nanumea (isl.), Tuv. 160/G5
Nanuque, Braz. 223/E3
Nanwon (res.), China 92/C4
Nanxi, China 98/E2
Nanxiang, China 92/L8
Nanxing, China 90/F5
Nanxun, China 92/L9
Nanyamba, Tanz. 137/B4
Nanyang, China 92/D4
Nanyang (lake), China 90/H4
Nanyang, China 92/C4
Nanyue, China 99/G3
Nanyuki, Kenya 137/B1
Nanzamu, China 93/C2
Nanzhang, China 92/B5
Nanzhao, China 92/C4
Nao, Cabo de la (cape), Sp. 53/F3
Não-Me-Toque, Braz. 225/F4
Naococane (lake), Qu, Can. 171/J3
Naogaon, Bang. 109/G3
Naokot, Pak. 104/A3
Naoli (riv.), China 91/L2
Naolinco, Mex. 205/N7
Naos, Namb. 140/C4
Naoua (falls), C.d'Iv. 132/D5
Náousa, Gre. 55/J4
Náousa, Gre. 55/H2
Naozhou (isl.), China 99/F4
Napa (riv.), Ca, US 197/K10
Napa (valley), Ca, US 197/K9
Napa (co.), Ca, US 197/K10
Napa, Ca, US 176/B4
Napa Junction, Ca, US 197/K10
Napak (peak), Ugan. 137/A1
Napakiak, Ak, US 201/F3
Napanee, On, Can. 191/H2
Napata (ruin), Sudan 159/F5
Napavine, Wa, US 174/C4
Nape, Laos 106/D2
Naperville, Il, US 190/B4
Napf (peak), Swi. 66/D4
Napido, Indo. 103/J4
Napier, SAfr. 142/L11
Napier, NZ 159/D2
Napier (pt.), Austl. 153/D2
Napier (mt.), Austl. 152/C4
Napier Broome (bay), Austl. 152/B3
Napierville (co.), Qu, Can. 189/N7
Napill, Eng, UK 36/A2
Napinka, Mb, Can. 186/D3
Naples (Napoli), It. 71/D6
Naples, Fl, US 195/H4
Naples, Id, US 174/F3
Naples, Me, US 191/L3
Naples, NY, US 191/H3
Naples, Tx, US 183/G4
Naples, Ut, US 177/J3
Naples Park, Fl, US 195/H4
Napo (prov.), Ecu. 216/B5
Napo (riv.), Ecu. 216/B5
Napo (riv.), Ecu.,Peru 209/B3
Napo (riv.), Peru 216/C5
Napo, China 105/J3
Napoleon, ND, US 186/E4
Napoleon, Oh, US 190/D4
Napoleon, Mi, US 190/D3
Napoleonville, La, US 194/C3
Napoli (gulf), It. 54/C2
Napoli (prov.), It. 71/D6
Napoli (Naples), It. 71/D6
Napoule (gulf), Fr. 70/C5
Nappa Merrie, Austl. 158/A4
Nappanee, In, US 190/C4
Napperby, Austl. 155/G2
Napton-on-the-Hill, Eng, UK 43/E2
Napuka (isl.), FrPol. 161/L6
Naqb Ghul (peak), Egypt 131/C5
Naqīl Sumārah (pass), Yem. 136/C2
Nara, Mali 132/D3
Nāra (riv.), Pak. 113/J4
Nara, Japan 95/J6
Nara Logna (pass), Nepal 111/D5
Naracoopa, Austl. 157/B4
Naracoorte, Austl. 156/B3
Naradhan, Austl. 157/C1
Narail, Bang. 109/G4
Naraini, India 108/C3
Nārāinpur, India 107/D2
Naramata, BC, Can. 174/E3
Naranbulag, Mong. 111/F2
Narang, Afg. 110/A2
Naranjal, Ecu. 216/B5
Naranjito, Ecu. 220/B1
Naranjos, Mex. 206/B1
Naranjos, Bol. 224/E1
Narāq, Iran 115/G3
Narasannapeta, India 107/E2
Narasapatnam (pt.), India 107/D2
Narasapur, India 107/D2
Narasaraopet, India 107/D2
Narashino, Japan 95/E2
Narat, China 111/D3
Narathiwat, Thai. 106/C5
Nārāyanganj, India 108/C4
Nārāyanganj, Bang. 109/H4
Nārāyani (zone), Nepal 109/E2
Narayani (riv.), Nepal 109/E2
Narbonne, Fr. 50/E5
Narceo (riv.), Sp. 52/B1
Narcoossee, Fl, US 194/N7
Nardò, It. 55/F2
Nare (pt.), Eng, UK 42/B6
Narellan, Austl. 158/G9
Narembeen, Austl. 154/C5
Naréna, Mali 132/C3
Nares (str.), Can.,Grld. 163/K2
Narew (riv.), Pol. 74/D5
Narganá, Pan. 216/B2
Narib, Namb. 140/C5
Narinda, Madg. 143/H6
Narinda (bay), Madg. 143/H6
Nariño (dept.), Col. 216/B4
Nariño, Col. 219/K7
Narita (int'l arpt.), Japan 97/G3
Narita, Japan 95/E2
Nariz (peak), Chile 191/C7
Narka, Ks, US 184/F4
Narkatiāganj, India 109/E2
Narmada (riv.), India 83/G7
Narman, Turk. 77/G4
Nærnes, Nor. 44/S8
Narni, It. 71/B2
Naro Moru, Kenya 137/B2
Naroch', Bela. 47/M4
Narodnaya (peak), Rus. 75/P2
Narok, Kenya 137/A2
Narón, Sp. 52/A1
Narooma, Austl. 157/E3
Narovlya, Bela. 78/E2
Nārowāl, Pak. 110/C3
Nærøy, Nor. 44/D2
Närpes (Närpiö), Fin. 74/D3
Närpiö (Närpes), Fin. 74/D3
Narra, Phil. 100/B3
Narrabri, Austl. 156/D1
Narrandera, Austl. 157/C2
Narre Warren North, Austl. 157/B3
Narriah (mtn.), Austl. 157/C1
Narrogin, Austl. 154/C5
Narromine, Austl. 156/D2
Narrows (dam), Ar, US 183/H3
Narrows (riv.), NY, US 199/J9
Narrows, Va, US 193/G2
Narsimhapur, India 108/B4
Narsingarh, India 104/C3
Narsinghdi, Bang. 109/H4
Narsī Patnam, India 107/D2
Nartuby (riv.), Fr. 70/C5
Narubis, Namb. 142/B2
Naruksovo, Rus. 75/K5
Narungombe, Tanz. 137/B4
Narusawa, Japan 95/B3
Naruto, Japan 96/D3
Narutō, Japan 95/E2
Narva (riv.), Est.,Rus. 74/E4
Narva (res.), Rus. 74/F4
Narva (bay), Est.,Rus. 47/M2
Narva, Est. 47/N2
Narva (riv.), Rus. 47/M2
Narva-Jõesuu, Est. 47/N2
Narvacan, Phil. 100/C1
Narvik, Nor. 44/F1
Narwāna, India 110/D5
Nar'yan-Mar, Rus. 75/M2
Naryn (riv.), Kyr. 80/H5
Naryn, Kyr. 111/C3
Naryn Khuduk, Rus. 77/H3
Narzole, It. 68/A3
NASA Test Center, Ms, US 194/D2
NASA Test Facility, NM, US 182/A4
NASA Wallops Space Ctr., Va, US 193/K2
Nasarawa, Nga. 133/G4
Năsăud, Rom. 57/G2
Naschel, Arg. 226/D2
Naschitti, NM, US 179/H2
Naseby, NZ 159/B4
Naselle, Wa, US 174/C4
Nash, Ok, US 183/E2
Nash, Eng, UK 43/F3
Nash (pt.), Wal, UK 42/C4
Nashoba, Ok, US 183/G3
Nashua, NH, US 191/L3
Nashua, Ia, US 185/H2
Nashua, Mt, US 175/L3
Nashville, Ar, US 183/H4
Nashville, Ga, US 195/G2
Nashville, In, US 190/C5
Nashville, Mi, US 190/D3
Nashville (int'l arpt.), Tn, US 192/D2
Nashville (cap.), Tn, US 192/D2
Nashville, Il, US 192/C1
Nashville, NC, US 193/J3
Nashwah, Egypt 131/C3
Našice, Cro. 56/D3
Nasielsk, Pol. 49/L2
Nasijärvi (lake), Fin. 47/K1
Nasikonis (cape), Indo. 152/A2
Nāşir, Sudan 135/G3
Nasīrābād, India 104/B2
Naso (pt.), Phil. 100/C3
Nason, Il, US 192/C1
Nasori (Suva) (int'l arpt.), Fiji 161/Y18
Nasorolevu (peak), Fiji 161/Z17
Nasosnyy, Azer. 77/J4
Nāsriganj, India 109/E3
Nass (riv.), BC, Can. 201/N4
Nassach (riv.), Ger. 64/D2
Nassau, Ger. 61/G3
Nassau (sound), Fl, US 195/H2
Nassau (cap.), Bahm. 203/F2
Nassau (isl.), Cookls. 161/J6
Nassau (bay), Chile 191/D7
Nassau, De, US 198/C6
Nassau (co.), NY, US 199/E2

Nassa – Newto
313

Nassau Bay, Tx, US 181/M9
Nassawadox, Va, US 193/K2
Nasser (lake), Egypt 119/E2
Nassereith, Aus. 67/G3
Nassian, C.d'Iv. 132/E4
Nässjö, Swe. 46/F3
Nassogne, Belg. 61/E3
Nassoukou, Ben. 133/F4
Nastapoka (isls.), Qu, Can. 171/J3
Nastätten, Ger. 61/G3
Næstved, Den. 46/D4
Nasu-dake (peak), Japan 97/F2
Nasugbu, Phil. 100/C2
Nat (peak), Myan. 98/C5
Nat'l West Coast Rec. Area, Namb. 140/B4
Nata, Bots. 140/E4
Natá, Pan. 216/A2
Natagaima, Col. 216/C4
Natal, Indo. 101/B2
Natal, Braz. 219/H4
Natalbany, La, US 194/C2
Natalia, Tx, US 181/E3
Naţanz, Iran 115/G3
Natashō, Japan 95/J5
Natashquan (riv.), Qu, Can. 171/K3
Natchez, La, US 194/B2
Natchez, Ms, US 194/C2
Natchez Trace (pkwy), Ms, US 183/J5
Natchez Trace, US 192/C4
Natchitoches, La, US 194/B2
Naters, Swi. 66/D5
Natewa (bay), Fiji 161/Z17
Nathalia, Austl. 157/B3
Nathalie, Va, US 193/H2
Nāthdwāra, India 104/B3
Nathenje, Malw. 141/G2
Nathrop, Co, US 179/J1
Natimuk, Austl. 156/B3
National Agriculture Rsch. Ctr., Md, US 198/B6
National Aquarium, Md, US 198/B5
National Archaeological Museum, Gre. 55/N8
National Atomic Musuem, NM, US 182/A3
National Capital District (cap. dist.), PNG 153/G2
National City, Ca, US 196/C5
National Elk (refuge), Wy, US 177/H2
National Exhibition Centre, Eng, UK 43/E2
National Institutes of Health, Md, US 198/A6
National Mine, Mi, US 187/L4
National Museum, Mona. 68/J8
National Security Agency, Md, US 198/B5
Natitingou, Ben. 133/F4
Natividade, Braz. 222/D1
Natkyizin, Myan. 106/B3
Natl, Jor. 117/D5
Nat'l Bison Range, Mt, US 175/G4
Nat'l Key Deer Refuge Nat'l Wild. Ref., Fl, US 195/H5
Nat'l Museum, NZ 159/H9
Natoma, Ks, US 184/E4
Nator, Bang. 109/G3
Natron (lake), Tanz. 137/A2
Nåttarö (isl.), Swe. 45/B2
Natternbach, Aus. 65/G6
Nattheim, Ger. 64/D5
Nättraby, Swe. 46/F3
Natuna (isls.), Indo. 83/K9
Natural Bridge Caverns, Tx, US 181/E3
Natural Bridges Nat'l Mon., Ut, US 179/H2
Naturaliste (chan.), Austl. 154/B3
Naturaliste (cape), Austl. 156/D4
Naturaliste (cape), Austl. 154/B5
Nature Center, Tx, US 180/K7
Nature Reserve, Austl. 154/C2
Nature Reserve, Austl. 154/C4
Nature Reserve, Austl. 154/C5
Nature Reserve, Austl. 154/E5
Naturita, Co, US 179/H1
Naturno (Naturns), It. 67/G4
Naturns (Naturno), It. 67/G4
Naubinway, Mi, US 190/D1
Naucalpan, Mex. 205/Q10
Naucelle, Fr. 50/E4
Naucratis (ruin), Egypt 131/B3
Nauders, Aus. 67/G4
Naudesnek (pass), SAfr. 142/E3
Nauen, Ger. 48/P6
Naugachhia, India 109/F3
Naugaon Sādāt, India 108/B1
Naugatuck, Ct, US 191/K4
Nauhcampatépetl (vol.), Mex. 205/M7
Nauheim, Ger. 64/B3
Naujamiestis, Lith. 47/L4
Naujan, Phil. 100/C2
Naujoji-Akmenė, Lith. 47/K3
Naumburg, Ger. 48/F3
Naumburg, Ger. 59/G6
Naunggala, Myan. 106/B2
Naunglon, Myan. 106/B2
Nauort, Ger. 61/G3
Nā'ūr, Jor. 117/D5
Nauru (ctry.) 160/F5
Nāushahra, India 110/C3
Naushahra Virkhan, Pak. 110/B4
Naushki, Rus. 90/F1
Nauta, Peru 220/C2
Nautla, Mex. 205/N6
Nauvo (Nagu), Fin. 47/J1
Nauvoo, Il, US 185/J3
Nauvoo, Al, US 192/D4
Nava, Mex. 180/D3
Nava del Rey, Sp. 52/C2
Navajo, Az, US 179/H3
Navajo Ind. Res., Az,NM, US 179/G2
Navajo Nat'l Mon., Az, US 179/G2
Navajo (peak), Co, US 179/J2
Navajo (riv.), Co,NM, US 182/A2
Navajo, Mt, US 186/B3
Navajo (dam), NM, US 179/J2
Navajo (lake), NM, US 179/J2
Naval, Phil. 100/D3
Naval Res., Ca, US 196/C4
Navalcarnero, Sp. 53/M9
Navalmoral de la Mata, Sp. 52/C3
Navalvillar de Pela, Sp. 52/C3
Navapolatsk, Bela. 47/N4
Navarin (cape), Rus. 81/T3
Navarino (isl.), Chile 191/C7
Navarra (reg.), Sp. 52/D1
Navarre, Oh, US 190/F4
Navarro, Ca, US 176/B4
Navarro, Arg. 191/J11
Navàs, Sp. 53/F2
Navas de San Juan, Sp. 52/D3
Navasota, Tx, US 181/F2
Navasota (riv.), Tx, US 205/F2
Navassa (isl.), Myan. 207/H2
Navax (pt.), Eng, UK 42/A6
Nave, It. 68/D2
Navenne, Fr. 66/C2
Navia, Sp. 52/B1
Navia (riv.), Sp. 52/B1
Navidad, Chile 226/N8
Navidad (riv.), Tx, US 181/F3
Naviraí, Braz. 225/F2
Navlya, Rus. 76/E1
Năvodari, Rom. 57/J3
Navojoa, Mex. 204/C3
Navolato, Mex. 204/D3
Navotas, Phil. 100/E6
Návpaktos, Gre. 55/G3
Návplion, Gre. 55/H4
Navrongo, Gha. 133/E4
Navy Board (inlet), Nun, Can. 171/H1
Navy Yard City, Wa, US 197/B2
Nawā, Syria 117/E3
Nawābganj, India 108/B1
Nawābganj, India 108/C2
Nawābganj, Bang. 109/G3
Nawābshāh, Pak. 113/J3
Nawāda, India 109/E3
Nawān Jandānwāla, Pak. 110/A3
Nawānshahr, India 110/C3
Nawāpāra, India 107/D1
Nawāshahr, India 110/D4
Nawāshahr, Pak. 110/B2
Nawnghkio, Myan. 98/C4
Nawngleng, Myan. 106/B1
Nawoiy, Uzb. 80/G5
Naxçıvan, Azer. 115/F2
Naxçivan Aut. Rep., Azer. 115/F2
Naxi, China 105/J2
Náxos, Gre. 55/J4
Náxos (isl.), Gre. 73/K3
Nāy Band, Iran 115/H5
Nāy Band, Iran 115/J3
Nay Pyi Taw (cap.), Myan. 98/C5
Naya, Col. 216/B4
Nayāgarh, India 107/E1
Nayarit (state), Mex. 204/D4
Nayland, Eng, UK 43/G3
Naylor, Mo, US 192/B2
Nayong, China 105/J2
Nayoro, Japan 94/C1
Nayramadlīn (peak), Mong. 111/E2
Naytahwaush, Mn, US 187/G4
Nayuci, Malw. 141/G2
Nayzatash (pass), Taj. 111/B4
Nazaré, Port. 52/A3
Nazaré, Braz. 218/E4
Nazaré da Mata, Braz. 219/H4
Nazaré do Piauí, Braz. 219/F4
Nazaré Paulista, Braz. 223/K8
Nazareth, Belg. 60/C2
Nazareth, Pa, US 198/C2
Nazas, Mex. 204/D3
Nazas (riv.), Mex. 204/D3
Nazca, Peru 220/C4
Naze, Japan 97/K6
Nazelles-Négron, Fr. 63/F6
Nazerat, Isr. 117/C3
Nazerat 'Illit, Isr. 117/C3
Nazilli, Turk. 114/B2
Nāzir Hāt, Bang. 109/H4
Nazko (riv.), BC, Can. 174/C1
Nazran', Rus. 77/H4
Nazrēt, Eth. 136/A3
Nazyvayevsk, Rus. 80/H4
Ncamasere (riv.), Bots. 140/D3
Nchanga, Zam. 141/E2
Nchelenge, Zam. 139/G5
Ncheu, Malw. 141/G2
Nchisi, Malw. 141/G2
Ncojane, Bots. 140/D4
Ndabala, Zam. 141/F2
Ndala, Tanz. 137/A3
Ndalatando, Ang. 138/C5
Ndali, Ben. 133/F4
Ndele, CAfr. 134/D3
Ndélélé, Camr. 138/C1
N'Dendé, Gabon 138/B3
Ndende (isl.), Sol. 160/F6
Ndengu, Tanz. 137/A4
Ndiago, Mrta. 132/A2
Ndikiniméki, Camr. 138/B1
Ndim, CAfr. 134/B4
Ndindi, Gabon 138/B3
N'Djamena (int'l arpt.), Chad 134/B2
N'Djili (int'l arpt.), D.R. Congo 138/C4
N'Djolé, Gabon 138/B3
Ndogo (lag.), Gabon 138/B3
Ndola, Zam. 141/F2
Ndolo Corner, Kenya 137/B2
Ndombi, D.R. Congo 139/E4
Ndouaniang, Gabon 138/B2
Ndouci, C.d'Iv. 132/D5
Ndougou, Gabon 138/B3
Ndrhamcha (lake), Mrta. 132/B2
Ndu, D.R. Congo 134/D4
Nduguti, Tanz. 137/A3
Nduli, Tanz. 137/A3
Ndumbwe, Tanz. 137/B4
Ndungu, Tanz. 137/B3
Né (riv.), Fr. 50/C4
Néa Alikarnassós, Gre. 55/J5
Néa Ankhíalos, Gre. 55/H3
Néa Artáki, Gre. 55/H3
Néa Ionía, Gre. 55/H3
Néa Ionía, Gre. 55/N8
Néa Kallikrátia, Gre. 55/H2
Néa Kíos, Gre. 55/H4
Néa Mikhanióna, Gre. 55/H2
Néa Moudhaniá, Gre. 55/H2
Néa Potídhaia, Gre. 55/H2
Néa Tríglia, Gre. 55/H2
Néa Víssa, Gre. 57/H5
Néa Zíkhni, Gre. 55/H2
Neagh (lake), NI, UK 40/B2
Neah Bay, Wa, US 174/B3
Neale (lake), Austl. 155/F3
Neales (riv.), Austl. 155/G3
Neamţ (prov.), Rom. 57/H2
Neaophli-le-Château, Fr. 36/H5
Neápolis, Gre. 55/J5
Neápolis, Gre. 55/H4
Neápolis, Gre. 55/G2
Near (isls.), Ak, US 201/A5
Neath, Wal, UK 42/C3
Neath (riv.), Wal, UK 42/C3
Neath Port Talbot (co.), Wal, UK 42/C3
Neavitt, Md, US 198/B6
Nebbi, Ugan. 139/G2
Nebel-Horn (peak), Ger. 67/G3
Nebikon, Swi. 66/D3
Nebin (peak), It. 70/D3
Nebish (isl.), Mi, US 190/D1
Nebitdag, Trkm. 115/H2
Neblina (peak), Braz. 217/E4
Nebo, Mo, US 183/H2
Nebo, SAfr. 141/F5
Nebo (mt.), Ut, US 177/H4
Nebo, Il, US 185/J4
Nebo (mt.), Austl. 158/E6
Nebraska (state), US 184/D3
Nebraska City, Ne, US 185/G3
Nebrodi (mts.), It. 54/C4
Necedah, Wi, US 185/J1
Necedah Nat'l Wild. Ref., Wi, US 185/J1
Nechako (riv.), BC, Can. 170/D3
Nechayane, Ukr. 78/F4
Neche, ND, US 186/F3
Neches (riv.), Tx, US 173/G5
Neches, Tx, US 180/G2
Nechisar NP, Eth. 135/H4
Nechranice (res.), Czh. 65/G2
Neckar (riv.), Ger. 48/D4
Neckarbischofsheim, Ger. 64/B4
Neckargemünd, Ger. 64/B4
Neckarsteinach, Ger. 64/B4
Neckarsulm, Ger. 64/C4
Necker (isl.), Hi, US 161/J2
Necochea, Arg. 226/F3
Necoclí, Col. 216/B2
Necropoli (ruin), It. 71/B3
Neda, Sp. 52/A1
Nedelino, Bul. 55/J2
Nedelišće, Cro. 56/C2
Nederland, Tx, US 181/H3
Nederweert, Neth. 58/C6
Nedlands (nbrhd.), Austl. 154/K6
Nedumangād, India 107/C4
Nee Soon (nbrhd.), Sing. 101/J6
Neede, Neth. 58/D4
Needham, Al, US 194/D2
Needham Market, Eng, UK 43/H2
Needingworth, Eng, UK 43/F2
Needle (mtn.), Wy, US 177/J1
Needles (pt.), NZ 159/C2
Needles, Ca, US 178/E3
Needles, BC, Can. 174/E3
Needles, The, Eng, UK 43/E5
Needville, Tx, US 181/G3
Neely Henry (lake), Al, US 192/D4
Neelyville, Mo, US 192/B2
Neembucú (dept.), Par. 224/E3
Neenah, Wi, US 185/K1
Neepawa, Mb, Can. 186/E2
Neerabup NP, Austl. 154/K6
Neerpelt, Belg. 58/C6
Neetze, Ger. 59/H2
Neetze (riv.), Ger. 59/H2
Nefas Mewch'a, Eth. 136/A3
Nefasīt, Erit. 136/A2
Neffelbach (riv.), Ger. 61/F2
Neftah, Tun. 72/E4
Neftçala, Azer. 115/G2
Neftegorsk, Rus. 77/J1
Neftegorsk, Rus. 79/K5
Neftekamsk, Rus. 75/M4
Neftekumsk, Rus. 77/H3
Nefud (des.), SAr. 83/B7
Nefyn, Wal, UK 40/D6
Nega Nega, Zam. 141/F2
Négala, Mali 132/C3
Negara, Indo. 101/F5
Negara, Indo. 102/E4
Negaunee, Mi, US 187/L4
Negba, Isr. 117/B5
Negēlē, Eth. 136/A4
Negēlē, Eth. 136/A4
Negeri Sembilan (state), Malay. 101/C2
Negev (reg.), Isr. 116/D4
Negoiu (peak), Rom. 57/G3
Negomano, Moz. 141/H1
Negoreloye, Bela. 47/M5
Negotin, Serb. 56/F3
Negotino, FYROM 55/H2
Negra (pt.), Belz. 206/D2
Negra (mesa), NM, US 179/J3
Negra (pt.), Peru 220/A2
Negrais (cape), Myan. 105/F4
Negrar, It. 69/D2
Negreet, La, US 194/B2
Negreira, Sp. 52/A1
Negreiros, Chile 224/B1
Negreşti, Rom. 78/D4
Negril, Jam. 207/G2
Negrillos, Bol. 224/B1
Negrine, Alg. 72/E4
Negritos, Peru 220/A2
Negro (peak), Arg. 226/C3
Negro (riv.), Uru. 191/J11
Negro (brook), Uru. 191/K10
Negro (riv.), Bol. 221/F4
Negro (riv.), Braz. 218/A3
Negro (riv.), Par. 224/E3
Negros (isl.), Phil. 83/M9
Neguac, NB, Can. 188/E2
Nehalem (riv.), Or, US 174/C5
Nehbandān, Iran 113/H2
Neheim-Hüsten, Ger. 59/E6
Nei Monggol (plat.), China 90/G3
Nei Monggol (aut. reg.), China 90/E3
Neiafu, Tonga 161/H6
Neiba, DRep. 203/G4
Neiba (mts.), DRep. 207/J2
Neiderösterreich (prov.), Aus. 51/L2
Neihart, Mt, US 175/J4
Neihuang, China 92/C4
Neijiang, China 98/E2
Neilburg, Sk, Can. 175/K1
Neillier (peak), Fr. 70/D4
Neillsville, Wi, US 185/J1
Neil's Harbour, NS, Can. 189/G2
Neilston, Sc, UK 39/B5
Neineis, Namb. 140/B4
Neiqiu, China 92/C3
Neira, Col. 219/K7
Neisse (riv.), Ger. 49/H3
Neiva, Col. 216/C4
Neixiang, China 92/B4
Nejanilini (lake), Mb, Can. 170/G3
Nejdek, Czh. 65/F2
Nejo, Eth. 135/G3
Nejrab (int'l arpt.), Syria 116/E1
Nekā, Iran 115/H2
Nekalagba, D.R. Congo 139/G2
Nek'emtē, Eth. 135/H3
Nekhayevskiy, Rus. 79/L2
Nekoosa, Wi, US 185/K1
Nekrasovo, Rus. 77/H2
Nekselø (isl.), Den. 45/H7
Neksø, Den. 46/F4
Nelas, Port. 52/B2
Nelidovo, Rus. 74/G4
Neligh, Ne, US 184/E2
Nellieburg, Ms, US 192/C4
Nellimarla, India 107/D2
Nellingen, Ger. 64/C5
Nellis Air Force Range, Nv, US 178/D2
Nellore, India 107/C3
Nelson, Arg. 224/D4
Nelson (cape), Austl. 156/B3
Nelson, BC, Can. 174/F3
Nelson (riv.), Mb, Can. 170/G3
Nelson (str.), Chile 191/B6
Nelson, NZ 159/C3
Nelson (cape), PNG 153/H2
Nelson, Eng, UK 41/F4
Nelson, Wal, UK 42/C3
Nelson (isl.), Ak, US 201/E3
Nelson, Az, US 179/F3
Nelson, Mo, US 185/H4
Nelson, Ne, US 184/E3
Nelson Bay, Austl. 156/E2
Nelson Forks, BC, Can. 170/D3
Nelson Lagoon, Ak, US 201/F4
Nelson Lakes NP, NZ 159/C3
Nelson-Miramichi, NB, Can. 188/E2
Nelsonville, Oh, US 190/E5
Nelspruit, SAfr. 141/F5
Néma, Mrta. 132/D2
Nemaha, Ne, US 185/G3
Neman, Rus. 47/K4
Neman (riv.), Rus. 49/M1
Neman (Nemunas) (riv.), Eur. 47/K4
Nembrala, Indo. 152/A2
Nembro, It. 68/C2
Neméa, Gre. 55/H4
Nemenčinė, Lith. 47/L4
Nemi, It. 71/B4
Nemingha, Austl. 156/D1
Nemira (peak), Rom. 57/H2
Nemocón, Col. 219/M7
Nemor (riv.), China 91/K2
Nemours, Fr. 50/E2
Nemunas (riv.), Lith. 74/D5
Nemunas (Neman) (riv.), Eur. 47/K4
Nemuro (str.), Japan,Rus. 91/P3
Nemuro (pen.), Japan 94/D2
Nemuro, Japan 94/D2
Nemyriv, Ukr. 78/B2
Nemyriv, Ukr. 78/E3
Nen (riv.), China 83/M5
Nenagh (riv.), Ire. 38/B4
Nenagh, Ire. 38/B4
Nenana, Ak, US 201/J3
Nenasi, Malay. 101/C2
Nendaz, Swi. 66/D5
Nene (riv.), Eng, UK 41/J6
Nenetskiy Aut. Okrug, Rus. 75/M2
Nenjiang, China 91/K2
Nentershausen, Ger. 61/G3
Nentershausen, Ger. 59/G6
Nenzing, Aus. 67/F3
Neola, Ut, US 177/H3
Neola, Ia, US 185/G3
Néon Petrítsion, Gre. 55/H2
Neoria Husainpur, India 108/B1
Néos Marmarás, Gre. 55/H2
Neosho, Mo, US 183/G2
Neosho (riv.), Ks,Ok, US 183/G2
Neosho Falls, Ks, US 183/G1
Nepal (ctry.) 108/D1
Nepālganj, Nepal 108/C1
Nepāltār, Nepal 109/F2
Nepanagar, India 104/C3
Nepean, On, Can. 191/J2
Nepean (riv.), Austl. 158/G8
Nepeña, Peru 220/B3
Nepessina (lake), Mi, US 197/F6
Nephi, Ut, US 177/H4
Nephin (peak), Ire. 38/A1
Nephin Beg (range), Ire. 38/A1
Nephin Beg (peak), Ire. 38/A1
Nepi, It. 71/B3
Nepisiguit (bay), NB, Can. 188/E2
Nepisiguit (riv.), NB, Can. 188/D2
Nepoko (riv.), D.R. Congo 139/G2
Nepomuceno, Braz. 222/D4
Nepomuk, Czh. 65/G4
Neptune City, NJ, US 199/D3
Nera (riv.), It. 51/K5
Nérac, Fr. 50/D4
Neratovice, Czh. 65/H2
Nercha (riv.), Rus. 90/H1
Nerchinsk, Rus. 90/H1
Nerekhta, Rus. 74/J4
Neresheim, Ger. 64/D5
Nereta, Lat. 47/L3
Nereto, It. 71/C2
Neretva (riv.), Bosn.,Cro. 56/D4
Neringa, Lith. 47/J4
Neris (riv.), Lith. 74/E5
Nerja, Sp. 52/D4
Ñermete (pt.), Peru 220/A2
Nerokoúros, Gre. 55/J5
Nerone (peak), It. 69/F6
Nerópolis, Braz. 222/C3
Nerpio, Sp. 52/D3
Nersingen, Ger. 64/D6
Nerva, Sp. 52/B4
Nervesa della Battaglia, It. 69/F2
Nervi, It. 68/C5
Nerviano, It. 68/B2
Neryungri, Rus. 81/N4
Nes, Nor. 46/C1
Nes, Nor. 46/D1
Nes, Neth. 58/C2
Nes Ziyyona, Isr. 117/B5
Nesbyen, Nor. 46/C1
Nescopeck (cr.), Pa, US 198/C1
Nesebŭr, Bul. 57/H4
Neshaminy (cr.), Pa, US 198/C3
Nesher, Isr. 117/C3
Neskaupstadhur, Ice. 44/Q6
Nesle, Fr. 60/B4
Nesles-la-Vallée, Fr. 36/J4
Nesodden, Nor. 44/S8
Nespelem, Wa, US 174/E3
Nesque (riv.), Fr. 70/B4
Nesquehoning, Pa, US 198/C2
Ness (riv.), Sc, UK 39/B2
Ness (lake), Sc, UK 39/B2
Ness City, Ks, US 182/E1
Nesselrode (mt.), Ak, US 201/M4
Nesselwang, Ger. 67/G2
Nesslau, Swi. 67/F3
Nesterovka, Rus. 77/K1
Neston, Eng, UK 41/E5
Nestor Falls, On, Can. 187/H3
Nestore (riv.), It. 71/B1
Nestórion, Gre. 55/G2
Néstos (riv.), Gre. 73/K2
Nesvizh, Bela. 76/C1
Net (riv.), Mi, US 187/K4
Netanya, Isr. 117/B4
Netarhāt, India 109/E4
Netarts, Or, US 174/C5
Netawaka, Ks, US 185/G4
Netcong, NJ, US 198/D2
Nethe (riv.), Ger. 59/G5
Netherend, Eng, UK 42/D3
Netherhill, Sk, Can. 175/K2
Netherlands (ctry.) 58/B5
Netherlands Antilles (isls.), StL. 203/H5
Netishyn, Ukr. 78/D2
Netivot, Isr. 117/B6
Netley, Eng, UK 43/E5
Netolice, Czh. 65/H4
Netphen, Ger. 61/H2
Netrakona, Bang. 109/H3
Netstal, Swi. 67/F3
Nett Lake, Mn, US 187/H3
Nett Lake Ind. Res. (lake), Mn, US 187/H3
Nette (riv.), Ger. 58/D6
Nettebach (riv.), Ger. 61/G3
Nettersheim, Ger. 61/F3
Nettetal, Ger. 58/D6
Nettilling (lake), Nun, Can. 171/J2
Nettleham, Eng, UK 41/H5
Nettleton, Ms, US 192/C3
Nettuno, It. 71/B5
Netzschkau, Ger. 65/F1
Neu Darchau, Ger. 59/H2
Neu Heusis, Namb. 140/C4
Neu Zittau, Ger. 48/Q7
Neu-Isenburg, Ger. 64/B2
Neu-Ostheim (Mannheim) (arpt.), Ger. 64/B4
Neu-Ulm, Ger. 64/D6
Neubiberg, Ger. 65/E6
Neubourg, Fr. 63/F2
Neubrandenburg, Ger. 49/G2
Neubrunn, Ger. 64/C3
Neubulach, Ger. 64/B5
Neuburg, Ger. 64/B5
Neuburg an der Donau, Ger. 64/E5
Neuburg an der Kammel, Ger. 67/G1
Neuchâtel (canton), Swi. 66/C4
Neuchâtel, Swi. 66/C4
Neuchâtel, de (lake), Fr. 72/E1
Neudorf, Sk, Can. 186/C2
Neuenbürg, Ger. 64/B5
Neuenburg am Rhein, Ger. 66/D2
Neuendettelsau, Ger. 64/D4
Neuendorf, Ger. 46/E4
Neuenhagen, Ger. 48/Q6
Neuenhaus, Ger. 58/D3
Neuenkirchen, Ger. 59/F3
Neuenkirchen, Ger. 59/F3
Neuenkirchen, Ger. 59/E4
Neuenrade, Ger. 59/E6
Neuenstadt am Kocher, Ger. 64/C4
Neuenstein, Ger. 64/C4
Neuerburg, Ger. 61/F3
Neuf-Brisach, Fr. 66/D1
Neufahrn bei Freising, Ger. 65/E6
Neufchâteau, Fr. 66/B1
Neufchâteau, Belg. 61/E4
Neufchâtel-en-Bray, Fr. 63/G1
Neufchâtel-Hardelot, Fr. 60/A2
Neufchelles, Fr. 36/M4
Neufmanil, Fr. 61/D4
Neufmoutiers-en-Brie, Fr. 36/L5
Neugablonz, Ger. 67/G2
Neuhaus am Inn, Ger. 65/G6
Neuhaus am Rennweg, Ger. 64/E1
Neuhaus-Schierschnitz, Ger. 64/E2
Neuhäusel, Ger. 61/G3
Neuhausen am Rheinfall, Swi. 67/E2
Neuhof, Ger. 64/C2
Neuhof an der Zenn, Ger. 64/D4
Neuhofen, Ger. 64/B4
Neuhofen an der Krems, Aus. 65/H6
Neuillé-Pont-Pierre, Fr. 63/F5
Neuilly-en-Thelle, Fr. 60/B5
Neuilly-L'Évêque, Fr. 66/B2
Neuilly-sur-Marne, Fr. 36/K5
Neuilly-sur-Seine, Fr. 36/J5
Neukirchen, Ger. 46/C4
Neukirchen an der Vöckla, Aus. 65/G6
Neukirchen vorm Wald, Ger. 65/G5
Neukölln, Ger. 48/Q7
Neumarkt (Enga), It. 67/H5
Neumarkt am Wallersee, Aus. 65/G7
Neumarkt im Mühlkreis, Aus. 65/H6
Neumarkt in der Oberpfalz, Ger. 65/E4
Neumarkt-Sankt Veit, Ger. 65/F6
Neumünster, Ger. 46/C4
Neung-sur-Beuvron, Fr. 63/G5
Neunkirch, Swi. 67/E2
Neunkirchen, Ger. 61/H2
Neunkirchen, Ger. 61/G5
Neunkirchen, Aus. 51/M3
Neunkirchen-Seelscheid, Ger. 61/G2
Neupotz, Ger. 64/B4
Neuquén, Arg. 226/C3
Neuquén (riv.), Arg. 226/C3
Neuquén (prov.), Arg. 226/C3
Neuruppin, Ger. 48/G2
Neusäss, Ger. 64/D6
Neuse (riv.), NC, US 193/J3
Neusiedl am See, Aus. 51/M3
Neusiedler (lake), Aus. 49/J5
Neusiedler (Fertő) (lake), Aus. 51/M3
Neuss, Ger. 58/D6
Neustadt, Ger. 48/G2
Neustadt, Ger. 61/G2
Neustadt am Rübenberge, Ger. 59/G3
Neustadt an der Aisch, Ger. 64/D3
Neustadt an der Donau, Ger. 65/E5
Neustadt an der Waldnaab, Ger. 65/F3
Neustadt an der Weinstrasse, Ger. 64/B4
Neustadt bei Coburg, Ger. 64/E2
Neustadt in Holstein, Ger. 46/D4
Neustift im Stubaital, Aus. 67/H3
Neustrelitz, Ger. 48/G2
Neutraubling, Ger. 65/F5
Neuvic, Fr. 50/E4
Neuville-aux-Bois, Fr. 63/H4
Neuville-sur-Saône, Fr. 66/A6
Neuville-sur-Sarthe, Fr. 63/F4
Neuvy-le-Roii, Fr. 63/F5
Neuwied, Ger. 61/G3
Neuzelle, Ger. 49/H2
Neva (riv.), Rus. 47/P2
Nevada (mts.), Col. 207/H4
Nevada (state), US 172/C4
Nevada, Ia, US 185/H2
Nevada, Mo, US 183/G2
Nevada, Tx, US 180/L6
Nevada City, Ca, US 176/C4
Nevada del Huila, PN, Col. 216/C4
Nevada Test Site, Nv, US 178/D2
Nevada, PN, Ven. 216/D2
Nevado de Chañi (peak), Arg. 224/C3
Nevado de Colima (peak), Mex. 204/E5
Nevado de Colima PN, Mex. 204/D5
Nevado de Cumbal (peak), Col. 216/B4
Nevado de Toluca, PN, Mex. 205/K7
Nevado del Candado (peak), Arg. 224/C3
Nevado del Huila (peak), Col. 216/C4
Nevado del Ruiz (peak), Col. 219/K8
Nevado del Tolima (peak), Col. 219/K8
Nevatim, Isr. 117/B6
Nevel', Rus. 47/N3
Nevele, Belg. 60/C1
Nevel'sk, Rus. 91/N2
Never, Rus. 91/J1
Nevers, Fr. 50/E3
Nevertire, Austl. 156/C1
Nevesinje, Bosn. 56/D4
Neville, Sk, Can. 175/L3
Nevinnomyssk, Rus. 79/L5
Nevis, Mn, US 187/G4
Nevis (isl.), UK 203/J4
Nevis (peak), StK. 203/N8
Nevola (riv.), It. 69/G5
Nevşehir, Turk. 114/C2
Nevşehir (prov.), Turk. 114/C2
New (riv.), Guy. 217/G4
New (riv.), NC, US 193/J3
New Abbey, Sc, UK 40/E2
New Albany, Ms, US 192/C3
New Albany, In, US 192/E1
New Alfresford, Eng, UK 43/E4
New Amsterdam, Guy. 217/G3
New Ancholme (riv.), Eng, UK 41/H4
New Angledool, Austl. 156/C1
New Ash Green, Eng, UK 36/D2
New Athens, Il, US 192/C1
New Auburn, Mn, US 185/G1
New Augusta, Ms, US 194/D2
New Baltimore, Mi, US 197/G6
New Barn, Eng, UK 36/E2
New Bedford, Ma, US 191/L4
New Berlin, NY, US 191/J3
New Berlin, Wi, US 197/P14
New Berlin, Pa, US 198/B2
New Berlinville, Pa, US 198/C3
New Bern, NC, US 193/J3
New Bethlehem, Pa, US 191/G4
New Bloomfield, Mo, US 183/H1
New Bloomfield, Pa, US 191/H4
New Boston, Tx, US 183/G4
New Boston, Oh, US 193/F1
New Braunfels, Tx, US 180/E3
New Bremen, Oh, US 190/D4
New Brighton, Mn, US 187/P6
New Britain (isl.), PNG 160/D5
New Britain, Ct, US 191/K4
New Britain, Pa, US 198/C3
New Brunswick (prov.), Can. 188/D2
New Brunswick, NJ, US 199/H10
New Buffalo, Mi, US 190/C4
New Buffalo, Pa, US 198/B3
New Buildings, NI, UK 40/A2
New Bussa, Nga. 133/G4
New Caledonia (terr.), Fr. 161/U11
New Caledonia (isl.), NCal., Fr. 161/U12
New Canaan, Ct, US 199/M7
New Carlisle, Qu, Can. 188/E1
New Castile (reg.), Sp. 72/C3
New Castle, In, US 190/D5
New Castle, Pa, US 190/F4
New Castle, Ky, US 192/E1
New Castle, Va, US 193/G2
New Castle, De, US 198/C4
New Castle (co.), De, US 198/C5
New Chicago, In, US 197/R16
New City, NY, US 199/K7
New Columbia, Pa, US 198/B1
New Columbus, Pa, US 198/B1
New Concord, Oh, US 190/F5
New Concord, Ky, US 192/C2
New Cordell (Cordell), Ok, US 182/E3
New Cumberland, WV, US 190/F4
New Cumberland, Pa, US 198/B3
New Cumnock, Sc, UK 39/B6
New Dayton, Ab, Can. 175/H3
New Deal, Tx, US 182/D4
New Deer, Sc, UK 39/D1
New Delhi (cap.), India 110/D5
New Denver, BC, Can. 174/F3
New Dorp (nbrhd.), NY, US 199/J9
New Edinburg, Ar, US 183/H4
New Effington, SD, US 186/F5
New Egypt, NJ, US 198/D3
New Ellenton, SC, US 193/G4
New England, ND, US 186/C4
New England NP, Austl. 156/E1
New Era, La, US 194/C2
New Exchequer (dam), Ca, US 178/B2
New Florence, Mo, US 185/J4
New Franklin, Mo, US 185/H4
New Freedom, Pa, US 198/B4
New Galloway, Sc, UK 40/D1
New Georgia (isls.), Sol. 160/E5
New Georgia (sound), Sol. 160/E5
New Germany, NS, Can. 188/E3
New Glasgow, NS, Can. 189/F3
New Glasgow, Qu, Can. 189/N6
New Gloucester, Me, US 191/L3
New Gretna, NJ, US 198/D4
New Guinea (isl.), Indo.,PNG 83/N10
New Hampshire (state), US 191/L3
New Hampton, Ia, US 185/H2
New Hanover (isl.), PNG 160/D5
New Hanover, SAfr. 143/E3
New Harbour, NS, Can. 189/G3
New Harmony, Ut, US 179/F2
New Harmony, In, US 192/D1
New Haven, Ct, US 191/K4
New Haven, In, US 190/D4
New Haven, Mi, US 197/G6
New Haven, WV, US 193/G1
New Haven, Il, US 192/C2
New Haven, Mo, US 185/J4
New Haven, Ky, US 192/E2
New Haven, Wy, US 184/B1
New Hebrides (isls.), Van. 160/F6
New Hebron, Ms, US 194/D2
New Hogan (dam), Ca, US 176/C4
New Holland, Pa, US 198/B3
New Holstein, Wi, US 190/B3
New Home, Tx, US 182/D4
New Hope, Ms, US 192/C4
New Hope, Al, US 192/D3
New Hope, Ga, US 193/L7
New Hope, Tx, US 180/L6
New Hope, NC, US 193/H3
New Hope, NC, US 193/J3
New Hope, Pa, US 198/D3
New Hradec, ND, US 186/C4
New Hyde Park, NY, US 199/L9
New Hythe, Eng, UK 36/E3
New Iberia, La, US 194/C2
New Ireland (isl.), PNG 160/E5
New Jersey (state), US 198/D3
New Johnsonville, Tn, US 192/D2
New Kensington, Pa, US 191/G4
New Kent, Va, US 193/J2
New Kowloon, China 99/L7
New Leipzig, ND, US 186/D4
New Lenox, Il, US 197/Q16
New Lexington, Oh, US 190/E5
New Lima, Ok, US 183/F3
New Lisbon, Wi, US 185/J2
New Lisbon, NJ, US 198/D4
New Liskeard, On, Can. 171/J4
New London, Ct, US 191/K4
New London, Wi, US 185/K1
New London, Mn, US 185/G1
New London, Mo, US 185/J4
New London, Tx, US 181/G1
New Lowell, On, Can. 190/G2
New Madrid, Mo, US 192/C2
New Market, Ia, US 185/G3
New Market, Al, US 192/D3
New Market, Va, US 193/H1
New Market, Md, US 198/A5
New Martinsville, WV, US 190/F5
New Meadows, Id, US 176/E1
New Mexico (state), US 172/E5
New Milford, NJ, US 199/J8
New Mills, Eng, UK 41/F5
New Norcia, Austl. 154/C4
New Norfolk, Austl. 156/C4
New Norway, Ab, Can. 175/H1
New Orleans, La, US 200/P17
New Orleans (Moisant Field) (int'l arpt.), La, US 200/P16
New Oxford, Pa, US 198/A4
New Paltz, NY, US 191/J4
New Paris, In, US 190/D4
New Pekin (Pekin), In, US 192/D1
New Philadelphia, Oh, US 190/F4
New Philadelphia, Pa, US 198/B2
New Pine Creek, Or, US 176/C3
New Pitsligo, Sc, UK 39/D1
New Plymouth, NZ 159/C2
New Plymouth, Id, US 176/E2
New Port Richey, Fl, US 194/K7
New Prague, Mn, US 185/H1
New Providence (isl.), Bahm. 203/F3
New Providence, NJ, US 199/H9
New Quay, Wal, UK 42/B2
New Radnor, Wal, UK 42/C2
New Richmond, Qu, Can. 188/E1
New Richmond, Wi, US 185/H1
New River Gorge Nat'l Riv., WV, US 193/G2
New Roads, La, US 194/C2
New Rochelle, NY, US 199/K8
New Rockford, ND, US 186/E4
New Romney, Eng, UK 43/G5
New Ross, Ire. 38/D5
New Ross, NS, Can. 188/E3
New Rossington, Eng, UK 41/G5
New Salem, ND, US 186/D4
New Sarepta, Ab, Can. 175/H1
New Schwabenland (phys. reg.), Ant. 228/Z
New Scone, Sc, UK 39/C4
New Shagunnu, Nga. 133/G4
New Sharon, Ia, US 185/H3
New Shoreham (Block Island), RI, US 199/G1
New Siberian (isls.), Rus. 83/N2
New Smyrna Beach, Fl, US 195/H3
New South Wales (state), Austl. 145/D4
New Straitsville, Oh, US 190/E5
New Strawn (Strawn), Ks, US 183/G1
New Stuyahok, Ak, US 201/G4
New Summerfield, Tx, US 180/G2
New Tazewell, Tn, US 192/F2
New Town, ND, US 186/C4
New Tredegar, Wal, UK 42/C3
New Tripoli, Pa, US 198/C2
New Ulm, Mn, US 185/G1
New Ulm, Tx, US 180/F3
New Vienna, Oh, US 190/E5
New Virginia, Ia, US 185/H3
New Washington, Oh, US 190/E4
New Waterford, NS, Can. 189/G2
New Westminster, BC, Can. 174/C3
New Whiteland, In, US 190/C5
New Windsor, Md, US 198/A4
New York, NY, US 199/K9
New York (state), US 191/J3
New York Mills, Mn, US 187/G4
New Zealand (ctry.) 191/*
Newala, Tanz. 137/B4
Newald, Wi, US 187/K5
Newark, Ar, US 183/J3
Newark, Ca, US 197/K11
Newark, De, US 198/C4
Newark, NJ, US 199/J9
Newark (bay), NJ, US 199/J9
Newark (int'l arpt.), NJ, US 199/J9
Newark, Il, US 185/K3
Newark, Oh, US 190/E4
Newark, Tx, US 180/K6
Newark Valley, NY, US 191/H3
Newark-on-Trent, Eng, UK 41/H5
Newaygo, Mi, US 190/D3
Newberg, Or, US 176/B1
Newbern, Tn, US 192/C2
Newberry, Fl, US 195/G3
Newberry, Mi, US 190/D1
Newberry, SC, US 193/G3
Newberry Nat'l Volcanic Mon., Or, US 176/C2
Newbiggin-by-the-Sea, Eng, UK 41/G1
Newbliss, Ire. 38/C1
Newbridge-on-Wye, Wal, UK 42/C2
Newburg, Ar, US 183/J2
Newburg, ND, US 186/D3
Newburgh, Sc, UK 39/E2
Newburgh, Sc, UK 39/C4
Newburgh, NY, US 191/J4
Newburn, Eng, UK 41/G2
Newbury, Eng, UK 43/E4
Newbury, Vt, US 191/K2
Newby Bridge, Eng, UK 41/F3
Newcastle, Austl. 157/E1
Newcastle, NB, Can. 188/E2
Newcastle (int'l arpt.), Eng, UK 41/G1
Newcastle, NI, UK 40/C3
Newcastle, Ire. 40/B5
Newcastle, Ire. 38/A5
Newcastle, SAfr. 143/E2
Newcastle, Ok, US 183/F3
Newcastle, Tx, US 183/E4
Newcastle, Ut, US 179/F2
Newcastle, Wy, US 184/B2
Newcastle upon Tyne, Eng, UK 41/G2
Newcastle upon Tyne (co.), Eng, UK 41/G1
Newcastle Waters, Austl. 152/D4
Newcastle-under-Lyme, Eng, UK 41/F6
Newcastleton, Sc, UK 41/F1
Newcomb, NM, US 179/H2
Newcomerstown, Oh, US 190/F4
Newdegate, Austl. 154/C5
Newdigate, Eng, UK 36/C3
Newe Yam, Isr. 117/B3
Newel, Ger. 61/F4
Newell, Austl. 158/B2
Newell, Ia, US 185/G2
Newellton, La, US 194/C1
Newenham (cape), Ak, US 201/F4
Newent, Eng, UK 42/D3
Newfane, Vt, US 191/K3
Newfane, NY, US 190/V9
Newfield, NJ, US 198/C4
Newfoundland (isl.), Can. 163/M5
Newfoundland and Labrador (prov.), Can. 171/K3
Newfoundland, NJ, US 199/H7
Newfoundland, Pa, US 198/C1
Newfoundland Evaporation (basin), Ut, US 177/G3
Newgulf, Tx, US 181/G3
Newhalem, Wa, US 174/D3
Newhalen, Ak, US 201/H4
Newham (bor.), Eng, UK 36/D2
Newhaven, Eng, UK 43/F5
Newhope, Ar, US 183/H3
Newick, Eng, UK 43/G5
Newington, Eng, UK 36/F3
Newington, Ga, US 193/G4
Newkirk, Ok, US 183/F2
Newland, NC, US 193/G2
Newlin, Tx, US 182/D3
Newllano, La, US 194/B2
Newlyn, Eng, UK 42/A6
Newmains, Sc, UK 39/C5
Newman, ND, US 186/F4
Newman, Il, US 190/C5
Newman, NM, US 179/J4
Newman (mt.), Austl. 154/C2
Newman, Austl. 154/C2
Newman Grove, Ne, US 184/F3
Newmarket (nbrhd.), Austl. 158/F6
Newmarket, On, Can. 191/G2
Newmarket, Ire. 38/A5
Newmarket (nbrhd.), NZ 159/F6
Newmarket, Eng, UK 43/G2
Newmarket, NH, US 191/L3
Newmarket on Fergus, Ire. 38/B4
Newmerella, Austl. 157/D3
Newmill, Sc, UK 39/D1
Newnan, Ga, US 192/E4
Newnans (lake), Fl, US 195/G3
Newnham, Eng, UK 42/D3
Newport, Qu, Can. 188/E1
Newport, Ire. 38/B4
Newport, Ire. 38/A2
Newport, Eng, UK 42/D1
Newport, Eng, UK 43/E5
Newport, Wal, UK 42/D3
Newport (co.), Wal, UK 42/D3
Newport, Wal, UK 42/B2
Newport, Ar, US 183/J3
Newport (bay), Ca, US 196/C3
Newport, De, US 198/C4
Newport, In, US 190/C5
Newport, Ky, US 190/D5
Newport, Mn, US 187/P7
Newport, NC, US 193/J3
Newport, NH, US 191/K3
Newport, NJ, US 198/C5
Newport, NY, US 191/J3
Newport, Or, US 176/A1
Newport, Pa, US 198/A3
Newport, RI, US 191/L4
Newport, Tn, US 193/F3
Newport, Vt, US 191/K2
Newport, Wa, US 174/F3
Newport Beach, Ca, US 196/G8
Newport Meadows (lake), NJ, US 198/C5
Newport News, Va, US 193/J2
Newport Pagnell, Eng, UK 43/F2
Newport-On-Tay, Sc, UK 39/D4
Newquay, Eng, UK 42/A6
Newquay Civil (arpt.), Eng, UK 42/A6
Newry (dist.), NI, UK 40/B3
Newry, NI, UK 40/B3
Newry (canal), NI, UK 40/B3
Newry, Austl. 152/C4
Newtok, Ak, US 201/F3
Newton, Eng, UK 42/D2
Newton, Sc, UK 41/E1
Newton, Ga, US 195/F2
Newton (co.), Ga, US 193/M7
Newton, Ia, US 185/H3
Newton, Il, US 192/C1
Newton, Ks, US 183/F1
Newton, Ma, US 191/L3
Newton, Ms, US 192/C4
Newton, NC, US 193/G3
Newton, NJ, US 198/D1
Newton, Tx, US 181/H2
Newton, Ut, US 177/H3
Newton Abbot, Eng, UK 42/C5
Newton Aycliffe, Eng, UK 41/G2
Newton Falls, NY, US 191/J2
Newton Mearns, Sc, UK 39/B5
Newton on the Moor, Eng, UK 39/E6
Newton Stewart, Sc, UK 40/D2
Newton Tors (hill), Eng, UK 39/D5
Newton-le-Willows, Eng, UK 41/F5
Newtonmore, Sc, UK 39/B2
Newtonville, NJ, US 198/D4
Newtown, Austl. 156/B3
Newtown, Ire. 38/B5
Newtown, Ct, US 191/K4
Newtown, Mo, US 185/H3
Newtown, Pa, US 198/D3
Newtown, Wal, UK 42/C1
Newtown Forbes, Ire. 38/C2
Newtown Mount Kennedy, Ire. 40/B5
Newtown Saint Boswells, Sc, UK 39/D5
Newtown Sandes, Ire. 38/A4
Newtown Square, Pa, US 198/C4
Newtownabbey, NI, UK 40/C2
Newtownards, NI, UK 40/C2
Newtownbutler, NI, UK 38/C1

314
Newto – Northa

Newtownhamilton, NI, UK 40/B3
Newtownstewart, NI, UK 40/A2
Newtyle, Sc, UK 39/C3
Newville, Al, US 195/F2
Nextlalpan, Mex. 205/Q9
Neyagawa, Japan 95/J6
Neyrīz, Iran 115/H4
Neyshābūr, Iran 113/G1
Neyva (riv.), Rus. 75/P4
Neyveli, India 107/C4
Neyyāttinkara, India 107/C4
Nez de Jobourg (pt.), Fr. 62/D1
Nez Perce Ind. Res., Id, US 174/F4
Nezahualcóyotl, Mex. 205/Q10
Nezlobnaya, Rus. 77/G3
Neznayka (riv.), Rus. 75/W9
Nezperce, Id, US 174/F4
Nezvěstice, Czh. 65/G3
Ngabang, Indo. 102/C3
Ngabé, Congo 138/D3
Ngabordamlu (cape), Indo. 152/D1
Ngabu, Malw. 141/G3
Ngabwe, Zam. 141/E2
Ngaga, Tanz. 137/B4
Ngahere, NZ 159/B3
Ngai-Ndethya Nat'l Rsv., Kenya 137/B2
Ngalipaeng, Indo. 103/G3
Ngaloua, Niger 134/B2
Ngalu, Indo. 103/F6
Ngama, Chad 134/C3
Ngamanu Bird Sanct., NZ 159/J8
Ngambé, Camr. 138/B1
Ngambwe (falls), Zam. 140/E3
Ngamda, China 98/C2
Ngami (lake), Bots. 140/D4
Ngamiland (dist.), Bots. 140/D3
Ngamring, China 109/F1
Nganda (peak), Malw. 137/A4
Ngangerabeli (plain), Kenya 137/B2
Ngangla Ringco (lake), China 111/D5
Ngangzê (lake), China 111/E5
Nganha, Montagne de (peak), Camr. 134/B4
Ngao, Thai. 106/B2
Ngaoundal, Camr. 134/B4
Ngaoundéré, Camr. 134/B4
Ngapara, NZ 159/B4
Ngara, Tanz. 139/G3
Ngaras, Indo. 101/D4
Ngarkat Consv. Park, Austl. 155/J5
Ngaruawahia, NZ 159/C2
Ngatapa, NZ 159/D2
Ngathainggyaung, Myan. 98/B5
Ngatik (isl.), Micr. 160/E4
Ngato, Camr. 138/C2
Ngau (isl.), Fiji 161/Y18
Ngauruhoe (vol.), NZ 159/C2
Ngawi, Indo. 101/E4
Ngele, D.R. Congo 138/D2
Ngerengere, Tanz. 137/B3
Nghia Dan, Viet. 106/D2
Nghia Lo, Viet. 106/D1
Ngidinga, D.R. Congo 138/C4
Ngiva, Ang. 140/B3
Ngo, Congo 138/C3
Ngoan Muc (pass), Viet. 106/E4
Ngoc Linh (peak), Viet. 105/J4
Ngofakiaha, Indo. 103/G3
Ngogwa, Tanz. 139/H3
Ngoïla, Camr. 138/C2
Ngoko (riv.), Camr. 138/C2
Ngolo, Chutes de (falls), CAfr. 134/D4
Ngom (falls), EqG. 138/B2
Ngom (falls), EqG. 138/B2
Ngomahuru, Zim. 141/F4
Ngomedzap, Camr. 138/B2
Ngomeni (cape), Kenya 137/C2
Ngong, Kenya 137/B2
Ngonye (falls), Zam. 140/D3
Ngoqumaima, China 111/E5
Ngora, Ugan. 137/A1
Ngoring (lake), China 90/D5
Ngorongoro Consv. Area, Tanz. 137/A2
Ngoto, CAfr. 138/D2
Ngotwane (riv.), Bots. 141/E5
Ngoulemakong, Camr. 138/B2
Ngounié (riv.), Gabon 138/B3
Ngounié (prov.), Gabon 138/B3
Ngoura, Chad 134/C2
Ngouri, Chad 134/B2
Ngourti, Niger 134/B2
N'Goutcheï (well), Chad 134/C1
Ngouyo, CAfr. 135/E4
Ngoywa, Tanz. 139/H4
Ngozi, Buru. 139/G3
Ngudu, Tanz. 137/A2
Nguélémendouka, Camr. 134/B4
Nguigmi, Niger 134/B2
Nguiu, Austl. 152/C2
Ngukurr, Austl. 152/D3
Ngulu (isl.), Micr. 160/C4
Ngumbe Sukani (pt.), Tanz. 137/B4
Ngundu Halt, Zim. 141/F4
Ngunga, Tanz. 137/A2
Ngunza, Ang. 140/B1
Ngurah Rai (int'l arpt.), Indo. 101/F5
Nguru (mts.), Tanz. 137/B3
Nguti, Camr. 133/H5
Nguyen Binh, Viet. 98/E4
Ngwedaung, Myan. 98/C5
Ngwenya (peak), Swaz. 143/E2
Ngwerere, Zam. 141/F2
Nha Trang, Viet. 106/E3
Nhamunda (riv.), Braz. 209/D3
Nhamundá, Braz. 218/B3
Nhandeara, Braz. 225/G2
Nhandugue (riv.), Moz. 141/G3
Nhangue-ia-Pepe, Ang. 138/C5
Nharêa, Ang. 140/C1
Nhia (riv.), Ang. 138/C5
Nhill, Austl. 156/B3
Nhlangano, Swaz. 143/E2
Nho Quan, Viet. 98/E4
Nhulunbuy, Austl. 153/E3
Nia-Nia, D.R. Congo 139/F2
Niabembe, D.R. Congo 139/F3
Niafounké, Mali 132/E3
Niagara, Wi, US 187/L5
Niagara (falls), Can.,US 190/U9
Niagara (co.), On, Can. 190/U9
Niagara (riv.), On, Can. 190/U9
Niagara Cave, Mn, US 185/H2
Niagara Falls, On, Can. 190/U9
Niagara Falls, NY, US 190/U9
Niagara-on-the-Lake, On, Can. 190/U9
Niagassola, Gui. 132/C3
Niakaramandougou, C.d'Iv. 132/D4
Niamey (int'l arpt.), Niger 133/F3
Niamey (cap.), Niger 133/F3
Niamey (dept.), Niger 133/F3
Niamtougou, Togo 133/F4
Niandan (riv.), Afr. 133/G5
Niangara, D.R. Congo 139/F2
Niangay (lake), Mali 132/E3
Niangoloko, Burk. 132/D4
Niangua (riv.), Mo, US 183/H2
Niangua, Mo, US 183/H2
Niangzi (pass), China 92/C3
Niantic, Ct, US 191/K4
Niari (pol. reg.), Congo 138/B3
Niari (riv.), Congo 138/C3
Nias (isl.), Indo. 83/J9
Niassa (prov.), Moz. 137/A4
Nibbar, Tun. 130/L6
Nibley, Ut, US 177/H3
Nibong Tebal, Malay. 101/C1
Nīca, Lat. 47/J3
Nicaragua (ctry.) 207/E3
Nicaragua (lake), Nic. 207/E4
Nicastro-Sambiase, It. 54/E3
Nicatous (lake), Me, US 188/C3
Nice, Fr. 70/D5
Niceville, Fl, US 195/E2
Nichelino, It. 70/D3
Nicheng, China 92/L9
Nichinan, Japan 96/B5
Nichlaul, India 108/D2
Nicholas (chan.), Bang. 207/F1
Nicholasville, Ky, US 192/E2
Nicholls, Ga, US 195/G2
Nichols, Fl, US 194/L8
Nichols, SC, US 193/H3
Nicholson (range), Austl. 154/C3
Nicholson, Austl. 152/C4
Nicholson (riv.), Austl. 153/E4
Nickby (Nikkilä), Fin. 45/F4
Nickelsville, Va, US 193/F2
Nickerie (dist.), Sur. 217/G3
Nickerie (riv.), Sur. 217/G3
Nickol (bay), Austl. 154/C2
Nicobar (isls.), India 83/J9
Nicodemus Nat'l Hist. Site, Ks, US 184/E4
Nicola Mameet Ind. Res., BC, Can. 174/D2
Nicolás Bravo, Mex. 206/D2
Nicolás Romero, Mex. 205/Q9
Nicolet, Qu, Can. 191/K1
Nicollet, Mn, US 185/G1
Nicolls (pt.), NY, US 199/E2
Nicosia, It. 54/D4
Nicosia (dist.), Cyp. 116/C2
Nicosia (cap.), Cyp. 116/C2
Nicotera, It. 54/D3
Nicoya, CR 207/E4
Nicoya (gulf), CR 207/E4
Nicoya (pen.), CR 207/E4
Nictau, NB, Can. 188/D2
Nictaux, NS, Can. 188/E3
Nidau, Swi. 66/D3
Nidd (riv.), Eng, UK 41/G3
Nidd (riv.), Eng, UK 41/G4
Nidda, Ger. 64/B2
Nidda (riv.), Ger. 48/E3
Niddatal, Ger. 64/B2
Nidder (riv.), Ger. 64/C2
Nideggen, Ger. 61/F2
Nidong, China 98/E3
Nidwalden (canton), Swi. 67/E4
Nidzica, Pol. 49/L2
Niebüll, Ger. 46/C4
Nied (riv.), Fr. 51/G2
Niedenstein, Ger. 59/G6
Nieder-Olm, Ger. 61/H4
Niederanven, Lux. 61/F4
Niederbipp, Swi. 66/D3
Niederbronn-les-Bains, Fr. 61/G6
Niedere Tauern (mts.), Aus. 73/G1
Niederfischbach, Ger. 61/G2
Niederlausitz (reg.), Ger. 49/G3
Niedernhausen, Ger. 64/B2
Niederösterreich (prov.), Aus. 56/B2
Niedersachsen (state), Ger. 46/C5
Niedersächsisches Wattenmeer NP, Ger. 59/E1
Niedersachswerfen, Ger. 59/H5
Niederstetten, Ger. 64/C4
Niederstotzingen, Ger. 64/D5
Niederurnen, Swi. 67/F3
Niederwerrn, Ger. 64/D2
Niederwinkling, Ger. 65/F5
Niederzier, Ger. 61/F2
Niederzissen, Ger. 61/G3
Niefang, EqG. 138/B2
Niefern-Öschelbronn, Ger. 64/B5
Niegocin (lake), Pol. 47/J5
Nieheim, Ger. 59/G5
Niélé, C.d'Iv. 132/D4
Niem, CAfr. 134/B4
Niemba, D.R. Congo 139/G4
Niemodlin, Pol. 49/J3
Nienburg, Ger. 59/G3
Nienhagen, Ger. 59/H3
Niénokoué (peak), C.d'Iv. 132/D5
Nieppe, Fr. 60/B2
Niéri (riv.), Sen. 132/B3
Niers (riv.), Ger. 61/F1
Nierstein, Ger. 64/B3
Niet Ban Tinh Xa, Viet. 106/D4
Nieuw Krai Ker, Indo. 152/D1
Nieuw-Amsterdam, Sur. 218/C1
Nieuw-Bergen, Neth. 58/D5
Nieuw-Buinen, Neth. 58/D3
Nieuw-Loosdrecht, Neth. 58/C4
Nieuw-Nickerie, Sur. 217/G3
Nieuw-Schoonebeek, Neth. 58/D3
Nieuw-Vossemeer, Neth. 58/B5
Nieuwe Pekela, Neth. 58/D2
Nieuwegein, Neth. 58/C4
Nieuwendam, Neth. 58/B4
Nieuwerkerk aan de Ijssel, Neth. 58/B5
Nieuweschans, Neth. 59/E2
Nieuwkoop, Neth. 58/B4
Nieuwleusen, Neth. 58/D3
Nieuwoudtville, SAfr. 142/B3
Nieuwpoort, Belg. 60/B1
Nieuwpoort-Bad, Belg. 60/B1
Nieve, Bol. 221/E4
Nieves, Mex. 204/E3
Nīfī Ya'qūb, WBnk. 117/C5
Niğde, Turk. 114/C2
Niğde (prov.), Turk. 114/C2
Nigel, SAfr. 142/E2
Niger (delta), Nga. 133/G5
Niger (riv.), Nga. 132/C4
Niger (ctry.) 119/C3
Niger (riv.), Afr. 119/C4
Niger, Mouths of the, Nga. 133/G5
Nigeria (ctry.) 119/C4
Nigg (bay), Sc, UK 39/B1
Nightcaps, NZ 159/B4
Nighthawk, Wa, US 174/E3
Nightmute, Ak, US 201/F3
Nigrán, Sp. 52/A1
Nigríta, Gre. 55/H2
Nīḩā (peak), Leb. 117/D1
Nihoa (isl.), Hi, US 161/J2
Nihonmatsu, Japan 97/G2
Nihtaur, India 108/B1
Nii (isl.), Japan 97/F3
Niigata, Japan 97/F2
Niigata (int'l arpt.), Japan 97/F2
Niigata (pref.), Japan 94/A4
Niihama, Japan 96/C4
Niihari, Japan 95/E1
Niihau (isl.), Hi, US 172/R10
Niimi, Japan 96/C3
Niitsu, Japan 97/F2
Niiza, Japan 95/D2
Níjar, Sp. 52/D4
Nijkerk, Neth. 58/C4
Nijlen, Belg. 61/D1
Nijmegen, Neth. 58/C5
Nijverdal, Neth. 58/D4
Níkaia, Gre. 55/H3
Nikel', Rus. 44/J1
Nikel'tau, Kaz. 77/L2
Nikiniki, Indo. 152/B2
Nikishka, Ak, US 201/H3
Nikísiani, Gre. 55/J2
Nikitovka, Rus. 79/K2
Nikki, Ben. 133/F4
Nikkilä (Nickby), Fin. 45/F4
Nikkō, Japan 97/F2
Nikkō NP, Japan 97/F2
Niklá al 'Inab, Egypt 131/B3
Niklasdorf, Aus. 51/L3
Nikolaevo, Bul. 57/G4
Nikolai, Ak, US 201/H3
Nikolayevka, Rus. 77/H1
Nikolayevka, Ukr. 78/F4
Nikolayevka, Ukr. 79/J3
Nikolayevo, Rus. 47/N2
Nikolayevsk, Rus. 77/H2
Nikolayevsk-na-Amure, Rus. 81/Q4
Nikol'sk, Rus. 77/H1
Nikolski, Ak, US 201/E5
Nikol'skiy Torzhok, Rus. 74/H4
Nikol'skoye, Rus. 77/H3
Nikol'skoye, Rus. 81/S4
Nikonga (riv.), Tanz. 139/G3
Nikonova Gora, Rus. 74/H3
Nikopol', Ukr. 79/H4
Nikopol, Bul. 57/G4
Niksar, Turk. 76/F4
Nīkshahr, Iran 113/H3
Nikšíc, Mont. 56/D4
Nikumaroro (Gardner) (isl.), Kiri. 161/H5
Nikunau (isl.), Kiri. 160/G5
Nikurān, India 110/D5
Nila (isl.), Indo. 152/C1
Niland, Ca, US 178/E4
Nilaveli, SrL. 107/D4
Nile (riv.), Afr. 119/F2
Nile (delta), Egypt 112/B2
Niles, Il, US 197/Q15
Niles, Mi, US 190/C4
Niles, Oh, US 190/F4
Ni'līn, WBnk. 117/C5
Nilo, Col. 219/L8
Nilópolis, Braz. 223/N7
Nilphāmāri, Bang. 109/G3
Nilsiä, Fin. 74/F3
Nilvange, Fr. 61/F5
Nīmach, India 104/B3
Nīmāj, India 104/B2
Niman (riv.), Rus. 91/L1
Nimba (co.), Libr. 132/C5
Nimba (peak), C.d'Iv. 132/C5
Nîmes, Fr. 50/F5
Nimmitabel, Austl. 157/D3
Nimpo Lake, BC, Can. 174/B1
Nimrod's Fortress (ruin), Syria 117/D2
Nimsbach (riv.), Ger. 61/F4
Nimu, India 110/D2
Nimule, Sudan 139/H2
Nimule NP, Sudan 139/G2
Nin, Cro. 56/B3
Ninaview, Co, US 182/C2
Nīnawā (gov.), Iraq 114/E3
Nīnawá (Nineveh) (ruin), Iraq 115/E2
Nine Point (mesa), Tx, US 180/C3
Ninepin Group (isls.), China 99/M8
Ninepipe Nat'l Wild. Ref., Mt, US 175/G4
Ninety Mile Beach (isl.), NZ 159/C1
Ninety Mile Beach (coast), Austl. 157/C4
Ninety Six, SC, US 193/F3
Ninety Six Nat'l Hist. Site, SC, US 193/F3
Nineveh (Nīnawá) (ruin), Iraq 115/E2
Ninfa (ruin), It. 71/B4
Ninfas (pt.), Arg. 226/D4
Ning'an, China 91/K3
Ningbo, China 92/E5
Ningerum, PNG 153/F1
Ninggang, China 99/G3
Ningguo, China 99/H2
Ninghe, China 92/H7
Ningjin, China 92/C3
Ningjin, China 92/D3
Ningjing (mts.), China 98/C2
Ninglang Yizu Zizhixian, China 98/D3
Ningling, China 92/C4
Ningming, China 99/E4
Ningwu, China 92/C3
Ningxia Zizhiqu (aut. reg.), China 90/F4
Ningyang, China 92/D4
Ningyuan, China 105/K2
Ninh Binh, Viet. 106/D1
Ninh Hoa, Viet. 106/E3
Ninian (riv.), Fr. 62/C4
Ninilchik, Ak, US 201/H3
Niningo (isls.), PNG 160/D5
Ninnescah (riv.), Ks, US 183/F2
Ninohe, Japan 94/B3
Ninomiya, Japan 95/C3
Ninove, Belg. 60/D2
Ninoy Aquino (int'l arpt.), Phil. 100/F6
Nioaque, Braz. 225/F2
Nioaque (riv.), Braz. 222/A4
Niobrara, Ne, US 184/E2
Niobrara (riv.), Ne,Wy, US 184/B2
Niokolo Koba, Sen. 132/B3
Niokolo-Koba, PN du, Sen. 132/B3
Nioku, India 98/B3
Niong (peak), Camr. 134/B4
Niono, Mali 132/D3
Nionsamoridougou, Gui. 132/C4
Nioro du Sahel, Mali 132/C3
Nioro-du-Rip, Sen. 132/B3
Niort, Fr. 50/C3
Nioumachoua, Com. 143/G6
Nipāni, India 107/B2
Nipawin, Sk, Can. 170/F3
Nipe (bay), Cuba 207/H1
Nipele (riv.), Namb. 140/C3
Nipigon (bay), On, Can. 187/K3
Nipigon (riv.), On, Can. 187/K3
Nipigon, On, Can. 187/K3
Nipigon (lake), On, Can. 170/G3
Nipissing (lake), On, Can. 171/J4
Nipomo, Ca, US 178/B3
Nippersink (cr.), Il, US 197/P15
Nipton, Ca, US 178/E3
Niqually (riv.), Wa, US 174/C4
Ñiquén, Chile 226/C3
Niquero, Cuba 207/G1
Nīr, Iran 115/F2
Nir Yizhaq, Isr. 117/A6
Nirasaki, Japan 97/F3
Nirayama, Japan 95/B3
Ñireguao, Chile 226/C5
Nirimba Army Afld., Austl. 158/G8
Nirmal, India 107/C2
Nirmāli, India 109/F2
Niš, Serb. 56/E4
Niš (int'l arpt.), Serb. 56/E4
Nişāb, SAr. 115/F4
Nişāb, Yem. 136/C2
Nišava (riv.), Serb. 55/H1
Niscemi, It. 54/D4
Nishiazai, Japan 95/K5
Nishibiwajima, Japan 95/L5
Nishiharu, Japan 95/L5
Nishikatsura, Japan 95/B2
Nishiki (riv.), Japan 96/B3
Nishiki, Japan 95/H5
Nishinomiya, Japan 95/H6
Nishino'omote, Japan 96/B5
Nishio, Japan 95/M6
Nishiwaki, Japan 95/G6
Nisko, Pol. 49/M3
Nisland, SD, US 184/C1
Nisporeni, Mol. 78/E4
Nisqually (riv.), Wa, US 197/B3
Nisqually, Wa, US 197/B3
Nisqually Ind. Res., Wa, US 197/B3
Nisqually Nat'l Wild. Ref., Wa, US 174/C4
Nisqually Reach (str.), Wa, US 197/B3
Nissan (isl.), PNG 160/E5
Nissan, Fr. 53/G1
Nisser (lake), Nor. 46/C2
Nisshin, Japan 95/M5
Nissum (bay), Den. 46/C3
Nisswa, Mn, US 187/G4
Nistru (riv.), Mol.,Ukr. 78/D3
Nistru (riv.), Mol. 57/H1
Nitelva (riv.), Nor. 44/S8
Niterói, Braz. 223/N7
Nith (riv.), Sc, UK 39/C6
Nith (riv.), Sc, UK 40/E1
Nithsdale (valley), Sc, UK 40/E1
Niti (pass), India 111/C5
Nítibe, ETim. 152/B2
Niton Junction, Ab, Can. 174/G1
Nitra (riv.), Slvk. 49/K4
Nitriansky (pol. reg.), Slvk. 49/K4
Nitsa (riv.), Rus. 75/P4
Nitta, Japan 95/C1
Nittedal, Nor. 46/D1
Nittel, Ger. 61/F4
Nittenau, Ger. 65/F4
Niuafo'ou (isl.), Tonga 161/H6
Niuatoputapu Group (isls.), Tonga 161/H6
Niubiziliang, China 111/F4
Niuchang, China 99/E3
Niue (terr.), NZ 161/H7
Niue (isl.), Niue 161/J6
Niulakita (isl.), Tuv. 160/G6
Niulan (riv.), China 105/H2
Niumaowu, China 93/C2
Niut (peak), Indo. 102/C3
Niutao (isl.), Tuv. 160/G5
Niutou (isl.), China 99/J2
Niutoudian, China 99/F1
Niuwudu (cape), Indo. 152/A2
Niuxintai, China 93/B2
Niuzhuang, China 93/B2
Nivå, Den. 45/J7
Nivelles, Belg. 61/D2
Nivernais (hill), Fr. 50/E3
Niverville, Mb, Can. 186/F3
Niverville, NY, US 191/K3
Niwot, Co, US 184/B3
Nixa, Mo, US 183/H2
Nixi, China 98/C3
Nixon, Nv, US 176/D4
Nixon, Tx, US 181/F3
Niya (riv.), China 111/D4
Niyodo (riv.), Japan 96/C4
Nizāmābād, India 107/C2
Nizhegorodskaya Oblast, Rus. 77/G1
Nizhnekama (res.), Rus. 75/M4
Nizhnekamsk, Rus. 75/L5
Nizhneudinsk, Rus. 81/K4
Nizhnevartovsk, Rus. 80/H3
Nizhneyansk, Rus. 81/P2
Nizhniy Baskunchak, Rus. 77/H2
Nizhniy Chir, Rus. 77/G2
Nizhniy Lomov, Rus. 77/G1
Nizhniy Novgorod, Rus. 75/K4
Nizhniy Tagil, Rus. 75/N4
Nizhniy Yenangsk, Rus. 75/K4
Nizhnyaya Pesha, Rus. 75/K2
Nizhnyaya Tura, Rus. 75/N4
Nizhnyaya Voch', Rus. 75/M3
Nizhyn, Ukr. 78/F2
Nizip, Turk. 114/D2
Nízke Tatry NP, Slvk. 76/A2
Nizwá, Oman 113/G4
Nizza Monferrato, It. 68/B4
Nizzanim, Isr. 117/B5
Njardhvík, Ice. 44/M7
Njombe, Tanz. 137/A4
Njombe (riv.), Tanz. 137/A3
Njoro, Kenya 137/A2
Nkandla, SAfr. 143/E3
Nkayi, Congo 138/C4
Nkeni (riv.), Congo 138/C3
Nkhata Bay, Malw. 141/G1
Nkhotakota, Malw. 141/G2
Nkomfap, Nga. 133/H5
Nkomi (lag.), Gabon 138/B3
Nkonde, Tanz. 139/G4
N'Kongsamba, Camr. 138/B1
Nkourala, Mali 132/D4
Nkout (peak), Camr. 138/C2
Nkululu (riv.), Tanz. 137/A3
Nkusi (riv.), Ugan. 139/G2
Nmai (riv.), Myan. 105/G2
Nnewi, Nga. 133/G5
Noailles, Fr. 60/B5
Noākhāli (pol. reg.), Bang. 109/H4
Noākhāli, Bang. 109/H4
Noale, It. 69/F2
Noāmundi, India 109/E4
Noank, Ct, US 199/F1
Noatak, Ak, US 201/F2
Noatak (riv.), Ak, US 201/F2
Nobber, Ire. 38/D2
Nobeoka, Japan 96/B4
Noble, Ok, US 183/F3
Noble, La, US 180/H2
Nobleford, Ab, Can. 175/H3
Noblesville, In, US 190/C4
Nobleton, Fl, US 194/L6
Nobleton, On, Can. 190/T8
Noboa, Ecu. 216/A5
Noboribetsu, Japan 94/B2
Nobres, Braz. 221/G4
Nocatee, Fl, US 195/H4
Noccundra, Austl. 158/A4
Noce (riv.), It. 67/G5
Nocelleto, It. 71/D5
Nocera Inferiore, It. 71/D6
Nocera Superiore, It. 71/D6
Nocera Umbra, It. 71/B1
Noceto, It. 68/D4
Noci, It. 55/E2
Nockamixon St. Park, Pa, US 198/C3
Nocona, Tx, US 183/F4
Noda, Japan 95/D2
Nodagawa, Japan 95/H4
Nodaway (riv.), Mo, US 185/G3
Nødebo, Den. 45/J7
Nodgrass (hill), Tn, US 192/D3
Noé (cape), Alg. 130/D2
Noel, Mo, US 183/G2
Noëlville, On, Can. 190/F1
Noetinger, Arg. 224/D5
Nogales, Az, US 179/G5
Nogales, Mex. 205/M8
Nogara, It. 69/E3
Nogara, Eth. 135/H2
Nogaro, Fr. 50/C5
Nogat (riv.), Pol. 47/H4
Nogata, Japan 96/B4
Nogent, Fr. 66/B1
Nogent-l'Artaud, Fr. 60/C6
Nogent-le-Roi, Fr. 63/G3
Nogent-le-Rotrou, Fr. 63/F4
Nogent-sur-Oise, Fr. 60/B5
Nogi, Japan 95/D1
Noginsk, Rus. 75/X9
Nogliki, Rus. 81/Q4
Nogoa (riv.), Austl. 158/B4
Nogodan-san (peak), SKor. 93/D5
Nogoonnuur, Mong. 111/F2
Nogoyá, Arg. 224/E5
Nógrád (co.), Hun. 49/K5
Nogwak-san (peak), SKor. 96/A2
Nohar, India 110/C5
Noheji, Japan 94/B3
Nohfelden, Ger. 61/G4
Nohkú, (pt.), Mex. 206/E2
Nohwa, SKor. 91/K5
Noi (riv.), Laos 106/D2
Noi (riv.), Viet. 105/J5
Noidans-lès-Vesoul, Fr. 66/C2
Noire (riv.), Qu, Can. 191/H1
Noireau (riv.), Fr. 63/E3
Noires, (mts.), Fr. 50/B2
Noirmoutier (isl.), Fr. 50/B3
Noisiel, Fr. 60/B6
Noisy-le-Grand, Fr. 36/K5
Noisy-le-Mec, Fr. 36/K5
Noisy-le-Roi, Fr. 36/J5
Nojima-zaki (pt.), Japan 97/F3
Nokaneng, Bots. 140/D3
Nokia, Fin. 47/K1
Nokilalaki (peak), Indo. 103/F4
Nokomis, Sk, Can. 186/B2
Nokomis, Il, US 185/K4
Nokou, Chad 134/B2
Nola, It. 71/D6
Nola, CAfr. 138/D2
Nolan (riv.), Tx, US 180/K7
Nolanville, Tx, US 180/F2
Nole, It. 70/D2
Nolensville, Tn, US 192/D3
Noli, It. 68/B5
Noli, Capo di (cape), It. 68/B5
Nolichucky (riv.), Tn, US 193/F2
Nolin River (lake), Ky, US 192/D2
Nolinsk, Rus. 75/L4
Noma, Fl, US 195/F2
Nomad, PNG 153/F1
Nomadgi NP, Austl. 156/D2
Nombre de Dios (mts.), Hon. 206/E3
Nombre de Dios, Mex. 204/D4
Nomburg, Rus. 75/L2
Nome, Ak, US 201/E3
Nome (cape), Ak, US 201/F3
Nomény, Fr. 61/F6
Nomexy, Fr. 66/C1
Nomgon, Mong. 90/F3
Nomo-misaki (cape), Japan 96/B5
Nomo-zaki (pt.), Japan 96/A4
Nomtsas, Namb. 140/C5
Non Sung, Thai. 106/C3
Nonacho (lake), NW, Can. 170/F2
Nonancourt, Fr. 63/G3
Nonantola, It. 69/E4
Nondalton, Ak, US 201/H4
Nondwa, Tanz. 137/A3
None, It. 70/D3
Nonette (riv.), Fr. 60/B5
Nong Bua Lamphu, Thai. 106/C2
Nong Chang, Thai. 106/B3
Nong Han (res.), Thai. 106/D2
Nong Het, Laos 106/C2
Nong Khai, Thai. 106/C2
Nong Pet, Laos 106/C2
Nong Phai, Thai. 106/C3
Nong'an, China 91/K3
Nongempulu, D.R. Congo 139/E3
Nongenturi, D.R. Congo 138/D3
Nongoma, SAfr. 143/E2
Nongstoin, India 109/H3
Nonnweiler, Ger. 61/F4
Nonoava, Mex. 204/D3
Nonogasta, Arg. 224/C4
Nonouti (isl.), Kiri. 160/G5
Nonri (isl.), China 92/E5
Nonsan, SKor. 93/D4
Nontron, Fr. 50/D4
Nooksack, Wa, US 174/C3
Noonan, ND, US 186/C3
Noonday, Tx, US 181/G1
Noonkanbah Abor. Land, Austl. 152/B4
Noord Holland (prov.), Neth. 58/B3
Noord-Brabant (prov.), Neth. 58/C5
Noordbeveland (isl.), Neth. 58/A5
Noorderhaaks (isl.), Neth. 58/B3
Noordhollandsch Kan. (riv.), Neth. 58/B3
Noordoewer, Namb. 142/B3
Noordostpolder (polder), Neth. 58/C3
Noordwijk aan Zee, Neth. 58/B4
Noordwijk-Binnen, Neth. 58/B4
Noordwijkerhout, Neth. 58/B4
Noordzeekan. (canal), Neth. 58/B4
Noormarkku, Fin. 47/J1
Noorvik, Ak, US 201/F2
Nóqui, Ang. 138/C4
Nor Achin, Arm. 115/F1
Nora, Swe. 46/F2
Nora, Va, US 193/F2
Nora (riv.), Rus. 91/L1
Norala, Phil. 100/D4
Noranside, Austl. 155/J2
Norassouba, Gui. 132/C4
Norberg, Swe. 46/F1
Norberto de la Riestra, Arg. 191/J11
Norborne, Mo, US 185/H4
Norcatur, Ks, US 184/D4
Norchia (ruin), It. 71/A3
Norcia, It. 71/C2
Norco, Ca, US 196/C3
Norcross, Ga, US 193/M7
Nord (prov.), Fr. 60/C3
Nord (prov.), Camr. 134/B3
Nord (riv.), Qu, Can. 189/M6
Nord, (canal), Fr. 60/B4
Nord-Ostsee (Kiel) (canal), Ger. 59/G1
Nord-Ouest (prov.), Camr. 133/H5
Nord-Ouest (pol. reg.), Mor. 130/B2
Nord-Pas-de-Calais (pol. reg.), Fr. 43/H6
Nord-Radde (riv.), Ger. 59/E3
Nord-Sud Kanal (canal), Ger. 59/E3
Nord-Trøndelag (co.), Nor. 44/E2
Nordborg, Den. 46/C4
Nordby, Den. 46/D4
Norddeich, Ger. 59/E1
Nordegg, Ab, Can. 174/F1
Nordegg (riv.), Ab, Can. 174/G1
Nordela (int'l arpt.), Azor., Port. 53/T13
Norden, Ger. 59/E1
Nordenham, Ger. 59/F1
Nordenskjöld (arch.), Rus. 80/J2
Norderney (isl.), Neth. 59/E1
Norderney (arpt.), Ger. 59/E1
Norderney, Ger. 59/E1
Norderstedt, Ger. 59/G1
Nordeste, Ang. 139/E4
Nordhausen, Ger. 48/F3
Nordheim, Tx, US 181/F3
Nordholz, Ger. 59/F1
Nordhorn, Ger. 59/E4
Nordhouse, Fr. 66/D1
Nordjylland (co.), Den. 46/C3
Nordkapp, Nor. 44/H1
Nordkapp (cape), Nor. 44/H1
Nordkinn (pt.), Nor. 44/H1
Nordkirchen, Ger. 59/E5
Nordland (co.), Nor. 44/E2
Nordland, Wa, US 174/C3
Nördlingen, Ger. 64/D5
Nordmaling, Swe. 44/F3
Nordreisa, Nor. 44/G1
Nordrhein-Westfalen (state), Ger. 46/E3
Nords Wharf, Austl. 157/E1
Nordwalde, Ger. 59/E4
Nore (riv.), Ire. 38/C4
Nore, Pic de (peak), Fr. 50/E5
Noresund, Nor. 46/C1
Norfolk (dam), Ar, US 183/H2
Norfolk, NY, US 191/J2
Norfolk (isl.), Austl. 160/F7
Norfolk (mt.), Austl. 156/C4
Norfolk, Ne, US 184/F2
Norfolk, Va, US 193/J2
Norfolk Broads (swamp), Eng, UK 43/H1
Norfolk Nav. Base, Va, US 193/J2
Norg, Neth. 58/D2
Norheimsund, Nor. 46/B1
Norias, Tx, US 181/F4
Norikura-dake (peak), Japan 97/E2
Noril'sk, Rus. 80/J3
Norland, On, Can. 191/G2
Norlina, NC, US 193/H2
Norma, It. 71/B4
Normal, Il, US 185/K3
Norman (riv.), Austl. 153/F4
Norman, Ar, US 183/H3
Norman (lake), NC, US 193/G3
Norman, Ok, US 183/F3
Norman Manley (int'l arpt.), Jam. 207/G2
Norman Park, Ga, US 195/G2
Norman Wells, NW, Can. 170/D2
Normanby, Austl. 158/B1
Normanby (isl.), PNG 160/E6
Normandale Japanese Garden, Mn, US 187/P7
Normandie, Collines de (hill), Fr. 63/E3
Normandin, Qu, Can. 188/A1
Normandy, Eng, UK 36/B3
Normandy (reg.), Fr. 50/C2
Normandy, Tx, US 180/D3
Normandy Beach, NJ, US 199/D4
Normandy Park, Wa, US 197/C3
Normangee, Tx, US 181/F2
Norman's Cove, Nf, Can. 189/L2
Normanton, Austl. 158/A2
Normanton South, Eng, UK 41/G4
Norotshama (peak), Namb. 142/B3
Norquay, Sk, Can. 186/C2
Ñorquinco, Arg. 226/C4
Norrbotten (co.), Swe. 44/F2
Nørre Alslev, Den. 46/D4
Nørre Nebel, Den. 46/C4
Nørre Vorupør, Den. 46/C3
Norridge, Il, US 197/Q16
Norris, Tn, US 192/E2
Norris (lake), Tn, US 192/F2
Norris City, Il, US 192/C2
Norristown, Pa, US 198/C3
Norrköping, Swe. 46/G2
Norrland (reg.), Swe. 44/F2
Norröra (isl.), Swe. 45/C1
Norrsunda, Swe. 45/A1
Norrsundet, Swe. 46/G1
Norrtälje, Swe. 47/H2
Nors, Den. 46/C3
Norseman, Austl. 154/D5
Norsjö, Swe. 44/F2
Norsup, Van. 160/F6
Nort-sur-Erdre, Fr. 62/D6
Norte (pt.), Arg. 191/F3
Norte (pt.), Arg. 226/E4
Norte de Santander (dept.), Col. 207/H4
Norte de Santander (dept.), Col. 207/H4
Norte Los Rodeos (int'l arpt.), Sp. 128/A3
Norte, Canal do (chan.), Braz. 218/D2
Norte, Serra do (mts.), Braz. 221/G3
Nortelândia, Braz. 221/G4
Nörten-Hardenberg, Ger. 59/G5
North (pt.), Austl. 154/B4
North (pt.), Austl. 156/C4
North (pt.), Austl. 157/C4
North (cape), NS, Can. 188/F2
North (cape), NS, Can. 189/G2
North (chan.), On, Can. 190/E1
North (isl.), Kenya 135/G4
North (cape), NZ 159/C1
North (isl.), NZ 159/C2
North (sound), Sc, UK 37/V14
North (sea), Sc, UK 39/D4
North (chan.), UK 40/C1
North (cape), Ak, US 201/D5
North (pt.), Mi, US 190/E2
North (bay), Me, US 188/C
North (pt.), Md, US 198/B5
North, SC, US 193/G4
North (lake), Tx, US 180/L7
North Adams, Ma, US 191/K3
North Albanian Alps (mts.), Alb.,Mont. 56/D4
North America (cont.) 163/*
North Amherst, Ma, US 191/K3
North Andaman (isl.), India 105/F5
North Anna (riv.), Va, US 193/J1
North Arlington, NJ, US 199/J8
North Ascot, Eng, UK 36/A2
North Atlanta, Ga, US 193/M7
North Augusta, SC, US 193/G4
North Aurora, Il, US 197/P16
North Ayrshire (co.), Sc, UK 39/A5
North Baldy (peak), Wa, US 174/F3
North Ballachulish, Sc, UK 39/A3
North Baltimore, Oh, US 190/E4
North Battleford, Sk, Can. 175/K1
North Bay, On, Can. 191/G1
North Bay, Wi, US 197/Q14
North Beach, Md, US 198/B6
North Beach Haven, NJ, US 199/D4
North Bellmore, NY, US 199/L9
North Bend, BC, Can. 174/D3
North Bend, Or, US 176/A2
North Bend, Pa, US 191/H4
North Bend, Wa, US 197/D3
North Benfleet, Eng, UK 36/E2
North Bergen, NJ, US 199/J8
North Berwick, Sc, UK 39/D4
North Bosque (riv.), Tx, US 181/F2
North Bourke, Austl. 156/C1
North Branch, NJ, US 198/D2
North Branford, Ct, US 199/F1
North Brunswick, NJ, US 198/D3
North Caicos (isl.), UK 207/J1
North Caldwell, NJ, US 199/J8
North Canadian (riv.), Ok, US 183/E2
North Canton, Oh, US 190/F4
North Cape May, NJ, US 198/D6
North Caribou (lake), On, Can. 170/H3
North Carolina (state), US 193/G3
North Cascades NP, Wa, US 174/D3
North Central (plain), Tx, US 205/F1
North Central (prov.), SrL. 107/D4
North Charleston, SC, US 193/H4
North Chicago, Il, US 190/C3
North Collins, NY, US 191/G3
North Concho (riv.), Tx, US 180/D2
North Cowichan, BC, Can. 174/C3
North Crossett, Ar, US 183/J4
North Dakota (state), US 186/D4
North Dandalup, Austl. 154/B5
North Decatur, Ga, US 193/M7
North Dorset Downs (uplands), Eng, UK 42/D5
North Down (dist.), NI, UK 40/C2
North Druid Hills, Ga, US 193/M7
North Eagle Butte, SD, US 184/D1
North East (pt.), Austl. 158/C3
North East, Md, US 198/C4
North East, Pa, US 191/G3
North Eastern (prov.), Kenya 136/B5
North Edwards, Ca, US 178/D3
North Elmham, Eng, UK 43/G1
North English, Ia, US 185/H3
North Enid, Ok, US 183/F2
North Entrance (inlet), PNG 153/F2
North Esk (riv.), Sc, UK 39/D3
North Fabius (riv.), Mo,Ia, US 185/H3
North Fond du Lac, Wi, US 190/B3
North Foreland (pt.), Eng, UK 43/H4
North Fork (riv.), Ok, US 182/E3
North Fork (cr.), Tx, US 183/G4
North Fork (riv.), Tx, US 182/D4
North Fork, Ca, US 178/C2
North Fork, Id, US 177/G1
North Fork Kuskokwim (riv.), Ak, US 201/H3
North Fork Village, Oh, US 190/E5
North Fort Myers, Fl, US 195/H4
North Fox (isl.), Mi, US 187/M5
North Frisian (isls.), Ger. 48/D1
North Front (int'l arpt.), UK 128/D1
North Gauhāti, India 109/H2
North Haledon, NJ, US 199/J8
North Harlowe, NC, US 193/J3
North Haven, Ct, US 191/K4
North Head, NB, Can. 188/D3
North Hero, Vt, US 191/K2
North Highlands, Ca, US 197/L9
North Hodge, La, US 194/B1
North Hollywood (nbrhd.), Ca, US 196/F7
North Holmwood, Eng, UK 36/C3
North Horr, Kenya 135/H5
North Hudson, Wi, US 187/Q7
North Hutchinson (isl.), Fl, US 195/H4
North Hykeham, Eng, UK 41/H5
North Judson, In, US 190/C4
North Killdeer (mtn.), ND, US 186/C4
North Kingsville, Oh, US 190/F4
North Korea (ctry.) 93/D2
North Lakhimpur, India 98/B3
North Lanarkshire (co.), Sc, UK 39/C5
North Las Vegas, Nv, US 178/E2
North Lincolnshire (co.), Eng, UK 41/H4
North Lindenhurst, NY, US 199/M9
North Little Rock, Ar, US 183/H3
North Logan, Ut, US 177/H3
North Long Beach (nbrhd.), Ca, US 196/F8
North Loup (riv.), Ne, US 184/D2
North Luangwa NP, Zam. 139/H5
North Madison, Oh, US 190/F4
North Manchester, In, US 190/D4
North Manitou (isl.), Mi, US 190/C2
North Manitou, Mi, US 190/D2
North Miami, Fl, US 194/P11
North Miami Beach, Fl, US 194/P11
North Minch (The Minch) (str.), Sc, UK 37/Q8
North (mtn.), Pa, US 198/B1
North Muskegon, Mi, US 190/C3
North Myrtle Beach, SC, US 193/H4
North New River (canal), Fl, US 194/P10
North Newton, Ks, US 183/F1
North Ogden, Ut, US 177/H3
North Olmsted, Oh, US 190/F4
North Pacific (ocean) 26/A4
North Palm Beach, Fl, US 194/P9
North Pease (riv.), Tx, US 182/D3
North Pelham, On, Can. 190/U9
North Petherton, Eng, UK 42/C4
North Pine (riv.), Austl. 158/E6
North Plainfield, NJ, US 199/H9
North Platte (riv.), Wy, US 177/K3
North Platte, Ne, US 184/D3
North Platte Nat'l Wild.Ref., Ne, US 184/C3
North Pole 228/G
North Pole, Magnetic 228/N
North Pole, Ak, US 201/J3
North Port, Fl, US 195/G4
North Portal, Sk, Can. 186/C3
North Potomac, Md, US 198/A5
North Powder, Or, US 176/E1
North Prairie, Wi, US 197/P14
North Puyallup, Wa, US 197/C3
North Raccoon (riv.), Ia, US 185/G2
North Redington Beach, Fl, US 194/K8
North Richland Hills, Tx, US 180/K7
North Rim, Az, US 179/F2
North Ronaldsay (isl.), Sc, UK 37/V14
North Rustico, PE, Can. 188/F2
North Saanich, BC, Can. 174/C3
North Saint Paul, Mn, US 187/Q6
North Saskatchewan (riv.), Ab,Sk, Can. 170/E3
North Saskatchewan (riv.), Sk, Can. 175/K1
North Shields, Eng, UK 41/G2
North Siberian Lowland (plain), Rus. 80/K2
North Sister (peak), Or, US 176/C1
North Skunk (riv.), Ia, US 185/H3
North Somercotes, Eng, UK 41/J5
North Somerset (co.), Eng, UK 42/D4
North Spirit Lake, On, Can. 187/H1
North Stratford, NH, US 191/L2
North Sulphur (riv.), Tx, US 183/F4
North Sunderland, Eng, UK 39/E5
North Sydney, NS, Can. 189/G2
North Taranaki Bight (bay), NZ 145/H6
North Terre Haute, In, US 190/C5
North Thompson (riv.), BC, Can. 174/E2
North Thoresby, Eng, UK 41/H5
North Tidworth, Eng, UK 43/E4
North Tolsta, Sc, UK 37/Q7
North Tonawanda, NY, US 190/V9
North Tunica, Ms, US 192/B3
North Tyne (riv.), Eng, UK 41/F1
North Uist (isl.), Sc, UK 37/Q8
North Umpqua (riv.), Or, US 176/B2
North Valley Stream, NY, US 199/L9
North Vancouver, BC, Can. 170/D4
North Vernon, In, US 190/D5
North Wales, Pa, US 198/C3
North Walsham, Eng, UK 43/H1
North Weald Bassett, Eng, UK 36/D1
North West (cape), Austl. 154/B2
North West Frontier (prov.), Pak. 111/B4
North West Highlands (uplands), Sc, UK 37/R8
North Western (prov.), SrL. 107/C5
North Wheatley, Eng, UK 41/H5
North Wichita (riv.), Tx, US 182/E4
North Wildwood, NJ, US 198/D6
North Wilkesboro, NC, US 193/G2
North Wilton, Ct, US 199/E1
North Windham, Me, US 191/L3
North Wingfield, Eng, UK 41/G5
North York (city), On, Can. 190/T8
North York Moors NP, Eng, UK 41/G3
North Yorkshire (co.), Eng, UK 41/G3
North-East (dist.), Bots. 141/E4
North-West (prov.), SAfr. 140/E5
North-West Frontier (co.), India 110/A3
Northallerton, Eng, UK 41/G3
Northam, Austl. 154/C4
Northam, Eng, UK 42/B4
Northampton, Austl. 154/B4
Northampton, Eng, UK 43/F2
Northampton, Ma, US 191/K3
Northampton (co.), Pa, US 198/C2
Northampton, Pa, US 198/C2
Northampton Uplands (uplands), Eng, UK 43/E2

Pende – Pingy
319

Pender, Ne, US 185/F2
Pender (bay), Austl. 152/A4
Pender Bay Abor. Land, Austl. 152/A4
Pendik (nbrhd.), Turk. 115/N7
Pendjari (riv.), Burk. 133/F4
Pendjari, PN de la, Ben. 133/F4
Pendle (hill), Eng, UK 41/F4
Pendleton, In, US 190/D5
Pendleton, Or, US 176/D1
Pendleton Mil. Res., Va, US 193/K2
Pendolo, Indo. 103/F4
Pendopo, Indo. 101/C3
Pendroy, Mt, US 175/H3
Pene-Mende, D.R. Congo 139/G4
Peneda-Gerês, PN, Port. 52/A2
Penedo, Braz. 223/F1
Penegoes, Wal, UK 42/C1
Penetanguishene, On, Can. 190/G2
Penfield, Pa, US 191/G4
Peng Xian, China 98/D2
Penganga (riv.), India 104/C4
Penge (nbrhd.), Eng, UK 36/C2
Penge, SAfr. 141/F5
Penge, D.R. Congo 139/F4
Penggong, China 92/K9
Penghu (isls.), Tai. 99/H4
Penghu, China 99/H3
Penghu (Pescadores) (isls.), China 99/H4
Penglai, China 92/E3
Penglaizhen, China 98/E2
Penguin, Austl. 156/C4
Penha, Braz. 225/G3
Penhalonga, Zim. 141/G3
Penhir (pt.), Fr. 62/A4
Penhold, Ab, Can. 175/H1
Penibético (mts.), Sp. 52/D4
Penice (peak), It. 68/C4
Peniche, Port. 52/A3
Penicuik, Sc, UK 39/C5
Peninsula (pt.), NY, US 191/H3
Peninsula de Paria, PN, Ven. 217/F2
Peñíscola, Sp. 53/F2
Peñita, Chile 224/B4
Penitente, Serra do (mts.), Braz. 219/E5
Penkridge, Eng, UK 42/D1
Penmaenmawr, Wal, UK 40/E5
Penmarc'h (pt.), Fr. 62/A5
Penmarch, Fr. 62/A5
Penn, ND, US 186/E3
Penn Forest (res.), Pa, US 198/C2
Penn Hills, Pa, US 191/G4
Penn Yan, NY, US 191/H3
Penna (peak), It. 71/B1
Penna, Punta della (cape), It. 71/D3
Pennant (pt.), NS, Can. 188/F3
Pennant, Sk, Can. 175/K2
Pennask (mt.), BC, Can. 174/D3
Penne (pt.), It. 55/E2
Penne, It. 71/C3
Pennell (mt.), Ut, US 179/G2
Penner (riv.), India 104/C5
Penney Farms, Fl, US 195/H3
Penniac, NB, Can. 188/D2
Pennine Alps (mts.), Swi. 51/G4
Pennine Chain (mts.), Eng, UK 41/F2
Pennington, NJ, US 198/D3
Pennington Gap, Va, US 193/F2
Pennino (peak), It. 71/B1
Penns (cr.), Pa, US 198/A2
Penns Creek (mtn.), Pa, US 198/A2
Penns Grove, NJ, US 198/C4
Penns Park, Pa, US 198/D3
Pennsauken, NJ, US 198/C4
Pennsboro, WV, US 190/F5
Pennsburg, Pa, US 198/C3
Pennsville, NJ, US 198/C4
Pennsylvania (hill), NY, US 191/H3
Pennsylvania (state), US 191/G4
Penny (str.), Nun, Can. 171/S7
Pennypack (cr.), Pa, US 198/C3
Penobscot (bay), Me, US 188/C3
Penobscot (riv.), Me, US 188/C3
Peñol, Col. 219/K6
Penola, Austl. 156/B3
Peñón Blanco, Mex. 204/D3
Penon de Al Hoceima (isl.), Sp. 130/C2
Penong, Austl. 155/G4
Penonomé, Pan. 216/A2
Penpont, Sc, UK 40/E1
Penrhyn (Tongareva) (isl.), Cookls. 161/J5
Penrhyn Mawr (pt.), IM, UK 40/D5
Penrhyn Mawr (pt.), Wal, UK 40/D6
Penrith, Eng, UK 41/F2
Penrith (nbrhd.), Austl. 158/G8
Penrose, Co, US 182/B1
Penryn, Eng, UK 42/A6
Pensacola (mts.), Ant. 228/X
Pensacola, Fl, US 194/E2
Pensacola (bay), Fl, US 194/E2
Pensacola (dam), Ok, US 183/G2
Pense, Sk, Can. 186/B2
Penshurst, Eng, UK 36/D3
Penshurst, Austl. 156/B3
Pensiangan, Malay. 100/B4
Pensilva, Eng, UK 42/B5
Pensilvania, Col. 219/K7
Pentagon Fed. Govt. Res., Va, US 198/A6
Pentecost (isl.), Van. 160/F6
Pentecoste, Braz. 219/G3
Penteleu (peak), Rom. 57/H3
Penthalaz, Swi. 66/C4
Penticton, BC, Can. 174/E3
Penticton Ind. Res., BC, Can. 174/E3
Pentire (pt.), Eng, UK 42/B5
Pentland (hills), Sc, UK 39/C5
Pentland, Austl. 158/B3
Pentland Firth (inlet), Sc, UK 37/V14
Pentwater, Mi, US 190/C3
Pentyrch, Wal, UK 42/C3
Peñuelas, PN, Chile 226/N8
Penvénan, Fr. 62/B3
Pènwègon, Myan. 106/B2
Penwell, Tx, US 180/C2
Penwith (pen.), Eng, UK 42/A6
Penza, Rus. 77/H1
Penzenskaya Oblast, Rus. 77/G1
Penzance, Eng, UK 42/A6
Penzance, Sk, Can. 175/M2
Penzberg, Ger. 67/H2
Penzé (riv.), Fr. 62/B3
Penzhina (riv.), Rus. 81/S3
Penzhina (bay), Rus. 81/S3
Penzing, Ger. 67/G1
Penzlin, Ger. 48/G2
Peoria, Az, US 179/F4
Peoria, Il, US 185/K3
Pepe (cape), Cuba 207/F1
Pepel, SLeo. 132/B4
Pepin (lake), Mn,Wi, US 185/H1
Pepinster, Belg. 61/E2
Peqin, Alb. 55/F2
Pequaming, Mi, US 187/K4
Pequannock, NJ, US 199/H8
Pequea (cr.), Pa, US 198/B4
Pequeña Isla del Maíz (isl.), Nic. 207/F3
Pequest (riv.), NJ, US 198/D2
Pequot Lakes, Mn, US 187/G4
Perabumulih, Indo. 101/D3
Perai-Tepuí, Ven. 217/F3
Perak (riv.), Malay. 101/C1
Perak (state), Malay. 101/C1
Perales (riv.), Sp. 53/M9
Peralta, Sp. 52/E1
Peralta, Uru. 191/K10
Peralta, NM, US 179/J3
Pérama, Gre. 55/J5
Pérama, Gre. 55/N9
Peranāmbattu, India 107/C3
Percé, Qu, Can. 188/E1
Percée (peak), Fr. 66/C6
Percha (dam), NM, US 179/J4
Perche, Collines du (hills), Fr. 50/D2
Perchtoldsdorf, Aus. 57/N7
Percilla, Tx, US 181/G2
Percival, Sk, Can. 186/C2
Percival (lakes), Austl. 154/E2
Percy, Fr. 63/D3
Percy, Il, US 192/C1
Percy (isls.), Austl. 145/E3
Percy Isles (chan.), Austl. 158/C3
Perdekop, SAfr. 143/E2
Pérdhika, Gre. 55/G3
Perdido, Al, US 194/E2
Perdido (mtn.), Sp. 50/D5
Perdões, Braz. 222/D4
Perdue, Sk, Can. 175/L1
Perechyn, Ukr. 49/M4
Peregian Beach, Austl. 158/D4
Perehins'ke, Ukr. 78/C3
Pereira, Col. 219/K8
Pereira Barreto, Braz. 225/G2
Pereiro, Braz. 219/G4
Perelló, Sp. 53/F2
Peremëtnoye, Kaz. 77/J2
Peremyshl', Rus. 74/H5
Peremyshlyany, Ukr. 78/C3
Perenjori, Austl. 154/C4
Peresechnaya, Ukr. 79/H2
Pereshchepyne, Ukr. 79/H3
Pereslavl'-Zalesskiy, Rus. 74/H4
Peretola (int'l arpt.), It. 69/E6
Perevolotskiy, Rus. 77/K2
Pereyaslav-Khmel'nyts'kyy, Ukr. 78/F2
Pereyaslavka, Rus. 91/M2
Perg, Aus. 65/H6
Pergamino, Arg. 226/E2
Pergamum (ruin), Turk. 76/C5
Pergine Valsugana, It. 67/H5
Perham, Mn, US 187/G4
Peri-Mirim, Braz. 219/E3
Periam, Rom. 56/E2
Péribonca (riv.), Qu, Can. 188/B1
Perico, Cuba 207/F1
Perico, Arg. 224/C3
Pericos, Mex. 204/D3
Pericos, Mex. 204/D4
Peridot, Az, US 179/G4
Périers, Fr. 62/D2
Périgueux, Fr. 50/D4
Perijá (mts.), Ven. 207/H4
Peringat, Malay. 101/C1
Perisher Village, Austl. 157/D3
Peristéra (isl.), Gre. 55/H3
Peristéri, Gre. 55/N8
Perito Moreno, Arg. 226/C5
Perito Moreno, PN, Arg. 191/B5
Periyakulam, India 107/C4
Perkasie, Pa, US 198/C3
Perkins, Ok, US 183/F3
Perkins, Mi, US 190/C2
Perkins, Ga, US 193/G4
Perkinston, Ms, US 194/D2
Perkiomen (cr.), Pa, US 198/C3
Perl, Ger. 61/F5
Perlas (lag.), Nic. 202/E5
Perlas, (pt.), Nic. 207/F3
Perleberg, Ger. 48/F2
Perlez, Serb. 56/E3
Perlis (state), Malay. 106/B5
Perm', Rus. 75/N4
Përmet, Alb. 55/G2
Permian Basin Petroleum Museum, Tx, US 180/C2
Permskaya Oblast, Rus. 75/N4
Pernambuco (state), Braz. 219/G5
Pernate, It. 68/B3
Pernell, Ok, US 183/F3
Pernes-les-Fontaines, Fr. 70/B4
Pernik, Bul. 56/F4
Perniö, Fin. 47/K1
Peron (pen.), Austl. 154/B3
Peron, North (isl.), Austl. 152/C3
Péronne, Fr. 60/B4
Perosa Argentina, It. 70/D3
Perote, Al, US 195/F2
Perote, Mex. 205/M7
Pérouges, Fr. 66/B6
Perovo (nbrhd.), Rus. 75/W9
Perranporth, Eng, UK 42/A6
Perray (riv.), Fr. 36/H6
Perriers-sur-Andelle, Fr. 63/G2
Perrigny, Fr. 66/B4
Perrin, Tx, US 183/E4
Perrine, Fl, US 194/P11
Perris, Ca, US 196/C3
Perris (res.), Ca, US 196/C3
Perris St. Rec. Area, Ca, US 196/C3
Perro (lag.), NM, US 182/B3
Perron des Encombres (peak), Fr. 70/C2
Perros-Guirec, Fr. 62/B3
Perry (riv.), Nun, Can. 170/F2
Perry, Fl, US 195/G2
Perry (lake), Ks, US 185/G4
Perry, Ga, US 192/F4
Perry, Ia, US 185/G3
Perry, Mo, US 185/J4
Perry, Ok, US 183/F2
Perry (co.), Pa, US 198/A3
Perry Hall, Md, US 198/B5
Perryman, Md, US 198/B5
Perrysburg, Oh, US 190/E4
Perryton, Tx, US 182/D2
Perrytown, Ar, US 183/H4
Perryville, Ak, US 201/G4
Perryville, Ar, US 183/H3
Perryville, Ky, US 192/E2
Perryville, Md, US 198/B4
Perryville, Mo, US 192/C2
Perryville, Tn, US 192/C3
Persan, Fr. 36/J4
Persepolis (ruin), Iran 115/H4
Perseverancia, Bol. 221/F4
Pershagen, Swe. 45/A1
Pershore, Eng, UK 42/D2
Pershotravens'k, Ukr. 78/D2
Pershotravnevoye, Ukr. 79/J4
Pershotravnevoye, Ukr. 78/D2
Persian (gulf), Asia 83/D7
Perstorp, Swe. 46/E3
Pertandangan (cape), Indo. 101/C2
Perth, Austl. 156/C4
Perth, Austl. 154/K6
Perth (int'l arpt.), Austl. 154/K6
Perth, On, Can. 191/H2
Perth, Sc, UK 39/C4
Perth Amboy, NJ, US 199/H9
Perth and Kinross (co.), Sc, UK 39/C4
Perth Zoo, Austl. 154/K6
Perth-Andover, NB, Can. 188/D2
Perthville, Austl. 157/D1
Pertokar, Erit. 135/H1
Pertuis, Fr. 70/B5
Pertuis Breton (inlet), Fr. 50/C3
Pertusato (cape), Fr. 54/A2
Peru (ctry.) 220/C3
Peru, Ks, US 183/F2
Peru, Il, US 185/K3
Peru, In, US 190/C4
Peru, Ne, US 185/G3
Perućačko (lake), Bosn. 56/D4
Perugia, It. 71/B1
Perugia (prov.), It. 71/B1
Peruíbe, Braz. 223/K9
Perushtitsa, Bul. 55/J1
Péruwelz, Belg. 60/C2
Pervari, Turk. 114/E2
Pervomaysk, Rus. 75/J5
Pervomays'k, Ukr. 78/F3
Pervomays'ke, Ukr. 79/G5
Pervomayskiy, Rus. 77/G1
Pervomayskiy, Rus. 77/J2
Pervomayskiy, Rus. 90/H1
Pervomayskoye, Rus. 77/H2
Pervomayskoye, Rus. 79/L3
Pervomays'kyy, Ukr. 79/J3
Pervoural'sk, Rus. 75/N4
Perwez, Belg. 61/D2
Péry, Swi. 66/D3
Pesa (riv.), It. 69/E5
Pesagi (peak), Indo. 101/D4
Pesaro, It. 69/F6
Pesaro E Urbino (prov.), It. 69/F5
Pescadero (pt.), Ca, US 178/A2
Pescadero, Ca, US 178/A2
Pescadore (chan.), Tai. 99/H4
Pescadores (Penghu) (isls.), China 99/H4
Pescantina, It. 69/D3
Pescara (riv.), It. 71/D3
Pescara (prov.), It. 71/C3
Pescara, It. 71/D3
Pescasseroli, It. 71/C4
Peschanokopskoye, Rus. 79/L4
Peschanyy (cape), Kaz. 77/J4
Peschici, It. 54/E2
Pescia, It. 69/D6
Pescina, It. 71/C3
Pescocostanzo, It. 71/D4
Peseux, Swi. 66/C4
Pesha (riv.), Rus. 75/L2
Peshawar (int'l arpt.), Pak. 110/A2
Peshāwar, Pak. 110/A2
Peshkopi, Alb. 55/G2
Peshtera, Bul. 55/J1
Peshtigo (riv.), Wi, US 187/L5
Peshtigo, Wi, US 190/C2
Peski, Rus. 74/H5
Peskovka, Rus. 75/M4
Pesmes, Fr. 66/B3
Peso da Régua, Port. 52/B2
Pesochnyy, Rus. 75/T6
Pesqueira, Braz. 219/G5
Pesquería (riv.), Mex. 180/D5
Pessac, Fr. 50/C4
Pest (co.), Hun. 49/K5
Pest (prov.), Hun. 56/D2
Pestovkoye (lake), Rus. 75/W8
Pestovo, Rus. 74/G4
Petacciato, It. 71/D4
Petah Tiqwa, Isr. 117/B4
Petal, Ms, US 194/D2
Petalión (gulf), Gre. 73/K3
Petaluma (riv.), Ca, US 197/J10
Petaluma, Ca, US 176/B4
Pétange, Lux. 61/E4
Petārbār, India 109/E4
Petare, Ven. 219/P7
Pétas, Gre. 55/G3
Petatlán, Mex. 205/E5
Petatlán (riv.), Mex. 204/D3
Petauke, Zam. 141/F2
Petawawa, On, Can. 191/H2
Petawawa (riv.), On, Can. 191/G2
Peten Itzá (lake), Guat. 206/D2
Petenwell (dam), Wi, US 185/J1
Peter (pond), Sk, Can. 170/F3
Peter (isl.), Nor., Ant. 228/U
Peterborough, Austl. 155/H5
Peterborough, On, Can. 191/G2
Peterborough, Eng, UK 43/F1
Peterborough (co.), Eng, UK 43/F1
Peterculter, Sc, UK 39/D2
Peterhead, Sc, UK 39/E1
Peterlee, Eng, UK 41/G2
Peterman, Al, US 194/E2
Petermann Aboriginal Land, Austl. 155/F3
Peteroa (vol.), Chile 226/C2
Petersaurach, Ger. 64/D4
Petersberg, Ger. 64/C1
Petersburg, Ak, US 201/M4
Petersburg, In, US 192/D1
Petersburg, Il, US 185/K3
Petersburg, ND, US 186/E3
Petersburg, Tx, US 182/D4
Petersburg, Va, US 193/J2
Petersburg, WV, US 193/H1
Petersburg Nat'l Bfld., Va, US 193/J2
Petersfield, Mb, Can. 186/F2
Petersfield, Eng, UK 43/F4
Petershagen, Ger. 59/F4
Petershagen, Ger. 48/Q6
Petershausen, Ger. 65/E6
Peterson (A.F.B.), Co, US 182/B1
Pétervására, Hun. 49/L4
Peterview, Nf, Can. 189/K1
Petilia Policastro, It. 54/E3
Pétionville, Haiti 207/H2
Petit Buëch (riv.), Fr. 70/B4
Petit Goâve, Haiti 207/H2
Petit Loango, PN du, Gabon 138/B3
Petit Mont Blanc (peak), Fr. 70/C2
Petit Rosne (riv.), Fr. 36/J4
Petit-Cap, Qu, Can. 188/E1
Petit-Couronne, Fr. 63/G2
Petit-de-Grat, NS, Can. 189/G3
Petit-Matane, Qu, Can. 188/D1
Petit-Noir, Fr. 66/B4
Petit-Saguenay, Qu, Can. 188/B1
Petitcodiac, NB, Can. 188/E3
Petite Miquelon (isl.), StP., Fr. 189/J2
Petite Nation (riv.), Qu, Can. 191/J1
Petite Rivière de l'Artibonite, Haiti 207/H2
Petite Rivière Noire (peak), Mrts. 143/T15
Petite-Rosselle, Fr. 61/F5
Petkeljärven NP, Fin. 74/F3
Petlād, India 113/K4
Petlalcingo, Mex. 206/B2
Peto, Mex. 206/D1
Petorca, Chile 226/C2
Petoskey, Mi, US 190/D2
Petra (isls.), Rus. 81/M2
Petre (pt.), On, Can. 191/H3
Petrel, Sp. 53/E3
Petrella (peak), It. 71/C5
Petrella Tifernina, It. 71/D4
Petretsovo, Rus. 75/N3
Petrey, Al, US 195/E2
Petrich, Bul. 55/H2
Petrified Forest NP, Az, US 179/H3
Petrikov, Bela. 76/D1
Petrila, Rom. 57/F3
Petritoli, It. 71/C1
Petrivka, Ukr. 78/F4
Petrodvorets, Rus. 75/S7
Petrograd (nbrhd.), Rus. 75/T7
Petrokhanski Prokhod (pass), Bul. 57/F4
Petrokrepost' (bay), Rus. 75/U7
Petrokrepost', Rus. 75/U7
Petrolândia, Braz. 219/G5
Petrolia, Tx, US 183/E3
Petrolia, On, Can. 190/E3
Petrolina, Braz. 219/F5
Petropavl, Kaz. 80/G4
Petropavlivka, Ukr. 79/J3
Petropavlovsk-Kamchatskiy, Rus. 81/R4
Petropavlovskoye, Rus. 77/H3
Petrópolis, Braz. 223/N7
Petros, Tn, US 192/E2
Petroşani, Rom. 57/F3
Petroso (peak), It. 71/C4
Petrovaradin, Serb. 56/D3
Petrovsk, Rus. 77/H1
Petrovsk-Zabaykal'skiy, Rus. 90/F1
Petrovskaya, Rus. 79/J5
Petrovs'ke, Ukr. 79/K3
Petrovskiy Yam, Rus. 74/G3
Petrovskoye, Rus. 77/L1
Petrozavodsk, Rus. 74/G3
Petrus Steyn, SAfr. 142/E2
Petrusburg, SAfr. 142/D3
Petrusville, SAfr. 142/D3
Petrykivka, Ukr. 79/H3
Pettenbach, Aus. 65/H7
Petteril (riv.), Eng, UK 41/F2
Pettibone, ND, US 186/E4
Pettigrew, Ar, US 183/H3
Pettus, Tx, US 180/F3
Petushki, Rus. 74/H5
Petworth, Eng, UK 43/F5
Petzeck (peak), Aus. 51/K3
Peuerbach, Aus. 65/G6
Peulik (mt.), Ak, US 201/G4
Peumo, Chile 226/N9
Peureulak, Indo. 101/B1
Pevek, Rus. 81/T3
Pevely, Mo, US 192/B1
Pevensey, Eng, UK 43/G5
Pewaukee, Wi, US 197/P13
Pewaukee (lake), Wi, US 197/X13
Pewsey, Eng, UK 43/E4
Peyia, Cyp. 116/C2
Peyk, Iran 115/G3
Peymeinade, Fr. 70/C5
Peyrehorade, Fr. 50/C5
Peyrins, Fr. 70/B2
Peyrolles-en-Provence, Fr. 70/B5
Peyruis, Fr. 70/B4
Peza (riv.), Rus. 75/K2
Pézenas, Fr. 50/E5
Pezu, Pak. 110/A3
Pfaffenhausen, Ger. 67/G1
Pfaffenhofen an der Ilm, Ger. 64/D6
Pfaffenhofen an der Ilm, Ger. 65/E5
Pfaffenhoffen, Fr. 61/G6
Pfäffikon, Swi. 67/E3
Pfaffing, Ger. 65/F6
Pfaffnau, Swi. 66/D3
Pfahl (ridge), Ger. 65/F4
Pfälzer Wald (mts.), Ger. 61/G5
Pfälzerwald (mts.), Ger. 64/A4
Pfalzgrafenweiler, Ger. 64/B5
Pfarrhof Esternberg, Aus. 65/G5
Pfarrkirchen, Ger. 65/F6
Pfatter, Ger. 65/F5
Pfeffenhausen, Ger. 65/E5
Pfettrach (riv.), Ger. 65/E5
Pfieffe (riv.), Ger. 59/G6
Pfinztal, Ger. 64/B5
Pflugerville, Tx, US 181/F2
Pforzheim, Ger. 64/B5
Pfreimd (riv.), Ger. 65/F3
Pfreimd, Ger. 65/F3
Pfronstetten, Ger. 67/F1
Pfronten, Ger. 67/G2
Pfroslkopf (peak), Aus. 67/G4
Pfullendorf, Ger. 67/F2
Pfunds, Aus. 67/G4
Pfungstadt, Ger. 64/B3
Phagwāra, India 110/C4
Phalaborwa, SAfr. 141/F4
Phalauda, India 110/D5
Phalempin, Fr. 60/C2
Phālia, Pak. 110/B3
Phalodi, India 113/K3
Phalombe, Malw. 141/G2
Phalsbourg, Fr. 61/G6
Phaltan, India 107/B2
Phan, Thai. 106/B2
Phan Rang Viet. 106/E4
Phan Thiet, Viet. 106/E4
Phanat Nikhom, Thai. 106/C3
Phang Hoei (range), Thai. 106/C3
Phangan (isl.), Thai. 105/H6
Phangnga, Thai. 106/B4
Phanom, Thai. 106/B4
Phanom Dongrak (mts.), Thai. 105/H5
Phāphlu, Nepal 109/F2
Pharr, Tx, US 181/E4
Phat Diem, Viet. 99/E4
Phatthalung, Thai. 106/C5
Phaya Fo (peak), Thai. 106/C2
Phayao, Thai. 106/B2
Pheasant (hills), Sk, Can. 186/C2
Phelan, Ca, US 196/C2
Phelps, Wi, US 187/K4
Phelps (lake), NC, US 193/J3
Phenix City, Al, US 192/E4
Phepane (riv.), SAfr. 140/D5
Phet Buri, Thai. 106/B3
Phetchabun, Thai. 106/C2
Phiafai, Laos 106/D3
Phibun Mangsahan, Thai. 106/D3
Phichai, Thai. 106/C2
Phichit, Thai. 106/C2
Phidim, Nepal 109/F2
Phil Campbell, Al, US 192/D3
Philadelphia, NY, US 191/J2
Philadelphia, Ms, US 192/C4
Philadelphia (int'l arpt.), Pa, US 198/C4
Philadelphia, Pa, US 198/C4
Philip, SD, US 184/D1
Philip S.W. Goldson (int'l arpt.), Belz. 206/D2
Philipp, Ms, US 192/B4
Philippeville, Belg. 61/D3
Philippi, WV, US 193/G1
Philippine (sea), Asia 83/M8
Philippines (ctry.) 132/*
Philippsburg, Ger. 64/B4
Philipsburg, Pa, US 191/G4
Philipsburg, Neth. 203/J4
Philipsburg, Mt, US 175/H4
Philipsdam (dam), Neth. 58/B5
Philipstown, Ire. 38/C3
Philipstown, SAfr. 142/D3
Phillaur, India 110/C4
Phillip (isl.), Austl. 157/B4
Phillips, Me, US 191/L2
Phillips, Wi, US 187/J5
Phillips Arm, BC, Can. 174/B2
Phillipsburg, Ga, US 195/G2
Phillipsburg, Ks, US 184/E4
Phillipsburg, Mo, US 183/H2
Phillipsburg, NJ, US 198/C2
Philo, Ca, US 176/B4
Philomath, Or, US 176/B1
Philoteris (ruin), Egypt 131/B6
Philpot, Ky, US 192/D2
Phimai, Thai. 106/C3
Phimai (ruin), Thai. 106/C3
Phipps (mtn.), Austl. 157/C3
Phitsanulok, Thai. 106/C2
Phnom Penh (Phnum Pénh) (cap.), Camb. 106/D4
Phnum Penh (int'l arpt.), Camb. 106/D4
Phnum Pénh (Phnom Penh) (cap.), Camb. 106/D4
Phnum Tbeng Meanchey, Camb. 106/D3
Pho (pt.), Thai. 106/C5
Phoenix (isls.), Kiri. 161/H5
Phoenix (cap.), Az, US 200/R19
Phoenix (mtn.), NC, US 193/G2
Phoenix, Or, US 176/B2
Phoenix (Rawaki) (isl.), Kiri. 161/H5
Phoenix Park, Ire. 40/B5
Phoenix Sky Harbor (int'l arpt.), Az, US 200/R19
Phoenixville, Pa, US 198/C3
Phon, Thai. 106/C3
Phon Phisai, Thai. 106/C2
Phon Thong, Thai. 106/C2
Phongsali, Laos 98/D4
Phou Bia (peak), Laos 106/C2
Phou Huatt (peak), Viet. 98/E5
Phou Khoun, Laos 106/C2
Phou Loi (peak), Laos 98/D4
Phou Xai Lai Leng (peak), Laos 106/D2
Phra Nakhon Si Ayutthaya, Thai. 106/C3
Phra Phutthabat, Thai. 106/C3
Phra Thong (isl.), Thai. 106/B4
Phrae, Thai. 106/C2
Phsar Ream, Camb. 106/C4
Phu Hin Rong Kla NP, Thai. 106/C2
Phu Hoi, Viet. 106/E4
Phu Kradung, Thai. 106/C2
Phu Kradung NP, Thai. 106/C2
Phu Loc, Viet. 106/D2
Phu Luong, Viet. 106/D1
Phu Luong (peak), Viet. 98/E4
Phu Ly, Viet. 106/D1
Phu My, Viet. 106/E3
Phu Nhon, Viet. 106/E3
Phu Phan NP, Thai. 106/D2
Phu Quoc (isl.), Camb. 105/H5
Phu Quoc (isl.), Viet. 106/C4
Phu Quoc, Viet. 106/C4
Phu Rieng Sron, Viet. 106/D4
Phu Rua NP, Thai. 106/C2
Phu Tho, Viet. 98/E4
Phu Vang, Viet. 106/D2
Phuc Loi, Viet. 106/D2
Phuc Yen, Viet. 98/E4
Phuket (isl.), Thai. 105/G6
Phuket, Thai. 106/B5
Phulabāni, India 107/E1
Phularwan, Pak. 110/B3
Phulbāri, Bang. 109/G3
Phulbāri, India 109/H3
Phuldungsei, India 98/B4
Phūlpur, India 108/D3
Phultala, Bang. 109/G4
Phumi Banam, Camb. 106/D4
Phumi Chhlong, Camb. 106/D3
Phumi Choan, Camb. 106/C4
Phumi Chuuk, Camb. 106/D4
Phumi Kampong Putrea Chas, Camb. 106/D3
Phumi Kampong Trabek, Camb. 106/D3
Phumi Kouk Kduoch, Camb. 106/C3
Phumi Krek, Camb. 106/D4
Phumi Labang Siek, Camb. 106/D3
Phumi Mlu Prey, Camb. 106/D3
Phumi O Pou, Camb. 106/D3
Phumi Phang, Camb. 106/C3
Phumi Phsa Romeas, Camb. 106/D3
Phumi Phsar, Camb. 106/D3
Phumi Prek Kak, Camb. 106/D3
Phumi Prek Preah, Camb. 106/D3
Phumi Samraong, Camb. 106/C3
Phumi Spoe Tbong, Camb. 106/D3
Phumi Sre Ta Chan, Camb. 106/D3
Phumi Ta Krei, Camb. 106/C3
Phumi Thma Pok, Camb. 106/C3
Phumi Toek Sok, Camb. 106/C3
Phumi Veal Renh, Camb. 106/C4
Phuntsholing, Bhu. 109/G2
Phutthaisong, Thai. 106/C3
Pi (riv.), China 90/H5
Pi Xian, China 98/D2
Pia, D.R. Congo 139/F2
Piaçabuçu, Braz. 223/F1
Piacenza, It. 68/C3
Piacenza (prov.), It. 68/C3
Piacoa, Ven. 217/F2
Piadena, It. 68/D3
Piaggine, It. 54/D2
Pian di Serra (peak), It. 69/F7
Pian-Upe Game Rsv., Ugan. 137/A1
Piancastagnaio, It. 54/B1
Pianella, It. 71/D3
Pianello val Tidone, It. 68/C4
Pianezza, It. 68/A2
Piangipane, It. 69/F5
Pianling, China 93/B2
Piano di Sorrento, It. 71/D6
Pianoro, It. 69/E5
Pianosa (isl.), It. 54/A1
Piaoli, China 99/F3
Piapot Ind. Res., Sk, Can. 186/B2
Piarco (int'l arpt.), Trin. 217/F2
Piasco, It. 70/D3
Piaseczno, Pol. 49/L2
Piatra Neamţ, Rom. 78/D4
Piauí (riv.), Braz. 219/F5
Piauí (state), Braz. 219/F4
Piave (riv.), It. 51/K3
Piazza, It. 68/D2
Piazza, It. 68/D2
Piazza al Serchio, It. 68/D5
Piazza Armerina, It. 54/D4
Piazza Brembana, It. 67/F6
Piazzola sul Brenta, It. 69/E2
Pibor (riv.), Sudan 135/G4
Pibor Post, Sudan 135/G4
Pic (isl.), On, Can. 187/L3
Pic (riv.), On, Can. 187/L3
Pica, Chile 224/B2
Picacho, Az, US 179/G4
Picacho del Centinela (peak), Mex. 180/C3
Picahos, Cerro Dos (peak), Mex. 204/B2
Picardie (pol. reg.), Fr. 50/E2
Picardy (reg.), Fr. 60/B4
Picatinny Arsenal, NJ, US 198/D2
Picauville, Fr. 62/D2
Picayune, Ms, US 194/D2
Piccaninny (cr.), Austl. 157/B3
Piccolo (lag.), It. 55/E2
Picentino (riv.), It. 71/D6
Pichacani, Peru 220/D5
Pichanal, Arg. 224/C2
Picher, Ok, US 183/G2
Pichidangui, Chile 226/C2
Pichidegua, Chile 226/N9
Pichilemu, Chile 226/B2
Pichincha (dept.), Ecu. 216/B4
Pichincha, Ecu. 216/B5
Pichkiryayevo, Rus. 77/G1
Pichl bei Wels, Aus. 65/G6
Pichor, India 108/B3
Pichucalco, Mex. 206/C2
Pickens, Ok, US 183/G3
Pickens, SC, US 193/F3
Pickens, Ms, US 192/C4
Pickering, Eng, UK 41/H3
Pickering, On, Can. 190/U8
Pickford, Mi, US 190/D1
Pickle Lake, On, Can. 187/J2
Pickton, Tx, US 183/G4
Pickwick (dam), Tn, US 192/C3
Pickwick (lake), Al,Ms, US 192/C3
Pickwick Dam, Tn, US 192/C3
Picnic Bay, Austl. 158/B2
Pico (isl.), Azor., Port. 53/S12
Pico da Neblina, PN do, Braz. 217/E4
Pico de Orizaba, PN, Mex. 205/M7
Pico de Salamanca, Arg. 226/D5
Pico Rivera, Ca, US 196/F8
Pico Truncado, Arg. 226/D5
Picos, Braz. 219/F4
Picota, Peru 220/B2
Picsi, Peru 220/B2
Picton, On, Can. 191/H3
Picton, NZ 159/C3
Picton, Austl. 157/E2
Pictou (isl.), NS, Can. 189/F3
Pictou, NS, Can. 189/F3
Picture Butte, Ab, Can. 175/H3
Picture Gorge (gorge), Or, US 176/D1
Picture Rock (pass), Or, US 176/C2
Picture Rocks, Pa, US 198/B1
Pictured Rocks Nat'l Lakeshore, Mi, US 187/L4
Picuí, Braz. 219/G4
Picuris Ind. Res., NM, US 179/K2
Pidcoke, Tx, US 180/F2
Piddle (riv.), Eng, UK 42/D5
Pidhorodne, Ukr. 79/H3
Pidi, D.R. Congo 139/F4
Pidurutagala (peak), SrL. 107/D5
Pidvolochys'k, Ukr. 78/D3
Pie (isl.), On, Can. 187/K3
Pie Town, NM, US 179/H3
Piedade, Port. 53/P10
Piedade do Rio Grande, Braz. 223/M6
Piedecuesta, Col. 216/C3
Piediluco (lake), It. 71/B2
Piedimulera, It. 67/E5
Piedmont, Al, US 192/E4
Piedmont, Ca, US 197/K11
Piedmont, Mo, US 192/B2
Piedmont, Ok, US 183/F3
Piedmont, SC, US 193/F3
Piedmont (upland), SC, US 193/G3
Piedmont, SD, US 184/C1
Piedmont NWR, Ga, US 192/F4
Piedra, Ca, US 178/C2
Piedra Grande, Ven. 216/D2
Piedra Sola, Uru. 225/E5
Piedrabuena, Sp. 52/C3
Piedrahita, Sp. 52/C2
Piedras (pt.), Arg. 191/K11
Piedras, Col. 219/L8
Piedras Coloradas, Uru. 191/K10
Piedras Negras, Mex. 205/N8
Piedras, Río de las (riv.), Peru 220/D3
Piedritas, Arg. 226/E2
Piekary Śląskie, Pol. 49/K3
Piekenierskloof (pass), SAfr. 142/L10
Pieksämäki, Fin. 74/E3
Pielinen (lake), Fin. 44/J3
Piemonte (pol.reg.), It. 51/G4
Pieniński NP, Pol. 49/L4
Piennes, Fr. 61/E5
Pieńsk, Pol. 49/H3
Piera, Sp. 53/K6
Pierce, Co, US 184/B3
Pierce (lake), Fl, US 194/M8
Pierce, Fl, US 194/M8
Pierce, Id, US 174/G4
Pierce, Ne, US 184/F2
Pierce (co.), Wi, US 187/Q7
Pierce City, Mo, US 183/G2
Pierceville, Ks, US 182/D2
Pieris, It. 69/G2
Piermont, NY, US 199/K7
Pierowall, Sc, UK 37/V14
Pierre (cap.), SD, US 184/D1
Pierre Menue (peak), It. 70/C2
Pierre Part, La, US 194/C3
Pierre Plate (peak), Fr. 70/D5
Pierre-de-Bresse, Fr. 66/B4
Pierre-Levée, Fr. 36/M5
Pierrefeu-du-Var, Fr. 70/C6
Pierrefitte-sur-Seine, Fr. 36/K5
Pierrefonds, Qu, Can. 189/N7
Pierrefontaine-les-Varans, Fr. 66/C3
Pierrelatte, Fr. 70/A4
Pierrelaye, Fr. 36/J4
Pierres, Fr. 63/G3
Pierrevert, Fr. 70/B5
Pierry, Fr. 60/C5
Pierson, Fl, US 195/H3
Piešt'any, Slvk. 49/J4
Piesting (riv.), Aus. 57/P7
Piet Retief, SAfr. 143/E2
Pietarsaari (Jakobstad), Fin. 74/D3
Pieterlen, Swi. 66/D3
Pietermaritzburg, SAfr. 143/E3
Pietersburg, SAfr. 141/F4
Pietra Ligure, It. 68/B5
Pietracatella, It. 71/D4
Pietralunga, It. 69/F7
Pietramelara, It. 71/D5
Pietrasanta, It. 68/D6
Pietravairano, It. 71/D5
Pietravecchia (peak), It. 68/A5
Pietrosul (peak), Rom. 57/G2
Pieve del Cairo, It. 68/B3
Pieve di Cento, It. 69/E4
Pieve di Soligo, It. 69/F2
Pieve di Teco, It. 68/A4
Pieve Emanuele, It. 68/C3
Pieve Ligure, It. 68/C5
Pieve Porto Morone, It. 68/C3
Pieve Santo Stefano, It. 69/F6
Pieve Vergonte, It. 67/E6
Pievepelago, It. 68/D5
Pigum (isl.), SKor. 93/C5
Pigeon (riv.), Can.,US 187/J3
Pigeon, Mi, US 190/E3
Pigeon (riv.), On, Can. 170/G4
Pigeon (lake), Ab, Can. 175/H1
Pigeon House (mtn.), Austl. 157/E2
Piggott, Ar, US 192/B2
Piggs Peak, Swaz. 143/E2
Piglio, It. 71/C4
Pigna, It. 70/D5
Pignataro Maggiore, It. 71/D5
Pigs (bay), Cuba 202/E3
Pigu, Gha. 133/E4
Pigüé, Arg. 226/E3
Pihāni, India 108/C2
Pijáo, Col. 219/K8
Pijijiapan, Mex. 206/C3
Pijnacker, Neth. 58/B4
Pijol (peak), Hon. 206/E3
Pike (co.), Pa, US 198/C1
Pikelot (isl.), Micr. 160/D4
Pikes (peak), Co, US 182/B1
Pikes Creek (res.), Pa, US 198/B1
Pikesville, Md, US 198/B5
Piketberg, SAfr. 142/L10
Piketon, Oh, US 193/F1
Pikeville, Ky, US 193/F2
Pikeville, Tn, US 192/E3
Pikit, Phil. 100/D4
Pikou, China 93/B3
Piła, Pol. 49/J2
Pila, Arg. 191/J12
Pilane, Bots. 140/E5
Pilanesberg (range), SAfr. 142/P12
Pilani, India 110/C5
Pilão Arcado, Braz. 223/E1
Pilar, Arg. 226/E1
Pilar, Arg. 224/D4
Pilar, Braz. 223/G1
Pilar, Par. 224/E3
Pilar, Phil. 103/F1
Pilatus (peak), Swi. 67/E4
Pilaya (riv.), Bol. 224/C2
Pilchuck (riv.), Wa, US 197/D1
Pilcomayo (riv.), SAm. 209/C5
Pilgrims Hatch, Eng, UK 36/D2
Pili, Phil. 100/C2
Pīlībhīt, India 108/B1
Pilica (riv.), Pol. 76/B2
Pílion (peak), Gre. 55/H3
Pilis (mts.), Hun. 57/R9
Pilis (peak), Hun. 57/Q9
Pilis, Hun. 56/D2
Piliscsaba, Hun. 57/Q9
Pilisvörösvár, Hun. 57/Q9
Pilkhua, India 110/D5
Pillar (cape), Austl. 156/C4
Pillar (peak), Eng, UK 41/E3
Pillar (pt.), Ca, US 197/J12
Pillar (pt.), Wa, US 174/B3
Pilliga, Austl. 156/D1
Pillow, Pa, US 198/B2
Pilões, Serra dos (mtn.), Braz. 225/H1
Pilon du Roi (peak), Fr. 70/B6
Pílos, Gre. 55/G4
Pilot (peak), Id, US 174/G5
Pilot (peak), Nv, US 176/E4
Pilot (mtn.), Tn, US 192/E2
Pilot (peak), Tn, US 192/E2
Pilot Butte, Sk, Can. 186/B2
Pilot Grove, Mo, US 183/H1
Pilot Grove (cr.), Tx, US 180/L6
Pilot Knob, Mo, US 192/B2
Pilot Mound, Mb, Can. 186/E3
Pilot Mountain, NC, US 193/G2
Pilot Point, Ak, US 201/G4
Pilot Point, Tx, US 183/F4
Pilot Rock, Or, US 176/D1
Pilot Station, Ak, US 201/F3
Pilottown, La, US 194/D3
Pilsting, Ger. 65/F5
Piltene, Lat. 47/J3
Piltown, Ire. 38/C5
Pilyugino, Rus. 77/K1
Pima, Az, US 179/H4
Pimamga-Moke, D.R. Congo 138/D3
Pimenta Bueno, Braz. 221/F3
Pimpi, Indo. 103/F3
Pimpri-Chinchwad, India 107/B2
Piña (pt.), Pan. 207/G5
Pinacate, Cerro (peak), Mex. 179/F5
Pináculo (peak), Arg. 191/B6
Pinaleno (mts.), Az, US 179/G4
Pinamalayan, Phil. 100/C2
Pinamar, Arg. 191/F3
Pinang (isl.), Malay. 102/A2
Pinang (cape), Malay. 101/B1
Pinangah, Malay. 100/B4
Pinar del Río, Cuba 207/F1
Pınarbaşı, Turk. 114/D2
Pınarhisar, Turk. 57/H5
Piñas, Ecu. 220/B1
Pinatubo (mt.), Phil. 100/C2
Pinawa, Mb, Can. 186/G2
Pinchbeck, Eng, UK 41/H6
Pincher Creek, Ab, Can. 175/H3
Pinckney, Mi, US 190/E3
Pinckneyville, Il, US 192/C1
Pinconning, Mi, US 190/E3
Pîncota, Rom. 56/E2
Pincourt, Qu, Can. 189/N7
Pińczów, Pol. 49/L3
Pind Dādan Khān, Pak. 110/B3
Pinda, Ang. 138/C5
Pindall, Ar, US 183/H2
Pindamonhangaba, Braz. 223/L7
Pindaré (riv.), Braz. 219/E4
Pindaré-Mirim, Braz. 219/E3
Píndhos NP, Gre. 55/G3
Pindi Bhattiān, Pak. 110/B4
Pindi Gheb, Pak. 110/B3
Pindiu, PNG 153/G1
Pindobaçu, Braz. 223/E1
Pindobal, Braz. 218/D3
Pindus (mts.), Gre. 73/J2
Pindwāra, India 104/B3
Pine (cape), Nf, Can. 189/L2
Pine, Az, US 179/G3
Pine, Co, US 182/B1
Pine (isl.), Fl, US 195/G4
Pine (pt.), Fl, US 195/G3
Pine, Id, US 177/F2
Pine (riv.), Mi, US 190/D3
Pine (hills), Ms, US 194/C2
Pine (ridge), Ne, US 184/C2
Pine (cr.), Pa, US 198/A1
Pine, Tx, US 183/G4
Pine Apple, Al, US 194/E2
Pine Barrens (phys. reg.), NJ, US 198/D4
Pine Bluff, Ar, US 183/H3
Pine Bluff Arsenal, Ar, US 183/H3
Pine Bluffs, Wy, US 184/B3
Pine Bush, NY, US 191/J4
Pine Castle, Fl, US 194/N7
Pine City, Mn, US 187/H5
Pine Creek (lake), Ok, US 183/G3
Pine Creek, Austl. 152/C3
Pine Creek (pt.), Ct, US 199/E1
Pine Dock, Mb, Can. 186/F2
Pine Falls, Mb, Can. 186/F2
Pine Flat (res.), Ca, US 178/C2
Pine Grove, La, US 194/C2
Pine Grove, Pa, US 198/B2
Pine Hill, Al, US 194/E2
Pine Hill, NJ, US 198/D4
Pine Island, Fl, US 194/K6
Pine Island, Mn, US 185/H1
Pine Island Bay (flat), Ant. 228/S
Pine Island Nat'l Wild. Ref., Fl, US 195/G4
Pine Knot, Ky, US 192/E2
Pine Level, Al, US 195/E1
Pine Mills, Tx, US 181/G1
Pine Point, NW, Can. 170/E2
Pine Prairie, La, US 194/B2
Pine Ridge, SD, US 184/C2
Pine Ridge Ind. Res., SD, US 184/C2
Pine River, Mn, US 187/G4
Pine River, Mb, Can. 186/D2
Pine Springs, Tx, US 180/B2
Pine Stump Junction, Mi, US 190/D1
Pine Valley, Ut, US 179/F2
Pine Valley, Ca, US 178/D4
Pine, South Branch (riv.), Mi, US 197/G6
Pinebluff, NC, US 193/H3
Pinecliff (lake), NJ, US 199/H7
Pinecreek, Mn, US 186/G3
Pinedale, Wy, US 177/J2
Pinedale, Ca, US 178/C2
Pinedale, Az, US 179/G3
Pinega (riv.), Rus. 80/E3
Pinega, Rus. 74/J2
Pinehurst, Ga, US 192/F4
Pinehurst, Id, US 174/F4
Pinehurst, NC, US 193/H3
Pinehurst, Tx, US 181/G2
Pineland, Fl, US 195/G4
Pineland, SC, US 193/G4
Pineland, Tx, US 181/H2
Pinelands, SAfr. 142/L10
Pinellas (co.), Fl, US 194/K8
Pinellas (pt.), Fl, US 194/K8
Pinellas Park, Fl, US 194/K8
Pineola, Fl, US 194/L6
Piñera, Uru. 191/K10
Pinerolo, It. 70/D3
Pinesdale, Mt, US 175/G4
Pineto, It. 71/D2
Pinetop-Lakeside, Az, US 179/H3
Pinetops, NC, US 193/J3
Pinetown, SAfr. 143/E3
Pinetta, Fl, US 195/G2
Pineuilh, Fr. 50/D4
Pineview, Ga, US 195/G1
Pineville, Ky, US 192/F2
Pineville, La, US 194/B2
Pineville, Mo, US 183/G2
Pineville, SC, US 193/G4
Pineville, WV, US 193/G2
Piney, Ar, US 183/H3
Piney (isl.), Fl, US 195/F2
Piney Green, NC, US 193/J3
Piney Point, Fl, US 194/K8
Piney Point, Md, US 193/J1
Piney Point Village, Tx, US 181/M9
Piney River, Va, US 193/H2
Ping (riv.), Thai. 105/G4
Ping (riv.), Myan. 106/B2
Ping Chau (isl.), China 99/M6
Pingbian Miaozu Zizhixian, China 98/D4
Pingchang, China 99/E2
Pingchao, China 99/J1
Pingding, China 92/C3
Pingdingshan, China 92/C4
Pingdu, China 92/D3
Pingelap (isl.), Micr. 160/F4
Pingelly, Austl. 154/C5
Ping'erguan, China 106/D1
Pingfa, China 99/E3
Pinggu, China 92/H6
Pingguo, China 105/J3
Pinghai, China 99/H3
Pinghai, China 99/G4
Pinghu, China 92/L9
Pingjing (pass), China 92/C5
Pingjinpu, China 99/E2
Pingle, China 99/F3
Pinglu, China 92/C3
Pinglu, China 92/B4
Pingquan, China 92/D2
Pingree, Id, US 177/G2
Pingsha, China 99/G4
Pingshan, China 92/C3
Pingshi, China 99/G3
Pingshun, China 92/C3
Pingtang, China 105/J2
Pingtou, China 90/F5
P'ingtung, Tai. 99/J4
Pingwang, China 92/L9
Pingxiang, China 99/E4
Pingxiang, China 99/G3
Pingxiang, China 92/C3
Pingxing Guan (pass), China 92/C3
Pingyang, China 91/J4
Pingyao, China 92/C3
Pingyi, China 92/D4
Pingyin, China 106/E1

Pingyin, China 92/D3
Pingyong, China 99/F3
Pingyu, China 92/C4
Pingyuan, Indo. 92/D3
Pinhal, Braz. 223/K7
Pinhal Novo, Port. 53/Q10
Pinheiro, Braz. 219/E3
Pinheiro Machado, Braz. 225/F4
Pinheiros, Braz. 219/F4
Pinhel, Port. 52/B2
Pinhook (swamp), Fl, US 195/G2
Pinhuã (riv.), Braz. 221/E2
Pini (isl.), Indo. 101/B2
Pinjar (lake), Austl. 154/B5
Pinjarra, Austl. 154/B5
Pink Hill, NC, US 193/J3
Pinkafeld, Aus. 56/C2
Pinkawillinnie Consv. Park, Austl. 155/G5
Pinkegat (chan.), Neth. 50/D1
Pinlebu, Myan. 105/G3
Pinnacles Nat'l Mon., Ca, US 196/B2
Pinnán, China
Pinnaroo, Austl. 155/J5
Pinnau (riv.), Ger. 59/G1
Pinneberg, Ger. 59/G1
Pino Hachado, (pass), Arg. 226/C3
Pino Torinese, It. 68/A2
Pinole, Ca, US 197/K10
Piñon, Co, US 182/B3
Piñon, NM, US 182/B4
Piñon, Az, US 179/G2
Pinon Hills, Ca, US 194/C3
Pinopolis, SC, US 191/G4
Pinopolis (dam), SC, US 191/G4
Pinos (mt.), Ca, US 178/C3
Pinos, Mex. 205/E4
Pinos, Isla de (Isla de la Juventud) (isl.), Cuba 202/E3
Pinos-Puente, Sp. 52/C4
Pinoso, Sp. 53/E3
Pinrang, Indo. 103/F4
Pinsdorf, Aus. 65/G7
Pinsk, Bela. 76/C1
Pinta, Isla (isl.), Ecu. 220/J6
Pintada Arroyo (cr.), NM, US 182/B3
Pintado, Uru. 191/K10
Pintados, Chile 224/B2
Pinto, Chile 226/C3
Pinto, Sp. 53/N9
Pintura, Ut, US 179/F2
Pintuyan, Phil. 100/D3
Pinzolo, It. 67/G5
Pio Xii, Braz. 219/E3
Piobbico, It. 69/F6
Pioche, Nv, US 178/E2
Piomba (riv.), It. 71/C2
Piombino, It. 54/B1
Piombino Dese, It.
Pioneer, La, US 183/J4
Pioneer (mts.), Mt, US 177/G1
Pioneer World, Austl. 154/L7
Pioner (isl.), Rus. 80/J2
Pionerskiy, Rus. 47/J4
Pionki, Pol. 49/L3
Piopio, NZ 159/G2
Piopolis, Qu, Can. 188/B3
Piorini (lake), Braz. 217/F3
Piorini (riv.), Braz. 221/F1
Piossasco, It. 70/D3
Piota (riv.), It. 68/B3
Piotrków Trybunalski, Pol. 49/K3
Piove di Sacco, It. 69/F3
Piovene-Rocchette, It. 69/E2
Pīpār, India
Piparia, India 108/B4
Pipe Spring Nat'l Mon., Az, US 179/F2
Pipersville, Pa, US 198/C2
Pipestem (cr.), ND, US 186/D3
Pipestone, Mb, Can. 186/D3
Pipestone, (riv.), On, Can. 170/G3
Pipestone, Mn, US 185/F1
Pipestone Nat'l Mon., Mn, US 185/F1
Piplān, Pak.
Pipmuacan (res.), Qu, Can. 171/J4
Pippingarra Abor. Land, Austl. 154/C2
Pipra, India 108/A3
Pipraich, India 108/D2
Pipriac, Fr. 62/D5
Piqanlik, China 111/D3
Piqua, Ks, US 183/G2
Piqua, Oh, US 190/D4
Piquet Carneiro, Braz. 219/E3
Piquete, Braz. 223/L7
Piquiri (riv.), Braz. 225/F3
Pīr Mahal, Pak. 110/B4
Pir Panjal (range), India 110/C3
Piracanjuba, Braz. 222/C3
Piracaua, Braz. 218/E3
Piracicaba, Braz. 223/F7
Piracuruca, Braz. 219/F2
Pirae-bong (peak), NKor. 93/C2
Pirai, Braz. 223/N7
Pirai do Sul, Braz. 225/F3
Piraiévs, Gre. 55/N9
Piraju, Braz. 225/G2
Pirajuí, Braz. 225/G2
Pirámide (peak), Chile 191/B6
Piran, Slov.
Pirané, Arg. 224/E3
Piranga, Braz. 223/E4
Piranhas (riv.), Braz. 219/G4
Piranhas, Braz. 222/C3
Pirapemas, Braz. 219/E3
Pirapora, Braz. 222/D3
Pirarajá, Uru. 191/G2
Pirassununga, Braz. 225/H2
Piratini, Braz. 225/F3
Piray (riv.), Bol. 221/F5
Pircas, Arg. 224/B3
Pirenópolis, Braz. 222/C2
Pires do Rio, Braz. 222/C3
Pīrganj, India 109/G3
Pírgos, Gre. 55/J5
Pírgos, Gre. 55/J5

Piri, Ang. 138/C5
Piriac-sur-Mer, Fr. 62/C6
Piriápolis, Uru. 191/G2
Piribebuy, Par. 225/E3
Pirimapun, Indo. 153/E1
Pirin NP, Bul. 55/H2
Pirin (peak), Bul. 55/H2
Pirin (mts.), Bul. 55/H2
Piritu, Ven. 216/D2
Piritiba, Braz. 223/E1
Pirmasens, Ger. 61/G5
Piru, Ca, US 196/B2
Piru (riv.), Ca, US 196/B1
Piru (lake), Ca, US 196/B1
Piryion, Gre. 55/J3
Pisa, It. 67/D6
Pisa (prov.), It. 54/D6
Pisac, Peru 220/D4
Pisagua, Chile 224/B1
Pisau (riv.), Malay. 100/B4
Piscataway, NJ, US 198/D2
Piscataway, Md, US 198/B6
Pisco, Peru 220/C4
Pisco (riv.), Peru 220/C4
Piscobamba, Peru 220/B3
Pisek, ND, US 186/F3
Pisek (peak), Czh. 65/H4
Pisgah, Oh, US 190/D5
Pishan, China 111/C4
Pishin, Pak. 78/E3
Pishín, Iran 113/H3
Pishvā, Iran
Piskavica, Bosn. 56/C3
Piskivka, Ukr. 78/E2
Piso Firme, Bol. 221/F4
Pisogne, It. 69/E2
Pisoniano, It. 71/B4
Pissila, Burk. 133/E3
Pissis (peak), Arg. 224/B3
Pistakee (lake), Il, US 197/P15
Pisticci, It. 54/E2
Pistoia, It. 69/D6
Pistoia (prov.), It. 69/D5
Pistol River, Or, US 176/B3
Pisuerga (riv.), Sp. 52/C1
Pisz, Pol. 49/L2
Pit (riv.), Ca, US 176/C3
Pita, Gui. 132/B4
Pitalito, Col. 216/C4
Pitanga, Braz. 225/G3
Pitangui, Braz. 223/D4
Pitcairn (isl.), Pitc. 161/N7
Pitcairn Islands (dpcy.) 49/L3
Pitch Place, Eng, UK 36/B3
Piteå, Swe. 44/G2
Piteälven (riv.), Swe. 44/F2
Piteşti, Rom. 57/G3
Pithāpuram, India 107/D3
Pithion, Gre. 57/H5
Pithiviers, Fr. 63/H4
Pithlachascotee (riv.), Fl, US 195/N7
Pithom (ruin) Egypt 131/D3
Pithoragarh, India 108/C1
Pitigliano, It. 54/B1
Pitimbu, Braz. 219/H4
Pitiquito, Mex. 204/B2
Pitjantjatjara Aboriginal Lands, Austl. 155/G3
Pitkas Point, Ak, US 201/F3
Pitkin, Co, US 179/J3
Pitkin (co.), Co, US 179/J3
Pitlochry, Sc, UK 39/C3
Pitman, NJ, US 198/C4
Pitmedden, Sc, UK 39/D2
Pitogo, Phil. 100/C2
Pitomača, Cro. 56/C2
Piton de la Fournaise (vol.), Reun. 143/S15
Piton des Neiges (peak), Reun. 143/S15
Pitowa, Camr. 134/B3
Pitres, Fr. 62/A3
Pitsea, Eng, UK 41/J7
Pitsunda, Geo. 76/A3
Pitt (str.), NZ 159/E4
Pitt (isl.), NZ 159/E4
Pitt (isl.), BC, Can. 174/C3
Pitt Water (bay), Austl. 158/H8
Pittem, Belg. 60/B1
Pitten (riv.), Aus. 56/C2
Pitts, Ga, US 191/G3
Pittsboro, Ms, US 187/K4
Pittsboro, NC, US 191/H3
Pittsburg, Ca, US 176/C4
Pittsburg, Ks, US 183/G3
Pittsburg, Mo, US 183/H2
Pittsburg, NH, US 191/L2
Pittsburg, Ok, US 183/G3
Pittsburg, Pa, US 190/G4
Pittsfield, Ma, US 191/K3
Pittsfield, Il, US 185/J4
Pittsfield, Vt, US 191/L3
Pittstown, NJ, US 198/D2
Pittsworth, Austl. 158/C4
Pitzbach (riv.), Aus. 67/G4
Piui, Braz. 219/E3
Piumazzo, It. 69/E4
Piura, Peru 220/A2
Piura (dept.), Peru 220/A2
Piute (res.), Ut, US 179/F3
Pivan', Rus. 91/M1
Pivijay, Col. 216/C2
Pivsko (lake), Mont. 56/D4
Pixoyal, Mex. 202/D4

Piz d'Err (peak), Swi. 67/F4
Pizarra, Sp. 52/C4
Pizarro, Peru 220/D5
Pizhma (riv.), Rus. 75/K4
Pizhou, Mo, US 185/G4
Pizol (peak), Swi. 67/F4
Pizzighettone, It. 68/C3
Pizzo, It. 54/E3
Pizzo dei Tre Signori, It.
Pizzo della Presolana, It.
Pizzo di Coca (peak), It. 67/G5
Pizzo di Vogorno, It.
Pizzoli, It. 71/C3
Plabennec, Fr. 62/A3
Plachkovtsi, Bul. 55/J3
Placencia, Nf, Can. 219/H4
Placentia, Ca, US 196/G8
Placentia (bay), Nf, Can. 189/K2
Placentia, Co, US 179/H1
Placer (riv.), Ca, US 196/B1
Placer (co.), Ca, US 177/M9
Placer, Phil. 100/C3
Placetas, Cuba 207/G1
Plácido de Castro, Braz. 221/E3
Placilla de Caracoles,
Plaffeien, Swi. 66/D4
Plai Mat (riv.), Thai. 106/C2
Plaidt, Ger. 61/G3
Plailly, Fr. 36/K4
Plain Dealing, La, US 183/H4
Plain of Jars, Laos 98/D5
Plainfield, In, US 190/C5
Plainfield, Il, US 197/P16
Plainfield, NJ, US 184/E3
Plainfield, Wi, US 185/K1
Plains, Tx, US 182/C4
Plains, Ga, US 191/G3
Plains, Mt, US 174/G4
Plains, Pa, US
Plains (West Plains), Ky, US 192/E1
Plampang, Indo. 103/E5
Planá, Czh.
Plan-de-Cuques, Fr. 70/B6
Plan-de-la-Tour, Fr. 69/D6
Plan-d'Orgon, Fr. 70/A5
Plana Cays (isls.), Bahm. 207/H1
Plánice, Czh.
Planada, Ca, US 196/C2
Planaltina, Col. 216/C3
Planaltina, Braz. 222/C2
Planalto da Borborema, Braz. 219/G4
Planalto da Huíla, Ang.
Planalto da Lichinga, Moz. 141/G2
Planalto do Bié, Ang.
Planalto do Chimoio, Moz. 141/G3
Planalto dos Macondes, Moz. 141/G3
Planchada, Chile 226/N8
Plancher-Bas, Fr.
Plancoët, Fr. 62/C3
Planet Ocean, Fl, US 194/P11
Planeta Rica, Col. 216/C2
Planken, Lcht. 67/F3
Plankinton, SD, US 185/H1
Plano, Il, US 185/K3
Plano, Tx, US 183/G4
Plantation, Fl, US 194/P10
Plantation Key, Fl, US 195/H5
Plantersville, Ms, US 187/K4
Plaquemine, La, US 194/C2
Plasencia, Sp. 52/B2
Plaster Rock, NB, Can. 189/D2
Plaster Rock-Renous Game Ref., Bots. 140/E5
Plasy, Czh.
Platani (riv.), It. 54/C4
Plateau, NS, Can. 189/G2
Plateau (state), Nga. 133/H4
Plateau Batéké,
Plateau de Manguéni, Niger 126/B4
Plateau de Tehiga'i, Niger
Plateau de Valensole, Fr. 70/B5
Plateau des Bolovens, Laos 106/D3
Plateau du Tademaït, Alg. 123/F3
Plateau of Yorubaland, Nga. 133/F4
Plateaux (pol. reg.), Congo 138/C3
Platinum, Ak, US 201/F4

Platteville, Co, US 184/B3
Platteville, Wi, US 185/J2
Plattling, Ger. 65/F5
Plattsburg, Mo, US 185/G4
Plattsburgh, NY, US 191/L2
Plattsmouth, Ne, US 185/G3
Plauen, Ger. 65/F1
Plav, Mont. 56/D4
Plavna Dadaint
Plaviņas, Lat. 47/L3
Plavsk, Rus.
Playa de los Muertos (ruin), Mex.
Playa del Carmen, Mex. 206/E1
Playa Noriega (lake), Mex. 204/C2
Playa Vicente, Mex. 206/C2
Playas, Ecu. 216/A5
Playas (lake), NM, US 179/H5
Plaza, ND, US 186/D3
Pleak, Tx, US 195/M9
Pleasant (mtn.),
Pleasant Bay, NS, Can. 189/G2
Pleasant Grove, Ut, US 177/H3
Pleasant Hill, Ca, US 197/K11
Pleasant Hill, La, US 194/B2
Pleasant Hill, Mo, US 183/G1
Pleasant Hills, Md, US 183/H2
Pleasant Hope, Mo, US 183/H2
Pleasant Point, Nf, Can. 189/K2
Pleasant Prairie, Wi, US 190/C4
Pleasant View, Ut, US 176/C4
Pleasant View, Tn, US 192/D2
Pleasantdale, Sk, Can. 175/M1
Pleasanton, Ca, US 197/L11
Pleasanton, Ks, US 183/G1
Pleasanton, Tx, US 180/E4
Pleasanton, Ne, US 184/E3
Pleasantville, Ia, US 185/H3
Pleasantville, NY, US 199/K7
Pleasantville, NJ, US 198/C1
Pleasantville, Oh, US 190/C4
Pleasure Ridge Park, Ky, US 192/E1
Pleaux, Fr. 50/E4
Pléchâtel, Fr. 62/C4
Plédran, Fr. 62/C4
Pleiku, Viet. 106/D3
Pleine-Fougères, Fr. 62/D3
Pleinfeld, Ger. 64/D4
Plélan-le-Grand, Fr. 62/C4
Plélan-le-Petit, Fr. 62/C4
Plémet, Fr. 36/H5
Pléneuf-Val-André, Fr. 62/C3
Pleniţa, Rom. 103/E5
Plenty (riv.), Austl. 156/G5
Plenty, Sk, Can. 175/K2
Plenty (bay), NZ 145/H6
Plérin, Fr. 62/C3
Plesetsk, Rus. 74/J3
Pleshchenitsy, Bela. 47/M4
Plesná (riv.), Czh. 65/F2
Plessé, Fr. 62/D5
Plessisville, Qu, Can. 188/B2
Plestin-les-Grèves, Fr. 62/B3
Pleszew, Pol. 49/J3
Plettenberg, Ger. 59/E6
Pleubian, Fr. 62/C3
Pleumartin, Fr.
Pleurtuit, Fr. 62/C3
Pleven, Bul. 57/G4
Plevna, Mt, US 186/B4
Pleyben, Fr. 62/B4
Pleyber-Christ, Fr. 62/B3
Plibo, Libr. 132/D5
Pliego, Sp. 53/E3
Plimmerton, NZ 159/H9
Pliska, Rus.
Plitvička Jezera, NP, Cro. 51/L4
Pljevlja, Mont. 56/D4
Plobsheim, Fr. 61/H6
Ploča, Rt (pt.), Cro. 56/B4
Plöcken (peak),
Plöckenstein,
Ploče, Cro. 56/C4
Ploemeur, Fr. 62/B4
Ploermel, Fr. 62/C4
Ploești, Rom. 57/H3
Plogastel-Saint-Germain, Fr.
Plogoff, Fr. 62/A4
Ploiești, Rom. 57/H3
Plomárion, Gre. 55/K3
Plombières-lès-Dijon, Fr. 66/A3
Plön, Ger. 46/D4
Plonéour-Lanvern, Fr. 62/A4
Plońsk, Pol. 49/K2
Plouagat, Fr. 62/C3
Plouaret, Fr. 62/B3
Plouay, Fr. 62/B4
Ploubalay, Fr. 62/C3
Ploubazlanec, Fr. 62/C3
Ploubezre, Fr. 62/B3
Ploudalmézeau, Fr. 62/A3
Ploudaniel, Fr. 62/A3
Plouescat, Fr. 62/A3
Plouézec, Fr. 62/C3
Plouézévédé, Fr. 62/A3
Plougasnou, Fr. 62/B3
Plougastel-Daoulas, Fr. 62/A4
Plougonven, Fr. 62/B3
Plouguenast, Fr. 62/C4
Plouguerneau, Fr. 62/A3
Plouguernével, Fr. 62/B4
Plouguiel, Fr. 62/B3
Plouha, Fr. 62/C3
Plouhinec, Fr. 62/A4
Plouider, Fr. 62/A3
Plouigneau, Fr. 62/B3
Ploumilliau, Fr. 62/B3
Plounéour-Trez, Fr. 62/A3
Plouray, Fr. 62/B4
Plourin-lès-Morlaix, Fr. 62/B3
Plouvorn, Fr. 62/A3
Plouzané, Fr. 62/A3
Plouzévédé, Fr. 62/A3

Plovdiv (pol. reg.), Bul. 55/J2
Plovdiv, Bul. 57/G4
Plovdiv (prov.), Hun.
Plover, Wi, US 185/K1
Plover Cove (res.), China 99/L7
Plozévet, Fr. 62/A4
Pluguffan, Fr. 62/A4
Pluguffan (int'l arpt.), Fr. 62/A4
Plum (isl.), NY, US 199/F1
Plum City, Wi, US 185/K1
Plum Coulee, Mb, Can. 186/F3
Plum Grove, Tx, US 181/G2
Plumas, Ca, US 186/C2
Plumaugat, Fr. 62/C4
Plumbridge, NI, US 40/A2
Plumerville, Ar, US 183/H3
Plumieux, Fr. 62/A3
Plumridge Lakes Nature Reserve, Austl. 154/E4
Plumsteadville, Pa, US 198/C2
Plumtree, Zim. 141/E4
Plungé, Lith. 47/J4
Plush, Or, US 176/D2
Pluvigner, Fr. 62/B4
Plymouth (cap.)
Plymouth, Monts. 203/N8
Plymouth (co.), Eng, UK 42/B6
Plymouth, Eng, UK 42/B6
Plymouth (arpt.), Eng, UK 42/B6
Plymouth, Ct, US
Plymouth, Fl, US 194/M6
Plymouth, Il, US 185/J3
Plymouth, In, US 190/C4
Plymouth, Ma, US 191/L4
Plymouth, Mn, US 187/P7
Plymouth, NC, US 193/J3
Plymouth, Ne, US 185/F3
Plymouth, NH, US 191/L3
Plymouth, Oh, US 190/C4
Plymouth, Pa, US 198/C1
Plymouth, Wi, US 192/D3
Plymouth (sound), Eng, UK 42/B6
Plymouth Rock, Ma, US 191/L4
Plynlimon
Point Mugu State Park, Ca, US 196/A2
Point Mugu Naval Air Sta., Ca, US 196/A2
Point Nepean NP, Austl. 156/A2
Point of Aire (pt.), Wal, UK 42/C2
Point of Ayre (pt.), IM, UK 40/D3
Point Pedro, SrL. 107/D4
Point Pelee NP, On, Can. 190/E4
Point Pleasant, NJ, US 198/C2
Point Pleasant, Oh, US 192/C1
Point Pleasant, WV, US 193/F1
Point Pleasant Beach, NJ, US 198/D3
Point Reyes National Seashore, Ca, US 184/M4
Point Roberts, Wa, US 174/C3
Point Salines (int'l arpt.), Gren. 217/F7
Point Salvation Abor. Rsv., Austl. 154/D4
Pointe à Gravois, Haiti 207/H2
Pointe à Raquette, Haiti 207/H2
Pointe au Baril Station, On, Can. 190/F2
Pointe d'Arcachon, Fr. 70/C1
Pointe d'Archeboc, Fr. 70/C1
Pointe de Calle-Rousse, Fr.
Pointe de Charbonnel, Fr. 70/D2
Pointe de Chassiron, Fr.
Pointe de la Coubre, Fr. 50/C4
Pointe de la Grande Casse, Fr.
Pointe des Issambres, Fr.
Pointe des Verres, Fr.
Pointe du Cap Roux, Fr.
Pointe du Cheval Blanc, Fr.
Pointe du Déffend, Fr.
Pointe du Hourdel, Fr.
Pointe Noir, Fr.
Pointe Ta'benghisa, Fr.
Pointe-à-la-Croix, Qu, Can. 188/D1
Pointe-à-Pitre, Guad. 203/N8
Pointe-au-Pic, Qu, Can. 188/B1
Pointe-aux-Outardes, Qu, Can. 188/D1
Pointe-aux-Trembles, Qu, Can. 189/N6
Pointe-Calumet, Qu, Can. 189/N6
Pointe-Claire, Qu, Can. 189/N7
Pointe-du-Lac, Qu, Can. 191/K1
Pointe-Noire, Congo 138/B4
Pointe-Verte, NB, Can. 188/E2
Poirino, It. 70/B2
Poison (cr.), Wy, US 177/A3
Poisson Blanc (lake), Qu, Can.
Poissonnier (pt.), Austl. 154/B2
Poissy, Fr. 36/J5
Poitiers, Fr. 50/D4
Poitou (reg.), Fr. 62/C1
Poitou-Charentes, Fr.
Poix-de-Picardie, Fr. 60/A4
Poix-Terron, Fr. 60/D4
Pojo, Bol. 221/F5
Pok Liu Chau (isl.), China 99/K8
Pokaran, India 113/K3
Pokataroo, Austl. 156/D1
Pokegama (lake),

Pograničnyy, Rus. 91/L3
Pogromni (mt.), Ak, US 201/F5
Pogromnoye, Rus. 77/K1
Poh, Indo. 103/F4
P'ohang-ri, NKor. 93/E2
P'ohang, SKor. 96/A2
Pohatcong (cr.), NJ, US 198/C2
Pohénégamook, Qu, Can. 188/C2
Pohja (Pojo), Fin. 47/K1
Pohjanmaa (reg.), Fin. 44/G3
Pohjois-Karjala, Fin.
Pohnpei (isl.), Micr. 160/C4
Pohong, China 99/E4
Pohri, India 108/C3
Poiana Mare, Rom. 78/B6
Poigny-la-Forêt, Fr. 36/H5
Poikkipuoliainen, Fin.
Poing, Ger. 65/E6
Point (lake), NW, Can. 170/E2
Poinsett (cape), Ant. 228/H4
Point, La, US 194/C2
Point, NY, US 191/J3
Point au Fer (pt.), La, US 194/C3
Point au Fer (isl.), La, US 194/C3
Point Baker, Ak, US 201/N4
Point Blank, Tx, US 181/G2
Point Comfort, Tx, US 180/F3
Point Edward, On, Can. 190/E3
Point Fortin, Trin. 217/E12
Point Hope, Ak, US 201/E2
Point Judith, RI, US 191/L4
Point Judith C. G. Station, RI, US
Point Lance, Nf, Can. 189/L2
Point Lay, Ak, US 201/F2
Point Lookout
Point Marion, Pa, US 191/G5
Point Mugu Naval Air Sta.,
Point Mugu State Park, Ca, US 196/A2
Point Nepean NP, Austl. 157/E4
Point of Aire (pt.), Wal, UK 42/C2
Point of Ayre (pt.), IM, UK 40/D3
Point Pedro, SrL. 107/D4
Point Pelee NP, On, Can. 190/E4
Point Pleasant, NJ, US 198/C1
Point Pleasant, Oh, US 192/C1
Point Pleasant, WV, US 193/F1
Point Pleasant Beach, NJ, US
Point Reyes National Seashore, Ca, US
Point Roberts, Wa, US 174/C3
Point Salines (int'l arpt.), Gren. 217/F7
Point Salvation Abor. Rsv., Austl. 154/D4
Poa (riv.), Ven. 217/E2
Poá, Braz. 223/R8
Poabli, Libr. 132/C5
Poatina, Austl. 156/C4
Pobé, Ben. 133/F5
Pobedy (peak), Kyr. 111/D3
Pobiedziska, Pol. 49/J2
Pobla de Segur, Sp. 53/F1
Poca, WV, US 193/G1
Pocahontas, Ar, US 192/B2
Pocahontas, Ia, US 185/G2
Poção de Pedra, Braz. 219/E4
Pocasse Nat'l Wild. Ref., SD, US 186/D5
Pocasset, Ok, US 183/F3
Pocatello, Id, US 177/G2
Pochayiv, Ukr. 78/C2
Pochep, Rus. 76/E1
Pochinki, Rus. 74/G5
Poch'ŏn, NKor. 93/E2
Pochinok, Rus. 76/E1
Poch'ŏn, SKor. 93/D2
Pochotoye, Rus. 79/G5
Pocinhos, Braz. 219/G4
Pöcking, Ger. 67/H2
Pocklington, Eng, UK 41/H4
Pocklington Reef, PNG 160/E6
Poço Fundo, Braz. 223/L6
Poções, Bol. 223/E1
Pocola, Bol. 224/C1
Pocomoke City, Md, US 193/K1
Poconchile, Chile 224/B1
Pocono (mts.), Pa, US 198/C1
Pocono (lake), Pa, US 198/C1
Pocono Pines, Pa, US 198/C1
Poços de Caldas, Braz. 223/L6
Pocrí, Pan. 216/A2
Podberez'ye, Rus. 47/P3
Podbořany, Czh. 65/G2
Podbor'ye, Rus. 75/N3
Poddar'ye, Rus. 47/P3
Podenzano, It. 68/D3
Podgorenskiy, Rus. 79/K2
Podkarpackie (prov.), Pol. 49/L4
Podlasie (reg.),
Podol'sk, Rus. 75/W9
Podolínec, Czh.
Podor, Sen. 132/B2
Podporozh'ye, Rus. 74/G3
Podravska Slatina, Cro. 56/C3
Podujevo, Serb. 56/E4
Poenari Burchi, Rom. 57/H3
Pofadder, SAfr. 140/C3
Pogibonsi, It. 69/E7
Poix-de-Picardie, Fr. 60/A4
Pogradec, Alb. 55/G2

Pokhvistnevo, Rus. 77/K1
Poko, D.R. Congo 139/F2
Pokrovka, Rus. 77/K1
Pokrovsk, Rus. 81/N3
Pokrovs'ke, Ukr. 79/J3
Pokrovs'ke, Ukr. 79/J4
Pokrovskoye, Rus. 76/F1
Pokrovskoye, Rus. 79/H4
Pol'ana (peak), Slvk. 76/A2
Pol-e Sefid, Iran 115/H2
Pole (inlet), Nun, Can. 171/U1
Pole of Inaccessibility, Ant. 228/E
Poleski NP, Pol. 49/M3
Polesella, It. 69/E3
Polesine (reg.), It. 69/E3
Polessk, Rus. 47/J4
Poles'ye, Bela. 76/D1
Polevskoy, Rus. 75/P4
Polgár, Hun. 73/D5
Poli, Camr. 134/B3
Poli (isl.), Gre. 55/J4
Poličastro (gulf), It. 54/E2
Police, Pol. 48/F2
Police, Pol.
Policoro, It. 54/E2
Polička, Czh.
Poligny, Fr. 66/B4
Políkastron, Gre. 55/H2
Políkhni, Gre. 55/H2
Poliízel NP, Gre. 49/H3
Polis, Cyp. 116/C2
Polis'ke, Ukr. 78/E2
Poliyiros, Gre. 55/H2
Polje, Slov. 51/L3
Polk, Ne, US 185/F3
Polk (co.), Fl, US 194/M8
Polkowice, Pol. 49/J3
Polkville, Ms, US 187/K4
Polkville, NC, US 193/G3
Pollāchi, India 107/C4
Pollár, Bol. 221/E5
Pollença, Sp. 53/G3
Pollica, It. 54/D2
Pollock, Id, US 176/D4
Pollock, La, US 194/B2
Pollock, SD, US 186/D3
Pollock Pines, Ca, US 176/C4
Pollockville, Ab, Can. 175/J2
Polo, Il, US 185/K3
Polo, Mo, US 185/G4
Polochic (riv.), Guat. 202/D3
Polohy, Ukr. 79/J4
Polomolok, Phil. 100/D4
Polonia (cape), Uru. 191/G2
Polonia, Ms, US 187/K1
Polonia (int'l arpt.), Indo. 101/B2
Polonne, Ukr. 78/C2
Polonnaruwa, SrL. 107/D4
Polperro, Eng, UK 42/B6
Polski Trümbesh, Bul. 57/G4
Polson, Mt, US 175/G4
Poltava, Ukr. 79/G2
Poltava (int'l arpt.), Ukr. 194/P10
Poltava Oblast, Ukr. 76/F2
Pöltsamaa, Est. 47/L2
Põlva, Est. 47/M2
Polvadera, NM, US 179/J3
Polvijärvi, Fin.
Polvoredas, Sp. 52/C1
Polyarnyy, Rus. 74/G1
Polyarnyy, Rus. 172/U12
Polynesia (reg.) 160/G4
Pomabamba, Peru 220/B3
Pomaria, SC, US 193/G3
Pomarico, It. 54/E2
Pomáz, Hun.
Pomerania (reg.), Pol.
Pomeranian (bay), Ger., Pol. 54/L7
Pomeroon-Supenaam (pol. reg.), Guy. 217/G2
Pomeroy, NI, UK 40/B2
Pomeroy, Oh, US 193/F1
Pomeroy, Wa, US 174/F4
Pomezia, It. 71/C5
Pomichna, Ukr. 78/F3
Pomigliano d'Arco, It. 71/D6
Pommelsbrunn, Ger.
Pommersfelden, Ger. 64/D3
Pomona, Ca, US 196/C2
Pomona, Mo, US 183/J2
Pomona (lake), Ks, US 185/G2
Pomona, Md, US 198/B6
Pomorie, Bul. 57/J4
Pomorskie (prov.), Pol. 49/J2
Pomos (pt.), Cyp. 116/C2
Pomozdino, Rus. 75/M3
Pompano Beach, Fl, US 194/P10
Pompei, It. 71/D6
Pompei (ruin), It. 71/D6
Pompéia, Braz. 225/G2
Pompey's Pillar Nat'l Mon., Mt, US 175/J4
Pompiano, It. 68/C3
Pompton (riv.), NJ, US 199/H8

Pompton Lakes, NJ, US 199/H8
Ponca (cr.), SD,Ne, US 184/E2
Ponca City, Ok, US 183/F2
Ponce, PR 203/M8
Ponce de Leon, Fl, US 195/F2
Ponce Inlet, Fl, US 195/H3
Poncha Springs, Co, US 179/J3
Ponchatoula, La, US 194/C2
Pond (inlet), Nun, Can. 171/U1
Pond (cape), Austl. 152/B3
Pond (lake), Mi, US 197/E6
Pond Creek, Ok, US 183/F2
Pond Inlet, Nun, Can. 171/U1
Ponderay, Id, US 174/F3
Pondicherry (terr.), India 104/B5
Ponferrada, Sp. 52/B1
Pong Nam Ron, Thai. 106/C3
Pongdong, SKor. 93/D5
Pongola (riv.), SAfr. 143/E2
Pongo (riv.), Sudan 135/E4
Poni (prov.), Burk. 132/E4
Ponnaiyar (riv.), India 104/C5
Ponnani, India 75/P4
Ponoka, Ab, Can. 175/H1
Ponoy (riv.), Rus. 74/J2
Ponza, It. 54/C2
Ponziane (isl.), It. 71/C6
Poole, Eng, UK 42/D5
Poole (co.), Eng, UK 42/D5
Poole (bay), Eng, UK 43/E5
Poolewe, Sc, UK 37/R8
Poona (Pune), India 113/K5
Poondinna (mt.), Austl. 155/F3
Poopó (lake), Bol. 209/C4
Poopó, Bol. 224/C1
Poortugaal, Neth. 58/B5
Pöössäpää (pt.), Est. 47/K2
Poosepatuck Ind. Res., NY, US 199/F2
Popa (peak), Myan. 98/B4
Popayán, Col. 216/B4
Poperinge, Belg. 60/B2
Popil'nya, Ukr. 78/E3
Popilta (lake), Austl. 155/J5
Popina, Bul. 57/H3
Popio (lake), Austl. 155/H5
Poplar, Mt, US 186/B3
Poplar (riv.), Mt, US 186/B3
Poplar Bluff, Mo, US 192/B2
Poplar Creek, BC, Can. 174/F2
Poplar Hill, 187/G1
Poplar Tent, NC, US
Poplar, West Fork
Poplar-Cotton Center, Ca, US
Poplarfield, Mb, Can. 186/F2
Poplarville, Ms, US 187/J5
Popocatépetl (vol.), Mex. 205/L7
Popokabaka, CAfr. 134/C4
Popoli, It. 71/C3
Popomanaseu (peak), Sol. 165/M7
Popondetta, PNG 153/H2
Popovo, Bul. 57/H4
Poppberg (peak), Ger. 65/E4
Poppenhausen, Ger. 58/E2
Poppenhausen, Ger. 64/D2
Poppi, It. 69/E6
Poprad (riv.), Slvk. 49/L4
Poprad, Slvk. 49/L4
Poquoson, Va, US 193/J2
Porangahau, NZ 159/D3
Porangatu, Braz. 222/C2
Porbandar, India 113/J4
Porce (riv.), Col. 216/C3
Porcheville, Fr. 36/H5
Porco, Bol. 224/C1
Porcuna, Sp. 52/C4
Porcupine (hills), Sk, Can. 186/C1
Porcupine (cr.), Mt, US 175/J3
Porcupine Gorge NP, Austl. 158/B3
Pordenone, It. 69/F2
Pordenone (prov.), It. 69/F2
Pordic, Fr. 62/C3
Pordim, Bul. 57/G4
Poreč, Cro. 69/G3
Pored'ye, Bela. 47/L5
Poretskoye, Rus. 75/K5
Porgera, PNG 153/F1
Pori (int'l arpt.), Fin. 47/J1
Pori, Fin.
Porirua (har.), NZ 159/H9
Porirua, NZ 159/H9
Porkhov, Rus. 47/N3
Porkkala, Fin. 45/E5

Plovdiv (pol. reg.), Bul. 55/J2
Ponte, It. 68/C3
Pontenure, It. 68/C3
Ponterwyd, Wal, UK 42/C2
Pontes e Lacerda, Braz. 222/G4
Pontesbury, Eng, UK 42/D1
Pontestura, It. 68/B3
Pontevedra, Sp. 52/A1
Pontevedra, Phil. 100/C3
Pontevico, It. 68/C3
Pontgouin, Fr. 63/G4
Ponthévrard, Fr. 36/H6
Ponthieu (reg.), Fr. 60/A3
Pontiac, Mi, US 190/D3
Pontiac (lake), Mi, US 197/E6
Pontiac, Il, US 185/K3
Pontianak, Indo. 102/C4
Pontinia, It. 71/C5
Pontivy, Fr. 62/C4
Pontlevoy, Fr. 63/G4
Ponto da Divisão, Braz. 218/B5
Pontoise, Fr. 36/J4
Pontonnyy, Rus. 75/T7
Pontorson, Fr. 62/D3
Pontotoc, Ms, US 192/C3
Pontotoc, Tx, US 180/E2
Pontremoli, It. 68/C5
Pontresina, Swi. 67/F5
Pontrhydfendigaid, Wal, UK
Pontrilas, Eng, UK 42/D2
Pontrilas, Sk, Can. 175/M1
Pontvallain, Fr. 63/F5
Pontybodkin, Wal, UK
Pontypool, On, Can. 191/G2
Pontypool, Wal, UK 42/D3
Pontypridd, Wal, UK 42/D3
Ponui (isl.), NZ 159/G6
Pony, Mt, US 177/H1
Ponza, It. 54/C2
Ponziane (isl.), It. 71/C6
Poole (bay), Eng, UK 43/E5
Poona (Pune), India 113/K5
Poondarrie,
Poondinna (mt.), Austl. 155/F3
Poopó (lake), Bol. 209/C4
Poor Man Ind. Res.,
Poortugaal, Neth. 58/B5
Pöössäpää (pt.), Est. 47/K2
Poosepatuck Ind. Res., NY, US 199/F2
Popa (peak), Myan. 98/B4
Popayán, Col. 216/B4
Poperinge, Belg. 60/B2
Popilta (lake), Austl. 155/J5
Popina, Bul. 57/H3
Popio (lake), Austl. 155/H5
Poplar, Mt, US 186/B3
Poplar (riv.), Mt, US 186/B3
Poplar Bluff, Mo, US 192/B2
Poplar Creek, BC, Can. 174/F2
Poplar Tent, NC, US
Poplar, West Fork
Poplar-Cotton Center, Ca, US
Popocatépetl (vol.), Mex. 205/L7
Popoli, It.
Popovo, Bul. 57/H4
Poppberg (peak), Ger. 65/E4
Poppenhausen, Ger. 64/D2
Poprad, Slvk. 49/L4
Poquonock, NKor. 93/D3
Porangahau, NZ 159/D3
Porbandar, India 113/J4
Porce (riv.), Col. 216/C3
Porco, Bol. 224/C1
Porcupine (hills), Sk, Can. 186/C1
Porcupine Gorge NP, Austl. 158/B3
Pordenone, It. 69/F2
Pordenone (prov.), It. 69/F2
Pordic, Fr. 62/C3
Pordim, Bul. 57/G4
Poreč, Cro. 69/G3
Pored'ye, Bela. 47/L5

Pontenure, It. 68/C3
Ponterwyd, Wal, UK 42/C2
Pontes e Lacerda, Braz. 222/G4
Pontesbury, Eng, UK 42/D1
Pontestura, It. 68/B3
Pontevedra, Sp. 52/A1
Pontevedra, Phil. 100/C3
Pontevico, It. 68/C3
Pontgouin, Fr. 63/G4
Ponthévrard, Fr. 36/H6
Ponthieu (reg.), Fr. 60/A3
Pontiac, Mi, US 190/D3
Pontiac (lake), Mi, US 197/E6
Pontiac, Il, US 185/K3
Pontianak, Indo. 102/C4
Pontinia, It. 71/C5
Pontivy, Fr. 62/C4
Pontlevoy, Fr. 63/G4
Ponto da Divisão, Braz. 218/B5
Pontoise, Fr. 36/J4
Pontonnyy, Rus. 75/T7
Pontorson, Fr. 62/D3
Pontotoc, Ms, US 192/C3
Pontotoc, Tx, US 180/E2
Pontremoli, It. 68/C5
Pontresina, Swi. 67/F5
Pontrhydfendigaid, Wal, UK
Pontrilas, Eng, UK 42/D2
Pontrilas, Sk, Can. 175/M1
Pontvallain, Fr. 63/F5
Pontybodkin, Wal, UK
Pontypool, On, Can. 191/G2
Pontypool, Wal, UK 42/D3
Pontypridd, Wal, UK 42/D3
Ponui (isl.), NZ 159/G6
Pony, Mt, US 177/H1
Ponza, It. 54/C2
Ponziane (isl.), It. 71/C6
Poole (bay), Eng, UK 43/E5
Poolewe, Sc, UK 37/R8
Poona (Pune), India 113/K5
Poondarrie, Austl. 156/B2
Poondinna (mt.), Austl. 155/F3
Poopó (lake), Bol. 209/C4
Poopó, Bol. 224/C1
Poor Man Ind. Res.,
Poortugaal, Neth. 58/B5
Pöössäpää (pt.), Est. 47/K2
Poosepatuck Ind. Res., NY, US 199/F2
Popa (peak), Myan. 98/B4
Popayán, Col. 216/B4
Poperinge, Belg. 60/B2
Popilta (lake), Austl. 155/J5
Popina, Bul. 57/H3
Popio (lake), Austl. 155/H5
Poplar, Mt, US 186/B3
Poplar (riv.), Mt, US 186/B3
Poplar Bluff, Mo, US 192/B2
Poplar Creek, BC, Can. 174/F2
Poplar Hill, 187/G1
Poplar Tent, NC, US
Poplar, West Fork
Poplar-Cotton Center, Can. 178/C2
Poplarfield, Mb, Can. 186/F2
Poplarville, Ms, US 187/J5
Popocatépetl (vol.), Mex. 205/L7
Popokabaka, CAfr. 134/C4
Popoli, It. 71/C3
Popomanaseu (peak), Sol. 165/M7
Popondetta, PNG 153/H2
Popovo, Bul. 57/H4
Poppberg (peak), Ger. 65/E4
Poppenhausen, Ger. 58/E2
Poppenhausen, Ger. 64/D2
Poppi, It. 69/E6
Poprad (riv.), Slvk. 49/L4
Poprad, Slvk. 49/L4
Poquoson, Va, US 193/J2
Porangahau, NZ 159/D3
Porbandar, India 113/J4
Porce (riv.), Col. 216/C3
Porcuna, Sp. 52/C4
Porcupine (cr.), Mt, US 175/J3
Porcupine Gorge NP, Austl. 158/B3
Pordenone, It. 69/F2
Pordenone (prov.), It. 69/F2
Pordic, Fr. 62/C3
Pordim, Bul. 57/G4
Pore, Cro. 69/G3
Pored'ye, Bela. 47/L5
Poretskoye, Rus. 75/K5
Porgera, PNG 153/F1
Pori (int'l arpt.), Fin. 47/J1
Pori, Fin.
Porirua, NZ 159/H9
Porkhov, Rus. 47/N3
Porkkala, Fin. 45/E5

Porkk – Puerto
321

Porkkalanselkä (bay), Fin. 45/E5
Porlamar, Ven. 217/F2
Porlezza, It. 67/F5
Porlock, Eng, UK 42/C4
Pormpuraaw Abor. Land, Austl. 153/F3
Pornainen (Borgnäs), Fin. 45/F4
Pornic, Fr. 50/B3
Pornichet, Fr. 62/C6
Poronaysk, Rus. 91/N2
Porongo (peak), Arg. 224/C4
Porongurup NP, Austl. 154/C5
Póros, Gre. 55/H4
Porozhsk, Rus. 75/M3
Porpoise (bay), Ant. 228/J
Porrentruy, Swi. 66/D3
Porretta Terme, It. 69/D5
Porriño, Sp. 52/A1
Porsangen (inlet), Nor. 44/H1
Porsgrunn, Nor. 46/C2
Porsuk (riv.), Turk. 76/D5
Port (isl.), Japan 95/H6
Port Adelaide (nbrhd.), Austl. 155/M8
Port Albert, Austl. 157/C4
Port Alexander, Ak, US 201/M4
Port Alfred, SAfr. 142/D4
Port Allegany, Pa, US 191/G4
Port Allen, La, US 194/C2
Port Angeles, Wa, US 174/C3
Port Antonio, Jam. 207/G2
Port Appin, Sc, UK 39/A3
Port Aransas, Tx, US 181/F4
Port Arthur, Tx, US 181/H3
Port Askaig, Sc, UK 37/Q9
Port au Port (pen.), Nf, Can. 189/H1
Port au Port (bay), Nf, Can. 189/H1
Port Augusta, Austl. 155/H5
Port Austin, Mi, US 190/E2
Port Bannatyne, Sc, UK 39/A5
Port Barre, La, US 194/C2
Port Blair, India 105/F5
Port Blakely, Wa, US 197/C2
Port Blandford, Nf, Can. 189/K1
Port Bolivar, Tx, US 181/N9
Port Bouet (Abidgan) (int'l arpt.), C.d'Iv. 132/E5
Port Broughton, Austl. 155/H5
Port Burwell, On, Can. 190/F3
Port Burwell, Qu, Can. 171/K2
Port Canning, India 109/G4
Port Carbon, Pa, US 198/B2
Port Carling, On, Can. 191/G2
Port Chalmers, NZ 159/B4
Port Charlotte, Fl, US 195/G4
Port Chester, NY, US 199/L8
Port Clements, BC, Can. 201/M5
Port Clinton, Oh, US 190/E4
Port Clinton, Pa, US 198/B2
Port Colborne, On, Can. 190/U10
Port Columbus (int'l arpt.), Oh, US 190/E5
Port Credit, On, Can. 190/T8
Port Darlington, On, Can. 190/V8
Port Davey (har.), Austl. 156/C4
Port Deposit, Md, US 198/B4
Port Dickson, Malay. 101/C2
Port Discovery (bay), Wa, US 197/B1
Port Douglas, Austl. 158/B2
Port Eads, La, US 194/D3
Port Edward, BC, Can. 201/M4
Port Edwards, Wi, US 185/K1
Port Elgin, On, Can. 188/E2
Port Elgin, On, Can. 190/F2
Port Elizabeth, SAfr. 142/D4
Port Elizabeth, NJ, US 198/D5
Port Ellen, Sc, UK 37/Q9
Port Elliot, Austl. 155/H5
Port Erin, IM, UK 40/D3
Port Fairy, Austl. 156/B3
Port Gamble, Wa, US 197/B2
Port Gamble Ind. Res., Wa, US 197/B2
Port Gibson, Ms, US 194/C2
Port Glasgow, Sc, UK 39/B5
Port Graham, Ak, US 201/H4
Port Harcourt (int'l arpt.), Nga. 133/G5
Port Harcourt, Nga. 133/G5
Port Hardy, BC, Can. 170/D3
Port Hawkesbury, NS, Can. 189/G3
Port Hedland (int'l arpt.), Austl. 154/C2
Port Hedland, Austl. 154/C2
Port Heiden, Ak, US 201/G4
Port Hood, NS, Can. 189/G2
Port Hope, Mi, US 190/E3
Port Hope, On, Can. 191/G3
Port Howard, UK 191/F6
Port Hueneme, Ca, US 196/A2
Port Huron, Mi, US 190/E3
Port İliç, Azer. 115/G2
Port Isaac (bay), Eng, UK 42/B5
Port Isaac, Eng, UK 42/B5
Port Isabel, Tx, US 180/F4
Port Jefferson, NY, US 199/E2
Port Jervis, NY, US 191/J4
Port Keats, Austl. 152/C3
Port Kembla, Austl. 157/E2
Port Kenny, Austl. 155/G5
Port Lambton, On, Can. 197/H6
Port Lavaca, Tx, US 180/F3
Port Leyden, NY, US 191/J3
Port Lincoln, Austl. 155/G5
Port Lions, Ak, US 201/H4
Port Loko, SLeo. 132/B4
Port Louis (cap.), Mrts. 143/T15
Port Ludlow, Wa, US 174/C4
Port Macdonnell, Austl. 156/B3
Port Macquarie, Austl. 156/E1
Port Madison Ind. Res., Wa, US 197/B2
Port Maria, Jam. 207/G2
Port Medway, NS, Can. 188/E3
Port Monmouth, NJ, US 199/J10
Port Moresby (cap.), PNG 153/G2
Port Neches, Tx, US 181/H3
Port Nicholson (bay), NZ 159/H9
Port Nolloth, SAfr. 142/B3
Port Norris, NJ, US 198/C5
Port O'Conner, Tx, US 180/F3
Port of Ness, Sc, UK 37/Q7
Port Orange, Fl, US 195/H3
Port Orchard, Wa, US 174/C4
Port Orford, Or, US 176/A2
Port Penn, De, US 198/C4
Port Phillip (bay), Austl. 156/C3
Port Pirie, Austl. 155/H5
Port Reading, NJ, US 199/J9
Port Renfrew, BC, Can. 174/B3
Port Republic, NJ, US 198/D4
Port Rexton, Nf, Can. 189/L1
Port Richey, Fl, US 194/K7
Port Richmond (nbrhd.), NY, US 199/J9
Port Rowan, On, Can. 190/F3
Port Royal, Pa, US 198/A2
Port Royal (sound), SC, US 193/G4
Port Said (Būr Sa'īd), Egypt 131/D2
Port Saint Joe, Fl, US 195/F3
Port Saint Johns, SAfr. 142/E3
Port Saint Lucie, Fl, US 195/H4
Port Saint Mary, IM, UK 40/D3
Port San Carlos, UK 191/F6
Port Seton, Sc, UK 39/D5
Port Shepstone, SAfr. 143/E3
Port Simpson, BC, Can. 201/M4
Port Stanley, On, Can. 190/F3
Port Stephens, UK 191/E7
Port Stevens (bay), Austl. 145/E4
Port Sudan (Būr Sūdān), Sudan 127/H5
Port Sulphur, La, US 194/D3
Port Townsend, Wa, US 174/C3
Port Union, Nf, Can. 189/L1
Port Victoria, Austl. 155/H5
Port Wakefield, Austl. 155/H5
Port Washington, Wi, US 190/C3
Port Washington, NY, US 199/L8
Port Weld, Malay. 101/C1
Port William, Sc, UK 40/D2
Port Williams, NS, Can. 188/E3
Port Wing, Wi, US 187/J4
Port-au-Prince (cap.), Haiti 207/H2
Port-Bergé, Madg. 143/H6
Port-Bouët, C.d'Iv. 132/E5
Port-Brillet, Fr. 63/E4
Port-Cartier, Qu, Can. 171/K3
Port-Cros Nat'l Park, Fr. 70/C7
Port-de-Bouc, Fr. 70/A6
Port-de-Paix, Haiti 207/H2
Port-en-Bessin-Huppain, Fr. 63/E2
Port-Eynon (pt.), Wal, UK 42/B3
Port-Gentil, Gabon 138/B3
Port-la-Nouvelle, Fr. 50/E5
Port-Louis, Fr. 62/B5
Port-Louis, Guad., Fr. 203/N8
Port-Menier, Qu, Can. 171/K4
Port-of-Spain (cap.), Trin. 217/F2
Port-Saint-Louis-du-Rhône, Fr. 70/A6
Port-sur-Saône, Fr. 66/C2
Port-Vila (cap.), Van. 160/F6
Porta Westfalica, Ger. 59/F4
Porta Westfalica (pass), Ger. 59/F4
Portachuelo, Bol. 221/F5
Portadown, NI, UK 40/B3
Portaferry, NI, UK 40/C3
Portage (bay), Mb, Can. 186/E2
Portage (lake), Mi, US 187/K4
Portage (pt.), Mi, US 190/C2
Portage, Mi, US 190/D3
Portage, Pa, US 191/G4
Portage, Wi, US 185/K2
Portage la Prairie, Mb, Can. 186/E3
Portage-du-Fort, Qu, Can. 191/H2
Portageville, Mo, US 192/C2
Portal, Az, US 179/H5
Portal, Ga, US 193/G4
Portal, ND, US 186/C3
Portalegre (dist.), Port. 52/B3
Portalegre, Port. 52/B3
Portales, NM, US 182/C3
Portarlington, Ire. 38/C3
Portarlington, Austl. 157/B4
Portavogie, NI, UK 40/C3
Portbail, Fr. 62/D2
Portbou, Sp. 50/E5
Portchester, Eng, UK 43/E5
Porteiras, Braz. 219/G4
Portel, Braz. 218/D3
Porteña, Arg. 224/D4
Porter, Ok, US 183/G3
Porter, Tx, US 181/M8
Porterdale, Ga, US 192/F4
Porters (lake), Pa, US 198/C1
Porters Lake, NS, Can. 188/F3
Porterville, SAfr. 142/L10
Porterville, Ca, US 178/C2
Portes d'Enfer, D.R. Congo 139/F4
Portes-lès-Valence, Fr. 70/A3
Portet-sur-Garonne, Fr. 50/D5
Portete (bay), Col. 207/J3
Portezuelo de Socompa (pass), Chile 224/B3
Portglenone, NI, UK 40/B2
Portgordon, Sc, UK 39/C1
Porth, Wal, UK 42/C3
Porthill, Id, US 174/F3
Porthleven, Eng, UK 42/A6
Portici, It. 71/D6
Portillo, Chile 226/N8
Portimão, Port. 52/A4
Portishead, Eng, UK 42/D4
Portknockie, Sc, UK 39/D1
Portland (cape), Austl. 156/C4
Portland, Austl. 157/E1
Portland, Austl. 156/B3
Portland, On, Can. 191/H2
Portland (pt.), Jam. 207/G2
Portland, NZ 159/C1
Portland, Eng, UK 42/D5
Portland, Ar, US 183/J4
Portland, Fl, US 195/E2
Portland, In, US 190/D4
Portland, Me, US 188/B4
Portland, ND, US 186/F4
Portland, Or, US 176/B1
Portland (int'l arpt.), Or, US 174/C5
Portland, Tn, US 192/D2
Portland, Tx, US 181/F4
Portland Canal (bay), BC, Can. 201/M4
Portland Jetport (int'l arpt.), Me, US 191/L3
Portlaoise, Ire. 38/C3
Portlaw, Ire. 38/C5
Portlethen, Sc, UK 39/D2
Portlock Reefs (reef), PNG 153/G2
Portmahomack, Sc, UK 39/C1
Portmarnock, Ire. 40/B5
Portmore, Jam. 207/G2
Portneuf (riv.), Qu, Can. 188/C1
Porto, Braz. 219/F3
Porto (gulf), Fr. 54/A1
Porto, Port. 52/A2
Porto (dist.), Port. 52/A2
Porto (int'l arpt.), Port. 52/A2
Porto Alegre, Braz. 225/G4
Porto Amboim, Ang. 138/C5
Porto Amboim (bay), Ang. 140/B1
Porto Azzurro, It. 54/B1
Porto Calvo, Braz. 219/H5
Porto Ceresio, It. 67/E6
Pôrto da Fôlha, Braz. 223/F1
Porto de Mós, Port. 52/A3
Porto de Moz, Braz. 218/C3
Porto de Pedras, Braz. 219/H5
Porto Empedocle, It. 54/C4
Porto Ercole, It. 54/B1
Porto Feliz, Braz. 225/H2
Porto Ferreira, Braz. 225/H2
Porto Franco, Braz. 219/E4
Porto Garibaldi, It. 69/F4
Porto Gole, GBis. 132/B4
Porto Inglês, CpV. 119/K10
Porto Moniz, Port. 128/A2
Porto Murtinho, Braz. 224/E2
Porto Nacional, Braz. 222/C1
Porto Novo, CpV. 119/J9
Porto Poet, Braz. 218/C2
Porto Potenza Picena, It. 69/G7
Porto Recanati, It. 69/G7
Porto Rico, Ang. 138/C4
Porto Rico, Braz. 225/F2
Porto San Giorgio, It. 71/C1
Porto Santo (isl.), Port. 128/A2
Porto Santo Stefano, It. 54/B1
Porto Seguro, Braz. 223/F3
Porto Tolle, It. 69/F4
Porto Torres, It. 54/A2
Porto União, Braz. 225/G3
Porto Valtravaglia, It. 67/E6
Porto Velho, Braz. 221/F3
Porto-Novo (cap.), Ben. 133/F5
Porto-Vecchio, Fr. 54/A2
Portobelo, PN, Pan. 207/G4
Portocannone, It. 71/D4
Portoferraio, It. 54/B1
Portofino, It. 68/C5
Portogruaro, It. 69/F2
Portola, Ca, US 176/C4
Portomaggiore, It. 69/E4
Portovenere, It. 68/C5
Portoviejo, Ecu. 216/A5
Portpatrick, Sc, UK 40/C2
Portree, Sc, UK 37/Q8
Portroe, Ire. 38/B4
Portrush, NI, UK 40/B1
Portsea (isl.), Eng, UK 43/E5
Portslade-by-Sea, Eng, UK 43/F5
Portsmouth, Dom. 203/N9
Portsmouth, Eng, UK 43/E5
Portsmouth (co.), Eng, UK 43/E5
Portsmouth (isl.), NC, US 193/J3
Portsmouth, Oh, US 193/F1
Portsmouth, Va, US 193/J2
Portsoy, Sc, UK 39/D1
Portstewart, NI, UK 40/B1
Portugal (ctry.) 52/A3
Portugalete, Bol. 224/C2
Portugalete, Sp. 50/B5
Portuguesa (riv.), Ven. 203/H6
Portuguesa (state), Ven. 216/D2
Portuguese Bend (nbrhd.), Ca, US 196/F8
Portumna, Ire. 38/B3
Porum, Ok, US 183/G3
Porvenir, Bol. 220/D3
Porvenir, Bol. 221/F4
Porvenir, Chile 191/C7
Porvenir, Peru 220/C2
Porvenir, Uru. 191/K10
Porvoo (Borgå), Fin. 47/L1
Porvoonjoki (riv.), Fin. 45/F4
Porz, Ger. 61/G2
Porzuna, Sp. 52/C3
Posada, It. 54/A2
Posadas, Sp. 52/C4
Posadas, Arg. 225/F3
Posavina (valley), Bosn.,Cro. 73/H1
Posavina (valley), Bosn. 56/C3
Poschiavo, Swi. 67/G5
Poseyville, In, US 192/D1
Poshnjë, Alb. 55/F2
Posht-e Bādām, Iran 115/H3
Posio, Fin. 74/F2
Positano, It. 71/D6
Poso (cr.), Ca, US 178/C3
Poso, Indo. 103/F4
Poso (lake), Indo. 103/F4
Posof, Turk. 77/G4
Posŏng (riv.), SKor. 93/D5
Posŏng, SKor. 93/D5
Posorja, Ecu. 216/A5
Pospelikha, Rus. 111/D1
Posse, Braz. 222/D2
Possel, CAfr. 134/C4
Possession (pt.), Wa, US 197/C2
Possession (sound), Wa, US 197/C2
Possum Kingdom (lake), Tx, US 181/E1
Post, Tx, US 182/D4
Post Falls, Id, US 174/F4
Postal (Burgstall), It. 67/H4
Poste Maurice Cortier (ruin), Alg. 129/F5
Postmasburg, SAfr. 142/C3
Postoak, Tx, US 183/E4
Postojna, Slov. 51/L4
Postolprty, Czh. 65/G2
Poston, Az, US 178/E4
Postrervalle, Bol. 224/D1
Postville, Ia, US 185/J2
Pot (mtn.), Id, US 174/G4
Pota, Indo. 103/F5
Potam, Mex. 204/C3
Potamós, Gre. 55/H5
Potaro (riv.), Guy. 218/B1
Potaro-Siparuni (pol. reg.), Guy. 217/G3
Potawatomi Ind. Res., Ks, US 185/F4
Potawatomi Ind. Res., Mi, US 187/L5
Potawatomi Ind. Res., Mi, US 190/C2
Potawatomi Ind. Res., Wi, US 187/K5
Potawatomi Ind. Res., Wi, US 185/K1
Potchefstroom, SAfr. 142/D2
Poteau, Ok, US 183/G3
Poteet, Tx, US 180/E3
Potengi, Braz. 219/G4
Potenza, It. 54/D2
Potenza (riv.), It. 54/C1
Potenza Picena, It. 69/G7
Potes, Sp. 52/C1
Potgietersrus, SAfr. 141/F5
Poth, Tx, US 181/E3
Potholes (res.), Wa, US 174/E4
P'ot'i, Geo. 77/G4
Poti (riv.), Braz. 219/F4
Potigny, Fr. 63/E3
Potlatch, Id, US 174/F4
Potomac, Il, US 190/C4
Potomac, Md, US 198/A5
Potomac (riv.), Md, US 193/J1
Potoru, SLeo. 132/C5
Potosi (mtn.), Nv, US 178/E3
Potosi, Mo, US 192/B2
Potosí (dept.), Bol. 224/C2
Potosí, Bol. 224/C1
Potosi, Tx, US 180/E1
Potrerillos, Chile 224/B3
Potrero, Ca, US 178/D4
Potro, Cerro del (peak), Arg.,Chile 224/B4
Potsdam, NY, US 191/J2
Potsdam, Ger. 48/Q7
Pottangi, India 107/D2
Pottenstein, Ger. 65/E3
Potter, Ne, US 184/C3
Potter Street, Eng, UK 36/D1
Potters Bar, Eng, UK 36/C1
Potterspury, Eng, UK 43/F2
Pottersville, Mo, US 183/H2
Pöttmes, Ger. 64/E5
Potton, Eng, UK 43/F2
Potts Camp, Ms, US 192/C3
Pottsboro, Tx, US 183/F4
Pottstown, Pa, US 198/C3
Pottsville, Pa, US 198/B2
Potwin, Ks, US 183/F2
Pouch Cove, Nf, Can. 189/L2
Poudre d'or, Mrts. 143/T15
Poughkeepsie, NY, US 191/K4
Pouilley-les-Vignes, Fr. 66/B3
Poulains (pt.), Fr. 62/B6
Poulan, Ga, US 195/G2
Poulaphouca (res.), Ire. 38/D3
Poulaphoucha (res.), Ire. 40/B5
Pouldreuzic, Fr. 62/A5
Poulsbo, Wa, US 174/C4
Poulter (riv.), Eng, UK 41/G5
Poultney, Vt, US 191/K3
Poulton-le-Fylde, Eng, UK 41/F4
Pouma, Camr. 138/B2
Poŭn, SKor. 93/D4
Pound, Wi, US 190/B2
Pounga-Nganda, Gabon 138/B3
Poungthak, Laos 106/D2
Poura, Burk. 132/E4
Pourri (peak), Fr. 70/C1
Pouru-Saint-Remy, Fr. 61/E4
Pouso Alegre, Braz. 223/L7
Pouss, Camr. 134/B3
Pouthisat, Camb. 106/C3
Pouthisat (riv.), Camb. 105/H5
Pouzauges, Fr. 50/C3
Považská Bystrica, Slvk. 49/K4
Povegliano Veronese, It. 69/D3
Povenets, Rus. 74/G3
Poverty Point Nat'l Mon., La, US 192/B4
Poviglio, It. 68/D4
Póvoa de Varzim, Port. 52/A2
Povoação, Azor., Port. 53/T13
Povorino, Rus. 79/M2
Povorotnyy, Mys (pt.), Rus. 91/L3
Povungnituk (riv.), Qu, Can. 171/J2
Povungnituk, Qu, Can. 171/J2
Powassan, On, Can. 191/G1
Poway, Ca, US 196/C5
Powder (riv.), Mt,Wy, US 172/E2
Powder River (pass), Wy, US 177/K1
Powder River, Wy, US 177/K2
Powder Springs, Ga, US 193/L7
Powder, North Fork (riv.), Wy, US 184/A2
Powder, South Fork (riv.), Wy, US 184/A2
Powderhorn, Co, US 179/J1
Powderly, Tx, US 183/G4
Powderville, Mt, US 186/B5
Powell (lake), Az,Ut, US 163/F6
Powell (cr.), Pa, US 198/B3
Powell, Tn, US 192/E2
Powell (riv.), Va, US 193/F2
Powell (mtn.), WV, US 193/G1
Powell, Wy, US 177/J1
Powell River, BC, Can. 174/B3
Powellton, WV, US 193/G1
Power (res.), NY, US 190/U9
Power, Mt, US 175/J4
Power Head (pt.), Ire. 38/B6
Powers (lake), Wi, US 197/P14
Powers, Or, US 176/A2
Powers Lake, ND, US 186/C3
Powhatan, Va, US 193/J2
Powhatan Point, Oh, US 190/F5
Powys (co.), Wal, UK 42/C2
Poxoreo, Braz. 222/B2
Poxoreu (riv.), Braz. 221/H5
Poy Sippi, Wi, US 185/K1
Poyang (lake), China 92/D5
Poygan (lake), Wi, US 185/K1
Poynette, Wi, US 185/K2
Poynor, Tx, US 181/G1
Poynton, Eng, UK 41/F5
Poyo, Sp. 52/A1
Poysdorf, Aus. 49/J4
Poza Rica, Mex. 205/M6
Požarevac, Serb. 56/E3
Požega, Serb. 56/E4
Pozhva, Rus. 75/N4
Poznań, Pol. 49/J2
Pozo Alcón, Sp. 52/D4
Pozo Almonte, Chile 224/B2
Pozo Colorado, Par. 224/E2
Pozo del Molle, Arg. 224/D5
Pozo del Tigre, Bol. 221/F5
Pozo Hondo, Arg. 224/C3
Pozoblanco, Sp. 52/C3
Pozohondo, Sp. 52/E3
Pozuelo de Alarcón, Sp. 53/N9
Pozuelos, Ven. 217/E2
Pozuelos (lag.), Arg. 224/C2
Pozuzo, Peru 220/C3
Pozza, It. 69/D4
Pozzallo, It. 54/D4
Pozzilli, It. 71/D4
Pozzolo Formigaro, It. 68/B4
Pozzoni (peak), It. 71/C2
Pozzonovo, It. 69/E3
Pozzuoli, It. 71/D6
Pozzuolo, It. 71/A1
Prabuty, Pol. 47/H5
Pracham Hiang (pt.), Thai. 106/B4
Prachatice, Czh. 65/H4
Prachin Buri, Thai. 106/C3
Prachin Buri (riv.), Thai. 106/C3
Prachuap Khiri Khan, Thai. 106/B4
Prad am Stilfserjoch (Prato allo Stelvio), It. 67/G4
Praděd (peak), Czh. 49/J3
Pradera, Col. 216/B4
Prado (dam), Ca, US 178/D4
Prado, Braz. 223/F3
Prado del Rey, Sp. 52/C4
Prado Flood Control (basin), Ca, US 196/C3
Pragelpass (pass), Swi. 67/E4
Prague, Ok, US 183/F3
Prague (Praha) (cap.), Czh. 65/H2
Praha (pol. reg.), Czh. 65/H2
Praha (peak), Czh. 65/G3
Prahova (prov.), Rom. 57/G3
Praia (int'l arpt.), CpV. 119/K11
Praia (cap.), CpV. 119/K11
Praia da Vitória, Azor., Port. 53/S12
Praia Grande, Braz. 223/K9
Prainha, Braz. 218/A4
Prainha, Braz. 218/C3
Prairie, Austl. 158/B3
Prairie (cr.), Ne, US 184/E3
Prairie City, SD, US 186/C5
Prairie Dog (cr.), Ks, US 184/D4
Prairie Dog Town Fk. (riv.), Tx, US 172/F4
Prairie du Chien, Wi, US 185/J2
Prairie Farm, Wi, US 187/J5
Prairie Grove, Il, US 197/P15
Prairie Island Ind. Res., Mn, US 185/H1
Prairie Point, Ms, US 192/C4
Prairie View, Tx, US 181/G2
Prairie, South (cr.), Wa, US 197/C3
Prairies (riv.), Qu, Can. 189/N6
Prairieville, Tx, US 181/F1
Prakhon Chai, Thai. 106/C3
Pralboino, It. 68/D3
Pralognan-la-Vanoise, Fr. 70/C2
Pralungo, It. 68/B2
Pram (riv.), Aus. 65/G6
Prambachkirchen, Aus. 65/G6
Prambanan (ruin), Indo. 101/E4
Pramort, Ger. 46/E4
Pran Buri (res.), Thai. 105/G5
Pran Buri, Thai. 106/B3
Prang, Gha. 133/E5
Prangins, Swi. 66/C5
Prānhita (riv.), India 104/C4
Prapat, Indo. 101/B2
Prasat Preah Vihear, Camb. 106/D3
Praskoveya, Rus. 77/H3
Præstø, Den. 46/E4
Praszka, Pol. 49/K3
Prat, Chile, Ant. 228/W
Prata, Braz. 219/G4
Prata di Pordenone, It. 69/F2
Prata di Principato Ultra, It. 71/D6
Prata do Piauí, Braz. 219/F4
Pratantico, It. 69/E7
Pratas (Dongsha) (isl.), China 99/H4
Pratas (reef), China 99/H4
Prätlgau (valley), Swi. 67/F4
Prato, It. 69/E6
Prato (Leventina), Swi. 67/E5
Prato allo Stelvio (Prad am Stilfserjoch), It. 67/G4
Pratola Peligna, It. 71/C3
Pratomagno (mts.), It. 69/E4
Pratovecchio, It. 69/E6
Pratt, Ks, US 183/E2
Pratt (isl.), Chile 191/B6
Pratteln, Swi. 66/D2
Prattsville, Ar, US 183/H3
Prattsville, NY, US 191/J3
Prattville, Al, US 192/D4
Prauthoy, Fr. 66/B2
Pravdinsk, Rus. 75/J4
Pravets, Bul. 55/H1
Pravia, Sp. 52/B1
Prawle (pt.), Eng, UK 42/C6
Praxedis G. Guerrero, Mex. 180/B2
Praya, Indo. 103/E5
Pré-en-Pail, Fr. 63/E4
Pré-Saint-Didier, It. 66/C6
Preah Vihear (ruin), Camb. 106/D3
Préalpes (upland), Fr. 70/B2
Précigné, Fr. 63/E5
Précy-sur-Oise, Fr. 60/B5
Predappio, It. 69/E5
Predazzo, It. 51/J3
Predeal, Rom. 57/G3
Predosa, It. 68/B4
Preeceville, Sk, Can. 186/C2
Prees, Eng, UK 41/F6
Preesall, Eng, UK 41/F4
Preetz, Ger. 46/D4
Preganziol, It. 69/F2
Pregarten, Aus. 65/H6
Pregolya (riv.), Pol. 47/J4
Pregolya (riv.), Rus. 49/L1
Pregonero, Ven. 216/D2
Preiļi, Lat. 47/M3
Prek Pouthi, Camb. 106/D4
Prelate, Sk, Can. 175/K2
Premana, It. 67/F5
Prémery, Fr. 50/E3
Premià de Mar, Sp. 53/L7
Premont, Tx, US 181/E4
Prenjas, Alb. 55/G2
Prentice, Wi, US 187/J5
Prentiss, Ms, US 194/D2
Prenzlau, Ger. 49/G2
Preobrazheniye, Rus. 91/L3
Přerov, Czh. 49/J4
Presanella (peak), It. 67/G5
Prescot, Eng, UK 41/F5
Prescott, On, Can. 191/J2
Prescott, Ar, US 183/H4
Prescott, Az, US 179/F3
Prescott, Ks, US 183/G1
Prescott, Ia, US 185/G3
Prescott, Wi, US 187/Q7
Prescott Valley, Az, US 179/F3
Preševo, Serb. 56/E4
Presidencia Roque Sáenz Peña, Arg. 224/D3
Presidente Bernardes, Braz. 222/C4
Presidente Dutra, Braz. 219/E4
Presidente Epitácio, Braz. 225/F2
Presidente Hayes (dept.), Par. 222/A4
Presidente Médici, Braz. 221/F3
Presidente Prudente, Braz. 225/G2
Presidente Venceslau, Braz. 225/G2
Presidential Lake Estates, NJ, US 198/D4
Presidio (riv.), Mex. 204/D4
Presidio, Tx, US 180/B3
Presidio La Bahia, Tx, US 181/F3
Preslav, Bul. 57/H4
Presles, Fr. 36/J4
Presles-en-Brie, Fr. 36/L5
Prešov, Slvk. 49/L4
Prešovský (pol. reg.), Slvk. 49/L4
Prespa (lake), Alb. 56/E5
Presqu'Île de Giens (pen.), Fr. 70/C6
Presque Isle, Wi, US 187/K4
Presque Isle (pt.), Mi, US 187/L4
Presque Isle, Mi, US 190/E2
Presque Isle, Me, US 171/K4
Presquile Nat'l Wild. Ref., Va, US 193/J2
Pressath, Ger. 65/E3
Pressbaum, Aus. 57/N7
Prestatyn, Wal, UK 41/E5
Prestea, Gha. 133/E5
Prestfoss, Nor. 46/C1
Přeštice, Czh. 65/G3
Preston (cape), Austl. 154/C2
Preston (nbrhd.), Austl. 156/G5
Preston, Eng, UK 42/D5
Preston, Eng, UK 41/F4
Preston, Ga, US 195/F1
Preston, Ia, US 185/J2
Preston, Id, US 177/H2
Preston, Ks, US 183/E2
Preston, Md, US 198/C6
Preston, Mn, US 185/H2
Preston, Ms, US 192/C4
Preston, Nv, US 177/F4
Preston, Ok, US 183/G3
Preston, Sc, UK 39/D5
Preston, Wa, US 197/D2
Prestonpans, Sc, UK 39/D5
Prestonsburg, Ky, US 193/F2
Prestwich, Eng, UK 41/F4
Prestwick, Sc, UK 39/B6
Prestwick (int'l arpt.), Sc, UK 39/B5
Prêto (riv.), Braz. 222/D3
Prêto do Igapó-Açu (riv.), Braz. 218/A4
Pretoria (cap.), SAfr. 142/E2
Pretoriuskop, SAfr. 141/F5
Pretty Boy (res.), Md, US 198/B4
Pretty Prairie, Ks, US 183/E2
Pretty Rock Nat'l Wild. Ref., ND, US 186/D4
Preussisch Olendorf, Ger. 59/F4
Prevalje, Slov. 51/L3
Préveza, Gre. 55/G3
Prévost, Qu, Can. 189/M6
Prewitt, NM, US 179/H3
Prey Veng, Camb. 106/D4
Priargunsk, Rus. 91/H1
Priazov Upland (upland), Ukr. 79/J4
Pribilof (isls.), Ak, US 201/D4
Priboj, Serb. 56/D4
Příbram, Czh. 65/H3
Price, Qu, Can. 188/C1
Price (falls), Ok, US 183/F3
Price (riv.), Ut, US 177/H4
Price, Ut, US 177/H4
Price, Md, US 198/C5
Pricedale, Ms, US 194/C2
Prichard, Al, US 194/D2
Prichsenstadt, Ger. 64/D3
Priddy, Tx, US 181/E2
Pridgen, Ga, US 195/G2
Priego, Sp. 52/D2
Priego de Córdoba, Sp. 52/C4
Priekulė, Lith. 47/J4
Priekule, Lat. 47/J3
Prien am Chiemsee, Ger. 65/F7
Prienai, Lith. 47/K4
Prieska, SAfr. 142/C3
Priest (riv.), Id, US 174/F3
Priest Rapids (dam), Wa, US 174/E4
Priest River, Id, US 174/F3
Prieta (mtn.), Sp. 52/C1
Prievidza, Slvk. 49/K4
Prignitz (reg.), Ger. 48/F2
Prijedor, Bosn. 56/C3
Prijepolje, Serb. 56/D4
Prikaspian (plain), Kaz.,Rus. 80/E5
Prikumsk, Rus. 77/H3
Prikumskiy, Rus. 77/H3
Prilep, FYROM 55/G2
Prilly, Swi. 66/C4
Prim, Ar, US 183/H3
Prima Porta, It. 71/B4
Primavera, Braz. 219/E3
Prime Hook NWR, De, US 198/C6
Primeira Cruz, Braz. 219/F3
Primero (cape), Chile 191/B6
Primero (riv.), Arg. 224/D4
Primero de Mayo, Mex. 180/D4
Primethorpe, Eng, UK 43/E1
Primghar, Ia, US 185/G2
Primorsk, Azer. 115/G1
Primorsk, Rus. 77/H2
Primorsk, Rus. 47/N1
Primorsk, Rus. 47/J4
Primorskiy Kray, Rus. 81/P5
Primorsko, Bul. 57/H4
Primorsko-Akhtarsk, Rus. 79/K4
Primorskoye, Ukr. 79/J4
Primorskoye, Ukr. 57/K3
Prims (riv.), Ger. 61/F4
Prince, Sk, Can. 175/K1
Prince Albert (sound), NW, Can. 170/E1
Prince Albert (pen.), NW, Can. 170/E1
Prince Albert, SAfr. 142/C4
Prince Albert NP, Sk, Can. 170/F3
Prince Alfred (cape), NW, Can. 171/Q7
Prince Charles (isl.), Nun, Can. 171/J2
Prince Edward (isls.), S.Afr. 27/L7
Prince Edward (isl.), Can. 163/L5
Prince Edward Island (prov.), Can. 188/F2
Prince Edward Island NP, PE, Can. 188/F2
Prince Frederick, Md, US 193/J1
Prince George, BC, Can. 170/D3
Prince George, Va, US 193/J2
Prince Georges (co.), Md, US 198/B6
Prince Gustav Adolf (sea), Nun, Can. 171/R7
Prince Leopold (isl.), Nun, Can. 170/G1
Prince of Wales (isl.), Austl. 153/F2
Prince of Wales (isl.), Nun, Can. 163/G2
Prince of Wales (str.), NW, Can. 170/E1
Prince of Wales (isl.), Ak, US 170/C3
Prince Olav (coast), Ant. 228/D
Prince Patrick (isl.), Can. 163/E2
Prince Regent (inlet), Nun, Can. 170/G1
Prince Regent Nature Rsv., Austl. 152/B3
Prince Rupert, BC, Can. 170/C3
Prince William, NB, Can. 188/D3
Prince William (sound), Ak, US 201/J3
Prince William Forest Park, Va, US 193/J1
Princenhof (lake), Neth. 58/C2
Princes Lake, In, US 190/C5
Princes Risborough, Eng, UK 43/F3
Princes Town, Trin. 203/J5
Princesa Isabel, Braz. 219/G4
Princess Anne, Md, US 193/K1
Princess Charlotte (bay), Austl. 145/D2
Princess Margaret (range), Nun, Can. 171/S6
Princess Royal (isl.), BC, Can. 170/C3
Princeton, BC, Can. 174/D3
Princeton, Il, US 185/K3
Princeton, In, US 192/D1
Princeton, Ks, US 183/G1
Princeton, Ky, US 192/D2
Princeton, La, US 183/H4
Princeton, Mi, US 187/L4
Princeton, Mn, US 187/H5
Princeton, Mo, US 185/H3
Princeton, NJ, US 198/D3
Princeton, Tx, US 180/L6
Princeton, WV, US 193/G2
Princeton Junction, NJ, US 198/D3
Princeville, Il, US 185/K3
Príncipe (isl.), SaoT. 138/A2
Prindle (mt.), Ak, US 201/K3
Prineville, Or, US 176/C1
Prineville (res.), Or, US 176/C1
Pringle, Tx, US 182/D3
Pringle, SD, US 184/C2
Pringsewu, Indo. 102/B5
Pringy, Fr. 66/C6
Prinsburg, Mn, US 185/G1
Prinsenbeek, Neth. 58/B5
Prinses Margriet (canal), Neth. 58/C3
Prinzapolka (riv.), Nic. 207/E3
Prinzapolka, Nic. 207/F3
Priolo di Gargallo, It. 54/D4
Prior (cape), Sp. 52/A1
Prior Lake, Mn, US 187/P7
Prior Lake Ind. Res., Mn, US 187/P7
Priore (peak), It. 71/C2
Priozernyy, Kaz. 111/D2
Priozersk, Rus. 47/P1
Pripet Marshes (swamp), Bela.,Ukr. 76/C1
Prlpyat' (riv.), Ukr. 76/C2
Prisdorf, Ger. 59/G1
Pristen', Rus. 79/J2
Priština, Serb. 56/E4
Pritchett, Co, US 182/C2
Prittriching, Ger. 67/G1
Pritzwalk, Ger. 48/G2
Privas, Fr. 70/A3
Priverno, It. 71/C5
Privokzal'nyy, Rus. 75/P4
Privolzhskiy, Rus. 77/H2
Privolzh'ye, Rus. 77/J1
Priyutnoye, Rus. 77/G3
Priyutovo, Rus. 77/K1
Prizren, Serb. 56/E4
Prnjavor, Serb. 56/D3
Prnjavor, Bosn. 56/C3
Probištip, FYROM 55/H1
Probolinggo, Indo. 101/F4
Probstzella, Ger. 65/E1
Procida, It. 71/D6
Proctor, Ok, US 183/G3
Proctor, Tx, US 180/E2
Proctor (lake), Tx, US 181/E1
Proctor, WV, US 190/F5
Proddatūr, India 107/C3
Proença-a-Nova, Port. 52/B3
Profondeville, Belg. 61/D3
Progreso, Mex. 180/D4
Progreso, Mex. 206/D1
Progreso, Mex. 205/K6
Progreso, Pan. 207/F4
Progreso, Uru. 191/K11
Progress, Rus. 91/K2
Progresso, It. 69/E4
Prokhladnyy, Rus. 77/G4
Prokhorovka, Rus. 79/J2
Prokop'yevsk, Rus. 111/E1
Prokuplje, Serb. 56/E4
Proletarsk, Rus. 79/L4
Proletarskiy, Rus. 79/H2
Promised Land (lake), Pa, US 198/C1
Promissão, Braz. 225/G2
Promissão (res.), Braz. 222/C4
Promontory, Ut, US 177/G3
Promyslovoye, Rus. 77/H3
Propriá, Braz. 223/F1
Propriano, Fr. 54/A2
Prorva, Kaz. 77/K3
Prosecco, It. 69/G2
Proserpine, Austl. 158/C3
Prosna (riv.), Pol. 49/J2
Prosotsáni, Gre. 55/H2
Prospect, Pa, US 190/F4
Prospect, Or, US 176/B2
Prospect (nbrhd.), Austl. 155/M8
Prospect Park, Pa, US 191/G4
Prospect Park, NJ, US 199/J8
Prospector (mt.), Yk, Can. 201/L3
Prosper, Tx, US 180/L6
Prosperidad, Phil. 100/D3
Prosperity, WV, US 193/G2
Prosperity, SC, US 193/G3
Prosperous, Ire. 38/D3
Prosser, Wa, US 174/E4
Prostějov, Czh. 49/J4
Proston, Austl. 158/C4
Proszowice, Pol. 49/L3
Protection, Ks, US 182/E2
Protivín, Czh. 65/H4
Protvino, Rus. 74/H5
Provadiya, Bul. 57/H4
Provencal, La, US 194/B2
Provence (int'l arpt.), Fr. 70/B6
Provence (reg.), Fr. 72/E2
Provence-Alpes-Côte D'Azur (pol. reg.), Fr. 53/H1
Provence-Alpes-Côte-D'Azur, Fr. 51/G4
Providence, Fl, US 194/M7
Providence (cape), NZ 159/A4
Providence, Ut, US 177/H3
Providence (mts.), Ca, US 178/E3
Providence, Ky, US 192/D2
Providence, Al, US 192/D4
Providence (cap.), RI, US 188/B5
Providence Bay, On, Can. 190/E2
Providencia, Isla de (isl.), Col. 202/E5
Providência, Serra de (mts.), Braz. 221/F3
Providenciales (isl.), Bahm. 207/H1
Provideniya, Rus. 201/D3
Provo, Ut, US 200/K13
Provo (riv.), Ut, US 200/K13
Provost, Ab, Can. 175/J1
Prozor, Bosn. 56/C4
Prudentópolis, Braz. 225/G3
Prudhoe, Eng, UK 41/G2
Prudhoe Bay, Ak, US 201/J1
Prudhoe (bay), Ak, US 201/J1
Prudnik, Pol. 49/J3
Prudyanka, Ukr. 79/J2
Prue, Ok, US 183/F2
Prüm, Ger. 61/F3
Prüm (riv.), Ger. 48/D4
Prunay-en-Yvelines, Fr. 36/H6
Prunedale, Ca, US 178/B2
Prunelli-di-Fiumorbo, Fr. 54/A1
Pruszcz Gdański, Pol. 46/H4
Pruszków, Pol. 49/L2
Prut (riv.), Eur. 80/C5
Prut (riv.), Rom. 73/K1
Prut (riv.), Ukr. 78/C3
Prutz, Aus. 67/G3
Pruzhany, Bela. 49/N2
Pryazovs'ke, Ukr. 79/H4
Prykolotne, Ukr. 79/J2
Pryluky, Ukr. 79/G1
Prymors'ke, Ukr. 79/J4
Prymors'kyy, Ukr. 79/H5
Pryor, Mt, US 177/J1
Pryor (cr.), Mt, US 177/J1
Pryor (Creek), Ok, US 183/G2
Prypyat', Ukr. 78/F2
Prypyats' (riv.), Bela. 80/C4
Przasnysz, Pol. 49/L2
Przemków, Pol. 49/H3
Przemyśl, Pol. 49/M4
Przeworsk, Pol. 49/M3
Przylądek Rozewie (cape), Pol. 46/H4
Przysucha, Pol. 49/L3
Psakhná, Gre. 55/H3
Psará (isl.), Gre. 55/J3
Psárion, Gre. 55/G4
Psebay, Rus. 77/G3
Psël (riv.), Rus.,Ukr. 76/E2
Psël (riv.), Ukr. 79/G3
Pskovskaya Oblast, Rus. 74/F4
Pskov (lake), Rus. 74/E5
Pskov, Rus. 47/N3
Pšovka (riv.), Czh. 65/H2
Pszczyna, Pol. 49/K4
Pt Morin (riv.), Fr. 50/E2
Pt. Reyes Nat'l Seashore, Ca, US 178/A1
Ptolemaís, Gre. 55/G2
Ptolemaïs (ruin), Libya 126/D1
Ptuj, Slov. 56/B2
Pu Xian, China 92/B3
Puan, SKor. 93/D5
Pu'an, China 98/E3
Puangue, Chile 226/N8
Puca Barranca, Peru 216/C5
Pucacaca, Peru 220/B2
Pucallpa, Peru 220/C3
Pucara, Bol. 224/C1
Pucará, Ecu. 220/B1
Pucará, Peru 220/D4
Pucará, Peru 220/B2
Pucarani, Bol. 224/B1
Pucaurco, Peru 216/D5
Puce, On, Can. 197/G7
Puchenau, Aus. 65/H6
Pucheng, China 92/B4
Puchheim, Ger. 65/E6
Puch'on, SKor. 93/F7
Puchuncaví, Chile 226/N8
Pucioasa, Rom. 57/G3
Puck, Pol. 46/H4
Puckaun, Ire. 38/B4
Puckaway (lake), Wi, US 185/K2
Puckeridge, Eng, UK 43/G3
Pucking, Aus. 65/H6
Pucón, Chile 226/C3
Pucusana, Peru 220/B4
Pudasjärvi, Fin. 74/E2
Puddletown, Eng, UK 42/D5
Pudem, Rus. 75/M4
Puderbach, Ger. 61/G2
Pudimoe, SAfr. 142/D2
Pudozh, Rus. 74/H3
Pudsey, Eng, UK 41/G4
Pudukkottai, India 107/C4
Puebla (state), Mex. 202/B4
Puebla, Mex. 205/L7
Puebla de Alcocer, Sp. 52/C3
Puebla de Don Fadrique, Sp. 52/D4
Puebla de la Calzada, Sp. 52/B3
Puebla de Sanabria, Sp. 52/B1
Puebla de Trives, Sp. 52/B1
Puebla del Caramiñal, Sp. 52/A1
Pueblillo, Mex. 205/M6
Pueblito, Col. 216/C2
Pueblo, Co, US 182/B1
Pueblo Army Depot, Co, US 184/B4
Pueblo de Taos Ind. Res., NM, US 182/B2
Pueblo de Taos Ind. Res., NM, US 179/K2
Pueblo Nuevo, Nic. 206/E3
Pueblo Nuevo, Ven. 216/D2
Pueblo West, Co, US 182/B1
Pueblo Yaqui, Mex. 204/C3
Puelches, Arg. 226/D3
Puelén, Arg. 226/D3
Puente (hills), Ca, US 196/G8
Puente Alto, Chile 226/N8
Puente Caldelas, Sp. 52/A1
Puente de Ixtla, Mex. 205/K8
Puente del Inca, Arg. 226/C2
Puente del Inca, Arg. 226/P8
Puente Nacional, Col. 216/C3
Puente Piedra, Peru 220/B3
Puente-Ceso, Sp. 52/A1
Puente-Genil, Sp. 52/C4
Puenteareas, Sp. 52/A1
Puentedeume, Sp. 52/A1
Puentes de García Rodríguez, Sp. 52/B1
Pu'er, China 98/D4
Puerco (riv.), Az,NM, US 179/H3
Puerto Abente, Par. 224/E2
Puerto Acosta, Bol. 220/D4
Puerto Aguirre, Chile 226/B5
Puerto Aisén, Chile 226/B5
Puerto Alegre, Bol. 221/F4
Puerto Almacen, Bol. 221/E4
Puerto América, Peru 220/B2
Puerto Ángel, Mex. 206/B3
Puerto Argentina, Col. 216/C4
Puerto Armuelles, Pan. 207/F4
Puerto Arturo, Bol. 221/F4
Puerto Arturo, Chile 191/C7
Puerto Arturo, Peru 216/C5
Puerto Asís, Col. 216/B4
Puerto Ayacucho, Ven. 217/E3
Puerto Ayora, Ecu. 220/J7
Puerto Bahía Negra, Par. 224/E2
Puerto Ballivián, Bol. 221/E4
Puerto Baquerizo Moreno, Ecu. 220/K7
Puerto Barrios, Guat. 206/D3
Puerto Bermúdez, Peru 220/C3
Puerto Berrío, Col. 216/C3
Puerto Bertrand, Chile 191/B5
Puerto Caballas, Peru 220/C4
Puerto Cabello, Ven. 216/D2
Puerto Cabezas, Nic. 207/F3
Puerto Calvimonte, Bol. 221/E4
Puerto Canoa, Bol. 221/E4
Puerto Carranza, Col. 216/D5
Puerto Carreño, Col. 217/E3
Puerto Casado, Par. 224/E2
Puerto Chacabuco, Chile 226/B5
Puerto Cisnes, Chile 226/B5
Puerto Coig, Arg. 191/C6
Puerto Colón, Par. 224/E2
Puerto Cortés, Hon. 206/E3
Puerto Cortés, Mex. 204/C3
Puerto Cumarebo, Ven. 216/D2
Puerto de la Cruz, Sp. 128/A3
Puerto de la Libertad, Mex. 204/B2
Puerto de Navacerrada (pass), Sp. 53/M8
Puerto del Rosario, Sp. 128/B3
Puerto del Son, Sp. 52/A1
Puerto Deseado, Arg. 191/D5
Puerto El Carmen, Ecu. 216/C4
Puerto Escondido, Col. 216/B2
Puerto Escondido, Mex. 206/B3
Puerto Esperanza, Arg. 225/F3

Puerto Esperanza, Par. 224/E2
Puerto Fonciere, Par. 224/E2
Puerto Frey, Bol. 221/F4
Puerto General Busch, Bol. 224/E1
Puerto General Ovando, Bol. 224/D3
Puerto Grether, Bol. 221/E5
Puerto Guadal, Chile 226/B5
Puerto Harberton, Arg. 191/D7
Puerto Heath, Peru 216/C4
Puerto Huitoto, Col. 216/C4
Puerto Iguazú, Arg. 225/F3
Puerto Inca, Peru 220/C3
Puerto Ingeniero Ibáñez, Chile 226/C5
Puerto Inírida, Col. 216/D3
Puerto Isabel, Bol. 224/E1
Puerto Izozog, Bol. 224/D3
Puerto José Pardo, Peru 220/B1
Puerto La Cruz, Ven. 217/E2
Puerto Leda, Par. 224/E2
Puerto Leguia, Peru 220/D4
Puerto Leguízamo, Col. 216/C5
Puerto Leigue, Bol. 221/E4
Puerto Lempira, Hon. 207/F3
Puerto Lobos, Arg. 226/D4
Puerto López, Col. 216/C3
Puerto López, Col. 216/C2
Puerto Lumbreras, Sp. 52/E4
Puerto Madero, Mex. 206/C3
Puerto Madryn, Arg. 226/D4
Puerto Magdalena, Mex. 204/B3
Puerto Maldonado, Peru 220/D4
Puerto Mamoré, Bol. 221/E5
Puerto Maria, Par. 224/E2
Puerto Mercedes, Col. 216/C4
Puerto Mihanovich, Arg. 224/E2
Puerto Montt, Chile 226/B4
Puerto Morazán, Nic. 206/E3
Puerto Morelos, Mex. 202/D3
Puerto Morín, Peru 220/B2
Puerto Napo, Ec. 216/C4
Puerto Natales, Chile 191/B6
Puerto Niño, Col. 219/L7
Puerto Nuevo, Col. 216/D3
Puerto Nuevo, Chile 191/C7
Puerto Obaldía, Pan. 216/B2
Puerto Ocopa, Peru 220/C3
Puerto Olaya, Col. 216/C3
Puerto Páez, Ven. 217/E3
Puerto Pando, Bol. 220/E4
Puerto Patiño, Bol. 224/E2
Puerto Peñasco, Mex. 179/F5
Puerto Pinasco, Par. 224/E2
Puerto Pirámides, Arg. 226/D4
Puerto Piray, Arg. 225/F3
Puerto Pirtu, Ven. 217/E2
Puerto Pizarro, Col. 216/C4
Puerto Portillo, Peru 220/C3
Puerto Prado, Peru 220/C3
Puerto Prat, Chile 191/B6
Puerto Princesa, Phil. 150/C4
Puerto Puyuguapi, Chile 226/B5
Puerto Real, Sp. 52/B4
Puerto Rico, Col. 216/C4
Puerto Rico, Col. 221/E3
Puerto Rico, Col. 216/C4
Puerto Rico (dpcy.), US 203/M7
Puerto Rico, Tx, US 181/E4
Puerto Rondón, Col. 216/D2
Puerto Ruiz, Arg. 191/J10
Puerto Saavedra, Chile 226/B3
Puerto Saiz, Col. 216/C3
Puerto Salgar, Col. 219/L7
Puerto Salinas, Bol. 224/D2
Puerto San Carlos, Mex. 204/B3
Puerto San Julián, Arg. 191/D6
Puerto Santa Cruz, Arg. 191/C6
Puerto Santa Maria, Phil. 150/C3
Puerto Sastre, Par. 224/E2
Puerto Saucedo, Bol. 224/E1
Puerto Serrano, Sp. 52/C4
Puerto Siles, Bol. 220/D3
Puerto Suárez, Bol. 224/E1
Puerto Supe, Peru 220/C3
Puerto Tacurú Pytá, Par. 225/E2
Puerto Tahuantisuyo, Peru 220/D4
Puerto Tejada, Col. 216/C5
Puerto Toledo, Col. 216/C5
Puerto Torno, Bol. 224/D2
Puerto Tunigrama, Peru 216/B5
Puerto Vallarta, Mex. 204/D4
Puerto Varas, Chile 226/B4
Puerto Vargas, Bol. 221/E4
Puerto Velarde, Bol. 221/E4
Puerto Victoria, Peru 220/C3
Puerto Viejo, CR 207/E4
Puerto Villamil, Ecu. 220/J7
Puerto Villarroel, Bol. 221/E4
Puerto Villazón, Bol. 221/F4
Puerto Wilches, Col. 216/C2
Puerto Williams, Chile 191/D7
Puerto Yartou, Chile 191/C7
Puertollano, Sp. 52/C3
Puesto Cunambo, Peru 220/B1
Puesto de Pailas, Bol. 224/D1
Pueyrredón (lake), Arg. 226/C5
Puffin (isl.), Wal, UK 40/D5
Pugachev, Rus. 77/J1
Pūgal, India 110/B5
Puge, Tanz. 137/A3
Puger, Indo. 101/L5
Puget (sound), Wa, US 172/B2
Puget-sur-Argens, Fr. 70/C5
Puget-Théniers, Fr. 70/C5
Puget-Ville, Fr. 70/C5
Puglia (pol. reg.), It. 54/E2
Puglia (prov.), It. 56/C5
Pugwash, NS, Can. 188/F3
Puhja, Est. 47/M2
Puigcerdà, Sp. 53/G2
Puigmal (peak), Sp. 53/G2
Puina, Bol. 220/D4
Puiseux-en-France, Fr. 36/K4
Pujaut, Fr. 70/A3
Pujehun, SLeo. 132/C6
Pujiang, China 98/M2
Pujili, Ecu. 216/B3
Pujōn, NKor. 93/D2
Pujut (cape), Indo. 101/K4
Pukaki (lake), NZ 159/B3

Puk'an-san (peak), SKor. 93/E4
Puk'an-san NP, SKor. 93/D4
Pukch'ang, NKor. 93/D3
Pukch'ŏng, NKor. 93/E2
Pukdae (riv.), NKor. 93/E2
Pukě (riv.), NKor. 93/E2
Pukch'ŏn (mtn.), NKor. 174/D4
Pukerua Bay, NZ 159/H9
Pukhan (riv.), SKor. 93/D4
Pukhǎyān, India 108/B2
Pukkila, Fin. 45/F4
Pukn-san, SKor. 93/F6
Pukovac, Serb. 56/E4
Pukp'ot'ae-san (peak), SKor. 93/E2
Puksoozero, Rus. 74/J3
Pukuatu (cape), Indo. 152/A2
Pula, Cro. 51/K4
Pulandian (bay), China 93/A3
Pulanduta (pt.), Phil. 103/F1
Pulangi (riv.), Phil. 100/D3
Pulāsar, India 110/C5
Pulaski, NY, US 191/H3
Pulaski, Tn, US 192/D3
Pulaski, Va, US 193/G2
Pulaw, Pol. 49/L3
Pulborough, Eng, UK 43/F5
Pulheim, Ger. 61/F2
Puli, Tanz. 137/A3
Pulicat (riv.), Guy. 217/G3
Pulivendla, India 110/C4
Pulkovo (int'l arpt.), Rus. 77/T7
Pullach im Isartal, Ger. 67/H7
Pullman, Mi, US 190/C3
Pullman, Wa, US 174/F4
Pully, Swi. 66/C5
Pulnitz (riv.), Ger. 49/G3
Pulog (mtn.), Phil. 103/G4
Pulpwood (riv.), On, Can. 190/E1
Pulsnitz, Ger. 49/G3
Pułtusk, Pol. 49/L2
Pulumur, Turk. 114/D2
Puluwat (isl.), Micr. 160/D4
Pulwama, India 110/C3
Puma (lake), China 109/H1
Pusur (riv.), Bang. 137/A3
Pumpkin (cr.), Mt, US 175/M4
Pumpsaint, Wal, UK 40/C4
Pumpville, Tx, US 180/D3
Pumu (riv.), Tai. 99/J4
Puna de Atacama (plat.), Arg. 224/C2
Punakaiki, NZ 159/B3
Punākha, Bhu. 109/G2
Punata, Bol. 224/C1
Punch, India 110/C3
Punch (riv.), India 110/C3
Punchaw, BC, Can. 174/C1
Püncogling, China 109/F1
Pūndri, India 110/D5
Pune (Poona), India 113/B5
Punelia (lake), Fin. 45/E4
Punggai (cape), Malay. 102/B3
Punggol, Sing. 101/E4
P'unggi, SKor. 93/E4
Pungo (riv.), NC, US 193/J3
Pungoè (riv.), Moz. 141/G3
Pungoteague, Va, US 193/K3
P'ungsan, NKor. 93/E2
P'ungsŏ, NKor. 93/E2
Puning, China 99/H4
Punjab (plain), Pak. 113/K2
Punjab (state), India 111/B5
Punjab (prov.), Pak. 113/J2
Puno, Peru 220/D4
Puno (dept.), Peru 220/D4
Puntaran, Al, US 194/D1
Punta, Peru 220/C4
Punta Allen, Mex. 202/D4
Punta Alta, Arg. 226/E3
Punta Arenas (pt.), Mex. 191/C7
Punta Arenas, Chile 191/C7
Punta Banda, Mex. 204/A2
Punta Cardón, Ven. 216/D2
Punta Celarain, Mex. 206/E1
Punta Colnett, Mex. 204/A2
Punta Colonet, Mex. 204/A2
Punta de Bombón, Peru 220/D5
Punta de Diaz, Chile 226/B2
Punta de Mata, Ven. 217/F2
Punta de Pietra, It. 106/B2
Puncta, Chile 226/B2
Puxi, China 99/H3
Puxico, Mo, US 194/E2
Puy de Sancy (peak), Fr. 50/E4
Puy-Saint-Vincent, Fr. 70/C4
Puyallup, Wa, US 197/C3
Puyallup Ind. Res., Wa, US 197/C3
Puyang, China 99/H3
Puyo Cliff Dwellings, NM, US 187/F3
Puyo, Ecu. 216/B4
Puysegur (pt.), NZ 159/E2
Puyuqao, NKor. 93/E2
P'warwŏn, NKor. 93/C3

Pwawi (prov.), Tanz. 137/B3
Pweto, D.R. Congo 139/G5
Pwllheli, Wal, UK 40/C4
Pyal'ma, Rus. 74/J2
Pyamalaw (riv.), Myan. 98/B5
Pyandzh, Taj. 101/E4
Pyandzh (Panj) (riv.), Afg., Taj. 107/E3
Pyaozero (lake), Rus. 44/J2
Pyapon, Myan. 105/G4
Pyasina (riv.), Rus. 80/J2
Pyatigorsk, Rus. 77/G3
Pyatykhatky, Ukr. 79/G3
Pye, Myan. 216/D5
Pyfara (riv.), Fr. 50/F4
Pyhä-Häkin NP, Fin. 74/E3
Pyhäjärvi, Fin. 47/K1
Pyhäjärvi (lake), Fin. 44/J2
Pyhäntä, Fin. 44/H2
Pyhätunturi (peak), Fin. 74/E2
Pyinga, Myan. 98/B4
Pyinmana, Myan. 98/C5
P'yŏktong, NKor. 93/C2
P'yŏngan-namdo (prov.), NKor. 93/C3
P'yŏngch'ang, SKor. 93/E4
P'yŏnggang, SKor. 93/D3
P'yŏngt'aek, SKor. 93/D4
P'yŏngsan, NKor. 93/C3
P'yŏngsong, NKor. 93/C3
P'yŏngt'aek, SKor. 93/D4
P'yŏngwŏn, NKor. 93/C3
P'yŏngyang (cap.), NKor. 93/C3
P'yŏngyang (int'l arpt.), NKor. 93/C3
P'yŏngyang-si (prov.), NKor. 93/C3
Pyŏnsanbando NP, SKor. 93/C4
Pyramid (mt.), BC, Can. 201/M4
Pyramid (riv.), India 115/G4
Pyramid (peak), Ca, US 172/C3
Pyramid (peak), Id, US 177/G1
Pyramid (peak), Nv, US 173/C2
Pyramid (peak), Wy, US 184/A2
Pyramid Lake Ind. Res., Nv, US 176/D3
Pyramids Of Jīzah, Egypt 131/C5
Pyrenees (range), Eur. 53/E1
Pyrenees (mts.), Fr.,Sp. 28/E6
Pyrénées Occidentales, PN, Fr. 74/H5
Pyryatyn, Ukr. 79/G1
Pyrzyce, Pol. 49/H2
Pyschug, Rus. 75/W8
Pys'menne, Ukr. 79/H3
Pyšpökladány, Hun. 56/E2
Pyu, Myan. 98/C5
Pyuntaza, Myan. 106/D2
Pyuthan, Nepal 108/D1

Q

Qā 'al Jafr (salt pan), Jor. 116/E4
Qabalah, WBnk. 117/C4
Qabb Ilyās, Leb. 117/D1
Qabātiyah, WBnk. 117/C4
Qachas Nek, Les. 142/E3
Qacha, China 98/D3
Qādeh, India 100/D4
Qadisiyah (well), Libya 126/D2
Qādub, India 110/C4
Qadīma, Isr. 117/B4
Qā'emshahr, Iran 115/H2
Qaen, Iran 113/G2
Qafa e Malit (pass), Alb. 55/G1
Qaffin, WBnk. 117/C4
Qafilah, Egypt 131/B2
Qagan (lake), China 97/J2
Qahā, Egypt 131/A4
Qāhar Youyi Qianqi, China 99/G2
Qahar Youyi Zhongqi, China 92/D2
Qaidam (basin), China 97/G5
Qal al Bīshah, SAr. 123/E4
Qala Da Nahl, Sudan 135/G2
Qala Sobha Singh, Pak. 110/C3
Qalansuwa, Isr. 117/B4
Qalāt, Afg. 107/J2
Qal'at al Aş Şanam, Tun. 130/L7
Qal'at Bishah, SAr. 123/E4
Qal'at Dizah, Iraq 115/H2
Qal'at Jandal, Syria 117/D2
Qalāt Şāleh, Iraq 115/H4
Qal'eh-ye Deh-e Bārez, Iran 113/G3
Qallābāt, Sudan 135/H2
Qalqīlyah, WBnk. 117/B4
Qamanittuaq (Baker Lake), Nun, Can. 171/H3
Qamīnis, Libya 126/D2
Qanā, Leb. 117/C2
Qanah (well), Isr. 117/C4
Qanat Junqoley (canal), Sudan 135/G3
Qandala, Som. 136/D3
Qantarah (peak), Egypt 131/B4
Qantarat Al Faḩş, Tun. 130/L6
Qapshagay, Kaz. 115/G3
Qapshaghay, Kaz. 111/C3
Qarabutaq, Kaz. 77/M2
Qarabulak, China 97/L3
Qarah, SAr. 123/E4
Qarah, China 115/G2
Qarānū (riv.), Iran 115/H4
Qārāt al Hayyirah (depr.), Libya 126/D2
Qārat al Jahannam, Egypt 131/D6
Qārat Jahannam, Egypt 131/D6

Qarqan (riv.), China 111/E4
Qarqaraly, Kaz. 80/H5
Qarrit (pass), Alb. 55/G2
Qarshi, Uzb. 107/H2
Qarţājannah (Carthage) (ruin), Tun. 130/M6
Qārūn (lake), Egypt 131/C5
Qaryat abu Nujaym, Libya 126/B2
Qaryat Abū Qurayn, Libya 126/C2
Qaryat az Zuwaytīnah, Libya 126/D2
Qāsim, Syria 117/E3
Qāsimwāla, Pak. 110/B4
Qaşr al Jady, Libya 126/E2
Qaşr al Kharānah, Jor. 117/E5
Qaşr al Khubbāz, Iraq 114/E3
Qaşr al Mushattá, Jor. 117/C3
Qaşr 'Amrah, Jor. 117/F5
Qaşr aş Şaghah (ruin), Egypt 131/B3
Qaşr Baghdād, Egypt 131/B3
Qaşr Farāfirah, Egypt 127/F3
Qaşr-e Qand, Iran 113/H3
Qaşr-e Shīrīn, Iran 115/H3
Qa'ţabah, Yem. 136/C2
Qaţanā, Syria 117/D3
Qatar (ctry.) 112/F3
Qattara Depression (depr.), Egypt 114/A4
Qaţţīnah (lake), Syria 116/E2
Qawz Abū Dulū (dune), Sudan 135/G2
Qaxi, China 111/D3
Qaysān, Sudan 135/G3
Qayü, China 98/D3
Qazaqtyng Usaqshoqzlyghy (uplands), Kaz. 80/H5
Qazax, Azer. 115/H2
Qāzi Ahmad, Pak. 107/J3
Qazimāmmād, Azer. 115/H2
Qazvīn, Iran 115/H2
Qeda, Isr. 117/B5
Qendrevica (peak), Alb. 55/F2
Qeqertarsuaq (Disko) (isl.), Grld. 171/L1
Qeshm, Iran 115/H5
Qeshm (isl.), Iran 115/H5
Qeydar, Iran 115/H2
Qezel Owzan (riv.), Iran 112/E1
Qi Xian, China 105/J2
Qian (mts.), China 92/C3
Qian (riv.), China 92/C3
Qian Gorlos Mongolzu, China 93/A2
Qiancun, China 99/J2
Qiandong, China 111/D3
Qianfodong, China 99/J2
Qiange, China 99/J3
Qianjiang, China 99/G3
Qianning, China 98/D2
Qianqing, China 92/L9
Qianqiu (pass), China 105/K2
Qianshanlaoba, China 111/D2
Qianxi, China 98/D3
Qiaodong, China 93/C2
Qiaojia, China 98/D3
Qiaomaidi, China 98/D3
Qiaoshe, China 99/G2
Qiaosi, China 92/L8
Qiaotouhe, China 99/G3
Qiaoxu, China 99/F4
Qibilī, Tun. 129/H2
Qibya, WBnk. 117/C4
Qidaogou, China 93/D2
Qidong, China 105/K2
Qidukou, China 90/D4
Qiemo, China 111/E4
Qifeng (pass), China 99/G2
Qihe, China 92/D3
Qikiqtarjuaq, Nun, Can. 171/K2
Qikou, China 92/D3
Qila Dīdār Singh, Pak. 110/D3
Qila Sobha Singh, Pak. 110/C3
Qilian (mts.), China 83/J6
Qiling, China 99/G3
Qilizhen, China 92/D3
Qimantag (mts.), China 90/C4
Qimen, China 99/H3
Qin (riv.), China 90/D4
Qin'an, China 92/C3
Qing'an, China 91/K2
Qingchengzi, China 92/C3
Qingdao, China 92/E3
Qinggang, China 91/K2
Qinghai (lake), China 90/D4
Qinghai (prov.), China 90/D5
Qinghe, China 111/D2
Qinghecheng, China 93/C2
Qinghemen, China 92/D3
Qinghua, China 111/B7
Qinglong, China 98/D3
Qingping, China 99/G4
Qingpu, China 92/L8
Qingquan, China 99/G2
Qingshan, China 99/G3
Qingshuihe, China 90/D5
Qingshuijiang (riv.), China 111/B7
Qingtongxia, China 92/C3
Qinguizi, China 92/D3
Qingyang, China 92/C3
Qingyuan, China 99/H2
Qingzhou, China 92/D3

Qingyuan (mts.), China 99/G4
Qingyuan (sound), BC, Can. 170/C3
Qing City, Tx, US 179/G4
Qinshui, China 92/C4
Qinyang, China 92/C4
Qinyuan, China 92/C3
Qionghai, China 105/K4
Qionglai (mts.), China 90/E5
Qiongshan, China 105/K4
Qiongzhong, China 106/E2
Qipan (pass), China 90/E1
Qiqihar, China 91/J2
Qiquanhu, China 111/E4
Qir, Iran 115/H4
Qira, China 111/D3
Qiryat Ata, Isr. 117/C3
Qiryat Bialik, Isr. 117/C3
Qiryat Gat, Isr. 117/B5
Qiryat Mal'akhi, Isr. 117/B5
Qiryat Motzkin, Isr. 117/C3
Qiryat Shemona, Isr. 117/D2
Qiryat Tiv'on, Isr. 117/C3
Qiryat Yam, Isr. 117/C3
Qishan, China 92/C4
Qishuyan, China 92/L8
Qitai, China 111/E3
Qiubei, China 98/D3
Qixia, China 92/E3
Qixing (riv.), China 81/P5
Qixing (pass), China 98/D3
Qixingpao, China 91/K2
Qixitian, China 99/H2
Qizhan, China 111/D3
Qizilqum (des.), Kaz. 80/G5
Qogir (peak), China 113/L1
Qom, Iran 115/H3
Qom (riv.), Iran 112/F2
Qomo, China 98/D2
Qomsheh, Iran 115/G3
Qondūz (riv.), Afg. 113/J1
Qondūz, Afg. 107/J1
Qonggyai, China 98/D2
Qoqalpoghiston Aut. Rep., Uzb. 77/L3
Qormi, Malta 54/L7
Qorveh, Iran 115/F3
Qoryooley, Som. 137/D1
Qostanay, Kaz. 77/M1
Qostanay (int'l arpt.), Kaz. 77/P5
Qostanay Oblast, Kaz. 77/P5
Qotbābād, Iran 115/G5
Qotbābād, Iran 113/G3
Qotür, Iran 115/F2
Qu (riv.), China 90/F5
Quabbin (res.), Ma, US 188/A4
Quail Gardens, Ok, US 187/E2
Quainton, Eng, UK 43/F3
Quairading, Austl. 154/C5
Quakenbrück, Ger. 59/E2
Quakertown, Pa, US 198/C2
Qualiano, It. 71/D6
Qualicum Beach, BC, Can. 199/G4
Quamba, Mn, US 187/H5
Quambatook, Austl. 156/B2
Quambone, Austl. 156/C1
Quamby, Austl. 155/G3
Quanah, Tx, US 182/E3
Quanbao (mtn.), China 99/G2
Quandialla, Austl. 157/C2
Quang Ngai, Viet. 106/E3
Quang Trach, Viet. 106/E2
Quang Tri, Viet. 106/D2
Quangjiao, China 99/J4
Quantico, Va, US 193/J3
Quantico M.C. Res., Va, US 193/J3
Quanyang, China 93/D2
Quanzhou, China 99/H3
Quapaw, Ok, US 183/G2
Qu'Appelle, Sk, Can. 186/C2
Qu'Appelle (riv.), Sk, Can. 186/C2
Qu'Appelle, Sk, Can. 186/D2
Quaraí, Braz. 225/E4
Quaregnon, Belg. 60/C2
Quarles (mts.), Indo. 83/J6
Quarona, It. 68/B2
Quarrata, It. 68/B2
Quarryville, Pa, US 198/B4
Quarto, It. 71/D6
Quarto d'Altino, It. 68/C2
Quartu Sant'elena, It. 54/A3
Quartz (peak), Ca, US 177/E4
Quartz Hill, Ca, US 196/C3
Quartzsite, Az, US 179/D4
Quatre Bornes, Mrts. 143/T15
Quatrevaux (peak), Swi. 67/G4
Quay, NM, US 182/C2
Quba, Azer. 115/J1
Qüchān, Iran 113/G1
Que Son, Viet. 106/E3
Queanbeyan, Austl. 157/D2
Quebec (prov.), Qu, Can. 188/B2
Québec (cap.), Qu, Can. 189/B2
Québec (int'l arpt.), Qu, Can. 188/B2
Quebec, Qu, Can. 189/B2
Quebra-Canalha (mts.), Braz. 223/L8
Quebrachos, Bol. 224/E1
Quebrada Honda, Bol. 224/D4
Quechisla, Bol. 224/C2
Quechultenango, Mex. 205/M8
Quedas do Iguaçu (falls), Braz. 225/G2
Quedgeley, Eng, UK 42/D3
Quedlinburg, Ger. 59/G3
Queen Alia (int'l arpt.), Jor. 117/C5
Queen Anne, Md, US 198/C6
Queen Annes (co.), Md, US 198/C5
Queen Bess (mt.), BC, Can. 174/B2
Queen Charlotte (isls.), Can. 170/A3
Queen Charlotte (str.), BC, Can. 170/C3
Queen Charlotte, BC, Can. 201/M4

Queen Charlotte (sound), BC, Can. 170/C3
Queen City, Tx, US 179/G4
Queen Creek, Az, US 179/E4
Queen Elizabeth (isls.), Can. 163/F2
Queen Mary, Eng, UK 36/B2
Queen Mary (coast), Ant. 227/G6
Queen Mary Land, Ant. 228/G6
Queen Maud (mts.), Ant. 228/P
Queen Maud (gulf), Nun, Can. 170/F2
Queen Maud Land, Ant. 229/L
Queen Victoria Spring Nature Reserve, Austl. 154/D4
Queenborough, Eng, UK 43/G4
Queens (chan.), Austl. 152/C2
Queens (co.), NY, US 199/E2
Queensberry (peak), SKor. 39/C6
Queensbury, Eng, UK 41/G4
Queenscliff, Austl. 156/B3
Queensferry, Wal, UK 40/E5
Queensferry, Sc, UK 39/C5
Queensland (state), Austl. 145/C3
Queenstown, On, Can. 190/U9
Queenstown, NZ 156/C4
Queenstown, Austl. 156/C4
Queenstown, Guy. 217/G3
Queenstown, SAfr. 142/D3
Queenstown, Md, US 198/C5
Queensville, Md, US 188/B6
Queguén (riv.), Arg. 226/F3
Queilén, Chile 226/B4
Queimadas, Braz. 219/H4
Queimadas, Braz. 223/F1
Quela, Ang. 140/B2
Queluz, Port. 53/P10
Quemado, Tx, US 180/D3
Quembo (riv.), Ang. 140/C2
Quemú Quemú, Arg. 226/E3
Quenington, Eng, UG 43/E3
Quepos, CR 207/E4
Quequén, Arg. 226/F3
Querencia (isl.), Braz. 219/H4
Querétaro (state), Mex. 205/E4
Querétaro de Arteaga, Mex. 205/E4
Quero, It. 69/E2
Querobabi, Mex. 204/C2
Quesada, CR 207/E4
Quesada, Sp. 52/D4
Queshan, China 92/C4
Quesnel, BC, Can. 170/D3
Quesnel (lake), BC, Can. 174/C1
Quesnoy-sur-Deûle, Fr. 60/C2
Quessoy, Fr. 63/B2
Questembert, Fr. 60/B2
Quetame, Col. 219/M8
Quetena, Col. 219/M8
Quetico (riv.), Mn, US 185/F1
Quetigny, Fr. 66/B3
Quetta, Pak. 113/J2
Quettehou, Fr. 63/F2
Queue (riv.), Fr. 62/D6
Quevedo, Ecu. 216/B3
Quevedo (riv.), Ecu. 216/B3
Queven, Fr. 60/B3
Quevenco (riv.), Belg. 60/C2
Quevy, Belg. 60/C2
Quezaltenango, Guat. 206/D3
Quezaltepeque, Guat. 206/D3
Quezon, China 100/D4
Quezon City, Phil. 100/E6
Quezon NP, Phil. 103/G5
Qufu, China 99/H3
Qui Nhon, Viet. 106/E4
Qui Parle (lake), Mn, US 185/F1
Quibala, Ang. 140/B2
Quibaxe, Ang. 140/B2
Quibdó, Col. 216/B2
Quiberon, Fr. 62/B6
Quiberon (pen.), Fr. 62/B6
Quibocolo, Ang. 140/B1
Quibor, Ven. 216/D2
Quibu, China 99/G3
Quicacha, Peru 220/D5
Quiché (dept.), Guat. 206/C3
Quickborn, Ger. 59/G1
Quidico, Chile 226/B3
Quidico (riv.), Chile 226/B3
Quierschied, Ger. 70/D2
Quijotoa, Az, US 179/E5
Quila, Mex. 204/D3
Quilán (cape), Chile 226/B4
Quilcene, Wa, US 197/C2
Quilengues, Ang. 140/B2
Quileute Ind. Res., Wa, US 174/A4
Quilimari, Chile 226/B2
Quilino, Arg. 226/D3
Quillacas, Bol. 224/C2
Quillacollo, Bol. 224/C1
Quillagua, Chile 224/C2
Quillan, Fr. 74/D6
Quillota, Chile 226/N8
Quilmaná, Peru 220/C4
Quilmes, Arg. 226/G3
Quilmes (peak), Arg. 224/C3

Quilty, Ire. 38/A4
Quimbaia, Ang. 138/C4
Quimbele, Ang. 138/D4
Quime, Bol. 224/C1
Quimili, Arg. 224/D3
Quimome, Bol. 224/D1
Quimper, Fr. 62/A4
Quimperlé, Fr. 62/B5
Quin, Ire. 38/B4
Quinault Ind. Res., Wa, US 171/S7
Quincampoix, Fr. 63/G1
Quince Mil, Peru 220/D4
Quincey, Fr. 66/C2
Quincy, Fl, US 195/F2
Quincy, Il, US 185/L4
Quincy, Ma, US 191/L3
Quincy, Mi, US 190/D4
Quincy, Wa, US 174/E4
Quincy-East Quincy, Ca, US 172/C3
Quincy-sous-Sénart, Fr. 36/K5
Quincy-Voisins, Fr. 36/L5
Quindío (dept.), Col. 216/C4
Quines, Arg. 224/C5
Quinhagak, Ak, US 201/F4
Quinlan, Tx, US 183/F4
Quinn (riv.), Nv, US 176/D3
Quinns Rocks, Austl. 154/K6
Quinta de la Serena, Sp. 52/B3
Quintana Roo (state), Mex. 202/D4
Quintanar de la Orden, Sp. 52/D3
Quintanar del Rey, Sp. 52/E3
Quinte (bay), On, Can. 191/H2
Quintenas, Fr. 68/A5
Quinter, Ks, US 184/D4
Quintin, Fr. 62/C4
Quinto, Swi. 67/F4
Quinto, Sp. 53/E2
Quinto di Treviso, It. 69/E2
Quinto di Valpantena, It. 69/E2
Quinton, NJ, US 198/C4
Quinwood, WV, US 193/G1
Quinzano d'Oglio, It. 68/C2
Quinzau, Ang. 138/C4
Quionga, Moz. 137/C4
Quipapá, Braz. 219/H5
Quipungo, Ang. 140/B2
Quirey, Col. 216/C3
Quirihue, Chile 226/B3
Quirima (arch.), Moz. 137/C4
Quirindi, Austl. 156/C1
Quirinópolis, Braz. 222/C2
Quiroga, Bol. 224/C1
Quiroga, Mex. 205/E5
Quiroga, Sp. 52/B1
Quirpon (isl.), Nf, Can. 189/K3
Quissico, Moz. 141/G5
Quita Sueno (bank), Col. 207/F3
Quitapak, Ak, US 201/E4
Quitapa, Ang. 138/D5
Quitilipi, Arg. 224/D3
Quitman, Ga, US 195/H4
Quitman, La, US 183/F4
Quito (cap.), Ecu. 216/B3
Quivilca, Peru 220/B3
Quiviro, Ven. 216/D2
Quixadá, Braz. 219/H4
Quixeramobim, Braz. 219/H4
Quixeré, Braz. 219/H4
Qujiang, China 99/G4
Qujie, China 99/H4
Qujing, China 98/D3
Qul Parle (lake), Mn, US 185/F1
Qulin, Mo, US 194/E2
Qumar (riv.), China 90/D4
Qumarrabdün, China 90/D4
Qumaym, Jor. 117/D3
Qumbu, SAfr. 142/D3
Qümishan, Iran 113/G3
Qunaitra, Syria 117/D3
Quorn, Austl. 155/H5
Quoile (riv.), NI, UK 40/C3
Quorndon, Eng, UK 43/F1
Quoro, Col. 216/C3
Qurayyat, Oman 112/G4
Qûrnat as Sawdā' (peak), Leb. 117/D1
Quşaybah (peak), SAr. 123/E4
Quşayr ad Daffah, SAr. 123/E4
Quseir, Egypt 127/G2
Qusmuryn, Kaz. 80/G4
Qusmuryn (lake), Kaz. 80/G4
Quttinirpaaq Nat'l Park, Nun, Can. 163/J1
Qutūr, Egypt 131/B4
Quwaysinā' (phys. reg.), Egypt 131/C3
Quwo, China 92/C4
Qüxü, China 109/H1
Quyon, Qu, Can. 188/B2
Quynh Nhai, Viet. 98/D4
Qüynhirot, Uzb. 80/F5
Qytet Stalin, Alb. 55/F2
Qyzylorda, Kaz. 80/G5
Qyzylorda Oblast, Kaz. 80/G5

R

Raab (riv.), Aus. 51/L3
Raab, Aus. 65/G6

Raabs an der Thaya, Aus. 49/H4
RAAF-Richmond (A.F.B.), Austl. 158/G8
Raahe, Fr. 74/E2
Raalte, Neth. 58/D4
Raamsdonk, Neth. 58/B5
Rääkkylä, Swe. 45/J7
Rään (riv.), Swe. 45/L7
Ra'ananna, Isr. 117/B4
Raanes (pen.), Nun, Can. 171/S7
Raas (isl.), Indo. 101/K4
Raas Jumbo, Som. 137/C2
Raasiku, Est. 47/L2
Rab, Cro. 51/K4
Rab (isl.), Cro. 51/K4
Rába (riv.), Hun. 56/C2
Rábafüzes, Hun. 56/C2
Rábahídvég, Hun. 56/C2
Rabai, Kenya 137/D2
Rabak, Sudan 135/G2
Rabastens, Fr. 53/F1
Rabat, Malta 54/L7
Rabat (Sale) (int'l arpt.), Mor. 130/A2
Rabat (Sale), Mor. 130/A2
Rabat (Victoria), Malta 54/L6
Rabbi (cr.), SD, US 184/C1
Rabbit (cr.), SD, US 184/C1
Rabbit Ear (peak), NM, US 182/C2
Rabbit Ears (pass), Co, US 177/K3
Rabbit Lake, Sk, Can. 175/L1
Rabgala (pass), China 109/F2
Rābigh, SAr. 112/C4
Rabil, Cyp. 119/K10
Rabinal, Guat. 206/D3
Rabiusa (riv.), Swi. 67/F4
Rabka, Pol. 49/K4
Rabkavi-Banhatti, India 113/L5
Rabocheostrovsk, Rus. 74/G2
Raby (pt.), On, Can. 190/V8
Raccoon (riv.), La, US 194/C3
Raccoon (cr.), Fl, US 194/K6
Rabyānah (des.), Libya 126/C3
Raceland, La, US 194/C3
Rach Gia (bay), Viet. 106/D4
Rachel Carson Nat'l Wild. Ref., Me, US 191/L3
Racibórz, Pol. 49/K3
Racine, La, US 194/C3
Racine, Wi, US 190/C3
Racine (co.), Wi, US 197/P14
Racola, Mo, US 192/B1
Radauti, India 110/D4
Rădăuți, Rom. 78/C4
Radbuza (riv.), Czh. 48/G4
Radchenskoye, Rus. 79/J3
Radcliff, Ky, US 192/E2
Radcliffe on Trent, Eng, UK 41/F4
Rade de Brest (har.), Fr. 62/A4
Radekhiv, Ukr. 78/C2
Radenthein, Aus. 51/K3
Radersburg, Mt, US 175/J4
Radevormwald, Ger. 59/E6
Radford, Va, US 193/G2
Rādhanpur, India 113/K4
Radisson, Wi, US 187/J5
Radium Hill, Austl. 155/J5
Radium Springs, NM, US 179/J4
Radlett, Eng, UK 36/B1
Radnevo, Bul. 57/G4
Radnor (co.), Wal, UK 41/D5
Radolfzell, Ger. 67/E2
Radom NP, Sudan 135/E2
Radom, Pol. 49/L3
Radomsko, Pol. 49/K3
Radomyshl', Ukr. 78/D2
Radovish, FYROM 55/H2
Radovljica, Slov. 51/J3
Radstadt, Aus. 49/G5
Radstock, Eng, UK 42/D4
Radviliškis, Lith. 47/K4
Radymno, Pol. 49/M3
Radziejów, Pol. 49/K2
Radzyń Podlaski, Pol. 49/M3
Radyr, Wal, UK 42/C3
Rae (isth.), Nun, Can. 170/H2
Rae Bareli, India 109/F2
Rae-Edzo, NW, Can. 170/D2
Raeford, NC, US 193/H3
Raeren, Belg. 61/F2
Raeside (lake), Austl. 154/D4
Raetihi, NZ 159/H8
Rafael J. Garcia, Mex. 205/M7
Rafael Núñez (int'l arpt.), Col. 216/C2
Rafaela, Arg. 224/D4
Rafah, SAr. 117/A5
Rafaï, CAfr. 134/D4
Rafaï, CAfr. 115/E4
Rafidīyah, WBnk. 117/C4
Rafiganj, India 109/E3
Rafina, Gre. 55/P8
Rafsaljan, India 113/B4
Rafsanjān, Iran 115/J4
Raft (pt.), Austl. 152/B2
Raft (riv.), Id, US 177/G3
Raga, Sudan 135/F3
Ragang (mt.), Phil. 103/G5
Ragay (gulf), Phil. 100/C2
Ragged (isl.), Me, US 188/F3
Ragged (isl.), Bahm. 207/G2
Ragged (pt.), Chile 191/B7
Ragland, Wal, UK 42/D3
Raglan, NZ 159/H7
Ragland, Al, US 192/D4
Rago NP, Nor. 44/E2
Ragstone (range), Eng, UK 36/D3

Rhode – Roose

324

Rhodes (Pódhos), Gre. 114/B2
Rhodope (mts.), Bul.,Gre. 73/J2
Rhome, Tx, US 180/K6
Rhön (mts.), Ger. 64/D1
Rhondda, Wal, UK 42/C3
Rhondda Cynon Taff (co.), Wal, UK 42/C3
Rhône (dept.), Fr. 66/A6
Rhone (glacier), Swi. 67/E4
Rhône (riv.), Fr. 29/E4
Rhône au Rhin (canal), Fr. 66/B3
Rhône-Alpes (pol. reg.), Fr. 66/B5
Rhonelle (riv.), Fr. 60/C3
Rhosllanerchrugog, Wal, UK 41/E6
Rhossili, Wal, UK 42/B3
Rhuddlan, Wal, UK 40/E5
Rhum (isl.), Sc, UK 37/Q8
Rhume (riv.), Ger. 59/H5
Rhumel, Oued el (riv.), Alg. 130/J4
Rhuys (pen.), Fr. 62/C6
Rhyddhywel (peak), Wal, UK 42/C2
Rhydowen, Wal, UK 42/B2
Rhyl, Wal, UK 40/E5
Rhynie, Sc, UK 39/D2
Rhyolite, Nv, US 178/D2
Riaba, EqG. 138/B2
Riachão, Braz. 219/E4
Riachão das Neves, Braz. 222/D1
Riachão do Jacuípe, Braz. 223/F1
Riacho de Santana, Braz. 223/E2
Riacho Monte Lindo (riv.), Arg. 224/E3
Riacho Pilagá (riv.), Arg. 224/E3
Riachuelo, Uru. 191/K11
Riachuelo, Braz. 219/H4
Riaillé, Fr. 62/D5
Riala, Swe. 45/B1
Rialto, Ca, US 196/C2
Riangnom, Sudan 135/F3
Rianjo, Sp. 52/A1
Riano, It. 71/B3
Riaño, Sp. 52/C1
Rians, Fr. 70/B5
Riāsi, India 110/C3
Riau (isls.), Indo. 102/B3
Riau (prov.), Indo. 101/C2
Riaza, Sp. 52/D2
Rib (mtn.), Wi, US 185/K1
Rib Lake, Wi, US 187/J5
Ribadeo, Sp. 52/B1
Ribadesella, Sp. 52/C1
Riban'i Manamby (mts.), Madg. 143/H9
Ribas do Rio Pardo, Braz. 225/F2
Ribauè, Moz. 141/H2
Ribble (riv.), Eng, UK 41/F4
Ribblesdale (valley), Eng, UK 41/F3
Ribe, Den. 46/C4
Ribe (co.), Den. 46/C4
Ribeauvillé, Fr. 66/D1
Ribécourt-Dreslincourt, Fr. 60/B4
Ribeira (riv.), Braz. 225/G3
Ribeira Brava, Port. 128/A2
Ribeira Brava, CpV. 119/J10
Ribeira de Pena, Port. 52/B2
Ribeira do Pombal, Braz. 223/F1
Ribeira Grande, CpV. 119/J9
Ribeira Grande, Azor., Port. 53/T13
Ribeirão, Braz. 219/H5
Ribeirão Preto, Braz. 225/H2
Ribeiro Gonçalves, Braz. 219/E4
Ribera, It. 54/C4
Ribera, NM, US 182/B3
Riberalta, Bol. 221/E3
Ribiers, Fr. 70/B4
Rîbnița, Mol. 78/E4
Ribnitz-Damgarten, Ger. 46/E4
Ribstone, Ab, Can. 175/J1
Ribstone (cr.), Ab, Can. 175/J1
Říčany u Prahy, Czh. 65/H3
Ricaurte, Col. 216/B4
Riccia, It. 71/D5
Riccione, It. 69/F6
Ricco'del Golfo, It. 68/C5
Rice, Mn, US 187/G5
Rice (lake), On, Can. 191/G2
Rice, Ca, US 178/E3
Rice, Wa, US 174/E3
Rice, Tx, US 181/F1
Rice Lake, Wi, US 187/J5
Rice Lake NWR, Mn, US 187/H4
Riceboro, Ga, US 195/H2
Riceville, Ia, US 185/H2
Rich (mtn.), Ar, US 183/G3
Rich, Mor. 128/D2
Rich Hill, Mo, US 183/G1
Rich Square, NC, US 193/J2
Richard B. Russell (dam), SC, US 193/F3
Richard Toll, Sen. 132/B2
Richards, Mo, US 183/G2
Richards (isl.), NW, Can. 170/C2
Richard's Bay, SAfr. 143/F3
Richards Landing, On, Can. 190/D1
Richardson, Tx, US 180/L7
Richardson Lakes (lakes), NH, US 188/B3
Richardton, ND, US 186/C4
Richboro, Pa, US 198/C3
Riche (cape), Austl. 154/C5
Richebourg, Fr. 36/G5
Richel (isl.), Neth. 58/C2
Richelieu (riv.), Qu, Can. 191/K2
Richelieu, Qu, Can. 189/P7
Richey, Mt, US 186/B4
Richfield, Ut, US 179/F1
Richfield, Id, US 177/F2
Richfield, Mn, US 187/P7
Richfield, Pa, US 198/A2
Richford, Vt, US 191/K2
Richhill, NI, UK 40/B3
Richibucto, NB, Can. 188/E2
Richland, Mo, US 183/H2
Richland, Ga, US 195/F1
Richland, Ms, US 192/B4
Richland, Tx, US 181/F2
Richland, Wa, US 174/E4
Richland, Pa, US 198/B3
Richland, NJ, US 198/D5
Richland Balsam (peak), NC, US 193/F3
Richland Center, Wi, US 185/J2
Richland Creek (res.), Tx, US 181/F2
Richland Hills, Tx, US 180/K7
Richland Springs, Tx, US 180/E2
Richlands, Va, US 193/G2
Richlands, NC, US 193/J3
Richlandtown, Pa, US 198/C3
Richmond, Austl. 158/A3
Richmond, BC, Can. 174/C3
Richmond, Qu, Can. 191/K2
Richmond, NZ 159/C3
Richmond, SAfr. 142/C3
Richmond, SAfr. 143/E3
Richmond, Eng, UK 41/G3
Richmond, Ar, US 183/G4
Richmond, Ks, US 183/G1
Richmond, Mn, US 187/G5
Richmond, In, US 190/D5
Richmond, Mi, US 190/E3
Richmond, Il, US 197/P15
Richmond, Ut, US 177/H3
Richmond, Ky, US 192/E2
Richmond, Mo, US 185/H4
Richmond, Tx, US 181/M9
Richmond (cap.), Va, US 193/J2
Richmond (co.), NY, US 199/J9
Richmond Beach-Innis Arden, Wa, US 197/B2
Richmond Dale, Oh, US 193/F1
Richmond Heights, Fl, US 194/P11
Richmond Hill, On, Can. 190/U8
Richmond Nat'l Bfld. Park, Va, US 193/J2
Richmond Park (bor.), Eng, UK 36/C2
Richmond Town (nbrhd.), NY, US 199/J9
Richmond Upon Thames (bor.), Eng, UK 36/B2
Richmond-Windsor, Austl. 158/G8
Richmondville, NY, US 191/J3
Richmound, Sk, Can. 175/K2
Richtersveld NP, SAfr. 142/B3
Richterswil, Swi. 67/E3
Richthofen (mt.), Co, US 184/B3
Richton, Ms, US 194/D2
Richville, NY, US 191/J2
Richwiller, Fr. 66/D2
Richwood, Tx, US 180/G3
Richwood, La, US 183/H4
Richwood, Oh, US 190/E4
Richwood, WV, US 193/G1
Richwoods, Mo, US 192/B1
Rickenbach, Ger. 66/D2
Ricketts Glen St. Park, Pa, US 198/B1
Rickman, Tn, US 192/E2
Rickmansworth, Eng, UK 36/B2
Ricla, Sp. 52/E2
Rico, Ga, US 193/L7
Ricse, Hun. 49/L4
Ridā', Yem. 136/C2
Riddells Creek, Austl. 157/B3
Ridderkerk, Neth. 58/B5
Riddle, Id, US 176/E2
Riddle, Or, US 176/B2
Rideau (riv.), On, Can. 191/J2
Rideau (lake), On, Can. 191/H2
Ridge, Mt, US 184/B1
Ridge Farm, Il, US 190/C5
Ridge Manor, Fl, US 194/L6
Ridge Spring, SC, US 193/G4
Ridgecrest, La, US 194/C2
Ridgecrest, Ca, US 178/D3
Ridgefield, NJ, US 199/K8
Ridgefield, Wa, US 174/C5
Ridgefield, Ct, US 199/E1
Ridgefield NWR, Or, US 174/C5
Ridgefield Park, NJ, US 199/J8
Ridgeland, Ms, US 192/B4
Ridgeland, SC, US 193/G4
Ridgely, Tn, US 192/C2
Ridgely, Md, US 198/C6
Ridgetown, On, Can. 190/F3
Ridgeville, SC, US 193/G4
Ridgeway, Mo, US 185/H3
Ridgeway, Va, US 193/H2
Ridgewood (nbrhd.), NY, US 199/K9
Ridgewood, NJ, US 199/J8
Ridgway, Pa, US 191/G4
Ridgway, Co, US 179/J1
Riding Mill, Eng, UK 41/G2
Riding Mountain NP, Mb, Can. 186/D2
Riding (mtn.), Mb, Can. 186/D2
Ridlees Cairn (hill), Eng, UK 39/D6
Ridley (cr.), Pa, US 198/C4
Riec-sur-Belon, Fr. 62/B5
Riecito (riv.), Col. 216/D3
Ried im Innkreis, Aus. 65/G6
Ried im Traunkreis, Aus. 65/H6
Riede, Ger. 59/F3
Riedenburg, Ger. 65/E5
Riedisheim, Fr. 66/D2
Riedlingen, Ger. 67/F1
Riegelsberg, Ger. 61/F5
Riegelsville, Pa, US 198/C2
Riegsee (lake), Ger. 67/H2
Riehen, Swi. 66/D2
Riemst, Belg. 61/E2
Rieneck, Ger. 64/C2
Rienzi, Ms, US 192/C3
Riesa, Ger. 49/G3
Rieschweiler-Mühlbach, Ger. 61/G5
Riesco (isl.), Chile 191/B7
Riese Pio X, It. 69/E2
Riet (riv.), SAfr. 142/D3
Rietavas, Lith. 47/J4
Rietberg, Ger. 59/F5
Rietbron, SAfr. 142/C4
Rietfontein, Namb. 140/D4
Rietfontein (riv.), Namb. 140/D4
Rieti, It. 71/B3
Rieti (prov.), It. 71/B3
Rievaulx, Eng, UK 41/G3
Riez, Fr. 70/C5
Riffe (lake), Wa, US 174/C4
Rifle, Co, US 177/K4
Rifsnes (pt.), Ice. 44/N6
Rift Valley (prov.), Kenya 137/A1
Rig-Rig, Chad 134/B2
Riga (gulf), Eur. 80/C4
Riga (Rīga) (cap.), Lat. 47/L3
Rigacikun, Nga. 133/G4
Rigby, Id, US 177/H2
Rīgestan (pol. reg.), Afg. 113/H2
Riggins, Id, US 176/E1
Rigi (peak), Swi. 67/E3
Rignano Flaminio, It. 71/B3
Rignano sull'Arno, It. 69/E6
Rigolet, Nf, Can. 171/L3
Rigside, Sc, UK 39/C5
Riguldi, Est. 47/K2
Riḩāb, Jor. 117/E4
Rihand (riv.), India 108/D3
Rihand (dam), India 108/D3
Rihand Sāgar (res.), India 104/D3
Riihimäki, Fin. 47/L1
Riiser-Larsen (pen.), Ant. 228/C
Riiser-Larsen Ice Shelf, Ant. 228/Y
Riisitunturin NP, Fin. 74/F2
Rijeka, Cro. 51/L4
Rijen, Neth. 58/B5
Rijksmuseum Kröller Müller, Neth. 58/C4
Rijnsburg, Neth. 58/B4
Rijsbergen, Neth. 58/B5
Rijssen, Neth. 58/D4
Rijswijk, Neth. 58/B4
Rikers (isl.), NY, US 199/K8
Rikitea, FrPol. 161/M7
Rikuchū-Kaigan NP, Japan 94/C4
Rikuzentakata, Japan 94/B4
Rila, Bul. 55/H1
Rila (mts.), Bul. 55/H1
Riley, Or, US 176/D2
Riley, Ks, US 185/F4
Riley Brook, NB, Can. 188/D2
Rillieux-la-Pape, Fr. 66/A6
Rillito, Az, US 179/G4
Rilski Manastir, Bul. 55/H1
Rīmah (wadi), SAr. 112/D3
Rimatara (isl.), FrPol. 161/K7
Rimavská Sobota, Slvk. 49/L4
Rimbach, Ger. 64/B3
Rimbey, Ab, Can. 175/G1
Rimbo, Swe. 45/B1
Rimé (riv.), Chad 134/C2
Rimersburg, Pa, US 191/G4
Rimforsa, Swe. 46/F2
Rimini, It. 69/F5
Rîmnicu Sărat, Rom. 57/H3
Rîmnicu Vîlcea, Rom. 57/G3
Rimogne, Fr. 61/D4
Rimouski, Qu, Can. 188/C1
Rimouski (riv.), Qu, Can. 188/C1
Rimouski-Est, Qu, Can. 188/C1
Rimpar, Ger. 64/C3
Rimpfischhorn (peak), Swi. 66/D5
Rimsting, Ger. 65/F7
Rimutaka (range), NZ 159/H9
Rimutaka Forrest Park, NZ 159/H9
Rinas (int'l arpt.), Alb. 55/F2
Rinbung, China 109/G1
Rinchnach, Ger. 65/G5
Rincon (peak), Az, US 179/G4
Rincón, Uru. 191/G2
Rincon, NM, US 179/J4
Rincón (peak), Arg.,Chile 224/C3
Rincon, Ga, US 193/G4
Rincón de la Vieja, PN, CR 202/D5
Rincón de Romos, Mex. 204/E4
Rinconada, Arg. 224/C2
Rindge, NH, US 191/K3
Ringarooma, Austl. 156/C4
Ringaskiddy, Ire. 38/B6
Ringboy (pt.), NI, UK 40/C3
Ringebu, Nor. 46/D1
Ringelspitz (peak), Swi. 67/F4
Ringgold, La, US 183/H4
Ringgold, Ga, US 192/E3
Ringim, Nga. 133/H3
Ringkøbing, Den. 46/C3
Ringkøbing (co.), Den. 46/B3
Ringkøbing (fjord), Den. 46/B3
Ringling, Mt, US 175/J4
Ringling, Ok, US 183/F3
Ringling Musuem of Art, Fl, US 195/G4
Ringmer, Eng, UK 43/G5
Ringoes, NJ, US 198/D3
Ringold, Ok, US 183/G3
Ringsend, NI, UK 40/B1
Ringsön (isl.), Swe. 45/A2
Ringsted, Den. 46/D4
Ringtown, Pa, US 198/B2
Ringvaart (riv.), Neth. 58/B4
Ringvassøy (isl.), Nor. 44/F1
Ringway (Manchester) (int'l arpt.), Eng, UK 41/F5
Ringwood, Austl. 155/G2
Ringwood (nbrhd.), Austl. 156/G5
Ringwood, Eng, UK 43/E5
Ringwood, NJ, US 199/H7
Ringwood State Park, NJ, US 199/H7
Rínia (isl.), Gre. 55/J4
Riñihue, Chile 226/B3
Rinteln, Ger. 59/G4
Rinxent, Fr. 60/A2
Rio, La, US 194/D2
Río Abiseo, PN, Peru 220/B2
Rio Azul, Braz. 225/G3
Rio Blanco, Co, US 177/K4
Río Blanco, Chile 226/N8
Río Blanco, Bol. 220/D5
Río Blanco, Mex. 205/M8
Rio Bonito, Braz. 223/P7
Rio Branco, Braz. 220/E3
Rio Branco, Uru. 225/F5
Rio Branco do Sul, Braz. 225/G3
Río Bravo, Mex. 181/E5
Rio Brilhante, Braz. 225/F2
Río Bueno, Chile 226/B4
Río Cauto, Cuba 207/G1
Río Ceballos, Arg. 224/C4
Río Chico, Arg. 191/C6
Río Clarillo, PN, Chile 226/N8
Rio Claro, Trin. 217/F2
Rio Claro, Braz. 223/M7
Rio Claro, Braz. 225/H2
Río Colorado, Arg. 226/D3
Río Cuarto, Arg. 226/D2
Río de Bavispe (riv.), Mex. 204/C2
Rio de Contas, Braz. 223/E2
Rio de Janeiro (int'l arpt.), Braz. 223/N7
Rio de Janeiro, Braz. 223/N7
Rio de Janeiro (state), Braz. 223/E4
Rio Dell, Ca, US 176/A3
Rio do Sul, Braz. 225/G3
Rio Frio, Port. 53/Q10
Río Gallegos, Arg. 191/C6
Río Grande, Arg. 191/D7
Rio Grande, Braz. 225/F5
Rio Grande (riv.), Mex.,US 172/G6
Rio Grande (canal), Co, US 182/A2
Rio Grande (plain), Tx, US 202/B2
Rio Grande, NJ, US 198/D5
Rio Grande, Oh, US 193/F1
Rio Grande City, Tx, US 181/E4
Rio Grande da Serra, Braz. 223/K8
Río Grande de Matagalpa (riv.), Nic. 202/D5
Río Grande de Santiago (riv.), Mex. 204/D4
Rio Grande do Norte (state), Braz. 219/G4
Rio Grande do Piauí, Braz. 219/F4
Rio Grande do Sul (state), Braz. 225/F4
Rio Grande Valley (int'l arpt.), Tx, US 181/F4
Rio Hondo, Tx, US 180/F4
Rio Jaú, PN do, Braz. 217/F5
Río Lagartos, Mex. 206/D1
Rio Largo, Braz. 219/H5
Rio Maior, Port. 52/A3
Río Mayo, Arg. 226/C5
Rio Muni (pol. reg.), EqG. 138/B2
Rio Negrinho, Braz. 225/G3
Río Negro, Chile 226/B4
Río Negro (prov.), Arg. 226/E3
Río Negro, Chile 226/B4
Río Negro (res.), Uru. 225/F5
Rio Negro, Braz. 225/F1
Río Negro (dept.), Uru. 225/F5
Rio Pardo, Braz. 225/F4
Rio Rancho, NM, US 179/J3
Rio Real, Braz. 223/F1
Rio Saliceto, It. 69/D4
Río Segundo, Arg. 224/D4
Río Simpson, PN, Chile 226/B5
Río Tala, Arg. 191/J10
Río Tercero, Arg. 224/C5
Río Tigre, Ecu. 216/B5
Rio Tinto, Braz. 219/H4
Río Verde, Chile 191/C7
Rio Verde, Braz. 222/C3
Río Verde, Mex. 205/F4
Rio Verde de Mato Grosso, Braz. 225/F1
Rio Vista, Ca, US 197/L10
Rio Vista, Tx, US 181/F1
Riobamba, Ecu. 216/B5
Ríohacha, Col. 216/C2
Rioja, Peru 220/B2
Riolo Terme, It. 69/E5
Riom, Fr. 50/E4
Riom-ès-Montagne, Fr. 50/E4
Riomaggiore, It. 68/C5
Rion-des-Landes, Fr. 50/C5
Riondel, BC, Can. 174/F3
Ríonegro, Col. 216/C3
Ríonegro, Col. 219/K6
Rionero in Vulture, It. 54/D2
Rionero Sannitico, It. 71/D4
Riorges, Fr. 50/F3
Ríos, Sp. 52/B2
Ríos (lake), Chile 226/B5
Ríosucio, Col. 216/B3
Ríosucio, Col. 219/K7
Rioz, Fr. 66/C3
Riozinho (riv.), Braz. 221/E2
Ripa Sottile (lake), It. 71/B3
Ripalimosano, It. 71/D4
Ripalti, Punta dei (pt.), It. 54/B1
Ripanj, Serb. 56/E3
Riparbella, It. 68/D7
Ripatransone, It. 71/C2
Ripky, Ukr. 78/F2
Ripley, Eng, UK 41/G5
Ripley, Eng, UK 36/B3
Ripley, Ca, US 178/E4
Ripley, Ms, US 192/C3
Ripley, Oh, US 192/F1
Ripley, Ok, US 183/F2
Ripley, Tn, US 192/C3
Ripley, WV, US 193/G1
Ripoll, Sp. 53/G1
Ripoll (riv.), Sp. 53/L6
Ripollet, Sp. 53/L6
Ripon, Eng, UK 41/G3
Ripon, Qu, Can. 191/J2
Ripon, Ca, US 178/B2
Ripon, Wi, US 185/K2
Riposto, It. 54/D4
Ripples, NB, Can. 188/D2
Rippon, WV, US 191/H5
Ripponden, Eng, UK 41/G4
Rippowam (riv.), Ct, US 199/L7
Riri Bāzār, Nepal 108/D2
Ris-Orangis, Fr. 36/K6
Risaralda (dept.), Col. 216/A4
Risaralda, Col. 219/K7
Risasi, D.R. Congo 139/F3
Rîşcani, Mol. 78/D4
Rishiri, Japan 94/B1
Rishiri (isl.), Japan 91/N2
Rishiri-Rebun-Sarobetsu NP, Japan 94/B1
Rishon Leẕiyyon, Isr. 117/B5
Rishrāsh (wadi), Egypt 131/C6
Rising Star, Tx, US 180/E1
Rising Sun, In, US 192/E1
Rising Sun, Md, US 198/B4
Rising Sun-Lebanon, De, US 198/C5
Riske Creek, BC, Can. 174/C2
Risle (riv.), Fr. 50/D2
Risley (Estell Manor), NJ, US 198/D5
Risnjak (peak), Cro. 51/L4
Risnjak NP, Cro. 56/B3
Rîşnov, Rom. 57/G3
Rison, Ar, US 183/H4
Risør, Nor. 46/C2
Risoul, Fr. 70/C3
Riss (riv.), Ger. 67/F1
Risse (riv.), Fr. 66/C5
Rişşū (peak), Egypt 131/B5
Risti, Est. 47/L2
Ristiina, Fin. 47/M1
Rita Blanca (cr.), Tx, US 182/C2
Ritacuba (peak), Col. 216/C3
Ritaiō (isl.), Japan 160/D2
Rito (cr.), NM, US 179/H3
Ritoio (peak), It. 69/E6
Ritterhude, Ger. 59/F2
Rittman, Oh, US 190/F4
Rittō, Japan 95/J5
Ritzville, Wa, US 174/E4
Riva, It. 67/G6
Riva Ligure, It. 68/A5
Riva Presso Chieri, It. 68/A3
Riva San Vitale, Swi. 67/E6
Rivadavia, Arg. 226/E2
Rivadavia, Arg. 224/D3
Rivadavia, Arg. 224/B4
Rival (riv.), Fr. 70/B2
Rivalta, It. 68/D3
Rivalta di Torino, It. 68/A2
Rivanazzano, It. 68/C4
Rivanna (riv.), Va, US 193/H2
Rivara, It. 70/D2
Rivarolo Canavese, It. 68/A2
Rivarolo Mantovano, It. 68/D3
Rivas, Nic. 206/E4
Rīvash, Iran 113/G1
Rive-de-Gier, Fr. 70/A1
River Bourgeois, NS, Can. 189/G3
River Cess, Libr. 132/C5
River Denys, NS, Can. 189/G3
River Edge, NJ, US 199/J8
River Falls, Al, US 194/E2
River Falls, Wi, US 187/Q7
River Hébert, NS, Can. 188/E3
River John, NS, Can. 188/F3
River Kwai Bridge, Thai. 106/B3
River Oaks, Tx, US 180/K7
River Rouge, Mi, US 197/F7
River Vale, NJ, US 199/J8
Rivera, Swi. 67/E5
Rivera (isl.), Chile 226/B5
Rivera, Arg. 226/E3
Rivera (dept.), Uru. 225/F4
Rivera, Uru. 225/F4
Riverdale, ND, US 186/D4
Riverdale, NJ, US 199/H8
Riverdale (nbrhd.), NY, US 199/K8
Riverdale, Ca, US 178/C2
Riverdale, Ga, US 193/M7
Rivergaro, It. 68/C4
Riverhead, NY, US 199/F2
Riverhurst, Sk, Can. 175/L2
Riverport, NS, Can. 188/E3
Rivers, Mb, Can. 186/D2
Rivers (state), Nga. 133/G5
Riversdale, SAfr. 142/C4
Riverside, Tx, US 181/G2
Riverside (co.), Ca, US 196/C3
Riverside, Ca, US 196/C3
Riverside, Or, US 176/D2
Riverside (canal), Co, US 184/B3
Riverside, Pa, US 198/B2
Riverside, NJ, US 198/D3
Riverside-Albert, NB, Can. 188/E3
Riverstone (nbrhd.), Austl. 158/G8
Riverstown, Ire. 38/B6
Riverstown, Ire. 38/B1
Riverton, Mb, Can. 186/F2
Riverton, NS, Can. 189/F3
Riverton, Austl. 155/H5
Riverton, NZ 159/B4
Riverton, Wy, US 177/J2
Riverton, Ut, US 177/H3
Riverview, NB, Can. 188/E2
Riverview, Mi, US 190/E3
Riverview, Fl, US 194/L8
Riverwoods, Il, US 197/Q15
Rîves, Fr. 70/B2
Riviera, Az, US 178/E3
Riviera, Tx, US 181/F4
Riviera Beach, Fl, US 194/P9
Riviera Beach, Md, US 198/B5
Rivière-à-Pierre, Qu, Can. 188/A2
Rivière-au-Renard, Qu, Can. 188/E1
Rivière-Bleue, Qu, Can. 188/C2
Rivière-du-Loup, Qu, Can. 188/C2
Rivière-Éternité, Qu, Can. 188/B1
Riviersonderendreeks (mts.), SAfr. 142/L11
Rivignano, It. 69/G2
Rivne, Ukr. 78/D2
Rivnens'ka Oblast, Ukr. 76/C2
Rivoli, It. 70/D2
Rivolta d'Adda, It. 68/C3
Rixensart, Belg. 61/D2
Rixheim, Fr. 66/D2
Riyadh (Ar Riyāḑ) (cap.), SAr. 112/E4
Rīyāq, Leb. 117/D1
Rizal, Phil. 100/C2
Rizal (prov.), Phil. 100/F6
Rize, Turk. 77/G4
Rizhao, China 92/D4
Rizokarpasso, Cyp. 116/D2
Rizzuto (cape), It. 54/E3
Rjukan, Nor. 46/C2
Rkîz, Mrta. 132/B2
Rkîz (lake), Mrta. 132/B2
Rö, Swe. 45/B1
Roa, Nor. 46/D1
Roa, Sp. 52/D2
Road Town (cap.), BVI 203/M8
Roade, Eng, UK 43/F2
Roadside, Sc, UK 39/D3
Roan (plat.), Ut, US 177/J4
Roan Fell (hill), Sc, UK 41/F1
Roan High (peak), NC, US 193/F2
Roanne (riv.), Fr. 70/B3
Roanne, Fr. 50/F3
Roanoke, Al, US 192/E4
Roanoke, Tx, US 180/K6
Roanoke (riv.), Va, US 193/H2
Roanoke (pt.), NY, US 199/F2
Roanoke, Va, US 193/H2
Roanoke Rapids, NC, US 193/J2
Roans Prairie, Tx, US 181/G2
Roaring (cr.), Pa, US 198/B2
Roaring Fk. (riv.), Co, US 177/K4
Roaring Springs, Tx, US 182/D4
Roatán (isl.), Hon. 202/D4
Roatán, Hon. 206/E2
Robards, Ky, US 192/D2
Robassomero, It. 70/D2
Robāţ Karīm, Iran 115/G3
Robāţ-e Khān, Iran 115/J3
Robāţ-e Sang, Iran 113/G1
Robb, Ab, Can. 174/F1
Robbiate, It. 68/C2
Robbins (isl.), Austl. 156/C4
Robbins, NC, US 193/H3
Robbinsville, NC, US 192/F3
Robbio, It. 68/B3
Robe (riv.), Ire. 38/A2
Robē, Eth. 136/A4
Robe (mt.), Austl. 156/B1
Robe, Austl. 156/A3
Robecchetto con Induno, It. 68/B2
Röbel, Ger. 46/E4
Röbel, Ger. 48/G2
Robersonville, NC, US 193/J3
Robert (peak), Fr. 66/B5
Robert Lee, Tx, US 180/D2
Roberta, Ga, US 192/E4
Roberts (mt.), Ak, US 201/E4
Roberts, Id, US 177/G2
Roberts, Il, US 190/B4
Roberts, Mt, US 177/J1
Roberts (Monrovia) (int'l arpt.), Libr. 132/C5
Roberts Creek (mtn.), Nv, US 176/E4
Roberts Creek, BC, Can. 174/C3
Robertsbridge, Eng, UK 43/G5
Robertsfors, Swe. 44/G2
Robertsganj, India 108/D3
Robertson, SAfr. 142/L10
Robertson, Wy, US 177/H3
Robertsport, Libr. 132/C5
Robertstown, Ire. 38/D3
Roberval, Qu, Can. 188/A1
Robesonia, Pa, US 198/B3
Robilante, It. 70/D4
Robin Hood's Bay, Eng, UK 41/H3
Robins (A.F.B.), Ga, US 193/F4
Robinson, Il, US 192/D1
Robinson, Tx, US 181/F2
Robinson (mtn.), Mt, US 174/G3
Robinson . (range), Austl. 145/A3
Robinson Crusoe (isl.), Chile 209/B6
Robinson Gorge NP, Austl. 158/C4
Robinson River, Austl. 153/E4
Robinson River, PNG 153/H2
Robinson River Abor. Land, Austl. 153/E4
Robinson Springs, Al, US 192/D4
Robinvale, Austl. 156/B2
Robion, Fr. 70/B5
Robledo (mtn.), NM, US 179/J4
Roblin, Mb, Can. 186/D2
Roboré, Bol. 224/E1
Robsart, Sk, Can. 175/K3
Robson (mt.), BC, Can. 174/E1
Robstown, Tx, US 181/F4
Roby, Mo, US 183/H2
Roby, Tx, US 180/D1
Roc (pt.), Fr. 62/D3
Roc de France (peak), Fr. 53/G1
Roc du Haut du Faite (peak), Fr. 66/D1
Roca Partida (isl.), Mex. 204/B5
Roca Partida, Punta (pt.), Mex. 206/C2
Roca, Cabo da (cape), Port. 53/P10
Rocafuerte, Ecu. 216/A5
Rocanville, Sk, Can. 186/D2
Rocas (isl.), Braz. 219/H3
Rocca di Mezzo, It. 71/C3
Rocca di Papa, It. 71/B4
Rocca San Casciano, It. 69/E5
Roccabianca, It. 68/D3
Roccagorga, It. 71/C4
Roccamandolfi, It. 71/D5
Roccamonfina, It. 71/C5
Roccarainola, It. 71/D6
Roccasecca, It. 71/C4
Roccastrada, It. 54/B1
Roccavione, It. 70/D4
Rocciamelone (peak), It. 70/D2
Rocha, Uru. 191/G2
Rocha (dept.), Uru. 191/G2
Rochambeau (int'l arpt.), FrG. 218/C1
Rochdale, Eng, UK 41/F4
Rochdale (co.), Eng, UK 41/F4
Roche, Swi. 66/C5
Roche, Eng, UK 42/B6
Roche Bernaude (peak), Fr. 70/C2
Roche de la Muzelle (peak), Fr. 70/C3
Roche du Sapin Sec (peak), Fr. 66/C1
Roche Faurio (peak), Fr. 70/C3
Roche-lez-Beaupré, Fr. 66/C3
Rochebrune, Pic de (peak), Fr. 70/C3
Rochefort, Belg. 61/E3
Rochefort, Fr. 50/C4
Rochefort-en-Terre, Fr. 62/C5
Rochefort-sur-Loire, Fr. 63/E6
Rochelaire, Pic de (peak), Fr. 70/C3
Rochelle, Ga, US 195/G2
Rochelle, Il, US 185/K3
Rochelle, Tx, US 180/E2
Rochelle Park, NJ, US 199/J8
Rochemaure, Fr. 70/A3
Rochers de la Tude (peak), Fr. 53/G1
Rochers du Bourbet (peak), Fr. 66/C3
Roches Blanches (peak), Fr. 70/C6
Rochester, Austl. 157/B3
Rochester, Eng, UK 43/G4
Rochester, NY, US 191/H3
Rochester, In, US 190/C4
Rochester, NH, US 191/L3
Rochester, Vt, US 191/K3
Rochester, Wi, US 197/P14
Rochester, Mi, US 197/F6
Rochester, Mn, US 185/H1
Rochester, Ky, US 192/D2
Rochester, Il, US 185/K4
Rochester Hills, Mi, US 190/E3
Rochford, Eng, UK 36/F2
Rochfortbridge, Ire. 38/C3
Rock (riv.), Ia,Mn, US 185/F2
Rock (riv.), Il, US 173/J3
Rock, Mi, US 187/L4
Rock (cr.), Mt, US 177/J1
Rock (lake), ND, US 186/E3
Rock Bluff, Fl, US 195/F2
Rock Cave, WV, US 193/G1
Rock Creek, Yk, Can. 201/L3
Rock Falls, Wi, US 185/J1
Rock Falls, Il, US 185/K3
Rock Forest, Qu, Can. 191/L2
Rock Glen, Pa, US 198/B2
Rock Hall, Md, US 198/B5
Rock Hill, SC, US 193/G3
Rock Island, Il, US 185/J3
Rock Island, Tx, US 180/F3
Rock Mills, Al, US 192/E4
Rock Port, Mo, US 185/G3
Rock Rapids, Ia, US 185/F2
Rock River, Wy, US 184/B3
Rock Springs, Wy, US 177/J3
Rock Springs, Mt, US 175/L4
Rock Valley, Ia, US 185/F2
Rockall (isl.), UK 29/C3
Rockaway (pt.), NY, US 199/K9
Rockaway (inlet), NY, US 199/K9
Rockaway (riv.), NJ, US 198/D2
Rockaway, NJ, US 198/D2
Rockaway (Rockaway Beach), Or, US 174/C5
Rockaway Beach (Rockaway), Or, US 174/C5
Rockaway Park (nbrhd.), NY, US 199/K9
Rockcorry, Ire. 38/C1
Rockdale, Il, US 197/P17
Rockdale (nbrhd.), Austl. 158/H8
Rockdale (co.), Ga, US 193/M7
Rockdale, Tx, US 181/F2
Rockefeller (plat.), Ant. 228/R
Rockenhausen, Ger. 61/G4
Rockett, Tx, US 180/L7
Rockfield, Ky, US 192/D2
Rockford, Al, US 192/D4
Rockford, Il, US 185/K2
Rockford, Oh, US 190/D4
Rockford, Wa, US 174/F4
Rockglen, Sk, Can. 175/M3
Rockhampton, Austl. 158/C3
Rockhampton Downs, Austl. 152/D4
Rockhill, Tx, US 180/L6
Rockingham, Vt, US 191/K3
Rockingham, Austl. 154/K7
Rockingham, NC, US 193/H3
Rockland, Id, US 177/G2
Rockland (co.), NY, US 199/D1
Rockland, On, Can. 191/J2
Rockland, Tx, US 181/G2
Rockland Lake, NY, US 199/K7
Rocklands (res.), Austl. 156/B3
Rockledge, Fl, US 195/H3
Rockledge, Pa, US 198/C3
Rocklin, Ca, US 176/C4
Rockmart, Ga, US 192/E3
Rockport, Ar, US 183/H3
Rockport, Ca, US 176/B4
Rockport, In, US 192/D2
Rockport, Ky, US 192/D2
Rockport, Ms, US 194/C2
Rockport, Tx, US 180/F3
Rockport, Wa, US 174/D3
Rocks (pt.), NZ 159/C3
Rocks, Md, US 198/B4
Rocksprings, Tx, US 180/D2
Rockstone, Guy. 217/G3
Rockton, Il, US 190/B3
Rockvale, Co, US 182/B1
Rockville, NS, Can. 188/D4
Rockville, In, US 190/C5
Rockville, Md, US 193/J1
Rockville, Ut, US 179/F2
Rockville Centre, NY, US 199/L9
Rockwall, Tx, US 180/L7
Rockwall (co.), Tx, US 180/L7
Rockwell, Ia, US 185/H2
Rockwell City, Ia, US 185/G2
Rockwood, On, Can. 190/S8
Rockwood, Me, US 191/M2
Rockwood, Tn, US 192/E3
Rockwood, Tx, US 180/E2
Rocky (pt.), Austl. 152/C2
Rocky (mts.), Can.,US 163/E4
Rocky (pt.), Namb. 140/B3
Rocky (mtn.), Ky, US 192/F2
Rocky (pt.), NY, US 199/F1
Rocky (riv.), NC, US 193/G3
Rocky, Ok, US 182/E3
Rocky Boys Ind. Res., Mt, US 175/K3
Rocky Cape NP, Austl. 156/C4
Rocky Ford, Co, US 182/C1
Rocky Ford, Ga, US 193/G4
Rocky Fork (lake), Oh, US 190/E5
Rocky Island (lake), On, Can. 190/E1
Rocky Mount, Mo, US 183/H1
Rocky Mount, NC, US 193/J3
Rocky Mount, Va, US 193/H2
Rocky Mountain Arsenal, Co, US 182/B1
Rocky Mountain House, Ab, Can. 174/G1
Rocky Mountain NP, Co, US 184/A3
Rocky Point, NC, US 193/J3
Rocky Reach (dam), Wa, US 174/D4
Rockyford, Ab, Can. 175/H2
Rockypoint, Wy, US 184/B1
Rocroi, Fr. 61/D4
Roda, Sp. 72/C3
Rodach (riv.), Ger. 65/E2
Rodach bei Coburg, Ger. 64/D2
Rodalben, Ger. 61/G5
Rodanthe, NC, US 193/K3
Rødberg, Nor. 46/C1
Rødbyhavn, Den. 46/D4
Rødbyvatn (lake), Nor. 44/S9
Rødding, Den. 46/C4
Roden (riv.), Eng, UK 41/F6
Rodenbach, Ger. 64/C2
Rodeo, Ca, US 197/K10
Rodeo, NM, US 179/H5
Rodeo, Mex. 204/D3
Roderfield, WV, US 193/G2
Rödermark, Ger. 64/B3
Rodessa, La, US 183/H4
Rodewisch, Ger. 65/F1
Rodez, Fr. 50/E4
Rodholívos, Gre. 55/H2
Ródhos (ruin), Gre. 114/B2
Ródhos (Rhodes), Gre. 114/B2
Rodigo, It. 68/D3
Roding (riv.), Eng, UK 36/D2
Roding, Ger. 65/F4
Rodinga (mt.), Austl. 155/G3
Rödinghausen, Ger. 59/F4
Rodney (cape), NZ 159/C2
Rodoč, Bosn. 56/C4
Rodolfo Sánchez Toboada, Mex. 204/A2
Rødovre, Den. 45/J7
Rodrigues, Braz. 220/C2
Rodríguez, Uru. 191/K11
Rødvig, Den. 45/J7
Rodyns'ke, Ukr. 79/J3
Roe (riv.), NI, UK 40/B2
Roebourne, Austl. 154/C2
Roebuck (bay), Austl. 145/B2
Roebuck, SC, US 193/G3
Roebuck Plains, Austl. 152/A4
Roedtan, SAfr. 141/F5
Roen (peak), It. 67/H5
Roer (riv.), Neth. 58/D6
Roermond, Neth. 58/C6
Roes Welcome Sound (str.), Nun, Can. 171/H2
Roeselare, Belg. 60/C2
Roesiger (lake), Wa, US 197/D2
Roff, Ok, US 183/F3
Rogač, Cro. 56/C4
Rogachev, Bela. 76/D1
Rogachëvka, Rus. 79/K2
Rogagua (lake), Bol. 221/E4
Rogaland (co.), Nor. 44/C4
Rogaška Slatina, Slov. 51/L3
Rogatica, Bosn. 56/D4
Rogers, BC, Can. 174/F2
Rogers, Ar, US 183/G2
Rogers, ND, US 186/E4
Rogers, Tx, US 180/F2
Rogers (mt.), Va, US 193/G2
Rogers City, Mi, US 190/E2
Rogersville, NB, Can. 188/E2
Rogersville, Al, US 192/D3
Rogersville, Mo, US 183/H2
Rogersville, Tn, US 193/F2
Roggwil, Swi. 66/D3
Rogliano, Fr. 54/A1
Roglio (riv.), It. 69/D5
Rognac, Fr. 70/B6
Rognes, Fr. 70/B5
Rognon (riv.), Fr. 50/F2
Rognonas, Fr. 70/A5
Rogo, Nga. 133/G4
Rogoaguado (lake), Bol. 221/E4
Rogoźno, Pol. 49/J2
Rogue (riv.), Or, US 176/A2
Rogue River, Or, US 176/B2
Rohatyn, Ukr. 78/C3
Rohl (riv.), Sudan 135/F4
Rohnert Park, Ca, US 176/B4
Rohr, Ger. 65/E5
Rohrbach bei Mattersburg, Aus. 56/C2
Rohrbach in Oberösterreich, Aus. 65/G5
Rohrbach-lès-Bitche, Fr. 61/G5
Rohri, Pak. 113/J3
Röhrmoos, Ger. 65/E6
Rohtak, India 110/D5
Rohtās, India 108/D3
Rohwer, Ar, US 183/J4
Roi Et, Thai. 106/C2
Roia (riv.), It. 70/D5
Roiffieux, Fr. 70/A2
Roine (lake), Fin. 47/L1
Roissy, Fr. 36/K5
Roissy-en-France, Fr. 36/K4
Roja, Lat. 47/K3
Rojas, Arg. 226/E2
Rojo (cape), PR 203/M8
Rojo, Cabo (cape), Mex. 206/B1
Roka, Kenya 137/B2
Rokan, Indo. 101/C2
Rokan (river), Indo. 101/C2
Rokan (riv.), Indo. 102/B3
Rokeby Croll Creek NP, Austl. 158/A1
Rokel (riv.), SLeo. 132/C4
Rokiškis, Lith. 47/L4
Rokkasho, Japan 94/B3
Rokkō-san (peak), Japan 95/H6
Rokot (cape), Indo. 101/B3
Rokugō, Japan 95/A3
Rokycany, Czh. 65/G3
Rokytka (riv.), Czh. 65/H2
Rokytne, Ukr. 78/D2
Rokytne, Ukr. 78/F3
Rolampont, Fr. 66/B2
Roland, Mb, Can. 186/F3
Roland, Ia, US 185/H2
Rolândia, Braz. 222/C4
Rolava (riv.), Czh. 65/F2
Røldal, Nor. 46/B2
Rolde, Neth. 58/D3
Rolette, ND, US 186/E3
Rolfe, Ia, US 185/G2
Rolim de Moura, Braz. 221/F3
Roll, Az, US 179/F4
Rolla, ND, US 186/E3
Rolla, Mo, US 183/J2
Rolle, Swi. 66/C5
Rolle, SAfr. 141/F5
Rolling Fork, Ms, US 192/B4
Rolling Hills, Ab, Can. 175/J2
Rolling Hills Estates, Ca, US 196/F8
Rolling Meadows, Il, US 197/P15
Rolling Prairies (plain), Tx, US 182/D4
Rollingbay, Wa, US 197/B2
Rolo, It. 69/D4
Rom (peak), Ugan. 135/G5
Roma, Austl. 158/C4
Roma (Rome) (cap.), It. 71/B4
Roma (prov.), It. 71/B4
Roma, Swe. 46/H3
Roma, Tx, US 180/E4
Romagna (reg.), It. 73/F1
Romagnano Sesia, It. 68/B2
Romagnat, Fr. 50/E4
Romain (cape), SC, US 193/H4
Romaine (riv.), Fr. 66/B2
Romaine (riv.), Qu, Can. 171/K3
Roman, Bul. 57/F4
Roman, Rom. 78/D4
Roman Kosh (peak), Ukr. 79/H5
Romanche (riv.), Fr. 70/C2
Romang (isl.), Indo. 152/B1
Romang (str.), Indo. 152/B1
Romania (ctry.) 57/F3
Romano (cape), Fl, US 195/H5
Romano Canavese, It. 68/A2
Romano d'Ezzelino, It. 69/E2
Romano di Lombardia, It. 68/C2
Romanovka, Rus. 77/H2
Romanovka, Rus. 90/G1
Romans d'Isonzo, It. 69/G2
Romans-sur-Isère, Fr. 70/B2
Romanshorn, Swi. 67/F2
Romanzof (cape), Ak, US 201/E3
Romashki, Rus. 77/H2
Rombas, Fr. 61/F5
Romblon, Phil. 100/C2
Rome (Roma) (cap.), It. 71/B4
Rome, Ga, US 192/E3
Rome, Il, US 185/K3
Rome, NY, US 191/J3
Rome, Or, US 176/E2
Rome, Pa, US 191/H4
Rome, Wi, US 197/N14
Romenay, Fr. 66/B4
Romeo, Mi, US 190/E3
Romeo, Co, US 179/K2
Romeoville, Il, US 197/P16
Romford (nbrhd.), Eng, UK 36/D2
Römhild, Ger. 64/D2
Romillé, Fr. 62/D4
Romilly-sur-Andelle, Fr. 63/G2
Rommani, Mor. 128/D2
Rommerskirchen, Ger. 61/F1
Romney, WV, US 191/G5
Romney Marsh (phys. reg.), Eng, UK 43/G4
Romny, Ukr. 79/G2
Rømø (isl.), Den. 46/C4
Romodan, Ukr. 79/G3
Romodanovo, Rus. 77/H1
Romoland, Ca, US 196/C3
Romont, Swi. 66/C4
Romorantin-Lanthenay, Fr. 63/G6
Romsey, Eng, UK 43/E5
Romsey, Austl. 157/B3
Rømskog, Nor. 46/D2
Romulus, Mi, US 190/E3
Ron, Viet. 106/D2
Ron (cape), Viet. 99/E5
Ron Phibun, Thai. 106/B4
Ronaldsway (Isle of Man) (arpt.), IM, UK 40/D3
Ronan, Mt, US 175/G4
Roncade, It. 69/F2
Roncador, Braz. 225/F3
Roncador Cay (isl.), Col. 203/F5
Roncador, Serra do (mts.), Braz. 222/B2
Ronceverte, WV, US 193/G2
Ronchamp, Fr. 66/C2
Ronchi dei Legionari (int'l arpt.), It. 69/G2
Ronchi dei Legionari, It. 69/G2
Ronciglione, It. 71/B3
Ronco (riv.), It. 69/F5
Ronco All'Adige, It. 69/E3
Ronco Scrivia, It. 68/B4
Roncoferraro, It. 69/D3
Roncq, Fr. 60/C2
Ronda, Sp. 52/C4
Rondane NP, Nor. 44/D3
Rondo, Ar, US 192/B3
Rondônia (state), Braz. 218/A5
Rondonópolis, Braz. 222/B3
Rondu, Pak. 110/C2
Rong (riv.), China 105/J2
Rong Kwang, Thai. 106/C2
Rong Xian, China 105/K3
Rong'an, China 99/F3
Rongchang, China 98/E2
Rongcheng, China 93/B4
Rongcheng, China 92/G7
Ronge (lake), Sk, Can. 170/F3
Rongelap (isl.), Mrsh. 160/F3
Rongerik (isl.), Mrsh. 160/F3
Rongjiang, China 99/F3
Rongjiawan, China 99/G2
Rongkou, China 99/H2
Rongshui Miaozu Zizhixian, China 105/J2
Rõngu, Est. 47/M2
Roniu (peak), FrPol. 161/X15
Ronkonkoma, NY, US 199/E2
Rønne, Den. 46/F4
Rönne (riv.), Swe. 45/K6
Ronne Ice Shelf, Ant. 228/W
Ronneby, Swe. 46/F3
Rønnede, Den. 45/J7
Ronnenberg, Ger. 59/G4
Rönninge, Swe. 45/A1
Ronquerolles, Fr. 36/J4
Ronsard (cape), Austl. 154/B3
Ronsberg, Ger. 67/G2
Ronse, Belg. 60/C2
Ronuro (plat.), Braz. 221/H4
Roodeport, SAfr. 142/P13
Roodhouse, Il, US 185/J4
Rooiberg (peak), Namb. 142/B2
Roosendaal, Neth. 58/B5
Roosevelt (isl.), Ant. 228/N
Roosevelt (riv.), Braz. 209/C4
Roosevelt (mt.), BC, Can. 170/D3
Roosevelt, Az, US 179/G4
Roosevelt, NJ, US 198/D3
Roosevelt, NY, US 199/L9

Roose – Sailo
325

Roosevelt (isl.), NY, US 199/K8
Roosevelt, Ok, US 182/E3
Roosevelt, Ut, US 177/J3
Roosville, BC, Can. 174/G3
Root (mt.), Ak, US 201/L4
Root (riv.), Wi, US 197/P14
Root, West Branch (riv.), Wi, US 197/P14
Roper (riv.), Austl. 152/D3
Roper, NC, US 193/J3
Roper Valley, Austl. 152/D3
Ropesville, Tx, US 182/C4
Roque Pérez, Arg. 191/J11
Roquebillière, Fr. 70/D4
Roquebrune-Cap-Martin, Fr. 70/D5
Roquebrune-sur-Argens, Fr. 70/C6
Roquefort-la-Bédoule, Fr. 70/B6
Roquemaure, Fr. 70/A4
Roquesteron, Fr. 70/D5
Roquetas de Mar, Sp. 52/D4
Roquevaire, Fr. 70/B6
Roraima (peak), Ven. 217/F3
Roraima (state), Braz. 217/F4
Rørby, Den. 45/H7
Rori, India 110/C5
Rorke's Drift, SAfr. 143/E3
Rorke's Drift Battlesite, SAfr. 143/E3
Rorketon, Mb, Can. 186/E2
Røros, Nor. 44/D3
Rorschach, Swi. 67/F3
Rosa (cape), Alg. 130/L6
Rosa (lake), Bahm. 207/H1
Rosà, It. 69/E2
Rosa, La, US 194/B2
Rosa Punta (pt.), Mex. 204/C3
Rosa Zárate, Ecu. 216/B4
Rosablanche (peak), Swi. 66/D5
Rosal, Sp. 52/A2
Rosales, Mex. 180/B3
Rosalia, Ks, US 183/F2
Rosalia, Wa, US 174/F4
Rosalie (lake), Fl, US 194/N8
Rosalina, Par. 225/F2
Rosamond, Ca, US 178/C3
Rosamorada, Mex. 204/D4
Rosanna (riv.), Aus. 67/G3
Rosans, Fr. 70/B4
Rosario, Arg. 226/E2
Rosario (riv.), Arg. 224/C3
Rosario, Bol. 221/E4
Rosário, Braz. 219/E3
Rosario, Mex. 204/D4
Rosario, Mex. 204/C3
Rosario, Par. 225/E3
Rosario, Phil. 100/C1
Rosario, Phil. 100/E7
Rosario, Uru. 191/K11
Rosario de la Frontera, Arg. 224/C3
Rosario de Lerma, Arg. 224/C3
Rosario del Tala, Arg. 191/J10
Rosário do Sul, Braz. 225/F4
Rosário Oeste, Braz. 221/G4
Rosarno, It. 54/D3
Rosas, Col. 216/B4
Rosas (gulf), Sp. 53/G1
Rosate, It. 68/C3
Rosay, Fr. 36/G5
Rosbach vor der Höhe, Ger. 64/B2
Rosche, Ger. 59/H3
Roscoe, Il, US 185/K2
Roscoe, Mo, US 183/H2
Roscoe, Tx, US 180/D1
Roscoff, Fr. 62/B3
Roscommon, Ire. 38/B2
Roscommon (co.), Ire. 38/B2
Roscommon, Mi, US 190/D2
Roscrea, Ire. 38/C4
Rosdorf, Ger. 59/G5
Rose (isl.), ASam. 161/J6
Rose (peak), Az, US 179/H4
Rose Belle, Mrts. 143/T15
Rose Bud, Ar, US 183/H3
Rose City, Mi, US 190/D2
Rose Hill, Ks, US 183/F2
Rose Hill, Ms, US 192/C4
Rose Hill, Va, US 193/F2
Rose Lodge, Or, US 176/B1
Rose Valley, Sk, Can. 186/C1
Roseau (cap.), Dom. 203/N9
Roseau, Mn, US 186/G3
Roseau (riv.), Mn, US 186/F3
Roseau River, Mb, Can. 186/F3
Roseaux, Haiti 207/H2
Rosebery, Austl. 156/C4
Roseboro, NC, US 193/H3
Rosebud (riv.), Ab, Can. 175/H2
Rosebud, Ga, US 193/N7
Rosebud, Mt, US 175/L4
Rosebud (cr.), Mt, US 175/L4
Rosebud, Tx, US 181/F2
Rosebud Ind. Res., SD, US 184/D2
Roseburg, Or, US 176/B2
Rosedale, Austl. 157/C4
Rosedale, Ca, US 178/C3
Rosedale, Md, US 198/B5
Rosedale, Ms, US 192/B4
Rosedale, Va, US 193/G2
Roseglen, ND, US 186/D4
Rosehearty, Sc, UK 39/D1
Roseira, Braz. 223/L7
Roseires (dam), Sudan 135/G3
Roseisle, Mb, Can. 186/E3
Roseland, La, US 194/C2
Roseland, NJ, US 199/H8
Roselette, Aiguille de (peak), Fr. 66/C6
Roselle, NJ, US 199/H9
Roselle, Il, US 197/P16
Roselle Park, NJ, US 199/H9
Rosemark, Tn, US 192/C3
Rosemead, Ca, US 196/F7
Rosemère, Qu, Can. 189/N6
Rosemount, Oh, US 193/F1
Rosemount, Mn, US 187/P7
Rosenberg, Ger. 64/D4
Rosenberg, Tx, US 181/G3
Rosenfeld, Ger. 67/E1
Rosenhayn, NJ, US 198/C5
Rosenhof, Sk, Can. 175/L2
Rosenort, Mb, Can. 186/F3
Rosepine, La, US 194/B2
Roses, Sp. 53/G1
Roseto, Pa, US 198/C2
Roseto degli Abruzzi, It. 71/D2
Rosetown, Sk, Can. 175/L2
Rosetta, Ms, US 194/C2
Rosetta (Massabb Rashīd) (mouth), Egypt 131/B1
Rosetta Branch (riv.), Egypt 116/B4
Roseville, Ca, US 176/C4
Roseville, Il, US 185/J3
Roseville, Mi, US 197/G6
Roseville, Mn, US 187/P6
Roseville, Oh, US 190/E5
Rosevine, Tx, US 181/H2
Rosewood, Austl. 152/C4
Rosh Ha'ayin, Isr. 117/B4
Rosh Hakarmel (pt.), Isr. 117/B3
Rosh Haniqra (pt.), Isr. 117/C2
Rosh Pina (arpt.), Isr. 117/D3
Rosh Pinah, Namb. 142/B2
Rosh Pinna, Isr. 117/D3
Rosharon, Tx, US 181/M9
Rosheim, Fr. 66/D1
Roshkhvār, Iran 113/G2
Rosholt, SD, US 186/F5
Rosholt, Wi, US 185/K1
Rosiclare, Il, US 192/C2
Rosières-en-Santerre, Fr. 60/B4
Rosignano Marittimo, It. 68/D7
Rosignano Solvay, It. 68/D7
Rosignol, Guy. 218/B1
Roşiori de Vede, Rom. 57/G3
Rositsa, Bul. 57/H4
Roskilde, Den. 46/E4
Roskilde (co.), Den. 46/D4
Roskilde (inlet), Den. 45/H7
Roslags-Bro, Swe. 45/B1
Roslags-Kulla, Swe. 45/B1
Roslags-Näsby, Swe. 45/B1
Roslavl', Rus. 76/E1
Roslev, Den. 46/C3
Roslyakova, Rus. 74/G1
Roslyatino, Rus. 75/K4
Roslyn, Wa, US 174/D4
Rosmalen, Neth. 58/C5
Rosmaninhal, Port. 52/B3
Rosneath, Sc, UK 39/B4
Rosny-sous-Bois, Fr. 36/K5
Rosny-sur-Seine, Fr. 63/G2
Rosolina, It. 69/F3
Rosolini, It. 54/D4
Rosporden, Fr. 62/B5
Rösrath, Ger. 61/G2
Ross (isl.), Ant. 228/M
Ross (sea), Ant. 228/P
Ross, Austl. 156/C4
Ross (pt.), On, Can. 190/V8
Ross, NZ 159/B3
Ross (mt.), NZ 159/C3
Ross (dist.), Sc, UK 39/C1
Ross, Tx, US 181/F2
Ross (lake), Wa, US 174/D3
Ross Barnett (res.), Ms, US 192/C4
Ross Carbery, Ire. 38/A6
Ross Ice Shelf, Ant. 228/N
Ross River, Yk, Can. 201/M3
Ross-on-Wye, Eng, UK 42/D3
Rossa, Swi. 67/F5
Rossa (peak), It. 51/K3
Rossall (pt.), Eng, UK 41/E4
Rossano Stazione, It. 54/E3
Rossano Veneto, It. 69/E2
Rossbach, Ger. 65/F5
Rossberg (peak), Fr. 66/D2
Rossburn, Mb, Can. 186/D2
Rossdorf, Ger. 64/B3
Rossel (isl.), PNG 160/E6
Rosselange, Fr. 61/F5
Rosser, Mb, Can. 186/F3
Rosser, Tx, US 180/L7
Rosshaupten, Ger. 67/G2
Rossie, NY, US 191/J2
Rossiglione, It. 68/B4
Rossignol (lake), NS, Can. 188/E3
Rössing, Namb. 140/B4
Rössjöholmsån (riv.), Swe. 45/J6
Rosskeeragh (pt.), Ire. 37/P9
Rossland, BC, Can. 174/F3
Rosslare, Ire. 38/D5
Rosslare (bay), Ire. 38/D5
Rosslare (pt.), Ire. 38/D5
Rosslea, NI, UK 38/C1
Rosslyn Village, On, Can. 187/K3
Rosso, Mrta. 132/B2
Rossosh', Rus. 79/K2
Rossport, On, Can. 187/L3
Rossstock (peak), Swi. 67/E4
Rosstal, Ger. 64/D4
Rosston, Ar, US 183/H4
Rossville, Il, US 190/C4
Røst, Nor. 44/E2
Rostāq, Iran 115/H5
Rostāq, Afg. 111/A4
Rostellan, Ire. 38/B6
Rosthern, Sk, Can. 175/L1
Rostock, Ger. 46/E4
Rostov, Rus. 74/H4
Rostov, Rus. 79/K4
Rostov (int'l arpt.), Rus. 79/K4
Rostovskaya Oblast, Rus. 77/G2
Rostrenen, Fr. 62/B4
Rostrevor, NI, UK 40/B3
Roswell, Ga, US 193/M6
Roswell, NM, US 182/B4
Rot (riv.), Ger. 48/E4
Rota (isl.), NMar. 160/D3
Rota, Sp. 52/B4
Rotan, Tx, US 182/D4
Rote Wand (peak), Aus. 67/F3
Rotebro, Swe. 45/A1
Rotenburg, Ger. 59/G2
Rotenburg an der Fulda, Ger. 59/G7
Roter Main (riv.), Ger. 48/F3
Rötgen, Ger. 61/F2
Roth (riv.), Ger. 67/G1
Roth bei Nürnberg, Ger. 64/E4
Rothaargebirge (mts.), Ger. 59/F6
Rothau, Fr. 66/D1
Rothbury, Eng, UK 39/E6
Röthenbach an der Pegnitz, Ger. 64/E4
Rothenberg, Ger. 64/B3
Rothenburg, Swi. 67/E3
Rothenburg ob der Tauber, Ger. 64/D4
Rothera, UK, Ant. 228/V
Rotherham, Eng, UK 41/G5
Rotherham (co.), Eng, UK 41/G5
Rothes, Sc, UK 39/C1
Rothesay, Sc, UK 39/A5
Rotheux-Rimière, Belg. 61/E2
Rothsay, Mn, US 186/F4
Rothschild, Wi, US 185/K1
Rothwell, Eng, UK 41/G4
Rothwell, Eng, UK 43/F2
Roti (isl.), Indo. 103/F6
Rotifunk, SLeo. 132/B4
Roto, Austl. 157/B1
Rotonda, Fl, US 195/G4
Rotondo (peak), It. 71/C2
Rotorua, NZ 159/D2
Rotselaar, Belg. 61/D2
Rott (riv.), Ger. 48/G4
Rott am Inn, Ger. 65/F7
Rottach-Egern, Ger. 48/F5
Rotte (riv.), Fr. 61/F6
Rotten (riv.), Swi. 66/E5
Rottenacker, Ger. 67/F1
Röttenbach, Ger. 64/E4
Rottenberg, Ger. 64/C2
Rottenburg am Neckar, Ger. 64/B6
Rottenburg an der Laaber, Ger. 65/F5
Rotterdam, Neth. 58/B5
Rotterdam (int'l arpt.), Neth. 58/B5
Rottershausen, Ger. 64/D2
Rotthalmünster, Ger. 65/G6
Rottingdean, Eng, UK 43/F5
Röttingen, Ger. 64/C3
Rottne, Swe. 46/F3
Rottnest (isl.), Austl. 154/B5
Rottofreno, It. 68/C3
Rottum (riv.), Ger. 67/F1
Rottumeroog (isl.), Neth. 58/D1
Rottumerplaat (isl.), Neth. 58/D1
Rottweil, Ger. 67/E1
Rotuma (isl.), Fiji 160/G6
Rötz, Ger. 65/F4
Roubaix, Fr. 60/C2
Roubion (riv.), Fr. 50/F4
Roudnice nad Labem, Czh. 65/H2
Rouen, Fr. 63/G2
Rouffach, Fr. 66/D2
Rougé, Fr. 62/D5
Rouge (riv.), Qu, Can. 171/J4
Rouge, Middle (riv.), Mi, US 197/F7
Rougemont, Fr. 66/C3
Rougemont-le-Château, Fr. 66/C2
Rough (riv.), Ky, US 192/D2
Rough River (lake), Ky, US 192/D2
Rouleau, Sk, Can. 186/B2
Roullet-Saint-Estèphe, Fr. 50/D4
Round (hill), In, US 192/E1
Round (hill), Ky, US 192/E2
Round (hill), Oh, US 190/F4
Round (hill), Pa, US 198/B3
Round Butte (dam), Or, US 176/C1
Round Hill (pt.), Austl. 158/C4
Round Lake, Il, US 197/P15
Round Lake Beach, Il, US 197/P15
Round Lake Park, Il, US 197/P15
Round Mountain, Nv, US 176/E4
Round Mountain, Tx, US 180/E2
Round Rock, Tx, US 181/F2
Round Spring, Mo, US 183/J2
Round Top, Tx, US 181/F2
Round Valley (res.), NJ, US 198/D2
Round Valley Ind. Res., Ca, US 176/B4
Roundup, Mt, US 175/K4
Roundway (hill), Eng, UK 42/E4
Rounthwaite, Mb, Can. 186/E3
Roura, FrG. 218/C1
Rousay (isl.), Sc, UK 37/V14
Rouse Hill (nbrhd.), Austl. 158/G8
Rouses Point, NY, US 191/K2
Rouseville, Pa, US 191/G4
Rousies, Fr. 60/D3
Rousínov, Czh. 49/J4
Rousset, Fr. 70/B6
Roussillon, Fr. 70/B5
Roussillon, Fr. 70/A2
Routhierville, Qu, Can. 188/D1
Rouvre (riv.), Fr. 63/E3
Rouvres, Fr. 36/M4
Rouvroy, Belg. 61/E4
Rouxmesnil-Bouteilles, Fr. 63/G1
Rouxville, SAfr. 142/D3
Rouyn-Noranda, Qu, Can. 171/J4
Rovaniemi (int'l arpt.), Fin. 74/E2
Rovaniemi, Fin. 74/E2
Rovasenda, It. 68/B2
Rovato, It. 68/C2
Roven'ki, Rus. 79/K3
Roven'ky, Ukr. 79/K3
Rover, Ar, US 183/H3
Rover, Mo, US 183/J2
Roverbella, It. 69/D3
Rovereto, It. 67/H6
Rovereto, It. 69/D4
Roviano, It. 71/C3
Rovieng Tbong, Camb. 106/D3
Rovigo, It. 69/E3
Rovigo (prov.), It. 69/E2
Rovinj, Cro. 69/G3
Rovira, Col. 219/K8
Rovnoye, Rus. 77/H2
Rovuma (riv.), Moz. 137/A4
Rowell, Ar, US 183/H4
Rowena, Austl. 156/D1
Rowena, Tx, US 180/D2
Rowland, NC, US 193/H3
Rowledge, Eng, UK 36/A3
Rowlett (cr.), Tx, US 180/L6
Rowlett, Tx, US 180/L7
Rowley (isl.), Nun, Can. 171/J2
Rowley Shoals (isl.), Austl. 145/A2
Rowta, India 109/J2
Roxa (isl.), GBis. 132/B4
Roxas, Phil. 100/C3
Roxas, Phil. 100/C1
Roxas, Phil. 100/B3
Roxboro, NC, US 193/H2
Roxborough, Trin. 217/F2
Roxburgh, NZ 159/B4
Roxbury, Ks, US 183/F1
Roxbury, NY, US 191/J3
Roxen (lake), Swe. 46/F2
Roxie, Ms, US 194/C2
Roxo (cape), Sen. 132/A3
Roxton, Tx, US 183/G4
Roxwell, Eng, UK 36/E1
Roy, Mt, US 175/K4
Roy, NM, US 182/B3
Roy, Ut, US 177/G3
Roy, Wa, US 197/B3
Roy Hill, Austl. 154/C2
Roya (riv.), Fr. 51/G5
Royal (canal), Ire. 40/B5
Royal Botanical Garden, On, Can. 190/T9
Royal Center, In, US 190/C4
Royal Chitwan NP, Nepal 109/E2
Royal City, Wa, US 174/E4
Royal (gorge), Co, US 182/B1
Royal Natal NP, SAfr. 142/E3
Royal NP, Austl. 156/D2
Royal Oak, Mi, US 197/F7
Royal Paekje Tombs, SKor. 93/D4
Royal Palm Beach, Fl, US 194/P9
Royal Pines, NC, US 193/F3
Royal Tombs, Viet. 106/D2
Royal Tunbridge Wells, Eng, UK 43/G4
Royalton, Mn, US 187/G5
Royalton, Pa, US 198/B3
Royalty, Tx, US 180/C2
Royalton, Vt, US 191/K3
Royan, Fr. 50/C4
Roydon, Eng, UK 36/D1
Roye, Fr. 66/C2
Roye, Fr. 60/B4
Royersford, Pa, US 198/C3
Røyken, Nor. 46/D2
Royse City, Tx, US 180/L7
Royston, BC, Can. 174/B3
Royston, Eng, UK 41/G4
Royston, Eng, UK 43/F2
Royston, Ga, US 193/F3
Royton, Eng, UK 41/F4
Rožaj, Serb. 56/E4
Rozay-en-Brie, Fr. 60/B6
Rozdil'na, Ukr. 78/F4
Rozdol'ne, Ukr. 79/G5
Rozel, Chl, UK 62/C2
Rozellville, Wi, US 185/J1
Rozenburg, Neth. 58/B5
Rozendo, Moz. 141/H3
Rozhaya (riv.), Rus. 75/W9
Rozhyshche, Ukr. 78/C2
Rozivka, Ukr. 79/J4
Rožmberk (lake), Czh. 65/H4
Rožmital pod Třemšínem, Czh. 65/G3
Rožňava, Slvk. 49/L4
Roztoczański PN, Pol. 78/B2
Roztoky, Czh. 65/H2
Rozzano, It. 68/C3
Rrëshen, Alb. 55/F2
Rrogozhinë, Alb. 55/F2
Rtishchevo, Rus. 77/G1
Ru (cape), Malay. 101/C2
Ruabon, Wal, UK 41/E6
Ruacana (falls), Ang. 140/B3
Ruacana, Namb. 140/B3
Ruaha NP, Tanz. 137/A3
Ruamahanga (riv.), NZ 159/J9
Ruapuke (isl.), NZ 159/B4
Ruatapu, NZ 159/B3
Ruawai, NZ 159/C2
Rub' al Khali (des.), SAr. 83/D7
Rubeho (mts.), Tanz. 137/B3
Rubelles, Fr. 36/L6
Rubeshibe, Japan 94/C2
Rubi (riv.), D.R. Congo 139/F2
Rubi, D.R. Congo 139/F2
Rubí, Sp. 53/L7
Rubiataba, Braz. 222/C2
Rubidoux, Ca, US 196/C3
Rubiera, It. 69/D4
Rubigen, Swi. 66/D4
Rubim, Braz. 223/E3
Rubizhne, Ukr. 79/K3
Rubondo NP, Tanz. 139/G3
Rubonia, Fl, US 194/K8
Rubottom, Ok, US 183/F4
Řubřina (riv.), Czh. 65/G4
Rubtsovsk, Rus. 111/D1
Rubuga, Tanz. 137/A3
Ruby, Ak, US 201/G3
Ruby, La, US 194/B2
Ruby (riv.), Mt, US 177/G1
Ruby (lake), Nv, US 176/F3
Ruby (mts.), Nv, US 176/F3
Ruby Lake NWR, Nv, US 176/F3
Ruby Valley, Nv, US 176/F3
Rubyvale, Austl. 158/B3
Rucava, Lat. 47/J3
Ruch'i, Rus. 74/J2
Rucphen, Neth. 58/B5
Ruda Woda (lake), Pol. 49/K2
Rudall River NP, Austl. 154/D2
Rūdarpur, India 108/D2
Rudauli, India 108/C2
Ruddell, Sk, Can. 175/L1
Ruddington, Eng, UK 41/G6
Rudensk, Bela. 47/M5
Rüdersdorf, Ger. 48/Q7
Rüdesheim, Ger. 61/G4
Rüdesheim, Ger. 61/G4
Rudewa, Tanz. 137/A4
Rudi, Tanz. 137/B3
Rudiano, It. 68/C3
Rūdiškės, Lith. 47/L4
Rudkøbing, Den. 46/D4
Rudky, Ukr. 78/B3
Rudnaya Pristan', Rus. 91/M3
Rudnik, Pol. 49/M3
Rudnya, Rus. 47/P4
Rudnytsya, Ukr. 78/E3
Rūdnyy, Kaz. 75/P5
Rudolf (isl.), Rus. 80/F1
Rudolf (Turkana) (lake), Kenya 119/F4
Rudolph, Wi, US 185/K1
Rudong, China 92/E4
Rudozem, Bul. 55/J2
Ruds-Vedby, Den. 45/H7
Rūdsar, Iran 115/G2
Rudston, Eng, UK 41/H3
Rudyard, Mi, US 190/D1
Rudyard, Mt, US 175/J3
Rue, Fr. 60/A3
Rue (pt.), NI, UK 40/B1
Rue, Swi. 66/C4
Rueda, Sp. 52/C2
Rueil-Malmaison, Fr. 36/J5
Ruell (riv.), Sc, UK 39/A4
Ruelle-sur-Touvre, Fr. 50/D4
Ruen (peak), Bul. 56/F4
Ruenya (riv.), Zim. 141/G3
Ruetzbach (riv.), Aus. 67/H3
Rufā'ah, Sudan 135/G2
Rufe, Ok, US 183/G3
Ruffano, It. 55/F3
Ruffec, Fr. 50/D3
Ruffin, SC, US 193/G4
Rufiji (riv.), Tanz. 119/F5
Rufina, It. 69/E6
Rufino, Arg. 226/E2
Rufisque, Sen. 132/A3
Rufunsa, Zam. 141/F2
Rufus Woods (lake), Wa, US 174/E3
Rugāji, Lat. 47/M3
Rugao, China 92/E4
Rugby, ND, US 186/E3
Rugby, Eng, UK 43/E2
Rugeley, Eng, UK 43/E1
Rügen (isl.), Ger. 46/E4
Ruggell, Lcht. 67/F3
Rugles, Fr. 63/F3
Ruhama, Isr. 117/B5
Ruhmannsfelden, Ger. 65/F5
Ruhnu saar (isl.), Lat. 47/K3
Ruhr (reg.), Ger. 48/E3
Ruhr (riv.), Ger. 48/D3
Ruhrgebiet (phys. reg.), Ger. 58/D6
Ruhstorf an der Rott, Ger. 65/F5
Ruicheng, China 92/B4
Ruidosa, Tx, US 180/B3
Ruidoso, NM, US 182/B4
Ruihong, China 99/H2
Ruinen, Neth. 58/D3
Ruins of Cahabra, Al, US 192/D4
Ruipa, Tanz. 137/B4
Ruiru, Kenya 137/B2
Ruiselede, Belg. 60/C1
Ruislip (nbrhd.), Eng, UK 36/B2
Ruiz, Mex. 204/D4
Rujen (peak), FYROM 55/H1
Rūjiena, Lat. 47/L3
Ruki (riv.), D.R. Congo 119/D5
Rukua, Indo. 152/B1
Rukumkot, Nepal 108/D1
Rukuru, South (riv.), Tanz. 141/G1
Rukwa (prov.), Tanz. 137/A3
Rukwa (lake), Tanz. 119/F5
Rule, Tx, US 182/E4
Ruleville, Ms, US 192/B4
Rulhieres (cape), Austl. 152/B3
Rulles (riv.), Belg. 61/E4
Rülzheim, Ger. 64/B4
Rum, Aus. 67/H3
Rum (riv.), Mn, US 187/H5
Rum Cay (isl.), Bahm. 203/G3
Rum Jungle, Austl. 152/C3
Ruma, Serb. 56/D3
Ruma Bāzār, Bang. 98/B4
Ruma NP, Kenya 137/A2
Rumāḩ, SAr. 112/E3
Rumán, Ven. 217/F3
Rumaylah, Sudan 135/G2
Rumaysh, Leb. 117/C2
Rumbalara, Austl. 155/G3
Rumbek, Sudan 135/F4
Rumeli Hisar, Turk. 115/N6
Rumelifeneri, Turk. 115/N6
Rumes, Belg. 60/C2
Rumia, Pol. 46/H4
Rumilly, Fr. 66/B6
Rümlang, Swi. 67/E3
Rumley, Tx, US 181/E2
Rumney, NH, US 191/L3
Rumney, Wal, UK 42/C3
Rumoi, Japan 94/B2
Rumphi, Malw. 137/A4
Rumson, NJ, US 199/E3
Rumst, Belg. 61/D1
Rumuruti, Kenya 137/B1
Run (riv.), Mn, US 185/H1
Runabay (pt.), NI, UK 40/B1
Runan, China 92/C4
Runanga, NZ 159/B3
Runaway (cape), NZ 159/D2
Runcorn, Eng, UK 41/F5
Rundēni, Lat. 47/M3
Runding, Ger. 65/F4
Rundu, Namb. 140/C3
Runere, Tanz. 137/A2
Runge, Tx, US 181/F3
Rungsted, Den. 45/J7
Rungu, D.R. Congo 139/F2
Rungwa (riv.), Tanz. 137/A3
Rungwa, Tanz. 137/A3
Rungwa, Tanz. 139/G4
Rungwa Game Reserve, Tanz. 137/A3
Rungwe (peak), Tanz. 137/A4
Runio (riv.), Fr. 62/C5
Runkel, Ger. 64/B2
Runmarö (isl.), Swe. 45/B1
Runn (lake), Swe. 46/F1
Runnelstown, Ms, US 194/D2
Runnemede, NJ, US 198/C4
Running (cr.), Co, US 182/B1
Running Springs, Ca, US 196/C2
Running Water Draw (riv.), Tx,NM, US 182/C3
Runwell, Eng, UK 36/E2
Ruo (riv.), China 81/K5
Ruokolahti, Fin. 47/N1
Ruoqiang, China 111/E4
Rupat (isl.), Indo. 102/B3
Rupea, Rom. 57/G2
Rupel (riv.), Belg. 61/D1
Rupert (riv.), Qu, Can. 171/J3
Rupert, Id, US 177/G2
Rupert, Ga, US 192/E4
Rupert, WV, US 193/G2
Rupert House (Waskaganish), Qu, Can. 171/J3
Rūpnagar, India 110/D4
Ruppichteroth, Ger. 61/G2
Rupt-sur-Moselle, Fr. 66/C2
Rupununi (riv.), Guy. 217/G4
Rur (riv.), Ger. 48/D3
Rur-Strasse (lake), Ger. 61/F2
Rural Hall, NC, US 193/G2
Rural Retreat, Va, US 193/G2
Rurrenabaque, Bol. 221/E4
Rurutu (isl.), FrPol. 161/K7
Rusagonis, NB, Can. 188/D3
Rusape, Zim. 141/G3
Rüschegg, Swi. 66/D4
Rüschlikon, Swi. 67/E3
Ruscom (riv.), On, Can. 197/G7
Ruse (pol. reg.), Bul. 55/K1
Ruse, Bul. 57/G4
Rusera, India 109/F3
Rush, Co, US 182/B1
Rush, Ire. 40/B4
Rush (cr.), Co, US 184/C4
Rush City, Mn, US 187/H5
Rush Springs, Ok, US 183/F3
Rushall, Eng, UK 43/E4
Rushan, China 92/E3
Rushden, Eng, UK 43/F2
Rushford, Mn, US 185/J2
Rushoon, Nf, Can. 189/K2
Rushville, Il, US 185/J3
Rushville, In, US 190/D5
Rushville, Ne, US 184/C2
Rushworth, Austl. 157/B3
Rusk, Tx, US 180/G2
Ruskin, Fl, US 194/L8
Ruskington, Eng, UK 41/H5
Ruskovce, Slvk. 56/C1
Rusnė, Lith. 47/J4
Russ, Fr. 66/D1
Russas, Braz. 219/G4
Russbach (riv.), Aus. 57/N7
Russell (isls.), Austl. 158/F7
Russell, Mb, Can. 186/D2
Russell (isl.), Nun, Can. 171/R7
Russell, On, Can. 191/J2
Russell, NZ 159/C1
Russell, Ks, US 182/E1
Russell, NY, US 191/J2
Russell (res.), SC, US 193/F3
Russell Cave Nat'l Mon., Al, US 192/E3
Russell Springs, Ky, US 192/E2
Russells Point, Oh, US 190/E4
Russellville, Al, US 192/D3
Russellville, Ar, US 183/H3
Russellville, Ky, US 192/D2
Russellville, Mo, US 183/H1
Russellville, Tn, US 193/F2
Rüsselsheim, Ger. 64/B3
Russi, It. 69/F5
Russia (ctry.) 80/H3
Russian (riv.), Ca, US 176/B4
Russian Mission, Ak, US 201/F3
Russkaya, Rus., Ant. 228/Q
Russkiy Brod, Rus. 76/F1
Rust'avi, Geo. 77/H4
Rustburg, Va, US 193/H2
Rustenburg, SAfr. 141/E5
Ruston, La, US 183/H4
Ruston, Wa, US 197/C3
Rusutjärvi, Fin. 45/E4
Rutana, Buru. 139/G3
Rute, Sp. 52/C4
Rutenga, Zim. 141/F4
Ruth, Ms, US 194/C2
Ruth, Nv, US 177/F4
Rüthen, Ger. 59/F6
Rutherford, Al, US 192/E4
Rutherford, NJ, US 199/J8
Rutherford, Tn, US 192/C2
Rutherfordton, NC, US 193/G3
Rutherglen, Sc, UK 39/B5
Rutherglen, On, Can. 191/G1
Rutherglen, Austl. 157/C3
Rutheron, NM, US 179/J2
Rüthi, Swi. 67/F3
Ruthin, Wal, UK 41/E5
Ruthven, On, Can. 197/G7
Rüti, Swi. 67/F4
Rüti, Swi. 67/E3
Rutland, ND, US 186/F4
Rutland, Oh, US 193/F1
Rutland, Vt, US 191/K3
Rutland Plains, Austl. 158/A1
Rutland Water (res.), Eng, UK 43/F1
Rutledge, Mn, US 187/H4
Rutledge, Tn, US 193/F2
Rutog, China 111/C5
Rutshuru (riv.), D.R. Congo 139/G3
Rutshuru, D.R. Congo 139/G3
Rutten, Neth. 58/C3
Ruukki, Fin. 74/E2
Ruurlo, Neth. 58/D4
Ruvo di Puglia, It. 54/E2
Ruvu (riv.), Tanz. 137/B3
Ruvu, Tanz. 137/B3
Ruvu, Tanz. 137/B3
Ruvubu (riv.), Buru. 139/G3
Ruvuma (prov.), Tanz. 137/B4
Ruvuma (riv.), Tanz. 119/F6
Ruwa, Zim. 141/F3
Ruwāndūz, Iraq 115/F2
Ruwenzori (range), Ugan. 139/G2
Ruwī, Oman 113/G4
Ruxton, Co, US 182/C2
Ruy, Fr. 70/B1
Ruya (riv.), Zim. 141/F3
Ruyang, China 92/C4
Ruyigi, Buru. 139/G3
Ruyuan Yaozu Zizhixian, China 99/G3
Ruzayevka, Rus. 77/H1
Ruzhany, Bela. 49/N2
Ruzhyn, Ukr. 78/E3
Ruzizi (riv.), D.R. Congo 139/G3
Ružomberok, Slvk. 49/K4
Ruzyně (int'l arpt.), Czh. 65/H2
Ruzzah (peak), Egypt 131/B4
Rwanda (ctry.) 139/G3
Rwenjaza, Ugan. 139/G2
Rwenzori NP, Ugan. 139/G3
Ryabobskiy, Rus. 79/L2
Ryan (mt.), Austl. 158/A1
Ryan (mt.), Austl. 157/D1
Ryan (inlet), Sc, UK 40/C2
Ryan, Ok, US 183/F3
Ryazan', Rus. 74/H5
Ryazanskaya Oblast, Rus. 74/H5
Ryazhsk, Rus. 76/G1
Rybachiy (pen.), Rus. 44/K1
Rybinsk, Rus. 74/H4
Rybinsk (res.), Rus. 29/J2
Rybnik, Pol. 49/K3
Rybnoye, Rus. 74/H5
Ryd, Swe. 46/F3
Rydaholm, Swe. 46/F3
Ryde, Ca, US 197/L10
Ryde (nbrhd.), Austl. 158/H8
Ryde, Eng, UK 43/E5
Rydebäck, Swe. 45/J7
Rydet, Swe. 46/D3
Rye, Eng, UK 43/G5
Rye (bay), Eng, UK 43/G5
Rye (riv.), Eng, UK 41/H3
Rye, Ar, US 183/J4
Rye, Co, US 182/B2
Rye, Tx, US 181/G2
Rye, NY, US 199/L8
Rye Brook, NY, US 199/L7
Rye Patch (dam), Nv, US 176/D3
Rye Patch (res.), Nv, US 176/D3
Ryegate, Mt, US 175/K4
Rygge, Nor. 46/D2
Ryki, Pol. 49/L3
Ryley, Ab, Can. 175/H1
Ryl'sk, Rus. 79/H2
Rylstone, Austl. 157/D1
Ryn-Peski (plain), Kaz. 77/J2
Ryōkami, Japan 95/B2
Ryökkä, Fin. 45/E4
Ryōtsu, Japan 97/F1
Ryōzen-yama (peak), Japan 95/K5
Rypin, Pol. 49/K2
Rysy (peak), Pol. 49/L4
Ryton, Eng, UK 41/G2
Ryton-on-Dunsmore, Eng, UK 43/E2
Rytterknægten (peak), Den. 46/F4
Ryttylä, Fin. 45/E4
Ryūgasaki, Japan 97/G3
Ryukyu (isls.), Japan 83/M7
Ryūō, Japan 95/K5
Ryūō, Japan 95/B2
Rzeszów, Pol. 49/M3
Rzhev, Rus. 74/G4
Rzhyshchiv, Ukr. 78/F3

S

's-Graveland, Neth. 58/C4
's Gravendeel, Neth. 58/B5
's-Gravenhage (The Hague) (cap.), Neth. 58/B4
's Heerenberg, Neth. 58/D5
's Hertogenbosch, Neth. 58/C5
S'ør-Trøndelag (co.), Nor. 44/D3
Sa, Thai. 106/C2
Şā al Ḩajar (ruin), Egypt 131/B3
Sa Dec, Viet. 106/D4
Sa Pa, Viet. 106/C1
Saab (int'l arpt.), Swe. 46/F2
Sa'ad, Isr. 117/B6
Sääksjärvi (lake), Fin. 47/K1
Saal an der Donau, Ger. 65/E5
Saalbach (riv.), Ger. 64/B4
Saaldorf, Ger. 65/E2
Saale (riv.), Ger. 48/F3
Saalfelden am Steinernen Meer, Aus. 51/K3
Saâne (riv.), Fr. 63/F1
Saane (riv.), Swi. 66/D5
Saanen, Swi. 66/D5
Saanta (peak), Kenya 137/B1
Saar (riv.), Ger. 61/F5
Saarbrücken, Ger. 61/F5
Saarbrücken (Ensheim) (arpt.), Ger. 61/G5
Saarburg, Ger. 61/F4
Sääre, Est. 47/K3
Saaremaa (isl.), Est. 74/D4
Saarland (state), Ger. 51/G2
Saarlouis, Ger. 61/F5
Saas, Swi. 67/F4
Saas Fee, Swi. 66/D5
Saastal (valley), Swi. 66/D5
Sa'ata, Sudan 135/F2
Saatlı, Azer. 115/G2
Saatta, Erit. 135/H1
Sab (riv.), Camb. 106/D3
Saba (isl.), NAm. 203/J4
Saba (isl.), NAnt. 203/N8
Šabac, Serb. 56/D3
Sabadell, Sp. 53/L6
Sabae, Japan 96/E3
Sabah (reg.), Malay. 83/L9
Sabalgarh, India 108/A2
Sabana, Cuba 207/H1
Sabana (arch.), Bang. 207/F1
Sabana de Uchire, Ven. 217/E2
Sabanalarga, Col. 216/C2
Sabanalarga, Col. 216/C3
Sabancuy, Mex. 206/D2
Sabaneta, Ven. 216/D2
Sabang, Indo. 101/A1
Sabanita, Pan. 207/G4
Sabará, Braz. 222/E3
Sabaragamuwa (prov.), SrL. 107/D5
Sabasţīyah, WBnk. 117/C4
Sabat (riv.), Sudan 119/F4
Sabato (riv.), It. 71/D5
Sabaudia, It. 71/C5
Sabaudia (lake), It. 71/C5
Sabaya, Bol. 224/B1
Sabbio Chiese, It. 68/D2
Sabbioneta, It. 68/D4
Sabdê, China 98/D2
Sabetha, Ks, US 185/G4
Sabhā, Libya 126/B3
Sabie (riv.), Moz. 143/F2
Sabierivier (riv.), SAfr. 141/F5
Sabile, Lat. 47/K3
Sabin, Mn, US 186/F4
Sabinal, Tx, US 180/E3
Sabinal (riv.), Tx, US 180/E3
Sabiñánigo, Sp. 53/E1
Sabinas, Mex. 180/D4
Sabinas (riv.), Mex. 180/D4
Sabinas Hidalgo, Mex. 180/D4
Sabine (lake), La,Tx, US 181/H3
Sabine (riv.), La,Tx, US 181/H2
Sabine NWR, La, US 181/H3
Sabine Pass, Tx, US 181/H3
Sabini, Monti (mts.), It. 54/C1
Sabirabad, Azer. 115/G1
Sabkhat al Bardawīl (lag.), Egypt 116/C4
Sabkhat al Hayshah (swamp), Libya 126/B2
Sabkhat al Milḩ (swamp), Libya 126/C2
Sabkhat ash Shuwayrib (swamp), Libya 126/C2
Sabkhat Ghuzayyil (swamp), Libya 126/C2
Sabkhat Shunayn (swamp), Libya 126/D2
Sablayan, Phil. 100/C2
Sable (cape), NS, Can. 188/E4
Sable (isl.), NS, Can. 171/L4
Sable (cape), Fl, US 202/E2
Sablé-sur-Sarthe, Fr. 63/E5
Sables (riv.), Qu, Can. 188/B1
Saboeiro, Braz. 219/G4
Sabon Gida, Nga. 133/H5
Sabongidda, Nga. 133/G5
Sabor (riv.), Port. 52/B2
Sabou, Burk. 133/E3
Saboyá, Col. 219/M7
Sabra (cape), Indo. 103/H4
Şabrātah, Libya 126/B1
Sabratha (ruin), Libya 126/B1
Sabrina (coast), Ant. 228/J
Sabrūm, India 109/H4
Sabual, India 98/B4
Sabugal, Port. 52/B2
Sabula, Ia, US 185/J2
Sabulubek, Indo. 101/B3
Şabyā, SAr. 112/D5
Sabzevār, Iran 115/J2
Sac City, Ia, US 185/G2
Sacaca, Bol. 224/C1
Sacajawea (peak), Or, US 176/E1
Sacajawea (lake), Wa, US 174/E4
Sácama, Col. 216/C3
Sacandica, Ang. 138/C4
Sacanta, Arg. 224/D4
Sacarnoochee (riv.), Ms, US 192/C4
Sacaton, Az, US 179/G4
Sacavém, Port. 53/P10
Saccarel (peak), Fr. 70/D4
Saccarello (peak), It. 68/A4
Sacco (riv.), It. 54/C2
Sacedón, Sp. 52/D2
Săcele, Rom. 57/G3
Sachanga, Ang. 140/C2
Sachigo (riv.), On, Can. 170/G3
Sachojere, Bol. 221/E4
Sachs Harbour, NW, Can. 170/D1
Sachse, Tx, US 180/L7
Sachseln, Swi. 67/E4
Sachsen (state), Ger. 48/G3
Sachsen-Anhalt (state), Ger. 48/F3
Sachsenbrunn, Ger. 64/D2
Sachsenhagen, Ger. 59/G4
Sacile, It. 69/F2
Säckingen, Ger. 66/D2
Sackville, NB, Can. 188/E3
Saclay, Fr. 36/J5
Saco, Al, US 195/F2
Saco, Me, US 191/L3
Saco (bay), Me, US 188/B4
Saco (riv.), Me, US 191/L3
Saco, Mt, US 175/L3
Saco do Giraul, Ang. 140/B2
Sacra di San Michele, It. 70/D2
Sacramento, Mex. 180/D4
Sacramento (co.), Ca, US 197/M10
Sacramento (riv.), Ca, US 172/B4
Sacramento (cap.), Ca, US 176/C4
Sacramento, Ky, US 192/D2
Sacramento (mts.), NM, US 172/E5
Sacramento Metropolitan (arpt.), Ca, US 197/L9
Sacramento NWR, Ca, US 176/B4
Sacramento River Deep Water Ship Canal, Ca, US 197/L10
Sacratif (cape), Sp. 52/D4
Sacriston, Eng, UK 41/G2
Sacro (peak), It. 54/E2
Sacro Monte, It. 68/B2
Sada, May., Fr. 143/H6
Sada, SAfr. 142/D4
Sádaba, Sp. 52/E1
Sadābād, India 108/B2
Sa'dah, Yem. 112/D5
Sadani, Tanz. 137/B3
Sadasar, India 104/B2
Sādāt Maḩalleh, Iran 115/G2
Sadd al Qir'awn (dam), Leb. 117/D1
Saddam (int'l arpt.), Iraq 115/F3
Saddle (mtn.), Az, US 179/G2
Saddle (riv.), NJ, US 199/J8
Saddle (mtn.), Or, US 174/C5
Saddle Brook, NJ, US 199/J8
Saddle Mtn. NWR, Wa, US 174/E4
Saddle River, NJ, US 199/J7
Saddle Rock, NY, US 199/K8
Saddleback (mesa), NM, US 182/C3
Saddlestring, Wy, US 177/K1
Saddleworth, Eng, UK 41/G4
Saddleworth, Austl. 155/H5
Sadêng, China 98/B2
Sādhaura, India 110/D4
Sadi, Eth. 135/G3
Sadīch, Iran 113/G3
Sadiola, Mali 132/C3
Sadiya, India 98/B3
Sadjoavato, Madg. 143/J6
Sadler, Tx, US 183/F4
Sado (riv.), Port. 52/A3
Sado (isl.), Japan 91/M4
Sadovo, Bul. 57/G4
Sadovoye, Rus. 77/H3
Sadowara, Japan 96/B4
Sādri, India 104/B2
Sadripante (mt.), Phil. 100/D3
Sādullāpur, Bang. 109/G3
Sadulshahar, India 110/C5
Saerbeck, Ger. 59/E4
Saeul, Lux. 61/E4
Safané, Burk. 132/E3
Safāpur, India 110/C2
Safed Koh (range), Pak. 110/A3
Safety Harbor, Fl, US 194/K8
Saffig, Ger. 61/G3
Säffle, Swe. 46/E2
Safford, Az, US 179/H4
Saffron Walden, Eng, UK 43/G2
Safi, Mor. 128/C2
Safi (cape), Mor. 128/C2
Safīd (riv.), Afg. 113/J1
Safid Khers (mts.), Afg. 113/K1
Safid Kūh (mts.), Afg. 113/H2
Safidon, India 110/D5
Safien, Swi. 67/F4
Safīpur, India 108/C2
Şāfītā, Syria 116/E2
Safonovo, Rus. 74/G5
Safranbolu, Turk. 76/E4
Şafţ al 'Inab, Egypt 131/B3
Şafţ al Mulūk, Egypt 131/B3
Şafţ Turāb, Egypt 131/C3
Sag Harbor, NY, US 199/F2
Saga, China 109/E1
Saga, Japan 96/B4
Saga (pref.), Japan 96/A4
Sagaba, Ang. 140/D1
Sagae, Japan 94/B4
Sagaing (div.), Myan. 105/F3
Sagaing, Myan. 98/B4
Sagami (bay), Japan 95/C3
Sagami (lake), Japan 95/C2
Sagami (riv.), Japan 95/C2
Sagami (sea), Japan 97/F3
Sagamihara, Japan 97/F3
Sagamiko, Japan 95/C2
Sagamore Hill Nat'l Hist. Site, NY, US 199/M8
Sagan, Indo. 103/H4
Sagana, Kenya 137/B2
Saganaga (lake), Can.,US 187/J3
Sāgar, India 108/B4
Sāgar, India 107/B3
Sagard, Ger. 46/E4
Sagarejo, Geo. 77/H4
Sagarmatha (zone), Nepal 109/F2
Sagarmatha (Everest) (mtn.), China,Nepal 109/F2
Sagarmatha NP, Nepal 109/F2
Sagata, Sen. 132/A3
Sagauli, India 109/E2
Sagavanirktok (riv.), Ak, US 201/J2
Sagay, Phil. 100/C3
Sagay, Phil. 100/D3
Sage, Ar, US 183/J2
Sage (cr.), Mt, US 175/J3
Sagemace (bay), Mb, Can. 186/D1
Saggart, Ire. 40/B5
Şaghīr (canal), Egypt 131/C2
Saginaw, Mi, US 190/E3
Saginaw (bay), Mi, US 190/E3
Saginaw, Or, US 176/B2
Saginaw, Tx, US 180/K7
Sagittario (riv.), It. 71/C4
Sagiz, Kaz. 77/K2
Sagle, Id, US 174/F3
Saglek (bay), Nf, Can. 171/K3
Sagola, Mi, US 187/K4
Sagone (gulf), Fr. 54/A1
Sagsay (riv.), Mong. 111/E2
Sagter Ems (riv.), Ger. 59/E2
Sagu, Indo. 152/A2
Sagua de Tánamo, Cuba 207/H1
Sagua la Grande, Cuba 207/F1
Saguache, Co, US 179/J1
Saguache (cr.), Co, US 179/J1
Saguaro NP, Az, US 179/G4
Saguia el Hamra (riv.), WSah. 128/C4
Sagunto, Sp. 53/E3
Sagy, Fr. 36/H4
Sa'gya, China 109/G1
Sagyz (riv.), Kaz. 77/K2
Saḩāb, Jor. 117/D5
Sahaba, Sudan 127/F5
Sahagún, Col. 216/C2
Sahagún, Mex. 205/L7
Sahagún, Sp. 52/C1
Saḩam, Jor. 117/D3
Sahand (mtn.), Iran 115/F2
Sahara (des.), Afr. 119/B2
Sahāranpur, India 110/D5
Saharsa, India 109/F3
Sahaspur, India 108/B1
Sahaswān, India 108/B1
Sahavato, Madg. 143/J8
Sahāwar, India 108/B2
Sahel (riv.), Alg. 130/H4
Sāhibganj, India 109/F3
Şahin, Turk. 57/H5
Şahinli, Turk. 57/H5
Sāhīwāl, Pak. 110/B4
Sahiwal, Pak. 110/B4
Şaḩneh, Iran 115/F3
Sahoué, Gabon 138/B2
Şahrajat al Kubrá, Egypt 131/C3
Sahrho, Jebel (mts.), Mor. 128/D3
Sahu, Indo. 103/G3
Sahuaripa, Mex. 204/C2
Sahuarita, Az, US 179/G5
Sahuayo de Morelos, Mex. 204/E4
Šahy, Slvk. 49/K4
Sai (riv.), India 108/C2
Sai (chan.), India 104/D2
Sai (riv.), Japan 96/E2
Sai Buri, Thai. 106/C5
Sai Kung, China 99/M7
Sai Yok, Thai. 106/B3
Sai Yok NP, Thai. 106/B3
Saibai (isl.), Austl. 153/F2
Sa'id Bundas, Sudan 135/E3
Saïda, Alg. 130/F5
Saïdia, Mor. 130/C2
Saidor, PNG 153/G1
Saidpur, India 108/D3
Saidpur, Bang. 109/G3
Saidu, Pak. 110/B2
Saignelégier, Swi. 66/D3
Saignon, Fr. 70/B5
Saigō, Japan 96/C2
Saigon, Viet. 106/D4
Saijō, Japan 96/C4
Saikai NP, Japan 96/A4
Saiki, Japan 96/B4
Saillans, Fr. 70/B3
Sailly, Fr. 36/H4
Sailly-sur-la-Lys, Fr. 60/B2
Sailolof, Indo. 103/H4

Sailu – Sakha
326

Sailu, India 104/C4
Saima, China 93/C2
Saimaa (lake), Fin. 44/J3
Sain Alto, Mex. 204/E4
Şā'īn Dezh, Iran 115/F2
Sainghin-en-Weppes, Fr. 60/B2
Sains-du-Nord, Fr. 60/D3
Saint (swamp), Fl, US 195/H3
Saint Mary's (riv.), NS, Can. 189/F3
Saint Abb's (pt.), Sc, UK 39/D5
Saint Abbs, Sc, UK 39/D5
Saint Adolphe, Mb, Can. 186/F3
Saint Agnes (pt.), Eng, UK 42/A6
Saint Agnes, Eng, UK 42/A6
Saint Alban's, Nf, Can. 189/K2
Saint Albans, Eng, UK 36/C1
Saint Albans, Vt, US 191/K2
Saint Albans, WV, US 193/G1
Saint Albert, Ab, Can. 175/H1
Saint Ambroise, Mb, Can. 186/E2
Saint Andrews, NB, Can. 188/D3
Saint Andrews, Sc, UK 39/D4
Saint Andrews (bay), Sc, UK 39/D4
Saint Andrew's, Nf, Can. 189/H2
Saint Ann (cape), SLeo. 132/B5
Saint Anne, Chl, UK 62/C1
Saint Ann's (pt.), Wal, UK 42/A3
Saint Anns, On, Can. 190/U9
Saint Ann's Bay, Jam. 203/F4
Saint Ansgar, Ia, US 185/H2
Saint Anthony, Nf, Can. 171/L3
Saint Anthony, Id, US 177/H2
Saint Anthony, ND, US 186/D4
Saint Arnaud, Austl. 156/B3
Saint Arthur, NB, Can. 188/D2
Saint Asaph, Wal, UK 40/E5
Saint Athan, Wal, UK 42/C4
Saint Aubin, Chl, UK 62/C2
Saint Aubin's (bay), UK 62/C2
Saint Augustine, Fl, US 195/H3
Saint Augustine Beach, Fl, US 195/H3
Saint Austell (bay), Eng, UK 42/B6
Saint Austell, Eng, UK 42/B6
Saint Bathans (mt.), NZ 159/B4
Saint Bees, Eng, UK 40/E3
Saint Bees (pt.), Eng, UK 40/E2
Saint Benedict, Sk, Can. 175/M1
Saint Blaize (cape), SAfr. 142/C4
Saint Boswells, Sc, UK 39/D5
Saint Briavels, Eng, UK 42/D3
Saint Bride's (bay), Wal, UK 42/A3
Saint Bride's, Nf, Can. 189/K2
Saint Brieux, Sk, Can. 175/M1
Saint Catharines, On, Can. 190/U9
Saint Catherine, Fl, US 194/L6
Saint Catherine (mt.), Gren. 217/F1
Saint Catherines (isl.), Ga, US 195/H2
Saint Catherine's (hill), Eng, UK 43/E5
Saint Catherine's (pt.), Eng, UK 43/E5
Saint Charles, Il, US 197/P16
Saint Charles, Mi, US 190/D3
Saint Charles, Mo, US 185/J4
Saint Charles, Mn, US 185/H2
Saint Charles, Md, US 193/J1
Saint Christoffel (peak), NAnt. 216/D1
Saint Clair (riv.), On, Can. 190/E3
Saint Clair (lake), Can.,US 197/G7
Saint Clair (co.), Mi, US 197/G6
Saint Clair, Mi, US 190/E3
Saint Clair, Mn, US 185/H1
Saint Clair, Pa, US 198/B2
Saint Clair Beach, On, Can. 197/G7
Saint Clair Shores, Mi, US 197/G6
Saint Clairsville, Oh, US 190/F4
Saint Cloud, Fl, US 194/N7
Saint Cloud, Mn, US 187/G5
Saint Columb Major, Eng, UK 42/B6
Saint Combs, Sc, UK 39/E1
Saint Croix, NB, Can. 188/D3
Saint Croix (riv.), Wi, US 187/H5
Saint Croix (riv.), Mn,Wi, US 185/H1
Saint Croix (co.), Wi, US 187/Q6
Saint Croix (isl.), USVI 203/M8
Saint Croix Ind. Res., Wi, US 187/H5
Saint Cyr (mt.), Yk, Can. 201/M3
Saint Cyrus, Sc, UK 39/D3
Saint David, Az, US 179/G5
Saint David's, Wal, UK 42/A3
Saint David's (pt.), Wal, UK 42/A3
Saint Edward, PE, Can. 188/E2
Saint Edward, Ne, US 184/F3
Saint Eleanors, PE, Can. 188/F2
Saint Elias (mts.), Ak, US 201/K3
Saint Elias (mt.), Ak, US 201/K3
Saint Elias (cape), Ak, US 201/K3
Saint Eustatius (isl.), NAnt. 203/N8
Saint Fergus, Sc, UK 39/E1
Saint Francis (cape), SAfr. 142/D4
Saint Francis (riv.), Ar,Mo, US 192/B2
Saint Francis, Ks, US 184/D4
Saint Francis, SD, US 184/D2
Saint Francis, Wi, US 197/Q14
Saint Francisville, La, US 194/C2
Saint Francisville, Il, US 192/D1
Saint Francois (mts.), Mo, US 183/J2
Saint François (riv.), Qu, Can. 191/L2
Saint Gabriel, La, US 194/C2
Saint Gallen (canton), Swi. 67/F3
Saint Geoirs (arpt.), Fr. 70/B2
Saint George, Austl. 158/C5
Saint George, NB, Can. 188/D3
Saint George (cape), Nf, Can. 189/H1
Saint George, On, Can. 190/S9
Saint George, Ak, US 201/E4
Saint George (isl.), Ak, US 201/E4
Saint George (cape), Fl, US 195/F3
Saint George, Ga, US 195/G2
Saint George (nbrhd.), NY, US 199/J9
Saint George, SC, US 193/G4
Saint George, Ut, US 179/F2
Saint George's (chan.) 40/C6
Saint George's (bay), Nf, Can. 189/H1
Saint George's, Nf, Can. 189/H1
Saint George's (cap.), Gren. 217/F1
Saint Georges, De, US 198/C4
Saint Georges Head (pt.), Austl. 157/E2
Saint Govan's (pt.), Wal, UK 42/B3
Saint Gregory (cape), Nf, Can. 189/H1
Saint Helen, Mi, US 190/D2
Saint Helena (isl.), Austl. 158/F6
Saint Helena (isl.), UK 26/J6
Saint Helena (bay), SAfr. 142/B4
Saint Helena (mt.), Ca, US 176/B4
Saint Helena, Ca, US 176/B4
Saint Helena (sound), SC, US 193/G4
Saint Helens, Austl. 156/D4
Saint Helens (pt.), Austl. 156/D4
Saint Helens, Eng, UK 41/F5
Saint Helens (co.), Eng, UK 41/F5
Saint Helens, Or, US 174/C5
Saint Helens (mt.), Wa, US 174/C4
Saint Helier, Chl, UK 62/C2
Saint Henry, Oh, US 190/D4
Saint Hilaire, Mn, US 186/F3
Saint Ignace (isl.), On, Can. 187/L3
Saint Ignace, Mi, US 190/D2
Saint Ignatius, Mt, US 175/G4
Saint Ives (nbrhd.), Austl. 158/H8
Saint Ives, Eng, UK 43/F2
Saint Ives (bay), Eng, UK 42/A6
Saint Ives, Eng, UK 42/A6
Saint Jacques (int'l arpt.), Fr. 62/D4
Saint James (cape), BC, Can. 170/C3
Saint James, Ar, US 183/J3
Saint James, Mi, US 190/D2
Saint James, Mn, US 185/G2
Saint James, Mo, US 183/J2
Saint James, NY, US 199/E2
Saint James City, Fl, US 195/G4
Saint Jo, Tx, US 183/F4
Saint Joe, Ar, US 183/H2
Saint Joe (riv.), Id,Wa, US 172/C2
Saint John, NB, Can. 188/D3
Saint John (riv.), NB, Can. 188/D3
SSaint John, Chl, UK 62/C2
Saint John, Ks, US 183/E1
aint John (lake), La, US 194/C2
Saint John (riv.), Me, US 171/K4
Saint John, ND, US 186/E3
Saint John, Wa, US 174/F4
Saint John (isl.), USVI 203/M8
Saint John's (cap.), Anti. 203/N8
Saint John's (cap.), Nf, Can. 189/L2
Saint John's (pt.), NI, UK 40/C3
Saint Johns, Az, US 179/H3
Saint Johns (riv.), Fl, US 195/H3
Saint Johns, Mi, US 190/D3
Saint Johnsbury, Vt, US 191/K2
Saint Jones (riv.), De, US 198/C5
Saint Joseph (isl.), On, Can. 190/E1
Saint Joseph (lake), On, Can. 170/G3
Saint Joseph, Fl, US 194/L7
Saint Joseph (pen.), Fl, US 195/F3
Saint Joseph (pt.), Fl, US 195/F3
Saint Joseph, La, US 194/C2
Saint Joseph (lake), La, US 194/C1
Saint Joseph, Mi, US 190/C3
Saint Joseph (riv.), Mi, US 190/D3
Saint Joseph, Mo, US 185/G4
Saint Joseph, Tn, US 192/D3
Saint Just, Eng, UK 42/A6
Saint Just-in-Roseland, Eng, UK 42/A6
Saint Kilda (isl.), UK 37/P8
Saint Kilda (nbrhd.), Austl. 156/F5
Saint Kitts (isl.), StK. 203/N7
Saint Kitts and Nevis (ctry.) 203/N7
Saint Landry, La, US 194/B2
Saint Laurent, Mb, Can. 186/F2
Saint Lawrence, Austl. 158/C3
Saint Lawrence (gulf), Can. 163/L5
Saint Lawrence (riv.), Can.,US 163/K5
Saint Lawrence, Nf, Can. 189/K2
Saint Lawrence Islands NP, On, Can. 191/H2
Saint Lawrence (riv.), NAm. 191/J2
Saint Lawrence, Eng, UK 43/E5
Saint Lawrence (isl.), Ak, US 201/D3
Saint Lawrence, Pa, US 198/C3
Saint Lawrence, Tx, US 180/D2
Saint Leo, Fl, US 194/L7
Saint Leon, Mb, Can. 186/E3
Saint Leonard (mt.), Austl. 156/G5
Saint Leonards, Austl. 157/B4
Saint Llorenc del Munt, PN, Sp. 53/K6
Saint Louis (lake), Qu, Can. 189/N7
Saint Louis, Sk, Can. 175/M1
Saint Louis (riv.), Mn, US 187/H4
Saint Louis, Mi, US 190/D3
Saint Louis, Mo, US 200/G8
Saint Louis Park, Mn, US 187/P7
Saint Lucia (ctry.) 203/N8
Saint Lucia (cape), SAfr. 143/F3
Saint Lucia (lake), SAfr. 143/F3
Saint Lucia (chan.), Mart.,StL. 203/N9
Saint Lucia Estuary, SAfr. 143/F3
Saint Lucie, Fl, US 195/H4
Saint Lucie (canal), Fl, US 195/H4
Saint Lucie (inlet), Fl, US 195/H4
Saint Maarten (isl.), NAnt. 203/N8
Saint Magnus (bay), Sc, UK 37/W13
Saint Malo, Mb, Can. 186/F3
Saint Margaret's at Cliffe, Eng, UK 60/A1
Saint Margaret's Hope, Sc, UK 37/V14
Saint Maries, Id, US 174/F4
Saint Marks, SAfr. 142/D4
Saint Marks, Fl, US 195/F2
Saint Marks NWR, Fl, US 195/F2
Saint Martin (lake), Mb, Can. 186/E2
Saint Martin (isl.), Mi, US 187/L5
Saint Martins, NB, Can. 188/E3
Saint Martins (isl.), Bang. 98/A4
Saint Martinville, La, US 194/C2
Saint Mary (peak), Austl. 155/H4
Saint Mary (riv.), BC, Can. 174/F3
Saint Mary (cape), NS, Can. 188/D3
Saint Mary (cape), Gam. 132/A3
Saint Mary's (bay), Ns., Can. 188/D3
Saint Mary's, Nf, Can. 189/L2
Saint Mary's, On, Can. 190/F3
Saint Mary's, Sc, UK 37/V14
Saint Mary's, Ak, US 201/F3
Saint Mary's, Zam. 141/E2
Saint Marys, Austl. 156/D4
Saint Marys (nbrhd.), Austl. 158/G8
Saint Marys, Ga, US 195/H2
Saint Marys (riv.), In, US 190/D4
Saint Marys, Ks, US 185/F4
Saint Marys, Mo, US 192/C2
Saint Marys, Oh, US 190/D4
Saint Marys, Pa, US 191/G4
Saint Marys, WV, US 190/F5
Saint Mary's Entrance (inlet), Ga,Fl, US 195/H2
Saint Matthew (isl.), Ak, US 201/D3
Saint Matthews, SC, US 193/G4
Saint Matthias Group (isls.), PNG 160/E5
Saint Maurice, La, US 194/B2
Saint Mawes, Eng, UK 42/A6
Saint Meinrad, In, US 192/D1
Saint Mellons, Wal, UK 42/C3
Saint Michael, Ak, US 201/F3
Saint Michael, Mn, US 187/N6
Saint Michaels, Md, US 198/B6
Saint Monance, Sc, UK 39/D4
Saint Moritz (Sankt Moritz), Swi. 51/H3
Saint Neots, Eng, UK 43/F2
Saint Nicholas Greek Orthodox Church, Fl, US 194/K7
Saint Niklaus, Swi. 66/D5
Saint Onge (peak), SD, US 184/C1
Saint Ouen's (bay), Chi., UK 62/C2
Saint Paris, Oh, US 190/E4
Saint Patrickswell, Ire. 38/B4
Saint Paul, Ab, Can. 170/E3
Saint Paul, Reun., Fr. 143/S15
Saint Paul (isl.), Fr. 27/N7
Saint Paul (cape), Gha. 133/F5
Saint Paul (riv.), Libr. 132/C5
Saint Paul, Ak, US 201/D4
Saint Paul (isl.), Ak, US 201/D4
Saint Paul, Ar, US 183/H3
Saint Paul, In, US 190/D5
Saint Paul, Ks, US 183/G2
Saint Paul (cap.), Mn, US 187/P7
Saint Paul, Ne, US 184/E3
Saint Paul, SC, US 193/G4
Saint Pauls, NC, US 193/H3
Saint Paul's Church Nat'l Hist. Site, NY, US 199/K8
Saint Peter (isl.), Austl. 155/G5
Saint Peter, Il, US 192/C1
Saint Peter, Ks, US 184/D4
Saint Peter, Mn, US 185/H1
Saint Peter and Saint Paul Rocks, (isl.), Braz. 26/H5
Saint Peter Port, Chl, UK 62/C2
Saint Peters, PE, Can. 189/F2
Saint Peters, NS, Can. 189/G3
Saint Peter's, Eng, UK 43/H4
Saint Peters, Mo, US 185/J4
Saint Peter's Basilica, VatC. 71/G7
Saint Peter's Square, VatC. 71/G7
Saint Petersburg, Rus. 75/T7
Saint Petersburg, Fl, US 194/K8
Saint Petersburg Beach, Fl, US 194/K8
Saint Petersburg-Clearwater International (arpt.), Fl, US 194/K8
Saint Philips, Sk, Can. 186/D2
Saint Pierre and Miquelon (dpcy.), Fr. 189/J2
Saint Pierre (isl.), StP., Fr. 189/J2
Saint Pierre-Jolys, Mb, Can. 186/F3
Saint Regis Ind. Res., NY, US 191/J2
Saint Sampson's, Chl, UK 62/C2
Saint Saviour, Chl, UK 62/C2
Saint Shotts, Nf, Can. 189/L2
Saint Simons (isl.), Ga, US 195/H2
Saint Simons Island, Ga, US 195/H2
Saint Stephen, NB, Can. 188/D3
Saint Stephen-in-Brannel, Eng, UK 42/B6
Saint Stephens, Al, US 194/D2
Saint Stephens, NC, US 193/G3
Saint Stephens Church, Va, US 193/J2
Saint Thomas, On, Can. 190/F3
Saint Thomas (isl.), USVI 203/H4
Saint Thomas, Mo, US 183/H1
Saint Thomas, ND, US 186/F3
Saint Victor, Sk, Can. 175/M3
Saint Vika, Swe. 45/A2
Saint Vincent (pt.), Austl. 156/C4
Saint Vincent, It. 68/A1
Saint Vincent (isl.), StV. 203/N9
Saint Vincent and the Grenadines (ctry.) 203/N8
Saint Vincent Nat'l Wild. Ref., Fl, US 195/F3
Saint Vincent Passage (chan.), StL.,StV. 203/N9
Saint Walburg, Sk, Can. 175/K1
Saint Xavier, Mt, US 177/K1
Saint-Affrique, Fr. 50/E5
Saint-Aignan, Fr. 63/G6
Saint-Alexis-de-Matapédia, Qu, Can. 188/D2
Saint-Alexis-des-Monts, Qu, Can. 191/K1
Saint-Amable, Qu, Can. 189/P6
Saint-Amand, Fr. 63/E2
Saint-Amand-les-Eaux, Fr. 60/C3
Saint-Amand-Longpré, Fr. 63/G5
Saint-Amand-Montrond, Fr. 50/E3
Saint-Amarin, Fr. 66/D2
Saint-Ambroise, Qu, Can. 188/B1
Saint-Amé, Fr. 66/C1
Saint-Andiol, Fr. 70/A5
Saint-André, NB, Can. 188/D2
Saint-André, Fr. 60/C2
Saint-André, Fr. 70/D5
Saint-André, Reun., Fr. 143/S15
Saint-André-de-Cubzac, Fr. 50/C4
Saint-André-de-l'Eure, Fr. 63/G3
Saint-André-le-Gaz, Fr. 70/B1
Saint-André-les-Alpes, Fr. 70/C5
Saint-André-les-Vergers, Fr. 50/F2
Saint-Anicet, Qu, Can. 191/J2
Saint-Antoine, NB, Can. 188/E2
Saint-Antoine, Qu, Can. 189/N6
Saint-Antonin, Qu, Can. 188/C2
Saint-Arnoult-en-Yvelines, Fr. 36/H6
Saint-Athanase, Qu, Can. 188/C2
Saint-Auban, Fr. 70/C5
Saint-Aubert, Qu, Can. 188/B2
Saint-Aubin, Fr. 66/B3
Saint-Aubin, Swi. 66/C4
Saint-Aubin-d'Aubigné, Fr. 62/D4
Saint-Aubin-du-Cormier, Fr. 62/D4
Saint-Aubin-lès-Elbeuf, Fr. 63/G2
Saint-Aubin-sur-Gaillon, Fr. 63/G2
Saint-Augustin, Madg. 143/G8
Saint-Augustin, Fr. 36/M5
Saint-Augustin, Qu, Can. 189/N6
Saint-Avé, Fr. 62/C5
Saint-Avertin, Fr. 63/F6
Saint-Avold, Fr. 61/F5
Saint-Baldoph, Fr. 70/B1
Saint-Barthélemy, Qu, Can. 191/K1
Saint-Barthélemy (isl.), Guad., Fr. 203/N8
Saint-Barthélemy, Pic de (peak), Fr. 50/D5
Saint-Barthélemy-d'Anjou, Fr. 63/E6
Saint-Basile, NB, Can. 188/C2
Saint-Benoît, Reun., Fr. 143/S15
Saint-Benoît, Fr. 50/D3
Saint-Benoît, Qu, Can. 189/M6
Saint-Berthevin, Fr. 63/E4
Saint-Blaise, Swi. 66/C3
Saint-Blaise, Qu, Can. 189/P7
Saint-Bonnet-de-Mure, Fr. 70/B1
Saint-Bonnet-en-Champsaur, Fr. 70/C3
Saint-Briac-sur-Mer, Fr. 62/C3
Saint-Brice-Courcelles, Fr. 60/C5
Saint-Brice-sous-Forêt, Fr. 36/K5
Saint-Brieuc, Fr. 62/C3
Saint-Brieuc (bay), Fr. 50/B2
Saint-Bruno (co.), Qu, Can. 189/P6
Saint-Bruno-de-Montarville, Qu, Can. 189/P6
Saint-Calais, Fr. 63/F5
Saint-Cannat, Fr. 70/B5
Saint-Canut, Qu, Can. 189/M6
Saint-Cassien (lake), Fr. 70/C5
Saint-Cast-le-Guildo, Fr. 62/C3
Saint-Céré, Fr. 50/D4
Saint-Cergue, Swi. 66/C5
Saint-Cergues, Fr. 66/C5
Saint-Chamas, Fr. 70/B5
Saint-Charles, NB, Can. 188/E2
Saint-Chef, Fr. 70/B1
Saint-Chély-d'Apcher, Fr. 50/E4
Saint-Chéron, Fr. 36/J6
Saint-Clair-de-la-Tour, Fr. 70/B1
Saint-Clair-du-Rhône, Fr. 70/A2
Saint-Claude, Fr. 66/B5
Saint-Cloud, Fr. 36/J5
Saint-Constant, Qu, Can. 189/N7
Saint-Cosme-de-Vair, Fr. 63/F4
Saint-Coulomb, Fr. 62/D3
Saint-Croix (lake), Fr. 70/C5
Saint-Cyprien, Qu, Can. 188/C2
Saint-Cyr-en-Val, Fr. 63/G5
Saint-Cyr-l'École, Fr. 36/J5
Saint-Cyr-sous-Dourdan, Fr. 36/J6
Saint-Cyr-sur-Loire, Fr. 63/F6
Saint-Cyr-sur-Mer, Fr. 70/B6
Saint-Cyr-sur-Morin, Fr. 36/M5
Saint-Cyrille, Qu, Can. 191/K2
Saint-Damase, Qu, Can. 188/D1
Saint-Damien-de-Buckland, Qu, Can. 188/B2
Saint-David-de-Falardeau, Qu, Can. 188/B1
Saint-Denis (cap.), Reun., Fr. 143/S15
Saint-Denis, Fr. 36/K5
Saint-Denis-en-Bugey, Fr. 66/B6
Saint-Denis-les-Ponts, Fr. 63/G4
Saint-Didier, Fr. 70/B5
Saint-Dié, Fr. 66/C1
Saint-Dizier, Fr. 61/D6
Saint-Donat, Qu, Can. 191/J1
Saint-Donat-sur-L'Herbasse, Fr. 70/A2
Saint-Doulchard, Fr. 50/E3
Saint-Édouard, Qu, Can. 189/N7
Saint-Égrève, Fr. 70/B2
Saint-Élie, FrG. 218/C1
Saint-Éloy-les-Mines, Fr. 50/E3
Saint-Esprit, Qu, Can. 189/N6
Saint-Estève, Fr. 50/E5
Saint-Étienne-au-Mont, Fr. 60/A2
Saint-Étienne-de-Baïgorry, Fr. 50/C5
Saint-Étienne-de-Cuines, Fr. 70/C2
Saint-Étienne-de-Montluc, Fr. 62/D6
Saint-Étienne-de-Tinée, Fr. 70/C4
Saint-Étienne-du-Grès, Fr. 70/A5
Saint-Étienne-du-Rouvray, Fr. 63/G2
Saint-Étienne-les-Orgues, Fr. 70/B4
Saint-Étienne-lès-Remiremont, Fr. 66/C1
Saint-Eusèbe, Qu, Can. 188/C2
Saint-Eustache, Qu, Can. 189/N6
Saint-Fabien, Qu, Can. 188/C1
Saint-Fargeau-Ponthierry, Fr. 36/K6
Saint-Félicien, Qu, Can. 188/A1
Saint-Félicien, Fr. 70/A2
Saint-Félix, Fr. 66/B6
Saint-Ferréol-les-Neiges, Qu, Can. 188/B2
Saint-Fidèle-de-Mont-Murray, Qu, Can. 188/C2
Saint-Firmin, Fr. 70/C3
Saint-Florent-le-Vieil, Fr. 63/D6
Saint-Florent-sur-Cher, Fr. 50/E3
Saint-Florentin, Fr. 50/E2
Saint-Fons, Fr. 70/A1
Saint-Four, Fr. 50/E4
Saint-François (riv.), Qu, Can. 188/A3
Saint-François-du-Lac, Qu, Can. 191/K1
Saint-Front, Sk, Can. 175/M1
Saint-Fulgence, Qu, Can. 188/B1
Saint-Gabriel, Qu, Can. 191/K1
Saint-Gaudens, Fr. 50/D5
Saint-Gaudens Nat'l Hist. Site, NH, US 191/K3
Saint-Gédéon, Qu, Can. 188/B3
Saint-Genis-Laval, Fr. 70/A1
Saint-Genis-Pouilly, Fr. 66/C5
Saint-Genix-sur-Guiers, Fr. 70/B1
Saint-Georges, Qu, Can. 188/B2
Saint-Georges, FrG. 218/D2
Saint-Georges-Buttavent, Fr. 63/E4
Saint-Georges-de-Cacouna, Qu, Can. 188/C2
Saint-Georges-des-Groseillers, Fr. 63/E3
Saint-Georges-du-Vièvre, Fr. 63/F2
Saint-Georges-sur-Cher, Fr. 63/G6
Saint-Georges-sur-Eure, Fr. 63/G4
Saint-Georges-sur-Loire, Fr. 63/E6
Saint-Géréon, Fr. 62/D6
Saint-Germain, Fr. 66/C2
Saint-Germain-de-la-Grange, Fr. 36/H5
Saint-Germain-du-Bois, Fr. 66/B4
Saint-Germain-du-Corbéis, Fr. 63/F4
Saint-Germain-du-Plain, Fr. 66/A4
Saint-Germain-en-Laye, Fr. 36/J5
Saint-Germain-lès-Corbeil, Fr. 36/K6
Saint-Germain-sous Doue, Fr. 36/M5
Saint-Germain-sur-Morin, Fr. 36/L5
Saint-Germer-de-Fly, Fr. 60/A5
Saint-Gervais, Fr. 36/H4
Saint-Gervais-la-Forêt, Fr. 63/G5
Saint-Gervais-les-Bains, Fr. 66/C6
Saint-Ghislain, Belg. 60/C3
Saint-Gildas-des-Bois, Fr. 62/C5
Saint-Gilles-Croix-de-Vie, Fr. 50/C3
Saint-Gingolph, Swi. 66/C5
Saint-Girons, Fr. 50/D5
Saint-Gobain, Fr. 60/C4
Saint-Godefroi, Qu, Can. 188/E1
Saint-Gratien, Fr. 36/J5
Saint-Grégoire, Fr. 62/D4
Saint-Guillaume-Nord, Qu, Can. 191/J1
Saint-Herblain, Fr. 62/D6
Saint-Hermas, Qu, Can. 189/M6
Saint-Herménégilde, Qu, Can. 188/B3
Saint-Hilaire-du-Harcouët, Fr. 63/D3
Saint-Hilarion, Fr. 36/H6
Saint-Hippolyte, Fr. 66/C3
Saint-Honorat (peak), Fr. 70/C4
Saint-Honoré, Qu, Can. 188/B3
Saint-Honoré, Qu, Can. 188/B1
Saint-Hubert, Belg. 61/E3
Saint-Hubert, Qu, Can. 188/C2
Saint-Hubert, Qu, Can. 189/P6
Saint-Hubert (pond), Fr. 36/H5
Saint-Hugues, Qu, Can. 191/K2
Saint-Hyacinthe, Qu, Can. 191/K2
Saint-Imier, Swi. 66/D3
Saint-Irénée, Qu, Can. 188/B2
Saint-Isidore, NB, Can. 188/E2
Saint-Isidore-de-Laprairie, Qu, Can. 189/N7
Saint-Ismier, Fr. 70/B2
Saint-Jacques, NB, Can. 188/C2
Saint-Jacques-de-la-Lande, Fr. 62/D4
Saint-Jacques-le-Mineur, Qu, Can. 189/P7
Saint-James, Fr. 62/D3
Saint-Jean (riv.), Qu, Can. 188/E1
Saint-Jean (lake), Qu, Can. 171/J4
Saint-Jean, FrG. 218/C1
Saint-Jean-Cap-Ferrat, Fr. 70/D5
Saint-Jean-d'Angély, Fr. 50/C4
Saint-Jean-de-Bboiseau, Fr. 62/D6
Saint-Jean-de-Bournay, Fr. 70/B2
Saint-Jean-de-Braye, Fr. 63/G5
Saint-Jean-de-Dieu, Qu, Can. 188/C1
Saint-Jean-de-la-Ruelle, Fr. 63/G5
Saint-Jean-de-Losne, Fr. 66/B3
Saint-Jean-de-Luz, Fr. 50/C5
Saint-Jean-de-Matha, Qu, Can. 191/K1
Saint-Jean-de-Muzols, Fr. 70/A2
Saint-Jean-en-Royans, Fr. 70/B2
Saint-Jean-Port-Joli, Qu, Can. 188/B2
Saint-Jean-sur-Richelieu, Qu, Can. 191/K2
Saint-Jeannet, Fr. 70/D5
Saint-Jeoire, Fr. 66/C5
Saint-Jêrôme, Qu, Can. 189/N6
Saint-Joachim, Fr. 62/C6
Saint-Joseph, NB, Can. 188/E3
Saint-Joseph, Reun., Fr. 143/S15
Saint-Joseph-de-Beauce, Qu, Can. 188/B2
Saint-Joseph-de-Madawaska, NB, Can. 188/C2
Saint-Joseph-de-Mékinac, Qu, Can. 188/A2
Saint-Jovite, Qu, Can. 191/J1
Saint-Juéry, Fr. 50/E5
Saint-Julien, Fr. 66/B3
Saint-Julien-de-Vouvantes, Fr. 62/D5
Saint-Julien-en-Genevois, Fr. 66/C5
Saint-Julien-les-Villas, Fr. 50/F2
Saint-Julien-Mont-Denis, Fr. 70/C2
Saint-Junien, Fr. 50/D4
Saint-Just-en-Chaussée, Fr. 60/B4
Saint-Juste-de-Bretenières, Qu, Can. 188/B2
Saint-Lambert, Qu, Can. 189/P6
Saint-Laurent, Qu, Can. 189/N6
Saint-Laurent du Maroni (dist.), FrG. 218/C1
Saint-Laurent du Maroni, FrG. 218/C1
Saint-Laurent-Blangy, Fr. 60/B3
Saint-Laurent-de-Cerdans, Fr. 50/E5
Saint-Laurent-de-Mure, Fr. 70/B1
Saint-Laurent-des-Arbres, Fr. 70/A4
Saint-Laurent-du-Pont, Fr. 70/B2
Saint-Laurent-du-Var, Fr. 70/D5
Saint-Laurent-en-Grandvaux, Fr. 66/B4
Saint-Laurent-Nouan, Fr. 63/G5
Saint-Laurent-sur-Saône, Fr. 66/A5
Saint-Lazare, Qu, Can. 188/B2
Saint-Lazare, Qu, Can. 189/M7
Saint-Léger, Belg. 61/E4
Saint-Léger-en-Yvelines, Fr. 36/H5
Saint-Léger-lès-Domart, Fr. 60/B3
Saint-Léonard, Fr. 60/A2
Saint-Léonard, Qu, Can. 189/N6
Saint-Leu, Reun., Fr. 143/S15
Saint-Leu-D'Esserent, Fr. 60/B5
Saint-Leu-la-Forêt, Fr. 36/J4
Saint-Liboire, Qu, Can. 188/A3
Saint-Lô, Fr. 63/D2
Saint-Louis, Fr. 66/D2
Saint-Louis (pol. reg.), Sen. 132/B3
Saint-Louis, Sen. 132/A2
Saint-Louis, Reun., Fr. 143/S15
Saint-Louis du Nord, Haiti 207/H2
Saint-Louis-de-Gonzague, Qu, Can. 189/N7
Saint-Louis-de-Kent, NB, Can. 188/E2
Saint-Loup-sur-Semouse, Fr. 66/C2
Saint-Lubin-des-Joncherets, Fr. 63/G3
Saint-Luc, Qu, Can. 189/P7
Saint-Lucien, Fr. 36/G6
Saint-Lunaire, Fr. 62/C3
Saint-Magloire-de-Bellechasse, Qu, Can. 188/B2
Saint-Maixent l'École, Fr. 50/C3
Saint-Malachie, Qu, Can. 188/B2
Saint-Malo, Fr. 62/C3
Saint-Malo (gulf), UK 50/B2
Saint-Malo-de-Guersac, Fr. 62/C6
Saint-Mandrier-sur-Mer, Fr. 70/B6
Saint-Marc, Haiti 207/H2
Saint-Marc-des-Carrières, Qu, Can. 188/A2
Saint-Marc-sur-Richelieu, Qu, Can. 189/P6
Saint-Marcel, Fr. 63/G2
Saint-Marcel, Fr. 66/A4
Saint-Marcel (peak), FrG. 218/C2
Saint-Marcel-d'Ardèche, Fr. 70/A4
Saint-Marcel-lès-Valence, Fr. 70/A3
Saint-Marcellin, Fr. 70/B2
Saint-Marcouf (isls.), Fr. 63/D1
Saint-Mard, Fr. 36/L4
Saint-Mars-la-Brière, Fr. 63/F4
Saint-Mars-la-Jaille, Fr. 63/D5
Saint-Martin, Swi. 66/D5
Saint-Martin (isl.), Guad., Fr. 203/N8
Saint-Martin-Boulogne, Fr. 60/A2
Saint-Martin-d'Ablois, Fr. 60/C6
Saint-Martin-de-Belleville, Fr. 70/C2
Saint-Martin-de-Crau, Fr. 70/A5
Saint-Martin-des-Champs, Fr. 62/B3
Saint-Martin-d'Hères, Fr. 70/B2
Saint-Martin-du-Tertre, Fr. 36/K4
Saint-Martin-du-Var, Fr. 70/D5
Saint-Martin-la-Garenne, Fr. 36/H4
Saint-Martin-Vésubie, Fr. 70/D4
Saint-Mathieu (pt.), Fr. 62/A4
Saint-Mathieu-de-Beloeil, Qu, Can. 189/N7
Saint-Maur-des-Fossés, Fr. 36/K5
Saint-Maurice, Swi. 66/D5
Saint-Maurice (riv.), Qu, Can. 188/A2
Saint-Maurice (riv.), Qu, Can. 171/J4
Saint-Maurice-L'Exil, Fr. 70/A2
Saint-Max, Fr. 61/F6
Saint-Maxime-du-Mont-Louis, Qu, Can. 188/E1
Saint-Maximin-la-Sainte-Baume, Fr. 70/B6
Saint-Méen-le-Grand, Fr. 62/C4
Saint-Memmie, Fr. 61/D6
Saint-Méry, Fr. 36/L6
Saint-Michel, Fr. 61/D4
Saint-Michel (mtn.), Fr. 62/B4
Saint-Michel-Chef-Chef, Fr. 62/C6
Saint-Michel-de-Maurienne, Fr. 70/C2
Saint-Michel-des-Saints, Qu, Can. 191/K1
Saint-Michel-sur-Meurthe, Fr. 66/C1
Saint-Michel-sur-Orge, Fr. 36/J6
Saint-Mihiel, Fr. 61/E6
Saint-Mitre-les-Remparts, Fr. 70/B6
Saint-Montant, Fr. 70/A4
Saint-Nabord, Fr. 66/C1
Saint-Nazaire, Fr. 62/C6
Saint-Nazaire, FrG. 218/C1
Saint-Nicolas, Belg. 61/E2
Saint-Nicolas-d'Aliermont, Fr. 63/G1
Saint-Nicolas-du-Pélem, Fr. 62/B4
Saint-Nom-la-Bretèche, Fr. 36/J5
Saint-Omer, Fr. 60/B2
Saint-Omer-en-Chaussée, Fr. 60/A4
Saint-Ouen, Fr. 63/G5
Saint-Ouen, Fr. 60/B3
Saint-Ouen-en-Brie, Fr. 36/L6
Saint-Ouen-L'Aumône, Fr. 36/J4
Saint-Pabu, Fr. 62/A3
Saint-Pacôme, Qu, Can. 188/C2
Saint-Pair-sur-Mer, Fr. 62/D3
Saint-Pamphile, Qu, Can. 188/C2
Saint-Pascal, Qu, Can. 188/C2
Saint-Paterne, Fr. 63/F4
Saint-Pathus, Fr. 36/L4
Saint-Paul, Fr. 70/D5
Saint-Paul, Fr. 70/C3
Saint-Paul-du-Nord, Qu, Can. 188/C1
Saint-Paul-en-Jarez, Fr. 70/A2
Saint-Paul-lès-Dax, Fr. 50/C5
Saint-Paul-Trois-Châteaux, Fr. 70/A4
Saint-Pé-de-Bigorre, Fr. 50/C5
Saint-Péray, Fr. 70/A3
Saint-Père-en-Retz, Fr. 62/C6
Saint-Philippe-de-Laprairie, Qu, Can. 189/P7
Saint-Pierre (pt.), Qu, Can. 188/E1
Saint-Pierre, StP., Fr. 189/J2
Saint-Pierre (lake), Qu, Can. 188/A2
Saint-Pierre, It. 70/D1
Saint-Pierre, Mart., Fr. 203/N9
Saint-Pierre, Reun., Fr. 143/S15
Saint-Pierre-d'Albigny, Fr. 70/C1
Saint-Pierre-d'Allevard, Fr. 70/C2
Saint-Pierre-de-Bœuf, Fr. 70/A2
Saint-Pierre-des-Corps, Fr. 63/F6
Saint-Pierre-des-Fleurs, Fr. 63/F2
Saint-Pierre-du-Mont, Fr. 50/C5
Saint-Pierre-du-Perray, Fr. 36/K6
Saint-Pierre-Église, Fr. 62/D1
Saint-Pierre-en-Faucigny, Fr. 66/C5
Saint-Pierre-en-Port, Fr. 63/F1
Saint-Pierre-la-Cour, Fr. 63/D4
Saint-Pierre-lès-Elbeuf, Fr. 63/G2
Saint-Pierre-Montlimart, Fr. 63/D6
Saint-Pierre-Quiberon, Fr. 62/B5
Saint-Pierre-sur-Dives, Fr. 63/E2
Saint-Point (lake), Fr. 66/C4
Saint-Pol-de-Léon, Fr. 62/B3
Saint-Pol-sur-Mer, Fr. 60/B1
Saint-Pol-sur-Ternoise, Fr. 60/B3
Saint-Pourçain-sur-Sioule, Fr. 50/E3
Saint-Prex, Swi. 66/C5
Saint-Priest, Fr. 70/A1
Saint-Prime, Qu, Can. 188/A1
Saint-Prix, Fr. 36/J4
Saint-Prosper, Qu, Can. 188/B2
Saint-Quay-Portrieux, Fr. 62/C3
Saint-Quentin, Fr. 60/C4
Saint-Quentin (pond), Fr. 36/H5
Saint-Quentin, Canal de (canal), Fr. 60/C4
Saint-Rambert-d'Albon, Fr. 70/A2
Saint-Rambert-en-Bugey, Fr. 66/B6
Saint-Raphaël, Qu, Can. 188/B2
Saint-Raphaël, Fr. 70/C6
Saint-Raymond, Qu, Can. 188/B2
Saint-Rémi, Qu, Can. 189/N7
Saint-Rémy-de-Provence, Fr. 70/A5
Saint-Rémy-lès-Chevreuse, Fr. 36/J5
Saint-Rémy-l'Honoré, Fr. 36/H5
Saint-Rémy-sur-Avre, Fr. 63/G3
Saint-Renan, Fr. 62/A4
Saint-René-de-Matane, Qu, Can. 188/D1
Saint-Roch-de-L'Achigan, Qu, Can. 189/N6
Saint-Romain-de-Colbosc, Fr. 63/F1
Saint-Romans, Fr. 70/B2
Saint-Saëns, Fr. 63/G1
Saint-Saturnin-lès-Apt, Fr. 70/B5
Saint-Saturnin-lès-Avignon, Fr. 70/A5
Saint-Saulve, Fr. 60/C3
Saint-Sauveur, Fr. 66/C2
Saint-Sauveur-des-Monts, Qu, Can. 189/M6
Saint-Sauveur-le-Vicomte, Fr. 62/D2
Saint-Sauveur-Lendelin, Fr. 62/D2
Saint-Savin, Fr. 70/B1
Saint-Sébastien, Qu, Can. 188/B3
Saint-Sébastien-sur-Loire, Fr. 62/D6
Saint-Sever, Fr. 50/C5
Saint-Sever-Calvados, Fr. 63/D3
Saint-Siméon-de-Bressieux, Fr. 70/B2
Saint-Soupplets, Fr. 36/L4
Saint-Sulpice, Fr. 50/D5
Saint-Sylvain-d'Anjou, Fr. 63/E5
Saint-Symphorien (arpt.), Fr. 63/F6
Saint-Symphorien-d'Ozon, Fr. 70/A1
Saint-Théodore-d'Acton, Qu, Can. 191/K2
Saint-Théophile, Qu, Can. 188/B3
Saint-Timothée, Qu, Can. 189/M7
Saint-Trivier-de-Courtes, Fr. 66/B5
Saint-Tropez (gulf), Fr. 70/C6
Saint-Tropez, Fr. 70/C6
Saint-Ubalde, Qu, Can. 188/A2
Saint-Urbain, Fr. 66/B1
Saint-Urbain, Qu, Can. 188/B2
Saint-Urbain-Premier, Qu, Can. 189/N7
Saint-Ursanne, Swi. 66/D3
Saint-Uze, Fr. 70/A2
Saint-Vaast-la-Hougue, Fr. 62/D1
Saint-Valery-en-Caux, Fr. 63/F1
Saint-Valery-sur-Somme, Fr. 60/A3
Saint-Vallier, Fr. 70/A2
Saint-Vallier, Fr. 50/F3
Saint-Vallier-de-Thiey, Fr. 70/C5
Saint-Vaury, Fr. 50/D3
Saint-Viâtre, Fr. 63/G5
Saint-Vigor-le-Grand, Fr. 63/E2
Saint-Vincent-de-Tyrosse, Fr. 50/C5
Saint-Vincent-des-Landes, Fr. 62/D5
Saint-Vit, Fr. 66/B3
Saint-Vith, Belg. 61/F3
Saint-Vrain, Fr. 36/K6
Saint-Wandrille-Rançon, Fr. 63/F1
Saint-Witz, Fr. 36/K4
Saint-Yrieix-la-Perche, Fr. 50/D4
Saint-Yvy, Fr. 62/B5
Saint-Zacharie, Fr. 70/B6
Saintala, India 107/D1
Sainte Agathe, Mb, Can. 186/F3
Sainte Amélie, Mb, Can. 186/E2
Sainte Anne, Mb, Can. 186/F3
Sainte Genevieve, Mo, US 192/B2
Sainte Rose du Lac, Mb, Can. 186/E2
Sainte-Adèle, Qu, Can. 191/J2
Sainte-Adresse, Fr. 63/F1
Sainte-Agathe-des-Monts, Qu, Can. 191/J1
Sainte-Anne-D'Auray, Fr. 62/C5
Sainte-Anne-de-Beaupré, Qu, Can. 188/B2
Sainte-Anne-de-Madawaska, NB, Can. 188/C2
Sainte-Anne-des-Monts, Qu, Can. 188/D1
Sainte-Anne-des-Plaines, Qu, Can. 189/N6
Sainte-Anne-du-Lac, Qu, Can. 191/J1
Sainte-Aulde, Fr. 36/M5
Sainte-Blandine, Qu, Can. 188/C1
Sainte-Cécile-les-Vignes, Fr. 70/A4
Sainte-Croix, Swi. 66/C4
Sainte-Croix, Qu, Can. 188/B2
Sainte-Croix-aux-Mines, Fr. 66/D1
Sainte-Florence, Qu, Can. 188/D1
Sainte-Foy-lès-Lyon, Fr. 70/A1
Sainte-Françoise, Qu, Can. 188/C1
Sainte-Gemmes-sur-Loire, Fr. 63/E6
Sainte-Geneviève-de-Batiscan, Qu, Can. 188/A2
Sainte-Geneviève-des-Bois, Fr. 36/K6
Sainte-Hénédine, Qu, Can. 188/B2
Sainte-Jamme-sur-Sarthe, Fr. 63/F4
Sainte-Julie, Qu, Can. 189/P6
Sainte-Julienne, Qu, Can. 191/K2
Sainte-Luce-sur-Loire, Fr. 62/D6
Sainte-Marie, Qu, Can. 188/B2
Sainte-Marie, Mart., Fr. 203/N9
Sainte-Marie-aux-Chênes, Fr. 61/F5
Sainte-Martine, Qu, Can. 189/N7
Sainte-Maxime, Fr. 70/C6
Sainte-Menehould, Fr. 61/D5
Sainte-Mère-Église, Fr. 62/D2
Sainte-Mesme, Fr. 36/H6
Sainte-Reine-de-Bretagne, Fr. 62/C6
Sainte-Rose-de-Watford, Qu, Can. 188/B2
Sainte-Rose-du-Nord, Qu, Can. 188/B1
Sainte-Sigolène, Fr. 50/F4
Sainte-Suzanne, Fr. 63/E4
Sainte-Thècle, Qu, Can. 188/A2
Sainte-Thérèse, Qu, Can. 189/N6
Sainte-Tulle, Fr. 70/B5
Sainte-Véronique, Qu, Can. 191/J1
Saintes, Fr. 50/C4
Saintfield, NI, UK 40/C3
Sainthia, India 109/F4
Saipan (isl.), NMar. 160/D3
Saipina, Bol. 224/C1
Sairakkala, Fin. 45/F4
Saiss (Fez) (int'l arpt.), Mor. 130/B3
Saitama (pref.), Japan 97/F2
Saito, Japan 96/B4
Saiwa Swamp NP, Kenya 137/A1
Sajama, Bol. 220/D5
Sajama (peak), Bol. 224/B1
Sajama NP, Bol. 224/B1
Sajānan, Tun. 130/L6
Sajószentpéter, Hun. 49/L4
Sak (riv.), SAfr. 142/C3
Sakado, Japan 95/C2
Sakae, Japan 95/E2
Sakahogi, Japan 95/L5
Sakai, Japan 97/F2
Sakai, Japan 96/E2
Sakai (riv.), Japan 95/C3
Sakai, Japan 95/C1
Sakaide, Japan 96/C3
Sakaigawa, Japan 95/B2
Sakaiminato, Japan 96/C3
Sakākah, SAr. 114/E4
Sakakawea (lake), ND, US 186/C4
Sakami (lake), Qu, Can. 171/J3
Sakania, D.R. Congo 141/F2
Sakar (isl.), PNG 153/G1
Sakaraha, Madg. 143/H8
Sakarya (riv.), Turk. 76/D4
Sakarya (prov.), Turk. 76/D4
Sakata, Japan 94/A4
Sakauchi, Japan 95/K4
Sakawa, Japan 96/C4
Sakay (riv.), Madg. 143/H7
Sakçagöze, Turk. 114/D2
Sakchu, NKor. 93/C2
Sakden, Bhu. 105/F2
Sake, D.R. Congo 139/G3
Sakeny (riv.), Madg. 143/H7
Saketa, Indo. 103/G4
Sakété, Ben. 133/F5
Sakhā, Egypt 131/B2
Sakha, Resp., Rus. 83/N3
Sakhalin (isl.), Rus. 83/P4
Sakhalin (gulf), Rus. 81/Q4

Sakha – San Mar
327

Sakhalinskaya Oblast, Rus. 81/Q4
Sakhnīn, Isr. 117/C3
Sakhnovshchyna, Ukr. 79/H3
Sakht Sar, Iran 115/G2
Šaki, Azer. 77/H4
Šakiai, Lith. 47/K4
Sākib, Jor. 117/D4
Sakishima (isl.), Japan 83/M7
Sakmara (riv.), Rus. 77/L1
Sakon Nakhon, Thai. 106/D2
Sakrand, Pak. 113/J3
Sakrivier, SAfr. 142/C3
Saksaul'skiy, Kaz. 80/G5
Sakti, India 108/D4
Saku, Japan 97/F2
Saku, Japan 95/A1
Sakura, Japan 95/E2
Sakura, Japan 95/E1
Sakuragawa, Japan 95/E2
Sakurai, Japan 95/J6
Saky, Ukr. 79/G5
Sakya Monastery, China 109/G1
Säkylä, Fin. 47/H1
Sal (isl.), CpV. 119/K10
Sal (pt.), Hon. 206/E3
Sal (riv.), Rus. 77/G3
Sal Rei, CpV. 119/K10
Sala, Swe. 46/G2
Sala, It. 71/D6
Šal'a, Slvk. 56/C1
Sala Baganza, It. 68/D4
Sala Consilina, It. 54/D2
Sala Mok, Laos 106/C1
Sala Pac Thu, Laos 106/C2
Salabangka, Indo. 102/D4
Salacgrīva, Lat. 47/L3
Salada (lake), Mex. 204/B1
Salada, Laguna (dry lake), Mex. 178/E4
Saladas, Arg. 224/E4
Saladillo (riv.), Arg. 191/J11
Saladillo, Arg. 226/F2
Saladillo (riv.), Arg. 224/C4
Salado (riv.), Arg. 209/C6
Salado (riv.), Cuba 207/G1
Salado (riv.), NM, US 179/J3
Salado, Tx, US 180/F2
Salado del Norte (riv.), Arg. 209/C5
Salaga, Gha. 133/E4
Salagle, Som. 137/C1
Şalaḩ Ad Din (gov.), Iraq 115/E3
Sala'ilua, Sam. 161/R9
Salaise-sur-Sanne, Fr. 70/A2
Sălaj (co.), Rom. 49/M5
Sălaj (prov.), Rom. 57/F2
Salal, Chad 134/C2
Salala, Libr. 132/C5
Şalālah, Sudan 127/H4
Şalālah, Oman 112/F5
Salamá, Guat. 206/D3
Salamajärven NP, Fin. 74/E3
Salamanca, Chile 224/B4
Salamanca, Mex. 205/E4
Salamanca, Sp. 52/C2
Salamanca, NY, US 191/G3
Salamat (pref.), Chad 134/D3
Salamatof, Ak, US 201/H3
Salamina, Col. 216/C2
Salamina, Col. 219/K7
Salamís, Gre. 55/H3
Salamís (isl.), Gre. 55/N9
Salamīyah, Syria 116/E2
Salāmūn, Egypt 131/C2
Salangen, Nor. 44/F1
Salantai, Lith. 47/J3
Salar de Arizaro, Arg. 224/B3
Salar de Ascotan, Bol. 224/B2
Salar de Atacama, Chile 224/B2
Salar de Coipasa, Bol. 224/B1
Salar de la Isla, Chile 224/B3
Salar de Pedernales, Chile 224/B3
Salar de Pipanaco, Arg. 224/C4
Salar de Punta Negra, Chile 224/B3
Salar de Uyuni, Bol. 224/B2
Salas, Sp. 52/B1
Salas, Peru 220/B2
Salas de los Infantes, Sp. 52/D1
Salat (riv.), Fr. 53/F1
Salatiga, Indo. 101/E4
Salavat, Rus. 78/K1
Salaverry, Peru 220/B3
Salbris, Fr. 63/H6
Salcantay (peak), Peru 220/C4
Salcedo, Phil. 100/D3
Šalčininkai, Lith. 47/L4
Salcombe, Eng, UK 42/C6
Saldaña, Sp. 52/C1
Saldanhabaai (bay), Safr. 142/K10
Saldus, Lat. 47/K3
Sale, Austl. 157/C4
Sale, Eng, UK 41/F5
Sale, It. 68/B4
Salé, Mor. 130/A2
Salé (prov.), Mor. 130/A3
Sale (Rabat) (int'l arpt.), Mor. 130/A2
Sale City, Ga, US 195/F2
Sale Marasino, It. 68/D2
Salebabu (isl.), Indo. 103/G3
Salebhatta, India 107/D1
Salekhard, Rus. 80/G3
Salem, Ger. 67/F2
Salem, India 107/C4
Salem, Namb. 140/B4
Salem, Swe. 45/A1
Salem, Ar, US 183/J2
Salem, Il, US 192/C1
Salem, In, US 192/D1
Salem, Ma, US 191/L3
Salem, Mi, US 197/E7
Salem, Mo, US 183/J2
Salem, NH, US 191/L3
Salem, NJ, US 198/C4
Salem (co.), NJ, US 198/C4
Salem (cr.), NJ, US 198/C4
Salem, NM, US 179/J4
Salem, Oh, US 190/F4
Salem (cap.), Or, US 176/B1
Salem, SD, US 184/F2
Salem, Va, US 193/G2
Salem, WV, US 190/F5
Salemi, It. 54/C4
Salentina (pen.), It. 73/H3
Salernes, Fr. 70/C5
Salerno, It. 71/D6
Salerno (gulf), It. 71/D6
Salerno (prov.), It. 71/D6
Sales (pt.), Eng, UK 43/G3
Saleux, Fr. 60/B4
Salfit, WBnk. 117/C4
Salford, Eng, UK 41/F5
Salford (co.), Eng, UK 41/F5
Salgado Filho (int'l arpt.), Braz. 225/G4
Salgan, Rus. 75/K5
Salgar, Col. 216/C3
Salgesch, Swi. 66/D5
Salgótarján, Hun. 49/K4
Salgueiro, Braz. 219/G5
Salhus, Nor. 46/A1
Sali, Cro. 56/B4
Salida, Co, US 179/K1
Salies-de-Béarn, Fr. 50/C5
Salies-du-Salat, Fr. 50/D5
Şalīf, Yem. 136/B2
Salihli, Turk. 114/B2
Salima, Malw. 141/G2
Salīmah (oasis), Sudan 127/F4
Salin, Myan. 98/B4
Salina (pt.), Bahm. 207/H1
Salina (isl.), It. 73/G3
Salina, Ks, US 183/F1
Salina, Ut, US 179/G1
Salina Cruz, Mex. 206/C2
Salina de Rincón, Chile 224/C2
Salinas, Ecu. 216/A5
Salinas (cape), Sp. 53/G3
Salinas, Ca, US 178/B2
Salinas (riv.), Ca, US 178/B2
Salinas de Ambargasta, Arg. 224/C4
Salinas de Garci Mendoza, Bol. 224/C1
Salinas de Hidalgo, Mex. 205/E4
Salinas Grande, Arg. 224/C2
Salinas Pueblo Missions Nat'l Mon., NM, US 179/J3
Salinas Victoria, Mex. 180/D5
Salinas Y Aguada Blanca, Res. Nacional, Peru 220/D4
Saline, It. 69/D7
Saline, Sc, UK 39/C4
Saline (riv.), Ks, US 184/E4
Saline, La, US 183/H4
Saline (lake), La, US 194/B2
Saline, Mi, US 190/E3
Saline Bayou (riv.), La, US 181/H1
Salinello (riv.), It. 71/C2
Salineno, Tx, US 180/E4
Salinópolis, Braz. 219/E3
Salins-les-Bains, Fr. 66/B4
Salins-les-Thermes, Fr. 70/C2
Salisbury, Austl. 155/M8
Salisbury, NB, Can. 188/E2
Salisbury (isl.), Nun, Can. 171/J2
Salisbury, Eng, UK 43/E4
Salisbury (plain), Eng, UK 42/D4
Salisbury, Ct, US 191/K4
Salisbury, Md, US 193/K1
Salisbury, Mo, US 185/H4
Salisbury, NC, US 193/G3
Salisbury, NY, US 191/J3
Salisbury, NY, US 199/L9
Salisbury Downs, Austl. 156/B1
Salish (mts.), Mt, US 174/G3
Salitpa, Al, US 194/D2
Salitre, Ecu. 216/B5
Salitre (riv.), Braz. 223/E1
Salka, Slvk. 56/D2
Salkehatchie (riv.), SC, US 193/G4
Salla, Fin. 74/F2
Salladasburg, Pa, US 198/A1
Sallanches, Fr. 66/C6
Salland (phys. reg.), Neth. 58/D4
Sallatouk (pt.), Gui. 132/B4
Sallaumines, Fr. 60/B3
Sallent, Sp. 53/F2
Salles, Belg. 61/D3
Sallins, Ire. 38/D3
Salliqueló, Arg. 226/E3
Sallisaw, Ok, US 183/G3
Sallūm, Sudan 127/H5
Sally (pass), Ire. 40/B5
Salm (riv.), Ger. 61/F3
Salmān Pāk, Iraq 115/F3
Salmās, Iran 115/F2
Salmo, Est. 47/K2
Salmo (riv.), BC, Can. 174/F3
Salmon (mts.), Ca, US 176/B3
Salmon, Id, US 177/G1
Salmon (dam), Id, US 177/F2
Salmon (riv.), Id, US 172/C2
Salmon (peak), Tx, US 180/D3
Salmon Arm, BC, Can. 174/E2
Salmon Cove, Nf, Can. 189/L2
Salmon Creek (res.), Id, US 177/F2
Salmon Creek, Wa, US 174/C5
Salmon Falls (cr.), Id, US 177/F2
Salmon Gums, Austl. 154/D5
Salmon River, NS, Can. 188/D3
Salmon River (mts.), Id, US 172/C2
Salmon Ruin, NM, US 179/H2
Salmon, Middle Fork (riv.), Id, US 177/F1
Salmon, South Fork (riv.), Id, US 176/F1
Salmtal, Ger. 61/F4
Salo, Fin. 47/K1
Salò, It. 68/D2
Salo, CAfr. 138/D2
Salole, Eth. 136/A4
Salome, Az, US 179/F4
Salon (riv.), Fr. 48/C5
Salon, India 108/C2
Salon-de-Provence, Fr. 70/B5
Salonga (riv.), D.R. Congo 139/E3
Salonga, PN de la, D.R. Congo 139/E3
Salonta, Rom. 56/E2
Salorno (Salurn), It. 67/H5
Salouël, Fr. 60/B4
Salpausselkä (mts.), Fin. 47/M1
Salpo, Peru 220/B3
Salses-le-Château, Fr. 50/E5
Sal'sk, Rus. 79/L4
Salso (riv.), It. 54/C4
Salsomaggiore Terme, It. 68/C4
Salt (range), Pak. 110/B3
Salt (riv.), SAfr. 142/C4
Salt, Sp. 53/G2
Salt (cr.), Il, US 185/K4
Salt (cr.), Mo, US 183/J1
Salt (lakes), Tx, US 180/B2
Salt (basin), Tx, US 182/B5
Salt Cay (isl.), UK 207/J1
Salt Draw (riv.), Tx, US 180/B2
Salt Fork (riv.), Ks,Ok, US 182/E2
Salt Lake City (cap.), Ut, US 200/K12
Salt Lake City (int'l arpt.), Ut, US 200/K12
Salt Meadow Nat'l Wild. Ref., Ct, US 199/F1
Salt Plains Nat'l Wildlife Res., Ok, US 183/E2
Salt, Middle Fork (riv.), Mo, US 185/H4
Salt, North (riv.), Mo, US 185/H4
Salta, Arg. 224/C3
Salta (int'l arpt.), Arg. 224/C3
Salta (prov.), Arg. 224/C3
Saltair, BC, Can. 174/C3
Saltaire, NY, US 199/E2
Saltash, Eng, UK 42/B6
Saltburn, Eng, UK 41/H2
Saltcoats, Sk, Can. 186/C2
Saltcoats, Sc, UK 39/B5
Saltdal, Nor. 44/E2
Saltee (isls.), Ire. 38/D5
Saltfjorden (inlet), Nor. 44/E2
Saltford, Eng, UK 42/D4
Saltholm (isl.), Den. 45/J7
Saltillo, Mex. 205/E3
Saltillo, Ms, US 192/C3
Saltillo, Tn, US 192/C3
Salto, Arg. 226/E2
Salto, Braz. 225/H2
Salto (lake), It. 71/C3
Salto (riv.), It. 71/B3
Salto, Uru. 224/E4
Salto (dept.), Uru. 225/E4
Salto da Divisa, Braz. 223/F3
Salto del Guairá, Par. 225/F3
Salto Grande (res.), Arg. 224/E4
Salto Santiago (res.), Braz. 225/F3
Salton Sea (lake), Ca, US 172/C5
Salton Sea Nat'l Wild. Ref., Ca, US 178/E4
Saltpond, Gha. 133/E5
Saltsjöbaden, Swe. 45/B1
Saltvik, Fin. 47/J1
Saltville, Va, US 193/G2
Saltykovka, Rus. 77/H1
Saluda (riv.), SC, US 193/G3
Saluda, SC, US 193/G3
Saluda, Va, US 193/J2
Salug, Phil. 100/C3
Saluggia, It. 68/B3
Salunga-Landisville, Pa, US 198/B3
Sālūr, India 107/D2
Salurn (Salorno), It. 67/H5
Salut (isls.), FrG. 218/C1
Saluta, Indo. 103/G3
Saluzzo, It. 70/D3
Salvación (bay), Chile 191/B6
Salvador (lake), La, US 194/C3
Salvador, Braz. 223/F2
Salvador, Sk, Can. 175/K1
Salvador Dali Museum, Fl, US 194/K8
Salvaleón de Higüey, DRep. 203/H4
Salvaterra, Braz. 218/D3
Salvaterra de Magos, Port. 52/A3
Salvatierra, Mex. 205/E4
Salvaterra de Miño, Sp. 52/A1
Salvisa, Ky, US 192/E2
Salween (riv.), Asia 83/J8
Salween (riv.), Myan.,Thai. 106/B2
Salween (Nu) (riv.), China 90/D5
Salyan, Azer. 115/G2
Salyan, Nepal 108/D1
Salyersville, Ky, US 193/F2
Salza (riv.), Aus. 49/H5
Salzach (riv.), Ger. 48/G5
Salzano, It. 69/F2
Salzbergen, Ger. 59/E4
Salzburg (prov.), Aus. 49/G5
Salzgitter, Ger. 59/H4
Salzhausen, Ger. 59/H2
Salzhemmendorf, Ger. 59/G4
Salzkotten, Ger. 59/F5
Salzwedel, Ger. 48/F2
Sam, Gabon 138/B2
Sam Houston Memorial Museum, Tx, US 181/G2
Sam Khok, Thai. 106/C3
Sam Ngao, Thai. 106/B2
Sam Rayburn (res.), Tx, US 181/G2
Sam Rayburn (dam), Tx, US 181/G2
Sam Sao (mts.), Laos,Viet. 106/C1
Sam Son, Viet. 106/D2
Sama, Sp. 52/C1
Samādūn, Egypt 131/B4
Samagaltay, Rus. 111/G1
Samaipata, Bol. 224/D1
Samak (cape), Indo. 101/D3
Samalayuca, Mex. 180/B2
Samales Group (isls.), Phil. 100/C4
Samālka, India 110/D5
Samālūţ, Egypt 127/F2
Samāna, India 110/D4
Samana (cay), Bahm. 203/H4
Samana (isl.), Bahm. 207/H1
Samaná, Col. 219/K7
Samanco, Peru 220/B3
Samandağı, Turk. 116/D1
Samandira, Turk. 115/N7
Samani, Japan 94/C2
Samaniego, Col. 216/B4
Samannūd, Egypt 131/C3
Samar (isl.), Phil. 83/M8
Samar (sea), Phil. 100/D3
Samar, Jor. 117/D3
Samara (int'l arpt.), Rus. 77/J1
Samara, Rus. 77/J1
Samara (riv.), Rus. 77/K1
Samaraskaya Oblast, Rus. 77/J1
Samarai, PNG 160/E6
Samarate, It. 68/B2
Samarga (riv.), Rus. 91/M2
Samaria (reg.), Isr. 117/C4
Samariapo, Ven. 216/E3
Samarinda, Indo. 103/E4
Samarqand, Uzb. 80/G6
Sāmarrā', Iraq 115/E3
Samarskoye, Rus. 77/L1
Samarskoye, Rus. 79/K4
Samasata, Pak. 110/A5
Samāstipur, India 109/E3
Samate, Indo. 103/H4
Samatigila, C.d'Iv. 132/D4
Şamaxi, Azer. 77/J4
Sāmba, India 110/C3
Samba, D.R. Congo 139/E2
Samba, D.R. Congo 139/F4
Samba Lucala, Ang. 138/C5
Sambaíba, Braz. 219/E4
Sambaïlo, Gui. 132/B3
Sambao (riv.), Madg. 143/H7
Sambar (cape), Indo. 102/D4
Sambas, Indo. 102/C3
Sambava, Madg. 143/J6
Samberbaba, Indo. 103/J4
Sambhal, India 108/B1
Sambili, D.R. Congo 134/D4
Sambir, Ukr. 49/M4
Sambo, Ang. 140/C2
Sambo, Indo. 103/E4
Sambong-ni, NKor. 93/E2
Sambor Prei Kuk (ruin), Camb. 106/D3
Samborombón (riv.), Arg. 191/K11
Samborombón (bay), Arg. 191/F2
Sambre (riv.), Fr. 48/C3
Sambre à l'Oise, Canal de (canal), Fr. 60/C4
Sambriāl, Pak. 110/C3
Sambro, NS, Can. 188/F3
Sambu, Japan 95/E2
Sambuceto, It. 71/D3
Samburu, Kenya 137/B2
Samburu Nat'l Rsv., Kenya 137/B1
Samchi, Bhu. 109/G2
Samch'ŏk, SKor. 96/A2
Samch'ŏnp'o, SKor. 93/E5
Samdrup Jongkhar, Bhu. 109/H2
Same, Tanz. 137/B3
Same, ETim. 155/E2
Samedan, Swi. 67/F4
Samer, Fr. 60/A2
Samfya Mission, Zam. 141/F1
Sámi, Gre. 55/G3
Sami, Myan. 98/B4
Saminskiy Pogost, Rus. 74/H3
Samiria (riv.), Peru 220/C2
Samit (cape), Camb. 106/C4
Samiyŏn, NKor. 93/E2
Samka, Myan. 106/B1
Şāmkir, Azer. 77/H4
Samkos (peak), Camb. 106/C3
Sammamish (lake), Wa, US 197/C2
Sammatti, Fin. 45/D4
Sammeron, Fr. 36/M5
Samnangjin, SKor. 96/A3
Samnaun, Swi. 67/G4
Samnorwood, Tx, US 182/D3
Samnū, Libya 126/B3
Samo Alto, Chile 224/B4
Samoa (ctry.) 161/R9
Samobor, Cro. 56/B3
Samoëns, Fr. 66/C5
Samoggia (riv.), It. 69/E4
Samokov, Bul. 57/F4
Samora (riv.), Port. 53/Q10
Samora Correia, Port. 53/Q10
Sámos, Gre. 114/A2
Sámos (isl.), Gre. 114/A2
Samothráki, Gre. 55/J2
Samouay, Laos 106/D2
Samoylovka, Rus. 77/G2
Sampacho, Arg. 226/D2
Sampang, Indo. 101/F4
Samper de Calanda, Sp. 53/E2
Sampeyre, It. 70/D3
Sampit (riv.), Indo. 102/D4
Sampit, Indo. 102/D4
Sampwe, D.R. Congo 139/F5
Samrāla, India 110/D4
Samrē, Eth. 136/A2
Samrong Thap, Thai. 106/C3
Sams, Co, US 179/J1
Samsang, China 111/D5
Samsø (isl.), Den. 46/D4
Samsø Bælt (chan.), Den. 46/D4
Samson, Al, US 195/E2
Samson (mt.), Austl. 158/E6
Samson Ind. Res., Ab, Can. 175/H1
Samsonvale (lake), Austl. 158/E6
Samsu, NKor. 93/E2
Samsun, Turk. 76/F4
Samsun (prov.), Turk. 76/E4
Samthar, India 108/B3
Samuel (mt.), Austl. 152/D4
Samuels, Id, US 174/F3
Samugheo, It. 54/A3
Samui (isl.), Thai. 105/H6
Samukawa, Japan 95/C3
Samundri, Pak. 110/B4
Samur (riv.), Azer.,Rus. 80/E5
Samur (riv.), Rus. 77/H4
Samut Prakan, Thai. 106/C3
Samut Sakhon, Thai. 106/C3
Samut Songkhram, Thai. 106/B3
Samye Monastery, China 109/H1
San, Mali 132/D3
San (riv.), Pol. 76/B2
San (riv.), Camb. 106/D3
San (riv.), China 91/H5
San Acacia, NM, US 179/J3
San Adrián, Cabo de (cape), Sp. 52/A1
San Agustín, Col. 216/B4
San Agustin (cape), Phil. 100/D4
San Agustín, Bol. 224/C2
San Agustín, Bol. 221/F5
San Agustin de Guadalix, Sp. 53/N8
San Agustín, Parque Arqeológico, Col. 216/B4
San Agustin, Plains of (plains), NM, US 179/H4
Şān al Ḩajar al Qiblīyah, Egypt 131/C3
San Ambrosio (isl.), Chile 209/B5
San Andreas (lake), Ca, US 197/J11
San Andreas, Ca, US 176/C4
San Andrés, Bol. 221/E4
San Andrés, Col. 207/F3
San Andrés, Col. 216/C3
San Andrés, Col. 216/C3
San Andrés (lake), Mex. 206/B1
San Andres, Phil. 100/D2
San Andres (mts.), NM, US 179/J4
San Andrés Cuexcontitlán, Mex. 205/Q10
San Andrés de Giles, Arg. 191/J11
San Andrés de Machaca, Bol. 220/D5
San Andrés del Rabanedo, Sp. 52/C1
San Andres Nat'l Wild Ref., NM, US 179/J4
San Andrés Tuxtla, Mex. 206/C2
San Andrés, Isla de (isl.), Col. 202/E5
San Angelo, Tx, US 180/D2
San Anselmo, Ca, US 197/J11
San Antonio (cape), Arg. 191/F3
San Antonio, Arg. 226/D2
San Antonio, Bol. 221/E4
San Antonio, Chile 226/N8
San Antonio, Ecu. 216/B4
San Antonio, Mex. 204/C4
San Antonio, Peru 220/B4
San Antonio, Phil. 100/C2
San Antonio, Uru. 191/K11
San Antonio, Ven. 217/E2
San Antonio, Ven. 217/F2
San Antonio (res.), Ca, US 178/B3
San Antonio (mt.), Ca, US 196/C2
San Antonio, Fl, US 194/L7
San Antonio, NM, US 179/J4
San Antonio (mtn.), NM, US 179/J2
San Antonio, Tx, US 200/U21
San Antonio (bay), Tx, US 181/F3
San Antonio (riv.), Tx, US 200/U20
San Antonio (riv.), Tx, US 181/F3
San Antonio Abad, Sp. 53/F3
San Antonio de Areco, Arg. 191/J11
San Antonio de Caparo, Ven. 216/D3
San Antonio de Lípez, Bol. 224/C2
San Antonio de los Cobres, Arg. 224/C3
San Antonio de Tabasca, Ven. 217/F2
San Antonio de Tamanaco, Ven. 219/P8
San Antonio del Golfo, Ven. 217/F2
San Antonio del Táchira, Ven. 216/C3
San Antonio Oeste, Arg. 226/D4
San Antonio, Punta (pt.), Mex. 204/B2
San Ardo, Ca, US 178/B2
San Augustin (pass), NM, US 179/J4
San Augustine, Tx, US 181/G2
San Bartolo, Peru 220/B4
San Bartolomé de Tirajana, Sp. 128/B4
San Bartolome Tlaltelulco, Mex. 205/Q10
San Bartolomeo in Bosco, It. 69/E4
San Bartolomeo in Galdo, It. 71/E5
San Bautista, Uru. 191/L11
San Benedetto (range), It. 69/E5
San Benedetto dei Marsi, It. 71/C3
San Benedetto del Tronto, It. 71/C2
San Benedetto in Alpe, It. 69/E6
San Benedetto Po, It. 69/D3
San Benedicto (isl.), Mex. 204/C5
San Benito (mtn.), Ca, US 178/B2
San Benito (riv.), Ca, US 178/B2
San Benito, Tx, US 180/F4
San Bernard (riv.), Tx, US 181/F3
San Bernard NWR, Tx, US 181/G3
San Bernardino, Swi. 67/F5
San Bernardino (mts.), Ca, US 196/C2
San Bernardino (co.), Ca, US 196/C2
San Bernardino, Ca, US 196/C2
San Bernardino (str.), Phil. 100/D2
San Bernardino Nat'l Forest, Ca, US 196/C2
San Bernardino Nat'l Wild. Ref., Az, US 179/H5
San Bernardo, Arg. 224/D3
San Bernardo (pt.), Col. 216/C2
San Bernardo, Chile 226/N8
San Bernardo, Col. 219/L8
San Blas, Mex. 180/D4
San Blas, Mex. 204/C3
San Blas, Mex. 204/D4
San Blas (cape), Fl, US 195/F3
San Bonifacio, It. 69/E3
San Borja, Bol. 221/E4
San Bruno, Ca, US 197/K11
San Bruno, Mex. 204/B3
San Buenaventura, Mex. 180/D4
San Buenaventura (Ventura), Ca, US 196/A2
San Candido (Innichen), It. 51/K3
San Carlos, Arg. 224/C3
San Carlos, Bol. 224/D1
San Carlos, Chile 226/C3
San Carlos, Col. 219/L6
San Carlos, Mex. 205/F3
San Carlos, Mex. 180/D3
San Carlos, Nic. 207/E4
San Carlos, Pan. 216/B2
San Carlos, Par. 225/E2
San Carlos, Phil. 100/C2
San Carlos, Ven. 216/D2
San Carlos, Uru. 191/G2
San Carlos, Az, US 179/G4
San Carlos, Ca, US 197/K11
San Carlos (lake), Az, US 179/G4
San Carlos de Bariloche, Arg. 226/C4
San Carlos de Bariloche (int'l arpt.), Arg. 226/C4
San Carlos de Río Negro, Ven. 217/E4
San Carlos del Zulia, Ven. 216/D2
San Carlos Ind. Res., Az, US 179/G4
San Casciano in Val di Pesa, It. 69/E6
San Casimiro, Ven. 219/N7
San Cataldo, It. 55/F2
San Cayetano, Arg. 226/F3
San Cayetano, Col. 219/L7
San Cesario sul Panaro, It. 69/E4
San Cipriano d'Aversa, It. 71/D5
San Ciro de Acosta, Mex. 205/F4
San Clemente, Ca, US 196/C4
San Clemente, Sp. 53/D3
San Clemente, Chile 226/C2
San Clemente (isl.), Ca, US 178/C4
San Clemente del Tuyú, Arg. 191/F3
San Clemente in Casauria, It. 71/C3
San Colombano al Lambro, It. 68/C3
San Cristóbal, Arg. 224/D4
San Cristóbal, Bol. 224/C2
San Cristóbal, Bol. 221/F4
San Cristóbal, Cuba 207/F1
San Cristóbal, Ecu. 220/K7
San Cristóbal (vol.), Nic. 206/E3
San Cristobal (isl.), Sol. 160/F6
San Cristobal, NM, US 182/B2
San Cristóbal, Ven. 216/C3
San Cristóbal de las Casas, Mex. 206/C2
San Cristobal Wash (riv.), Az, US 179/F4
San Damiano d'Asti, It. 68/B4
San Damiano Macra, It. 70/D4
San Demetrio ne'Vestini, It. 71/C3
San Diego (cape), Arg. 191/D7
San Diego, Bol. 221/F5
San Diego, Bol. 224/C2
San Diego (co.), Ca, US 196/C4
San Diego (bay), Ca, US 196/C5
San Diego (aqueduct), Ca, US 196/C4
San Diego, Ca, US 196/C5
San Diego (riv.), Ca, US 178/D4
San Diego, Tx, US 181/E4
San Diego International-Lindbergh Field (int'l arpt.), Ca, US 196/C5
San Diego Naval Station, Ca, US 196/C5
San Diego Wild Animal Park, Ca, US 196/C4
San Diego Zoo, Ca, US 196/C5
San Diequito (riv.), Ca, US 196/C5
San Dimas, Ca, US 196/C2
San Donà di Piave, It. 69/F2
San Donato Val di Comino, It. 71/C4
San Donnino, It. 69/E6
San Dorligo della Valle, It. 69/G2
San Elizario, Tx, US 180/A2
San Estanislao, Par. 225/E3
San Esteban de Gormaz, Sp. 52/D2
San Fabián de Alico, Chile 226/C3
San Felice a Cancello, It. 71/D6
San Felice Circeo, It. 71/C5
San Felice del Benaco, It. 68/D2
San Felice sul Panaro, It. 69/E4
San Felipe, Ven. 216/C2
San Felipe, Ven. 216/D2
San Felipe (cr.), Ca, US 178/D4
San Felipe, Chile 226/N8
San Felipe, Mex. 204/B2
San Felipe de Puerto Plata, DRep. 203/G4
San Felipe de Vichayal, Peru 220/A2
San Felipe Ind. Res., NM, US 179/J3
San Felipe Jalapa de Díaz, Mex. 205/F5
San Felipe Pueblo, NM, US 179/J3
San Felipe Torres Mochas, Mex. 205/E4
San Felix (isl.), Chile 209/A5
San Fernando, Arg. 191/J11
San Fernando, Arg. 224/C3
San Fernando, Chile 226/C2
San Fernando, Phil. 100/C2
San Fernando, Phil. 100/C1
San Fernando, Phil. 100/C2
San Fernando, Sp. 52/B4
San Fernando, Trin. 217/F2
San Fernando (valley), Ca, US 196/B2
San Fernando, Ca, US 196/F7
San Fernando de Apure, Ven. 217/E3
San Fernando de Atabapo, Ven. 216/E3
San Fernando de Henares, Sp. 53/N9
San Fernando de Presas, Mex. 205/F3
San Fidel, NM, US 179/J3
San Fior di Sopra, It. 69/F2
San Francesco al Campo, It. 68/A2
San Francisco (riv.), Arg. 224/C2
San Francisco, Arg. 224/D4
San Francisco, Bol. 221/E4
San Francisco, Bol. 224/E1
San Francisco, Col. 219/L8
San Francisco, Col. 216/B4
San Francisco, ESal. 206/D3
San Francisco, Phil. 100/C2
San Francisco, Phil. 100/D3
San Francisco (mts.), Az, US 179/G3
San Francisco (riv.), Az, US 179/H4
San Francisco (bay), Ca, US 178/A2
San Francisco (co.), Ca, US 197/K11
San Francisco (cr.), Tx, US 180/C3
San Francisco, Ven. 216/D2
San Francisco Acuautla, Mex. 205/R10
San Francisco Bay NWR, Ca, US 197/K11
San Francisco Chimalpa, Mex. 205/Q10
San Francisco de la Paz, Hon. 206/E3
San Francisco de Macorís, DRep. 203/G4
San Francisco de Mostazal, Chile 226/N8
San Francisco de Tiznados, Ven. 219/N8
San Francisco del Chañar, Arg. 224/D4
San Francisco del Mezquital, Mex. 204/D4
San Francisco del Monte de Oro, Arg. 226/D2
San Francisco del Oro, Mex. 204/D3
San Francisco del Rincón, Mex. 205/E4
San Francisco Telixtlahuaca, Mex. 202/B4
San Francisco, Cabo de (cape), Ecu. 216/A4
San Francisco, Paso de (pass), Arg.,Chile 224/B3
San Fratello, It. 54/D3
San Gabriel, Chile 226/N8
San Gabriel, Ecu. 216/B4
San Gabriel, (pt.), Mex. 204/B2
San Gabriel, Ca, US 196/F7
San Gabriel (mts.), Ca, US 178/C3
San Gabriel (res.), Ca, US 196/C2
San Gabriel (riv.), Ca, US 196/C2
San Gavino Monreale, It. 54/A3
San Gemini, It. 71/B2
San Genaro, Arg. 224/D5
San Germán, Cuba 207/G1
San Germano Vercellese, It. 68/B3
San Giacomo (Sankt Jakob), It. 67/H4
San Gil, Col. 216/C3
San Gimignano, It. 69/E7
San Ginesio, It. 71/C1
San Giorgio a Cremano, It. 71/D6
San Giorgio del Sannio, It. 71/D5
San Giorgio delle Pertiche, It. 69/E2
San Giorgio di Piano, It. 69/E4
San Giorgio Ionico, It. 55/E2
San Giorgio Piacentino, It. 68/C4
San Giovanni al Natisone, It. 69/G2
San Giovanni Bianco, It. 68/C2
San Giovanni Gemini, It. 54/C4
San Giovanni in Croce, It. 68/D3
San Giovanni in Fiore, It. 54/E3
San Giovanni in Marignano, It. 69/F6
San Giovanni in Persiceto, It. 69/E4
San Giovanni in Venere, It. 71/D3
San Giovanni Lupatoto, It. 69/E3
San Giovanni Rotondo, It. 54/D2
San Giovanni Valdarno, It. 69/E6
San Giuliano, It. 68/B4
San Giuliano Terme, It. 68/D6
San Giuseppe Vesuviano, It. 71/D6
San Giustino, It. 69/F6
San Giusto Canavese, It. 68/A2
San Gorgonio (mtn.), Ca, US 178/D3
San Gottardo, Passo del (pass), Swi. 67/E4
San Gregorio, Arg. 226/E2
San Gregorio, Uru. 191/L10
San Gregorio, Uru. 191/K10
San Gregorio, Ca, US 197/K12
San Guiliano Milanese, It. 68/C3
San Guillermo, Arg. 224/D4
San Hipólito Punta (pt.), Mex. 204/B3
San Ignacio, Belz. 206/D2
San Ignacio, Bol. 221/E4
San Ignacio, Bol. 221/F5
San Ignacio, Bol. 224/D1
San Ignacio, Chile 226/B3
San Ignacio (riv.), Mex. 204/B2
San Ignacio, Mex. 204/D4
San Ignacio, Mex. 204/B3
San Ignacio, Par. 225/E3
San Ignacio, Peru 220/B2
San Ildefonso, Sp. 52/D2
San Ildefonso (cape), Phil. 100/C1
San Isidro, CR 207/F4
San Isidro, Nic. 206/E3
San Isidro de Curuguaty, Par. 225/F3
San Jacinto, Col. 216/C2
San Jacinto, Phil. 100/C2
San Jacinto, Uru. 191/L11
San Jacinto, Ca, US 178/D4
San Jacinto, Nv, US 177/F3
San Jacinto (dam), Tx, US 181/M9
San Jacinto Battleground, Tx, US 181/M9
San Jaime, Arg. 224/E4
San Javier, Arg. 226/E4
San Javier, Arg. 224/E4
San Javier, Bol. 221/F5
San Javier, Bol. 221/E4
San Javier, Chile 226/C2
San Javier, Sp. 53/E4
San Javier, Uru. 191/J10
San Jerónimo, Col. 219/K6
San Jerónimo, Mex. 204/E3
San Joaquin, Ca, US 178/B2
San Joaquin (co.), Ca, US 197/L11
San Joaquin (hills), Ca, US 196/G8
San Joaquin (riv.), Ca, US 178/B2
San Joaquin (valley), Ca, US 178/B2
San Joaquín (riv.), Bol. 221/F4
San Joaquín, Col. 216/C3
San Joaquín (peak), Ecu. 220/K7
San Joaquín, Bol. 221/E4
San Joaquín, Par. 225/E3
San Joaquín, Ven. 219/N7
San Joaquin, South Fork (riv.), Ca, US 178/C2
San Jorge, Arg. 224/D4
San Jorge (cape), Arg. 226/D5
San Jorge (gulf), Arg. 209/C7
San Jorge (riv.), Col. 207/H5
San Jorge (bay), Mex. 204/B2
San Jorge (gulf), Sp. 72/D2
San José, Arg. 224/C4
San José (gulf), Arg. 226/D4
San José (cap.), CR 207/E4
San José, Col. 216/B4
San José (isl.), Mex. 204/C3
San José, Peru 220/B2
San José, Peru 220/D4
San Jose, Phil. 100/C2
San Jose, Phil. 100/C3
San José, Sp. 53/F3
San José (dept.), Uru. 191/K11
San José, Ven. 216/E3
San Jose (riv.), Uru. 191/K10
San Jose (hills), Ca, US 196/G7
San Jose, Il, US 185/K3
San Jose (riv.), NM, US 179/J3
San Jose (isl.), Tx, US 181/F4
San José de Amacuro, Ven. 217/F2
San José de Aura, Mex. 180/D4
San José de Chiquitos, Bol. 224/D1
San José de Feliciano, Arg. 224/E4
San José de Guanipa, Ven. 217/E2
San José de Guaribe, Ven. 217/E2
San José de Jáchal, Arg. 224/B4
San Jose de la Banda (int'l arpt.), Bol. 224/C1
San José de la Esquina, Arg. 226/E2
San Jose de Los Molinos, Peru 220/C4
San José de los Remates, Nic. 206/E3
San José de Maipo, Chile 226/N8
San José de Mayo, Uru. 191/K11
San José de Raíces, Mex. 205/E3
San José de Río Chico, Ven. 219/P7
San José de Seque, Ven. 216/D2
San José de Tiznados, Ven. 219/N8
San José del Cabo, Mex. 204/C4
San José del Guaviare, Col. 216/C4
San Jose del Monte, Phil. 100/F6
San José del Ocuné, Col. 216/D3
San José Iturbide, Mex. 205/E4
San José Viejo, Mex. 204/C4
San Juan (cape), Arg. 191/E7
San Juan (prov.), Arg. 224/B4
San Juan, Arg. 224/B4
San Juan (riv.), Bol. 224/C1
San Juan, Bol. 224/E1
San Juan (riv.), Col. 216/B3
San Juan (cape), EqG. 138/B2
San Juan (pt.), ESal. 206/D3
San Juan (riv.), Nic. 202/E5
San Juan, Peru 220/C4
San Juan, Peru 220/C4
San Juan, Phil. 100/C2
San Juan, Phil. 100/D3
San Juan, PR 203/M8
San Juan (cr.), Ca, US 196/C4
San Juan (mts.), Co, US 172/E4
San Juan (basin), NM, US 179/H2
San Juan, NM, US 179/J4
San Juan (isl.), Wa, US 174/C3
San Juan Abajo, Mex. 204/D4
San Juan Bautista, Ca, US 178/B2
San Juan Bautista, Par. 225/E3
San Juan Bautista Coixtlahuaca, Mex. 206/B2
San Juan Bautista de Ñeembucú, Par. 224/E3
San Juan Bautista Tuxtepec, Mex. 206/B2
San Juan Bautista Valle Nacional, Mex. 206/B2
San Juan Capistrano, Ca, US 196/C3
San Juan de Alicante, Sp. 53/E3
San Juan de Aznalfarache, Sp. 52/B4
San Juan de la Costa, Mex. 204/C3
San Juan de Lima, (pt.), Mex. 204/E5
San Juan de los Cayos, Ven. 216/D2
San Juan de los Lagos, Mex. 204/E4
San Juan de los Morros, Ven. 219/N8
San Juan de Manapiare, Ven. 217/E3
San Juan de Ríoseco, Col. 219/L8
San Juan del Norte, Nic. 207/F4
San Juan del Piray, Bol. 224/C2
San Juan del Potrero, Bol. 224/C1
San Juan del Río, Mex. 205/F4
San Juan Guichicovi, Mex. 202/B4
San Juan Hot Springs, Ca, US 196/C3
San Juan Ixcaquixtla, Mex. 205/M8
San Juan Juquila Mixes, Mex. 206/C2
San Juan Nat'l Wild. Ref., Wa, US 174/C3
San Juan Nepomuceno, Col. 216/C2
San Juan Nepomuceno, Par. 225/F3
San Juan Pueblo, NM, US 179/J2
San Juanico, Mex. 204/B3
San Juanico Punta (pt.), Mex. 204/B3
San Juanito, Mex. 204/D2
San Justo, Arg. 224/D4
San Lázaro, Par. 224/E2
San Lázaro (cape), Mex. 204/B3
San Lazzaro, It. 69/E5
San Leandro (res.), Ca, US 197/K11
San Leandro, Ca, US 197/K11
San Leon, Tx, US 181/N9
San Leonardo in Passiria (Sankt Leonhard in Passeier), It. 67/H4
San Lorenzo, Bol. 221/E4
San Lorenzo, Bol. 221/F5
San Lorenzo, Bol. 224/C2
San Lorenzo (peak), Chile 191/B5
San Lorenzo, Ecu. 216/B4
San Lorenzo, Hon. 206/E3
San Lorenzo (cape), It. 54/A3
San Lorenzo (isl.), Mex. 204/D3
San Lorenzo, Nic. 206/E3
San Lorenzo, Peru 220/D3
San Lorenzo, Ca, US 197/K11
San Lorenzo, NM, US 179/J4
San Lorenzo al Mare, It. 68/A5
San Lorenzo de El Escorial, Sp. 53/M8
San Lorenzo in Campo, It. 69/F6
San Lucas, Nic. 206/E3
San Lucas, Bol. 224/C2
San Lucas, Cabo (cape), Mex. 204/C4
San Luis, Arg. 226/D2
San Luis (prov.), Arg. 224/C5
San Lucas, Ca, US 178/B2
San Luis (lake), Bol. 221/E4
San Luis, Bol. 224/E1
San Luis, Col. 219/K8
San Luis, Col. 219/L6
San Luis, Cuba 207/H1
San Luis, Guat. 206/D2
San Luis, Peru 220/B4
San Luis, Ven. 216/D2
San Luis, Az, US 178/E4
San Luis (dam), Ca, US 178/B2
San Luis (res.), Ca, US 178/B2
San Luis (cr.), Co, US 179/K1
San Luis, Co, US 182/B2
San Luis (valley), Co, US 179/J2
San Luis Acatlán, Mex. 206/B2
San Luis al Medio, Uru. 191/G2
San Luis Archaeological Site, Fl, US 195/F2
San Luis de la Paz, Mex. 205/E4
San Luis NWR, Ca, US 178/B2
San Luis Obispo, Ca, US 178/B3
San Luis Potosí (state), Mex. 202/A3
San Luis Potosí, Mex. 205/E4
San Luis Rey (riv.), Ca, US 196/C4
San Luis Rey, Ca, US 196/C4
San Manuel, Az, US 179/G4
San Manuel, Chile 224/B3
San Marcello Pistoiese, It. 69/D5
San Marco (peak), It. 71/D5
San Marco dei Cavoti, It. 71/D5
San Marco la Catola, It. 71/D4
San Marcos, Col. 216/C2
San Marcos, CR 207/E4
San Marcos, Guat. 206/D3
San Marcos, Mex. 202/B4
San Marcos, Peru 220/B2
San Marcos, Peru 220/B3
San Marcos, Ca, US 196/C4

Santi – Scrap
329

Santisteban del Puerto, Sp. 52/D3
Santō, Japan 95/K5
Santō, Japan 95/G5
Santo, Tx, US 181/E1
Santo Amaro, Braz. 223/F2
Santo Amara (isl.), Braz. 223/K8
Santo Amaro (isl.), Braz. 223/K8
Santo Amaro das Brotas, Braz. 223/F1
Santo Anastácio, Braz. 225/G2
Santo André, Braz. 223/K8
Santo Ângelo, Braz. 225/F4
Santo Antão (isl.), CpV. 119/J9
Santo António, SaoT. 138/A2
Santo Antônio do Içá, Braz. 216/E5
Santo Antônio do Leverger, Braz. 222/A2
Santo Antônio do Sudoeste, Braz. 225/F3
Santo Antônio dos Lopes, Braz. 219/E4
Santo Augusto, Braz. 225/F3
Santo Corazón, Bol. 224/E1
Santo Domingo, Bol. 221/E3
Santo Domingo, Cuba 207/F1
Santo Domingo, Chile 226/N8
Santo Domingo (cap.), DRep. 203/H4
Santo Domingo (pt.), Mex. 204/B3
Santo Domingo, Mex. 205/E4
Santo Domingo de la Calzada, Sp. 50/B5
Santo Domingo de los Colorados, Ecu. 216/B5
Santo Domingo Petapa, Mex. 206/C2
Santo Domingo Pueblo, NM, US 179/J3
Santo Domingo Tehuantepec, Mex. 206/C2
Santo Domingo Zanatepec, Mex. 206/C2
Santo Stefano (isl.), It. 71/C6
Santo Stefano Belbo, It. 68/B4
Santo Stefano d'Aveto, It. 68/C4
Santo Stefano di Magra, It. 68/C5
Santo Stino di Livenza, It. 69/F2
Santo Tomás (vol.), Ecu. 220/J7
Santo Tomás, Mex. 204/A2
Santo Tomás, (pt.), Mex. 204/A2
Santo Tomas (mt.), Phil. 100/C1
Santo Tomás, Peru 220/B2
Santo Tomás, Peru 220/C4
Santo Tomé, Arg. 225/E4
Santo Tomé, Arg. 224/D4
Santoña, Sp. 50/B5
Sant'Onofrio, It. 71/G8
Sant'Oreste, It. 71/B3
Santorso, It. 69/E2
Santos, Braz. 223/K8
Santos Dumont (int'l arpt.), Braz. 223/N7
Santos Dumont, Braz. 223/N6
Santos Mercado, Bol. 221/E3
Santos Reyes Nopala, Mex. 206/B2
Santuario, Col. 219/K7
Santuario, Col. 219/K6
Santuario di Crea, It. 68/B3
Santuario di Monte Vergine, It. 71/D6
Santuario di Oropa, It. 68/A1
Santunying, China 92/J6
Şānūr, WBnk. 117/C4
Sanwa, Japan 95/D1
Sanxing, China 92/L8
Sanya, China 99/F5
Sanyang, China 99/H2
Sanyati (riv.), Zim. 141/F3
Sanyuanba, China 99/E1
Sanyuanpu, China 93/C1
Sanza Pombo, Ang. 138/C4
São Bartolomeu (riv.), Braz. 222/D3
São Benedito, Braz. 219/F4
São Benedito do Rio Prêto, Braz. 219/F3
São Bento, Braz. 219/G4
São Bento, Braz. 219/E3
São Bento do Sapucaí, Braz. 223/L7
São Bento do Sul, Braz. 225/G3
São Bento do Una, Braz. 219/G5
São Bernardo do Campo, Braz. 223/K8
São Borja, Braz. 225/F4
São Braz, Cabo de (cape), Ang. 138/C5
São Carlos, Braz. 225/H2
São Cristóvão, Braz. 223/F1
São Desidério, Braz. 222/D2
São Domingos, Braz. 222/D2
São Domingos (riv.), Braz. 222/D2
São Domingos, GBis. 132/A3
São Domingos do Capim, Braz. 218/E3
São Domingos do Maranhão, Braz. 219/E4
São Félix do Araguaia, Braz. 222/C1
São Félix do Piauí, Braz. 219/F4
São Félix do Xingu, Braz. 218/D4
São Fidélis, Braz. 223/E4
São Filipe, CpV. 119/J11
São Francisco (riv.), Braz. 209/F3
São Francisco (isl.), Braz. 225/G3
São Francisco, Braz. 222/D2
São Francisco do Sul, Braz. 225/G3
São Fransisco de Assis, Braz. 225/F4
São Fransisco de Paula, Braz. 225/G4
São Gabriel, Braz. 225/F4
São Gabriel da Palha, Braz. 223/E3
São Gonçalo, Braz. 223/N7
São Gonçalo do Sapuçaí, Braz. 223/L6
São Gotardo, Braz. 225/H1
Sao Hill, Tanz. 137/A4
São Joachim da Barra, Braz. 225/H2
São João Batista, Braz. 219/E3
São João Batista, Braz. 225/G3
São João da Aliança, Braz. 222/D2
São João da Boa Vista, Braz. 223/K6
São João da Madeira, Port. 52/A2
São João da Pesqueira, Port. 52/B2
São João da Ponte, Braz. 222/D2
São João das Lampas, Port. 53/P10
São João de Meriti, Braz. 223/N7
São João del Rei, Braz. 222/D4
São João do Araguaia, Braz. 218/D4
São João do Jaguaribe, Braz. 219/G4
São João do Paraíso, Braz. 223/E2
São João do Piauí, Braz. 219/F5
São João dos Patos, Braz. 219/F4
São João Evangelista, Braz. 223/E3
São João Nepomuceno, Braz. 223/N6
São João, Serra de (mts.), Braz. 221/F3
São Joaquim, Braz. 225/G4
São Joaquim, PN de, Braz. 225/G4
São Jorge (isl.), Azor., Port. 53/S12
São José, Braz. 225/G3
São José da Laje, Braz. 219/G5
São José de Mipibu, Braz. 219/H4
São José de Ribamar, Braz. 219/E3
São José do Belmonte, Braz. 219/G4
São José do Campestre, Braz. 219/H4
São José do Egito, Braz. 219/G4
São José do Gurupi, Braz. 219/E3
São José do Norte, Braz. 225/F5
São José do Peixe, Braz. 219/F4
São José do Rio Pardo, Braz. 223/K6
São José do Rio Prêto, Braz. 225/G2
São José dos Campos, Braz. 223/L8
São José dos Pinhais, Braz. 225/G3
São Julião, Braz. 219/F4
São Lourenço, Port. 53/P11
São Lourenço, Braz. 223/L7
São Lourenço (riv.), Braz. 221/G5
São Lourenço da Mata, Braz. 219/H5
São Lourenço do Sul, Braz. 225/G4
São Lourenço d'Oeste, Braz. 225/F3
São Lucas, Ang. 138/D5
São Luís, Braz. 219/E3
São Luís de Montes Belos, Braz. 222/C3
São Luís do Curu, Braz. 219/G3
São Luís do Quitunde, Braz. 219/H5
São Luís Gonzaga, Braz. 225/F4
São Mamede, Braz. 219/G4
São Marcos (bay), Braz. 209/E3
São Marcos (riv.), Braz. 222/D3
São Martinho do Porto, Port. 52/A3
São Mateus, Braz. 223/F3
São Mateus (riv.), Braz. 223/E3
São Mateus do Maranhão, Braz. 219/E4
São Mateus do Sul, Braz. 225/G3
São Miguel (isl.), Azor., Port. 53/T13
São Miguel, Braz. 219/G4
São Miguel do Araguaia, Braz. 222/C2
São Miguel do Guamá, Braz. 219/E3
São Miguel do Tapuio, Braz. 219/F4
São Miguel d'Oeste, Braz. 225/F3
São Miguel dos Campos, Braz. 223/F1
São Nicolau (isl.), CpV. 119/J10
São Paulo, Braz. 223/K8
São Paulo (state), Braz. 222/C4
São Paulo de Olivença, Braz. 220/D1
São Paulo do Potengi, Braz. 219/H4
São Pedro do Piauí, Braz. 219/F4
São Pedro do Sul, Port. 52/A2
São Pedro do Sul, Braz. 225/F4
São Rafael, Braz. 219/G4
São Raimundo das Mangabeiras, Braz. 219/E4
São Raimundo Nonato, Braz. 219/F5
São Romão, Braz. 222/D3
São Roque (cape), Braz. 219/H4
São Roque do Pico, Azor., Port. 53/S12
São Sebastião, Braz. 223/L8
São Sebastião (isl.), Braz. 222/D4
São Sebastião (pt.), Moz. 141/G4
São Sebastião da Boa Vista, Braz. 218/D3
São Sebastião do Paraíso, Braz. 225/H2
São Sebastião do Tocantins, Braz. 218/D4
São Sebastião do Umbuzeiro, Braz. 219/G5
São Simão, Braz. 222/C3
São Simão (riv.), Braz. 221/F4
São Simão (res.), Braz. 222/C3
São Teotónio, Port. 52/A4
São Tiago (isl.), CpV. 119/K10
São Tomé (cap.), SaoT. 138/A2
São Tomé (int'l arpt.), SaoT. 138/A2
São Tomé (isl.), SaoT. 138/A2
São Tomé and Príncipe (ctry.) 138/A2
São Tomé, Cabo de (cape), Braz. 223/E4
São Vicente (cape), Port. 52/A4
São Vicente, Braz. 223/K8
São Vicente (isl.), CpV. 119/J10
São Vicente Ferrer, Braz. 219/E3
Saône (riv.), Fr. 72/E1
Saône-et-Loire (dept.), Fr. 66/B4
Saori, Japan 95/L5
Saouru, Oued (riv.), Alg. 129/E3
Sapāhār, Bang. 109/G3
Sápai, Gre. 55/J2
Sapallanga, Peru 220/C4
Sapanca, Turk. 57/K5
Saparua, Indo. 103/G4
Sapatgrām, India 109/H2
Sapawe, On, Can. 187/J3
Sapé, Braz. 219/H4
Sapele, Nga. 133/G5
Sapelo (isl.), Ga, US 195/H2
Şaphane, Turk. 76/D5
Sapiéndza (isl.), Gre. 55/G4
Sapkyo, SKor. 93/D4
Sapo (mts.), Pan. 207/G5
Sapo NP, Libr. 132/C5
Sapo-Sapo, D.R. Congo 139/E4
Saponé, Burk. 133/E3
Saposoa, Peru 220/B2
Sapozhok, Rus. 77/G1
Sappa (cr.), Ks, US 184/D4
Sappa, Middle Fork (cr.), Ks, US 182/D1
Sappa, South Fork (cr.), Ks, US 182/D1
Sappemeer, Neth. 58/D2
Sapphire, Austl. 158/B3
Sapporo, Japan 94/B2
Sapri, It. 54/D2
Sapsi (isl.), SKor. 93/D3
Sapt Kosi (riv.), Nepal 109/F2
Sapucaí (riv.), Braz. 223/L7
Sapucai (riv.), Braz. 225/H2
Sapucaia, Braz. 223/P6
Sapudi (isl.), Indo. 101/F4
Sapulpa, Ok, US 183/F3
Sapulut, Malay. 100/B4
Sāqiyat Sīdī Yūsuf, Tun. 130/L6
Saqqez, Iran 115/F2
Saquena, Peru 220/C2
Saquisilí, Ecu. 216/B5
Šar (mts.), Serb. 56/E4
Sar Dasht, Iran 115/F2
Sara, Phil. 100/C3
Sara Buri, Thai. 106/C3
Sarāb, Iran 115/F2
Sarābiyūm, Egypt 131/D3
Saraceno (peak), It. 71/D5
Saraf Doungous, Chad 134/C2
Sarafjagān, Iran 115/G3
Saragosa, Tx, US 180/C2
Saragossa (Zaragoza), Sp. 53/E2
Saraguro, Ecu. 220/B1
Sarāi Alamgir, Pak. 110/B3
Sarāi Sidhu, Pak. 110/A4
Saraikela, India 109/E4
Sarāil, Bang. 109/H3
Saraipāli, India 107/D1
Sarajevo (cap.), Bosn. 56/D4
Saraktash, Rus. 77/L2
Saraland, Al, US 194/D2
Saramabila, D.R. Congo 139/F4
Saramacca (dist.), Sur. 217/H3
Saramati (peak), India 98/B3
Sarampiuni, Bol. 220/D4
Saran, Fr. 63/G5
Saran (peak), Indo. 102/D4
Saran', Kaz. 111/B2
Saranac Lake, NY, US 191/J2
Saranda, Tanz. 137/A3
Sarandapótamos (riv.), Gre. 81/N8
Sarandë, Alb. 55/G3
Sarandi, Braz. 225/F3
Sarandí de Navarro, Uru. 191/K10
Sarandí del Yi, Uru. 191/G2
Sarandí Grande, Uru. 191/K10
Sārangagada, India 107/E1
Sarangami (isls.), Phil. 103/G2
Sarangani (isls.), Phil. 100/D4
Sārangarh, India 107/D1
Sārangpur, India 104/C3
Saranley, Som. 137/C1
Saransk, Rus. 77/H1
Sarapul, Rus. 75/M4
Sarare (riv.), Ven. 216/D3
Sāraskheri, India 108/A3
Sarasota, Fl, US 195/G4
Sarata, Ukr. 57/J2
Saratoga, Ca, US 197/K12
Saratoga, Wy, US 177/K3
Saratoga Nat'l Hist. Park, NY, US 191/K3
Saratoga Springs, NY, US 191/K3
Saratok, Malay. 102/D3
Saratov (res.), Rus. 77/J1
Saratov, Rus. 77/H2
Saratovskaya Oblast, Rus. 77/H2
Saravan, Laos 106/D3
Sarawaget (range), PNG 153/G1
Sarawak (reg.), Malay. 83/L9
Saray, Turk. 57/H5
Saraya, Sen. 132/C3
Sarayacu, Ecu. 216/B5
Sarāyan (riv.), India 108/C2
Sarayköy, Turk. 114/B2
Sarayönü, Turk. 114/C2
Sarbāz, Iran 113/H3
Sarbhāng, Bhu. 109/H2
Sárbogárd, Hun. 56/D2
Sarcari, Bol. 224/C2
Sarcelles, Fr. 36/K5
Sarco, Chile 224/B4
Sarcoxie, Mo, US 183/G2
Sārda (riv.), India 108/C1
Sārda (canal), India 108/C2
Sarda (riv.), India 104/D2
Sardara, It. 54/A3
Sardārpura, India 110/B5
Sardārshahar, India 110/C5
Sardegna (prov.), It. 54/A2
Sardhana, India 110/D5
Sardinata, Col. 216/C2
Sardinia (isl.), It. 54/A2
Sardinia, Oh, US 192/F1
Sardis (dam), Ms, US 192/C3
Sardis, Ms, US 192/C3
Sardis, Tx, US 180/L7
Sardis, Ga, US 193/G4
Sardis (lake), Ms, US 192/C3
Sareks NP, Swe. 44/F2
Sarektjåkko (peak), Swe. 44/F2
Sarempaka (peak), Indo. 103/E4
Sārenga, India 109/F4
Sarentino, It. 67/H4
Sarepta, La, US 183/H4
Sarezzo, It. 68/D2
Sargans, Swi. 67/F3
Sargents, Co, US 179/J1
Sargodha, Pak. 110/B3
Sarh, Chad 134/C3
Sārī, Iran 115/H2
Sari (cape), Malay. 101/C2
Sari-Solenzara, Fr. 54/A2
Saria, India 110/C3
Saribi (cape), Indo. 103/J4
Sarigan (isl.), NMar. 160/D3
Sarigazi (arpt.), Turk. 115/N7
Sarıgöl, Turk. 114/B2
Sarıkamış, Turk. 114/E1
Sarikaya (prov.), Turk. 76/E5
Sarıkaya, Turk. 76/E5
Sarikei, Malay. 102/D3
Sarina, Austl. 158/C3
Sarine (riv.), Swi. 51/G3
Sariñena, Sp. 53/E2
Sarīr Kalanshiyū (des.), Libya 126/D3
Sarīr Kalanshiyū ar Ramlī al Kabīr (des.), Libya 126/D2
Sarīr Tibasti (des.), Libya 126/C4
Sarita, Tx, US 181/F4
Sariwŏn, NKor. 93/C3
Sarju (riv.), India 108/C1
Sark (isl.), Fr. 62/C2
Sark (isl.), Chl, UK 50/B2
Sarkad, Hun. 56/E2
Sarkant, Kaz. 80/H5
Särkijärvi (lake), Fin. 45/D4
Şarkîkaraağaç, Turk. 114/B2
Şarkışla, Turk. 114/D2
Şarköy, Turk. 57/H5
Sarlat-la-Canéda, Fr. 50/D4
Sarleinsbach, Aus. 65/G5
Sarmato, It. 68/C3
Sarmeola, It. 69/E3
Sarmi, Indo. 103/J4
Sarmiento, Arg. 226/C5
Sarmiento (peak), Chile 191/C7
Särna, Swe. 46/E1
Sarnano, It. 71/C1
Sarnen, Swi. 67/E4
Sarnia, On, Can. 190/E3
Sarnico, It. 68/C2
Sarno, It. 71/D6
Sarny, Ukr. 78/D2
Saroako, Indo. 103/F4
Sarolangun, Indo. 101/C3
Saroma (lake), Japan 94/C1
Saronic (gulf), Gre. 73/J3
Saronno, It. 68/C2
Saros (gulf), Turk. 76/C4
Sárospatak, Hun. 49/L4
Sarpsborg, Nor. 46/D2
Sarralbe, Fr. 61/G6
Sarras, Fr. 70/A2
Sarratt, Eng, UK 36/B1
Sarre (riv.), Fr. 60/F6
Sarre-Union, Fr. 61/G6
Sarrebourg, Fr. 61/G6
Sarreguemines, Fr. 61/G5
Sarria, Sp. 52/B1
Sarrians, Fr. 70/A4
Sarroch, It. 54/A3
Sarry, Fr. 61/D6
Sarsāwa, India 110/D4
Sarsina, It. 69/F6
Särsö (isl.), Swe. 45/B1
Sarstedt, Ger. 59/G4
Sarstsún (riv.), Guat. 206/D3
Sartang (riv.), Rus. 81/P3
Sarteano, It. 54/B1
Sartell, Mn, US 187/G5
Sartène, Fr. 54/A2
Sarthe (dept.), Fr. 63/F4
Sarthe (riv.), Fr. 50/C3
Sarthon (riv.), Fr. 63/E4
Sartilly, Fr. 62/D3
Sartrouville, Fr. 36/J5
Sarufutsu, Japan 94/C1
Saruhanlı, Turk. 76/C5
Şärur, Azer. 115/F2
Sárvár, Hun. 56/C2
Sarvestān, Iran 115/H4
Sárvíz (riv.), Hun. 56/D2
Sary Ishikotrau (des.), Kaz. 111/C2
Saryagach, Kaz. 111/A3
Sarybasat, Kaz. 77/M3
Sarych (cape), Ukr. 79/G5
Saryg-Sep, Rus. 111/G1
Sarygamysh Köli (lake), Trkm. 77/L4
Saryshaghan, Kaz. 111/B2
Sarysu (riv.), Kaz. 80/G5
Sarzana, It. 68/C5
Sarzeau, Fr. 62/C5
Sas Van Gent, Neth. 60/C1
Sa'sa', Syria 117/E2
Sasabe, Az, US 179/G5
Sasaginnigack (lake), Mb, Can. 187/G2
Sasak, Indo. 101/B2
Sasarām, India 109/E3
Sasayama, Japan 95/H5
Sasayama (riv.), Japan 95/H5
Sásd, Hun. 56/D2
Sasebo, Japan 96/A4
Sashima, Japan 95/D1
Saskatchewan (riv.), Can. 163/G4
Saskatchewan (prov.), Can. 170/F3
Saskatoon, Sk, Can. 175/L1
Saslaya (mtn.), Nic. 207/E3
Saslaya, PN, Nic. 207/E3
Sāsni, India 108/B2
Sasolburg, SAfr. 142/D2
Sasoma, India 110/D2
Sasovo, Rus. 77/G1
Sassafras (peak), Tn, US 192/E3
Sassafras (mtn.), SC, US 193/F3
Sassafras, Md, US 198/C5
Sassafras (riv.), Md, US 198/B5
Sassandra, C.d'Iv. 132/D5
Sassandra (riv.), C.d'Iv. 132/D5
Sassari, It. 54/A2
Sasse (riv.), Fr. 70/C4
Sassello, It. 68/B5
Sassenage, Fr. 70/B2
Sassenberg, Ger. 59/F4
Sassenheim, Neth. 58/B4
Sasser, Ga, US 195/F2
Sassnitz, Ger. 46/E4
Sasso Marconi, It. 69/E5
Sassocorvaro, It. 69/F6
Sassoferrato, It. 69/F7
Sassoumbouroum, Niger 133/H3
Sasstown, Libr. 132/C5
Sassuolo, It. 69/D4
Sástago, Sp. 53/E2
Sastre, Arg. 224/D4
Sasykkol (lake), Kaz. 111/D2
Sata-misaki (cape), Japan 96/B5
Satadougou Tintiba, Mali 132/C3
Satara, SAfr. 141/F5
Satawan (isl.), Micr. 160/E4
Satellite Beach, Fl, US 195/H3
Satema, CAfr. 134/D4
Säter, Swe. 46/F1
Saticoy, Ca, US 196/A2
Satilla (riv.), Ga, US 195/G2
Satillieu, Fr. 70/A2
Satipo, Peru 220/C3
Satis, Rus. 75/J5
Sātkānia, Bang. 109/J4
Sātkhira, Bang. 109/G4
Satley, Eng, UK 41/G2
Satna, India 108/C3
Satolas (Lyon) (int'l arpt.), Fr. 66/B6
Sátoraljaújhely, Hun. 49/L4
Satpayev, Kaz. 111/A2
Satpura (range), India 104/C3
Sætre, Nor. 44/S8
Satsuma, Al, US 194/D2
Satsuma, Tx, US 181/M9
Sattahip, Thai. 106/C3
Satte, Japan 95/D1
Satteins, Aus. 67/F3
Satteldorf, Ger. 64/D4
Sattleberg, PNG 153/G1
Sättra, Swe. 45/A1
Satu Mare, Rom. 49/M5
Satu Mare (co.), Rom. 49/M5
Satuk, Thai. 106/C3
Satun, Thai. 106/C5
Satupaitea, Sam. 161/R9
Saturna, BC, Can. 174/C3
Sauce, Arg. 224/E4
Sauce, Peru 220/B2
Sauce de Luna, Arg. 224/E4
Sauce Grande (riv.), Arg. 226/E3
Saucedo, Uru. 224/E4
Saucier, Ms, US 194/D2
Saucillo, Mex. 204/D2
Sauda, Nor. 46/B2
Saudhárkrókur, Ice. 44/N6
Saudi Arabia (ctry.) 112/D4
Sauer (riv.), Ger. 59/F5
Sauerlach, Ger. 67/H2
Sauerland (reg.), Ger. 48/D3
Sauêruiná (riv.), Braz. 221/G4
Saugatuck, Mi, US 190/C3
Saugatuck (riv.), Ct, US 199/E1
Saugeen (riv.), On, Can. 190/F2
Saugeen Ind. Res., On, Can. 190/F2
Saugerties, NY, US 191/K3
Sauiá, Braz. 218/B3
Saujon, Fr. 50/C4
Sauk (riv.), Mn, US 185/G1
Sauk Centre, Mn, US 187/G5
Sauk City, Wi, US 185/K2
Sauk Rapids, Mn, US 187/G5
Saukkola, Fin. 45/D4
Saül, FrG. 218/C2
Sauland, Nor. 46/C2
Saulce-sur-Rhône, Fr. 70/A3
Sauldre (riv.), Fr. 50/D3
Saulgau, Ger. 67/F1
Saulheim, Ger. 64/B3
Saulieu, Fr. 50/F3
Saulkrasti, Lat. 47/L3
Saulnierville, NS, Can. 188/D3
Sault, Fr. 70/B4
Sault aux Cochons (riv.), Qu, Can. 188/C1
Sault Sainte Marie, On, Can. 190/D1
Sault Sainte Marie, Mi, US 190/D1
Sault-lès-Rethel, Fr. 61/D5
Saulx, Fr. 66/C2
Saulx (riv.), Fr. 48/C4
Saulxures-sur-Moselotte, Fr. 66/C2
Saumlaki, Indo. 152/C1
Saumur, Fr. 63/E6
Saunders (cape), NZ 159/B4
Saunders (peak), Austl. 154/E3
Saundersfoot, Wal, UK 42/B3
Saura (riv.), India 109/F3
Saurimo, Ang. 139/E5
Sausalito, Ca, US 197/J11
Sausseron (riv.), Fr. 36/J4
Sausset-les-Pins, Fr. 70/B6
Sausu, Indo. 103/F4
Saut-Tigre, FrG. 218/C1
Sautatá, Col. 216/B3
Sautet (lake), Fr. 70/B3
Sauteurs, Gren. 217/F1
Sautron, Fr. 62/D6
Sauzon, Fr. 62/B6
Sava, It. 54/E2
Sava (riv.), Eur. 73/J1
Savá, Hon. 206/E3
Savage, Mt, US 186/B4
Savage (mtn.), Md, US 191/G5
Savage (dam), Ca, US 196/D5
Savage, Mn, US 187/P7
Savage River, Austl. 156/C4
Savai'i (isl.), Sam. 161/H6
Savalou, Ben. 133/F5
Savanna, Ok, US 183/G3
Savanna, Il, US 185/J2
Savanna-la-Mar, Jam. 207/G2
Savannah (riv.), Ga,SC, US 193/G4
Savannah, Mo, US 185/G4
Savannah, Tn, US 192/C3
Savannah (brook), Austl. 154/L6
Savannah, Ga, US 193/G4
Savannah NWR, Ga, US 195/H1
Savannah River Plant, SC, US 193/G4
Savannakhet, Laos 106/D2
Savant (lake), On, Can. 187/J2
Savant Lake, On, Can. 187/J2
Sävar, Swe. 44/G3
Savaştepe, Turk. 76/C5
Savate, Ang. 140/C3
Savé, Ben. 133/F4
Save (riv.), Moz. 119/F7
Save (riv.), Zim. 141/G4
Sāveh, Iran 115/G3
Savena (riv.), It. 69/E4
Savenay, Fr. 62/D6
Săveni, Rom. 78/D4
Saverdun, Fr. 50/D5
Saverne, Fr. 61/G6
Savièse, Swi. 66/D5
Savigliano, It. 70/D3
Savignano sul Panaro, It. 69/E5
Savignano sul Rubicone, It. 69/F5
Savigné-L'Évêque, Fr. 63/F4
Savigny-le-Temple, Fr. 36/K6
Savigny-sur-Braye, Fr. 63/F5
Savigny-sur-Orge, Fr. 36/K5
Savines-le-Lac, Fr. 70/C3
Saviniemi, Fin. 45/E3
Sävja, Swe. 46/G2
Savognin, Swi. 67/F4
Savoie (dept.), Fr. 66/C6
Savona, It. 68/B5
Savona (prov.), It. 68/B4
Savona, BC, Can. 174/D2
Savonburg, Ks, US 183/G2
Savoonga, Ak, US 201/D3
Savoy, Tx, US 183/F4
Savoy, Il, US 190/B4
Savoy (reg.), Fr. 72/E1
Savoy, SD, US 184/C1
Savoy, Mt, US 175/K3
Savoy Alps (mts.), Fr. 66/C6
Saxman, Ak, US 201/M4
Şavşat, Turk. 77/G4
Sävsjö, Swe. 46/F3
Savu (sea), Phil. 83/M10
Savusavu, Fiji 161/Z17
Sawahlunto, Indo. 101/C3
Sawākin, Sudan 127/H5
Sawang Daeh Din, Thai. 106/C2
Sawankhalok, Thai. 106/B2
Sawara, Japan 97/G3
Sawasaki-bana (pt.), Japan 97/F2
Sawatch (range), Co, US 184/A4
Sawbridgeworth, Eng, UK 43/G3
Sawdā', Jabal (peak), SAr. 112/D5
Sawdirī, Sudan 134/F2
Saweba (cape), Indo. 103/H4
Sawel (mtn.), NI, UK 40/A2
Sawena, Eth. 136/B4
Sāwi, India 105/F6
Sawkanah, Libya 126/B2
Sawmills, Zim. 141/F3
Sawpit, Co, US 179/H2
Sawston, Eng, UK 43/G2
Sawtell, Austl. 156/E1
Sawtooth (range), Id, US 177/F1
Sawtooth (mtn.), Mt, US 175/K3
Sawtooth Nat'l Rec. Area, Id, US 177/F1
Sawu, Indo. 152/A2
Sawu (isl.), Indo. 152/A2
Sawu (isls.), Indo. 103/F6
Sawyer, ND, US 186/D3
Sawyer, Ks, US 183/E2
Sawyers Bar, Ca, US 176/B3
Sax, Sp. 53/E3
Saxån (riv.), Swe. 45/K7
Saxarfjärden (sound), Swe. 45/B1
Saxilby, Eng, UK 41/H5
Saxis, Va, US 193/K2
Saxmundham, Eng, UK 43/H2
Saxon, Swi. 66/D5
Say, Niger 133/F3
Say-Utes, Kaz. 77/K3
Saya, Japan 95/L5
Saya, Bol. 224/C1
Sayabec, Qu, Can. 188/D1
Sayak, Kaz. 80/H5
Sayama, Japan 97/F3
Sayama, Japan 95/J6
Sayán, Peru 220/B3
Sayansk, Rus. 90/E1
Şaydā (Sidon), Leb. 117/C1
Şaydnāyā, Syria 117/E1
Sayḩūt, Yem. 136/D2
Sayil (ruin), Mex. 206/D1
Sayingpan, China 98/D3
Saykhin, Kaz. 77/H2
Saylah, Egypt 131/B6
Saynbach (riv.), Ger. 61/G2
Sayner, Wi, US 187/K5
Sayram (lake), China 111/D3
Sayre, Ok, US 182/E3
Sayre, Pa, US 191/H4
Sayreville, NJ, US 199/H10
Saysu, China 111/F3
Sayula, Mex. 204/E5
Sayville, NY, US 199/E2
Saywūn, Yem. 136/D2
Sazan (isl.), Alb. 55/F2
Sazan (isl.), Gre. 56/D5
Sazdy, Kaz. 77/J3
Sazīn, Pak. 110/B2
Sazli Dere (riv.), Turk. 115/M6
Sbaa, Alg. 129/E3
Sbeitla, Tun. 130/L7
Scaër, Fr. 62/B4
Scafati, It. 71/D6
Scafell Pikes (peak), Eng, UK 41/E3
Scalasaig, Sc, UK 37/Q8
Scalby, Eng, UK 41/H3
Scald Law (peak), Sc, UK 39/C5
Scalea, It. 54/D3
Scalino (peak), It. 67/F5
Scalloway, Sc, UK 37/W13
Scammon Bay, Ak, US 201/E3
Scandia, Ab, Can. 175/H2
Scandia, Ks, US 184/F4
Scandia, Mn, US 187/Q6
Scandia, Wa, US 197/B2
Scandiano, It. 69/D4
Scandicci, It. 69/E6
Scanlon, Mn, US 187/H4
Scanno, It. 71/C4
Scapa Flow (chan.), Sc, UK 37/V14
Scar Water (riv.), Sc, UK 40/E1
Scarborough, Eng, UK 41/H3
Scarborough, Trin. 217/F2
Scarborough (nbrhd.), Austl. 154/K6
Scarborough (co.), On, Can. 190/U8
Scarborough Shoal (isl.), Phil. 100/B2
Scardovari, It. 69/F4
Scarinish, Sc, UK 37/Q8
Scarpe (riv.), Fr. 48/B3
Scarperia, It. 69/E6
Scarriff, Ire. 38/B4
Scarsdale, NY, US 199/K7
Scatarie (isl.), Ns., Can. 189/H3
Scattery (isl.), Ire. 38/A4
Scauri, It. 71/C5
Sceaux, Fr. 36/J5
Scerni, It. 71/D3
Scey-sur-Saône-et-St-Albin, Fr. 66/B2
Schaefferstown, Pa, US 198/B3
Schaerbeek, Belg. 61/D2
Schaffer, Mi, US 187/L5
Schaffhausen, Swi. 67/E2
Schaffhausen (canton), Swi. 67/E2
Schäftlarn, Ger. 67/H2
Schagen, Neth. 58/B3
Schaijk, Neth. 58/C5
Schalchen, Aus. 65/G6
Schalkau, Ger. 64/E2
Schalksmühle, Ger. 59/E6
Schaller, Ia, US 185/G2
Schanck (cape), Austl. 157/B4
Schangnau, Swi. 66/D4
Scharans, Swi. 67/F4
Schardenberg, Aus. 65/G5
Schärding, Aus. 65/G6
Scharfreiter (peak), Aus. 67/H3
Scharhorn (isl.), Ger. 59/F1
Scharnebeck, Ger. 59/H2
Scharnhorst (pt.), PNG 153/G1
Scharnitz (pass), Ger. 67/H3
Scharnstein, Aus. 65/G7
Schashagen, Ger. 48/F1
Schattdorf, Swi. 67/E4
Schauenstein, Ger. 65/E2
Schaumburg, Il, US 197/P15
Scheemda, Neth. 58/D2
Scheer, Ger. 67/F1
Scheessel, Ger. 59/G2
Schefferville, Qu, Can. 171/K3
Scheibbs, Aus. 49/H4
Scheidegg, Ger. 67/F2
Scheinfeld, Ger. 64/D3
Schelde (riv.), Belg. 60/C2
Scheldt (riv.), Belg. 50/E1
Schelklingen, Ger. 64/C6
Schell City, Mo, US 183/G1
Schell Creek (range), Nv, US 177/F4
Schellerten, Ger. 59/H4
Schellville, Ca, US 197/K10
Schenectady, NY, US 191/K3
Schenefeld, Ger. 59/G1
Schererville, In, US 190/C4
Schermbeck, Ger. 58/D5
Scherpenzeel, Neth. 58/C3
Schertz, Tx, US 181/E3
Schesaplana (peak), Aus. 67/F3
Schesslitz, Ger. 64/E3
Scheveningen, Neth. 58/B4
Scheyern, Ger. 65/E5
Schiedam, Neth. 58/B5
Schieder-Schwalenberg, Ger. 59/G5
Schiehallon (peak), Sc, UK 39/B3
Schier Monnikoog (isl.), Neth. 48/D2
Schierling, Ger. 65/F5
Schiermonnikoog (isl.), Neth. 58/D1
Schiermonnikoog, Neth. 58/D2
Schiers, Swi. 67/F4
Schifferstadt, Ger. 64/B4
Schiffweiler, Ger. 61/G5
Schijndel, Neth. 58/C5
Schilde, Belg. 58/B6
Schildmeer (lake), Neth. 58/D2
Schillighörn (cape), Ger. 59/F1
Schillingfürst, Ger. 64/D4
Schiltach, Ger. 67/E1
Schiltigheim, Fr. 66/D1
Schinnen, Neth. 61/E2
Schinznach-Dorf, Swi. 66/E3
Schio, It. 69/E2
Schipbeek (riv.), Neth. 58/D4
Schiphol, Neth. 58/B4
Schipol (Amsterdam) (int'l arpt.), Neth. 58/B4
Schirmeck, Fr. 66/D1
Schkumbin (riv.), Alb. 55/G2
Schladen, Ger. 59/H4
Schladming, Aus. 51/K3
Schlanders (Silandro), It. 67/G4
Schlangen, Ger. 59/F5
Schlangenbad, Ger. 64/B2
Schlater, Ms, US 192/B4
Schleiden, Ger. 61/F2
Schleitheim, Swi. 67/E2
Schleiz, Ger. 65/E1
Schlema, Ger. 65/F1
Schleswig, Ger. 46/C4
Schleswig, Ia, US 185/G2
Schleswig-Holstein (state), Ger. 46/B4
Schleswig-Holsteinisches Wattenmeer NP, Ger. 46/C4
Schleuse (riv.), Ger. 64/D2
Schleusingen, Ger. 64/D1
Schliengen, Ger. 66/D2
Schlierbach, Aus. 65/H7
Schlieren, Swi. 67/E3
Schloss Herrenchiemsee, Ger. 65/F7
Schloss Holte-Stukenbrock, Ger. 59/F5
Schloss Sansoucci, Ger. 48/Q7
Schloss Wilhelmstein, Ger. 59/G4
Schlotheim, Ger. 59/H6
Schluchsee, Ger. 66/E2
Schlüchtern, Ger. 64/C2
Schluderns (Sluderno), It. 67/G4
Schlüsselfeld, Ger. 64/D3
Schlüsslberg, Aus. 65/G6
Schmallenberg, Ger. 59/F6
Schmeich (riv.), Ger. 64/C6
Schmelz, Ger. 61/F5
Schmiech (riv.), Ger. 67/F1
Schmitten, Swi. 66/D4
Schmitten, Ger. 64/B2
Schmutter (riv.), Ger. 64/D5
Schnaitsee, Ger. 65/F6
Schnaittach, Ger. 65/E3
Schnaittenbach, Ger. 65/F3
Schnarrtanne, Ger. 65/F1
Schnecksville, Pa, US 198/C2
Schneeberg (peak), Ger. 65/E2
Schneeberg, Ger. 65/F1
Schneeberg, Ger. 64/C3
Schneifel (upland), Ger. 48/D3
Schneverdingen, Ger. 59/G2
Schoenchen, Ks, US 182/E1
Schofield, Wi, US 185/K1
Schoharie, NY, US 191/J3
Scholle, NM, US 179/J3
Schollene, Ger. 48/G2
Schöllkrippen, Ger. 64/C2
Schömberg, Ger. 67/E1
Schömberg, Ger. 64/B5
Schönaich, Ger. 64/C5
Schönau im Schwarzwald, Ger. 66/D2
Schönberg, Ger. 46/D4
Schönberg, Ger. 65/G5
Schönbrunn, Ger. 64/D1
Schondorf am Ammersee, Ger. 67/H1
Schondra (riv.), Ger. 64/C2
Schönebeck, Ger. 48/F2
Schöneck, Ger. 64/B2
Schöneck, Ger. 65/F2
Schönecken, Ger. 61/F3
Schönefeld (int'l arpt.), Ger. 48/Q7
Schöneiche, Ger. 48/Q7
Schongau, Ger. 67/G2
Schöningen, Ger. 48/F2
Schönow, Ger. 48/Q6
Schönsee, Ger. 65/F3
Schonungen, Ger. 64/D2
Schönwald, Ger. 65/E2
Schoolcraft, Mi, US 190/D3
Schoonebeek, Neth. 58/D3
Schoonhoven, Neth. 58/B5
Schoorl, Neth. 58/B3
Schopfheim, Ger. 66/D2
Schopfheim, Ger. 61/G4
Schopfloch, Ger. 64/D4
Schöppenstedt, Ger. 59/H4
Schörfling, Aus. 65/G7
Schorndorf, Ger. 64/C5
Schortens, Ger. 59/E1
Schoten, Belg. 58/B6
Schotten, Ger. 64/C1
Schouten (isls.), Indo. 160/C5
Schouten (isl.), Austl. 156/D4
Schouwen (isl.), Neth. 58/A5
Schramberg, Ger. 67/E1
Schrankogel (peak), Aus. 67/H3
Schreckhorn (peak), Swi. 66/E4
Schreiber, On, Can. 187/L3
Schriesheim, Ger. 64/B4
Schriever, La, US 194/C3
Schrobenhausen, Ger. 64/E5
Schroeder, Mn, US 187/J4
Schroffenstein (peak), Namb. 142/B2
Schrozberg, Ger. 64/C4
Schruns, Aus. 67/F3
Schübelbach, Swi. 67/E3
Schuby, Ger. 46/C4
Schulenburg, Tx, US 181/F3
Schuler, Ab, Can. 175/J2
Schulter, Ok, US 183/G3
Schulzendorf, Ger. 48/Q7
Schunter (riv.), Ger. 59/H4
Schüpfheim, Swi. 66/E4
Schurz, Nv, US 176/D4
Schussen (riv.), Ger. 67/F2
Schussenried, Ger. 67/F1
Schutter (riv.), Ger. 64/A6
Schutterwald, Ger. 66/D1
Schüttorf, Ger. 59/E4
Schuyler, Ne, US 185/F3
Schuylkill (riv.), Pa, US 198/C3
Schuylkill (co.), Pa, US 198/B2
Schuylkill Haven, Pa, US 198/B2
Schwabach, Ger. 64/D4
Schwabhausen bei Dachau, Ger. 65/E6
Schwäbisch Gmünd, Ger. 64/C5
Schwäbisch Hall, Ger. 64/C4
Schwäbische Alb (range), Ger. 48/E4
Schwabmünchen, Ger. 67/G1
Schwaig bei Nürnberg, Ger. 64/E4
Schwaigern, Ger. 64/C4
Schwalbach, Ger. 61/F5
Schwalbach am Taunus, Ger. 64/B2
Schwalm (riv.), Ger. 48/E3
Schwalmtal, Ger. 58/D6
Schwanden, Swi. 67/F4
Schwandorf im Bayern, Ger. 65/F4
Schwanebeck, Ger. 48/Q6
Schwanenstadt, Aus. 65/G6
Schwaner (mts.), Indo. 102/D4
Schwanewede, Ger. 59/F2
Schwanfeld, Ger. 64/D3
Schwangau, Ger. 67/G2
Schwarmstedt, Ger. 59/G3
Schwartz Elster (riv.), Ger. 49/G3
Schwartzerberg (peak), Namb. 142/B2
Schwarza (riv.), Ger. 64/E1
Schwarzach, Ger. 65/F5
Schwarzach (riv.), Ger. 65/E4
Schwarzach im Pongau, Aus. 51/K3
Schwarze Laber (riv.), Ger. 65/E4
Schwarzenbach am Wald, Ger. 65/E2
Schwarzenbek, Ger. 59/H1
Schwarzenberg, Ger. 65/F1
Schwarzenbruck, Ger. 64/E4
Schwarzenburg, Swi. 66/D4
Schwarzenfeld, Ger. 65/F4
Schwarzer Mann (peak), Ger. 61/F3
Schwarzhorn (peak), Aus. 67/H3
Schwarzrand (mts.), Namb. 140/C5
Schwarzwald (Black Forest) (for.), Ger. 64/B6
Schwaz, Aus. 51/J3
Schwebheim, Ger. 64/D3
Schwechat, Aus. 57/N7
Schwechat (int'l arpt.), Aus. 57/P7
Schwedt, Ger. 49/H2
Schwegenheim, Ger. 64/B4
Schweich, Ger. 61/F4
Schweighouse-sur-Moder, Fr. 61/G6
Schweinfurt, Ger. 64/D2
Schweitenkirchen, Ger. 65/E5
Schweizer-Reneke, SAfr. 142/D2
Schwelm, Ger. 59/E6
Schwendi, Ger. 67/F1
Schwenksville, Pa, US 198/C3
Schwerin, Ger. 46/D5
Schweriner (lake), Ger. 48/F2
Schwertberg, Aus. 65/H6
Schwerte, Ger. 59/E6
Schwetzingen, Ger. 64/B4
Schwinge (riv.), Ger. 59/G1
Schwörstadt, Ger. 66/D2
Schwülme (riv.), Ger. 59/G5
Schwülper, Ger. 59/H4
Schwyz (canton), Swi. 67/E3
Schwyz, Swi. 67/E3
Sciacca, It. 54/C4
Scicli, It. 54/D4
Science Hill, Ky, US 192/E2
Science Museum of Minnesota, Mn, US 187/P7
Scilly (isls.), Eng, UK 37/Q11
Ścinawa, Pol. 49/J3
Scio, Or, US 176/B1
Scionzier, Fr. 66/C5
Sciota, Pa, US 198/C2
Scioto (riv.), Oh, US 193/F1
Sclater, Mb, Can. 186/D2
Scobey, Mt, US 175/M3
Scofield (res.), Ut, US 177/H4
Scolt (pt.), Eng, UK 43/G1
Scone, Austl. 156/D2
Scooba, Ms, US 192/C4
Scopello, It. 68/B2
Scordia, It. 54/D4
Scorff (riv.), Fr. 62/B5
Scorzè, It. 69/F2
Scotch Corner, Eng, UK 41/G3
Scotch Creek, BC, Can. 174/E2
Scotch Plains, NJ, US 199/H9
Scotchman (peak), Id, US 174/F3
Scotia (sea) 228/W
Scotia, Ca, US 176/A3
Scotland, UK 40/D1
Scotland, Tx, US 183/E4
Scotland Neck, NC, US 193/J2
Scots Bay, NS, Can. 188/E3
Scotstown, Ire. 38/C1
Scott (cape), Austl. 152/C3
Scott (cape), BC, Can. 170/D3
Scott (cape), NW, Can. 171/R7
Scott (lake), NW, Can. 170/F2
Scott, Sk, Can. 175/K1
Scott, NZ, Ant. 228/M
Scott (riv.), Ca, US 176/B3
Scott (A.F.B.), Il, US 185/K4
Scott (co.), Mn, US 187/N7
Scott (mt.), Ok, US 183/E3
Scott City, Ks, US 182/D1
Scott City, Mo, US 192/C2
Scott NP, Austl. 154/B5
Scott (reef), Austl. 152/A3
Scottburgh, SAfr. 143/E3
Scottdale, Pa, US 191/G4
Scottdale, Ga, US 193/M7
Scottish Borders (co.), Sc, UK 39/C5
Scotts (cr.), Austl. 155/M9
Scotts Bluff Nat'l Mon., Ne, US 184/C3
Scotts Hill, Tn, US 192/C3
Scotts Peak (dam), Austl. 156/C4
Scottsbluff, Ne, US 184/C3
Scottsboro, Al, US 192/D3
Scottsburg, In, US 192/E1
Scottsdale, Austl. 156/C4
Scottsdale, Az, US 179/G4
Scottsmoor, Fl, US 195/H3
Scottsville, Ky, US 192/D2
Scottville, Mi, US 190/C3
Scotty's Castle, Ca, US 178/D2
Scoudouc, NB, Can. 188/E2
Scourie, Sc, UK 37/R7
Scranton, ND, US 186/C4
Scranton, Pa, US 191/J4
Scranton, SC, US 193/H4
Scraper, Ok, US 183/G2

Screv – Shche

330

Screven, Ga, US 195/G2
Scribner, Ne, US 185/F3
Scripps Aquarium/Museum, Ca, US 196/C5
Scrivia (riv.), It. 68/B3
Scunthorpe, Eng, UK 41/H4
Scuol, Swi. 67/G4
Scuppernong (riv.), Wi, US 197/N14
Scurdie Ness (pt.), Sc, UK 39/D3
Scurry, Tx, US 180/L7
Scutari (lake), Alb.,Mont. 56/D4
Scye (riv.), Fr. 62/D2
Sea (isls.), Ga, SC, US 193/G5
Sea Cliff, Ca, US 196/A2
Sea Cliff, NY, US 199/L8
Sea Girt, NJ, US 199/D3
Sea Isle City, NJ, US 198/D5
Sea Lake, Austl. 156/B2
Sea Pines, SC, US 193/G4
Sea Ranch Lakes, Fl, US 194/P10
Sea World of Florida, Fl, US 194/N7
Sea-Tac, Wa, US 197/C3
Seabeck, Wa, US 197/B2
Seaboard, NC, US 193/J2
Seabold, Wa, US 197/B2
Seabra, Braz. 223/E2
Seabrook, NH, US 191/L3
Seabrook, NJ, US 198/C5
Seabrook, SC, US 193/G4
Seabrook, Tx, US 181/M9
Seadrift, Tx, US 180/F3
Seaford, Eng, UK 43/G5
Seaford, NY, US 199/M9
Seaford, De, US 193/K1
Seaforde, NI, UK 40/C3
Seaforth, On, Can. 190/F3
Seaforth, Austl. 158/C3
Seagoville, Tx, US 180/L7
Seagraves, Tx, US 182/C4
Seaham, Eng, UK 41/G2
Seahorse (pt.), Nun, Can. 171/J2
Seahurst, Wa, US 197/C3
Seal (isl.), Me, US 188/C4
Seal, Eng, UK 36/D3
Seal (riv.), MB, Can. 170/G3
Seal (pt.), Chile 226/B5
Seal (cape), SAfr. 142/C4
Seal Beach, Ca, US 196/F8
Seal Beach NWR, Ca, US 196/F8
Seal Cove, NS, Can. 188/D3
Seal Cove, Nf, Can. 189/J2
Seale, Eng, UK 36/A3
Seale, Al, US 192/E4
Sealy, Tx, US 180/F3
Seaman, Oh, US 192/F1
Seamer, Eng, UK 41/H3
Seano, It. 69/E6
Searchlight, Nv, US 178/E3
Searchmont, On, Can. 190/D1
Searcy, Ar, US 183/J3
Seascale, Eng, UK 40/E3
Seaside, Ca, US 178/B2
Seaside, Or, US 174/C5
Seaside Heights, NJ, US 199/D4
Seaside Park, NJ, US 199/D4
Seaton, Eng, UK 42/C5
Seaton (riv.), Eng, UK 42/B6
Seaton Carew, Eng, UK 41/G2
Seattle, Wa, US 174/C4
Seattle Art Museum, Wa, US 197/C2
Seattle Center, Wa, US 197/C2
Seattle-Tacoma (int'l arpt.), Wa, US 174/C4
Seatuck Nat'l Wild. Ref., NY, US 199/E2
Seba, Indo. 152/A2
Sébaco, Nic. 206/E3
Sebago (lake), Me, US 191/L3
Sebaou (riv.), Alg. 130/H4
Sebastian, Fl, US 195/H4
Sebastian, Tx, US 181/F4
Sebastián Vizcaíno (bay), Mex. 204/B2
Sebastopol, Austl. 157/A3
Sebastopol, Ca, US 176/B4
Sebastopol, Ms, US 192/C4
Sebastopol, Tx, US 181/G2
Sebatik (isl.), Malay. 100/B4
Sebayan (peak), Indo. 102/D4
Sebderat, Erit. 134/H2
Sebdou, Alg. 130/D2
Sébé (riv.), Gabon 138/C3
Sebec (lake), Me, US 188/C3
Sebeka, Mn, US 187/G4
Sébékoro, Mali 132/C3
Seben, Turk. 57/K5
Sebeş, Rom. 57/F3
Sebeta, Eth. 136/A3
Sebewaing, Mi, US 190/E3
Sebezh, Rus. 47/N3
Sebina, Bots. 141/E4
Şebinkarahisar, Turk. 114/D1
Sebiş, Rom. 56/F2
Sebkhet al Kalīyah (drylake), Alg. 130/M7
Sebkhet Kelbia (swamp), Tun. 130/M7
Seblat, Indo. 101/C3
Sebnitz, Ger. 49/H3
Seboruco, Ven. 216/C2
Seboto (pt.), Phil. 100/C4
Sebou (riv.), Mor. 130/B2
Sebou, Oued (riv.), Mor. 128/D2
Seboyeta, NM, US 179/J3
Sebree, Ky, US 192/D2
Sebring, Fl, US 195/H4
Sebuku (isl.), Indo. 103/E4
Sebuku (bay), Indo. 100/B5
Secaucus, NJ, US 199/J8
Secchia (riv.), It. 51/J4
Sechelt, BC, Can. 174/C3
Sechura, Peru 220/A2
Sechura (bay), Peru 220/A2
Sechura, Desierto de (des.), Peru 220/A2
Seclin, Fr. 60/C2
Seco (riv.), Arg. 191/D6
Seco (riv.), Mex.,US 179/G5
Seco (cr.), Tx, US 180/E3
Second Cataract (falls), Sudan 127/F4
Second Mesa, Az, US 179/G3
Second Mountain (mtn.), Pa, US 198/B3
Second San Diego Aqueduct (riv.), Ca, US 196/C4
Second Watchung (mtn.), NJ, US 199/H9
Section, Al, US 192/E3
Secunda, SAfr. 142/E2
Secure (riv.), Bol. 221/E4
Security-Widefield, Co, US 182/B1
Seda, Lith. 47/K3
Sedalia, Mo, US 183/H1
Sedalia, Ab, Can. 175/J2
Sedan, Ks, US 183/F2
Sedan, NM, US 182/C2
Sedan, Fr. 61/D4
Sedano, Sp. 52/D1
Sedaung (mtn.), Myan. 106/B3
Sedayu, Indo. 101/F4
Sedbergh, Eng, UK 41/F3
Seddenga Temple (ruin), Sudan 127/F4
Seddon, NZ 159/C3
Seddonville, NZ 159/B3
Seddülbahir, Turk. 81/K2
Sedeh, Iran 113/G2
Sederot, Isr. 117/B5
Sedgefield, Eng, UK 41/G2
Sedgewick, Ab, Can. 175/J1
Sedgwick (mt.), Yk, Can. 201/L2
Sedgwick, Ks, US 183/F2
Sedhiou, Sen. 132/B3
Sedlčany, Czh. 65/H3
Sedlo (peak), Czh. 65/H1
Sedona, Az, US 179/G3
Sedot Yam, Isr. 117/B4
Sedrata, Alg. 130/K6
Sedro-Woolley, Wa, US 174/C3
Šeduva, Lith. 47/K4
Sędziszów, Pol. 49/L3
Sędziszów Małopolski, Pol. 78/A2
Sée (riv.), Fr. 50/C2
Seeb (int'l arpt.), Oman 113/G4
Seebe, Ab, Can. 174/G2
Seeboden, Aus. 51/K3
Seedskadee NWR, Wy, US 177/J3
Seefeld in Tirol, Aus. 67/H3
Seefin (peak), Ire. 38/A6
Seefin (peak), Ire. 38/C5
Seeg, Ger. 67/G2
Seehausen, Ger. 48/F2
Seeheim, Namb. 142/B2
Seeheim-Jugenheim, Ger. 64/B3
Seeis, Namb. 140/C4
Seekirchen Markt, Aus. 65/G7
Seekooi (riv.), SAfr. 142/D3
Seeley, Ca, US 178/E4
Seeley Lake, Mt, US 175/H4
Seelow, Ger. 49/H2
Seeon-Seebruck, Ger. 65/F7
Seer Green, Eng, UK 36/B2
Sées, Fr. 63/F3
Seesen, Ger. 59/H5
Seeshaupt, Ger. 67/H2
Seeve (riv.), Ger. 59/G2
Seewalchen, Aus. 65/G7
Seewis im Prättigau, Swi. 67/F4
Séez, Fr. 70/C1
Şefaatlı, Turk. 114/C2
Seffner, Fl, US 194/L8
Sefhare, Bots. 141/E4
Sefīd Rūd (riv.), Iran 115/G2
Sefrou, Mor. 130/B3
Sefton (mt.), NZ 159/B3
Sefton (co.), Eng, UK 41/E4
Segag, Eth. 136/B4
Segama (riv.), Malay. 100/B4
Segamat, Malay. 101/C2
Segarcea, Rom. 57/F3
Ségbana, Ben. 133/F4
Ségélo-Koro, C.d'Iv. 132/D4
Segelstad Bru, Nor. 46/D1
Segen Wenz (riv.), Eth. 134/H4
Seget, Indo. 103/H4
Segezha, Rus. 74/G3
Segni, It. 71/C4
Segorbe, Sp. 53/E3
Ségou, Mali 132/D3
Ségou (pol. reg.), Mali 132/D3
Segovia, Col. 216/C3
Segovia, Sp. 52/C2
Segovia, Tx, US 180/E2
Segozero (lake), Rus. 74/G3
Segrate, It. 68/C3
Segré, Fr. 63/E5
Segre (riv.), Sp. 53/F2
Seguam (isl.), Ak, US 201/D5
Seguam Pass (Str.), Ak, US 201/D5
Séguédine, Niger 126/B4
Séguéla, C.d'Iv. 132/D5
Séguénéga, Burk. 133/E3
Seguin, Tx, US 181/F3
Segundo (riv.), Arg. 224/D4
Segura (riv.), Sp. 72/C3
Segusino, It. 69/E2
Sehithwa, Bots. 140/D4
Sehnde, Ger. 59/G4
Sehonghong, Les. 142/E3
Sehore, India 104/C3
Sehwān, Pak. 113/J3
Seibersbach, Ger. 61/G4
Seiche (riv.), Fr. 62/D5
Seiches-sur-le-Loir, Fr. 63/E5
Seiersberg, Aus. 56/B2
Seika, Japan 95/J6
Seiling, Ok, US 182/E2
Seille (riv.), Fr. 48/C5
Seinäjoki, Fin. 74/D3
Seine (riv.), On, Can. 187/J3
Seine (bay), Fr. 50/C2
Seine (riv.), On, Can. 170/G4
Seine (riv.), Fr. 29/E4
Seine-et-Marne (dept.), Fr. 60/B5
Seine-Maritime (dept.), Fr. 60/A4
Seine-St-Denis (dept.), Fr. 60/B6
Seitenstetten, Aus. 65/H6
Seiwa, Japan 95/K7
Seix, Fr. 50/D5
Seixal, Port. 53/P10
Seixas (pt.), Braz. 219/H4
Sejaka, Indo. 103/E4
Sejerø (isl.), Den. 46/D4
Sejero (flat), Den. 45/H7
Sejny, Pol. 47/K4
Sekayu, Indo. 101/C3
Seke, Tanz. 137/A2
Seke-Banza, D.R. Congo 138/C4
Sekenke, Tanz. 137/A3
Seki (riv.), Turk. 116/A1
Seki, Japan 95/L5
Seki, Japan 95/K6
Sekigahara, Japan 95/K5
Sekijo, Japan 95/D1
Sekiyado, Japan 95/D1
Sekoma, Bots. 140/D5
Sekondi, Gha. 133/E5
Sek'ot'a, Eth. 136/A2
Sel, Nor. 44/D3
Selah, Wa, US 174/D4
Selama, Malay. 101/C1
Selangor (state), Malay. 101/C2
Selaön (isl.), Swe. 45/A1
Selaphum, Thai. 106/C2
Selargius, It. 54/A3
Selaru (isl.), Indo. 103/H5
Selatan (cape), Indo. 102/D4
Selawik, Ak, US 201/F2
Selawik (lake), Ak, US 201/F2
Selayar (isl.), Indo. 103/F5
Selb, Ger. 65/F2
Selbitz, Ger. 65/E2
Selbitz (riv.), Ger. 65/E2
Selbu, Nor. 44/D3
Selby, SD, US 186/D5
Selby, Eng, UK 41/G4
Selby-On-The-Bay, Md, US 198/B6
Selci, It. 69/F6
Selçuk, Turk. 114/A2
Selden, Ks, US 184/D4
Selden, NY, US 199/E2
Seldovia, Ak, US 201/H4
Sele (riv.), It. 54/D2
Selebi-Phikwe, Bots. 141/E4
Seleka, Bots. 141/E4
Selela (pt.), Moz. 141/J2
Seleli (hill), Tanz. 139/H5
Selemdzha (riv.), Rus. 81/N4
Selenča, Serb. 56/D3
Selenduma, Rus. 90/F1
Selenga (riv.), Rus. 90/F1
Selenge (prov.), Mong. 90/F2
Selenge (riv.), Mong. 90/F2
Selenginsk, Rus. 90/F1
Selenicë, Alb. 55/F2
Sélestat, Fr. 66/D1
Seletar (res.), Sing. 101/J6
Selety (riv.), Kaz. 111/B1
Seletyteniz (lake), Kaz. 111/B1
Seleznëvo, Rus. 47/N1
Selfoss, Ice. 44/N7
Selfridge, ND, US 186/D4
Sélia (well), Chad 134/C2
Sélibabi, Mrta. 132/B3
Seligenstadt, Ger. 64/B2
Seliger (lake), Rus. 74/G4
Seligman, Mo, US 183/H2
Seligman, Az, US 179/F3
Selim River, Malay. 101/C2
Selimbau, Indo. 102/D3
Selimiye, Turk. 114/A2
Selinsgrove, Pa, US 198/B2
Seljord, Nor. 46/C2
Selkan (tun.), Japan 94/B3
Selkirk, Sc, UK 39/D5
Selkirk, Mb, Can. 170/G3
Selkirk (mts.), BC, Can. 174/E2
Selleck, Wa, US 197/D3
Sellers, Al, US 195/E1
Sellersville, Pa, US 198/C3
Selles-sur-Cher, Fr. 63/G6
Sellières, Fr. 66/B4
Sells, Az, US 179/G5
Selly Oak, Eng, UK 42/E2
Sellye, Hun. 56/C3
Selm, Ger. 59/E5
Selma, Al, US 192/D4
Selma, Ar, US 183/J4
Selma, Ca, US 178/C2
Selma, NC, US 193/H3
Selman, Ok, US 182/E2
Selmer, Tn, US 192/C3
Selommes, Fr. 63/G5
Selongey, Fr. 66/B2
Selouma, Gui. 132/C4
Selous (mt.), Yk, Can. 201/M3
Selous, Zim. 141/F3
Selous Game Reserve, Tanz. 137/B4
Selsey, Eng, UK 43/F5
Selsey Bill (pt.), Eng, UK 43/F5
Selsingen, Ger. 59/G2
Sel'tso, Rus. 76/E1
Seltz, Fr. 64/B5
Selu (isl.), Indo. 152/C1
Sélune (riv.), Fr. 50/C2
Selvas (for.), Braz. 209/C3
Selvik, Nor. 44/R9
Selway (riv.), Id, US 177/F1
Selway (falls), Id, US 174/G4
Selwyn, Austl. 158/A3
Selwyn (range), Austl. 153/F5
Selydove, Ukr. 79/J3
Selz (riv.), Ger. 51/H2
Semara, WSah. 128/C4
Semarang, Indo. 101/E4
Semarsot, India 108/D4
Semau (isl.), Indo. 152/A2
Sembakung (riv.), Indo. 100/B4
Sembawang (nbrhd.), Sing. 101/J6
Sembé, Congo 138/C2
Sembehun, SLeo. 132/B5
Sembera (riv.), Czh. 65/H2
Semberong (riv.), Malay. 101/C2
Şemdinli, Turk. 115/F2
Séméac, Fr. 50/D5
Semelle (riv.), Fr. 63/F4
Semendua, D.R. Congo 138/D3
Semenivka, Ukr. 78/G1
Semenivka, Ukr. 79/G3
Semenov, Rus. 75/K4
Semeru (peak), Indo. 101/F5
Semey, Kaz. 111/D1
Semidi (isls.), Ak, US 201/G4
Semikarakorsk, Rus. 79/L4
Semilovo, Rus. 74/J5
Semiluki, Rus. 79/K2
Seminole, Fl, US 194/K8
Seminole (lake), Ga, US 195/F2
Seminole, Ok, US 183/F3
Seminole, Tx, US 180/C1
Seminoe (dam), Wy, US 177/K2
Seminoe (res.), Wy, US 177/K2
Seminole Draw (riv.), Tx, US 180/C1
Seminole Ind. Res., Fl, US 195/H4
Semipalatinsk (int'l arpt.), Kaz. 111/D1
Semirara (isl.), Phil. 100/C3
Semīrom, Iran 115/G4
Semisopochnoi (isl.), Ak, US 201/B5
Semitau, Indo. 102/D4
Semliki (riv.), D.R. Congo 139/G2
Semnān, Iran 115/H3
Semnān (gov.), Iran 115/H3
Semnon (riv.), Fr. 50/C3
Semois (riv.), Belg. 50/F2
Semouse (riv.), Fr. 66/C2
Semoy, Fr. 63/G5
Semoy (riv.), Fr. 61/D4
Sempach, Swi. 66/E3
Sempacher (lake), Swi. 66/D3
Semporna, Malay. 100/B4
Semprevisa (peak), It. 71/C4
Semsales, Swi. 66/C4
Semskefjellet (peak), Nor. 44/E2
Sen (riv.), Camb. 105/H5
Sen-san (peak), Japan 95/G7
Sena, Thai. 106/C3
Sena, Bol. 221/E3
Sena Madureira, Braz. 218/E5
Senador Pompeu, Braz. 219/G4
Senador Sá, Braz. 219/F3
Sen'afē, Erit. 136/A2
Senai, Malay. 101/C2
Senaja, Malay. 100/B4
Senaki, Geo. 77/G4
Senanga, Zam. 140/D3
Sénas, Fr. 70/B5
Senate, Sk, Can. 175/K3
Senath, Mo, US 192/B2
Senatobia, Ms, US 192/C3
Sence (riv.), Eng, UK 43/E1
Send, Eng, UK 36/B3
Sendafa, Eth. 136/A3
Sendai (riv.), Japan 96/D3
Sendai, Japan 97/G1
Sendai (int'l arpt.), Japan 97/G1
Sendai, Japan 96/B5
Sendai (bay), Japan 94/B4
Sendal (riv.), Japan 96/B5
Senden, Ger. 64/D6
Senden, Ger. 59/E5
Sendenhorst, Ger. 59/E5
Sendhwa, India 107/B1
Senebui, Indo. 101/C2
Senebui (cape), Indo. 101/C2
Senec, Slvk. 49/J4
Seneca, Mo, US 183/G2
Seneca (lake), NY, US 191/H3
Seneca, Or, US 176/D1
Seneca, SC, US 193/F3
Seneca, Ks, US 185/F4
Seneca Creek State Park, Md, US 198/A5
Seneca Falls, NY, US 191/H3
Seneca Rocks NRA, WV, US 193/H1
Senecaville (lake), Oh, US 190/F5
Seneffe, Belg. 61/D2
Senegal (ctry.) 132/B3
Sénégal (riv.), Afr. 132/B2
Senekal, SAfr. 142/D3
Seney, Mi, US 190/D1
Seney NWR, Mi, US 187/L4
Senezhskoye (lake), Rus. 75/W8
Senfi, Gha. 133/E5
Senftenberg, Ger. 49/H3
Senga Hill Mission, Zam. 139/G5
Sengenthal, Ger. 65/E4
Sênggê (riv.), China 111/D5
Sengilev, Rus. 77/J1
Sengor, Bhu. 109/H2
Senguer (riv.), Arg. 226/D3
Sengwe (riv.), Zim. 141/F3
Senhor do Bonfim, Braz. 223/E1
Senica, Slvk. 49/J4
Senirkent, Turk. 114/B2
Senise, It. 54/E2
Senj, Cro. 51/L4
Senja (isl.), Nor. 44/F1
Senkaku-Shotō (isl.), Japan 97/G8
Şenkaya, Turk. 114/E1
Senkevychivka, Ukr. 78/C2
Şenköy, Turk. 116/E1
Senlac, Sk, Can. 175/K1
Senlis, Fr. 60/B5
Senmonoron, Camb. 106/D3
Sennan, Japan 95/H7
Sennar (dam), Sudan 134/G2
Senne (riv.), Belg. 61/D2
Sennecy-le-Grand, Fr. 66/A4
Sennfeld, Ger. 64/D2
Senno, Bela. 47/N4
Sennoy, Rus. 77/G2
Sennoy, Rus. 77/H1
Sennwald, Swi. 67/F3
Sennybridge, Wal, UK 42/C3
Séno (prov.), Burk. 133/F3
Senonches, Fr. 63/G3
Senones, Fr. 66/C1
Senorbì, It. 54/A3
Senovo, Bul. 57/H4
Sens, Fr. 50/E2
Sens-de-Bretagne, Fr. 62/D4
Sensuntepeque, ESal. 206/D3
Senta, Serb. 56/E3
Sentani, Indo. 103/K4
Sentery, D.R. Congo 139/F4
Sentinel, Ok, US 182/E3
Sentinel, Az, US 179/F4
Sentosa (isl.), Sing. 101/J6
Sentrum, SAfr. 141/E5
Senya Beraku, Gha. 133/E5
Senyavin (isls.), Micr. 160/E4
Senzig, Ger. 48/Q7
Seohārā, India 108/B1
Seon, Swi. 66/E3
Seondha, India 108/B2
Seoni, India 108/B4
Seonī Mālwā, India 108/A4
Seoul (Sŏul) (cap.), SKor. 91/K4
Seoul Grand Park, SKor. 93/G7
Seoul Jikhalsi (prov.), SKor. 93/D4
Sepang (pt.), Malay. 101/D2
Sepanjang (isl.), Indo. 101/F4
Separ, NM, US 179/H4
Separation (pt.), NZ 159/C3
Sepatini (riv.), Braz. 221/E3
Sepetiba (bay), Braz. 223/M8
Sepik (riv.), PNG 160/D5
Sepino, It. 71/D5
Sep'o, NKor. 93/D3
Sepo, Indo. 103/G3
Sępólno Krajeńskie, Pol. 49/J2
Sepopa, Bots. 140/D3
Sept-Îles, Qu, Can. 171/K3
Septèmes-les-Vallons, Fr. 70/B6
Septemvri, Bul. 55/J1
Septeuil, Fr. 63/G3
Sepulveda (dam), Ca, US 196/F7
Sequeros, Sp. 52/B2
Sequim (bay), Wa, US 197/A1
Sequim, Wa, US 174/C3
Sequoia NP, Ca, US 178/C2
Sequoyah Nat'l Wildlife Res., Ok, US 183/G3
Sera (isl.), Indo. 152/C1
Serafimovich, Rus. 79/M3
Seraincourt, Fr. 36/H4
Seraing, Belg. 61/E2
Serambe, Sudan 135/E2
Serampore, India 109/G4
Sèran (riv.), Fr. 66/B6
Serang, Indo. 101/D4
Serangoon (nbrhd.), Sing. 101/J6
Serasan (str.), Indo.,Malay. 102/C3
Serasan, Indo. 102/C3
Seravezza, It. 68/D6
Serbeulangit (mts.), Indo. 101/B2
Serbia (reg.), Serb. 56/E3
Serbia and Montenegro (Yugoslavia) (ctry.) 56/D3
Serbin, Tx, US 181/F2
Serchhīp, India 98/B4
Serchio (riv.), It. 68/D4
Serdang (cape), Indo. 101/D4
Serdo, Eth. 136/B3
Serdobsk, Rus. 77/H1
Serebryansk, Kaz. 80/J5
Serednikovo, Rus. 74/H5
Seredžius, Lith. 47/K4
Seregno, It. 68/C2
Serein (riv.), Fr. 48/D4
Serémange-Erzange, Fr. 61/F5
Seremban, Malay. 101/C2
Serengeti (plain), Tanz. 137/A2
Serengeti NP, Tanz. 137/A2
Serenje, Zam. 141/F2
Serere, Ugan. 137/A1
Sergach, Rus. 75/K5
Sergeantsville, NJ, US 198/D3
Sergen, Turk. 57/H5
Sergeya Kirova (isls.), Rus. 80/J2
Sergeyevka, Kaz. 75/Q5
Sergipe (state), Braz. 223/F1
Sergiyev Posad, Rus. 74/H4
Sergnano, It. 68/C3
Seria, Bru. 102/D3
Seriate, It. 68/C2
Sérifontaine, Fr. 60/A5
Sérifos, Gre. 55/J4
Sérifos (isl.), Gre. 55/J4
Sérignan, Fr. 50/E5
Serik, Turk. 116/B1
Serikbuya, China 111/C4
Seringa, Serra da (mts.), Braz. 218/D4
Serinyol, Turk. 116/E1
Serio (riv.), It. 68/C2
Serkout (peak), Alg. 129/G5
Sermaises, Fr. 63/H4
Sermaize-les-Bains, Fr. 61/D6
Sermata (isls.), Indo. 152/C2
Sermide, It. 69/E4
Sermoneta, It. 71/B4
Sernaglia della Battaglia, It. 69/F2
Sernovodsk, Rus. 77/J1
Sernur, Rus. 75/L4
Serón, Sp. 52/D4
Serós, Sp. 53/F2
Serottini (peak), It. 67/G5
Serov, Rus. 80/G4
Serowe, Bots. 141/E4
Serpa, Port. 52/B4
Serpeddi (peak), It. 54/A3
Serpent Mound, Oh, US 193/F1
Serpent's Mouth (str.), Trin.,Ven. 217/F2
Serpentine (dam), Austl. 156/C4
Serpentine Lakes, Austl. 155/F4
Serpukhov, Rus. 74/H5
Serquigny, Fr. 63/F2
Serra (peak), It. 68/D6
Serra, Braz. 223/E4
Serra Branca, Braz. 219/G4
Serra da Bocaina, PN, Braz. 225/H2
Serra da Bocaina, PN da, Braz. 222/D4
Serra da Canastra, PN, Braz. 225/H2
Serra da Canastra, PN da, Braz. 222/D4
Serra da Capivara, PN da, Braz. 223/E1
Serra da Capivara, PN da, Braz. 219/F5
Serra da Chela (mts.), Ang. 140/B3
Serra da Estrela (peak), Port. 52/B2
Serra da Estrela (mts.), Port. 52/A3
Serra do Cipó, PN da, Braz. 223/E3
Serra do Congo (mts.), Ang. 138/C4
Serra do Navio, Braz. 218/C2
Serra dos Órgãos, PN da, Braz. 223/N7
Serra Negra do Norte, Braz. 219/G4
Serra San Bruno, It. 54/E3
Serra San Quirico, It. 69/G7
Serra Talhada, Braz. 219/G4
Sérrai, Gre. 55/H2
Serralta di San Vito (peak), It. 54/E3
Serramanna, It. 54/A3
Serramazzoni, It. 69/D5
Serrana Bank (isl.), Col. 203/F5
Serranía de la Cerbatana (mts.), Ven. 217/E3
Serranía de la Neblina, PN, Ven. 217/E4
Serranías del Burro (mts.), Mex. 204/E2
Serranilla Bank (isl.), Col. 203/F4
Serrano, Arg. 226/E2
Serranópolis, Braz. 222/B3
Serrat (cape), Tun. 130/L6
Serravalle, It. 69/F4
Serravalle, SMar. 69/F6
Serravalle di Chienti, It. 71/B1
Serravalle Scrivia, It. 68/B4
Serravalle Sesia, It. 68/B2
Serre (riv.), Fr. 48/B4
Serre Chevalier (peak), Fr. 70/C3
Serre-Ponçon (lake), Fr. 70/C3
Serrenti, It. 54/A3
Serres, Fr. 70/B4
Serrières, Fr. 70/A2
Serrinha, Braz. 223/F1
Serris, Fr. 36/L5
Serrita, Braz. 219/G4
Sêrro, Braz. 225/J1
Sersale, It. 54/E3
Sertã, Port. 52/A3
Sertânia, Braz. 219/G5
Sertãozinho, Braz. 225/H2
Sertavul (pass), Turk. 116/C1
Serteng (mts.), China 90/C4
Sēru, Eth. 136/B4
Serui, Indo. 103/J4
Serule, Bots. 141/E4
Serurumi (riv.), Bots. 140/E4
Seruwai, Indo. 101/B1
Seruyan (riv.), Indo. 102/D4
Servance, Fr. 66/C2
Servel (Lannion) (arpt.), Fr. 62/B3
Servi, Turk. 114/E2
Sérvia, Gre. 55/G2
Serviceton, Austl. 156/B3
Servigliano, It. 71/C1
Serwaru, Indo. 152/B2
Sesayap (riv.), Indo. 100/B5
Sese (isls.), Ugan. 139/G3
Sesebi (ruin), Sudan 127/F4
Sesepe, Indo. 103/G4
Sesfontein, Namb. 140/B3
Sesheke, Zam. 140/E3
Sesia (riv.), It. 51/H4
Sesimbra, Port. 53/P11
Seskar (isl.), Rus. 47/N1
Sespe, Ca, US 196/B2
Sespe (cr.), Ca, US 196/A1
Sespe Condor Sanctuary, Ca, US 178/C3
Sessa Aurunca, It. 71/C5
Sesser, Il, US 192/C1
Sesslach, Ger. 64/D2
Sesto Calende, It. 68/B2
Sesto Campano, It. 71/D5
Sesto Fiorentino, It. 69/E6
Sesto San Giovanni, It. 68/C2
Sesto Ulteriano, It. 68/C3
Sestola, It. 69/D5
Sestra (riv.), Rus. 75/W8
Sestri Levante, It. 68/C5
Sestroretsk, Rus. 75/S6
Sestroretskiy (lake), Rus. 75/T6
Sestu, It. 54/A3
Sesvenna (peak), It. 67/G4
Sesvete, Cro. 56/C3
Šeta, Lith. 47/L4
Setana, Japan 94/A2
Sète, Fr. 50/E5
Sete Cidades, PN de, Braz. 219/F4
Sete Lagoas, Braz. 222/D3
Seth, WV, US 193/G1
Sethārja, Pak. 113/J3
Seti (riv.), Nepal 108/C1
Seti (zone), Nepal 108/C1
Sétif, Alg. 130/H4
Sétif (wilaya), Alg. 130/H4
Seto, Japan 95/M5
Seto-Naikai NP, Japan 96/C4
Setouchi, Japan 97/K6
Settat, Mor. 128/D2
Setté-Cama, Gabon 138/B3
Settecamini, It. 71/B4
Settepani (peak), It. 68/B5
Settimo Torinese, It. 68/A2
Settimo Vittone, It. 68/A1
Settle, Eng, UK 41/F3
Settsu, Japan 95/J6
Setúbal (dist.), Port. 52/A3
Setúbal (bay), Port. 52/A3
Setúbal, Port. 53/Q10
Seubersdorf, Ger. 65/E4
Seudre (riv.), Fr. 50/C4
Seugne (riv.), Fr. 50/C4
Seuil-D'Argonne, Fr. 61/E6
Seul (lake), On, Can. 170/G3
Seulimeum, Indo. 101/A1
Seulles (riv.), Fr. 63/E2
Seurre, Fr. 66/B4
Seuzach, Swi. 67/E2
Sevan, Arm. 115/F1
Sevana (lake), Arm. 80/E5
Sevastopol', Ukr. 79/G5
Sevelen, Swi. 67/F3
Seven (riv.), Eng, UK 41/H3
Seven (cr.), Ab, Can. 175/J3
Seven Heads (pt.), Ire. 38/B6
Seven Oaks, Tx, US 181/G2
Seven Sisters Falls, Mb, Can. 186/F2
Seven Valleys, Pa, US 198/B4
Sevenmile (hill), Ne, US 184/D2
Sevenoaks, Eng, UK 36/D3
Sevenoaks Weald, Eng, UK 36/D3
Seventy Mile House, BC, Can. 174/D2
Séveraisse (riv.), Fr. 70/C3
Severn (riv.), Wal, UK 41/F6
Severn (riv.), On, Can. 170/G3
Severn (riv.), Md, US 198/B5
Severn, Md, US 198/B5
Severna Park, Md, US 198/B5
Severnaya Osetiya-Alaniy, Resp., Rus. 81/Q6
Severnaya Sos'va (riv.), Rus. 75/N3
Severnaya Zemlya (isls.), Rus. 80/J2
Severnyy, Rus. 75/P2
Severo-Kuril'sk, Rus. 81/R4
Severo-Yeniseyskiy, Rus. 80/K3
Severobaykal'sk, Rus. 81/L4
Severočeský (pol. reg.), Czh. 51/L1
Severodvinsk, Rus. 74/H2
Severomoravský (pol. reg.), Czh. 51/M1
Severomorsk, Rus. 74/G1
Severomuysk, Rus. 81/M4
Severoural'sk, Rus. 75/N3
Seversk, Ukr. 79/K3
Severskaya, Rus. 79/K5
Severukha, Rus. 75/P4
Severy, Ks, US 183/F2
Seveso, It. 68/C2
Sevier (lake), Ut, US 177/G4
Sevier (des.), Ut, US 177/G4
Sevier, Ut, US 179/F1
Sevier (riv.), Ut, US 172/D4
Sevier (plat.), Ut, US 179/F1
Sevier, East Fork (riv.), Ut, US 179/F2
Sevierville, Tn, US 193/F3
Sevilla, Col. 219/K8
Seville, Sp. 52/C4
Seville, Austl. 156/G5
Sevilleta Nat'l Wild. Ref., NM, US 179/J3
Sevlievo, Bul. 57/G4
Sevnica, Slov. 56/B2
Sevojno, Serb. 56/D4
Sevran, Fr. 36/K5
Sevsk, Rus. 79/H1
Sewa (riv.), SLeo. 132/C5
Sewall, BC, Can. 201/M5
Sewanee, Tn, US 192/E3
Seward (pen.), Ak, US 201/E2
Seward, Ak, US 201/J3
Seward, Ne, US 185/F3
Sewaren, NJ, US 199/J9
Sewell, Chile 226/N9
Sewell Inlet, BC, Can. 201/M5
Sextons Creek, Ky, US 192/F2
Seyah Cheshmeh, Iran 115/F2
Seybaplaya, Mex. 206/D2
Seybouse, Oued (riv.), Alg. 130/K6
Seydhisfjördhur, Ice. 44/Q6
Seydişehir, Turk. 114/B2
Seyhan (dam), Turk. 116/D1
Seyhan (riv.), Turk. 116/D1
Seyitgazi, Turk. 114/B2
Seylac, Som. 136/B3
Seym (riv.), Rus. 76/E2
Seymour, Austl. 157/B3
Seymour, Ia, US 185/H3
Seymour, In, US 192/E1
Seymour, Mo, US 183/H2
Seymour, Tx, US 182/E4
Seymour, Wi, US 190/B2
Seymour Arm, BC, Can. 174/E2
Seymour Johnson (A.F.B.), NC, US 193/J3
Seyne, Fr. 70/C4
Seynod, Fr. 66/C6
Seyssel, Fr. 66/B6
Seyssinet-Pariset, Fr. 70/B2
Şeytan (riv.), Turk. 115/M6
Sežana, Slov. 51/K4
Sézanne, Fr. 60/C6
Sezimovo Ústí, Czh. 65/H4
Sezze, It. 71/C5
Sfax, Tun. 129/H2
Sfax (gov.), Tun. 129/H2
Sfîntu Gheorghe, Rom. 57/J3
Sfîntu Gheorghe, Rom. 57/G3
Sfîntu Gheorghe Branch (riv.), Rom. 57/J3
Sfizef, Alg. 130/E5
Sgurr a' Chaorachain (peak), Sc, UK 39/A2
Sgurr a' Choire Ghlais (peak), Sc, UK 39/B2
Sgurr a' Mhuilinn (peak), Sc, UK 39/B1
Sgurr Mór (peak), Sc, UK 39/A1
Sgurr na Ciche (peak), Sc, UK 39/A2
Sgurr na Lapaich (peak), Sc, UK 39/A2
Sha (riv.), China 92/C4
Sha Tau Kok, China 99/L6
Sha Tin, China 99/L7
Shaanxi (prov.), China 90/F5
Shab'ā, Leb. 117/D2
Shaba Nat'l Rsv., Kenya 137/B1
Shābah, Egypt 131/B2
Shabās al Milḩ, Egypt 131/B2
Shabās ash Shuhadā', Egypt 131/B2
Shabās 'Umayr, Egypt 131/B2
Shabashah, Sudan 134/G2
Shābāzpur (riv.), Bang. 109/H4
Shabla, Bul. 57/J4
Shabo, Ukr. 78/F4
Shabqadar, Pak. 110/A2
Shabunda, D.R. Congo 139/F3
Shabwah, Yem. 136/C2
Shache, China 111/C4
Shackan Ind. Res., BC, Can. 174/D2
Shackleford, Eng, UK 36/B3
Shadaogou, China 99/F2
Shade (mtn.), Pa, US 198/A2
Shadehill (dam), SD, US 186/C5
Shadehill, SD, US 186/C5
Shadeland, In, US 190/C4
Shadrinsk, Rus. 75/P4
Shaduzup, Myan. 98/C3
Shady Cove, Or, US 176/B2
Shady Grove, Fl, US 195/G2
Shady Spring, WV, US 193/G2
Shadyside, Oh, US 190/F5
Shafer (lake), In, US 190/C4
Shafranovo, Rus. 75/M5
Shafter, Ca, US 178/C3
Shafter, Nv, US 177/F3
Shafter, Tx, US 180/B3
Shaftesbury, Eng, UK 42/D4
Shaftsbury, Vt, US 191/K3
Shag Harbour, NS, Can. 188/E4
Shagamu, Nga. 133/F5
Shagan (riv.), Kaz. 111/C2
Shagang, China 93/B2
Shagany (lake), Urk. 78/E5
Shagany (lake), Rom. 57/J3
Shageluk, Ak, US 201/G3
Shagonar, Rus. 90/C1
Shah Alam, Malay. 101/C2
Shāh Kot, Pak. 110/B4
Shāhābād, India 110/D4
Shāhābād, India 108/B2
Shāhābād, India 108/B1
Shāhābād, India 108/A3
Shahbā', Syria 117/F3
Shāhbandar, Pak. 113/J4
Shahdād, Iran 113/G2
Shāhdādkot, Pak. 113/J3
Shāhdādpur, Pak. 113/J3
Shāhdara, Pak. 110/C4
Shāhdasht, Iran 115/F4
Shahdol, India 108/C4
Shahekan, China 90/F5
Shāhganj, India 108/D2
Shaḩḩāt, Libya 126/D1
Shāhjahānpur, India 108/B2
Shāhpur, Pak. 110/B3
Shāhpur, India 110/D3
Shāhpur, India 108/A4
Shāhpur Chākar, Pak. 104/A2
Shāhpura, India 108/C4
Shahr Sultān, Pak. 110/A5
Shahr-e Bābak, Iran 115/H4
Shahr-e Kord, Iran 115/G3
Shahr-e Monjān, Afg. 110/A1
Shahrak, Iran 115/G3
Shāhrūd, Iran 115/G3
Shahryār, Iran 115/G3
Shāhzādpur, India 110/D4
Shāhzādpur, Bang. 109/G3
Shā'ib al Banāt (peak), Egypt 127/G3
Shaikhpura, India 109/E3
Shāistāganj, Bang. 109/H3
Shājāpur, India 104/C3
Shaji, China 90/F4
Shajian, China 99/H3
Shajianzi, China 93/C2
Shakargarh, Pak. 110/C3
Shakaskraal, SAfr. 143/E3
Shakawe, Bots. 140/D3
Shakespeare (isl.), On, Can. 187/K3
Shakhbuz, Azer. 77/H5
Shakhtars'k, Ukr. 79/K3
Shakhtërsk, Rus. 91/N2
Shakhtinsk, Kaz. 80/H5
Shakhty, Rus. 79/L4
Shakhun'ya, Rus. 75/K4
Shaki, Nga. 133/F4
Shakīso, Eth. 136/A4
Shakopee, Mn, US 187/N7
Shakotan (pen.), Japan 94/B2
Shaksha, Rus. 75/N5
Shaktoolik, Ak, US 201/F3
Shāl, Iran 115/G3
Shala (lake), Eth. 136/A4
Shalaanbood, Som. 137/D1
Shalbuzdag (peak), Rus. 77/H4
Shaldon, Eng, UK 42/C5
Shalford, Eng, UK 36/B3
Shali, Rus. 77/H4
Shaling, China 93/B2
Shallotte, NC, US 193/H4
Shallow Reach (inlet), Austl. 155/M8
Shallowater, Tx, US 182/D4
Shalqar, Kaz. 77/L3
Shal'skiy, Rus. 74/H3
Shaluli (mts.), China 90/D5
Shalyhyne, Ukr. 79/H2
Shama (riv.), Tanz. 137/A3
Shamary, Rus. 75/N4
Shamattawa (riv.), On, Can. 171/H3
Shambe, Sudan 134/F4
Shambu, Eth. 134/H3
Shambungu, D.R. Congo 138/D4
Shāmgarh, India 104/C3
Shamīl, Iran 115/J5
Shāmli, India 110/D5
Shammar, Jabal (mts.), SAr. 112/D3
Shamokin (cr.), Pa, US 198/B2
Shamokin, Pa, US 198/B2
Shamokin Dam, Pa, US 198/B2
Shāmpur, India 108/A2
Shamrock, Tx, US 182/D3
Shamrock Dome (mt.), Yk, Can. 201/L3
Shamsābād, India 108/A4
Shamsābād, India 108/B2
Shamva, Zim. 141/F3
Shan (state), Myan. 105/G3
Shan (plat.), Myan. 105/G3
Shan (pass), China 99/H3
Shan-Ngaw (range), Myan. 98/C3
Shanagolden, Ire. 38/A4
Shanchengzhen, China 93/C1
Shandī, Sudan 134/G1
Shandon, Ca, US 178/B3
Shandong (prov.), China 91/H4
Shandong (pen.), China 91/H4
Shandong (isl.), China 92/E3
Shangani, Zim. 141/F3
Shangani (riv.), Zim. 141/F3
Shangcai, China 92/C4
Shangcheng, China 92/C5
Shangchuan (isl.), China 99/G4
Shangdu, China 99/G3
Shangdu, China 90/G3
Shangfang, China 99/H2
Shanghai (prov.), China 91/J5
Shanghai, China 92/L8
Shanghe, China 92/D3
Shanghekou, China 93/C2
Shangjiahe, China 93/C2
Shangjiaodao, China 99/H2
Shangjing, China 99/H3
Shangliang, China 90/F5
Shanglin, China 105/J3
Shangolume, D.R. Congo 139/F5
Shangombo, Zam. 140/D3
Shangping, China 99/G3
Shangqiu, China 92/C4
Shangrao, China 99/H2
Shangshui, China 92/C4
Shangsi, China 106/D1
Shangyi, China 92/C2
Shangyou (riv.), China 99/G3
Shanhua, Tai. 99/J4
Shani, Nga. 134/B3
Shanklin, Eng, UK 43/E5
Shankou, China 99/F2
Shanks, WV, US 191/G5
Shanmatang (mtn.), China 99/F3
Shanmen, China 99/F3
Shannawona (peak), Ire. 38/A3
Shannon, Qu, Can. 188/B2
Shannon (int'l arpt.), Ire. 38/B4
Shannon (riv.), Ire. 38/B4
Shannon, NZ 159/C3
Shannon, Ga, US 192/E3
Shannon, Ms, US 192/C3
Shannon (lake), Wa, US 174/C3
Shannon Hills, Ar, US 183/H3
Shannonbridge, Ire. 38/B3
Shanshan, China 90/C3
Shanshūr, Egypt 131/C4
Shantangyi, China 99/F3
Shanţānūf, Egypt 131/C4
Shantar (isl.), Rus. 83/N4
Shantar (isls.), Rus. 81/P4
Shantou, China 99/H4
Shanty Bay, On, Can. 191/G2
Shanwa, Tanz. 137/A2
Shanxi (prov.), China 90/G4
Shanyang, China 99/H3
Shanyao, China 99/H3
Shanyin, China 92/C3
Shaodong, China 99/F3
Shaoguan, China 99/G3
Shaoshan, China 99/G3
Shaoxing, China 99/J2
Shaoyang, China 99/F3
Shap, Eng, UK 41/F2
Shapa, China 99/F4
Shapki, Rus. 47/P2
Shapkina (riv.), Rus. 75/M2
Shaqiuhe, China 111/E2
Shaqlāwah, Iraq 115/F2
Shaqrā', SAr. 112/E3
Shaqrā', Yem. 136/C2
Sharafkhāneh, Iran 115/F2
Sharan, Rus. 75/M5
Sharanga, Rus. 75/K4
Sharbot Lake, On, Can. 191/H2
Sharga, Mong. 90/D2
Sharhorod, Ukr. 78/E3
Shari, Japan 94/D2
Sharïngol, Mong. 90/F2
Sharjah (int'l arpt.), UAE 113/G3
Shark (bay), Austl. 145/A3
Shark River (inlet), NJ, US 199/D3
Sharkovshchina, Bela. 47/M4
Sharlyk, Rus. 77/K1
Sharm ash Shaykh, Egypt 127/G3
Sharnbrook, Eng, UK 43/F2
Sharnūb, Egypt 131/B2
Sharon, Ct, US 191/K4
Sharon, Pa, US 190/F4
Sharon, Tn, US 192/C2
Sharon, Vt, US 191/K3
Sharon Springs, Ks, US 182/D1
Sharonville, Oh, US 190/D5
Sharovka, Ukr. 79/H2
Sharpe (lake), SD, US 184/E1
Sharpes, Fl, US 195/H3
Sharpsburg, Ky, US 192/F1
Sharqpur, Pak. 110/C4
Shar'ya, Rus. 75/K4
Shasha, Eth. 134/G4
Shashe, Bots. 141/E4
Shashe (riv.), Bots. 141/F4
Shashemenē, Eth. 136/A4
Shashi, China 99/G2
Shasta (lake), Ca, US 176/B3
Shasta (mt.), Ca, US 176/B3
Shasta (dam), Ca, US 176/B3
Shatalovo, Rus. 74/G5
Shāţi (wadi), Libya 126/B3
Shatsk, Rus. 77/G1
Shatsk, Bela. 47/M5
Shatskiy NP, Ukr. 49/M3
Shatt al Arab (riv.), Iraq 112/E2
Shattāy, Sudan 134/D2
Shattuck, Ok, US 182/E2
Shaughnessy, Ab, Can. 175/H3
Shaunavon, Sk, Can. 175/K3
Shavano Park, Tx, US 181/E3
Shave Ziyyon, Isr. 117/C3
Shaver Lake, Ca, US 178/C2
Shaw, La, US 194/C2
Shaw, Ms, US 192/B4
Shaw, Eng, UK 43/E4
Shaw (A.F.B.), SC, US 193/G4
Shawan, China 99/H3
Shawano, Wi, US 185/K1
Shawbury, Eng, UK 42/D1
Shawnee, Co, US 182/B1
Shawnee, Oh, US 190/E5
Shawnee, Ok, US 183/F3
Shawneetown, Il, US 192/C2
Shawnī, Egypt 131/B3
Shawville, Qu, Can. 191/H2
Shaxi, China 99/F3
Shay Gap, Austl. 154/D2
Shaykh Miskīn, Syria 117/E3
Shaykh Sa'd, Iraq 115/F3
Shaykh 'Uthmān, Yem. 136/C2
Shaykhān, Iraq 115/E2
Shaymak, Taj. 111/B4
Shazaoyuan, China 90/C4
Shazipo, China 99/F2
Shchara (riv.), Bela. 76/C1
Shchastya, Ukr. 79/K3
Shchedok, Rus. 77/G3
Shchekino, Rus. 76/F1
Shchelkovo, Rus. 75/W9
Shchel'yabozh, Rus. 75/N2
Shchel'yayur, Rus. 75/M2

Shcherbakty, Kaz. 80/H4
Shcherbinka, Rus. 75/W9
Shchigry, Rus. 79/J2
Shchors, Ukr. 78/F2
Shchuchin, Bela. 47/L5
Shchūchīnsk, Kaz. 111/B1
Shchuch'ye, Rus. 75/P5
She Xian, China 99/H2
Shea Stadium, NY, US 199/K9
Sheaville, Or, US 134/H4
Shebē, Eth. 134/H4
Shebekino, Rus. 79/J2
Sheberghān, Afg. 113/J1
Sheppey, Isle of
Sheboygan, Wi, US 190/C3
Sheboygan Falls, Wi, US 190/C3
Shebunino, Rus. 91/N2
Shedd, Or, US 176/F1
Shediac, NB, Can. 188/E2
Shee (riv.), Sc, UK 39/C3
Sheelin, Ire. 40/A4
Sheep (mt.), Ak, US 201/F2
Sheep (mts.), Nv, US 178/E2
Sheep (riv.), Ab, Can. 174/G2
Sheep Mountain (peak), SD, US 184/C2
Sheepshead Bay (nbrhd.), NY, US 199/G3
Sheerness, Eng, UK 43/G4
Sheerness, Ab, Can. 175/J2
Sheet Harbour, NS, Can. 189/F3
Shefar'am, Isr. 117/C3
Shefayim, Isr. 117/F4
Sheffield, Austl. 156/C4
Sheffield, Eng, UK 41/G5
Sheffield (co.), Eng, UK 41/G5
Sheffield, Al, US 199/M7
Sheffield (isl.), Ct, US 199/M7
Sheffield, Ma, US 191/K3
Sheffield, Tx, US 180/D2
Shefford, Eng, UK 43/F2
Shegamishu, China 99/G2
Shegovary, Rus. 74/J3
Shēh Ḩusēn, Eth. 136/B4
Shehēt, Eth. 136/A2
Shehuen (riv.), Arg. 191/C6
Shehy (mts.), Ire. 38/A6
Sheikh, Som. 136/C3
Sheila, NB, Can. 188/E2
Shejiaping, China 92/B3
Shek Uk (peak), China 99/M7
Shekhūpura, Pak. 110/B4
Shelagskiy (cape), Rus. 81/S2
Shelbina, Mo, US 185/K4
Shelburne (bay), Austl. 153/F2
Shelburne, NS, Can. 189/F3
Shelburne, On, Can. 188/D2
Shelburn, In, US 190/C5
Shelburne, Vt, US 191/K2
Shelburne Falls, Ma, US 191/J2
Shelby, Ia, US 185/G3
Shelby, Mi, US 190/C3
Shelby, Ms, US 192/B4
Shelby, Mt, US 175/J3
Shelby, NC, US 193/G3
Shelby, Ne, US 184/F3
Shelby, Oh, US 188/D4
Shelbyville, Il, US 185/K4
Shelbyville, Il, US 185/K4
Shelbyville (lake), Il, US 185/K4
Shelbyville, Ky, US 192/E1
Shelbyville, Mo, US 185/K4
Shelbyville, Tn, US 192/D3
Shelbyville, Tx, US 181/G2
Sheldon, Ia, US 185/G2
Sheldon, Il, US 190/C4
Sheldon, Mo, US 183/G2
Sheldon, ND, US 186/F4
Sheldon, Tx, US 181/M9
Sheldon, Vt, US 191/K2
Sheldon, Wi, US 187/J5
Sheldon Antelope Range, Nv, US 176/D3
Sheldon Point, Ak, US 201/F3
Shelekhov (gulf), Rus. 83/Q3
Shelikof (str.), Ak, US 201/H4
Shell (pt.), Ak, US 184/E4
Shell (cr.), Ne, US 184/F3
Shell Keys Nat'l Wild. Ref., La, US 181/J3
Shell Lake, Sk, Can. 175/L1
Shell Lake, Wi, US 187/J5
Shell Rock Nat'l Wild. Ref., ND, US 186/F4
Shell Rock, Ia, US 185/H2
Shellbrook, Sk, Can. 175/L1
Shelley, Id, US 177/G2
Shelley, Pa, US 188/B3
Shellharbour, Austl. 157/E2
Shellman, Ga, US 195/F2
Shelly, Mn, US 186/F4
Shelter I., NY, US 199/F1
Shelter Island (sound), NY, US 199/F1
Shelton, Ct, US 199/E1
Shelton, Ne, US 184/F3
Shelton, Wa, US 174/C4
Shemgang, Bhu. 109/H2
Shemya, Ak, US 201/A5
Shen Xian, China 92/C3
Shenandoah, Ia, US 185/G3
Shenandoah (riv.), Va, US 193/H1
Shenandoah, Va, US 193/H1
Shenandoah, Pa, US 198/B2
Shenandoah NP, Va, US 193/H1
Shenandoah, South Fork
Shenchi, China 92/C3
Shendam, Nga. 138/C3
Shenge (pt.), SLeo. 132/B5
Shengena (peak), Tanz. 137/B3
Shengfang, China 92/H7
Shengjiaqiao, China 99/H2
Shengjin, Alb. 55/F2
Shengjing (pass), China 111/E3
Shengli (pass), China 111/F3
Shengze, China 92/L9
Shenhu, China 99/H3
Shenkursk, Rus. 74/J3
Sheno, Eth. 136/A3
Shenqiu, China 99/H3
Shenstone, Eng, UK 43/E1
Shenyang, China 93/B2
Shenzao, China 91/J5

Shenzhen, China 99/G4
Sheoganj, India 104/B2
Sheopur, India 104/C2
Shepard, Ab, Can. 175/H2
Shepetivka, Ukr. 78/D2
Shepherd, Tx, US 181/G2
Shepherd (isls.), Van. 160/F6
Shepherdsville, Ky, US 192/E2
Sheppard 199/K9
Shepparton, Austl. 157/B3
Shepshed, Eng, UK 43/E1
Shepton Mallet, Eng, UK 42/D4
Sherborne, Eng, UK 42/D5
Sherbro (isl.), SLeo. 132/B5
Sherbrooke, Qu, Can. 191/L2
Sherbrooke, NS, Can. 189/G3
Sherburn, Eng, UK 41/G2
Sherburn, Mn, US 185/H3
Sherburne Nat'l Wild. Ref., Kenya 137/B3
Shimabara, Japan 96/B4
Shimada, Japan 97/F3
Shimagahara, Japan 95/K6
Shimamoto, Japan 95/J6
Shimane (pref.), Japan 96/C3
Shimamasi, Japan 41/G2
Shimba Hills Nat'l Rsvs., Kenya 137/B3
Shimbara (riv.), Japan 96/B4
Shimber Berris (peak), Som. 133/H4
Shimen, China 92/H6
Shimenqiao, China 99/F2
Shimizu, Japan 97/F3
Shimizu, Japan 109/J2
Shimizu, Japan 109/E3
Shimo-koshiki, Japan 96/C3
Shimobe, Japan 95/A3
Shimoda, Japan 97/F3
Shimodate, Japan 95/A3
Shimofusa, Japan 95/C2
Shimoichi, Japan 95/J7
Shimokita (pen.), Japan 94/B3
Shimonita, Japan 95/A3
Shimonoseki, Japan 96/B4
Shimotsuma, Japan 95/A3
Shimoyama, Japan 95/M5
Shimsk, Rus. 47/P2
Shin (lake), Sc, UK 37/E7
Shin, Japan 95/C1
Shinano (riv.), Japan 91/M4
Shinano, China 106/E1
Shinās, Oman 113/G4
Shinch'ŏrwon, SKor. 93/D3
Shindo, SKor. 93/F6
Shiner, China 107/C4
Shingbwiyang, Myan. 98/C3
Shingleton, Mi, US 190/C1
Shingū, Japan 96/D4
Shingwidzi, SAfr. 141/F4
Shinhyŏn, SKor. 96/A3
Shinji (lake), Japan 96/C3
Shinjō, Japan 95/G1
Shinjō, Japan 95/J7
Shinkawa, Japan 95/L5
Shinminato, Japan 97/E2
Shinnecock (bay), NY, US 199/F2
Shinnecock Ind. Res., NY, US 199/F2
Shinnston, WV, US 190/F5
Shinrone, Ire. 38/C4
Shinsei, Japan 95/L5
Shintoku, Japan 94/C2
Shinyanga, Tanz. 137/A2
Shinyanga (prov.), Tanz. 137/A2
Shio-no-misaki, Japan 96/D4
Shiogama, Japan 97/G1
Shioya-saki (pt.), Japan 97/G2
Ship (isl.), Ms, US 194/D2
Ship Bottom, NJ, US 199/D3
Shipai, China 99/H3
Shipbourne, Eng, UK 36/D3
Shipeng, China 95/B3
Shippagan, NB, Can. 188/E2
Shippensburg, Pa, US 191/H4
Shippingport, Pa, US 188/E2
Shiprock, NM, US 179/H2
Shiqiao, China 99/H3
Shiqiao, China 99/H3
Shiqijie, China 91/K3
Shir (mtn.), Iran 115/H4
Shirakami-misaki (chan.), Japan 94/B2
Shirakawa, Japan 99/H3
Shirakawa, Japan 97/G2
Shirakawa-tōge 111/B3
Shiriya-zaki (pt.), Japan 94/B3
Shirley, Ar, US 183/H3
Shirley, NY, US 199/F2
Shiro, Tx, US 181/G2
Shiroishi, Japan 95/E2
Shirone, Japan 97/G1
Shīrvān, Iran 115/J2
Shu'āt, WBnk. 117/C5
Shu'aldin (vol.), Ak, US 201/F5
Shishan, China 99/H3
Shīshgarh, India 108/B1

Shilabo, Eth. 136/C4
Shilbottle, Eng, UK 39/E6
Shildon, Eng, UK 41/G2
Shilpu, China 99/G2
Shilka (riv.), Rus. 83/L4
Shilka, Rus. 90/H1
Shillelagh, Ire. 38/D4
Shillington, Pa, US 198/C3
Shillong, India 105/F2
Shiloango (riv.), Congo 157/B3
Shiting, China 198/C5
Shilou, China 92/B3
Shilovo, Rus. 77/G1
Shivacheve, Bul. 57/H1
Shivalaya, Bang. 109/G4
Shiven (riv.), China 38/D3
Shivers, China 77/G1
Shivpurī, India 104/A3
Shivpurī NP, India 108/A3
Shivwits 90/D3
Shixing, China 99/G3
Shiyan, China 92/B4
Shizhong, China 98/D3
Shizipu, China 99/H3
Shizong, China 98/D3
Shizugawa, Japan 94/B4
Shizuishan, Japan 92/H6
Shizukuishi, Japan 94/B4
Shizunai, Japan 94/C2
Shizuoka, Japan 97/F3
Shizuoka (pref.), Japan 97/F3
Shizigouhou, China 95/J5
Shizong, China 99/J2
Shizuka, China 99/H3
Shkoder, Alb. 55/F1
Shkumbin (riv.), Alb. 56/E5
Shoal (cr.), Il, US 185/K3
Shoal (pt.), Austl. 153/G3
Shoal Harbour, Nf, Can. 189/L1
Shoal Lake, Mb, Can. 186/D2
Shoalhaven Heads, Austl. 157/E2
Shoals, In, US 192/D1
Shoalwater Ind. Res., Wa, US 174/B4
Shōbara, Japan 96/C3
Shōbu, Japan 95/D1
Shōdo (isl.), Japan 96/D3
Shoe (mtn.), Ok, US 183/G4
Shoeburyness, Eng, UK 43/G3
Shoemakersville, Pa, US 198/C3
Shomron (ruin), WBnk. 117/C4
Shonto, Az, US 179/G2
Shōnan, Japan 95/C2
Shoreacres, BC, Can. 174/F3
Shoreham, Eng, UK 36/C4
Shoreham, Mi, US 190/C4
Shoreham, Vt, US 191/K3
Shoreham-by-Sea, Eng, UK 43/F5
Shoreview, Mn, US 187/P6
Shorewood, Il, US 197/P16
Shorewood, Wi, US 197/Q13
Shorkot, Pak. 110/B4
Shorkot Road, Pak. 110/B4
Shorncliffe 153/F3
Short (mtn.), Tn, US 192/D3
Shorten, Il, US 192/F4
Shorter, Al, US 192/F4
Shorterville, Al, US 195/F2
Shortland (isls.), Sol. 159/V15
Shortland (isl.), Sol. 159/V15
Shorwell, Eng, UK 43/E5
Shoshone (lake), 177/H1
Shoshone, Ca, US 178/D3
Shoshone (mts.), Nv, US 176/E4
Shoshone (riv.), Wy, US 177/J1
Shoshone, Id, US 177/F2
Shoshone (falls), Id, US 177/F2
Shoshong, Bots. 141/E4
Shoshoni, Wy, US 177/J2
Shostka, Ukr. 79/G2
Shotley, Eng, UK 43/H3
Shotton, Eng, UK 41/G2
Shotts, Sc, UK 39/C5
Shou Xian, China 92/D4
Shouguang, China 99/G2
Shouyang, China 92/C3
Shoval, Isr. 117/B6
Show Low, Az, US 179/G3
Shōwa, Japan 95/B2
Shoyna, Rus. 75/K2
Shozhma, Rus. 74/J3
Shpakovskoye, Rus. 79/M5
Shpanberga 141/F3
Shpikov, Ukr. 78/E3
Shpola, Ukr. 78/F3
Shreveport, La, US 180/H1
Shrewsbury, Eng, UK 42/D1
Shrewsbury, Ma, US 198/G2
Shriner (mtn.), Pa, US 198/A2
Shropshire (co.), Eng, UK 41/E6
Shropshire Union (canal), Eng, UK 41/F6
Shrule, Ire. 38/A2
Shū, Kaz. 80/H5
Shū (riv.), China 99/J2
Shu'bah (wadi), Libya 126/D2
Shuangbai, China 98/D3
Shuangcheng, China 81/N5
Shuangchang, China 141/D3
Shuangliao, China 92/E2
Shuangpaishan, China 99/H2
Shuangxi, China 99/H3
Shuangyang, China 93/B2
Shuangyashan, China 81/P5
Shubarkuduk, Kaz. 77/L2
Shubarshi, Kaz. 77/L2
Shubenacadie, NS, Can. 189/F3
Shubuta, Ms, US 194/D2
Shucheng, China 99/D2
Shuguang, China 99/E2
Shuguang, China 92/C3
Shuguorovo, Rus. 75/M5
Shuibatang, China 99/E2
Shuibei, China 99/H3

Shishhid 136/C4
Shishmaref, Ak, US 201/E2
Shishou, China 99/G2
Shisht al An'ām, Egypt 83/L4
Shisui, Japan 38/D4
Shitang, China 99/J2
Shitang, China 198/C3
Shithātha, Iraq 115/E3
Shiting (riv.), China 98/E2
Shituan, China 99/M5
Shivachevo, Bul. 57/H1
Shivalaya, Bang. 109/G4
Shiven (riv.), China 38/D3
Shivurī NP, India 108/A3
Shizhong, China 98/D3
Shizipu, China 99/H3
Shizong, China 98/D3
Shōbara, Japan 96/C3
Shōbu, Japan 95/D1
Shōdo (isl.), Japan 96/D3
Shoe (mtn.), Ok, US 183/G4
Shoeburyness, Eng, UK 43/G3
Shoemakersville, Pa, US 198/C3
Shomron (ruin), WBnk. 117/C4
Shonto, Az, US 179/G2
Shōnan, Japan 95/C2
Shoreacres, BC, Can. 174/F3
Shoreham, Eng, UK 36/C4
Shoreham, Mi, US 190/C4
Shoreham, Vt, US 191/K3
Shoreham-by-Sea, Eng, UK 43/F5
Shoreview, Mn, US 187/P6
Shorewood, Il, US 197/P16
Shorewood, Wi, US 197/Q13
Shorkot, Pak. 110/B4
Shorkot Road, Pak. 110/B4
Shorncliffe 153/F3
Short (mtn.), Tn, US 192/D3
Shorten, Il, US 192/F4
Shorter, Al, US 192/F4
Shorterville, Al, US 195/F2
Shortland (isls.), Sol. 159/V15
Shorwell, Eng, UK 43/E5
Shoshone (lake) 177/H1
Shoshone, Ca, US 178/D3
Shoshone (mts.), Nv, US 176/E4
Shoshone (riv.), Wy, US 177/J1
Shoshone, Id, US 177/F2
Shoshone (falls), Id, US 177/F2
Shoshong, Bots. 141/E4
Shoshoni, Wy, US 177/J2
Shostka, Ukr. 79/G2
Shotley, Eng, UK 43/H3
Shotton, Eng, UK 41/G2
Shotts, Sc, UK 39/C5
Shou Xian, China 92/D4
Shouguang, China 99/G2
Shouyang, China 92/C3
Shoval, Isr. 117/B6
Show Low, Az, US 179/G3
Shōwa, Japan 95/B2
Shoyna, Rus. 75/K2
Shozhma, Rus. 74/J3
Shpakovskoye, Rus. 79/M5
Shpanberga 141/F3
Shpikov, Ukr. 78/E3
Shpola, Ukr. 78/F3
Shreveport, La, US 180/H1
Shrewsbury, Eng, UK 42/D1
Shrewsbury, Ma, US 198/G2
Shriner (mtn.), Pa, US 198/A2
Shropshire (co.), Eng, UK 41/E6
Shropshire Union (canal), Eng, UK 41/F6
Shrule, Ire. 38/A2
Shū, Kaz. 80/H5
Shū (riv.), China 99/J2
Shu'bah (wadi), Libya 126/D2
Shuangbai, China 98/D3
Shuangcheng, China 81/N5
Shuangchang, China 141/D3
Shuangliao, China 92/E2
Shuangpaishan, China 99/H2
Shuangxi, China 99/H3
Shuangyang, China 93/B2
Shuangyashan, China 81/P5
Shubarkuduk, Kaz. 77/L2
Shubarshi, Kaz. 77/L2
Shubenacadie, NS, Can. 189/F3
Shubuta, Ms, US 194/D2
Shucheng, China 99/D2
Shuguang, China 99/E2
Shuguang, China 92/C3
Shuguorovo, Rus. 75/M5
Shuibatang, China 99/E2
Shuibei, China 99/H3

Shuiche, China 99/H3
Shuiji, China 99/H3
Shuijing, China 99/F2
Shuikou, China 99/E2
Shuikou, China 99/G4
Shuikouguan, China 106/D1
Shuiluo (riv.), China 98/D2
Shuimenzi, China 93/B3
Shuinan, China 99/F2
Shuiping, China 90/F5
Shujāābād, Pak. 110/A5
Shukan, China 99/H3
Shule (riv.), China 80/K6
Shule, China 90/D3
Shulehe, China 98/A2
Shulerville, SC, US 193/H4
Shulu, China 92/C3
Shumanay, Uzb. 77/L4
Shumen, Bul. 57/H4
Shumerlya, Rus. 75/K5
Shumikha, Rus. 75/P5
Shums'k, Ukr. 78/D2
Shuna (isl.), Sc, UK 39/A3
Shūnak (wadi), Egypt 127/E2
Shūnak (peak), Kaz. 111/B2
Shūnat Nimrīn, Jor. 117/D5
Shun'ga, Rus. 74/G3
Shungnak, Ak, US 201/G2
Shunyi, China 92/H6
Shuo Xian, China 92/C3
Shuoliang, China 99/E4
Shuolong, China 106/D1
Shupiyan, India 110/C3
Shuqualak, Ms, US 192/C4
Shūr (riv.), Iran 113/G2
Shūr Āb, Iran 115/G3
Shurayk, Sudan 130/B2
Shurugwi, Zim. 141/F3
Shūsh, Iran 115/F3
Shushenskoye, Rus. 111/F1
Shūshtar, Iran 115/G3
Shuswap 130/A2
Shuswap (lake), BC, Can. 174/E2
Shuwak, Sudan 134/G2
Shuwaykah, WBnk. 117/C4
Shuya, Rus. 74/J4
Shuya, Rus. 74/J4
Shuyang, China 92/D4
Shuyeretskoye, Rus. 74/G2
Shwebandaw, Myan. 98/B5
Shwebo, Myan. 98/B3
Shwedaung, Myan. 98/B5
Shwegun, Myan. 98/C5
Shwegyin, Myan. 98/C4
Shweli (riv.), Myan. 98/C3
Shwemawdaw Pagoda, Myan. 98/C5
Shwethalyaung (Reclining Buddha), Myan. 98/C5
Shyghys Qazaqstan Oblast, (obl.), Kaz. 80/J5
Shymkent, Kaz. 111/A3
Shyok, India 110/C2
Shyok (riv.), India 110/C2
Shyroke, Ukr. 79/G4
Shyshaky, Ukr. 79/G3
Si Chiang Mai, Thai. 106/C2
Si (riv.), Ger. 51/G1
Si Kiu, Thai. 106/B4
Si Khiu, Thai. 106/C3
Si Piso-Piso (falls), Indo. 101/B2
Si Racha, Thai. 106/C3
Si Satchanalai, Thai. 106/B2
Si Xian, China 92/D4
Siah Koh (mts.), Afg. 113/H2
Siāh Kūh (mts.), India 102/C3
Siakslriinderapura, Indo. 101/C2
Siālkot, Pak. 110/C2
Siargao (isl.), Phil. 103/F1
Siasi, Phil. 100/C4
Siasconset, Ma, US 189/G2
Siatista, Gre. 55/G2
Siau (isl.), Indo. 103/G1
Siauliai (prov.), Lith. 47/K4
Siavonga, Zam. 141/E3
Sibalom, Phil. 103/G3
Sibanyati, Zam. 141/E3
Sibasa, SAfr. 141/F4
Sibay, Rus. 77/L1
Sibbhultan (riv.), Swe. 45/L6
Sibbo (Sipoo), Fin. 45/J3
Sibdey, NJ, US 187/J5
Sibay, Rus. 77/L1
Sibi, Pak. 113/J3
Sibidiri, PNG 153/F2
Sibigo, Indo. 101/A2
Sibiloi NP, Kenya 134/H4
Sibiti, Congo 138/C3
Sibiu (prov.), Rom. 57/G2
Sibiu, Rom. 57/G3
Sible Hedingham, Eng, UK 43/G3
Sibley, Ia, US 185/G2
Sibley (peak), Sp. 52/B1
Sibolga, Indo. 101/B2
Siboluton, Indo. 103/B2
Siborongborong, Indo. 101/B2
Sibsāgar, India 105/H2
Sibu, Malay. 102/D3
Sibuan, Indo. 103/G1
Sibubuan (bay), China 99/H3
Sibuco, Phil. 100/C4
Sibut, CAfr. 138/D3
Sibutu Passage (chan., Malay/Phil.) 100/C1
Sibuyan (isl.), Phil. 103/F1
Sicamous, BC, Can. 174/E2
Sicapoo (mt.), Phil. 100/C1

Sichifulo (riv.), Zam. 140/E3
Sichuan (prov.), China 90/E5
Sicié (cape), Fr. 70/B6
Sicily (pol. reg.), It. 54/C4
Sicily (str.), It. 73/F3
Sicily Island, La, US 194/C2
Sicily Island 29/F5
Sicuani, Peru 220/D4
Sico (riv.), Hon. 69/G2
Sid, Serb. 56/D3
Sidamo (prov.), Eth. 134/H4
Sidaogou, China 134/H4
Sidcup (nbrhd.), Eng, UK 36/D2
Sidéradougou, Burk. 132/D4
Siderno Marina, It. 54/E3
Sidhi, India 90/D3
Sidhīrokastron, Gre. 55/H2
Sidhirókastron, Gre. 55/H2
Sidi Aïssa, Alg. 130/G5
Sīdī Barrānī, Egypt 127/E2
Sidi Bel-Abbes, Alg. 129/H3
Sidi Bennour, Mor. 128/C2
Sīdī Bū Zīd 74/G3
Sīdī Ghāzī, Egypt 131/C2
Sidi Ifni, Mor. 128/C3
Sidi Kacem, Mor. 130/B2
Sidi Kacem (prov.), Mor. 130/B2
Sīdī Nājī, Tun. 130/M6
Sīdī Sālim, Egypt 131/C2
Sidi Slimane, Mor. 130/B2
Sidi 'Umar Bū Ḩajalah, 130/M7
Sīdī Yahya du Rharb, Mor. 130/M7
Sidikalang, Indo. 101/A2
Sidlaw (hills), Sc, UK 39/C3
Sidmouth, Eng, UK 42/C5
Sidnaw, Mi, US 187/K4
Sidney (riv.), BC, Can. 174/E2
Sidney, Mb, Can. 186/D3
Sidney, Ar, US 183/J2
Sidney, Il, US 185/K4
Sidney, Mt, US 186/B4
Sidney, Ne, US 184/D3
Sidney, NY, US 191/J3
Sidney, Oh, US 188/D4
Sidney Draw 184/C2
Sidney Lanier (riv.), Co, US 184/C2
Sidon (Şaydā), Leb. 117/C1
Sidra, Libya 125/J2
Sidrolândia, Braz. 225/F2
Sidvokodvo, Swaz. 143/E2
Sieci, It. 69/E6
Siedlce, Pol. 49/M2
Siegiswil, Swi. 69/E4
Sieg (riv.), Ger. 51/G1
Siegburg, Ger. 50/G6
Siegel (mtn.), Mt, US 174/G4
Siegen, Ger. 26/C1
Siegenburg, Ger. 65/E5
Siegendorf im Burgenland, Aus. 56/C2
Sielo, Libr. 132/C4
Siemianówka (lake), Pol. 49/M2
Siemiatycze, Pol. 49/M2
Siempang, Camb. 106/D2
Siemreab, Camb. 106/C3
Siena, It. 69/E6
Siena, It. 51/J5
Sienne (riv.), Fr. 50/C2
Sieradz, Pol. 49/K3
Sierning, Aus. 65/H6
Sierpc, Pol. 49/K2
Sierra Army Depot, Ca, US 196/C3
Sierra Blanca, Tx, US 180/B2
Sierra Chilengue 141/E3
Sierra City, Ca, US 176/C4
Sierra Colorada, Arg. 226/D4
Sierra de Amambay 226/E1
Sierra de Calalaste (chan.), Peru 221/B7
Sierra de Juarez 224/C4
Sierra de Misiones 225/F3
Sierra de Olte 216/D3
Sierra de Perijá 203/D3
Sierra de S. Luis 226/D2
Sierra de San Jonquín 225/F3
Sierra de la Giganta 224/B3
Sierra de la Macarena, Col. 216/C4
Sierra Gorda, Chile 220/D4
Sierra Grande, Arg. 226/D4
Sierra Leone (ctry.) 132/B4
Sierra Leone (cape), SLeo. 132/B5
Sierra Madre (mts.) 100/C1
Sierra Madre, Ca, US 196/C2
Sierra Madre al Khaymah 131/C4
Sierra Madre del Sur (chan., Malay/Phil.) 103/F1
Sierra Madre Occidental 204/B2
Sierra Madre Oriental 204/C2

Sierra Maestra (mts.), Cuba 207/G2
Silla (mts.) 70/B6
Sierra Nacimiento 73/H3
Silla (str.), It. 54/C4
Sierra Nevada (mts.), Sp. 52/D4
Sillajguay (peak), Chile 224/B1
Sierra Nevada (mts.), Ca, Nv, US 172/B4
Sillamäe, Est. 47/M2
Sierra Nevada de Santa Marta, Col. 207/H4
Sillé-le-Guillame, Fr. 63/E4
Sierra Nevada de Santa Marta, PN, Col. 203/D5
Silleda, Sp. 52/A1
Sillen (lake), Swe. 45/A2
Sierra San Pedro Martir (mts.), Mex. 204/B2
Silloth, Eng, UK 41/E2
Sierra Vieja 132/D4
Sillustani (ruin) 220/D4
Sierra Vista, Az, US 179/G5
Silly-le-Long, Fr. 36/L4
Sierra Vizcaíno (mts.), Mex. 204/B3
Silo, Oh, US 188/D4
Sierras Bayas, Arg. 226/E3
Silsbee, Tx, US 181/G2
Sierras de Córdoba 224/C4
Silsden, Eng, UK 41/F3
Siesta Key (isl.), Fl, US 195/G4
Silton, Sk, Can. 186/B2
Siete Picos (peak), Sp. 52/M8
Siltou (well), Chad 134/B1
Siete Tazas, PN, Chile 226/C2
Siluas, Indo. 102/C3
Sieve (riv.), It. 69/E5
Siluko, Nga. 133/G5
Sif Fatima, Alg. 129/H3
Silute, Lith. 47/J4
Sīfenī, Iran 136/B2
Silva, Mo, US 192/B2
Siffray, Gui. 132/C4
Silvani, India 108/B4
Sifié, C.d'Iv. 132/D5
Silvania, It. 66/E5
Sifnos (isl.), Gre. 55/J4
Silvania, Braz. 222/C3
Sīga, Alg. 130/E5
Silvaplana, Swi. 67/F5
Siga (hills), Tanz. 137/A2
Silver (mtn.), Ca, US 196/C1
Sigean, Fr. 50/E5
Silver (cr.), Il, US 185/G3
Siggiewi, Malta 54/L7
Silver (cr.), Or, US 176/D2
Sighetu Marmatiei, Rom. 78/B4
Silver (lake), Or, US 176/C2
Sighișoara, Rom. 57/G2
Silver Bay, Mn, US 187/J4
Sighty Crag (hill), Eng, UK 41/F1
Silver Bell, Az, US 179/G4
Sigillo, It. 69/F7
Silver City, NM, US 179/H4
Sigli, Indo. 101/A1
Silver City, SD, US 184/C1
Sigli (cape), Alg. 130/H4
Silver Cliff, Co, US 182/B1
Siglufjördhur, Ice. 44/N6
Silver Creek, Yk, Can. 201/L3
Sigmaringen, Ger. 67/E6
Silver Creek, NY, US 191/G3
Sigmarszell, Ger. 67/F2
Silver Lake, Or, US 176/D2
Signa, It. 69/E6
Silver Lake, Wi, US 197/P14
Signal (hill), SD, US 184/C2
Silver Lake NWR 183/J2
Signal de la Mère Boitier (peak), Fr. 70/A1
Silver Lake-Fircrest, Wa, US 197/C2
Signal de Saint-Andre 186/B4
Silver Meadow 70/A1
Signal de Toussaines 70/A1
Silver Run, Md, US 198/A4
Signal d'Écouves 62/B4
Silver Spring, Md, US 198/A6
Signal Hill, Ca, US 196/F8
Silver Springs, Fl, US 195/G3
Signes, Fr. 70/B6
Silver Star, Mt, US 177/G1
Signy-l'Abbaye, Fr. 61/D4
Silver Water, On, Can. 190/E2
Signy-le-Petit, Fr. 61/D4
Silverado, Ca, US 196/C2
Signy-Signets, Fr. 36/M5
Silverdale, Wa, US 174/C4
Sigourney, Ia, US 185/J3
Silverdale, Austl. 157/E1
Siguatepeque, Hon. 206/E3
Silverstone, Eng, UK 43/E2
Siguë, Ecu. 216/B4
Silverton, Austl. 156/B1
Sigüenza, Sp. 52/D2
Silverton, Co, US 179/J2
Siguiri, Gui. 132/C4
Silverton, NJ, US 199/D3
Sigulda, Lat. 47/L3
Silverton, Tx, US 180/D3
Sigura Gura 56/C2
Silverton, Wa, US 174/D3
Sihl (riv.), Swi. 67/E3
Silverwood
Sihlsee (lake), Swi. 67/E3
Silves, Braz. 218/B3
Sihochac, Mex. 206/D2
Silves, Port. 52/A4
Sikanni Chief (riv.), BC, Can. 170/D3
Silvi, It. 71/D2
Sikandarābād, India 108/A1
Silvia, Col. 216/B4
Sikandarpur, India 108/A1
Silvies (riv.), Or, US 176/D3
Sikandra Rao, India 108/B2
Silvretta (mts.), Aus. 67/G4
Sikar, India 104/B2
Sili'īr, WBnk. 117/C5
Sikasso, Mali 132/D4
Silz, Aus. 67/G3
Sikasso (pol. reg.), Mali 132/D4
Sim (cape), Mor. 128/C3
Sikaw, Myan. 98/B3
Sima, Com. 143/H6
Sikeston, Mo, US 192/C2
Sima, Congo
Sikhote-Alin' (mts.), Rus. 81/P5
Simão Dias, Braz. 223/F1
Sikinos (isl.), Gre. 55/J4
Simão Pereira
Sikinssa, C.d'Iv. 132/D5
Simbach am Inn, Ger. 65/J6
Sikkim (state), India 109/F2
Simbai, PNG 153/G1
Siklós, Hun. 56/D3
Simbel (mts.), Eth. 134/H2
Sikóurion, Gre. 55/H3
Simdega, Tanz. 139/E2
Sikyakh, Rus. 81/N3
Simeto (riv.), It. 73/G3
Sikuati, Malay. 103/F1
Simeulue (isl.), Indo. 83/J9
Sikwane, Bots. 140/E5
Simeyzia, Ukr. 79/H5
Silai (riv.), India 109/F4
Simferopol, Ukr. 79/H5
Silālē, Lith. 47/K4
Simferopol', Ukr. 79/H5
Silandro (Schlanders), It. 51/H4
Simga, India 108/C3
Silao, India 109/E3
Simi (mts.), Eth. 134/H2
Silao, Mex. 204/E4
Simi Valley, Ca, US 196/B2
Sīlat Az Zahr, WBnk. 117/C4
Simijaca, Col. 216/B3
Silay, Phil. 103/F1
Silchar, India 105/H3
Simikot, Nepal 109/D2
Silda, India 109/E4
Similaun (peak) 51/H4
Sīle, Turk. 57/J5
Simla, India 108/B1

Silksworth, Eng, UK 41/G2
Simojovel de Allende, Mex. 206/D2
Silla, Sp. 53/E3
Simón Bolívar 206/D2
Silla Tombs, SKor. 96/A3
Simón Bolívar (int'l arpt.), Ecu. 216/B5
Sillajhuay (peak), Bol. 172/B4
Simoncello (peak), It. 219/P7
Sillamäe, Est. 47/M2
Simonds, NB, Can. 188/D2
Sillānwāli, Pak. 110/B4
Simonstown, SAfr. 142/L11
Silleda, Sp. 52/A1
Simonton, Tx, US 181/L3
Sillen (lake), Swe. 45/A2
Simpang Tiga
Sillian, Aus. 51/K3
Simpang (int'l arpt.), Indo. 101/C2
Silloth, Eng, UK 41/E2
Simpang-kiri 101/B2
Sills (riv.), Aus. 67/H3
Simpangulim, Indo. 101/B1
Sillustani (ruin) 220/D4
Simpelveld, Indo. 61/E2
Silly-le-Long, Fr. 36/L4
Simplicio Mendes, Braz. 219/F4
Silo, Oh, US 188/D4
Simplon, Swi. 66/E5
Silsbee, Tx, US 181/G2
Simplonpass (pass), Swi. 66/E5
Silsden, Eng, UK 41/F3
Simpson (isl.), On, Can. 187/L3
Silton, Sk, Can. 186/B2
Simpson (pen.), Nun. Can. 170/G2
Siltou (well), Chad 134/B1
Simpson (riv.), Nun. Can. 170/G2
Siluas, Indo. 102/C3
Simpson Desert Consv. Park, Austl. 155/H3
Siluko, Nga. 133/G5
Simpson Desert NP, Austl. 155/H3
Silute, Lith. 47/J4
Simpsons Gap NP, Austl. 155/G2
Silva, Mo, US 192/B2
Simrishamn, Swe. 46/F4
Silvani, India 108/B4
Sims, Ar, US 183/H3
Silvania, It. 66/E5
Sims Bayou (riv.), Tx, US 181/M9
Silvania, Braz. 222/C3
Simunul (isl.), Phil. 100/B4
Silvaplana, Swi. 67/F5
Simupu (isl.), Indo. 152/A1
Silver (mtn.), Ca, US 196/C1
Sin-le-Noble, Fr. 60/C3
Silver (cr.), Il, US 185/G3
Sinabang, Indo. 101/B2
Silver (cr.), Or, US 176/D2
Sinadhago, Som. 136/C4
Silver (lake), Or, US 176/C2
Sinai (pen.), Egypt 127/G2
Silver Bay, Mn, US 187/J4
Sinaia, Rom. 57/G3
Silver Bell, Az, US 179/G4
Sinait, Phil. 100/C1
Silver City, NM, US 179/H4
Sinaloa (state), Mex. 204/C3
Silver City, SD, US 184/C1
Sinaloa de Leyva, Mex. 204/C3
Silver Cliff, Co, US 182/B1
Sinalunga, It. 51/J5
Silver Creek, Yk, Can. 201/L3
Sinarca (riv.), It. 71/D4
Silver Creek, NY, US 191/G3
Sināwin, Libya 129/H3
Silver Lake, Or, US 176/D2
Sinazongwe, Zam. 141/E3
Silver Lake, Wi, US 197/P14
Sincé, Col. 216/C2
Silver Lake NWR 198/E3
Sincelejo, Col. 216/C2
Silver Lake-Fircrest, Wa, US 197/C2
Sinceny, Fr. 60/C4
Silver Meadow
Sinch'ŏn, NKor. 93/C3
Silver Run, Md, US 198/A4
Sinch'ŏn, NKor. 93/C3
Silver Spring, Md, US 198/A6
Sinclair (pt.), Austl. 155/G5
Silver Springs, Fl, US 195/G3
Sinclair (res.), Ga, US 193/F4
Silver Star, Mt, US 177/G1
Sind (riv.), India 104/C2
Silver Water, On, Can. 190/E2
Sindal, Den. 46/D3
Silverado, Ca, US 196/C2
Sindangan, Phil. 100/D3
Silverdale, Wa, US 174/C4
Sindangbarang, Indo. 101/D4
Silverdale, Austl. 157/E1
Sindelfingen, Ger. 64/C5
Silverstone, Eng, UK 43/E2
Sindhulimādi, Nepal 109/E2
Silverton, Austl. 156/B1
Sindi, Est. 47/L2
Silverton, Co, US 179/J2
Sindirgi, Turk. 76/D5
Silverton, NJ, US 199/D3
Sindri, India 109/E3
Silverton, Tx, US 180/D3
Sinegorskiy, Rus. 79/J3
Silverton, Wa, US 174/D3
Sinepuxent (bay), Md, US 198/D5
Silverwood
Singapore City 101/J6
Silves, Braz. 218/B3
Singapore (ctry.) 101/J6
Silves, Port. 52/A4
Singar, India 104/B2
Silvi, It. 71/D2
Singaraja, Indo. 101/F5
Silvia, Col. 216/B4
Singar
Simão Dias, Braz. 223/F1
Singida, Tanz. 137/A3
Simão Pereira, Braz. 139/F2
Simbach am Inn, Ger. 65/J6
Singida (prov.), Tanz. 137/A3
Simbai, PNG 153/G1
Singitic (gulf), Gre. 73/G2
Simbei, Myan. 141/D3
Singkaling Hkamti, Myan. 98/B3
Simcoe, On, Can. 190/F3
Singkang, Indo. 103/F4
Simcoe (lake), On, Can. 188/D2
Singkawang, Indo. 102/C3
Simdega, India 109/E4
Singkel, Indo. 101/B2
Simen (mts.), Eth. 134/H2
Singkuang, Indo. 101/B2
Simen Mountains NP, Eth. 134/H2
Singleton, Austl. 157/E1
Simferopol, Ukr. 79/H5
Singleton (mt.), Austl. 155/F2
Simferopol', Ukr. 79/H5
Singleton, Eng, UK 154/C4
Simga, India 108/C3
Singleton, Rés. Tot. de Faune Du, Burk. 157/H3
Simi (mts.), Eth. 134/H2
Singra, Bang. 109/G3
Simi Valley, Ca, US 196/B2
Singuédeze (riv.), Moz. 141/F4
Simijaca, Col. 216/B3
Sinhū, Gre. 93/D3
Simikot, Nepal 109/D2
Singou, Rés. Tot. de Faune du, Burk. 133/F4
Similaun (peak) 51/H4
Sinhkung, NKor. 93/D2
Sīle, Turk. 57/J5
Sinhūng, NKor. 93/D2
Silchar, India 105/H3
Siniloa, China 137/A3
Sīlat Az Zahr, WBnk. 117/C4
Siniye Lipyagi, Rus. 79/K2
Silda, India 109/E4
Sinjah, Sudan 134/G2
Sile, Turk. 57/J5
Sinjär, Iraq 114/E2
Sileby, Eng, UK 43/E1
Sinjil, WBnk. 117/C4
Silel (riv.), Col. 216/C3
Sinkät, Sudan 127/H4
Silenen, Swi. 67/E4
Sinking, Turk. 76/E1
Siler City, NC, US 193/H3
Sinlumkaba, Myan. 105/G2
Silesia (ctry.) 132/B4
Sinnamary (riv.), FrG. 218/C1
Siletz, Or, US 176/B1
Sinnamary, FrG. 218/C1
Sili'īr, WBnk. 117/C5
Sinnar, India
Siligurimādi, Nepal 130/L6
Sinnicolau Mare, Rom. 56/F2
Siling (lake), China 111/E5
Sinnūris, Egypt 131/B4
Silistra, Bul. 57/H3
Sinnyŏng, SKor. 93/E4
Silivri, Turk. 57/J5
Sinoe (lake), Libr. 73/J1
Siljan (lake), Swe. 46/F1
Sinop (prov.), Turk. 76/E1
Siljansnäs, Swe. 46/F1
Sinop (pt.), Turk. 76/E1
Silkeborg, Den. 46/C3
Simões Filho, Braz. 223/F2
Sinop, Turk. 76/E4

Sinos – Sorse
332

Sinos, Rio dos (riv.), Braz. 225/G4
Sinp'a-ŭp, NKor. 93/D2
Sinp'o, NKor. 93/E2
Sinp'yŏng, NKor. 93/D3
Sinsheim, Ger. 64/B4
Sint Annaland, Neth. 58/B5
Sint Hubert, Neth. 58/C5
Sint Jacobiparochie, Neth. 58/C2
Sint Maartensdijk, Neth. 58/B5
Sint-Genesius-Rode, Belg. 61/D2
Sint-Gillis-Waas, Belg. 58/B6
Sint-Katelijne-Waver, Belg. 61/D1
Sint-Laureins, Belg. 60/C1
Sint-Martens-Voeren, Belg. 61/E2
Sint-Michielsgestel, Neth. 58/C5
Sint-Niklaas, Belg. 58/B6
Sint-Oedenrode, Neth. 58/C5
Sint-Pieters-Leeuw, Belg. 61/D2
Sint-Truiden, Belg. 61/E2
Sint'ae-ri, NKor. 93/E2
Sint'aein, SKor. 93/D5
Sintang, Indo. 102/D3
Sinton, Tx, US 181/F3
Sintra (range), Port. 53/P10
Sintra, Port. 53/P10
Sinú (riv.), Col. 203/F6
Sinŭiju, NKor. 93/C2
Sinujif, Som. 136/D3
Sinwŏn, NKor. 93/C3
Sinyang, NKor. 93/D3
Sinyavino, Rus. 75/U7
Sinzheim, Ger. 64/B5
Sinzig, Ger. 61/G2
Sió (riv.), Hun. 56/D2
Sio, Kenya 137/A1
Siocon, Phil. 100/C4
Siófok, Hun. 56/D2
Sioma Ngwezi NP, Zam. 140/D3
Sion, Swi. 66/D5
Sion Mills, NI, UK 37/Q9
Sion-les-Mines, Fr. 62/D5
Sioule (riv.), Fr. 50/E4
Sioux Center, Ia, US 185/F2
Sioux City, Ia, US 185/F2
Sioux Falls, SD, US 185/F2
Sioux Lookout, On, Can. 187/J2
Sioux Narrows, On, Can. 187/G3
Sioux Rapids, Ia, US 185/G2
Sipalay, Phil. 100/C3
Sipaliwini (riv.), Sur. 217/G4
Sipaliwini (dist.), Sur. 217/H4
Siparia, Trin. 217/F2
Sipí, Col. 216/B3
Siping, China 92/F2
Sipitang, Malay. 100/A4
Sipiwesk (lake), Mb, Can. 170/G3
Siple (isl.), Ant. 228/R
Sipocot, Phil. 100/C2
Siponto (ruin), It. 54/D2
Sipoo (Sibbo), Fin. 47/L1
Sipoonselkä (bay), Fin. 45/F4
Sipsey (riv.), Al, US 192/D4
Sipura (isl.), Indo. 102/A4
Sipura (str.), Indo. 101/B3
Siqueira Campos, Braz. 225/G2
Siquia (riv.), Nic. 202/E5
Siquijar (isl.), Phil. 100/C3
Siquisique, Ven. 216/D2
Sir Edward Pellew Group (isls.), Austl. 153/E3
Sir James Macbrien (mt.), NW, Can. 170/D2
Sir James Mitchell NP, Austl. 154/C5
Sir John (cape), Austl. 157/C5
Sir Muttra, India 108/A2
Sir Sandford (mt.), BC, Can. 174/F2
Sir Seewoosagur Ramgoolam (int'l arpt.), Mrts. 143/T15
Sir Seretse Khama (Gaborone) (int'l arpt.), Bots. 140/E5
Sir Thomas (mt.), Austl. 155/F3
Sira (riv.), Nor. 44/C4
Sīra, India 107/C3
Sirac (peak), Fr. 70/C3
Siracusa (Syracuse), It. 54/D4
Sirājganj, Bang. 109/G3
Şiran, Turk. 114/D1
Sīrē, Eth. 136/A3
Siren, Wi, US 187/H5
Sirente (peak), It. 71/C3
Siret (riv.), Rom. 76/C3
Siret, Rom. 78/D4
Sirha, Nepal 109/F2
Sirhind, India 110/D4
Sīrīk, Iran 115/J5
Sirik (cape), Malay. 102/D3
Sirikit (res.), Thai. 98/D5
Sirinhaém, Braz. 219/H5
Sīrīs, WBnk. 117/C4
Sirit (res.), Thai. 105/H4
Sirius Point (cape), Ak, US 201/B5
Sīrjān, Iran 115/H4
Sirmione, It. 68/D3
Sirnach, Swi. 67/F3
Şırnak, Turk. 114/E2
Sirohi, India 104/B3
Sirolo, It. 69/G6
Sirombu, Indo. 101/B2
Sironj, India 108/A3
Síros (isl.), Gre. 55/J4
Sirotinskaya, Rus. 79/M3
Siroua (peak), Mor. 128/D3
Sırpsındığı, Turk. 57/H5
Sirs al Layyānah, Egypt 131/B4
Sirsa, India 110/C5
Sirsāganj, India 108/B2
Sirsi, India 108/B1
Sirtica (reg.), Libya 126/C2
Siruma, Phil. 100/C2
Sīrvān (riv.), Iran 115/F3
Širvintos, Lith. 47/L4
Sisak, Cro. 56/C3
Sisaket, Thai. 106/D3
Sishen, SAfr. 142/C2
Sishui, China 92/D4
Sisian, Arm. 115/F2
Sisib (lake), Mb, Can. 186/E1
Sisikon, Swi. 67/E4
Siskiyou (mts.), Or, US 176/B2
Sisophon, Camb. 106/C3
Sissach, Swi. 66/D3
Sisséla, Gui. 132/C4
Sisseton, SD, US 186/F5
Sisseton-Wahpeton Ind. Res., SD, US 185/F1
Sissili (prov.), Burk. 133/E4
Sissonne, Fr. 60/C4
Sissonville, WV, US 193/G1
Sister Bay, Wi, US 190/C2
Sister Grove (cr.), Tx, US 180/L6
Sisteron, Fr. 70/B4
Sistersville, WV, US 190/F5
Sistina, It. 69/G2
Sistine Chapel, VatC. 71/G7
Sisto (riv.), It. 71/C5
Siswā Bāzār, India 108/D2
Sitacocha, Peru 220/B2
Sītākunda, Bang. 105/F3
Sitalike, Tanz. 139/G4
Sītāmarhi, India 109/E2
Sītāpur, India 108/C2
Sitārganj, India 108/B1
Siteki, Swaz. 143/E2
Sitges, Sp. 53/K7
Sithoniá (pen.), Gre. 76/C5
Sitía, Gre. 73/K4
Sitian, China 90/C3
Sitidgi (lake), NW, Can. 201/M2
Siting, China 99/E3
Sítio d'Badia, Braz. 222/D2
Sítio Novo do Grajaú, Braz. 219/E4
Sitka, Ak, US 201/L4
Sitno (peak), Slvk. 56/D1
Sito Ganno, India 110/C4
Sitoti, Zam. 140/D3
Sittard, Neth. 61/E2
Sittensen, Ger. 59/G2
Sitter (riv.), Swi. 67/F3
Sittingbourne, Eng, UK 43/G4
Sitton (peak), Ca, US 196/C3
Sittwe (Akyab), Myan. 105/F3
Situbondo, Indo. 101/F4
Siuntio (Sjundeå), Fin. 45/E4
Siuslaw (riv.), Or, US 176/B2
Sivac, Serb. 56/D3
Sivakāsi, India 107/C4
Sivaki, Rus. 91/K1
Sīvand, Iran 115/H4
Sivas, Turk. 114/D2
Sivas (prov.), Turk. 76/F5
Sivash (sound), Ukr. 79/H4
Sivé, Mrta. 132/B3
Siverek, Turk. 114/D2
Siverskiy, Rus. 47/P2
Siviriez, Swi. 66/C4
Sivomaskinskiy, Rus. 75/P2
Sivrihisar, Turk. 114/B2
Sivry-Courtry, Fr. 36/L6
Siwa, Indo. 103/F4
Siwa Oasis (oasis), Egypt 127/E2
Sīwah, Egypt 127/E2
Siwālik (range), India,Nepal 104/D2
Siwān, India 109/E2
Siwāni, India 110/C5
Six Flags Great Adventure, NJ, US 198/D3
Six Flags Great America, Il, US 197/Q15
Six Flags Magic Mountain, Ca, US 196/B2
Six Flags Over Georgia, Ga, US 193/L7
Six Flags Over Texas, Tx, US 180/K7
Six-Fours-la-Plage, Fr. 70/B6
Sixes, Or, US 176/A2
Sixmile (lake), La, US 194/C3
Sixmilebridge, Ire. 38/B4
Sixmilecross, NI, UK 40/A2
Sixth Cataract (falls), Sudan 134/G1
Sixtymile, Yk, Can. 201/K3
Siyabuswa, SAfr. 141/F5
Siyāna, India 108/B1
Siyang, China 92/D4
Siyäzän, Azer. 77/J4
Siyichang, China 98/E2
Siyitang, China 90/F3
Sizhoutou, China 99/J2
Siziano, It. 68/C3
Sizun, Fr. 62/A4
Sizyahsk, Rus. 75/M2
Sjælland (isl.), Den. 45/H7
Sjællands (pen.), Den. 45/H7
Sjenica, Serb. 56/E4
Sjöberg, Swe. 45/A1
Sjöbo, Swe. 46/E4
Sjónfridh (peak), Ice. 44/M6
Sjösa, Swe. 45/A2
Sjundeå (Siuntio), Fin. 45/E4
Sjuntorp, Swe. 46/E2
Skadovs'k, Ukr. 78/G4
Skaftafell NP, Ice. 44/P7
Skagen, Den. 46/D3
Skagens (The Skaw) (cape), Den. 46/D3
Skagern (lake), Swe. 46/F2
Skagerrak (str.), Den.,Nor. 46/C3
Skaget (peak), Nor. 46/C1
Skagit (riv.), Wa, US 174/D3
Skagway, Ak, US 201/L3
Skaidi, Nor. 44/H1
Skaistkalne, Lat. 47/L3
Skála, Gre. 55/H4
Skälderviken (bay), Swe. 46/E3
Skálfandafljót (riv.), Ice. 44/P7
Skalica, Slvk. 49/J4
Skalice (riv.), Czh. 51/K2
Skalka (res.), Czh. 65/F2
Skælskør, Den. 46/D4
Skanderborg, Den. 46/C3
Skåne (reg.), Swe. 46/E4
Skaneateles, NY, US 191/H3
Skanes (int'l arpt.), Tun. 54/B5
Skånland, Nor. 44/F1
Skänninge, Swe. 46/F2
Skanör, Swe. 46/E4
Skantzoura (isl.), Gre. 55/J3
Skara, Swe. 46/E2
Skaraborg (co.), Swe. 44/E4
Skärblacka, Swe. 46/F2
Skārdu, Pak. 110/C2
Skåre, Swe. 46/E2
Skärholmen, Swe. 45/A1
Skarszewy, Pol. 46/H4
Skarven (lake), Swe. 45/A1
Skarżysko-Kamienna, Pol. 49/L3
Skateraw, Sc, UK 39/D5
Skattkärr, Swe. 46/E2
Skaudvilė, Lith. 47/K4
Skavaböle (Hyrylä), Fin. 45/F4
Skævinge, Den. 45/J7
Skaw, The (Skagens) (cape), Den. 46/D3
Skawina, Pol. 49/K4
Skederid, Swe. 45/B1
Skedviken (lake), Swe. 45/B1
Skeena (mts.), BC, Can. 170/D3
Skeena (riv.), BC, Can. 170/D3
Skegemog (lake), Mi, US 190/D2
Skegness, Eng, UK 41/J5
Skeleton Coast Park, Namb. 140/B3
Skellefteå, Swe. 44/G2
Skellefteälven (riv.), Swe. 74/C2
Skelleftehamn, Swe. 44/G2
Skellytown, Tx, US 182/D3
Skelmanthorpe, Eng, UK 41/G4
Skelmersdale, Eng, UK 41/F4
Skelmorlie, Sc, UK 39/B5
Skelton, Eng, UK 41/H2
Skerne (riv.), Eng, UK 41/G2
Skerries, Ire. 40/B4
Skhimatárion, Gre. 55/H3
Skhirat, Mor. 130/A3
Skhirat Temara (prov.), Mor. 130/A3
Skhiza (isl.), Gre. 55/G4
Skhodnya (riv.), Rus. 75/W9
Ski, Nor. 46/D2
Skíathos, Gre. 55/H3
Skiatook, Ok, US 183/F2
Skibbereen, Ire. 38/A6
Skibby, Den. 45/H7
Skidaway Island, Ga, US 195/H2
Skidegate, BC, Can. 201/M5
Skidel', Bela. 47/L5
Skídhra, Gre. 55/H2
Skidmore, Mo, US 185/G3
Skidmore, Tx, US 180/F3
Skidway Lake, Mi, US 190/D2
Skien, Nor. 46/C2
Skierniewice (prov.), Pol. 49/K3
Skierniewice, Pol. 49/L3
Skiff, Ab, Can. 175/J3
Skikda, Alg. 130/K6
Skillet Fork (riv.), Il, US 192/C1
Skinári (cape), Gre. 55/G4
Skinnskatteberg, Swe. 46/F2
Skipness, Sc, UK 39/A5
Skipperville, Al, US 195/F2
Skipsea, Eng, UK 41/H4
Skipton, Eng, UK 41/F4
Skiptvet, Nor. 44/T9
Skirfare (riv.), Eng, UK 41/F3
Skíros, Gre. 55/J3
Skivarpsån (riv.), Swe. 45/K7
Skive, Den. 46/C3
Skjærhollen, Nor. 46/D2
Skjeberg, Nor. 46/D2
Skjelåtinden (peak), Nor. 44/E2
Skjern, Den. 46/C4
Skjern (riv.), Den. 46/C4
Škofja Loka, Slov. 51/L3
Skoger, Nor. 44/R8
Skoghall, Swe. 46/E2
Skogstorp, Swe. 46/G2
Skokholm (isl.), Wal, UK 42/A3
Skokie, Il, US 190/C3
Skokie (riv.), Il, US 197/Q15
Skokloster, Swe. 46/G2
Skokomish Ind. Res., Wa, US 174/C4
Sköldvik, Fin. 45/F4
Skole, Ukr. 78/B3
Sköllersta, Swe. 46/F2
Skolniki Park, Rus. 75/W9
Skomer (isl.), Wal, UK 42/A3
Skon, Camb. 106/D3
Skookumchuck, BC, Can. 174/G3
Skópelos, Gre. 55/H3
Skópelos (isl.), Gre. 55/H3
Skopin, Rus. 76/F1
Skopje (cap.), FYROM 55/G2
Skopje (int'l. arpt.), FYROM 55/G2
Skorodnoye, Bela. 78/E2
Skorodnoye, Rus. 79/J2
Skotterud, Nor. 46/E2
Skoútari, Gre. 55/H2
Skövde, Swe. 46/E2
Skovorodino, Rus. 91/J1
Skownan, Mb, Can. 186/E2
Skrīveri, Lat. 47/L3
Skrudaliena, Lat. 47/M4
Skrunda, Lat. 47/K3
Skukum (mt.), Yk, Can. 201/L3
Skukuza, SAfr. 141/F5
Skull, Ire. 38/A6
Skull (valley), Ut, US 177/G3
Skull Valley, Az, US 179/F3
Skull Valley Ind. Res., Ut, US 177/G3
Skultorp, Swe. 46/E2
Skultuna, Swe. 46/G2
Skunk (riv.), Ia, US 185/J3
Skuodas, Lith. 47/J3
Skurup, Swe. 49/G1
Skutskär, Swe. 46/G1
Skvyra, Ukr. 78/E3
Skwentna, Ak, US 201/H3
Skwierzyna, Pol. 49/H2
Skye (isl.), Sc, UK 37/Q8
Skykomish (riv.), Wa, US 174/D4
Skykomish, Wa, US 174/D4
Skyring (sound), Chile 191/B7
Skytop, Pa, US 198/C1
Slade NWR, ND, US 186/E4
Sladkovskoye, Rus. 75/Q4
Sladt (pt.), Austl. 153/F2
Slagelse, Den. 46/D4
Slagle, La, US 194/B2
Slaidburn, Eng, UK 41/F4
Slakovský Les (for.), Czh. 65/F2
Slamannan, Sc, UK 39/C5
Slamet (peak), Indo. 101/E4
Slaná (riv.), Slvk. 49/L4
Slana, Ak, US 201/K3
Slane, Ire. 40/B4
Slangerup, Den. 45/J7
Slănic, Rom. 57/G3
Slănic-Moldova, Rom. 57/H2
Slantsy, Rus. 47/N2
Slaný, Czh. 65/H2
Slapy (res.), Czh. 65/H3
Śląskie (prov.), Pol. 49/K3
Slate (isls.), On, Can. 187/L3
Slatedale, Pa, US 198/C2
Slater, Ia, US 185/H3
Slater, Mo, US 185/H4
Slatina, Rom. 57/G3
Slatington, Pa, US 198/C2
Slaton, Tx, US 182/D4
Slattum, Nor. 46/D1
Slaughter, La, US 194/C2
Slaughter Beach, De, US 198/C6
Slaughterville, Ok, US 183/F3
Slave (coast), Afr. 133/F5
Slave (riv.), NW, Can. 170/E2
Slave (riv.), Can. 163/F3
Slave Lake, Ab, Can. 170/E3
Slavgorod, Rus. 111/C1
Slavkov u Brna, Czh. 51/M2
Slavonia (reg.), Cro. 56/C3
Slavonska Požega, Cro. 56/C3
Slavonski Brod, Cro. 56/D3
Slavuta, Ukr. 78/D2
Slavyanka, Rus. 91/L3
Slavyanovo, Bul. 57/G4
Slavyansk-na-Kubani, Rus. 79/K5
Sławno, Pol. 46/G4
Slayton, Mn, US 185/G2
Sleaford, Eng, UK 41/H6
Sleen, Neth. 58/D3
Sleeper (isls.), On, Can. 171/H3
Sleeping Bear Dunes Nat'l Lakeshore, Mi, US 190/C2
Sleepy Eye, Mn, US 185/G1
Sleepy Hollow, Il, US 197/P15
Sleepy Hollow, NY, US 199/K7
Sleetmute, Ak, US 201/G3
Slemp, Ky, US 193/F2
Sliabh na Caillighe (peak), Ire. 38/C2
Slide (mtn.), NY, US 191/J4
Slidell, La, US 194/D2
Slidre, Nor. 46/C1
Sliedrecht, Neth. 58/B5
Sliema, Malta 54/M7
Slieve Anierin (peak), Ire. 38/C1
Slieve Aughty (mts.), Ire. 38/B3
Slieve Bernagh (peak), Ire. 38/B4
Slieve Binnian (peak), NI, UK 40/C3
Slieve Bloom (mts.), Ire. 38/C4
Slieve Car (peak), Ire. 38/A1
Slieve Croob (peak), NI, UK 40/C3
Slieve Donard (peak), NI, UK 40/C3
Slieve Elva (peak), Ire. 38/A3
Slieve Fyagh (peak), Ire. 38/A1
Slieve Gamph (mts.), Ire. 38/A1
Slieve Gamph (Ox) (mts.), Ire. 38/A1
Slieve Gullion (peak), NI, UK 40/B3
Slieve Martin (peak), UK 38/D1
Slieve Snaght (peak), Ire. 40/A1
Slievecallan (peak), Ire. 38/A4
Slievecarran (peak), Ire. 38/A3
Slievefelim (mts.), Ire. 38/B4
Slievekimalta (peak), Ire. 38/B4
Slievenamon (hill), Ire. 38/C5
Slieverve, Ire. 38/C5
Sligo, Ire. 38/B1
Sligo (bay), Ire. 38/B1
Sligo (arpt.), Ire. 38/B1
Sligo (co.), Ire. 38/B1
Slioch (peak), Sc, UK 39/A1
Slite, Swe. 47/H3
Sliven, Bul. 57/H4
Slivnitsa, Bul. 56/F4
Sloan, Nv, US 178/E3
Sloan, Ia, US 185/F2
Sloan, NY, US 190/V10
Sloatsburg, NY, US 199/J7
Slobidka, Ukr. 78/E4
Slobodskoy, Rus. 75/L4
Slobozia, Rom. 57/H3
Slobozia, Mol. 78/E4
Slocan (lake), BC, Can. 174/F3
Slocan, BC, Can. 174/F3
Slocan Park, BC, Can. 174/F3
Slochteren, Neth. 58/D2
Slocomb, Al, US 195/F2
Slocum, Tx, US 180/G2
Sloten, Neth. 58/C3
Sloterdijk, Neth. 58/C4
Slotermeer (lake), Neth. 58/C3
Slottskogen, Swe. 45/A1
Slough, Eng, UK 36/B2
Slough (co.), Eng, UK 36/B2
Slovakia (ctry.) 49/K4
Slovechne, Ukr. 78/E2
Slovenia (ctry.) 56/B3
Slovenj Gradec, Slov. 56/B2
Slovenska Bistrica, Slov. 56/B2
Slovenska L'upča, Slvk. 49/K4
Slovenske Konjice, Slov. 56/B2
Slovenské Rudohorie (mts.), Slvk. 49/L4
Slov'yans'k, Ukr. 79/J3
Słowiński PN, Pol. 46/G4
Słubice, Pol. 49/H2
Sluch' (riv.), Ukr. 76/C2
Sluderno (Schluderns), It. 67/G4
Sluis, Neth. 60/C1
Słupca, Pol. 49/J2
Słupia (riv.), Pol. 46/G4
Słupsk, Pol. 46/G4
Slutsk, Bela. 76/C1
Slyne Head (pt.), Ire. 36/F10
Slyudyanka, Rus. 90/E1
Smackover, Ar, US 183/H4
Smålandsstenar, Swe. 46/E3
Small, Id, US 177/G1
Smallfield, Eng, UK 36/C3
Smallwood (res.), Can. 163/L4
Smarden, Eng, UK 36/F3
Smaylovskiy, Kaz. 77/M1
Smearlagh (riv.), Ire. 38/A5
Smederevo, Serb. 56/E3
Smederevska Palanka, Serb. 56/E3
Smedjebacken, Swe. 46/F1
Smendou (riv.), Alg. 130/J4
Smethport, Pa, US 191/G4
Smidovich, Rus. 91/L2
Śmigiel, Pol. 49/J2
Smila, Ukr. 78/F3
Smilax, Ky, US 193/F2
Smilde, Neth. 58/D3
Smiley, Tx, US 181/F3
Smiley, Sk, Can. 175/K2
Smiltene, Lat. 47/L3
Smirnykh, Rus. 91/N2
Smith (isl.), Nun., Can. 171/J2
Smith (isl.), Md, US 193/J1
Smith, Nv, US 176/D4
Smith (pt.), Tx, US 181/N9
Smith (riv.), Va, US 192/G2
Smith Center, Ks, US 184/E4
Smith Mountain (dam), Va, US 193/H2
Smith Mountain (lake), Va, US 193/H2
Smith River, Ca, US 176/A3
Smithburg, NJ, US 199/D3
Smithdale, Ms, US 194/C2
Smithers, BC, Can. 170/D3
Smithers (lake), Tx, US 181/M9
Smithfield, Ut, US 177/H3
Smithfield, NC, US 193/H3
Smithland, Ky, US 192/C2
Smiths, Al, US 192/E4
Smiths Creek, Mi, US 197/G6
Smiths Falls, On, Can. 191/H2
Smiths Grove, Ky, US 192/D2
Smithton, Mo, US 183/H1
Smithton, Austl. 156/C4
Smithtown, NY, US 199/E2
Smithtown (bay), NY, US 199/E2
Smithville, On, Can. 190/T9
Smithville, In, US 190/C5
Smithville, Ga, US 195/F2
Smithville, Mo, US 185/G4
Smithville (lake), Mo, US 185/G4
Smithville, Ok, US 183/G3
Smithville, Tn, US 192/E3
Smithville, Tx, US 180/F2
Smoke Creek (des.), Nv, US 176/D3
Smoky (cape), Austl. 156/E1
Smoky (riv.), Ab, Can. 170/E3
Smoky (riv.), Ab, Can. 174/E1
Smoky (hills), Ks, US 184/E4
Smoky Bay, Austl. 155/G5
Smoky Hill (riv.), Ks, US 172/F4
Smoky Hill, North Fork (riv.), Co, Ks, US 182/C1
Smoky Hill, North Fork (riv.), Co, Ks, US 184/C4
Smøla (isl.), Nor. 44/C3
Smolan, Ks, US 183/F1
Smolensk, Rus. 74/G5
Smolenskaya Oblast, Rus. 74/F5
Smolevichi, Bela. 47/N4
Smólikas (peak), Gre. 55/G2
Smolnaya (arpt.), Rus. 75/T7
Smolyan, Bul. 55/J2
Smoot, Wy, US 177/H2
Smorgon', Bela. 47/M4
Smrčina (peak), Czh. 65/G5
Smutná (riv.), Czh. 65/H4
Smuts, Sk, Can. 175/L1
Smyadovo, Bul. 57/H4
Smyrna, Tn, US 192/D3
Smyrna, Ga, US 193/L7
Smyrna (riv.), De, US 198/C5
Smyrna, De, US 198/C5
Snaefell (peak), IM, UK 40/D3
Snake (isl.), Austl. 157/C4
Snake (riv.), US 172/D3
Snake (cr.), SD, US 184/E1
Snake Indian (riv.), Ab, Can. 174/E1
Snake River (plain), Id, US 177/G2
Snake River Birds Of Prey Natural Area, Id, US 176/E2
Snares (isls.), NZ 159/A5
Snåsa, Nor. 44/E2
Sneads, Fl, US 195/F2
Sneads Ferry, NC, US 193/J3
Snedsted, Den. 46/C3
Sneedville, Tn, US 193/F2
Sneek, Neth. 58/C2
Sneekermeer (lake), Neth. 58/C2
Sneeuberg (peak), SAfr. 142/B4
Sneeuberg (mts.), SAfr. 142/D3
Sneeuwkop (peak), SAfr. 142/L11
Sneffels (mt.), Co, US 179/J1
Snejbjerg, Den. 46/C3
Snelgrove, On, Can. 190/T8
Snellville, Ga, US 193/M7
Snettisham, Eng, UK 43/G1
Snezhnogorsk, Rus. 80/J3
Sněžka (peak), Czh. 49/H3
Snežnik (peak), Slov. 51/L4
Śniardwy (lake), Pol. 49/L2
Snihurivka, Ukr. 79/G4
Snilow (int'l arpt.), Ukr. 78/B3
Snina, Slvk. 78/B3
Snizhne, Ukr. 79/K3
Snodland, Eng, UK 43/G4
Snøhetta (peak), Nor. 44/D3
Snohomish, Wa, US 197/C2
Snohomish (co.), Wa, US 197/C2
Snohomish (riv.), Wa, US 197/C2
Snook, Tx, US 180/F2
Snoqualmie, Wa, US 197/D2
Snoqualmie (falls), Wa, US 197/D2
Snoqualmie (riv.), Wa, US 197/D2
Snoqualmie Falls, Wa, US 197/D2
Snoqualmie, Middle Fk. (riv.), Wa, US 197/D2
Snoqualmie, North Fork (riv.), Wa, US 197/D2
Snoqualmie, South Fork (riv.), Wa, US 197/D3
Snøtind (peak), Nor. 44/E2
Snow, Ok, US 183/G3
Snow (mtn.), Me, US 191/L2
Snow (peak), Wa, US 174/E3
Snow Hill, NC, US 193/J3
Snow Hill, Md, US 193/K1
Snowcrest (mtn.), BC, Can. 174/F3
Snowdon (peak), IM, UK 40/D5
Snowdonia NP, Wal, UK 40/D6
Snowdoun, Al, US 192/D4
Snowflake, Mb, Can. 186/E3
Snowflake, Az, US 179/G3
Snowtown, Austl. 155/H5
Snowville, Ut, US 177/G3
Snowy (mtn.), NY, US 191/J3
Snowy Peak (mt.), Ak, US 201/K2
Snyatyn, Ukr. 78/C3
Snyder, Ar, US 183/J4
Snyder, Ok, US 182/E3
Snyder (co.), Pa, US 198/A2
Snyder, Tx, US 180/D1
Snydertown, Pa, US 198/B2
Soacha, Col. 219/L8
Soalala, Madg. 143/H7
Soalara, Madg. 143/G8
Soamanonga, Madg. 143/H8
Soana (riv.), It. 70/D1
Soanierana-Ivongo, Madg. 143/J7
Soanindrariny, Madg. 143/H7
Soar (riv.), Eng, UK 41/G6
Soavina, Madg. 143/H8
Soavina, Madg. 143/J8
Soavinandriana, Madg. 143/H7
Soba, Nga. 133/H4
Sobaek (mts.), SKor. 93/D5
Soberanía, Bol. 221/E4
Sobernheim, Ger. 61/G4
Soběslav, Czh. 65/H4
Sobger (riv.), Indo. 103/K4
Sobhādero, Pak. 113/J3
Sobradinho (res.), Braz. 209/E3
Sobradinho, Braz. 222/D2
Sobral, Braz. 219/F3
Sobrance, Slvk. 78/B3
Sobretta (peak), It. 67/G5
Sobue, Japan 95/L5
Soc Trang, Viet. 106/D4
Socabaya, Peru 220/D5
Socastee, SC, US 193/H4
Sochaczew, Pol. 49/L2
Sochi, Rus. 76/F4
Sŏch'ŏn, SKor. 93/D4
Söchtenau, Ger. 65/F7
Soci, It. 69/E6
Social Circle, Ga, US 192/F4
Society (isls.), FrPol. 161/K6
Society Hill, SC, US 193/H3
Socompa (vol.), Arg.,Chile 224/B3
Socorro, Braz. 223/K7
Socorro, Col. 216/C3
Socorro, NM, US 179/J3
Socorro, Tx, US 180/A2
Socorro (isl.), NM, Mex. 204/C5
Socotá, Col. 216/C3
Socota, Peru 220/B2
Socotra (isl.), Yem. 83/E8
Socrum, Fl, US 194/L7
Socuéllamos, Sp. 52/D3
Soda (lake), Ca, US 178/D3
Soda Creek, BC, Can. 174/C1
Soda Springs, Id, US 177/H2
Sodankylä, Fin. 74/E2
Soddy-Daisy, Tn, US 192/E3
Sodegaura, Japan 95/D3
Söderbärke, Swe. 46/F1
Söderby-Karl, Swe. 45/B1
Söderfors, Swe. 46/G1
Söderhamn, Swe. 46/G1
Söderköping, Swe. 46/G2
Södermanland (co.), Swe. 44/E4
Söderöra (isl.), Swe. 45/C1
Södersvik, Swe. 45/B1
Södertälje, Swe. 46/G2
Sodo, Eth. 134/H4
Södra Sandby, Swe. 45/K7
Sŏdu (riv.), NKor. 93/E2
Sodus Point, NY, US 191/H3
Sodwana Bay NP, SAfr. 143/F2
Soe, Indo. 152/B2
Soekmekaar, SAfr. 141/F4
Soest, Ger. 59/F5
Soest, Neth. 58/C4
Soeste (riv.), Ger. 48/D2
Soesterberg, Neth. 58/C4
Soeurs, Passage des (chan.), Fr. 62/C6
Sofádhes, Gre. 55/H3
Sofala (prov.), Moz. 141/G3
Sofia (int'l arpt.), Bul. 57/F4
Sofia (riv.), Madg. 143/J6
Sofiya (prov.), Bul. 55/H1
Sofiya (cap.), Bul. 57/F4
Sofiyivka, Ukr. 79/G3
Sofiysk, Rus. 91/L1
Sofporog, Rus. 74/F2
Sogakofe, Gha. 133/F5
Sogamoso (riv.), Col. 216/C3
Sogamoso, Col. 216/C3
Sögel, Ger. 59/E3
Sogeri, PNG 153/F1
Şoghād, Iran 115/H4
Sogn Og Fjordane (co.), Nor. 44/C3
Sognafjorden (inlet), Nor. 44/C3
Sogndal, Nor. 46/B1
Søgne, Nor. 46/B2
Sogod, Phil. 100/D3
Soğuksu NP, Turk. 76/E4
Söğüt, Turk. 114/B1
Söğütlü, Turk. 57/K5
Sogwass (peak), Ugan. 134/G5
Sŏgwip'o, SKor. 91/K5
Soh, Iran 115/G3
Sohāgī, India 108/C3
Sohāgpur, India 108/B4
Soham, Eng, UK 43/G2
Sohren, Ger. 61/G4
Sŏhŭng, NKor. 93/D3
Soignies, Belg. 61/D2
Soignolles-en-Brie, Fr. 36/L6
Soila, China 98/C2
Soings-en-Sologne, Fr. 63/G6
Soissons, Fr. 60/C5
Sōja, Japan 96/C3
Sojat, India 104/B2
Sŏjosŏn (bay), NKor. 93/C3
Sok (riv.), Rus. 77/J1
Sok (pt.), Thai. 106/C3
Sōka, Japan 95/D2
Sokal', Ukr. 78/C2
Sokch'o, SKor. 93/E3
Söke, Turk. 114/A2
Sokh, Uzb. 111/B4
Sokhor (peak), Rus. 90/F1
Sokhós, Gre. 55/H2
Sokhumi, Geo. 77/G4
Sokna, Nor. 46/C1
Soko (isls.), China 99/K8
Soko Banja, Serb. 56/E4
Sokodé, Togo 133/F4
Sokol (peak), Czh. 65/G4
Sokol, Rus. 74/J4
Sokółka, Pol. 49/M2
Sokolo, Mali 132/D3
Sokolov, Czh. 65/F2
Sokolovo-Kundryuchenskoye, Rus. 79/K4
Sokołów Podlaski, Pol. 49/M2
Sokoto (state), Nga. 133/G3
Sokoto (riv.), Nga. 133/G3
Sokoto (plain), Nga. 133/G4
Sokoto, Nga. 133/G3
Sokyryany, Ukr. 78/D3
Sol'-Iletsk, Rus. 77/K2
Sola, Nor. 46/A2
Sola (int'l arpt.), Nor. 46/A2
Solana, Phil. 100/C1
Solana Beach, Ca, US 196/C5
Solânea, Braz. 219/H4
Solano (pt.), Col. 216/B3
Solano, Phil. 100/C1
Solano (co.), Ca, US 197/L10
Solano, Ven. 217/E4
Solarolo, It. 69/E5
Solca, Rom. 78/C4
Sölden, Aus. 67/H4
Soldier (riv.), Ia, US 185/G3
Soldiers Grove, Wi, US 185/J2
Soldotna, Ak, US 201/H3
Solec Kujawksi, Pol. 49/K2
Soledad, Col. 216/C2
Soledad, Ca, US 178/B2
Soledad, Ven. 217/F2
Soledad Canyon (canyon), Ca, US 196/B2
Soledad de Doblado, Mex. 205/N7
Soledad de Graciano, Mex. 205/E4
Soledade, Braz. 219/G4
Soledade, Braz. 225/F4
Soleduck (riv.), Wa, US 174/B3
Solen, ND, US 186/D4
Solenzo, Burk. 132/D3
Solesino, It. 69/E3
Solesmes, Fr. 63/E5
Solesmes, Fr. 60/C3
Soleuvre (peak), Lux. 61/E4
Solferino, It. 68/D3
Solhan, Turk. 114/E2
Soliera, It. 69/D4
Soligalich, Rus. 74/J4
Soligo, It. 69/F2
Solihull, Eng, UK 43/E2
Solihull (co.), Eng, UK 43/E2
Solikamsk, Rus. 75/N4
Solimões (riv.), Braz. 217/E5
Solingen, Ger. 58/E6
Solitaire, Namb. 140/C4
Sollefteå, Swe. 44/F3
Sollentuna, Swe. 46/G2
Sóller, Sp. 53/G3
Søllerød, Den. 45/J7
Sollerön, Swe. 46/F1
Solliès-Pont, Fr. 70/C6
Solling (mts.), Ger. 48/E3
Sollum (gulf), Egypt,Libya 127/E2
Solmsbach (riv.), Ger. 64/B2
Søln (peak), Nor. 44/D3
Solna, Swe. 45/B1
Solnan (riv.), Fr. 50/F3
Solnechnogorsk, Rus. 75/W8
Solntsevo, Rus. 75/W9
Solntsevo, Rus. 79/J2
Solo (riv.), Indo. 102/D5
Solofra, It. 71/D6
Solok, Indo. 101/C3
Solokh-Aul, Rus. 76/F4
Sololá, Guat. 206/D3
Solomon (sea), PNG,Sol. 160/D5
Solomon, Ak, US 201/F3
Solomon, Az, US 179/H4
Solomon, Ks, US 183/F1
Solomon (riv.), Ks, US 184/E4
Solomon Islands (ctry.) 160/E6
Solomon, North Fork (riv.), Ks, US 184/D4
Solomon, South Fork (riv.), Ks, US 184/D4
Solon, China 91/J2
Solonchak Goklenkui (swamp), Trkm. 77/L4
Solonópole, Braz. 219/G4
Solopaca, It. 71/D5
Solor (isl.), Indo. 152/A2
Solor (isls.), Indo. 152/A2
Solothurn, Swi. 66/D3
Solothurn (canton), Swi. 66/D3
Solotvyna, Ukr. 78/B4
Solovetskiy (isls.), Rus. 74/G2
Solov'yevsk, Rus. 91/J1
Solre-le-Château, Fr. 61/D3
Solsona, Sp. 53/F2
Solt, Hun. 56/D2
Šolta (isl.), Cro. 54/E1
Solţānābād, Iran 115/J2
Soltau, Ger. 59/G3
Sol'tsy, Rus. 47/P2
Soltustik Qazaqstan Oblast, Kaz. 80/G4
Soltvadkert, Hun. 56/D2
Solunska (peak), FYROM 55/G2
Solva (riv.), Wal, UK 42/A3
Solvang, Ca, US 178/B3
Sölvesborg, Swe. 46/F3
Solway Firth (inlet), Eng.,Sc, UK 40/E2
Solwezi, Zam. 141/E2
Solymár, Hun. 57/Q9
Som Det, Thai. 106/C2
Soma, Turk. 76/C5
Sōma, Japan 97/G2
Somabhula, Zim. 141/F3
Somain, Fr. 60/C3
Somalia (ctry.) 119/G4
Sombor, Serb. 56/D3
Sombra, On, Can. 197/H6
Sombreffe, Belg. 61/D2
Sombrerete, Mex. 204/E4
Sombrio, Braz. 225/G4
Somercotes, Eng, UK 41/G5
Someren, Neth. 58/C6
Somero, Fin. 47/K1
Somers, Austl. 157/B4
Somers, Mt, US 175/G3
Somers, Wi, US 197/Q14
Somers Point, NJ, US 198/D5
Somerset (isl.), Can. 163/H2
Somerset, Mb, Can. 186/E3
Somerset (isl.), Nun, Can. 170/G1
Somerset (co.), Eng, UK 42/D4
Somerset, Ky, US 192/E2
Somerset, La, US 194/C1
Somerset, Ma, US 191/L4
Somerset, NJ, US 198/D3
Somerset (co.), NJ, US 198/D2
Somerset, NY, US 190/V9
Somerset, Oh, US 190/E5
Somerset, Pa, US 191/G4
Somerset, Wi, US 187/Q6
Somerset East, SAfr. 142/D4
Somerset West, SAfr. 142/L11
Somersham, Eng, UK 43/G2
Somersworth, NH, US 191/L3
Somerton, Eng, UK 42/D4
Somerton, Az, US 178/E4
Somerville, Austl. 157/B4
Somerville, NJ, US 198/D2
Somerville (lake), Tx, US 181/F2
Somerville, Tn, US 192/C3
Somerville, Tx, US 180/F2
Someş (riv.), Rom. 76/B3
Someşul Mare (riv.), Rom. 57/G2
Someswar (range), India 109/E2
Somis, Ca, US 196/B2
Sŏmjin (riv.), SKor. 93/D5
Somma Lombardo, It. 68/B2
Sommacampagna, It. 69/D3
Sommam (riv.), Alg. 130/H4
Sommariva del Bosco, It. 68/A3
Somme (riv.), Fr. 48/B3
Somme (dept.), Fr. 60/B4
Somme (bay), Fr. 50/D1
Somme, Canal de la (canal), Fr. 60/B4
Somme-Leuze, Belg. 61/E3
Somme-Soude (riv.), Fr. 61/D6
Sommedieue, Fr. 61/E5
Sommeiller (peak), Fr. 70/C2
Sommelsdijk, Neth. 58/B5
Sommen (lake), Swe. 46/F2
Sommet de Finiels (peak), Fr. 50/E4
Sommet des Bains (peak), Fr. 70/C3
Sommet du Caduc (peak), Fr. 70/C4
Sommevoire, Fr. 66/A1
Somogy (prov.), Hun. 56/C2
Somonauk, Il, US 190/B4
Somoto, Nic. 206/E3
Somovo, Rus. 79/K2
Son, Nor. 44/S9
Son (riv.), India 104/D3
Son, Neth. 58/C5
Son Ha, Viet. 106/E3
Son La, Viet. 98/D4
Son Servera, Sp. 53/G3
Son Tay, Viet. 98/E4
Sona, It. 69/D3
Sona-Bata, D.R. Congo 138/C4
Sonāmarg, India 110/C2
Sonāmukhi, India 109/F4
Sonāmukhi, Bang. 109/G3
Sonāmura, India 109/H4
Sonār (riv.), India 108/B4
Sonātala, Bang. 109/G3
Sonbarsa, India 109/E2
Sonchamp, Fr. 36/H6
Sŏnch'ŏn, NKor. 93/C3
Soncino, It. 68/C3
Sondalo, It. 67/G5
Sondby, Fin. 45/F4
Sønder Nissum, Den. 46/C3
Sønderborg, Den. 46/C4
Sonderborg (int'l arpt.), Den. 46/C4
Sonderend (riv.), SAfr. 142/L11
Sønderjylland (co.), Den. 46/C4
Sondica (int'l arpt.), Sp. 50/B5
Søndre Strømfjord, Grld. 171/L2
Sondrio, It. 67/F5
Sondrio (dept.), It. 67/F5
Sone Ka Gurja, India 108/A2
Song (peak), China 92/C4
Song Cau, Viet. 106/E3
Song Dinh, Viet. 106/D4
Song Ma, Viet. 98/D4
Song Phi Nong, Thai. 106/C3
Song Xian, China 92/C4
Song-Kel' (lake), Kyr. 111/C3
Sŏngch'ŏn, NKor. 93/D3
Songcun, China 99/H2
Songea, Tanz. 137/A4
Songeons, Fr. 60/A4
Songhua (riv.), China 83/M5
Songhwa, NKor. 93/C3
Sŏnghwan, SKor. 93/D4
Songi (isl.), SKor. 93/C5
Songino, Mong. 90/D2
Songjiang, China 92/L8
Songjianghe, China 93/D1
Songjŏng, SKor. 93/D5
Sŏngju, SKor. 93/E5
Songkhla, Thai. 106/C5
Songkhram (riv.), Thai. 105/H4
Songling, China 91/J2
Songmen, China 99/J2
Songming, China 98/D3
Sŏngnam, SKor. 93/G7
Songnim, NKor. 93/C3
Songo, Ang. 138/C4
Songo, Moz. 141/G2
Songololo, D.R. Congo 138/C4
Songsak, India 109/H3
Songshan, China 99/F4
Songshu, China 93/B3
Songshuzhen, China 93/D1
Songt'an, SKor. 93/D4
Songtao, China 99/F5
Songtao Miaozu Zizhixian, China 99/F2
Songwŏn, NKor. 93/C2
Songxi, China 99/H3
Songxia, China 99/H3
Songyan, China 99/E3
Songzi (pass), China 92/C5
Songzi, China 99/F2
Songzi Hudu (riv.), China 99/G2
Sonhāt, India 108/D4
Soni, Japan 95/K6
Sonīpat, India 110/D5
Sonmiāni, Pak. 113/J3
Sonneberg, Ger. 64/E2
Sonnefeld, Ger. 64/E2
Sonning, Eng, UK 43/F4
Sonnino, It. 71/C5
Sonnjoch (peak), Aus. 67/H3
Sonntagshorn (peak), Ger. 51/K3
Sonobe, Japan 95/H5
Sonoita, Az, US 179/G5
Sonoma (cr.), Ca, US 197/J10
Sonoma (mts.), Ca, US 197/J10
Sonoma (co.), Ca, US 197/J10
Sonoma, Ca, US 176/B4
Sonoma (lake), Ca, US 176/B4
Sonora (state), Mex. 204/C2
Sonora (riv.), Mex. 204/C2
Sonora (pass), Ca, US 176/D4
Sonora, Tx, US 180/D2
Sonoran Desert Nat'l Mon., Az, US 179/F4
Sonoyta, Mex. 179/F5
Sonoyta (riv.), Mex. 204/B2
Sonpur, India 109/E3
Sonqor, Iran 115/F3
Sŏnsan, SKor. 93/E4
Sonsbeck, Ger. 58/D5
Sonseca, Sp. 52/D3
Sonsón, Col. 219/K7
Sonsonate, ESal. 206/D3
Sonsorol (isls.), Palau 160/C4
Sonta, Serb. 56/D3
Sontag, Ms, US 194/C2
Sontheim, Ger. 67/G2
Sontheim an der Brenz, Ger. 64/D5
Sonthofen, Ger. 67/G2
Sontra, Ger. 59/G6
Sonvico, Swi. 67/E5
Sook, Malay. 100/B4
Sooner (lake), Ok, US 183/F2
Sooyaac, Som. 137/C1
Sop Hao, Laos 106/D1
Sop Kai, Laos 106/C1
Sop Nhom, Laos 106/C1
Sop Prap, Thai. 106/B2
Soper, Ok, US 183/G3
Soperton, Ga, US 193/F4
Sopetrán, Col. 216/C3
Sophie, FrG. 218/C2
Sopi (cape), Indo. 103/G3
Sopka, Laos 106/C1
Sopo (riv.), Sudan 135/E3
Sopó, Col. 219/M8
Sopor, India 110/C2
Sopot, Pol. 46/H4
Sopot, Bul. 57/G4
Sopron, Hun. 56/C2
Soquel, Ca, US 178/B2
Sôr (riv.), Wal, UK 42/D3
Sor Karatuley (salt pan), Kaz. 77/K3
Sor Kaydak (swamp), Kaz. 77/K3
Sor Mertvyy Kultuk (swamp), Kaz. 77/K3
Sør-Varanger, Nor. 44/J1
Sora, It. 71/C4
Sorae, SKor. 93/F7
Soragna, It. 68/D4
Sŏrak-san (peak), SKor. 93/E3
Sŏraksan Nat'l Pk., SKor. 93/E3
Sŏraksan NP, SKor. 96/A1
Sorata, Bol. 220/D4
Sorbas, Sp. 52/D4
Sorbolo, It. 68/D4
Sorcy-Saint-Martin, Fr. 61/E6
Sorel (pt.), Chl, UK 62/C2
Sorel, Qu, Can. 191/K1
Sorell-Midway Point, Austl. 156/C4
Soresina, It. 68/C3
Sörforsa, Swe. 46/G1
Sorfta, Eth. 136/A4
Sorgues, Fr. 70/A5
Sorgun, Turk. 114/C2
Sori, It. 68/C5
Soria, Sp. 52/D2
Soriano (dept.), Uru. 226/G3
Soriano, Uru. 191/J10
Soriano nel Cimino, It. 71/B3
Sorigny, Fr. 63/F6
Sorikmerapi (peak), Indo. 101/B2
Soritor, Peru 220/B2
Sørmarka (reg.), Nor. 44/S8
Sormonne (riv.), Fr. 61/D4
Sorø, Den. 46/D4
Soro, Rio do (riv.), Braz. 222/D1
Soroca, Mol. 78/E3
Sorocaba, Braz. 225/H2
Sorochinsk, Rus. 77/K1
Sorol (isl.), Micr. 160/D4
Soron, India 108/B2
Sorong, Indo. 103/H4
Sororieng (mtn.), Guy. 218/B1
Soroti, Ugan. 137/A1
Sørøya (isl.), Nor. 44/G1
Sørøysundet (chan.), Nor. 44/G1
Sorpestausee (lake), Ger. 59/E6
Sorraia (riv.), Port. 52/A3
Sorrento, It. 71/D6
Sorrento, La, US 194/C2
Sorrento, Fl, US 194/M6
Sorrento, BC, Can. 174/E2
Sorris-Sorris, Namb. 140/B4
Sorsele, Swe. 44/F2

Sorso, It. 54/A2
Sorsogon, Phil. 100/C2
Sort, Sp. 53/F1
Sorunda, Swe. 45/A1
Sõrve (pt.), Est. 47/K3
Sos del Rey Católico, Sp. 52/E1
Sosa, Ger. 65/F1
Sŏsan, SKor. 93/D4
Sŏsan Haean NP, SKor. 93/C4
Sösdala, Swe. 46/E3
Söse (riv.), Ger. 59/H5
Sosenskiy, Rus. 76/E1
Soshanguve, SAfr. 141/F5
Soskovo, Rus. 76/E1
Sosna (riv.), Rus. 76/F1
Sosneado (peak), Arg. 226/C2
Sosnivka, Ukr. 78/C2
Sosnogorsk, Rus. 75/M3
Sosnovets, Rus. 74/G2
Sosnovka, Rus. 77/G1
Sosnovka, Rus. 75/L4
Sosnovka, Rus. 74/J2
Sosnovo, Rus. 47/P1
Sosnovo-Ozerskoye, Rus. 90/G1
Sosnovskoye, Rus. 74/J5
Sosnovyy Bor, Rus. 47/N2
Sosnowiec, Pol. 49/K3
Sosnytsya, Ukr. 79/G1
Soso, Ms, US 194/D2
Soso, CAfr. 138/C2
Sosonpal, India 107/D2
Sospel, Fr. 70/D5
Sospiro, It. 68/D3
Sosúa, DRep. 203/G4
Sos'va (riv.), Rus. 80/G3
Sot (riv.), India 108/B1
Sotik, Kenya 137/A2
Sotkajärvi (lake), Fin. 45/E4
Soto del Real, Sp. 53/N8
Soto la Marina, Mex. 205/F4
Sotouboua, Togo 133/F4
Sotteville-lès-Rouen, Fr. 63/G2
Sottrum, Ger. 59/G2
Sotuta, Mex. 206/D1
Souanké, Congo 138/C2
Soubre, C.d'Iv. 132/D5
Soudan, Austl. 153/E5
Soudan, Fr. 62/D5
Soudan, Ar, US 192/B3
Soudan, Mn, US 187/H4
Soude (riv.), Fr. 61/D6
Souderton, Pa, US 198/C3
Soúdha, Gre. 55/J5
Souellaba (pt.), Camr. 138/B2
Souesmes, Fr. 63/H6
Souffelweyersheim, Fr. 61/G6
Soufflenheim, Fr. 61/G6
Souffles, Pic des (peak), Fr. 70/C3
Souflíon, Gre. 57/H5
Soufrière (peak), StV. 203/N9
Soufrière (peak), Guad. 203/N8
Sougéta, Gui. 132/B4
Souillac, Mrts. 143/T15
Souillac, Fr. 50/D4
Souk Ahras (wilaya), Alg. 130/K6
Souk Ahras, Alg. 130/K6
Souk el Arba du Rharb, Mor. 130/A2
Sŏul (Seoul) (cap.), SKor. 91/K4
Soulanges (co.), Qu, Can. 189/M7
Soulijärvi (lake), Fin. 45/E4
Soulles (riv.), Fr. 62/D2
Soultz-Haut-Rhin, Fr. 66/D2
Soultz-sous-Forêts, Fr. 64/A5
Soum (prov.), Burk. 133/E3
Soumagne, Belg. 61/E2
Sound of Bute (sound), Sc, UK 39/A5
Sounding (lake), Ab, Can. 175/J1
Sounding (cr.), Ab, Can. 175/J2
Souppes-sur-Loing, Fr. 50/E2
Sour El Ghozlane, Alg. 130/G4
Sour Lake, Tx, US 181/G2
Sourbaral (peak), Chad 134/D2
Sources, Mont aux (peak), Les. 142/E3
Sourdeval, Fr. 63/E3
Sourdough (peak), Id, US 176/F1
Soure, Port. 52/A2
Soure, Braz. 218/D3
Souris (riv.), Can.,US 170/F4
Souris, Mb, Can. 186/D3
Souris, PE, Can. 189/F2
Souris (riv.), Sk, Can. 175/N3
Souris, ND, US 186/D3
Souris (riv.), ND, US 186/D3
Sourou (prov.), Burk. 132/E3
Sours, Fr. 63/G4
Sous, Oued (riv.), Mor. 128/C3
Sousa, Braz. 219/G4
Sousse, Tun. 130/M7
Sousse (gov.), Tun. 130/M6
Sout (riv.), SAfr. 142/C3
South (cr.), Austl. 158/G8
South (mts.), NS, Can. 188/E3
South (bay), Nun, Can. 197/H2
South (sound), Ire. 38/A4
South (isl.), NZ 145/H7
South (cape), NZ 159/A4
South (pt.), La, US 194/C3
South (riv.), NC, US 193/H3
South (mtn.), Pa, US 198/A3
South Africa (ctry.) 119/E7
South Alligator (riv.), Austl. 152/D3
South Amboy, NJ, US 199/H10
South America (cont.) 202/*
South Anna (riv.), Va, US 193/H2
South Augusta, Ga, US 193/F4
South Australia (state), Austl. 145/C3
South Ayrshire (co.), Sc, UK 39/B6
South Bay, Fl, US 195/H4
South Baymouth, On, Can. 190/E2
South Beloit, Il, US 185/K2
South Bend, In, US 190/C4
South Bend, Tx, US 183/E4
South Bend, Wa, US 174/C4
South Benfleet, Eng, UK 43/G3
South Berwick, Me, US 191/L3
South Boston, Va, US 193/H2
South Branch, Nf, Can. 189/H2
South Brent, Eng, UK 42/C6
South Brook, Nf, Can. 189/J1
South Burlington, Vt, US 191/K2
South Caicos (isl.), UK 207/J1
South Carolina (state), US 193/G3
South Charleston, WV, US 193/G1
South China (sea), Asia 83/L8
South Cle Elum, Wa, US 174/D4
South Coffeyville, Ok, US 183/G2
South Colby, Wa, US 197/B2
South Colton, NY, US 191/J2
South Dakota (state), US 184/D1
South Dorset Downs (uplands), Eng, UK 42/D5
South Dos Palos, Ca, US 178/B2
South Downs (hills), Eng, UK 43/F5
South Dum Dum, India 109/G4
South East (pt.), Austl. 157/C4
South East (cape), Austl. 145/D5
South Elgin, Il, US 197/P16
South Elmsall, Eng, UK 41/G4
South Entrance (inlet), PNG 153/F2
South Esk (riv.), Sc, UK 39/C3
South Fallsburg, NY, US 191/J4
South Farmingdale, NY, US 199/M9
South Foreland (pt.), UK 60/A1
South Fork, Co, US 179/J2
South Fork Ind. Res., Nv, US 176/F3
South Fork Koyukuk (riv.), Ak, US 201/H2
South Fork Kuskokwim (riv.), Ak, US 201/H3
South Fox (isl.), Mi, US 187/M5
South Fulton, Tn, US 192/C2
South Gate, Ca, US 196/F8
South Gate, Md, US 198/B5
South Georgia (isl.), UK 26/H8
South Glamorgan (co.), Wal, UK 42/C4
South Gloucestershire (co.), Eng, UK 42/D3
South Grand (riv.), Mo, US 183/G1
South Grand (riv.), Mo, US 185/G4
South Hams (plain), Eng, UK 42/C6
South Haven, Mi, US 190/C3
South Heart, ND, US 186/C4
South Hill, Va, US 193/H2
South Holland, Il, US 197/Q16
South Holmwood, Eng, UK 36/C3
South Horr, Kenya 137/B1
South Houston, Tx, US 181/M9
South Hutchinson, Ks, US 183/F1
South Island NP, Kenya 137/B1
South Kinangop, Kenya 137/B2
South Kirkby, Eng, UK 41/G4
South Kitui Nat'l Rsv., Kenya 137/B2
South Koel (riv.), India 109/E4
South Korea (ctry.) 93/D4
South Lake Tahoe, Ca, US 176/D4
South Lanarkshire (co.), Sc, UK 39/C5
South Llano (riv.), Tx, US 180/D2
South Loup (riv.), Ne, US 184/E3
South Luangwa NP, Zam. 141/F2
South Lyon, Mi, US 197/E7
South Magnetic Pole, Ant. 228/K
South Manitou (isl.), Mi, US 190/C2
South Miami, Fl, US 194/P11
South Mills, NC, US 193/J2
South Milwaukee, Wi, US 190/C3
South Molton, Eng, UK 42/C4
South Monroe, Mi, US 190/E4
South Naknek, Ak, US 201/G4
South Nation (riv.), On, Can. 191/J2
South New River (canal), Fl, US 194/P10
South Normanton, Eng, UK 41/G5
South Nyack, NY, US 199/K7
South Ockenden, Eng, UK 36/D2
South Ogden, Ut, US 177/H3
South Ohio, NS, Can. 188/D4
South Orange, NJ, US 199/H9
South Orkney (isls.), UK 228/X
South Ossetia (reg.), Geo. 77/G4
South Oxhey, Eng, UK 36/B2
South Oyster (bay), NY, US 199/M9
South Pacific (ocean) 26/B7
South Padre Island, Tx, US 180/F4
South Palm Beach, Fl, US 194/P9
South Para (res.), Austl. 155/M8
South Paris, Me, US 191/L2
South Pasadena, Fl, US 194/K8
South Pasadena, Ca, US 196/F7
South Pekin, Il, US 185/K3
South Perth (nbrhd.), Austl. 154/K6
South Petherton, Eng, UK 42/D5
South Pine (riv.), Austl. 158/E6
South Plainfield, NJ, US 199/H9
South Plains, Tx, US 182/D3
South Platte (riv.), Co, Ne, US 184/C3
South Platte (riv.), Co, US 184/B4
South Platte, Middle Fork (riv.), Co, US 182/A1
South Polar (plat.), Ant. 228/Y
South Pole, Ant. 228/A
South Portland, Me, US 191/L3
South Prairie, Wa, US 197/C3
South Prong South Alafia (riv.), Fl, US 194/L8
South Pugwash, NS, Can. 188/F3
South Range Refuge, Ut, US 177/G4
South River, On, Can. 191/G2
South River, NJ, US 199/H10
South Rockwood, Mi, US 197/F7
South Ronaldsay (isl.), Sc, UK 37/V14
South Saint Paul, Mn, US 187/P7
South San Francisco, Ca, US 197/K11
South Sandwich (isls.), UK 26/H8
South Saskatchewan (riv.), Sk, Can. 170/E3
South Seaville, NJ, US 198/D5
South Shetland (isls.), UK 228/W
South Shields, Eng, UK 41/G2
South Shore, SD, US 185/F1
South Shore, Ky, US 193/F1
South Sioux City, Ne, US 185/F2
South Sister (peak), Or, US 176/C1
South Skunk (riv.), Ia, US 185/H2
South Sulphur (riv.), Tx, US 181/G1
South Sulphur (riv.), Tx, US 183/G4
South Taranaki Bight (bay), NZ 159/C2
South Tucson, Az, US 179/G4
South Tyne (riv.), Eng, UK 41/F2
South Ubian, Phil. 100/C4
South Uist (isl.), Sc, UK 37/Q8
South Umpqua (riv.), Or, US 176/B2
South Valley Stream, NY, US 199/L9
South West (cape), Austl. 156/C4
South West (cape), NZ 159/A4
South West City, Mo, US 183/G2
South West NP, Austl. 156/C4
South West Port Mouton, NS, Can. 188/E4
South West Rocks, Austl. 156/E1
South Whittier, Ca, US 196/F8
South Wichita (riv.), Tx, US 182/D4
South Williamsport, Pa, US 198/B1
South Woodham Ferrers, Eng, UK 36/E2
South Yorkshire (co.), Eng, UK 41/G5
South Zanesville, Oh, US 190/E5
Southall (nbrhd.), Eng, UK 36/B2
Southam, Eng, UK 43/E2
Southampton, On, Can. 190/F2
Southampton (isl.), Nun, Can. 197/H2
Southampton (cape), Nun, Can. 197/H2
Southampton (isl.), Can. 163/J3
Southampton, Eng, UK 43/E5
Southampton (co.), Eng, UK 43/E5
Southampton, NY, US 199/F2
Southampton Water (inlet), Eng, UK 43/E5
Southaven, Ms, US 192/B3
Southborough, Eng, UK 43/G4
Southbourne, Eng, UK 43/F5
Southbridge, Ma, US 191/K3
Southbridge, NZ 159/C3
Southbury, Ct, US 191/K4
Southeast (pt.), Bahm. 207/H1
Southeast (dist.), Bots. 140/E5
Southeast (pt.), Jam. 207/G2
Southeast (cape), Ak, US 201/E3
Southend, Sc, UK 40/C1
Southend (int'l arpt.), Eng, UK 43/G3
Southend-on-Sea, Eng, UK 43/G3
Southend-on-Sea (co.), Eng, UK 43/G3
Southern (riv.), Austl. 154/K7
Southern (dist.), Bots. 140/E5
Southern (dist.), Isr. 116/D4
Southern, Malw. 141/G2
Southern (mts.), NZ 145/G7
Southern (prov.), SLeo. 132/B5
Southern (prov.), SrL. 107/D5
Southern (prov.), Zam. 141/E3
Southern Cook (isls.), Cookls. 161/J6
Southern Cross, Austl. 154/C4
Southern Harbour, Nf, Can. 189/L2
Southern Highlands (prov.), PNG 153/F1
Southern Indian (lake), Mb, Can. 170/G3
Southern NP, Sudan 134/F4
Southern Pines, NC, US 193/H3
Southern Shores, NC, US 193/K2
Southern Uplands (hills), Sc, UK 40/D1
Southern Ural (mts.), Rus. 75/N5
Southern Ute Ind. Res., Co, US 179/H2
Southery, Eng, UK 43/G1
Southesk Tablelands (plat.), Austl. 145/B2
Southey, Sk, Can. 186/B2
Southfield, Mi, US 190/E3
Southgate, Mi, US 190/E3
Southgate (nbrhd.), Eng, UK 36/C2
Southgate (riv.), BC, Can. 174/B2
Southlake, Tx, US 180/K7
Southland, Tx, US 182/D4
Southminster, Eng, UK 43/G3
Southold, NY, US 199/F1
Southport, Eng, UK 41/E4
Southport, Fl, US 195/F2
Southport, NY, US 191/H3
Southport, NC, US 193/H4
Southside, Al, US 192/D4
Southside, Tn, US 192/D2
Southside Place, Tx, US 181/M9
South Tyneside (co.), Eng, UK 41/G2
Southwark (bor.), Eng, UK 36/A1
Southwell, Eng, UK 41/H5
Southwold, Eng, UK 43/H2
Southwood NP, Austl. 158/C4
Southworth, Wa, US 197/C3
Soutpansberg (mts.), SAfr. 141/F4
Sovata, Rom. 57/G2
Soverato Marina, It. 54/E3
Sovere, It. 68/D2
Sovetsk, Rus. 75/L4
Sovetsk, Rus. 47/J4
Sovetskaya, Rus. 79/L5
Sovetskaya Gavan', Rus. 91/N2
Sovetskiy, Rus. 75/L4
Sovetskoye, Rus. 77/H3
Sovets'kyy, Ukr. 79/H5
Sōwa, Japan 95/D1
Sowa Pan (salt pan), Bots. 140/E4
Sowerby Bridge, Eng, UK 41/G4
Soweto, SAfr. 142/D2
Sōya-misaki (cape), Japan 94/B1
Soyana (riv.), Rus. 74/J2
Soyang (lake), SKor. 96/A2
Soyaux, Fr. 50/D4
Soyen, Ger. 65/F6
Soyhières, Swi. 66/D3
Soyo, Ang. 138/C4
Sozh (riv.), Bela. 76/D1
Sozopol, Bul. 57/H4
Spa, Belg. 61/E3
Spaceport USA, Fl, US 195/H3
Spada (lake), Wa, US 197/D2
Spaichingen, Ger. 67/E1
Spain (ctry.) 52/C2
Spakenburg, Neth. 58/C4
Spalding, Austl. 155/H5
Spalding, Sk, Can. 175/M1
Spalding, Eng, UK 41/H6
Spalding, Mi, US 190/C2
Spallumcheen, BC, Can. 174/E2
Spalt, Ger. 64/D4
Spanaway, Wa, US 174/C4
Spangenberg, Ger. 59/G6
Spangle, Wa, US 174/F4
Spangler, Pa, US 191/G4
Spanish (pt.), Ire. 38/A4
Spanish Fork, Ut, US 177/H3
Spanish Fort, Al, US 194/E2
Spanish River Ind. Res., On, Can. 190/E1
Spanish Town, Jam. 207/G2
Spannort (peak), Swi. 67/E4
Spar City, Co, US 179/J2
Sparanise, It. 71/D5
Sparkman, Ar, US 183/H4
Sparks, Ga, US 195/G2
Sparks, Nv, US 176/D4
Sparks, Tx, US 180/F2
Sparlingville, Mi, US 197/G6
Sparreholm, Swe. 46/G2
Sparta, Ga, US 193/F4
Sparta, Il, US 192/C1
Sparta, Mo, US 183/H2
Sparta, Mi, US 190/D3
Sparta, NJ, US 198/D1
Sparta, NC, US 193/G2
Sparta, Tn, US 192/E3
Sparta, Wi, US 185/J2
Sparta (Spárti), Gre. 55/H4
Spartanburg, SC, US 193/G3
Spartel (cape), Mor. 130/B2
Spárti (Sparta), Gre. 55/H4
Spartivento (cape), It. 54/E4
Sparwood, BC, Can. 174/G3
Spas-Demensk, Rus. 74/G5
Spassk-Dal'niy, Rus. 91/L3
Spasskaya Guba, Rus. 74/G3
Spáta, Gre. 81/N9
Spátha (cape), Gre. 55/H5
Spavinaw, Ok, US 183/G2
Spay, Ger. 61/G3
Spean (riv.), Sc, UK 39/B3
Spean Bridge, Sc, UK 39/B3
Spearfish, SD, US 184/C1
Spearman, Tx, US 182/D2
Spearville, Ks, US 182/E2
Speculator, NY, US 191/J3
Speedway, In, US 190/C5
Speer (peak), Swi. 67/F3
Speers, Sk, Can. 175/L1
Speicher, Swi. 67/F3
Speicher, Ger. 61/F4
Speichersdorf, Ger. 65/E3
Speke, Eng, UK 41/F5
Speke (int'l arpt.), Eng, UK 41/F5
Speke (gulf), Tanz. 137/A2
Spelle, Ger. 59/E4
Spello, It. 71/B2
Spence Bay, Nun, Can. 170/G2
Spencer (cape), Austl. 155/H5
Spencer (gulf), Austl. 145/C4
Spencer (cape), Ak, US 201/E2
Spencer, In, US 190/C5
Spencer, Ia, US 185/G2
Spencer, NC, US 193/G3
Spencer, Tn, US 192/E3
Spencer, Wi, US 185/J1
Spencer, WV, US 193/G1
Spencerville, Ok, US 183/G3
Spencerville, Oh, US 190/D4
Spences Bridge, BC, Can. 174/D2
Spenge, Ger. 59/F4
Spennymoor, Eng, UK 41/G2
Spentrup, Den. 46/D3
Sperkhiás, Gre. 55/H3
Sperkhíos (riv.), Gre. 55/H3
Sperlonga, It. 71/C5
Sperrin (mts.), NI, UK 40/A2
Spessart (range), Ger. 64/C3
Spétsai, Gre. 55/H4
Spey (bay), Sc, UK 39/C1
Spey (riv.), Sc, UK 39/B2
Speyer, Ger. 64/B4
Speyerbsch (riv.), Ger. 64/B4
Speyside, On, Can. 190/T8
Spezzano Albanese, It. 54/E3
Špičák (peak), Czh. 65/F2
Spicer (isls.), Nun, Can. 197/H2
Spicer, Mn, US 185/G1
Spicewood, Tx, US 180/E2
Spickard, Mo, US 185/H3
Spiddle, Ire. 38/A3
Spiekeroog (isl.), Ger. 59/E1
Spiez, Swi. 66/D4
Spigno Monferrato, It. 68/B4
Spijkenisse, Neth. 58/B5
Spike (mt.), Ak, US 201/K2
Spilamberto, It. 69/E4
Spílion, Gre. 55/J5
Spillersboda, Swe. 45/B1
Spillimacheen (riv.), BC, Can. 174/F2
Spillimacheen, BC, Can. 174/F2
Spilsby, Eng, UK 41/J5
Spilve (int'l arpt.), Lat. 47/L3
Spina (peak), It. 54/A2
Spinea, It. 69/F3
Spinetta Marengo, It. 68/B4
Spino d'Adda, It. 68/C3
Spirano, It. 68/C2
Spirit, Wi, US 187/J5
Spirit (lake), Ia, US 185/G2
Spirit Lake, Ia, US 185/G2
Spirit Lake, Id, US 174/F4
Spirit, North (lake), On, Can. 187/H1
Spiritwood, Sk, Can. 175/L1
Spiro, Ok, US 183/G3
Spišská Nová Ves, Slvk. 49/L4
Spitak, Arm. 77/H4
Spiti (riv.), India 110/D3
Spitsbergen (isl.), Sval. 80/B2
Spittal an der Drau, Aus. 51/K3
Spivey, Ks, US 183/E2
Spivey (lake), Ga, US 193/M7
Splendora, Tx, US 181/G2
Split, Cro. 56/C4
Split (int'l arpt.), Cro. 56/C4
Split (lake), Mb, Can. 170/G3
Split (mtn.), Ca, US 178/C2
Splitrock (res.), NJ, US 199/H8
Spluga, Passo dello (pass), Swi. 67/F5
Splügen, Swi. 67/F4
Špoģi, Lat. 47/M3
Spokane, Mo, US 183/H2
Spokane, Wa, US 174/F4
Spokane Ind. Res., Wa, US 174/E4
Spokoynaya, Rus. 79/L5
Spöl (riv.), It. 67/G5
Spoleto, It. 71/B2
Spoltore, It. 71/D3
Spook Cave, Ia, US 185/J2
Spoon (riv.), Il, US 185/K3
Spooner, Wi, US 187/J5
Spotorno, It. 68/B5
Spotswood, NJ, US 199/H10
Spotsylvania Courthouse, Va, US 193/J1
Sprague, Mb, Can. 187/G3
Sprague (riv.), Or, US 176/C2
Sprague, Wa, US 174/F4
Sprang, Neth. 58/C5
Spranger (mt.), BC, Can. 174/D1
Spratly (isls.) 102/D2
Spray, Or, US 176/D1
Spree (riv.), Ger. 49/H2
Sprendlingen, Ger. 61/G4
Spresiano, It. 69/F2
Sprimont, Belg. 61/E3
Spring (riv.), Ar, US 192/B2
Spring (lake), Ca, US 178/D3
Spring (cr.), Nv, US 176/E3
Spring (cr.), Ne, US 184/D3
Spring (mts.), Nv, US 178/E2
Spring, Tx, US 181/M8
Spring City, Pa, US 198/C3
Spring City, Tn, US 192/E3
Spring City, Ut, US 177/H4
Spring Grove, Il, US 197/P15
Spring Grove, Mn, US 185/J2
Spring Grove, Pa, US 198/B4
Spring Hill, Ar, US 183/H4
Spring Hill, Fl, US 194/K7
Spring Hill, Ks, US 183/G1
Spring Hill, Tn, US 192/D3
Spring Lake, Fl, US 194/L7
Spring Lake, NJ, US 199/D3
Spring Lake, NC, US 193/H3
Spring Valley, Ca, US 196/D5
Spring Valley, NY, US 199/J7
Spring Valley, Mn, US 185/H2
Spring Valley, Tx, US 181/M9
Springbok, SAfr. 142/B3
Springbokvlatke (valley), SAfr. 141/F5
Springboro, Oh, US 190/D5
Springdale, Ar, US 183/G2
Springdale, Ut, US 179/F2
Springdale, Wa, US 174/F3
Springdale, SC, US 193/G3
Springe, Ger. 59/G4
Springer, Ok, US 183/F3
Springer, NM, US 182/B2
Springerville, Az, US 179/H3
Springfield, Co, US 182/C2
Springfield, Fl, US 195/F2
Springfield, Ga, US 193/G4
Springfield, Ky, US 192/E2
Springfield, Ma, US 191/K3
Springfield, Mi, US 190/D3
Springfield, Mo, US 183/H2
Springfield, Oh, US 190/E5
Springfield, NJ, US 199/H9
Springfield, Or, US 176/B1
Springfield, SD, US 184/F2
Springfield, Mn, US 185/G1
Springfield (cap.), Il, US 185/K4
Springfield, Tn, US 192/D2
Springfield, Va, US 198/A6
Springfield, Vt, US 191/K3
Springfontein, SAfr. 142/D3
Springhill, NS, Can. 188/E3
Springhill, La, US 183/H4
Springs, SAfr. 142/E2
Springs, NY, US 199/F1
Springside, Sk, Can. 186/C2
Springsure, Austl. 158/C4
Springtown, Tx, US 180/K7
Springvale, Me, US 191/L3
Springvale (nbrhd.), Austl. 156/G5
Springview, Ne, US 184/E2
Springville, NY, US 191/G3
Springville, Ut, US 177/H3
Springville, Al, US 192/D4
Springville, Ia, US 185/J2
Springwater, NY, US 191/H3
Springwater, Sk, Can. 175/K2
Springwater Nat'l Wild. Ref., ND, US 186/D4
Sprockhövel, Ger. 59/E6
Sprowston, Eng, UK 43/H1
Spruce (mtn.), Nv, US 177/F3
Spruce (peak), WV, US 193/H1
Spruce Knob NRA, WV, US 193/H1
Spruce Lake, Sk, Can. 175/K1
Spruce Pine, NC, US 193/F3
Spruce Run (res.), NJ, US 198/C2
Sprucewoods, Mb, Can. 186/E3
Spui (riv.), Neth. 58/B5
Spur, Tx, US 182/D4
Spurn (pt.), Eng, UK 41/J4
Spuzzum, BC, Can. 174/D3
Spydeberg, Nor. 44/T9
Spydeberg (peak), Nor. 44/S9
Squa Pan (lake), Me, US 188/C2
Squamish (riv.), BC, Can. 174/C3
Squamish, BC, Can. 174/C3
Square Butte, Mt, US 175/J4
Squaw Creek Nat'l Wild. Ref., Mo, US 185/G3
Squaw Harbor, Ak, US 201/F4
Squaw Lake, Mn, US 187/G4
Squaw Valley, Ca, US 178/C2
Squaxin Island Ind. Res., Wa, US 197/A3
Squinzano, It. 55/F2
Squire, WV, US 193/G2
Squires (mt.), Austl. 155/E3
Squires, Mo, US 183/H2
Srbobran, Serb. 56/D3
Sre Ambel, Camb. 106/C4
Sre Khtum, Camb. 106/D3
Sre Noy, Camb. 106/D3
Srebrenica, Bosn. 56/D3
Sredna (mts.), Bul. 55/J1
Srednebelaya, Rus. 91/K1
Srednekolymsk, Rus. 81/R3
Sredniy Ikorets, Rus. 79/K2
Srednogorie, Bul. 57/G4
Srednyaya Akhtuba, Rus. 77/H2
Śrem, Pol. 49/J2
Sremčica, Serb. 56/E3
Sremska Mitrovica, Serb. 56/D3
Sreng (riv.), Camb. 106/C3
Srepok (riv.), Camb. 106/D3
Sretensk, Rus. 91/H1
Sri Dungargarh, India 113/K3
Sri Gangānagar, India 110/B5
Sri Jayewardenepura Kotte (cap.), SrL. 107/C5
Sri Kshetra (ruin), Myan. 98/B5
Sri Lanka (ctry.) 104/D6
Srikākulam, India 107/D2
Srimangal, Bang. 109/H3
Srīnagar, India 110/C2
Srīrampur, India 107/B2
Srīvardhan, India 107/B2
Środa Śląska, Pol. 49/J3
Środa Wielkopolska, Pol. 49/J2
St-Floris, PN de, CAfr. 134/D3
Staaten (riv.), Austl. 153/F4
Staaten River NP, Austl. 153/F4
Stabbursdalen NP, Nor. 44/H1
Staberhuk (pt.), Ger. 46/D4
Stabroek, Belg. 58/B6
Stacyville, Ia, US 185/H2
Stadbroke, North (isl.), Austl. 145/E3
Stade, Ger. 59/G1
Staden, Belg. 60/C2
Stadl-Paura, Aus. 65/G6
Stadskanaal, Neth. 58/D3
Stadtbergen, Ger. 64/D6
Stadthagen, Ger. 59/G4
Stadtlauringen, Ger. 64/D2
Stadtlohn, Ger. 58/D5
Stadtoldendorf, Ger. 59/G5
Stadtsteinach, Ger. 65/E2
Stäfa, Swi. 67/E3
Staffanstorp, Swe. 46/E4
Staffelberg (peak), Ger. 64/E2
Staffelegg (pass), Swi. 66/E3
Staffelsee (lake), Ger. 67/H2
Staffelstein, Ger. 64/D2
Staffhorst, Ger. 59/F3
Staffora (riv.), It. 68/C3
Stafford, Eng, UK 41/F6
Stafford, Ct, US 191/K4
Stafford, Tx, US 181/M9
Stafford, Va, US 193/J1
Stagno, It. 68/D6
Stagnone, Isole della (isl.), It. 54/C4
Stahnsdorf, Ger. 48/Q7
Staicele, Lat. 47/L3
Staindrop, Eng, UK 41/G2
Staines, Eng, UK 36/B2
Stains, Fr. 36/K5
Stakes (mt.), Ca, US 197/M12
Stäket, Swe. 45/A1
Stakhanov, Ukr. 79/K3
Stalbridge, Eng, UK 42/D5
Stalden, Swi. 66/D5
Stalham, Eng, UK 43/H1
Stallarholmen, Swe. 45/A1
Stallworthy (cape), Nun, Can. 197/S6
Stalowa Wola, Pol. 49/M3
Stalwart, Sk, Can. 175/M2
Stalybridge, Eng, UK 41/F5
Stambaugh, Mi, US 187/K4
Stamboliyski, Bul. 55/J1
Stamford, Austl. 158/A3
Stamford, Eng, UK 43/F1
Stamford, Ct, US 199/L7
Stamford, NY, US 191/J3
Stamford, Tx, US 182/E4
Stamford (lake), Tx, US 180/E1
Stamford Bridge, Eng, UK 41/H4
Stampa, Swi. 67/F5
Stampede (res.), Ca, US 176/C4
Stampriet, Namb. 140/C5
Stamps, Ar, US 183/H4
Stamullen, Ire. 40/B4
Stanardsville, Va, US 193/H1
Stanberry, Mo, US 185/G3
Stanchfield, Mn, US 187/H5
Standard, Ab, Can. 175/H2
Standerton, SAfr. 142/E2
Standing Indian (peak), NC, US 193/F3
Standing Rock, Al, US 192/E4
Standing Rock Ind. Res., SD, US 184/D1
Standish, Mi, US 190/E3
Standish, Me, US 191/L3
Standish-with-Langtree, Eng, UK 41/F4
Stanfield, Az, US 179/G4
Stanfield, Or, US 174/E5
Stanford, Ky, US 192/E2
Stanford, Mt, US 175/J4
Stanford Rivers, Eng, UK 36/D1
Stanford-le-Hope, Eng, UK 43/G3
Stange, Nor. 46/D1
Stangelville, Wi, US 190/C2
Stanger, SAfr. 143/E3
Stanghella, It. 69/E3
Stanhope, Eng, UK 41/F2
Stanhope, NJ, US 198/D2
Stanišić, Serb. 56/D3
Stanislaus (co.), Ca, US 197/M12
Stanislaus (riv.), Ca, US 176/C4
Stanke Dimitrov, Bul. 55/H1
Stanley, NB, Can. 188/D2
Stanley, ND, US 186/C3
Stanley, Sc, UK 39/C4
Stanley, Eng, UK 41/G2
Stanley, Austl. 156/C4
Stanley, NM, US 179/K3
Stanley, Wi, US 185/J1
Stanley (mt.), Austl. 155/F2
Stanley (res.), India 104/C5
Stanley (cap.), Falk. 191/F6
Stanley, China 99/L8
Stanley (mt.), Austl. 157/B5
Stanleytown, Va, US 193/H2
Stanleyville, NC, US 193/G2
Stanovo, Serb. 56/E4
Stanovoy (range), Rus. 83/M4
Stans, Swi. 67/E4
Stanstead Plain, Qu, Can. 191/K2
Stansted, Eng, UK 36/D3
Stansted (int'l arpt.), Eng, UK 43/G3
Stansted Mountfitchet, Eng, UK 43/G3
Stanthorpe, Austl. 158/C5
Stanton, Eng, UK 43/G2
Stanton, Al, US 192/D4
Stanton, Ca, US 196/G8
Stanton, De, US 198/C4
Stanton, Ky, US 192/F2
Stanton, Ia, US 185/G3
Stanton, Mi, US 190/D3
Stanton, ND, US 186/D4
Stanton, Ne, US 185/F3
Stanton, NJ, US 198/D2
Stanton, Tn, US 192/C3
Stanton, Tx, US 180/D1
Stanwell, Eng, UK 36/B2
Stanwood, Wa, US 174/C3
Stanychno-Luhans'ke, Ukr. 79/K3
Staphorst, Neth. 58/D3
Stapleford, Eng, UK 43/E4
Stapleford Abbotts, Eng, UK 36/D2
Staplehurst, Ne, US 185/F3
Staplehurst, Eng, UK 43/G4
Staples, Mn, US 187/G4
Staples, On, Can. 197/G7
Stapleton, Al, US 194/E2
Stapleton, Ga, US 193/F4
Stapleton, Ne, US 184/D3
Stąporków, Pol. 49/L3
Star', Rus. 76/E1
Star, Tx, US 181/E2
Star City, Sk, Can. 175/M1
Star City, Ar, US 183/J4
Star Lake, NY, US 191/J2
Stara Pazova, Serb. 56/E3
Stara Planina (mts.), Serb. 56/F3
Stara Vyzhivka, Ukr. 78/C2
Stara Zagora, Bul. 57/G4
Starachowice, Pol. 49/L3
Staranzano, It. 69/G2
Staraya Racheyka, Rus. 77/J1
Staraya Russa, Rus. 47/P2
Starbuck, Mb, Can. 186/F3
Starbuck, Mn, US 187/G5
Starbuck (isl.), Kiri. 161/K5
Starcke NP, Austl. 158/B1
Stargard Szczeciński, Pol. 46/F5
Stari Grad, Cro. 56/C4
Stark, Ks, US 183/G2
Starke, Fl, US 195/G3
Starkey, Or, US 176/D1
Starkville, Ms, US 192/C4
Starkweather, ND, US 186/E3
Starnberg, Ger. 65/E6
Starnbergersee (lake), Ger. 67/H2
Starobil's'k, Ukr. 79/K3
Staroderevyankovskaya, Rus. 79/K4
Starodub, Rus. 76/E1
Starogard Gdański, Pol. 46/H5
Starokostyantyniv, Ukr. 78/D3
Starominskaya, Rus. 79/K4
Staronizhestebliyevskaya, Rus. 79/K5
Staroshcherbinovskaya, Rus. 79/K4
Starotitarovskaya, Rus. 79/J5
Starovelichkovskaya, Rus. 79/K5
Start (bay), Eng, UK 42/C6
Start (pt.), Eng, UK 42/C6
Start (pt.), Sc, UK 37/V14
Start, La, US 183/J4
Startup, Wa, US 197/D2
Staryy Kistruss, Rus. 74/J5
Staryy Krym, Ukr. 79/H5
Staryy Oskol', Rus. 79/J2
Staryy Studenets, Rus. 75/L5
Staryye Dorogi, Bela. 76/D1
Staszów, Pol. 49/L3
State College, Pa, US 191/H4
State Fair Park (Cotton Bowl), Tx, US 180/L7
State Fairgrounds, De, US 198/C6
State Line, Ms, US 194/D2
Staten (isl.), NY, US 199/J9
Statenville, Ga, US 195/G2
States (int'l arpt.), Chl, UK 62/C2
Statesboro, Ga, US 193/G4
Statesville, NC, US 193/G3
Statham, Ga, US 192/F4
Statts Mills, WV, US 193/G1
Statue of Liberty Nat'l Mon., NY, US 199/J9
Staufen im Breisgau, Ger. 66/D2
Staufenberg, Ger. 48/E3
Staunton, Il, US 185/K4
Staunton, Eng, UK 42/D3
Staunton, Va, US 193/H1
Staunton on Wye, Eng, UK 42/D2
Stavanger, Nor. 46/A2
Staveley, Eng, UK 41/F3
Staveley, Eng, UK 41/G5
Stavelot, Belg. 61/E3
Stavely, Ab, Can. 175/H2
Staveren, Neth. 58/C3
Stavern, Nor. 46/D2
Stavropol', Rus. 79/M5
Stavropol'skiy Kray, Rus. 80/E5
Stavrós, Gre. 55/H2
Stavsnäs, Swe. 45/B1
Stavyshche, Ukr. 78/F3
Stawell, Austl. 156/B3
Stayner, On, Can. 190/F2
Stayton, Or, US 176/B1
Steamboat Slough (riv.), Ca, US 197/L10
Steamboat Springs, Co, US 177/K3
Stearns, Ky, US 192/E2
Stebbins, Ak, US 201/F3
Stebnyk, Ukr. 78/B3
Steckborn, Swi. 67/E2
Stederau (riv.), Ger. 59/H3
Steeg, Aus. 67/G3
Steel (mtn.), Id, US 177/F2
Steele, ND, US 186/E4
Steele, Mo, US 192/C2
Steele (cr.), Austl. 156/F5
Steele's Knowe (hill), Sc, UK 39/C4
Steeleville, Il, US 192/C1
Steelpoortrivier (riv.), SAfr. 143/E2
Steelton, Pa, US 198/B3
Steelville, Mo, US 183/J2
Steenbergen, Neth. 58/B5
Steenkool, Indo. 103/H4
Steens Mtn. Recreation Lands, Or, US 176/D2
Steensby (inlet), Nun, Can. 197/J1
Steenvoorde, Fr. 60/B2
Steenwijk, Neth. 58/D3
Steep (pt.), Austl. 154/B3
Steep Holm (isl.), Eng, UK 42/C4
Steep Rock, Mb, Can. 186/E2
Steeping (riv.), Eng, UK 41/J5
Ştefăneşti, Rom. 78/D4
Stefansson (isl.), Nun, Can. 170/F1
Steffen (peak), Chile 226/C5
Steffisburg, Swi. 66/D4
Steg, Swi. 66/D5
Stege, Den. 46/E4
Steglitz, Ger. 48/Q7
Steiermark (prov.), Aus. 49/H5
Steigerwald (for.), Ger. 51/J2
Steilacoom, Wa, US 197/B3
Steilloopbrug, SAfr. 141/F4
Steimbke, Ger. 59/G3
Stein, Neth. 61/E2
Stein (riv.), BC, Can. 174/D2
Stein am Rhein, Swi. 67/E2
Stein bei Nünnberg, Ger. 64/E4
Steina (riv.), Ger. 67/E2
Steinach, Ger. 64/E2
Steinach (riv.), Ger. 64/E2
Steinach, Ger. 65/F5
Steinach am Brenner, Aus. 67/H3
Steinau an der Strasse, Ger. 64/C2
Steinbach, Mb, Can. 186/F3
Steinbach an der Steyr, Aus. 65/H7
Steinbourg, Fr. 61/G6
Steinen, Ger. 66/D2
Steinen (riv.), Braz. 221/H4
Steinerkirchen an der Traun, Aus. 65/G6
Steinfeld, Ger. 64/B4
Steinfeld, Ger. 64/C3
Steinfeld, Ger. 59/F3
Steinfort, Lux. 61/E4
Steingaden, Ger. 67/G2
Steinhagen, Ger. 59/F4
Steinhatchee, Fl, US 195/G3
Steinhausen, Swi. 67/E3
Steinhausen, Namb. 140/C4
Steinhausen an der Rottum, Ger. 67/F1
Steinheid, Ger. 64/D2
Steinheim, Ger. 59/G5
Steinheim am Albuch, Ger. 64/D5
Steinheim an der Murr, Ger. 64/C5
Steinhorst, Ger. 59/H3
Steinhuder (lake), Ger. 59/G4
Steinkjer, Nor. 44/D2
Steinsland, Nor. 46/A1
Steinstücken, Ger. 48/Q7
Steinweiler, Ger. 64/B4
Stekene, Belg. 58/B6
Steklyanka, Rus. 74/J4
Stella (peak), It. 67/F5
Stella, SAfr. 142/D2
Stella, Ne, US 185/G3
Stellarton, NS, Can. 189/F3
Stelle, Ger. 59/H2
Stellenbosch, SAfr. 142/L10
Stello (peak), Fr. 54/A1
Stelvio, Passo di (pass), It. 67/G4
Stelvio, PN dello (nat'l park), It. 51/J3
Stenay, Fr. 61/E5
Stendal, Ger. 48/F2
Stende, Lat. 47/K3
Steneto NP, Bul. 57/G4
Stenhamra, Swe. 45/A1
Stenhousemuir, Sc, UK 39/C4
Stenlille, Den. 45/H7
Stenløse, Den. 45/J7
Stensån (riv.), Swe. 45/K6
Stenungsund, Swe. 46/D2
Step'anavan, Arm. 77/H4
Stepaside, Ire. 40/B5
Stephan, SD, US 184/E1
Stephansposching, Ger. 65/F5
Stephens, Ar, US 183/H4
Stephens City, Va, US 193/H1
Stephens Creek, Austl. 156/B1
Stephensburg, Ky, US 192/D2
Stephenson, Mi, US 190/C2
Stephenville, Nf, Can. 189/H1
Stephenville, Tx, US 181/E1
Stephenville Crossing, Nf, Can. 189/H1
Stepnoy, Rus. 75/P5
Stepnoye, Rus. 77/H3
Stepnoye, Rus. 77/H2
Steptoe (valley), Nv, US 177/F4
Steptoe, Wa, US 174/F4
Sterkspruit, SAfr. 142/D3
Sterkstroom, SAfr. 142/D3
Sterling, Ak, US 201/H3
Sterling, Co, US 184/C3
Sterling, Ga, US 195/H2
Sterling, Il, US 185/K3
Sterling, Ks, US 183/E1
Sterling, Mi, US 190/D2
Sterling City, Tx, US 180/D2
Sterling Heights, Mi, US 190/E3
Sterlington, La, US 183/H4
Sterlitamak, Rus. 77/K1
Sternstein (peak), Aus. 65/H5
Sterzing (Vipiteno), It. 67/H4
Stęszew, Pol. 49/J2
Štěti, Czh. 65/H2
Stetsonville, Wi, US 185/J1
Stettler, Ab, Can. 175/H1
Steubenville, Oh, US 190/F4
Stevenage, Eng, UK 43/F3
Stevens Point, Wi, US 185/K1
Stevens Village, Ak, US 201/J2
Stevenson (cr.), Austl. 155/G3
Stevenson, Al, US 192/E3
Stevenson, Wa, US 174/D5
Stevenson Entrance (Str.), Ak, US 201/H4
Stevenston, Sc, UK 39/B5
Stevensville, Mi, US 190/C3
Stevensville, Mt, US 175/G4
Stevensville, Md, US 198/B6
Stevinsluizen (dam), Neth. 58/C3
Stewardson, Il, US 192/C1
Stewart (mt.), Ab, Can. 174/F1
Stewart, BC, Can. 201/N4
Stewart (riv.), Yk, Can. 170/C2
Stewart (isl.), NZ 145/G7
Stewart, Al, US 192/D4
Stewart, Ms, US 192/C4
Stewart Crossing, Yk, Can. 201/L3
Stewart Lake Nat'l Wild. Ref., ND, US 186/C4
Stewart River, Yk, Can. 201/L3
Stewart Valley, Sk, Can. 175/L2
Stewarton, Sc, UK 39/B5
Stewartstown, NI, UK 40/B2
Stewartstown, Pa, US 198/B4
Stewartville, Mn, US 185/H2
Stewiacke, NS, Can. 188/F3
Steyning, Eng, UK 43/F5
Steynrus, SAfr. 142/D2
Steynsburg, SAfr. 142/D3
Steyr (riv.), Aus. 49/H5
Steyr, Aus. 65/H6
Steyregg, Aus. 65/H6
Steytlerville, SAfr. 142/D4
Stia, It. 69/E6
Stiava, It. 68/D6
Stickney (mt.), Wa, US 197/D2
Stiens, Neth. 58/C2
Stigler, Ok, US 183/G3
Stigtomta, Swe. 46/G2
Stikine, BC, Can. 201/M4
Stikine (riv.), BC, Can. 201/M4
Stilbaai, SAfr. 142/C4
Stiles, Tx, US 180/D2
Stiles, Wi, US 190/B2
Stilfontein, SAfr. 142/D2
Stilís, Gre. 55/H3
Still Creek (res.), Pa, US 198/C2
Still Pond, Md, US 198/B5
Stilling, Den. 46/D3
Stillmore, Ga, US 193/F4
Stillwater, Ok, US 183/F2
Stillwater (res.), NY, US 191/J3
Stillwater (riv.), Mt, US 177/J1
Stillwater (range), Nv, US 176/D4
Stillwater, Mn, US 187/Q6
Stillwater (lake), Pa, US 198/C1
Stillwater, Pa, US 198/B1
Stillwater NWR, Nv, US 176/D4
Stilo (cape), It. 54/E3
Stilwell, Ok, US 183/G3
Štimlje, Serb. 56/E4
Stimpfach, Ger. 64/D4
Stimson (mt.), Mt, US 175/H3
Stinchar (riv.), Sc, UK 40/D1
Stinking Water (cr.), Ne, US 184/D3
Stinnett, Tx, US 182/D3
Štip, FYROM 55/H2

Swallow (falls), Md, US 191/G5
Swalmen, Neth. 58/D6
Swan (riv.), Mb,Sk, Can. 186/D4
Swan (lake), Mb, Can. 186/D1
Swan (isls.), Hon. 202/E4
Swan (cr.), Mi, US 197/F7
Swan (riv.), Austl. 154/C4
Swan (hills), Ab, Can. 170/E3
Swan (falls), Id, US 176/E2
Swan (lake), Mn, US 185/G1
Swan (mt.), Austl. 155/G2
Swan (range), Mt, US 175/G3
Swan (riv.), Mt, US 175/H4
Swan Hill, Austl. 156/B2
Swan Lake, Mt, US 175/H4
Swan Lake Nat'l Wildlife Res., Mo, US 183/H1
Swan Lake NWR, Mo, US 185/H4
Swan Plain, Sk, Can. 186/C1
Swan Reach, Austl. 155/H5
Swan River, Mb, Can. 186/D1
Swan River NWR, Mt, US 175/H4
Swan, North Branch (cr.), Mi, US 197/E7
Swanage, Eng, UK 43/E5
Swanley, Eng, UK 36/D2
Swanlinbar, Ire. 38/C1
Swannanoa, NC, US 193/F3
Swanquarter, NC, US 193/J3
Swanquarter NWR, NC, US 193/J3
Swans (isl.), Me, US 188/C3
Swanscombe, Eng, UK 36/D2
Swansea, Austl. 156/D4
Swansea (bay), Eng, UK 42/C3
Swansea, Wal, UK 42/C3
Swansea (co.), Wal, UK 42/B3
Swanson (res.), Ne, US 184/D3
Swanton, Oh, US 190/E4
Swanton, Vt, US 191/K2
Swanville, Mn, US 187/G5
Swart Kei (riv.), SAfr. 142/D3
Swarthmore, Pa, US 198/C4
Swartruggens, SAfr. 141/E5
Swartswood (lake), NJ, US 198/D1
Swartz (cr.), Mi, US 197/E6
Swartz Creek, Mi, US 190/E3
Swarzędz, Pol. 49/J2
Swarzenbach an der Sächsischen Saale, Ger. 65/E2
Swarzrand (mts.), Namb. 142/B2
Swāt (riv.), Pak. 110/B2
Swatara, Mn, US 187/H4
Swatara (cr.), Pa, US 198/B3
Swatragh, NI, UK 40/B2
Swauk (pass), Wa, US 174/D4
Sway, Eng, UK 43/E5
Swayambhunath, Nepal 109/E2
Swaziland (ctry.) 143/E2
Sweden (ctry.) 44/E3
Swedesboro, NJ, US 198/C4
Swedru, Gha. 133/E5
Sweeden, Ky, US 192/D2
Sweeny, Tx, US 180/G3
Sweers (isl.), Austl. 153/E4
Sweet Grass Ind. Res., Sk, Can. 175/K1
Sweet Home, Or, US 176/B1
Sweet Home, Tx, US 181/F3
Sweet Springs, Mo, US 185/H4
Sweet Water, Al, US 194/E1
Sweetwater (res.), Ca, US 196/D5
Sweetwater, Fl, US 194/P11
Sweetwater (lake), ND, US 186/E3
Sweetwater, Ok, US 182/E3
Sweetwater, Tn, US 192/E3
Sweetwater, Tx, US 180/D1
Sweetwater (riv.), Wy, US 177/J2
Swellendam, SAfr. 142/C4
Świdnica, Pol. 49/J3
Świdnik, Pol. 49/M3
Świdwin, Pol. 46/F5
Świebodzice, Pol. 49/J3
Świebozin, Pol. 49/H2
Świecie, Pol. 49/K2
Świętokrzyskie (prov.), Pol. 49/K3
Świętokrzysky NP, Pol. 49/L3
Swift (riv.), BC, Can. 174/C1
Swift Current, Sk, Can. 175/L2
Swifterbant, Neth. 58/C3
Swifton, Ar, US 192/B3
Swiftown, Ms, US 192/B4
Swifts Creek, Austl. 157/C3
Swilly, Lough (inlet), Ire. 37/Q9
Swimming River (res.), NJ, US 199/D3
Swindmish Ind. Res., Wa, US 174/C3
Swindon, Eng, UK 43/E3
Swindon (co.), Eng, UK 43/E3
Swineford, Ire. 38/B2
Swineshead, Eng, UK 41/H6
Świnoujście, Pol. 46/F5
Swinton, Eng, UK 41/G5
Swisshome, Or, US 176/B1
Swist Bach (riv.), Ger. 61/F2
Switzerland (ctry.) 66/D4
Sword Beach, Fr. 63/E2
Swords, Ire. 40/B5
Swoyersville, Pa, US 198/C1
Syābru, Nepal 109/E1
Syamozero (lake), Rus. 74/G3
Syas'stroy, Rus. 47/Q1
Syava, Rus. 75/K4
Sycamore, Al, US 192/D4
Sycamore, Ga, US 195/G2
Sycamore, Il, US 185/K3
Sycan (riv.), Or, US 176/C2
Syców, Pol. 49/J3
Sydney, Austl. 158/H8
Sydney, NS, Can. 189/G2
Sydney (Manra) (isl.), Kiri. 161/H5
Sydney, Fl, US 194/L8
Sydney, ND, US 186/E4
Sydney-Kingsford Smith (int'l arpt.), Austl. 158/H8
Syeverodonets'k, Ukr. 79/K3
Sykäri (lake), Fin. 45/F4
Syke, Ger. 59/F3
Sykeston, ND, US 186/E4
Sykesville, Md, US 198/B5
Sykkylven, Nor. 44/C3
Syktyvkar, Rus. 75/L3
Sylacauga, Al, US 192/D4
Sylarna (peak), Swe. 44/E3
Sylhet (pol. reg.), Bang. 109/H3
Sylhet, Bang. 105/F3
Sylling, Nor. 44/R8
Sylva (riv.), Rus. 75/N4
Sylva, NC, US 193/F3
Sylvan Grove, Ks, US 183/E1
Sylvan Lake, Ab, Can. 175/G1
Sylvan Lake, Mi, US 197/F6
Sylvania, Sk, Can. 175/M1
Sylvania, Al, US 192/E3
Sylvania, Ga, US 193/G4
Sylvania, Oh, US 190/E4
Sylvenstein-Stausee (lake), Ger. 67/H2
Sylvester (lake), Austl. 153/E4
Sylvester, Ga, US 195/G2
Sylvester, Tx, US 180/D1
Sylvia, Ks, US 183/E2
Synel'nykove, Ukr. 79/H3
Synnott (range), Austl. 152/B4
Syntagma, Gre. 81/N8
Synya, Rus. 75/N2
Syosset, NY, US 199/L8
Syowa, Japan, Ant. 228/C
Syracuse, In, US 190/D4
Syracuse, Ks, US 182/D2
Syracuse, Ne, US 185/F3
Syracuse, NY, US 191/H3
Syracuse (Siracusa), It. 54/D4
Syracuse Hancock (int'l arpt.), NY, US 191/H3
Syrdarīya (riv.), Kaz. 83/F5
Syria (ctry.) 114/D3
Syriam, Myan. 105/G4
Syrian (des.), Jor. 112/C2
Syrskiy, Rus. 76/F1
Sysmä, Fin. 47/L1
Sysola (riv.), Rus. 75/L3
Syston, Eng, UK 43/E1
Sytkivtsi, Ukr. 78/E3
Syzran', Rus. 77/J1
Szabolcs-Szatmár-Bereg (co.), Hun. 49/L4
Szamotuły, Pol. 49/J2
Szarvas, Hun. 56/E2
Százhalombatta, Hun. 57/Q10
Szczebrzeszyn, Pol. 49/M3
Szczecin, Pol. 46/F5
Szczecinek, Pol. 46/G5
Szczytna, Pol. 49/J3
Szczytno, Pol. 49/L2
Szeged, Hun. 56/E2
Szeghalom, Hun. 56/E2
Székesfehérvár, Hun. 56/D2
Szekszárd, Hun. 56/D2
Szendro, Hun. 56/E1
Szent László-Vize (riv.), Hun. 57/Q10
Szentendre, Hun. 57/R9
Szentes, Hun. 56/E2
Szentlorinc, Hun. 56/C2
Szerencs, Hun. 49/L4
Szeskie (peak), Pol. 47/K4
Sziget-Szentmiklós, Hun. 57/R10
Szigetvár, Hun. 56/C2
Szirák, Hun. 49/K5
Szolnok, Hun. 56/E2
Szombathely, Hun. 56/C2
Szprotawa, Pol. 49/H3
Sztum, Pol. 47/H5
Szubin, Pol. 49/J2
Szydłowiec, Pol. 49/L3

T

T'aipei (cap.), Tai. 99/J3
Ta Fou San, Laos 106/C1
Ta Khmau, Camb. 106/D4
Ta Phraya, Thai. 106/C3
Ta Seng, Camb. 106/D3
Ta Waewae (bay), NZ 159/A4
Tabaco, Phil. 100/C2
Tabanan, Indo. 101/F5
Tabango, Phil. 100/D3
Tabaquite, Trin. 217/F2
Ţabarqah, Tun. 130/L6
Ţabas, Iran 115/J3
Tabasará (mts.), Pan. 207/F4
Tabasco (state), Mex. 202/C4
Tabatinga, Serra da (mts.), Braz. 222/D1
Tabayama, Japan 95/B2
Tabbs (bay), Tx, US 181/M9
Tabda, Som. 137/C1
Tabelbala, Alg. 128/E3
Tabelbalet (well), Alg. 129/G4
Taber, Ab, Can. 175/H3
Tabernes de Valldigna, Sp. 53/E3
Tabiang, Kiri. 160/F5
Tabibuga, PNG 153/G1
Tabing (int'l arpt.), Indo. 101/C3
Tabio, Col. 219/L8
Tabira, Braz. 219/G4
Tabiteuea (isl.), Kiri. 160/G5
Tabitta, Austl. 157/B2
Tablas (isl.), Phil. 103/F1
Tablas (str.), Phil. 100/C2
Tablas de Daimiel, PN, Sp. 52/D3
Table (mtn.), Ire. 38/D3
Table (bay), SAfr. 142/B4
Table (mtn.), SAfr. 142/L10
Table (cape), NZ 159/D2
Table (mtn.), Wa, US 174/D4
Table Rock (dam), Mo, US 183/H2
Table Rock (lake), Mo, US 183/G2
Tableland Station, Austl. 152/B4
Tabletop (mt.), PNG 153/G1
Tabligbo, Togo 133/F5
Tábor, Czh. 65/H4
Tabor City, NC, US 193/H3
Tabora, Tanz. 139/H4
Tabora, Tanz. 137/B4
Tabora (prov.), Tanz. 137/A3
Tabory, Rus. 75/P4
Tabou, C.d'Iv. 132/D5
Tabrīz, Iran 115/F2
Tabuaeran (Fanning) (isl.), Kiri. 161/K4
Tabubil, PNG 103/K5
Tabūk, SAr. 127/H2
Tabuk, Phil. 100/C1
Tabuleiro do Norte, Braz. 219/G4
Taburno (peak), It. 71/D5
Tabursuq, Tun. 130/L6
Tabuyung, Indo. 101/B2
Tabwemasana (peak), Van. 160/F6
Täby, Swe. 45/B1
Tacabamba, Peru 220/B2
Tacámbaro de Codallos, Mex. 205/E5
Tacaná (vol.), Mex. 206/C3
Tacaratu, Braz. 219/G5
Tacarcuna (mtn.), Pan. 216/B2
Tacheng, China 111/D2
Tachia (riv.), Tai. 99/J3
Tachibana (bay), Japan 96/A4
Tachikawa, Japan 97/F3
Tachinger (lake), Ger. 65/F7
Tachira (state), Ven. 207/H5
Tachoshui, Tai. 99/J3
Tachov, Czh. 65/F3
Tacipi, Indo. 103/F4
Tacloban, Phil. 100/D3
Tacna, Az, US 179/F4
Tacna, Peru 224/B1
Tacna (dept.), Peru 220/D5
Tacobamba, Bol. 224/C1
Tacoma, Wa, US 174/C4
Tacopaya, Bol. 224/C1
Tacora (vol.), Chile 224/B1
Tacotalpa, Mex. 206/C2
Tacuarembó (dept.), Uru. 191/G2
Tacuarembó, Uru. 225/F4
Tacuarembo (dept.), Uru. 225/F5
Tacurong, Phil. 100/D4
Tacutu (riv.), Braz. 217/F4
Tadaoka, Japan 95/H7
Tadcaster, Eng, UK 41/G4
Ta'Delimara (pt.), Malta 54/M7
Tādepallegūdem, India 107/D2
Tadine, NCal., Fr. 161/V12
Tadjoura, Djib. 136/B3
Tadley, Eng, UK 43/E4
Tadmur, Syria 114/D3
Tadmur (Palmyra) (ruin), Syria 114/D3
Tadó, Col. 216/B3
Tado, Japan 95/L5
Tadohae Hasang NP, SKor. 93/C5
Tadotsu, Japan 96/C3
Tadoussac, Qu, Can. 188/C1
Tādpatri, India 107/C3
Tadrart (mts.), Alg.,Libya 126/H4
Taduno, Indo. 103/F4
Tadworth, Eng, UK 36/C3
Tadzewu, Gha. 133/F5
T'aean, SKor. 93/D4
T'aebaek, SKor. 93/E4
T'aebaek (mts.), NKor.,SKor. 91/K4
Taebudo (isl.), SKor. 93/F7
Taech'ŏng (isl.), SKor. 93/C4
Taech'ŏn, SKor. 93/D4
T'aech'ŏn, NKor. 93/C3
Taedŏk, SKor. 93/D5
Taedong (riv.), NKor. 93/D3
Taedong, NKor. 93/C3
Taegang-got (pt.), NKor. 93/D3
Taegu, SKor. 93/E5
Taegu-jikhalsi (prov.), SKor. 96/A3
Taegwan, NKor. 93/C2
Taehŭksan (isl.), SKor. 93/C5
Taehŭng, NKor. 93/D2
Taehwa (isl.), NKor. 93/C3
T'aein, SKor. 93/D5
Taejŏn, SKor. 93/D4
Taejŏn-jikhalsi (prov.), SKor. 93/D4
Taeryŏng (riv.), NKor. 93/C2
T'aet'an, NKor. 93/C3
Tafalla, Sp. 50/C5
Ţafas, Syria 117/E3
Tafassasset, Oued (riv.), Alg. 129/H4
Taff (riv.), Wal, UK 42/C3
Tafí Viejo, Arg. 224/C3
Tafiré, C.d'Iv. 132/D4
Tafraout, Mor. 128/C3
Tafresh, Iran 115/G3
Taft, Iran 115/H4
Taft, Ok, US 183/G3
Taft, Fl, US 194/N7
Taft, Ca, US 178/C3
Taft, Phil. 100/D3
Taft, Tx, US 181/F4
Taftān (mtn.), Iran 113/H3
Taga, Japan 95/K5
Taga Dzong, Bhu. 109/G2
Taganrog, Rus. 79/K4
Tagant (pol. reg.), Mrta. 132/C2
Tagarav (peak), Trkm. 115/J2
Tagawa, Japan 96/B4
Tagbilaran, Phil. 100/C3
Taggia, It. 68/A5
Taghit, Alg. 129/E3
Taghmon, Ire. 38/D5
Tagish, Yk, Can. 201/M3
Tagliacozzo, It. 71/C3
Tagliamento (riv.), It. 51/K3
Taglio di Po, It. 69/F4
Tagolo (pt.), Phil. 100/C3
Tagoloan, Phil. 100/D3
Tagounit, Mor. 128/D3
Taguasco, Cuba 207/G1
Taguatinga, Braz. 222/D2
Taguatinga, Braz. 222/C2
Tagudin, Phil. 100/C1
Taguig, Phil. 100/F6
Tagula (isl.), PNG 160/E6
Tagum, Phil. 100/D4
Tagun (riv.), Rus. 75/P4
Tagus (riv.), Port.,Sp. 72/B3
Tagus (riv.), Sp. 29/D5
Tagus (Tajo) (riv.), Sp. 52/C3
Tagus Rio Tejo (lake), Port. 53/P10
Tahakopa, NZ 159/B4
Tahan (peak), Malay. 101/C1
Tahanea (isl.), FrPol. 161/L6
Tahanroz'ka (gulf), Rus.,Ukr. 76/F3
Tahar-Souk, Mor. 130/B3
Tahara, Japan 95/M6
Tahat (peak), Alg. 129/G5
Tahat, Oued et (riv.), Alg. 130/F5
Tahe, China 91/J1
Tahilt, Mong. 90/D2
Tahir (pass), Turk. 114/E2
Tahiti (isl.), FrPol. 161/L6
Tahkuna (pt.), Est. 47/K2
Tahlequah, Ok, US 183/G3
Tahmoor, Austl. 157/E2
Tahnaout, Mor. 128/D3
Tahoe (lake), Ca,Nv, US 170/D5
Tahoka, Tx, US 182/D4
Taholah, Wa, US 174/B4
Tahoua, Niger 133/G3
Tahoua (dept.), Niger 133/G3
Tahquamenon (falls), Mi, US 190/D1
Tahţā, Egypt 127/F3
Tahua, Bol. 220/E4
Tahuamanu (riv.), Peru 220/D3
Tahuamanú, Peru 220/D3
Tahuata (isl.), FrPol. 161/L6
Tahulandang (isl.), Indo. 103/G3
Tahuna, Indo. 103/G3
Tahuya (riv.), Wa, US 197/B3
Tahuya, Wa, US 197/A3
Ţahwāy, Egypt 131/B4
Taï, C.d'Iv. 132/D5
Tai (lake), China 91/J5
Tai Long Wan (bay), China 99/M7
Tai Mo Shan (peak), China 99/L7
Tai O, China 99/K8
Tai Po, China 99/L7
Tai Xian, China 92/E4
Taï, PN de, C.d'Iv. 132/D5
Taiama, SLeo. 132/B4
Tai'an, China 93/B2
Tai'an, China 92/D3
Tai'angang, China 92/L8
Taiarapu (pen.), FrPol. 161/X15
Taiaret (well), Mor. 128/B5
Taibai (peak), China 90/F5
Taibus, China 90/H3
Taicang, China 92/L8
T'aichung, Tai. 99/J3
Taiei, Japan 95/E2
Taigu, China 92/C3
Taihang (mts.), China 92/C3
Taihape, NZ 159/C2
Taihe, China 92/C4
Taihsi, Tai. 99/J4
Taihu, China 99/H2
Taikang, China 92/C4
Taiki, Japan 94/C2
Tailai, China 91/J2
Taileleo, Indo. 101/B3
Tailem Bend, Austl. 155/H5
Tailfingen, Ger. 64/B5
Taima, Japan 95/J6
Tain, Sc, UK 39/B1
Tain-L'Hermitage, Fr. 70/A2
T'ainan, Tai. 99/J4
Taínaron (cape), Gre. 55/H4
Taingainony, Madg. 143/H8
Taino, It. 68/B2
Taió, Braz. 225/G3
Taiobeiras, Braz. 223/E2
Taiohae, FrPol. 161/L5
Taiping, China 106/D1
Taiping, Malay. 101/C1
Taiping, China 99/F4
Taiping, China 99/H2
Taiping, China 99/G1
Taiping (peak), China 91/J2
Taipinggou, China 91/L2
Taipingshao, China 93/C2
Taipu, Braz. 219/H4
Tais, Indo. 101/C4
Taisha, Japan 96/C3
Taishan, China 99/G4
Taishi, Japan 95/J6
Taishun, China 99/H3
Taiskirchen im Innkreis, Aus. 65/G6
Taissy, Fr. 61/D5
Taitao (pen.), Chile 209/B7
Taiti (peak), Kenya 137/A1
T'aitung, Tai. 99/J4
Taiwan (ctry.) 99/J3
Taiwan (str.), China,Tai. 99/H3
Taixing, China 92/E4
Taíyetos (mts.), Gre. 55/H4
Taiyuan, China 92/C3
Taizhao, China 98/B2
Taizhou, China 92/D4
Taizi (riv.), China 92/F2
Ta'izz, Yem. 136/C2
Tāj Mahal, India 108/B2
Tajarhī, Libya 126/B3
Tajikistan (ctry.) 80/H6
Tajima, Japan 97/F2
Tajimi, Japan 95/M5
Tajique, NM, US 179/J3
Tajiri, Japan 95/H7
Tājirwīn, Tun. 130/L7
Tajo (Tagus) (riv.), Sp. 52/C3
Tājpur, India 108/B1
Tajrīsh, Iran 115/G3
Tajumulco (vol.), Guat. 206/D3
Tajuña (riv.), Sp. 52/D2
Tājūrā, Libya 126/B1
Tak, Thai. 106/B2
Takāb, Iran 115/F2
Takahagi, Japan 97/G2
Takahama, Japan 95/J5
Takahama, Japan 95/L6
Takahashi (riv.), Japan 96/C3
Takahashi, Japan 96/C3
Takahata, Japan 97/G1
Takaishi, Japan 95/H6
Takajärvi (lake), Fin. 45/E3
Takaka, NZ 159/C3
Takama, Guy. 218/B1
Takamatsu, Japan 96/D3
Takami-yama (peak), Japan 95/K7
Takanabe, Japan 96/B4
Takane, Japan 95/A2
Takanosu, Japan 94/B3
Takanosu-yama (peak), Japan 95/C2
Takaoka, Japan 97/E2
Takapau, NZ 159/D3
Takapuna, NZ 159/F6
Takarazuka, Japan 95/H6
Takaroa (isl.), FrPol. 161/L6
Takasaki, Japan 97/F2
Takashima, Japan 95/K5
Takatomi, Japan 95/L5
Takatori, Japan 95/J7
Takatsuki, Japan 95/K5
Takatsuki, Japan 95/J6
Takaungu, Kenya 137/B2
Takayama, Japan 97/E2
Takefu, Japan 96/E3
Takehara, Japan 96/C3
Tākestān, Iran 115/G2
Taketa, Japan 96/B4
Taketoyo, Japan 95/L6
Takev, Camb. 106/D4
Takh, India 110/D3
Takhatgarh, India 104/B2
Takhatpur, India 108/C4
Takhli, Thai. 106/C3
Takht-i-Bhāi, Pak. 110/A2
Takhta, Rus. 79/M5
Takhta-Bazar, Trkm. 80/G6
Takhtamygda, Rus. 91/J1
Taki, Japan 95/L7
Takiéta, Niger 133/H3
Takijuq (lake), Nun, Can. 170/E2
Takikawa, Japan 94/B2
Takingeun, Indo. 101/B1
Takino, Japan 95/G6
Takla Makan (des.), China 83/H6
Tāknis, Libya 126/D1
Tako, Japan 95/E2
Takoradi, Gha. 133/E5
Takouch (cape), Alg. 130/K6
Takoukout, Niger 133/H3
Taksimo, Rus. 81/M4
Taksony, Hun. 57/R10
Takum, Nga. 133/H5
Takundi, D.R. Congo 138/D4
Tala, Kenya 137/B2
Talā, Egypt 131/B3
Tala, Uru. 191/L11
Tala, Mex. 204/E4
Tala Mugongo, Ang. 138/D5
Talacasto, Arg. 224/B4
Talacre, Wal, UK 41/E5
Talagang, Pak. 110/B3
Talagante, Chile 226/N8
Tālah, Tun. 130/L7
Talaimannar, SrL. 107/C4
Talāja, India 113/K4
Talak (phys. reg.), Niger 133/G2
Talala, Ok, US 183/G2
Talalayivka, Ukr. 79/G2
Talamanca (mts.), CR 207/F4
Talamba, Pak. 110/B4
Talamona, It. 67/F5
Talang (peak), Indo. 101/C3
Talanga, Hon. 206/E3
Talangbatu, Indo. 101/D4
Talangbetutu, Indo. 101/D3
Talange, Fr. 61/F5
Talant, Fr. 66/A3
Talara, Peru 220/A2
Talas, Turk. 114/C2
Talas (riv.), Kaz. 111/B3
Talas, Kyr. 111/B3
Talata Ampano, Madg. 143/H8
Talata Mafara, Nga. 133/G3
Talaud (isl.), Phil. 83/M9
Talavera de la Reina, Sp. 52/C3
Talawakele, SrL. 107/D5
Talawdī, Sudan 134/F3
Talawgyi, Myan. 98/C3
Talayuela, Sp. 52/C3
Talbingo (dam), Austl. 157/D2
Talbingo (res.), Austl. 157/D2
Talbingo, Austl. 157/D2
Talbot (mt.), Austl. 154/E3
Talbot, Ab, Can. 175/J1
Talbot (co.), Md, US 198/B6
Talbotton, Ga, US 192/E4
Talca, Chile 226/C2
Talcahuano, Chile 226/B3
Tālcher, India 107/E1
Talcho, Niger 133/F3
Talco, Tx, US 183/G4
Talcott, WV, US 193/G2
Taldan, Rus. 91/J1
Taldykuduk, Kaz. 77/J2
Taldyqorghan, Kaz. 111/C3
Taleex, Som. 136/D3
Talence, Fr. 50/C4
Talent (riv.), Swi. 66/C4
Talent, Or, US 176/B2
Tālesh, Iran 115/G2
Talfer (Talvera) (riv.), It. 67/H4
Talgar, Kaz. 80/H5
Tali Post, Sudan 134/F4
Taliabu (isl.), Indo. 103/F4
Tālibwāla, Pak. 110/B4
Talihina, Ok, US 183/G3
T'alin, Arm. 115/E1
Talinay, PN, Chile 224/B4
Taliouine, Mor. 128/D3
Talipaw, Phil. 100/C4
Talisayan, Indo. 103/E3
Talisayan, Phil. 100/D3
Talitsa, Rus. 75/P4
Taliwang, Indo. 103/E5
Tal'ka, Bela. 47/N5
Talkeetna, Ak, US 201/H3
Ţalkhā, Egypt 131/C2
Tall 'Afar, Iraq 114/E2
Tall al Muqayyar (ruin), Iraq 112/E2
Tall ar Rub' (ruin), Egypt 131/C3
Tall 'Āsūr (peak), WBnk. 117/C5
Tall Kayf, Iraq 115/E2
Tall Kūjik, Syria 114/E2
Tall Rāk, Egypt 131/C3
Tall Timay (ruin), Egypt 131/C3
Talladega, Al, US 192/D4
Tallaght, Ire. 40/B5
Tallahala (cr.), Ms, US 194/D1
Tallahassee (cap.), Fl, US 195/F2
Tallahatchie (riv.), Ms, US 192/B3
Tallangatta, Austl. 157/C3
Tallanstown, Ire. 40/B4
Tallapoosa (riv.), Al, US 192/E4
Tallapoosa, Ga, US 192/E4
Tallard, Fr. 70/C4
Tallassee, Al, US 192/E4
Tallering (peak), Austl. 154/B4
Talleyville, De, US 198/C4
Tallgrass Prairie Nat'l Prsv., Ks, US 185/F4
Tallinn (cap.), Est. 47/L2
Tallmadge, Oh, US 190/F4
Tallman Mountain State Park, NY, US 199/K7
Talloires, Fr. 66/C6
Tallow, Ire. 38/B5
Tallowa (dam), Austl. 157/E2
Talmage, Ut, US 177/H3
Talmassons, It. 69/G2
Talmoon, Mn, US 187/H4
Tal'ne, Ukr. 78/F3
Talo (peak), Eth. 134/H3
Taloda, India 107/B1
Taloga, Ok, US 182/E2
Tāloqān, Afg. 113/J1
Talovaya, Rus. 79/L2
Talpa, Tx, US 180/E2
Talpa de Allende, Mex. 204/D4
Talshand, Mong. 90/D2
Talsi, Lat. 47/K3
Talsperre Pöhl (res.), Ger. 65/F1
Taltal, Chile 224/B3
Taltson (riv.), NW, Can. 170/E2
Talty, Tx, US 180/L7
Taluk, Indo. 101/C3
Talukbayur, Indo. 103/E3
Talumphuk (pt.), Thai. 106/C4
Talut (pt.), Fr. 62/B5
Talvera (Talfer) (riv.), It. 67/H4
Talwandi Bhāi, India 110/C4
Talwandi Sābo, India 110/C5
Talwāra, India 110/C4
Taly, Rus. 79/L3
Ţalyā, Egypt 131/C4
Tam Ky, Viet. 106/E3
Tam Le, Viet. 106/D2
Tam Quan, Viet. 106/E3
Tama (riv.), Japan 95/D2
Tama, Japan 95/C2
Tama Abu (range), Malay. 100/A5
Tamagawa, Japan 95/C2
Tamaha, Ok, US 183/G3
Tamaho, Japan 95/B2
Tamaki (str.), NZ 159/F6
Tamaki, Japan 95/L7
Tamalameque, Col. 216/C2
Ţamalāy, Egypt 131/B3
Tamale, Gha. 133/E4
Tamamura, Japan 95/C1
Taman', Rus. 79/J5
Taman (bay), Rus. 79/J5
Taman, Indo. 102/D5
Taman Negara NP, Malay. 101/C1
Taman-Rasset, Oued (riv.), Alg. 129/F5
Tamaná (peak), Col. 216/B3
Tamana (isl.), Kiri. 160/G5
Tamanaco (riv.), Ven. 219/P8
Tamanar, Mor. 128/C3
Tamanghasset (pol. reg.), Alg. 133/F1
Tamanghasset, Oued (riv.), Alg. 129/F5
Tamanhint, Libya 126/B3
Tamanrasset, Alg. 129/G5
Tamanrasset (wilaya), Alg. 129/F4
Tamanthi, Myan. 98/B3
Tamaqua, Pa, US 198/C2
Tamar (riv.), Eng, UK 42/B5
Tamara (isl.), Japan 97/H8
Tamarac, Fl, US 194/P10
Tamarack, Mn, US 187/H4
Tamarak NWR, Mn, US 187/G4
Tamari, Japan 95/E1
Tamarike, Indo. 153/F2
Tamarindo Nat'l Wild. Ref., CR 206/E4
Tamarite de Litera, Sp. 53/F2
Tamaro (peak), Swi. 67/E5
Tamási, Hun. 56/D2
Tamassoumît, Mrta. 132/B2
Tamatama, Ven. 217/E4
Tamatsukuri, Japan 95/E1
Tamaulipas (state), Mex. 202/B3
Tamazula de Gordiano, Mex. 204/E5
Tamazunchale, Mex. 206/B1
Tamba, Japan 95/H5
Tamba (uplands), Japan 95/H5
Tambach, Kenya 137/A1
Tambacounda (pol. reg.), Sen. 132/B3
Tambacounda, Sen. 132/B3
Tambakara, Mali 132/C3
Tambaoura, Falaise de (cliff), Mali 132/C3
Tambar Springs, Austl. 156/D1
Tambara, Moz. 141/G3
Tambawel, Nga. 133/G3
Tambea, Indo. 103/F4
Tambelan (isls.), Indo. 102/C3
Tambellup, Austl. 154/C5
Tambey, Rus. 80/H2
Tambisan, Malay. 100/B4
Tambo (peak), Swi. 67/F5
Tambo, Austl. 158/B4
Tambo (riv.), Peru 220/C3
Tambo (riv.), Austl. 157/C3
Tambo Colorado (ruin), Peru 220/C4
Tambo de Mora, Peru 220/B4
Tambo Grande, Peru 220/A2
Tambobamba, Peru 220/C4
Tambohorano, Madg. 143/G7
Tambopata (riv.), Peru 220/D4
Tambora (peak), Indo. 103/E5
Tambores, Uru. 225/E4
Tamboril, Braz. 219/F4
Tamboritha (mt.), Austl. 157/C3
Tambov, Rus. 77/G1
Tambovskaya Oblast, Rus. 77/G1
Tambre (riv.), Sp. 52/A1
Tambu, Indo. 103/E4
Tambul, PNG 153/F1
Tambunan, Malay. 100/B4
Tambura, Sudan 135/E4
Tamchaket, Mrta. 132/C2
Tame, Col. 216/D3
Tame (riv.), Eng, UK 43/E1
Tameside (co.), Eng, UK 41/F5
Támega (riv.), Port. 52/B2
Tamel Aike, Arg. 191/C6
Tamentit, Alg. 129/E4
Támesis, Col. 219/K7
Tamgak (peak), Niger 133/H2
Tamghas, Nepal 108/D1
Tamiahua, Mex. 206/B1
Tamiahua (lag.), Mex. 206/B1
Tamiami (canal), Fl, US 195/H5
Tamiami, Fl, US 194/P11
Tamiang (pt.), Indo. 101/B1
Tamil Nādu (state), India 104/C5
Taminango, Col. 216/B4
Tamines, Belg. 61/D3
Ţāmiyah, Egypt 131/B6
Tamkuhi, India 109/E2
Tamlūk, India 109/F4
Tāmma, India 98/B3
Tammany (mt.), NJ, US 198/C2
Tammaro (riv.), It. 71/D5
Tammela, Fin. 47/K1
Tammisaari (Ekenäs), Fin. 47/K2
Ţammūn, WBnk. 117/C4
Tamo, Ar, US 183/J3
Tampa, Ks, US 183/F1
Tampa, Fl, US 194/L8
Tampa (bay), Fl, US 194/K8
Tampa (int'l arpt.), Fl, US 194/K8
Tampalakamam, SrL. 107/D4
Tampang, Indo. 101/D4
Tampere, Fin. 47/K1
Tampere-Pirkkala (int'l arpt.), Fin. 47/K1
Tampico, Mex. 206/B1
Tampin, Malay. 101/C2
Tampines (nbrhd.), Sing. 101/J6
Tampoc (riv.), FrG. 217/H4
Tampon Ambohitra (peak), Madg. 143/J6
Tampulonanjing (peak), Indo. 101/B2
Tamra, Isr. 117/C3
Tamrah, SAr. 112/E4
Tamsalu, Est. 47/M2
Tamshiyacu, Peru 220/C2
Tamuín, Mex. 206/B1
Tamuín (riv.), Mex. 206/B1
Tāmulpur, India 109/H2
Tamur (riv.), Nepal 109/F2
Tamworth, Austl. 156/D1
Tamworth, Eng, UK 43/E1
Tamyang, SKor. 93/D5
Tan (riv.), China 105/K3
Tan An, Viet. 106/D4
Tan-Tan, Mor. 128/C3
Tana (riv.), Fin. 80/C3
Tana (riv.), Nor. 44/H1
Tana, Nor. 44/J1
Tana (lake), Eth. 119/F3
Tana (riv.), Kenya 119/G5
Tana River Primate Nat'l Rsv., Kenya 137/C2
Tanabe, Japan 96/D4
Tanabe, Japan 95/J6
Tanabi, Braz. 225/G2
Tanacross, Ak, US 201/K3
Tanafjorden (estu.), Nor. 44/J1
Tanaga (isl.), Ak, US 201/C6
Tanaga (mt.), Ak, US 201/C6
Tanagura, Japan 97/G2
Tanahbala (isl.), Indo. 102/A4
Tanahmasa (isl.), Indo. 101/B3
Tanahmerah, Indo. 153/F1
Tanahputih, Indo. 101/C2
Tanakpur, India 108/C1
Tanambe, Madg. 143/J7
Tanami, Austl. 152/C4
Tanami (des.), Austl. 145/C2
Tanami Desert Wildlife Sanctuary, Austl. 152/C5
Tanana, Ak, US 201/H2
Tanana (riv.), Ak, US 201/J3
Tanandava, Madg. 143/G8
Tanangozi, Tanz. 137/A3
Tanaro (riv.), It. 51/G4
Tancacha, Arg. 224/D5
Tancarville, Fr. 63/F2
Tancheng, China 92/D4
Tanch'ŏn, NKor. 93/E2
Tancítaro, Pico de (peak), Mex. 204/E5
Tancitaro, PN de, Mex. 202/A4
Tandā, India 108/D2
Tanda, C.d'Iv. 132/E5
Tanda (lake), Mali 132/D3
Tānda, India 108/B1
Tandag, Phil. 100/D3
Tandaltī, Sudan 134/F2
Ţăndărei, Rom. 57/H3
Tāndi, India 110/D3
Tandian, China 93/C2
Tandil, Arg. 226/F3
Tandjilé (pref.), Chad 134/C3
Tandjoaré, Togo 133/F4
Tāndliānwāla, Pak. 110/B4
Tando Ādam, Pak. 113/J3
Tando Allāhyār, Pak. 113/J3
Tando Muhammad Khān, Pak. 113/J3
Tandou (lake), Austl. 145/D4
Tandragee, NI, UK 40/B3
Tandrano, Madg. 143/H8
Taneatua, NZ 159/D2
Tanega (isl.), Japan 91/L5
Tanem (range), Myan.,Thai. 105/G4
Taneytown, Md, US 191/H5
Taneyville, Mo, US 183/H2
Tanezrouft (des.), Alg. 119/B2
Tanezrouft-n-Ahenet (des), Alg. 129/F5
Tang (riv.), China 92/C4
Tanga (prov.), Tanz. 137/B3
Tanga, Tanz. 137/B3
Tangail, Bang. 109/G3
Tangail (pol. reg.), Bang. 109/G3
Tangalī, Iran 115/H2
Tangali, Gui. 132/C4
Tangang, China 99/G2
Tanganyika (lake), D.R. Congo 119/F5
Tangará da Serra, Braz. 221/G4
Tangdan, China 98/D3
Tangent (pt.), Ak, US 201/G1
Tanger, Mor. 130/B2
Tanger (prov.), Mor. 130/A2
Tangerang, Indo. 101/D4
Tangerhütte, Ger. 48/F2
Tangerine, Fl, US 194/M6
Tangermünde, Ger. 48/F2
Tangfang, China 92/J7
Tanggula (pass), China 111/F5
Tanggula (mts.), China 111/E5
Tanghe, China 92/C4
Tangi, Pak. 110/A2
Tangier, Va, US 193/K2
Tangier (sound), Md, US 193/J1
Tangier (Boukhalf) (int'l arpt.), Mor. 130/B2
Tangipahoa (riv.), Ms, US 194/C2
Tangipahoa, La, US 194/C2
Tangjin, SKor. 93/D4
Tangkak, Malay. 101/C2
Tanglewilde-Thompson Place, Wa, US 197/B3
Tangmai, China 98/B2
Tango, Ang. 138/C5
Tangqi, China 92/L9
Tangra (lake), China 111/E5
Tangshan, China 92/J7
Tangtou, China 99/F3
Tangub, Phil. 100/C3
Tanguiéta, Ben. 133/F4
Tangwan, China 99/F3
Tangxi, China 99/H2
Tangyan (riv.), China 99/F2
Tangyin, China 92/C4
Tangyuan, China 91/K2
Tanhaçu, Braz. 223/E2
Taniantaweng (mts.), China 98/C2
Tanigumi, Japan 95/L4
Tanimbar (isl.), Indo. 83/N10
Taninges, Fr. 66/C5
Tanintharyi (div.), Myan. 105/G5
Tanis (ruin), Egypt 131/C3
Taniwel, Indo. 103/G4
Tanjay, Phil. 100/C3
Tanjiachang, China 99/F2
Tanjong Malim, Malay. 101/C2
Tanjung, Indo. 102/E4
Tanjung Sedano (pt.), Indo. 101/F4
Tanjungbalai, Indo. 101/B2
Tanjungbatu, Indo. 101/C2
Tanjungenim, Indo. 101/C3
Tanjungkarang-Telukbetung, Indo. 101/D4
Tanjungpandan, Indo. 102/C4
Tanjungpinang, Indo. 101/D2
Tanjungpura, Indo. 101/B2
Tanjunguban, Indo. 101/D2
Tānk, Pak. 110/A3
Tankersley, Tx, US 180/D2
Tankwa Karoo NP, SAfr. 142/B4
Tann, Ger. 65/F6
Tanna (isl.), Van. 160/F6
Tanna, Ger. 65/E1
Tannan, Japan 95/H5
Tannersville, Pa, US 198/C1
Tannheim, Aus. 67/G3
Tannu-Ola (mts.), Rus. 90/C1
Tano (riv.), Gha. 133/E5
Tânout, Niger 133/H3
Tanqiu, China 99/G3
Tanque Verde, Az, US 179/G4
Tanquián de Escobedo, Mex. 206/B1
Tansen, Nepal 108/D2
Tānsing, Nepal 108/D2
Ţanţā, Egypt 131/B3
Tantabin, Myan. 98/C5
Tantallon, Sk, Can. 186/D2
Tantallon, Md, US 198/A6
Tantangara (dam), Austl. 157/D2
Tantō, Japan 95/G5
Tantou, China 99/H2
Tantoyuca, Mex. 206/B1
Tantu, China 91/J2
Tanuku, India 107/D2
Tanumshede, Swe. 46/D2
Tanunda, Austl. 156/A2
Tanxu, China 106/E1
Tanyang, SKor. 93/E4
Tanza, Phil. 100/E7
Tanzania (ctry.) 119/F5
Tanzawa-yama (peak), Japan 95/C3
Tanzishan, China 99/G3
Tao (riv.), China 90/E5
Tao (isl.), Myan. 106/B4
Taochuan, China 99/F3
Tao'er (riv.), China 91/J2
Taolañaro, Madg. 143/H9
Taole, China 90/F4
Taolin, China 99/G3
Taonan, China 91/J2
Taormina, It. 54/D4
Tāoru, India 110/D5
Taos, NM, US 182/B2
Taos, Mo, US 183/H1
Taoudenni, Mali 128/E5
Taounate, Mor. 130/B2
Taounate (town), Mor. 130/B2
Taourirt, Alg. 129/F4
Taourirt, Mor. 130/C2
Taoxi, China 99/H2
Taoyuan, China 105/K2
T'aoyüan, Tai. 99/J3
Tap Mun Chau (isl.), China 99/M7
Tap O'Noth (hill), Sc, UK 39/D2
Tapa, Est. 47/L2
Tapacarí, Bol. 224/C1
Tapachula, Mex. 206/C3
Tapah, Malay. 101/C1
Tapajós (riv.), Braz. 209/D3
Tapajós (Amazônia), PN de, Braz. 221/G2
Tapaktuan, Indo. 101/B2
Tapan, Indo. 101/C3
Tapanahoni (riv.), Sur. 217/H4
Tapanti Nat'l Wild. Ref., CR 207/F4
Tapanui, NZ 159/B4
Tapará, Serra da (mts.), Braz. 218/C3
Tapauá (riv.), Braz. 221/E2
Tapauá, Braz. 221/E2
Tapaz, Phil. 100/C3
Tapenagá (riv.), Arg. 224/E3
Taperoá, Braz. 219/G4
Tapeta, Libr. 132/C5
Taphan Hin, Thai. 106/C2
Tapi Aike, Arg. 191/C6
Tapia de Casariego, Sp. 52/B1
Tapiche (riv.), Peru 220/C2
Tapili, D.R. Congo 139/F2
Tapilula, Mex. 206/C2
Taping (riv.), Myan. 98/C3
Tapini, PNG 153/G2
Tapis (peak), Malay. 101/C1
Tāplejun, Nepal 109/F2
Tapo, Peru 220/C3
Tapoa (prov.), Burk. 133/F3
Tapolca, Hun. 56/C2
Tappahannock, Va, US 193/J2
Tappan (lake), Oh, US 190/F4
Tappan, NY, US 199/K7
Tappan Zee (riv.), NY, US 199/K7
Tappan Zee (lake), NY, US 199/E1
Tappanahoni (riv.), Sur. 218/C2
Tappen, ND, US 186/E4
Tappi-zaki (pt.), Japan 94/B3
Tappino (riv.), It. 71/D4
Tapps (lake), Wa, US 197/C3
Tāpti (riv.), India 104/B3
Tapul Group (isls.), Phil. 100/C4
Tapun, India 98/C3
Taqab, Sudan 127/F5
Taqātu' Hayyā, Sudan 112/C5
Taqian, China 99/H2
Taquari, Braz. 225/G4
Taquari (riv.), Braz. 222/A3
Taquari (riv.), Braz. 225/F1
Taquaritinga, Braz. 225/G2
Taquarituba, Braz. 225/G2
Taquaruçu (res.), Braz. 222/B4
Taquil, Ecu. 220/B1
Tar (riv.), Ire. 38/B5
Tar (riv.), Kyr. 111/B3
Tar (riv.), NC, US 193/J3
Tara, Austl. 158/C4
Tara, Rus. 80/H4
Tara (riv.), Bosn.,Mont. 56/D4
Tara, Zam. 141/E3
Taraba (state), Nga. 133/H5
Taraba (riv.), Nga. 133/H4
Tarabuco, Bol. 224/C1
Ţarābulus, Leb. 116/D2
Ţarābulus (Tripoli) (cap.), Libya 126/B1
Taraclia, Mol. 57/J3
Taradale, NZ 159/D2
Tarairí, Bol. 224/D2
Tarakan (int'l arpt.), Indo. 103/E3
Tarakan, Indo. 103/E3
Tarakit (peak), Kenya 137/A1
Taraklı, Turk. 57/K5
Tārākot, Nepal 108/D1
Taraku (isl.), Rus. 94/E2
Taralga, Austl. 157/D2
Taramana, Indo. 152/B2
Taranagar, India 110/C5
Tarancón, Sp. 52/D2
Tarangire NP, Tanz. 137/A2
Taranna, Austl. 156/C4
Taranto, It. 54/E2
Taranto (gulf), It. 73/H2
Tarapacá, Col. 216/D5
Tarapacá (pol. reg.), Chile 224/B1
Tarapoa, Ecu. 216/B5
Tarapoto, Peru 220/B2
Tarare, Fr. 50/F4
Tarariras, Uru. 191/K11
Tararua (range), NZ 159/J9
Tarascon, Fr. 70/A5
Tarascon-sur-Ariège, Fr. 50/D5
Tarashcha, Ukr. 78/F3
Tarata, Bol. 224/C1
Tarata, Peru 224/B1
Tarauacá, Braz. 220/D3
Tarauacá (riv.), Braz. 220/D2
Taravai (isl.), FrPol. 161/M7
Tarawa (isl.), Kiri. 160/G4
Tarawa (cap.), Kiri. 160/G4
Tarawera (vol.), NZ 159/D2
Tarazona, Sp. 52/E2
Tarazona, Sp. 52/E3
Tarbagatay (mts.), Kaz. 111/D2
Tarbaj, Kenya 137/C1
Tarbat Ness (pt.), Sc, UK 39/C1
Tarbela (res.), Pak. 110/B2
Tarbela (dam), Pak. 110/B2
Tarbela (res.), India 111/B5
Tarbert, Sc, UK 37/Q8
Tarbert, Ire. 38/A4
Tarbes, Fr. 50/D5
Tarbolton, Sc, UK 39/B5
Tarboro, Ga, US 195/H2
Tarboro, NC, US 193/J3
Tarbûl Abu Khashîrât (peak), Egypt 131/C6
Tarcento, It. 51/K3
Tarcoola, Austl. 155/G4
Tarcutta, Austl. 157/C2
Tardes (riv.), Fr. 50/E3
Tardienta, Sp. 53/E2
Tardoire (riv.), Fr. 50/D4
Tardoki-Jani (peak), Rus. 91/M2
Taree, Austl. 156/E1
Tarf Water (riv.), Sc, UK 40/D2
Ţarfā' (wadi), Egypt 127/F2
Tarfaya, Mor. 128/B4
Target Rock Nat'l Wild. Ref., NY, US 199/M8
Targuist, Mor. 130/B2
Tarhūnah, Libya 126/B1
Tari, PNG 153/F1
Tariana, Col. 216/D4
Tarīf, UAE 112/F4
Tarifa, Sp. 52/C4
Tarifa, Ecu. 220/B1
Tarija (dept.), Bol. 224/C2
Tarija (int'l arpt.), Bol. 224/C2
Tarija, Bol. 224/C2
Tariku (riv.), Indo. 103/J4
Tariku-Taritatu (plain), Indo. 103/J4
Tarim (riv.), China 80/J5
Tarim (basin), China 80/J6
Tarīm, Yem. 136/D1
Tarim Liuchang, China 111/E3
Tarime, Tanz. 137/A2
Tarin (riv.), Afg. 113/J2
Tarin (Torino), It. 51/G4
Taring, Indo. 101/B2
Taritatu (riv.), Indo. 103/J4
Tarkastad, SAfr. 142/D4
Tarkhankut (cape), Ukr. 79/G5

Thiou – Tor
337

Thiou, Burk. 133/E3
Thíra, Gre. 55/J4
Thíra (isl.), Gre. 73/K3
Third Cataract (falls), Sudan 127/F5
Third Lake, Il, US 197/Q15
Thirlmere (lake), Eng, UK 41/E2
Thirlmere, Austl. 157/E2
Thiron Gardais, Fr. 63/G4
Thironne (riv.), Fr. 63/G4
Thirsk, Eng, UK 41/G3
Thirsty (mt.), Austl. 154/D5
Thirtymile (pt.), NY, US 190/W9
Thiruvananthapuram, India 107/C4
Thise, Fr. 66/C3
Thisted, Den. 46/C3
Thistilfjördhur (estu.), Ice. 44/P6
Thistle (isl.), Austl. 155/H5
Thistle (mt.), Yk, Can. 201/L3
Thithia (isl.), Fiji 161/Y18
Thívai, Gre. 55/H3
Thiverval-Grignon, Fr. 36/H5
Thjósa (riv.), Ice. 44/N7
Thlanship, India 98/B3
Thlewiaza (riv.), Nun, Can. 170/G2
Thoen, Thai. 106/B2
Thoeng, Thai. 106/C2
Thohoyandou, SAfr. 141/F4
Thoi Binh, Viet. 106/D4
Thoiry, Fr. 36/H5
Tholen (isl.), Neth. 58/B5
Tholen, Neth. 58/B5
Tholey, Ger. 61/G5
Thomas, Ok, US 183/E3
Thomas, WV, US 193/H1
Thomasboro, Il, US 190/B4
Thomaston, Al, US 192/D4
Thomaston, Ga, US 192/E4
Thomastown, Ire. 38/C4
Thomastown, Ms, US 192/C4
Thomasville, Al, US 194/E2
Thomasville, Ga, US 195/G2
Thomasville, Mo, US 183/J2
Thomasville, NC, US 193/G3
Thomasville, Pa, US 198/B4
Thomes (cr.), Ca, US 176/B4
Thompson (peak), NM, US 182/B3
Thompson, ND, US 186/F4
Thompson, Mi, US 190/C2
Thompson, Ct, US 191/L4
Thompson, Ut, US 179/H1
Thompson, Mb, Can. 170/G3
Thompson (peak), Ca, US 176/B3
Thompson (riv.), Ia,Mo, US 185/G3
Thompson (lake), Austl. 154/K7
Thompson (riv.), BC, Can. 174/D2
Thompson Falls, Mt, US 174/G4
Thompsonville, Mi, US 190/D2
Thompsonville, Il, US 192/C2
Thomsen (riv.), NW, Can. 170/E1
Thomson, Ga, US 193/F4
Thomson, Il, US 185/J3
Thomson (riv.), Austl. 145/D3
Thon Lac Nghiep, Viet. 106/E4
Thon Song Pha, Viet. 106/E4
Thongwa, Myan. 106/B2
Thonnance-lès-Joinville, Fr. 66/B1
Thonon-les-Bains, Fr. 66/C5
Thonotosassa, Fl, US 194/L7
Thonotosassa (lake), Fl, US 194/L7
Thoreau, NM, US 179/H3
Thorens-Glières, Fr. 66/C6
Thorigny-sur-Marne, Fr. 36/L5
Thorlákshöfn, Ice. 44/N7
Thorn (cr.), Il, US 197/Q16
Thornaby-on-Tees, Eng, UK 41/G2
Thornbury, On, Can. 190/F2
Thornbury, Eng, UK 42/D3
Thorndale, Tx, US 181/F2
Thorndale, Pa, US 198/C4
Thorne, Eng, UK 41/H4
Thorne, On, Can. 191/G1
Thorne Bay, Ak, US 201/M4
Thornfield, Mo, US 183/H2
Thornhill, Sc, UK 40/E1
Thornhill, Sc, UK 39/B4
Thornhurst, Pa, US 198/C1
Thornley, Eng, UK 41/G2
Thornthwaite, Eng, UK 41/G3
Thornton, Ar, US 183/H4
Thornton, Ca, US 197/M10
Thornton, Co, US 184/B4
Thornton, Tx, US 181/F2
Thornton Cleveleys, Eng, UK 41/E4
Thornton Dale, Eng, UK 41/H3
Thorntonville, Tx, US 180/C2
Thorntown, In, US 190/C4
Thornwood Common, Eng, UK 36/D1
Thorold, On, Can. 190/U9
Thorold South, On, Can. 190/U9
Thorp, Wi, US 185/J1
Thorp, Wa, US 174/D4
Thorpe, Eng, UK 36/B2
Thorpe Thewles, Eng, UK 41/G2
Thorpe-le-Soken, Eng, UK 43/H3
Thorsby, Al, US 192/D4
Thorsby, Ab, Can. 175/G1
Thórshöfn, Ice. 44/P6
Thouarcé, Fr. 63/E6
Thouaré-sur-Loire, Fr. 62/D6
Thoubāl, India 98/B3
Thouet (riv.), Fr. 50/C3
Thourotte, Fr. 60/B5
Thousand (isl.), On, Can. 191/H2
Thousand Oaks, Ca, US 196/B2
Thousand Springs (cr.), Nv, US 177/F3
Thowa (riv.), Kenya 137/B2
Thrace (reg.), Bul.,Gre. 73/K2
Thracian (sea), Gre. 76/C4
Thread (cr.), Mi, US 197/E6
Thredbo Village, Austl. 157/D3
Three Bridges, NJ, US 198/D2
Three Creek, Id, US 177/F2
Three Forks, Mt, US 175/J5
Three Guardsmen (mt.), Yk, Can. 201/L3
Three Hills, Ab, Can. 175/H2
Three Kings (isls.), NZ 159/B1
Three Lakes, Wi, US 187/K5
Three Mile (isl.), Pa, US 198/B3
Three Mile Plains, NS, Can. 188/E3
Three Notch, Al, US 195/F1
Three Oaks, Mi, US 190/C4
Three Pagodas (pass), Myan. 106/B3
Three Points (cape), Gha. 133/E5
Three Rivers, Austl. 154/C3
Three Rivers, Mi, US 190/D4
Three Rivers, NM, US 179/J4
Three Springs, Austl. 154/B4
Three Valley, BC, Can. 174/E2
Threehills (cr.), Ab, Can. 175/H2
Thrifty, Tx, US 180/E2
Throckmorton, Tx, US 182/E4
Throssel (lake), Austl. 145/B3
Thrums, BC, Can. 174/F3
Thrumster, Sc, UK 37/S7
Thrushel (riv.), Eng, UK 42/B5
Thu Dau Mot, Viet. 106/D4
Thu Duc, Viet. 106/D4
Thud (pt.), Austl. 153/F3
Thuin, Belg. 61/D3
Thuir, Fr. 50/E5
Thulba (riv.), Ger. 64/C2
Thule Air Base, Den. 171/T7
Thun, Swi. 66/D4
Thunder (bay), On, Can. 187/K3
Thunder (mtn.), Wi, US 187/K5
Thunder Bay, On, Can. 187/K3
Thunder Butte (cr.), SD, US 184/C1
Thundersley, Eng, UK 36/E2
Thuner (lake), Swi. 51/G3
Thung Chang, Thai. 106/C2
Thung Salaeng Luang NP, Thai. 106/C2
Thung Song, Thai. 106/B4
Thüngersheim, Ger. 64/C3
Thunkar, Bhu. 109/H2
Thur (riv.), Swi. 51/H3
Thurgau (canton), Swi. 67/E2
Thüringen, Aus. 67/F3
Thüringen (state), Ger. 51/J1
Thüringer Schiefergebirge (mts.), Ger. 64/E2
Thüringer Wald (for.), Ger. 48/F3
Thurlaston, Eng, UK 43/E2
Thurles, Ire. 38/C4
Thurloo Downs, Austl. 156/B1
Thurlow, Mt, US 175/L4
Thurmont, Md, US 191/H5
Thurnau, Ger. 65/E2
Thurø By, Den. 46/D4
Thurrock (co.), Eng, UK 43/G3
Thursday Island, Austl. 153/F2
Thursley, Eng, UK 36/A3
Thurso, Qu, Can. 191/J2
Thurso, Sc, UK 37/V14
Thurston (co.), Wa, US 197/A3
Thurston (isl.), Ant. 228/T
Thury-en-Valois, Fr. 36/M4
Thury-Harcourt, Fr. 63/E3
Thusis, Swi. 67/F4
Thyez, Fr. 66/C5
Thyolo, Malw. 141/G3
Ti-m-Merhsoï (riv.), Niger 133/G2
Ti-n-Essako, Mali 133/F2
Ti-n-Jedane, Oued (riv.), Alg. 129/G4
Ti-n-Toumma (reg.), Niger 134/A1
Ti-n-Zaouâtene, Mali 133/F2
Ti-Tree Abor. Land, Austl. 155/G2
Tia, Austl. 156/D1
Tiahuanco (ruin), Bol. 224/B1
Tian Shan (mts.), China 83/H5
Tianbao, China 99/H3
Tiancang, China 90/D3
Tianchang, China 92/D4
Tiandeng, China 99/E4
Tian'e, China 105/J2
Tianguá, Braz. 219/F3
Tianguistenco, Mex. 205/Q10
Tianhua, China 99/G3
Tianjin (prov.), China 91/H4
Tianjin, China 92/H7
Tianlin, China 105/J3
Tianmen, China 99/G2
Tianmu (mts.), China 92/K9
Tianping, China 99/F3
Tianqiao, China 99/F2
Tianshifu, China 93/C2
Tianshui, China 90/F5
Tianshuihai, China 111/C4
Tianzhen, China 92/C2
Tianzhu, China 99/F3
Tianzhuangtai, China 93/B2
Tiaret, Alg. 130/F5
Tiassalé, C.d'Iv. 132/D5
Tiatucurá, Uru. 191/K10
Tiavea, Sam. 161/S9
Tibagi (riv.), Braz. 222/C4
Tibagi, Braz. 225/G3
Tibaná, Col. 216/C3
Tibati, Camr. 134/B4
Tibba, Pak. 110/A5
Tibbee (cr.), Ms, US 192/C4
Tibberton, Eng, UK 42/D1
Tibbie, Al, US 194/D2
Tibble, Swe. 45/A1
Tibé, Pic de (peak), Gui. 132/C4
Tiber (riv.), It. 73/G2
Tiber (dam), Mt, US 175/J3
Tiber (Tevere) (riv.), It. 51/K5
Tiberias (lake), Isr. 116/D3
Tiberias, Isr. 117/D3
Tibert (peak), It. 70/D4
Tibesti (mts.), Chad 119/D3
Tibet (reg.), China 83/H6
Tibet (Xizang) (aut. reg.), China 90/C5
Tibiri, Niger 133/G3
Tibnīn, Leb. 117/C2
Tibooburra, Austl. 155/J4
Tibro, Swe. 46/F2
Tibshelf, Eng, UK 41/G5
Tiburon (cape), Haiti 203/G4
Tiburon, Ca, US 197/K11
Tiburón, Isla (isl.), Mex. 204/B2
Ticaco, Peru 220/D5
Ticehurst, Eng, UK 43/G4
Tichigan (lake), Wi, US 197/P14
Tîchît, Mrta. 132/C2
Tichla, Mor. 128/B5
Tichnor, Ar, US 183/J3
T'īcho, Eth. 136/A4
Ticino (canton), Swi. 67/E5
Ticino (riv.), Swi. 67/E6
Tickfaw, La, US 194/C2
Ţicleni, Rom. 57/F3
Ticllos, Peru 220/B3
Ticonderoga, NY, US 191/K3
Ticul, Mex. 206/D1
Tīdah, Egypt 131/B2
Tidaholm, Swe. 46/E2
Tiddim, Myan. 98/B4
Tideswell, Eng, UK 41/G5
Tidikelt (plain), Alg. 129/F4
Tidioute, Pa, US 191/G4
Tidjikdja, Mrta. 132/C2
Tidone (riv.), It. 68/C3
Tidore (isl.), Indo. 103/G3
Tidsit (lake), WSah. 128/B5
Tie Plant, Ms, US 192/C4
Tiébélé Corabie, Burk. 133/E4
Tiébissou, C.d'Iv. 132/D5
Tiéboro, Chad 126/C4
Tiechang, China 93/D2
Tiede, PN del, Sp. 128/A3
Tiefencastel, Swi. 67/F4
Tiefensee, Ger. 48/Q6
Tiéfinzo, C.d'Iv. 132/D4
Tiège, Belg. 61/E2
Tiel, Neth. 58/C5
Tieli, China 91/K2
Tieling, China 92/E2
Tielt, Belg. 60/C2
Tielt-Winge, Belg. 61/D2
Tiemba (riv.), C.d'Iv. 132/D4
Tiemen (pass), China 111/E3
Tien Yen, Viet. 106/D1
Tien Yen, Viet. 106/D2
Tienen, Belg. 61/D2
Tiénigbe, C.d'Iv. 132/D4
Tieniu (pass), China 99/H3
Tiercé, Fr. 63/E5
Tieri, Austl. 158/C3
Tieroko (peak), Chad 126/C4
Tierp, Swe. 46/G1
Tierra Amarilla, NM, US 179/J2
Tierra Amarilla, Chile 224/B3
Tierra Blanca (cr.), Tx,NM, US 182/C3
Tierra Blanca, Mex. 205/N8
Tierra Colorada, Mex. 205/F5
Tierra del Fuego (isl.), Arg. 209/C8
Tierra del Fuego, Antártida e Islas del Atlántico Sur, Arg. 191/C7
Tierra del Fuego, PN, Chile 191/C7
Tierradentro, Col. 216/B4
Tierranueva, Mex. 205/E4
Tiétar (riv.), Sp. 52/C2
Tietê (riv.), Braz. 209/D5
Tieton, Wa, US 174/D4
Tieton (peak), Wa, US 174/D4
Tieyon, Austl. 155/G3
Tifariti, WSah. 128/C4
Tiffany, Co, US 179/J2
Tiffany (mtn.), Wa, US 174/E3
Tiffin (riv.), Oh, US 190/D4
Tiffin, Oh, US 190/E4
Tiflet, Mor. 130/A3
Tifton, Ga, US 195/G2
Tigapuluh (mts.), Indo. 101/C3
Tigeaux, Fr. 36/L5
Tiger (hills), Mb, Can. 186/D3
Tiger (lake), Fl, US 194/N8
Tigerton, Wi, US 185/K1
Tighina (Bendery), Mol. 78/E4
Tighvein (hill), Sc, UK 39/A6
Tigil', Rus. 81/R4
Tignall, Ga, US 193/F4
Tignère, Camr. 134/B4
Tignieu-Jameyzieu, Fr. 66/B6
Tignish, PE, Can. 188/E2
Tigray (prov.), Eth. 134/H2
Tigre (riv.), Ven. 203/J6
Tigre (riv.), Ven. 217/F2
Tigre, Arg. 191/J11
Tigres (bay), Ang. 140/A3
Tigris (riv.), Iraq 83/C6
Tiguent, Mrta. 132/A2
Tigui (well), Chad 126/C5
Tiguidit, Falaise de (cliff), Niger 133/G2
Tigy, Fr. 63/H5
Tigzirt, Alg. 130/H4
Tihamat al Yaman (valley), Yem. 136/B1
Tihosuco, Mex. 206/D1
Tihuatlán, Mex. 206/B1
Tiilikkajärven NP, Fin. 74/F3
Tijāra, India 108/A2
Tijger (falls), Sur. 218/B2
Tījī, Libya 126/A1
Tijuana, Mex. 196/C5
Tijuca, PN da, Braz. 223/N7
Tijucas, Braz. 225/G3
Tijuco (riv.), Braz. 222/C3
Tikal (ruin), Guat. 206/D2
Tikal, Guat. 205/H5
Tīkamgarh, India 108/B3
Tikanlik, China 111/E3
Tikarapāra, India 107/D1
Tikaré, Burk. 133/E3
Tikchik Lakes, Ak, US 201/G3
Tikehau (isl.), FrPol. 161/L6
Tikhoretsk, Rus. 79/L5
Tikhvin, Rus. 74/G4
Tiko, Camr. 138/B1
Tikrīt, Iraq 115/E3
Tiksi, Rus. 81/N2
Tikveš (lake), FYROM 55/H2
Tila, Mex. 206/C2
Tiläänjärvi (lake), Fin. 45/F4
Tilburg, Neth. 58/C5
Tilbury, On, Can. 190/E3
Tilbury, Eng, UK 36/E2
Tilcha, Austl. 155/J4
Tilden, Il, US 192/C1
Tilden, Tx, US 181/E3
Tilford, Eng, UK 36/A3
Tilford, SD, US 184/C1
Tilghman, Md, US 198/B6
Tilghman (isl.), Md, US 198/B6
Tilhar, India 108/B2
Tilin, Myan. 98/B4
Tilisarao, Arg. 226/D2
Till (riv.), Eng, UK 39/D5
Tillabéry, Niger 133/F3
Tillamook (bay), Or, US 176/A1
Tillamook, Or, US 174/C5
Tillar, Ar, US 183/J4
Tille (riv.), Fr. 48/C5
Tillery (lake), NC, US 193/G3
Tilley, Sk, Can. 175/J2
Tillicoultry, Sc, UK 39/C4
Tillières-sur-Avre, Fr. 63/G3
Tillmans Corner, Al, US 194/D2
Tillsonburg, On, Can. 190/F3
Tilly-sur-Seulles, Fr. 63/E2
Tilomar, ETim. 152/B2
Tilomonte, Chile 224/B2
Tilopozo, Chile 224/B2
Tilpa, Austl. 156/C1
Tilst, Den. 46/D3
Tilston, Mb, Can. 186/D3
Tilt (riv.), Sc, UK 39/C3
Tiltagara, Austl. 156/C1
Tiltil, Chile 226/N8
Tilton, Il, US 190/C4
Tim, Den. 46/C3
Tim, Rus. 79/J2
Ţimā, Egypt 114/B5
Timan (ridge), Rus. 80/F3
Timaná, Col. 216/C4
Timane (riv.), Par. 224/D2
Timanfaya, PN de, Sp. 128/B3
Timaru, NZ 159/B4
Timashevo, Rus. 77/J1
Timashevsk, Rus. 79/K5
Timbákion, Gre. 55/J5
Timbalier (bay), La, US 194/C3
Timbaúba, Braz. 219/H4
Timbédra, Mrta. 132/C2
Timber (mtn.), Tx, US 180/C2
Timber Lake, SD, US 186/D5
Timberlake, Va, US 193/H2
Timberville, Va, US 193/H1
Timbiquí, Col. 216/B4
Timbiras, Braz. 219/F4
Timbo, Gui. 132/C4
Timbó, Braz. 225/G3
Timboon, Austl. 156/B3
Timbué (pt.), Moz. 141/H3
Timbuni (riv.), Indo. 103/H4
Timehri (int'l arpt.), Guy. 217/G3
Timelkam, Aus. 65/G6
Timenocalin (well), Libya 126/A3
Timetrine, Mali 133/E2
Timetrout (peak), Mor. 72/B4
Timfristós (peak), Gre. 55/G3
Timgad (ruin), Alg. 72/E4
Tîmia, Niger 133/H2
Timimoun, Alg. 129/F3
Timiris (cape), Mrta. 132/A2
Timiş (riv.), Rom. 76/B3
Timiş (prov.), Rom. 56/E3
Timişoara (int'l arpt.), Rom. 56/E3
Timişoara, Rom. 56/E3
Timmins, On, Can. 197/H4
Timmonsville, SC, US 193/H3
Timms (hill), Wi, US 187/J5
Timoleague, Ire. 38/B6
Timon, Braz. 219/F4
Timonium, Md, US 198/B5
Timor (isl.), Indo. 83/M10
Timor (sea), Asia,Austl. 83/M11
Timor Timur (prov.), Indo. 152/A2
Timóteo, Braz. 223/E3
Timpas, Co, US 182/C2
Timpson, Tx, US 181/G2
Timpton (riv.), Rus. 81/N4
Tims Ford (dam), Tn, US 192/D3
Tims Ford (lake), Tn, US 192/D3
Timsāḩ (lake), Egypt 131/D3
Timsher, Rus. 75/M3
Timucuan Nat'l Prsv., Fl, US 195/H2
Timurnī, India 108/A4
Tin Can Bay, Austl. 158/D4
Tin Shui Wai, China 99/K7
Tina (riv.), SAfr. 142/B1
Tinaca (pt.), Phil. 100/D4
Tinaco, Ven. 216/D2
Tinahely, Ire. 38/D4
Tinca, Rom. 56/E2
Tinchebray, Fr. 63/E3
Tincup, Co, US 179/J1
Tinderry (mtn.), Austl. 157/D2
Tindivanam, India 107/C3
Tindouf (wilaya), Alg. 128/D3
Tindouf, Alg. 128/C4
Tiné, Oued (riv.), Chad 134/D2
Tinée (riv.), Fr. 70/C4
Tineo, Sp. 52/B1
Ting (riv.), China 99/H3
Tinga (peak), CAfr. 134/D3
Tingalpa (res.), Austl. 158/F7
Tingaringy NP, Austl. 156/D3
Tingha, Austl. 156/D1
Tingi (mts.), SLeo. 132/C4
Tingjegaon, Nepal 108/D1
Tinglin, China 92/L9
Tingmerkpuk (mt.), Ak, US 201/F2
Tingo María, Peru 220/C3
Tingping, China 99/F3
Tingréla, C.d'Iv. 132/D4
Tingri, China 109/F1
Tingsryd, Swe. 46/F3
Tinguiririca (vol.), Chile 226/C2
Tinh Gia, Viet. 106/D2
Tinharé (isl.), Braz. 223/F2
Tinian (isl.), NMar. 160/D3
Tinicum Nat'l Consv. Area, Pa, US 198/C4
Tinker (A.F.B.), Ok, US 183/F3
Tinkisso (riv.), Gui. 132/C4
Tinley Park, Il, US 197/Q16
Tinogasta, Arg. 224/C4
Tínos, Gre. 55/J4
Tínos (isl.), Gre. 73/K3
Tinqueux, Fr. 60/C5
Tinrhir, Mor. 128/D3
Tinsman, Ar, US 183/H4
Tinsukia, India 98/B3
Tinta, Peru 220/D4
Tintagel, Eng, UK 42/B5
Tintagel (pt.), Eng, UK 42/B5
Tîntâne, Mrta. 132/C2
Tinténiac, Fr. 62/D4
Tintern Abbey (ruin), Eng, UK 42/D3
Tintigny, Belg. 61/E4
Tintina, Arg. 224/D3
Tintinara, Austl. 156/B2
Tinto (peak), Sc, UK 39/C5
Tinto (riv.), Sp. 52/B4
Tinton Falls (New Shrewsbury), NJ, US 199/D3
Tintwistle, Eng, UK 41/G5
Tinui, NZ 159/D3
Tinyahuarco, Peru 220/B3
T'i'o, Erit. 136/B2
Tioga (peak), Ca, US 178/C2
Tioga, ND, US 186/C3
Tioga, Tx, US 183/F4
Tioga, WV, US 193/G1
Tiom, Indo. 103/J4
Tioman (isl.), Malay. 102/B3
Tione di Trento, It. 67/G5
Tionesta, Pa, US 191/G4
Tip Top (mt.), On, Can. 187/L3
Tipac (hill), Braz. 218/D2
Tipasa, Alg. 130/G4
Tipasa (wilaya), Alg. 130/F4
Tipp City, Oh, US 190/D5
Tipperary, Ire. 38/B5
Tipperary (co.), Ire. 38/C4
Tippettville, Ga, US 195/G1
Tipton, Ok, US 182/E3
Tipton, Mo, US 183/H1
Tipton, Pa, US 191/G4
Tipton, In, US 190/C4
Tipton, Ks, US 184/E4
Tipton, Ia, US 185/J3
Tiptonville, Tn, US 192/C2
Tiptree, Eng, UK 43/G3
Tiptūr, India 107/C3
Tiputa, FrPol. 161/L6
Tir Rhiwiog (peak), Wal, UK 42/C1
Tira, Tx, US 183/G4
Tīra Sujānpur, India 110/D4
Tiracambu, Serra do (mts.), Braz. 219/E4
Tiran (isl.), SAr. 127/G3
Tiran (str.), Egypt, SAr. 127/G3
Tiran Sinafir (isl.), SAr. 114/C5
Tiranë (cap.), Alb. 55/F2
Tirano, It. 67/G5
Tiraque, Bol. 224/C1
T'irarē Shet' (riv.), Eth. 136/A2
Tirari (des.), Austl. 155/H4
Tiraspol, Mol. 78/E4
Tirat Karmel, Isr. 117/B3
Tirat Ẕevi, Isr. 117/D4
Tire, Turk. 114/A2
Tirebolu, Turk. 76/F4
Tiree (isl.), Sc, UK 37/Q8
Tirest (well), Mali 133/F1
Tirgol, Eth. 134/G4
Tîrgovişte, Rom. 57/G3
Tîrgu Bujor, Rom. 57/H3
Tîrgu Cărbuneşti, Rom. 57/F3
Tîrgu Frumos, Rom. 78/D4
Tîrgu Jiu, Rom. 57/F3
Tîrgu Lăpuş, Rom. 57/F2
Tîrgu Mureş, Rom. 57/G2
Tîrgu Neamţ, Rom. 78/D4
Tîrgu Ocna, Rom. 57/H2
Tîrgu Secuiesc, Rom. 57/H2
Tiris (reg.), WSah. 128/B5
Tiris Zemmour (pol. reg.), Mrta. 128/C4
Tiritiri Matangi (isl.), NZ 159/F6
Tirlyanskiy, Rus. 75/N5
Tîrnava Mare (riv.), Rom. 57/G2
Tîrnava Mică (riv.), Rom. 57/F2
Tîrnăveni, Rom. 57/G2
Tírnavos, Gre. 55/H3
Tiro, Gui. 132/C4
Tirol (prov.), Aus. 48/F5
Tirrenia, It. 68/D6
Tirschenreuth, Ger. 65/F3
Tirso (riv.), It. 72/F2
Tirstup (int'l arpt.), Den. 46/D3
Tirúa, Chile 226/B3
Tiruchendūr, India 107/C4
Tiruntán, Peru 220/C2
Tirupati (int'l arpt.), India 107/C3
Tirūr, India 107/B4
Tiruttani, India 104/C3
Tiruvalla, India 107/C4
Tiruvannāmalai, India 107/C3
Tisa (riv.), Serb. 56/E3
Tisbury, Eng, UK 42/D4
Tisdale, Sk, Can. 175/M1
Tishkovo, Rus. 77/J3
Tishomingo, Ok, US 183/F3
Tishomingo, Ms, US 192/C3
Tishomingo Nat'l Wildlife Res., Ok, US 183/F3
Ţīsīyah, Syria 117/E4
Tissa, Mor. 130/B2
Tissemsilt, Alg. 130/F5
Tissemsilt (wilaya), Alg. 130/F5
Tissø (lake), Den. 45/H7
Tista (riv.), Bang. 109/G2
Tisvilde, Den. 45/J6
Tisza (riv.), Hun. 76/B3
Tiszaföldvár, Hun. 56/E2
Tiszafüred, Hun. 56/E2
Tiszakécske, Hun. 56/E2
Tiszalök, Hun. 56/E1
Tiszavasvári, Hun. 49/L5
Tit, Alg. 129/F4
Titano (peak), SMar. 69/F6
Titao, Burk. 133/E3
Titay, Phil. 100/C4
Titel, Serb. 56/E3
Titerno (riv.), It. 71/D5
Titi, Congo 138/C3
Titicaca (lake), Bol.,Peru 209/B4
Titistee-Neustadt, Ger. 66/E2
Titlagarh, India 107/D1
Titlis (peak), Swi. 67/E4
Tito, It. 54/D2
Titov vrh (peak), FYROM 55/G2
Titsey, Eng, UK 36/D3
Titting, Ger. 64/E5
Tittmoning, Ger. 65/F6
Titu, Rom. 57/G3
Titule, D.R. Congo 139/F2
Titusville, Fl, US 195/H3
Titusville, NJ, US 198/D3
Titusville, Pa, US 191/G4
Tiuni, India 110/D4
Tiva (riv.), Kenya 137/B2
Tivaouane, Sen. 132/A3
Tivat, Mont. 56/D4
Tiverton, On, Can. 190/F2
Tiverton, Eng, UK 42/C5
Tivoli, It. 71/B4
Tivoli, Tx, US 181/F3
Tiwanacu, Bol. 224/B1
Ţīwī, Oman 113/G4
Tixán, Ecu. 220/B1
Tixtla de Guerrero, Mex. 205/F5
Tizayuca, Mex. 205/L7
Tizi Ouzou (wilaya), Alg. 130/H4
Tizi Ouzou, Alg. 130/H4
Tizimín, Mex. 206/D1
Tizmant ash Sharqīyah, Egypt 131/C6
Tiznados (riv.), Ven. 219/N8
Tiznap (riv.), China 113/L1
Tiznit, Mor. 128/C3
Tjæreborg, Den. 46/C4
Tjeldstø, Nor. 46/A1
Tjeukemeer (lake), Neth. 58/C3
Tjøme, Nor. 46/D2
Tjorn (isl.), Den. 46/D3
Tkhab (peak), Rus. 79/K5
Tkibuli, Geo. 77/G4
Tlachichuca, Mex. 205/M7
Tlacolula de Matamoros, Mex. 206/B2
Tlacotalpan, Mex. 205/P8
Tlacotepec, Mex. 205/F5
Tlalixcoyan, Mex. 205/N8
Tlalmanalco, Mex. 205/Q10
Tlalnepantla, Mex. 205/Q9
Tláloc (vol.), Mex. 205/Q10
Tlalpan (nbrhd.), Mex. 205/Q10
Tlaltenango de Sánchez Román, Mex. 204/E4
Tlaltizapan, Mex. 205/K8
Tlapa de Comonfort, Mex. 206/B2
Tlapacoya (ruin), Mex. 205/Q10
Tlapacoyan, Mex. 205/M7
Tlapehuala, Mex. 205/E5
Tlaquepaque, Mex. 204/E4
Tlaquiltenango, Mex. 205/K8
Tlatlauquitepec, Mex. 205/M7
Tlaxcala (state), Mex. 202/A5
Tlaxcala, Mex. 205/L7
Tlaxco, Mex. 205/L7
Tlaxcoapan, Mex. 205/K6
Tlell, BC, Can. 201/M5
Tlemcen, Alg. 130/D2
Tlokweng, Bots. 140/E5
Tmassah, Libya 126/B3
To-grenda, Nor. 44/S8
Toa Payoh (nbrhd.), Sing. 101/J6
Toabré, Pan. 216/A2
Toaca (peak), Rom. 57/G2
Toachi (riv.), Ecu. 216/B4
Toadlena, NM, US 179/H2
Toamasina, Madg. 143/J7
Toamasina (prov.), Madg. 143/J7
Toandos (pen.), Wa, US 197/B2
Toasi, Gha. 133/E5
Toast, NC, US 193/G2
Toau (isl.), FrPol. 161/L6
Toay, Arg. 226/D3
Toba (lake), Indo. 102/A3
Toba, China 90/D5
Toba, Japan 95/L7
Toba (inlet), BC, Can. 174/B2
Toba (riv.), BC, Can. 174/B2
Toba Kākar (range), Pak. 113/J2
Toba Tek Singh, Pak. 110/B4
Tobago (isl.), Trin. 203/J5
Tobarra, Sp. 52/E3
Tobbio (peak), It. 68/B4
Tobeatic Game Sanct., NS, Can. 188/E3
Tobercurry, Ire. 38/B1
Tobermore, NI, UK 40/B2
Tobermorey, Austl. 155/H2
Tobermory, On, Can. 190/F2
Tōbetsu, Japan 94/B2
Tobias, Ang. 138/C5
Tobias Barreto, Braz. 223/F1
Tobin (lake), Austl. 145/B3
Tobique (riv.), NB, Can. 188/D2
Tobishima, Japan 95/L5
Toblol (riv.), Kaz.,Rus. 83/F4
Toboali, Indo. 101/D3
Toboł (riv.), Rus. 75/Q5
Tobol, Kaz. 77/M1
Tobruk (Ţubruq), Libya 126/D1
Tobseda, Rus. 75/M1
Tobu, Japan 95/A1
Toburdanovo, Rus. 75/K5
Tobyhanna (lake), Pa, US 198/C1
Tobyhanna (riv.), Pa, US 198/C1
Tobyhanna, Pa, US 198/C1
Tobyhanna St. Park, Pa, US 198/C1
Tobyl (riv.), Kaz.,Rus. 80/G4
Tobysh (riv.), Rus. 75/L2
Tocache, Peru 220/B3
Tocaima, Col. 219/L8
Tocantínia, Braz. 218/D5
Tocantinópolis, Braz. 219/E4
Tocantins (riv.), Braz. 209/E4
Tocantins (state), Braz. 218/D5
Tocco da Casauria, It. 71/C3
Toccoa, Ga, US 193/F3
Toccoa (riv.), Ga, US 192/E3
Toce (riv.), It. 51/H3
Tochigi (pref.), Japan 97/F2
Tochigi, Japan 97/F2
Tochimilco, Mex. 205/L8
Tochio, Japan 97/F2
Tocina, Sp. 52/C4
Töcksfors, Swe. 46/D2
Toco, Tx, US 183/G4
Toco, Trin. 217/F2
Tocomechi, Bol. 224/D1
Tocopilla, Chile 224/B2
Tocumen, Pan. 216/B2
Tocumwal, Austl. 157/B2
Tocuyito, Ven. 216/D2
Tocuyo (riv.), Ven. 203/H5
Toda, Japan 95/D2
Toda Bhīm, India 104/C2
Toddington, Eng, UK 43/F3
Todenyang, Kenya 134/G4
Tödi (peak), Swi. 67/E4
Todi, It. 71/B2
Todmorden, Eng, UK 41/F4
Todos os Santos (bay), Braz. 223/F2
Todos Santos, Bol. 224/B1
Todos Santos, Bol. 221/E4
Todos Santos, Bol. 224/C1
Todos Santos, Mex. 204/C4
Todt Hill (nbrhd.), NY, US 199/J9
Todtmoos, Ger. 66/E2
Todtnau, Ger. 66/D2
Toe (pt.), Ire. 38/A7
T'oejo, NKor. 93/D3
Toffal (hill), Mrta. 128/C5
Toffo, Ben. 133/F5
Tofield, Ab, Can. 175/H1
Tofte, Nor. 44/S9
Tofua (isl.), Tonga 161/H6
Tōgane, Japan 95/E2
Togatax, China 111/D4
Togba (well), Mrta. 132/C2
Toggenburg (valley), Swi. 67/F3
Togher, Ire. 40/B5
Togiak, Ak, US 201/F4
Töging am Inn, Ger. 65/F6
Togo (ctry.) 133/F4
Togo, Sk, Can. 186/D2
Tōgō, Japan 95/M5
Tögrög, Mong. 90/C2
Togtoh, China 92/B2
Tŏgyu-san NP, SKor. 93/D5
Togyz, Kaz. 77/M3
Tohāna, India 110/C5
Tohatchi, NM, US 179/H3
Tohickon (cr.), Pa, US 198/C3
Tohivea (peak), FrPol. 161/X15
Tōhoku (prov.), Japan 97/F1
Tohom, China 90/F3
Tohopekaliga (lake), Fl, US 195/H3
Tohopekaliga, East (lake), Fl, US 194/N7
Tohor (cape), Malay. 101/C2
Tohoun, Togo 133/F5
Toi, Japan 97/F3
Toibalawe, India 105/F5
Toijala, Fin. 45/D3
Tōin, Japan 95/L5
Toiyabe (range), Nv, US 176/E4
Tojō, Japan 96/C3
Tōjō, Japan 95/H6
Tok, Ak, US 201/K3
Tokachi (riv.), Japan 94/C2
Tōkai, Japan 95/L5
Tokaj, Hun. 49/L4
Tōkamachi, Japan 97/F2
Tokanui, NZ 159/B4
Tokar, Sudan 127/H5
Tokar Game Reserve, Sudan 127/H5
Tokar Nat'l Rsv., Sudan 127/F4
Tokara (isls.), Japan 160/B1
Tokarevka, Rus. 77/G2
Tokat, Turk. 114/D1
Tokat (prov.), Turk. 76/F4
Tŏkchŏk (arch.), NKor. 93/C4
Tŏkchŏk (isl.), NKor. 93/C4
Tŏkch'ŏn, NKor. 93/D3
Tokeen, Ak, US 201/M4
Tokeland, Wa, US 174/C4
Tokelau (terr.), NZ 161/H5
Toki (riv.), Japan 95/M5
Toki, Japan 95/M5
Tokigawa, Japan 95/C2
Tokio, ND, US 186/E4
Tokkya Chaung, Myan. 106/B3
Tokmak, Ukr. 79/H4
Tokmok, Kyr. 80/H5
Tokomaru Bay, NZ 159/D2
Tokoname, Japan 95/L6
Tokonou, Gui. 132/C4
Tokoro, Japan 94/D1
Tokoro (riv.), Japan 94/C2
Tokoroa, NZ 159/C2
Tokorozawa, Japan 97/F3
Tŏksŏng, NKor. 91/K3
Toksook Bay, Ak, US 201/E3
Toksovo, Rus. 75/T6
Toksun, China 111/E3
Toktogul (res.), Kyr. 111/B3
Toktogul, Kyr. 111/B3
Tokuno (isl.), Japan 97/K7
Tokunoshima, Japan 97/K7
Tokur, Rus. 91/L1
Tokushima, Japan 96/D3
Tokushima (pref.), Japan 96/C4
Tokuyama, Japan 96/B3
Tokwe (riv.), Zim. 141/F3
Tōkyō (bay), Japan 95/D2
Tōkyō (cap.), Japan 97/F3
Tōkyō (pref.), Japan 97/F3
Tōkyō Disneyland, Japan 95/D2
Tola, Nic. 206/E4
Tolaga Bay, NZ 159/D2
Tolar, Tx, US 181/F1
Tolar Grande, Arg. 224/C3
Tolbazy, Rus. 75/M5
Tolbo, Mong. 90/C2
Toledo, Bol. 224/C1
Toledo, Braz. 225/F3
Toledo, Col. 216/C3
Toledo, Phil. 100/C3
Toledo, Sp. 52/C3
Toledo, Uru. 191/K11
Toledo, Ia, US 185/H3
Toledo, Il, US 192/C1
Toledo, Oh, US 190/E4
Toledo, Or, US 176/B1
Toledo, Wa, US 174/C4
Toledo Bend (dam), Tx, US 181/H2
Toledo Bend (res.), Tx, US 181/H2
Toledo, Montes de (mts.), Sp. 52/C3
Tolentino, It. 71/C1
Tolfa, It. 71/A3
Tolfaccia (peak), It. 71/A3
Tolhuaca, PN, Chile 226/C3
Toli, China 111/D2
Toliara, Madg. 143/G8
Toliara (prov.), Madg. 143/G8
Tolima, Col. 216/C5
Tolima (dept.), Col. 216/C4
Tolitoli, Indo. 103/F3
Tolka (riv.), Ire. 40/B5
Tolkis (Tolkkinen), Fin. 45/F4
Tolkkinen (Tolkis), Fin. 45/F4
Tolland, Ab, Can. 175/J1
Tollarp, Swe. 45/K7
Tollette, Ar, US 183/H4
Tolley, ND, US 186/D3
Tollo, It. 71/D3
Tølløse, Den. 45/H7
Tolmezzo, It. 51/K3
Tolna, ND, US 186/E4
Tolna (prov.), Hun. 56/D2
Tolna, Hun. 56/D2
Tolo, D.R. Congo 138/D3
Tolo (gulf), Indo. 103/F4
Tolo (chan.), China 99/L7
Tolochin, Bela. 47/N4
Tolokiwa (isl.), PNG 153/G1
Tolongoina, Madg. 143/H8
Tolono, Il, US 190/B5
Tolosa, Sp. 50/B5
Tolsan (isl.), SKor. 93/D5
Tolstoy, SD, US 184/E1
Tolt (riv.), Wa, US 197/D2
Tolt (res.), Wa, US 197/D2
Tolt, North Fork (riv.), Wa, US 197/D2
Tolt, South Fork (riv.), Wa, US 197/D2
Toltén, Chile 226/B3
Toltén (riv.), Chile 226/B3
Tolú, Col. 216/C2
Toluca, Il, US 185/K3
Toluca, Mex. 205/Q10
Tolúviejo, Col. 216/C2
Tol'yatti, Rus. 77/J1
Tolybay, Kaz. 77/M2
Tom' (riv.), Rus. 80/J4
Tom, Ok, US 183/G4
Tom Price, Austl. 154/C2
Tom White (mt.), Ak, US 201/K3
Toma, Burk. 132/E3
Toma, PNG 153/G2
Tomah, Wi, US 185/J2
Tomahawk, Wi, US 187/K5
Tomahawk, Ab, Can. 174/G1
Tomakin, Austl. 157/E2
Tomakivka, Ukr. 79/H4
Tomakomai, Japan 94/B2
Tomamae, Japan 94/B1
Tomanao, Phil. 100/D4
Tomanivi (peak), Fiji 161/Y18
Tomar, Port. 52/A3
Tomari, Rus. 91/N2
Tómaros (peak), Gre. 55/G3
Tomarpaån (riv.), Swe. 45/L7
Tomarza, Turk. 114/C2
Tomás, Peru 220/C4
Tomás Barrón, Bol. 224/C1
Tomás de Berlanga, Ecu. 220/J7
Tomashëvka, Bela. 49/M3
Tomaszów Lubelski, Pol. 49/M3
Tomaszów Mazowiecki, Pol. 49/L3
Tomat, Sudan 135/E3
Tomatin, Sc, UK 39/C2
Tomatlán, Mex. 204/D5
Tomave, Bol. 224/C2
Tomb of Qinshihuang, China 92/B4
Tombador, Serra do (mts.), Braz. 221/G3
Tomball, Tx, US 181/M8
Tombe, Sudan 134/F4
Tombigbee (riv.), Al, Ms, US 173/J5
Tomboco, Ang. 138/C4
Tombolo, It. 69/E2
Tombouctou (pol. reg.), Mali 128/D5
Tombouctou, Mali 132/E2
Tombstone, Az, US 179/G5
Tombua, Ang. 140/A2
Tomé (isl.), Fr. 50/B2
Tomé, Chile 226/B3
Tome, NM, US 179/J3
Tomé-Açu, Braz. 218/D3
Tomea (isl.), Indo. 152/A1
Tomelilla, Swe. 46/E4
Tomelloso, Sp. 52/D3
Tomika, Japan 95/L5
Tomina, Bol. 224/C1
Tomingley, Austl. 157/D1
Tomini (gulf), Indo. 83/M10
Tominian, Mali 132/D3
Tomiño, Sp. 52/A2
Tomintoul, Sc, UK 39/C2
Tomioka, Japan 95/B1
Tomisato, Japan 95/E2
Tomiura, Japan 95/D3
Tomiyama, Japan 97/F3
Tomizawa, Japan 95/A3
Tommot, Rus. 81/N4
Tomo (riv.), Col. 216/D3
Tomorlog, China 111/F4
Tompa, Hun. 56/D2
Tompe, Indo. 103/E4
Tompkins, Sk, Can. 175/K2
Tompkinsville, Ky, US 192/E2
Tompo, Indo. 103/F3
Toms (riv.), NJ, US 199/D3
Toms River, NJ, US 199/D4
Tomsk, Rus. 80/J4
Tomskaya Oblast, Rus. 80/J4
Tömük, Turk. 116/D1
Tonalá, Mex. 206/C2
Tonale, Passo del (pass), It. 67/G5
Tonalea, Az, US 179/G2
Tonasket, Wa, US 174/E3
Tonate, FrG. 218/C1
Tonawanda (cr.), NY, US 190/V9
Tonawanda (res.), NY, US 190/V9
Tonawanda, NY, US 190/V9
Tonbridge, Eng, UK 36/D3
Tonckens (falls), Sur. 218/B1
Toncontín (int'l arpt.), Hon. 206/E3
Tondabayashi, Japan 95/J7
Tondano, Indo. 103/F3
Tondi Kiwindi, Niger 133/F3
Tondo, D.R. Congo 138/D3
Tondon, Gui. 132/B4
Tondoro, Namb. 140/C3
Tondu (peak), Fr. 66/C6
Tone (riv.), Japan 97/G3
Tone, Japan 95/E2
Tone (riv.), Eng, UK 42/C5
Tonekābon, Iran 115/G2
Tonelagee (peak), Ire. 40/B5
Tong (riv.), China 90/F5
Tong Fuk, China 99/K8
Tong Xian, China 92/H7
Tonga, Sudan 134/F3
Tonga (ctry.) 161/H7
Tongaat, SAfr. 143/E3
Tongala, Austl. 157/B3
Tong'an, China 99/H3
Tongareva (Penrhyn) (isl.), Cookls. 161/J5
Tongariro (vol.), NZ 159/C2
Tongariro NP, NZ 159/C2
Tongatapu (isl.), Tonga 161/H7
Tongbai, China 92/C4
Tongbei, China 91/K2
Tongbu, SKor. 93/G6
Tongbu (nbrhd.), SKor. 93/G6
Tongch'ang, NKor. 93/C2
Tongcheng, China 92/D5
Tongcheng, China 99/G2
T'ongch'ŏn, NKor. 93/D3
Tongchuan, China 92/B4
Tongdaemun (nbrhd.), SKor. 93/G6
Tongdao Dongzu Zizhixian, China 99/F3
Tongduch'on, SKor. 93/G6
Tongeren, Belg. 61/E2
Tonggou, China 93/C2
Tonggu, China 105/K2
Tonggu (peak), China 99/H3
Tonghae, SKor. 93/E4
Tongham, Eng, UK 36/A3
Tonghua, China 93/C2
Tonghua, China 93/C2
Tongjiadian, China 91/J3
Tongliao, China 92/E2
Tongling, China 99/H2
Tongmu, China 99/G3
Tongnae, SKor. 93/E5
Tongnan, China 98/E2
Tongnim, NKor. 93/C3
Tongno (riv.), NKor. 93/D2
Tongo, Austl. 156/B1
Tongo (peak), Indo. 103/E5
Tongobory, Madg. 143/H8
Tongren, China 99/F3
Tongsa (riv.), Bhu. 109/H2
Tongsa Dzong, Bhu. 109/H2
Tongshan, China 99/G2
Tongsin, NKor. 93/D2
Tongtian (riv.), China 90/D5
Tongue, Sc, UK 37/R7
Tongue (riv.), Mt, US 172/E2
Tongxu, China 92/C4
Tongyu, China 91/J3
Tongyuan, China 99/H2
Tongyuanpu, China 93/B2
Tonino-Anivskiy (pen.), Rus. 94/C1
Tönisvorst, Ger. 58/D6
Tonj (riv.), Sudan 134/F4
Tonj, Sudan 134/F4
Tonk, India 104/C2
Tonkawa, Ok, US 183/F2
Tonkin (gulf), China,Viet. 83/K7
Tonkoui (peak), C.d'Iv. 132/D5
Tonle Sap (lake), Camb. 105/H5
Tonneins, Fr. 50/D4
Tonnerre, Fr. 50/E3
Tönning, Ger. 46/C4
Tōno, Japan 94/B4
Tonopah, Az, US 179/F4
Tonoshō, Japan 96/D3
Tonosí, Pan. 216/A3
Tonota, Bots. 141/E4
Tons (riv.), India 108/C3
Tønsberg, Nor. 46/D2
Tonstad, Nor. 46/B2
Tonsina, Ak, US 201/J3
Tonto Nat'l Mon., Az, US 179/G4
Tontouta (Noumea) (int'l arpt.), NCal., Fr. 161/V13
Tonya, Turk. 76/F4
Toodyay, Austl. 154/C4
Tooele, Ut, US 177/G3
Tooele Army Dep., Ut, US 177/G3
Tooke (lake), Fl, US 194/K6
Tool, Tx, US 181/F1
Tooleybuc, Austl. 156/B2
Toomsboro, Ga, US 193/F4
Toomuc (cr.), Austl. 156/G6
Toomyvara, Ire. 38/B4
Tooradin, Austl. 156/C3
Tooraweenah, Austl. 156/D1
Tooromt, Mong. 90/C1
Toosey Ind. Res., BC, Can. 174/C2
Toot Hill, Eng, UK 36/D1
Tootsi, Est. 47/L2
Toowoomba, Austl. 158/C4
Top (mt.), Austl. 155/G2
Top of the World (peak), Wy, US 184/B2
Top Springs, Austl. 152/C4
Topaipí, Col. 219/L7
Topanaga State Park, Ca, US 196/B2
Topanga, Ca, US 196/B2
Topanga Beach, Ca, US 196/E7
Topawa, Az, US 179/G5
Tope de Coroa (mtn.), CpV. 119/J10
Topeka, In, US 190/D4
Topeka (cap.), Ks, US 185/G4
Topia, Mex. 204/D3
Topkapi Palace, Turk. 115/M6
Topliţa, Rom. 78/C4
Topock, Az, US 178/E3
Topohoco, Bol. 220/D5
Topol'čany, Slvk. 49/K4
Topol'níky, Slvk. 56/C2
Topolobampo, Mex. 204/C3
Topoloveni, Rom. 57/G3
Topolovgrad, Bul. 57/H4
Topozero (lake), Rus. 44/J2
Toppenish, Wa, US 174/D4
Toppenish (cr.), Wa, US 174/D4
Toprakkale, Turk. 116/E1
Topsham, Eng, UK 42/C5
Topton, Pa, US 198/C3
Toquepala, Peru 220/D5
Toquerville, Ut, US 179/F2
Toquima (range), Nv, US 176/E4
Tor, Eth. 134/G4

Tor – Tumba

Tor (bay), Eng., UK 42/C6
Tor Lupara, It. 71/B4
Tora, D.R. Congo 139/G2
Torahime, Japan 95/K5
Torata, Peru 220/D5
Torawitan (cape), Indo. 103/G3
Torbalı, Turk. 114/A2
Torbat-e Ḩeydarīyeh, Iran 113/G1
Torbay, Nf., Can. 189/L2
Torbay (co.), Eng., UK 42/C6
Torbeck, Haiti 207/H2
Torbert (mt.), Ak., US 190/D2
Torbeyevo, Rus. 77/G1
Torch (lake), Mi., US 190/D2
Torcy, Fr. 36/K5
Tordera (riv.), Sp. 53/L6
Tordesillas, Sp. 52/C2
Tordino, It. 71/C2
Töreboda, Swe. 46/F2
Torekov, Swe. 45/J6
Torelló, Sp. 53/G1
Torez, Ukr. 79/K3
Torfaen (co.), Wal., UK 42/C6
Torgelow, Ger. 46/G4
Torghay, Kaz. 82/E4
Torghay, Kaz. 80/G5
Torhamnsudde (pt.), Swe. 46/F3
Torhout, Belg. 60/C1
Tori, India 109/E4
Tori-shima (isl.), Japan 160/D1
Toride, Japan 95/E2
Torigni-sur-Vire, Fr. 63/E2
Torii-tōge (pass), Japan 97/E3
Toriñana (cape), Sp. 52/A1
Torino (riv.), It. 70/D2
Torino (Tarin), It. 51/G4
Torino (Turin), It. 68/A2
Torino di Sangro, It. 71/D3
Torit, Sudan 139/G2
Torkestān (mts.), Afg. 113/H1
Tormes (riv.), Sp. 52/C2
Torndirrup NP, Austl. 154/C6
Torne (riv.), Eng., UK 41/H4
Torneälven (riv.), Swe. 42/D2
Tornesch, Ger. 59/G1
Tornik (peak), Serb. 106/A3
Tornillo, Tx., US 180/A2
Tornio, Fin. 44/H2
Tornionjoki (riv.), Fin. 44/H2
Toro, Sp. 52/C2
Torö, Swe. 45/A2
Torö (isl.), Swe. 45/A2
Toro (peak), Ca., US 178/D4
Toro Nat'l Rsv., Ugan. 139/G2
Toro, Cerro del (peak), Arg./Chile 224/B4
Toro, PN, Ven. 216/D2
Torodi, Niger 133/F3
Torok, Chad 134/B3
Törökbálint, Hun. 57/Q10
Törökszentmiklós, Hun. 56/E2
Toromélun, Gui. 132/B4
Toronaic (gulf), Gre. 55/H2
Toronao (pt.), Arg. 224/C2
Torondoy, Ven. 216/C2
Toronto (cap.), On., Can. 190/U8
Toronto (city), On., Can. 190/U8
Toronto (isl.), On., Can. 190/U8
Toronto (lake), Ks., US 183/G2
Toropets, Rus. 47/P3
Tororo, Ugan. 137/A1
Toroshino, Rus. 47/N3
Torote (riv.), Sp. 53/N8
Torotoro, Bol. 224/C1
Torp (int'l arpt.), Nor. 46/D2
Torpa, Sc. 46/E3
Torphins, Sc., UK 39/G4
Torpoint, Eng., UK 42/B6
Torqebeh, Iran 113/G1
Torquay, Sk., Can. 186/C3
Torquay, Eng., UK 42/C6
Torquay, Austl. 157/B4
Torquemada, Sp. 52/C1
Torr (pt.), NI, UK 40/B1
Torrance, Ca., US 196/F8
Torrazza Piemonte, It. 68/A2
Torre Annunziata, It. 71/D6
Torre de Moncorvo, Port. 52/B2
Torre de' Passeri, It. 71/C3
Torre del Campo, Sp. 52/D4
Torre del Greco, It. 71/D6
Torre del Lago Puccini, It. 68/D2
Torre Gaia, It. 71/B4
Torre Maggiore (peak), It. 70/D2
Torre Pellice, It. 70/D3
Torre-Pacheco, Sp. 53/E4
Torrebelvicino, It. 69/E2
Torreblanca, Sp. 53/F2
Torredonjimeno, Sp. 52/D4
Torregaveta, It. 71/D6
Torreglia, It. 69/E2
Torrejón de Ardoz, Sp. 53/N9
Torrejoncillo, Sp. 52/B3
Torrelaguna, Sp. 52/D2
Torrelavega, Sp. 52/C1
Torrelodones, Sp. 53/N8
Torremaggiore, It. 54/D2
Torremolinos, Sp. 52/C4
Torrens (cr.), Austl. 153/G5
Torrens (lake), Austl. 145/C4
Torrens (isl.), Austl. 155/M8
Torrens (riv.), Austl. 155/M8
Torrente, Sp. 53/E3
Torreón, NM, US 179/J3
Torreón, Mex. 204/D3
Torreperogil, Sp. 52/D3
Torres (str.), Austl., PNG 153/G2
Torres (isl.), Van. 160/F6
Tôrres, Braz. 225/G4
Torres del Paine, PN, Chile 191/B6
Torres Martinez Ind. Res., Ca, US 178/D4
Torres Novas, Port. 52/A3
Torres Straight Island Abor. Land, Austl. 153/F2
Torres Vedras, Port. 52/A3
Torrevieja, Sp. 53/E4
Torrey, Ut., US 179/G3
Torri di Quartesolo, It. 69/E2
Torricella Peligna, It. 71/D3
Torridge (riv.), Eng., UK 42/C6
Torrijos, Sp. 52/C3
Torrington, Ct, US 191/K4

Torrington, Wy, US 184/B2
Torrington, Ab., Can. 175/H2
Torrita di Siena, It. 53/G1
Tors Cove, Nf., Can. 189/L2
Torsa (riv.), Bhu. 109/G2
Torsåker, Swe. 45/A2
Torsby, Swe. 46/E1
Torsdby, Den. 29/D2
Torteval, Chl., UK 36/E3
Tortilla Flat, Az., US 179/G4
Tortola (riv.), It. 67/F5
Tortola, I., UK 203/J4
Tortoli, It. 54/A3
Tortona, It. 68/B4
Tortoreto Lido, It. 71/C2
Tortosa (cape), Sp. 53/F2
Tortosa, Sp. 53/F2
Tortuga (isl.), Haiti 203/H5
Tortuguero, PN, CR 207/H4
Tortum, Turk. 77/G4
Torūd, Iran 115/H3
Torul, Turk. 114/D1
Toruń, Pol. 49/K2
Torup, Swe. 46/K2
Torvaianica, It. 71/B4
Torysa (riv.), Slvk. 49/L4
Torzhok, Rus. 74/G4
Tosa, Japan 96/C4
Tosa (bay), Japan 91/L5
Tosashimizu, Japan 96/C4
Toscana (reg.), It. 68/C4
Toscanella, It. 69/E5
Toscanini, Namb. 140/D4
Toscolano-Maderno, It. 68/D2
Toshi (isl.), Japan 95/L6
Toshibetsu (riv.), Japan 94/A2
Toshka (lake), Egypt 137/U3
Toshviska, Rus. 75/M2
Tosno, Rus. 47/P2
Toson (inlet), NJ, US 198/D3
Tosontsengel, Mong. 90/D4
Toson (lake), China 90/D4
Töss (riv.), Swi. 51/H3
Tosson (hill), Eng., UK 39/E6
Tostado, Arg. 224/D4
Tostedt, Ger. 59/H2
Tosu, Japan 96/B4
Tosya, Turk. 76/E4
Totana, Sp. 52/E4
Toteng, Bots. 140/D4
Tôtes, Fr. 63/G1
Tot'ma, Rus. 74/J4
Totnes, Eng, UK 42/C6
Totness, Sur. 217/G3
Totoral, Uru. 191/K10
Totoral, Chile 224/B3
Totoras, Arg. 224/D5
Totowa, NJ, US 199/J8
Totoya, Japan 96/D3
Toto'oka, Japan 97/K1
Tottenham 65/H6
Tottenham, Austl. 156/C2
Tottenville 46/E3
Totton, Eng, UK 42/D6
Tottori (pref.), Japan 96/C3
Tottori, Japan 96/D3
Touajil, Mrta. 130/B2
Touat (riv.), Alg. 129/E4
Tra Bong, Viet. 106/E3
Tra Cu, Viet. 132/B3
Tra Linh, Viet. 99/E2
Tra Mi, Viet. 106/E4
Tra On, Viet. 106/D4
Tra Vinh, Viet. 106/D4

Tourves, Fr. 70/B6
Tourville-la-Rivière, Fr. 51/J5
Tous (res.), Sp. 53/E3
Toussaint (peak), Chad 132/D4
Toussidé (peak), Chad 126/C4
Toussière (peak), Fr. 68/A5
Toussoro (peak), CAfr. 134/D3
Toutes, Fr. 63/G1
Touwrivier, SAfr. 142/M10
Tövo (prov.), Mong. 90/F2
Tovar, Ven. 216/D2
Tovarkovskiy, Rus. 76/F1
Tove (riv.), Eng, UK 43/E2
Tovil, Eng, UK 36/E3
Tovste, Ukr. 78/C3
Tovuz, Azer. 77/H4
Tow Law, Eng, UK 41/G2
Towaco, NJ, US 199/H8
Towada, Japan 95/G1
Towada (lake), Japan 94/B3
Towada-Hachimantai NP, Japan 94/B3
Towamba (riv.), Austl. 157/D2
Towanda, Pa, US 207/F4
Towang, India 109/H2
Towaoc, Co, US 179/H3
Towcester, Eng, UK 43/F2
Tower (mtn.), Or, US 176/B1
Tower, Ire. 38/B6
Tower (falls), Wy, US 177/H1
Tower City, ND, US 186/F4
Tower City, Pa, US 198/B2
Tower Hamlets 36/C2
Tower Hill, Il, US 185/K4
Tower of London, 36/C2
Town Bluff (dam), Tx, US 181/G2
Town 'n' Country, Fl, US 194/K7
Townend, Wi, US 187/K5
Townsend (mt.), Wa, US 197/A2
Townsend, Wi, US 187/K5
Townsend, Mt, US 175/J4
Townsend, De, US 198/C5
Townsend, Ma, US 193/K2
Townsends, 47/P2
Townshend (cape), 158/C3
Townsville, Austl. 158/B2
Towot, Sudan 139/G4
Town Kham, Afg. 110/A2
Towson, Md, US 198/B5
Towuti (lake), Indo. 103/F4
Toya (lake), Japan 94/B2
Toyah, Tx, US 180/C2
Toyahvale, Tx, US 180/C2
Toyama (pref.), Japan 97/F3
Toyama, Japan 42/C6
Toyama (bay), Japan 91/M4
Toyama, SKor. 93/D5
Toyohashi, Japan 95/M5
Toyohashi, Japan 97/E3
Tréburden, Fr. 62/B3
Trébeurden, Fr. 62/B3
Trebinje, Bosn. 56/D4
Trébisacce, It. 54/E3
Trebnje, Slov. 65/H4
Trebon, Czh. 65/G1
Trebonne, Austl. 158/B2
Trebujena, Sp. 52/B4
Trebur, Ger. 64/B3
Trecase, It. 71/D6
Trecate, It. 68/B3

Trancoso, Port. 52/B2
Tranebjerg, Den. 46/D4
Tranemo, Swe. 46/E3
Tranent, Sc, UK 39/G5
Tranet (peak), Fr. 61/D4
Trang, Thai. 106/B5
Trangan (isl.), Indo. 103/H5
Trangie (isl.), Austl. 156/C2
Trängsletsjön (lake), 46/E1
Trani, It. 54/E2
Tranoroa, Madg. 143/H9
Tranqueras, Uru. 225/F4
Tranquebar, India 112/B5
Transantarctic 228/W
Transilvania (reg.), Rom. 73/J1
Transsylvanian Alps 107/F2
Trans-en-Provence, Fr. 70/C5
Transantarctic 228/W
Tranzano, Mex. 68/D3
Treorky, Wal, UK 42/C3
Trapassey, Nf, Can. 189/L2
Trapani, It. 54/C4
Trapeang Veng, Camb. 106/D3
Trapper (peak), Mt, US 174/G5
Trappers, Fr. 36/J5
Trás Algarrobos, Arg. 226/C4
Trás Árboles, Uru. 191/K10
Trás Arroyos, Arg. 226/E1
Trás Coraçõns, Braz. 223/L6
Trás Cruces, 36/J5
Trás de Maio, Braz. 225/F3
Trás Esquinas, Col. 216/C4
Três Irmãos (res.), Braz. 222/C4
Três Isletas, Arg. 224/D3
Trás Lagoas, Braz. 225/G2
Trás Lagos, Arg. 191/C6
Trás Lomas, Arg. 226/E3
Três Mapajos, Bol. 221/E3
Trino, It. 68/B3
Trás Marias, Mex. 205/Q10
Trás Marias (range), Nv, US 179/G3
Trás Marias, 222/D3
Trás Montes (cape), Chile 191/B5
Trás Morros, Alto de (peak), Col. 216/B3
Trás Passos, Braz. 225/F3
Trás Pontas, It. 69/E2
Trás Pontas, It. 68/B2
Três Piedras, NM, US 179/J4
Tristan da Cunha (isl.), StH. 26/J7
Trás Puntas, Arg. 226/E3
Trisuli (riv.), Nepal 109/E2
Trisuli Bāzār, Nepal 109/E2
Trittau, Ger. 59/H1
Triúnfo, Braz. 219/G4
Triúnfo, Bol. 221/E3
Trivandrum (int'l arpt.), India 107/C4
Trivento, It. 71/D4
Trivero, It. 68/B2
Trkmenbashi (Krasnovodsk), Trkm. 86/E5
Trobovlje, Slov. 51/L3
Trochov, Ab, Can. 175/H2
Trochu, Ab, Can. 175/H2
Trochu, Ab, Can. 175/H2
Tróchtelfingen, Ger. 64/C5
Tróia, It. 71/B2
Tróia, Port. 52/A3
Trois-Pistoles, Qu, Can. 188/C1
Trois-Rivières, Qu, Can. 191/K1
Troisdorf, Ger. 64/E1
Troisorrents, Swi. 66/C5
Troisvierges, Lux. 60/F3

Trentola-Ducenta, It. 71/D6
Trenton, Fl, US 195/G3
Trenton, Ga, US 192/H3
Trenton, Ky, US 192/D2
Trenton, Mo, US 185/H3
Trenton, NC, US 193/J3
Trenton (isl.), Ca, US 226/E1
Trenton, Nf, Can. 189/H2
Trenton, NS, Can. 189/H2
Trenton, On, Can. 191/H2
Trenton, Co, US 182/B2
Trenton, Tn, US 192/D3
Trenzano, It. 68/D3
Trepassey, Nf, Can. 189/L2
Trepton, Ger. 48/07
Trepuzzi, It. 55/F2
Trés, It. 55/G1
Tres Algarrobos, Arg. 226/C4
Tres Árboles, Uru. 191/K10
Tres Arroyos, Arg. 226/E1
Três Corações, Braz. 223/L6
Tres Cruces, 36/J5
Tres de Maio, Braz. 225/F3
Tres Esquinas, Col. 216/C4
Três Irmãos (res.), Braz. 222/C4
Tres Isletas, Arg. 224/D3
Tres Lagoas, Braz. 225/G2
Tres Lagos, Arg. 191/C6
Tres Lomas, Arg. 226/E3
Três Mapajos, Bol. 221/E3
Trino, It. 68/B3
Tres Marias, Mex. 205/Q10
Tres Marias (range), Nv, US 179/G3
Três Marias, 222/D3
Tres Montes (cape), Chile 191/B5
Tres Morros, Alto de (peak), Col. 216/B3
Tres Passos, Braz. 225/F3
Três Pontas, It. 69/E2
Três Pontas, It. 68/B2
Três Pontas, Cabo das (cape), Ang. 138/C5
Tres Puntas, Arg. 226/E3
Trisuli (riv.), Nepal 109/E2
Trisuli Bāzār, Nepal 109/E2
Trittau, Ger. 59/H1
Triúnfo, Braz. 219/G4
Triúnfo, Bol. 221/E3
Trivandrum (int'l arpt.), India 107/C4
Trivento, It. 71/D4
Trivero, It. 68/B2
Trkmenbashi (Krasnovodsk), Trkm. 86/E5

Třinec, Czh. 49/K4
Tring, Eng, UK 43/F3
Tring-Jonction, Qu, Can. 188/B2
Trinidad, Col. 216/D3
Trinidad (isl.), Arg. 226/E1
Trinidad, In, US 192/D2
Trinidad (chan.), Chile 191/B6
Trinidad (gulf), Chile 191/B6
Trinidad (isl.), Trin. 203/J5
Trinidad, Ven. 207/K10
Trinidad, On, Can. 191/H2
Trinidad, Co, US 182/B2
Trinidad, Tn, US 192/D3
Trinidad and Tobago (ctry.), 203/R9
Trinity, Nf, Can. 189/L1
Trinity, Tx, US 181/G2
Trinity, Vt, US 191/K2
Trinity (isl.), Ak, US 201/H4
Trinity, Al, US 192/D3
Trinity (dam), Ca, US 176/B2
Trinity (range), Nv, US 176/C2
Trinity (riv.), Tx, US 181/G2
Trinity, Ca, US 176/B2
Trinity Center, Ca, US 176/B2
Trinity S. Fk. (res.), Ca, US 176/B2
Trinity Site, NM, US 179/J4
Trinity, West Fork 183/E4
Trudeau (Logan) (mt.), 179/J4
Trinkitat, Sudan 137/U6
Trino, It. 68/B3
Trinta-e-um de Janeiro, (res.), Braz. 222/D3
Trion, Ga, US 192/G3
Triplet, Va, US 193/J2
Tripoli (int'l arpt.), Libya 126/B1
Tripoli (Ṭarābulus) (cap.), Libya 126/B1
Tripolis, Gre. 55/H4
Tripolitania (reg.), Libya 126/B1
Trippstadt, Ger. 61/G5
Tripunittura, India 107/C4
Tripura (state), India 105/F3
Trisanna (riv.), Aus. 67/G4
Trissino, It. 69/E2
Tristan da Cunha (isl.), StH. 26/J7
Trisuli (riv.), Nepal 109/E2

Trowutta, Austl. 156/C4
Troxelville, Pa, US 198/A2
Troy (Ilium) (ruin), Turk. 81/K3
Troy, Al, US 192/D3
Troy, Kan, Ca, US 176/D4
Troy, In, US 192/D2
Troy, Ks, US 185/J4
Troy, Mi, US 190/E3
Troy, Mo, US 185/K4
Troy, NY, US 191/K3
Troy, Oh, US 191/F1
Troy, Or, US 174/F5
Troy, Tx, US 181/G2
Troy Center, Wi, US 197/N14
Troyanski Prokhod 57/G4
Troyebratskiy, Kaz. 72/05
Troyes, Fr. 50/F2
Troyits'ke, Ukr. 79/K3
Trstenik, Serb. 106/B3
Trub, Swi. 66/D4
Trübbach, Swi. 51/H3
Trubchёvsk, Rus. 76/E1
Truchas (peak), NM, US 179/J4
Truckee (riv.), Nv, US 176/D4
Trudovanovo, Rus. 75/M2
Trufanovo, Rus. 75/K2
Truitt Peak (mt.), 201/M3
Trujillo, Hon. 206/E3
Trujillo, Sp. 52/C3
Trujillo, Peru 220/B3
Trujillo, Ven. 216/D2
Truk (isls.), Micr. 160/F4
Trulben, Ger. 61/G5
Truman, Mn, US 185/G2
Trumann, Ar, US 192/B3
Trumau, Aus. 57/N8
Trumbauersville, Pa, US 198/C3
Trumbull (mt.), Az, US 179/F2
Trumbull, Tx, US 180/L7
Trumbull, Ct, US 199/F2
Trün, Bul. 57/F4
Trün, Bul. 57/F4
Trundle, Austl. 157/C1
Truth Or Consequences, NM, US 179/J4
Trung Khanh, Viet. 99/E1
Trunovskoye, Rus. 79/M5
Truro, NS, Can. 189/H3
Truro, Ia, US 185/H3
Truro, Eng, UK 42/A6
Truscott, Tx, US 182/D4
Truskavets', Ukr. 78/B3
Truskmore (peak), Ire. 37/P9
Trüstenik, Bul. 57/F4
Trustrup, Den. 45/G6
Truth Or Consequences, NM, US 179/J4

Tshilenge, D.R. Congo 139/E4
Tshimbulu, D.R. Congo 139/E4
Tshinsenda, D.R. Congo 141/F2
Tshipise, SAfr. 141/F4
Tshisenga, D.R. Congo 139/E4
Tshokwe, Zim. 141/F2
Tsholotsho, Zim. 141/E3
Tshopo, 139/F2
Tshuapa, 139/D4
Tshuapa (riv.), D.R. Congo 139/F2
Tshuapa (riv.), D.R. Congo 119/E5
Tsiafajavona, 143/H7
Tsiafahy, 143/H7
Tsiigehtchic, NW, Can. 201/M2
Tsil'ma (riv.), Rus. 75/L2
Tsimlyansk Reservoir 79/M4
Tsimlyansk, Rus. 80/E5
Tsineng, SAfr. 142/C2
Tsineng Yi, China 99/L7
Tsinjomitondraka, 143/H9
Tsiombe, Madg. 143/H9
Tsiroanomandidy, 143/H7
Tsirombihina (riv.), Madg. 143/H7
Tsitondroina, Madg. 143/H8
Tsitsikamma Forest and Coastal NP, SAfr. 142/C4
Tsivil'sk, Rus. 75/K5
Tsivory, Madg. 143/H9
Tskhaltubo, Geo. 77/G4
Tskhinvali, Geo. 77/G4
Tsna (riv.), Rus. 74/G4
Tsnori, Geo. 206/E3
Tsodilo (hills), Bots. 140/D3
Tsolo (riv.), Mong. 90/F2
Tsomo, SAfr. 142/D4
Tsomog, Mong. 90/F2
Tsu (isl.), Japan 81/N6
Tsu, Japan 95/L6
Tsubame, Japan 97/G2
Tsukuyu, Tanz. 137/A4
Tsuchiura, Japan 95/K6
Tsuchiyama, Japan 95/K6
Tsugaru, Japan 94/B3
Tsugaru (pen.), Japan 94/B3
Tsukidate, Japan 95/G3
Tsukigase, Japan 95/K6
Tsukuba, Japan 95/E1
Tsukude, Japan 95/M6
Tsukui, Japan 95/M6
Tsukumi, Japan 96/B4
Tsumbe, Namb. 140/C3
Tsumkwe, Namb. 140/D3
Tsuna, Japan 96/D3
Tsurib, Rus. 77/H4
Tsuru, Japan 95/M5
Tsuruga, Japan 96/E3
Tsurugashima, Japan 95/L5
Tsurugi, Japan 96/E2
Tsurugi-san (mt.), Japan 96/D3
Tsuruoka, Japan 94/B4
Tsuruta, Japan 94/B3
Tsushima, Japan 95/L5
Tsushima, Japan 96/E3
Tsuyama, Japan 96/D3
Tsuyung (riv.), Bots. 140/D4
Tswaane, Bots. 140/D4
Tswapong (hills), Bots. 141/E4
Tsyurupyns'k, Ukr. 79/G4
Tua (riv.), Port.,Sp. 52/B2
Tuakau, NZ 159/N6
Tual, Indo. 103/H5
Tuam, Ire. 38/B5
Tuam (isl.), PNG 160/C4
Tuamapu (chan.), Chile 226/B4
Tuamotu (arch.), FrPol. 161/L6
Tuan (pt.), Indo. 106/B4
Tuan (cape), Malay. 106/B4
Tuan Giao, Viet. 98/D4
Tuan (riv.), China 92/B4
Tuapse, Rus. 79/K4
Tuatapere, NZ 159/A4
Tuba City, Az, US 179/G4
Tuba (riv.), Rus. 85/K4
Tuban (riv.), Yem. 112/D6
Tubarão, Braz. 225/G4
Tübās, WBnk. 117/C4
Tubbataha Reefs 167/U3
Tubbergen, Neth. 60/D3
Tubinal (peak), 143/H7
Tubingen, Germany 64/C5
Tubize, Belg. 60/D2
Tubmanburg, Libr. 132/C5
Tubou, Fiji 160/H6
Tubuai (bay), Wal, UK 40/B6
Tubuai (Tobruk), Libya 126/D1
Tubuai Islands (Austral Islands), FrPol. 161/K7
Tubuala, Pan. 216/B2
Tubutama, Mex. 204/C2
Tuburan, Phil. 167/U3
Tuchola, Pol. 49/J2
Tuckahoe, NY, US 199/K8
Tuckahoe, NJ, US 198/D5
Tuckahoe (riv.), NJ, US 198/D5
Tuckahoe (cr.), Md, US 198/C6
Tuckasegee 206/D2
Tucker, NC, US 193/F3
Tucker, Ga, US 193/M7
Tuckerman, Ar, US 192/B3
Tuckerton, NJ, US 199/D4
Tucopia (isl.), Sol. 160/H5
Tucquegnieux, Fr. 61/F5
Tucson, Az, US 179/G4
Tucu Tucu, Arg. 191/C6
Tucumán (prov.), Arg. 224/C3
Tucumari, NM, US 180/B3
Tucunaré, Braz. 224/D1
Tucunuco, Arg. 224/C4
Tucupita, Ven. 217/F2
Tucuruí, Braz. 218/D3
Tucuruí, Braz. 218/D3

Tudeä (riv.), Den. 45/H7
Tudela, Sp. 52/E1
Tudela de Duero, Sp. 52/C2
Tudeley, Eng, UK 36/E3
Tudu, Est. 47/M2
Tudun Wada, Nga. 133/H4
Tuen Mun, China 99/K7
Tuenno, It. 67/H5
Tuena, Austl. 157/D2
Tufanbeyli, Turk. 114/D2
Tuffé, Fr. 63/F4
Tufi, PNG 153/E2
Tufino, It. 71/D6
Tug Fork 193/F1
Tugaloo 193/F3
Tugao, Ga, SC, US 193/F3
Tugao, China 90/F4
Tugaung Yi, China 143/E3
Tugela, SAfr. 143/E3
Tugela (falls), SAfr. 142/E3
Tughlakabad (ruin), India 110/D5
Tugnug (pt.), Phil. 100/D3
Tuguaria, Indo. 98/D3
Tuguegarao, Phil. 100/C1
Tugulym, Rus. 75/Q4
Tugun (pt.), Bots. 141/F4
Tuhembarua, Indo. 101/B2
Tuibo, China 91/K3
Tuichi (riv.), Bol. 196/F7
Tuijunga 178/G2
Tuineje, Sp. 142/C2
Tukangbesi (isls.), Indo. 103/F5
Tukayel, Eth. 136/C3
Tukh Dalakah, Egypt 131/C3
Tükh, Egypt 131/C3
Tukh al Qāim, Egypt 131/C3
Tuko, D.R. Congo 139/F2
Tukobo, Gha. 133/C5
Tukoyaktuk, NW, Can. 201/M2
Tuktums, Lat. 47/K3
Tukung (peak), Indo. 102/D4
Tukuyu, Tanz. 137/A4
Tukwila, Wa, US 197/C3
Tula (riv.), Kenya 137/B2
Tula, Rus. 76/F1
Tula, Mex. 205/K6
Tula, Mex. 205/K6
Tula, PN, Mex. 205/K6
Tulagt Ar (riv.), China 111/F4
Tulalip Bay, Wa, US 174/C3
Tulalip Ind. Res., Wa, US 174/C3
Tulameen, BC, Can. 174/D3
Tulancingo, Mex. 205/K6
Tulangbawang (riv.), Indo. 101/D4
Tulangbawang, Indo. 101/D4
Tulare, Ca, US 178/C2
Tulare, SD, US 184/E1
Tulare Lake Bed, Ca, US 178/C2
Tularosa (valley), NM, US 180/A1
Tularosa, NM, US 180/A1
Tulayjät al Ghassūl, Jor. 117/D3
Tulcán, Ecu. 216/B4
Tulcea, Rom. 57/J3
Tulcea (prov.), Rom. 57/J3
Tulchyn, Ukr. 78/E3
Tule (canal), Ca, US 197/L3
Tule (riv.), Ca, US 178/C2
Tule Lake NWR, 176/C3
Tule River Ind. Res., Ca, US 178/C2
Tuli Block 141/E4
Tuli (riv.), Zim. 141/F3
Tuli (riv.), Zim. 141/F3
Tulia, Tx, US 182/D3
Tulik (isl.), Ak, US 201/E5
Tuliszków, Pol. 160/E5
Tulip, Ar, US 183/H3
Tulip Tree 183/H3
Tülkarm, WBnk. 117/C4
Tulla, Ire. 38/B5
Tullahoma, Tn, US 192/D3
Tullamarine (int'l arpt.), Austl. 156/F5
Tullamore, Austl. 157/C1
Tullamore, Ire. 38/C4
Tullaroan, Ire. 38/C5
Tulle, Fr. 50/D4
Tullibigeal, Austl. 157/C1
Tullibody, Sc, UK 39/C4
Tulln, Aus. 57/N7
Tullnerbach, Aus. 57/N7
Tulloch (res.), Ca, US 176/C5
Tullow, Ire. 38/D4
Tullus, Sudan 135/G2
Tully, NY, US 191/H3
Tully, Austl. 158/B2
Tullytown, Pa, US 198/D3
Tuloma (riv.), Rus. 80/D3
Tulpehocken 198/B3
Tulpios 198/B3
Tulsa, Ok, US 183/G2
Tulsequah, BC, Can. 201/M4
Tulsipur, Nepal 108/D1
Tulu Bolo, Eth. 136/A3
Tultepec, Mex. 205/Q9
Tultitlán, Mex. 205/Q9
Tuluksak, Ak, US 201/F3
Tulum (ruin), Mex. 206/E1
Tulun, Rus. 81/L4
Tulungagung, Indo. 101/E5
Tulungselapan, Indo. 101/D4
Tumacácori, Az, US 179/G5
Tumacácori Nat'l Mon., 179/G5
Tumaco, Col. 216/B4
Tumanovo, Rus. 76/F1
Tumatumari, Guy. 217/G3
Tumba (lake), D.R. Congo 138/D3
Tumba, Swe. 46/G2
Tumbangkaman, Indo. 102/D4

Tumba – Urugu
339

Tumbangsenamang, Indo. 102/D4
Tumbarumba, Austl. 157/D2
Tumbes, Peru 220/A1
Tumbes (dept.), Peru 220/A1
Tumblong, Austl. 157/D2
Tumbot (peak), Camb. 106/C3
Tumbwe, D.R. Congo 141/E1
Tumby Bay, Austl. 155/H5
Tumd Youqi, China 92/B2
Tumd Zuoqi, China 92/B2
Tumen (riv.), China 93/E1
Tumen, China 91/K3
Tumenzi, China 90/E4
Tumeremo, Ven. 217/F3
Tumereng, Guy. 217/F3
Tummel (riv.), Sc, UK 39/C3
Tumnin (riv.), Rus. 91/M1
Tump, Pak. 113/H3
Tumpaan, Indo. 103/F3
Tumpat, Malay. 101/C1
Tumpu (peak), Indo. 103/F4
Tumtum, Wa, US 174/F4
Tumu, Gha. 133/E4
Tumuc-Humac (mts.), Braz. 217/H4
Tumudibandh, India 107/D2
Tumupasa, Bol. 220/E4
Tumusla, Bol. 224/C2
Tumut, Austl. 157/D2
Tumwater, Wa, US 174/C4
Tuna, Gha. 133/E4
Tunadal, Swe. 74/C3
Tunbridge, Vt, US 191/K3
Tunceli, Turk. 114/D2
Tunceli (prov.), Turk. 114/D2
Tunchang, China 99/F5
Tunda Chissococua, Ang. 140/C1
Tundazi (hill), Zim. 141/F3
Tundla, India 108/B2
Tunduma, Tanz. 139/H5
Tunduru, Tanz. 137/B4
Tundyk (riv.), Kaz. 111/C1
Tundzha (riv.), Bul. 73/K2
Tune, Den. 45/J7
Tung Chung, China 99/K7
Tung Lung (riv.), China 99/M8
Tungabhadra (riv.), India 104/C4
Tungabhadra (res.), India 104/C4
Tungamah, Austl. 156/C3
Tungaru, Sudan 134/F3
Tungawan, Phil. 100/C4
Tungelsta, Swe. 45/B1
Tungku, Malay. 100/B4
Tŭngsan-got (pt.), NKor. 93/C4
Tungshih, Tai. 99/J3
Tungsten, NW, Can. 170/D2
Tungurahua (prov.), Ecu. 216/B5
Tünhel, Mong. 90/F2
Tuni, India 107/D2
Tunica, La, US 194/C2
Tunica, Ms, US 192/B3
Tūnis (cap.), Tun. 130/M6
Tūnis (gov.), Tun. 130/M6
Tunisia (ctry.) 129/H2
Tunjá, Col. 216/C3
Tunkhannock, Pa, US 191/J4
Tunku Abdul Rahman NP, Malay. 100/B4
Tunliu, China 92/C3
Tunnel Creek NP, Austl. 152/B4
Tunnels of Vinh Moc, Viet. 106/D2
Tuntum, Braz. 219/E4
Tuntutuliak, Ak, US 201/F3
Tunungayualuk (isl.), Nf, Can. 171/K3
Tunuyán (riv.), Arg. 226/C2
Tunuyán, Arg. 226/C2
Tuo (riv.), China 90/E5
Tuokou, China 99/F3
Tuolu, China 99/E4
Tuolumne (riv.), Ca, US 176/D5
Tuolumne Grove, Ca, US 178/C2
Tuong Duong, Viet. 106/D2
Tuoniang (riv.), China 105/J3
Tuoro sul Trasimeno, It. 71/B1
Tuotuo (riv.), China 111/F5
Tuotuoheyan, China 90/C5
Tūp Āghāj, Iran 115/F2
Tupã, Braz. 225/G2
Tupaciguara, Braz. 225/G1
Tupai (isl.), FrPol. 161/K6
Tupambaé, Uru. 191/G2
Tupanatinga, Braz. 219/G5
Tupanciretã, Braz. 225/F4
Tuparro (riv.), Col. 216/D3
Tupelo, Ok, US 183/F3
Tupelo, Ms, US 192/C3
Tupelo Nat'l Bfld., Ms, US 192/C3
Tupi Paulista, Braz. 225/G2
Tupik, Rus. 74/G5
Tupinambarana (isl.), Braz. 218/B3
Tupiza, Bol. 224/C2
Tupman, Ca, US 178/C3
Tupper Lake, NY, US 191/J2
Tupungato, Arg. 226/C2
Tupungato (peak), Arg. 226/P8
Tuquan, China 91/J2
Tura (riv.), Rus. 80/G4
Tura, Rus. 81/L3
Tura, India 109/H3
Tura, China 111/E4
Ṭurá, Egypt 131/C5
Turabah, SAr. 112/D4
Turakina, NZ 159/C3
Turan, Rus. 90/C1
Tur'ān, Isr. 117/C3
Turan Lowland (plain), Uzb. 80/G5
Turana (mts.), Rus. 91/L1
Turanganui (riv.), NZ 159/J9
Turangi, NZ 159/C2
Turano (riv.), It. 71/B3
Ṭurayf, SAr. 114/D4
Turbaco, Col. 216/C2
Turbat, Pak. 113/H3
Turbenthal, Swi. 67/E3
Turbeville, SC, US 193/G4
Turbo, Col. 216/B2
Turbotville, Pa, US 198/B1
Turckheim, Fr. 66/D1
Turda, Rom. 57/F2
Tureia (isl.), FrPol. 161/M7
Turek, Pol. 49/K2
Turenki, Fin. 45/E4
Tŭrgovishte, Bul. 57/H4
Turgutlu, Turk. 114/A2
Turhal, Turk. 114/D1
Türi, Est. 47/L2
Turiaçu (bay), Braz. 219/E3
Turiaçu, Braz. 219/E3
Turiamo, Ven. 219/N7
Turin (Torino), It. 68/A2
Turiys'k, Ukr. 78/C2
Turka, Ukr. 49/M4
Turka, Rus. 90/F1
Turkana (Rudolf) (lake), Kenya 119/F4
Turkana Nat'l Rsv., Kenya 137/A1
Türkeli, Turk. 76/E4
Túrkeve, Hun. 56/E2
Turkey (ctry.) 114/C2
Turkey (riv.), Ia, US 185/J2
Turkey (cr.), Tx, US 180/E3
Turkey Creek (lake), La, US 194/C2
Turkey Creek, Austl. 152/C4
Türkheim, Ger. 67/G1
Turki, Rus. 79/M2
Türkistan, Kaz. 111/A3
Türkmenabat, Trkm. 80/G6
Turkmen-Kala, Trkm. 113/H1
Turkmenistan (ctry.) 80/F6
Türkoğlu, Turk. 114/D2
Turks (isls.), Haiti 203/G3
Turks and Caicos (isls.), UK 163/K7
Turks Island Passage (chan.), UK 207/J1
Turku (int'l arpt.), Fin. 47/K1
Turku (Åbo), Fin. 47/K1
Turku Ja Pori (prov.), Fin. 44/G3
Turkwel (riv.), Kenya 137/A1
Turley, Ok, US 183/G2
Turlingua (cr.), Tx, US 180/C3
Turlock, Ca, US 178/B2
Turmalina, Braz. 223/E3
Turmantas, Lith. 47/M4
Turmero, Ven. 219/N7
Turnagain (cape), NZ 159/D3
Turnberry, Sc, UK 39/B6
Turnbull (dry lake), Or, US 176/E2
Turnbull (mt.), Az, US 179/G4
Turnbull NWR, Wa, US 174/F4
Turneffe (isls.), Belz. 202/D4
Turner (mt.), Austl. 154/C2
Turner, Me, US 191/L2
Turner, Mt, US 175/K3
Turner Valley, Ab, Can. 174/G2
Turnersville, NJ, US 198/C4
Turnersville, Tx, US 180/F2
Turnhouse (int'l arpt.), Sc, UK 39/C5
Turnhout, Belg. 58/B6
Turnov, Czh. 49/H3
Turnu Măgurele, Rom. 57/G4
Turon, Ks, US 183/E2
Turon (riv.), Austl. 157/D1
Tuross Head, Austl. 157/E3
Turov, Bela. 78/D1
Turpan, China 111/E3
Turquino (peak), Cuba 207/G2
Turrell, Ar, US 192/B3
Turretot, Fr. 63/F1
Turriaco, It. 69/G2
Turriers, Fr. 70/C4
Turriff, Sc, UK 39/D1
Tursunzoda, Taj. 80/G6
Turt, Mong. 90/E1
Turtle (riv.), ND, US 186/F3
Turtle (isls.), SLeo. 132/B5
Turtle (cr.), SD, US 184/E1
Turtle (pt.), Austl. 152/C3
Turtle Lake, ND, US 186/D4
Turtle Mountain Ind. Res., ND, US 186/E3
Turtle River, Mn, US 187/G4
Turtleford, Sk, Can. 175/K1
Turton, Eng, UK 41/F4
Turton, SD, US 184/E1
Turukhansk, Rus. 80/J3
Turvo (riv.), Braz. 222/C4
Tuscaloosa, Al, US 192/D4
Tuscaloosa (lake), Al, US 192/D4
Tuscano (arch.), Fr. 54/B1
Tuscano (arch.), It. 72/F2
Tuscany (reg.), It. 72/F2
Tuscarawas (riv.), Oh, US 190/F4
Tuscarora, Nv, US 176/E3
Tuscarora (mtn.), Pa, US 198/A3
Tuscola, Il, US 190/B5
Tuscola, Tx, US 180/E1
Tuscumbia, Mo, US 183/H1
Tuscumbia, Al, US 192/D3
Tushar (mts.), Ut, US 179/F1
Tushino (nbhd.), Rus. 75/W9
Tushka, Ok, US 183/F3
Tuskahoma, Ok, US 183/G3
Tuskegee, Al, US 192/E4
Tuskegee Institute Nat'l Hist. Site, Al, US 192/E4
Tusket, NS, Can. 188/E4
Tussy, Ok, US 183/F3
Tustin, Ca, US 196/G8
Tuszyn, Pol. 49/K3
Tutak, Turk. 115/E2
Tutayev, Rus. 74/H4
Tutbury, Eng, UK 41/G6
Tutin, Serb. 56/E4
Tutóia, Braz. 219/F3
Tutong, Bru. 100/A4
Tutrakan, Bul. 57/H3
Tuttle, ND, US 186/E4
Tuttle, Ok, US 183/F3
Tuttle Creek (res.), Ks, US 183/F1
Tuttlingen, Ger. 67/E2
Tutuala, ETim. 152/B2
Tutubu, Tanz. 139/H4
Tutuila (isl.), ASam. 161/T10
Ṭuṭūn, Egypt 131/B6
Tutupaca (vol.), Peru 220/D5
Tututalak (mt.), Ak, US 201/F2
Tutwiler, Ms, US 192/B3
Tutzing, Ger. 67/H2
Tuul (riv.), Mong. 90/F2
Tuulos, Fin. 45/E3
Tuusula, Fin. 47/L1
Tuusulajärvi (lake), Fin. 45/E4
Tuvalu (ctry.) 160/G5
Ṭuwayq, Jabal (mts.), SAr. 112/E3
Tuxford, Sk, Can. 175/M2
Tuxford, Eng, UK 41/H5
Tuxpan, Mex. 204/D4
Tuxpan, Mex. 204/E5
Tuxpan de Rodríguez Cano, Mex. 206/B1
Tuxtla Gutiérrez, Mex. 206/C2
Túy, Sp. 52/A1
Tuy (riv.), Ven. 219/P7
Tuy An, Viet. 106/E3
Tuy Hoa, Viet. 106/E3
Tuyen Hoa, Viet. 106/D2
Tuyen Quang, Viet. 106/D1
Tuymazy, Rus. 75/M5
Tūysarkān, Iran 115/G3
Tuyuk, Kaz. 111/C3
Tuz (lake), Turk. 114/C2
Ṭūz Khurmātū, Iraq 115/F3
Tuzha, Rus. 75/K4
Tuzigoot Nat'l Mon., Az, US 179/F3
Tuzla, Turk. 116/D1
Tuzla, Bosn. 56/D3
Tuzla, Turk. 115/N7
Tuzluca, Turk. 115/E1
Tuzlukçu, Turk. 114/B2
Tuzly, Ukr. 57/K3
Tuzule, D.R. Congo 139/E4
Tvååker, Swe. 46/E3
Tvedestrand, Nor. 46/C2
Tver', Rus. 74/G4
Tverskaya Oblast, Rus. 47/P3
Tvertsa (riv.), Rus. 74/G4
Tvŭrditsa, Bul. 57/G4
Twapia, Zam. 141/F2
Twardogóra, Pol. 49/J3
Tway, Sk, Can. 175/M1
Tweed (riv.), Sc, UK 39/C5
Tweed, On, Can. 191/H2
Tweed Heads, Austl. 158/D5
Tweed-New Haven (arpt.), Ct, US 199/F1
Tweedmouth, Eng, UK 39/D5
Tweedsmuir, Sc, UK 39/C5
Twello, Neth. 58/D4
Twente (pol. reg.), Neth. 58/D4
Twente (canal), Neth. 58/D4
Twenty Mile (cr.), On, Can. 190/T9
Twentynine Palms, Ca, US 178/D3
Twentynine Palms Marine Corps Base, Ca, US 178/D3
Twig, Mn, US 187/H4
Twin (falls), Id, US 177/F2
Twin Bridges, Mt, US 177/G1
Twin Buttes (res.), Tx, US 180/D2
Twin City, Ga, US 193/F4
Twin Falls, Id, US 177/F2
Twin Hills, Ak, US 201/F4
Twin Lake, Mi, US 190/C3
Twin Lakes, Wi, US 197/P14
Twin Rivers, NJ, US 198/D3
Twin Rocks, Or, US 174/C5
Twin Valley, Mn, US 186/F4
Twin, North (lake), Wi, US 187/K4
Twingi, Zam. 141/F1
Twist, Ger. 58/E3
Twiste (riv.), Ger. 59/G6
Twistringen, Ger. 59/F3
Twitchell (res.), Ca, US 178/B3
Two Butte (cr.), Co, US 182/C2
Two Harbors, Mn, US 187/J4
Two Hills, Ab, Can. 175/J1
Two Medicine (riv.), Mt, US 175/H3
Two Rivers (res.), NM, US 182/B4
Two Rivers, Wi, US 190/C2
Twodot, Mt, US 175/J4
Twyfelfontein Rock Engravings, Namb. 140/B4
Twyford, Eng, UK 43/F4
Twymyn (riv.), Wal, UK 42/C1
Twynholm, Sc, UK 40/D2
Tyachiv, Ukr. 78/B3
Tyao (riv.), India 98/B4
Tyatya (vol.), Rus. 94/E1
Tybee Nat'l Wild. Ref., Ga, US 195/H1
Tychy, Pol. 49/K3
Tydd Saint Giles, Eng, UK 43/G1
Tye, Tx, US 180/E1
Tyémé, C.d'Iv. 132/D4
Tyendinaga, On, Can. 191/H2
Tygart (lake), WV, US 193/H1
Tygda, Rus. 91/K1
Tyger (riv.), SC, US 193/G3
Tygh Valley, Or, US 176/C1
Tyi Grounto (plat.), Niger 126/B4
Tyldesley, Eng, UK 41/F4
Tyler, Mn, US 185/F1
Tyler, Tx, US 181/G1
Tylers Green, Eng, UK 36/A2
Tylertown, Ms, US 194/C2
Tylersville, Pa, US 198/A2
Tymovskoye, Rus. 91/N1
Týn, Czh. 49/H4
Tynagh, Ire. 38/B3
Tynan, Tx, US 180/F3
Tynda, Rus. 81/N4
Tyndall, Mb, Can. 186/F2
Tyndall (A.F.B.), Fl, US 195/F2
Tyndall, SD, US 184/E2
Tyndrum, Sc, UK 39/B4
Tyne (riv.), Eng, UK 39/D5
Tyne and Wear (co.), Eng, UK 41/G2
Tyne Valley, PE, Can. 188/F2
Tynemouth, Eng, UK 41/G1
Tyner, Ky, US 193/F2
Tynset, Nor. 44/D3
Tyonek, Ak, US 201/H3
Tyre (Ṣūr), Leb. 117/C2
Tyresö, Swe. 45/B1
Tyrifjorden (lake), Nor. 46/C1
Tyringe, Swe. 46/E3
Tyrma (riv.), Rus. 91/L2
Tyrnyauz, Rus. 77/G4
Tyro, Ks, US 183/G2
Tyrone, Ok, US 182/D2
Tyrone, Pa, US 191/G4
Tyrone, NM, US 179/H4
Tyrone, Ga, US 193/L8
Tyronza, Ar, US 192/B3
Tyrrell (cr.), Austl. 156/B2
Tyrrellspass, Ire. 38/C3
Tyrrhenian (sea), It. 29/F4
Tyshkivka, Ukr. 78/F3
Tysnes, Nor. 46/A1
Tysnesøy (isl.), Nor. 46/A2
Tysons Corner, Va, US 198/A6
Tysse, Nor. 46/A1
Tystberga, Swe. 46/G2
Tytuvėnai, Lith. 47/K4
Tyub-Karagan (pt.), Kaz. 77/J3
Tyulen'i (isls.), Rus. 77/J3
Tyuleniy (isl.), Rus. 77/H3
Tyumenskaya Oblast, Rus. 75/Q4
Tyumen', Rus. 75/Q4
Tyumen (int'l arpt.), Rus. 75/Q4
Tyup, Kyr. 111/C3
Tyva Resp., Rus. 80/K4
Tywi (riv.), Wal, UK 42/B3
Tywyn, Wal, UK 42/B1
Tzaneen, SAfr. 141/F4
Tzucacab, Mex. 206/D1

U

U S Army Ammunition Plant, Ok, US 183/F3
U. S. Naval Weapons Station, Ca, US 196/F8
U.C.-Irvine, Ca, US 196/G8
U.K. Sovereign Base Area (gov.), Cyp. 116/C2
U.S.S. Alabama Battleship Park, Al, US 194/E2
Ua Huka (isl.), FrPol. 161/M5
Ua Pou (isl.), FrPol. 161/L5
Uad Assag (riv.), WSah. 128/B4
Uad Atui (riv.), WSah. 128/B5
Uad el Jat (riv.), WSah. 128/B4
Uad Tenuaiur (riv.), WSah. 128/A5
Uadi Uadaimo (wadi), Som. 136/D3
Uamba (riv.), D.R. Congo 138/D4
Uamh Bheag (peak), Sc, UK 39/B4
Uanda, Austl. 158/B3
Uato-Lari, ETim. 152/B2
Uatuma (riv.), Braz. 218/B3
Uatumã (riv.), Braz. 217/G5
Uauá, Braz. 223/F1
Uaupés (riv.), Braz. 216/D4
Uaxactún (ruin), Guat. 206/D2
Ub, Serb. 56/E3
Ubá, Braz. 223/E4
Uba, Nga. 134/B3
Ubach over Worms, Neth. 61/F2
Übach-Palenberg, Ger. 61/F2
Ubagan (riv.), Kaz. 75/Q5
Ubaitaba, Braz. 223/F2
Ubajara, Braz. 219/F3
Ubajara, PN de, Braz. 219/F3
Ubangi (riv.), D.R. Congo 119/D4
Ubatã, Braz. 223/F2
Ubaté, Col. 219/M7
Ubatuba, Braz. 223/L8
Ubay, Phil. 100/D3
Ubaye (riv.), Fr. 51/G4
Ubbergen, Neth. 58/C5
Ube, Japan 96/B4
Úbeda, Sp. 52/D3
Uberaba, Braz. 225/H1
Uberaba (lake), Braz. 221/G5
Überherrn, Ger. 61/F5
Uberlândia, Braz. 222/C3
Überlingen, Ger. 67/F2
Überlingersee (lake), Ger. 67/E2
Ubia (peak), Indo. 103/J4
Ubiaja, Nga. 133/G5
Ubina, Bol. 224/C2
Ubinas, Peru 220/D5
Ubly, Mi, US 190/E3
Ubombo, SAfr. 143/F2
Ubon Ratchathani, Thai. 106/D3
Ubrique, Sp. 52/C4
Ubundu, D.R. Congo 139/F3
Ubute, D.R. Congo 139/F3
Ucar, Azer. 115/F1
Ucayali (riv.), Peru 209/B3
Ucayali (dept.), Peru 220/C3
Uccle, Belg. 61/D2
Uch, Pak. 110/A5
Uch-Adzhi, Trkm. 113/H1
Uch-Aral, Kaz. 80/J5
Ucha (riv.), Rus. 75/W8
Uchab, Namb. 140/C3
Uchaly, Rus. 75/N5
Uchāna, India 110/D5
Ucharonidge, Austl. 152/D4
Uchinskoye (res.), Rus. 75/W8
Uchiura (bay), Japan 91/N3
Uchiza, Peru 220/B3
Uchkeken, Rus. 79/M6
Uchquduq, Uzb. 80/G5
Uchte (riv.), Ger. 48/F2
Uchte, Ger. 59/F3
Uchumarca, Peru 220/B2
Uchumayo, Peru 220/D5
Uchur (riv.), Rus. 81/P4
Ücker (riv.), Ger. 46/E5
Uckermark (reg.), Ger. 49/G2
Uckfield, Eng, UK 43/G5
Ucluelet, BC, Can. 174/B3
Ucon, Id, US 177/H2
Üçpınar, Turk. 116/C1
Ucross, Wy, US 177/K1
Ucua, Ang. 138/C5
Ucumasi, Bol. 224/C1
Uda (riv.), Rus. 81/M4
Udaipur, India 104/B3
Udaipur Garhi, Nepal 109/F2
Udaipura, India 108/B4
Udamalpet, India 107/C4
Udara, Nga. 133/G4
Uddevalla, Swe. 46/D2
Uddingston, Sc, UK 39/B5
Uddjaure (lake), Swe. 44/F2
Üdem, Ger. 58/D5
Uden, Neth. 58/C5
Udenhout, Neth. 58/C5
Uder, Ger. 59/H6
Udgīr, India 107/C2
Udhampur, India 110/C3
Udi, Nga. 133/G5
Udimskiy, Rus. 75/K3
Udine (prov.), It. 69/G1
Udine, It. 51/K3
Udmurtiya Resp., Rus. 80/F4
Udomlya, Rus. 74/G4
Udon (riv.), Fr. 63/E3
Udon Thani, Thai. 106/C2
Ueckermünde, Ger. 46/F5
Ueda, Japan 97/F2
Uele (riv.), D.R. Congo 119/E4
Uelen, Rus. 201/D2
Uelsen, Ger. 58/D3
Uelzen, Ger. 59/H3
Ueno, Japan 95/K6
Ueno, Japan 95/B1
Uenohara, Japan 97/F3
Uere (riv.), D.R. Congo 135/E4
Uetendorf, Swi. 66/D4
Uetersen, Ger. 59/G1
Uetze, Ger. 59/H4
Ufa, Rus. 75/M5
Ufa (riv.), Rus. 75/N5
Uffenheim, Ger. 64/D3
Uffing, Ger. 67/H2
Uffington, Eng, UK 43/E3
Ufra, Trkm. 115/H2
Ugab (riv.), Namb. 140/B4
Ugāle, Lat. 47/K3
Ugalla (riv.), Tanz. 139/G4
Ugalla, Tanz. 139/G4
Ugalla River Game Rsv., Tanz. 139/G4
Uganda (ctry.) 119/F4
Ugbobo Ani, Nga. 133/G5
Ugento, It. 55/F3
Ugep, Nga. 133/H5
Ughelli, Nga. 133/G5
Ugie (riv.), Sc, UK 39/E1
Ugine, Fr. 66/C6
Uglegorsk, Ukr. 79/K3
Uglegorsk, Rus. 91/N2
Ugleural'skiy, Rus. 75/N4
Uglich, Rus. 74/H4
Ugljan (isl.), Cro. 51/L4
Uglovoye, Rus. 91/L3
Ugod, Hun. 56/C2
Ugol'nyye Kopi, Rus. 81/T3
Ugra (riv.), Rus. 74/G5
Ugŭrchin, Bul. 57/G4
Ugweno, Tanz. 137/B2
Uherské Hradiště, Czh. 49/J4
Uhingen, Ger. 64/C5
Uhland, Tx, US 180/F3
Úhlava (riv.), Czh. 49/G4
Úhlavka (riv.), Czh. 65/F3
Uhrichsville, Oh, US 190/F4
Uia di Ciamarella (peak), It. 70/D2
Uiangombe, Ang. 138/C5
Uig, Sc, UK 37/Q7
Uig, Sc, UK 37/Q8
Uíge, Ang. 138/C4
Uíge (prov.), Ang. 138/C4
Ŭihŭng, SKor. 93/E4
Ŭijŏngbu, SKor. 93/G6
Ŭiju, NKor. 93/C2
Uil, Kaz. 77/K2
Uil (riv.), Kaz. 77/K2
Uilkraal (riv.), SAfr. 142/L11
Uilpata (Gora Peak), Rus. 77/G4
Uinta (basin), Ut, US 177/H3
Uinta (mts.), Ut, US 177/H3
Uinta and Ouray Ind. Res., Ut, US 177/H3
Uiraúna, Braz. 219/G4
Ŭiryŏng, SKor. 93/E5
Ŭisŏng, SKor. 96/A2
Uitenhage, SAfr. 142/D4
Uitgeest, Neth. 58/B3
Uithoorn, Neth. 58/B4
Uithuizen, Neth. 58/D2
Uiwang, SKor. 93/F7
Ujae (isl.), Mrsh. 160/F4
Ujelang (isl.), Mrsh. 160/F4
Újfehértó, Hun. 49/L5
Ujhāni, India 108/B1
Uji (riv.), Japan 96/D3
Uji, Japan 95/J6
Ujiji, Tanz. 139/G4
Ujitawara, Japan 95/J6
Ujjain, India 104/C3
Ujohbilang, Indo. 102/E3
Ujung Pandang, Indo. 103/E5
Ujunggading, Indo. 101/B2
Ujunggenteng, Indo. 101/D4
Ukara (isl.), Tanz. 137/A2
Ukata, Nga. 133/G4
Ukerewe (isl.), Tanz. 137/A2
Ukhiya, Bang. 105/F3
Ukhta, Rus. 75/M3
Ukiah, Ca, US 176/B4
Ukiah, Or, US 176/D1
Uklāna, India 110/C5
Ukmergė, Lith. 47/L4
Ukraine (ctry.) 78/F4
Ukwama, Tanz. 137/A4
Ukwatutu, D.R. Congo 135/E4
Ul Bend NWR, Mt, US 175/L4
Ula, Turk. 73/L3
Ulaan-Uul, Mong. 90/G3
Ulaanbaatar (cap.), Mong. 90/F2
Ulaanbaatar (int'l arpt.), Mong. 90/F2
Ulaandel, Mong. 90/G2
Ulaangom, Mong. 111/F2
Ulaanjirem, Mong. 90/F2
Ulan Erge, Rus. 77/H3
Ulan Ul (lake), China 111/F5
Ulan-Burgasy (mts.), Rus. 90/F1
Ulan-Khol, Rus. 77/H3
Ulan-Ude, Rus. 90/F1
Ulangati, D.R. Congo 139/F3
Ulanhot, China 91/J2
Ulatis (cr.), Ca, US 197/L10
Ulaya, Tanz. 137/B3
Ulchin, SKor. 96/A2
Ulcinj, Mont. 56/D5
Ulcumayo, Peru 220/C3
Uldz (riv.), Mong. 90/G2
Ulefoss, Nor. 46/C2
Ulemiste (int'l arpt.), Est. 47/L2
Ulen, Mn, US 186/F4
Ulgain (riv.), China 91/H2
Ulhāsnagar, India 107/B2
Uliastay, Mong. 90/D2
Ulindi (riv.), D.R. Congo 139/F3
Ulithi (isl.), Micr. 160/C3
Uljma, Serb. 56/E3
Ulla, Bela. 47/N4
Ulla (riv.), Sp. 52/A1
Ulla Ulla, Bol. 220/D4
Ulla Ulla, Res. Nacional, Bol. 220/D4
Ulladulla, Austl. 157/E2
Ullāpāra, Bang. 109/G3
Ullapool, Sc, UK 37/R8
Ullared, Swe. 46/E3
Ulldecona, Sp. 53/F2
Ullensvang, Nor. 46/B1
Ullerslev, Den. 45/G7
Üllő, Hun. 57/R10
Ulloma, Bol. 224/B1
Ullsfjorden (estu.), Nor. 44/F1
Ullswater (lake), Eng, UK 41/F2
Ullŭng (isl.), SKor. 91/L4
Ŭllyul, NKor. 93/C3
Ulm, Ger. 64/C6
Ulm, Ar, US 183/J3
Ulman, Mo, US 183/H1
Ulmarra, Austl. 156/E1
Ulmen, Ger. 61/F3
Ulonguè, Moz. 141/G2
Ulricehamn, Swe. 46/E3
Ulrichen, Swi. 67/E5
Ulrichsberg, Aus. 65/G5
Ulrichstein, Ger. 64/C1
Ulrum, Neth. 58/D2
Ulsan, SKor. 96/A3
Ulstein, Nor. 44/C3
Ulster (reg.), Ire. 40/A3
Ulster, Pa, US 191/H4
Ulster (riv.), Ger. 64/C1
Ulster American Folk Park, NI, UK 40/A2
Ulu, Indo. 103/G3
Ulu, Sudan 134/G3
Ulua (riv.), Hon. 206/E3
Uluçınar, Turk. 116/D1
Uludağ (peak), Turk. 114/B1
Uludoruk (peak), Turk. 115/F2
Uluguru (mts.), Tanz. 137/B3
Ulukışla, Turk. 114/C2
Ulundi, SAfr. 143/E3
Ulungur (riv.), China 90/B2
Ulungur (lake), China 90/B2
Uluru (Ayers Rock) (peak), Austl. 155/F3
Uluru NP, Austl. 155/F3
Ulutau (peak), Kaz. 111/A2
Ulverston, Eng, UK 41/E3
Ulverstone, Austl. 156/C4
Ulvik, Nor. 46/B1
Ulvila, Fin. 47/J1
Ul'yanovka, Rus. 47/P2
Ul'yanovka, Ukr. 78/F3
Ul'yanovo, Rus. 76/E1
Ul'yanovsk, Rus. 75/L5
Ul'yanovskaya Oblast, Rus. 77/H1
Ulysses, Ks, US 182/D2
Ulysses, Pa, US 191/H4
Ulysses, Ne, US 185/F3
Um Dafuq, Sudan 134/D3
Umala, Bol. 224/C1
Uman', Ukr. 78/F3
Umán, Mex. 206/D1
Umanum (pt.), Phil. 100/D3
Umari, Braz. 219/G4
Umarizal, Braz. 219/G4
Umarkot, India 107/D2
Umāsi La (pass), India 110/D3
Umatilla, Fl, US 195/H3
Umatilla, Or, US 174/E5
Umatilla (riv.), Or, US 176/D1
Umatilla Ind. Res., Or, US 176/D1
Umatilla NWR, Or, US 176/D1
Umba, Rus. 74/G2
Umbakumba, Austl. 153/E3
Umbeara, Austl. 155/G3
Umberto I, Arg. 224/D4
Umbogintwini, SAfr. 143/E3
Umboi (isl.), PNG 160/D5
Umbrail (peak), Swi. 67/G4
Umbrailpass (pass), Swi. 67/G4
Umbria (pol. reg.), It. 69/F6
Umbria (prov.), It. 51/K5
Umbuluze (riv.), Afr. 141/F5
Ume (riv.), Swe. 80/B3
Ume (riv.), Zim. 141/F3
Umeå, Swe. 44/G3
Umeälven (riv.), Swe. 44/F2
Umedpur, Bang. 109/G4
Umët, Rus. 77/G1
Umfolozi (riv.), SAfr. 143/E3
Umfreville (lake), On, Can. 187/G2
Umfuli (riv.), Zim. 141/F3
Umgeni (riv.), SAfr. 143/E3
Umhausen, Aus. 67/G3
Umiat, Ak, US 201/H2
Umkirch, Ger. 66/D1
Umkomaas, SAfr. 143/E3
Umm al Abīd, Libya 126/B3
Umm al Arānib, Libya 126/B3
Umm al Birak, SAr. 112/C4
Umm al Ghirbāl (well), Libya 126/B2
Umm al Khashab, SAr. 112/D5
Umm al Qaywayn, UAE 113/G3
Umm Buru, Sudan 134/D2
Umm Dam, Sudan 134/F2
Umm Dhibbān, Sudan 134/G2
Umm Dhibbān, Sudan 134/F2
Umm Durmān (Omdurman), Sudan 134/G2
Umm el Faḥm, Isr. 117/C3
Umm Inderaba, Sudan 134/F2
Umm Jawzah, Jor. 117/D4
Umm Kaddādah, Sudan 135/E2
Umm Lajj, SAr. 127/H3
Umm Qaṣr, Iraq 115/F4
Umm Qawzayn, Sudan 135/E2
Umm Qays (Gedara) (ruin), Jor. 117/D3
Umm Ruwābah, Sudan 134/F2
Umm Sayyālah, Sudan 134/F2
Ummendorf, Ger. 67/F1
Umnak (isl.), Ak, US 201/E5
Umnak Pass (str.), Ak, US 201/E5
Umniati, Zim. 141/F3
Umniati (riv.), Zim. 141/F3
Umphang, Thai. 106/B2
Umpqua (riv.), Or, US 172/B3
Umpqua, Or, US 176/B2
Umpulo, Ang. 140/C2
Umraniye, Turk. 114/B2
Umred, India 107/C1
Ŭmsŏng, SKor. 93/D4
Umtata, SAfr. 142/E3
Umu Duru, Nga. 133/G5
Umuahia, Nga. 133/G5
Umuarama, Braz. 225/F2
Umuda (isl.), PNG 153/F2
Umunede, Nga. 133/G5
Umurbey, Turk. 81/K2
Umzimvubu (riv.), SAfr. 142/E3
Umzingwani (riv.), Zim. 141/F4
Umzinto, SAfr. 143/E3
Una, Braz. 223/F2
Una (riv.), Bosn.,Cro. 56/B3
Una, India 110/D4
Una (mt.), NZ 159/C3
Unadilla, Ga, US 192/F4
Unadilla, NY, US 191/J3
Unaí, Braz. 222/D3
Unaka (mts.), Tn, US 193/F2
Unalakleet, Ak, US 201/F3
Unalaska, Ak, US 201/E5
Unalaska (isl.), Ak, US 201/E5
Unas (isl.), Fin. 45/F4
'Unayzah, SAr. 112/D3
Uncastillo, Sp. 53/E1
Unchahra, India 108/C3
Uncompaghre (riv.), Co, US 177/K4
Uncompaghre (plat.), Co, US 177/J4
Uncompahgre (peak), Co, US 179/J1
Undaunda, Zam. 141/F2
Unden (lake), Swe. 46/F2
Undenheim, Ger. 64/B3
Underberg, SAfr. 142/E3
Underbool, Austl. 156/B2
Underwood, ND, US 186/D4
Underwood-Petersville, Al, US 192/D3
UNDOF Zone, Syria 117/D2
Undu (pt.), Fiji 161/Z17
Unduavi, Bol. 220/E5
Une, Col. 219/L8
Unecha, Rus. 76/E1
Unga (isl.), Ak, US 201/F4
Ungama (bay), Kenya 137/C2
Ungarie, Austl. 157/C1
Ungava (bay), Can. 171/K3
Ungava (pen.), Qu, Can. 171/J2
Unggi, NKor. 91/L3
Ungheni, Mol. 78/D4
Ungwariba (pt.), Austl. 153/E3
Unhošt, Czh. 65/H2
Unhŭng, NKor. 93/E2
União, Braz. 219/F4
União da Vitória, Braz. 225/G3
União dos Palmares, Braz. 219/G5
Unimak (isl.), Ak, US 201/E5
Unimak (str.), Ak, US 201/E5
Unini (riv.), Braz. 217/F5
Unini, Peru 220/C3
Unión, Arg. 226/D2
Unión, Par. 225/E3
Union (canal), Sc, UK 39/C5
Union, Al, US 192/D4
Union (mt.), Az, US 179/F3
Union, Mo, US 192/B1
Union, Ms, US 192/C4
Union, NJ, US 199/H9
Union (lake), NJ, US 198/C5
Union, Oh, US 190/D5
Union, Or, US 176/E1
Union, SC, US 193/G3
Union, WV, US 193/G2
Union Beach, NJ, US 199/J10
Union Bridge, Md, US 198/A4
Union Center, SD, US 184/C1
Union City, Ca, US 197/K11
Union City, Ga, US 193/L7
Union City, In, US 190/D4
Union City, Mi, US 190/D3
Union City, NJ, US 199/J8
Union City, Ok, US 183/F3
Union City, Pa, US 191/G4
Union City, Tn, US 192/C2
Union Creek, Or, US 176/B2
Unión de Reyes, Cuba 207/F1
Unión de Tula, Mex. 204/D5
Union Flat (cr.), Wa, US 174/F4
Union Grove, Wi, US 190/B3
Unión Hidalgo, Mex. 206/C2
Union Mills, Md, US 198/A4
Union Park, Fl, US 194/N6
Union Pier, Mi, US 190/C4
Union Point, Ga, US 193/F4
Union Springs, Al, US 192/E4
Union Springs, NY, US 191/H3
Uniondale, SAfr. 142/C4
Uniondale, NY, US 199/L9
Unionhall, Ire. 38/A6
Uniontown, Al, US 192/D4
Uniontown, Ar, US 183/G3
Uniontown, Ky, US 192/D2
Uniontown, Md, US 198/A4
Uniontown, Pa, US 191/G5
Unionville, Ga, US 195/G2
Unionville, In, US 190/C5
Unionville, Mi, US 190/E3
Unionville, Mo, US 185/H3
Unionville, Nv, US 176/D3
Unionville, On, Can. 190/U8
Unionville, Va, US 193/J1
Unita (riv.), Ut, US 177/J3
United Arab Emirates (ctry.) 112/F4
United Kingdom (ctry.) 37/*
United Nations, NY, US 199/K9
United Nations Mem. Cemetery, SKor. 96/A3
United States (ctry.) 172/*
United States (range), Nun, Can. 171/T6
United States Coast Guard Receiving Center, NJ, US 198/D6
United States Department of Energy, Md, US 198/A5
United States Naval Academy, Md, US 198/B6
United States Naval Reservation Mil. Res., PR 203/M8
Unitsa, Rus. 74/G3
Unity, Sk, Can. 175/K1
Unity (pond), Me, US 188/C3
Unity, Or, US 176/D1
Unity, Wi, US 185/J1
Universal City, Tx, US 180/E3
Universal Studios Florida, Fl, US 194/M7
University of Minnesota Landscape Arboretum, Mn, US 187/N7
University Park, NM, US 179/J4
University Park, Tx, US 180/L7
University Place, Wa, US 197/B3
Unjha, India 113/K4
Unjŏn, NKor. 93/C3
Unkel, Ger. 61/G2
Unkurda, Rus. 75/N5
Unley (nbrhd.), Austl. 155/M8
Unna, Ger. 59/E5
Unnão, India 108/C2
Ŭnp'a, NKor. 93/C3
Unsan, NKor. 93/C2
Ŭnsan-ŭp, NKor. 93/D3
Unshin (riv.), Ire. 38/B1
Unst (isl.), Sc, UK 37/W13
Unsu-Nodongjagu, NKor. 93/D2
Unter Pleichfeld, Ger. 64/D3
Unterägeri, Swi. 67/E3
Unterargen (riv.), Ger. 67/F2
Untergriesbach, Ger. 65/G5
Unterhaching, Ger. 65/E6
Unteriberg, Swi. 67/E3
Unterkulm, Swi. 66/E3
Unterlüss, Ger. 59/H3
Unterschleissheim, Ger. 65/E6
Untersee (lake), Swi. 67/E2
Unterseen, Swi. 66/D4
Untersiggenthal, Swi. 67/E3
Unterthingau, Ger. 67/G2
Untervaz, Swi. 67/F4
Unterweissenbach, Aus. 65/H6
Unuli Horog, China 111/F4
Unverre, Fr. 63/G4
Ünye, Turk. 76/F4
Unzen-Amakusa NP, Japan 96/A4
Unzen-dake (peak), Japan 96/B4
Unzha (riv.), Rus. 80/E4
Unzimkulu, SAfr. 143/E3
Uonquén, Ven. 217/F3
Uozu, Japan 97/E2
Upala, CR 207/E4
Upalco, Ut, US 177/H3
Upanema, Braz. 219/G4
Upata, Ven. 217/F2
Upemba (lake), D.R. Congo 139/F5
Upemba, PN de l', D.R. Congo 139/F5
Uphall, Sc, UK 39/C5
Upi, Phil. 100/D4
Upington, SAfr. 142/C3
Upinniemi (Obbnäs), Fin. 45/E4
Upiriwombe, Zam. 137/A4
Upland, In, US 190/D4
Upland, Pa, US 198/C4
Upleta, India 113/K4
Upminster (nbrhd.), Eng, UK 36/D2
Upolu (isl.), Sam. 161/S9
Upolu (pt.), Hi, US 172/S9
Upper (lake), Ca, US 176/C3
Upper (pen.), Mi, US 173/J2
Upper (bay), NJ,NY, US 199/J9
Upper (falls), Wy, US 177/H1
Upper Arlington, Oh, US 190/E4
Upper Arrow (lake), BC, Can. 174/F2
Upper Blackville, NB, Can. 188/E2
Upper Darby, Pa, US 198/C4
Upper Demerara-Berbice (pol. reg.), Guy. 217/G3
Upper Dicker, Eng, UK 43/G5
Upper East (pol. reg.), Gha. 133/E4
Upper Engadine (valley), Swi. 67/F5
Upper Fairmount, Md, US 193/K1
Upper Falls, Md, US 198/B5
Upper Ganges (canal), India 108/A1
Upper Hale, Eng, UK 36/A3
Upper Hutt, NZ 159/J9
Upper Iowa (riv.), Ia, US 185/J2
Upper Klamath (lake), Or, US 176/B2
Upper Klamath NWR, Or, US 176/C2
Upper Lake, Ca, US 176/B4
Upper Lough Erne (lake), NI, UK 37/Q9
Upper Marlboro (Marlboro), Md, US 198/B6
Upper Mesa (falls), Id, US 177/H1
Upper Missouri River Breaks Nat'l Mon., Mt, US 175/K4
Upper Ouachita NWR, La, US 181/H1
Upper Peoria (lake), Il, US 185/K3
Upper Red (lake), Mn, US 187/G3
Upper Rouge (riv.), Mi, US 197/F7
Upper Saddle River, NJ, US 199/J7
Upper Sandusky, Oh, US 190/E4
Upper Sioux Ind. Res., Mn, US 185/G1
Upper Souris NWR, ND, US 186/D3
Upper Takutu-Upper Essequibo (pol. reg.), Guy. 217/G4
Upper Thames (valley), Eng, UK 43/E3
Upper Trajan's Wall (wall), Mol. 76/D3
Upper Vaughan, NS, Can. 188/E3
Upper West (pol. reg.), Gha. 133/E4
Upper Yarra (res.), Austl. 157/B3
Upperglade, WV, US 193/G1
Upperlands, NI, UK 40/B2
Uppingham, Eng, UK 43/F1
Upplands-Bro, Swe. 45/A1
Upplands-Väsby, Swe. 46/G2
Uppsala (co.), Swe. 44/F3
Uppsala, Swe. 46/G2
Upsala, On, Can. 187/J3
Upshi, India 110/D3
Upson, Wi, US 187/J4
Upstart (cape), Austl. 158/B2
Upstart (bay), Austl. 153/G4
Upton, Wy, US 184/B1
Upton, Ky, US 192/E2
Upton upon Severn, Eng, UK 42/D2
Urabá (gulf), Col. 207/G4
Uracoa, Ven. 217/F2
Urad Qianqi, China 92/B2
Uraga (chan.), Japan 95/D3
Urahoro, Japan 94/C2
Urajärvi (lake), Fin. 45/F3
Urakawa, Japan 94/C2
Ural (riv.), Kaz.,Rus. 77/J2
Ural (mts.), Rus. 80/F3
Ural (Zhāyya) (riv.), Kaz.,Rus. 77/J2
Uralla, Austl. 156/D1
Ural'skiy, Rus. 77/J2
Ural'skoye, Rus. 77/L1
Urambo, Tanz. 139/H4
Urana (lake), Austl. 157/C2
Urana, Austl. 157/C2
Urangeline (cr.), Austl. 157/C2
Urania, La, US 194/B2
Uranium City, Sk, Can. 170/F3
Uranquinty, Austl. 157/C2
Urapunga, Austl. 152/D3
Uraras, Namb. 140/B4
Uraricoera (riv.), Braz. 217/F4
Uraricoera, Braz. 217/F4
Urasoe, Japan 97/J7
Uravan, Co, US 179/H1
Urawa, Japan 97/F3
Uray, Rus. 80/G3
Urayasu, Japan 95/D2
Urazovka, Rus. 75/K5
Urazovo, Rus. 79/K2
Urbach, Ger. 64/C5
Urbana, Mo, US 183/H2
Urbana, Il, US 190/B4
Urbana, Md, US 198/A5
Urbana, Oh, US 190/E4
Urbandale, Ia, US 185/H3
Urbania, It. 69/F6
Urbano Santos, Braz. 219/F3
Urbenville, Austl. 158/D5
Urbino, It. 69/F6
Urcos, Peru 220/D4
Urda, Kaz. 77/H2
Urda, Sp. 52/D3
Urdinarrain, Arg. 191/J10
Urdorf, Swi. 67/E3
Urdzhar, Kaz. 111/D2
Ure (riv.), Eng, UK 41/G3
Urein, Egypt 131/B3
Ureki, Geo. 77/G4
Urengoy, Rus. 80/H3
Ures, Mex. 204/C2
Ureshino, Japan 95/K6
Ureterp, Neth. 58/D2
Urewera NP, NZ 159/D2
Urfa, Turk. 114/D2
Urfa (prov.), Turk. 114/D2
Urft (lake), Ger. 61/F2
Urft (riv.), Ger. 59/G6
Urgal, Rus. 91/L1
Urganch, Uzb. 80/G5
Urgnano, It. 68/C2
Urho Kekkosen NP, Fin. 44/H1
Uri, India 110/C2
Uri-Rotstock (peak), Swi. 67/E4
Uriah, Al, US 194/E2
Uriangato, Mex. 205/E4
Uribante (riv.), Ven. 216/D3
Uribia, Col. 216/C2
Uricani, Rom. 78/B5
Urich, Mo, US 183/G1
Urie (riv.), Sc, UK 39/D2
Urim, Isr. 117/B6
Urimán, Ven. 217/F3
Uriménil, Fr. 66/C1
Uriondo, Bol. 224/C2
Urique (riv.), Mex. 204/D3
Uriranteriña, Ven. 217/F3
Uritskiy, Kaz. 80/G4
Urjala, Fin. 47/K1
Urk, Neth. 58/C3
Urla, Turk. 76/C5
Urlaţi, Rom. 57/H3
Urlingford, Ire. 38/C4
Urman, Rus. 75/N5
Urmar, India 110/C4
Urmi (riv.), Rus. 90/L2
Urmia (lake), Iran 115/F2
Urmitz, Ger. 61/G3
Urmston, Eng, UK 41/F5
Urnäsch, Swi. 67/F3
Urnersee (lake), Swi. 67/E4
Uroševac, Serb. 56/E4
Urr Water (riv.), Sc, UK 40/E1
Urrin (riv.), Ire. 38/D4
Ursensollen, Ger. 65/E4
Ursulo Galván, Mex. 205/N7
Urtazym, Rus. 77/L1
Uru Uru (lake), Bol. 224/C1
Uruaçu, Braz. 222/C2
Uruapan, Mex. 178/D5
Uruapan, Mex. 204/E5
Urubamba, Peru 220/C4
Urubamba (riv.), Peru 220/C3
Urubichá, Bol. 221/F4
Urubu (riv.), Braz. 217/G5
Urubuquara (hill), Braz. 218/C3
Uruburetama, Braz. 219/G3
Urucará, Braz. 218/B3
Urucu (riv.), Braz. 221/E2
Uruçuí, Braz. 219/E4
Uruçuí Preto (riv.), Braz. 219/E5
Uruçuí, Serra do (mts.), Braz. 219/E5
Urucuia (riv.), Braz. 222/D3
Urucurituba, Braz. 218/B3
Uruguai (riv.), Braz. 225/F3

Urugu – Verno
340

Uruguaiana, Braz. 225/E4
Uruguay (ctry.) 209/D6
Uruguay (riv.), SAm. 209/D5
Urumaco, Ven. 216/D2
Ürümqi (int'l arpt.), China 111/E3
Ürümqi, China 111/E3
Urunga, Austl. 156/E1
Uruoca, Braz. 219/F3
Urup (isl.), Rus. 83/Q5
Ururi, It. 71/E4
Urus-Martan, Rus. 77/H4
Urussanga, Braz. 225/G4
Urussu, Rus. 77/K1
Uruwira, Tanz. 139/G4
Uruyén, Ven. 217/F3
Uryumkan (riv.), Rus. 91/H1
Uryupinsk, Rus. 79/M2
Urzhum, Rus. 75/L4
Urziceni, Rom. 57/H3
Us, Fr. 36/H4
Us (riv.), Rus. 90/C1
Usa (riv.), Rus. 80/F3
Usa, Japan 96/B4
USAF Academy, Co, US 184/B4
USAF Res., Tn, US 192/D3
Usagara, Tanz. 137/A2
Uşak, Turk. 114/B2
Uşak (prov.), Turk. 114/B2
Usakos, Namb. 140/B4
Usborne (mt.), UK 191/F6
Uscio, It. 68/C5
Usedom (isl.), Ger. 46/E4
Usedom, Ger. 46/E5
Useldange, Lux. 61/E4
Useless Loop, Austl. 154/B3
Usevia, Tanz. 139/G4
'Usfān, SAr. 112/C4
Ushachi, Bela. 47/N4
Ushaki, Rus. 47/P2
Ushashi, Tanz. 137/A2
'Ushayrah, SAr. 112/D4
Ushetu, Tanz. 139/H4
Ushibori, Japan 95/F2
Ushibuka, Japan 96/B4
Ushiku, Japan 95/E2
Ushirombo, Tanz. 139/G3
Ushkovo, Rus. 75/S6
Ushtobe, Kaz. 111/C2
Ushuaia, Arg. 191/C7
Ushumun, Rus. 91/K1
Usi, NKor. 93/C2
Usibelli, Ak, US 201/J3
Usicayos, Peru 220/D4
Usilampatti, India 104/C6
Usinge, Tanz. 139/G4
Usingen, Ger. 64/B2
Usino, PNG 153/G1
Usinsk, Rus. 80/E4
Üsküdar (nbrhd.), Turk. 115/N7
Üsküp, Turk. 57/H5
Uslar, Ger. 59/G5
Usman', Rus. 76/F1
Usoke, Tanz. 139/H4
Usol'ye-Sibirskoye, Rus. 90/E1
Uson, Phil. 100/C2
Uspallata, Arg. 226/C2
Uspallata, Paso de (pass), Chile 226/N8
Uspenka, Ukr. 79/K3
Usquil, Peru 220/B2
Ussel, Fr. 50/E4
Ussel (riv.), Ger. 64/D5
Usses (riv.), Fr. 66/C5
Ussoque, Ang. 140/B2
Ussure, Tanz. 137/A3
Ussuri (riv.), China,Rus. 81/P5
Ussuriysk, Rus. 91/L3
Ussy-sur-Marne, Fr. 36/M5
Ust'-Barguzin, Rus. 90/F1
Ust'-Ilimsk, Rus. 81/L4
Ust'-Ishim, Rus. 80/H4
Ust'-Kamchatsk, Rus. 81/S4
Ust'-Karsk, Rus. 91/H1
Ust'-Kulom, Rus. 75/M3
Ust'-Kut, Rus. 81/L4
Ust'-Kuyga, Rus. 81/P2
Ust'-Labinsk, Rus. 79/K5
Ust'-Luga, Rus. 47/N2
Ust'-Man'ya, Rus. 75/P3
Ust'-Maya, Rus. 81/P3
Ust'-Nera, Rus. 81/Q3
Ust'-Ocheya, Rus. 75/L3
Ust'-Olenëk, Rus. 81/M2
Ust'-Omchug, Rus. 81/Q3
Ust'-Ordynskiy, Rus. 90/E1
Ust'-Ordynskiy Buryatskiy Aut. Okrug, Rus. 81/Q6
Ust'-Pinega, Rus. 74/J2
Ust'-Port, Rus. 80/J3
Ust'-Pozhva, Rus. 75/N4
Ust'-Tsil'ma, Rus. 75/M2
Ust'-Uda, Rus. 90/E1
Ústecký (pol. reg.), Czh. 49/G3
Úštěk, Czh. 65/H1
Uster, Swi. 67/E3
Ustica, It. 54/C3
Ustica (isl.), It. 73/G3
Ustka, Pol. 46/G4
Ustrzyki Dolne, Pol. 49/M4
Ust'ya (riv.), Rus. 75/K3
Ustyurt (plat.), Kaz. 83/D5
Ustyuzhna, Rus. 74/H4
Usu, China 111/D3
Usuda, Japan 95/A1
Usuki, Japan 96/B4
Usulután, ESal. 206/D3
Usuma, D.R. Congo 135/E4
Usumacinta (riv.), Mex. 202/C4
Uta, Indo. 103/J4
Utah (state), US 172/D4
Utah (lake), Ut, US 177/G3
Utah Beach, Fr. 62/D2
Utah Test and Training Range, Ut, US 177/G3
Utale, Malw. 141/G2
Utangan (riv.), India 108/A2
Utano, Japan 95/J7
Utashinai, Japan 94/C2
'Utaybah (lake), Syria 117/F1
Ute (cr.), NM, US 182/C2
Ute Mountain Ind. Res., Co, US 179/H2
Utembo (riv.), Ang. 140/D3
Utena, Lith. 47/L4
Utengule, Tanz. 137/A4
Utero (peak), It. 71/C2
Uterský (riv.), Czh. 65/G3
Utete, Tanz. 137/B3
Uthai Thani, Thai. 106/C3
Utica, NY, US 191/J3
Utica, Oh, US 190/E4
Utica, Mi, US 197/F6
Utica, Mo, US 185/H4
Utica, Ne, US 185/F3
Utica, Ms, US 192/B4
Utiel, Sp. 52/E3
Utila (isl.), Hon. 206/E2
Utinga, Braz. 223/E2
Utirik (isl.), Mrsh. 160/G3
Utiroa, Kiri. 160/G5
Utlyukskiy Estuary (estu.), Ukr. 79/H4
Utmānzai, Pak. 110/A2
Utnūr, India 107/C2
Utö (isl.), Swe. 45/B2
Utö, Swe. 45/B2
Utopia, Austl. 155/G2
Utopia, Tx, US 180/E3
Utopia Abor. Land, Austl. 155/G2
Utorgosh, Rus. 47/P2
Utraulā, India 108/D2
Utrecht (prov.), Neth. 58/C4
Utrecht, Neth. 58/C4
Utrecht, SAfr. 143/E2
Utrera, Sp. 52/C4
Utsunomiya, Japan 97/F2
Utta, Rus. 77/H3
Uttar Patiata, Bang. 109/G3
Uttar Pradesh (state), India 111/C6
Uttaradit, Thai. 106/C2
Uttaranchal (state), India 108/B1
Uttendorf, Aus. 65/G6
Uttenweiler, Ger. 67/F1
Uttoxeter, Eng, UK 41/G6
Utuado, PR 203/M8
Utupua (isl.), Sol. 160/F6
Uturoa, FrPol. 161/K6
Utzenstorf, Swi. 66/D3
Uulu, Est. 47/L2
Üür (riv.), Mong. 90/E1
Üüreg (lake), Mong. 90/C1
Uusikaupunki, Fin. 47/J1
Uusimaa (prov.), Fin. 44/H3
Uva (riv.), Col. 216/D4
Uva (prov.), SrL. 107/D5
Uvalda, Ga, US 195/G1
Uvalde, Tx, US 180/E3
Uvarovo, Rus. 77/G2
Uvel'skiy, Rus. 75/P5
Uverito, Ven. 217/E2
Uvinza, Tanz. 139/G4
Uvira, D.R. Congo 139/G3
Uvongo, SAfr. 143/E3
Uvs (lake), Mong. 90/C1
Uvs (prov.), Mong. 90/C2
Uvs Nuur (lake), Mong. 111/F1
Uwajima, Japan 96/C4
'Uwaybid (peak), Egypt 131/D4
Uwayl, Sudan 135/E3
Uwekuli, Indo. 103/F4
Uwimmerah (riv.), Indo. 103/K5
Uxbridge (nbrhd.), Eng, UK 36/B2
Uxin Qi, China 92/B3
Uxmal (ruin), Mex. 206/D1
Üydzin, Mong. 90/F3
Uyo, Nga. 133/G5
Üyönch, Mong. 90/C2
Uyu (riv.), Myan. 98/B3
Uyuni, Bol. 224/C2
Uzbekistan (ctry.) 80/G5
Uzcudún, Arg. 226/D5
Uzein (int'l arpt.), Fr. 50/C5
Uzel, Fr. 62/C4
Uzen', Kaz. 77/K4
Uzerche, Fr. 50/D4
Uzès, Fr. 50/F4
Uzhhorod, Ukr. 49/M4
Uzhok (pass), Ukr. 49/M4
Užice, Serb. 56/D4
Uzlovaya, Rus. 76/F1
Uznach, Swi. 67/E3
Üzümlü, Turk. 114/D2
Uzunköprü, Turk. 57/H5
Užventis, Lith. 47/K4
Uzwil, Swi. 67/F3
Uzyn, Ukr. 78/F3

V

V.P. Rosales, PN, Chile 226/B4
Vääksy, Fin. 45/F3
Vaal (riv.), SAfr. 119/E7
Vaala, Fin. 44/H2
Vaalbos NP, SAfr. 142/D3
Vaaldam (res.), SAfr. 142/D2
Vaals, Neth. 61/F2
Vaalserberg (hill), Neth. 61/E2
Vaalwater, SAfr. 141/F5
Vaas, Fr. 63/F5
Vaasa (int'l arpt.), Fin. 44/G3
Vaasa (prov.), Fin. 44/G3
Vaasa (Vasa), Fin. 44/G3
Vaassen, Neth. 58/C4
Vabalninkas, Lith. 47/L4
Vác, Hun. 56/D2
Vaca (mt.), Ca, US 197/K10
Vaca (mts.), Ca, US 197/K10
Vacacai (riv.), Braz. 225/F4
Vacaria, Braz. 225/G4
Vacaria (riv.), Braz. 222/B4
Vacaville, Ca, US 176/C4
Vaccares (swamp), Fr. 70/A6
Vachères (peak), Fr. 70/B3
Vachères (riv.), Fr. 70/C3
Vachi, Rus. 77/H4
Vachon (riv.), Qu, Can. 171/J2
Vacov, Czh. 65/G4
Vad, Rus. 75/K5
Vada, It. 68/D7
Vaden, Ar, US 183/H4
Vadheim, Nor. 46/A1
Vado, NM, US 180/A1
Vado Ligure, It. 68/B5
Vadodara (Baroda), India 104/B3
Vadret (peak), Swi. 67/F4
Vadsø, Nor. 44/J1
Vadstena, Swe. 46/F2
Vadul lui Voda, Mol. 78/E4
Vaduz (cap.), Lcht. 67/F3
Vaernes (int'l arpt.), Nor. 44/D3
Vaga (riv.), Rus. 74/J3
Vågå, Nor. 44/D3
Vågan, Nor. 44/E1
Vaganski Vrh (peak), Cro. 56/B3
Vagay (riv.), Rus. 75/R4
Vaggeryd, Swe. 46/F3
Vagney, Fr. 66/C1
Vagnhärad, Swe. 45/A2
Vagos, Port. 52/A2
Vågsøy, Nor. 44/C3
Vah (riv.), Slvk. 49/J4
Vahermanjärvi (lake), Fin. 45/E4
Vahitahi (isl.), FrPol. 161/M6
Vaiano, It. 69/E6
Vaiano Cremasco, It. 68/C3
Vaich (lake), Sc, UK 39/B1
Vaiden, Ms, US 192/C4
Vaige (riv.), Fr. 63/E5
Vaiges, Fr. 63/E4
Vaihingen an der Enz, Ger. 64/B5
Vaijāpur, India 113/K5
Väike-Maarja, Est. 47/M2
Vail, Az, US 179/G4
Vailate, It. 68/C3
Vailsburg (nbrhd.), NJ, US 199/J9
Vaiņode, Lat. 47/J3
Vair (riv.), Fr. 66/B1
Vairano Patenora, It. 71/D5
Vaire (riv.), Fr. 70/C4
Vaisali (riv.), India 108/B2
Vaison-la-Romaine, Fr. 70/B4
Vaitupu (isl.), Tuv. 160/G5
Vaivre-et-Montoille, Fr. 66/C2
Vakaga (pref.), CAfr. 134/D3
Vakfıkebir, Turk. 76/F4
Vakh (riv.), Rus. 80/J3
Vākhān (mts.), Afg. 113/K1
Vakhrushev, Rus. 91/N2
Vakhrushi, Rus. 75/L4
Vakhsh (riv.), Taj. 113/J1
Vakhtan, Rus. 75/K4
Vál, Hun. 56/D2
Val de Cans (int'l arpt.), Braz. 218/D3
Val Lagarina (valley), It. 69/D1
Val Marie, Sk, Can. 175/L3
Val Venosta (valley), It. 67/G4
Val Verde, Ca, US 196/B2
Val-Brillant, Qu, Can. 188/D1
Val-d'Oise (dept.), Fr. 63/G2
Val-David, Qu, Can. 191/J1
Val-de-Marne (dept.), Fr. 60/B6
Val-de-Reuil, Fr. 63/G2
Val-des-Monts, Qu, Can. 191/J2
Val-d'Isère, Fr. 70/C2
Val-d'Or, Qu, Can. 171/J4
Valais (canton), Swi. 66/D5
Valajärvi (lake), Fin. 45/E4
Valaská Belá, Slvk. 49/K4
Valbo, Swe. 46/G1
Valburg, Neth. 58/C5
Valcheta, Arg. 226/D4
Valcourt, Qu, Can. 191/K2
Valdagno, It. 69/E2
Valdahon, Fr. 66/C3
Valdai (hills), Rus. 74/G4
Valdarno (valley), It. 69/E5
Valday, Rus. 74/G4
Valdecañas (res.), Sp. 52/C3
Valdemarpils, Lat. 47/K3
Valdemarsvik, Swe. 46/G2
Valdemorillo, Sp. 53/M8
Valdense, Uru. 191/K11
Valdepeñas, Sp. 52/D3
Valderas, Sp. 52/C1
Valderrobres, Sp. 53/F2
Valdés (pen.), Arg. 209/C7
Valdeverdeja, Sp. 52/C3
Valdez, Ecu. 216/B4
Valdez, Ak, US 201/J3
Valdivia, Col. 216/C3
Valdivia, Chile 226/B3
Valdobbiadene, It. 69/F2
Valdoie, Fr. 66/C2
Valdosta, Ga, US 195/G2
Valdoviño, Sp. 52/A1
Vale, Chl, UK 62/C2
Vale, Geo. 77/G4
Vale, Or, US 176/E2
Vale of Conwy (valley), Wal, UK 40/E5
Vale of Evesham (valley), Eng, UK 42/D2
Vale of Glamorgan (co.), Wal, UK 42/C4
Vale of Pickering (valley), Eng, UK 41/H3
Vale of Powys (valley), Wal, UK 42/C1
Vale of St. Albans (valley), Eng, UK 36/B1
Vale of Sussex (valley), Eng, UK 43/F4
Vale of York (valley), Eng, UK 41/G3
Valea lui Mihai, Rom. 49/M5
Valeggio sul Mincio, It. 69/D3
Valemount, BC, Can. 174/E1
Valença, Port. 52/A1
Valença, Braz. 223/N7
Valença, Braz. 223/F2
Valença do Piauí, Braz. 219/F4
Valence, Fr. 70/A3
Valence, Fr. 50/D4
Valence-sur-Baïse, Fr. 50/D5
Valencia, Ecu. 216/B5
Valencia (isl.), Ire. 36/P11
Valencia, Phil. 100/D4
Valencia, Phil. 100/D3
Valencia, Sp. 53/E3
Valencia (state), Sp. 52/E2
Valencia (int'l arpt.), Sp. 53/E3
Valencia, NM, US 179/J3
Valencia, Ven. 219/M7
Valencia (lake), Ven. 219/N7
Valencia (int'l arpt.), Ven. 219/N7
Valencia de Alcántara, Sp. 52/B3
Valencia de Don Juan, Sp. 52/C1
Valenciennes, Fr. 60/C3
Valendas, Swi. 67/F4
Vălenii de Munte, Rom. 57/H3
Valensole, Fr. 70/B5
Valentigney, Fr. 66/C3
Valentin, Rus. 91/L3
Valentine, Az, US 179/F3
Valentine, Ne, US 184/D2
Valentine, Tx, US 180/B2
Valentine Nat'l Wild. Ref., Ne, US 184/D2
Valentines, Uru. 191/G2
Valentines, Va, US 193/J2
Valenton, Fr. 36/K5
Valenza, It. 68/B3
Valenzuela, Phil. 100/E6
Våler, Nor. 46/D2
Våler, Nor. 46/D1
Valera, Ven. 216/D2
Valfabbrica, It. 71/B1
Valff, Fr. 66/D1
Valga, Est. 47/M3
Valhalla, NY, US 199/K7
Valier (peak), Fr. 53/F1
Valier, Il, US 192/C1
Valier, Mt, US 175/H3
Valinco (gulf), Fr. 54/A2
Valinhos, Braz. 223/J7
Valjevo, Serb. 56/D3
Valka, Lat. 47/M3
Valkeakoski, Fin. 47/K1
Valkeala, Fin. 47/M1
Valkenburg, Neth. 61/E2
Valkenswaard, Neth. 58/C6
Valkininkai, Lith. 47/L4
Valky, Ukr. 79/H3
Vall de Uxó, Sp. 53/E3
Valladolid, Mex. 206/D1
Valladolid, Sp. 52/C2
Valladolid (int'l arpt.), Sp. 52/C2
Vallangoujard, Fr. 36/J4
Vallauris, Fr. 70/D5
Valle, Nor. 46/B2
Valle, Ecu. 216/B5
Valle d Aosta (pol.reg.), It. 51/G4
Valle D'Aosta (pol. reg.), It. 70/D1
Valle d'Aosta (valley), It. 70/D1
Valle de Bravo, Mex. 205/E5
Valle de Cauca (dept.), Col. 216/B4
Valle de Encantado, PN, Chile 224/B4
Valle de Guanape, Ven. 217/E2
Valle de La Pascua, Ven. 219/P8
Valle de Santiago, Mex. 205/E4
Valle Fértil (valley), Arg. 224/C4
Valle Hermoso, Mex. 205/F3
Valle Lomellina, It. 68/B3
Valle, Río del (riv.), Arg. 224/C4
Valle Mosso, It. 68/B2
Vallecas (nbrhd.), Sp. 53/N9
Vallecillo, Mex. 180/E4
Vallecitos, NM, US 179/J2
Vallecitos de Zaragoza, Mex. 205/E5
Vallecorsa, It. 71/C5
Vallecrosia, It. 70/D5
Valledupar, Col. 216/C2
Valleé de l'Azaouak (riv.), Mali 133/G2
Vallée du Ferlo (riv.), Sen. 132/B3
Valleé du Mboune (riv.), Sen. 132/B3
Valleé du Saloum (riv.), Sen. 132/B3
Valleé du Serpent (riv.), Mali 132/C3
Vallée-Jonction, Qu, Can. 188/B2
Vallegrande, Bol. 224/C1
Vallehermoso, Sp. 128/A3
Vallejo, Ca, US 176/B4
Vallenar, Chile 224/B4
Vallendar, Ger. 61/G3
Vallentuna, Swe. 45/B1
Vallerano, It. 71/B3
Valleroy, Fr. 61/E5
Valles Mines, Mo, US 192/B1
Valletta (cap.), Malta 54/M7
Valley, Al, US 192/E4
Valley, Wa, US 174/F3
Valley Center, Ca, US 196/C4
Valley Centre, Sk, Can. 175/L2
Valley City, ND, US 186/E4
Valley Cottage, NY, US 199/K7
Valley East, On, Can. 190/F1
Valley Falls, Or, US 176/C2
Valley Falls, Ks, US 185/G4
Valley Farms, Az, US 179/G4
Valley Forge Nat'l Hist. Park, Pa, US 198/C3
Valley Head, Al, US 192/E3
Valley Head, WV, US 193/G1
Valley Mills, Tx, US 180/F2
Valley of Desolation, SAfr. 142/D4
Valley of the Kings, Egypt 127/G3
Valley Park, Ms, US 192/B4
Valley River, Mb, Can. 186/D2
Valley Spring, Tx, US 181/E2
Valley Springs, Ar, US 183/H2
Valley Stream, NY, US 199/L9
Valley View, Tx, US 183/F4
Valleyfair, Mn, US 187/N7
Valleyford, Wa, US 174/F4
Valleyview, Ab, Can. 170/E3
Vallière (riv.), Fr. 66/B4
Vallimanca, Arroyo (stream), Arg. 226/E3
Vallo della Lucania, It. 54/D2
Valloire, Fr. 70/C2
Vallorbe, Swi. 66/C4
Valls, Sp. 53/F2
Valluga (peak), Aus. 67/G3
Valmayor (res.), Sp. 53/M8
Valme (riv.), Ger. 59/F6
Valmiera, Lat. 47/L3
Valmondois, Fr. 36/J4
Valmont, NM, US 180/B1
Valmontone, It. 71/B4
Valmy, Wi, US 190/C2
Valmy, Nv, US 176/E3
Valognes, Fr. 62/D2
Valois (reg.), Fr. 60/B5
Valona, Ga, US 195/H2
Valpaços, Port. 52/B2
Vālpārai, India 107/C4
Valparaiso, In, US 190/C4
Valparaiso, Fl, US 195/E2
Valparaíso (pol. reg.), Chile 226/C2
Valparaiso, Ne, US 185/F3
Valparaíso, Col. 219/K7
Valparaíso, Chile 226/N8
Valparaíso, Mex. 204/E4
Valperga, It. 70/D2
Valpovo, Cro. 56/D3
Valréas, Fr. 70/A4
Valrico, Fl, US 194/L8
Vals, Swi. 67/F4
Vals (cape), Indo. 153/E2
Vals (riv.), SAfr. 142/D2
Vals-les-Bains, Fr. 50/F4
Valsaquillo (res.), Mex. 205/L8
Valsbaai (bay), SAfr. 142/B4
Valserine (riv.), Fr. 66/B5
Valserrhein (riv.), Swi. 67/F4
Valsura (riv.), It. 67/G4
Valtellina (valley), It. 67/F5
Valuyki, Rus. 79/K2
Valverde, Sp. 128/A4
Valverde del Camino, Sp. 52/B4
Valyermo, Ca, US 196/C2
Våmhus, Swe. 46/F1
Vamizi (isl.), Moz. 141/J1
Vammala, Fin. 47/K1
Vamori Wash (riv.), Az, US 179/F5
Vámos, Gre. 55/J5
Vámosmikola, Hun. 56/D2
Vámospércs, Hun. 56/E2
Van, Turk. 115/E2
Van (lake), Turk. 80/E6
Van (pt.), Fr. 62/A4
Van, Or, US 176/D2
Van, WV, US 193/G2
Van (prov.), Turk. 115/E2
Van, Tx, US 181/G1
Van Alstyne, Tx, US 183/F4
Van Buren, Ar, US 183/G3
Van Buren, Mo, US 192/B2
Van Cortlandt Park, NY, US 199/K8
Van Diemen (cape), Austl. 153/E4
Van Diemen (cape), Austl. 152/C2
Van Diemen (gulf), Austl. 145/C2
Van Harinxmakanaal (riv.), Neth. 58/C2
Van Hoa, Viet. 106/D1
Van Horn, Tx, US 180/B2
Van Lear, Ky, US 193/F2
Van Ninh, Viet. 106/E3
Van Norman Lakes, Ca, US 196/B2
Van Nuys (nbrhd.), Ca, US 196/F7
Van Rees (mts.), Indo. 103/J4
Van Vleck, Tx, US 181/G3
Van Wert, Oh, US 190/D4
Van Wert, Ia, US 185/H3
Van Yen, Viet. 106/D1
Vana-Javesi (lake), Fin. 47/K1
Vanadzor, Arm. 77/H4
Vananda, Mt, US 175/L4
Vanavara, Rus. 81/L3
Vanavaro (isl.), FrPol. 161/L7
Vance (A.F.B.), Ok, US 183/F2
Vanceboro, NC, US 193/J3
Vanceburg, Ky, US 193/F1
Vancon (riv.), Fr. 70/C4
Vancourt, Tx, US 180/D2
Vancouver (cape), Austl. 154/C5
Vancouver, BC, Can. 174/C3
Vancouver (isl.), BC, Can. 170/D4
Vancouver (int'l arpt.), BC, Can. 174/C3
Vancouver (mt.), Yk, Can. 201/L3
Vancouver, Wa, US 174/C5
Vandalia, Oh, US 190/D5
Vandalia, Il, US 192/C1
Vandalia, Mo, US 185/J4
Vandalia, Mt, US 175/L3
Vandans, Aus. 67/F3
Vandenberg (A.F.B.), Ca, US 178/B3
Vanderbijlpark, SAfr. 142/D2
Vanderbilt, Tx, US 181/F3
Vanderbilt Museum, NY, US 199/E2
Vanderhoof, BC, Can. 170/D3
Vanderlin (isl.), Austl. 153/E3
Vanderlin Abor. Land, Austl. 153/E3
Vandervoort, Ar, US 183/G3
Vandœuvre-Lès-Nancy, Fr. 61/F6
Vändra, Est. 47/L2
Vandra (riv.), It. 71/D4
Vandysh, Rus. 74/J3
Vandžiogala, Lith. 47/K4
Vanegas, Mex. 205/E4
Vänern (lake), Swe. 80/B4
Vänersborg, Swe. 46/E2
Vanga, Kenya 137/B3
Vangaindrano, Madg. 143/H8
Vanguard, Sk, Can. 175/L3
Vanier, On, Can. 191/J2
Vanier (isl.), Nun, Can. 171/R7
Vanikolo (isl.), Sol. 160/F6
Vanil Noir (peak), Swi. 66/D4
Vanimo, PNG 160/D5
Vanino, Rus. 91/N2
Vännäs, Swe. 44/F3
Vanndale, Ar, US 192/B3
Vanne (riv.), Fr. 50/E2
Vannes, Fr. 62/C5
Vanoise, PN, Fr. 51/G4
Vanreenenpas (pass), SAfr. 142/E3
Vanrhynsdorp, SAfr. 142/B3
Vanrook, Austl. 158/A2
Vansant, Va, US 193/F2
Vansbro, Swe. 46/F1
Vanscoy, Sk, Can. 175/L1
Vanse, Nor. 46/B2
Vansittart (isl.), Nun, Can. 171/H2
Vansittart (bay), Austl. 152/B3
Vantaa, Fin. 47/L1
Vantage, Sk, Can. 175/L3
Vantage, Wa, US 174/E4
Vanua Levu (isl.), Fiji 160/G6
Vanuatu (ctry.) 160/F6
Vanwyksvlei, SAfr. 142/C3
Vanzant, Mo, US 183/H2
Vapnyarka, Ukr. 78/E3
Var (dept.), Fr. 70/C5
Var (riv.), Fr. 51/G5
Vara, Swe. 46/E2
Vara (riv.), It. 68/C4
Varadero, Cuba 207/F1
Varades, Fr. 63/D6
Varaita (riv.), It. 68/A3
Varaita (riv.), Fr. 70/D3
Varakļāni, Lat. 47/M3
Varalé, C.d'Iv. 132/E4
Varallo, It. 68/B2
Varāmīn, Iran 115/G3
Vārānāsi, India 108/D3
Varandey, Rus. 75/N1
Varanger-Halvøya (pen.), Nor. 44/J1
Varangerfjorden (estu.), Nor. 44/J1
Varangéville, Fr. 61/F6
Varano (lake), It. 54/D2
Varano Borghi, It. 68/B2
Varaždin, Cro. 56/C2
Varazze, It. 68/B5
Varberg, Swe. 46/E3
Varces-Allières-et-Risset, Fr. 70/B2
Vardaman, Ms, US 192/C4
Vardar (riv.), FYROM 73/J2
Varde, Den. 46/C4
Vardenis, Arm. 115/F1
Várdha, Gre. 55/G3
Vardø, Nor. 44/J1
Varel, Ger. 59/F2
Varėna, Lith. 47/L4
Varengeville-sur-Mer, Fr. 63/F1
Varenikovskaya, Rus. 79/J5
Varenne (riv.), Fr. 50/C2
Varennes, Qu, Can. 189/P6
Varennes-Jarcy, Fr. 36/K5
Varennes-Vauzelles, Fr. 50/E3
Vareš, Bosn. 56/D3
Varese (prov.), It. 67/E6
Varese, It. 68/B2
Varese Ligure, It. 68/C5
Varèze (riv.), Fr. 70/A2
Vårgårda, Swe. 46/E2
Vargem Grande, Braz. 219/F3
Vargem Grande do Sul, Braz. 223/K6
Varginha, Braz. 223/L6
Varik, Neth. 58/C5
Varilhes, Fr. 50/D5
Varillas, Chile 224/B3
Varkala, India 107/C4
Värmdö, Swe. 45/B1
Värmdölandet (isl.), Swe. 45/B1
Värmeln (lake), Swe. 46/E2
Värmland (co.), Swe. 44/E3
Varna, Bul. 57/H4
Varna (int'l arpt.), Bul. 57/H4
Varna (pol. reg.), Bul. 57/H4
Varna, Rus. 75/P5
Värnamo, Swe. 46/F3
Varnek, Rus. 75/N1
Varniai, Lith. 47/K4
Varnville, SC, US 193/G4
Varois-et-Chaignot, Fr. 66/B3
Varoška Rijeka, Bosn. 56/C3
Várpalota, Hun. 56/D2
Varraddes, Fr. 36/L5
Vars, Fr. 70/C3
Varsi, It. 68/C4
Värska, Est. 47/M3
Vårsta, Swe. 46/G2
Vartashen, Azer. 77/H4
Vartholomión, Gre. 55/G4
Varto, Turk. 114/E2
Vartry (res.), Ire. 40/B5
Vartry (riv.), Ire. 40/B5
Varva, Ukr. 79/G1
Varzaneh, Iran 115/H3
Várzea Alegre, Braz. 219/G4
Várzea da Palma, Braz. 222/D3
Várzea Grande, Braz. 222/A2
Várzea Grande, Braz. 219/F4
Varzi, It. 68/C4
Varzo, It. 67/E5
Varzuga (riv.), Rus. 74/H2
Vas (prov.), Hun. 56/C2
Vasa (Vaasa), Fin. 44/G3
Vasa Barris (riv.), Braz. 223/F1
Vasai (Bassein), India 113/K5
Vasanello, It. 71/B3
Vásárosnamény, Hun. 49/M4
Vaşcău, Rom. 56/F2
Vashka (riv.), Rus. 75/K2
Vashon (isl.), Wa, US 197/C3
Vashon, Wa, US 197/C3
Vasile Roaită, Rom. 57/J3
Vasilevichi, Bela. 78/E1
Vasiliká, Gre. 55/H2
Vasil'yevskiy (isl.), Rus. 75/T7
Vaslui, Rom. 78/D4
Vaslui (prov.), Rom. 57/H2
Vassar, Mb, Can. 186/G3
Vassar, Mi, US 190/E3
Vassdalsegga (peak), Nor. 46/B2
Vassés (Bassae) (ruin), Gre. 55/G4
Vassouras, Braz. 223/N7
Vassy, Fr. 63/E3
Västerås, Swe. 46/G2
Västerbotten (co.), Swe. 44/F2
Västerdalälven (riv.), Swe. 46/E1
Västerhaninge, Swe. 45/B1
Västerljung, Swe. 45/A2
Västernorrland (co.), Swe. 44/F3
Västervik, Swe. 46/G3
Västmanland (co.), Swe. 44/E3
Vasto, It. 71/D3
Västra Silen (lake), Swe. 46/E2
Vasvár, Hun. 56/C2
Vasylivka, Ukr. 79/H4
Vasyl'kiv, Ukr. 78/F2
Vasyl'kivka, Ukr. 79/J3
Vasyurinskaya, Rus. 79/K5
Vaterstetten, Ger. 65/E6
Vatican City (ctry.) 71/F7
Vatican Gardens, VatC. 71/G7
Vatican Museums, VatC. 71/G7
Vatnajökull (glacier), Ice. 44/P7
Vatneyri, Ice. 44/M6
Vatö (isl.), Swe. 45/B1
Vatomandry, Madg. 143/J7
Vatra Dornei, Rom. 78/C4
Vättern (lake), Swe. 44/E4
Vatukoula, Fiji 161/Y18
Vatutine, Ukr. 78/F3
Vaucluse (dept.), Fr. 70/A4
Vaucluse, SC, US 193/G4
Vaucluse, Monts de (mts.), Fr. 70/B5
Vaucouleurs (riv.), Fr. 36/H5
Vaud (canton), Swi. 66/C4
Vaudelle (riv.), Fr. 63/E4
Vaudoy-en-Brie, Fr. 36/M5
Vaudreuil (co.), Qu, Can. 189/M7
Vaudreuil-Dorion, Qu, Can. 189/M7
Vaughan, Ms, US 192/B4
Vaughan, On, Can. 190/T8
Vaughn, NM, US 182/B3
Vaughn, Mt, US 175/J4
Vaughn, Wa, US 197/B3
Vaulruz, Swi. 66/C4
Vaulx-en-Velin, Fr. 66/A6
Vaunoise (riv.), Fr. 62/D4
Vaupés (dept.), Col. 216/D4
Vaupés (riv.), Col. 209/B2
Vauréal, Fr. 36/J4
Vauvert, Fr. 50/F5
Vauvillers, Fr. 66/C2
Vaux (riv.), Fr. 48/C4
Vaux-sur-Seine, Fr. 36/H4
Vaux-sur-Sûre, Belg. 61/E4
Vauxhall, Ab, Can. 175/H2
Vavatenina, Madg. 143/J7
Vava'u Group (isls.), Tonga 161/H6
Vavenby, BC, Can. 174/E2
Vavoua, C.d'Iv. 132/D5
Vawkavysk, Bela. 49/N2
Vawn, Sk, Can. 175/K1
Vaxholm, Swe. 45/B1
Vaxjo (int'l arpt.), Swe. 46/F3
Växjö, Swe. 46/F3
Vay, Fr. 62/D5
Vaygach (isl.), Rus. 80/F3
Vazante, Braz. 222/D3
Vázea Paulista, Braz. 223/K8
Vazhgort, Rus. 75/K2
Vazuza (res.), Rus. 74/G5
Vazzola, It. 69/F2
Veberöd, Swe. 45/K7
Veblen, SD, US 186/F5
Vecchiano, It. 68/D6
Vechelde, Ger. 59/H4
Vechigen, Swi. 66/D4
Vecht (riv.), Neth. 58/D3
Vechta, Ger. 59/F3
Vechte (riv.), Ger. 58/D3
Veckholm, Swe. 45/A1
Vecpiebalga, Lat. 47/L3
Vecsés, Hun. 56/D2
Vecumnieki, Lat. 47/L3
Vedano Olona, It. 68/B2
Veddige, Swe. 46/E3
Vedelago, It. 69/F2
Vedène, Fr. 70/A5
Vedia, Arg. 226/E2
Vedra, Sp. 52/A1
Veedersburg, In, US 190/C4
Veendam, Neth. 58/D2
Veenendaal, Neth. 58/C4
Veenhuizen, Neth. 58/D2
Veere, Neth. 58/A5
Veerse Meer (res.), Neth. 58/A5
Vefsn, Nor. 44/E2
Véga (riv.), Fr. 70/A1
Vega (isl.), Nor. 44/D2
Vega, Swe. 45/B1
Vega (pt.), Ak, US 201/B6
Vega, Tx, US 182/C3
Vega de Alatorre, Mex. 205/N6
Vegafjorden (estu.), Nor. 44/D2
Vegeån (riv.), Swe. 45/J6
Vegesack, Ger. 59/F2
Veghel, Neth. 58/C5
Vegorítis (lake), Gre. 55/G2
Vègre (riv.), Fr. 63/E4
Vègreville, Ab, Can. 175/H1
Végueta, Peru 220/B3
Veguita, NM, US 179/J3
Vehkalahti, Fin. 47/M1
Vehne (riv.), Ger. 59/F2
Veigné, Fr. 63/F6
Veikkola, Fin. 45/E4
Veilsdorf, Ger. 64/D2
Veinticinco de Mayo, Arg. 226/E2
Veinticinco de Mayo, Arg. 226/D3
Veinticinco de Mayo, Uru. 191/K11
Veintiocho de Mayo, Ecu. 220/B1
Veintiocho de Noviembre, Arg. 191/B6
Veio (ruin), It. 71/B3
Veisiejai, Lith. 47/K4
Veitsch, Aus. 56/B2
Veitshöchheim, Ger. 64/C3
Vejen, Den. 46/C4
Vejer de la Frontera, Sp. 52/C4
Vejle, Den. 46/C4
Vejle (co.), Den. 46/C4
Vejprnice, Czh. 65/G3
Vejprty, Czh. 65/G2
Vejrø (isl.), Den. 45/G7
Vela Luka, Cro. 56/C4
Vela, Cabo de la (pt.), Col. 216/C1
Velaines, Fr. 61/E6
Vélan (peak), Swi. 66/D6
Velarde, NM, US 179/K2
Velardeña, Mex. 204/E3
Velas, Azor., Port. 53/S12
Velasco Ibarra, Ecu. 216/B5
Velaux, Fr. 70/B5
Velázquez, Uru. 191/G2
Velbert, Ger. 58/E6
Velburg, Ger. 65/E4
Velddrif, SAfr. 142/L10
Velden, Ger. 65/F6
Velden, Neth. 58/D6
Velden am Wörthersee, Aus. 51/L3
Veldhoven, Neth. 58/C6
Velen, Ger. 58/D5
Velenje, Slov. 56/B2
Veles, FYROM 55/G2
Velešta, FYROM 55/G2
Velestínon, Gre. 55/H3
Vélez, Col. 216/C3
Vélez-Blanco, Sp. 52/D4
Vélez-Málaga, Sp. 52/C4
Vélez-Rubio, Sp. 52/D4
Velhas, Rio das (riv.), Braz. 222/D3
Velika Gorica, Cro. 56/C3
Velika Kladuša, Bosn. 56/B3
Velika Lepetykha, Ukr. 79/G4
Velika Novosilka, Ukr. 79/J4
Velika Plana, Serb. 56/E3
Velikaya (riv.), Rus. 74/F4
Veliki Birky, Ukr. 78/C3
Velikiy Ustyug, Rus. 75/K3
Velikiye Luki, Rus. 47/P3
Veliko Tŭrnovo, Bul. 57/G4
Velikodvorskiy, Rus. 74/J5
Velikovisochnoye, Rus. 75/M2
Velille, Peru 220/D4
Vélingara, Sen. 132/B3
Vélingara, Sen. 132/B3
Velingrad, Bul. 55/J1
Velino (peak), It. 71/C3
Velino (riv.), It. 71/C3
Velizh, Rus. 47/P4
Vélizy-Villacoublay, Fr. 36/J5
Velké Meziříčí, Czh. 49/J4
Velké Žernoseky, Czh. 65/H1
Vel'ký Krtíš, Slvk. 49/K4
Velký Zvon (peak), Czh. 65/F3
Vellberg, Ger. 64/C4
Velleron, Fr. 70/B5
Velletri, It. 71/B4
Vellinge, Swe. 46/E4
Vellinge, Swe. 45/K7
Vellmar, Ger. 59/G6
Vellón (res.), Sp. 53/N8
Velma, Ok, US 183/F3
Vélon, Gre. 55/H4
Velp, Neth. 58/C5
Velsen-Noord, Neth. 58/B4
Vel'sk, Rus. 74/J3
Velten, Ger. 48/Q6
Veluwe (phys. reg.), Neth. 58/C4
Veluwemeer (lake), Neth. 58/C4
Veluwezoom, NP, Neth. 58/C4
Velva, ND, US 186/D3
Velvary, Czh. 65/H2
Velvendós, Gre. 55/H2
Velykodolyns'ke, Ukr. 78/F4
Velykyy Bereznyy, Ukr. 49/M4
Velykyy Burluk, Ukr. 79/J2
Velykyy Lyubin', Ukr. 78/B3
Vémars, Fr. 36/K4
Vemb, Den. 46/C3
Vembādi Shola (peak), India 107/C4
Véménd, Hun. 56/D2
Ven (isl.), Swe. 45/J7
Vena Park, Austl. 158/A2
Venachar (lake), Sc, UK 39/B4
Venadillo, Col. 219/L8
Venado Tuerto, Arg. 226/E2
Venados, Mex. 205/L6
Venafro, It. 71/D5
Venamo (peak), Ven. 217/F3
Venâncio Aires, Braz. 225/F4
Venango, Ne, US 184/C3
Venaria, It. 70/D2
Venarotta, It. 71/C2
Vence, Fr. 70/D5
Venceslau Brás, Braz. 225/G2
Vendas Novas, Port. 52/A3
Vendelsö, Swe. 45/B1
Vendôme, Fr. 63/G5
Vendrell, Sp. 53/F2
Vendrest, Fr. 36/M4
Venecia, Col. 219/K7
Venelles, Fr. 70/B5
Vénéon (riv.), Fr. 70/C2
Veneta (lake), It. 69/F2
Veneta, Or, US 176/B1
Venetie, Ak, US 201/J2
Veneto (pol. reg.), It. 51/J4
Venëv, Rus. 76/F1
Venezia (gulf), Eur. 73/G1
Venezia (prov.), It. 69/F1
Venezia (Venice), It. 69/F3
Venezuela (ctry.) 217/E3
Venezuela (gulf), Col.,Ven. 209/B1
Veniaminof (mt.), Ak, US 201/G4
Venice (Venezia), It. 69/F3
Venice (nbrhd.), Ca, US 196/F8
Venice, Fl, US 195/G4
Venice, Ut, US 179/F1
Vénissieux, Fr. 70/A1
Venjan, Swe. 46/E1
Venjansjön (lake), Swe. 46/E1
Venkatāpuram, India 107/D2
Venlo, Neth. 58/D6
Venn, Sk, Can. 175/M2
Vennesla, Nor. 46/B2
Veno (bay), Den. 46/C3
Venoge (riv.), Swi. 66/C4
Venosa, It. 54/D2
Venray, Neth. 58/C5
Venta (riv.), Lat.,Lith. 47/J3
Venta de Baños, Sp. 52/C2
Ventabren, Fr. 70/B5
Ventersburg, SAfr. 142/D3
Ventersdorp, SAfr. 142/D2
Venterspos, SAfr. 142/P13
Venterstad, SAfr. 142/D3
Ventimiglia, It. 70/D5
Ventiseri, Fr. 54/A2
Ventnor, Eng, UK 43/E5
Ventnor City, NJ, US 198/D5
Ventotene (isl.), It. 71/C6
Ventoux (peak), Fr. 70/B4
Ventspils, Lat. 47/J3
Ventuari (riv.), Ven. 217/E3
Ventura (co.), Ca, US 196/A2
Ventura (riv.), Ca, US 196/A2
Ventura (San Buenaventura), Ca, US 196/A2
Venturina, It. 54/B1
Venturosa, Braz. 219/G5
Vénus (pt.), FrPol. 161/X15
Venus, Tx, US 180/K7
Venustiano Carranza, Mex. 202/C4
Venustiano Carranza (res.), Mex. 205/E3
Véore (riv.), Fr. 70/B3
Vép, Hun. 56/C2
Ver-sur-Launette, Fr. 36/L4
Vera, Arg. 224/D4
Vera, Sp. 52/E4
Vera, Tx, US 182/E4
Vera Cruz, Pan. 216/B2
Veracruz, Mex. 205/N7
Veracruz-Llave (state), Mex. 202/B3
Veranópolis, Braz. 225/G4
Verāval, India 113/K4
Verbania, It. 67/E6
Verbena, Al, US 192/D4
Verberie, Fr. 60/B5
Verbicaro, It. 54/D3
Verbovskiy, Rus. 74/J5
Vercelli (prov.), It. 66/E6
Vercelli, It. 68/B3
Verchères (co.), Qu, Can. 189/P6
Verchères, Qu, Can. 189/P6
Vercors (upland), Fr. 70/B3
Verda, Ky, US 193/F2
Verdal, Nor. 44/D3
Verde (bay), Arg. 226/E3
Verde (riv.), Az, US 179/F3
Verde (riv.), Braz. 225/F2
Verde (riv.), Braz. 221/F4
Verde (riv.), Braz. 225/G1
Verde (riv.), Mex. 205/F4
Verde (cape), It. 68/A5
Verde (coast), Sp. 52/B1
Verde Grande (riv.), Braz. 223/E2
Verde Island Passage (chan.), Phil. 100/C2
Verden, Ger. 59/G3
Verdhikoússa, Gre. 55/G3
Verdigris (riv.), Ks, US 183/G2
Verdon (riv.), Fr. 50/F5
Verdugo (mts.), Ca, US 196/F7
Verdun, Qu, Can. 189/N7
Verdun, Fr. 61/E5
Verdunville, WV, US 193/F2
Vereeniging, SAfr. 142/D2
Veregin, Sk, Can. 186/C2
Verena (peak), It. 67/H6
Vereshchagino, Rus. 75/M4
Veretskiy (pass), Ukr. 49/M4
Verga (cape), Gui. 132/B4
Vergara, Uru. 191/G2
Vergara, Arg. 191/K11
Vergas, Mn, US 186/G4
Vergato, It. 69/E5
Vergennes, Vt, US 191/K2
Vergiate, It. 68/B2
Vergína (ruin), Gre. 55/H2
Verhknyaya Toyma, Rus. 75/K3
Veribest, Tx, US 180/D2
Verigenstadt, Ger. 67/F1
Verín, Sp. 52/B2
Veriora, Est. 47/M3
Verkaån (riv.), Swe. 45/K7
Verkhazovka, Rus. 77/J2
Verkhivtseve, Ukr. 79/H3
Verkhnebakanskiy, Rus. 79/J5
Verkhnedneprovskiy, Rus. 74/G5
Verkhnedvinsk, Bela. 47/M4
Verkhnetulomskiy (res.), Rus. 74/F1
Verkhneural'sk, Rus. 75/N5
Verkhni Rohachyk, Ukr. 79/H4
Verkhniy At Uryakh, Rus. 81/R3
Verkhniy Baskunchak, Rus. 77/H2
Verkhniy Mamon, Rus. 79/L2
Verkhniy Tagil, Rus. 75/N4
Verkhniy Ufaley, Rus. 75/N4
Verkhniye Kigi, Rus. 75/N5
Verkhniye Osel'ki, Rus. 75/T6
Verkhn'odniprovs'k, Ukr. 79/H3
Verkhnyaya Orlyanka, Rus. 77/J1
Verkhnyaya Pyshma, Rus. 75/P4
Verkhnyaya Salda, Rus. 75/P4
Verkhnyaya Sinyachikha, Rus. 75/P4
Verkhnyaya Tura, Rus. 75/N4
Verkhnyaya Zolotitsa, Rus. 74/J2
Verkhoyansk, Rus. 81/P3
Verkhoyansk (range), Rus. 83/M2
Verl, Ger. 59/F5
Verlo, Sk, Can. 175/K2
Vermenagna (riv.), It. 68/A4
Vermenagna (riv.), Fr. 70/D4
Vermilion, Ab, Can. 175/J1
Vermilion (riv.), Ab, Can. 175/J1
Vermilion (hills), Sk, Can. 175/L2
Vermilion (bay), La, US 181/H3
Vermilion (lake), Mn, US 187/H4
Vermilion (range), Mn, US 187/H4
Vermilion Bay, On, Can. 187/H3
Vermilion Lake Ind. Res., Mn, US 187/H4
Vermillion (riv.), Il, US 185/F2
Vermillion, SD, US 185/F2
Vermillion (cr.), Wy, US 177/J3
Vermillion Cliffs Nat'l Mon., Az, US 179/F2
Vermillion, East Fork (riv.), SD, US 185/F2
Vermillion, West Fork (riv.), SD, US 185/F2
Vermont (state), US 191/K3
Vermont, Il, US 185/J3
Vermontville, Mi, US 190/D3
Vern-sur-Saiche, Fr. 62/D4
Vernāg, India 110/C3
Vernaison (riv.), Fr. 70/B3
Vernal, Ut, US 177/J3
Vernante, It. 70/D4
Vernantes, Fr. 63/F6
Vernayaz, Swi. 66/D5
Vernazza, It. 68/C5
Verndale, Mn, US 187/G4
Verneuil-sur-Avre, Fr. 63/F3
Verneuil-sur-Seine, Fr. 36/H5
Verneukpan (salt pan), SAfr. 142/C3
Vernier, Swi. 66/C5
Vernon, BC, Can. 174/E2
Vernon, Fr. 63/G2
Vernon, Al, US 192/C4
Vernon, Ct, US 191/K4
Vernon, Fl, US 195/F2
Vernon, In, US 192/E1
Vernon (lake), La, US 194/B2
Vernon, Tx, US 182/E3
Vernon Hills, Il, US 197/Q15
Vernon Valley, NJ, US 198/D1

Vuca, Eth. 135/G4
Vučitrn, Serb. 56/E4
Vught, Neth. 58/C5
Vukovar, Cro. 54/D3
Vulcan, Ab, Can. 175/H2
Vulcan, Rom. 57/F3
Vulcan, Mo, US 183/J2
Vulcăneşti, Mol. 57/J3
Vulcano (isl.), It. 54/D3
Vülchedrüm, Bul. 57/F4
Vülchi Dol, Bul. 57/H4
Vulci (ruin), It. 54/B1
Vung Tau, Viet. 106/D4
Vunisea, Fiji 160/G6
Vuntut NP, Yk., Can. 201/K2
Vuoggatjålme, Swe. 44/F2
Vuohijärvi (lake), Fin. 47/M1
Vuollerim, Swe. 44/G2
Vuoska (lake), Rus. 47/N1
Vuotso, Fin. 74/E1
Vürbitsa, Bul. 57/H4
Vuria (peak), Kenya 137/B2
Vurnary, Rus. 75/K5
Vürshets, Bul. 57/F4
Vuruena, Res. Florestal do, Braz. 222/A1
Vuyyūru, India 107/D2
Vvedenka, Kaz. 75/P5
Vwawa, Tanz. 139/H5
Vyāra, India 104/B3
Vyatka (riv.), Rus. 80/E4
Vyatskiye Polyany, Rus. 75/L4
Vyatskoye, Rus. 74/J4
Vyazemskiy, Rus. 91/L2
Vyaz'ma, Rus. 74/G5
Vyazovaya, Rus. 75/N5
Vyborg (nbrhd.), Rus. 75/T7
Vyborg (bay), Rus. 47/N1
Vyborg, Rus. 47/N1
Vychegda (riv.), Rus. 80/F3
Vygozero (lake), Rus. 74/G3
Vyhorlat (peak), Slvk. 49/M4
Vyksa, Rus. 74/J5
Vylkove, Ukr. 57/J3
Vym' (riv.), Rus. 75/L3
Vynnyky, Ukr. 78/C3
Vynohradiv, Ukr. 49/M4
Vypolzovo, Rus. 74/G4
Vyritsa, Rus. 47/P2
Vyrnwy (riv.), Wal, UK 42/C1
Vyselki, Rus. 79/K5
Vyshgorodok, Rus. 47/N3
Vyshhorod, Ukr. 78/F2
Vyshniy Volochek, Rus. 74/G4
Vyshnivets', Ukr. 78/C3
Vyškov, Czh. 49/J4
Vyškovce nad Ipl'om, Slvk. 56/D1
Vysokogornyy, Rus. 91/M1
Vysokopillya, Ukr. 79/G4
Vysokovsk, Rus. 74/H4
Vysokoye, Bela. 49/M2
Vysotsk, Rus. 47/N1
Vyšší Brod, Czh. 65/H5
Vytegra, Rus. 74/H3
Vyyeznoye, Rus. 75/J5
Vyzhnytsya, Ukr. 78/C3
Vzmor'ye, Rus. 91/N2

W

W du Benin, PN du, Ben. 133/F4
W du Burkino Faso, PN du, Burk. 133/F4
W du Niger, PN du, Niger 133/F3
W.F. George (res.), Al,Ga, US 192/E5
Wa, Gha. 133/E4
Waadi Luud (wadi), Som. 136/D3
Waajid, Som. 136/B5
Waal, Ger. 67/G2
Waal (riv.), Neth. 48/C3
Waal (riv.), Neth. 58/C5
Waalre, Neth. 58/C6
Waalwijk, Neth. 58/C5
Waany-Garawa Aboriginal Land, Austl. 153/E4
Waarschoot, Belg. 60/C1
Waasis, NB, Can. 188/D3
Wabag, PNG 153/F1
Wabamun, Ab, Can. 174/G1
Wabamun (lake), Ab, Can. 174/G1
Wabana, Nf, Can. 189/L2
Wabasca (riv.), Ab, Can. 170/E3
Wabash, In, US 190/D4
Wabash (riv.), Il, In, US 173/J4
Wabasha, Mn, US 185/H1
Wabasso, Mn, US 185/G1
Wabē Gestro Wenz (riv.), Eth. 136/B4
Wabē Shebelē Wenz (riv.), Eth. 119/G4
Wabeno, Wi, US 187/K5
Wabern, Ger. 59/G6
Wabigoon (lake), On, Can. 187/H3
Wabigoon, On, Can. 187/H3
Wąbrzeźno, Pol. 49/K2
Wabu, SKor. 93/G6
Wabu (lake), China 92/D4
Wabuda (isl.), PNG 153/F2
Waccamau (riv.), SC, US 193/H4
Waccasassa (bay), Fl, US 195/G3
Wachenheim an der Weinstrasse, Ger. 64/B4
Wachi, Japan 95/H5
Wach'īlē, Eth. 136/A4
Wachtebeke, Belg. 60/C1
Wachtendonk, Ger. 58/D6
Wächtersbach, Ger. 64/C2
Wackernheim, Ger. 64/B3
Wackersdorf, Ger. 65/F4
Waco, Tx, US 181/F2
Waconda (lake), Ks, US 184/E4
Waconia, Mn, US 187/N7
Waconia (lake), Mn, US 187/N7
Wad al Ḩaddād, Sudan 135/G2
Wad an Nail, Sudan 135/G2
Wad Bandah, Sudan 135/E2
Wad Ḩāmid, Sudan 135/G1
Wad Medanī, Sudan 135/G2
Wada, Japan 95/E3
Wadayama, Japan 95/G5
Waddān, Libya 126/C2
Waddell (dam), Az, US 179/F4
Waddenzee (sound), Neth. 48/C2
Waddington, Eng, UK 41/H5
Waddington, Eng, UK 41/F4
Waddinxveen, Neth. 58/B4
Waddy (pt.), Austl. 158/D4
Wade, Ok, US 183/F4
Wadebridge, Eng, UK 42/B5
Wadena, Sk, Can. 186/C2
Wadena, Mn, US 187/G4
Wädenswil, Swi. 67/E3
Wadern, Ger. 61/F4
Wadersloh, Ger. 59/F5
Wadesboro, NC, US 193/G3
Wadgassen, Ger. 61/F5
Wadhurst, Eng, UK 43/G4
Wādī an Natrūn, Egypt 131/B4
Wādī As Sīr, Jor. 117/D5
Wādī Az Zarqā', Tun. 130/L6
Wādī Ḩalfā', Sudan 127/F4
Wādī Mūsá, Jor. 116/D4
Wading (riv.), NJ, US 198/D4
Wading River, NY, US 199/F2
Wadley, Ga, US 193/F4
Wadowice, Pol. 49/K4
Wadsworth, Tx, US 181/G3
Wadsworth, Oh, US 190/F4
Wadsworth, Il, US 197/Q15
Waegwan, SKor. 93/E5
Waelder, Tx, US 181/F3
Wafangdian, China 93/A3
Wafangdian, China 99/F1
Wafania, D.R. Congo 138/E3
Waffenrod, Ger. 64/D2
Wāgah, Pak. 110/C4
Wagait Abor. Land, Austl. 152/C3
Wagaru, Myan. 106/B3
Wagat, Ouadi (riv.), Chad 134/D2
Wagener, SC, US 193/G4
Wagenfeld-Hasslingen, Ger. 59/F3
Wageningen, Sur. 218/B1
Wageningen, Neth. 58/C5
Wager (bay), Nun, Can. 170/G2
Wagga Wagga, Austl. 157/C2
Waggrakine, Austl. 154/B4
Waghäusel, Ger. 64/B4
Wagin, Austl. 154/C5
Waging am See, Ger. 65/F7
Waginger (lake), Ger. 65/F7
Wägitaler-see (lake), Swi. 67/E3
Wagna, Aus. 56/B2
Wagner, SD, US 184/E2
Wagoner, Ok, US 183/G3
Wagontire, Or, US 176/D2
Wągrowiec, Pol. 49/J2
Wāh, Pak. 110/B3
Wah Wah (mts.), Ut, US 177/G4
Wahai, Indo. 103/G4
Wāḩāt ad Dākhilah (oasis), Egypt 127/F3
Wāḩāt al Farāfirah (oasis), Libya,Egypt 127/E3
Wahkon, Mn, US 187/H4
Wahlern, Swi. 66/D4
Wahoo, Ne, US 185/F3
Wahpeton, ND, US 186/F4
Wahrenholz, Ger. 59/H3
Wai, India 107/B2
Waialua, Hi, US 172/S9
Waiau (riv.), NZ 159/C3
Waiau, NZ 159/C3
Waibamiao, China 92/D2
Waiblingen, Ger. 64/C5
Waibstadt, Ger. 64/B4
Waidhaus, Ger. 65/F3
Waidhofen an der Thaya, Aus. 51/L2
Waidhofen an der Ybbs, Aus. 65/H7
Waigeo (isl.), Indo. 103/H3
Waigolshausen, Ger. 64/D3
Waigoumen, China 90/H3
Waiheke (isl.), NZ 159/G6
Waihou (riv.), NZ 159/C2
Waika, D.R. Congo 139/F3
Waikabubak, Indo. 103/E5
Waikanae, NZ 159/C3
Waikari, NZ 159/C3
Waikato (riv.), NZ 145/H6
Waikerie, Austl. 155/H5
Waikouaiti, NZ 159/B4
Wailuo, China 99/F4
Waimangaroa, NZ 159/B3
Waimate, NZ 159/B4
Waimes, Belg. 61/F3
Wainfleet, On, Can. 190/U10
Wainfleet All Saints, Eng, UK 41/J5
Waingangā (riv.), India 104/C3
Waingapu, Indo. 103/F5
Waini (riv.), Guy. 217/G2
Wainuiomata, NZ 159/H9
Wainuiomata (riv.), NZ 159/H9
Wainwright, Ab, Can. 175/J1
Wainwright, Ak, US 201/F1
Wainwright, Ok, US 183/G3
Waiohine (riv.), NZ 159/J8
Waipahu, Hi, US 172/S9
Waipapa (pt.), NZ 159/B4
Waipara, NZ 159/C3
Waipawa, NZ 159/D2
Waipio, Hi, US 172/S9
Waipiro, NZ 159/D2
Waipukurau, NZ 159/D2
Wairarapa (lake), NZ 159/J9
Wairau (riv.), NZ 159/C3
Wairoa (riv.), NZ 159/C1
Wairoa, NZ 159/D2
Waischenfeld, Ger. 65/E3
Waitakere, NZ 159/F6
Waitakere (range), NZ 159/F6
Waitaki (riv.), NZ 159/B4
Waitangi, NZ 159/E3
Waitara, NZ 159/C2
Waitemata (har.), NZ 159/F6
Waitotara, NZ 159/C2
Waitsburg, Wa, US 174/E4
Waiuku, NZ 159/C2
Waiyevu, Fiji 161/Z17
Waizenkirchen, Aus. 65/G6
Wajima, Japan 97/E2
Wajir, Kenya 137/C1
Waka, D.R. Congo 138/E2
Waka, Eth. 135/H4
Waka, D.R. Congo 138/E3
Waka (cape), Indo. 103/G4
Wakakusa, Japan 95/A2
Wakapitu (lake), NZ 159/B4
Wakarusa, In, US 190/C4
Wakasa, Japan 96/D3
Wakasa (bay), Japan 95/H4
Wakaw, Sk, Can. 175/M1
Wakayama, Japan 96/D3
Wakayama (pref.), Japan 96/D4
Wake (isl.), Pac., US 160/F3
Wakeeney, Ks, US 182/E1
Wakefield, Eng, UK 41/G4
Wakefield (co.), Eng, UK 41/G4
Wakefield, Ks, US 185/F4
Wakefield, Mi, US 187/K4
Wakefield, Ne, US 185/F2
Wakefield, Oh, US 193/F1
Wakema, Myan. 98/B5
Waki, Japan 96/D3
Wakita, Ok, US 183/F2
Wakkanai, Japan 94/B1
Wakool, Austl. 157/B2
Wakpala, SD, US 186/D5
Waku Kungo, Ang. 140/B1
Wakulla, Fl, US 195/F2
Wakuya, Japan 94/B4
Wal (peak), Camr. 134/B4
Wal Athiang, Sudan 135/F4
Wala (riv.), Tanz. 137/A3
Walachia (reg.), Rom. 73/K1
Walagan, China 91/J1
Walagunya Abor. Land, Austl. 154/D2
Walamba, Zam. 141/F2
Walan, Austl. 157/B3
Wałbrzych, Pol. 49/J3
Walbury (hill), Eng, UK 43/E4
Walcha, Austl. 156/D1
Walcheren (isl.), Neth. 58/A5
Walcott, ND, US 186/F4
Walcott (lake), Id, US 177/G2
Walcott, Wy, US 177/K3
Walcourt, Belg. 61/D3
Wałcz, Pol. 49/J2
Wald, Swi. 67/E3
Wald, Ger. 65/E4
Waldbillig, Lux. 61/F4
Waldbreitbach, Ger. 61/G2
Waldbröl, Ger. 61/G2
Waldbronn, Ger. 64/B5
Waldbrunn, Ger. 64/C3
Waldburg, Ger. 67/F2
Waldeck, Sk, Can. 175/L2
Walden, On, Can. 190/F1
Waldenbuch, Ger. 64/C5
Waldenburg, Swi. 66/D3
Waldenburg, Ger. 64/C4
Waldershof, Ger. 65/F3
Walderslade, Eng, UK 36/E3
Waldesch, Ger. 61/G3
Waldfischbach-Burgalben, Ger. 61/G5
Waldheim, Sk, Can. 175/L1
Waldighofen, Fr. 66/D2
Walding, Aus. 65/H6
Waldkappel, Ger. 59/G6
Waldkirch, Ger. 66/D1
Waldkraiburg, Ger. 65/F6
Waldmohr, Ger. 61/G5
Waldmünchen, Ger. 65/F4
Waldnaab (riv.), Ger. 65/F3
Waldo, Ar, US 183/H4
Waldo, Fl, US 195/G3
Waldo (lake), Or, US 176/B2
Waldorf, Md, US 193/J1
Waldport, Or, US 176/A1
Waldrach, Ger. 61/F4
Waldron, Ar, US 183/G3
Waldron, In, US 190/D5
Waldsassen, Ger. 65/F3
Waldshut-Tiengen, Ger. 67/E2
Waldstetten, Ger. 64/C5
Waldviertel (reg.), Aus. 49/H4
Waldwick, NJ, US 199/J8
Walea (str.), Indo. 103/F4
Waleabahi (isl.), Indo. 103/F4
Walensee (lake), Swi. 67/F3
Walenstadt, Swi. 67/F3
Wales (isl.), Nun, Can. 171/H2
Wales, UK 42/B3
Wales, Ak, US 201/E2
Wales, Ut, US 177/H4
Wales, Wi, US 197/P14
Walewale, Gha. 133/E4
Walferdange, Lux. 61/F4
Walgett, Austl. 156/D1
Walhalla, Ger. 65/F4
Walhalla, Mi, US 190/C3
Walhalla, ND, US 186/F3
Walhalla, SC, US 193/F3
Walhalla Historical Site, ND, US 186/F3
Walikale, D.R. Congo 139/G3
Walker (bay), SAfr. 142/L11
Walker, Mn, US 187/G4
Walker, Mo, US 183/G2
Walker, Mi, US 190/D3
Walker (lake), Nv, US 176/D4
Walker (riv.), Nv, US 176/D4
Walker Art Center, Mn, US 187/P7
Walker River Ind. Res., Nv, US 176/D4
Walker, West (riv.), Ca, Nv, US 176/D4
Walkerburn, Sc, UK 39/C5
Walkers Ferry, Malw. 141/G2
Walkerston, Austl. 158/C3
Walkersville, Md, US 191/H5
Walkerton, On, Can. 190/F2
Walkerton, In, US 190/C4
Walkertown, NC, US 193/G2
Walkill (riv.), NY, US 198/D1
Wall, SD, US 184/C2
Wall, Tx, US 180/D2
Wall Of Ghenghis Khan (wall), Mong. 90/G2
Walla Walla, Wa, US 174/E4
Walla Walla, Austl. 157/C2
Wallace, Ca, US 176/C4
Wallace, Id, US 174/G4
Wallace, Ks, US 182/D1
Wallace, Ne, US 184/D3
Wallace, NS, Can. 188/F3
Wallace Lake, Mb, Can. 187/G2
Wallaceburg, On, Can. 190/E3
Wallacia, Austl. 157/E1
Wallaga Lake NP, Austl. 157/E3
Wallal Downs, Austl. 154/D1
Wallaroo, Austl. 155/H5
Wallasey, Eng, UK 41/E5
Walldorf, Ger. 64/B4
Walldorf, Ger. 64/D1
Walldürn, Ger. 64/C3
Walled (lake), Mi, US 197/F6
Walled City Hist. Site, SKor. 93/G7
Walled Lake, Mi, US 197/F6
Wallendbeen, Austl. 157/D2
Wallenhorst, Ger. 59/F4
Wallenpaupack (lake), Pa, US 191/J4
Waller, Tx, US 181/G2
Wallerawang, Austl. 157/E1
Wallern im Burgenland, Aus. 56/C2
Wallers, Fr. 60/C3
Wallersdorf, Ger. 65/F5
Wallersee (lake), Aus. 65/G7
Wallerstein, Ger. 64/D5
Wallingford, Ct, US 191/K4
Wallingford, Eng, UK 43/E3
Wallington, NJ, US 199/J8
Wallis (isls.), Wall., Fr. 161/H6
Wallis and Futuna (dpcy.), Fr. 160/G6
Wallisellen, Swi. 67/E3
Wallisville, Tx, US 181/N9
Walloon Brabant (prov.), Belg. 61/D2
Wallowa (mts.), Or, US 176/E1
Wallowa (riv.), Or, US 176/E1
Walls, Sc, UK 37/W13
Wallsend, Eng, UK 41/G2
Wallula, Wa, US 174/E4
Wallumbilla, Austl. 158/C4
Walney, Isle of (isl.), Eng, UK 41/E3
Walnut, Ca, US 196/G7
Walnut (cr.), Ga, US 193/M8
Walnut, Il, US 185/K3
Walnut (cr.), Ks, US 184/E4
Walnut (riv.), Ks, US 183/F2
Walnut, Ms, US 192/C3
Walnut Canyon Nat'l Mon., Az, US 179/G3
Walnut Creek, Ca, US 197/K11
Walnut Grove, Al, US 192/D3
Walnut Grove, Ga, US 192/F4
Walnut Grove, Mo, US 183/H2
Walnut Grove, Ms, US 192/C4
Walnut Park, Ca, US 196/F8
Walnut Ridge, Ar, US 192/B2
Walnut Springs, Tx, US 180/F1
Walnutport, Pa, US 198/C2
Walpole, Austl. 154/C5
Walpole, NH, US 191/K3
Walpole Island. Ind. Res., On, Can. 190/E3
Walpole-Nornalup NP, Austl. 154/C5
Walrus (isls.), Ak, US 201/F4
Walsall, Eng, UK 42/E1
Walsall (co.), Eng, UK 43/E1
Walsenburg, Co, US 182/B2
Walsh, Co, US 182/C2
Walsh, Austl. 158/A2
Walsingham (cape), Nun, Can. 171/K2
Walsingham, Eng, UK 43/G1
Walsrode, Ger. 59/G3
Walt Disney World, Fl, US 194/M7
Waltenhofen, Ger. 67/G2
Walter F. George (res.), Ga, US 195/F2
Walterboro, SC, US 193/G4
Walters, Ok, US 183/E3
Walters, La, US 194/C2
Walter's Ash, Eng, UK 36/A2
Walterville, Or, US 176/B1
Walthall, Ms, US 192/C4
Waltham Abbey, Eng, UK 36/D1
Waltham Forest (bor.), Eng, UK 36/A1
Waltham Saint Lawrence, Eng, UK 36/A2
Walthill, Ne, US 185/F2
Walthourville, Ga, US 195/H2
Waltman, Wy, US 177/K2
Walton, In, US 190/C4
Walton, Ky, US 192/E1
Walton, NY, US 191/J3
Walton, WV, US 193/G1
Walton-le-Dale, Eng, UK 41/F4
Walton-on-Thames, Eng, UK 36/B2
Walton-on-the-Naze, Eng, UK 43/H3
Waltrop, Ger. 59/E5
Walungchung Gola, Nepal 109/F2
Walvis Bay, Namb. 140/B4
Walworth, Wi, US 197/N14
Walworth (co.), Wi, US 197/N14
Walyahmoning (peak), Austl. 154/C4
Walyunga NP, Austl. 154/L6
Walzenhausen, Swi. 67/F3
Wama, Ang. 140/B2
Wamac, Il, US 192/C1
Wamaza, D.R. Congo 139/F4
Wamba, Nga. 133/H4
Wamba, D.R. Congo 139/F2
Wamba, Kenya 137/B1
Wamberal, Austl. 157/E1
Wamego, Ks, US 185/F4
Wamel, Neth. 58/C5
Wamena, Indo. 103/J4
Wami (riv.), Tanz. 137/B3
Wamic, Or, US 176/C1
Wampool (riv.), Eng, UK 41/E2
Wampsville, NY, US 191/J3
Wamsutter, Wy, US 177/K3
Wān Hsa-la, Myan. 106/B1
Wān Hwè-ün, Myan. 98/C5
Wanaaring, Austl. 156/C1
Wanaka, NZ 159/B4
Wanaka (lake), NZ 159/B4
Wanamassa, NJ, US 199/D3
Wanamingo, Mn, US 185/H1
Wanapum (dam), Wa, US 174/E4
Wanaque, NJ, US 199/H7
Wanaque (res.), NJ, US 199/H7
Wanblee, SD, US 184/D2
Wanci, Indo. 152/A1
Wanda (mts.), China 91/L2
Wandering, Austl. 154/C5
Wandi, Ugan. 139/G2
Wanding, China 98/C3
Wandlitz, Ger. 48/Q6
Wando, SKor. 93/D5
Wandoan, Austl. 158/C4
Wandong, Austl. 157/B3
Wandsbek, Ger. 59/H1
Wandsworth (bor.), Eng, UK 36/C2
Wanette, Ok, US 183/F3
Wanfried, Ger. 59/H6
Wanfu, China 93/B2
Wang (riv.), Thai. 105/G4
Wang Hip (peak), Thai. 106/B4
Wang Noi, Thai. 106/C3
Wang Saphung, Thai. 106/C2
Wanganella, Austl. 157/B2
Wanganui, NZ 159/C2
Wangaratta, Austl. 157/C3
Wangasi Turu, Gha. 133/E4
Wangcun, China 99/F2
Wangdu, China 92/C3
Wangdü Phodrang, Bhu. 109/G2
Wangen, Ger. 67/F2
Wangen an der Aare, Swi. 66/D3
Wangen bei Olten, Swi. 66/D3
Wangerooge (isl.), Ger. 59/E1
Wangerooge (arpt.), Ger. 59/E1
Wanggamet (peak), Indo. 103/F6
Wanggao, China 99/F3
Wanghai Shan (peak), China 93/A2
Wängi, Swi. 67/E3
Wangiwangi (isl.), Indo. 152/A1
Wangjiang, China 99/H2
Wangjiapu, China 93/B2
Wangkui, China 91/K2
Wangling, China 99/G3
Wangmao, China 99/F4
Wangmo Bouyeizu Miaozu Zizhixian, China 98/E3
Wangolodougou, C.d'Iv. 132/D4
Wangou, China 93/D1
Wangpan (bay), China 92/E5
Wangpang (sea), China 99/J2
Wangqing, China 91/K3
Wangqingmen, China 93/C2
Wangtan, China 99/J2
Wangting, China 92/L8
Wani (peak), Indo. 103/F4
Wanica (dist.), Sur. 217/H3
Wanie-Rukula, D.R. Congo 139/F2
Wanilla, Austl. 155/G5
Wanipitie (lake), On, Can. 190/F1
Wanjiabu, China 99/G2
Wanjialing, China 93/B3
Wank (peak), Ger. 67/H2
Wankie (Hwange) NP, Zim. 141/E3
Wanle Weyne, Som. 137/D1
Wann, Ok, US 183/G2
Wannaska, Mn, US 187/G3
Wannān (spr.), Libya 126/B2
Wanning, China 105/K4
Wanouchi, Japan 95/L5
Wanquan (lake), China 111/D5
Wanquan, China 92/C3
Wanquan (riv.), China 99/F5
Wanrong, China 92/B4
Wansbeck (riv.), Eng, UK 41/G1
Wanshengchang, China 99/E2
Wansra, Indo. 103/H4
Wanstead (nbrhd.), Eng, UK 36/D2
Wantage, Eng, UK 43/E3
Wantagh, NY, US 199/M9
Wantan, China 99/F2
Wanwei, China 106/E1
Wanxian, China 99/F2
Wanze, Belg. 61/E2
Wao, Phil. 100/D4
Wapakoneta, Oh, US 190/D4
Wapanocca NWR, Ar, US 192/B3
Wapanucka, Ok, US 183/F3
Wapato, Wa, US 174/D4
Wapella, Sk, Can. 186/D2
Wapello, Ia, US 185/J3
Wapenamanda, PNG 153/F1
Wapinda, D.R. Congo 139/E2
Wapiti, Wy, US 177/J1
Waples, Tx, US 180/K7
Wapoga (riv.), Indo. 103/J4
Wappapello (lake), Mo, US 192/B2
Wappingers Falls, NY, US 191/K4
Wapsipinicon (riv.), Ia, US 185/H2
Wapske, NB, Can. 188/D2
Wapwallopen (cr.), Pa, US 198/B1
Wapwallopen, Pa, US 198/B1
Wāqid, Egypt 131/B3
Waqqāş, Jor. 117/D3
War, WV, US 193/G2
War Horse Nat'l Wild. Ref., Mt, US 175/K4
Warabi, Japan 95/D2
Waranga (basin), Austl. 157/B3
Waratah, Austl. 156/C4
Waratah (bay), Austl. 157/C4
Warba, Mn, US 187/H4
Warboys, Eng, UK 43/F2
Warburg, Ger. 59/G6
Warburg, Ab, Can. 174/G1
Warburton, Pak. 110/B4
Warburton, Austl. 154/E3
Warburton (cr.), Austl. 145/C3
Warburton (Central Australia) Abor. Rsv., Austl. 155/E3
Warburton Range Abor. Reserve, Austl. 154/E3
Warche (riv.), Belg. 61/F3
Ward, NZ 159/C3
Ward Cove, Ak, US 201/M4
Ward Hunt (cape), PNG 153/H2
Warden (pt.), Eng, UK 43/G4
Warden, SAfr. 142/E2
Warden, Wa, US 174/E4
Wardenburg, Ger. 59/F2
Wardlow, Ab, Can. 175/J2
Wardo, Indo. 103/J4
Ward's Stone (peak), Eng, UK 41/F3
Wardsville, Mo, US 183/H1
Ware, Eng, UK 43/F3
Ware Shoals, SC, US 193/F3
Waregem, Belg. 60/C2
Wareham, Eng, UK 42/D5
Waremme, Belg. 61/E2
Waren, Ger. 46/E5
Waren, Indo. 103/J4
Warendorf, Ger. 59/E5
Waretown, NJ, US 199/D4
Warffum, Neth. 58/D2
Warfield, BC, Can. 174/F3
Wargrave, Eng, UK 43/F4
Warialda, Austl. 156/D1
Warin Chamrap, Thai. 106/D3
Waring, Tx, US 181/E3
Waringstown, NI, UK 40/B3
Wark, Eng, UK 41/F1
Warka, Pol. 49/L3
Warkworth, On, Can. 191/H2
Warkworth, NZ 159/C2
Warlingham, Eng, UK 36/C3
Warlmanpa Abor. Land, Austl. 155/G2
Warlmanpa Aboriginal Land, Austl. 152/D4
Warm Lake, Id, US 176/F1
Warm Springs, Or, US 176/C1
Warm Springs (res.), Or, US 176/D2
Warm Springs, Va, US 193/H1
Warm Springs Ind. Res., Or, US 176/C1
Warman, Sk, Can. 175/L1
Warmbad, SAfr. 141/F5
Warmbad, Namb. 142/B3
Warme Bode (riv.), Ger. 59/H5
Warmebach (riv.), Ger. 59/G6
Warmenhuizen, Neth. 58/B3
Warmeriville, Fr. 61/D5
Warmia (reg.), Pol. 49/K1
Warmińsko-Mazurskie (prov.), Pol. 49/L2
Warminster, Eng, UK 42/D4
Warminster, Pa, US 198/C3
Warnemünde, Ger. 46/E4
Warner (mts.), Ca, US 176/C3
Warner, Ok, US 183/G3
Warner, SD, US 186/E5
Warner Robins, Ga, US 192/F4
Warnes, Bol. 224/D1
Warnow (riv.), Ger. 46/D5
Warnsveld, Neth. 58/D4
Waroona, Austl. 154/B5
Waropko, Indo. 153/F1
Warrabri, Austl. 155/G2
Warrabri Abor. Land, Austl. 152/D5
Warragamba, Austl. 157/B3
Warragamba, Austl. 157/E1
Warragul, Austl. 157/B4
Warrakunta (pt.), Austl. 153/D3
Warrandirinna (lake), Austl. 155/H3
Warrandyte (nbrhd.), Austl. 156/G5
Warrego (range), Austl. 145/D3
Warrego (riv.), Austl. 145/D3
Warren, Austl. 156/C1
Warren (riv.), Austl. 154/C5
Warren, Ar, US 183/H4
Warren, Id, US 176/F1
Warren, In, US 190/D4
Warren, Mi, US 190/E3
Warren, Mn, US 186/F3
Warren (peak), Mt, US 175/H5
Warren (co.), NJ, US 198/C2
Warren, NJ, US 198/D2
Warren, Oh, US 190/F4
Warren, Or, US 174/C5
Warren, Pa, US 191/G4
Warren, RI, US 191/L4
Warrenpoint, NI, UK 40/B3
Warrens, Wi, US 185/J1
Warrensburg, Mo, US 183/H1
Warrensburg, NY, US 191/K3
Warrenton, SAfr. 142/D3
Warrenton, Ga, US 193/F4
Warrenton, Mo, US 185/J4
Warrenton, NC, US 193/H2
Warrenton, Or, US 174/C4
Warrenton, Va, US 193/J1
Warrenville, Il, US 197/P16
Warri, Nga. 133/G5
Warrina, Austl. 155/G4
Warringah, Austl. 157/E1
Warrington, Eng, UK 41/F5
Warrington (co.), Eng, UK 41/F5
Warrington, Fl, US 194/E2
Warrior, Al, US 192/D4
Warrior Reefs (reef), Austl. 153/F2
Warrnambool, Austl. 156/B3
Warroad, Mn, US 187/G3
Warrumbungle NP, Austl. 156/D1
Warsaw (Warszawa) (cap.), Pol. 49/L2
Warsaw, In, US 190/D4
Warsaw, Mo, US 183/H1
Warsaw, NY, US 191/G3
Warsaw, Ky, US 192/E1
Warsaw, Va, US 193/J2
Warsaw, NC, US 193/H3
Warscheneck (peak), Aus. 56/B2
Warshiikh, Som. 136/C5
Warslow, Eng, UK 41/G5
Warsop, Eng, UK 41/G5
Warstein, Ger. 59/F6
Warszawa (Warsaw) (cap.), Pol. 49/L2
Warta (riv.), Pol. 76/A1
Wartberg an der Krems, Aus. 65/H7
Wartberg ob der Aist, Aus. 65/H6
Wartburg, Tn, US 192/E2
Warthen, Ga, US 193/F4
Wartrace, Tn, US 192/D3
Waru, Indo. 103/H4
Warwick, Austl. 158/D5
Warwick, Eng, UK 43/E2
Warwick, Ga, US 195/G2
Warwick, Md, US 198/C5
Warwick, NY, US 199/D1
Warwick, RI, US 191/L4
Warwickshire (co.), Eng, UK 43/E2
Wasa, BC, Can. 174/G3
Wasagu, Nga. 133/G4
Wasatch (range), Ut, US 172/D4
Wasāwwāla, Pak. 110/B4
Wasbank, SAfr. 143/E3
Wasburn (riv.), Eng, UK 41/G4
Wascana (riv.), Sk, Can. 175/M2
Wasco, Ca, US 178/C3
Wascott, Wi, US 187/J4
Waseca, Mn, US 185/H1
Wash, The (bay), Eng, UK 41/J6
Washaw (bay), Mb, Can. 186/F1
Washburn (lake), Nun, Can. 170/F1
Washburn, ND, US 186/D4
Washburn, Wi, US 187/J4
Washdyke, NZ 159/B4
Washimiya, Japan 95/D1
Washingborough, Eng, UK 41/H5
Washington, Eng, UK 41/G2
Washington (state), US 174/D4
Washington (cap.), US 198/A6
Washington (int'l arpt.), DC, US 198/A6
Washington, Ga, US 193/F4
Washington, Ia, US 185/J3
Washington, Il, US 185/K3
Washington, In, US 192/D1
Washington, Ks, US 185/F4
Washington, Ky, US 192/F1
Washington, La, US 194/B2
Washington (isl.), Mi, US 190/C2
Washington (co.), Mn, US 187/Q6
Washington, Mo, US 185/J4
Washington, Ms, US 194/C2
Washington, NJ, US 198/D2
Washington, Pa, US 190/F4
Washington, Tx, US 181/F2
Washington, Ut, US 179/F2
Washington, Va, US 193/H1
Washington (lake), Wa, US 197/C2
Washington (mt.), Wa, US 174/C4
Washington, NC, US 193/J3
Washington (isl.), Wi, US 187/L5
Washington, WV, US 193/G1
Washington (Teraina) (isl.), Kiri. 161/J4
Washington Court House (Washington), Oh, US 190/E5
Washington Dulles (int'l arpt.), DC, US 193/J1
Washingtonville, Pa, US 198/B1
Washita (riv.), Ok,Tx, US 182/D3
Washita Battlefield Nat'l Hist. Site, Ok, US 182/E3
Washita Nat'l Wildlife Res., Ok, US 182/E3
Washtenaw (co.), Mi, US 197/E7
Washtucna, Wa, US 174/E4
Wasilków, Pol. 49/M2
Wasilla, Ak, US 170/B2
Wāsiṃt (gov.), Iraq 115/F3
Wasior, Indo. 103/H4
Wasiri, Indo. 152/B1
Wasjabo, Sur. 218/B1
Waskada, Mb, Can. 186/D3
Waskaganish (Rupert House), Qu, Can. 171/J3
Waskasa (bay), Japan 96/D3
Waskey (mt.), Ak, US 201/G4
Wasletan, Indo. 152/C1
Waspán, Nic. 207/F3
Wassau Nat'l Wild Ref., Ga, US 195/H2
Wasselonne, Fr. 61/G6
Wassen, Swi. 67/E4
Wassenaar, Neth. 58/B4
Wassenberg, Ger. 61/F1
Wasser, Namb. 142/B2
Wasserbillig, Lux. 61/F4
Wasserburg, Ger. 64/D6
Wasserburg am Inn, Ger. 65/F6
Wasserkuppe (peak), Ger. 64/C2
Wasserliesch, Ger. 61/F4
Wassertrüdingen, Ger. 64/D4
Wassou, Gui. 132/B4
Wassuk (range), Nv, US 172/C4
Wassy, Fr. 66/A1
Wast Water (lake), Eng, UK 41/E3
Wasu, PNG 153/G1
Wat Bot, Thai. 106/C2
Wat Mahathat, Thai. 98/C5
Wat Phra Si Ratana Mahathat, Thai. 98/D5
Wat Phu, Laos 106/D3
Wat Xieng Thong, Laos 98/D5
Wataga, Il, US 185/J3
Watampone, Indo. 103/F4
Watarai, Japan 95/L7
Watarase (riv.), Japan 97/F2
Watari, Japan 97/G1
Watauga, Tx, US 180/K7
Watauga (lake), Tn, US 193/G2
Watch Hill (pt.), RI, US 199/G1
Watchet, Eng, UK 42/C4
Watchfield, Eng, UK 43/E3
Watchung (mts.), NJ, US 199/H9
Watchung, NJ, US 199/H9
Water of Ae (riv.), Sc, UK 40/E1
Water of Girvan (riv.), Sc, UK 40/D1
Water of Girvan (riv.), Sc, UK 39/B6
Water of Ken (riv.), Sc, UK 40/D1
Water Valley, Ky, US 192/C2
Water Valley, Ms, US 192/C3
Water Valley, Ab, Can. 174/G2
Waterbeach, Eng, UK 43/G2
Waterberg, Namb. 140/C4
Waterberg Plateau Park, Namb. 140/C4
Waterberge (mts.), SAfr. 141/E5
Waterbury, Vt, US 191/K2
Waterbury, Ct, US 191/K4
Waterdown, On, Can. 190/T9
Wateree (lake), SC, US 193/G3
Waterfall, Austl. 157/E2
Waterflow, NM, US 179/H2
Waterford (arpt.), Ire. 38/C5
Waterford, Ire. 38/C5
Waterford (har.), Ire. 38/C5
Waterford (co.), Ire. 38/C5
Waterford, Mi, US 190/E3
Waterford, Wi, US 190/B3
Waterford, Ct, US 199/F1
Waterford Works, NJ, US 198/D4
Watergate (bay), Eng, UK 42/A6
Watergrasshill, Ire. 38/B5
Waterhen (lake), Mb, Can. 186/E1
Waterhouse (riv.), Austl. 152/D3
Wateringbury, Eng, UK 36/E3
Waterloo, Austl. 152/C4
Waterloo, Belg. 61/D2
Waterloo, On, Can. 190/F3
Waterloo, Qu, Can. 191/K2
Waterloo, NY, US 191/H3
Waterloo, Ia, US 185/H2
Waterloo, Il, US 192/B1
Waterloo Battlesite, Belg. 61/D2
Waterloo Village, NJ, US 198/D2
Waterlooville, Eng, UK 43/E5
Watermael-Boitsfort, Belg. 60/D2
Waterproof, La, US 194/C2
Watersmeet, Mi, US 187/K4
Waterton Lakes NP, Ab, Can. 175/G3
Waterton Lkes. Nat'l Pk., Ab, Can. 170/E4
Waterton Park, Ab, Can. 175/H3
Waterton-Glacier International Peace Park, Can.,US 175/H3
Watertown, NY, US 191/J3
Watertown, Fl, US 195/G2
Watertown, Wi, US 185/K2
Watertown, SD, US 185/F1
Watertown, Mn, US 187/N7
Waterval-Boven, SAfr. 141/F5
Waterville, Ire. 36/N11
Waterville, Ks, US 185/F4
Waterville, NY, US 191/J3
Waterville, Oh, US 190/E4
Waterville, Wa, US 174/D4
Watervliet, Belg. 60/C1
Watervliet, NY, US 191/K3
Watford, On, Can. 190/F3
Watford, Eng, UK 36/B1
Watford City, ND, US 186/C4
Wa'th, Sudan 135/G3
Wath-upon-Dearne, Eng, UK 41/G4
Watheroo, Austl. 154/C4
Watheroo NP, Austl. 154/B4
Wāṭī Kulīyāh (wadi), Egypt 131/D4
Watkins Glen, NY, US 191/H3
Watkinsville, Ga, US 193/F4
Watling (San Salvador) (isl.), Bahm. 203/G3
Watlington, Eng, UK 43/F3
Watmuri, Indo. 152/C1
Watonga, Ok, US 183/E3
Watonwan (riv.), Mn, US 185/G1
Watowato (peak), Indo. 103/G3
Watrous, NM, US 182/B3
Watrous, Sk, Can. 175/M2
Watsa, D.R. Congo 139/G2
Watseka, Il, US 190/C4
Watson, Ar, US 183/J4
Watson, Ok, US 183/G3
Watson, Il, US 192/C1
Watson, Sk, Can. 175/M1
Watson Lake, Yk, Can. 170/D2
Watsontown, Pa, US 198/B1
Watsonville, Ca, US 178/B2
Watten, Fr. 60/B2
Wattenheim, Ger. 64/B3
Wattens, Aus. 67/H3
Wattignies, Fr. 60/C2
Watton, Eng, UK 43/G1
Wattrelos, Fr. 60/C2
Watts Bar (dam), Tn, US 192/E3
Watts Bar (lake), Tn, US 192/E3
Wattwil, Swi. 67/F3
Wau, PNG 153/G1
Waubay, SD, US 186/F5
Waubay (lake), SD, US 184/F1
Waubay NWR, SD, US 185/F1
Waubun, Mn, US 186/G4
Wauchope, Austl. 156/E1
Wauchula, Fl, US 195/H4
Wauconda, Il, US 197/P15
Waugh (mtn.), Id, US 177/F1
Waukarlycarly (lake), Austl. 145/B3
Waukegan, Il, US 190/C3
Waukesha, Wi, US 190/B3
Waukesha (co.), Wi, US 197/P14
Waukomis, Ok, US 183/F2
Waukon, Ia, US 185/J2
Waun Fâch (peak), Wal, UK 42/C3
Waun-Oer (peak), Wal, UK 42/C1
Wauna, Wa, US 197/B3
Wauneta, Ne, US 184/D3
Waupaca, Wi, US 185/K1
Waupun, Wi, US 185/K2
Waurika, Ok, US 183/F3
Waurika (lake), Ok, US 183/E3
Wausau, Wi, US 185/K1
Wausaukee, Wi, US 190/C2
Wauseon, Oh, US 190/D4
Wautoma, Wi, US 185/K1
Wauwatosa, Wi, US 190/B3
Wave Hill, Austl. 152/C4
Waveland, Ar, US 183/H3
Waveland, Ms, US 194/D2
Waveney (riv.), Eng, UK 43/H2
Waver (riv.), Eng, UK 41/E2
Waverley, Austl. 157/C4
Waverley, NS, Can. 188/F3
Waverley, NZ 159/C2
Waverley Downs, Austl. 156/B1
Waverly, Fl, US 194/M8
Waverly, Ga, US 195/H2
Waverly, Ia, US 185/H2
Waverly, Ks, US 183/G1
Waverly, La, US 183/J4
Waverly, Ne, US 185/F3
Waverly, NY, US 191/H3
Waverly, Oh, US 193/F1
Waverly, Tn, US 192/D2
Waverly (nbrhd.), Austl. 156/G5
Waverly Hall, Ga, US 192/E4
Wavre, Belg. 61/D2
Wavrin, Fr. 60/B2
Wāw, Sudan 135/E4
Wāw al Kabīr, Libya 126/C3
Wawa, On, Can. 171/H4
Wawa, Nga. 133/G4
Wawa (riv.), Nic. 207/E3
Wawanesa, Mb, Can. 186/E3
Wawasang (peak), Nic. 207/E3
Wawayanda St. Park, NJ, US 198/D1
Wawo, Indo. 103/F4
Wawoi (riv.), PNG 153/F1
Wawota, Sk, Can. 186/C3
Waxahachie, Tx, US 180/L7
Waxahachie (cr.), Tx, US 180/L7
Waxxari, China 111/E4
Wayabula, Indo. 103/G4
Wayamli, Indo. 103/G3
Wayatinah, Austl. 156/C4
Waycross, Ga, US 195/G2
Waygay, Indo. 103/G4
Wayhaya, Indo. 103/F4
Wayland, NY, US 191/H3
Wayland, Mi, US 190/D3
Wayne, Il, US 197/P16
Wayne, Mi, US 197/F7
Wayne, Ne, US 185/F2
Wayne, NY, US 191/H3
Wayne, NJ, US 199/J8
Wayne, WV, US 193/F1
Wayne, Ok, US 183/F3
Wayne, Pa, US 198/C3
Wayne (co.), Pa, US 198/C3
Wayne City, Il, US 192/C1
Waynesboro, Ga, US 193/F4
Waynesboro, Tn, US 192/D3
Waynesboro, Va, US 193/H1
Waynesboro, Ms, US 194/D2
Waynesboro, Pa, US 191/H5
Waynesburg, Pa, US 190/F5
Waynesville, Mo, US 183/H2
Waynesville, NC, US 193/F3
Waynoka, Ok, US 182/E2
Wayside, Ms, US 192/B4
Wayuan, China 99/G3
Waza, Camr. 134/B3
Waza, PN de, Camr. 134/B3
Waziers, Fr. 60/C3
Wazīrābād, Pak. 110/C3
Wazuka, Japan 95/J6
Wda (riv.), Pol. 49/K2
Wé, NCal., Fr. 161/V12
We (isl.), Malay. 101/A1
Weald, The (grsld.), Eng, UK 43/F4
Weam, PNG 153/F2
Wear (riv.), Eng, UK 41/G2
Wear (riv.), Eng, UK 41/F2
Wear Head, Eng, UK 41/F2
Weare, NH, US 191/L3
Weatherford, Ok, US 183/E3
Weatherford (lake), Tx, US 180/K7
Weatherford, Tx, US 181/F1
Weatherly, Pa, US 198/C2
Weaubleau, Mo, US 183/H2
Weaver (lake), Mb, Can. 186/F1
Weaver (riv.), Eng, UK 41/F5
Weaverville, Ca, US 176/B3
Weaverville, NC, US 193/F3
Webb, Al, US 195/F2
Webb, Ms, US 192/B4
Webb, Sk, Can. 175/K2
Webb (A.F.B.), Tx, US 180/D1
Webb City, Mo, US 183/G2
Webber, Ks, US 184/E4
Webbers Falls, Ok, US 183/G3
Webberville, Mi, US 190/D3
Weber (mt.), Mn, US 187/J4
Weber (riv.), Ut, US 177/H3
Webi Jubba (riv.), Som. 119/G4
Webi Shabeelle (riv.), Som. 136/C4
Webster, Fl, US 194/L6
Webster, Mt, US 186/B4
Webster, Ma, US 191/L3
Webster, SD, US 186/F5
Webster, Tx, US 181/M9
Webster City, Ia, US 185/H2
Webster Groves, Mo, US 185/J4
Webster Springs (Addison), WV, US 193/G1
Webuye, Kenya 137/A1
Wedde-Warden, Ger. 59/F1
Weddell (sea) 228/X
Weddell (isl.), Mald. 191/E6
Wedderburn, Austl. 156/B3
Weddin Mountains NP, Austl. 157/C1
Weddington, NC, US 193/G3
Wedel, Ger. 59/G1
Wedemark, Ger. 59/G3
Wedge (mt.), BC, Can. 174/C2
Wedgeport, NS, Can. 188/E4
Wedmore, Eng, UK 42/D4
Wednesbury, Eng, UK 42/D1
Wednesfield, Eng, UK 42/D1
Wedowee, Al, US 192/E4
Weduar (cape), Indo. 152/D1
Wedweil, Sudan 135/E3
Wedza, Zim. 141/F3
Wee Waa, Austl. 156/D1
Weed, Ca, US 176/B3
Weedon Bec, Eng, UK 43/E2
Weedon-Centre, Qu, Can. 191/L2
Weedpatch (hill), In, US 190/C5
Weedville, Pa, US 191/G4
Weehawken, NJ, US 199/J8
Weekapaug, RI, US 199/G1
Weekes, Sk, Can. 186/C1
Weeki Wachee, Fl, US 194/K6
Weeki Wachee Springs, Fl, US 194/K6
Weeks, La, US 194/C3
Weeksbury, Ky, US 193/F2
Weeksville, NC, US 193/J2
Weenen, SAfr. 143/E3
Weeping Water, Ne, US 185/F3
Weerselo, Neth. 58/D4
Weert, Neth. 58/C6
Weesatche, Tx, US 181/F3
Weesen, Swi. 67/F3

Yuzhnyy, Rus. 79/L4
Yuzhnyy, Rus. 111/D1
Yvel (riv.), Fr. 62/C4
Yvelines (dept.), Fr. 63/G3
Yverdon, Swi. 66/C4
Yvetot, Fr. 63/F1
Yvette (riv.), Fr. 60/B6
Yvoir, Belg. 61/D3
Yvonand, Swi. 66/C4
Yvron (riv.), Fr. 36/L6
Ywathit, Myan. 106/B2
Yxlan (isl.), Swe. 45/B1
Yxlö (isl.), Swe. 45/B2
Yzeron (riv.), Fr. 70/A1
Yzeure, Fr. 50/E3

Z

Za (riv.), China 90/D5
Za (riv.), Mor. 130/C2
Zaachila, Mex. 206/B2
Zaandam, Neth. 48/C2
Zaandijk, Neth. 58/B4
Zaanstad, Neth. 58/B4
Zabaykal'sk, Rus. 91/H2
Žabbar, Malta 54/M7
Zaber (riv.), Ger. 64/C4
Zabīd, Yem. 135/H4
Zabīd (wadi), Yem. 136/B2
Ząbki, Pol. 49/L2
Ząbkowice Śląskie, Pol. 49/J3
Žabljak, Mont. 56/D4
Zābolī, Iran 113/H3
Zabré, Burk. 133/E4
Zábřeh, Czh. 49/J4
Zabrze, Pol. 49/K3
Zaburun'ye, Rus. 77/J3
Zabzuga, Gha. 133/F4
Zacapa, Guat. 206/D3
Zacapoaxtla, Mex. 205/M7
Zacapu, Mex. 204/E4
Zacatecas (state), Mex. 202/A3
Zacatecas, Mex. 204/E4
Zacatecoluca, ESal. 206/D3
Zacatepec, Mex. 205/L7
Zacatepec, Mex. 205/K8
Zacatlán, Mex. 205/M7
Zachary, La, US 194/C2
Zachodnio-Pomorskie (prov.), Pol. 49/H2
Zacoalco de Torres, Mex. 204/E4
Zacualtipán, Mex. 206/B1
Zadar, Cro. 56/B3
Zadetkyi (isl.), Myan. 102/A2
Zadi (riv.), Ang. 138/D5
Zadi, Myan. 106/B3
Zadoi, China 90/D5
Zadonsk, Rus. 76/F1
Żafar al Qadīmah, Egypt 131/C3
Zafarwāl, Pak. 110/C3
Zafra, Sp. 52/B3
Żagań, Pol. 49/H3
Žagarė, Lith. 45/J3
Zagarolo, It. 71/B4
Zāgheh-ye Pa'īn, Iran 115/G3
Zaghouan, Tun. 130/M6
Zaghouan (gov.), Tun. 130/L6
Zagorá, Gre. 55/H4
Zagora, Mor. 128/D3
Zagorje ob Savi, Slov. 51/L3
Zagreb (cap.), Cro. 56/B3
Zagros (mts.), Iran 80/F6
Za'gya (riv.), China 90/D4
Zāhedān, Iran 113/H3
Zahirābād, India 107/C2
Zahlah, Leb. 117/D1
Záhony, Hun. 49/M4
Zahrez Chergui (dry lake), Alg. 130/G5
Zahrez Rharbi (dry lake), Alg. 72/D4
Zai NP, Jor. 117/D4
Zaidín, Sp. 53/F2
Zaidpur, India 108/C2
Zaima, China 99/F3
Zaïo, Mor. 130/D2
Zaire (see Democratic Republic of the Congo) */°
Zaječar, Serb. 56/F3
Zaka, Zim. 141/F4
Zakamensk, Rus. 90/D5
Zakháro, Gre. 55/G4
Zakhodnyaya Dzvina (riv.), Bela. 74/E5
Zākhū, Iraq 115/E2

Zaki Biam, Nga. 133/H5
Zākinthos, Gre. 55/G4
Zākinthos (isl.), Gre. 55/G4
Zakopane, Pol. 49/K4
Zakouma, Chad 134/C3
Zakouma, PN de, Chad 134/C3
Zalaegerszeg, Hun. 106/B2
Zalamea de la Serena, Sp. 52/C3
Zalamea la Real, Sp. 52/B4
Zalanga, Nga. 133/H4
Zalantun, China 91/J2
Zalari, Rus. 90/E1
Zalaszentgrót, Hun. 56/C2
Zalău, Rom. 57/F2
Žalec, Slov. 56/B2
Zalim, SAr. 206/B2
Zalingei, Sudan 134/C2
Zalishchyky, Ukr. 78/C3
Zaltan (well), Libya 126/C2
Zaltan, Libya 126/C2
Zaltbommel, Neth. 58/C5
Zara, Turk. 114/D2
Zarafshon, Uzb. 98/B5
Zaragoza, Col. 216/C3
Zaragoza, Mex. 205/M7
Zamālat As Sawāsī, Libya 130/M7
Žabljak, Zam. 108/D3
Žábolī, Sp. 140/D2
Zambezi (riv.), Ang. 139/E5
Zambezi (riv.), Afr. 141/G3
Zambezi (riv.), Moz. 119/E6
Zambezi Escarpment, Zam. 77/J3
Zambézia (prov.), Moz. 141/H3
Zaraza, Ven. 217/E2
Zárate, Arg. 227/J11
Zarauz, Sp. 50/B5
Zaraza, Ven. 217/E2
Zarechensk, Rus. 115/H3
Zárda, Azer. 115/F1
Zardab, Azer. 115/F1
Zareh Sharan, Afg. 113/J2
Zaria, Nga. 133/G4
Zarinsk, Rus. 117/D1
Zarmast (pass), Afg. 113/H2
Zaros, Gre. 55/J5
Zarqā' (riv.), Jor. 117/D3
Zarrīn Shahr, Iran 115/G3
Zarrīneh (riv.), Iran 115/F2
Zaruma, Ecu. 220/A1
Zarumilla, Peru 220/A1
Żary, Pol. 49/H3
Zarzaïtine, Alg. 129/H3
Zarzal, Col. 216/B3
Zarzis, Tun. 129/H2
Zasa, Lat. 46/E3
Záskär (riv.), India 110/D3
Záskär (range), India 111/C5
Zaslavl', Bela. 77/M4
Zasul'ye, Pol. 75/K2
Žatec, Czh. 65/G2
Zauche (reg.), Ger. 48/P7
Zauche, Tx, US 180/G2
Žemaičių Naumiestis,
Zemaitija NP, 47/J3
Zembra (isls.), Tun. 130/M6
Zemdasam, China 90/E5
Zemen, Bul. 56/F4
Zemetchino, Rus. 77/L2
Zemio, CAfr. 135/E4
Zemmer, Ger. 61/F4
Zemmora, Alg. 72/C4
Zémongo, Rsv. de Faune de, CAfr. 135/E4
Zempoala (peak), Mex. 205/Q10
Zempoaltepec, Cerro
Zemst, Belg. 61/D2

Zazafotsy, Madg. 143/H8
Zāzamt (wadi), Libya 126/B2
Zazárida, Ven. 216/D2
Zbarazh, Ukr. 78/C3
Zbąszyń, Pol. 49/H2
Zbiroh, Czh. 65/G3
Zboriv, Ukr. 78/C3
Zbůch, Czh. 65/G3
Ždár nad Sázavou, Czh. 49/H4
Zdice, Czh. 65/G3
Zdolbuniv, Ukr. 78/D2
Zdrojowa Wola, Pol. 49/K3
Zealand, NB, Can. 188/D2
Zeballos (peak), Arg. 227/C5
Zebbuġ, Malta 54/L7
Zebediela, SAfr. 141/F5
Zebulon, Ga, US 192/E4
Zeddam, Neth. 58/D5
Zedelgem, Belg. 60/C1
Zeebrugge, Belg. 60/C1
Zeeland, Mi, US 190/C3
Zeeland (prov.), Neth. 58/A5
Zeeland, Neth. 58/C5
Zeewolde, Neth. 58/C4
Zefat, Isr. 117/D3
Zeguo, China 99/J2
Zehdenick, Ger. 60/C1
Zehlendorf, Ger. 48/Q7
Zehner, Sk, Can. 186/B2
Zeigler, Il, US 192/C2
Zeil (mt.), Austl. 155/G2
Zeil (mt.), Austl. 47/M4
Zeiselmauer, Aus. 57/N7
Zeist, Neth. 58/C4
Zeitz, Ger. 48/G3
Zele, Belg. 60/D1
Zelenchukskaya, Rus. 77/G4
Zelenoborskiy, Rus. 74/G2
Zelenodol'sk, Rus. 75/L5
Zelenodol'sk, Rus. 78/G4
Zelenogorsk, Rus. 75/S6
Zelenograd, Rus. 75/W8
Zelenokumsk, Rus. 77/G3
Zelhem, Neth. 58/D4
Zelimai, Libr. 132/C5
Zell, Swi. 66/D3
Zell, Swi. 67/E3
Zell, Ger. 61/G3
Zell, SD, US 184/E1
Zell am Harmersbach,
Zell am Main, Ger. 64/C3
Zell am Moos, Aus. 65/G7
Zell am See, Aus. 51/K3
Zell an der Pram, Aus. 65/G5
Zell in Wiesental, Ger. 66/D2
Zellersee (lake), Aus. 64/G7
Zellersee (lake), Aus. 67/E2
Zellingen, Ger. 64/C2
Zellwood, Fl, US 194/M6
Zelouw, Pol. 49/K3
Zeltingen-Rachtig, Ger. 61/G4
Zeltweg, Aus. 51/L3
Zelzate, Belg. 60/C1
Žemaičių Naumiestis, 47/J4
Zematija NP, 47/J3
Zembra (isls.), Tun. 130/M6
Zemdasam, China 90/E5
Zemen, Bul. 56/F4
Zemetchino, Rus. 77/L2
Zemio, CAfr. 135/E4
Zemmer, Ger. 61/F4
Zemmora, Alg. 72/C4
Zenda, China 90/D5
Zenica, Bosn. 56/D3
Zenith, Wa, US 197/C3
Zenn (riv.), Ger. 64/D2
Zenne (riv.), Belg. 61/D1

Zenon Park, Sk, Can. 175/N1
Zentsūji, Japan 96/C3
Zenza do Itombe, Ang. 216/D2
Zeona, SD, US 186/C5
Zepernick, Ger. 48/Q6
Žepče, Bosn. 56/D3
Zephyr, Tx, US 180/E2
Zephyr Cove, Nv, US 176/D4
Zephyrhills, Fl, US 194/L7
Zeralda, Alg. 130/G4
Zermatt, Swi. 66/D5
Zernez, Swi. 67/H2
Zernien, Ger. 59/H2
Zernograd, Rus. 79/L4
Zero Branco, It. 69/F2
Zerqan, Alb. 55/G2
Zestap'oni, Geo. 77/G4
Zêtang, China 109/H1
Zetel, Ger. 59/E2
Zeulenroda, Ger. 64/F1
Zeuthen, Ger. 48/Q7
Zeven, Ger. 59/G2
Zevenaar, Neth. 58/D5
Zevenbergen, Neth. 58/B5
Zevio, It. 117/B6
Ze'elim, Isr. 117/B6
Zeya (riv.), Rus. 81/N4
Zeya (res.), Rus. 83/M4
Zeya, Rus. 91/K1
Zeya-Bureya
Zeytindağ, Turk. 76/C5
Zezere (riv.), Port. 52/A3
Zhetybay, Kaz. 77/K4
Zhewang, China 91/H4
Zhezqazghan, Kaz. 111/A2
Zhezqazghan, Kaz. 111/A2
Zhicheng, China 99/G3
Zhigalovo, Rus. 81/K4
Zhigansk, Rus. 81/N3
Zhigulevsk, Rus. 77/J1
Zhigung, China 109/H1
Zhijiang, China 99/F2
Zhanatas, Kaz. 80/G5
Zhangaqazaly, Kaz. 80/G5
Zhangguangcai

Zheleznogorsk, Rus. 76/E1
Zheleznogorsk-Ilimskiy, Rus. 81/L4
Zheleznovodsk, Rus. 77/G3
Zhelin, China 92/L9
Zhěltoye, Rus. 77/L2
Zhenchang, China 99/G3
Zhenfeng Bouyeizu Miaozu
Zhytkavichy, Bela. 78/E3
Zhengguo, China 92/C3
Zhenglan, China 99/H2
Zhengyang, China 99/G3
Zhengzhou, China 99/G3
Zhenkang, China 105/G2
Zhenlai, China 91/J2
Zhenlong, China 99/F4
Zhenning Bouyeizu Miaozu
Zhenping, China 90/F5
Zhenping, China 99/H3
Zhenxiong, China 99/H3
Zhenyuan, China 92/L9
Zhenze, China 92/L9
Zherdevka, Rus. 79/L2
Zhestyanka, Rus. 77/M1
Zhetiqara, Kaz. 77/K4
Zhibo, China 99/F3
Zhijiang, China 99/F2
Zhijin, China 99/E3
Zhongba, China 111/D6
Zhongdian, China 99/D3
Zhonghe, China 92/L8
Zhongjiang, China 99/E2
Zhongshan, China 99/G4
Zhongxian, China 105/K2
Zhongxin, China 99/G4
Zhongyang, China 99/G2
Zhouhu, China 99/G3
Zhoukou, China 99/H3
Zhoulichang, China 92/C4
Zhoupu, China 92/L8
Zhouzhou, China 92/G7
Zhouzhou, China 92/G2
Zhovkva, Ukr. 78/B2
Zhovti Vody, Ukr. 79/G2
Zhovtneve, Ukr. 79/H4
Zhuanghe, China 93/B3
Zhuangzi, China 81/N3
Zhuanghe, China 93/B3
Zhucheng, China 93/D3
Zimatlán de Álvarez,
Zugdidi, Geo. 77/G4
Zugspitze, Ger. 67/F5
Zuhres, Rus. 79/K3
Zhuji (isl.), China 77/J2
Zhujiang Kou
Zhumadian, China 99/H3
Zhuozhou, China 99/G3
Zhuozi, China 75/X9
Zhushan, China 92/B4

Zhutan, China 99/G2
Zhuxi, China 99/H2
Zhuxi, China 92/B4
Zhuyu, China 77/G3
Zhuyuanba, China 92/L9
Zhuzhou, China 99/G3
Zhuzhou, China 99/G3
Zhydachiv, Ukr. 78/C3
Zhytomyr, Ukr. 78/E2
Zhytomyrs'ka Oblast, Ukr. 76/C2
Zi (riv.), China 90/D5
Zia (int'l arpt.), Bang. 111/H3
Zia Ind. Res., NM, US 179/A3
Zia Town, Libr. 132/C5
Zibo, China 99/H3
Zibyu (hills), Myan. 98/B4
Zičbice, Pol. 49/J3
Ziegenrück, Ger. 65/E1
Zielona Góra, Pol. 49/H2
Ziemetshausen, Ger. 67/G1
Zienzu, Lith. 132/C5
Zierenberg, Ger. 59/G6
Zierikzee, Neth. 58/A5
Ziftá, Egypt 131/C3
Zigey, Chad 134/B2
Zigon, Myan. 98/B2
Zigong, China 105/G2
Zigui, China 92/B5
Ziguinchor, Sen. 132/A3
Ziguinchor (pol. reg.), Sen. 132/A3
Zihuatanejo, Mex. 205/C6
Zijing (mtn.), China 92/B3
Zijingguan, China 99/F3
Zijingguan, China 92/G7
Zikhron Ya'aqov, Isr. 117/L1
Zilair, Rus. 77/L1
Zile, Turk. 114/C1
Zilote, Ukr. 79/J1
Zilina, Slvk. 49/K4
Zillah, China 126/C2
Zillah, Wa, US 174/D4
Ziller (riv.), Aus. 67/F2
Zillisheim, Fr. 66/D2
Zilupe, Lat. 47/N3
Zim, Mn, US 187/H4
Zima, Rus. 90/E1
Zimapán, Mex. 205/F4
Zimatlán de Álvarez, Mex. 206/B2
Zimba, Zam. 140/E3
Zimbabwe (ctry.) 141/F3
Zimla (well), Alg. 126/B5
Zimmerman, Mn, US 187/H5
Zimnitsa, Bul. 57/H4
Zimnyatskiy, Rus. 81/P2
Zimoviniki, Rus. 79/M4
Zinapécuaro de Figueroa, Mex. 205/F5
Zinave, PN de, Moz. 141/G4
Zinder (dept.), Niger 133/H3
Zinder, Niger 133/H3
Zinga, CAfr. 138/D2
Ziniaré, Burk. 133/E3
Zinjibār, Yem. 136/C2
Zinnik, Ukr. 79/H2
Zinnowitz, Ger. 46/E4
Zion NP, Ut, US 198/C4
Zion, Md, US 196/C6
Zion, Il, US 193/F6
Zionville, NC, US 193/G2
Zionz Lake, On, Can. 187/J2
Zipaquirá, Col. 219/M7
Zippori, Isr. 117/C3
Zirc, Hun. 56/C2
Zirco Schorlau, Ger. 65/F1
Ziro, India 98/B3
Zirzow, Ger. 60/D4
Zitácuaro, Mex. 205/K7
Žitava (riv.), Slvk. 49/K5
Zittau, Ger. 49/H3
Živinice, Bosn. 56/D3
Ziway (lake), Eth. 136/A3
Zixing, China 99/G3
Ziya (riv.), China 99/H3
Ziyang, China 92/C4
Ziyun Miaozu Bouyeizu
Zizhixian, China 99/G1

Zlatograd, Bul. 55/J2
Zlatorsko (lake), Serb. 56/D4
Zlatoust, Rus. 92/B4
Zlatoustovsk, Rus. 91/L1
Zlín, Czh. 49/J4
Zlin, Czh. 98/E1
Zlínsky (pol. reg.), Czh. 49/J4
Zlínský (pol. reg.), Slvk. 49/K4
Zlīṭan, Libya 126/B1
Zliv, Czh. 65/H4
Zlocieniec, Pol. 49/J2
Zlot, Serb. 56/E3
Złotoryja, Pol. 49/H3
Złotów, Pol. 49/J2
Žlutice, Czh. 65/G2
Żmigród, Pol. 49/J3
Znamenka, Rus. 76/E1
Znamensk, Rus. 47/J4
Znam'yanka, Ukr. 78/G3
Znam'yanka Druha, Ukr. 78/G3
Žnin, Pol. 49/J2
Znojmo, Czh. 49/J4
Zoar, D.R. Congo 139/F2
Zobia, D.R. Congo 139/F2
Zocca, It. 69/D5
Zoétélé, Camr. 138/B2
Zofingen, Swi. 66/D3
Zofu, D.R. Congo 139/F4
Zogang, China 105/G2
Zogno, It. 68/C2
Zoggën, China 99/E1
Zohreh (riv.), Iran 112/F2
Zoissa, Tanz. 137/B3
Zola, Fr. 69/E5
Zola (lake), Fr. 70/B5
Zolfo Springs, Fl, US 195/M4
Zollikon, Swi. 99/E3
Zolochiv, Ukr. 78/C3
Zolochiv, Ukr. 79/H2
Zolonogou, China 90/F5
Zolote, Ukr. 79/L2
Zolotonosha, Ukr. 78/G3
Zolotukhino, Rus. 79/J1
Zomba, Malw. 141/G2
Zone (pt.), Eng, UK 42/A6
Zongjiafangzi, China 90/D4
Zongo, D.R. Congo 134/C4
Zongolica, Mex. 205/N8
Zonguldak (prov.), Turk. 76/F4
Zonhoven, Belg. 61/E2
Zonza, Fr. 68/A4
Zoo Baba (well), Niger 126/B5
Zorge (riv.), Ger. 59/G6
Zorgo, Burk. 133/E3
Zorneding, Ger. 67/F1
Zornheim, Ger. 64/B3
Zornotza, Sp. 52/D1
Zorritos, Peru 220/A1
Zorzor, Libr. 132/C5
Zossen, Ger. 48/G3
Zottegem, Belg. 60/C2
Zou Xian, China 92/C4
Zouar, Chad 128/B5
Zound-Wéogo 190/C3
Zoupa, China 99/G4
Zoufana, Oued 128/D2
Zoutkamp, Neth. 58/D2
Zoutleeuw, Belg. 61/E2
Zrenjanin, Serb. 56/E2
Zschopau (riv.), Ger. 65/F1
Zschorlau, Ger. 65/F1
Zuata, Ven. 217/E2
Zubia, Sp. 52/D4
Zubiri, Sp. 53/E1
Zubübā, Isr. 117/C3
Zuckerhütl (peak), Aus. 67/H4
Zuera, Sp. 53/E2
Zug, Swi. 66/E3
Zufayat Mashtūl, Egypt 131/C4
Zwolen

165° W	150° W	135° W	120° W	105° W	90° W	75° W	60° W	45° W	30° W	15° W	0°
1 A.M.	2 A.M.	3 A.M.	4 A.M.	5 A.M.	6 A.M.	7 A.M.	8 A.M.	9 A.M.	10 A.M.	11 A.M.	NOON

ARCTIC   OCEAN

GREENLAND

NOON

11 A.M.

6 A.M.

3 A.M.
ALASKA

Anchorage

5 A.M.   6 A.M.

7 A.M.

Nuuk

Reykjavík   ICELAND

1 A.M.

Whitehorse

CANADA

NORW

Edmonton

Seattle

Winnipeg

Montréal

NEWFOUNDLAND
8:30 A.M.

St. Pierre
& Miquelon
9 A.M.

IRELAND

UNITED
KINGDOM

London   NETH.
BELG.

Boise

UNITED   STATES

Chicago   Detroit

Halifax

Paris
FRANCE

San Francisco

Denver

New York
Washington

PORTUGAL   SPAIN

Madrid

Los Angeles

Phoenix

Atlanta

BERMUDA

AZORES

Algiers

Honolulu

HAWAII

Houston

MEXICO

Miami   BAHAMAS

CUBA

ATLANTIC

CANARY IS.

MOROCCO

ALGERIA

Mexico

HAITI DOM.
REP.

PUERTO
RICO

CAPE
VERDE

Dakar
SENEGAL

GAMBIA

MAURITANIA

MALI

1 A.M.

PACIFIC

GUATEMALA   BELIZE
HONDURAS

JAMAICA

ANTIGUA & BARBUDA
DOMINICA

W. SAHARA

GUINEA-BISSAU

BURKINA
FASO

N

EL SALVADOR   NICARAGUA

GRENADA

BARBADOS

GUINEA

BENIN

Midnight

Kiribati

INT'L DATE LINE

COSTA RICA

PANAMA

VENEZUELA

TRINIDAD & TOBAGO

GUYANA

SIERRA LEONE

CÔTE
D'IVOIRE   GHANA

Lag

LIBERIA

TOGO

COLOMBIA

SUR. FR. GUIANA

São Tomé
&
Príncipe

Bogotá

OCEAN

ECUADOR

OCEAN

ASCENSION

GÁLAPAGOS IS.

Manaus

Recife

French   Polynesia

Marquesas Is.
2:30 A.M.

PERU

Lima

BRAZIL

La Paz
BOLIVIA

Pitcairn Is.

Easter I.

PARAGUAY

Rio de Janeiro

CHILE

Santiago

Buenos
Aires

URUGUAY

TRISTAN DA CUNHA

ARGENTINA

FALKLAND
IS.

S. GEORGIA

Time Zones of the World						
Standard Time Zones	3 A.M.	4 A.M.	5 A.M.	6 A.M.		
Areas Using Half Hour Deviations	5:30 P.M.					

1 A.M.	2 A.M.	3 A.M.	4 A.M.	5 A.M.	6 A.M.	7 A.M.	8 A.M.	9 A.M.	10 A.M.	11 A.M.	NOON